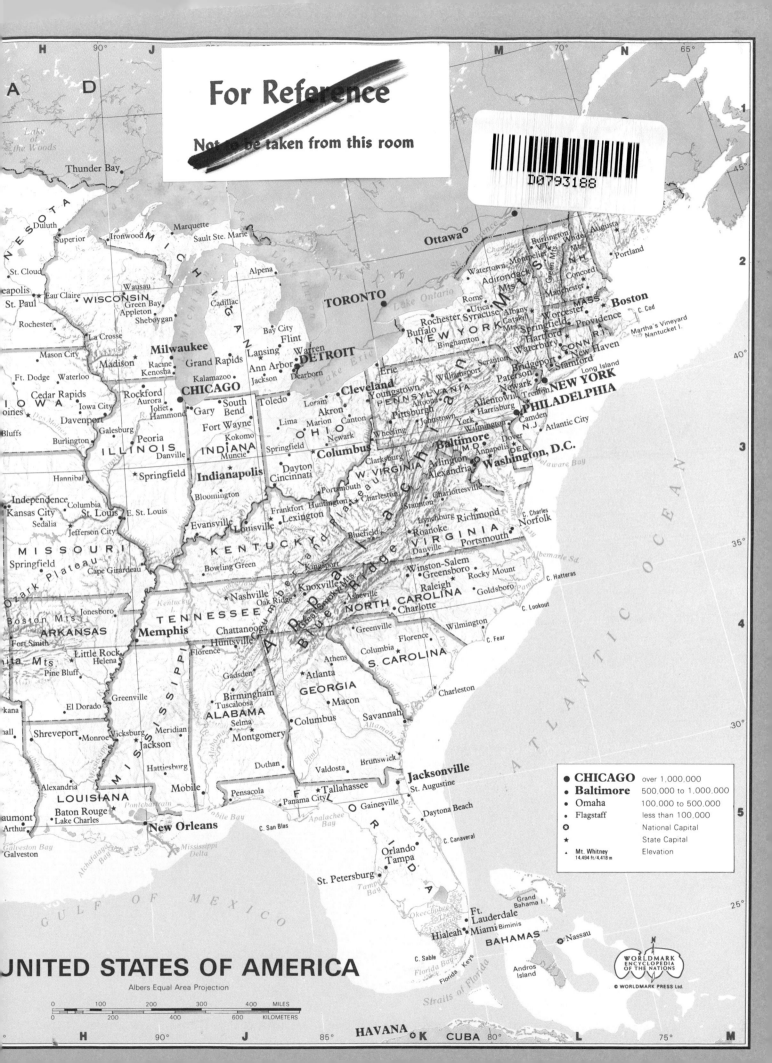

UNITED STATES OF AMERICA

Albers Equal Area Projection

● **CHICAGO**	over 1,000,000
● **Baltimore**	500,000 to 1,000,000
● Omaha	100,000 to 500,000
▪ Flagstaff	less than 100,000
⊛	National Capital
★	State Capital
▲ Mt. Whitney 14,494 ft/4,418 m	Elevation

WORLDMARK ENCYCLOPEDIA OF THE NATIONS
© WORLDMARK PRESS Ltd.

0   100   200   300   400 MILES
0   200   400   600 KILOMETERS

WORLDMARK ENCYCLOPEDIA OF THE STATES

WORLDMARK
ENCYCLOPEDIA
OF THE STATES

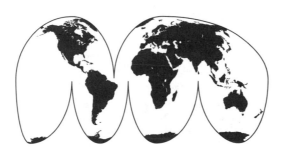

Formerly published by Worldmark Press, Ltd.

GALE

DETROIT · NEW YORK · TORONTO · LONDON

Gale Research Staff

Andrea Kovacs Henderson, Project Editor
Leslie Joseph, Allison McNeill, Contributing Editors
Jolen Marya Gedridge, Camille Killens, Gerda-Ann Raffaelle,
Stephanie Samulski, Karen Uchic, Associate Editors
Catherine Goldstein, Assistant Editors
Lawrence W. Baker, Managing Editor

Mary Beth Trimper, Production Director
Evi Seoud, Production Manager
Shanna P. Heilveil, Production Assistant

Cynthia Baldwin, Production Design Manager
Barbara J. Yarrow, Graphic Services Manager
Gary W. Leach, Desktop Publisher

Library of Congress Cataloging-in-Publication Data

Worldmark encyclopedia of the States. -- 4th ed.
   p. cm
   Includes bibliographical references.
   ISBN 0-7876-0080-6 (alk. paper)
   1. U.S. states—Encyclopedias.   2. United States—Territories and possesions—Encyclopedias.
E156.W67   1997
973' .03—dc21

          97-31432
          CIP

ISBN 0-7876-0080-6
Printed in the United States of America
10 9 8 7 6 5 4 3 2 1

CONTENTS

EDITORIAL STAFF

REVIEWERS

CONTRIBUTORS

TO THE FOURTH EDITION

ALABAMA

Jason Blackman, Department of Transportation; Delia Clenney, Research and Statistics Division, Department of Industrial Relations; Nancy Gouce, Executive Director, Council on Arts and Humanities; John Hyden, Deputy Commissioner, Department of Insurance; L. Louis Hyman, Resource Planning, Forestry Commission; Grover T. Jacobs, Financial Advisor; Bettye McMosen, Department of Education; Fred Neighbors, Public Library Service; John O'Connell, Research Division, Department of Revenue; Dennis Wright, Chief, Consumer Affairs, Office of the Attorney General

ALASKA

John Boucher, Department of Labor; Jay Kerttula, Division of Agriculture, Department of Natural Resources; Ross A. Kinney, Deputy Commissioner, Treasury, Department of Revenue; Steve McMains, Alaska Oil and Gas Conservation Commission; Patty L. Olson, Administrative Manager, Division of Insurance, Department of Commerce and Economic Division; Jeff Ottesen, Statewide Planning Chief, Department of Transportation and Public Facilities, Division of Statewide Planning; Kristi Peel, Division of Banking, Securities and Corp., Department of Commerce and Economic Development

ARIZONA

Lloyd Brown, Public Information Officer, Department of Agriculture; Sydney K. Davis, Chief Counsel, Consumer Protection and Advocacy Section, Office of the Attorney General; Jack Dillenberg, D.D.S., M.P.H., Director, Department of Health Services; Al Hendricks, Forest Management Section Chief, State Land Department; Teresa Hilton, Commission Secretary, Industrial Commission of Arizona; Mark Hope, Energy Office, Department of Commerce; Mark W. Killian, Director, Department of Revenue; Sharon C. Mayes, Assistant Director, Division of Human Resources/Development, Department of Corrections; Bill McCullough, Office of the Treasurer; Robert Rocha, State Comptroller, Department of Administration, Financial Services Division; Victor Rodarte, Acting Director, Securities Section, Corporation Commission; Donald Sneed, Sr., Planner, Department of Transportation, Advance Planning; Judy Seymour, State Banking Department

ARKANSAS

Don R. Clark, Assistant Bank Commissioner, State Bank Department; Dan Flowers, Director of Highways and Transportation, State Highway Commission; Jim Grant, Forestry Commission; Alma Holbrook, Employment Security Department, Labor Market Information Section; Jim Mitchell, Director, State Arts Council; Sandra Nichols, Director, Department of Health; F. Mike Stormes, Director, Department of Finance and Administration; Don Zern, Taxpayer Information Officer, Revenue Division, Department of Finance and Administration

CALIFORNIA

Patrick C. Carroll, Program Analyst, State Banking Department; Delaine Eastin, State Superintendent of Public Instruction, Department of Education; Richard A. Elbrecht, Supervising Attorney, Legal Services Unit, Department of Consumer Affairs; Liz Gibson, Bureau Chief, Library Development Services, State Library; Kevin Herglotz, Assistant Secretary for Public Affairs, Department of Food and Agriculture; C. Jane McKendry, Chief, Vital Statistics Section, Department of Health Services; Greg Pochy, Research Analyst, California Trade and Commerce Agency; Denise Quade, Public Affairs Office, Franchise Tax Board; Carl Rogers, Program Budget Manager, Department of Finance; Tiang-Ting Shih, Forest Economist, Department of Forestry and Fire Protection; Hugh Slayden, Special Assistant, External Affairs, Youth and Adult Correctional Agency; Dale Trenschel, Fuels Planning Office, California Energy Commission

COLORADO

Ken Anderson; Barbara K. Berg, State Forest Service, Colorado State University; Zaida Birkhofer, General Division of Business Regulation, Department of Law; Nancy Bolt, Assistant Commissioner, Department of Education; Beverly J. Day, Chief, Financial Affairs, Division of

Insurance, Department of Regulatory Agencies; **Clifford W. Hall,** State Controller, Division of Accounts and Control, Department of Administration; **Fred J. Joseph,** Deputy Securities Commissioner, Division of Securities, Department of Regulatory Agencies; **Jo Ann Keith,** Research and Evaluation, Department of Education; **Tom Kourlis,** Commissioner, Department of Agriculture; **Jennifer Harrison Lane,** Communications Coordinator, Office of Energy Conservation; **Bill Owens,** State Treasurer; **Susan P. Piatt,** Manager of Research and Special Projects, Office of Business Development; **Carl T. Sorrentino,** Public Relations Officer, Department of Transportation; **Stan Williams,** Department of Revenue

CONNECTICUT

Cynthia Antanaitis, Assistant Director, Securities and Business Investments Division, Department of Banking; **John J. Armstrong,** Commissioner, Department of Correction; **Paul M. Hughes,** Senior Vice President, Connecticut Development Authority; **Julianne Konopka,** Director, Program Support and Information Management, Department of Public Health; **Kyle Miasek,** Budget Division, Office of Policy and Management; **June S. Neal,** Director of Communications, Department of Consumer Protection; **Ron Olsen,** Department of Agriculture; **Rie Poirier,** Director of Marketing, Department of Labor; **Susan Reynolds,** Director of Communications, Department of Transportation; **K. Marilyn Ware,** Administrative Assistant, Examination Division, Insurance Department

DELAWARE

Anthony R. Farina, Chief of Media Relations, Department of Correction; **Pascal Forgione,** Superintendent, Department of Public Instruction; **Herb Macia,** Division of Management Services, Health and Social Services; **Timothy R. McTaggart,** State Bank Commissioner; **Evelyn Pearson,** State Data Center; **William Remington,** Director, Division of Revenue, Department of Finance; **E. Austin Short, III,** State Forester, Department of Agriculture; **Tom W. Sloan,** State Librarian, Division of Libraries; **Whitney T. Sweeney,** Deputy Principal Assistant, Department of Finance

DISTRICT OF COLUMBIA

Mohamed Hassan, Department of Revenue; **F. Alexis H. Roberson,** Director, Department of Employment Services

FLORIDA

Robert B. Bradley, Director, Office of Planning and Budgeting; **Bob Crawford,** Commissioner of Agriculture, Department of Agriculture and Consumer Services; **Catherine Deans,** Office of Media Relations, Enterprise Florida; **Kathy Engerran,** Division of Cultural Affairs, Department of State; **Thomas J. Hill,** Professional Services Coordinator, Department of Transportation, Office of the State Transportation Planner; **Eric Karplus,** Full Circle Energy Project, Inc.; **John O'Meara,** State Lands Supervisor, Forest Management Bureau, Department of Forestry; **Don Pride,** Director of Communications, Press Office, Department of Insurance; **Kathy Reeves,** Statistician II, Executive Office of the Governor; **Rebeccca Rust,** Chief, Bureau of Labor Market Information, Department of Labor and Employment Security; **Julia Smith,** Director, Education Accountablility Reports Services; **Susan A. Tedcastle,** Financial Specialist, Bureau of Research, Planning and Staff Development, Division of Banking; **Christian O. Weiss,** Chief Economist, Department of Revenue; **Tony Welch,** Director, Office of Communications and Health Promotion, Department of Health; **Barratt Wilkins,** State Librarian; **Gwendolyn B. Worlds,** Chief, Bureau of Consumer Assistance., Department of Agriculture and Consumer Services

GEORGIA

Bill Alred, Help Desk, Department of Education; **Susan Brown,** Department of Banking and Finance; **Peggy Chambliss,** Office of Public Library Services, Department of Technical and Adult Education; **Jarrod K. Collins,** Supervisor, Property and Casualty Regulatory Services Section; **Sam Hall,** Director of Communications, Department of Labor; **David K. Imahara,** Associate, Legal Services Office, Department of Corrections; **Tommy Irvin,** Commissioner, Department of Agriculture; **Janet Jackson,** Director Business Services and Regulations, Office of Secretary of State; **Tommy Loggins,** Chief, Forest Products UM&D, Forestry Commission; **Patrick J. Meehan,** M.D., Director, Division of Public Health, Department of Human Resources; **Elizabeth Sparrow Robertson,** Georgia Energy Res., Environmental Facilities Authority; **John S. Smith, III,** Counsel and Division Director, Governor's Office of Consumer Affairs

HAWAII

Lorraine H. Akiba, Director, State Department of Labor and Industrial Relations; Earl I. Anzai, Director of Finance, Department of Budget and Finance; Michael G. Buck, Administrator, Forestry and Wildlife Division, Department of Land and Natural Resources; Joan F. Church, Communications Office, Department of Education; Fern Elizares, Department of Taxation; Kazu Hayashida, Director of Transportation, Department of Transportation; Maurice H. Kaya, Program Administrator, Energy, Resources and Technology Division, Business, Economic Development and Tourism; Paul A. Mark, Information Specialist, State Librarian's Office; Don Martin, Agricultural Statistics Service, Department of Agriculture; Lawrence Miike, Director, Department of Health; Chief Justice Moon, Supreme Court of Hawaii; Gary L. Ruby, Regulation Analyst, Division of Financial Institutions, Department of Commerce and Consumer Affairs; Jo Ann M. Uchida, Executive Director, Office of Consumer Protection

IDAHO

Pamela Bradshaw, State Library; Mark Carnopis, Department of Corrections; Brett T. DeLange, Deputy Attorney General; Gavin Gee, Director, Department of Finance; Bill Hargrove, Office of the Superintendent of Public Instruction, Department of Education; Bob Hoppie, Administrator, Energy Division, Department of Water Resources; Daniel D. John, Tax Policy Manager, State Tax Commission; Candie Kinch, Sr. Financial Examiner, Department of Insurance; Davalee Leavitt, Deputy State Registrar; Bill Love, Chief, Bureau of Forestry Assistance, Department of Lands; Larry Sohlicht, Division of Financial Management

ILLINOIS

John Dickey, Legislative Liason, State Treasurer's Office; David A. Gillespie, Section Manager, Field Operations, Department of Natural Resources; Mike Klemens, Communications Office, Department of Revenue; Carolyn Lorton, State Board of Higher Education; Nan Nases, Director, Department of Insurance; Therese Oxtoby, Securities Department; Tom Schafer, Director's Office, Department of Public Health; Erin N. Tepen, Department of Agriculture; Winnie Tuthill, Department Of Communications, State Board of Education; Joan E. Walters, Director, Bureau of the Budget, Office of the Governor; Barb Welk, Department of Transportation, Office of Public Affairs

INDIANA

John Christopher Bailey, Commissioner, State Board of Health; Roberta Brooker, Library Development Office, State Library; H. Christian DeBruyn, Commissioner, Department of Correction; Department of Revenue, Office of the Secretary of State; Patti Fralich, Deputy Commissioner, Department of Labor; Stu Huffman, Communication Specialist, Department of Education; Charles W. Phillips, Director, Department of Financial Institutions; Jeff Settle, Forest Products Specialist, Indiana Forestry; Shea Ward, Department of Transportation; Julia A. Wickard, Natural Resources Director, Office of the Commissioner of Agriculture

IOWA

Larry L. Bean, Administrator, Energy and Geological Resources Division, Department of Natural Resources; Michael E. Brandrup, Chief, Forestry Services Bureau, Department of Natural Resources; Dale Cochran, Secretary, Department of Agriculture; Mary Fehring, Division of Banking, Department of Commerce; Craig Goettsch, Superintendent, Securities Division, Department of Commerce; A. Harder, Insurance Division, Department of Commerce; Sha Khan, Labor Market Analyst, Research and Information Services, Iowa Workforce Development; Karl C. Koch, Chief Finance Officer, Treasurer of State's Office; Patti Schroeder, Department of Management, Department of Revenue and Finance; Sharman B. Smith, State Librarian, Department of Education; Susan Wallace, Staff of the Director, Department of Transportation

KANSAS

Raymond G. Aslin, State Forester, Kansas Forest Service; E. Dean Carlson, Secretary of Transportation, Department of Transportation; Lori J. Forster, Energy Office, Kansas Corporation Commission; Jim Janosek, Department of Commerce and Housing; Amy Johnson, Office of the State Bank Commissioner; Carole Jordan, Department of Agriculture; Robert L. Kennedy, Jr., Assistant Commissioner, Kansas Insurance Department; John LaFaver, Secretary of Revenue; Rachel Lindbloom, MA, LSCSW, Health Planning Consultant, Department of Health and Environment; C. Steven Rarrick, Deputy Attorney General, Consumer Protection Division; Gloria Timmer, Director of the Budget; Andy Tompkins, Commissioner of Education, State Board of Education; Joan Wingerson, Arts Program Consultant, Kansas Arts Commission

KENTUCKY

Jay Bank, Office of State Librarian and Commissioner, Department for Libraries and Archives; Teresa Fisher, Department of Financial Institutions, Public Protection and Regulation Cabinet; Rice C. Leach, Commissioner, Department for Health Services, Cabinet for Human Resources; Joe Lilly, Communications Director, Cabinet for Economic Development; Mark Matuszews, Natural Resources and Environmental Protection Cabinet, Division of Forestry; John McCarty, Secretary, Finance and Administration Cabinet; Bruce McCutchen, Tax Consultant, Division of Tax Policy and Research, Revenue Cabinet; Fred Mudge, Secretary, Transportation Cabinet; Doug Sapp, Commissioner, Department of Corrections, Justice Cabinet; Billy Ray Smith, Commissioner of Agriculture, Department of Agriculture

LOUISIANA

Nancy Beverly, Tax Research Analyst, Research and Technical Division, Department of Revenue and Taxation; Mark C. Drennen, Commissioner of Administration, Division of Administration, Office of Planning and Budget; Ken Duncan, State Treasurer, Department of Treasurer; Paul D. Frey, Assistant Commissioner, Office of Forestry, Department of Agriculture and Forestry; Joseph P. Gardner, Savings and Loan Division, Office of Financial Institutions; Gerri Hobdy, Assistant Secretary, Department of Culture, Recreation and Tourism; Nancy Johnson, State Department of Transportation and Development, Public Affairs Office; Bryce Malone, Assistant Commissioner, Department of Agriculture and Forestry; Christine McColloster, Louisiana Center for Health Statistics, Department of Health and Hospitals; Cecil J. Picard, State Superintendent, Department of Education; Judy Smith, Head, Louisiana Section, State Library

MAINE

John Bradley, Budget Analyst, Bureau of the Budget, Department of Adm. and Financial Services; James F. Connors, Senior Policy Planner, State Planning Office; Michael Higgins, Director of Special Projects, Department of Education; Rosalie Howes, Bureau of Insurance, Professional and Financial Regulation; Valerie R. Landry, Commissioner, Department of Labor; William N. Lund, Superintendent, Office of Consumer Credit Regulation; Bonnie E. Russell, Securities Registration Supervisor, Department of Professional and Financial Reg., Bureau of Banking; State Judiciary Department; Craig W. Ten Broeck, Senior Planner, Department of Agriculture, Food and Rural Resources

MARYLAND

H. Denise Adams, Economist, Bureau of Revenue Estimates; Patrick Arnold, Director, Office of Labor Market Analysis and Information, Department of Labor, Licensing, and Regulation; Neil Bergsman, Deputy Director, Division of Budget Analysis, Department of Budget and Management; Marvin A. Bond, Assistant State Comptroller, Office of the Comptroller of the Treasury; Rebecca Bowman, Chief, Consumer Protection Division, Office of the Attorney General; Audrey Brown, State Division of Corrections; Nancy S. Grasmick, State Superintendent, State Department of Education; Harold K. Kanarek, Department of Agriculture; Robert N. McDonald, Securities Commissioner, Securities Division, Office of the Attorney General; Barbara N. Rice, Forestry Education Coordinator, Department of Natural Resources Forest Service; Peter Trapp, Maryland Energy Administration; Maurice Travillian, Assistant State Superintendent, Division of Library Development and Services, Department of Education; Martin P. Wasserman, M.D., J.D., Secretary, Department of Health and Mental Hygiene

MASSACHUSETTS

Angelo R. Buonopane, Director, Department of Labor and Workforce Development; David Flaherty, Research Coordinator, Department of Economic Development; Joyce Golin, Division of Energy Resources, Department of Economic Development; Joseph A. Leonard, Jr., Deputy Commissioner of Banks and General Counsel, Office of the Commissioner of Banks; Robert E. Moore, Jr., Securities Division, Office of Secretary of Commonwealth

MICHIGAN

Robin Bertsch, Forest Development Executive, Forest Management Division, Department of Natural Resources; Amy Byrd, Forms and Manuals Analyst, State Court Administrative Office; Michael T. Jackson, Research and Consumer Services, Michigan Insurance Bureau; Margaret Kavanagh, Michigan Jobs Commission; Dan Kitchel, Department of Treasury; Linda Krieger, Department of Management and Budget; Pat McQueen, Commissioner, Financial Institutions Bur., Department of Commerce; Robin Pannecouk, Administrator, Department of Transportation, Office of Communications

MINNESOTA

Doug Blanke, Policy Director of Consumer Enforcement, Office of the Attorney General; **Janice Feye-Stukas,** Assistant Director, Library Development and Services; **Michael Hunst,** State Statistician, Agricultural Statistics Service; **Lyn Isaacson,** Administrative Assistant, Department of Transportation; **Daniel P. O'Brien,** Assistant to the Commissioner, Department of Corrections; **Nancy J. Rooney,** Budget Research and Analysis; **K. Sterns,** Research and Statistics, Minnesota DES; **Paul A. Wilson,** Senior Research Analyst, Department of Revenue

MISSISSIPPI

Trey Bobinger, Director, Consumer Protection Division, Office of the Attorney General; **Deb Collier,** Office of Budget and Fund Management, Department of Finance and Administration; **Bill Colusis,** State Forestry Commission; **Purvie Green,** Special Assistant, Department of Agriculture and Commerce; **Marianne T. Hill, Ph.D.,** Senior Economist, Mississippi Institutions of Higher Learning; **Linda Irby,** State Department of Education; **Ricky Jackson,** State Department of Banking and Consumer Finance; Mississippi State Law Library; **Shep Montgomery,** Department of Insurance; **Robert L. Robinson,** Executive Director, Department of Transportation; **Eva Throckmorton,** Director of Regulation, Securities Division; **Marilyn J. Wash,** Energy Division, Department of Economic and Community Development

MISSOURI

Terry Ball, Attorney General's Office; **Greg Barlow,** Division of Finance, Department of Economic Development; **Marvin Brown,** Division of Forestry, Department of Conservation; **Rebecca McDowell Cook,** Secretary of State; **Don Dyer,** Program Specialist, Arts Council, Department of Economic Development; **Amy W. Gardner,** Senior Public Affairs Specialist, Department of Transportation; **Andrei Kuznetsov,** Department of Corrections, Planning, Research, and Evaluation Unit; **Janette M. Lohman,** Director, Department of Revenue; **Mark L. Mehmert,** State Treasurer's Office; **Jim Muench,** Division Information Officer, Division of Energy; **Bill Niblack,** Research and Analysis, Department of Labor and Industrial Relations; **Sally Oxenhandler,** Public Information Officer, Department of Agriculture; **Richard Speidel,** Designated Principal Assistant, Department of Insurance; **Nancy Worts,** Administrative Assistant, Office of the Commissioner of Education

MONTANA

Don Artley, Administrator, Forestry Division, Department of Natural Resources and Conservation; **Annie Bartos,** Chief Legal Counsel, Department of Commerce, Office of Consumer Affairs; **Jane Clack,** Department of Commerce; **Greg Clark,** Marketing Intern; **Jo Ann Walsh Dotson, RN, MSN,** Primary Care Office, Department of Public Health and Human Services; **Donald W. Hutchinson,** Commissioner, Division of Banking and Financial Institutions, Department of Commerce; **Zia Kazimi,** Department of Transportation, Transportation Planning Division; **Dave Martin,** Department of Commerce, Census and Economic Information Center; **Nancy McLane,** Research Specialist, Department of Environmental Quality; **Dori Nielson,** Office of Public Instruction; **Mark O'Keefe,** Auditor; **Dan Seman,** Insurance Division, Office of the State Auditor; **Cathy Shenkle,** Research and Analysis Bureau, Department of Labor and Industry

NEBRASKA

M. Berri Balka, State Tax Commissioner, Department of Revenue; **Marilyn Bath,** Consumer Protection Division, Office of the Attorney General; **Marilyn Crane,** Labor Market Information, Department of Labor; **Tom Doering,** Department of Economic Development; **Jack E. Herstein,** Assistant Director, Department of Banking and Finance; **Mark B. Horton,** Director, Health and Human Services System; **Brenda Linder,** Department of Agriculture; **Pam Nielsen,** Data Center, Department of Education; **Jennifer Severin,** Executive Director, Nebraska Arts Council; **Rod Wagner,** Director, Nebraska Library Commission; **Tom Wardle,** Department of Forestry, Fisheries, and Wildlife, University of Nebraska–Lincoln

NEVADA

Bill Anderson, State Treasurer's Office; **Thomas J. Fronapfel, P.E.,** Assistant Director, Planning, State Department of Transportation; **Carol A. Jackson,** Director, Department of Employment, Training and Rehabilitation; **Joan G. Kerschner,** Director, Museums, Library and Arts Department; **Mary Peterson,** Superintendent, Department of Education; **Roberta E. Reese,** Chief Accountant, Office of the State Controller; **Donald Reis,** Deputy Secretary of State, Securities Division; **Luana J. Ritch, MPA, CHES,** Public Health Education and Information Officer, Department of Human Resources, Health Division; **Bonnie Vivant,** Assistant Chief, Department of Taxation, Revenue Division; **L. Scott Walshaw,** Commissioner, Division of Financial Institutions, Department of Business and Industry

NEW HAMPSHIRE

Bill Boynton, Public Information Officer, Department of Transportation; Charles Danielson, Director, Division of Public Health Services; Bruce DeMay, New Hampshire Economic and Labor Market Information Bureau; John Sargent, Director, Forest and Lands Division, Department of Resources and Economic Development; Kendall F. Wiggin, State Librarian, State Library, Department of Cultural Affairs

NEW JERSEY

Winnie Comfort, Director, Office of Public Affairs, Department of Banking and Insurance; Rod DeSmet, Agricultural Statistics Service, Department of Agriculture; Lynn M. Fleeger, Chief Information Officer, New Jersey Turnpike Authority; Mark C. Fulcomer, Director, Center for Health Statistics, Department of Health and Senior Services; Linda Furlong, Division of Economic Development, Department of Commerce and Economic Development; Mark S. Herr, Director, Bureau of Securities, Division of Consumer Affairs; Richard L. Kaluzny, Chief, Office of Tax Analysis, Department of Treasury, Division of Taxation; Robert Lupp, Office of the State Librarian, Division of State Library, Department of Education; Gregory A. Marshall, Director, Division of Parks and Forestry, Department of Environmental Protection; Betsy Pugh, Director, Office of Management and Budget, Department of Treasury; Faith Sarafin, Manager, Office of Information, Department of Education; Vivien Shapiro, Assistant Commissioner, Department of Labor; Nina Stack, Communications Director, Council on the Arts, Department of State; John Traier, Deputy Commissioner, Department of Banking and Insurance, Division of Banking

NEW MEXICO

Larry Blackwell, Chief, Economic Research and Analysis Bureau, Department of Labor; John Chavez, Secretary, Taxation and Revenue Department; David W. Harris, Cabinet Secretary, Department of Finance and Administration; Kay Hatton, Mining and Minerals Division, Energy, Minerals and Natural Resources Department; John B. Hiatt, Director, Consumer Protection and Economic Crimes, Office of the Attorney General; Legal Department, State Corrections Department; Don Ortega, Statistical Analyst III, Department of Health; Dave Post, Chief Examiner, Financial Institutions Division

NEW YORK

Richard H. Cate, Chief Operating Officer, State Education Department; Michelle Cummings, Deputy Commissioner, Department of Taxation and Finance; John Daily, Commissioner, Department of Transportation; Glenn S. Goord, Department of Correctional Services; Michael C. Greason, Acting Chief, Bureau of Private Land Services, State Department of Environmental Conservation; Carol Huxley, State Education Department, Office of Cultural Education; Jack Kinnicutt, Assistant Deputy Commission for External Affairs, State Department of Economic Development; Joseph Meany, State Museum; William J. O'Reilly, Associate Accountant, Office of State Comptroller, Bureau of Financial Reporting; Michael Rothman, Public Affairs Group, Department of Health; Randall T. Sawyer, Public Information Officer, Department of Agriculture and Markets; John E. Sweeney, Commissioner, Department of Labor

NORTH CAROLINA

Sandra Cooper, Director, State Library, Department of Cultural Resources; Coleman Doggett, State Forest Service, Department of Environment, Health, and Natural Resources; Michael F. Easley, Attorney General, Department of Justice; Deborah B. Lamm, Energy Emergency Preparedness Manager, Energy Division, Department of Commerce; Hal Lingerfelt, Commissioner, Banking Comm., Department of Commerce; Jean McLaughlin, Director, Statewide Initiatives, North Carolina Arts Council, Department of Cultural Resources; Kathy M. Newbern, Information Specialist, Public Schools of North Carolina; Janice C. Pearce, Economist, Labor Market Information Division, Employment Security Commission; Francine J. Stephenson, Office of State Planning; Conni Tucker, Business/Industry Development Division, Department of Commerce; Vicky T. Young, Department of Transportation, Public Affairs Division

NORTH DAKOTA

Rod Backman, Director, Office of Management and Budget; Linda Fiechtner, Department of Economic Development and Finance; Larry A. Kotchman, State Forester, North Dakota Forest Service; Gary Preszler, Commissioner, Department of Banking and Financial Institutions; Ted Quanrud, Public Information Officer, Department of Agriculture; Dr. Jon R. Rice, State Health Officer, Department of Health; Wayne G. Sanstead, Department of Public Instruction; Norlyn Schmidt, Transportation Planner, Department of Transportation, Planning Division; Timothy Schuetzle, Warden, State Penitentiary; Carol Siegert, Deputy, State Treasurer; Kathy Strombeck, State Tax Department

OHIO

Ronald G. Abraham, Chief, Division of Forestry, Department of Natural Resources; **Darla Cottrill**, Data Coordinator, State Library; **Harold Duryee**, Director, Department of Insurance; **Deb Edwards**, Agricultural Statistics Service, Department of Agriculture; **Omar Farooq**, Office of Energy Efficiency, Department of Development; **Thomas E. Geyer**, Commissioner of Securities, Department of Commerce; **Donald Jakeway**, Director, Department of Development; **Michael Miguel**, Office of the Treasurer; **Ronald A. Mucha**, Administrator, Tax Analysis and Local Government Distribution, Department of Taxation; **Ron Poole**, Public Information Specialist, ODOT Communications, Department of Transportation; **Shelly Thrash**, Communications Office, Department of Education; **Robert S. Tongren**, Consumers' Counsel, Office of Consumers' Counsel; **Steve Van Dine**, Department of Rehabilitation and Corrections

OKLAHOMA

Keesa Crouch, Administrative Assistant, Office of the Secretary of Energy; **Roger L. Davis**, Director Division of Forestry, Department of Agriculture; **Nancy A. Huff**, Public Information Director, Oklahoma Arts Council; **Ann Dee Lee**, Department of Commerce; **J.R. Nida, M.D.**, Commissioner of Health, State Department of Health; **Nancy Tarr**, Director, Office of State Finance; **Bob Zapffe**, Executive Assistant, Research and Evaluation, Department of Corrections

OREGON

Bruce Andrews, Director, Department of Agriculture; **Doug Bray**, State Judicial Department; **Tanya Gross**, Education Program Specialist, Department of Education; **Richard Nockleby**, Division of Finance and Corp. Securities, Department of Consumer and Business Services; **Sandy Salter**, State Department of Corrections; **Lou Torres**, Public Affairs Specialist, Department of Forestry; **Monte R. Turner**, Public Information Representative, Department of Transportation; **David Yamaka**, Program Coordinator, Oregon Employment Department

PENNSYLVANIA

Merlin Benner, Wildlife Biologist, Bureau of Forestry, Department of Conservation and Natural Resources; **Charles C. Brosius**, Secretary, Department of Agriculture; **Joanna Cummings**, Pennsylvania Securities Commission; **Richard D. DeMartino**, Director, Bureau of Supervision and Enforcement, Department of Banking; **Joseph K. Goldberg**, Director, Office of the Attorney General, Bureau of Consumer Protection; **Robert E. Greenwood**, Deputy Secretary of the Budget, Office of the Budget; **Michele Haskins**, Office of Press and Communications, Department of Education; **Crystal L. Hull**, Press Secretary, Insurance Department; **Mary Ann Regan**, Director, Bureau of Research and Statistics, Department of Labor and Industry; **Shawn Skelly**, Department of Health; **Wendi Taylor**, Legislative Office/Press Office, Department of Revenue

PUERTO RICO

Isidra Albino, Undersecretary of Education, Department of Education; **Cesar Almodovar**, Secretary, Department of Labor and Human Resources; **Nydia Cotto**, Secretary, Department of Correction and Rehabilitation; **Ana Maria Cruz**, Director, Office of Agricultural Statistics; Staff, Forest Service Bureau, Department of Natural and Environmental Resources; **Ana E. Ortiz**, Director, Office of Budget and Management; **Carlos I. Pesquera**, Secretary, Department of Transportation and Public Works; **José M. Rosario**, Assistant Commissioner, Office Financial Institutions

RHODE ISLAND

Erin Barrette, Rhode Island Economic Development Corporation; **R. Gary Clark**, Tax Administrator, Division of Taxation; **Karolye Cunha**, State Council on the Arts; **Thomas Dryden**, State Department of Environmental Management; **Maria D'Alessandro Piccirilli**, Associate Director and Superintendent of Securities, Department of Business Regulation; **Peg Tormey**, Administrator, Consumer Protection Unit, Department of Attorney General; **Dennis Ziroli**, Division of Banking, Department of Business Regulation

SOUTH CAROLINA

Debbie Anderson, Administrative Assistant, State Library; **John Barkley**, Office of Executive Affairs, Department of Corrections; **Camille T. Brown**, Coordinator of MIS, Commission on Higher Education; **Dean Carson**, State Forestry Comm.; **Richard Eckstrom**, State Treasurer's Office, Board of Economic Advisors; **Robert A. Ehrlich**, Financial Analyst, Department of Insurance; **Robert W. Martin**, Econometrician/Program Manager, Board of Economic Advisors; **Tracy A. Meyers**, Deputy Securities Commissioner, Office of the Attorney General; **Kay Thomas Packett**, Special Assistant, Public Affairs; **Vicki Ringer**, Public Affairs, Department of Revenue and Taxation; **Ray Sharpe**, Rate Analyst, Utilities Department, Public Service Commission; **Stanley L. Shealy,** Director of Publications and Media Resources, Department of Transportation; **Clay Williams,** Assistant Director of Public Information, Department of Agriculture

SOUTH DAKOTA

Melita Bisbee-Hauge, Division of Securities, Department of Commerce and Regulation; **Barbara E. Buhler,** Public Information Officer, Office of Administrative Services, Department of Health; **Mary Carney,** Governor's Office of Economic Development; **Cheryl Chick,** Administrative Assistant, Office of the Attorney General; **David Erickson,** Division Staff Specialist, Prairie and Urban Forestry Programs, Division of Resource Conservation and Forestry; **Dennis Holub,** Executive Director, South Dakota Arts Council; **Wendell Madson,** Division of Insurance, Department of Commerce and Regulation; **Bernie Moran,** Labor Market Information Center, Department of Labor; **Jeffery R. Moser,** Deputy State Treasurer; **Susan Ryan,** DECA, Office of Finance and Management, Department of Education and Cultural Affairs; US Department of Agriculture, National Agricultural Statistics Service; **Ron Wheeler,** Secretary, Department of Transportation

TENNESSEE

Hazel Albert, Acting Commissioner, Department of Employment Security; **Dwight D. Barnett,** Staff Forester, Division of Forestry, Department of Agriculture; **Larry D. Burton,** Chief, Broker, Dealer Registration, Securities Division, Department of Commerce and Insurance; **Talmadge Gilley,** Commissioner, Department of Financial Institutions; **Gary A. Lukowski, Ph.D.,** Assistant to the Commissioner, Department of Correction; **Isaac Nevaise,** Research Section, Department of Revenue; **Sidney Owen,** Department of Education; **Bruce Saltsman,** Commissioner, Department of Transportation; **Fran Schell,** Assistant Director, State Library and Archives; **Bennett Tarleton,** Director, Tennessee Arts Commission; **Mark Williams,** Director, Division of Consumer Affairs

TEXAS

Greg Barrow, Executive Services, Department of Criminal Justice; **Beverly Boyd,** Deputy Assistant Commissioner, Communications, Department of Agriculture; **Patty Davis,** Library Systems Administrator, State Library and Archives Commission; **Glen D. Hunt,** Director, Research and Policy Development, Office of Comptroller of Public Accounts; **Lee Jones,** Department of Insurance; **Philip A. Lena,** Financial Analyst, Department of Banking; **Dan Morales,** Attorney General; **Patti J. Patterson, M.D.,** Commissioner of Health, Department of Health; **Katy Hall Rachui,** Forest Information Officer, Texas Forest Service, Texas A and M Univ. System; **Debbie Graves Ratcliffe,** Division of Communications, Texas Education Agency; **Linda L. Ribble,** Department of Transportation, Public Information Office; **John Sharp,** Comptroller of Public Accounts

U.S. VIRGIN ISLANDS

Joanne Bozzuto, Director, Bureau of Internal Revenue

UTAH

Michael Deily, Director, Division of Health Care Financing, Department of Health; **R. Lee Ellertson,** Chair, Utah State Industrial Commission; **J. Matthew Jenkins,** Division of Securities, Department of Commerce; **Craig Kennedy,** Department of Financial Institutions; **Larry Lewis,** State Department of Agriculture and Food; **Rodney G. Marrelli,** Executive Director, State Tax Commission; **Susan Rutherford,** Governor's Office of Planning and Budget; **Kim Thorne,** Director, Finance Department; **Jilene Whitby,** Administrative Assistant, State Insurance Department

VERMONT

Jeff Carr, Economic and Policy Resources, Inc.; **Richard S. Cortese,** Deputy Commissioner, Department of Banking, Insurance and Securities; **Leon C. Graves,** Commissioner, Department of Agriculture; **Maggie Moran Green,** Deputy Commissioner, Department of Health; **Mike Griffin,** Department of Employment and Training; **Edward Haase,** Commissioner, Department of Taxes, Agency of Administration; **Kenneth L. McGuckin,** Director of Company Licensing and Examinations, Department of Banking, Insurance and Securities; Office of Court Administrator, State of Vermont; **Richard B. Radford,** Office of the Commissioner, Department of Banking, Insurance and Securities; **Douglas R. Walker,** Acting Commissioner, Department of Education

VIRGINIA

Mary M. Bannister, Deputy Commissioner of Insurance, State Corporation Commission, Bureau of Insurance; **Theron J. Bell,** Commissioner, Department of Labor and Industry; **Robert**

T. Benton, Ph.D., Assistant Commissioner, Office of Fiscal Research, Department of Taxation; J. Carlton Courter III, Commissioner, Department of Agriculture and Consumer Services; Larry D. Dodd, Department of Transportation; Susan FitzPatrick, Virginia Commission for the Arts; Shirley Hughes, Analyst, Planning, Evaluation, and Certification, Department of Commerce; Ronald S. Hyman, Director, Center for Health Statistics, Department of Health; James S. Jones, Jr., Exec. Assistant to the Director, Department of Corrections; William E. Landsidle, Comptroller, Commonwealth of Virginia; Don Lillywhite, Labor Market and Demographic Analysis, Virginia Employment Commission, EIS Division; Irvine L. Reaves, Senior Research Analyst, State Corporation Commission, Bureau of Insurance; Margaret Roberts, Department of Education; William R. Shelton, Jr., Chief of Registration, State Corporation Commission, Division of Securities and Retail Franchising; Wayne L. Sterling, Director, Department of Economic Development; Stephen A. Walz, Department of Mines, Minerals and Energy

WASHINGTON

John Bley, Director, Department of Financial Institutions, Division of Banks; Debra Bortner, Administrator, Securities Division, Department of Financial Institutions; Candice Espesith, Office of Financial Management; Gary Kaunincera, Office of Information Services, State Employment Security Division; Janice Marich, Chief Deputy Attorney General, Office of the Attorney General; Bruce Miyahara, Secretary, Department of Health; Sid Morrison, Secretary, Department of Transportation; Alan Mountjoy-Venning, Washington State University Cooperative Extension; Gary M. Perkins, Public Information Officer, Department of Agriculture; Greg Potegal, Taxpayer Information Specialist, Taxpayer Information and Education Sec., Department of Revenue; Chase Riveland, Secretary, Department of Corrections; Kirsten Taylor, State Library; Zhi Xu, Economist, Office of Policy Analysis and Research, Department of Natural Resources

WEST VIRGINIA

Nancy E. Brown, Assistant Director, Taxpayer Services Division, Department of Tax and Revenue; S. Radley Edwards, Deputy State Statistician, State Department of Agriculture; Beth L. Kimble, Division of Banking; William Maxey, Director, Division of Forestry; Jill L. Miles, Deputy Attorney General, Division of Consumer Protection, Office of the Attorney General; Joan E. Ohl, Secretary, Department of Health and Human Resources; Randall A. Price, Auditor/ Assistant Director, Financial Conditions Division, West Virginia Insurance Commission; R. H. Rosswurm, State Supreme Court Administration Office; William E. Schneider, Deputy Commissioner of Securities; Paul F. Wilkinson, Director, Department of Transportation, Division of Transportation Planning; Bill Willis, Program Specialist, Energy Efficiency Program

WISCONSIN

Acting Superintendent, Superintendent of Public Instruction; Dean Amhaus, Executive Director, Arts Board, Department of Administration; Kenneth L. Hojnacki, Director, Licensing and Compliance Section; William J. Raftery, State Controller, Department of Administration; Nathaniel E. Robinson, Administrator, Energy and Intergovernmental Relations, Department of Administration; June M. Suhling, Division Administrator, Department of Workforce Development; Charles H. Thompson, Secretary, Department of Transportation; Alan T. Tracy, Secretary, Department of Agriculture, Trade and Consumer Protection; Cate Zeuske, Secretary of Revenue

WYOMING

Johnnie Burton, Director, Department of Revenue; Thomas Cook, Planner/State Intermodal Planning Coordinator, Department of Transportation; Mike Evans, Employment Resources Division, Department of Employment, Research and Planning; David G. Ferrari, State Auditor, Capitol Building; Michael Gagen, State Forester, State Forestry Division; Dale S. Hoffman, Energy Section, Division of Economic and Community Development; Rick Hunnicutt, Business Development Officer, Division of Economic and Community Development; Wayne Liu, Economic Analysis Division, Administration and Information; John P. McBride, Commissioner, Department of Insurance; Ron Micheli, Department of Agriculture; Don Rolston, Director, Department of Health; Sheila Russell, Public Information Specialist, State Library Publications and Marketing Office; Shirley R. Winter, Data/Technology Unit, Department of Education

CONTRIBUTORS

TO THE FIRST EDITION

ALLEN, HAROLD B. Emeritus Professor of English and Linguistics, University of Minnesota (Minneapolis–St. Paul). LANGUAGES.***

BASSETT, T.D. SEYMOUR. Former University Archivist, University of Vermont (Burlington). VERMONT.**

BENSON, MAXINE. Curator of Document Resources, Colorado Historical Society. COLORADO.**

BROWN, RICHARD D. Professor of History, University of Connecticut (Storrs). MASSACHUSETTS.**

CASHIN, EDWARD J. Professor of History, Augusta College. GEORGIA.*

CHANNING, STEVEN A. Professor of History, University of Kentucky (Lexington). KENTUCKY.**

CLARK, CHARLES E. Professor of History, University of New Hampshire (Durham). MAINE.*

COGSWELL, PHILIP, JR. Forum Editor, *The Oregonian*. OREGON.*

CONLEY, PATRICK T. Professor of History and Law, Providence College. RHODE ISLAND.**

CORLEW, ROBERT E. Dean, School of Liberal Arts, Middle Tennessee State University (Murfreesboro). TENNESSEE.*

CREIGH, DOROTHY WEYER. Author and historian; member, Nebraska State Board of Education. NEBRASKA.**

CUNNINGHAM, JOHN T. Author and historian. NEW JERSEY.**

FISHER, PERRY. Director, Columbia Historical Society. DISTRICT OF COLUMBIA.**

FRANTZ, JOE B. Professor of History, University of Texas (Austin). TEXAS.**

GOODELL, LELE. Member, Editorial Board, *Hawaiian Journal of History*. HAWAII (in part).**

GOODRICH, JAMES W. Associate Director, State Historical Society of Missouri. MISSOURI.**

HAMILTON, VIRGINIA. Professor of History, University of Alabama (Birmingham). ALABAMA.**

HAVIGHURST, WALTER. Research Professor of English Emeritus, Miami University (Oxford). OHIO.**

HINTON, HARWOOD P. Editor, *Arizona and the West*, University of Arizona (Tucson). ARIZONA.**

HOOGENBOOM, ARI. Professor of History, Brooklyn College of the City University of New York. PENNSYLVANIA.**

HOOVER, HERBERT T. Professor of History, University of South Dakota (Vermillion). SOUTH DAKOTA.**

HUNT, WILLIAM R. Historian; former Professor of History, University of Alaska. ALASKA.*

JENSEN, DWIGHT. Author and historian. IDAHO.*

JENSEN, RICHARD J. Professor of History, University of Illinois (Chicago). ILLINOIS.*

LARSON, ROBERT W. Professor of History, University of Northern Colorado (Greeley). NEW MEXICO.**

MAPP, ALF J., JR. Author, lecturer, and historian; Professor of English, Creative Writing, and Journalism, Old Dominion University (Norfolk). VIRGINIA.**

MAY, GEORGE S. Professor of History, Eastern Michigan University (Ypsilanti). MICHIGAN.*

MEYER, GLADYS. Professor emeritus, Columbia University. ETHNIC GROUPS.***

MOODY, ERIC N. Historian, Nevada Historical Society. NEVADA.**

MUNROE, JOHN A. H. Rodney Sharp Professor of History, University of Delaware. DELAWARE.**

MURPHY, MARIAM. Associate Editor, *Utah Historical Quarterly*. UTAH.**

O'BRIEN, KATHLEEN ANN. Project Director, Upper Midwest Women's History Center for Teachers. MINNESOTA.**

PADOVER, SAUL K. Distinguished Service Professor Emeritus, Graduate Faculty, New School (New York City). UNITED STATES OF AMERICA.**

PECKHAM, HOWARD H. Professor emeritus, University of Michigan. INDIANA.**

PRYOR, NANCY. Research consultant and librarian, Washington State Library. WASHINGTON.**

RAWLS, JAMES J. Instructor of History, Diablo Valley College (Pleasant Hill). CALIFORNIA.**

RICE, OTIS K. Professor of History, West Virginia Institute of Technology (Montgomery). WEST VIRGINIA.*

RICHMOND, ROBERT W. Assistant Executive Director, Kansas State Historical Society. KANSAS.**

RIGHTER, ROBERT W. Assistant Professor of History, University of Wyoming (Laramie). WYOMING.**

ROTH, DAVID M. Director, Center for Connecticut Studies, Eastern Connecticut State College (Willimantic). CONNECTICUT.*

SCHEFFER, BARBARA MOORE. Feature Writer. OKLAHOMA (in part).*

SCHEFFER, WALTER F. Regents' Professor of Political Science and Director, Graduate Program in Public Administration, University of Oklahoma (Norman). OKLAHOMA (in part).*

SCHMITT, ROBERT C. Hawaii State Statistician. HAWAII (in part).**

SCUDIERE, PAUL J. Senior Historian, New York State Education Department. NEW YORK.**

SKATES, JOHN RAY. Professor of History, University of Southern Mississippi (Hattiesburg). MISSISSIPPI.**

SMITH, DOUG. Writer, *Arkansas Gazette* (Little Rock). ARKANSAS.**

STOUDEMIRE, ROBERT H. Professor of State and Local Government and Senior Research Associate, Bureau of Governmental Research, University of South Carolina (Columbia). SOUTH CAROLINA.*

SULLIVAN, LARRY E. Librarian, New York Historical Society. MARYLAND.**

TAYLOR, JOE GRAY. Professor of History, McNeese State University (Lake Charles). LOUISIANA.**

TEBEAU, CHARLTON W. Emeritus Professor of History, University of Miami. FLORIDA.**

THOMPSON, WILLIAM FLETCHER. Director of Research, State Historical Society of Wisconsin. WISCONSIN.**

VIVO, PAQUITA. Author and consultant. PUERTO RICO.**

WALL, JOSEPH FRAZIER. Professor of History, Grinnell College. IOWA.**

WALLACE, R. STUART. Assistant Director/Editor, New Hampshire Historical Society. NEW HAMPSHIRE.**

WATSON, HARRY L. Assistant Professor of History, University of North Carolina (Chapel Hill). NORTH CAROLINA.*

WEAVER, KENNETH L. Associate Professor of Political Science, Montana State University (Bozeman). MONTANA.**

WILKINS, ROBERT P. Professor of History, University of North Dakota (Grand Forks). NORTH DAKOTA.**

WOODS, BOB. Editor, *Sierra Club Wildlife Involvement News.* FLORA AND FAUNA.***

*Full contributor.
**Consultant contributor.
***Special contributor.

PREFACE

In 1980, editor and publisher Moshe Y. Sachs set out to create the *Worldmark Encyclopedia of the Nations,* a new kind of reference work that would view every nation of the world as if through a "world mirror" and not from the perspective of any one country or group of countries. In 1981, a companion volume, the *Worldmark Encyclopedia of the States,* was introduced. It was selected as an "Outstanding Reference Source" by the Reference Sources Committee of the American Library Association, Reference and Adult Services Division. Gale Research now offers a revised and updated fourth edition of the *Worldmark Encyclopedia of the States.*

The fitness of the United States of America as a subject for encyclopedic study is plain. No discussion of world politics, economics, culture, technology, or military affairs would be complete without an intensive examination of the American achievement. What is not so obvious is why the editors chose to present this work as an encyclopedia of the *states* rather than of the United States. In so doing, they emphasize the fact that the United States is a federal union of separate states with divergent histories, traditions, resources, laws, and economic interests.

Every state, large or small, is treated in an individual chapter, within a framework of 50 standard subject headings; generally, the more populous the state, the longer the article. The District of Columbia and the Commonwealth of Puerto Rico each have their own chapters, and two additional articles describe in summary the other Caribbean and Pacific dependencies. The concluding chapter is an overview of the nation as a whole. Supplementing this textual material are tables of conversions and abbreviations, a glossary, and more than 50 black-and-white maps prepared especially for this encyclopedia.

Publication of this encyclopedia was a collective effort that enlisted the talents of scholars, government agencies, editor-writers, artists, cartographers, typesetters, proofreaders, and many others. Perhaps only those involved in the production of reference books fully appreciate how complex that endeavor can be. Readers customarily expect that a reference book will be correct in every particular; and yet, by the time it has been on the shelves for a few months, a conscientious editor may already have a long list of improvements and corrections to be made in a subsequent edition. We invite you, the reader, to add your suggestions to our list.

Send comments to:

Worldmark Encyclopedia of the States
Gale Research
835 Penobscot Bldg.
Detroit, MI 48226

The Editors

NOTES

GENERAL NOTE: In producing the fourth edition of *Worldmark Encyclopedia of the States,* the editors contacted hundreds of government officials and others with special expertise. In response, over 540 individuals, representing every state in the nation, contributed to this fourth edition by rewriting entries or submitting new, up-to-date information that was used by *Worldmark* editors to revise state articles. Another 36 individuals, many from state libraries, reviewed completed articles for accuracy and quality of content. Space does not permit listing of the hundreds of documents which were consulted for each state's entry. Listed below are notable sources of data which were used in revising a majority of entries.

MAPS: The maps of the states were produced by the University of Akron Laboratory for Cartographic and Spatial Analysis under the direction of Joseph W. Stoll. The maps originated from the United States Geological Survey 1:2,000,000 Digital Line Graphs (DLG). Additional sources used to determine and verify the positioning of text and symbols include 1990 United States Census Data, U.S.G.S. 1:500,000 Topographic State Maps, brochures and maps from the state visitor bureaus, and the 1995 *Rand McNally United States Road Atlas.*

WEIGHTS AND MEASURES: Recognizing the trend toward use of the metric system throughout the United States, the text provides metric equivalents for customary measures of length and area, and both Fahrenheit and Centigrade expressions for temperature. Production figures are expressed exclusively in the prevailing customary units.

LOCATION, SIZE, AND EXTENT: The lengths of interstate boundary segments and the total lengths of state boundaries appear in roman type when derived from official government sources; italic type indicates data derived from other sources. Discrepancies in the boundary lengths of neighboring states as specified by official sources arise from divergent methodologies of measurement.

FLORA AND FAUNA: Discussions of endangered species are based on the *List of Endangered and Threatened Wildlife and Plants* maintained by the Fish and Wildlife Service of the US Department of the Interior, and on data supplied by the states.

POPULATION: Population figures are from the 1990 *Decennial Census of Population,* the 1996 *Current Population Survey,* and the 1995 *Time Series of Resident Population of Places: April 1, 1990 to July 1, 1994.* Tables of counties, county seats, county areas, and county populations accompany the articles on the 14 most populous states; the editors regret that space limitations prevented the publication of such a table for each state. Because of rounding, county areas in these tables may not add to the total.

LANGUAGES: Examples of lexical and pronunciation patterns cited in the text are meant to suggest the historic development of principal linguistic features and should not be taken as a comprehensive statement of current usage. Data on languages spoken in the home were obtained from the "Listing of Selected Languages Spoken by Persons 3 Years Old and Over by State: 1990 Census," issued by the US Bureau of the Census.

JUDICIAL SYSTEM: *Uniform Crime Reports for the United States,* published annually by the Federal Bureau of Investigation and embodying the FBI Crime Index (tabulations of offenses known to the police), was the principal source for the crime statistics cited in the text.

ARMED FORCES: Estimates published by the Veterans Administration of the number of veterans of US military service in each state represent extrapolations from 1990 census data.

ENERGY AND POWER: Data for proved reserves and production of fossil fuels were derived from publications of the American Gas Association, American Petroleum Institute, National Coal Association, and US Department of Energy. Data on nuclear power facilities were obtained from the Nuclear Information and Resource Service and from state sources.

HEALTH: The principal statistical sources for hospitals and medical personnel were annual publications of the American Dental Association, American Hospital Association, and American Medical Association.

LIBRARIES AND MUSEUMS: In most cases, library and museum names are listed in the *American Library Directory* by R. R. Bowker, and the *Official Museum Directory*, compiled by the National Register Publishing Co. in cooperation with the American Association of Museums.

PRESS: Circulation data follow the 1997 *Editor & Publisher International Yearbook*.

FAMOUS PERSONS: Entries are current through July 1997. Where a person described in one state is known to have been born in another, the state of birth follows the personal name, in parentheses.

BIBLIOGRAPHY: Bibliographies are intended as a guide to landmark works on each state for further research and not as a listing of sources in preparing the articles. Such listings would have far exceeded space limitations.

GUIDE TO STATE ARTICLES

All information contained within a state article is uniformly keyed by means of small superior numerals to the left of the subject headings. A heading such as "Population," for example, carries the same key numeral (6) in every article. Thus, to find information about the population of Alabama, consult the table of contents for the page number where the Alabama article begins and look for section 6 thereunder.

Introductory matter for each state includes: Origin of state name
Nickname
Capital
Date and order of statehood
Song
Motto
Flag
Official seal
Symbols (animal, tree, flower, etc.)
Legal holidays
Time zone

FLAG COLOR SYMBOLS

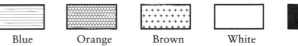

| Yellow | Red | Green | Blue | Orange | Brown | White | Black |

SUBJECT HEADINGS IN NUMERICAL ORDER

1 Location, size, and extent
2 Topography
3 Climate
4 Flora and fauna
5 Environmental protection
6 Population
7 Ethnic groups
8 Languages
9 Religions
10 Transportation
11 History
12 State government
13 Political parties
14 Local government
15 State services
16 Judicial system
17 Armed forces
18 Migration
19 Intergovernmental cooperation
20 Economy
21 Income
22 Labor
23 Agriculture
24 Animal husbandry
25 Fishing
26 Forestry
27 Mining
28 Energy and power
29 Industry
30 Commerce
31 Consumer protection
32 Banking
33 Insurance
34 Securities
35 Public finance
36 Taxation
37 Economic policy
38 Health
39 Social welfare
40 Housing
41 Education
42 Arts
43 Libraries and museums
44 Communications
45 Press
46 Organizations
47 Tourism, travel, and recreation
48 Sports
49 Famous persons
50 Bibliography

SUBJECT HEADINGS IN ALPHABETICAL ORDER

Agriculture 23
Animal husbandry 24
Armed forces 17
Arts 42
Banking 32
Bibliography 50
Climate 3
Commerce 30
Communications 44
Consumer protection 31
Economic policy 37
Economy 20
Education 41
Energy and power 28
Environmental protection 5
Ethnic groups 7
Famous persons 49
Fishing 25
Flora and fauna 4
Forestry 26
Health 38
History 11
Housing 40
Income 21
Industry 29
Insurance 33
Intergovernmental cooperation 19
Judicial system 16
Labor 22
Languages 8
Libraries and museums 43
Local government 14
Location, size, and extent 1
Migration 18
Mining 27
Organizations 46
Political parties 13
Population 6
Press 45
Public finance 35
Religions 9
Securities 34
Social welfare 39
Sports 48
State government 12
State services 15
Taxation 36
Topography 2
Tourism, travel, and recreation 47
Transportation 10

EXPLANATION OF SYMBOLS

A fiscal split year is indicated by a stroke (e.g. 1994/95).
A dollar sign ($) stands for US$ unless otherwise indicated.
Note that 1 billion = 1,000 million = 10^9.
The use of a small dash (e.g., 1990–94) normally signifies the full period of calendar years covered (including the end year indicated).

CONVERSION TABLES*

LENGTH
1 centimeter ....0.3937 inch
1 centimeter .... 0.03280833 foot
1 meter (100 centimeters) ....3.280833 feet
1 meter...1.093611 US yards
1 kilometer (1,000 meters) ....0.62137 statute mile
1 kilometer.................................0.539957 nautical mile
1 inch ....2.540005 centimeters
1 foot (12 inches) ....30.4801 centimeters
1 US yard (3 feet) ....0.914402 meter
1 statute mile (5,280 feet; 1,760 yards) .... 1.609347 kilometers
1 British mile .... 1.609344 kilometers
1 nautical mile (1.1508 statute miles
or 6,076.10333 feet) .... 1.852 kilometers
1 British nautical mile (6,080 feet) .... 1.85319 kilometers

AREA
1 sq centimeter .... 0.154999 sq inch
1 sq meter (10,000 sq centimeters) ....10.76387 sq feet
1 sq meter ....1.1959585 sq yards
1 hectare (10,000 sq meters) ....2.47104 acres
1 sq kilometer (100 hectares) ....0.386101 sq mile
1 sq inch ....6.451626 sq centimeters
1 sq foot (144 sq inches) .... 0.092903 sq meter
1 sq yard (9 sq feet)................................. 0.836131 sq meter
1 acre (4,840 sq yards) .... 0.404687 hectare
1 sq mile (640 acres) ....2.589998 sq kilometers

VOLUME
1 cubic centimeter ....0.061023 cubic inch
1 cubic meter
(1,000,000 cubic centimeters) ....35.31445 cubic feet
1 cubic meter...1.307943 cubic yards
1 cubic inch ....16.387162 cubic centimeters
1 cubic foot (1,728 cubic inches).............................0.028317 cubic meter
1 cubic yard (27 cubic feet) ....0.764559 cubic meter

LIQUID MEASURE
1 liter .... 0.8799 imperial quart
1 liter .... 1.05671 US quarts
1 hectoliter ....21.9975 imperial gallons
1 hectoliter .... 26.4178 US gallons
1 imperial quart .... 1.136491 liters
1 US quart... 0.946333 liter
1 imperial gallon ....0.04546 hectoliter
1 US gallon..0.037853 hectoliter

WEIGHT
1 kilogram (1,000 grams) ....35.27396 avoirdupois ounces
1 kilogram...32.15074 troy ounces
1 kilogram..................................2.204622 avoirdupois pounds
1 quintal (100 kg) ....220.4622 avoirdupois pounds
1 quintal.......................................1.9684125 hundredweights
1 metric ton (1,000 kg) ....1.102311 short tons

1 metric ton.. 0.984206 long ton
1 avoirdupois ounce .... 0.0283495 kilogram
1 troy ounce .... 0.0311035 kilogram
1 avoirdupois pound .... 0.453592 kilogram
1 avoirdupois pound .... 0.00453592 quintal
1 hundred weight (cwt., 112 lb) .... 0.50802 quintal
1 short ton (2,000 lb) ....0.907185 metric ton
1 long ton (2,240 lb) ....1.016047 metric tons

ELECTRIC ENERGY
1 horsepower (hp) .... 0.7457 kilowatt
1 kilowatt (kw) .... 1.34102 horsepower

TEMPERATURE
Celsius (C)..Fahrenheit–32 x 5/9
Fahrenheit (F) .... 9/5 Celsius + 32

BUSHELS

	LB	METRIC TON	BUSHELS PER METRIC TON
Barley (US)	48	0.021772	45.931
(UK)	50	0.022680	44.092
Corn (UK, US)	56	0.025401	39.368
Linseed (UK)	52	0.023587	42.396
(Australia, US)	56	0.025401	39.368
Oats (US)	32	0.014515	68.894
(Canada)	34	0.015422	64.842
Potatoes (UK, US)	60	0.027216	36.743
Rice (Australia)	42	0.019051	52.491
(US)	45	0.020412	48.991
Rye (UK, US)	56	0.025401	39.368
(Australia)	60	0.027216	36.743
Soybeans (US)	60	0.027216	36.743
Wheat (UK, US)	60	0.027216	36.743

BAGS OF COFFEE

	LB	KG	BAGS PER METRIC TON
Brazil, Columbia Mexico, Venezuela	132.28	60	16.667
El Salvador	152.12	69	14.493
Haiti	185.63	84.2	11.876

BALES OF COTTON

	LB	METRIC TON	BALES PER METRIC TON
India	392	0.177808	5.624
Brazil	397	0.180000	5.555
US (net)	480	0.217724	4.593
US (gross)	500	0.226796	4.409

PETROLEUM
One barrel = 42 US gallons = 34.97 imperial gallons = 158.99 liters = 0.15899 cubic meter (or 1 cubic meter = 6.2898 barrels).

*Includes units of measure cited in the text, as well as certain other units employed in parts of the English-speaking world.

GENERAL NOTE: In producing the fourth edition of *Worldmark Encyclopedia of the States,* the editors contacted hundreds of government officials and others with special expertise. In response, over 540 individuals, representing every state in the nation, contributed to this fourth edition by rewriting entries or submitting new, up-to-date information that was used by *Worldmark* editors to revise state articles. Another 36 individuals, many from state libraries, reviewed completed articles for accuracy and quality of content. Space does not permit listing of the hundreds of documents which were consulted for each state's entry. Listed below are notable sources of data which were used in revising a majority of entries.

MAPS: The maps of the states were produced by the University of Akron Laboratory for Cartographic and Spatial Analysis under the direction of Joseph W. Stoll. The maps originated from the United States Geological Survey 1:2,000,000 Digital Line Graphs (DLG). Additional sources used to determine and verify the positioning of text and symbols include 1990 United States Census Data, U.S.G.S. 1:500,000 Topographic State Maps, brochures and maps from the state visitor bureaus, and the 1995 *Rand McNally United States Road Atlas.*

WEIGHTS AND MEASURES: Recognizing the trend toward use of the metric system throughout the United States, the text provides metric equivalents for customary measures of length and area, and both Fahrenheit and Centigrade expressions for temperature. Production figures are expressed exclusively in the prevailing customary units.

LOCATION, SIZE, AND EXTENT: The lengths of interstate boundary segments and the total lengths of state boundaries appear in roman type when derived from official government sources; italic type indicates data derived from other sources. Discrepancies in the boundary lengths of neighboring states as specified by official sources arise from divergent methodologies of measurement.

FLORA AND FAUNA: Discussions of endangered species are based on the *List of Endangered and Threatened Wildlife and Plants* maintained by the Fish and Wildlife Service of the US Department of the Interior, and on data supplied by the states.

POPULATION: Population figures are from the 1990 *Decennial Census of Population,* the 1996 *Current Population Survey,* and the 1995 *Time Series of Resident Population of Places: April 1, 1990 to July 1, 1994.* Tables of counties, county seats, county areas, and county populations accompany the articles on the 14 most populous states; the editors regret that space limitations prevented the publication of such a table for each state. Because of rounding, county areas in these tables may not add to the total.

LANGUAGES: Examples of lexical and pronunciation patterns cited in the text are meant to suggest the historic development of principal linguistic features and should not be taken as a comprehensive statement of current usage. Data on languages spoken in the home were obtained from the "Listing of Selected Languages Spoken by Persons 3 Years Old and Over by State: 1990 Census," issued by the US Bureau of the Census.

JUDICIAL SYSTEM: *Uniform Crime Reports for the United States,* published annually by the Federal Bureau of Investigation and embodying the FBI Crime Index (tabulations of offenses known to the police), was the principal source for the crime statistics cited in the text.

ARMED FORCES: Estimates published by the Veterans Administration of the number of veterans of US military service in each state represent extrapolations from 1990 census data.

ENERGY AND POWER: Data for proved reserves and production of fossil fuels were derived from publications of the American Gas Association, American Petroleum Institute, National Coal Association, and US Department of Energy. Data on nuclear power facilities were obtained from the Nuclear Information and Resource Service and from state sources.

HEALTH: The principal statistical sources for hospitals and medical personnel were annual publications of the American Dental Association, American Hospital Association, and American Medical Association.

LIBRARIES AND MUSEUMS: In most cases, library and museum names are listed in the *American Library Directory* by R. R. Bowker, and the *Official Museum Directory,* compiled by the National Register Publishing Co. in cooperation with the American Association of Museums.

PRESS: Circulation data follow the 1997 *Editor & Publisher International Yearbook*.

FAMOUS PERSONS: Entries are current through July 1997. Where a person described in one state is known to have been born in another, the state of birth follows the personal name, in parentheses.

BIBLIOGRAPHY: Bibliographies are intended as a guide to landmark works on each state for further research and not as a listing of sources in preparing the articles. Such listings would have far exceeded space limitations.

GUIDE TO STATE ARTICLES

All information contained within a state article is uniformly keyed by means of small superior numerals to the left of the subject headings. A heading such as "Population," for example, carries the same key numeral (6) in every article. Thus, to find information about the population of Alabama, consult the table of contents for the page number where the Alabama article begins and look for section 6 thereunder.

Introductory matter for each state includes: Origin of state name
Nickname
Capital
Date and order of statehood
Song
Motto
Flag
Official seal
Symbols (animal, tree, flower, etc.)
Legal holidays
Time zone

FLAG COLOR SYMBOLS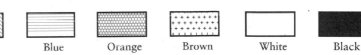

Yellow   Red   Green   Blue   Orange   Brown   White   Black

SUBJECT HEADINGS IN NUMERICAL ORDER

1 Location, size, and extent	27 Mining
2 Topography	28 Energy and power
3 Climate	29 Industry
4 Flora and fauna	30 Commerce
5 Environmental protection	31 Consumer protection
6 Population	32 Banking
7 Ethnic groups	33 Insurance
8 Languages	34 Securities
9 Religions	35 Public finance
10 Transportation	36 Taxation
11 History	37 Economic policy
12 State government	38 Health
13 Political parties	39 Social welfare
14 Local government	40 Housing
15 State services	41 Education
16 Judicial system	42 Arts
17 Armed forces	43 Libraries and museums
18 Migration	44 Communications
19 Intergovernmental cooperation	45 Press
20 Economy	46 Organizations
21 Income	47 Tourism, travel, and
22 Labor	recreation
23 Agriculture	48 Sports
24 Animal husbandry	49 Famous persons
25 Fishing	50 Bibliography
26 Forestry	

SUBJECT HEADINGS IN ALPHABETICAL ORDER

Agriculture	23	Intergovernmental	
Animal husbandry	24	cooperation	19
Armed forces	17	Judicial system	16
Arts	42	Labor	22
Banking	32	Languages	8
Bibliography	50	Libraries and museums	43
Climate	3	Local government	14
Commerce	30	Location, size, and extent	1
Communications	44	Migration	18
Consumer protection	31	Mining	27
Economic policy	37	Organizations	46
Economy	20	Political parties	13
Education	41	Population	6
Energy and power	28	Press	45
Environmental protection	5	Public finance	35
Ethnic groups	7	Religions	9
Famous persons	49	Securities	34
Fishing	25	Social welfare	39
Flora and fauna	4	Sports	48
Forestry	26	State government	12
Health	38	State services	15
History	11	Taxation	36
Housing	40	Topography	2
Income	21	Tourism, travel, and	
Industry	29	recreation	47
Insurance	33	Transportation	10

EXPLANATION OF SYMBOLS

A fiscal split year is indicated by a stroke (e.g. 1994/95).
A dollar sign ($) stands for US$ unless otherwise indicated.
Note that 1 billion = 1,000 million = 10^9.
The use of a small dash (e.g., 1990–94) normally signifies the full period
of calendar years covered (including the end year indicated).

CONVERSION TABLES*

LENGTH
1 centimeter ....0.3937 inch
1 centimeter .... 0.03280833 foot
1 meter (100 centimeters).....................................3.280833 feet
1 meter..1.093611 US yards
1 kilometer (1,000 meters) ....0.62137 statute mile
1 kilometer...0.539957 nautical mile
1 inch..2.540005 centimeters
1 foot (12 inches) .... 30.4801 centimeters
1 US yard (3 feet) ....0.914402 meter
1 statute mile (5,280 feet; 1,760 yards) .... 1.609347 kilometers
1 British mile .... 1.609344 kilometers
1 nautical mile (1.1508 statute miles
or 6,076.10333 feet) .... 1.852 kilometers
1 British nautical mile (6,080 feet) .... 1.85319 kilometers

AREA
1 sq centimeter .... 0.154999 sq inch
1 sq meter (10,000 sq centimeters) ....10.76387 sq feet
1 sq meter ....1.1959585 sq yards
1 hectare (10,000 sq meters) ....2.47104 acres
1 sq kilometer (100 hectares) ....0.386101 sq mile
1 sq inch...6.451626 sq centimeters
1 sq foot (144 sq inches) .... 0.092903 sq meter
1 sq yard (9 sq feet).. 0.836131 sq meter
1 acre (4,840 sq yards) .... 0.404687 hectare
1 sq mile (640 acres) ....2.589998 sq kilometers

VOLUME
1 cubic centimeter ....0.061023 cubic inch
1 cubic meter
(1,000,000 cubic centimeters) ....35.31445 cubic feet
1 cubic meter...1.307943 cubic yards
1 cubic inch..16.387162 cubic centimeters
1 cubic foot (1,728 cubic inches)............................0.028317 cubic meter
1 cubic yard (27 cubic feet) ....0.764559 cubic meter

LIQUID MEASURE
1 liter .... 0.8799 imperial quart
1 liter .... 1.05671 US quarts
1 hectoliter ....21.9975 imperial gallons
1 hectoliter ....26.4178 US gallons
1 imperial quart .... 1.136491 liters
1 US quart.. 0.946333 liter
1 imperial gallon ....0.04546 hectoliter
1 US gallon...0.037853 hectoliter

WEIGHT
1 kilogram (1,000 grams)..............................35.27396 avoirdupois ounces
1 kilogram...32.15074 troy ounces
1 kilogram...2.204622 avoirdupois pounds
1 quintal (100 kg) ....220.4622 avoirdupois pounds
1 quintal...1.9684125 hundredweights
1 metric ton (1,000 kg) .... 1.102311 short tons
1 metric ton.. 0.984206 long ton
1 avoirdupois ounce .... 0.0283495 kilogram
1 troy ounce .... 0.0311035 kilogram
1 avoirdupois pound .... 0.453592 kilogram
1 avoirdupois pound .... 0.00453592 quintal
1 hundred weight (cwt., 112 lb) .... 0.50802 quintal
1 short ton (2,000 lb) .... 0.907185 metric ton
1 long ton (2,240 lb) ....1.016047 metric tons

ELECTRIC ENERGY
1 horsepower (hp) .... 0.7457 kilowatt
1 kilowatt (kw).. 1.34102 horsepower

TEMPERATURE
Celsius (C)..Fahrenheit–32 x 5/9
Fahrenheit (F).. 9/5 Celsius + 32

BUSHELS

	LB	METRIC TON	BUSHELS PER METRIC TON
Barley (US)	48	0.021772	45.931
(UK)	50	0.022680	44.092
Corn (UK, US)	56	0.025401	39.368
Linseed (UK)	52	0.023587	42.396
(Australia, US)	56	0.025401	39.368
Oats (US)	32	0.014515	68.894
(Canada)	34	0.015422	64.842
Potatoes (UK, US)	60	0.027216	36.743
Rice (Australia)	42	0.019051	52.491
(US)	45	0.020412	48.991
Rye (UK, US)	56	0.025401	39.368
(Australia)	60	0.027216	36.743
Soybeans (US)	60	0.027216	36.743
Wheat (UK, US)	60	0.027216	36.743

BAGS OF COFFEE

	LB	KG	BAGS PER METRIC TON
Brazil, Columbia Mexico, Venezuela	132.28	60	16.667
El Salvador	152.12	69	14.493
Haiti	185.63	84.2	11.876

BALES OF COTTON

	LB	METRIC TON	BALES PER METRIC TON
India	392	0.177808	5.624
Brazil	397	0.180000	5.555
US (net)	480	0.217724	4.593
US (gross)	500	0.226796	4.409

PETROLEUM
One barrel = 42 US gallons = 34.97 imperial gallons = 158.99 liters = 0.15899 cubic meter (or 1 cubic meter = 6.2898 barrels).

*Includes units of measure cited in the text, as well as certain other units employed in parts of the English-speaking world.

ALABAMA

State of Alabama

ORIGIN OF STATE NAME: Probably after the Alabama Indian tribe. **NICKNAME:** The Heart of Dixie. **CAPITAL:** Montgomery. **ENTERED UNION:** 14 December 1819 (22d). **SONG:** "Alabama." **MOTTO:** *Audemus jura nostra defendere* (We dare defend our rights). **COAT OF ARMS:** Two eagles, symbolizing courage, support a shield bearing the emblems of the five governments (France, England, Spain, Confederacy, US) that have held sovereignty over Alabama. Above the shield is a sailing vessel modeled upon the ships of the first French settlers of Alabama; beneath the shield is the state motto. **FLAG:** Crimson cross of St. Andrew on a square white field. **OFFICIAL SEAL:** Map of Alabama, including names of major rivers and neighboring states, surrounded by the words "Alabama Great Seal." **BIRD:** Yellowhammer. **FISH:** Tarpon. **FLOWER:** Camellia. **TREE:** Southern (longleaf) pine. **STONE:** Marble. **MINERAL:** Hematite. **LEGAL HOLIDAYS:** New Year's Day, 1 January; Birthdays of Robert E. Lee and Martin Luther King, Jr., 3d Monday in January; George Washington's/Thomas Jefferson's Birthdays, 3d Monday in February; Mardi Gras, February or March; Confederate Memorial Day, 4th Monday in April; Jefferson Davis's Birthday, 1st Monday in June; Independence Day, 4 July; Labor Day, 1st Monday in September; Columbus Day, 2d Monday in October; Veterans Day, 11 November; Thanksgiving Day, 4th Thursday in November; Christmas Day, 25 December. **TIME:** 6 AM CST = noon GMT.

¹LOCATION, SIZE, AND EXTENT

Located in the eastern south-central US, Alabama ranks 29th in size among the 50 states.

The total area of Alabama is 51,705 sq mi (133,915 sq km), of which land constitutes 50,767 sq mi (131,486 sq km) and inland water 938 sq mi (2,429 sq km). Alabama extends roughly 200 mi (320 km) E-W; the maximum N-S extension is 300 mi (480 km). Alabama is bordered on the N by Tennessee; on the E by Georgia (with part of the line formed by the Chattahoochee River); on the s by Florida (with part of the line defined by the Perdido River) and the Gulf of Mexico; and on the w by Mississippi (with the northernmost part of the line passing through the Tennessee River).

Dauphin Island, in the Gulf of Mexico, is the largest offshore island. The total boundary length of Alabama is 1,044 mi (1,680 km). The state's geographic center is in Chilton County, 12 mi (19 km) sw of Clanton.

²TOPOGRAPHY

Alabama is divided into four major physiographic regions: the Gulf Coastal Plain, Piedmont Plateau, Ridge and Valley section, and Appalachian (or Cumberland) Plateau. The physical characteristics of each province have significantly affected settlement and industrial development patterns within the state.

The coastal plain, comprising the southern half of Alabama, consists primarily of lowlands and low ridges. Included within the coastal plain is the Black Belt—historically, the center of cotton production and plantation slavery in Alabama—an area of rich, chalky soil that stretches across the entire width of central Alabama. Just to the north, the piedmont of east-central Alabama contains rolling hills and valleys. Alabama's highest elevation, Cheaha Mountain, 2,407 feet (734 meters) above sea level, is located at the northern edge of this region. North and west of the piedmont is a series of parallel ridges and valleys running in a northeast-southwest direction. Mountain ranges in this area include the Red, Shades, Oak, Lookout, and other noteworthy southern extensions of the Appalachian chain; elevations of 1,200 feet (366 meters) are found as far south as Birmingham. The Appalachian Plateau covers most of northwestern Alabama, with a portion of the Highland Rim in the extreme north near the Tennessee border. The floodplain of the Tennessee River cuts a wide swath across both these northern regions.

The largest lake wholly within Alabama is Guntersville Lake, covering about 108 sq mi (280 sq km) and formed during the development of the Tennessee River region by the Tennessee Valley Authority (TVA). The TVA lakes—also including Wheeler, Pickwick, and Wilson—are all long and narrow, fanning outward along a line that runs from the northeast corner of the state westward to Florence.

The longest rivers are the Alabama, extending from the mid-central region to the Mobile River for a distance of about 160 mi (260 km); the Tennessee, which flows across northern Alabama for about the same distance; and the Tombigbee, which flows south from north-central Alabama for some 150 mi (240 km). The Alabama and Tombigbee rivers, which come together to form the Mobile River, and the Tensaw River flow into Mobile Bay, an arm of the Gulf of Mexico.

About 450 million years ago, Alabama was covered by a warm, shallow sea. Over millions of years, heavy rains washed gravel, sand, and clay from higher elevations onto the rock floor of the sea to help form the foundation of modern Alabama. The skeletons and shells of sea animals, composed of limy material from rocks that had been worn away by water, settled into great thicknesses of limestone and dolomite, Numerous caves and sinkholes formed as water slowly eroded the limestone subsurface of northern Alabama. Archaeologists believe that Russell Cave, in northeastern Alabama, was the earliest site of human habitation in the southeastern US. Other major caves in northern Alabama are Manitou and Sequoyah; near Childersburg is DeSoto Caverns, a huge onyx cave once considered a sacred place by Creek Indians.

Wheeler Dam on the Tennessee River is now a national historic monument. Other major dams include Guntersville, Martin, Millers Ferry, Jordan, Mitchell, and Holt.

³CLIMATE

Alabama's three climatic divisions are the lower coastal plain, largely subtropical and strongly influenced by the Gulf of Mexico; the northern plateau, marked by occasional snowfall in winter; and the Black Belt and upper coastal plain, lying between the two extremes. Among the major population centers, Birmingham has an annual mean temperature of 62°F (17°C), with a normal July daily maximum of 90°F (32°C) and a normal January daily minimum of 34°F (1°C). Montgomery has an annual mean of 65°F (18°C), with a normal July daily maximum of 91°F (33°C) and a normal January daily minimum of 37°F (3°C). The mean in Mobile is 67°F (19°C), with a normal July daily maximum of 91°F (33°C) and a normal January daily minimum of 41°F (51°C). The record low temperature for the state is −27°F (−33°C), registered at New Market, in the northeastern corner, on 30 January 1966; the all-time high is 112°F (44°C), registered at Centreville, in the state's midsection, on 5 September 1925. Mobile, one of the rainiest cities in the US, recorded an average precipitation of 65 in (165 cm) a year between 1951 and 1980.

Two of the most destructive hurricanes to hit Alabama were Camille in August 1969 and Frederic in September 1979, the latter causing extensive property damage in the Mobile Bay area. In 1995, the state was hit by 37 tornadoes.

⁴FLORA AND FAUNA

Alabama was once covered by vast forests of pine, which still form the largest proportion of the state's forest growth. Alabama also has an abundance of poplar, cypress, hickory, oak, and various gum trees. Red cedar grows throughout the state; southern white cedar is found in the southwest, hemlock in the north. Other native trees include hackberry, ash, and holly, with species of palmetto and palm in the Gulf Coast region. There are more than 150 shrubs, mountain laurel and rhododendron among them. Cultivated plants include wisteria and camellia, the state flower.

In a state where large herds of bison, elk, bear, and deer once roamed, only the white-tailed deer remains abundant. Other mammals still found are the Florida panther, bobcat, beaver, muskrat, and most species of weasel. The fairly common raccoon, opossum, rabbit, squirrel, and red and gray foxes are also native, while nutria and armadillo have been introduced to the state. Alabama's birds include golden and bald eagles, osprey and various other hawks, yellowhammer or flicker (the state bird), and black and white warblers; game birds include quail, duck, wild turkey, and goose. Freshwater fish such as bream, shad, bass, and sucker are common. Along the Gulf Coast there are seasonal runs of tarpon (the state fish), pompano, redfish, and bonito.

Endangered or threatened animals include the fine-rayed and shiny pigtoe, 8 kinds of pearly mussels, 3 kinds of darters, chub spotfin, Alabama cavefish, red hills salamander, eastern indigo snake, American alligator, ivory-billed and red-cockaded woodpecker, bald eagle, brown pelican, wood stork, red wolf, and Florida panther.

⁵ENVIRONMENTAL PROTECTION

Under the 1982 Alabama Environmental Management Act, the Alabama Environmental Management Commission was created and the Alabama Department of Environmental Management (ADEM) was established. The ADEM absorbed several commissions, programs, and agencies that had been responsible for Alabama's environment.

The Environmental Commission, whose seven members are appointed to six year terms by the governor and approved by the Alabama Senate, is charged with managing the state's land, air, and water resources. The ADEM administers all major federal environmental groups including the Clean Air Act, Safe Drinking Water Act, and solid and hazardous waste laws. The most active environmental groups in the state are the Alabama Environmental Council, Sierra Club, League of Women Voters, Alabama Audubon Council, and Alabama Rivers Alliance.

Major concerns of environmentalists in the state are the improvement of land-use planning and the protection of groundwater. Another issue is the transportation, storage, and disposal of hazardous wastes. In 1995, there were 13 superfund sites in Alabama. One of the nation's five largest commercial hazardous waste sites is in Emelle, in Sumter County. Alabama's solid waste stream is 4.500 tons a year (1.10 tons per capita). There are 108 municipal land fills and 8 curbside recycling programs in the state. Air quality is generally satisfactory, with only one area of the state (the Birmingham metropolitan area, including Jefferson and Shelby counties) not meeting the ozone standard as of 1997; ADEM is in the process of requesting that the US EPA classify the city as having achieved air quality attainment.

⁶POPULATION

Alabama ranked 22d in population among the 50 states in 1990 with a census total of 4,040,587, a 3.8% increase since 1980. In 1996 Alabama had an estimated population of 4,273,084, a 5.8% increase over 1990.

Alabama experienced its greatest population growth between 1810 and 1820, following the defeat of the Creek Nation by General Andrew Jackson and his troops. Population in what is now Alabama boomed from 9,046 in 1810 to 127,901 in 1820, as migrants from older states on the eastern seaboard poured into the territory formerly occupied by the Creek Indians. Thousands of farmers, hoping to find fertile land or to become wealthy cotton planters, brought their families and often their slaves into the young state, more than doubling Alabama's population between 1820 and 1830. By 1860, Alabama had almost 1,000,000 residents, nearly one-half of whom were black slaves. The Civil War brought Alabama's population growth almost to a standstill, largely because of heavy losses on the battlefield. The total population gain between 1860 and 1870 was only about 30,000; whereas between 1870 and 1970, Alabama's population rose 150,000–300,000 every decade. During the 1980s the population increased 148,000.

In 1990, Alabama had a population density of 79.6 persons per sq mi (30.6 per sq km). About 2 out of every 3 Alabamians lived in urban areas in 1990. First in size among Alabama's metropolitan areas comes greater Birmingham, which had 881,761 residents in 1995. Other major metropolitan areas were greater Mobile, 517,611; and greater Montgomery, 315,332. Birmingham proper had a population of 264,527 in 1994. The next largest cities in 1994 were Mobile proper, 204,490; Montgomery proper, 195,471; and Huntsville, 160,325.

⁷ETHNIC GROUPS

Alabama's population is largely divided between whites of English and Scotch-Irish descent, and blacks descended from African slaves. The 1990 census counted about 17,000 Indians, mostly of Creek or Cherokee descent. Creek Indians are centered around the small community of Poarch in southern Alabama; most of the Cherokee live in the northeastern part of the state.

The black population of Alabama in 1990 was estimated at 1,021,000, about 25% of the total population. As of 1990, Birmingham was 64% nonwhite, Mobile 40%, and Montgomery 43%. As before the Civil War, rural blacks are most heavily represented in the Black Belt of central Alabama.

In 1990, Alabama had 3,686 Asian Indians, 3,969 Koreans, and 3,529 Chinese; the population of Hispanic origin was about 25,000. All told, the foreign-born numbered 43,533 (1% of the state's population) in 1990. Among persons reporting a single

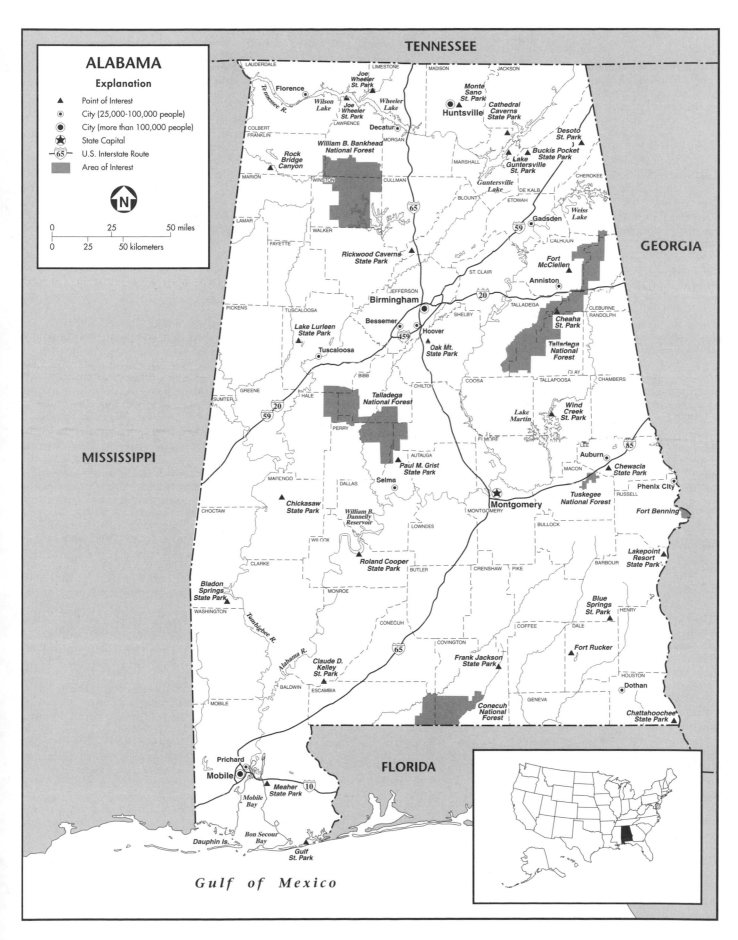

ALABAMA

Explanation

▲ Point of Interest
◉ City (25,000-100,000 people)
◉ City (more than 100,000 people)
★ State Capital
—65— U.S. Interstate Route
■ Area of Interest

N

0   25   50 miles
0   25   50 kilometers

TENNESSEE

LAUDERDALE
Florence
LIMESTONE
Wilson Lake
Joe Wheeler St. Park
Wheeler Lake
Joe Wheeler St. Park
Decatur
LAWRENCE
COLBERT
FRANKLIN
MORGAN
MADISON
Monte Sano St. Park
Huntsville
JACKSON
Cathedral Caverns State Park
Desoto St. Park
Buckis Pocket State Park
Lake Guntersville St. Park
Guntersville Lake
MARSHALL
DE KALB
CHEROKEE

William B. Bankhead National Forest

MARION
Rock Bridge Canyon
WINSTON
CULLMAN
BLOUNT
ETOWAH
Weiss Lake
Gadsden
CALHOUN
59
GEORGIA

LAMAR
FAYETTE
WALKER
Rickwood Caverns State Park
ST. CLAIR
Fort McClellen
Anniston

PICKENS
TUSCALOOSA
JEFFERSON
Birmingham
Bessemer
Hoover
459
SHELBY
20
TALLADEGA
Cheaha St. Park
CLEBURNE
RANDOLPH
Talladega National Forest

Lake Lurleen State Park
Tuscaloosa
Oak Mt. State Park
BIBB
CHILTON
COOSA
CLAY
CHAMBERS

GREENE
HALE
PERRY
Talladega National Forest
Lake Martin
Wind Creek St. Park
TALLAPOOSA

SUMTER
20
59

MARENGO
DALLAS
AUTAUGA
Paul M. Grist State Park
Selma
ELMORE
MACON
LEE
85
Auburn
Chewacla State Park
Phenix City
RUSSELL

CHOCTAW
Chickasaw State Park
William B. Dannelly Reservoir
LOWNDES
Montgomery
MONTGOMERY
BULLOCK
Tuskegee National Forest
Fort Benning

WILCOX
CLARKE
MONROE
Roland Cooper State Park
BUTLER
CRENSHAW
PIKE
BARBOUR
Lakepoint Resort State Park

Bladon Springs State Park
WASHINGTON
Tombigbee R.
CONECUH
Blue Springs St. Park
HENRY

Alabama R.
Claude D. Kelley St. Park
BALDWIN
ESCAMBIA
65
COVINGTON
COFFEE
DALE
Fort Rucker
Frank Jackson State Park
HOUSTON

MOBILE
Conecuh National Forest
GENEVA
Dothan
Chattahoochee State Park

Prichard
Mobile
Meaher State Park
10
FLORIDA

Mobile Bay
Dauphin Is.
Bon Secour Bay
Gulf St. Park

Gulf of Mexico

ancestry group, the leaders were Irish, 617,065; and English, 479,499.

Alabama's Cajuns, of uncertain racial origin (Anglo-Saxon, French, Spanish, Choctaw, Apache, and African elements may all be represented), are ethnically unrelated to the Cajuns of Louisiana. Numbering perhaps 5,700, they live primarily in the pine woods area of upper Mobile and lower Washington counties. Many Alabama Cajuns suffer from poverty, poor health, and malnutrition.

8LANGUAGES

Four Indian tribes—the Creek, Chickasaw, Choctaw, and Cherokee—occupied the four quarters of Alabama as white settlement began, but by treaty agreement they were moved westward between 1814 and 1835, leaving behind such place-names as Alabama, Talladega, Mobile, and Tuscaloosa.

Alabama English is predominantly Southern, with a transition zone between it and a smaller area into which South Midland speech was taken across the border from Tennessee. Some features common to both dialects occur throughout the state, such as *croker sack* (burlap bag), *batter cakes* (made of cornmeal), *harp* (harmonica), and *snap beans*. In the major Southern speech region are found the decreasing loss of final /r/, the /boyd/ pronunciation of *bird, soft peach* (freestone), *press peach* (clingstone), *mosquito hawk* (dragonfly), *fire dogs* (andirons), and *gopher* (burrowing turtle). In the northern third of the state are found South Midland *arm* and *barb* rhyming with *form* and *orb, redworm* (earthworm), *peckerwood* (woodpecker), *snake doctor* and *snake feeder* (dragonfly), *tow sack* (burlap bag), *plum peach* (clingstone), *French harp* (harmonica), and *dog irons* (andirons).

Alabama has experienced only minor foreign immigration, and 97.1% of all residents five years old or older spoke only English at home in 1990. Principal languages other than English spoken at home were as follows:

Spanish	42,653	Korean	3,232
French	17,965	Italian	2,853
German	14,603	Japanese	2,480
Chinese	3,728	Greek	1,957

9RELIGIONS

Although predominantly Baptist today, Alabama was officially Roman Catholic throughout most of the 18th century, under French and Spanish rule. A century passed between the building of the first Catholic church in 1702 and the earliest sustained efforts by Protestant evangelists. The first Baptist church in the state, the Flint River Church in Madison County, was organized in 1808; the following year, the Old Zion Methodist Church was founded in the Tombigbee area.

During the second decade of the 19th century, settlers from the southeastern states brought the influence of the Great Revival to Alabama, along with the various Methodist, Presbyterian, and Baptist sects that had developed in its wake. The first black church in Alabama probably dates from 1820. As in other southern states, black slaves who had previously attended the churches of their masters formed their own churches after the Civil War. One of the earliest of these, the Little Zion Methodist Church, was established in 1867 in Mobile. Most freed blacks became Baptists, however.

As of 1990, the major Protestant denominations were the Southern Baptist Convention, with 1,313,907 adherents; the United Methodist Church, with 332,029; and Churches of Christ, 118,561. In 1990, Roman Catholics in Alabama numbered 137,834, and there were an estimated 8,350 Jews.

10TRANSPORTATION

The first rail line in the state—the Tuscumbia Railroad, chartered in 1830—made its first run, 44 mi (71 km) around the Muscle Shoals from Tuscumbia to Decatur, on 15 December 1834. By 1852, however, Alabama had only 165 mi (266 km) of track, less than most other southern states. Further development awaited the end of the Civil War. Birmingham, as planned by John T. Milner, chief engineer of the South and North Railroad, was founded in 1871 as a railroad intersection in the midst of Alabama's booming mining country; it subsequently became the state's main rail center, followed by Mobile. As of the end of 1992, Alabama had 3,628 rail mi (5,838 km) of track. In 1991, the state was 2d (after Georgia) in originated pulp and paper tonnage handled by rail. Coal is the major commodity sent by rail—38% of all rail tonnage originating from and 42% of all rail tonnage terminating within the state was coal in 1991. An Amtrak passenger rail connected Birmingham, Anniston, and Tuscaloosa with Washington and New Orleans. Other passenger service included a route connecting Montgomery and Mobile with Birmingham and New Orleans. Total Alabama ridership was 98,992 in 1991/92.

In settlement days the principal roads into Alabama were the Federal Road, formerly a Creek horse path, from Georgia and South Carolina; and the Natchez Trace, bought by the federal government (1801) from the Choctaw and Chickasaw, leading from Kentucky and Tennessee. Throughout most of the 19th century, road building was in the hands of private companies. Only after the establishment of a state highway department in 1911 and the securing of federal aid for rural road building in 1916 did Alabama begin to develop modern road systems.

As of 1995 there were 93,313 mi (150,141 km) of public streets, roads, and highways. In the same year, the state had 1,842,094 registered automobiles, 1,702,290 trucks, and 8,451 buses. There were 3,506,766 licensed drivers in May 1997. Most of the major interstate highways in Alabama intersect at Birmingham: I-65, running from the north to Montgomery and Mobile; and I-59 from the northeast and I-20 from the east, which, after merging at Birmingham, run southwestward to Tuscaloosa and into Mississippi. Route I-85 connects Montgomery with Atlanta; and I-10 connects Mobile with New Orleans and Tallahassee, FL. In 1995, total expenditures on roads and highways by all units of government amounted to just over $1.3 billion.

In 1995, there were five class I railroads operating in the state, with 3,351 rail miles (5,392 km). Total rail tonnage handled that year was 141.5 million tons. Amtrak operates two long distance trains through Alabama (one via Birmingham and one via Mobile); ridership in 1995/96 was 40,088.

The coming of the steamboat to Alabama waters, beginning in 1818, stimulated settlement in the Black Belt; however, the high price of shipping cotton by water contributed to the eventual displacement of the steamboat by the railroad. Thanks to the Tennessee Valley Authority, the Tennessee River has been transformed since the 1930s into a year-round navigable waterway, with three locks and dams in Alabama. The 234-mi (377-km), $2-billion Tennessee-Tombigbee project, which opened in 1985, provided a new barge route, partly through Alabama, from the Midwest to the Gulf of Mexico, for which the US Army Corps of Engineers cut a 39-mi (63-km) canal and built 10 locks and dams. This was not only the largest civilian engineering project in the US during the early 1980s but also by far the largest earth-moving project in US history, displacing more earth than was moved to build the Panama Canal.

The Alabama-Coosa and Black Warrior-Tombigbee systems also have been made navigable by locks and dams: river barges carry bulk cargoes. There are 1,600 mi (2,600 km) of navigable inland water and 50 mi (80 km) of Gulf coast. The only deepwater port is Mobile, with a large ocean-going trade; total tonnage in 1996 was 17.6 million tons. The Alabama State Docks also operates a system of 10 inland docks; and there are several privately run inland docks.

In 1996, Alabama had 99 public-use airports, of which 8 were for commercial service, 3 were relief airports for Birmingham, and the rest were for general aviation. Mobile, on the Gulf of Mexico, is Alabama's only international port. The largest and busiest facility is Birmingham Municipal Airport, where 1,045,671 passengers enplaned during 1994.

¹¹HISTORY

The region now known as Alabama has been inhabited for some 9,000–10,000 years. The earliest evidence of human habitation, charcoal from an ancient campfire at Russell Cave in northeastern Alabama, is about 9,000 years old. These early peoples, probably descended from humans who crossed from Asia to North America via the Bering Strait, moved from caves and open campsites to permanent villages about AD 1000. Some of their descendants, popularly called Mound Builders, erected huge earthen temple mounds and simple huts along Alabama's rivers, beginning around 1100. Moundville (near Tuscaloosa), one of the most important Mound Builder sites in the southeastern US, includes 20 "platform mounds" for Indian buildings, dating from 1200 to 1500. When the first Europeans arrived, Alabama was inhabited by Indians, half of them either Creek or members of smaller groups living within the Creek confederacy. The Creeks resided in central and eastern Alabama; Cherokee Indians inhabited northeastern Alabama, the Chickasaws lived in the northwest, and the Choctaws settled in the southwest.

During the 16th century, five Spanish expeditions entered Mobile Bay or explored the region now called Alabama. The most extensive was that of Hernando de Soto, whose army marched from the Tennessee Valley to the Mobile Delta in 1540. In 1702, two French naval officers—Pierre Le Moyne, Sieur d'Iberville; and Jean Baptiste Le Moyne, Sieur de Bienville— established Ft. Louis de la Mobile, the first permanent European settlement in present-day Alabama. Mobile remained in French hands until 1763, when it was turned over to the British under the terms of the Treaty of Paris. Because a British garrison held Mobile during the American Revolution, that city was captured in 1780 by the forces of Spain, an ally of the rebellious American colonists. In 1803, the United States claimed the city as part of the Louisiana Purchase, but in vain. Spanish control of Mobile lasted until the city was again seized during the War of 1812, this time by American troops in 1813. West Florida, including Mobile, was the only territory added to the US as a result of that war.

At the start of the 19th century, Indians still held most of present-day Alabama. War broke out in 1813 between American settlers and a Creek faction known as the Red Sticks, who were determined to resist white encroachment. After General Andrew Jackson and his Tennessee militia crushed the Red Sticks in 1814 at the Battle of Horseshoe Bend in central Alabama, he forced the Creek to sign a treaty ceding some 40,000 sq mi (103,600 sq km) of land to the US, thereby opening about three-fourths of the present state to white settlement. By 1839, nearly all Alabama Indians had been removed to Indian Territory.

From 1814 onward, pioneers, caught up by what was called "Alabama fever," poured out of the Carolinas, Virginia, Georgia, Tennessee, and Kentucky into what Andrew Jackson called "the best unsettled country in America." Wealthy migrants came in covered wagons, bringing their slaves, cattle, and hogs. But the great majority of pioneers were ambitious farmers who moved to the newly opened area in hopes of acquiring fertile land on which to grow cotton. Cotton's profitability had increased enormously with the invention of the cotton gin. In 1817, Alabama became a

territory; on 2 August 1819, a state constitution was adopted; and on the following 14 December, Alabama was admitted to statehood. Alabama, then as now, was sparsely populated. In 1819, its residents comprised 1.3% of the US population. That percentage had grown to only 2% in 1980.

During the antebellum era, 95% of white Alabamians lived and worked in rural areas, primarily as farmers. Although "Cotton was king" in 19th-century Alabama, farmers also grew corn, sorghum, oats, and vegetables, as well as razorback hogs and cattle. By 1860, 80% of Alabama farmers owned the land they tilled. Only about 33% of all white Alabamians were slave-owners. Whereas in 1820 there were 85,451 whites and 41,879 slaves, by 1860 the number of slaves had increased to 435,080, constituting 45% of the state population. Large planters (owners of 50 slaves or more) made up less than 1% of Alabama's white population in 1860. However, they owned 28% of the state's total wealth and occupied 25% of the seats in the legislature. Although the preponderance of the wealth and the population in Alabama was located in the north, the success of Black Belt plantation owners at forging coalitions with industrialists enabled planters to dominate state politics both before and after the Civil War. The planters led the secessionist movement, and most other farmers, fearing the consequences of an end to slavery, eventually followed suit. However, 2,500 white Alabamians served in the Union Army, and an estimated 8,000–10,000 others acted as Union scouts, deserted Confederate units, or hid from conscription agents.

Alabama seceded from the Union in January 1861 and shortly thereafter joined the Confederate States of America. The Confederacy was organized in Alabama's senate chamber in Montgomery, and Jefferson Davis was inaugurated president on the steps of the capitol. Montgomery served as capital of the Confederacy until May, when the seat of government was moved to Richmond, VA.

Remote from major theaters of war, Alabama experienced only occasional Union raids during the first three years of the conflict. In the summer of 1864, however, Confederate and Union ships fought a major naval engagement in Mobile Bay, which ended in surrender by the outnumbered southern forces. During the Confederacy's dying days in the spring of 1865, federal troops swept through Tuscaloosa, Selma, and Montgomery. Their major goal, Selma, one of the Confederacy's main industrial centers, was left almost as heavily devastated as Richmond or Atlanta. Estimates of the number of Alabamians killed in the Civil War range from 25,000 upward.

During Reconstruction, Alabama was under military rule until it was readmitted to the Union in 1868. For the next six years, Republicans held most top political positions in the state. With the help of the Ku Klux Klan, Democrats regained political control of the state in November 1874.

Cotton remained the foundation of the Alabama economy in the late 19th and early 20th centuries. However, with the abolition of slavery it was now raised by sharecroppers—white and black landless farmers who paid for the land they rented from planters with the cotton they harvested. Alabama also attempted to create a "New South" in which agriculture would be balanced by industry. In the 1880s and 1890s, at least 20 Alabama towns were touted as ironworking centers. Birmingham, founded in 1871, became the New South's leading industrial center. Its promoters invested in pig iron furnaces, coal mines, steel plants, and real estate. Small companies merged with bigger ones, which were taken over, in turn, by giant corporations. In 1907, Birmingham's Tennessee Coal, Iron, and Railroad Co. was purchased by the nation's largest steelmaker, US Steel.

Another major Alabama enterprise was cotton milling. By 1900, 9,000 men, women, and children were employed in Alabama mills; most of these white workers were farm folk who had lost their land after the Civil War because of mounting debts and low cotton prices. Wages in mills were so low that entire families had to work hours as long as those they had endured as farmers.

The rise in the rate of farm tenancy produced a corresponding increase in social and political unrest. Discontented farmers and factory workers allied during the 1890s in the Populist Party in an attempt to overthrow the Bourbon Democrats who had dominated Alabama politics for two decades. Although a number of Populists were elected to the Alabama legislature, no Populist candidate succeeded in winning the governorship, primarily because Democrats manipulated the black vote to their own advantage. In 1901, Alabama adopted a new state constitution containing numerous restrictions on voting, supposedly to end vote manipulation and restore honest elections. The tangible result of these new rules was to disenfranchise almost all Alabama black voters and thousands of poor whites. For example, the total of blacks registered in 14 counties fell from 78,311 in 1900 to 1,081 in 1903. As recently as 1941, fewer than 25% of Alabama adults were registered voters. In 1960, no blacks voted in Lowndes or Wilcox counties, 80% and 78% black, respectively.

As one of the poorest states in the country, Alabama benefited disproportionately from the New Deal. Yet, like other southern states, Alabama viewed the expansion of the national government's role with mixed feelings. Alabamians embraced federal aid, even lobbying for military bases, while seeing federal power as a threat to the "Southern way of life" that included racial segregation.

During the 1950s and 1960s, national attention focused on civil rights demonstrations in Alabama, including the Montgomery bus boycott of 1955, the Birmingham and University of Alabama demonstrations of 1963, and the voting rights march from Selma to Montgomery in 1965. The primary antagonists were Dr. Martin Luther King, Jr., head of the Southern Christian Leadership Conference; and Governor George C. Wallace, an opponent of integration. These black protests and the sometimes violent reactions to them, such as the 1963 bombing of a church in Birmingham in which four young black girls were killed, helped influence the US Congress to pass the Civil Rights Act of 1964 and the Voting Rights Act of 1965.

Once the most tightly segregated city in the nation, Birmingham has become thoroughly integrated in public facil-ities, and in 1979 the city elected its first black mayor, Richard Arrington. The civil rights era brought other momentous changes to Alabama. Hundreds of thousands of black voters are now an important force in state politics. Blacks attend school, colleges, and universities of their choice and enjoy equal access to all public facilities. New racial attitudes among most whites have contributed to a vast improvement in the climate of race relations since 1960. Indeed, a significant amount of black support contributed to Wallace's election to a fourth term as governor in 1982. In 1984 there were 314 black elected officials, including 25 mayors, 19 lawmakers in the Alabama state legislature, and an associate justice of the state supreme court. In 1990, 704 blacks held elective office.

In many respects Alabama has resisted change more success-fully than any other state in the deep South. The state's tax system remains the most regressive in the country. In 1982, the state legislature passed a law prohibiting taxation of land owned by timber companies at market value (timber comprises the state's largest industry). In part because none of its property taxes are devoted to education, Alabama spends less than almost any other state on its school system: its expenditures on education placed it 47th among the states in 1990. The state continues to be plagued by a high infant mortality rate, owing in part to widespread

poverty. In 1990, over one-fifth of its citizens lived below the federal poverty level of $12,500 for a family of four.

A strange turn of events in 1986 resulted in the election of the first Republican governor since Reconstruction. The Democratic candidate, State Attorney General Charles Graddick, was stripped of his party's nomination by a federal panel because of crossover Republican voting in the Democratic primary. His replacement, Lieutenant Governor Bill Baxley, lost the election to a little-known pro-business Republican and former Baptist preacher, Guy Hunt. Hunt was reelected in 1990 but was confronted early in his second term with accusations of financial misdeeds, including personal use of official resources and mismanagement of public funds. In 1992 Hunt was indicted on 13 separate felony counts. The following year, he was found guilty of fraud and conspiracy charges and forced to resign the governorship, becoming the fourth governor in the nation's history to be convicted of criminal charges while in office.

In 1995 Alabama was one of five southern states in which a string of fires were set at predominantly black churches. Early in 1996, Attorney General Janet Reno announced that the federal government planned to investigate the fires.

[12]STATE GOVERNMENT

Alabama has had six constitutions, the most recent one dating from 1901. That document was 172,000 words long by the end of 1983—longer than that of any other state—and had been amended 443 times.

Alabama's bicameral legislature consists of a 35-seat senate and a 105-seat house of representatives, all of whose members are elected at the same time for four-year terms. Senators must be at least 25 years of age; representatives, 21. Under federal pressure, the legislature in 1983 approved a reapportionment plan, effective in 1986, that was expected to increase black repre-sentation. In 1984 there were 24 black legislators. In 1995 Alabama's legislators received a per diem salary of $10 during regular sessions.

Elected executive officials are the governor and lieutenant-governor (separately elected), secretary of state, attorney general, treasurer, auditor, eight members of the Board of Education, and three members of the Public Service Commission. The governor, who serves for four years, must be at least 30 years of age and must have been a US citizen for 10 years and a citizen of the state for 7. The governor is limited to a maximum of two consecutive terms. In 1996 Alabama's governor earned a salary of $81,151.

A bill becomes a law when it is passed by at least a majority of a quorum of both houses and is either signed by the governor or left unsigned for 6 days while the legislature is in session, or passed over the governor's veto by a majority of the elected members of each house. The governor may pocket veto a measure submitted fewer than 5 days before adjournment by not signing it within 10 days after adjournment. The submission of a constitu-tional amendment to the electorate requires the approval of three-fifths of the membership of each house, but such amendments can also be adopted by initiative and referendum, or by a constitu-tional convention.

Voters in Alabama must be US citizens, at least 18 years of age, and must have resided in the state at least one day prior to the election.

[13]POLITICAL PARTIES

The major political parties in Alabama are the Democratic and Republican parties, each affiliated with the national party organi-zation. The Republicans are weak below the federal-office level.

Pre-Civil War political divisions in the state reflected those elsewhere in the South. Small and subsistence farmers, especially in the northern hill country and pine forest areas, tended to be Jacksonian Democrats, while the planters of the Black Belt and the river valleys often voted Whig. After a period of Radical Republican rule during Reconstruction, the Bourbon Democrats, whose party then served largely the interests of wealthy property owners, business people, and white supremists, ran the state for the rest of the century, despite a challenge in the 1890s by the Populist Party.

During the 20th century, the Democratic Party has continued to command virtually every statewide office, major and minor. In the 1996 presidential elections, 50% of the vote went to Republican Bob Dole; 43% to Democrat Bill Clinton; and 6% to independent Ross Perot. Richard Shelby was reelected to the Senate as a Democrat in 1992, but switched his affiliation to Republican on 9 November 1994, the day after the Republicans swept into power in the Senate. In 1996 Democratic Senator Howell Heflin retired, and his seat was won by Republican Jeff B. Sessions. Alabama's delegation of US Representatives in 1996 consisted of two Democrats and five Republicans. Democrat James Folsom was elected Lieutenant Governor in 1990 and became Governor in April of 1993 when Governor Guy Hunt was convicted of illegally using money from his inauguration for personal expenses. Folsom lost his election bid for governor to Fob James, Jr., in 1994. James had served as governor of the state from 1979–83 as a Democrat, but he switched party affiliations for the 1994 election and upset Folsom in a narrow victory. The state legislature in 1997 consisted of 22 Democrats and 12 Republicans in the state senate and 72 Democrats and 33 Republicans in the state house. Minority elected officials in 1993 included 699 blacks. There were 8 women serving in the state legislature and in the executive branch in 1995.

On two occasions, 1948 and 1964, the Alabama Democratic Party bolted the national Democratic ticket, each time because of disagreement over civil rights. Barry Goldwater in 1964 was the first Republican presidential candidate in the 20th century to carry Alabama. In 1968, George Wallace carried Alabama overwhelmingly on the American Independent Party slate.

[14]LOCAL GOVERNMENT

Alabama has 67 counties, 438 municipalities, 129 school districts, and at least 487 special districts. Counties are governed by county commissions, usually consisting of three to seven commissioners, elected by district. Other county officials include a clerk, assessor, tax collector, sheriff, and superintendent of education. Elections for municipal officers are held every four years.

Until the late 1970s, the predominant form of municipal government, especially in the larger cities, was the commission, whose members are elected either at-large or by district. Partly in response to court orders requiring district elections in order to permit the election of more black officials, there has since been a trend toward the mayor-council form, although the US Supreme Court ruled in May 1980 that Mobile may elect its public officials at-large.

An alteration in local government had a significant effect on the racial climate in Birmingham during the 1960s, when the Young Men's Business Club led a movement to change to the mayor-council system, in order to oust a commission (including Eugene "Bull" Connor as public safety commissioner) that for nearly a decade had reacted negatively to every black demand. After a narrow vote in favor of the change, a moderate was

Alabama Presidential Vote by Political Parties, 1948–96

YEAR	ELECTORAL VOTE	ALABAMA WINNER	DEMOCRAT	REPUBLICAN	STATES' RIGHTS DEMOCRAT	PROHIBITION	PROGRESSIVE
1948	11	Thurmond (SRD)	—	40,930	171,443	1,026	1,522
1952	11	Stevenson (D)	275,075	149,231	—	1,814	—
1956	11	Stevenson (D)	279,542	195,694	UNPLEDGED 20,323	—	—
1960	11	*Kennedy (D)	318,303	236,110	NAT'L STATES' RIGHTS 4,367	—	—
1964	10	Goldwater (R)	—	479,085	UNPLEDGED DEMOCRAT 210,782	—	—
1968	10	Wallace AI)	195,918	146,591	AMERICAN IND. 687,664	AM. IND. DEMOCRAT 3,814	10,518
1972	9	*Nixon (R)	256,923	728,701	AMERICAN 11,928	8,559	—
1976	9	*Carter (D)	659,170	504,070	AMERICAN IND. 9,198	6,669	COMMUNIST 1,954
1980	9	*Reagan (R)	636,730	654,192	—	—	—
1984	9	*Reagan (R)	551,899	872,849	LIBERTARIAN 9,504	—	—
1988	9	*Bush (R)	549,506	815,576	8,460	3,311	
1992	9	Bush (R)	690,080	804,283	5,737	2,161	IND.(PEROT) 183,109
1996	9	Dole (R)	662,165	769,044	5,290	—	92,149

*Won US presidential election.

elected mayor in April 1963, but the former commissioners then contested the initial vote that had changed the system. At the height of Birmingham's racial troubles, both the former commissioners and the newly elected council claimed to govern Birmingham, but neither did so effectively. When peace came, it was as the result of an unofficial meeting held between local black leaders and 77 of the city's most influential whites, with federal officials serving as mediators. Although the council, like the commissioners, publicly opposed these negotiations, once they were over and the council's election confirmed, the new moderate leadership permitted peaceful racial accommodation to go forward.

[15]STATE SERVICES

Alabama's Ethics Commission administers the state's ethics law, makes financial disclosure records available to the public, and receives monthly reports from lobbyists. Educational services are administered primarily by the Department of Education and the Alabama Commission on Higher Education. The Alabama Public Library Service supports and promotes the development of public libraries. The Department of Aeronautics, Highway Department, and Public Service Commission (PSC) administer transportation services; the PSC supervises, regulates, and controls all transportation companies doing business in the state. Drivers' licenses are issued by the Department of Public Safety.

Health and welfare services are offered primarily through the Department of Public Health, Department of Mental Health, Department of Veterans Affairs, the Commission on Aging, Department of Youth Services, and Department of Pensions and Security. Planning for the state's future health-care needs is carried out by the Health Planning and Development Agency.

Public protection services are administered by the Military Department, Board of Corrections, Alabama Law Enforcement Planning Agency, and Department of Public Safety, among other agencies. Numerous government bodies offer resource protection services: the Department of Conservation and Natural Resources, Department of Environmental Management, Alabama Forestry Commission, Oil and Gas Board, Surface Mining Reclamation Commission, and Alabama State Soil and Water Conservation Committee.

[16]JUDICIAL SYSTEM

The high court of Alabama is the supreme court, consisting of a chief justice and eight associate justices, all elected for staggered six-year terms. It issues opinions on constitutional issues, and hears cases appealed from the lower courts. The court of civil appeals has exclusive appellate jurisdiction in all suits involving sums up to $10,000; its three judges are elected for six-year terms, and the one who has served the longest is the presiding judge. The five judges of the court of criminal appeals are also elected for six-year terms; they choose the presiding judge by majority vote.

Circuit courts, which encompassed 40 districts and 127 judgeships in 1997, have exclusive original jurisdiction over civil actions involving sums of more than $5,000, and over criminal prosecutions involving felony offenses. They also have original jurisdiction, concurrent with the district courts, in all civil matters exceeding $500. They have appellate jurisdiction over most cases from district and municipal courts. A new system of district courts replaced county and juvenile courts as of January 1977, staffed by judges who serve six-year terms. Municipal court judges are appointed by the municipality. Alabama had 9,436 practicing attorneys in 1996, an increase of 7% since 1994.

At the end of 1995, 17,943 prisoners were held in 31 state and federal prisons in Alabama, an increase of 44% since 1990. Alabama had an incarceration rate of 422 per 100,000 population. In 1976, US District Court Judge Frank M. Johnson, Jr., ruled that conditions in Alabama prisons inflicted "cruel and unusual punishment" upon inmates, spurring the process of prison reform.

Alabama had an FBI Crime Index rate in 1995 of 4,848.1 crimes per 100,000 population, including 632.4 violent crimes and 4,215.7 property crimes. Alabama has a death penalty and has executed 147 persons since 1930, 12 since 1977. There were 143 persons under sentence of death in 1995.

An Alabama case that became internationally notorious was that of the nine "Scottsboro boys," eight of whom were sentenced to death and one to life imprisonment in 1931 for the alleged rape of two white girls, one of whom later recanted her charges. After multiple appeals and reversals, five indictments were subsequently dropped; of the four remaining defendants, all sentenced to lengthy jail terms, three were paroled and one escaped to Michigan, which refused extradition.

[17]ARMED FORCES

The US Department of Defense had 14,616 active military personnel in Alabama during fiscal year 1995/96. The major installation in terms of expenditures was the US Army's Redstone Arsenal at Huntsville, with 1,479 military and 7,777 civilian personnel. Redstone is the center of the Army's missile and rocket programs and contains the George C. Marshall Space Flight Center of the National Aeronautics and Space Administration, which directs all private contractors for the space program. Among the spacecraft developed there were the Redstone rocket, which launched the first US astronaut; Explorer I, the first US earth-orbiting satellite; and the Saturn rocket, which boosted the Apollo missions to the moon. Other installations include Ft. Rucker (near Enterprise); Ft. McClellan (Anniston—scheduled to be closed in September 1999), site of recruit training; the Anniston Army Depot; Maxwell Air Force Base (Montgomery), site of the US Air University, Air War Colleges, and national headquarters for the Civil Air Patrol; and Gunter Air Force Base (also in Montgomery). During fiscal year 1995/96, Alabama firms received defense contract awards totaling over $1.8 billion.

There were 421,000 veterans of US military service in Alabama as of 1 July 1996, less than 500 of whom served in World War I, 93,000 in World War II, 78,000 in the Korean conflict, 122,000 during the Vietnam era, and 31,000 in the Persian Gulf War. During fiscal year 1995/96, benefits paid to Alabama veterans amounted to $826 million. As of 1996, Alabama reserve and National Guard units had a strength of 41,101. In 1993, the Alabama Department of Public Safety employed 586 full-time sworn officers, or one per 10,000 residents.

[18]MIGRATION

After 1814, Alabama was the mecca of a great migratory wave, mainly of whites of English and Scotch-Irish descent (some with their black slaves) from Virginia, Georgia, and the Carolinas. Since the Civil War, migration to Alabama has been slight. Many blacks left Alabama from World War I (1914–18) through the 1960s to seek employment in the East and Midwest, and the proportion of blacks in Alabama's population fell from 35% in 1940 to 25.3% in 1990. Following the civil rights revolution, the trend began to reverse; more blacks chose to remain in the state, and some who had gone elsewhere returned. Overall, Alabama may have lost as many as 944,000 residents through migration between 1940 and 1970, but enjoyed a net gain from migration of over 143,000 between 1970 and 1990, and an additional 99,156 in domestic and international migration between 1990 and 1996.

As of 1990, about 76% of Alabamians were born in the state. Of state residents over 5 years of age in 1990 who lived in a different house than in 1985, 79% reported intrastate movements, over 75% of which were within the same county.

[19]INTERGOVERNMENTAL COOPERATION

Among the interstate compacts and commissions in which Alabama participates are the Gulf States Marine Fisheries Compact, Interstate Mining Compact, Interstate Oil and Gas Compact, Southeastern Forest Fire Protection Compact, Southern Growth Policies Compact, Southern Interstate Energy Compact, Southern Regional Education Compact, and Tennessee-Tombigbee Waterway Development Compact. The Office of State Planning and Federal Programs coordinates planning efforts by all levels of government. During fiscal year 1995/96, Alabama received federal grants amounting to $3.33 billion.

[20]ECONOMY

Cotton dominated Alabama's economy from the mid-19th century to the 1870s, when large-scale industrialization began. The coal, iron, and steel industries were the first to develop, followed by other resource industries such as textiles, clothing, paper, and wood products. Although Alabama's prosperity has increased, particularly in recent decades, the state still lags in wage rates and per capita income. One factor that has hindered the growth of the state's economy is declining investment in resource industries owned by large corporations outside the state. Between 1974 and 1983, manufacturing grew at little more than half the rate of all state goods and services. Industries such as primary metals, once the backbone of Alabama's economy, were clearly losing importance. The 1980–82 recession hit the state economy harder than the nation as a whole: 39,000 jobs were lost in manufacturing alone, and real output in manufacturing fell by 10.5%. In 1994, Alabama's gross state product was $88,661 million, consisting of private goods-producing industries, $26,050 million; private services-producing industries, $48,166 million; and government, $14,445 million. In 1996, there were 31,672 bankruptcy filings.

[21]INCOME

Alabama's per capita personal income in 1996 was $20,055, for a rank of 39th among the 50 states. Between 1960 and 1978, per capita income rose from 69% of the US average to 80%, and in 1996 it was 83%. Median household income in 1996 was estimated at $25,991, and disposable per capita personal income was $17,785. Total disposable income rose from $72.6 billion in 1995 to $76 billion in 1996. In 1995, 20.1% of all Alabamians were living below the federal poverty level.

[22]LABOR

Alabama's civilian labor force at the start of 1997 numbered 2,125,400. Alabama's total employment was 1,981,000 in 1996, yielding an unemployment rate of 5.1%. Employment patterns for nonfarm industry groups in Alabama were as follows at the beginning of 1996 and 1997 (in thousands):

	1996	1997
Total nonfarm employment	1,815.8	1,837.3
Mining	10.7	10.5
Construction	91.6	97.8
Manufacturing	387.6	382.5
Durable goods	194.7	195.8
Nondurable goods	192.9	186.7
Transportation, Communications, Public Utilities	90.5	90.0
Trade	415.9	421.3
Wholesale	93.4	94.7
Retail	322.5	326.6
Finance, Insurance, Real Estate	80.4	82.9
Services	396.6	409.7
Government	342.5	342.6

In 1871, James Thomas Rapier, a black Alabamian who would later serve a term as a US representative from the state, organized the first black labor union in the South, the short-lived Labor Union of Alabama. The Knights of Labor began organizing in the state in 1882. A serious obstacle to unionization and collective bargaining was the convict leasing system, which was not ended officially until 1923, and in practice, not until five years later. In 1888, the Tennessee Coal, Iron, and Railroad Co. (later taken over by US Steel) was granted an exclusive 10-year contract to use the labor of all state convicts, paying the state $9–18 per person per month.

Child labor was also exploited. Alabama had limited a child's working day to 8 hours in 1887, but a Massachusetts company that was building a large mill in the state secured the repeal of that law in 1895. A weaker measure passed 12 years later limited the child's workweek to 60 hours and set the minimum working age at 12.

As of 1995, 235,500 Alabamians belonged to labor unions, or about 13.6% of all employees; unions were especially strong in the northern industrial cities and in Mobile. About 19.5% of all manufacturing workers were unionized—one of the highest rates among states with right-to-work laws.

[23]AGRICULTURE

Alabama ranked 26th among the 50 states in farm marketing in 1995, with $2.9 billion, of which only $740 million came from crops.

There was considerable diversity in Alabama's earliest agriculture. By the mid-19th century, however, cotton had taken over, and production of other crops dropped so much that corn and other staples, even work animals, were often imported. In 1860, cotton was grown in every county, and one-crop agriculture had already worn out much of Alabama's farmland.

Diversification began early in the 20th century, a trend accelerated by the destructive effects of the boll weevil on cotton growing. In 1996, only 540,000 acres (218,500 hectares) were planted in cotton, compared to 3,500,000 acres (1,400,000 hectares) in 1930. As of 1996 there were some 45,000 farms in Alabama, occupying approximately 10.2 million acres (4.1 million hectares), or roughly 30% of the state's land area. Soybeans and livestock are raised in the Black Belt; peanuts in the southeast; vegetables, livestock, and timber in the southwest; and cotton and soybeans in the Tennessee River Valley.

In 1996, Alabama ranked 3rd in the US in production of peanuts, with 456,950,000 lb (207,272,500 kg), worth about $120,635,000. Other crops included soybeans, 10,710,000 bushels, $71,757,000; corn, 22,960,000 bushels, $82,656,000; wheat, 3,520,000 bushels, $15,840,000; tomatoes for fresh market, 425,000 hundredweight (19,278,000 kg), $9,350,000; sweet potatoes, 774,000 hundredweight (35,108,640 kg), $11,300,000; and pecans, 15,000,000 lb (6,804,000 kg), $7,995,000. The 1996 cotton crop of 810,000 bales, 8th highest in the nation, was valued at $277,603,000.

[24]ANIMAL HUSBANDRY

The principal livestock-raising regions of Alabama are the far north, the southwest, and the Black Belt, where the lime soil provides excellent pasturage. During 1995, Alabama produced 544.9 million lb (247.2 million kg) of cattle and calves, valued at $283.8 million, and 182.6 million lb (82.8 million kg) of hogs, valued at $65.8 million. There were 1,750,000 cattle and 200,000 hogs and pigs on Alabama farms and ranches. In addition, 34,000 milk cows yielded 482 million lb (219 million kg) of milk in 1995.

Alabama is a leading producer of chickens, broilers, and eggs. In broiler production, the state was surpassed only by Arkansas and Georgia in 1995, with 3.7 billion lb (1.7 billion kg), valued at

$1.4 billion. That year, Alabama ranked 5th in chicken production, with 63.9 million lb (28.9 billion kg), worth $6.3 million; and 11th in egg production, with 2.7 billion lb (1.2 billion kg), worth $215.6 million.

25FISHING

Alabama's commercial fish catch was 28,741,000 lb (13,037,000 kg), worth $49,656,000, in 1995. The principal fishing port is Bayou La Batre, which brought in about 22,100,000 lb (10,025,000 kg), worth $37,500,000, 12th-highest by value in the nation. Catfish farming is of growing importance. As of January 1997, there were 245 catfish farms (down from 370 in 1990) covering 21,000 acres (8,500 hectares) of water surface, with an average farm size of about 88 acres (36 hectares). Altogether, Alabama growers had an inventory of 49.1 million stocker-size and 36.8 million fingerling/fry catfish. There were 92 processing and 19 wholesaling plants, with a combined total of about 1,700 employees in 1995. There were 546,440 sport fishing licenses issued by Alabama in 1995/96, and the US Fish and Wildlife Service spent over $2.9 million for the Sport Fish Restoration Program in 1995/96, mostly for area and facility maintenance. Two federal fish hatcheries distributed 8,664 lb (3,930 kg) of trout and catfish to Alabama waters in 1995/96.

26FORESTRY

Forestland in Alabama, predominantly pine, covering 21,974,000 acres (8,893,000 hectares), was nearly 3% of the nation's total in 1992, and 67% of the state's land area. Nearly all of that was classified as commercial timberland, 95% of it privately owned. Four national forests covered a gross area of 1,272,017 acres (516,404 hectares) in 1996, of which 48% was privately held. Shipments of lumber and wood products were valued at $3.6 billion in 1995; of paper and allied products, $8.5 billion. Production of softwoods and hardwood lumber totaled $1.9 billion board feet in 1996.

Alabama has a program in place, called TREASURE Forest, to recognize and certify sustainable forestry management on private lands. this program has already certified over 1.57 million acres (635,000 hectares).

27MINING

In 1995 Alabama's nonfuel mineral industry mined and processed an estimated $676 million of mineral commodities (2% of the US total), according to statistics related by the US Geological Survey. This was an increase of $50 million over the value reported by the state's 230+ mineral producers in 1994. Value increased for cement, clay, sand, gravel, and stone, the mineral commodities used in construction.

In 1995, Alabama produced 4.2 million metric tons of portland cement valued at $264 million, 3.8 billion metric tons of clay worth $35.4 million, 12.1 million metric tons of construction sand and gravel valued at $46.6 million, and 33.4 million metric tons of crushed stone worth $170 million. Portland cement, crushed stone, lime, and construction sand and gravel accounted for 86% of the total nonfuel mineral value in 1995.

The State ranked 18th nationally in total mineral production, and remained 1st in bauxite, 2d in common clays, gemstones and kaolin clays, 3d in fire clays, and 4th in masonry cement.

28ENERGY AND POWER

Electrical generating plants in Alabama had an installed capacity of 21.8 million kW in 1996, and production totaled 99.6 billion kWh in 1995. About half of the capacity and production came from private sources (the Alabama Power Company and Alabama Electric Cooperative), with most of the remainder attributable to the Tennessee Valley Authority, which also owned three of the state's five nuclear reactors.

Significant petroleum finds in southern Alabama date from the early 1950s. The 1996 output was 16,868,000 barrels; proved reserves as of 31 December 1995 totaled 43,000,000 barrels. During 1995, 519.7 billion cu feet of natural gas were extracted from 3,526 wells, leaving reserves of 4,868 billion cu feet. Coal production, which began in the 19th century, reached 24,345,000 tons in 1996, 8th among the states, of which all was bituminous and about 70% was surface mined. Coal reserves in 1995 totaled 510 million tons.

29INDUSTRY

Alabama's industrial boom, which began in the 1870s with the exploitation of the coal and iron fields in the north, quickly transformed Birmingham into the leading industrial city in the South, producing pig iron more cheaply than its American and English competitors. An important stimulus to manufacturing in the north was the development of ports and power plants along the Tennessee River. Although Birmingham remains highly dependent on steel, the state's industry has diversified considerably since World War II (1939–45).

By the late 1970s, the older smokestack industries were clearly in decline, but Birmingham received a boost in 1984 when US Steel announced it would spend $1.3 billion to make its Fairfield plant the newest fully integrated steel mill in the nation.

In 1997, Mercedes Benz began manufacturing its sport utility vehicle at a new facility in Vance.

As of 1994, the principal employers among industry groups were food and kindred products, textile mill products, apparel and other textile products, primary metal industries, industrial machinery and equipment, electronic equipment, and transportation equipment. Electrical machinery, computer equipment, and transportation equipment in Alabama are typically exported to Canada, Mexico, and Germany. In 1995 there were 346 US patents issued to Alabama residents.

30COMMERCE

According to the 1992 Census of Wholesale Trade, Alabama had 7,066 wholesale establishments, with sales of $31,971 million. Of the total amount, durable goods accounted for 68.5% of the establishments and 78.5% of the sales. Retail establishments numbered 24,059 with sales of $27,732.6 million (25th in the US), or 1.5% of the national total.

The leading types of retail businesses by number of establishments were eating and drinking places (5,326), food stores (3,128), and miscellaneous retail (4,274). Automotive dealers, general merchandise stores, and eating and drinking places accounted for 22.3%, 14.1%, and 9% of all sales, respectively. Alcoholic beverages, except for beer, are sold in ABC (Alcoholic Beverage Control) stores, run by the state. Prohibition is by local option; 26 of the 67 counties were dry in 1994, but some dry counties had wet cities.

Exporters located in Alabama exported $3,702.5 million in merchandise during 1996, when $5,169.5 million of goods produced within the state were exported from across the nation.

31CONSUMER PROTECTION

The Office of Consumer Assistance, established in 1972, was transferred to the Office of the Attorney General in 1979. The major duties of the office are to enforce the Deceptive Trade Practices Act and other criminal laws to combat consumer fraud; and to offer programs in consumer education. In response to a myriad of inquiries, complaints, and fraudulent schemes, recent attorneys general have expanded the Division's role in their administrations, and it has become one of the most effective arms of the Attorney General's law enforcement efforts.

The Consumer Protection Office also acts as a mediator or negotiator in response to approximately 3,000 consumer complaints received each year, three-quarters of which are registered by residents over age 65. In this capacity, the Attorney General undertakes to assist the complaining consumer and the business or person complained against in resolving the dispute. These complaints are submitted to the Attorney General in writing and made available to the business for a response. If a business or person fails to respond to the Attorney General's request for cooperation in addressing the problem, the Attorney General possesses subpoena power to compel these persons to appear at his or her office for this purpose. About 75% of such cases are resolved through the Consumer Protection Office.

[32]BANKING

As of 1996, Alabama's 186 insured commercial banks had assets of $56.3 billion; outstanding loans totaled $36.9 billion, and deposits were over $41 billion. There were 18 insured savings institutions in 1996, with combined assets of $2.4 billion. In 1996, the state's insured savings institutions had $1.5 billion in mortgage loans. At the end of 1995, the Resolution Trust Corporation had resolved 11 Alabama savings and loan institutions which had $4.0 billion in assets and $3.3 billion in deposits through 498,000 accounts.

[33]INSURANCE

In 1995 there were 8,499,000 policies in force with a total value of $192.2 billion. The average coverage per family was $119,300.

Property and liability insurers wrote premiums amounting to $3.434 billion in 1995, of which automobile physical damage accounted for $875.36 million; automobile liability, $687 million; and homeowners insurance, $448 million.

[34]SECURITIES

Alabama has no securities exchanges. The state has approximately 1,000 securities brokers and dealers registered to do business within Alabama, with over 30,000 registered agents. There are nearly 500 businesses that provide securities investment advice services, with over 3,000 registered agents.

[35]PUBLIC FINANCE

The Division of the Budget within the Department of Finance prepares and administers the state budget, which the governor submits to the legislature for amendment and approval. The fiscal year runs from 1 October through 30 September. The following table summarizes revenues for fiscal year 1996 in millions.

REVENUES	
General fund	$ 897.5
Other State, Federal and Local Funds	4,329.2
Special educational trust fund, of which:	3,346.4
Income tax	1,779.8
Sales tax	1,086.4
Utility tax	231.1
Other receipts	1,457.8
Special Mental Health Trust Fund	117.3
TOTALS	$9,971.3

EXPENDITURES	
Special educational trust fund	$2,781.0
Department of Transportation	768.2
Health, Physical and Mental	4,228.8
Department of Economic and Community Affairs	383.6
Department of Corrections	458.3
Other outlays	695.8
TOTALS	$9,315.7

As of mid-1994, the total debt of Alabama state government was $1.443 billion, or $357.03 per capita.

[36]TAXATION

Alabama state tax collections in 1996 were $5.2 billion. Per capita tax revenues of all state and local governments—$1,230 in 1994—were less than those of every other state except (just as in 1982) Arkansas and Mississippi, and receipts from property taxes ($31.42 per capita) were still the lowest in the nation. The state tax burden ($1,232 per capita) in 1994 was 43d among the states.

As of the end of 1994, the personal income tax, which is designated for education, ranged from 2% to 5%, depending on income and marital status. The tax on corporate net income was 5% for most enterprises, but 6% for financial institutions. The state also imposes a sales tax of 4%; localities may charge up to an additional 3%. Other state levies include a value-added tax, utility tax, use tax, and taxes on oil production, oil and gas, cigarettes, beer, and whiskey.

Alabama residents paid $12.1 billion in federal taxes in 1995. The state received federal expenditures totaling $22.7 billion—a ratio of $0.53 in taxes for every $1 received.

[37]ECONOMIC POLICY

Alabama seeks to attract out-of-state business by means of tax incentives and plant-building assistance. The Alabama Development Office plans for economic growth through industrial development. It also extends loans, issues bonds, and offers other forms of financing to growing companies, to firms that create permanent jobs, and to small businesses. The Alabama Industrial Development Training Institute, within the Department of Education, provides job training especially designed to suit the needs of new or expanding industries in the state. Alabama offers zero-interest loans and grants to rural economic development projects. In an effort to attract new industries or help existing companies grow, the state helps counties and municipalities pay for site improvements, and assists communities in financing infrastructures such as water and sewer lines or access roads. The state Foreign Trade Relations Commission seeks to promote international markets for Alabama products.

[38] HEALTH

Alabama's infant death rate for the 12 months ending December 1995—10.2 per 1,000 live births—was one of the highest in the US. The abortion rate of 14 per 1,000 live births in 1992 was lower than the US average.

The state's overall death rate in 1995—996.1 deaths per 100,000 population—included a death rate from heart disease of 314.2 per 100,000, compared to the national rate of 280.7. Alabama ranked 46th out of 52 for its high cardiovascular disease mortality rate in 1992. Alabama also ranked above the national rate in death rates from cancer, cerebrovascular diseases, accidents, traffic fatalities, and suicide. The mortality rate from HIV infection was 9.2 per 100,000 population. There were 581 documented AIDS cases in 1994. The current AIDS rate per 100,000 population is 13.42, 53% lower than the national average in 1995.

Alabama had 115 hospitals in 1995; there were 17,174 beds and 639,311 admissions. Hospital personnel included 15,123 registered nurses. The average expense to hospitals in the state for care in 1994 was $781 per inpatient day and $4,895 per stay, both figures being close to 17% below the US average. Alabama had 7,294 physicians in 1994, and 33,400 registered nurses in 1994. In 1994, there were 175 physicians per 100,000 population.

In 1995, 15.9% of Alabamians were uninsured. Medicare and Medicaid payments in 1994 were $2.7 billion and $1.3 billion respectively.

Smoking prevalence was 24.1% of persons aged 18–30 years. The projected number of persons aged 0–17 who will become smokers and die prematurely as adults because of smoking-related illness for 1995 was 83,404 people.

39 SOCIAL WELFARE

Public welfare expenditures in Alabama are still low by national standards. The weekly unemployment benefit check was $138.51 in 1995. Payments of approximately $97 million were made in 1996 to 108,269 recipients of aid to families with dependent children; the average monthly payment was $194 per family. In 1996 509,214 recipients received monthly food stamp allowances averaging $71.92. Alabama's participation in the national school lunch program in 1996 cost the federal government $109.3 million.

With the enactment of the Personal Responsibility and Work Opportunity Reconciliation Act of 1996, the US government has changed the form and regulations for many of its social welfare programs; most significantly, it replaces Aid to Families with Dependent Children (AFDC), an open-ended entitlement program, with Temporary Assistance for Needy Families (TANF), a limited system of assistance funded largely through federal block grants. The reform act also impacts the food stamp program, the Supplemental Security Income program, and the child nutrition program. The law took effect on 1 July 1997 and provided $16.38 billion in block grants for fiscal years 1997–2002. The grants are to be divided among the states based on an equation involving the numbers of former AFDC recipients in each state. Because many of the bills provisions have yet to be implemented into state-by-state policy, it was not possible to include the details of each state's programs for this edition of this work.

During 1996, Social Security benefits were paid to 775,670 Alabamians. The average monthly payment to retired workers (excluding persons with special benefits) was $671 per month. Federal Supplemental Security Income payments in 1995 went to 165,093 residents, averaging $313 a month.

40 HOUSING

In October 1996, there were an estimated 1,783,000 housing units in Alabama, of which 1,602,000 were occupied. As of 1996, about 71% of all housing units were owner-occupied.

A total of 19,868 new privately owned units valued at $1,508 million were authorized in 1996. During 1995/96, Alabama received $308.9 million in aid from the US Department of Housing and Urban Development (HUD), including $59.1 million in HUD community development block grants. In 1990, the most recent year for which the government has estimates, the median home value was $53,700. Median monthly costs for owners (with a mortgage) and renters in 1990 were $555 and $325, respectively.

The Fairhope Single Tax Corp., near Point Clear, was founded in 1893 by Iowans seeking to put into practice the economic theories of Henry George. Incorporated under Alabama law in 1904, this oldest and largest of US single-tax experiments continues to lease land in return for the payment of a rent (the "single tax") based on the land's valuation; the combined rents are used to pay taxes and to provide and improve community services.

41 EDUCATION

In 1995, 72% of Alabamians age 25 and older were high school graduates, the third-lowest rate in the nation. Approximately 10% of adult Alabamians had no education beyond the eighth grade.

The total enrollment in Alabama's public schools as of December of the 1995/96 school year was 736,825. Of these, 529,985 attended schools from kindergarten through grade eight, and 206,840 attended high school. In fall 1993, estimated enrollment in nonpublic schools was 35,000. In December 1995/96, 36.5% of all minority public school students were in schools with less than 50% minority group enrollment; 23.6% were in schools with 99–100% minority enrollment.

As of 1993/94, there were 64 institutions of higher education in Alabama: 48 public and 16 private. Thirty-two of the public schools are two-year institutions, many of them founded under former Governor George Wallace. The largest state universities are Auburn University, with a fall 1993 enrollment of 21,363; and the three University of Alabama campuses, including the main campus in Tuscaloosa, with 19,480 students; Birmingham, 15,913; and Huntsville, 8,232. Tuskegee University, founded as a normal and industrial school in 1881 under the leadership of Booker T. Washington, became one of the nation's most famous black colleges. Its fall 1993 enrollment was 3,371. The fall 1994 total enrollment in institutions of higher education was 229,511.

42 ARTS

The Alabama Council on the Arts and Humanities, established by the legislature in 1967, provides aid to local nonprofit arts organizations; there were 70 local arts councils in 1980. From 1987 to 1991, federal and state arts funding amounted to $12,510,407. The funding provided arts training for 29,000 school children. The grants supported the efforts of 125,390 artists and more than 400 arts associations.

A community arts development and residency program is financed by a state income tax check-off and private contributions. The Alabama Shakespeare Festival State Theater performs in Montgomery. The festival has been attended by over 1 million people. It has also generated $9.4 million and 337 jobs for the city of Montgomery. The Birmingham Festival of Arts was founded in 1951, and the city's Alabama School of Fine Arts has been state-supported since 1971. The arts have brought $53.9 million to Birmingham along with 515 full-time jobs. Huntsville, Montgomery, and Tuscaloosa have symphony orchestras.

Sacred Harp a cappella "sings" of old hymn tunes are held regularly. The Tennessee Valley Old Time Fiddlers Convention takes place in October at Athens State College. Every June, the annual Hank Williams Memorial Celebration is held near the country singer's birthplace at the Olive West Community.

43 LIBRARIES AND MUSEUMS

As of 1995, Alabama had 20 county and multicounty regional library systems. Alabama public libraries had a combined total of 7,252,492 volumes in 1995, when the total circulation was 15,053,076. The Amelia Gayle Gorgas Library of the University of Alabama had 1,661,003 volumes; the Birmingham Public and Jefferson County Free Library had 19 branches and 973,936 volumes. The Alabama Department of Archives and History Library, at Montgomery, had 35,000 cu ft (990 cu m) of records and special collections on Alabama history and government. Collections on aviation and space exploration in Alabama's libraries, particularly its military libraries, may be the most extensive in the US outside of Washington, D.C. In 1997 the Alabama Public Library Service and its regional library for the blind and physically handicapped had over 450,000 books, videos, and audio tapes, including more than 25,000 books in braille. Memorabilia of Wernher von Braun are in the library at the Alabama Space and Rocket Center at Huntsville; the Redstone Arsenal's Scientific Information Center holds over 240,000 volumes and 1,800,000 technical reports.

Alabama had 74 museums in 1995. The most important art museum is the Birmingham Museum of Art. Other museums include the George Washington Carver Museum at Tuskegee Institute, the Women's Army Corps Museum and Military Police Corps Museum at Ft. McClellan, the US Army Aviation Museum at Ft. Rucker, the Pike Pioneer Museum at Troy, the Museum of the City of Mobile, and the Montgomery Museum of Fine Arts. Also in Montgomery are Old Alabama Town and the F. Scott and Zelda Fitzgerald home. Russell Cave National Monument has an archaeological exhibit. In Florence is the W.C. Handy Home; at Tuscumbia, Helen Keller's birthplace, Ivy Green.

44COMMUNICATIONS
In March 1993, 92.6% of Alabama's 1,587,000 occupied housing units had telephones.

During 1996, Alabama had 294 operating radio stations (149 AM, 145 FM) and 39 television stations, of which 6 were noncommercial educational broadcast stations. In 1993, 11 large cable systems served the state.

45PRESS
The earliest newspaper in Alabama, the short-lived *Mobile Centinel* (sic), made its first appearance on 23 May 1811. The oldest newspaper still in existence in the state is the *Mobile Register,* founded in 1813.

As of 1997, Alabama had 14 morning dailies; 11 evening dailies; and 30 Sunday papers. The following table shows the leading dailies with their 1997 circulations:

AREA	NAME	DAILY	SUNDAY
Birmingham	*News* (e,S)	158,880	201,023
	Post–Herald (m)	57,030	
Huntsville	*Times* (e,S)	59,795	79,082
Mobile	*Register* (m)	74,333	
	Press (e)	26,893	
	Press Register (S)	118,862	
Montgomery	*Advertiser* (m)	60,073	74,063
Tuscaloosa	*News* (m,S)	38,239	40,373

46ORGANIZATIONS
The 1992 US Census of Service Industries counted 843 organizations in Alabama, including 201 business associations; 468 civic, social, and fraternal associations; and 174 other membership organizations. National organizations with headquarters in Alabama include Civitan International (Birmingham); the National Speleological Society (Huntsville); and Klanwatch and the Southern Poverty Law Center, both located in Montgomery. The last-named is one of the major civil rights organizations active in Alabama, along with the Southern Christian Leadership Conference (SCLC) and the National Association for the Advancement of Colored People (NAACP). Two branches of the Ku Klux Klan are also active in Alabama.

47TOURISM, TRAVEL, AND RECREATION
A top tourist attraction is the Alabama Space and Rocket Center at Huntsville, home of the US Space Camp. Other attractions include many antebellum houses and plantations: Magnolia Grove (a state shrine) at Greensboro; Gaineswood and Bluff Hall at Demopolis; Arlington in Birmingham; Oakleigh at Mobile; Sturdivant Hall at Selma; Shorter Mansion at Eufaula; and the first White House of the confederacy at Montgomery.

The celebration of Mardi Gras in Mobile, which began in 1704, predates that in New Orleans and now occupies several days before Ash Wednesday. Gulf beaches are a popular attraction, and Point Clear, across the bay from Mobile, has been a fashionable resort, especially for southerners, since the 1840s. The state fair is held at Birmingham every October.

During 1995, 1,039,796 tourists visited Alabama's four national park sites, which include Tuskegee Institute National Historic Site and Russell Cave National Monument, an almost continuous archaeological record of human habitation from at least 7000 BC to about AD 1650. During 1995, a smaller number of tourists (3,951,01) visited Alabama's 23 state parks covering a total of 49,710 acres (20,118 hectares). Tannehill Historical State Park features ante- and postbellum dwellings, a restored iron furnace over a century old, and a museum of iron and steel.

The Alabama Deep Sea Fishing Rodeo at Dauphin Island attracts thousands of visitors. In 1995, 305,556 hunting licenses and 593,133 fishing licenses were issued to visitors and state residents.

Alabama's Robert Trent Jones Golf Trail is a major tourist attraction, with seven championship courses located from Huntsville to Mobile.

48SPORTS
There are no major-league professional sports teams in Alabama. There are minor-league baseball clubs at Birmingham and Mobile, and minor-league hockey teams at Birmingham, Huntsville, and Mobile. Two major professional stock car races, the Winston 500 and Talladega 500, in May and July, respectively, are held at Alabama International Motor Speedway in Talladega. Dog-racing was legalized in Mobile in 1971. Four of the major hunting-dog competitions in the US are held annually in the state.

Football reigns supreme among collegiate sports. The University of Alabama finished number one in 1961, 1965 (with Michigan State), 1978 (with USC), 1979, and 1992 and is a perennial top 10 entry. Competing in the Southeastern Conference, Alabama's Crimson Tide won the Sugar Bowl in 1962, 1964, 1967, 1978, 1979, 1980, and 1993; the Orange Bowl in 1943, 1953, 1963, and 1966; the Cotton Bowl in 1942 and 1981; the Sun Bowl in 1983 and 1988; the Gator Bowl in 1993; and the Florida Citrus Bowl in 1995. Auburn University, which also competes in the Southeastern Conference, won the Sugar Bowl in 1984, the Florida Citrus Bowl in 1982 and 1987; the Gator Bowl in 1954, 1971, and 1972; the Peach Bowl in 1990; the Hall of Fame Bowl in 1990; and the Sun Bowl in 1968. The Blue-Gray game, an all-star contest, is held at Montgomery on Christmas Day, and the Senior-South game is played in Mobile. Additionally, Alabama-Huntsville won NCAA Division II hockey championships in 1996 and 1997.

Boat races include the Lake Eufaula Summer Spectacular Boat Race in August, and the Dixie Cup Regatta in Guntersville in July. The Alabama Sports Hall of Fame is located at Birmingham.

49FAMOUS ALABAMIANS
William Rufus De Vane King (b.North Carolina, 1786–1853) served as a US senator from Alabama and as minister to France before being elected US vice president in 1852 on the Democratic ticket with Franklin Pierce; he died six weeks after taking the oath of office. Three Alabamians who served as associate justices of the US Supreme Court were John McKinley (b.Virginia, 1780–1852), John A. Campbell (b.Georgia, 1811–89), and Hugo L. Black (1886–1971). Campbell resigned from the court in 1861, later becoming assistant secretary of war for the Confederacy; Black, a US senator from 1927 to 1937, served one of the longest terms (1937–71) in the history of the court and is regarded as one of its most eminent justices.

Among the most colorful figures in antebellum Alabama was William Lowndes Yancey (b.Georgia, 1814–63), a fiery orator who was a militant proponent of slavery, states' rights, and eventually secession. During the early 20th century, a number of Alabamians became influential in national politics. Among them were US senators John Hollis Bankhead (1842–1920) and John Hollis Bankhead, Jr. (1872–1946); the latter's brother, William B.

Bankhead (1874–1940), who became speaker of the US House of Representatives in 1936; and US Senator Oscar W. Underwood (b.Kentucky, 1862–1929), a leading contender for the Democratic presidential nomination in 1912 and 1924. Other prominent US senators from Alabama have included (Joseph) Lister Hill (1894–1984) and John Sparkman (1899–1985), who was the Democratic vice presidential nominee in 1952. Alabama's most widely known political figure is George Corley Wallace (b.1919), who served as governor in 1963–67 and 1971–79, and was elected to a fourth term in 1982. Wallace, an outspoken opponent of racial desegregation in the 1960s, was a candidate for the Democratic presidential nomination in 1964; four years later, as the presidential nominee of the American Independent Party, he carried five states. While campaigning in Maryland's Democratic presidential primary on 15 May 1972, Wallace was shot and paralyzed from the waist down by a would-be assassin. In 1976, Wallace made his fourth and final unsuccessful bid for the presidency.

Civil rights leader Martin Luther King, Jr. (b.Georgia, 1929–68), winner of the Nobel Peace Prize in 1964, first came to national prominence as leader of the Montgomery bus boycott of 1955; he also led demonstrations at Birmingham in 1963 and at Selma in 1965. His widow, Coretta Scott King (b.1927) is a native Alabamian. Federal judge Frank M. Johnson, Jr. (b.1918), has made several landmark rulings in civil rights cases.

Helen Keller (1880–1968), deaf and blind as the result of a childhood illness, was the first such multihandicapped person to earn a college degree; she later became a world-famous author and lecturer. Another world figure, black educator Booker T. Washington (b.Virginia, 1856–1915), built Alabama's Tuskegee Institute from a school where young blacks were taught building, farming, cooking, brickmaking, dressmaking, and other trades into an internationally known agricultural research center. Tuskegee's most famous faculty member was George Washington Carver (b.Missouri, 1864–1943), who discovered some 300 different peanut products, 118 new ways to use sweet potatoes, and numerous other crop varieties and applications. Among Alabama's leaders in medicine was Dr. William Crawford Gorgas (1854–1920), head of sanitation in Panama during the construction of the Panama Canal; he later served as US surgeon general. Brought to the US after World War II (1939–45), the internationally known scientist Wernher von Braun (b.Germany, 1912–77) came to Alabama in 1950 to direct the US missile program.

Two Alabama writers, (Nelle) Harper Lee (b.1926) and Edward Osborne Wilson (b.1929), have won Pulitzer Prizes. Famous musicians from Alabama include blues composer and performer W(illiam) C(hristopher) Handy (1873–1958), singer Nat "King" Cole (1917–65), and singer-songwriter Hank Williams (1923–53). Alabama's most widely known actress was Tallulah Bankhead (1903–68), the daughter of William B. Bankhead.

Among Alabama's sports figures are track and field star Jesse Owens (James Cleveland Owens, 1913–80), winner of four gold medals at the 1936 Olympic Games in Berlin; boxer Joe Louis (Joseph Louis Barrow, 1914–81), world heavyweight champion from 1937 to 1949; and baseball stars Leroy Robert "Satchel" Paige (1906?–82), Willie Mays (b.1931), and (Louis) Henry Aaron (b.1934), all-time US home-run leader.

[50]BIBLIOGRAPHY

Barnard, William D. *Dixiecrats and Democrats: Alabama Politics, 1942–1950.* University, Ala.: University of Alabama Press, 1974.

Carter, Dan T. *Scottsboro. A Tragedy of the American South.* Baton Rouge: Louisiana State University Press, 1969.

Lofton, J. Mack. *Voices from Alabama: A Twentieth-Century Mosaic.* Tuscaloosa: University of Alabama Press, 1993.

Marks, Henry S., and Marsha Marks. *Alabama Past Leaders.* Huntsville, Ala.: Strode, 1981.

Martin, David L. *Alabama's State and Local Government.* University, Ala.: University of Alabama Press, 1985.

Permaloff, Anne. *Political Power in Alabama: The More Things Change—.* Athens: University of Georgia Press, 1995.

Rogers, William Warren, and Robert David Ward. *August Reckoning: Jack Turner and Racism in Post-Civil War Alabama.* Baton Rouge: Louisiana State University Press, 1973.

Rosengarten, Theodore. *All God's Dangers: The Life of Nate Shaw.* New York: Knopf, 1974.

Van De Veer Hamilton, Virginia. *Hugo Black: The Alabama Years.* Baton Rouge: Louisiana State University Press, 1972.

ALASKA

State of Alaska

ORIGIN OF STATE NAME: From the Aleut world *alakshak*, meaning "peninsula" or "mainland." **CAPITAL:** Juneau. **ENTERED UNION:** 3 January 1959 (49th). **SONG:** "Alaska's Flag." **MOTTO:** North to the Future. **FLAG:** On a blue field, eight gold stars form the Big Dipper and the North Star. **OFFICIAL SEAL:** In the inner circle symbols of mining, agriculture, and commerce are depicted against a background of mountains and the northern lights. In the outer circle are a fur seal, a salmon, and the words "The Seal of the State of Alaska." **BIRD:** Willow ptarmigan. **FISH:** King salmon. **FLOWER:** Wild forget-me-not. **TREE:** Sitka spruce. **GEM:** Jade. **MINERAL:** Gold. **SPORT:** Dogteam racing (mushing). **LEGAL HOLIDAYS:** New Year's Day, 1 January; Birthday of Martin Luther King, Jr., 3d Monday in January; Lincoln's Birthday, 12 February; Washington's Birthday, 3d Monday in February; Seward's Day, last Monday in March; Memorial Day, last Monday in May; Independence Day, 4 July; Labor Day, 1st Monday in September; Alaska Day, 18 October; Veterans Day, 11 November; Thanksgiving Day, 4th Thursday in November; Christmas Day, 25 December. **TIME:** noon GMT = 3 AM Alaska Standard Time, 2 AM Hawaii-Aleutian Standard Time.

¹LOCATION, SIZE, AND EXTENT

Situated at the northwest corner of the North American continent, Alaska is separated by Canadian territory from the coterminous 48 states. Alaska is the largest of the 50 states, with a total area of 591,004 sq mi (1,530,699 sq km). Land takes up 570,833 sq mi (1,478,456 sq km) and inland water 20,171 sq mi (52,243 sq km). Alaska is more than twice the size of Texas, the next-largest state, and occupies 16% of the total US land area; the E-W extension is 2,261 mi (3,639 km); the maximum N-S extension is 1,420 mi (2,285 km).

Alaska is bounded on the N by the Arctic Ocean and Beaufort Sea; on the E by Canada's Yukon Territory and province of British Columbia; on the S by the Gulf of Alaska, Pacific Ocean, and Bering Sea; and on the w by the Bering Sea, Bering Strait, Chukchi Sea, and Arctic Ocean.

Alaska's many offshore islands include St. Lawrence, St. Matthew, Nunivak, and the Pribilof group in the Bering Sea; Kodiak Island in the Gulf of Alaska; the Aleutian Islands in the Pacific; and some 1,100 islands constituting the Alexander Archipelago, extending SE along the Alaska panhandle.

The total boundary length of Alaska is 8,187 mi (13,176 km), including a general coastline of 6,640 mi (10,686 km); the tidal shoreline extends 33,904 mi (54,563 km). Alaska's geographic center is about 60 mi (97 km) NW of Mt. McKinley. The northern-most point in the US—Point Barrow, at 71°23′30″N, 156°28′30″W—lies within the state of Alaska, as does the western-most point—Cape Wrangell on Attu Island in the Aleutians, at 52°55′30″N, 172°28′E. Little Diomede Island, belonging to Alaska, is less than 2 mi (3 km) from Big Diomede Island, belonging to the Soviet Union.

²TOPOGRAPHY

Topography varies sharply among the six distinct regions of Alaska. In the southeast is a narrow coastal panhandle cut off from the main Alaskan landmass by the St. Elias Range. This region, featuring numerous mountain peaks of 10,000 feet (3,000 meters) in elevation, is paralleled by the Alexander Archipelago. South-central Alaska, which covers a 700-mi (1,100-km) area along the Gulf of Alaska, includes the Kenai Peninsula and Cook Inlet, a great arm of the Pacific penetrating some 200 mi (320

km) to Anchorage. The southwestern region includes the Alaska Peninsula, filled with lightly wooded, rugged peaks; and the 1,700-mi (2,700-km) sweep of the Aleutian islands, barren masses of volcanic origin. Western Alaska extends from Bristol Bay to the Seward Peninsula, an immense tundra dotted with lakes and containing the deltas of the Yukon and Kuskokwim rivers, the longest in the state at 1,900 mi (3,058 km) and 680 mi (1,094 km), respectively. Interior Alaska extends north of the Alaska Range and south of the Brooks Range, including most of the drainage of the Yukon and its major tributaries, the Tanana and Porcupine rivers. The Arctic region extends from Kotzebue, north of the Seward Peninsula, east to Canada. From the northern slopes of the Brooks Range, the elevation falls to the Arctic Ocean.

The 11 highest mountains in the US—including the highest in North America, Mt. McKinley (20,320 feet—6,194 meters), located in the Alaska Range—are in the state, which also contains half the world's glaciers; the largest, Malaspina, covers more area than the entire state of Rhode Island. Ice fields cover 4% of the state. Alaska has more than 3 million lakes larger than 20 acres (8 hectares), and more than one-fourth of all the inland water wholly within the US lies inside the state's borders. The largest lake is Iliamna, occupying about 1,000 sq mi (2,600 sq km).

The most powerful earthquake in US recorded history, measuring 8.5 on the Richter scale, struck the Anchorage region on 27 March 1964, resulting in 114 deaths and $500 million in property damage in Alaska and along the US west coast.

³CLIMATE

Americans, who called Alaska "Seward's icebox" when it was first purchased from the Russians, were unaware of the variety of climatic conditions within its six topographic regions. Although minimum daily winter temperatures in the Arctic region and in the Brooks Range average –20°F (–29°C) and the ground at Point Barrow is frozen permanently to 1,330 feet (405 meters), summer maximum daily temperatures in the Alaskan lowlands average above 60°F (16°C) and have been known to exceed 90°F (32°C). The southeastern region is moderate, ranging from a daily average of 30°F (–1°C) in January to 56°F (13°C) in July; the south-central zone has a similar summer range, but winters are somewhat harsher, especially in the interior. The Aleutian Islands have chilly, damp winters and rainy, foggy weather for most of the year; western Alaska is also rainy and cool. The all-time high for the state was 100°F (38°C), recorded at Ft. Yukon on 27 June 1915; the reading of –79.8°F (–62°C) registered at Prospect Creek Camp, in the northwestern part of the state, on 23 January 1971 is the lowest temperature ever officially recorded in the US.

Juneau receives an average of 53 in (135 cm) of precipitation each year, but the entire southeastern region of Alaska has a wide range of microclimates with varying levels of precipitation; Juneau's metropolitan area precipitation ranges from 40 in (need cm) to over 100 in (need cm) per year.

[4]FLORA AND FAUNA

Life zones in Alaska range from grasslands, mountains, and tundra to thick forests, in which Sitka spruce (the state tree), western hemlock, tamarack, white birch, and western red cedar predominate. Various hardy plants and wild flowers spring up during the short growing season on the semiarid tundra plains. Species of poppy and gentian are endangered.

Mammals abound amid the wilderness. Great herds of caribou migrate across some northern areas of the state. Moose move within ranges they establish, but do not migrate seasonally or move in herds as do caribou. Reindeer were introduced to Alaska as herd animals for Alaska Natives, and there are no free-ranging herds in the state. Kodiak, polar, black, and grizzly bears, Dall sheep, and an abundance of small mammals are also found. The sea otter and musk ox have been successfully reintroduced. Round Island, along the north shore of Bristol Bay, has the world's largest walrus rookery. North America's largest population of bald eagles nest in Alaska, and whales migrate annually to the icy bays. Pristine lakes and streams are famous for trout and salmon fishing. In all, 386 species of birds, 430 fishes, 105 mammals, 7 amphibians, and 3 reptiles have been found in the state. Endangered species include the Eskimo curlew, American and Arctic peregrine falcons, Aleutian Canada goose, and short-tailed albatross; numerous species considered endangered in the conterminous US remain common in Alaska.

[5]ENVIRONMENTAL PROTECTION

In 1997, Alaska's number one environmental health problem was the unsafe water and sanitation facilities in over 135 of Alaska's communities—mostly Alaska Native villages. The people of these communities must carry their water from streams or watering points to their homes; people must use "honey buckets" or privies for disposal of human waste; and solid waste lagoons are usually a collection of human waste, trash, and junk, infested with flies and other carriers of disease. Governor Tony Knowles has established a goal of "putting the honey bucket in museums" by the year 2005. To accomplish this goal he has established the "Rural Sanitation Task force" to guide the effort and has committed approximately $40 million per year in state and federal funds to finance new water, sewer, and solid waste facilities.

A tremendous backlog of contaminated sites from World War II (1939–45) military installations exists, and some of these sites many years later were discovered to be the source of contamination of groundwater, drinking water, and fisheries habitat. Sites have been identified and prioritized and an aggressive state/federal cleanup effort is underway. Two former pulp mill sites in southeast Alaska are also the subject of major cleanup efforts.

The 1989 Exxon Valdez oil spill highlighted the need for better prevention and response abilities. Since then these capabilities have been increased through stronger laws and more clearly defined roles among all the various governments and communities and greatly enhanced state regulatory agency capabilities. State-of-the-art tugs are now escorting tankers in Prince William Sound; these tankers are constantly monitored to ensure that they stay on course, and their crews have been increased to ensure redundancy of critical positions.

Oil development on the North Slope and in Cook Inlet, mining throughout the state, and timber harvesting largely in the southern regions continue to be areas of focus for environmental protection, as do winter violations of air quality standards for carbon monoxide in Anchorage and Fairbanks.

Compliance assistance efforts in conjunction with voluntary pollution prevention programs in the business community, in addition to the protection afforded through laws and permit requirements, have helped ensure maintenance or enhancement of Alaska's incomparable environment.

[6]POPULATION

Alaska, with a land area one-fifth the size of the conterminous US, ranked 49th in population in 1990 with a census figure of 550,043. In 1996, Alaska's estimated population was 607,007. Regions of settlement and development constitute less than 0.001% of Alaska's total land area. The population density was 1 person per sq mi in 1990 (0.4 persons per sq km), and Alaska has now surpassed Wyoming's population total. The increase of 36.9% from 1980 to 1990 made Alaska the second-fastest-growing state during the period (behind only Nevada). Between 1990 and 1996, Alaska's population grew by 10.4%.

Historically, population shifts in Alaska have directly reflected economic and political changes. The Alaska gold rush of the 1890s resulted in a population boom from 32,052 in 1890 to 63,592 a decade later; by the 1920s, however, when mining had declined, Alaska's population had decreased to 55,036. The region's importance to US national defense during the 1940s led to a rise in population from 72,524 to 128,643 during that decade. Oil development, especially the construction of the Alaska pipeline, brought a 78% population increase between 1960 and 1980. Almost all of this gain was from migration; as of 1990, over 60% of all state residents had been born in another state. The state's population is much younger than that of the nation as a whole (the median age was only 31.5 in 1990), and only 4.1% of all Alaskans were 65 years of age or older in 1990—by far the lowest such percentage in any state. Alaska is also one of the few states where men outnumber women (by 12.5% in 1989).

About half of Alaska's residents live in and around Anchorage, whose population was about 251,335 in 1995. The 1990 populations of other leading metropolitan areas were Fairbanks, 77,720; and Juneau, 26,751. Only about 10% of the population lives in Western Alaska.

[7]ETHNIC GROUPS

Indians—primarily Athabaskan, Tlingit, Haida, and small numbers of Tsimshian—living in southeastern Alaska (Alaska Panhandle) numbered around 34,000 in 1990. Eskimos (42,024) and Aleuts (10,244), the other native people, live mostly in scattered villages to the north and northwest. Taken together, Alaska Natives numbered about 86,000 in 1996, 16% of the population. The Native Claims Settlement Act of 1971 gave 13 native corporations nearly $1 billion in compensation for exploration, mining, and drilling rights, and awarded them royalties on oil and the rights to nearly 12% of Alaska's land area.

In 1990, blacks numbered around 22,000, or 4% of the population. Among those of Asian and Pacific Islands origin were 8,584 Filipinos, 3,009 Japanese, and 4,349 Koreans. Out of Alaska's total population, about 18,000 individuals were of Hispanic origin, with 6,888 of those claiming Mexican ancestry. Foreign-born persons numbered 24,814 in 1990, 4.4% of the population.

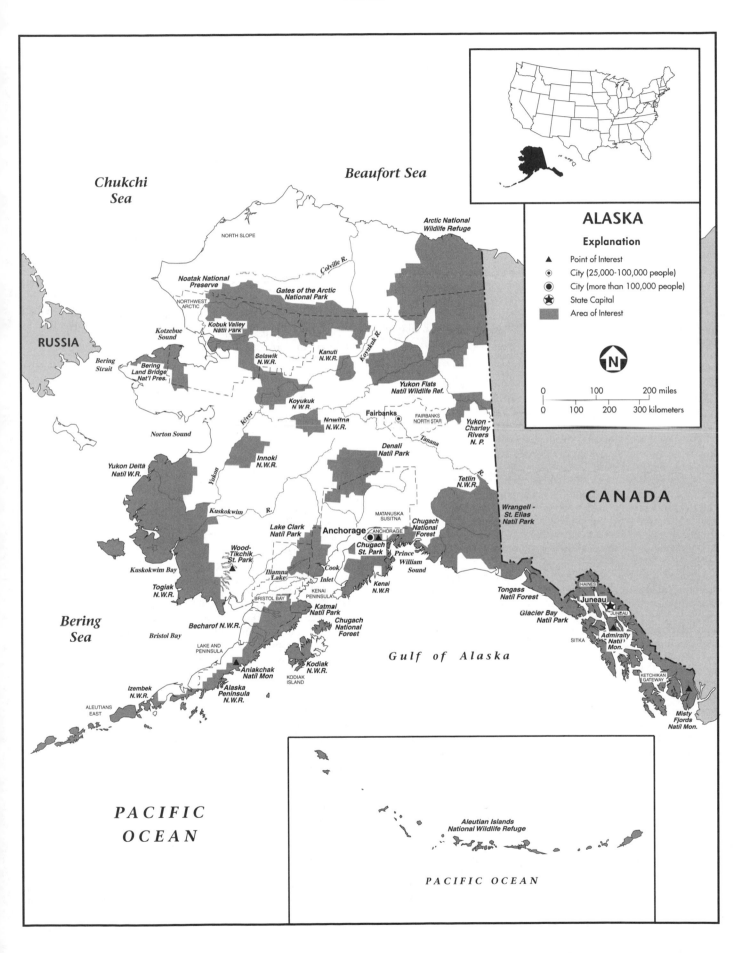

Chukchi
Sea

Beaufort Sea

RUSSIA

ALASKA

Explanation

▲ Point of Interest

⊙ City (25,000-100,000 people)

◉ City (more than 100,000 people)

★ State Capital

Area of Interest

| 0 | 100 | 200 miles |
| 0 | 100 | 200 | 300 kilometers |

NORTH SLOPE

Arctic National
Wildlife Refuge

Colville R.

Noatak National
Preserve

Gates of the Arctic
National Park

NORTHWEST
ARCTIC

Kobuk Valley
Nat'l Park

Kotzebue
Sound

Koyukuk R.

Kanuti
N.W.R.

Selawik
N.W.R.

Bering
Land Bridge
Nat'l Pres.

Bering
Strait

Yukon Flats
Nat'l Wildlife Ref.

Koyukuk
N W R

Yukon -
Charley
Rivers
N. P.

Norton Sound

River

Nowitna
N.W.R.

Fairbanks

FAIRBANKS
NORTH STAR

Innoki
N.W.R.

Yukon Delta
Nat'l W.R.

Yukon

Tanana

Denali
Nat'l Park

Tetlin
N.W.R.

R.

CANADA

Wrangell -
St. Elias
Nat'l Park

Kuskokwim

R.

Lake Clark
Nat'l Park

MATANUSKA
SUSITNA

Chugach
National
Forest

Wood-
Tikchik
St. Park

Anchorage
◉ ANCHORAGE ▲

Chugach
St. Park

Prince
William
Sound

Kuskokwim Bay

Iliamna
Lake

Cook
Inlet

KENAI
PENINSULA

BRISTOL BAY

Kenai
N.W.R

Tongass
Nat'l Forest

HAINES

Juneau
JUNEAU ★

Togiak
N.W.R.

Katmai
Nat'l Park

Chugach
National
Forest

Glacier Bay
Nat'l Park

Becharof N.W.R.

Bering
Sea

Bristol Bay

LAKE AND
PENINSULA

Admiralty
Nat'l
Mon.

SITKA

Aniakchak
Nat'l Mon

Kodiak
N.W.R.

KODIAK
ISLAND

Gulf of Alaska

KETCHIKAN
GATEWAY

Izembek
N.W.R.

Alaska
Peninsula
N.W.R.

ALEUTIANS
EAST

Misty
Fjords
Nat'l Mon.

**PACIFIC
OCEAN**

Aleutian Islands
National Wildlife Refuge

PACIFIC OCEAN

[8]LANGUAGES

From the Tlingit, Haida, and Tsimshian groups of lower Alaska almost no language influence has been felt, save for *hooch* (from Tlingit *hoochino*); but some native words have escaped into general usage, notably Eskimo *mukluk* and Aleut *parka*. Native place-names abound: Skagway and Ketchikan (Tlingit), Kodiak and Katmai (Eskimo), and Alaska and Akutan (Aleut).

In 1990, 87.9% of the population five years old and older was reported to speak only English in the home. Other major languages spoken in the home, and the number of people speaking them, included various Native American and Aleut languages, 26,780; Spanish, 10,020; and Tagalog, 5,124.

[9]RELIGIONS

The largest religious organization in the state is the Roman Catholic Church, which had 45,203 members in 1990. Southern Baptists constituted the largest Protestant denomination, with 28,718 adherents in 1990. Other major groups were the Latter-day Saints (Mormons), 15,751; Assembly of God, 8,779; United Presbyterians, 6,307; and Episcopalians, 7,540. There is a very small Jewish population as of 1997.

Many Aleuts were converted to the Russian Orthodox religion during the 18th century, and small Russian Orthodox congregations are still active on the Aleutian Islands, in Kodiak and southeastern Alaska, and along the Yukon River.

[10]TRANSPORTATION

The first rail transportation networks in Alaska were constructed to serve mining interests. The 110-mile-long (177-km-long) White Pass and Yukon Railway (WP&YRR), originally constructed during the Klondike Gold Rush and completed in 1900, constituted the key link between tidewater at Skagway, the Yukon River, and the gold fields. Today, this line runs as a summer-only tourist attraction and provides service between Skagway and Fraser, British Columbia. Shortly after the turn of the century, the Guggenheims financed the construction of the Copper River & Northwestern Railway, which connected Cordova and McCarthy to service the Kennicott Copper Mining Company.

Regular passenger and freight railroad service began in 1923, when the Alaska Railroad began operation. The Alaska Railroad links communities between Whittier, Seward, Anchorage, and Fairbanks. This railroad of 480 route miles (772 km) is not connected to any other North American line (although rail-barge service provides access to the rest of the US rail network). The Alaska Railroad was federally operated until 1985 when it was bought by the state government for $22.3 million. The railroad carries volumes of coal from Healy north to Fairbanks (600,000 tons/year) and south to Seward for export (800,000 tons/year). The railroad also carries large volumes of gravel to Anchorage (2.3 million tons from Palmer in 1993) and petroleum products (1.3 million tons from Mapco's North Pole refinery) to Anchorage and various military bases in the area. The railroad is increasing summer passenger travel, often by hauling dome/dining rail cars owned by tour companies.

The Alaska Highway, which extends 1,523 miles (2,451 km) from Dawson Creek, British Columbia, to Fairbanks, is the only total road link with the rest of the US. In-state roads are few and far between: although Fairbanks, Anchorage, and Seward are linked, Juneau, the state capital, has no road link. In total, 13,486 mi (21,706 km) of roads were in use in 1995, including 1,880 mi (3,025 km) of roads in national parks and forests. During the same year, the state had 542,186 registered vehicles and 405,588 licensed drivers. The largest public transit system, that of Anchorage, accommodated 3.1 million unlinked passenger trips in 1994.

The Alaska Marine Highway System (AMHS) provides year-round scheduled ferry service to 32 communities throughout southeast and southwest Alaska. Service extends from Bellingham, Washington, and Prince Rupert, British Columbia. This nine-vessel ferry system extends over 3,500 route miles (5,632 km) and connects communities with each other, with regional centers, and with the continental road system.

Water transport in Alaska is dominated by Valdez, which annually ships about 100 million tons of crude petroleum from the Trans-Alaska Pipeline Terminal. Kenai/Nikishka is the state's second-largest freight-handling port and also has petroleum as its principal commodity. Anchorage is the state's largest general cargo port with over 2.7 million tons per year.

Air travel is the primary means of intrastate transportation, with regional carriers serving remote communities. The state operates 258 airports, including two major international airports in Anchorage and Fairbanks. In addition, there are 854 other airports in the state. In 1991, there were 9,678 active pilots and 6,616 registered aircraft in the state, with about 995,000 hours flown—3.3% of the nation's total. Anchorage International Airport (AIA) is a major refueling stop for international freight airplanes and is a freight hub for Federal Express and United Parcel Service. It is the nation's largest cargo airport as measured by maximum gross weight of annual aircraft landings.

[11]HISTORY

At some time between 10,000 and 40,000 years ago, the ancestors of all of America's aboriginal peoples trekked over a land bridge that connected northeastern Siberia with northwestern America. These early hunter-gatherers dispersed, eventually becoming three distinct groups: Aleut, Eskimo, and Indian.

Ages passed before overseas voyagers rediscovered Alaska. Separate Russian parties led by Aleksei Chirikov and Vitas Bering (who had sailed in 1728 through the strait that now bears his name) landed in Alaska in 1741. Within a few years, the discoverers were followed by the exploiters, who hunted the region's fur-bearing animals. In 1784, the first permanent Russian settlement was established on Kodiak Island: 15 years later, the Russian American Company was granted a monopoly over the region. Its manager, Aleksandr Baranov, established Sitka as the company's headquarters. In 1802, the Tlingit Indians captured Sitka, but two years later lost the town and the war with the Russian colonizers. Fluctuations in the fur trade, depletion of the sea otter, and the Russians' inability to make their settlements self-sustaining limited their development of the region. Increasingly, the czarist government viewed the colonies as a drain on the treasury. In 1867, as a result of the persistence of Secretary of State William H. Seward, a devoted American expansionist, Russia agreed to sell its American territories to the US for $7,200,000. From 1867 until the first Organic Act of 1884, which provided for a federally appointed governor, Alaska was administered first by the US Army, then by the US Customs Service.

The pace of economic development quickened after the discovery of gold in 1880 at Juneau. Prospectors began moving into the eastern interior after this success, leading to gold strikes on Forty Mile River in 1886 and at Circle in 1893. But it was the major strike in Canada's Klondike region in 1896 that sparked a mass stampede to the Yukon Valley and other regions of Alaska, including the Arctic. The gold rush led to the establishment of permanent towns in the interior for the first time.

Subsequent development of the fishing and timber industries increased Alaska's prosperity and prospects, although the region suffered from a lack of transportation facilities. A significant achievement came in 1914, when construction started on the Alaska Railroad connecting Seward, a new town with an ice-free port, with Anchorage and Fairbanks. Politically there were advances as well. In 1906, Alaskans were allowed to elect a nonvoting delegate to Congress for the first time. Congress granted territorial status to the region in 1912, and the first statehood bill was introduced in Congress four years later.

Mineral production declined sharply after 1914. Population declined too, and conditions remained depressed through the 1920s, although gold mining was helped by a rise in gold prices in 1934. World War II (1939–45) provided the next great economic impetus for Alaska; the Aleutian campaign that followed the Japanese invasion of the islands, though not as pivotal as the combat in other areas of the Pacific, did show American policymakers that Alaska's geography was in itself an important resource. Thus the spurt of federal construction and movement of military personnel continued even after the war ended, this time directed at the Soviet Union—only 40 mi (64 km) across the Bering Strait—rather than Japan.

The US government built the Alaska Highway and many other facilities, including docks, airfields, and an extension of the Alaska Railroad. Population soared as thousands of civilian workers and military personnel moved to the territory. The newcomers added impetus to a new movement for statehood, and the Alaska Statehood Act was adopted by Congress in June 1958 and ratified by Alaska voters that August. On 3 January 1959, President Dwight Eisenhower signed the proclamation that made Alaska the 49th state.

In 1971, the Native Claims Settlement Act provided an extensive grant to the state's natives but also precipitated a long federal–state controversy over land allocations. A major oil field was discovered in 1968, and in 1974, over the opposition of many environmentalists, construction began on the 789-mi (1,270-km) Trans-Alaska Pipeline from Prudhoe Bay to Valdez. The oil that began flowing through the pipeline in 1977 made Alaska almost immediately one of the nation's leading energy producers.

Alaska's extraordinary oil wealth enabled it to embark on a heavy program of state services and to abolish the state income tax. However, state spending failed to stimulate the private sector to the degree expected. Further, the state's dependence on oil—82% of its revenue came from oil industry taxes and royalties—became a disadvantage when overproduction in the Middle East drove the price of oil down from $36 a barrel at the peak of Alaska's oil boom in 1980–81 to $13.50 a barrel in 1988. In 1986, the state's revenues had declined by two-thirds. Alaska lost 20,000 jobs between 1985 and 1989. The economy's collapse forced 10,000 properties into foreclosure in those years. At the same time, the state rapidly depleted its oil reserves. In 1981, the Interior Department estimated that 83 billion barrels of undiscovered oil existed. By 1989, that estimate had dropped to 49.

On 24 March 1989, the *Exxon Valdez*, a 987-ft (300-m) oil tanker, hit a reef and ran aground. The tanker spilled 11 million gallons of crude oil. The oil eventually contaminated 1,285 mi (2,068 km) of shoreline, fouling Prince William Sound and its wildlife sanctuary, the Gulf of Alaska, and the Alaska Peninsula. In the settlement of the largest environmental suit in US history brought by the state and federal governments, Exxon was fined $1.025 billion in civil and criminal penalties. By 1992, some $2 billion had been spent cleaning up Prince William Sound.

In the early 1990s, oil production in Prudhoe Bay was declining, a development that forced Governor Tony Knowles to implement cutbacks in state spending and brought a renewal of proposals to open the 1.5-million-acre (607,000-hectare) Arctic National Wildlife Refuge to oil and gas exploration. Republican control of Congress offered renewed hope to those backing such a measure, although President Clinton vowed to veto any legislation opening the refuge to commercial development.

12STATE GOVERNMENT

Under Alaska's first and only constitution—adopted in 1956, effective since the time of statehood, and amended 19 times by the end of 1983—the house of representatives consists of 40 members elected for two-year terms; the senate has 20 members elected for staggered four-year terms. The minimum age is 21 for a representative, 25 for a senator; legislators must have resided in the state for at least three years before election and in the district at least one year. In 1995, legislators' salaries were $24,012.

Alaska's executive branch, modeled after New Jersey's, features a strong governor who appoints all cabinet officers (except the commissioner of education) and judges subject to legislative confirmation. The lieutenant governor is the only other elected executive. The governor must be at least 30 years of age, and must have been a US citizen for seven years and an Alaska resident for seven years. The term of office is four years, and the governor is limited to two consecutive terms. The qualifications for the lieutenant governor are the same as for the governor. In 1996, the governor's salary was $81,648.

After a bill has been passed by the legislature, it becomes law if signed by the governor; if left unsigned for 15 days (Sundays excluded) while the legislature is in session, or for 20 days after it has adjourned; or if passed by a two-thirds vote of the combined houses over a gubernatorial veto (to override a veto of an appropriations bill requires a three-fourths vote). Constitutional amendments require a two-thirds vote of the legislature and ratification by the electorate. Any US citizen at least 18 years of age who has been a resident of a voting district for 30 days may register to vote in that district.

Between 1993 and 1995, the Constitutional Revision Task Force studied alternatives to existing methods of revising the state constitution, recommending the appointment of a permanent advisory commission to submit proposals to the state legislature.

13POLITICAL PARTIES

When Congress debated the statehood question in the 1950s, it was assumed that Alaska would be solidly Democratic, but this expectation has not been borne out; as of 1994, of 306,440 registered voters, only 15% were Democrat, while 22% were Republican, and 59% were unaffiliated. In 1990, a member of the Alaskan Independent party, Walter J. Hickel, was elected governor. Democrat Tony Knowles won the governorship in the November 1994 election. Two Republicans, Frank Murkowski and Ted Stevens, were reelected to the US Senate in 1992 and 1996, respectively.

Alaska Presidential Vote by Major Political Parties, 1960–96

YEAR	ELECTORAL VOTE	ALASKA WINNER	DEMOCRAT	REPUBLICAN
1960	3	Nixon (R)	29,809	30,953
1964	3	*Johnson (D)	44,329	22,930
1968	3	*Nixon (R)	35,411	37,600
1972	3	*Nixon (R)	32,967	55,349
1976	3	Ford (R)	44,058	71,555
1980	3	*Reagan (R)	41,842	86,112
1984	3	*Reagan (R)	62,007	138,377
1988	3	*Bush (R)	72,584	119,251
1992**	3	Bush (R)	78,294	102,000
1996***	3	Dole (R)	80,380	122,746

* Won US presidential election.

** Independent candidate Ross Perot received 73,481 votes.

*** Independent candidate Ross Perot received 26,333 votes.

In 1996, Alaska's US Representative, Republican Don Young, was also reelected. In presidential elections since 1968, Alaskans have voted Republican eight consecutive times. Alaskans gave Bob Dole 51% of the vote in 1996, while Bill Clinton received 33% and independent Ross Perot garnered 11%. In 1997 Alaska's state legislature consisted of 7 Democrats and 13 Republicans in the state senate, and 15 Democrats, 25 Republicans, and 1 Independent in the state house. Alaska had 3 black elected officials in 1993, and 15 women holding statewide public office in 1995

14LOCAL GOVERNMENT

Unlike most other states, Alaska has no counties. Instead, the needs of its small, scattered population were met in 1992 by 12 boroughs (covering 40% of the state) governed by elected assemblies; the rest of the state was considered an unorganized borough. As of 1992 there were 148 cities, most of them governed by elected mayors and councils. Juneau, Sitka, and Anchorage, known as Alaska's three unified municipalities, have consolidated city and borough functions.

15STATE SERVICES

By law, Alaska's government may contain no more than 20 administrative departments. As of 1994 there were 14: Administration, Commerce and Economic Development, Community and Regional Affairs, Education, Environmental Conservation, Fish and Game, Health and Social Services, Labor, Law, Military Affairs, Natural Resources, Public Safety, Revenue, and Transportation and Public Facilities. In addition, the state has an ombudsman with limited powers to investigate citizen complaints against state agencies.

16JUDICIAL SYSTEM

The supreme court, consisting of a chief justice and 4 associate justices, hears appeals for civil matters from the 15 superior courts, whose 30 judges are organized among the four state judicial districts, and for criminal matters from the 3-member court of appeals. The superior court has original jurisdiction in all civil and criminal matters, and it hears appeals from the district court. The lowest court is the district court, of which there are 56 in four districts. All judges are appointed by the governor from nominations made by the Judicial Council, but are thereafter subject to voter approval; supreme court justices serve terms of 10 years; court of appeals and superior court judges, 6 years; and district judges, 4 years. Alaska had 2,196 practicing attorneys in 1996.

In 1995, the crime rate was 5,753.8 crimes per 100,000 population; murder and non-negligent manslaughter, 9.1; forcible rape, 80.3. Alaska has no capital punishment statute. There were 3,132 inmates in 20 state and federal prisons at the end of 1995. Alaska had an incarceration rate of 519 per 100,000 inhabitants.

17ARMED FORCES

A huge buildup of military personnel occurred after World War II (1939–45), as the Cold War with the Soviet Union led the US to establish the Distant Early Warning (DEW) System, Ballistic Missile Early Warning System, and Joint Surveillance System in the area. Later years saw a cutback in personnel, however, from a high of 40,214 in 1962 to 16,625 in 1996, 9,504 of them in the Air Force. Anchorage is the home of both the largest Army base, Ft. Richardson, and the largest Air Force base, Elmendorf. In the Aleutians are several Navy facilities and the Shemya Air Force Base. Alaska firms received defense contracts worth $564 million in 1995/96.

About 64,000 veterans were living in Alaska as of 1 July 1996, of whom fewer than 10 served in World War (1914–18), 8,000 in World War II (1939–45), 8,000 during the Korean conflict (1950–53), 30,000 during the Vietnam era (1954–75), and 3,000 in the Persian Gulf War (1990–91). Expenditures on veterans amounted to $120 million in 1995/96.

The Alaska State Troopers provide police protection throughout the state, except in the larger cities, where municipal police forces have jurisdiction. In 1993, the Alaska State Troopers employed 300 full-time sworn officers, or 6 per 10,000 residents. Army Reserve and National Guard personnel numbered 3,908 in 1996, and Air National Guard and Reserve strength was 2,450 during the same year.

18MIGRATION

The earliest immigrants to North America, more than 10,000 years ago, likely came to Alaska via a land bridge across what is now the Bering Strait. The Russian fur traders who arrived during the 1700s found Aleuts, Eskimos, and Indians already established there. Despite more than a century of Russian sovereignty over the area, however, few Russians came, and those that did returned to the mother country with the purchase of Alaska by the US in 1867.

Virtually all other migration to Alaska has been from the continental US—first during the gold rush of the late 19th century, and most recently during the oil boom of the 1970s. Between 1970 and 1983, Alaska's net gain from migration was 78,000, but Alaska suffered net losses in domestic migration of over 37,500 from 1985 to 1990, and 11,160 between 1990 and 1996.

Mobility is a way of life in Alaska. In 1990, only 41% of those 5 years or older were living in the same house as in 1985, and 37% of those who reported living in a different house in 1985 did so in another state. Urbanization increased with migration during the 1980s; the urban population increased from 64.5% in 1980 to 67.5% of the total population in 1990. In the 1980s, migration added 36,000 people to the state, or 34% of the total population increase. Only 34% of the 1990 population was born within the state, a lower percentage than any other state but Florida and Nevada.

19INTERGOVERNMENTAL COOPERATION

Alaska participates with Washington, Oregon, and Idaho in the Pacific Marine Fisheries Compact. Alaska also belongs to other western regional agreements covering energy, corrections, and education. The most important federal–state effort, the Joint Federal-State Land Use Planning Commission, was involved with the Alaska lands controversy throughout the 1970s. Federal aid to Alaska was $1.1 billion in 1995/96.

20ECONOMY

When Alaska gained statehood in 1959, its economy was almost totally dependent on the US government. Fisheries, limited mining (mostly gold and gravel), and some lumber production made up the balance. That all changed with development of the petroleum industry during the 1970s. Construction of the Trans–Alaska Pipeline brought a massive infusion of money and people into the state. Construction, trade, and services boomed—only to decline when the pipeline was completed.

In the mid-1980s, the economy was heavily dependent on government spending, especially by the state, and on the oil industry, which by 1984 supplied 85% of state revenues. The collapse of the oil prices in the mid-1980s hit Alaska hard. Employment dropped 9.4% between 1986 and 1988. By 1990, a recovery was underway. Accumulated gains in employment, while small, more than compensated for the losses of a few years before.

One area of growth in the 1980s and early 1990s was the Alaska groundfish industry. Commercial fishing is one of the bulwarks of the Alaska economy. The seafood industry had wholesale values of more than $3 billion in 1990, and Alaska's fishery accounts for 50% of the total annual US catch. The volume of Alaska groundfish catches rose from 69 million lb (31.3 million kg) in 1980 to 4.8 billion lb (2.2 billion kg) in 1990. Employment in seafood harvesting grew from 45,000 in 1980 to 54,000 in 1991, although the boom has slowed somewhat since.

Other industries, however, continued to suffer. Retrenchment of oil and gas companies reduced mining jobs by 11% in 1992. Log exports began to decline in 1990 and are expected to drop 50% by 1997 as the supply of timber shrinks. In 1993, the state sued the federal government for violating the Statehood Act. The act had entitled Alaska to 90% of the revenues from mineral leasing on federal lands. Since passage of the Act, however, half of the federal lands had been withdrawn from mineral leasing. In 1994, Alaska's gross state product was $22,712 billion, of which private goods-producing industries provided $6,800 million; private services-producing industries, $11,178 million; and government, $4,742 million. In 1996, there were 1,226 bankruptcy filings, almost a 30% increase from the previous year.

21INCOME

Alaska's per capita income ranked 19th among the US states at $24,558 in 1996, $327 above the national average. Alaska was among the 10 states with the lowest growth between 1995 and 1996, at 2.1%, compared to 4.5% for the US as a whole. The median household income in 1995 was $47,954, and the median income for four-person families was $56,045.

Living costs are high: in 1995, Anchorage, Fairbanks, and Juneau all had a cost of living some 25–35% above the US urban average. A total of 7.1% of all Alaskans were living below the federal poverty level in 1995. Alaskans had a per capita disposable income of $21,277 in 1996.

22LABOR

Alaska has a very seasonal economy, with extreme fluctuations in employment and unemployment. Of the 315,900 persons in the civilian labor force in 1996, 24,700 were unemployed. The rate of 7.8% was the second-highest in the US, and the rate for Alaskan natives was much higher. Due to seasonality, the statewide rate fluctuated from 9.8% in January to 5.9% in August.

A federal survey in 1995 revealed the following earnings and employment pattern projection for major industry groups in Alaska:

	EARNINGS (IN $MILLIONS)	EMPLOYMENT IN THOUSANDS
Total	11,775.4	372.5
Farm	11.9	0.7
Nonfarm	11,763.5	371.8
Private	8,209.4	277.6
Agricultural service, forestry, fisheries	248.8	14.9
Mining	911.1	11.6
Construction	928.8	19.5
Manufacturing	662.7	19.1
Nondurable goods	455.8	14.5
Durable goods	206.9	4.6
Transportation and public utilities	1,181.3	27.9
Wholesale trade	349.4	9.9
Retail Trade	1,136.8	57.7
Finance, insurance, and real estate	425.1	21.2
Services	2,365.4	95.8
Government and government enterprises	3,554.1	94.2

About 23.1% of all workers belonged to labor unions in 1995, the third-highest percentage in the US. The International Brotherhood of Teamsters is especially strong in the state, covering a range of workers from truck drivers to school administrators.

Wage rates averaged $464 per week for production workers in December 1996.

23AGRICULTURE

A short but intense growing season provides good potential for Alaska commercial agriculture, although the expense of getting agricultural products to market is a limiting factor. International export opportunities are being developed. Farm income in 1997 was approximately $30.2 million. Hay, potatoes, lettuce, cabbage, carrots, beef, pork, dairy products, and greenhouse and nursery items are common commodities produced. In 1996, hay production was 14,400 tons, valued at $2,736,000; potatoes, 129,000 hundredweight (5,851,440 kg), $2,490,000); and barley for grain, 285,000 tons, $926,000. In 1997, there were about 520 farms and 920,000 acres (370,000 hectares) in farms; the leading farming regions are the Matanuska Valley, northeast of Anchorage, and Delta Junction, north of Fairbanks.

24ANIMAL HUSBANDRY

Dairy and livestock products account for about 22% of Alaska's agricultural income. In 1995, an estimated 11.3 million lb (5.1 million kg) of milk, valued at $2.3 million, were produced by 700 milk cows. Meat and poultry production is negligible by national standards.

25FISHING

Alaska was the leading fishing state in terms of earnings and in the total weight of catch in 1995. The salmon catch, the staple of the industry, amounted to 1.1 billion lb (0.5 billion kg) of fish valued at $495.9 million in 1995. The distribution of Alaska salmon landings by species that year was sockeye, 32%; pink, 39%; chum, 24%; coho, 4%; and chinook, 1%. The cod catch in 1995 was a record 589,695,000 lb (267,485,650 kg), valued at $109,034,000. Concerns of possible exhaustion of wild pollock stocks have resulted in a reduction in the total allowable catch for pollock. Crab, a major export item, had recently declined in availability; the sablefish harvest, however, was over 47.4 million lb (21.5 million kg) in 1995, accounting for 72% of the US sablefish catch in 1995. In all, Alaska's commercial catch in 1995 totaled over 5.4 billion lb (2.5 billion kg, down from the record high of 5.9 billion lb, or 2.7 billion kg, in 1993), valued at $1.4 billion—providing 55% of the total commercial landing of the US. In that year, Dutch Harbor–Unalaska ranked 1st and Kodiak 2d among US fishing ports for both quantity (684.6 million lb/ 310.5 million kg, 362.4 million lb/164.4 million kg) and value ($146.2 million, $105.4 million). Alaska had 321 processing and wholesale plants with an average of about 10,778 employees during 1994, as well as a commercial fishing fleet of 16,277 boats and vessels that year.

Anglers are attracted by Alaska's abundant stocks of salmon and trout. There were over 402,400 sport anglers licensed in Alaska in 1995/96.

26FORESTRY

In 1992, Alaska's forested area was 129.1 million acres (52.2 million hectares), far more than any other state. However, the area of harvestable timberland was only 15.1 million acres (6.1 million hectares), 15th among the states. Some 9.8 million acres (4 million hectares) of forestland were privately held in 1994. Alaska contains the nation's largest natural forests, Tongass in the southeast (17.4 million acres—7 million hectares) and Chugach along the Gulf Coast (6.6 million acres—2.7 million hectares).

Timber companies harvest logs from the two national forests with the majority from the Tongass National Forest (annual harvest, 220 million board feet). The timber is made available for harvest through a competitive bidding process.

Lumbering and related industries employed about 10,500 workers in 1995. In that same year, the value added by manufacture from the lumber and wood products industry was $443.7 million, with shipments of $1.056 million.

27MINING

The US Geological Survey estimated the 1995 value for Alaska nonfuel mineral production at $594 million, about 15% more than the $519 million reported in 1994. Metallic minerals accounted for 86% of Alaska's total nonfuel mineral production in 1995. Increases in zinc and lead production at the Red Dog Mine in northwestern Alaska were the main causes for the increased mineral value. The Red Dog Mine is the largest producer of zinc in the world, supplying 8% of the world's mined zinc in 1995.

In 1995, Alaska produced 4 million metric tons of crushed stone, valued at $25 million; 200,000 oz (5,630 kg) gold, $67.6 million; 15.5 million metric tons of sand and gravel, $56.6 million. The state ranked 21st nationally in the value of mineral production. Its ranking among the states for specific minerals was: zinc (1st), lead (2d), silver (5th), and gold (7th of 14 states).

State estimates show that 3,406 people were employed in all aspects of the mineral industry during 1995, compared to about 3,083 employed in 1994.

Exploration continued to focus on gold prospects and formerly producing gold mines. There is renewed interest in both copper-molybdenum and sulfide base-metal exploration in several areas. This interest arises in part in anticipation of steady demand for industrial metals.

Late in 1992, the Alaska Department of Natural Resources (DNR) began to select its final 20 million acres (8 million hectares) of land from the federal government as part of the 1959 Alaska Statehood Act. When Alaska became a state it was awarded 105.3 million acres (42.6 million hectares) of land; state government researched natural resource values in order to make its final decisions by a January 1994 deadline. The DNR presents reclamation awards to mining firms for exemplary work in returning disturbed ground to useful condition as required by state law. In 1995, the awards went to 10 placer operations and 1 hardrock mining company.

28ENERGY AND POWER

As of 1996, Alaskan production of crude oil was 24% of the nation's total, and 2d only to that of Texas. Of the 510.8 million barrels produced, 97% came from the vast North Shore fields and 3% from the Cook Inlet area. The Trans-Alaska Pipeline, which runs 789 mi (1,270 km) from the North Slope oil fields to the port of Valdez on the southern coast, carried l,450,000 barrels of crude oil a day in 1996. Most of Alaska's energy products are produced and refined locally. Proved reserves as of 31 December 1996 in Alaska totaled 7.3 billion barrels, or about one-quarter of national reserves.

Natural gas production in 1996 was 490.6 billion cu ft (13.9 billion cu m), 7th among states. In 1996, proved reserves were 32.8 trillion cu ft (1 trillion cu m). Electric power production totaled over 4.8 billion kWh in 1995; installed capacity was nearly 1.9 million kW, and almost all generating facilities were government-owned. Alaska also had proved coal reserves totaling 6.5 billion tons in 1996. Production of coal in 1996 was 1,481,000 tons, from a single mine at Healy. Alaska's total consumption of energy per capita was 1,001.6 million Btu (252.4 kcal) in 1993, over three times greater than the national average.

29INDUSTRY

Alaska's small but growing manufacturing sector is centered on petroleum refining and the processing of lumber and food products, especially seafood.

Of Alaska's 10 top employers, 5 are engaged in the petroleum industry: ARCO Alaska, VECO, BP Exploration, Alyeska Pipeline Service, and Alaska Petroleum Contractors. Other principal employers among industry groups are food and kindred products, lumber and wood products, and printing and publishing. In 1995, there were 48 US patents issued to Alaskan residents.

30COMMERCE

Alaska had 908 wholesale trade establishments in 1992, according to the Census of Wholesale Trade, with sales of $3,599.9 million. Durable goods accounted for 64.4% of wholesale establishments and for 35.3% of sales. That year, the Census of Retail Trade counted 3,693 retail establishments in the state, with $4,981.9 million in sales. More than 71% of all retail sales were in the Anchorage metropolitan area. Food stores accounted for 23.2% of all sales, followed by automotive dealers, 15.7%; department stores, 14.1%; eating and drinking places, 13.1%; and others, 33.9%.

During 1994, Anchorage area exporters sold $198.2 million of merchandise. Many of Alaska's resource products, including the salmon and crab catch, pass through the Seattle customs district. By federal law, Alaskan petroleum cannot be exported, a provision many Alaskans would like to see repealed. Exports of goods manufactured in Alaska came to $2.88 billion in 1996. Exporters located in Alaska had sales of $850.4 million in 1996. One-third of Alaska's manufactured goods were exported to other countries, the highest ratio of all the states, with paper and food products being the leading items. Alaska was the leading fish-exporting state and the largest exporter of salmon.

31CONSUMER PROTECTION

The State of Alaska does not maintain a Consumer Protection Office that can process consumer complaints from the public. Callers are referred to the Better Business Bureau of Alaska, Inc.

32BANKING

As of the end of 1996, Alaska had 8 insured commercial banks; the state's insured commercial banks had assets exceeding $5.8 billion. There was also 1 state-chartered mutual savings bank and 1 federal savings and loan association. Alaska's state-chartered banks are under the regulatory authority of the Department of Commerce and Economic Development's Division of Banking, Securities, and Corporations. The nationally chartered banks are under the regulatory authority of the Office of the Comptroller of the Currency. The federal savings and loan is regulated by the Office of Thrift Supervision.

33INSURANCE

In 1995, one life insurance company, Hospital and Medical Services Corp., and six property/casualty insurance companies were domiciled in Alaska. Premiums written in 1995 totaled $1.4 billion, including $736.8 million for property and casualty; $223 million for life insurance; and $412 million for health insurance and individual annuities. The insurance industry is regulated by the Department of Commerce and Economic Development's Division of Insurance.

34SECURITIES

There are no securities exchanges in Alaska. As of 1994, Alaska had 670 registered securities brokers and dealers, with nearly 19,000 agents. There were also 169 investment advisor firms registered to provide services within the state.

The Alaska Securities Act of 1959 serves as the foundation for the regulation of the sale of securities through a triple-tiered system of registration for brokers and dealers, as well as through anti-fraud provisions.

35PUBLIC FINANCE

Alaska's annual budget is prepared by the Division of Budget and Management, within the Office of the Governor, and submitted by the governor to the legislature for amendment and approval. The fiscal year runs from 1 July through 30 June. The following table summarizes actual revenues and expenditures for the 1995 fiscal year, in thousands of dollars, for the general fund, including capital projects funding:

REVENUES (IN THOUSANDS)	
Taxes	$1,922,463
Insurance trust	905,812
Federal grants-in-aid	980,048
Miscellaneous	4,177,013
TOTAL	$ 8,288,036

EXPENDITURES (IN THOUSANDS)	
Department of Transportation and Public Facilities	$ 579,041
Department of Education	1,257,989
Department of Health and Social Services	786,854
Debt Service	275,631
Other outlays	1,301,671
TOTAL	$5,599,033

As of 1995, the outstanding debt of Alaska state and local governments was more than $3.2 billion, or about $5,351 per capita.

36TAXATION

The large sums generated by the sale of oil leases and by oil and gas royalties make Alaska's tax structure highly atypical. Petroleum revenue accounted for 78% of total general fund unrestricted revenue in 1995/96. General fund unrestricted revenue was approximately $2.1 billion in 1995/96. General fund unrestricted revenue does not include federal funds, state corporation receipts (e.g., the Alaska Railroad), or income from the permanent or constitutional budget reserve funds. Nongeneral fund unrestricted revenue was approximately $4.4 billion in 1995/96. There is no state sales tax or personal income tax, but some localities impose a sales tax, as well as a property tax. The corporate tax rate in 1996 ranged from 1% on the first $10,000 of taxable income to 9.4% on amounts over $90,000. Other taxes include ones on alcoholic beverages, motor fuels and vehicles, estates, cigarettes, insurance companies, and fisheries. Alaska had the lowest individual tax burden of all states in 1996, according to *Money* magazine. A two-career family with an income of $88,764 would pay $2,982 in taxes in Alaska, as opposed to $14,005 in New York. Each Alaska resident also receives a permanent fund dividend from the state (in 1996, the permanent fund dividend was $1,130).

37ECONOMIC POLICY

The Alaska Industrial Development Authority, a public corporation of the state, provides long-term financing for capital investments and loans for most commercial and industrial activities, including manufacturing, small business, tourism, mining, commercial fishing, and other enterprises. The Alaska Science and Technology Foundation offers grants for basic and applied research. The Alaska Resources Corporation, another state public corporation, provides developmental capital for the establishment and expansion of small enterprises in resource industries. The state imposes no taxes on income, sales, gross receipts or inventories. It offers an investment tax credit for the development of gas-processing projects and for the mining of minerals and other natural deposits, except oil and gas.

38HEALTH

Alaska's birthrate of 17.0 per 1,000 population in 1995 was higher than the national average. The infant mortality rate of 6.7 per 1,000 live births for the year ending with December 1995 was below the national average. The abortion ratio was 152 per 1,000 births in 1992.

Alaska's overall death rate of 423 per 100,000 population in 1995 was less than half the US rate, but the death rate from accidents (56.2 per 100,000) was the highest in the US and over twice the national rate, and the suicide rate of 17.1 was above the national average of 11.9. The commercial fishing industry has one of the highest occupational fatality rates in Alaska; during 1991 and 1992 the annual occupational fatality rate for the fishing industry was 200 per 100,000 workers. The fatality rate for the shellfish industry was 530 per 100,000. Among Alaskan adults 18 to 30 years old, 29.7% were current smokers. The projected number of deaths from smoking-related illness was 17,999 in 1995. The death rate of 24.0 per 100,000 for cerebrovascular diseases was significantly lower than the national rate of 60.1, due to the relative youth of the state's population. Deaths due to heart disease were also much fewer (90.6 per 100,000 population) than the US average of 280.7. There were only 59 AIDS cases in 1995. The AIDS incidence rate was 13.03 per 100,000 in 1995.

Alaska's 17 hospitals (1 federal) in 1995 had 1,191 beds and 39,935 admissions; hospital personnel included 1,654 registered nurses in 1991. The average daily expense to Alaskan hospitals per inpatient amounted to $775 in 1994. Alaska had 1,092 federal and nonfederal physicians and 431 federal and nonfederal dentists in 1995, and 592 nurses per 100,000 population in 1994. Alaska had only 143 physicians per 100,000 residents in 1994. In 1995, only 13.3% of the Alaskan population was uninsured. Payments made to cover the health costs of Medicare and Medicaid recipients in 1994 were $2.7 billion and $1.3 billion, respectively. Alaska's Pioneer Homes, operated by the state's Department of Administration, are residential facilities for Alaskans over 65 (with at least one year of residency in the state) that offer five levels of care from independent living to full medical care, including Alzheimer's units. As of 1997, a total of 600 residents are being served at 6 locations.

39SOCIAL WELFARE

In 1996, approximately 35,000 Alaskans received aid for families with dependent children, with an average monthly payment of $1,025. The school lunch program had a federal cost of $14.8 million, and 46,233 Alaskans used food stamps in 1996.

With the enactment of the Personal Responsibility and Work Opportunity Reconciliation Act of 1996, the US government has changed the form and regulations for many of its social welfare programs; most significantly, it replaces Aid to Families with Dependent Children (AFDC), an open-ended entitlement program, with Temporary Assistance for Needy Families (TANF), a limited system of assistance funded largely through federal block grants. The reform act also impacts the food stamp program, the Supplemental Security Income program, and the child nutrition program. The law took effect on 1 July 1997 and provided $16.38 billion in block grants for fiscal years 1997–2002. The grants are to be divided among the states based on an equation involving the numbers of former AFDC recipients in each state. Because many of the bills' provisions have yet to be implemented into state-by-state policy, it was not possible to include the details of each state's programs for this edition of this work.

The weekly unemployment check averaged $172.88 in 1995. Social Security benefits were received by 44,500 retired Alaskans in 1995, averaging $708 a month. That year, 6,879 Alaskans received federal Supplemental Security Income, averaging $334 a month. In 1979, Alaska became the first state to withdraw its government workers from the Social Security system.

40HOUSING

Despite the severe winters, housing designs in Alaska do not differ notably from those in other states. Builders do usually provide thicker insulation in walls and ceilings, but the high costs of construction have not encouraged more energy-efficient adaptation to the environment. In 1980, the state legislature passed several measures to encourage energy conservation in housing and in public buildings. In native villages, traditional dwellings like the half-buried huts of the Aleuts and others have long since given way to conventional, low-standard housing. In point of fact, Alaska's Eskimos never built snow houses as did those of Canada; in the Eskimo language, the word *igloo* refers to any dwelling.

In 1996, there were an estimated 239,000 housing units, 62% of which were owner-occupied. From 1970 to 1978, 43,009 building permits were issued, as construction boomed during the years of pipeline building. In 1996, the state authorized 2,640 new privately owned housing units, valued at $316.4 million. During 1995/96, Alaska received $70.4 million in aid from the US Department of Housing and Urban Development, including $6.6 billion in community development block grants. The median house value was $94,400 in 1990, down 22.1% from 1980 after adjusting for inflation. The median monthly cost for an owner-occupied unit with a mortgage was $1,059 (fourth highest in the US) in 1990, the most recent year for which the government has estimates; the median rent was $559 per month.

The Alaska State Housing Authority acts as an agent for federal and local governments in securing financial aid for construction and management of low-rent and moderate-cost homes.

41EDUCATION

As of 1995, 92% of the population 25 years or older had completed high school. Alaska spent $8,353 per public school pupil during the 1995/96 school term.

Enrollment in public schools was 132,379 in the fall of 1995. Private school enrollment was 4,581 in 1993/94.

The University of Alaska is the state's leading higher educational institution. The main campus at Fairbanks, established in 1917, had 5,072 students in 1993, while the Anchorage campus had 13,519. Private institutions included two colleges with four-year programs, a theological seminary, and Alaska Pacific University. The University of Alaska's Rural Education Division has a network of education centers and offers 90 correspondence courses in 22 fields of study.

42ARTS

The Council on the Arts sponsors tours by performing artists, supports artists' residences in the schools, aids local arts projects, and purchases the works of living Alaskans for display in state buildings. The National Endowment for the Arts awarded $2,690,000 to the Alaska State Council on the Arts. The funds were used for arts education and assistance for the 88,589 artists who contributed to Alaska's art programs.

By 1996, there were 250 arts-related associations in Alaska, and 32 local art groups. In 1996, the National Endowment for the Arts awarded the Alaska State Council on the Arts $595,000 in Arts Education grants and $869,000 worth of grants through the State and Regional Program. Fairbanks, Juneau, and Anchorage have symphony orchestras, and Anchorage has a civic opera. The Alaska Repertory Theater tours the state.

43LIBRARIES AND MUSEUMS

Alaska public libraries had an estimated combined book stock of 1,879,830 and a circulation of 3,731,830 in 1994; facilities are located in seven boroughs and in most larger towns. Anchorage had the largest public library system, with five branches and 431,353 volumes in 1994. Also notable are the State Library in Juneau and the library of the University of Alaska at Fairbanks. Alaska had 46 museums in 1995. The Alaska State Museum in Juneau offers an impressive collection of native crafts and Alaskan artifacts. Sitka National Historical Park features Indian and Russian items, and the nearby Museum of Sheldon Jackson College holds important native collections. Noteworthy historical and archaeological sites include the Totem Heritage Center in Ketchikan. Anchorage has the Anchorage Museum of History and Art and the Alaska Zoo.

44COMMUNICATIONS

Considering the vast distances traveled and the number of small, scattered communities, the US mail is a bargain for Alaskans. In March 1993, 90.4% of the state's 191,000 residences had telephones. There were 83 radio stations (36 AM, 47 FM) in 1996, along with 17 television stations (5 noncommercial educational). Prime Cable of Alaska is the state's major cable carrier.

45PRESS

Alaska's most widely-read newspaper, among its seven dailies and two Sunday papers, is the *Anchorage Daily News*. Below are the leading newspapers with their circulations.

Anchorage Daily News	(m) 71,239	(S) 91,863
Fairbanks Daily News-Miner	(m) 17,786	(S) 22,769

The *Tundra Times*, also published in Anchorage, is a statewide weekly devoted to native concerns. There are about 30 publishers in Alaska, including the University of Alaska Press, Denali Press, Alaska Geographic, Rainforest Publishers, and Inside Passage Press.

46ORGANIZATIONS

The 1992 Census of Service Industries counted 342 organizations in Alaska, including 70 business associations; 217 civic, social, and fraternal associations; and 55 other membership organizations. There are no major national organizations based in Alaska. The largest statewide organization, the Alaska Federation of Natives, with headquarters in Anchorage, represents the state's Eskimos, Aleuts, and Indians.

47TOURISM, TRAVEL, AND RECREATION

With thousands of miles of unspoiled scenery and hundreds of mountains and lakes, Alaska has vast tourist potential. A total of 1,835,752 travelers visited Alaska in 1996. Alaska's tourism industry was estimated at over $1 billion in 1996. Cruise travel along the Gulf of Alaska is one of the fastest growing sectors in the tourist trade. One of the most popular tourist destinations is Glacier Bay National Monument. In 1995, millions of visits were paid to the state's national parks, preserves, historical parks, and monuments, which totaled 52.9 million acres (21.7 million hectares). Licenses were held by 184,826 fishermen and 216,977 hunters in 1995.

48SPORTS

There are no major-league professional sports teams in Alaska. Sports in Alaska generally revolve around the outdoors, including skiing, fishing, hiking, mountain biking, and camping. Perhaps the biggest sporting event in the state is the Iditarod Trail Sled Dog Race, covering 1,159 mi (1,865) from Anchorage to Nome. The race is held in March, and men and women compete against each other. With a $50,000 purse, it is the richest sled dog race in the world.

Other annual sporting events include the Great Alaska Shootout, in which college basketball teams from around the country compete in Anchorage in November, and the World Eskimo-Indian Olympics in Fairbanks in July.

49FAMOUS ALASKANS

Alaskan's best-known federal officeholder was Ernest Gruening (b.New York, 1887–1974), a territorial governor from 1939 to 1953 and US senator from 1959 to 1969. Alaska's other original US senator was E. L. "Bob" Bartlett (1904–68). Walter Hickel (b.Kansas, 1919), the first Alaskan to serve in the US cabinet, left the governorship in 1969 to become secretary of the interior. Among historical figures, Vitus Bering (b.Denmark, 1680–1741), a seaman in Russian service who commanded the discovery expedition in 1741, and Aleksandr Baranov (b.Russia, 1746–1819), the first governor of Russian America, are outstanding. Secretary of State William H. Seward (b.New York, 1801–72), who was instrumental in the 1867 purchase of Alaska, ranks as the state's "founding father," although he never visited the region.

Sheldon Jackson (b.New York, 1834–1909), a Presbyterian missionary, introduced the reindeer to the region and founded Alaska's first college in Sitka. Carl Ben Eielson (1897–1929), a famed bush pilot, is a folk hero. Benny Benson (1913–72), born at Chignik, designed the state flag at the age of 13.

50BIBLIOGRAPHY

Alaska, State of. *The Alaska Economy*. Vol. 7. Juneau: Department of Commerce and Economic Development, Division of the Economic Enterprises, 1979.

Alaska, State of. *Alaska Blue Book 1983*. Juneau: Department of Education, Division of State Libraries and Museums, 1983.

Brooks, Alfred Hulse. *Blazing Alaska's Trails*. Fairbanks: University of Alaska Press, 1972.

Gruening, Ernest. *State of Alaska*. New York: Random House, 1968.

Haycox, Stephen W., and Mary Childers Mangusso, ed. *An Alaska Anthology: Interpreting the Past*. Seattle: University of Washington Press, 1996.

Hedin, Robert, and Gary Holthaus (eds.). *The Great Land: Reflections on Alaska*. Tucson: University of Arizona Press, 1994.

Hunt, William R. *Alaska: A Bicentennial History*. New York: Norton, 1976.

Hunt, William R. *North of 53°: The Wild Days of the Alaska-Yukon Mining Frontier*. New York: Macmillan, 1974.

Kizzia, Tom. *The Wake of the Unseen Object: Among the Native Cultures of Bush Alaska*. New York: Henry Holt, 1992.

McBeath, Gerald A. *Alaska Politics & Government*. Lincoln: University of Nebraska Press, 1994.

McPhee, John. *Coming into the Country*. New York: Farrar, Straus & Giroux, 1977.

Naske, Claus M. *A History of Alaska Statehood*. Lanham, Md.: University Press of America, 1985.

Naske, Claus M., and Herman E. Slotnick. *Alaska: A History of the 49th State*. 2d ed. Norman: University of Oklahoma, 1987.

Oswalt, Wendell H. *Alaskan Eskimos*. San Francisco: Chandler, 1967.

Ryan, Alan, ed. *The Reader's Companion to Alaska*. San Diego, Calif.: Harcourt Brace, 1997.

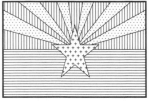

ARIZONA

State of Arizona

ORIGIN OF STATE NAME: Probably from the Pima or Papago Indian word *arizonac,* meaning "place of small springs." **NICKNAME:** The Grand Canyon State. **CAPITAL:** Phoenix. **ENTERED UNION:** 14 February 1912 (48th). **SONGS:** "Arizona March Song" and "Arizona." **MOTTO:** *Ditat Deus* (God enriches). **FLAG:** A copper-colored five-pointed star symbolic of the state's copper resources rises from a blue field; six yellow and seven red segments radiating from the star cover the upper half. **OFFICIAL SEAL:** Depicted on a shield are symbols of the state's economy and natural resources, including mountains, a rising sun, and a dam and reservoir in the background; irrigated farms and orchards in the middle distance; and a quartz mill, a miner, and cattle in the foreground; as well as the state motto. The words "Great Seal of the State of Arizona 1912" surround the shield. **BIRD:** Cactus wren. **FLOWER:** Blossom of the saguaro cactus. **TREE:** Paloverde. **OFFICIAL NECKWEAR:** Bola tie. **LEGAL HOLIDAYS:** New Year's Day, 1 January; Birthday of Martin Luther King, Jr., 3d Monday in January; Lincoln's Birthday, 1st Monday in February; Washington's Birthday, 3d Monday in February; Memorial Day, last Monday in May; Independence Day, 4 July; Labor Day, 1st Monday in September; Columbus Day, 2d Monday in October; Veterans Day, 11 November; Thanksgiving Day, 4th Thursday in November; Christmas Day, 25 December. **TIME:** 5 AM MST = noon GMT.

¹LOCATION, SIZE, AND EXTENT

Located in the Rocky Mountains region of the southwestern US, Arizona ranks 6th in size among the 50 states.

The total area of Arizona is 114,000 sq mi (295,260 sq km), of which land takes up 113,508 sq mi (293,986 sq km) and inland water 492 sq mi (1,274 sq km). Arizona extends about 340 mi (547 km) E–W; the state's maximum N–S extension is 395 mi (636 km).

Arizona is bordered on the N by Utah and on the E by New Mexico (with the two borders joined at Four Corners, the only point in the US common to four states); on the S by the Mexican state of Sonora; and on the W by the Mexican state of Baja California Norte, California, and Nevada (with most of the line formed by the Colorado River). The total boundary length of Arizona is 1,478 mi (2,379 km). The state's geographic center is in Yavapai County, 55 mi (89 km) ESE of Prescott.

²TOPOGRAPHY

Arizona is a state of extraordinary topographic diversity and beauty. The Colorado Plateau, which covers two-fifths of the state in the north, is an arid upland region characterized by deep canyons, notably the Grand Canyon, a vast gorge more than 200 mi (320 km) long, up to 18 mi (29 km) wide, and more than 1 mi (1.6 km) deep. Also within this region are the Painted Desert and Petrified Forest, as well as Humphreys Peak, the highest point in the state, at 12,633 feet (3,850 meters).

The Mogollon Rim separates the northern plateau from a central region of alternating basins and ranges with a general northwest–southeast direction. Ranges in the Mexican Highlands in the southeast include the Chiricahua, Dos Cabezas, and Pinaleno mountains. The Sonora Desert, in the southwest, contains the lowest point in the state, 70 feet (21 meters) above sea level, on the Colorado River near Yuma.

The Colorado is the state's major river, flowing southwest from Glen Canyon Dam on the Utah border through the Grand Canyon and westward to Hoover Dam, then turning south to form the border with Nevada and California. Tributaries of the Colorado include the Little Colorado and Gila rivers. Arizona has few natural lakes, but there are several large artificial lakes formed by dams for flood control, irrigation, and power development. These include Lake Mead (shared with Nevada), formed by Hoover Dam; Lake Powell (shared with Utah); Lake Mohave and Lake Havasu (shared with California), formed by David Dam and Parker Dam, respectively; Roosevelt Lake, formed by Theodore Roosevelt Dam; and the San Carlos Lake, created by Coolidge Dam.

³CLIMATE

Arizona has a dry climate, with little rainfall. Temperatures vary greatly from place to place, season to season, and day to night. Average daily temperatures at Yuma, in the southwestern desert range from 43° to 67°F (6° to 19°C) in January, and from 81° to 106°F (27° to 41°C) in July. At Flagstaff, in the interior uplands, average daily January temperatures range from 14° to 41°F (–10° to 5°C), and average daily July temperatures range from 50° to 81°F (10° to 27°C). The maximum recorded temperature was 128°F (53°C), registered at Lake Havasu City on 29 June 1994; the minimum, –40°F (–40°C), was set at Hawley Lake on 7 January 1971.

The highest elevations of the state, running diagonally from the southeast to the northwest, receive between 25 and 30 in (63 to 76 cm) of precipitation a year, and the rest, for the most part, between 7 and 20 in (18 to 51 cm). The driest area is the extreme southwest, which receives less than 3 in (8 cm) a year. Snow, sometimes as much as 100 in (254 cm), falls on the highest peaks each winter but is rare in the southern and western lowlands.

The greatest amount of sunshine is registered in the southwest, with the proportion decreasing progressively toward the northeast; overall, the state receives more than 80% of possible sunshine, among the highest in the US, and Phoenix's 86% is higher than that of any other major US city.

4FLORA AND FAUNA

Generally categorized as desert, Arizona's terrain also includes mesa and mountains; consequently, the state has a wide diversity of vegetation. The desert is known for many varieties of cacti, from the saguaro, whose blossom is the state flower, to the cholla and widely utilized yucca. Desert flowers include the night-blooming cereus; among medicinal desert flora is the jojoba, also harvested for its oil-bearing seeds. Below the tree line (about 12,000 ft, or 3,658 m) the mountains are well timbered with varieties of spruce, fir, juniper, ponderosa pine, oak, and piñon. Rare plants, some of them endangered or threatened, include various cacti of commercial or souvenir value.

Arizona's fauna range from desert species of lizards and snakes to the deer, elk, and antelope of the northern highlands. Mountain lion, jaguar, coyote, and black and brown bears are found in the state, along with the badger, black-tailed jackrabbit, and gray fox. Small mammals include various cottontails, mice, and squirrels; prairie dog towns dot the northern regions. Rattlesnakes are abundant, and the desert is rife with reptiles such as the collared lizard and chuckwalla. Native birds include the thick-billed parrot, white pelican, and cactus wren (the state bird). Arizona counts the osprey, desert bighorn, desert tortoise, spotted bat, and Gila monster among its threatened wildlife. Officially listed as endangered or threatened are the southern bald eagle, masked bobwhite (quail), peregrine falcon, Yuma clapper rail, Sonoran pronghorn, ocelot, jaguarundi, black-footed ferret, bonytail chub, humpback chub, Colorado River squawfish, woundfin, Apache trout, Gila topminnow, and fat pocketbook clam.

5ENVIRONMENTAL PROTECTION

Aside from Phoenix, whose air quality is poorer than that of most other US cities, Arizona has long been noted for its clear air, open lands, and beautiful forests. The main environmental concern of the state is to protect these resources in the face of growing population, tourism, and industry.

State agencies with responsibility for the environment include the State Land Department, which oversees natural resource conservation and land management; the Game and Fish Commission, which administers state wildlife laws; the Department of Health Services, which supervises sewage disposal, water treatment, hazardous and solid waste treatment, and air pollution prevention programs; and the Department of Water Resources, formed in 1980, which is concerned with the development, management, use, and conservation of water.

Legislation enacted in 1980 attempts to apportion water use among cities, mining, and agriculture, the last of which, through irrigation, accounts for about 85.8% of Arizona's annual water consumption. Less than 1% of Arizona's land is wetlands. As of 1995, Arizona had 10 hazardous waste sites.

6POPULATION

Arizona ranked 24th in the US, with a 1990 census population of 3,665,228, 34.8% more than in 1980. The state's estimated 1996 population was 4,428,068, up 20.8% from 1990. Arizona's population growth rate has been one of the nation's highest for two decades.

Arizonans 65 years of age or older increased from 12.7% of the population in 1984 to 13.1% in 1990, reflecting to some extent the state's continuing popularity among retirees. Over 60% of the 1990 population had been born outside the state. Despite its rapid population growth, Arizona still had a population density of only 32.3 persons per sq mi (12.4 per sq km) in 1990.

Three out of four Arizonans live in metropolitan areas. The largest cities are Phoenix, with a 1994 estimated population of 1,048,949; Tucson, 434,726; Mesa, 313,649; Glendale, 168,439;

Scottsdale, 152,439; and Tempe, 144,289. More than half the state's population resides in Maricopa County, which includes every leading city except Tucson. Phoenix was the nation's 7th-largest city in 1990.

7ETHNIC GROUPS

Arizona has by far the nation's greatest expanse of Indian lands: the state's 22 reservations have a combined area of 19.1 million acres (7.7 million hectares)—26% of the total state area.

The largest single American Indian nation, the Navaho, with a registered 1991 reservation population of 96,494 (and an estimated 1995 population of 125,691) in Arizona, is located primarily in the northeastern part of the state. The Navaho reservation, covering 14,221 sq mi (36,832 sq km) within Arizona, extends into Utah and New Mexico and comprises desert, mesa, and mountain terrain. Herders by tradition, the people are also famous for their crafts. Especially since 1965, the Navaho have been active in economic development; reservation resources in uranium and coal have been leased to outside corporations, and loans from the US Department of Commerce have made possible roads, telephones, and other improvements. There are at least 12 and perhaps 17 other tribes (depending on definition). After the Navaho, the leading tribes are the Papago in the south, Apache in the east, and Hopi in the northeast. All together, the Indian population was about 204,000 in 1990.

The southern part of Arizona has most of the state's largest ethnic majority, a Hispanic population estimated at 668,000 (18% of the population) in 1990. There are some old, long-settled Spanish villages, but the bulk of Hispanics are of Mexican origin. Raul Castro, a Mexican-American, served as governor in 1975–77. There were 111,000 black Americans in Arizona in 1990. Filipinos, Chinese, Japanese, and other Asian and Pacific Island peoples made up 1.5% of the population.

8LANGUAGES

With the possible exception of the Navaho word *hogan* (earth-and-timber dwelling), the linguistic influence of Arizona's Papago, Pima, Apache, Navaho, and Hopi tribes is almost totally limited to some place-names: Arizona itself, Yuma, Havasu, Tucson, and Oraibi. Indian loan-words spreading from Arizona derive from the Nahuatl speech of the Mexican Aztecs—for example, *coyote, chili, mesquite,* and *tamale.* Spanish, dominant in some sections, has given English *mustang, ranch, stampede, rodeo, marijuana, bonanza, canyon, mesa, patio,* and *fiesta.*

English in the state represents a blend of North Midland and South Midland dialects without clear regional differences, although new meanings developed in the north and east for meadow and in the southern strip for swale as terms for flat mountain valleys. The recent population surge from eastern states has produced an urban blend with a strong Northern flavor. In 1990, 2,674,519 Arizonans—79.2% of all residents five years old and older—spoke only English at home. Other languages spoken at home, and the number of people speaking them, included Spanish, 478,234; various Native American languages, 110,559; and German, 21,344.

9RELIGIONS

The first religions of Arizona were the sacred beliefs and practices of the Indians. Catholic missionaries began converting Arizona Indians (Franciscans among the Hopi, and Jesuits among the Pima) to the Christian faith in the late 17th century. By the late 18th century, the Franciscans were the main missionary force, and the Roman Catholic Church was firmly established. In 1990, the state had 655,665 Catholics.

The Church of Jesus Christ of Latter-day Saints (Mormons) constitutes the 2d-largest Christian denomination. Mormons were among the state's earliest Anglo settlers; in 1990, there were

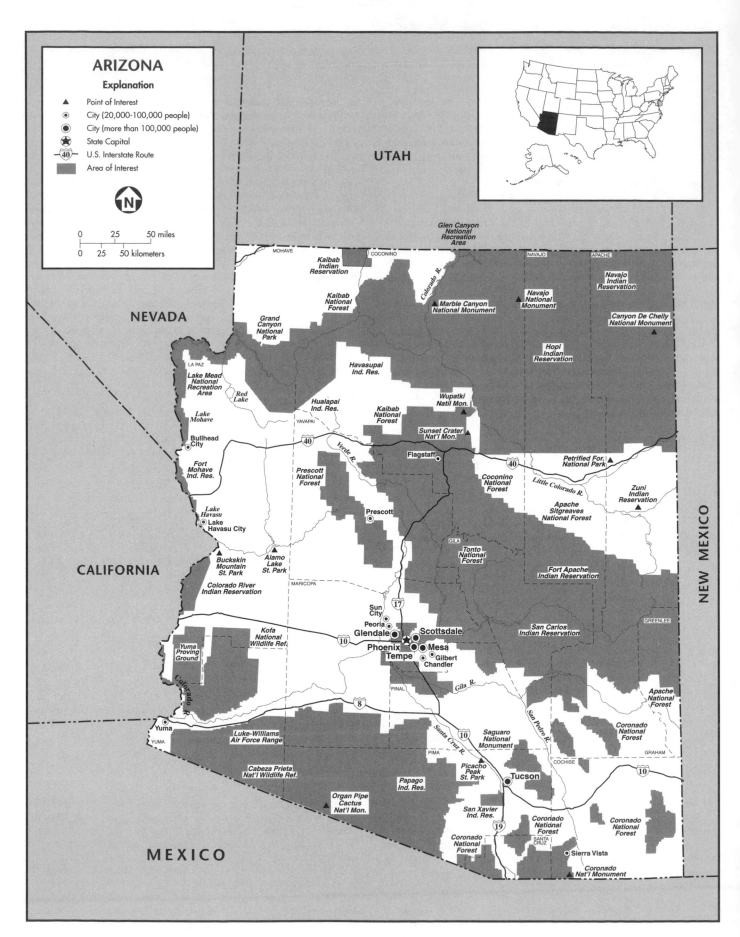

199,761 known Mormon adherents. Other major denominations include the Southern Baptist Convention, 162,887; and the United Methodist Church, 59,504.

In 1990, Arizona's estimated Jewish population was 70,850, virtually all of whom lived in the Phoenix or Tucson metropolitan areas.

[10]TRANSPORTATION

Until the last decade of the 19th century, the principal reason for the development of transportation in Arizona was to open routes to California. The most famous early road was El Camino de Diablo (The Devil's Highway), opened by the missionary Eusebio Kino in 1699. The first wagon road across Arizona was the Gila Trail (Cooke's Wagon Road), opened in 1846 as a southern route to California: Beale's Road was inaugurated in 1857. Also in 1857, the first stagecoach began operations. Until the coming of the railroads in the 1880s, however, the bulk of territorial commerce was by water transport on the Colorado River. Railroad construction reached its peak in the 1920s and declined rapidly thereafter.

Railroad trackage totaled 1,972.8 rail mi (3,174 km) in 1996, with 13 railroads operating in the state. The state's 2 Class I railroads, Burlington Northern Santa Fe and Union Pacific, controlled about two-thirds of Arizona's total rail miles. In 1994, the top rail tonnage commodities originating from within the state included metallic ores and acid. That year, over half the rail tonnage terminating within the state was coal/coke. Amtrak provides limited passenger service through Flagstaff, Kingman, and other cities in the north, and through Tucson, Phoenix, and Yuma on the southern route. Total ridership in the state was 100,149 in 1994/95.

In 1994, the state had 55,322.3 mi (89,014 km) of public streets and roads, of which 41,979.6 mi (67,545 km) were classified as rural and 13,342.7 mi (21,468 km) as urban. Interstate highways in Arizona totaled 1,221 mi (1,965 km). Of the 3,302,227 motor vehicles registered in 1995, there were 2,612,512 passenger vehicles, 297,076 commercial vehicles, 320,147 trailers, 70,067 motorcycles, 362 mopeds, and 2,063 buses/taxis. There were 1,273,599 licensed drivers in 1995/96, of whom 53% were male. Total highway expenditures in 1995/96 were $508.5 million. Arizona received $219.9 million in federal aid highway apportionment funds in 1995/96.

Arizona had 302 airports and 89 heliports in 1996. The leading air terminal was Phoenix Sky Harbor International Airport, which handled 13,875,000 arriving and departing passengers (10th-highest in the nation); Tucson International Airport ranked second with 1,758,000 (65th-highest). In the same year, there were 15,738 active pilots in Arizona.

[11]HISTORY

Evidence of a human presence in Arizona dates back more than 12,000 years. The first Arizonans—the offshoot of migrations across the Bering Strait—were large-game hunters: their remains have been found in the San Pedro Valley in the southeastern part of the state. By AD 500, their descendants had acquired a rudimentary agriculture from what is now Mexico and divided into several cultures. The Basket Makers (Anasazi) flourished in the northeastern part of the state; the Mogollon hunted and foraged in the eastern mountains; the Hokoham, highly sophisticated irrigators, built canals and villages in the central and southern valleys: and the Hakataya, a less-advanced river people, lived south and west of the Grand Canyon. For reasons unknown—a devastating drought is the most likely explanation—these cultures were in decay and the population much reduced by the 14th century. Two centuries later, when the first Europeans arrived, most of the natives were living in simple shelters in fertile river valleys, dependent on hunting, gathering,

and small-scale farming for subsistence. These Arizona Indians belonged to three linguistic families: Uto-Aztecan (Hopi, Paiute, Chemehuevi, Pima-Papago), Yuman (Yuma, Mohave, Cocopa, Maricopa, Yavapai, Walapai, Havasupai), and Athapaskan (Navaho-Apache). The Hopi were the oldest group, their roots reaching back to the Anasazi; the youngest were the Navaho-Apache, migrants from the Plains, who were not considered separate tribes until the early 18th century.

The Spanish presence in Arizona involved exploration, missionary work, and settlement. Between 1539 and 1605, four expeditions crossed the land, penetrating both the upland plateau and the lower desert in ill-fated attempts to find great riches. In their footsteps came Franciscans from the Rio Grande to work among the Hopi; and Jesuits from the south, led by Eusebio Kino in 1692, to proselytize among the Pima. Within a few years, Kino had established a major mission station at San Xavier del Bac, near present-day Tucson. In 1736, a rich silver discovery near the Pima village of Arizonac, about 20 mi (32 km) southwest of present-day Nogales, drew Spanish prospectors and settlers northward. To control the restless Pima, Spain in 1752 placed a military outpost, or presidio, at Tubac on the Santa Cruz River north of Nogales. This was the first major European settlement in Arizona. The garrison was moved north to the new fort at Tucson, also on the Santa Cruz, in 1776. During these years, the Spaniards gave little attention to the Santa Cruz settlements, administered as part of the Mexican province of Sonora, regarding them merely as way stations for colonizing expeditions traveling overland to the highly desirable lands of California. The end of the 18th century and the beginning of the 19th were periods of relative peace on the frontier; mines were developed and ranches begun. Spaniards removed hostile Apache bands onto reservations and made an effort to open a road to Santa Fe.

When Mexico revolted against Spain in 1810, the Arizona settlements were little affected. Mexican authorities did not take control at Arizpe, the Sonoran capital, until 1823. Troubled times followed, characterized by economic stagnation, political chaos, and renewed war with the Apache. Sonora was divided into *partidos* (counties), and the towns on the Santa Cruz were designated as a separate partido, with the county seat at Tubac. The area north of the Gila River, inhabited only by Indians, was vaguely claimed by New Mexico. With the outbreak of the Mexican War in 1846, two US armies marched across the region: Col. Stephen W. Kearny followed the Gila across Arizona from New Mexico to California, and Lt. Col. Philip Cooke led a Mormon battalion westward through Tucson to California. The California gold rush of 1849 saw thousands of Americans pass along the Gila toward the new El Dorado. In 1850, most of present-day Arizona became part of the new US Territory of New Mexico; the southern strip was added by the Gadsden Purchase in 1853.

Three years later, the Sonora Exploring and Mining Co. organized a large party, led by Charles D. Poston, to open silver mines around Tubac. A boom followed, with Tubac becoming the largest settlement in the valley; the first newspaper, the *Weekly Arizonian*, was launched there in 1859. The great desire of California for transportation links with the rest of the Union prompted the federal government to chart roads and railroad routes across Arizona, erect forts there to protect Anglo travelers from the Indians, and open overland mail service. Dissatisfied with their representation at Santa Fe, the territorial capital, Arizona settlers joined those in southern New Mexico in 1860 in an abortive effort to create a new territorial entity. The outbreak of the Civil War in 1861 saw the declaration of Arizona as Confederate territory and abandonment of the region by the Union troops. A small Confederate force entered Arizona in 1862 but was driven out by a volunteer Union army from California. On 24 February 1863, President Abraham Lincoln signed into law a measure creating the new Territory of Arizona. Prescott became the capital in 1864, Tucson in 1867, Prescott again in 1877, and finally Phoenix in 1889.

During the early years of territorial status, the development of rich gold mines along the lower Colorado River and in the interior mountains attracted both people and capital to Arizona, as did the discovery of silver bonanzas in Tombstone and other districts in the late 1870s. Additional military posts were constructed to protect mines, towns, and travelers. This activity, in turn, provided the basis for a fledgling cattle industry and irrigated farming. Phoenix, established in 1868, grew steadily as an agricultural center. The Southern Pacific Railroad, laying track eastward from California, reached Tucson in 1880, and the Atlantic and Pacific (later acquired by the Santa Fe), stretching west from Albuquerque through Flagstaff, opened service to California in 1883. By 1890, copper had replaced silver as the principal mineral extracted in Arizona. In the Phoenix area, large canal companies began wrestling with the problem of supplying water for commercial agriculture. This problem was resolved in 1917 with the opening of the Salt River Valley Project, a federal reclamation program that provided enormous agricultural potential.

As a creature of the Congress, Arizona Territory was presided over by a succession of governors, principally Republicans, appointed in Washington. In reaction, the populace was predominantly Democratic. Within the territory, a merchant-capitalist class, with strong ties to California, dominated local and territorial politics until it was replaced with a mining-railroad group whose influence continued well into the 20th century. A move for separate statehood began in the 1880s but did not receive serious attention in Congress for another two decades. In 1910, after Congress passed an enabling act that allowed Arizona to apply for statehood, a convention met at Phoenix and drafted a state constitution. On 14 February 1912, Arizona entered the Union as the 48th state.

During the first half of the 20th century, Arizona shook off its frontier past. World War I (1914–18) spurred the expansion of the copper industry, intensive agriculture, and livestock production. Goodyear Tire and Rubber established large farms in the Salt River Valley to raise pima cotton. The war boom also generated high prices, land speculation, and labor unrest; at Bisbee and Jerome, local authorities forcibly deported more than 1,000 striking miners during the summer of 1917. The 1920s brought depression: banks closed, mines shut down, and agricultural production declined. To revive the economy, local boosters pushed highway construction, tourism, and the resort business. Arizona also shared in the general distress caused by the Great Depression of the 1930s and received large amounts of federal aid for relief and recovery. A copper tariff encouraged the mining industry, additional irrigation projects were started, and public works were begun on Indian reservations, in parks and forests, and at education institutions. Prosperity returned during World War II (1939–45) as camps for military training, prisoners of war, and displaced Japanese-Americans were built throughout the state. Meat, cotton, and copper markets flourished, and the construction of processing and assembly plants suggested a new direction for the state's economy.

Arizona emerged from World War II as a modern state. War industries spawned an expanding peacetime manufacturing boom that soon provided the principal source of income, followed by tourism, agriculture, and mining. During the 1950s, the political scene changed. Arizona Republicans captured the governorship, gained votes in the legislature, won congressional seats, and brought a viable two-party system to the state. The rise of Barry Goldwater of Phoenix to national prominence further encouraged Republican influence. Meanwhile, air conditioning changed lifestyles, prompting a significant migration to the state.

For many years Arizona had seen its water diverted to California. In 1985, however, the state acted to bring water from the Colorado river to its own citizens by building the Central Arizona Project (CAP). The CAP was a $3 billion network of canals, tunnels, dams and pumping stations which had the capacity to bring 2.8 million acre-feet of water a year from the Colorado River to Arizona's desert lands, cities, and farms. By 1994, however, many considered the project to be a failure, as little demand existed for the water it supplied. Farmers concluded that water-intensive crops such as cotton were not profitable, and Arizona residents complained that the water provided by the CAP was dirty and undrinkable.

Arizona politics in recent years has been rocked by the discovery of corruption in high places. In 1988, Governor Evan Mecham was impeached on two charges of official misconduct. In 1989, Senators John McCain and Dennis DeConcini were indicted for interceding in 1987 with federal bank regulators on behalf of Lincoln Savings and Loan Association. Lincoln's president, Charles Keating, Jr., had contributed large sums to the Senators' reelection campaigns. In 1990, Peter MacDonald, the leader of the Navajo Nation, was convicted in the Navajo Tribal Court of soliciting $400,000 in bribes and kickbacks from corporations and individuals who sought to conduct business with the tribe in the 1970s and 1980s. A year later, seven members of the Arizona state legislature were charged with bribery, money laundering, and filing false election claims as the result of a sting operation. The legislators were videotaped accepting thousands of dollars from a man posing as a gaming consultant in return for agreeing to legalize casino gambling.

The most recent in Arizona's series of political scandals was the investigation and 1996 indictment of Governor Fife Symington on 23 counts of fraud and extortion in connection with his business ventures before he became governor in 1991, and his filing of personal bankruptcy. The case went to trial in May 1997.

12STATE GOVERNMENT

The current constitution of Arizona, drafted in 1910 at the height of the Progressive era, contained reform provisions that were very advanced for the time: initiative, referendum, workers' compensation, short terms for elected officials, suffrage for women, and the barring of trusts and monopolies from the state.

Legislative authority is vested in a 30-member senate and a 60-member house of representatives. All senators and representatives serve 2-year terms and are chosen at the general election in November of each even-numbered year. A legislator must be a US citizen, at least 25 years of age, and must have been an Arizona resident for at least 3 years. The legislative salary in 1995 was $15,000.

Chief executive officials elected statewide include the governor, secretary of state, treasurer, attorney general, and superintendent of public instruction, all of whom serve 4-year terms. The three members of the Corporation Commission, which regulates public services and utilities, are elected for staggered 6-year terms, and the state mine inspector is elected for 2 years. Candidates for executive office must have been US citizens for at least 10 years, must be at least 25 years of age, and must have been residents or citizens of Arizona for at least 5 years. In 1996 the governor's salary was $75,000.

Bills may originate in either house of the legislature and must be passed by both houses and approved by the governor in order to become law. A two-thirds vote in each house is necessary to override the governor's veto. Under the initiative procedure, legislation and proposed constitutional amendments can be placed on the ballot by petition.

In order to vote in Arizona, a person must be 18 years of age, must be a US citizen, and must have been a resident of the state for 50 days.

13POLITICAL PARTIES

Of Arizona's 17 territorial governors, all federally appointed, 14 were Republicans and 3 Democrats. Statehood meant a prolonged period of Democratic dominance. From 1912 through 1950, the state had 9 Democratic and 3 Republican governors; during that 49-year period, Republicans held the statehouse for only 6 years.

Republican Party fortunes improved dramatically after 1950, largely because of the rise to state and national prominence of a conservative Republican, Barry Goldwater, first elected to the US Senate in 1952. From 1951 to 1994, 8 Republican governors occupied the state house for 26 years, and 5 Democratic governors for 18 years. Several Arizona Republicans were appointed to high office during the Nixon years, and in 1973, another Republican, John J. Rhodes, became minority leader in the US House of Representatives. Democrat and former governor Bruce Babbitt was named Secretary of the Interior for the Clinton administration in 1992.

Arizonans elected a Republican, Fife Symington, as governor in 1991 in a special run-off election; he was reelected in 1994. In 1996 Bill Clinton ended 40 years of Republican presidential victories in Arizona, becoming the first Democratic winner since 1952, with 47% of the vote to Bob Dole's 44% and 8% for Independent Ross Perot. Democrat Dennis DeConcini won reelection to the Senate in 1988; he retired in 1994, and his seat was won by Republican Jon Kyl. John McCain, a Republican, was reelected Senator in 1992. Following the November 1994 election, Arizona's delegation of US Representatives went from 3 Democrats and 3 Republicans to 1 Democrat and 5 Republicans, a balance that was retained in 1996. In 1995, Arizona's state legislature consisted of 18 Republicans and 12 Democrats in the state senate, and 38 Republicans and 22 Democrats in the state house. There were 19 black elected officials in 1993, and 30 women serving in the state legislature and in elective executive office in 1995.

14LOCAL GOVERNMENT

Each of Arizona's 15 counties has a sheriff, county attorney, county recorder, treasurer, assessor, superintendent of schools, and three or five supervisors, each elected to a four-year term.

Local governmental units include towns, cities, and charter cities. Towns generally follow the council-mayor form of government. All of Arizona's largest cities are charter cities. In all, there were 591 local government units in 1992, of which 86 were municipal governments. There were 228 school districts and 261 special districts.

Each of the 22 Indian reservations in Arizona has a tribal council or board with members elected by the people.

15STATE SERVICES

The Arizona Department of Education regulates the school system. The Arizona Board of Regents governs the state's three public universities. The Department of Transportation administers the state's highway and air-transport systems, among other functions.

The Department of Health Services operates programs for environmental health, behavioral health (including alcohol abuse, drug abuse, and mental-illness treatment facilities), and family health services. The National Guard falls under the jurisdiction of the Department of Emergency and Military Affairs, while prisons and rehabilitation programs are administered by the State Department of Corrections and the Board of Pardons and Paroles. The Department of Public Safety oversees the state highway patrol.

Natural resources are the responsibility of several agencies, including the Game and Fish Commission, Department of Mines and Mineral Resources, Oil and Gas Conservation Commission, Parks Board, and Department of Water Resources. The Department of Economic Security handles employment services and public-assistance programs.

16JUDICIAL SYSTEM

The supreme court is the highest court in Arizona and has administrative responsibility over all other courts in the state. The five supreme court justices, appointed by the governor for staggered six-year terms, choose a chief justice and vice-chief justice to preside over the court.

The court of appeals, established in 1964, is organized in two geographical divisions which together have 22 judges. Appeals court judges are appointed for terms of six years.

The superior court is the general trial court of the state, and there must be at least one superior court judge in every Arizona county. In 1997 there were 137 superior court judges in the state's 15 counties. In counties with populations over 150,000, superior court judges are appointed by the governor; they hold office for

Arizona Presidential Vote by Political Party, 1948–96

YEAR	ELECTORAL VOTE	ARIZONA WINNER	DEMOCRAT	REPUBLICAN	PROGRESSIVE
1948	4	*Truman (D)	95,251	77,597	3,310
1952	4	*Eisenhower (R)	108,528	152,042	—
1956	4	*Eisenhower (R)	112,880	176,990	—
1960	4	Nixon (R)	176,781	221,241	—
1964	5	Goldwater (R)	237,753	242,535	—
					AMERICAN IND.
1968	5	*Nixon (R)	170,514	266,721	46,573
					AMERICAN
1972	6	*Nixon (R)	198,540	402,812	21,208
1976	6	Ford (R)	295,602	418,642	7,647
1980	6	*Reagan (R)	246,843	529,688	18,784
1984	7	*Reagan (R)	333,854	681,416	10,585
1988	7	*Bush (R)	454,029	702,541	13,351
					IND. (PEROT)
1992	8	Bush (R)	543,086	572,086	353,741
1996	8	*Clinton (D)	653,288	622,073	112,072

*Won US presidential election.

terms ending 60 days following the next regular general election after expiration of a two-year term. Those seeking retention run at the next general election on a nonpartisan ballot. In counties with populations of under 150,000, superior court judges are elected by nonpartisan ballot to four-year terms.

Counties are divided into precincts, each of which has a justice court. Every incorporated city and town has a police court. The jurisdiction of justice courts and police courts is limited to minor civil and criminal cases. Local judges are elected for terms of four years.

According to the FBI Crime Index of 1995, Arizona had a crime rate of 8,039.2 per 100,000 population. Rates for murder were 10.4; rape, 32.8; robbery, 169.6; aggravated assault, 480.9; burglary, 1,376.4; larceny-theft, 4,794.6; and motor vehicle theft, 1,138.2. In 1996 federal and state institutions held 25,405 prisoners at year-end (2,708 federal and 22,697 state prisoners). At the end of 1996, 123 prisoners were under sentence of death. In 1996, there were 10,104 practicing attorneys.

17ARMED FORCES
In 1996, 21,842 active-duty federal military personnel were stationed at 9 military installations in Arizona. Major military installations include the Army's Fort Huachuca at Sierra Vista; the Air Force's Williams base near Phoenix, and the Luke and Davis-Monthan bases, near Phoenix and Tucson, respectively; and the Marine Corps' Yuma Air Station. Defense Department expenditures in Arizona were $4.8 billion in 1995/96, $2.9 billion for contracts, and about $1.9 billion for payroll.

As of 1996, 455,000 veterans lived in the state: 24,000 saw service in the Persian Gulf War (1990–91); 146,000 during the Vietnam era (1954–75); 82,000 in the Korean conflict (1950–53); 133,000 in World War II (1939–45); and fewer than 500 in World War I (1914–18). On 10 September 1992, Nathan E. Cook, the last veteran of the Spanish-American War (1898–1902), died in Phoenix at the age of 106. Veterans' benefits totaled $764 million in 1995/96.

In 1996 there were 22,053 Reserve and National Guard personnel in Arizona. In 1993, the Arizona Department of Public Safety employed 889 full-time sworn officers, or 2 for every 10,000 citizens.

18MIGRATION
Arizona's first migrants were the ancient peoples who came from Asia across the Bering Strait more than 12,000 years ago. Hispanic settlers began arriving in the late 17th century. Anglo migration, especially from the South, became significant as the US developed westward to California, and increased at an even faster rate with the building of the railroads during the 1880s. Migration has accelerated since World War II (1939–45), and Arizona showed a net gain of 296,449 immigrants from 1985 to 1990, and 458,876 in domestic and international migration from 1990 to 1996. Mexico is the main source of foreign immigrants. In the 1980s, half of Arizona's total population increase was from migration; about 530,000 persons moved there during that time. By 1990, only 34.2% of state residents had been born in Arizona; only three other states had a lower proportion. Only 43% of state residents age 5 or older in 1990 lived in the same house as in 1985; of those who lived in a different house in 1985, 35% did so in another state (predominantly California or Texas). Partly as a result of migration, the urban population increased from 83.8% of Arizona's population in 1980 to 87.5% of the state population in 1990. In 1996, 8,900 immigrants from foreign countries arrived in Arizona, bringing the foreign-born population to 472,000, or about 11% of the state's total population. As of 1994, the number of undocumented immigrants was estimated at between 50 and 68.

19INTERGOVERNMENTAL COOPERATION
Arizona is a signatory to a boundary agreement with California (1963) and to such interstate accords as the Colorado River Compact, Interstate Oil and Gas Compact, Upper Colorado River Basin Compact, and Western Interstate Energy Compact.

The most important federal project in the state has been the Central Arizona Project, approved by Congress in 1968 and designed to divert water from the Colorado River to the Phoenix and Tucson areas for agriculture, energy, and other purposes. Federal aid totaled $3.1 billion in 1995/96.

20ECONOMY
Mining and cattle-raising were the principal economic activities in Arizona during the territorial period. With the introduction of irrigation in the early 1900s, farming assumed a greater importance. Improvements in transportation later in the 20th century led to the development of manufacturing and tourism. State and federal sources estimated the value of manufacturing in 1983 at $6.95 billion; tourism and travel, $4.8 billion; mining, $1.5 billion; and agriculture (including livestock), $1.6 billion. Leading products include electronic components and nonelectrical machinery from the manufacturing sector, copper from the mining sector, and cattle and cotton from the farming sector.

Arizona's economy compiled an impressive growth record during the 1970s and early 1980s. Between 1973 and 1983, the state population increased by 39% (4th in the US); nonfarm wage and salary employment grew by 49% (5th in the US); and total personal income by 218% (6th in the US). Arizona's gross state product in 1994 was $94,093 million, to which private goods-producing industries contributed $21,686 million; private services-producing industries, $59,327 million; and government, $13,081 million. In 1996, there were a total of 20,284 bankruptcy filings.

21INCOME
In 1996, Arizona ranked 36th among the 50 states with a per capita personal income of $20,989. In 1996, total disposable income rose to $81.1 billion, up from $75.8 billion in 1995. The median household disposable income was estimated at $30,863 in 1995. The vast majority of total personal income is concentrated in Maricopa County and in Pima County (the Tucson metropolitan area). The other 13 counties, all rural and including most of the state's Indian lands, account for the rest. Except in Yavapai County, per capita income in these counties was far below that in Maricopa and Pima. In 1995, about 16.1% of the population was below the federal poverty level.

22LABOR
In December 1996, the labor force totaled 2,177,200. The unemployment rate was 4.6% at that time.

The Arizona Department of Economic Security forecasted 1997 nonfarm employment at 1,990,300, of which manufacturing accounted for 10.4%; mining, 0.1%; construction, 6.6%; transportation, communications, and utilities, 4.9%; trade, 24.7%; finance, insurance, and real estate, 6.2%; services, 30.5%; and government, 16.6%.

Organized labor has a long history in Arizona. A local of the Western Federation of Miners was founded in 1896, and labor was a powerful force at the constitutional convention in 1910. Nevertheless, the state's work force is much less organized than that of the nation as a whole. In 1995, 145,500 Arizonans belonged to labor unions, or about 8% of all workers. The state has a right-to-work law.

23AGRICULTURE

Arizona's agricultural output (including livestock products) was valued at $1.9 billion in 1995 (32d in the US). Cash receipts from farming alone amounted to $1.0 billion.

In 1995 there were about 7,400 farms covering 35.4 million acres (14.3 million hectares), or about 46.8% of the state's total area, but only 1,650,000 acres (667,800 hectares), or 2.1% of the state, were actually farmed for crops in 1995. Arizona's farmed cropland is intensely cultivated and highly productive. In 1995, Arizona was second among all states in cotton yield per acre (1,008 lb per acre, or 1,130 kg per hectare). About 95% of all farmland is dependent on irrigation provided by dams and water projects.

Cotton is the leading cash crop in Arizona. In 1995 the state produced 865,200 bales of cotton on 413,100 acres (167,180 hectares), with a total value of $355,447,000. (In 1994, 862,400 bales were produced, with a value of $304,754,000.) Vegetables, especially head lettuce, accounted for a value of $353,908,000 in 1995. Hay is also an important item; total hay production was 1,392,000 tons in 1995, for a value of $108,576,000. Other crops are wheat, sorghum, barley, grapes, and citrus fruits.

24ANIMAL HUSBANDRY

The total inventory of cattle and calves was 790,000 in 1997, with a value of $458 million. In 1995, the state had 107,000 sheep and lambs. In 1996, the state had 150,000 hogs and pigs valued at $15 million.

A total of 2.2 billion lb (1 billion kg) of milk was produced in 1995.

25FISHING

Arizona has no commercial fishing. The state's lakes and mountain streams lure the state's 468,500 licensed anglers and are an increasingly important tourist attraction. In 1995/96, over 217,700 lb (98,750 kg) of live fish and 3 million fish eggs were distributed within the state by federal authorities.

26FORESTRY

The lumber industry in Arizona began during the 19th century, when the building of the transcontinental railroad created a demand for railroad ties. Production of lumber from Arizona's forests remained strong until the 1990s, during which the primary emphasis shifted to conservation and recreation.

The main forest regions stretch from the northwest to the southeast, through the center of the state. Altogether, in 1992 there were 19,595,000 acres (7,930,000 hectares) of forestland in Arizona, 27% of the state's area and 2.5% of the US total. Commercial timberland accounted for only 3,968,000 acres (1,606,000 hectares). National forests covered nearly 11,235,316 acres (4,681,382 hectares) as of 1990. Lumber production remains an important emphasis on the Kaibab, Coconino, and Apache-Sitgreaves National Forests, and on the Hualapai, Navajo, Ft. Apache, and San Carlos Apache Indian Reservations.

27MINING

Arizona continued to lead the nation in nonfuel mineral production value, thanks to the state's copper industry. According to US Geological Survey estimates, nonfuel mineral production in Arizona during 1995 was valued at $4.18 billion (11% of the US total), up $900 million from 1994. Copper represented 87% of the nonfuel mineral production value in 1995; industrial minerals, 8%; and the remaining 5% was divided between molybdenum, silver, and gold. Productions and values in 1995 for principal minerals are as follows: copper, 1.2 million metric tons ($3.6 billion); sand and gravel, 37 million metric tons ($180 million); silver, 194 metric tons ($33.1 million); gold, 68,440 oz or 1,940 kg ($23.3 million); and crushed stone, 5.4 million metric tons ($27.5 million).

Arizona continued to lead the country in copper production in 1995, a rank it has held for more than 80 years. The state also ranks first in production of molybdenum; second in silver and perlite; and fifth in pumice and iron oxide pigments.

The Morenci Mine in Greenlee County is the nation's largest copper producer and the second-largest copper mine in the world. New drillings in 1994 added another 687 million metric tons to the Morenci copper reserve.

Population growth and freeway construction projects in metropolitan Phoenix have contributed to Arizona's ranking as the nation's sixth-largest producer of sand and gravel. Employment in mining was about 12,600 in December 1996.

28ENERGY AND POWER

In 1995, Arizona produced 45.6 billion kWh of electric power; installed capacity was 16.7 million kW in 1996. The state had 33 power plants, of which 14 were hydroelectric, accounting for 12% of power output. Electric energy sales in the state were 45.6 billion kWh; the surplus production was exported to other states, primarily California.

Arizona's fossil-fuel potential remains largely undeveloped, though oil and natural-gas exploration began in the 1980s. In 1995, the state marketed 68.0 billion cu ft (2 billion cu m) of natural gas. Coal production in 1995 was 11,968,000 metric tons, all of it from two surface mines.

Energy resource development in the state is encouraged by the Department of Mines and Mineral Resources, Oil and Gas Conservation Commission, and Department of Water Resources.

29INDUSTRY

Manufacturing, which has grown rapidly since World War II (1939–45), became the state's leading economic activity in the 1970s. Factors contributing to this growth included a favorable tax structure, available labor, plentiful electric power, and low land costs. The major manufacturing centers are the Phoenix and Tucson areas. Principal industries include nonelectrical machinery, electrical and electronic equipment (computers, semiconductors, communication equipment), aircraft equipment, food products, and printing and publishing. Military equipment accounts for much of the output. The total value added by manufacturing in 1995 amounted to an estimated $21 billion. Principal manufacturers of electronic and technology-intensive equipment in Arizona include: Motorola, Allied Signal Aerospace, Honeywell, Hughes Missile Systems Co., and Intel. Intel expanded its operations in Arizona with the construction of a $1.3 billion plant in 1994.

In 1995, there were 1,101 US patents issued to Arizona residents.

30COMMERCE

Arizona had 6,518 wholesale trade establishments in 1992, according to the Census of Wholesale Trade, with sales of $27,974.5 million. Durable goods accounted for 67.4% of the establishments and 53.1% of sales. Most wholesale establishments were concentrated in Maricopa and Pima Counties. Retail trade was conducted by 21,351 establishments in 1992, with sales of $29,365.9 million. Automotive dealers accounted for 21.7% of retail sales; food stores, 21%; general merchandise stores, 13.2%; eating and drinking places, 10.3%; and other establishments, 33.8%. In 1996, exports originally produced in Arizona amounted to $10.5 billion. Goods worth $9.9 billion were sold by exporters within Arizona in 1996.

[31]CONSUMER PROTECTION

The Arizona Attorney General has primary enforcement powers regarding consumer protection.

[32]BANKING

As of February 1996, there were 30 commercial banks in Arizona. Total domestic assets of commercial banks were $31.6 billion. There were 2 insured federal savings banks, with total assets of $515 million. Deposits in all Arizona federally insured commercial banks exceeded $26.8 billion at the close of 1996, and outstanding loans of commercial banks exceeded $22.3 billion in 1996.

The banking industry in Arizona is regulated by the Department of Banking.

[33]INSURANCE

In 1995, Arizona policyholders paid $5.1 billion in premiums for life, health, automobile, homeowner, and all other types of insurance. Premiums for life insurance totaled $1,008 million; accident and health, $48 million; automobile liability and physical damage, $1.8 billion; and homeowners, $385.2 million.

Purchases of ordinary life insurance in Arizona totaled over $14.1 billion in 1995, and the total amount of life insurance in force was $99.6 billion, covering 1.7 million policies. The average amount of life insurance per family increased from $82,800 in 1991 to $97,800 in 1995. Life insurance companies paid $2,188.5 million in benefits and annuities in 1995, including $422.3 million in death payments. In 1995 there were 482 life insurance companies and 43 property and casualty insurance companies with home offices in Arizona. The Department of Insurance regulates the state's insurance industry and examines and licenses agents and brokers.

[34]SECURITIES

Arizona has the Arizona Stock Exchange. The exchange is an electronic call market which trades equity securities, including many Arizona-based companies. In 1996, securities transactions were conducted by approximately 1,500 broker-dealers and 67,000 designated agents registered to do business in the state.

[35]PUBLIC FINANCE

Governmental Type Funds (appropriated and nonappropriated) for fiscal years 1994/95 and 1995/96 are as follows:

	1994/95	1995/96
REVENUES		
Taxes	$6,378,271	$6,881,734
Earnings on investments	118,767	152,795
Licenses, fees, and permits	159,890	173,311
Other revenues	3,424,960	3,500,449
TOTAL REVENUES	$10,081,888	$10,708,289
EXPENDITURES		
General government	$ 1,189,562	$ 1,277,101
Health and welfare	3,644,541	3,790,039
Inspection and regulation	91,954	95,675
Education	2,033,675	2,220,246
Protection and safety	533,166	571,325
Transportation	1,008,472	1,287,309
Natural resources	81,669	87,252
Capital outlay	192,337	253,753
Other	126,619	155,214
TOTAL EXPENDITURES	$8,901,995	$9,737,914

Total bonded indebtedness and certificates of participation issued as of June 1996 amounted to $3.2 million.

[36]TAXATION

State tax receipts for the general fund in 1995/96 came to slightly more than $4.3 billion. The personal income tax ranged from 3% to 5.6%, with further rate reductions to occur for tax year 1997. For corporations the rate was 9.0% on net income, with a minimum tax of $50. Arizona has a state transaction privilege tax, with the retail sales tax rate at 5%. An estate tax, luxury tax, parimutuel tax, insurance premium tax, and transport fuel tax are also levied. The state also receives tax revenue from collections of the motor-vehicle license tax, and it has a lottery. In 1995, Arizona's share of the federal income tax burden was $9.2 billion.

[37]ECONOMIC POLICY

The Department of Commerce has primary responsibility for attracting business and industry to Arizona, aiding existing business and industry, and assisting companies engaged in international trade. Its programs emphasize job opportunities, energy conservation, support of small businesses, and development of the film industry.

[38]HEALTH

In 1995, there were 72,386 live births and 35,428 deaths in Arizona. Infant mortality for the year ending with December 1995 was 7.6 per 1,000 live births. There were 11,738 legal abortions in 1995; the ratio of 162 per 1,000 live births was far below the national ratio of 335. Arizona's overall death rate (846.6 per 100,000 population) was below the US norm in 1995, and was especially low for heart disease and cardiovascular diseases. Deaths from accidents and suicide were above average, however. Serious public-health problems include multidrug-resistant tuberculosis and San Joaquin Valley fever (coccidioidomycosis), especially among older adults.

In 1995, there were 85 state-licensed hospitals, with 10,521 beds. Hospital personnel included 9,186 registered nurses. The state had 12,465 physicians (283 per 100,000 people) and 2,127 dentists in 1995. In that same year, the average expense to a hospital for care provided per inpatient day was $2,731. In 1993, 557,000 people received $2,910 each in Medicare benefits.

[39]SOCIAL WELFARE

In 1996, 171,600 Arizonans received $418 a month in aid to families with dependent children. Some 427,000 Arizonans participated in the federal food stamp program, and 231,810 pupils took part in the school lunch program at a cost to the federal government of $93.1 million in 1996.

With the enactment of the Personal Responsibility and Work Opportunity Reconciliation Act of 1996, the US government has changed the form and regulations for many of its social welfare programs; most significantly, it replaces Aid to Families with Dependent Children (AFDC), an open-ended entitlement program, with Temporary Assistance for Needy Families (TANF), a limited system of assistance funded largely through federal block grants. The reform act also impacts the food stamp program, the Supplemental Security Income program, and the child nutrition program. The law took effect on 1 July 1997 and provided $16.38 billion in block grants for fiscal years 1997–2002. The grants are to be divided among the states based on an equation involving the numbers of former AFDC recipients in each state. Because many of the bills provisions have yet to be implemented into state-by-state policy, it was not possible to include the details of each state's programs for this edition of this work.

In 1995, Social Security was paid to 702,510 beneficiaries; the average monthly benefit was $728. About 72,961 Arizonans received $343 monthly in federal Supplemental Security Income benefits during 1995. The weekly unemployment check averaged $148.57 in 1995.

⁴⁰HOUSING

In October 1996, an estimated 1,826,000 units of year-round housing were in Arizona, of which 1,551,000 were occupied and 98% had complete plumbing facilities. As of 1996, 62% of all housing units were owner-occupied.

From 1980 to 1990, the housing boom in Arizona caused the number of housing units to increase by 55%; about 38% of all housing structures in Arizona were built in the 1980s, and only 3.2% were built before 1940. During 1995/96, Arizona received $241.1 million in aid from the US Department of Housing and Urban Development, including nearly $50 million in community development block grants. The median value of a home in Arizona was $80,100 in 1990, the most recent year for which the government has estimates, down 7.9% from 1980 after adjusting for inflation. An owner-occupied unit with a mortgage had a median monthly cost of $769 in 1990; the median cost for a rental unit was $438. In the greater Phoenix vicinity, where 40% of all housing units were built during the 1980s, an owner-occupied unit (including mortgage) had a median monthly cost of $821, while a rental unit had a median cost of $466 per month. In 1996, 53,715 units were authorized. Building permits valued at $5.4 billion were authorized in that year for privately owned housing units.

⁴¹EDUCATION

In 1996, 82.5% of Arizonans 25 years old and over were high school graduates, and 21.4% were college graduates. Some 32,361 Arizonans graduated from high school in the 1995/96 school year.

The first public school in the state opened in 1871 at Tucson, with 1 teacher and 138 students. In the fall of 1995, enrollment at public schools was 762,096. There were 39,550 public-school teachers in the 1995/96 school year. Private schools enrolled 41,957 students in 1993.

The leading public higher educational institutions, the University of Arizona at Tucson and Arizona State University (originally named the Arizona Territorial Normal School) at Tempe, were both established in 1885. As of 1993, the state had 12 colleges and universities and 17 community colleges, with a total enrollment of 291,985 students. The American Graduate School of International Management, a private institution, is located in Glendale.

⁴²ARTS

Arizona has traditionally been a center for Indian folk arts and crafts. The Arizona State Museum (Tucson), Colorado River Indian Tribes Museum (Parker), Heard Museum of Anthropology and Primitive Art (Phoenix), Mohave Museum of History and Arts (Kingman), Navaho Tribal Museum (Window Rock), and Pueblo Grande Museum (Phoenix) all display Indian creations, both historic and contemporary. Modern Arizona artists are featured at the Tucson Museum of Art and the Yuma Art Center.

Musical and dramatic performances are presented in Phoenix, Tucson, Scottsdale, and other major cities. Phoenix and Tucson have symphony orchestras, and the Arizona Opera Company performs in both cities.

From 1991 to 1996, federal and state funding for the arts amounted to $1,055,000. The National Endowment for the Arts awarded $269,000 to artists in the state, and $840,000 to the Arizona Commission on the Arts. Contributions from the state to arts-related institutions have reached 85,958 artists. Arts education programs have been provided for 77,600 children. By 1996, Arizona's arts associations numbered 350.

⁴³LIBRARIES AND MUSEUMS

In 1994, Arizona's public libraries had a combined book stock of 8,836,288 volumes, and total circulation was 26 million. Spending on libraries per capita was approximately $10.00 in 1994. Principal public libraries include the Phoenix Public Library and the State Library and Department of Archives in Phoenix, and the Arizona Historical Society Library in Tucson. The largest university libraries are located at the University of Arizona and Arizona State University.

Arizona has more than 111 museums and historic sites. Attractions in Tucson include the Arizona State Museum, University of Arizona Museum of Art, Arizona Historical Society, Arizona-Sonora Desert Museum, Flandreau Planetarium, and Gene C. Reid Zoological Park. Phoenix has the Heard Museum (anthropology and primitive art), Arizona Mineral Resources Museum, Phoenix Art Museum, Phoenix Zoo, Pueblo Grande Museum, and Desert Botanical Garden. The Museum of Northern Arizona and Lowell Observatory are in Flagstaff. Kitt Peak National Observatory is in Tucson.

Archaeological and historical sites include the cliff dwellings at the Canyon de Chelly, Casa Grande Ruins, Montezuma Castle, Tonto, and Tuzigoot national monuments; the town of Tombstone, the site of the famous O. K. Corral gunfight in the early 1880s; and the restored mission church at Tumacacori National Monument and San Xavier del Bac Church near Tucson.

⁴⁴COMMUNICATIONS

Almost 94% of the 1,483,000 housing units had telephones in March 1993. There were 163 radio stations broadcasting in Arizona in 1996 (67 AM and 96 FM). The state also had 27 television stations in 1996 (including 4 noncommercial educational), of which 9 were in Phoenix, 8 in Tucson, and 3 in Flagstaff. Phoenix and Tucson each had 1 station broadcasting in Spanish in 1993. In that same year, 7 large cable television systems provided service.

⁴⁵PRESS

The *Weekly Arizonian*, started in 1859, was the first newspaper in the state. The *Daily Arizona Miner*, the state's first daily, was founded at Prescott in 1866. As of 1997 there were 12 morning dailies and 11 evening dailies; 13 dailies had Sunday editions. There were 41 weekly newspapers. The following table shows 1997 circulations for leading dailies:

AREA	NAME	DAILY	SUNDAY
Phoenix	*Arizona Republic* (m,S)	399,830	597,255
	Gazette (e)	62,929	
Tucson	*Citizen* (e)	48,215	
	Arizona Daily Star (m,S)	100,429	186,257

Among the most notable magazines and periodicals published in Arizona were *Phoenix Magazine*, *Phoenix Living*, and *Arizona Living*, devoted to the local and regional life-style; *American West*, dedicated to the Western heritage; *Arizona and the West*, published quarterly by the University of Arizona Library in Tucson; and *Arizona Highways*, a beautifully illustrated monthly published by the Department of Transportation in Phoenix.

⁴⁶ORGANIZATIONS

The 1992 Census of Service Industries counted 886 organizations in Arizona, including 177 business associations; 522 civic, social, and fraternal associations; and 187 other membership organizations. Among the organizations headquartered in Arizona are the National Foundation for Asthma (Tucson), the Pianists Foundation of America (Tucson), the National Indian Athletic Association (Mesa), the Kampground Owners Association (Phoenix), the American Science Fiction Association (Scottsdale), the Southwest Parks and Monuments Association (Globe), and Up With People (Tucson).

47TOURISM, TRAVEL, AND RECREATION

Tourism and travel is a leading industry in Arizona. In 1993, tourism and travel accounted for $5,525,000 in domestic travel within the state.

There are 22 national parks and monuments located entirely within Arizona. By far the most popular is Grand Canyon National Park, which had over 5 million visitors in 1995. Petrified Forest National Park and Saguaro National Monument are also popular national parks. There are also 14 state parks, which attracted 1,571,480 visitors in 1995.

Arizona offers excellent camping on both public and private land, and there are many farm vacation sites and dude ranches, particularly in the Tucson and Wickenburg areas. Popular for sightseeing and shopping are the state's Indian reservations, particularly those of the Navaho and Hopi. Boating and fishing on Lake Mead, Lake Powell, Lake Mohave, Lake Havasu, the Colorado River, and the Salt River lakes are also attractions. Licenses were held by 372,228 hunters and 656,485 anglers in 1995.

48SPORTS

There are three major-league professional teams in Arizona, all in Phoenix: the Cardinals of the National Football League, the Suns of the National Basketball Association, and the Coyotes of the National Hockey League. Additionally, the expansion Arizona Diamondbacks will begin play in Major League Baseball in 1998. Several major-league baseball teams hold spring training in Arizona, and Phoenix and Tucson have entries in the Pacific Coast League—the Firebirds and the Toros, respectively. There is horse-racing at Turf Paradise in Phoenix, and dog-racing at Phoenix, Tucson, and Yuma. Auto-racing is held at Manzanita Raceway and International Raceway, in Phoenix. Both Phoenix and Tucson have hosted tournaments on the Professional Golfers Association's nationwide tour.

The first organized rodeo that awarded prizes and charged admission was held in Prescott on 4 July 1988 and rodeos continue to be held throughout the state. Phoenix hosts the Rodeo of Rodeos, while Tucson has La Fiesta de los Vaqueros (The Festival of the Cowboys).

Both Arizona State and the University of Arizona joined the Pacific 10 Conference in 1978. The Sun Devils won the Rose Bowl in their first appearance in 1987, and also appeared in 1997. The Wildcats captured NCAA Division I baseball championships in 1975, 1980, and 1986, and the NCAA Division I men's basketball championship in 1997. The Sun Devils won the championship in 1981. College football's Fiesta Bowl is held annually at Sun Devil Stadium in Tempe.

Other annual sporting events include the Thunderbird Invitational Hot Air Balloon Races in Glendale in November.

49FAMOUS ARIZONIANS

Although Arizona entered the Union relatively late (1912), many of it citizens have achieved national prominence, especially since World War II (1939–45). William H. Rehnquist (b.Wisconsin, 1924) was appointed associate justice of the US Supreme Court in 1971 and chief justice in 1986; in 1981 Sandra Day O'Connor (b.Texas, 1930) became the first woman to serve on the Supreme Court. Arizona natives who became federal officeholders include Lewis Douglas (1894–1974), a representative who served as director of the budget in 1933–34 and ambassador to the Court of St. James's from 1947 to 1950; Stewart L. Udall (b.1920), secretary of the interior, 1961–69; and Richard B. Kleindienst (b.1923), attorney general, 1972–73, who resigned during the Watergate scandal. Another native son was Carl T. Hayden

(1877–1972), who served in the US House of Representatives from statehood in 1912 until 1927 and in the US Senate from 1927 to 1969, thereby setting a record for congressional tenure. Barry Goldwater (b.1909), son of a pioneer family, was elected to the US Senate in 1952, won the Republican presidential nomination in 1964, and returned to the Senate in 1968. His Republican colleague, John J. Rhodes (b.Kansas, 1916), served in the US House of Representatives for 30 years and was House minority leader from 1973 to 1980. Raul H. Castro (b.Mexico, 1916), a native of Sonora, came to the US in 1926, was naturalized, served as Arizona governor from 1975 to 1977, and has held several ambassadorships to Latin America. Morris K. Udall (b.1922), first elected to the US House of Representatives in 1960, contended for the Democratic presidential nomination in 1976.

Prominent state officeholders include General John C. Frémont (b.Georgia, 1813–90), who was territorial governor of Arizona from 1878 to 1883, and George W. P. Hunt (1859–1934), who presided over the state constitutional convention in 1910 and was elected governor seven times during the early decades of statehood. Eusebio Kino (b.Italy, 1645?–1711) was a pioneer Jesuit who introduced missions and European civilization to Arizona. Also important to the state's history and development were Charles D. Poston (1825–1902), who in the late 1850s promoted settlement and separate territorial status for Arizona; Chiricahua Apache leaders Cochise (1812?–74) and Geronimo (1829–1909), who, resisting the forced resettlement of their people by the US government, launched a series of raids that occupied the Army in the Southwest for over two decades; Wyatt Earp (b.Illinois, 1848–1929), legendary lawman of Tombstone during the early 1880s; John C. Greenway (1872–1926), copper magnate and town builder who was a nominee on the Democratic ticket in 1924 for US vice president; and Frank Luke, Jr. (1897–1918), a World War I flying ace who was the first American airman to receive the Medal of Honor.

Distinguished professional people associated with Arizona have included James Douglas (b.Canada, 1837–1918), metallurgist and developer of the Bisbee copper district; Percival Lowell (b.Massachusetts, 1855–1916), who built the Lowell Observatory in Flagstaff; and Andrew Ellicott Douglass (b.Vermont, 1867–1962), astronomer, university president, and inventor of dendrochronology, the science of dating events and environmental variations through the study of tree rings and aged wood. Cesar Chavez (1927–93) was president of the United Farm Workers of America.

Writers whose names have been associated with Arizona include novelist Harold Bell Wright (b.New York, 1872–1944), who lived for an extended period in Tucson; Zane Grey (b.Ohio, 1875–1939), who wrote many of his Western adventure stories in his summer home near Payson; and Joseph Wood Krutch (b.Tennessee, 1893–1970), an essayist and naturalist who spent his last two decades in Arizona. Well-known performing artists from Arizona include singers Marty Robbins (1925–1970), and Linda Ronstadt (b.1946). Joan Ganz Cooney (b.1929), president of the Children's Television Workshop, was one of the creators of the award-winning children's program, *Sesame Street*.

50BIBLIOGRAPHY

Alampi, Gary, ed. *Gale State Rankings Reporter*. Detroit: Gale Research, Inc., 1994.

Arizona: Its People and Resources. 2d rev. ed., rev. Tucson: University of Arizona Press, 1972.

Arizona Yearbook, 1979–80: A Guide to Government in Arizona. Yuma: Arizona Informational Press, 1979.

Barnes, Will C. *Arizona Place Names*. Revised by Byrd H. Granger. Tucson: University of Arizona Press, 1960.

Comeaux, Malcolm. *Arizona: A Geography*. Boulder: Westview Press, 1981.

Council of State Governments. *The Book of the States, 1994–1995 Edition*. Vol. 30. Lexington, Ky.: The Council of State Governments, 1994.

Faulk, Odie B. *Arizona: A Short History*. Norman: University of Oklahoma Press, 1970.

FDIC, Division of Research and Statistics. *Statistics on Banking: A Statistical Profile of the United States Banking Industry*. Washington, D.C.: Federal Deposit Insurance Corporation, 1993.

Federal Writers' Project. *Arizona: The Grand Canyon State*. 1940. Reprint, New York: Hastings House, 1968

Fireman, Bert M. *Arizona: Historic Land*. New York: Knopf, 1982.

Goldwater, Barry. *Arizona*. New York: Random House, 1978.

Lamar, Howard R. *The Far Southwest, 1846–1912: A Territorial History*. New Haven: Yale University Press, 1966.

Powell, Lawrence C. *Arizona: A Bicentennial History*. New York: Norton, 1976.

Schmittroth, Linda, and Mary Kay Rosteck, ed. *Cities of the United States*. 2d ed. Detroit: Gale Research, Inc., 1994.

Sheridan, Thomas E. *Arizona: A History*. Tucson: University of Arizona Press, 1995.

University of Arizona Library. *The Arizona Index: A Subject Index to Periodical Articles about the State*. Boston: Hall Library, 1978.

US Department of Education, National Center for Education Statistics. Office of Educational Research and Improvement. *Digest of Education Statistics, 1993*. Washington, D.C.: US Government Printing Office, 1993.

US Department of the Interior, US Fish and Wildlife Service. *Endangered and Threatened Species Recovery Program*. Washington, D.C.: US Government Printing Office, 1990.

Valley National Bank of Arizona. *Arizona Statistical Review*. 40th ed. Phoenix, 1984.

Wagoner, Jay J. *Arizona's Heritage*. Layton, Utah: Peregrine Smith, 1977.

———. *Arizona Territory 1863–1912*. Tucson: University of Arizona Press, 1970.

———. *Early Arizona: Prehistory to Civil War*. University of Arizona Press, 1975.

Walker, Henry P., and Don Bufkin. *Historical Atlas of Arizona*. 2d ed. Norman: University of Oklahoma Press, 1986.

Wallace, Andrew, ed. *Sources and Readings in Arizona History*. Tucson: Arizona Pioneers' Historical Society, 1965.

Wyllys, Rufus K. *Arizona: The History of a Frontier State*. Phoenix: Hobson and Herr, 1950.

ARKANSAS

State of Arkansas

ORIGIN OF STATE NAME: French derivation of *Akansas* or *Arkansas,* a name given to the Quapaw Indians by other tribes. **NICKNAME:** The Natural State. **CAPITAL:** Little Rock. **ENTERED THE UNION:** 15 June 1836 (25th). **SONG:** "Arkansas." **MOTTO:** *Regnat populus* (The people rule). **COAT OF ARMS:** In front of an American eagle is a shield displaying a steamboat, plow, beehive, and sheaf of wheat, symbols of Arkansas's industrial and agricultural wealth. The angel of mercy, the goddess of liberty encircled by 13 stars, and the sword of justice surround the eagle, which holds in its talons an olive branch and three arrows, and in its beak a banner bearing the state motto. **FLAG:** On a red field, 25 stars on a blue band border a white diamond containing the word "Arkansas" and 4 blue stars. **OFFICIAL SEAL:** Coat of arms surrounded by the words "Great Seal of the State of Arkansas." **BIRD:** Mockingbird. **INSECT:** Honeybee. **FLOWER:** Apple blossom. **TREE:** Pine. **GEM:** Diamond. **LEGAL HOLIDAYS:** New Year's Day, 1 January; Robert E. Lee's birthday, 19 January; Birthday of Martin Luther King, Jr., 3d Monday in January; George Washington's Birthday, 3d Monday in February; Memorial Day, last Monday in May, Independence Day, 4 July; Labor Day, 1st Monday in September; Veterans Day, 11 November; Thanksgiving Day, 4th Thursday in November; Christmas Eve, 24 December; Christmas Day, 25 December. **TIME:** 6 AM CST = noon GMT.

¹LOCATION, SIZE, AND EXTENT

Located in the western south-central US, Arkansas ranks 27th in size among the 50 states.

The total area of Arkansas is 53,187 sq mi (137,754 sq km), of which land takes up 52,078 sq mi (134,882 sq km); and inland water, 1,109 sq mi (2,872 sq km). Arkansas extends about 275 mi (443 km) E-W and 240 mi (386 km) N-S.

Arkansas is bordered on the N by Missouri; on the E by Missouri, Tennessee, and Mississippi (with part of the line passing through the St. Francis and Mississippi rivers); on the S by Louisiana; on the SW by Texas (with part of the line formed by the Red River), and on the W by Oklahoma. The total boundary length of Arkansas is 1,168 mi (1,880 km). The state's geographic center is in Pulaski County, 12 mi (19 km) NW of Little Rock.

²TOPOGRAPHY

The Boston Mountains (an extension of the Ozark Plateau, sometimes called the Ozark Mountains) in the northwest and the Ouachita Mountains in the west-central region not only constitute Arkansas's major uplands but also are the only mountain chains between the Appalachians and the Rockies. Aside from the wide valley of the Arkansas River, which separates the two chains, the Arkansas lowlands belong to two physiographic regions: the Mississippi Alluvial Plain and the Gulf Coastal Plain. The highest elevation in Arkansas, at 2,753 feet (839 meters), is Magazine Mountain, standing north of the Ouachitas in the Arkansas River Valley. The state's lowest point, at 55 feet (17 meters), is on the Ouachita River in south-central Arkansas.

Arkansas's largest lake is the artificial Lake Ouachita, covering 63 sq mi (163 sq km); Lake Chicot, in southeastern Arkansas, and oxbow of the Mississippi River, is the state's largest natural lake, with a length of 18 mi (29 km). Bull Shoals Lake, occupying 71 sq mi (184 sq km), is shared with Missouri. Principal rivers include the Mississippi, forming most of the eastern boundary; the Arkansas, beginning in Colorado and flowing 1,450 mi (2,334 km) through Kansas and Oklahoma and across central Arkansas to the Mississippi; and the Red, White, Ouachita, and St. Francis rivers, all of which likewise drain south and southeast into the Mississippi. Numerous springs are found in Arkansas, of which the best known are Mammoth Springs, near the Missouri border, one of the largest in the world, with a flow rate averaging 9 million gallons (34 million liters) an hour, and Hot Springs in the Ouachitas.

Crowley's Ridge, a unique strip of hills formed by sedimentary deposits and windblown sand, lies west of and parallel to the St. Francis River for about 180 mi (290 km). The ridge is rich in fossils and has an unusual diversity of plant life.

³CLIMATE

Arkansas has a temperate climate, warmer and more humid in the southern lowlands than in the mountainous regions. At Little Rock, the normal daily temperature ranges from 40°F (4°C) in January to 81°F (27°C) in July. A record low of –29°F (–34°C) was set on 13 February 1905 at the Pond weather station, and a record high of 120°F (49°C) was recorded on 10 August 1936 at the Ozark station.

Average yearly precipitation is approximately 45 in (114 cm) in the mountainous areas and greater in the lowlands; Little Rock receives an annual average of 49 in (124 cm) and has an average relative humidity ranging from 84% at 7 AM to 57% at 1 PM. Snowfall in the capital averages 5.4 in (13.7 cm) a year. In 1995, there were 24 tornadoes.

⁴FLORA AND FAUNA

Arkansas has at least 2,600 native plants, and there are many naturalized exotic species. Cypresses, water oak, hickory, and ash grow in the Mississippi Valley, while the St. Francis Valley is home to the rare cork tree. Crowley's Ridge is thick with tulip trees and beeches. A forest belt of oak, hickory, and pine stretches across south-central and southwestern Arkansas, including the Ozark and Ouachita mountains. The Mexican juniper is common along the White River's banks. The state has at least 26 native varieties of orchid; the passion flower is so abundant that it was once considered for designation as the state flower, but the apple blossom was finally chosen instead.

Arkansas's native animals include 15 varieties of bat and 3 each of rabbit and squirrel. Common throughout the state are mink, armadillo, white-tailed deer, and eastern chipmunk. Black bear roam the swamp and mountain regions. Among 300 native birds are such game birds as the eastern wild turkey, mourning dove, and bobwhite quail. Among local fish are catfish, gar, and the unusual paddle fish. Arkansas counts 20 frog and toad species, 23 varieties of salamander, and 36 kinds of snake.

The Arkansas Game and Fish Commission lists the leopard darter and fat pocketbook pearly mussel as threatened species. The peregrine falcon and American alligator are listed as endangered, along with the Indiana and gray bats and eastern puma. In 1983, Arkansas established the Non-Game Preservation Committee to promote sound management, conservation, and public awareness of the state's nongame animals and native plants.

[5]ENVIRONMENTAL PROTECTION

In 1949, the Arkansas General Assembly created the Arkansas Pollution Control Commission. This legislation was amended in later years to be known as the Arkansas Water and Air Pollution Control Act. Under an extensive reorganization of state government in 1971, the Arkansas Department of Pollution Control and Ecology (ADPC&E) was created as a cabinet-level agency and the Commission was renamed the Arkansas Pollution Control and Ecology Commission. Although the terms are frequently confused or used interchangeably by persons not connected with either governmental unit, the Commission and the Department are two separate, but related, entities. The Commission, with guidance from the governor and the Arkansas General Assembly, determines the environmental policies for the state, and the Department employees are responsible for implementing those policies. In 1996, the Arkansas General Assembly voted to change the name of the Department to the Arkansas Department of Environmental Quality on 31 March 1999. The initial authority to regulate water and air sources has been expanded to open-cut mining, solid waste, hazardous waste, and underground storage tanks.

In 1987, the state adopted some of the first "ecoregion" water quality standards in the nation. These standards recognize the distinct physical, chemical, and biological properties of the six geographical regions of the state and establish separate water quality standards within each region.

The US Environmental Protection Agency (EPA) has delegated responsibility for its clean-air programs to the ADPC&E. These programs include New Source Performance Standards (NSPS), National Emission Standards for Hazardous Air Pollutants (NESHAPS), Prevention of Significant Deterioration (PSD), and State Implementation Plan (SIP).

Citizens' groups actively involved with environmental issues include: the Arkansas Native Plant Society, Arkansas Audubon Society, Arkansas Canoe Club, Arkansas Herpetological Society, Arkansas Wildlife Federation, Audubon Society of Central Arkansas, League of Women Voters, Ozark Society, Sierra Club—Arkansas Chapter, and National Water Center. The Arkansas Environmental Federation presents industry's viewpoints on environmental issues.

The Buffalo River, designated as a national river, flows through northern Arkansas. One of the wildest areas in the state is the 113,000-acre (46,000-hectare) White River Refuge, which contains more than 100 small lakes. The Department of Arkansas Natural and Cultural Heritage (now called the Department of Heritage) was established in 1975 for, among other purposes, the preservation of rivers and other natural areas in an unspoiled condition.

Arkansas's solid waste stream is 2,000 tons a year (0.84 tons per capita). There are 64 municipal landfills in the state and 2 curbside recycling programs. Arkansas had 12 hazardous waste sites in 1995.

[6]POPULATION

At the time of the 1990 census, Arkansas had a population of 2,350,725 (33d in the US), an increase of 2.8% from the 1980 population of 2,286,000. Estimates for 1996 show Arkansas with 2,509,793 residents; the average population density is 45 per sq mi (17 per sq km).

As of 1989, Arkansas and Rhode Island were tied for 3rd behind Florida, Iowa, and Pennsylvania (the latter two being tied for 2d) in percentage of population aged 65 or over—14.8%—partially reflecting the large number of retirees who settled in the state during the 1970s and early 1980s.

Over 40% of all state residents lived in metropolitan areas in 1990. The largest city in Arkansas is Little Rock, which had an estimated 1994 population of 178,136. Estimates for other major cities in 1994 included Ft. Smith, 74,480; North Little Rock, 62,197; Pine Bluff, 57,971; and Fayetteville, 49,219. The Little Rock–North Little Rock metropolitan area had an estimated 543,568 residents in 1994.

[7]ETHNIC GROUPS

Arkansas's population is predominantly white, composed mainly of descendants of immigrants from the British Isles. The largest minority group consists of black Americans, numbering 374,000, or 15.9% of the population, in 1990, followed by American Indian, 13,000 (0.5%). About 20,000 Arkansans were of Hispanic origin. The 1990 census listed 1,788 Vietnamese, 1,575 Chinese, 2,166 Filipinos, 1,202 Asian Indians, and 754 Japanese. The foreign-born population numbered 24,867, or 1% of all Arkansas residents, in 1990.

[8]LANGUAGES

A few place-names—such as Arkansas itself, Choctaw, Caddo, and Ouachita—attest to the onetime presence of American Indians in the Territory of Arkansas, mostly members of the Caddoan tribe, with the Cherokee the most influential.

Arkansas English is essentially a blend of Southern and South Midland speech, with South Midland dominating the mountainous northwest; and Southern, the southeastern agricultural areas. Common in the east and south are *redworm* (earthworm) and *mosquito hawk* (dragonfly). In the northwest appear south Midland *whirlygig* (merry-go-round) and *sallet* (garden greens).

In 1990, 2,125,884 Arkansans—97.2% of the residents five years old or older—spoke only English at home. Other languages spoken at home included:

Spanish	27,351 (up 101% from 1980)	Vietnamese	1,701
French	8,210	Chinese	1,387
German	7,059	Italian	1,279

[9]RELIGIONS

Although French Roman Catholic priests had worked as missionaries among the Indians since the early 18th century, the state's first mission was founded among the Cherokee by a Congregationalist, Cephas Washburn, in 1820. When the Cherokee were removed to Indian Territory (present-day Oklahoma), the mission moved there as well, remaining active through the Civil War. William Patterson may have been the first Methodist to preach in Arkansas, around 1800, in the area of Little Prairie: the first Methodist circuit, that of Spring River, was organized in 1815. The first Baptist church was likely that of the Salem congregation, begun in 1818 near what is now Pochahontas.

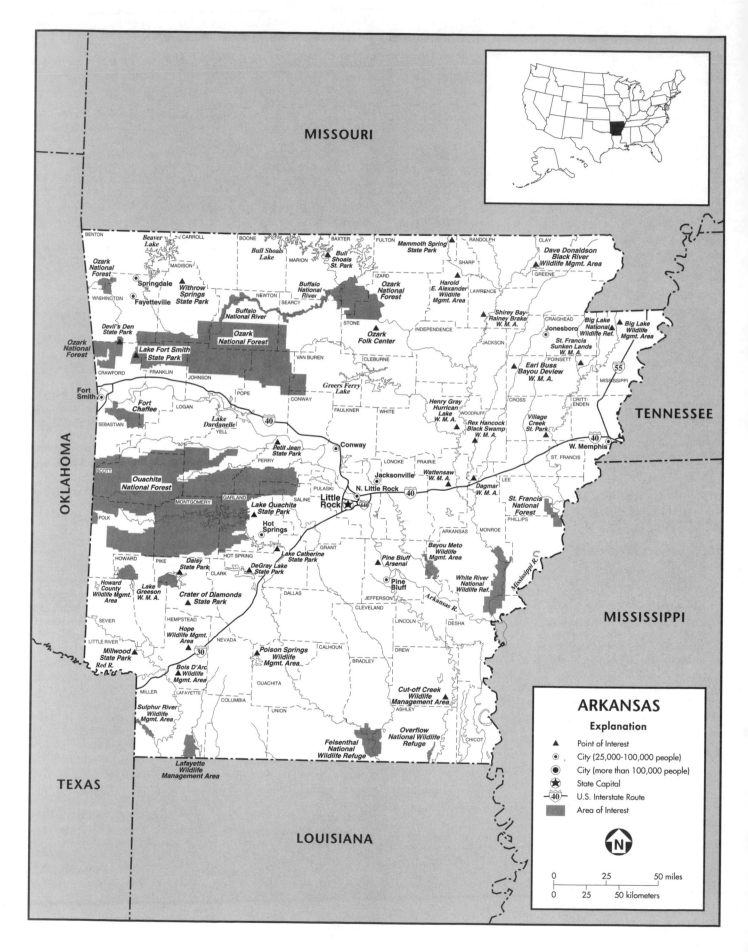

MISSOURI

TENNESSEE

OKLAHOMA

MISSISSIPPI

TEXAS

LOUISIANA

BENTON
Beaver Lake
CARROLL
Ozark National Forest
MADISON
Springdale
Fayetteville
WASHINGTON
Withrow Springs State Park
NEWTON
Bull Shoals Lake
MARION
BOONE
Buffalo National River
SEARCY
BAXTER
Bull Shoals St. Park
Mammoth Spring State Park
FULTON
IZARD
Ozark National Forest
SHARP
RANDOLPH
Dave Donaldson Black River Wildlife Mgmt. Area
CLAY
GREENE
Harold E. Alexander Wildlife Mgmt. Area
LAWRENCE
Shirey Bay Rainey Brake W. M. A.
Jonesboro
CRAIGHEAD
Big Lake National Wildlife Ref.
Big Lake Wildlife Mgmt. Area
Devil's Den State Park
Ozark National Forest
CRAWFORD
Lake Fort Smith State Park
FRANKLIN
JOHNSON
Buffalo National River
Ozark National Forest
VAN BUREN
STONE
Ozark Folk Center
CLEBURNE
INDEPENDENCE
JACKSON
St. Francis Sunken Lands W. M. A.
POINSETT
Earl Buss Bayou Deview W. M. A.
CROSS
MISSISSIPPI
55
Fort Smith
Fort Chaffee
SEBASTIAN
LOGAN
Lake Dardanelle
YELL
POPE
CONWAY
Greers Ferry Lake
FAULKNER
WHITE
Henry Gray Hurrican Lake W. M. A.
WOODRUFF
Rex Hancock Black Swamp W. M. A.
Village Creek St. Park
CRITTENDEN
40
Ouachita National Forest
SCOTT
MONTGOMERY
PERRY
Petit Jean State Park
GARLAND
Conway
LONOKE
PRAIRIE
Jacksonville
Wattensaw W. M. A.
N. Little Rock
PULASKI
SALINE
Lake Quachita State Park
Little Rock
440
40
Dagmar W. M. A.
LEE
ST. FRANCIS
W. Memphis
40
St. Francis National Forest
PHILLIPS
POLK
Hot Springs
Lake Catherine State Park
GRANT
ARKANSAS
MONROE
HOWARD
PIKE
Daisy State Park
DeGray Lake State Park
CLARK
Pine Bluff Arsenal
Bayou Meto Wildlife Mgmt. Area
HOT SPRING
Howard County Wildlife Mgmt. Area
Lake Greeson W. M. A.
Crater of Diamonds State Park
DALLAS
Pine Bluff
JEFFERSON
CLEVELAND
LINCOLN
DESHA
White River National Wildlife Ref.
SEVIER
HEMPSTEAD
Hope Wildlife Mgmt. Area
NEVADA
Poison Springs Wildlife Mgmt. Area
CALHOUN
DREW
LITTLE RIVER
Millwood State Park
Red R.
30
Bois D'Arc Wildlife Mgmt. Area
OUACHITA
BRADLEY
MILLER
LAFAYETTE
COLUMBIA
UNION
Cut-off Creek Wildlife Management Area
ASHLEY
CHICOT
Sulphur River Wildlife Mgmt. Area
Felsenthal National Wildlife Refuge
Overflow National Wildlife Refuge
Lafayette Wildlife Management Area
Arkansas R.
Mississippi R.

ARKANSAS

Explanation

▲ Point of Interest

⊙ City (25,000-100,000 people)

◉ City (more than 100,000 people)

★ State Capital

—40— U.S. Interstate Route

▮ Area of Interest

Ⓝ

0   25   50 miles

0   25   50 kilometers

The largest denomination in Arkansas is the Southern Baptist Convention, which had 617,524 known adherents in 1990. Other leading Protestant groups are the United Methodist Church, with 197,402 adherents in 1990 and the Baptist Missionary Association of America, with 78,121. As of 1990, the Roman Catholic population of Arkansas was 72,952 and the estimated Jewish population was 2,389.

¹⁰TRANSPORTATION

Although railroad construction began in the 1850s, not until after the Civil War (1861–65) were any lines completed. The most important railroad—the St. Louis, Iron Mountain, and Southern line—reached Little Rock in 1872 and was subsequently acquired by financier Jay Gould, who added the Little Rock and Ft. Smith line to it in 1882. By 1890, the state had about 2,200 mi (3,500 km) of track; in 1974, trackage totaled 3,559 mi (5,728 km). As of 1995, Arkansas was served by four major railroads, and had 2,643 rail mi (4,280 km) of track. In 1995, nonmetallic minerals accounted for 25% of the rail tonnage originating within the state, and coal made up 52% of the rail tonnage terminating within Arkansas. Amtrak passenger trains serviced Little Rock, Walnut Ridge, Malvern, Arkadelphia, and Texarkana en route from St. Louis to Dallas. In 1995/96, Arkansas ridership amounted to 16,005.

Intensive road building began in the 1920s, following the establishment of the State Highway Commission and the inauguration of a gasoline tax. By 1995, Arkansas had 77,222 mi (125,100 km) of public roads, streets, and highways. During the same year, 807,233 automobiles and 800,305 trucks were registered in Arkansas, and there were 1,769,012 licensed drivers. In 1995, private and commercial automobiles in the state came only to 32 per every 100 residents, fewer than in any other state.

Beginning in the 1820s, steamboats replaced keelboats and flatboats on Arkansas rivers. Steamboat transportation reached its peak during 1870–90, until supplanted by the railroads that were opened during the same two decades. Development of the Arkansas River, completed during the early 1970s, made the waterway commercially navigable all the way to Tulsa.

In 1995, Arkansas had 181 airports and 73 heliports. The principal airport in the state, Adams Field at Little Rock, enplaned 1,142,292 passengers and handled 19,189 departures in 1994.

¹¹HISTORY

Evidence of human occupation of Arkansas reaches back to about 10,000 BC. The bluff dwellers of the Ozark Plateau were among the first human beings to live in what is now Arkansas, making their homes in caves and beneath overhanging rock cliffs along the banks of the upper White River. Farther south are the remains of another primitive people, the Mound Builders. The most significant of the Stone Age monuments they left are those of the Toltec group in Lonoke County, some 25 mi (40 km) southeast of Little Rock. Eventually, both ancient peoples vanished, for reasons that remain unclear.

Foremost among the Indian tribes in Arkansas were the Quapaw (meaning "downstream people" or "South Wind people"), agriculturists who had migrated to southern Arkansas in the early 16th century; the Caddo, fighters from Texas, who claimed the western region between the Red and Arkansas rivers; the warlike Osage, who hunted north of the Arkansas River and in present-day Missouri; and the Choctaw. Another prominent tribe, the Cherokee, arrived in the early 19th century, after federal and state authorities had taken their land east of the Mississippi and driven them westward. Nearly all these Indians had been expelled to what is now Oklahoma by the time Arkansas became a state.

The first Europeans to set foot in Arkansas were Spaniards, led by Hernando de Soto. They crossed the Mississippi River, probably near present-day Helena, in the spring of 1541, roamed the land for a year or so, and then returned to the mighty river, where De Soto was buried in 1542. More than 100 years later, in 1673, a small band of Frenchmen led by Jacques Marquette, a Jesuit missionary, and Louis Jolliet, a fur trader and explorer, ended their voyage down the Mississippi at the mouth of the Arkansas River and returned north after being advised by friendly Indians that hostile tribes lay to the south. Nine years later, Robert Cavelier, Sieur de la Salle, led an expedition from Canada down the Mississippi to the Gulf of Mexico, stopping at Indian villages in Arkansas along the way and, on 9 April 1682, claiming all the Mississippi Valley for his king, Louis XIV.

Henri de Tonti, who had been second in command to La Salle, came back to Arkansas in 1686 to claim a land grant at the confluence of the Arkansas and White rivers, a few miles inland from the Mississippi. He left six men there; the log house they built was the beginning of Arkansas Post, the first permanent white settlement in the lower Mississippi Valley. Though tiny and isolated, Arkansas Post upheld the French claim to the Mississippi Valley until 1762, when France ceded the territory to Spain. Restored to France in 1800, the territory was sold to the US in the Louisiana Purchase of 1803. White settlers soon began arriving in Arkansas, and in 1806, the Louisiana territorial legislature created the District of Arkansas as a separate entity. When the Louisiana Purchase was further subdivided, Arkansas became part of the Missouri Territory. In 1819, Arkansas gained territorial status in its own right, and its boundaries were fixed by Congress. The territorial capital was moved from Arkansas Post to Little Rock in 1821. By 1835, Arkansas Territory had a population of 52,240, including 9,838 slaves. It was admitted to the Union in 1836 as a slave state, paired with the free state of Michigan in accordance with the Missouri Compromise.

Increasing numbers of slaves were brought into the largely agricultural state as the cultivation of cotton spread. Arkansas, like the rest of the South, was headed for secession, although it waited to commit itself until the Civil War (1861–65) had begun. There was considerable Union sentiment in the state, especially in the hilly northern and western counties, which lacked the large plantations and the slaves of southern and eastern Arkansas. But the pro-Union sympathies crumbled after Confederate guns fired on Ft. Sumter, SC, and the secession convention was held at Little Rock on 6 May 1861. The final vote to leave the Union was 69–1: the lone holdout was Isaac Murphy of Madison County, who became the first Unionist Democrat governor at the end of the war.

The largest Civil War battle fought in Arkansas, and one of the most significant battles of the war west of the Mississippi, was at Pea Ridge, in the northwest corner of the state. After three days of fighting, the Union forces retreated, and then the Confederate forces relinquished the field. By September 1863, the Union Army had taken Little Rock, and the Confederate capital was moved to Washington, in Hempstead County, until the conclusion of hostilities in 1865. Like virtually all white southerners, Arkansas's white majority hated the postwar Reconstruction government and repudiated it thoroughly at the first opportunity. Reconstruction officially ended in 1874, when the reenfranchised white Democratic majority adopted a new state constitution, throwing out the carpetbagger constitution of 1868. The most colorful figure in postwar Arkansas was federal judge Isaac C. Parker, known as the Hanging Judge. From his court at Ft. Smith, he had sole jurisdiction over Indian Territory, which had become a gathering place for the nation's worst cutthroats. Parker and his deputy marshals fought them relentlessly. From 1875 through 1896, the judge hanged 79 men on his Ft. Smith gallows. The struggle was not one-sided: 65 of Parker's deputy marshals were killed.

Industrialization, urbanization, and modernization did not come to Arkansas until after the depression of the 1930s. Following World War II (1939–45), the state became the first in the South to integrate its public colleges and universities. Little Rock's school board decided in 1954 to comply with the US Supreme Court's desegregation decision. Nevertheless, in September 1957, Governor Orval E. Faubus called out the National Guard to block the integration of Central High School at Little Rock. US President Dwight D. Eisenhower enforced a federal court order to integrate the school by sending in federal troops. The 1957 crisis brought years of notoriety to Arkansas, as Faubus, then in his second term, was elected to a third term and then to three more.

By the end of the Faubus administration, the public mood had changed, and the contrast between Faubus and his successor could not have been greater. Winthrop Rockefeller, millionaire scion of a famous family, moved to Arkansas from New York in the early 1950s, established himself as a gentleman rancher, and devoted himself to luring industry into his adopted state and building a Republican Party organization in one of the most staunchly Democratic states in the Union. Elected governor in 1966, Rockefeller thus became the first Republican to capture the Arkansas statehouse since Reconstruction. The specific accomplishments of his two terms were relatively few—he and the Democratic-controlled legislature warred incessantly—but he helped immeasurably in bringing a new image and a new spirit to the state.

Rockefeller's successors have continued the progressive approach he took. Governor Bill Clinton, who became United States President in 1992, introduced a number of reforms. These included investment tax credits to help corporations modernize their facilities and thereby to create jobs. Clinton also signed a "bare bones" health insurance law which dropped state requirements for some of the more costly coverages and thus made health insurance affordable for small businesses. He increased expenditures for education and passed legislation requiring competency tests for teachers. But Clinton, like other governors before him, remained hampered in his efforts to improve Arkansas's economy and standard of living by the state constitutional requirement that any increase in the state income tax obtain approval of two-thirds of the legislature. Arkansas continued to rank among the poorest states in the nation, with a per capita income in 1990 of only $14,000 (46th among the states).

In 1994, a federal special prosecutor began to investigate the actions of several members of Little Rock's Rose law firm, in which First Lady Hillary Rodham Clinton had been a partner, in connection with the failed Whitewater real estate venture. Governor Jim Guy Tucker resigned from office in July 1996 after his conviction on fraud and conspiracy charges stemming from his bank dealings.

12STATE GOVERNMENT

Arkansas's fourth constitution (not counting the territorial period), enacted in 1874 and amended many times, has survived several efforts to replace it with a more modern charter. In November 1980, voters turned down yet another proposed new constitution. In May 1995, the Governor's Task Force for a New Constitution was appointed in anticipation of a proposed 1996 constitutional convention. However, in December 1995, a referendum authorizing the convention was defeated by the voters.

Arkansas's bicameral legislature, the general assembly, consists of a 35-member senate and a 100-member house of representatives. Senators serve four-year terms and must be at least 25 years of age; representatives serve for two years and must be at least

21. Each legislator must be a US citizen and have resided for at least two years in the state and one year in the county or district prior to election. Legislators' salaries in 1995 were $12,500.

Under the 1874 constitution, the executive officers elected statewide are the governor, secretary of state, treasurer, auditor, and state land commissioner, all of whom serve two-year terms. In the 1920s, a constitutional amendment provided for the election of the lieutenant governor as well. In 1986, Arkansas initiated its first four-year term for elected officials. The governor and lieutenant governor, who run separately, must be US citizens, must be at least 30 years old, and must have resided in Arkansas for seven years. In 1996, the governor's salary was $60,000.

A bill passed by both houses of the legislature becomes law if signed by the governor, if passed over his veto by a majority of all elected members of each house, or if neither signed nor returned by the governor within five days when the legislature is in session. Under an initiative procedure, 8% of those who voted for governor in the last election may propose a law, and 10% may initiate a constitutional amendment; initiative petitions must be filed at least four months before the general election in order to be voted upon at that time. A referendum on any measure passed by the general assembly or any item of an appropriations bill or other measure may be petitioned by 6% of the voters; referendum petitions must be filed within 90 days of the session in which the act in question was passed. A successful referendum measure may be repealed by a two-thirds vote of all elected members of the general assembly. Constitutional amendments may also be proposed by the general assembly or by constitutional convention, subject to ratification by the electorate.

To vote in Arkansas, one must be a US citizen at least 18 years of age; registration closes 20 days before an election.

13POLITICAL PARTIES

The principal political groups in Arkansas are the Democratic Party and the Republican Party, each affiliated with the national party organizations.

Before the Civil War (1861–65), politics in Arkansas were fraught with violence. Republicans ruled during Reconstruction, which officially ended in Arkansas after the constitution of 1874 had been adopted by the new Democratic majority. During the election of 1872, the Liberal Republicans, nicknamed Brindletails, opposed the Radical Republicans, or Minstrels. After the Minstrel candidate, Elisha Baxter, was elected, he proved so independent a governor that some of the party leaders who had supported him attempted to oust him through a court order in April 1874, declaring his defeated opponent, Joseph Brooks, the winner. Supported by a militia of about 300 blacks under white command, Brooks took over the statehouse; Baxter, bolstered by his own 300-man black army, set up his headquarters three blocks away. The so-called Brooks-Baxter War finally ended with President Ulysses S. Grant's proclamation of Baxter as the lawful governor. Baxter did not seek reelection—instead Augustus H. Garland was elected, the first of a long series of Bourbon Democrats who were to rule the state well into the 20th century.

After Reconstruction, blacks in Arkansas continued to vote and to be elected to public office; under what became known as the fusion principle, black Republican and white Democratic leaders in the plantation belt often agreed not to oppose each other's candidates. Segregation in public places was still outlawed, and Little Rock was perhaps the most integrated city in the South. During the 1890s, however, as in the rest of the South, Democrats began to pass laws imposing segregation and disfranchising blacks as well as poor whites. In 1906, the Democrats instituted a nominating primary for whites only.

On the rocky path to progressive government, Arkansans elected several governors who stand out as progressive: George Donaghey (1909–13), Charles Brush (1917–21), Thomas McRae

(1921–25), Carl Bailey (1935–39) and Sidney McMath (1948–53). Although elected to the governorship as a progressive in 1954, McMath's protégé Orval Faubus took a segregationist stand in 1957. In subsequent years, poor whites tended to support Faubus, while blacks and more affluent whites opposed him. Faubus's successor, progressive Republican Winthrop Rockefeller, was strongly supported by blacks. Rockefeller was followed by three more progressives, all Democrats: Dale Bumpers, David Pryor, and—after Bumpers and Pryor had graduated to the US Senate—Bill Clinton. In a major upset, Clinton was defeated in 1980 by Republican Frank White, but he recaptured the statehouse in 1982 and won reelection in 1984, 1986, and 1990. Clinton ran for and won the presidency in 1992 with a plurality of 53% in Arkansas. Clinton won presidential reelection in 1996, gaining 54% of the vote, against 37% for Republican challenger Bob Dole and 8% for Independent Ross Perot. On 8 November 1994, Democratic governor Jim Guy Tucker was one of the few of his party nationwide to resist a Republican challenge. However, in 1996 Tucker was forced to resign following his conviction on charges related to the Whitewater prosecution, and the governorship was assumed by Lieutenant Governor Mike Huckabee.

Senator Dale Bumpers, a Democrat, was reelected in 1992. In 1996, the vacated Senate seat of Democrat David Pryor was won by US Representative Tim Hutchinson, a Republican. Arkansas's US Representatives in 1996 included 2 Republicans and 2 Democrats. Following the November 1996 election, the state legislature had 28 Democrats and 6 Republicans in the state senate, and 86 Democrats and 13 Republicans in the state house. In 1993 there were 380 black elected officials, and in 1995 there were 19 women serving in the state legislature and in elective executive office. As of 1994, 3 Hispanics held elective office.

14LOCAL GOVERNMENT

There are 75 counties in Arkansas, ten of them with two county seats. Each county is governed by a quorum court, consisting of 9–15 justices of the peace, elected for two-year terms; the county judge, who presides, does not vote but has veto power, which may be overridden by a three-fifths vote of the total membership. Elected county executives, who serve two-year terms, include the sheriff, assessor, coroner, treasurer, and county supervisor. In 1992, Arkansas had 489 municipalities, 561 special districts, and 321 school districts.

15STATE SERVICES

Educational services in Arkansas are administered primarily by the Department of Education and the Department of Higher Education. The State Highway and Transportation Department has primary responsibility for roads, rails, and public transit; the offices of motor vehicle registration and driver services are in the Department of Finance and Administration.

Health and welfare services are under the jurisdiction of the Department of Health and the Department of Human Services. Public protection is provided primarily through the Department of Public Safety—which includes the Office of Emergency Services, State Police, National Guard, and Civil Air Patrol—and the Department of Correction, which operates three prisons and three work-release centers. The Public Service Commission, within the Department of Commerce, regulates utilities in the state. Housing services are provided through the Housing Development Agency and the Department of Local Services, whose Division of Manpower offers employment and training programs.

16JUDICIAL SYSTEM

Arkansas's highest court is the supreme court, consisting of a chief justice and six associate justices, elected for staggered eight-year terms. An appeals court of six judges, also elected for eight-year terms, was established in 1978.

Arkansas's courts of original jurisdiction are the circuit courts (law) and the chancery courts (equity), of which there are 24 circuits each; their judges are elected for four-year terms. Courts of limited jurisdiction include justice of the peace, county, municipal, and police courts, and courts of common pleas. There were 6,900 practicing attorneys in 1996, a 53% increase since 1994.

Arkansas had an FBI Crime Index rate of 4,690.9 per 100,000 population in 1995. The state's once notorious prisons, which had been under federal jurisdiction for more than a decade, were returned in 1978 to state authority, subject to monitoring by an independent ombudsman. By then, the decaying system of the 1960s had been almost entirely replaced by modern facilities. In 1995 there were 8,318 prisoners in 15 state and federal correc-

Arkansas Presidential Vote by Political Parties, 1948–96

YEAR	ELECTORAL VOTE	ARKANSAS WINNER	DEMOCRAT	REPUBLICAN	STATES' RIGHTS DEMOCRAT
1948	9	*Truman (D)	149,659	50,959	40,068
1952	8	Stevenson (D)	226,300	177,155	—
					CONSTITUTION
1956	8	Stevenson (D)	213,277	186,287	7,008
					NAT'L STATES' RIGHTS
1960	8	*Kennedy (D)	215,049	184,508	28,952
1964	6	*Johnson (D)	314,197	243,264	2,965
					AMERICAN IND.
1968	6	Wallace (AI)	188,228	190,759	240,982
					AMERICAN
1972	6	*Nixon (R)	199,892	448,541	2,887
1976	6	*Carter (D)	498,604	267,903	—
					LIBERTARIAN
1980	6	*Reagan (R)	398,041	403,164	8,970
1984	6	*Reagan (R)	388,646	534,774	2,2221
1988	6	*Bush (R)	349,237	466,578	3,297
					IND. (Perot)
1992	6	*Clinton (D)	505,823	337,324	99,132
1996	6	*Clinton (D)	475,171	325,416	69,884

* Won US presidential election.

tional institutions, an incarceration rate of 335 per 100,000 inhabitants. Arkansas has a death penalty and has executed 129 persons since 1930, including 2 in 1995. There were 38 persons under sentence of death in 1995.

17ARMED FORCES

As of 1996, there were five military installations in Arkansas, the principal ones being Little Rock Air Force Base and the Army's Pine Bluff Arsenal. Military personnel in the state numbered 4,994 in 1996. Firms in the state received $249 million in defense contract awards in 1995/96.

As of 1996, some 255,000 Arkansans were veterans of US military service; fewer than 500 saw service in World War I (1914–18); 74,000 in World War II (1939–45); 45,000 during the Korean conflict (1950–53); 79,000 during the Vietnam era (1954–75); and 22,000 in the Persian Gulf War (1990–91). Arkansas veterans received $634 million in benefits in 1995/96. There were 16,167 Army Reserve and National Guard in 1996, and 3,107 Air Force Reserve and Air National Guard personnel. In 1993 the Arkansas State Police had 485 full-time sworn officers, or 2 per 10,000 residents.

18MIGRATION

Near the end of the 18th century, Indians from east of the Mississippi, displaced by white settlement, entered the area now known as Arkansas. However, as the availability of cheap land in Louisiana Territory drew more and more white settlers—in particular, veterans of the War of 1812, who had been promised 160-acre (65-hectare) tracts—the Indians were pressured to cross the border from Arkansas to present-day Oklahoma.

After the end of the Mexican War, thousands of Arkansans emigrated to Texas, and others were attracted to California in 1849 by the gold rush. Because of a law passed in 1859 requiring free blacks to leave the state by the end of the year or risk being enslaved, Arkansas's population of free blacks dropped from 682 in 1858 to 144 in 1860. During Reconstruction, the state government encouraged immigration by both blacks and whites. Literature sent out by the Office of State Lands and Migration, under the tenure of William H. Grey, a black leader, described the state as a new Africa. Railroads, seeking buyers for the lands they had acquired through government grants, were especially active in encouraging immigration after Reconstruction. Later immigrants included Italians and, in the early 1900s, Germans.

During the Depression era (1930s) and thereafter, Arkansas lost a substantial proportion of its farm population, and many blacks left the state for the industrial cities of the Midwest and the east and west coasts. The net loss from migration totaled 919,000 between 1940 and 1970. Between 1970 and 1980, however, the state gained 180,000 residents through migration, as the Ozarks became one of the fastest-growing rural areas in the US. The state experienced a small net decline of 2,000 in migration between 1980 and 1983. Net migration from 1985 to 1990 amounted to a gain of nearly 36,600. Between 1990 and 1996, there were net gains of 94,972 in domestic migration and 5,963 in international migration. As of 1990, just over two-thirds of all Arkansans had been born in the state. Some 54% of state residents (age 5 and older) lived in the same house in 1990 as in 1985. Of those who lived in a different house in 1985, 76% did so in Arkansas, of which nearly three-fourths moved within the same county.

19INTERGOVERNMENTAL COOPERATION

Among the many interstate agreements in which Arkansas participates are the Arkansas River Basin Compact of 1970 (with Oklahoma), Interstate Oil and Gas Compact, Red River Compact, South Central Forest Fire Protection Compact, Southern Growth Policies Compact, Southern Interstate Energy Compact, and Southern Regional Education Compact. There are boundary agreements with Mississippi, Missouri, and Tennessee.

In 1995/96, Arkansas received federal aid totaling $2.1 billion.

20ECONOMY

During the 19th century, Arkansas's economic growth was hindered by credit problems. When the state's two central banks, the Arkansas State Bank and the Real Estate Bank, failed during the 1840s, the government defaulted on bonds issued by the latter and amended the constitution to prohibit all banking in Arkansas. Although banking was restored after the Civil War (1861–65), the state defaulted on its obligations once more in 1877, this time following a decision by the Arkansas supreme court that $10 million worth of railroad bonds issued during Reconstruction were unconstitutional. Not until 1917 did New York banks again accept Arkansas securities.

Cotton dominated Arkansas's agricultural economy until well into the 20th century, when rice, soybeans, poultry, and fish farming diversified the output. Coal mining began in the 1870s, bauxite mining near the turn of the century, and oil extraction in the 1920s; lumbering developed in the last quarter of the 19th century, reached its peak about 1909, and then declined until the 1920s, when reforestation started. Industrialization was limited, however, and resources were generally shipped out of state for processing. Not until the 1950s did Arkansas enjoy significant success in attracting industry, thanks in large part to the efforts of Winthrop Rockefeller. Although the Little Rock integration crisis of 1957 was a severe setback to industrial growth in its own Pulaski County the following year, development resumed during the following decades.

By the mid-1990s, Arkansas's principal industries had become manufacturing, dominated by lumber and wood products companies; agriculture; forestry; and tourism. Five Fortune 500 firms are headquartered in Arkansas: Wal-Mart Stores, Tyson Foods, Dillard Department Stores, Beverly Enterprises, and Alltel. Contributing to Arkansas's gross state product of $50,575 million in 1994 were private goods-producing industries, $17,155 million; private services-producing industries, $27,375 million; and government, $6,045 million.

Arkansas's per capita income was $18,101 in 1995, ranking it 48th in the nation. In 1996, there were 13,194 bankruptcies filed in the state, which was nearly 41% more than the previous year.

21INCOME

Total disposable personal income was $42.1 billion in 1996, up from $40 billion in 1995. In 1996, the per capita disposable household income was estimated at $16,783. In 1996, Arkansas ranked 47th among the 50 states in per capita personal income. The personal per capita income figure of $18,928 represented 78% of the US average per capita income for that year, which was a large improvement over the 62% recorded in 1960 and the 43% registered in 1929. From 1995 to 1996, total personal income grew by 5.7%, slightly above the national average of 5.4%. An estimated 15% of the population were living below the federal poverty level in 1995. In 1995, median household income was $25,814.

22LABOR

Arkansas's civilian labor force totaled 1,234,400 in 1996. Of the total labor force, the Little Rock metropolitan area accounted for 24.3%; Fayetteville-Springdale-Rogers, 11.3%; Fort Smith, 7.6%; Pine Bluff, 3%; and other areas, 53.8%. A total of 1,167,800 Arkansans were employed and 66,600 unemployed, for an overall unemployment rate of 5.4% in 1996.

Employment and earnings of workers covered by the Arkansas Employment Security Law, by major industry, for 1995 are shown below:

	EARNINGS (IN MILLIONS)	EMPLOYMENT (IN THOUSANDS)
Nonfarm	22,510.6	1,042.5
Private	18,564.2	878.4
Agricultural service, forestry, fisheries	269.3	15.3
Mining	104.0	3.5
Construction	984.2	44.1
Manufacturing	6,153.9	258.5
Transportation and public utilities	1,760.5	59.4
Wholesale trade	1,359.3	49.5
Retail trade	2,616.6	193.3
Finance, insurance, and real estate	1,061.4	40.1
Services	4,255.0	214.7
Government	3,946.4	164.1

Chartered in 1865, the Little Rock Typographical Union, consisting of *Arkansas Gazette* employees, was the first labor union in the state. The United Mine Workers was established in the Ft. Smith area by 1898; six years later, the UMW led in the founding of the Arkansas Federation of Labor. Between 1904 and World War I (1914–18), a series of progressive labor laws was enacted, including a minimum wage, restrictions on child labor, and prohibitions against blacklisting and payment of wages in scrip. Union strength waned after the war, however, and the labor movement is not a powerful force in the state today. Union membership was about 79,400 in 1995, or 8% of all workers. Unionization among private manufacturers was 4.9% in 1995. Arkansas has a right-to-work law.

23AGRICULTURE

Farm marketings in Arkansas were over $5 billion in 1996 (13th in the US), with crops and livestock accounting for about 40% and 60%, respectively. The state is the nation's leading producer of rice and is among the leaders in cotton, soybeans, and grain sorghum.

Cotton was first grown in the state about 1800, along the river valleys. Confined mainly to slaveholding plantations before the Civil War (1861–65), cotton farming became more widespread in the postwar period, expanding into the hill country of the northwest and eventually into the deforested areas of the northeast, which proved to be some of the most fertile farmland in the nation. As elsewhere in the postbellum South, share-cropping by tenant farmers predominated well into the 20th century, until mechanization and diversification gradually brought an end to the system. Rice was first grown commercially in the early 1900s; by 1920, Arkansas had emerged as a poultry and soybean producer.

During 1996, Arkansas produced 112,000,000 bushels of soybeans, valued at $795,200,000; 66,960,000 bushels of wheat, worth $294,624,000; 2,310,000 tons of hay, worth $131,550,000; and 16,280,000 bushels of sorghum for grain, valued at $48,840,000. The rice harvest in 1996 was 71,945,000 hundredweight (3,263,425,200 kg), worth $701,464,000. The cotton crop in 1996, 1,600,000 bales, was worth $549,888,000.

24ANIMAL HUSBANDRY

Poultry farms are found throughout Arkansas, but especially in the northern and western regions. Arkansas was the top-ranked broiler-producing state in the US in 1995; 1.1 billion broilers were valued at $1.7 billion.

In 1996 it was estimated that Arkansas produced 3.4 million eggs. In 1995 Arkansas produced 535.6 million lb (243 million kg) of turkey valued at $241 million. Arkansas sold 117 million lb (53 million kg) of chickens valued at $15 million; Arkansas was the top-ranking chicken-producing state in 1995.

The dairy yield of the state's 60,000 milk cows in 1995 was 732 million lb (332 million kg) of milk. In 1997 Arkansas had 1.9 million cattle and calves valued at $703 million. In 1996 Arkansas had 825,000 hogs and pigs valued at $82 million.

25FISHING

Aquaculture is of greater economic importance to Arkansas than is traditional commercial fishing. As of 1997, the state ranked 1st in the US in minnow farming, and 2d only to Mississippi in catfish farming. As of 1 January 1997, there were 180 catfish operations covering 28,500 acres (11,534 hectares) of water surface, with 124.3 million stocker-size and 130.6 million fingerling/fry catfish. Some producers rotate fish crops with row crops, periodically draining their fish ponds and planting grains in the rich and well-fertilized soil. Arkansas had 590,782 licensed anglers in 1995/96.

26FORESTRY

Forestland comprised 18,778,600 acres (7,599,700 hectares), or 56% of the state's total land area, in 1995. Of that total, 18,382,000 acres (7,439,000 hectares) were commercial timberland, 78% of Arkansas's total forestland. The southwest and central plains, the state's timber belt, constitute one of the most concentrated sources of yellow pine in the US. In 1997, there were 1,036 lumber and wood products establishments in Arkansas. Three national forests in Arkansas covered a total of 2,263,300 acres (915,960 hectares) in 1995.

27MINING

The US Geological Survey estimate of the value of mineral production in Arkansas in 1995 was $451 million, an increase of $14 million from the figure reported by the state's more than 200 mineral producers in 1994.

In 1995, 21,500,000 metric tons of crushed stone were produced, valued at $128,000,000; 207,000 metric tons of bromine worth $185,000,000; and 10,800,000 metric tons of construction sand and gravel with a value of $44,800,000.

Increased value of production in 1995 came primarily from crushed stone. Arkansas continues to be the leading bromine-producing state, accounting for most US production. Arkansas also ranked 3rd in gemstones in 1995, with a value of $4.7 million.

28ENERGY AND POWER

Although Arkansas possesses substantial and varied energy resources—petroleum, natural gas, coal, and water—the state was slow to develop them. As late as 1935, only 1% of Arkansas farms had electric power. The struggle that began during the 1930s over whether Arkansas's rivers would be publicly developed for the production of electricity (in the manner of the Tennessee Valley Authority) was won by the advocates of private power development. As of 1996, Arkansas power plants had a combined capacity of 9.8 million kW, of which about three-fourths was privately owned; production totaled 39.5 billion kWh in 1995.

During 1996, 8,814,000 barrels of crude petroleum were produced. At the beginning of 1996, proved reserves were 48,000,000 barrels. Production of natural gas was 187.2 billion cu ft (5.3 billion cu m) in 1995, with 1.56 trillion cu ft (0.04 trillion cu m) of reserves remaining. About 21,000 tons of bituminous coal were mined in 1996.

29INDUSTRY

Manufacturing in Arkansas is diverse, ranging from blue jeans to bicycles, though resource industries such as rice processing and woodworking still play a major role. The total value of shipments of manufactured goods in 1995 was nearly $43 billion, of which food and kindred products contributed $10.726 billion; lumber and wool, $3.111 billion; paper and allied products, $4.474 billion; primary metal industries, $3.9 billion; industrial machinery and equipment, $3.178 billion. In 1995, the US government issued 143 patents to Arkansas citizens. The following table shows value of shipments for selected industries in 1995:

Meat product	$5,123,500,000
Grain-mill products	1,827,200,000
Preserved fruits and vegetables	1,343,100,000
Motor vehicles and equipment	1,254,200,000
Household appliances	568,000,000
Household furniture	325,000,000

30COMMERCE

In 1992, Arkansas had a total of 4,296 wholesale establishments, with sales of over $18 billion. Durable goods accounted for 61.7% of establishments and 35.2% of sales. There were a total of 14,866 retail establishments in 1992, with sales of $15,925.3 million (32d in the US). The leading retail categories for sales were automotive dealers, 23.5%; food stores, 19.2%; general merchandise, 17.3%; and gasoline service stations, 8.5%.

During 1996, exports of goods produced within the state were valued at $2 billion.

31CONSUMER PROTECTION

Under the mandate of Consumer Protection Act of 1971, the Consumer Protection Division of the Office of the Attorney General has principal responsibility for consumer affairs.

32BANKING

In 1836, the first year of statehood, the legislature created the Arkansas State Bank; and the Real Estate Bank, which was intended to promote the plantation system. Fraud, mismanagement, and the consequences of the financial panic of 1837 ruined both banks and led to the passage in 1846 of a constitutional amendment prohibiting the incorporation of any lending institution in Arkansas. Money grew scarce, with credit being rendered largely by suppliers and brokers to farmers and planters until after the Civil War (1861–65), when the prohibition was removed.

Arkansas had 233 insured commercial banks in 1996. At the end of 1996, the state's insured commercial banks had $31 billion in assets and $26 billion in deposits. The combined assets of 16 insured savings and loans amounted to $3.4 billion at the end of 1996; they held nearly $2.6 billion in deposits. As of the early 1980s, Arkansas's usury law, imposing a 10% ceiling on interest rates, was among the most rigid in the US; the US Supreme Court upheld the 10% limit in 1981. The rise of the federal discount rate above that limit, beginning in mid-1979, caused a considerable outflow of capital from Arkansas. The Arkansas Usury Law was changed in December 1992, with Amendment 60. Amendment 60 to the Arkansas Constitution provides that the maximum interest rate on general loans is 5% above the Federal Reserve Discount Rate. The Arkansas Supreme Court has interpreted Amendment 60 to provide that the rate on consumer loans is 5% above the discount rate or 17%, whichever is lower. Amendment 60 became effective 2 December 1982.

33 INSURANCE

Arkansans held 1.6 million life insurance policies worth $57.2 billion at the close of 1995. The average of $96,300 in life insurance per family was the fifth-lowest of all the states. Benefits paid in 1995 amounted to $926.1 million, including $244.5 million in death payments. During the same year, premiums were written for $664.2 million in private passenger and commercial automobile liability insurance, $402.3 million for automobile physical-damage coverage, and $225.3 million for homeowners' insurance.

34SECURITIES

There are no securities exchanges in Arkansas, although New York Stock Exchange member firms have sales offices and registered representatives in the state.

35PUBLIC FINANCE

Under the 1874 constitution, state expenditures may not exceed revenues. The mechanism adopted each biennium to prevent deficit spending is a Revenue Stabilization Act. This Act provides the funding for state appropriations by assigning levels of funding priority to the appropriations. All appropriations in a higher level must be fully funded before any appropriations in a lower level are funded. In the event of insufficient revenues to fund appropriations, each agency reduces its appropriations, to correspond to the general revenues allocated to the agency.

Revenues and expenditures for the General Fund for the fiscal year ended 30 June 1996, in millions, are as follows:

REVENUES	
Taxes	$3,713,893
Licenses, Fees and Permits	355,742
Investment Earnings	66,033
Intergovernmental	2,213,786
Other	361,376
TOTAL	$6,710,830

EXPENDITURES	
Current:	
Education	$1,690,844
Health and Human Resources	2,297,385
Transportation	579,417
Law, Justice, and Public Safety	241,228
Recreation and Resource Development	178,519
General Government	783,378
Regulation of Businesses and Professionals	130,339
Debt Service	27,413
Capital Outlay	94,874
TOTAL	$6,023,397

The total outstanding debt of State government at 30 June 1996 was $2.16 billion.

36TAXATION

As of 1996, Arkansas's state tax revenue per capita was $1,477, the 34th-lowest in the US. In 1996, the state income tax ranged from 1% to 7%; the corporate income tax ranged from 1% on the first $3,000 to 6% on amounts over $25,000. Corporate taxpayers with a net income of $100,000 or greater pay a flat rate of 6.5%. The state sales tax is 4.625%, effective 1 July 1997. The state also imposes severance taxes on oil, natural gas, and other natural resources, along with levies on liquor, gasoline, and cigarettes. City and county property taxes in Arkansas are among the lowest in the nation.

Arkansas taxpayers paid $1.162 billion in state income tax in 1995.

37ECONOMIC POLICY

First as chairman of the Arkansas Industrial Development Commission and later as governor of the state from 1967–71, Winthrop Rockefeller succeeded in attracting substantial and diverse new industries to Arkansas. In 1979, Governor Bill Clinton formed the Department of Economic Development from the former Arkansas Industrial Development Commission for the purpose of stimulating the growth of small business and finding new export markets.

[38]HEALTH

The infant death rate for the year ending December 1995 was 9.0 per 1,000 live births. There were 5,886 legal abortions performed in 1995, when the state's abortion ratio was 16.7 per 1,000 live births. During the same year, however, Arkansas's death rate, 1,110.3 per l00,000 population, was well above the national rate of 880.0, and the incidence of cerebrovascular disease was 94.3 per 100,000 population. Death rates from heart disease, cancer, accidents, and motor vehicle accidents also exceeded the national average. The number of AIDS cases in 1995 decreased from 1994 (137 vs. 285). The HIV death rate in Arkansas is much lower than the national average of 16.4 per 100,000 population in 1995. In 1993 there was a stroke mortality rate of 39.1 per 100,000 population. Of persons 18–30 years old, 24% were current smokers. The estimated deaths from smoking-related diseases for those who will become smokers is 49,821 (1995 calculation). The unintentional death rate has increased from 46.9 to 47.5 deaths per 100,000 population (1992 vs. 1993).

Arkansas's 85 hospitals had 9,352 beds and recorded 337,892 admissions in 1995. Hospital expenses for services provided in 1994—$1263 per inpatient day and $8,168 per stay—were higher than the US average. In 1994, the state had 4,027 nonfederal physicians, 18,500 active registered nurses, and 999 professionally active dentists (1995).

[39]SOCIAL WELFARE

Social welfare payments in Arkansas generally fall well below national norms. During 1996, aid to families with dependent children was given to 59,000 recipients; the average payment per family was $247 monthly. The food stamp program had an average monthly participation of 273,900; and the school lunch program had a federal outlay of $63.7 million in 1996.

With the enactment of the Personal Responsibility and Work Opportunity Reconciliation Act of 1996, the US government has changed the form and regulations for many of its social welfare programs; most significantly, it replaces Aid to Families with Dependent Children (AFDC), an open-ended entitlement program, with Temporary Assistance for Needy Families (TANF), a limited system of assistance funded largely through federal block grants. The reform act also impacts the food stamp program, the Supplemental Security Income program, and the child nutrition program. The law took effect on 1 July 1997 and provided $16.38 billion in block grants for fiscal years 1997–2002. The grants are to be divided among the states based on an equation involving the numbers of former AFDC recipients in each state. Because many of the bills provisions have yet to be implemented into state-by-state policy, it was not possible to include the details of each state's programs for this edition of this work.

Some 503,330 Arkansans received Social Security benefits in 1995, averaging $655 monthly. Supplemental Security Income payments were made to 94,486 persons, averaging $298 a month. The weekly unemployment check averaged $167.73 in 1995.

[40]HOUSING

In October 1996, there were an estimated 1,054,000 housing units in Arkansas, 938,000 of them year-round units. From 1980 to 1990, the number of housing units in Arkansas increased by 11%; about one-quarter of all housing structures were built in the 1980s. 1995/96, the Department of Housing and Urban Development awarded $193.9 million in grants to Arkansas, including $36 million in community development block grants and $18.2 million in housing assistance for residents with low incomes.

In 1990, the most recent year for which the government has estimates, the median value of a home in Arkansas was $46,300, lower than in 47 other states, and down 6.3% from 1980 after adjusting for inflation. The median monthly cost for an owner-occupied unit (including a mortgage) was $514; a rental unit had a median monthly cost of $328 in 1990.

[41]EDUCATION

In 1990, 68.7% of all Arkansans 25 years of age and older were high school graduates (41st-lowest in the US). Only 16% had completed four or more years of college, the 10th-lowest rate among the states. In 1983, in an effort to raise the quality of education in Arkansas, the state legislature approved a comprehensive program that included smaller classes, more high-school-level courses, and competency tests for teachers.

Public school enrollment in 1995 totaled 451,877. The 1994/95 expenditure for public elementary and secondary schools was $3,980 per pupil. In some ways, Little Rock was an unlikely site for the major confrontation over school integration that occurred in 1957. The school board had already announced its voluntary compliance with the Supreme Court's desegregation decision, and during Governor Faubus's first term (1955–56), several public schools in the state had been peaceably integrated. Nevertheless, on 5 September 1957, Faubus, claiming that violence was likely, ordered the National Guard to seize Central High School to prevent the entry of nine black students. When a mob did appear following the withdrawal of the National Guardsmen in response to a federal court order later that month, President Dwight Eisenhower dispatched federal troops to Little Rock, and they patrolled the school grounds until the end of the 1958 spring semester. Although Faubus's stand encouraged politicians in other southern states to resist desegregation, in Arkansas integration proceeded at a moderate pace. By 1980, Central High School had a nearly equal balance of black and white students, and the state's school system was one of the most integrated in the South.

In 1984, Arkansas had 35 institutions of higher education, 19 public and 16 private, of which the largest, the University of Arkansas at Fayetteville (established in 1871), had a fall 1983 enrollment of 13,483. In 1994, Arkansas had 96,294 students enrolled in institutions of higher education. Student aid is provided by the State Scholarship Program within the Department of Higher Education, by the Arkansas Student Loan Guarantee Foundation, and by the Arkansas Rural Endowment Fund, Inc.

[42]ARTS

Little Rock is the home of the Arkansas Symphony, Ballet Arkansas, and the Arkansas Arts Center, which holds art exhibits and classes, and children's theater performances. The best-known center for traditional arts and crafts is the Ozark Folk Center at Mountain View; every evening from late spring through October, folk music of the Ozarks may be heard. The Arkansas Folk Festival is held there during two weekends in April, and the Family Harvest Festival for three weeks in October. Lyon College at Batesville sponsors two-week summer workshops in Ozark crafts, music, and folklore in association with the center. The Grand Prairie Festival of Arts is held at Stuttgart in September.

From 1991 to 1996, arts funding in Arkansas amounted to $1,055,000. The National Endowment for the Arts (NEA) provided $480,000 for state artists and $753,000 for the Arkansas Arts Council through selected programs by state and outlying agencies. The Council also used funding from the State of Arkansas to support arts organizations. Funding for the arts reached 71,576 artists. There were 66,500 school children who participated in arts education programs. By 1996, there were 55 arts-related associations in Arkansas and 25 local groups. The Arkansas Arts Council received funding in arts education grants from the NEA, as well as monies through the NEA's state and regional program.

⁴³LIBRARIES AND MUSEUMS

During 1994, Arkansas had 72 county or regional libraries and 15 municipal libraries. That year, public libraries held a total of 4,890,373 volumes and circulation amounted to 9,074,119. Important collections include those of the University of Arkansas at Fayetteville (1,452,137 volumes), Arkansas State University at Jonesboro (508,077), the Central Arkansas Library System of Little Rock (516,491), and the News Library of the Arkansas Gazette, also in Little Rock.

There were 71 museums in 1994 and a number of historic sites. Principal museums include the Arkansas Arts Center and the Museum of Science and History, both at Little Rock; the Arkansas State University Museum at Jonesboro; and the University of Arkansas Museum at Fayetteville, specializing in archaeology, anthropology, and the sciences. Also of interest are the Stuttgart Agricultural Museum; the Arkansas Post County Museum at Gillett, whose artifacts are housed in re-created plantation buildings; Hampson Museum State Park, near Wilson, which has one of the largest collections of Mound Builder artifacts in the US; the Mid-American Museum at Hot Springs, which has visitor-participation exhibits; and the Saunders Memorial Museum at Berryville, with an extensive collection of firearms.

Civil War battle sites include the Pea Ridge National Military Park, the Prairie Grove Battlefield State Park, and the Arkansas Post National Memorial. The Ft. Smith National Historic Site includes buildings and museums from the days when the town was a military outpost on the border of Indian Territory.

⁴⁴COMMUNICATIONS

In March 1993, 88.6% of the state's 929,000 occupied housing units had telephones, among the lowest rates in the nation. There were 229 radio stations (83 AM, 146 FM) and 23 television stations, 5 of which were noncommercial educational. Cable television service was supplied by 4 large systems in 1996.

⁴⁵PRESS

The first newspaper in Arkansas, the *Arkansas Gazette*, established at Arkansas Post in 1819 by William E. Woodruff, is the state's most widely read and influential journal. In 1997, there were 10 morning dailies, 21 evening papers, and 16 Sunday papers. In 1992, Little Rock's two major dailies, the *Arkansas Democrat* and the *Democrat Gazette*, merged. The following table shows the 1997 circulations of the leading dailies:

AREA	NAME	DAILY	SUNDAY
Ft. Smith	*Southwest Times Record* (all day, S)	40,799	45,060
Little Rock	*Arkansas Democrat* (m,S)	179,609	292,057

⁴⁶ORGANIZATIONS

The 1992 Census of Service Industries counted 659 organizations in Arkansas, including 146 business associations; 322 civic, social, and fraternal associations; and 191 other organizations. Among the national organizations with headquarters in Arkansas are the American Crossbow Association in Huntsville; the American Fish Farmers Federation in Lonoke; and the Ozark Society, the American Parquet Association, the Federation of American Hospitals, and the Civil War Round Table Associates, all located in Little Rock.

ACORN, the Association of Community Organizations for Reform Now, was founded in Little Rock in 1970 and has since spread to some 20 other states and has become one of the most influential citizens' lobbies in the US.

⁴⁷TOURISM, TRAVEL, AND RECREATION

During 1992, tourists trips spent over $2.7 billion during trips to and through Arkansas. In 1995, Arkansas's five national parks had 2,468,449 visitors.

Leading attractions are the mineral waters and recreational facilities at Hot Springs, Eureka Springs, Mammoth Spring, and Heber Springs. The Crater of Diamonds, near Murfreesboro, is the only known public source of natural diamonds in North America. For a fee, visitors may hunt for diamonds and keep any they find; more than 100,000 diamonds have been found in the area since 1906, of which the two largest are the 40.42-carat Uncle Sam and the 34.25-carat Star of Murfreesboro.

During 1995, licenses were held by 515,979 hunters and 731,060 anglers who used the state's fishing and hunting resources. The World's Championship Duck Calling Contest is held at the beginning of the winter duck season in Stuttgart.

⁴⁸SPORTS

Arkansas has no major-league professional sports teams but has a minor-league baseball team, the Travellers, in Little Rock. Oaklawn Park in Hot Springs has a 62-day thoroughbred-racing season each spring, and dog-races are held in West Memphis from April through November. Several major rodeos take place in summer and fall, including the Rodeo of the Ozarks in Springdale in early July and the southeast Arkansas Rodeo and Livestock Show in Pine Bluff each September.

The University of Arkansas has competed in the Southeastern Conference since 1990, when it ended its 76-year affiliation with the Southwest Conference. The Razorback football team won the Cotton Bowl in 1947, 1965, and 1976; the Orange Bowl in 1978; the Sugar Bowl in 1969; and the Bluebonnet Bowl in 1982. The men's basketball team won the NCAA Division I basketball championship in 1994; won or shared the Southwest Conference championship in 1977, 1978, 1979, 1981, and 1982; and won the Southeastern Conference in 1994.

⁴⁹FAMOUS ARKANSANS

Arkansas has produced one president of the United States, William Jefferson Clinton (b. 1946). Clinton, a Democrat, defeated President George Bush in the 1992 presidential election and was reelected in 1996. Clinton's wife is the former Hillary Rodham (b. Illinois 1947). Arkansas has yet to produce a vice president or a Supreme Court justice, although one Arkansan came close to reaching both offices: US Senator Joseph T. Robinson (1872–1937) was the Democratic nominee for vice president in 1928, on the ticket with Al Smith; later, he was Senate majority leader under President Franklin D. Roosevelt. At the time of his death, Robinson was leading the fight for Roosevelt's bill to expand the Supreme Court's membership and had reportedly been promised a seat on the court if the bill passed. Robinson's colleague, Hattie W. Caraway (b.Tennessee, 1878–1950), was the first woman elected to the US Senate, serving from 1931 to 1945.

After World War II (1939–45), Arkansas's congressional delegation included three men of considerable power and fame: Senator John L. McClellan (1896–1977), investigator of organized labor and organized crime and champion of the Arkansas River navigation project; Senator J. William Fulbright (b.Missouri, 1905–95), chairman of the Senate Foreign Relations Committee; and Representative Wilbur D. Mills (1909–92), chairman of the House Ways and Means Committee until scandal ended his political career in the mid-1970s.

Other federal officeholders include Brooks Hays (1898–1981), former congressman and special assistant to Presidents John F. Kennedy and Lyndon B. Johnson, as well as president of the Southern Baptist Convention, the nation's largest Protestant denomination; and Frank Pace, Jr. (1912–88), secretary of the Army during the Truman administration.

General Douglas MacArthur (1880–1964), supreme commander of Allied forces in the Pacific during World War II, supervised the occupation of Japan and was supreme commander of UN troops in Korea until relieved of his command in April 1951 by President Truman.

Orval E. Faubus (1910–94) served six terms as governor (a record), drew international attention during the 1957 integration crisis at Little Rock Central High School, and headed the most powerful political machine in Arkansas history. Winthrop Rockefeller (b.New York, 1917–73) was Faubus's most prominent successor. At the time of his election in 1978, Bill Clinton was the nation's youngest governor.

Prominent business leaders include the Stephens brothers, W. R. "Witt" (b.1907) and Jackson T. (b.1923), whose Stephens, Inc., investment firm in Little Rock is the largest off Wall Street; and Kemmons Wilson (b.1913), founder of Holiday Inns.

Other distinguished Arkansans are Edward Durrell Stone (1902–78), renowned architect; C. Vann Woodward (b.1908), Sterling Professor Emeritus of History at Yale University; and the Right Reverend John M. Allin (b.1921), presiding bishop of the Episcopal Church of the United States. John H. Johnson (b.1918), publisher of the nation's leading black-oriented magazines—*Ebony, Jet,* and others—is an Arkansan, as is Helen Gurley Brown (b.1922), former editor of *Cosmopolitan.*

Harry S. Ashmore (b.South Carolina, 1916) won a Pulitzer Prize for his *Arkansas Gazette* editorials calling for peaceful integration of the schools during the 1957 crisis; the *Gazette* itself won a Pulitzer for meritorious public service that year. Paul Greenberg (b.Louisiana, 1937), of the *Pine Bluff Commercial,* is another Pulitzer Prize-winning journalist. John Gould Fletcher (1886–1950) was a Pulitzer Prize-winning poet. Other Arkansas writers include Dee Brown (b.Louisiana, 1908), Maya Angelou (b.Missouri, 1928), Charles Portis (b.1933), and Eldridge Cleaver (b.1935).

Arkansas planter Colonel Sanford C. Faulkner (1803–74) is credited with having written the well-known fiddle tune "The Arkansas Traveler" and its accompanying dialogue. Perhaps the best-known country music performers from Arkansas are Johnny Cash (b.1932) and Glen Campbell (b.1938). Film stars Dick Powell (1904–63) and Alan Ladd (1913–64) were also Arkansans.

Notable Arkansas sports personalities include Jerome Herman "Dizzy" Dean (1911–74) and Bill Dickey (1907–93), both members of the Baseball Hall of Fame; Brooks Robinson (b.1937), considered by some the best-fielding third baseman in baseball history; and star pass-catcher Lance Alworth (b.Missis-sippi, 1940), a University of Arkansas All-American and member of the Professional Football Hall of Fame.

[50]BIBLIOGRAPHY

Alampi, Gary, ed. *Gale State Rankings Reporter.* Detroit: Gale Research, Inc., 1994.

Angelou, Maya. *I Know Why the Caged Bird Sings.* New York: Bantam, 1971.

Arkansas, University of. Industrial Research and Extension Center. *Arkansas State and County Economic Data.* Little Rock: University of Arkansas, 1984.

Ashmore, Harry S. *Arkansas: A Bicentennial History.* New York: Norton, 1978.

Council of State Governments. *The Book of the States, 1994–1995 Edition.* Vol. 30. Lexington, Ky.: The Council of State Governments, 1994.

Du Vall, Leland. *Arkansas: Colony and State.* Little Rock: Rose, 1973.

FDIC, Division of Research and Statistics. *Statistics on Banking: A Statistical Profile of the United States Banking Industry.* Washington, D.C.: Federal Deposit Insurance Corporation, 1993.

Federal Writers' Project. *Arkansas: A Guide to the State.* 1941. Reprint, New York: Somerset, n.d.

Fletcher, John Gould. *Arkansas.* Fayetteville: University of Arkansas Press, 1989.

Gatewood, Willard B., and Jeannie Whayne, ed. *The Arkansas Delta: Land of Paradox.* Fayetteville: University of Arkansas Press, 1993.

Moroe, Waddy William, ed. *Arkansas in the Guilded Age.* Little Rock: Rose, 1976.

Ross, Margaret. *Arkansas Gazette: The Early Years, 1819–66.* Little Rock: Arkansas Gazette Foundation, 1969.

Schmittroth, Linda, and Mary Kay Rosteck, ed. *Cities of the United States.* 2d ed. Detroit: Gale Research, Inc., 1994.

Taylor, Orville, W. *Negro Slavery in Arkansas.* Durham, N.C.: Duke University Press, 1958.

US Department of Education, National Center for Education Statistics. Office of Educational Research and Improvement. *Digest of Education Statistics, 1993.* Washington, D.C.: US Government Printing Office, 1993.

US Department of the Interior, US Fish and Wildlife Service. *Endangered and Threatened Species Recovery Program.* Washington, D.C.: US Government Printing Office, 1990.

Whayne, Jeannic M. *A New Plantation South: Land, Labor, and Federal Favor in Twentieth-Century Arkansas.* Charlottesville: University Press of Virginia, 1996.

Williams, C. Filed. *A Documentary History of Arkansas.* Fayetteville: University of Arkansas Press, 1983.

CALIFORNIA REPUBLIC

CALIFORNIA

State of California

ORIGIN OF STATE NAME: Probably from the mythical island California in a 16th-century romance by Garci Ordónez de Montalvo. **NICKNAME:** The Golden State. **CAPITAL:** Sacramento. **ENTERED UNION:** 9 September 1850 (31st). **SONG:** "I Love You California." **MOTTO:** Eureka (I have found it). **FLAG:** The flag consists of a white field with a red star at upper left and a red stripe and the words "California Republic" across the bottom; in the center, a brown grizzly bear stands on a patch of green grass. **OFFICIAL SEAL:** In the foreground is the goddess Minerva; a grizzly bear stands in front of her shield. The scene also shows the Sierra Nevada, San Francisco Bay, a miner, a sheaf of wheat, and a cluster of grapes, all representing California's resources. The state motto and 31 stars are displayed at the top. The words "The Great Seal of the State of California" surround the whole. **COLORS:** Yale blue and golden yellow. **ANIMAL:** California grizzly bear (extinct). **BIRD:** California valley quail. **FISH:** South Fork golden trout. **MARINE MAMMAL:** California gray whale. **REPTILE:** California desert tortoise. **INSECT:** California dog-face butterfly (flying pansy). **FLOWER:** Golden poppy. **TREE:** California redwood. **ROCK:** Serpentine. **MINERAL:** Native gold. **FOSSIL:** California saber-toothed cat. **LEGAL HOLIDAYS:** New Year's Day, 1 January; Birthday of Martin Luther King, Jr., 3d Monday in January; Lincoln's Birthday, 12 February; Presidents' Day, 3d Monday in February; Memorial Day, last Monday in May; Independence Day, 4 July; Labor Day, 1st Monday in September; Admission Day, 9 September; Columbus Day, 2d Monday in October; Veterans Day, 11 November; Thanksgiving Day, 4th Thursday in November; Christmas Day, 25 December. **TIME:** 4 AM PST = noon GMT.

¹LOCATION, SIZE, AND EXTENT

Situated on the Pacific coast of the southwestern US, California is the nation's 3d-largest state (after Alaska and Texas).

The total area of California is 158,706 sq mi (411,048 sq km), of which land takes up 156,299 sq mi (404,814 sq km) and inland water 2,407 sq mi (6,234 sq km). California extends about 350 mi (560 km) E-W; its maximum N-S extension is 780 mi (1,260 km).

California is bordered on the N by Oregon; on the E by Nevada; on the SE by Arizona (separated by the Colorado River); on the S by the Mexican state of Baja California Norte; and on the W by the Pacific Ocean.

The eight Santa Barbara islands lie from 20 to 60 mi (32–97 km) off California's southwestern coast; the small islands and islets of the Farallon group are about 30 mi (48 km) W of San Francisco Bay. The total boundary length of the state is 2,050 mi (3,299 km), including a general coastline of 840 mi (1,352 km); the tidal shoreline totals 3,427 mi (5,515 km). California's geographic center is in Madera County, 38 mi (61 km) E of the city of Madera.

²TOPOGRAPHY

California is the only state in the US with an extensive seacoast, high mountains, and deserts. The extreme diversity of the state's landforms is best illustrated by the fact that Mt. Whitney (14,495 ft—4,418 m), the highest point in the contiguous US, is situated no more than 80 mi (129 km) from the lowest point in the entire country, Death Valley (282 ft, or 86 m, below sea level). The mean elevation of the state is about 2,900 ft (900 m).

California's principal geographic regions are the Sierra Nevada in the east, the Coast Ranges in the west, the Central Valley between them, and the Mojave and Colorado deserts in the southeast. The mountain-walled Central Valley, more than 400 mi (640 km) long and about 50 mi (80 km) wide, is probably the

state's most unusual topographic feature. It is drained in the north by the Sacramento River, about 320 mi (515 km) long, and in the south by the San Joaquin River, about 350 mi (560 km). The main channels of the two rivers meet at and empty into the northern arm of San Francisco Bay, flowing through the only significant break in the Coast Ranges, a mountain system that extends more than 1,200 mi (1,900 km) alongside the Pacific. Lesser ranges, including the Siskiyou Mountains in the north and the Tehachapi Mountains in the south, link the two major ranges and constitute the Central Valley's upper and lower limits.

California has 41 mountains exceeding 10,000 ft (3,050 m). After Mt. Whitney, the highest peaks in the state are Mt. Williamson, in the Sierra Nevada, at 14,375 ft (4,382 m) and Mt. Shasta (14,162 ft—4,317 m), an extinct volcano in the Cascades, the northern extension of the Sierra Nevada. Lassen Peak (10,457 ft—3,187 m), also in the Cascades, is a dormant volcano.

Beautiful Yosemite Valley, a narrow gorge in the middle of the High Sierra, is the activities center of Yosemite National Park. The Coast Ranges, with numerous forested spurs and ridges enclosing dozens of longitudinal valleys, vary in height from about 2,000 to 7,000 ft (600–2,100 m).

Melted snow from the Sierra Nevada feeds the state's principal rivers, the Sacramento and San Joaquin. The Coast Ranges are drained by the Klamath, Eel, Russian, Salinas, and other rivers. In the south, most rivers are dry creek beds except during the spring flood season; they either dry up from evaporation in the hot summer sun or disappear beneath the surface, like Death Valley's Amargosa River. The Salton Sea, in the Imperial Valley of the southeast, is the state's largest lake, occupying 374 sq mi (969 sq km). This saline sink was created accidentally in the early 1900s when Colorado River water, via an irrigation canal, flooded a natural depression 235 ft (72 m) below sea level in the Imperial Valley. Lake Tahoe, in the Sierra Nevada at the angle of the California-Nevada border, covers 192 sq mi (497 sq km).

The California coast is indented by two magnificent natural harbors, San Francisco Bay and San Diego Bay, and two smaller bays, Monterey and Humboldt. Two groups of islands lie off the California shore: the Santa Barbara Islands, situated west of Los Angeles and San Diego; and the rocky Farallon Islands, off San Francisco.

The Sierra Nevada and Coast Ranges were formed more than 100 million years ago by the uplifting of the earth's crust. The Central Valley and the Great Basin, including the Mojave Desert and Death Valley, were created by sinkage of the earth's crust; inland seas once filled these depressions but evaporated over eons of time. Subsequent volcanic activity, erosion of land, and movement of glaciers until the last Ice Age subsided some 10,000 years ago and gradually shaped the present topography of California. The San Andreas Fault, extending from north of San Francisco Bay for more than 600 mi (970 km) southeast to the Mojave Desert, is a major active earthquake zone and was responsible for the great San Francisco earthquake of 1906. Damage from that earthquake amounted to $24 million, with an additional $350–500 in fire losses (total losses would amount to about $6 billion in current dollars). More recently, the 1994 earthquake in Northridge caused damage estimated at $13–20 billion, making it the costliest earthquake in US history.

Because water is scarce in the southern part of the state and because an adequate water supply is essential both for agriculture and for industry, more than 1,000 dams and reservoirs have been built in California. By 1993, there were 1,336 reservoirs in the state. Popular reservoirs for recreation are located along the tributaries of the Sacramento and San Joaquim rivers. Clair Lake Eagle, also known as Trinity Lake, is located on the Trinity River. The reservoir has a surface area of 16,400 acres (6,640 hectares). Lake Shasta, located on the Sacramento River, has a surface area of 15,800 acres (6,397 hectares). Lake Berryessa, located on Putah Creek, has a surface area of 19,250 acres (7,794 hectares). Lake New Melones, located on the Stanislaus River, has a surface area of 12,500 acres (5,061 hectares). The San Luis Reservoir, fed by the California Aqueduct, has a surface area of 12,500 acres (5,061 hectares). Don Pedro Lake, located on the Toulumme River, has a surface area of 13,000 acres (5,263 hectares).

³CLIMATE

Like its topography, California's climate is varied and tends toward extremes. Generally there are two seasons—a long, dry summer, with low humidity and cool evenings, and a mild, rainy winter—except in the high mountains, where four seasons prevail and snow lasts from November to April. The one climatic constant for the state is summer drought.

California has four main climatic regions. Mild summers and winters prevail in central coastal areas, where temperatures are more equable than virtually anywhere else in the US; in the area between San Francisco and Monterey, for example, the difference between average summer and winter temperatures is seldom more than 10°F (6°C). During the summer there are heavy fogs in San Francisco and all along the coast. Mountainous regions are characterized by milder summers and colder winters, with markedly low temperatures at high elevations. The Central Valley has hot summers and cool winters, while the Imperial Valley is marked by very hot, dry summers, with temperatures frequently exceeding 100°F (38°C).

Average annual temperatures for the state range from 47°F (8°C) in the Sierra Nevada to 73°F (23°C) in the Imperial Valley. The highest temperature ever recorded in the US was 134° (57°C), registered in Death Valley on 10 July 1913. Death Valley has the hottest average summer temperature in the Western Hemisphere, at 98°F (37°C). The state's lowest temperature was –45°F (–43°C), recorded on 20 January 1937 at Boca, near the Nevada border.

Among the major population centers, Los Angeles has an average annual temperature of 63°F (17°C), with an average January minimum of 48°F (9°C) and an average July maximum of 75°F (24°C). San Francisco has an annual average of 57°F (14°C), with a January average minimum of 42°F (6°C) and a July average maximum of 72°F (22°C). The annual average in San Diego is 64°F (18°C), the January average minimum 49°F (9°C), and the July average maximum 76°F (24°C). Sacramento's annual average temperature is 61°F (16°C), with January minimums averaging 38°F (3°C) and July maximums of 93°F (34°C).

Annual precipitation varies from only 2 in (5 cm) in the Imperial Valley to 68 in (173 cm) at Blue Canyon, near Lake Tahoe. San Francisco has a normal annual precipitation of 20 in (51 cm), Sacramento 17 in (43 cm), Los Angeles 12 in (30 cm), and San Diego 9 in (23 cm). The largest one-month snowfall ever recorded in the US—390 in (991 cm)—fell in Alpine County in January 1911. Snow averages between 300 and 400 in (760 to 1,020 cm) annually in the high elevations of the Sierra Nevada, but is rare in the coastal lowlands.

Sacramento has the greatest percentage (79%) of possible annual sunshine among the state's largest cities; Los Angeles has 73% and San Francisco 67%. San Francisco is the windiest, with an average annual wind speed of 11 mph (18 km/hr). Tropical rainstorms occur often in California during the winter.

⁴FLORA AND FAUNA

Of the 48 conterminous states, California embraces the greatest diversity of climate and terrain. The state's six life zones are the lower Sonoran (desert); upper Sonoran (foothill regions and some coastal lands); transition (coastal areas and moist northeastern counties); and the Canadian, Hudsonian, and Arctic zones, comprising California's highest elevations.

Plant life in the arid climate of the lower Sonoran zone features a diversity of native cactus, mesquite, and paloverde. The Joshua tree (*Yucca brevifolia*) is found in the Mojave Desert. Flowering plants include the dwarf desert poppy and a variety of asters. Fremont cottonwood and valley oak grow in the Central Valley. The upper Sonoran zone includes the unique chaparral belt, characterized by forests of small shrubs, stunted trees, and herbaceous plants. Nemophila, mint, phacelia, viola, and the golden poppy (*Eschscholtzia californica*)—the state flower—also flourish in this zone, along with the lupine, more species of which occur here than anywhere else in the world.

The transition zone includes most of the state's forests, with such magnificent specimens as the redwood (*Sequoia sempervirens*) and "big tree" or giant sequoia (*Sequoia gigantea*), among the oldest living things on earth (some are said to have lived at least 4,000 years). Tanbark oak, California laurel, sugar pine, madrona, broad-leaved maple, and Douglas fir are also common. Forest floors are carpeted with swordfern, alumroot, barrenwort, and trillium, and there are thickets of huckleberry, azalea, elder, and wild currant. Characteristic wild flowers include varieties of mariposa, tulip, and tiger and leopard lilies.

The high elevations of the Canadian zone are abundant with Jeffrey pine, red fir, and lodgepole pine. Brushy areas are covered with dwarf manzanita and ceanothus; the unique Sierra puffball is also found here. Just below timberline, in the Hudsonian zone, grow the whitebark, foxtail, and silver pines. At approximately 10,500 ft (3,200 m) begins the Arctic zone, a treeless region whose flora includes a number of wild flowers, including Sierra primrose, yellow columbine, alpine buttercup, and alpine shooting star.

Common plants introduced into California include the eucalyptus, acacia, pepper tree, geranium, and Scotch broom. Among the numerous species found in California that are federally classified as endangered are the Contra Costa wallflower, Antioch Dunes evening primrose, Solano Grass, San

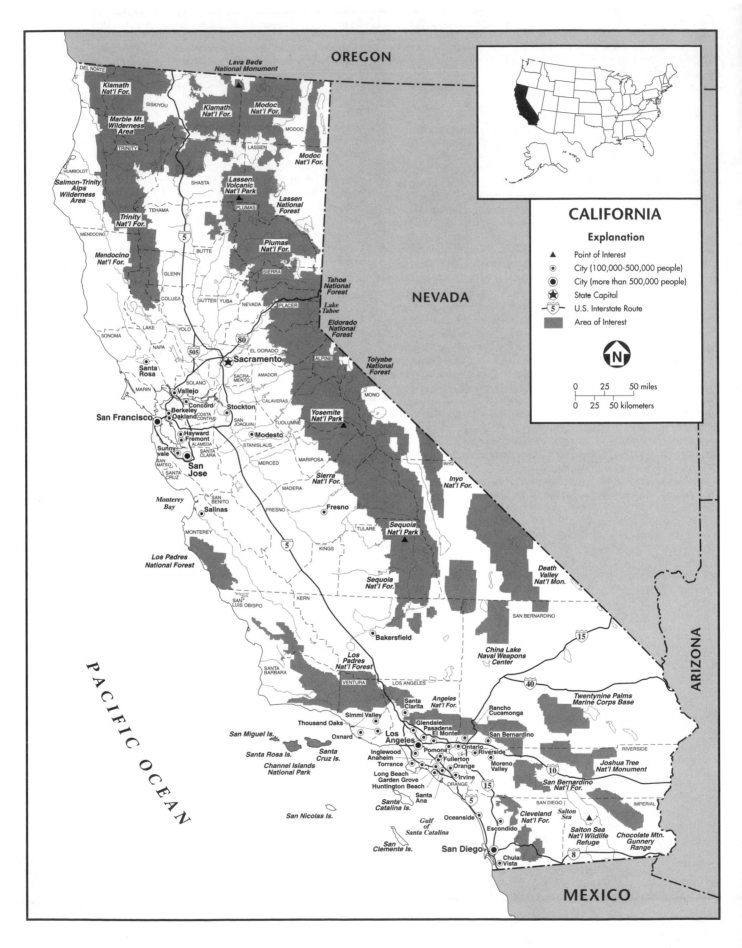

OREGON

Lava Beds
National Monument

DEL NORTE

Klamath
Nat'l For.

SISKIYOU

Klamath
Nat'l For.

Modoc
Nat'l For.

Marble Mt.
Wilderness
Area

TRINITY

MODOC

LASSEN

Modoc
Nat'l For.

HUMBOLDT

SHASTA

Lassen
Volcanic
Nat'l Park

Salmon-Trinity
Alps
Wilderness
Area

TEHAMA

PLUMAS

Lassen
National
Forest

Trinity
Nat'l For.

Mendocino
Nat'l For.

BUTTE

Plumas
Nat'l For.

MENDOCINO

GLENN

SIERRA

Tahoe
National
Forest

COLUSA

SUTTER YUBA

NEVADA

NEVADA

PLACER

Lake
Tahoe

LAKE

YOLO

Eldorado
National
Forest

SONOMA

NAPA

Sacramento

SACRA-
MENTO

EL DORADO

ALPINE

Toiyabe
National
Forest

Santa
Rosa

SOLANO

MARIN

Vallejo

Concord

Berkeley
Oakland

Stockton

AMADOR

CALAVERAS

MONO

San Francisco

COSTA
CONTRA

SAN
JOAQUIN

Hayward
Fremont

ALAMEDA

Modesto

TUOLUMNE

Yosemite
Nat'l Park

Sunny-
vale

SANTA
CLARA

STANISLAUS

San Jose

SAN
MATEO

SANTA
CRUZ

MERCED

MARIPOSA

Monterey
Bay

SAN
BENITO

MADERA

Sierra
Nat'l For.

Inyo
Nat'l For.

INYO

Salinas

FRESNO

Fresno

MONTEREY

Sequoia
Nat'l Park

Los Padres
National Forest

Death
Valley
Nat'l Mon.

TULARE

KINGS

Sequoia
Nat'l For.

SAN
LUIS OBISPO

KERN

SAN BERNARDINO

Bakersfield

China Lake
Naval Weapons
Center

SANTA
BARBARA

Los
Padres
Nat'l Forest

VENTURA

LOS ANGELES

Twentynine Palms
Marine Corps Base

Santa
Clarita

Angeles
Nat'l For.

Rancho
Cucamonga

Simmi Valley

Thousand Oaks

Glendale
Pasadena
El Monte

San Bernardino

San Miguel Is.

Oxnard

Los
Angeles

Ontario
Pomona

Riverside

RIVERSIDE

Santa Rosa Is.

Santa
Cruz Is.

Inglewood
Anaheim
Torrance

Fullerton
Orange

Moreno
Valley

Joshua Tree
Nat'l Monument

Channel Islands
National Park

Long Beach
Garden Grove
Huntington Beach

Irvine

ORANGE

San Bernardino
Nat'l For.

Santa
Ana

Santa
Catalina Is.

SAN DIEGO

IMPERIAL

San Nicolas Is.

Oceanside

Cleveland
Nat'l For.

Salton
Sea

Salton Sea
Nat'l Wildlife
Refuge

Chocolate Mtn.
Gunnery
Range

Gulf
of
Santa Catalina

Escondido

San Clemente Is.

San Diego

Chula
Vista

PACIFIC OCEAN

ARIZONA

MEXICO

Clemente Island larkspur, salt marsh bird's beak, McDonald's rock-cress, and Santa Barbara Island live forever.

Mammals found in the deserts of the lower Sonoran zone include the jackrabbit, kangaroo rat, squirrel, and opossum. The Texas night owl, roadrunner, cactus wren, and various species of hawk are common birds, and the sidewinder, desert tortoise, and horned toad represent the area's reptilian life. The upper Sonoran zone is home to such mammals as the antelope, brown-footed woodrat, and ring-tailed cat. Birds distinctive to this zone are the California thrasher, bush tit, and California condor.

Animal life is abundant amid the forests of the transition zone. Colombian black-tailed deer, black bear, gray fox, cougar, bobcat, and Roosevelt elk are found. Garter snakes and rattle-snakes are common, as are such amphibians as the water-puppy and redwood salamander. The kingfisher, chickadee, towhee, and hummingbird represent the bird life of this region.

Mammals of the Canadian zone include the mountain weasel, snowshoe hare, Sierra chickaree, and several species of chipmunk. Conspicuous birds include the blue-fronted jay, Sierra hermit thrush, water ouzel, and Townsend solitaire. Birds become scarcer as one ascends to the Hudsonian zone, and the wolverine is now regarded as rare. Only one bird is native to the high Arctic region—the Sierra rosy finch—but others often visit, including the hummingbird and Clark nutcracker. Principal mammals of this region are also visitors from other zones, through the Sierra coney and white-tailed jackrabbit make their homes here. The bighorn sheep also lives in this mountainous terrain. Among fauna found throughout several zones are the mule deer, coyote, mountain lion, red-shafted flicker, and several species of hawk and sparrow.

Aquatic life in California is abundant, from the state's mountain lakes and streams to the rocky Pacific coastline. Many trout species are found, among them rainbow, golden, and Tahoe; migratory species of salmon are also common. Deep-sea life-forms include sea bass, yellowfin tuna, barracuda, and several types of whale. Native to the cliffs of northern California are seals, sea lions, and many types of shorebirds, including several migratory species.

The Resources Agency of California's Department of Fish and Game is especially active in listing and providing protection for rare, threatened, and endangered fauna. Joint efforts by state and federal wildlife agencies have established an ambitious—if somewhat controversial—recovery program to revitalize the dwindling population of the majestic condor, the largest bird native to the US.

As of 31 October 1996, over 40 California animals were on the federal endangered list. These include the San Joaquin kit fox, California gray whale (the official state marine mammal), Point Arena mountain beaver, Pacific pocket mouse, salt marsh harvest mouse, Morro Bay kangaroo rat (and four other species of kangaroo rat), Amargosa vole, California least tern, California condor, San Clemente loggerhead shrike and sage sparrow, San Francisco garter snake, desert slender salamander, Santa Cruz long-toed salamander, Mohave tui chub, and Owens River pupfish. Seven butterflies listed as endangered on the federal list are California species. Among threatened animals are the coastal California gnatcatcher, Paiute cutthroat trout, and Southern sea otter. California has a total of 290,821 acres (117,6791 hectares) of National Wildlife Refuges.

⁵ENVIRONMENTAL PROTECTION

Efforts to preserve natural wilderness areas in California go back at least to 1890, when the US Congress created three national parks in the Sierra Nevada: Sequoia, Grant (now part of Kings Canyon), and Yosemite. Three years later, some 4 million acres (1.6 million hectares) of the Sierra Nevada were set aside in national forests. In 1892, naturalist John Muir and other wilderness lovers founded the Sierra Club which, with other private groups of conservationists, has been influential in saving the Muir Woods and other stands of redwoods from the lumbermen's axes.

California's primary resource problem is water: the southern two-thirds of the state accounts for about 75% of annual water consumption but only 30% of the supply. Water has been diverted from the Sierra Nevada snow runoff and from the Colorado River to the cities and dry areas largely by means of aqueducts, some 700 mi (1,100 km) of which have been constructed in federal and state undertakings. In 1960, California embarked on one of the largest public works programs ever undertaken in the US when voters approved a bond issue to construct the California Water Project, designed to deliver 1.4 trillion gallons of water annually to central and southern California for residential, industrial, and agricultural use. Other purposes of the project were to provide flood control, generate electric power, and create recreation areas.

Maintaining adequate water resources continued to be a problem in the 1990s. As the result of a US Supreme Court decision, southern California lost close to 20% of its water supply in December 1985, when a portion of the water it had been permitted to draw from the Colorado River was diverted to Arizona. In 1982, California voters turned down a proposal to build a canal that would have delivered water that flows into San Francisco Bay to southern California; no other plans to cope with the impending shortage were approved at that time. In December 1994 the state and federal governments joined together to form the Bay Delta Accord, intended to restore the environmentally threatened area through a combination of better conservation efforts and public and private investment. In November 1996 voters approved a bond issue valued at nearly $1 billion to implement the Accord.

Air pollution has been a serious problem since July 1943, when heavy smog enveloped Los Angeles for the first time; smog conditions in October 1954 forced the closing of the city's airport and harbor. Smog is caused by an atmospheric inversion of cold air that traps unburned hydrocarbons at ground level; perhaps two-thirds of the smog particles are created by automobile exhaust emissions. In 1960, the state legislature passed the first automobile antismog law in the nation, requiring that all cars be equipped with antismog exhaust devices within three years. (Federal laws controlling exhaust emissions on new cars came into effect in the 1970s.) The city's smog problem has since been reduced to manageable proportions, but pollution problems from atmospheric inversions still persist there and in other California cities. Nonetheless there is reason for optimism—in 1996, for example, Southern California had the best air quality ever measured in the post–World War II era. A key factor was intro-duction of a reformulated gasoline touted as the cleanest-burning in the world—which reduced polluting emissions by 15% when put into use in 1996. The state inspection-and-maintenance program is also being reformed and updated, focusing on the small number of cars linked to as much as 50% of vehicular pollution in the state.

In early 1995, the EPA approved a California ozone-reduction plan that orders car manufacturers to design and produce cars that will be 50% to 84% cleaner than the ones sold in 1990. Also, the plans call for a zero-emission car by 1998. By the year 2003, California expects 10% of the cars offered for sale will be zero emission.

State land-reclamation programs have been important in providing new agricultural land and controlling flood damage. One of the earliest such programs, begun shortly before 1900, reclaimed 500,000 acres (200,000 hectares) by means of a network of dams, dikes, and canals in the swampy delta lying within the fork of the Sacramento and San Joaquin rivers. In

1887, a state law created irrigation districts in the southeastern region; the Imperial Valley was thus transformed from a waterless, sandy basin into some of the most productive agricultural land in the US.

Flood control was one of the main purposes of the $2.6 billion Feather River Project in the Central Valley, completed during the 1970s. Ironically, in the western portion of the Central Valley, farmland is now threatened by irrigation water tainted by concentrated salts and other soil minerals, for which current drainage systems are inadequate. One drainage system, the San Luis Drain, originally intended to carry the water to San Francisco Bay, was stopped short of completion and goes only as far as the Kesterson National Wildlife Refuge, where, according to the US Fish and Wildlife Service, the tainted water has caused birth defects in birds.

In the 1980s, the state legislature enacted stringent controls on toxic waste. California has also been a leader in recycling waste products—for example, using acid waste from metal-processing plants as a soil additive in citrus orchards.

The California Department of Water Resources is responsible for maintaining adequate groundwater levels, enforcing water-quality standards, and controlling floodwaters. The state Department of Conservation has overall responsibility for conservation and protection of the state's soil, mineral, petroleum, geothermal, and marine resources. The California Coastal Commission, created in 1972, is designated by federal law to review projects that effect California's coastline, including offshore oil leasing, which has become a source of concern in recent years.

6POPULATION

About 12% of all Americans live in California, which ranks 1st in population among the 50 states. California replaced New York as the decennial census leader in 1970, with a total of 19,971,069 residents and has lengthened its lead ever since. In 1996, California had an estimated population of 31,878,234, up 7.1% from 1990. Los Angeles is the 2d most populous city in the US and Los Angeles County ranks 1st in population among all US counties.

When Europeans first arrived in California, at least 300,000 Indians lived in the area. By 1845, the Indian population had been reduced to about 150,000. Although Spanish missions and settlements were well established in California by the late 18th century, the white population numbered only about 7,000 until the late 1840s. The gold rush brought at least 85,000 adventurers to the San Francisco Bay area by 1850, however, and the state's population increased rapidly thereafter. California's population grew to 379,994 by 1860 and had passed the 1 million mark within 30 years. Since 1890, the number of state residents just about doubled every two decades until the 1970s, when the population increased by 18.5%, down from the 27.1% increase of the 1960s. However, the total growth rate during the 1980s was 25.7%, reflecting a population increase of over 6 million. Projections indicate a steady increase to nearly 34 million by 2000.

In 1990, California was 2d only to New Jersey in the proportion of residents living in metropolitan areas, more than 95%. At the 1990 census, the population of 29,760,021 was 49.6% male and 50.4% female. The population density in 1985 was 165 persons per sq mi (64 per sq km); by 1990, the density was 190.8 per sq mi (73.3 per sq km). Densities in urban areas were much higher—7,427 per sq mi (2,868 per sq km) in Los Angeles in 1990, and 15,502 per sq mi (5,985 per sq km) in San Francisco. In 1989, only 10.6% of all Californians were over 65, lower than the national average of 12.5%. Californians are highly mobile: according to the 1990 census, only 55.6% of state residents five years of age or older lived in the same house they

had lived in five years earlier. Over 59% of all Californians in 1990 had been born in the state, an increase of 14% over 1980. California gained 1,573,000 people through migration during the 1970s and about 1,629,000 through net natural increase. The birthrate per 1,000 residents dropped from 23.7 in 1960 to 14.7 in 1978, but then rose to 17.3 in 1983 and to 19.8 by 1990. The death rate declined from 8.6 in 1960 to about 7.1 in 1991.

California Counties, County Seats, and County Areas and Populations

COUNTY	COUNTY SEAT	LAND AREA (SQ MI)	POPULATION (1996 EST.)
Alameda	Oakland	735	1,328,139
Alpine	Markleeville	739	1,232
Amador	Jackson	589	33,315
Butte	Oroville	1,646	192,507
Calaveras	San Andreas	1,021	38,437
Colusa	Colusa	1,153	18,443
Contra Costa	Martinez	730	881,490
Del Norte	Crescent City	1,007	26,947
El Dorado	Placerville	1,715	151,706
Fresno	Fresno	5,978	751,272
Glenn	Willows	1,319	26,202
Humboldt	Eureka	3,579	123,023
Imperial	El Centro	4,173	147,651
Inyo	Independence	10,223	18,433
Kern	Bakersfield	8,130	622,729
Kings	Hanford	1,392	113,351
Lake	Lakeport	1,262	55,261
Lassen	Susanville	4,553	31,431
Los Angeles	Los Angeles	4,070	9,127,751
Madera	Madera	2,145	110,481
Marin	San Rafael	523	233,230
Mariposa	Mariposa	1,456	15,869
Mendocino	Ukiah	3,512	83,298
Merced	Merced	1,944	192,311
Modoc	Alturas	4,064	9,673
Mono	Bridgeport	3,019	10,497
Monterey	Salinas	3,303	339,047
Napa	Napa	744	116,512
Nevada	Nevada City	960	89,016
Orange	Santa Ana	798	2,636,888
Placer	Auburn	1,416	213,227
Plumas	Quincy	2,573	20,597
Riverside	Riverside	7,214	1,417,425
Sacramento	Sacramento	971	1,117,275
San Benito	Hollister	1,388	44,503
San Bernardino	San Bernardino	20,064	1,598,358
San Diego	San Diego	4,212	2,655,463
San Francisco	San Francisco*	46	735,315
San Joaquin	Stockton	1,415	533,392
San Luis Obispo	San Luis Obispo	3,308	229,437
San Mateo	Redwood City	447	686,909
Santa Barbara	Santa Barbara	2,748	385,573
Santa Clara	San Jose	1,293	1,599,604
Santa Cruz	Santa Cruz	446	237,821
Shasta	Redding	3,786	161,740
Sierra	Downieville	959	3,409
Siskiyou	Yreka	6,281	44,193
Solano	Fairfield	834	365,536
Sonoma	Santa Rosa	1,604	420,872
Stanislaus	Modesto	1,506	415,786
Sutter	Yuba City	602	75,650
Tehama	Red Bluff	2,953	54,108
Trinity	Weaverville	3,190	13,418
Tulare	Visalia	4,808	349,922
Tuolumne	Sonora	2,234	52,196
Ventura	Ventura	1,862	714,733
Yolo	Woodland	1,014	149,925
Yuba	Marysville	640	60,905
TOTALS		156,299	31,878,234

*The city and county of San Francisco are coterminous.

Three out of four Californians live in urban areas located within 20 mi (32 km) of the ocean; 70% reside in metropolitan San Francisco and Los Angeles. Los Angeles had an estimated 1994 population of 3,448,613; San Diego, 1,151,977; San Jose, 816,884; San Francisco, 734,676; Long Beach, 433,852; Fresno, 386,551; Sacramento, 373,964; Oakland, 366,926; Santa Ana, 290,827; and Anaheim, 282,133. The first four all placed among the nation's 15 most populous cities in 1990.

Los Angeles, which expanded irregularly and lacks a central business district, nearly quadrupled its population from 319,000 in 1910 to 1,240,000 in 1930, and then doubled it to 2,479,000 by 1960. A major component of the city's population growth was the upsurge in the number of blacks after World War II, especially between 1960 and 1970, when the number of blacks increased from 335,000 to 504,000, many of them crowded into the deteriorating Watts section.

In 1990, the Los Angeles-Anaheim-Riverside urban complex, with a total population of 14,532,000, was the 2d most populous metropolitan area in the US (after New York City). In 1994, its estimated population was 15,362,165. Other estimates for that year include the San Francisco–Oakland–San Jose area, 6,539,602; metropolitan San Diego, 2,644,132; and metropolitan Sacramento, 1,456,955.

[7]ETHNIC GROUPS

At least 32% of all foreign-born persons in the US live in California. The state has the nation's largest populations of those born in: Mexico, the Philippines, Canada, Germany, the United Kingdom, Korea, Vietnam, China, El Salvador, India, Japan, Taiwan, Guatemala, Iran, Laos, Hong Kong, Peru, France, Cambodia, Honduras, and Thailand. California also has the most American Indians and Asian Indians, more blacks than any state except New York, more Eskimos and Aleuts than any state except Alaska, and more native Hawaiians than any state except Hawaii.

The westward movement of American settlers in the third quarter of the 19th century, followed by Germans, Irish, North Italians, and Italian Swiss immigrants, overshadowed but did not obliterate California's Spanish heritage. In 1990, 7,688,000 (25.8%) of the state's residents were of Hispanic origin, more than any other state and 34% of the US total. The majority— 5,322,170—were Mexican-Americans; in 1990 there were also 113,548 Puerto Ricans, 143,017 Guatemalans, and 300,102 Salvadorans. The number of Hispanic residents was estimated at 9,623,000 in 1996. After World War II, the Hispanic communities of Los Angeles, San Diego, and other southern California cities developed strong political organizations. Increasing numbers of Mexican-Americans have won local, state, and federal elective office, though their potential remains unrealized.

Nearly 50% of all Mexican-Americans in the US are farm laborers. In California, with its large corporate growers, fewer than 10% of the growers employ three-fourths of the laborers; it was this concentration of labor that made possible the successful unionization of field workers.

California had 2,846,000 Asians and Pacific Islanders in 1990, over 39% of the US total and more than four times the number in New York State. The Asian/Pacific Islander population was estimated at 3,784,000 in 1996.

Chinese workers were imported into the state between 1849 and 1882, when the Chinese Exclusion Act was passed by Congress. In 1990, the state's Chinese population was 641,250, more than double that of New York State and by far the highest in the US. The nation's oldest and largest Chinatown is in San Francisco. Although Chinese-Americans, as they prospered, moved to suburban areas, the seats of the powerful nationwide and worldwide merchant and clan associations are in that city. Los Angeles also has a Chinese district.

The Japanese, spread throughout the western seaboard states, were engaged mainly in agriculture, along with fishing and small business, until their removal and internment during World War II. After the war, some continued in market gardening and other family agriculture, but most, deprived of their landholdings, entered urban occupations, including the professions; many dispersed to other regions of the country. In 1990 there were 353,251 Japanese in California.

While the Chinese and Japanese communities in California are the oldest in the state, they were not the most populous in 1990; this distinction was held by the Filipino community, which numbered 709,599 that year. There were also 260,822 Koreans, 242,946 Vietnamese, 112,560 Asian Indians, 43,418 native Hawaiians, 26,444 Samoans, and 19,820 Guamanians.

Native Americans numbered around 242,000 in 1990, of which 1,854 were Eskimos and 1,091 were Aleuts. The 1996 Native American population was estimated at 257,000. The figure for American Indians includes Indians native to California and many others coaxed to resettle there under a policy that sought to terminate tribal status. Along with the remaining indigenous tribes in California, there is also a large urban Indian population, especially in Los Angeles, which has more Indians than any other US city. Many of the urban Indians were unprepared for the new kind of life and unable to earn an adequate living; militant Indians have made dramatic, but on the whole unsuccessful, protests aimed at bettering their condition.

Black Americans constitute a smaller proportion of California's population than of the nation's as a whole: less than 8% in 1990 (and an estimated 7% in 1996). Considerable migration of blacks took place during World War II, when defense industries on the West Coast offered new opportunities.

[8]LANGUAGES

The speakers of Russian, Spanish, and English who first came to what is now California found an amazing diversity of Indian cultures, ranging from the Wiyot in the north to the Yokuts in the Central Valley and the Diegueño in the south, and of Indian languages, representing four great language families— Athapaskan, Penutian, Kokan-Siouan, and Aztec. Yet, except for place names such as Shasta, Napa, and Yuba, they have not lent any of their words to California speech.

As in much of the West, California English is a composite of the eastern dialects and subdialects brought by the continuing westward migration from the eastern states, first for gold and timber, then for farming, for diversified manufacture, for Hollywood, and for retirement. The interior valley is Midland-oriented with such retained terms as *piece* (a between-meals lunch), *quarter till, barn lot* (barnyard), *dog irons* (andirons), and *snake feder* and *snake doctor* (dragonfly), but generally, in both northern and southern California, Northern dominates the mixture of North Midland and South Midland speech in the same communities. Northern *sick to the stomach,* for example, dominates Midland *sick at* and *sick in,* with a 46% frequency; Northern *angleworm* has 53% frequency, as compared with 21% for Midland *fishworm;* and Northern *string beans* has 80% frequency, as compared with 17% North Midland *green beans* and South Midland and Southern *snap beans.* Northern *comforter* was used by 94% of the informants interviewed in a state survey; Midland *comfort* by only 21%. Dominant is Northern /krik/ as the pronunciation of *creek,* but Midland *bucket* has a greater frequency than Northern *pail,* and the Midland /greezy/ for *greasy* is scattered throughout the state. Similarly, the distinction between the /wh/ in *wheel* and the /w/ of *weal* is lost in the use of simple /w/ in both words, and *cot* and *caught* sound alike, as do *caller* and *collar.*

There are some regional differences. San Francisco, for instance has *sody* or *soda water* for a soft drink; there the large sandwich is a *grinder,* while in Sacramento it is either a *poor Joe* or a *submarine.* Notable is the appearance of *chesterfield* (meaning sofa or davenport), found in the Bay region and from San Jose to Sacramento; this sense is common in Canada but now found nowhere else in the US. Boonville, a village about 100 mi (160 km) north of San Francisco, is notorious for "Boontling," a local dialect contrived in the mid-19th century by Scotch-Irish settlers who wanted privacy and freedom from obscenities in their conversation. Now declining in use, Boontling has about 1,000 vocabulary replacements of usual English words, together with some unusual pronunciations and euphemisms.

As the nation's major motion picture, radio, and television entertainment center, Los Angeles has influenced English throughout the nation—even the world—by making English speakers of many dialects audible and visible and by making known new terms and new meanings. It has thus been instrumental in reducing dialectal extremes and in developing increased language awareness.

California's large foreign-language populations have posed major educational problems. In 1974, a landmark San Francisco case, *Lau v. Nichols,* brought a decision from the US Supreme Court that children who do not know English should not thereby be handicapped in school, but should receive instruction in their native tongue while learning English. California's Chacon-Moscone law required native-language instruction, but the law expired in 1987. Since then, the state legislature has not adopted any reforms or modifications to the bilingual education requirement. In 1997, a federal judge ruled against an injunction that had blocked English immersion classes in Orange County. The ruling ended the bilingual education program in the school district and opened the possibility for a statewide vote in June 1998 to decide if non-English-speaking students will be permitted to learn English upon entering public schools.

In 1990, 18,764,213 Californians—or 68.5% of the population five years old or over—reported speaking only English at home. Other languages spoken at home included the following:

Spanish	5,478,712
Chinese	575,447
Tagalog	464,644
Vietnamese	233,074
Korean	215,845
German	165,962
Japanese	174,451
French	132,657
Indic	119,318
Italian	111,133
Mon-Khmer	59,622
Russian	44,978
Greek	32,889
Other various Indo-European	231,654
Other various West-Germanic	34,433
Arabic	73,738
Portuguese	78,232

9RELIGIONS

The first Roman Catholics in California were Spanish friars, who established 21 Franciscan missions from San Diego to Sonoma between 1769 and 1823. After an independent Mexican government began to secularize the missions in 1833, the Indian population at the missions declined from about 25,000 to only about 7,000 in 1840. With the American acquisition of California in 1848, the Catholic Church was reorganized to include the archdiocese of San Francisco. Protestant ministers accompanied migrant miners during the gold rush, founding 32 churches in San Francisco by 1855. These early Protestants included Baptists, Congregationalists, Methodists, Presbyterians, Episcopalians, and Unitarians; a group of Mormons had arrived

by ship via Cape Horn in 1846. Small Jewish communities were established throughout California by 1861 and, in 1880, the Jewish population was estimated at 18,580. The midwesterners who began arriving in large numbers in the 1880s were mostly Protestants who settled in southern California. By 1900, the number of known Christians in the state totaled 674,000, out of a population of nearly 1,500,000.

The mainstream religions did not satisfy everybody's needs, however, and in the early 20th century, many dissident sects sprang up, including such organizations as Firebrands for Jesus, the Psychosomatic Institute, the Mystical Order of Melchizedek, the Infinite Science Church, and Nothing Impossible, among many others. Perhaps the best-known founder of a new religion was Canadian-born Aimee Semple McPherson, who preached her Foursquare Gospel during the 1920s at the Angelus Temple in Los Angeles, won a large radio audience and thousands of converts, and established 240 branches of her church throughout the state before her death in 1944. She was typical of the many charismatic preachers of new doctrines who gave—and still give—California its exotic religious flavor. Since World War II, religions such as Zen Buddhism and Scientology have won enthusiastic followings, along with various cults devoted to self-discovery and self-actualization.

Nevertheless, the large majority of religious adherents in California continue to follow traditional faiths. In 1990, there were 7,142,067 Roman Catholics and 4,524,337 known Protestant adherents. The largest non-Catholic Christian denominations were the Church of Jesus Christ of Latter-Day Saints with 533,741 adherents; Southern Baptist, 504,516; United Methodist, 266,306; United Presbyterian, 258,854; American Baptist, 184,723; Assembly of God, 263,059; Episcopal, 178,263; and the Lutheran Church-Missouri Synod, 143,987. In 1990, the Jewish population was estimated at 918,935, nearly two-thirds of whom lived in the Los Angeles metropolitan area.

10TRANSPORTATION

California has—and for decades has had—more motor vehicles than any other state, and ranked 2d only to Texas in interstate highway mileage in 1995. An intricate 8,300-mi (13,400-km) network of urban interstate highways, expressways, and freeways is one of the engineering wonders of the modern world—but the traffic congestion in the state's major cities during rush hours may well be the worst in the country.

In pioneer days, the chief modes of transportation were sailing ships and horse-drawn wagons; passage by sea from New York took three months, and the overland route from Missouri was a six-week journey. The gold rush spurred development of more rapid transport. The state's first railroad, completed in 1856, was a 25-mi (40-km) line from Sacramento northeast to Folsom, in the mining country. The Central Pacific–Union Pacific transcontinental railroad, finished 13 years later, was financed in part by several Sacramento business leaders, including Leland Stanford, who became governor of the state in 1861, the same year he assumed the presidency of the Central Pacific. Railroad construction crews, mostly imported Chinese laborers, started from Sacramento and dug and blasted the route through the solid granite of the Sierra Nevada and then across the Nevada desert, linking up with the Union Pacific at Promontory, Utah, on 10 May 1869; Stanford himself helped drive the golden spike that marked the historic occasion. The Southern Pacific completed a line from Sacramento to Los Angeles in 1876, and another to Texas the following year. Other railroads took much longer to build; the coastal railroad from San Francisco to Los Angeles was not completed until 1901, and another line to Eureka was not finished until 1914. The railroads dominated transportation in the state until motor vehicles came into widespread use in the 1920s.

As of 1995, California had 6,544 rail mi (10,601 km) of track, with Class I track constituting 75%; class I railroads operating within the state in 1995 included Atchison, Topeka & Santa Fe, Burlington Northern, Southern Pacific, and Union Pacific. Amtrak passenger trains connect the state's major population centers with an average of 38 intercity trains and an additional 170 commuter trains every day. In 1995–96, ridership through Los Angeles and San Diego amounted to 1,012,095 and 655,195, respectively; ridership throughout the state totaled 7,273,350.

Urban transit began in San Francisco in 1861 with horse-drawn streetcars. Cable-car service was introduced in 1873; a few cable cars are still in use, mainly for the tourist trade. The 71-mi (114-km) Bay Area Rapid Transit System, or BART, connects San Francisco with Oakland by high-speed, computerized subway trains via a 3.6-mi (5.8-km) tunnel under San Francisco Bay and runs north-south along the San Francisco peninsula. Completed in the 1970s despite many mechanical problems and costly delays, BART carried an average of 219,000 weekday passengers as of December 1984.

Public transit in the Los Angeles metropolitan area was provided by electric trolleys beginning in 1887. By the early 1930s, the Los Angeles Railway carried 70% of the city's transit passengers, and in 1945, its trolleys transported 109 million passengers. Competition from buses—which provided greater mobility, but aggravated the city's smog and congestion problems—forced the trolleys to end service in 1961. Los Angeles is currently constructing a regional transportation system similar to BART, which will extend to Long Beach as well as north of the city.

California's extensive highway system had its beginning in the mid-19th century, when stagecoaches began hauling freight to the mining camps from San Francisco, Sacramento, and San Jose. In the early 1850s, two stagecoach lines, Adams and Wells Fargo, expanded their routes and began to carry passengers; by 1860, some 250 stagecoach companies were operating in the state. The decline of stagecoach service corresponded with the rise of the railroads. In 1910, at a time when only 36,000 motor vehicles were registered in the state, the California Highway Commission was established. Among its first acts was the issuance of $18 million in bonds for road construction, and the state's first paved highway was constructed in 1912. The number of automobiles surged to 604,000 by 1920; by 1929, about 1 of every 11 cars in the US belonged to a Californian. Ironically, in view of the state's subsequent traffic problems, the initial effect of the automobile was to disperse the population to outlying areas, thus reducing traffic congestion in the cities.

The Pasadena Freeway, the first modern expressway in California, opened in 1941. During the 1960s and 1970s, the state built a complex toll-free highway network linking most cities of more than 5,000 population, tying in with the federal highway system, and costing more than $10 billion. Local, state, and federal authorities combined spent over $9.1 billion on California highways in 1992, nearly $2 billion of that amount for maintenance. In 1994/95, federal aid to California from the Highway Trust fund totaled about $2 billion, or about 10% of the Fund's total that year.

The new freeways, by providing easy access to beach and mountain recreation areas, and in combination with the favorable climate and low price of gasoline, further encouraged the use of the automobile—and led to massive traffic tie-ups, contributed to the decline of public transit, and worsened the coastal cities' air-pollution problems. Los Angeles County claims more automobiles, more miles of streets, and more intersections than any other city in the US. The greatest inducement to automobile travel in and out of San Francisco was the completion in 1936 of the 8-mi (13-km) San Francisco–Oakland Bay Bridge. The following year saw the opening of the magnificent Golden Gate Bridge, which at 4,200 ft (1,280 m) was the world's longest suspension bridge until New York's Verrazano–Narrows Bridge opened to traffic in 1964.

In 1995, California had 170,389 mi (276,030 km) of public roads. Included in this total were 17,676 mi (28,458 km) of federal highways, 18,251 mi (29,384 km) of state highways, 66,774 mi (107,506 km) of county roads, and 67,678 mi (108,962 km) of city streets. In that year, the state registered 22,431,749 motor vehicles, 1st in the nation and 11% of the US total—about 46 for every 100 state residents—including 14,849,807 automobiles, 7,539,043 trucks, and 42,899 buses. California also leads the nation in private and commercial motorcycle registrations, at 518,927 in 1995, 14% of the US total. There were 20,139,586 California drivers' licenses in force in 1995. In that year, California led the nation in number of traffic injuries, 304,940 persons; pedestrian fatal injuries, 825; and vehicular fatalities, 4,192; but the state's death rate per 100 million vehicle miles—1.52—was less than the US average of 1.73.

The large natural harbors of San Francisco and San Diego monopolized the state's maritime trade until 1912, when Los Angeles began developing port facilities at San Pedro by building a breakwater that eventually totaled 8 mi (13 km) in length. In 1924, Los Angeles surpassed San Francisco in shipping tonnage handled, and became one of the busiest ports on the Pacific coast. In 1995, the port at Long Beach handled 53.2 million tons of cargo (9th), including 17.5 million tons of exports, for a total value of over $71.9 billion (2d). The port at Los Angeles handled 46.8 million tons (17th) for a total value of over $74.1 billion (1st). Other main ports and their 1995 cargo quantities are: Richmond, 20.8 million tons; Oakland, 13.2 million tons; and San Francisco, with 1.3 million tons; the latter two also ranked high in total cargo value, with $29.7 billion (5th), and $1 billion (27th), respectively.

In 1995, California had 946 aircraft facilities, including 552 airports, 379 heliports, 12 seaplane bases, and 3 stolports. More than 33,100 general aviation aircraft, greater than the number in any other state and over 12% of the US total, were registered in California. California's most active air terminal—and the nation's 4th most active—is Los Angeles International Airport, which handled 203,001 departing passenger aircraft and enplaned 19,885,450 passengers in 1994. Also among the nation's 20 busiest air traffic control towers in 1995 were those at Van Nuys, Oakland, Long Beach, Santa Ana, and San Francisco.

11HISTORY

The region now known as California has been populated for at least 10,000 years, and possibly far longer. Estimates of the prehistoric Indian population have varied widely, but it is clear that California was one of the most densely populated areas north of Mexico. On the eve of European discovery, at least 300,000 Indians lived there. This large population was divided into no fewer than 105 separate tribes or nations speaking at least 100 different languages and dialects, about 70% of which were as mutually unintelligible as English and Chinese. No area of comparable size in North America, and perhaps the world, contained a greater variety of native languages and cultures than did aboriginal California.

In general, the California tribes depended for their subsistence on hunting, fishing, and gathering the abundant natural food resources. Only in a few instances, notably along the Colorado River, did the Indians engage in agriculture. Reflecting the mild climate of the area, their housing and dress were often minimal. The basic unit of political organization was the village community, consisting of several small villages, or the family unit. For the most part, these Indians were sedentary people: they occupied village sites for generations, and only rarely warred with their neighbors.

European contact with California began early in the Age of Discovery, and was a product of the two great overseas enterprises of 16th-century Europe: the search for a western passage to the East and the drive to control the riches of the New World. In 1533, Hernán Cortés, Spanish conqueror of the Aztecs, sent a naval expedition northward along the western coast of Mexico in search of new wealth. The expedition led to the discovery of Baja California (now part of Mexico), mistakenly described by the pilot of the voyage, Fortún Jiménez, as an island. Two years later, Cortés established a settlement on the peninsula at present-day La Paz, but because Baja California seemed barren of any wealth, the project was soon abandoned. The only remaining interest in California was the search for the western mouth of the transcontinental canal—a mythical waterway the Spanish called the Strait of Anian. In 1542, Juan Rodriquez Cabrillo led a voyage of exploration up the western coast in a futile search for the strait. On 28 September, Cabrillo landed at the bay now known as San Diego, thus becoming the first European discoverer of Alta (or Upper) California.

European interest in the Californias waned in the succeeding decades, and California remained for generations beyond the periphery of European activity in the New World. Subsequent contact was limited to occasional landfalls by Manila galleons, such as those of Pedro de Unamuno (1587) and Sebastián Cermeno (1595), and the tentative explorations of Sebastián Vizcaino in 1602–3.

Spanish interest in California revived during the late 18th century, largely because Spain's imperial rivals were becoming increasingly aggressive. For strategic and defensive reasons, Spain decided to establish permanent settlements in the north. In 1769, José de Gálvez, visitor-general in New Spain, selected the president of the Franciscan missions in Baja California, Father Junípero Serra, to lead a group of missionaries on an expedition to Alta California. Accompanying Serra was a Spanish military force under Gaspar de Portolá. This Portolá-Serra expedition marks the beginning of permanent European settlement in California. Over the next half-century, the 21 missions established by the Franciscans along the Pacific coast from San Diego to San Francisco formed the core of Hispanic California. Among the prominent missions were San Diego de Alcalá (founded in 1769), San Francisco de Asis (1776), Santa Barbara (1786), and San José (1797). During most of the Spanish period, Mission San Carlos Borromeo (1770), at Carmel, was the ecclesiastical headquarters of the province, serving as the residence of the president-general of the Alta California missions.

These missions were more than just religious institutions. The principal concern of the missionaries was to convert the Indians to Christianity—a successful enterprise, if the nearly 88,000 baptisms performed during the mission period are any measure. The Franciscans also sought to bring about a rapid and thorough cultural transformation. The Indians were taught to perform a wide variety of new tasks: making bricks, tiles, pottery, shoes, saddles, wine, candles, and soap; herding horses, cattle, sheep, and goats; and planting, irrigating, and harvesting. In addition to transforming the way of life of the California Indians, the missions also reduced their number by at least 35,000. About 60% of this decline was due to the introduction of new diseases, especially those of the nonepidemic and venereal type.

Spain also established several military and civilian settlements in California. The four military outposts, or presidios, at San Diego (1769), Monterey (1770), San Francisco (1776), and Santa Barbara (1783) served to discourage foreign influence in the region and to contain Indian resistance. The presidio at Monterey also served as the political capital, headquarters for the provincial governors appointed in Mexico City. The first civilian settlement, or pueblo, was established at San José de Guadalupe in 1777, with 14 families from the Monterey and San Francisco presidios. The pueblo settlers, granted supplies and land by the government, were expected to provide the nearby presidios with their surplus agricultural products. The second pueblo was founded at Los Angeles (1781), and a third, Branciforte, was established near present-day Santa Cruz in 1797.

During the 40 years following the establishment of the Los Angeles pueblo, Spain did little to strengthen its outposts in Alta California. The province remained sparsely populated and isolated from other centers of Hispanic civilization. During these years, the Spanish-speaking population of 600 grew nearly fivefold, but this expansion was almost entirely due to natural increase rather than immigration.

Spanish control of California ended with the successful conclusion of the Mexican Revolution in 1821. For the next quarter-century, California was a province of the independent nation of Mexico. Although California gained a measure of self-rule with the establishment of a provincial legislature, the real authority still remained with the governor appointed in Mexico City. The most important issues in Mexican California were the secularization of the missions, the replacement of the Franciscans with parish or "secular" clergy, and the redistribution of the vast lands and herds the missions controlled. Following the secularization proclamation of Governor José Figueroa in 1834, the Mexican government authorized more than 600 rancho grants in California to Mexican citizens. The legal limit of an individual grant was 11 square leagues (about 76 sq mi, 197 sq km), but many large landholding families managed to obtain multiple grants.

The rancho economy, like that of the missions, was based on the cultivation of grain and the raising of huge herds of cattle. The rancheros traded hides and tallow for manufactured goods from foreign traders along the coast. As at the missions, herding, slaughtering, hide tanning, tallow rendering, and all the manual tasks were performed by Indian laborers. By 1845, on the eve of American acquisition, the non-Indian population of the region stood at about 7,000.

During the Mexican period, California attracted a considerable minority of immigrants from the US. Americans first came to California in the late 18th century in pursuit of the sea otter, a marine mammal whose luxurious pelts were gathered in California waters and shipped to China for sale. Later, the hide and tallow trade attracted Yankee entrepreneurs, many of whom became resident agents for American commercial firms. Beginning in 1826, with the arrival overland of Jedediah Strong Smith's party of beaver trappers, the interior of California also began to attract a growing number of Americans. The first organized group to cross the continent for the purpose of settlement in California was the Bidwell-Bartleson party of 1841. Subsequent groups of overland pioneers included the ill-fated Donner party of 1846, whose members, stranded by a snowstorm near the Sierra Nevada summit, resorted to cannibalism so that 47 of the 87 travelers could survive.

Official American efforts to acquire California began during the presidency of Andrew Jackson in the 1830s, but it was not until the administration of James K. Polk that such efforts were successful. Following the American declaration of war against Mexico on 13 May 1846, US naval forces, under command of Commodores John D. Sloat and Robert F. Stockton, launched an assault along the Pacific coast, while a troop of soldiers under Stephen W. Kearny crossed overland. On 13 January 1847, the Mexican forces in California surrendered. More than a year later, after protracted fighting in central Mexico, a treaty of peace was signed at Guadalupe-Hidalgo on 2 February 1848. Under the terms of the treaty, Mexico ceded California and other territories to the US in exchange for $15 million and the assumption by the US of some $3 million in claims by Mexican citizens.

Just nine days before the treaty was signed, James Wilson Marshall discovered gold along the American River in California. The news of the gold discovery, on 24 January 1848, soon spread around the globe, and a massive rush of people poured into the region. By the end of 1848, about 6,000 miners had obtained $10 million worth of gold. During 1849, production was two or three times as large, but the proceeds were spread among more than 40,000 miners. In 1852, the peak year of production, about $80 million in gold was mined in the state, and during the century following its discovery, the total output of California gold amounted to nearly $2 billion.

California's census population quadrupled during the 1850s, reaching nearly 380,000 by 1860, and continued to grow at a rate twice that of the nation as a whole in the 1860s and 1870s. The new population of California was remarkably diverse. The 1850 census found that nearly a quarter of all Californians were foreign-born, while only a tenth of the national population had been born abroad. In succeeding decades, the percentage of foreign-born Californians increased, rising to just under 40% during the 1860s.

One of the most serious problems facing California in the early years of the gold rush was the absence of adequate government. Miners organized more than 500 "mining districts" to regulate their affairs; in San Francisco and other cities, "vigilance committees" were formed to combat widespread robbery and arson. The US Congress, deadlocked over the slavery controversy, failed to provide any form of legal government for California from the end of the Mexican War until its admission as a state in the fall of 1850. Taking matters into their own hands, 48 delegates gathered at a constitutional convention in Monterey in September 1849 to draft a fundamental law for the state. The completed constitution contained several unique features, but most of its provisions were based on the constitutions of Iowa and New York. To the surprise of many, the convention decided by unanimous vote to exclude slavery from the state. After considerable debate, the delegates also established the present boundaries of California. Adopted on 10 October, the constitution was ratified by the voters on 13 November 1849; at the same time, Californians elected their first state officials. California soon petitioned Congress for admission as a state, having bypassed the preliminary territorial stage, and was admitted after southern objections to the creation of another free state were overcome by adoption of the stringent new Fugitive Slave Law. On 9 September 1850, President Millard Fillmore signed the admission bill, and California became the 31st state to enter the union.

The early years of statehood were marked by racial discrimination and considerable ethnic conflict. Indian and white hostilities were intense; the Indian population declined from an estimated 150,000 in 1845 to less than 30,000 by 1870. In 1850, the state legislature enacted a foreign miners' license tax, aimed at eliminating competition from Mexican and other Latin American miners. The Chinese, who replaced the Mexicans as the state's largest foreign minority, soon became the target of a new round of discrimination. By 1852, 25,000 Chinese were in California, representing about a tenth of the state's population. The legislature enacted new taxes aimed at Chinese miners, and passed an immigration tax (soon declared unconstitutional) on Chinese immigrants.

Controversy also centered on the status of the Mexican ranchos, those vast estates created by the Mexican government that totaled more than 13 million acres (5 million hectares) by 1850. The Treaty of Guadalupe-Hidalgo had promised that property belonging to Mexicans in the ceded territories would be "inviolably protected." Nevertheless, in the early years of statehood, thousands of squatters took up residence on the rancho lands. Ultimately, about three-fourths of the original Mexican grants were confirmed by federal commissions and courts; however, the average length of time required for confirmation was 17 years. During the lengthy legal process, many of the grantees either sold parts of their grants to speculators or assigned portions to their attorneys for legal fees. By the time title was confirmed, the original grantees were often bankrupt and benefited little from the decision.

Despite the population boom during the gold rush, California remained isolated from the rest of the country until completion of the transcontinental railroad in 1869. Under terms of the Pacific Railroad Act of 1862, the Central Pacific was authorized by Congress to receive long-term federal loans and grants of land, about 12,500 acres per mi (3,100 hectares per km) of track, to build the western link of the road. The directors of the California corporation—Leland Stanford, Collis P. Huntington, Charles Crocker, and Mark Hopkins, who became known as the Big Four—exercised enormous power in the affairs of the state. Following completion of the Central Pacific, the Big Four constructed additional lines within California, as well as a second transcontinental line, the Southern Pacific, providing service from southern California to New Orleans.

To a degree unmatched anywhere in the nation, the Big Four established a monopoly of transportation in California and the Far West. Eventually the Southern Pacific, as the entire system came to be known after 1884, received from the federal government a total of 11,588,000 acres (4,690,000 hectares), making it the largest private landowner in the state. Opponents of the railroad charged that it had established not only a transportation monopoly but also a corrupt political machine and a "land monopoly" in California. Farmers in the San Joaquin Valley became involved in a protracted land dispute with the Southern Pacific, a controversy that culminated in a bloody episode in 1880, known as the Battle of Mussel Slough, in which seven men were killed. This incident, later dramatized by novelist Frank Norris in *The Octopus* (1901), threw into sharp relief the hostility between many Californians and the state's largest corporation.

In the late 19th century, California's economy became more diversified. The early dependence on gold and silver mining was overcome through the development of large-scale irrigation projects and the expansion of commercial agriculture. Southern California soon was producing more than two-thirds of the nation's orange crop, and more than 90% of its lemons. The population of southern California boomed in the 1880s, fueled by the success of the new citrus industry, an influx of invalids seeking a warmer climate, and a railroad rate war between the Southern Pacific and the newly completed Santa Fe. For a time, the tariff from Kansas City to Los Angeles fell to a dollar a ticket. Real estate sales in Los Angeles County alone exceeded $200 million in 1887.

During the early 20th century, California's population growth became increasingly urban. Between 1900 and 1920, the population of the San Francisco Bay area doubled, while residents of metropolitan Los Angeles increased fivefold. On 18 April 1906, San Francisco's progress was interrupted by the most devastating earthquake ever to strike California. The quake and the fires that raged for three days killed at least 452 people, razed the city's business section, and destroyed some 28,000 buildings. The survivors immediately set to work to rebuild the city, and completed about 20,000 new buildings within three years.

By 1920, the populations of the two urban areas were roughly equal, about 1 million each. As their population grew, the need for additional water supplies became critical, and both cities became involved in bitter "water fights" with other state interests. Around the turn of the century, San Francisco proposed the damming of the Tuolumne River at the Hetch Hetchy Valley to form a reservoir for the city's water system. Conservationist John Muir and the Sierra Club objected strongly to the proposal, arguing that the Hetch Hetchy was as important a natural landmark as neighboring Yosemite Valley. The conservationists lost the battle, and the valley was flooded. (The dam there is named for Michael O'Shaughnessy, San Francisco's city engineer from 1912 to 1932 and the builder of many of California's water systems.) When Los Angeles began its search for new water supplies, it soon became embroiled in a long controversy over access to the waters of the Owens River. The city constructed a 250-mi (400-km) aqueduct that eventually siphoned off nearly the entire flow of the river, thus jeopardizing the agricultural development of Owens Valley. Residents of the valley dramatized their objection to the project by dynamiting sections of the completed aqueduct.

Important movements for political reform began simultaneously in San Francisco and Los Angeles in the early 20th century. Corruption in the administration of San Francisco Mayor Eugene Schmitz led to a wide-ranging public investigation and to a series of trials of political and business leaders. Meanwhile, in Los Angeles, a coalition of reformers persuaded the city to adopt a new charter with progressive features such as initiative, referendum, and recall. Progressive Republican Hiram Johnson won the governorship in 1910, and reformers gained control of both houses of the state legislature in 1911. Subsequent reform legislation established effective regulation of the railroads and other public utilities, greater governmental efficiency, female suffrage, closer regulation of public morality, and workers' compensation.

During the first half of the 20th century, California's population growth far outpaced that of the nation as a whole. The state's climate, natural beauty, and romantic reputation continued to attract many, but new economic opportunities were probably most important. In the early 1920s, major discoveries of oil were made in the Los Angeles Basin, and for several years during the decade, California ranked 1st among the states in production of crude oil. The population of Los Angeles County more than doubled during the decade, rising to 2,208,492 by 1930. Spurred by the availability and low price of petroleum products and by an ever expanding system of public roadways, Los Angeles also became the most thoroughly motorized and automobile-conscious city in the world. By 1925, Los Angeles had one automobile for every three persons—more than twice the national average.

Even during the 1930s, when California shared in the nationwide economic depression, hundreds of thousands of refugees streamed into the state from the dust bowl of the southern Great Plains. The film industry, which offered at least the illusion of prosperity to millions of Americans, continued to prosper during the depression. By 1940 there were more movie theaters in the US than banks, and the films they showed were almost all California products.

Politics in the Golden State in the 1930s spawned splinter movements like the Townsend Plan and the "Ham 'n' Eggs" Plan, both of which advocated cash payments for the elderly. In 1934, Socialist author Upton Sinclair won the Democratic gubernatorial nomination with a plan called End Poverty In California (EPIC), but he lost the general election to the Republican incumbent, Frank Merriam.

During World War II, the enormous expansion of military installations, shipyards, and aircraft plants attracted millions of new residents to California. The war years also saw an increase in the size and importance of ethnic minorities. By 1942, only Mexico City had a larger urban Mexican population than Los Angeles. During the war, more than 93,000 Japanese-Americans in California—most of whom were US citizens and American-born—were interned in "relocation centers" throughout the Far West.

California continued to grow rapidly during the postwar period, as agricultural, aerospace, and service industries provided new economic opportunities. Politics in the state were influenced by international tensions, and the California legislature expanded the activities of its Fact-Finding Committee on Un-American Activities. The University of California became embroiled in a loyalty-oath controversy, culminating in the dismissal in 1950 of 32 professors who refused to sign an anti-communist pledge. Blacklisting became common in the film industry. The early 1950s saw the rise to the US vice presidency of Richard Nixon, whose early campaigns capitalized on fears of communist subversion.

At the beginning of 1963, California (according to census estimates) became the nation's most populous state; its population continued to increase at a rate of 1,000 net migrants a day through the middle of the decade. By 1970, however, California's growth rate had slowed considerably. During the 1960s, the state was beset by a number of serious problems that apparently discouraged would-be immigrants. Economic opportunity gave way to recessions and high unemployment. Such rapid-growth industries as aerospace experienced a rapid decline in the late 1960s and early 1970s. Pollution of air and water called into question the quality of the California environment. The traditional romantic image of California was overshadowed by reports of mass murders, bizarre religious cults, extremist social and political movements, and racial and campus unrest.

The political importance of California's preeminence in population can be measured in the size of its congressional delegation and electoral votes. Defeated in his quest for the presidency in 1960, former vice president Nixon in 1968 became the first native Californian to win election to the nation's highest office. Both Ronald Reagan, governor of the state from 1967 to 1975, and Edmund G. Brown, Jr., elected governor in 1974 and reelected in 1978, were active candidates for the US presidency in 1980. Reagan was the Republican presidential winner that year and in 1984.

Assisted by the Reagan administration's military build-up, which invested billions of dollars into California manufacturers of bombers, missiles, and spacecraft as well as into its military bases, the California economy rebounded in the early and mid-1980s, bringing increases in total output, personal income, and employment which surpassed the national average. By the late 1980s and early 1990s, however, a recession and cuts in military spending, combined with existing burdens of expensive commercial and residential real estate, strict environmental regulations, and the effects of a savings and loan scandal, produced a dramatic economic decline. In 1992, the state's unemployment rate climbed to 10.1%. Jobs in the California aerospace and manufacturing sector dropped by 24%. For the first time in the state's history, substantial numbers of Californians migrated—over a million left between 1991 and 1994. Although such factors as air pollution, traffic congestion, and earthquakes were cited as reasons for this exodus, research has shown that most left in search of better job opportunities.

California's economic woes were matched by civil disorders. In 1991, an onlooker released a seven minute videotape which showed a group of police officers beating a black motorist with nightsticks. The driver had pulled over after giving chase. In a jury trial which took place in a mostly white suburb northwest of Los Angeles, four police officers who had been charged with unnecessary brutality were acquitted. The verdict set off riots in South Central Los Angeles, killing 60 people and causing an estimated one billion dollars in property damage.

In the late 1980s and early 1990s California was also hit by two severe earthquakes. The first, which struck the San Francisco area in 1989, measured 7.1 on the Richter scale. The quake caused the collapse of buildings, bridges, and roadways, including the upper level of Interstate Highway 880 in Oakland and a 30-foot section of the Bay Bridge. As many as 270 people were killed and 100,000 houses were damaged. The quake caused $5–7 billion worth of property damage. In 1994, an earthquake measuring 6.7 on the Richter scale occurred 20 mi northwest of downtown Los Angeles. Three major overpasses ruptured and 680,000 people were left without electricity. The quake produced $13–20 million in property damage.

In 1994, anger over illegal immigration led to passage of Proposition 187, which would bar illegal aliens from welfare, education, and nonemergency health services. The measure was approved by a 59% to 41% margin. Passage of the measure prompted immediate challenges in the courts by the opposition. The following year, Governor Pete Wilson signed an executive order limiting the application of affirmative action in hiring and contracting by the state. He also approved the elimination of affirmative action in university admissions, a policy implemented by the Board of Regents and effective as of January 1997. In November 1996, the California Civil Rights Initiative (Proposition 209) passed with 55% of the vote, banning the use of racial and sex-based preferences in state-run affirmative action programs. Three weeks later, a federal judge blocked the enforcement of the initiative, claiming that it might be unconstitutional. In April 1997, however, a federal appeals court upheld the constitutionality of Proposition 209.

12STATE GOVERNMENT

The first state constitution, adopted in 1849, outlawed slavery and was unique in granting property rights to married women in their own name. A new constitution, drafted in 1878 and ratified the following year, sought to curb legislative abuses—even going so far as to make lobbying a felony—and provided for a more equitable system of taxation, stricter regulation of the railroads, and an eight-hour workday. Of the 152 delegates to the 1878 constitutional convention, only 2 were natives of California, and 35 were foreign-born; no Spanish-speaking persons or Indians were included. This second constitution, as amended, is the basic document of state government today. In April 1994 the California Constitutional Revision Commission was appointed to make recommendations to the governor and legislature for constitutional revisions affecting budget process, governmental structure, local government duties, and other areas. Final recommendations were to be submitted in 1996.

The California legislature consists of a 40-member senate and an 80-member assembly. Senators are elected to four-year terms, half of them every two years, and assembly members are elected to two-year terms. As a result of a 1972 constitutional amendment, the legislature meets in a continuous two-year session, thus eliminating the need to reintroduce or reprint bills proposed in the first year of the biennium. Each session begins with an organizational meeting on the first Monday in December of even-numbered years; then, following a brief recess, the legislature reconvenes on the first Monday in January. Special sessions may be called by the governor to consider certain specific matters. Members of the senate and assembly must be over 18 years of age, and have been US citizens and residents of the state for at least three years and residents of the districts they represent for at least one year prior to election. Legislative salaries in 1994 were $52,500 annually.

Bills, which may be introduced by either house, are referred to committees, and must be read before each house three times. Legislation must be approved by an absolute majority vote of each house, except for appropriations bills, certain urgent measures, and proposed constitutional amendments, which require a two-thirds vote for passage. Gubernatorial vetoes may be overridden by two-thirds majority votes in both houses. In the 1973/74 session, the legislature overrode a veto for the first time since 1946, but overrides have since become more common.

Constitutional amendments and proposed legislation may also be placed on the ballot through the initiative procedure. For a constitutional amendment, petitions must be signed by at least 8% of the number of voters who took part in the last gubernatorial election; for statutory measures, 5%. In each case, a simple majority vote at the next general election is required for passage.

Officials elected statewide include the governor and lieutenant governor (who run separately), secretary of state, attorney general, controller, treasurer, and superintendent of public instruction. Each serves a four-year term, without limitation. As chief executive officer of the state, the governor is responsible for the state's policies and programs, appoints department heads and members of state boards and commissions, serves as commander in chief of the California National Guard, may declare states of emergency, and may grant executive clemency to convicted criminals. The governor's annual salary in 1996 was $120,000.

The lieutenant governor acts as president of the senate and may assume the duties of the governor in case of the latter's death, resignation, impeachment, inability to discharge the duties of the office, or absence from the state. The annual salary of the lieutenant governor was $90,000 in 1996. In order to vote in California, one must be a US citizen, at least 18 years old, and have been a resident of the state for at least 29 days prior to the election.

13POLITICAL PARTIES

As the state with the largest number of US representatives, 52, in 1996, and electoral votes, 47, California plays a key role in national and presidential politics.

In 1851, the year after California entered the Union, the state Democratic Party was organized. But the party soon split into a pro-South faction, led by US Senator William Gwin, and a pro-North wing, headed by David Broderick. A political leader in San Francisco, Broderick became a US senator in 1857 but was killed in a duel by a Gwin stalwart two years later. This violent factionalism helped switch Democratic votes to the new Republican Party in the election of 1860, giving California's four electoral votes to Abraham Lincoln. This defeat, followed by the Civil War, demolished Senator Gwin's Democratic faction, and he fled to exile in Mexico.

The Republican party itself split into liberal and conservative wings in the early 1900s. Progressive Republicans formed the Lincoln-Roosevelt League to espouse political reforms, and succeeded in nominating and electing Hiram Johnson as governor on the Republican ticket in 1910. The following year, the legislature approved 23 constitutional amendments, including the initiative, referendum, recall, and other reform measures. Johnson won reelection on a Progressive Party line in 1915. After Johnson's election to the US Senate in 1916, Republicans (both liberal and conservative) controlled the state house uninterruptedly for 22 years, from 1917 to 1939. Democratic fortunes sank so low that in 1924 the party's presidential candidate, John W. Davis, got only 8% of the state's votes, leading humorist Will Rogers to quip, "I don't belong to any organized political party—I am a California Democrat." An important factor in the Progressive Republicans' success was the cross-filing system, in effect from 1913 to 1959, which blurred party lines by permitting candidates to appear on the primary ballots of several parties. This favored such Republican moderates as Earl Warren, who won an unprecedented three terms as governor—in 1946, he won both Republican and Democratic party primaries—before being elevated to US chief justice in 1953.

Political third parties have had remarkable success in California since the secretive anti-foreign, anti-Catholic Native

American Party—called the Know-Nothings because party members were instructed to say they "knew nothing" when asked what they stood for—elected one of their leaders, J. Neely Johnson, as governor in 1855. The Workingmen's Party of California, as much anti-Chinese as it was anti-monopolist and pro-labor, managed to elect about one-third of the delegates to the 1878 constitutional convention. The most impressive third-party triumph came in 1912, when the Progressive Party's presidential candidate, Theodore Roosevelt, and vice-presidential nominee, Governor Hiram Johnson, defeated both the Republican and Democratic candidates among state voters. The Socialist Party also attracted support in the early 20th century. In 1910, more than 12% of the vote went to the Socialist candidate for governor, J. Stitt Wilson. Two years later, Socialist congressional nominees in the state won 18% of the vote, and a Socialist assemblyman was elected from Los Angeles. In 1914, two Socialist assemblymen and one state senator were elected. During the depression year of 1934, the Socialist Party leader and author Upton Sinclair won the Democratic nomination for governor on his End Poverty In California program and received nearly a million votes while losing to Republican Frank Merriam. Nonparty political movements have also won followings: several southern California congressmen were members of the ultraconservative John Birch Society during the 1960s, and in 1980 the Grand Dragon of the Ku Klux Klan won the Democratic Party nomination for a US House seat. Even when they lost decisively, third parties have won enough votes to affect the outcome of elections. In 1968, for example, George Wallace's American Independent Party received 487,270 votes, while Republican presidential candidate Richard Nixon topped Democrat Hubert Humphrey by only 223,346. In 1992, Ross Perot picked up 20.6% of the vote.

As of 1994, California had 15,101,673 registered voters, including 7,410,914 Democrats, or 49%; 5,593,555 Republicans, or 37%; and 2,097,204 unaffiliated, or 14%. Even with an advantage in voter registration, however, the Democrats managed to carry California in presidential elections only three times between 1948 and 1992, and to elect only two governors—Edmund G. "Pat" Brown (in 1958 and 1962) and his son, Edmund G. "Jerry" Brown, Jr. (in 1974 and 1978)—during the same period. Three times Californians gave their electoral votes to a California Republican, Richard Nixon, though they turned down his bid for governor in 1962. They elected one former film actor, Republican George Murphy, as US senator in 1964, and another, Republican Ronald Reagan, as governor in 1966 and 1970 and as president in 1980 and 1984. Democratic nominee Bill Clinton garnered 51% of the popular vote in 1996, while Republican Bob Dole received 38% and Independent Ross Perot picked up just under 7%.

Both Senators in 1996 were women: Democrat Barbara Boxer, who won election in 1992; and Dianne Feinstein, elected in 1992 to replace Senator Pete Wilson, who was elected governor in 1990. Both Feinstein and Wilson won reelection in 1994. Following the 1996 elections, California's delegation of US Representatives consisted of 30 Democrats and 22 Republicans, a gain of 2 seats by the Democrats. In 1997, the Democrats kept control of the state senate (23–16) and house (43–37).

The state's direct primary law had a salutary effect on local politics by helping to end the power of political machines in the large cities. In 1910, Los Angeles voters adopted the nonpartisan primary and overthrew the corrupt rule of Mayor A. C. Harper in favor of reformer George Alexander. At the same time, voters were revolting against bossism and corruption in San Francisco, Sacramento, Oakland, and other cities.

Minority groups of all types are represented in California politics. As of 1993, elected officials included 273 blacks, and 796 Hispanics held office in 1994. In 1995 there were 27 women serving in the state legislature and in elective executive office. Two of the most prominent black elected officials include Los Angeles Mayor Thomas Bradley, who served from 1973–90, and San Francisco Mayor Willie L. Brown, Jr., whose term expires in 1999. Organized groups of avowed homosexuals began to play an important political role in San Francisco during the 1970s.

[14]LOCAL GOVERNMENT

As of 1992, California had 57 counties, about 1,078 school districts, and 2,797 special districts. There were 460 municipal governments in 1992.

County government is administered by an elected board of supervisors, which also exercises jurisdiction over unincorporated towns within the county. Government operations are administered by several elected officials, the number varying according to the population of the county. Most counties have a district attorney, assessor, treasurer-tax collector, superintendent of schools, sheriff, and coroner. Larger counties may also have an elected planning director, public defender, public works director, purchasing agent, and social welfare services director.

Municipalities are governed under the mayor-council, council-manager, or commission system. Most large cities are run by councils of from 5 to 15 members, elected to four-year terms, the councils being responsible for taxes, public improvements, and the budget. An elected mayor supervises city departments and appoints most city officials. Other elected officials usually include the city attorney, treasurer, and assessor. Los Angeles and San Francisco have the mayor-council form of government, but in San Francisco, the city and county governments are consolidated under an elected board of supervisors, and the mayor appoints a manager who has substantial authority. San Diego and San Jose have both an elected mayor and city manager chosen by an elected city council.

[15]STATE SERVICES

In accordance with the Political Reform Act of 1974, the Fair Political Practices Commission investigates political campaign irregularities, regulates lobbyists, and enforces full disclosure of political contributions and public officials' assets and income.

Educational services are provided by the Department of Education, which administers the public school system. The department, which is headed by the superintendent of public instruction, also regulates special schools for blind, deaf, and disabled children. The University of California system is governed by a board of regents headed by the governor.

Transportation services are under the direction of the Department of Transportation (CALTRANS), which oversees mass transit lines, highways, and airports. Intrastate rate regulation of pipelines, railroads, buses, trucks, airlines, and waterborne transportation is the responsibility of the Public Utilities Commission, which also regulates gas, electric, telephone, water, sewer, and steam-heat utilities. The Department of Motor Vehicles licenses drivers, road vehicles, automotive dealers, and boats.

Health and welfare services are provided by many state departments, most of which are part of the Health and Welfare Agency. The Department of Health Services provides health care for nearly 3 million persons through the state's Medi–Cal program. The department's public health services include controlling infectious disease, conducting cancer research, safeguarding water quality, and protecting the public from unsafe food and drugs. The department also has licensing responsibility for hospitals, clinics, and nursing homes. Care for the mentally ill is provided through the Department of Mental Health by means of state hospitals and community outpatient clinics. Disabled people receive counseling, vocational training, and other aid through the Department of Rehabilitation. Needy families receive income maintenance aid and food stamps from the Department of Social Services. Senior citizens can get help from the Department of Aging, which allocates federal funds for the elderly. The Commission on the Status of Women reports to the legislature on women's educational and employment needs, and on statutes or practices that infringe on their rights. The Youth Authority, charged with the rehabilitation of juvenile offenders, operates training schools and conservation camps. The Department of Alcohol and Drug Programs coordinates prevention and treatment activities.

Public protection services are provided by the Military Department, which includes the Army and Air National Guard and the California Cadet Corps, and by the Youth and Adult Correctional Agency, which maintains institutions and programs to control and treat convicted felons and narcotics addicts. The California Highway Patrol has its own separate department within the Business, Transportation and Housing Agency. This agency also includes the Department of Housing and Community Development. The State and Consumer Services Agency has jurisdiction over the Department of Consumer Affairs, the Department of Veterans Affairs, and several other state departments. A state innovation was the establishment in 1974 of the Seismic Safety Commission to plan public safety programs in connection with California's continuing earthquake problem.

Programs for the preservation and development of natural resources are centralized in the Resources Agency. State parks and recreation areas are administered by the Department of Parks and Recreation. California's vital water needs are the responsibility of the Department of Water Resources. In 1975, as a result of a national oil shortage, the state established the Energy Resources Conservation and Development Commission to develop contingency plans for dealing with fuel shortages, to forecast the state's energy needs, and to coordinate programs for energy conservation. The California Conservation Corps provides employment opportunities for young people in conservation work.

The Department of Industrial Relations has divisions dealing with fair employment practices, occupational safety and health standards, and workers' compensation. The Employment Development Department provides unemployment and disability benefits and operates job-training and work-incentive programs.

16 JUDICIAL SYSTEM

California has a complex judicial system and a very large correctional system.

The state's highest court is the supreme court, which may review appellate court decisions and superior court cases involving the death penalty. The high court has a chief justice and six associate justices, all of whom serve 12-year terms; justices are appointed by the governor, confirmed or disapproved by the Commission on Judicial Appointments (headed by the chief justice), and then submitted to the voters for ratification. The chief justice also chairs the Judicial Council, which seeks to expedite judicial business and to equalize judges' caseloads.

Courts of appeal, organized in six appellate districts, review decisions of superior courts and, in certain cases, of municipal and justice courts. There are 88 district appeals court judgeships. All district court judges are appointed by the governor, reviewed by the Commission on Judicial Appointments, and subject to popular election for 12-year terms.

Superior courts in each of the 58 county seats have original jurisdiction in felony, juvenile, probate, and domestic relations cases, as well as in civil cases involving more than $15,000. They also handle some tax and misdemeanor cases and appeals from lower courts. Municipal courts, located in judicial districts with populations of more than 40,000, hear misdemeanors (except those involving juveniles) and civil cases involving $15,000 or less. In districts with less than 40,000 population, justice courts have jurisdiction similar to that of municipal courts. All trial court judges are elected to six-year terms. There were 113,615 attorneys licensed to practice law in 1996.

As of 1997 there were 149,079 prisoners in state and federal prisons in California, an increase of almost 8% over 1996. The State Department of Corrections maintains 32 state prisons and 38 minimum custody facilities located in wilderness areas where inmates are trained as wildland firefighters. As of 1997, California had 42,406 state and local corrections personnel, including about 26,000 sworn peace officers.

California Presidential Vote by Political Parties, 1948–96

YEAR	ELECTORAL VOTE	CALIFORNIA WINNER	DEMOCRAT	REPUBLICAN	STATES' RIGHTS	PROGRESSIVE	SOCIALIST	PROHIBITION
1948	25	*Truman (D)	1,913,134	1,895,269	1,228	190,381	3,459	16,926
					CONSTITUTION		SOC. LABOR	
1952	32	*Eisenhower (R)	2,197,548	2,897,310	3,504	24,692	273	16,117
1956	32	*Eisenhower (R)	2,420,135	3,027,668	6,087		300	11,119
1960	32	Nixon (R)	3,224,099	3,259,722			1,051	21,706
1964	40	*Johnson (D)	4,171,877	2,879,108			489	
					AMERICAN IND.		PEACE & FREEDOM	
1968	40	*Nixon (R)	3,244,318	3,467,664	487,270		27,707	
						AMERICAN	PEOPLE'S	LIBERTARIAN
1972	45	*Nixon (R)	3,475,847	4,602,096		232,554	55,167	980
						COMMUNIST		
1976	45	Ford (R)	3,742,284	3,882,244	51,096	12,766	41,731	56,388
						CITIZENS	PEACE & FREEDOM	
1980	45	*Reagan (R)	3,039,532	4,444,044		9,687	60,059	17,797
1984	47	*Reagan (R)	3,922,519	5,467,009	39,265	NEW ALLIANCE	26,297	49,951
1988	47	*Bush (R)	4,702,233	5,054,917	27,818	31,181		70,105
						IND. (Perot)		
1992	54	*Clinton (D)	5,121,325	3,630,574	12,711	2,296,006	18,597	48,139
							GREEN (Nader)	
1996	54	*Clinton (D)	5,119,835	3,828,380		697,847	237,016	73,600

*Won US presidential election.

According to the FBI, California's crime rate in 1995 was 5,831.1 crimes per 100,000 population. In that year, 1,841,984 crimes were reported to the police, including 305,154 violent crimes and 1,536,830 crimes against property. The 1995 rate per 100,000 population included murder and manslaughter, 11.2; forcible rape, 33.4; robbery, 331.2; assault, 590.3; burglary, 1,120.3; larceny-theft, 2,856.9; and motor vehicle theft, 887.9. In 1995, Los Angeles reported 266,204 crimes (including 849 murders), San Francisco 60,474 (99 murders), and San Diego 64,235 (91 murders). In 1965, California became the first state to institute a victim compensation program.

California's death penalty statute received its most serious challenge after the 1948 conviction of Carl Chessman on a charge of forcible rape. Chessman served 12 years on death row at San Quentin, got eight stays of execution, and wrote a best-seller about his ordeal. Despite highly publicized attempts to overturn capital punishment and save Chessman's life, the legislature refused to act, and he was executed in 1960. The death penalty was carried out 292 times in California from 1930 to 1977, but only twice between 1977 and 1995. California had 420 persons under sentence of death in 1995, more than any other state in the nation.

17ARMED FORCES

California leads the 50 states in defense contracts received, numbers of National Guardsmen and military veterans, veterans' benefit payments, and funding for police forces.

In 1996, the US Department of Defense had 314,662 personnel in California, including 118,839 active-duty military and 84,651 civilians. Army military personnel totaled 15,627; the Navy (including Marines), 132,041; and the Air Force, 44,002. Army bases are located at Oakland and San Francisco. Naval facilities in the San Diego area had more than 47,000 personnel in 1991/92; there are weapons stations at Concord and Seal Beach, and supply depots at Oakland and San Pedro. The Marine Corps training base, Camp Pendleton at Oceanside had 32,391 personnel. The Air Force operates three main bases—McClellan AFB at Sacramento, Travis AFB at Fairfield, and Norton AFB at San Bernardino—and numerous smaller installations. In 1995/96, California companies were awarded $18.2 billion in defense contracts, more than two times the total for Texas (which ranked 2d), and more than 20% of the US total.

As of 1 July 1996, 2,783,000 veterans of US military service, nearly 11% of the national total, were living in California. Of those 1,000 served in World War I, 721,000 in World War II, 483,000 in the Korean conflict, 940,000 during the Vietnam era, and 139,000 in the Persian Gulf War. Veterans' benefits paid to Californians in 1995/96 exceeded $3.7 billion.

California's military forces consist of the Army and Air National Guard, the naval and state military reserve (militia), and the California Cadet Corps. Total Reserve and National Guard strength was 111,172 in 1996.

In 1993, the California Highway Patrol employed 5,803 full-time sworn officers, or 2 per 10,000 residents.

18MIGRATION

A majority of Californians today are migrants from other states. The first great wave of migration, beginning in 1848, brought at least 85,000 prospectors by 1850. Perhaps 20,000 of them were foreign-born, mostly from Europe, Canada, Mexico, and South America, as well as a few from the Hawaiian Islands and China. Many thousands of Chinese were brought in during the latter half of the 19th century to work on farms and railroads. When Chinese immigration was banned by the US Congress in 1882, Japanese migration provided farm labor. These ambitious workers soon opened shops in the cities and bought land for small farms. By 1940, about 94,000 Japanese lived in California.

During the depression of the 1930s, approximately 350,000 migrants came to California, most of them looking for work. Many thousands of people came there during World War II to take jobs in the burgeoning war industries; after the war, some 300,000 discharged servicemen settled in the state. All told, between 1940 and 1990 California registered a net gain from migration of 12,426,000, representing well over half of its population growth during that period.

In the 1990s California has registered net losses in domestic migration, peaking with a loss of 444,186 in 1993/94. Altogether net losses in domestic migration between 1990 and 1996 totaled 1.87 million people. During the same period, net gains in international migration totaled 1.63 million. As of 1996, nearly 22% of all foreign immigrants in the US were living in California, a higher proportion than in any other state. Although the 1970s brought an influx of refugees from Indochina, and, somewhat later, from Central America, the bulk of postwar foreign immigration has come from neighboring Mexico. At first, Mexicans—as many as 750,000 a year—were imported legally to supply seasonal labor for California growers. Later, hundreds of thousands—perhaps even millions—of illegal Mexican immigrants crossed the border in search of jobs and then, unless they were caught and forcibly repatriated, stayed on. In 1996, California was the intended residence of 201,529 foreign immigrants (more than any other state and 22% of the US total that year). Counting these state residents for census purposes is extremely difficult, since many of them are unwilling to declare themselves for fear of being identified and deported. As of 1990, California's foreign-born population was reported at 8,055,000, or 25% of the state's total. As of 1994, the number of undocumented immigrants was estimated at between 1,321 and 1,784—the highest number of any state and close to 40% of the total number thought to be residing in the US.

Intrastate migration has followed two general patterns: rural to urban until the mid-20th century, and urban to suburban thereafter. In particular, the percentage of blacks increased in Los Angeles, San Francisco, and San Diego between 1960 and 1970 as black people settled or remained in the cities while whites moved into the surrounding suburbs. In the 1970s and 1980s, the percentage of blacks in Los Angeles and San Francisco decreased slightly; in San Diego, the percentage of blacks increased from 8.9% to 9.4%. California's net gain from migration during 1970–80 amounted to about 1,573,000. In the 1980s, migration accounted for 54% of the net population increase, with about 2,940,000 new residents. By 1990, 46.4% of all state residents had been born in California. Only 44% of all Californians (age 5 and older) lived in the same house in 1990 as in 1985; of those who lived in a different house in 1985, 86% resided within California.

19INTERGOVERNMENTAL COOPERATION

The Colorado River Board of California represents the state's interests in negotiations with the federal government and other states over utilization of Colorado River water and power resources. California also is a member of the Western States Water Council, the Klamath River Compact Commission (with Oregon), and the Tahoe Regional Planning Compact (with Nevada). Regional agreements signed by the state include the Pacific Marine Fisheries Compact, Western Corrections Compact, Western Interstate Energy Compact, and Western Regional Education Compact. The Arizona-California boundary accord dates from 1963. California also is a member of the Commission of the Californias, along with the State of Baja California Norte and the territory of Baja California Sur, both in Mexico.

During the 1995/96 fiscal year, federal aid to California exceeded $26.4 billion, the most received by any state.

20ECONOMY

California leads the 50 states in economic output and total personal income. In the 1960s, when it became the nation's most populous state, California also surpassed Iowa in agricultural production and New York in value added by manufacturing.

The gold rush of the mid-19th century made mining (which employed more people than any other industry in the state until 1870) the principal economic activity and gave impetus to agriculture and manufacturing. Many unsuccessful miners took up farming or went to work for the big cattle ranches and wheat growers. In the 1870s, California became the most important cattle-raising state and the 2d-leading wheat producer. Agriculture soon expanded into truck farming and citrus production, while new manufacturing industries began to produce ships, metal products, lumber, leather, cloth, refined sugar, flour, and other processed foods. Manufacturing outstripped both mining and agriculture to produce goods valued at $258 million by 1900, and 10 times that by 1925. Thanks to a rapidly growing work force, industrial output continued to expand during and after both world wars, while massive irrigation projects enabled farmers to make full use of the state's rich soil and favorable climate.

By the late 1970s, one of every four California workers was employed in high-technology industry. California has long ranked 1st among the states in defense procurement, and in 1984/85, defense contracts awarded to southern California firms surpassed the combined totals of New York and Texas.

From its beginnings in the late 18th century, California's wine industry has grown to encompass some 500 wineries. In 1981, they accounted for about 90% of total US production. By 1985, California had surpassed Chicago to rank 2d in advertising among the states.

A highly diversified economy makes California less vulnerable to national recession than most other states. During the first half of the 1980s, the state generally outperformed the national economy. In 1984, California enjoyed an estimated increase of 12.1% in personal income and a 6.1% increase in nonagricultural employment, and reduced the unemployment rate from 9.7% to an estimated 7.8%. The boom was short-lived, however. Cuts in the military budget in the late 1980s, a decline in Japanese investment, and the national recession in the early 1990s had a devastating impact on the state, particularly on southern California. Unemployment in 1992 rose to 9.1%, up from 5.1% in 1989. The aerospace and construction industries suffered disproportionately. Employment in aerospace declined 22.3% between May of 1990 and September of 1992; construction lost 20% of its jobs in the same period. The gross state product in 1994 was $875,697 million. Contributing to the GSP were private goods-producing industries, $173,884 million; private services-producing industries, $595,035 million; government, $106,778 million. California's per capita personal income in 1995 was $24,073, placing it 11th in the nation. In 1996, there were 183,630 filings for bankruptcy in California.

21INCOME

With a per capita personal income of $25,144 in 1996, California ranked 12th among the 50 states. Total personal income exceeded $800 billion—over 50% more than in New York, and about double the total for Texas. The growth from 1995 to 1996 in personal per capita income was 4.4%, slightly below the national average of 4.5%. Median household income was $37,009 in 1995.

Despite California's relatively high average personal income, 16.7% of the population was below the federal poverty level in 1995. In the Los Angeles vicinity, the poverty rate was 18.6% in 1995.

California is justly noted for its large number of wealthy residents, particularly in the Los Angeles and San Francisco metropolitan areas. The cost of living in these areas, however, was some 30% higher than the national average in 1993. In 1995, the median household income was about $37,009, 8th in the nation.

In 1996, total disposable income, after state and federal income taxes, amounted to $693.7 billion, or $21,760 per capita.

22LABOR

California has the largest work force in the nation and the greatest number of employed workers. During the 1970s, California's work force also grew at a higher annual rate than that of any other state.

In early 1997, the state's civilian labor force totaled 15,446,200, of whom 14,483,200 (93.8%) were employed and 963,000 (6.2%) unemployed.

A large majority of the labor force is employed in metropolitan areas, including, as of the beginning of 1997, 4,382,500 in the Los Angeles–Long Beach area, 2,028,900 in the San Francisco–Oakland area, 1,308,600 in the Riverside–San Bernardino area, 888,400 in metropolitan San Jose, and 1,226,700 in the San Diego metropolitan area.

Seasonally adjusted employment patterns for major industry groups in California at the beginning of 1996 and 1997 were as follows (in thousands):

	1996	1997
Total nonfarm employment	12,591.1	12,960.1
Mining	30.1	29.6
Construction	503.5	537.8
Manufacturing	1,825.7	1,870.4
Durable goods	1,118.2	1,146.6
Nondurable goods	707.5	723.8
Transportation, communications, utilities	635.1	651.6
Trade	2,941.7	2,983.8
Wholesale trade	727.0	754.9
Retail trade	2,214.7	2,228.9
Finance, insurance, real estate	730.8	732.3
Services	3,821.1	4,015.6
Government	2,103.1	2,139.0

As of 1995, California's 44,100 employees in the guided missiles and space vehicle sector accounted for 49% of the total nationwide.

The unemployment rate during the 1970s and early 1980s ranged from the 1973 low of 7% to a high of 9.9% in 1975 and 1982. From 1967 to 1976, an average of 226,000 Californians entered the labor market each year, but the economy generated only about 175,000 jobs annually, so unemployment rose steadily.

The labor movement in California was discredited by acts of violence during its early years. On 1 October 1910, a bomb explosion at a Los Angeles Times plant killed 21 workers, resulting in the conviction and imprisonment of two labor organizers a year later. Another bomb explosion, this one killing 10 persons in San Francisco on 22 July 1916, led to the conviction of two radical union leaders, Thomas Mooney and Warren Billings; the death penalty for Mooney was later commuted to life imprisonment (the same sentence Billings had received), and after evidence had been developed attesting to his innocence, he was pardoned in 1939. These violent incidents led to the state's Criminal Syndicalism Law of 1919, which forbade "labor violence" and curtailed militant labor activity for more than a decade.

Unionism revived during the depression of the 1930s. In 1934, the killing of two union picketers by San Francisco police during a strike by the International Longshoremen's Association led to a three-day general strike that paralyzed the city, and the union eventually won the demand for its own hiring halls. In Los Angeles, unions in such industries as automobiles, aircraft, rubber, and oil refining obtained bargaining rights, higher wages, and fringe benefits during and after World War II. In 1958, the California Labor Federation was organized, and labor unions have since increased both their membership and their benefits. As of 1995, 17.7% of all workers belonged to labor unions; 12.1% of all private sector manufacturing workers in California belonged to a labor union.

Of all working groups, migrant farm workers have been the most difficult to organize because their work is seasonal and because they are largely members of minority groups, mostly Mexicans, with few skills and limited job opportunities. During the 1960s, a Mexican-American "stoop" laborer named Cesar Chavez established the National Farm Workers Association (later the United Farm Workers Organizing Committee, now the United Farm Workers of America), which, after a long struggle, won bargaining rights from grape, lettuce, and berry growers in the San Joaquin Valley. Chavez's group was helped by a secondary boycott against these California farm products at some grocery stores throughout the US. When his union was threatened by the rival Teamsters Union in the early 1970s, Chavez got help from the AFL-CIO and from Governor Brown, who in 1975 pushed through the state legislature a law mandating free elections for agricultural workers to determine which union they wanted to represent them. The United Farm Workers and Teamsters formally settled their jurisdictional dispute in 1977. In January 1996, there were 162,000 farm laborers in California.

In 1996, production workers in manufacturing industries worked an average of 42.6 hours per week and earned average weekly wages of $556.78, ranging from an average low of $468.13 in the Fresno area to an average high of $685.61 in the San Jose area.

[23]AGRICULTURE

California has led the United States in agriculture for nearly 50 years with a diverse economy of over 250 crop and livestock commodities. With only 3.9% of the nation's farms and 3.1% of the nation's farm acreage, the state accounts for over 11.6% of US gross cash farm receipts. Famous for its specialty crops, California produces virtually all (99% or more) of the following crops grown commercially in the US: almonds, artichokes, avocados, clovers, dates, figs, kiwifruit, olives, persimmons, pistachios, prunes, raisins, and English walnuts. California's total cash farm receipts for 1995 amounted to $22.1 billion and generated nearly $70 billion in related economic activity.

Agriculture has always thrived in California. The Spanish missions and Mexican ranchos were farming centers until the mid-19th century, when large ranches and farms began to produce cattle, grain, and cotton for the national market. Wheat was a major commodity by the 1870s, when the citrus industry was established and single-family farms in the fertile Central Valley and smaller valleys started to grow large quantities of fruits and vegetables. European settlers planted vineyards on the slopes of the Sonoma and Napa valleys, beginning California's wine industry, which today produces over 90% of US domestic wines. Around 1900, intensive irrigation transformed the dry, sandy Imperial Valley in southeastern California into a garden of abundance for specialty crops. Since World War II, corporate farming, or agribusiness, has largely replaced small single-family farms. Today, the state grows approximately 55% of all fruits and vegetables marketed in the US.

In 1995, California devoted nearly one-third (29 million acres/ 17.7 million hectares) of its 100 million acres (40.5 million hectares) to agricultural production with 80,000 farms comprising 30 million acres (12 million hectares). According to US Department of Agriculture estimates, the average size of a farm in 1995 was 375 acres (152 hectares). One-fourth of all farmland represents crop growth, and currently 10% of all cropland uses irrigation.

Irrigation is essential for farming in California. Agriculture consumes 28% of the state's annual water supply. A major irrigation system was implemented, including the Colorado River Project, which irrigated 500,000 acres (200,000 hectares) in the Imperial Valley in 1913; the Central Valley Project, completed by 1960, which harnessed the runoff of the Sacramento River; and the Feather River Project, also in the Central Valley, which was finished during the 1970s. Largest of all is the California Water Project, begun in 1960 and completed in 1973. During 1983, this project delivered 1.3 million acre-feet of water.

On 16 June 1980, the US Supreme Court ended 13 years of litigation by ruling that federally subsidized irrigation water in the Imperial Valley could not be limited to family farms of fewer than 160 acres (56 hectares) but must be made available to all farms regardless of size; the ruling represented a major victory for agribusiness interests.

The leading crops in 1995 were grapes, nursery products, and cotton. The following table shows the farm product, commodity ranking, value in thousands of dollars, and percent of total production in 1995 for the top 20 California agricultural commodities:

FARM PRODUCT	VALUE $1,000	PERCENT OF TOTAL	COMMODITY RANKING
Milk and cream	3,078,480	13.7	1
Grapes	1,838,900	8.2	2
Nursery products	1,500,000	6.7	3
Cattle and calves	1,289,756	5.7	4
Cotton lint	1,063,505	4.7	5
Lettuce, head	986,952	4.4	6
Almonds	857,771	3.8	7
Hay	847,050	3.8	8
Tomatoes, processing	672,472	3.0	9
Flowers and foliage	671,904	3.0	10
Strawberries	551,698	2.5	11
Oranges	458,130	2.0	12
Chickens	384,208	1.7	13
Rice	318,168	1.4	14
Broccoli	317,604	1.4	15
Walnuts	313,560	1.4	16
Eggs, chicken	288,369	1.3	17
Carrots	287,070	1.3	18
Celery	246,229	1.1	19
Cantaloupe	237,319	1.1	20

California is the top agricultural exporter in the US with $11.7 billion in 1995. California outpaced China, Canada, Brazil, and Australia as the 6th largest exporter of agricultural products in 1995. Japan accounted for more than 25% of all California agricultural exports in 1995, and the entire Pacific Rim accounted for more than half their total exports at $6.4 billion. Export markets hold the greatest potential for expanding sales of California agriculture products.

[24]ANIMAL HUSBANDRY

California is a leading producer of livestock and dairy products.

In 1997 there was an estimated 4.5 million cattle and calves valued at $3.1 billion. There were 210,000 hogs and pigs on California farms and ranches in 1996, valued at $27.3 million. In 1995 California produced 60 million lb (27.2 million kg) of sheep and lambs for a gross income of $69.7 million.

In 1995 California was the leading milk producer among the 50 states with 25 billion lb (11.3 million kg) of milk produced. Milk cows, raised mainly in the southern interior, totaled 1.254 million head in 1995.

California ranked 1st among the 50 states in egg production in 1996, with an output of 6.5 billion eggs. In 1995, California produced 462 million lb (209.6 million kg) of turkey, which was valued at $212 million. In 1995, the state produced 1.179 billion lb (530 million kg) of broilers valued at $383 million.

25FISHING

The Pacific whaling industry, with its chief port at San Francisco, was important to the California economy in the 19th century, and commercial fishing is still central to the food-processing industry. In 1995, California ranked 4th in the US in commercial fishing, with a catch of 432.5 million lb (196.2 million kg); the value of the catch, $166.5 million, ranked 7th and only accounted for 4.4% of the national value. Los Angeles ranked 6th among fishing ports in 1995, with landings totaling 168.5 million lb (76.4 million kg).

In 1994, the California fishing fleet numbered 6,250 vessels. In 1995, principal commercial species included squid, 154.8 million lb (70.2 million kg); dungeness crab, 9.1 million lb (4.1 million kg); shrimp, 7.6 million lb (3.4 million kg); salmon, 6.6 million lb (3 million kg); sablefish, 6.1 million lb (2.8 million kg); and jack mackerel, 3.8 million lb (1.7 million kg). California accounted for 92% of US landings of jack mackerel in 1995, and 67% of squid landings.

Deep-sea fishing is a popular sport. As of June 1984, world records for giant sea bass, California halibut, white catfish, and sturgeon had been set in California. The Coleman National Fish Hatchery distributed over 21.8 million coldwater fish (mostly Chinook salmon) within the state in 1995/96. There were over 2.3 million anglers licensed in the state in 1995/96, when federal authorities spent over $9.8 million on sport fish restoration, through development of artificial reefs, barrier construction, and shoreline stabilization. In 1995, an estimated 534,000 coastal residents, 101,000 inland residents, and 81,000 residents of other states participated in recreational fishing off the coast of northern California. Sport fishing off the coast of southern California involved an estimated 902,000 coastal residents, 9,000 inland Californians, and 161,000 persons from other states in 1995. In 1995, marine recreational anglers caught an estimated 26 million fish along the Pacific coast of California, with Pacific mackerel and kelp bass the principal species.

26FORESTRY

California has more forests than any other state except Alaska. Forested lands in 1994 covered 39,673,000 acres (16,056,000 hectares). Nearly 42% of the state's forested area is used to produce commercial timber.

Forests are concentrated in the northwestern part of the state and in the eastern Sierra Nevada. Commercial forestland in private hands was estimated at 7,437,000 acres (3,010,000 hectares) in 1994; an additional 8,783,000 acres (3,554,000 hectares) were US Forest Service lands, and 430,000 acres (174,000 hectares) were public lands other than national forests. In 1994, the volume of sawtimber on commercial forest land totaled 258 billion board feet, mostly of such softwoods as fir, pine, cedar, and redwood.

About half of the state's forests are protected as national forests and state parks or recreational areas. Although stands of coast redwood trees have been preserved in national and state parks since the late 19th century, only about 46% of the original 2 million acres (800,000 hectares) of redwoods between Monterey Bay and southern Oregon remain.

Reforestation of public lands is supervised by the National Forest Service and the California Department of Forestry. In 1924–25, more than 1.5 million redwood and Douglas fir seedlings were planted in the northwestern corner of the state. During the 1930s, the Civilian Conservation Corps replanted trees along many mountain trails, and the California Conservation Corps performed reforestation work in the 1970s. In 1993/94, 69,552 acres (28,148 hectares) were reforested.

As of 1995, there were 21 national forests with all or part of their acreage in California. Total area within their boundaries in California amounted to 24,225,542 acres (9,804,077 hectares), of which 85% was National Forest System land.

27MINING

According to data compiled by the US Geological Survey, California was the 3d-leading state in the nation in the value of nonfuel minerals produced during 1995, accounting for more than 7% of the US total. The value of the nonfuel mineral commodities produced in the state during the year was estimated to be $2.68 billion, a 3% increase from the $2.59 billion of 1994. Industrial minerals accounted for 87% of the nonfuel mineral production value. California led all other states in the production of boron minerals, (546,000 metric tons, valued at $462 million), portland cement (9.2 million metric tons, worth $515 million), diatomite, construction sand and gravel (93 million metric tons, valued at $512 million), rare earth concentrates, natural sodium sulfate, asbestos, and tungsten.

More than 20 industrial minerals are produced in California. Portland cement was the most valuable commodity produced followed in order by construction sand and gravel, boron, gold (29,500 kg, valued at $354 million), and crushed stone (48 million short tons, worth $307 million). Gold accounts for more than 95% of metal production value. California is the sole source of domestic boron mineral production. Also in 1995, California was second among the states in the production of gold, soda ash, and titanium (ilmenite); third in potash, perlite, and mercury; fourth in pumice; and fifth in feldspar.

Mining permits are granted by the California Department of Conservation, Division of Mines and Geology. Siting and permitting of mining operations throughout California often generate local controversies. The leading issues involve intense land use competition and wide-ranging environmental concerns, along with the typical noise, dust, and truck-traffic issues in populated areas. Mining employment was about 28,200 in December 1996.

28ENERGY AND POWER

In 1994, petroleum supplied an estimated 46% of the state's energy needs, natural gas 32%, coal 7%, nuclear power 6%, geothermal 4%, hydroelectric power 2%, and other sources about 3%. California ranks 4th among the 50 states in energy input to electric utilities, 4th in crude oil, and 10th in natural gas. California utilities own and operate coal-fired power plants across the southwest. This electricity shows up as "imports" in federal accounting. California utilities buy electricity from out-of-state suppliers if it is less expensive than in-state operation.

Installed electric capacity in 1991 was 44 million kW in 1996. In 1994, electrical output totaled 214.4 billion kWh. About 12% was generated from hydroelectric plants, 44% from natural gas, less than 1% from oil, 18% from nuclear power plants, 12% from coal, and about 13% from geothermal and other sources.

Originally ordered by the Pacific Gas and Electric Co. in 1966, the Diablo Canyon nuclear power plant near San Luis Obispo has been a source of controversy ever since 1971, when an earthquake fault line was discovered offshore, 2.5 mi (4 km) from the plant. After years of delays and demonstrations by environmental groups, the first unit of the plant began operation in November 1984, the second reactor in 1985 making a total of four reactors at two plants operating in the state, with a net capacity of over 4,500 MW.

In 1994, sales of electric power in the state totaled 213.7 billion kWh, of which 40% went to commercial businesses, 32%

to home consumers, and 28% to industries. In part because of the mild California climate and the state's aggressive 20-year effort to improve energy efficiency, utility bills are lower than in many other states. In 1993, per capita energy consumption in California was 237.8 million Btu, or 49th among the states; energy expenditures per capita were $1,564, or 50th.

In 1994 petroleum and natural gas supplied 78% of California's energy demand. In-state resources accounted for 47% of oil supply and 12% of gas supply. Domestic oil sources accounted for 45% of oil supply with foreign sources representing the remaining 8%. Domestic sources of natural gas accounted for 70% of the state's gas supply with foreign sources representing the remaining 18%.

Crude oil was discovered in Humboldt and Ventura counties as early as the 1860s with the first year of commercial production occurring in 1876. It was not until the 1920s, however, that large oil strikes were made at Huntington Beach, near Los Angeles, and at Santa Fe Springs and Signal Hill, near Long Beach. These fields added vast pools of crude oil to the state's reserves, which were further augmented in the 1930s by the discovery of large offshore oil deposits in the Long Beach area. In 1995 there were 212 and 88 active oil and gas fields, respectively.

The state's attempts to retain rights to tideland oil reserves as far as 30 mi (48 km) offshore were denied by the US Supreme Court in 1965; state claims were thus restricted to Monterey Bay and other submerged deposits within a 3-mi (5-km) offshore limit. In 1994, however, California banned any further oil drilling in state offshore waters because of environmental concerns, high operating costs, and resource limitations. In 1995, state and federal offshore resources accounted for 25% and 19% of state oil and gas production, respectively. Production from state waters alone represented 6% and 2% of total California oil and gas production, respectively. The state's largest oil companies include Chevron, with headquarters in San Francisco, and Los Angeles-based Atlantic Richfield.

California's proved oil reserves as of 31 December 1995 were estimated at more than 3.5 billion barrels, 15% of the US total and 3d behind Alaska and Texas. Petroleum production in 1995 totaled 351.3 million barrels, representing nearly 15% of the domestic output. Production of natural gas totaled 289.6 billion cu ft, 1.5% of the US total, and proved reserves were nearly 4.3 trillion cu ft (2.6%). In 1995 there were 14,217 active oil wells and 1,172 active natural gas wells in the state. About 90% of the coal consumed for electric power generation occurs out of state.

California has been a leader in developing solar and geothermal power as alternatives to fossil fuels. As of the end of 1994, geothermal, wind, and solar energy electric generation amounted to 26.8 billion kWh, or nearly 13% of the total electric generation for the state. Over 98% of the geothermal, wind, and solar electric capacity nationally comes from California.

[29]INDUSTRY

California is the nation's leading industrial state, ranking 1st in almost every general manufacturing category: number of establishments, number of employees, total payroll, value added by manufacture, value of shipments, and new capital spending. Specifically, California ranks among the leaders in machinery, fabricated metals, agricultural products, food processing, computers, aerospace technology, and many other industries.

With its shipyards, foundries, flour mills, and workshops, San Francisco was the state's first manufacturing center. The number of manufacturing establishments in California nearly doubled between 1899 and 1914, and the value of manufactures increased almost tenfold from 1990 to 1925. New factories for transportation equipment, primary metal products, chemicals and food products sprang up in the state during and after World War II. Second to New York State in industrial output for many years,

California finally surpassed that state in most manufacturing categories in the 1972 Census of Manufacturers.

According to the 1995 Annual Survey of Manufacturers, value added by manufacture totaled $178.358 billion, the value of shipments by manufactures was $348.765 billion, and new capital expenditures amounted to $12.879 billion. Of the total value added, food and kindred products accounted for $47.864 billion; printing and publishing, $19.263 billion; chemicals and allied products, $18 billion; industrial machinery and equipment, $48.494 billion; electronic and other electric equipment, $54.263 billion. The following table shows value of shipments by manufacturers for selected industries in 1995.

Aircraft and parts	$13,526,700,000
Computer and office equipment	30,817,400,000
Petroleum refining	16,881,800,000
Electronic components	28,799,200,000
Guided missiles and space vehicles	8,706,200,000
Search and navigation equipment	6,374,500,000
Measuring and controlling devices	10,145,200,000
Medical instruments and supplies	8,461,000,000
Motor vehicles and equipment	8,347,600,000
Communications equipment	13,203,200,000
Fabricated structural metal products	5,105,100,000
Grain mill products	4,136,900,000

California's industrial workforce is mainly located in the two major manufacturing centers: almost three-fourths work in either the Los Angeles–Long Beach–Orange County area or the San Francisco–Oakland–San Jose area. Although the state workforce has a wide diversity of talents and products, about 11% is in each of the three leading categories: food and food products, electronic and other electrical equipment, and transportation equipment. Three other categories each have between 8–9% of the workforce: apparel, and fabricated and industrial machinery.

Computers and aerospace manufacturers stand out among California's largest publicly owned corporations. Hewlett-Packard, Sun Microsystems, Tandem Computers, Varian Associates, and Silicon Graphics are leading names of the Silicon Valley (Santa Clara County) area just south of San Francisco. Southern California's manufacturing leaders are Rockwell International, Lockheed, Northrop, and Computers Sciences. In 1991, 59% of Californians employed in the aerospace industry lived in Los Angeles County, and 76% in six southern Californian counties.

Leading manufacturers on the list of California private companies are Levi Strauss, Del Monte, Sunkist Growers, and Ernest and Julio Gallo Winery, showing the continuing strength that the Golden State has historically maintained in apparel and food production and processing.

Of the $24 billion in prime defense contracts received by all California firms during federal fiscal year 1991–92, 22% went for missile and space systems, 27% for military aircraft, and 15% for electronic and communication equipment.

In 1987, California's motion picture industry, based primarily in Los Angeles, had receipts of at least $11.8 billion—more than 59% of the US total. A 1992 research report shows the film and TV production industry generating an annual payroll of $7.4 billion and paying $8.9 billion to suppliers while providing jobs to 35,000 Californians.

In 1995, there were 10,672 patents issued to Californians.

[30]COMMERCE

California's wholesale trade in 1992 was $432.9 billion from 58,437 establishments. Durable goods accounted for 58.8% of wholesale sales, and nondurable goods for the remaining 41.2%. Of the total sales of durable goods in that year, motor vehicles and automotive parts made up 27.2%; professional and commercial equipment, 23.6%; electrical goods, 10.3%; metals and minerals (excluding petroleum), 3.5%; furniture and home furnishings, 3.1%; and other categories, 32%. Of the nondurable goods, groceries and related products accounted for more than 37%; petroleum products, 15.6%; paper and paper products, 7.3%; chemicals and allied products, 6.7%; and other items, 33.4%.

The state's 1992 retail sales amounted to $224.6 billion (1st). Of total 1992 sales in establishments with payrolls, food stores accounted for 20.1%; automobile dealers, 19.4%; general merchandise stores, 12.8%; eating and drinking places, 11.4%; gasoline service stations, 6.5%; and other establishments, 29.8%. Retail sales in the Los Angeles–Riverside–Orange County area totaled $107.6 billion, 48% of the state total and 5.7% of the US total. San Francisco–Oakland–San Jose accounted for 23.4% of the state's retail sales in 1992, and 2.8% of US retail sales.

Foreign trade is important to the California economy. In 1996, goods exported from California were valued at an estimated $98.6 billion (1st) and goods originally produced in California and exported from anywhere in the US were valued at $93.4 billion. The Los Angeles metropolitan area handled $22.2 billion in exports during 1994. About 15.8% of the nations's exports were distributed from California in 1996. California's major markets are Japan, Canada, South Korea, Mexico, the European Community, and the industrializing countries of East Asia.

Leading exports include data-processing equipment, electrical tubes and transistors, scientific equipment, measuring instruments, optical equipment, and aircraft parts and spacecraft. California's leading agricultural export is cotton.

California's customs districts are the ports of Los Angeles, San Francisco, and San Diego. San Francisco and San Jose have been designated as federal foreign-trade zones, where imported goods may be stored duty-free for reshipment abroad, or customs duties avoided until the goods are actually marketed in the US.

31CONSUMER PROTECTION

Numerous California state and local government agencies protect, promote, and serve the interests of consumers.

The California Department of Consumer Affairs comprises 36 entities (4 bureaus, 3 programs, 22 boards, 6 committees, and 1 commission) that license more than 2.1 million Californians in more than 180 occupations and professions. These entities establish minimum qualifications and levels of competency for licensure; license, register, or certify practitioners; investigate complaints; and discipline violators.

The California Department of Consumer Affairs also administers the Consumer Affairs Act (consumer information, education, complaints, and advocacy), the Arbitration Review Program (auto warranty dispute resolution), and the Dispute Resolution Programs Act (funding of local dispute resolution programs). It helps carry out the Small Claims Act by publishing materials for those who administer and use the Small Claims Court, and by training small claims advisors and attorneys who serve as judges.

Other state agencies that serve consumers include the Department of Fair Employment and Housing (unlawful employment and housing discrimination), the Department of Real Estate (licensing of real estate brokers and sales agents), the Department of Corporations (licensing of personal finance companies), the Department of Insurance (licensing and conduct of insurance companies), and the State Banking Department (licensing and conduct of banks and other lenders).

Consumers are also assisted by a variety of state and local law enforcement agencies that enforce the state's laws on false and deceptive advertising, unfair and deceptive trade practices, unfair competition, and other laws. These agencies include the California Attorney General, the District Attorneys of most counties, the City Attorneys of San Francisco, Los Angeles, and San Diego counties, and county consumer affairs departments.

32BANKING

In 1848, California's first financial institution—the Miners' Bank—was founded in San Francisco. Especially since 1904, when A. P. Giannini founded the Bank of Italy, now known as the Bank of America, California banks have pioneered in branch banking for families and small businesses. Today, California is among the leading states in branch banking, savings and loan associations, and credit union operations.

In 1996 there were 331 insured commercial banks in California. Of these, 110 were national banks and 221 state banks. In 1996, banking offices for insured banks in the state totaled 4,447. As of 31 December 1996, insured commercial banks in California had total assets of $411 billion, 2d only to New York State, and held about 9% of all US commercial bank assets; state banks had about 20% of the total, and national banks 80%. Loans in 1996 totaled $269.8 billion. In 1996, commercial bank deposits were over $316.5 billion.

Until 30 June 1997, the State Banking Department administered laws and regulations governing state-chartered banks, foreign banks, trust companies, issuers of payment instruments, issuers of travelers' checks, and transmitters of money abroad.

On 1 July 1997 a new department began supervising all of California's depository institutions. The Department of Financial Institutions now supervises commercial banks, credit unions, industrial loan companies, savings and loans, and other licensees formerly supervised by the State Banking Department.

33INSURANCE

Insurance companies provide a major source of California's investment capital by means of premium payments collected from policyholders. Life insurance companies also invest heavily in real estate; in 1995, life insurance firms held an estimated $39.2 billion in mortgage debt on California properties.

In 1996 there were 43 life insurance companies domiciled in California; these and out-of-state companies doing business in the state paid benefits of $16.1 billion (1st in the US), including $3.1 billion in death benefits. Total premiums received by California life insurance companies amounted to over $29.5 billion, second only to New York. Nearly 10.3 million policies were in force, with a total value of $1,305.3 billion. The average family held $114,900 worth of life insurance, 7% below the US norm.

Property and casualty companies, 166 of which were domiciled in California in 1995, offer automobile, homeowners', and other types of insurance. In 1995, $32.3 billion in direct premiums were written in the state, including $8.9 billion in private passenger and commercial automobile liability insurance, $4.94 billion in automobile physical damage insurance, about $2.9 billion in homeowners' insurance, and $926 million in earthquake insurance (69% of the US total).

34SECURITIES

California's Pacific Stock Exchange (PSE), the largest securities market in the US outside New York City and the third-largest stock options marketplace in the world, is an association of some 500 member brokers who provide an auction market for the stocks, options, and bonds of national and local corporations. The exchange, which operates trading floors in Los Angeles and San Francisco, traces its roots to the San Francisco Stock and Bond Exchange formed in 1882. In 1957, the Los Angeles Oil Exchange merged with the Pacific Stock Exchange. Between 1957 and 1983, the volume of shares traded increased 30-fold, to more than 1 billion. In 1996, nearly 1,800 securities, and options on 354 underlying stocks and indexes, are traded on the PSE. By

2000, the PSE plans to relocate from its historic Art Deco building that has been its headquarters since the 1930s.

Because of the time difference between the east and west coasts, the PSE begins trading at 6:30 AM PST and stays open until 1:30 PM PST, a half hour after the New York exchanges have closed.

35PUBLIC FINANCE

The Governor's Budget is prepared by the Department of Finance (DOF) and presented by the governor to the legislature for approval. The state's fiscal year begins 1 July and ends 30 June. The Governor's Budget is the result of a process that begins more than one year before the budget becomes law. When presented to the legislature by 10 January of each year, the Governor's Budget incorporates revenue and expenditure estimates based upon the most current information available through late December.

The DOF proposes adjustments to the Governor's Budget through "Finance Letters" in March. These adjustments are to update proposals made in January or to submit any new proposal of significant importance that has arisen since the fall process.

By 14 May, the DOF submits revised expenditure and revenue estimates for both the current and budget years to the legislature. This revision incorporates changes in enrollment, caseload, and population estimates. This update process is referred to as the May Revision.

The following table summarizes 1997/98 estimated revenues and expenditures (in millions), as of the 1997/98 May Revision:

REVENUE SOURCES	GENERAL FUND	SPECIAL FUNDS
Personal income tax	$ 25,500	—
Sales tax	17,230	$1,953
Bank and corporation tax	5,920	—
Highway users tax	—	2,946
Motor vehicle fees	37	5,434
Insurance tax	1,213	—
Estate taxes	695	—
Liquor tax	262	—
Tobacco taxes	165	481
Horse racing fees	46	36
Other	892	3,202
TOTAL	$ 51,960	$ 14,052

EXPENDITURES BY FUNCTION	GENERAL FUND	SPECIAL FUNDS	BOND FUNDS
Education (K–12)	$ 22,082	$ 58	$135
Health and welfare	14,551	3,349	—
Higher education	6,589	667	549
Youth and adult corrections	4,300	10	21
Business, transportation and housing	260	4,257	1,014
Trade and commerce	98	15	—
Courts	502	—	—
Tax relief	461	—	—
Local government subventions	116	3,621	—
Resources	782	899	198
Environmental protection	150	516	90
State and consumer services	394	394	78
Other	1,407	651	1
TOTAL	$ 51,692	$ 14,437	$ 2,086

36TAXATION

In the mid-1970s, Californians were paying more in taxes than residents of any other state. On a per capita basis, California ranked 3d among the 50 states in state and local taxation in 1977, but this heavy tax burden was reduced by the passage in 1978 of Proposition 13. By 1982, California ranked 5th in per capita state and local taxes. The state ranked 12th in federal tax burden per capita in 1990. In the same year, California's revenues from state taxes and fees totaled more than $44.8 billion.

The state's progressive income tax rates as of May 1997 ranged from 1% to 9.3% on net taxable income. Low-income tax credits exempted single people with gross income of less than $10,160 and married couples with gross income less than $20,320 from paying state income taxes. Personal income tax has been indexed since 1978. The state corporate income tax on general corporations is 8.84% of net income from California sources; a minimum franchise tax of $800 is applied to all firms except banks and financial corporations, whose net income is taxed at rates 2% above the general corporation rate.

The state sales tax as of 1 January 1997 was 7.25% on retail sales (excepting food for home consumption, prescription medicines, gas, water, electricity, and certain other exempt products); of that 7.25%, 6.0% represented the basic state rate, 1.0% was designated for localities, and 0.25% was a county tax for the support of county transit systems. Other state taxation includes inheritance and gift taxes, insurance tax, motor vehicle fees, cigarette tax, alcohol beverage tax, and pari-mutuel betting fees.

Localities derive most of their revenue from property taxes, which were limited in 1978 by Proposition 13 to 1% of market value, with annual increases in the tax not to exceed 2%. The drastic revision reduced property tax collections by about 57% to an estimated $4.9 billion in the 1978/79 fiscal year. The tax rate per $100 of assessed property value for Los Angeles County fell from $12.40 in 1977/78 to $4.78 in 1978/79; for San Francisco County, from $11.82 to $5.06; and for Alameda County, from $12.59 to $5.19.

In 1995 California's share of the federal tax burden contributed $163 billion in federal taxation. But California also received more federal expenditures than any other state—$152.5 billion.

37ECONOMIC POLICY

The California Trade and Commerce Agency is the state's lead agency for promoting economic development, job creation, and business retention. Created in 1992 by Governor Pete Wilson, this cabinet-level agency consolidated the former Department of Commerce, the World Trade Commission, and the state's overseas offices. The agency oversees all state economic development efforts, international commerce, and tourism.

In fulfilling its mission to improve California's business climate, the agency works closely with domestic and international businesses, economic development corporations, chambers of commerce, regional visitor and convention bureaus, and the various permit-issuing state and municipal government agencies.

The International Trade and Investment Division is headquarters for California's international offices and the Offices of Foreign Investment, Export Finance, and Export Development. The Agency also houses the Tourism Division, and the Economic Development Division, which includes the Offices of Business Development, Small Business, Strategic Technology, Permit Assistance, Major Corporate Projects, and the California Film Commission.

California offers a broad array of state economic development incentives, including a business assistance program, including guidance through regulatory and permitting processes. California also has a statewide network of small business development centers. California has an enterprise zone program with 39 zones offering various tax credits, deductions, and exemptions. The zones focus on rural and economically distressed areas.

There are nine foreign trade zones in the state, and an Office of Foreign Investment with incentives to attract foreign companies. In addition, the state has 10 foreign offices in Asia, Europe, Mexico, Africa, and the Middle East.

In the 1990s, California lowered many of its business taxes, reduced workers' compensation premiums, offered research and development tax credits and manufacturer's investment credits, and restructured its electric utility industry. The state developed programs for the conversion of defense-related technology to new product lines, and incentives for businesses locating to former military bases.

38HEALTH

Despite California's reputation for unconventional lifestyles, the vital statistics for state residents have grown closer to national norms in recent years. In 1990, there were 7.9 marriages per 1,000 population, less than the US rate of 9.8. California's divorce rate in 1990 was 4.3 per 1000 population, slightly less than the national rate. California's abortion rate of 47 per 1,000 women 15–44 years of age was highest among the states. Its ratio of 564 abortions to 1,000 live births was also higher than any other state in 1992.

Because of its large population, California led the nation in live births in 1995 with 551,226. The California birthrate in 1995 was 17.2 per 1,000 population, higher than the national rate of 14.8. The infant death rate for the 12 months ending with 1995 was 6.3 per 1,000 live births, well below the US norm of 9.0.

California registered 222,626 deaths in 1995, including 4,623 infant deaths and 2,795 neonatal deaths. California ranked below the national death rate in 1991 for 5 of the 6 leading causes of death (the exception was suicide, which was equivalent to the US rate). Principal causes of death and their rates per 100,000 population during 1991 (and percentages of all deaths) included diseases of the heart, 68,329 (547; 31.3%); malignant neoplasms, 50,144 (165.1; 23.3%); cerebrovascular diseases, 16,239 (51.4); accidents and adverse effects, 9,253 (29.3); and suicide, 3,694 (11.7). From 1981 to 1995, California recorded 83,397 AIDS cases, second only after New York.

In 1995, 16.5% of the population 18–30 years old were smokers. The projected number of deaths attributed to smoking-related illness in 1995 was 462,896.

As of 1995, there were 70 psychiatric hospitals, including three institutions for the mentally retarded. In recent years, an increasing number of patients have been treated through community mental health programs rather than in state hospitals.

In 1995, California's accredited health-care facilities included 495 general-care hospitals, with 78,442 beds. In 1991, the state's 552 certified hospitals admitted 3,319,929 patients. In 1991, hospital personnel included 87,044 registered nurses and 14,923 licensed practical nurses. The average expense per inpatient day for a hospital in the state amounted to $1,301, and was $7,252 per hospital stay—both higher than the US average. The average hospital stay cost 16% more in California than the US average. Medical personnel licensed to practice in California in 1995 included 103,130 nonfederal physicians and 26,979 dentists in 1995. There were 254,161 active registered nurses in the state during 1995.

Medi-Cal is a statewide program that pays for the medical care of persons who otherwise could not afford it. California has also been a leader in developing new forms of health care, including the health maintenance organization (HMO), which provides preventive care, diagnosis, and treatment for which the patient pays a fixed annual premium. During 1992, there were 3,434,524 Medicare enrollees who collected an estimated $15.6 billion in benefits.

A large portion of California's population, 22.7%, remained uninsured in 1995.

39SOCIAL WELFARE

Payments in aid to families with dependent children (AFDC) went to an average of 2.6 million recipients in 1996. AFDC payments were $723 a month that year, second only to Alaska. In 1996, the food stamp program had an average monthly participation of 3.14 million, and students benefited from $694.2 million spent on the school lunch program. Federal Social Security benefits were paid in 1995 to 3,983,540 persons, averaging $735 a month.

With the enactment of the Personal Responsibility and Work Opportunity Reconciliation Act of 1996, the US government has changed the form and regulations for many of its social welfare programs; most significantly, it replaces Aid to Families with Dependent Children (AFDC), an open-ended entitlement program, with Temporary Assistance for Needy Families (TANF), a limited system of assistance funded largely through federal block grants. The reform act also impacts the food stamp program, the Supplemental Security Income program, and the child nutrition program. The law took effect on 1 July 1997 and provided $16.38 billion in block grants for fiscal years 1997–2002. The grants are to be divided among the states based on an equation involving the numbers of former AFDC recipients in each state. Because many of the bills provisions have yet to be implemented into state-by-state policy, it was not possible to include the details of each state's programs for this edition of this work.

As of 1995, 1,031,872 Californians were enrolled in federal Supplemental Security Income (SSI) and state supplemental income programs, averaging $446 a month. The weekly unemployment check averaged $153.55 in 1995.

40HOUSING

California had long led the US both in the number of housing units built annually and in the value of their construction, but by 1982 it was overtaken by Texas in both categories and by Florida in the former. However, California still ranks 1st in the number of housing units (11,727,000 in 1996). Housing construction boomed at record rates during the 1970s but slowed down at the beginning of the 1980s because rising building costs and high mortgage interest rates made it difficult for people of moderate means to enter the housing market. From 1990 to 1992, there were 206,700 housing unit completions in the greater Los Angeles area (including Anaheim and Riverside), of which 57% were one-family houses. During that same period, the Sacramento area saw 43,400 housing unit completions (79% single-family houses); the San Diego area had 38,700 new housing unit completions (51% single-family houses).

The earliest homes in southern California were Spanish colonial structures renowned for their simplicity and harmony with the landscape. These houses were one story high and rectangular in plan, with outside verandas supported by wooden posts; their thick adobe walls were covered with whitewashed mud plaster. In the north, the early homes were usually two stories high, with thick adobe walls on the ground floor, balconies at the front and back, and tile roofing. Some adobe houses dating from the 1830s still stand in coastal cities and towns, particularly Monterey.

During the 1850s, jerry-built houses of wood, brick, and stone sprang up in the mining towns, and it was not until the 1870s that more substantial homes, in the Spanish mission style, were built in large numbers in the cities. About 1900, the California bungalow, with overhanging eaves and low windows, began to sweep the state and then the nation. The fusion of Spanish adobe structures and traditional American wooden construction appeared in the 1930s, and "California style" houses gained great popularity throughout the West. Adapted from the functional international style of Frank Lloyd Wright and other innovative architects, modern domestic designs, emphasizing split-level surfaces and open interiors, won enthusiastic acceptance in California. Wright's finest California homes include the Freeman house in Los Angeles and the Millard house in Pasadena. One of Wright's disciples, Viennese-born Richard Neutra, was especially influential in adapting modern design principles to California's economy and climate.

Between 1960 and 1990, some 6.3 million houses and apartments were built in the state, comprising more than 56% of California housing stock. The total number of housing units in the state increased by 53% during 1940–50; 52%, 1950–60; 28% 1960–70; 33%, 1970–80; and 20%, 1980–90. In 1993, 84,341 housing units were authorized, of which 82% were single family units and 18% were multi-dwelling structures.

Of the state's estimated 11,727,000 housing units in 1996, nearly 10.9 million were occupied. Of 1990 year-round housing units, 99.4% had complete plumbing facilities. During the 1980s, the housing stock grew by over 20%, so that as of 1990, about 23% of all housing units in California were built in the 1980s. The median monthly cost for a mortgaged, owner-occupied housing unit in 1990, the last year for which figures are available, was $1,077; the median monthly rent for a housing unit was $620. Median monthly rents in 1990 for some of California's greater metropolitan areas include: Sacramento, $528; Riverside, $562; San Diego, $611; Los Angeles, $626; San Francisco, $709; San Jose, $773; and Anaheim, $790.

California housing policies have claimed national attention on several occasions. In 1964, state voters approved Proposition 14, a measure repealing the Fair Housing Act and forbidding any future restrictions on the individual's right to sell, lease, or rent to anyone of his own choosing. The measure was later declared unconstitutional by state and federal courts. In March 1980, a Los Angeles city ordinance banned rental discrimination on the basis of age. A municipal court judge had previously ruled it was illegal for a landlord to refuse to rent an apartment to a couple simply because they had children. Ordinances banning age discrimination had previously been enacted in the cities of San Francisco, Berkeley, and Davis, and in Santa Monica and Santa Clara counties. During 1995/96, the US Department of Housing and Urban Development awarded $2.5 billion in aid to California, including nearly $650 million in community development block grants.

41EDUCATION

California ranks 1st among the states in enrollment in public schools and in institutions of higher learning. However, in fall 1995, California had the highest public school pupil/teacher ratio (24.1%), according to the National Education Association (NEA). California's expenditure on public schools in 1995/96 was estimated at $4,977 per pupil—41st in the US based on student membership.

The history of public education in California goes back at least to the 1790s, when the governor of the Spanish colony assigned retired soldiers to open one-room schools at the Franciscan mission settlements of San Jose, Santa Barbara, San Francisco, San Diego, and Monterey. Most of these schools, and others opened during the next three decades, were short-lived, however. During the 1830s, a few more schools were established for Spanish children, including girls, who were taught needlework. Easterners and midwesterners who came to California in the 1840s laid the foundation for the state's present school system. The first American school was opened in an old stable at the Santa Clara mission in 1846, and the following year a schoolroom was established in the Monterey customhouse. San Francisco's first school was founded in April 1848 by a Yale graduate, Thomas Douglass, but six weeks later, caught up in the gold rush fever, he dropped his books and headed for the mines.

Two years after this inauspicious episode, the San Francisco city council passed an ordinance providing for the first free public school system in California. Although the first public high school was opened in San Francisco in 1856, the California legislature did not provide for state financial support of secondary schools until 1903.

The state's first colleges, Santa Clara College (now the University of Santa Clara), founded by Jesuits, and California Wesleyan (now the University of the Pacific), located in Stockton, both opened in 1851. A year later, the Young Ladies' Seminary (now Mills College) was founded at Benicia. The nucleus of what later became the University of California was established at Oakland in 1853 and moved to nearby Berkeley in 1873. Subsequent landmarks in education were the founding of the University of Southern California (USC) at Los Angeles in 1880 and of Stanford University in 1885, the opening of the first state junior colleges in 1917, and the establishment in 1927 of the Department of Education, which supervised the vast expansion of the California school system in the years following.

Almost 80% of the state's adult population 25 years old and over had completed four years of high school by 1996; in addition, about 5.3 million Californians had completed four or more years of college, representing 26.8% of the adult population. During the 1995/96 school year, California's 7,872 public schools enrolled 5,467,224 pupils. In fall 1996, enrollment was up to 5,612,965; kindergarten through grade eight had 4,053,885 pupils; and grades nine through twelve had 1,559,080 pupils. In 1995 there were 232,488 teachers and 34,055 other professionals in the public school system. In 1996, the number of public high school graduates was 259,0071; private, 26,998. In 1996/97, 4,323 private schools enrolled 615,011 pupils and had 39,728 full-time teachers. As of 1 January 1997, there were 594 Roman Catholic elementary schools with 176,133 pupils and 101 Roman Catholic high schools with 65,768 pupils. As of December 1996, 590,000 students per year participated in special education programs, at a cost of about $3.4 billion.

NEA preliminary data for California shows revenues for public schools in 1995/96 totaled $30.7 billion, of which it is estimated state aid furnished 57%, local sources 34.2%, and federal assistance 8.8%. Public school teachers were paid an average salary of $43,114 (8th highest in the nation, according to a 1995/96 NEA report).

As of fall 1992, the University of California, a state university, enrolled 165,804 students, 156,029 of them full-time. The California state college and university system—which should not be confused with the University of California—had 313,900 students (199,800 full-time). In addition, private colleges and universities that reported enrollments to the state had 165,520 students (119,933 full-time); public community colleges, 1,518,918 in 1991 (376,099 full-time); private two-year colleges, 1,354 (723 full-time); and other public institutions, 3,568 (3,546 full-time). The University of California has its main campus at Berkeley and branches at Davis, Irvine, Los Angeles (UCLA), Riverside, San Diego, San Francisco, Santa Barbara, and Santa Cruz. California's 19 state universities include those at Los Angeles, Sacramento, San Diego, San Francisco, and San Jose; state colleges are located at Bakersfield, San Bernardino, and Stanislaus.

Privately endowed institutions with the largest student enrollments are the University of Southern California (USC), with 29,657 students in 1990, and Stanford University (13,758). Other independent institutions are Occidental College in Los Angeles, Mills College at Oakland, Whittier College, Claremont University Center (including Harvey Mudd College, Pomona College, and Claremont Men's College), and the California Institute of Technology at Pasadena. California has 16 Roman

Catholic colleges and universities, including Loyola Marymount University of Los Angeles.

California's public school system is directed by the Department of Education, which is headed by the state superintendent of public instruction, elected on a nonpartisan ballot every four years. The University of California is governed separately by a board of regents which includes, ex officio, the state governor, lieutenant governor, speaker of the assembly, and superintendent of public instruction, along with the university president and the president and vice president of the alumni association. The four state officials also serve on the board of trustees which administers the state colleges and universities. The California Student Aid Commission supervises three financial assistance programs. The commission also administers the California Guaranteed Student Loan Program and the State Graduate Fellowship Program. All recipients must have been California residents for at least 12 months.

Revenues for the public schools in 1989–90 totaled $24,320,281, of which state aid furnished about 67%, local property taxes 26.5%, and federal assistance 6.6%; between 1977–78 and 1990–91, local contributions fell by 50%, and state aid increased by 68% as a result of Proposition 13. Teachers at public institutions of higher education were paid an average of $55,613 in 1990/91.

[42]ARTS

The arts have always thrived in California—at first in the Franciscan chapels with their religious paintings and church music, later in the art galleries, gas-lit theaters, and opera houses of San Francisco and Los Angeles, and today in seaside artists' colonies, regional theaters, numerous concert halls, and, not least, in the motion picture studios of Hollywood.

In the mid-19th century, many artists came from the East to paint western landscapes, and some stayed on in California. The San Francisco Institute of Arts was founded in 1874; the E. B. Crocker Art Gallery was established in Sacramento in 1884; and the Monterey-Carmel artists' colony sprang up in the early years of the 20th century. Other art colonies developed later in Los Angeles, Santa Barbara, Laguna Beach, San Diego, and La Jolla. Notable art museums and galleries include the Los Angeles County Museum of Art (founded in 1910), Huntington Library, Art Gallery and Botanical Gardens at San Marino (1919), San Francisco Museum of Modern Art (1921), Norton Simon Museum of Art at Pasadena (1924), and San Diego Museum of Art (1925).

The theater arrived in California as early as 1846 in the form of stage shows at a Monterey amusement hall. The first theater building was opened in 1849 in Sacramento by the Eagle Theater Co. Driven out of Sacramento by floods, the company soon found refuge in San Francisco; by 1853, that city had seven theaters. During the late 19th century, many famous performers, including dancer Isadora Duncan and actress Maude Adams, began their stage careers in California. Today, California theater groups with national reputations include the American Conservatory Theater of San Francisco, Berkeley Repertory Theater, Mark Taper Forum in Los Angeles, and Old Globe Theater of San Diego.

The motion picture industry did not begin in Hollywood—the first commercial films were made in New York City and New Jersey in the 1890s—but within a few decades this Los Angeles suburb had become synonymous with the new art form. California became a haven for independent producers escaping an East Coast monopoly on patents related to film making. (If patent infringements were discovered, the producer could avoid a lawsuit by crossing the border into Mexico.) In 1908, an independent producer, William Selig, completed in Los Angeles a film he had begun in Chicago, *The Count of Monte Cristo*, which is now recognized as the first commercial film produced in California. He and other moviemakers opened studios in Los Angeles, Santa Monica, Glendale, and—finally—Hollywood, where the sunshine was abundant, land was cheap, and the work force plentiful. These independent producers developed the full-length motion picture and the star system, utilizing the talents of popular actors like Mary Pickford, Douglas Fairbanks, and Charlie Chaplin again and again. In 1915, D. W. Griffith produced the classic "silent" *The Birth of a Nation*, which was both a popular and an artistic success. Motion picture theaters sprang up all over the country, and an avalanche of motion pictures was produced in Hollywood by such increasingly powerful studios as Warner Brothers, Fox, and Metro-Goldwyn-Mayer. Hollywood became the motion picture capital of the world. By 1923, film production accounted for one-fifth of the state's annual manufacturing value; in 1930, the film industry was one of the 10 largest in the US.

Hollywood flourished by using the latest technical innovations and by adapting itself to the times. Sound motion pictures achieved a breakthrough in 1927 with *The Jazz Singer*, starring Al Jolson; color films appeared within a few years; and Walt Disney originated the feature-length animated cartoon with *Snow White and the Seven Dwarfs* (1937). Whereas most industries suffered drastically from the depression of the 1930s, Hollywood prospered by providing, for the most part, escapist entertainment on a lavish scale. The 1930s saw the baroque spectacles of Busby Berkeley, the inspired lunacy of the Marx Brothers, and the romantic historical drama *Gone with the Wind* (1939). During World War II, Hollywood offered its vast audience patriotic themes and pro-Allied propaganda.

In the postwar period, the motion picture industry fell on hard times because of competition from television, but it recovered fairly quickly by selling its old films to television and producing new ones specifically for home viewing. In the 1960s, Hollywood replaced New York City as the main center for the production of television programs. Fewer motion pictures were made, and those that were produced were longer and more expensive, including such top box-office attractions as *The Sound of Music* (1965), *Star Wars* (1977), *E.T.—The Extra-Terrestrial* (1982), and *Jurassic Park* (1993). No longer are stars held under exclusive contracts, and the power of the major studios has waned as the role of independent filmmakers like Francis Ford Coppola, Steven Spielberg, and George Lucas has assumed increased importance.

Among the many composers who came to Hollywood to write film music were Irving Berlin, George Gershwin, Kurt Weill, George Antheil, Ferde Grofe, and Erich Korngold; such musical luminaries as Igor Stravinsky and Arnold Schoenberg were longtime residents of the state. Symphonic music is well established. In addition to the renowned Los Angeles Philharmonic, whose permanent conductors have included Zubin Mehta and Carlo Maria Giulini, there are the San Francisco Symphony and other professional symphonic orchestras in Oakland and San Jose. Some 180 semiprofessional or amateur orchestras have been organized in other communities. Resident opera companies perform regularly in San Francisco and San Diego. Annual musical events include the Sacramento and Monterey Jazz Festivals and summer concerts at the Hollywood Bowl.

California has also played a major role in the evolution of popular music since the 1960s. The "surf sound" of the Beach Boys dominated California pop music in the mid-1960s. By 1967, the "acid rock" of bands like the Grateful Dead, Jefferson Airplane (later Jefferson Starship), and the Doors had started to gain national recognition—and that year the heralded "summer of love" in San Francisco attracted young people from throughout the country. It was at the Monterey International Pop Festival, also in 1967, that Jimi Hendrix began his rise to stardom. During the 1970s, California was strongly identified with a group of resident singer-songwriters, including Neil Young, Joni Mitchell, Randy Newman, Jackson Browne, and Warren Zevon, who brought a new sophistication to rock lyrics. Los Angeles is a main center of the popular music industry, with numerous recording studios and branch offices of the leading record companies. Los Angeles-based Motown Industries, the largest black-owned company in the US, is a major force in popular music.

California has nurtured generations of writers, many of whom moved there from other states. In 1864, Mark Twain, a Missourian, came to California as a newspaperman. Four years later, New York-born Bret Harte published his earliest short stories, many set in mining camps, in San Francisco's *Overland Monthly*. The writer perhaps most strongly associated with California is Nobel Prize-winner John Steinbeck, a Salinas native. Hollywood's film industry has long been a magnet for writers, and San Francisco in the 1950s was the gathering place for a group, later known as the Beats (or "Beat Generation"), that included Jack Kerouac and Allen Ginsberg. The City Lights Bookshop, owned by poet Lawrence Ferlinghetti, was the site of readings by Beat poets during this period.

A California law, effective 1 January 1977, is the first in the nation to provide living artists with royalties on the profitable resale of their work.

From 1991 to 1996, aid to the arts amounted to $1,606,000. The National Endowment for the Arts gave $75,950 to artists in the state and $73,850 to the California Arts Council. The Council also used state financial resources to promote arts organizations.

In 1996, arts associations numbered 1,400 with 230 local programs for the promotion of the arts. The California Arts Council received funds for arts education programs and grants through the NEA's state and regional program.

43LIBRARIES AND MUSEUMS

As of 1994/95, California had 172 public library jurisdictions and 516 academic libraries that held a total of 121.5 million volumes. Of the public libraries, 161 were centralized libraries; 106 of the 172 public libraries had branches; and 60 of California's libraries had bookmobiles. In 1994–95, the book stock was nearly 50 million volumes.

California has three of the largest public library systems in the nation, along with some of the country's finest private collections. The Los Angeles Public Library System had 5,855,534 volumes in 1994/95; the San Francisco Public Library, 2,085,889; and the San Diego Public Library, 2,380,714.

Outstanding among academic libraries is the University of California's library at Berkeley, with its Bancroft collection of western Americana. Stanford's Hoover Institution has a notable collection of research materials on the Russian Revolution, World War I, and worldwide relief efforts thereafter. Numerous rare books, manuscripts, and documents are held in the Huntington Library in San Marino.

California has nearly 520 museums and 50 public gardens. Outstanding museums include the California Museum of Science and Industry, Los Angeles County Museum of Art, and Natural History Museum, all in Los Angeles; the San Francisco Museum of Modern Art, Fine Arts Museums of San Francisco, and Asian Art Museum of San Francisco; the San Diego Museum of Man; the California State Indian Museum in Sacramento; the Norton Simon Museum in Pasadena; and the J. Paul Getty Museum at Malibu. Among historic sites are Sutter's Mill, northeast of Sacramento, where gold was discovered in 1848, and a restoration of the Mission of San Diego de Alcala, where in 1769 the first of California's Franciscan missions was established. San Diego has an excellent zoo, and San Francisco's Strybing Arboretum and

Botanical Gardens has beautiful displays of Asian, Mediterranean, and California flora.

44COMMUNICATIONS

Mail service in California, begun in 1851 by means of mule-drawn wagons, was soon taken over by stagecoach companies. The need for speedier delivery led to the founding in April 1860 of the Pony Express, which operated between San Francisco and Missouri. On the western end, relays of couriers picked up mail in San Francisco, carried it by boat to Sacramento, and then conveyed it on horseback to St. Joseph, Mo., a hazardous journey of nearly 2,000 mi (3,200 km) within 10 days. The Pony Express functioned for only 16 months, however, before competition from the first transcontinental telegraph line (between San Francisco and New York) put it out of business; telegraph service between San Francisco and Los Angeles had begun a year earlier.

California has more telephones than any other state. In March 1993, 95.4% of the state's 11,187,000 occupied housing units had telephones.

The state's first radio broadcasting station, KQW in San Jose, began broadcasting speech and music on an experimental basis in 1912. California stations pioneered in program development with the earliest audience-participation show (1922) and the first "soap opera," *One Man's Family* (1932). When motion picture stars began doubling as radio performers in the 1930s, Hollywood emerged as a center of radio network broadcasting. Similarly, Hollywood's abundant acting talent, experienced film crews, and superior production facilities enabled it to become the principal production center for television programs from the 1950s onward.

California ranks 1st in the US in the number of commercial television stations, and 2d only to Texas in radio stations. There were 96 radio stations with a Spanish language format in the state in 1996, which represented about 20% of the nation's total. In 1996 there were 239 AM and 439 FM radio stations and 102 television stations (including 18 public stations); Los Angeles alone had 15 television stations, including 4 that broadcast in Spanish. Los Angeles is also the home of the Pacifica Foundation, which operated 6 listener-sponsored FM radio stations (2 in Berkeley, 1 in Los Angeles, and 3 outside the state). Affiliates of the Public Broadcasting System serve Los Angeles, San Francisco, and Sacramento. In 1996, 81 large systems provided cable television service; Los Angeles alone had 2,997,230 cable television households that year.

45PRESS

California's newspapers rank 1st in number and 2d in circulation among the 50 states. Los Angeles publishes one of the nation's most influential dailies, the *Los Angeles Times*, and San Francisco has long been the heart of the influential Hearst newspaper chain.

In August 1846, the state's first newspaper, the *Californian*, first published in Monterey, printed (on cigarette paper—the only paper available) the news of the US declaration of war on Mexico. The *Californian* moved to San Francisco in 1847 to compete with a new weekly, the *California Star*. When gold was discovered, both papers failed to mention the fact, and both soon went out of business as their readers headed for the hills. On the whole, however, the influx of gold seekers was good for the newspaper business. In 1848, the *Californian* and the *Star* were resurrected and merged into the *Alta Californian*, which two years later became the state's first daily newspaper; among subsequent contributors were Mark Twain and Bret Harte. Four years later there were 57 newspapers and periodicals in the state.

The oldest continuously published newspapers in California are the *Sacramento Bee* (founded in 1857), San Francisco's *Examiner* (1865) and *Chronicle* (1868), and the *Los Angeles Times* (1881). *Times* owner and editor Harrison Gray Otis quickly made his newspaper preeminent in Los Angeles—a tradition continued by his son-in-law, Henry Chandler, and by the Otis-Chandler family today. Of all California's dailies, the *Times* is the only one with a depth of international and national coverage to rival the major east coast papers. In 1887, young William Randolph Hearst took over his father's *San Francisco Daily Examiner* and introduced human interest items and sensational news stories to attract readers. The *Examiner* became the nucleus of the Hearst national newspaper chain, which later included the *News-Call Bulletin* and *Herald Examiner* in Los Angeles. The *Bulletin,* like many other newspapers in the state, ceased publication in the decades following World War II because of rising costs and increased competition for readers and advertisers.

In 1997 there were 72 morning dailies and 35 evening dailies, plus 61 Sunday newspapers. The *Los Angeles Times* is the only California paper whose daily circulation exceeds 1 million. The following table shows California's leading newspapers, with their 1997 circulations:

AREA	NAME	DAILY	SUNDAY
Fresno	*Bee* (m,S)	156,309	189,855
Long Beach–Huntington Beach	*Press-Telegram* (all day,S)	109,255	125,577
Los Angeles	*Times* (m,S)	1,021,121	1,391,076
Oakland	*Tribune* (m,S)	87,066	85,017
Orange County–Santa Ana	*Register* (all day,S)	352,173	419,401
Riverside	*Press-Enterprise* (m,S)	169,231	175,367
Sacramento	*Bee* (m,S)	282,594	352,712
San Diego	*Union Tribune* (m,S)	376,511	453,891
San Francisco	*Chronicle* (m,S)	493,942	—
	Examiner (e,S)	115,184	646,171
San Jose	*Mercury-News* (all day,S)	288,792	350,199
Woodland Hills	*Daily News* (d,S)	212,252	227,054

California has more book publishers—about 225—than any state except New York. Among the many magazines published in the state are *Architectural Digest, Bon Appetit, Motor Trend, PC World, Runner's World,* and *Sierra.*

46ORGANIZATIONS

Californians belong to thousands of nonprofit societies and organizations, many of which have their national headquarters in the state. The 1992 Census of Service Industries counted 6,694 such organizations in California, including 1,353 business associations; 3,796 civic, social, and fraternal organizations; and 1,545 other membership organizations.

National service organizations operating out of California include the National Assistance League and Braille Institute of America, both in Los Angeles, and Knights of the Round Table International, Pasadena. Cultural and educational groups headquartered in the state are the American Aviation Historical Society, Garden Grove; American Battleships Association, San Diego; and American Society of Zoologists, Thousand Oaks.

Environmental and scientific organizations include the Sierra Club, Friends of the Earth, and Save-the-Redwoods League, all with headquarters in San Francisco; Animal Protection Institute of America, Sacramento; Geothermal Resources Council, Davis; and Seismological Society of America, Berkeley.

Among entertainment-oriented organizations centered in the state are the Academy of Motion Picture Arts and Sciences and the Academy of Television Arts and Sciences, both in Beverly Hills; Directors Guild of America and Writers Guild of America (West), both in Los Angeles; Screen Actors Guild and American Society of Cinematographers, both in Hollywood; and the National Academy of Recording Arts and Sciences, Burbank. Other commercial and professional groups are the Institute of Mathematical Statistics, San Carlos; Manufacturers' Agents National Association, Irvine; National Association of Civil Service Employees, San Diego; and Pacific Area Travel Association, San Francisco.

The many national sports groups with California headquarters include the Association of Professional Ball Players of America (baseball), Garden Grove; US Hang Gliding Association, Los Angeles; National Hot Rod Association, North Hollywood; Professional Karate Association, Beverly Hills; United States Youth Soccer Association, Castro Valley; Soaring Society of America, Santa Monica; International Softball Congress, Anaheim Hills; American Surfing Association, Huntington Beach; and US Swimming Association, Fresno.

California also has Gamblers Anonymous, Los Angeles; Overeaters Anonymous, Torrance; and the National Investigations Committee on UFOs, Van Nuys.

47TOURISM, TRAVEL, AND RECREATION

California's cornucopia of scenic wonders attracts millions of state residents, out-of-state visitors, and foreign tourists each year. From 1995–96, there was a 2% decrease in the number of visitors to national recreational sites within California; there were 34,569,619 visitors to the state's 21 national parks.

While the state's mild, sunny climate and varied scenery of seacoast, mountains, and desert lure many visitors, the San Francisco and Los Angeles metropolitan areas offer the most popular tourist attractions. San Francisco's Fisherman's Wharf, Chinatown, and Ghirardelli Square are popular for shopping and dining; tourists also frequent the city's unique cable cars, splendid museums, Opera House, and Golden Gate Bridge. The Golden Gate National Recreation Area, comprising 68 sq mi (176 sq km) on both sides of the entrance to San Francisco Bay, includes Fort Point in the Presidio park, Alcatraz Island (formerly a federal prison) in the bay, the National Maritime Museum with seven historic ships, and the Muir Woods, located 17 mi (27 km) north of the city. South of the city, the rugged coastal scenery of the Monterey peninsula attracts many visitors; to the northeast, the wineries of the Sonoma and Napa valleys offer their wares for sampling and sale.

The Los Angeles area has the state's principal tourist attractions: the Disneyland amusement center at Anaheim, and Hollywood, which features visits to motion picture and television studios and sightseeing tours of film stars' homes in Beverly Hills. One of Hollywood's most popular spots is Mann's (formerly Grauman's) Chinese Theater, where the impressions of famous movie stars' hands and feet (and sometimes paws or hooves) are embedded in concrete. The New Year's Day Tournament of Roses at Pasadena is an annual tradition. Southwest of Hollywood, the Santa Monica Mountain National Recreation Area was created by Congress in 1978 as the country's largest urban park, covering 150,000 acres (61,000 hectares). The Queen Mary ocean liner, docked at Long Beach, is now a marine-oceanographic exposition center and hotel-convention complex.

The rest of the state offers numerous tourist attractions, including some of the largest and most beautiful national parks in the US. In the north are Redwood National Park and Lassen Volcanic National Park. In east-central California, situated in the Sierra Nevada, are Yosemite National Park, which drew over 4 million visitors in 1995; towering Mt. Whitney in Sequoia National Park, which had 838,060 visitors; and Lake Tahoe, on the Nevada border. About 80 mi (129 km) east of Mt. Whitney is Death Valley. Among the popular tourist destinations in southern California are the zoo and Museum of Man in San Diego's Balboa Park and the Mission San Juan Capistrano, to which, according to tradition, the swallows return each spring. The San Simeon mansion and estate of the late William Randolph Hearst are now a state historical monument.

In 1995, the state issued 3,290,014 fishing licenses and 925,780 hunting licenses.

48SPORTS

There are 19 major-league professional sports teams in California, considerably more than in any other state. Of these, five play baseball, five play basketball, and three each are in football and hockey. The baseball teams are the Los Angeles Dodgers, the San Francisco Giants, the San Diego Padres, the Oakland Athletics, and the Anaheim Angels. The Oakland Raiders, the San Francisco 49ers, and the San Diego Chargers play in the National Football League. In basketball the Los Angeles Lakers, the Los Angeles Clippers, the Golden State Warriors, and the Sacramento Kings play in the National Basketball Association. The Los Angeles Sparks and Sacramento Monarchs are in the Women's NBA. The Los Angeles Kings, the Anaheim Mighty Ducks, and the San Jose Sharks are members of the National Hockey League. The Los Angeles Galaxy and San Jose Clash play in Major League Soccer.

Since moving from Brooklyn, NY, in 1959, the Dodgers have won the National League Pennant ten times, going on to win the World Series in 1959, 1963, 1965, 1981, and 1988. The Athletics won the American League Pennant six times, going on to win the World Series in 1972, 1973, 1974, and 1980. The Giants, who moved from New York City in 1959, won the National League Pennant in 1962 and 1989, losing both World Series. The Padres won the National League Pennant in 1984 and lost the World Series. The Lakers won the NBA Championship in 1972, 1980, 1982, 1985, 1987, and 1988. The Warriors won the Championship in 1975. The Los Angeles Rams, who moved to St. Louis in 1996, played in NFL title games in 1949, 1950, 1951, 1955, 1974, 1975, 1976, 1978, and 1978. They won in 1951, and lost the Super Bowl in 1980. The Raiders won the Super Bowl three times; twice from Oakland, in 1977 and 1981, and once from Los Angeles, in 1984. The Raiders returned to Oakland in 1996. The 49ers were the 1980's most successful NFL team, winning the Super Bowl in 1982, 1985, 1989, 1990, and 1995. The Kings became the first California hockey team to make it to the Stanley Cup Finals in 1993, but they lost to the Montreal Canadiens.

Another popular professional sport is horse racing at such well-known tracks as Santa Anita and Hollywood Park. Because of the equitable climate, there is racing virtually the whole year round.

California's teams have fielded powerhouses in collegiate sports. The University of Southern California's baseball team won five consecutive national championships between 1970 and 1974. Its football team was number one in the nation in 1928, 1931, 1932, 1962, 1967, and 1972, and was a co-national champion in 1974 and 1978. USC has won the Rose Bowl 20 times, most recently in 1996. The UCLA basketball team won 10 NCAA titles, while the Bruins football team won Rose Bowls in 1966, 1976, 1983, 1984, and 1986. Additionally, Stanford has won five Rose Bowl titles, and California, two. Stanford also won the NCAA men's basketball championship in 1942, and women's championships in 1990 and 1992. Cal won the men's title in 1959. All four schools compete in the PAC-10 Conference.

49FAMOUS CALIFORNIANS

Richard Milhous Nixon (1913–94) is the only native-born Californian ever elected to the presidency. Following naval service in World War II, he was elected to the US House of Representatives in 1946, then to the US Senate in 1950. He served as vice president during the Eisenhower administration (1953–61) but failed, by a narrow margin, to be elected president as the Republican candidate in 1960. Returning to his home state, Nixon ran for the California governorship in 1962 but was defeated. The next year he moved his home and political base to New York, from which he launched his successful campaign for the presidency in 1968. As the nation's 37th president, Nixon withdrew US forces from Vietnam while intensifying the US bombing of Indochina, established diplomatic relations with China, and followed a policy of détente with the Soviet Union. In 1972, he scored a resounding reelection victory, but within a year his administration was beset by the Watergate scandal. On 9 August 1974, after the House Judiciary Committee had voted articles of impeachment, Nixon became the first president ever to resign the office.

The nation's 31st president, Herbert Hoover (b.Iowa, 1874–1964), moved to California as a young man. There he studied engineering at Stanford University and graduated with its first class (1895) before beginning the public career that culminated in his election to the presidency on the Republican ticket in 1928. Former film actor Ronald Reagan (b.Illinois, 1911) served two terms as state governor (1967–75) before becoming president in 1981. He was elected to a second presidential term in 1984.

In 1953, Earl Warren (1891–1974) became the first Californian to serve as US chief justice (1953–69). Warren, a native of Los Angeles, was elected three times to the California governorship and served in that office (1943–53) longer than any other person. Following his appointment to the US Supreme Court by President Eisenhower, Warren was instrumental in securing the unanimous decision in *Brown v. Board of Education of Topeka* (1954) that racial segregation was unconstitutional under the 14th Amendment. Other cases decided by the Warren court dealt with defendants' rights, legislative reapportionment, and First Amendment freedoms.

Before the appointment of Earl Warren, California had been represented on the Supreme Court continuously from 1863 to 1926. Stephen J. Field (b.Connecticut, 1816–99) came to California during the gold rush, practiced law, and served as chief justice of the state supreme court from 1859 to 1863. Following his appointment to the highest court by President Lincoln, Field served what was at that time the longest term in the court's history (1863–97). Joseph McKenna (b.Pennsylvania, 1843–1926) was appointed to the Supreme Court to replace Field upon his retirement. McKenna, who moved with his family to California in 1855, became US attorney general in 1897 and was then elevated by President McKinley to associate justice (1898–1925).

Californians have also held important positions in the executive branch of the federal government. Longtime California resident Victor H. Metcalf (b.New York, 1853–1936) served as Theodore Roosevelt's secretary of commerce and labor. Franklin K. Lane (b.Canada, 1864–1921) was Woodrow Wilson's secretary of the interior, and Ray Lyman Wilbur (b.Iowa, 1875–1949) occupied the same post in the Hoover administration. Californians were especially numerous in the cabinet of Richard Nixon. Los Angeles executive James D. Hodgson (b.Minnesota, 1915) was secretary of labor; former state lieutenant governor Robert H. Finch (b.Arizona, 1925) and San Francisco native Caspar W. Weinberger (b.1917) both served terms as secretary of health, education, and welfare; and Claude S. Brinegar (b.1926) was secretary of transportation. Weinberger and Brinegar stayed on at their respective posts in the Ford administration; Weinberger later served as secretary of defense under Ronald Reagan. An important figure in several national administrations, San Francisco-born John A. McCone (1902–91) was chairman of the Atomic Energy Commission (1958–60) and director of the Central Intelligence Agency (1961–65).

John Charles Frémont (b.Georgia, 1813–90) led several expeditions to the West, briefly served as civil governor of California before statehood, became one of California's first two US senators (serving only until 1851), and ran unsuccessfully as the Republican Party's first presidential candidate in 1856. Other prominent US senators from the state have included Hiram Johnson (1866–1945), who also served as governor from 1911 to 1917; William F. Knowland (1908–74); and, more recently, former college president and semanticist Samuel Ichiye Hayakawa (b.Canada, 1906–1992) and former state controller Alan Cranston (b.1914). Governors of the state since World War II include Reagan, Edmund G. "Pat" Brown (1905–96), 4th-generation Californian Edmund G. "Jerry" Brown, Jr. (b.1938), and George Deukmejian (b.New York, 1928). Other prominent state officeholders are Rose Elizabeth Bird (b.Arizona, 1936), the first woman to be appointed chief justice of the state supreme court, and Wilson Riles (b.Louisiana, 1917), superintendent of public instruction, the first black Californian elected to a state constitutional office. Prominent among mayors are Thomas Bradley (b.Texas, 1917) of Los Angeles, Pete Wilson (b.Illinois, 1933) of San Diego, Dianne Feinstein (b.1933) of San Francisco, and Janet Gray Hayes (b.Indiana, 1926) of San Jose.

Californians have won Nobel Prizes in five separate categories. Linus Pauling (b.Oregon, 1901–94), professor at the California Institute of Technology (1927–64) and at Stanford (1969–74), won the Nobel Prize for chemistry in 1954 and the Nobel Peace Prize in 1962. Other winners of the Nobel Prize in chemistry are University of California (Berkeley) professors William Francis Giauque (b.Canada, 1895–1982), in 1949; Edwin M. McMillan (1907–91) and Glenn T. Seaborg (b.Michigan, 1912), who shared the prize in 1951; and Stanford Professor Henry Taube (b.Canada, 1915), in 1983. Members of the Berkeley faculty who have won the Nobel Prize for physics include Ernest Orlando Lawrence (b.South Dakota, 1901–58), in 1939; Emilio Segré (b.Italy, 1905–89) and Owen Chamberlain (b.1920), who shared the prize in 1959; and Luis W. Alvarez (1911–88), in 1968. Stanford professor William Shockley (b.England, 1910–89) shared the physics prize with two others in 1956; William A. Fowler (b.Pennsylvania, 1911–95), professor at the California Institute of Technology, won the prize in 1983. The only native-born Californian to win the Nobel Prize for literature was novelist John Steinbeck (1902–68), in 1962. Gerald Debreu (b.France, 1921), professor at the University of California at Berkeley, won the 1983 prize for economics.

Other prominent California scientists are world-famed horticulturist Luther Burbank (b.Massachusetts, 1849–1926) and nuclear physicist Edward Teller (b.Hungary, 1908). Naturalist John Muir (b.Scotland, 1838–1914) fought for the establishment of Yosemite National Park. Influential California educators include college presidents David Starr Jordan (b.New York, 1851–1931) of Stanford, and Robert Gordon Sproul (1891–1975) and Clark Kerr (b.Pennsylvania, 1911) of the University of California.

Major figures in the California labor movement were anti-Chinese agitator Denis Kearney (b.Ireland, 1847–1907); radical organizer Thomas Mooney (b.Illinois, 1882–1942); and Harry Bridges (b.Australia, 1901–90), leader of the San Francisco general strike of 1934. The best-known contemporary labor leader in California is Cesar Chavez (b.Arizona, 1927–93).

The variety of California's economic opportunities is reflected in the diversity of its business leadership. Prominent in the development of California railroads were the men known as the Big Four: Charles Crocker (b.New York, 1822–88), Mark Hopkins (b.New York, 1813–78), Collis P. Huntington (b.Connecticut, 1821–1900), and Leland Stanford (b.New York, 1824–93). California's long-standing dominance in the aerospace industry is a product of the efforts of such native Californians as John Northrop (1895–1981) and self-taught aviator Allen Lockheed (1889–1969), along with Glenn L. Martin (b.Iowa, 1886–1955); the San Diego firm headed by Claude T. Ryan (b.Kansas, 1898–1982), built the monoplane, *Spirit of St. Louis,* flown by Charles Lindbergh across the Atlantic in 1927. Among the state's banking and financial leaders was San Jose native Amadeo Peter Giannini (1870–1949), founder of the Bank of America. Important figures in the development of California agriculture include Edwin T. Earl (1856–1919), developer of the first ventilator-refrigerator railroad car, and Mark J. Fontana (b.Italy, 1849–1922), whose California Packing Corp., under the brand name of Del Monte, became the largest seller of canned fruit in the US. Leaders of the state's world-famous wine and grape-growing industry include immigrants Ágostan Haraszthy de Mokcsa (b.Hungary, 1812?–69), Charles Krug (b.Prussia, 1830–94), and Paul Masson (b.France, 1859–1940), as well as two Modesto natives, Ernest (b.1910) and Julio (1911–93) Gallo. It was at the mill of John Sutter (b.Baden, 1803–80) that gold was discovered in 1848.

Leading figures among the state's newspaper editors and publishers were William Randolph Hearst (1863–1951), whose publishing empire began with the *San Francisco Examiner,* and Harrison Gray Otis (b.Ohio, 1837–1917), longtime owner and publisher of the *Los Angeles Times.* Pioneers of the state's electronics industry include David Packard (b.Colorado, 1912–96) and William R. Hewlett (b.Michigan, 1913); Stephen Wozniak (b.1950) and Steven Jobs (b.1955) were cofounders of Apple Computer. Other prominent business leaders include clothier Levi Strauss (b.Germany, 1830–1902), paper producer Anthony Zellerbach (b.Germany, 1832–1911), cosmetics manufacturer Max Factor (b.Poland, 1877–1938), and construction and manufacturing magnate Henry J. Kaiser (b.New York, 1882–1967).

California has been home to a great many creative artists. Native California writers include John Steinbeck, adventure writer Jack London (1876–1916), novelist and dramatist William Saroyan (1908–81), and novelist-essayist Joan Didion (b.1934). One California-born writer whose life and works were divorced from his place of birth was Robert Frost (1874–1963), a native of San Francisco. Many other writers who were residents but not natives of the state have made important contributions to literature. Included in this category are Mark Twain (Samuel Langhorne Clemens, b.Missouri, 1835–1910); local colorist Bret Harte (b.New York, 1836–1902); author-journalist Ambrose Bierce (b.Ohio, 1842–1914); novelists Frank Norris (b.Illinois, 1870–1902), Mary Austin (b.Illinois, 1868–1934), and Aldous Huxley (b.England, 1894–1963); novelist-playwright Christopher Isherwood (b.England, 1904–86); and poets Robinson Jeffers (b.Pennsylvania, 1887–1962) and Lawrence Ferlinghetti (b.New York, 1920). California has been the home of several masters of detective fiction, including Raymond Chandler (b.Illinois, 1888–1959), Dashiell Hammett (b.Connecticut, 1894–1961), Erle Stanley Gardner (b.Massachusetts, 1889–1970), creator of Perry Mason, and Ross Macdonald (1915–83). Producer-playwright David Belasco (1853–1931) was born in San Francisco.

Important composers who have lived and worked in California include natives Henry Cowell (1897–1965) and John Cage (1912–92), and immigrants Arnold Schoenberg (b.Austria, 1874–1951), Ernest Bloch (b.Switzerland, 1880–1959), and Igor Stravinsky (b.Russia, 1882–1971). Immigrant painters include landscape artists Albert Bierstadt (b.Germany, 1830–1902) and William Keith (b.Scotland, 1839–1911), as well as abstract painter Hans Hofmann (b.Germany, 1880–1966). Contemporary artists working in California include Berkeley-born Elmer Bischoff (b.1916–91), Wayne Thiebaud (b.Arizona, 1920), and Richard Diebenkorn (b.Oregon, 1922–93). San Francisco native Ansel Adams (1902–84) is the best known of a long line of California photographers that includes Edward Curtis (b.Wisconsin, 1868–1952), famed for his portraits of American Indians, and Dorothea Lange (b.New Jersey, 1895–1965), chronicler of the 1930s migration to California.

Many of the world's finest performing artists have also been Californians: Violinist Ruggiero Ricci (b.1918) was born in San Francisco, while fellow virtuosos Yehudi Menuhin (b.New York, 1916) and Isaac Stern (b.Russia, 1920) were both reared in the state. Another master violinist, Jascha Heifetz (b.Russia, 1901–84), made his home in Beverly Hills. California jazz musicians include Dave Brubeck (b.1920) and Los Angeles-reared Stan Kenton (b.Kansas, 1912–79).

Among the many popular musicians who live and record in the state are California natives David Crosby (b.1941), Randy Newman (b.1943), and Beach Boys Brian (b.1942) and Carl (b.1946) Wilson.

The list of talented and beloved film actors associated with Hollywood is enormous. Native Californians on the screen include child actress Shirley Temple (Mrs. Charles A. Black, b.1928) and such greats as Gregory Peck (b.1916) and Marilyn Monroe (Norma Jean Baker, 1926–62). Other longtime residents of the state include Douglas Fairbanks (b.Colorado, 1883–1939), Mary Pickford (Gladys Marie Smith, b.Canada, 1894–1979), Harry Lillis "Bing" Crosby (b.Washington, 1904–77), Cary Grant (Archibald Leach, b.England, 1904–86), John Wayne (Marion Michael Morrison, b.Iowa, 1907–79), Bette Davis (b.Massachusetts, 1908–89), and Clark Gable (b.Ohio, 1901–60). Other actors born in California include Clint Eastwood (b.1930), Robert Duvall (b.1931), Robert Redford (b.1937), Kevin Costner (b.1955), and Dustin Lee Hoffman (b. 1937).

Hollywood has also been the center for such pioneer film producers and directors as D. W. Griffith (David Lewelyn Wark Griffith, b.Kentucky, 1875–1948), Cecil B. DeMille (b.Massachusetts, 1881–1959), Samuel Goldwyn (b.Poland, 1882–1974), Frank Capra (b.Italy, 1897–1991), and master animator Walt Disney (b.Illinois, 1901–66).

California-born athletes have excelled in every professional sport. A representative sampling includes Baseball Hall of Famers Joe Cronin (1906–1984), Vernon "Lefty" Gomez (1908–89), and Joe DiMaggio (b.1914), along with John Donald "Don" Budge (b.1915), Richard A. "Pancho" Gonzales (b.1928), Maureen "Little Mo" Connelly (1934–69), and Billie Jean (Moffitt) King (b.1943) in tennis, Gene Littler (b.1930) in golf, Frank Gifford (b.1930) and Orenthal James "O. J." Simpson (b.1947) in football, Mark Spitz (b.1950) in swimming, and Bill Walton (b.1952) in basketball. Robert B. "Bob" Mathias (b.1930) won the gold medal in the decathlon at the 1948 and 1952 Olympic Games.

[50]BIBLIOGRAPHY

Bean, Walton, and James J. Rawls. *California: An Interpretive History*. 4th ed. New York: McGraw-Hill, 1982.

California, State of. Department of Finance. *California Statistical Abstract, 1984*. Sacramento, 1984.

Caughey, John W. *California: A Remarkable State's Life-History. 4th ed.* Englewood Cliffs, N.J.: Prentice-Hall, 1982.

Davie, Michael. *California: The Vanishing Dream*. New York: Dodd Mead, 1972.

Finson, Bruce, ed. *Discovering California*. San Francisco: California Academy of sciences, 1983.

Hart, James D. *A Companion to California*. Rev. ed. Berkeley: University of California Press, 1987.

Hesse, Georgia I. *California and the West 1985*. Robert C. Fisher, ed. New York: NAL, 1984.

Hoeber, Thomas R., and Charles Price, eds. *California Government and Politics Annual 1984–85*. Sacramento: California Journal, 1984.

Hohm, Charles F., ed. *California's Social Problems*. New York: Longman in collaboration wiith the California Sociological Association, 1997.

Hyink, Bernard L., et al. *Politics and Government in California*. 11th ed. New York: Harper & Row, 1985.

Jackson, Donald Dale. *Gold Dust*. New York Knopf, 1980.

Kahrl, William L. *Water and Power: The Conflict over Los Angeles's Water Supply in the Owens Valley*. Berkeley: University of California Press, 1982.

Lavender, David. *California: Land of New Beginnings*. New York: Harper & Row, 1972.

———. *California: A Bicentennial History*. New York: Norton, 1976.

McWilliams, Carey. *California: The Great Expectation*. Layton, Utah: Gibbs M. Smith, 1976.

Martin, Stoddard. *California Writers: Jack London, John Steinbeck, the Tough Guys*. New York: St. Martin's Press, 1984.

Miller, Crane S., and Richard S. Hysolp. *California: The Geography of Diversity*. Palo Alto, Calif.: Mayfield, 1983.

Muir, John. *Mountains of California*. New York: Penguin, 1985.

Nash, Gerald D. *The American West in the Twentieth Century*. Englewood Cliffs, N.J.: Prentice Hall, 1973.

———. *State Government and Economic Development: A History of Administrative Politics in California, 1849-1933*. Reprint. Salem, N.H.: Ayer, 1979.

Rawls, James J. *Indians of California: The Changing Image*. Norman: University of Oakland, 1984.

Robinson, W. W. *Los Angeles: From the Days of the Pueblo*. San Francisco: California Press, 1979.

Ross, Michael J. *California: Its Government and Politics*. 2d ed. Monterey, Calif.: Brooks/Cole, 1983.

Starr, Kevin. *The Dream Endures: California Enters the 1940s*. New York: Oxford University Press, 1997.

———. *Inventing the Dream: California Through the Progressive Era*. New York: Oxford University Press, 1985.

Watkins, T. H. *California: An Illustrated History*. New York: Outlet, 1983.

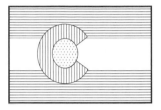

COLORADO

State of Colorado

ORIGIN OF STATE NAME: From the Spanish word *colorado*, meaning red or reddish brown. **NICKNAME:** The Centennial State. **CAPITAL:** Denver. **ENTERED UNION:** 1 August 1876 (38th). **SONG:** "Where the Columbines Grow." **MOTTO:** *Nil sine numine* (Nothing without providence). **COAT OF ARMS:** The upper portion of a heraldic shield shows three snow-capped mountains surrounded by clouds; the lower portion has a miner's pick and shovel, crossed. Above the shield are an eye of God and a Roman fasces, symbolizing the republican form of government; the state motto is below. **FLAG:** Superimposed on three equal horizontal bands of blue, white, and blue is a large red "C" encircling a golden disk. **OFFICIAL SEAL:** The coat of arms surrounded by the words "State of Colorado 1876." **ANIMAL:** Rocky Mountain bighorn sheep. **BIRD:** Lark bunting. **FLOWER:** Rocky Mountain columbine. **TREE:** Colorado blue spruce. **GEM:** Aquamarine. **FOSSIL:** Stegasaurus. **LEGAL HOLIDAYS:** New Year's Day, 1 January; Birthday of Martin Luther King, Jr., 3d Monday in January; Lincoln's Birthday, 12 February; Washington's Birthday, 3d Monday in February; Memorial Day, last Monday in May; Independence Day, 4 July; Colorado Day, 1st Monday in August; Labor Day, 1st Monday in September; Columbus Day, 2d Monday in October; Election Day, 1st Tuesday after 1st Monday in November in even-numbered years; Thanksgiving Day, 4th Thursday in November; Christmas Day, 25 December. **TIME:** 5 AM MST = noon GMT.

¹LOCATION, SIZE, AND EXTENT

Located in the Rocky Mountain region of the US, Colorado ranks 8th in size among the 50 states.

The state's total area is 104,091 sq mi (269,596 sq km), of which 103,595 sq mi (268,311 sq km) consists of land and 496 sq mi (1,285 sq km) comprise inland water. Shaped in an almost perfect rectangle, Colorado extends 387 mi (623 km) E–W and 276 mi (444 km) N–S.

Colorado is bordered on the N by Wyoming and Nebraska; on the E by Nebraska and Kansas; on the S by Oklahoma and New Mexico; and on the W by Utah (with the New Mexico and Utah borders meeting at Four Corners). The total length of Colorado's boundaries is 1,307 mi (2,103 km). The state's geographic center lies in Park County, 30 mi (48 km) NW of Pikes Peak.

²TOPOGRAPHY

With a mean average elevation of 6,800 feet (2,100 meters), Colorado is the nation's highest state. Dominating the state are the Rocky Mountains. Colorado has 54 peaks 14,000 feet (4,300 meters) or higher, including Elbert, the highest in the Rockies at 14,433 feet (4,399 meters), and Pikes Peak, at 14,110 feet (4,301 meters), one of the state's leading tourist attractions.

The entire eastern third of the state is part of the western Great Plains, a high plateau that rises gradually to the foothills of the Rockies. Colorado's lowest point, 3,350 feet (1,021 meters), on the Arkansas River, is located in this plateau region. Running in a ragged north-south line, slightly west of the state's geographic center, is the Continental Divide, which separates the Rockies into the Eastern and Western slopes. The Eastern Slope Front (Rampart) Range runs south from the Wyoming border and just west of Colorado Springs. Also on the Eastern Slope are the Park, Mosquito, Medicine Bow, and Laramie mountains. Western Slope ranges include the Sawatch, Gore, Elk, Elkhead, and William Fork mountains. South of the Front Range, crossing into New Mexico, is the Sangre de Cristo Range, separated from the San Juan Mountains to its west by the broad San Luis Valley. Several glaciers, including Arapahoe, St. Mary's, Andrews, and Taylor,

are located on peaks at or near the Continental Divide. Colorado's western region is mostly mesa country—broad, flat plateaus accented by deep ravines and gorges, with many subterranean caves. Running northwest from the San Juans are the Uncompahgre Plateau, Grand Mesa, Roan Plateau, the Flat Tops, and Danforth Hills. The Yampa and Green gorges are located in the northwestern corner of the state.

Blue Mesa Reservoir in Gunnison County is Colorado's largest lake. Six major river systems originate in Colorado: the Colorado River, which runs southwest from the Rockies to Utah; the South Platte, northeast to Nebraska; the North Platte, north to Wyoming; the Rio Grande, south to New Mexico; and the Arkansas and Republican, east to Kansas. Dams on these rivers provide irrigation for the state's farmland and water supplies for cities and towns. Eighteen hot springs are still active in Colorado; the largest is at Pagosa Springs.

³CLIMATE

Abundant sunshine and low humidity typify Colorado's highland continental climate. Winters are generally cold and snowy, especially in the higher elevations of the Rocky Mountains. Summers are characterized by warm, dry days and cool nights.

The average annual temperature statewide ranges from 54°F (12°C) at Lamar and at John Martin Dam to about 32°F (0°C) at the top of the Continental Divide; differences in elevation account for significant local variations on any given day. Denver's annual average is 50°F (10°C); normal temperatures range from 16° to 43°F (−9 to 6°C) in January and from 59° to 88°F (15 to 31°C) in July. Bennett recorded the highest temperature in Colorado, 118°F (48°C), on 11 July 1888; the record low was −61°F (−52°C), in Moffat County on 1 February 1985.

Annual precipitation ranges from a low of 7 in (18 cm) in Alamosa to a high of 25 in (64 cm) in Crested Butte, with Denver receiving about 15 in (38 cm). Denver's snowfall averages 59 in (150 cm) yearly. The average snowfall at Cubres in the southern mountains is nearly 300 in (762 cm); less than 30 mi (48 km) away at Manassa, snowfall is less than 25 in (64 cm). On 14–15

April 1921, Silver Lake had 76 in (193 cm) of snowfall, the highest amount ever recorded in North America during a 24-hour period. Colorado had 48 tornadoes in 1995.

4FLORA AND FAUNA

Colorado's great range in elevation and temperature contributes to a variety of vegetation, distributed among five zones: plains, foothills, montane, subalpine, and alpine. The plains teem with grasses and as many as 500 types of wildflowers. Arid regions contain two dozen varieties of cacti. Foothills are matted with berry shrubs, lichens, lilies, and orchids, while fragile wild flowers, shrubs, and conifers thrive in the montane zone. Aspen and Engelmann spruce are found up to the timberline.

In 1983, Colorado counted 747 nongame wildlife species and 113 sport-game species. Principal big-game species are the elk, mountain lion, Rocky Mountain bighorn sheep (the state animal), antelope, black bear, and white-tailed and mule deers; the mountain goat and the moose—introduced in 1948 and 1975, respectively—are the only nonnative big-game quarry. The lark bunting is the state bird; blue grouse and mourning doves are numerous, and 28 duck species have been sighted. Colorado has about 100 sport-fish species. Scores of lakes and rivers contain bullhead, kokanee salmon, and a diversity of trout. Rare Colorado fauna include the golden trout, white pelican, and wood frog. The lesser prairie chicken and razorback sucker are listed among threatened species. The greater prairie chicken, Canada lynx, wolverine, river otter, and bonytail are among endangered species.

5ENVIRONMENTAL PROTECTION

The Department of Natural Resources and the Department of Health share responsibility of state environmental programs. The first efforts to protect Colorado's natural resources were the result of federal initiatives. On 16 October 1891, US President Benjamin Harrison set aside the White River Plateau as the first forest reserve in the state. Eleven years later, President Theodore Roosevelt incorporated six areas in the Rockies as national forests. By 1906, 11 national forests covering about one-fourth of the state had been created. Mesa Verde National Park, founded in 1906, and Rocky Mountain National Park (1915) were placed under the direct control of the National Park Service. In 1978, Colorado became the first state in the US to encourage taxpayers to allocate part of their state income tax refunds to wildlife conservation. In addition, a state lottery was approved in the late 1980s, with proceeds approved for Great Outdoors Colorado (GOCO) to be used for parks improvement and wildlife and resource management.

Air pollution, water supply problems, and hazardous wastes head the list of Colorado's current environmental concerns. The Air Quality Control Commission, within the Department of Health, has primary responsibility for air pollution control. Because of high levels of carbon monoxide, nitrogen dioxide, and particulates in metropolitan Denver, Colorado Springs, Pueblo, and other cities, a motor vehicle emissions inspection system was inaugurated in January 1982 for gasoline-powered vehicles and in January 1985 for diesel-powered vehicles. The high altitudes of Colorado almost double auto emissions compared to auto emissions at sea level. The high level of particulates in the air is because of frequent temperature inversions along Colorado's Front Range. The state has launched an aggressive campaign to improve air quality. Cars must use oxygenated fuels, and pass tough vehicle emissions controls, and driving is discouraged on high pollution days.

Formal efforts to ensure the state's water supply date from the Newlands Reclamation Act of 1902, a federal program designed to promote irrigation projects in the semiarid plains areas; its first effort, the Uncompahgre Valley Project, reclaimed 146,000 acres (59,000 hectares) in Montrose and Delta counties. One of the largest undertakings, the Colorado–Big Thompson Project, started in the 1930s, diverts a huge amount of water from the Western to the Eastern Slope. Colorado's efforts to obtain water rights to the Vermejo River in the Rockies were halted in 1984 by the US Supreme Court, which ruled that New Mexico would retain these rights. Some 98% of Colorado's drinking water complies with federal and state standards. Federal standards for local water supply have stiffened in recent years. The Colorado Department of Health works with local officials to ensure federal standards for drinking water are met. Isolated aquifers are generally in good condition in Colorado, though a few are contaminated. Colorado's ground water quality is generally high.

Colorado's rapid population growth during the 1970s and early 1980s taxed an already low water table, especially in the Denver metropolitan area. The Department of Natural Resources' Water Conservation Board and Division of Water Resources are responsible for addressing this and other water-related problems.

The Department of Health has primary responsibility for hazardous waste management. In the spring of 1984, the department, along with federal agencies, began cleaning up nearly 7,000 contaminated sites in Grand Junction and other parts of Mesa County; these sites—homes and properties—were contaminated during the 1950s and 1960s by radioactive mill tailings that had been used as building material and that were not considered hazardous at the time. (It is now known that the low-level radiation emitted by the mill tailings can cause cancer and genetic damage.) In the fall of 1984, Aspen was placed on the federal Environmental Protection Agency's list of dangerous waste sites because potentially hazardous levels of cadmium, lead, and zinc were found in Aspen's streets, buildings, and water. Cadmium, lead, and zinc mill tailings had been used as filling material during the construction of the popular resort. Also in the mid-1980s, Rocky Flats, a former plutonium production site near Golden, was closed and a major cleanup was begun. The site was the focus of many protests during the 1970s, and has been a major newsmaker since the start of the cleanup. In 1995 the state had 18 hazardous waste sites; 1.5% of the state's land is covered with wetlands, a 50% decrease over the last two centuries.

6POPULATION

Colorado rose from 30th in population in 1970 to 28th in 1980, and 26th in 1990, with a 14% increase in population during the 1980s. The 1990 census population was 3,294,394; the 1996 estimate, 3,822,676, an increase of 16% over 1990. In 1990, 81.5% lived in metropolitan areas. The population density in 1990 was 31 per sq mi (12 per sq km). The estimated median age in 1990 was 32.2 years; nearly 24% of the population was under 16 years of age, and less than 10% was over 65. The 2000 population is projected to be 3,424,000.

Denver is the state's largest city and was, in 1990, the 26th largest US city. Its 1994 population was 493,559, but its metropolitan area (including Boulder and Greeley) encompassed 2,233,172 or more than half the state's population. Other major cities, with their estimated 1994 population figures, are Colorado Springs, 316,480; Aurora, 250,717; Lakewood, 126,031; and Pueblo, 100,471.

7ETHNIC GROUPS

Once the sole inhabitants of the state, American Indians in 1990 numbered 28,000, including 303 Eskimos and 67 Aleuts. The black population is also small, 4% in 1990; the figure for Denver, however, was 12.8%. Of far greater importance to the state's history, culture, and economy are its Hispanic residents, of whom there were 424,000 in 1990, comprising nearly 13% of the population. Among residents of Denver, 23% were Hispanics. Of

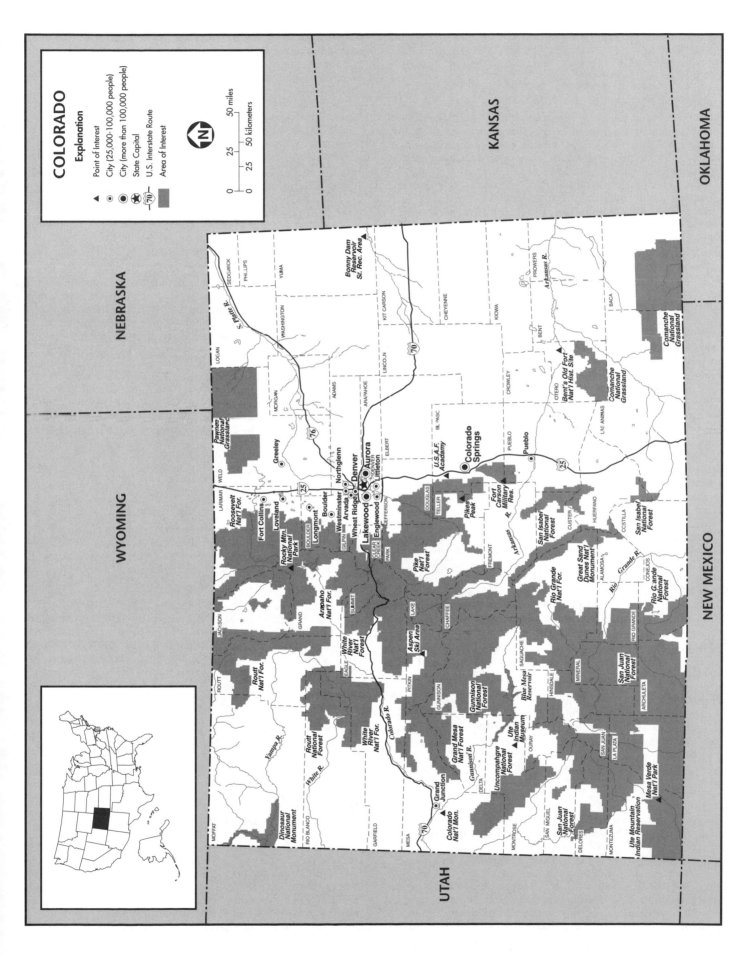

COLORADO

over 60,000 Asians and Pacific Islanders, 15,198 were Japanese, 12,490 Korean, 6,679 Vietnamese, 9,117 Chinese, and 7,270 Filipino. In all 142,434 persons, or 4.3% of the state population, were foreign-born in 1990.

8LANGUAGES

The first whites to visit Colorado found Arapaho, Kiowa, Comanche, and Cheyenne Indians roaming the plains and often fighting the Ute in the mountains. Despite this diverse heritage, Indian place-names are not numerous: Pagosa Springs, Uncompahgre, Kiowa, and Arapahoe.

Colorado English is a mixture of the Northern and Midland dialects, in proportions varying according to settlement patterns. Homesteading New Englanders in the northeast spread *sick to the stomach, pail,* and *comforter* (tied and filled bedcover), which in the northwest and the southern half are Midland *sick at the stomach, bucket,* and *comfort.* South Midland *butter beans* and *snap beans* appear in the eastern agricultural strip. Denver has *slat fence,* and *Heinz dog* (mongrel). In the southern half of the state, the large Spanish population has bred many loanwords such as *arroyo* (small canyon or gulley) and *penco* (pet lamb).

In 1990, 2,722,355 Coloradans—89.5% of the residents five years old and older—spoke only English at home. Other languages spoken at home, and the number of speakers, included Spanish, 203,896; German, 30,460; French, 12,855; and Korean, 8,306.

9RELIGIONS

The Spanish explorers who laid claim to (but did not settle in) Colorado were Roman Catholic, but the first American settlers were mostly Methodists, Lutherans, and Episcopalians. Some evangelical groups sought to proselytize the early mining camps during the mid-19th century.

Roman Catholics comprise the single largest religious group in the state, with 482,892 in 1990. The largest Protestant denomination in 1990 was the United Methodist Church, with 91,310 adherents. Other major denominations included Southern Baptist, 81,627; United Presbyterian, 50,831; Church of Jesus Christ of Latter-day Saints, 70,313; Lutheran Church–Missouri Synod, 47,262; and Episcopal, 36,119. The World Evangelical Fellowship and the Focus on the Family are both headquartered in Colorado Springs.

According to the 1990 estimates there were 48,550 Jews in Colorado, nearly all of them in the Denver area.

10TRANSPORTATION

As the hub of the Rocky Mountain states, Colorado maintains extensive road and rail systems.

Because of its difficult mountain terrain, Colorado was bypassed by the first transcontinental railroads. In 1870, however, the Denver Pacific built a line from Denver to the Union Pacific's cross-country route at Cheyenne, Wyoming. Several intrastate lines were built during the 1870s, connecting Denver with the mining towns. In particular, the Denver and Rio Grande built many narrow-gauge lines through the mountains. Denver finally became part of a main transcontinental line in 1934. As of 1995 there were 3,088 rail mi (4,968 km) of track in the state, utilized by 12 railroads. This included two Class I railroads (which by definition carry more than $250 million a year in freight revenue). AMTRAK trains in Colorado had a ridership of 247,071 persons in 1995.

Colorado has an extensive network of roads, including 29 mountain passes. As of 1996 there were 84,195 mi of roadway in Colorado: 9,137 on the state highway system, 57,310 on the county system, 11,065 in communities, 6,282 mi administered by the US Forest Service, and 401 mi under the jurisdiction of the Bureau of Indian Affairs. The major state roads are Interstate 70,

US 40, and US 50 crossing the state from east to west, and Interstate 25 running north–south along the Front Range of the Rocky Mountains between Raton Pass and Cheyenne, Wyoming. Interstate 76 connects Denver on a northeasterly diagonal with Nebraska's I-80 to Omaha.

Of the 2,680,000 motor vehicles registered in 1995, 1,646,000 were automobiles and 1,034,000 were trucks or buses. There were 2,764,000 licensed drivers that year.

A total of 79 public-use airfields served the state in 1996. Denver International Airport (DIA) replaced the former Stapleton International Airport in 1994 as the state's largest and busiest. In 1996, DIA handled 16,177,987 departing passengers (32,296,174 total) and 288,076 tons of cargo.

11HISTORY

A hunting people lived in eastern Colorado at least 20,000 years ago, but little is known about them. The Basket Makers, who came to southwestern Colorado after 100 BC, grew corn and squash and lived in pit houses. By AD 800 there were Pueblo tribes who practiced advanced forms of agriculture and pottery making. From the 11th through the 13th centuries (when they migrated southward), the Pueblo Indians constructed elaborate apartment-like dwellings in the cliffs of the Colorado canyons and planted their crops both on the mesa tops and in the surrounding valleys.

In the 1500s, when Spanish conquistadors arrived in the Southwest, northeastern Colorado was dominated by the Cheyenne and Arapaho, allied against the Comanche and Kiowa to the south. These plains-dwellers also warred with the mountain-dwelling Ute Indians, who were divided into the Capote, Moache, and Wiminuche in the southwest; the Yampa, Grand River, and Uintah in the northwest; and the Tabeguache and Uncompahgre along the Gunnison River.

The exact date of the first Spanish entry into the region now called Colorado is undetermined; the explorer Juan de Onate is believed to have traveled into the southeastern area in 1601. More than a century later, in 1706, Juan de Uribarri claimed southeastern Colorado for Spain, joining it with New Mexico. Meanwhile, French traders did little to stake out their claim to the Colorado region, which included most of the area east of the Rocky Mountains. In 1763, France formally ceded the Louisiana Territory to Spain, which returned it to the French in 1801. Two years later, as part of the Louisiana Purchase, Colorado east of the Rockies became US land; the rest of Colorado still belonged to Spain.

Formal boundaries had never been demarcated between the lands of French Louisiana and Spanish New Mexico. In 1806, the US government sent out a group led by Lt. Zebulon M. Pike to explore this southwestern border. Pike's group reached Pueblo on 23 November 1806 and then attempted without success to scale the peak that now bears his name. Not until 1819 did the US and Spain agree to establish the boundary along the Arkansas River and then northward along the Continental Divide. The following year, Maj. Stephen Long explored this new border, and Dr. Edwin James made the first known ascent of Pikes Peak.

Eastern Colorado remained a wilderness for the next few decades, although traders and scouts like Charles and William Bent, Kit Carson, and Jim Bridger did venture into the largely uncharted and inhospitable land, establishing friendly relations with the Indians. It was in 1840 at Bent's Fort, the area's major trading center, that the four major eastern tribes ended their warfare and struck an alliance, a bond that lasted through their later struggle against the white settlers and US government. Between 1842 and 1853, John C. Frémont led five expeditions into the region, the first three for the US government. In 1842, he traveled along the South Platte River; on the next two trips, he crossed the Rockies. In his fourth expedition, he and a few of his party barely survived severe winter conditions. Finally, in 1853, Frémont led an expedition over a route traveled by Capt. John Gunnison earlier that year through the San Luis Valley over Cochetopa Pass and along the Gunnison River. The 1853 trips were made five years after western and southern Colorado had come into US possession through the Mexican War.

The magnet that drew many Americans to Colorado was the greatly exaggerated report of a gold strike in Cherry Creek (present-day Denver) in July 1858. Within a year, thousands of prospectors had crossed the plains to seek their fortune. Many were disappointed and headed back east, but those who stayed benefited from a second strike at North Clear Creek, some 40 mi (64 km) to the west. The subsequent boom led to the founding of such mining towns as Central City, Tarryall, Golden, Blackhawk, Boulder, Nevadaville, Colorado City, and Gold Hill. By 1860, the population exceeded 30,000. A bill to organize a territory called Colorado, along the lines of the state's present-day boundaries, was passed by the US Congress on 28 February 1861. Colorado City, Golden, and Denver served at various times as the territorial capital until 1867, when Denver was selected as the permanent site. Colorado sided with the Union during the Civil War, though some settlers fought for the Confederacy. Union troops from Colorado helped defeat a contingent led by Confederate Gen. Henry H. Sibley at La Glorieta Pass in New Mexico in 1862.

The 1860s also saw the most serious conflict between Indians and white settlers in Colorado history. Cheyenne and Arapaho chiefs had ceded most of their tribal holdings to the US government in 1861. Sent to a reservation in the Arkansas Valley, these nomadic tribes were expected to farm the land. Unsuccessful at farming, the Indians rebelled against the poor rations supplied them by the US government, and sought to resume a nomadic life-style, hunting buffalo, raiding towns, and attacking travelers along the Overland and Sante Fe trails. Col. John Chivington was placed in charge of controlling the Indian unrest in the summer of 1864, as Territorial Governor John Evans departed for Washington, DC, leaving the situation in the hands of the military. On 29 November of that year, Chivington led his forces to Sand Creek, on the reservation's northeastern border, where they brutally massacred perhaps 200 Indian men, women, and children who thought they were under the protection of US military forces at nearby Ft. Lyon. Five more years of warfare followed, with the Indians finally defeated at Beecher Island (1868) and Summit Spring (1869). By 1874, most Plains Indians were removed to reservations in what is now Oklahoma. After gold and silver were discovered in areas belonging to the Ute in 1873, they too were forced off the land. By 1880, a series of treaties limited the Ute to a small reservation in the barren mesa country.

The first bill to admit Colorado to statehood was vetoed in 1866 by President Andrew Johnson, who at that time was in the midst of an impeachment fight and feared the entry of two more Republicans into the US Senate. Colorado finally entered the Union as the 38th state on 1 August 1876 less than a month after the nation's 100th birthday during the presidency of Ulysses S. Grant.

In the early years of statehood, silver strikes at Leadville and Aspen brought settlers and money into Colorado. Rail lines, smelters, and refineries were built, and large coalfields were opened up. The High Plains attracted new farmers, and another new industry, tourism, emerged. As early as the 1860s, resorts had opened near some of the state's mineral springs. By the mid-1870s, scenic canyons and towns became accessible by train. One of the first major spas, Colorado Springs, recorded 25,000 tourists in 1878, and by the mid-1880s, Denver was accommodating up to 200,000 visitors a year. Colorado's boom years ended with a depression during the early 1890s. Overproduction of silver coupled with the US government's decision to adopt a gold standard in 1893 wiped out the silver market, causing the closing of mines, banks, and some businesses. Coinciding with this economic disaster was a drought that led to the abandonment of many farms. A more positive development was a gold find at Cripple Creek in 1891.

By the dawn of the 20th century, farmers were returning to the land and making better use of it. Immigrants from Germany and Russia began to grow sugar beets in the Colorado, Arkansas, and South Platte river valleys. Huge reclamation projects brought water to semiarid cropland, and dry-land farming techniques also helped increase yields. The development of the automobile and good roads opened up more of the mountain areas, bringing a big boom in tourism by the 1920s.

Following World War I, the agricultural and mining sectors fell into depression. From 1920 to 1940, statewide employment declined, and the population growth rate lagged behind that of the US as a whole. World War II (1939–45) brought military training camps, airfields, and jobs to the state. Colorado also became the site of several major POW camps as well as relocation centers for Japanese Americans (Nisei), especially the northeastern and southeastern areas of the state. After the war, the expansion of federal facilities in Colorado led to new employment opportunities. The placement of both the North American Air Defense Command and the US Air Force Academy in Colorado Springs helped stimulate the growth of defense, federal research, and aerospace-related industries in the state. As these and other industries grew, so too did Colorado's population and income: between 1960 and 1983, the state's population growth rate was more than twice that of the nation as a whole; and between 1970 and 1983, Colorado moved from 18th to 9th rank among the states in personal income per capita. It was expected that the construction of the Air Force's $1.2 billion Space Operations Center at Colorado Springs, announced in 1983, would accelerate Colorado's economic and population growth.

In the 1970s and early 1980s, Colorado experienced a boom in its oil, mining and electronics industries. Its prosperity attracted immigrants from other states, and for about a decade Colorado's population increased at an average of 3% a year. The economy began to shrink, however, in the mid-1980s with the drop in oil prices and the closing of mines. Business starts declined by 23% between 1987 and 1988. However, Colorado's economy rebounded in the late 1980s and early 1990s. Major challenges facing Colorado in the mid-1990s included industrial pollution of its air and water, overcrowding on the eastern slope of the Rockies (home to four-fifths of its population), water shortages, and job losses caused by cutbacks in defense spending.

12STATE GOVERNMENT

Colorado's state constitution, ratified on 1 July 1876, is a complex and extremely detailed document specifying the duties and structure of state and local government. Despite numerous amendments and revisions, some anachronistic legislation—people who have been caught dueling, for example, may not hold office—still remains on the books.

The general assembly, which meets annually from early January to mid-May, consists of a 35-member senate and 65-member house of representatives. There is no constitutional limit to the length of a session, and the legislature may call special sessions by request of two-thirds of the members of each house. The governor may also call a special session of the legislature. Members of the legislature must be US citizens, at least 25 years old, and have been Colorado residents for at least one year. The legislative salary in 1995 was $17,500.

The executive branch is headed by the governor, who submits the budget and legislative programs to the general assembly, and appoints judges, department heads, boards, and commissions.

The governor must be a US citizen, at least 30 years old, and have been a resident of the state for two years or more. Elected with the governor is the lieutenant governor, who assumes the governor's duties in the governor's absence. Other elective officers include the secretary of state, attorney general, and state treasurer, all of whom serve four-year terms. In 1996 the governor's salary was $70,000.

Bills may originate in either house of the general assembly and become law when passed by majority vote of each house and signed by the governor; a bill may also become law if the governor fails to act on it within 10 days after receiving it. A two-thirds vote in each house is needed to override a gubernatorial veto.

The state constitution may be amended in several ways. An amendment may be introduced in the legislature, passed by a two-thirds majority in both houses, and submitted to the voters for approval. Alternatively, an initiative amendment, signed by a number of eligible voters equaling at least 5% of the number of votes cast for secretary of state in the previous election and then published in every county, may be filed no later than four months before the general election. If approved by the voters, it then becomes law.

Any US citizen 18 or older who is a resident of a Colorado county 32 days prior to an election may register to vote.

13POLITICAL PARTIES

The Democratic and Republican parties are the major political organizations in Colorado. Although both parties were in existence when Colorado achieved statehood, the Republicans controlled most statewide offices prior to 1900. Since then, the parties have been more evenly balanced. Of the 2,003,379 registered voters in 1994, 680,777, or 34% were Democrats; 668,051, or 33% were Republicans; and 654,551, or 33% were unaffiliated. Following the election in November 1996, the state had two Republican US senators, and four Republican and two Democratic US representatives. In 1997 the Republicans controlled the state senate (20 Republicans to 15 Democrats) and the state house (41 Republicans to 24 Democrats). Colorado's governor, Democrat Roy Romer, was elected to a four-year term

in 1990 and was reelected in 1994. In 1996, 46% of all Coloradan voters cast their ballots for Republican Bob Dole; Democrat Bill Clinton won 44% of the vote; Independent Ross Perot received 7% of the vote. Republican Ben Nighthorse Campbell, a Native American, was elected Senator in 1992, and fellow Republican Wayne Allard was elected to the Senate in 1996. In 1993, Colorado had 20 black elected officials, and 201 Hispanic American elected officials in 1994. In 1995 there were 34 women serving in the state legislature and in elective executive office.

14LOCAL GOVERNMENT

As of 1992 there were 62 counties, 266 municipal governments, cities, towns, and designated places, 180 school districts, and 1,252 special districts. The administrative and policymaking body in each county is the board of county commissioners, whose three to five members (dependent on population) are elected to staggered four-year terms. Other county officials include the county clerk, treasurer, assessor, sheriff, coroner, superintendent of schools, surveyor, and attorney.

Statutory cities are those whose structure is defined by the state constitution. Power is delegated by the general assembly to either a council-manager or mayor-council form of government. Colorado municipalities have increasingly opted for home rule, taking control of local functions from the state government. Towns, which generally have fewer than 2,000 residents, are governed by a mayor and a six-member board of trustees. The major source of revenue for both cities and towns is the property tax.

Denver, the only city in Colorado that is also a county, exercises the powers of both levels of government. It is run by a mayor and city council; a city auditor, independently elected, serves as a check on the mayor.

15STATE SERVICES

The Department of Education, under the direction of the State Board of Education, supervises and makes policy decisions for all public elementary and secondary schools. The State Board is made up of seven elected representatives from the state's congres-

Colorado Presidential Vote by Political Parties, 1948–96

YEAR	ELECTORAL VOTE	COLORADO WINNER	DEMOCRAT	REPUBLICAN	PROGRESSIVE	SOCIALIST	SOC. LABOR
1948	6	*Truman (D)	267,288	239,714	6,115	1,678	—
						CONSTITUTION	
1952	6	*Eisenhower (R)	245,504	379,782	1,919	2,181	—
1956	6	*Eisenhower (R)	263,997	394,479	—	759	3,308
						SOC. WORKERS	
1960	6	Nixon (R)	330,629	402,242	—	563	2,803
1964	6	*Johnson (D)	476,024	296,767		2,537	—
					AMERICAN IND.		
1968	6	*Nixon (R)	335,174	409,345	60,813	235	3,016
					AMERICAN		
1972	7	*Nixon (R)	329,980	597,189	17,269	666	4,361
							LIBERTARIAN
1976	7	Ford (R)	460,801	584,278	397	1,122	5,338
					STATESMAN	CITIZENS	
1980	7	*Reagan (R)	368,009	652,264	1,180	5,614	25,744
1984	8	Reagan (R)	454,975	821,817	NEW ALLIANCE	—	11,257
1988	8	*Bush (R)	621,453	728,177	2,491	—	15,482
					IND. (PEROT)		
1992	8	*Clinton (D)	629,681	562,850	366,010	1,608	8,669
						GREEN (NADER)	
1996	8	Dole (R)	671,152	691,848	99,629	25,070	12,392

* Won US presidential election.

sional districts, plus the Commissioner of Education, who is hired by the State Board. The Board of Regents of the University of Colorado governs the operations of that institution as well as its affiliates, the Colorado University Hospital, Children's Diagnostic Center, Psychiatric Hospital, and schools of medicine, nursing, and dentistry. All other state-run colleges, as well as the Colorado Historical Society, Council on the Arts and Humanities, and Advanced Technology Institute, are under the jurisdiction of the Department of Higher Education.

The Department of Highways builds, operates, and maintains state roads. The Department of Social Services administers welfare, medical assistance, rehabilitation, and senior-citizens programs. Human resource planning and development are under the Department of Labor and Employment, and health conditions are monitored by the Department of Health. The Department of Institutions oversees mental health, youth services, and developmental disabilities programs. The state's correctional facilities are administered by the Department of Corrections.

All programs concerned with the protection and control of Colorado's natural resources are the responsibility of the Department of Natural Resources. Other state agencies include the Department of Agriculture, Department of Military Affairs, Department of Regulatory Agencies, Department of Public Safety, and Department of Law.

[16]JUDICIAL SYSTEM

The supreme court, the highest court in Colorado, consists of 7 justices elected on a nonpartisan ballot. The number of justices may be increased to 9 upon request of the court and concurrence of two-thirds of the members of the General Assembly. The justices select a chief justice, who also serves as the supervisor of all Colorado courts. The next highest court, the court of appeals, consists of 10 judges, and is confined to civil matters. The 22 district courts have original jurisdiction in civil, criminal, juvenile, mental health, domestic relations, and probate cases, except in Denver, where probate and mental health matters are heard by the probate court and all juvenile matters by the juvenile court.

All judges in state courts are appointed to 2-year terms by the governor from a list of names recommended by a judicial nominating commission. The appointees must then be elected by the voters: supreme court justices for 10-year terms, appeals court judges for 8 years, and district court judges for 6. Colorado had 15,383 practicing attorneys in 1996.

County courts hear minor civil disputes and misdemeanors. Appeals from the Denver county courts are heard in Denver's superior court. Municipal courts throughout the state handle violations of municipal ordinances. Colorado's FBI Crime Index crime rate in 1995 was 5,396.3 per 100,000 people; the violent crime rate was 440.2, below the US average of 684.6; the property crime rate was 4,956.1, above the US average of 4,593. Denver's metropolitan area crime rate was 5,591.3 per 100,000: the violent crime rate was 513.4, the property crime rate 5,077.9.

In 1995 there were 8,117 prisoners held in 20 state and federal facilities, an incarceration rate of 217 per 100,000 inhabitants. Colorado has a death penalty and has executed 47 persons since 1930. The last execution in the state was in the early 1960s. One death row inmate was scheduled to be executed in October 1997, and 5 other persons were under sentence of death in 1997.

[17]ARMED FORCES

As of 1996, 67,570 personnel, of whom 12,451 were civilians, were stationed at the nine military facilities in the state. The largest Army base is Ft. Carson in Colorado Springs, headquarters of the 4th Infantry Division, with 16,053 personnel. At the Army's Rocky Mountain Arsenal near Denver chemical weapons have been produced and stored. Colorado Springs is the

site of the US Air Force Academy. Peterson Air Force Base is also located in Colorado Springs, as is the North American Air Defense Command (NORAD). Defense contracts awarded in 1995/96 totaled nearly $2.04 billion.

About 379,000 veterans lived in Colorado as of 1 July 1996. Of those who served in wartime, less than 500 were veterans of World War I, 85,000 of World War II, 64,000 of the Korean conflict, 145,000 of the Vietnam era, and 23,000 of the Persian Gulf War. Veterans benefits paid in the state in 1995/96 were $685 million.

As of September 1992, 11,880 Coloradans served in the state's Army Reserve or National Guard; 8,312 served in the Air National Guard or Reserve at that time as well. In 1993 the Colorado State Patrol employed 538 full-time sworn officers, or 2 per 10,000 residents.

[18]MIGRATION

The discovery of gold in 1858 brought an avalanche of prospectors. Some of these migrants later moved westward into the Rockies and Colorado River canyons. In 1873, another gold strike brought settlers into the Ute territory, eventually driving the Indians into a small reservation in the southwestern corner of the state. During the late 19th and early 20th centuries, the sparsely populated eastern plains were settled by farmers from Kansas and Nebraska and by immigrants from Scandinavia, Germany, and Russia. Five years of drought, from 1933 to 1938, helped drive many rural Coloradans off the land into the cities or westward to California.

Since the end of World War II, net migration into the state has been substantial, amounting to over 880,000 between 1950 and 1990. Between 1990 and 1996, Colorado had net gains of 283,049 in domestic migration and 41,241 in international migration. In 1996 8,895 foreign immigrants were admitted to the state. As of 1994 the number of undocumented immigrants was estimated at between 22 and 29. Growth has been evident in both urban and rural areas, but the largest increase has been in the Denver metropolitan area. A number of migrant workers, mostly Mexican Americans, work seasonally in the western orchards and fields. In the 1980s, migration accounted for 27% of the net population increase, with some 117,000 persons, even though there was a net loss from migration every year from 1986 to 1990. In 1990, native Coloradans made up 43.3% of the population. Only 45% of state residents 5 years or older were living in the same house in 1990 as in 1985; of those who lived in a different house in 1985, 29% did so in a different state.

[19]INTERGOVERNMENTAL COOPERATION

Among the most important interstate agreements for Coloradans are those governing water resources. Colorado participates with New Mexico in the Animas–La Plata Project, Costilla Creek, and La Plata River compacts; with Kansas in the Arkansas River Compact of 1949; and with Nebraska in the South Platte River Compact. Multistate compacts allocate water from the Colorado and Republican rivers and the Rio Grande. Colorado also is a signatory to such regional agreements as the Interstate Oil and Gas Compact.

The Western Interstate Commission for Higher Education has its headquarters in Boulder, as does the National Conference of State Legislatures. Federal grants to Colorado totaled over $2.4 billion in 1995/96.

[20]ECONOMY

During the late 1880s, Colorado was the nation's leading silver producer, and an important source of gold. With its abundant reserves of coal, natural gas, and other minerals—and the economic potential of its vast oil-shale deposits—Colorado remains a major mining state, although the mineral industry's share of the state economy has declined throughout this century. Agriculture, primarily livestock, retains its historic importance.

Trade, services, government, and manufacturing were responsible for more than 75% of new jobs created between 1975 and 1985.

A driving force behind Colorado's economy is the US government, which in 1984 employed 93,000 civilian and military personnel in the state. Mining and construction suffered the greatest losses of employment between 1982 and 1992. Mining jobs declined 53% in that decade and construction jobs dropped 29%. Employment in services, in contrast, rose 36% in those years, and jobs in finance, insurance and real estate increased by 15%. Tourism has also expanded rapidly in all areas of the state. Colorado's gross state product in 1994 was $99,767 million, to which private goods-producing industries contributed $20,879 million; private services-producing industries, $64,843 million; and government, $14,045 million. Colorado's per capita personal income in 1995 was $23,961, or 15th in the nation. In 1996 there were 16,403 bankruptcy filings in Colorado.

21INCOME

In 1996, Colorado ranked 13th among the 50 states in per capita personal income, with $25,084. Total disposable personal income in 1996 reached $81.3 billion, up from $76.6 billion in 1995. In 1994, Denver ranked 30th among the largest US metropolitan areas in per capita income.

About 8.8% of all Coloradans were below the federal poverty level in 1995. Median household income was estimated at $40,706 in 1995. Pitkin County (Aspen) was one of the highest in per capita personal income of any US county in 1994, at $41,889 or 193% of the national average.

22LABOR

Colorado's labor history has been marked by major disturbances in the mining industry. From 1881 to 1886, the Knights of Labor led at least 35 strikes in the mines; during the 1890s, the Western Federation of Miners struck hard-rock mines in Telluride and Cripple Creek. The United Mine Workers, who came into the state in 1899, shut down operations at numerous mines in 1900 and 1903. Violence was common in these disputes. In one well-known episode, after striking miners and their families set up a tent colony at Ludlow, near Trinidad, the governor called out the militia; in the ensuing conflict, on 20 April 1914, the miners' tents were burned, killing 2 women and 11 children, an event that touched off a rebellion in the whole area. Federal troops restored order in June, and the strike ended with promises of improved labor conditions. In 1917, the state legislature created the Colorado Industrial Commission, whose purpose is to investigate all labor disputes.

In 1996, an average of 2,013,100 Coloradans were employed in the civilian labor force. Unemployment was 4.2% or 88,800 persons.

Employment for major nonfarm industry groups at the beginning of 1996 and 1997 was as follows (in thousands):

	1996	1997
Total nonfarm employment	1,868.4	1,922.0
Mining	13.8	13.2
Construction	106.0	111.7
Manufacturing	195.5	196.8
Durable goods	120.8	123.0
Nondurable goods	74.7	73.8
Transportation, communications, utilities	120.8	118.0
Trade	459.3	467.6
Wholesale trade	96.1	99.0
Retail trade	363.2	368.6
Finance, insurance, real estate	115.8	119.9
Services	550.8	581.5
Government	306.4	313.3

In 1995 there were about 170,000 union members, or 9.9% of all employees. Unionization among private sector manufacturing firms was 9.2%.

23AGRICULTURE

Colorado ranked 17th among the 50 states in agricultural income in 1995, with $3.98 billion, of which more than $1.3 billion came from crops.

As of 1996 there were 24,500 farms and ranches covering about 32.5 million acres (13 million hectares); the average farm (including ranches) was 1,326 acres (537 hectares). The major crop-growing areas are the east and east-central plains for sugar beets, beans, potatoes, and grains; the Arkansas Valley for grains and peaches; and the Western Slope for grains and fruits.

Colorado ranked 5th in the US in production of dry edible beans in 1995, with 2,555,000 hundredweight; 9th in sugar beets, with 715,000 tons; 7th in barley, with 10 million bushels; and 7th in wheat, with 10 million bushels. Other field crops include corn, hay, and sorghum. In 1996, Colorado produced 300,100 tons of fresh market vegetables, 9,500 tons of vegetables for processing, 55 million lb (24.9 million kg) of commercial apples, and 17 million lb (7.7 million kg) of peaches. About 1.2 million lb (544,308 kg) of tart cherries were harvested in 1996. Colorado is also a major grower of roses.

24ANIMAL HUSBANDRY

A leading sheep-producing state, Colorado is also a major area for cattle and other livestock.

From 1858 to about 1890, cattle drives were a common sight in Colorado, as a few cattle barons had their Texas longhorns graze on public-domain lands along the eastern plains and Western Slope. This era came to an end when farmers in these regions fenced in their lands, and the better-quality shorthorns and Herefords took over the market. Today, huge tracts of pasture-land are leased from the federal government by both cattle and sheep ranchers, with cattle mostly confined to the eastern plains and sheep to the western part of the state.

Preliminary estimates of the number of cattle and calves for 1997 was 3,150,000 with an estimated total value at $1,795,500. Colorado had an estimated 630,000 hogs and pigs with an estimated total value at $63 million. In 1995 Colorado produced 68.4 million lb of sheep and lambs at a gross income of $105 million. Colorado was estimated to have produced 3.96 million lb of shorn wool at an estimated value of $4.3 million for 1995.

Other livestock products in 1995 included chickens, at an estimated 7.88 million lb; and milk, estimated at 1.468 billion lb. In 1996, the state produced an estimated 827 million lb of eggs.

25FISHING

There is virtually no commercial fishing in Colorado. The many warm-water lakes lure the state's 736,200 licensed sport anglers with perch, black bass, and trout, while walleyes are abundant in mountain streams. In 1995/96, federal hatcheries distributed 3.1 million coldwater and warmwater species fish and 4.7 million fish eggs within the state.

26FORESTRY

Approximately 21,338,000 acres (8,635,000 hectares) of forested lands are located in Colorado. In spite of this wood resource, however, commercial forestry is not a major element of the state's economy. In Colorado, forestry emphasis occurs in diverse areas: traditional forest management and stewardship; urban and community forestry; resource protection (from wildfire, insects, and disease); and tree planting and care.

27MINING

According to US Geological Survey estimates, the value of 1995 nonfuel mineral production was about $448 million, up $38 million from the $410 million reported in 1994. The major factors in the increase in Colorado's nonfuel mineral value were increases in the values of molybdenum, zinc, lead, silver, grade-A helium, and gemstones.

In 1995 Colorado ranked second in the nation in production of molybdenum. In 1994 improving economies in East Asia and Europe resulted in an increase in the demand for molybdenum, leading to higher prices.

The State ranked 28th among the 50 states in total nonfuel mineral production value with more than 1% of the national total. In 1995, Colorado mined 27,500,000 metric tons of sand and gravel ($106,000,000), 8,200,000 metric tons of crushed stone ($51,300,000), 4,340 kilograms of gold ($52,000,000), and 288,000,000 metric tons of clay ($2,020,000). Construction of the Denver International Airport recently contributed to the increased demand for cement.

28ENERGY AND POWER

An abundant supply of coal, oil, and natural gas makes Colorado a major energy-producing state.

During 1995, 33 billion kWh of electricity were generated in Colorado, about 94% of that in coal-fired plants; installed capacity was 6.7 million kW.

Petroleum production in 1996 was 24,954,000 barrels; proved reserves were 252,000,000 barrels. Natural gas marketed production in 1995 was 523 billion cu feet; reserves were nearly 7.2 trillion cu feet.

Colorado's coal output, which reached a peak of some 19 million short tons in 1981, had declined during the 1980s, but rose back to 24.1 million short tons in 1996.

Colorado holds the major portion of the nation's proved oilshale reserves. Because of its ample sunshine and wind, Colorado is also well suited to renewable energy development. Among the many energy-related facilities in the state is the National Renewable Energy Laboratory in Golden.

29INDUSTRY

Colorado is the main manufacturing center of the Rocky Mountain states; value of shipments by manufacturers in 1995 was $37.5 billion. The major sectors for value of shipments by manufacturers were food and food products, $7.624 billion; printing and publishing, $3.144 billion; industrial machinery and equipment, $7.110 billion; electronic and other electric equipment, $2.743 billion; transportation equipment, $3.479 billion; and instruments and related products, $4.996 billion.

High-technology research and manufacturing grew substantially in Colorado during the 1980s and early 1990s. Storage Technology in Louisville is the largest high-tech company with headquarters in the state, but many large out-of-state companies—including Apple Computer, IBM, Hewlett-Packard, Eastman Kodak, Digital Equipment, Ball Aerospace, Martin-Lockheed Corporation, MCI Telecommunications, TCI Cable, and Cobe Laboratories—have divisions there.

There are three Fortune 500 companies headquartered in Colorado: US West, Tele-Communications, and Cyprus Amax Minerals. In 1995 there were 1,218 US patents issued to Colorado residents.

30COMMERCE

Colorado is the leading wholesale and retail distribution center for the Rocky Mountain states. In 1992 there were 7,554 wholesale establishments, with sales of $46,871.5 million. Durable goods accounted for 57% of sales; nondurable goods, 43%. Retail sales in 1992 totaled $28,532.6 million from 22,921 establishments. Colorado ranked 22nd in retail sales, with 1.5% of the US total in 1992. Major retail sectors by sales volume included food stores, 19.6%; automotive dealers, 21.1%; eating and drinking places, 10.9%; and general merchandise stores, 12.7%.

Colorado's foreign exports in 1996 included nearly $4.9 billion in goods produced within the state.

31CONSUMER PROTECTION

Colorado Attorney General's Consumer Protection Office is responsible for enforcing the state consumer protection laws including the Colorado Consumer Protection Act, the Unfair Trade Practices Act, the Fair Debt Collection Practices Act, the Uniform Consumer Credit Code, the Credit Services Organization Act and the Rental Purchase Agreement Act. The office also represents the interests of consumers, small business, and agriculture before the Public Utilities Commission in matters involving electric, gas, and telephone utility services.

32BANKING

In 1996, Colorado had 231 insured commercial banks, with assets of $37.4 billion, and 16 insured savings institutions with assets of $2.7 billion. Most of these institutions were concentrated in metropolitan Denver, the leading banking center between Kansas City and the Pacific.

33INSURANCE

As of the end of 1996, 21 property/casualty insurance companies were domiciled in Colorado. There were 2,700,000 policies in force worth $180.8 billion in 1996.

Property and liability insurers wrote premiums amounting to about $4 billion in 1995. Automobile physical damage insurance accounted for $1,297.8 billion; automobile liability insurance, $691.3 billion; and homeowners' coverage, $448.4 billion.

34SECURITIES

There are no stock or commodity exchanges in Colorado. As of 31 March 1997, there were 2,049 securities dealers licensed to do business in Colorado, with 84,513 brokers.

35PUBLIC FINANCE

The governor's annual budget is presented to the general assembly on 1 November. The fiscal year runs from 1 July to 30 June. In 1992 Colorado's citizens passed a constitutional amendment, entitled the Taxpayer's Bill of Rights (TABOR), that restricts state expenditures based on population growth and inflation. The amendment also requires a vote of the people for any new or increased taxes. The following table summarizes the general fund budget revenues and expenditures (in $ millions):

	FY 1994/95	FY 1995/96
REVENUES		
Individual Income Taxes	2,106.4	2,318.5
Sales and Use Taxes	1,222.9	1,312.5
Corporate Income Taxes	191.1	205.7
Insurance Taxes	105.1	110.4
Other Excise Taxes	93.1	93.9
All other Taxes/Fees	277.9	218.8
TOTALS	3,996.4	4,268.8
EXPENDITURES		
Education	2,041.7	2,172.0
Public Health and Environment	672.9	709.5
Public Safety	380.0	420.8
Human Services	326.5	355.4
General Government	52.8	48.1
Business, Community, and Consumer Affairs	28.8	31.9
Natural Resources	20.2	22.4

	FY 1994/95	FY 1995/96
Capital Construction	231.7	254.9
Other	139.9	179.2
TOTALS	3,913.9	4,390.4
Revenues Over/(Under) Expenditures	82.47	(121.7)
Prior Year's Beginning Balance	414.6	497.1
Ending Balance	497.1	375.4

36TAXATION

As of 1996, Colorado's state income tax had a flat rate of 5.0%. The corporate income tax was 5% of net income, based on a formula taking into consideration both total profits and those derived solely from state sources. The state also imposed a 3% sales and use tax, along with taxes on cigarettes, alcoholic beverages, pari-mutuel racing, fossil fuel production, motor fuel sales, and insurance premiums. Property taxes are the major source of revenue for local governments. Colorado municipalities are also allowed to levy sales and use taxes. In 1995, Colorado paid almost $18.4 billion in federal income taxes.

37ECONOMIC POLICY

Colorado's economic programs are aimed at encouraging new industry, helping existing companies expand and compete, and providing assistance to small businesses and to farmers. Economic development in rural areas is a priority. It offers real estate loans to help companies purchase or expand existing buildings or to construct new buildings. It assists employers with training programs for newly created and existing jobs. Colorado seeks to aid small businesses by contributing to lenders' reserve funds for small commercial and agricultural loans, by extending to small businesses loans with fixed interest rates, by giving grants to small technology-based firms for research and development projects, and by offering capital loans and credit to small export/import companies. The state offers a variety of loan programs for economic development and manages a number of loan programs for farmers and agricultural producers. A limited program of grants are earmarked for agriculture feasibility studies, technology, and defense conversion programs.

38HEALTH

Colorado's birthrate was 14.5 per 1,000 people in 1995. The infant mortality rate (7.1 per 1,000 live births in 1995) was well below it. There were 10,607 legal abortions in 1992. Colorado's death rate from all causes was only four-fifths of the national rate; specific death rates for heart disease, cancer, and cerebrovascular diseases were far below the US norm, while those for accidents were about the same. The suicide rate of 17.5 per 100,000 was considerably higher than the US rate of 11.9 in 1995. In 1995 there were 19.64 AIDS cases per 100,000 population, slightly lower than the US average of 28.48 that year. The mortality rate from heart disease was one of the lowest in the country at 172.1 per 100,000 people in 1995.

In 1994, Colorado had 88 accredited hospitals, with 13,677 beds; hospital personnel including 30,500 registered nurses. In 1994 the average cost per inpatient day to community hospitals providing services in Colorado was $993, higher than the US average of $931. The state had 7,960 nonfederal physicians in 1994, there were 2,509 practicing dentists. The state's only medical school is the University of Colorado Medical Center in Denver. The percentage of uninsured in Colorado in 1995 was 16.0%.

The per capita personal health care expenditure in 1991 was $2,447. The most costly services were hospital services, physician services, and drugs and other nondurables. Over 396,000 Medicare and 281,000 Medicaid recipients received $1.4 and $.9 billion respectively in health services during 1993.

39SOCIAL WELFARE

In 1996, 99,700 individuals were recipients of aid to families with dependent children; the monthly payment averaged $432. In 1996 the food stamp program had an average monthly participation of 243,592. The school lunch program cost the federal government $53.3 million.

With the enactment of the Personal Responsibility and Work Opportunity Reconciliation Act of 1996, the US government has changed the form and regulations for many of its social welfare programs; most significantly, it replaces Aid to Families with Dependent Children (AFDC), an open-ended entitlement program, with Temporary Assistance for Needy Families (TANF), a limited system of assistance funded largely through federal block grants. The reform act also impacts the food stamp program, the Supplemental Security Income program, and the child nutrition program. The law took effect on 1 July 1997 and provided $16.38 billion in block grants for fiscal years 1997–2002. The grants are to be divided among the states based on an equation involving the numbers of former AFDC recipients in each state. Because many of the bills provisions have yet to be implemented into state-by-state policy, it was not possible to include the details of each state's programs for this edition of this work.

Social Security benefits averaging $700 per month were paid to 495,320 retired Coloradans in 1991. The weekly unemployment benefit check averaged $202.49 in 1995.

40HOUSING

In October 1996, there were an estimated 1,582,000 housing units, an increase of about 30% from 1980. Of the total, 1,461,000 units were occupied. In 1996, 41,135 new privately-owned housing units were authorized with a total value of over $4.2 billion. During 1995/96, Colorado received $291.3 million in aid from the US Department of Housing and Urban Development, including $37.8 million in community development block grants. The Denver-Boulder area is Colorado's primary region of housing growth, with some 23,000 housing units completed from 1990 to 1992. In 1990, the last year for which figures are available, the median home value was $82,700, down 18.8% from 1980 after adjusting for inflation.

41EDUCATION

Colorado residents are better educated than the average American. According to the 1990 census, 27.0% of the adult population of Colorado had completed four years of college, ranking 1st among the 50 states; almost 84.5% of all adult Coloradans were high school graduates (3d in the US).

In fall 1996, Colorado's public elementary and secondary schools had 67,343 pupils. There were 36,397 elementary and secondary school teachers that year, with an average salary of $36,271. Nonpublic school enrollment was about 49,078 for all grades.

More than 241,295 students were enrolled in 35 colleges and universities in the fall of 1994. The oldest state school is the Colorado School of Mines, founded in Golden in 1869. Although chartered in 1861, the University of Colorado did not open until 1876; its Boulder campus is now the largest in the state. Colorado State University, founded at Ft. Collins in 1870, had 21,210 students in 1992. The University of Denver, chartered in 1864 as the Colorado Seminary of the Methodist Episcopal Church, had 8,213 students.

42ARTS

From its earliest days of statehood, Colorado has been receptive to the arts. Such showplaces as the Tabor Opera House in Leadville and the Tabor Grand Opera House in Denver were among the most elaborate buildings in the Old West. Newer centers are Denver's Boettcher Concert Hall, which opened in 1978 as the home of the Denver Symphony, and the adjacent Helen G. Bonfils Theater Complex, which opened in 1980 and houses a repertory theater company.

Other artistic organizations include the Colorado Springs Symphony and Colorado Opera Festival of Colorado Springs; the Central City Opera House Association, which sponsors a summer opera season in this old mining town; and the Four Corners Opera Association in Durango. Aspen is an important summer music center. The amphitheater in Red Rocks Park near Denver, formed by red sandstone rocks, provides a natural and acoustically excellent concert area.

In 1996, Colorado generated significant state funds for the development of the arts. The National Endowment for the Arts (NEA) provided $1,606,000 of the total. The State of Colorado also provided a sizeable share of the total for the support of the artists. In this four-year period, audiences for arts programs totaled 22,332,000 people. Colorado's arts programs included the contributions of 103,694 artists. Arts education programs were presented to 11,000 school children. By 1991, there were 600 arts associations in Colorado.

In 1996, Colorado Council on the Arts received $37,100 in federal grants for its arts education programs. The Council also received $17,000 from the NEA's State and Regional Program. Since 1988, arts organizations in Denver successfully supported a proposal to contribute 0.1% of the area's sales tax to the development of the arts.

43LIBRARIES AND MUSEUMS

In 1995, public libraries in the state held nearly 9.5 million volumes and circulated more than 31 million. The largest system was the Denver Public Library with 1,938,062 million volumes in 21 branches. The leading academic library is at the University of Colorado at Boulder, with over 2.5 million volumes.

Colorado has more than 156 museums and historic sites. One of the most prominent museums in the West is the Denver Art Museum, with its large collection of American Indian, South Seas, and Oriental art. Another major art museum is the Colorado Springs Fine Arts Center, specializing in southwestern and western American art.

Other notable museums include the Denver Museum of Natural History, University of Colorado Museum in Boulder, Western Museum of Mining and Industry in Colorado Springs, and the Colorado Ski Museum–Ski Hall of Fame in Vail. Museums specializing in state history include the Colorado Heritage Center of the Colorado Historical Society in Denver, Ute Indian Museum in Montrose, Ft. Carson Museum of the Army in the West, Bent's Old Fort National Historic Site in La Junta, Georgetown–Silver Plume Historic District, Healy House–Dexter Cabin and Tabor Opera House Museum in Leadville, and Ft. Vasquez in Platteville.

44COMMUNICATIONS

Colorado's first mail and freight service was provided in 1859 by the Leavenworth and Pikes Peak Express. Over 96% of the state's 1,363,000 occupied housing units had telephones as of March 1993. Of the 187 radio stations in operation in 1996, 75 were AM and 112 FM. There were 26 commercial and 4 educational television stations; 9 large cable television systems also were in operation that year.

45PRESS

As of 1997, there were 16 morning dailies, 13 afternoon dailies, and 12 Sunday papers. The leading newspapers were the *Rocky Mountain News,* 333,471 mornings and 439,295 Sundays; and the *Denver Post,* 316,027 mornings and 456,057 Sundays.

46ORGANIZATIONS

The 1992 Census of Service Industries counted 1,252 organizations in Colorado, including 285 business associations; 638 civic, social, and fraternal associations; and 329 other membership organizations.

Among the environmental associations located in the state are the National Environmental Health Association and the American Humane Association, both in Denver. The International Association of Meteorology and Atmospheric Physics and the American Solar Energy Society are in Boulder. Among the many professional and trade groups in the state are the Geological Society of America in Boulder; National Cattlemen's Association in Englewood; and the American School Food Service Association, American Sheep Producers Council, College Press Service, and National Livestock Producers Association, all in Denver. Colorado Springs is the home of several important sports organizations, including the US Olympic Committee, Amateur Basketball Association of the USA, Amateur Hockey Association of the US, Professional Rodeo Cowboys Association, and the US Ski Association. The Sports Car Club of America is in Englewood.

47TOURISM, TRAVEL, AND RECREATION

Scenery, history, and skiing combine to make Colorado a prime tourist mecca. Annually, travel and tourism generate over $6 billion in expenditures in the state.

Vail is the most popular ski resort center, followed by Keystone and Steamboat. Skiing aside, the state's most popular attraction is the US Air Force Academy near Colorado Springs. Nearby are Pikes Peak, the Garden of the Gods (featuring unusual red sandstone formations), and Manitou Springs, a resort center. Besides its many museums, parks, and rebuilt Larimer Square district, Denver's main attraction is the US Mint.

All nine national forests in Colorado are open for camping, as are the state's two national parks: Rocky Mountain, encompassing 265,000 acres (107,000 hectares) in the Front Range; and Mesa Verde, 52,000 acres (21,000 hectares) of mesas and canyons in the southwest.

Other attractions include the fossil beds at Dinosaur National Monument, Indian cliff dwellings at Mesa Verde, Black Canyon of the Gunnison, Colorado National Monument at Fruita, Curecanti National Recreation Area, Florissant Fossil Beds, Great Sand Dunes, Hovenweep National Monument, Durango-Silverton steam train, and white-water rafting on the Colorado, Green, and Yampa rivers. In 1995, licenses were held by 604,129 hunters and 907,060 anglers who used the state's game and fishing resources.

48SPORTS

There are five major-league professional sports teams in Colorado, all in Denver; the Broncos of the National Football League, the Nuggets of the National Basketball Association, the Avalanche of the National Hockey League, and the Colorado Rockies of Major League Baseball, and the Colorado Rapids of Major League Soccer. The Broncos won the American Football Conference Championship in 1978, 1987, 1988, and 1990, losing each year in the Super Bowl. The Avalanche, who moved to Denver from Quebec after the 1995 season, won the Stanley Cup in 1996. The Colorado Springs Sky Sox compete in the Pacific Coast division of minor league baseball and are the AAA farm team for the Colorado Rockies.

Colorado is home to some of the world's finest alpine skiing resorts, such as Vail, Aspen, and Steamboat Springs.

The Buffaloes of the University of Colorado produced some excellent football teams in the late 1980s and early 1990s, and they were named National Champions in 1990 (with Georgia Tech). Colorado won the Orange Bowl in 1957 and 1991, the Fiesta Bowl in 1995, and the Cotton Bowl in 1996. The Buffaloes have won or shared five Big Eight titles, the last one in 1991.

[49]FAMOUS COLORADANS

Ft. Collins was the birthplace of Byron R. White (b.1917), who as an associate justice of the US Supreme Court since 1962, has been the state's most prominent federal officeholder. Colorado's first US senator, Henry M. Teller (b.New York, 1830–1914), also served as secretary of the interior. Gary Hart (b.Kansas, 1937) was a senator and a presidential candidate in 1984 and 1988.

Charles Bent (b.Virginia, 1799–1847), a fur trapper and an early settler in Colorado, built a famous fort and trading post near present-day La Junta. Early explorers of the Colorado region include Zebulon Pike (b.New Jersey, 1779–1813) and Stephen Long (b.New Hampshire, 1784–1864). John Evans (1814–97) was Colorado's second territorial governor and founder of the present-day University of Denver. Ouray (1820–83) was a Ute chief who ruled at the time when mining districts were being opened. Silver magnate Horace Austin Warner Tabor (b.Vermont, 1830–99) served as mayor of Leadville and lieutenant governor of the state, spent money on lavish buildings in Leadville and Denver, but lost most of his fortune before his death. The story of Tabor and his second wife Elizabeth McCourt Doe Tabor (1862–1935), is portrayed in Douglas Moore's opera *The Ballad of Baby Doe* (1956). Willard F. Libby (1909–80), winner of the Nobel Prize for chemistry in 1960, and Edward L. Tatum (1909–75), co-winner of the 1958 Nobel Prize for physiology or medicine, were born in Colorado. Among the performers born in the state were actors Lon Chaney (1883–1930) and Douglas Fairbanks (1883–1939), and band leader Paul Whiteman (1891–1967). Singer John Denver (Henry John Deutschendorf, Jr., b.New Mexico, 1943) is closely associated with Colorado and lives in Aspen.

Colorado's most famous sports personality is Jack Dempsey (1895–1983), born in Manassa and nicknamed the "Manassa Mauler," who held the world heavyweight boxing crown from 1919–26.

[50]BIBLIOGRAPHY

Abbott, Carl. *Colorado: A History of the Centennial State.* 3d ed. Boulder: Colorado Associated University Press, 1994.

Athearn, Robert G. *The Coloradans.* Albuquerque: University of New Mexico Press, 1982.

Aylesworth, Thomas G. *The Southwest: Colorado, New Mexico, Texas.* Chicago: Chelsea House Publishers, 1996.

Babb, Sanora. *An Owl on Every Post.* New York: McCall, 1970.

Baggs, Mae Lacy. *Colorado, the Queen Jewel of the Rockies—A Description of its Climate and of its Mountains, Rivers, Forests and Valleys.* Denver: The Page Company, 1918.

Casewit, Curtis W. *Colorado.* New York: Viking, 1973.

Cronin, Thomas E. *Colorado Politics & Government: Governing the Centennial State.* Lincoln, Nebr.: University of Nebraska Press, 1993.

Federal Writers' Project. *Colorado: A Guide to the Highest State.* Reprint. New York: Somerset, 1987 (orig. 1941).

Harris, Katherine. *Long Vistas: Women and Families on Colorado Homesteads.* Niwot, Colo.: University of Colorado Press, 1993.

Mahoney, Paul F., Thomas J. Noel, and Richard E. Stevens. *Historical Atlas of Colorado.* Norman, Okla., University of Oklahoma Press, 1994.

Sprague, Marshall. *Colorado: A Bicentennial History.* New York: Norton, 1976.

Ubbelohde, Carol, Maxine Benson, and Duane A. Smith. *A Colorado History.* 5th ed. Boulder: Pruett, 1982.

Walton, Roger A. *Colorado: A Practical Guide to Its Government and People.* Ft. Collins: Publishers Consultants, 1976.

CONNECTICUT

State of Connecticut

ORIGIN OF STATE NAME: From the Mahican word *quinnehtukqut,* meaning "beside the long tidal river." **NICKNAME:** The Constitution State. (Also: the Nutmeg State.) **CAPITAL:** Hartford. **ENTERED UNION:** 9 January 1788 (5th). **SONG:** "Yankee Doodle." **MOTTO:** *Qui transtulit sustinet* (He who transplanted still sustains). **COAT OF ARMS:** On a rococo shield, three grape vines, supported and bearing fruit, stand against a white field. Beneath the shield is a streamer bearing the state motto. **FLAG:** The coat of arms appears on a blue field. **OFFICIAL SEAL:** The three grape vines and motto of the arms surrounded by the words *Sigillum reipublicae Connecticutensis* (Seal of the State of Connecticut). **ANIMAL:** Sperm whale. **BIRD:** American robin. **INSECT:** European praying mantis. **FLOWER:** Mountain laurel. **TREE:** White oak. **MINERAL:** Garnet. **SHIP:** *USS Nautilus.* **LEGAL HOLIDAYS:** New Year's Day, 1 January; Birthday of Martin Luther King, Jr., 3d Monday in January; Lincoln's Birthday, 12 February; Washington's Birthday, 3d Monday in February; Good Friday, March or April; Memorial Day, last Monday in May; Independence Day, 4 July; Labor Day, 1st Monday in September; Columbus Day, 2d Monday in October; Veterans Day, 11 November; Thanksgiving Day, 4th Thursday in November; Christmas Day, 25 December. **TIME:** 7 AM EST = noon GMT.

¹LOCATION, SIZE, AND EXTENT

Located in New England in the northeastern US, Connecticut ranks 48th in size among the 50 states.

The state's area, 5,018 sq mi (12,997 sq km), consists of 4,872 sq mi (12,619 sq km) of land and 146 sq mi (378 sq km) of inland water. Connecticut has an average length of 90 mi (145 km) E-W, and an average width of 55 mi (89 km) N-S.

Connecticut is bordered on the N by Massachusetts; on the E by Massachusetts and Rhode Island (with part of the line formed by the Pawcatuck River); on the S by New York (with the line passing through Long Island Sound); and on the W by New York. On the SW border, a short panhandle of Connecticut territory juts toward New York City. The state's geographic center is East Berlin in Hartford County. Connecticut has a boundary length of 328 mi (528 km) and a shoreline of 253 mi (407 km).

²TOPOGRAPHY

Connecticut is divided into four main geographic regions. The Connecticut and Quinnipiac river valleys form the Central Lowlands, which bisect the state in a north-south direction. The Eastern Highlands range from 500 feet (150 meters) to 1,100 feet (335 meters) near the Massachusetts border and from 200 feet (60 meters) to 500 feet (150 meters) in the southeast. Elevations in the Western Highlands, an extension of the Green Mountains, range from 200 feet (60 meters) in the south to more than 2,000 feet (600 meters) in the northwest; within this region, near the Massachusetts border, stands Mt. Frissell, the highest point in the state at 2,380 feet (725 meters). The Coastal Lowlands, about 100 mi (160 km) long and generally 2–3 mi (3–5 km) wide, consist of rocky peninsulas, shallow bays, sand and gravel beaches, salt meadows, and good harbors at Bridgeport, New Haven, New London, Mystic, and Stonington.

Connecticut has more than 6,000 lakes and ponds. The two largest bodies of water—both artificial—are Lake Candlewood, covering about 5,000 acres (2,000 hectares), and Barkhamsted Reservoir, a major source of water for the Hartford area. The main river is the Connecticut, New England's longest river at 407 mi (655 km), of which 69 mi (111 km) lie within Connecticut; this waterway, which is navigable as far north as Hartford by means of a 15-foot (5-meter) channel, divides the state roughly in half before emptying into Long Island Sound. Other principal rivers include the Thames, Housatonic, and Naugatuck.

Connecticut's bedrock geology and topography are the product of a number of forces: uplift and depression, erosion and deposit, faulting and buckling, lava flows, and glaciation. About 180 million years ago, the lowlands along the eastern border sank more than 10,000 feet (3,000 meters); the resultant trough or fault extends from northern Massachusetts to New Haven Harbor and varies in width from about 20 mi (32 km) to approximately 4 mi (6 km). During the Ice Ages, the melting Wisconsin glacier created lakes, waterfalls, and sand plains, leaving thin glaciated topsoil and land strewn with rocks and boulders.

³CLIMATE

Connecticut has a generally temperate climate, with mild winters and warm summers. The January mean temperature is 27°F (–3°C) and the July mean is 70°F (21°C). Coastal areas have warmer winters and cooler summers than the interior. Norfolk, in the northwest, has a January mean temperature of 22°F (–6°C) and a July mean of 66°F (19°C), while Bridgeport, on the shore, has a mean of 30°F (–1°C) in January and of 71°F (22°C) in July. The highest recorded temperature in Connecticut was 106°F (41°C) in Danbury on 15 July 1995; the lowest, –32°F (–36°C) in Falls Village on 16 February 1943. The annual rainfall is about 44 to 48 in (112 to 122 cm) and is evenly distributed throughout the year. The state receives some 25 to 60 in (64 to 150 cm) of snow each year, with heaviest snowfall in the northwest.

Weather annals reveal a remarkable range and variety of climatic phenomena. Severe droughts were experienced in 1749, 1762, 1929–33, the early 1940s, 1948–50, and 1956–57. The worst recent drought, which occurred in 1963–66, resulted in a severe forest-fire hazard, damage to crops, and rationing of water. Downtown Hartford was inundated by a flood in March 1936. On 21 September 1938, a hurricane struck west of New Haven and followed the Connecticut Valley northward, causing 85 deaths and property losses of more than $125 million. Severe flooding occurred in 1955 and again in 1982. In the latter year, property damage exceeded $266 million.

⁴FLORA AND FAUNA

Connecticut has an impressive diversity of vegetation zones. Along the shore of Long Island Sound are tidal marshes with salt grasses, glasswort, purple gerardia, and seas lavender. On slopes fringing the marshes are black grass, switch grass, marsh elder, and sea myrtle.

The swamp areas contain various ferns, abundant cattails, cranberry, tussock sedge, skunk cabbage, sweet pepperbush, spicebush, and false hellebore. The state's hillsides and uplands support a variety of flowers and plants, including mountain laurel (the state flower), pink azalea, trailing arbutus, Solomon's seal, and Queen Anne's lace. Endangered species in the state include showy lady's slipper, ginseng, showy aster, sickle-leaved golden aster, nodding pogonia, goldenseal, climbing fern, and chaffseed.

The first Englishmen arriving in Connecticut in the 1630s found a land teeming with wildlife. Roaming the forests and meadows were black bear, white-tailed deer, red and gray foxes, timber wolf, cougar, panther, raccoon, and enough rattlesnakes to pose a serious danger. The impact of human settlement on Connecticut wildlife has been profound, however. Only the smaller mammals—the woodchuck, gray squirrel, cottontail, eastern chipmunk, porcupine, raccoon, and striped skunk—remain common. Snakes remain plentiful but are mostly harmless, except for the northern copperhead and timber rattlesnake. Freshwater fish are abundant, and aquatic life in Long Island Sound even more so. Common birds include the robin (the state bird), blue jay, song sparrow, wood thrush, and many species of waterfowl; visible in winter are the junco, pine grosbeak, snowy owl, and winter wren.

Threatened or endangered wildlife listed by the US Department of the Interior include Atlantic and shortnose sturgeon, bog or Muhlenberg's turtle, American peregrine falcon, Indiana bat, bald eagle, and eastern cougar.

⁵ENVIRONMENTAL PROTECTION

The Department of Environmental Protection, established in 1971, is responsible for protecting natural resources and controlling water, air, and land pollution.

Its fiscal 1997 estimated expenditures for all programs from all sources will be approximately $90,400,000. State funds of $37,500,000 total less than 1% of the overall state budget.

Since the Connecticut Clean Water Act was passed in 1967, upgrading of sewage treatment plants, correction of combined sewer overflows, and improved treatment, at and sewage treatment tie-ins, by industrial facilities have resulted in significant water quality improvement in many state rivers. In 1997, about 75% of the state's 900 miles of major streams meet federal "swimmable-fishable" standards. The Connecticut Clean Water Fund was created in 1986 to provide grants and low interest loans to municipalities to finance more than $1 billion in municipal sewerage infrastructure improvements over 20 years. Connecticut was the first state in the country to adopt, in 1980, a comprehensive statewide groundwater quality management system.

In 1994 the governors of Connecticut and New York formally adopted a comprehensive plan to manage Long Island Sound, an "estuary of national significance."

The Tidal Wetlands Act (1969) and the Inland Wetlands and Watercourses Act (1972) put the state in the forefront in wetland protection. In 1997 the DEP estimates permitted tidal wetland losses at less than one acre per year and inland wetland losses at about 630 acres per year. Two thousand or more acres of wetlands and watercourses have been restored.

For five of six criteria for air pollutants (lead, carbon monoxide, particulates, nitrogen dioxide, sulfur dioxide), Connecticut has virtually eliminated violations of health-based federal standards, and levels of these pollutants continue to decrease. The state exceeds the national standard for ozone but has reduced the number of days the standard is exceeded each year by 60% since the early 1970s. Vehicle-related emissions of ozone precursors have been reduced by almost 50%, and the state is working closely with other northeastern and mid-Atlantic states on regional ozone reduction.

In 1986 the state adopted a hazardous air pollutant regulation that covers over 850 substances. Permitting and enforcement processes and voluntary reductions have resulted in at least a 68% reduction in toxics emitted to the air.

In 1987 Connecticut adopted statewide mandatory recycling. As of 1997 the state has achieved a recycling rate of 23%, with its goal 40% recycling by the year 2000.

Since 1986, five regional resource recovery facilities have begun operation, while dozens of landfills closed as they became full or federal regulations prohibited continued operation. The combination of resource recovery, recycling, and reduction of waste by consumers has resulted in landfilled garbage declining from 1,400 pounds per capita in 1986 to about 300 in 1996.

Connecticut DEP has been a pioneer in efforts to restore anadromous fish runs and extirpated species such as wild turkeys and fishers and to document and preserve habitats for numerous plant and animal species.

⁶POPULATION

The 1990 census total for Connecticut was 3,287,116, representing 1.32% of the total US population. The state had a population gain of 5.8% (about 180,000 residents) for the entire decade of the 1980s, compared with a US population growth of 9.7%. One sign of the population lag is that in 1990 Connecticut had the 11th lowest birthrate in the US, 14.5 live births per 1,000 population.

By 1996, Connecticut had an estimated population of 3,274,238, a decrease of 0.4% from 1990. Connecticut ranked 4th among the 50 states in population density in 1990 with 678.4 persons per sq mi (260.7 per sq km). About 79.1% of all Connecticut residents lived in urban areas and 20.9% in rural areas.

Major cities with 1994 population estimates are Bridgeport, 132,919; Hartford, 124,196; New Haven, 119,604; Waterbury, 103,523, and Stamford, 107,199. The three largest cities each had either a slight net growth or remained stable in population from 1980 to 1990, helping to reverse their losses during the 1960s and 1970s due to an exodus to the suburbs, which had increased rapidly in population. For example, Bloomfield, to the north of Hartford, gained in population from 5,700 in 1950 to 19,023 in 1984; and Trumbell, near Bridgeport, increased from 8,641 in 1950 to 33,285 in 1984.

⁷ETHNIC GROUPS

Connecticut has large populations of second-generation European descent. The biggest groups came from Italy, Ireland, Poland, and Quebec, Canada. Most of these immigrants clustered in the cities of New Haven, Hartford, Bridgeport, and New London. The number of Roman Catholic newcomers drew the hostility of many native-born Connecticuters, particularly during the decade 1910–20, when state officials deported 59 "dangerous aliens" on scant evidence of radicalism and Ku Klux Klan chapters enrolled some 20,000 members.

Since 1950, ethnic groups of non-Yankee ancestry have exercised leadership roles in all facets of Connecticut life, especially in politics. Connecticut elected a Jewish governor in 1954, and its four subsequent governors were of Irish or Italian ancestry. A wave of newcomers to the state during and after World War II consisted chiefly of blacks and Hispanics seeking employment opportunities. In 1990, the black population numbered 274,000, about 8.3% of the state total. According to

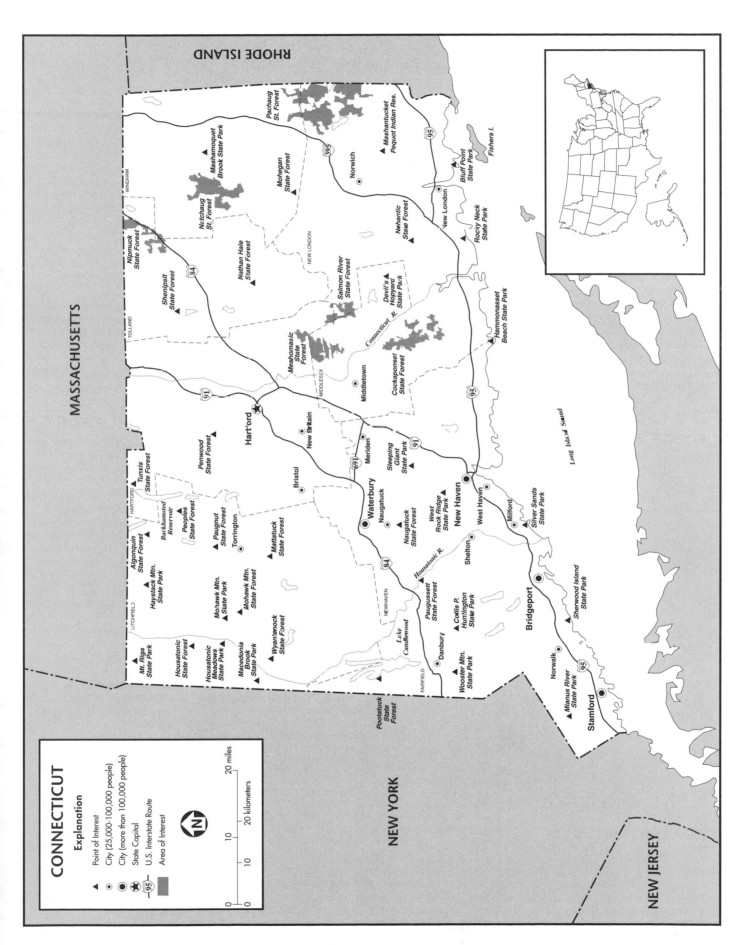

CONNECTICUT

Explanation

▲ Point of Interest
⊙ City (25,000-100,000 people)
◉ City (more than 100,000 people)
★ State Capital
[95] U.S. Interstate Route
▨ Area of Interest

0   10   20 miles
0   10   20 kilometers

N

RHODE ISLAND

MASSACHUSETTS

NEW YORK

NEW JERSEY

Pachaug St. Forest
Mashamoquet Brook State Park
Mashantucket Pequot Indian Res.
Mohegan State Forest
Norwich
Bluff Point State Park
Fishers I.
Netchaug St. Forest
Nipmuck State Forest
WINDHAM
Nehantic State Forest
New London
Rocky Neck State Park
Shenipsit State Forest
Nathan Hale State Forest
NEW LONDON
Salmon River State Forest
Devil's Hopyard State Park
84
TOLLAND
Meshomasic State Forest
Cockaponset State Forest
Connecticut R.
Hammonasset Beach State Park
91
MIDDLESEX
Middletown
Hartford
New Britain
Penwood State Forest
Bristol
Meriden
Sleeping Giant State Park
91
New Haven
West Haven
Milford
Silver Sands State Park
Algonquin State Forest
Tunxis State Forest
HARTFORD
Barkhamsted Reservoir
Peoples State Forest
Paugnut State Forest
Torrington
Waterbury
Naugatuck
West Rock Ridge State Park
Mattatuck State Forest
Naugatuck State Forest
Shelton
Long Island Sound
Haystack Mtn. State Park
Mohawk Mtn. State Park
Mohawk Mtn. State Forest
84
NEWHAVEN
Paugussett State Forest
Collis P. Huntington State Park
Bridgeport
Sherwood Island State Park
Mt. Riga State Park
Housatonic State Forest
Housatonic Meadows State Park
Macedonia Brook State Park
Wyantenock State Forest
Lake Candlewood
Housatonic R.
Danbury
Wooster Mtn. State Park
FAIRFIELD
Norwalk
Stamford
Mianus River State Park
Pootatuck State Forest
LITCHFIELD
95

the 1990 federal census, there were also about 213,000 residents of Hispanic origin, of whom 93,608 were Puerto Ricans. In addition Connecticut had 7,000 American Indians and 51,000 Asians and Pacific Islanders. About 279,000 Connecticut residents, or 8.5% of the population, were foreign-born in 1990.

8LANGUAGES

Connecticut English is basically that of the Northern dialect, but features of the eastern New England subdialect occur east of the Connecticut River. In the east, *half* and *calf* have the vowel of *father: box* is /bawks/ and *cart* is /kaht/; *yolk* is /yelk/; *care* and *chair* have the vowel of *cat;* and many speakers have the intrusive /r/, as in *swaller it* (swallow it). In the western half, *creek* is /krik/; *cherry* may be /chirry/; *on* has the vowel of *father;* and /r/ is heard after a vowel, as in *cart.* Along the Connecticut river, *butcher* is /boocher/, and *tomorrow* is pronounced /tomawro/. Along the coast, the wind may be *breezing on,* and a *creek* is a saltwater inlet. The sycamore is *buttonball,* one is *sick to his stomach,* gutters are *eavestroughs,* a lunch between meals is a *bite,* and in the northwest, an earthworm is an *angledog.*

In 1990, 2,593,825 Connecticuters (84.8% of the resident population 5 years old and older) spoke only English at home. Other languages spoken at home, and the number of people who spoke them, included:

Spanish	167,007	German	17,344
Italian	71,309	Greek	10,554
French	53,586	Hungarian	6,152
Polish	40,306	Chinese	8,234
Portuguese	24,936	Other Indo-European	10,024

9RELIGIONS

Connecticut's religious development began in the 1630s with the designation of the Congregational Church as the colony's "established church." The Puritan fathers enacted laws decreeing church attendance on Sundays and other appointed days, and requiring all residents to contribute to the financial maintenance of local Congregational ministers. Educational patterns, business practices, social conduct, and sexual activities were all comprehensively controlled in accordance with Puritan principles. "Blue Laws" provided penalties for offenses against God's word, such as profanation of the Sabbath and swearing, and capital punishment was mandated for adultery, sodomy, bestiality, lesbianism, harlotry, rape, and incest.

Connecticut authorities harassed and often persecuted such non-Congregationalists as Quakers, Baptists, and Anglicans. However, the church was weakened during the 18th century by increasing numbers of dissenters from the Congregational order. A coalition of dissenters disestablished the church by the Connecticut constitution of 1818. The final blow to Congregational domination came in the late 19th and early 20th centuries, with the arrival of many Roman Catholic immigrants.

Since World War I, Roman Catholics have been the most numerous religious group in the state. As of 1990, there were 1,374,747 Roman Catholics and 557,439 known adherents of Protestant denominations. Leading groups included Congregationalists (United Church of Christ), 135,231; Episcopalians, 78,804; and United Methodists, 56,372. In 1990, the state's estimated Jewish population was 115,460.

10TRANSPORTATION

Because of both the state's traditional conservatism and the opposition of turnpike and steamboat companies, rail service did not fully develop until the 1840s. Hartford and New Haven were connected in 1839, and in 1850 that line was extended to Northampton, MA. In the 1840s and the 1850s, a network of lines connected Hartford with eastern Connecticut communities. Railroad expansion peaked during the 1890s, when total

trackage reached 1,636 mi (2,633 km). The giant in Connecticut railroading from the 1870s until its second and final collapse in 1961 was the New York, New Haven and Hartford Railroad.

In the late 1960s, the Interstate Commerce Commission required that the assets of the bankrupt New York, New Haven and Hartford Railroad be included into the Penn Central Transportation Company, which was formed by the merger of the New York Central and Pennsylvania Railroads. In 1970, Penn Central went bankrupt. In 1976, Penn Central's profitable assets were merged with the profitable assets of other northeast bankrupt railroads to form the Consolidated Rail Corporation (Conrail). As of 1997, Conrail had divested itself of most of its services in Connecticut, which is now served by eight regional and short line railroads. Currently there are approximately 570 route miles of railroad in Connecticut.

In October of 1970 the Connecticut Department of Transportation (CDOT) and the Metropolitan Transportation Authority of New York (MTA) entered an agreement (effective 1 January 1971) with the Trustees of Penn Central to oversee the operation of the New Haven Line Commuter Rail Service between New Haven and Grand Central Terminal in New York City and to jointly fund the operating deficit. In 1976 Conrail succeeded Penn Central as the operator of the New Haven Line and operated it until the end of 1982, when CDOT and MTA decided to operate the New Haven Line themselves.

On 1 January 1983, the Metro-North Railroad, which had been created as a subsidiary of the MTA, took over the operations of the New Haven Line in New York. CDOT and MTA continue to jointly oversee the operations of the New Haven Line service and fund the operating deficit. The costs of New Haven Line capital projects in Connecticut are funded by Connecticut, and the costs of capital projects in New York are funded by MTA. CDOT and MTA share the capital costs of rolling stock rehabilitation and acquisition. In 1985, CDOT purchased from Penn Central the Connecticut portion of the New Haven Line's main line and the three branch lines in Connecticut, including the right of way and support facilities.

On an average weekday, over 240 trains serve almost 100,000 New Haven Line customers from Connecticut and New York. In the mid-1990s, the on-time performance of New Haven Line trains ranged between 94.5% and 96.2%.

In 1990 CDOT contracted with Amtrak to operate the Shore Line East Commuter Rail Service between Old Saybrook and New Haven. Following a period of free service between 29 May and 29 June 1990, weekday only revenue service was implemented on 2 July 1990. In February of 1996, Shore Line East service was extended to New London. CDOT oversees the operation, and provides the rolling stock, maintenance facilities, and funding necessary to cover the operating deficit. On an average weekday, 18 revenue trains serve about six hundred customers. In the mid-1990s, the on-time performance of Shore Line East trains ranged between 90.0% and 96.3%.

Since 1971, Amtrak has provided intercity passenger service to Connecticut on the Northeast Corridor main line (Boston-New Haven-New York City-Philadelphia-Washington,D.C.) and on the Springfield Line (New Haven-Hartford-Springfield). In 1996 Amtrak served 927,805 customers at 12 Connecticut stations.

Local bus systems provide intracity transportation. These services are generally subsidized by the state and, in some instances, by the Federal Transit Administration. Intercity bus service (not subsidized by the state or the federal government) is provided in 31 municipalities by 28 companies.

Connecticut has an extensive system of expressways, state highways, and local roads, aggregating 20,252 mi (32,591 km) in 1995; over 99% of the roads are either paved or hard-surfaced. Major highways include I-95, the John Davis Lodge Turnpike, which crosses the entire length of the state near the shore; I-91, linking New Haven and Springfield, MA; and I-84 from the Massachusetts Turnpike southwestward through Hartford, Waterbury, and Danbury to New York State. Over the past 13 years, Connecticut has embarked on an ambitious infrastructure renewal program. Almost $2.2 billion has been expended to rehabilitate or replace over 1,866 of the 3,820 bridges that the state maintains. Approximately $927 million was used to resurface an average of 475 two-lane miles of state highway per year.

As of 1996 there were 1,934,776 automobiles, 374,500 commercial vehicles, 50,560 motorcycles, and 10,129 buses registered in the state. Connecticut had 2,314,364 licensed drivers during the same year.

Presently, most of Connecticut's waterborne traffic is handled through the two major ports of New Haven and Bridgeport, which collectively handled approximately three quarters of a million metric tons of cargo in 1996. In addition, 10.8 million tons of liquid cargo came into the State of Connecticut in 1996, of which 54% of the liquid volume was handled in New Haven. The New London State Pier is currently under reconstruction, and the east side is expected to reopen in the fall of 1997 with Logistec Connecticut, Inc. in charge of operations.

Currently, there are 124 civil and joint-use air facilities in Connecticut including 55 airports, 61 heliports, 1 stolport, and 7 seaplane bases. Connecticut's principal air terminal is Bradley International Airport in Windsor Locks, located 14 mi (23 km) north of Hartford. Served by nine major airlines and nine commuter lines, Bradley handled 5.3 million passengers during 1996.

11HISTORY

The first people known to have lived in the area now called Connecticut were American Indians, whose forebears may have come to New England as many as 10,000 years ago. By the early 17th century, Connecticut had between 6,000 and 7,000 Indians organized into 16 tribes, all members of the lose Algonquian Confederation. The most warlike of these tribes were the Pequot, who apparently had migrated not long before from the Hudson River region to escape the Mohawk and had settled along the Connecticut coast. There was also a heavy concentration of Indian groups in the Connecticut River Valley, but fear of Mohawk hunting parties kept them from occupying most of western and northwestern Connecticut.

Because of their fear of the Pequot along the shore and of the Mohawk to the west, most of Connecticut's Indians sought the friendship of English newcomers in the 1630s. The Indians sold land to the English and provided instruction in New World agricultural, hunting, and fishing techniques. The impact of English settlers on Connecticut's friendly Indians was devastating, however. The Indians lost their land, were made dependents in their own territory, and were decimated by such European imports as smallpox and measles. The Pequot, who sought to expel the English from Connecticut by a series of attacks in 1636–37, were defeated during the Pequot War by a Connecticut-Massachusetts force, aided by a renegade Pequot named Uncas. By the 1770s, Connecticut's Indian population was less than 1,500.

The first recorded European penetration of Connecticut was in 1614 by the Dutch mariner Adriaen Block, who sailed from Long Island Sound up the Connecticut River, probably as far as the Enfield Rapids. The Dutch established two forts on the Connecticut River, but they were completely dislodged by the English in 1654.

The early English settlers were part of a great migration of some 20,000 English Puritans who crossed the treacherous Atlantic to New England between 1630 and 1642. The Puritans declared that salvation could be achieved only by returning to the simplicity of the early Christian Church and the truth of God as revealed in the Bible. They sailed to America in order to establish a new society that could serve as a model for the rest of Christendom. Attracted by the lushness of the Connecticut River Valley, the Puritans established settlements at Windsor (1633), Wethersfield (1634), and Hartford (1636). In 1639, these three communities joined together to form the Connecticut Colony, choosing to be governed by the Fundamental Orders, a relatively democratic framework for which the Reverend Thomas Hooker was largely responsible. (According to some historians, the Fundamental Orders comprised the world's first written constitution, hence the state nickname, adopted in 1959.) A separate Puritan colony was planted at New Haven in 1638 under the leadership of John Davenport, a Puritan minister, and Theophilus Eaton, a successful merchant.

In 1662, the Colony of Connecticut secured legal recognition by England. Governor John Winthrop, Jr., persuaded King Charles II to grant a charter that recognized Connecticut's existing framework of government and established its north and south boundaries as Massachusetts and Long Island Sound and its east and west borders as Narragansett Bay and the Pacific Ocean. In 1665, New Haven reluctantly became part of the colony because of economic difficulties and feat of incorporation into Anglican New York.

Connecticut had acrimonious boundary disputes with Massachusetts, Rhode Island, New York, and Pennsylvania. The most serious disagreement was with New York, which claimed the entire area from Delaware Bay to the Connecticut River. The issue was resolved in 1683 when the boundary was set 20 mi (32 km) east of and parallel to the Hudson River, although it was not until 1881 that Connecticut, New York, and Congress established the exact line.

Connecticut functioned throughout the colonial period much like an independent republic. It was the only American colony that generally did not follow English practice in its legislative proceedings, nor did it adopt a substantial amount of English common and statute law for its legal code. Connecticut's autonomy was threatened in 1687 when Sir Edmund Andros, appointed by King James II as the governor of the Dominion of New England, arrived in Hartford to demand surrender of the 1662 charter. Connecticut leaders protected the colony's autonomy by hiding the charter in an oak tree, which subsequently became a landmark known as the Charter Oak.

With its Puritan roots and historic autonomy, Connecticut was a Patriot stronghold during the American Revolution. Tories numbered no more than 7% of the adult male population 2,000 to 2,500 out of a total of 38,000 males. Connecticut sent some 3,600 men to Massachusetts at the outbreak of fighting at Lexington and Concord in April 1775. Jonathan Trumbull, who served as governor from 1769 to 1784, was the only colonial governor in office in 1775 who supported the Patriots. He served throughout the Revolutionary War, during which Connecticut troops participated in most of the significant battles. Connecticut's privateers captured more than 500 British merchant vessels, and its small but potent fleet captured at least 40 enemy ships. Connecticut also produced arms and gunpowder for state and Continental forces, thus beginning an arms-making tradition that would lead to the state's unofficial designation as the "arsenal of the nation." It was also called the Provisions State, in large part because of the crucial supplies of foodstuffs it sent to General George Washington throughout the war. The state's most famous Revolutionary War figure was Nathan Hale, executed as a spy by the British in New York City in 1776.

On 9 January 1788, Connecticut became the 5th state to ratify the Constitution. Strongly Federalist during the 1790s, Connecticut ardently disagreed with the foreign policy of presidents Thomas Jefferson and James Madison, opposed the War of

1812, and even refused to allow its militia to leave the state. Connecticut's ire over the war was exacerbated by the failure of the government to offer significant help when the British attacked Essex and Stonington in the spring and summer of 1814. The politically vulnerable Federalists were defeated in 1817 by the Toleration Party. This coalition of Republicans and non-Congregationalists headed the drive for the new state constitution (1818) that disestablished the Congregational Church, a Federalist stronghold.

Long before the Civil War, Connecticut was stoutly antislavery. In the early years of independence, the general assembly enacted legislation providing that every black born after 1 March 1784 would be free at age 25. Connecticut had a number of antislavery and abolition societies whose members routed escaped slaves to Canada via the Underground Railroad. The state's pro-Union sentiment was reflected in the enormous support given to the Union war effort; some 55,000 Connecticut men served in the Civil War, suffering more than 20,000 casualties. Arms manufacturers such as Colt and Winchester produced desperately needed rifles and revolvers, and the state's textile, brass, and rubber firms turned out uniforms buttons, ponchos, blankets, and boots for Union troops.

The contributions by Connecticut industries to the war effort signaled the state's emergence as a manufacturing giant. Its industrial development was facilitated by abundant waterpower, the growth of capital held by banks and insurance companies, a sophisticated transportation network, and, most important, the technological and marketing expertise of the people. The first American hat factory was established in Danbury in 1780, and the nation's brass industry had its roots in Naugatuck Valley between 1806 and 1809. Connecticut clocks became known throughout the world. Micah Rugg organized the first nut and bolt factory in Marion in 1840; Elias Howe invented the first practical sewing machine in Hartford in 1843. Perhaps the most important figure in the development of Connecticut manufacturing was Eli Whitney, best known for inventing the cotton gin (1793).

Seventy-five years after Whitney's death, Connecticut was a leader in the production of hats, typewriters, electrical fixtures, machine tools, and hardware. The state's textile industry ranked 6th in the nation in 1900, with an annual output of $50 million. By 1904, Connecticut's firearms industry was producing four-fifths of the ammunition and more than one-fourth of the total value of all firearms manufactured by nongovernment factories in the US. These great strides in manufacturing transformed Connecticut from a rural, agrarian society in the early 1800s to an increasingly urban state.

The state's contribution to the Allied forces in World War I more than equaled its Civil War effort. Four Liberty Loan drives raised $437 million, more than the contribution from any other state. About 66,000 Connecticuters served in the armed forces, and the state's manufacturers produced 450,000 Enfield rifles, 45,000 Browning automatic rifles, 2 million bayonets, and much other war materiel. By 1917–18, four-fifths of Connecticut's industry was involved in defense production.

The prosperity sparked by World War I continued, for the most part, until 1929. During the 1920s, Connecticuters enjoyed a rising standard of living, as the state became a national leader in the production of specialty parts for the aviation, automotive, and electric power industries. However, from 1919 to 1929, Connecticut lost 14 of its 47 cotton mills to southern states.

The stock market crash of 1929 and the subsequent depression of the 1930s hit highly industrialized Connecticut hard. By the spring of 1932, the state's unemployed totaled 150,000 and cities such as Bridgeport fell deeply in debt. The economic reversal led to significant political change: the ousting of a business-oriented Republican administration, which had long dominated the state,

by a revitalized Democratic Party under the leadership of Governor Wilbur L. Cross (1931–39). During his tenure, Connecticut reorganized its state government, improved facilities in state hospitals and penal institutions, and tightened state regulations of business.

Connecticut was pulled out of the unemployment doldrums in 1939, when the state's factories were once again stimulated by defense contracts. The value of war contracts placed in Connecticut was $8 billion by May 1945, and industrial employment increased from 350,000 in 1939 to 550,000 by late 1944. Connecticut's factories turned out submarines, Navy Corsair fighter aircraft, helicopters, 80% of all ball bearings manufactured in the US, and many thousands of small arms. Approximately 220,000 Connecticut men and women served in the US armed forces.

Since 1945, Connecticut has seen substantial population growth, economic diversification with a greater proportion of service industries, the expansion of middle-class suburbs, and an influx of black and Hispanic migrants to the major cities. Urban renewal projects in Hartford and New Haven have resulted in expanded office and recreational facilities, but not much desperately needed new housing. A major challenge facing Connecticut in the 1980s was once again how to effect the social and economic integration of this incoming wave of people and industries.

Connecticut became the nation's wealthiest state during the 1980s, achieving the highest per capita income in 1986, a position still held in 1992 when its residents' per capita income of $26,797 was 35% above the average for the United States. The state's prosperity came in part from the expansion of the military budget, as 70% of Connecticut's manufacturing sector was defense related. The end of the cold war, however, brought cuts in military spending which reduced the value of defense related contracts in Connecticut from $6 billion in 1989 to $4.2 billion in 1990. By 1992, manufacturing jobs had declined by 25% while jobs in such service industries as retail, finance, insurance and real estate increased by 23%. The total number of jobs, however, dropped by 10%. In 1991 the state imposed a controversial personal income tax.

In the 1980s and early 1990s, Connecticut witnessed an increasing contrast between the standard of living enjoyed by urban and suburban residents, blacks and whites, and the wealthy and the poor. In 1992, the median family income in many of the state's suburbs was nearly twice that of families living in urban areas. Lowel L. Weicker, governor from 1990 to 1994, implemented a program to modify state funding formulas so that urban communities received a larger share. In the mid-1990s, Connecticut's economy was on the upswing, and its employment outlook had improved, although there was a shortage of skilled applicants for certain high-tech jobs. Projections indicated that Connecticut's population would be evenly divided among whites, blacks and Hispanics by the year 2015.

12 STATE GOVERNMENT

Connecticut has been governed by four basic documents: the Fundamental Orders of 1639; the Charter of the Colony of Connecticut of 1662; the constitution of 1818 (which remained in effect until 1964, when a federal district court, acting on the basis of the US Supreme Court's "one person, one vote" ruling, ordered Connecticut to reapportion and redistrict its legislature); and the constitution of 1965. This last document adjusted representation to conform with population, and provided for mandatory reapportionment every 10 years.

The state legislature is the general assembly, consisting of a 36-member senate and 151-member house of representatives. Legislators, who must be 18 years old and qualified voters in Connecticut, are elected to both houses for two-year terms from single-member districts of substantially equal populations. Legislators received $16,760 in 1995.

Elected members of the executive branch are the governor and lieutenant governor (who run jointly and must each be at least 30 years of age), secretary of state, treasurer, comptroller, and attorney general. All are elected for four-year terms and may be reelected. The governor, generally with the advice and consent of the general assembly, selects the heads of state departments, commissions, and offices. In 1996 the governor's salary was $78,000.

A bill becomes law when approved by both houses of the general assembly and signed by the governor. If the governor fails to sign it within 5 days when the legislature is in session, or within 15 days when it has adjourned, the measure also becomes law. A bill vetoed by the governor may be overridden by a two-thirds vote of the members of each house.

A constitutional amendment may be passed in a single legislative session if approved by three-fourths of the total membership of each house. If approved in one session by a majority but by less than three-fourths, the proposed amendments requires approval by majority vote in the next legislative session following a general election. After passage by the legislature, the amendment must be ratified by the voters in the next even-year general election in order to become part of the state constitution.

To vote in state elections, residents must be US citizens, at least 18 years of age, and must satisfy a 21-day registration requirement.

13POLITICAL PARTIES

Connecticut's major political groups during the first half of the 19th century were successively the Federalist Party, the Democratic-Republican coalition, the Democrats, and the Whigs. The political scene also included a number of minor political parties—the Anti-Masonic, Free Soil, Temperance, and Native American (Know-Nothing) parties—of which the Know-Nothings were the most successful, holding the governorship from 1855 to 1857. The Whig Party collapsed during the controversy over slavery in the 1850s, when the Republican Party emerged as the principal opposition to the Democrats.

From the 1850s to the present, the Democratic and Republican parties have dominated Connecticut politics. The Republicans held power in most of the years between the Civil War and the 1920s. Republican hegemony ended in 1930, when the Democrats elected Wilbur L. Cross as governor. Cross greatly strengthened the Connecticut Democratic Party by supporting organized labor and providing social legislation for the aged and the needy. The success of the increasingly liberal Democrats in the 1930s prodded Connecticut Republicans to become more forward-looking, and the two parties were fairly evenly matched between 1938 and 1954. Connecticut's Democrats have held power in most years since the mid-1950s. As of 1994, Democratic Party registration in Connecticut was 736,914, or 38%; Republican, 506,115, or 26%, and Independent, 721,239, or 37%.

Republican presidential candidates carried Connecticut for five successive elections starting in 1972 and ending with the victory of Democrat Bill Clinton in 1992. In the November 1996 elections, Clinton again carried the state with 53% of the popular vote; Republican Bob Dole won 35%, and Independent Ross Perot received 10%. In 1997 Republicans controlled the state senate, 19–17, and Democrats formed a majority in the state house (95–56). Following the 1996 elections, Connecticut's delegation of US Representatives consisted of four Democrats and two Republicans. Both of Connecticut's US senators are Democrats: Christopher J. Dodd, elected in 1992, and Joseph I. Lieberman, elected in 1994. In 1993 there were 62 black elected officials, and there were 26 Hispanic public officials in 1994. As of 1995, 52 women served in the state legislature and in elective executive office.

In 1994, Republican John G. Rowland was elected governor on a platform that included a promise to repeal the state income tax. US Representative Gary Franks, the first black member of the US House of Representatives from Connecticut and the first black House Republican in 55 years, was unseated in 1996, in his bid for a fourth term.

14LOCAL GOVERNMENT

As of 1992, Connecticut had 8 counties, and 29 municipal governments, 17 school districts, and 368 special districts. Counties in Connecticut have been geographical subdivisions without governmental functions since county government was abolished in 1960.

Connecticut's cities generally use the council-manager or mayor-council forms of government. The council-manager system provides for an elected council that determines policy, enacts local legislation, and appoints the city manager. The mayor-council system employs an elected chief executive with extensive appointment power and control over administrative agencies.

In most towns, an elected, three-member board of selectmen heads the administrative branch; the town meeting, in which all registered voters may participate, is the legislative body. Boroughs are generally governed by an elected warden, and borough meetings exercise major legislative functions.

15STATE SERVICES

The Department of Education administers special programs for the educationally disadvantaged, the emotionally and physically disabled, and non-English-speaking students. The Department of Transportation operates state-owned airports, oversees bus system operations, and provides for snow removal from state highways and roads. The Department of Human Resources has a variety of social programs for state residents, including special services for the physically disabled. The Department of Children and Youth Services investigates cases of child abuse and administers programs dealing with child protection, adoption, juvenile corrections and rehabilitation, and prevention of delinquency. The Department on Aging has state and regional ombudsmen to handle problems involving nursing homes. Among programs sponsored by the Health Services Department are ones that help people to stop smoking, increase their nutritional awareness, and improve their dental health. The Labor Department provides a full range of services to the unemployed, to jobseekers, and to disadvantaged workers. Other departments deal with consumer protection, economic development, environmental protection, housing, mental retardation, and public safety.

16JUDICIAL SYSTEM

Connecticut's judicial system has undergone significant streamlining in recent years, with the abolition of municipal courts (1961), the circuit court (1974), the court of common pleas (1978), and the juvenile court (1978), and the creation of an appellate court (1983). Currently, the Connecticut judicial system consists of the supreme court, appellate court, superior court, and probate courts.

The supreme court comprises the chief justice, five associate justices, and two senior associate justices. The high court hears cases on appeal, primarily from the appellate court but also from the superior court in certain special instances, including the review of a death sentence, reapportionment, election disputes, invalidation of a state statute, or censure of a probate judge. Justices of the supreme court, as well as appellate and superior court judges, are nominated by the governor and appointed by the general assembly for eight-year terms.

The superior court, the sole general trial court, has the authority to hear all legal controversies except those over which the probate courts have exclusive jurisdiction. The superior court sits in 12 state judicial districts and is divided into trial divisions for civil, criminal, and family cases. As of 1994 there were 150 superior court trial judges.

Connecticut has 132 probate courts. These operate on a fee basis, with judges receiving their compensation from fees paid for services rendered by the court. Each probate district has one probate judge, elected for a four-year term. There were 16,500 licensed attorneys in 1996.

Connecticut had an inmate population of 9,517 at the end of 1995. State law provides for the death penalty (by electrocution). There were 21 executions performed between 1930 and 1995. Five persons were under sentence of death in 1995. The total crime rate in 1996 was 4,503.2 per 100,000 inhabitants. That total includes 405.9 for violent crime and 4,097.3 for property crime.

17ARMED FORCES

In 1996, there were 5,806 active duty military personnel stationed in Connecticut. The principal military installation in the state is the US Navy submarine base at Groton, with 5,616 military and civilian personnel in 1996. Across the Thames River in New London is one of the nation's four service academies—the US Coast Guard Academy. Founded in 1876 and located at its present site since 1932, this institution offers a four-year curriculum leading to a BS degree and a commission as ensign in the Coast Guard.

In fiscal year 1996, the value of defense contracts was $2.6 billion, and total defense-oriented expenditures amounted to $3.2 billion.

As of 1 July 1996, some 334,000 veterans were living in Connecticut, of whom fewer than 500 were veterans of World War I, 98,000 of World War II, 56,000 of the Korean conflict, 98,000 of the Vietnam era, and 16,000 of the Persian Gulf War. Veterans' benefits in fiscal year 1996 totaled $407 million.

In 1996, the Connecticut National Guard and Reserves had a total personnel of 12,855. In 1993, the Connecticut State Police employed 972 full-time sworn officers, or three per 10,000 residents.

18MIGRATION

Connecticut has experienced four principal migrations: the arrival of European immigrants in the 17th century, the out-migration of many settlers to other states beginning in the 18th century, renewed European immigration in the late 19th century, and the intrastate migration of city dwellers to the suburbs since 1945.

Although the first English settlers found an abundance of fertile farmland in the Connecticut Valley, later newcomers were not so fortunate. It is estimated that in 1800, when Connecticut's population was 250,000, nearly three times that many people had moved away from the state, principally to Vermont, western New York, Ohio, and other midwestern states.

The influx of European immigrants increased the number of foreign-born in the state from 38,518 in 1850 to about 800,000 by World War I. After World War II, the rush of middle-class whites (many from neighboring states) to Connecticut suburbs, propelled in part by the "baby boom" that followed the war, was accompanied by the flow of minority groups to the cities. All told, Connecticut had a net increase from migration of 561,000 between 1940 and 1970, followed by a net loss of 113,000 from 1970 to 1990. Between 1990 and 1996, the state had a net loss of 175,792 residents in domestic migration, and a net gain of 46,833 in international migration. As of 1994, the number of undocumented immigrants was estimated at between 31 and 46. In 1990, 57% of all Connecticut residents had been born in the state, and 57% (age 5 and older) lived in the same house as in 1985. Of those who lived in a different house in 1985, nearly 24% did so in another state.

19INTERGOVERNMENTAL COOPERATION

Among the regional interstate agreements to which Connecticut belongs are the Atlantic States Marine Fisheries Compact, the New England Higher Education Compact, and the New England Corrections Compact. Boundary agreements are in effect with Massachusetts, New York, and Rhode Island. Connecticut partic-

Connecticut Presidential Vote by Political Parties, 1948–96

YEAR	ELECTORAL VOTE	CONNECTICUT WINNER	DEMOCRAT	REPUBLICAN	PROGRESSIVE	SOCIALIST
1948	8	Dewey (R)	423,297	437,754	13,713	6,964
1952	8	*Eisenhower (R)	481,649	611,012	1,466	2,244
1956	8	*Eisenhower (R)	405,079	711,837	—	—
1960	8	*Kennedy (D)	657,055	565,813	—	—
1964	8	*Johnson (D)	826,269	390,996		
					AMERICAN IND.	
1968	8	Humphrey (D)	621,561	556,721	76,660	—
						AMERICAN
1972	8	*Nixon (R)	555,498	810,763	—	17,239
						US LABOR
1976	8	Ford (R)	647,895	719,261	7,101	1,789
					LIBERTARIAN	CITIZENS
1980	8	*Reagan (R)	541,732	677,210	8,570	6,130
					CONN-ALLIANCE	COMMUNIST
1984	8	*Reagan (R)	569,597	890,877	1,274	4,826
					LIBERTARIAN	NEW ALLIANCE
1988	8	*Bush (R)	676,584	750,241	14,071	2,491
						IND. (PEROT)
1992	8	*Clinton (D)	682,318	578,313	5,391	348,771
1996	8	*Clinton (D)	735,740	483,109	5,788	139,523

* Won US presidential election.

ipates with New York in the Railroad Passenger Transportation Compact.

In fiscal year 1996, federal aid to Connecticut was almost $3.1 billion.

[20]ECONOMY

Connecticut has had a strong economy since the early 19th century, when the state, unable to support its population by farming, turned to a variety of nonagricultural pursuits. Shipbuilding and whaling were major industries; in the 1840s and 1850s. New London ranked behind only New Bedford and Nantucket, Mass., among US whaling ports. Connecticut has been a leader of the insurance industry since the 1790s.

Connecticut's most important economic pursuit is manufacturing. In 1984, Connecticut was a leader in the manufacture of aircraft engines and parts, bearings, hardware, submarines, helicopters, typewriters, electronic instrumentation, electrical equipment, guns and ammunition, and optical instruments.

Because defense production has traditionally been important to the state, the economy has fluctuated with the rise and fall of international tensions. Connecticut's unemployment rate stood at 8.7% in 1949, dropped to 3.5% in 1951 during the Korean conflict, and rose sharply after the war to 8.3% in 1958. From 1966 to 1968, during the Viet-Nam war, unemployment averaged between 3.1% and 3.7%, but the rate subsequently rose to 9.5% in 1976. In 1984, in the midst of the Reagan administration's military build-up, Connecticut's unemployment rate dropped below 5%, becoming the lowest in the country. Connecticut has lessened its dependence on the defense sector somewhat by attracting nonmilitary domestic and international firms to the state. As of 1984, more than 250 international companies employed more than 30,000 Connecticut workers. Nevertheless, Connecticut was hit hard by cuts in military spending in the late 1980s and early 1990s. In 1992, 70% of manufacturing was defense related, either through direct federal contracts, subcontracts with other companies, or in the manufacturing of basic metals used for weaponry. A year earlier, in 1991, defense related prime contract awards had dropped 37.7% from the 1990 level. Pratt and Whitney, the jet engine maker, and General Dynamics' Electric Boat division, manufacturer of submarines, announced in 1992 that they would lay off a total of 16,400 workers over the next six years. Unemployment in 1993 was 7.3%.

Despite its dependence on military contracts, Connecticut's economy underwent a restructuring during the 1980s and 1990s. Between 1984 and 1991, manufacturing employment declined 22.4%, while nonmanufacturing jobs rose by 11.6%. This shift had been in process for several decades, however—the ratio of manufacturing employment to total employment dropped from 49.6% in 1950 to 20.1% in 1992. At the end of 1996, services was the largest employer, with 483,500 workers. Wholesale and retail trade was second with 359,600; manufacturing was third with 277,900; followed by government with 231,200; finance, insurance, real estate with 129,800; transportation and public utilities with 73,500. Contributing to the gross state product of $110,449 million in 1994 were private goods-producing industries with $23,080 million; private services-producing industries with $76,962 million; and government with $10,407 million. Connecticut had the nation's highest per capita personal income with $31,776 in 1995. In 1996, there were a total of 11,307 bankruptcies filed in the state, an increase of 23.6% from the previous year.

[21]INCOME

Connecticut is one of the wealthiest states, ranking first among the 50 states in 1996 in per capita personal income, which was $33,189. In 1996, total disposable income was $90.7 billion, up from $87.4 billion in 1995. Nationally, total personal income increased 5.4% from 1995 to 1996; in Connecticut the increase was 4.4% for the same period. Median household income in Connecticut was $40,243 in 1995.

Only 9.7% of all state residents were below the federal poverty level in 1992.

[22]LABOR

The state's civilian labor force in early 1997 totaled 1,723,900. The unemployment rate at that time was 5.9%, ranging from a high of 6.9% in the Bridgeport area to a low of 3.8% in the Danbury area.

In 1995, annual average employment (in thousands) and total wages (in millions of dollars) in Connecticut were as follows:

	WAGES	EMPLOYMENT
Total	53,992.8	1,537.3
Agricultural service, forestry, fisheries	302.5	14.0
Construction and mining	1,873.7	51.1
Manufacturing	12,437.3	278.3
Nondurable goods	3,690.0	82.6
Durable goods	8,747.3	195.7
Transportation and public utilities	2,833.1	69.5
Wholesale trade	3,717.6	78.1
Retail trade	4,593.8	263.4
Finance, insurance, and real estate	6,971.3	132.0
Services	13,882.8	448.1
Government	7,283.8	200.1

During the early 20th century, Connecticut was consistently antiunion and was one of the leading open-shop states in the northeastern US. But great strides were made by organized labor in the 1930s with the support of New Deal legislation recognizing union bargaining rights. In 1995, labor union membership totaled 287,900 (2.2% of all workers). All workforce services—recruiting, training, workplace regulation, labor market information, and unemployment insurance—are offered through a statewide partnership of Connecticut's Department of Labor, Regional Workforce Development Boards, and state and community organizations.

[23]AGRICULTURE

Agriculture is no longer of much economic importance in Connecticut. The number of farms declined from 22,241 in 1945 to 3,800 in 1996, when the average farm covered 100 acres (40 hectares). Cash receipts from all agricultural sales totaled $484.5 million in 1995.

Cash receipts from crop sales in 1995 were $227.7 million. Tobacco production was 3,498,000 lb. (1,586,693 kg) in 1996. In 1995, the state ranked fifth in mushroom production and eighth in pears. Nursery and greenhouse products were valued at $200 million and $130 million, respectively, in 1995. Other principal crops are hay, silage, potatoes, sweet corn, tomatoes, apples, and peaches.

[24]ANIMAL HUSBANDRY

There were an estimated 71,000 cattle and calves on Connecticut farms in 1997. Their estimated value was $53.96 million. In 1996 there were an estimated 4,000 hogs and pigs, valued at $480,000. During 1995, Connecticut dairy farmers produced an estimated 526 million lb. (236 million kg) of milk. Also during 1995, poultry farmers received an estimated $315,000 from the sale of 12.3 million lb. (5.6 million kg) of chicken, and $364,000 for turkeys. Connecticut produced an estimated 944,000 eggs in 1995 at an estimated value of $81.8 million.

[25]FISHING

Commercial fishing does not play a major role in the economy. In 1995, the value of commercial landings was $56.7 million for a catch of 21,914,00 lb (9,940,000 kg) of edible finfish and shellfish. Commercial cod landings in 1995 totaled 20,000 lb (9,072 kg), valued at $27,000.

During 1995/96, programs to restore the Atlantic salmon and trout populations continued on the Connecticut River. Streams also were surveyed that year to update the trout stocking program. Connecticut had nearly 189,700 sport fishing license holders in 1995/96.

26FORESTRY

By the early 20th century, the forests that covered 95% of Connecticut in the 1630s were generally destroyed. Woodland recovery has been stimulated since the 1930s by an energetic reforestation program. More than half of the state's 1,819,000 acres (736,000 hectares) of forestland in 1994 was wooded with new growth. Shipments of lumber and wood products were valued at $300.4 million in 1995; shipments of paper and paper products were valued at $2,152.8 million.

State woodlands include 91 state parks and 30 state forests covering some 168,000 acres (69,055 hectares).

27MINING

The value of nonfuel mineral production in Connecticut in 1995 was estimated by the US Geological Survey to be nearly $80.9 million. Crushed stone (5.9 million short tons, worth $53.1 million) and construction sand and gravel (5.3 million short tons, valued at $27.8 million), the state's two leading mineral commodities, accounted for nearly all the value. Other commodities produced included clays, industrial sand, and dimension stone. The total production value reported was artificially low because information was withheld to avoid disclosing company proprietary data. Crushed stone production (predominantly Jurassic-age basalt, which is commonly called traprock) increased by 31% from the output in 1994. Crushed stone value also rose by 4% over the same period. In October 1995, a new law came into effect allowing towns to protect traprock ridges within their borders from development, including quarrying.

Demand for virtually all of the state's mineral output is dependent on a healthy construction industry, the main consumer of aggregates.

28ENERGY AND POWER

In 1994, Connecticut's fuel bill was $6.6 billion, of which 45% was for petroleum products, 13% for natural gas, and 3% for coal and nuclear fuel. In 1994, prices were 69% higher than the national average for natural gas, 47% higher for electricity, and about 12% higher for petroleum products.

Production of electricity increased from 23.9 billion kWh in 1983 to 26.9 billion kWh in 1995; installed capacity increased from 6.1 million kW to 7.0 million kW during the same years. The use of coal to generate electric power declined from 85% of the total fuel used in 1965 to 8% in 1995 because of the increased utilization of nuclear energy and oil. As of 1996, Connecticut had four nuclear reactors, one at Haddam Neck (600,300 kw) and three at Waterford (totaling 2,824,500 kw). Energy input totals at utilities amounted to 222.3 trillion Btu in 1970 and steadily rose to levels over 391.8 trillion Btu in 1988 but fell back to 299.8 trillion Btu in 1994.

Having no petroleum or gas resources of its own, Connecticut must rely primarily on imported oil from Saudi Arabia, Venezuela, Nigeria, and other countries. Most of the natural gas used in Connecticut is piped in from Texas and Louisiana.

29INDUSTRY

Connecticut is one of the most industrialized states, and it has recently diversified toward a broader economic portfolio. Six diverse industry clusters drive the state's economy: aerospace and

advanced manufacturing; communications, information, and education; financial services; health and biomedical; business services; and tourism and entertainment.

The state's value of shipments of manufactured goods totaled $44 billion in 1995. The following table shows the value of shipments for Connecticut's major industries in that year:

Transport equipment	$8,134,500,000
Electric and electronic equipment	$3,588,300,000
Fabricated metal products	$4,529,800,000
Chemicals and allied products	$4,561,700,000
Instruments and related products	$3,946,500,000
Primary metals	$2,044,000,000
Printing and publishing	$2,849,000,000
Food and food products	$2,064,500,000
Paper and allied products	$2,152,800,000
Rubber and plastic products	$1,731,600,000
Apparel and other textile products	$408,000,000

Leading industrial and service corporations with headquarters in Connecticut include, in order of 1993 sales, General Electric, United Technologies, GTE, Xerox, American Brands, Champion International, Union Carbide, Dun & Bradstreet, Deloitte and Touche, Pitney Bowes, Northeast Utilities, Praxair, and Ultramar. In 1997, 22 Connecticut-based companies appeared on *Fortune* magazine's list of the 500 biggest industrial companies in the US. In 1995, there were 1,776 US patents issued to Connecticut residents.

30COMMERCE

Considering its small size, Connecticut is a busy commercial state. In 1992, Connecticut had 6,262 wholesale establishments, with sales of $46,871.5 million. Some 68% of all wholesale establishments sold durable goods, with sales of $39,673.8 million. Retail sales in 1992 totaled $27,753.7 million, from 21,012 establishments. Of total retail sales in 1992, food stores accounted for 19.7%, automotive dealers 18%, department stores 10.7%, restaurants and taverns 8.9%, and other establishments 42.7%. The estimated value of Connecticut's goods exported abroad was $6.1 billion in 1996. Shipments of transport equipment, nonelectrical machinery, electric and electronic equipment, and instruments accounted for most of the state's foreign sales. Tobacco is the major agricultural export.

31CONSUMER PROTECTION

Since 1959, the Connecticut Department of Consumer Protection has been protecting consumers from injury by product use or merchandising deceit. The department conducts regular inspections of wholesale and retail food establishments, drug-related establishments, liquor retailers, bedding and upholstery dealers and manufacturers, and commercial establishments that use weighing and measuring devices. The department conducts investigations into alleged fraudulent activities, provides information and referral services to consumers, and responds to their complaints. It also licenses most professional and occupational trades and registers home improvement contractors. The Lemon Law Arbitration program and consumer guarantee funds in the areas of home improvement, real estate, and health clubs have returned millions of dollars to aggrieved consumers.

32BANKING

The first banks in Connecticut were established in Hartford, New Haven, Middletown, Bridgeport, Norwich, and New London between 1792 and 1805. By 1850, the state had 45 commercial and 15 savings banks. As of 1996, Connecticut's banking institutions included 9 national banks, 30 state banks and trust companies, and 59 savings banks. Assets of the state's insured commercial banks amounted to $34.0 billion in 1996; their outstanding loans totaled $19.9 billion in 1996.

At the start of 1996 there were 59 (FDIC-insured) savings institutions, with combined assets of $38.8 billion. The Resolution Trust Corporation resolved eight Connecticut savings institutions by the end of 1995 at a cost of $191 million.

Banking operations are regulated by the state department of banking.

33INSURANCE

Connecticut's preeminence in the insurance field and Hartford's title as "insurance capital" of the nation date from the late 18th century, when state businessmen agreed to bear a portion of a shipowner's financial risks in return for a share of the profits. Marine insurance companies were established in Hartford and major port cities between 1797 and 1805. The state's first insurance company had been formed in Norwich in 1795 to provide fire insurance. The nation's oldest fire insurance firm is Hartford Fire Insurance, active since 1810. Subsequently, Connecticut companies have been leaders in life, accident, casualty, automobile, and multiple-line insurance.

In 1996 there were 120 insurance companies domiciled in Connecticut. Property and casualty insurers wrote premiums totaling $4.4 billion, of which automobile insurance accounted for $2.0 billion, and homeowners' insurance $432 million. The insurance industry is regulated by the state department of insurance.

34SECURITIES

There are no securities or commodities exchanges in Connecticut. Securities broker-dealers registered to do business within the state numbered 2,076 as of December 31, 1996, and 79,764 of their agents were similarly registered. At that time, there were also 1,156 investment advisory firms registered to provide services within Connecticut, with 10,546 investment adviser agents registered.

35PUBLIC FINANCE

In 1991, the state of Connecticut underwent a massive restructuring of its revenue stream; the cornerstone of the restructuring was the enactment of a broad-based personal income tax at a rate of 4.5%. Also included in the revenue restructuring was a 25% drop in the sales tax rate (from 8% to 6%) and a reduction in the corporate tax rate from 13.8% to 11.5%.

As part of the income tax bill, the state also enacted a statutory spending cap, while a constitutional expenditure cap was approved by the electorate in November 1992. The statutory cap requires a balanced budget and limits appropriations in all state funds to the growth in the consumer price index for the most recent twelve months or the five-year average growth in personal income, whichever is greater. The expenditure cap has had significant impact on the budgeting process since its inception. The imposition of the cap has resulted in the state making difficult choices about where to spend available dollars, ending some programs, and restricting growth in others.

The 1991 legislature also revised the debt limit statute. The current law limits authorized plus outstanding bonds payable from the general fund to not more than 1.6 times estimated general fund net tax revenues. The new limit has brought discipline to the capital budget process and has significantly reduced the level of new general obligation bond authorizations.

By the close of fiscal 1996, the state finished with a surplus in excess of $160 million, making it the fifth consecutive year-end surplus. The recovery, although moderate, allowed the state to set aside roughly $240,000 in its Budget Reserve Fund due to healthy revenue growth and modest expenditure increases. The revenue stream also provided the means for the governor and the general

assembly to enact laws cutting state taxes during the last biennium.

In 1995, the legislature voted to reduce the state's income tax for all taxpayers. This was accomplished by reducing the tax rate from 4.5% to 3% for taxable income below a certain threshold, depending on type of filer, coupled with the introduction of a $100 tax credit incorporated into the income tax code for those individuals owning property within the state. Also enacted during the same session was a seven-year phase-out of the state's inheritance tax, followed up by both an acceleration of the scheduled phase-down in corporate taxes, and a further decrease in the corporate tax rate to 7.5% by 2000.

The state budget is prepared biennially by the Budget and Financial Management Division of the Office of Policy and Management and submitted by the governor to the general assembly for consideration. In odd-numbered years, the governor transmits a budget document setting forth his financial program for the ensuing biennium with a separate budget for each of the two fiscal years in the biennium. In the even numbered years, the governor transmits a report on the status of the budget enacted in the previous year and recommendations for adjustments and revisions. The fiscal year in Connecticut runs from July 1st to June 30th.

The following is a summary of final revenues and expenditures for fiscal year 1995 and 1996 (in millions of dollars):

REVENUES	1994/95	1995/96
Net Taxes	6,250.7	6,758.2
Other Revenues	718.4	751.6
Other Sources	1,510.6	1,601.3
TOTALS	8,479.7	9,111.1
EXPENDITURES		
Legislative	37.3	37.8
General Government	365.5	387.7
Regulation & Protection	82.5	82.3
Conservation & Development	42.8	49.9
Health & Hospitals	681.0	710.5
Human Services	3,212.0	3,234.1
Education, Libraries & Museums	1,984.3	2,075.7
Corrections	653.1	693.4
Judicial	169.0	178.4
Debt Service	580.9	645.7
Miscellaneous	798.4	730.4
TOTALS	8,616.9	8,846.1

36TAXATION

Connecticut's 1996 tax revenue was $6.7 billion, or $2,072 per capita. Principal taxes are a sales and use tax levied at a rate of 6%, a corporation business tax levied at the basic rate of 10.75%, and a motor fuels tax of 35 cents per gallon of gasoline. Other state taxes are levied on cigarettes, alcoholic beverages, and theater admissions.

In 1995, Connecticuters paid more than $22 billion in federal income taxes.

37ECONOMIC POLICY

Connecticut's principal economic goal is to strengthen employment in the manufacturing sector and urban areas. The state offers low-interest loans and grants for capital expenditures, machinery, land, building, training, and recruiting. In 1996, Connecticut began a plan to reduce the corporate tax rate from 10.7% to 7.5% by 2000. Connecticut offers tax credits and abatements for machinery and equipment and has enterprise zones with favorable tax regulations for businesses. Connecticut Innovations is the state's technology development corporation.

The Connecticut Economic Resource Center, Inc., coordinates business-to-business marketing and recruitment on behalf of the state. Business recruitment missions have been sent to industrialized Europe and Japan to stimulate the state's export program.

[38]HEALTH

The infant mortality rate in 1995 was 7.3 per 1,000 live births, below the national rate of 7.5. There were 11,325 legal abortions in 1995, when there were 44,388 live births. The two leading causes of death in 1995 were heart disease and cancer. Death rates for heart disease, cancer, cerebrovascular diseases, chronic liver disease and cirrhosis, accidents and adverse effects, motor vehicle accidents, homicide, and suicide were below their respective national rates in 1995.

In 1995, Connecticut had 33 non-federal acute care hospitals, with 10,919 licensed beds and 8,192 staffed beds. In 1996, there were 40,585 personnel working in Connecticut hospitals. In 1996, there were 48,864 registered nurses in the state. Hospital expenses in 1995 averaged $1,928 per day and $10,523 per stay. Connecticut had 12,217 physicians in 1996, and 2,957 dentists in 1996. Outstanding medical schools are those of Yale University and the University of Connecticut. Most people in Connecticut are insured; only 10.1% of the population went without insurance in 1995. Some 22% of the population aged 18–30 were smokers, and 56,160 deaths from smoking-related illness were projected for 1995. The AIDS prevalence rate of 32.55 per 100,000 was above the US average of 28.48 in 1995.

[39]SOCIAL WELFARE

In 1996, aid to families with dependent children was paid to 161,000 state residents. The average monthly benefit was $639. The national school lunch program cost the federal government $42.4 million in 1996. In that year, the food stamp program had an average monthly participation of 222,758. In 1995, 566,320 retired state residents received federal Social Security benefits, averaging $789 a month. Medicare programs provided health care and helped subsidize nutritional programs, senior-citizen centers, and home-care services. The Department of Human Resources provides a wide range of social services to individuals of all ages.

With the enactment of the Personal Responsibility and Work Opportunity Reconciliation Act of 1996, the US government has changed the form and regulations for many of its social welfare programs; most significantly, it replaces Aid to Families with Dependent Children (AFDC), an open-ended entitlement program, with Temporary Assistance for Needy Families (TANF), a limited system of assistance funded largely through federal block grants. The reform act also impacts the food stamp program, the Supplemental Security Income program, and the child nutrition program. The law took effect on 1 July 1997 and provided $16.38 billion in block grants for fiscal years 1997–2002. The grants are to be divided among the states based on an equation involving the numbers of former AFDC recipients in each state. Because many of the bills provisions have yet to be implemented into state-by-state policy, it was not possible to include the details of each state's programs for this edition of this work.

As of 1995, unemployment insurance in Connecticut provided recipients with an average weekly benefit of $214.29.

[40]HOUSING

In October 1996 there were 1,353,000 housing units in Connecticut, 1,223,000 of which were occupied. New privately owned housing units authorized in 1996 numbered 8,537, the vast majority of which (7,590) were single-family residences. In total, new housing constructed was valued at $987 million for the year.

As of 1990, the last year for which figures were available, year-round housing units in Connecticut had a median monthly mortgage and owner cost of $1,096 and a median monthly rent of $598 and 2.59 people per unit. In 1990, Connecticut had the second-highest median cost for owners with a mortgage (after New Jersey), and the third-highest median rent cost (after Hawaii and California) of any state. The proportion of all housing units having full plumbing facilities was 99.6%. During 1995/96, the state received $311.4 million in aid from the US Department of Housing and Urban Development, including $51.8 million in community development block grants.

[41]EDUCATION

Believing that the Bible was the only true source of God's truths, Connecticut's Puritan founders viewed literacy as a theological necessity. A law code in 1650 required a town of 50 families to hire a schoolmaster to teach reading and writing, and a town of 100 families to operate a school to prepare students for college. Despite such legislation, many communities in colonial Connecticut did not provide sufficient funding to operate first-rate schools. Public education was greatly strengthened in the 19th century by the work of Henry Barnard, who advocated free public schools, state supervision of common schools, and the establishment of schools for teacher training. By the late 1860s and early 1870s, all of Connecticut's public elementary and high schools were tuition free. In 1865, the Board of Education was established.

As of 1990, 81.9% of adult state residents were high school graduates, and 29.4% had completed four or more years of college. As of fall 1995, Connecticut's public schools had 36,273 teachers and 518,078 students. During 1980, nonpublic schools had 88,404 students. In 1984, Connecticut had 201 Roman Catholic parochial schools (including 6 colleges and 30 high schools) with 71,984 pupils. The state's private preparatory schools include Choate Rosemary Hall (Wallingford), Taft (Waltertown), Westminster (Simsbury), Loomis Chaffee (Windsor), and Miss Porter's (Farmington).

Fall enrollment in institutions of higher education was 159,990 in 1994. Public institutions of higher education include the University of Connecticut at Storrs, with 25,497 students in 1990; four divisions of the Connecticut State University, at New Britain, New Haven, Danbury, and Willimantic; 12 regional community colleges; and 5 state technical colleges.

Connecticut's 23 private four-year colleges and universities had 40,060 students in 1990. Among the oldest institutions are Yale, founded in 1701 and settled in New Haven between 1717 and 1719; Trinity College (1823) in Hartford; and Wesleyan University (1831) in Middletown. Other private institutions include the University of Hartford, University of Bridgeport, Fairfield University, and Connecticut College in New London.

A characteristic of public-school financing in Connecticut has been high reliance on local support for education. Differences among towns in their wealth bases and taxation were compounded by the mechanism used to distribute a majority of state funds for public education—the flat-grant-per-pupil formula. After the Connecticut supreme court in *Horton v. Meskill* (1978) declared this funding mechanism to be unconstitutional, the general assembly in 1979 replaced it with an equity-based model in order to reduce the disparity among towns in expenses per pupil. The 1994/95 school year per pupil expenditure for public elementary and secondary schools was $8,152.

[42]ARTS

Art museums in Connecticut include the Wadsworth Atheneum in Hartford, the oldest (1842) free public art museum in the US; the Yale University Art Gallery and the Yale Center for British Art in New Haven; the New Britain Museum of American Art; and the

Lyman Allyn Museum of Connecticut College in New London. The visual arts are easily accessible through numerous other art museums, galleries, and more than 150 annual arts shows and festivals. The Connecticut Commission on the Arts, established in 1965, has 20 members appointed by the general assembly and 5 by the governor. It administers a state art collection and establishes policies for an art bank program.

The theater is vibrant in contemporary Connecticut, which has numerous dinner theaters, at least 100 community theater groups, and many college and university theater groups. Professional theaters include the American Shakespeare Festival Theater in Stratford, the Long Wharf Theater and the Yale Repertory Theater in New Haven, the Hartford Stage Company, and the Eugene O'Neill Memorial Theater Center in Waterford.

The state's foremost metropolitan orchestras are the Hartford and New Haven symphonies. Professional opera is presented by the Stanford State Opera and by the Connecticut Opera in Hartford. Prominent dance groups include the Connecticut Dance Company in New Haven, the Hartford Ballet Company, and the Pilobolus Dance Theater in the town of Washington. In 1996, Connecticut received $371,000 in federal and state funds to develop the arts. The National Endowment for the Arts contributed $11,980 to the arts in Connecticut and $62,900 to the Connecticut Commission on the Arts.

The state's arts programs had a total audience attendance of 18,750,000 people in 1991, and the number of participating artists totaled 80,235. Connecticut's arts education programs were offered to 23,100 school children. By 1992, there were 900 arts associations in the state and 65 local arts groups. The Connecticut Commission on the Arts received federal grants for its arts education programs and funding through the NEA's state and regional program.

43LIBRARIES AND MUSEUMS

As of 1993/94, Connecticut had 194 public libraries. The leading public library is the Connecticut State Library (Hartford), which houses about 938,982 bound volumes and over 2,451 periodicals as well as the official state historical museum. Connecticut's most distinguished academic collection is the Yale University library system (nine million volumes), headed by the Sterling Memorial Library and the Beinecke Rare Book and Manuscript Library. Special depositories include the Hartford Seminary Foundation's impressive material on Christian-Muslim relations; the Connecticut Historical Society's especially strong collection of materials pertaining to state history and New England genealogy; the Trinity College Library's collection of church documents; the Indian Museum in Old Mystic; the maritime history collections in the Submarine Library at the US Navy submarine base in Groton; and the G. W. Blunt White Library at Mystic Seaport. In all, Connecticut libraries held 12.9 million volumes in 1993/94 and had a combined circulation of 24.4 million.

Connecticut has more than 150 museums, in addition to its historic sites. The Peabody Museum of Natural History at Yale includes an impressive dinosaur hall. Botanical gardens include Harkness Memorial State Park in Waterford, Elizabeth Park in West Hartford, and Hamilton Park Rose Garden in Waterbury. Connecticut's historical sites include the Henry Whitfield House in Guilford (1639), said to be the oldest stone house in the US; the Webb House in Wethersfield, where George Washington met with the Comte de Rochambeau in 1781 to plan military strategy against the British; Noah Webster's birthplace in West Hartford; and the Jonathan Trumbull House in Lebanon.

44COMMUNICATIONS

As of March 1993, 97.4% of the state's 1,236,000 occupied housing units had telephones.

In 1996, Connecticut had 38 AM and 56 FM radio stations, and 13 television stations. There were educational television stations in Bridgeport, Hartford, and Norwich. In addition, 16 large cable television systems served the state.

45PRESS

The *Hartford Courant*, founded in 1764, is generally considered to be the oldest US newspaper in continuous publication. The leading Connecticut dailies in 1997 were the *Courant*, with an average morning circulation of 207,816 (Sundays, 306,058), and the *New Haven Register*, with an average evening circulation of 100,261 (Sundays, 120,252). Statewide, in 1997 there were 10 morning newspapers, 8 evening newspapers, and 10 Sunday newspapers. In 1997, Connecticut also had 57 weekly newspapers.

Leading periodicals are *American Scientist, Connecticut Magazine, Fine Woodworking, Golf Digest,* and *Tennis.*

46ORGANIZATIONS

The 1992 Census of Service Industries counted 1,090 organizations in Connecticut, including 149 business associations; 697 civic, social, and fraternal associations; and 244 other membership organizations. National organizations with headquarters in Connecticut included the Knights of Columbus (New Haven), the American Institute for Foreign Study (Greenwich), Junior Achievement (Stanford), the International Association of Approved Basketball Officials (West Hartford), and Save the Children Federation (Westport).

47TOURISM, TRAVEL, AND RECREATION

Tourism has become an increasingly important part of the state economy in recent decades. Popular tourist attractions include the Mystic Seaport restoration and its aquarium, the Mark Twain House and state capitol in Hartford, the American Clock and Watch Museum in Bristol, the Lock Museum of America in Terryville, and the Yale campus in New Haven. Outstanding events are the Harvard–Yale regatta held each June on the Thames River in New London, and about 50 fairs held in Guilford and other towns between June and October.

Connecticut abounds in outdoor recreational facilities. The state issued licenses to 150,755 hunters and 189,696 fishermen who used its wildlife resources in 1995.

48SPORTS

Connecticut's only major league professional team, the Hartford Whalers of the National Hockey League, moved to North Carolina following the 1996/97 season. New Haven has a minor league baseball franchise, the Red Sox. Auto racing takes place at Lime Rock Race Track, Salisbury.

The state licenses off-track betting facilities for horse racing (not actually held in the state) and pari-mutuel operations for greyhound racing and jai alai.

Connecticut schools, colleges, and universities provide amateur athletic competitions, highlighted by Ivy League football games on autumn Saturdays at the Yale Bowl in New Haven. While Yale has won 12 Ivy League football titles, the University of Connecticut has become a force in men's and women's basketball. The Huskies' women's team won the NCAA championship in 1995 and has advanced to two other Final Four tournaments. The men's team won the National Invitational Tournament in 1988 and has made 37 NCAA Tournament appearances. Other annual sporting events include the US Eastern Ski Jumping Championships in Salisbury in February, and the Greater Hartford Open Golf Tournament in Cromwell in July.

[49]FAMOUS CONNECTICUTERS

Although Connecticut cannot claim any US president or vice president as a native son, John Moran Bailey (1904–75), chairman of the state Democratic Party (1946–75) and of the national party (1961–68), played a key role in presidential politics as a supporter of John F. Kennedy's successful 1960 campaign.

Two Connecticut natives have served as chief justice of the US: Oliver Ellsworth (1745–1807) and Morrison R. Waite (1816–88). Associate justices include Henry Baldwin (1780–1844), William Strong (1808–95), and Stephen J. Field (1816–99). Other prominent federal officeholders were Oliver Wolcott (1760–1833), secretary of the treasury; Gideon Welles (1802–78), secretary of the navy; Dean Acheson (1893–1971), secretary of state; and Abraham A. Ribicoff (b.1910), secretary of health, education, and welfare. An influential US senator was Orville H. Platt (1827–1905), known for his authorship of the Platt Amendment (1901), making Cuba a virtual protectorate of the United States. Also well known are Connecticut senator Ribicoff (served 1963–81) and former governor Lowell P. Weicker, Jr. (b.France, 1931 and served 1991–95), the latter first brought to national attention while a US Senator by his work during the Watergate hearings in 1973.

Notable colonial and state governors include John Winthrop, Jr. (b.England, 1606–76), Jonathan Trumbull (1710–85), William A. Buckingham (1804–75), Simeon Eben Baldwin (1840–1927), Marcus Holcomb (1844–1932),Wilbur L. Cross (1862–1948), Chester Bowles (1901–86), Ribicoff, and Ella Tambussi Grasso (1919–81), elected in 1974 and reelected in 1978 but forced to resign for health reasons at the end of 1980 (Grasso was the first woman governor in the US who did not succeed her husband in the post).

In addition to Winthrop, the founding fathers of Connecticut were Thomas Hooker (b.England, 1586–1647), who was deeply involved in establishing and developing Connecticut Colony, and Theophilus Eaton (b.England, 1590–1658) and John Davenport (b.England, 1597–1670), cofounders and leaders of the strict Puritan colony of New Haven. Other famous historical figures are Israel Putnam (b.Massachusetts, 1718–90), Continental Army major general at the Battle of Bunker Hill, who supposedly admonished his troops not to fire "until you see the whites of their eyes"; diplomat Silas Deane (1737–89); and Benedict Arnold (1741–1801), known for his treasonous activity in the Revolutionary War but also remembered for his courage and skill at Ft. Ticonderoga and Saratoga. Roger Sherman (b.Massachusetts, 1721–93), a signatory to the Articles of Association, Declaration of Independence (1776), Articles of Confederation (1777), Peace of Paris (1783), and the US Constitution (1787), was the only person to sign all these documents; at the Constitutional Convention, he proposed the "Connecticut Compromise," calling for a dual system of congressional representation. Connecticut's most revered Revolutionary War figure was Nathan Hale (1755–76), the Yale graduate who was executed for spying behind British lines. Radical abolitionist John Brown (1800–1859) was born in Torrington.

Connecticuters prominent in US cultural development include painter John Trumbull (1756–1843), son of Governor Trumbull, known for his canvases commemorating the American Revolution. Joel Barlow (1754–1812) was a poet and diplomat in the early national period. Lexicographer Noah Webster (1758–1843) compiled the *American Dictionary of the English Language* (1828). Frederick Law Olmsted (1822–1903), the first American landscape architect, planned New York City's Central Park. Harriet Beecher Stowe (1811–96) wrote one of the most widely read books in history, *Uncle Tom's Cabin* (1852). Mark Twain (Samuel L. Clemens, b.Missouri, 1835–1910) was living in Hartford when he wrote *The Adventures of Tom Sawyer* (1876),

The Adventures of Huckleberry Finn (1885), and *A Connecticut Yankee in King Arthur's Court* (1889). Charles Ives (1874–1954), one of the nation's most distinguished composers, used his successful insurance business to finance his musical career and to help other musicians. Eugene O'Neill (b.New York, 1888–1953), the playwright who won the Nobel Prize for literature in 1936, spent summers in New London during his early years. A seminal voice in modern poetry, Wallace Stevens (b.Pennsylvania, 1879–1955), wrote the great body of his work while employed as a Hartford insurance executive. James Merrill (b.New York, 1926–95), a poet whose works have won the National Book Award (1967), Bollingen Prize (1973), and numerous other honors, lived in Stonington.

Native Connecticuters important in the field of education include Eleazar Wheelock (1711–79), William Samuel Johnson (1727–1819), Emma Willard (1787–1870), and Henry Barnard (1811–1900). Shapers of US history include Jonathan Edwards (1703–58), a Congregationalist minister who sparked the 18th-century religious revival known as the Great Awakening; Samuel Seabury (1729–96), the first Episcopal bishop in the US; Horace Bushnell (1802–76), said to be the father of the Sunday school; Lyman Beecher (1775–1863), a controversial figure in 19th-century American Protestantism who condemned slavery, intemperance, Roman Catholicism, and religious intolerance with equal fervor; and his son Henry Ward Beecher (1813–87), also a religious leader and abolitionist.

Among the premier inventors born in Connecticut were Abel Buel (1742–1824), who designed the first American submarine; Eli Whitney (1765–1825), inventor of the cotton gin and a pioneer in manufacturing; Charles Goodyear (1800–60), who devised a process for the vulcanization of rubber; Samuel Colt (1814–62), inventor of the six-shooter; Frank Sprague (1857–1934), who designed the first major electric trolley system in the US; and Edwin H. Land (1909–91), inventor of the Polaroid Land Camera. The Nobel Prize in physiology or medicine was won by three Connecticuters: Edward Kendall (1886–1972) in 1949, John Enders (1897–1985) in 1954, and Barbara McClintock (1902–92) in 1983.

Other prominent Americans born in Connecticut include clock manufacturer Seth Thomas (1785–1859), circus impresario Phineas Taylor "P. T." Barnum (1810–91), jeweler Charles Lewis Tiffany (1812–1902), financier John Pierpont Morgan (1837–1913), pediatrician Benjamin Spock (b.1903), cartoonist Al Capp (1909–79), soprano Eileen Farrell (b.1920), and consumer advocate Ralph Nader (b.1934). Leading actors and actresses are Ed Begley (1901–70), Katherine Hepburn (b.1909), Rosalind Russell (1911–76), and Robert Mitchum (1917–97).

Walter Camp (1859–1925), athletic director of Yale University who helped formulate the rules of US football, was a native of Connecticut.

[50]BIBLIOGRAPHY

Anderson, Ruth O.M. *From Yankee to American: Connecticut, 1865–1914*. Chester, Conn.: Pequot Press, 1975.

Bachman, Ben. *Upstream: A Voyage on the Connecticut River*. Boston: Houghton Mifflin, 1985.

Bingham, Harold J. *History of Connecticut*. 4 vols. New York: Lewis, 1962.

Bixby, William. *Connecticut: A New Guide*. New York: Scribner, 1974.

Bushman, Richard L. *From Puritan to Yankee: Character and the Social Order in Connecticut, 1690–1765*. Cambridge: Harvard University Press, 1967.

Connecticut, State of. Secretary of State. *Register and Manual 1984*. Hartford, 1984.

Dayton, Cornelia Hughes. *Women Before the Bar: Gender, Law, and Society in Connecticut, 1839–1789*. Chapel Hill, N.C.:

University of North Carolina Press, 1995.

Hamblen, Charles P. *Connecticut Yankees at Gettysburg.* Kent, Ohio: Kent State University Press, 1993.

Janick, Herbet F. *A Diverse People: Connecticut, 1914 to the Present.* Chester, Conn.: Pequot Press, 1975.

Lee, W. Storrs. *The Yankee of Connecticut.* New York: Holt, 1957.

Morse, Jarvis Means, *A Neglected Period of Connecticut's History: 1818–1850.* New Haven: Yale University Press, 1933.

Niven, John. *Connecticut for the Union: The Role of the State in the Civil War.* New Haven: Yale University Press, 1965.

Peirce, Neal R. *The New England States: People, Politics, and Power in the Six New England States.* New York: Norton, 1976.

Rose, Gary L. *Connecticut Politics at the Crossroads.* Lanham, Md.: University Press of America, 1992.

Roth David, M., and Freeman Myer. *From Revolution to Constitution: Connecticut, 1763–1818.* Chester, Conn.: Pequot Press, 1975.

Stuart, Patricia. *Units of Local Government in Connecticut.* Storrs: Institute of Public Service. University of Connecticut, 1979.

Taylor, Robert J. *Colonial Connecticut.* Milkwood, N.Y.: KTO Press, 1979.

Trecker, Janice Law. *Preachers, Rebels, and Traders: Connecticut, 1818–1865.* Chester, Conn.: Pequot Press, 1975.

Van Dusen, Albert E. *Connecticut.* New York: Random House, 1961.

———. *Puritans Against the Wilderness: Connecticut to 1763.* Chester, Conn.: Pequot Press, 1975.

Warren, William L. *Connecticut Art and Architecture: Looking Backwards Two Hundred Years.* Hartford: American Revolution Bicentennial Commission of Connecticut, 1976.

Whipple, Chandler. *The Indian in Connecticut.* Stockbridge, Mass.: Berkshire Traveler Press, 1972.

Zeichner, Oscar. *Connecticut's Years of Controversy, 1775–1776.* Chapel Hill: University of North Carolina Press, 1949.

DELAWARE

State of Delaware

ORIGIN OF STATE NAME: Named for Thomas West, Baron De La Warr, colonial governor of Virginia: the name was first applied to the bay. **NICKNAMES:** The First State; the Diamond State. **CAPITAL:** Dover. **ENTERED UNION:** 7 December 1787 (1st). **SONG:** "Our Delaware." **COLORS:** Colonial blue and buff. **MOTTO:** Liberty and Independence. **COAT OF ARMS:** A farmer and a rifleman flank a shield that bears symbols of the state's agricultural resources—a sheaf of wheat, an ear of corn, and a cow. Above is a ship in full sail; below, a banner with the state motto. **FLAG:** Colonial blue with the coat of arms on a buff-colored diamond; below the diamond is the date of statehood. **OFFICIAL SEAL:** The coat of arms surrounded by the words "Great Seal of the State of Delaware 1793, 1847, 1907." The three dates represent the years in which the seal was revised. **BIRD:** Blue hen's chicken. **FISH:** Sea trout. **INSECT:** Ladybug. **FLOWER:** Peach blossom. **TREE:** American holly. **ROCK:** Sillimanite. **LEGAL HOLIDAYS:** New Year's Day, 1 January; Birthday of Martin Luther King, Jr., 3d Monday in January; Lincoln's Birthday, 1st Monday in February; Washington's Birthday, 3d Monday in February; Good Friday, March or April; Memorial Day, last Monday in May; Independence Day, 4 July; Labor Day, 1st Monday in September; Columbus Day, 2d Monday in October; Veterans Day, 11 November; General Election Day, 1st Tuesday after the 1st Monday in November in even-numbered years; Thanksgiving Day, 4th Thursday in November; Christmas Day, 25 December. **TIME:** 7 AM EST = noon GMT.

[1] LOCATION, SIZE, AND EXTENT

Located on the eastern seaboard of the US, Delaware ranks 49th in size among the 50 states. The state's total area is 2,044 sq mi (5,295 sq km), of which land takes up 1,932 sq mi (5,005 sq km) and inland water 112 sq mi (290 sq km). Delaware extends 35 mi (56 km) E-W at its widest; its maximum N-S extension is 96 mi (154 km).

Delaware is bordered on the N by Pennsylvania; on the E by New Jersey (with the line passing through the Delaware River into Delaware Bay) and the Atlantic Ocean; and on the S and W by Maryland.

The boundary length of Delaware, including a general coastline of 28 mi (45 km), totals 200 mi (322 km). The tidal shoreline is 381 mi (613 km). The state's geographic center is in Kent County, 11 mi (18 km) S of Dover.

[2] TOPOGRAPHY

Delaware lies entirely within the Atlantic Coastal Plain except for its northern tip, above the Christina River, which is part of the Piedmont Plateau. The state's highest elevation is 442 feet (135 meters) on Ebright Road, near Centerville, New Castle County. The rolling hills and pastures of the north give way to marshy regions in the south (notably Cypress Swamp), with sandy beaches along the coast. Delaware's mean elevation, 60 feet (18 meters), is the lowest in the US.

Of all Delaware's rivers, only the Nanticoke, Choptank, and Pocomoke flow westward into Chesapeake Bay. The remainder—including the Christina, Appoquinimink, Leipsic, St. Jones, Murderkill, Mispillion, Broadkill, and Indian—flow into Delaware Bay. There are dozens of inland freshwater lakes and ponds.

[3] CLIMATE

Delaware's climate is temperate and humid. The normal daily mean temperature in Wilmington is 54°F (12°C), ranging from 31°F (–1°C) in January to 76°F (24°C) in July. Both the record low and the record high temperatures for the state were established at Millsboro: –17°F (–27°C) on 17 January 1893 and 110°F (43°C) on 21 July 1930. The average annual precipitation is 41 in (104 cm), and about 21 in (53 cm) of snow falls each year. Wilmington's average share of sunshine is 57%—one of the lowest percentages among leading US cities.

[4] FLORA AND FAUNA

Delaware's mixture of northern and southern flora reflects its geographical position. Common trees include black walnut, hickory, sweetgum, and tulip poplar. Shadbush and sassafras are found chiefly in southern Delaware. Two subspecies of orchid are threatened, and one member of the sedge family is endangered.

Mammals native to the state include the white-tailed deer, red and gray foxes, eastern gray squirrel, muskrat, raccoon, woodcock, and common cottontail. The quail, robin, wood thrush, cardinal, and eastern meadowlark are representative birds, while various waterfowl, especially Canada geese, are common. The southern bald eagle and the Delmarva Peninsula fox squirrel are endangered species.

[5] ENVIRONMENTAL PROTECTION

The Coastal Zone Act of 1971 outlaws new industry "incompatible with the protection of the natural environment" of shore areas, but in 1979 the act was amended to permit offshore oil drilling and the construction of coastal oil facilities. The traffic of oil tankers into the Delaware Bay represents an environmental hazard.

In 1982, Delaware enacted a bottle law requiring deposits on most soda and beer bottles; deposit for aluminum cans were made mandatory in 1984. In that year, Delaware became the first state to administer the national hazardous waste program at the state level. The state's municipal governments have constructed 3 municipal land fills to handle the solid waste produced by the state's 670,000 residents.

State environmental protection agencies include the Department of natural resources and Environmental Control, Coastal Zone Industrial Control Board, and Council on Soil and Water Conservation.

6POPULATION

Delaware ranked 46th among the 50 states in January 1990, with a population of 666,168; the population density was 340.8 people per square mile (131 per sq km). The estimated population in 1996 was 724,842, an 8.8% increase.

About 66% of all Delawareans live in metropolitan areas. The largest cities in 1994 were Wilmington, with an estimated 72,799, and Dover, the capital, with 28,876. The greater Wilmington urbanized area of Delaware had a population of 407,962 in 1990.

7ETHNIC GROUPS

Black Americans constitute Delaware's largest racial minority, numbering 112,000 in 1990 and comprising about 17% of the population. Approximately 16,000, or 2.4% of the total population is of Hispanic origin.

The 22,275 foreign-born made up 3.3% of the state's population in 1990. The United Kingdom, Germany, India, Italy, and Canada were the leading places of origin.

8LANGUAGES

English in Delaware is basically North Midland, with Philadelphia features in Wilmington and the northern portion. In the north, one wants off a bus, lowers curtains rather than blinds, pronounces wharf without /h/, and says /noo/ and /doo/ for new and due and /krik/ for creek. In 1990, 575,393 Delawareans —of the resident population 3 years of age or older—spoke only English at home. Other languages spoken at home, and the number of speakers, included Spanish, 15,302, and German, 4,206.

9RELIGIONS

The earliest permanent European settlers in Delaware were Swedish and Finnish Lutherans and Dutch Calvinists. English Quakers, Scotch-Irish Presbyterians, and Welsh Baptists arrived in the 18th century, though Anglicization was the predominant trend. The Great Awakening, America's first religious revival, began at Lewes with the arrival of George Whitefield, an Anglican preacher, on 30 October 1739, and the colony soon became a center of early Methodist activity. The Methodist Church was the largest denomination in Delaware by the early 19th century. Subsequent immigration brought Lutherans from Germany, Roman Catholics from Ireland, Germany, Italy, and Poland, and Jews from Germany, Poland, and Russia; most of the Catholic and Jewish immigrants settled in cities, Wilmington in particular.

There were 116,341 Catholics and an estimated 9,500 Jews in Delaware in 1990. Protestantism has the largest number of adherents; in 1990, the leading groups were the United Methodist Church, 61,091; the Episcopal Church, 13,307; and the United Presbyterian Church, 15,401.

10TRANSPORTATION

The New Castle and Frenchtown Railroad, a portage route, was built in 1832; the state's first passenger line—the Philadelphia, Wilmington, and Baltimore Railroad—opened six years later. As of 1995 there were 274 rail mi (441 km) of track. In 1995, Delaware's five railroads carried over 12.4 million tons of freight within the state—58% of the rail tonnage originating from within the state were chemicals. In 1995/96 Amtrak operated approximately 70 daily trains through Delaware and served both Newark (ridership: 3,840) and Wilmington (ridership: 649,832). Consoli-

dated Rail and CSX are Delaware's main freight carriers. The Delaware Authority for Regional Transit (DART) provides state-subsidized bus service.

In 1995, the state had 5,631 mi (9,066 km) of public highways, roads, and streets. In the same year, there were 591,908 registered vehicles and 524,992 licensed drivers. Delaware's first modern highway—and the first dual highway in the US—running about 100 mi (160 km) from Wilmington to the southern border, was financed by industrialist T. Coleman du Pont between 1911 and 1924. The twin spans of the Delaware Memorial Bridge connect Delaware highways to those in New Jersey; The Delaware Turnpike section of the John F. Kennedy Memorial Highway links the bridge system with Maryland. The Lewes–Cape May Ferry provides auto and passenger service between southern Delaware and New Jersey.

In 1995, New Castle, Delaware's chief port, handled 12,455,809 tons of goods, followed by Wilmington, with a tonnage of 4,272,719 that year. The Delaware River is the conduit for much of the oil brought by tanker to the US east coast.

Delaware had 36 airfields (23 airport, 12 heliports, 1 seaplane base) at the beginning of 1995, of which Greater Wilmington Airport was the largest and busiest.

11HISTORY

Delaware was inhabited nearly 10,000 years ago, and a succession of various cultures occupied the area until the first European contact. At that time, the Leni-Lenape (Delaware) Indians occupied northern Delaware, while several tribes, including the Nanticoke and Assateague, inhabited southern Delaware. The Dutch in 1631 were the first Europeans to settle in what is now Delaware, but their little colony (at Lewes) was destroyed by Indians. Permanent settlements were made by the Swedes in 1638 (at Wilmington, under the leadership of a Dutchman, Peter Minuit) and by the Dutch in 1651 (at New Castle). The Dutch conquered the Swedes in 1655, and the English conquered the Dutch in 1664. Eighteen years later, the area was ceded by the duke of York (later King James II), its first English proprietor, to William Penn. Penn allowed Delaware an elected assembly in 1704, but the colony was still subject to him and to his deputy governor in Philadelphia; ties to the Penn family and Pennsylvania were not severed until 1776. Boundary quarrels disturbed relations with Maryland until Charles Mason and Jeremiah Dixon surveyed the western boundary of Delaware (and the Maryland-Pennsylvania boundary) during the period 1763–68. By this time, virtually all the Indians had been driven out of the territory.

In September 1777, during the War for Independence, British soldiers marched through northern Delaware, skirmishing with some of Washington's troops at Cooch's Bridge, near Newark, and seizing Wilmington, which they occupied for a month. In later campaigns, Delaware troops with the Continental Army fought so well that they gained the nickname "Blue Hen's Chicken," after a famous breed of fighting gamecocks. On 7 December 1787, Delaware became the first state to ratify the federal Constitution. Although Delaware had not abolished slavery, it remained loyal to the Union during the Civil War. By that time, it was the one slave state in which a clear majority of blacks (about 92%) were already free. However, white Delawareans generally resented the Reconstruction policies adopted by Congress after the Civil War, and by manipulation of registration laws denied blacks the franchise until 1890.

The key event in the state's economic history was the completion of a railroad between Philadelphia and Baltimore through Wilmington in 1838, encouraging the industrialization of northern Delaware, Wilmington grew so rapidly that by 1900 it encompassed 41% of the state's population. Considerable

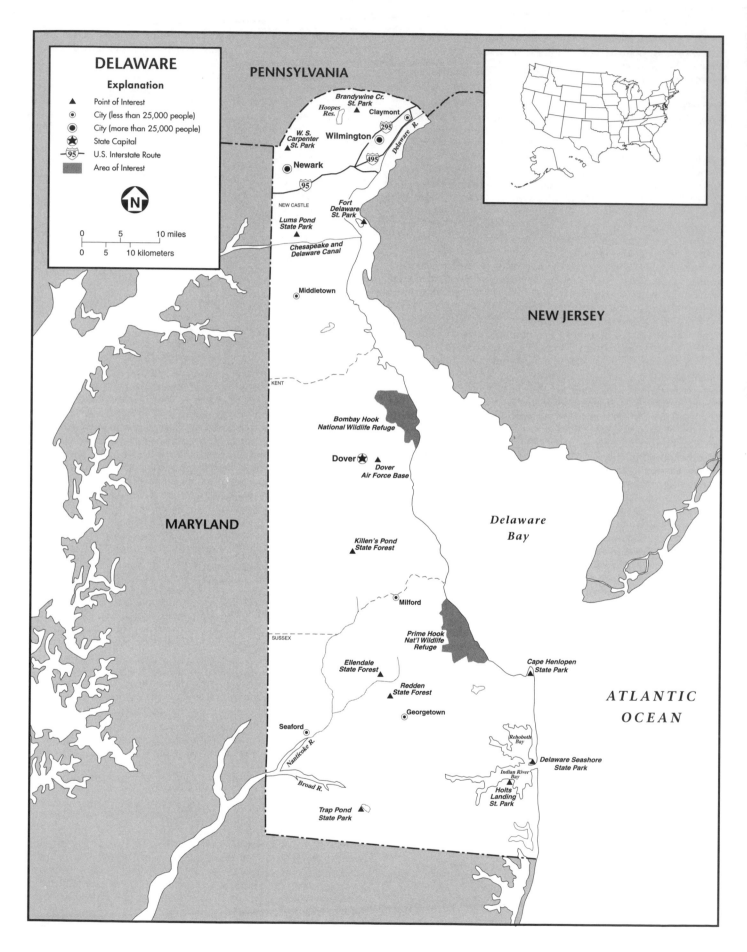

DELAWARE

Explanation

▲ Point of Interest
⊙ City (less than 25,000 people)
◉ City (more than 25,000 people)
★ State Capital
95 U.S. Interstate Route
Area of Interest

N

0   5   10 miles
0   5   10 kilometers

PENNSYLVANIA

Brandywine Cr. St. Park
Hoopes Res.
Claymont
W. S. Carpenter St. Park
Wilmington
Delaware R.
295
495
Newark
95
NEW CASTLE
Fort Delaware St. Park
Lums Pond State Park
Chesapeake and Delaware Canal
Middletown

NEW JERSEY

KENT

Bombay Hook National Wildlife Refuge

Dover ★ ▲ Dover Air Force Base

Delaware Bay

MARYLAND

Killen's Pond State Forest

Milford

SUSSEX

Prime Hook Nat'l Wildlife Refuge

Ellendale State Forest

Redden State Forest

Cape Henlopen State Park

Georgetown

ATLANTIC OCEAN

Seaford

Nanticoke R.

Rehoboth Bay

Delaware Seashore State Park

Indian River Bay

Broad R.

Holts Landing St. Park

Trap Pond State Park

foreign immigration contributed to this growth, largely from the British Isles (especially Ireland) and Germany in the mid-19th century and from Italy, Poland, and Russia in the early 20th century.

Flour and textile mills, shipyards, carriage factories, iron foundries, and morocco leather plants were Wilmington's leading enterprises for much of the 19th century. By the early 1900s however, E. I. du Pont de Nemours and Co., founded near Wilmington in 1802 as a gunpowder manufacturer, made the city famous as a center for the chemical industry.

During the same period, Delaware's agricultural income rose. Peaches and truck crops flourished in the 19th century, along with corn and wheat; poultry and soybeans became major sources of agricultural income in the 20th century. Another economic stimulus was improved transportation.

During the 1950s, Delaware's population grew by an unprecedented 40%. The growth was greatest around Dover, site of a large air base, and on the outskirts of Wilmington. Wilmington itself lost population after 1945 because of the proliferation of suburban housing developments, offices, and factories, including two automobile assembly plants and an oil refinery. Although many neighborhood schools became racially integrated during the 1950s, massive busing was instituted by court order in 1978 to achieve a racial balance in schools throughout northern Delaware.

The 1980s ushered in a period of dramatic economic improvement. According to state sources, Delaware was one of only two states to improve its financial strength during the recession that plagued the early part of the decade. In 1988, Delaware enjoyed an unemployment rate of 3.3%, the second lowest in the country. The state's revenues grew at an average of 7.7% in the early 1980s, even while it successively cut the personal income tax. Some of Delaware's prosperity came from a 1981 state law which raised usury limits and lowered taxes for large financial institutions. More than 30 banks established themselves in Delaware, including Chase Manhattan Bank and Manufacturers Hanover. The state also succeeded in using its simplified incorporation procedures to attract foreign companies, bringing in an estimated $1 million in incorporation fees from Asian companies in the late 1980s. The state's efforts to attract industry have not been confined to financial institutions. Delaware has built two industrial parks in Sussex, its southernmost county, and a third industrial complex in the center of the state.

While business has fared well in Delaware, the state lags behind in social welfare indicators. Delaware's rates of teenage pregnancy and infant mortality are among the highest in the country, while its welfare benefits are lower than those of any other mid-Atlantic state with the exception of West Virginia. Other problems in the mid-1990s included housing shortages, urban sprawl, and pollution.

12STATE GOVERNMENT

Delaware has had four state constitutions, adopted in 1776, 1792, 1831, and 1897. Under the 1897 document, as amended, the legislative branch is the general assembly, consisting of a 21-member senate and a 41-member house of representatives. Senators are elected for four years, representatives for two. Legislators earned $26,000 annually in 1995.

Delaware's major elected executives include the governor and lieutenant governor (separately elected), treasurers, attorney general, auditor of accounts, and insurance commissioner. All serve four-year terms, except the treasurer and auditor, who are elected for two years. The governor, who may be reelected only once, must be at least 30 years of age and must have been a US citizen for 12 years and a state resident for 6 years before taking office. In 1996 the governor's salary was $95,000. The legislature

may override a gubernatorial veto by a three-fifths vote of the elected members of each house. An amendment to the state constitution must be approved by a two-thirds vote in each house of the general assembly in two successive sessions with an election intervening; Delaware is the only state in which amendments need not be ratified by the voters.

Voters must be US citizens at least 18 years of age. There is no minimum residency requirement, and mail registration is allowed.

13POLITICAL PARTIES

The Democrats were firmly entrenched in Delaware for three decades after the Civil War; a subsequent period of Republican dominance lasted until the depression of the 1930s. Since then, the two parties have been relatively evenly matched.

As of 1994, 142,542 voters were registered as members of the Democratic party, accounting for 43% of the total number of registered voters, while 125,829, or 37% were registered as Republicans. There were 67,717 voters registered as independents or with minor parties. In November 1996, Delaware gave the Democratic incumbent, Bill Clinton, 52% of the vote. Republican Bob Dole received 37%, and Independent Ross Perot collected 11%. Democrat Thomas R. Carper won reelection to the governor's office, Republican William Roth was reelected Senator in 1988 and 1994, and Democrat Joseph Biden won reelection to the Senate in 1990 and 1996. Republican Michael Castle won reelection in 1994 and 1996 to remain Delaware's sole US Representative. In 1997 there were 13 Democrats and 8 Republicans in the state senate, and 27 Republicans and 14 Democrats in the state house. In 1994 there was one Hispanic in public office, and 23 blacks held elected office. As of 1995, 17 women held statewide elective office.

Delaware Presidential Vote by Major Political Parties, 1948–96

YEAR	ELECTORAL VOTE	DELAWARE WINNER	DEMOCRAT	REPUBLICAN
1948	3	DEWEY (R)	67,813	69,588
1952	3	*EISENHOWER (R)	83,315	90,059
1956	3	*EISENHOWER (R)	79,421	98,057
1960	3	*KENNEDY (D)	99,590	96,373
1964	3	*JOHNSON (D)	122,704	78,078
1968	3	*NIXON (R)	89,194	96,714
1972	3	*NIXON (R)	92,283	140,357
1976	3	*CARTER (D)	122,596	109,831
1980	3	*REAGAN (R)	105,700	111,185
1984	3	*REAGAN (R)	101,656	152,190
1988	3	*BUSH (R)	108,647	139,639
1992**	3	*CLINTON(D)	126,054	102,313
1996**	3	*CLINTON(D)	140,355	99,062

* Won US presidential election.

** Independent Ross Perot received 59,213 votes in 1992 and 28,719 votes in 1996.

14LOCAL GOVERNMENT

Delaware is divided into three counties. In New Castle, voters elect a county executive and a county council; in Sussex, the members of the elective county council choose a county administrator, who supervises the executive departments of the county government. Kent operates under an elected levy court, which sets tax rates and runs the county according to regulations spelled out by the assembly. Most of Delaware's 57 municipalities elect a mayor and council. In 1992 Delaware had 19 school districts and 196 special districts.

15STATE SERVICES

Public education is supervised by state boards of education and vocational education. Highways are the responsibility of the

Department of Transportation, while medical care, mental health facilities, drug- and alcohol-abuse programs, and help for the aging fall within the jurisdiction of the Department of Health and Social Services. Public protection services are provided primarily through the Department of Public Safety and Department of Correction. The Department of Labor has divisions covering employment services, vocational rehabilitation, unemployment insurance, and equal employment opportunity. Other services include those of the Department of Services to Children, Youth and Their Families and the Department of Community Affairs.

[16]JUDICIAL SYSTEM

Delaware's highest court is the supreme court, composed of a chief justice and 4 associate justices, all appointed by the governor and confirmed by the senate for 12-year terms, as are all state judges. Other state courts include the court of chancery, comprising a chancellor and two vice-chancellors, and the superior court, which has a president judge and 10 associate judges. There are 7 judges on the Court of Common Pleas in Wilmington. There were 2,178 practicing attorneys in 1996.

Delaware was the last state to abolish the whipping post. During the 1900–1942 period, 1,604 prisoners (22% of the state's prison population) were beaten with a cat-o'-nine-tails. The whipping post, nicknamed "Red Hannah," was used for the last time in 1952 but was not formally abolished until 1972. The death penalty is authorized in Delaware, with lethal injection as the method of execution. Delaware has executed 17 persons since 1930. In 1995 there were 14 persons under sentence of death. In 1995, Delaware had a total crime rate of 5,158.7 per 100,000, which included 725 for violent crime and 4,433.8 for property crime. In 1995 there were 4,618 inmates held in 8 state and federal correctional facilities, an incarceration rate of 644 inmates per 100,000 inhabitants.

[17]ARMED FORCES

Delaware's main defense facility is the military airlift wing at Dover Air Force Base, with 4,001 military personnel in 1996. There were some 78,000 veterans living in Delaware as of 1 July 1996; fewer than 500 were veterans of World War I, 21,000 of World War II, 13,000 of the Korean conflict, 24,000 of the Vietnam era, and 6,000 of the Persian Gulf War. Veterans' benefits totaled $127 million in 1995/96.

The Delaware National Guard and Reserve had 6,868 members in 1996. In 1993 the Delaware state police employed 489 full-time sworn officers, or 7 per 10,000 residents.

[18]MIGRATION

Delaware has attracted immigrants from a variety of foreign countries: Sweden, Finland, and the Netherlands in the early days; England, Scotland, and Ireland during the later colonial period; and Italy, Poland, and Russia, among other countries, during the first 130 years of statehood. The 1960s and 1970s saw the migration of Puerto Ricans to Wilmington. Delaware enjoyed a net gain from migration of 122,000 persons between 1940 and 1970. Between 1970 and 1990, however, there was a net migration of only about 25,000. Net domestic migration between 1990 and 1996 totaled 23,000, while net international migration for the same period totaled 5,733. Half of all residents in 1990 had been born within the state. About 46% of state residents (age 5 and older) lived in a different house in 1985 than in 1990; of those who moved, 34% moved to another state.

[19]INTERGOVERNMENTAL COOPERATION

Among the interstate agreements to which Delaware subscribes are the Delaware River and Bay Authority Compact, Delaware River Basin Compact, Atlantic States Marine Fisheries Compact, and Southern Interstate Energy Compact.

Federal aid to Delaware was $600 million in 1995/96, least among all the states.

[20]ECONOMY

Since the 1930s, and particularly since the mid-1970s, Delaware has been one of the nation's most prosperous states. Although manufacturing—preeminently the chemical and automotive industries—is the major contributor to the state's economy, it is the third largest employer after services and trade. Tourism also plays a major role in the state's economy.

Delaware's gross state product in 1994 was $26,697 million, to which private goods-producing industries contributed $6,586 million; private services-producing industries, $17,746 million; and government, $2,364 million. Delaware's per capita personal income in 1995 was $26,273, or 6th in the US. In 1996 there were a total of 2,044 bankruptcy filings in the state.

[21]INCOME

Average personal income per capita in Delaware was $33,189 in 1996, 5th highest among the 50 states. Median household income was $34,928 in 1995. Total personal income increased by 6.3% to $20 billion in 1996, up from $18.8 billion in 1995. In 1995, 10.3% of the state's residents were living below the federal poverty level. In 1996, per capita disposable income was $23,654.

[22]LABOR

The labor force totaled 388,500 at the beginning of 1997. In January 1997, 5.6% of all Delawareans were unemployed. At the end of 1996, there were 102,300 Delaware residents in the service industry; 88,200 in wholesale and retail trade; 57,600 in manufacturing; 21,600 in construction; 16,400 in transportation, communications, and utilities; 51,300 in government; and 43,400 in finance, insurance, and real estate. A federal survey in 1994 revealed the following 1995 earning and employment pattern projection for major industry groups in Delaware:

	EARNINGS (IN MILLIONS OF 1982 DOLLARS)	EMPLOYMENT IN THOUSANDS
Total	8,670.3	435.9
Farm	148.6	5.5
Nonfarm	8,521.6	430.5
Private	7,435.9	371.9
Agricultural service, forestry, fisheries	35.9	3.2
Mining	8.4	0.2
Construction	698.3	28.2
Manufacturing	2,412.8	73.0
Nondurable goods	1,873.1	54.9
Durable goods	539.7	18.2
Transportation and public utilities	446.8	18.6
Wholesale trade	372.1	14.7
Retail trade	770.8	73.3
Finance, insurance, and real estate	777.6	45.4
Services	1,913.3	115.2
Government and government enterprises	1,085.7	58.6

Some 42,900 Delawareans—about 13% of all employees—belonged to labor unions in 1995. Unionization among workers in the private manufacturing sector was 18.7%.

[23]AGRICULTURE

Though small by national standards, Delaware's agriculture is efficient and productive. In 1995, Delaware's total farm marketings were $675.6 million (40th in the US), and its income from crops was $159.1 million.

Tobacco was a leading crop in the early colonial era, but was soon succeeded by corn and wheat. Peaches were a mainstay during the mid-19th century, until the orchards were devastated by "the yellows," a tree disease. Today, the major field crops are corn, soybeans, barley, wheat, melons, potatoes, mushrooms, lima beans, and green peas. Production in 1996 included corn for grain, 21,450,000 bushels, valued at $61,133,000; soybeans, 7,595,000 bushels, $52,406,000; wheat, 4,134,000 bushels, $17,776,000; and barley, 1,564,000 bushels, $4,614,000.

24ANIMAL HUSBANDRY

In 1995 an estimated 10,000 milk cows produced 146 million lb of milk. Also during 1995 an estimated 5.3 million lb of chicken were produced and an estimated 1.39 billion lb of broilers were produced and valued at an estimated $474 million. Delaware produced an estimated 138 million eggs valued at around $13 million.

25FISHING

Fishing, once an important industry in Delaware, has declined in recent decades. The total commercial landings in 1995 were 10,108,000 lb, worth $7,858,000. Clams, plentiful until the mid-1970s, are in short supply because of overharvesting. Delaware issued 26,798 sport fishing licenses in 1995/96.

26FORESTRY

Delaware has approximately 365,000 acres of forest land of which approximately 90% is classified as commercial forest land. Nonindustrial private landowners own over 80% of Delaware's forests, while approximately 10% is publicly owned and 9% is owned by forest industry.

Southern Delaware contains many loblolly pine forests as well as the northernmost stand of bald cypress. Northern Delaware contains more hardwoods, such as oak and yellow poplar. Other common species are gum, maple, and American holly, which is Delaware's state tree. Delaware has approximately 10,000 acres (4,050 hectares) of state forests, which are managed on a multiple-use basis and are open to the public.

27MINING

The value of nonfuel mineral production in Delaware in 1995 was about $8.9 million (50th), according to estimated data compiled by the U.S. Geological Survey. Production of construction sand and gravel was 2.6 million metric tons, valued at $8.9 million. However, the Delaware Geological Survey estimated that the state's total nonfuel mineral–related activity is approximately $30 million annually. Demand for sand and gravel was at an all-time high because of a $770 million state highway construction program. Delaware also produced magnesium compounds for use in chemical and pharmaceutical manufacturing. The State was one of only six states that produced magnesium compounds in the US (extracted from seawater close to the mouth of the Delaware Bay near Lewes), which with aluminum hydroxides are used in the manufacture of antacid product.

28ENERGY AND POWER

Installed electric capacity totaled 2.29 million kW in 1996; production of electric power reached 8.5 billion kWh in 1995. Most of the power is supplied by coal- and oil-fired plants. Delaware has no nuclear reactors, nor does it have any fossil fuel resources.

29INDUSTRY

From its agricultural beginnings, Delaware has developed into an important industrial state. Today, Wilmington is called the "Chemical Capital of the World," largely because of E. I. du Pont de Nemours and Co., a chemical industry giant originally founded as a powder mill in 1802. As of 1997 the company was the 10th largest US industrial corporation, with sales of $39.689 billion.

The Chrysler Corp. is another leading employer. During the 1994 model year, 232,314 cars were assembled in Delaware. Notable Delaware manufactures, in addition to chemicals and transportation equipment, include apparel, processed meats and vegetables, paper, printing and publishing, scientific instruments, and plastic products.

The total value of shipments by manufacturers in 1995 were:

Chemicals, chemical products	$3,524,700,000
Food, food products	2,252,400,000
Rubber, miscellaneous plastic products	849,800,000
Instruments and related products	807,800,000
Paper, allied products	636,700,000

In 1995 there were 419 US patents issued to Delaware residents.

30COMMERCE

Wholesale trade in Delaware totaled $12,258 million, conducted by 1,088 establishments. Durable goods accounted for 67% of wholesale establishments and 17.8% of wholesale sales. Retail sales in 1992 totaled $6,491.9 million, conducted by 4,865 establishments. The leading retail sectors by sales were food stores, 18.1%; automotive dealers, 19.1%; and department stores, 14.9%.

In 1996, Delaware exported $1.6 billion worth of products to foreign markets. Exporters located in Delaware had sales of nearly $4.6 billion in 1996.

31CONSUMER PROTECTION

The Consumer Protection Unit of the Attorney General's Office is responsible for enforcing state consumer protection laws. It investigates consumer complaints; mediates resolution, when appropriate; and takes enforcement, when warranted. It also provides consumer education programs.

32BANKING

As of December 1996, there were 59 financial institutions in Delaware, including full-service commercial banks, credit card banks, non-deposit and limited-purpose trust companies, wholesale banks, and federal and state savings banks. Delaware credit card banks accounted for 63% of securitized credit card loans for the top credit card banks in the nation. Delaware is home to 7 of the top 15 credit card banks with assets greater than $500 million and home to 6 of the 15 most profitable credit card banks in the nation. Total assets as of 31 December 1996 for Delaware's 59 financial institutions were $128 billion.

33INSURANCE

As of 1995, a total of 494,000 life insurance policies valued at almost $24.5 billion were in force. The average of $196,100 in life insurance per family ranked 1st among the 50 states and was surpassed only by the District of Columbia. Life insurance benefits totaling $657.9 million were paid in 1991; death payments constituted 27% of the total.

34SECURITIES

Delaware has no securities exchanges. There are over 1,000 broker and dealer firms registered to sell securities within the state.

35PUBLIC FINANCE

Delaware's annual state budget is prepared by the Office of the Budget and submitted by the governor to the general assembly for amendment and approval. The fiscal year runs from 1 July through 30 June. The following table summarizes state general revenues and expenditures for 1995/96 (budgeted) in millions:

	1995	1996
REVENUES		
Individual Income Taxes	$ 588.6	$ 631.4
Franchise Taxes	302.9	319.3
Business & Occupational Gross Receipts	112.0	110.9
Corporation Income Taxes	86.8	75.1
Other Receipts	511.1	519.5
TOTALS	$ 1,601.4	$ 1,656.2
EXPENDITURES		
Public Education	$ 496.0	$ 521.8
Higher Education	152.4	157.5
Health, Social Services	372.9	412.7
Transportation*	0.0	0.0
Other Outlays	519.7	559.0
TOTALS	$ 1,541.0	$ 1,651.0

*Includes all transportation sources

At the close of fiscal year 1996, the outstanding debt of Delaware state and local governments was more than $3.4 billion, or $4,644 per capita.

[36]TAXATION
Delaware's state tax revenues come primarily from levies on personal and corporate income, incorporations, inheritance and estates, motor fuels, cigarettes, state lottery, and alcoholic beverages.

Delaware's corporate tax rate was 8.7% as of 1 January 1994, and its individual income tax rate, as of 1 January 1994, ranged from 0.0 to 7.1%. There is no state sales tax.

Delaware paid $4.4 billion in federal taxes in 1995 and received $3.2 billion in federal expenditures, for a spending/tax ratio of 0.7.

[37]ECONOMIC POLICY
Legislation passed in 1899 permits companies to be incorporated and chartered in Delaware even if they do no business in the state and hold their stockholders' meetings elsewhere. Another incentive to chartering in Delaware is the state's court of chancery, which has extensive experience in dealing with corporate problems.

The Delaware Economic Development Office seeks to create jobs by helping existing businesses to grow and by encouraging out-of-state companies to relocate to Delaware. The Development Office offers a variety of financing programs for small businesses, including assistance with land acquisition, loans and tax credits for capital investments, and state grants to match federal awards for research and development. The Delaware Innovation Fund is a private, non-profit public/private initiative to assist companies with pre-startup seed money, with long-term loans for establishing patents, business plans, and to begin commercialization ($10,000–$150,000).

[38]HEALTH
Infant mortality for 1994 was 6.7 per 1,000 live births. With an overall death rate of 898.1 per 100,000 residents, Delaware had lower death rates than the nation as a whole for heart diseases, cerebrovascular diseases, accidents and adverse effects, motor vehicle accidents, and suicide, but higher death rates for cancer.

Delaware's 7 private acute care hospitals had 86,091 admissions and 1,711 beds in 1995. The average expense of a community hospital for care was $1,790 per inpatient day and $9,289 per hospital stay in 1995. Delaware has 2,613 licensed

physicians, 10,450 licensed registered nurses, and 365 licensed dentists.

In Delaware, 17.1% of the population was uninsured. Many of Delaware's residents aged 18–30 (approximately 29%) were smokers in 1995. The heart disease death rate was somewhat lower than the US average. In 1995, 276.1 per 100,000 people died from heart disease. The unintentional injury death rate improved slightly from 37.8 in 1992 to 36.8 per 100,000 population in 1993.

In 1995, the AIDS prevalence rate in Delaware (44.31 cases per 100,000 population) was higher than the US average (28.48 per 100,000 population).

[39]SOCIAL WELFARE
Delaware does not have a history of expansive social programs. A survey made in 1938 found that the state, which then ranked 4th nationally in per capita income, spent little more than the poorest southern states on public assistance. By 1991, however, the state ranked 25th in terms of public aid recipients as a percentage of population.

Aid to families with dependent children was given to 23,000 residents in 1996, averaging $407 a month. In 1996 the food stamp program had an average monthly participation of 57,836; the school lunch program cost the federal government $11.5 million.

With the enactment of the Personal Responsibility and Work Opportunity Reconciliation Act of 1996, the US government has changed the form and regulations for many of its social welfare programs; most significantly, it replaces Aid to Families with Dependent Children (AFDC), an open-ended entitlement program, with Temporary Assistance for Needy Families (TANF), a limited system of assistance funded largely through federal block grants. The reform act also impacts the food stamp program, the Supplemental Security Income program, and the child nutrition program. The law took effect on 1 July 1997 and provided $16.38 billion in block grants for fiscal years 1997–2002. The grants are to be divided among the states based on an equation involving the numbers of former AFDC recipients in each state. Because many of the bills provisions have yet to be implemented into state-by-state policy, it was not possible to include the details of each state's programs for this edition of this work.

Social Security benefits went to 121,580 retired state residents in 1995; the average monthly payment was $747. The weekly unemployment check averaged $195.34 in 1996.

[40]HOUSING
In October 1996 there were approximately 314,000 housing units in Delaware, of which 269,000 were occupied. In that year, there were 4,370 new privately owned housing units authorized for construction, the vast majority of which (4,218) were single-family units. In total, newly constructed housing units in 1996 were valued at $351 million. In 1990, the last year for which figures are available, the median value of a home in Delaware was $100,100, up 42% from 1980 after adjusting for inflation. In 1990, the median rent for a housing unit was $495 per month. The median monthly owner costs were $763 with a mortgage and $200 without one. During 1995/96, Delaware received $43.6 million in aid from the US Department of Housing and Urban Development, including $8.1 million in community development block grants.

[41]EDUCATION
The development of public support and financing for an adequate public educational system was the handiwork of industrialist-Progressive Pierre S. du Pont, who undertook the project in 1919. Today's schools compare favorably with those of neighboring

states. Nearly 80.1% of adult Delawareans were high school graduates in 1992.

In 1996, 110,549 students were enrolled in public elementary and secondary schools, and 24,712 students were enrolled in public institutes of higher education. Delaware ranked 7th among the states in per capita state government expenditures for all education in 1993/94. Delaware has two public four-year institutions: the University of Delaware (Newark), with a total undergraduate enrollment of 15,359 in 1996; and Delaware State College (Dover), with an enrollment of 3,175. Alternatives to these institutions include Widener University and the Delaware Technical and Community College, which has four campuses. There are three independent colleges: Goldey Beacon (Wilmington), Wesley (Dover), and Wilmington.

42ARTS

Wilmington has a local symphony orchestra, opera society, and drama league. The Playhouse, located in the Du Pont Building in Wilmington, shows first-run Broadway plays. The restored Grand Opera House in Wilmington, Delaware's Center for the Performing Arts, is the home of the Delaware Symphony and the Delaware Opera Guild as well as host to performances of popular music and ballet. In 1996, Delaware received $54,000,000 in federal funds for the development of the arts. The National Endowment for the Arts (NEA) contributed $361,000 directly to the arts and $908,000 to the Delaware Division of the Arts.

By 1991, there were 60 art associations and three local associations in Delaware. The state's arts programs attracted an audience of 3,755,000 people. The number of contributing artists was 34,544. During 1991 art education programs were made available to 16,000 school children. Numbers for 1996 are unavailable.

In 1996 the Delaware Division of the Arts received a small grant from the federal government for the development of its arts programs. The Division of Arts also received monies through the NEA's state and regional programs.

43LIBRARIES AND MUSEUMS

Delaware had 30 public libraries and branches in 1995, with 1,319,821 books and other materials and a circulation of 2,957,030. The University of Delaware's Hugh M. Morris Library, with 2,213,548 volumes, is the largest academic library in the state. Other distinguished libraries include the Eleutherian Mills Historical Library, the Winterthur Library, and the Historical Society of Delaware Library (Wilmington). The Delaware™ Library Information connects all types of libraries through a statewide computer/telecommunication system.

Notable among the state's 24 museums and numerous historical sites are the Hagley Museum and Delaware Art Museum, both in Wilmington, where the Historical Society of Delaware maintains a museum in the Old Town Hall. The Henry Francis du Pont Winterthur Museum features a collection of American antiques and decorative arts. The Brandywine Zoo, adjacent to Rockford Park, is popular with Wilmington's children. The Delaware State Museum is in Dover.

44COMMUNICATIONS

In March 1993, about 269,000 (96.9%) of Delaware's housing units had telephones. The state had 8 AM and 20 FM radio stations and 1 commercial and 2 educational television stations in 1996. Philadelphia and Baltimore commercial television stations are within range. The state also had three large cable systems in 1996.

45PRESS

The *Wilmington Morning News* and the *Wilmington Evening Journal* merged with the *News Journal* in 1989. The paper's daily circulation is 124,669 (149,517 on Sunday). In the State's capitol is the *Delaware State News* with a daily circulation of 21,304 (34,000 on Sunday), as of 1997. Statewide, there were 3 morning and 3 Sunday papers in 1997.

46ORGANIZATIONS

The 1992 Census of Service Industries counted 225 organizations in Delaware, including 39 business associations; 148 civic, social, and fraternal associations; and 38 other membership organizations. Among national organizations headquartered in Delaware are the International Reading Association, the Jean Piaget Society, and the American Philosophical Association, all located in Newark.

47TOURISM, TRAVEL, AND RECREATION

Delaware's travel and recreation industry is second only to manufacturing in economic importance. In 1993, travel and tourism generated $836 million in revenue.

Rehoboth Beach on the Atlantic Coast bills itself as the "Nation's Summer Capital" because of the many federal officials and foreign diplomats who summer there; annual festivities include an Easter sunrise service. Among other events are the Delaware Kite Festival at Cape Henlopen State Park (east of Lewes) every Good Friday, Old Dover Days during the first weekend in May, and Delaware Day ceremonies (7 December, commemorating the day in 1787 when Delaware was the first of the original 13 states to ratify the Constitution) throughout the state.

Fishing, clamming, crabbing, boating, and swimming are the main recreational attractions. In 1995, Delaware had 36,631 licensed hunters and 35,167 licensed fishermen who hunted and/or fished in the state.

48SPORTS

Delaware has two major horse racing tracks: Harrington, which has harness racing, and Dover Downs, which also has a track for auto racing. The Delaware 500 stock car race on the 3rd Sunday in September. Thoroughbred races are held at Delaware Park in Wilmington. Wilmington has a minor league baseball team, the Blue Rocks, in the Carolina League.

49FAMOUS DELAWAREANS

Three Delawareans have served as US secretary of state: Louis McLane (1786–1857), John M. Clayton (1796–1856), and Thomas F. Bayard (1828–98). Two Delawareans have been judges on the Permanent Court of International Justice at The Hague: George Gray (1840–1925) and John Bassett Moore (1860–1947). James A. Bayard (b.Pennsylvania, 1767–1815), a US senator from Delaware from 1805 to 1813, was chosen to negotiate peace terms for ending the War of 1812 with the British.

John Dickinson (b.Maryland, 1732–1808), the "Penman of the Revolution," and Caesar Rodney (1728–84), wartime chief executive of Delaware, were notable figures of the Revolutionary era. George Read (b.Maryland, 1733–98) and Thomas McKean (b.Pennsylvania, 1734–1817) were, with Rodney, signers for Delaware of the Declaration of Independence. Naval officers of note include Thomas Macdonough (1783–1825) in the War of 1812 and Samuel F. du Pont (b.New Jersey, 1803–65) in the Civil War.

Morgan Edwards (b.England, 1722–95), Baptist minister and historian, was a founder of Brown University. Richard Allen (b.Pennsylvania, 1760–1831) and Peter Spencer (1779–1843) established separate denominations of African Methodists. Welfare worker Emily P. Bissell (1861–1948) popularized the Christmas seal in the US, and Florence Bayard Hilles (1865–1954) was president of the National Woman's Party.

Among scientists and engineers were Oliver Evans (1755–1819), inventor of a high-pressure steam engine; Edward Robinson Squibb (1819–1900), physician and pharmaceuticals manufacturer; Wallace H. Carothers (b.Iowa, 1896–1937), developer of nylon at Du Pont; and Daniel Nathans (b.1928), who shared the Nobel Prize in medicine in 1978 for his research on molecular genetics. Eleuthère I. du Pont (b.France, 1771–1834) founded the company that bears his name; Pierre S. du Pont (1870–1954) was architect of its modern growth.

Delaware authors include Robert Montgomery Bird (1806–54), playwright; Hezekiah Niles (b.Pennsylvania, 1777–1839), journalist; Christopher Ward (1868–1944), historian; Henry Seidel Canby (1878–1961), critic; and novelist Anne Parrish (b.Colorado, 1888–1957). Howard Pyle (1853–1911) was known as a writer, teacher, and artist-illustrator.

[50]BIBLIOGRAPHY

Essah, Patience. *A House Divided: Slavery and Emancipation in Delaware, 1638–1865.* Charlottesville, Va.: University Press of Virginia, 1996.

Federal Writers Project. *Delaware: A Guide to the First State.* Reprint. New York: Somerset, 1955 (orig. 1938).

Hoffecker. Carol E. *Delaware: A Bicentennial History.* New York: Norton, 1977.

Mosley, Leonard. *Blood Relations: The Rise and Fall of Du Ponts of Delaware.* New York: Atheneum, 1980.

Munroe, John A. *Colonial Delaware: A History.* Millwood, N.Y.: KTO Press, 1978.

———. *History of Delaware.* 3rd ed. Newark: University of Delaware Press, 1993.

Vessels, Jane. *Delaware: Small Wonder.* New York: Abrams, 1984.

FLORIDA

State of Florida

ORIGIN OF STATE NAME: Named in 1513 by Juan Ponce de León, who landed during *Pascua Florida*, the Easter festival of flowers. **NICKNAME:** The Sunshine State. **CAPITAL:** Tallahassee. **ENTERED UNION:** 3 March 1845 (27th). **SONG:** "Old Folks at Home" (also known as "Swannee River"). **POET LAUREATE:** Dr. Edmund Skellings. **MOTTO:** In God We Trust. **FLAG:** The state seal appears in the center of a white field, with four red bars extending from the seal to each corner; the flag is fringed on three sides. **OFFICIAL SEAL:** In the background, the sun's rays shine over a distant highland; in the foreground are a sabal palmetto palm, a steamboat, and an Indian woman scattering flowers on the ground. The words "Great Seal of the State of Florida" and the state motto surround the whole. **ANIMAL:** Florida panther. **MARINE MAMMALS:** Manatee, dolphin (saltwater). **BIRD:** Mockingbird. **FISH:** Largemouth bass (freshwater), Atlantic sailfish (saltwater). **FLOWER:** Orange blossom. **TREE:** Sabal palmetto palm. **GEM:** Moonstone. **STONE:** Agatized coral. **SHELL:** Horse conch. **BEVERAGE:** Orange juice. **LEGAL HOLIDAYS:** New Year's Day, 1 January; Robert E. Lee's Birthday, 19 January; Birthday of Martin Luther King, Jr., 3d Monday in January; Lincoln's Birthday, 12 February; Susan B. Anthony's Birthday, 15 February; Washington's Birthday, 3d Monday in February; Shrove Tuesday, February or March; Good Friday, March or April; Pascua Florida Day, 2 April; Confederate Memorial Day, 26 April; Memorial Day, last Monday in May; Jefferson Davis's Birthday, 3 June; Independence Day, 4 July; Labor Day, 1st Monday in September; Columbus Day and Farmers' Day, 2d Monday in October; General Election Day, 1st Tuesday after the 1st Monday in November in even-numbered years; Veterans Day, 11 November; Thanksgiving Day, 4th Thursday in November; Christmas Day, 25 December. **TIME:** 7 AM EST = noon GMT; 6 AM CST = noon GMT.

¹LOCATION, SIZE, AND EXTENT

Located in the extreme southeastern US, Florida is the 2d-largest state (after Georgia) east of the Mississippi River, and ranks 22d in size among the 50 states.

The total area of Florida is 58,664 sq mi (151,939 sq km), of which land takes up 54,153 sq mi (140,256 sq km) and inland water 4,511 sq mi (11,683 sq km). Florida extends 361 mi (581 km) E–W; its maximum N–S extension is 447 mi (719 km). The state comprises a peninsula surrounded by ocean on three sides, with a panhandle of land in the NW.

Florida is bordered on the N by Alabama and Georgia (with the line in the NE formed by the St. Marys River); on the E by the Atlantic Ocean; on the S by the Straits of Florida; and on the W by the Gulf of Mexico and Alabama (separated by the Perdido River).

Offshore islands include the Florida Keys, extending form the state's southern tip into the Gulf of Mexico. The total boundary length of Florida is 1,799 mi (2,895 km). The state's geographic center is in Hernando County, 12 mi (19 km) NNW of Brooksville.

²TOPOGRAPHY

Florida is a huge plateau, much of it barely above sea level. The highest point in the state is believed to be a hilltop in the panhandle, 345 feet (105 meters) above sea level, near the city of Lakewood, in Walton County. No point in the state is more than 70 mi (113 km) from saltwater.

Most of the panhandle region is gently rolling country, much like that of southern Georgia and Alabama, except that large swampy areas cut in from the Gulf coast. Peninsular Florida, which contains extensive swampland, has a relatively elevated central spine of rolling country, dotted with lakes and springs. Its east coast is shielded from the Atlantic by a string of sandbars. The west coast is cut by numerous bays and inlets, and near its

southern tip are the Ten Thousand Islands, a mass of mostly tiny mangrove-covered islets. Southwest of the peninsula lies Key West, which, at 24°33′N, is the southernmost point of the US mainland.

Almost all the southeastern peninsula and the entire southern end are covered by the Everglades, the world's largest sawgrass swamp, with an area of approximately 5,000 sq mi (13,000 sq km). The Everglades is, in a sense, a huge river, in which water flows south-southwest from Lake Okeechobee to Florida Bay. No point in the Everglades is more than 7 feet (2 meters) above sea level. Its surface is largely submerged during the rainy season—April to November—and becomes a muddy expanse in the dry months. Slight elevations, known as hammocks, support clumps of cypress and the only remaining stand of mahogany in the continental US. To the west and north of the Everglades is Big Cypress Swamp, covering about 2,400 sq mi (6,200 sq km), which contains far less surface water.

Lake Okeechobee, in south-central Florida, is the largest of the state's approximately 30,000 lakes, ponds, and sinks. With a surface area of about 700 sq mi (1,800 sq km), it is the 4th-largest natural lake located entirely within the US. Like all of Florida's lakes, it is extremely shallow, having a maximum depth of 15 feet (5 meters), and was formed through the action of groundwater and rainfall in dissolving portions of the thick limestone layer that underlies Florida's sandy soil. The state's numerous underground streams and caverns were created in a similar manner. Because of the high water table, most of the caverns are filled, but some spectacular examples thick with stalactites can be seen in Florida Caverns State Park, near Marianna. More than 200 natural springs send up some 7 billion gallons of groundwater a day through cracks in the limestone. Silver Springs, near Ocala in north-central Florida, has the largest average flow of all inland springs, 823 cu feet (23 cu meters) per second.

Florida has more than 1,700 rivers, streams, and creeks. The longest river is the St. Johns, which empties into the Atlantic 19 mi (42 km) east of Jacksonville: estimates of its length range from 273 to 318 mi (439 to 512 km), an exact figure being elusive because of the swampy nature of the headwaters. Other major rivers are the Suwannee, which flows south from Georgia for 177 mi (285 km) through Florida and empties into the Gulf of Mexico; and the Apalachicola, formed by the Flint and Chattahoochee rivers at the Florida-Georgia border, and flowing southward across the panhandle for 94 mi (151 km) to the Gulf. Jim Woodruff Lock and Dam is located on the Apalachicola about 1,000 feet (300 meters) below the confluence of the two feeder rivers. Completed in 1957, the dam created Lake Seminole, most of which is in Georgia.

More than 4,500 islands ring the mainland. Best known are the Florida Keys, of which Key Largo—about 29 mi (47 km) long and less than 2 mi (3 km) wide—is the largest. Key West—less than 4 mi (6 km) long and 2 mi (3 km) wide—a popular resort, is the westernmost.

For much of the geological history of the US, Florida was under water. During this time, the shells of countless millions of sea animals decayed to form the thick layers of limestone that now blanket the state. The peninsula rose above sea level perhaps 20 million years ago. Even then, the southern portion remained largely submerged, until the buildup of coral and sand around its rim blocked out the sea, leaving dense marine vegetation to decay and form the peaty soil of the present-day Everglades.

³CLIMATE

A mild, sunny climate is one of Florida's most important natural resources, making it a major tourist center and a retirement home for millions of transplanted northerners. Average annual temperatures range from 65° to 70°F (18° to 21°C) in the north, and from 74° to 77°F (23° to 25°C) in the southern peninsula and on the Keys. At Jacksonville, the average annual temperature is 68°F (20°C); the average low is 57°F (14°C), the average high 79°F (26°C). At Miami, the annual average is 76°F (24°C), with a low of 69°F (21°C) and a high of 83°F (28°C). Key West has the highest annual average temperature in the US, at 78.2°F (25.7°C). The record high temperature, 109°F (43°C), was registered at Monticello on 29 June 1931; the record low, –2°F (–19°C), at Tallahassee on 13 February 1899.

Florida's proximity to the Atlantic and the Gulf of Mexico, and the state's many inland lakes and ponds, together account for the high humidity and generally abundant rainfall, although precipitation can vary greatly from year to year and serious droughts have occurred. At Jacksonville, the average annual precipitation is 53 in (135 cm), with an average of 116 days of precipitation a year. At Miami, precipitation averages 58 in (147 cm), with 130 rainy days a year. Rainfall is unevenly distributed throughout the year, more than half generally occurring from June through September; periods of extremely heavy rainfall are common. The highest 24-hour total ever recorded in the US, 38.7 in (98.3 cm), fell at Yankeetown, west of Ocala on the Gulf coast, on 5–6 September 1950. Despite the high annual precipitation rate, the state also receives abundant sunshine—62% of the maximum possible at Jacksonville, and 73% at Miami. Snow is virtually unheard of in southern Florida but does fall on rare occasions in the panhandle and the northern peninsula.

Winds are generally from the east and southeast in the southern peninsula; in northern Florida, winds blow from the north in winter, bringing cold snaps, and from the south in summer. Average wind velocities are 8.2 mph (13.2 km/hr) at Jacksonville and 9.2 mph (14.8 km/hr) at Miami. Florida's long coastline makes it highly vulnerable to hurricanes and tropical

storms, which may approach from either the Atlantic or the Gulf coast, bringing winds of up to 150 mph (240 km/hr). Hurricane Donna, which struck the state 9–10 September 1960, and until 1992 was considered the most destructive in Florida's history, caused an estimated $300 million in damage. On 23–24 August 1992, Hurricane Andrew caused over $10 billion in damage in Florida, making it the most costly insured disaster in US history. In addition to hurricanes and tropical storms, tornadoes and waterspouts are not uncommon in Florida; in 1995, 95 tornadoes were recorded statewide.

⁴FLORA AND FAUNA

Generally, Florida has seven floral zones: flatwoods, scrublands, grassy swamps, savannas, salt marshes, hardwood forests (hammocks), and pinelands. Flatwoods consist of open forests and an abundance of flowers, including more than 60 varieties of orchid. Small sand pines are common in the scrublands; other trees here are the saw palmetto, blackjack, and water oak. The savannas of central Florida support water lettuce, American lotus, and water hyacinth. North Florida's flora includes longleaf and other pines, oaks, and cypresses; one giant seminole cypress is thought to be 3,500 years old. The state is known for its wide variety of palms, but only 15 are native and more than 100 have been introduced; common types include royal and coconut. Although pine has the most commercial importance, dense mangrove thickets grow along the lower coastal regions, and northern hardwood forests include varieties of rattan, magnolia, and oak. Numerous rare plants have been introduced, among them bougainvillea and oleander. All species of cacti and orchids are regarded as threatened, as are most types of ferns and palms. Endangered species include the prickly apple, key tree cactus, cowhorn orchid, Chapman rhododendron, Harper's beauty, and Florida torreya.

Florida once claimed more than 80 land mammals. Today the white-tailed deer, wild hog, and gray fox can still be found in the wild; such small mammals as the raccoon, eastern gray and fox squirrels, and cottontail and swamp rabbits remain common. Florida's bird population includes many resident and migratory species. The mockingbird was named the state bird in 1927; among game birds are the bobwhite quail, wild turkey, and at least 30 duck species. Several varieties of heron are found, as well as coastal birds such as gulls, pelicans, and frigates. The Arctic tern stops in Florida during its remarkable annual migration between the North and South poles.

Common Florida reptiles are the diamondback rattler and various water snakes. Turtle species include mud, green, and loggerhead, and various lizards abound. More than 300 native butterflies have been identified. The peninsula is famous for its marine life: scores of freshwater and saltwater fish, rays, shrimps, live coral reefs, and marine worms.

All of Florida's lands have been declared sanctuaries for the bald eagle, of which Florida has about 350 pair (2d only to Alaska among the 50 states). The state's unusually long list of threatened and endangered wildlife includes the American crocodile, American alligator, shortnose sturgeon, Atlantic ridley turtle, brown pelican, dusky seaside sparrow, red-cockaded and ivory-billed woodpeckers, Florida panther, Key deer, West Indian (Florida) manatee, Key Largo cotton mouse, Key Largo woodrat, Everglade kite, Cape Sable seaside sparrow, Bachman's warbler, Atlantic salt marsh snake, eastern indigo snake, Okaloosa darter, Stock Island snail, Bahama swallowtail butterfly, and Schaus swallowtail butterfly.

⁵ENVIRONMENTAL PROTECTION

Throughout the 20th century, a rapidly growing population, the expansion of agriculture, and the exploitation of such resources

ALABAMA

GEORGIA

ATLANTIC
OCEAN

Gulf of Mexico

FLORIDA

Explanation

▲ Point of Interest

⊙ City (50,000–100,000 people)

◉ City (more than 100,000 people)

★ State Capital

—95— U.S. Interstate Route

▓ Area of Interest

N

| 0 | 25 | 50 miles |
| 0 | 25 | 50 kilometers |

ESCAMBIA, SANTA ROSA, OKALOOSA, WALTON, HOLMES, JACKSON
Blackwater River State For., Florida Caverns State Park ▲
Eglin A.F. Base ▲
Pensacola
Gulf Islands National Seashore
WASHINGTON, CALHOUN, GADSDEN, LEON, JEFFERSON, MADISON, HAMILTON
St. Andrews State Recreational Area ▲
BAY, GULF, LIBERTY
Apalachicola Nat'l For.
FRANKLIN
★ Tallahassee
St. Marks National Wildlife Ref.
TAYLOR, SUWANNEE
Osceola Nat'l For.
BAKER, NASSAU, DUVAL
Fort Clinch State Park
◉ Jacksonville
CLAY
95
COLUMBIA, UNION, ST. JOHNS
BRADFORD, ALACHUA
◉ Gainesville
PUTNAM, FLAGLER
LAFAYETTE, DIXIE, GIL-CHRIST, LEVY
Lower Suwannee Nat'l Wildlife Ref. ▲
Manatee Springs State Park ▲
MARION
Ocala Nat'l For.
VOLUSIA
Daytona Beach
CITRUS, SUMTER, LAKE
SEMINOLE
Cape Canaveral Air Force Station ▲
HERNANDO, PASCO
Lake Louisa State Park ▲
ORANGE
◉ Orlando
OSCEOLA
4
Melbourne
Palm Bay
PINELLAS, HILLSBOROUGH, POLK
Clearwater
Largo
◉ Tampa
Lakeland
BREVARD, INDIAN RIVER
St. Petersburg
Avon Park A.F. Range ▲
MANATEE, HARDEE, HIGHLANDS
ST. LUCIE
Port St. Lucie
Sarasota
Highlands Hammock State Park ▲
SARASOTA, DE SOTO, OKEECHOBEE
MARTIN
95
Brighton Seminole Indian Res.
Lake Okeechobee
PALM BEACH
West Palm Beach
CHARLOTTE, GLADES
LEE, HENDRY
Arthur R. Marshall Loxahatchee National Wildlife Refuge
Boca Raton
Cape Coral
Coral Springs
Pompano Beach
Big Cypress National Preserve
BROWARD
Sunrise
Plantation
Fort Lauderdale
Pembroke Pines
Hollywood
COLLIER
Hialeah
Miami Beach
MONROE
Miami
Everglades National Park
DADE
Florida Bay
Florida Keys

as timber and minerals have put severe pressure on Florida's natural environment.

The state agency principally responsible for safeguarding the environment is the Department of Environmental Protection (DEP), created in 1993 by the merger of the Departments of Natural Resources and Environmental Regulation. Its duties include implementing state pollution control laws, and improving water-resource management. The Department oversees and coordinates the activities of the state's five water-management districts, which have planning and regulatory responsibilities. The Department also protects the state's coastal and marine resources. Its Division of State Lands acquires environmentally endangered tracts of land in what has been called the nation's largest environmental land-buying program. More than 1.2 million acres of environmentally important lands have been purchased. The Department also administers state parks and wilderness lands.

The Department of Agriculture and Consumer Services' Division of Forestry manages four state forests plus the Talquin State Lands. The Game and Fresh Water Fish Commission manages nature preserves and regulates hunting and fishing.

State spending for environmental protection in 1995/96 was more than $1.2 billion. Federal aid included $98 million from the Environmental Protection Agency (EPA) and more than $6.6 million from the Department of the Interior for land and water conservation, fish and wildlife restoration and management, and the construction of urban parks. Growth, contamination of groundwater and control of stormwater (non-point sources) are the state's most serious environmental problems. Groundwater supplies 90% of the drinking water in the state, as well as 8.2% of industry's needs and 53% of agricultural uses. Groundwater, surface water, and soil contamination have been found across the state. Among the major contaminants were the pesticides ethylene dibromide (EDB) (2,300 wells statewide) and other chemicals (about 1,000 additional wells). The state's program to clean groundwater contaminated by leaking underground storage tanks is one of the nation's largest and pioneered the pattern followed by many other states. Florida's groundwater quality standards are among the most stringent in the nation.

Contamination of groundwater is not the state's only water problem. The steadily increasing demand for water for both residential and farm use has reduced the subterranean runoff of fresh water into the Atlantic and the Gulf of Mexico. As a result, saltwater from these bodies has begun seeping into the layers of porous limestone that hold Florida's reserves of fresh water. This problem has been aggravated in some areas by the cutting of numerous inlets by developers of coastal property.

The DEP and South Florida Water Management District are undertaking, with various federal agencies, a massive restoration program for the Kissimmee River, Lake Okeechobee, the Everglades, and Florida Bay. This undertaking resulted from the settlement of a lawsuit brought by the federal government. The restoration effort includes: rechannelization of the Kissimmee River canal to restore its floodplains and prevent water pollution from entering Lake Okeechobee; other measures to reduce suficants in the lake caused by agricultural operations around its edges; creation of large stormwater treatment areas within the Everglades to treat nutrient-rich agricultural waters that are upsetting the ecological balance of the Everglades; and hydrological corrections to improve water delivery to the Everglades and Florida Bay.

In 1960, the only undersea park in the US, the John Pennekamp Coral Reef State Park, was established in a 75-sq-mi (194-sq-km) sector off the Atlantic coast of Key Largo, in an effort to protect a portion of the beautiful reefs, rich in tropical fish and other marine life, that adjoin the Keys. Untreated sewage from the Miami area, runoff water polluted by pesticides and other chemicals, dredging associated with coastal development,

and the removal of countless pieces of live coral by growing numbers of tourists and souvenir dealers have severely damaged large areas of the reefs. However, most of the Keys is now a National Marine Sanctuary and efforts are being made to improve water quality.

[6]POPULATION

Florida, the most populous state in the southeastern US, is also one of the fastest growing of the 50 states. In 1960, it was the 10th most populous state; by 1980, it ranked 7th with a population of 9,746,324; and by 1990, it ranked 4th, with a population of 12,937,926. US Census Bureau projections indicate that Florida had 14,399,985 residents in 1996, up 11.3% from 1990.

The first US census to include Florida, in 1830, recorded a total population of only 34,730. By 1860, on the eve of the Civil War, the population had more than quadrupled, to 140,424 people; about 80% of them lived in the state's northern rim, where cotton and sugarcane plantations flourished. Newcomers migrating southward in the late 19th century through the early 1920s sharply increased the state's population; the 1930 census was the first in which the state passed the million mark. Migration from other states, especially of retirees, caused a population explosion in the post–World War II period, with much of the increase occurring along the south Atlantic coast. From 1950 to 1960, Florida's population increased 79%—the fastest rate of all the states. From 1960 to 1970, the growth rate was 37%; from 1970 to 1980, 44%; and from 1980 to 1990, 33%.

Of the 1990 population, 90.8% lived in metropolitan areas; the average population density in 1990 was 240 per sq mi (92.2 per sq km). Females constituted 52% of the population in 1990, males 48%. Over 18% of the 1989 population was 65 years of age or over, the highest such percentage of all the states and nearly 50% above the US average.

The most populous city in Florida is Jacksonville, the 15th largest city in the US in 1990. Its population in 1994 was estimated at 665,070. Miami is Florida's 2d-largest city, with an estimated 1994 population of 373,024. The Miami–Ft. Lauderdale metropolitan area, the state's largest metropolitan region, had an estimated 3,443,501 residents in 1995; the Jacksonville metropolitan area's population was 979,045. Florida's 2d-largest metropolitan area was Tampa–St. Petersburg–Clearwater, with an estimated 2,180,484 residents; the city of Tampa had an estimated 285,523 people in 1994, and St. Petersburg had 238,585. Ft. Lauderdale had an estimated population of 162,842 in 1994. Tallahassee, the state capital, had a population of 133,718.

[7]ETHNIC GROUPS

Florida's population consists mainly of whites of northern European stock, blacks, and Hispanics. European immigrants came primarily from Germany and the United Kingdom. Germans were particularly important in the development of the citrus fruit industry. Since World War II, the development of southern Florida as a haven for retired northerners has added new population elements to the state, a trend augmented by the presence of numerous military bases.

The largest group of first- and second-generation residents are Cubans, who represented 4% of Florida's population in 1990. The state also has the highest number of foreign-born Nicaraguans, and is second behind New York as a residence of individuals from Jamaica, Colombia, Haiti, and Trinidad and Tobago. There were 1,574,000 individuals of Hispanic origin in 1990, including 541,011 Cubans (more than 100,000 of whom arrived on Florida shores as refugees in 1980), 174,445 Puerto Ricans, and 134,161 Mexicans. In 1996, the number of

Hispanics was estimated at 2,411,000, including 590,000 Cubans and 145,000 Mexicans.

The nonwhite population, as reported in 1990, was 2,189,000, or almost 17% (rising to 2,416,000 in 1996 estimates). Black-white relations in the 20th century have been tense. There were race riots following World War I, and the Ku Klux Klan was openly active until World War II. One of the worst race riots in US history devastated black areas of Miami in the spring of 1980.

Florida's indigenous inhabitants resisted encroachment from settlers longer and more militantly than tribes in other seaboard states. The leaders in resistance were the Seminole, most of whom by the 1850s had been killed or removed to other states, had fled to the Florida swamplands, or had been assimilated as small farmers. No peace treaty was signed with the Seminole until 1934, following the Indian Reorganization Act that attempted to establish tribal integrity and self-government for Indian nations. In 1939, the Native American population was reported as only 600, but the 1990 census reported a figure of 42,619 Native Americans from 34 tribes (with a somewhat lower 1996 estimate of 38,000). The difference is too large to be explained by natural increase, and there is no evidence of marked in-migration; presumably, then, it reflects a growing consciousness of Indian identity. There are seven Indian reservations: five for the Seminole—Big Cypress, Hollywood, Brighton, Immokalee, and Tampa, and two for the Miccosuckee—one on the Tamiami Trail and one north of Alligator Alley near Big Cypress.

Florida has the 9th-largest population of Asian and Pacific Islanders of the 50 states, estimated at 193,000 in 1996. In 1990 there were 37,531 Filipinos, 28,787 Chinese, 22,240 Asian Indians, 14,586 Vietnamese, 15,401 Japanese, 14,722 Koreans, and 3,075 Hawaiians.

8LANGUAGES

Spanish and English settlers found what is now Florida inhabited by Indians recently separated from the Muskogean Creeks, who, with the addition of escaped black slaves and remnants of the Apalachee Indians of the panhandle, later became known as the Seminole Indians. Although the bulk of the Seminole were removed to Indian Territory in the 1840s, enough remained to provide the basis of the present population. Florida has such Indian place-names as Okeechobee, Apalachicola, Kissimmee, Sarasota, Pensacola, and Hialeah.

The rapid population change that has occurred in Florida since World War II makes accurate statements about the language difficult. Massive migration from the North Central and North Atlantic areas, including a large number of speakers of Yiddish, has materially affected the previously rather uniform Southern speech of much of the state. Borrowing from the Spanish of the expanding number of Cubans and Puerto Ricans in the Miami area has had a further effect.

Representative words in the Southern speech of most native-born Floridians are *light bread* (white bread), *pallet* (temporary bed on the floor), *fairing off* (clearing up), *serenade* (shivaree), *tote* (carry), *snap beans* (green beans); *mosquito hawk*

Florida Counties, County Seats, and County Areas and Populations

COUNTY	COUNTY SEAT	LAND AREA (SQ MI)	POPULATION (1996 EST.)	COUNTY	COUNTY SEAT	LAND AREA (SQ MI)	POPULATION (1996 EST.)
Alachua	Gainesville	901	196,525	Lake	Tavares	954	186,631
Baker	MacClenny	585	20,556	Lee	Ft. Myers	803	380,001
Bay	Panama City	758	144,637	Leon	Tallahassee	676	215,593
Bradford	Starke	293	24,130	Levy	Bronson	1,100	30,296
Brevard	Titusville	995	453,998	Liberty	Bristol	837	6,542
Broward	Ft. Lauderdale	1,211	1,438,228	Madison	Madison	710	17,513
Calhoun	Blountstown	568	12,217	Manatee	Bradenton	747	232,285
Charlotte	Punta Gorda	690	130,426	Marion	Ocala	1,610	230,068
Citrus	Inverness	629	109,389	Martin	Stuart	555	112,527
Clay	Green Cove Springs	592	128,912	Monroe	Key West	1,034	80,730
Collier	East Naples	1,994	188,187	Nassau	Fernandina Beach	649	52,079
Columbia	Lake City	796	49,291	Okaloosa	Crestview	936	165,873
Dade	Miami	1,955	2,076,175	Okeechobee	Okeechobee	770	30,894
De Soto	Arcadia	636	25,253	Orange	Orlando	910	758,980
Dixie	Cross City	701	12,352	Osceola	Kissimmee	1,350	135,812
Duval	Jacksonville	776	721,139	Palm Beach	West Palm Beach	1,993	992,840
Escambia	Pensacola	660	277,634	Pasco	Dade City	738	311,556
Flagler	Bunnell	491	42,142	Pinellas	Clearwater	280	868,887
Franklin	Apalachicola	545	10,271	Polk	Bartow	1,823	440,954
Gadsden	Quincy	518	43,787	Putnam	Palatka	733	69,704
Gilchrist	Trenton	354	12,871	St. Johns	St. Augustine	617	106,503
Glades	Moore Haven	763	7,851	St. Lucie	Ft. Pierce	581	174,728
Gulf	Port St. Joe	559	13,327	Santa Rosa	Milton	1,024	108,186
Hamilton	Jasper	517	12,288	Sarasota	Sarasota	573	296,518
Hardee	Wauchula	637	20,130	Seminole	Sanford	298	335,468
Hendry	La Belle	1,163	29,821	Sumter	Bushnell	561	35,948
Hernando	Brooksville	1.163	121,266	Suwannee	Live Oak	690	30,901
Highlands	Sebring	1,029	74,836	Taylor	Perry	1,058	18,173
Hillsborough	Tampa	1,053	897,522	Union	Lake Butler	246	12,451
Holmes	Bonifay	488	18,174	Volusia	DeLand	1,113	414,322
Indian River	Vero Beach	497	96,490	Wakulla	Crawfordville	601	18,105
Jackson	Marianna	942	44,728	Walton	De Funiak Springs	1,066	35,255
Jefferson	Monticello	609	13,260	Washington	Chipley	590	19,212
Lafayette	Mayo	545	6,237	TOTALS		54,153	14,399,985

(dragonfly), *crocus sack* (burlap bag), *pullybone* (wishbone), and *comforter* (tied and filled bedcover), especially in south Florida. Largely limited to the northern half of the state are *pinder* (peanut), *croker sack* instead of crocus sack, *fire dogs* (andirons); also, in the Tampa Bay area, *comfort* (tied and filled bedcover), and, in the panhandle, *whirlygig* (merry-go-round). Some north-Florida terms are clearly imported from Georgia: *mutton corn* (green corn), *light-wood* (kindling), and *co-wench!* (a call to cows).

In 1990, 9,996,969 Floridians—82.7% of the resident population five years old and older—spoke only English at home. Other languages spoken at home included:

Spanish	1,447,747	Yiddish	27,363
French	194,783	Polish	27,314
German	81,033	Greek	21,396
Italian	70,636	Chinese	20,839

⁹RELIGIONS

Protestant denominations claim the majority of church members in Florida. The state also has sizable Roman Catholic and Jewish populations.

Dominican and Franciscan friars, intent on converting the Indians, arrived with the Spanish conquistadores and settlers in the 1500s, and for some 200 years Florida's white population was overwhelmingly Catholic. Protestant colonists from Britain arrived in the late 1700s, and significant influx of Protestant settlers from the southern US followed in the early 1800s. Sephardic Jews from the Carolinas also moved into Florida around this time, although the largest influx of Jews has occurred during the 20th century.

The largest Protestant denominations in 1990 were Southern Baptist Convention, with 786,276 members (1980); United Methodist Church, 462,174; Episcopal Church, 120,332 (1980); Presbyterian Church in the US, 166,255; Assembly of God, 134,297; United Presbyterian Church in the USA, 35,998; and Lutheran Church Missouri Synod, 67,645. The Roman Catholic population of Florida in 1990 was 1,598,457. The state has one archdiocese (Miami) and six dioceses (Orlando, Palm Beach, Pensacola, Tallahassee, St. Augustine, St. Petersburg, and Venice). A Greek Orthodox community is centered in Tarpon Springs.

¹⁰TRANSPORTATION

Railroad building in the 19th century opened southern Florida to tourism and commerce. During the 20th century, long-distance passenger trains and, more recently, planes and automobiles have brought millions of visitors to the state each year.

The first operating railway in Florida was the St. Joseph Railroad, which inaugurated service on an 8-mi (13-km) track between St. Joseph Bay and Lake Wimico on 14 April 1836—using mules to pull the train. The railroad soon put into operation the state's first steam locomotive, on 5 September 1836. By the time the Civil War broke out, railroads connected most of northern Florida's major towns, but the rapid expansion of the state's railroad system—and with it the development of southern Florida—awaited two late-19th-century entrepreneurs, Henry B. Plant and Henry M. Flagler. Plant's South Florida Railroad extended service to Tampa in 1884. Flagler consolidated a number of small lines in the 1880s into the Florida East Coast Railway with service as far south as Daytona. He then extended service down the Atlantic coast, reaching Palm Beach in 1894, Miami in 1896, and, after construction of an extensive series of bridges, Key West in 1912. The "overseas" railway down the Keys was abandoned in 1935 after a hurricane severely damaged the line.

On 1 January 1997, there was a total of 2,888 rail mi (4,650 km) of track in Florida, operated by 13 railroads. In 1995, Florida-originated rail tonnage of nonmetallic minerals (40.2 million tons), accounting for 50.9% of the total tonnage originated within the state. Burlington Northern, CSX Transportation, and Norfolk Southern were the state's operating Class I railroads in 1996, with about 1,700 route mi (2,735 km) of Class I track between them. As of 1 January 1997, Amtrak provided passenger rail service to 29 Florida stations; 1,049,906 Florida passengers rode the Amtrak system in 1996.

On 7 June 1979, construction began on a surface rail system for Miami and surrounding areas of Dade County. The first stage of this $1.1-billion mass transit system (known as Metrorail), a 20.5-mi (33-km) line serving Hialeah, Miami International Airport, downtown Miami, and areas to the south, was opened on 20 May 1984.

In 1995, Florida had 113,778 mi (183,108 km) of public roads. Of this total, 11,921 mi (19,185 km) constituted the state highway system, including 1,472 mi (2,369 km) of interstate highways and the 327-mi (526-km) Florida Turnpike, a toll road. The turnpike's 265-mi (426-km) main section extends from Wildwood in north-central Florida to Ft. Pierce on the Atlantic coast and then south to Miami; a 50-mi (80-km) extension runs between Miramar and Homestead. The Overseas Highway down the Keys, including the famous Seven Mile Bridge (which is actually 35,716 feet, or 10,886 meters—6.8 mi—in length), is part of the state highway system. In 1983, 37 of the 44 bridges connecting the Florida Keys were replaced at a cost of $189 million. Florida also had 69,045 mi (111,117 km) of county roads as of 1995, along with 31,352 mi (50,746 km) of city streets.

Florida had 12,062,731 registered motor vehicles in 1995. As of 1995, 12,019,156 people held active Florida drivers' licenses.

Inland waterways in Florida include the southernmost section of the Atlantic Intracoastal Waterway and the easternmost section of the Gulf Intracoastal Waterway, encompassing approximately 1,200 navigable miles; federally maintained coastal channels for commercial vessels and pleasure craft. Construction began on 27 February 1964 on a barge canal across northern Florida to connect the two intracoastal systems; however, work was ordered stopped by President Richard Nixon on 19 January 1971 because of the threat the canal posed to flora and fauna in the surrounding area.

Florida has several commercially important ports. By far the largest in terms of gross tonnage is Tampa, which handled 51.9 million tons of cargo in 1995, making it the 10th busiest in the US. Other major ports and their 1995 tonnage handled include Jacksonville, 18.9 million; Port Everglades in Ft. Lauderdale, 20.2 million; Pensacola, 0.7 million; Miami, 5.6 million; Panama City, 0.6 million; Port Canaveral, 3.7 million; and Palm Beach, 3.7 million.

Florida is the 3d-ranking state in terms of aircraft, pilots, and airline passengers. In addition to civil aviation activity, Florida has 26 military airfields. There are 12,336 active aircraft based in the state, as well as 47,630 licensed pilots. During 1995, more than 47,000,000 passengers took off from Florida's 19 commercial service airports. There are 132 public airports; Florida's busiest airport is Miami International, which enplaned 16,065,673 passengers in 1995. The same year, Orlando International enplaned 10,583,166 passengers; Tampa International, 5,567,950 passengers; and Ft. Lauderdale–Hollywood International, 4,787,467 passengers.

¹¹HISTORY

Indians entered Florida from the north 10,000 to 12,000 years ago, and had reached the end of the peninsula by 1400 BC. As they grew in number, the Indians developed more complex economic and social organization. In northeastern Florida and nearby Georgia, they apparently invented pottery independently about 2000 BC, some 800 years earlier than any other Indian group in North America.

In north Florida, an agricultural and hunting economy organized around village life was typical by this time. South of Tampa Bay and Cape Canaveral, Indians lived mostly along the coast and relied heavily on wild plants and on a large variety of aquatic and land animals for meat. The southern groups did not practice agriculture until about 450 BC, when they began to plant corn in villages around Lake Okeechobee.

As they spread over Florida and adjusted to widely different local conditions, the Indians fell into six main divisions, with numerous subgroups and distinctive cultural traits. When Europeans arrived in the early 16th century, they found nearly 100,000 Indians: 25,000 Apalachee around Tallahassee; 40,000 Timucua in the northeast; on Tampa Bay, 7,000 Tocobaga; on the southwest coast and around Lake Okeechobee, 20,000 Calusa; on the lower southeast coast, 5,000 Tequesta; and in the Jupiter area, 2,000 Ais and Jeaga.

The Spanish who began arriving in the 16th century found the Indians in upper Florida to be relatively tractable, but those in the lower peninsula remained uniformly hostile and resisted to the last. The Spaniards sought to Christianize the Indians and settle them around missions to grow food, to supply labor, and to help defend the province. By 1674, 70 Franciscan friars were working in dozens of missions and stations in a line running west from St. Augustine and north along the sea island coast to Carolina.

The impact of the Europeans on the Indian population was, on the whole, disastrous. Indians died of European-introduced diseases, were killed in wars with whites or with other Indians, or moved away. Raids from South Carolina by the Creeks, abetted by the British, between 1702 and 1708 completely destroyed the missions. When the Spanish departed Florida in 1763, the remaining 300 of the original 100,000 Indians left with them.

As early as 1750, however, small groups of Creek tribes from Georgia and Alabama had begun to move into the north Florida area vacated by the first Indian groups. Called Seminole, the Creek word for runaway or refugee, these Indians did not then constitute a tribe and had no common government or leadership until resistance to white plans to resettle them brought them together. They numbered only 5,000 when Florida became part of the US.

Pressures on the US president and Congress to remove the Seminole intensified after runaway black slaves began seeking refuge with the Indians. In 1823, the Seminole accepted a reservation north of Lake Okeechobee. Nine years later, an Indian delegation signed a document pledging the Seminole to move within three years to lands in present-day Oklahoma. The Indians' subsequent resistance to removal resulted in the longest and most costly of Indian wars, the Seminole War of 1835–42. The warfare and the Indians' subsequent forced migration left fewer than 300 Seminole in Florida.

The history of the twice-repeated annihilation of Florida Indians is, at the same time, the history of white settlers' rise to power. After Christopher Columbus reached the New World at Hispaniola in 1492, the Caribbean islands became the base for wider searches, one of which brought Juan Ponce de León to Florida. Sailing from Puerto Rico in search of the fabled island of Bimini, he sighted Florida on 27 March 1513 and reached the coast a week later. Ponce de León claimed the land for Spain and named it La Florida, for *Pascua Florida,* the Easter festival of flowers; sailing southward around Florida, he may have traveled as far as Apalachicola, on the shore of the panhandle. In 1521, he returned to found a colony at Charlotte Harbor, on the lower Gulf coast, but the Indians fought the settlers. After Ponce was seriously wounded, the expedition sailed for Cuba, where he died the same year.

Other Spaniards seeking treasure and lands to govern came after Ponce. Pánfilo de Narváez arrived in 1528, landing near Tampa Bay and marching inland and northward to Tallahassee. Hernando de Sota, a rich and famous associate of Francisco Pizarro in the conquest of Peru, found many men eager to try the same with him in Florida. Appointed governor of Cuba and *adelantado* (loosely, conqueror) of Florida, he followed the route of Narváez to Tallahassee in 1539, finding some food but no promise of wealth. In 1559, Spain sought to establish a settlement on Pensacola Bay, but it was abandoned at the end of two years.

In 1562, Jean Ribault, with a small expedition of French Huguenots, arrived at the St. Johns River, east of present-day Jacksonville, and claimed Florida for France. Another group of French Huguenot settlers built Ft. Caroline, 5 mi (8 km) upriver, two years later. In the summer of 1565, Ribault brought in naval reinforcements, prepared to defend the French claim against the Spaniards, who had sent Pedro Menéndez de Avilés to find and oust the intruders. Menéndez selected St. Augustine as a base, landing on 28 August, and with the aid of a storm withstood the French effort to destroy him. He then marched overland to take Ft. Caroline by surprise, killing most of the occupants and later captured Ribault and his shipwrecked men, most of whom he slaughtered. St. Augustine, the first permanent European settlement in the US, served primarily, under Spanish rule, as a military outpost, maintained to protect the wealth of New Spain. The Spanish established a settlement at Pensacola in 1698, but it too remained only a small frontier garrison town. In 1763, when Spain ceded Florida to England in exchange for Cuba, about 3,000 Spaniards departed from St. Augusta and 800 from Pensacola, leaving Florida to the Seminole.

British Florida reached from the Atlantic to the Mississippi River and became two colonies, East and West Florida. Settlers established farms and plantations, traded with the Indians, and moved steadily toward economic and political self-sufficiency. These settlers did not join the American Revolution, but Florida was affected by the war nonetheless, as thousands of Loyalists poured into East Florida. In 1781, Spain attacked and captured Pensacola. Two years later, Britain ceded both Floridas back to Spain, whereupon most of the Loyalists left for the West Indies.

The second Spanish era was only nominally Spanish. English influence remained strong, and US penetration increased. Florida west of the Perdido River was taken over by the US in 1810, as part of the Louisiana Purchase (1803). Meanwhile, renegade whites, runaway slaves, pirates, and political adventures operated almost at will.

Present-day Florida was ceded to the US in 1821, in settlement of $5 million in claims by US citizens against the Spanish government. At this time, General Andrew Jackson who three years earlier had led a punitive expedition against the Seminole and their British allies came back to Florida as military governor. His main tasks were to receive the territory for the US and to set up a civilian administration, which took office in 1822. William P. DuVal of Kentucky was named territorial governor, and a legislative council was subsequently elected. The new council met first in Pensacola and in St. Augustine, and then, in 1824, in the newly selected capital of Tallahassee, located in the wilderness of north-central Florida, from which the Indians had just been removed. Middle Florida, as it was called, rapidly became an area of slave-owning cotton plantations, and was for several decades the fastest-growing part of the territory. The war to remove the Seminole halted the advance of frontier settlement, however, and the Panic of 1837 bankrupted the territorial government and the three banks whose notes it had guaranteed. Floridians drew up a state constitution at St. Joseph in 1838–39, but, being proslavery, had to wait until 1845 to enter the Union paired with the free state of Iowa.

In 1861, Florida, with only 140,000 people, about 40% of them blacks (mostly slaves), only 400 mi (644 km) of railroad, and no manufacturing, seceded from the Union and joined the Confederacy. Some 15,000 whites (one-third of whom died) served in the Confederate army, and 1,200 whites and almost as many blacks joined the Union army. Bitterness and some violence accompanied the Republican Reconstruction government in 1868–76. The conservative Bourbon Democrats then governed for the rest of the century. They encouraged railroad building and other forms of business, and they kept taxes low by limiting government services. Cotton production never recovered to prewar levels, but cattle raising, citrus and vegetable cultivation, forestry, phosphate mining, and, by late in the century, a growing tourist industry took up the slack.

The Spanish-American War in 1898, during which Tampa became the port of embarkation for an expedition to Cuba, stimulated the economy and advertised the state nationwide, not always favorably. Naval activity at Key West and Pensacola became feverish. Lakeland, Miami, Jacksonville, and Fernandina were briefly the sites of training camps.

In 1904, Napoleon Bonaparte Broward was elected governor on a moderately populist platform, which included a program to drain the Everglades lands which the state had received under the Swamp and Overflowed Lands Act of 1850. Drainage did lower water levels, and settlements grew around Lake Okeechobee, developments whose full environmental impact was recognized only much later. By the time Broward took office, Jacksonville had become the state's largest city, with Pensacola and Tampa not far behind, and Key West had dropped from 1st to 4th. During World War I, more than 42,030 Floridians were in uniform.

Boom, bust, and depression characterized the 1920s. Feverish land speculation brought hundreds of thousands of people to Florida in the first half of the decade. Cresting in 1925, the boom was already over in 1926, when a devastating hurricane struck Miami, burying all hope of recovery. Yet population jumped by more than 50% during the decade, and Miami rose from 4th to 2d place among Florida cities. Florida's choice of Republican Herbert Hoover over Al Smith in the 1928 presidential election reflected the Protestant and prohibitionist attitudes of most of the state voters at that time.

The 1930s were marked first by economic depression, then by recovery, new enterprise, and rapidly growing government activity. Bank and business failures, as well as defaults on city and county bond issues and on mortgage payments, produced growing economic distress. The state joined the federal government in assuming responsibility for relief and recovery. The legalization of parimutuel betting in 1931 created a new industry and a new tax source. The state's first paper mill opened in the same year, revolutionizing the forest industry. Private universities in Miami, Tampa, and Jacksonville were started during the Depression years.

The 1940s opened with recovery and optimism, arising from the stimulus of production for World War II, production that began well before the actual entry of the US into the war. New army and navy installations and training programs brought business growth. After 1941, Florida seemed to become a vast military training school. The number of army and navy airfield flying schools increased from 5 to 45. Tourist facilities in all major cities became barracks, mess halls, and classrooms, with 70,000 rooms in Miami Beach alone being used to house troops in 1942. Families of thousands of trainees visited the state. Florida was on the eve of another boom.

First discovered but nearly last to be developed, Florida reached a rank of 27th in population only in 1940. Migration brought Florida's ranking to 4th in 1990, increasing its population to more than 12.8 million people. In 1986, Florida absorbed 1,000 arrivals a day. Until the early 1980s, many of those migrants were 65 years of age or over, swelling the proportion of senior citizens in Florida to 50% above the national average. In the mid-1980s, however, the preponderance of newcomers was somewhat younger—25 to 44 years old. They came in search of the opportunities provided by Florida's growing and diversifying economy. Whereas Florida once depended on the three industries of tourism, citrus, and construction for its survival, military spending increased the presence of high tech, banking, and service industries. In 1990, only 10% of Florida workers held jobs in the manufacturing industry, in contrast to 19% of the labor force nationwide.

The management of growth in Florida—the resolution of conflicts between developers and those who seek to preserve the natural beauty of the state, particularly in the northern part of Florida—has dominated state politics in the postwar era. While growth costs money in additional state services—each new migrant costs Florida $10,000 worth of public services—it also provides a ready source of needed revenues.

Racial and ethnic relations have become another central issue. Efforts to reapportion Florida's 23 congressional districts and the state legislature's 40 senate and 120 house seats have been complicated by battles between blacks and Hispanics over the number and character of minority districts. The absence of black congressmen or senators, and the paucity of black officials at the state and local levels have provoked demands for the creation of "safe districts" for blacks that will thereby ensure their representation. Likewise Hispanics, whose numbers grew in the 1980s from 8.8% to 12.2% of the state population, have called for Hispanic districts. However, in the 1990s, Florida's third congressional district, which had a majority of black voters, was declared unconstitutional and ordered redrawn by the US Supreme Court. The tensions between blacks and Hispanics led to violence in 1989 when a Hispanic police officer shot and killed a black motorcyclist who was speeding and driving erratically. Riots broke out in the predominantly black Overton section of Miami and continued for three days. Six people died and 27 stores were set on fire. The riots expressed blacks' anger at police brutality and at perceived preferential treatment of Hispanic immigrants.

Tropical storms and hurricanes have periodically struck Florida. In August 1992, Hurricane Andrew caused over $10 billion in damages in south Florida, primarily in and around Homestead. In October 1995, Hurricane Opal caused an estimated $2.1 billion in damage in the Pensacola area, damaging marinas and shipyards with waves that reached 15 ft in some areas.

Florida has the unwelcome distinction of leading the nation in violent crime. The state's crime level received nationwide attention when a series of foreign tourists were murdered in the early 1990s.

12 STATE GOVERNMENT

Florida's first constitutional convention, which met from December 1838 to January 1839, drew up the document under which the state entered the Union in 1845. A second constitutional convention, meeting in 1861, adopted the ordinance of secession that joined Florida to the Confederacy. After the war, a new constitution was promulgated in 1865, but not until still another document was drawn up and ratified by the state—the Fourteenth Amendment to the US Constitution—was Florida readmitted to statehood in 1868. A fifth constitution was framed in 1885; extensively revised in 1968, this is the document under which the state is now governed.

The 1968 constitutional revision instituted annual (rather than biennial) regular sessions of the legislature, which consists of a 40-member senate and a 120-member house of representatives. Senators serve four-year terms, with half the senate being elected every two years; representatives serve two-year terms. All legislators must be US citizens, must be at least 21 years of age, must have been residents of Florida for at least two years, and must be registered voters and residents of the district. The maximum length of a regular legislative session is 60 calendar days, unless it is extended by a three-fifths vote of each house. Special sessions may be called by the governor or by joint action of the presiding officers of the two houses (the president of the senate and speaker of the house of representatives). In addition, a special session may be convened by a three-fifths vote of all legislators, the poll being conducted by mail by the secretary of state upon a written request from at least 20% of the members. The legislative salary in 1995 was $23,244.

The governor is elected for a four-year term; a two-term limit is in effect. The lieutenant governor is elected on the same ticket as the governor. A six-member cabinet—consisting of the secretary of state, attorney general, comptroller, insurance commissioner and treasurer, commissioner of agriculture, and commissioner of education—is independently elected. Each of its officials must be at least 30 years old, a US citizen, and a registered voter, and must have been a resident of Florida for at least seven years; in addition, the attorney general must have been a member of the Florida bar for at least five years. In 1996 the governor's salary was $101,764.

Each cabinet member heads an executive department. The governor appoints the heads of 10 departments and shares supervision of 7 additional departments with the cabinet. The governor and cabinet also share management of or membership in several other state agencies. These provisions make Florida's elected cabinet one of the strongest such bodies in any of the 50 states.

The Public Service Commission (PSC), an arm of the legislative branch with quasi-judicial powers, sets rates for and otherwise regulates (consistent with Interstate Commerce Commission rulings) railroads, telephone companies, and privately owned electric, gas, water, and sewer utilities. The PSC's five members are appointed by the governor from lists prepared by the Florida Public Service Nominating Council, a nine-member body selected, for the most part, by the legislative leadership.

Passage of legislation requires a majority vote of those present and voting in both houses. A bill passed by the legislature becomes law if it is signed by the governor; should the governor take no action on it, it becomes law 7 days (including Sundays) after receipt if the legislature is still in session, or 15 days (including Sundays) after presentation to the governor if the legislature has adjourned. The governor may veto legislation and, in general appropriations bills, may veto individual items. Gubernatorial vetoes may be overridden by a two-thirds vote of the legislators present in each house.

Amendments to the constitution may originate in three ways: by a joint resolution of the legislature passed by a three-fifths majority of the membership of each house; by action of a constitutional revision commission which, under the constitution, must be periodically convened; or by initiative petition, which may call for a constitutional convention. A proposed amendment becomes part of the constitution if it receives a majority vote in a statewide election.

To be eligible to vote in state elections, a person must be at least 18 years of age, a US citizen, and a resident in the county of registration. The registration books close 30 days before a general election.

13POLITICAL PARTIES

The Democratic and Republican parties are Florida's two principal political organizations. The former is the descendant of one of the state's first two political parties, the Jeffersonian Republican Democrats; this party, along with the Florida Whig Party, was organized shortly before statehood.

Florida's Republican Party was organized after the Civil War and dominated state politics until 1876, when the Democrats won control of the statehouse. Aided from 1889 to 1937 by a poll tax, which effectively disfranchised most of the state's then predominantly Republican black voters, the Democrats won every gubernatorial election but one from 1876 through 1962; the Prohibition Party candidate was victorious in 1916.

By the time Republican Claude R. Kirk, Jr., won the governorship in 1966, Florida had already become, for national elections, a two-party state, although Democrats retained a sizable advantage in party registration. Beginning in the 1950s, many registered Democrats became "presidential Republicans," crossing party lines to give the state's electoral votes to Dwight D. Eisenhower in 1952 and 1956 and to Richard M. Nixon in 1960.

A presidential preference primary, in which crossover voting is not permitted, is held on the 2d Tuesday in March of presidential election years. Because it occurs so early in the campaign season, this primary is closely watched as an indicator of candidates' strength. Primaries to select state and local candidates are held in early September, with crossover voting again prohibited; runoff elections are held on the Tuesday five weeks before the general election.

As of 1994, the state had 3,318,565 registered Democrats, accounting for 51% of the total number of registered voters; 2,672,968 Republicans, 41%; and 523,292 unaffiliated, 8%. In addition to the Democratic and Republican parties, organized groups include the Citizens and Libertarian parties. Minor parties running candidates for statewide office can qualify by obtaining petition signatures from 3% of the state's voters.

Former US senator and Democrat Lawton Chiles was elected governor in 1990 and reelected in 1994. Connie Mack, a Republican, was reelected to a second US senatorial term in 1994, and Democrat Robert Graham was reelected to the Senate in 1992.

Florida's US House delegation in 1996 had 15 Republicans and 8 Democrats. The state senate in 1997 contained 17 Democrats and 23 Republicans, and the state house of representatives had 61 Republicans and 59 Democrats. In the 1996 presidential election, Florida backed a Democrat for the first time in 20 years, giving 48% of the vote to Bill Clinton; 42% to Republican Bob Dole; and 9% to Independent Ross Perot.

In 1994 there were 200 black elected officials and 64 Hispanic public officials. In 1995, 32 women served in the state legislature and in elective executive office.

14LOCAL GOVERNMENT

In 1992, Florida had 66 counties, 390 municipalities, 95 school districts, and 462 special districts.

Generally, legislative authority within each county is vested in a five-member elected board of county commissioners, which also has administrative authority over county departments, except those headed by independently elected officials. In counties without charters, these elected officials usually include a sheriff, tax collector, property appraiser, supervisor of elections, and clerk of the circuit court. County charters may provide for a greater or lesser number of elected officials, and for a professional county administrator (analogous to a city manager). Much state legislation restricting county government operations has been repealed since 1968. Counties may generally enact any law not inconsistent with state law. However, the taxing power of county and other local governments is severely limited.

Municipalities are normally incorporated and chartered by an act of the state legislature. Except where a county charter specifies otherwise, municipal ordinances override county laws. Municipal governments may provide a full range of local services, but as populations rapidly expand beyond municipal boundaries, many of these governments have found that they lack the jurisdiction to deal adequately with area problems. Annexations of surrounding territory are permissible but difficult under state law. Some municipal governments have reached agreements with county or other local governments for consolidation of overlapping or redundant services or for provision of service by one local government to another on a contract basis. Complete consolidation of a municipal and a county government is authorized by the state constitution, requiring state legislation and voter approval in the area affected. As of 1985, one such consolidation effort had been successful, involving Jacksonville and Duval County.

The problem of overlapping and uncoordinated service is most serious in the case of special districts. These districts, established by state law and by approval of the voters affected, provide a specified service in a specified geographic area. An urban area may have dozens of special districts. State legislation in the 1970s attempted to deal with this problem by permitting counties to set up their own special-purpose districts, whose operations could be coordinated by the county government.

Regional planning councils resulted from the need to cope with problems of greater than local concern. These councils deal with such issues as land management, resource management, and economic development.

15STATE SERVICES

A "Sunshine" amendment to the constitution and a statutory code of ethics require financial disclosure by elected officials and top-level public employees; the code prohibits actions by officials and employees that would constitute a conflict of interest. The Commission on Ethics, established in 1974, is empowered to investigate complaints of breach of public trust or violation of the code of ethics. In addition, an auditor general appointed by the legislature conducts financial and performance audits of state agencies.

Educational services are provided by the State Department of Education, which sets overall policy and adopts comprehensive objectives for public education, operates the state university and community college systems, and issues bonds (as authorized by the state constitution) to finance capital projects. The Department of Transportation is responsible for developing long-range transportation plans and for construction and maintenance of the state highway system. The Department of Highway Safety and Motor Vehicles licenses drivers, regulates the registration and sale of motor vehicles, and administers the Florida Highway Patrol.

Health and welfare services are the responsibility primarily of the Department of Health and Rehabilitative Services. In 1994, this department operated 16 major institutions and 71 other facilities, including mental hospitals, institutions for the mentally retarded, alcoholic treatment centers, and training schools for juvenile delinquents. In addition, the department administers such social welfare programs as Medicaid, aid to families with dependent children, food stamps, home health care, and foster care and adoption. It is also responsible for disease prevention and for assisting localities in performing health services.

The Department of Corrections maintained 46 major correctional institutions as of October 1994; two new facilities were scheduled to be completed by January 1995, raising the total to 48. The Department of Law Enforcement is responsible for maintaining public order and enforcing the state criminal code; enforcement activities emphasize combating organized crime, vice, and racketeering. The state's Army and Air National Guard are under the jurisdiction of the Department of Military Affairs. The Florida Highway Patrol, within the Department of Highway Safety and Motor Vehicles, is the only statewide uniformed police force.

The Housing Finance Agency, created in 1980, encourages the investment of private capital in residential housing through the use of public financing. The Northwest Florida Regional Housing Authority provides housing for low-income and other residents of that area. The Florida Housing Advisory Council assists the Department of Community Affairs in carrying out its duties related to housing. The Division of Local Resource Management is designated as the state's housing and urban development agency.

The Department of Labor and Employment Security enforces legislation protecting the state's workers (including child labor and industrial safety laws) and administers the federally funded workers' compensation and unemployment insurance programs and the State Employment Service, whose offices provide employment counseling and assist in job placement. Included in the department are the Division of Employment and Training and the Division of Employment Security. The Department of Administration includes the Division of Personnel, Office of Career

Florida Presidential Vote by Political Parties, 1948–96

YEAR	ELECTORAL VOTE	FLORIDA WINNER	DEMOCRAT	REPUBLICAN	STATES' RIGHTS DEMOCRAT	PROGRESSIVE
1948	8	*Truman (D)	281,988	194,280	89,755	11,620
1952	10	*Eisenhower (R)	444,950	544,036		
1956	10	*Eisenhower (R)	480,371	643,849		
1960	10	Nixon (R)	748,700	795,476		
1964	14	*Johnson (D)	948,540	905,941		
					AMERICAN IND.	
1968	14	*Nixon (R)	676,794	886,804	624,207	
1972	17	*Nixon (R)	718,117	1,857,759		
					AMERICAN	
1976	17	*Carter (D)	1,636,000	1,469,531	21,325	
						LIBERTARIAN
1980	17	*Reagan (R)	1,417,637	2,043,006		30,457
1984	21	*Reagan (R)	1,448,816	2,730,350		744
					NEW ALLIANCE	
1988	21	*Bush	1,656,701	2,618,885	6,665	19,796
					IND. (PEROT)	
1992	25	Bush (R)	2,072,798	2,173,310	1,053,067	15,079
1996	25	*Clinton (D)	2,546,870	2,244,536	483,870	23,965

*Won US presidential election.

Service and State Retirement Commissions, Florida Commission on Human Relations, and Division of Veterans Affairs.

The Department of State manages state historic sites, archives, museums, libraries, and fine arts centers.

[16]JUDICIAL SYSTEM

The state's highest court is the supreme court, a panel of seven justices that sits in Tallahassee; every two years, the presiding justices elect one of their number as chief justice. All justices are appointed to six-year terms by the governor upon the recommendation of a judicial nominating commission. They may seek further six-year terms in a yes-no vote in a general election; if the incumbent justice does not receive a majority of "yes" votes, the governor appoints another person to fill the vacancy from the recommended list of qualified candidates.

The supreme court has appellate jurisdiction only. The state constitution, as amended, prescribes certain types of cases in which an appeal must be heard, including those in which the death penalty has been ordered and those in which a lower appellate court has invalidated a state law or a provision of the state constitution. The court also hears appeals of state agency decisions on utility rates and may, at its discretion, hear appeals in many other types of cases.

Below the supreme court are five district courts of appeal, which sit in Tallahassee, Lakeland, Miami, West Palm Beach, and Daytona Beach. There are 57 district court judges; the method of their selection and retention in office is the same as for supreme court justices. District courts hear appeals of lower court decisions and may review the actions of executive agencies. District court decisions are usually final, since most requests for supreme court review are denied.

The state's principal trial courts are its 20 circuit courts, which have original jurisdiction in many types of cases, including civil suits involving more than $5,000, felony cases, and all cases involving juveniles. Circuit courts may also hear appeals from county courts if no constitutional question is involved. Circuit court judges are elected for six-year terms and must have been members of the Florida bar for at least five years before election.

Each of Florida's 67 counties has a county court with original jurisdiction in misdemeanor cases, civil disputes involving $5,000 or less, and traffic-violation cases. County court judges are elected for four-year terms and must be members of the bar only in counties with populations of 40,000 or more.

Florida has one of the highest crime rates in the US. In 1995, the total crime rate was 7,701.5 per 100,000. This total included 1,021.0 for violent crimes and 6,630.6 for property crimes. In 1995, Miami had 59,170 index offenses; Jacksonville had 61,129, and Tampa had 41,112. As of 1995, a total of 42,306 persons were serving prison sentences in 98 state and federal institutions run by Florida's correctional authorities, a rate of 436 inmates per 100,000 inhabitants. The state has a capital punishment statute, which was upheld by the US Supreme Court in 1976. The first execution under the statute took place in the state on 25 May 1979. Between 1979 and 1995, 36 other people were executed. In 1995 Florida had 362 persons under sentence of death, the third-largest number after California and Texas. There were 43,635 practicing attorneys in 1996.

[17]ARMED FORCES

In 1996, there were 56,108 active-duty military personnel stationed in Florida. Military and civilian personnel numbered 12,610 at facilities in Pensacola, 6,404 in Orlando, 14,091 in Jacksonville, and 11,986 at Eglin AFB. In October 1979, the Key West Naval Air Station was made the headquarters of a new Caribbean Joint Task Force, established to coordinate US military activities in the Caribbean. The state had 27,086 active-duty Air Force personnel in 1996; the largest Air Force bases were Eglin,

in Valparaiso; MacDill, near Tampa; and Tyndall, west of Tallahassee. The US Air Force Missile Test Center at Cape Canaveral (called Cape Kennedy from 1963 to 1973) has been the launching site for most US space flights, including all manned flights. US Department of Defense procurement contracts in Florida in 1995/96 totaled $5.8 billion.

Some 1,698,000 US military veterans lived in Florida as of 1 July 1996; 1,000 served during World War I, 587,000 during World War II, 314,000 during the Korean conflict, 486,000 during the Vietnam era, and 93,000 during the Persian Gulf War. US Veterans Administration spending in Florida in 1995/96 totaled $2.5 billion.

The state's reserve and national guard contained approximately 64,406 officers and enlisted personnel in 1996. Of that total, 33,906 came from the army, 20,697 from the navy and marine corps, and 9,797 from the air force.

In 1993, the Florida Highway Patrol employed 1,610 full-time sworn officers, or one per 10,000 residents.

[18]MIGRATION

Florida is populated mostly by migrants. In 1990, only 30.5% of all state residents were Florida-born, compared with 61.8% for the US as a whole. Only Nevada had a lower proportion of native residents. Migration from other states accounted for more than 85% of Florida's population increase in the 1970s. From 1985 to 1990, net migration gains added another 1,461,550 new residents, and net domestic migration added 77,030 between 1990 and 1996, while international migration added 373,362 during the same period. Only 45% of those age five and older were living in the same house in 1990 as in 1985. Of those who lived in a different house in 1985, 34% did so in another state.

The early European immigrants to Florida—first the Spanish, then the English—never populated the state in significant numbers. Immigration from southern states began even before the US acquisition of Florida, and accelerated thereafter. In the 20th century, US immigrants to Florida have come, for the most part, from the Northeast and Midwest. Their motivation has often been to escape harsh northern winters, and a large proportion of the migrants have been retirees and other senior citizens. Between 1970 and 1980, the number of Floridians 65 or over increased by 70%, compared with a 44% increase for the US population as a whole.

Since the 1960s, Florida has also experienced large-scale migration from the Caribbean and parts of Latin America. Although the state has had a significant Cuban population since the second half of the 19th century, the number of immigrants surged after the Cuban revolution of 1959. From December 1965 to April 1973, an airlift agreed to by the Cuban and US governments landed a quarter of a million Cubans in Miami. Another period of large-scale immigration from Cuba, beginning in April 1980, brought more than 100,000 Cubans into Florida harbors. At the same time, Haitian "boat people" were arriving in Florida in significant numbers—often reaching the southern peninsula in packed, barely seaworthy small craft. The number of ethnic Haitians in Florida was reported at 105,495 in 1990. By 1990, a reported 541,011 ethnic Cubans were living in southern Florida, mostly in and around Miami, where the Cuban section had become known as "Little Havana." The US government classified some of them as illegal aliens, fleeing extreme poverty in their native country, but the immigrants claimed to be political refugees and sued to halt deportation proceedings against them. As of 1994, the total number of illegal aliens in Florida was estimated at between 243 and 385. As of 1996, a reported 2,186,000 Floridians (15%) were foreign-born.

In 1996, 76,461 foreign immigrants were admitted into Florida, the 4th-highest total of any state, accounting for over 8% of all foreign immigration that year.

[19]INTERGOVERNMENTAL COOPERATION

In 1953, Florida became a signatory to the Alabama-Florida Boundary Compact. Among the interstate regional compacts in which Florida participates are the Southern Interstate Energy Compact, Southeastern Forest Fire Protection Compact, Atlantic States Marine Fisheries Compact, and Gulf States Marine Fisheries Compact. The Central and South American and Caribbean Trade and Development Commission, within Florida's Department of Commerce, was created in 1978 to foster cooperation between Florida and Latin America.

Federal aid to Florida in 1995/96 totaled over $8.4 billion.

[20]ECONOMY

Farming and the lumbering and naval stores industries, all concentrated in northern Florida, were early mainstays of the economy. In the late 19th century, the extension of the railroads down the peninsula opened up an area previously populated only by Indians; given the favorable climate, central and southern Florida soon became major agricultural areas. Tourism, aggressively promoted by the early railroad builders, became a major industry after World War I and remains so today.

Tourists and winter residents with second homes in Florida contribute billions of dollars annually to the state economy and make retailing and construction particularly important economic sectors. However, this dependence on discretionary spending by visitors and part-time dwellers also makes the economy—and especially the housing industry—highly vulnerable to recession. The economic downturn of the early 1980s hit Florida harder than the US generally. New housing starts, for example, which fell by about 2% in the US from 1981 to 1982, dropped by more than 20% in Florida during the same period.

An extremely low level of unionization among Florida workers encouraged growth in manufacturing in the 1970s and early 1980s—but may also help explain Floridians' below-average income levels. Florida ranked 15th in manufacturing employment in 1991. Its per capita personal income of $19,397 in 1992, however, placed it 20th in the nation.

The arms build-up during the Reagan administration helped to expand Florida's aerospace and electronics industries. Even in 1991, after the reduction of the military budget in the late 1980s and early 1990s, Florida ranked 7th nationally in the value of Department of Defense contracts awarded. The state's economy—particularly that of the Miami area— has also benefited from an influx of Latin American investment funds. Miami is said to have one of the largest "underground economies" in the US, a reference both to the sizable inflow of cash from illicit drug trafficking and to the large numbers of Latin American immigrants working for low, unreported cash wages. Florida's gross state product in 1994 totaled $317,829 million, of which the private goods-producing industries contributed $48,049 million; private services-producing industries contributed $229,103 million; and government contributed $40,677 million. In 1996, there were 59,354 bankruptcy filings in the state, up almost 30% from the previous year.

[21]INCOME

In 1996, Florida's per capita personal income was $24,104, 20th among the 50 states and 2d in the Southeast. Total personal income rose from $326.7 billion in 1995 to $347 billion in 1996, an increase of 6.3%. Non-farm personal income grew from $324.7 billion in 1995 to $345.2 billion in 1996, up 6.3%. Florida's median household income in 1995 was $29,745. In 1995, 10.3% of all Floridians lived below the federal poverty level.

In 1994, the West Palm Beach Metropolitan Statistical Area (MSA) ranked second highest in per capita personal income (at $33,518) of all metropolitan areas in the nation; the Naples area

ranked 5th (at $30,906). In 1994, per capita income for some of Florida's metropolitan areas included: Pensacola, $17,519; Daytona Beach, $17,591; Orlando, $20,119; Jacksonville, $20,938; Miami, $20,014; Tampa, $21,358; and Ft. Lauderdale, $24,706.

[22]LABOR

Florida's civilian labor force averaged 6,938,000 in 1996. Of that total, 6,586,000 were employed and 352,000 unemployed, for an unemployment rate of 5.1%. As in the US generally, unemployment was higher among nonwhites and teenagers than among white adults—and highest among black teenagers.

In 1996, about 62% of the state's civilian noninstitutionalized population 16 years of age or older was in the labor force, compared with 66.8% for the US as a whole. The major reason for the difference is the extremely low participation rate for Floridians 65 or older, reflecting the fact that many people migrate to the state for their retirement years.

Reflecting the importance of tourism to Florida's economy, a higher proportion of the state's workers are employed in the trade and service industries than for the US as a whole; the proportion of workers in manufacturing is a little over half the US average. A federal survey revealed the following 1995 earnings and employment patterns for major industry groups in Florida:

	TOTAL ANNUAL WAGES (IN MILLIONS OF DOLLARS)	EMPLOYMENT (IN THOUSANDS)
Total	$148,506.5	6,009.3
Private	123,088.4	5,106.9
Agriculture	2,138.2	152.9
Mining	254.5	6.9
Construction	7,653.9	304.5
Manufacturing	14,886.9	480.4
Nondurable goods	5,672.2	198.6
Durable goods	9,214.6	281.8
Transportation, Communications, and Public Utilities	9,550.8	294.6
Wholesale trade	10,879.3	318.2
Retail trade	18,579.1	1,229.4
Finance, insurance, real estate	12,270.6	372.2
Services	46,022.8	1,916.5
Nonclassified	672.2	31.4
Government	25,418.1	902.5

The federal survey excluded the self-employed and several other employment categories. In 1995, 902,454 workers were employed in government: 582,980 by local governments, 199,223 by the state, and 119,427 by the federal government. The remaining 823 were employed by foreign governments.

In 1995, the average annual pay of Florida nonagricultural workers was $24,962. The average weekly earnings for manufacturing in 1995 were $595.94. Some 430,000 workers belonged to labor unions in 1996, about 7.5% of the total employed (about half the national average). There were 131 labor unions operating in Florida in 1997. The state has a right-to-work law.

[23]AGRICULTURE

Florida's most important agricultural products, and the ones for which it is most famous, are its citrus fruits. Florida continues to supply the vast majority of orange juice consumed in the US. Florida produced 71.7% of the nation's oranges and 72.4% of its grapefruits in 1995. It is also an important producer of other fruits, vegetables, and sugarcane.

The total value of Florida's crops in 1995 exceeded $4.7 billion, 5th highest among the 50 states. Total farm marketings, including livestock marketings and products, exceeded $5.8 billion in 1995 (9th in the US). There were about 39,000 farms covering some 10.5 million acres (4.25 million hectares) in 1995; the total represented nearly 30% of the state's entire land area.

The orange was introduced to Florida by Spanish settlers around 1570. Oranges had become an important commercial crop by the early 1800s, when the grapefruit was introduced. In 1886, orange production for the first time exceeded 1 million boxes (one box equals 90 lb/41 kg). Much of this production came from groves along the northern Atlantic coast and the St. Johns River, which offered easy access to maritime shipping routes north. The expansion of the railroads and severe freezes in the 1890s encouraged the citrus industry to move farther south. In the 1990s, Polk, St. Lucie, Indian River, Hendry, and Hardee counties in central Florida were the largest producers of citrus fruits.

The orange crop totaled 205,400,000 90-lb (41-kg) boxes in the 1994/95 season. The grapefruit crop was 55,700,000 85-lb (39-kg) boxes; tangerines, 3,550,000 95-lb (43-kg) boxes; and tangelos and temple oranges, 4,760,000 90-lb (41-kg) boxes. There are about 50 processing plants in Florida where citrus fruits are processed into canned or chilled juice, frozen or pasteurized concentrate, or canned fruit sections. Production of frozen concentrate orange juice totaled 1,194,419,448 gallons in the 1994/95 season. Stock feed made from peel, pulp, and seeds is an important by-product of the citrus-processing industry; annual production is nearly 1 million tons. Other citrus by-products are citrus molasses, D-limonene, alcohol, wines, preserves, and citrus seed oil.

Florida is the country's 2d leading producer of vegetables. Vegetable farming is concentrated in central and southern Florida, especially in the area south of Lake Okeechobee, where drainage of the Everglades left exceptionally rich soil. In 1994/5, Florida farmers harvested 1,606,000 hundredweight of tomatoes; they sold 8,957,000 hundredweight of potatoes. Florida's tomato and vegetable growers, who had at one time enjoyed a near-monopoly of the US winter vegetable market, began in the 1990s to face increasing competition from Mexican growers, whose lower-priced produce had captured about half the market by 1995. About 67% of all farm laborers in 1995 were hired hands.

Florida's major field crop is sugarcane (mostly grown near Lake Okeechobee), which enjoyed a sizable production increase in the 1960s and 1970s, following the cutoff of imports from Cuba. In 1995, Florida's sugarcane production was 14,445,000 tons. Florida's 2d-largest field crop is peanuts (193,590,000 lb/8,781,048 kg in 1995), followed by cotton, hay, corn, tobacco, soybeans, and wheat. Florida leads the nation in the production of watermelons.

24ANIMAL HUSBANDRY

Florida is an important cattle-raising state. The Kissimmee Plain, north of Lake Okeechobee, is the largest grazing area. In 1997, Florida had an estimated 1.97 million cattle and calves valued at an estimated $847 million. During 1996, Florida had an estimated 65,000 hogs and pigs valued at around $6.2 million. An estimated 2.37 billion eggs were produced in 1995, worth $95 million. Florida had an estimated 162,000 milk cows in 1995 that produced around 2.4 billion lb (1 billion kg) of milk. Also during 1995, Florida poultry farmers produced 25.4 million lb (11.5 million kg) of chicken and sold them for around $1 million.

25FISHING

Florida's extensive shoreline and numerous inland waterways make sport fishing a major recreational activity. Commercial fishing is also economically important.

In 1995, Florida's commercial fish catch was 133,483,000 lb (60,546,553 kg), worth $198,067,000. The most important commercial species of shellfish are shrimp, spiny lobster, and crabs. Landings of spiny lobster in 1995 totaled 6.5 million lb (2.9 million kg) with a value of $29.4 million, accounting for 91% of the volume and 85% of the value for the US spiny lobster catch that year. Gulf coast shrimp landings totaled 18.8 million lb (8.5 million kg) in 1995. Florida accounted for the total US landings of calico scallops that year, at 957,000 lb/434,000 kg (valued at $1.2 million). Valuable finfish species include grouper, swordfish, and snapper. Florida's commercial fishing fleet had 10,779 boats and vessels in 1994. In 1995, Florida had 178 Atlantic and 273 Gulf coast processing and wholesale plants employing on average 2,094 and 2,649 employees, respectively.

Both freshwater and saltwater fishing are important sports. Tarpon, sailfish, and redfish are some of the major saltwater sport species; largemouth bass, panfish, sunfish, catfish, and perch are leading freshwater sport fish. In 1995/96, federal hatcheries distributed about 1.5 million (2,656 lb/1,204 kg) warmwater fish within the state. Florida had 1,049,704 sport fishing license holders in 1995/96 (coastal marine fishing does not require a license). In 1995/96, the US Fish and Wildlife Service spent over $5.1 million on several sport fish restoration projects.

26FORESTRY

About 47% of Florida's land area—16,221,197 acres (6,564,718 hectares)—was forested in 1995 when the state had about 2.2% of all forested land in the US. A total of 4,601,483 acres (1,862,220 hectares) was owned by forest industries. The most common tree is the pine, which occurs throughout the state but is most abundant in the north.

Florida's forestry industry, concentrated in the northern part of the state, shipped $7.9 billion worth of lumber and wood products in 1993. The most important forestry product is pulpwood for paper manufacturing; production in 1995 was 4.5 million cords. Lumber production that year was 805 million board feet, 769 million board feet of softwoods and 36 million board feet of hardwoods. In 1993, the payroll in the forestry and major wood-using industries, including paper and furniture manufacturing, exceeded $1.25 billion.

Four national forests—Apalachicola, Ocala, Osceola, and Choctawatchee—covering 1,224,611 acres (495,584 hectares) are located in Florida. The Division of Forestry operates 35 state forests covering 687,450 acres (278,200 hectares). Three of the main activities of state forests are forest management, outdoor recreation, and wildlife management.

Virtually all of Florida's natural forest had been cleared by the mid-20th century; the forests existing today are thus almost entirely the result of reforestation. Since 1928, more than 5.6 billion seedlings have been planted in the state.

27MINING

According to the US Geological Survey, Florida's estimated nonfuel mineral production in 1995 was valued at nearly $1.4 billion (9th among the states and 4% of the US total). This was $50 million more than that reported by the state's 200-plus mineral producers in 1994. Since reaching the record high of $1.61 billion in 1989, Florida's mineral value has been on a downward trend. The phosphate industry usually has the greatest impact on the state's nonfuel mineral economy. The increase in Florida's mineral production value in 1995 resulted mainly from a large increase in the value of phosphate rock. This increase was offset by declines in portland cement, zircon concentrates, and titanium concentrates.

The 1994 increase in the tonnage and value of cement, sand and gravel, and crushed stone, the raw materials of the construction industry, signaled a reversal in the multiyear downward spiral experienced by this sector. Florida leads the nation in phosphate rock, mineral sands, and peat output and ranks among the top three states in crushed stone and masonry cement production.

Phosphate rock was again the leading mineral commodity, in terms of value, accounting for over 50% of the estimated value in 1995. The state continued as the world's leader in phosphate rock production and led the nation in heavy-mineral output. Rising phosphate production has led to increased employment in the sector. Although most of the phosphate rock produced during 1995 was sold domestically, exports of phosphate fertilizers continued to be important for the industry's vitality. The largest foreign consumers of Florida phosphate are China, India, and the countries of Eastern Europe and the former Soviet Union. Crushed stone, sales of which were estimated at $343 million, was the second leading mineral commodity, accounting for almost 25% of Florida's mineral value. Portland cement ranked third; the $200 million in sales accounted for approximately 14% of the state's total mineral value. Sand, gravel, and clays rounded out the top five commodities in terms of reportable value. Approximately 7,300 persons were employed in mining in December 1996. Of these, 3,900 worked in the Lakeland–Winter Haven area, where the phosphate industry is concentrated.

28 ENERGY AND POWER

In 1994, a total of 3,296.7 trillion Btu of energy was consumed in Florida. About 36.1% of that total was used in transportation, 27.5% in residences, 21.8% by commercial establishments, and 14.6% by industry. The sources of the energy consumed were petroleum, 51.1%; natural gas, 11.9%; coal, 19.5%; nuclear power, 8.6%, and hydroelectric power, less than 0.1%.

Per capita energy use in 1994 was 236.2 million Btu. Although Florida produces some oil and natural gas, it is a net importer of energy resources. Its mild climate and abundant sunshine offer great potential for solar energy development, but this potential has not been extensively exploited.

In 1996, Florida had an installed electric energy generating capacity of 39,563 Mw; net generation in 1995 was 147.2 billion kWh. In 1994, 19% of electricity produced came from residual fuel oil, 35.3% from coal, 16.5% from nuclear, and 10.6% from natural gas; hydroelectricity and distillate fuels totaled less than 0.6%. Nuclear generating capacity increased by 27% in August 1983, when the state's fifth nuclear plant, the 830,000-kW St. Lucie 2 facility, operated by the Florida Power and Light Co., south of Ft. Pierce, began commercial operation. Three other nuclear plants owned by Florida Power and Light are St. Lucie 1, with a capacity of 830,000 kW, and Turkey Point Units 3 and 4, each with a capacity of 693,000 kW, located in Dade County. Florida Power Corp. operates the state's other nuclear power plant, the 830,000-kW Crystal River 3 facility, on the northern Gulf coast. Residential customers used 51% of all electricity sold by utilities in 1994, commercial customers 39%, and industrial customers 10%. The transportation sector used slightly over 0.02%.

Florida ranked 19th in oil production and 22d in natural gas production in 1994. In 1996, the state produced 6,292,000 barrels of crude oil; proved reserves as of 31 December 1995 were 71 million barrels. Natural gas marketed production in 1995 was 6,463 million cu feet, or 1.3% of consumption for that year; proved reserves were 92 billion cu feet in 1995.

29 INDUSTRY

Florida is not a center of heavy industry, and many of its manufacturing activities are related to agriculture and exploitation of natural resources. Leading industries include food processing, electric and electronic equipment, transportation equipment, and chemicals. The value of manufacturing shipments in 1995 totaled $73.574 billion for the state. Florida's major industrial categories, in terms of value of shipments, were food and food products, $12.378 billion; paper and allied products, $4.429 billion; printing and publishing, $6.341 billion; chemicals

and allied products, $6.881 billion; electronic and other electric equipment, $8.676 billion; transportation equipment, $6 billion; and instruments and related products, $6.267 billion.

From 1980 to 1990, manufacturing grew by 14.4% in Florida, while declining 6% nationwide. In 1993, Florida ranked 8th among the states in the number of manufacturing plants, with 15,600. Florida ranks 2d only to California in both employment and number of firms engaged in the manufacture of guided missiles and space vehicles; 10% of all US aircraft engines and engine parts are manufactured in Florida. Nearly 20% of the nation's boat manufacturers are located in the state. Electric components are primarily manufactured in three east coast counties (Brevard, Palm Beach, and Broward), where 56% of the state's electronic component workers reside. Since the perfection of the laser by Martin-Marietta in Orlando in the 1950s, the greater Orlando area has grown to have the 3d-highest concentration of electro-optics and laser manufacturers in the US.

The cigar-making industry, traditionally important in Florida, has declined considerably with changes in taste and the cutoff of tobacco imports from Cuba. In the late 1930s, the Tampa area alone had well over 100 cigar factories, employing some 10,000 people. The 1987 Census of Manufactures found just 35 plants statewide.

Manufacturing is currently concentrated in and around Florida's largest cities, such as Miami, Tampa–St. Petersburg, Ft. Lauderdale–Hollywood, and Orlando. Dade and Broward counties (Greater Miami), Hillsborough County (Tampa), Pinellas County (St. Petersburg), Duval County (Jacksonville), Orange County (Orlando), and Palm Beach County accounted for almost two-thirds of all manufacturing employment in 1982.

In 1995, there were 2,435 US patents issued to Florida residents. In 1997, there were 13 Fortune 500 companies headquartered in Florida.

30 COMMERCE

Wholesale trade in 1992 totaled $132.6 billion, conducted by 30,137 establishments. Of that total, durable goods accounted for 65.4% of the establishments and 51.4% of sales. According to the 1992 US Census of Retail Trade, the state ranked 4th in retail sales, with 6.3% of the US total. The fashionable shops lining Palm Beach's Worth Avenue make it one of the nation's most famous shopping streets.

In 1992 retail sales totaled $118.7 billion, conducted by 87,653 establishments. At least 25.8% of all retail establishments were restaurants, cafeterias, bars, and similar businesses—a reflection, in part, of the importance of the travel business in Florida's economy. Sales at eating and drinking places represented 10.2% of total retail sales. Food stores accounted for 17.8%; automotive dealers, 25.2%; department, variety, and other general merchandise stores, 11.9%; furniture, home furnishing, and equipment stores, 5.2%; building material, and other establishments, 29.7%.

The value of all exports sent from Florida was over $19.6 billion in 1996. Florida's exports of goods produced within the state totaled $20.7 billion in 1996. Duty-free goods for reshipment abroad pass through Port Everglades, Miami, Orlando, Jacksonville, Tampa, and Panama City—free-trade zones established to bring international commerce to the state. The Miami metropolitan area had exports of over $9.2 billion in 1994; Tampa–St. Petersburg–Clearwater, $1.8 billion.

In the 1970s and early 1980s, Florida was believed to be the principal entry point for marijuana, cocaine, and other illicit drugs being smuggled into the US from Latin America.

31 CONSUMER PROTECTION

The Division of Consumer Services, Department of Agriculture and Consumer Services, is the state's clearinghouse for consumer complaints and information and performs the initial review under the Motor Vehicle Warranty Enforcement Act—the so-called "Lemon Law." The division also regulates ballroom dance studios, charitable organizations, health studios, motor vehicle repair shops, pawnshops, sellers of travel, sellers of business opportunities, and telemarketers, and maintains the state's No Sales Solicitation Calls list. The Florida Consumers' Council advises the commissioner of agriculture on consumer issues.

The public counsel to the Public Service Commission (PSC), appointed by a joint committee of the legislature, represents the public interest in commission hearings on utility rates and other regulations. The public counsel can also seek judicial review of PSC rulings, and may appear before other state and federal bodies on the public's behalf in utility and transportation matters.

The Department of Business Regulation oversees parimutuel betting; land sales; the operations of condominiums, cooperative apartments, hotels, and restaurants; and the regulation and licensing of alcoholic beverage and tobacco sales.

In 1983, the state legislature enacted the Motor Vehicle Warranty Enforcement Act, which forces automobile dealers to replace new cars or refund the purchase price if the cars are in constant need of repairs.

32BANKING

The Florida Department of Banking and Finance, Division of Banking, has regulatory and supervisory authority over state-chartered financial institutions in Florida, including commercial banks and nondeposit trust companies, credit unions, savings associations, offices of foreign banks operating in Florida, and money transmitters.

At year end 1996, there were 324 insured commercial banks (including nondeposit trust companies) in Florida, of which 194 were state-chartered and 130 were nationally chartered. A total of 158 banks were members of the Federal Reserve System as of year-end 1996.

Assets of Florida's commercial banks as of 31 December 1996 totaled $160.7 billion; deposits totaled $130.5 billion, and liabilities totaled $147.1 billion.

The state had 57 state and federally chartered savings institutions at year-end 1996. Their total assets as of 31 December 1996 exceeded $16.8 billion. Thrift institutions in Florida made a total of $12.2 billion in loans and leases, of which almost 70% were secured by one to four family residential properties.

International banking grew in Florida during the late 1970s and early 1980s with the establishment of the Edge Act banks in Miami. These banks have headquarters outside Florida and must engage exclusively in international banking. As of year-end 1996, there were a total of 68 foreign banking offices in Florida, including state-licensed international bank agencies, representative offices, and administrative offices.

The Florida Department of Banking and Finance, Division of Finance, has regulatory and supervisory authority over mortgage brokers and mortgage lenders, consumer finance companies, motor vehicle sales finance companies, commercial and consumer debt collection agencies, cemeteries, and abandoned property.

33INSURANCE

In 1995, 51 life insurance companies and 127 property and casualty insurance companies were domiciled in Florida. Insurance premiums written in 1995 totaled $26.8 billion.

More than 12.8 million life insurance policies were in force in 1995, carrying a total face value of $541.05 billion. Claims and benefits paid during the year were approximately $10.77 billion, consisting of the following: death payments, $1.796 billion; annuity payments, $2.151 billion; matured endowments, $30.6 million; surrender values, $3.616 billion; aggregate write-ins for miscellaneous, $3.131 billion; and all other benefits, except A &

H, $44.2 million. Policy and contract dividends totaled $752.4 million.

Premiums written by property/casualty insurance companies totaled nearly $15.81 billion in 1995, of which private passenger and commercial liability accounted for over $4.25 billion; automobile physical damage, $2.14 billion; homeowners insurance, $1.68 billion; and commercial multiple-peril policies, $1.2 billion. Florida ranked 1st in the US in flood insurance in 1995, with 1,421,251 policies in force worth $151.85 billion, or over 44% of the US total. Marine insurance accounted for over $515 million (77% inland, 23% ocean) in premiums written in 1995.

The insurance industry is regulated by the state's Department of Insurance.

34SECURITIES

No securities exchanges are located in Florida, but there are thousands of registered brokers and dealers doing business in the state. A large portion of the industry's total employment was concentrated in the three Gold Coast counties—Dade, Broward, and Palm Beach.

The Department of Banking and Finance's Division of Securities, headed by the comptroller, oversees the securities industry.

35PUBLIC FINANCE

The Office of Planning and Budget of the Governor's Office prepares and submits to the legislature the budget for each fiscal year, which runs from 1 July to 30 June. The largest expenditure items are education, health and social concerns, general government, and transportation. By prohibiting borrowing to finance operating expenses, Florida's constitution requires a balanced budget. The following table shows the governor's recommended general revenues and allocations for the 1997/98 fiscal year (in thousands):

REVENUES	1997/98
From federal government	$ 10,712.7
From own sources	31,902.6
Taxes	
Sales and gross receipts	$15,426.5
Income	1,290.1
Total taxes	16,716.6
Charges and miscellaneous	15,186.0
TOTAL	$ 42,615.3
ALLOCATIONS	
Education	$ 12,467.3
Health and social concerns	4,604.1
Financial administration	2,245.0
Transportation (highways)	3,127.4
Public safety (police)	3.961.8
Natural resources	1,705.4
Community development	742.6
Other	13,156.9
TOTAL GENERAL EXPENDITURE	$ 42,010.5

The issuance of state bonds is overseen by the State Board of Administration, which consists of the governor, the state treasurer, and the comptroller. Three principal types of bonds are issued. The first consists of bonds backed by the "full faith and credit" of the state and payable from general revenue. Issuance of such bonds generally requires voter approval. The second type consists of revenue bonds, payable from income derived from the capital project financed, for example, from bridge or highway tolls. The third type consists of bonds payable from a constitutionally specified source, for example, higher education bonds backed by the state gross receipts tax, or elementary and secondary education bonds backed by the motor vehicle license tax.

The total indebtedness of Florida state government in 1996 exceeded $11 billion. The state debt outstanding at the end of 1996 was $768 per capita.

36TAXATION

Florida ranked 31st among the 50 states in per capita state taxation in 1994 with a tax burden of $2,107 per person. The 6% sales and use tax is the largest single source of state revenue; property taxes make up the bulk of local receipts. The state constitution prohibits a personal income tax. The legislature increased the sales tax in 1982 to 5% and in 1988 to the current 6%. During the 1980s and early 1990s, taxes on cigarettes, alcoholic beverages, fuel, and stock holdings were increased. For 1996, school districts levied $5.28 billion in property taxes.

The state sales tax applies to most retail items (but excludes groceries, medicines, and certain other items), as well as to car and hotel room rentals and theater admissions. The use tax is levied on wholesale items brought into Florida for sale. A 5.5% tax is levied on corporations' net income over $5,000. Other taxes include those on gasoline and other motor fuels, cigarettes, alcoholic beverages, drivers' licenses and motor vehicles, and parimutuel betting. An estate tax is also levied, but only up to the federal credit.

In 1995, Floridians paid nearly $51.7 billion in federal income taxes.

37ECONOMIC POLICY

From the late 1980s into the late 1990s, Florida intensified its efforts to attract high-tech, high-wage industries such as silicon technologies and aviation/aerospace industries. Florida became the first state in the nation to close its Department of Commerce. All of the state's economic development and international trade strategies are now handled through a partnership of business and government, Enterprise Florida. This new approach calls for collaboration among leaders in government, business, and academia. Enterprise Florida and its regional and local partner organizations provide a statewide network of business assistance resources in the areas of capital acquisition, technology commercialization, manufacturing competitiveness, training, minority and rural business development, incentives, site selection, permitting, and trade development. Florida businesses interested in the global marketplace can take advantage of Enterprise Florida's offices in Frankfurt, Germany; London, England; Taipei, Republic of China; Toronto, Canada; Seoul, South Korea; Mexico City, Mexico; Tokyo, Japan; and Sao Paolo, Brazil.

Florida is the 5th-largest economy among the 34 market economies of the Americas and the 15th-largest in the world. It has 14.5 million consumers, a gross state product of nearly $370 billion, and over $56 billion in international trade. It ranks consistently among the leading states in terms of business incorporations, corporate relocations, and business expansions.

Florida has 14 deep-water commercial seaports; 5 barge ports; 9 major shallow-water ports; 4 river ports; and 16 customs ports of entry.

With more than 17,000 manufacturing firms, Florida ranks 2d behind California in the number of aerospace and defense-related businesses. Florida ranks first in the nation in production of electromedical equipment and second in guided missiles, space vehicle equipment, and ophthalmic goods.

38HEALTH

Reflecting the age distribution of the state's population, Florida has a relatively low birthrate and a high death rate. Florida's birthrate was 13 per 1,000 population in 1996, well below the overall figure of 16.3. The state's 1996 infant mortality rate was 7.35 per 1,000 live births, below the US average. Some 80,040 legal abortions were performed in Florida in 1996; there were 424 abortions per 1,000 live births, slightly below the US average, and 28 abortions per 1,000 women aged 15–44 (about the same as the US average).

Florida's 1996 death rate, 1,041.7 per 100,000 population, was the 2d highest of all the states and 19% above the national norm, due in part to the state's considerable geriatric population. A better measure is the age-adjusted death rate. For 1995, the age-adjusted death rate for Florida was 483 per 100,000 persons, substantially below the national average. In 1991, Florida exceeded the national rate in deaths from heart disease, cancer, cerebrovascular disease, accidents, and suicide. The leading causes of death in 1996 were cardiovascular disease and cancer. The former accounted for 41% of all deaths in the state, 62,338 out of 150,809. Cancer claimed 36,897 lives, just over 24% of the total. In 1995, Florida had the lowest rate of mortality due to congestive heart failure of all the states, at just 7.3 per 100,000 population.

In 1996, there were 281 hospitals in Florida. The total number of beds available was 58,590; admissions totaled 1,751,754 in 1994. Florida's hospitals had 194,410 full-time equivalent employees in 1994. There were a total of 119,962 registered nurses and 42,906 licensed practical nurses in Florida as of 1993.

As of 1994, the total number of nonfederal licensed physicians in the state was 29,817. There were 252 physicians per 100,000 population in 1993. About 18% of all physicians were practicing in Dade County. There were 7,558 licensed dentists in the state in 1993.

In 1995, the preliminary average cost per hospital stay (estimated from charges) was $7,298; per inpatient day, $1,311. Florida ranked 4th among the 50 states in number of Medicaid recipients in 1996, with 1,560,700; Medicaid payments came to $6.139 million. In 1992, Florida ranked 2d in number of residents enrolled in the Medicare program. As of 1996, 2,667,000 Floridians were Medicare beneficiaries, with estimated payments exceeding $11,721,988 in 1993.

39SOCIAL WELFARE

More than one-fifth of all Floridians receive Social Security payments. Florida residents numbering 2.9 million received benefits averaging $718 per month in 1995. That year, 338,246 Floridians were receiving Supplemental Security Income. The average weekly unemployment benefit in Florida was $171.94 in 1995.

With the enactment of the Personal Responsibility and Work Opportunity Reconciliation Act of 1996, the US government has changed the form and regulations for many of its social welfare programs; most significantly, it replaces Aid to Families with Dependent Children (AFDC), an open-ended entitlement program, with Temporary Assistance for Needy Families (TANF), a limited system of assistance funded largely through federal block grants. The reform act also impacts the food stamp program, the Supplemental Security Income program, and the child nutrition program. The law took effect on 1 July 1997 and provided $16.38 billion in block grants for fiscal years 1997–2002. The grants are to be divided among the states based on an equation involving the numbers of former AFDC recipients in each state. Because many of the bills provisions have yet to be implemented into state-by-state policy, it was not possible to include the details of each state's programs for this edition of this work.

During fiscal years 1989–92, AFDC cases increased from 121,600 to 134,124 annually. In 1996, the number had increased to 575,000, with an average monthly check of $364.

In 1996, the food stamp program had an average monthly participation of 1.37 million. Also, students were taking part in the national school lunch program that year; federal spending for this program came to $293.5 million.

40 HOUSING

Florida's housing market fluctuated widely in the 1970s and early 1980s. During the mid-1970s recession, home buying dropped off markedly, and much newly completed housing could not be sold. By late in the decade, however, the unused housing stock had been depleted, and a new building boom was under way. The number of housing units in Florida increased 73.2% between 1970 and 1980, but only by 39.4% between 1980 and 1990. In 1990, 35% of all housing units had been built in the previous decade; only 3.7% were built before 1940.

In October 1996, there were an estimated 6,654,000 housing units in Florida, 5,527,000 of which were occupied. In 1996, 125,020 new privately owned housing units were authorized for construction, 91,040 of which were single-family units. Total value of newly constructed housing for 1996 was estimated at $11.4 billion. From 1990 to 1992, the number of housing unit completions for the Jacksonville area was 21,400 (of which 86% were single-family houses); greater Miami–Ft. Lauderdale, 61,100 (53% single-family houses); greater Orlando, 47,500 (65% single-family units); and the Tampa Bay area (includes St. Petersburg and Clearwater), 37,300 (71% single-family houses). Multifamily housing ranges from beachfront luxury high rises along the Gold Coast to dilapidated residential hotels in the South Beach section of Miami Beach. In 1990, the last year for which figures are available, the median monthly cost for an owner-occupied housing unit with a mortgage was $718, and for a unit without a mortgage it was $186. That year, the median rent for a housing unit was $481. During 1995/96, Florida received $748.9 million in aid from the US Department of Housing and Urban Development, including $193 million in community development block grants.

The Division of Florida Land Sales and Condominiums, within the Department of Business Regulation, registers all sellers of subdivided land and oversees the advertising and selling of land, condominiums, and cooperatives. A major controversy involving condominiums in the early 1970s centered on "rec leases." Until the practice was outlawed in mid-decade, condominium developers often retained ownership of such recreational facilities as the swimming pool, clubhouse, and tennis courts, requiring apartment purchasers to pay rent for their use. The rents were generally set quite low at the time of sale, but raised sharply soon after.

41 EDUCATION

In the 1970s, Florida was an innovator in several areas of education, including competency testing, expansion of community colleges, and school finance reform. Further advances were made in 1983 and 1984, when the state increased taxes to help fund education, raised teachers' salaries, initiated the nation's strictest high school graduation requirements, and reformed the curriculum.

Student achievement in reading, writing, and mathematics is measured by national norm-referenced tests selected at the district level, and by the High School Competency Test (HSCT), measuring communication and math skills of 11th-grade students. In 1996, 77% of students who took the test passed the communications part and 75% passed the mathematics part. A total of 91,653 high school diplomas were awarded in 1995/96. In 1990, 78.6% of Floridians 25 years of age or older were high school graduates; 19.4% had four or more years of college.

There were 119,388 public school teachers in 1996. The full-time equivalent enrollment was 2,176,930. The basic education total consisted of 51,629 students in pre-kindergarten, 1,562,396 students in grades K–8, and 562,905 in grades 9–12. In 1995/96, 57.5% of public school students were white non-Hispanic, 25.3% black non-Hispanic, and over 15.3% Hispanic; there were small percentages of Asian and American Indian students. In Dade County, 50.6% of the student body was Hispanic.

Florida has 9 state universities, with a total fall 1994 enrollment of 155,232. The largest, the University of Florida (Gainesville), had a fall 1994 enrollment of 38,277. Also part of the state university system are special university centers, such as the University of Florida's Institute of Food and Agricultural Science, which provide advanced and graduate courses. The State University System also offers instruction at strategic sites away from the regular campuses. In 1972, Florida completed a community college system that put a public two-year college within commuting distance of virtually every resident. The state's 29 community colleges had a fall 1994 enrollment of more than 326,782.

Of Florida's 76 private institutions of higher education, by far the largest is the University of Miami (Coral Gables).

The Board of Education, consisting of the governor and the cabinet, is responsible for the state's educational system. The commissioner of education (a cabinet member) is also the administrative head of the Department of Education. The policy-making body for the state university system is the Board of Regents; the chancellor is the system's chief administrative officer.

In 1994/95, the state government provided about 50.1% of the funding for public schools; local governments, 42.4%; and the federal government, 7.5%. Estimated operating expenditures in 1994/95 were $11.1 billion. Spending per pupil in average daily attendance was $4,879 in 1994/95. Florida's school finance law, the Florida Education Finance Act of 1973, establishes a funding formula aimed at equalizing both per-pupil spending statewide and the property tax burdens of residents of different school districts.

42 ARTS

Florida is home to a vibrant and diverse cultural community. The not-for-profit cultural industry in Florida contributes a total of over $1.1 billion to the state's economy, not including associated expenditures such as cultural tourism, which generates an additional $3.3 billion. Florida ranks 2d nationally in state funding for culture and the arts, with a total annual budget in 1996/97 of over $27 million. Cultural organizations thrive in virtually every county and include museums, galleries, symphonies, dance and opera companies, and literary organizations. Offerings range from the Miami Book Fair International at one end of the state, to the widely renowned Jacksonville Jazz Festival, to the Naval Aviation Museum in Pensacola at the other end. According to the 1990 US Census, Florida ranks 4th nationally in the number of individual artists living and working in the state. Key West has long been a gathering place for creative artists, ranging from John James Audubon and Winslow Homer to Ernest Hemingway and Tennessee Williams.

Regional and metropolitan symphony orchestras include the Florida Philharmonic Orchestra (Fort Lauderdale), Florida Orchestra (Tampa), Jacksonville Symphony, and the Florida West Coast Symphony (Sarasota). Opera companies include the Florida Grand Opera (Miami) and the Sarasota Opera. The four state theater companies are the Caldwell Theatre Company (Boca Raton), Hippodrome State Theatre (Gainesville), Coconut Grove Playhouse (Miami), and the Asolo Theatre Company (Sarasota).

Florida is also home to premier museums and performing arts halls, such as the John and Mable Ringling Museum of Art (Sarasota), the Norton Gallery (West Palm Beach), the Miami Art Museum, Orlando Museum of Art, Philharmonic Center for the

Arts (Naples), Tampa Bay Performing Arts Center, and the Kravis Center for the Performing Arts (West Palm Beach).

Truly unique cultural institutions also located in Florida include Fairchild Tropical Garden (Miami), the Atlantic Center for the Arts (New Smyrna Beach), and Bok Tower Gardens (Lake Wales), which has a working carillon.

From 1993 to 1997, the State of Florida's Division of Cultural Affairs awarded $116,454,670 in grants to both cultural organizations and individual artists. In 1996, Florida received $897,000 from the NEA. Over 30 million people attend cultural events each year in Florida.

In addition to a wide range of cultural grants programs offered by the State of Florida, the Florida Department of State, Division of Cultural Affairs also coordinates a touring program, a public art program that acquires artwork for new state buildings, an arts license plate program, and the Florida Artists Hall of Fame, which includes such luminaries as Zora Neale Hurston, Ernest Hemingway, Ray Charles, Marjorie Kinnan Rawlings, and Robert Rauschenberg.

43 LIBRARIES AND MUSEUMS

Florida had 9 multi-county library systems and 40 county systems in 1995. The book stock was 32.4 million, and circulation totaled 70.1 million.

The largest public library systems are those of Miami–Dade County (3,359,122 volumes in 1995) and Jacksonville (2,420,294 volumes). The State Library in Tallahassee housed 286,645 volumes, as well as 289,970 microfiche and 282,070 state and federal documents in 1995; the State Library also distributes federal aid to local libraries and provides other assistance. In 1995 federal aid under the Library Services and Construction Act to Florida public libraries totaled $5.5 million; state aid to public libraries was $25 million. The largest university library in the state is that of the University of Florida, with holdings of more than 3.2 million volumes in 1996. Other major university libraries are those of the University of Miami (2.1 million volumes) and Florida State University (2.2 million).

Florida has about 239 museums, galleries, and historical sites, as well as numerous public gardens. One of the best-known museums is the John and Mabel Ringling Museum of Art (Sarasota), a state owned facility which houses the collection of the late circus entrepreneur, featuring Italian and North European Renaissance paintings. Also in Sarasota are the Ringling Museum of the Circus and the Circus Hall of Fame, and Ca'd'Zan, the Ringling mansion. The estates and homes of a number of prominent former Florida residents are now open as museums. The Villa Vizcaya Museum and Gardens in Miami, originally the estate of International Harvester founder James R. Deering, displays his collection of 15th–18th-century antiques. Railroad developer Henry Morrison Flagler's home in Palm Beach is now a museum in his name. The Society of the Four Arts is also in Palm Beach. On Key West, Ernest Hemingway's home is also a museum. The John James Audubon house in Key West and Thomas Edison's house in Ft. Myers are two of Florida's other great homes.

The Metrozoo-Miami, with an average annual attendance of 840,000, and the Jacksonville Zoological park, 260,000, are among the state's leading zoos. Both Busch Gardens (Tampa) and Sea World of Florida (Orlando) report average annual attendances of 3,000,000.

The largest historic restoration in Florida is in St. Augustine, where several blocks of the downtown area have been restored to their 18th-century likeness under the auspices of the Historic St. Augustine Preservation Board, a state agency. Castillo de San Marcos, the 17th-century Spanish fort at St. Augustine, is now a national monument under the jurisdiction of the National Park Service and is open to the public. Other Florida cities having

historic preservation boards are Pensacola, Tallahassee, and Tampa.

44 COMMUNICATIONS

As of March 1993, 93.7% of the state's 5,578,000 occupied housing units had telephones.

Florida's first radio station was WFAW (later WQAM) in Miami, which went on the air in 1920. In 1996, the state had 198 AM stations and 262 FM. Miami was also the site of the state's first television station, WTVJ, which began broadcasting on 27 January 1949.

Film and television production in Florida is a billion-dollar per year industry with over 5,000 production companies providing more than 66,000 jobs. There were 92 TV stations in Florida in 1996; Miami, with 11 stations, had more than any other Florida city. Educational television stations numbered 18 in 1996, serving virtually the entire state. Ft. Lauderdale and Miami each had one television station broadcasting in Spanish in 1996. In 1993, Florida had 48 large cable television systems.

45 PRESS

The *East Florida Gazette,* published in St. Augustine in 1783–84, was Florida's earliest newspaper. The oldest paper still publishing is the *Jacksonville Times-Union* (now *Florida Times-Union,*) which first appeared in February 1883.

In 1997, the state had 33 morning papers, 9 evening papers, and 33 Sunday papers. The leading English-language dailies and their circulations in 1997 were:

AREA	NAME	DAILY	SUNDAY
Ft. Lauderdale	*Sun-Sentinel*(m)	272,258	391,063
Jacksonville	*Florida Times-Union* (m, S)	197,706	251,256
Miami	*Herald* (m, S)	378,195	500,654
Orlando	*Sentinel* (all day, S)	273,689	396,244
St. Petersburg	*Times* (m, S)	364,810	462,103
Sarasota	*Herald-Tribune* (m,S)	122,198	151,255
Tampa	*Tribune* (all day)	269,349	371,086
West Palm Beach	*Palm Beach Post* (m,S)	188,996	239,531

There were 223 weekly newspapers in 1997. Fifteen black newspapers and 4 Spanish-language newspapers were also published in Florida. The most widely read periodical published in Florida is the sensationalist *National Enquirer.* There were 30 book publishers in Florida in 1997, including Academic Press and University Presses of Florida.

46 ORGANIZATIONS

The 1992 Census of Service Industries counted 3,499 organizations in Florida, including 661 business associations; 2,214 civic, social, and fraternal associations; and 624 other membership organizations.

Commercial, trade, and professional organizations based in Florida include the American Accounting Association (Sarasota), American Welding Society (Miami), American Electroplaters' Society (Winter Park), Florida Citrus Mutual (Lakeland), and Florida Fruit and Vegetable Association (Orlando).

Sports groups include the National Association for Stock Car Auto Racing, better known as NASCAR (Daytona Beach), American Surfing Association (Lake Worth), American Water Ski Association (Winter Haven), International Game Fish Association (Ft. Lauderdale), and International Swimming Hall of Fame (Ft. Lauderdale).

Among other organizations with headquarters in Florida are the American Sunbathing Association, formerly the International Nudist Conference (Kissimmee), and the National Head Start Association (Bradenton).

⁴⁷TOURISM, TRAVEL, AND RECREATION

Tourism is a mainstay of the state's economy. In 1996, Florida experienced an 18% decline in visitors to its national parks and recreational areas. Almost 6 million travelers in 1995 spent nearly $29 million on day trips and overnight stays away from home. Most of Florida's tourists are from elsewhere in the US, although, in the 1990s, Miami was attracting large numbers of affluent Latin American travelers, lured at least in part by the Latin flavor the large Cuban community has given the city. In 1995, Florida was rated the number one vacation destination for overseas tourists to the United States.

Hundreds of thousands of Floridians worked in tourist- and recreation-related businesses in 1995, and the state ranked 2d in the nation in the number of travel and tourism employees. In 1993, the state had 1,350 licensed hotels and 1,793 motels. More than half of all hotels were located in Dade County, where hotels and other tourist accommodations stretch for miles along Collins Avenue in Miami Beach, in the heart of the state's tourist industry.

Florida's biggest tourist attractions are its sun, sand, and surf. According to the state's Department of Commerce, leisure-time activity is the principal reason why more than four-fifths of auto travelers enter the state. A major tourist attraction is Walt Disney World, a huge amusement park near Orlando; in 1982, EPCOT Center, a futuristic exhibition and amusement park, was opened at Disney World. Other major attractions are the Kennedy Space Center at Cape Canaveral and the St. Augustine historic district.

Nine parks and other facilities in Florida operated by the National Park Service draw millions of visitors annually. The most popular destination is the Gulf Islands National Seashore, located near Pensacola (1.9 million visitors), followed by the Canaveral National Seashore. Almost 6.6 million people visited 92 facilities operated by the Division of Recreation and Parks of the state's Department of Natural Resources. These facilities included 28 state parks, 28 state recreation areas, and 18 state historical sites.

Fishing and boating are major recreational activities. In 1995, licenses were held by 1,532,979 anglers and 331,742 hunters who visited the state.

In the 1970s and early 1980s, the Miami Beach tourist hotels faced increasing competition from Caribbean and Latin American resorts. The city's business community, seeking to boost tourism, strongly backed a 1978 statewide referendum to authorize casino gambling along part of Collins Avenue in Miami Beach and Hollywood; however, the proposal was defeated by a wide margin. In a local advisory referendum in March 1980, Miami Beach voters approved development in South Beach of an $850 million, 250-acre (100-hectare) complex that included hotels and a convention center. Off-track betting, horse racing, dog racing, jai alai, and bingo are all legalized and operative forms of gaming.

⁴⁸SPORTS

Florida has 10 major-league professional sports teams: the Miami Dolphins, Tampa Bay Buccaneers, and Jacksonville Jaguars of the National Football League; the Miami Heat and the Orlando Magic of the National Basketball Association; the Tampa Bay Lightning and the Florida Panthers of the National Hockey League; the Florida Marlins and, beginning in 1998, the Tampa Bay Devil Rays of Major League Baseball; and Tampa Bay has a Major League Soccer team. Of the football teams, the Dolphins have been by far the most successful, winning the Super Bowl in 1973 (following the NFL's only undefeated season) and 1974, and appearing in three other Super Bowls (in 1972, 1983, and 1985). Many Major League Baseball teams have their training camps in Florida and play exhibition games (in the "Grapefruit League") in the spring.

Several tournaments on both the men's and women's professional golf tours are played in Florida. In auto racing, the Daytona 500 is a top race on the NASCAR circuit, while the 24 Hours of Daytona is one of the top sports car races in the world. Three of the major collegiate football bowl games are played in the state: the Orange Bowl in Miami, the Gator Bowl in Jacksonville, and the Florida Citrus Bowl in Orlando.

In collegiate sports, football dominates. The University of Florida, Florida State, and the University of Miami all emerged as nationally ranked powerhouses in the 1980s and 1990s. Miami won the Orange Bowl in 1946, 1984, 1988, 1989, and 1992, the Sugar Bowl in 1990, and the Cotton Bowl in 1991. The Hurricanes were named national champions in 1983, 1987, 1989, and 1991 (with Washington). Florida State won the Orange Bowl in 1993, 1994, and 1996, the Sugar Bowl in 1989, and the Cotton Bowl in 1992. The Seminoles were named national champions in 1993. The University of Florida won the Orange Bowl in 1967, the Gator Bowl in 1984 and 1993, the Sugar Bowl in 1994, and defeated Florida State in the 1997 Sugar Bowl to win the national championship.

Other annual sporting events include rodeos in Arcadia and Kissimmee and the Firecracker 400 Auto Race in Daytona Beach, all on the Fourth of July weekend.

⁴⁹FAMOUS FLORIDIANS

The first Floridian to serve in a presidential cabinet was Alan S. Boyd (b.1922), named the first secretary of transportation (1967–69) by President Lyndon Johnson. Florida also produced one of the major US military figures of World War II, General Joseph Warren Stilwell (1883–1946), dubbed "Vinegar Joe" for his strongly stated opinions. Graduated from West Point in 1904, he served in France during World War I. First posted to China in the 1920s, he became chief of staff to General Chiang Kai-shek and commander of US forces in the China-Burma-India theater during World War II. He was promoted to full general in 1944 but forced to leave China because of his criticism of the Chiang Kai-shek regime. Janet Reno (b.1938), Attorney General of the United States in the Clinton administration, was born in Miami.

David Levy Yulee (b.St. Thomas, 1810–86) came to Florida in 1824 and, after serving in the US House of Representatives, was appointed one of the state's first two US senators in 1845, thereby becoming the first Jew to sit in the Senate. He resigned in 1861 to serve in the Confederate Congress. Yulee built the first cross-state railroad, from Fernandina to Cedar Key, in the late 1860s. Ruth Bryan Owen Rohde (b.Illinois, 1885–1954), a longtime Miami resident and member of the US House of Representatives (1929–33), in 1933 became the first woman to head a US diplomatic office abroad when she was named minister to Denmark.

Prominent governors of Florida include Richard Keith Call (b.Virginia, 1792–1862), who came to Florida with General Andrew Jackson in 1821 and remained to become governor of the territory in 1826–39 and 1841–44. In the summer of 1836, Call commanded the US campaign against the Seminole. Although a southerner and a slaveholder, he steadfastly opposed secession. Napoleon Bonaparte Broward (1857–1910) was, before becoming governor, a ship's pilot and owner of St. Johns River boats. He used one of these, *The Three Friends*, a powerful seagoing tug, to run guns and ammunition to Cuban rebels in 1896. As governor (1905–9), he was noted for a populist program that included railroad regulation, direct elections, state college reorganization and coordination, and drainage of the Everglades under state auspices. As governor in 1955–61, Thomas LeRoy Collins (1909–91), met the desegregation issue by advocating moderation and respect for the law, helping the state avoid violent confrontations. He served as chairman of both the southern and national governors' conferences, and he was named by President Johnson as the first director of the Community Relations Service under the 1964 Civil Rights Act.

Military figures who have played a major role in Florida's history include the Spanish conquistadors Juan Ponce de León (c.1460–1521), the European discoverer of Florida, and Pedro Menéndez de Avilés (1519–74), founder of the first permanent settlement, St. Augustine. Andrew Jackson (b.South Carolina, 1767–1845), a consistent advocate of US seizure of Florida, led military expeditions into the territory in 1814 and 1818 and, after US acquisition, served briefly in 1821 as Florida's military governor before leaving for Tennessee. During the Seminole War of 1835–42, one of the leading military tacticians was Osceola (c.1800–1838), who, although neither born a chief nor elected to that position, rose to the leadership of the badly divided Seminole by force of character and personality. He rallied them to fierce resistance to removal, making skillful use of guerrilla tactics. Captured under a flag of truce in 1837, he was imprisoned; already broken in health, he died in Fort Moultrie in Charleston harbor. During the Civil War, General Edmund Kirby Smith (1824–93), a native of St. Augustine who graduated from West Point in 1845, served as commander (1863–65) of Confederate forces west of the Mississippi River. He surrendered the last of the southern forces at Galveston, Texas, on 26 May 1865.

Among the late-19th-century entrepreneurs who played significant roles in Florida's development, perhaps the most important was Henry Morrison Flagler (b.New York, 1830–1913). Flagler made a fortune in Ohio as an associate of John D. Rockefeller in the Standard Oil Co. and did not even visit Florida until he was in his fifties. However, in the 1880s he began to acquire and build railroads down the length of Florida's east coast and to develop tourist hotels at various points, including St. Augustine, Palm Beach, and Miami, helping to create one of the state's major present-day industries. Henry Bradley Plant (b.Connecticut, 1819–99) did for Florida's west coast what Flagler did for the east. Plant extended railroad service to Tampa in 1884, built a huge tourist hotel there, developed the port facilities, and established steamship lines.

Among Floridians prominent in science was Dr. John F. Gorrie (b.South Carolina, 1802–55), who migrated to Apalachicola in 1833 and became a socially and politically prominent physician, specializing in the treatment of fevers. He blew air over ice brought in by ship from the north to cool the air in sickrooms, and he independently developed a machine to manufacture ice, only to have two others beat him to the patent office by days.

The noted labor and civil rights leader A. Philip Randolph (1889–1979) was a native of Crescent City. Mary McLeod Bethune (b.South Carolina, 1875–1955) was an advisor to President Franklin D. Roosevelt on minority affairs, became the first president (1935) of the National Council of Negro Women, and was a consultant at the 1945 San Francisco Conference that founded the UN. A prominent black educator, she opened a school for girls at Daytona Beach in 1904. The school merged with Cookman Institute in 1923 to become Bethune-Cookman College, which she headed until 1942 and again in 1946–47.

Prominent Florida authors include James Weldon Johnson (1871–1938), perhaps best known for his 1912 novel *Autobiography of an Ex-Colored Man*. He was also the first black to be admitted to the Florida bar (1897) and was a founder and secretary of the NAACP. Marjory Stoneman Douglas (b.Minnesota, 1890), who came to Miami in 1915, is the author of several works reflecting her concern for the environment, including *The Everglades: River of Grass* (first published in 1947), *Hurricane* (1958), and *Florida: The Long Frontier* (1967). Marjorie Kinnan Rawlings (b.Washington, D.C., 1895–1953) came to Florida in 1928 to do creative writing. After her first novel, *South Moon Under* (1933), came the Pulitzer Prize–winning *The Yearling* (1938), the poignant story of a 12-year-old

boy on the Florida frontier in the 1870s. Zora Neale Hurston (1901–60), born in poverty in the all-Negro town of Eatonville and a graduate of Barnard College, spent four years collecting folklore, which she published in *Mules and Men* (1935) and *Tell My Horse* (1938).

Entertainers born in Florida include Sidney Poitier (b.1927), Charles Eugene "Pat" Boone (b.1934), Faye Dunaway (b.1941), and Ben Vereen (b.1946).

Florida's most famous sports figure is Chris Evert Lloyd (Christine Marie Evert, b.1953), who became a dominant force in women's tennis in the mid-1970s. After turning pro in 1973, she won the Wimbledon singles title in 1974, 1976, and 1981, and the US Open from 1975 to 1978 and in 1980 and 1982. She retired from tennis in 1990.

[50]BIBLIOGRAPHY

Bennett, Charles E. *Florida's French Revolution, 1793–1795.* Gainesville: University Presses of Florida, 1981.

Daver, Manning J., ed. *Florida Politics and Government.* 2d ed. Gainesville: University Presses of Florida, 1984.

Douglas, Marjory Stoneman. *The Everglades: River of Grass.* Rev. ed. Miami: Banyan, 1978.

Federal Writers's Project. *Florida: A Guide to the Southernmost State.* Reprint. New York: Somerset, 1981 (orig. 1939).

Florida, University of. College of Business Administration. Bureau of Business and Economic research. *1984 Florida Abstract.* Gainesville: University Presses of Florida, 1984.

Gannon, Michael, ed. *The New History of Florida.* Gainesville, Fla.: University Presses of Florida, 1996.

Hanna, Kathryn T. Abbey. *Florida: Land of Change.* Chapel Hill: University of North Carolina Press, 1948.

Harris, Michael H. *Florida History: A Bibliography.* Metuchen, N.J.: Scarecrow Press, 1972.

Jahoda, Gloria. *Florida: A Bicentennial History.* New York: Norton, 1976.

Johns, John E. *Florida During the Civil War.* Gainesville: University Presses of Florida, 1963.

Lyon, Eugene. *The Enterprise of Florida: Pedro Menèndez de Avilès and the Spanish Conquest of 1565–68.* Gainesville: University Presses of Florida, 1976.

MacDonald, John D. *Condominium.* Philadelphia: Lippincott, 1977.

Mahon, John K. *The Second Seminole War.* Gainesville: University Presses of Florida, 1967.

McGovern, Bernie, ed. *Florida Almanac 1997–1998.* Greta, La.: Pelican, 1997.

Morris, Allen (comp.) *The Florida Handbook 1985–86.* Tallahassee: Peninsular Publishing, 1985.

Patrick, Rembert W. *Florida Under Five Flags.* Gainesville: University Presses of Florida, 1960.

Rawlings, Marjorie Kinnan. *The Yearling.* New York: Scribner, 1938.

Shofner, Jerrell M. *Nor Is It Over Yet: Florida in the Era of Reconstruction, 1863–77.* Gainesville: University Presses of Florida, 1974.

Smiley, Nixon. *Knights of the Fourth Estate: The Story of the Miami Herald.* Miami: Seeman, 1974.

———. *Yesterday's Florida.* Miami: Seeman, 1974.

Tebeau, Charlton. *A History of Florida.* Coral Gables: University of Miami Press, 1981 (orig. 1971).

Thompson, Ralph B., ed. *Florida Statistical Abstract 1984.* 18th ed. Gainesville: University Presses of Florida, 1984.

Wood, Roland, and Edward A. Fernald. *The New Florida Atlas: Patterns of the Sunshine State.* Tampa: Trend House, 1974.

Wright J. Leitch, Jr. *Florida in the American Revolution.* Gainesville: University Presses of Florida, 1975.

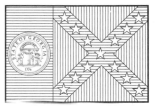

GEORGIA

State of Georgia

ORIGIN OF STATE NAME: Named for King George II of England in 1732. **NICKNAME:** The Empire State of the South. (also Peach State.) **CAPITAL:** Atlanta. **ENTERED UNION:** 2 January 1788 (4th). **SONG:** "Georgia." **MOTTO:** Wisdom, Justice, Moderation. **COAT OF ARMS:** Three columns support an arch inscribed with the word "Constitution"; intertwined among the columns is a banner bearing the state motto. Right of center stands a soldier with a drawn sword, representing the aid of the military in defending the Constitution. Surrounding the whole are the words "State of Georgia 1776." **FLAG:** At the hoist, on a blue bar, is the coat of arms. The remainder comprises the battle flag of the Confederacy. **OFFICIAL SEAL:** OBVERSE: same as the coat of arms. REVERSE: a sailing vessel and a smaller boat are offshore; on land, a man and horse plow a field, and sheep graze in the background. The scene is surrounded by the words "Agriculture and Commerce 1776." **BIRD:** Brown thrasher. **FISH:** Largemouth bass. **INSECT:** Honeybee. **FLOWER:** Cherokee rose. **WILDFLOWER:** Azalea. **TREE:** Live oak. **GEM:** Quartz. **FOSSIL:** Shark tooth. **LEGAL HOLIDAYS:** New Year's Day, 1 January; Robert E. Lee's Birthday, 19 January; Birthday of Martin Luther King, Jr., 3d Monday in January; Washington's Birthday, 3d Monday in February; Confederate Memorial Day, 26 April; National Memorial Day, last Monday in May; Jefferson Davis's Birthday, 3 June; Independence Day, 4 July; Labor Day, 1st Monday in September; Columbus Day, 2d Monday in October; Veterans Day, 11 November; Thanksgiving Day, 4th Thursday in November; Christmas Day, 25 December. **TIME:** 7 AM EST = noon GMT.

¹LOCATION, SIZE, AND EXTENT

Located in the southeastern US, Georgia is the largest state east of the Mississippi River, and ranks 21st in size among the 50 states.

The total area of Georgia is 58,910 sq mi (152,576 sq km), of which land comprises 58,056 sq mi (150,365 sq km) and inland water 854 sq mi (2,211 sq km). Georgia extends 254 mi (409 km) E-W; the maximum N-S extension is 320 mi (515 km).

Georgia is bordered on the N by Tennessee and North Carolina; on the E by South Carolina (with the line formed by the Chattooga, Tugaloo, and Savannah rivers) and by the Atlantic Ocean; on the S by Florida (with the line in the SE defined by the St. Marys River); and on the W by Alabama (separated in the SW by the Chattahoochee River). The state's geographic center is located in Twiggs County, 18 mi (29 km) SW of Macon.

The Sea Islands extend the length of the Georgia coast. The state's total boundary length is 1,039 mi (1,672 km).

²TOPOGRAPHY

Northern Georgia is mountainous, the central region is characterized by the rolling hills of the Piedmont Plateau, and southern Georgia is a nearly flat coastal plain.

The Blue Ridge Mountains tumble to an end in northern Georgia, where Brasstown Bald, at 4,784 feet (1,458 meters), is the highest point in the state. The piedmont slopes slowly to the fall line, descending from about 2,000 feet (610 meters) to 300 feet (90 meters) above sea level. Stone Mountain, where a Confederate memorial is carved into a mass of solid granite 1,686 feet (514 meters) high, is the region's most famous landmark.

The piedmont region ends in a ridge of sand hills running across the state from Augusta to Columbus. The residue of an ancient ocean was caught in the vast shallow basin on the Florida border, known as the Okefenokee Swamp, which filled with fresh water over the centuries. The coastal plain, thinly populated except for towns at the mouths of inland rivers, ends in marshlands along the Atlantic Ocean. Lying offshore are the Sea Islands, called the Golden Isles of Georgia, the most important of

which are, from north to south, Tybee, Ossabaw, St. Catherines, Sapelo, St. Simons, Sea Island, Jekyll, and Cumberland.

Two great rivers rise in the northeast: the Savannah, which forms part of the border with South Carolina, and the Chattahoochee, which flows across the state to become the western boundary. The Flint joins the Chattahoochee at the southwestern corner of Georgia to form the Apalachicola, which flows through Florida into the Gulf of Mexico. The two largest rivers of central Georgia, the Ocmulgee and Oconee, flow together to form the Altamaha, which then flows eastward to the Atlantic. Perhaps the best-known Georgia river, though smaller than any of the above, is the Suwannee, flowing southwest through the Okefenokee Swamp, across Florida, and into the Gulf of Mexico, and famous for its evocation by Stephen Foster in the song "Old Folks at Home." Huge lakes created by dams on the Savannah River are Clark Hill Reservoir and Hartwell Lake; artificial lakes on the Chattahoochee River include Lake Seminole, Walter F. George Reservoir, Lake Harding, West Point Reservoir, and Lake Sidney Lanier.

³CLIMATE

The Chattahoochee River divides Georgia into separate climatic regions. The mountain region to the northwest is colder than the rest of Georgia, averaging 39°F (4°C) in January and 78°F (26°C) in July. The state experiences mild winters, ranging from a January average of 44°F (7°C) in the piedmont to 54°F (12°C) on the coast. Summers are hot in the piedmont and on the coast, with July temperatures averaging 80°F (27°C) or above. The record high is 113°F (45°C) at Greenville on 27 May 1978; the record low is −17°F (−27°C), registered in Floyd County on 27 January 1940.

Humidity is high, ranging from 83% in the morning to 57% in the afternoon in Atlanta. Rainfall varies considerably from year to year, but averages 50 in (127 cm) annually in the lowlands, increasing to 75 in (191 cm) in the mountains; snow falls occasionally in the interior. Tornadoes (22 recorded in 1995) are an annual threat in mountain areas, and Georgia beaches are exposed to hurricane tides.

The growing season is approximately 185 days in the mountains and a generous 300 days in southern Georgia.

⁴FLORA AND FAUNA

Georgia has some 250 species of trees, 90% of which are of commercial importance. White and scrub pines, chestnut, northern red oak, and buckeye cover the mountain zone, while loblolly and shortleaf (yellow) pines and whiteback maple are found throughout the piedmont. Pecan trees grow densely in southern Georgia, and white oak and cypress are plentiful in the eastern part of the state. Trees found throughout the state include red cedar, scaly-bark and white hickories, red maple, sycamore, yellow poplar, sassafras, sweet and black gums, and various dogwoods and magnolias. Common flowering shrubs include yellow jasmine, flowering quince, and mountain laurel. Spanish moss grows abundantly on the coast and around the streams and swamps of the entire coastal plain. Kudzu vines, originally from Asia, are ubiquitous.

The state lists 58 protected plants, of which 23—including buckthorn, golden seal, spiderlily, fringed campion, and starflower—are endangered.

Prominent among Georgia fauna is the white-tailed (Virginia) deer, found in some 50 counties. Other common mammals are the black bear, muskrat, raccoon opossum, mink, common cottontail, and three species of squirrel—fox, gray, and flying. No fewer than 160 birds species breed in Georgia, among them the mockingbird, brown thrasher (the state bird), and numerous sparrows; the Okefenokee Swamp is home to the sandhill piper, snowy egret, and white ibis. The bobwhite quail is the most popular game bird. There are 79 species of reptile, including such poisonous snakes as the rattler, copperhead, and cottonmouth moccasin. The state's 63 amphibian species consist mainly of various salamanders, frogs, and toads. The most popular fresh-water game fish are trout, bream, bass, and catfish, all but the last of which are produced in state hatcheries for restocking. Dolphins, porpoises, shrimp, oysters, and blue crabs are found off the Georgia coast.

Rare or threatened animals include the indigo snake and Georgia's blind cave salamander. The state protects 23 species of wildlife, among them the colonial and Sherman's pocket gophers, right and humpback whales, manatee, brown pelican, American alligator, three species of sea turtles, shortnose sturgeon, and southern cave fish.

⁵ENVIRONMENTAL PROTECTION

In the early 1970s, environmentalists pointed to the fact that the Savannah River had been polluted by industrial waste and that an estimated 58% of Georgia's citizens lived in districts lacking adequate sewage treatment facilities. In 1972, at the prodding of Governor Jimmy Carter, the general assembly created the Environmental Protection Division (EPD) within the Department of Natural Resources (DNR). This agency administers 21 state environmental laws, most of them passed during the 1970s: the Water Quality Control Act, the Safe Drinking Water Act, the Groundwater Use Act, the Surface Water Allocation Act, the Air Quality Act, the Safe Dams Act, the Asbestos Safety Act, the Vehicle Inspection and Maintenance Act, the Hazardous Site Response Act, the Comprehensive Solid Waste Management Act, the Scrap Tire Amendment, the Underground Storage Tank Act, the Hazardous Waste Management Act, the Sedimentation and Erosion Control Act, the River Basin Management Plans, The Water Well Standards Act, the Oil and Hazardous Materials Spill Act, the Georgia Environmental Policy Act, the Surface Mining Act, and the Oil and Gas and the Deep Drilling Act. The EPD issues all the environmental permits, with the exception of those required by the Marshlands Protection and Shore Assistance Acts, which are enforced by the Coastal Resources Division of the DNR. Georgia's greatest environmental problems are an increasingly scarce water supply, nonpoint source water pollution, and hazardous waste sites. In 1995 hazardous waste sites numbered 14. As of 1997 the state had 7.7 million acres of wetlands.

⁶POPULATION

Georgia ranked 11th among the 50 states in 1990 with a population of 6,478,216. The 1996 population was estimated at 7,353,225, up 13.5% from 1990. The population density was 112 per sq mi (43 per sq km) in 1990.

During the first half of the 18th century, restrictive government policies discouraged settlement. In 1752, when Georgia became a royal colony, the population numbered only 3,500, of whom 500 were blacks. Growth was rapid thereafter, and by 1773 there were 33,000 people, almost half of them black. The American Revolution brought free land and an influx of settlers, so that by 1800 the population has swelled to 162,686. Georgia passed the million mark by 1860, the 2 million mark by 1900, and by 1960, the population had doubled again. Georgia's population increased 19% between 1980 and 1990.

According to the 1990 census, the population was 51.5% female and 48.5% male. With a median age of 26.7, Georgia residents were somewhat younger than the national average. Over 66% of all residents were born in Georgia, and 50.6% of the Georgians five years of age or older counted in the 1990 census had lived in a different house in 1985.

About 65% of all Georgians lived in urban areas in 1990, and 35% in rural areas. There has always been a strained relationship between rural and urban Georgians, and the state's political system long favored the rural population. Since before the American Revolution, the city people have called the country folk "crackers," a term that implies a lack of good manners and which may derive from the fact that these pioneers drove their cattle before them with whips.

The state's four largest cities in 1994 were Atlanta, with an estimated population of 396,052; Columbus, 186,470; Savannah, 140,597; and Macon, 109,191. The Atlanta metropolitan area had an estimated population of 3,431,983 in 1995.

⁷ETHNIC GROUPS

Georgia has been fundamentally a white/black state, with minimal ethnic diversity. Most Georgians are of English or Scotch-Irish descent. The number of Georgians who were foreign-born in 1990 was low—173,126 (or 2.6% of the population). However this was a considerable increase over 91,480 foreign-born Georgians in 1980, and 33,000 in 1970. Between 1970 and 1990, the number of Georgians from Asia or the Pacific Islands increased from 8,838 in 1970 to 24,461 in 1980 to 76,000 in 1990. By 1990, 6,284 Vietnamese had resettled in Georgia.

Georgia's black population declined from a high of 47% of the total population in 1880 to about 26% in 1970, when there were 1,187,149 blacks. Black citizens accounted for 27% of the total population and numbered 1,747,000 in 1990. Atlanta, which had 264,000 black residents (67.1%) in 1990, has been a significant center for the development of black leadership, especially at Atlanta University. With its long-established black elite, Atlanta has also been the locus of some large black-owned business enterprises. There are elected and appointed blacks in the state government, and in 1973, Atlanta elected its first black mayor, Maynard Jackson. By 1984 there were 13 black mayors, including Andrew J. Young of Atlanta.

There were only 13,000 American Indians in Georgia in 1990. The great Cherokee nation and its collateral linguistic relatives had been effectively removed from the state 150 years earlier.

GEORGIA
Explanation

▲ Point of Interest
◉ City (25,000-100,000 people)
◉ City (more than 100,000 people)
★ State Capital
—95— U.S. Interstate Route
▨ Area of Interest

N

0   25   50 miles
0   25   50 kilometers

TENNESSEE

NORTH CAROLINA

SOUTH CAROLINA

ALABAMA

ATLANTIC OCEAN

FLORIDA

Gulf of Mexico

Chattahoochee National Forest

Chattahoochee National Forest

Dalton

Rome

Roswell
Marietta
Smyrna
Atlanta
East Point

Hartwell Reservoir

Bobby Brown St. Park

Athens
Ft. Yargo State Park
Lake Sidney Lanier

Oconee Nat. For.

Martinez
Augusta

John Tanner State Park

Oconee Nat'l For.
High Falls S. P.

Hamburg State Park

Fort Gordon Mil. Res.

LaGrange
Franklin D. Roosevelt State Park

Piedmont N.W.R.

Magnolia Springs State Park

West Point Lake

Macon

George L. Smith State Park

Columbus
Fort Benning Mil. Res.

Warner Robins

Eufaula National Wildlife Ref.

Georgia Veterens Mem. State Park

Little Ocmulgee State Park

Fort Stewart Mil. Res.

Savannah N. W. R.

Savannah

Tybee National Wildlife Ref.

Wassaw National Wildlife Refuge

St. Catherines Sound

Walter F. George Reservoir

Albany

Kolomoki Mounds State Park

General Coffee State Park

Blackbeard Is. Wilderness Area

Blackbeard Island Nat'l Wildlife Ref.

Wolf Island Nat'l Wildlife Ref.

Saint Simons Sound

St. Andrews Sound

Red Bingham St. Park

Dixon Mem. State Forest

Cumberland Is. Nat'l Seashore

Seminole State Park

Valdosta

Okefenokee Nat'l. Wildlife Refuge and Wilderness Area

Kings Bay Naval Submarine Support Base

Lake Seminole

Chattahoochee R.

Savannah R.

Georgia Counties, County Seats, and County Areas and Populations

COUNTY	COUNTY SEAT	LAND AREA (SQ MI)	POPULATION (1996 EST.)	COUNTY	COUNTY SEAT	LAND AREA (SQ MI)	POPULATION (1996 EST.)
Appling	Baxley	510	16,333	Jenkins	Millen	353	8,471
Atkinson	Pearson	344	7,022	Johnson	Wrightsville	307	8,252
Bacon	Alma	286	10,344	Jones	Gray	394	22,330
Baker	Newton	347	3,686	Lamar	Barnesville	186	14,029
Baldwin	Milledgeville	258	41,947	Lanier	Lakeland	194	6,610
Banks	Homer	234	11,918	Laurens	Dublin	816	43,342
Barrow	Winder	163	37,407	Lee	Leesburg	358	20,705
Bartow	Cartersville	456	66,293	Liberty	Hinesville	517	59,063
Ben Hill	Fitzerald	254	17,322	Lincoln	Lincolnton	196	8,026
Berrien	Nashville	456	15,784	Long	Ludowici	402	8,151
Bibb	Macon	253	155,573	Loundes	Valdosta	507	83,982
Bleckley	Cochran	219	10,930	Lumpkin	Dahlonega	287	17,286
Brantley	Nahunta	444	13,048	Macon	Oglethorpe	404	13,141
Brooks	Quitman	491	15,820	Madison	Danielsville	285	24,192
Bryan	Pembroke	441	22,286	Marion	Buena Vista	366	6,345
Bulloch	Statesboro	678	49,328	McDuffie	Thomson	256	21,474
Burke	Waynesboro	833	21,542	McIntosh	Darien	425	9,592
Butts	Jackson	187	16,583	Meriwether	Greenville	506	22,944
Calhoun	Morgan	284	4,844	Miller	Colquitt	284	6,144
Camden	Woodbine	649	42,798	Mitchell	Camilla	512	20,990
Candler	Metter	248	8,676	Monroe	Forsyth	397	19,368
Carroll	Carrollton	502	79,307	Montgomery	Mt. Vernon	244	7,700
Catoosa	Ringgold	163	48,541	Morgan	Madison	349	14,171
Charlton	Folkston	780	9,293	Murray	Chatsworth	345	30,777
Chatham	Savannah	444	226,961	Muscogee	Columbus	218	183,394
Chattahoochee	Cusseta	250	16,137	Newton	Covington	277	52,709
Chattooga	Summerville	314	22,953	Oconee	Watkinsville	186	22,410
Cherokee	Canton	424	121,496	Oglethorpe	Lexington	442	10,899
Clarke	Athens	122	90,602	Paulding	Dallas	312	64,072
Clay	Ft. Gaines	197	3,360	Peach	Ft. Valley	151	23,529
Clayton	Jonesboro	148	202,427	Pickens	Jasper	232	17,570
Clinch	Homerville	821	6,582	Pierce	Blackshear	344	15,270
Cobb	Marjetta	343	538,832	Pike	Zebulon	219	11,702
Coffee	Douglas	602	33,188	Polk	Cedartown	312	35,370
Colquitt	Moultrie	556	38,960	Pulaski	Hawkinsville	249	8,268
Columbia	Appling	290	86,173	Putnam	Eatonton	344	16,511
Cook	Adel	232	14,351	Quitman	Georgetown	146	2,463
Coweta	Newman	444	76,295	Rabun	Clayton	370	13,013
Crawford	Knoxville	328	10,514	Randolph	Cuthbert	431	7,989
Crisp	Cordele	275	20,643	Richmond	Augusta	326	193,784
Dade	Trenton	176	14,486	Rockdale	Conyers	132	65,219
Dawson	Dawsonville	210	13,016	Schley	Ellaville	169	3,763
Decatur	Bainbridge	586	26,529	Screven	Sylvania	655	14,286
DeKalb	Decatur	270	589,796	Seminole	Donalsonville	225	9,252
Dodge	Eastman	504	17,936	Spalding	Griffin	199	57,713
Dooly	Vienna	397	10,416	Stephens	Toccoa	177	25,246
Dougherty	Albany	330	96,581	Stewart	Lumpkin	452	5,532
Douglas	Douglasville	203	84,463	Sumter	Americus	488	30,668
Early	Blakely	516	12,149	Talbot	Talbotton	395	6,865
Echols	Statenville	420	2,325	Taliaferro	Crawfordville	196	1,861
Effingham	Springfield	482	33,363	Tattnall	Reidsville	484	18,728
Elbert	Elberton	367	19,286	Taylor	Butler	382	8,189
Emanuel	Swainsboro	688	21,030	Telfair	MacRae	444	11,662
Evans	Claxton	186	9,519	Terrell	Dawson	337	11,092
Fannin	Blue Ridge	384	17,745	Thomas	Thomasville	551	41,908
Fayette	Fayetteville	199	81,891	Tift	Tifton	268	36,850
Floyd	Rome	519	84,422	Toombs	Lyons	371	25,463
Forsyth	Cumming	226	69,127	Towns	Hiawassee	165	7,990
Franklin	Carnesville	264	18,184	Treutlen	Soperton	202	5,903
Fulton	Atlanta*	534	718,336	Troup	La Grange	415	58,568
Gilmer	Ellijay	427	16,868	Turner	Ashburn	289	9,003
Glascock	Gibson	144	2,429	Twiggs	Jeffersonville	362	9,873
Glynn	Brunswick	412	65,608	Union	Blairsville	320	14,923
Gordon	Calhoun	355	39,369	Upson	Thomaston	326	26,923
Grady	Cairo	459	21,454	Walker	La Fayette	446	61,163
Greene	Greensboro	390	13,010	Walton	Monroe	330	49,307
Gwinnett	Lawrenceville	435	478,001	Ware	Waycross	970	35,568
Habersham	Clarkesville	278	30,794	Warren	Warrenton	286	6,001
Hall	Gainesville	379	113,033	Washington	Sandersville	683	19,910
Hancock	Sparta	469	9,023	Wayne	Jesup	647	24,636
Haralson	Buchanan	283	23,871	Webster	Perston	210	2,242
Harris	Hamilton	464	21,303	Wheeler	Alamo	299	4,933
Hart	Hartwell	230	21,005	White	Cleveland	242	16,140
Heard	Franklin	292	9,855	Whitefield	Dalton	291	80,296
Henry	McDonough	321	90,969	Wilcox	Abbeville	382	7,320
Houston	Perry	380	101,384	Wilkes	Washington	470	10,583
Irwin	Ocilla	362	8,871	Wilkinson	Irwinton	451	10,801
Jackson	Jefferson	342	35,230	Worth	Sylvester	575	22,003
Jasper	Monticello	371	9,556				
Jeff Davis	Hazlehurst	335	12,612		TOTALS	58,056	7,353,225
Jefferson	Louisville	529	17,860	*Atlanta city limits extend into DeKalb County			

[8]LANGUAGES

The first Europeans entering what is now Georgia found it occupied almost entirely by Creek Indians of the Muskogean branch of Hokan-Siouan stock. Removed by treaty to Indian Territory after their uprising in 1813, the Creek left behind only such places-names as Chattahoochee, Chattooga, and Okefenokee. Except for the South Midland speech of the extreme northern up-country, Georgia English is typically Southern. Loss of /r/ after a vowel in the same syllable is common. The diphthong /ai/ as in *right* is so simplified that Northern speakers hear the word as *rat*. *Can't* rhymes with *paint*, and *borrow*, *forest*, *foreign*, and *orange* all have the /ah/ vowel as in *father*. However, a highly unusual variety of regional differences, most of them in long vowels and diphthongs, makes a strong contrast between northern up-country and southern low-country speech. In such words as *care* and *stairs*, for example, many up-country speakers have a vowel like that in *cat*, while many low-country speakers have a vowel like in *pane*.

In general, northern Georgia *snake doctor* contrasts with southern Georgia *mosquito hawk* (dragonfly), *goobers* with *pinders* (peanuts), *French harp* with *harmonica*, *plum peach* with *press peach* (both clingstone peaches), *nicker* with *whicker* for a horse's neigh, and *sallet* with *salad*. In Atlanta a big sandwich is a *poorboy*; in Savannah, a peach pit is a *kernel*.

A distinctive variety of black English, called Gullah, is spoken in the islands off the Georgia and South Carolina coast, to which Creole-speaking slaves escaped from the mainland during the 17th and 18th centuries. Characteristic grammatical features include lack of inflection in the personal pronoun, the invariant form of the *be* verb, and the absence of the final *s* in the third person singular of the present tense. Many of the private personal names stem directly from West African languages.

In 1990, 5,699,642 Georgians—95.2% of the population five years old and older—spoke only English at home. Other languages spoken at home, and the number of people who spoke them, were as follows:

Spanish	122,295	Chinese	11,181
French	34,422	Indic	9,785
German	29,480	Vietnamese	6,483
Korean	13,433	Italian	4,686

[9]RELIGIONS

The Church of England was the established church in colonial Georgia. During this period, European Protestants were encouraged to immigrate, and German Lutherans and Moravians took advantage of the opportunity. Roman Catholics were barred and Jews were not welcomed, but persons of both denominations came anyway. In the mid-18th century, George Whitefield, called the Great Itinerant, helped touch off the Great Awakening, the religious revival out of which came the Methodist and Baptist denominations. Daniel Marshall, the first "separate" Baptist in Georgia, established a church near Kiokee Creek in 1772. Some 16 years later, James Asbury formed the first Methodist Conference in Georgia.

The American Revolution resulted in the lessening of the authority of Anglicanism and a great increase in the number of Baptists, Methodists, and Presbyterians. During the 19th century, fundamentalist sects were especially strong among blacks. Roman Catholics from Maryland, Ireland, and Hispaniola formed a numerically small but important element in the cities, and Jewish citizens were active in the leadership of Savannah and Augusta. Catholics and Jews enjoyed general acceptance from the early 1800s until the first two decades of the 20th century, when they became the targets of political demagogues, notably Thomas E. Watson.

In 1990 there were 3,447,800 known Protestant adherents. The leading denominations were Southern Baptist Convention, 1,582,520; United Methodist, 530,076; Presbyterian, 101,274; Church of God (Cleveland, Tenn.), 96,173; and Episcopal, 62,738. In 1990, Georgia had 210,210 Roman Catholics and an estimated 72,747 Jews.

[10]TRANSPORTATION

Georgia's location between the Appalachian Mountains and the Atlantic Ocean makes it the link between the eastern seaboard and the Gulf states. In the 18th century, Carolina fur traders crossed the Savannah River at the site of Augusta and followed trails to the Mississippi River. Pioneer farmers soon followed the same trails and used the many river tributaries to send their produce to Savannah, Georgia's first great depot. Beginning in 1816, steamboats plied the inland rivers, but they never replaced the older shallow-drafted Petersburg boats, propelled by poles.

From the 1830s onward, businessmen in the eastern cities of Savannah, Augusta, and Brunswick built railroads west to maintain their commerce. The two principal lines, the Georgia and the Central of Georgia, were required by law to make connection with a state-owned line, the Western and Atlantic, at the new town of Atlanta, which thus became in 1847 the link between Georgia and the Ohio Valley. By the Civil War, Georgia, with more miles of rail than any other Deep South state, was a vital link between the eastern and western sectors of the Confederacy. After the war, the railroads contributed to urban growth as towns sprang up along their routes. Trackage increased from 4,532 mi (7,294 km) in 1890 to 7,591 mi (12,217 km) in 1920. But with competition from motor carriers, the total trackage declined to 4,602 rail mi (7,409 km) in 1995 (8th highest among the states), and CSX and Norfolk Southern were the only Class I railroads operating within the state. As of 1995/96, Amtrak operated five long-distance trains through the state, with east-west routes through Atlanta, and north-south routes through Savannah. Total Georgia ridership in 1995/96 was 131,998. In 1979, Atlanta inaugurated the first mass-transit system in the state, including the South's first subway.

Georgia's old intracoastal waterway carries about 1 million tons of shipping annually and is also used by pleasure craft and fishing vessels. Savannah's modern port facilities handled 17,379,724 million tons of cargo in 1995; the coastal cities of Brunswick and St. Marys also have deepwater docks.

In the 1920s, Georgia became the gateway to Florida for motorists. Today, I-75 is the main route from Atlanta to Florida, and I-20 is the major east-west highway; both cross at Atlanta with I-85, which proceeds southeast from South Carolina to Alabama. I-95 stretches along the coast from South Carolina through Savannah to Jacksonville, Florida. During the 1980s, Atlanta invested $1.4 billion in a freeway expansion program that permitted capacity to double. In 1995, Georgia had 111,273 mi (179,150 km) of public roads, 6,120,197 registered motor vehicles, and 4,840,495 licensed drivers. Hartsfield International Airport in Atlanta is the hub of air traffic in the Southeast and was the 3rd busiest airport in the US in 1994/95; it enplaned 25,669,559 passengers and handled 198,494 tons of freight and mail in 1995. In 1995 there were 267 private and 138 public airports in Georgia.

[11]HISTORY

The history of what is now Georgia was influenced by two great prehistoric events: first, the upheaval that produced the mountains of the north, and second, the overflow of an ancient ocean that covered and flattened much of the rest of the state. Human beings have inhabited Georgia for at least 12,000 years. The first nomadic hunters were replaced by shellfish eaters who lived along the rivers. Farming communities later grew up at these sites, reaching their height in the Master Farmer culture about AD 800. These Native Americans left impressive mounds at Ocmulgee, near Macon, and at Etowah, north of Atlanta.

During the colonial period, the most important Indian tribes were the Creek, who lived along the central and western rivers, and the Cherokee, who lived in the mountains. By clever diplomacy, the Creek were able to maintain their position as the fulcrum of power between the English on the one hand and the French and Spanish on the other. With the ascendancy of the English and the achievement of statehood, however, the Creek lost their leverage and were expelled from Georgia in 1826. The Cherokee sought to adopt the white man's ways in their effort to avoid expulsion or annihilation. Thanks to their remarkable linguist Sequoyah, they learned to write their own language, later running their own newspaper, the *Cherokee Phoenix*, and their own schools. Some even owned slaves. Unfortunately for the Cherokee, gold was discovered on their lands; the Georgia state legislature confiscated their territory and outlawed the system of self-government the Cherokee had developed during the 1820s. Despite a ruling by the US Supreme Court, handed down by Chief Justice John Marshall, that Georgia had acted illegally, federal and state authorities expelled the Cherokee between 1832 and 1838. Thousands died on the march to Indian Territory (Oklahoma), known ever since as the Trail of Tears.

Georgia's first European explorer was Hernando de Soto of Spain, who in 1540 crossed the region looking for the fabled Seven Cities of Gold. French Huguenots under Jean Ribault claimed the Georgia coast in 1562 but were driven out by the Spanish captain Pedro Menéndez Avilés in 1564, who by 1586 had established the mission of Santa Catalina de Gaule on St. Catherines Island. (The ruins of this mission—the oldest European settlement in Georgia—were discovered by archaeologists in 1982.) By 1700, Jesuit and Franciscan missionaries had established an entire chain of missions along the Sea Islands and on the lower Chattahoochee.

From Charles Town, in Carolina colony, the English challenged Spain for control of the region, and by 1702 they had forced the Spaniards back to St. Augustine, Fla. In 1732, after the English had become convinced of the desirability of locating a buffer between the valuable rice-growing colony of Carolina and Indian-held lands to the south and west, King George II granted a charter to a group called the Trustees for Establishing the Colony of Georgia in America. The best known of the trustees was the soldier-politician and philanthropist James Edward Oglethorpe. His original intention was to send debtors from English prisons to Georgia, but Parliament refused to support the idea. Instead, Georgia was to be a place where the industrious poor would produce those things England needed, such as silk and wine, and would guard the frontier. Rum and slavery were expressly prohibited.

Oglethorpe and the first settlers landed at Yamacraw Bluff on 12 February 1733 and were given a friendly reception by a small band of Yamacraw Indians and their chief, Tomochichi. Oglethorpe is best remembered for laying out the town of Savannah in a unique design, featuring numerous plazas that still delight tourists today; however, as a military man, his main interest was defending the colony against the Spanish. After the war declared in 1739, Oglethorpe conducted an unsuccessful siege of St. Augustine. The Spaniards counterattacked at Oglethorpe's fortified town of Frederica on St. Simons Island in July 1742 but were repulsed in a confused encounter known as the Battle of Bloody Marsh, which ended Spanish threats to the British colonies. Soon afterward, Oglethorpe returned permanently to England.

The trustees' restrictions on rum and slavery were gradually removed, and in 1752, control over Georgia reverted to Parliament. Georgia thus became a royal colony, its society, like

that of Carolina, shaped by the planting of rice, indigo, and cotton. After the French and Indian War, settlers began to pour into the Georgia backcountry above Augusta. Because these backcountry pioneers depended on the royal government for protection against the Indians, they were reluctant to join the protests by Savannah merchants against new British mercantile regulations. When war came, however, the backcountry seized the opportunity to wrest political control of the new state away from Savannah.

Georgians spent the first three years of the Revolutionary War in annual attempts to invade Florida, each of them unsuccessful. The British turned their attention to Georgia late in 1778, reestablishing control of the state as far as Briar Creek, midway between Savannah and Augusta. After a combined French and American force failed to retake Savannah in October 1779, the city was used by the British as a base from which to recapture Charleston, in present-day South Carolina, and to extend their control further inland. For a year, most of Georgia was under British rule, and there was talk of making the restoration permanent in the peace settlement. However, Augusta was retaken in June 1781, and independent government was restored. A year later, the British were forced out of Savannah.

With Augusta as the new capital of Georgia, a period of rapid expansion began. Georgia ratified the US Constitution on 2 January 1788, the 4th state to do so. The invention of the cotton gin by Eli Whitney in 1793 made cotton cultivation profitable in the lands east of the Oconee River, relinquished by the Creek Indians under the Treaty of New York three years earlier. A mania for land speculation was climaxed by the mid–1790s Yazoo Fraud, in which the state legislature sold 50 million acres (20 million hectares), later the states of Alabama and Mississippi, to land companies of which many of the legislators were members.

Georgia surrendered its lands west of the Chattahoochee River to the federal government in 1802. As the Indians were removed to the west, the lands they had occupied were disposed of by successive lotteries. The settlement of the cotton lands brought prosperity to Georgia, a fact that influenced Georgians to prefer the Union rather than secession during the constitutional crises of 1833 and 1850, when South Carolina was prepared to secede.

After South Carolina did secede in 1860, Georgia also withdrew from the Union and joined the Confederate States of America. Union troops occupied the Sea Islands during 1862. Confederate forces defeated the Union Army's advance into northern Georgia at Chickamauga in 1863, but in 1864, troops under General William Tecumseh Sherman moved relentlessly upon Atlanta, capturing it in September. In November, Sherman began his famous "march to the sea," in which his 60,000 troops cut a swath of destruction 60 mi (97 km) wide. Sherman presented Savannah as a Christmas present to President Abraham Lincoln.

After ratifying the 14th and 15th amendments, Georgia was readmitted to the Union on 15 July 1870. Commercial interests were strong in antebellum Georgia, but their political power was balanced by that of the great planters. After the Democrats recovered control of the state in 1871, business interests dominated politics. Discontented farmers supported an Independent Party in the 1870s and 1880s, and then the Populist Party in the 1890s. Democratic Representative Thomas E. Watson, who declared himself a Populist during the early 1890s, was defeated three times in congressional races by the party he had deserted. Watson subsequently fomented anti-black, anti-Jewish, and anti-Catholic sentiment in order to control a bloc of rural votes with which he dominated state politics for 10 years. In 1920, Watson finally was elected to the US Senate, but he died in 1922. Rebecca L. Felton was appointed to succeed him, thus becoming the first woman to serve in the US Senate, although she was replaced after one day.

Franklin D. Roosevelt learned the problems of Georgia farmers firsthand when he made Warm Springs his second home in 1942. However, his efforts to introduce the New Deal to Georgia after he became president in 1933 were blocked by Governor Eugene Talmadge, who advertised himself as a "real dirt farmer." It was not until the administration of Eurith D. Rivers (1937–41) that progressive social legislation was enacted. Governor Ellis Arnall gained national attention for his forward-looking administration (1943–47), which revised the outdated 1877 state constitution and gave the vote to 18-year-olds. Georgia treated the nation to the spectacle of three governors at once when Eugene Talmadge was elected for a fourth time in 1946 but died before assuming office. His son Herman was then elected by the legislature, but the new lieutenant governor, M. E. Thompson, also claimed the office, and Arnall refused to step aside until the issue was resolved. The courts finally decided in favor of Thompson.

The Supreme Court order to desegregate public schools in 1954 provided Georgia politicians with an emotional issue they exploited to the hilt. A blow was dealt to old-style politics in 1962, however, when the US Supreme Court declared the county-unit system unconstitutional. Under this system, state officers and members of Congress had been selected by county units instead of by popular vote since 1911; the new ruling made city voters as important as those in rural areas. During the 1960s, Atlanta was the home base for the civil-rights efforts of Martin Luther King, Jr., though his campaign to end racial discrimination in Georgia focused most notably on the town of Albany. Federal civil-rights legislation in 1964 and 1965 changed the state's political climate by guaranteeing the vote to black citizens. A black man, Julian Bond, was elected to the state legislature in 1965; in 1973, Maynard Jackson was elected major of Atlanta, thus becoming the first black mayor of a large southern city. For decades the belief that defense of segregation was a prerequisite for state elective office cost white southerners any chance they might have had for national leadership. Governor Jimmy Carter's unequivocal renunciation of racism in his inaugural speech in 1971 thus marked a turning point in Georgia politics and was a key factor in his election to the presidency in 1976.

Another black, former US Ambassador to the United Nations Andrew Young, succeeded Jackson as mayor of Atlanta in 1981, when that city—and the state—was experiencing an economic boom. The prosperity of Atlanta in the 1970s and 1980s stemmed largely from its service-based economy, which was centered on such industries as the airlines, telecommunications, distribution and insurance. The decline of service industries in the early 1990s, however, pulled Atlanta and the state of Georgia as a whole into a recession. That decline was epitomized by the collapse in 1991 of one of the two airlines that used Atlanta as its hub, Eastern Airlines, which cost Atlanta 10,000 jobs. While Atlanta's economic expansion produced a more mature economy, it also raised the price of labor, diminishing Georgia's appeal to business. Nevertheless, as the decade progressed, the state's economy rebounded. By the end of 1996, Georgia's gross state product was nearly double the gross domestic product of the US, and its unemployment rate was about 1% lower than the national average.

In July 1994 record flooding in central and southwest Georgia over a 10–day period caused 31 deaths and millions of dollars in damage, including extensive crop damage. Two years later, Atlanta hosted the 26th Summer Olympic Games, which marked the 100th anniversary of the modern games. This event was marred by the explosion on July 27 of a homemade pipe bomb in Centennial Olympic Park, killing one person and injuring dozens of others.

12STATE GOVERNMENT

Georgia's first constitution, adopted in 1777, was considered one of the most democratic in the new nation. Power was concentrated in a unicameral legislature; a senate was added in 1789. The Civil War period brought a flurry of constitution making in 1861, 1865, and 1868. When the Democrats displaced the Republicans after Reconstruction, they felt obliged to replace the constitution of 1868 with a rigidly restrictive one. This document, adopted in 1877, modified by numerous amendments, and revised in 1945 and 1976, continued to govern the state until July 1983, when a new constitution, ratified in 1982, took effect.

The legislature, called the general assembly, consists of a 56-seat senate and a 180-seat house of representatives; all the legislators serve two-year terms. The legislature convenes on the 2d Monday in January and stays in session for 40 legislative days. Recesses called during a session may considerably extend its calendar length. During the 1960s and 1970s, the legislature engaged in a series of attempts to redistrict itself to provide equal representation based on population; it was finally redistricted in 1981 on the basis of 1980 census results. Legislators received a salary of $10,854 in 1995.

Elected executives include the governor, lieutenant governor, secretary of state, attorney general, state school superintendent, comptroller general, commissioner of agriculture, and commissioner of labor. Each serves a four-year term. To be eligible for office, the governor and lieutenant governor, who are elected separately, must have been US citizens for 15 years, Georgia citizens for 6 years preceding the election, and at least 30 years of age. In 1996 the governor's salary was $103,074.

To become law, a bill must be passed by both houses of the legislature and approved by the governor or passed over the executive veto by a two-thirds vote in both houses. All revenue measures originate in the house, but the senate can propose, or concur in, amendments to these bills. Amendments to the constitution may be proposed by two-thirds votes of the elected members of each chamber and must then be ratified by popular vote.

To vote, a person must be a citizen of the US, at least 18 years old, and must have resided in the state for at least 30 days immediately preceding the election.

13POLITICAL PARTIES

The first political group to emerge in the state was the Federalist Party, but it was tainted by association with the Yazoo Fraud of the 1790s. The reform party at this time was the Democratic-Republican Party, headed in Georgia by James Jackson (whose followers included many former Federalists), William Crawford, and George Troup. During the presidency of Andrew Jackson (1829–37), one wing, headed by John Clark, supported the president and called itself the Union Party. The other faction, led by Troup, defended South Carolina's right to nullify laws and called itself the States' Rights Party. Subsequently the Union Party affiliated with the Democrats, and the States' Rights Party merged with the Whigs. When the national Whig Party collapsed, many Georgia Whigs joined the Native American (Know-Nothing) Party. During Reconstruction, the Republican Party captured the governor's office, but Republican hopes died when federal troops were withdrawn from the state in 1870.

Georgia voted solidly Democratic between 1870 and 1960, despite challenges from the Independent Party in the 1880s and the Populists in the 1890s. Georgia cast its electoral votes for the Democratic presidential candidate in every election until 1964, when Republican Barry Goldwater won the state. Four years later, George C. Wallace of the American Independent Party received Georgia's 12 electoral votes. Republican Richard Nixon carried the state in 1972, as the Republicans also became a viable party at the local level. In 1976, Georgia's native son Jimmy

Carter returned the state to the Democratic camp in presidential balloting. Another native Georgian and former Georgia governor, Lester Maddox, was the American Independent candidate in 1976.

Republican Bob Dole won 47% of the vote, and Democratic incumbent Bill Clinton won 46% in the 1996 presidential election, while Independent Ross Perot won 6%. Zell Miller, a Democrat, won the gubernatorial race in 1990 and was reelected in 1994. In 1996, four-term US Senator Democrat Sam Nunn vacated his Senate seat, which was won by Democrat Max Cleland, a Vietnam War veteran and triple amputee who had formerly headed the Veterans Administration. Georgia's other senator in 1996 was Paul Coverdell, elected in 1992 in a special runoff election. Georgia congressman Newt Gingrich, Speaker of the US House of Representatives, was also reelected and retained his position as Speaker in the Republican-controlled House. After the 1994 elections, Gingrich became the first Republican to hold that position in 40 years. Following the 1996 elections, Georgia's delegation to the House comprised eight Republicans and three Democrats. The Georgia state legislature remained under Democratic control, although by a less overwhelming margin than in the past. There were 34 Democrats and 22 Republicans in the state senate, and 106 Democrats and 74 Republicans in the state house. In 1993, there were 545 blacks holding elective office, and in 1995 44 women served in the state legislature and in elective executive office.

14LOCAL GOVERNMENT

In 1758, colonial Georgia was divided into eight parishes, the earliest political districts represented in the royal assembly. By the constitution of 1777, the parishes were transformed into counties, and as settlement gradually expanded, the number of counties grew to 159. The Georgia constitution of 1877 granted counties from one to three seats in the house of representatives, depending on population. This county-unit system was used in counting votes for elected state and congressional offices until ruled unconstitutional by the US Supreme Court in 1962. Originally administered by judges of county courts, all Georgia counties but one, Towns County, have since adopted a commission system, although some are administered by a single commissioner. In 1992, Georgia had 157 counties, 536 municipal governments, 183 school districts, and 421 special districts. In 1965, the legislature passed a home-rule law permitting these local governments to amend their own charters. The traditional and most common form of municipal government is the mayor-council form. But city managers are employed by some communities, and a few make use of the commission system.

During the 1970s there were efforts to merge some of the larger cities with their counties. However, most county voters showed an unwillingness to be burdened with city problems.

The Department of Community Affairs serves as the governor's representative to local governments.

15STATE SERVICES

In 1977, the State Ethics Commission was renamed the Campaign and Financial Disclosure Commission. As the title indicates, this commission is charged with providing procedures for public disclosure of all state and local campaign contributions and expenditures.

Educational services are provided by the Board of Education, which exercises jurisdiction over all public schools, including teacher certification and curriculum approval. The superintendent of schools is the board's executive officer. The public colleges are operated by the Board of Regents of the University System of Georgia, whose chief administrator is the chancellor. Air, water, road, and rail services are administered by the Department of Transportation.

The Reorganization Act of 1972 made the Department of Human Resources a catch-all agency for health, rehabilitation, and social-welfare programs. The department offers special services to the mentally ill, drug abusers and alcoholics, neglected and abused children and adults, juvenile offenders, the handicapped, the aged, and the poor.

Public protection services are rendered through the Department of Public Safety. Responsibility for natural-resource protection is lodged with the Department of Natural Resources, into which 33 separate agencies were consolidated in 1972. The Environmental Protection Division is charged with maintaining air, land, and water quality standards; the Game and Fish Division manages wildlife resources; and the Parks and Historic Sites Division administers state parks, recreational areas, and historic sites. Labor services are provided by the Department of Labor, which oversees workers' compensation programs.

Georgia Presidential Vote by Political Parties, 1948–96

YEAR	ELECTORAL VOTE	GEORGIA WINNER	DEMOCRAT	REPUBLICAN	STATES' RIGHTS DEMOCRAT	PROGRESSIVE
1948	12	*TRUMAN (D)	254,646	76,691	85,136	1,636
1952	12	STEVENSON (D)	456,823	198,961		
1956	12	STEVENSON (D)	444,6878	222,778		
1960	12	*KENNEDY (D)	458,638	274,472		
1964	12	GOLDWATER (R)	522,163	616,584		
1968	12	WALLACE (AI)	334,440	380,111	535,550	
1972	12	*NIXON (R)	289,529	881,490		
1976	12	*CARTER (D)	979,409	483,743	**1,071	1,1681
					LIBERTARIAN	
1980	12	CARTER (D)	890,955	654,168	15,627	
1984	12	*REAGAN (R)	706,628	1,068,722	1521	
						NEW ALL.
1988	12	*BUSH (R)	714,792	1,081,331	8,435	5,099
						IND. (PEROT)
1992	13	*CLINTON (D)	1,008,966	995,252	7,110	309,657
1996	13	DOLE (R)	1,053,849	1,080,843	17,870	146,337

* Won US presidential election.
** Write-in votes.

16JUDICIAL SYSTEM

Georgia's highest court is the supreme court, created in 1845 and consisting of a chief justice, presiding justice (who exercises the duties of chief justice in his absence), and five associate justices. They are elected by the people to staggered six-year terms in nonpartisan elections.

Georgia's general trial courts are the superior courts, which have exclusive jurisdiction in cases of divorce and land title, and in felony cases. As of 1996 there were 190 superior court judges, all of them elected for four-year terms in nonpartisan elections. Cases from local courts can be carried to the court of appeals, consisting of 10 judges elected for staggered six-year terms in nonpartisan elections. Each county has a probate court; there are also separate juvenile courts. Most judges of the county and city courts are appointed by the governor with the consent of the senate. There were 22,612 practicing attorneys in 1996.

The prison population in Georgia numbered 35,139 by the end of 1996, producing a ratio of 509 prisoners per 100,000 population. The prison population increased by over 60% from 1990 to 1995. Between 1930 and 1996 Georgia executed 380 persons, second only to Texas. Executions are carried out by electrocution.

According to the FBI Crime Index, the crime rate per 100,000 inhabitants for 1995 was 5,785.4. This total included 633.4 for violent crime and 5,152.0 for property crime.

17ARMED FORCES

In 1996 there were 62,989 active-duty military personnel stationed in Georgia. Major facilities include Dobbins Air Force Base, Ft. Gillem, Ft. McPherson, and the Atlanta Naval Air Station, all located in the Atlanta area; Ft. Stewart and Hunter Army Airfield near Savannah; Ft. Gordon at Augusta; Moody Air Force Base at Macon; Ft. Benning, a major Army training installation at Columbus; Robins Air Force Base, between Columbus and Macon; and a Navy Supply School in Athens. In 1995/96, Georgia firms received defense contracts worth $3.9 billion.

There were 677,000 veterans of the US armed forces living in Georgia as of 1 July 1996. Of these fewer than 500 served in World War I, 143,000 in World War II, 106,000 in the Korean conflict, 246,000 during the Vietnam era, and 51,000 in the Persian Gulf War. In all, 77,000 Georgians fought and 1,503 died in World War I, and 320,000 served and 6,754 were killed in World War II. In 1995/96, Georgia veterans received benefits amounting to $1.1 billion.

The Reserve and National Guard consisted of 49,711 members during 1996. In 1993 the Georgia State Police employed 864 full-time sworn officers, or one per 10,000 residents. The Georgia Bureau of Investigation, part of the Department of Public Safety, operates the Georgia Crime Laboratory, one of the oldest and largest in the US.

18MIGRATION

During the colonial period, the chief source of immigrants to Georgia was England; other important national groups were Germans, Scots, and Scotch-Irish. The number of African slaves increased from 1,000 in 1752 to nearly 20,000 in 1776. After the Revolution, a large number of Virginians came to Georgia, as well as lesser numbers of French refugees from Hispaniola and immigrants from Ireland and Germany. Following the Civil War, there was some immigration from Italy, Russia, and Greece. The greatest population shifts during the 20th century have been from country to town and, after World War I, of black Georgians to northern cities. Georgia suffered a net loss through migration of 502,000 from 1940 to 1960, but enjoyed a net gain of 329,000 during 1970–80 and about 500,000 during 1980-90. From 1985–90, Georgia's net gain through migration was greater than that of any other state except California and Florida. There were net gains of 437,030 in domestic migration and 67,788 in international migration between 1990 and 1996. From 1980 to 1990, the proportion of native-born residents in Georgia fell from 71% to 64.5%. In 1996 Georgia admitted 12,608 immigrants from foreign countries. As of 1994 the number of undocumented immigrants was estimated at between 29 and 36. Just over 50% of all Georgians age 5 and over lived in a different house in 1985 as in 1990, of which 27% did so in another state (primarily Florida, Texas, or Alabama).

19INTERGOVERNMENTAL COOPERATION

Multistate agreements in which Georgia participates include the Southern Regional Education Compact, Southeastern Forest Fire Protection Compact, Southern Interstate Energy Compact, and Southern Growth Policies Compact. In 1995/96, federal aid to Georgia totaled $5.4 billion.

20ECONOMY

According to the original plans of Georgia's founders, its people were to be sober spinners of silk. The reality was far different, however; during the period of royally appointed governors, Georgia became a replica of Carolina, a plantation province producing rice, indigo, and cotton. After the Revolution, the invention of the cotton gin established the plantation system even more firmly by making cotton planting profitable in the piedmont. Meanwhile, deerskins and other furs and lumber were produced in the backcountry; rice remained an important staple along the coast; turnpikes, canals, and railroads were built; and textile manufacturing became increasingly important, especially in Athens and Augusta.

At the end of the Civil War, the state's economy was in ruins, and tenancy and sharecropping were common. Manufacturing, especially of textiles, was promoted by "New South" spokesmen like Henry Grady of Atlanta and Patrick Walsh of Augusta. Atlanta, whose nascent industries included production of a thick sweet syrup called Coca-Cola, symbolized the New South idea—then as now. Farmers did not experience the benefits of progress, however. Many of them flocked to the mills while others joined the Populist Party in an effort to air their grievances. To the planters' relief, cotton prices rose from the turn of the century through World War I. Meanwhile, Georgians lost control of their railroads and industries to northern corporations. During the 1920s, the boll weevil wrecked the cotton crops, and farmers resumed their flight to the cities. Not until the late 1930s did Georgia accept Social Security, unemployment compensation, and other relief measures.

Georgia's economy underwent drastic changes as a result of World War II. The raising of poultry and livestock became more important than crop cultivation, and manufacturing replaced agriculture as the chief source of income. In 1982, only about 2.4% of the employed labor force was working in agriculture; 33.4% were blue-collar workers, 17.5% clerical workers, 15.5% professional or technical workers, and 12.6% service workers. Georgia is a leader in the making of paper products, tufted textile products, processed chickens, naval stores, lumber, and transportation equipment.

After World War II, many northern industries moved to Georgia to take advantage of low wages and low taxes, conditions that meant low benefits for Georgians. A chronic problem for workers in the textile industry has been how to organize labor unions for the purpose of collective bargaining. As of 1985, national unions had not been very successful in their attempts to organize mill workers. A recent barrier to the employment of economically disadvantaged Georgians has been the gradual movement of manufacturing plants from the inner cities to the suburbs.

Textile manufacturing, Georgia's oldest industry, remains its most important source of income. However, that sector has grown slowly in recent years, while most durable-goods industries, such as electrical machinery and appliances, have grown rapidly. Exports have become increasingly important to Georgia's economy. From 1977 to 1981, the value of Georgia's exported manufactures increased 76%—considerably faster than the 44% rate of increase in the state's manufacturing. The state economy suffered in the national recession of the early 1980s but performed better during the expansion of the latter part of the decade than the nation as a whole. Service industries grew dramatically, particularly health and business as well as finance, insurance and real estate. Georgia's gross state product in 1994 was $183,042 million, to which private goods-producing industries contributed $43,294 million; private services-producing industries, $115,477 million; and government, $24,270 million. Georgia's per capita personal income was $24,741 in 1995, ranking it 25th in the nation. In 1996 there were 55,339 filings for bankruptcy, up 20% from the previous year.

21INCOME
The per capita income of Georgians has been low historically, at least since the Civil War. In 1940, the average income was below $350 a year; the average doubled during World War II and stood at $1,034 in 1950. In relative terms, Georgians in 1940 received only 57% as much as other Americans, but by 1950 they were earning nearly 70% of the national average. During the next two decades, Georgia continued to close the gap until, by 1970, per capita income averaged $3,318, or 84% of the national level.

Georgia's per capita personal income rose to $22,709 in 1996, boosting the state's national rank to 26th. Per capita disposable personal income in 1996 was $19,664. Growth from 1995 to 1996 in per capita personal income was 4.6%, just above the national average of 4.5%. The median household income was $34,099 in 1995. In 1995, about 12.1% of all state residents were living below the poverty level.

22LABOR
Georgia's civilian labor force was estimated at 3,753,094 in 1996. Of this total, 173,000 workers, or 4.6%, were unemployed. The most remarkable change in the labor force since World War II has been the rising proportion of women, whose share increased from less than 28% in 1940 to an estimated 47% in 1996.

The trend during the 1970s, 1980s, and so far into the 1990s has been toward increased employment in trade and service industries and toward multiple job holding. Employment in agriculture, the leading industry prior to World War II, continued its long-term decline. One indication of declining employment was the decrease in farm population, which went from 515,000 in 1960 to 228,000 in 1970 and from 121,000 in 1980, and 73,647 in 1990. Georgia's farm employment in 1996 totaled about 42,000. The mining, construction, and manufacturing industries registered employment increases but declined in importance relative to such sectors as trade and services.

Between 1982 and 1996, durable goods employment increased four times faster than that of Georgia's traditional nondurable industries, such as apparel, textiles, and food. The weakest link in the nondurable sector is apparel, where 27,200 jobs have been lost. Of Georgia's total nonfarm employment of 3,579,600 at the beginning of 1997, mining accounted for 0.2%; construction, 4.5%; manufacturing, 16.5%; transportation, communications, and utilities, 6.3%; trade, 26%; finance, insurance, and real estate, 5%; services, 25%; and government, 16.5%.

Georgia is not considered to be a unionized state. Among state laws strictly regulating union activity is a right-to-work law enacted in 1947. Although union membership in Georgia grew from 273,000 in 1970 to 323,000 in 1980, the proportion of union members in the employed nonagricultural labor force was only about 5% in 1996. There were about 55 local unions located in Georgia, with about 175,000 members

In 1962, the Georgia legislature denied state employees the right to strike. Strikes in Georgia tend to be fewer than in most heavily industrialized states.

One of the earliest state labor laws was an 1889 act requiring employers to provide seats for females to use when resting. A child-labor law adopted in 1906 prohibited the employment of children under 10 years of age in manufacturing. A general workers' compensation law was enacted in 1920.

23AGRICULTURE
In 1995, Georgia's farm marketings totaled $5.17 billion (14th in the US). Georgia ranked 1st in the production of peanuts and pecans, harvesting 40% of all the pecans grown in the US in 1996 and 39% of the peanuts.

Cotton, first planted near Savannah in 1734, was the mainstay of Georgia's economy through the early 20th century, and the state's plantations also grew corn, rice, tobacco, wheat, and sweet potatoes. World War I stimulated the cultivation of peanuts along with other crops. By the 1930s, tobacco and peanuts were challenging cotton for agricultural supremacy, and Georgia had also become an important producer of peaches, a product for which the "peach state" is still widely known.

After 1940, farm mechanization and consolidation were rapid. The number of tractors increased from 10,000 in 1940 to 85,000 by 1955. In 1940, 6 out of 10 farms were tenant-operated; by the mid-1960s, this proportion had decreased to fewer than 1 in 6. The number of farms declined from 226,000 in 1945 to 43,000 in 1996, when the average farm size was 274 acres (111 hectares). Georgia's farmland area of 11.8 million acres (4.8 million hectares) represents 32% of its land area.

The following table shows preliminary production and value for leading crops in 1996:

	PRODUCTION	VALUE
Peanuts	1,439,100,000	$388,557,000
Cotton	2,100,000 bales	735,840,000
Tobacco	113,620,000 lb	NA
Corn	49,875,000 bu	177,056,000
Pecans	100 million lb	99,900,000
Soybeans	10,140,000 bu	66,924,000
Peaches	160 million lb	29,657,000
Wheat	16,800,000 bu	73,920,000

Nursery, greenhouse, and turf sales in 1995 amounted to $206.6 million.

24ANIMAL HUSBANDRY
In 1997, Georgia had an estimated 1.49 million cattle and calves valued at around $611 million, and an estimated 800,000 hogs and pigs valued at around $69 million. Cows kept for milk production numbered an estimated 100,000 in 1995, when Georgia dairies produced around 1.5 billion lb of milk. Poultry farmers sold an estimated $1.772 billion worth of broilers and $289.5 million worth of eggs in 1995; the total egg production was 4.37 billion. The 1.45 million turkeys produced in 1995 had an estimated value of $19,331,000. Georgia ranked 2nd only to Arkansas in production from chickens and broilers in 1995.

25FISHING
Georgia's total commercial catch of fish and shellfish in 1995 was 20,341,000 lb, valued at $35,268,000—a volume representing only 0.2% of the national catch. Commercial fishing in Georgia involves more shellfish—mainly shrimp and crabs—than finfish, the most important of which are caught in the nets of shrimp

trawlers. Leading finfish are snappers, groupers, tilefish, and porgy.

In brisk mountain streams and sluggish swamps, anglers catch bass, catfish, jackfish, bluegill, crappie, perch, and trout. In 1995/96, over 4.6 million (133,808 lb) coldwater species fish and 3.1 million fish eggs were distributed within the state by federal hatcheries. Georgia issued 653,189 sport fishing licenses in 1995/96.

26FORESTRY

Georgia, which occupies 1.6% of the total US land area, has nearly 3.4% of the nation's forestland and 5.1% of the nation's commercial forests. Georgia's forest area totals 24,136,737 acres (9,768,137 hectares) of which 23,631,214 acres (9,563,552 hectares) are commercial forest.

Forests cover 65% of the state's land area. The most densely wooded counties are in the piedmont hills and northern mountains. Ware and Charlton counties in southeastern Georgia, containing the Okefenokee Swamp, are almost entirely forested. In 1994, 91% of Georgia's commercial forestland was privately owned.

In 1995 there were an estimated 1,400 logging contractors in Georgia, and 144 sawmills and planing mills. The chief products of Georgia's timber industry are pine lumber and pine panels for the building industry, hardwood lumber for the furniture industry, and pulp for the paper and box industry. In 1995, Georgia produced approximately 2.9 billion board feet of lumber, of which 89.7% was softwood (pine). In 1995, the state produced 8.4 million cords of pulpwood, of which 68.6% was softwood. In 1995/96 366,742 acres (148,420 hectares) were reforested, 46% by the forest industry.

The chief recreational forest areas are in the Chattahoochee-Oconee National Forest, consisting of two main tracts in the northern and central part of the state. Georgia has 872,479 acres (353,080 hectares) of National Forest System lands, 99% of which are within the boundaries of the two major tracts.

The Georgia Forest Commission employs about 750 persons, including approximately 85 professional foresters. In 1995/96, there were 10,668 fires in Georgia forests. The commission produced approximately 50 million genetically superior seedlings in state nurseries in 1995/96. The commission's budget for 1995/96 provided for the reforestation of 83,000 acres (33,600 hectares).

27MINING

Statistics released by the US Geological Survey indicated that the estimated value of nonfuel minerals produced in Georgia in 1995 was $1.67 billion, an 8% increase over the value produced in 1994.

Kaolin clay is Georgia's foremost nonfuel mineral commodity, accounting for 62% of the total nonfuel mineral value in 1995. The value of kaolin production increased 8% in 1995. Crushed stone, representing 23% of the 1995 total production value, also rose in value by 14% at that time. Other minerals increasing in value included dimension stone, barite, kaolin crushed stone, fuller's earth, construction sand and gravel, masonry cement, industrial sand and gravel, and feldspar. Mineral commodities showing decreases in value in 1995 included portland cement, common clays, mica, and bauxite.

Clays, valued at $1.13 billion, accounted for 67.7% of the total estimated value of minerals produced in Georgia. The state once again in 1995 was the national leader in the quantity of both kaolin and dimension stone. Georgia also ranked 2d of only two bauxite-producing states, 3d in mica and iron oxide pigments, 4th in feldspar, and 9th in masonry cement. Blue-gray granite, known as "Elberton granite," is the mainstay of the industry—the granite is commonly used for road curbing in the northeastern US. Overall, the estimated quantity of dimension stone produced increased to 217,000 metric tons. Crushed stone, Georgia's second leading mineral commodity, increased 11% to 61 million short tons valued at $381 million, a 15% increase. The state also ranked second nationally in the quantity and value of barite produced, which was used by the chemical and the industrial filler and pigments industries.

Highway and building construction increased in 1995, in preparation for the 1996 Summer Olympics in Atlanta, causing increased demand for crushed stone and construction sand and gravel.

28ENERGY AND POWER

Georgia is an energy-dependent state which produces only a small proportion of its energy needs, most of it through hydroelectric power. There are no commercially recoverable petroleum or natural-gas reserves, and the state's coal deposits are of no more than marginal importance. Georgia does have large amounts of timberland, however, and it has been estimated that 20–40% of the state's energy demands could be met by using wood that is currently wasted. The state's southern location and favorable weather conditions also make solar power an increasingly attractive energy alternative. Georgia's extensive river system also offers the potential for further hydroelectric development.

In 1994, Georgia's energy consumption per capita was 336.9 million Btu, slightly less than the national average of 341; the state's 1994 energy expenditure per capita was $1,952, slightly above the national average of $1,938.

In 1995, Georgia produced 102 billion kWh of electricity and had an installed capacity of 24.4 million kW. As of 1 January 1996 the Georgia Power Co. had two atomic reactors near Baxley with a combined capacity of 1,630,000 kW; two more reactors were at Waynesboro with a combined capacity of 2,320,000 kW. All utilities are regulated by the Georgia Public Service Commission, which must approve their rates.

Petroleum accounted for 39% of all fuel used in Georgia in 1994, coal for 29%, and natural gas for 15%. Exploration for oil is currently in progress off the coast, but the state's offshore oil resources are expected to be slight.

29INDUSTRY

Georgia had 9,771 manufacturing firms in 1992. Important products include textiles, clothing, aircraft, soft drinks, paper, paints and varnishes, bricks and tiles, glassware, and ceramics.

Georgia was primarily an agrarian state before the Civil War, but afterward the cities developed a strong industrial base by taking advantage of abundant waterpower to operate factories. Textiles have long been dominant, but new industries have also been developed. Charles H. Herty, a chemist at the University of Georgia, discovered a new method of extracting turpentine which worked so well that Georgia led the nation in producing turpentine, tar, rosin, and pitch by 1982. Herty also perfected an economical way of making newsprint from southern pines, which was adopted by Georgia's paper mills. With the onset of World War II, meat-processing plants were built at rail centers, and fertilizer plants and cottonseed mills were expanded.

The state's—and Atlanta's—most famous product was created in 1886, when druggist John S. Pemberton developed a formula which he sold to Asa Griggs Candler, who in 1892 formed the Coca-Cola Co. In 1919, the Candlers sold the company to a syndicate headed by Ernest Woodruff, whose son Robert made "Coke" into the world's most widely known commercial product. The transport equipment, chemical, food-processing, apparel, and forest-products industries today rival textiles in economic importance.

The total value of shipments by manufacturers in 1995 was $112 billion.

Georgia's heavily forested northern region is dominated by carpet mills, especially around Dalton. In the piedmont plateau, manufacturing is highly diversified, with textiles and transportation equipment the most significant.

In 1997, 13 of the nation's 500 largest industrial corporations listed by *Fortune* magazine had headquarters in Georgia. In 1995, 1,031 US patents were issued to Georgia residents.

30COMMERCE

Georgia's wholesale establishments numbered 14,608 in 1992, with sales of $113.8 billion. Durable goods accounted for 65% of the establishments by type and for 57.2% of the sales. The state ranked 10th in retail trade in 1992, with retail sales totaling $49.9 billion. Retail sales in the Atlanta area accounted for 53.1% of the state's total. The most important categories (and their sales shares) were automotive dealers, 21.9%; food stores, 18.7%; general merchandise stores, 13.2%, and eating and drinking places, 10.8%. In 1994, the sale of distilled spirits was legal countywide in over one-fourth of Georgia's counties.

Georgia exported goods worth $8.6 billion in 1996, while exports of goods produced in Georgia totaled $11 billion. Savannah is Georgia's most important export center; in 1994 it handled exports valued at $423.3 million.

31CONSUMER PROTECTION

Georgia's basic consumer protection law is the Fair Business Practices Act of 1975, which forbids representing products as having official approval when they do not, outlaws advertising without the intention of supplying a reasonable number of the items advertised, and empowers the administrator of the law to investigate and resolve complaints and seek penalties for unfair practices. The administrator heads the Office of Consumer Affairs, which now also administers five other laws that regulate charitable solicitation, offers to sell or buy business opportunities buying services or clubs, transient merchants, and promotional contests.

In 1997, a number of changes were made in Georgia's basic consumer protection laws. The Consumer's Utility Counsel became a division of the Office of Consumer Affairs; the Counsel represents the interests of consumers and small businesses before the Georgia Public Service Commission. Telemarketing, internet, and home remodeling/home repair fraud became criminal offenses under the jurisdiction of the Office of Consumer Affairs, with maximum sentences of up to 10 years. Finally, multilevel marketing is now covered along with business opportunities.

32BANKING

The state's first bank was the branch of the Bank of the United States established at Savannah in 1802. Eight years later, the Georgia legislature chartered the Bank of Augusta and the Planters' Bank of Savannah, with the state holding one-sixth of the stock of each bank. The state also subscribed two-thirds of the stock of the Bank of the State of Georgia, which opened branches throughout the region. To furnish small, long-term agricultural loans, the state in 1828 established the Central Bank of Georgia, but this institution collapsed in 1856 because the state kept dipping into its reserves. After the Civil War, the lack of capital and the high cost of credit forced farmers to borrow from merchants under the lien system. By 1900 there were 200 banks in Georgia; with an improvement in cotton prices, their number increased to nearly 800 by World War I. During the agricultural depression of the 1920s, about half these banks failed, and the number has remained relatively stable since 1940. Georgia banking practices came under national scrutiny in 1979, when Bert Lance, President Carter's former budget director and the former president of the National Bank of Georgia, was indicted on 33 counts of bank fraud. The federal government dropped its case after Lance was acquitted on 9 of the charges, and most of the rest were dismissed.

At the end of 1996 there were 355 insured commercial banks in Georgia, of which 71, including the 61 national banks, were members of the Federal Reserve System. At the end of 1996, the state's 35 insured savings institutions had total assets of $5.8 billion. All of these institutions were stock corporations except one which was a mutual corporation. All of these institutions were federally chartered. Additionally, at the end of 1996 there were 247 credit unions in Georgia having total assets of $7.3 billion; 88 credit unions were state chartered with total assets of $4.2 billion, while 159 were federally chartered with total assets of $3.1 billion.

33INSURANCE

At the end of 1996 there were 22 life insurance companies domiciled in Georgia. Life insurance in force in 1996 totaled more than $369.9 billion. Direct benefit payments, which include death benefits, matured endowments, annuity benefits, surrender values, and other miscellaneous claims and benefits, totaled $3.2 billion in 1996. Direct insurance premiums written totaled $2.3 billion and direct insurance losses incurred totaled $1.5 billion.

Premiums written by other types of insurance firms in 1996 included nearly $1.9 billion for automobile liability coverage, $1.6 billion for automobile physical damage coverage, $712 million for homeowners insurance, and nearly $445 million for commercial multiple-peril insurance. There were 38 property/casualty insurance companies domiciled in Georgia in early 1997.

34SECURITIES

There are no stock or commodity exchanges in Georgia. In April 1997, registered securities brokers and dealers numbered 1,933; agents, 83,057. Some 1,108 securities investment advisory businesses were registered by the state at that time.

35PUBLIC FINANCE

Since the Georgia constitution forbids the state to spend more than it takes in from all sources, the governor attempts to reconcile the budget requests of the state department heads with the revenue predicted by economists for the coming fiscal year. The governor's Office of Planning and Budget prepares the budget, which is then presented to the general assembly at the beginning of each year's session. The assembly may decide to change the revenue estimate, but it usually goes along with the governor's forecast. The fiscal year begins on 1 July, and the first question for the assembly when it convenes the following January is whether to raise or lower the current year's budget estimate. If the revenues are better than expected, the legislators enact a supplemental budget; if the income is below expectations, cuts can be made.

The following table summarizes state revenues and expenditures for 1995 (actual):

REVENUES	1995
From own sources	$20,283,513
Taxes	
property	8,255,139
sales and gross receipts	5,645,044
income	3,841,595
SUBTOTAL	9,486,639
Charges and Miscellaneous	
current charges	1,329,672
Interest earnings	1,082,859
Other	129,204
Total	2,541,735
TOTALS	$20,283,513

EXPENDITURES	1995
Education	$ 7,340,676
Health and social concerns	5,831,052
Financial administration	396,094
Transportation (highways)	1,325,497
Public Safety (police)	902,222
Natural resources	358,856
Other	3,001,260
TOTALS	$19,154,482

Georgia's state debt totaled more than $5.6 billion in 1995. Total state indebtedness in 1995 amounted to $780 per capita.

³⁶TAXATION

Georgia was the last of the 13 original colonies to tax its citizens, but today its state tax structure is among the broadest in the US. The first comprehensive state tax was provided by the Property Tax Act of 1852, which allocated 50% of the tax to the counties; as of 1994, less than 1% of property taxes went to the state. Motor vehicle license fees began in 1910; motor fuel has been taxed since 1921, tobacco since 1923. In 1929, Georgia began taxing incomes; a withholding tax on incomes has been required since 1960. In 1951, Georgia enacted what at that time was the most all-inclusive sales tax in the US; this 4% tax is now the state's second-largest source of revenue. State law allows counties to charge an additional 1% local-option sales tax and to use the money to roll back property taxes. In 1994, only 29 counties did not impose an additional sales tax.

As of January 1996, the personal income tax ranged from 1% to 6%; the basic corporate tax rate was 6%. Georgians paid $30.3 billion in federal taxes in 1995. Georgia ranked 30th in per capita federal tax burden in 1996.

³⁷ECONOMIC POLICY

Since the time of journalist Henry Grady (1851–89), spokesman for the New South, Georgia has courted industry. Corporate taxes have traditionally been low, wages also low, and unions weak. Georgia's main attractions for new businesses are a favorable location for air, highway, and rail transport, a mild climate, a rapidly expanding economy, tax incentives, and competitive wage scales, and an abundance of recreational facilities. During the 1980s and 1990s, Georgia governors aggressively sought out domestic and foreign investors, and German, Japanese, and South American corporations were lured to the state. The state offers loans to businesses unable to obtain conventional financing, provides venture capital to start-up companies, and extends loans to small businesses and to companies in rural areas.

The Department of Industry and Trade promotes international trade, cultivates new industry, and is responsible for developing tourism. The state funds city and county development plans, aids recreational projects, promotes research and development, and supports industrial training programs.

³⁸HEALTH

Georgia's public health facilities developed only after the turn of the century. The Ellis Health Law of 1914 placed the responsibility for public health with the counties, but by 1936 only 36 of the state's 159 counties had full-time health departments. Not until after federal funds became available during the 1940s was malaria, one of the oldest afflictions in Georgia, brought under control through the eradication of mosquito breeding places. Federal funds also enabled every county to receive public health nursing services and X-ray clinics.

Georgia's birthrate declined to a record low of 15.9 per 1,000 population in 1976; the 1995 birthrate was 15.8. Fetal abortions have increased dramatically since 1973, when abortion laws were changed. There were 32,369 legal abortions performed in Georgia in 1995, for a rate of 19.1 per 1,000 women 15–44 years old and a ratio of 288 per 1,000 live births. Georgia's infant mortality rate in 1995 was 9.4 per 1,000 live births. Heart disease, cancer, and cerebrovascular disease were the leading causes of death in 1995. Of the population aged 18–30, 21.3% were classified as smokers. There were an estimated 131,112 deaths caused by smoking-related illness in 1995.

In 1995 there were 158 general hospitals in Georgia, which had a total of 837,963 admissions; 5,074,150 outpatient visits; 2,867,717 emergency room visits; and 187,700 observation visits. The number of hospital beds increased from 9,673 in 1950 to 24,756 beds in 1995. The average expense of general hospitals for care in 1995 was $1,509 per inpatient day and $9,617 per stay. In 1995 Georgia had 316 active licensed dentists, 12,801 practicing nonfederal physicians, and 48,400 registered nurses.

In 1995, 20% of Georgia's population went uninsured.

The Medical College of Georgia, established at Augusta in 1828, is one of the oldest medical schools in the US and the center of medical research in the state. The Federal Centers for Disease Control (CDC) were established in Atlanta in 1973.

³⁹SOCIAL WELFARE

As a responsibility of state government, social welfare came late to Georgia. The state waited two years before agreeing to participate in the federal Social Security system in 1937. Eighteen years later, Georgia was distributing only $62 million to the aged, blind, and disabled, and to families with dependent children. By 1970, the amount had risen to $150 million, but the state still lagged far behind the national average.

In 1996, 367,000 Georgians received an average of $330 per month in Aid to Families with Dependent Children (AFDC). In 1996 the food stamp program had an average monthly participation of 792,502. Pupils took part in the federal school lunch program, which cost about $192.6 million.

With the enactment of the Personal Responsibility and Work Opportunity Reconciliation Act of 1996, the US government has changed the form and regulations for many of its social welfare programs; most significantly, it replaces AFDC, an open-ended entitlement program, with Temporary Assistance for Needy Families (TANF), a limited system of assistance funded largely through federal block grants. The reform act also impacts the food stamp program, the Supplemental Security Income program, and the child nutrition program. The law took effect on 1 July 1997 and provided $16.38 billion in block grants for fiscal years 1997–2002. The grants are to be divided among the states based on an equation involving the numbers of former AFDC recipients in each state. Because many of the bills provisions have yet to be implemented into state-by-state policy, it was not possible to include the details of each state's programs for this edition of this work.

The average monthly Social Security benefit for Georgia's 1.01 million recipients was $679. Supplemental Security Income benefits were distributed to 198,933 Georgians. In 1995, unemployment insurance benefits averaged $161.67 weekly.

⁴⁰HOUSING

Post–World War II housing developments provided Georgia families with modern, affordable dwellings. The home-loan guarantee programs of the Federal Housing Administration and the Veterans Administration made modest down payments, low interest rates, and long-term financing the norm in Georgia. The result was a vast increase in both the number of houses constructed and the percentage of families owning their own homes.

Between 1940 and 1970, the number of housing units in the state doubled to 1,470,754. In 1940, only 3 in 10 Georgia homes were owner-occupied; by 1990, nearly 6 in 10 were. In 1970, 13% of all Georgians were still living in units that lacked full plumbing; in 1990, 1.1% were.

In October 1996 there were an estimated 2,929,000 housing units in Georgia, of which 2,645,000 were occupied. In that year, 74,874 privately owned housing units were authorized for construction, 59,397 of which were single-family. Total value of newly constructed housing in 1996 was $5.5 billion. The median cost for housing to owners with a mortgage was $737 per month in 1990, the last year for which figures are available, and $182 per month for those without a mortgage; the median monthly rent for renter-occupied housing was $433. These figures are comparable to the median national costs. In 1990, the median cost for owner-occupied housing by mortgage holders in Atlanta was $745 per month; for those without a mortgage, $240. Both figures are slightly higher than the median US costs. During 1995/96 Georgia received $575.7 million in aid from the US Department of Housing and Urban Development, including $98.3 million in community development block grants.

41EDUCATION

During the colonial period, education was in the hands of private schoolmasters. Georgia's first constitution called for the establishment of a school in each county. The oldest school in the state is Richmond Academy (Augusta), founded in 1788. The nation's oldest chartered public university, the University of Georgia, dates from 1784. Public education was inadequately funded, however, until the inauguration of the 3% sales tax in 1951, now 4%. By 1960, rural one-teacher schools had disappeared, and children were riding buses to consolidated schools. In the 1953/54 school year, Georgia spent $190 per white student and $132 per black student. In 1995/96, expenditures per student amounted to $6,102. Funding for elementary and secondary schools totaled $8 billion, of which 57% was by the state, 36.7% local, and 6.3% federal.

Georgia has continued to make great strides in education in recent years, with the most comprehensive pre-kindergarten program for four-year-olds in any of the 50 states, the "HOPE" (Helping Outstanding Pupils Educationally) scholarship program, and programs administered by the Georgia Department of Technical and Adult Education. Student test scores on norm-referenced tests are at or above the national average. In 1990, 71% of the population age 25 or older had a high school diploma; 204,332 Georgians were enrolled in college compared to 30,000 in 1960. Georgia students gained 26 points on the SAT compared to nine points for all SAT takers in the US in the decade 1983 to 1993. The state offers full-day kindergarten statewide, and preschool for all four-year-olds. Every school has a satellite dish for long-distance learning, and computers are being provided to every school, with extensive technology services, both instructional and administrative. High school graduation requirements have been strengthened to require 21 units for graduation, including four years of English, three each of math, science and social studies, plus other required courses. The Board of Regents of the state university system also increased its requirements for students starting college after 1988.

In 1996, Georgia public schools enrolled 1,311,126 students, of whom 445,510 were in grades 8 to 12. In 1995/96 there were 1,109 elementary, 281 middle, 267 high and 119 combination and special public schools. Additionally, instructional services are provided for hearing- and sight-impaired students at three state schools: Atlanta Area School for the Deaf, Georgia Academy for the Blind, and Georgia School for the Deaf.

Georgia had 111 institutions of higher learning, 66 public and 45 private, with a total of 251,810 students in 1990/91. Thirty-four public colleges are components of the University System of Georgia; the largest of these is the University of Georgia (Athens),

with a fall 1996 enrollment of 29,404. The largest private university is Emory (Atlanta), with 10,367 students in 1992/93. A scholarship program was established in 1978 for minority students seeking graduate and professional degrees.

42ARTS

During the 20th century, Atlanta has replaced Savannah as the major art center of Georgia, while Athens, the seat of the University of Georgia, has continued to share in the cultural life of the university. The state has eight major art museums, as well as numerous private galleries; especially notable is the High Museum of Art in Atlanta, dedicated in 1983. The Atlanta Memorial Arts Center was dedicated in 1968 to the 100 members of the association who lost their lives in a plane crash. The Atlanta Art Association exhibits the work of contemporary Georgia artists; Georgia's Art Bus Program delivers art exhibits to Georgia communities, mostly in rural areas, for three-week periods.

The theater has enjoyed popular support since the first professional resident theater troupe began performing in Augusta in 1790. Atlanta has a resident theater, and there are community theaters in some 30 cities and counties. Georgia has actively cultivated the film making industry, and an increasing number of films for cinema and television are being produced in the state—15 in 1983/84.

Georgia has at least 11 symphony orchestras, ranging from the Atlanta Symphony to community and college ensembles throughout the state. Atlanta and Augusta have professional ballet touring companies, Augusta has a professional opera company, and choral groups and opera societies perform in all major cities. Macon has become a major recording center, especially for popular music. The north Georgia mountain communities retain their traditional folk music.

In 1996, the state of Georgia generated $855,000 from federal sources for support of the arts. The National Endowment for the Arts (NEA) contributed $1,660,000 to Georgia's arts programs and $838,000 to the Georgia Council for the Arts. Resources provided by the State of Georgia amounted to $15,710,203. During 1987–1996, nearly 200,000 artists contributed to the state's arts programs; about 73,000,000 people attended them. Georgia's arts education programs were offered to about 21,600 students. By 1991, there were 200 arts associations in Georgia along with 30 local arts groups.

Other NEA grants were given to promote the Summer Atlanta Jazz Series and the Chamber Music Rural Residencies. The Augusta Opera received financial support from the Georgia Council for the Arts. In 1996, the NEA contributed to the Center for Puppetry Arts, Inc. The NEA also provided support for the arts through state and regional programs.

43LIBRARIES AND MUSEUMS

In 1996, the Georgia public library system included 33 regional and 2 county systems, each operating under its own board.

The holdings of all public libraries totaled 15,899,878 materials in 1996, and the combined circulation was 32,653,018 materials, or 4.52 per capita. The University of Georgia had by far the largest academic collection, including 3,303,268 books in addition to government documents, microfilms, and periodicals. Emory University, in Atlanta, has the largest private academic library, with about 1,208,615 bound volumes.

Georgia has at least 157 museums, including the Telfair Academy of Arts and Sciences in Savannah, the Georgia State Museum of Science and Industry in Atlanta, the Columbus Museum of Arts and Sciences, and Augusta-Richmond County Museum in Augusta. Atlanta's Cyclorama depicts the 1864 Battle of Atlanta. The Crawford W. Long Medical Museum in Jefferson is a memorial to Dr. Long, a pioneer in the use of anesthetics. A museum devoted to gold mining is located at Dahlonega.

Georgia abounds in historic sites, 100 of which were selected for acquisition in 1972 by the Georgia Heritage Trust Commission. Sites administered by the National Park Service include the Chickamauga and Chattanooga National Military Park, Kennesaw National Battlefield Park, Ft. Pulaski National Monument, and Andersonville National Monument near Americus, all associated with the Civil War, as well as the Ft. Frederica National Monument, an 18th-century English barracks on St. Simons Island. Also of historic interest are Factors Wharf in Savannah, the Hay House in Macon, and Franklin D. Roosevelt's "Little White House" at Warm Springs. The Martin Luther King, Jr., National Historic Site was established in Atlanta in 1980. Also in Atlanta is President Jimmy Carter's library, museum, and conference center complex. The state's most important archaeological sites are the Etowah Mounds at Cartersville, the Kolomoki Mounds at Blakely, and the Ocmulgee Indian village near Macon.

44COMMUNICATIONS

Airmail service was introduced to Georgia about 1930, and since then the quantity of mail has increased enormously.

As of March 1993, there were 2,378,000 Georgian residences (93.5%) with telephones.

That same year, Georgia had 373 radio stations, 176 AM and 197 FM. There were 37 commercial and 8 educational television stations in 1996. There were 20 large cable systems in 1996.

Fifteen large cable television systems were operating in 1993. On 1 June 1980, Atlanta businessman Ted Turner inaugurated the independent Cable News Network (CNN), which made round-the-clock news coverage available to 4,100 cable television systems throughout the US. By 1985, CNN was available to 32.3 million households in the US through 7,731 cable television systems and was broadcast to 22 other countries. By the late 1980s, CNN had become well known worldwide. In addition, Turner broadcasts CNN Headline News.

45PRESS

Georgia's first newspaper was the *Georgia Gazette,* published by James Johnston from 1763 until 1776. When royal rule was temporarily restored in Savannah, Johnston published the *Royal Georgia Gazette;* when peace came, he changed the name again, this time to the *Gazette of the State of Georgia.* After the state capital was moved to Augusta in 1785, Greensburg Hughes, a Charleston printer, began publishing the *Augusta Gazette.* Today's *Augusta Chronicle* traces its origin to this paper and claims the honor of being the oldest newspaper in the state. In 1817, the *Savannah Gazette* became the state's first daily. After the Indian linguist Sequoyah gave the Cherokee a written language, Elias Boudinot gave them a newspaper, the *Cherokee Phoenix,* in 1828. Georgia authorities suppressed the paper in 1835, and Boudinot joined his tribe's tragic migration westward.

After the Civil War, Henry Grady made the *Atlanta Constitution* the most famous newspaper in the state, with his "New South" campaign. Joel Chandler Harris's stories of Uncle Remus appeared in the *Constitution,* as did the weekly letters of humorist Charles Henry Smith, writing under the pseudonym of Bill Arp. In 1958, Ralph E. McGill, editor and later publisher of the *Constitution,* won a Pulitzer Prize for his editorial opposition to racial intolerance.

As of 1997, Georgia had 17 morning dailies, 15 evening dailies, and 15 Sunday newspapers. The following table shows leading daily newspapers with their 1997 circulations:

AREA	NAME	DAILY	SUNDAY
Atlanta	*Journal* and *Constitution* (m,S)	525,189	715,397
Augusta	*Chronicle* (m,S)	91,349	100,992
Columbus	*Ledger-Enquirer* (m,S)	52,456	67,942
Macon	*Telegraph* (m,S)	74,555	102,408
Savannah	*Morning News* (m,S)	55,039	81,262
	Evening Press (e)	12,466	
	News-Press (M,S)	69,533	77,176

Periodicals published in Georgia in 1994 included *Golf World, Atlanta Weekly, Industrial Engineering, Robotics World,* and *Southern Accents.* Among the nation's better-known scholarly presses is the University of Georgia Press, which publishes the *Georgia Review.*

46ORGANIZATIONS

The 1992 Census of Service Industries counted 1,445 organizations in Georgia, including 346 business associations; 694 civic, social, and fraternal associations, and 105 other membership organizations. National organizations headquartered in Georgia include the National Association of College Deans, Registrars, and Admissions Officers, located in Albany, and the Association of Information and Dissemination Centers, the American Risk and Insurance Association, and the American Business Law Association, located in Athens. The many organizations headquartered in Atlanta include the Industrial Development Research Council, the Southern Association of Colleges and Schools, the Southern Education Foundation, the Southern Regional Council, the Southern Christian Leadership Conference, the American Rheumatism Association, the Arthritis Foundation, the American Academy of Psychotherapists, the Federation of Southern Cooperatives, the International Association of Financial Planning, the National Association of Market Developers, and the Textile Quality Control Association.

47TOURISM, TRAVEL, AND RECREATION

Georgia's travel industry earned $9.6 billion in 1990; tourists spent nearly $26.3 million per day.

Major tourist attractions include national forests, national parks, state parks, and historic areas. Other places of interest include the impressive hotels and convention facilities of downtown Atlanta; the Okefenokee Swamp in southern Georgia; Stone Mountain near Atlanta; former President Jimmy Carter's home in Plains; the birthplace, church, and gravesite of Martin Luther King, Jr., in Atlanta; and the historic squares and riverfront of Savannah. The varied attractions of the Golden Isles include fashionable Sea Island; primitive Cumberland Island, now a national seashore; and Jekyll Island, owned by the state and leased to motel operators and to private citizens for beach homes. Since 1978, the state, under its Heritage Trust Program, has acquired Ossabaw and Sapelo islands, and strictly regulates public access to these wildlife sanctuaries.

Georgia has long been a hunters' paradise. Waynesboro calls itself the "bird dog capital of the world," and Thomasville in South Georgia is a mecca for quail hunters. In 1995, Georgia licensed 818,846 fishermen and 1,011,348 hunters.

48SPORTS

There are three major-league professional sports teams in Georgia, all in Atlanta. Turner Stadium and the Georgia Dome, main venues for the 1996 Summer Olympic Games hosted by the city, serve as the home field for two professional teams: baseball's Atlanta Braves, for whom Henry Aaron hit many of his record 755 home runs, and the Atlanta Falcons of the National Football League. The Omni International Sports Complex houses the Atlanta Hawks of the National Basketball Association. The

Atlanta Braves won the National League Pennant in 1991, 1992, 1995, and 1996. The Braves went on to win their only World Series championship since moving to Atlanta, defeating the Cleveland Indians in 1995. The Braves lost the Series to the New York Yankees in 1996, and to the Toronto Blue Jays in 1991 and 1992.

The Atlanta 500 is one of the NASCAR Winston Cup auto races. The Masters, brainchild of golf great Bobby Jones, has been played at the Augusta National Golf Club since 1934. The Atlanta Golf Classic is also listed on the professional golfers' tour.

Football and basketball dominate college sports. The University of Georgia Bulldogs, who play in the Southeastern Conference, were named National Champions in football in 1980, and advanced to the Final Four in basketball in 1983. Georgia Tech's Yellow Jackets of the Atlantic Coast Conference are a perennial basketball power. The Peach Bowl has been an annual post-season football game in Atlanta since 1968.

Professional fishing, sponsored by the Bass Anglers Sportsman's Society, is one of the fastest-growing sports in the state. A popular summer pastime is rafting. Massive raft races on the Chattahoochee at Atlanta and Columbus, and on the Savannah Rive at Augusta, draw many spectators and participants.

Atlanta hosted the 1996 Summer Olympic Games, at a cost of more than $1 billion.

49 FAMOUS GEORGIANS

James Earl "Jimmy" Carter (b.1924), born in Plains, was the first Georgian to serve as president of the US. He was governor of the state (1971–75) before being elected to the White House in 1976. Georgia has not contributed any US vice presidents; Alexander H. Stephens (1812–83) was vice president of the Confederacy during the Civil War.

Georgians who served on the US Supreme Court include James M. Wayne (1790–1867), John A. Campbell (1811–89), and Joseph R. Lamar (1857–1916). Supreme Court Justice Clarence Thomas, appointed to the court during the Bush administration, was born in Savannah on 23 June 1948. Several Georgians have served with distinction at the cabinet level: William H. Crawford (b.Virginia, 1772–1834), Howell Cobb (1815–68), and William G. McAdoo (1863–1941) as secretaries of the treasury; John M. Berrien (b.New Jersey, 1781–1856) as attorney general; John Forsyth (1781–1841) and Dean Rusk (1909–94) as secretaries of state; George Crawford (1798–1872) as secretary of war; and Hoke Smith (b.North Carolina, 1855–1931) as secretary of the interior.

A leader in the US Senate before the Civil War was Robert Toombs (1810–85). Notable US senators in recent years were Walter F. George (1878–1957), Richard B. Russell (1897–1971), Herman Talmadge (b.1913), and Sam Nunn (b.1938). Carl Vinson (1883–1981) was chairman of the House Armed Services Committee.

Many Georgians found fame in the ranks of the military. Confederate General Joseph Wheeler (1836–1906) became a major general in the US Army during the Spanish-American War. Other Civil War generals included W. H. T. Walker (1816–64), Thomas R. R. Cobb (1823–62), who also codified Georgia's laws, and John B. Gordon (1832–1904), later a US senator and governor of the state. Gordon, Alfred Colquitt (1824–94), and wartime governor Joseph E. Brown (b.South Carolina, 1821–94) were known as the "Bourbon triumvirate" for their domination of the state's Democratic Party from 1870 to 1890. Generals Courtney H. Hodge (1887–1966) and Lucius D. Clay (1897–1978) played important roles in Europe during and after World War II.

Sir James Wright (b.South Carolina 1714–85) was Georgia's most important colonial governor. Signers of the Declaration of Independence for Georgia were George Walton (b.Virginia, 1741–1804), Button Gwinnett (b.England, 1735–77), and Lyman Hall (b.Connecticut, 1724–90). Signers of the US Constitution were William Few (b.Maryland, 1748–1828) and Abraham Baldwin (b.Connecticut, 1754–1807). Revolutionary War hero James Jackson (b.England, 1757–1806) organized the Democratic-Republican Party (today's Democratic Party) in Georgia.

The first Georgians, the Indians, produced many heroes. Tomochichi (c.1664–1739) was the Yamacraw chief who welcomed Oglethorpe and the first Georgians. Alexander McGillivray (c.1759–93), a Creek chief who was the son of a Scottish fur trader, signed a treaty with George Washington in a further attempt to protect the Creek lands. Osceola (1800–1838) led his Seminole into the Florida swamps rather than move west. Sequoyah (b.Tennessee, 1773–1843) framed an alphabet for the Cherokee, and John Ross (Coowescoowe, b.Tennessee, 1790–1866) was the first president of the Cherokee republic.

Among influential Georgian educators were Josiah Meigs (b.Connecticut, 1757–1822), the first president of the University of Georgia, and Milton Antony (1784–1839), who established the Medical College of Georgia in Augusta in 1828. Crawford W. Long (1815–78) was one of the first doctors to use ether successfully in surgical operations. Paul F. Eve (1806–77) was a leading teacher of surgery in the South, and Joseph Jones (1833–96) pioneered in the study of the causes of malaria.

Distinguished black Georgians include churchmen Henry M. Turner (b.South Carolina, 1834–1915) and Charles T. Walker (1858–1921), educators Lucy Laney (1854–1933) and John Hope (1868–1936), and civil-rights activists William Edward Burghardt DuBois (b.Massachusetts, 1968–1963) and Walter F. White(1893–1955). One of the best-known Georgians was Martin Luther King, Jr. (1929–68), born in Atlanta, leader of the March on Washington in 1963, and winner of the Nobel Peace Prize in 1964 for his leadership in the campaign for civil rights; he was assassinated in Memphis, Tenn., while organizing support for striking sanitation workers. Black Muslim leader Elijah Muhammad (Elijah Poole, 1897–1975) was also a Georgian. Other prominent black leaders include Atlanta mayor and former UN ambassador Andrew Young (b.Louisiana, 1932), former Atlanta Mayor Maynard Jackson (b.Texas, 1938), and Georgia Senator Julian Bond (b.Tennessee, 1940).

Famous Georgia authors include Sidney Lanier (1842–81), Joel Chandler Harris (1848–1908), Lillian Smith (1857–1966), Conrad Aiken (1889–1973), Erskine Caldwell (b.1902), Caroline Miller (1903–92), Frank Yerby (1916–91) Carson McCullers (1917–67), James Dickey (1923–97), and Flannery O'Connor (1925–64). Also notable is Margaret Mitchell (1900–49), whose Pulitzer Prize–winning *Gone with the Wind* (1936) typifies Georgia to many readers.

Entertainment celebrities include songwriter Johnny Mercer (1909–76); actors Charles Coburn (1877–1961) and Oliver Hardy (1877–1961); singers and musicians Harry James (1916–83), Ray Charles (Ray Charles Robinson, b.1930), James Brown (b.1933), Little Richard (Richard Penniman, b.1935), Jerry Reed (b.1937), Gladys Knight (b.1944), and Brenda Lee (b.1944); and actors Melvyn Douglas (1901–81), Sterling Holloway (1905–92), Ossie Davis (b.1917), Barbara Cook (b.1927), Jane Withers (b.1927), Joanne Woodward (b.1930), and Burt Reynolds (b.1936).

Major sports figures include baseball's "Georgia peach," Tyrus Raymond "Ty" Cobb (1886–1961); Jack Roosevelt "Jackie" Robinson (1919–72), the first black to be inducted into the Baseball Hall of Fame; and Robert Tyre "Bobby" Jones (1902–71), winner of the "grand slam" of four major golf tournaments in 1930.

Robert E. "Ted" Turner (b.Ohio, 1939), an Atlanta businessman-broadcaster, owns the Atlanta Hawks and the Atlanta Braves and skippered the *Courageous* to victory in the America's Cup yacht races in 1977. Architect John C. Portman, Jr. (b.South Carolina, 1924), was the developer of Atlanta's Peachtree Center.

⁵⁰BIBLIOGRAPHY

Bartley, Numan V. *From Thurmond to Wallace: Political Tendencies in Georgia, 1948–68.* Baltimore: John Hopkins University Press, 1970.

Brook, Diane L. *Georgia: A Geography.* Boulder, Colo.: Westview, 1985.

Coleman, Kenneth, et al. *A History of Georgia.* 2nd ed. Athens: University of Georgia Press, 1991.

Grady, Henry W. *The New South.* Savannah: Beehive Press, 1971.

Grant, L. Donald. *The Way It Was in the South: The Black Experience in Georgia.* Secaucus, N.J.: Carol Publishing Group, 1993.

Hepburn, Lawrence R. *The Georgia History Book.* Athens: University of Georgia Institute of Government, 1982.

Inscoe, John C., ed. *Georgia in Black and White: Explorations in the Race Relations of a Southern State, 1865–1950.* Athens: University of Georgia Press, 1994.

King, Coretta Scott. *My Life with Martin Luther King.* Rev. ed. New York: H. Holt, 1993.

Lane, Mills. *The People of Georgia: An Illustrated History.* 2d ed. Savannah: Library of Georgia, 1992.

Maguire, Jane. *On Shares: Ed Brown's Story.* New York: Norton, 1976.

Malone, Henry. *Cherokees of the Old South.* Athens: University of Georgia Press, 1956.

Martin, Harold H. *Georgia: A Bicentennial History.* New York: Norton, 1977.

Reidy, Joseph P. *From Slavery to Agrarian Capitalism in the Cotton Plantation South: Central Georgia, 1800–1880.* Chapel Hill: University of North Carolina Press, 1992.

Saye, Albert B. *Georgia History and Government.* Austin: Steck Vaughn, 1973.

Woodward, C. Vann. *Tom Watson: Agrarian Rebel.* New York: Oxford Press, 1970 (orig. 1938).

HAWAII

State of Hawaii

ORIGIN OF STATE NAME: Unknown. The name may stem from Hawaii Loa, traditional discoverer of the islands, or from Hawaiki, the traditional Polynesian homeland. **NICKNAME:** The Aloha State. **CAPITAL:** Honolulu. **ENTERED UNION:** 21 August 1959 (50th). **SONG:** "Hawaii Ponoi." **MOTTO:** *Ua mau ke ea o ka aina i ka pono* (The life of the land is perpetuated in righteousness). **COAT OF ARMS:** The heraldic shield of the Hawaiian kingdom is flanked by the figures of Kamehameha I, who united the islands, and Liberty, holding the Hawaiian flag. Below the shield is a phoenix surrounded by taro leaves, banana foliage, and sprays of maidenhair fern. **FLAG:** Eight horizontal stripes, alternately white, red, and blue, represent the major islands, with the British Union Jack (reflecting the years that the islands were under British protection) in the upper left-hand corner. **OFFICIAL SEAL:** Same as coat of arms, with the words "State of Hawaii 1959" above and the state motto below. **BIRD:** Nene (Hawaiian goose). **FLOWER:** Pua aloalo (hibiscus). **TREE:** Kukui (candlenut). **ISLAND EMBLEMS:** Each of the eight major islands has its own color and emblem. **HAWAII:** red; lehua (ohia blossom). **KALHOOLAWE:** gray; hinahina (beach heliotrope). **KAUAI:** purple; mokihana (fruit capsule of the *Pelea anisata*). **LANAI:** orange; kaunaoa *(Cuscuta sandwichiana)*. **MAUI:** pink; lokelani (pink cottage rose). **MOLOKAI:** green; kukui (candlenut) blossom. **NIIHAU:** white; white pupu shell. **OAHU:** yellow; ilima *(Sida fallax)*. **LEGAL HOLIDAYS:** New Year's Day, 1 January; Birthday of Martin Luther King, Jr., 3d Monday in January; Presidents' Day, 3d Monday in February; Kuhio Day, 26 March; Good Friday, March or April; Memorial Day, last Monday in May; Kamehameha Day, 11 June; Independence Day, 4 July; Admission Day, 3d Friday in August; Labor Day, 1st Monday in September; Discoverers Day, 2d Monday in October; Election Day, 1st Tuesday after 1st Monday in November; Veterans Day, 11 November; Thanksgiving Day, 4th Thursday in November; Christmas Day, 25 December. **TIME:** 2 AM Hawaii-Aleutian Standard Time = noon GMT.

¹LOCATION, SIZE, AND EXTENT

The State of Hawaii is an island group situated in the northern Pacific Ocean, about 2,400 mi (3,900 km) wsw of San Francisco. The smallest of the five Pacific states, Hawaii ranks 47th in size among the 50 states.

The 132 Hawaiian Islands have a total area of 6,470 sq mi (16,758 sq km), including 6,425 sq mi (16,641 sq km) of land and only 45 sq mi (117 sq km) of inland water. The island chain extends over 1,576 mi (2,536 km) N-S and 1,425 mi (2,293 km) E-W. The largest island, Hawaii (known locally as the "Big Island") extends 76 mi (122 km) E-W and 93 mi (150 km) N-S; Oahu, the most populous island, extends 44 mi (71 km) E-W and 30 mi (48 km) N-S.

The eight largest islands of the Hawaiian group are Hawaii (4,035 sq mi—10,451 sq km), Maui (734 sq mi—1,901 sq km), Oahu (617 sq mi—1,598 sq km), Kauai (558 sq mi—1,445 sq km), Molokai (264 sq mi—684 sq km), Lanai (141 sq mi—365 sq km), Niihau (73 sq mi—189 sq km), and Kahoolawe (45 sq mi—117 sq km). The general coastline of the island chain is 750 mi (1,207 km); the tidal shoreline totals 1,052 mi (1,693 km). The state's geographic center is off Maui, at 20°15'N, 156°20'w.

²TOPOGRAPHY

The 8 major and 124 minor islands that make up the State of Hawaii were formed by volcanic eruptions. Mauna Loa, on the island of Hawaii, is the world's largest active volcano, at a height of 13,675 feet (4,168 meters). Kilauea, on the eastern slope of Mauna Loa, is the world's largest active volcanic crater: beginning on 24 May 1969, it spewed forth 242 million cu yards (185 million cu meters) of lava, spreading over an area of 19.3 sq mi (50 sq km). The longest volcanic eruption in Hawaii lasted 867 days. Further indications of Hawaii's continuing geological

activity are the 14 earthquakes, each with a magnitude of 5 or more on the Richter scale, that shook the islands from 1969 to 1979; one quake, at Puna, on Hawaii in 1975, reached a magnitude of 7.2.

Hawaii, Maui, Kauai, and Molokai are the most mountainous islands. The highest peak in the state is Mauna Kea (13,796 feet—4,205 meters), on Hawaii; the largest natural lake, Halulu (182 acres—74 hectares), Niihau; the largest artificial lake, Waiia Reservoir (422 acres—171 hectares), Kauai; and the longest rivers, Kaukonahua Stream (33 mi—53 km) in the north on Oahu and Wailuku River (32 mi—51 km) on Hawaii. While much of the Pacific Ocean surrounding the state is up to 20,000 feet (6,100 meters) deep, Oahu, Molokai, Lanai, and Maui stand on a submarine bank at a depth of less than 2,400 feet (730 meters).

³CLIMATE

Hawaii has a tropical climate cooled by trade winds. Normal daily temperatures in Honolulu average 72°F (22°C) in February and 78°F (26°C) in August; the average wind speed is a breezy 11.8 mph (19 km/hr). The record high for the state is 100°F (38°C), set at Pahala on 27 April 1931, and the record low is 12°F (–11°C), set at Mauna Kea Observatory on 17 May 1979.

Rainfall is extremely variable, with far more precipitation on the windward (northeastern) than on the leeward side of the islands. Mt. Waialeale, Kauai, is reputedly the rainiest place on earth, with a mean annual total of 486 in (1,234 cm). Kukui, Maui, holds the US record for the most precipitation in one year—739 in (1,878 cm) in 1982. In the driest areas—on upper mountain slopes and in island interiors, as in central Maui—the average annual rainfall is less than 10 in (25 cm). Snow falls at the summits of Mauna Loa, Mauna Kea, and Haleakala—the

152

highest mountains. The highest tidal wave (tsunami) in the state's history reached 56 feet (17 meters).

⁴FLORA AND FAUNA

Formed over many centuries by volcanic activity, Hawaii's topography—and therefore its flora and fauna—have been subject to constant and rapid change. Relatively few indigenous trees remain; most of the exotic trees and fruit plants have been introduced since the early 19th century. Of 2,200 species and subspecies of flora, more than half are endangered, threatened, or extinct; the koa is an indigenous tree under state protection.

The only land mammal native to the islands is the Hawaiian hoary bat, now endangered; there are no indigenous snakes. The endangered humpback whale migrates to Hawaiian waters in winter; other marine animals abound. Listed as threatened are Newell's shearwater turtle and the green sea turtle. Among threatened birds are several varieties of honeycreeper and the Hawaiian goose (nene), crow, and hawk. The nene (the state bird), once close to extinction, now numbers in the hundreds and is on the increase. Animals considered endangered by the state but not on the federal list include the Hawaiian storm petrel, Hawaiian owl, Maui 'amakihi (Loxops virens wilsoni), and 'i'iwi (Vestiaria coccinea).

⁵ENVIRONMENTAL PROTECTION

Environmental protection responsibilities are vested in the Department of Land and Natural Resources and in the Environmental Management Division of the Department of Health. The Hawaii Environmental Policy Act of 1974 established environmental policies and guidelines for state agencies. Also enacted in 1974 was the Environmental Impact Statement Law, which mandated environmental assessments for all state and county projects and some private projects. Noise pollution requirements for the state are among the strictest in the US, and air and water purity levels are well within federal standards.

The federal Environmental Protection Agency banned the use of ethylene dibromide (EDB), a pesticide used in the state's pineapple fields, after high levels of the chemical were found in wells on the island of Oahu in 1983; irrigation accounted for more than 42% of the state's water usage in 1992. In 1996, there were seven municipal landfills. In 1993, there were 2,000 tons of hazardous waste generated in Hawaii.

⁶POPULATION

According to the 1990 census, Hawaii had a resident population of 1,108,229, 15% more than in 1980 and 39th among the 50 states. Estimates for 1996 give a population of 1,183,723; Census Bureau projections indicate that Hawaii will have a population of 1,362,000 in the year 2000. Almost four-fifths of the population lives on Oahu, primarily in the greater Honolulu metropolitan area, which had a density of 4,412 persons per sq mi (1,703 per sq km) in 1990; the figure for the entire state was 172.5 per sq mi (66.3 per sq km) in 1990.

In 1900, 74.5% of Hawaii's inhabitants were rural; by 1990, only 11% lived outside urban areas. By far the largest city is Honolulu, with an estimated 1994 population of 385,881. The greater metropolitan Honolulu area had an estimated 877,198 residents in 1995. The city of Honolulu is coextensive with Honolulu County.

⁷ETHNIC GROUPS

According to federal census data, Hawaii ranked 2d only to California in number of ethnic Filipino residents in 1990, and placed 3d behind California and New York in ethnic Chinese and Japanese inhabitants. Of the state's 1.1 million residents, 685,000 are Asian or Pacific Islanders, 370,000 are white, 27,000 are black, and 5,000 are American Indian, Eskimo, or Aleut. About

81,000 individuals of that total are of Hispanic origin. In 1990, ethnic composition in Hawaii for those who claimed at least one specific ancestry group included: Japanese, 23,6%; Filipino, 15.9% Hawaiian, 14.1%; Chinese, 8.6%; Korean, 2.6%; and Samoan, 1.3%.

The earliest Asian immigrants, the Chinese, were superseded in number in 1900 by the Japanese, who have since become a significant factor in state politics. The influx of Filipinos and other Pacific island peoples is largely a 20th-century phenomenon. In recent decades, ethnic Hawaiians have been increasingly intent on preserving their cultural identity.

⁸LANGUAGES

Although massive immigration from Asia and the US mainland since the mid-19th century has effectively diluted the native population, the Hawaiian lexical legacy in English is conspicuous. Newcomers soon add to their vocabulary *aloha* (love, good-bye), *haole* (white foreigner), *malihini* (newcomer), *lanai* (porch), *tapa* (bark cloth), *mahimahi* (a kind of fish), *ukulele*, *muumuu*, and the common directional terms *mauka* (toward the mountains) and *makai* (toward the sea), customarily used instead of "north," "east," "west," and "south." Native place-names are numerous—Waikiki, Hawaii, Honolulu, Mauna Kea, and Molokai for example.

Most native-born residents of Hawaiian ancestry speak one of several varieties of Hawaiian pidgin, a lingua franca incorporating elements of Hawaiian, English, and other Asian and Pacific languages. In 1990, 75.2% of Hawaiians 5 years old or older spoke only English at home. Other languages spoken at home, and the number of speakers, were as follows:

Japanese	69,587
Tagalog	55,341
Chinese	26,366
Korean	14,636
Spanish	13,729
Vietnamese	4,620
German	4,066
French	3,921

⁹RELIGIONS

Congregationalist missionaries arrived in 1820, and Roman Catholics in 1827; the constitution of 1840 guaranteed freedom of worship for all religions. Subsequent migration brought Mormons and Methodists, and Anglican representatives were invited by King Kamehameha IV in 1862. Confucianism, Taoism, and Buddhism arrived with the Chinese during the 1850s; by the turn of the century, Shinto and five forms of Mahayana Buddhism were being practiced by Japanese immigrants.

Figures derived from a 1990 census of churches and church membership by the National Council of the Churches of Christ in the USA showed that an estimated 232,750 Hawaiians considered themselves Roman Catholic, and 158,047 Protestant. Mormons numbered about 38,303 in 1990.

¹⁰TRANSPORTATION

Hawaii has only two railroads: the non-profit Hawaiian Railway Society, with 6.5 mi (10.5 km) of track on Oahu, and the commercial-recreational Lahaina, Kaanapali & Pacific on Maui, with 6 mi (10 km) of track. The islands of Oahu, Hawaii, Maui, and Kauai have public bus systems. In 1996, Hawaii's 733,500 licensed drivers traversed 4,100 mi (6,600 km) of roads and streets, 95.2% paved, and 72% of that on the two most populous islands. There were about 703,100 passenger cars registered in 1996, along with 160,000 trucks and 3,500 buses.

Most scheduled inter-island passenger traffic and most transpacific travel is by air. The state has 6 military and 29 civilian aircraft facilities, including 3 semi-private civilian heliports. The

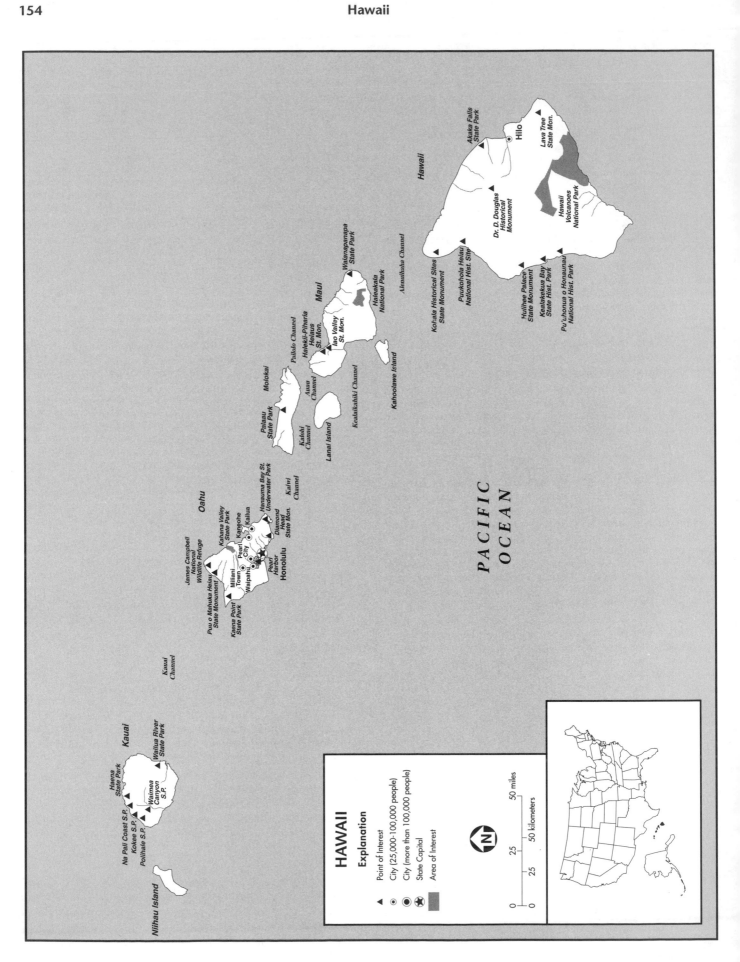

Hawaii

Akaka Falls State Park
Hilo
Lava Tree State Mon.
Dr. D. Douglas Historical Monument
Hawaii Volcanoes National Park
Kohala Historical Sites State Monument
Puukohola Heiau National Hist. Site
Hulihee Palace State Monument
Kealakekua Bay State Hist. Park
Pu'uhonua o Honaunau National Hist. Park

Waianapanapa State Park
Haleakala National Park
Maui
Halekii-Pihana Heiaus St. Mon.
Iao Valley St. Mon.

Alenuihaha Channel

Pailolo Channel
Molokai
Palaau State Park
Auau Channel
Kahoolawe Island
Kealaikahiki Channel
Kaohi Channel
Lanai Island

James Campbell National Wildlife Refuge
Kahana Valley State Park
Oahu
Kaneohe
Kailua
Hanauma Bay St. Underwater Park
Diamond Head State Mon.
Kaiwi Channel
Puu o Mahuka Heiau State Monument
Mililani Town
Pearl City
Waipahu
Pearl Harbor
Honolulu
Kaena Point State Park

PACIFIC OCEAN

Kauai Channel

Kauai
Haena State Park
Wailua River State Park
Na Pali Coast S.P.
Kokee S.P.
Polihale S.P.
Waimea Canyon S.P.

Niihau Island

HAWAII
Explanation

Point of Interest ▲
City (25,000-100,000 people) ◉
City (more than 100,000 people) ◉
State Capital ✪
Area of Interest ▨

N

50 miles
25
0

50 kilometers
25
0

busiest air terminal, Honolulu International Airport, serves about 64% of the state's passengers using Hawaii's civilian aircraft facilities. In 1995, enplaned and deplaned passengers numbered about 23,672,900, making Honolulu International Airport the 17th busiest air terminal in the nation.

¹¹HISTORY

Hawaii's earliest inhabitants were Polynesians who came to the islands in double-hulled canoes between 1,000 and 1,400 years ago, either from Southeast Asia or from the Marquesas in the South Pacific. The Western world learned of the islands in 1778, when an English navigator, Captain James Cook, sighted Oahu; he named the entire archipelago the Sandwich Islands after his patron, John Montagu, 4th Earl of Sandwich. At that time, each island was ruled by a hereditary chief under a caste system called *kapu*. Subsequent contact with European sailors and traders exposed the Polynesians to smallpox, venereal disease, liquor, firearms, and Western technology—and fatally weakened the *kapu* system. Within 40 years of Cook's arrival, one of the island chiefs, Kamehameha (whose birth date, designated as 11 June, is still celebrated as a state holiday), had consolidated his power on Hawaii, conquered Maui and Oahu, and established a royal dynasty in what became known as the Kingdom of Hawaii.

The death of Kamehameha I in 1819 preceded by a year the arrival of Protestant missionaries. One of the first to come was the Reverend Hiram Bingham, who, as pastor in Honolulu, was instrumental in the christianizing of Hawaii. Even before Bingham arrive, however, Liholiho, successor to the throne under the title of Kamehameha II, had begun to do away with the *kapu* system. After the king's death from measles while on a state trip to England in 1824, another son of Kamehameha I, Kauikeaouli, was proclaimed King Kamehameha III. His reign saw the establishment of public schools, the first newspapers, the first sugar plantation, a bicameral legislature, and the establishment of Honolulu as the kingdom's capital city. Hawaii's first written constitution was promulgated in 1840, and in 1848 a land reform called the Great Mahele abolished the feudal land system and legitimized private landholdings, in the process fostering the expansion of sugar plantations. The power behind the throne during this period was Dr. Gerrit P. Judd, a medical missionary who served as finance minister and interpreter for Kamehameha III.

Diplomatic maneuverings during the 1840s and 1850s secured recognition of the kingdom from the US, Britain, and France. As the American presence on the islands increased, however, so did pressure for US annexation—a movement opposed by Alexander Liholiho, who ruled as Kamehameha IV after his father's death in 1854. His brief reign and that of his brother Lot (Kamehameha V) witnessed the arrival of Chinese contract laborers and of the first Japanese immigrants, along with the continued growth of Hawaii as an international port of call (especially for whalers) and of the increasing influence of American sugar planters. Lot's death in 1872 left no direct descendant of Kamehameha, and the legislature elected a new king, whose death only a year later required yet another election. The consequent crowning of Kalakaua, known as the Merry Monarch, inaugurated a stormy decade during which his imperial schemes clashed with the power of the legislature and the interests of the planters. The most significant event of Kalakaua's unstable reign was the signing of a treaty with the US in 1876, guaranteeing Hawaii an American sugar market. The treaty was renewed in 1887 with a clause leasing Pearl Harbor to the US.

Kalakaua died during a visit to San Francisco in 1891 and was succeeded by his sister, Liliuokalani, the last Hawaiian monarch. Two years later, after further political wrangling, she was deposed in an American-led revolution that produced a provisional government under the leadership of Sanford B. Dole. The new regime immediately requested annexation by the US, but the treaty providing for it bogged down in the Senate, and died after the inauguration of President Grover Cleveland, an opponent of expansionism. The provisional government then drafted a new constitution and on 4 July 1894 proclaimed the Republic of Hawaii, with Dole as president. The Spanish-American War, which fanned expansionist feelings in the US and pointed up the nation's strategic interests in the Pacific, gave proponents of annexation the opportunity they had been seeking. The formal transfer of sovereignty took place on 12 August 1898, and Dole became Hawaii's first territorial governor when the act authorizing the annexation became effective in June 1900.

Notable in the territorial period were a steady US military buildup, the creation of a pineapple canning industry by James D. Dole (the governor's cousin), the growth of tourism (spurred in 1936 by the inauguration of commercial air service), and a rising desire for statehood, especially after passage of the Sugar Act of 1934, which lowered the quota on sugar imports from Hawaii. The Japanese attack on Pearl Harbor on 7 December 1941, crippling the US Pacific fleet and causing some 4,000 casualties, quickly turned Hawaii into an armed camp, under martial law. The record of bravery compiled by Nisei of the 442d Regiment on the European front did much, on the other hand, to allay the mistrust that some mainlanders felt about the loyalties of Hawaiians of Japanese ancestry. Hawaii also bore a disproportionate burden during the Korean conflict, suffering more casualties per capita than any of the 48 states.

Hawaiians pressed for statehood after World War II, but Congress was reluctant, partly because of racial antipathy and partly because of fears that Hawaii's powerful International Longshoremen's and Warehousemen's Union was Communist-controlled. The House of Representatives passed a statehood bill in 1947, but the Senate refused. Not until 1959, after Alaska became the 49th state, did Congress vote to let Hawaii enter the Union. President Eisenhower signed the bill on 18 March, and the question was then put to the Hawaiian electorate, who voted for statehood on 27 June 1959 by a margin of about 17 to 1. Hawaii became the 50th state on 21 August 1959. Since then, defense, tourism, and food processing have been mainstays of Hawaii's economy, with the state playing an increasingly important role as an economic, educational, and cultural bridge between the US and the nations of Asia and the Pacific. In the 1900s Hawaiians faced the challenge of preserving the natural beauty of their environment while accommodating a growing population (especially on Oahu) and a thriving tourist industry. A prominent political issue in recent years has been the achievement of some form of sovereignty by native Hawaiians. In 1994 the US returned jurisdiction over the island of Kahoolawe to the state.

¹²STATE GOVERNMENT

The constitution of the state of Hawaii was written by the constitutional convention of 1950, ratified by the people of the Territory of Hawaii that year, and then amended by the 1959 plebiscite on the statehood question.

There is a bicameral legislature of 25 senators elected from eight senatorial districts for four-year terms, and 51 representatives elected for two-year terms. The legislature meets annually on the 3d Wednesday in January. To be eligible to serve as a legislator, a person must have attained the age of majority, be an American citizen, have been a resident of the state for at least three years, and be a qualified voter of his district. The legislative salary in 1995 was $32,000.

The governor and lieutenant governor are elected for concurrent four-year terms and must be of the same political party. They are the only elected officers of the executive branch, except for members of the Board of Education. In 1996 the governor's salary was $94,780. There are 17 executive departments, each under the supervision of the governor and headed by a single appointed executive.

Voters in Hawaii must be US citizens at least 18 years of age; there is no minimum residency requirement.

13POLITICAL PARTIES

Both Republicans and Democrats established party organizations early in the 20th century when Hawaii was still a territory. Before statehood, the Republican Party dominated the political scene; since the 1960s, however, Hawaii has been solidly Democratic. As of 1994, Hawaii's governor, majorities of both houses of the state legislature, its two US Senators, and its two US Representatives were all Democrats. Democrat Bill Clinton won just under 57% of the vote in the presidential election in 1996, while Republican Bob Dole garnered nearly 32%, and Independent Ross Perot received over 7%. Hawaii's governor is Democrat Benjamin J. Cayetano. Its US Senators are Daniel K. Akaka and Senate veteran Daniel K. Inouye, most recently re-elected in 1992. In 1997 there were 23 Democrats and 2 Republicans in the state senate, and 39 Democrats and 12 Republicans in the state house. As of 1995, 17 women held elective state office.

Hawaii Presidential Vote by Major Political Parties, 1960–96

YEAR	ELECTORAL VOTE	HAWAII WINNER	DEMOCRAT	REPUBLICAN
1960	3	*Kennedy (D)	92,410	92,295
1964	4	*Johnson (D)	163,249	44,022
1968	4	Humphrey (D)	141,324	91,425
1972	4	*Nixon (R)	101,433	168,933
1976	4	*Carter (D)	147,375	140,003
1980	4	Carter (D)	135,879	130,112
1984	4	*Reagan (R)	147,154	185,050
1988	4	Dukakis (D)	192,364	158,625
1992**	4	*Clinton (D)	179,310	136,822
1996**	4	*Clinton (D)	205,012	113,943

*Won US presidential election.
**Independent candidate Ross Perot received 53,003 votes in 1992 and 27,358 votes in 1996.

14LOCAL GOVERNMENT

The state is divided into four principal counties: Hawaii, including the island of Hawaii; Maui, embracing the islands of Maui, Kahoolawe, Lanai, and Molokai; Honolulu, coextensive with the city of Honolulu and covering all of Oahu and the northwestern Hawaiian Islands, from Nihoa to Kure Atoll; and Kauai, including the islands of Kauai and Niihau. Because there are no further subdivisions, the counties provide some services traditionally performed in other states by cities, towns, and villages, notably fire and police protection, refuse collection, and street maintenance and lighting. On the other hand, the state government provides many functions normally performed by counties on the mainland. Each principal county has an elected council and a mayor.

A fifth county of Kalawao forms that part of Molokai more commonly known as the Kalaupapa Settlement, primarily for the care and treatment of persons suffering from leprosy. Kalawao is entirely under the jurisdiction of the Department of Health; the only county officer is an appointed sheriff.

15STATE SERVICES

Hawaii's first ombudsman, empowered to investigate complaints by the public about any officer or employee of state or county government, took office in 1969. The State Ethics Commission, a legislative agency, implements requirements for financial disclosure by state officials and investigates alleged conflicts of interest and other breaches of ethics.

The Department of Education (headed by an elected Board of Education) operates 226 regular public schools and 7 special schools for the physically and mentally disabled. It administers the statewide public library system, regulates private schools, and certifies teachers. The Board of Regents of the University of Hawaii oversees the state's higher educational institutions. Highways, airports, harbors, and other facilities are the concern of the Department of Transportation.

The Department of Health operates 10 public hospitals, the Kalaupapa leper colony, and various programs for the mentally ill, the mentally retarded, and alcoholics. Civil defense and the Air and Army national guards are under the jurisdiction of the Department of Defense.

The Corrections Division of the Department of Social Services and Housing operates the state prison system, along with programs for juvenile offenders. Also within this department are divisions of public welfare and vocational rehabilitation, as well as the Hawaii Housing Authority. The Executive Office on Aging works with state and county departments to coordinate programs for senior citizens. Unemployment insurance, occupational safety and health laws, and workers' compensation programs are run by the Department of Labor and Industrial Relations.

16JUDICIAL SYSTEM

The supreme court, the highest in the state, consists of a chief justice and four associate justices, all of them appointed by the governor with the advice and consent of the senate. All serve 10-year terms, up to the mandatory retirement age of 70.

The state is divided into four judicial circuits with 22 circuit court judges and 4 intermediate appellate court judges, also appointed by the governor with the advice and consent of the senate to 10-year terms. Circuit courts are the main trial courts, having jurisdiction in most civil and criminal cases. District courts, whose judges are appointed by the chief justice with the advice and consent of the senate to 6-year terms, function as inferior courts within each judicial circuit; district court judges may also preside over family court proceedings. Hawaii also has a land court and a tax appeal court. There were approximately 3,960 practicing attorneys as of February 1997.

According to the FBI Crime Index, Hawaii's crime rate in 1995 totaled 7,246.2 per 100,000 inhabitants, including 297.6 for violent crimes and 6,948.6 for property crimes. There were 3,599 practicing attorneys in 1994.

There were 3,312 inmates held in 8 state and federal correctional institutions; a rate of 279 inmates per 100,000 inhabitants. The prison population increased by almost 30% from 1990 to 1995. Hawaii does not have a death penalty.

17ARMED FORCES

Hawaii is the nerve center of US defense activities in the Pacific. CINCPAC (Commander-in-Chief Pacific), headquartered at Camp H. M. Smith in Honolulu, directs the US Pacific Command, largest of the six US unified commands and responsible for all US military forces in the Pacific and Indian oceans and southern Asia. Total US Defense Department expenditures in Hawaii in fiscal year 1996 were $3.3 billion. Military prime contract awards totaled $928 million.

As of 1996, Hawaii was home base for 63,596 Department of Defense military and civilian personnel on 7 military installations and properties. The US Navy accounted for 25,984 personnel; the Army, 27,495; the Air Force, 9,068; and other defense agencies, 1,049. Pearl Harbor is home port for 40 ships. The major Army bases, all on Oahu, are Schofield Barracks, Ft. Shafter, and Ft. DeRussy; Air Force bases include Hickam and Wheeler. Military reservations occupy nearly one-fourth of Oahu's land area.

In 1996, there were 115,000 veterans living in Hawaii: 26,000 of World War II; 20,000 of the Korean conflict; 42,000 of the

Vietnam era; and 7,000 of the Persian Gulf War. Veterans' benefits totaled $184 million in fiscal year 1996. Hawaii's Reserve and National Guard had 12,358 personnel in 1996.

[18]MIGRATION

The US mainland and Asia have been the main sources of immigrants to Hawaii since the early 19th century. Immigration remains a major source of population growth: between 1950 and 1980, Hawaii's net gain from migration was 91,000, and between 1980 and 1983, 15,000. In the 1980s, migration accounted for 23% of the net increase in population.

Since the early 1970s, about 40,000 mainland Americans have come each year to live in Hawaii. More than half are military personnel and their dependents, on temporary residence during their term of military service. From 1985 to 1990, Hawaii suffered a net loss from migration within the US, but experienced an overall net gain in migration due to immigration from abroad. Between 1990 and 1996, the net loss from domestic migration was 55,900. During the same period there was a net gain of 37,501 from international migration. In fiscal 1996, 8,436 foreign immigrants arrived in Hawaii. As of 1994, it was estimated that there were fewer than 25 undocumented immigrants in the state. Residents born within Hawaii made up 56.1% of the population in 1990. Just under 50% of state residents age 5 and older lived in a different house in 1985 than they did in 1990, 37% in a different state (mostly in California and Texas).

[19]INTERGOVERNMENTAL COOPERATION

Among the interstate accords in which Hawaii participates are the Western Corrections Compact and the Compact for Education. Federal aid was estimated at $1.1 billion in fiscal year 1996.

[20]ECONOMY

Tourism remains Hawaii's leading employer, revenue producer, and growth sector. However, agricultural diversification (including the cultivation of flowers and nursery products, papaya, and macadamia nuts), aquaculture, manganese nodule mining, and film and television production have broadened the state's economic base. Hawaii's gross state product in 1994 was $36,718 million to which private goods-producing industries contributed $3,785 million and private services-producing industries, $7,811 million. In 1996, Hawaii's per capita personal income was $25,159, which was ranked 11th in the US. In 1996, there were 3,092 filings for bankruptcy, up almost 52% from the previous year.

[21]INCOME

Average per capita personal income in Hawaii in 1996 was $25,159 (11th in the US). Average per capita personal income grew only 1.7% from 1995 to 1996, well below the national average of 4.5% The median household income in 1996 was $42,851. Although Hawaii's per capita income was above the US average, the cost of living on the islands is substantially higher than on the mainland.

As of 1995, 10.3% of all Hawaii residents were living below the federal poverty level.

[22]LABOR

The civilian labor force in 1996 averaged 590,900, of whom 553,200 were employed and 37,700 were unemployed, for an unemployment rate of 6.4%.

The state's Department of Labor and Industrial Relations tabulated employment and wages for major industries in 1995 as follows:

INDUSTRY	TOTAL WAGES (MILLIONS OF $)	AVERAGE
Total, including government	$14,456.3	535,750
Total, excluding government	11,099.6	428,058
Agricultural services, forestry fisheries	234.1	10,330
Construction	1,081.6	25,942
Manufacturing	494.3	16,950
Transportation, communication, and utilities	1,352.0	40,718
Wholesale trade	671.4	21,615
Retail trade	1,900.9	114,404
Finance, insurance, and real estate	1,168.3	37,041
Services	4,170.76	160,374
Government	3,356.7	107,692

Hawaii had approximately 7,000 hired farm laborers in January 1996. Unionization was slow to develop in Hawaii. After World War II, however, the International Longshoremen's and Warehousemen's Union (ILWU) organized workers in the sugar and pineapple industries and then on the docks. The Teamsters Union is also well established. Altogether, 117,100 Hawaiian workers belonged to labor unions in 1995, or about 24.6% of all employees, giving Hawaii the second highest unionization rate among the states.

[23]AGRICULTURE

Export crops—especially sugar cane and pineapple—dominate Hawaiian agriculture, which had farm receipts exceeding $491 million in 1995. The following table shows data for crops in 1995:

	ACREAGE (1,000)	VOLUME (TONS)	SALES
Sugar cane	48.5	3,953,000	127,700,000
Pineapples	20.8	345,000	87,360,000
Vegetables	6.0	44,550	38,604,000
Macadamia nuts	20.3	25,000	37,000,000

The islands of Hawaii (Maui, Molokai, Oahu, and Kauai) are the only places in the US where coffee is grown commercially; another tropical product, papaya, has also become a substantial export crop, as well as macadamia nuts and tropical flowers. Taro (coco yam) used for making poi, is also grown; production in 1996 was 5.9 million pounds, valued at $2,891,000. Banana production in 1996 was 13 million pounds (valued at $5,070,000).

[24]ANIMAL HUSBANDRY

Hawaii had an estimated 166,000 cattle and calves worth $68 million in 1997. In 1996, the estimated number of hogs and pigs was 28,000 worth $4.2 million. Poultry farms produced an estimated 186 million eggs in 1995 worth $13.5 million. Most of the eggs were for domestic consumption, making eggs one of the very few farm commodities in which the state is close to self-sufficient. Most of the state's cattle farms are in Hawaii and Maui counties.

[25]FISHING

Although expanding, Hawaii's commercial catch remains surprisingly small—29.9 million pounds, worth $59.8 million, in 1995. The most valuable commercial species are swordfish and bigeye tuna. There were 3,070 commercial fishing vessels in 1994. Sport fishing is extremely popular, with bass, bluegill, tuna, and marlin among the most sought-after varieties by the state's 7,552 sport fishing license holders in 1995/96.

26FORESTRY

As of 1997, Hawaii had 1,748,000 acres (707,940 hectares) of forestland and water reserves, with 700,000 acres (283,500 hectares) classified as commercial timberland, most of it located on the island of Hawaii. The majority of the locally grown wood is used in the manufacture of furniture, flooring, and craft items. As the sugar industry downsizes, there is an initiative to expand the forest industry by planting trees on lands formerly planted in sugar cane.

27MINING

The value of Hawaii's nonfuel mineral production in 1995 was estimated to be $106 million, an 8% increase from the $116 million reported in 1994. The State ranked 43rd nationally in the value of 1995 nonfuel mineral production. Crushed stone, construction sand and gravel, and portland cement were the principal mineral commodities produced, with values of $85,000,000, $5,700,000, and $15,100,000 respectively. Small amounts of masonry cement ($316,000) and gemstone production were also reported. Portland cement production has declined since the record high of 522,000 metric tons in 1992, valued at $54 million.

Mineral production in Hawaii is mainly for local construction usage. The rapid growth in construction throughout the state slowed somewhat in 1991, but government policy aimed at expanding the housing industry and at raising public construction levels offset the anticipated drop in private construction, resulting in a modest increase in mineral production. However, between 1993 and 1994, mineral production value decreased by 16.5%.

28ENERGY AND POWER

Devoid of indigenous fossil fuels and nuclear installations, Hawaii depends on imported petroleum for 87% of its energy needs; hydroelectric power, natural gas, windmills, geothermal energy, and sugar cane wastes contribute only 13%. In 1995, Hawaii's electric production from geothermal was 2.1%, hydro was 1.0%, wind was 0.2%, sugar/bagasse was 2.8%, municipal solid waste was 3.6%, coal was 15.8%, and methane was 0.1%. Transportation accounts for 52% of energy consumption in Hawaii, industry 29%, residences 9%, and commercial establishments 10%.

Generation of electricity accounts for 29% of the state's fuel consumption. Installed capacity reached 2.2 million kW in 1995, when sales totaled 10.56 billion kWh. The utilities' installed capacity was 1.7 million kW, and independent power producers with power contracts with the utilities owned another 0.5 million kW.

All of Hawaii's electric power plants are privately owned.

29INDUSTRY

Food and food products account for about one-third of the total annual value of shipments by manufacturers. Other major industries are clothing; stone, clay, and glass products; fabricated metals; and shipbuilding.

Hawaii's publicly held corporations include Amfac, involved in food processing, merchandising, and land development; and Castle & Cooke, which owns the Dole and Bumble Bee food product lines. Other corporations are Dillingham, which is involved in maritime industries and land development, and Brewer (owned by IU International), which produces 20% of the state's sugar and more than half the world's macadamia nuts.

In 1995, there were 75 US patents issued to Hawaii residents.

30COMMERCE

In 1996, Hawaii's personal income earnings from wholesale trade amounted to $811 million. Retail establishments had personal income from sales totaling $2.7 billion in 1996. The leading shopping centers, all on Oahu, are the Ala Moana Center, Pearlridge Center, and Kahala Mall.

Hawaii's central position in the Pacific ensures a sizable flow of goods through the Honolulu Customs District. Foreign imports to Hawaii totaled $3.2 billion in 1994, while exports exceeded $980 million. Hawaii's major trading partners are Japan for exports and Japan, Singapore and Indonesia for imports.

Hawaii had 2,202 wholesale establishments in 1992, with sales of over $8 billion. Retail sales that year totaled $11.25 billion (38th) from 7,807 establishments. Food stores, general merchandise stores and eating and drinking establishments accounted for 18.5%, 16.6%, and 16.4% of retail sales, respectively.

31CONSUMER PROTECTION

Hawaii's Office of Consumer Protection, a division of the Department of Commerce and Consumer Affairs, enforces the state's consumer protection laws and provides information regarding landlord-tenant matters.

32BANKING

In 1996, Hawaii had 15 FDIC-insured commercial banks (one nationally chartered and 14 state-chartered) with combined assets of $21.7 billion—$12.2 billion in deposits, and $13.5 billion in outstanding loans. The state's five savings institutions, three federally chartered and two state-chartered, had $6.3 billion in assets and $3.9 billion in outstanding mortgage loans in 1996.

33INSURANCE

The 4 life insurance and 45 property/casualty insurance companies headquartered in the state, as well as others authorized to do business in Hawaii, received premiums in 1995 of $2.11 billion.

Hawaii residents held about 620,000 life policies with a face value of $66.5 billion in 1995; the average family coverage was $166,000. Life insurance and annuity payouts totaled $707.8 million, of which $136.4 million was in death payments. Property and casualty companies wrote premiums in 1995 for $517.7 million in automotive liability insurance, $156.5 million in automotive physical damage insurance, and $124.3 million in homeowners' coverage. A total of $114 billion in flood insurance was in effect as of 1995.

34SECURITIES

The Honolulu Stock Exchange, established in 1898, discontinued trading on 30 December 1977.

35PUBLIC FINANCE

Development and implementation of Hawaii's biennial budget are the responsibility of the Department of Budget and Finance. The fiscal year runs from 1 July through 30 June. The following table summarizes operating revenues and expenditures for fiscal year (in millions):

	95/96
REVENUES (IN MILLIONS)	
Taxes	$2,947.0
Interest and investment income	93.5
Charges for current services	204.3
Intergovernmental revenues	1,127.9
Other revenues	178.7
TOTAL	$4,550.4

EXPENDITURES (IN MILLIONS)	95/96
General government	$ 458.6
Public safety	173.7
Conservation of natural resources	35.5
Health	284.6
Welfare	1,241.0
Education	1,015.8
Culture and recreation	68.5
Urban redevelopment and housing	41.8
Economic development and assistance	246.5
Social security and pension contribution	222.1
Highways	281.8
Other expenditures	15.9
Intergovernmental expenditures	2.8
Debt service	416.1
TOTAL	$4,504.7

The debt of the Hawaii state government at the end of fiscal 1996 was $5 billion, or $4,190 per capita.

36TAXATION

Hawaii's per capita tax burden is one of the highest in the US. The personal income tax ranges from 2% to 10%; there is a maximum capital gains tax of 7.25%. The corporate income tax is 4.4% on taxable income up to $25,000, 5.4% on taxable income over $25,000 but not over $100,000 less $250, and 6.4% on taxable income over $100,000 less $1,250. There is a broad-based general excise tax of 0.5% on wholesaling and manufacturing activities and 4% on retail sales of goods and services. Taxes on estates, fuel, liquor, and tobacco are also levied, and the property tax is a major source of county income. Hawaii's total federal tax burden in fiscal year 1995 was $6.4 billion, or $5,400 per capita.

37ECONOMIC POLICY

Business activity in Hawaii is limited by physical factors: land for development is scarce, living costs are relatively high, heavy industry is environmentally inappropriate, and there are few landbased mineral operations. On the other hand, Hawaii is well-placed as a trading and communications center, and Hawaii's roles as a defense outpost and tourist mecca seem secure for the foreseeable future. The state has actively encouraged tourism and aquaculture. A free trade zone, authorized by the US government in 1966, is managed and promoted by the Foreign Trade Zone, a division of the Department of Planning and Economic Development.

38HEALTH

The infant mortality rate in Hawaii for 1995 was 5.7 per 1,000 live births. In 1995, the birth rate was 18.5 per 1,000 population, and the death rate was 6.3 per 1,000 population. Death rates from heart diseases, cancer, cerebrovascular diseases, accidents, and suicide were all below their respective national rates in 1995. The AIDs rate in Hawaii was less than the US average (22.32 vs. 28.48 per 100,000) in 1995. Hawaii residents had the 3rd lowest coronary disease death rates in 1993 (80.9 per 100,000 population). Smoking prevalence was 20.9% among Hawaiians aged 18–30 years in 1995.

In 1995, Hawaii had 26 hospitals, including one psychiatric hospital, which together provided 4,106 beds and had a total of 129,000 hospital discharges. As of 1995 there were 2,945 physicians and surgeons, and 9,800 registered nurses in Hawaii. In 1995 there were 1045 licensed dentists. The average expense for hospital care provided in 1995 ranged from $1631 to $3149 (average $2,379) per inpatient day.

Only 10.2% of Hawaiians were uninsured in 1995.

39SOCIAL WELFARE

Some 66,900 Hawaiians received aid to families with dependent children (AFDC) in 1996, with an average monthly payment of $859. In 1996, the food stamp program had an average monthly participation of 130,344. The school lunch program served low-income students with a federal subsidy of $25.1 million. Social Security benefits averaging $709 a month were paid to 166,020 residents in 1995. The average weekly unemployment check was $270.03 in 1995.

With the enactment of the Personal Responsibility and Work Opportunity Reconciliation Act of 1996, the US government has changed the form and regulations for many of its social welfare programs; most significantly, it replaces Aid to Families with Dependent Children (AFDC), an open-ended entitlement program, with Temporary Assistance for Needy Families (TANF), a limited system of assistance funded largely through federal block grants. The reform act also impacts the food stamp program, the Supplemental Security Income program, and the child nutrition program. The law took effect on 1 July 1997 and provided $16.38 billion in block grants for fiscal years 1997–2002. The grants are to be divided among the states based on an equation involving the numbers of former AFDC recipients in each state. Because many of the bill's provisions have yet to be implemented into state-by-state policy, it was not possible to include the details of each state's programs in this edition of this work.

40HOUSING

Although statehood set off a building surge in Hawaii, housing remained in short supply throughout the 1970s and early 1980s. In 1996 there were an estimated 425,000 housing units, 385,000 of which were owner occupied. In 1996, 3,927 privately owned housing units, valued at $486 million, were authorized for construction, 2,698 of which were single-family units. The median monthly cost of housing for owners with a mortgage in 1990 (the last year for which figures are available) in the greater Honolulu area was $1,121; for owners without a mortgage, $185. The median monthly rent in greater Honolulu was $663 in 1990. Renters throughout Hawaii had a median monthly cost of $650, higher than in any other state. During fiscal year 1996, Hawaii received $116.7 million in aid from the US Department of Housing and Urban Development, including $14.6 million in community development block grants.

41EDUCATION

Education has developed rapidly in Hawaii: 92% of all state residents 25 years of age or older had completed high school by 1993.

Hawaii's single, unified public school system, the only one in the US, was founded in 1840. In the 1996/97 school year, there were 245 regular education and 3 special education public schools, with 11,668 teachers and 188,485 students. The University of Hawaii maintains three campuses—Manoa (by far the largest), Hilo, and West Oahu—with a total enrollment of 50,229 in the fall of 1993. Six community colleges enrolled 26,563 the same year. Three private colleges—Brigham Young University–Hawaii Campus, Chaminade University of Honolulu, and Hawaii Pacific College—had a combined enrollment of 8,601 in 1990.

42ARTS

The Neal Blaisdell Center in Honolulu has a 2,100-seat theater and concert hall, an 8,400-seat arena, and display rooms. Other performance facilities in Honolulu are the John F. Kennedy Theater at the University of Hawaii, the Waikiki Shell for outdoor concerts, and the Hawaii Opera Theater, which presents three operas each season. The Honolulu Symphony Orchestra performs both on Oahu and on the neighboring islands. Other Oahu cultural institutions are the Honolulu Community Theater, Honolulu Theater for Youth, Windward Theater Guild, and Polynesian Cultural Center.

From 1987 to 1991, the state of Hawaii generated $632,000 in public funds for the development of its arts programs. The NEA contributed $669,000 directly to the programs and $917,000 to the Hawaii Foundation on Culture and the Arts.

The Hawaii Youth Symphony received state funds to support its activities. The NEA continued to support the State Foundation on Culture and the arts in developing Arts education programs in 1996.

43 LIBRARIES AND MUSEUMS

The Hawaii State Public Library System (HSPLS) had 49 libraries (23 on Oahu) and 5 bookmobiles in fiscal year 1995/96, with a combined book collection of 3,517,989 and total circulation of 7,374,583. During the same year, the University of Hawaii library system had approximately 3 million volumes, five-sixths of them on the Manoa campus.

Hawaii has 37 major museums and cultural attractions. Among the most popular sites are the National Memorial Cemetery of the Pacific, USS *Arizona* Memorial at Pearl Harbor, Polynesian Cultural Center, Sea Life Park, Bernice P. Bishop Museum (specializing in Polynesian ethnology and natural history), and Honolulu Academy of Arts. Outside Oahu, the Kilauea Visitor Center (Hawaii Volcanoes National Park) and Kokee Natural History Museum (Kauai) attract the most visitors.

44 COMMUNICATIONS

Commercial inter-island wireless service began in 1901, and radiotelephone service to the mainland was established in 1931. In March 1993, 93.5% of Hawaii's 407,000 occupied housing units had telephones. Hawaii had 23 AM radio stations and 38 FM stations as of 1996, as well as 23 television stations (21 commercial and 2 educational). Two large cable television systems were operating in 1996.

45 PRESS

In 1997, Hawaii had six English-language daily newspapers: the *Honolulu Advertiser* (109,624 daily; 194,728 Sundays), *Honolulu Star-Bulletin* (74,886 daily), *Hawaii Tribune-Herald* (19,548 daily; 23,193 Sundays), *Maui News* (21,604 daily; 24,291 Sundays), *West Hawaii Today* (11,022 daily; 13,851 Sundays), and *The Garden Island* (8,101 daily; 7,838 Sundays).

46 ORGANIZATIONS

The 1992 Census of Service Industries counted 343 organizations in Hawaii, including 72 business associations; 194 civic, social, and fraternal associations; and 77 other membership organizations. The leading organization headquartered in Honolulu is the East-West Center, a vehicle of scientific and cultural exchange.

47 TOURISM, TRAVEL, AND RECREATION

Jet air service has fueled the Hawaii travel boom in recent decades. Some 243,000 travelers visited Hawaii in 1959, and more than 1,527,000 in 1969. In 1995, domestic travelers in the state spent $5,866,000 on overnight and day trips. A total of 7,740 fishing licenses and 10,863 hunting licenses were issued to sportsmen in 1995. Visitors come for scuba diving, snorkeling, swimming, fishing, and sailing; for the hula, luau, lei, and other distinctive island pleasures; for the tropical climate and magnificent scenic beauty; and for a remarkable variety of recreational facilities, including (as of 1995) 7 national parks and historic sites, 74 state parks, 626 county parks, 17 public golf courses, and 1,600 recognized surfing sites.

48 SPORTS

Hawaii has no major-league professional sports teams. Since 1982, the Aloha Bowl, a major college football postseason game played on Christmas Day, has been played in Aloha Stadium in Honolulu. The Pro Bowl (the National Football League's all-star game) is also played in Honolulu, on the weekend following the Super Bowl. Hawaii is also the site of an annual Professional Golfers' Association tournament, the yearly Duke Kahanamoku and Makaha surfing meets, and the world-famous Ironman Triathlon competition. The Transpacific Yacht Race is held biennially from California to Honolulu. Kona is the site of the International Billfish Tournament, and the Hawaii Big Game Fishing Club holds statewide tournaments each year. Football, baseball, and basketball are the leading collegiate sports.

49 FAMOUS HAWAIIANS

Hawaii's best-known federal officeholder is Daniel K. Inouye (b.1924), a US senator since 1962 and the first person of Japanese ancestry ever elected to Congress. Inouye, who lost an arm in World War II, came to national prominence during the Senate Watergate investigation of 1973, when he was a member of the Select Committee on Presidential Campaign Activities. George R. Ariyoshi (b.1926), who was elected governor of Hawaii in 1974, was the first Japanese-American to serve as chief executive of a state.

Commanding figures in Hawaiian history are King Kamehameha I (1758?–1819), who unified the islands through conquest, and Kamehameha III (Kauikeaouli, 1813–54), who transformed Hawaii into a constitutional monarchy. Two missionaries who shaped Hawaiian life and politics were Hiram Bingham (b.Vermont, 1789–1869) and Gerrit Parmele Judd (b.New York, 1803–73). Sanford B. Dole (1844–1926) and Lorrin Andrews Thurston (1858–1931) were leaders of the revolutionary movement that overthrew Queen Liliuokalani (1838–1917), established a republic, and secured annexation by the US. Dole was the republic's first president and the territory's first governor. Another prominent historical figure is Bernice Pauahi Bishop (1831–88), of the Kamehameha line, who married an American banker and left her fortune to endow the Kamehameha Schools in Honolulu; the Bishop Museum was founded by her husband in her memory. Honolulu-born Luther Halsey Gulick (1865–1918), along with his wife, Charlotte Vetter Gulick (b.Ohio, 1865–1928), founded the Camp Fire Girls.

Don Ho (b.1930) is a prominent Hawaiian-born entertainer; singer-actress Bette Midler (b.1945) was also born in Hawaii. Duke Kahanamoku (1889–1968) held the Olympic 100-meter free-style swimming record for almost 20 years.

50 BIBLIOGRAPHY

Daws, Gavan. *Shoal of Time: A History of the Hawaiian Islands.* Honolulu: University of Hawaii Press, 1974.

Fuchs, Lawrence H. *Hawaii Pono: A Social History.* San Diego: Harcourt Brace Jovanovich, 1984.

Hawaii, State of. Department of Planning and Economic Development. *The State of Hawaii Data Book 1984—A Statistical Abstract.* Honolulu, 1985.

Kuykendall, Ralph S., and A. Grove Day. *Hawaii: A History—From Polynesian Kingdom to American State.* Rev. ed. Englewood Cliffs, N.J.: Prentice-Hall, 1961.

Pratt, Richard C., and Zachary A. Smith, eds. *Politics and Public Policy in Hawaii.* Albany: State University of New York Press, 1992.

Trask, Haunani-Kay. From *A Native Daughter: Colonialism and Sovereignty in Hawaii.* Monroe, ME: Common Courage, 1993.

Wooden, Wayne S. *Return to Paradise: Continuity and Change in Hawaii.* Lanham, Md.: University Press of America, 1995.

IDAHO

State of Idaho

ORIGIN OF STATE NAME: Apparently coined by a lobbyist-politician, George M. Willing, who claimed the word came from an Indian term meaning "gem of the mountains." **NICKNAME:** The Gem State. **CAPITAL:** Boise. **ENTERED UNION:** 3 July 1890 (43d). **SONG:** "Here We Have Idaho." **MOTTO:** *Esto perpetua* (May it endure forever). **FLAG:** On a blue field with gilt fringe, the state seal appears in the center with the words "State of Idaho" on a red band below. **OFFICIAL SEAL:** With cornucopias at their feet, a female figure (holding the scales of justice in one hand and a pike supporting a liberty cap in the other) and a miner (with pick and shovel) stand on either side of a shield depicting mountains, rivers, forests, and a farm; the shield rests on a sheaf of grain and is surmounted by the head of a stag above whose antlers is a scroll with the state motto. The words "Great Seal of the State of Idaho" surround the whole. **BIRD:** Mountain bluebird. **HORSE:** Appaloosa. **FLOWER:** Syringa. **TREE:** Western white pine. **GEM:** Star garnet. **LEGAL HOLIDAYS:** New Year's Day, 1 January; Birthday of Martin Luther King, Jr., 3d Monday in January; Washington's Birthday, 3d Monday in February; Memorial Day, last Monday in May; Independence Day, 4 July; Labor Day, 1st Monday in September; Columbus Day, 2d Monday in October; Veterans Day, 11 November; Thanksgiving Day, 4th Thursday in November; Christmas Day, 25 December. **TIME:** 5 AM MST = noon GMT; 4 AM PST = non GMT.

¹LOCATION, SIZE, AND EXTENT

Situated in the northwestern US, Idaho is the smallest of the eight Rocky Mountain states and 13th in size among the 50 states.

The total area of Idaho is 83,564 sq mi (216,431 sq km), of which land comprises 82,412 sq mi (213,447 sq km) and inland water 1,152 sq mi (2,984 sq km). With a shape described variously as a hatchet, a snub-nosed pistol, and a pork chop, Idaho extends a maximum of 305 mi (491 km) E-W and 479 mi (771 km) N-S.

Idaho is bordered on the N by the Canadian province of British Columbia; on the NE by Montana; on the E by Wyoming; on the S by Utah and Nevada; and on the W by Oregon and Washington (with part of the line formed by the Snake River). The total boundary length of Idaho is 1,787 mi (2,876 km). The state's geographic center is in Custer County, SW of Challis.

²TOPOGRAPHY

Idaho is extremely mountainous. Its northern two-thirds consists of a mountain massif broken only by valleys carved by rivers and streams, and by two prairies: the Big Camas Prairie around Grangeville and the Palouse Country around Moscow. The Snake River Plain extends east–west across Idaho from Yellowstone National Park to the Boise area, curving around the southern end of the mountain mass. A verdant high-mountain area encroaches into the southeastern corner; the rest of Idaho's southern edge consists mostly of low, dry mountains. Among the most important ranges are the Bitterroot (forming the border with Montana), Clearwater (the largest range), Salmon River, Sawtooth, Lost River, and Lemhi mountains. More than 40 peaks rise above 10,000 feet (3,000 meters), of which the highest is Mt. Borah, at 12,662 feet (3,859 meters), in the Lost River Range. Idaho's lowest point is 710 feet (216 meters) near Lewiston, where the Snake River leaves the Idaho border and enters Washington.

The largest lakes are Pend Oreille (180 sq mi/466 sq km), Coeur d'Alene, and Priest in the panhandle, and Bear on the Utah border. The Snake River—one of the longest in the US, extending

1,038 mi (1,671 km) across Wyoming, Idaho, and Washington—dominates the southern part of the state. The Salmon River—the "River of No Return," a salmon-spawning stream that flows through wilderness of extraordinary beauty—separates northern from southern Idaho. The Clearwater, Kootenai, Bear, Boise, and Payette are other major rivers. There are ice caves near Shoshone and American Falls, and a large scenic cave near Montpelier. Near Arco is an expanse of lava, craters, and caves called the Craters of the Moon, another scenic attraction. At Hell's Canyon in the northernmost part of Adams County, the Snake River cuts the deepest gorge in North America, 7,913 feet (2,412 meters) deep.

³CLIMATE

The four seasons are distinct in all parts of Idaho, but not simultaneous. Spring comes earlier and winter later to Boise and Lewiston, which are protected from severe weather by nearby mountains and call themselves "banana belts." Eastern Idaho has a more continental climate, with more extreme temperatures; climatic conditions there and elsewhere vary with the elevation. Mean temperatures in Boise range from 29°F (–2°C) in January to 74°F (23°C) in July. The record low, –60°F (–51°C), was set at Island Park Dam on 16 January 1943; the record high, 118°F (48°C), at Orofino on 28 July 1934. The corresponding extremes for Boise are –23°F (–31°C) and 111°F (44°C).

Humidity is low throughout the state. Precipitation in southern Idaho averages 13 in (33 cm) per year; in the north, over 30 in (76 cm). Boise gets more than 21 in (53 cm) of snow per year, with much greater accumulations in the mountains.

⁴FLORA AND FAUNA

With 10 life zones extending from prairie to mountaintop, Idaho has some 3,000 native plants. Characteristic evergreens are Douglas fir and western white pine (the state tree); oak/mountain mahogany, juniper/piñon, ponderosa pine, and spruce/fir constitute the other main forest types. Syringa is the state flower. MacFarlane's four-o'clock is listed as endangered.

Classified as game mammals are the elk, moose, white-tailed and mule deer, pronghorn antelope, bighorn sheep, mountain goat, black bear, mountain lion, cottontail, and pigmy rabbit. Several varieties of pheasant, partridge, quail, and grouse are the main game birds, and there are numerous trout, salmon, bass, and whitefish species in Idaho's lakes and streams. Rare animal species include the wolverine, kit fox, and pika. The grizzly bear is listed as threatened, while the woodland caribou, gray (timber) wolf, bald eagle, Arctic and American peregrine falcons, and whooping crane are endangered. There were six national wildlife refuges covering 133,456 acres (54,009 hectares) in the early 1990s.

5ENVIRONMENTAL PROTECTION

The environmental protection movement in Idaho dates from 1897, when President Grover Cleveland established the Bitterroot Forest Preserve, encompassing much of the northern region. In the early 1930s, the US Forest Service set aside some 3 million acres (1.2 million hectares) of Idaho's roadless forestland as primitive areas. The Taylor Grazing Act of 1934 regulated grazing on public lands, providing for the first time some relief from the overgrazing that had transformed much Idaho grassland into sagebrush desert. Thirty years later, Idaho Senator Frank Church was floor sponsor for the bill creating the National Wilderness System, which now contains most of the primitive areas set aside earlier. Many miles of Idaho streams are now in the Wild and Scenic Rivers System, another congressional accomplishment in which Senator Church played a leading role. In 1970, Governor Cecil Andrus (later, US secretary of the interior) was elected partly on a platform of environmental protection.

The Department of Health and Welfare's Division of Environment is responsible for enforcing environmental standards. Air quality improved greatly between 1978 and 1997, following the passage of federal regulations strengthening the Clean Air Act. Vehicle emissions were responsible for high carbon monoxide levels in the Boise area in the late 1970s and 1980s. Emissions have dropped to the point that no carbon monoxide violations have occurred for several years.

Water quality is generally good. Most of the existing problems stem from runoff from agricultural lands. Water quality is rated as only fair in the Upper Snake River Basin and in the Southwest Basin around Boise, and as poor in the Bear River Basin, partly because of municipal effluents from Soda Springs and Preston. The state has 386,000 acres of wetlands. The Idaho Department of Fish and Game has implemented plans to acquire privately owned wetlands deemed to be in danger. The plan runs from 1991 to 2005.

Since 1953, nuclear waste has been buried at the Idaho National Engineering Laboratory west of Idaho Falls or discharged in liquid form into the underground aquifer; some isotopes are migrating toward the boundaries of the site. Tailings from a former uranium-ore milling operation near Lowman are a potential health hazard. A top-priority site for hazardous-waste cleanup is Bunker Hill Mining at Smelterville; two sites in Pocatello are also considered candidates for cleanup. In 1995, the state had 10 hazardous waste sites.

6POPULATION

Idaho's population at the 1990 census was 1,006,749, 42nd among the 50 states. The 6.7% population increase between 1980 and 1990 was a significant drop from the 32.4% increase of the previous decade, even though in 1990 only 52% of the population had been born in Idaho. By 1996, population was estimated at 1,189,251 (an 18.1% increase from 1990). The population projection for 2000, however, drops to 1,008,000.

As of 1990, the ratio of males to females in Idaho was virtually equal. The median age was 31.5, and the state 57.4%

"urban" —although no part of Idaho except Boise is genuinely urban, and even Boise does not have much of a central city. Boise's estimated 1994 population was 145,987, a 16% increase since the 1990 census; Pocatello was next with 49,634; Idaho Falls had 49,928; Nampa, 35,333; Lewiston, 30,097, and Twin Falls, 31,568, Boise's metropolitan area (Ada County) had an estimated 360,341 inhabitants in 1995.

7ETHNIC GROUPS

The 1990 census included 14,000 American Indians. There are five reservations; the most extensive is that of the Nez Percé in northern Idaho with an estimated population of 1,839 in 1995.

There is a very small population of black Americans (about 3,000 in 1990) and a somewhat larger number (9,000) of Asian-Pacific peoples, over 3,800 of them Japanese. There were 53,000 persons of Hispanic origin (35,591 of Mexican heritage) and a very visible Basque community in the Boise area, with an organization devoted to preserving their language and culture.

The foreign-born (28,905) accounted for about 2.8% of Idaho's population in 1990. The three most common countries of birth for foreign-born Idahoans were Mexico, 12,343; Canada, 3,349; and Germany, 1,579.

8LANGUAGES

In the general word stock, only a few place-names, such as Nampa, Pocatello, and Benewah, reflect the presence of Idaho Indians. In Idaho, English reflects a merger of Northern and North Midland features, with certain Northern pronunciations marking the panhandle. More than 93% of the people 5 years old or older spoke only English in the home in 1990. The number of persons speaking other languages at home included the following:

Spanish	37,081	French	2,839
German	5,148	various Native American	2,327

9RELIGIONS

Roman Catholic and Presbyterian missionaries first came to Idaho between 1820 and 1840. The church of Jesus Christ of Latter-day Saints (Mormon) has been the leading religion in Idaho since 1860; with about a quarter of the population, the number of Mormons in Idaho is 2d only to that in Utah. Catholicism predominates north of Boise. According to 1990 estimates, Idaho has about 268,060 Mormons, 13,303 members of various Lutheran denominations, and 20,979 United Methodists. In 1990 there were 232,780 Roman Catholics and an estimated 320 Jews.

10TRANSPORTATION

In 1995, Idaho had 59,783 mi (96,170 km) of public roads and streets, 94% of them rural. The major east–west highways are I-90, I-84 (formerly I-80N), and US 12; US 95, Idaho 55, US 93, and I-15 are among the most traveled north–south routes. Idaho had 1,043,074 registered vehicles—including 586,566 automobiles, 453,147 trucks, and 3,361 buses—in 1995, when there were 805,911 licensed drivers. In 1995, about 34% of all highway expenditures ($431.5 million) went for maintenance. Boise has the only mass transit system—a bus line.

There were 2,023 rail mi (3,031 km) used by the seven railroads operating within the state in 1995. Among the two Class I railroads, the Union Pacific Railroad serves southern Idaho, and the Burlington Northern crosses the panhandle. Amtrak provides limited passenger service to Pocatello, Boise, Shoshone, Nampa, and Sandpoint on two Chicago–Seattle trains. Boise's modern airport—the busiest of the state's 183 airports, 31 heliports, and 5 seaplane bases, and 1 stolport—enplaned 901,538 passengers during 1994. Other transport facilities are 6,100 mi (9,800 km) of pipeline, carrying virtually all the natural gas and most of the gasoline consumed in Idaho, and a Snake

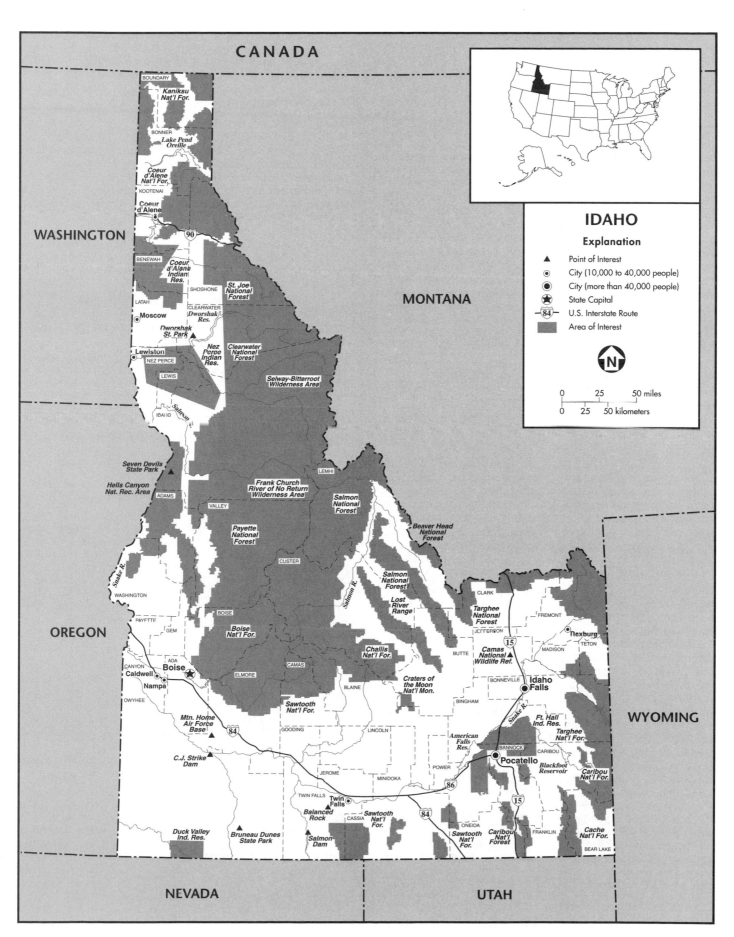

CANADA

WASHINGTON

MONTANA

OREGON

WYOMING

NEVADA

UTAH

BOUNDARY

Kaniksu Nat'l For.

BONNER

Lake Pend Oreille

Coeur d'Alene Nat'l For.

KOOTENAI

Coeur d'Alene

BENEWAH

Coeur d'Alene Indian Res.

SHOSHONE

St. Joe National Forest

LATAH

CLEARWATER

Dworshak Res.

Moscow

Dworshak St. Park ▲

Nez Perce Indian Res.

Clearwater National Forest

Lewiston

NEZ PERCE

LEWIS

Selway-Bitterroot Wilderness Area

IDAHO

Salmon R.

LEMHI

Seven Devils State Park ▲

Hells Canyon Nat. Rec. Area

ADAMS

Frank Church River of No Return Wilderness Area

VALLEY

Salmon National Forest

Beaver Head National Forest

Payette National Forest

CUSTER

Salmon National Forest

Lost River Range

CLARK

Targhee National Forest ▲

FREMONT

JEFFERSON

Rexburg

MADISON

TETON

GEM

BOISE

Challis Nat'l For.

Camas National Wildlife Ref. ▲

BONNEVILLE

Idaho Falls

Boise Nat'l For.

ELMORE

CAMAS

BUTTE

Craters of the Moon Nat'l Mon.

BINGHAM

Ft. Hall Ind. Res.

Targhee Nat'l For.

WASHINGTON

PAYETTE

Boise

ADA

Caldwell

Nampa

CANYON

OWYHEE

Mtn. Home Air Force Base ▲

Sawtooth Nat'l For.

BLAINE

GOODING

LINCOLN

American Falls Res.

CARIBOU

BANNOCK

Pocatello

Blackfoot Reservoir

Caribou Nat'l For.

POWER

C.J. Strike Dam ▲

JEROME

MINIDOKA

TWIN FALLS

Twin Falls

Balanced Rock

Sawtooth Nat'l For.

CASSIA

Duck Valley Ind. Res.

Bruneau Dunes State Park ▲

▲ *Salmon Dam*

ONEIDA

Caribou Nat'l Forest

Sawtooth Nat'l For.

FRANKLIN

Cache Nat'l For.

BEAR LAKE

Snake R.

Snake R.

IDAHO

Explanation

▲ Point of Interest

⊙ City (10,000 to 40,000 people)

◉ City (more than 40,000 people)

★ State Capital

─84─ U.S. Interstate Route

▨ Area of Interest

Ⓝ

0   25   50 miles

0   25   50 kilometers

River port at Lewiston that links Idaho, Montana, and the Dakotas with the Pacific via 464 mi (747 km) of navigable waterways in Washington State.

11HISTORY

Human beings came to the land now known as Idaho about 15,000 years ago. Until 1805, only Indians and their ancestors had ever lived in the area, eking out a bare living from seeds and roots, insects, small animals, and what fishing and big-game hunting they could manage. At the time of white penetration, Shoshone and Northern Paiute lived in the south, as well as two linked tribal families, the Salishan and Shapwailutan (including the Nez Percé, who greeted the Lewis and Clark expedition when it entered Idaho in 1805; it was their food and canoes that helped these explorers reach the Columbia River and the Pacific).

Fur trappers—notably David Thompson, Andrew Henry, and Donald Mackenzie—followed within a few years. Missionaries came later; Henry Harmon Spalding founded a mission among the Nez Percé in 1836. The Oregon Trail opened in 1842, but for two decades, people merely crossed Idaho over it; virtually no one settled. In 1860, 14 years after Idaho had officially become US land through the Oregon Treaty with the United Kingdom, Mormons from Utah established Franklin, Idaho's first permanent settlement, and began farming. Gold was discovered that summer in northern Idaho; a gold rush, lasting several years, led directly to the organizing of Idaho Territory on 10 July 1863.

Boise became the capital of Idaho in 1864, and the following decade saw the inauguration of telegraph service, the linking of Franklin with the transcontinental railway, and the birth of the territory's first daily newspaper. Idaho's population nearly doubled between 1870 and 1880, and the pressure of white settlement impinging on Indian hunting and fishing grounds touched off a series of wars in the late 1870s. The most famous of those was the Nez Percé War, culminating in Chief Joseph's surrender in Montana on 5 October 1877 and in the subsequent confinement of Idaho Indians to reservations.

Lead and silver were discovered in south-central Idaho in 1880 and in the panhandle in 1884, touching off yet another stampede of would-be miners. With a population of 88,548 in 1890, Idaho was eligible to enter the Union, becoming the 43d state on 3 July. Statehood came to Idaho at a time of turmoil, when Mormons and non-Mormons were contending for political influence, the Populist Party was challenging the established political organizations, and violent labor disputes were sweeping the mining districts. In 1907, in a case that grew out of the labor conflict, William "Big Bill" Haywood (defended by Clarence Darrow) was acquitted on charges that he conspired to assassinate former Idaho Governor Frank Steunenberg, murdered on 30 December 1905.

From 1895 onward, federal land and irrigation projects fostered rapid economic growth. The modern timber industry began in 1906 with the completion of one of the nation's largest sawmills at Potlatch. By World War I, agriculture was a leading enterprise; however, a farm depression of the 1920s lasted up to the Great Depression of the 1930s and ended only with the onset of World War II. After the war, an agro-industrial base was established, with fertilizers and potato processing leading the way. Idaho has also developed a thriving tourist industry, with large numbers of vacationers visiting the Sun Valley ski resort and the state's other scenic areas. Population expansion and the push for economic growth have collided with a new interest in the environment, creating controversies over land-use planning, mineral development, and water supply and dam construction. On 5 June 1976, the new, earth-filled Teton Dam in eastern Idaho collapsed, flooding the region and, in the process, claiming 10 lives and causing at least $400 million in damage to property and livestock.

Governor Cecil Andrus was a strong advocate of environmental preservation for over two decades. In the 1990s a major environmental issue has been nuclear waste contamination. Idaho celebrated its 100th year of statehood in 1990.

12STATE GOVERNMENT

Idaho's 1889 constitution, amended 102 times as of 1983, continues to govern the state today. The bicameral legislature, consisting of a 35-seat senate and a 70-member house of representatives, regularly meets for 60–90 days a year; special sessions, summoned by the governor, last 20 days. All legislators serve two-year terms. In 1995 the legislative salary was $12,360. The executive branch is headed by seven elected officials: the governor and lieutenant governor (who run separately), secretary of state, attorney general, auditor, treasurer, and superintendent of public instruction. All serve four-year terms. The governor, who must be at least 30 years of age and must have been a state resident for at least two years prior to election, can sign or veto a bill or let it become law without his signature. Vetoes may be overridden by a two-thirds vote of each house. In 1996 the governor's salary was $85,000.

The state constitution may be amended with the consent of two-thirds of each house and a majority of the voters at the next general election. Provisions for initiative, referendum, and recall were added by amendment to the state constitution in 1912 but not implemented by the legislature until 1933. The initiative procedure was employed in 1974 to pass the Sunshine Act, mandating registration by lobbyists and campaign financing disclosures by candidates for public office. An Idaho voter must be at least 18 years of age, a US citizen, and a resident of the state for at least 30 days.

13POLITICAL PARTIES

Registered voters numbered 502,740 in 1994; there is no party registration. Idahoans usually vote Republican in presidential elections, but sometimes elect Democrats to Congress or the statehouse. While the state has become increasingly conservative politically since the early 1960s, Democrats have been elected governor since 1970. The dominant Republican in the 20th century was US Senator William E. Borah, an isolationist-progressive who opposed US entry into the League of Nations but advocated world disarmament and supported prohibition, the graduated income tax, and some New Deal reforms; as chairman of the Senate Foreign Relations Committee from 1924 to 1940, he was one of the most influential legislators in the nation.

One measure of the conservatism of Idaho voters in the 1960s and 1970s was the showing by George Wallace's American Independent Party in 1968 (12.6% of the total vote) and his American Party in 1972 (9.3%, the highest of any state). In 1996 Republican Bob Dole received 52% of the vote, while Democrat Bill Clinton won 34% and Independent Ross Perot captured 13%.

A Democrat, Cecil Andrus, served four terms as governor, retiring in 1994. In winning the governor's office in November 1994, Republican Phil Batt ended 24 years of Democratic control of that office. Following the November 1996 elections, the state legislature had 30 Republicans and 5 Democrats in the state senate, and 59 Republicans and 11 Democrats in the state house. Idaho's US Representatives, both re-elected in 1996, were both Republicans, Helen Chenoweth and Mike Crapo. Its senators, Larry Craig, re-elected in 1996, and Dirk Kempthorne, elected in 1992, were also both Republicans. In 1992, there were two Hispanics holding public office, and in 1995 there were 32 women serving in the state legislature and in elective executive office.

Idaho Presidential Vote by Major Political Parties, 1948–96

YEAR	ELECTORAL VOTE	IDAHO WINNER	DEMOCRAT	REPUBLICAN
1948	4	*Truman (D)	107,370	101,514
1952	4	*Eisenhower (R)	395,081	180,707
1956	4	*Eisenhower (R)	105,868	166,979
1960	4	Nixon (R)	138,853	161,597
1964	4	*Johnson (D)	148,920	143,557
1968	4	*Nixon (R)	389,273	165,369
1972	4	*Nixon (R)	380,826	199,384
1976	4	Ford (R)	126,549	204,151
1980	4	*Reagan (R)	110,192	290,699
1984	4	*Reagan (R)	108,510	297,523
1988	4	*Bush (R)	147,272	253,881
1992**	4	Bush (R)	137,013	202,645
1996**	4	Dole (R)	165,443	256,595

* Won US presidential election
** Independent candidate Ross Perot received 130,395 votes in 1992 and 62,518 votes in 1996.

14LOCAL GOVERNMENT

As of 1992, Idaho had 44 counties, 199 municipal governments, 115 school districts, and 728 special districts or authorities. Most counties elect three commissioners and other officers, usually including an assessor, treasurer, coroner, and sheriff. Nearly all cities have an elected mayor and council of 4 to 6 members. School districts have elected board members.

15STATE SERVICES

Executive agencies concerned with education are the State Board of Education and the Department of Education. Under the heading of human resources are the Departments of Health and Welfare, Employment, Correction, and Law Enforcement, which includes the Idaho State Police. Under the general rubric of natural resources come the Department of Lands, Water Resources, Fish and Game, and Parks and Recreation. Self-governing agencies (7 commodity commissions and 15 professional licensing and regulating boards and commissions) and the Departments of Agriculture, Finance, Insurance, Labor and Industrial Services, and Transportation oversee economic development and regulation. Within the Executive Office of the Governor are a number of funds, divisions, boards, commissions, and other bodies.

16JUDICIAL SYSTEM

Idaho's highest court, the supreme court, consists of five justices, each elected at large on a nonpartisan ballot, to a six-year term; the justice with the shortest remaining term automatically becomes chief justice. There is a three-member court of appeals. The district court, with 34 judges, is the main trial court in civil and criminal matters, while magistrates' courts handle traffic, misdemeanor, and minor civil cases and preliminary hearings in felony cases. Like supreme court justices, appeals court justices and district court judges are elected by nonpartisan ballot, for six years and four years, respectively. Magistrates are appointed by a commission and run for four-year terms in the first general election succeeding the 18-month period followed appointment. In 1996, there were 2,756 practicing attorneys in the state.

Idaho's crime rates are low in almost every category. The total rate in 1994 was 4,077 per 100,000, which included 285 for violent crime and 3,792 for property crime. The rate for the Boise metropolitan area was 7,416 per 100,000. A few murderers have been hanged, but none since the 1950s. The state permits execution by lethal injection, and since 1930 has executed 4 persons. In 1995 there were 19 persons under sentence of death. The prison population increased by over 60% from 1990 to 1995. In 1991 there were 2,138 inmates in state and federal prisons, or 206 prisoners per 100,000 in population.

17ARMED FORCES

Mountain Home Air Force Base, about 50 mi (80 km) southeast of Boise, has 3,909 officers and enlisted personnel. In 1996, 4,009 active duty military personnel were stationed in Idaho. Defense contract awards to Idaho firms in fiscal year 1996 totaled $132 million. Idaho casualties in recent US wars include 1,419 in World War II, 132 in Korea, and 187 in Viet Nam. As of 1 July 1996, 111,000 veterans of military service were living in Idaho, including from World War I, fewer than 500; World War II, 30,000; the Korean conflict, 18,000; the Viet Nam era, 36,000; and the Persian Gulf War, 9,000. Benefits paid to Idaho veterans totaled $161 million in fiscal year 1996.

The Army Reserve and National Guard had 5,804 personnel in 1996; the Air National Guard and Reserve had 1,697 that same year. In 1993, the Idaho State Police employed 189 full-time sworn officers, or two per 10,000 residents.

18MIGRATION

Idaho's first white immigrants came from Utah, California, and Oregon in the early 1860s. By the end of the Civil War, the chief sources of immigrants were the southern and border states. Homesteaders from the Midwest, Utah, and Scandinavia arrived at the end of the 19th century.

Since 1960, immigrants have come largely from California. Idaho suffered a net loss from migration of 109,000 persons between 1940 and 1970, but had a net gain of 110,000 persons in the 1970s. During the 1980s, Idaho had a net loss of 28,000 persons from migration. Between 1990 and 1996, the state had net gains of 111,704 in domestic migration, and 11,622 in international migration. In 1996, 1,825 immigrants from foreign countries arrived in Idaho. Just under 50% of residents age 5 and older lived in a different house in 1990 than they did in 1985; of those, 31% had moved to another state.

19INTERGOVERNMENTAL COOPERATION

Idaho participates with Utah and Wyoming in the Bear River Compact; with Oregon, Washington, and Alaska in the Pacific Marine Fisheries Compact; with Wyoming in the Snake River Compact; with Washington, Oregon, Idaho, and Montana in the Northwest Power Planning Council; and in numerous other interstate compacts. Federal aid in fiscal year 1996 was estimated at $887 million.

20ECONOMY

Fur trapping was Idaho's earliest industry. Agriculture and mining began around 1860, with agriculture dominating since the 1870s. Timber became important after 1900, tourism and manufacturing—especially food processing and forest products—after 1945. Currently, agriculture, mining, forest products, and food processing are Idaho's largest industries.

The Idaho economy prospered in the 1970s. Machinery and transportation equipment manufacturing grew 20% between 1970 and 1980, and services expanded 7.5%. The early 1980s, in contrast, brought a national recession in which Idaho lost 8% of its employment base. Recovery, which required a restructuring of Idaho's mining, forest products, and agricultural industries, has come slowly. Some industries posted significant gains in employment in the 1980s. Chemical manufacturing employment grew 36% in the early and mid-1980s, and jobs in the paper industry increased 30%. Travel and tourism employment rose 35% between 1982 and 1991, and high-tech jobs increased 50% between 1986 and 1990. The labor force in other sectors of the economy, however, has permanently shrunk. Modernization in lumber and wood products eliminated hundreds of jobs. Mining employment has fluctuated, dropping in the early 1980s, improving in the late 1980s, and declining again in the early nineties.

Idaho's gross state product, which totaled $24,185 million in 1994, consisted of private goods–producing industries, $7,853 million; private services–producing industries, $13,002 million; and government, $3,330 million.

Idaho enjoys the highest rate of growth in the nation in wages and employment, ranging from 3.3% during the 1991 recession to 5.3% in 1989. The growth was distributed fairly evenly across industries. Electronics continued to grow, as evidenced by expansions announced by Hewlett Packard, Micron, and Zilog. Construction employment increased 10.4% in 1992, although its growth rate dropped to 4.8% in 1993. In contrast, mining jobs dropped 25% in 1992.

Disputes with the federal government over the management of federal lands remain central to discussion of Idaho's economic policy, as the federal government owns 60% of Idaho's public land. The disputes center on such matters as grazing fees, costs of water from government projects, species protection, and mining regulations.

In 1996, there were 5,426 filings for bankruptcy, up 31.7% from the previous year.

21INCOME
Per capita personal income in Idaho in 1996 was $19,539, 43d in the US. Per capita personal income increased 3.6% between 1995 and 1996, compared to 4.5% for the nation. Total disposable personal income rose from $13.6 billion in 1990 to $19.9 billion in 1996.

Median household income in 1996 was $32,676, when 14.5% of all state residents were below the federal poverty level.

22LABOR
Of Idaho's civilian labor force of 613,600 at the beginning of 1997, the Boise area accounted for 34%. Unemployment, which reached a high of 10.7% in October 1982, averaged only 5.2% in 1996, below the national average of 5.4%.

At the end of 1996, 2,900 Idaho residents worked in mining; 33,00 in construction; 74,300 in manufacturing; 23,800 in transportation, communications, and public utilities; 131,000 in wholesale and retail trade; 25,500 in finance, insurance, and real estate; 117,800 in services; and 99,100 in government. In 1991, there were 39,790 farmers in the state.

Idaho was a pioneer in establishing the eight-hour day and in outlawing yellow-dog contracts. By 1995 there were some 37,700 union members in Idaho, accounting for 8.1% of all workers. Unionization among private sector workers in manufacturing was 11.6%. In 1958, Idaho voters rejected right-to-work legislation; Governor John Evans vetoed similar legislation in 1982, but Idaho is now a right-to-work state.

23AGRICULTURE
Receipts from farm marketings totaled $3.16 billion in 1995 (22d in the US); farm industry income was about $1.95 billion. As of 1996, Idaho led the US in potato production; was 2d in sugar beets and barley; 3d in hops, peppermint oil, and spearmint oil; and 4th in dry edible beans.

Development of the russet potato in the 1920s gave Idaho its most famous crop. In 1996, the state produced 139,960,000 hundredweight of potatoes (28.1% of the US total); some 90% were grown on about 110,000 acres (45,000 hectares) of irrigated land on the Snake River plain. About three-fourths of the crop is processed into frozen french fries, instant mashed potatoes, and other products. Other leading crops were hay, 4,760,000 tons, valued at $425,880,000; wheat, 119,200,000

bushels (6th), $471,520,000; barley, 53,290,000 bushels (2d), $162,535,000; and sugar beets, 4,545,000 tons (2d) $4,545,000.

As of 1996, Idaho had 13.5 million acres (5.5 million hectares) in farms, 26% of the state's land area; an estimated 22,000 farms, (including ranches) averaged about 614 acres (248 hectares). Over 3.2 million acres (1.3 hectares) of land were irrigated. Idaho had the highest proportion of irrigated farm land, at 63.7% of all land used for farming in 1992.

24ANIMAL HUSBANDRY
In 1997, there was an estimated 1.75 million cattle and calves worth around $1 billion. In 1996, Idaho had an estimated 33,000 hogs and pigs worth around $3 million. Idaho had an estimated 232,000 dairy cows, which produced 4.2 billion lb of milk in 1995. In 1995, Idaho produced an estimated 1.9 million lb of chicken that sold for $57,000 and the state produced an estimated 238 million eggs worth $12 million. Also during 1995, the state produced an estimated 25.8 million lb of sheep and lambs, which grossed $18.25 million for Idaho farmers. Shorn wool production in 1995 totaled an estimated 2.16 million lb.

25FISHING
In 1995/96, there were some 420,002 licensed sport fishermen catching trout along with salmon, steelhead, bass, and 32 other game-fish species. Idaho is a leading producer of farm-raised trout. Idaho hatcheries shipped 7.3 million fish and 4 million fish eggs in 1995/96, mostly trout, salmon, and steelhead. The US Fish and Wildlife Service apportioned over $3.4 million for sport fish restoration programs in 1995/96.

26FORESTRY
As of 1993, Idaho forests covered 21,727,000 acres (8,793,000 hectares), or 41% of the land area, with 14,474,000 acres (5,858,000 hectares) classified as commercial timberland. Of the total forest area in 1992, the federal government controlled 79%; state government, 5%; and private owners, 16%. National forest system lands in Idaho totaled 21,674,000 acres (8,771,000 hectares) in 1991. Idaho forests are used increasingly for ski areas, hunting, and other recreation, as well as for timber and pulp. The total lumber production is nearly 2 billion board feet annually, almost all softwoods. Shipments of lumber and wood products in 1995 were valued at $2,380 million.

27MINING
The estimated value of nonfuel mineral production for Idaho in 1995 was $399 million, an increase of 15% from that of 1994. Industrial minerals, led by phosphate rock and construction sand and gravel, accounted for almost 58% of the state's nonfuel mineral production value, ranking Idaho 32d nationally. In 1995 Idaho was the only state to produce vanadium ore and antimony; first of two garnet-producing states; second in phosphate; third in silver, lead and pumice; fourth in molybdenum; sixth in feldspar; eighth in zinc; and ninth in copper. Of 14 gold-producing states, Idaho ranked 10th in 1995. In 1995, the state's production of sand and gravel for construction was 14.7 million metric tons valued at $49.2 million, and crushed stone, 4 million metric tons ($19.4 million).

Molybdenum had the largest single effect on the value of Idaho's overall nonfuel mineral production from 1992 to 1995. In late 1992, production ceased at the state's only molybdenum mine at Thompson Creek, but the mine reopened in mid-1994. Molybdenum production and value increased by 140% for 1994 to 1995, the first full year of production since 1991.

28ENERGY AND POWER
Installed electrical capacity exceeded 2.37 million kW in 1996; production in 1995 (95.25% hydroelectric) totaled 10 billion

kWh. About half of Idaho's irrigation depends on electric pumping, and electrical energy consumption regularly exceeds the state's supply. Large dams used to generate electricity include the Dworshak on the north fork of the Clearwater, the Anderson Ranch on the south fork of the Boise, and the Brownlee on the Snake at the Oregon border.

Idaho's large size, widespread and relatively rural population, and lack of public transportation foster reliance on motor vehicles and imported petroleum products. Natural gas is also imported. Hot water from thermal springs is used to heat buildings in Boise.

29INDUSTRY

Resource industries—food processing, chemical manufacturing, and lumber production—form the backbone of manufacturing in Idaho. Value added by manufacture increased from $1.4 billion in 1977 to $3.9 billion in 1991. In 1995, the value of shipments by major industries was $16.484 billion, of which, food and food products contributed $3.603 billion; lumber and wood products contributed $2.380 billion; industrial machinery and equipment contributed $3.451 billion; and electronic and other electric equipment contributed $4.315 billion.

Nonelectrical machinery increased by over 500% in value added between 1977 and 1983; during this period, many northern California computer companies, including Hewlett Packard, opened or expanded plants in Idaho. Other major manufacturers of electronic equipment include Micron Technology (Boise), Advanced Input Devices (Coeur d'Alene), Gould Electronics (Pocatello), and Zilog (Nampa).

Ore-Ida Foods is a leading potato processor, and J. R. Simplot engages in food processing and fertilizer production. Boise Cascade (with headquarters at Boise), Potlatch, and Louisiana-Pacific dominate the wood-products industry. Morrison-Knudsen, a diversified engineering and construction company that also has forest-products interests, has its headquarters in Boise.

In 1995, there were 363 US patents issued to Idaho residents.

30COMMERCE

In 1992 Idaho's wholesale establishments registered nearly $8.9 million in sales. Durable goods accounted for 38.65 of wholesale sales. Retail sales in 1992 totaled $7.7 billion (42D), with automotive dealers accounting for 25% and general merchandise stores, 11.6%. Boise is the headquarters of the Albertson's supermarket chain, a major retailer. About two-thirds of Idaho's wheat crop and a substantial amount of its fertilizer, peas, lentils, beans, potatoes, and barley are exported abroad. Natural gas and sulfate are imported from Canada in significant quantities. Foreign exports of goods originating within Idaho were valued at $1,570.6 million in 1996 (41st in the US).

31CONSUMER PROTECTION

The Idaho attorney general's office is responsible for investigating consumer complaints and enforcing most consumer laws. The Department of Finance administers the Idaho Credit Code and resolves consumer credit complaints under that law. The legislature has enacted Idaho's consumer protection, telephone solicitation, and pay-per-telephone call acts for purposes of protecting both consumers and businesses against unfair or deceptive acts in trade and commerce, and to provide efficient and economical procedures to secure such protection. The Idaho Consumer Protection Unit seeks to fulfill this charge through education, mediation, and enforcement efforts.

32BANKING

As of 1996, 18 insured commercial banks (14 state-chartered) had $12.9 billion in assets, $9.4 billion in deposits, and $9.0 billion in outstanding loans. The state's four savings institutions had nearly $570 million in assets in 1996 and $336 million in outstanding mortgage loans at the start of 1996.

33INSURANCE

At the beginning of 1997, 13 property/casualty and 5 life insurance companies had home offices in Idaho. A total of 7,117,848 policies in effect at the end of 1995 had a combined value of $41.7 billion; payouts reached $507.6 million, including $110.3 million in death payments. Property and liability companies wrote $174.7 million for automobile physical damage insurance, $273.7 million for automobile liability insurance, and $86.1 million for homeowners' coverage in 1995.

34SECURITIES

Although Idaho has no stock exchanges, there were nevertheless 1,110 broker/dealer firms and 35,314 salesmen licensed to sell securities in the state as of 31 March 1997. As of the same date, 364 investment advisor firms and 2,275 investment advisor representatives held licenses allowing them to provide advice to Idaho residents relating to securities investments.

35PUBLIC FINANCE

Idaho's annual budget, prepared by the Division of Financial Management, is submitted by the governor to the legislature for amendment and approval. The fiscal year runs from 1 July to 30 June.

The following table summarizes proposed revenues and expenditures for 1997/98 as contained in the legislature's appropriation:

REVENUES	
Personal income tax	$ 732.2 million
Corporate income tax	123.3 million
Sales tax	514.3 million
Other general revenues	78.6 million
Federal funds	387.2 million
Dedicated funds	508.0 million
Other funds	470.4 million
TOTAL	$3,315.5 billion

EXPENDITURES	
Public schools	$ 1,042.2 billion
Other education	408.6 million
Health and social services	782.9 million
Public safety	194.3 million
Natural resources	164.3 million
General government	95.4 million
Economic development & infrastructure	617.2 million
TOTAL	$3,304.9 billion

The state has no outstanding general obligation debt. There are three independent public entities created by the state which have outstanding debt. These entities and their respective debts as of 31 December 1996 are: Idaho Housing Agency with $1,113.5 billion; Idaho Health Facilities Authority with $256.2 million; and Idaho State Building Authority with $51.2 million.

36TAXATION

Idaho's original revenue base of property taxes and a variety of local business license fees has been essentially abandoned. The state instituted an income tax in 1931 and a sales tax in 1965; as of 1994, the personal income tax ranged from 2% to 8.2%, the corporate income tax was 8.0%, and the general sales tax was 5%. The state also levies taxes on inheritances, alcoholic beverages, cigarettes and tobacco products, motor fuels, insurance premiums, hotel/motel rooms and campgrounds, ores mined and extracted, oil and gas produced, and electric utilities. Property taxes are the only major source of local revenue. Per capita state taxes came to only $1,486.40 in 1995.

In 1995, Idaho paid federal taxes totaling $5.1 billion and received federal outlays of $5.3 billion, a highly favorable ratio.

37ECONOMIC POLICY

The Division of Economic and Community Affairs, within the office of the governor, seeks to widen markets for Idaho products and goods and services, encourage film production in the state, attract new business and industry to Idaho, expand and enhance existing enterprises, and promote the state travel industry. Incentives for investment include conservative state fiscal policies and a pro-business regulatory climate. Idaho offers industrial revenue bonds to assist companies with the financing of land, buildings, and equipment used in manufacturing. The state extends loans to businesses seeking to start up or expand and for energy conservation improvements. To help distressed areas, there are matching grants for economic development as well as training in strategic planning and economic diversification techniques. Cities and counties may also apply for community development block grants.

38HEALTH

Idaho's infant mortality rate of 6.1 per 1,000 births was below the national rate for 1995. The live birthrate in 1995 was 15.5 per 1,000 population. The death rate was 7.3 in 1995. There were 970 legal abortions in Idaho in 1995, with 55 abortions performed per 1,000 live births. (In 1992, the latest year for which nationwide data are available, Idaho's ration of 80 abortions per 1,000 live births was second lowest after Wyoming.) Death rates for accidents and adverse effects, motor vehicle accidents, and suicide were above the respective national rates in 1995. Death rates for heart disease, cancer, and cerebrovascular diseases were below their corresponding national rates in 1995. The high birthrate and low death rate reflect Idaho's younger-than-average population.

In all, 52 hospitals had 3,142 licensed beds in 1995; with 105,404 admissions; community hospital personnel included 3,027 registered nurses with an additional 94 registered nurses employed in psychiatric facilities. The average expense to hospitals for care provided in 1995 was $718.57 per inpatient day and $4,686.06 per stay (data source: Idaho Hospital Association). There were 1,104 physicians in October 1995, and 613 active licensed dentists in November 1995. In 1995, 72.6% of the state's 8,799 registered nurses were employed in nursing. Five counties (Boise, Camas, Clark, Lewis, and Owyhee) had no physician active in patient care in 1995.

39SOCIAL WELFARE

Recipients of aid to families with dependent children (AFDC) averaged 23,500, with an average monthly payment of $382.00 per person, in 1991. In 1996, the food stamp program had an average monthly participation of 79,855; students took part in the school lunch program at a federal cost of $22.8 million. Unemployment insurance benefits came to $175.14 a week during 1995.

With the enactment of the Personal Responsibility and Work Opportunity Reconciliation Act of 1996, the US government has changed the form and regulations for many of its social welfare programs; most significantly, it replaces Aid to Families with Dependent Children (AFDC), an open-ended entitlement program, with Temporary Assistance for Needy Families (TANF), a limited system of assistance funded largely through federal block grants. The reform act also impacts the food stamp program, the Supplemental Security Income program, and the child nutrition program. The law took effect on 1 July 1997 and

provided $16.38 billion in block grants for fiscal years 1997–2002. The grants are to be divided among the states based on an equation involving the numbers of former AFDC recipients in each state. Because many of the bill's provisions have yet to be implemented into state-by-state policy, it was not currently possible to include the details of each state's programs.

Social Security benefits averaging $699 a month were paid to 177,850 residents in 1995; Supplemental Social Security provided an average monthly income of $324 to 16,605 residents.

40HOUSING

Single-family housing predominates in Idaho. In 1996 there were an estimated 463,000 housing units, 415,000 of which were occupied. In 1996, 10,755 privately owned housing units, valued at just over $1 billion, were authorized for construction. The median monthly expense for owner-occupied housing by mortgage holders ($561) and median gross monthly rent ($330) were below the national averages. During fiscal year 1996, Idaho received nearly $91 million in aid from the US Department of Housing and Urban Development, including $10.2 million in community development block grants.

41EDUCATION

Idaho's state and local per-pupil expenditure on education, $4,055 in 1995/96, is one of the lowest among the states. Nevertheless, as of 1990, nearly 80% of Idahoans over 25 were high school graduates, well above the national average.

As of fall 1996, public educational institutions enrolled 129,525 elementary school students (including kindergarten) and 115,727 secondary school (7th through 12th grade). The enrollment totals for nonpublic schools were 5,534 and 3,592, respectively. Idaho's 11 institutions of higher learning had 59,904 students in the fall of 1996. The leading public higher educational institutions are the University of Idaho at Moscow, with 11,133 students in the fall of 1996; Idaho State University (Pocatello), with an enrollment of 12,139; and Boise State University, 15,137; and Lewis-Clark State College in Lewiston with 2,967. There are two public community colleges and five private institutions. The State Board of Education offers scholarships to graduates of accredited Idaho high schools.

42ARTS

The Boise Philharmonic is Idaho's leading professional orchestra; other symphony orchestras are in Coeur d'Alene, Moscow, Pocatello, and Twin Falls. Boise and Moscow have seasonal theaters. The Idaho Commission on the Arts and Humanities, founded in 1966, offers grants to support both creative and performing artists. It has also cut records of folk music, mounted a folk art exhibit, and prepared a slide-tape series on Idaho folk life and folk art. In 1996, arts programs in Idaho received $624,000 from federal sources. The NEA contributed $400,000 to arts associations and $468,000 to the Idaho Commission on the Arts. The Commission also received $1,770,500 from the state to support its art programs. Idaho's arts education programs were offered to 9,000 school children. Audiences for the state's art programs amounted to about 2,460,000 people. There were 28,516 contributing artists. In 1991, Idaho had 55 arts associations and 26 local art groups.

The NEA also supported the development of an environmental project and the improvement of the Spokane and Inland Railway Building. The Idaho Commission of the Arts continues to develop arts education programs through state and federal grants.

43LIBRARIES AND MUSEUMS

Idaho's 110 public libraries had a combined book stock of nearly 3,253,835 volumes in 1996/97 and a total circulation of more than 6,247,003. The largest public library system was the Boise

Public Library and Information Center, with about 318,832 volumes; the leading academic library, at the University of Idaho (Moscow), had 958,235 volumes.

The state also has 30 museums, notably the Boise Art Museum, Idaho State Historical Museum (Boise), and the Idaho Museum of Natural History (Pocatello). The University of Idaho Arboretum is at Moscow, and there is a zoo at Boise and an animal park in Idaho Falls. Major historical sites include Cataldo Mission near Kellogg, Spalding Mission near Lapwai, and Nez Percé National Historical Park in north-central Idaho.

44COMMUNICATIONS

As of 1996, 96.1% of Idaho's 440,000 occupied housing units had telephones. Idaho's first radio station, built by a Boise high school teacher and his students, began transmitting in 1921, was licensed in 1922, and six years later was sold and given the initials KIDO—the same call letters later assigned to Idaho's first permanent television station, which began broadcasting in 1953 and subsequently became KTVB. As of 1996, the state had 81 operating radio stations (37 AM, 44 FM), 11 commercial television stations, and 3 noncommercial educational TV stations. Several large cable systems serviced the state in 1996.

45PRESS

Idaho, site of the first printing press in the Northwest, had 12 daily newspapers in 1997 (6 morning and 6 evening), and 9 Sunday papers. There were 51 weeklies. The most widely read newspaper was the (morning) *Idaho Statesman,* published in Boise, with a circulation of 66,325 daily and 88,308 Sundays in 1997. Caxton Printers, founded in 1902, is the state's leading publishing house.

46ORGANIZATIONS

The 1992 US Census of Service Industries counted 337 organizations in Idaho, including 84 business associations; 187 civic, social, and fraternal associations; and 66 other membership organizations. Among the few national organizations with headquarters in Idaho are the Food Industries Suppliers Association (Caldwell) and the Appaloosa Horse Club (Moscow).

47TOURISM, TRAVEL, AND RECREATION

In 1993, domestic travel and tourism generated $1.4 million in business revenues. Tourists come to Idaho primarily for outdoor recreation—river trips, skiing, camping, hunting, fishing, and hiking. There are 19 ski resorts, of which by far the most famous is Sun Valley, which opened in 1936. Licenses were held by 627,185 hunters and 457,798 fishermen in 1995.

Tourist attractions include two US parks, the Craters of the Moon National Monument and the Nez Percé National Historical Park, and the Hell's Canyon and Sawtooth national recreational areas. A sliver of Yellowstone National Park is also in Idaho. There were 9 recreation areas in early 1995, covering 31,383 acres (19,270 hectares).

48SPORTS

Idaho has no major league professional team, although the Atlanta Braves have a farm team in Idaho Falls. In college sports,

the Idaho State Bengals and the University of Idaho Vandals play Division I basketball and Division I-A football in the Big Sky and Big West Conferences, respectively. Boise State University is the largest university in the Big West Conference, with a football team in Division I. Most county seats hold pari-mutuel quarter-horse racing a few days a year, and Boise's racing season (including thoroughbreds) runs three days a week for five months. World chariot racing championships have been held at Pocatello, as are the National Circuit Rodeo Finals. Polo was one of Boise's leading sports from 1910 through the 1940s. Idaho cowboys have won numerous riding, roping, and steer-wrestling championships. Skiing is very popular throughout the state, and there is a world-class resort at Sun Valley. Golf is also quite popular.

49FAMOUS IDAHOANS

Leading federal officeholders born in Idaho include Ezra Taft Benson (b.1899), secretary of agriculture from 1953 to 1961, and Cecil D. Andrus (b.Oregon, 1931), governor of Idaho from 1971 to 1977 and 1987 to 1995, and secretary of the interior from 1977 to 1981. Maverick Republican William E. Borah (b.Illinois, 1865–1940) served in the US Senate from 1907 until his death. Frank Church (1924–84) entered the US Senate in 1957 and became chairman of the Senate Foreign Relations Committee in 1979; he was defeated in his bid for a fifth term in 1980. Important state officeholders were the nation's first Jewish governor, Moses Alexander (b.Germany, 1853–1932), and New Deal governor C. Ben Ross (1876–1946).

Author Vardis Fisher (1895–1968) was born and spent most of his life in Idaho, which was also the birthplace of poet Ezra Pound (1885–1972). Nobel Prize–winning novelist Ernest Hemingway (b.Illinois, 1899–1961) is buried at Ketchum. Gutzon Borglum (1871–1941), the sculptor who carved the Mt. Rushmore National Memorial in South Dakota, was an Idaho native. Idaho is the only state in the US with an official seal designed by a woman, Emma Edwards Green (b.California, 1856–1942).

Baseball slugger Harmon Killebrew (b.1936) and football star Jerry Kramer (b.1936) are Idaho's leading sports personalities.

50BIBLIOGRAPHY

Arrington, Leonard J. *History of Idaho.* Moscow, Idaho: University of Idaho Press, 1994.

Domitz, Gary, and Leonard Hitchcock, eds. *Idaho History: A Bibliography.* Centennial ed. Pocatello, Idaho: Idaho State University Press, 1991.

Beal, Merrill D., and Merle W. Wells. *History of Idaho.* 3 vols. New York: Lewis, 1959.

Federal Writers' Project. *Idaho: A Guide in Word and Picture.* Reprint. New York: Somerset, n.d. (orig. 1937).

Peterson, F. Ross. *Idaho: A Bicentennial History.* New York: Norton, 1976.

Walker, Deward E., Jr. *American Indians of Idaho.* Moscow, Idaho: University of Idaho Press, 1971.

Young, Virgil. *The Story of Idaho.* Moscow, Idaho: University of Idaho Press, 1984.

ILLINOIS

State of Illinois

ORIGIN OF STATE NAME: French derivative of *Iliniwek,* meaning "tribe of superior men," an Indian group formerly in the region. **NICKNAME:** The Prairie State. **SLOGAN:** Land of Lincoln. **CAPITAL:** Springfield. **ENTERED UNION:** 3 December 1818 (21st). **SONG:** "Illinois." **MOTTO:** State Sovereignty–National Union. **FLAG:** The inner portion of the state seal and the word "Illinois" on a white field. **OFFICIAL SEAL:** An American eagle perched on a boulder holds in its beak a banner bearing the state motto; below the eagle is a shield resting on an olive branch. Also depicted are the prairie, the sun rising over a distant eastern horizon, and, on the boulder, the dates 1818 and 1868, the years of the seal's introduction and revision, respectively. The words "Seal of the State of Illinois Aug. 26th 1818" surround the whole. **ANIMAL:** White-tailed deer. **BIRD:** Cardinal. **FISH:** Bluegill. **INSECT:** Monarch butterfly. **FLOWER:** Violet. **TREE:** White oak. **MINERAL:** Fluorite. **LEGAL HOLIDAYS:** New Year's Day, 1 January; Birthday of Martin Luther King, Jr., 3d Monday in January; Lincoln's Birthday, 12 February; George Washington's Birthday, 3d Monday in February; Memorial Day, last Monday in May; Independence Day, 4 July; Labor Day, 1st Monday in September; Columbus Day, 2d Monday in October; Election Day, 1st Tuesday after the 1st Monday in November in even-numbered years; Veterans Day, 11 November; Thanksgiving Day, 4th Thursday in November; Christmas Day, 25 December. **TIME:** 6 AM CST = noon GMT.

¹LOCATION, SIZE, AND EXTENT

Situated in the eastern north-central US, Illinois ranks 24th in size among the 50 states. Its area totals 56,345 sq mi (145,934 sq km), of which land comprises 55,645 sq mi (144,120 sq km) and inland water 700 sq mi (1,814 sq km). Illinois extends 211 mi (340 km) E-W; its maximum N-S extension is 381 mi (613 km).

Illinois is bounded on the N by Wisconsin; on the E by Lake Michigan and Indiana (with the line in the SE defined by the Wabash River); on the extreme SE and S by Kentucky (with the line passing through the Ohio River); and on the W by Missouri and Iowa (with the entire boundary formed by the Mississippi River).

The state's boundaries total 1,297 mi (2,088 km). The geographic center of Illinois is in Logan County, 28 mi (45 km) NE of Springfield.

²TOPOGRAPHY

Illinois is flat. Lying wholly within the Central Plains, the state exhibits a natural topographic monotony relieved mainly by hills in the northwest (an extension of Wisconsin's Driftless Area) and throughout the southern third of the state, on the fringes of the Ozark Plateau. The highest natural point, Charles Mound, tucked into the far northwest corner, is only 1,235 feet (376 meters) above sea level—far lower than Chicago's towering skyscrapers. The low point, at the extreme southern tip along the Mississippi River, is 279 feet (85 meters) above sea level. The average elevation is about 600 feet (180 meters).

Although some 2,000 rivers and streams totaling 9,000 mi (14,500 km) crisscross the land, pioneers in central Illinois confronted very poor drainage. The installation of elaborate and expensive networks of ditches and tiled drains was necessary before commercial agriculture became feasible. Most of the 2,000 lakes of 6 acres (2.4 hectares) or more were created by dams. The most important rivers are the Wabash and the Ohio, forming the southeastern and southern border; the Mississippi, forming the western border; and the Illinois, flowing northeast-southwest across the central region and meeting the Mississippi at Grafton,

just northwest of the junction between the Mississippi and the Missouri rivers. The artificial Lake Carlyle (41 sq mi—106 sq km) is the largest body of inland water. Illinois also has jurisdiction over 1,526 sq mi (3,952 sq km) of Lake Michigan.

³CLIMATE

Illinois has a temperate climate, with cold, snowy winters and hot, wet summers—ideal weather for corn and hogs. The seasons are sharply differentiated: mean winter temperatures are 22°F (–6°C) in the north and 37°F (3°C) in the south; mean summer temperatures are 70°F (21°C) in the north and 77°F (25°C) in the south. The record high, 117°F (47°C), was set at East St. Louis on 14 July 1954; the record low, –35°F (–37°C), was registered at Mt. Carroll on 22 January 1930.

The average farm sees rain one day in three, for a total of 36 in (91 cm) of precipitation a year. An annual snowfall of 37 in (94 cm) is normal for northern Illinois, decreasing to 24 in (61 cm) or less in the central and southern regions. Chicago's record 90 in (229 cm) of snow in the winter of 1978/79 created monumental transportation problems, enormous personal hardship, and even a small political upheaval when incumbent Mayor Michael Bilandic lost a primary election to Jane Byrne in February 1979 partly because of his administration's slowness in snow removal.

Chicago is nicknamed the "Windy City" because in the 1800s New York journalists labeled Chicagoans as "the windy citizenry out west" and called some Chicago leaders "loudmouth and windy"—not because of fierce winds. In fact, the average wind speed, 10.3 mph (16.6 km/hr), is lower than that of Boston, Honolulu, Cleveland, and 16 other major US cities. The flat plains of Illinois are favorable to tornado activity; the state recorded 76 tornadoes in 1995.

⁴FLORA AND FAUNA

Urbanization and commercial development have taken their toll on the plant and animal resources of Illinois. Northern and central Illinois once supported typical prairie flora, but nearly all the land has been given over to crops, roads, and suburban lawns.

About 90% of the oak and hickory forests that once were common in the north have been cut down for fuel and lumber. In the forests that do remain, mostly in the south, typical trees are black oak, sugar maple, box elder, slippery elm, beech, shagbark hickory, white ash, sycamore, black walnut, sweet gum, cottonwood, black willow, and jack pine. Characteristic wildflowers are the Chase aster, French's shooting star, lupine, primrose violet, purple trillium, small fringed gentian, and yellow fringed orchid. Tamarack and ginseng are considered threatened, and the small-whorled pogonia is endangered.

Before 1800, wildlife was abundant on the prairies, but the bison, elk, bear, and wolves that once roamed freely have long since vanished. The white-tailed deer (the state animal) disappeared in 1910 but was successfully reintroduced in 1933 by the Department of Conservation. Among the state's fur-bearing mammals are opossum, raccoon, mink, red and gray foxes, and muskrat. More than 350 birds have been identified, with such game birds as ruffed grouse, wild turkey, and bobwhite quail especially prized. Other indigenous birds are the cardinal (the state bird), horned lark, blue jay, purple martin, black-capped chickadee, tufted titmouse, bluebird, cedar waxwing, great crested flycatcher, and yellow-shafted flicker. Mallard and black ducks are common, and several subspecies of Canada goose are also found. The state claims 17 types of native turtle, 46 kinds of snake, 19 varieties of salamander, and 21 types of frog and toad. Heavy industrial and sewage pollution have eliminated most native fish, except for the durable carp and catfish. Coho salmon were introduced into Lake Michigan in the 1960s, thus reviving sport fishing.

In 1973, the Department of Conservation established an endangered and threatened species protection program. Included among threatened animals are the river otter, bobcat, Swainson's warbler, western hog-nosed snake, and lake sturgeon. Endangered species include the gray and Indiana bats, eastern woodrat, white-tailed jackrabbit, little blue heron, red-shouldered hawk, greater prairie chicken, barn owl, bigeye chub, bluebreast darter, dusky salamander, and Higgins' eye pearly mussel.

5ENVIRONMENTAL PROTECTION

The history of conservation efforts in Illinois falls into three stages. From 1850 to the 1930s, city and state parks were established and the beauty of Chicago's lakefront was successfully preserved. During the next stage, in the 1930s, federal intervention through the Civilian Conservation Corps and other agencies focused on upgrading park facilities and, most important, on reversing the severe erosion of soils, particularly in the hilly southern areas. Soil conservation laws took effect in 1937, and within a year the first soil conservation district was formed. By 1970, 98 districts, covering 44% of the state's farmland, promoted conservation cropping systems, contour plowing, and drainage.

The third stage of environmentalism began in the late 1960s, when Attorney General William J. Scott assumed the leadership of an antipollution campaign; he won suits against steel mills, sanitary districts, and utility companies, and secured passage of clean air and water legislation. The Illinois Environmental Protection Act of 1970 created the Pollution Control Board to set standards and conduct enforcement proceedings, and the Environmental Protection Agency to establish a comprehensive program for protecting environmental quality. In 1980, the Department of Nuclear Safety was established. The federal Environmental Protection Agency has also helped upgrade water and air quality in Illinois.

The years since the enactment of specific environmental laws and regulations have seen a noticeable improvement in environmental quality. Dirty air has become less prevalent. The Illinois EPA maintains more than 200 air-monitoring stations to measure different types of pollutants. Many of these stations are in the Chicago area. The agency also conducts about 2,500 facility inspections each year to verify compliance with air regulations. Since Illinois formerly produced about 6 million tons of hazardous wastes annually, the state agency tried to pinpoint and clean up abandoned hazardous waste sites. In 1984, Illinois began a three-year, $20 million program to eliminate the 22 worst sites and to evaluate nearly 1,000 other potential hazardous waste sites. Thanks to that program, 64 sites were cleaned up as of 1993. Since 1990, progress has been made toward the voluntary cleanup of contaminated sites; as of 1997, the Illinois General Assembly enacted a law developing a state underground storage tank program. As of May 1997, over 14,800 releases from underground storage tanks have been reported, 5,800 of which have completed remediation under the new initiative.

6POPULATION

At the 1990 census, Illinois ranked 6th among the 50 states, with a population of 11,430,602, or 205.6 persons per sq mi (79 per sq km), having ceded 3d place to California by 1950 and 4th place to Texas during the 1960s. The estimated 1996 population was 11,846,544; but the projection for the year 2000 indicates a loss at 11,722,000.

The population of Illinois was only 12,282 in 1810. Ten years later, the new state had 55,211 residents. The most rapid period of growth came in the mid-19th century, when heavy immigration made Illinois one of the fastest-growing areas in the world. Between 1820 and 1860, the state's population doubled every 10 years. The rate of increase slowed somewhat after 1900, especially during the 1930s, although the population more than doubled between 1900 and 1960. Population growth was very slow in the 1970s, about 0.3% a year; the rate of growth from 1980 to 1990 was a tiny 0.04%.

The age distribution of the state's population in 1990 closely mirrored the national pattern, with 26% under age 18 and more than 12% aged 65 or older. The number of households was 4,228,00 in 1983, up from 3,502,000 in 1970; nearly all the increase was in families headed by women and in households composed of unmarried persons. The number of husband-wife households fell slightly from 2,405,000 in 1970 to 2,378,000 in 1980. By 1992, the number of households was 4,244,700. Illinois population was 48.6% male and 51.4% female in 1990.

The rapid rise of Chicago meant that a large proportion of the state's population was concentrated in cities from a relatively early date. Thus, by 1895, 50% of Illinoisans lived in urban areas, whereas the entire country reached that point only in 1920. By 1990, 83% of the population lived in metropolitan areas, compared with 75.2% nationally. With a population of 8,066,000 in 1990, Greater Chicago was the 3d-largest metropolitan area in the nation and alone accounted for just over 70% of the total state population. The state's other major metropolitan areas, with their estimated 1995 populations, were Peoria, 345,555; and Rockford, 350,538. The largest city in 1994 was Chicago, with an estimated 2,731,743 residents, followed by Rockford, 143,263; Peoria, 112,878; Aurora, 112,313; Springfield, 105,938; Naperville, 101,163; Decatur, 83,105; Joliet, 79,492; and Evanston, 73,433.

7ETHNIC GROUPS

The Indian population of Illinois had disappeared by 1832 as a result of warfare and emigration. By 1990, however, Indian migration from Wisconsin, Minnesota, and elsewhere had brought the Native American population to 22,000, concentrated in Chicago. (The 1996 estimate was 23,000.)

French settlers brought in black slaves from the Caribbean in the mid-18th century; in 1752, one-third of the small non-Indian

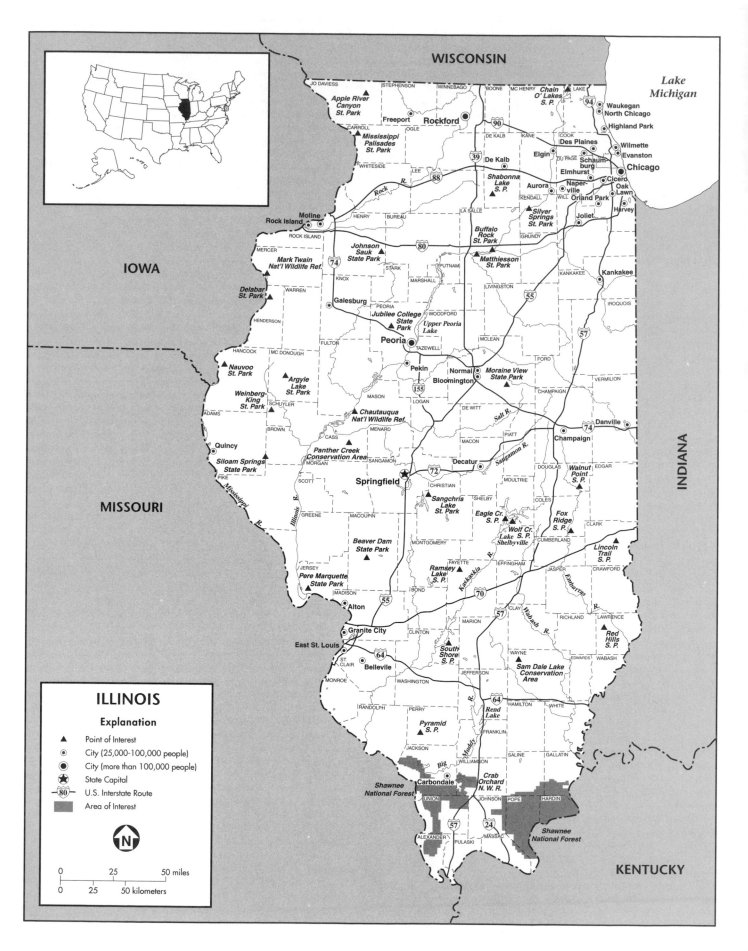

ILLINOIS

Explanation

▲ Point of Interest
◉ City (25,000-100,000 people)
◉ City (more than 100,000 people)
★ State Capital
⑧⓪ U.S. Interstate Route
▨ Area of Interest

N

0   25   50 miles
0   25   50 kilometers

population was black. Slavery was slowly abolished in the early 19th century. For decades, however, few blacks entered the state, except to flee slavery in neighboring Kentucky and Missouri. Freed slaves did come to Illinois during the Civil War, concentrating in the state's southern tip and in Chicago. By 1900, 109,000 blacks lived in Illinois. Most held menial jobs in the cities or eked out a precarious existence on small farms in the far south. Large-scale black migration, mainly to Chicago, began during World War I. By 1940, Illinois had a black population of 387,000; extensive wartime and postwar migration brought the total in 1990 to 1,694,000, of whom about 64% lived within the city of Chicago, which was about 40% black. Smaller numbers of black Illinoisans lived in Peoria, Rockford, and certain Chicago suburbs. In 1996, the black population was estimated at 1,932,000

The Hispanic population did not become significant until the 1960s. In 1990, the number of Illinoisans of Hispanic origin was 904,000, chiefly in Chicago. There were 557,536 persons of Mexican origin, 121,871 Puerto Ricans, and 14,625 Cubans; most of the remainder came from other Caribbean and Latin American countries. Estimates placed the Hispanic population at 1,003,000 in 1996.

In 1990 there were 44,077 Chinese in Illinois, 26,579 Japanese, 66,984 Filipinos, 42,167 Koreans, and 8,550 Vietnamese. In 1996, the total Asian/Pacific Islander population was estimated at 355,000.

Illinois Counties, County Seats, and County Areas and Populations

COUNTY	COUNTY SEAT	LAND AREA (SQ MI)	POPULATION (1996 EST.)	COUNTY	COUNTY SEAT	LAND AREA (SQ MI)	POPULATION (1996 EST.)
Adams	Quincy	852	67,816	Livingston	Pontiac	1,046	40,597
Alexander	Cairo	236	10,228	Logan	Lincoln	619	31,499
Bond	Greenville	377	17,069	Macon	Decatur	581	115,416
Boone	Belvidere	282	37,389	Macoupin	Carlinville	865	48,994
Brown	Mt. Sterling	306	6,400	Madison	Edwardsville	728	256,007
Bureau	Princeton	869	35,739	Marion	Salem	573	42,295
Calhoun	Hardin	250	5,011	Marshall	Lacon	388	12,789
Carroll	Mt. Carroll	444	16,907	Mason	Havana	536	16,820
Cass	Virginia	374	13,284	Massac	Metropolis	241	15,336
Champaign	Urbana	998	167,392	McDonough	Macomb	590	34,152
Christian	Taylorville	710	34,730	McHenry	Woodstock	606	230,555
Clark	Marshall	506	17,571	McLean	Bloomington	1,185	139,133
Clay	Louisville	469	14,397	Menard	Petersburg	315	12,359
Clinton	Carlyle	472	35,368	Mercer	Aledo	559	17,605
Coles	Charleston	509	51,186	Monroe	Waterloo	388	25,388
Cook	Chicago	958	5,096,540	Montgomery	Hillsboro	705	31,059
Crawford	Robinson	446	21,071	Morgan	Jacksonville	568	36,252
Cumberland	Toledo	346	11,169	Moultrie	Sullivan	325	14,319
DeKalb	Sycamore	634	82,703	Ogle	Oregon	759	50,107
DeWitt	Clinton	397	16,795	Peoria	Peoria	621	183,337
Douglas	Tuscola	417	19,799	Perry	Pinckneyville	443	21,498
DuPage	Wheaton	337	859,310	Piatt	Monticello	439	16,357
Edgar	Paris	623	20,106	Pike	Pittsfield	830	17,251
Edwards	Albion	223	7,129	Pope	Golconda	374	4,735
Effingham	Effingham	478	33,337	Pulaski	Mound City	203	7,348
Fayette	Vandalia	709	21,362	Putnam	Hennepin	160	5,715
Ford	Paxton	486	14,164	Randolph	Chester	583	34,240
Franklin	Benton	414	40,948	Richland	Olney	360	16,767
Fulton	Lewistown	871	38,650	Rock Island	Rock Island	423	148,640
Gallatin	Shawneetown	325	6,753	Saline	Harrisburg	385	26,476
Greene	Carrollton	543	15,733	Sangamon	Springfield	866	191,771
Grundy	Morris	423	32,712	Schuyler	Rushville	436	7,702
Hamilton	McLeansboro	436	8,622	Scott	Winchester	251	5,615
Hancock	Carthage	796	21,205	Shelby	Shelbyville	747	22,660
Hardin	Elizabethtown	181	5,068	Stark	Toulon	288	6,402
Henderson	Oquawka	373	8,526	St. Clair	Belleville	672	264,419
Henry	Cambridge	824	51,807	Stephenson	Freeport	564	49,167
Iroquois	Watseka	1,118	31,625	Tazewell	Pekin	650	128,366
Jackson	Murphysboro	590	61,154	Union	Jonesboro	414	18,079
Jasper	Newton	496	10,635	Vermillion	Danville	900	85,260
Jefferson	Mt. Vernon	570	39,090	Wabash	Mt. Carmel	224	12,681
Jersey	Jerseyville	373	21,308	Warren	Monmouth	543	18,901
Jo Daviess	Galena	603	21,783	Washington	Nashville	563	15,204
Johnson	Vienna	346	12,954	Wayne	Fairfield	715	17,049
Kane	Geneva	524	370,361	White	Carmi	497	15,840
Kankakee	Kankakee	679	101,949	Whiteside	Morrison	682	60,225
Kendall	Yorkville	322	47,894	Will	Joliet	844	427,818
Knox	Galesburg	720	55,936	Williamson	Marion	427	60,764
Lake	Waukegan	454	582,983	Winnebago	Rockford	516	254,873
La Salle	Ottawa	1,139	109,462	Woodford	Eureka	527	34,798
Lawrence	Lawrenceville	374	15,865				
Lee	Dixon	725	35,959	TOTALS		55,651	11,846,544

Members of non-British European ethnic groups are prevalent in all the state's major cities and in many farming areas. In 1990, 952,272 persons were foreign-born, including 288,199 Europeans, 225,339 Asians, 347,437 from other North, Central, or South American countries (81% Mexican), 12,388 Africans, and 1,819 from Oceanic countries. The most common European countries of origin were Poland (80,594), Germany (39,920), Italy (33,812), the former Yugoslavia (20,953), and the former Soviet Union (19,507). There were also significant numbers of Scandinavians, Irish, Lithuanians, Serbs, East European Jews, Ukrainians, Slovaks, Hungarians, Czechs, Greeks, and Dutch. Except for the widely dispersed Germans, most of these ethnic groups lived in and around Chicago.

Most ethnic groups in Illinois maintain their own newspapers, clubs, festivals, and houses of worship. These reminders of their cultural heritage are now largely symbolic for the European ethnics, who have become highly assimilated into a "melting pot" society. Such was not always the case, however. In 1889, the legislature attempted to curtail foreign-language schools, causing a sharp political reaction among German Lutherans, German Catholics, and some Scandinavians. The upshot was the election of a German-born Democrat, John Peter Altgeld, as governor in 1892. During World War I, anti-German sentiment was intense in the state, despite the manifest American loyalty of the large German element, then about 25% of the state's population. The Germans responded by rapidly abandoning the use of their language and dissolving most of their newspapers and clubs. At about the same time, the US government, educators, social workers, and business firms sponsored extensive "Americanization" programs directed at the large numbers of recent arrivals from Poland, Italy, and elsewhere. The public schools especially played a major role in the assimilation process, as did the Catholic parochial schools, which sought to protect the immigrants' religious but not their ethnic identities.

8LANGUAGES

A number of place-names—Illinois itself, Chicago, Peoria, Kankakee, and Ottawa—attest to the early presence of various Algonkian-speaking tribes, such as the Kickapoo, Sauk, and Fox, and particularly those of the Illinois Federation, the remnants of which moved west of the Mississippi River after the Black Hawk War of 1832.

Nineteenth-century western migration patterns determined the rather complex distribution of regional language features. Excepting the Chicago metropolitan area and the extreme northwestern corner of Illinois, the northern quarter of the state is dominated by Northern speech. An even greater frequency of Northern features appears in the northeastern quadrant; in this region, speakers get *sick to the stomach, catch cold* (take cold), use *dove* as the past tense of dive, pronounce *hog, fog, frog, crop,* and *college* with the vowel /ah/, and sound a clear /h/ in *whine, wheel,* and *wheat.*

Settlement from Pennsylvania and Ohio led to a mix of Northern and North Midland speech in central Illinois, with such dominating Northern features as *white bread, pail, greasy* with an /s/ sound, and *creek* rhyming with *stick.* Here appear Midland *fishworm* (earthworm), *firebug* (firefly), *wait on* (wait for), *dived* as the past tense of *dive, quarter til four* (3:45), and *sick at one's stomach* (but *sick on the stomach* in German communities near East St. Louis).

Migration from South Midland areas in Indiana and Kentucky affected basic speech in the southern third of Illinois, known as Egypt. Here especially occur South Midland and Southern *pullybone* (wishbone), *dog irons* (andirons), *light bread* (white bread), and, in extreme southern countries, *loaf bread, snake doctor* (dragonfly), *redworm* (earthworm), *ground squirrel* (chipmunk), *plum peach* (clingstone peach), *to have a crow to*

pick (to have a bone to pick) with someone, and the pronunciations of *coop* with the vowel of *put* and of *greasy* with a /z/ sound. Such speech is found also in the northwestern corner around Galena, where Kentucky miners who came to work in the lead mines brought such pronunciations as *bulge* with the vowel of *put, soot* with the vowel of *but,* and /yelk/ for *yolk.*

Metropolitan Chicago has experienced such complex inmigration that, although it still has a basic Northern/Midland mix, elements of almost all varieties of English appear somewhere. The influx since World War II of speakers of black English, a Southern dialect, and of nonstandard Appalachian English has aggravated language problems in the schools. Foreign-language schools were common in the 1880s and 1890s, but by 1920 all instruction was in English. The policy of monolingual education came into question in the 1970s, when the state legislature mandated bilingual classes for immigrant children, especially Spanish speakers.

In Chicago, rough-and-tumble politics has created a new meaning for *clout; prairie* means a vacant lot, *porch* includes the meaning of *stoop,* and *cornbread* has been generalized to include the meanings of *corn pone* and *hush puppies.* A fuel and food stop on the Illinois tollway system is an *oasis.*

In 1990, English was spoken at home by 85.8% of all state residents 5 years of age and older. Speakers of other languages were as follows:

Spanish	728,380	Greek	42,976
Polish	143,480	French	43,070
German	84,625	Chinese	41,807
Italian	66,903	Tagalog	46,453

9RELIGIONS

Before 1830, little religion of any sort was practiced on the Illinois frontier. Energetic Protestant missionaries set out to evangelize this un-Christian population, and they largely succeeded. By 1890, 36% of the adults in Illinois were affiliated with evangelical denominations—chiefly Methodist, Disciples of Christ, Baptist, Congregationalist, and Presbyterian—while 35%, mostly immigrants, belonged to liturgical denominations (chiefly Roman Catholic, Lutheran, and Episcopal). The remaining adults acknowledged no particular denomination. Illinois has had episodes of religious bigotry: at Carthage in 1844 the Mormon founder Joseph Smith was killed by a mob, and strong but brief waves of anti-Catholicism developed in the 1850s (the "Know-Nothing" movement) and 1920s (the Ku Klux Klan). Robert Green Ingersoll, a self-proclaimed agnostic, was appointed attorney general of Illinois in 1867–69, but his identity as an agnostic prevented him from ever being elected into politics. Nevertheless, tolerance of religious diversity has been the norm for most of the state's history.

Today, the largest Christian denomination is the Roman Catholic Church, with 3,611,033 members in 1990. The largest Protestant denomination in 1990 was the United Methodist Church, with 440,681 adherents, followed by the Lutheran Church—Missouri Synod 222,985; Southern Baptist Convention, 292,644; United Presbyterian Church, 158,320; and United Church of Christ 185,558. Protestants are most numerous in the Chicago suburbs and in smaller cities and towns downstate. The Jewish population was estimated at 269,188 in 1990.

10TRANSPORTATION

The fact that Illinois is intersected by several long-distance transportation routes has been of central importance in the state's economic development for a century and a half. East access by way of the major rivers and the Great Lakes system facilitated extensive migration to Illinois even before the coming of the railroads in the 1850s. Most of the nation's rail lines converge on Illinois, and Chicago and St. Louis (especially East St. Louis) have been the two main US railroad centers since the late 19th century. Interstate highways, notably the main east-west routes, also cross the state, and Chicago's central location in the United States has made it a major transfer point for airline connections.

After several false starts in the 1830s and 1840s, the state's railroad system was begun in the 1850s. The Illinois Central aided by the first federal land grants, opened up the prairie lands in the years before the Civil War. By 1890, about 10,000 mi (16,000 km) of track crisscrossed the state, placing 90% of all Illinois farms no more than 5 mi (8 km) from a rail line. The railroads stimulated not only farming but also coal mining, and in the process created tens of thousands of jobs in track and bridge construction, maintenance, traffic operations, and the manufacture of cars, rails, and other railroad equipment.

The rise of automobile and truck traffic in the 1920s and 1930s dealt the railroads a serious blow, but their utter ruin was staved off by complex mergers that incorporated bankrupt or threatened lines into ever-larger systems. By 1974, the state had 10,607 mi (17,070 km) of track, 2d only to Texas. Shedding their unprofitable passenger business in the 1970s (except for important commuter lines around Chicago which were taken over by public agencies), the railroads concentrated on long-distance freight traffic. The bankruptcy of the Penn Central, Rock Island, and Milwaukee Road systems during the 1970s impelled some companies, notably the Illinois Central Gulf and the Chicago & North Western, to shift their attention to real estate and manufacturing. Abandoned railroad tracks and right-of-ways are reverting to the private sector in the 1990s and being developed into public bicycle trails, walking paths, and greenways to take advantage of the scenic beauty of the state. Chicago is the hub of Amtrak's passenger service, which operated approximately 20 train routes through Illinois in 1996. Total ridership through the state's 35 stations amounted to 2,526,721 that year. There were 44 railroad companies operating 7,700 route mi (12,714 km) of track within the state at the end of 1996; in 1996, the state ranked 1st in rail carloads handled, total tons carried by rail, and total railroad employment.

Mass transit is of special importance to Chicago, where subways, buses, and commuter railroads are essential to daily movement. The transit systems were built privately but eventually were acquired by the city and regional transportation authorities. Ridership declines every year, as fewer people work in the central city and as more people choose the privacy and convenience of travel by automobile. Federal aid to mass transit, beginning in 1964, and state aid, initiated in 1971, have only partly stemmed the decline. Outside Chicago, transit service is available in some of the older, larger cities.

The road system of Illinois was inadequate until the 1920s, when an elaborate program to build local and trunk highways first received heavy state aid. In 1995, 138,821 mi (223,502 km) of public roadway served 8,973,009 registered vehicles—including 6,611,668 automobiles and 2,344,913 trucks—operated by 7,860,000 licensed drivers. The main east–west routes are I-90, I-88, I-80, I-74, I-72, I-70, and I-64. I-94 links Chicago with Milwaukee to the north and Indiana to the east, while I-57 and I-55 connect Chicago with the south and southwest (St. Louis), respectively. The Interstate Highway System totaled 2,163 mi (3,482 km) in the state as of 31 December 1995.

Barge traffic along the Mississippi, Ohio, and Illinois rivers remains important, especially for the shipment of grain. The Port of Chicago no longer harbors the sailing ships that brought lumber, merchandise, and people to a fast-growing city. However, the port is still the largest on the Great Lakes, handling 25.3 million tons of cargo in 1995, mostly grain and iron ore. Midway Airport in Chicago became the world's busiest after World War II, but was superseded by O'Hare Airport, which opened in the late 1950s. With 31,433,002 arriving and departing travelers in 1995,

O'Hare was the busiest airport in the country. In 1992, air traffic controllers at O'Hare performed 900,302 operations, more than at any other airport, according to the Federal Aviation Administration. With 687 airports and 283 heliports, Illinois is also an important center for general aviation. There were 18,693 licensed pilots and 6,177 operating aircraft in the state in as of May 1997.

[11]HISTORY

Different tribes of paleo-Indians lived in Illinois as long ago as 8000 BC. By 2000 BC, the cultivation of plants and use of ceramics were known to village dwellers; the first pottery appeared during the Woodland phase, a millennium later. Between 500 BC and AD 500, skilled Hopewellian craftsmen practiced a limited agriculture, developed an elaborate social structure, and constructed burial mounds. Huge mounds, which still exist, were built along the major rivers by the Middle Mississippian culture, about AD 900.

It is not known why the early native civilizations died out, but by the time white explorers arrived in the 17th century, the state was inhabited by seminomadic Algonkian-speaking tribes. The Kickapoo, Sauk, and Fox lived in the north, while the shores of Lake Michigan were populated by the Potawatomi, Ottawa, and Ojibwa. The Kaskaskia, Illinois (Iliniwek), and Peoria tribes roamed across the central prairies, and the Cahokia and Tamoroa lived in the south. Constant warfare with tribes form neighboring areas, plus disease and alcohol introduced by white fur traders and settlers, combined to decimate the Native American population. Warfare with the whites led to a series of treaties, the last in 1832, that removed all of the Indians to lands across the Mississippi.

French missionaries and fur traders from Quebec explored the rivers of Illinois in the late 17th century. Father Jacques Marquette and trader Louis Jolliet were the first to reach the area now known as the state of Illinois in 1673, when they descended the Mississippi as far as the Arkansas River and then returned by way of the Illinois River. The first permanent settlement was a mission built by French priests at Cahokia, near present-day St. Louis, in 1699. It was followed by more southerly settlements at Kaskaskia in 1703 and Ft. Chartres in 1719. In 1765, pursuant to the Treaty of Paris (1763) that ended the French and Indian War, the British took control of the Illinois country, but they established no settlements of their own. Most of the French settlers were Loyalists during the American Revolution. However, they put up no resistance when Virginia troops, led by George Rogers Clark, captured the small British forts at Cahokia and Kaskaskia in 1778. Virginia governed its new territory in desultory fashion, and most of the French villagers fled to Missouri. In 1784, Virginia relinquished its claim to Illinois, which three years later became part of the newly organized Northwest Territory. In 1800, Illinois was included in the Indiana Territory. Nine years later the Illinois Territory, including the present state of Wisconsin, was created; Kaskaskia became the territorial capital, and Ninian Edwards was appointed territorial governor by President James Madison. A territorial legislature was formed in 1812. During the War of 1812, British and Indian forces combined in a last attempt to push back American expansion into the Illinois country, and much fighting took place in the area. On 3 December 1818, Illinois was formally admitted to the Union as the 21st state. The capital was moved to Vandalia in 1820 and to Springfield in 1839.

Apart from a few thousand nomadic Indians and the remaining French settlers and their slaves, Illinois was largely uninhabited before 1815; two years after statehood, the population barely exceeded 55,000. The withdrawal of British influence after the War of 1812 and the final defeat of the Indian tribes in the Black Hawk War of 1832 opened the fertile prairies to settlers from the south, especially Kentucky. The federal government owned most of the land, and its land offices did a fast business on easy terms. Before the 1830s, most of the pioneers were concerned with acquiring land titles and pursuing subsistence agriculture, supplemented by hunting and fishing. An effort in 1824 to call a constitutional convention to legalize slavery failed because of a widespread fear that rich slaveholders would seize the best land, squeezing out the poor yeoman farmers. Ambitious efforts in the 1830s to promote rapid economic development led to fiscal disaster. Three state banks failed; a lavish program of building roads, canals, and railroads totally collapsed, leaving a heavy state debt that was not paid off until 1880. Despite these setbacks, the steady influx of land-hungry poor people and the arrival after 1840 of energetic Yankee entrepreneurs, all attracted by the rich soil and excellent water routes, guaranteed rapid growth.

Although Illinois gradually eliminated French slavery and even served as a conduit to Canada for slaves escaping from the South, the state was deeply divided over the slavery issue and remained unfriendly territory for blacks and their defenders. The abolitionist leader Elijah P. Lovejoy was killed in Alton in 1837, and as late as 1853 the state passed legislation providing that free blacks entering Illinois could be sold into slavery. In 1856, however, the new Republican Party nominated and Illinois voters elected a governor, William H. Bissell, on a reform program that included support for school construction, commercial and industrial expansion, and abolition of slavery. During the Civil War, Illinois sent half its young men to the battlefield and supplied the Union armies with huge amounts of food, feed, and horses. The strong-handed wartime administration of Republican Governor Richard Yates guaranteed full support for the policies of Abraham Lincoln, who had been prominent in Illinois political life since the 1840s and had been nominated for the presidency in 1860 at a Republican convention held in Chicago. Democratic dissenters were suppressed, sometimes by force, leaving a legacy of bitter feuds that troubled the "Egypt" section (the southern third of the state) for decades thereafter.

Economic and population growth quickened after 1865, as exemplified by the phenomenal rise of Chicago to become the principal city of the Midwest. Responding to opportunities presented by the coming of the railroads, boosters in hundreds of small towns and cities built banks, grain elevators, retail shops, small factories, ornate courthouses, and plain schools, in an abundance of civic pride. The Democrats sought the support of the working class and small farmers, assuming an attitude of hostility toward banks, high railroad freight rates, protective tariffs, and antiunion employers, but they failed to impose any significant restraints on business expansion. They were more successful, however, in opposing prohibition and other "paternalistic" methods of social control demanded by reformers such as Frances Willard, a leader in the Women's Christian Temperance Union, and the Prohibition Party. In Chicago and other cities the Democrats were less concerned with social reform than with building lucrative political machines on the backs of the poor Irish, Polish, and Czech Catholic immigrants, who kept arriving in large numbers. Statewide, Illinois retained a highly competitive two-party system, even as the excitement and high voter turnouts characteristic of 19th-century elections faded rapidly in the early 20th century.

During the second half of the 19th century, Illinois was a center of the American labor movement. Workers joined the Knights of Labor in the 1870s and 1880s and fought for child-labor laws and the eight-hour day. Union organizing led to several spectacular incidents, including the Haymarket riot in 1886 and the violent Pullman strike in 1894, suppressed by federal troops at the behest of President Grover Cleveland. A coalition of Germans, labor, and small farmers elected John Peter Altgeld to the governorship in 1892. After the turn of the century,

Illinois became a center of the Progressive movement, led by Jane Addams and Republican Governor Frank Lowden. Lowden reorganized the state government in 1917 by placing experts in powerful positions in state and municipal administrations.

After the great fire of 1871 destroyed Chicago's downtown section (but not its main residential or industrial areas), the city's wealthy elite dedicated itself to rebuilding Chicago and making it one of the great metropolises of the world. Immense steel mills, meat-packing plants, and factories sprang up, and growth was spectacular in the merchandising, banking, and transportation fields. Their fortunes made, Chicago's business leaders began building cultural institutions in the 1890s that were designed to rival the best in the world: the Chicago Symphony, the Art Institute, and the Field Museum of Natural History. The World's Columbian Exposition of 1893 was a significant international exhibition of the nation's technological achievements, and it focused worldwide attention on what was by then the 2d-largest American city. A literary renaissance, stimulated by the new realism that characterized Chicago's newspapers, flourished for a decade or two before World War I, but the city was recognized chiefly for its contributions in science, architecture, and (in the 1920s) jazz.

The first three decades of the 20th century witnessed almost unbroken prosperity in all sections except Egypt, the downstate region where poor soil and the decline of the coal industry produced widespread poverty. The slums of Chicago were poor, too, because most of the hundreds of thousands of new immigrants arrived virtually penniless. After 1920, however, large-scale immigration ended, and the immigrants' steady upward mobility, based on savings and education, became apparent. During the prohibition era, a vast organized crime empire rose to prominence, giving Chicago and Joliet a reputation for gangsterism, violence, and corruption; the most notorious gangster was Al Capone. Money, whether legally or illegally acquired, mesmerized Illinois in the 1920s as never before—and never since.

The Great Depression of the 1930s affected the state unevenly, with agriculture hit first and recovering first. Industries began shutting down in 1930 and did not fully recover until massive military contracts during World War II restored full prosperity. The very fact of massive depression brought discredit to the pro-business Republican regime that had run the state with few exceptions since 1856. Blacks, white ethnics, factory workers, and the undereducated, all of whom suffered heavily during the early years of the Depression, responded enthusiastically to Franklin Roosevelt's New Deal. They elected Henry Horner, a Democrat, to the governorship in 1932, reelected him in 1936, and flocked to the new industrial unions of the Congress of Industrial Organizations, founded in 1938.

World War II and its aftermath brought prosperity, as well as new anxiety about national security in a nuclear age. The chilling events of the 1960s and 1970s—assassinations, the Viet Nam war, the race riots, and the violence that accompanied the 1968 Democratic National Convention in Chicago—helped reshape many people's attitudes in Illinois. The problems attendant on heavy industrialization, particularly air and water pollution and urban decay, began to be addressed for the first time. This transformation was perhaps best exemplified in Chicago, where voters elected Jane Byrne the city's first woman mayor in 1979 and chose Harold Washington as its first black mayor in 1983.

The economy of Illinois, like those of other Rust Belt states, suffered a severe recession in the early eighties. Hit hard by foreign competition, producers of steel, machine tools, and automobiles engaged in massive layoffs. By the end of the decade, the economy had begun to rebound, but many industrial jobs were permanently lost, as industries sought to improve their efficiency and productivity through automation. In 1990, the unemployment rate in Illinois was 7.2%, in contrast to the national average of 5.2%.

In 1992, the 60-mile maze of tunnels that lay beneath downtown Chicago ruptured. Water from the Chicago River entered the tunnels and flooded basements and sub-basements of buildings in the city's central "loop" district. The flooding filled basements with up to 30 feet of water, forcing the temporary closure of such institutions as Chicago Board of Trade, City Hall, and the Marshall Fields department store. A year later, in the spring and summer of 1993, flooding of the Mississippi and Illinois rivers caused $1.5 billion of damage in the western part of the state and forced 12,800 people to evacuate their homes.

In 1991 Jim Thompson retired from office after 14 years as the governor of Illinois. The following year, Carol Moscley Braun became the first black woman elected to the US Senate. By the 1990s, the industrial losses of the 1980s had slowed, and the state had adjusted to the dominance of service industries in the US economy, as well as to the newer high-tech industries, which had gained a strong foothold in the area surrounding Cook County.

12 STATE GOVERNMENT

Illinois has had four constitutions. The first, written in 1818, was a short document modeled on those of New York, Kentucky, and Ohio. An attempt to rewrite the charter to allow slavery failed in a bitterly contested referendum in 1824. A new constitution in 1848 democratized government by providing for the popular election of judges. A third constitution, enacted in 1870, lasted a century; its unique feature was a voting system for the lower house of the state legislature that virtually guaranteed minority party representation in each electoral district. Important amendments in 1884 and 1904, respectively, gave the governor an item veto over appropriation bills and provided a measure of home rule for Chicago. In 1970, a fourth constitution streamlined state offices somewhat, improved accounting procedures, reformed the state tax system, and gave the state, rather than local governments, the major responsibility for financing education. The state bill of rights was expanded to include provisions banning discrimination in housing and employment and recognizing women's rights. An elected judiciary and the state's unique representational system were retained.

Under the 1970 constitution, as amended, the upper house of the general assembly consists of a senate of 59 members, who are elected on a two-year cycle to four-year terms. Until 1980, the lower house, the house of representatives, consisted of 177 members, with 3 representatives elected for two-year terms from each district. Each voter was empowered to cast three ballots for representatives, giving one vote to each of three candidates, one and a half votes to each of two, or all three to one candidate; each party never nominated more than two candidates in any single district. In November 1980, however, Illinois voters chose to reduce the size of house membership to 118 (2 representatives from each district) and to eliminate the proportional system. The legislative salary was $42,265 in 1995.

The executive officers elected statewide are the governor and lieutenant governor (who run jointly), secretary of state, treasurer, comptroller, and attorney general. Each serves a four-year term and is eligible for re-election. An important revision of appointive offices in 1917 made most agency heads responsible to the governor. In the 1970s, the governor's office expanded its control over the budget and the higher education complex, further augmenting an already strong executive position. The governor must be a US citizen, at least 25 years of age, and must have been a state resident for three years prior to election. In 1996 the governor's salary was $119,439.

Bills passed by both houses of the legislature become law if signed by the governor, if left unsigned for 60 days while the legislature is in session or 90 days after it adjourns, or if vetoed by the governor but passed again by three-fifths of the elected members of each house. Constitutional amendments require a three-fifths vote by the legislature for placement on the ballot; either a simple majority of those voting in the election or three-fifths of those voting on the amendment is sufficient for ratification.

Qualified voters must be US citizens at least 18 years of age. There is a 30-day district residency requirement.

13 POLITICAL PARTIES

The Republican and Democratic parties have been the only major political groups in Illinois since the 1850s. Illinois is a closely balanced state, with a slight Republican predominance from 1860 to 1930 giving way in seesaw fashion to a highly competitive situation statewide. In Chicago and Cook County, an equally balanced division before 1930 gave way to heavy Democratic predominance forged during the New Deal.

Illinois Presidential Vote by Political Parties, 1948–96

YEAR	ELECTORAL VOTE	ILLINOIS WINNER	DEMOCRAT	REPUBLICAN	SOCIALIST LABOR	PROHIBITION	COMMUNIST	SOCIALIST
1948	28	*Truman (D)	1,994,715	1,961,103	3,118	11,959	—	11,522
1952	27	*Eisenhower (R)	2,013,920	2,457,327	9,363	—	—	—
1956	27	*Eisenhower (R)	1,775,682	2,623,327	8,342	—	—	—
1960	27	*Kennedy (D)	2,377,846	2,368,988	10,560	—	—	—
1964	26	*Johnson (D)	2,796,833	1,905,946	—	—	—	—
						AMERICAN IND.		
1968	26	*Nixon (R)	2,039,814	2,174,774	13,878	390,958	—	—
						AMERICAN		
1972	26	*Nixon (R)	1,913,472	2,788,179	12,344	2,471	4,541	—
						LIBERTARIAN		SOC. WORKERS
1976	26	Ford (R)	2,271,295	2,364,269	2,422	8,057	9,250	3,615
					CITIZENS			
1980	26	*Reagan (R)	1,981,413	2,358,094	10,692	38,939	9,711	1,302
1984	24	*Reagan (R)	2,086,499	2,707,103	2,716	10,086	—	—
1988	24	*Bush (R)	2,215,940	2,310,939	10,276	14,944	—	—
					NEW ALLIANCE		IND. (PEROT)	POPULIST
1992	22	*Clinton (D)	2,453,350	1,734,096	5,267	9,218	840,515	3,577
1996	22	*Clinton (D)	2,341,744	1,587,021	–	22,548	346,408	—

* Won US presidential election.

The Democrats, organized by patronage-hungry followers of President Andrew Jackson in the 1830s, dominated state politics to the mid-1850s. They appealed to subsistence farmers, former southerners, and poor Catholic immigrants. Though they advocated minimal government intervention, Democratic officials were eager for the patronage and inside deals available in a fast-growing state. Their outstanding leader, Stephen Douglas, became a major national figure in the 1850s, but never lost touch with his base of support. After Douglas died in 1861, many Illinois Democrats began to oppose the conduct of the Civil War and became stigmatized as "Copperheads." The success of the Republican war policies left the Democrats in confusion in the late 1860s and early 1870s. Negative attitudes toward blacks, banks, railroads, and prohibition kept a large minority of Illinoisans in the Democratic fold, while the influx of Catholic immigrants replenished the party's voter base. However, the administration of Governor Altgeld (1893–97), coinciding with a deep depression and labor unrest, split the party, and only one other Democrat held the governorship between 1852 and 1932. The intraparty balance between Chicago and downstate changed with the rise of the powerful Cook County Democratic organization in the 1930s. Built by Mayor Anton Cermak and continued from 1955 to 1976 by six-term Mayor Richard J. Daley, the Chicago Democratic machine totally controlled the city, dominated the state party, and exerted enormous power at the national level. However, the machine lost its clout with the election in 1979 of independent Democrat Jane Byrne as Chicago's first woman mayor, and again in 1983 when Harold Washington became its first black mayor. Although Richard Daley's son, also named Richard Daley, won the mayoralty in 1989, the machine has never recovered the power it once enjoyed.

The Republican Party, born amid the political chaos of the 1850s, brought together most former Whigs and some Democrats who favored industrialization and opposed slavery. Abraham Lincoln, aided by many talented lieutenants, forged a coalition of commercial farmers, businessmen, evangelical Protestants, skilled craftsmen, professionals, and later, patronage holders and army veterans. Ridiculing the Democrats' alleged parochialism, the GOP called for vigorous prosecution of the Civil War and Reconstruction and for an active policy of promoting economic growth by encouraging railroads and raising tariffs. However, such moralistic crusades as the fight for prohibition frequently alienated large voting blocs (especially the Germans) from the Republicans.

In the early 20th century, Republican politicians built their own ward machines in Chicago and succumbed to corruption. William "Big Bill" Thompson, Chicago's Republican mayor in the 1910s and 1920s, openly allied himself with the gangster Al Capone. Moralistic Republicans, who were strongest in the smaller towns, struggled to regain control of their party. They succeeded in the 1930s, when the Republican political machines in Chicago collapsed or switched their allegiance to the Democrats.

Since then, the Republicans have become uniformly a party of the middle and upper-middle classes, hostile to machine politics, welfare, and high taxes, but favorable to business, education, and environmental protection. Although the GOP has a stronger formal organization in Illinois than in most other states, its leading candidates have exuded an aura of independence. Republican James R. Thompson, elected to the governorship in 1976 and reelected in 1978 and 1982, served in that office longer than any other. Thompson was followed by Republican Jim Edgar in 1990.

The Whigs usually ran a close second to the Democrats from 1832 to 1852. Taken over in the 1840s by a group of professional organizers under Lincoln's leadership, the Whigs simply vanished after their crushing defeat in 1852. Notable among the smaller

parties was the Native American ("Know-Nothing") Party, which controlled Chicago briefly in the 1850s. The Prohibitionists, Greenbackers, Union Labor, and Populist parties were weak forces in late-19th-century Illinois. The Socialist Party, strongest among coal miners and central European immigrants, grew to a minor force in the early 20th century and elected the mayor of Rockford for many years.

Illinois provided two important leaders of the national GOP in the 1860s—Abraham Lincoln and Ulysses S. Grant. The only major-party presidential nominee from the state between 1872 and 1976, however, was Governor Adlai Stevenson, the unsuccessful Democratic candidate in 1952 and 1956. In 1980, three native-born Illinoisans pursued the Republican Party nomination. The first, US Representative Philip Crane, was the earliest to declare his candidacy but failed in the primaries. The second, US Representative John Anderson, dropped out of the GOP primaries to pursue an independent candidacy, ultimately winning more than 6% of the popular vote nationally and in Illinois, but no electoral votes. The third, Ronald Reagan, a native of Tampico, won both the Republican nomination and the November election, becoming the 40th president of the US; he was elected by a heavy majority of Illinois voters in 1980 and re-elected in 1984.

There is no party registration. In the 1996 presidential election, Democrat Bill Clinton won 54% of the vote, Republican Bob Dole received 37%, and Independent Ross Perot garnered 8%. As of the November 1996 elections, Republicans held the governorship, Democrats held both US Senate seats, and each party had 10 of the 20 US House seats. Democratic Congressman Richard J. Durbin won the race to succeed retiring senator Paul Simon. In the 1994 elections, the once powerful chairman of the House Ways and Means Committee, Dan Rostenkowski, was defeated by a relative unknown, Michael P. Flanagan. Rostenkowski, an 18-term Chicago Democrat, had been indicted on corruption charges, a fact that did not go unnoticed by an electorate already in an anti-incumbent mood. Following the 1996 elections, there were 31 Republicans and 28 Democrats in the state senate, and 60 Democrats and 58 Republicans in the state house.

Illinois elected its first black female senator, Carol Moseley Braun, in 1992. In 1994, there were 465 black elected officials and 881 Hispanics in public office. In 1995 there were 44 women serving in the state legislature and in elective executive office.

¹⁴LOCAL GOVERNMENT

Illinois has more units of local government (most with property-taxing power) than any other state. In 1992 there were 102 counties, 1,282 municipalities, 1,433 townships, 985 school districts, and 2,920 special districts.

County government in Illinois dates from 1778, when Virginia, claiming authority over the territory, established the earliest counties. The major county offices are elective: the county board chairman, the county clerk (chief administrative officer), clerk of the circuit court, sheriff, state's attorney, treasurer, coroner, and superintendent of schools. Cook County controls hospital and welfare programs in Chicago, thus spreading the cost over both the city's own tax base and that of the more affluent suburbs. The New England township system was made optional by the 1848 constitution, and eventually 85 counties, including Cook County, adopted the idea. Townships, which elect local judges and administrators, also handle tax collection.

Chicago is governed by an elected mayor, clerk, treasurer, and city council composed of 50 aldermen. The mayor's power depends more on control of the city's Democratic Party organization than on formal authority. Independent candidates get elected to the city council from time to time, but the Democratic machine generally staffs the city with its own members.

Other cities may choose either the commission or aldermanic system: most are administered by nonpartisan city managers.

15STATE SERVICES

Officials responsible to the governor of Illinois and the members of Congress, as well as to the mayor of Chicago, actively provide ombudsman service, although there is no state office by that name. Illinois has a board of ethics, but the US attorney's office in Chicago has far more potent weapons at its disposal: many top political leaders were indicted and convicted in the 1970s, including federal judge and former Governor Otto Kerner and, in 1980, Attorney General William Scott.

Educational services provided by the Illinois Office of Education include teacher certification and placement, curriculum development, educational assessment and evaluation, and programs for the disadvantaged, gifted, handicapped, and ethnic and racial minorities. The Board of Higher Education and the Illinois Community College Board oversee postsecondary education. The Department of Transportation handles highways, traffic safety, and airports.

Among state agencies offering health and welfare services are the Department of Children and Family Services, which focuses on foster care, the deaf, the blind, and the handicapped; and the Department of Public Aid, which supervises Medicaid, food stamps, and general welfare programs. The Mental Health and Developmental Disabilities Department operates homes and outpatient centers for the retarded and the mentally ill; it also offers an alcoholism program. Established in 1973, the Department on Aging provides nutritional and field services. The Board of Vocational Rehabilitation operates programs to retrain the disabled, while the Department of Veterans' Affairs administers bonus and scholarship programs and maintains four veterans' homes with nursing facilities, including one with an Alzheimer's Unit, and three with 300 or more beds.

State responsibility for public protection is divided among several agencies: the Office of the Attorney General, Department of Corrections (prisons and parole), Department of Law Enforcement (including the State Police and Bureau of Investigation), Dangerous Drugs Commission, and Military and Naval Department. Resource protection is supervised by the Department of Conservation, which oversees fish hatcheries, state parks, nature reserves, game preserves, and forest fire protection. The Department of Mines and Minerals handles mine safety and land reclamation programs. The Department of Labor mediates disputes and handles unemployment compensation. The Department of Human Rights, established in 1980, seeks to ensure equal employment, housing, and credit opportunities.

16JUDICIAL SYSTEM

The state's highest court is the supreme court, consisting of seven justices elected by judicial districts for 10-year terms; the justices elect one of their number as chief justice for three years. The supreme court has appellate jurisdiction generally, but has original jurisdiction in cases relating to revenue, mandamus, and habeas corpus. The chief justice, assisted by an administrative director, has administrative and supervisory authority over all other courts. The appellate court is divided into five districts; appellate judges, also elected for 10-year terms, hear appeals from the 22 circuit courts, which handle civil and criminal cases. Circuit judges are elected for 6-year terms. Repeated efforts to remove the state's judgeships from partisan politics have failed in the face of strong party opposition.

The penal system, under the general supervision of the Department of Corrections (established in 1970), includes large prisons at Joliet (1860), Pontiac (1871), Menard (1878), and Stateville (1919), near Joliet, plus juvenile facilities and an active parole division. The Cook County House of Corrections is highly

active, as are federal facilities in Chicago and Marion. Illinois had 28,941 prisoners in 1991, or 246 prisoners per 100,000 in population. Prisoner unrest, demands for legal rights, gang activity, and low guard morale continue to be serious problems in the state's penal institutions.

Illinois has a reputation for lawlessness, born of the gang warfare in Chicago during the prohibition era. In the 19th century, southern Illinois was ravaged by numerous bands of outlaws, and one county still carries the nickname "Bloody Williamson" because of its history of murders, massacres, and assassinations. As of 1992, the number of violent crimes in Illinois was 670,564, for a rate of 5,765.3 per 100,000 population. Crime rates statewide were murder, 11.4; forcible rape, 37.1; robbery, 412.5; aggravated assault, 516.4; burglary, 1,077.3; larceny-theft, 3,091.9; and motor vehicle theft, 618.8. In 1994, Illinois had an estimated 60,501 practicing attorneys.

17ARMED FORCES

The most important military installations in Illinois are the Great Lakes Naval Training Center near Chicago and Scott Air Force Base near Belleville. Total active duty military personnel numbered 28,976 in 1996, when Illinois firms received defense contract awards amounting to $1.25 billion.

About 1 million Illinoisans served in World War II, of whom 30,000 were killed. As of 1 July 1996, 1,057,000 veterans were living in Illinois, of whom fewer than 500 saw service in World War I, 299,000 in World War II, 175,000 in the Korean Conflict, 319,000 during the Viet Nam era, and 67,000 in the Persian Gulf War. Veterans' benefits reached $1.4 billion in 1995/96.

Illinois's national guard and reserve comprised 52,025 men and women in 1996. Police forces are relatively large, totaling 39,890 men and women in 1991 and costing $1.604 million; the ratio of 3.5 police employees per 1,000 population was one of the highest in the US. In 1993, the Illinois State Police employed 1,897 full-time officers, or two per 10,000 residents.

18MIGRATION

Apart from the small French settlements along the Mississippi River that were formed in the 18th century, most early white migration into Illinois came from the South, as poor young farm families trekked overland to southern Illinois from Kentucky, Tennessee, and the Carolinas between 1800 and 1840. After 1830, migration from Indiana, Ohio, and Pennsylvania filled the central portion of the state, while New Englanders and New Yorkers came to the northern portion.

Immigration from Europe became significant in the 1840s and continued in a heavy stream for about 80 years. Before 1890, most of the new arrivals came from Germany, Ireland, Britain, and Scandinavia. These groups continued to arrive after 1890, but they were soon outnumbered by heavy immigration from southern and eastern Europe. The opening of prairie farms, the burgeoning of towns and small cities, and the explosive growth of Chicago created a continuous demand for unskilled and semiskilled labor. Concern for the welfare of these newcomers led to the establishment by Jane Addams in Chicago of Hull House (1889), which served as a social center, shelter, and advocate for immigrants. Hull House launched the settlement movement in America, and its activities helped popularize the concept of cultural pluralism. The University of Chicago was one of the first major universities to concern itself with urban ecology and with the tendency to "ghettoize" culturally and economically disadvantaged populations.

The outbreak of World War I interrupted the flow of European immigrants but also increased the economy's demand for unskilled labor. The migration of blacks from states south of Illinois—especially from Arkansas, Tennessee, Louisiana, Mississippi, and Alabama—played an important role in meeting the demand for labor during both world wars. After World War II, the further collapse of the cotton labor market drove hundreds of thousands more blacks to Chicago and other northern cities.

In contrast to the pattern of foreign and black migration to Illinois was the continued westward search by native-born whites for new farmland, a phenomenon that produced a net outflow by this group from 1870 to 1920. After World War II, native whites again left the state in large numbers, with southern California a favorite mecca. After 1970 for the first time, more blacks began leaving than entering Illinois.

The major intrastate migration pattern has been from farms to towns. Apart from blacks, who migrated considerable distances from farms in the South, most ex-farmers moved only 10–30 mi (16–48 km) to the nearest town or city.

During the 1970s the state lost 649,000 persons in net migration, for an annual rate of 0.5%. From 1980 to 1983, the net loss from migration totaled 212,000, or 0.6% annually. From 1985 to 1990, the net loss from migration came to 139,360. Between 1990 and 1996, there was a net loss of 359,460 persons from domestic migration and a net gain of 240,204 from international migration. In 1996, 42,517 immigrants from foreign countries arrived in Illinois, the 6th highest number for any state and over 4% of all foreign immigration to the US for that year. As of 1994, the number of undocumented immigrants in Illinois was estimated at between 157 and 225. Some 69% of all state residents had been born in Illinois as of 1990. About 56% of state residents age 5 and older lived in the same house in 1990 as in 1985. Of those who lived in a different house in 1985, only 15% did so in another state. In 1996, the number of foreign-born residents totaled 1,062, or 9% of the state's total population. The greatest number of foreign-born residents came from Mexico.

[19]INTERGOVERNMENTAL COOPERATION

Illinois participates in 25 interstate compacts, including such regional accords as the Great Lakes Basin Compact and Ohio River Valley Water Sanitation Compact. In 1985, Illinois and seven other states formed the Great Lakes Charter to protect the lakes' water supply. Federal grants to Illinois totaled $9.2 billion in 1995/96.

[20]ECONOMY

The economic development of Illinois falls into four periods: the frontier economy, up to 1860; the industrial transition, 1860–1900; industrial maturity, 1900–1950; and the transition to a service economy, 1950 to the present.

In the first phase, subsistence agriculture was dominant; the cost of transportation was high, cities were small and few, and cash markets for farm products hardly existed. The main activity was settling and clearing the land. A rudimentary market economy developed at the end of the period, with real estate and land speculation the most lucrative activities.

The industrial transition began about 1860, stimulated by the construction of the railroad network, which opened up distant markets for farm products and rural markets for manufactured items. The Civil War stimulated the rapid growth of cash farming, commercial and financial institutions, and the first important factories. The last quarter of the 19th century saw the closing of the agricultural frontier in Illinois and the rapid growth of commercial towns and industrial cities, especially Chicago.

Industrial maturity was reached in the early 20th century. Large factories grew, and small ones proliferated. Chicago's steel industry, actually centered in Gary, Ind., became second in size only to Pittsburgh's, while the state took a commanding lead in food production, agricultural implement manufacture, and agricultural finance. The depression of the 1930s stifled growth in the state and severely damaged the coal industry, but with the

heavy industrial and food demands created by World War II, the state recovered its economic health.

Since 1950, the importance of manufacturing has declined, but a very strong shift into services—government, medicine, education, law, finance, and business—has underpinned the state's economic vigor.

Trends in the 1970s showed declines in the relative importance of manufacturing and construction, little relative change in transportation and agriculture, and significant proportional increases in the other sectors. Severe competition from Japan wreaked havoc in the state's steel, television, and automotive industries, while Illinois's high-wage, high-cost business climate encouraged the migration of factories to the southern states. Meat-packing, once the most famous industry in Illinois, dwindled after the closing of the Chicago stockyards in 1972. Chicago remained the nation's chief merchandising center during the early 1980s, and an influx of huge international banks boosted the city's financial strength. Currently, Illinois's major industries include primary and secondary metals; industrial and farm equipment; electric equipment and appliances; electronic components; food processing; and printing equipment.

The gross state product reached $332,853 million in 1994, consisting of private goods–producing industries, $82,637 million; private services–producing industries, $216,235 million; and government, $33,918 million. In 1995, Illinois's per capita personal income was $5,225, which ranked the state 8th nationally. In 1996, there were 54,498 filings for bankruptcy, up 27% from the previous year.

[21]INCOME

Illinois is a rich state and has been for the last century. In per capita personal income, it ranked 7th in 1996. Total disposable personal income increased from $256.7 billion in 1995 to $269.8 billion in 1996. Nonfarm personal income rose 6.67% from $279.9 billion in 1994 to $298.3 billion in 1995. In the same year, per capita income was $25,225, and the median household income was $38,071.

In 1995, 12.4% of the population lived below the poverty level, down 2.9% from the 1991 rate.

Income levels vary by race and geography. The average income for white families is somewhat higher than the mean income for black and Hispanic families. Residents of southern Illinois tend to have lower income than those living in central and northern Illinois.

[22]LABOR

In early 1997, the Illinois labor force numbered 6,175,700 persons, with the Chicago area accounting for 67% of the total.

In 1996, the average unemployment rate was 5.3%. Of the total nonfarm employment of 5,727,600 at the start of 1997, mining accounted for 0.2%; construction, 3.9%; manufacturing, 17.1%; transportation, communication, and utilities, 5.8%; trade, 23.6%; finance, insurance, and real estate, 6.8%; services, 28.5%; and government, 14.1%.

The first labor organizations sprang up among German tailors, teamsters, and carpenters in Chicago in the 1850s, and among British and German coal miners after the Civil War. The period of industrialization after the Civil War saw many strikes, especially in coal mining and construction, many of them spontaneous rather than union-related. The Knights of Labor organized extensively in Chicago, Peoria, and Springfield in the 1870s and 1880s, reaching a membership of 52,000 by 1886. However, in the aftermath of the Haymarket Riot—at which a dynamite blast at a labor rally killed seven policemen and four civilians—the Knights faded rapidly. More durable was the Chicago Federation of Labor, formed in 1877 and eventually absorbed by the American Federation of Labor (AFL). Strongest in the highly skilled construction, transportation, mining, and printing industries, the federation stood aside from the 1894 Pullman strike, led by industrial union organizer Eugene V. Debs, a bitter struggle broken by federal troops over the protest of Governor Altgeld.

Today, labor unions are powerful in Chicago but relatively weak downstate. In 1995, 1,041,700 persons, or 20.2% of all workers, belonged to unions. Unionization among private sector manufacturing workers was 23.5% The major unions are the International Brotherhood of Teamsters, the United Steelworkers of America, the International Association of Machinists, the United Automobile Workers, the United Brotherhood of Carpenters, and the American Federation of State, County, and Municipal Employees. The Illinois Education Association, though not strictly a labor union, has become one of the state's most militant employee organizations, often calling strikes and constituting the most active lobby in the state. In 1983, a new law granted all public employees except police and firemen the right to strike.

23AGRICULTURE

Total agricultural income in 1995 reached $7.9 billion in Illinois, 5th behind California, Texas, Iowa, and Nebraska. Crops accounted for nearly 78% of the value of farm marketings, with soybeans and corn the leading cash commodities.

Prior to 1860, agriculture was the dominant occupation, and food for home consumption was the leading product. Enormous effort was devoted to breaking the thick prairie soil in the northern two-thirds of the state. Fences and barns were erected, and in the 1870s and 1880s the drainage of low-lying areas in central Illinois was a major concern. Commercial agriculture was made possible by the extension of the railroad network in the 1860s and 1870s. Corn, wheat, hogs, cattle, and horses were the state's main products in the 19th century. Since then, wheat and poultry have declined greatly in significance, while soybeans and, to a lesser extent, dairy products and vegetables have played an increasingly important role. The mechanization and electrification of agriculture, beginning about 1910, proceeded at an unmatched pace in Illinois. Strong interest in scientific farming, including the use of hybrid corn, sophisticated animal-breeding techniques, and chemical fertilizers, has also fostered a steady, remarkable growth in agricultural productivity.

The number of farms reached a peak at 264,000 in 1900 and began declining rapidly after World War II, down to 76,000 in 1996. Total acreage in farming was 28.1 million acres (11.4 million hectares) in 1996, down from 32.8 million acres (13.3 million hectares) in 1990. The average farm size has more than doubled from 124 acres (50 hectares) in 1900 to 368 acres (150 hectares) in 1996. The farm population, which averaged 1.2 million persons from 1880 to 1900, declined to 314,000 in 1980; by then, moreover, about half the people who lived on farms commuted to work in stores, shops, and offices.

The major agricultural region is the corn belt, covering all of central and about half of northern Illinois. Among the 50 states, Illinois ranked 2d only to Iowa in production of corn and soybeans in 1996. The following table shows output and value of leading field crops in that year:

	VOLUME (MILLION BUSHELS)	VALUE (MILLIONS)
Corn for grain	1,468.9	$ 3,965.8
Soybeans	398.9	2,772.5
Wheat	41.8	171.4
Hay (millions tons)	3.0	278.3
Oats	4.6	9.9
Sorghum for grain	18.5	40.6

Agriculture is big business in the state, though very few farms are owned by corporations (except "family corporations," a tax

device). The financial investment in agriculture is enormous, largely because of the accelerating cost of land. The value of land quadrupled during the 1970s to an average of $2,013 per acre in 1980, fell to $1,536 per acre by 1992, but rose to $2,064 by 1996.

24ANIMAL HUSBANDRY

Livestock is raised almost everywhere in Illinois, but production is concentrated especially in the west-central region. In 1997, Illinois farms had an estimated 1.68 million cattle and calves worth around $957 million. Illinois farms had an estimated 4.4 million hogs and pigs worth around $422 million. The dairy belt covers part of northern Illinois. Milk production in 1995 totaled and estimated 2.5 billion lb. During 1995, Illinois poultry farmers sold an estimated 12.4 million lb of chicken. An estimated 762 million eggs were produced in 1995, worth around $43.4 million.

25FISHING

Commercial fishing is insignificant in Illinois: only 235,000 lb of fish, valued at $444,000, made up the commercial catch in 1995, down from 405,000 lb and $566,000 in 1994. Sport fishing is of modest importance in southern Illinois and in Lake Michigan. Some 450 lakes and ponds and 200 streams and rivers are open to the public. In 1995/96, over 840,000 sport anglers were licensed in Illinois. The US Fish and Wildlife Service dedicated over $4 million to sport fish restoration programs. Federal hatcheries distributed 135,900 fish (6,727 lb) and 22.2 million fish eggs within the state in 1995/96.

26FORESTRY

Forestland covering 4,900,000 acres (1,983,000 hectares) comprises about 13.5% of the state's land area. Forests in the northern two-thirds of the state are predominately located in the northwestern part of the state and along major rivers and streams. The majority of Illinois's forests are located in the southern one-third of the state. Some 4,150,000 acres (1,680,000 hectares) are classified as commercial forests and are 90% privately owned. The Shawnee National Forest encompasses over 270,000 acres (109,000 hectares). In 1995, the value of shipments by the lumber and wood products industry was $1,271.1 million.

27MINING

The value of nonfuel mineral production for Illinois in 1995 was estimated to be $820 million, a decrease from the $823 million reported in 1994. Increased sales of lime, clay, and fuller's earth offset decreased sales of crushed stone and construction sand and gravel.

Illinois was the nation's only producer of fluorspar and ranked 1st in industrial sand and gravel (4.4 million metric tons, worth $65.8 million), 7th in the production of crushed stone (59.5 million metric tons, worth $340 million), and 8th in both portland cement (2.6 million metric tons, worth $152 million) and common clays (1.07 billion metric tons, worth $4.1 million). Nationally, the state continued to rank 16th in nonfuel mineral production value in 1995.

Of the state's five leading nonfuel mineral commodities (crushed stone, portland cement, construction sand and gravel, industrial sand, and clay), only portland cement and clay increased in value compared with 1994 figures. Clay production increased by 117% from 1994 to 1995, and its value rose by 254%. Crushed stone, the state's leading nonfuel mineral commodity, accounted for about 416% of Illinois nonfuel mineral value in 1995.

Illinois was the only state with reported fluorspar production in the United States in 1995. A combination of increased competition from foreign imports and a decrease in the use of chlorofluorocarbons (because of environmental concerns) has been mostly responsible for the decline in domestic production. Fluorspar has been mined commercially in Hardin County since 1870, and in 1995 the last two operating fluorspar mines in the US were scheduled to be closed (making it difficult to obtain fluorite, the state mineral). Fluorspar is used in making steel, enamels, aluminum, toothpaste, specialty glass, and a variety of chemicals.

There were 12,900 employees in the Illinois mining industry at the end of December 1996, down from 13,100 in December 1995.

28 ENERGY AND POWER

Illinois is one of the nation's leading energy producers and consumers. Electric power production totaled 145.1 billion kWh (4th in the US) in 1995; installed capacity was 37 million kW in 1996, nearly all of it privately owned. Consumption of energy in 1994 amounted to 3,694.7 trillion Btu (7th), of which industry accounted for 36%, residences 24%, commercial establishments 19%, and transportation 21%. Commonwealth Edison and Northern Illinois Light and Power are the largest suppliers. Coal-fired plants account for about 43% of the state's power production; nuclear power is also important, particularly for the generation of electricity in the Chicago area. The state's six operating nuclear power plants in 1996 with 13 reactors were all owned by Commonwealth Edison.

In 1995, Illinois ranked 4th in natural-gas usage, with 1,078 billion cu ft delivered to 3.7 million customers. People's Gas, a diversified energy conglomerate based in Chicago, is the largest firm. Petroleum production, though steadily declining, totaled 15.58 million barrels in 1996; reserves were 119 million barrels.

Illinois ranked 6th in the US in coal production in 1996, with 46 million tons; recoverable reserves were estimated at 882.3 million tons. Coal is abundant throughout the state, with the largest mines in the south and central regions. Coal mining reached its peak in the 1920s, but suffered thereafter from high pricing policies, the depression of the 1930s, and the environmental restrictions against burning high-sulfur coal in the 1970s. In 1995 there were 31 productive coal mines—11 surface (strip) mines and 20 underground mines.

29 INDUSTRY

Manufacturing in Illinois, concentrated in but not limited to Chicago, has always been diverse. Before 1860s, small gristmills, bakeries, and blacksmith shops handled what little manufacturing was done. Industry tripled in size in the 1860s, doubled in the 1870s, and doubled again in the 1880s, until manufacturing employment leveled off at 10–12% of the population. Value added by manufacture grew at a compound annual rate of 8.1% between 1860 and 1900, and at a rate of 6.3% until 1929. The chief industries in 1929 were iron and steel, printing, food, electrical equipment, and machinery.

In 1995, the value of shipments by manufacturers totaled $193 billion. Food and food products contributed $29.7 billion; industrial machinery and equipment, $26.8 billion; chemicals and allied products, $20.8 billion; electronics and other electronic equipment, $17.6 billion; and transportation equipment, $16.2 billion. The following table shows value of shipments by manufacturers for selected industries in 1995:

Petroleum refining	$ 8,147,900,000
Construction machinery	6,220,600,000
Communications equipment	8,634,300,000
Fats and oils	3,880,700,000
Meat products	4,444,300,000
Paper and allied products	6,820,500,000
Grain mill products	5,684,100,000
Commercial printing	5,617,600,000

By far the leading industrial center is Chicago, followed by Rockford, the East St. Louis area, Rock Island and Moline in the Quad Cities region, and Peoria.

As of 1997, there were 39 Fortune 500 companies headquartered in Illinois. In 1995, there were 3,407 US patents issued to residents of Illinois.

30 COMMERCE

Chicago is the leading wholesaling center of the Midwest. In 1992, the state's 24,637 wholesale establishments had sales of $219.4 billion. Chicago is an especially important trade center for furniture, housewares, and apparel. Durable goods accounted for 52.5% of wholesale sales in 1992. The state's 64,826 retail stores recorded sales of $85.8 billion in 1992. The principal retail store groups and their respective sales shares were automotive dealers, 21.4%; foodstores, 17.4%; general merchandise stores, 12.3%; and eating and drinking places, 10.6%. Leading Illinois-based retailing companies in 1996 were Sears, Roebuck, with nationwide revenues of $38.2 billion; Household International, $5 billion; McDonald's, $10.7 billion; and Walgreen, $11.8 billion.

Illinois ranked 5th among the states in exports with estimated exports of $32.2 billion in 1996. Exports produced in Illinois amounted to $24.2 billion in 1996.

In 1994, 3.3% of the nation's exports passed through the Chicago customs district, covering most of the Midwest; total volume of exports through the district was $17.3 billion.

31 CONSUMER PROTECTION

Statewide, the Office of the Attorney General is the most active protector of consumers with its Consumer Fraud Section and Consumer Protection Division. The governor controls the Consumer Advocate's Office, and the Department of Insurance also has a Consumer Division. The Department of Human Rights was established in 1979 to protect individuals in regard to employment, public accommodations, and other areas.

32 BANKING

Banking was highly controversial in 19th-century Illinois. Modernizers stressed the need for adequate venture capital and money supplies, but traditionalist farmers feared they would be impoverished by an artificial "money monster." Efforts to create a state bank floundered in confusion, while the dubious character of most private banknotes inspired the state to ban private banks altogether. The major breakthrough came during the Civil War, when federal laws encouraged the establishment of strong national banks in all the larger cities, and Chicago quickly became the financial center of the Midwest. Apart from the 1920s and early 1930s, when numerous neighborhood and small-town banks folded, the banking system has flourished ever since.

There were 864 commercial banks in Illinois in 1996 (2d only to Texas), an unusually large number attributable to regulations restricting branch banking. Until the 1970s, even the largest banks were allowed only one office. At the end of 1996, commercial banks held $238.7 billion in assets and deposits of $146.8 billion. By 1995, the Resolution Trust Corporation (RTC) assisted 49 Illinois institutions out of insolvency, at a cost of $1.5 billion.

In 1996, Illinois had 149 insured savings institutions, with total assets of $52.9 billion and outstanding mortgage loans of $30.3 billion. The largest associations are First Federal, Talman, and Home Federal, all of Chicago.

33 INSURANCE

Illinois is a major center of the insurance industry. In 1995, the state's 91 life insurance companies collected $23.6 billion in premiums. In 1995, the average family had $137,200 in life insurance coverage.

Illinois fire and casualty companies are among the US leaders. State Farm is based in Bloomington, and Allstate, a subsidiary of Sears, Roebuck is in Chicago. Within the state, fire and casualty underwriters wrote premiums totaling $12.5 billion in 1995, including $2.9 billion in automotive liability insurance, $2.0 billion in automobile physical-damage insurance, and $1,060 million in homeowners' coverage. In the same year, 38,110 policies covered flood insurance, totaling $2.8 billion. Blue Cross–Blue Shield, the nation's largest hospital and medical insurance program, is headquartered in Chicago.

34SECURITIES

Chicago, home of the Midwest Stock Exchange, ranks 2d only to New York as a center for securities trading. As of March 1997, there were 2,300 broker and dealer firms registered to sell securities in Illinois via 108,000 registered agents. Some 1,500 securities investment advisor firms were registered to do business in the state in March 1997.

The most intensive trading in Chicago takes place on the three major commodity exchanges. The Chicago Board of Trade has set agricultural prices for the world since 1848, especially in soybeans, corn, and wheat. The Chicago Mercantile Exchange specializes in pork bellies (bacon), live cattle, potatoes, and eggs; since 1972, it has also provided a market for world currency futures. The Mid-America Commodity Exchange, the smallest of the three, has a colorful ancestry dating from 1868. It features small-lot futures contracts on soybeans, silver, corn, wheat, and live hogs.

35PUBLIC FINANCE

Among the larger states, Illinois is known for its low taxes and conservative fiscal policy. The Bureau of the Budget, under the governor's control, has major responsibility for the state's overall fiscal program, negotiating annually with key legislators, cabinet officers, and outside pressure groups. The governor then submits the budget to the legislature for amendment and approval. The fiscal year runs from 1 July to 30 June. The following table summarizes consolidated revenues and appropriations for 1996/97 (estimated) and 1997/98 (projected) (in millions):

REVENUES	1996/97	1997/98
Sales tax	$ 5,426	5,649
Personal income tax	6,009	6,309
Corporate income tax	996	1,036
Public utility tax	860	860
Cigarette tax	419	419
Liquor tax	56	56
Inheritance tax	190	200
Other taxes	1,860	1,884
Federal receipts	8,156	8,197
Other receipts and designated funds	4,992	4,907
TOTALS	$ 28,964	29,517

APPROPRIATIONS	1996/97	1997/98
Highways and transportation	$ 5,281	4,908
Public welfare	7,542	9,361
Primary and secondary education	5,379	5,740
Higher education	2,704	2,382
Mental health	1,546	—
Capital development	1,054	1,123
Environmental protection	773	697
Public health	519	190
Other outlays	10,022	10,178
TOTALS	$ 34,820	34,579

Spending against appropriations is estimated to be $29 billion in 1996/97 and $29.6 billion in 1997/98.

36TAXATION

Illinoisans have fiercely resisted the imposition of new and higher taxes. The levying of the first 1% sales tax in 1933 to finance relief programs was bitterly resented, and the inauguration of a state personal income tax in 1970 led to the defeat of Governor Richard Ogilvie in his 1972 re-election campaign. Total state revenue from 1995 general revenue sources was $29.1 billion, or $2,456.7 per capita.

As of 1996, the state personal income tax was a flat 3%. The corporate income tax was 7.3% and the sales tax 6.25%, with few exemptions. Excise taxes included charges on cigarettes and on gasoline.

Local levies, chiefly property taxes, are relatively light. Low state and local taxes were counterbalanced by high federal payments and a very low return of federal dollars to Illinois. In 1995, Illinois per capita federal tax payments averaged $5,694.1. The federal government collected $74.4 billion in Illinois for 1994, and sent back $50.96 billion.

37ECONOMIC POLICY

The state's policy toward economic development has engendered political controversy since the 1830s. Before the Civil War, the Democrats in power usually tried to slow, though not reverse, the tide of rapid industrial and commercial growth. The Republican ascendancy between the 1850s and the 1930s (with a few brief interruptions) produced a generally favorable business climate, which in turn fostered rapid economic growth. The manufacturing sector eroded slowly in the 1960s and 1970s, as incentives and tax credits for new industry were kept at a modest level. In 1989, however, the state began to aggressively encourage companies undergoing modernization or commercializing new technologies by enacting the Technology Advancement and Development Act, which invests in companies developing advanced technologies for commercial purposes.

The Department of Commerce and Community Affairs promotes economic development, describing itself as the "sales department for Illinois." It maintains offices in Washington (DC), Brussels, Hong Kong, São Paulo, and Osaka. The promotion of jobs, tourism, minority owned enterprises, and foreign markets for Illinois products is the department's major responsibility. The assistance by the DCCA includes equity capital and low interest loans for small businesses; low-interest financing to communities undergoing infrastructure improvements which help create or retain jobs; tax-exempt bonds for companies expanding or renovating their physical plant; and grants for employee training and retraining.

38HEALTH

In 1995, infant mortality was 9.3 per 1,000 live births. Although the infant mortality rate fell from 21.5 in 1970 to 13.9 in 1981 to 10.7 in 1991, it did not decline as rapidly as elsewhere. Since the late 1960s, Illinois has had a slightly higher infant mortality rate than the rest of the country; the 1993/94 rate was the 5th highest among the states. The number of legal abortions performed in 1995 was 52,300, down from 72,000 in 1977.

Illinois's marriage and divorce rates were both below the US norms, but the birthrate, 25.7 per 1,000 population in 1995, was marginally higher, as was the death rate, 9.1 per 1,000 residents in that same year. At that time Illinois ranked above the national average in deaths due to heart disease, cancer, and cerebrovascular disease, but below the average in accidents and adverse effects and suicide. In 1993, Illinois had a coronary artery disease mortality rate of 108.4 per 100,000. In 1995, there were 35.3 breast cancer deaths per 100,000 women, fourth highest among the states. Major public health problems in the 1980s included rapidly increasing rates of venereal disease and drug abuse. Alcoholism has always been a major problem in Illinois. The state also has a high proportion of residents receiving psychiatric care. The latest census documents report over 3 million smokers, or 26% of the adults 18–30 years of age, in Illinois. The AIDS rate of 23.70 per 100,000 population was slightly below the national average in 1995.

Hospitals abound in Illinois, with Chicago serving as a diagnostic and treatment center for patients throughout the Midwest. With 227 facilities (many quite large) and 52,934 beds, Illinois hospitals recorded 1,538,969 admissions in 1994. In January 1994, the state had 27,388 physicians. In 1993, there were 7,188 professionally active dentists. At least 11% of Illinois residents had no insurance in 1994. Per capita personal health expenditures in 1991 were higher than the US average of $2,648.

[39]SOCIAL WELFARE

Prior to the 1930s, social welfare programs were the province of county government and private agencies. Asylums, particularly poor farms, were built in most counties following the Civil War; they provided custodial care for orphans, the very old, the helpless, sick, and itinerant "tramps." Most people who needed help however, turned to relatives, neighbors, or church agencies. The local and private agencies were overwhelmed by the severe depression of the 1930s, forcing first the state and then the federal government to intervene. Social welfare programs are implemented by county agencies, but funded by local and state taxes and federal aid. In the early 1990s, the annual outlays for the five largest welfare programs in Illinois totaled more than $2 billion; $421.05 per capita in state government expenditures.

In 1996, 663,212 children and adults received aid to families with dependent children, averaging $414 a month in 1996.

The federal food stamp program had an average monthly participation of 1.1 million in 1996. The federal school lunch program's federal outlays totaled $208.6 million.

With the enactment of the Personal Responsibility and Work Opportunity Reconciliation Act of 1996, the US government has changed the form and regulations for many of its social welfare programs; most significantly, it replaces Aid to Families with Dependent Children (AFDC), an open-ended entitlement program, with Temporary Assistance for Needy Families (TANF), a limited system of assistance funded largely through federal block grants. The reform act also impacts the food stamp program, the Supplemental Security Income program, and the child nutrition program. The law took effect on 1 July 1997 and provided $16.38 billion in block grants for fiscal years 1997–2002. The grants are to be divided among the states based on an equation involving the numbers of former AFDC recipients in each state. Because many of the bills provisions have yet to be implemented into state-by-state policy, it was not possible to include the details of each state's programs for this edition of this work.

Social Security monthly payments averaged $760 for the state's 1.6 million retired workers in 1995. In addition, total Supplemental Security Income payments averaging $370 a month covered 266,563 disabled, aged, and blind persons.

Unemployment insurance is slightly more generous in Illinois than in most other states; the average weekly benefit in 1995 was $207.62 to eligible state residents.

[40]HOUSING

Flimsy cabins and shacks provided rude shelter for many Illinoisans in pioneer days. Later, the balloon-frame house, much cheaper to build than traditional structures, became a trademark of the Prairie State. After a third of Chicago's wooden houses burned in 1871, the city moved to enforce more stringent building codes. The city's predominant dwelling then became the three- or five-story brick apartment house. Great mansions were built in elite areas of Chicago (first Prairie Avenue, later the Gold Coast), and high-rise lakefront luxury apartments first became popular in the 1920s. In the 1970s, Chicago pioneered the conversion of luxury apartment buildings to condominiums, which numbered 242,653 (5.4% of all housing units) in 1990.

In 1996 there were an estimated 4,679,000 housing units in Illinois, of which 4,335,000 were occupied. In 1996, 45,592 new privately owned units valued at nearly $5.2 billion were authorized for construction, 35,912 of which were single-family units. The median monthly cost for owners with a mortgage in 1990, the last year for which figures were available, was $767, and $241 for owners without a mortgage; the same costs in the greater Chicago area of Illinois were $889 and $284, respectively. The median monthly rent in 1990 throughout the state was $445; in the greater Chicago area it was $491. From 1990 to 1992, the Chicago vicinity of Illinois saw 47,200 new units completed, of which 65% were single-family houses.

During 1995/96 Illinois received $1.4 billion in aid from the US Department of Housing and Urban Development, including nearly $240 million in community development block grants.

[41]EDUCATION

In 1854, Ninian Edwards became the first superintendent of public education. His first and most difficult task was to convince pioneer parents that a formal education was a necessary item in the lives of their children. By the mid 1870s, education in Illinois had become a going enterprise. Edwards helped create an outstanding public school system, although the city of Chicago was hard pressed to construct enough school buildings to serve the growing numbers of students until foreign immigration subsided in the 1920s. The dedication of these educators continued to improve the quality of education, but it was not until the development of a good highway system and state funding for the transporting of students, that rural Illinois was to see the demise of one-room school houses. In one decade, 1944–54, state mandated school consolidation/reorganization reduced the number of school districts from 11,955 to 2,607. Today, there are 906 operational public school districts providing the leadership/training necessary to guarantee high-quality public education to all children in Illinois.

In 1993, Illinois had slightly higher literacy levels than the national averages. In 1990, 76.2% of the Illinois adult population held high school diplomas with nearly 21% continuing their education and earning a bachelor's degree or higher.

In 1995, Illinois had 2,598 public elementary schools, 588 junior high schools, 639 high schools, and 273 special education and other schools. Enrollment at the elementary level was 1,641,653 in 1995/96; enrollment at the secondary level was 624,413 in 1995/96. Over 36% of all public school students are minorities: Black, 21.1%; Hispanic, 12.2%; Asian, 3.0%; and Native Americans, 0.1%. The 1995/96 elementary pupil-teacher ratio was 19.5; secondary ratio, 17.9. The 1995/96 median salary for Illinois elementary teachers was $35,639; secondary salary, $41,081.

Nonpublic schools, dominated by Chicago's extensive Roman Catholic school system, have shown a slight decrease since the early 1980s. Total nonpublic enrollment in Illinois private schools was 320,880 in 1995/96. Rising tuition fees, caused in part by higher salaries for lay teachers and a drop in the number of teaching sisters, threatened the parochial schools. The Chicago/Cook County nonpublic schools had 130,300 primary pupils and 43,258 high school students in the 1996/97 school year. High-tuition private schools continue to flourish in Chicago, however.

In the fall of 1995 the 183 Illinois public and private colleges had a total enrollment of 721,575. The state's 12 public universities enrolled 192,532 students in the fall of 1995, or almost 27% of total higher education enrollment. Together these universities offered a full range of educational opportunities, including nearly 700 bachelor's degree programs, more than 550 master's degree programs, and nearly 200 doctoral programs, plus professional degrees in law, medicine, veterinary medicine, and dentistry. The University of Illinois system has both the largest and smallest public university campuses. Champaign-Urbana was the state's most populous campus with 38,420 students, and the University of Illinois at Springfield, formerly Sangamon State University, enrolled 4,702 students in fall 1995.

Nearly half of all Illinois college students attend one of the state's 49 public community colleges, which in 1995 enrolled 337,716 students.

Private institutions enroll about 25% of Illinois college students, a total of 191,327 in 1995. Private sector institutions are broken down into two broad categories—not-for-profit and proprietary. There are 103 independent, not-for-profit colleges and universities.

For fiscal year 1997, the board of higher education, the coordinating agency for all sectors of Illinois higher education, recommended and the governor and general assembly appropriated, a total of $2.6 billion for higher education operations and grants.

Revenues for Illinois public schools for 1995/96 were $12,458.3 million. Illinois education is financed through a combination of state ($3,994.8 million), local ($7,339.8 million), and federal funds ($1.123.7 million). In 1991/92, the Illinois per capita school expenditure was $808 (41st among the states). The estimated mean expenditure per student in 1995/96 was $5,530 (33rd among the states); the average United States expenditure was $6,103.

[42]ARTS

Chicago emerged in the late 19th century as the leading arts center of the Midwest, and it continues to hold this premier position. The major downstate facilities include the Krannert Center at the University of Illinois (Champaign-Urbana) and the Lakeview Center in Peoria.

In 1996, the state of Illinois generated $908,000 from federal sources to develop its art programs. The NEA contributed $2,472,000 to the arts and $4,964,000 to the Illinois Arts Council. The state also provided $44,900,054. Private sources provided an additional $154 million. A total of 944,628 artists contributed to Illinois's art programs. Audiences for the events totaled about 250,293,000.

Architecture is the outstanding art form in Illinois, and Chicago—where the first skyscrapers were built in the 1880s—has been a mecca for modern commercial and residential architects ever since the fire of 1871. The Art Institute of Chicago, incorporated in 1879, is the leading art museum in the state. Although its holdings, largely donated by wealthy Chicagoans, cover all the major periods, its French Impressionist collection is especially noteworthy. The most recent example of bold architecture is the $172-million State of Illinois Center in Chicago, which opened in 1985.

The state's arts education programs were offered to 850,000 school children. By 1991, Illinois had 2,200 arts associations and 83 local associations. The Illinois Arts Council continues to develop its arts education programs through the NEA's state and regional program.

Theater groups abound—there were 116 theatrical producers in 1982—notably in Chicago, where the Second City comedy troupe and the Steppenwolf Theatre are located; the city's best playwrights and performers, however, often gravitate to Broadway or Hollywood. Film production was an important industry in Illinois before 1920, when operations shifted to the sunnier climate and more opulent production facilities of southern California. By the early 1980s, however, the Illinois Film Office had staged an impressive comeback, and television films and motion pictures were being routinely shot in the state.

The Chicago Symphony Orchestra, organized by Theodore Thomas in 1891, quickly acquired world stature; its permanent conductors have included Frederick Stock, Fritz Reiner, and Sir George Solti, who regularly took the symphony on triumphant European tours. German immigrants founded many musical societies in Chicago in the late 19th century, when the city also became a major center of musical education. Opera flourished in Chicago in the early 20th century, collapsed during the early 1930s, but was reborn through the founding of the Lyric Opera in 1954. Chicago's most original musical contribution was jazz, imported from the South by black musicians in the 1920s. Such jazz greats as King Oliver, Louis Armstrong, Jelly Roll Morton, Benny Goodman, and Gene Krupa all worked or learned their craft in the speakeasies and jazz houses of the city's South Side. More recently, Chicago became the center of an urban blues movement, using electric rather than acoustic guitars and influenced by jazz.

The seamy side of Chicago has fascinated writers throughout the 20th century. Among well-known American novels set in Chicago are two muckraking works, Frank Norris's *The Pit* (1903) and Upton Sinclair's *The Jungle* (1906), as well as James T. Farrell's *Studs Lonigan* (1935) and Saul Bellow's *The Adventures of Augie March* (1953). Famous American plays associated with Chicago are *The Front Page* (1928), by Ben Hecht and Charles MacArthur, and *A Raisin in the Sun* (1959), by Lorraine Hansberry.

[43]LIBRARIES AND MUSEUMS

Libraries and library science are particularly strong in Illinois. In 1997 there were 637 public libraries, nearly all of them members of 12 regional systems, which had a combined book stock in 1993 of 32,517,717. The facilities in Peoria, Oak Park, Evanston, Rockford, and Quincy are noteworthy, and the Chicago Public Library system now operates the Harold Washington Library Center, two regional centers, 79 branch libraries, and the Illinois Regional Library for the Blind and Physically Handicapped. The outstanding libraries of the University of Illinois (Champaign-Urbana) and the University of Chicago (with 8,096,040 and 5,854,014 volumes in 1996/97, respectively) constitute the state's leading research facilities, and the University of Illinois has a famous library school. Principal historical collections are at the Newberry Library in Chicago, the Illinois State Historical Society in Springfield, and the Chicago Historical Society.

Illinois has 267 museums and historic sites. Chicago's Field Museum of Natural History, founded in 1893, has sponsored numerous worldwide expeditions in the course of acquiring some 13 million anthropological, zoological, botanical, and geological specimens. The Museum of Science and Industry, near the University of Chicago, attracts 5 million visitors a year, mostly children, to see its exhibits of industrial technology. Also noteworthy are the Adler Planetarium, Shedd Aquarium, and the Oriental Institute Museum of the University of Chicago. The Brookfield Zoo, near Chicago, opened in 1934; smaller zoos can be found in Chicago's Lincoln Park and in Peoria, Elgin, and other cities.

Just about every town has one or more historic sites authenticated by the state. The most popular is New Salem, near Springfield, where Abraham Lincoln lived from 1831 to 1837. Its reconstruction, begun by press magnate William Randolph Hearst in 1906, includes one original cabin and numerous replicas. The most important archaeological sites are the Dixon Mounds, 40 mi (64 km) south of Peoria, and the Koster Excavation in Calhoun County, north of St. Louis, Mo.

44COMMUNICATIONS

Illinois has an extensive communications system. The state's households with telephones numbered about 4,268,000 in March 1993, or 93.7% of all households.

Illinois had 125 AM and 255 FM commercial radio stations in 1996, when 38 commercial television stations and 11 educational stations served the state. The state's 25 large cable systems have brought good television reception to the small towns. In 1979, WGN-TV in Chicago became a "superstation," with sports programs, movies, and advertising. Although the three major networks own stations in Chicago, they originate very little programming from the city. However, as a major advertising center, Chicago produces many commercials and industrial films. Most educational broadcasting in Illinois comes from state universities and the Chicago public and Catholic school systems.

45PRESS

The state's first newspaper, the *Illinois Herald,* was begun in Kaskaskia in 1814. From the 1830s through the end of the 19th century, small-town weeklies exerted powerful political influence. After 1900, however, publishers discovered that they needed large circulations to appeal to advertisers, and so they toned down their partisanship and began adding a broad range of features to attract a wider audience.

As of 1997, Illinois had 23 morning newspapers (including all-day papers), 46 evening dailies, and 28 Sunday papers. The Illinois editions of St. Louis newspapers are also widely read. The following table shows the state's leading dailies with their 1997 circulations:

AREA	NAME	DAILY	SUNDAY
Chicago	*Sun-Times* (m,S)	505,115	469,161
	Tribune (all day,S)	667,908	1,060,393
Peoria	*Journal Star* (all day,S)	75,244	104,610
Rockford	*Register Star* (all day,S)	75,228	87,916
Springfield	*State Journal–Register* (m,S)	65,631	75,319

The most popular magazines published in Chicago are *Playboy* and *Ebony.* Many specialized trade and membership magazines, such as the *Lion* and the *Rotarian,* are published in Chicago, which is also the printing and circulation center for many magazines edited in New York. The popular *Cricket Magazine* for children is published in LaSalle-Peru.

46ORGANIZATIONS

Before the Civil War, Yankee-dominated towns and cities in northern Illinois sponsored lyceums, debating circles, women's clubs, temperance groups, and antislavery societies. During the 20th century, Chicago's size and central location attracted the headquarters of numerous national organizations, though far fewer than New York or, more recently, Washington, D.C. The 1992 Census of Service Industries counted 3,273 organizations in Illinois, including 700 business associations; 1,795 civic, social, and fraternal organizations; and 778 other membership organizations. Major national service and fraternal bodies with headquarters in Chicago or nearby suburbs include the Benevolent and Protective Order of Elks of the USA, Lions Clubs International, Loyal Order of Moose, and Rotary International.

Chicago has long been a center for professional organizations, among them the most powerful single US medical group, the American Medical Association, founded in 1847, and the American Hospital Association, begun in 1898. Other major groups include associations of surgeons, dentists, veterinarians, osteopaths, and dietitians, as well as the Blue Cross and Blue Shield Association and the National Easter Seal Society.

The American Bar Association has its headquarters in Chicago, as do several smaller legal groups, including the American Judicature Society and the Commercial Law League of America. Librarians also have a base in Chicago: the American Library Association, the Society of American Archivists, and the associations of law and medical librarians. The National Parent-Teacher Association is the only major educational group.

A variety of trade organizations, such as the American Marketing Association, are based in Chicago, though many have moved to Washington, D.C. The American Farm Bureau Federation operates out of Park Ridge. The National Women's Christian Temperance Union, one of the most important of all US pressure groups in the 19th century, has its headquarters in Evanston.

47TOURISM, TRAVEL, AND RECREATION

The tourist industry is of special importance to Chicago, the nation's leading convention center. The city's chief tourist attractions are its museums, restaurants, and shops. Chicago also boasts the world's tallest building, the Sears Tower, 110 stories and 1,454 feet (443 meters) high.

For the state as a whole, tourism generated $13.8 billion in revenue in 1993. There are 42 state parks, 4 state forests, 36,659 campsites, and 25 state recreation places. The Lincoln Home National Historic Site in Springfield, one of the state's most popular tourist attractions, had 412,524 visitors in 1993.

Swimming, bicycling, hiking, camping, horseback riding, fishing, and motorboating are the most popular recreational activities. Licenses were issued to 908,496 fishermen and 1,176,950 hunters who were state residents in 1995. Even more popular than hunting is wildlife observation, an activity that engages nearly 3 million Illinoisans annually.

48SPORTS

Illinois has five major league professional sports teams, all of which play in Chicago: the Cubs and the White Sox of major league baseball, the Bears of the National Football League, the Bulls of the National Basketball Association, and the Blackhawks of the National Hockey League.

The Cubs last won a World Series in 1908, the White Sox in 1917. The Bears won the Super Bowl in 1986. The Bulls established a remarkable basketball dynasty fueled by the play of Michael Jordan, perhaps the best athlete in the history of basketball, winning NBA championships in 1991, 1992, 1993, 1996, and 1997. They were the first basketball team to win three consecutive championships since the Boston Celtics set the probably unbreakable record of eight consecutive titles from 1959 to 1966. The Blackhawks won the Stanley Cup in 1934, 1938, and 1961. The state also has minor league baseball, basketball, and hockey.

The White Sox built a new ballpark, which opened in 1993. Horse racing is very popular in the state, with pari-mutuel betting allowed. The Golden Glove Boxing Tournament is held annually in February in Chicago.

In collegiate sports the emphasis is on basketball and football. The University of Illinois and Northwestern compete in the Big Ten conference. Illinois won the Rose Bowl in 1947, 1952, and 1964, and was named national champion in 1923. In a remarkable revival of its football program, Northwestern won its first Big Ten title (winning against Ohio State) in 46 years in 1995. The Wildcats played in the Rose Bowl for the first time since 1949, when they recorded their only victory in the New Year's Day game. Southern Illinois won the National Invitational Tournament in basketball in 1967. The DePaul Blue Demons of the Great Midwest Conference consistently rank high among college basketball teams.

[49]FAMOUS ILLINOISANS

Abraham Lincoln (b.Kentucky, 1809–65), 16th president of the US, is the outstanding figure in Illinois history, having lived and built his political career in the state between 1830 and 1861. The only Illinois native to be elected president is Ronald Reagan (b.1911), who left the state after graduating from Eureka College to pursue his film and political careers in California. Ulysses S. Grant (b.Ohio, 1822–85), the nation's 18th president, lived in Galena on the eve of the Civil War. Adlai E. Stevenson (b.Kentucky, 1835–1914), founder of a political dynasty, served as US vice president from 1893 to 1897, but was defeated for the same office in 1900. His grandson, also named Adlai E. Stevenson (b.California, 1900–65), served as governor of Illinois from 1949 to 1953, was the Democratic presidential nominee in 1952 and 1956, and ended his career as US ambassador to the United Nations. Charles Gates Dawes (b.Ohio, 1865–1951), a Chicago financier, served as vice president from 1925 to 1929 and shared the 1925 Nobel Peace Prize for the Dawes Plan to reorganize German finances. William Jennings Bryan (1860–1925), a leader of the free-silver and Populist movements, was the Democratic presidential nominee in 1896, 1900, and 1908.

US Supreme Court justices associated with Illinois include David Davis (b.Maryland, 1815–86); John M. Harlan (1899–1971); Chicago-born Arthur Goldberg (1908–90), who also served as secretary of labor and succeeded Stevenson as UN ambassador; Harry A. Blackmun (1908–97); and John Paul Stevens (b.1920). Melville Fuller (b.Maine, 1833–1910) served as chief justice from 1888 to 1910.

Many other politicians who played important roles on the national scene drew their support form the people of Illinois. They include Stephen Douglas (b.Vermont, 1813–61), senator from 1847 to 1861, Democratic Party leader, 1860 presidential candidate, but equally famous as Lincoln's opponent in a series of debates on slavery in 1858; Lyman Trumbull (b.Connecticut, 1813–96), senator from 1855 to 1873, who helped secure passage of the 13th and 14th amendments to the US Constitution; Joseph "Uncle Joe" Cannon (b.North Carolina, 1836–1926), Republican congressman from Danville for half a century and autocratic speaker of the House from 1903 to 1911; Henry Rainey (1860–1934), Democratic speaker of the House during 1933–34, Everett McKinley Dirksen (1896–1969), senator and colorful Republican leader during the 1950s and 1960s; Charles H. Percy (b.Florida, 1919), Republican senator from 1967 to 1985; John B. Anderson (b.1922), Republican congressman for 20 years and an independent presidential candidate in 1980; and Robert H. Michel (b.1923), House Republican leader in the 1980s.

Among noteworthy governors of the state, in addition to Stevenson, were Richard Yates (b.Kentucky, 1815–73), who maintained Illinois's loyalty to the Union during the Civil War; John Peter Altgeld (b.Germany, 1847–1902), governor from 1893 to 1897; and Republican-Progressive leader Frank Lowden (b.Minnesota, 1861–1943). Richard J. Daley (1902–76) was Democratic boss and mayor of Chicago from 1955 to 1976. Jane Byrne (b.1934), a Daley protégé, became mayor in 1979; she was succeeded in 1983 by Harold Washington (1922–87), the city's first black mayor. Richard Michael Daley (b. 1942), son of Richard Daley, also became mayor.

Phyllis Schlafly (b.Missouri, 1924) of Alton became nationally known as an antifeminist conservative crusader during the 1970s. An outstanding Illinoisan was Jane Addams (1860–1935), founder of Hull House (1889), author, reformer, prohibitionist, feminist, and tireless worker for world peace; in 1931, she shared the Nobel Peace Prize. Winners of the Nobel Prize in physics include Albert Michelson (b.Germany, 1852–1931), Robert Millikan (1868–1953), Arthur Holly Compton (b.Ohio, 1892–1962), Enrico Fermi (b.Italy, 1901–54), John Bardeen (b.Wisconsin, 1908), John R. Schrieffer (b.1931), and James W. Cronin (b.1931). Chemistry prizes went to Robert Mulliken (b.Massachusetts, 1896–1986), Wendell Stanley (b.Indiana, 1904–71), Willard Libby (b.Colorado, 1908–80), and Stanford Moore (1913–82). Nobel Prizes in physiology or medicine were won by Charles Huggins (b.Canada, 1901), George Beadle (b.Nebraska 1903–89), and Robert W. Holley (1922–93). A Nobel award in literature went to Saul Bellow (b.Canada, 1915), and the economics prize was given to Milton Friedman (b.New York, 1912), leader of the so-called Chicago school of economists, and to Theodore Schultz (b.South Dakota, 1902) in 1979.

Some of the most influential Illinoisans have been religious leaders; many of them also exercised social and political influence. Notable are Methodist circuit rider Peter Cartwright (b.Virginia, 1785–1872); Dwight Moody (b.Massachusetts, 1837–99), leading force in the National Women's Christian Temperance Union and the feminist cause; Mother Frances Xavier Cabrini (b.Italy, 1850–1917), the first American to be canonized; Bishop Fulton J. Sheen (1895–1979), influential spokesman for the Roman Catholic Church; Elijah Muhammad (Elijah Poole, b.Georgia, 1897–1975), leader of the Black Muslim movement; and Jesse Jackson (b.North Carolina, 1941), civil rights leader and one of the most prominent black spokesmen of the 1980s and 1990s.

Outstanding business and professional leaders who lived in Illinois include John Deere (b.Vermont, 1804–86), industrialist and inventor of the steel plow; Cyrus Hall McCormick (b.Virginia, 1809–84), inventor of the reaping machine; Nathan Davis (1817–1904), the "father of the American Medical Association", railroad car inventor George Pullman (b.New York 1831–97); meat-packer Philip Armour (b.New York, 1832–1901); merchant Marshall Field (b.Massachusetts, 1834–1906); merchant Aaron Montgomery Ward (b.New Jersey, 1843–1913); sporting-goods manufacturer Albert G. Spalding (1850–1915); breakfast-food manufacturer Charles W. Post (1854–1911); William Rainey Harper (b.Ohio, 1856–1906), first president of the University of Chicago; lawyer Clarence Darrow (b.Ohio, 1857–1938); public utilities magnate Samuel Insull (b.England, 1859–1938); Julius Rosenwald (1862–1932), philanthropist and executive of Sears, Roebuck; advertising executive Albert Lasker (b.Texas, 1880–1952); and *Chicago Tribune* publisher Robert R. McCormick (1880–1955). Thomas R. Cech (b.Illinois 1937) was a recipient of the 1989 Nobel prize for chemistry. Jerome Friedman (b.1930), 1990 co-recipient of the Nobel Prize for physics, in Chicago. Harry M. Markowitz (b.Illinois 1927) won the Nobel prize for economics in 1990. Michael Bishop (b.Illinois 1936) was a recipient of the 1989 Nobel Prize for physiology or medicine.

Artists who worked for significant periods in Illinois (usually in Chicago) include architects William Le Baron Jenney (b.Massachusetts, 1832–1907), Dankmar Adler (b.Germany, 1844–1900), Daniel H. Burnham (b.New York, 1846–1912), John Wellborn Root (b.Georgia, 1850–91), Louis Sullivan (b.Massachusetts, 1856–1924), Frank Lloyd Wright (b.Wisconsin, 1869–1959), and Ludwig Mies van der Rohe (b.Germany, 1886–1969). Important writers include humorist Finley Peter Dunne (1867–1936), creator of the fictional saloon-keeper-philosopher Mr. Dooley; and novelists Hamlin Garland (b.Wisconsin, 1860–1940), Edgar Rice Burroughs (1875–1950), John Dos Passos (1896–1970), Ernest Hemingway (1899–1961), and James Farrell (1904–79). Poets include Harriet Monroe (1860–1936); Edgar Lee Masters (b.Kansas, 1869–1950); biographer-poet Carl Sandburg (1878–1967); Nicholas Vachel Lindsay (1879–1931); Archibald MacLeish (1892–1982), also librarian of Congress and assistant secretary of state; and Gwendolyn Brooks (b.Kansas, 1917), the first black woman to win a Pulitzer Prize. Robert Butler (b. 1945) was the 1993 winner of the Pulitzer Prize for fiction. Performing artists connected with the state include opera stars Mary Garden (b.Scotland, 1877–1967) and Sherrill Milnes (b.1935); clarinetist Benny Goodman (1909–86); pop singers Mel Torme (b.1925) and Grace Slick (b.1939); jazz musician Miles Davis (b.1926–91); showmen Gower Champion (1921–80) and Robert Louis "Bob" Fosse (b.1927–87); comedians Jack Benny (Benjamin Kubelsky, 1894–1974), Harvey Korman (b.1927), Bob Newhart (b.1929), and Richard Pryor (b.1940); and a long list of stage and screen stars, including Gloria Swanson (1899–1983), Ralph Bellamy (b.1904–91), Robert Young (b.1907), Karl Malden (Malden Sekulovich, b.1913), William Holden (1918–81), Jason Robards, Jr. (b.1922), Charlton Heston (b.1922), Rock Hudson (Roy Fitzgerald, 1925–85), Donald O'Connor (b.1925), Bruce Dern (b.1936), and Raquel Welch (Raquel Tejeda, b.1942). Dominant figures in the Illinois sports world include Ernest "Ernie" Banks (b.Texas, 1931) of the Chicago Cubs; Robert "Bobby" Hull (b.Canada, 1939) of the Chicago Black Hawks; owner George Halas (1895–83) and running backs Harold Edward "Red" Grange (b.Pennsyl-vania, 1903–91), Gale Sayers (b.Kansas, 1943), and Walter Payton (b.Mississippi, 1954) of the Chicago Bears; and collegiate football coach Amos Alonzo Stagg (b.New Jersey, 1862–1965).

[50]BIBLIOGRAPHY

Carrier, Lois. *Illinois: Crossroads of a Continent*. Urbana: University of Illinois Press, 1993.

Gove, Samuel Kimball. *Illinois Politics & Government: The Expanding Metropolitan Frontier*. Lincoln: University of Nebraska, 1996.

Illinois, State of. Department of Commerce and Community Affairs. *Illinois Data Book*, Springfield. 1994.

Illinois, State of. Secretary of State. *Illinois Blue Book*. Springfield.

Jensen, Richard J. *Illinois: A Bicentennial History*. New York: Norton, 1978.

Petterchak, Janice A., ed. *Illinois History: An Annotated Bibliography*. Westport, Conn.: Greenwood, 1995.

INDIANA

State of Indiana

ORIGIN OF STATE NAME: Named "land of Indians" for the many Indian tribes that formerly lived in the state. **NICKNAME:** The Hoosier State. **CAPITAL:** Indianapolis. **ENTERED UNION:** 11 December 1816 (19th). **SONG:** "On the Banks of the Wabash, Far Away." **MOTTO:** The Crossroads of America. **FLAG:** A flaming torch representing liberty is surrounded by 19 gold stars against a blue background. The word "Indiana" is above the flame. **OFFICIAL SEAL:** In a pioneer setting, a farmer fells a tree while a buffalo flees from the forest and across the prairie; in the background, the sun sets over distant hills. The words "Seal of the State of Indiana 1816" surround the scene. **BIRD:** Cardinal. **FLOWER:** Peony. **TREE:** Tulip tree (yellow poplar). **STONE:** Indiana limestone. **POEM:** "Indiana." **LEGAL HOLIDAYS:** New Year's Day, 1 January; Birthday of Martin Luther King, Jr., 3d Monday in January; Lincoln's Birthday, 12 February; Washington's Birthday, 3d Monday in February; Good Friday, March or April; Primary Election Day, 1st Tuesday after 1st Monday in May in even-numbered years; Memorial Day, last Monday in May; Independence Day, 4 July; Labor Day, 1st Monday in September; Columbus Day, 2d Monday in October; Election Day, 1st Tuesday after 1st Monday in November in even-numbered years; Veterans Day, 11 November; Thanksgiving Day, 4th Thursday in November; Christmas Day, 25 December. **TIME:** 7 AM EST = noon GMT; 6 AM CST = noon GMT.

¹LOCATION, SIZE, AND EXTENT

Situated in the eastern north-central US, Indiana is the smallest of the 12 midwestern states and ranks 38th in size among the 50 states.

Indiana's total area is 36,185 sq mi (93,720 sq km), of which land takes up 35,932 (93,064 sq km) and water the remaining 253 sq mi (656 sq km). Shaped somewhat like a vertical quadrangle, with irregular borders on the s and w, the state extends about 160 mi (257 km) E-W and about 280 mi (451 km) N-S.

Indiana is bordered on the N by Michigan (with part of the line passing through Lake Michigan); on the E by Ohio; on the SE and s by Kentucky (the entire line formed by the north bank of the Ohio River); and on the w by Illinois (with the line in the sw demarcated by the Wabash River). The total boundary length of Indiana is 1,696 mi (2,729 km).

Indiana's geographical center is located in Boone County, 14 mi (23 km) NNW of Indianapolis.

²TOPOGRAPHY

Indiana has two principal types of terrain: slightly rolling land in the northern half of the state and rugged hills in the southern, extending to the Ohio River. The highest point in the state, a hill near Lynn (Randolph County) on the eastern boundary, is 1,257 feet (383 meters) above sea level; the lowest point, on the Ohio River, is 320 feet (98 meters). The richest soil is in the north-central region, where the retreating glacier during the last Ice Age enriched the soil, scooped out lakes, and cut passageways for rivers.

Four-fifths of the state's land is drained by the Wabash River, which flows westward across the north-central region and turns southward to empty into the Ohio, and by its tributaries, the White, Eel, Mississinewa, and Tippecanoe rivers. The northern region is drained by the Maumee River, which flows into Lake Erie at Toledo, Ohio, and by the Kankakee River, which joins the Illinois River in Illinois. In the southwest, the two White River

forks empty into the Wabash, and in the southeast, the White-water River flows into the Ohio.

In addition to Lake Michigan on the northwestern border, there are more than 400 lakes in the northern part of the state. The largest lakes include Wawasee, Maxinkuckee, Freeman, and Shafer. There are mineral springs at French Lick and West Baden in Orange County, and two large caves at Wyandotte and Marengo in adjoining Crawford County.

The underlying rock strata found in Indiana were formed from sediments deposited during the Paleozoic era, when the land was submerged. About 400 million years ago, the first uplift of land, the Cincinnati arch, divided the Indiana region into two basins, a small one in the north and a large one in the southwest. The land was steadily elevated and at one time formed a lush swamp, which dried up some 200 million years ago when the climate cooled. During the Ice Ages, about five-sixths of the land lay under ice some 2,000 feet (600 meters) thick. The retreat of the glacier more than 10,000 years ago left excellent topsoil and drainage conditions in Indiana.

³CLIMATE

Temperatures vary from the extreme north to the extreme south of the state; the annual mean temperature is 49°F–58°F (9°C–12°C) in the north and 57°F (14°C) in the south. The annual mean for Indianapolis is 52°F (11°C). Although Indiana sometimes has temperatures below 0°F (–18°C) during the winter, the average temperatures in January range between 17°F (–8°C) and 35°F (2°C). Average temperatures during July vary from 63°F (17°C) to 88°F (31°C). The record high for the state was 116° F (47° C) set on 14 July 1936 at Collegeville, and the record low was –36° F (–38° C) on 19 January 1994 at New Whiteland.

The growing season averages 155 days in the north and 185 days in the south. Rainfall is distributed fairly evenly throughout the year, although drought sometimes occurs in the southern region. The average annual precipitation in the state is 40 in (102 cm), ranging from about 35 in (89 cm) near Lake Michigan to 45 in (114 cm) along the Ohio River; Indianapolis has an average of

39 in (99 cm) per year. The annual snowfall in Indiana averages less than 22 in (56 cm). Average wind speed in the state is 8 mph (13 km/hr), but gales sometimes occur along the shores of Lake Michigan, and there are occasional tornadoes in the interior.

⁴FLORA AND FAUNA
Because the state has a relatively uniform climate, plant species are distributed fairly generally throughout Indiana. There are 124 native tree species, including 17 varieties of oak, as well as black walnut, sycamore, and tulip tree (yellow poplar), the state tree. Fruit trees—apple, cherry, peach, and pear—are common. Local indigenous species—now reduced because of industrialization and urbanization—are the persimmon, black gum, and southern cypress along the Ohio River; tamarack and bog willow in the northern marsh; and white pine, sassafras, and pawpaw near Lake Michigan. American elderberry and bittersweet are common shrubs, while various jack-in-the-pulpits and spring beauties are among the indigenous wild flowers. The peony is the state flower. Mountain laurel is considered threatened, the prairie white-fringed orchid endangered.

Although the presence of wolves and coyotes has been reported occasionally, the red fox is Indiana's only common carnivorous mammal. Other native mammals are the common cottontail, muskrat, raccoon, opossum, and several types of squirrel. Many waterfowl and marsh birds, including the black duck and great blue heron, inhabit northern Indiana, while the field sparrow, yellow warbler, and red-headed woodpecker nest in central Indiana. Various catfish, pike, bass, and sunfish are native to state waters.

The state provides protection for the following animals, considered to be rare and endangered: bobcat, badger, otter, Indiana bat, gray myotis, southeastern myotis, and big-eared bat. In keeping with federal statutes, Indiana lists as endangered the eastern timber wolf, Arctic peregrine falcon, Kirtland's warbler, bald eagle, longjaw cisco, and eight types of mussel.

⁵ENVIRONMENTAL PROTECTION
During the 19th century, early settlers cut down much of Indiana's forests for farms, leaving the land vulnerable to soil erosion and flood damage, particularly in the southern part of the state. In 1919, the legislature created the State Department of Conservation (which in 1965 became the Department of Natural Resources) to reclaim worn-out soil, prevent further erosion, and control pollution of rivers and streams. In 1986 the Indiana Department of Environmental Management was initiated as a watchdog over the environmental laws and regulations designated to preserving the environmental well being of the state. Still, almost 85% of Indiana's original wetlands have been lost and, in 1997, it was estimated that the state continues to lose 1–3% of its remaining wetlands a year.

The Department of Natural Resources regulates the use of Indiana's lands, waters, forests, and wildlife resources. Specifically, the department manages land subject to flooding, preserves natural rivers and streams, grants mining permits and regulates strip-mining, plugs and repairs faulty/abandoned oil and gas wells, administers existing state parks and preserves and buys land for new ones, regulates hunting and fishing, and examines any damage to fish and wildlife by investigating industrial accidents. Also, the department is responsible for preventing soil erosion and flood damage, and for conserving and disposing of water in the state's watersheds.

The Indiana Department of Environmental Management (IDEM) seeks to protect public health through the implementation and management of various environmental programs. The focus of the environmental programs is to protect Indiana's air, land and water resources, since the proper management of these resources contribute to the health and well being of the citizens of Indiana. Prior to April 1986, these environmental programs were under the auspices of the State Board of Health (ISBH).

In addition to IDEM and the Department of Natural Resources the following boards exist to aid in environmental involvement: Air Pollution Control Board, Water Pollution Control Board, Pollution Prevention Control Board, and the Solid Waste Management Board.

In 1990, Indiana lawmakers passed landmark legislation that created an Office of Pollution Prevention and Technical Assistance within IDEM. OPPTA's long-term goal is to ensure that all Indiana industries use pollution prevention techniques as the preferred method for reducing waste and protecting the environment. This policy, along with programs that encourage reuse and recycling and discourage landfilling and incineration, will help conserve natural resources.

In March 1990, Indiana's Water Pollution Control Board adopted some of the strictest water quality standards in the nation. The standards set criteria for more than 90 chemicals and designated almost all water bodies for protection of aquatic life and recreational use. These standards will help improve and protect the quality of water in Indiana's lakes, rivers, and streams.

IDEM devotes much attention to identifying, cleaning up, and remediating all forms of toxic contamination. On 31 January 1986 the agency gained federal delegation for the Resource Conservation and Recovery Act (RCRA), which governs the generation, storage, treatment, transport, and disposal of all hazardous waste. Beyond RCRA, IDEM encourages companies to examine their production cycles and to adopt processes that won't create hazardous waste. the Department of Environmental Management offers technical assistance for the installation of pollution prevention equipment, and encourages consumers to rethink their use and disposal of hazardous household goods and chemicals. Indiana is the 10th largest producer of hazardous waste in the country. When that waste is not properly handled and disposed of, expensive remediation is often required.

Since IDEM was established in 1986, enforcement activity has increased fivefold. This is due, in part, to its unified Office of Enforcement, which consolidated enforcement staff who had been working separately in offices for air, solid waste, hazardous waste, and water. A key strategy in enforcement actions is to encourage violators to adopt pollution prevention practices or restore environmental damage as part of their penalty.

Some of the state's most serious environmental challenges lie in Lake and Porter counties in Northwest Indiana. A century of spills, emissions and discharges to the environment there require comprehensive, regionally coordinated programs. In 1991, IDEM opened a regional office in Gary to act as a liaison with local officials, concerned citizens, and industry. This office is helping drive the development of a comprehensive remediation plan, including the involvement of concerned citizens through the Citizen's Advisory for the Remediation of the Environment (CARE) committee. The Northwest Indiana Remedial Action Plan (RAP) is a three-phased program designed especially for the Grand Calumet River and the Indiana Harbor Ship Canal. Both waterways are heavily contaminated and, if left in their current state, would certainly degrade the waters of Lake Michigan, the primary source of drinking water for the Northwest Indiana area.

The RAP is a direct result of treaties of the International Joint Commission, a coalition formed to protect the waters between the United States and Canada.

IDEM now offers expertise and approval for voluntary cleanup plans. When a voluntary cleanup is completed properly, IDEM will issue a certificate of completion, and the governor will provide a covenant not to sue for further action involving the damage revealed to IDEM. This innovative program has led to many cleanups at virtually no cost to Indiana citizens.

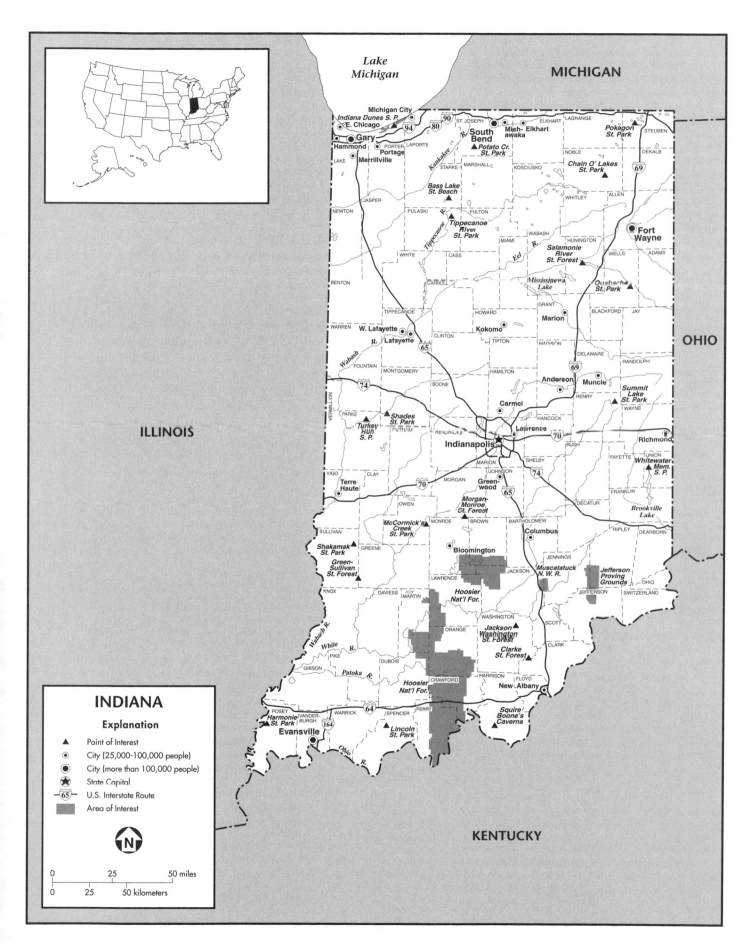

Lake Michigan

MICHIGAN

Michigan City
Indiana Dunes S. P.
E. Chicago
Gary
Hammond
Portage
Merrillville

ST. JOSEPH
South Bend
Mish-awaka
Elkhart
LAGRANGE
Pokagon St. Park
STEUBEN

Potato Cr. St. Park
NOBLE
DEKALB

Chain O' Lakes St. Park
ALLEN
69

Bass Lake St. Beach

Tippecanoe River St. Park
Fort Wayne

Salamonie River St. Forest

Mississinewa Lake
Ouabache St. Park

Marion

W. Lafayette
Lafayette
Kokomo
Anderson
Muncie
Summit Lake St. Park

Carmel

Terre Haute
Turkey Run S. P.
Shades St. Park
Indianapolis
Lawrence
Richmond
Whitewater Mem. S. P.

ILLINOIS

OHIO

Greenwood

Morgan-Monroe St. Forest
Brookville Lake

McCormick's Creek St. Park
Columbus

Shakamak St. Park
Bloomington
Muscatatuck N. W. R.
Jefferson Proving Grounds

Green-Sullivan St. Forest

Hoosier Nat'l For.
Jackson Washington St. Forest
Clarke St. Forest

Hoosier Nat'l For.
New Albany
Squire Boone's Caverns

Harmonie St. Park
Evansville
Lincoln St. Park

KENTUCKY

INDIANA

Explanation

▲ Point of Interest
⊙ City (25,000-100,000 people)
◉ City (more than 100,000 people)
★ State Capital
65 U.S. Interstate Route
▨ Area of Interest

N

0   25   50 miles
0   25   50 kilometers

[6]POPULATION

In 1990, Indiana had a population of 5,544,149 and ranked 14th in population among the 50 states; the population density was 155 persons per sq mi (59.5 per sq km). In 1996 the estimated population was 5,840,528, up 5.3%.

Although the French founded the first European settlement in Indiana in 1717, the census population was no more than 5,641 in 1800, when the Indiana Territory was established. Settlers flocked to the state during the territorial period, and the population rose to 24,520 by 1810. After Indiana became a state in 1816, its population grew even more rapidly, reaching 147,178 in 1820 and 988,416 in 1850. At the outbreak of the Civil War, Indiana had 1,350,428 inhabitants and ranked 5th in population among the states.

Indiana was relatively untouched by the great waves of European immigration that swept the US from 1860 to 1880. In 1880, when the state's population was 1,978,301, Indiana had fewer foreign-born residents (about 7% of its population) than any other northern state. Indiana doubled its 1900 population to 5,193,669 by the time of the 1970 census.

Of the 1990 census population, 64.9% lived in urban areas and 35.1% resided in rural areas. Indianapolis, the capital and largest city, expanded its boundaries in 1970 to coincide with those of Marion County, thereby increasing its area to 388 sq mi (1,005 sq km) and its population by some 50% (the city and county limits also include four self-governing communities). The estimated population was 752,279 in 1994, and the Indianapolis metropolitan area had an estimated population of 1,476,865 in 1995. Other cities with 1994 populations estimated at more than 100,000 were Fort Wayne, 183,359; Evansville, 129,452; Gary, 114,256; and South Bend, 105,092. All of these cities suffered population declines in the 1970s and early 1980s.

[7]ETHNIC GROUPS

Originally an agricultural state, Indiana was settled by Native Americans moving west, by a small group of French Creoles, and

Indiana Counties, County Seats, and County Areas and Populations

COUNTY	COUNTY SEAT	LAND AREA (SQ MI)	POPULATION 1996 EST	COUNTY	COUNTY SEAT	LAND AREA (SQ MI)	POPULATION 1996 EST.
ADAMS	DECATUR	340	32,686	MADISON	ANDERSON	453	132,782
ALLEN	FORT WAYNE	659	310,803	MARION	INDIANAPOLIS	396	817,525
BARTHOLOMEW	COLUMBUS	409	68,441	MARSHALL	PLYMOUTH	444	45,173
BENTON	FOWLER	407	9,669	MARTIN	SHOALS	339	10,581
BLACKFORD	HARDFORD CITY	166	14,134	MIAMI	PERU	369	32,686
BOONE	LEBANON	424	42,453	MONROE	BLOOMINGTON	385	116,176
BROWN	NASHVILLE	312	15,485	MONTGOMERY	CRAWFORDSVILLE	505	36,349
CARROLL	DELPHI	372	19,643	MORGAN	MARTINSVILLE	409	63,244
CASS	LOGANSPORT	414	38,829	NEWTON	KENTLAND	401	14,611
CLARK	JEFFERSONVILLE	376	92,530	NOBLE	ALBION	413	41,449
CLAY	BRAZIL	360	26,491	OHIO	RISING SUN	87	5,490
CLINTON	FRANKFORT	405	32,876	ORANGE	PAOLI	408	19,221
CRAWFORD	ENGLISH	307	10,559	OWEN	SPENCER	386	20,158
DAVIES	WASHINGTON	432	28,760	PARKE	ROCKVILLE	444	16,339
DEARBORN	LAWRENCEBURG	307	45,236	PERRY	CANNELTON	481	19,210
DECATUR	GREENSBURG	373	25,105	PIKE	PETERSBURG	341	12,569
DEKALB	AUBURN	364	38,272	PORTER	VALPARAISO	419	142,363
DELAWARE	MUNCIE	392	118,600	POSEY	MT. VERNON	410	26,505
DUBOIS	JASPER	429	39,088	PULASKI	WINAMAC	435	13,103
ELKHART	GOSHEN	466	168,941	PUTNAM	GREENCASTLE	482	33,451
FAYETTE	CONNERSVILLE	215	26,237	RANDOLPH	WINCHESTER	454	27,530
FLOYD	NEW ALBANY	150	70,746	RIPLEY	VERSAILLES	447	26,932
FOUNTAIN	COVINGTON	398	18,207	RUSH	RUSHVILLE	408	18,285
FRANKLIN	BROOKVILLE	385	21,530	ST. JOSEPH	SOUTH BEND	459	257,740
FULTON	ROCHESTER	369	20,223	SCOTT	SCOTTSBURG	192	22,652
GIBSON	PRINCETON	490	32,058	SHELBY	SHELBYVILLE	412	42,951
GRANT	MARION	415	73,469	SPENCER	ROCKPORT	400	20,540
GREENE	BLOOMFIELD	546	32,942	STARKE	KNOX	309	23,399
HAMILTON	NOBLESVILLE	398	147,719	STEUBEN	ANGOLA	308	30,831
HANCOCK	GREENFIELD	307	52,000	SULLIVAN	SULLIVAN	452	20,115
HARRISON	CORYDON	486	33,349	SWITZERLAND	VEVAY	224	8,380
HENDRICKS	DANVILLE	409	89,343	TIPPECANOE	LAFAYETTE	502	138,324
HENRY	NEW CASTLE	395	49,135	TIPTON	TIPTON	261	16,453
HOWARD	KOKOMO	293	84,126	UNION	LIBERTY	163	7,345
HUNTINGTON	HUNTINGTON	366	37,024	VANDERBURGH	EVANSVILLE	236	167,716
JACKSON	BROWNSTOWN	514	40,467	VERMILLION	NEWPORT	260	16,791
JASPER	RENSSELAER	561	28,368	VIGO	TERRE HAUTE	405	106,389
JAY	PORTLAND	384	21,733	WABASH	WABASH	398	34,661
JEFFERSON	MADISON	363	31,039	WARREN	WILLIAMSPORT	366	8,188
JENNINGS	VERNON	378	26,747	WARRICK	BOONVILLE	391	50,070
JOHNSON	FRANKLIN	321	104,280	WASHINGTON	SALEM	516	26,689
KNOX	VINCENNES	520	39,667	WAYNE	RICHMOND	404	72,017
KOSCIUSKO	WARSAW	540	69,932	WELLS	BLUFFTON	370	26,651
LAGRANGE	LAGRANGE	380	32,103	WHITE	MONTICELLO	506	25,081
LAKE	CROWN POINT	501	479,940	WHITLEY	COLUMBIA CITY	336	29,863
LAPORTE	LAPORTE	600	109,604				
LAWRENCE	BEDFORD	452	45,361		TOTALS	35,932	5,840,528

by European immigrant farmers. Although railroad building and industrialization attracted other immigrant groups—notably the Irish, Hungarians, Italians, Poles, Croats, Slovaks, and Syrians—foreign immigration to Indiana declined sharply in the 20th century. As of 1990, foreign-born Hoosiers numbered 94,263, or less than 2% of the state total. The major ancestry groups among foreign-born Indiana residents were Mexican (10,294), German (8,866), British (6,498), Canadian (5,715), and Asian Indian (4,590).

Restrictions on foreign immigration and the availability of jobs spurred the migration of black Americans to Indiana after World War I; by 1990, the state had 432,000 blacks, representing about 7.7% of the total population. Approximately 22% of all Indiana blacks live in the industrial city of Gary, which was 80.6% black in 1990.

In 1990, approximately 1.8% (99,000) of Indiana's population was of Hispanic origin. That year, Indiana's Asian residents included 6,093 Indians, 6,128 Chinese, 5,354 Filipinos, 6,298 Koreans, 6,338 Japanese, and 2,420 Vietnamese.

The natives of early 19th-century Indiana came from a variety of Algonkian-speaking tribes, including Delaware, Shawnee, and Potawatomi. By 1846, however, all Indian lands in the state had been seized or ceded, and most Indians had been removed. In 1990, there were 13,000 Native Americans.

8 LANGUAGES

Several Algonkian Indian tribes, including some from the east, met the white settlers who arrived in Indiana in the early 1800s. The heritage of the Delaware, Potawatomi, Miami, and other groups survives in many place-names, from Kokomo to Nappanee, Muncie, and Shipshewana.

Except for the dialect mixture in the industrial northwest corner and for the Northern-dialect fringe of counties along the Michigan border, Indiana speech is essentially that of the South Midland pioneers from south of the Ohio River, with a transition zone toward North Midland north of Indianapolis. Between the Ohio River and Indianapolis, South Midland speakers use *evening* for late afternoon, eat *clabber cheese* instead of cottage cheese, are wary of *frogstools* rather than toadstools, once held that *toadfrogs* and not plain toads caused warts, eat *goobers* instead of peanuts at a ball game, and may therefore be *sick at the stomach*. In the same region, some Hoosiers use a few Midland words that also occur north of Indianapolis, such as *rock fence* (stone wall), *French harp* (harmonica), *mud dauber* (wasp), *shucks* (leaves on an ear of corn), and perhaps even some expanding North Midland words, such as *run* (a small stream), *teetertotter* (seesaw), and *fishworm*. North of Indianapolis, speakers with a Midland Pennsylvania background wish on the *pullybone* of a chicken, may use a *trestle* (sawhorse), and are likely to get their hands *greezy* rather than *greasy*. Such was the Hoosier talk of James Whitcomb Riley.

In 1990, 95.2% of all Hoosiers 5 years old and older spoke only English at home. Other languages spoken at home were as follows:

Spanish	90,146
German	46,034
French	20,578
Polish	11,552
Other West Germanic	11,956
Various South Slavic	7,091

Chinese, Indic, Greek, Italian, and Korean were also reported.

9 RELIGIONS

The first branch of Christianity to gain a foothold in Indiana was Roman Catholicism, introduced by the French settlers in the early 18th century. The first Protestant church was founded near Charlestown by Baptists from Kentucky in 1798. Three years later, a Methodist church was organized at Springville; in 1806, Presbyterians established a church near Vincennes; and the following year, Quakers built their first meetinghouse at Richmond. The Disciples of Christ, Lutherans, the United Brethren, Mennonites, and Jews were among the later 19th-century arrivals.

A dissident religious sect, the Shakers, established a short-lived community in Sullivan County in 1808. In 1815, some German separatists, led by George Rapp, founded a community called the Harmonie Society, which flourished briefly. Rapp moved his followers to Pennsylvania and sold the town to a Scottish social reformer, Robert Owen, in 1825. Owen renamed the town New Harmony and tried to establish a nonreligious utopia there, but the experiment failed after three years. A group of religious dissidents founded the Pentecostal Church of God at Beaver Dam in 1881; the world headquarters of the church, which had 22,569 adherents in 1990, is now at Anderson. The Youth for Christ movement started in Indianapolis in 1943.

In addition to a sizable Roman Catholic population, the largest Protestant denominations were the United Methodists, Churches of Christ, American Baptist Churches in USA, Lutheran Church–Missouri Synod, and United Presbyterian Church. The estimated Jewish population of the state was 20,314 as of 1990.

10 TRANSPORTATION

Indiana's central location in the US and its position between Lake Michigan to the north and the Ohio River to the south gave the state its motto, "The Crossroads of America." Historically, the state took advantage of its strategic location by digging canals to connect Indiana rivers and by building roads and railroads to provide farmers access to national markets.

The success of the state's first railroad, completed in 1847 between Madison and Indianapolis, led to a tenfold increase in track mileage during the 1850s, and more railroad expansion took place after the Civil War. In December 1992, there were 29 railroads operating on 4,185 rail mi (6,734 km) of track; Class I railroads operated 3,323 route mi (5,347 km) of track in Indiana. Over 60% of the rail freight terminating within the state in 1991 was coal. Regularly scheduled Amtrak passenger trains served Indianapolis, Fort Wayne, Hammond/Whiting, South Bend, and 10 other stations in the state, with a total ridership in Indiana of 89,663 persons during 1995/96. Indianapolis and other major cities have public transit systems subsidized heavily by the state and federal governments. The South Shore commuter railroad connects South Bend, Gary, and East Chicago with Chicago, Ill.

The east-west National Road (US 40) reached Indiana in 1827, and the north-south Michigan road (US 421) was built in the late 1830s. In 1995, Indiana had 1,172 miles (1,887 km) of interstate highways—more than other states of comparable size. In that year, there were 11,315 mi (18,217 km) of state highways and 81,162 mi (131,162 km) of country and municipal roads. In 1992, motor vehicle registrations totaled 4,515,850, including 3,300,636 passenger cars and 1,192,763 trucks. Several of the nation's largest moving companies have their headquarters in Indiana.

Water transportation has been important from the earliest years of European settlement. The Wabash and Erie Canal, constructed in the 1830s from Fort Wayne east to Toledo, Ohio, and southwest to Lafayette, was vital to the state's market economy. In 1836, the state legislature earmarked $10 million for an ambitious network of canals, but excessive construction costs and the financial panic of 1837 caused the state to go virtually bankrupt and default on its bonds. Nevertheless, the Wabash canal was extended to Terre Haute and Evansville by the early 1850s.

The transport of freight via Lake Michigan and the Ohio River helped to spark Indiana's industrial development. A deepwater port on Lake Michigan, which became operational in 1970, provided access to world markets via the St. Lawrence Seaway. Indiana Harbor handled 15.7 million tons of goods in 1995, and the tonnage at the port of Gary was over 9.59 million.

In 1997, there were 675 public and private airports in the state. The number of active general aviation aircraft in Indiana was 4,194 in 1996.

¹¹HISTORY

When the first human beings inhabited Indiana is not known. Hundreds of sites used by primitive hunters, fishermen, and food gatherers before 1000 BC have been found in Indiana. Burial mounds of the Woodland culture (1000 BC to AD 900), when the bow and arrow appeared, have been located across the state. The next culture, called Mississippian and dating about AD 900 to 1500, is marked by gardens, ceramics, tools, weapons, trade, and social organization. It is well illustrated by remains of an extensive village on the north side of the Ohio River near Newburgh. The unidentified inhabitants are believed to have come up from the south about 1300, for reasons not known, and to have migrated back before 1500, again for unknown reasons.

The next Indian invaders, and the first to be seen by white men, were the Miami and Potawatomi tribes that drifted down the west side of Lake Michigan and turned across the northern sector of what is now Indiana after the middle of the 17th century. The Kickapoo and Wea tribes pushed into upper Indiana from northern Illinois. The southern two-thirds of the present state was a vast hunting ground, without villages.

The first European penetration was made in the 1670s by the French explorers Father Jacques Marquette and René-Robert Cavelier, Sieur de la Salle. After the founding of Detroit in 1701, the Maumee-Wabash river route to the lower Ohio was discovered. At the portage between the two rivers, Jean Baptiste Bissot, Sieur de Vincennes, lived at Kekionga, the principal village of the Miami and the present site of Fort Wayne. The first French fort was built farther down the Wabash among the Wea, near modern Lafayette, in 1717. Three years later, Fort Miami was erected. Vincennes's son constructed another fort on the Wabash in 1732, at the site of the town later named for him.

English traders venturing down the Ohio River disputed the French trade monopoly, and as a result of the French and Indian War, French Canada was given up to the British in 1760. Indians under Chief Pontiac captured the two forts in northern Indiana, and the area was not securely in English hands until 1765. The pre-Revolutionary turbulence in the Atlantic seaboard colonies was hardly felt in Indiana, although the region did not escape the Revolutionary War itself. Colonel George Rogers Clark, acting for Virginia, captured Vincennes from a British garrison early in 1779 after a heroic march. Two years later, a detachment of 108 Pennsylvanians, passing down the Ohio to reinforce Clark, was surprised by a force of French Canadians and Indians under Mohawk Captain Joseph Brant; most of the Pennsylvanians were killed during the battle or after capture.

Following the Revolutionary War, the area northwest of the Ohio River was granted to the new nation; known as the Northwest Territory, it included present-day Indiana, Ohio, Illinois, Michigan, Wisconsin, and part of Minnesota. The first US settlement in Indiana was made in 1784 on land opposite Louisville, Ky., granted to Clark's veterans by Virginia. (The new town, called Clarksville, still exists.) Americans also moved into Vincennes. Government was established by the Continental Congress under the Northwest Ordinance of 1787. Again, Indiana unrest endangered all settlements north of the Ohio, and the small US army, with headquarters at Cincinnati, met defeat at what is now Fort Wayne in 1790 and disaster in neighboring

Ohio in 1791. General Anthony Wayne was put in command of an enlarged army and defeated the Indians in 1794 at Fallen Timbers (near Toledo, Ohio). British meddling was ended by Jay's treaty later the same year. Wayne then build a new fort—named for him—among the Miami.

In 1800, as Ohio prepared to enter the Union, the rest of the Northwest Territory was set off and called Indiana Territory, with its capital at Vincennes. There Elihu Stout established a newspaper, the *Indiana Gazette,* in 1804. After Michigan Territory was detached in 1805, and Illinois Territory in 1809, Indiana assumed its present boundaries. The federal census counted 24,520 people in Indiana in 1810, including a new Swiss colony on the Ohio, where settlers planted vineyards and made wine.

William Henry Harrison was appointed first governor and, with a secretary and three appointed judges, constituted the government of Indiana Territory. Under the Northwest Ordinance, when the population reached 5,000 adult males, it was allowed to elect an assembly and nominate candidates for an upper house. When the population totaled 60,000—as it did in 1815—the voters were allowed to write a state constitution and to apply for admission to the Union. A short constitution excluding slavery and recommending public schools was adopted and Indiana became the 19th state on 11 December 1816.

Meanwhile, Indiana had seen Governor Harrison lead US troops up the Wabash in 1811 and beat off an Indian attack at Tippecanoe. The War of 1812 took Harrison away from Indiana, and battles were fought in other theaters. Hoosiers suffered Indian raids, and two forts were besieged for a few days. After the war, new settlers began pouring into the state from the upper South and in fewer numbers from Ohio, Pennsylvania, New York, and New England. A group of German Pietists under George Rapp settled Harmonie on the lower Wabash in 1815 and stayed 10 years before selling out to Robert Owen, a visionary with utopian dreams that failed at the village he renamed New Harmony. In 1816, Tom Lincoln brought his family from Kentucky, and his son Abe grew up in southern Indiana from age 7 to 21.

Unlike most other states, Indiana was settled from south to north. The inhabitants were called Hoosiers; the origin of the word is obscure, but the term may have come from an Anglo-Saxon word for hill dwellers. Central and northern Indiana were opened up as land was purchased from the Indians. The Potawatomi were forced to go west in 1838, and the Miami left in 1846. Commerce flowed south to the Ohio River in the form of corn, hogs, whiskey, and timber. Indianapolis was laid out as a planned city and centrally located capital in 1820, but 30 years passed before its population caught up to the size of Madison and New Albany on the Ohio.

An overambitious program of internal improvements (canals and roads) in the 1830s plunged the state into debts it could not pay. Railroads, privately financed, began to tie Indiana commercially with the East. The Irish came to dig canals and lay the rails, and Germans, many of them Catholics, came to do woodworking and farming. Levi Coffin, a Quaker who moved to Fountain City in 1826, opened a different kind of road, the Underground Railroad, to help escaping slaves from the South.

A new constitution in 1851 showed Jacksonian preferences for more elective offices, shorter terms, a one-term governorship, limited biennial legislative sessions, county government, obligatory common schools, and severe limits on state debt. But this constitution also prohibited blacks from entering the state.

Hoosiers showed considerable sympathy with the South in the 1850s, and there was considerable "copperhead" activity in the early 1860s. Nevertheless, Indiana remained staunchly in the Union under Governor Oliver P. Morton, sending some 200,000 soldiers to the Civil War. The state suffered no battles, but

General John Hunt Morgan's Confederate cavalry raided the southeastern sector of Indiana in July 1863.

After the Civil War, small local industries expanded rapidly. The first nonfarm enterprises were gristmills, sawmills, meat-packing plants, distilleries and breweries, leatherworking shops, furniture factories, and steamboat and carriage makers. Wagons made by Studebaker in South Bend won fame during the war, as did Van Camp's canned pork and beans from Indianapolis. Discovery of natural gas in several northeastern counties in 1886, and the resultant low fuel prices, spurred the growth of glass factories. Elwood Haynes of Kokomo designed a one-cylinder horseless carriage in 1894 and drove it. As America became infatuated with the new autos, 375 Indiana factories started turning them out. A racetrack for testing cars was built outside Indianapolis in 1908, and the famous 500-mi (805-km) race on Memorial Day weekend began in 1911. Five years earlier, US Steel had constructed a steel plant at the south end of Lake Michigan. The town built by the company to house the workers was called Gary, and it grew rapidly with the help of the company and the onset of World War I. Oil refineries were developed in the same area, known as the Calumet region.

Of the millions of immigrants who flocked to the US from 1870 to 1914, very few settled in Indiana. The percentage of foreign-born residents declined from 9% in 1860 to 7% in 1880, all of them from northern Europe and over half from Germany. By 1920, the percentage was down to 5%, although some workers from southern and eastern Europe had gravitated to the industries of the Calumet.

Although many Hoosiers of German and Irish descent favored neutrality when World War I began, Indiana industries eventually boomed with war orders, and public sympathy swung heavily toward the Allies. Indiana furnished 118,000 men and women to the armed forces and suffered the loss of 3,370—a much smaller participation than in the Civil War, from a population more than twice the size.

After 1920, only about a dozen makes of cars were still being manufactured in Indiana, and those factories steadily lost out to the Big Three car makers in Detroit. The exception was Studebaker in South Bend, which grew to more than 23,000 employees during World War II. The company finally closed its doors in 1965. Auto parts continued to be a big business, however, along with steelmaking and oil refining in the Calumet. Elsewhere there was manufacturing of machinery, farm implements, railway cars, furniture, and pharmaceuticals. Meat-packing, coal mining, and limestone quarrying continued to be important. With increasing industrialization, cities grew, particularly in the northern half of the state, and the number of farms diminished. The balance of rural and urban population, about even in 1920, tilted in favor of urban dwellers.

World War II had a greater impact on Indiana than did World War I. Most factories converted to production of war materials; 300 held defense orders in 1942. Du Pont built a huge powder plant near Charlestown. The slack in employment was taken up, women went into factories, more rural families moved to cities, and military training facilities were created. The enormous Jefferson Proving Ground tested ammunition and parachutes.

After the war, many locally small industries were taken over by national corporations, and their plants were expanded. By 1984, the largest employer in Indiana was General Motors, with 47,800 employees in six cities. Inland Steel, with 18,500 workers, was second, followed by US Steel with 13,800 workers. Although the state's population in the mid-1980s was about two-thirds urban and one-third rural, agriculture retained much of its importance.

Nostalgia for an older, simpler, rural way of life pervades much Hoosier thinking. The state stands high in conservation, owing to the vision of Richard Lieber, a state official who from 1933 to 1944 promoted the preservation of land for state parks and recreational areas as well as for state and federal forests.

The percentage of registered voters in Indiana who participate in elections generally exceeded the national average by a wide margin. The evenness of strength between the two major political parties during much of its history has frequently made Indiana a swing state, eagerly courted by Democrats and Republicans alike. In 1967, Democrat Richard Hatcher became one of the nation's first blacks to serve as head of a major city when he was elected mayor of Gary. In 1988 Indiana native son J. Danforth Quayle, then a US senator, was elected vice president of the United States on the Republican ticket with George Bush.

The state legislature was dominated by rural interests until reapportionment in 1966 gave urban counties more representation. Biennial sessions were then changed to annual, although they are still limited in duration. Indianapolis has extended its boundaries to cover the county, and much of city and county government's unified. The direct primary for nomination of governor, lieutenant governor, and US senator was mandated in 1975.

In the early 1980s, Indiana, along with the other Rust Belt states, suffered a recession, compounded by declining farm prices and high operating costs for farmers. Later in the decade, the state's economy improved with the expansion of service industries and the introduction of high-tech industries, both of which continued into the 1990s.

Educational reform based on increased funding has played a prominent role in Indiana public policy in the 1990s.

12 STATE GOVERNMENT

The first state constitution took effect when Indiana became a state in 1816. Reportedly written by convention delegates beneath a huge elm tree in Corydon, the first state capital, the brief document prohibited slavery and recommended a free public school system, including a state university.

This constitution did not allow for amendment, however, and a new constitution that did so was adopted in 1851. The second constitution authorized more elective state officials, gave greater responsibility to county governments, and prohibited the state from going into debt (except under rare circumstances). It also established biennial rather than annual sessions of the state legislature, a provision not repealed until 1971. With amendments, the second constitution is still in effect today.

The Indiana general assembly consists of a 50-member senate elected to four-year terms, with half the senators elected every two years, and a 100-member house of representatives elected to two-year terms. A member of the general assembly must be a US citizen and have been a resident of Indiana for at least one year. A senator must be at least 25 years of age, a representative at least 21 years old. Senators and representatives are paid the same base salary and allowances; legislative leaders receive additional compensation. The legislative salary was $11,600 in 1995.

The state's chief executive is the governor, elected to a 4-year term and eligible for reelection, although ineligible to serve more than 8 years in a 12-year period. A governor must be at least 30 years old, a US citizen, and a state resident for 5 years prior to election. The governor may call special sessions of the legislature and may veto bills passed by the legislature, but his veto can be overridden by a majority vote in each house. In 1996 the governor's salary was $77,199.

Indiana's other top elected officials are the lieutenant governor, secretary of state, treasurer, auditor, attorney general, and superintendent of public instruction. Each is elected to a four-year term. The lieutenant governor is constitutionally empowered to preside over the state senate and to act as governor if the office should become vacant or the incumbent is unable to discharge his duties. By statute, the lieutenant governor also serves as executive director of the Department of Commerce and as commissioner of agriculture.

Legislation may be introduced in either house of the general assembly, although bills for raising revenue must originate in the house of representatives. A bill approved by both houses goes to the governor for signing into law; if the governor declines to sign it within seven days, the bill becomes law, but if the governor vetoes it, majorities of at least 26 votes in the senate and 51 votes in the house are required to override the veto. Should the governor veto a bill after the end of a legislative session, it must be returned to the legislature when that body reconvenes.

An amendment to the state constitution must be approved by two successive legislatures and be submitted to the voters for approval or rejection at the next general election.

In order to vote in Indiana, a person must be a US citizen, be at least 18 years old, and have been a resident of the voting precinct for 30 days.

13POLITICAL PARTIES

The Democratic Party has been one of the two major political parties since Indiana became a state in 1816, as has the Republican Party since its inception in 1854. In that year, Hoosiers voted for Democrat James Buchanan for president, but in 1860, the voters supported Republican Abraham Lincoln. After voting Republican in four successive presidential elections, Indiana voted Democratic in 1876 and became a swing state. More recently, a Republican trend has been evident: the state voted Republican in 11 out of 12 presidential elections between 1940 and 1984.

Third-party movements have rarely succeeded in Indiana. Native son Eugene Debs, the Socialist Party leader who was personally popular in Indiana, received only 36,931 votes in the state in 1912, while garnering more than 900,000 votes nationally. Even in 1932, during the Great Depression, Socialist candidate Norman Thomas won only 21,388 votes in Indiana. The most successful third-party movement in recent decades was George Wallace's American Independent Party, which took 243,108 votes (11.5% of the Indiana total) in 1968. In each of the four presidential elections of the 1970s and early 1980s, minority party candidates together received only 1.1% or less of the votes cast.

In 1996, Indiana gave 47% of the vote to Republican Bob Dole, 42% to Democrat Bill Clinton, and 11% to Independent Ross Perot. Democrat Frank L. O'Bannon was elected to succeed two-term Democratic governor Evan Bayh. Richard Lugar, a Republican, won election to his fourth term in the Senate in 1994, and Daniel Coats, also a Republican, was re-elected in 1992. Coats had first been elected Senator in 1990 to replace Senator Dan Quayle when Quayle resigned to become vice-president. Indiana's delegation to the US House of Representatives following the 1996 elections included four Democrats and six Republicans. In the state senate Republicans numbered 31; Democrats, 19. Control of the state house was split, with 50 Democrats and 50 Republicans.

In 1994, there were 72 black and 8 Hispanic elected officials. In 1995, 37 women served in the state legislature and in elective executive office.

14LOCAL GOVERNMENT

In 1816, when Indians controlled central and northern Indiana. the state had only 15 counties. By 1824, the number of counties had grown to 49. All but one of Indiana's 92 counties were established by 1851. The last county—Newton, in the state's northwest corner—was created in 1859.

Counties in Indiana have traditionally provided law enforcement in rural areas, operated county courts and institutions, maintained county roads, administered public welfare programs, and collected taxes. Under a "home rule" law enacted by the state in 1980, they also have "all the power they need for the effective operation of government as to local affairs," or, in effect, all powers not specifically reserved to the state. In 1984, counties were given the power to impose local income taxes.

The county's business is conducted by a board of county commissioners, consisting of three members elected to four-year terms. Nine officials also elected to four-year terms exercise executive functions: the county auditor, treasurer, recorder, clerk, surveyor, sheriff, prosecuting attorney, coroner, and assessor. The county's appointed officials include the county superintendent of schools, highway supervisor, highway engineer, extension agent, attorney, and physician. An elected seven-member county council exercises taxing power and acts as a check on the Board of county commissioners. The major exception to this general

Indiana Presidential Vote by Political Parties, 1948–96

YEAR	ELECTORAL VOTES	INDIANA WINNER	DEMOCRAT	REPUBLICAN	PROGRESSIVE	PROHIBITION
1948	13	Dewey (R)	807,833	821,079	9,649	14,711
1952	13	*Eisenhower (R)	801,530	1,136,259	1,222	15,335
1956	13	*Eisenhower (R)	783,908	1,182,811	—	6,554
1960	13	*Nixon (R)	952,358	1,175,120	—	6,746
1964	13	*Johnson (D)	1,170,848	911,118	—	8,266
					AMERICAN IND.	
1968	13	*Nixon (R)	806,659	1,067,885	243,108	4,616
					PEOPLE'S	SOC. WORKERS
1972	13	*Nixon (R)	708,568	1,405,154	4,544	5,575
					AMERICAN	
1976	13	Ford (R)	1,014,714	1,185,958	14,048	5,695
					CITIZENS	LIBERTARIAN
1980	13	*Reagan (R)	844,197	1,255,656	4,852	19,627
1984	12	*Reagan (R)	841,481	1,377,230	—	6,741
					NEW ALLIANCE	
1988	12	*Bush (R)	860,643	1,297,763	10,215	—
					Ind.(Perot)	
1992	12	Bush (R)	848,420	989,375	455,934	7,936
1996	12	Dole (R)	887,424	1,006,693	224,299	15,632

*Won US presidential election.
*Won US presidential election.

pattern is Marion County, which in 1970 was consolidated with the city of Indianapolis and is governed by an elected mayor and council of 29 members.

Townships (1,008 in 1992) provide assistance for the poor and assess taxable property. Each township is administered by a trustee elected to a four-year term. In a few townships, the trustee oversees township schools, but most public schools are now run by community school corporations.

Indiana had 566 municipal governments in 1992. They are governed by elected city councils varying in membership from 5 to 25 persons. City officials elected for four-year terms are the mayor and (except in Indianapolis) the city clerk or clerk-treasurer. (In Indianapolis, the city clerk is appointed for a one-year term.) In 1992 Indiana had 294 school districts and 939 special districts.

15STATE SERVICES

In 1971, Indiana's state legislature created the State Ethics and Conflicts of Interest Commission to formulate and regulate a code of ethics for state officials. The commissioner investigates reported cases of misconduct or violations of the code of ethics by any state official or employee. After holding hearings, the commission reports violations to the governor and makes its findings public. Top-level state officials and heads of state departments must provide statements of their financial interests to the commission.

In 1977, the state established an Interdepartmental board for the coordination of human service programs. Members include the chief administrative officers of state agencies for senior citizens and community services, mental health, health, corrections, and public welfare. The board provides assistance to persons and families requiring help from one of these agencies and monitors federal service programs in the state. The Indiana Office of Social Services Fiscal Office administers programs for the board. An executive assistant to the governor serves as chairperson of the board, which also includes the director of the state budget agency.

Educational services are provided by the Commission for Higher Education, the Indiana Educational Services Foundation, and the Commission for Postsecondary Proprietary Education, which accredits private vocational, technical, and trade schools in the state. A public counselor, appointed by the governor, represents the public at hearings of the Public Service Commission, which regulates public transportation agencies and public utilities. Health services are supplied by the state board of health, department of mental health, and emergency medical services commission. Disabled citizens are assisted by the Indiana Rehabilitation Services Agency. The Civil Rights Commission enforces state antidiscrimination laws.

16JUDICIAL SYSTEM

The Indiana supreme court consists of five justices who are appointed by the governor from names submitted by a nonpartisan judicial nominating committee. To qualify for selection, a nominee must have practiced law in the state for at least 10 years or have served as judge of a lower court for at least 5 years. A justice serves for 2 years and then is subject to approval by referendum in the general election; if approved by the voters, the justice serves a 10-year term before again being subject to referendum. The chief justice of the Indiana supreme court is chosen by the nominating commission and serves a 5-year term.

The state court of appeals consists of 15 justices; they serve 10-year terms. The court exercises appellate jurisdiction under rules set by the state supreme court. Both the clerk and the reporter for the state's high courts are chosen in statewide elections for 4-year terms.

Superior courts, probate courts, and circuit courts all function as general trial courts and are presided over by 242 judges who serve a term of six years. When the justice of the peace system in the counties was abolished by the state legislature in 1976, small-claims dockets (civil cases involving up to $1,500) were added to circuit and county courts. In 1995, Indiana had 14,044 practicing attorneys.

Indiana had a prison population of 35,324 in 1991, or 378 per 100,000. For 1992, the FBI Crime Index reported 28,791 instances of violent crime, or 508.5 per 100,000. These included murder and manslaughter, 454 (8.2 per 100,000 inhabitants); forcible rape, 545 (8.2 per 100,000); and aggravated assault, 19,008 (335.7 per 100,000). Indiana has a death penalty and since 1930 has executed 44 persons. There were 46 persons under sentence of death in 1995.

17ARMED FORCES

US defense installations in Indiana had 1,194 active duty military personnel in 1996. Army installations include the Jefferson Proving Ground; Grissom Air Force Base which had been the state's only Air Force base was closed in 1994. The navy operates a weapons support center at Crane and an avionics center at Indianapolis. The state was awarded $1.5 billion in prime defense contracts in fiscal year 1996.

Indiana supported the Union during the Civil War; about 200,000 Hoosiers served in Northern armies, and some 24,400 died while in service. During World War I, a Hoosier reportedly was the first American soldier to fire a shot, and the first American soldier killed was from Indiana; in all, about 118,000 Indiana citizens served and 3,370 lost their lives. In World War II, about 338,000 Hoosiers served in the armed forces and some 10,000 died in line of duty. In 1996, 587,000 veterans were living in Indiana, of whom fewer than 500 served during World War I, 152,000 in World War II, 95,000 during the Korean Conflict, 181,000 during the Vietnam era, and 41,000 in the Persian Gulf War. After World War II, the state paid a bonus to veterans for the first time; in fiscal year 1996, veterans' benefits in Indiana totaled $614 million.

Indiana's national guard units served in World War II, the Korean conflict, and the Vietnam war. In 1996 there were 34,375 reserve and national guard personnel in the state. In 1993, the Indiana state police employed 1,046 full-time sworn officers, or two per 10,000 residents.

18MIGRATION

Indiana's early settlers were predominantly northern Europeans who migrated from eastern and southern states. The influx of immigrants to the US in the late 19th and early 20th centuries had little impact on Indiana. In 1860, only 9% of the state's population was foreign-born, mostly Germans and Irish. The percentage was only 5.6% in 1900 and had further declined to 5.2% by 1920, and to just 1.7% by 1990. The principal migratory pattern since 1920 has been within the state, from the farms to the cities.

In 1860, more than 91% of the population lived in rural areas; the percentage fell to 67% in 1900, 50% in 1920, and 40% in 1960. In 1990, 65% of the population was urban, and only 35% was rural.

Since World War II, Indiana has lost population through a growing migratory movement to other states, mostly to Florida and the Southwest. From 1960 to 1970, Indiana suffered a net loss of about 16,000 persons through migration, and from 1970 to 1983, a net total of 340,000 left the state. From 1985 to 1990, however, there was a net gain in migration of over 35,000, 90% of whom came from abroad. Between 1990 and 1996, the state had a net gain of 76,279 persons through domestic migration and a net gain of 16,913 in international migration. In 1996, 4,692 foreign immigrants arrived in Indiana. As of 1990, 71.1% of all state residents had been born in Indiana. In 1990, 56% of residents age 5 and over lived in the same house as in 1985. Of those who lived in a different house in 1985, 19% did so in another state.

[19]INTERGOVERNMENTAL COOPERATION

Indiana's Commission on Interstate Cooperation promotes cooperation with other states and with the federal government. It acts largely through the Council of State Governments. Indiana is a member of such interstate regulatory bodies as the Great Lakes Commission, the Ohio River Basin Commission, and the Ohio River Valley Water Sanitation Commission. The Indiana-Kentucky Boundary Compact was signed by Indiana in 1943 and received congressional approval the same year. In 1985, Indiana joined seven other states in signing a Great Lakes Charter, aimed at further protecting the lakes' resources.

Federal aid to Indiana totaled $3.6 billion in fiscal year 1996.

[20]ECONOMY

Indiana is both a leading agricultural and industrial state. The economy was almost entirely agricultural until after the Civil War. By 1900, rapid industrial development had tripled the number of factories in the state to 18,000, employing a total of 156,000 workers. During that period, the mechanization of agriculture resulted in the doubling of the number of farms to a peak of 220,000 in 1900. Metals and other manufacturing industries surged during and after World War I, lagged during the Great Depression of the 1930s, then surged again during and after World War II. Between 1940 and 1950, the number of wage earners in the state nearly doubled. Job opportunities brought in many workers from other states and encouraged the growth of labor unions. It ranked 10th among the states in farm marketings in 1983, and 9th in value of manufacturing shipments in 1981.

The state's industrial development in Indianapolis, Gary, and other cities has been based on its plentiful natural resources—coal, natural gas, timber, stone, and clay—and on good transportation facilities. The northwestern corner of the state is the site of one of the world's greatest concentrations of heavy industry, especially steel. In 1994, the gross state product for the state was $138,190 million, of which private good-producing industries contributed $51,459 million; private services-producing industries, $72,297 million; and government, $14,434 million. Indiana's per capita personal income in 1995 was $21,433, which ranked 28th in the nation. In 1996, there were 29,891 filings for bankruptcy.

[21]INCOME

In 1996, Indiana ranked 29th among the 50 states in per capita income, with an average of $22,440 per capita. Total disposable personal income in 1996 amounted to $113.5 billion, up 5.5% from $108.5 billion in 1995.

The median household income in 1995 was $33,385. About 10% of the population had incomes below the federal poverty level in 1995. In 1992, just over 1% (26,000) of all Hoosier households had a disposable income exceeding $125,000.

[22]LABOR

At the beginning of 1997, the state's civilian labor force was estimated at 3,055,300 persons, with the Indianapolis area accounting for 26.3% of the total.

Of the total nonfarm employment of 2,805,700 at the beginning of 1997, mining accounted for 0.2%; construction 4.7%; manufacturing, 24.2%; transportation, communication, and utilities, 5%; trade, 24.4%; finance, insurance, and real estate, 4.8%; services, 22.9%; and government, 13.8%.

In 1996, the unemployment rate averaged 4.1%. Unemployment rates are usually higher than the state average around Terre Haute and Gary (5.3% and 4%, respectively, in December 1996), and lower than the state average in the Bloomington area (1.8%).

Most industrial workers live in Indianapolis and the Calumet area of northwestern Indiana. The AFL first attempted to organize workers at the US Steel Company's plant in Gary in 1919, but a strike to get union recognition failed. Other strikes by Indiana coal miners and railway workers in 1922 had limited success. By 1936, however, the CIO had won bargaining rights and the 40-hour workweek from US Steel, and union organization spread to other industries throughout the state.

In 1995, labor unions had 443,100 members in Indiana, or 16.5% of the total number of workers. Unionization among private sector workers in manufacturing was 29.9%, second highest among the states. The majority of the workers belonged to unions affiliated with the AFL-CIO.

[23]AGRICULTURE

Agriculture in Indiana is a large and diverse industry that plays a vital role in the economic stability of Indiana, with 60,000 farms containing 15,900,000 acres (6,400,000 hectares) of farmland. In 1995, cash receipts from the sale of all commodities (crops and livestock) reached $5 billion. In the same year, Indiana ranked 14th in the United States in cash receipts from the sale of all commodities; crop sales amounted to $3.4 billion (10th in the nation); and livestock sales totaled $1.74 billion (17th in the nation). Over 80% of Indiana's farm operators live on the farm, while more than 51% of farmers have a principal occupation other than farming. The average age for Indiana farmers is 51 years old and the average farm size is 265 acres (107 hectares).

Indiana's principal field crops are as follows, based upon 1995 crop production:

COMMODITY	QUANTITY	% OF U.S.	U.S. RANK
Corn for popcorn	163,200,000 lbs.	22.9%	1st
Spearmint	180,000 lbs.	7.9%	3rd
Tomatoes for processing	157,450 tons	1.4%	3rd
Soybeans	196,710,000 bu.	9.0%	4th
Peppermint	999,000 lbs.	10.6%	4th
Cantaloupes	544,000 cwt.	2.6%	5th
Corn for grain	598,900,000 bus.	8.1%	5th

[24]ANIMAL HUSBANDRY

Indiana ranked 5th in the number of hogs and pigs in 1996 and 7th in turkey production in 1995.

Indiana dairy farmers produced an estimated 2.2 billion lbs of milk from 144,000 milk cows in 1995. The state's poultry farmers sold an estimated 28.4 million lbs of chicken and an estimated 335 million lbs of turkey during 1995.

In 1997, Indiana had an estimated 1.15 million cattle and calves worth around $644 million.

[25]FISHING

Fishing is not of commercial importance in Indiana; in 1995, only 1,025,000 lbs of fish valued at $2,225,000 were landed. Fishing for bass, pike, perch, catfish, and trout is a popular sport with Indiana anglers. In 1995/96, there were some 650,620 sport fishing licenses issued by the state. Federal sportfish restoration program expenditures amounted to over $3.1 million in 1995/96.

[26]FORESTRY

About 19% of Indiana's total land area was forested in 1992. Indiana has 4,439,200 acres (1,820,072 hectares) of forestland, of which 97%, or 4,295,800 acres (1,761,278 hectares), is considered commercial timberland. Of the commercial timberland, 534,900 acres (219,309 hectares) are publicly owned as follows: Hoosier National Forest, 166,000 acres (68,060 hectares); miscellaneous federal ownerships, 162,600 acres (66,666 hectares); state-owned, including 145,000 acres (59,450 hectares) on 13 state forests, 177,400 acres (72,734 hectares); and county and municipal ownerships, 28,900 acres (11,849 hectares).

Seventy-four percent of the commercial forestland is located in the southern half of Indiana, where oak, hickory, beech, maple, yellow poplar, and ash predominate in the uplands. Soft maple, sweetgum, pin oak, cottonwood, sycamore, and river birch are the most common species found in wetlands and drainage corridors. Of all the commercial forestland in Indiana, 85% was privately owned in 1994.

Approximately 25,400 Hoosiers were employed in Indiana's lumber and wood products industry in 1995, which paid over $568.4 million in wages that year. The paper and allied products industry employed another 16,800 persons in 1995, with a payroll of $486.8 million. Indiana's wood-using industries manufacture everything from the "crinkle" center lining in cardboard boxes to the finest furniture in the world. Products such as pallets, desks, fancy face veneer, millwork, flooring, mobile homes, and even recreational vehicles use about 500 million board feet of lumber each year.

Indiana has always been noted for the quality of its hardwood forests and the trees it produces. It presently is the third leading producer of hardwood lumber, following only Pennsylvania and North Carolina.

27MINING

The value of nonfuel mineral production in Indiana in 1995 was about $574 million (up 3% from 1994), and the highest ever recorded in the state. Crushed stone and cement production in 1995 offset the drop in value for dimension stone.

Employment in mining was approximately 6,600 in December 1996.

Nationally, Indiana ranks 23d in value of nonfuel mineral production. The state's top two mineral commodities, crushed stone and cement, respectively account for approximately 40% and 23% of Indiana's total nonfuel value. In 1995, Indiana ranked 11th and 12th, respectively, in output of both of these commodities, 2nd in dimension stone and masonry cement, 7th in gypsum, and 10th in construction sand and gravel in 1995.

28ENERGY AND POWER

Indiana is largely dependent on fossil fuels for its energy supplies. In recent years, petroleum has become an important power source for automobiles, home heating, and electricity. Nevertheless, coal has continued to be the state's major source of power, meeting about half of Indiana's energy needs.

In 1994, Indiana's gross energy consumption totaled 2,523.6 trillion Btu, of which 51% was provided by coal, 35% by petroleum products, 10% by dry natural gas, and 4% by other sources.

The state has no nuclear power plants. In 1984, construction of the planned Marble Hill nuclear power plant on the Ohio River near Madison was permanently suspended by the Public Service Co. of Indiana because of escalating construction costs; total cost estimates had risen from $1.4 billion during the planning stage in 1973 to more than $7 billion. Per capita energy consumption in the state in 1994 was 438.5 million Btu, the 10th highest in the US. Indiana also ranks high in energy expenditures per capita—$2,229 in 1994.

Electric power produced in Indiana in 1995 totaled 105.2 billion kWh; total installed capacity was 23.1 million kW in 1996, 90% of it provided by coal-fired plants. Privately owned power plants account for nearly all of Indiana's production and installed capacity. Of total electricity sales in 1995, roughly 48% was sold to industries, 30% to residences, 21% to commercial users, and 1% to others. The major electric utilities were Northern Indiana Public Service Co., Indiana & Michigan Electric Co., Public Service Co. of Indiana, Indianapolis Power & Light Co., and Southern Indiana Gas & Electric Co.

At the end of 1995, Indiana's estimated proved reserves of petroleum totaled 13 million barrels, and production of crude petroleum totaled 2.5 million barrels in 1996.

In 1995 there were 4 underground coal mines and 38 strip mines active in the state. Indiana's coal production in 1996 was estimated at 29.8 million tons of coal, 9th in the US. Recoverable reserves totaled 324 million short tons.

29INDUSTRY

The industrialization of Indiana that began in the Civil War era was spurred by technological advances in processing agricultural products, manufacturing farm equipment, and improving transportation facilities. Meat-packing plants, textile mills, furniture factories, and wagon works—including Studebaker wagons—were soon followed by metal foundries, machine shops, farm implement plants, and a myriad of other durable-goods plants.

New industries included a pharmaceutical house started in Indianapolis in 1876 by a druggist named Eli Lilly, and several automobile-manufacturing shops established in South Bend and other cities by 1900. In 1906, the US Steel Co. laid out the new town of Gary for steelworkers and their families.

In 1995, the estimated total value of shipments by manufacturers in Indiana was $131 billion. The leading industry groups in 1995, and the estimated value of their shipments were as follows:

Transportation equipment	$26,477,900,000
Primary metal products	19,801,000,000
Chemicals and chemical products	11,799,900,000
Food and food products	10,0969,700,000
Electrical and electronic equipment	9,475,400,000
Industrial machinery	11,099,300,000
Fabricated metal products	10,417,300,000
Rubber and plastic products	7,206,500,000
Printing and publishing	3,910,700,000
Furniture and fixtures	2,640,900,000
Lumber and wood products	3,157,800,000

Indiana is a leading producer of storage batteries, small motors and generators, mobile homes, household furniture, burial caskets, and musical instruments. Most manufacturing plants are located in and around Indianapolis and in the Calumet region. As of 1997, there were six Fortune 500 companies headquartered in Indiana. In 1995, there were 1,293 US patents issued to Indiana residents.

30COMMERCE

There were a total of 10,624 wholesale establishments in Indiana during 1992, with $52.4 billion in sales. Durable goods accounted for 50.9% of sales.

The 1995, there were 14,462 wholesale establishments in Indiana. Of the total sales, merchant wholesalers accounted for 61.7%. Principal goods traded included food and related products, machinery, equipment, and supplies, farm product raw materials, petroleum and petroleum products, and electrical goods.

Retail establishments in 1992 had sales of $42,373.5 million, from 33,448 establishments. Indiana ranked 14th in the nation in retail sales, with 2.25% of the US total. Automotive dealers accounted for 20.9% of sales; food stores, 17.3%; general merchandise stores, 14%; and eating and drinking places, 10.3%.

Indiana ranked 16th among the 50 states in exports during 1995, when its goods shipped abroad were valued at $11.96 billion. Major farm exports are soybeans; feed grains; wheat; meat (including poultry) and meat products; fats, oils, and greases; and hides and skins. Principal nonfarm exports include transportation equipment, electric and electronic equipment, nonelectric machinery, primary metals products, chemicals and allied products, food and kindred products, and fabricated metal products.

31CONSUMER PROTECTION

The Division of Consumer Protection of the Office of the Attorney General, created in 1971, is empowered to investigate consumer complaints, initiate and prosecute civil actions, and warn consumers about deceptive sales practices. Indiana also has a public counselor, who appears on behalf of the public at hearings of the Public Service Commission in regard to rates charged by public utilities and transportation agencies. The public counselor is appointed by the governor to a four-year term and is aided by a 20-member staff and 11-member advisory council.

In early 1980, the first criminal prosecution of an American corporation because of alleged product defects was brought against the Ford Motor Co. at Winamac. A jury found the company not guilty of reckless homicide in a rear-end collision involving a Pinto automobile in which three young women were killed.

32BANKING

The large-scale mechanization of agriculture in Indiana after 1850 encouraged the growth of banks to lend money to farmers to buy farm machinery, using their land as collateral. The financial panic of 1893 caused most banks in the state to suspend operations, and the depression of the 1930s caused banks to foreclose many farm mortgages and dozens of banks to fail. The nation's subsequent economic recovery, together with the federal reorganization of the banking system, helped Indiana banks to share in the state's prosperity during and after World War II.

In December 1996 there were 214 insured commercial banks in the state, of which 71 were members of the Federal Reserve System (51 of these had national charters and 20 were state-chartered). The total assets of insured commercial banks amounted to $67.8 billion; their liabilities included time and savings deposits of $53.1 billion as of 31 December 1996.

At the end of 1996, the state's 66 insured savings institutions held $9.1 billion in mortgage loans and $9.7 billion in savings accounts; their total assets amounted to $14.9 billion.

The Department of Financial Institutions regulates the operations of Indiana-chartered banks, savings and loan associations, and credit unions, and monitors observance of a Uniform Consumer Credit Code. The department is headed by a seven-member board, each board member serves a four-year term and no more than four members may be of the same political party. A full-time director, also appointed by the governor to a four-year term, is the department's chief executive and administrative officer.

33INSURANCE

As of 1995 there were 124 state-licensed property/casualty insurance companies with home offices in Indiana, and 50 life insurance companies.

In 1991, life insurance companies in the state had in force a total of 3.9 million policies and paid total benefits of $1.7 billion. In that year, life insurance policies were valued at $261 billion; the average amount of life insurance held by families was $116,300.

Some 790,985 people were enrolled in Medicare in 1992 and received benefit payments of $2.4 billion. There were 506,829 Medicaid recipients in 1992, with expenditures of over $2.2 billion, or $4,390 per recipient.

Property and liability companies in 1995 wrote premiums for $2.42 billion in automobile liability and physical damage coverage, $528.8 million in homeowners' insurance, and $68.7 million in farmowners' insurance.

The Department of Insurance licenses insurance carriers and agents in Indiana, and it enforces regulations governing the issuance of policies.

34SECURITIES

There are no securities exchanges in Indiana. As of May 1992, there were 1,636 securities brokers and dealers registered to conduct transactions in Indiana by means of 64,005 registered agents. Investment advisor firms and their agents also register with the state. Laws governing the trading and sale of corporate securities are administered by the secretary of state, who also regulates franchise sales and corporate takeover attempts.

35PUBLIC FINANCE

The State Budget Agency acts as watchdog over state financial affairs. The agency prepares the budget for the governor and presents it to the general assembly. The budget director, appointed by the governor, serves with four legislators (two from each house) on the state budget committee, which helps to prepare the budget. The state budget agency receives appropriations requests from the heads of state offices, estimates anticipated revenues for the biennium, and administers the budget.

The fiscal year runs from 1 July to 30 June of the following year. Budgets are prepared for the biennium beginning and ending in odd-numbered years.

The following is a summary of total estimated revenues and requested expenditures for 1995 (in thousands):

REVENUES	
Federal government	$3,438,489
Own resources	12,822,026
Taxes income	3,257,299
Property	1,412,442
Sales and gross receipts	4,788,454
TOTAL	9,548,195
CHANGES AND MISCELLANEOUS	
Current charges	2,032,941
Special miscellaneous	1,330,890
TOTAL	3,363,831
TOTAL REVENUE	$16,260,515
EXPENDITURES	
Education	$5,840,259
Health and social concerns	4,157,194
Financial administration	332,933
Transportation (highways)	1,398,483
Utilities	0
Public safety (police)	469,519
Natural resources	190,344
Other	2,975,573
TOTAL GENERAL EXPENDITURES	$15,248,083

The total indebtedness of the state government was nearly $5.5 billion in 1995.

36TAXATION

The first state property tax in Indiana was levied in 1852 to support public schools. In 1923, a state gasoline tax of 2 cents per gallon was introduced. (It ranged from 11.1 cents to 14 cents in 1984, depending on average prices in a specified month.) In 1992 the gasoline tax was 15 cents a gallon. In 1933, Indiana instituted the personal income tax, which was the major source of state revenue until 1963, when a 2% retail sales tax was enacted. Also in 1933, with the end of Prohibition, taxes were imposed on the manufacture and sale of alcoholic beverages. In 1973, the state sales tax was doubled to 4% and optional local income taxes of up to 1% were initiated, while local property taxes were reduced by at least 20% to ease the tax burden on property owners. In 1996, the state sales tax was 5%, and the state tax on cigarettes was 15.5 cents per pack. The state's personal income tax was 3.4% of adjusted gross income.

In the 1996 fiscal year, Indiana's state tax revenue totaled $8 billion; the tax per capita was about $1,444.

The total federal income tax burden in Indiana for 1995 amounted to $26.1 billion, or $4,501 per capita; the state ranked 29th among the 50 states in per capita tax burden in 1996.

37ECONOMIC POLICY

The state's early economic policy was to provide farmers with access to markets by improving transportation facilities. During the Civil War era, however, Indiana began to encourage industrial growth. In modern times, the state has financed extensive highway construction, developed deepwater ports on Lake Michigan and the Ohio River, and worked to foster industrial growth and develop its tourist industry. Tax incentives to business include a 15-year phaseout, beginning in 1979, of the "intangibles" tax on stocks, bonds, and notes.

In the 1980s and 1990s, the state government focused on a series of economic development initiatives. These included programs offering job training and retraining, the promotion of new businesses and tourism, the development of infrastructure, and the provision of investment capital for start-up companies—as well as programs providing additional tax incentives. The Department of Commerce, which has sole responsibility for economic development, solicits new businesses to locate in Indiana, promotes sales of exports abroad, plans the development of energy resources, continues to foster the expansion of agriculture, and helps minority-group owners of small businesses. The department's Industrial Development Fund makes loans to municipalities for the purchasing or leasing of property for industrial development.

38HEALTH

Mortality rates are above the national average and infant death rates are close to the national average in Indiana. In 1995, the provisional live-birth rate for the state was 14.5 per 1,000 population; the provisional infant mortality rate for 1995 was 8.3 per 1,000 live births. In 1995, the legal abortion ratio was 144.1 per 1,000 live births.

The principal causes of death, with rates of death per 100,000 population in 1994, were heart disease, 312.9 (158.9 age-adjusted); cancer, 218.1 (141.4 age-adjusted); cerebrovascular diseases, 72.5 (32.4 age-adjusted); injury and poisoning, 57.1 (51.5 age-adjusted); of which motor vehicle injuries accounted for 17.6 (17.2 age-adjusted) and suicide, 12.9 (12.2 age-adjusted). The crude total death rate was 944.7 (542.6 age-adjusted), higher than the national average of 875.4 (507.4 age-adjusted).

In 1994, the Indiana State Department of Health identified public health priorities that will be used to develop agency-wide integrated work plans and evaluate the effectiveness of disease intervention and prevention strategies. These priorities are:

Chronic Disease (breast and lung cancer, coronary heart disease, diabetes); Communicable Disease (HIV and STDs, vaccine preventable diseases, emerging conditions—The AIDS prevalence was 9.11 per 100,000 in 1995); Environmental (foodborne and waterborne disease, lead exposure, oral health); Infant Mortality (infant mortality and high-risk pregnancy); and Injury (intentional and unintentional)

Indiana had 135 acute-care hospitals in 1995, with 19,823 beds; discharges from these hospitals totaled 707,266 in that year, and there were 12,269,459 outpatient visits. A total of 88,546 full-time equivalent employees worked in Indiana hospitals as of 1995. The average expense for care per discharged stay in 1995 was $8,647, and the average expense per patient day came to $1,524. The state had 10,125 active, non-federal licensed physicians and 3,046 active, licensed dentists in 1995.

At least 14% of the Indiana population had no insurance in 1995.

39SOCIAL WELFARE

Public assistance payments to 147,000 families with dependent children averaged $346 a month in 1996. In 1996, the food stamp program had an average monthly participation of 389,537. School lunches were provided to pupils at a cost to the federal government of $87.6 million.

With the enactment of the Personal Responsibility and Work Opportunity Reconciliation Act of 1996, the US government has changed the form and regulations for many of its social welfare programs; most significantly, it replaces Aid to Families with Dependent Children (AFDC), open-ended entitlement program, with Temporary Assistance for Needy Families (TANF), a limited system of assistance funded largely through federal block grants. The reform act also impacts the food stamp program, the Supplemental Security Income program, and the child nutrition program. The law took effect on 1 July 1997 and provided $16.38 billion in block grants for fiscal years 1997–2002. The grants are to be divided among the states based on an equation involving the numbers of former AFDC recipients in each state. Because many of the bill's provisions have yet to be implemented into state-by-state policy, it was not currently possible to include the details of each state's programs.

In 1996, the average monthly Social Security payment of $655 was paid to 962,370 residents. Supplemental Security Income was provided to 87,757 recipients in 1995, averaging $341 a month.

Weekly payments to unemployed workers averaged $178.71 in 1995.

40HOUSING

The great majority of Indiana families enjoy adequate housing, particularly in newly built suburbs, but inadequate housing exists in the deteriorating central cores of large cities.

In 1996, the state had an estimated 2,401,000 housing units, 2,183,000 of which were occupied. In 1996, 37,291 privately owned housing units, valued at $3.7 billion, were authorized for construction; 29,863 were single family units. In 1990, the last year for which figures are available, about 51% of all owner occupied units had mortgages; the median monthly payment for mortgage and other selected costs was $561, and the median monthly cost for owners without a mortgage was $188. Median monthly rent was $374.

During fiscal year 1996, Indiana received $329.1 million in aid from the US Department of Housing and Urban Development, including $76.7 million in community development block grants.

41EDUCATION

Although the 1816 constitution recommended establishment of public schools, the state legislature did not provide funds for education. The constitution of 1851 more specifically outlined the state's responsibility to support a system of free public schools. Development was rapid following passage of this document; more than 2,700 schoolhouses were built in the state from 1852 to 1857, and an adult literacy rate of nearly 90% was achieved by 1860. The illiteracy rate was reduced to 5.2% for the adult population in 1900, to 1.7% in 1950, and to only 0.7% in 1970, when Indiana ranked 14th among the 50 states. In 1990, 76% of those aged 25 years and over were high school graduates, and 15% had completed four years of college.

In the fall of 1995, Indiana had 976,604 pupils enrolled in public elementary and secondary schools, and 55,702 teachers, or about 17.2 pupils per teacher, compared with a national average of 17.5. The average public school teacher drew an annual salary of $36,405 in 1996/97, about $300 below the national average. As of 1995/96, total nonpublic school enrollment came to 112,150.

In the 1992/93 academic year there were 384,842 students attending colleges and universities in the state. Indiana University, the state's largest institution of higher education, was founded in 1820. It is one of the largest state universities in the US, with a total 1992/93 enrollment on seven campuses of 121,290; the Bloomington campus alone had 45,455 students. Other major state universities and their 1992/93 enrollments were Purdue University (Lafayette), 43,212; Ball State University (Muncie), 27,042; and Indiana State University (Terre Haute), 15,805. Well-known private universities in the state include Notre Dame (at South Bend), with 11,343 students, and Butler (Indianapolis), with 5,600 students. Small private colleges and universities include DePauw (Greencastle), Earlham (Richmond), Hanover (Hanover), and Wabash (Crawfordsville).

In 1992/93 the state provided about $50 million in need-based financial aid to 80,557 full-time resident undergraduate students attending public and independent colleges and universities.

The state superintendent of public instruction is elected for a four-year term. The superintendent serves as chairperson of the 11-member state board of education, which is appointed by the governor. The board sets basic policy for the public school system.

In fiscal year 1995, Indiana spent more than $4.7 billion on public schools, for an average expenditure of $5,322 per student (34th in the US).

42ARTS

The earliest center for artists in Indiana was the Art Association of Indianapolis, founded in 1883. It managed the John Herron Art Institute, consisting of a museum and art school (1906–08). Around 1900, art colonies sprang up in Richmond, Muncie, South Bend, and Nashville. Indianapolis remains the state's cultural center, especially after the opening in the late 1960s of the Lilly Pavilion of the Decorative Arts; the Krannert Pavilion, which houses the paintings originally in the Herron Museum; the Clowes Art Pavilion; and the Grace Showalter Pavilion of the Performing Arts (all collectively known as the Indianapolis Museum of Art). Since 1969, the Indiana Arts Commission has taken art—and artists—into many Indiana communities; the commission also sponsors biennial awards to artists in the state. Indiana has over 450 arts associations.

The state's first resident theater company established itself in Indianapolis in 1840, and the first theater building, the Metropolitan, was opened there in 1858. Ten years later, the Academy of Music was founded as the center for dramatic activities in Indianapolis. In 1875, the Grand Opera House opened there, and the following year it was joined by the English Opera House, where touring performers such as Sarah Bernhardt, Edwin Booth, and Ethel Barrymore held the stage. Amateur theater has been popular since the founding in 1915 of the nation's oldest amateur

drama group, the Little Theater Society, which later became the Civic Theater of Indianapolis.

Music has flourished in Indiana. Connersville reportedly was the first American city to establish a high school band, while Richmond claims the first high school symphony orchestra. The Indianapolis Symphony Orchestra was founded in 1930. There are 23 other symphony orchestras in the state. The Arthur Jordan College of Music is part of Butler University in Indianapolis. From 1991 to 1996, federal and state funding for the arts in Indiana amounted to $701,000. The NEA contributed $671,000 to the state's art programs and $1,233,000 to the Indiana Arts Commission. Financial resources from the state amounted to $10,936,019. Private sources provided $34 million. Indiana's arts programs had a total audience of 86,068,000 people. The number of contributing artists amounted to 190,403.The Indiana Arts Commission also received funds from state and regional programs.

43LIBRARIES AND MUSEUMS

The state constitution of 1816 provided for the establishment of public libraries. A majority of Indiana cities opened such libraries but neglected to provide adequate financing. Semiprivate libraries did better: workingmen's libraries were set up by a bequest at New Harmony and 14 other towns. After the state legislature provided for township school libraries in 1852, more than two-thirds of the townships established them, and the public library system has thrived ever since. In 1996 there were 56 county libraries, and every county received some form of library service. Federal grants-in-aid to all public libraries totaled $2,642,678; state grants, $2,607,936. The largest book collections are at public libraries in Indianapolis, Fort Wayne, Gary, Evansville, Merrillville, and Hammond; the total book stock of all Indiana public libraries was 21,671,191 volumes in 1996.

The Indiana State Library has a strong collection of documents about Indiana's history and a large genealogical collection. The Indiana University Library has special collections on American literature and history and an extensive collection of rare books; the University of Notre Dame has a noteworthy collection on medieval history; and Purdue University Libraries contain outstanding industrial and agricultural collections, as well as voluminous materials on Indiana history.

Private libraries and museums include those maintained by historical societies in Indianapolis, Fort Wayne, and South Bend. Also of note are the General Lew Wallace Study museum in Crawfordsville and the Elwood Haynes Museum of early technology in Kokomo. In all, Indiana had 170 museums in 1997 registered with the American Association of Museums. Many county historical societies maintain smaller museums, such as the Wayne County Historical Museum.

Indiana's historic sites of most interest to visitors are the Lincoln Boyhood National Memorial near Gentryville, the Levi Coffin Home (one of the Underground Railroad stops) in Fountain City, the Benjamin Harrison Memorial Home and the James Whitcomb Riley Home in Indianapolis, and the Grouseland Home of William Henry Harrison in Vincennes. Among several archaeological sites are two large mound groups: one at Mounds State Park near Anderson, which dates from about AD 800–900, and a reconstructed village site at Angel Mounds, Newburgh, which dates from 1300–1500.

44COMMUNICATIONS

About 91% of all households had telephone service in March 1993. The state's first radio station was licensed in 1922 at Purdue University, Lafayette. Indiana had 875 AM and 201 FM radio stations and 31 commercial and 8 educational television stations as of 1996. Powerful radio and television transmissions from Chicago and Cincinnati also blanket the state. In 1993, fifteen large cable systems served the state.

45PRESS

The first newspaper in Indiana was published at Vincennes in 1804, and a second pioneer weekly appeared at Madison nine years later. By 1830, newspapers were also being published in Terre Haute, Indianapolis, and 11 other towns; the following year, the state's oldest surviving newspaper, the *Richmond Palladium*, began publication. Most pioneer newspapers were highly political and engaged in acrimonious feuds; in 1836, for example, the *Indianapolis Journal* referred to the editors of the rival *Democrat* as "the Lying, Hireling Scoundrels." By the time of the Civil War, Indiana had 154 weeklies and 13 dailies.

The last third of the 19th century brought a sharp increase in both the number and the quality of newspapers. Two newspapers which later became the state's largest in circulation, the *Indianapolis News* and the *Star*, began publishing in 1869 and 1903, respectively. In 1941 there were 294 weekly and 98 daily newspapers in Indiana; the number declined after World War II because of fierce competition for readers and advertising dollars, rising operating costs, and other financial difficulties. In 1997, the state had 19 morning dailies and 52 evening dailies; Sunday papers numbered 23. In 1997, the Indianapolis morning *Star* had a daily circulation of 231,299 (Sunday circulation, 404,614); the Indianapolis evening *News* had a daily circulation of 62,726; and the Gary evening *Post-Tribune's* circulation averaged 67,355 daily and 76,026 on Sundays.

A number of magazines are published in Indiana, including *Children's Digest* and *The Saturday Evening Post*.

Indiana is noted for its literary productivity. The list of authors claimed by Indiana up to 1966 showed a total of 3,600. Examination of the 10 best-selling novels each year from 1900 to 1940 (allowing 10 points to the top best-seller, down to 1 point for the 10th best-selling book) showed Indiana with a score of 213 points, exceeded only by New York's 218.

Many Hoosier authors were first published by Indiana's major book publisher, Bobbs-Merrill. Indiana University Press is an important publisher of scholarly books.

46ORGANIZATIONS

The 1992 US Census of Service Industries counted 2,127 organizations in Indiana, including 282 business associations; 1,436 civic, social, and fraternal associations; and 409 other membership organizations. National organizations with headquarters in the state include the American Camping Association, located in Martinsville, and the Amateur Athletic Union of the US, the American Legion, the US Gymnastics Federation, and Kiwanis International, all in Indianapolis.

Philanthropic foundations headquartered in Indiana include the Eugene V. Debs Foundation (Terre Haute) and the Irwin Sweeny-Miller Foundation (Columbus)

47TOURISM, TRAVEL, AND RECREATION

Tourism is of moderate economic importance to Indiana. In 1996, 1,792,103 visitors spent their vacations at the state's three national parks. Residents spent $4,220,000 on domestic overnight and day trips in the state.

Summer resorts are located in the north, along Lake Michigan and in Steuben and Kosciusko counties, where there are nearly 200 lakes. Popular tourist sites include the reconstructed village of New Harmony, site of famous communal living experiments in the early 19th century; the Indianapolis Motor Speedway and Museum; and the George Rogers Clark National Historic Park at Vincennes. In addition to the Indiana State Museum there are 15 state memorials, including the Wilbur Wright State Memorial at his birthplace near Millville, the Ernie Pyle birthplace near Dana,

and the old state capitol at Corydon. Among the natural attractions are the Indiana Dunes National Lakeshore on Lake Michigan (12,534 acres/5,072 hectares); the state's largest waterfall, Cataract Falls, near Cloverdale; and the largest underground cavern, at Wyandotte.

Indiana has 23 state parks, comprising 59,292 acres (21,800 hectares). The largest state park is Brown County (15,543 acres/16,290 hectares), near Nashville. There are 15 state fish and wildlife preserves, totaling about 75,200 acres (30,400 hectares). The largest are Pigeon River, near Howe, and Willow Slough, at Morocco. Game animals during the hunting season include deer, squirrel, and rabbit; ruffed grouse, quail, ducks, geese, and partridge are the main game birds. In 1995, licenses were held by 754,185 anglers and 738,076 hunters.

48SPORTS

Indiana is represented in professional sports by the Indiana Pacers of the National Basketball Association and by the National Football League's Colts, who moved to Indianapolis from Baltimore in 1984. Indianapolis is also represented in baseball's Class AAA American Association.

The state's biggest annual sports event is the Indianapolis 500, which has been held at the Indianapolis Motor Speedway on Memorial Day every year since 1911 (except for the war years 1917 and 1942–45). The race is now part of a three-day Indiana festival held over Memorial Day weekend that attracts crowds of over 300,000 spectators, the largest crowd for any sporting event anywhere in the world.

The state's most popular amateur sport is basketball. The high school boys' basketball tournament culminates on the last Saturday in March, when the four finalists play afternoon and evening games to determine the winner. A tournament for girls' basketball teams began in 1976. Basketball is also popular at the college level: Indiana University won the NCAA Division I basketball championship in 1940, 1953, 1976, 1981, and 1987, and the National Invitational Tournament (NIT) in 1979; Purdue University won the NIT title in 1974; and Evansville College won the NCAA Division II championships in 1959–60, 1964–65, and 1971.

Collegiate football in Indiana has a colorful tradition stretching back to at least 1913, when Knute Rockne of Notre Dame unleashed the forward pass as a potent football weapon. Notre Dame, which competes as an independent, was recognized as National Champions in 1946–47, 1949, 1966, 1973 (with Alabama), 1977, and 1988. It won the following string of bowl games: the Orange Bowl in 1975 and 1990, and the Cotton Bowl in 1971, 1978, 1979, 1993, and 1994, the Sugar Bowl in 1973 and 1992, and the Fiesta Bowl in 1989. Indiana and Purdue compete in the Big Ten. Purdue won the Rose Bowl in 1967. Indiana State is part of the Missouri Valley Conference.

The Little 500, a 50-mi (80-km) bicycle race, is held each spring at Indiana University's Bloomington campus. The US Open Clay Court Tennis Championships are held annually in Indianapolis.

Other annual sporting events include the National Muzzle-loading Rifle Association Championship Shoot which is held in Friendship in August, and the Sugar Creek canoe race which is held in Crawfordsville in April.

49FAMOUS INDIANANS

Indiana has contributed one US president and four vice presidents to the nation. Benjamin Harrison (b.Ohio, 1833–1901), the 23d president, was a Republican who served one term (1889–93) and then returned to Indianapolis, where his home is now a national historic landmark. Three vice presidents were Indiana residents: Thomas Hendricks (b.Ohio, 1819–85), who served only eight months under President Cleveland and died in office; Schuyler

Colfax (b.New York, 1823–85), who served under President Grant; and Charles Fairbanks (b.Ohio, 1852–1918), who served under Theodore Roosevelt. Two vice presidents were native sons: Thomas Marshall (1854–1925), who served two four-year terms with President Wilson and J(ames) Danforth Quayle of Indianapolis (b. 1947), President George Bush's running mate in the 1988 presidential election. Marshall, remembered for his wit, originated the remark, "What this country needs is a good five-cent cigar."

Other Indiana-born political figures include Eugene V. Debs (1855–1926), Socialist Party candidate for president five times, and Wendell L. Willkie (1892–1944), the Republican candidate in 1940.

A dozen native and adoptive Hoosiers have held cabinet posts. Hugh McCulloch (b.Maine, 1808–95) was twice secretary of the treasury, in 1865–69 and 1884–85. Walter Q. Gresham (b.England, 1832–95) was successively postmaster general, secretary of the treasury, and secretary of state. John W. Foster (1836–1917) was an editor and diplomat before service as secretary of state under President Benjamin Harrison. Two other postmasters general came from Indiana: Harry S. New (1858–1937) and Will H. Hays (1879–1954). Hays resigned to become president of the Motion Picture Producers and Distributors (1922–45), and enforced its moral code in Hollywood films through what became widely known as the Hays Office. Two Hoosiers served as secretary of the interior: Caleb B. Smith (b.Massachusetts, 1808–64) and John P. Usher (b.New York, 1816–89). Richard W. Thompson (b.Virginia, 1809–1900) was secretary of the Navy. William H. H. Miller (b.New York, 1840–1917) was attorney general. Two native sons and Purdue University alumni have been secretaries of agriculture: Claude R. Wickard (1873–1967) and Earl Butz (b.1909). Paul V. McNutt (1891–1955) was a governor of Indiana, high commissioner to the Philippines, and director of the Federal Security Administration.

Only one Hoosier, Sherman Minton (1890–1965), has served on the US Supreme Court. Ambrose Burnside (1824–81) and Lew Wallace (1827–1905) were Union generals during the Civil War; Wallace later wrote popular historical novels. Oliver P. Morton (1823–77) was a strong and meddlesome governor during the war, and a leader of the radical Republicans during the postwar Reconstruction. Colonel Richard Owen (b.England, 1810–90) commanded Camp Morton (Indianapolis) for Confederate prisoners; after the war, some of his grateful prisoners contributed to place a bust of Owen in the Indiana statehouse. Rear Admiral Norman Scott (1889–1942) distinguished himself at Guadalcanal during World War II. Nearly 70 Hoosiers have won the Medal of Honor.

Dr. Hermann J. Muller (b.New York, 1890–1967), of Indiana University, won the Nobel Prize in physiology or medicine in 1946 for proving that radiation can produce mutation in genes. Harold C. Urey (1893–1981) won the Nobel Prize in chemistry in 1934, and Wendell Stanley (1904–71) won it in 1946. The Nobel Prize in economics was awarded to Paul Samuelson (b. 1915) in 1970. The Pulitzer Prize in biography was awarded in 1920 to Albert J. Beveridge (b.Ohio, 1862–1927) for his *Life of John Marshall*. Beveridge also served in the US Senate. Booth Tarkington (1869–1946) won the Pulitzer Prize for fiction in 1918 and 1921. A. B. Guthrie (b.1901) won it for fiction in 1950. The Pulitzer Prize in history went to R. C. Buley (1893–1968) in 1951 for *The Old Northwest*.

Aviation pioneer Wilbur Wright (1867–1912) was born in Millville. Other figures in the public eye were chemist Harvey W. Wiley (1844–1930), who was responsible for the Food and Drug Act of 1906; Emil Schram (b.1893-1897), president of the New York Stock Exchange from 1931 to 1951; and Alfred C. Kinsey (b.New Jersey, 1894–1956), who investigated human sexual

behavior and issued the two famous "Kinsey reports" in 1948 and 1953.

Indiana claims such humorists as George Ade (1866–1944), Frank McKinney "Kin" Hubbard (b.Ohio, 1868–1930), and Don Herold (1889–1966). Historians Charles (1874–1948) and Mary (1876–1958) Beard, Claude Bowers (1878–1958), and Glenn Tucker (1892–1976) were Hoosiers. Maurice Thompson (1844–1901) and George Barr McCutcheon (1866–1928) excelled in historical romances. The best-known poets were James Whitcomb Riley (1849–1916) and William Vaughn Moody (1869–1910). Juvenile writer Annie Fellows Johnston (1863–1931) produced the "Little Colonel" series.

Other Indiana novelists include Edward Eggleston (1837–1902), Meredith Nicholson (1866–1947), David Graham Phillips (1868–1911) Gene Stratton Porter (1868–1924), Theodore Dreiser (1871–1945), Lloyd C. Douglas (1877–1951), Rex Stout (1886–1975), William E. Wilson (b.1906), Jessamyn West (1907–84), and Kurt Vonnegut (b.1922). Well-known journalists were news analyst Elmer Davis (1890–1958), war correspondent Ernie Pyle (1900–45), and columnist Janet Flanner (1892–1978), "Genet" of *The New Yorker*.

Among the few noted painters Indiana has produced are Theodore C. Steele (1847–1928), William M. Chase (1851–1927), J. Ottis Adams (1851–1927), Otto Stark (1859–1926), Wayman Adams (1883–1959), Clifton Wheeler (1883–1953), Marie Goth (1887–1975), C. Curry Bohm (1894–1971), and Floyd Hopper (b.1909).

Composers of Indiana origin have worked mainly in popular music: Paul Dresser (1857–1906), Cole Porter (1893–1964), and Howard Hoagland "Hoagy" Carmichael (1899–1981). Howard Hawks (1896–1977) was a renowned film director. Entertainers from Indiana include actor and dancer Clifton Webb (Webb Hollenbeck, 1896–1966); orchestra leader Phil Harris (b.1904); comedians Ole Olsen (1892–1963), Richard "Red" Skelton (b.1913), and Herb Shriner (b.Ohio, 1918–70); actresses Marjorie Main (1890–1975) and Carole Lombard (Jane Peters, 1908–42); and singer Michael Jackson (b.1958).

Hoosier sports heroes include Knute Rockne (b.Norway, 1888–1931), famed as a football player and coach at Notre Dame. Star professionals who played high school basketball in Indiana include Oscar Robertson (b.Tennessee, 1938) and Larry Bird (b.1956), who at Indiana State University in 1978/79 was honored as college basketball's player of the year.

[50]BIBLIOGRAPHY

Banta, R. E. *Indiana Authors and Their Books, 1816–1916.* Crawfordville, Ind.: Wabash College, 1949.

——. *The Wabash.* New York: Farrar & Rinehart, 1950.

Barnhart, John D., and Donald F. Carmony. *Indiana from Frontier to Industrial Commonwealth.* 4 vols. New York: Lewis Historical Publishing, 1954.

Barnhart, John D., and Dorothy L. Riker. *Indiana to 1816: The Colonial Period.* Indianapolis: Indiana Historical Society, 1971.

Buley, R. C. *The Old Northwest: Pioneer Period, 1815–1840.* Indianapolis: Indiana Historical Society, 1950.

Carter, Jared, and Darryl Jones. *Indiana.* Portland, Ore.: Graphic Arts Center Publishing Co., 1984.

Cayton, Andrew R.L. *Frontier Indiana.* Bloomington: Indiana University Press, 1996.

Dorson, Ron. *The Indy Five Hundred.* New York: Norton, 1974.

Federal Writers' Project. *Indiana: A Guide to the Hoosier State.* Reprint. New York: Somerset, n.d. (orig. 1941).

Indiana State Chamber of Commerce. *Here Is Your Indiana Government.* Indianapolis, 1983.

Latta, William C. *Outline History of Indiana Agriculture.* Lafayette: Purdue University and Indiana County Agricultural

Agents Association, 1938.

Leibowitz, Irving. *My Indiana*. Englewood Cliffs, N.J.: Prentice-Hall, 1964.

Lilly, Eli. *Prehistoric Antiquities of Indiana*. Indianapolis: Indiana Historical Society, 1937.

Lindley, Harlow, ed. *Indiana as Seen by Early Travelers*. Indianapolis: Indiana Historical Commission, 1916.

McCord, Shirley S., ed. *Travel Accounts of Indiana, 1679–1961*. Indianapolis: Indiana Historical Bureau, 1970.

Martin, John Bartlow. *Indiana: An Interpretation*. New York: Knopf, 1947.

Nicholson, Meredith. *The Hoosiers*. New York: Macmillan, 1900.

Nolan, Jeanette C. *Hoosier City: The Story of Indianapolis*. New York: Messner, 1943.

Peat, Wilbur D. *Pioneer Painters of Indiana*. Indianapolis: Art Association of Indianapolis, 1954.

Shumaker, Arthur W. *A History of Indiana Literature*. Indianapolis: Indiana Historical Society, 1962.

Starr, George W. *Industrial Development of Indiana*. Bloomington: Indiana University Press, 1937.

Thompson, Donald E. *Indiana Authors and Their Books, 1916–66*. Crawfordsville, Ind.: Wabash College, 1974.

Thornbrough, Emma Lou. *Indiana in the Civil War Era, 1850–80*. Indianapolis: Indiana Historical Society, 1965.

Wilson William E. *The Angel and the Serpent: The Story of New Harmony*. Bloomington: Indiana University Press, 1964.

———. *Indiana: A History*. Bloomington: Indiana University Press, 1966.

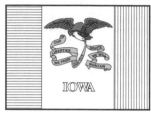

IOWA

State of Iowa

ORIGIN OF STATE NAME: Named for Iowa Indians of the Siouan family. **NICKNAME:** The Hawkeye State. **CAPITAL:** Des Moines. **ENTERED UNION:** 28 December 1846 (29th). **SONG:** "The Song of Iowa." **MOTTO:** Our Liberties We Prize and Our Rights We Will Maintain. **FLAG:** There are three vertical stripes of blue, white, and red; in the center a spreading eagle holds in its beak a blue ribbon with the state motto. **OFFICIAL SEAL:** A sheaf and field of standing wheat and farm utensils represent agriculture; a lead furnace and a pile of pig lead are to the right. In the center stands a citizen-soldier holding a US flag with a liberty cap atop the staff in one hand and a rifle in the other. Behind him is the Mississippi River with the steamer *Iowa* and mountains; above him an eagle holds the state motto. Surrounding this scene are the words "The Great Seal of the State of Iowa" against a gold background. **BIRD:** Eastern goldfinch. **FLOWER:** Wild rose. **TREE:** Oak. **STONE:** Geode. **LEGAL HOLIDAYS:** New Year's Day, 1 January; Birthday of Martin Luther King, Jr., 3d Monday in January; Lincoln's Birthday, 12 February; Washington's Birthday, 3d Monday in February; Memorial Day, last Monday in May; Independence Day, 4 July; Labor Day, 1st Monday in September; Veterans Day, 11 November; Thanksgiving Day, 4th Thursday in November; Christmas Day, 25 December. **TIME:** 6 AM CST = noon GMT.

¹LOCATION, SIZE, AND EXTENT

Located in the western north-central US, Iowa is the smallest of the midwestern states situated W of the Mississippi River, and ranks 25th in size among the 50 states.

The total area of Iowa is 56,275 sq mi (145,752 sq km), of which land takes up 55,965 sq mi (144,949 sq km) and inland water 310 sq mi (803 sq km). The state extends 324 mi (521 km) E-W; its maximum extension N-S is 210 mi (338 km).

Iowa is bordered on the N by Minnesota; on the E by Wisconsin and Illinois (with the line formed by the Mississippi River); on the S by Missouri (with the extreme southeastern line defined by the Des Moines River); and on the W by Nebraska and South Dakota (with the line demarcated by the Missouri River and a tributary, the Big Sioux).

The total boundary length of Iowa is 1,151 mi (1,853 km). The state's geographic center is in Story County near Ames.

²TOPOGRAPHY

The topography of Iowa consists of a gently rolling plain that slopes from the highest point of 1,670 feet (509 meters) in the northwest to the lowest point of 480 feet (146 meters) in the southeast at the mouth of the Des Moines River. About two-thirds of the state lies between 800 feet (244 meters) and 1,400 feet (427 meters) above sea level; the mean elevation of land is 1,100 feet (335 meters).

Supremely well suited for agriculture, Iowa has the richest and deepest topsoil in the US and an excellent watershed. Approximately two-thirds of the state's area is drained by the Mississippi River, which forms the entire eastern boundary, and its tributaries. The western part of the state is drained by the Missouri River and its tributaries. Iowa has 13 natural lakes. The largest are Spirit Lake (9 mi, or 14 km, long) and West Okoboji Lake (6 mi. or 10 km. long), both near the state's northwest border.

The Iowa glacial plain was formed by five different glaciers. The last glacier, which covered about one-fifth of the state's area, retreated from the north-central region some 10,000 years ago, leaving the topsoil as its legacy. Glacial drift formed the small lakes in the north. The oldest rock outcropping, located in the state's northwest corner, is about 1 billion years old.

³CLIMATE

Iowa lies in the humid continental zone and generally has hot summers, cold winters, and wet springs.

Temperatures vary widely during the year, with an annual average of 49°F (9°C). The state averages 166 days of full sunshine and 199 cloudy or partly cloudy days. Des Moines, in the central part of the state, has a normal daily maximum temperature of 86°F (30°C) in July and a normal daily minimum of 10°F (–4°C) in January. The record low temperature for the state is –47°F (–44°C), established at Washta on 12 January 1912; the record high is 118°F (48°C), registered at Keokuk on 20 July 1934. Rainfall averages 32 in (81 cm) annually; snowfall, 30 in (76 cm); and relative humidity, 72%. There were 42 tornadoes in 1995.

⁴FLORA AND FAUNA

Although most of Iowa is under cultivation, such unusual wild specimens as bunchberry and bearberry can be found in the northeast, where the loess soil supports tumblegrass, western beard-tongue, and prickly pear cactus. Other notable plants are pink lady's slipper and twinleaf in the eastern woodlands, arrowgrass in the northwest, and erect dryflower and royal and cinnamon ferns in sandy regions. More than 80 native plants can no longer be found, and at least 35 others are confined to a single location. The federal government classified the northern wild monkshood as threatened as of 1984.

Common Iowa mammals include red and gray foxes, raccoon, opossum, woodchuck, muskrat, common cottontail, gray fox, and flying squirrel. The bobolink and purple martin have flyways over the state; the cardinal, rose-breasted grosbeak, and eastern goldfinch (the state bird) nest there. Game fish include rainbow trout, smallmouth bass, and walleye; in all, Iowa has 140 native fish species.

Rare animals include the pygmy shrew, ermine, black-billed cuckoo, and crystal darter. The state lists as endangered the red-backed vole, black bear, bobcat, red-shouldered hawk, piping plover, burrowing owl, northern copperhead, and lake sturgeon. The Indiana bat and peregrine falcon, both indigenous to Iowa, are on the federal endangered species list.

[5]ENVIRONMENTAL PROTECTION

Because this traditionally agricultural state's most valuable resource has been its topsoil, Iowa's conservation measures beginning in the 1930s were directed toward preventing soil erosion and preserving watershed runoff. In the 1980s and 1990s, Iowans were particularly concerned with improving air quality, preventing chemical pollution, and preserving water supplies. In 1997, wetlands covered 12% of Iowa. The Wetlands Reserve Program of the 1990 Food, Agriculture, Conservation and Trade Act was created to reclaim some of the state's lost wetlands.

On 1 July 1983, the Department of Water, Air and Waste Management came into operation, with responsibility for environmental functions formerly exercised by separate state agencies. Functions of the new department include regulating operation of the state's 2,900 public water supply systems, overseeing nearly 1,200 municipal and industrial wastewater treatment plants, inspecting dams, and establishing chemical and bacterial standards to protect the quality of lakes. The department also enforces laws prohibiting open dumping of solid wastes, regulates the construction and operation of 140 solid waste disposal projects, and monitors the handling of hazardous wastes. It also establishes standards for air quality and regulates the emission of air pollutants from more than 600 industries and utilities.

Iowa had 17 hazardous waste sites in 1995.

[6]POPULATION

Iowa, the 25th in size of the 50 states, ranked 30th in state population at the 1990 census, with 2,776,755 residents. In 1996, Iowa's population was estimated at 2,851,792, an increase of 2.7% from 1990. Population density in 1990 was 49.7 persons per sq mi (19 per sq km).

Iowa's population growth was rapid during the early years of settlement. When the first pioneers arrived in the early 19th century, an estimated 8,000 Indians were living within the state's present boundaries. From 1832 to 1840, the number of white settlers increased from fewer than 50 to 43,112. The population had almost doubled to more than 80,000 by the time Iowa became a state in 1846. The great influx of European immigrants who came via other states during the 1840s and 1850s caused the new state's population to soar to 674,913 at the 1860 census. By the end of the next decade, the population had reached nearly 1,200,000; by 1900, it had surpassed 2,200,000.

The state's population growth leveled off in the 20th century. In 1990, Iowa's population was 51.2% female and 48.8% male, and 60.6% of all Iowans lived in urban areas. Of the total 1990 population, over 98% was native-born. Iowa is tied for second at 15.1% with Pennsylvania and behind only Florida in the concentration of population over 65.

In 1994, the largest cities were: Des Moines, 193,965; Cedar Rapids, 113,438; Davenport, 96,964; Sioux City, 80,500; Waterloo, 66,537; Dubuque, 59,084; and Iowa City, 60,655. In 1995, the Des Moines metropolitan area had 421,447 residents; the Davenport metropolitan area had 358,243 residents that year.

[7]ETHNIC GROUPS

In 1990, there were 48,000 black Americans, 7,000 American Indians, and 33,000 people of Hispanic origin living in Iowa. Among Iowans of European descent, there were 1,394,542 Germans; 536,720 English, Scottish, or Welsh; 527,428 Irish; and 152,084 Norwegians. The foreign-born population numbered 43,316 in 1990. Primary countries of origin included Germany, Mexico, Laos, Canada, Korea, and Vietnam.

[8]LANGUAGES

A few Indian place-names are the legacy of early Siouan Iowa Indians and the westward-moving Algonkian Sauk and Fox tribes who pushed them out: Iowa, Ottumwa, Keokuk, Sioux City, Oskaloosa, Decorah.

Iowa English reflects the three major migration streams: Northern in that half of the state above Des Moines and North Midland in the southern half, with a slight South Midland trace in the extreme southeastern corner. Although some Midland features extend into upper Iowa, rather sharp contrasts exist between the two halves. In pronunciation, Northern features contrast directly with Midland: /hyumor/ with /yumor/, /ah/ in on and fog with /aw/, the vowel of but in bulge with the vowel of put, and /too/ with /tyoo/ for two. Northern words also contrast with Midland words: crab with crawdad, corn on the cob with roasting ears, quarter to with quarter till, barnyard with barn lot, and gopher with ground squirrel

In 1990, 96.1% of all Iowans aged five or more spoke only English at home. The following are other languages reported by Iowans, and the number speaking each at home.

Spanish	31,620
German	21,429
French	7,941
Various Scandinavian	4,579
Other West Germanic	3,833
Chinese	3,450

[9]RELIGIONS

The first church building in Iowa was constructed by Methodists in Dubuque in 1834; a Roman Catholic church was built in Dubuque the following year. By 1860, the largest religious sects were the Methodists, Presbyterians, Catholics, Baptists, and Congregationalists. Other religious groups who came to Iowa during the 19th century included Lutherans, Dutch Reformers, Quakers, Mennonites, Jews, and the Community of True Inspiration, or Amana Society, which founded seven communal villages.

There were more than 1,154,034 Protestants, including 272,098 adherents of the United Methodist Church, 1,810 members of the American Lutheran Churches, 124,021 adherents of the Lutheran Church-Missouri Synod, and 50,771 adherents of the Disciples of Christ (Christian Church).

Roman Catholic church membership totaled 520,322 and the Jewish population 6,701 in 1990.

[10]TRANSPORTATION

The early settlers came to Iowa by way of the Ohio and Mississippi rivers and the Great Lakes, then traveled overland on trails via wagon and stagecoach. The need of Iowa farmers to haul their products to market over long distances prompted the development of the railroads, particularly during the 1880s. River traffic still plays a vital role in the state's transport.

As of 31 December 1995, Iowa ranked 9th among the 50 states in total rail miles, with 4,246 mi, including 3,569 route miles of Class I track operated by six railroads. Amtrak operates the long-distance California Zephyr (Chicago to Oakland, CA), and Southwest Chief (Chicago to Los Angeles, CA) serving six major stations in Iowa with an Iowa ridership of 43,016 in 1996/96.

Iowa ranked 11th among the states in road mileage in 1995, with 103,365 mi (166,418 km) of rural and 9,337 mi (15,033 km) of urban roads, including 781 mi (1,257 km) of interstate highways. In 1995, there were 1,993,287 registered automobiles and 760,275 trucks and buses in the state (not including truck tractors), with 2,058,335 licensed drivers.

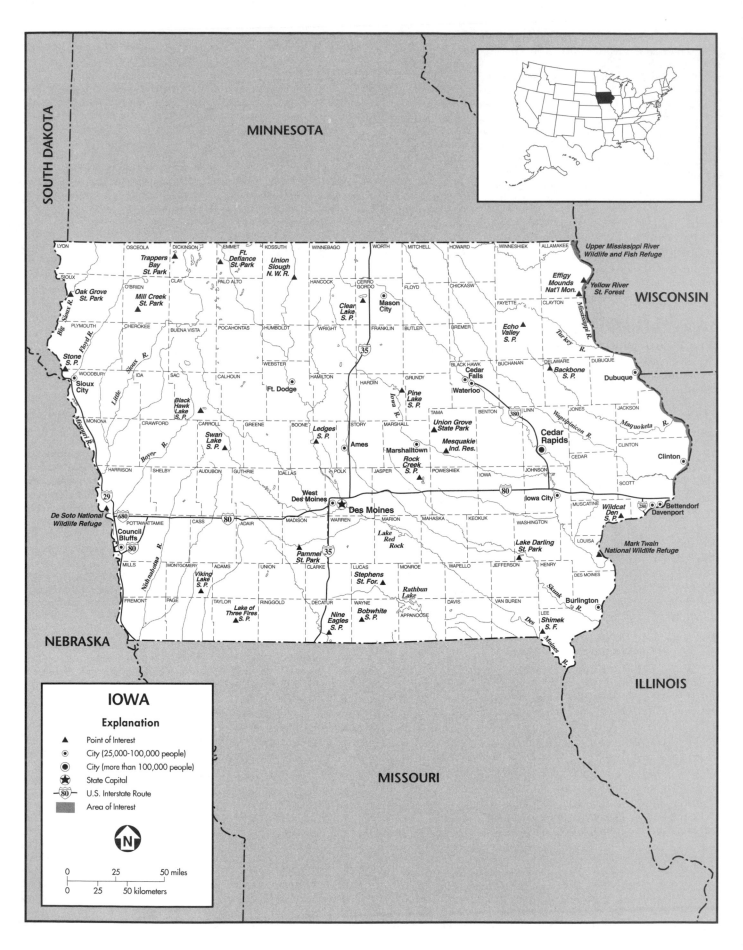

MINNESOTA

SOUTH DAKOTA

WISCONSIN

Upper Mississippi River
Wildlife and Fish Refuge

LYON · OSCEOLA · DICKINSON · EMMET · KOSSUTH · WINNEBAGO · WORTH · MITCHELL · HOWARD · WINNESHIEK · ALLAMAKEE

Trappers
Bay
St. Park

Ft.
Defiance
St. Park

Union
Slough
N. W. R.

Effigy
Mounds
Nat'l Mon.

Yellow River
St. Forest

SIOUX · O'BRIEN · CLAY · PALO ALTO · HANCOCK · CERRO GORDO · FLOYD · CHICKASW · FAYETTE · CLAYTON

Oak Grove
St. Park

Mill Creek
St. Park

Clear
Lake
S. P.

Mason
City

Echo
Valley
S. P.

PLYMOUTH · CHEROKEE · BUENA VISTA · POCAHONTAS · HUMBOLDT · WRIGHT · FRANKLIN · BUTLER · BREMER

Big Sioux R.
Floyd R.

Stone
S. P.

Sioux
City

WEBSTER

Ft. Dodge

Cedar
Falls

Waterloo

Backbone
S. P.

DELAWARE · DUBUQUE

Dubuque

WOODBURY · IDA · SAC · CALHOUN · HAMILTON · HARDIN · GRUNDY · BLACK HAWK · BUCHANAN

Sioux R.

Little Sioux R.

Black
Hawk
Lake
S. P.

Pine
Lake
S. P.

Iowa R.

TAMA · BENTON · LINN · JONES · JACKSON

MONONA · CRAWFORD · CARROLL · GREENE · BOONE · STORY · MARSHALL

Swan
Lake
S. P.

Ledges
S. P.

Ames

Union Grove
State Park

Mesquakie
Ind. Res.

Cedar
Rapids

Maquoketa R.

Missouri R.

Boyer R.

Marshalltown

Rock
Creek
S. P.

Wapsipinicon R.

CLINTON

Clinton

HARRISON · SHELBY · AUDUBON · GUTHRIE · DALLAS · POLK · JASPER · POWESHIEK · IOWA · JOHNSON · CEDAR · SCOTT

De Soto National
Wildlife Refuge

West
Des Moines

Des Moines

Iowa City

Wildcat
Den
S. P.

Bettendorf
Davenport

Council
Bluffs

POTTAWATTAMIE · CASS · ADAIR · MADISON · WARREN · MARION · MAHASKA · KEOKUK · WASHINGTON · MUSCATINE

Lake
Red
Rock

Lake Darling
St. Park

Mark Twain
National Wildlife Refuge

Pammel
St. Park

MILLS · MONTGOMERY · ADAMS · UNION · CLARKE · LUCAS · MONROE · WAPELLO · JEFFERSON · HENRY · DES MOINES

Nishnabotna R.

Viking
Lake
S. P.

Stephens
St. For.

Rathbun
Lake

Burlington

Skunk R.

FREMONT · PAGE · TAYLOR · RINGGOLD · DECATUR · WAYNE · APPANOOSE · DAVIS · VAN BUREN · LEE

Lake of
Three Fires
S. P.

Nine
Eagles
S. P.

Bobwhite
S. P.

Shimek
S. F.

Des Moines R.

NEBRASKA

ILLINOIS

MISSOURI

IOWA

Explanation

▲   Point of Interest

◉   City (25,000–100,000 people)

◉   City (more than 100,000 people)

★   State Capital

🛡80   U.S. Interstate Route

  Area of Interest

N

| 0 | 25 | 50 miles |
| 0 | 25 | 50 kilometers |

Iowa is bordered by two great navigable rivers, the Mississippi and the Missouri. They provided excellent transport facilities for the early settlers via keelboats and paddle-wheel steamers. Today, rivers remain an important part of Iowa's intermodal transportation system. In 1996, nearly 43 million tons of cargo moved on the Mississippi past Davenport, including over 26 million tons of grain. Important terminal ports on the Mississippi are Dubuque and Davenport; on the Missouri, Sioux City and Council Bluffs. These rivers provide shippers a gateway to an extensive inland waterway system that has access to ports in St. Paul, Chicago, Pittsburgh, Houston and New Orleans. Most docks in Iowa are privately owned, and all are privately operated.

In 1991, Iowa had 290 aircraft facilities of all types. The busiest airfield is Des Moines Municipal Airport, which handled 14,412 commercial operations and 905,405 enplaned passengers in 1996.

11HISTORY

The fertile land now known as the State of Iowa was first visited by primitive hunting bands of the Paleo-Indian period some 12,000 years ago. The first permanent settlers of the land were the Woodland Indians, who built villages in the forested areas along the Mississippi River, introduced agriculture, and left behind only their animal-shaped burial mounds.

Not until June 1673 did the first known white men come to the territory. When Louis Jolliet, accompanied by five French voyageurs and a Jesuit priest, Jacques Marquette, stopped briefly in Iowa on his voyage down the Mississippi, the region was uninhabited except for the Sioux in the west and a few outposts of Illinois and Iowa Indians in the east. Iowa was part of the vast, vaguely defined Louisiana Territory that extended from the Gulf of Mexico to the Canadian border and was ruled by the French until title was transferred to Spain in 1762. Napoleon took the territory back in 1800 and then promptly sold all of Louisiana Territory to the amazed American envoys who had come to Paris seeking only the purchase of New Orleans and the mouth of the Mississippi. After Iowa had thus come under US control in 1803, the Lewis and Clark expedition worked its way up the Missouri River to explore the land that President Thomas Jefferson had purchased so cheaply. Iowa looked as empty as it had to Jolliet 130 years earlier. The only white man who had come to explore its riches before the American annexation was an enterprising former French trapper, Julien Dubuque. Soon after the American Revolution, he had obtained from the Fox Indians the sole right to work the lead mines west of the Mississippi, and for 20 years Dubuque was the only white settler in Iowa.

The first wave of migrants into Iowa were the Winnebago, Sauk, and Fox, driven there by the US Army, which was clearing Wisconsin and Illinois of their Indian populations to make way for white farmers. Although President Andrew Jackson had intended that Louisiana Territory lying north of Missouri should forever be Indian land, the occupation of Iowa by the Indians was brief. Following the abortive attempt by an aging Sauk chieftain, Black Hawk, to win his lands in Illinois, the Sauk and Fox were driven westward in 1832 and forced to cede their lands in eastern Iowa to the incoming white settlers.

Placed under the territorial jurisdiction of Michigan in 1834, and then two years later under the newly created Territory of Wisconsin, Iowa became a separate territory in 1838. The first territorial governor, Robert Lucas, extended county boundaries and local government westward, planned for a new capital city to be located on the Iowa River, resisted Missouri's attempt to encroach on Iowa territory, and began planning for statehood by drawing boundary lines that included not only the present State of Iowa but also southern Minnesota up to present-day Minneapolis.

Because a new state seeking admission to the Union at that time could expect favorable action from Congress only if accompanied by a slave state, Iowa was designed to come into the Union with Florida as its slaveholding counterpart. A serious dispute over how large the state would be delayed Iowa's admission into the Union until 28 December 1846, but by the delay the people of Iowa got what they wanted—all the land between the Mississippi and Missouri rivers—even though they had to abandon Lucas's northern claim.

The settlement of Iowa was rapidly accomplished. With one-fourth of the nation's fertile topsoil located within its borders, Iowa was a powerful magnet that drew farmers by the thousands from Indiana, Ohio, and Tennessee, and even from faraway Virginia, the Carolinas, New York, and New England. Except for German and Irish immigrants along the eastern border and later Scandinavian immigrants during the 1870s and 1880s, Iowa was settled primarily by Anglo-American stock. The settlers were overwhelmingly Protestant in religion and remarkably homogeneous in ethnic and cultural backgrounds. Although New Englanders made up only 5% of Iowa's early population, they had a cultural influence that far exceeded their numbers. Many small Iowa towns—with their large frame houses, elm-lined streets, and Congregational churches—looked like New England villages faithfully replicated on the prairie.

Fiercely proud of its claim to be the first free state created out of the Louisiana Purchase, Iowa was an important center of abolitionist sentiment throughout the 1850s. The Underground Railroad for fugitive slaves from the South ran across the southern portion of Iowa to the Mississippi River. Radical abolitionist John Brown spent the winters of 1857 and 1859 in the small Quaker village of Springdale, preparing for his attack on the US arsenal at Harpers Ferry, in western Virginia.

Although the Democrats had a slight edge over their Whig opposition in the early years of statehood, a majority of Iowa voters in 1856 supported the new Republican Party and, for the most part, did so in succeeding years. A Republican legislative majority in 1857 scrapped the state's first constitution, which had been written by Jacksonian Democrats 12 years earlier. The new document moved the state capital from Iowa City westward to Des Moines, but it provided that the state university would remain forever in Iowa City.

When the Civil War came, Iowa overwhelmingly supported the Union cause. Iowans fought not only for their ideals, the abolition of slavery and the preservation of the Union, but also for the very practical objective of keeping open the Mississippi River, the main artery for transport of agricultural products.

In the decades following the Civil War, Iowans on the national scene, most notably US Senators James Harlan and his successor William B. Allison belonged to the conservative Republican camp, but they frequently faced liberal Republican and Populist opposition inside the state. The railroad had been lavishly welcomed by Iowans in the 1850s; by the 1870s, Iowa farmers were desperately trying to free themselves from the stranglehold of the rail lines. The National Grange was powerful enough in Iowa to put through the legislature the so-called Granger laws to regulate the railroads. At the turn of the century, as the aging Allison's hold on the state weakened, Iowa became a center for Republican progressivism.

Following World War I, the conservatives regained control of the Republican Party. They remained in control until, during the 1960s, new liberal leadership was forced on the party because of the debacle of Barry Goldwater's 1964 presidential campaign, controversy over US involvement in Viet Nam, and effective opposition from a revitalized Democratic Party led by Harold Hughes. After Hughes gave up the governorship in 1969 to become a US senator, Republicans once more dominated the executive branch, but Democrats gained control of the state legislature and made strong inroads at the top levels of state government.

Iowa's economy suffered in the 1980s from a combination of high debt, high interest rates, numerous droughts, and low crop prices. Businesses departed or automated and shrank their work forces. The population dropped by 7.9%. By the 1990s, however, the companies that had survived were in a much stronger position, and diversification efforts in both the agricultural and manufacturing sectors had ushered in a period of cautious prosperity. The number of jobs in the service sector grew by 10%, and the state's unemployment rate in 1992 was 4.7%, substantially lower than the national average.

A debilitating drought hit Iowa in 1988, reducing corn and soybean harvests to their lowest levels in 14 years and prompting Governor Terry Branstad to declare a statewide emergency. In 1993, unusually heavy spring and summer rains produced record floods along the Mississippi River by mid-July. Countless levees, or earthen berms designed to raise the height of river banks, collapsed or were overrun. The entire state of Iowa was declared a disaster area. Highways were closed and train service temporarily halted. The floods forced 11,200 people to evacuate their homes and produced $2.2 billion dollars worth of damage. The floods were followed by an early frost. Altogether, it was estimated that 40 million acres of farmland were severely damaged and 500,00 acres permanently ruined. It was expected that the area would not recover fully until the year 2000.

12STATE GOVERNMENT

Iowa has had two state constitutions. The constitution of 1857 replaced the original constitution of 1846 and is still in effect.

The state legislature, or general assembly, consists of a 50-member senate and a 100-member house of representatives. Senators serve four-year terms, with half the members elected every two years. Representatives are elected to two-year terms. The legislature convenes each year on the 2d Monday in January. Special sessions may be called by the governor or initiated by petition of two-thirds of the members of each house. Each house may introduce or amend legislation, with a simple majority vote required for passage. The governor's veto of a bill may be overridden by a two-thirds majority in both houses. Legislators must be US citizens and must have resided in the state for a year;

a representative must be at least 21 years of age, and a senator 25. The legislative salary was $18,800 in 1995.

The state's only elected executives are the governor, lieutenant governor, secretary of state, auditor, treasurer, attorney general, and secretary of agriculture; since 1974, these have been elected to four-year terms. The governor and lieutenant governor each must be a US citizen, at least 30 years old, and a resident of the state for two years. In 1996 the governor's salary was $98,200.

To vote in Iowa, one must be a US citizen, at least 18 years old, and a state resident. A voter must register at least 10 days before an election and remains permanently registered if there is no change of residency.

13POLITICAL PARTIES

For 70 years following the Civil War, a majority of Iowa voters supported the Republicans over the Democrats in nearly all state and national elections. During the Great Depression of the 1930s, Iowa briefly turned to the Democrats, supporting Franklin D. Roosevelt in two presidential elections. But from 1940 through 1992, the majority of Iowans voted Republican in 10 of 12 presidential elections. Republicans won 34 of the 42 gubernatorial elections from 1900 through 1990 and controlled both houses of the state legislature for 112 of the 130 years from 1855 to 1984.

In the 1960s, Iowa showed signs of a Democratic upsurge. Harold Hughes, a liberal Democrat, revitalized the party in Iowa and was elected governor for three two-year terms before moving on to the US Senate. During the post-Watergate period of the mid-1970s, Democrats captured both US Senate seats, five of the six congressional seats, and both houses of the Iowa legislature.

By the early and mid-1990s, a balance had reasserted itself. In 1996, Iowa gave Democrat Bill Clinton 50% of the vote, while Republican Bob Dole received just under 40%, and Independent Ross Perot picked up over 8%. Republicans had a 4–1 edge in the US House delegation. Terry Branstad, a Republican, won election to a fourth term as governor in 1994. As of 1996, a Democrat and a Republican both served in the US Senate—Republican Charles Grassley, who won election to a third term in 1992, and Democrat Tom Harkin, who won re-election in 1996. After the November 1996 elections, there were 29 Republicans and 21 Democrats in the state senate, and 54 Republicans and 46 Democrats in the state house. In 1993 there were 12 black elected

Iowa Presidential Vote by Political Parties, 1948–96

YEAR	ELECTORAL VOTE	IOWA WINNER	DEMOCRAT	REPUBLICAN	PROGRESSIVE	PROHIBITION	SOCIALIST LABOR
1948	10	*Truman (D)	522,380	494,018	12,125	3,382	4,274
1952	10	*Eisenhower (R)	451,513	808,906	5,085	2,882	—
							CONSTITUTION
1956	10	*Eisenhower (R)	501,858	729,187	—	—	3,202
1960	10	Nixon (R)	550,565	722,381	—	—	—
1964	9	*Johnson (D)	733,030	449,148	—	1,902	—
					SOC. WORKERS	AMERICAN IND.	
1968	9	*Nixon (R)	476,699	619,106	3,377	66,422	—
						AMERICAN	PEACE AND FREEDOM
1972	8	*Nixon (R)	496,206	706,207	—	22,056	1,332
							LIBERTARIAN
1976	8	Ford (R)	619,931	632,863	—	3,040	1,452
					CITIZENS		
1980	8	*Reagan (R)	508,672	676,026	2,191	NA	12,324
1984	8	*Reagan (R)	605,620	703,088	—		—
1988	8	Dukakis (D)	670,557	545,355	755	540	2,494
					IND. (Perot)		
1992	7	*Clinton (D)	586,353	504,891	253,468	3,079	1,177
1996	7	*Clinton (D)	620,258	492,644	105,159	-	2,315

* Won US presidential election.

officials; in 1995 there were 28 women serving in the state legislature and in elective executive office.

Iowa's presidential caucuses are held in January of presidential campaign years, earlier than any other state, thus giving Iowans a degree of influence in national politics.

14LOCAL GOVERNMENT

The state's 99 counties are governed by boards of supervisors consisting of three to five members. In general, county officials are elected to four-year terms. They enforce state laws, collect taxes, supervise welfare activities, and manage roads and bridges.

Local government was exercised by 952 municipal units in 1992. The mayor-council system functioned in the great majority of these municipalities. Iowa's towns and cities derive their local powers from the state constitution, but the power to tax is authorized by the general assembly. In 1992 there were 441 school districts and 388 special districts.

15STATE SERVICES

The Department of Public Instruction is responsible for educational services in Iowa. It assists local school boards in supplying special educational programs and administers local education agencies.

Transportation services are directed by the Department of Transportation, which is responsible for the safe and efficient operation of highways, motor vehicles, airports, railroads, public transit, and river transportation. The department's motor vehicle division licenses drivers, road vehicles, and car dealers.

Health and welfare services are provided by the Department of Health, the Iowa Mental Health Authority, and the Department of Social Services. Public protection is the responsibility of the Departments of Public Defense and of Public Safety. Housing programs are supported by the Iowa Housing Finance Authority.

16JUDICIAL SYSTEM

The Iowa supreme court consists of nine justices who are appointed by the governor and confirmed to eight-year terms by judicial elections held after they have served on the bench for at least one year. Judges may stand for reelection before their terms expire. The justices select one of their number as chief justice. The court exercises appellate jurisdiction in civil and criminal cases, supervises the trial courts, and prescribes rules of civil and appellate procedure. The supreme court transfers certain cases to the court of appeals, a five-member appellate court that began reviewing civil and criminal cases in 1977, and may review its decisions. Judges on the court of appeals are appointed and confirmed to six-year terms in the same manner as supreme court justices; they elect one of their members as chief judge.

The state is divided into eight judicial districts, each with a chief judge appointed to a two-year term by the chief justice of the supreme court. District court judges are appointed to six-year terms by the governor from nominations submitted by district nominating commissions. Appointees must stand for election after they have served as judges for at least one year. The state had 6,289 active attorneys in 1996.

As of 1995 there were 6,746 prisoners in federal and state institutions, or 237 per 100,000 inhabitants. The prison population increased by almost 50% from 1990 to 1995. Iowa's total crime rate in 1995 was 4,101.9 per 100,000 population, including 354 violent crimes and 3,747 property crimes.

Iowa does not have a death penalty.

17ARMED FORCES

In 1996, 374 active duty military personnel were stationed in Iowa, nearly all of whom were in the army.

Iowa residents as of 1 July 1996 included an estimated 287,000 veterans, of whom fewer than 500 saw service during World War I, 82,000 during World War II, 51,000 in the Korean conflict, 86,000 during the Vietnam era, and 21,000 in the Persian Gulf War. The federal government expended $410 million for veterans' benefits in Iowa during fiscal year 1996.

The Iowa National Guard provides reserve units for the US Army and Air Force in case of a national emergency or war. As of 1992, National Guard and Reserve units stationed in Iowa had a total assigned strength of 19,253. In 1993, the Iowa State Patrol employed 558 full-time sworn officers, or two per 10,000 residents.

18MIGRATION

Iowa was opened, organized, and settled by a generation of native migrants from other states. According to the first federal census of Iowa in 1850, 31% of the total population of 192,214 came from nearby midwestern states (Illinois, Wisconsin, Indiana, Michigan, and Ohio), 14% from the five southern border states, and 13% from the Middle Atlantic states.

Another 10% of the state's 1850 population consisted of immigrants from northern Europe. The largest group were Germans who had fled military conscription; the next largest group had sought to escape the hardships of potato famine in Ireland or of agricultural and technological displacement in Scotland, England, and Wales. They were joined in the 1850s by Dutch immigrants seeking religious liberty, and in the 1860s and 1870s by Norwegians and Swedes. During and immediately after the Civil War, some former slaves fled the South for Iowa, and more blacks settled in Iowa cities after 1900.

But many of the migrants who came to Iowa did not stay long. Some Iowans left to join the gold rush, and others settled lands in the West. Migration out of the state has continued to this day, as retired Iowans seeking warmer climates have moved to California and other southwestern states; from 1970 through 1990, Iowa's net loss through migration amounted to over 266,000.

An important migratory trend within the state has been from the farm to the city. Although Iowa has remained a major agricultural state, the urban population surpassed the rural population by 1960 and increased to over 60.6% of the total population by 1990. As of 1990, 77.6% of all state residents had been born in Iowa; only Pennsylvania and Louisiana had higher proportions. Between 1990 and 1996, Iowa had a net loss of 1,667 in domestic migration and a net gain of 12,681 in international migration. In 1996, 3,037 foreign immigrants arrived in the state. In 1990, some 58% of residents age five and older lived in the same house as in 1985. Of those who lived in a different house in 1985, 82% did so in Iowa; 70% of the reported intrastate residence changes took place within the same county.

19INTERGOVERNMENTAL COOPERATION

Iowa is a signatory to the Midwest Nuclear Compact, the Iowa-Missouri and Iowa-Nebraska boundary compacts, and 11 other major interstate compacts and agreements. Federal aid to the Iowa state government amounted to $2 billion in fiscal year 1996.

20ECONOMY

Iowa's economy is based on agriculture. Although the value of the state's manufactures exceeds the value of its farm production, manufacturing is basically farm-centered. The major industries are food processing and the manufacture of agriculture-related products, such as farm machinery.

Periodic recessions—and especially the Great Depression of the 1930s—have afflicted Iowa farmers and adversely affected the state's entire economy. But technological progress in agriculture and the proliferation of manufacturing industries have enabled Iowans to enjoy general prosperity since World War II.

Because the state's population is scattered, the growth of light manufacturing has extended to hundreds of towns and cities.

In the late 1970s, the state's major economic problem was inflation, which boosted the cost of farm equipment and fertilizers. In the early 1980s, high interest rates and falling land prices created serious economic difficulties for farmers and contributed to the continuing decline of the farm population. By 1992, the state had recovered. Iowa's gross state product in 1994 was $68,298 million, which could be broken down into: private goods-producing industries, $24,346 million; private services-producing industries, $35,793 million; and government, $8,159 million. At the end of 1996, employment in Iowa was distributed as follows: 364,100 Iowans worked in services; 355,500 worked in wholesale and retail trade; 251,600 in manufacturing; 235,800 in government; 78,300 in finance, insurance, and real estate; 63,800 in transportation and public utilities; 56,400 in construction; 2,000 in mining. In 1996, there were 8,715 filings for bankruptcy.

21INCOME
With a personal income per capita of $22,560 in 1996, Iowa ranked 28th among the 50 states. The state's total disposable personal income was $56.2 billion in 1996, up from $52 billion in 1995. The median household income in 1995 was $35,519. Some 12.2% of the population was below the federal poverty level in 1995.

22LABOR
Since 1950, Iowa has consistently ranked above the national average in employment of its work force. Iowa's unemployment rate of 3.8% for 1996 was below the overall US rate of 5.4%.

During the first quarter of 1997, the civilian labor force was estimated at 1,600,800, of whom 1,533,400 were employed and 67,400 (4.2%) were unemployed. Of the total nonfarm employment at that time, mining accounted for 0.1%; construction, 3.3%; manufacturing, 16.1%; transportation, communication, and utilities, 4.2%; wholesale trade, 5.2%; retail trade, 16.5%; finance, insurance, and real estate, 5%; services, 23.9%; and government, 15.2%. Agriculture accounted for most of the remaining 10.5%.

The labor movement generally has not been strong in Iowa, and labor unions have had little success in organizing farm laborers. The Knights of Labor, consisting mostly of miners and railroad workers, was organized in Iowa in 1876 and enrolled 25,000 members by 1885. But the Knights practically disappeared after 1893, when the American Federation of Labor (AFL) established itself in the state among miners and other workers. The Congress of Industrial Organizations (CIO) succeeded in organizing workers in public utilities, meat packing, and light industries in 1937. After 1955, when the AFL and CIO merged, the power and influence of labor unions increased in the state. In 1995, the number of labor union members in Iowa was 152,100, or about 12.1% of all employees.

Iowa did not forbid the employment of women in dangerous occupations or prohibit the employment of children under 14 years of age in factories, shops, or mines until the early 1900s. A right-to-work law was enacted in 1947.

23AGRICULTURE
Iowa recorded a (realized) gross farm income of $11.7 billion in 1995. More than half of all cash receipts from marketing came from the sale of livestock and meat products; about one-fifth derived from the sale of feed grains. In that year, Iowa ranked 1st in output of corn for grain and soybeans and 5th for oats.

The early settlers planted wheat. Iowa ranked 2d in wheat production by 1870, but as the wheat belt moved farther west, the state's farmers turned to raising corn to feed their cattle and hogs. Two important 20th-century developments were the introduction in the 1920s of hybrid corn and the utilization on a massive scale during World War II of soybeans as a feed grain. Significant postwar trends included the rapid mechanization of farming and the decline of the farm population.

In 1995, Iowa had 99,000 farms, with an average size of 332 acres (134 hectares) per farm. This total represents a decrease of 41,000 farms since 1970, although the amount of land being farmed has only declined 0.6% to 33,200,000 acres (13,400,000 hectares) over the same period.

Nearly all of Iowa's land is tillable, and more than nine-tenths of it is given to farmland. Corn is grown practically everywhere; wheat is raised in the southern half of the state and in counties bordering the Mississippi and Missouri rivers.

In 1995, production of corn for grain totaled 1.402 billion bushels, valued at $3.368 billion; soybeans, 398 million bushels, $2.51 billion; oats, 14.6 million bushels; and hay, 5.66 million tons.

24ANIMAL HUSBANDRY
Iowa had an estimated 3.9 million cattle and calves in 1997, worth around $2.2 billion. In that year, Iowa was ranked 1st among the 50 states in the number of hogs and pigs with 12.2 million, worth around $1.1 billion.

Pigs, calves, lambs, and chickens are raised throughout the state, particularly in the Mississippi and Missouri river valleys, where good pasture and water are plentiful. Iowa farmers are leaders in applying modern livestock breeding methods to produce lean hogs, tender corn-fed cattle, and larger-breasted chickens and turkeys.

In 1995, Iowa farmers produced an estimated $28.8 million lb of sheep and lambs, which grossed a total of around $27 million. Also during 1995, Iowa farmers produced 72 million lb of broilers, worth around $25 million, and 227 million lb of turkeys, worth $88.6 million. An estimated 4 billion eggs were produced, worth around $145.8 million in 1995.

Iowa dairy farmers produced 4 billion pounds of milk from 251,000 dairy cows in 1995.

25FISHING
Fishing has little commercial importance in Iowa. Game fishing in the rivers and lakes is a popular sport—there were 414,336 sport fishermen licensed in the state in 1995/96. Federal hatcheries distributed 314,323 (1,146 lb) of fish and 2.1 million fish eggs within the state in 1995/96.

26FORESTRY
Lumber and woodworking were important to the early settlers, but the industry has since declined in commercial importance. In 1992, Iowa had 2 million acres of forestland, which represents 5.7% of the state's land area. This was a 31% increase in forest area when compared to the 1974 survey's 1.6 million acres. The lumber and wood products industry employed more than 8,600 people and generated over $469 million of value added to the Iowa economy in 1995. The state's lumber industry annually produces over 70 million board feet of lumber.

27MINING
The value of nonfuel mineral production in Iowa was estimated at $484 million in 1995, an increase of nearly $33 million over the $451 million reported in 1994. Estimated values in 1995 for crushed stone ($219 million), portland cement ($181 million), crude gypsum ($12.9 million), and construction sand and gravel ($53.9 million) were all increases over 1994 levels. Combined values of crushed stone, portland cement, and construction sand and gravel accounted for over 93% of the total mineral value produced in 1995. Crushed stone (predominantly limestone-

dolomite) continued as the state's leading mineral commodity, accounting for almost 45% of the estimated total nonfuel mineral value. Estimated production increased about 2.5% over reported 1994 totals. In 1995 Iowa ranked 2d of 20 states producing crude gypsum, which constituted 2.7% of the state's estimated total nonfuel mineral value, an increase of about 1.6% over the amount produced in 1994. Iowa ranked 26th nationally in nonfuel mineral value and seventh in the production of portland cement.

Employment in the mining industry in December 1996 was approximately 2,000 workers.

28ENERGY AND POWER

Although Iowa's fossil fuel resources are extremely limited, the state's energy supply has been adequate. In 1994, Iowa consumed 363.8 million Btu per capita, to rank 21st among the states. According to 1994 estimates, oil supplied about 34% of the state's energy requirements; natural gas, 24%; coal 36%; nuclear energy, hydropower, and ethanol, 6%.

The state's production of electricity totaled 33.5 billion kWh in 1995; installed capacity was 8.0 million kW. Coal-fired plants supplied 28.4 billion kWh of electricity; nuclear power plants supplied 3.7 billion kWh; and hydroelectric plants less than 1 billion kWh.

Extensive coalfields in southeastern Iowa were first mined in 1840. The boom town of Buxton, in Monroe County, mined sufficient coal in 1901 to support a population of 6,000 people, of whom 5,500 were transplanted southern blacks, but the mines closed in 1918 and Buxton became a ghost town. The state's annual bituminous coal production reached nearly 9 million tons in 1917–18. Coal output in 1994 was only 46,000 tons; demonstrated reserves totaled 2.1 billion tons.

29INDUSTRY

Because Iowa was primarily a farm state, the first industries were food processing and the manufacture of farm implements. These industries have retained a key role in the economy. In recent years, Iowa has added a variety of other manufactures—including pens, washing machines, even mobile homes.

The estimated total value of shipments by manufacturers was $59 billion in 1995. The following table shows value of shipments for selected industries in that year:

Food and kindred products	$20,722,300,000
Industrial machinery	9,921,800,000
Chemicals and allied products	4,734,000,000
Electric and electronic equipment	4,297,800,000
Printing and publishing	2,808,600,000
Fabricated metal products	2,775,000,000
Primary metal products	3,031,000,000
Rubber and plastic products	2,118,500,000
Transportation equipment	2,036,100,000
Paper and allied products	1,590,300,000
Stone, clay, and glass products	1,163,000,000

More than 120 of *Fortune* magazine's "Top 500" industrial corporations have plants in Iowa, including Caterpillar Tractor, General Motors, Mobil, General Electric, General Foods, Procter & Gamble, and US Steel. In 1995, there were 469 US patents issued to Iowa residents.

30COMMERCE

Wholesale establishments numbered 6,971 in 1992, with sales of $29.4 billion. About 50% of the establishments and 27.5% of the sales dealt with durable goods. The most valuable categories of goods traded were agricultural raw materials, durable goods, groceries and related products, and farm supplies.

Retail sales totaled $20 billion (30th in the nation) in 1992, conducted by 19,732 establishments. Of the total sales, automotive dealers accounted for 22.1%; food stores, 20.5%; general merchandise, 14%; and eating and drinking places, 9.3%.

The leading exported commodities are feed grains and products, soybeans and soybean products, and meats and meat products. Exports of goods originating within Iowa in 1996 had an estimated value of $4.4 billion.

31CONSUMER PROTECTION

Iowa has laws prohibiting fraud and misrepresentation in sales and advertising and harassment in debt collecting. There is a cooling-off period of three days for door-to-door purchases.

32BANKING

As of 31 December 1996, Iowa had 469 insured commercial banks; total commercial bank assets amounted to $42.4 billion and total deposits to $35 billion as of 31 December 1996. The state's 30 insured savings institutions had assets totaling $4.2 billion at the end of 1996.

The Division of Banking supervises and regulates the state's chartered banks, loan companies, and mortgage bankers/brokers.

33INSURANCE

In 1991, Iowa had 35 life insurance companies. Life insurance in force as of 31 December 1995 totaled $330.8 billion. The 190 fire, casualty, and multiple-line insurance companies operating in the state had premiums totaling $3.2 billion. In 1995, $1.0 billion of automobile liability and physical damage insurance premiums were written in the state.

The commissioner of insurance, appointed by the governor, supervises all insurance business transacted in the state.

34SECURITIES

There are no securities exchanges in Iowa. Securities are sold through 1,300 registered brokers and dealers, involving 45,546 registered agents as of April 1997.

35PUBLIC FINANCE

The public budget is prepared by the Department of Management with the governor's approval and is adopted or revised by the general assembly. Each budget is prepared for the biennium of the upcoming fiscal year and the one following; the fiscal year runs from 1 July to 30 June.

Iowa's estimated fiscal years 1995 and 1996 budget was as follows (in millions):

REVENUES	1995	1996
Personal income tax	$1,875.0	$2,000.9
Sales tax	1,147.3	1,213.0
Inheritance, use, and insurance taxes	387.3	408.0
Corporate income taxes	267.7	277.6
Tobacco and alcohol taxes	133.8	137.4
Other revenues	342.9	367.6
TOTALS	$4,154.0	$4,404.5

EXPENDITURES		
Administration and local tax credits	308.2	366.9
Agriculture and natural resources	42.9	44.7
Economic development	25.4	28.0
Education	2,134.8	2,248.4
Health and human services	801.7	810.2
Justice and corrections	240.7	260.0
Regulation, transportation and public safety	87.6	97.2
TOTALS	$3,641.3	$3,855.4

36TAXATION

In 1996, Iowa's personal income tax ranged from 0.4% to 9.98%. The corporate tax rate ranged from 6% on the first $25,000 of net income to 12% on amounts over $250,000. Iowa's retail sales tax was 5% in 1993. The state also taxed gasoline, cigarettes, alcoholic beverages, insurance premiums, inheritances, chain stores, and business franchises.

As of 1995, Iowan's federal benefits amounted to $4,567 per capita.

37ECONOMIC POLICY

Since World War II, the state government has attracted new manufacturing industries to Iowa by granting tax incentives and by encouraging a favorable business climate. The Iowa Department of Economic Development helps local communities diversify their economies, assists companies already in the state, and helps exporters to sell their products abroad. In the 1980s and 1990s, the Iowa state government stressed such development goals as agricultural diversification, increased small-business support, creation of high-tech jobs, and expansion of tourism. Iowa offers financial assistance programs to businesses for programs to retain or create jobs, capital investment, to utilize agricultural commodities, to establish or expand minority and women-owned enterprises, to support low income and disabled entrepreneurs, to build or improve a community's infrastructure (railroads, roads, etc.), and to foster construction of new industrial facilities.

38HEALTH

Infant mortality for the 12 months ending December 1995 was 6.6 per 1,000 live births, well below the national average. In 1992, 6,759 legal abortions were performed, a rate of 176 per 1,000 live births. The unintentional death rate was higher than the national average. The death rate was 1,024 (1996) per 100,000 population, higher than the US average. Leading causes of death, heart disease, diabetes, and cancer were all higher than the national average. An estimated 53,602 smoking-related deaths occurred in 1995. The smoking prevalence was 23.1% of all Iowans aged 18–30.

In 1995, Iowa's 116 hospitals admitted 347,932 patients. In 1994, hospital expenses amounted to $672 per inpatient day and $5,077 per stay.

As of 1995, there were an estimated 5,463 licensed medical doctors and 29,000 active registered nurses (1994). Fewer than half of physicians were primary care physicians in 1995. As of 1995, there were 1,524 active licensed dentists in Iowa.

39SOCIAL WELFARE

In 1996, aid to families with dependent children (AFDC) in Iowa was given to 91,700 recipients and averaged $495 per month. In 1995, 539,920 residents received Social Security benefits averaging $719 a month. Participation in the federal school lunch program in 1996, which cost $51.7 million, and the food stamp program had an average combined monthly participation of 177,283.

With the enactment of the Personal Responsibility and Work Opportunity Reconciliation Act of 1996, the US government has changed the form and regulations for many of its social welfare programs; most significantly, it replaces Aid to Families with Dependent Children (AFDC) an open-ended entitlement program with Temporary Assistance for Needy Families (TANF), a limited system of assistance funded largely through federal block grants. The reform act also impacts the food stamp program, the Supplemental Security Income program, and the child nutrition program. The law took effect on 1 July 1997 and provided $16.38 billion in block grants for fiscal years 1997–2002. The grants are to be divided among the states based on an equation involving the numbers of former AFDC recipients in each state. Because many of the bill's provisions have yet to be implemented into state-by-state policy, it was not possible to include the details of each state's programs in this edition of this work.

Unemployment insurance benefits in 1995 were $194.11 per person weekly.

40HOUSING

Iowa ranks high in the number of housing units that are family owned and occupied. In 1996, there were 1,186,000 housing units in Iowa, of which 1,090,000 were occupied. In 1996, 12,027 privately-owned housing units, valued at just over $1 billion, were authorized for construction, 7,923 of them single-family units. The median monthly cost for owners with a mortgage in 1990, the last year for which figures are available, was $553, one of the lowest amounts in the nation. The monthly median cost of housing for renters in 1990 was $336, well below the $447 national median. The median value of a home in 1990 was $45,900, lower than any state except Mississippi and South Dakota. In terms of constant 1990 dollars, home values declined by 28.8% during the 1980s. During fiscal year 1996, Iowa received $207.3 million in aid from the US Department of Housing and Urban Development, including $68.9 million in community development block grants.

41EDUCATION

Iowa's progressive public school system has been an innovator in school curriculum development, teaching methods, educational administration, and school financing.

In the fall of 1995, Iowa had a total of 502,343 pupils enrolled in the public school system. The number of teachers in the 1995/96 school year was 32,360. In addition, the state's nonpublic elementary and secondary schools enrolled 60,658 pupils in 1989/90.

In fall 1994, 172,450 students were enrolled in institutions of higher learning. Iowa has three state universities, with 67,957 students; 35 private colleges; and 23 vocational schools and area community colleges. Since the public community college system began offering vocational and technical training in 1960, total enrollment has increased rapidly, and the number of different career programs has grown.

Iowa's small liberal arts colleges and universities include Briar Cliff College, Sioux City; Coe College, Cedar Rapids; Cornell College, Mt. Vernon; Drake University, Des Moines; Grinnell College, Grinnell; Iowa Wesleyan College, Mt. Pleasant; Loras College, Dubuque; and Luther College, Decorah.

Public schools are administered by the state superintendent of public instruction, who is appointed by a nine-member state board to a four-year term. Iowa's $5,249 in per-pupil expenditures for public schools in 1994/95 ranked in the middle range among the states.

42ARTS

Beginning with the public lecture movement in the late 19th century and the Chautauqua shows in the early 20th century, cultural activities have gradually spread throughout the state. Today there is an opera company in Des Moines, and there are art galleries, little theater groups, symphony orchestras, and ballet companies in the major cities and college towns. In 1991, the University of Iowa received $24,000 from the NEA to support the development of its music and theater activities.

The Des Moines Arts Center is a leading exhibition gallery for native painters and sculptors. There are regional theater groups in Des Moines, Davenport, and Sioux City. The Writers' Workshop at the University of Iowa has an international reputation. One problem for the arts in Iowa is the continued migration of native artists to cultural centers in New York, California, and elsewhere. In (1996) the State of Iowa generated $820,000 from federal sources to support its art programs. The NEA contributed $538,000 to Iowa's art programs and $716,000 to the Iowa Arts Council. The state also contributed to the efforts of the Arts Council and private sources provided additional funding. Iowa's arts programs had a total audience of 6,698,000 people. There were 36,024 contributing artists for the programs. The state offered arts education to 117,900 school children. By 1991, there were 826 art associations in Iowa and 78 local art associations.

43LIBRARIES AND MUSEUMS

Beginning with the founding in 1873 of the state's first tax-supported library at Independence, Iowa's public library system has grown to include 536 public libraries with total book holdings of 857,932 volumes in 1992. Among the principal libraries in Iowa are the State Library in Des Moines, the State Historical Society Library in Iowa City, the libraries of the University of Iowa (also in Iowa City), and the Iowa State University Library in Ames.

Iowa had 125 museums and zoological parks in 1996/97. The Herbert Hoover National Historical Site, in West Branch, houses the birthplace and grave of the 31st US president and a library and museum with papers and memorabilia. Other historic sites include the grave of French explorer Julien Dubuque, near the city named for him; the girlhood home at Charles City of suffragist Carrie Chapman Catt; and the seven communal villages of the Amana colonies.

44COMMUNICATIONS

The first post office in Iowa was established at Augusta in 1836. Mail service developed slowly with the spread of population, and rural free delivery of mail did not begin until 1897.

The first telegraph line was built between Burlington and Bloomington (now Muscatine) in 1848. Telegraph service throughout the state is provided by Western Union. In March 1993, about 1,069,000 housing units, or 96.1% of all occupied units, had telephones.

Among the first educational radio broadcasting stations in the US was one established in 1919 at the State University in Iowa City and another in 1921 at Iowa State University in Ames. The first commercial radio station west of the Mississippi, WDC at Davenport, began broadcasting in 1921. In 1996 there were 211 radio stations, including 73 AM stations and 138 FM stations. In 1996, Iowa had a total of 19 commercial television stations and 9 educational stations. In that year, 5 large cable television systems served the state.

45PRESS

Iowa's first newspaper, the *Dubuque Visitor*, was founded in 1836 but lasted only a year. The following year, the *Fort Madison Patriot* and the *Burlington Territorial Gazette* were established; the latter paper, now the *Hawk Eye*, is the oldest newspaper in the state. In 1860, the *Iowa State Register* was founded. As the *Des Moines Register and Tribune*, it grew to be the state's largest newspaper. The *Tribune* ceased publication in 1982; the *Register* remains preeminent, with a morning circulation of 174,842 and a Sunday circulation of 294,510 as of 1997. The *Dubuque Telegraph Herald* circulates 29,926 daily papers and 35,507 Sunday papers.

Overall, Iowa had 36 dailies (24 evening, 12 morning, and 9 Sunday papers in 1997. Also published in Iowa were 127 periodicals, among them *Better Homes and Gardens* (circulation 7.4 million) and *Successful Farming* (500,000).

46ORGANIZATIONS

The 1992 Census of Service Industries counted 1,193 organizations in Iowa, including 262 business associations; 618 civic, social, and fraternal associations; and 313 other membership organizations. Among the organizations headquartered in Iowa are the National Farmers Organization (Corning), the American College Testing Program (Iowa City), and the Antique Airplane Association (Ottumwa).

47TOURISM, TRAVEL, AND RECREATION

The Mississippi and Missouri rivers offer popular water sports facilities for both out-of-state visitors and resident vacationers. Iowa's "Little Switzerland" region in the northeast, with its high bluffs of woodland overlooking the Mississippi, is popular for hiking and camping. Notable tourist attractions in the area include the Effigy Mounds National Monument (near Marquette), which has hundreds of prehistoric Indian mounds and village sites, and the Buffalo Ranch (at Fayette), with its herd of live buffalo. Tourist sites in the central part of the state include the state capitol and the Herbert Hoover National Historic Site, with its Presidential Library and Museum. The Hoover Site attracted 241,757 visits in 1996.

Iowa has about 85,000 acres (34,400 hectares) of lakes and reservoirs and 19,000 mi (30,600 km) of fishing streams. There are 52 state parks, covering 33,811 acres, and 7 state forests, covering 25,000 acres (10,000 hectares); these and other state recreational areas attract numerous visitors every year. The state had 789,268 hunting-license holders and 444,657 holders of fishing licenses in 1995.

48SPORTS

Iowa has no major league professional sports teams, but minor league baseball and basketball teams make their home in Des Moines, Cedar Rapids, Clinton, Burlington, and the Quad Cities. The Iowa Cubs of the Triple-A American Association play in Des Moines. High school and college basketball and football teams draw thousands of spectators, particularly to the state high school basketball tournament at Des Moines in March. Large crowds also fill stadiums and fieldhouses for the University of Iowa games in Iowa City and Iowa State University games in Ames. In intercollegiate competition, the University of Iowa Hawkeyes belong to the Big Ten Conference. They have a legendary wrestling program that has won the NCAA Championship 15 times since 1969. Iowa went to the Rose Bowl in 1957, 1959, 1982, 1986, and 1991, winning in 1957 and 1959. The Iowa State University Cyclones are in the Big Twelve Conference. A popular track-and-field meet for college athletes is the Drake Relays, held every April in Des Moines. Horse racing is popular at state and county fairgrounds, as is stock car racing at small-town tracks. The Register's Annual Great Bicycle Ride Across Iowa is held each July. There are rodeos in Sidney and Fort Madison, and the National Hot Air Balloon Classic is held in Indianola.

49FAMOUS IOWANS

Iowa was the birthplace of Herbert Clark Hoover (1874–1964), the first US president born west of the Mississippi. Although he was orphaned and left the state for Oregon at the age of 10, he always claimed Iowa as his home. His long and distinguished career included various relief missions in Europe, service as US secretary of commerce (1921–29), and one term in the White House (1929–33). Hoover was buried in West Branch, the town of his birth. Iowa has also produced one US vice president, Henry A. Wallace (1888–1965), who served in that office during Franklin D. Roosevelt's third term (1941–45). Wallace also was secretary of agriculture (1933–41) and of commerce (1945–47);

he ran unsuccessfully as the Progressive Party's presidential candidate in 1948.

Two Kentucky-born members of the US Supreme Court were residents of Iowa prior to their appointments: Samuel F. Miller (1816–90) and Wiley B. Rutledge (1894–1949). Iowans who served in presidential cabinets as secretary of the interior were James Harlan (b.Illinois, 1820–99), Samuel J. Kirkwood (b.Maryland, 1813–94), Richard Ballinger (1858–1922), and Ray Lyman Wilbur (1875–1949). Ray Wilbur's brother Curtis (1867–1954) was secretary of the Navy, and James W. Good (1866–1929) was secretary of war. Appropriately enough, Iowans have dominated the post of secretary of agriculture in this century. They included, in addition to Wallace, James "Tama Jim" Wilson (b.Scotland, 1835–1920), who served in that post for 16 years and set a record for longevity in a single cabinet office; Henry C. Wallace (b.Illinois, 1866–1924), the father of the vice president; and Edwin T. Meredith (1876–1928). Harry L. Hopkins (1890–1946) was Franklin D. Roosevelt's closest adviser in all policy matters, foreign and domestic, and served in a variety of key New Deal posts. Prominent US senators from Iowa have included James W. Grimes (b.New Hampshire, 1816–72), whose vote, given from a hospital stretcher, saved President Andrew Johnson from being convicted of impeachment charges in 1868; earlier, Grimes had been governor of the state when its 1857 constitution was adopted. William Boyd Allison (b.Ohio, 1829–1908) was the powerful chairman of the Senate Appropriations Committee for nearly 30 years.

Among Iowa's most influential governors were the first territorial governor, Robert Lucas (b.Virginia, 1781–1853); Cyrus C. Carpenter (b.Pennsylvania, 1829–98); William Larrabee (b.Connecticut, 1832–1912); Horace Boies (b.New York, 1827–1923); and, in recent times, Harold Hughes (b.1922) and Robert D. Ray (b.1928).

Iowa has produced a large number of radical dissenters and social reformers. Abolitionists, strong in Iowa before the Civil War, included James W. Grimes, Josiah B. Grinnell (b.Vermont, 1821–91), and Asa Turner (b.Massachusetts, 1799–1885). George D. Herron (b.Indiana, 1862–1925) made Iowa a center of the Social Gospel movement before helping to found the Socialist Party. William "Billy" Sunday (1862–1935) was an evangelist with a large following among rural Americans. James B. Weaver (b.Ohio, 1833–1912) ran for the presidency on the Greenback-Labor ticket in 1880 and as a Populist in 1892. John L. Lewis (1880–1969), head of the United Mine Workers, founded the Congress of Industrial Organizations (CIO).

Iowa can claim two winners of the Nobel Peace Prize: religious leader John R. Mott (b.New York, 1865–1955) and agronomist and plant geneticist Norman E. Borlaug (b.1914). Three other distinguished scientists who lived in Iowa were George Washington Carver (b.Missouri 1864–1943), Lee De Forest (1873–1961), and James Van Allen (b.1914). George H. Gallup (1904–84), a public-opinion analyst, originated the Gallup Polls.

Iowa writers of note include Hamlin Garland (b.Wisconsin, 1860–1940), Octave Thanet (Alice French, b.Massachusetts, 1850–1934), Bess Streeter Aldrich (1881–1954), Carl Van Vechten (1880–1964), James Norman Hall (1887–1951), Thomas Beer (1889–1940), Ruth Suckow (1892–1960), Phillip D. Strong (1899–1957), MacKinlay Kantor (1904–77), Wallace Stegner (1909–93), and Richard P. Bissell (1913–77). Iowa's poets include Paul H. Engle (b.1908–91), who directed the University of Iowa's famed Writers' Workshop, and James S. Hearst (b.1900). Two Iowa playwrights, Susan Glaspell (1882–1948) and her husband, George Cram Cook (1873–1924), were instrumental in founding influential theater groups.

Iowans who have contributed to America's musical heritage include popular composer Meredith Willson (1902–84), jazz musician Leon "Bix" Beiderbecke (1903–31), and bandleader Glenn Miller (1904–44). Iowa's artists of note include Grant Wood (1892–1942), whose *American Gothic* is one of America's best-known paintings, and printmaker Mauricio Lasansky (b.Argentina, 1914).

Iowa's contributions to the field of popular entertainment include William F. "Buffalo Bill" Cody (1846–1917); circus impresario Charles Ringling (1863–1926) and his four brothers; the reigning American beauty of the late 19th century, Lillian Russell (Helen Louise Leonard, 1860–1922); and one of America's best-loved movie actors John Wayne (Marion Michael Morrison, 1907–79). Johnny Carson (b. 1925), host of the Tonight Show for many years, was born in Corning. Iowa sports figures of note are baseball Hall of Famers Adrian C. "Cap" Anson (1851–1922) and Robert "Bob" Feller (b.1918) and football All-American Nile Kinnick (1918–44).

50BIBLIOGRAPHY

Bogue, Allen G. *From Prairie to Cornbelt*. Chicago: University of Chicago Press, 1963.

Federal Writers' Project. *Iowa: A Guide to the Hawkeye State*. Reprint. New York: Somerset, n.d. (orig. 1938).

Gue, Benjamin F. *History of Iowa*. 4 vols. New York: Century History Co., 1903.

Hamilton, Carl. *In No Time at All*. Ames: Iowa State University Press, 1974.

Iowa Development Commission. *1985 Statistical Profile of Iowa*. Des Moines, 1985.

Morain, Thomas J., ed. *Family Reunion: Essays on Iowa*. Ames: Iowa State University Press, 1995.

Offenburger, Chuck. *Ah, You Iowans!: At Home, At Work, At Play, At War*. Ames: Iowa State University Press, 1992.

Riley, Glenda, ed. *Prairie Voices: Iowa's Pioneering Women*. Ames: Iowa State University Press, 1996.

Ross, Earle D. *Iowa Agriculture*. Iowa City: State Historical Society, 1951.

Sage, Leland. *A History of Iowa*. Ames: Iowa State University Press, 1974.

Schwieder, Dorothy, ed. *Patterns and Perspectives in Iowa History*. Ames: Iowa State University Press, 1973.

Swierenga, Robert P. *Pioneers and Profits*. Ames: Iowa State University Press, 1968.

Wall, Joseph Frazier. *Iowa: A Bicentennial History*. New York: Norton, 1978.

State of Kansas

ORIGIN OF STATE NAME: Named for the Kansa (or Kaw) Indians, the "people of the south wind." **NICKNAME:** The Sunflower State. (Also: the Wheat State; the Jayhawk State.) **CAPITAL:** Topeka. **ENTERED UNION:** 29 January 1861 (34th). **SONG:** "Home on the Range." **MARCH:** "The Kansas March." **MOTTO:** *Ad astra per aspera* (To the stars through difficulties). **FLAG:** The flag consists of a dark blue field with the state seal in the center; a sunflower on a bar of twisted gold and blue is above the seal, the word "Kansas" is below it. **OFFICIAL SEAL:** A sun rising over mountains in the background symbolizes the east; commerce is represented by a river and a steamboat. In the foreground, agriculture, the basis of the state's prosperity, is represented by a settler's cabin and a man plowing a field; beyond this is a wagon train heading west and a herd of buffalo fleeing from two Indians. Around the top is the state motto above a cluster of 34 stars; the circle is surrounded by the words "Great Seal of the State of Kansas, January 29, 1861." **ANIMAL:** American buffalo. **BIRD:** Western meadowlark. **INSECT:** Honeybee. **REPTILE:** Ornate box turtle. **FLOWER:** Wild native sunflower. **TREE:** Cottonwood. **LEGAL HOLIDAYS:** New Year's Day, 1 January; Birthday of Martin Luther King, Jr., 3d Monday in January; Lincoln's Birthday, 12 February; Washington's Birthday, 3d Monday in February; Memorial Day, last Monday in May; Independence Day, 4 July; Labor Day, 1st Monday in September; Columbus Day, 2d Monday in October; Veterans Day, 11 November; Thanksgiving Day, 4th Thursday in November; Christmas Day, 25 December. **TIME:** 6 AM CST = noon GMT; 5 AM MST = noon GMT.

¹LOCATION, SIZE, AND EXTENT

Located in the western north-central US, Kansas is the 2d-largest midwestern state (following Minnesota) and ranks 14th among the 50 states.

The total area of Kansas is 82,277 sq mi (213,097 sq km), of which 81,778 sq mi (211,805 sq km) are land, and the remaining 499 sq mi (1,292 sq km) inland water. Shaped like a rectangle except for an irregular corner in the NE, the state has a maximum extension E-W of about 411 mi (661 km) and an extreme N-S distance of about 208 mi (335 km).

Kansas is bounded on the N by Nebraska, on the E by Missouri (with the line in the NE following the Missouri River), on the S by Oklahoma, and on the W by Colorado, with a total boundary length of 1,219 mi (1,962 km). The geographic center of Kansas is in Barton County, 15 mi (24 km) NE of Great Bend.

²TOPOGRAPHY

Although the popular image of the state is one of unending flatlands, Kansas has a diverse topography. Three main land regions define the state. The eastern third consists of the Osage Plains, Flint Hills, Dissected Till Plains, and Arkansas River Lowlands. The central third comprises the Smoky Hills (which include the Dakota sandstone formations, Greenhorn limestone formations, and chalk deposits) to the north and several lowland regions to the south. To the west are the Great Plains proper, divided into the Dissected High Plains and the High Plains. Kansas generally slopes eastward from a maximum elevation of 4,039 feet (1,231 meters) at Mt. Sunflower (a mountain in name only) on the Colorado border to 680 feet (207 meters) by the Verdigris River at the Oklahoma border. More than 50,000 streams run through the state, and there are hundreds of artificial lakes. Major rivers include the Missouri, which defines the state's northeastern boundary; the Arkansas, which runs through Wichita; and the Kansas (Kaw), which runs through Topeka and joins the Missouri at Kansas City.

The geographic center of the 48 contiguous states is located in Smith County, in north-central Kansas, at 39°50' N and 98°35'w. Forty miles (64 km) south of this point, in Osborne County at 39°13'27" N and 98°32'31" w, is the North American geodetic datum, the controlling point for all land surveys in the US, Canada, and Mexico. Extensive beds of prehistoric ocean fossils lie in the chalk beds of two western counties, Logan and Gove.

³CLIMATE

Kansas's continental climate is highly changeable. The average mean temperature is 55°F (13°C). The record high is 121°F (149°C), recorded near Alton on 24 July 1936, and the record low, –40°F (–40°C), was registered at Lebanon on 13 February 1905. The normal annual precipitation ranges from slightly more than 40 in (101.6 cm) in the southeast to as little as 16 in (40.6 cm) in the west. The overall annual average is 27 in (68.6 cm), although years of drought have not been uncommon. About 70–77% of the precipitation falls between 1 April and 30 September. The annual mean snowfall ranges from about 36 in (91.4 cm) in the extreme northwest to less than 11 in (27.9 cm) in the far southeast. Tornadoes are a regular fact of Kansas life; in 1995, 72 tornadoes were recorded. Dodge City is said to be the windiest city in the US, with an average wind speed of 14 mph (23 kph).

⁴FLORA AND FAUNA

Native grasses, consisting of 60 different groups subdivided into 194 species, cover one-third of Kansas, which is much overgrazed. Bluestem—both big and little—which grows in most parts of the state, has the greatest forage value. Other grasses include buffalo grass, blue and hairy gramas, and alkali sacaton. One native conifer, eastern red cedar, is found generally throughout the state. Hackberry, black walnut, and sycamore grow in the east, while box elder and cottonwood predominate in western Kansas. There are no native pines. The wild native sunflower, the state flower, is found throughout the state. Other characteristic wildflowers include wild daisy, ivy-leaved morning glory, and smallflower verbena. The prairie white-fringed orchid and Mead's milkweed are protected under federal statutes.

Kansas's indigenous mammals include the common cottontail, black-tailed jackrabbit, black-tailed prairie dog, muskrat, opossum, and raccoon; the white-tailed deer is the state's only big-game animal. There are 12 native species of bat, 2 varieties of shrew and mole, and 3 types of pocket gopher. The western meadowlark is the state bird. Kansas has the largest flock of prairie chickens remaining on the North American continent. The black-footed ferret, gray bat, and bald eagle are on the threatened or endangered list.

5ENVIRONMENTAL PROTECTION

No environmental problem is more crucial for Kansas than water quality, and its protection remains a primary focus of the state's environmental efforts, which include active regulatory and remedial programs for both surface and groundwater sources. Maintenance of air quality is also a primary effort, and the state works actively with the business community to promote pollution prevention.

Strip mining for coal is decreasing in southeast Kansas, and the restoration of resources damaged by previous activities is ongoing.

The state has sufficient capacity for handling solid waste, although the total number of solid waste facilities has decreased in recent years. In 1995, Kansas had 13 hazardous waste sites. In 1996, the state had 435,000 acres of wetlands.

6POPULATION

With a population in 1990 of 2,477,574 (4.8% more than in 1980), Kansas ranked 32d among the states. The estimated population in 1996 was 2,563,618 (a 3.8% increase over 1990); the population density in 1990 was 30 per sq mi (12 per sq km).

When it was admitted to the Union in 1861, Kansas's population was 107,206. During the decade that followed, the population grew by 240%, more than 10 times the US growth rate. Steady growth continued through the 1930s, but in the 1940s the population declined by 4%. Since then, the population has risen, though at a slower pace than the national average.

Of the 1990 population, 49% was male and 51% female. About 69.1% lived in urban areas and 30.9% in rural areas, reversing the percentages recorded 70 years earlier. In 1990, 13.7% of all Kansas were over 65, higher than the national average of 12.5%.

Whereas the populations of Wichita and Topeka grew 8.6% and 1.0% respectively, the population of Kansas City dropped 7.1% during the 1980s. Estimates for 1994 showed about 310,236 residents for Wichita, and 142,630 for Kansas City. That part of the Kansas City metropolitan area in Kansas had a population of 480,249 in 1990. In 1995, the Wichita metropolitan area had an estimated 508,224 residents, and the Topeka metropolitan area had 165,062.

7 ETHNIC GROUPS

White settlers began to pour into Kansas in 1854, dispersing the 36 Indian tribes living there and precipitating a struggle over the legal status of slavery. Remnants of six of the original tribes still make their homes in the state. Some Indians live on three reservations covering 30,000 acres (12,140 hectares); others live and work elsewhere, returning to the reservations several times a year for celebrations and observances. There were 22,000 Indians in Kansas as of 1990.

Black Americans in Kansas numbered 143,000—more than 5% of the population—in 1990, when the state also had 94,000 residents of Hispanic origin. The 1990 census recorded 32,000

Asian-Pacific residents, the largest group being 6,001 Vietnamese, followed by 5,406 Laotians and 4,298 Cambodians.

The foreign-born numbered only 62,840 (2.5% of the population) in 1990, the most common lands of origin being Mexico, Germany, and Viet Nam. Among persons who reported descent from a single ancestry group, the leading nationalities were German (968,078), English (405,709), and Irish (435,784).

8LANGUAGES

Plains Indians of the Macro-Siouan group originally populated what is now Kansas; their speech echoes in such place-names as Kansas, Wichita, Topeka, Chetopa, and Ogallah.

Regional features of Kansas speech are almost entirely those of the Northern and North Midland dialects, reflecting the migration into Kansas in the 1850s of settlers from the East. Kansans typically use *fish(ing) worms* as bait, play as children on a *teetertotter,* see a *snakefeeder* (dragonfly) over a /krik/ (creek), make *white bread* sandwiches, carry water in a *pail,* and may designate the time 2:45 as a quarter *to,* or *of,* or *till* three.

The migration by southerners in the mid-19th century is evidenced in southeastern Kansas by such South Midland terms as *pullybone* (wishbone) and *light bread* (white bread); the expression *wait on* (wait for) extends farther westward.

In 1990, 2,158,011 Kansans—94.3% of the residents 5 years old or older—spoke only English at home. The number of Kansans who spoke another language at home included:

Spanish	62,059	Vietnamese	5,625
German	22,887	Korean	3,221
French	7,851	Chinese	4,272

9RELIGIONS

Protestant missions played an important role in early Kansas history. Isaac McCoy, a Baptist minister, was instrumental in founding the Shawnee Baptist Mission in Johnson County in 1831. Later Baptist, Methodist, Quaker, Presbyterian, and Jesuit missions became popular stopover points for pioneers traveling along the Oregon and Santa Fe trails. Mennonites were drawn to the state by a law passed in 1874 allowing exemptions from military service on religious grounds.

Religious freedom is specifically granted in the Kansas constitution, and a wide variety of religious groups is represented in the state. The leading Protestant denominations in 1990 were United Methodists, 238,029; Southern Baptist Convention, 96,524; and Christian Church (Disciples of Christ), 58,314. Roman Catholics constitute the largest single religious group in the state, with 369,241 adherents in 1990. Kansas's estimated Jewish population that year was 9,151.

10TRANSPORTATION

In the heartland of the nation, Kansas is at the crossroads of US road and railway systems. In 1995, Kansas had 25,919 bridges (3d in the nation). The state had 133,322 mi (214,515 km) of public roads (4th in the nation), of which 123,631 mi (198,922 km) were rural, 9,691 mi (15,593 km) were urban, and 872 mi (1,403 km) were part of the Interstate Highway System. There were 1,346,319 autos, 641,292 pickups and trucks, 113,414 trailers, and 44,041 motorcycles registered in Kansas in 1995.

In the late 1800s, the two major railroads, the Kansas Pacific (now the Union Pacific) and the Santa Fe (now the Burlington Northern-Santa Fe) acquired more than 10 million acres (4 million hectares) of land in the state and then advertised for immigrants to come and buy it. By 1872, the railroads stretched across the state, creating in their path the towns of Ellsworth, Newton, Caldwell, Wichita, and Dodge City. One of the first "cow towns" was Abilene, the terminal point for all cattle shipped to the East.

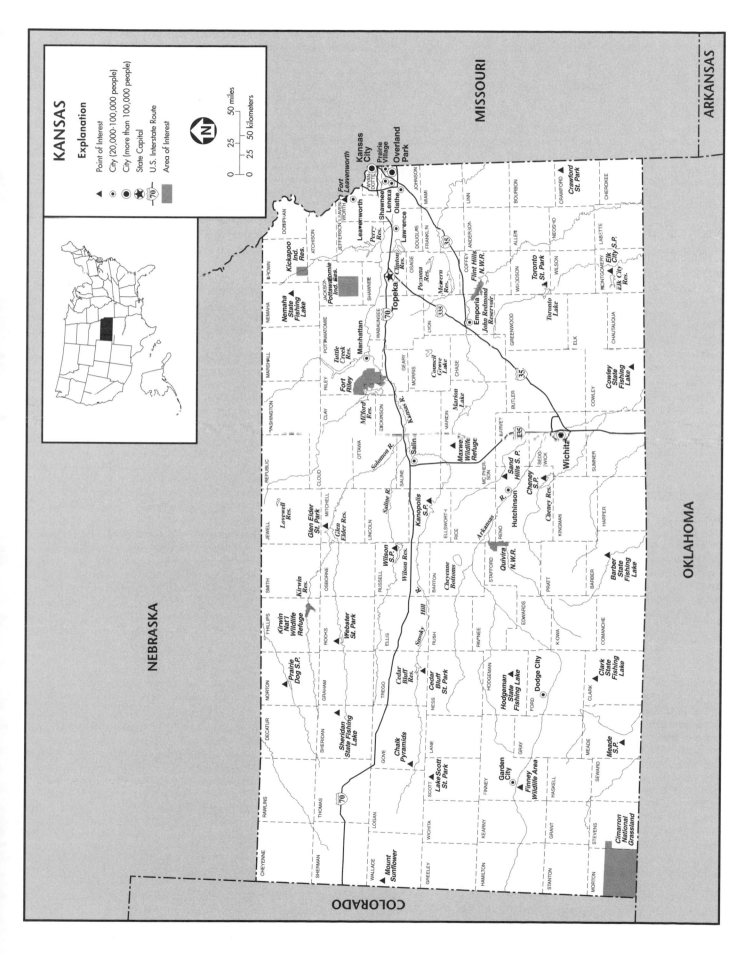

KANSAS

Explanation

Point of Interest ▲

City (20,000-100,000 people) ⊙

City (more than 100,000 people) ◉

State Capital ★

U.S. Interstate Route 70

Area of Interest ▢

50 miles

50 kilometers

N

NEBRASKA

COLORADO

OKLAHOMA

MISSOURI

ARKANSAS

Kickapoo Ind. Res.

Pottawatomie Ind. Res.

Nemaha State Fishing Lake

Leavenworth

Fort Leavenworth

Kansas City

Prairie Village

Overland Park

Shawnee

Lenexa

Olathe

Lawrence

Perry Res.

Clinton Res.

Topeka

Pomona Res.

Melvern Res.

Flint Hills N.W.R.

Emporia

John Redmond Reservoir

Toronto St. Park

Toronto Lake

Crawford St. Park

Elk City S.P.

Elk City Res.

Cowley State Fishing Lake

Manhattan

Tuttle Creek Res.

Fort Riley

Milford Res.

Council Grove Lake

Marion Lake

Maxwell Wildlife Refuge

Wichita

Sand Hills S.P.

Cheney S.P.

Cheney Res.

Hutchinson

Salina

Lovewell Res.

Glen Elder St. Park

Glen Elder Res.

Wilson S.P.

Wilson Res.

Kanopolis S.P.

Cheyenne Bottoms

Quivira N.W.R.

Barber State Fishing Lake

Kirwin Res.

Kirwin Nat'l Wildlife Refuge

Webster St. Park

Cedar Bluff Res.

Cedar Bluff St. Park

Hodgeman State Fishing Lake

Dodge City

Clark State Fishing Lake

Prairie Dog S.P.

Sheridan State Fishing Lake

Chalk Pyramids

Lake Scott St. Park

Garden City

Finney Wildlife Area

Meade S.P.

Mount Sunflower

Cimarron National Grassland

Counties

DONIPHAN, BROWN, NEMAHA, MARSHALL, WASHINGTON, REPUBLIC, JEWELL, SMITH, PHILLIPS, NORTON, DECATUR, RAWLINS, CHEYENNE, SHERMAN, THOMAS, SHERIDAN, GRAHAM, ROOKS, OSBORNE, MITCHELL, CLOUD, CLAY, RILEY, POTTAWATOMIE, JACKSON, ATCHISON, LEAVENWORTH, JEFFERSON, SHAWNEE, WABAUNSEE, OSAGE, DOUGLAS, JOHNSON, WYANDOTTE, MIAMI, FRANKLIN, LINN, ANDERSON, COFFEY, LYON, MORRIS, GEARY, DICKINSON, SALINE, OTTAWA, LINCOLN, RUSSELL, ELLIS, TREGO, GOVE, LOGAN, WALLACE, GREELEY, WICHITA, SCOTT, LANE, NESS, RUSH, BARTON, ELLSWORTH, RICE, MCPHERSON, MARION, CHASE, GREENWOOD, WOODSON, ALLEN, BOURBON, CRAWFORD, CHEROKEE, LABETTE, MONTGOMERY, WILSON, NEOSHO, ELK, CHAUTAUQUA, COWLEY, BUTLER, SEDGWICK, HARVEY, RENO, STAFFORD, PAWNEE, HODGEMAN, FINNEY, KEARNY, HAMILTON, STANTON, GRANT, HASKELL, GRAY, FORD, EDWARDS, KIOWA, PRATT, KINGMAN, HARPER, SUMNER, BARBER, COMANCHE, CLARK, MEADE, SEWARD, STEVENS, MORTON

Solomon R.

Kansas R.

Saline R.

Smoky Hill R.

Arkansas R.

In 1995, the state had 5,912 route mi (9,512 km) of railroad track (4th in the nation). That same year Kansas ranked 2d in the nation in the total amount of originated rail-tons of farm products.

An Amtrak passenger train crosses Kansas en route from Chicago to Los Angeles. Total ridership through the state in 1995/96 was 32,944.

In 1995, the state had 386 airports. The busiest airport, Wichita Mid-Continent, had 544,439 total passenger enplanements in 1994. Approximately two-thirds of all business and private aircraft in the United States are built in Kansas, according to 1994 data.

River barges move bulk commodities along the Missouri River. The chief river ports are Atchison, Leavenworth, Lansing, and Kansas City.

11HISTORY

Present-day Kansas was first inhabited by Paleo-Indians approximately 10,000 years ago. They were followed by several prehistoric cultures, forerunners of the Plains tribes—the Wichita, Pawnee, Kansa, and Osage—that were living or hunting in Kansas when the earliest Europeans arrived. These tribes were buffalo hunters who also farmed and lived in small permanent communities. Around 1800, they were joined on the Central Plains by the nomadic Cheyenne, Arapaho, Comanche, and Kiowa.

The first European, explorer Francisco Coronado, entered Kansas in 1541, searching for riches in the fabled land of Quivira. He found no gold but was impressed by the land's fertility. A second Spanish expedition to the Plains was led by Juan de Onate in 1601. Between 1682 and 1739, French explorers established trading contacts with the Indians. France ceded its claims to the area to Spain in 1762, but received it back from Spain in 1800.

Most of Kansas was sold to the US by France as part of the Louisiana Purchase of 1803. (The extreme southwestern corner was gained after the Mexican War.) Lewis and Clark examined the country along the Missouri River in 1804, and expeditions under the command of Zebulon Pike (1806) and Stephen Long (1819) traversed the land from east to west. Pike and Long were not impressed with the territory's dry soil, the latter calling the area "unfit for civilization, and of course uninhabitable by a people depending on agriculture for their subsistence."

Largely because of these negative reports, early settlement of Kansas was sparse, limited to a few thousand eastern Indians who were removed from their lands and relocated in what is now eastern Kansas. Included were such once-powerful tribes as the Shawnee, Delaware, Ojibwa, Wyandot, Ottawa, and Potawatomi. They were joined by a number of Christian missionaries seeking to transform the Indians into Christian farmers.

William Becknell opened the Santa Fe Trail to wagon traffic in 1822, and for 50 years that route, two-thirds of which lay in Kansas, was of commercial importance to the West. During the 1840s and 1850s, thousands of migrants crossed northeastern Kansas on the California-Oregon Trail. In 1827, Ft. Leavenworth was established, followed by Ft. Scott (1842) and Ft. Riley (1853). Today, Ft. Leavenworth and Ft. Riley are still the two largest military installations in the state.

Kansas Territory was created by the Kansas-Nebraska Act (30 May 1854), with its western boundary set at the Rocky Mountains. Almost immediately, disputes arose as to whether Kansas would enter the Union as a free or slave state. Both free-staters and proslavery settlers were brought in, and a succession of governors tried to bring order out of the chaos arising from the two groups' differences. Free-staters established an extralegal government at Topeka following the establishment of a territorial capital at Lecompton.

Because of several violent incidents, the territory became known as Bleeding Kansas. One of the most memorable attacks came in May 1856, when the town of Lawrence was sacked by proslavery forces. John Brown, an abolitionist who had recently arrived from upstate New York, retaliated by murdering five proslavery settlers. Guerrilla skirmishes continued for the next few years along the Kansas-Missouri border. The final act of violence was the Marais des Cygnes massacre in 1858, which resulted in the death of several free-staters. In all, about 50 people were killed in the territorial period—not an extraordinary number for a frontier community.

After several attempts to write a constitution acceptable to both anti- and proslavery groups, the final document was drafted in 1859. Kansas entered the Union on 29 January 1861 as a free state. Topeka was named the capital, and the western boundary was moved to its present location.

Although Kansas lay west of the major Civil War action, more than two-thirds of its adult males served in the Union Army and gave it the highest military death rate among the northern states. Kansas units saw action in the South and West, most notably at Wilson's Creek, Cane Hill, Prairie Grove, and Chickamauga. The only full-scale battle fought in Kansas was at Mine Creek in 1864, at the end of General Sterling Price's unsuccessful Confederate campaign in the West. The most tragic incident on Kansas soil came on 21 August 1863, when Confederate guerrilla William C. Quantrill raided Lawrence, killing at least 150 persons and burning the town.

Following the Civil War, settlement expanded in Kansas, particularly in the central part of the state. White settlers encroached on the hunting grounds of the Plains tribes, and the Indians retaliated with attacks on white settlements. Treaty councils were held, the largest at Medicine Lodge in 1867, but not until 1878 did conflict cease between Indians and whites. Most of the Indians were eventually removed to the Indian Territory in what is now Oklahoma. Also during this period, buffalo, slaughtered for food and hides, all but disappeared from the state.

By 1872, both the Union Pacific and the Santa Fe railroads had crossed Kansas, and other lines were under construction. Rail expansion brought more settlers, who established new communities. It also led to the great Texas cattle drives that meant prosperity to a number of Kansas towns—including Abilene, Ellsworth, Wichita, Caldwell, and Dodge City—from 1867 to 1885. This was when Bat Masterson, Wyatt Earp, Doc Holliday, and Wild Bill Hickok reigned in Dodge City and Abilene—the now romantic era of the Old West.

A strain of hard winter wheat that proved particularly well suited to the state's soil was brought to Kansas in the 1870s by Russian Mennonites fleeing czarist rule, and Plains agriculture was thereby transformed. There were also political changes: the state adopted limited female suffrage in 1887. Prohibition, made part of the state constitution in 1880, was a source of controversy until its repeal in 1948.

Significant changes in agriculture, industry, transportation, and communications came after 1900. Mechanization became commonplace in farming, and vast areas were opened to wheat production, particularly during World War I. Some automobile manufacturing took place, and the movement for "good roads" began. The so-called agrarian revolt of the late 19th century, characterized politically by populism, evolved into the Progressive movement of the early 1900s, which focused attention on control of monopolies, public health, labor legislation, and more representative politics. Much of the Progressive leadership came from Kansas; Kansan newspaper editor and national Progressive leader William Allen White devoted considerable energy to Theodore Roosevelt's Bull Moose campaign in 1912.

Kansas suffered through the Great Depression of the 1930s. The state's western region, part of the Dust Bowl, was hardest hit. Improved weather conditions and the demands of World War II revived Kansas agriculture in the 1940s. The World War II era also saw the development of industry, especially in transportation. Wichita had been a major center of the aircraft industry in the 1920s and 1930s, and its plants became vital to the US war effort. Other heavy industry grew, and mineral production—oil, natural gas, salt, coal, and gypsum—expanded greatly. In 1952, a native Kansan, Dwight D. Eisenhower, was elected to the first of two terms as president of the United States. Two years later, Topeka became the focal point of a landmark in US history—the US Supreme Court ruling in the *Brown v. Board of Education* case that banned racial segregation in the nation's schools.

Since World War II, Kansas has become increasingly urban. Agriculture has become highly commercialized, and there are dozens of large industries that process and market farm products and supply materials to crop producers. Livestock production, especially in closely controlled feedlots, is a major enterprise. The recession of the 1980s led to a period of crisis for Kansas farmers. Agricultural banks failed, and many farms were lost and their owners forced into bankruptcy. Recent governors have worked to expand international exports of Kansas products. In 1993, Kansas signed a trade agreement with the St. Petersburg region of Russia.

The late 1980s and early 1990s brought dramatic extremes of weather. Kansas received less than 25 percent of its normal average rainfall in 1988. Topsoil erosion damaged 865,000 acres (354,650 hectares), and drought drove up commodity prices and depleted grain stocks. From April through September of 1993, Kansas experienced the worst floods of the century. Some 13,500 people evacuated their homes, and the floods caused $574 million dollars worth of damage. In the 1990s, in response to the economic problems created by the drought and to a slowdown in industrial growth, the state government implemented a number of measures to bolster economic development, including block grants to cities.

In 1996, native son and US Senate majority leader Robert Dole won the Republican presidential nomination but was defeated by Democratic incumbent Bill Clinton, although Dole carried his home state with 54% of the vote to Clinton's 36%.

12 STATE GOVERNMENT

The form of Kansas's constitution was a matter of great national concern, for the question of whether Kansas would be a free or slave state was in doubt throughout the 1850s. After three draft constitutions failed to win popular support or congressional approval, a fourth version, banning slavery, was drafted in July 1859 and ratified by Kansas voters that October. Signed by President James Buchanan on 29 January 1861, this constitution (with 79 subsequent amendments, as of 1983) has governed Kansas to the present day.

The Kansas legislature consists of a 40-member senate and a 125-member house of representatives. Senators serve four-year terms and house members serve for two years; elections are held in even-numbered years. Legislative sessions are limited to 90 days in even-numbered years but are unlimited in odd-numbered years. In 1995, legislators received a per diem salary of $63 during regular sessions.

Officials elected statewide are the governor, lieutenant governor, secretary of state, attorney general, treasurer, and commissioner of insurance. Members of the state Board of Education are elected by districts. All serve four-year terms. The governor cannot serve more than two consecutive terms. Every office in the executive branch is controlled by either the governor or another elected official. The governor appoints the heads

(secretaries) of all state departments. In 1996, the governor's salary was $80,340.

A bill becomes law when it has been approved by 21 senators and 63 representatives and signed by the governor. A veto can be overridden by one more than two-thirds of the members of both houses.

To vote in the state, a person must be a US citizen, 18 years old at the time of the election, and a resident of Kansas for at least 20 days. Registration closes 20 days before all elections, and mail registration is allowed.

13 POLITICAL PARTIES

Kansas was dominated by the Republican Party for the first three decades of statehood. Although the Republicans remain the dominant force in state politics, the Democrats controlled several state offices in the mid-1990s.

The Republican Party of early Kansas espoused the abolitionist ideals of the New England settlers who sought to ban slavery from the state. After the Civil War, the railroads played a major role in Republican politics and won favorable tax advantages from the elected officials. The party's ranks swelled with the arrival of immigrants from Scandinavia and Germany, who tended to side with the party's by then strongly conservative beliefs.

The Republicans' hold over state life was shaken by the Populist revolt toward the end of the 19th century. The high point of Populist Party power came in 1892, when the insurgents won all the statewide elective offices and also took control of the senate. When electoral irregularities denied them control of the house, they temporarily seized the house chambers. The two parties then set up separate houses of representatives, the Populists meeting one day and the Republicans the next. This continued for six weeks, until the Kansas supreme court ruled that the Republicans constituted the rightful legal body. After a Republican sweep in 1894, the Populists returned to office in 1896, but the party declined rapidly thereafter.

The Democrats rose to power in the state as a result of the split between the conservative and progressive wings of the Republican Party in 1912. Nevertheless, the Democrats were very much a minority party until after World War II. Democrats held the governorship for 18 of the 28 years between 1957 and 1985; the most recent Democratic governor was Joan Finney, elected in 1990. Republicans have regularly controlled the legislature, however Republican Bill Graves was elected to the governorship in 1994. In 1994, the state had 587,303 registered Republicans (43% of registered voters) and 424,478 registered Democrats (31%). The remaining 26% included independents and members of minor parties.

In 1988 and 1992, Kansans voted for George Bush in the presidential elections. In the 1996 election, native Kansan Bob Dole won 54% of the vote; Clinton received 36%; and Independent Ross Perot garnered 9%. Dole, first elected to the US Senate in 1968 and elected Senate majority leader in 1984, reclaimed the post of majority leader when the Republicans gained control of the Senate in the elections of 1994. In a surprise move in May 1996, Dole suddenly retired from the Senate to concentrate on his presidential campaign. In November, the race to fill his remaining term was won by Republican Sam Brownback. Kansas's other Republican senator, Nancy Landon Kassebaum, also vacated her seat in 1996; it was won by Republican Congressman Pat Roberts. Prior to the November 1994 elections, the state's US congressional delegation was split between Republicans and Democrats (two Republicans, two Democrats); following the 1994 and 1996 elections, Republicans held all four seats. In the state legislature in 1997, there were 27 Republicans and 13 Democrats in the senate and 77 Republicans and 48 Democrats in the state house. In 1994, 21 blacks and 7

Hispanics held elective office. As of 1995, there were 50 women serving in the state legislature and in elective executive office.

¹⁴LOCAL GOVERNMENT

As of 1992, Kansas had 105 counties, 627 incorporated cities, 1,353 townships, 324 school districts, and 1,482 special districts. The total number of local government bodies was 3,918 in 1992. By law, no county can be less than 432 sq mi (1,119 sq km).

Each county government is headed by three elected county commissioners (although two counties, Johnson and Sedgwick, each have five commissioners). Other county officials include the county clerk, treasurer, register of deeds, attorney, sheriff, clerk of district court, and appraiser. Most cities are run by mayor-council systems.

¹⁵STATE SERVICES

All education services, including community colleges, are handled by the state Board of Education; the state university system lies within the jurisdiction of the Board of Regents. The Department of Human Resources administers employment and worker benefit programs; the Department of Economic Development operates housing and business planning programs. Social, vocational, and children's and youth programs are run by the Department of Social and Rehabilitation Services; the Department of Health and Environment supervises health, environment, and laboratory services.

A "Sunset Law" automatically abolishes specified state agencies at certain times unless they receive renewed statutory authority.

¹⁶JUDICIAL SYSTEM

The supreme court, the highest court in the state, is composed of a chief justice and six other justices. All justices are appointed by the governor but after one year must run for election at the next general election. They then are elected for six-year terms. In case of rejection by the voters, the vacancy is filled by appointment. An intermediate-level court of appeals consists of a chief judge and six other judges appointed by the governor; like supreme court justices, they must be elected to full terms, in this case for four years.

In January 1977, probate, juvenile, and county courts, as well as magistrate courts of countywide jurisdiction, were replaced by district courts.The 31 district courts are presided over by 149 district and associate district judges and 69 district magistrate judges. Kansas has a death penalty and has executed 15 persons since 1930.

The Department of Corrections administers the state correctional system. Kansas had a prison population of 6,844 in 1995, or 267 per 100,000. A federal prison is located at Leavenworth. Kansas's crime rate was 4,886.9 per 100,000 inhabitants in 1995, including 420.7 violent crimes and 4,466.2 property crimes. Kansas had 6,024 active attorneys in 1994.

¹⁷ARMED FORCES

The US Army's 1st Infantry Division, known as the Big Red One, is located at Ft. Riley in Junction City and had 10,902 military personnel in 1992. The Army's Command and General Staff College is housed at Ft. Leavenworth, which had 3,174 military personnel in 1996; McConnell Air Force Base, located in Wichita, had 2,913. A total of 17,230 military personnel were stationed in Kansas in 1996. In 1995/96, over $762 million in defense contracts was awarded to state firms, down from $2.4 billion in 1983/84.

Kansas had 259,000 veterans in 1996. Of these fewer than 500 were veterans of World War I, 72,000 of World War II, 44,000 of the Korean conflict, 86,000 of the Viet Nam era, and 15,000 of the Persian Gulf War. During fiscal year 1996, $468 million was paid in veterans benefits.

In 1996, Kansas had 2,967 members of the Air National Guard and Reserve and 13,652 members of the Army Reserve and National Guard. In 1993, the Kansas Highway Patrol employed 554 full-time sworn officers, or two per 10,000 residents.

¹⁸MIGRATION

By the 1770s, Kansas was inhabited by a few thousand Indians, mainly from five tribes: the Kansa (Kaw) and the Osage, both of whom had migrated from the east, the Pawnee from the north, and the Wichita and Comanche, who had come from the southwest. In 1825, the US government signed a treaty with the Kansa and Osage that allowed eastern Indians to settle in the state.

The first wave of white migration came during the 1850s with the arrival of New England abolitionists who settled in Lawrence, Topeka, and Manhattan. They were followed by a much larger wave of emigrants from the eastern Missouri and the upper Mississippi Valley, drawn by the lure of wide-open spaces and abundant economic opportunity.

Kansas Presidential Vote by Political Parties, 1948–96

YEAR	ELECTORAL VOTE	KANSAS WINNER	DEMOCRAT	REPUBLICAN	PROGRESSIVE	SOCIALIST	PROHIBITION
1948	8	Dewey (R)	351,902	423,039	4,603	2,807	6,468
1952	8	*Eisenhower (R)	273,296	616,302	6,038	530	6,038
1956	8	*Eisenhower (R)	296,317	566,878	—	—	3,048
1960	8	Nixon (R)	363,213	561,474	—	—	4,138
1964	7	*Johnson (D)	464,028	386,579		1,901	5,393
					AMERICAN IND.		
1968	7	*Nixon (R)	302,996	478,674	88,921	—	2,192
1972	7	*Nixon (R)	270,287	619,812	21,808	—	4,188
						LIBERTARIAN	
1976	7	Ford (R)	430,421	502,752	4,724	3,242	1,403
1980	7	*Reagan (R)	326,150	566,812	7,555	14,470	—
1984	7	*Reagan (R)	333,149	677,296	—	3,329	—
1988	7	*Bush (R)	422,636	554,049	3,806	12,553	—
					IND. (Perot)		
1992	6	Bush (R)	390,434	449,951	312,358	4,314	—
1996	6	Dole (R)	387,659	583,245	92,639	4,557	—

* Won US presidential election.

The population swelled as a result of the Homestead Act of 1862, which offered land to anyone who would improve it and live on it for five years. The railroads promoted the virtues of Kansas overseas and helped sponsor immigrant settlers. By 1870, 11% of the population was European. More than 30,000 blacks, mostly from the South, arrived during 1878–80. Crop failures caused by drought in the late 1890s led to extensive out-migration from the western half of the state. Another period of out-migration occurred in the early 1930s, when massive dust storms drove people off the land. From 1980 to 1990, Kansas had a net loss of 63,411 from migration. Only 10 of Kansas's 105 counties recorded a net gain from migration in the 1980s. Between 1990 and 1996, the state had a net loss of 19,677 in domestic migration and a gain of 16,577 in international migration. In 1996, 4,303 foreign immigrants arrived in the state. As of 1990, 61.3% of all Kansans had been born within the state. In 1990, about 52% of residents age 5 and older lived in the same house as in 1985. Nearly three-fourths of those who lived in a different house in 1985 did so within Kansas. Steady migration from farms to cities has been a feature of Kansas life throughout this century, with urban population surpassing farm population after World War II. From 1980 to 1990, the urban population increased from 66.7% to 69.1% of the state's total.

19INTERGOVERNMENTAL COOPERATION

Kansas is a member of the Midwestern Conference, Arkansas River Compact of 1949, Arkansas River Compact of 1965, Big Blue River Compact, Kansas City Area Transportation Compact, Kansas-Missouri Waterworks Compact, Missouri River Toll Bridge Compact, Republican River Compact, Multistate Tax Compact, and other interstate bodies. The Interstate Cooperation Commission assists state officials and employees in maintaining contact with governmental units in other states. In fiscal year 1996, Kansas received $1.7 billion in federal assistance.

20ECONOMY

Although wheat production has long been the mainstay of the Kansas economy, efforts to bring other industries into the state began as early as the 1870s, when the railroads linked Kansas to eastern markets. Today, agricultural products and meat-packing industries are rivaled by the large aircraft industry centered in Wichita. Kansas leads all states and trails only seven countries in wheat production.

Three Kansas companies, all located in Wichita, manufacture two-thirds of the world's general aviation aircraft. The Kansas City metropolitan area is a center of automobile production and printing. Metal fabrication, printing, and mineral products industries predominate in the nine southeastern counties. In 1994, contributions to the gross state product of $61,758 million consisted of private goods–producing industries, $16,822 million; private services–producing industries, $35,779 million; and government, $9,158 million.

In 1993, the Kansas economy suffered from cuts of 9.1%—a result of 4,400 job cutbacks in aircraft manufacturing, most of which came from layoffs at Boeing; the closing of major firms; and extensive flood damage. While mining employment dropped 8.1% between 1992 and 1993, service jobs increased by 7% from 1991 to 1993.

In 1996, there were 11,312 filings for bankruptcy in the state. In 1995, Kansas's per capita personal income was $21,841, which was ranked 23rd nationally.

21INCOME

In 1996, Kansas's per capita income was $23,281 (22nd in the US). Total disposable personal income was $52 billion in 1996, up from $48.8 billion in 1995. Median household income in

1995 was $30,346. About 11% of all Kansans lived below the federal poverty level in 1995.

22LABOR

Kansas has traditionally had a fairly low unemployment rate. In 1996, the civilian labor force was 1,364,300, of whom 1,314,200 were employed, yielding an unemployment rate of 3.7%. The urban areas of Wichita, Topeka, and Lawrence contained 20%, 7%, and 3.8% of the labor force, respectively,

At the end of 1996, distribution of nonfarm employment by industry was as follows: mining, 8,100; construction, 55,800; manufacturing, 199,300; transportation, communication, and utilities, 70,800; wholesale and retail trade, 316,300; finance, insurance, and real estate, 59,500; and government, 245,800.

In 1995, 110,600 workers, or 10.2% of the work force, belonged to labor unions. Kansas has a right-to-work law.

23AGRICULTURE

Known as the Wheat State and the breadbasket of the nation, Kansas typically produces more wheat than any other state. It ranked 6th in total farm income in 1995, with cash receipts of $7.5 billion.

Because of fluctuating prices, Kansas farmers have always risked economic disaster. During the 1920s, depressed farm prices forced many new farmers out of business. By World War II, Kansas farmers were prospering again, as record prices coincided with record yields. Since then, improved technology has favored corporate farms at the expense of small landholders. Between 1940 and 1996, the number of farms declined from 159,000 to 66,000, while the average size of farms more than doubled (to 724 acres/293 hectares). In 1992, about 25,213,000 acres (10,203,700 hectares) were used for crops, of which 2,680,000 acres (1,085,000 hectares) were irrigated. Income from crops in 1995 totaled $2.8 billion. The following table shows several leading crops in 1996:

	VALUE	PRODUCTION(BU)	US RANK
Sorghum (grain)	$796,950,000	354,200,000	1
Wheat	1,199,440,000	255,200,000	2
Corn (grain)	1,018,020,000	357,200,000	7
Soybeans	492,100,000	74,000,000	10

Other leading crops are alfalfa, hay, oats, barley, popcorn, rye, dry edible beans, corn and sorghums for silage, wild hay, red clover, and sugar beets.

24ANIMAL HUSBANDRY

In 1995, Kansas dairy farmers had an estimated 82,000 milk cows which produced 1.18 billion lb of milk. Also during 1995 Kansas poultry farmers sold an estimated 1.6 million lb of chicken, and produced 325 million eggs worth around $11.9 million.

In 1997, Kansas farmers had an estimated 6.55 million cattle and calves worth $3.275 billion, which was ranked 3rd out of the 50 states. Kansas farmers had an estimated 1.45 million hogs and pigs worth around $129 million in 1996. An estimated 12.1 million lb of sheep and lambs were produced by Kansas farmers in 1995 and sold for $11.6 million.

25FISHING

There is little commercial fishing in Kansas. Sport fishermen can find bass, crappie, catfish, perch, and pike in the state's reservoirs and artificial lakes. In 1995/96, there were 306,943 fishing licenses issued by the state. The Kansas Department of Wildlife and Parks' objectives for fisheries include provision of 11.7 million angler trips annually on Kansas reservoirs, lakes, streams, and private waters, while maintaining the quantity and quality of the catch.

[26]FORESTRY

Kansas was at one time so barren of trees that early settlers were offered 160 acres (65 hectares) free if they would plant trees on their land. This program was rarely implemented, however, and today much of Kansas is still treeless.

Kansas has 1,546,200 acres (569,000 hectares) of forestland, 2.9% of the total state area. There are 1,491,700 acres (491,000 hectares) of commercial timberland, of which 96% are privately owned.

[27]MINING

The value of nonfuel mineral production in Kansas was estimated at $486 million in 1995. This was an $11 million decrease from the $497 million reported in 1994 caused by decreases in salt and crushed stone values. Grade-A helium and salt were two leading nonfuel mineral commodities, accounting for 22% and 21%, respectively, of the total nonfuel mineral production value in 1995. Kansas continued to rank first of two states producing crude helium. The state also ranked first of four states producing grade-A helium (55 million cu m/1,942 million cu ft, valued at $108 million), which constituted 22.2% of the state's total nonfuel mineral value in 1995, an increase of about 2 million cu m (71 million cu ft) over 1994. Mineral values that increased in 1995 included grade-A helium, crude helium, crude gypsum, industrial sand and gravel, bentonite clays, and pumice and pumicite. Combined values of salt, grade-A helium, crushed stone, and portland cement accounted for almost 64% of the total mineral value reported in 1995, when Kansas ranked 25th nationally in nonfuel mineral value. Total employment in mining was about 8,100 in December 1996.

[28]ENERGY AND POWER

The state ranked 13th in energy consumption per capita, with 420.1 million Btu, and 14th in energy expenditures per capita, with $2,113.

In 1996, Kansas had an installed electrical generating capacity of 10,476,000 kW. Electrical output was 38.9 billion kWh, 68% coalfired. Sales in 1995 totaled 30.4 billion kWh, of which 34% was for residences, 34% for commercial establishments, 31% for industrial plants, and 1% for other purposes.

In 1996, Kansas was the nation's 8th-leading oil producer. Output totaled 41,789,000 barrels of crude petroleum. There were proved reserves of 275,000,000 barrels at the end of 1995.

Natural gas marketed production was 721.4 billion cu ft (20 billion cu m) in 1995, when six gas companies served 888,766 customers. The average well head price per 1,000 cu ft that year was $1.36. About 45% of total consumption went for industrial purposes, 26% for residential use, 19% for commercial applications, and 10% for utilities.

One surface mine produced 232,373 tons of bituminous coal in 1996. Demonstrated coal reserves were estimated at 975 million tons.

[29]INDUSTRY

Industries are concentrated in Douglas, Johnson, Sedgwick, Shawnee, and Wyandotte counties. The estimated value of shipments for all state manufacturing totaled $42,640.8 billion in 1995. The following table shows the estimated value of shipments for major industries in 1995:

	(MILLIONS)
Food and kindred products	$12,530.8
Transportation equipment	8,600.5
Printing and publishing	3,338.8
Petroleum and coal products	2,669.5
Chemicals and allied products	2,216.9
Electrical and electronics equipment	1,960.3
Fabricated metal products	1,224.6
Stone, clay, and glass products	1,025.6

Kansas is a world leader in aviation, claiming a large share of both US and world production and sales of commercial aircraft. Wichita is the home of Beech, Cessna, and Learjet, which combined manufacture two-thirds of the world's general aviation aircraft. In 1995, there were 315 US patents issued to Kansas residents.

[30]COMMERCE

Domestically, Kansas is not a major commercial state. In 1992, Kansas had a total of 5,854 wholesale establishments with sales of $34.87 billion. Durable goods accounted for 39.5% of the sales. Retail sales in 1992 totaled $17.6 billion (31st). Automotive dealers had sales of over $3.9 billion; food stores, $3.4 billion; general merchandise stores, $2.7 billion; and eating and drinking places, $1.7 billion. In 1993, personal income from wholesale trade totaled $2.4 billion. Manufacturing of nondurables accounted for $6.39 billion in personal income in 1993, with food and kindred products at $2.49 billion. Durable goods accounted for $3.9 billion in income, with transportation equipment at $1.73 billion (primarily aircraft). In both agricultural and manufactured exports, Kansas plays an important role in US foreign trade. Exports of goods originating within Kansas totaled $3.8 billion in 1996, or just 0.6% of the US total.

[31]CONSUMER PROTECTION

The attorney general's consumer protection division enforces the Kansas consumer protection act, which protects consumers against fraud and false advertising. The consumer credit commissioner is responsible for administering the state's investment and common credit codes.

[32]BANKING

Kansas's 416 commercial banks had assets of $28,608 million in 1996. In 1996, 22 insured savings institutions reported $7,785 million in assets.

Records of all banks and trust companies in the state are examined once a year either by the state bank commissioner, the Office of Comptroller of Currency, the Federal Deposit Insurance Corporation, or by a federal reserve bank. The state savings and loan commissioner's office was merged into the state bank commissioner's office in 1993. However, currently there are no Kansas state-chartered savings and loans.

[33]INSURANCE

In 1997, 12 life insurance companies were headquartered in Kansas. In 1995, $3.7 billion in premiums was written by all life and health insurers, and benefit payments totaled $2.6 billion. There are 25 property and casualty insurers based in Kansas. All property and casualty insurers wrote $2.5 billion in premiums, of which $604 million was in automobile liability insurance, $463 million in automobile physical damage insurance, and $292 million in homeowner's insurance. These amounts do not include amounts paid by employers and individuals in "self-insured" or nontraditional insurance benefit plans, pools, or funds.

[34]SECURITIES

There are no stock exchanges in Kansas. There are approximately 1,000 brokers and dealers and nearly 500 investment advisory firms registered to do business in the state.

[35]PUBLIC FINANCE

The state budget is prepared by the Division of the Budget and is submitted by the governor to the legislature for approval. The fiscal year runs from 1 July to 30 June.

The following is a summary of state general fund net receipts and expenditures for fiscal years 1997 (actual) and 1998 (estimated):

	1997	1998
RECEIPTS		
Taxes	$3,549,200,000	$3,648,900,000
Net transfers	−19,820,000	−40,390,000
Other revenues, not including federal grants	112,700,000	116,100,000
TOTALS	$3,642,080,000	$3,724,610,000
Education	$2,259,068,954	$2,509,682,220
Human resources	673,419,192	667,015,614
General government	252,465,554	257,472,440
Public safety	239,654,299	272,464,260
Agriculture	39,286,382	31,579,809
Transportation	94,915,339	96,596,359
TOTALS	$3,558,809,720	$3,384,790,702

Generally, according to state law, no Kansas governmental unit may issue revenue bonds to finance current activities—these must operate on a cash basis. Bonds may be issued for such capital improvements as roads and buildings. The total indebtedness of state government exceeded $934.5 million as of 30 June 1996.

36 TAXATION

Kansas ranked 29th in state taxes per capita in 1991, at $1,120.80.

In the fiscal year that ended June 1996, Kansans paid $2,565 in state and local taxes per capita.

The state individual income tax rates range from 3.5% to 7.75%. The corporate tax rate is 4.0% with a 3.35% surtax on Kansas taxable income in excess of $50,000. Receipts from individual income tax in fiscal year 1996 were $1.392 billion. Receipts from corporate income tax in fiscal year 1996 were $219 million.

A statewide 3% sales tax was adopted in 1965. The current state sales tax rate is 4.9%, enacted in June 1992. Cities and counties can vote to adopt an additional 1% local sales tax. For special projects, counties may also assess an additional 1% local sales tax. The state also collects liquor and bingo enforcement taxes, cigarette and tobacco products taxes, inheritance taxes, motor vehicle and motor carrier taxes, motor fuel taxes, and royalty and excise taxes on oil, natural gas, and other minerals and other excise taxes.

The total amount of state taxes collected in fiscal year 1996, including individual and corporate income taxes, was $3.954 billion.

Local units of government collected tax revenue of $2.199 billion in fiscal year 1996. Property taxes are the largest source of income for local governments. Of the state and local taxes collected, 45% go for education.

In 1995, Kansans paid almost $10 billion in federal taxes.

37 ECONOMIC POLICY

The first state commission to promote industrial development was formed in 1939. In 1986, this commission was reorganized into the Kansas Department of Commerce, and in 1992 it became the Department of Commerce & Housing. The department now consists of five divisions: Small Business Development, Community Development, Travel, Tourism, and Film Services, Business Development, and Trade Development.

Kansas Inc., created by the state in 1986, is a public corporation with membership from both the private and public sectors. It conducts research and strategic planning in economic development and also serves as an advisory board to the Kansas Department of Commerce & Housing.

Kansas has a duty-free foreign trade zone and provides tax-exempt bonds to help finance business and industry. Specific tax incentives include job expansion and investment tax credits; tax exemptions or moratoriums on land, capital improvements, and specific machinery; and certain corporate income tax exemptions.

38 HEALTH

The birthrate in Kansas in 1995 was 14.5 per 1,000 population. Infant mortality rate in 1995 was 6.9 per 1,000 live births. Kansans reported 11,149 legal abortions. Heart disease, the leading cause of death in the state, accounted for 32.1% of all deaths in 1995. Topeka, a major US center for psychiatric treatment, is home to the world-famous Menninger Clinic.

In 1995, Kansas had 128 community hospitals with 11,728 beds and 269,127 admissions. The same year, the state had 15,329 nurses. There were 5,791 physicians in February 1997, and 1,274 licensed active dentists in 1996. Elk, Hodgeman, and Chase counties each had no practicing physician.

The University of Kansas has the state's only medical and pharmacology schools. The university's Mid-America Cancer Center and Radiation Therapy Center are the major cancer research and treatment facilities in the state. The Menninger Foundation has a research and treatment center for mental health.

39 SOCIAL WELFARE

Public assistance and social programs are coordinated through the Department of Human Resources and the Department of Social and Rehabilitation Services.

Aid to Families with Dependent Children (AFDC) payments averaging $471 a month went to 70,700 Kansans in 1996. In 1995, Social Security benefits were paid to 433,950 Kansans; additionally, 37,352 residents received Supplemental Security Income checks averaging $332. In 1996, the food stamp programs had an average monthly participation of 171,831, and the government spent a total of $48.3 million for school lunches. The average weekly unemployment benefit was $195.95 in 1995.

With the enactment of the Personal Responsibility and Work Opportunity Reconciliation Act of 1996, the US government has changed the form and regulations for many of its social welfare programs; most significantly, it replaces Aid to Families with Dependent Children (AFDC), an open-ended entitlement program, with Temporary Assistance for Needy Families (TANF), a limited system of assistance funded largely through federal block grants. The reform act also impacts the food stamp program, the Supplemental Security Income program, and the child nutrition program. The law took effect on 1 July 1997 and provided $16.38 billion in block grants for fiscal years 1997–2002. The grants are to be divided among the states based on an equation involving the numbers of former AFDC recipients in each state. Because many of the bills provisions have yet to be implemented into state-by-state policy, it was not possible to include the details of each state's programs for this edition of this work.

40 HOUSING

Kansas has relatively old housing stock. According to the 1990 census, 25% of all dwellings were built before 1940, and only 17% were built in the 1980s. The overwhelming majority were one-unit structures, and 61% were owner-occupied. By 1996, there were an estimated 1,095,000 housing units in Kansas. In 1996, 14,676 privately-owned units, valued at $1.3 billion, were authorized for construction, 10,121 of which were single-family dwellings. The median monthly cost in 1990 (the last year for which figures are available) of housing for owners with a mortgage was $628; the median monthly rent was $372. The median value of a house was $52,200; during the 1980s, the median value of a home fell 13% (in terms of 1990 dollars). During 1995/96, Kansas received $169.8 million in aid from the

US Department of Housing and Urban Development, including $41.9 million in community development block grants.

41 EDUCATION

Kansans are, by and large, better educated than most other Americans. In 1996, there were 25,786 public high school graduates, or 1.13% of all those graduating in the US. In 1995, 25.8% of the Kansas population had completed four or more years of college as compared to the national percentage of 23%.

Enrollment in the state's 1,479 public schools in 1995/96 was 463,018: 133,448 students were in high school, 14,442 in junior high school, 68,107 in middle school, 245,686 in elementary school (including kindergarten), and 1,335 in special purpose schools. There were about 16,423 elementary-school teachers and 14,306 secondary-school teachers. The dropout rate was 3.1% of grades 7–12 enrollment. Attendance at nonpublic schools in the fall of 1995 was 30,688, of whom 26,487 were in Catholic schools.

In 1996 there were 6 state universities, 19 two-year community colleges, 5 private two-year colleges, 17 church-affiliated universities and four-year colleges, and 12 vocational-technical schools and 4 technical colleges (4 community colleges have vocational-technical divisions). In addition, Kansas has a state technical institute, a municipal university (Washburn University, Topeka), and an American Indian university. Kansas State University was the nation's first land-grant university. Washburn University and the University of Kansas have the state's two law schools. In 1994, 170,603 students were enrolled in institutions of higher education. The Kansas Board of Regents offers scholarships and tuition grants to needy Kansas students.

During 1995/96, Kansas spent $5,435 per pupil (24th in the US) for elementary and secondary education. Total expenditures for elementary and secondary education in Kansas were $2.75 billion.

State residents made up 79% of all freshmen enrolled in Kansas in the fall of 1994 who had graduated from high school in the previous year; 87% of all Kansas residents who were freshmen attended college in their home state. Students averaged 21.3 on the ACT, which was taken by an estimated 70% of high school seniors in Kansas.

In 1954, Kansas was the focal point of a US Supreme Court decision that had enormous implications for US public education. The court ruled, in *Brown v. Board of Education of Topeka,* that Topeka's "separate but equal" elementary schools for black and white students were inherently unequal, and it ordered the school system to integrate.

The oldest higher-education institution in Kansas is Highland Community College, which was chartered in 1857. The oldest four-year institution is Baker University, a United Methodist institution, which received its charter just three days after Highland's was issued.

42 ARTS

The Kansas Arts Commission is a state arts agency governed by a 12-member panel of commissioners appointed for four-year rotating terms by the governor. The commission's annual budget of approximately $1.8 million is made up of funds appropriated by the Kansas legislature (approximately $1.3 million) and grants awarded to the agency by the National Endowment for the Arts (NEA), approximately $500,000.

The commission. awards grants and provides technical assistance for community-based nonprofit organizations and public agencies that provide opportunities for all citizens of Kansas to participate in the arts. Commission grant programs offer support in a variety of categories, including operational support of arts organizations, arts in education programs, arts projects, Kansas

touring artists programs, and arts programs for underserved constituents.

Grants are awarded annually by the commission to more than 300 organizations, based on recommendations by a panel of citizens. Grant applicants are required to provide local matching funds, with each dollar of state and federal funds being matched by more than $15 in local support. Participants in arts events for which the commission provided support totaled 3,786,560 in 1996.

43 LIBRARIES AND MUSEUMS

The Dwight D. Eisenhower Library in Abilene houses the collection of papers and memorabilia from the 34th president; there is also a museum. The Menninger Foundation Museum and Archives in Topeka maintains various collections pertaining to psychiatry. The Kansas State Historical Society Library (Topeka) contains the state's archives. Volumes of books and documents on the Old West are found in the Cultural Heritage and Arts Center Library in Dodge City. Kansas had 338 public libraries in 1996, with 9,594,318 volumes and a circulation of 19,041,494. Additionally, there were 35 county and regional libraries, 10 bookmobiles, 28 college libraries, and 24 junior college libraries. Seven regional library systems serve state residents who have no local library service.

Almost 153 museums, historical societies, and art galleries were scattered across the state in 1996. The Dyche Museum of Natural History at the University of Kansas, Lawrence, draws many visitors. The Kansas State Historical Society maintains an extensive collection of ethnological and archaeological materials in Topeka.

Among the art museums are the Mulvane Art Center in Topeka, the Helen Foresman Spencer Museum of Art at the University of Kansas, and the Wichita Art Museum. The Dalton Museum in Coffeyville displays memorabilia from the famed Dalton family of desperadoes. La Crosse is the home of the Barbed Wire Museum, displaying more than 500 varieties of barbed wire. The Emmett Kelly Historical Museum in Sedan honors the world-famous clown born there. The US Cavalry Museum is on the grounds of Ft. Riley. The Sedgwick County Zoo in Wichita and the Topeka Zoo are the largest of seven zoological gardens in Kansas.

The entire town of Nicodemus, where many blacks settled after the Civil War, was made a national historic landmark in 1975. The chalk formations of Monument Rocks in western Kansas constitute the state's only national natural landmark. Ft. Scott and Ft. Larned are national historic parks.

44 COMMUNICATIONS

About 96.5% of all households had telephone service in March 1993, about 2.3% higher than the US average.

The state had 53 AM and 113 FM radio stations, 21 commercial television stations, and 4 public television stations in 1996. As of 1996 there were four large cable television systems.

45 PRESS

Starting with the *Shawnee Sun,* a Shawnee-language newspaper founded by missionary Jotham Meeker in 1833, the press has played an important role in Kansas history. The most famous Kansas newspaperman was William Allen White, whose *Emporia Gazette* was a leading voice of progressive Republicanism around the turn of the century. Earlier, John J. Ingalls launched his political career by editing the *Atchison Freedom's Champion.* Captain Henry King came from Illinois to found the *State Record* and *Daily Capital* in Topeka.

In 1997, Kansas had 47 daily newspapers and 15 Sunday papers. Leading newspapers and their circulations in 1997 were as follows:

AREA	NAME	DAILY	SUNDAY
Topeka	*Capital–Journal* (m,S)	64,721	72,164
Wichita	*Eagle* (m,S)	100,932	177,402

The *Kansas City* (Missouri) *Star* (285,086 daily; 425,337 Sundays) is widely read in the Kansas as well as in the Missouri part of the metropolitan area.

⁴⁶ORGANIZATIONS

The 1992 Census of Service Industries counted 1,107 organizations in Kansas, including 190 business associations; 581 civic, social, and fraternal associations; and 336 other membership organizations. Among the organizations headquartered in Kansas are the National Collegiate Athletic Association (NCAA) and the Junior College Athletic Association.

⁴⁷TOURISM, TRAVEL, AND RECREATION

During 1993, domestic travel and tourism generated $2.5 million from overnight and day trips. Kansas has 23 state parks, 2 national historic sites, 24 federal reservoirs, 48 state fishing lakes, more than 100 privately owned campsites, and more than 304,000 acres (123,000 hectares) of public hunting and game management lands. Over 1.5 million visitors use the state park system yearly. The two national historic sites, Ft. Larned and Ft. Scott, both 19th century army bases on the Indian frontier, had 94,391 visitors in 1993.

Topeka features a number of tourist attractions, including the state capitol, state historical museum, and Menninger Foundation. Dodge City offers a reproduction of Old Front Street as it was when the town was the "cowboy capital of the world." Historic Wichita Cowtown is another frontier-town reproduction. In Hanover stands the only remaining original and unaltered Pony Express station. A recreated "Little House on the Prairie," near the childhood home of Laura Ingalls Wilder, is 13 mi (21 km) southwest of Independence. The Eisenhower Center in Abilene contains the 34th president's family home, library, and museum. The state fair is held in Hutchinson. In 1995, the state issued 306,943 fishing licenses and 187,110 hunting licenses.

⁴⁸SPORTS

There are no major professional sports teams in Kansas. The minor league Wichita Wranglers play in the Double-A Texas League. During spring, summer, and early fall, horses are raced at Eureka Downs. The national Greyhound Association Meet is held in Abilene.

The University of Kansas and Kansas State both play collegiate football in the Big 12 Conference. Kansas went to the Orange Bowl in 1948 and 1969, losing both times. The Jayhawks won the Aloha Bowl in 1992 and 1995. Kansas State played in the Cotton Bowl in 1996 and 1997, winning in 1996. In basketball, Kansas won the NCAA Championship in 1952 and 1988 and has appeared in 10 Final Fours. The National Junior College Basketball Tournament is held in Hutchinson each March. The Kansas Relays take place at Lawrence in April. The Flint Hills Rodeo in Strong City is one of many rodeos held statewide.

A US sporting event unique to Kansas is the International Pancake Race, held in Liberal each Shrove Tuesday. Women wearing housedresses, aprons, and scarves run along an S-shaped course carrying skillets and flipping pancakes as they go.

⁴⁹FAMOUS KANSANS

Kansas claims only one US president and one US vice president. Dwight D. Eisenhower (b.Texas, 1890–1969) as elected the 34th president in 1952 and reelected in 1956; he had served as the supreme commander of Allied Forces in World War II. He is buried in Abilene, his boyhood home. Charles Curtis (1860–1936) was vice president during the Hoover administration.

Two Kansans have been associate justices of the US Supreme Court: David J. Brewer (1837–1910) and Charles E. Whittaker (1901–73). Other federal officeholders from Kansas include William Jardine (1879–1955), secretary of agriculture; Harry Woodring (1890–1967), secretary of war; and Georgia Neese Clark Gray (1900–95), treasurer of the US. Prominent US senators include Edmund G. Ross (1826–1907), who cast a crucial acquittal vote at the impeachment trial of Andrew Johnson; John J. Ingalls (1833–1900), who was also a noted literary figure; Joseph L. Bristow (1861–1944), a leader in the Progressive movement; Arthur Caper (1865–1951), a former publisher and governor; Robert Dole (b.1923), who was the Republican candidate for vice president in 1976, twice served as Senate majority leader and was his party's presidential candidate in 1996; and Nancy Landon Kassebaum (b.1932), elected to the US Senate in 1978. Among the state's important US representatives were Jeremiah Simpson (1842–1905), a leading Populist, and Clifford R. Hope (1893–1970), important in the farm bloc. Gary Hart, a senator and a presidential candidate in 1984 and 1988, was born in Ottowa, Kansas, on 28 November 28 1936.

Notable Kansas governors include George W. Glick (1827–1911); Walter R. Stubbs (1858–1929); Alfred M. Landon (1887–1984), who ran for US president on the Republican ticket in 1936; and Frank Carlson (1893–1984). Other prominent political figures were David L. Payne (1836–84), who helped open Oklahoma to settlement; Carry Nation (1846–1911), the colorful prohibitionist; and Frederick Funston (1865–1917), hero of the Philippine campaign of 1898 and a leader of San Francisco's recovery after the 1906 earthquake and fire.

Earl Sutherland (1915–74) won the Nobel Prize in 1971 for physiology or medicine. Other leaders in medicine and science include Samuel J. Crumbine (1862–1954), a public health pioneer; the doctors Menninger—C. F. (1862–1953), William (1899–1966), and Karl (1893–1990)—who established the Menninger Foundation, a leading center for mental health; Arthur Hertzler (1870–1946), a surgeon and author; and Clyde Tombaugh (b.1906), who discovered the planet Pluto.

Kansas also had several pioneers in aviation including Clyde Cessna (1880–1954), Glenn Martin (1886–1955), Walter Beech (1891–1950), Amelia Earhart (1898–1937), and Lloyd Stearman (1898–1975). Cyrus K. Holliday (1826–1900) founded the Santa Fe railroad; William Coleman (1870–1957) was an innovator in lighting; and Walter Chrysler (1875–1940) was a prominent automotive developer.

Most famous of Kansas writers was William Allen White (1868–1944), whose son William L. White (1900–73) also had a distinguished literary career; Damon Runyon (1884–1946) was a popular journalist and storyteller. Novelists include Edgar Watson Howe (1853–1937), Margaret Hill McCarter (1860–1938), Dorothy Canfield Fisher (1879–1958), Paul Wellman (1898–1966), and Frederic Wakeman (b.1909). Gordon Parks (b.1912) has made his mark in literature, photography, and music. William Inge (1913–73) was a prize-winning playwright who contributed to the Broadway stage. Notable painters are Sven Birger Sandzen (1871–1954), John Noble (1874–1934), and John Steuart Curry (1897–1946). Sculptors include Robert M. Gage (b.1892), Bruce Moore (b.1905), and Bernard Frazier (1906–76). Among composers and conductors are Thurlow Lieurance (b.Iowa 1878–1963), Joseph Maddy (1891–1966), and Kirke L. Mechem (b.1926). Jazz great Charlie "Bird" Parker (Charles Christopher Parker, Jr., 1920–55) was born in Kansas City.

Stage and screen notables include Fred Stone (1873–1959), Joseph "Buster" Keaton (1895–1966), Milburn Stone (1904–1980), Charles "Buddy" Rogers (b.1904), Vivian Vance (1912–79), Edward Asner (b.1929), and Shirley Knight (b.1937). The clown Emmett Kelly (1898–1979) was a Kansan. Operatic performers include Marion Talley (b.1906) and Kathleen Kersting (1909–65).

Glenn Cunningham (1909–1988) and Jim Ryun (b.1947) both set running records for the mile. Also prominent in sports history were James Naismith (1861–1939), the inventor of basketball; baseball pitcher Walter Johnson (1887–1946); and Gale Sayers (b.1943), a football running back.

50BIBLIOGRAPHY

Boyer, Richard O. *The Legend of John Brown*. New York: Knopf, 1973.

Davis, Kenneth S. *Kansas: A Bicentennial History*. New York: Norton, 1976.

———. *Soldier of Democracy: A Biography of Dwight Eisenhower*. New York: Doubleday, 1945. 1952.

Frederickson, H. George, ed. *Public Policy and the Two States of Kansas*. Lawrence, Kans.: University Press of Kansas, 1992.

Howes, Charles C. *This Place Called Kansas*. Norman: University of Oklahoma Press, 1984.

Kansas, University of. Center for Public Affairs. *Kansas Statistical Abstract 1983–84*. 19th ed. Lawrence, 1984.

Richard, Robert W. *Kansas: A Land of Contracts*. St. Charles. Mo.: Forum Press, 1977.

Shortridge, James R. *Peopling the Plains: Who Settled Where in Frontier Kansas*. Lawrence, Kans.: University Press of Kansas, 1995.

Socolofsky, Homer, and Huber Self. *Historical Atlas of Kansas*. Norman: University of Oklahoma Press, 1972.

———, and Virgil W. Dean. *Kansas History: An Annotated Bibliography*. New York: Greenwood, 1992.

KENTUCKY

Commonwealth of Kentucky

ORIGIN OF STATE NAME: Derived from the Wyandot Indian word *Kah-ten-tah-teh* (land of tomorrow). **NICKNAME:** The Bluegrass State. **CAPITAL:** Frankfort. **ENTERED UNION:** 1 June 1792 (15th). **SONG:** "My Old Kentucky Home." **MOTTO:** United We Stand, Divided We Fall. **FLAG:** A simplified version of the state seal on a blue field. **OFFICIAL SEAL:** In the center, two men exchange greetings; above and below them is the state motto. On the periphery are two sprigs of goldenrod and the words "Commonwealth of Kentucky." **COLORS:** Blue and gold. **BIRD:** Cardinal. **WILD ANIMAL:** Gray squirrel. **FISH:** Bass. **FLOWER:** Goldenrod. **TREE:** Tulip poplar. **FOSSIL:** Brachiopod. **LEGAL HOLIDAYS:** New Year's Day, 1 January, plus one extra day; Birthday of Martin Luther King, Jr., 3d Monday in January; Washington's Birthday, 3d Monday in February; Good Friday, March or April, half-day holiday; Memorial Day, last Monday in May; Independence Day, 4 July; Labor Day, 1st Monday in September; Thanksgiving Day, 4th Thursday in November, plus one extra day; Christmas Day, 25 December, plus one extra day. **TIME:** 7 AM EST = noon GMT; 6 AM CST = noon GMT.

¹LOCATION, SIZE, AND EXTENT

Located in the eastern south-central US, the Commonwealth of Kentucky is the smallest of the eight south-central states and ranks 37th in size among the 50 states.

The total area of Kentucky is 40,409 sq mi (104,659 sq km), of which land makes up 39,669 sq mi (102,743 sq km) and inland water 740 sq mi (1,917 sq km). Kentucky extends about 350 mi (563 km) E-W; its maximum N-S extension is about 175 mi (282 km).

Kentucky is bordered on the N by Illinois, Indiana, and Ohio (with the line roughly following the north bank of the Ohio River); on the NE by West Virginia (with the line formed by the Big Sandy and Tug Fork rivers); on the SE by Virginia; on the S by Tennessee; and on the W by Missouri (separated by the Mississippi River). Because of a double bend in the Mississippi River, about 10 sq mi (26 sq km) of SW Kentucky is separated from the rest of the state by a narrow strip of Missouri.

After 15 years of litigation, Kentucky in 1981 accepted a US Supreme Court decision giving Ohio and Indiana control of at least 100 feet (30 meters) of the Ohio River from the northern shore. This in effect returned Kentucky's border to what it was in 1792, when Kentucky entered the Union.

The total boundary length of Kentucky is 1,290 mi (2,076 km). The state's geographic center is in Marion County, 3 mi (5 km) NW of Lebanon.

²TOPOGRAPHY

The eastern quarter of the state is dominated by the Cumberland Plateau, on the western border of the Appalachians. At its western edge, the plateau meets the uplands of the Lexington Plain (known as the Bluegrass region) to the north and the hilly Pennyroyal to the south. These two regions, which together make up nearly half the state's area, are separated by a narrow curving plain known as the Knobs because of the shapes of its eroded hills. The most level area of the state consists of the western coalfields bounded by the Pennyroyal to the east and the Ohio River to the north. In the far west are the coastal plains of the Mississippi River; this region is commonly known as the Purchase, having been purchased from the Chickasaw Indians.

The highest point in Kentucky is Black Mountain on the southeastern boundary in Harlan County, at 4,145 feet (1,263 meters). The lowest point is 257 feet (78 meters), along the Mississippi River in Fulton County. The state's mean altitude is 750 feet (229 meters).

The only large lakes in Kentucky are artificial. The biggest is Cumberland Lake (79 sq mi/205 sq km); Kentucky Lake, Lake Barkley, and Dale Hollow Lake straddle the border with Tennessee.

Including the Ohio and Mississippi rivers on its borders and the tributaries of the Ohio, Kentucky claims at least 3,000 mi (4,800 km) of navigable rivers—sometimes said to have more water than any other state except Alaska. Among the most important of Kentucky's rivers are the Kentucky, 259 mi (417 km); the Cumberland, partly in Tennessee; the Tennessee, also in Tennessee and Alabama; and the Big Sandy, Green, Licking, and Tradewater rivers. All, except for a portion of the Cumberland, flow northwest into the Ohio and thence to the Mississippi. Completion in 1985 of the Tennessee-Tombigbee Waterway, linking the Tennessee and Tombigbee rivers in Alabama, gave Kentucky's Appalachian coalfields direct water access to the Gulf of Mexico for the first time.

Drainage through porous limestone rock has honeycombed much of the Pennyroyal with underground passages, the best known of which is Mammoth Cave, now a national park. The Cumberland Falls, 92 feet (28 meters) high and 100 feet (30 meters) wide, are located in Whitely County.

³CLIMATE

Kentucky has a moderate, relatively humid climate, with abundant rainfall.

The southern and lowland regions are slightly warmer than the uplands. In Louisville, the normal monthly mean temperature ranges from 33°F (1°C) in January to 76°F (24°C) in July. The record high for the state was 114°F (46°C), registered in Greensburg on 28 July 1930; the record low, −34°F (−37°C), in Cynthiana on 28 January 1963.

Average daily relative humidity in Louisville ranges from 60% to 80%. The normal annual precipitation is 43 in (109 cm);

snowfall totals about 18 in (46 cm) a year. Kentucky had 30 tornadoes in 1995.

⁴FLORA AND FAUNA

Kentucky's forests are mostly of the oak/hickory variety, with some beech/maple stands. Four species of magnolia are found, and the tulip poplar, eastern hemlock, and eastern white pine are also common; the distinctive "knees" of the cypress may be seen along riverbanks. Kentucky's famed bluegrass is said to be actually blue only in May, when dwarf iris and wild columbine are in bloom. Rare plants include the swamp loosestrife and showy gentian.

Game mammals include the raccoon, muskrat, opossum, mink, gray and red foxes, and beaver; the eastern chipmunk and flying squirrel are common small mammals. At least 300 bird species have been recorded, of which 200 are common. Blackbirds are a serious pest, with some roosts numbering 5–6 million; more desirable avian natives include the cardinal (the state bird), robin, and brown thrasher, while eagles are winter visitors. More than 100 types of fish have been identified.

Rare animal species include the swamp rabbit, black bear, raven *(Corvus corax),* and mud darter. Among Kentucky's threatened species are the river otter, common shrew, and osprey. The Indiana bat, cougar, brown bear, Kirtland's warbler, bald eagle, whooping crane, peregrine falcon, and orange-footed and pink mucket pearly mussels are listed as endangered.

⁵ENVIRONMENTAL PROTECTION

The National Resources and Environmental Protection Cabinet, with broad responsibility, includes the departments of Natural Resources, Environmental Protection, and Surface Mining Reclamation and Enforcement, as well as the Kentucky Nature Preserves Commission. The Environmental Quality Commission, created in 1972 to serve as a watchdog over environmental concerns, is a citizen's group of seven members appointed by the governor.

The most serious environmental concern in Kentucky is repairing and minimizing damage to land and water from stripmining. Efforts to deal with such damage are relatively recent. The state has had a strip-mining law since 1966, but the first comprehensive attempts at control did not begin until the passage in 1977 of the Federal Surface Mining Control and Reclamation Act.

Also active in environmental matters is the Department of Environmental Protection, consisting of four divisions. The Division of Water administers the state's Safe Drinking Water and Clean Water acts and regulation of sewage disposal. The Division of Waste Management oversees solid waste disposal systems in the state. The Air Pollution Control Division monitors industrial discharges into the air and other forms of air pollution. Most air pollution has declined since the 1970s, with lead air concentrations down by 97% since 1970. A special division is concerned with Maxey Flats, a closed nuclear waste disposal facility in Fleming County, where leakage of radioactive materials was discovered.

There are 15 major dams in Kentucky, and more than 900 other dams. Flooding is a chronic problem in southeastern Kentucky, where strip-mining has exacerbated soil erosion. Kentucky's solid waste stream averaged 17 million lb a day in 1996 (4.4 lb a day per capita). There were 24 municipal landfills, and 115 of the state's 120 counties have recycling centers. Kentucky had 20 hazardous waste sites in 1995, when the state generated 6.5 million tons of such waste annually.

⁶POPULATION

Kentucky ranked 23d in population among the states in 1990 with a census population of 3,685,296. The estimated population in 1996 was 3,856,877, up 5% from 1990.

During the early decades of settlement, population grew rapidly, from a few hundred in 1780 to 564,317 in 1820, by which time Kentucky was the 6th most populous state. By 1900, however, when the population was 2,147,174, growth had slowed considerably. For most of the 20th century, Kentucky's growth rate has been significantly slower than the national average.

At the time of the 1990 census, Kentucky's population was 51% urban, far below the national norm of 75.2%. The population density in 1990 was 92.8 persons per sq mi (35.6 per sq km).

Louisville, the state's largest city, had an estimated 1996 population of about 270,308, down from 298,694 in 1980 and 361,706 in 1970. Lexington-Fayette urban county was next with 237,612 residents. Owensboro, with 53,645 residents was the state's third most populous city. The population of the Louisville (Ky.-Ind.) metropolitan area was 987,102. Population in the Lexington metropolitan area was estimated at 435,736 in 1995, up from 317,548 in 1980.

⁷ETHNIC GROUPS

Though a slave state, Kentucky never depended on a plantation economy. In 1830, almost 25% of the population was black. After the Civil War, a lack of jobs and migration to the industrial cities of the Midwest in the 1890s may have accounted for a dwindling black population. In 1990 the black population of Kentucky was relatively low at 263,000 (7.1%). Kentucky was a center of the American (or Know-Nothing) Party, a pre–Civil War movement whose majority were staunchly anti-immigration and anti-Catholic. With relatively little opportunity for industrial employment, Kentucky attracted small numbers of foreign immigrants in the 19th and 20th centuries. The state had only 34,119 foreign-born residents in 1990, accounting for 0.9% of the total population. Among persons reporting a single ancestry in the 1990 census, a total of 552,802 claimed English descent, 798,001 German, 695,853 Irish, 222,428 African-American, and 92,588 French.

There were 208,938 reporting American Indian origins in 1990. The 1990 census also found 4,264 Koreans, 2,367 Asian Indians, 3,275 Japanese, 1,340 Vietnamese, and 3,137 Chinese. A total of 22,000 state residents were of Hispanic origin, with 6,823 reporting Mexican ancestry and 2,692 Puerto Rican ancestry.

⁸LANGUAGES

Kentucky was a fought-over hunting ground for Ohio Shawnee, Carolina Cherokee, and Mississippi Chickawaw Indians, Placenames from this heritage include Etowah (Cherokee) and Paducah (Chickasaw).

Speech patterns in the state generally reflect the first settlers' Virginia and Kentucky backgrounds. South Midland features are best preserved in the mountains, but some common to Midland and Southern are widespread.

Other regional features are typically both South Midland and Southern. After a vowel, the /r/ may be weak or missing. *Coop* has the vowel of *put,* but *root* rhymes with *boot.* In southern Kentucky, earthworms are *redworms,* a burlap bag a *tow sack* or the Southern *grass sack,* and green beans *snap beans.* A young man may *carry,* not escort, his girlfriend to a party. Subregional terms appear in abundance. In the east, kindling is *pine,* a seesaw is a *ridyhorse,* and the freestone peach is an *openstone peach.* In central Kentucky, a moth is a *candlefly.*

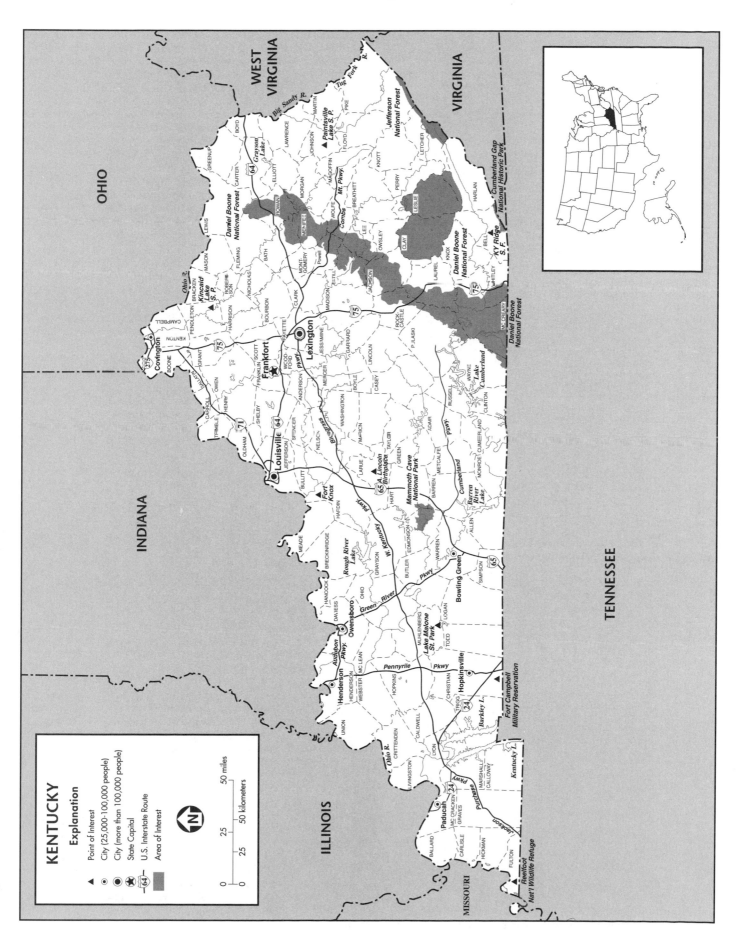

In 1990, 97.5% of all residents 5 years old and older spoke only English at home. The number of people who spoke other languages at home included:

Spanish	31,293	Korean	2,676
German	15,677	Chinese	2,596
French	13,543	Japanese	2,306

[9]RELIGIONS

Throughout its history, Kentucky has been predominantly Protestant. A group of New Light Baptists who, in conflict with established churches in Virginia, immigrated to Kentucky under the leadership of Lewis Craig, built the first church in the state in 1781, near Lancaster. The first Methodist Church was established near Danville in 1783; within a year, Roman Catholics had also built a church, and a presbytery of 12 churches had been organized. There were 42 churches in Kentucky by the time of statehood, with a total membership of 3,095.

Beginning in the last few years of the 18th century, the Great Revival sparked a new religious fervor among Kentuckians, a development that brought the Baptists and Methodists many new members. The revival, which had begun among the Presbyterians, led to a schism in that sect. Presbyterian minister Barton W. Stone organized what turned out to be the era's largest frontier revival meeting, at Cane Ridge (near Paris), in August 1801. Differences over doctrine led Stone and his followers to withdraw from the Synod of Kentucky in 1803, and they formed their own church, called simply "Christian." The group later formed an alliance with the sect now known as the Christian Church (Disciples of Christ).

As of 1990 there were 1,847,667 known Protestant adherents in Kentucky, of whom 962,945 belonged to the Southern Baptists Convention, 227,143 to the United Methodist Church, 66,798 to the Christian Church (Disciples of Christ), and 90,520 to the Christian Churches and Churches of Christ. The Roman Catholic Church, with 365,270 members at the beginning of 1990, is a large denomination in the state. There were an estimated 14,810 Jews in Kentucky in 1990.

[10]TRANSPORTATION

Statewide transportation developed slowly in Kentucky. Although freight and passengers were carried by river and later by rail during the 19th century, mountains and lack of good roads made land travel in eastern Kentucky so arduous that the region was for a long time effectively isolated from the rest of the state.

The first railroad in Kentucky, the Lexington and Ohio, opened on 15 August 1832 with a 26-mi (42-km) route from Lexington to Frankfort. Not until 1851 did the railroad reach the Ohio River. In November 1859, Louisville was connected with Nashville, Tenn., by the Louisville and Nashville Railroad; heavily used by the Union, it was well maintained during the Civil War. Railroad construction increased greatly after the conflict ended. By 1900, Kentucky had three times the track mileage it had had in 1870. As of December 1995, Kentucky had 2,892 rail mi (4,656 km), of which about 80% was Class I track. As of 1996, there were six Class I railroads operating in the state—that year, over 90% of the rail tonnage originating within Kentucky was coal. Rail service to the state, nearly all of which was freight, was provided by 17 railroads. There are four Amtrak stations in Kentucky; total ridership was 7,330 in 1995/96.

The trails of Indians and buffalo became the first roads in Kentucky. Throughout the 19th century, counties called on their citizens to maintain some roads, although maintenance was haphazard. The best roads were the toll roads. This system came to an end as a result of the "tollgate war" of the late 19th and early 20th centuries—a rebellion in which masked Kentuckians, demanding free roads, raided tollgates and assaulted their

keepers. Not until 1909, however, was a constitutional prohibition against the spending of state funds on highways abolished. In 1912, a state highway commission was created, and by 1920, roads had improved considerably. In 1996, Kentucky had 72,981 mi (117,427 km) of public roads. Local government controlled 45,123 mi (72,603 km) of Kentucky's roads; the state government 27,367 mi (44,034 km); and the federal government 491 mi (790 km). There were 763 mi (1,228 km) of interstate highway. In 1995, 1,629,780 automobiles, 989,989 trucks, and 32,996 motorcycles were registered in the state.

Until displaced by the railroads in the late 1800s, the Ohio River and its tributaries, along with the Mississippi, were Kentucky's primary commercial routes for trade with the South and the West. The Kentucky Port and River Development Commission was created by the legislature in 1966 to promote river transportation. Louisville, on the Ohio River, is the chief port. In 1995, traffic through the port totaled 9,603,218 tons, up from a 1982 low of only 5,701,896 tons. Paducah is the outlet port for traffic on the Tennessee River.

In 1996 there were 70 airports and 28 heliports in Kentucky. The largest of these is Cincinnati/Northern Kentucky International Airport, which enplaned 6,107,000 passengers in 1996.

[11]HISTORY

Six distinctive Indian cultures inhabited the region now known as Kentucky. The earliest nomadic hunters occupied the land for several thousand years, and were followed by the seminomadic Woodland and Adena cultures (1000 BC–AD 1000). Remains of the Mississippian and Fort Ancient peoples (AD 1000–1650) indicate that they were farmers and hunters who often dwelled in stockaded villages, subsisting on plentiful game and fish supplemented by crops of beans, corn, and squash.

No Indian nations resided in central and eastern Kentucky when these areas were first explored by British-American surveyors Thomas Walker and Christopher Gist in 1750 and 1751. The dominant Shawnee and Cherokee tribes utilized the region as a hunting ground, returning to homes in the neighboring territories of Ohio and Tennessee. Early descriptions of Kentucky generated considerable excitement about the fertile land and abundant wildlife. The elimination of French influence after the French and Indian War intensified pressures to open the region to American settlement—pressures that were initially thwarted by Britain's Proclamation of 1763, barring such western migration until Native American interests could be protected. This artificial barrier proved impossible to maintain, however, and the first permanent white settlement in Kentucky was finally established at Harrodstown (now Harrodsburg) in 1774 by a group of settlers from Virginia and Pennsylvania.

The most ambitious settlement scheme involved the Transylvania Land Company, a creation of North Carolina speculator Richard Henderson, assisted by the famed woodsman Daniel Boone. Henderson purchased a huge tract of land in central Kentucky from the Cherokee and established Fort Boonesborough. The first political meeting by whites in Kentucky, held at Fort Boonesborough on 23 May 1775, provided for rule by the Transylvania proprietors and a representative assembly. Henderson then sought approval for creation of a 14th colony, but the plan was blocked by Virginians determined to claim Kentucky as a possession of the Old Dominion. On 1 December 1776, the new state of Virginia incorporated its new County of Kentucky.

Kentucky's image soon changed from "western Eden" to "dark and bloody ground," as it became the scene of frequent clashes between Ohio-based Indians and the growing number of white settlements dotting the central Bluegrass region. Nevertheless, immigrants continued to come westward, down the Ohio River and through the Cumberland Gap. Kentucky became the principal conduit for migration into the Mississippi Valley. By the late 1780s, settlements were gaining in population, wealth, and maturity, and it was obvious that Kentucky could not long remain under the proprietorship of distant Virginia. Virginia yielded permission for the drafting of a Kentucky state constitution, and in June 1792, Kentucky entered the Union as the 15th state.

Over the next several decades, Kentucky prospered because of its diverse agricultural and processing industries. Although there were 225,483 slaves in the state in 1860, Kentucky was spared the evils of one-crop plantation agriculture. Nevertheless, its economy was tightly linked to the lower South's, a tie facilitated by the completion in 1829 of a canal around the Ohio River falls at Louisville. Hemp was one such connection; the plant was the principal source of rope and bagging used to bind cotton bales. Kentucky was also a major supplier of hogs, mules, workhorses, prepared meats, salt, flour, and corn for the plantation markets of the South. The state became a center for breeding and racing fine thoroughbred horses, an industry that thrives today on Bluegrass horse farms as virtually the state symbol. More important was the growing and processing of tobacco, an enterprise accounting for half the agricultural income of Kentucky farmers by 1860. Finally, whiskey began to be produced in vast quantities by the 1820s, culminating in the standardization of a fine, aged amber-red brew known throughout the world as bourbon, after Bourbon County.

Despite this economic development, several social and cultural problems disturbed the state. Much of the agricultural productivity came from farms employing slave labor, while the less affluent majority of white families often dwelled on less fertile upland farms. Efforts were repeatedly made to consider the slavery question. Leaders such as Henry Clay, Reverend Robert J. Breckinridge, and the fiery antislavery advocate Cassius Marcellus Clay urged an end to the "peculiar institution." Because of racial phobias and hostility to "Yankee meddling," the appeal was rejected. During the Civil War, Kentuckians were forced to choose sides between the Union, led in the north by Kentucky native Abraham Lincoln, and the Confederacy, led in the South by Kentucky native Jefferson Davis.

Although the state legislature finally opted for the Union side, approximately 30,000 men went south to Confederate service, while up to 100,000—including nearly 24,000 black soldiers—served in the Union army. For four years the state was torn with conflict over the collapse of slavery and wracked with guerrilla warfare and partisan feuds. Vigilantism and abuse of black people continued into the turbulent Reconstruction period, until legislative changes in the early 1870s began to restrain Ku Klux Klan violence and bring increased civil rights to black people.

The decades to 1900 saw other progress. Aided by liberal tax exemptions, railroad construction increased threefold, and development of timber and coal reserves began in eastern Kentucky. Industrial employment and productivity increased by more than 200%, drawing rural folk into the growing cities of Louisville and Lexington. In 1900, Kentucky ranked 1st among southern states in per capita income.

An economic and political crisis was developing, however, that would send shock waves across the state. Farmers, especially western Kentucky "dark leaf" tobacco farmers, were feeling the brunt of a prolonged price depression. The major national farm protest movements—the Grange, the Farmers' Alliance, and the Populist Party—all found support here, for by 1900 a third of all Kentucky farmers were landless tenants, and the size of the average family farm had fallen below 10 acres (40 hectares). Calls for currency inflation, reform of corporate monopolies, and improved rights for industrial workers reached a climax in the gubernatorial election of 1899. Republican William S. Taylor narrowly defeated the more reform-minded Democrat William

Goebel and was sworn into office. Democrats, claiming electoral fraud, instituted a recount. On 30 January 1900, Goebel, a state senator, was shot while approaching the capitol; as he lingered near death, the legislature, controlled by Democrats, declared him governor. Goebel died immediately thereafter, and his lieutenant governor, J. C. W. Beckham, was administered the oath of office. Further bloodshed was averted, the courts upheld the Goebel-Beckham election, and "Governor" Taylor fled the state.

Goebel's assassination weighed heavily, however. The state was polarized, outside investment plummeted, and Kentucky fell into a prolonged economic and moral depression. By 1940, the state ranked last among the 48 states in per capita income and was burdened by an image of clan feuding and homicide, poverty, and provincial courthouse politics. The Great Depression hit the state hard, though an end to Prohibition revived the dormant whiskey industry.

Kentucky has changed greatly since World War II. Between 1945 and 1980, the farm population decreased by 76% and the number of farms by 53%. In addition, tobacco has come under attack as a menace to public health. Although Kentucky remains one of the poorest states in the nation, positive change is evident even in relatively isolated rural communities—a result of better roads, education, and government programs. In response to lawsuits by a coalition of school systems in the 1980s, Kentucky's supreme court ruled in 1990 that the state's public education system was unconstitutional and ordered the legislature to design a new system of school funding and administration. The Kentucky Education Reform Act (KERA) was passed in 1990 and implemented over the next five years.

In 1983, Kentucky elected its first woman governor, former Lieutenant Governor Martha Layne Collins, a Democrat. In the early nineties, public corruption became a major issue in Kentucky politics. In a sting operation code-named Bobtrot, legislators were filmed by hidden cameras accepting payments from lobbyists. Fifteen state legislators, lobbyists and public figures were convicted or charged with bribery, extortion, fraud and racketeering. In response, the legislature passed major reform measures in 1993 to ensure a stricter code of ethics.

12STATE GOVERNMENT

Kentucky's current and fourth constitution was adopted on 28 September 1891. As of 31 December 1983, it had been amended 25 times. Earlier constitutions were adopted in 1792, 1799, and 1849.

The state legislature, called the general assembly, consists of the house of representatives, which has 100 members elected for two-year terms, and the senate, with 38 members elected for staggered four-year terms. A constitutional amendment approved by the voters in November 1979 provided for the election of legislators in even-numbered years, a change scheduled for completion by November 1988. The assembly meets in regular sessions of no more than 60 legislative days, beginning in January of each even-numbered year. The governor may also call special sessions. Except for revenue-raising measures, which must be introduced in the house of representatives, either chamber may introduce or amend a bill. Most bills may be passed by voting majorities equal to at least two-fifths of the membership of each house. Measures requiring an absolute majority in each house include those that appropriate money or create a debt, summon a constitutional convention, or enact emergency measures to take effect immediately. A majority of the members of each house is required to override the governor's veto.

A member of the senate must have been a citizen and resident of Kentucky for six years preceding election, a representative for two. A senator must be at least 30 and a representative at least 24. The constitutional limit of $12,000 for salaries of public officials, which is thought to apply to legislators, has been interpreted by the courts in terms of 1949 dollars and thus may be increased considerably—and has been. However, most legislators in Kentucky probably receive less than $12,000 per year, including travel and expense allowances, based on per diem in-session salaries of $100 and per diem expense allowances of $75.

The elected executive officers of Kentucky are the governor and lieutenant governor (who must run as a slate), secretary of state, attorney general, treasurer, auditor of public accounts, commissioner of agriculture, and three members of the Railroad Commission. All serve four-year terms, and a recent constitutional amendment allows a second term for those offices. The governor and lieutenant governor must each be 30 years old, US citizens, and residents of Kentucky for six years. As of 1996, the governor's salary was $88,645, and the lieutenant governor's $75,361.

A three-fifths majority of each house plus a voting majority of the electorate must approve any proposed constitutional amendment. Before a constitutional convention may be called, two regular sessions of the general assembly must approve it, and the call must be ratified at the polls by a majority voting on the proposal and equal to at last one-fourth the number of voters who cast ballots in the last general election.

To vote in Kentucky, one must be a US citizen, be at least 18 years of age, and have been a resident in the state for 30 days.

13POLITICAL PARTIES

A rift was created in Kentucky politics by the presidential election of 1824, which had to be determined in the US House of Representatives because neither John Quincy Adams nor Andrew Jackson won a majority of the Electoral College. Representative Henry Clay voted for Adams, despite orders by the Kentucky general assembly to support Jackson, thereby splitting the state into two factions: supporters of Clay, who became Whigs, and supporters of Jackson, who became Democrats. The Whigs dominated Kentucky politics until Clay's death in 1852, after which, as the Whigs divided over slavery, most Kentuckians turned first to the Native American (or Know-Nothing) Party and then to the Democrats. Regional divisions in party affiliation during the Civil War era, according to sympathy with the South and slavery (Democrats) or with the Union and abolition (Republicans), have persisted in the state's voting patterns. In general, the poorer mountain areas tend to vote Republican, while the more

affluent lowlanders in the Bluegrass and Pennyroyal tend to vote Democratic.

In 1994, Kentucky had 1,418,835 registered Democrats or 67% of the total number of registered voters; 615,732 registered Republicans, or 30% and 86,072 independents or 3%. In 1983, Martha Layne Collins, a Democrat, defeated Republican candidate Jim Bunning to become Kentucky's first woman governor. Democrat Paul E. Patton was elected governor in 1995. Democratic presidential incumbent Bill Clinton defeated Republican Bob Dole by a narrow margin in 1996—45.84% to 44.88%. After the November 1996 elections, Democrats held 20 seats in the state senate, Republicans 18; the Democrats continued to dominate the house of representatives, with 64 seats to the Republicans' 36. At the national level, Kentucky was represented by four-term Democratic Senator Wendell H. Ford, most recently reelected in 1992; Republican Senator Mitch McConnell, re-elected in 1996; and, in the US House of Representatives, by one Democrat and five Republicans. The 1996 elections marked only the third time in history that Republicans controlled the Congressional delegation (the second time was in 1994).

In 1993, there were 63 blacks holding public office. As of 1995, 12 women held statewide elected office.

14LOCAL GOVERNMENT

The form of Kentucky's county government is of English origin. The chief governing body is the fiscal court, consisting of the county judge executive and of the state's 120 counties, three to eight magistrates or commissioners. Other elected officials are the sheriff, jailer, attorney, and court clerk. All are elected for four-year terms; a 1984 constitutional amendment allows the sheriff to succeed himself in office. Except for jailers, many county officials earn their living by collecting a share of the fees for the services they render. In 1992, Kentucky had 120 counties, 435 municipalities, 176 school districts, and 590 special districts.

Cities are assigned by the general assembly to one of six classes on the basis of population. First-class cities have populations of 100,000 or more; second, 20,000 to 99,999; third, 8,000 to 19,999; fourth, 3,000 to 7,999; fifth, 1,000 to 2,999; and sixth, 999 to fewer. Kentucky has two first-class cities, Louisville and Lexington. There are 14 second-class cities and 22 third. The mayor or other chief executive officer in the top three classes must be elected; in the bottom classes, the executive may be either

Kentucky Presidential Vote by Political Parties, 1948–96

YEAR	ELECTORAL VOTE	KENTUCKY WINNER	DEMOCRAT	REPUBLICAN	STATES' RIGHTS DEMOCRAT	PROHIBITION	PROGRESSIVE	SOCIALIST
1948	11	*Truman (D)	466,756	341,210	10,411	1,245	1,567	1,284
1952	10	Stevenson (D)	495,729	495,029	—	1,161	—	—
1956	10	*Eisenhower (R)	476,453	572,192	—	2,145	—	—
1960	10	Nixon (R)	521,855	602,607	—	—	—	—
					STATES' RIGHTS			
1964	9	*Johnson (D)	669,659	372,977	3,469	—	—	—
					AMERICAN IND.			SOC. WORKERS
1968	9	*Nixon (R)	397,541	462,411	193,098			2,843
						AMERICAN	PEOPLE'S	
1972	9	*Nixon (R)	371,159	676,446	—	17,627	1,118	
1976	9	*Carter (D)	615,717	531,852	2,328	8,308	—	—
							LIBERTARIAN	CITIZENS
1980	9	*Reagan (R)	617,417	635,274	—	—	5,531	1,304
1984	9	*Reagan (R)	539,539	821,702	—	—	1,776	599
1988	9	*Bush (R)	580,368	734,281	4,994	1,256	2,118	—
					IND. (Perot)			
1992	8	*Clinton (D)	665,104	617,178	203,944	430	4,513	989
1996	8	*Clinton (D)	636,614	623,283	120,396	—	4,009	

*Won US presidential election.

elected by the people or appointed by a city council or commission. Mayors serve four-year terms; members of city legislative boards, also provided for in the state constitution, are elected for terms of two years. City officials must be residents of the cities and of the districts in which they are elected.

Other units of local government in Kentucky include urban counties and special-purpose districts, including districts for sewer and flood control and the 15 area-development districts for regional planning. The general assembly may create new local government units, although its power to create new counties is restricted. (Since 1912, it has created only one new county, McCreary.)

15 STATE SERVICES

An ombudsman in the Cabinet for Human Resources receives citizens' complaints concerning services offered by that agency. The Financial Disclosure Review Board was established in 1975 to review the financial status of constitutional officers and government management personnel in order to prevent conflicts of interest.

Educational services are provided through the Education, Arts, and Humanities Cabinet, and the Department of Education. The Council on Postsecondary Education oversees the state-supported colleges, universities, and technical schools. The Human Rights Commission and the Commission on Women are administered by the governor's office. Rehabilitation services, including the Eastern Kentucky Comprehensive Rehabilitation Center, are under the jurisdiction of the Department of Education. Transportation services are administered by the Transportation Cabinet. Health, welfare, and other human services are provided primarily by two cabinet divisions, the Cabinet for Families and Children and the Cabinet for Health Services. Among the agencies that provide public protection services are the Department of Military Affairs, the Public Protection and Regulation Cabinet, and the Consumer Protection Division of the Department of Law. Corrections and parole were transferred in 1981 from the Department of Justice to the Corrections Cabinet. The Department of State Police is part of the Justice Cabinet.

Housing rights for members of minority groups are provided by the Commission on Human Rights. The Department of Economic Development oversees industrial and community development programs within the Commerce Cabinet. Also assisting in community development are programs within the Department of Local Government, which was organized as an independent agency of the office of the governor in 1982.

Natural resource protection services are provided by the separate departments of Natural Resources, Environmental Protection, and Surface Mining Reclamation and Enforcement, all within the Natural Resources and Environmental Protection Cabinet. The Kentucky state park system is administered by the Department of Parks in the Tourism Cabinet, which also includes the Department of Travel Development, Kentucky Horse Park, and the Department of Fish and Wildlife Resources. The Energy Cabinet, created in 1978, is within the Department of Energy Research and Development.

Labor services are administered by the Labor Cabinet; its areas of concern include labor-management relations, occupational safety and health, and occupational injury and disease compensation.

16 JUDICIAL SYSTEM

In accordance with a constitutional amendment approved in 1975 and fully implemented in 1978, judicial power in Kentucky is vested in a unified court of justice. The highest court is the supreme court, consisting of a chief justice and six associate justices. It has appellate jurisdiction and also bears responsibility for the budget and administration of the entire system. Justices

are elected from seven supreme court districts for terms of eight years; they elect one of their number to serve for the remaining term as chief justice.

The court of appeals consists of 14 judges, 2 elected from each supreme court district. The court divides itself into panels of at least 3 judges which may sit anywhere in the state. The judges also serve eight-year terms and elect one of their number to serve a four-year term as chief judge.

Circuit courts, with original and appellate jurisdiction, are held in each county. There are 56 judicial circuits. Circuit court judges are elected for terms of eight years. In circuits with more than one judge, the judges elect one of their number as chief judge for a two-year term. Under the revised judicial system, district courts, which have limited and original jurisdiction, replaced various local and county courts. There is no mandatory retirement age. A total of 12,179 attorneys were actively practicing as of 1997.

In 1997 there were 13,559 prisoners in state prisons in Kentucky. Between 1990 and 1995 Kentucky's prison population increased by almost 45%. The Department of Corrections maintains 12 correctional institutions, including a career development center, a forestry camp, and two farm centers. There are also 3 private minimum-custody prisons. In 1980, the department entered into a consent decree to eliminate overcrowding and provide more humane conditions at the state reformatory and penitentiary. Death by electrocution is the only method of execution. The state's first execution since 1976 took place in 1997; 28 prisoners were under sentence of death as of 29 April that year.

In the past, Kentucky had a reputation for lawlessness. In 1890, more homicides were reported in Kentucky than in any other state except New York; blood feuds among Kentucky families were notorious throughout the country. In recent years, however, crime rates have diminished to a comparatively low level. The total crime rate in 1995 was 3,351.7 crimes per 100,000, including 364.7 violent crimes and 2,987 property crimes.

17 ARMED FORCES

The US Department of Defense had 66,386 personnel in Kentucky in 1996, including 33,448 active-duty military and 10,097 civilians. US Army installations in the state include Ft. Knox (site of the US gold depository) near Louisville, with 14,297 military and civilian personnel, and Ft. Campbell (partly in Tennessee), with 26,217 military and civilian personnel. Kentucky received $874 million in prime federal defense contracts in 1995/96.

As of 1 July 1996 there were 364,000 veterans of US military service living in Kentucky. Of these, World War I veterans numbered fewer than 500; World War II, 98,000; Korean conflict, 61,000; Viet Nam era, 117,000; and Persian Gulf War, 28,000. Kentucky veterans received more than $630 million in benefits during 1995/96.

Kentucky national guard and reserve units had 22,846 personnel in 1996. In 1993, the Kentucky State Police employed 900 full-time sworn officers, or two per 10,000 residents.

18 MIGRATION

During the frontier period, Kentucky first attracted settlers from eastern states, especially Virginia and North Carolina. Prominent among early foreign immigrants were people of English and Scotch-Irish ancestry, who tended to settle in the Kentucky highlands, which resembled their Old World homelands.

Kentucky's black population increased rapidly during the first 40 years of statehood. By the 1830s, however, slavery had become less profitable in the state, and many Kentucky owners either moved to the Deep South or sold their slaves to new owners in that region. During the 1850s, nearly 16% of Kentucky's slave population—more than 43,000 blacks—were sold or moved from the state. A tiny percentage of Kentucky's blacks, probably fewer than 200, emigrated to Liberia under the auspices of the Kentucky Colonization Society.

The waves of European immigration that inundated many states during the late 19th century left Kentucky virtually untouched. In 1890, Kentucky's population was nearly 98% native-born. At that time, there were more than 284,000 blacks in the state—a number that was to fall precipitously until the 1950s because of migration to industrial cities in the Midwest.

Until the early 1970s there was a considerable out-migration of whites, especially from eastern Kentucky to industrial areas of Ohio, Indiana, and other nearby states. The state's net loss to migration from 1960 to 1970 totaled 153,000 persons. This tide of out-migration was temporarily reversed during the 1970s, with Kentucky recording a net migration gain of 131,000 persons. From 1980 to 1990, net loss to migration came to about 22,000. Between 1990 and 1996, Kentucky had net gains of 74,010 in domestic migration and 9,729 in international migration. In 1996, 2,019 foreign immigrants arrived in the state. As of 1990, 77.4% of the state's residents had been born in Kentucky. About 57% of the residents age 5 and older lived in the same house in 1990 as in 1985. Of those who lived in a different house, only 19% did so in another state.

19 INTERGOVERNMENTAL COOPERATION

Among the many interstate regional commissions in which Kentucky participates are the Appalachian Regional Commission, Interstate Mining Compact, Interstate Oil and Gas Compact, Southern Growth Policies Compact, Ohio River Valley Water Sanitation Compact, and Tennessee-Tombigbee Waterway Compact. Kentucky also participates in the Tennessee Valley Authority. The Council of State Governments, founded in 1925 to foster interstate cooperation, has its headquarters in Lexington.

In 1995/96, Kentucky received $3.4 billion in federal aid.

20 ECONOMY

Between statehood and the Civil War, Kentucky was one of the preeminent agricultural states, partly because of good access to river transportation down the Ohio and the Mississippi to southern markets. Coal mining had become an important part of the economy by the late 19th century. Although agriculture is still important in Kentucky, manufacturing has grown rapidly since World War II and was, by the mid-1980s, the most important sector of the economy as a source of both employment and personal income. Kentucky leads the nation in the production of bituminous coal and whiskey, and ranks 2d in tobacco output.

In contrast to the generally prosperous Bluegrass area and the growing industrial cities, eastern Kentucky, highly dependent on coal mining, has long been one of the poorest regions in the US. Beginning in the early 1960s, both the state and federal governments undertook programs to combat poverty in Appalachian Kentucky. Per capita personal income increased faster in this region than in the US as a whole between 1965 and 1976, and unemployment decreased between 1970 and 1978; however, personal income was still much lower, and unemployment higher, than in the rest of the state.

In 1979, 29% of the people living in the state's 49 Appalachian counties were below the federal poverty level, compared to 17% of the people in Kentucky's other counties; in 1983, 34 of the 49 Appalachian counties had unemployment rates greater than the state average of 11.6%.

In 1994, contributions to Kentucky's gross state product of $86,485 million were as follows: private goods–producing indus-

tries, $31,900 million; private services–producing industries, $42,711 million; and government, $11,874 million.

In 1995, Kentucky's per capita personal income was $18,849, which ranked 42nd nationally. In 1996, there were 18,794 bankruptcy filings in the state, up almost 31% from the previous year.

21 INCOME

Kentucky has long been one of the poorest of the 50 states, and in 1996, per capita personal income was $19,687 for a rank of 42nd among the 50 states.

Total disposable personal income rose to $66.8 billion in 1996 from $63.8 billion in 1995. Median household income in 1995 was $29,810. Incomes were highest in the Louisville and Lexington-Fayette metropolitan areas; in Kentucky's share of the Cincinnati, Ohio, and Evansville, Ind., metropolitan regions; and in Franklin County (Frankfort). In the state as a whole, 14.7% of all Kentuckians were below the federal poverty line in 1995.

22 LABOR

According to federal statistics, Kentucky's civilian labor force in December 1996 was about 1,893,500. A total of 1,790,300 persons held jobs and 103,200 were unemployed, for an unemployment rate of 5.5%. The urban areas of Louisville, Lexington, and Owensboro together contained only 44% of the labor force.

At the end of 1996, the wholesale and retail trade industry was the largest nonfarm employer in Kentucky, with 419,700 employees, followed by the services industry with 414,400 employees; manufacturing, 310,000; government, 294,600; transportation, communications, and public utilities, 95,100; construction, 75,600; finance, insurance, and real estate, 67,300; and mining, 24,500.

Although a small number of trade unions existed in Kentucky before the 1850s, it was not until after the Civil War that substantial unionization took place. During the 1930s, there were long, violent struggles between the United Mine Workers (UMW) and the mine owners of eastern Kentucky. The UMW won bargaining rights in 1938, but after World War II the displacement of workers because of mechanization, a drastic drop in the demand for coal, and evidence of mismanagement and corruption within the UMW served to undercut the union's position. Following the announcement by the UMW in 1962 that its five hospitals would be sold or closed, unemployed mine workers began protracted picketing of nonunion mines. Episodes of violence accompanied the movement, which succeeded in closing the mines but not in keeping them closed. The protests dissipated when public works jobs were provided for unemployed fathers among the miners, beginning in late 1973. Increased demand for coal in the 1970s led to a substantial increase in jobs for miners, and the UMW, under different leaders, began a new drive to organize the Cumberland Plateau.

Union membership amounted to 12.6% of the labor force in 1995, and 22% among private sector workers in manufacturing.

23 AGRICULTURE

With cash receipts totaling $3 billion—$1.4 million from crops and $1.6 billion from livestock—Kentucky ranked 25th among the 50 states in farm marketings in 1996.

Kentucky tobacco, first marketed in New Orleans in 1787, quickly became the state's most important crop. Kentucky ranked 1st among tobacco-producing states until it gave way to North Carolina in 1929. Corn has long been one of the state's most important crops, not only for livestock feed but also as a major ingredient in the distilling of whiskey. Although hemp is no longer an important crop in Kentucky, its early significance to Kentucky farmers, as articulated in Congress by Henry Clay, was partly responsible for the establishment by the US of a protective tariff system. From 1849 to 1870, the state produced nearly all the hemp grown in the US.

In 1995 there were approximately 88,000 farms in Kentucky (down from 91,000 in 1991), with an average size of 159 acres (64 hectares). In 1990, almost half of Kentucky's population was considered rural. There are approximately 422,000 agriculture-related jobs in Kentucky, which means about one-fourth of the state's population owes its living to agriculture. In 1995 Kentucky farms produced some 302,250,000 lb of tobacco (down from 420,000,000 in 1994). Leading field crops in 1996 (in bushels) included corn for grain, 123,120,000; soybeans, 41,400,000; wheat, 24,380,000; sorghum, 1,848,000; and barley, 1,050,000. Farmers also harvested 5,790,000 tons of hay, including 1,170,000 tons of alfalfa.

24ANIMAL HUSBANDRY

Since early settlement days, livestock raising has been an important part of Kentucky's economy. The Bluegrass region, which offers excellent pasturage and drinking water, has become renowned as a center for horse breeding and racing.

In 1985 there were 223,000 horses in Kentucky, including thoroughbreds, quarter horses, American saddle horses, Arabians, and standardbreds. In 1989, over 8,050 thoroughbred foals were produced, more than in any other state.

In 1997, Kentucky had an estimated 2.55 million cattle and calves worth $1.02 billion. In 1996, Kentucky farmers had an estimated 625,000 hogs and pigs, worth around $51 million. Kentucky produced an estimated 2.02 billion lb of milk from 162,000 dairy cows in 1995.

25FISHING

Fishing is of little commercial importance in Kentucky. Federal hatcheries distributed 777,324 (218,041 lb) coldwater species fish (mostly rainbow trout) and 2 million fish eggs within the state in 1995/96, when Kentucky had over 581,858 fishing license holders.

26FORESTRY

In 1992 there were 12,714,000 acres (5,145,000 hectares) of forested land in Kentucky—50% of the state's land area. Some 97% of the forestland is classified as commercially viable for timber production.

The most heavily forested areas are in the river valleys of eastern Kentucky, in the Appalachians. In 1995, Kentucky produced 883.5 million board feet of lumber, nearly all of it in hardwoods. The Division of Forestry of the Department of Natural Resources manages approximately 30,000 acres (12,300 hectares) of state-owned forestland and operates two forest tree nurseries producing 7–9 million seedling trees a year.

There are two national forests—the Daniel Boone and the Jefferson on Kentucky's eastern border—enclosing two national wilderness areas. National parks in the state include the Mammoth Cave National Park and the Cumberland Gap National Historical Park on Kentucky's eastern border.

27MINING

The value of nonfuel mineral production in Kentucky in 1995 was about $401 million, down nearly $27 million from the 1994 record level, primarily because of a 12% drop in the production of crushed stone. Nationally, Kentucky's position was 31st in nonfuel value, compared to 28th the year before.

Crushed stone accounted for about 57% ($230 million) of Kentucky's nonfuel mineral production value in 1995. Nationally, the state ranked 3d in ball clays and 11th in crushed stone. The state's mines also produce significant quantities of construction sand and gravel, masonry cement, and common clays.

28ENERGY AND POWER

At the end of 1995, Kentucky had 37 electric generating plants. Total installed capacity was 17.8 million kW in 1995, when 86.16 billion kWh of power were produced. Southern Kentucky shares in the power produced by the Tennessee Valley Authority, which supports a coal-fired steam electric plant in Kentucky at Paducah.

Most of Kentucky's coal came from the western fields of the interior coal basin until late in the 19th century, when the lower-sulfur Cumberland Plateau coal reserves of the Appalachian region were discovered. In 1996, eastern Kentucky produced an estimated 114,908,000 tons of coal, and western Kentucky 35,155,000. Kentucky, with 598 active mines in 1995, has more mines than any other state. All coal mined is bituminous. Much of the mining in Kentucky is done by out-of-state companies; a number of oil companies have acquired coal companies as a hedge against declining petroleum resources. Recoverable coal reserves as of 1995 were estimated at 516 million tons in western Kentucky and 763 million tons in eastern Kentucky, or 6.3% of the nation's reserves.

In 1996, Kentucky produced 3,602,000 barrels of crude petroleum and was estimated to have about 24,000,000 barrels of proved oil reserves. The oil industry was centered in Henderson County. In 1995, Kentucky marketed 74.7 billion cu ft of natural gas. As of the beginning of 1996, the state was estimated to have proved reserves totaling 1,044 billion cu ft of natural gas.

Oil shale is found in a band stretching from Lawrence County in the northeast through Madison and Washington counties in central Kentucky to Jefferson County in the north-central region.

29INDUSTRY

Although primarily an agricultural state during the 19th century, Kentucky was a leading supplier of manufactures to the South before the Civil War. Kentucky ranked 20th among the 50 states with shipments of manufactured goods valued at $53.5 billion in 1991. Manufacturing activities are largely concentrated in Louisville and Jefferson County and other cities bordering the Ohio River. In 1993, Kentucky was the leading producer of American whiskey. It also produced 9.5% of the nation's trucks in assembly plants at Louisville (480,522 units) as well as 256,638 automobiles at Bowling Green and Georgetown. In 1995, the value of shipments for manufacturers in Kentucky totaled $79.405 billion.

The following table shows value of shipments in 1995 for selected major industries:

Transportation equipment	$24,240,600,000
Chemical and allied products	6,775,500,000
Industrial machinery and equipment	6,324,600,000
Primary metal industries	5,743,000,000
Electronic and other electronic equipment	5,269,400,000
Fabricated metal products	3,760,000,000
Tobacco products	3,542,800,000

In 1997, Kentucky was the headquarters for 5 Fortune 500 companies: Ashland, Humana, Providian, LG&E Energy, and Vencor.

In 1995, there were 351 US patents awarded to Kentucky citizens.

30COMMERCE

In 1994, Kentucky had 6,118 wholesale establishments, with a total personal income of $2.5 billion. Wholesale sales totaled $31.6 billion in 1992, and retail sales totaled $25.3 billion, 26th in the nation. Personal income from retail sales totaled $5.1 billion in 1994. The KFC Corp., which owns and franchises Kentucky Fried Chicken restaurants, has its headquarters in Louisville, as does Papa John's, another restaurant chain.

Kentucky's exports to foreign countries in 1996 totaled $6.9 billion.

31CONSUMER PROTECTION

The Consumer Protection Division of the Attorney General's Office was created in 1972 to assist consumers with disputes in the marketplace through the mediation of consumer complaints; the litigation of violators of the Consumer Protection Statute; and the education of consumers. The mediation branch handles consumer complaints.

32BANKING

Kentucky had 276 insured commercial banks, as of 1996. Total assets stood at $49.6 billion. Loans amounted to $33.3 billion; insured deposits totaled $37.9 billion.

As of 1996 there were 51 insured savings institutions in Kentucky.

33INSURANCE

In 1996, Kentuckians held some 2.5 million life insurance policies, with a total value of $142.3 billion. The average amount of life insurance per family was $93,200. In 1996 Kentuckians received life insurance benefits of $420.2 million.

Premiums written by property and liability insurance companies in 1996 totaled $3.2 billion.

34SECURITIES

There are no securities exchanges in Kentucky. As of May 1997, there were 1,304 securities brokers and dealers (involving 41,376 registered agents), and 357 investment advisory organizations registered to conduct business in the state.

35PUBLIC FINANCE

The Kentucky biennial state budget is prepared by the Governor's Office for Policy and Management late in each odd-numbered year and submitted by the governor to the general assembly for approval. The fiscal year runs from July 1 to June 30. The following is a summary of revenues (available funds) and appropriations for fiscal years 1996/97 and 1997/98 from the enacted 1996–98 Budget of the Commonwealth (in millions):

AVAILABLE FUNDS	1996/97	1997/98
General fund	$ 5,495.3	$ 5,729.0
Road fund	989.1	981.4
Agency funds	2,451.1	2,502.8
Federal funds	3,896.9	3,949.9
Other funds	1,043.1	429.3
TOTALS	$13,875.4	$13,592.4
APPROPRIATIONS		
Human resources	$ 5,788.8	$ 4,054.1
Education and humanities	2,775.7	2,852.5
Higher education	2,019.9	2,076.3
Transportation	1,496.6	1,323.7
Other appropriations	3,794.4	3,285.8
TOTALS	$13,875.4	$13,592.4

For fiscal 1996/97, the total appropriation-supported state debt was more than $3.5 billion. Per capita appropriation-supported state debt is $777.

36TAXATION

Kentucky collected more than $5.975 billion in state taxes in 1996. As of 1997, the tax rate on personal income ranged from 2% on the first $3,000 to 6% on the amount over $8,000. Corporate income was taxed at a rate of 4% to 8.25%. Kentucky imposes a license tax on oil, a severance tax on natural gas, and severance and processing taxes on coal and other materials, all at a rate of 4.5%. Kentucky also levies a 6% sales and use tax (excluding food and drugs), motor fuels taxes, an inheritance tax (excluding Class A beneficiaries after 30 June 1998), taxes on motor vehicles, and excise taxes on alcoholic beverages and cigarettes.

In 1995, Kentucky's total share of the federal income tax burden was $5.6 billion.

37ECONOMIC POLICY

The Kentucky Cabinet for Economic Development seeks to encourage businesses to locate in Kentucky and to expand through its job creation program. Various available programs offer companies tax credits totaling as much as 100% of their investment. Low interest loans and bonds also are available. Additional incentives are available to qualified businesses for locating in one of Kentucky's enterprise zones or in Kentucky's federal empowerment zone, one of only three in the nation. Incentives also are available for tourist attractions that locate in Kentucky. Regional industrial parks are currently being developed to provide available, accessible, and marketable land in areas where an abundant labor force is available.

38HEALTH

In 1995, Kentucky's birthrate was 13.5 per 1,000 inhabitants, below the national average of 14.8. The state's death rate was 9.6 per 1,000 inhabitants, higher than the national average of 8.8. The infant mortality rate was 7.5 per 1,000 live births for 1994/95. In 1995, 7,438 legal abortions were performed in Kentucky, for a ratio of 143 per 1,000 live births. In the same year, Kentucky ranked higher than the national averages in death rates from heart diseases, 313.2 per 100,000 residents; cancer, 229.4; cerebrovascular diseases, 65.0; accidents and adverse effects, 42.6 (of which motor vehicle accidents accounted for 21.7); and suicide, 12.5. There were 8.13 AIDS cases per 100,000 population in 1995 according to the Centers for Disease Control. Black lung (pneumoconiosis) has been recognized as a serious work-related illness among coal miners.

In 1995, Kentucky's 124 hospitals had 17,352 beds and recorded 524,647 admissions. At the start of 1995 there were 7,671 physicians in Kentucky. In 1995, there were 2,608 active licensed dentists in the state.

There were 575,000 Medicare and 638,000 Medicaid recipients in 1994 receiving $2.2 and $1.8 billion in health care, respectively. At least 15% of Kentucky residents were uninsured during 1994.

39SOCIAL WELFARE

In 1996, 176,600 recipients received aid to families with dependent children. Payments averaged $285/month in that year. In 1996, the food stamp program had an average monthly participation of 478,425. Kentucky children participated in the school lunch program in 1996, at a federal cost of $95.9 million.

With the enactment of the Personal Responsibility and Work Opportunity Reconciliation Act of 1996, the US government has changed the form and regulations for many of its social welfare programs; most significantly, it replaces Aid to Families with Dependent Children (AFDC), an open-ended entitlement program, with Temporary Assistance for Needy Families (TANF), a limited system of assistance funded largely through federal block grants. The reform act also impacts the food stamp program, the Supplemental Security Income program, and the child nutrition program. The law took effect on 1 July 1997 and provided $16.38 billion in block grants for fiscal years 1997–2002. The grants are to be divided among the states based on an equation involving the numbers of former AFDC recipients in each state. Because many of the bill's provisions have yet to be implemented into state-by-state policy, it was not possible to include the details of each state's programs for this edition of this work.

In 1996, 711,770 Kentuckians received Social Security benefits; their average monthly payment was $669. Federal Supplemental Security Income payments went to 165,286 persons in 1996, averaging $336 a month.

There is no employee payroll deduction for unemployment insurance. All unemployment benefits were derived from the tax on employer payrolls collected by the state for the Federal Unemployment Insurance Fund. The average unemployment benefit check was $167.26 in 1995.

40HOUSING

In 1996, Kentucky had 1,610,000 year-round housing units, 1,456,000 of which were occupied. In 1996, 18,778 privately owned units, valued at $15 billion, were authorized for construction, 14,056 of which were single-family dwellings. About 16% of all year-round housing units were built before 1939, 20% between 1980 and 1990. In 1993 just under 3% of all housing units lacked full plumbing facilities, well above the national average of 1.1%. The median cost for an owner with a mortgage was $536 per month in 1990, the last year for which figures are available. Median rent was $319 per month. During 1995/96, Kentucky received $288.9 million in aid from the US Department of Housing and Urban Development, including $54.4 million in community development block grants.

41EDUCATION

Kentucky was relatively slow to establish and support its public education system and has consistently ranked below the national average in per capita spending on education and in the educational attainments of its citizens. In 1990 the US Department of Labor reported that only 68.7% of all adults, 41st in the nation, had completed four years of high school, far below the national average of 77.6%; only 15.3% had completed four or more years of college, placing Kentucky 41st among the states and well below the national average of 21.3%. Expenditures per pupil on education by state and local governments totaled $5,051 in 1994/95, ranking Kentucky 30th among the states and below the national average of $5,526.

In 1995, 639,251 students attended public schools in Kentucky, and the number of teachers was 37,407. The estimated average salary of a public school teacher in 1994/95 was $34,232, ranking Kentucky 28th among the states and below the national average of $38,442.

During 1992/93, Kentucky's higher education facilities included 26 colleges and universities, 3 junior colleges, and 14 community colleges. In the fall of 1994, total enrollment at these institutions was over 182,577 students. The University of Kentucky, established in 1865 at Lexington, is the state's largest public institution, with an enrollment on the Lexington campus of 24,200 in 1992/93. The state-supported University of Louisville (1798) had an enrollment of 23,635. Loans and grants to Kentucky students are provided by the Kentucky Higher Education Assistance Authority.

In 1990 the Kentucky Education Reform Act established SEEK (Support Education Excellence in Kentucky). SEEK is a program that balances the available education dollars among poor and wealthy counties. The government allocated $2.8 billion to SEEK in 1993 and 1994.

42ARTS

The Actors Theater of Louisville holds a yearly festival of new American plays. The city also has a resident ballet company. The Louisville Orchestra has recorded numerous works by contemporary composers. The Kentucky Arts Council, a division of the Kentucky Department of the Arts within the Commerce Cabinet, is authorized to promote the arts through such programs as Arts in Education and the State Arts Resources Program.

Bluegrass, a form of country music performed on fiddle and banjo and played at a rapid tempo, is named after the style pioneered by Kentuckian Bill Monroe and his Blue Grass Boys.

Kentucky generated $589,000 from federal sources in support of its art programs. The NEA contributed $663,000 to arts programs and $764,000 to the Kentucky Arts Council. The Council also received $11,972,600 from the state. Private source contributions were $41 million. The state offered arts education to 23,100 school children. As of 1991, Kentucky had 200 arts associations and 51 local art associations. Audiences for Kentucky's art programs totaled 41,200,000. There were 188,589 contributing artists.

Project Outreach 1992, sponsored by the Kentucky Arts Council and the Ashland Oil Foundation, contributed financial resources to support the American Dance Ensemble of Lexington and New York. In 1991/92, the NEA contributed $25,000 to support cultural events in the Cumberland area featuring mountain music, theater, and dance. The Kentucky Arts Council received funding from the state to develop its arts education programs.

43LIBRARIES AND MUSEUMS

In 1995/96 there were 116 public libraries, 70 branches, and 107 bookmobiles in Kentucky, with a total of 7,109,315 volumes, including those in bookmobiles. The regional library system of 14 districts included university libraries and the state library at Frankfort, as well as city and county libraries. The Kentucky Historical Society in Frankfort also maintains a research library of more than 80,000 volumes.

The state has more than 103 museums. Art museums include the University of Kentucky Art Museum and the Headley-Whitney Museum in Lexington, the Allen R. Hite Art Institute at the University of Louisville, and the J. B. Speed Art Museum, also in Louisville. Among Kentucky's equine museums are the International Museum of the Horse and the American Horse Museum, both in Lexington, and the Kentucky Derby Museum in Louisville. The John James Audubon Museum is located in Audubon State Park at Henderson.

Leading historical sites include Abraham Lincoln's birthplace at Hodgenville and the Mary Todd Lincoln and Henry Clay homes in Lexington. The Kentucky Historical Society in Frankfort operates three museums and supports a mobile museum system that brings exhibits on Kentucky history to schools, parks, and local gatherings, and aids over 400 local historical organizations.

44COMMUNICATIONS

Only 90.9% of all occupied housing units in the state had a telephone in March 1993.

In 1922, Kentucky's first radio broadcasting station, WHAS, was established. By 1996 there were 297 radio stations, 124 AM and 173 FM. That year there were 24 commercial and 13 public television broadcasting stations. As of 1993 there were seven large cable television systems serving Kentucky.

45PRESS

In 1997, Kentucky had 22 daily newspapers (5 morning, 17 evening), and 14 Sunday papers. The following table shows the leading Kentucky newspapers with their 1997 circulations:

AREA	NAME	DAILY	SUNDAY
Frankfort	*State Journal* (e,S)	10,609	—
Lexington	*Herald–Leader* (m)	115,369	165,795
Louisville	*Courier–Journal* (m,S)	236,864	323,697

46ORGANIZATIONS

The 1992 US Census of Service Industries counted 823 organizations in Kentucky, including 203 business associations; 414 civic, social, and fraternal associations; and 206 other membership organizations. Notable organizations with headquarters in Kentucky include the Thoroughbred Club of America and the Burley Tobacco Growers Cooperative Association (both in Lexington); the Burley Auction Warehouse Association (Mt. Sterling); and the Association of Dark Leaf Tobacco Dealers and Exporters and the American Saddlebred Horse Association (both in Louisville).

47TOURISM, TRAVEL, AND RECREATION

Travelers staying for a day or overnight spent over $3.5 million in 1993 within Kentucky. One of the state's top tourist attractions is Mammoth Cave National Park, which contains an estimated 150 mi (241 km) of underground passages. Other units of the national park system in Kentucky include a re-creation of Abraham Lincoln's birthplace in Hodgenville and Cumberland Gap National Historical Park, which extends into Tennessee and Virginia.

As of 1994, the state operated 15 resort parks (13 of them year round). The state also operates 15 recreational parks and 9 shrines. Breaks Interstate Park, on the Kentucky-Virginia border, is noted for the Russell Fork River Canyon, which is 1,600 feet (488 meters) deep; the park is supported equally by the two states.

In 1979, the Kentucky Horse Park opened in Lexington. The Kentucky State Fair is held every August at Louisville. In 1995, 519,040 hunters and 650,561 fishermen were licensed.

48SPORTS

There are no major league professional sports teams in Kentucky. There is a minor league baseball team in Louisville, the Redbirds of the Triple-A American Association; however, the team was scheduled to leave the city by 1998.

The first known horse race in Kentucky was held in 1783. The annual Kentucky Derby, first run on 17 May 1875, has become the single most famous event in US thoroughbred racing. Held on the 1st Saturday in May at Churchill Downs in Louisville, the Derby is one of three races for three-year-olds constituting the Triple Crown and offers a gross purse of $985,900. Keeneland Race Course in Lexington is the site of the Blue Grass Stakes and other major thoroughbred races. The Kentucky Futurity, an annual highlight of the harness racing season, is usually held on the 1st Friday in October at the Red Mile in Lexington.

Rivaling horse racing as a spectator sport is collegiate basketball. The University of Kentucky Wildcats won NCAA Division I basketball championships in 1948–49, 1951, 1958, 1978, and 1996, and the National Invitation Tournament in 1946 and 1976. The University of Louisville Cardinals captured the NCAA crown in 1980 and 1986, having won an NIT title in 1956. Kentucky Wesleyan, at Owensboro, was the NCAA Division II titleholder in 1966, 1968–69, 1973, 1987, and 1990.

49FAMOUS KENTUCKIANS

Kentucky has been the birthplace of one US president, four US vice presidents, the only president of the Confederacy, and several important jurists, statesmen, writers, artists, and sports figures.

Abraham Lincoln (1809–65) the 16th president of the US, was born in Hodgenville, Hardin (now Larue) County, and spent his developing years in Indiana and Illinois. Elected as the first Republican president in 1860 and reelected in 1864, Lincoln reflected his Kentucky roots in his opposition to secession and the expansion of slavery, and in his conciliatory attitude toward the defeated southern states. His wife, Mary Todd Lincoln (1818–82), was a native of Lexington.

Kentucky-born US vice presidents have all been Democrats. Richard M. Johnson (1780–1850) was elected by the Senate after a deadlock in the Electoral College; John C. Breckinridge (1821–75) in 1857 became the youngest man ever to hold the office; Adlai E. Stevenson (1835–1914) served in Grover Cleveland's second administration. The best-known vice president was Alben W. Barkley (1877–1956), who, before his election with President Harry S Truman in 1948, was a US senator and longtime Senate majority leader.

Frederick M. Vinson (1890–1953) was the only Kentuckian to serve as chief justice of the US. Noteworthy associate justices were John Marshall Harlan (1833–1911), famous for his dissent from the segregationist *Plessy v. Ferguson* decision (1896), and Louis B. Brandeis (1856–1941), the first Jew to serve on the Supreme Court and a champion of social reform.

Henry Clay (b.Virginia, 1777–1852) came to Lexington in 1797 and went on to serve as speaker of the US House of Representatives, secretary of state, and US senator; he was also a three-time presidential candidate. Other important federal officeholders from Kentucky include attorneys general John Breckinridge (b.Virginia, 1760–1806) and John J. Crittenden (1787–1863), who also served with distinction as US senator; treasury secretaries Benjamin H. Bristow (1830–96) and John G. Carlisle (1835–1910); and US senator John Sherman Cooper (b.1901). Zachary Taylor (1784–1850), 12th US president, spent much of his adult life in Kentucky and is buried there.

Among noteworthy state officeholders, Isaac Shelby (b.Maryland 1750–1826) was a leader in the movement for statehood and the first governor of Kentucky. William Goebel (1856–1900) was the only US governor assassinated in office. Albert B. ("Happy") Chandler (1898–1991), twice governor, also served as US senator and as commissioner of baseball.

A figure prominently associated with frontier Kentucky is the explorer and surveyor Daniel Boone (b.Pennsylvania, 1734–1820). Other frontiersmen include Kit Carson (1809–68) and Roy Bean (1825?–1903). During the Civil War, Lincoln's principal adversary was another native Kentuckian, Jefferson Davis (1808–89). Davis moved south as a boy to a Mississippi plantation home, subsequently serving as US senator from Mississippi, US secretary of war, and president of the Confederate States of America.

Other personalities of significance include James G. Birney (1792–1857) and Cassius Marcellus Clay (1810–1903), both major antislavery spokesmen. Clay's daughter Laura (1849–1941) and Madeline Breckinridge (1872–1920) were important contributors to the women's suffrage movement. Henry Watterson (1840–1921) founded and edited the *Louisville Courier-Journal* and was a major adviser to the Democratic Party. Carry Nation (1846–1911) was a leader of the temperance movement. During the 1920s, Kentuckian John T. Scopes (1900–70) gained fame as the defendant in the "monkey trial" in Dayton, Tenn.; Scopes was prosecuted for teaching Darwin's theory of evolution. Whitney M. Young (1921–71), a prominent black leader, served as head of the National Urban League.

Thomas Hunt Morgan (1866–1945), honored for his work in heredity and genetics, was a Nobel Prize winner. Journalists born in Kentucky include Irvin S. Cobb (1876–1944), who was also a humorist and playwright, and Arthur Krock (1887–1974), a winner of four Pulitzer Prizes. Notable businessmen include Harland Sanders (b.Indiana, 1890–1980), founder of Kentucky Fried Chicken restaurants.

Kentucky has produced several distinguished creative artists. These include painters Matthew Jouett (1787–1827), Frank Duveneck (1848–1919), and Paul Sawyer (1865–1917); folk song collector John Jacob Niles (1891–1980); and novelists Harriette Arnow (1908–86) and Wendell Berry (b.1934). Robert Penn Warren (1905–89), a novelist, poet, and critic, won the Pulitzer

Prize three times and was the first author to win the award in both the fiction and poetry categories.

Among Kentuckians well recognized in the performing arts are film innovator D. W. Griffith (David Lewelyn Wark Griffith, 1875–1948), Academy Award–winning actress Patricia Neal (b.1926), and country music singer Loretta Lynn (b.1932). Kentucky's sports figures include basketball coach Adolph Rupp (b.Kansas, 1901–77), shortstop Harold ("Pee Wee") Reese (b.1919), football great Paul Hornung (b.1935), and world heavyweight boxing champions Jimmy Ellis (b.1940) and Muhammad Ali (Cassius Clay, b.1942).

50BIBLIOGRAPHY

Alvey, R. Gerald. *Kentucky Bluegrass Country*. Jackson: University Press of Mississippi, 1992.

Axton, W. F. *Tobacco and Kentucky*. Lexington: University Press of Kentucky, 1976.

Channing, Steven A. *Kentucky: A Bicentennial History*. New York: Norton, 1977.

Clark, Thomas Dionysius. *The Kentucky*. Lexington: University Press of Kentucky, 1992.

Fuller, Paul E. *Laura Clay and the Woman's Rights Movement*. Lexington: University Press of Kentucky, 1975.

Harrison, Lowell Hayes, and James C. Klotter. *A New History of Kentucky*. Lexington: University Press of Kentucky, 1997.

Hollingsworth, Kent. *The Kentucky Thoroughbred*. Lexington: University Press of Kentucky, 1985.

Kentucky Cabinet for Economic Development. Division of Research. *1997 Kentucky Deskbook of Economic Statistics*. Frankfort, 1997.

Kleber, John E., ed. *The Kentucky Encyclopedia*. Lexington: University Press of Kentucky, 1992.

Miller, Penny M. *Kentucky Politics & Government: Do We Stand United?* Lincoln: University of Nebraska Press, 1994.

Rennick, Robert M. *Kentucky Place Names*. Lexington: University Press of Kentucky, 1984.

Williams, Rob, comp. *A Citizen's Guide to the Kentucky Constitution*. Rev. ed. Frankfort: Legislative Research Commission, 1995.

LOUISIANA

State of Louisiana

ORIGIN OF STATE NAME: Named in 1682 for France's King Louis XIV. **NICKNAME:** The Pelican State. **CAPITAL:** Baton Rouge. **ENTERED UNION:** 30 April 1812 (18th). **SONGS:** "Give Me Louisiana"; "You are My Sunshine." **MOTTO:** Union, Justice, and Confidence. **COLORS:** Gold, white, and blue. **FLAG:** On a blue field, a white pelican feeds her three young, symbolizing the state providing for its citizens; the state motto is inscribed on a white ribbon. **OFFICIAL SEAL:** A pelican, with its head turned to the left, sits in a nest with three young. Around the inner circle are inscribed "Union," "Justice," and under the nest, "Confidence." **BIRD:** Eastern brown pelican. **CRUSTACEAN:** Crawfish. **DOG:** Catahoula leopard. **FLOWER:** Magnolia grandiflora. **WILDFLOWER:** Louisiana iris. **TREE:** Bald cypress. **GEM:** Agate. **FOSSIL:** Petrified palmwood. **INSECT:** Honeybee. **LEGAL HOLIDAYS:** New Year's Day, 1 January; Battle of New Orleans Day, 8 January; Birthday of Martin Luther King, Jr., 3d Monday in January; Robert E. Lee's Birthday, 19 January; Washington's Birthday, 3d Monday in February; Good Friday, March or April; National Memorial Day, last Monday in May; Confederate Memorial Day and Jefferson Davis's Birthday, 3 June; Independence Day, 4 July; Huey Long's Birthday, 30 August, by proclamation of the governor; Labor Day, 1st Monday in September; Columbus Day, 2d Monday in October; All Saints' Day, 1 November; Veterans Day, 11 November; Thanksgiving Day, 4th Thursday in November; Christmas Day, 25 December. Legal holidays in New Orleans, Jefferson, St. Bernard, St. Charles, and East Baton Rouge parishes also include Mardi Gras, February or March. **TIME:** 6 AM CST = noon GMT.

¹LOCATION, SIZE, AND EXTENT

Situated in the western south-central US, Louisiana ranks 31st in size among the 50 states. The total area of Louisiana is 47,751 sq mi (123,675 sq km), including 44,521 sq mi (115,309 sq km) of land and 3,230 sq mi (8,366 sq km) of inland water. The state extends 237 mi (381 km) E-W; its maximum N-S extension is 236 mi (380 km). Louisiana is shaped roughly like a boot, with the heel in the SW corner and the toe at the extreme SE.

Louisiana is bordered on the N by Arkansas; on the E by Mississippi (with part of the line formed by the Mississippi River and part, in the extreme SE, by the Pearl River); on the S by the Gulf of Mexico; and on the W by Texas (with part of the line passing through the Sabine River and Toledo Bend Reservoir). The state's geographic center is in Avoyelles Parish, 3 mi (5 km) SE of Marksville. The total boundary length of Louisiana is 1,486 mi (2,391 km). Louisiana's total tidal shoreline is 7,721 mi (12,426 km).

²TOPOGRAPHY

Louisiana lies wholly within the Gulf Coastal Plain. Alluvial lands, chiefly of the Red and Mississippi rivers, occupy the north-central third of the state. East and west of this alluvial plain are the upland districts, characterized by rolling hills sloping gently toward the coast. The coastal-delta section, in the southernmost portion of the state, consists of the Mississippi Delta and the coastal lowlands. The highest elevation in the state is Driskill Mountain at 535 feet (163 meters), in Bienville Parish; the lowest, 5 feet (2 meters) below sea level, in New Orleans.

Louisiana has the most wetlands of all the states, about 11,000 sq mi (28,000 sq km) of floodplains and 7,800 sq mi (20,200 sq km) of coastal swamps, marshes, and estuarine waters. The largest lake, actually a coastal lagoon, is Lake Pontchartrain, with an area of more than 620 sq mi (1,600 sq km). Toledo Bend Reservoir, an artificial lake along the Louisiana-Texas border, has an area of 284 sq mi (736 sq km).

The most important rivers are the Mississippi, Red, Pearl, Atcha-falaya, and Sabine. Most drainage takes place through swamps between the bayous, which serve as outlets for overflowing rivers and streams. Louisiana has nearly 2,500 coastal islands covering some 2,000 sq mi (5,000 sq km).

³CLIMATE

Louisiana has a relatively constant semitropical climate. Rainfall and humidity decrease, and daily temperature variations increase, with distance from the Gulf of Mexico. The normal daily temperature in New Orleans is 68°F (20°C), ranging from 52°F (11°C) in January to 82°F (28°C) in July. The all-time high temperature is 114°F (46°C), recorded at Plain Dealing on 10 August 1936; the all-time low, –16°F (–27°C), was set at Minden on 13 February 1899. New Orleans has sunshine 59% of the time, and the average annual rainfall is 60 in (152 cm). Snow falls occasionally in the north, but rarely in the south.

Prevailing winds are from the south or southeast. During the summer and fall, tropical storms and hurricanes frequently batter the state, especially along the coast. Among the most severe hurricanes in recent decades were Audrey, which entered Cameron Parish on 28 June 1957, causing 400–500 deaths and property damage of $150 million; Betsy, which entered the coast near Grand Isle on 9 September 1965, causing 58 deaths and damages of $1.2 billion; and Andrew, which landed on 25 August 1992 after devastating southern Florida two days earlier. There were 51 tornadoes in 1995.

⁴FLORA AND FAUNA

Forests in Louisiana consist of four major types: shortleaf pine uplands, slash and longleaf pine flats and hills, hardwood forests in alluvial basins, and cypress and tupelo swamps. Important commercial trees also include beech, eastern red cedar, and black walnut. Among the state's wild flowers are the ground orchid and several hyacinths. Spanish moss (actually a member of the pineapple family) grows profusely in the southern regions but is rare in the north. Two types of orchid are threatened, and the *Schwalbea americana* is endangered. Louisiana's varied habitats—tidal marshes, swamps woodlands, and prairies—offer a diversity of fauna. Deer, squirrel, rabbit, and bear are hunted as game, while muskrat, nutria, mink, opossum, bobcat, and skunk are commercially significant furbearers. Prized game birds include quail, turkey, woodcock, and various waterfowl, of which the mottled duck and wood duck are native. Coastal beaches are inhabited by sea turtles, and whales may be seen offshore. Freshwater fish include bass, crappie, and bream; red and white crawfishes are the leading commercial crustaceans. Threatened animal species include both the green and loggerhead sea turtles. The American alligator is on the federal endangered species list. Other endangered animals are the sei and sperm whales, Florida panther, gray wolf, eastern brown pelican (the state bird), whooping crane, and red-cockaded woodpecker.

5ENVIRONMENTAL PROTECTION

Louisiana's earliest and most pressing environmental problem was the chronic danger of flooding by the Mississippi River. In April and May 1927, the worst flood in the state's history inundated more than 1,300,000 acres (526,000 hectares) of agricultural land, left 300,000 people homeless, and would have swept away much of New Orleans had levees below the city not been dynamited. The following year, the US Congress funded construction of a system of floodways and spillways to divert water from the Mississippi when necessary. These flood control measures, and dredging for oil and gas exploration, created another environmental problem—the slowing of the natural flow of silt into the wetlands. As a results, salt water from the Gulf of Mexico has seeped into the wetlands.

In 1984, Louisiana consolidated much of its environmental protection efforts into a new state agency—The Department of Environmental Quality (DEQ). Among its responsibilities are maintenance of air and water quality, solid-waste management, hazardous waste disposal, and control of radioactive materials. According to the Louisiana Environmental Action Plan (LEAP to 2000 Project), toxic air pollution, industrial and municipal wastewater discharges, and coastal wetland loss head the list of state residents' environmental concerns. Louisiana's problem in protecting its wetlands differs from that of most other states in that its wetlands are more than wildlife refuges—they are central to the state's agriculture and fishing industries. Assessment of the environmental impact of various industries on the wetlands has been conducted under the Coastal Zone Management Plan of the Department of Natural Resources.

The two largest wildlife refuges in the state are the Rockefeller Wildlife Refuge, comprising 84,000 acres (34,000 hectares) in Cameron and Vermilion parishes, and the Marsh Island Refuge, 82,000 acres (33,000 hectares) of marshland in Iberia Parish. Both are managed by the Department of Wildlife and Fisheries. Louisiana's coastal marshes represent almost 40% of such lands in the country.

With approximately 100 major chemical and petrochemical manufacturing and refining facilities located in Louisiana, many DEQ programs deal with the regulation of hazardous waste generation, management and disposal, and chemical releases to the air and water. Trends in air monitoring have, for example, continued to show decreases in criteria pollutants. In 1993, Louisiana became one of the first states in the nation to receive federal approval for stringent new solid waste landfill regulations, and the department has developed a Statewide Solid Waste Management Plan which encourages waste reduction. Of the total river miles in the state impacted by pollution, 69% of the pollution is due to nonpoint sources such as agricultural and urban runoff. Efforts by DEQ to curb nonpoint source pollution

have included the support and cooperation of the agricultural community and other state and federal agencies.

Among the most active citizen's groups on environmental issues are the League of Women Voters, the Sierra Club (Delta Chapter), and the Louisiana Environmental Action Network (LEAN). Curbside recycling programs exist 28 parishes. In 1995, the state had 17 hazardous waste sites. In 1996, wetlands, which once covered more than half the state, accounted for about one-third of Louisiana's land.

6POPULATION

At the time of the 1980 census, Louisiana ranked 19th among the 50 states, with a population of 4,203,972, representing an increase of more than 15% since 1970. By 1990 however, the population was 4,219,973 representing only a 0.3% gain, and a rank of 21st of the 50 states. The US Census Bureau estimated Louisiana's population at 4,350,579 in 1996, nearly 3.1% higher than in 1990. As of 1990, 51% of Louisianians were female and 49% male. In 1990 80% of all state residents had been born in the state. Louisiana's population density in 1990 was 97 persons per sq mi (37 per sq km).

About 69% of Louisianians lived in metropolitan areas in 1990. New Orleans is the largest city, with an estimated 1996 population of 480,260, followed by Baton Rouge, 231,219; and Shreveport, 201,270. Baton Rouge, the capital, had grown with exceptional speed since 1940, when its population was 34,719; however, since 1980, the population has decreased 0.4%. Among the state's largest metropolitan areas in 1990 were New Orleans, 1,315,294; and Baton Rouge, 563,994.

7ETHNIC GROUPS

Louisiana, most notably the Delta region, is an enclave of ethnic heterogeneity in the South. At the end of World War II, the established population of the Delta, according to descent, included blacks, French, Spanish (among them Central and South Americans and Islenos, Spanish-speaking migrants from the Canary Islands), Filipinos, Italians, Chinese, American Indians, and numerous other groups.

Blacks made up about 30% of the population in 1990. They include descendants of "free people of color," some of whom were craftsmen and rural property owners before the Civil War (a few were slaveholding plantation owners). Many of these, of mixed blood, are referred to locally as "colored Creoles" and have constituted a black elite in both urban and rural Louisiana. The black population of New Orleans constituted 61.9% of its residents in 1990; the city elected its first black mayor, Ernest N. "Dutch" Morial, in 1977.

Two groups that have been highly identified with the culture of Louisiana are Creoles and Acadians (also called Cajuns). Both descend primarily from early French immigrants to the state, but the Cajuns trace their origins from the mainly rural people exiled from Acadia (Nova Scotia) in the 1740s, while the Creoles tend to be city people from France and, to a lesser extent, from Nova Scotia or Hispaniola. (The term "Creole" also applies to the relatively few early Spanish settlers and their descendants.) Although Acadians have intermingled with Spaniards and Germans, they still speak a French patois and retain a distinctive culture and cuisine. In 1990, 432,549 residents claimed Acadian/Cajun ancestry.

At the time of the 1990 census, 87,407 Louisianians (2% of the population) were foreign-born. France, Germany, Ireland, and the United Kingdom provided Louisiana with the largest ancestry groups. As of 1990, there were 19,000 American Indians in Louisiana, along with 41,000 Pacific Islanders and Asians, including 14,696 Vietnamese.

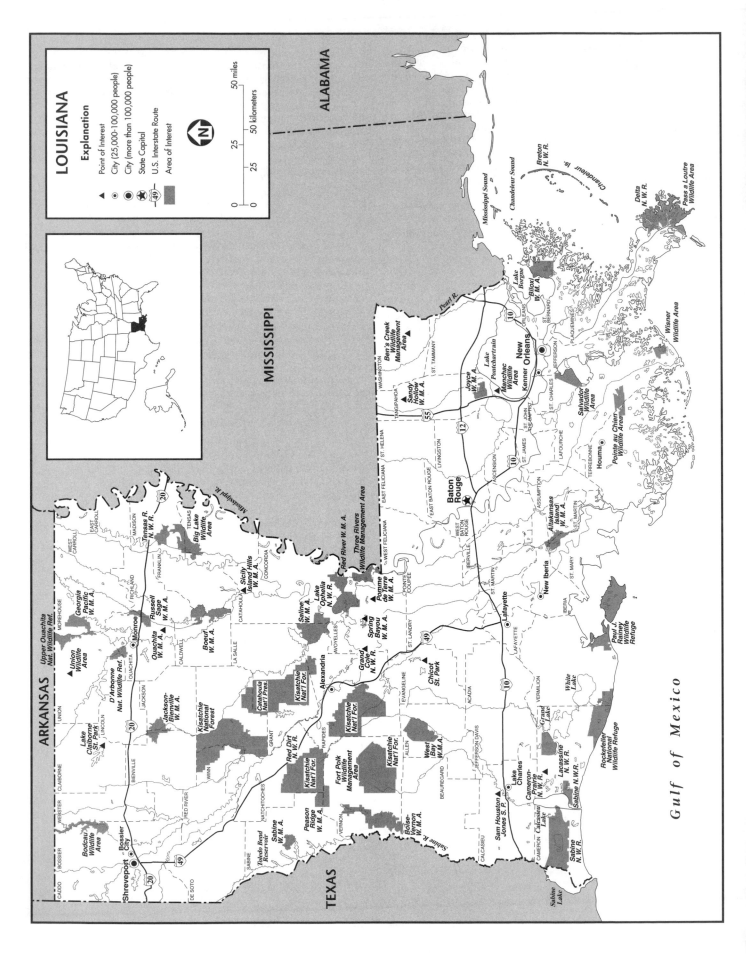

ALABAMA

MISSISSIPPI

ARKANSAS

TEXAS

Gulf of Mexico

Chandeleur Sound

Breton N.W.R.

Chandeleur Is.

Delta N.W.R.

Pass a Loutre Wildlife Area

Mississippi Sound

Lake Borgne

Biloxi W.M.A.

Wisner Wildlife Area

Pearl R.

Ben's Creek Wildlife Management Area

Sandy Hollow W.M.A.

Joyce W.M.A.

Lake Pontchartrain

Manchac Wildlife Area

New Orleans

Kenner

Salvador Wildlife Area

Pointe au Chien Wildlife Area

Houma

Baton Rouge

Attakapas I. W.M.A.

New Iberia

Paul J. Rainey Wildlife Refuge

Lafayette

White Lake

Grand Lake

Rockefeller National Wildlife Refuge

Upper Ouachita Nat. Wildlife Ref.

Georgia Pacific W.M.A.

Tensas R. N.W.R.

Big Lake Wildlife Area

Mississippi R.

Russell Sage W.M.A.

Sicily Island Hills W. M. A.

Fred River W. M. A.

Three Rivers Wildlife Management Area

Union Wildlife Area

D'Arbonne Nat. Wildlife Ref.

Monroe

Ouachita W.M.A.

Boeuf W.M.A.

Saline W.M.A.

Lake Ophelia N.W.R.

Pomme de Terre W.M.A.

Spring Bayou W.M.A.

Grand Cote N.W.R.

Chicot St. Park

Lake Claiborne St. Park

Jackson-Bienville W. M. A.

Catahoula Nat'l Pres.

Kisatchie Nat'l For.

Alexandria

Kisatchie National Forest

Kisatchie Nat'l For.

West Bay W.M.A.

Lake Charles

Bodcau Wildlife Area

Bossier City

Shreveport

Toledo Bend Reservoir

Sabine W.M.A.

Red Dirt N.W.R.

Peason Ridge W.M.A.

Fort Polk Wildlife Management Area

Kisatchie Nat'l For.

Boise Vernon W.M.A.

Sam Houston Jones S.P.

Cameron Prairie N.W.R.

Calcasieu Lake

Lacassine N.W.R.

Sabine N.W.R.

Sabine N.W.R.

Sabine Lake

Sabine R.

CADDO, BOSSIER, WEBSTER, CLAIBORNE, DE SOTO, BIENVILLE, LINCOLN, UNION, MOREHOUSE, OUACHITA, JACKSON, WINN, NATCHITOCHES, SABINE, VERNON, RAPIDES, GRANT, CALDWELL, LA SALLE, CATAHOULA, FRANKLIN, RICHLAND, MADISON, EAST CARROLL, WEST CARROLL, TENSAS, CONCORDIA, AVOYELLES, EVANGELINE, ACADIA, JEFFERSON DAVIS, CALCASIEU, BEAUREGARD, ALLEN, CAMERON, VERMILION, IBERIA, ST. MARTIN, ST. LANDRY, POINTE COUPEE, WEST FELICIANA, EAST FELICIANA, ST. HELENA, TANGIPAHOA, WASHINGTON, ST. TAMMANY, LIVINGSTON, ASCENSION, ST. JAMES, ST. JOHN THE BAPTIST, ST. CHARLES, JEFFERSON, ST. BERNARD, PLAQUEMINES, TERREBONNE, LAFOURCHE, ASSUMPTION, ST. MARY, IBERVILLE, WEST BATON ROUGE, EAST BATON ROUGE, BERVILLE

8 LANGUAGES

White settlers in Louisiana found several Indian tribes of the Caddoan confederacy, from at least five different language groups. In 1990, about 495 Louisiana residents spoke an American Indian language at home. Place-names from this heritage include Coushatta, Natchitoches, and Ouachita.

Louisiana English is predominantly Southern. Notable features of the state's speech patterns are *pen* and *pin* as sound-alikes and, in New Orleans, the so-called Brooklyn pronunciation of *bird* as /boyd/. A pecan sugar candy is well known as *praline*.

In 1990, 3,494,359 Louisiana residents—89.9% of the population five years old and older—spoke only English at home. Other languages spoken at home included:

French	261,678	German	8,588
Spanish	72,173	Italian	4,933
Vietnamese	14,352	Chinese	4,727

Unique to Louisiana is a large enclave, west of New Orleans, where a variety of French called Acadian (Cajun) is the first language. From it, and from early colonial French, English has taken such words as *pirogue* (dugout canoe), *armoire* (wardrobe), *boudin* (blood sausage), and *lagniappe* (extra gift).

9 RELIGIONS

Spanish missionaries brought Roman Catholicism to Louisiana in the early 16th century, and many of them were killed in their attempts to convert the Indians. During the early days, the most active religious orders were the Jesuits, Capuchins, and Ursuline nuns. Until the Louisiana Purchase, the public practice of any but the Catholic religion was prohibited, and Jews were entirely banned.

Joseph Willis, a mulatto preacher who conducted prayer meetings at what is now Lafayette in 1804, organized the first Baptist church west of the Mississippi, at Bayou Chicot in 1812. In the Opelousas region, in 1806, the first Methodist church in the state was organized. The first Episcopal church was established in New Orleans in 1805, a Methodist church in 1813, a Presbyterian church in 1817, a synagogue in 1828, and a Baptist church in 1834. After the Civil War, blacks withdrew from white-dominated churches to form their own religious groups, mainly Baptist and Methodist.

As of 1990, the Roman Catholic Church was the largest Christian denomination, with 1,369,154 church members. The leading Protestant denominations in 1990 were Southern Baptist, 757,639; United Methodist, 172,676; Episcopal, 33,423; and Presbyterian, 27,105. In 1990, 15,625 Jews resided in Louisiana, about 70% of them in New Orleans. Voodoo, in some cases blended with Christian ritual, is more widespread in Louisiana than anywhere else in the US, although the present number of practitioners is impossible to ascertain.

10 TRANSPORTATION

New Orleans is a major center of domestic and international freight traffic. In volume of domestic and foreign cargo handled, it is the busiest port on the Gulf of Mexico and leading port in the US. Although Louisiana's roads remained poor until the 1930s, the state was one of the nation's major rail centers by the end of the 19th century, and New Orleans was one of the first cities to develop a mass transit system.

Several short-run railroads were built in Louisiana during the 1830s. The first of these, and the first rail line west of the Alleghenies, was the Pontchartrain Railroad, which opened, using horse-drawn vehicles, on 23 April 1831. New Orleans was connected with New York before the Civil War, with Chicago by 1873, and with California in 1883 via a line that subsequently became part of the Southern Pacific. Railroads soon rivaled the Mississippi River in the movement of goods to and from New Orleans, and, even today, the long-distance freight service provided by New Orleans' six trunk lines is a major reason for the preeminence of the port. There were seven Class I line-haul railroads in Louisiana in 1995, and as of December 1995, total railroad mileage was 2,786 route mi (4,485 km), of which about 90% was Class I track. That same year, the state ranked 2d in originated tonnage of chemicals transported by rail, at over 19 million tons. As of 1995/96, Amtrak provided passenger links with Los Angeles, Chicago, and New York and carried 165,888 passengers from nine stations through the state. The New Orleans and Carrollton Railroads, a horse-drawn trolley system, began service in 1835; 59 years later, electric trolleys came into use.

Louisiana's first road-building boom began after Huey Long entered the statehouse. When Long took office in 1928, the state had no more than 300 mi (480 km) of paved roads; by 1931 there were 1,583 mi (2,548 km). At the end of 1995, Louisiana had a total of 60,119 mi (96,791 km) of public roads, 77% of them rural. In 1995, 1,958,314 automobiles and 1,306,922 trucks were registered in the state, and 2,593,509 drivers' licenses were in force.

Early in the nation's history, the Mississippi River emerged as the principal route for north-south traffic, and New Orleans soon became the South's main port. The advent of the steamboat in 1812 solved the problem of upstream navigation, which previously had required three or four months for a distance that could be covered downstream in 15 days. (Barges moved by towboats eventually supplanted steamboats as cargo carriers.) An important breakthrough in international transportation was the deepening of the channel at the mouth of the Mississippi by means of jetties, the first of which were completed in 1879. The port of New Orleans is served by more than 100 steamship lines and by 20 common carrier and about 100 contract carrier barge lines. The Louisiana Offshore Oil Port (LOOP), the first deepwater oil port in the US, was opened in 1981. Located south of New Orleans in the Gulf of Mexico, the supertanker facility has a designed capacity of 1,400,000 barrels of oil a day. LOOP offloaded 300,490,028 barrels of crude oil from 279 supertankers in 1996, handling 13% of the nation's crude oil imports. Large ports include Baton Rouge (4th), with a tonnage of over 83.6 million tons in 1995; New Orleans (6th), 76.9 million tons; and the Port of Plaquemine (7th) with 72.9 million tons of cargo in 1995.

As of the beginning of 1995, Louisiana had a total of 323 private and 110 public airfields. The busiest was New Orleans International Airport, which enplaned 3,915,453 passengers and 21,592 tons of freight. Louisiana also has 207 heliports, including one in Morgan City with 46 landing pads.

11 HISTORY

The region now known as Louisiana is largely the creation of the Mississippi River; the process of land building still goes on in the Atchafalaya Basin and below New Orleans on the Mississippi Delta. Louisiana was never densely inhabited in prehistoric times, and at no time, probably, did as many as 15,000 Indians live inside the present boundaries of the state. The main relic of prehistoric inhabitants is the great earthwork at Poverty Point, near Marksville, but other Indian mounds are to be found in alluvial and coastal regions.

When white exploration and settlement of North America began, various tribes of Caddo Indians inhabited northwestern Louisiana, and small Tunican-speaking groups lived in the northeast. In the southwest were a number of rather primitive people of the Atakapa group; in south-central Louisiana, the Chitimacha ranged through the marshes and lowlands. Various small Muskogean tribes, related to the Choctaw, lived east of the

Mississippi in the "Florida parishes," so called because they were once part of Spanish West Florida. The Natchez Indians, whose main villages were in present-day Mississippi near the city that still bears their name, fought with the French settlers in Louisiana's early history but were exterminated in the process.

Several Spanish explorers sailed along the coast of Louisiana, but Hernando de Sota was probably the first to penetrate the state's present boundaries, in 1541. Almost a century and a half passed before Robert Cavelier, Sieur de la Salle, departing from Canada, reached the mouth of the Mississippi on 9 April 1682, named the land there Louisiana in honor of King Louis XIV, and claimed it for France. La Salle's later attempt at a permanent settlement failed, but in 1699 an expedition headed by Pierre le Moyne, Sieur d'Iberville, made a settlement on Biloxi Bay. In 1714, Louis Juchereau de St. Denis established Natchitoches, the first permanent European settlement in Louisiana; Iberville's brother, the Sieur de Bienville, established New Orleans four years later.

Louisiana did not thrive economically under French rule, either as a royal colony or, from 1712 to 1731, under the proprietorship first of Antoine Crozat and then of John Law's Company of the Indies. On the other hand, French culture was firmly implanted there, and non-French settlers, especially Germans from Switzerland and the Rhineland, were quickly Gallicized. In 1762, on the verge of losing the rest of its North American empire to Great Britain in the French and Indian War, France ceded Louisiana to Spain. Governed by Spaniards, the colony was much more prosperous, although it was a burden on the Spanish treasury. New settlers—Americans, Spaniards, Canary Islanders, and, above all, Acadian refugees from Nova Scotia—added to the population. By 1800 there were about 50,000 inhabitants, a considerable number of them black slaves imported from Africa and the West Indies. The availability of slave labor, Eli Whitney's invention of the cotton gin, and Étienne de Boré's development of a granulation process for making cane sugar set the stage for future prosperity, though not under Spanish auspices. In 1800, by the secret Treaty of San Ildefonso, Napoleon forced the feeble Spanish government to return Louisiana to France. Three years later, having failed to reestablish French rule and slavery in Haiti, Napoleon sold Louisiana to the US to keep it from falling into the hands of Great Britain.

President Thomas Jefferson concluded what was probably the best real estate deal in history, purchasing 800,000 sq mi (2,100,000 sq km) for $15,000,000 and thus more than doubling the size of the US at a cost of about 3 cents per acre. He made William C. C. Claiborne the governor of the huge new acquisition. The next year, that part of the purchase south of 33°N was separated from the remainder and designated the Territory of Orleans. The people of the territory then began the process of learning self-government, something with which they had had no experience under France and Spain. After the census of 1810 showed that the population had risen to 76,556, the people were authorized by Congress to draw up a state constitution. The constitutional convention met under the presidency of Julian Poydras in a coffeehouse in New Orleans and adopted, with a few changes, the constitution then in effect in Kentucky. In the meantime, in 1810, a revolt against Spain had taken place in West Florida. When the proposed Louisiana constitution reached Washington, Congress added that part of West Florida between the Mississippi and Pearl rivers to the new state, which entered the Union on 30 April 1812.

The key event in the Americanization of Louisiana was the campaign for New Orleans in December 1814 and January 1815, actually fought after the War of 1812 had ended. A force of British veterans under General Sir Edward Pakenham sailed into Lake Borgne and established itself below New Orleans at Chalmette. There they were met by detachments of Creoles,

Acadians, blacks, and even Jean Lafitte's pirates, all from Louisiana, as well as Tennesseans, Kentuckians, and Choctaw Indians, with the whole army under the command of Andrew Jackson. After several preliminary battles, the British were bloodily defeated when they launched an all-out assault on Jackson's line.

From 1815 to 1861, Louisiana was one of the most prosperous states in the South, producing sugar and cotton on its rich alluvial lands and grazing hogs and cattle in the wooded hills of the north and on the prairies of the southwest. Yeoman farmers and New Orleans workers far outnumbered the wealthy planters but the planters, whose slaves made up almost half the population, dominated Louisiana politically and economically. When the secession crisis came in 1861, the planters led Louisiana into the Confederacy and, after four bloody years, to total defeat. The state suffered crippling economic losses during the Civil War, but the greatest loss was the lives of tens of thousands of young white men who died in defense of the South, and of thousands of blacks who died seeking and fighting for freedom. Louisiana did not fully recover from this disaster until the mid-20th century.

After the Civil War, radical Republican governments elected by black voters ruled the state, but declining support from the North and fierce resistance from Louisiana whites brought the Reconstruction period to an end. Black people and their few white allies lost control of state government, and most of the former slaves became laborers on sugar plantations or sharecroppers in the cotton fields. There, as the years passed, they were joined by more and more landless whites. In 1898, blacks were disfranchised almost entirely by a new state constitution drawn up primarily for that purpose. This constitution also significantly reduced the number of poorer whites who voted in Louisiana elections.

The vast majority of Louisiana whites—whether hill farmers, Cajuns along the southern rivers and bayous, lumbermen in the yellow pine forests, or workers in New Orleans—were little better off than the black or white sharecroppers. Many economic changes had taken place: rice had become a staple crop on the southwestern prairies, and an oil boom had begun after the turn of the century. But just as before the Civil War, large landowners—combined with New Orleans bankers, businessmen, and politicians—dominated state government, effectively blocking political and social reform. The Populist movement, which succeeded in effecting some change in other southern states, was crushed in Louisiana.

Not until 1928, with the election of Huey P. Long as governor, did the winds of change strike Louisiana; having been so long delayed, they blew with gale force. The years from 1928 through 1960 could well be called the Long Era: three Longs—Huey, who was assassinated in 1935; his brother Earl, who served as governor three times; and Huey's son Russell, who became a powerful US senator—dominated state politics for most of the period. From a backward agricultural state, Louisiana evolved into one of the world's major petrochemical-manufacturing centers. Offshore drilling sent clusters of oil wells 60 mi (97 km) out into the Gulf. The pine lands were reforested, and soybeans provided a new source of income. What had been one of the most parsimonious states became one of the most liberal in welfare spending, care for the aged, highway building, and education. The state could afford these expanding programs because of ever-increasing revenues from oil and gas.

In the mid-1980s, a drop in world oil prices rocked Louisiana's economy, hurting both the oil exploration and service industries and raising the state's unemployment rate in 1986 to 13%, the highest in the nation. In the 1990s, in spite of an increase in service-sector and high-tech jobs, Louisiana had more people living in poverty than any other state in the country. Other problems confronting the state included racial and labor tensions, inadequate disposal sites for toxic wastes from the petrochemical industry, and (despite important new discoveries) the depletion of oil and gas resources.

Meanwhile, the announcement in February 1985 by Russell B. Long, senator since 1948, that he would not seek reelection in 1986, and the indictment of former Governor Edwin W. Edwards by a federal grand jury on conspiracy charges during the same month, caused turmoil in Louisiana's political arena. Edwards was defeated in 1987 by Buddy Roemer, a young, well-educated Republican who promised to clean up government. Roemer directed his efforts at overhauling the state's archaic taxation system, under which 85% of residential homeowners paid no property taxes. In an attempt to attract businesses to Louisiana, Roemer sought to shift the tax burden from reliance on sales taxes and on corporations, which paid 96% of property taxes, to middle and high income individuals. The voters, however, rejected such reforms, voting 55 to 45% against Roemer's tax initiative

In 1989, racial tensions surfaced when white supremacist David Duke, running as a Republican, narrowly won a seat in the Louisiana state legislature. Almost immediately after he assumed office, Duke entered the race for US Senate. While Duke lost to state senator J. Bennett Johnston, his showing of 44% among voters overall, over half of which came from white voters, was interpreted both as evidence of his potency as a political force and as an expression of the discontent of working class and middle class whites. In opposing affirmative action and minority set-asides, Duke appealed to whites' frustrations with the high unemployment brought by the collapse of oil prices in the mid- and late eighties. In 1991, Duke ran again for public office, this time for governor. Although Duke's appeal remained strong, he was defeated by former governor Edwin Edwards. In the same year, Louisiana's legislature passed one of the toughest antiabortion laws in the country, virtually prohibiting abortions altogether and imposing harsh penalties for performing them.

In 1992 Hurricane Andrew killed 11 people in Louisiana and caused roughly $1 billion in damage.

12STATE GOVERNMENT

Louisiana has had 11 constitutions (more than any other state), the most recent of which was enacted in 1974. The state legislature consists of a 39-member senate and a 105-member house of representatives. All legislators are elected for concurrent four-year terms; they must be US citizens, be at least 18 years old, and have resided in the state for two years and in their districts for at least one year preceding election. The legislative salary in 1995 was $16,800.

Major elected executive officials include the governor and lieutenant governor (independently elected), secretary of state, attorney general, treasurer, superintendent of education, commissioner of agriculture, commissioner of insurance, and commissioner of elections. All are elected for four-year terms. The governor must be a qualified elector, be at least 25 years old, and have been a US and Louisiana citizen for five years preceding election; after two consecutive terms, a governor may not succeed himself. The same eligibility requirements apply to the lieutenant governor, except that there is no limit on succession to the latter office. In 1996 the governor's and lieutenant governor's salaries were each $85,000. Other executive agencies are the State Board of Elementary and Secondary Education, whose eight elected members and three appointed members serve four-year terms, and the Public Service Commission, whose five members serve for six years.

To become law, a bill must receive majority votes in both the senate and the house and be signed by the governor, be left unsigned but not vetoed by the governor, or be passed again by two-thirds votes of both houses over the governor's veto. Appropriation bills must originate in the house but may be amended by the senate. The governor has an item veto on appropriation bills. Constitutional amendments require approval by two-thirds of the elected members of each house and ratification by a majority of the people voting on it at the next general election. Voters in Louisiana must be US citizens, be 18 years of age, and have registered at least 24 days before a general election (30 days before a primary election).

13POLITICAL PARTIES

The major political organizations are the Democratic Party and the Republican Party, each affiliated with the national party. However, differences in culture and economic interests have made Louisiana's politics extremely complex. Immediately following statehood, the primary political alignment was according to ethnic background, Anglo or Latin. By the 1830s, however, Louisiana politics reflected the national division of Jacksonian Democrats and National Republicans, who were by mid-decade replaced by the Whigs. By and large, the Whigs were favored by the Anglo-Americans while the Democrats were favored by those of French and Spanish descent. When the Whig Party fell apart over slavery, many former Whigs supported the Native American (Know Nothing) Party.

Louisiana was one of the three southern states whose disputed electoral votes put Republican Rutherford B. Hayes in the White House in 1877, in return for his agreement to withdraw federal troops from the South, thus putting an end to Reconstruction. The ensuing period of Bourbon Democratic dominance in Louisiana, a time of reaction and racism in politics (though a few blacks continued to hold office), lasted until the early 1890s, when worsening economic conditions inspired Populists and Republicans to challenge Democratic rule. The attempt failed largely because Democratic landowners were able to control the ballots of their black sharecroppers and "vote" them Democrat. The recognition that it was the black vote, however well-controlled, that held the balance in Louisiana politics impelled the Democrats to seek its elimination as an electoral factor. The constitution of 1898 imposed a poll tax, a property requirement, a literacy test, and other measures that succeeded in reducing the number of registered black voters from 130,000 at the beginning of 1897 to 5,320 in March 1900 and 1,342 by 1904. White registration also declined, from 164,000 in 1897 to 92,000 in 1904, because the new constitutional requirements tended to disfranchise poor whites as well as blacks.

Between 1900 and 1920, the New Orleans Ring, or Choctaw Club, was the dominant power in state politics. Growing political discontent led 5,261 Louisianians (6.6% of those voting) to cast their ballots for the Socialist presidential candidate in 1912. A few Socialists won local office that year in Winn Parish, a center of Populist activity in the 1890s and the birthplace of Huey Long in 1893.

During his relatively brief career as a member of the Railroad Commission, governor, and US senator, Long committed government resources to public service to an extent without precedent in the state. He also succeeded in substituting for the traditional Democratic Party organization a state machine geared primarily toward loyalty to himself and, after his assassination in 1935, to the Long family name, which kept its hold on the voters despite a series of scandals that publicized the corruption of his associates. When blacks began voting in increasing numbers during the 1940s, they tended to favor Democratic candidates from the Long camp. The Longs repaid their loyalty: when race became a bitterly divisive issue in the late 1940s and 1950s—Louisiana gave its presidential vote to the States' Rights "Dixiecrat" candidate in 1948—the Longs supported the national Democratic ticket.

The 1960s and 1970s saw a resurgence of the Republican Party and the election in 1979 of David C. Treen, the state's first Republican governor since Reconstruction. Treen was succeeded by Democrat Edwin Edwards in 1983, Democrat Charles Roemer in 1987, and Edwin Edwards again in 1991. As of 1994 there were 1,169,653 registered Democrats, or 72%, 424,150 registered Republicans, or 19%, and 210,085 unaffiliated, or 9%. In 1995, Louisiana elected another Republican governor—Murphy J. "Mike" Foster. Both US senators—John Breux and Mary L. Landrieu, who replaced retiring J. Bennett Johnston, Jr.—were Democrats in 1996. Landrieu is the daughter of former New Orleans mayor Moon Landrieu. Louisiana's delegation of US representatives consisted of two Democrats and five Republicans. In 1997, 25 of the state senators were Democrats, and 14 were Republicans; 78 of the state representatives were Democrats, 27 were Republicans, and one was an Independent.

In 1996, Louisianians gave Democrat Bill Clinton 52% of the vote in the presidential election, while Republican Bob Dole received just under 40%, and Ross Perot collected nearly 7%.

Minority representation in public office in 1994 included 636 blacks and 12 Hispanics. There were 16 women serving in the state legislature and in elective executive office in 1995.

[14]LOCAL GOVERNMENT

The ecclesiastical districts, called parishes, into which Louisiana was divided in the late 17th century remain the primary political divisions in the state, serving functions similar to those of counties in other states.

In 1994 there were 64 parishes, many of them governed by police jury. Juries for parishes of over 10,000 population have 5 to 15 members, or the number authorized as of 13 May 1974, whichever is greater; smaller parishes have at least 3 members on their juries. All police jury members are elected for four-year terms. Parishes without police juries include East Baton Rouge, Jefferson, Orleans, Plaquemines, St. Charles, St. James, and St. Tammany, all of which are governed by other means. Other parish officials are the sheriff, clerk of court, assessor, and coroner. Each parish elects a school board whose members generally serve six-year terms; all other officers serve four-year terms.

As of 1992, Louisiana also had 301 municipal governments, 66 school districts, and 30 special districts. Prominent local officials include the mayor, chief of police, and a council or board of aldermen.

[15]STATE SERVICES

Louisiana's ethics laws are administered by the Commission on Ethics for Public Employees and the Board of Ethics for Elected Officials, both under the Department of Civil Service.

Educational services are provided through the Department of Education, which has jurisdiction over elementary, secondary, higher, and vocational-technical instruction, as well as the state schools for the visually impaired, hearing-impaired, and other handicapped children. Highways, waterways, airports, and mass transit are the province of the Department of Transportation and Development. Environmental affairs, conservation, forestry, and mineral resources are the responsibility of the Department of Natural Resources. The Motor Vehicle Office, Fire Protection Office, Emergency Preparedness Office, and Alcoholic Beverage Control Office are all within the Department of Public Safety.

Health and welfare services are administered mainly through the Department of Health and Hospitals (DHH), which provides welfare services under the Office of Family Security, services for the blind and vocational rehabilitation through the Department of Social Services Office of Rehabilitation Services, and special training for the mentally handicapped under the Office for Citizens with Developmental Disabilities/DHH. The Head Start program for preschool age children is administered by the Department of Education. Such programs as supplemental food and summer youth recreation are administered by the Department of Social Services, which also helps develop and administer housing and urban renewal programs.

[16]JUDICIAL SYSTEM

Louisiana's legal system is the only one in the US to be based on civil or Roman law, specifically the Code Napoléon of France. Under Louisiana state law, cases may be decided by judicial interpretation of the statutes, without reference to prior court cases, whereas in other states and in the federal courts the common law prevails, and decisions are generally based on previous judicial

Louisiana Presidential Vote by Political Parties, 1948–96

YEAR	ELECTORAL VOTE	LOUISIANA WINNER	DEMOCRAT	REPUBLICAN	STATES' RIGHTS DEMOCRAT	PROGRESSIVE	AMERICAN INDEPENDENT
1948	10	Thurmond (SRD)	136,344	72,657	204,290	3,035	—
1952	10	Stevenson (D)	345,027	306,925	—	—	—
					UNPLEDGED		
1956	10	*Eisenhower (R)	243,977	329,047	44,520	—	—
					NAT'L. STATES' RIGHTS		
1960	10	*Kennedy (D)	407,339	230,980	169,572	—	—
1964	10	Goldwater (R)	387,068	509,225	—	—	—
1968	10	Wallace (AI)	309,615	257,535	—	—	530,300
					AMERICAN	SOC. WORKERS	
1972	10	*Nixon (R)	298,142	686,852	44,127	12,169	—
					LIBERTARIAN	COMMUNIST	
1976	10	*Carter (D)	661,365	587,446	3,325	7,417	10,058
						CITIZENS	
1980	10	*Reagan (R)	708,453	792,853	8,240	1,584	10,333
1984	10	*Reagan (R)	651,586	1,037,299	1,876	9,502	—
						POPULIST	N ALLIANCE
1988	10	*Bush (R)	717,460	883,702	4,115	18,612	2,355
					IND. (PEROT)		AMERICA FIRST
1992	9	*Clinton (D)	815,971	733,386	3,155	211,478	18,545
1996	9	*Clinton (D)	927,837	712,586	7,499	123,293	—

* Won US presidential election.

interpretations and findings. In actual practice, Louisiana laws no longer differ radically from US common law, and most Louisiana lawyers and judges now cite previous cases in their arguments and rulings.

The highest court in Louisiana is the supreme court, with appellate jurisdiction. It consists of a chief justice who is chosen by seniority of service, and 6 associate justices, all of them elected from 6 supreme court districts (the first district has 2 judges) for staggered 10-year terms. There are 5 appellate circuits in the state, each divided into 3 districts; the 5 circuits are served by 54 judges, all of them elected for overlapping 10-year terms. Each of the state's district courts serves at least 1 parish and has at least 1 district judge, elected for a 6-year term; there are 207 district judges. District courts have original jurisdiction in criminal and civil cases. City courts are the principal courts of limited jurisdiction.

Louisiana may have been the first state to institute a system of leasing convict labor; large numbers of convicts were leased, especially after the Civil War, until the practice was discontinued in the early 1900s. The abuses entailed in this system may be suggested by the fact that, of 700 convicts leased in 1882, 149 died in service. As of 1995, 16,206 prisoners were in Louisiana's state and federal prisons—a ratio of 373 per 100,000 inhabitants.

According to the FBI Crime Index in 1995, Louisiana had a crime index total of 6,676 per 100,000, including a violent crime rate of 1,007.4 and a property crime rate of 5,668.6. Louisiana's rates of murder were 17.0 (per 100,000); forcible rape, 42.7; robbery, 268.6; assault, 679; burglary, 1,231.7; larceny-theft, 3,838.5; and motor vehicle theft, 598.4.

Louisiana has a death penalty law; 22 people were executed between 1977 and 1995, and 57 were under sentence of death. Judges may impose sentences of hard labor. Louisiana had 14,816 active attorneys in 1996.

17ARMED FORCES

In 1996, there were 16,339 active duty military personnel stationed in Louisiana. There was one major army installation in the state, Ft. Polk at Leesville, with 11,051 military and civilian personnel; an Air Force base at Barksdale near Bossier City; and a naval air station and support station in the vicinity of New Orleans. During fiscal year 1996, Louisiana firms received defense contracts totaling just over $1 billion.

There were 368,000 veterans of US military service in Louisiana on 1 July 1996, of whom fewer than 500 had served in World War I, 103,00 in World War II, 62,000 during the Korean conflict, 117,000 in the Vietnam era, and 34,000 in the Persian Gulf War. Veterans' benefits during fiscal year 1996 amounted to $713 million.

National Guard and Reserve forces in Louisiana totaled 35,826 in 1996. In 1993, the Louisiana State Police employed 703 full-time sworn officers, or two per 10,000 residents.

18MIGRATION

Louisiana was settled by an unusually diverse assortment of immigrants. The Company of the Indies, which administered Louisiana from 1717 until 1731, at first began importing French convicts, vagrants, and prostitutes because of the difficulty of finding willing colonists. Next the company turned to struggling farmers in Germany and Switzerland, who proved to be more suitable and productive settlers. The importation of slaves from Africa and the West Indies began early in the 18th century.

Attracted by generous land grants, perhaps 10,000 Acadians, or Cajuns—people of French descent who had been exiled from Nova Scotia (Acadia) during the 1740s—migrated to Louisiana after the French and Indian War. They settled in the area of Lafayette and Breaux Bridge and along Bayou Lafourche and the Mississippi River. Probably the second largest group to migrate in

the late 18th century came from the British colonies and, after the Revolution, from the US. Between 1800 and 1870, Americans settled the area north of the Red River. Small groups of Canary Islanders and Spaniards from Malaga also settled in the south, and in 1791, a number of French people fled to Louisiana during the slave insurrection on Hispaniola.

During the 1840s and 1850s, masses of Irish and German immigrants came to New Orleans. In the late 1880s, a large number of midwestern farmers migrated to the prairies of southwestern Louisiana to become rice farmers. Louisiana did not immediately begin losing much of its black population after the Civil War. In fact, the number of blacks who migrated to Louisiana from the poorer southeastern states during the postwar years may have equaled the number of blacks who migrated before the war or were brought into the state as slaves. In 1879, however, "Kansas fever" struck blacks from the cotton country of Louisiana and Mississippi, and many of them migrated to the Wheat State; however, many later returned to their home states.

Beginning in World War II, large numbers of both black and white farm workers left Louisiana and migrated north and west. During the 1960s, the state had a net out-migration of 15% of its black population, but the trend had slowed somewhat by 1975.

Recent migration within the state has been from north to south, and from rural to urban areas, especially to Shreveport, Baton Rouge, and the suburbs of New Orleans. From 1980 to 1990, however, the state's urban population fell from 68.6% to 68.1% Overall, Louisiana suffered a net loss from migration of about 368,000 from 1940 to 1990. Between 1990 and 1996, the state had a net loss of 86,038 in domestic migration and a net gain of 18,979 in international migration. In 1996, 4,092 foreign immigrants arrived in Louisiana. By 1990, 79% of all state residents were native-born, a proportion exceeded only by Pennsylvania. About 59% of Louisianians age five and older lived in the same house in 1990 as in 1985; of those who lived in a different house in 1985, only 14% did so in another state.

19INTERGOVERNMENTAL COOPERATION

Among the interstate and regional efforts in which Louisiana participates are the Interstate Oil and Gas Compact, Interstate Compact on Juveniles, Interstate Compact on Placement of Children, Gulf States Marine Fisheries Compact, Red River Compact, Sabine River Compact, South Central Forest Fire Protection Compact, Southern Growth Policies Compact, Southern Interstate Energy Compact, and Southern Regional Education Compact.

Federal aid to Louisiana during fiscal year 1996 was over $4.7 billion.

20ECONOMY

Before the Civil War, when Louisiana was one of the most prosperous of southern states, its economy depended primarily on two then-profitable crops—cotton and sugar—and on its position as the anchor of the nation's principal north–south trade route. But the upheaval and destruction wrought by the war, combined with severe flood damage to cotton crops, falling cotton prices, and the removal of the federal bounty on sugar, left the economy stagnant through the end of the 19th century, although New Orleans retained its commercial importance as an exporter of cotton and grain.

With the addition of two major crops, rice and soybeans, the rebirth of the timber industry as a result of reforestation, the demand for pine for paper pulp, and most dramatically, the rise of the petrochemical industry, Louisiana's economy has regained much of its former vitality. Today, Louisiana ranks 2d only to Texas in the value of its mineral products, and in value per capita it exceeds that much larger and more populous state. As of 1982, the value of mineral production (including fossil fuels) was $31.4

billion, accounting for 18% of the value of mineral production in the US.

Unfortunately, not all of Louisiana's citizens share in this newfound wealth. Wages have been rising—the average manufacturing wage is among the top third in the nation—but the state's unemployment rate has been higher than the national average, and the rate for women is especially high. In 1995 Louisiana's per capita personal income, at $18,827, placed it 39th in the nation.

Louisiana is primarily an industrial state, but its industries are to a large degree based on its natural resources, principally oil, water, and timber. A booming oil industry fueled an expansion in the Louisiana economy during the 1970s. That expansion ended in the early 1980s, when the price of oil dropped from $37 a barrel in 1981 to $15 a barrel in 1986. Employment in oil and gas extraction dropped from 100,000 to 55,000. Energy-related industries such as barge building, machinery manufacturing, and rig/platform production also suffered. At the same time that oil prices dropped, natural gas prices rose, forcing a contraction in the chemical industry which uses large quantities of natural gas. Chemicals were also hurt by a leap in the exchange value of the dollar in the mid-1980s, as Louisiana exports 25% of its chemical production. A subsequent drop in the dollar's exchange value in the late 1980s and early 1990s has enabled the chemical industry not only to rebound but to expand. In an attempt to offset losses in employment, Louisiana planned to build several riverboat casinos and a land-based casino in 1994–95 which were expected to add 6,900 jobs.

Louisiana's gross state product in 1994 was $101,101 million, to which private goods-producing industries contributed $33,140 million; private services-producing industries contributed $55,559 million; and government contributed $12,402 million.

Louisiana's per capita personal income of $19,824 placed it 40th in the nation in 1996.

In 1996, there were 20,437 filings for bankruptcy, up almost 39% from the previous year.

21INCOME

Louisiana's per capita personal income in 1970 was $3,023, for a rank of 46th in the US. By 1983, largely because of the oil boom, per capita income had risen to $10,406 (34th), and by 1996 it was $19,824 (40th). Total personal disposable income rose from $74.2 billion in 1995 to $77.4 billion in 1996. Median household income in 1997 was $34,400.

Income, although increasing, is unequally distributed. In 1995, about 19.7% of all Louisianians were below the federal poverty level. About 115,000 (8%) households in Louisiana had a disposable income greater than $75,000 in 1992, including about 25,000 (1.7%) whose disposable incomes exceeded $125,000.

22LABOR

In 1996, Louisiana had a total civilian labor force of 1,997,000 or about 62% of the working-age population. The average number of employed Louisianians in 1996 was 1,863,000, and 135,000 were unemployed, for an average annual unemployment rate of 6.7%.

At the beginning of 1997, Louisiana had an estimated 1,811,200 nonfarm employees, with mining accounting for 2.7%; construction, 6.2%; manufacturing, 10.4%; transportation, communications, and public utilities, 6%; wholesale and retail trade, 23.9%; finance, insurance and real estate, 4.4%; services, 26.6%; and government, 19.8%.

During the ante-bellum period, Louisiana had both the largest slave market in the US—New Orleans—and the largest slave revolt in the nation's history, in St. Charles and St. John the Baptist parishes in January 1811. New Orleans also had a relatively large free black population, and many of the slaves in the city were skilled workers, some of whom were able to earn their freedom by outside employment. Major efforts to organize Louisiana workers began after the Civil War. There were strikes in the cane fields in the early 1880s, and in the mid-1880s, the Knights of Labor began to organize the cane workers. The strike they called in 1886 was ended by hired strikebreakers, who killed at least 30 blacks. Back in New Orleans, the Knights of Labor led a general strike in 1892. The Brotherhood of Timber Workers began organizing in 1910, but had little to show for their efforts except the scars of violent conflict with the lumber-mill owners.

In 1995, 114,400 workers belonged to labor unions, or about 7% of all employees. Only 16.8% of all manufacturing workers were union members. A right-to-work law was passed in 1976, partly as a result of violent conflict between an AFL-CIO building trades union and an independent union over whose workers would build a petrochemical plant near Lake Charles. In 1979, a police strike began in New Orleans on the eve of Mardi Gras, causing the cancellation of most of the parades, but it collapsed the following month.

23AGRICULTURE

With a farm income of $2.03 billion in 1995—66% from crops—Louisiana ranked 32d among the 50 states. Nearly every crop grown in North America can be raised somewhere in Louisiana. In the south are strawberries, oranges, sweet potatoes, and truck crops; in the southeast, sugarcane; and in the southwest, rice and soybeans. Soybeans—which were introduced into Louisiana after World War I—are also raised in the cotton-growing area of the northeast and in a diagonal belt running east-northwest along the Red River. Oats, alfalfa, corn, potatoes, and peaches are among the other crops grown in the north.

As of 1996, there were an estimated 27,000 farms covering 8.7 million acres (3.5 million hectares) with an average farm size of 322 acres (130 hectares). Louisiana ranked 2nd in the US in sugar cane production. Cash receipts for the sugar crop in 1995 amounted to $257,394,000 for 10,240,000 tons. Louisiana ranked 3d in the value of its rice production in 1995, $196,860,000 for 26,209,000 hundredweight (a unit of measure equal to 100 lb); 6th for upland cotton in 1995, $537,805,000 for 1,375,000 bales; and 16th for soybeans in 1995, $168,427,000 for 26,000,000 bushels.

24ANIMAL HUSBANDRY

In the mid-19th century, before rice production began there, southwestern Louisiana was a major cattle-raising area. Today, cattle are raised mainly in the southeast (between the Mississippi and Pearl rivers), in the north-central region, and in the west.

In 1997, there were an estimated 1 million cattle and calves worth $410 million. In 1996, Louisiana had an estimated 40,000 hogs and pigs worth around $4 million. Dairy farmers had an estimated 79,000 milk cows, which produced 905 million pounds of milk in 1995. Also during 1995, poultry farmers produced an estimated 10 million pounds of chicken, which sold for $589,000 and an estimated 472 million eggs worth around $38.7 million.

Fur trapping has some local importance. In 1981, a month-long statewide alligator season was held for the first time in 18 years.

25FISHING

In 1995, Louisiana was second behind only Alaska in the size of its commercial landings, with more than 1.1 billion lb, and ranked 2d by value of catch at $290.5 million. Empire-Venice was 3d highest of all US ports in 1995 with a catch of 298.1 million lb. The ports of Cameron and Intercoastal City ranked 4th and 5th respectively, together accounting for another 459.2 million lb.

The most important species caught in Louisiana are shrimp, menhaden, and oysters. In 1995, shrimp landings amounted to 88,300,000 lb, 29% of the US total.

Louisiana produces most of the US crawfish harvest. With demand far exceeding the natural supply, crawfish farming began about 1959. In 1995, crawfish farms covered some 100,000 acres (40,500 hectares). Spring water levels of the state's Atchafalaya Basin cause the wild crawfish harvest to vary from year to year. The rapid increase in imports of low-priced frozen crawfish meat from China between 1992 and 1995 greatly concerned the Louisiana crawfish industry. Catfish are also cultivated in Louisiana, on 108 farms covering some 14,300 acres (5,790 hectares) in January 1997, with an inventory of about 34 million fingerlings and 99.8 million stocker-sized catfish. Cash receipts from aquacultural sales were $51.9 million in 1995.

Louisiana had 621,283 sport fishing license holders in 1995/96, when the state was apportioned $3.3 million by the US Fish and Wildlife Service for sportfish restoration programs. More than 1.2 million fish and 100,000 fish eggs were distributed within the state by federal hatcheries in 1995/96.

26FORESTRY

As of 1992, there were 13,864,000 acres (5,611,000 hectares) of forestland in Louisiana, representing almost half the state's land area and 2% of all US forests. The principal forest types are loblolly and shortleaf pine in the northwest, longleaf and slash pine in the south, and hardwood in a wide area along the Mississippi River. More than 99% of Louisiana's forests—some 13,855,000 acres (5,607,000 hectares) in 1992—are commercial timberland, over 90% of it privately owned. In 1996, forest landowner income from sales of timber was estimated at $594.9 million. The value of shipments by the lumber and wood products industry was $2.5 billion in 1995; by the paper and allied products industry, $5.4 billion.

Louisiana has one national forest, Kisatchie, with a gross area of 1,022,703 acres (413,875 hectares) within its boundaries and almost 600,000 acres (242,800 hectares) of National Forest System lands. Near the boundaries of Kisatchie's Evangeline Unit is the Alexander State Forest, established in 1923.

27MINING

The US Geological Survey's 1995 estimate of Louisiana's nonfuel mineral value totaled $387 million, $33 million above the figure reported by the state's mineral producers in 1994. The estimated value increased by 51% from 1993 to 1994, but was still less than the record $584 million produced in 1980. The leading mineral commodities, in terms of reported value, were salt, $158,000,000; construction sand and gravel, $55,400,000; and industrial sand and gravel, $9,320,000. Louisiana is the leading state in salt and sulfur production. Salt brine is produced in Ascension, Assumption, Calcasieu, Iberville, and Lafourche Parishes. Rock salt is produced in Iberia and St. Mary Parishes, with Iberia Parish contributing 63% to the state's total salt production in 1995. All sulfur production comes from a mine 27 km (17 mi) off the Louisiana coast. According to the Louisiana Geological Survey, more than 148 mineral producers were mining in 51 of the state's 64 parishes in 1995. Employment in mining was approximately 48,300 in December 1996, with 14,200 in the New Orleans area. The state's national ranking in mineral value rose one position to 33d in 1995.

28ENERGY AND POWER

Oil and gas production has expanded greatly since World War II, but production reached its peak in the early 1970s and proved reserves are declining.

At the beginning of 1996, power plants in Louisiana had a total installed capacity of 18.37 million kW. In 1995, total electrical generation was 65.56 billion kWh. Energy consumption in 1994 was 3,817 trillion Btu—884.3 million Btu per capita. Louisiana ranked 2d nationally in per capita energy consumption in 1994. About 44% of the state's energy needs were supplied by natural gas, 41% by oil, and 15% by other sources. As of 1996, Louisiana had two nuclear power plants: Waterford 3 in St. Charles Parish (capacity, 1,199,900 kW), which received a low-power operating license on 18 December 1984, and River Bend I in West Feliciana Parish (1,036,000 kW), which began commercial operation in December 1985.

Louisiana produced 132,151,000 barrels of crude oil during 1996: 22,141,000 from offshore wells and 110,010,000 from the rest of the state. Production that year was approximately 5.6% of the US total. At the end of 1995, remaining proven reserves of oil in Louisiana amounted to 637 million barrels (2.8% of the US total), down about 12 million barrels from a year earlier, continuing a trend that began in 1971.

Louisiana accounts for 27% of US gross withdrawals of natural gas. Marketed production in 1995 was 5.1 trillion cu feet, leaving proven reserves of 9.2 trillion cu feet of any natural gas. There were 14,169 producing gas wells in 1991, down from 16,889 in 1990. Energy conservation plans in Louisiana call for development of untapped energy sources, such as the state's lignite and geothermal reserves.

29INDUSTRY

The Standard Oil Refinery (now owned by Exxon) that is today the largest in North America began operations in Louisiana in 1909, the same year construction started on the state's first long-distance oil pipeline. Since then, a huge and still-growing petrochemical industry has become a dominant force in the state's economy. Other expanding industries are wood products and, especially since World War II, shipbuilding.

In 1995, the total value of shipments of manufactured goods was $74,492,800,000.

The following table shows value of shipments in 1995 for selected industry groups:

Chemicals and allied products	$24,765,500,000
Petroleum coal products	22,772,000,000
Food and food products	5,611,900,000
Paper and allied products	5,364,100,000
Transportation equipment	4,302,100,000
Lumber and wood products	2,539,100,000

The principal industrial regions extend along the Mississippi River from north of Baton Rouge to New Orleans, and also include the Monroe, Shreveport, Morgan City, and Lake Charles areas.

In 1995, 407 US patents were issued to Louisiana residents.

30COMMERCE

Louisiana had 7,347 wholesale establishments in 1992, with sales of $37.3 billion (including $12.8 billion in durable goods). Retail trade amounted to $27.8 billion (23d) in 1992, conducted by 22,644 establishments. The leading retail categories were food stores, with 22.2% of total sales; automotive dealers, 21%; general merchandise stores, 15.7%; eating and drinking places, 9.8%.

31CONSUMER PROTECTION

The Consumer Protection Section, Department of Justice, investigates and mediates consumer complaints, takes action against companies allegedly engaging in unfair business practices, distributes consumer publications, and registers multi-level marketing, telemarketing, and charitable organizations. It does not handle the areas of insurance, banking, or utilities.

32BANKING

As of 31 December 1996, Louisiana had 172 insured commercial banks with assets totaling $46.97 billion, comprised of 143 state-chartered banks with assets totaling $16.98 billion, and 29 nationally chartered banks, with assets totaling $29.99 billion.

As of 31 December 1996, Louisiana banks had total loans of $27.73 billion, investment securities of $12.79 billion, deposits of $38.25 billion, Tier 1 capital of $4.48 billion, and an aggregate Tier 1 Capital Ratio of 9.53%. Aggregate net income for calendar year 1996 was $570 million, or a return on average assets of 1.27%.

Louisiana banks remain in sound financial condition. Calendar year 1996 was characterized by slightly reduced but continued solid earnings, some asset growth, modest capital increases, and continued strong loan growth. Loan demand increased during the year, as banks continued to shift assets from lower-yielding investment securities to loans. Earnings decreased slightly during 1996, but remained strong. All but 4 of 172 Louisiana banks showed operating profits during 1996.

Although the number of banks in Louisiana continues to decline, aggregate assets are increasing. Between year-end 1992 and year-end 1996, the total number of banks decreased from 221 to 172, or by approximately 22%. However, total assets increased from $39.27 billion to $46.97 billion, or an increase of approximately 20%. Louisiana remains one of the most active states in the southeast region of the United States in merger and acquisition activity, and such activity is expected to continue at a moderate pace in 1997.

Louisiana state-chartered banks are regulated by the Office of Financial Institutions under the Department of Economic Development. Nationally chartered banks are regulated by the Office of the Comptroller of the Currency.

33INSURANCE

There were 74 life insurance companies domiciled in the state in mid-1995. That year, Louisianians held 2,967,000 life insurance policies with a total value of $173.2 billion; the average family held $107,900 in coverage. Total benefits paid that year amounted to $1,868.2 million, of which $568.8 million represented death benefits.

As of the end of 1994, 31 property/casualty insurance companies had headquarters in Louisiana. Premiums written by these and out-of-state insurance firms in 1995 totaled $4.5 billion, of which automobile liability coverage accounted for $1.9 billion; automobile physical damage insurance, $644.6 million; and homeowners' insurance, $505.9 million. At the end of 1991, over $25.7 billion in flood insurance was in force, 3d behind Florida and Texas among the 50 states. The Department of Insurance administers Louisiana's laws governing the industry.

34SECURITIES

There are no securities or commodities exchanges in Louisiana. As of May 1997, Louisiana had 1,000 brokers and 50,000 agents registered to sell securities in Louisiana.

35PUBLIC FINANCE

The budget is prepared by the state executive budget director and submitted annually by the governor to the legislature for amendment and approval. The fiscal year runs from 1 July through 30 June. The following table shows revenues and expenditures for fiscal years 1995 and 1996 (in millions):

	1995	1996
REVENUES		
Intergovernmental revenues	$4,777	$4,335
Taxes	4,926	5,180
Use of money and property	784	909
Licenses, permits and fees	368	431
Sales of commodities and services	539	548
Other receipts	299	253
TOTALS	$9,533	11,656
EXPENDITURES		
Public education	$2,643	$2,698
Health and human resources	4,733	4,266
Aid to local governments	326	385
Transportation and development	235	237
(Insurance Operations)	467	578
Corrections	358	378
Public safety	168	178
Other appropriations and requirements	44	41
Debt service	693	643
Capital outlays	635	665
TOTALS	$11,303	$10,974

In 1996, the state's general obligation debt service requirements to maturity was $2.9 billion. The general obligation bonded debt per capita in 1995 was $777 per capita.

36TAXATION

For most of the state's history, Louisianians paid little in taxes. Despite increases in taxation and expenditures since the late 1920s, when Huey Long introduced the graduated income tax, Louisiana's state tax burden per capita, $1,077 in 1995, is still well below the national average.

Income taxes yielded $1.19 billion in state revenues in 1996. As of 1996, the individual income tax ranged from 2% to 6%. The corporate income tax ranged from 4% on the first $25,000 up to 8% on net income over $200,000.

The state's sales and use tax, which yielded over $1.96 billion to the state in 1996, was raised from 3% to 4% in 1984. Parishes and municipalities may impose additional sales taxes. Louisiana has natural resource severance taxes, whose rates vary according to the resource. The state also taxes gasoline sales (this tax doubled from 8 cents a gallon to 16 cents in 1984, and was 20 cents as of 1992), gifts and inheritances, soft drinks, alcoholic beverages, and tobacco products, among other items. Taxes on beer and chain stores contribute to local revenues, as does the property tax, although Louisiana relies less on this than do most other states. The Louisiana Stadium and Exposition District, and the New Orleans Exhibition Hall Authority impose a tax on hotel and motel room occupancy in the greater New Orleans area. In addition, local taxing authorities may impose a tax on hotel and motel room occupancy.

In fiscal 1995, Louisiana had a federal tax burden of $16.6 billion, or $3,830 per capita.

37ECONOMIC POLICY

The Office of Commerce and Industry in the Department of Economic Development seeks to encourage investment and create jobs in the state and to expand the markets for Louisiana products. Financial assistance services for industrial development include state and local tax incentives and state "Enterprise Zone" legislation. The Louisiana Small Business Equity Corporation and the Louisiana Minority Business Development Authority offer financial assistance.

38HEALTH

There were 65,574 live births in Louisiana in 1995, for a crude birth rate of 14.7 per 1,000 population. Of these births, 37,348 (56.9%) were to Whites, 26,807 (40.9%) were to African-Americans, and 1,419 (2.2%) to women classified under the racial category "Others." Teen births accounted for 12,548 (19.1%) of the total number of live births. Among the teenaged mothers, the highest birth rate was among the mothers aged 15 through 19 at a rate of 72.8 per 1,000 population. The number and the rate of births to unmarried mothers continues to increase in Louisiana. In 1995, 42% of the live births were to unmarried mothers. Of all the births to whites, 22% were to unmarried mothers compared with 72% for African-Americans. Of all the births to unmarried women, 37% were among teenagers. The timely receipt of prenatal care has improved by 15% since 1987. In 1995, 80% of mothers began prenatal care in the first trimester. However, only 69% of African-American mothers and 50% of teens received any prenatal care in the first trimester of pregnancy.

In 1995, life expectancy at birth for the total population of Louisiana was 73.9 years, approximately two years below the national life expectancy of 75.5 years. Examination of the life expectancies among the different race-sex groups shows that black males have the lowest life expectancy (65.2 years). This was nine years below the life expectancy of black females (74.2 years). The life expectancy of white females was 79.2 versus 72.8 for white males, a difference of 6.4 years.

The infant mortality rate in 1995 was 9.9 per 1,000 live births accounting for 2.4% of total deaths. Major causes of infant deaths include birth trauma, disorders relating to abnormal gestation, intrauterine hypoxia, and birth asphyxia. Other leading causes of infant death were congenital anomalies (1.7 per 2,000) and pneumonia (0.23 per 1,000). Age-adjusted death rates from heart disease (163.21 per 100,000), malignant neoplasms (151.2 per 100,000), suicide (11.7 per 100,000) cerebrovascular diseases (31.3 per 100,000), accidents and adverse effects (38 per 100,000) for the entire population of Louisiana were above the US median. The overall age-adjusted death rate, 584.8 per 100,000 population was also above the national rate of 513.3.

In 1991, the 170 hospitals in Louisiana had a total of 23,818 beds and recorded 658,714 admissions. Hospital personnel included 14,785 registered nurses. The average expense to hospitals in the state in 1991 was $5,044 per stay and $764 per inpatient day, both below the national average. There were 9,316 physicians in 1991, and 1,856 active licensed dentists in the state in 1993.

39SOCIAL WELFARE

During the governorships of Huey and Earl Long, Louisiana developed a relatively progressive welfare system. In 1996, 239,200 residents received AFDC payments averaging $234 a month. In 1996, the food stamp program had an average monthly participation of 670,034. Pupils benefited from the school lunch program in 1996, at a federal cost of $144.8 million.

With the enactment of the Personal Responsibility and Work Opportunity Reconciliation Act of 1996, the US government has changed the form and regulations for many of its social welfare programs; most significantly, it replaces Aid to Families with Dependent Children (AFDC), an open-ended entitlement program, with Temporary Assistance for Needy Families (TANF), a limited system of assistance funded largely through federal block grants. The reform act also impacts the food stamp program, the Supplemental Security Income program, and the child nutrition program. The law took effect on 1 July 1997 and provided $16.38 billion in block grants for fiscal years 1997–2002. The grants are to be divided among the states based on an equation involving the numbers of former AFDC recipients in each state. Because many of the bill's provisions have yet to be implemented into state-by-state policy, it was not possible to include the details of each state's programs for this edition of this work.

During 1996, Social Security benefits were paid to 701,790 Louisianians. Supplemental Security Income payments that year went to 182,104 residents, averaging $336 a month. In 1995, weekly unemployment insurance benefits averaged $121.38.

40HOUSING

The Indians of Louisiana built huts with walls made of clay kneaded with Spanish moss and covered with cypress bark or palmetto leaves. The earliest European settlers used split cypress boards filled with clay and moss; a few early 18th-century houses with clay and moss walls remain in the Natchitoches area. Examples of later architectural styles also survive, including buildings constructed of bricks between heavy cypress posts, covered with plaster; houses in the raised cottage style, supported by brick piers and usually including a wide gallery and colonettes; the Creole dwellings of the Vieux Carre in New Orleans, built of brick and characterized by balconies and French windows; and urban and plantation houses from the Greek Revival period of ante bellum Louisiana.

In 1996 there were 1,761,000 housing units, of which 1,556,000 were occupied. In 1996, 17,998 privately owned units, valued at $1.4 billion, were authorized for construction; of these, 14,422 were single-family. In 1990, New Orleans had 264,146 housing units, 7.2% of which had been built during the previous decade. The median value of a home in Louisiana fell by 14.3 (in terms of 1990 dollars) during the 1980s, to $58,500 in 1990. Owner-occupied monthly costs (including mortgage) had a median of $595 in 1990, the last year for which figures are available, and the median monthly rent was $352. During fiscal year 1996, Louisiana received $362.9 million in aid from the US Department of Housing and Urban Development, including $87.8 million in community development block grants.

41EDUCATION

Most education in Louisiana was provided through private (often parochial) schools until Reconstruction. Not until Huey Long's administration, when spending for education increased greatly and free textbooks were supplied, did education become a high priority of the state. As of 1990, only 68.7% of adult Louisianians had completed high school, and 15.3% had completed four or more years of college.

In fall 1995, total enrollment in Louisiana's public elementary and secondary schools was 785,433. In the 1995/96 school year, expenditure per pupil was $4,468.

Integration of New Orleans public schools began in 1960; two years later, the archbishop of New Orleans required that all Catholic schools under his jurisdiction be desegregated. However, it took a federal court order in 1966 to bring about integration in public schools throughout the state. By 1980, 36% of minority students in Louisiana were in schools with under 50% minority enrollment, and 25% were in schools with 99–100% minority enrollment. The civil rights revolution also affected other aspects of Louisiana education. In 1946/47, combined salaries of principals and teachers averaged $1,765 for whites and $936 for blacks. By 1996, the average salary for all teachers was $26,800 with very little, if any, discrepancy between blacks and whites.

As of 1990, in addition to 53 vocational-technical schools, there were 34 institutions of higher education in Louisiana, of which 22 were public and 12 private. The center of the state university system is Louisiana State University (LSU), founded at Baton Rouge in 1855 and having a 1990/91 enrollment of 26,112; LSU also has campuses at Alexandria, Eunice, and

Shreveport, and includes the University of New Orleans, with 15,322 students. Tulane University, founded in New Orleans in 1834, is one of the most distinguished private universities in the South, as is Loyola University, also in New Orleans. As of the early 1990s, Southern University Agricultural and Mechanical System at Baton Rouge (1881) was the largest predominantly black university in the country; other campuses were in New Orleans and Shreveport. Another mainly black institution is Grambling State University (1901).

The Governor's Special Commission on Education Services administers state loan, grant, and scholarship programs. The state Council for the Development of French in Louisiana (CODOFIL) organizes student exchanges with Quebec, Belgium, and France and aids Louisianians studying French abroad.

Total state and local expenditures on public schools in 1989/90 exceeded $2.8 billion.

42ARTS

New Orleans has long been one of the most important centers of artistic activity in the South. The earliest theaters were French, and the first of these was started by refugees from Hispaniola, who put on the city's first professional theatrical performance in 1791. The American Theater, which opened in 1824, attracted many of the finest actors in America, as did the nationally famous St. Charles. Showboats traveled the Mississippi and other waterways, bringing dramas, musicals, and minstrel shows to river towns and plantations as early as the 1840s, with their heyday being the 1870s and 1880s.

In the mid-1990s, principal theaters included the New Orleans Theater of the Performing Arts, the Saenger Theater in New Orleans, one of the "grand old theaters," Le Petit Theatre du Vieux Carre, and the Tulane Theater. Junebug Productions is a black touring company based in New Orleans. LSU at Baton Rouge has theaters for both opera and drama. Baton Rouge, Shreveport, Monroe, Lake Charles, and Hammond are among the cities with little theaters, and Baton Rouge, Lafayette, and Lake Charles have ballet companies. There are symphony orchestras in most of the larger cities, the Louisiana Philharmonic Orchestra being the best known.

It is probably in music that Louisiana has made its most distinctive contributions to culture. Jazz was born in New Orleans around 1900; among its sources was the music played by brass bands at carnivals and at Negro funerals, and its immediate precursor was the highly syncopated music known as ragtime. Early jazz in the New Orleans style is called Dixieland; the transformation of jazz from the Dixieland ensemble style to a medium for solo improvisation was pioneered by Louis Armstrong. Traditional Dixieland may still be heard in New Orleans at Preservation Hall, Dixieland Hall, and the New Orleans Jazz Club. Equally distinctive is Cajun music, dominated by the sound of the fiddle and accordion. The French Acadian Music Festival, held in Abbeville, takes place in April.

Louisiana provides grants for arts projects and also created and maintains the Louisiana State Museum. Arts projects are funded in every parish (county) in the state through the Louisiana Division of the Arts' Decentralized Arts Funding Program.

Visual arts in the state continue to flourish, especially in New Orleans, where the New Orleans Museum of Southern Art is slated to open in 1998.

43LIBRARIES AND MUSEUMS

Louisiana's 64 parishes were served by 65 public libraries in 1995. That year, the public library system held 10,488,371 volumes and had a total circulation of 18,682,170. The New Orleans Public Library, with 11 branches and 1,003,274 books, features a special collection on jazz and folk music, and the Tulane University Library (1,470,549 volumes) has special collec-

tions on jazz and Louisiana history. Among the libraries with special black-studies collections are those of Grambling State University, Southern University Agricultural and Mechanical System at Baton Rouge, Xavier University of Louisiana at New Orleans, and the Amistad Collection at Tulane University. The library of Northwestern State University at Natchitoches has special collections on Louisiana history, folklore, Indians, botany, and oral history.

As of 1996, Louisiana had 152 museums, historic sites, and public gardens, as well as 27 art collections. Leading art museums are the New Orleans Museum of Art, the Lampe Gallery in New Orleans, and the R. W. Norton Art Gallery at Shreveport. The art museum of the Louisiana Arts and Science Center at Baton Rouge is located in the renovated Old Illinois Central Railroad Station. The oldest and largest museum in the state is the Louisiana State Museum, an eight-building historic complex in the Vieux Carre. There is a military museum in Beauregard House at Chalmette National Historical Park, on the site of the Battle of New Orleans, and a Confederate Museum in New Orleans. The Bayou Folk Museum at Cloutierville is in the restored home of author Kate Chopin; the Longfellow-Evangeline State Commemorative Area has a historical museum on its site. Among the state's scientific museums are the Lafayette Natural History Museum, Planetarium, and Nature Station, and the Museum of Natural Science in Baton Rouge. Audubon Park and Zoological Gardens are in New Orleans. The "Louisiana and Lower Mississippi Valley Collection" at LSU is an extensive collection of Louisiana history, photographs, and manuscripts.

44COMMUNICATIONS

The second rural free delivery route in the US, and the first in Louisiana, was established on 1 November 1896 at Thibodaux. As of March 1993, 90.3% of Louisiana's 1,540,000 occupied housing units had telephones.

In 1996, the state had 211 radio broadcasting stations (84 AM and 127 FM) as well as 28 commercial and 8 educational television stations. That year, there were nine large cable television systems.

45PRESS

At one time, New Orleans had as many as 9 daily newspapers (4 English, 3 French, 1 Italian, and 1 German), but by 1997 there was only 1, the *Times-Picayune*. In 1997, Louisiana had a total of 13 morning dailies, 12 evening dailies, and 18 Sunday papers. The following table shows the principal dailies with their 1997 circulations:

AREA	NAME	DAILY	SUNDAY
Baton Rouge	*Advocate* (m,S)	99,960	137,368
New Orleans	*Times-Picayune*	262,462	311,264
Shreveport	*Times* (m,S)	79,605	99,035

Two influential literary magazines originated in the state. The *Southern Review* was founded at LSU in the 1930s by Robert Penn Warren and Cleanth Brooks. The *Tulane Drama Review*, founded in 1955, moved to New York University in 1967 but is still known by its original acronym, TDR.

46ORGANIZATIONS

The 1992 Census of Service Industries counted 857 organizations in Louisiana, including 203 business associations; 456 civic, social, and fraternal associations, as well as 198 other membership organizations. Among business or professional organizations with headquarters in Louisiana are the Federated Pecan Growers' Associations of the US and the Louisiana Historical Association, currently in Lafayette; the National Rice Growers Association at Jennings; and the Federal Court Clerks Association and the Southern Forest Products Association, both in New Orleans. Blue Key, a national honor society, has its headquarters in Metairie.

Civil rights groups represented in the state include the National Association for the Advancement of Colored People (NAACP) and the Urban League. Especially active during the 1970s were the local branches of the American Civil Liberties Union, the Louisiana Coalition on Jails and Prisons, and its legal arm, the Southern Prisoners Defense Council, and the Fishermen's and Concerned Citizens Association of Plaquemines Parish, which organized a campaign against the continued domination of the parish by the descendants of Leander Perez, a racist judge who ruled there for 50 years until his death in 1969.

The Invisible Empire, Knights of the Ku Klux Klan, is headquartered in Denham Springs.

[47]TOURISM, TRAVEL, AND RECREATION

In 1996, 849,136 tourists visited Louisiana's Chalmette National Historic Park. Domestic visitors spent an estimated $4.8 million on overnight and day trips in the state in 1993.

New Orleans is one of the major tourist attractions in the US. Known for its fine restaurants, serving such distinctive fare as gumbo, jambalaya, crawfish, and beignets, along with an elaborate French-inspired haute cuisine, New Orleans also offers jazz clubs, the graceful buildings of the French Quarter, and a lavish carnival called Mardi Gras ("Fat Tuesday"). Beginning on the Wednesday before Shrove Tuesday, parades and balls staged by private organizations called krewes are held almost nightly. In other towns, people celebrate Mardi Gras in their own, no less uproarious, manner.

Among the many other annual events that attract visitors to the state are the blessing of the shrimp fleet at the Louisiana Shrimp and Petroleum Festival in Morgan City on Labor Day weekend and the blessing of the cane fields during the Louisiana Sugar Cane Festival at New Iberia in September. October offers the International Rice Festival (including the Frog Derby) at Crowley, Louisiana Cotton Festival at Ville Platte (with a medieval jousting tournament), the Louisiana Yambilee Festival at Opelousas, and the Louisiana State Fair at Shreveport. Attractions of the Natchitoches Christmas Festival include 170,000 Christmas lights and spectacular fireworks displays.

Louisiana's 34 state parks and recreation sites totaled 39,000 acres (15,800 hectares) that year. In 1995, sport licenses were held by 556,378 hunters and 914,549 anglers.

[48]SPORTS

Louisiana has one major league professional sports team: the Saints of the National Football League. The Super Bowl has been held in New Orleans five times: in 1978, 1981, 1986, 1990, and 1997.

New Orleans also has a minor league baseball team, the Zephyrs, of the Triple-A American Association. In Shreveport, the Captains compete in the Double-A Texas League.

During the 1850s, New Orleans was the horse-racing center of the US, and racing is still popular in the state. The principal tracks are the Louisiana Jockey Club at the Fair Grounds in New Orleans, and Evangeline Downs at Lafayette. Gambling has long been widespread in Louisiana, particularly in steamboat days, when races along the Mississippi drew huge wagers.

From the 1880s to World War I, New Orleans was the nation's boxing capital, and in 1893, the city was the site of the longest bout in boxing history, between Andy Bowen and Jack Burke, lasting 7 hours and 19 minutes, 110 rounds, and ending in a draw. The New Orleans Open golf tournament, held in April, has been won by Billy Casper (twice), Gary Player, and Jack Nicklaus, among others.

In 1935, Tulane University inaugurated the Sugar Bowl (which they won that year for the first and only time), an annual New Year's Day event and one of the most prestigious bowl games in college football. Louisiana State University (LSU) won the Sugar Bowl in 1959, 1965, and 1968. They were named National Champions in 1958. The LSU Tigers baseball team won the College World Series in 1991, 1993, 1996, and 1997—more than any other college baseball team.

[49]FAMOUS LOUISIANIANS

Zachary Taylor (b.Virginia, 1784–1850) is the only US president to whom Louisiana can lay claim. Taylor, a professional soldier who made his reputation as an Indian fighter and in the Mexican War, owned a large plantation north of Baton Rouge, which was his residence before his election to the presidency in 1848. Edward Douglass White (1845–1921) served first as associate justice of the US Supreme Court and then as chief justice.

Most other Louisianians who have held national office won more fame as state or confederate officials. John Slidell (b.New York, 1793–1871), an antebellum political leader, also played an important role in Confederate diplomacy. Judah P. Benjamin (b.West Indies, 1811–84), of Jewish lineage, was a US senator before the Civil War; during the conflict he held three posts in the Confederate cabinet, after which he went to England and became a leading barrister. Henry Watkins Allen (b.Virginia, 1820–66) was elected governor of Confederate Louisiana in 1864, after he had been maimed in battle; perhaps the best administrator in the South, he installed a system of near-socialism in Louisiana as the fortunes of the Confederacy waned. During and after the Civil War, many Louisianians won prominence as military leaders. Leonidas Polk (b.North Carolina, 1806–64), the state's first Episcopal bishop, became a lieutenant general in the Confederate Army and died in the Atlanta campaign. Zachary Taylor's son Richard (b.Kentucky, 1826–79), a sugar planter who also became a Confederate lieutenant general, is noted for his defeat of Nathaniel P. Bank's Union forces in the Red River campaign of 1864. Pierre Gustave Toutant Beauregard (1818–93) attained the rank of full general in the Confederate Army and later served as director of the Louisiana state lottery, one of the state's major sources of revenue at that time. In the modern era, General Claire Chennault (b.Texas 1893–1958) commanded the famous "Flying Tigers" and then the US 14th Air Force in China during World War II.

Throughout the 20th century, the Longs have been the first family of Louisiana politics. Without question, the most important state officeholder in Louisiana history was Huey P. Long (1893–1935), a latter-day Populist who was elected to the governorship in 1928 and inaugurated a period of social and economic reform. In the process, he made himself very nearly an absolute dictator within Louisiana. After his election to the US Senate, the "King Fish" became a national figure, challenging Franklin D. Roosevelt's New Deal with his "Share the Wealth" plan and flamboyant oratory. Huey's brother Earl K. Long (1895–1960) served three times as governor. Huey's son, US Senator Russell B. Long (b.1918), was chairman of the Finance Committee—and, consequently, one of the most powerful men in Congress—from 1965 to 1980.

Also prominent in Louisiana history were Robert Cavelier, Sieur de la Salle (b.France, 1643–87), who was the first to claim the region for the French crown; Pierre le Moyne, Sieur d'Iberville (b.Canada, 1661–1706), who commanded the expedition that first established permanent settlements in the lands La Salle had claimed; his brother, Jean Baptiste le Moyne, Sieur de Bienville (b.Canada, 1680–1768), governor of the struggling colony and founder of New Orleans; and Bernardo de Galvez (b.Spain, 1746–86), who, as governor of Spanish Louisiana during the last years of the American Revolution, conquered British-held Florida in a series of brilliant campaigns. William Charles Coles Claiborne (b.Virginia, 1775–1817) was the last territorial and first state governor of Louisiana. The state's first Republican governor, Henry Clay Warmoth (b.Illinois, 1842–1932), came there as a Union officer before the end of the Civil War and was sworn in at age 26. Jean Étienne de Boré (b.France, 1741–1820) laid the foundation of the Louisiana sugar industry by developing a process for granulating sugar from cane; Norbert Rillieux (birthplace unknown, 1806–94), a free black man, developed the much more efficient vacuum pan process of refining sugar.

Andrew Victor Schally (b.Poland, 1926), a biochemist on the faculty of the Tulane University School of Medicine, shared the Nobel Prize for medicine in 1977 for his research on hormones. Among other distinguished Louisiana professionals have been historian T. Harry Williams (1909–79), who won the Pulitzer Prize for his biography of Huey Long; architect Henry Hobson Richardson (1838–86); and four doctors of medicine: public health pioneer Joseph Jones (b.Georgia, 1833–96), surgical innovator Rudolph Matas (1860–1957), surgeon and medical editor Alton V. Ochsner (b.South Dakota, 1896–1981), and heart specialist Michael De Bakey (b.1908).

Louisiana's important writers include George Washington Cable (1844–1925), an early advocate of racial justice; Kate O'Flaherty Chopin (b.Missouri, 1851–1904); playwright and memoirist Lillian Hellman (1905–84); and novelists Walker Percy (b.Alabama 1916–1990); Truman Capote (1924–84); Ernest Gaines (b.1933), author of *The Autobiography of Miss Jane Pittman;* Shirley Ann Grau (b.1929); and John Kennedy Toole (1937–69), the last two being winners of the Pulitzer Prize.

Louisiana has produced two important composers, Ernest Guiraud (1837–92) and Louis Gottschalk (1829–69). Jelly Roll Morton (Ferdinand Joseph La Menthe, 1885–1941), Pete Fountain (b.1930), and Sidney Bechet (1897–1959) were important jazz musicians, and Louis "Satchmo" Armstrong (1900–1971) was one of the most prolific jazz innovators and popular performers in the nation. The distinctive rhythms of pianist and singer Professor Longhair (Henry Byrd, 1918–80) were an important influence on popular music. Other prominent Louisianians in music are gospel singer Mahalia Jackson (1911–72), pianist-singer-songwriter Antoine "Fats" Domino (b.1928), and pop singer Jerry Lee Lewis (b.1935).

Louisiana baseball heroes include Hall of Famer Melvin Thomas "Mel" Ott (1909–58) and pitcher Ron Guidry (b.1950).

Terry Bradshaw (b.1948), a native of Shreveport, quarterbacked the Super Bowl champion Pittsburgh Steelers during the 1970s. Player-coach William F. "Bill" Russell (b.1934) led the Boston Celtics to 10 National Basketball Association championships between 1956 and 1969. Chess master Paul Morphy (1837–84) was born in New Orleans.

[50]BIBLIOGRAPHY

Bell, Caryn Cossé. *Revolution, Romanticism, and the Afro-Creole Protest Tradition in Louisiana, 1718–1868.* Baton Rouge: Louisiana State University Press, 1997.

Fairclough, Adam. *Race & Democracy: The Civil Rights Struggle in Louisiana, 1915–1972.* Athens: University of Georgia Press, 1995.

Hair, William Ivy. *Bourbonism and Agrarian Protest in Louisiana, 1877–1900.* Baton Rouge: Louisiana State University Press, 1965.

Jackson, Joy. *New Orleans in the Gilded Age: Politics and Urban Progress, 1880–96.* Baton Rouge: Louisiana State University Press, 1969.

Louisiana, State of. Secretary of State. *Roster of Officials, 1997.* Baton Rouge, 1997.

Louisiana Almanac, 1997–98. Gretna, La.: Pelican Publishing Co., 1997.

Schafer, Judith Kelleher. *Slavery, the Civil Law, and the Supreme Court of Louisiana.* Baton Rouge: Louisiana State University Press, 1994.

Shugg, Roger W. *Origins of Class Struggle in Louisiana: A Social History of White Farmers and Laborers During Slavery and After, 1840–75.* Baton Rouge: Louisiana State University Press, 1968 (orig. 1939).

Taylor, Joe Gray. *Louisiana: A Bicentennial History.* New York: Norton, 1976.

——. *Louisiana Reconstructed, 1863–77.* Baton Rouge: Louisiana State University Press, 1974.

Williams, T. Harry. *Huey Long,* New York: Random House, 1981.

Winters, John D. *The Civil War in Louisiana.* Baton Rouge: Louisiana State University Press, 1979.

MAINE

State of Maine

¹LOCATION, SIZE, AND EXTENT

Situated in the extreme northeastern corner of the US, Maine is the nation's most easterly state, the largest in New England, and 39th in size among the 50 states.

The total area of Maine is 33,265 sq mi (86,156 sq km), including 30,995 sq mi (80,277 sq km) of land and 2,270 sq mi (5,879 sq km) of inland water. Maine extends 207 mi (333 km) E–W; the maximum N–S extension is 322 mi (518 km).

Maine is bordered on the N by the Canadian provinces of Quebec (with the line passing through the St. Francis River) and New Brunswick (with the boundary formed by the St. John River); on the E by New Brunswick (with the lower eastern boundary formed by the Chiputneticook Lakes and the St. Croix River); on the SE and S by the Atlantic Ocean; and on the W by New Hampshire (with the line passing through the Piscataqua and Salmon Falls rivers in the SW) and Quebec.

Hundreds of islands dot Maine's coast. The largest is Mt. Desert Island; others include Deer Isle, Vinalhaven, and Isle au Haut. The total boundary length of Maine is 883 mi (1,421 km).

The state's geographic center is in Piscataquis County, 18 mi (29 km) N of Dover-Foxcroft. The easternmost point of the US is West Quoddy Head, at 66°57'W.

²TOPOGRAPHY

Maine is divided into four main regions: coastal lowlands, piedmont, mountains, and uplands.

The narrow coastal lowlands extend, on average, 10–20 mi (16–32 km) inland from the irregular coastline, but occasionally disappear altogether, as at Mt. Desert Island and on the western shore of Penobscot Bay. Mt. Cadillac on Mt. Desert Island rises abruptly to 1,532 feet (467 meters), the highest elevation on the Atlantic coast north of Rio de Janeiro, Brazil. The transitional hilly belt, or piedmont, broadens from about 30 mi (48 km) wide in the southwestern part of the state to about 80 mi (129 km) in the northeast.

Maine's mountain region, the Longfellow range, is at the northeastern end of the Appalachian Mountain system. This zone, extending into Maine from the western border for about 150 mi (250 km) and averaging about 50 mi (80 km) wide, contains nine peaks over 4,000 feet (1,200 meters), including Mt. Katahdin, which at 5,268 feet (1,607 meters) is the highest point in the state. The summit of Katahdin marks the northern terminus of the 2,000-mi (3,200-km) Appalachian Trail. Maine's uplands form a high, relatively flat plateau extending northward beyond the mountains and sloping downward toward the north and east. The eastern part of this zone is the Aroostook potato-farming region; the western part is heavily forested.

Of Maine's more than 2,200 lakes and ponds, the largest are Moosehead Lake, 117 sq mi (303 sq km), and Sebago Lake, 13 mi (21 km) by 10 mi (16 km). Of the more than 5,000 rivers and streams, the Penobscot, Androscoggin, Kennebec, and Saco rivers drain historically and commercially important valleys. The longest river in Maine is the St. John, but it runs for most of its length in the Canadian province of New Brunswick.

³CLIMATE

Maine has three climatic regions: the northern interior zone, comprising roughly the northern half of the state, between Quebec and New Brunswick; the southern interior zone; and the coastal zone. The northern zone is both drier and cooler in all four seasons than either of the other zones, while the coastal zone is more moderate in temperature year-round than the other two.

The annual mean temperature in the northern zone is about 40°F (5°C); in the southern interior zone, 44°F (7°C); and in the coastal zone, 46°F (8°C). Record temperatures for the state are –48°F (–44°C), registered at Van Buren on 19 January 1925, and 105°F (41°C) at North Bridgton on 10 July 1911. The mean annual precipitation increases from 40.2 in (102 cm) in the north to 41.5 in (105 cm) in the southern interior and 45.7 in (116 cm) on the coast. Average annual snowfall is 78 in (198 cm).

⁴FLORA AND FAUNA

Maine's forests are largely softwoods, chiefly red and white spruces, balsam fir (*Abies balsamea*), eastern hemlock, and white and red pine. Important hardwoods include beech, yellow and white birches, sugar and red maples, white oak, black willow, black and white ashes, and American elm, which has fallen victim in recent years to Dutch elm disease. Maine is home to most of the flowers and shrubs common to the north temperate zone, including an important commercial resource, the low-bush blueberry. Maine has 17 rare orchid species, of which 4 are considered threatened; one species, the small whorled pogonia, is on the federal endangered list. The Furbish lousewart is also classified as endangered.

About 30,000 white-tailed deer are killed by hunters in Maine each year, but the herd does not appear to diminish. Moose hunting was banned in Maine in 1935; however, in 1980, 700 moose-hunting permits were issued for a six-day season, and moose hunting has continued despite attempts by some residents to ban the practice. Other common forest animals include the bobcat, beaver, muskrat, river otter, mink, fisher, raccoon, red fox, and snowshoe hare. The woodchuck is a conspicuous inhabitant of pastures, meadows, cornfields, and vegetable gardens. Seals, porpoises, and occasionally finback whales are found in coastal waters, along with virtually every variety of North Atlantic fish and shellfish, including the famous Maine lobster. Coastal waterfowl include the osprey, herring and great black-backed gulls, great and double-crested cormorants, and various duck species. Matinicus Rock, a small uninhabited island about 20 mi (32 km) off the coast near the entrance to Penobscot Bay, is the only known North American nesting site of the common puffin, or sea parrot.

Endangered species include the cougar, bald eagle, peregrine and Arctic falcons, shortnose sturgeon, and Indiana bat.

5ENVIRONMENTAL PROTECTION

The Department of Environmental Protection administers laws regulating the development of large residential, commercial, and industrial sites; the protection and improvement of air and water quality; the prevention and cleanup of oil spills; the control of hazardous wastes; the licensing of oil terminals; the protection of state-significant natural resources (including wetlands, rivers, streams and brooks, and fragile mountain areas); and mining. The Land Use Regulation Commission, established in 1969, extends the principles of town planning and zoning to Maine's 411 unorganized townships, 313 "plantations," and numerous coastal islands that have no local government and might otherwise be subject to ecologically unsound development.

6POPULATION

Maine's 1990 census population was 1,227,928 (38th among the 50 states), a 9.2% increase from 1980. The population was estimated at 1,243,316 in 1996, a 1.3% gain from 1990.

The area that now comprises the state of Maine was sparsely settled throughout the colonial period. At statehood, Maine had 298,335 residents. The population doubled by 1860, but then grew slowly until the 1970s, when its growth rate outstripped the nation's.

The population density for 1990 was 40 per sq mi (15 per sq km); more than half the population lives on less than one-seventh of the land within 25 mi (40km) of the Atlantic coast, and almost half the state is virtually uninhabited. Although almost half of Maine's population is classified as urban (44.6%), much of the urban population lives in towns and small cities. The state's major cities are Portland, with an estimated 61,982 people in 1994; Bangor, 32,004; and Lewiston-Auburn, 37,385.

7ETHNIC GROUPS

Maine's population is primarily Yankee, both in its English and Scotch-Irish origins and in its retention of many of the values and folkways of rural New England. The largest minority group consists of French-Canadians. Among those reporting at least one specific ancestry group in 1990, 372,042 claimed English ancestry; 223,653 French (not counting 123,857 who claimed

Canadian or French-Canadian); and 217,226 Irish. There were 32,296 foreign-born.

The most notable ethnic issue in Maine during the 1970s was the legal battle of the Penobscot and Passamaquoddy Indians—living on two reservations covering 27,546 acres (11,148 hectares)—to recover 12,500,000 acres (5,059,000 hectares) of treaty lands. A compromise settlement in 1980 awarded them $81.5 million, two-thirds of which went into a fund enabling the Indians to purchase 300,000 acres (121,000 hectares) of timberland. In 1995, Maine's American Indian population included the following groups living on or near reservations (with population estimates): the Penobscot Tribe (1,206); the Aristook Band of Micmac (1,155); Pleasant Point (878); the Passamaquoddy (722); and the Houlton Band of Maliseets (331).

As of 1990, Maine had 6,000 Indians, 5,000 Blacks, 7,000 Asians and Pacific Islanders, and 7,000 residents of Hispanic origin.

8LANGUAGES

Descendants of the Passamaquoddy and Penobscot Indians of the Algonkian family who inhabited Maine at the time that European settlers arrived still lived there in the mid-1980s. Algonkian place-names abound: Saco, Millinocket, Wiscasset, Kennebec, Skowhegan.

Maine English is celebrated as typical Yankee speech. Final /r/ is absent, a vowel sound between /ah/ and the /a/ in cat appears in car and garden, aunt and calf. Coat and home have a vowel that to outsiders sounds like the vowel in cut. Maple syrup comes from rock or sugar maple trees in a sap or sugar orchard; cottage cheese is curd cheese; and pancakes are fritters.

In 1990, 90.8% of Maine residents five years old or older reported speaking only English in the home; 81,012 residents spoke French, down from 95,181 in 1980.

The decline of parochial schools and a great increase in the number of young persons attending college have begun to erode the linguistic and cultural separateness that marks the history of the Franco-American experience in Maine.

9RELIGIONS

Maine had 264,943 Roman Catholics and an estimated 8,160 Jews in 1990. The leading Protestant denominations were United Methodist, with 36,164; American Baptist USA, with 32,549; United Church of Christ, 33,265; and Episcopal 16,375.

10TRANSPORTATION

Railroad development in Maine, which reached its peak in 1924, has declined rapidly since World War II, and passenger service has been dropped altogether. Although Maine had no Class I railroads in 1995, seven regional and local railroads operated on 1,270 rail mi (2,045 km) of track.

About three-quarters of all communities and about half the population depend entirely on highway trucking for the overland transportation of freight. In 1995, Maine had 22,577 mi (36,349 km) of public roads. There were 966,845 registered motor vehicles and 864,447 licensed drivers in 1995. The Maine Turnpike and I-95, which coincide between Portland and Kittery, are the major highways.

River traffic has been central to the lumber industry; only since World War II has trucking replaced seasonal log drives downstream from timberlands to the mills, a practice that is now outlawed for environmental reasons. Maine has 10 established seaports, with Portland and Searsport being the main depots for overseas shipping. In 1995, Portland harbor handled 11,456,007 tons; Bucksport, 1,237,542; and Searsport, 1,262,712. Crude oil, fuel oil, and gasoline were the chief commodities. There were 152 airfields in 1994; Portland International Jetport was the largest and most active, enplaning 460,596 passengers.

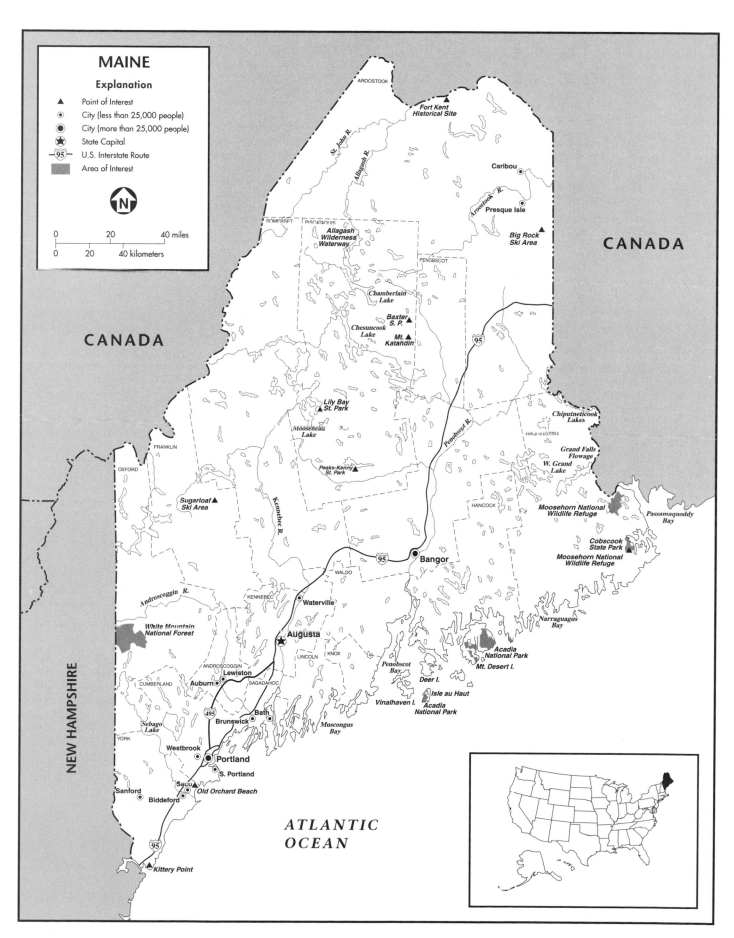

MAINE

Explanation

▲ Point of Interest
◉ City (less than 25,000 people)
◉ City (more than 25,000 people)
★ State Capital
—95— U.S. Interstate Route
▨ Area of Interest

N

0   20   40 miles
0   20   40 kilometers

CANADA

CANADA

AROOSTOOK

Fort Kent
Historical Site

Caribou

St. John R.

Allagash R.

Aroostook R.

Presque Isle

Big Rock
Ski Area

SOMERSET

PISCATAQUIS

Allagash
Wilderness
Waterway

PENOBSCOT

Chamberlain
Lake

Baxter
S. P.

Chesuncook
Lake

Mt.
Katahdin

Lily Bay
St. Park

Chiputneticook
Lakes

WASHINGTON

Mooseheud
Lake

Penobscot R.

Grand Falls
Flowage

W. Grand
Lake

FRANKLIN

Peaks-Kenny
St. Park

HANCOCK

Mooseborn National
Wildlife Refuge

Passamaquoddy
Bay

OXFORD

Sugarloaf
Ski Area

Cobscook
State Park

Mooseborn National
Wildlife Refuge

Kennebec R.

95

Bangor

Androscoggin R.

KENNEBEC

WALDO

Waterville

Narraguagus
Bay

White Mountain
National Forest

Augusta

LINCOLN

KNOX

Penobscot
Bay

Acadia
National Park

Mt. Desert I.

ANDROSCOGGIN

Lewiston

SAGADAHOC

Deer I.

Isle au Haut

Auburn

CUMBERLAND

495

Bath

Vinalhaven I.

Acadia
National Park

Brunswick

Muscongus
Bay

Sebago
Lake

YORK

Westbrook

Portland

S. Portland

Saco

Old Orchard Beach

Sanford

Biddeford

ATLANTIC
OCEAN

95

Kittery Point

NEW HAMPSHIRE

[11]HISTORY

The first inhabitants of Maine—dating from 3000 to 1000 BC—are known to archaeologists as the Red Paint People because of the red ocher that has been found in their graves. This Paleolithic group had evidently disappeared long before the arrival of the Algonkian-speaking Abnaki (meaning "living at the sunrise"), or Wabanaki. Just at the time of European settlement, an intertribal war and a disastrous epidemic of smallpox swept away many of the Abnaki, some of whom had begun peaceful contacts with the English. After that, most Indian contacts with Europeans were with the French.

The first documented visit by a European to the Maine coast was that of Giovanni da Verrazano during his voyage of 1524, but one may infer from the record that the Abnaki he met there had encountered white men before. Sometime around 1600, English expeditions began fishing the Gulf of Maine regularly. The first recorded attempts to found colonies, by the French on an island in the St. Croix River in 1604 and by the English at Sagadahoc in 1607, both failed. By 1630, however, there were permanent English settlements on several islands and at nearly a dozen spots along the coast.

The first grant of Maine lands was to Sir Ferdinando Gorges from the Council from New England, a joint-stock company that received and made royal grants of New England territory and which Gorges himself dominated. He and Captain John Mason received the territory between the Merrimack River (in present-day New Hampshire and Massachusetts) and the Kennebec River in 1622. Seven years later, the two grantees divided their land at the Piscataqua River, and Gorges became sole proprietor of the "Province of Maine." The source of the name is not quite clear. It seems likely that some connection with the historical French province of the same name was intended, but the name was also used to distinguish the mainland from the islands.

Sir Ferdinando's various schemes for governing the territory and promoting a feudal-style settlement never worked. A few years after his death in 1647, the government of the Massachusetts Bay Colony began absorbing the small Maine settlements. Massachusetts purchased the title to Maine from the Gorges heirs in 1677, and Maine became a district of Massachusetts with the issuance of a new royal charter in 1691. During the first hundred years of settlement, Maine's economy was based entirely on fishing, trading, and exploitation of the forests. The origin of the Maine shipbuilding industry, the early settlement of the interior parts of southern Maine, and the beginning of subsistence farming all date from about the time that New England's supply center of white-pine masts for the Royal Navy moved from Portsmouth, N.H., to Falmouth (now the city of Portland).

The first naval encounter of the Revolutionary War occurred in Machias Bay, when, on 12 June 1775, angry colonials captured the British armed schooner *Margaretta*. On 8 October 1775, a British naval squadron shelled and set fire to Falmouth. Wartime Maine was the scene of two anti-British campaigns, both of which ended in failure: an expedition through the Maine woods in the fall of 1775 intended to drive the British out of Quebec, and a disastrous 1779 expedition in which a Massachusetts amphibious force, failing to dislodge British troops at Castine, scuttled many of its own ships near the mouth of the Penobscot River.

The idea of separation from Massachusetts began surfacing as early as 1785, but popular pressure for such a movement did not mount until the War of 1812. The overwhelming vote for statehood in an 1819 referendum was a victory for William King, who would become the first governor, and his fellow Jeffersonian Democratic-Republicans. Admission of Maine as a free state was joined with the admission of Missouri as a slave state in the Missouri Compromise of 1820.

Textile mills and shoe factories came to Maine between 1830 and 1860 as part of the industrialization of Massachusetts. After the Civil War, the revolution in papermaking that substituted wood pulp for rags brought a vigorous new industry to Maine. By 1900, Maine was one of the leading papermaking states in the US, and the industry continues to dominate the state today. The rise of tourism and the concurrent and often conflicting concerns for economic development and environmental protection have been the main themes since the 1940s. Shipbuilding has joined paper manufacturing as a leading employer in the state, enjoying a boom in government contracts in the 1980s. Tourism has also grown substantially in the 1980s and 1990s, especially in the state's coastal and ski areas. In the 1990s, Maine's environmental concerns included hazardous waste disposal, sewage treatment, deforestation, overfishing, and acid rain caused by pollution from the Midwest.

In 1972, the Penobscot and Passamaquoddy Indians filed a land claims suit against the federal government for property that amounted to the northern two-thirds of Maine, claiming that a 1794 treaty, under which the Passamaquoddy handed over most of its land while receiving nothing in exchange, had not been ratified by Congress, and therefore violated the Indian Non-Intercourse Act of 1790. The Government settled the suit in 1980 by paying the tribes $81.5 million, which was allocated to purchase commercial and industrial properties in Maine.

In 1992, Independent presidential candidate Ross Perot won 30% of the vote in Maine, coming in ahead of Republican incumbent George Bush in spite of the fact that Bush maintained a summer home in the state. The Maine vote was Perot's strongest showing in any state.

[12]STATE GOVERNMENT

The Maine constitution, based on that of Massachusetts but incorporating a number of more democratic features, was adopted in 1819 and amended 150 times by the end of 1983.

The bicameral legislature, consisting of a senate of from 31 to 35 members, depending on the number of districts, and a 151-member house of representatives, convenes biennially in joint session to elect the secretary of state, attorney general, and state treasurer. All legislators serve two-year terms. The legislative salary in 1996 was $7,500.

The governor, who serves a four-year term and is limited to two consecutive terms, is the only official elected statewide. A gubernatorial veto may be overridden by a two-thirds vote of members present and voting in each legislative chamber. In 1996, the governor's salary was $69,992.

The state constitution may be amended by a two-thirds vote of the legislature and a majority vote at the next general election. To vote in Maine, one must be a US citizen and at least 18 years of age; there is no minimum residency requirement.

[13]POLITICAL PARTIES

Maine's two major political parties are the Democratic and the Republican, each affiliated with the national party. Minor parties have not figured in Maine elections in this century, although an independent candidate, James B. Longley, beat the candidates of both major parties in the gubernatorial election of 1974.

During the early decades of statehood, Jeffersonian and Jacksonian Democrats remained in power quite consistently. In 1854, however, reformers rallied around the new Republican Party, which dominated Maine politics for the next hundred years. Maine's strong Republican tradition continued into the middle and late 1950s, when Margaret Chase Smith distinguished herself in the US Senate as a leader of national importance. The rise of Democrat Edmund S. Muskie, elected governor in 1954 and 1956 and to the first of four terms in the US Senate in 1960, signaled a change in Maine's political complexion. Muskie appealed personally to many traditionally Republican voters, but his party's resurgence was also the result of demographic changes, especially an increase in the proportion of French-Canadian voters. In 1994 there were 272,089 registered Democrats, or 33% of the total number of registered voters; 246,277 registered Republicans, or 30%, and 306,292 unaffiliated registered voters, or 37%.

In the November 1994 elections, Independent Angus King became the governor. With his win, Maine became the only state in the nation with an Independent governor. In 1994, Republican Olympia Snowe won the US Senate seat vacated by retiring Democrat George J. Mitchell; in 1996 Republican Susan E. Collins won the seat left vacant by retiring three-term senator William S. Cohen, also a Republican. Following the 1996 elections, both of Maine's two US House of Representatives seats were held by Democrats. In 1996 Democrat Bill Clinton won 52% of the presidential vote, Republican Bob Dole received 31%, and Independent Ross Perot won 14%. Following the November 1996 elections, the state house of representatives comprised 81 Democrats and 69 Republicans (compared to the Democrats' 93-58 margin in 1992), while the state senate had 19 Democrats and 15 Republicans. In 1993, there was one black elected official, and in 1995, 50 women served in the state legislature.

Maine Presidential Vote by Major Political Parties, 1948–96

YEAR	ELECTORAL VOTE	MAINE WINNER	DEMOCRAT	REPUBLICAN
1948	5	Dewey (R)	111,916	150,234
1952	5	*Eisenhower (R)	118,806	232,353
1956	5	*Eisenhower (R)	102,468	249,238
1960	5	*Eisenhower (R)	102,468	249,238
1960	5	Nixon (R)	181,159	240,608
1964	4	*Johnson (D)	262,264	118,701
1968	4	Humphrey (D)	217,312	169,254
1972	4	*Nixon (R)	160,584	256,458
1976	4	Ford (R)	232,279	236,320
1980	4	*Reagan (R)	220,974	238,522
1984	4	*Reagan (R)	214,515	336,500
1988	4	*Bush (R)	243,569	307,131
1992**	4	*Clinton (D)	263,420	206,504
1996**	4	*Clinton (D)	312,788	186,378

*Won US presidential election.

**Independent candidate Ross Perot received 206,820 votes in 1992 and 85,970 votes in 1996.

14LOCAL GOVERNMENT

The principal units of local government in 1992 were the 22 cities and 468 towns; in all, there were 797 local government units, 91 school districts, and 199 special districts. As is customary in New England, the basic instrument of town government is the annual town meeting, with an elective board of selectmen supervising town affairs between meetings; some of the larger towns employ full-time town managers. There is no local government in roughly half the state. Maine's 16 counties function primarily as judicial districts.

15STATE SERVICES

There were 20 state executive departments in 1984. The State Board of Education and Department of Educational and Cultural Services supervise the public education system. The Department of Transportation, established in 1972, includes divisions responsible for aviation and railroads, a bureau to maintain highways and bridges, the Maine Port Authority, the State Ferry Advisory Board, and the Maine Aeronautical Advisory Board.

Various agencies responsible for health and social welfare were combined into the Department of Human Services in 1975. The Maine State Housing Authority, established in 1969, provides construction loans and technical assistance and conducts surveys of the state's housing needs. The Commission on Governmental Ethics and Election Practices, an advisory and investigative body, was created in 1975 to serve as a watchdog over the legislature.

16JUDICIAL SYSTEM

The highest state court is the supreme judicial court, with a chief justice and six associate justices appointed by the governor, with the consent of the legislature, for seven-year terms (as are all other state judges). The supreme judicial court has statewide appellate jurisdiction in all civil and criminal matters. The 16-member superior court, which has original jurisdiction in cases involving trial by jury and also hears some appeals, holds court sessions in all 16 counties. The district courts hear non-felony criminal cases and small claims and juvenile cases, and have concurrent jurisdiction with the superior court in divorce and civil cases involving less than $30,000. A probate court judge is elected in each county. In 1996, there were 3,110 practicing lawyers.

Maine's crime rate in 1995 was 3,284.7 per 100,000 persons, which included 131.4 violent crimes and 3,153.3 property crimes.

There were 1,460 state and federal prisoners in 1995, or 118 per 100,000, a decline of almost 3% between 1990 and 1995.

Maine does not have a death penalty.

17ARMED FORCES

The largest US military installation in Maine is the Naval Air Station at Brunswick, home of a wing of antisubmarine patrol squadrons. Defense Department personnel in Maine totaled 1,817 active military and 5,539 civilians. In 1995/96, state firms received $797 million in defense contracts, of which General Dynamics, a division of which builds warships and is the state's largest private employer, received $672 million.

There were 153,000 veterans of US military service living in Maine as of 1 July 1996, including fewer than 500 veterans of World War I, 38,000 of World War II, 25,000 of the Korean conflict, 51,000 from the Vietnam era, and 11,000 from the Persian Gulf War. A total of $259 million in veterans' benefits were paid in 1995/96.

The Maine National Guard and Reserves consisted of 9,260 personnel during 1996; 4,928 in the Army, 2,713 in the Navy and Marine Corps, and 1,619 in the Air Force. In 1993, the Maine State Police employed 321 full-time sworn officers, or three per 10,000 residents.

18MIGRATION

Throughout the colonial, Revolutionary, and early national periods, Maine's population grew primarily by immigration from elsewhere in New England. About 1830, after agriculture in the state had passed its peak, Maine farmers and woodsmen began moving west. Europeans and French Canadians came to the state, but not in sufficient numbers to offset this steady emigration.

Net losses from migration have continued through most of this century. Between 1940 and 1970, for example, the net loss was 163,000. However, there was a net gain of about 80,000 from 1970 to 1990. Between 1990 and 1996, the state had a net loss of 13,212 in domestic migration and a net gain of 2,167 in international migration. As of 1990, some 68.5% of all state residents had been born in Maine. In 1990, about 44% of residents age five and older lived in a different house than in 1985, of which

27% did so in another state. From 1980 to 1990, Maine's urban population declined from 47.5% to 44.6% of the state's total.

19INTERGOVERNMENTAL COOPERATION

Regional agreements in which Maine participates include the Maine New Hampshire School District Compact, which authorizes interstate public school districts. Maine also takes part in the New England Interstate Water Pollution Control Compact.

In 1996/97, Maine received over $1.3 billion in federal grants.

20ECONOMY

Maine's greatest economic strengths, as they have been since the beginning of European settlement, are its forests and waters, yielding wood products, water power, fisheries, and ocean commerce. Today, the largest industry by far is paper manufacturing, for which both forests and water power are essential.

Maine's greatest current economic weakness is its limited access to the national transportation network that links major production and manufacturing centers with large metropolitan markets. On the other hand, this relative isolation, combined with the state's traditional natural assets, has contributed to Maine's attractiveness as a place for tourism and recreation.

In 1994, the gross state product was $26,069 million, to which private goods-producing industries contributed $6,281 million; private services-producing industries, $16,091 million; and government, $3,697 million. In 1995, Maine's per capita personal income was 36th in the nation with $20,105. In 1996, there were 3,073 filings for bankruptcy, up 40% from the previous year.

21INCOME

Personal income in 1996 was $20,826 per capita, 37th in the US and the lowest in New England. Total disposable personal income rose from 1995 to 1996, from $22 billion to $22.7 billion.

22LABOR

Maine's civilian labor force totaled 669,000 in 1996; 52.5% of the work force was male and 47.5% female in 1995. The unemployment rate in 1996 was 5.1%, and the number of unemployed was 34,000. In 1995, earnings and jobs for major industry groups in Maine were:

	1995 EARNINGS (MILLIONS)	1995 JOBS (THOUSANDS)
Total	16,585.1	716.1
Farm	112.0	11.7
Nonfarm	16,473.1	704.4
Private	13,650.0	602.9
Agricultural services, forestry, fisheries	203.1	14.0
Mining	3.5	0.4
Construction	999.9	43.3
Manufacturing	3,284.5	100.2
Nondurable goods	1,691.7	51.1
Durable goods	1,592.8	49.1
Transportation and public utilities	943.0	28.6
Wholesale trade	855.5	27.9
Retail trade	2,000.4	138.5
Finance, insurance, and real estate	969.4	40.8
Services	4,390.6	209.3
Government	2,823.2	101.5

The paper and allied products industry employed 13,800 persons in 1995. In 1995, the average Maine production worker on a manufacturing payroll earned $493.07 per week. Labor union membership among Maine's workers in 1995 amounted to 43,639. There were 60 labor unions operating in Maine in 1995.

23AGRICULTURE

Maine's gross farm income in 1995 was $479 million (44th in the US). There were 7,600 farms in 1995, with an estimated 1,350,000 acres (546,000 hectares) of land.

Maine's agriculture and food processing industries contribute over $1 billion annually to the state's economy. Maine produces more food crops for human consumption than any other New England state. Maine ranks first in the world in the production of blueberries, producing over 25% of the total blueberry crop and over 50% of the world's wild blueberries. Maine is also home to the largest bio-agricultural firm in the world, which produces breeding stock for the broiler industry worldwide. In New England, Maine ranks first in potato production and second in the production of milk and apples. Nationally, Maine ranks third in maple syrup and eighth in potatoes. The greenhouse/nursery and wild blueberry sectors have also shown steady growth in total sales since 1990. Cranberry production has recently enjoyed a resurgence in Maine; 70 acres (28 hectares) have been brought into production through a $1.4 million capital investment.

24ANIMAL HUSBANDRY

In 1997, Maine had an estimated 116,000 cattle and calves worth around $77.7 million. Dairy farmers had an estimated 40,000 milk cows, which produced 641 million lb of milk in 1995. Poultry farmers sold an estimated 19.7 million lb of chickens for $570,000 in 1995. South-central Maine is the leading poultry region.

25FISHING

Fishing has been important to the economy of Maine since its settlement. In 1995, 231.8 million lb of finfish and shellfish worth $216.5 million were landed at Maine ports, ranking the state 8th and 4th in the nation, respectively. Rockland and Portland accounted for 44.5 million lb and 66.7 million lb, respectively, of the state's landings in 1995. The most valuable Maine fishery product is the lobster. In 1995, Maine led in landings of American lobster for the 14th consecutive year, with 36.5 million lb, valued at $102.3 million. Flounder, halibut, scallops, and shrimp are also caught. Cod landings in 1995 totaled 5,259,000 lb, valued at $5,034,000. The state sought during the late 1970s and early 1980s to conserve and restore Atlantic salmon stocks in Maine's inland waterways. In 1995/96, federal hatcheries distributed over 3 million (107,957 lb) coldwater species fish and nearly 1.4 million fish eggs within the state, mostly Atlantic salmon. Average employment in 359 processing and wholesaling plants was 2,792 in 1994.

26FORESTRY

Maine's 17.5 million acres (7 million hectares) of forest in 1992 contained an estimated 3.6 billion trees and covered 89% of the state's land area, the largest percentage of any state in the US. About 16,987,000 acres (6,874,000 hectares) are classified as commercial timberland, over 90% of it privately owned, and half of that by a dozen large paper companies and land managing corporations. Principal commercial hardwood include ash, hard maple, white and yellow birch, beech, and oak; commercially significant softwoods include white pine, hemlock, cedar, spruce, and fir. The total roundwood harvest in 1993 was 776.4 million cu ft (12th among the states and 3.4% of the US total), of which

65% was softwood. Lumber and wood products establishments employed 9,800 persons in 1995; value added by manufacture was $588.9 million, and value of shipments was $1.67 billion.

27MINING

The value of nonfuel mineral production in Maine in 1995 was estimated to be $58.7 million, representing an decrease of $2.3 million over that of 1994. Decreases were reported for construction sand and gravel and portland and masonry cements. However, the values of crushed stone, dimension stone, and gemstones increased. Leading mineral commodities, in terms of value, were construction sand and gravel, $21,000,000; crushed stone, $16,900,000; and cement. Other mineral commodities produced included clay, peat, dimension stone, and gemstones. Maine ranked 46th in the nation in total nonfuel mineral production value in 1995.

28ENERGY AND POWER

For more than three centuries, Maine has been exploiting its enormous waterpower potential. In recent decades, however, waterpower has been surpassed in importance by oil-fired steam plants and, most recently, by nuclear power. In 1995, the Maine Yankee Atomic Power Co. station in Wiscasset generated 7.4% of the state's electric power (down from 74% in 1994); in referendums in 1980 and 1982, voters decided that the station should remain open and that future nuclear power development should be allowed. However, as of 1997, Maine Yankee and other nuclear plants in the region were offline and may remain so pending thorough reviews by the Nuclear Regulatory Commission. Oil-fired steam units accounted for 30% of electric power generation in 1995, and hydroelectric units for 62%.

Installed generating capacity in 1996 totaled 2,468,000 kW, consisting of 386,000 kW in hydroelectric plants, 1,130,000 kW in conventional steam plants, 920,000 kW in the Wiscasset nuclear plant, and 32,000 kW in other renewable sources. Power production in 1995 totaled 2.67 billion kWh (down from 9 billion kWh in 1994).

All fuel oil and coal must be imported; natural gas, piped into the southwest corner of the state, is available in Portland and the Lewiston-Auburn area.

The Office of Energy Resources provides tax incentives and research and development grants to encourage use of solar power and energy conservation. The late 1970s and early 1980s saw some Maine homeowners switch to wood for heating as an alternative to oil.

29INDUSTRY

Manufacturing in Maine has always been related to the forests. From the 17th century through much of the 19th, the staples of Maine industry were shipbuilding and lumber; today they are papermaking and wood products, but footwear, textiles and apparel, shipbuilding, and electronic components and accessories are also important items.

Maine has the largest paper-production capacity of any state in the nation. There are large papermills and pulpmills in more than a dozen towns and cities; major companies include International Paper, Boise-Cascade, Scott Paper, US Gypsum, and Great Northern Nekoosa. Wood-related industries—paper, lumber, wood products—accounted for 43% of the value of manufacturers shipments in 1991.

Estimated value of manufacturers' shipments in 1995 exceeded $14.4 billion.

The following table shows value of shipments for selected industries in 1995:

Paper and allied products	$4,938,000,000
Lumber and wood products	1,670,000,000
Transportation equipment	1,566,100,000
Electric and other electric equipment	1,088,000,000
Leather and leather products	918,400,000
Textile mill products	527,600,000

In 1997, Maine was the headquarters for two Fortune 500 companies: UNUM and Hannaford Bros.

In 1995, there were 142 US patents issued to Maine residents.

30COMMERCE

In 1992, Maine had 1,974 wholesale establishments with $6.5 billion in sales, and durable goods accounted for 38% of the sales. In 1995, Maine's workers' earnings from employment in wholesale trade totaled $855 million. Retail sales totaled $10.3 billion (41st) in 1992, from 9,270 establishments. Food stores accounted for 22.6% of sales; automotive dealers, 16.9%; general merchandise stores, 10.3%; and eating and drinking places, 8.4%. Earnings in retail sales employment came to $2 billion in 1995, with food stores accounting for 15.6%, automotive dealers and service stations 16.0%, eating and drinking places 21.7%, general merchandise stores 9.0%, and building materials and garden equipment 6.1%.

Maine has shipping facilities located in Portland, Searsport, and Easport. Exports originating or produced in Maine totaled $1.4 billion in 1996. Maine's largest trading partners are Canada, Japan, and Malaysia.

31CONSUMER PROTECTION

The Public Protection Unit of the Attorney General's Office protects consumers through enforcement of a wide variety of laws including Maine's Unfair Trade Practices Act. The office also provides a consumer mediation service which uses volunteer mediators to resolve disputes between businesses and consumers.

The Office of Consumer Credit Regulation was established in 1974 to protect state residents from unjust and misleading consumer credit practices, particularly in relation to the federal Truth-in-Lending Act. The agency also administers state laws regulating collection agencies, credit reporting agencies, mortgage companies, loan brokers, rent-to-own companies, pawn brokers, money order issuers, check cashers, and money transmitters.

32BANKING

In 1996, Maine had 49 federally insured depository institutions, of which 20 were commercial banks, 20 state banks, and 9 national banks, with a combined total of 3 Federal Reserve members. Commercial banks had assets of $9 billion and deposits of over $6.7 billion at the end of 1996. There were 29 savings institutions at the end of 1996, with $7 billion in assets.

33INSURANCE

Two life insurance companies were domiciled in Maine in mid-1996, when 980,058 policies worth $47,233,067,391 were in force. The average coverage per family was $81,200, the lowest of any northeastern state. Property and liability insurers wrote $1,110,706,297 in premiums in 1996, of which 35% was for private passenger automotive coverage.

34SECURITIES

As of June 1996, there were 928 broker-dealer firms and 31,158 sales representatives licensed to sell in Maine; 402 investment advisors were licensed as well. In 1995/96, the state received 8,782 applications to register or exempt securities offerings.

35PUBLIC FINANCE

Maine's biennial budget is prepared by the Bureau of the Budget, within the Department of Administrative and Financial Services, and submitted by the Governor to the Legislature for consideration. The fiscal year extends from 1 July to 30 June. The following table shows revenues and expenditures for governmental funds for the fiscal year ending 30 June 30 1995:

REVENUES	
Sales and use tax	$716,199,000
Individual income tax	637,516,000
Corporate income tax	63,032,000
Other taxes	553,480,000
Federal revenues	1,104,096,000
Other revenues and resources	307,009,000
TOTAL	$3,381,332,000

EXPENDITURES	
Human services	$1,536,796,187
Education and culture	959,367,295
General government	362,172,228
Transportation	308,040,032
Natural resources	115,905,717
Economic development	92,458,587
Labor	62,406,550
Public protection	56,640,292
TOTAL	$3,493,786,888

36TAXATION

The individual income tax in 1994 ranged from 2% to 8.5%; the corporate income tax rates ranged from 3.5% of the first $25,000 of net income to 8.93% of net income in excess of $250,000. Other state levies include taxes on utilities, inheritance and estate taxes, liquor and cigarette taxes, and a tax on gasoline, fuel, and motor carriers. Counties do not assess taxes, but they do make levies on municipalities and unorganized territories to meet county budgets. In 1995, federal expenditures in the state were over $6.5 billion. Federal expenditures traditionally outstrip the state's federal tax burden by a large amount.

37ECONOMIC POLICY

The Finance Authority of Maine (FAME) encourages industrial and recreational projects by insuring mortgage loans, selling tax-exempt bonds to aid industrial development and natural-resource enterprises, authorizing municipalities to issue such revenue bonds, and guaranteeing loans to small businesses, veterans, and natural-resource enterprises. A corporate franchise tax was repealed in December 1974, and the personal property tax on business inventories in April 1977. The State Development Office provides technical, financial, training, and marketing assistance for existing Maine businesses and companies interested in establishing operations in the state.

38HEALTH

The death rate of 944.1 per 100,000 in 1995 was slightly higher than the US rate of 879.0, reflecting a higher than average population in the upper age levels. The birth rate in 1995 was 11.2 per 1,000 population. The infant mortality rate was 6.1 per 1,000 live births. During 1995, 2,819 legal abortions were performed in Maine. In 1995, the AIDS prevalence was 11.21 per 100,000 population, well below the US average of 28.48. The 1995 rates for the major causes of death were: heart disease, 293.2 per 100,000; cancer, 241.9; and cerebrovascular disease, 60.0. The suicide rate of 12.9 per 100,000 population was above the national rate in 1995. During 1980–89, the average annual rate of traumatic occupational fatalities in Maine was 7.6 per

100,000. The fatality rate for the risky sea-urchin harvesting industry in 1993 was 278 per 100,000 workers.

In 1995, Maine had 44 hospitals, with 4,376 beds. The average per-inpatient charge for hospital care for the year ending June 1996 was $1,632 per day and $8,580 per stay. Active, licensed medical personnel included 2,200 allopathic physicians (1995–96), 298 osteopathic physicians (1995–96), 387 active dentists (1994), 8,785 registered nurses (1990), and 917 licensed practical nurses (1987).

At least 13.1% of Maine residents had no insurance in 1995. Both Medicare and Medicaid reimbursements increased in the years 1993–1994 to $625 and $807 million respectively.

39SOCIAL WELFARE

Despite Maine's relatively low personal income and large proportion of residents below the poverty level, welfare payments per capita generally fall short of the national norms.

In 1996, for example, payments averaging $526 a month went to Maine's 56,000 recipients of AFDC. In 1996, the food stamp program had an average monthly participation of 130,872, and students took part in the school lunch program, costing $18.8 million.

With the enactment of the Personal Responsibility and Work Opportunity Reconciliation Act of 1996, the US government has changed the form and regulations for many of its social welfare programs; most significantly, it replaces Aid to Families with Dependent Children (AFDC), an open-ended entitlement program, with Temporary Assistance for Needy Families (TANF), a limited system of assistance funded largely through federal block grants. The reform act also impacts the food stamp program, the Supplemental Security Income program, and the child nutrition program. The law took effect on 1 July 1997 and provided $16.38 billion in block grants for fiscal years 1997–2002. The grants are to be divided among the states based on an equation involving the numbers of former AFDC recipients in each state. Because many of the bill's provisions have yet to be implemented into state-by-state policy, it was not possible to include the details of each state's programs for this edition of this work.

In 1996, Social Security payments averaging $664 a month were paid for 237,140 state residents. Supplemental Security Income benefits reached 30,841 residents, averaging $277 a month. Payments for unemployment insurance averaged $166.10 weekly in 1995.

40HOUSING

Housing for Maine families has improved substantially since 1960, when the federal census categorized 57,000 of Maine's 364,650 housing units as deteriorated or dilapidated. Between 1970 and 1980, over 115,000 new units were built. About 3.5% of all occupied units in 1990 lacked full plumbing, however.

There were an estimated 620,000 housing units in Maine in 1996, up from 587,045 at the time of the 1990 census. In 1996, 4,685 privately owned units, valued at $436 million, were authorized for construction. Of these, 4,463 were single-family units. About one-seventh of all Maine homes are for seasonal rather than year-round use. During the 1980s, the median home value in Maine increased by 45.2% to $87,400 in 1990. Maine had the lowest median owner (including mortgage) and renter costs in New England in 1990, the most recent year for which figures are available, at $664 and $419 per month, respectively. During 1996/97, Maine received $198 million in US Department of Housing and Urban Development aid, including $23.4 million in community development block grants.

41EDUCATION

Maine has a long and vigorous tradition of education at all levels, both public and private. Maine fourth- and eighth-grade students have achieved highest in the nation status in academic performance in reading, mathematics, and science on tests administered by the National Assessment of Educational Progress (NAEP). The NAEP compared Maine students in 1994 and 1996 assessments to their peers in 43 states. In the fall of 1996, Maine's public school enrollment was 218,560.

Since 1968, the state's public colleges and universities have been incorporated into a single University of Maine System, which in the fall of 1996 had 30,931 undergraduate, graduate, and doctoral students. The original land grant campus is at Orono; the other major campus in the system is the University of Southern Maine at Portland and Gorham. The state also operates the Maine Maritime Academy at Castine and the Maine Technical College System, comprised of six technical colleges. Of the state's 16 private colleges and professional schools, Bowdoin College in Brunswick, Colby College in Waterville, and Bates College in Lewiston are the best known.

42ARTS

Maine has long held an attraction for painters and artists, Winslow Homer and Andrew Wyeth among them. The state abounds in summer theaters, the oldest and most famous of which is at Ogunquit. The Portland Symphony is Maine's leading orchestra; another ensemble is in Bangor.

In 1979, Maine became the first state to allow inheritance taxes to be paid with acceptable art. The Department of Educational and Cultural Services has an Arts and Humanities Bureau that provides funds to artists in residence, Maine touring artists, and community arts councils. In 1996, the State of Maine generated a total of $447,000 from federal sources to support its arts programs. The NEA contributed $501,000 to the programs and $602,000 to the Maine Arts Commission. Funds came from the state and other private sources. Audiences for Maine's arts programs totaled 14,923,000, and there were 22,536 contributing artists. Arts education was offered by the state to about 11,600 school children. The state also made 287 grants available to rural arts groups. The Maine Arts Commission also received funding for the state's arts education programs from the NEA's State and Regional Program.

43LIBRARIES AND MUSEUMS

In 1996/97, Maine public libraries had 4,766,104 volumes and a combined circulation of 7,410,748. Leading libraries and their book holdings in 1996 included the Maine State Library at Augusta (150,000 volumes), the University of Maine at Orono (876,000), Bowdoin College at Brunswick (827,974), and the University of Southern Maine at Portland (365,248).

Maine has at least 113 museums and historic sites. The Maine State Museum in Augusta houses collections in history, natural history, anthropology, marine studies, mineralogy, science, and technology. The privately supported Maine Historical Society in Portland maintains a research library and the Wadsworth Longfellow House, the boyhood home of Henry Wadsworth Longfellow. The largest of several maritime museums is in Bath.

44COMMUNICATIONS

In March 1993, 96.9% of the 490,000 occupied housing units had telephones.

Maine had 107 commercial radio stations (29 AM, 78 FM) in 1996, along with 14 commercial and 4 noncommercial educational television stations. Educational television stations broadcast from Augusta, Biddeford, Calais, Orono, and Presque Isle. In 1996, three large cable television systems served the state.

45PRESS

Maine had seven daily newspapers in 1997. The most widely read newspaper was the *Bangor Daily News* (mornings, 69,779; weekend, 85,648), though its circulation was surpassed by the combined circulations of the *Portland Press Herald* (mornings, 71,861), published daily in Portland by Gannett Publishing Co. Gannett also publishes Maine's largest Sunday newspaper, the *Maine Sunday Telegram* (128,442). The capital is served by the *Augusta Kennebec Journal* (16,702 daily; 14,327 Sundays).

46ORGANIZATIONS

The 1992 US Census of Service Industries counted 474 organizations in Maine, including 108 business associations; 264 civic, social, and fraternal associations; and 102 other membership organizations. Among the organizations with headquarters in Maine are the Maine Potato Council (Presque Isle); the Maine Lobstermen's Association (Stonington); and the Potato Association of America (Orono).

47TOURISM, TRAVEL, AND RECREATION

Calling itself "Vacationland," the State of Maine is a year-round resort destination. Expenditures by tourists were estimated at over $1.2 billion in 1982. Travel and tourism was the state's largest employer, generating 38,000 jobs.

Most out-of-state visitors continue to come in the summer, when the southern coast offers sandy beaches, icy surf, and several small harbors for sailing and saltwater fishing. Northeastward, the scenery becomes more rugged and spectacular, and sailing and hiking are the primary activities. Hundreds of lakes, ponds, rivers, and streams offer opportunities for freshwater bathing, boating, and fishing. Whitewater canoeing lures the adventurous along the Allagash Wilderness Waterway in northern Maine. Maine has always attracted hunters, especially during the fall deer season. Wintertime recreation facilities include nearly 60 ski areas and countless opportunities for cross-country skiing. In 1995, 217,553 hunters and 285,329 fishermen used the state's wildlife resources.

In 1995, there were 12 state parks and beaches. Baxter State Park, in central Maine, includes Mount Katahdino. In 1996, Acadia National Park, a popular attraction, drew 2,704,831 visitors. There are other wildlife areas, refuges, and forests.

The state fair is held at Bangor.

48SPORTS

Maine has no major league professional sports team. The Portland Pirates (a minor league) of the American Hockey League play on their home ice at the Cumberland County Civic Center in Portland. Minor League baseball's Dogs of the Double-A Eastern League play their games at Hadlock Field, which opened in 1994. Harness racing is held at Scarborough Downs and other tracks and fairgrounds throughout the state. Sailing is a popular participant sport with a Windsummer Festival held each July at Boothbay Harbor and a Retired Skippers Race at Castine in August.

49FAMOUS MAINERS

The highest federal officeholders born in Maine were Hannibal Hamlin (1809–91), the nation's first Republican vice president, under Abraham Lincoln, and Nelson A. Rockefeller (1908–79), governor of New York State from 1959 to 1973 and US vice president under Gerald Ford. James G. Blaine (b.Pennsylvania, 1830–93), a lawyer and politician, served 13 years as a US representative from Maine and a term in the Senate; on his third try, he won the Republican presidential nomination in 1884 but lost to Grover Cleveland, later serving as secretary of state (1889–92) under Benjamin Harrison. Edmund S. Muskie (b.1914), leader of the Democratic revival in Maine in the 1950s, followed two successful terms as governor with 21 years in the Senate until appointed secretary of state by President Jimmy Carter in 1980.

Other conspicuous state and national officeholders have included Rufus King (1755–1827), a member of the Continental Congress and Constitutional Convention and US minister to Great Britain; William King (1768–1852), leader of the movement for Maine statehood and the state's first governor; Thomas Bracket Reed (1839–1902), longtime speaker of the US House of Representatives; and Margaret Chase Smith (b.1897), who served longer in the US Senate—24 years—than any other woman.

Names prominent in Maine's colonial history include those of Sir Ferdinando Gorges (b.England, 1566–1647), the founder and proprietor of the colony; Sir William Phips (1651–95), who became the first American knight for his recovery of a Spanish treasure, later serving as royal governor of Massachusetts; and Sir William Pepperrell (1696–1759), who led the successful New England expedition against Louisburg in 1745, for which he became the first American-born baronet.

Maine claims a large number of well-known reformers and humanitarians: Dorothea Lynde Dix (1802–87), who led the movement for hospitals for the insane; Elijah Parish Lovejoy (1802–37), an abolitionist killed while defending his printing press from a proslavery mob in St. Louis, Missouri; Neal Dow (1804–97), who drafted and secured passage of the Maine prohibition laws of 1846 and 1851, later served as a Civil War general, and ran for president on the Prohibition Party ticket in 1880; and Harriet Beecher Stowe (b.Connecticut, 1811–96), whose *Uncle Tom's Cabin* (1852) was written in Maine.

Other important writers include poet Henry Wadsworth Longfellow (1807–82), born in Portland while Maine was still part of Massachusetts; humorist Artemus Ward (Charles Farrar Browne, 1834–67); Sarah Orne Jewett (1849–1909), novelist and short-story writer; Kate Douglas Wiggin (1856–1923), author of *Rebecca of Sunnybrook Farm;* Kenneth Roberts (1885–1957), historical novelist; and Robert Peter Tristram Coffin (1892–1955), poet, essayist, and novelist. Edwin Arlington Robinson (1869–1935) and Edna St. Vincent Millay (1892–1950) were both Pulitzer Prize-winning poets, and novelist Marguerite Yourcenar (b.Belgium, 1903–1987), a resident of Mt. Desert Island, became in 1980 the first woman ever elected to the Académie Française. Winslow Homer (b.Massachusetts, 1836–1910) had a summer home at Prouts Neck, where he painted many of his seascapes.

[50]BIBLIOGRAPHY

Alampi, Gary, ed. *Gale State Rankings Reporter.* Detroit: Gale Research, Inc., 1994.

Bearse, Ray, ed. *Maine: A Guide to the Vacation State.* 2d ed., rev. Boston: Houghton Mifflin, 1969.

Churchill, Edwin A., Joel W. Eastman, and Richard W. Judd, eds. *Maine: The Pine Tree State from Prehistory to the Present.* Orono: University of Maine Press, 1995.

Clark, Charles E. *Maine: A Bicentennial History.* New York: Norton, 1977.

Council of State Governments. *The Book of the States, 1994–1995 Edition.* Vol. 30. Lexington, Kentucky: The Council of State Governments, 1994.

FDIC, Division of Research and Statistics. *Statistics on Banking: A Statistical Profile of the United States Banking Industry.* Washington, D.C.: Federal Deposit Insurance Corporation, 1993.

Gould, John. *Maine's Golden Road: A Memoir.* New York: Norton, 1995.

Isaacson, Dorris, ed. *Maine: A Guide "Down East."* 2d ed. Rockland: Courier-Gazette, Inc., for the Maine League of Historical Societies and Museums, 1970 (orig. 1937).

Maine, State of. State Development Office. *Maine: A Statistical Summary.* Augusta, 1984.

Morris, Gerald E., ed. *The Maine Bicentennial Atlas.* Portland: Maine Historical Society, 1976.

Osborn, William C. *The Paper Plantation.* New York: Grossman, 1974.

Palmer, Kenneth T. *Maine Politics & Government.* Lincoln: University of Nebraska Press, 1992.

Rich, Louise Dickinson. *State O' Maine.* New York: Harper & Row, 1964.

Rowe, William H. *The Maritime History of Maine.* New York: Norton, 1948.

U.S. Department of the Interior, U.S. Fish and Wildlife Service. *Endangered and Threatened Species Recovery Program.* Washington, D.C.: U.S. Government Printing Office, 1990.

U.S. Department of Education, National Center for Education Statistics. Office of Educational Research and Improvement. *Digest of Education Statistics, 1993.* Washington, D.C.: U.S. Government Printing Office, 1993.

Schmittroth, Linda, ed. *Cities of the United States.* 3rd ed. Detroit: Gale Research, Inc., 1997.

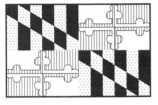

MARYLAND

State of Maryland

ORIGIN OF STATE NAME: Named for Henrietta Maria, queen consort of King Charles I of England. **NICKNAME:** The Old Line State; Free State. **CAPITAL:** Annapolis. **ENTERED UNION:** 28 April 1788 (7th). **SONG:** "Maryland, My Maryland." **MOTTO:** *Fatti maschii, parole femine* (Manly deeds, womanly words). **FLAG:** Bears the quartered arms of the Calvert and Crossland families (the paternal and maternal families of the founders of Maryland). **OFFICIAL SEAL:** REVERSE: A shield bearing the arms of the Calverts and Crosslands is surmounted by an earl's coronet and a helmet and supported by a farmer and fisherman. The state motto (originally that of the Calverts) appears on a scroll below. The circle is surrounded by the Latin legend *Scuto bon voluntatis tu coronasti nos*, meaning "With the shield of thy favor hast thou compassed us," and "1632," the date of Maryland's first charter. OBVERSE: Lord Baltimore is seen as a knight in armor on a charger. The surrounding inscription, in Latin, means "Cecilius, Absolute Lord of Maryland and Avalon New Foundland, Baron of Baltimore." **BIRD:** Baltimore oriole. **FISH:** Rockfish. **REPTILE:** Diamondback terrapin. **CRUSTACEAN:** Blue crab. **DOG:** Chesapeake Bay retriever. **INSECT:** Baltimore checkerspot butterfly. **FLOWER:** Black-eyed Susan. **TREE:** White oak. **SPORT:** Jousting. **BOAT:** The skipjack. **LEGAL HOLIDAYS:** New Year's Day, 1 January; Birthday of Martin Luther King, Jr., 3d Monday in January; Lincoln's Birthday, 12 February; Washington's Birthday, 3d Monday in February; Maryland Day, 25 March; Good Friday, March or April; Memorial Day, 30 May; Independence Day, 4 July; Labor Day, 1st Monday in September; Defenders' Day, 12 September; Columbus Day, 12 October; Election Day, 1st Tuesday after 1st Monday in November, even-numbered years; Veterans Day, 11 November; Thanksgiving Day, 4th Thursday in November; Christmas Day, 25 December. **TIME:** 7 AM EST = noon GMT.

¹LOCATION, SIZE, AND EXTENT

Located on the eastern seaboard of the US in the South Atlantic region, Maryland ranks 42d in size among the 50 states.

Maryland's total area—10,460 sq mi (27,092 sq km)—comprises 9,837 sq mi (25,478 sq km) of land and 623 sq mi (1,614 sq km) of inland water. The state extends 199 mi (320 km) E-W and 126 mi (203 km) N-S.

Maryland is bordered on the N by Pennsylvania; on the E by Delaware and the Atlantic Ocean; on the S and SW by Virginia, the District of Columbia, and West Virginia (with the line passing through the Chesapeake Bay and Potomac River); and on the extreme W by West Virginia. Important islands in Chesapeake Bay, off Maryland's Eastern Shore (the Maryland sector of the Delmarva Peninsula), include Kent, Bloodsworth, South Marsh, and Smith.

The total boundary length of Maryland is 842 mi (1,355 km), including a general coastline of 31 mi (50 km); the total tidal shoreline extends 3,190 mi (5,134 km). The state's geographic center is in Prince George's County, 4.5 mi (7.2 km) NW of Davidsonville.

²TOPOGRAPHY

Three distinct regions characterize Maryland's topography. The first and major area, falling within the Atlantic Coastal Plain, is nearly bisected by the Chesapeake Bay, dividing Maryland into the Eastern Shore and the Western Shore. The Piedmont Plateau, west of the coastal lowlands, is a broad, rolling upland with several deep gorges cut by rivers. Farther west, from the Catoctin Mountains in Frederick County to the West Virginia border, is the Appalachian Mountain region, containing the state's highest hills. Backbone Mountain, in Garrett County in westernmost Maryland, is the state's highest point, at 3,360 ft (1,024 m).

A few small islands lie in the Chesapeake Bay, Maryland's dominant waterway. Extending 195 mi (314 km) inland from the Atlantic and varying in width from 3 to 20 mi (5–32 km), the bay comprises 3,237 sq mi (8,384 sq km), of which 1,726 sq km (4,470 sq km) are under Maryland's jurisdiction. Principal rivers include the Potomac, forming much of the southern and western border; the Patapsco, which runs through Baltimore; the Patuxent, draining the Western Shore; and the Susquehanna, crossing the Pennsylvania border and emptying into the Chesapeake Bay in northeastern Maryland. The state has 23 rivers and other bays, as well as many lakes and creeks, none of any great size.

³CLIMATE

Despite its small size, Maryland exhibits considerable climatic diversity. Temperatures vary from an annual average of 48°F (9°C) in the extreme western uplands to 59°F (15°C) in the southeast, where the climate is moderated by the Chesapeake Bay and the Atlantic Ocean. The daily mean temperature for Baltimore is 55°F (13°C), ranging from 33°F (1°C) in January to 77°F (25°C) in July. The record high temperature for the state is 109°F (43°C), set on 10 July 1936 in Cumberland and Frederick counties; the record low, –40°F (–40°C), occurred on 13 January 1912 at Oakland in Garrett County.

Precipitation averages about 49 in (124 cm) annually in the southeast, but only 36 in (91 cm) in the Cumberland area west of the Appalachians; Baltimore averages 41 in (104 cm) each year. As much as 100 in (254 cm) of snow falls in western Garrett County, while 8–10 in (20–25 cm) is average for the Eastern Shore; and Baltimore receives about 22 in (56 cm).

[4]FLORA AND FAUNA

Maryland's three life zones—coastal plain, piedmont, and Appalachian—mingle wildlife characteristic of both North and South. Most of the state lies within a hardwood belt in which red and white oaks, yellow poplar, beech, blackgum, hickory, and white ash are represented; shortleaf and loblolly pines are the leading softwoods. Honeysuckle, Virginia creeper, wild grape, and wild raspberry are also common. Wooded hillsides are rich with such wild flowers as Carolina cranesbill, trailing arbutus, Mayapple, early blue violet, wild rose, and goldenrod; *Trillium virginiana* is an endangered plant.

The white-tailed (Virginia) deer, eastern cottontail, raccoon, and red and gray foxes are indigenous to Maryland, although urbanization has sharply reduced their habitat. Common small mammals are the woodchuck, eastern chipmunk, and gray squirrel. The brown-headed nuthatch has been observed in the extreme south, the cardinal and tufted titmouse are common in the piedmont, and the chestnut-sided warbler and rose-breasted grosbeak are native to the Appalachians. Among saltwater species, shellfish—especially oysters, clams, and crabs—have the greatest economic importance. The Indiana bat, eastern cougar, Maryland darter, southern bald eagle, and Delmarva Peninsula fox squirrel are listed as endangered fauna in the state.

[5]ENVIRONMENTAL PROTECTION

The Maryland Department of the Environment (MDE) serves as the state's primary environmental protection agency. MDE protects and restores the quality of Maryland's land, air, and water by assessing, preventing and controlling sources of pollution for the benefit of public health, the environment and future generations. MDE regulations control the storage, transportation, and disposal of hazardous wastes and ensure long-term, environmentally sound solid waste recycling and disposal capabilities. As of 1995, Maryland had 14 hazardous waste sites.

MDE has broad regulatory, planning, and management responsibility for water quality, air quality, solid and hazardous waste management, stormwater management, sediment control, wetlands and waterways management, and water allocation. MDE also plays a pivotal role in Maryland's initiatives to protect and restore the Chesapeake Bay and has divided the state into ten major tributary watershed basins, each of which have specific nutrient reduction strategies designed to give the Bay added protection from the effects of stormwater run-off, airborne pollutants, and direct discharges. Additionally, Maryland's Department of Natural Resources manages water allocation, fish and wildlife, state parks and forests, land reclamation and open space.

MDE operates an innovative infrastructure financing program that leverages federal, state, and local funds to upgrade wastewater treatment plants, connect residents to public sewer systems, and improve water supply facilities. In addition, the Maryland Environmental Service, a quasi-public agency, contracts with local governments to design, construct, finance, and operate wastewater treatment plants, water supply systems, and recycling facilities.

The Maryland Department of Natural Resources (DNR) is responsible for the management, enhancement, and preservation of the state's living and natural resources. Utilizing an ecosystem approach to land, waterway, and species management, DNR programs and services support the health of the Chesapeake Bay and its tributaries, sustainable populations of fishery and wildlife species, and an integrated network of public lands and open space.

The Maryland Office of Planning's mission is to plan for the most effective development of the state and all of its resources. The Office assists state agencies and local governments to more effectively achieve environmental, agricultural, and natural resource objectives by integrating them with comprehensive planning and land use management. The state has recently embarked on a Neighborhood Conservation and Smart Growth initiative to encourage population and economic growth in priority funding areas, and to use a Rural Legacy Program to preserve agricultural, forest, and other rural lands from development.

[6]POPULATION

The enormous expansion of the federal government and exodus of people from Washington, D.C., to the surrounding suburbs contributed to the rapid growth that made Maryland the 17th most populous state in 1980, with 4,216,446 residents. As of 1990, Maryland holds the 19th ranking, with 4,781,468 people. The state's population doubled between 1940 and 1970, increased 7.5% between 1970 and 1980, and 13.4% from 1980 to 1990. The population then increased 6.1% by 1996, to an estimated 5,071,604, and it was estimated that the population would be 5,608,000 by 2000. The population density in 1990 was 489 per sq mi (188 per sq km).

Almost all the growth since World War II has occurred in the four suburban counties around Washington, D.C., and Baltimore. As of 1980, about 54% of the state's population resided there, and more than 81% of the total population was urban. Metropolitan Baltimore, embracing Carroll, Howard, Hartford, Anne Arundel, and Baltimore counties, expanded from 2,244,700 to 2,382,000 between 1984 and 1990 (18th in the US); the city of Baltimore, on the other hand, declined from 763,570 to 736,000 during the same period, and to an estimated 702,979 in 1995. Baltimore is the state's only major city; several west-central counties belong to the Washington metropolitan area, and Cecil County, in the northeast, is part of metropolitan Wilmington, Delaware.

[7]ETHNIC GROUPS

Black Americans, numbering 1,190,000 in 1990, constitute the largest racial minority in Maryland. About 36% of the blacks lived in the city of Baltimore. According to 1996 estimates, Maryland's black population was 1,462,000.

Hispanic Americans, mostly from Puerto Rico and Central America, numbered 125,000 in 1990 and an estimated 141,000 in 1996. The Asian population was relatively large: 29,471 Koreans, 26,479 Chinese, 21,086 Filipinos, 10,067 Japanese, and 7,809 Vietnamese.

Foreign-born residents numbered 313,494, or 6.5% of the population in 1990, many having immigrated to Maryland in the 1970s. In 1996, estimates placed this figure at 412,000, or 8% of the total population. The leading countries of origin in 1990 were Korea, India, El Salvador, Germany, and the Philippines; a significant proportion of the German, Polish, and Russian immigrants were Jewish refugees arriving just before and after World War II. In 1996, the combined Native American population (including Eskimos and Aleuts) was estimated at 21,000.

[8]LANGUAGES

Several Algonkian tribes originally inhabited what is now Maryland. There are some Indian place-names, such as Potomac, Susquehanna, and Allegheny.

The state's diverse topography has contributed to unusual diversity in its basic speech. Geographical isolation of the Delmarva Peninsula, proximity to the Virginia piedmont population, and access to southeastern and central Pennsylvania helped to yield a language mixture that now is dominantly Midland and yet reflects earlier ties to Southern English.

Regional features occur as well. In the northeast are found eastern Pennsylvania *pavement* (sidewalk) and *baby coach* (baby carriage). In the north and west are *poke* (bag), *quarter till, sick*

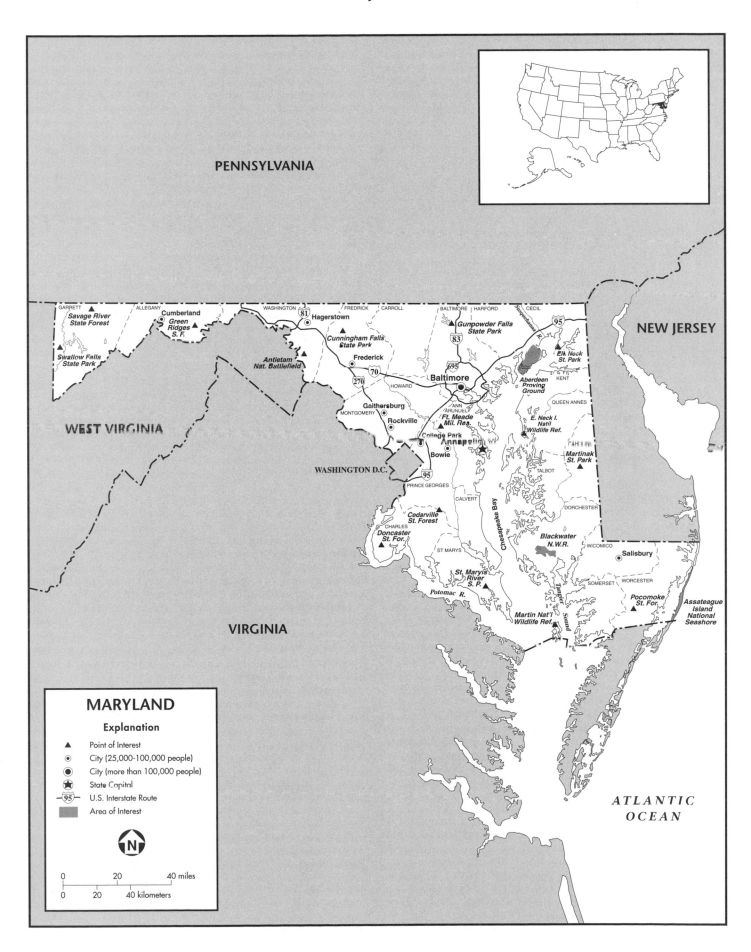

MARYLAND

Explanation

▲ Point of Interest

◉ City (25,000-100,000 people)

◉ City (more than 100,000 people)

★ State Capital

95 U.S. Interstate Route

Area of Interest

0   20   40 miles

0   20   40 kilometers

on the stomach, openseed peach (freestone peach), and Pennsylvania German *ponhaws* (scrapple). In the southern portion are found *light bread* (white bread), *curtain* (shade), *carry* (escort), *crop* as /krap/, and *bulge* with the vowel of *put*. East of Chesapeake Bay are *mosquito hawk* (dragonfly), *paled fence* (picket fence), *poor* (rhyming with *mower)*, and *Mary* with the vowel of *mate*. In central Maryland, an earthworm is a *baitworm*.

In 1990, 4,030,234 residents, or 91.1% of the population five years old or older, spoke only English at home. Other languages spoken at home, with the number of speakers, included:

Spanish (up 116% from 1980)	122,871	Greek	13,146
French	39,484	Chinese	24,508
German	26,454	Korean	23,563
Italian	15,980	Indic	20,096

⁹RELIGIONS

Maryland was founded as a haven for Roman Catholics, and they remain the state's leading religious group, although their political supremacy ended in 1692, when Anglicanism became the established religion. Laws against "popery" were enacted by 1704, and Roman Catholic priests were harassed; the state constitution of 1776, however, placed all Christian faiths on an equal footing. The state's first Lutheran church was built in 1729, the first Baptist church in 1742, and the earliest Methodist church in 1760. Jews settled in Baltimore in the early 1800s, with a much larger wave of Jewish immigration in the late 19th century.

As of 1990, there were 832,763 Roman Catholics in Maryland. Adherents of the major Protestant denominations included United Methodist Church, 310,008; Southern Baptist Convention, 131,627; Lutheran Church, 31,393; and Episcopal Church, 82,714. In 1990, there were an estimated 210,965 Jews.

¹⁰TRANSPORTATION

Some of the nation's earliest efforts toward the development of a reliable transportation system began in Maryland. In 1695, a public postal road was opened from the Potomac River through Annapolis and the Eastern Shore to Philadelphia. Construction on the National Road (now US 40) began at Cumberland in 1811; within seven years, the road was a conduit for settlers in Ohio. The first commercial steamboat service from Baltimore started in 1813, and steamboats were active all along the Chesapeake during the 1800s. The Delaware and Chesapeake Canal, linking Chesapeake Bay and the Delaware River, opened in 1829.

Maryland's first railroad, the Baltimore and Ohio (B&O), was started in 1828; in 1835, it provided the first passenger train service to Washington, D.C., and Harpers Ferry, Va. (now W.Va.). By 1857, the line was extended to St. Louis, and its freight capacity helped build Baltimore into a major center of commerce. In the 1850s, the Pennsylvania Railroad began to buy up small Maryland lines and provide direct service to northern cities.

Today Consolidated Rail, CSX Transportation, and Norfolk Southern are the Class I railroads operating in the state, along with 2 regional, 3 local, and 3 switching and terminal railroads. As of 1995, total rail miles in Maryland amounted to 866 mi (1,394 km), including about 675 mi (1,085 km) of Class I track. Amtrak operated about 70 daily trains through the state in 1995/96, carrying 1,471,381 passengers from six stations. The Maryland Transportation Department's Railroad Administration subsidizes four commuter lines, as well as freight lines in western Maryland and on the Eastern Shore.

The Maryland Mass Transit Administration inaugurated Baltimore's first subway line on 21 November 1983. The combined underground-elevated line ran for 8 mi (13 km) from downtown Baltimore to Reisterstown Plaza; later, the Baltimore Metro was extended for 6 mi (10 km) to Owings Mills, just outside the city limits. The Metro cost nearly $1 billion to build.

In 1984, the Washington, D.C., mass transit system was extended to the Maryland suburbs, including Bethesda and Rockville.

About half of Maryland's roads serve metropolitan Baltimore and Washington. As of 1995 there were 29,680 mi (47,785 km) of roadway. Interstate highways in Maryland totaled 482 mi (776 km) that year; the major toll road is the John F. Kennedy Memorial Highway (I-95), linking Baltimore with Wilmington, Delaware, and the New Jersey Turnpike. There were 3,344,125 licensed drivers and 3,654,199 motor vehicles registered in Maryland in 1995.

The Port of Baltimore, the nation's 19th busiest, handled 31,597,443 tons of foreign cargo, and 13,098,369 tons of domestic cargo in 1995. That year, the port handled 14,359,323 tons of imports as well as 17,238,120 tons of exports, valued at $6.3 billion (10th highest value in US). There are 146 airports in Maryland. The Department of Transportation operates Baltimore–Washington International (BWI) Airport, the major air terminal in the state. In 1994, it handled 79,315 aircraft departures with 5,524,703 passengers. Another 57 airfields (53 heliports, 1 stolport, and 3 seaplane bases) also served the state in 1994.

¹¹HISTORY

The Indian tribes living in the region that was to become Maryland were Algonkian-speakers: the Accomac, Nanticoke, and Wicomico on the Eastern Shore, and the Susquehannock, Yacomico, and Piscataway on the Western Shore. The Susquehannock, the most powerful tribe at the time of English colonization, claimed all the land lying between the Susquehanna and Potomac rivers. Although the Algonkian Indians hunted for much of their food, many tribes (including the Susquehannock) also had permanent settlements where they cultivated corn (maize), vegetables, tobacco, and other crops. George Alsop, in his *Character of the Province of Maryland* (1666), noted that Susquehannock women "are the Butchers, Cooks, and Tillers of the ground but the men think it below the honour of a Masculine to stoop to any thing but that which their Gun, or Bow and Arrows can Command." European penetration of the Chesapeake region began early in the 16th century, with the expeditions of Giovanni da Verrazano, a Florentine navigator, and the Spaniard Lucas Vázquez de Ayllón. Captain John Smith, leader of the English settlement at Jamestown, Virginia, was the first English explorer of Chesapeake Bay (1608) and produced a map of the area that was used for years.

The founding of Maryland is intimately tied to the career of another Englishman, George Calvert. A favorite of King James I, Calvert left the Church of England in 1624 to become a Roman Catholic. He announced his conversion in 1625 and—because Catholics were not allowed to hold public office in England at that time—then resigned his post as secretary of state and, against the king's wishes, retired from the royal court. As a reward for Calvert's service, the king bestowed upon him large Irish estates and a peerage with the title of Baron of Baltimore. Two years later, Calvert sailed for the New World, landing in Newfoundland, to which he had received title in 1621. After a severe winter, however, Calvert decided to seek his fortunes where the weather was warmer—in Virginia. Not well-received there because of his religion, Calvert returned to England and asked King Charles I (James's successor) for land south of Virginia; instead he received a grant north of the Potomac. Virginia's agents in England contested Calvert's right to this land strenuously but unsuccessfully, and when he died in 1632, the title passed to his son Cecilius Calvert, 2d Baron Baltimore (usually called Lord Baltimore), who named the region Maryland after the queen consort of Charles I, Henrietta Maria. At this time, the land grant embraced not only present-day Maryland but also the present State of Delaware, a large part of Pennsylvania, and the valley between the north and south branches of the Potomac River. Not until the 1760s was the final boundary between Pennsylvania and Maryland (as surveyed by Charles Mason and Jeremiah Dixon) established by royal decree, and nearly a century passed before Maryland conceded to Virginia the land between the north and south branches of the Potomac.

The government of provincial Maryland was absolute, embodying the most extensive grant of royal powers to a colonial settlement. Lord Baltimore's main source of income as lord proprietary was the quitrents settlers paid for their land; in return for his authority, Calvert had to give the king only two Indian arrows yearly. Lord Baltimore assigned to his half-brother, Leonard Calvert, the task of organizing the settlement of the colony. On 22 November 1633, Calvert and approximately 250 settlers, including many Roman Catholics and two Jesuit priests, set sail for America on two ships, the *Ark* and the *Dove*. They landed at St. Clements Island on 25 March 1634. Two days later, Calvert purchased a site from the Indians, named it St. Marys (the first capital of Maryland), and assumed the governorship of the colony.

The early days of settlement were tumultuous. The refusal by a Virginia colonist, William Claiborne of Kent Island, to acknowledge Lord Baltimore's charter led to a small war that ended in 1638 with a temporary victory for Governor Calvert. The conflict in England during the 1640s found an echo in the struggle between Puritans and Roman Catholics in Maryland, a conflict that saw the two-year exile of Governor Calvert to Virginia, the assumption of power by English representatives (including Claiborne and one of the Puritan leaders) in 1652, a subsequent civil war, and finally the recognition of Lord Baltimore's charter by Oliver Cromwell in 1657.

Cecilius Calvert died in 1675. His successor was Charles Calvert, 3d Baron Baltimore and the next lord proprietary. His tenure, which lasted until 1715, saw a decisive change in the character of the province. In 1689, with Protestants ascendant in both England and Maryland, the British crown assumed direct control over the province, and in 1692, the Church of England became Maryland's established religion. When Charles Calvert died, his successor, Benedict Leonard Calvert, 4th Baron Baltimore, was granted full proprietary rights—but only because he had embraced the Protestant faith. Proprietary rule continued through his legitimate heirs until the eve of the American Revolution.

Throughout this period, the upper and lower houses of the colonial assembly—consisting, respectively, of the governor and his council and of delegates elected from the counties—quarreled over taxation and the extension of English statutes to free Marylanders. Having already secured most rights from the proprietor, the lower house was somewhat reluctant to vote for independence from the British crown, on whose authority the proprietary government now rested. After its initial hesitancy, however, Maryland cast its lot with the Revolution and sent approximately 20,000 soldiers to fight in the war. The Continental Congress met in Baltimore from December 1776 to March 1777 and in Annapolis from November 1783 to June 1784. These cities were thus among the eight that served as US capitals before the designation of a permanent seat of government in Washington, D.C.

Maryland was one of the last states to sign the Articles of Confederation, not ratifying them until other states dropped their claims to what later became the Northwest Territory. On 28 April 1788, Maryland became the 7th state to ratify the federal Constitution. The state constitution, drawn up in 1776, was weighted heavily in favor of propertyholders and the rural counties, at the expense of the propertyless and the city of Baltimore; the legislature removed the property qualifications in 1810.

Maryland's prosperity during the colonial and early federal period waxed and waned according to the world price of tobacco, the staple crop of tidewater and southern Maryland. Planters increasingly employed slave labor on farms and plantations, and the black population grew rapidly in the 18th century. German immigrants began moving into western Maryland, where wheat became the primary crop. The cultivation of wheat also helped make Baltimore's fortune. Founded in 1729 and incorporated in 1796, the city of Baltimore was blessed with a harbor well suited to the export and import trade. As commerce developed, shipbuilding emerged as a major economic activity. By the early 19th century, Baltimore was already the state's major center of commerce and industry.

The city and harbor were the site of extensive naval and military operations during the War of 1812. It was during the bombardment of Ft. McHenry in 1814 that Francis Scott Key, detained on the British frigate, composed "The Star-Spangled Banner," which became the US national anthem in March 1931.

After the War of 1812, Maryland history was marked by the continued growth of Baltimore and increasing division over immigration, slavery, and secession. The chartering in 1827 of the Baltimore and Ohio (B&O) Railroad, which eventually linked Maryland with the markets of the Ohio Valley and the West, added to the city's economic vitality. But distrust of the thousands of newcomers—especially of Irish immigrants and their Roman Catholicism—and fear of the economic threat they supposedly represented spurred the rise of nativist political groups, such as the Know-Nothings, who persecuted the immigrants and dominated Maryland politics in the 1850s.

Although not many Marylanders were in favor of secession, they were hostile to the idea of using force against the secessionist states. On 19 April 1861, as the 6th Massachusetts Regiment passed through Baltimore, it was attacked by a mob of southern sympathizers in a riot that left 4 soldiers and 12 civilians dead. Ten days later, the Maryland house of delegates, following the lead of Governor Thomas Hicks, rejected a bill of secession. Throughout the Civil War, Maryland was largely occupied by Union troops because of its strategic location and the importance for the northern cause of the B&O Railroad. Marylanders fought on both sides during the war, and one major battle took place on Maryland soil—the Battle of Antietam (1862), during which a Union army thwarted a Confederate thrust toward the north, but at an enormous cost to both sides. Confederate armies invaded the state on two other occasions, when General Robert E. Lee brought his troops through the state on the way to Gettysburg in 1863 and when Lieutenant general Jubal Early ravaged the Hagerstown area and threatened Baltimore in 1864. The Maryland legislature, almost totally pro-Union by 1864, passed a new constitution, which among other things abolished slavery.

The state's economic activity increased during Reconstruction, as Maryland, and especially Baltimore, played a major role in rebuilding the South. Maryland's economic base gradually shifted from agriculture to industry, with shipbuilding, steelmaking, and the manufacture of clothing and shoes leading the way. The decades between the Civil War and World War I were also notable for the philanthropic activities of such wealthy businessmen as John Hopkins, George Peabody, and Enoch Pratt, who endowed some of the state's most prestigious cultural and educational institutions. The years after World War I saw the emergence of a political figure without equal in Maryland's more recent history: Albert C. Ritchie, a Democrat who won election to the governorship in 1919 and served in that office until 1935, just one year before his death. Stressing local issues, states' rights, and opposition to prohibition, Ritchie remained in power until Harry W. Nice, a Republican but an advocate of New Deal reforms, defeated him in 1934.

The decades since World War II have been marked by significant population growth. From 1980 to 1990 alone, Maryland grew by 13.4%, well above the national rate of 9.8%. The state has also witnessed political scandal in recent years and the passage of open housing and equal opportunity laws to protect Maryland's black citizens. Perhaps the most significant occurrence has been the redevelopment of Baltimore, which, though still the hub of the state's economy, had fallen into decay. Much of Baltimore's downtown area and harbor facilities were revitalized by many urban rejuvenation projects, begun in the late 1970s and continued into the 1980s. These featured the Charles Center development and the waterfront renovation of the Inner Harbor. Oriole Park at Camden Yards opened in 1992, and a new $150 million convention center was slated to open at the Inner Harbor in 1997. Although Maryland's economy declined less than those of other states during the recession of the late 1980s, the state has suffered from the contraction of defense and technology industries. Nevertheless, service industry employment, primarily in the Baltimore–Washington corridor, still gave Maryland the fifth highest state income in the country as of the mid-1990s. Federal government and high-tech employment accounted for many of these jobs. The environmental clean-up of the Chesapeake Bay, begun in the mid-1980s, is slated to continue into the 21st century.

12STATE GOVERNMENT

Maryland's first state constitution was enacted in 1776. Subsequent constitutions were ratified in 1851, 1864, and 1867.

Under the 1867 constitution, as amended, the general assembly, Maryland's legislative body, consists of two branches: a 47-member senate and a 141-member house of delegates. All legislators serve four-year terms and must have been residents of the state for at least a year and of their district for at least six months prior to election. Senators must be at least 25 years of age, delegates 21. The legislative salary was $28,840 in 1995.

Executives elected statewide are the governor and lieutenant governor (who run jointly), the comptroller of the treasury, and the attorney general; all serve four-year terms. The state treasurer is elected by joint ballot of the general assembly, while the secretary of state is appointed by the governor. The governor, who may serve no more than two four-year terms in succession, also appoints other members of the executive council (cabinet) and the heads of major boards and commissions. The chief executive must be a US citizen at least 30 years of age and must have been a resident of Maryland for five years before election. In 1996, the governor's salary was $120,000.

Bills passed by majority vote of both houses of the assembly become law when signed by the governor or if left unsigned for 6 days while the legislature is in session or 30 days if the legislature has adjourned. The only exception is the budget bill, which becomes effective immediately upon legislative passage. Gubernatorial vetoes may be overridden by three-fifths votes in both houses. Proposed constitutional amendments also require approval by three-fifths of both houses of the legislature before submission to the voters at the next general election.

US citizens who are at least 18 years of age and have been residents of the state for 30 days prior to the election are eligible to vote.

13POLITICAL PARTIES

The Republican and Democratic parties are the dominant political groups in Maryland. Before the Civil War, the Democrats drew much of their strength from the slaveholding Eastern Shore, while their opponents, the Whigs, were popular in Baltimore and other centers of antislavery activity. The collapse of the Whigs on both the national and local levels corresponded with the rise in Maryland of the Native American ("Know-Nothing") Party, whose anti-immigrant and anti-Catholic attitudes appealed to Marylanders who saw their livelihood threatened by Roman Catholic immigrants. The Know-Nothings swept Baltimore in 1855 and won the governorship in 1857; Maryland was the only state to cast its electoral votes for the Know-Nothing presidential candidate, former President Millard Fillmore, in 1856. The Native American Party declined rapidly, however, and by 1860, Maryland was back in the Democratic column, voting for the secessionist John Breckinridge.

As of 1994, there were 2,463,010 registered voters, of whom 61% were Democrats, 29% Republicans, and 10% Independents and members of minor parties. Maryland was one of the few states carried by President Jimmy Carter in the November 1980 presidential election, but four years later the state went for President Ronald Reagan in the national Republican landslide. In 1996, Maryland gave 54% of its vote to Democrat Bill Clinton, 38% to Republican Bob Dole, and 7% to Independent Ross Perot.

Maryland Presidential Vote by Political Parties, 1948–96

YEAR	ELECTORAL VOTE	MARYLAND WINNER	DEMOCRAT	REPUBLICAN	PROGRESSIVE	STATE'S RIGHTS DEMOCRAT	SOCIALIST
1948	8	Dewey (R)	286,521	294,814	9,983	2,467	2,941
1952	9	*Eisenhower (R)	395,337	499,424	7,313	—	—
1956	9	*Eisenhower (R)	372,613	559,738	—	—	—
1960	9	*Kennedy (D)	565,808	489,538	—	—	—
1964	10	*Johnson (D)	730,912	385,495	—	—	—
					AMERICAN IND.		
1968	10	Humphrey (D)	538,310	517,995	178,734	—	—
					AMERICAN		
1972	10	*Nixon (R)	505,781	829,305	18,726	—	—
1976	10	*Carter (D)	759,612	672,661	—	—	—
						LIBERTARIAN	
1980	10	Carter (D)	726,161	680,606	—	14,192	—
1984	10	*Reagan (R)	787,935	879,918	—	5,721	—
1988	10	*Bush (R)	826,304	876,167	5,115	6,748	—
							IND. (PEROT)
1992	10	*Clinton (D)	988,571	707,094	2,786	4,715	281,414
1996	10	*Clinton (D)	966,207	681,530	—	8,765	115,812

* Won US presidential election.

Revelations of influence peddling and corruption afflicted both major parties during the 1970s. In 1973, Republican Spiro T. Agnew, then vice president of the US, was accused of taking payments from people who had done business with the state government while he was Baltimore County executive and then governor of Maryland until 1969. Agnew pleaded *nolo contendere* to a federal charge of income tax evasion and resigned from the vice-presidency on 10 October 1973. His gubernatorial successor, Democrat Marvin Mandel, was convicted of mail fraud and racketeering in 1977 for having used the powers of his office to assist the owners of a now-defunct racetrack in exchange for $350,000 in gifts and favors; he served 20 months of a 36-month prison sentence before receiving a presidential pardon in 1981.

In 1994, the governor's race, one of the closest in Maryland history, was won by Democrat Parris N. Glendening, a three-term Prince George's county executive. The two senators from Maryland, Barbara Mikulski and Paul S. Sarbanes, both Democrats, were re-elected in 1992 and 1994, respectively.

Following the November 1996 elections, Maryland's congressional delegation consisted of four Democrats and four Republicans; there were 32 Democrats and 15 Republicans in the state senate, and 100 Democrats and 41 Republicans in the state house.

In 1994, there were 140 blacks and 2 Hispanics holding public office. As of 1995, 55 women served in the state legislature.

14LOCAL GOVERNMENT

As of 1992, there were 23 counties, 152 incorporated cities and towns, and 155 municipal governments in Maryland. Eight counties had charter governments, with (in most cases) elected executives and county councils, and 15 had elected boards of county commissioners. County government is highly developed in Maryland, and there are numerous appointed county officials with responsibilities ranging from civil defense to liquor licensing.

The city of Baltimore is the only one in Maryland not contained within a county. It provides the same services as a county, and shares in state aid according to the same allocation formulas. The city (not to be confused with Baltimore County, which surrounds the city of Baltimore but has its county seat at Towson) is governed by a mayor and a nine-member city council. Other cities and towns are each governed by a mayor, with or without a council, depending on the local charter.

15STATE SERVICES

The State Ethics Commission, established in 1979, monitors compliance by state officeholders and employees with the Maryland public ethics law in order to avoid conflicts of interest; the Joint Committee on Legislative Ethics, created in 1972, has similar responsibilities with respect to general assembly members. The Fair Campaign Financing Commission provides for the public financing of elections and sets campaign spending limits.

The State Board of Education is an independent policymaking body whose nine members are appointed by the governor; its responsibilities include selection of a superintendent of schools to run the Education Department. The growth and development of postsecondary institutions are the responsibility of the State Board for Higher Education. The Department of Transportation oversees air, road, rail, bridge, and mass transit. The Department of Health and Mental Hygiene coordinates public health programs, regulates in-state medical care, and supervises the 24 local health departments. Social services and public assistance programs as well as employment security lie within the jurisdiction of the Department of Human Resources. The Department of Business and Economic Development advances job opportunities and works to bring new businesses into the state. It also serves in a public relations capacity at home and abroad to stimulate international trade and tourism, and also invests in the arts and promotes sports events.

Maryland's s Department of Public Safety and Correctional Services has statewide responsibility for the supervision and rehabilitation of adjudicated individuals, while the Department of Labor, Licensing, and Regulation supervises employment training, job match services, unemployment insurance, and many of the state's licensing and regulatory boards for businesses and trades. The Department of State Police enforces state motor vehicle and criminal laws, preserves public peace, maintains safe traffic on public streets and highways, enforces laws relating to narcotics, and incorporates the office of the State Fire Marshal.

16JUDICIAL SYSTEM

The court of appeals, the state's highest court, comprises a chief judge and six associate judges. Each is appointed to the court by the governor but must be confirmed by the voters within two years of appointment. Most criminal appeals are decided by the court of special appeals, consisting of a chief judge and 12 associate judges, selected in the same manner as judges of the high court; each case must be heard by a panel of at least three judges of the high court. All state judges serve 10-year terms.

In 1971, 12 district courts took the place of all justices of the peace, county trial judges, magistrates, people's courts, and the municipal court of Baltimore. District courts handle all criminal, civil, and traffic cases, with appeals being taken to one of eight circuit courts. Circuit court judges are appointed by the governor and stand for election to 15-year terms; district court judges are appointed by the governor and confirmed by the senate to 10-year terms. The city of Baltimore and all counties except Montgomery and Hartford have orphans' courts composed of two judges and one chief judge, all of them elected to four-year terms. In 1996, there were 17,698 licensed attorneys.

According to the FBI Crime Index for 1996, Maryland had a violent crime rate of 986.9 per 100,000 population and a property crime rate of 5,307.9. Rates for specific crimes were: murder and non-negligent homicide, 11.8; forcible rape, 42.2; robbery, 423.1; aggravated assault, 509.7; burglary, 1,057.5; larceny/theft, 3,532.8; and motor vehicle theft, 717.6. Baltimore had a violent crime rate of 1,335.9. Maryland has the death penalty, and 17 prisoners were being held under the death sentence as of 30 May 1997. No prisoner had been executed since 1977 until John Thanos was executed on 17 May 1994 by lethal injection. There were 20,907 prisoners in state and federal prisons in 1995, a rate of 415 prisoners per 100,000 inhabitants.

17ARMED FORCES

As of 1996, there were 29,877 active US military personnel in Maryland. Ft. Meade in Baltimore had 5,777, and 2,960 were stationed at the Aberdeen Proving Ground in Harford County. Perhaps Maryland's best-known defense installation is Andrews Air Force Base in Camp Springs, a military airlift center that had 5,802 active military personnel in 1996. Annapolis is the home of the US Naval Academy, which in 1992 had 5,392 active military personnel. Total military personnel at all naval facilities, including the National Naval Medical Center at Bethesda, was 14,588 in 1996. Federal defense contract awards to Maryland firms exceeded $4.1 billion in 1995/96.

Some 526,000 veterans were living in the state as of 1 July 1996, with wartime service as follows: World War I, fewer than 500; World War II, 126,000; Korean conflict, 84,000; Vietnam era, 173,000; Persian Gulf War, 32,000. Veterans' benefits during 1995/96 totaled $645 million. In 1996, Maryland's National Guard and Reserve numbered 32,379 members; the Army, 20,164; the Navy and Marine Corps, 5,513; and the Air Force, 6,702. In 1993, the Maryland State Police employed 1,547 full-time sworn officers, or 3 per 10,000 residents.

[18]MIGRATION

Maryland's earliest white settlers were English; many of them farmed lands on the Eastern Shore. As tobacco crops wore out the soil, these early immigrants moved on to the fertile Western Shore and piedmont. During the 19th century, Baltimore ranked 2d only to New York as a port of entry for European immigrants. First to come were the Germans, followed by the Irish, Poles, East European Jews, and Italians; a significant number of Czechs settled in Cecil County during the 1860s. After the Civil War, many blacks migrated to Baltimore, both from rural Maryland and from southern states.

Since World War II, intrastate migration has followed the familiar urban/suburban pattern: both the Baltimore metropolitan area and the Maryland part of the metropolitan Washington, D.C., area have experienced rapid growth, while the inner cities have lost population. Overall, Maryland experienced a net loss from migration of about 36,000 between 1970 and 1980, much of it to Pennsylvania, Virginia, and Florida; the outmigration stopped during the 1980s, however, with a net gain of over 200,000 from 1980 to 1990. Between 1990 and 1996, Maryland had a net loss of 24,974 in domestic migration and a net gain of 79,358 in international migration. In 1996, 20,732 foreign immigrants arrived in the state—the ninth highest total of any state for that year. As of 1994, it was estimated that Maryland had between 29 and 63 undocumented immigrants. Maryland's foreign-born population totaled 412,000, or 8% of the total population, in 1996. By 1990, just under 50% of all Maryland residents had been born in the state, down from 53.7% in 1980. About 48% of residents age five and older lived in a different house in 1985 than in 1990, of which 27% did so in a different state.

[19]INTERGOVERNMENTAL COOPERATION

Maryland is active in several regional organizations, including the Southern Regional Education Board, Atlantic States Marine Fisheries Commission, Susquehanna River Basin Commission (with Pennsylvania and New York), and the Potomac River Fisheries Commission (with Virginia). Representatives of Maryland, Virginia, and the District of Columbia form the Washington Metropolitan Area Transit Authority, which coordinates regional mass transit. The Delmarva Advisory Council, representing Delaware, Maryland, and Virginia, works with local organizations on the Delmarva Peninsula to develop and implement economic improvement programs. In 1995/96, federal aid to Maryland totaled over $3.5 billion.

[20]ECONOMY

Throughout the colonial period, Maryland's economy was based on one crop—tobacco. Not only slaves but also indentured servants worked the fields, and when they earned their freedom, they too secured plots of land and grew tobacco for the European market. By 1820, however, industry was rivaling agriculture for economic preeminence. Shipbuilding, metalworking, and commerce transformed Baltimore into a major city; within 60 years, it was a leading manufacturer of men's clothing and had the largest steelmaking plant in the US.

Although manufacturing output continues to rise, the biggest growth areas in Maryland's economy are government, construction, trade, and services. Manufacturing, which has shifted toward high technology, information, and health-related products, lost 39,000 jobs between 1981 and 1991. With the expansion of federal employment in the Washington metropolitan area by 40% from 1961 to 1980, many US government workers settled in suburban Maryland, primarily Prince George's and Montgomery counties; construction and services in those areas expanded accordingly. Between 1982 and 1992, the number of jobs grew 24%, somewhat above the national average of 21%

for that period. From 1981 to 1991, services added 243,800 jobs, reaching a total of 567,052 in 1991. During that decade, retail trade increased by 82,000 jobs to 401,333 in 1991; finance gained 37,000 jobs, totaling 132,989; and construction acquired 30,400 jobs, reaching a total of 163,717. The growth of state government boosted employment in Anne Arundel and Baltimore counties. Also of local importance are fishing and agriculture (primarily dairy and poultry farming) on the Eastern Shore and coal mining in Garrett and Allegheny counties.

Maryland's gross state product was $132,703 million in 1994, to which private goods-producing industries contributed $19,300 million; private services-producing industries, $89,914 million; government, $27,226 million. In 1996, Maryland's per capita personal income was $26,333, which ranked 6th nationally. In 1996, there were 24,347 filings for bankruptcy, up almost 36% from the year before.

[21]INCOME

Per capita personal income rose by more than 14% from 1986 to 1996, in terms of 1992 constant dollars. As of 1996, Maryland ranked 6th in per capita income with $27,221. Total earned income by place of work was up 4.2% to $86 billion in 1996 from $82.6 billion in 1995. Nonfarm personal income grew from $126.4 billion in 1995 to $132.6 billion in 1996 for an increase of 4.9%.

Montgomery County had one of the highest personal income amounts per capita of all US counties in 1994 ($35,536). About 273,691 (16%) households in Maryland had total household income of $75,000 or greater in 1989. The state's median household income in 1995 was $41,041. An estimated 509,000 Marylanders—10.1% of the population—were below the federal poverty level in 1995.

[22]LABOR

Maryland's civilian labor force in 1996 averaged 2,786,000, of whom 2,650,000 were employed and 136,000 unemployed, for an annual unemployment rate of 4.9%.

The following table shows annual average nonfarm employment, total wages, and average weekly wages per worker in 1995:

	ANNUAL AVERAGE EMPLOYMENT	TOTAL WAGES ($ MILLIONS)	AVERAGE WEEKLY WAGES PER WORKER
Total employment	$2,145,713	$62,527.0	560
Private sector	1,738,381	48,364.7	535
Construction	127,262	3,788.8	573
Manufacturing	175,790	6,451.1	706
Transportation, Communications, Utilities	101,530	3,617.4	685
Wholesale trade	106,840	4,008.6	722
Retail trade	421,182	6,705.3	306
Finance, insurance, real estate	128,597	4,659.5	697
Services	655,309	18,865.1	548
Other	21,871	448.9	395
Government	406,932	14,162.2	669

Baltimore was a leading trade union center by the early 1830s, although union activity subsided after the Panic of 1837. The Baltimore Federation of Labor was formed in 1889, and by 1900, the coal mines had been organized by the United Mine Workers. In 1902, Maryland passed the first workers' compensation law in the US; it was declared unconstitutional in 1904 but subsequently revived. As of 1995, there were 350,700 workers who were members of labor unions in the state, or about 14.9% of all employees. Unionization among manufacturing workers in the private sector was 20.1%.

23AGRICULTURE

Maryland ranked 32nd among the 50 states in agricultural income in 1995, with estimated receipts of $1,658 million, about 40% of that in crops.

Until the Revolutionary War, tobacco was the state's only cash crop; in 1995, Maryland produced an estimated 11,475,000 lb of tobacco (12th in the US). Corn and cereal grains are grown mainly in southern Maryland. Production in 1995 included 42,000,000 bushels of corn for grain; 11,730,000 bushels of soybeans, $75,442,000; 14,400,000 bushels of wheat, $56,447,000, and 5,022,000 bushels of barley, $6,374,000. Fresh vegetables, cultivated primarily on the Eastern Shore, were valued at $6,494,000 in 1995. Fruits are also cultivated.

Maryland had some 14,300 farms covering 2,200,000 acres (890,688 hectares) in 1995. The number of farm operators declined from 7,882 in 1987 to 6,980 in 1992.

24ANIMAL HUSBANDRY

The Eastern Shore is an important dairy and poultry region; cattle are raised in north-central and western Maryland, while the central region is notable for horse breeding. In 1995, poultry farmers produced an estimated 22 million lb of chickens for around $1 million, and 1.36 billion lb of broilers for around $462 million which ranked 8th among the 50 states in broiler production. Also in 1995, Maryland farmers produced an estimated 1 billion eggs worth around $53 billion.

An estimated 1.3 billion lb of milk was produced in 1995 from 92,000 dairy cows. Maryland farms and ranches had around 270,000 cattle and calves worth an estimated $186 million in 1997. In 1996, there were an estimated 64,000 hogs and pigs, worth $5.9 million.

25FISHING

A leading source of oysters, clams, and crabs, Maryland had a total commercial catch in 1995 of 68,030,000 lb, valued at $60,570,000 (1.6% of US total). Ocean City is the state's leading fishing port, with landings of 12.5 million lb in 1995. Shellfish landings in 1995 included blue crab, 40.3 million lb; surf clams, 5.7 million lb; and soft clams, 367,000 lb. Bigeye and yellowfin tuna together are the most important finfish, followed by menhaden, dogfish shark, swordfish, and sea bass. The state's 85 seafood-processing and wholesale plants employed 1,676 persons during 1995.

The Fisheries Administration of the Department of Natural Resources monitors fish populations and breeds and implants oysters; it also stocks inland waterways with finfish. Maryland had 554,252 licensed sport anglers in 1995/96, when the state was apportioned $2.1 million by the US Fish and Wildlife Service for sport fish restoration programs.

26FORESTRY

Maryland's 2,700,000 acres (1,100,000 hectares) of forestland covers 43% of the state's land area. More than 89% of that was classified as commercial forest, 90% of it privately owned. Hardwoods predominate, with red and white oaks and yellow poplar among the leading hardwood varieties.

Forest management and improvement lie within the jurisdiction of the Maryland Department of Natural Resources Forest Service.

27MINING

The value of nonfuel mineral production in Maryland in 1995 was about $341 million, ranking 35th among the states and accounting for almost 1% of the national nonfuel mineral production value.

Crushed stone is the leading nonfuel mineral commodity, accounting for nearly 50% of the value in 1995, followed by portland cement (26%), and construction sand and gravel (17%). In 1995, output of crushed stone was 24.8 million metric tons; portland cement, 1.68 million metric tons; and construction sand and gravel, 8.4 million metric tons. Maryland was 3d among the states in masonry cement production in 1995, and also produced significant quantities of dimension stone. Employment in mining was about 1,100 in December 1996.

28ENERGY AND POWER

Maryland's installed electrical capacity was 11.76 million kW in 1997; production of electricity exceeded 44.6 billion kWh in 1995. More than 99% of the generating capacity was privately owned, and about 58% of the state's electricity was produced by coal-fired plants. The Calvert Cliffs Nuclear Plant in Lusby, operated by Baltimore Gas and Electric, had a capacity of 1,828.7 Mw and produced about 28% of the state's electricity in 1995.

Coal, Maryland's lone fossil fuel resource, is mined in Allegheny and Garrett counties, along the Pennsylvania border. Recoverable reserves in 1995 were estimated at 58 million tons of bituminous coal; the 1996 output of 20 coal mines totaled 3.9 million tons. About 212 trillion cu ft of natural gas from out of state was sold to 908,347 Maryland consumers in 1995.

29INDUSTRY

During the early 1800s, Maryland's first industries centered around the Baltimore shipyards. Small ironworks cast parts for sailing vessels, and many laborers worked as shipbuilders. By the 1850s, Baltimore was also producing weather-measuring instruments and fertilizers, and by the 1930s, it was a major center of metal refining. The city remains an important manufacturer of automobiles and parts, steel, and instruments.

Value of shipments by manufacturers in 1995 was $34,478 million. The following table shows value of shipments by selected industry groups in 1995:

Food and food products	$5,601,200,000
Chemicals and allied products	4,992,400,000
Transportation equipment	3,705,100,000
Printing and publishing	2,950,400,000
Instruments and related products	2,761,600,000
Industrial machinery and equipment	2,624,000,000
Primary metal industries	2,459,700,000

About one-third of all manufacturing activity (by value) takes place in the city of Baltimore, followed by Baltimore County, Montgomery County, and Prince George's County. Maryland is the headquarters for six Fortune 500 companies: Lockheed Martin, Marriott International, Black and Decker, Giant Food, USF&G, and BG&E. In 1995, there were 1,126 US patents issued to Maryland residents.

30COMMERCE

In 1992, wholesale sales totaled $52.9 billion, with durable goods accounting for 60.7%. Maryland's 7,443 wholesale establishments generated $3.7 billion in total payroll among 108,655 employees during 1994. Durable goods account for almost 5,000 of these establishments, a figure more than double the number of non-durable establishments (2,391). Professional and commercial equipment (e.g., computers, software and related peripherals, ophthalmic goods, photographic equipment, etc.); motor vehicles, parts and supplies; and machinery, equipment lead in number of establishments. Groceries and related products, paper and paper goods, and petroleum and petroleum products lead in establishments among the non-durables.

Retail sales in 1992 totaled $37.6 billion (18th). The state's 28,249 retail establishments in 1994 had $5.9 billion in annual wages. More than 75% of Maryland's retail facilities are located in the Baltimore metropolitan area and Montgomery and Prince George's counties surrounding Washington, D.C. Leading retail activity centers on food stores, automobiles and services stations, and apparel and accessory stores. These counties are home to about 90% of Maryland's 5 million residents. The Washington-Baltimore Consolidated Metropolitan Statistical Area is the nation's fourth largest retail market, with sales of $54.3 billion in 1992.

The value of imports through the Port of Baltimore in 1995 was $12.2 billion. Nearly half of these imports came from Europe, while almost one-quarter originated in Japan. Exports by Maryland companies totaled a record $6.22 billion in 1995, an increase of 6.4% over the previous year. While export activities in established markets such as Europe and Canada are still predominant, strong inroads have been made in targeted trade areas of Asia and Latin America.

31CONSUMER PROTECTION

The state agency responsible for controlling unfair and deceptive trade practices is the Division of Consumer Protection within the Attorney General's Office. Under the division's jurisdiction is the Maryland Consumer Council, comprising representatives of consumer groups, business groups, and other interests. The consumer credit commissioner, within the Department of Licensing and Regulation, is responsible for enforcing the state's Credit Deregulation Act, Retail Credit Accounts Law, Retail Installment Sales Act, and Equal Credit Opportunity Act (except for those provisions that apply to banks, over which the state banking commissioner has sole jurisdiction). The Consumer Services Division of the Motor Vehicle Administration, under the Department of Transportation, licenses motor vehicle dealers and manufacturers and professional driving schools; the division is also responsible for school bus safety inspections.

32BANKING

Maryland's 91 insured commercial banks in 1996 reported total assets of $68.8 billion; outstanding loans exceeded $44.6 billion; and deposits of $52.2 billion.

In 1996, there were 79 federally insured savings institutions with total assets of $17.4 billion. Fourteen savings institutions in Maryland were enrolled in the Resolution Trust Corporations (RTC) joint regulatory oversight program—these institutions had combined assets of over $8 billion and combined deposits exceeding $5.5 billion through nearly 842,000 accounts. In 1995, the RTC successfully resolved 14 institutions, at a cost of $1.5 billion.

All state-chartered savings and loan associations are regulated by the Board of Savings and Loan Associations, within the Department of Licensing and Regulation.

33INSURANCE

Life insurance in force as of 31 December 1991 included 3,375,000 policies worth $277.2 billion. Payments of $33.2 billion were made, including $679.2 million in death benefits. The average value of life insurance per family was $144,600 in 1995.

Property and liability insurers wrote premiums in 1991 totaling $4.9 billion, including $1.8 billion in automobile liability insurance, $365.1 million in automobile physical damage insurance, and $434.7 million in homeowners' coverage. Federal flood insurance totaling $3.7 billion was in effect as of 1995.

The Maryland Automobile Insurance Fund, a quasi-independent agency created in 1972, pays claims against uninsured motorists (i.e., hit-and-run drivers, out-of-state uninsured motorists, and state residents driving in violation of Maryland's compulsory automobile insurance law), and sells policies to Maryland drivers unable to obtain insurance from private companies.

The State Insurance Division of the Department of Licensing and Regulation licenses all state insurance companies, agents, and brokers, and must approve all policies for sale in the state.

34SECURITIES

There are no securities or commodities exchanges in Maryland. As of June 1996, there were 1,800 broker-dealers registered to sell securities in Maryland by means of 76,300 registered agents. Some 1,100 investment advisory companies were registered to provide services in June 1996 through 10,600 representatives. Securities dealers in Maryland are regulated by the Division of Securities within the Attorney General's Office.

35PUBLIC FINANCE

The state budget, prepared by the Department of Budget and Management, is submitted annually by the governor to the general assembly for amendment and approval. The fiscal year runs from 1 July to 30 June. The following table shows recommended revenues and expenditures for fiscal year 1997/98 (in millions of dollars):

EXPENDITURES	
Education	$ 5,311.2
Health and hospitals	3,412.8
Transportation	2,311.6
Human resources	1,248.7
Public safety and corrections	689.2
Judiciary	253.6
State police	218.3
Natural resources	175.5
Economic and employment development	77.3
Environment	150.5
Housing and community development	116.7
Juvenile services	120.7
General services	38.5
Agriculture	39.5
Retirement	16.1
Debt service	418.3
"Rainy day" fund	30.2
Other	814.8
TOTAL	$ 15,443.5

REVENUES	
Income taxes*	$ 4,125.4
Federal aid	3,449.8
Retail sales and use tax	2,171.3
Educational institutions	1,392.0
Motor vehicle tax and licenses	257.5
Business franchise taxes and fees	365.9
State lottery	406.1
Transportation receipts	668.0
Property tax	239.0
Other taxes and fees	1,383.8
Other receipts	178.7
TOTAL	$ 15,257.9

*Includes corporate income tax.

The outstanding state debt exceeded $4.2 billion as of 1996. The per capita debt of the state and local governments was $2,597 in 1995.

36TAXATION

Among the taxes levied by the state in 1997 were an individual income tax, ranging from 2% to 5%; a corporate income tax of 7%; a 5% sales and use tax; a state property tax; a motor vehicle use tax; a franchise tax; a pari-mutuel tax; a cigarette tax; and an alcoholic beverage tax. All county and some local governments levy property taxes. The counties also tax personal income at rates ranging from 30% to 60% of those imposed by the state; the city of Baltimore taxes personal income at rates equal to 50% of the state levy.

Marylanders paid $34.4 billion in federal income taxes in 1995 and received $36.8 billion in federal funding, or $7,307 per capita.

37ECONOMIC POLICY

The Department of Economic and Employment Development, created in 1970, encourages new firms to locate in Maryland and established firms to expand their in-state facilities, promotes the tourist industry, and disseminates information about the state's history and attractions. The department helps secure industrial mortgage loans for businesses that create new jobs, and also provides small-business loans, low-interest construction loads, assistance in plant location and expansion, and an Office of Business and Industrial Development to allow companies to maximize their use of state services. In addition, the department assists local governments in attracting federal funds for economic development and maintains programs to encourage minority businesses, the marketing of seafood, and the use of Ocean City Convention Hall. The Division of Economic Development maintains a representative in Brussels to promote European investment in Maryland. The Department of State Planning oversees state and regional development programs and helps local governments develop planning goals.

During the 1930s, Maryland pioneered in urban design with the new town of Greenbelt, in Prince George's County. A wholly planned community, Columbia, was built in Howard County during the 1960s. More recently, redevelopment of Baltimore's decaying inner city has been aggressively promoted. Harborplace, a waterside pavilion featuring hundreds of shops and restaurants, formally opened in 1980, and an industrial park was developed in a high-unemployment section of northwest Baltimore during the early 1980s. Not far from Harborplace are the 33-story World Trade Center and the National Aquarium. Urban restoration has also been encouraged by urban homesteading: a Baltimorean willing to make a commitment to live in an old brick building and fix it up can submit a closed bid to buy it. An analogous "shopsteading" program to attract merchants has also been encouraged.

In 1982, Maryland initiated a program of state enterprise zones to encourage economic growth by focusing state and local resources on designated areas requiring economic stimulus. Five of these enterprise zones were located in western Maryland, four in the central part of the state, and one on the Eastern Shore.

38HEALTH

The infant mortality rate for the 12 months ending with February 1994 was 9.5 per 1,000 live births, slightly below the US average. There were 19,860 legal abortions in 1992—a rate of 17 per 1,000 women aged 15–44, or about 255 for every 1,000 live births.

Maryland's birthrate in 1995 (14.4 per 1,000 population) was above the US norm of 14.8, while the death rate (8.3) was below the national norm of 8.8. The death rates for the leading causes of death in 1995 were: heart disease, 236.4 per 100,000 population; cancer, 201.6; and cerebrovascular diseases, 52.5—rates all below or nearly equal to the US average for these categories. Death from diabetes mellitus and HIV were higher than the national average in 1995. Among persons 18–30 years old, 21.1% were current smokers in 1995. The projected deaths from smoking-related illness for those (0–17) who become smokers was 85,720 (1995 estimate). The Alcoholism Control Administration monitors rehabilitation programs for alcoholics, while the Drug Abuse Administration oversees all drug treatment programs.

In 1996, Maryland had 50 acute care hospitals, with 13,871 beds and 614,083 patient admissions; hospital personnel included 17,599 registered nurses. The average daily census of hospital patients was 8,062; the bed occupancy rate was about 58%. The average expense of hospitals for care in 1996 was $1,159 per inpatient day and $5,950 per stay, slightly lower than the national average. In 1994, 12.6% of Maryland residents were uninsured. The per capita personal health care expenditures were $2,793 (1991), slightly above the national average.

Maryland's two medical schools are at Johns Hopkins University, which operates in connection with the Johns Hopkins Hospital and has superbly equipped research facilities, and at the University of Maryland—both located in Baltimore. Federal health centers located in Bethesda include the National Institutes of Health and the National Naval Medical Center. Maryland had 16,744 non-federal physicians as of January 1994, and 3,682 licensed active dentists as of 1995.

39SOCIAL WELFARE

About 207,800 Marylanders received public assistance under the Aid to Families with Dependent Children (AFDC) program in 1996, averaging $450 a month. In 1996, the food stamp program had an average monthly participation of 374,512. In the same year, the school lunch program served students at a federal cost of $72.3 million. The city of Baltimore accounts for a clear majority of public assistance recipients in the state.

With the enactment of the Personal Responsibility and Work Opportunity Reconciliation Act of 1996, the US government changed the form and regulations for many of its social welfare programs; most significantly, it replaced AFDC, an open-ended entitlement program, with Temporary Assistance for Needy Families (TANF), a limited system of assistance funded largely through federal block grants. The reform act also impacted the food stamp program, the Supplemental Security Income program, and the child nutrition program. The law took effect on 1 July 1997 and provided $16.38 billion in block grants for fiscal years 1997–2002. The grants were to be divided among the states based on an equation involving the numbers of former AFDC recipients in each state. Because many of the bill's provisions have yet to be implemented into state-by-state policy, it was not possible to include the details of each state's programs for this edition of this work.

In 1995, Social Security benefits went to approximately 678,930 Marylanders, including 433,190 retirees, averaging $721 a month. During 1995, unemployment insurance benefits averaged $185.76 a week per recipient.

40HOUSING

Maryland has sought to preserve many of its historic houses. Block upon block of two-story brick row houses, often with white stoops, fill the older parts of Baltimore, and stone cottages built to withstand rough winters are still found in the western counties. Greenbelt and Columbia exemplify changing modern concepts of community planning.

There were an estimated 2,023,000 year-round housing units in Maryland in 1996, of which 1,852,000 were occupied. In 1996, 25,108 privately owned units, valued at $2.2 billion, were authorized for construction; of these, 22,594 were single-family. Statewide, 21.6% of all units were built between 1980 and 1990. According to the 1990 census, 60% of Maryland houses were owner-occupied and less than 1% lacked full plumbing facilities. In 1990, the median value of a home was $116,500, up by 25.8% (in terms of 1990 dollars) from 1980.

The Department of Housing and Community Development, formed in 1987, oversees all housing and cultural resource areas, providing neighborhood rehabilitation and revitalization, development financing, historical and cultural programs, and information technology. The Maryland Housing Fund of the Department insures qualified lending institutions against losses on home mortgage loans.

The median monthly cost for housing for owners with a mortgage in 1990 (the last year for which figures are available) was $919, and $235 for owners without a mortgage. The median monthly rent throughout the state was $548 in 1990. In the Maryland suburbs of Washington, D.C., the median monthly cost of housing including a mortgage was $1,068, and the median rent was $675; for the greater Baltimore area, the median costs were $855 and $490, respectively. During 1995/96, Maryland received $444 million in aid from the US Department of Housing and Urban Development, including $78.9 million in community development block grants.

41EDUCATION

Partly because of Maryland's large number of government and professional workers, educational attainments compare favorably with those of the other South Atlantic states. As of 1992, 81% of all Marylanders had completed high school, and 25% had at least four years of college (the US average was 21.4%). Maryland students must pass state competency exams in order to graduate from high school.

There are 791 elementary and 202 secondary schools serving the state. Public schools enrollment in 1996/97 for grades pre-K through 12 was 818,583. Baltimore's total public school enrollment is 108,759 for the city, 104,073 for the county. Statewide, there were 48,970 public school teachers, earning average salaries of $41,679 in 1996.

The institutions of higher education in Maryland are organized as follows: (1) the public four-year colleges and universities, (2) the community colleges, (3) the independent colleges and universities, and (4) the private career schools.

The State's public four-year institutions include: The University of Maryland System, Morgan State University, and St. Mary's College of Maryland. The University of Maryland System is comprised of 11 separate degree-granting institutions located throughout the state. In addition, there are two research and public service institutions reporting to the System—the Center for Environmental and Estuarine Studies and the University of Maryland Biotechnology Institute. These institutions are governed by a single board of regents and a system administration. Morgan State University, the designated public urban teaching university, is governed by a single board of regents. Morgan is one of Maryland's four historically black institutions. St. Mary's College of Maryland, the State's public honors college, is the state's only "state-related" institution. As such, the college has more operational autonomy than the other public four-year institutions, particularly concerning procurement, budget, and personnel administration. The college's annual state funding is calculated by applying the implicit price deflator for state and local governments to the prior year's appropriation.

The 18 community colleges are two-year, open-admission institutions with courses and programs leading to certificates and associate degrees, as well as career-oriented and continuing education/community service programs. There are 17 local community colleges. They receive their funding from three sources: 1) state funding through a funding formula; 2) local funding through a negotiated budget process; and 3) students' tuition and fees. Baltimore City Community College became a

state institution in 1990/91 and receives the majority of its funding from the State.

The state provides funding to 15 independent colleges and universities in Maryland under a statutory formula. Eligible independent institutions must meet certain standards concerning the date of establishment, type of degrees conferred, accreditation, and affirmative action programs.

Private career schools in Maryland provide job preparatory training for students in a wide variety of fields, including business, computers, travel, truck driving, mechanics, electronics, allied health, cosmetology, and barbering. In 1996/97, approximately 100 private career schools reported a total enrollment of nearly 20,000 students in over 200 separate training programs.

The Maryland Higher Education Commission serves as the state's agency which provides, as part of its primary mission, coordination, regulatory oversight, and program approval for Maryland's post-secondary education system.

The State Scholarship Administration oversees 18 different state scholarship programs. Scholarships amounting to over $45 million were awarded in 1996/97 to students attending community colleges, private institutions, the state's public four-year campuses, as well as private career schools. Scholarship assistance is available for students attending full-time or part-time at the undergraduate or graduate level. Legislative scholarships are available for use out-of-state if a student's major is unique. Financial assistance is provided to students on the basis of financial need as well as academic excellence.

42ARTS

Although close to the arts centers of Washington, D.C., Maryland has its own cultural attractions. Baltimore, a major theatrical center in the 1800s, still contains many legitimate theaters. Center Stage in Baltimore is the designated state theater of Maryland, and the Olney Theatre in Montgomery County is the official state summer theater. Arts organizations are aided by the 11-member Maryland Arts Council.

The state's leading orchestra is the Baltimore Symphony. Baltimore is also the home of the Baltimore Opera Company, and its jazz clubs were the launching pads for such musical notables as Eubie Blake, Ella Fitzgerald, and Cab Calloway. The Peabody Institute of Johns Hopkins University in Baltimore is one of the nation's most distinguished music schools. Both the Maryland Ballet Company and Maryland Dance Theater are nationally known.

Maryland generated $588,000 in arts funding from federal sources in 1996. The NEA contributed $1,676,000 to the state's arts programs and $3,235,000 to the Maryland State Arts Council. The state also provided funding for the Council's activities. Private sources also contributed.

Audiences for Maryland's arts programs totaled 61,000,000 in 1996, and there were 507,000 contributing artists. The state made arts education available to 169,000 school children. In 1996, there were 1,000 arts associations in Maryland; there were also 24 local art associations. In the mid-1990s, the State Arts Council supported theater productions by "Shakespeare on Wheels." The Council also provided financial resources for the Baltimore Festival of the Arts.

The Maryland Arts Council received grants from the NEA's arts education funds and the NEA's state and regional program.

43LIBRARIES AND MUSEUMS

Maryland's public libraries held 16,366,682 volumes in 1996/97 and had a combined circulation of 45,374,960. The center of the state library network is the Enoch Pratt Free Library in the city of Baltimore; founded in 1886, it had 28 branches, 2,773,011 volumes, and a circulation of 1,518,524 in 1996. Each county also has its own library system. The largest academic libraries are those of Johns Hopkins University (2,201,033 volumes in 1992) and the University of Maryland at College Park (2,174,628). The Maryland Historical Society Library specializes in genealogy, heraldry, and state history. The Maryland State Archives houses government records, private manuscripts, maps, and photographs. Maryland is also the site of several federal libraries, including the National Agricultural Library at Beltsville, with 2,104,735 volumes; the National Library of Medicine at Bethesda, 4,730,000; and the National Oceanic and Atmospheric Administration Library at Rockville, 800,000.

Of the approximately 135 museums and historic sites in the state, the major institutions are the US Naval Academy Museum in Annapolis and Baltimore's Museum of Art, National Aquarium Seaport and Maritime Museum, Maryland Academy of Sciences, the Maryland Historical Society Museum, and Peale Museum, the oldest museum building in the US. Important historic sites include Ft. McHenry National Monument and Shrine in Baltimore (inspiration for "The Star-Spangled Banner") and Antietam National Battlefield Site near Sharpsburg.

⁴⁴COMMUNICATIONS

In March 1993, 95.8% of Maryland's 1,871,000 occupied housing units had telephones.

The state had 53 AM and 66 FM radio stations in 1996. Seven of the state's 16 television stations are in Baltimore. Maryland Public Broadcasting operates six noncommercial television stations—in Annapolis, Baltimore, Frederick, Hagerstown, Oakland, and Salisbury. There were 14 large cable television systems in Maryland as of 1996. Maryland also receives the signals of many Washington, D.C. broadcast stations.

⁴⁵PRESS

The *Maryland Gazette,* established at Annapolis in 1727, was the state's first newspaper. Not until 1773 did Baltimore get its first paper, the *Maryland Journal and Baltimore Advertiser,* but by 1820 there were five highly partisan papers in the city. The *Baltimore Sun,* founded in 1837, reached its heyday after 1906, when H. L. Mencken became a staff writer. Mencken, who was also an important editor and critic, helped found the *American Mercury* magazine in 1924.

As of 1997, Maryland had 11 morning and 5 afternoon dailies, as well as 8 Sunday papers, 7 semiweekly newspapers, and 88 weeklies. The most influential newspaper published in Baltimore is the *Sun* (daily, 337,292; Sunday, 488,562). The *Washington Post* (834,641 daily; 1,140,564 Sundays) is also widely read in Maryland.

⁴⁶ORGANIZATIONS

The 1992 US Census of Service Industries counted 1,281 organizations in Maryland, including 232 business associations; 708 civic, social, and fraternal associations; and 341 other membership organizations.

National medically oriented organizations with headquarters in Maryland include the National Federation of the Blind and American Urological Association, both in Baltimore; the American Association of Colleges of Pharmacy, American Institute of Nutrition, and National Foundation for Cancer Research, Bethesda; the American Speech-Language-Hearing Association and Cystic Fibrosis Foundation, Rockville; and the National Association of the Deaf, Silver Spring.

Leading commercial, professional, and trade groups include the Aircraft Owners and Pilots Association and American Fisheries Society, Bethesda; International Association of Chiefs of Police, Gaithersburg; and Retail Bakers of America, Hyattsville. Lacrosse, a major sport in the state, is represented by the Lacrosse Foundation in Baltimore and the US Intercollegiate Lacrosse Association in Chestertown.

⁴⁷TOURISM, TRAVEL, AND RECREATION

Although not a tourist mecca, Maryland attracted 3,485,313 visitors to its parks, historical sites, and national seashore (Assateague Island) in 1995. Domestic travelers spent nearly $5 million on overnight and day trips within the state in 1995. The tourist industry provides an estimated 124,000 jobs.

Among the state's attractions is Annapolis, the state capital and site of the US Naval Academy. On Baltimore's waterfront are monuments to Francis Scott Key and Edgar Allan Poe, historic Ft. McHenry, and many restaurants serving the city's famed crab cakes and other seafood specialties. Ocean City is the state's major seaside resort, and there are many resort towns along Chesapeake Bay.

There are 19 state parks with camping facilities and 10 recreation areas. In 1995, licenses were held by 534,835 fishermen and 226,428 hunters.

⁴⁸SPORTS

Maryland has two major league professional sports teams: the Baltimore Orioles of major league baseball, and the Baltimore Ravens of the National Football League. The Ravens (formerly the Browns) moved from Cleveland after the 1995 season, and were scheduled to begin playing in a new downtown stadium near Oriole Park at Camden Yards in 1998. The NFL's Washington Redskins will begin play in a new stadium in Landover, but will still be considered a team of the District of Columbia. The Orioles won the World Series in 1966, 1970, and 1983, and American League titles in 1969, 1971, and 1979.

There are also minor league hockey teams in Baltimore and Upper Marlboro, and a minor league baseball teams in Bowie, Frederick and Salisbury.

Ever since 1750, when the first Arabian thoroughbred horse was imported by a Maryland breeder, horse racing has been a popular state pastime. The major tracks are Pimlico (Baltimore), Bowie, and Laurel; Pimlico is the site of the Preakness, the second leg of racing's Triple Crown. Harness racing is held at Ocean Downs in Ocean City; quarter-horse racing takes place at several tracks throughout the state; and several steeplechase events, including the prestigious Maryland Hunt Cup, are held annually.

In collegiate basketball, the University of Maryland won the National Invitation Tournament in 1972, and Morgan State took the NCAA Division II title in 1974. Another major sport is lacrosse: Johns Hopkins, Navy, the University of Maryland, and Washington College in Chestertown all have performed well in intercollegiate competition.

Every weekend from April to October, Marylanders compete in jousting tournaments held in four classes throughout the state. In modern jousting, designated as the official state sport, horseback riders attempt to pick up small rings with long, lance-like poles. The state championship is held in October.

⁴⁹FAMOUS MARYLANDERS

Politicians

Maryland's lone US vice president was Spiro Theodore Agnew (b.1918), who served as governor of Maryland before being elected as Richard Nixon's running mate in 1968. Reelected with Nixon in 1972, Agnew resigned the vice-presidency in October 1973 after a federal indictment had been filed against him. Roger Brooke Taney (1777–1864) served as attorney general and secretary of the treasury in Andrew Jackson's cabinet before being confirmed as US chief justice in 1836; his most historically significant case was the *Dred Scott* decision in 1856, in which the Supreme Court ruled that Congress could not exclude slavery from any territory.

Three associate justices of the US Supreme Court were also born in Maryland. Thomas Johnson (1732–1819), a signer of the

Declaration of Independence, served as the first governor of the State of Maryland before his appointment to the Court in 1791. Samuel Chase (1741–1811) was a Revolutionary leader, another signer of the Declaration of Independence, and a local judicial and political leader before being appointed to the high court in 1797; impeached in 1804 because of his alleged hostility to the Jeffersonians, he was acquitted by the Senate the following year. As counsel for the National Association for the Advancement of Colored People, Thurgood Marshall (1908–93), argued the landmark *Brown v. Board of Education* school desegregation case before the Supreme Court in 1954; President Lyndon Johnson appointed him to the Court 13 years later.

Other major federal officeholders born in Maryland include John Hanson (1721–83), a member of the Continental Congress and first president to serve under the Articles of confederation (1781–82); Charles Carroll of Carrollton (1737–1832), a signer of the Declaration of Independence and US senator from 1789 to 1792; John Pendleton Kennedy (1795–1870), secretary of the Navy under Millard Fillmore and a popular novelist known by the pseudonym Mark Littleton; Reverdy Johnson (1796–1876), attorney general under Zachary Taylor; Charles Joseph Bonaparte (1851–1921) secretary of the Navy and attorney general in Theodore Roosevelt's cabinet; and Benjamin Civiletti (b.New York, 1935), attorney general under Jimmy Carter. Among the many important state officeholders are William Paca (1740–99), a signer of the Declaration of Independence and later governor; Luther Martin (b.New Jersey, 1748–1826), Maryland's attorney general from 1778 to 1805 and from 1818 to 1822, as well as defense counsel in the impeachment trial of Chase and in the treason trial of Aaron Burr; John Eager Howard (1752–1827), Revolutionary soldier, governor, and US senator; and Albert C. Ritchie (1876–1936), governor from 1919 to 1935. William D. Schaefer (b.1921) was mayor of Baltimore from 1971–87; he was elected governor in 1987.

Lawyer and poet Francis Scott Key (1779–1843) wrote "The Star-Spangled Banner"—now the national anthem—in 1814. The prominent abolitionists Frederick Douglass (Frederick Augustus Washington Bailey, 1817?–95) and Harriet Tubman (1820?–1913) were born in Maryland, as was John Carroll (1735–1815), the first Roman Catholic bishop in the US and founder of Georgetown University. Elizabeth Ann Bayley Seton (b.New York, 1774–1821), canonized by the Roman Catholic Church in 1975, was the first native-born American saint. Stephen Decatur (1779–1820), a prominent naval officer, has been credited with the toast "Our country, right or wrong!"

Business Leaders

Prominent Maryland business leaders include Alexander Brown (b.Ireland, 1764–1834), a Scotch-Irish immigrant who built the firm that is now the 2d-oldest private investment banking house in the US; George Peabody (b.Massachusetts, 1795–1869), founder of the world-famous Peabody Conservatory of Music (now the Peabody Institute of Johns Hopkins University); and Enoch Pratt (b.Masachusetts, (1808–96) who endowed the Enoch Pratt Free Library in Baltimore. Benjamin Banneker (1731–1806), a free black, assisted in surveying the new District of Columbia and published almanacs from 1792 to 1797. Ottmar Mergenthaler (b.Germany, 1854–99), who made his home in Baltimore, invented the linotype machine.

Educators and Physicians

Financier-philanthropist Johns Hopkins (1795–1873) was a Marylander, and educators Daniel Coit Gilman (b.Connecticut, 1831–1908) and William Osler (b.Canada, 1849–1919, also a famed physician), were prominent in the establishment of the university and medical school named in Hopkins' honor. Peyton

Rous (1879–1970) won the 1966 Nobel Prize for physiology or medicine.

Writers

Maryland's best-known modern writer was H(enry) L(ouis) Mencken (1880–1956), a Baltimore newspaper reporter who was also a gifted social commentator, political wit, and student of the American language. Edgar Allan Poe (b.Massachusetts, 1809–49), known for his poems and eerie short stories, died in Baltimore, and novelist-reformer Upton Sinclair (1878–1968) was born there. Other writers associated with Maryland include James M. Cain (1892–1976), Leon Uris (b.1924), John Barth (b.1930), and Russell Baker (b.1925). Painters John Hesselius (b.Pennsylvania, 1728–78) and Charles Willson Peale (1741–1827) are also linked with the state.

Actors and Musicians

Most notable among Maryland actors are Edwin Booth (1833–93) and his brother John Wilkes Booth (1838–65), notorious as the assassin of President Abraham Lincoln. Maryland was the birthplace of several jazz musicians, including James Hubert "Eubie" Blake (1883–1983), William Henry "Chick" Webb (1907–39), and Billie Holiday (1915–59).

Sports Figures

Probably the greatest baseball player of all time, George Herman "Babe" Ruth (1895–1948) was born in Baltimore. Other prominent ballplayers include Robert Moses "Lefty" Grove (1900–75), James Emory "Jimmy" Foxx (1907–67), and Al Kaline (b.1934). Former lightweight boxing champion Joe Gans (1874–1910) was a Maryland native.

[50]BIBLIOGRAPHY

Alampi, Gary (ed.). *Gale State Rankings Reporter.* Detroit: Gale Research, Inc., 1994

Bode, Carl. *Maryland: A Bicentennial History.* New York: Norton, 1978.

Cohen, Richard M., and Jules Witcover. *A Heartbeat Away: The Investigation and Resignation of Vice President Spiro T. Agnew.* New York: Viking, 1974.

Council of State Governments. *The Book of the States, 1994–1995 Edition.* Vol. 30. Lexington, Ky.: The Council of State Governments, 1994.

Dozer, Donald. *Portrait of the Free State: A History of Maryland.* Cambridge, Md.: Tidewater, 1976.

FDIC, Division of Research and Statistics. *Statistics on Banking: A Statistical Profile of the United States Banking Industry.* Washington, D.C.: Federal Deposit Insurance Corporation, 1993.

Fields, Barbara J. *Slavery and Freedom on the Middle Ground: Maryland during the Nineteenth Century.* New Haven, Conn.: Yale University Press, 1985.

Harvey, Katherine. *The Best-Dressed Miners: Life and Labor in the Maryland Coal Region, 1835–1910.* Ithaca, N.Y.: Cornell University Press, 1969.

Maryland, State of. Department of Economic and Community Development. *Maryland Statistical Abstract 1993–94.* Annapolis: State of Maryland, 1995.

Maryland, State of. Department of General Services. Hall of Records Commission. Archives Division. *Maryland Manual 1985–1986.* Edited by Gregory A. Stiverson. Annapolis: State of Maryland, 1985.

Mencken, H. L. *A Choice of Days: Essays from "Happy Days," "Newspaper Days," and "Heathen Days."* Selected by Edward L. Galligan. New York: Knopf, 1980.

Papenfuse, Edward C. et al. *Maryland: A New Guide to the Old Line State.* Baltimore: Johns Hopkins University Press, 1976.

Schmittroth, Linda, and Mary Kay Rosteck (eds.). *Cities of the United States*. 2d ed. Detroit: Gale Research, Inc., 1994.

U.S. Department of Education, National Center for Education Statistics. Office of Educational Research and Improvement. *Digest of Education Statistics, 1993*. Washington, D.C.: U.S. Government Printing Office, 1993.

U.S. Department of the Interior, U.S. Fish and Wildlife Service. *Endangered and Threatened Species Recovery Program*. Washington, DC: U.S. Government Printing Office, 1990.

Walsh, Richard, and William Lloyd Fox (eds.). *Maryland: A History*. Baltimore: Maryland Hall of Records, 1983.

Warner, William. *Beautiful Swimmers: Watermen, Crabs, and the Chesapeake Bay*. Boston: Little, Brown, 1976.

MASSACHUSETTS

Commonwealth of Massachusetts

ORIGIN OF STATE NAME: Derived from the name of the Massachuset Indian tribe that lived on Massachusetts Bay; the name is thought to mean "at or about the Great Hill." **NICKNAME:** The Bay State. **CAPITAL:** Boston. **ENTERED UNION:** 6 February 1788 (6th). **SONG:** "All Hail to Massachusetts." **FOLK SONG:** "Massachusetts." **POEM:** "Blue Hills of Massachusetts." **MOTTO:** *Ense petit placidam sub libertate quietem* (By the sword we seek peace, but peace only under liberty). **COAT OF ARMS:** On a blue shield an Indian depicted in gold holds in his right hand a bow, in his left an arrow pointing downward. Above the bow is a five-pointed silver star. The crest shows a bent right arm holding a broadsword. Around the shield beneath the crest is a banner with the state motto in green. **FLAG:** The coat of arms on a white field. **OFFICIAL SEAL:** Same as the coat of arms, with the inscription *Sigillum Reipublicae Massachusettensis* (Seal of the Republic of Massachusetts). **HEROINE:** Deborah Sampson. **BIRD:** Chickadee. **HORSE:** Morgan horse. **DOG:** Boston terrier. **MARINE MAMMAL:** Right whale. **FISH:** Cod. **INSECT:** Ladybug. **FLOWER:** Mayflower (ground laurel). **TREE:** American elm. **GEM:** Rhodonite. **MINERAL:** Babingtonite. **ROCK:** Roxbury pudding stone. **HISTORICAL ROCK:** Plymouth Rock. **EXPLORER ROCK:** Dighton Rock. **BUILDING AND MONUMENT STONE:** Granite. **FOSSIL:** Theropod dinosaur tracks. **BEVERAGE:** Cranberry juice. **LEGAL HOLIDAYS:** New Year's Day, 1 January; Birthday of Martin Luther King, Jr., 3d Monday in January; Washington's Birthday, 3d Monday in February; Patriots' Day, 3d Monday in April; Lafayette Day, 20 May; Memorial Day, last Monday in May; Independence Day, 4 July; Labor Day, 1st Monday in September; Columbus Day, 2d Monday in October; Veterans Day, 11 November; Thanksgiving Day, appointed by the governor, customarily the 4th Thursday in November; Christmas Day, 25 December. **TIME:** 7 AM EST = noon GMT.

¹LOCATION, SIZE, AND EXTENT

Located in the northeastern US, Massachusetts is the 4th largest of the six New England states and ranks 45th in size among the 50 states.

The total area of Massachusetts is 8,284 sq mi (21,456 sq km), of which land comprises 7,824 sq mi (20,265 sq km) and inland water occupies 460 sq mi (1,191 sq km). Massachusetts extends about 190 mi (306 k) E-W; the maximum N-S extension is about 110 mi (177 km). Massachusetts is bordered on the N by Vermont and New Hampshire; on the E by the Atlantic Ocean; on the S by the Atlantic Ocean and by Rhode Island and Connecticut; and on the W by New York.

Two important islands lie south of the state's fishhook-shaped Cape Cod peninsula: Martha's Vineyard (108 sq mi or 280 sq km) and Nantucket (57 sq mi or 148 sq km). The Elizabeth Islands, SW of Cape Cod and NW of Martha's Vineyard, consist of 16 small islands separating Buzzards Bay from Vineyard Sound. The total boundary length of Massachusetts is 515 mi (829 km), including a general coastline of 192 mi (309 km); the tidal shoreline, encompassing numerous inlets and islands, is 1,519 mi (2,444 km). The state's geographic center is located in Worcester County, in the northern section of the city of Worcester.

²TOPOGRAPHY

Massachusetts is divided into four topographical regions: coastal lowlands, interior lowlands, dissected uplands, and residuals of ancient mountains. The coastal lowlands, located on the state's eastern edge, extend from the Atlantic Ocean 30–50 mi (48–80 km) inland and include Cape Cod and the offshore islands. The northern shoreline of the state is characterized by rugged high slopes, but at the southern end, along Cape Cod, the ground is flatter and covered with grassy heaths.

The Connecticut River Valley, characterized by red sandstone, curved ridges, meadows, and good soil, is the main feature of west-central Massachusetts. The Berkshire Valley to the west is filled with streams in its northern end, including the two streams that join below Pittsfield to form the Housatonic River.

East of the Connecticut River Valley are the eastern uplands, an extension of the White Mountains of New Hampshire. From elevations of 1,100 feet (335 meters) in midstate, this ridge of heavily forested hills slopes down gradually toward the rocky northern coast.

In western Massachusetts, the Taconic Range and Berkshire Hills (which extend southward from the Green Mountains of Vermont) are characterized by numerous hills and valleys. Mt. Greylock, close to the New York border, is the highest point in the state, at 3,491 feet (1,064 meters). Northeast of the Berkshires is the Hoosac Range, an area of plateau land. Its high point is Spruce Hill, at 1,974 feet (602 meters).

There are more than 4,230 mi (6,808 km) of rivers in the state. The Connecticut River, the longest, runs southward through west-central Massachusetts; the Deerfield, Westfield, Chicopee, and Millers rivers flow into it. Other rivers of note include the Charles and the Mystic, which flow into Boston harbor; the Taunton, which empties into Mount Hope Bay at Fall River; the Blackstone, passing through Worcester on its way to Rhode Island; the Housatonic, winding through the Berkshires; and the Merrimack, flowing from New Hampshire to the Atlantic Ocean via the state's northeast corner. Over 1,100 lakes dot the state; the largest, the artificial Quabbin Reservoir in central Massachusetts, covers 24,704 acres (9,997 hectares). The largest natural lake is Assawompset Pond in southern Massachusetts, occupying 2,656 acres (1,075 hectares).

Hilly Martha's Vineyard is roughly triangular in shape, as is Nantucket Island to the east. The Elizabeth Islands are characterized by broad, grassy plains.

Millions of years ago, three mountainous masses of granite rock extended northeastward across the state. The creation of the Appalachian Mountains transformed limestone into marble, mud and gravel into slate and schist, and sandstone into quartzite. The new surfaces were worn down several times. Then, during the last Ice Age, retreating glaciers left behind the shape of Cape Cod as well as a layer of soil, rock, and boulders.

3CLIMATE

Although Massachusetts is a relatively small state, there are significant climatic differences between its eastern and western sections. The entire state has cold winters and moderately warm summers, but the Berkshires in the west have both the coldest winters and the coolest summers. The normal January temperature in Pittsfield in the Berkshires is 22°F (–6°C), while the normal July temperature is 68°F (20°C). The interior lowlands are several degrees warmer in both winter and summer; the normal July temperature is 71°F (22°C). The coastal sections are the warmest areas of the state; the normal January temperature for Boston is 30°F (–1°C), and the normal July temperature is 74°F (23°C). The record high temperature in the state is 107°F (42°C), established at Chester and New Bedford on 2 August 1975; the record low is –35°F (–37°C), registered at Chester on 12 January 1981.

Precipitation ranges from 39 to 46 in (99 to 117 cm) annually, with an average for Boston of 43.8 in (111 cm); Worcester, 45.4 in (115 cm), and Pittsfield, 44.4 in (113 cm). The average snowfall for Boston is 42 in (107 cm), with the range in the Berkshires considerably higher. Boston's average wind speed is 13 mph (21 km/hr).

4FLORA AND FAUNA

Maple, birch, beech, oak, pine, hemlock, and larch cover the Massachusetts uplands. Common shrubs include rhodora, mountain laurel, and shadbush. Various ferns, maidenhair and osmund among them, grow throughout the state. Typical wildflowers include the Maryland meadow beauty and false loosestrife, as well as several varieties of orchid, lily, goldenrod, and aster. Listed among rare and endangered plants are Eaton's quillwort, climbing fern, burhead, needlegrass, pipewort, mountain alder, white-water crowfoot, Seneca snakeroot, prickly pear, and small whorled pogonia.

Massachusetts had 76 species of mammals in 1993, of which 74 were native species. Common native mammals include the white-tailed deer, bobcat, river otter, striped skunk, mink, ermine, fisher, raccoon, black bear, gray fox, muskrat, porcupine, beaver, red and gray squirrels, snowshoe hare, little brown bat, and masked shrew. Among the Bay State's 336 resident bird species are the mallard, ruffed grouse, bobwhite quail, ring-necked pheasant, herring gull, great horned and screech owls, downy woodpecker, blue jay, mockingbird, cardinal, and song sparrow. Native inland fish include brook trout, chain pickerel, brown bullhead, and yellow perch; brown trout, carp, and smallmouth and largemouth bass have been introduced. Native amphibians include the Jefferson salamander, red-spotted newt, eastern American toad, gray tree frog, and bullfrog. Common reptiles are the snapping turtle, stinkpot, spotted turtle, northern water snake, and northern black racer. The venomous timber rattlesnake and northern copperhead are found mainly in Norfolk, Hampshire, and Hampden counties. The Cape Cod coasts are rich in a variety of shellfish, including clams, mussels, shrimps, and oysters. Among endangered mammals are the sperm, blue, sei, finback, right, and humpback whales; among reptiles, the red-bellied turtle (found only in Plymouth County).

5ENVIRONMENTAL PROTECTION

All environmentally related programs are administered by the Executive Office of Environmental Affairs (EOEA) and its five agencies: the Department of Environmental Management (DEM); the Department of Environmental Protection (DEP); the Department of Fisheries, Wildlife and Environmental Law Enforcement (DFWELE); the Department of Food and Agriculture (DFA); and the Metropolitan District Commission (MDC).

EOEA agencies protect the state's more than 3,100 lakes and ponds covering about 150,000 acres (61,000 hectares); some 2,000 rivers and streams flowing 10,700 mi (17,200 km); 810,000 acres (about 328,000 hectares) of medium- and high-yield aquifers underlying about a sixth of the state; a half-million acres (about 200,000 hectares) of wetlands covering about a tenth of the state; and 1,500 mi (2,400 km) of coastal capes, coves, and estuaries.

With disposal of treated sewage sludge in Boston Harbor halted in 1991 and with improved sewage treatment, the harbor today is markedly cleaner than before. In 1988, 10% of the flounder caught in Boston Harbor had liver tumors caused by toxic chemicals; as of 1993, no flounder tested had tumors. In 1994, the state opened a new primary water treatment plant, and in 1996, a second new treatment facility also began operation.

Between 1978 and 1985, Massachusetts averaged 24 air pollution (i.e., ozone) violation days per year; between 1985 and 1993, the average dropped to 14. Since 1990, the state has averaged 7 violation days per year. With the adoption of Massachusetts acid rain legislation in 1985, sulfur dioxide output from Massachusetts sources has been cut by 17%. Additional decreases, particularly from out-of-state power plants, are expected to further cut sulfur dioxide emissions in half by 2000. In response to the Massachusetts Toxic Use Reduction Program and certain federal requirements, toxic air emissions were reduced by about a third between 1989 and 1996.

The state's solid waste recycling and composting rate stood at 28% in 1994; its goal for 2000 is 46%. In 1994, 341 of the state's 351 communities had some type of recycling program, and in 1994, about 49% of solid waste was incinerated. Active landfills dropped in number from 220 in 1988 to 119 in 1994. In 1995, there were 30 hazardous waste sites.

Of the state's native vertebrate animals, 17% are endangered or threatened; among reptiles 55% are so listed. Wildlife management has restored populations of wild turkeys, white-tailed deer, bears, peregrine falcons, bald eagles, ospreys, Atlantic sturgeon, and Atlantic salmon.

Since about 1900, the Commonwealth has protected 528,400 acres (208,730 hectares) through acquisitions or restrictions, an area equal to 10% of the total land mass of the state. In 1993/94, the state added 8,930 acres (3,614 hectares) to its stock of protected land, expending $41 million in the effort. Federal, county, local, and private nonprofit agencies and organizations provide another 375,680 acres (152,038 hectares) of open space.

6POPULATION

As New England's most populous state, Massachusetts has seen its population grow steadily since colonial times. However, since the early 1800s, its growth rate has often lagged behind the rest of the nation's. Massachusetts's population, according to the 1990 federal census, was 6,016,425 (13th in the US), an increase of 4.9% over 1980, and much better than the 0.8% growth rate of the 1970s. The estimated population for the state in 1996 was 6,092,352, a change of 1.3% since 1990. Reasons behind the population lag include a birthrate (13.2 per 1,000 in 1982) well below the US average, and a net out-migration of 301,000 people between 1970 and 1983, the largest drop of all New England states.

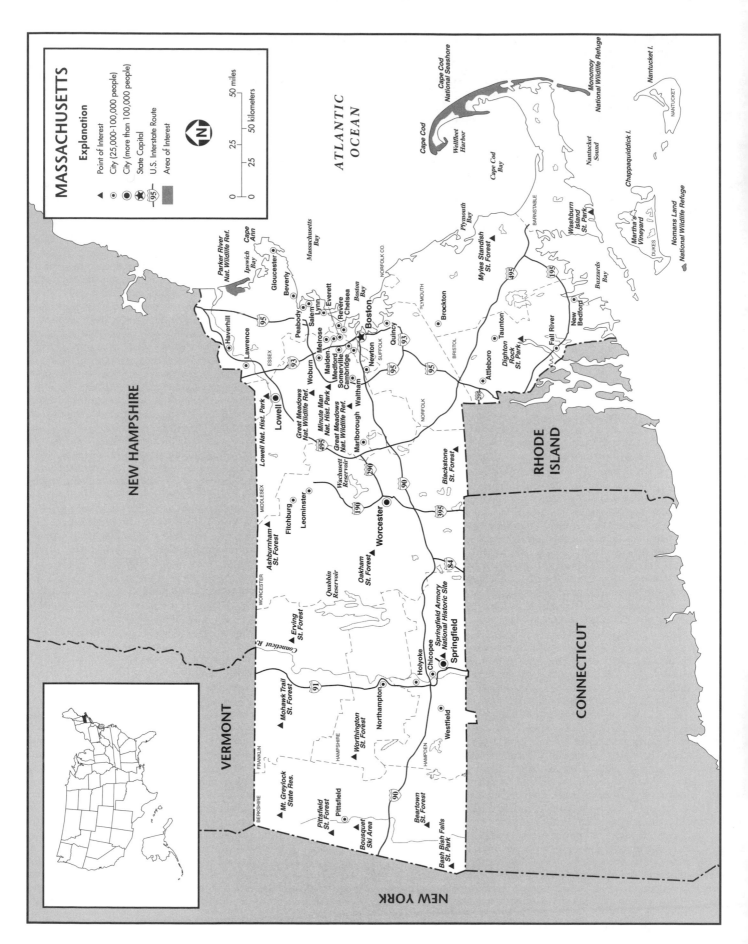

MASSACHUSETTS

Explanation

▲ Point of Interest
◉ City (25,000–100,000 people)
◉ City (more than 100,000 people)
✪ State Capital
95 U.S. Interstate Route
▓ Area of Interest

50 miles
50 kilometers
N

ATLANTIC OCEAN

Cape Cod National Seashore
Monomoy National Wildlife Refuge
Nantucket I.
Cape Cod
Wellfleet Harbor
Cape Cod Bay
Nantucket Sound
Chappaquiddick I.
NANTUCKET
BARNSTABLE
Plymouth Bay
Washburn Island St. Park
Martha's Vineyard
Nomans Land National Wildlife Refuge
DUKES

NEW HAMPSHIRE

Parker River Nat. Wildlife Ref.
Cape Ann
Ipswich Bay
Gloucester
Beverly
Massachusetts Bay
NORFOLK CO.
Myles Standish St. Forest
Haverhill
95
Lawrence
ESSEX
93
Peabody
Salem
Lynn
Revere
Chelsea
Everett
Melrose
Malden
Medford
Somerville
Cambridge
Boston
Boston Bay
PLYMOUTH
Brockton
Taunton
Buzzards Bay
New Bedford
Woburn
Waltham
Newton
Quincy
93
SUFFOLK
95
95
Dighton Rock St. Park
Fall River
Great Meadows Nat. Wildlife Ref.
Minute Man Nat. Hist. Park
Great Meadows Nat. Wildlife Ref.
Marlborough
NORFOLK
BRISTOL
Attleboro
495
195
Lowell Nat. Hist. Park
Lowell
495
590
Wachusett Reservoir
Blackstone St. Forest
MIDDLESEX
Fitchburg
Leominster
190
590
90
RHODE ISLAND
Ashburnham St. Forest
WORCESTER
Worcester
395
Quabbin Reservoir
Oakham St. Forest
84
Erving St. Forest
Connecticut R.
Springfield Armory National Historic Site
Springfield
Chicopee
Holyoke
91
Mohawk Trail St. Forest
Worthington St. Forest
Northampton
Westfield
HAMPSHIRE
HAMPDEN
FRANKLIN
90
Beartown St. Forest
Mt. Greylock State Res.
Pittsfield St. Forest
Pittsfield
Bousquet Ski Area
Bash Bish Falls St. Park
BERKSHIRE

VERMONT

CONNECTICUT

NEW YORK

In 1990, about 84.3% of the state was urban and 15.7% rural. A density of 767 people per sq mi (295 per sq km) in 1990 made Massachusetts the 3d most densely populated state. A population of 6,159,000 is projected for 2000.

The state's biggest city is Boston, which ranked 20th among the largest US cities with a population of 574,000 in 1990, a rise of just 0.6% since 1984. This figure declined 4.6% to an estimated 547,725 by 1994. Other large cities (with their 1994 estimated populations) are Worcester, 165,387; Springfield, 149,164; and New Bedford, 94,623. More than 70% of all state residents live in the Greater Boston area, which in 1990 had a metropolitan population of 4,172,000 (7th largest in the US). The estimated population for 1996 was 5,768,968.

Massachusetts Counties, County Seats, and County Areas and Populations

COUNTY	COUNTY SEAT(S)*	LAND AREA (SQ MI)	POPULATION (1996 EST)
Barnstable	Barnstable	400	201,970
Berkshire	Pittsfield	929	134,788
Bristol	New Bedford, Taunton, Fall River	557	513,899
Dukes	Edgartown	102	13,259
Essex	Lawrence, Salem, Newburyport	495	686,774
Franklin	Greenfield	702	71,209
Hampden	Springfield	618	442,194
Hampshire	Northampton	528	149,610
Middlesex	Cambridge (East), Lowell	822	1,412,561
Nantucket	Nantucket	47	7,267
Norfolk	Dedham	400	637,688
Plymouth	Plymouth, Brockton	655	456,820
	Suffolk**	57	645,068
Worcester	Worcester, Fitchburg	1,514	719,545
	TOTALS	7,824	6,092,352

* Officially designated "shire town."
** No shire town. Suffolk County includes the city of Boston.

7ETHNIC GROUPS

Early industrialization helped make Massachusetts a mecca for many European migrants, particularly the Irish. As late as 1990 more than half of the population identified with at least one single ancestry group, the largest being the Irish (26% of the population), English (15%), Italian (14%), French (10%), Portuguese (5%), and Polish (6%). In that year, 9.5% of the state's population was foreign-born.

Massachusetts has always had some black population, and has contributed such distinguished figures as poet Phillis Wheatley and NAACP founder W.E.B. DuBois (the first black Ph.D. from Harvard) to US cultural and public life. A sizable class of black professionals has developed, and the 20th century has seen an influx of working-class blacks from southern states. In 1990 there were 300,000 black Americans in Massachusetts, 5% of the population; blacks constituted more than 25% of Boston's population. By 1996, the state's black population numbered an estimated 458,000. The state also had 288,000 people of Hispanic ancestry in 1990, predominantly Puerto Rican and Dominican. Estimates for 1996 showed a decline to 284,000.

Greater Boston has a small, well-organized Chinatown; in the suburbs reside many business and professional Chinese, as well as those connected with the region's numerous educational institutions. Statewide, there were 47,245 Chinese in 1990, 12,878 Koreans, 10,662 Japanese, and 13,101 Vietnamese. In 1996, the total Asian/Pacific Islander population was estimated at 198,000.

The Native American population (including Eskimos and Aleuts) totaled an estimated 2,000.

Cape Cod has settlements of Portuguese fisherman, as has New Bedford.

8LANGUAGES

Some general Algonkian loanwords and a few place-names—such as Massachusetts itself, Chicopee, Quebbin, and Naukeag—are the language echoes of the Massachuset, Pennacook, and Mahican Indians so historically important in the founding of Massachusetts Bay Colony and Old Colony, now Plymouth.

On the whole, Massachusetts English is classed as Northern, but early migration up the Connecticut River left that waterway a sometimes sharp, sometimes vague boundary, setting off special variations within the eastern half of the state. Two conspicuous but now receding features long held prestige because of the cultural eminence of Boston: the absence of /r/ after a vowel, as in *fear* and *port*, and the use of a vowel halfway between the short /a/ of *cat* and /ah/ in *half* and *past* as well as in *car* and *park*. Eastern Massachusetts speakers are likely to have /ah/ in *orange* and to pronounce *on* and *fog* with the same vowel as in *form*. In the east, a sycamore is a *buttonwood*, a tied and filled quilt is a *comforter*, a *creek* is a saltwater inlet, and pancakes may be called *fritters*.

Around Boston are heard the intrusive /r/ as in "the lawr of the land," the /oo/ vowel in *butcher*, *tonic* for soft drink, *submarine* for a large sandwich, and *milkshake* for a concoction lacking ice cream. West of the Connecticut River are heard the /aw/ sound in *orange*, /ah/ in *on* and *fog*, and the short /a/ of *cat* in *half* and *bass*; *buttonball* is a sycamore, and *comfortable* is a tied quilt.

In 1990, 84.8% of the population 5 years of age or older spoke only English at home. Principal other languages spoken at home were as follows:

Spanish	228,458	Polish	37,769
Portuguese	133,373	Greek	33,006
French	124,973	German	20,872
Italian	81,987	Arabic	13,128
Chinese	43,248	Indic	12,971

9RELIGIONS

While Protestant sects have contributed greatly to the state's history and development, more than half the state's population is Roman Catholic, a fact that has had a profound effect on Massachusetts politics and policies.

Both the Pilgrims, who landed on Plymouth Rock in 1620, and the Puritans, who formed the Massachusetts Bay Company in 1629, came to the land to escape harassment by the Church of England. These early communities were based on strict religious principles and forbade the practice of differing religions. Religious tolerance was included in the Charter of 1692, to protect the Baptists, Anglicans, and Catholics who had by then arrived in the colony.

The major influx of Roman Catholics came in the 1840s with the arrival of the Irish in Boston. By the 1850s, they had migrated to other towns and cities and formed the backbone of the state's industrial workforce. Later migration by Italian Catholics, German Catholics, and Eastern European Jews turned the state, by 1900, into a melting pot of religions and nationalities, although many of these minorities did not win substantial acceptance from the Protestant elite until the World War II era.

As of 1990, there were 2,961,259 Roman Catholics in Massachusetts, more than half the total population. The largest Protestant denominations were: United Church of Christ, 135,983 adherents; Episcopal, 122,190; American Baptist (USA), 66,156; United Methodist, 71,858; Unitarian, 35,787; Lutheran Church Missouri Synod, 7,053; and Congregationalist, 9,931. In

1990, most of the state's estimated Jewish population of 107,116 lived in Boston.

Although small, the Church of Christ, Scientist is significant to Massachusetts's history. Its first house of worship was founded in 1879 in Boston by Mary Baker Eddy, who, four years earlier, had published the Christian Science textbook, *Science and Health with Key to the Scriptures.* In Boston, the church continues to publish an influential newspaper, the *Christian Science Monitor.*

10 TRANSPORTATION

The first rail line in the US, a 3-mi (5-km) stretch from the Neponset River to the granite quarries in Quincy, was built in 1826. The first steam railroad in New England, connecting Boston and Lowell, was completed seven years later. By the late 1830s, tracks were laid from Boston to Worcester and to Providence, R.I., and during the next two decades, additional railroad lines opened up new cities for industrial expansion.

As of 1995, 12 railroads transported freight through Massachusetts: Consolidated Rail, the state's sole Class I railroad; Central Vermont, Providence & Worcester, and Springfield Terminal, the state's regional railroads; and 7 other local and switching and terminal railroads. Boston is the northern terminus of Amtrak's Northeast Corridor, linking New England with Washington, D.C. via New York City and Philadelphia. At the end of 1995, the state had 912 rail mi (1,468 km), almost half of it regional road, and about 45% Class I road. In 1995/96, Amtrak operated about 30 daily trains through the state, with a total ridership of 1,265,022.

Commuter service is coordinated by the Massachusetts Bay Transportation Authority (MBTA), formed in 1964 to consolidate bus, commuter rail, high-speed trolley, and subway services to the 79 cities and towns in the Greater Boston area. The Boston subway, which began operation in 1897, is the oldest subway system in the US. Boston also is one of the few cities in the US with an operating trolley system. About 40% of all Bostonians commute to work by public transportation, the 2d-highest percentage in the nation, following New York City.

In 1995, 30,751 mi (49,509 km) of paved roadways crisscrossed the state. The major highways, which extend from and through Boston like the spokes of a wheel, include I-95, which runs north–south; the Massachusetts Turnpike (I-90), which runs west to the New York State border; I-93, which leads north to New Hampshire; State Highway 3 to Cape Cod; and State Highway 24 to Fall River. The other major road in the state is I-91, which runs north–south through the Connecticut River Valley. The interstate highway network in Massachusetts totaled 565 mi (910 km) in 1995. Some $2.5 billion was spent by all units of government for highways in 1995. The same year, 4,501,969 motor vehicles were registered in the state, of which 3,507,025 were automobiles, 984,018 were trucks, and 10,926 were buses; there also were 74,243 motorcycles. The state issued 4,211,029 driver's licenses in 1995.

Because it is the major American city closest to Europe, Boston is an important shipping center for both domestic and foreign cargo. In 1995, 16,744,386 tons of cargo, of which 6,363,958 tons were imports, passed through the Port of Boston. All port activity is under the jurisdiction of the Massachusetts Port Authority, which also operates Logan International Airport and Hanscom Field in Bedford. Other important ports and their 1995 cargo totals were Fall River, 3,279,988 tons (720,330 imported), and Salem, 1,197,416 tons (801,732 imported).

There were 84 airports and 126 heliports in the state as of 31 December 1994. Logan International, near Boston, was the 16th-busiest airport in the nation in 1994, when it handled 158,746 departing aircraft, enplaning 10,667,886 passengers, and processed 128,746 tons of freight.

11 HISTORY

Some 15,000 years ago, when the last of the glaciers receded form the land we call Massachusetts, what remained was a rocky surface scoured of most of its topsoil. In time, however, forests grew to support a rich variety of wildlife. When the first Indians arrived from the south, game abounded and fish were plentiful in streams and along the coast. These first Indians were hunter-gatherers; their successors not only foraged for food but also cleared fields for planting corn (maize) and squash. Periodically they burned away the woodland underbrush, a technique of forest management that stimulated the vegetation that supported game. When English settlers arrived, they encountered five main Algonkian tribes: the Nauset, a fishing people on Cape Cod; the Wampanoag in the southeast; the Massachusetts in the northeast; the Nipmuc in the central hills; and the Pocumtuc in the west.

The earliest European explorers—including the Norsemen, who may have reached Cape Cod—made no apparent impact on these Algonkian groups, but in the wake of John and Sebastian Cabot's voyages (1497 and following), fishermen from England, France, Portugal, and Spain began fishing off the Massachusetts coast. By the mid-16th century, they were regularly going ashore to process and pack their catch. Within 50 years, fur trading with the Indians was established.

Permanent English settlement, which would ultimately destroy the Algonkian peoples, began in 1620 when a small band of Puritans left their haven at Leiden in the Netherlands to start a colony in the northern part of Virginia lands, near the Hudson River. Their ship, the *Mayflower,* was blown off course by an Atlantic storm, and they landed on Cape Cod before settling in an abandoned Wampanoag village they called Plymouth. Ten years later, a much larger Puritan group settled the Massachusetts Bay Colony, some miles to the north in Salem. Between 1630 and 1640, about 20,000 English people, chiefly Puritans, settled in Massachusetts with offshoots moving to Connecticut and Rhode Island.

The leaders of the Massachusetts settlement, most notably John Winthrop, a country gentleman with some legal training, intended to make their colony an exemplary Christian society. Though church and state were legally separate, they were mutually reinforcing agencies; thus, when Roger Williams and Anne Hutchinson were separately found guilty of heresy in the 1630s, they were banished by the state. All male church members had a voice in both church and state leadership, though both institutions were led by college-educated men. In order to provide for future leaders, Harvard College (now Harvard University) was founded in 1636.

After the beginning of the English revolution in 1640, migration to Massachusetts declined abruptly. Farming soon overtook fishing and fur trading in economic importance; after the trade in beaver skins was exhausted, the remaining Indian tribes were decimated in King Philip's War (1675–76). Shipbuilding and Atlantic commerce also brought prosperity to the Massachusetts Bay Colony, which was granted a new charter by King William and Queen Mary in 1692, merging Massachusetts and the colony of Plymouth. In that year, 19 people were executed for witchcraft on the gallows at Salem before Massachusetts authorities put a stop to the proceedings.

During the 18th century, settlement spread across the entire colony. Boston, the capital, had attained a population of 15,000 by 1730; it was an urbane community of brick as well as wooden buildings, with nearly a dozen church spires distinguishing its skyline by the 1750s. Religious revivals, also occurring elsewhere in America, swept Massachusetts in the 1730s and 1740s, rekindling piety and dividing the inhabitants into competing camps. Although the conflicts had ebbed by the 1750s, Massachusetts did not achieve unity again until the resistance to British imperial actions during the next two decades.

Up to this time, imperial government had rested lightly on Massachusetts, providing more advantages than drawbacks for commerce. The colony had actively supported British expeditions against French Canada, and supply contracts during the French and Indian War had enriched the economy. But the postwar recession after 1763 was accompanied by a new imperial policy that put pressure on Massachusetts as well as other colonies. None of the crown's three objectives—tight regulation of trade, the raising of revenue, and elimination of key areas of colonial political autonomy—were popular among the merchants, tradespeople, and farmers of Massachusetts. From 1765, when Bostonians violently protested the Stamp Act, Massachusetts was in the vanguard of the resistance.

At first, opposition was largely confined to Boston and surrounding towns, although the legislature, representing the entire colony, was active in opposing British measures. By December 1773, when East India Company tea was dumped into Boston harbor to prevent its taxation, most of the colony was committed to resistance. Newspaper polemics composed by Samuel Adams and his cousin John, among others, combined with the persuasive activities of the Boston Committee of Correspondence, helped convince a majority of Massachusetts residents that the slogan "no taxation without representation" stood for the preservation of their communities. When Parliament retaliated for the Tea Party by closing the port of Boston in 1774, rescinding the colony's 1692 charter, and remaking the government to put it under London's control, Massachusetts was ready to rebel. Military preparations began immediately on both sides. After almost a year of confrontation, battle began at Lexington and Concord on 19 April 1775. By this time, Massachusetts had the backing of the Continental Congress.

For Massachusetts, the battlefield experience of the Revolution was largely confined to 1775, the climaxes being the Battle of Bunker Hill and the British evacuation of Boston the following year. Thereafter, Massachusetts soldiers were active throughout the colonies, but the theater of action shifted southward. A new republican constitution, adopted in 1780, was the first state constitution to be submitted to the electorate for ratification.

Social and economic conditions in post-Revolutionary Massachusetts were much like those of the colonial era. Although the Shays Rebellion, an uprising of central and western farmers led by Daniel Shays in 1786–87, challenged the political hegemony of commercially oriented eastern leaders, the latter succeeded in maintaining their hold on the state. Massachusetts, which entered the Union on 6 February 1788, was the center of Federalism from 1790 until the mid-1820s. Although Jeffersonian Republicans and Jacksonian Democrats achieved substantial followings, Federalist policies, embodied in the Whigs in the 1830s and the Republicans from the late 1850s, were dominant. This political continuity was based on the importance of national commercial and industrial development to the state.

Even before 1800, it was clear that Massachusetts could not sustain growth in agriculture. Its soil had never been excellent, and the best lands were tired, having been worked for generations with little regard for conservation. Much of the state's population departed for New York, Ohio, and beyond during the first decades of the 19th century. Those who stayed maintained productive agriculture, concentrating more and more on fruits and dairying, but they also developed commerce and industry. At Waltham, Lowell, and Lawrence the first large-scale factories in the US were erected, and smaller textile mills throughout the state helped to make Massachusetts a leader in the cloth industry. At Springfield and Watertown, US armories led the way in metalworking, while shoes and leather goods brought prosperity to Lynn, and whale products and shipbuilding to New Bedford. By the 1850s, steam engines and clipper ships were both Bay State products.

The industrial development of Massachusetts was accompanied by a literary and intellectual flowering that was partly in reaction to the materialism and worldliness associated with urban and industrial growth. Concord, the home of Ralph Waldo Emerson, Henry David Thoreau, and a cluster of others, became the center of the transcendentalist movement in philosophy. Social reform also represented an assertion of moral values, whether in the field of education, health care, temperance, or penology. Abolitionism, the greatest of the moral reform efforts, found some of its chief leaders in Massachusetts, among them William Lloyd Garrison and Wendell Phillips, as well as a host of supporters.

In the years following the Civil War, Massachusetts emerged as an urban industrial state. Its population, fed by immigrants from England, Scotland, Germany, and especially Ireland, grew rapidly in the middle decades of the century. Later, between 1880 and 1920, another wave of immigrants came from French Canada, Italy, Russia, Poland, Scandinavia, Portugal, Greece, and Syria. Still later, between 1950 and 1970, black southerners and Puerto Ricans settled in the cities.

From the election of Lincoln in 1860 through the 1920s, Massachusetts was led by Protestant Yankee Republicans; most Democrats were Catholics. Class, ethnic, and religious tensions were endemic, occasionally erupting into open conflict. Three such episodes gained national attention. In 1912, immigrant textile workers in Lawrence were pitted against Yankee capitalists. A highly publicized strike of 1919 had the largely Irish-American police force rebelling against Yankees in city and state government, and brought Governor Calvin Coolidge—who suppressed the strike and refused to reinstate the striking policemen—to national prominence. In 1921, Nicola Sacco and Bartolomeo Vanzetti, Italian immigrant anarchists, were convicted for a payroll robbery and murder, though there was bitter controversy regarding the quality of the evidence against them. Before they were executed in 1927, their case and the issues it raised polarized political opinion throughout the US. Subsequently, electoral competition between Democrats and Republicans emerged as a less divisive outlet for class and ethnic tensions. Since 1959, the Democrats have enjoyed ascendance statewide, and Republicans have won only when their candidates stood close to the Democrats on the issues. Party loyalties as such have waned, however.

The Massachusetts economy, relatively stagnant between 1920 and 1950, revived in the second half of the 20th century through a combination of university talent, capital resources, a skilled work force, and political clout. As the old industries and the mill cities declined, new high-technology manufacturing developed in Boston's suburban perimeter, centering on start-up manufacturing firms along Route 128 outside Boston. Electronics, computers, and defense-oriented industries led the way, stimulating a general prosperity in which service activities such as banking, insurance, health care, and higher education were especially prominent. As a result, white-collar employment and middle-class suburbs flourished, though run-down mill towns and Yankee dairy farms and orchards still dotted the landscape.

In this respect, as in its politics, Massachusetts resembled many other areas of the Northeast. It was a multiracial state in which the general welfare was defined by shifting coalitions of ethnic groups and special interests. From a national perspective, Massachusetts voters appeared liberal; the Bay State was the only one to choose Democrat George McGovern over President Richard M. Nixon in 1972, and was a perennially secure base for Senator Edward M. Kennedy, a leading liberal Democrat, from the 1970s onward. Yet Boston was also the site of some of the most extreme anti-integration tension during the same era;

Massachusetts was simultaneously a center of efforts in favor of the Equal Rights Amendment and against abortion.

Massachusetts's defiance of political categories continued into the 1990s. In 1990, blaming the current governor, Democrat Michael Dukakis, for the economy's decline, Massachusetts voters elected a Republican, William Weld, as governor. Yet Weld in fact espoused a blend of liberal and conservative positions. A fiscal conservative who called for cutting taxes and reducing programs such as Medicaid and state employee pension plans, Weld took a liberal stance on social issues, supporting gay rights, abortion rights, and strict protection of the environment. In August 1997, Weld resigned as governor to pursue an appointment as ambassador to Mexico.

Beginning in 1989, the Massachusetts economy declined dramatically, losing 14% of its total jobs in three years. Like other parts of New England, Massachusetts was hit hard by the recession of the early 1990s, and the state's economic woes were aggravated by the collapse in the late 1980s of speculative real estate ventures. The saturation of the real estate market forced retrenchments not only of that industry but of construction as well. By 1992, a number of indications suggested that a recovery had begun to take hold, aided in part by the privatization of highway maintenance, prison health care, and some other state-run operations.

By the mid-1990s, the Massachusetts economy was in the midst of a vigorous upturn, credited largely to the strength of its leading local industries, including software and mutual funds, and the health of the US economy as a whole. In 1996 the state's unemployment level fell to 4%, the lowest it had been since 1989. Its 1995 per capita income of $28,021 was the third highest in the nation.

12STATE GOVERNMENT

The first state constitution, drawn up soon after the signing of the Declaration of Independence, was rejected by the electorate. A revised draft was not approved by the state voters until 15 June 1780, following two constitutional conventions. This constitution, as amended, governs Massachusetts and is, according to the state, the oldest written constitution in the world still in effect. The legislature of Massachusetts, known as the General Court, is composed of a 40-member senate and 160-member house of representatives, all of whom are elected every two years in even-numbered years. Members of the senate must have resided in their home district for at least five years; representatives, at least one year. The legislative salary was $46,410 in 1995.

The governor and lieutenant governor are elected jointly every four years. The governor appoints all state and local judges, as well as the heads of the 10 executive offices. Both the governor and lieutenant governor must have resided in the state for at least seven years. In 1996 the governor's salary was $75,000. Other elected officials include the attorney general, secretary of the commonwealth, treasurer and receiver-general, and auditor of the commonwealth. All serve four-year terms.

Massachusetts also has an eight-member executive council, elected every two years by district. The council has the power to review the governor's judicial appointments and pardons, and to authorize expenditures from the state treasury. The lieutenant governor also has a vote on the executive council except when the governor is absent, in which case the lieutenant governor presides over it as a nonvoting participant. Members of the council must have resided in the state for five years.

Any Massachusetts citizen may file a bill through a state legislator, or a bill may be filed directly by a legislator or by the governor. To win passage, a bill must gain a majority vote of both houses of the legislature. After a bill is passed, the governor has 10 days in which to sign it, return it for reconsideration (usually with amendments), veto it, or refuse to sign it ("pocket veto"). A veto may be overridden by a two-thirds majority in both houses.

Amendments to the constitution may be introduced by any house or senate member (legislative amendment) or by a petition signed by at least 25,000 qualified voters (initiative amendment) that is presented in a joint session of the General Court. If it is approved by two successive sessions of the legislature, the amendment is then submitted to the voters at the next general election.

To vote in a Massachusetts district, a person must be a US citizen, at least 18 years old, and a resident of that district; there is no time requirement for residency.

13POLITICAL PARTIES

The Federalist Party, represented nationally by John Adams, dominated Massachusetts in the late 18th and early 19th centuries. The state turned to the Whig Party in the second quarter of the 19th century. Predominantly Yankee in character, the Whigs supported business growth, promoted protective tariffs, and favored such enterprises as railroads and factories. The new Republican Party, to which most Massachusetts Whigs gravitated when their party split in the 1850s, was a prime mover of abolitionism and played an important role in the election of Abraham Lincoln as president in 1860. Republicans held most of the major state elective offices, as well as most US congressional seats, until the early 1900s.

The Democratic Party's rise starting in the 1870s was tied directly to massive Irish immigration. Other immigrant groups also gravitated toward the Democrats, and in 1876, the state's first Democratic congressman was elected. In 1928, the state voted for Democratic presidential candidate Alfred E. Smith, a Roman Catholic, the first time the Democrats won a majority in a Massachusetts presidential election. Democrats have subsequently, for the most part, dominated state politics. In 1960, John F. Kennedy, who had been a popular US senator from Massachusetts, became the first Roman Catholic president in US history. Since then the state has voted for all Democratic presidential candidates except Republican Ronald Reagan in 1980 and 1984; in 1972, it was the only state carried by Democrat George McGovern. Massachusetts chose its native son, Democratic Governor Michael Dukakis, for president in 1988 and voted again for a Democrat in the next two elections, giving Bill Clinton 61% of the vote, Republican Bob Dole 28%, and Independent Ross Perot almost 9%.

As of 1994, there were 1,346,097 registered Democrats, or 40% of the total number of registered voters; 447,181 Republicans, or 13%; and 1,558,640 independents, or 47%. From 1990–97, the governorship was held by a Republican, William Weld. Weld resigned in 1997 to pursue an appointment as ambassador to Mexico. The US Senate seats for Massachusetts were held by Democrats, Edward Kennedy and John Kerry. In the 1996 elections, Kerry retained his Senate seat in the face of a strong challenge by then-Governor Weld. The 10-member US House delegation following the 1996 elections consisted entirely of Democrats. The Massachusetts state senate had 33 Democrats and seven Republicans, while the state house of representatives had 129 Democrats and 29 Republicans. As of 1994, there were 30 black elected officials and one Hispanic holding public office. In 1995, there were 48 women serving in the state legislature.

14LOCAL GOVERNMENT

As of 1992, Massachusetts had 13 counties, 39 cities, and 312 towns, 84 school districts, and 396 special districts.

In 12 of the 13 counties, executive authority was vested in three county commissioners elected to four-year terms. The exception was Suffolk County—where executive powers are exercised by the mayor and city council of Boston, the board of aldermen in Chelsea, the city council of Revere, and the board of selectmen of Winthrop. Other county officials include the register of probate and family court, sheriff, clerk of courts, county treasurer, and register of deeds.

All Massachusetts cities are governed by mayors and city councils. Towns are governed by selectmen, who are usually elected to either one- or two-year terms. Town meetings—a carryover from the colonial period, when every taxpayer was given an equal voice in town government—still take place regularly. By state law, to be designated a city, a place must have at least 12,000 residents. Towns with more than 6,000 inhabitants may hold representative town meetings limited to elected officials.

[15]STATE SERVICES

State services are provided through the 12 executive offices and major departments that constitute the governor's cabinet. The heads of these departments are appointed by the governor.

Educational services are administered by the Executive Office of Education. Included under its jurisdiction are the State Board of Education and Board of Regents of Higher Education, the Massachusetts community college and state college systems, the University of Massachusetts, the Council of the Arts and Humanities, and the State Library.

The Executive Office of Transportation and Construction supervises the Department of Public Works and has responsibility for the planning and development of transportation systems within the state, including the Massachusetts Port Authority, the Massachusetts Turnpike Authority, the Massachusetts Bay Transportation Authority, and the Massachusetts Aeronautics Commission.

All public health, mental health, youth, and veterans' programs are administered by the Executive Office of Human Services. Also under its jurisdiction are the Department of Public Welfare and the Department of Correction. The Executive Office of Public Safety includes the Division of Civil Defense, Registry of Motor Vehicles, and Highway Safety Bureau.

The Executive Office of Consumer Affairs and Business Regulation regulates state standards and registers professional workers. The Department of Public Utilities and Alcoholic Beverages Control Commission are also part of this office, as are the divisions regulating banks and insurance. Housing services

are provided through the Executive Office of Communities and Development. This office administers the Massachusetts Home Mortgage Finance Agency, the Housing Finance Agency, and the Bureaus of Housing Development and of Housing Management and Tenant Services.

The Executive Office of Environmental Affairs protects the state's marine and wildlife, and monitors the quality of its air, water, and food.

Labor and industrial relations are monitored through the Executive Office of Labor, whose Department of Labor and Industries administers the minimum wage law, occupational safety laws, and child labor laws, among others. The Executive Office of Economic Affairs helps to improve the economic climate in the state and promotes exports and tourism. The Department of Elder Affairs plans and implements programs for the elderly, including nutrition, home care, and education programs.

[16]JUDICIAL SYSTEM

All statewide judicial offices are filled by the governor, with the advice and consent of the executive council.

The supreme judicial court, composed of a chief justice and six other justices, is the highest court in the state. It has appellate jurisdiction in matters of law and also advises the governor and legislature on legal questions. The superior courts, actually the highest level of trial court, have a chief justice and 55 other justices; these courts hear law, equity, civil, and criminal cases, and make the final determination in matters of fact. The appeals court, consisting of a chief justice and nine other justices, hears appeals of decisions by district and municipal courts. There are 90 district and municipal courts and 320 trial court judges. Other court systems in the state include the land court, probate and family court, housing court (with divisions in Boston and Hampden counties), and juvenile court (with divisions in Boston, Springfield, Worcester, and Bristol counties). In 1996, there were 38,912 active attorneys.

Massachusetts's total crime rate per 100,000 inhabitants was 4,341.6. Specific figures for 1996 were murder and non-negligent manslaughter, 3.6 per 100,000 inhabitants; forcible rape, 29; robbery, 150.4; aggravated assault, 504.2; burglary, 817.7; larceny-theft, 2,232.2; and motor vehicle theft, 604.5. In 1995, a total of 263,710 crimes were reported in the state, of which

Massachusetts Presidential Vote by Political Party, 1948–96

YEAR	ELECTORAL VOTE	MASSACHUSETTS WINNER	DEMOCRAT	REPUBLICAN	SOCIALIST LABOR	PROGRESSIVE
1948	16	*Truman (D)	1,151,788	909,370	5,535	38,157
1952	16	*Eisenhower (R)	1,083,525	1,292,325	1,957	4,636
1956	16	*Eisenhower (R)	948,190	1,393,197	5,573	—
1960	16	*Kennedy (D)	1,487,174	976,750	3,892	—
1964	14	*Johnson (D)	1,786,422	549,727	4,755	—
						AMERICAN IND.
1968	14	Humphrey (D)	1,469,218	766,844	6,180	87,088
					SOC. WORKERS	AMERICAN
1972	14	McGovern (D)	1,332,540	1,112,078	10,600	2,877
1976	14	*Carter (D)	1,429,475	1,030,276	8,138	7,555
					LIBERTARIAN	
1980	14	*Reagan (R)	1,048,562	1,054,213	21,311	—
1984	13	*Reagan	1,239,600	1,310,936	—	—
						NEW ALLIANCE
1988	13	Dukakis (D)	1,401,415	1,194,635	24,251	9,561
						IND. (PEROT)
1992	12	*Clinton (D)	1,318,639	805,039	9,021	630,731
1996	12	*Clinton (D)	1,571,763	718,107	20,426	227,217

*Won US presidential election.

41,739 were violent crimes. Massachusetts does not have a death penalty. Under Massachusetts gun control laws, all guns must be registered, and there is a mandatory one-year jail sentence for possession without a permit.

As of 1995 there were 10,755 prisoners in state and federal correctional institutions, a rate of 177 prisoners per 100,000 inhabitants.

[17] ARMED FORCES

The military installations located in Massachusetts in 1996 had 3,037 active-duty military personnel. The largest installation in the state is the Laurence G. Hanscom Air Force Base in Bedford, housing 1,700 active duty personnel. Other installations include the Army reserve and development center at Natick, the Navy's South Weymouth Naval Air Station, and Westover Air Force Base. The state ranked 6th among the 50 states in the value of defense contracts awarded in FY1996, with a total of about $4.6 billion.

Approximately 515,000 military veterans were living in the state in 1996. Veterans of World War I numbered less than 500; World War II, 181,000; the Korean conflict, 101,000; the Vietnam era, 165,000; and the Persian Gulf War, 27,000. About $1.1 billion was paid in veterans' benefits in 1995/96.

The Massachusetts National Guard and Reserve had 36,104 members in 1996; 18,816 in the army, 5,036 in the navy and marine corps, and 6,252 in the air force.

In 1993, the Massachusetts State Police employed 1,975 full-time sworn officers, or 3 per 10,000 residents.

[18] MIGRATION

Massachusetts was founded by the migration of English religious groups to its shores, and for over a century their descendants dominated all activity in the state. The first great wave of non-English to enter Massachusetts were the Irish, who migrated in vast numbers during the 1840s and 1850s. By 1860, one-third of Boston's population was Irish, while nearly one-fourth of Middlesex and Norfolk counties and one-fifth of the inhabitants of Berkshire, Bristol, Essex, and Hampden counties were Irish-born. Other ethnic groups—such as the Scottish, Welsh, Germans, and Poles—were also entering the state at this time, but their numbers were small by comparison. During the late 1880s and 1890s, another wave of immigrants—from Portugal, Spain, Italy, Russia, and Greece—arrived. Irish and Italians continued to enter the state during the 20th century.

A slow but steady migration from Massachusetts farm communities began during the mid–1700s and continued well into the 1800s. The first wave of farmers resettled in northern Connecticut, Vermont, New Hampshire, and Maine. Later farmers moved to New York's Mohawk Valley, Ohio, and points farther west. Out migration has continued to recent times: from 1970 to 1990, Massachusetts lost nearly 400,000 residents in net migration to other states, but experienced an overall net increase from migration of 59,000 due to migration from abroad. Between 1990 and 1996, the state had a net loss of 213,844 in domestic migration and a net gain of 104,576 in international migration. In 1996, Massachusetts's foreign-born population numbered 591,000, or nearly 10% of the state's total population. In the same year, 23,085 foreign immigrants arrived in Massachusetts, the 6th highest total of any state for that year. As of 1994, there were an estimated 42–106 undocumented immigrants living in the state. As of 1990, 68.7% of all state residents had been born in Massachusetts. In 1990, 58% of the residents lived in the same house as in 1985. About 20% of those who lived in a different house in 1985 did so in another state.

The only significant migration from other areas of the US to Massachusetts has been the influx of southern blacks since World War II. According to census estimates, Massachusetts gained 84,000 blacks between 1940 and 1975; in 1990, it had a black population of about 300,000 persons, mostly in the Boston area.

[19] INTERGOVERNMENTAL COOPERATION

Massachusetts participates in numerous regional agreements, including the New England Corrections Compact, New England Police Compact, New England Higher Education Compact, New England Radiological Health Protection Compact, and New England Interstate Water Pollution Control Compact. The state is also a party to the Atlantic States Marine Fisheries Compact, the Northeastern Forest Fire Protection Compact, and the Connecticut River Valley Flood Control Compact.

Border agreements include the Connecticut-Massachusetts Boundary Compact (ratified by Massachusetts in 1908), the Massachusetts-New York Compact of 1853, and the Massachusetts-Rhode Island Compact of 1859. During 1995/96, the state received over $6.8 billion in federal aid.

[20] ECONOMY

From its beginnings as a farming and seafaring colony, Massachusetts became one of the most industrialized states in the country in the late 19th century and, more recently, a leader in the manufacture of high-technology products.

During the colonial and early national periods, the towns of Salem, Gloucester, Marblehead, and Boston, among others, gave the state strong fishing and shipbuilding industries. Boston was also an important commercial port and a leading center of foreign commerce. Agriculture was important, but productivity of the rocky soil was limited, and by the mid-1800s, farming could not sustain the expanding population. The opening of the Erie Canal, and subsequent competition with cheaper produce grown in the West, hastened agriculture's decline in the Bay State.

Massachusetts's rise as a center of manufacturing began in the early 1800s, when cottage industries developed in small farming communities. Large factories were then built in towns with water power. The country's first "company town," Lowell, was built in the early 1820s to accommodate the state's growing textile industry. Throughout the rest of the 19th century, the state supplied the nation with most of its shoes and woven goods.

Underbid by cheap labor in the south and in other countries, the shoe and textile industries died a slow and painful death. Manufacturing remained central to Massachusetts's economy, however. Fueled in part by a dramatic increase in the Pentagon's budget during the Reagan administration which focused on high-technology weaponry, as well as by significant advances in information technology, high-tech companies sprung up around the periphery of Boston in the 1970s and early 1980s. Wholesale and retail trade, transportation and public utilities also prospered. In the late 1980s, the boom ended. The minicomputer industry failed to innovate at the same pace as its competitors elsewhere at the same time that the market became increasingly crowded, and defense contractors suffered from cuts in military spending. Between 1988 and 1991, jobs in both high-tech and non–high tech manufacturing declined by 17%. The early 1980s had also seen the rise of speculative real estate ventures which collapsed at the end of the decade when the market became saturated. Employment in construction dropped 44% between 1988 and 1991, and real estate jobs declined 23.8%. Wholesale and retail trade lost 100,000 jobs. Hurt by unsound loans, banks were forced to retrench. Unemployment rose to 9% in 1991. The economy has begun to make a recovery, as evidenced by several banks' announcement of new lending programs as well as a reduction in the unemployment rate to 4.0% in 1997. Massachusetts's gross state product in 1994 was $186,199 million, to which private goods-producing industries contributed $37,516 million; private services-producing industries, $131,067 million; and government, $17,616 million.

In 1995, the state per capita personal income was $28,021, which ranked 3d nationally.

In 1996, there were 17,744 filings for bankruptcy, up 19% from the previous year.

21INCOME

In 1996, Massachusetts ranked 3d among the 50 states in per capita personal income, with $33,189. During the same year, total disposable personal income was $150.6 billion, an increase from $143.6 billion in 1995. The median household income in 1995 was $38,574.

As of 1995, 11% of all Bay Staters had incomes below the federal poverty line. As of 1992, some 363,000 (16%) households in the Bay State had disposable incomes exceeding $75,000, including about 66,000 with $125,000 or more in disposable income.

22LABOR

In 1996, the state's labor force numbered 3,189,100 persons, of whom 3,051,800 were employed and 137,300 were unemployed. The unemployment rate for all workers in 1996 was 4.3%.

In 1996, the state Department of Labor and Workforce Development tabulated actual nonfarm employment as follows:

	EMPLOYMENT IN THOUSANDS
Total nonfarm	3,036.4
Private	2,636.1
Mining	1.2
Construction	93.9
Manufacturing	444.1
Nondurable goods	167.6
Durable goods	276.4
Transportation and public utilities	129.2
Wholesale trade	166.9
Retail trade	529.6
Finance, insurance, and real estate	208.6
Services	1,062.6
Government	400.2

As of 1996, production workers in manufacturing on the average earned $13.04 per hour, and average hours worked totaled 41.8 per week.

Some of the earliest unionization efforts took place in Massachusetts in the early 1880s, particularly in the shipbuilding and construction trades. However, the most important trade unions to evolve were those in the state's textile and shoe industries. The workers had numerous grievances: shoebinders' salaries of $1.60–$2.40 a week during the 1840s, workdays of 14 to 17 hours, wages paid in scrip that could be cashed only at company stores (which charged exorbitantly high prices), and children working at dangerous machinery. In 1867, a seven-week-long shoemakers' strike at Lynn, the center of the shoe business, was at that time the longest strike in US history.

After the turn of the century, the state suffered a severe decline in manufacturing, and employers sought to cut wages to make up for lost profits. This resulted in a number of strikes by both the United Textile Workers and the Boot and Shoe Workers Union. The largest strike of the era was at Lawrence in 1912, when textile workers (led by a radical labor group, the Industrial Workers of the World) closed the mills, and the mayor called in troops in an attempt to reopen them. Although the textile and shoe businesses are no longer major employers in the state, the United Shoe Workers of America, the Brotherhood of Shoe and Allied Craftsmen, the United Textile Workers, and the Leather Workers International Union of America have their headquarters in Massachusetts. As of 1995, about 427,900 persons, or nearly 16.2% of all workers, were unionized.

Massachusetts was one of the first states to enact child labor laws. In 1842, it established the 10-hour day for children under 12; in 1867, it forbade employment for children under 10. The nation's first Uniform Child Labor Law, establishing an 8-hour day for children aged 14 to 16, was enacted by Massachusetts in 1913. Massachusetts was also the first state to enact minimum wage guidelines (1912).

23AGRICULTURE

As of 1996, there were 6,200 farms in Massachusetts, covering 570,000 acres (231,000 hectares). Farming was mostly limited to the western Massachusetts counties of Hampshire, Franklin, and Berkshire, and southern Bristol County. Total agricultural income for 1995 was estimated at $430,377,000 (45th of the 50 states), of which crops provided 76%. Although the state is not a major farming area, it is the largest producer of cranberries in the US; production for 1996 was 181 million lb, about 39% of the US total. Output totals for other crops in 1996 were as follows: corn for silage, 527,000 tons; hay, 190,000 tons; and tobacco, 1,225,000 lb. While of local economic importance, these figures are tiny fractions of US totals.

24ANIMAL HUSBANDRY

Massachusetts is not a major producer of livestock. In 1997, the state had 62,000 cattle and calves worth around $47 million, and had an estimated 64,000 hogs and pigs worth $5.9 million in 1996. During 1995, the state produced 459,000 lb of sheep and lamb, which grossed $724,000 in income, and around 2 million lb of turkeys worth $2.6 million. Also during 1995, poultry farmers sold 3 million lb of chickens for $87,000, and the state produced an estimated 133 million eggs, worth around $11 million. An estimated 28,000 milk cows produced 448 million lb of milk in 1995.

25FISHING

Massachusetts's fish catch in 1995 was the 8th largest in the US, but the fishing industry is not as important to the state economy as it once was.

The early settlers earned much of their income from the sea. The first shipyard in Massachusetts opened at Salem Neck in 1637, and during the years before independence the towns of Salem, Newburyport, Plymouth, and Boston were among the colonies' leading ports. By 1807, Massachusetts's fishing fleet made up 88% of the US total; for much of the 19th century, Nantucket and, later, New Bedford were the leading US whaling centers. But with the decline of the whaling industry came a sharp drop in the importance of fishing to the livelihood of the state. By 1978, the fishing industry ranked 13th in importance of the 15 industries monitored by the state. However, the fishing ports of New Bedford and Gloucester were still among the busiest in the US in 1995, with the 3d and 29th most valuable catches, respectively. That same year, there were 311 fish processing and wholesale plants with an annual average of 3,627 employees in the state.

The value of the commercial catch in 1995—$224,361,000—was the highest among the New England states and the 3d highest in the US at 204,255,000 lb. In 1995, the lobster catch totaled 15.8 million lb, valued at $62.7 million, and cod landings amounted to 20.9 million lb, valued at $19.9 million. About 7.7 million lb of sea scallops were landed in 1995.

The state's long shoreline and many rivers make sport fishing a popular pastime for both deepsea and freshwater fishermen. The fishing season runs from mid-April through late October, with the season extended through February for bass, pickerel, panfish, and trout. In 1995/96, there were 227,691 fishing license holders.

26 FORESTRY

Forestry is a minor industry in the state. Forested lands cover about 3,203,000 acres (1,296,000 hectares), 85% of which are private lands. Wooded areas lost to urbanization in recent years have been offset by the conversion of inactive agricultural areas into forests. Red oak and white ash are found in the west; specialty products include maple syrup and Christmas trees. The wood and paper products industries require more pulp than the state currently produces.

Massachusetts has the 6th-largest state park system in the nation, with 38 state parks and 74 state forests totaling some 273,000 acres (110,000 hectares). There are no national forests in Massachusetts.

27 MINING

The value of nonfuel mineral production in Massachusetts in 1995 was estimated at $213 million. This value represents an increase of 20% from 1994, which followed a 10.8% increase from 1993 to 1994. Crushed stone and construction sand and gravel are the state's two leading mineral commodities. In 1995, there were 13.5 million metric tons of crushed stone and 10.5 million metric tons of sand and gravel produced, worth $128 million and $52 million, respectively. Other mineral commodities produced include common clay, lime and peat; industrial sand; and dimension stone. Nationally, the state ranked 39th in the production of nonfuel minerals, and 5th in dimension stone. Industrial minerals processed or manufactured in the state include abrasives, graphite, gypsum, perlite, and vermiculite.

28 ENERGY AND POWER

Massachusetts depends on oil for about one-third of its electric generation and almost one-half of its home heating. Energy costs in the state are among the highest in the US. Nevertheless, this is an improvement from the early 1980s, when as much as 81% of the state's electric power output was generated from oil.

In 1995, about 34.8 billion kWh of electric power was generated in state, and installed capacity was over 9.5 million kW. Almost all generating capacity in the state is privately owned. Of the 46.6 billion kWh sold in 1995, 34% was for residential use, 42% commercial, 22% industrial, and 2% for other purposes. Boston Edison supplies electricity to the city of Boston; the rest of the state is served by 13 other companies, although a few municipalities do generate their own power. Power companies are regulated by the Department of Public Utilities, which establishes rates and monitors complaints from customers.

Massachusetts has no proved oil or coal reserves. After a lengthy court battle, oil exploration off the coast of Cape Cod began in 1979. Environmentalists and fishermen had sought to prevent development of an oil industry in the region, which is one of the richest fishing grounds in the country.

The state consumes but does not produce natural gas. In 1995 about 360.4 billion cu ft of natural gas were delivered. Almost 35% of the gas sold was for residential use, 40% for industries and electricity generation, and 25% for commercial use.

There is one nuclear power plant in Plymouth, with an average operating capacity of 665 Mw. Two pumped-storage hydro-electric plants, one at Bear Swamp and the other at Northfield Mountain, have a combined capacity of 1,446 Mw. Altogether there were 40 hydroelectric generators, which produced 2.5 million Mw in 1994.

The state encourages energy conservation and the development of alternative energy systems by granting tax credits to qualifying industries. Private researchers and the state have established demonstration projects for solar energy systems and other alternatives to fossil fuels.

29 INDUSTRY

Massachusetts was the nation's first major industrial state, and during the later part of the 19th century, it was the US leader in shoemaking and textile production. By 1860, the state was a major producer of machinery and milled nearly one-fourth of the country's paper.

Massachusetts remains an important manufacturing center, placing 13th among the 50 states in the value of manufacturers' shipments in 1982. Nearly all the major manufacturing sectors had plants in Massachusetts's eastern counties. Significant concentrations of industrial machinery employment are in Attleboro, Wilmington, Worcester, and the Springfield area. Much of the manufacturing industry is located along Route 128, a superhighway that circles Boston from Gloucester in the north to Quincy in the south and is unique in its concentration of high-technology enterprises. Although Massachusetts ranked 15th among the states in manufacturing employment in 1991 (at 484,500), nearly 189,000 manufacturing jobs had been lost from 1980 to 1991.

Massachusetts's future as a manufacturing center depends on its continued preeminence in the production of computers, optical equipment, and other sophisticated instruments. In 1995, the value of shipments by manufacturers was $75.249 billion, of which electronic and other electronic equipment contributed $11.023 billion; instruments and related products, $10.104 billion; industrial machinery and equipment, $8.987 billion; printing and publishing, $6,811 billion; chemicals and allied products, $6,291 billion; food and food products, $5.073 billion; fabricated metals, $4.809 billion. As of 1997, the state was the headquarters for 16 Fortune 500 companies. In 1995, there were 2,484 US patents issued to residents of Massachusetts.

30 COMMERCE

Massachusetts's machinery and electrical goods industries are important components of the state's wholesale trade, along with motor vehicle and automotive equipment, and paper and paper products. Overall, in 1992, 10,950 establishments produced about $86.7 billion in sales. Durable goods accounts for 50.7% of the sales. More than one-fourth of the wholesale establishments were located in Middlesex County.

The state ranked 13th in retail sales in 1992, at $47.7 billion, in 38,491 stores of all types. Food stores accounted for 19.8% of sales; automotive dealers, 17.5%; eating and drinking places, 11.4%; and general merchandise stores, 10.3%.

In 1994, the Boston customs district handled about $7.1 billion in exports. Foreign exports of the state's own products totaled $14.5 billion in 1996 (11th in the US).

31 CONSUMER PROTECTION

The cabinet-level Executive Office of Consumer Affairs and Business Regulation serves as an information and referral center for consumer complaints and oversees the activities of many regulatory agencies. The Office of the Attorney General also has a Consumer Protection Division that handles consumer complaints. The Massachusetts Consumer Council advises the governor and legislature; there are many local consumer councils.

32 BANKING

By the mid-1800s, Boston had developed into a major banking center whose capital financed the state's burgeoning industries. Today banking remains an important sector of the state's economy; in 1992, 1,966 insured financial institutions employed 58,600 workers, with an annual payroll of nearly $1.8 billion. As of 31 December 1995, there were 31 insured state-chartered commercial banks, known as trust companies in Massachusetts. Assets of these state-chartered trust companies totaled $39.7 billion and deposits $27.1 billion at the end of 1995. As of 31

December 1995, Massachusetts had 186 state-chartered savings banks and co-operative banks with assets of $45.4 billion and deposits of $38.3 billion.

State chartered savings banks, trust companies, co-operative banks, credit unions, and over 2,000 other financial service providers, including mortgage lenders and brokers, debt collection agencies, foreign transmittal agencies, check cashers, and credit grantors, are examined by the state Division of Banks and Loan Agencies, within the Office of Consumer Affairs and Business Regulation. The division administers the state's banking laws and oversees bank and financial institution practices and policies.

[33]INSURANCE

Insurance is an important business in Massachusetts, and some of the largest life and property/casualty insurance companies in the nation have their headquarters in Boston.

The state's 16 life insurance companies had in force 5,275,000 life policies worth $341.5 billion in 1995. The average amount of life insurance per family was $140,800 and payments to 74,000 beneficiaries amounted to $5,715 million. New England Mutual Life Insurance Co. of Boston was the first mutual company to be chartered in the US and remains one of the largest firms in the business. John Hancock Mutual Life, also of Boston, is one of the largest life insurance companies in the US.

There are 59 mutual property/casualty companies in Massachusetts. Direct premiums written by these companies at the end of 1995 totaled $7.6 billion, of which automobile liability premiums accounted for 34%, automobile physical damage premiums 13%, and homeowners' premiums 10%. In 1971, Massachusetts became the first state in the US to implement a no-fault automobile insurance law.

All aspects of the insurance business in Massachusetts, including the licensing of agents and brokers and the examination of all insurance companies doing business in the state, are controlled by the Division of Insurance, under the Executive Office of Consumer Affairs and Business Regulation.

[34]SECURITIES

The Boston Stock Exchange, founded in 1846, is the only stock exchange in Massachusetts. In March 1997, there were 2,040 securities brokers and dealers registered to conduct transactions in Massachusetts via 87,541 registered agents. Mutual funds originated in Boston during the 1920s.

The Securities Division of the Office of the Secretary of the Commonwealth is responsible for licensing and monitoring all brokerage firms in the state.

[35]PUBLIC FINANCE

The Massachusetts budget is prepared by the Executive Office of Administration and Finance and is presented by the governor to the legislature for revision and approval. The fiscal year runs from 1 July to 30 June.

The following is a summary of estimated expenses and revenues for the 1994/95 (in thousands of dollars):

REVENUES

From federal government	$ 5,758,080
From own sources	18,342,464
Taxes:	
Property	2,564,429
Sales and receipts)	3,170,447
Income	5,974,201
TOTAL	$11,601,135

CHARGES AND MISCELLANEOUS:

Current charges	$ 1,621,748
Interest earnings	2,490,022
Special assessments	65,130
Other	2,564,429
TOTAL	6,741,329
TOTAL REVENUES	$ 24,100,544

EXPENDITURES

Education	$ 4,101,910
Health and social concerns	8,186,364
Financial administration	1,078,732
Transportation (highways	1,703,039
Utilities	96,690
Public safety	907,199
Natural resources	281,478
Other	7,926,990
TOTAL EXPENDITURES	$ 24,282,382

The total debt of state and local governments as of 1995 was more than $27 billion, or $4,566 per capita.

[36]TAXATION

Massachusetts's tax burden on a per capita basis as of 1996 was $2,044 (6th among the states). Total tax revenues received in fiscal year 1996 were the 10th highest in the country at $12.45 billion. As of 1997, the state levied a 12% tax on interest, dividends, and short-term capital gains, a 5% tax rate on capital gains from assets held between one and two years, a 4% rate on capital gains from assets held longer than two years, and a flat 5.95% rate on all other taxable income. The corporate income tax rate was 9.5%. For the 1997 tax year, commercial banks and other banking and trust companies paid an 11.32% tax on net income; public utilities, 6.5%.

Since 1975 the gross receipts tax on sales has been 5%, but such necessities as food, clothing, and home heating fuel are exempt. In 1997, the estate tax changed from a separate system of estate taxation, in which estates were taxed from 5% to 16%, to a "sponge tax" system, which is currently used by the majority of states; a "sponge tax" is a term used to describe an estate tax system whereby the amount of estate tax due is a portion of, or all of, the credit for state death taxes allowed by the federal government. Effective for dates of death on or after 1 January 1997, the Massachusetts estate tax is imposed only on estates worth $600,000 or more. The Massachusetts estate tax is equal to the amount of the maximum federal credit for state death taxes.

Other levies include a room occupancy tax of 5.7%, with a local option of up to 4%, a cigarette tax of 76 cents per pack (increased from 51 cents, effective 1 October 1996), a gasoline tax of 21 cents per gallon, a deeds tax of $2.28 per $500 of the sales price (less mortgage assumed) of real estate, and a motor vehicle excise tax of $25 for every $1,000 of valuation.

In November 1980, Bay Staters voted to lower their local property taxes by approving the so-called Proposition 2½, which limited the maximum tax levy to 2.5% of the value of all taxable property, both real and personal. The effect was to lower property taxes by $400 million for 1982/83, when total levies were actually lower than those for 1977/78. As a result of the reduced revenues, many municipalities reduced the number of public employees, including police, firemen, and teachers.

Massachusetts's share of federal funding in fiscal year 1995 was $35.82 billion; this figure includes Department of Defense funding, salaries and wages, grant awards, direct payments for individuals, procurement contract awards, and other federal assistance such as direct loans and guaranteed loans and insurance. Bay Staters paid federal income taxes totaling $18.69 billion in tax year 1995, or $3,075 per capita.

37ECONOMIC POLICY

The Department of Economic Development is responsible for setting economic policy, promoting Massachusetts as a place to do business, increasing the job base, and generating economic activity in the Commonwealth.

The following agencies are within the Department of Economic Development: Division of Energy Resources, Massachusetts Office of Business Development, Massachusetts Office of International Trade and Investment, Massachusetts Office of Travel and Tourism, Office of Film and Video Development, and State Office of Minority and Women Business Assistance. The department also works closely with the Department of Labor and Workforce Development and the Department of Housing and Community Development.

Among the many tax incentives offered to businesses are a 3% investment tax credit; research and development tax credit; property and sales tax exemptions for some machinery, parts, and inventory; credits against the state excise tax; real-estate tax reductions for building facilities in certain urban areas; and a 10% abandoned building tax deduction.

The Massachusetts Economic Development Incentive Program (EDIP), launched in 1993, is a series of initiatives geared to stimulate job creation, attract new businesses, and help firms expand. There are 34 Economic Target Areas (ETAs) throughout the state. Cities and towns, in partnership with the Commonwealth and private enterprises, are also developing economic programs to attract new business.

38HEALTH

Massachusetts recorded 13.4 live births per 1,000 population in 1995. Infant mortality was 5.5 per 1,000 live births in 1995, far below the US rate. In 1992, there were 34,527 abortions, for a rate of 396 per 1,000 live births, far above the US average.

The age-adjusted death rate was 446 per 100,000 population in 1996, below the US average. The death rate from cancer in 1995 was above the US average. The major causes of death and their rates per 100,000 population were heart diseases, 275.8; cancer, 231.9; cerebrovascular diseases, 57.0; accidents and adverse effects, 20.1; and suicide, 8.1. In 1990, Massachusetts ranked 3d (after New Jersey and Rhode Island) in the proportion of breast cancer deaths per 100,000 women, at 31.2. The AIDS rate of 23.11 per 100,000 population was 19% less than the national average.

Programs for treatment and rehabilitation of alcoholics are administered by the Division of Alcoholism of the Department of Health, under the Executive Office of Human Services. The Division of Communicable Disease Control operates venereal disease clinics throughout the state and provides educational material to schools and other groups. The Division of Drug Rehabilitation administers drug treatment from a statewide network of hospital agencies and self-help groups. The state also runs a lead-poisoning prevention program. Smoking rates among women (21%) and men (22.5%) were similar in 1995.

Massachusetts had 96 hospitals, with 18,056 beds and 743,906 admissions in 1995. In addition, the state had 16 nursing homes with 804 beds. Among the best-known institutions are Massachusetts General Hospital, a leading research and treatment center, and the Massachusetts Eye and Ear Infirmary, a Boston clinic. In 1994 there were 22,397 non-federal active physicians; in 1995, 4,532 professionally active dentists. Four prominent medical schools are located in the state: Harvard Medical School, Tufts University School of Medicine, Boston University School of Medicine, and the University of Massachusetts School of Medicine. The average expense per stay was $7,018 in a Massachusetts community hospital in 1994, and the average cost per day was $1,131. There were 710,000 Medicaid patients, who received $3.1 billion in benefits during fiscal 1994. Medicare enrollees in fiscal 1994 totaled 923,000 and collected an estimated $4.9 billion.

All health-care facilities are registered by the Department of Public Health. The Division of Health Care Quality inspects and licenses hospitals, clinics, school infirmaries, and blood banks every two years. Licensing of nursing homes is also under its control.

39SOCIAL WELFARE

Some two-thirds of the state's budget for human services went to the Medicaid and Aid to Families with Dependent Children (AFDC) programs, although federal payments reimbursed the state for more than half the cost of these programs. AFDC expenditures increased by 21% from 1970 to 1981, but then fell by 25% in 1981–83 as federal cuts in the program were felt. In 1996, 242,500 persons received AFDC, and the monthly payment was $668 per family.

In 1996, the food stamp program had an average monthly participation of 373,599. In that year, students who took part in the school lunch program cost the federal government $83.1 million.

With the enactment of the Personal Responsibility and Work Opportunity Reconciliation Act of 1996, the US government changed the form and regulations for many of its social welfare programs; most significantly, it replaced Aid to Families with Dependent Children (AFDC), an open-ended entitlement program, with Temporary Assistance for Needy Families (TANF), a limited system of assistance funded largely through federal block grants. The reform act also impacted the food stamp program, the Supplemental Security Income program, and the child nutrition program. The law took effect on 1 July 1997 and provided $16.38 billion in block grants for fiscal years 1997–2002. The grants were to be divided among the states based on an equation involving the numbers of former AFDC recipients in each state. Because many of the bill's provisions have yet to be implemented into state-by-state policy, it was not possible to include the details of each state's programs for this edition of this work.

Social Security benefits were paid to some 1.05 million persons, averaging $723 a month.

The 163,528 Massachusetts residents receiving Supplemental Security Income in 1995 received an average monthly allowance of $372. In 1995, the average weekly unemployment benefit was $240.40.

40HOUSING

Massachusetts's housing stock, much older than the US average, reflects the state's colonial heritage and its ties to English architectural traditions. According to the 1990 census, 39% of the state's housing was built before 1940. Two major styles are common: colonial, typified by a wood frame, two stories, center hall entry, and center chimney; and Cape Cod, one-story houses built by fishermen, typified by shallow basements, shingled roofs, clapboard fronts, and unpainted shingled sides weathered gray by the salt air. Many new houses are also built in these styles.

As of 1996, there were an estimated 2,521,000 housing units in the state, of which 2,291,000 were occupied. Over 99% of all structures had plumbing. In 1996, 17,261 new housing units were authorized, with a value of over $1.8 billion; of these, 15,077 were single-family. Monthly cost for owners with a mortgage in 1990, the last year for which figures are available, was $985 and $298 for those without a mortgage; median monthly rent was $580. In the Boston vicinity of Massachusetts, these median monthly costs were $1,090, $332, and $640, respectively. In 1990, the median value of a home in Massachusetts was $162,800 (4th highest of any state); the median home value increased by 111.7% from 1980 to 1990 (in terms of 1990 dollars). During 1995/96, Massachusetts received $971.9 million in aid from the US Department of Housing and Urban Development, including $112.6 million in community development block grants.

The Executive Office of Communities and Development administers federal housing programs for the state. The Massachusetts Housing Finance Agency finances the construction and rehabilitation of housing by private and community groups.

41EDUCATION

Massachusetts has a long history of support for education. The Boston Latin School opened in 1635 as the first public school in the colonies. Harvard College—the first college in the US—was founded the following year. In 1647, for the first time, towns with more than 50 people were required by law to establish tax-supported school systems. More firsts followed: the country's first board of education, compulsory school attendance law, training school for teachers, state school for the retarded, and school for the blind. The drive for quality public education in the state was intensified through the efforts of educator Horace Mann, who during the 1830s and 1840s was also a leading force for the improvement of school systems throughout the US. Today the state boasts some of the most highly regarded private secondary schools and colleges in the country.

As of the 1990 census, 78.6% of state residents age 25 or older were high school graduates and 29.1% had completed four or more years of college. As of fall 1995, there were 914,726 students enrolled in public schools, and 36,273 public school teachers whose average salary was $51,770, ranked first in the country, well above the mean of $38,442.

Violence broke out in the South Boston schools when they were integrated in the mid-1970s. Between then and the fall of 1984, the percentage of black students increased from 34% to 48%, while the percentage of non-Hispanic white students decreased from 57.2% to 26.5%.

The early years of statehood saw the development of private academies, where the students could learn more than the basic reading and writing skills that were taught in the town schools at the time. Some of these private preparatory schools remain, including such prestigious institutions as Andover, Deerfield, and Groton. Enrollment in private schools in October 1992 totaled 123,305.

There are 116 colleges and universities in the state. The major public university system is the University of Massachusetts, with campuses at Amherst, Boston, Dartmouth, Lowell, and a medical school at Worcester. The Amherst campus, established in 1863, had an enrollment of 21,912 in the fall of 1992; the Boston campus, established in 1965, had 10,797 students. The state's 14 public colleges and universities had 110,031 students in 1990, while the Massachusetts Board of Regional Community Colleges had 74,641 students at its 17 campuses.

Harvard University, which was established in Cambridge originally as a college for clergymen and magistrates, has grown to become one of the country's premier institutions; its 1992 student population was 18,556. Also located in Cambridge are Radcliffe College (whose enrollment is included in Harvard's), founded in 1879, and the Massachusetts Institute of Technology, or MIT (1861), with 9,790 students in 1992. Mount Holyoke College, the first US college for women, was founded in 1837 and had a 1992 enrollment of 1,952. Other prominent private schools, their dates of origin, and their 1992 enrollments are Amherst College (1821), 1,585; Boston College (1863), 14,440; Boston University (1869), 28,594; Brandeis University (1947), 3,938; Clark University (1887), 2,706; Hampshire College (1965),1,079; the

New England Conservatory of Music (1867), 696; Northeastern University (1898), 30,510; Smith College (1871), 3,000; Tufts University (1852), 7,998; Wellesley College (1875), 2,340; and Williams College (1793), 2,125.

Among the tuition assistance programs available to state residents are the Massachusetts General Scholarships, awarded to thousands of college students annually; Massachusetts Honor Scholarships, for outstanding performance on the Scholastic Aptitude Test; special scholarships for war orphans and the children of deceased members of fire, police, and corrections departments; and the Higher Education Loan Plan, offered by the Massachusetts Higher Education Assistance Corp.

The State Board of Education establishes standards and policies for the public schools throughout the state; its programs are administered by the Department of Education. Higher education planning and programs are under the control of the Higher Education Coordinating Council. State and local expenditures for public elementary and secondary pupils in 1994/95 averaged $8,152 per pupil, ranked 4th in the country, well above the mean of $5,526.

The landmark Education Reform Act of 1993 established new systems of financial support for public elementary and secondary schools and instituted major reforms in governance, professional development, student educational goals, curricula, and assessments.

42ARTS

Boston is the center of artistic activity in Massachusetts, and Cape Cod and the Berkshires are areas of significant seasonal artistic activity. In 1979, Massachusetts became the first state to establish a lottery solely for funding the arts ($3.3 million in 1984). Boston is the home of several small theaters, some of which offer previews of shows bound for Broadway. Well-known local theater companies include the American Repertory Theatre and the Huntington Theatre. Of the regional theaters scattered throughout the state, the Williamstown Theater in the Berkshires and the Provincetown Theater on Cape Cod are especially noteworthy.

The Boston Symphony, one of the major orchestras in the US, was founded in 1881, and its principal conductors have included Serge Koussevitzky, Charles Munch, Erich Leinsdorf, and Seiji Ozawa. Emmanuel Church in Boston's Back Bay is known for its early music concerts, and chamber music by first-rate local and internationally known performers is presented at the New England Conservatory's Jordan Hall and other venues throughout the city. During the summer, the Boston Symphony is the main attraction of the Berkshire Music Festival at Tanglewood in Lenox. An offshoot of the Boston Symphony, the Boston Pops Orchestra, gained fame under the conductorship of Arthur Fiedler. Its mixture of popular, jazz, and light symphonic music continued under the direction of Fiedler's successors, John Williams and Keith Lockhart. Boston is also the headquarters of the Boston Lyric Opera. Prominent in the world of dance are the Boston Ballet Company and the Jacob's Pillow Dance Festival in the Berkshires.

The Massachusetts Cultural Council provides grants and services to support public programs in the arts, sciences, and the humanities. Grants are made to organizations, schools, communities and artists. The state appropriation to the Council as of 1997 is $14.1 million. The NEA contribution is $3.0 million.

43LIBRARIES AND MUSEUMS

The first public library in the US was established in Boston in 1653. Massachusetts has one of the most important university libraries in the country, and numerous museums and historical sites commemorate the state's rich colonial history.

Three regional library systems served 351 towns and cities with a total library circulation of over 35 million in 1996/97. The major city libraries are in Boston, Worcester, and Springfield. Statewide in 1996/97 there were 30,069,578 volumes in all public libraries. State funding for public libraries was $10.5 million in 1996/97; total library income amounted to $133,679,478 million.

The Boston Athenaeum, with 650,000 volumes, is the most noteworthy private library in the state. The American Antiquarian Society in Worcester has a 670,000-volume research library of original source material dating from colonial times to 1876.

Harvard University's library system is one of the largest in the world, with 13,143,330 volumes in 1996. Other major academic libraries are those of Boston University, the University of Massachusetts (Amherst), Smith College, and Boston College.

Boston houses a number of important museums, among them the Museum of Fine Arts with vast holdings of artwork including extensive Far East and French impressionists collections and American art and furniture, the Isabella Stewart Gardner Museum, the Museum of Science, the Massachusetts Historical Society, and the Children's Museum. Harvard University's museums include the Fogg Art Museum, the Peabody Museum of Archaeology and Ethnology, the Museum of Comparative Zoology, and the Botanical Museum. Other museums of note are the Whaling Museum in New Bedford, the Essex Institute in Salem, the Worcester Art Museum, the Clark Art Institute in Williamstown, the Bunker Hill Museum near Boston, and the National Basketball Hall of Fame in Springfield. In addition, many towns have their own historical societies and museums, including Historic Deerfield, Framingham Historical and Natural History Society, Ipswich Historical Society, Lexington Historical Society, and Marblehead Historical Society. Plymouth Plantation in Plymouth is a re-creation of life in the 17th century, and Old Sturbridge Village, a working historical farm, displays 18th- and 19th-century artifacts. The state had over 328 museums in 1996/97.

44COMMUNICATIONS

The first American post office was established in Boston in 1639. Alexander Graham Bell first demonstrated the telephone in 1876 in Boston. As of March 1993, 97.6% of the state's 2,316,000 occupied housing units had telephones, the highest percentage of any state.

The state had 67 AM stations and 106 FM stations in 1995, when 15 commercial and 4 educational television stations were also in operation. Boston alone accounts for 9 of the state's television stations, with WGBH a major producer of programming for the Public Broadcasting Service. In 1996 there were 21 large cable television systems.

45PRESS

Milestones in US publishing history that occurred in the state include the first book printed in the English colonies (Cambridge, 1640), the first regularly issued American newspaper, the *Boston News-Letter* (1704), and the first published American novel, William Hill Brown's *The Power of Sympathy* (Worcester, 1789). During the mid-1840s, two noted literary publications made their debut, the *North American Review* and the *Dial*, the latter under the editorial direction of Ralph Waldo Emerson and Margaret Fuller. *The Atlantic*, which began publishing in 1857, *Harvard Law Review, Harvard Business Review*, and *New England Journal of Medicine* are other influential publications.

As of 1997 there were 33 daily newspapers in the state (including 10 morning, 23 evening). The *Boston Globe*, the most widely read newspaper in the state, has won numerous awards for journalistic excellence on the local and national levels. The

Christian Science Monitor is highly respected for its coverage of national and international news. Major newspapers and their average daily circulations in 1994 were:

AREA	NAME	DAILY	SUNDAY
Boston	*Christian Science Monitor* (m)	87,257	
	Globe (m,S)	486,403	777,902
	Herald (m,S)	294,507	203,977

Massachusetts is also a center of book publishing, with more than 100 publishing houses. Among them are Little, Brown and Co., Houghton Mifflin, Merriam-Webster, and Harvard University Press.

46ORGANIZATIONS

The 1992 US Census of Service Industries counted 1,744 organizations in Massachusetts, including 309 business associations; 1,086 civic, social, and fraternal associations; and 349 other membership organizations.

Headquartered in Massachusetts are the National Association of Independent Schools, the National Commission for Cooperative Education, both in Boston, and the National Bureau of Economic Research in Cambridge. The Union of Concerned Scientists in Cambridge and International Physicians for the Prevention of Nuclear War in Boston—recipient of the 1985 Nobel Peace Prize—are the major public affairs associations based in the state.

Academic and scientific organizations headquartered in Boston include the American Meteorological Society, American Society of Law and Medicine, American Surgical Association, and Optometric Research Institute. The American Academy of Arts and Science is located in Cambridge, the National Association of Emergency Medical Technicians is in Newton Highlands, and the Protestant Guild for the Blind is in Belmont.

Among the many professional, business, and consumer organizations based in Massachusetts are the American Institute of Management in Quincy, Wood Products Manufacturers Association in Gardner, and the National Consumer Law Center, Northern Textile Association, and Wool Manufacturers Council in Boston. The American Orchid Society and the Nieman Foundation are in Cambridge, the Shoe Suppliers Association of America is in East Bridgewater, and the United Textile Workers of America is in Lawrence.

The headquarters of the John Birch Society, an archconservative political association, is in Belmont. Oxfam-America, the US affiliate of the international humanitarian relief agency, is located in Boston. Major sports associations in the state are the Eastern College Athletic Conference in Centerville and the American Hockey League in Springfield. The International Friendship League, which matches pen pals in 139 countries, has its headquarters in Boston.

47TOURISM, TRAVEL, AND RECREATION

Massachusetts beaches are a popular destination for summer travelers, but other areas have their own attractions.

In 1993, domestic travelers spent nearly $8 million in the state. It was estimated that about 39% of annual visits were for recreation and entertainment, 37% to see friends or relatives, 19% for business and conventions, and 5% for other personal reasons. Tourist-related industries employ 164,000 workers yearly. The largest employment was on Nantucket Island, followed by Martha's Vineyard and Cape Cod.

The largest number of visitor-days are spent in Barnstable County (Cape Cod); in 1996, the Cape Cod National Seashore attracted nearly 5,000,000 visitors. Among its many attractions are beaches, fishing, good dining spots, several artists' colonies with arts and crafts fairs, antique shops, and summer theaters.

Beaches, fishing, and quaint villages are also the charms of Nantucket and Martha's Vineyard.

Boston is the second most popular area for tourists. A trip to the city might include visits to such old landmarks as the Old North Church, the USS *Constitution,* and Paul Revere's House, and such newer attractions as the John Hancock Observatory, the skywalk above the Prudential Tower, Quincy Market, Faneuil Hall, and Copley Place. Boston Common, one of the oldest public parks in the country, is the most noteworthy municipal park.

The Berkshires are the summer home of the Berkshire Music Festival at Tanglewood and the Jacob's Pillow Dance Festival in Lee, and during the winter also provide recreation for cross-country and downhill skiers. Essex County on the North Shore of Massachusetts Bay offers many seaside towns and the art colony of Rockport. Its main city, Salem, contains the Witch House and Museum as well as Nathaniel Hawthorne's House of Seven Gables. Middlesex County, to the west of Boston, holds the university city of Cambridge as well as the battlegrounds of Lexington and Concord. In Concord are the homes of Henry David Thoreau, Ralph Waldo Emerson, and Louisa May Alcott. Norfolk County, south of Boston, has the homes of three US presidents: John Adams and John Quincy Adams in Quincy and John F. Kennedy in Brookline. The seaport town and former whaling center of New Bedford and the industrial town of Fall River are in Bristol County. Plymouth County offers Plymouth Rock, Plimoth Plantation, and a steam-train ride through some cranberry bogs.

In 1996, Massachusetts had about 79 operational state parks. In 1996, 264,668 hunters and 458,448 fishermen held licenses.

⁴⁸SPORTS

There are five major-league professional sports teams in Massachusetts: the Boston Red Sox of Major League Baseball, the New England Patriots of the National Football League, the Boston Celtics of the National Basketball Association, the Boston Bruins of the National Hockey League, and the New England Revolution of Major League Soccer.

The Red Sox last won the World Series in 1918 but have appeared in it and lost five times since, most recently in 1986. The Patriots won the American Football Conference Championship in 1986 and 1997, but lost Super Bowls to the Chicago Bears and the Green Bay Packers, respectively. The Celtics are the winningest team in NBA history; they have won the championship 16 times including the seemingly unbeatable record of eight consecutive titles from 1959 to 1966. They last won an NBA championship in 1986. The Bruins won the Stanley Cup in 1929, 1939, 1941, 1970, and 1972. Additionally, there are minor league hockey teams in Springfield and Worcester.

Suffolk Downs in East Boston features thoroughbred horse racing; harness racing takes place at the New England Harness Raceway in Foxboro. Dog racing can be seen at Raynham Park in Raynham, Taunton Dog Track in North Dighton, and Wonderland Park in Revere.

Probably the most famous amateur athletic event in the state is the Boston Marathon, a race of more than 26 mi (42 km) held every Patriots' Day (3d Monday in April). It attracts many of the world's top long-distance runners. During the summer, a number of boat races are held, including the Colorado Cup Races off Martha's Vineyard. Rowing is also popular. Each October the traditional sport is celebrated in a regatta on the Charles River among college students in the Boston/Cambridge area.

In collegiate sports, the University of Massachusetts has become a nationally ranked basketball power; Boston College has appeared in four bowl games, winning the Cotton Bowl in 1985; and the annual Harvard-Yale football game is one of the traditional rites of autumn.

⁴⁹FAMOUS BAY STATERS

Massachusetts has produced an extraordinary collection of public figures. Its four US presidents were John Adams (1735–1826), a signer of the Declaration of Independence; his son John Quincy Adams (1767–1848); John Fitzgerald Kennedy (1917–63), and George Herbert Walker Bush (b. Milton, 12 June 1924). All four served in Congress. John Adams was also the first US vice president; John Quincy Adams served as secretary of state under James Monroe, Calvin Coolidge (b.Vermont, 1872–1933) was governor of Massachusetts before his election to the vice-presidency in 1920 and his elevation to the presidency in 1923. George Bush was elected vice president on the Republican ticket in 1980 and reelected in 1984. Bush was elected president in 1988. Two others who held the office of vice president were another signer of the Declaration of Independence, Elbridge Gerry (1744–1814), for whom the political practice of gerrymandering is named, and Henry Wilson (b.New Hampshire, 1812–75), a US senator from Massachusetts before his election with Ulysses S. Grant.

Massachusetts's great jurists include US Supreme Court Justices Joseph Story (1779–1845), Oliver Wendell Holmes, Jr. (1841–1935), Louis D. Brandeis (b.Kentucky, 1856–1941), and Felix Frankfurter (b.Austria, 1882–1965). David Souter (b.1939), a Supreme Court justice appointed during the Bush administration, was born in Melrose. Stephen Breyer (b.California, 1939), another Supreme Court justice, was a Circuit Court of Appeals judge in Boston before his appointment. Important federal officeholders at the cabinet level were Henry Knox (1750–1806), the first secretary of war; Timothy Pickering (1745–1820), the first postmaster general and later secretary of war and secretary of state under George Washington and John Adams; Levi Lincoln (1749–1820), attorney general under Jefferson; William Eustis (1753–1825), secretary of war under Madison; Jacob Crowninshield (1770–1808), secretary of the navy under Jefferson, and his brother Benjamin (1772–1851), who held the same office under Madison; Daniel Webster (b.New Hampshire, 1782–1852), US senator from Massachusetts who served as secretary of state under William Henry Harrison, John Tyler, and Millard Fillmore; Edward Everett (1794–1865), a governor and ambassador who served as secretary of state under Fillmore; George Bancroft (1800–1891), a historian who became secretary of the Navy under James K. Polk; Caleb Cushing (1800–1879), attorney general under Franklin Pierce; Charles Devens (1820–91), attorney general under Rutherford B. Hayes; Christian Herter (1895–1966), secretary of state under Dwight Eisenhower; Elliot L. Richardson (b.1920), secretary of health, education and welfare, secretary of defense, and attorney general under Richard Nixon; Henry Kissinger (b.Germany, 1923), secretary of state under Nixon and Gerald Ford and a Nobel Peace Prize winner in 1973; and Robert F. Kennedy (1925–68), attorney general under his brother John and later US senator from New York.

Other federal officeholders include some of the most important figures in American politics. Samuel Adams (1722–1803), the Boston Revolutionary leader, served extensively in the Continental Congress and was later governor of the Bay State. John Hancock (1737–93), a Boston merchant and Revolutionary, was the Continental Congress's first president and later became the first elected governor of the state. In the 19th century, Massachusetts sent abolitionist Charles Sumner (1811–74) to the Senate. As ambassador to England during the Civil War, John Quincy Adams's son Charles Francis Adams (1807–86) played a key role in preserving US-British amity. At the end of the century, Henry Cabot Lodge (1850–1924) emerged as a leading Republican in the US Senate, where he supported regulatory legislation, protectionist tariffs, and restrictive immigration laws, and opposed women's suffrage and the League of Nations; his grandson, also Henry Cabot Lodge (1902–85), was an internationalist who held numerous federal posts and was a US senator. Massachusetts has provided two US House speakers: John W. McCormack (1891–1980) and Thomas P. "Tip" O'Neill, Jr. (1912–94). Other well-known legislators include Edward W. Brooke (b.1919), the first black US senator since Reconstruction, and Edward M. Kennedy (b.1932), President Kennedy's youngest brother and a leading Senate liberal. Paul Tsongas (1941–97), a senator and presidential candidate during the 1992 election, was born in Lowell, Massachusetts. Michael S. Dukakis (b.1933), a former governor of the state and the 1988 Democratic nominee for president, was born in Brookline.

Among other historic colonial and state leaders were John Winthrop (b.England, 1588–1649), a founder of Massachusetts and longtime governor; William Bradford (b.England, 1590–1657), a founder of Plymouth, its governor, and author of its classic history; Thomas Hutchinson (1711–80), colonial lieutenant governor and governor during the 1760s and 1770s; and Paul Revere (1735–1818), the Patriot silversmith-courier, who was later an industrial pioneer.

Literary genius has flourished in Massachusetts. In the 17th century, the colony was the home of poets Anne Bradstreet (1612–72) and Edward Taylor (1645–1729) and of the prolific historian, scientist, theologian, and essayist Cotton Mather (1663–1728). Eighteenth-century notables include the theologian Jonathan Edwards (b.Connecticut, 1703–58), poet Phillis Wheatley (b.Senegal, 1753–84), and numerous political essayists and historians. During the 1800s, Massachusetts was the home of novelists Nathaniel Hawthorne (1804–64), Louisa May Alcott (b.Pennsylvania, 1832–88), Horatio Alger (1832–99), and Henry James (b.New York, 1843–1916); essayists Ralph Waldo Emerson (1803–82) and Henry David Thoreau (1817–62); and such poets as Henry Wadsworth Longfellow (b.Maine, 1807–82), John Greenleaf Whittier (1807–92), Oliver Wendell Holmes, Sr. (1809–94), James Russell Lowell (1819-91), and Emily Dickinson (1830–86). Classic historical writings include the works of George Bancroft, William Hickling Prescott (1796–1859), John Lothrop Motley (1814–77), Francis Parkman (1823–93), and Henry B. Adams (1838–1918). Among 20th-century notables are novelists John P. Marquand (b.Delaware, 1893–1960) and John Cheever (1912–82); poets Elizabeth Bishop (1911–79), Robert Lowell (1917–77), Anne Sexton (1928–74), and Sylvia Plath (1932–63); and historian Samuel Eliot Morison (1887–1976). In philosophy, Charles Sanders Peirce (1839–1914) was one of the founders of pragmatism; Henry James's elder brother, William (b.New York, 1842–1910), was a pioneer in the field of psychology; and George Santayana (b.Spain, 1863–1952), philosopher and author, grew up in Boston. Mary Baker Eddy (b.New Hampshire, 1821–1910) founded the Church of Christ, Scientist, during the 1870s.

Reformers have abounded in Massachusetts, especially in the 19th century. William Lloyd Garrison (1805–79), Wendell Phillips (1811–84), and Lydia Maria Child (1802–80) were outstanding abolitionists. Lucretia Coffin Mott (1793–1880), Lucy Stone (1818–93), Abigail Kelley Foster (1810–87), Margaret Fuller (1810–50), and Susan Brownell Anthony (1820–1906) were leading advocates of women's rights. Horace Mann (1796–1859), the state secretary of education, led the fight for public education; and Mary Lyon (1797–1849) founded Mount Holyoke, the first women's college.

Efforts to improve the care and treatment of the sick, wounded, and handicapped were led by Samuel Gridley Howe (1801–76), Dorothea Lynde Dix (1802–87), and Clara Barton (1821–1912), founder of the American Red Cross. The 20th-century reformer and NAACP leader William Edward Burghardt Du Bois (1868–1963) was born in Great Barrington.

Leonard Bernstein (1918–90) was a composer and conductor of worldwide fame. Arthur Fiedler (1894–79) was the celebrated conductor of the Boston Pops Orchestra. Composers include William Billings (1746–1800), Carl Ruggles (1876–1971), and Alan Hovhaness (b.1911). Charles Bulfinch (1763–1844), Henry H. Richardson (b.Louisiana, 1838–86), and Louis Henri Sullivan (1856–1924) have been among the nation's important architects. Painters include John Singleton Copley (1738–1815), James Whistler (1834–1903), Winslow Homer (1836–1910), and Frank Stella (b.1936); Horatio Greenough (1805–52) was a prominent sculptor.

Among the notable scientists associated with Massachusetts are Nathaniel Bowditch (1773–1838), a mathematician and navigator; Samuel F. B. Morse (1791–1872), inventor of the telegraph; and Robert Hutchins Goddard (1882–1945), a physicist and rocketry pioneer.

Two professors at the Massachusetts Institute of Technology, in Cambridge, have won the Nobel Prize in economics—Paul A. Samuelson (b.Indiana, 1915), in 1970, and Franco Modigliani (b.Italy, 1918), in 1985. Other winners of the Nobel Prize include: Mertun Miller (b.1923), in economics; William Sharpe (b.1934), in economics; Douglass C. North (b.1920), 1993 co-recipient in economics; Elias James Carey (b.1928); Henry Kendall (b.1926), 1990 co-recipient in physics; and Joseph E. Murray (b.1919), the 1990 winner in medicine or physiology.

Massachusetts's most famous journalist has been Isaiah Thomas (1750–1831). Its great industrialists include textile entrepreneurs Francis Lowell (1775–1817) and Abbott Lawrence (1792–1855). Elias Howe (1819–67) invented the sewing machine.

Massachusetts was the birthplace of television journalists Mike Wallace (b.1918) and Barbara Walters (b.1931). Massachusetts-born show business luminaries include director Cecil B. DeMille (1881–1959); actors Walter Brennan (1894–1974), Jack Haley (1901–79), Ray Bolger (1904-84), Bette Davis (1908–84), and Jack Lemmon (b.1925); and singers Donna Summer (b.1948) and James Taylor (b.1948). Outstanding among Massachusetts-born athletes was world heavyweight boxing champion Rocky Marciano (Rocco Francis Marchegiano, 1925–69), who retired undefeated in 1956.

[50]BIBLIOGRAPHY

Andrews, Charles McLean. *The Colonial Period in American History.* New Haven, Conn.: Yale University Press, 1934.

Bailyn, Bernard. *The Ordeal of Thomas Hutchinson.* Cambridge, Mass.: Harvard University Press, 1974.

Bedford, Henry F., ed. *Their Lives and Numbers: The Condition of Working People in Massachusetts, 1870–1900.* Ithaca: Cornell University Press, 1995.

Boyer, Paul, and Stephen Nissenbaum. *Salem Possessed: The Social Origins of Witchcraft.* Cambridge, Mass.: Harvard University Press, 1974.

Brown, Richard D. *Massachusetts: A Bicentennial History.* New York: Norton, 1978.

Butterfield, L.H., et al., ed. *Diary and Autobiography of John Adams.* Cambridge, Mass.: Harvard University Press, 1962.

Federal Writers' Project. *Massachusetts: A Guide to Its Places and People.* Reprint. New York: Somerset (orig. 1937).

Gibney, Fred J. *Monograph of the Commonwealth of Massachusetts.* Boston: Massachusetts Office of Economic Affairs, 1980.

Gross, Robert. *The Minutemen and Their World.* New York: Hill and Wang, 1976.

Handlin, Oscar. *Boston's Immigrants.* Rev. ed. Cambridge, Mass.: Harvard University Press, 1979.

Hart, Albert, and Albert Bushnell, eds. *Commonwealth History of Massachusetts: Colony, Province, and State.* 5 vols. New York: Russell, 1967 (orig. 1927–30).

Haskell, John D., Jr., ed. *Massachusetts A Biography of Its History.* Boston: G. K. Hall, 1976.

Mandell, Daniel R. *Behind the Frontier: Indians in Eighteenth-Century Eastern Massachusetts.* Lincoln: University of Nebraska Press, 1996.

Massachusetts, Commonwealth of. Secretary of the Commonwealth. Citizen Information Service. *Citizen's Guide to State Services: A Selective Listing of Government Agencies and Programs.* Boston, 1984.

Morison, Samuel Eliot. *The Maritime History of Massachusetts, 1783–1860.* Boston: Northeastern University Press, 1979.

Porter, Susan L., ed. *Women of the Commonwealth: Work, Family, and Social Change in Nineteenth-Century Massachusetts.* Amherst: University of Massachusetts Press, 1996.

Rothenberg, Winifred Barr. *From Market-Places to a Market Economy: The Transformation of Rural Massachusetts.* Chicago: University of Chicago Press, 1992.

Russell, Francis. *A City in Terror—1919: The Boston Police Strike.* New York: Viking, 1975.

Whitehall, Walter M., and Norman Kotker. *Massachusetts: A Pictorial History.* New York: Scribner, 1981.

MICHIGAN

State of Michigan

ORIGIN OF STATE NAME: Possibly derived from the Fox Indian word *mesikami,* meaning "large lake." **NICKNAME:** The Wolverine State. **CAPITAL:** Lansing. **ENTERED UNION:** 26 January 1837 (26th). **SONG:** "Michigan, My Michigan" (unofficial). **MOTTO:** *Si quaeris peninsulam amoenam circumspice* (If you seek a pleasant peninsula, look about you). **COAT OF ARMS:** In the center, a shield depicts a peninsula on which a man stands, at sunrise, holding a rifle. At the top of the shield is the word "Tuebor" (I will defend), beneath it the state motto. Supporting the shield are an elk on the left and a moose on the right. Over the whole, on a crest, is an American eagle beneath the US motto, *E pluribus unum.* **FLAG:** The coat of arms centered on a dark blue field, fringed on three sides. **OFFICIAL SEAL:** The coat of arms surrounded by the words "The Great Seal of the State of Michigan" and the date "AD MDCCCXXXV" (1835, the year the first state constitution was adopted). **BIRD:** Robin. **FISH:** Trout. **REPTILE:** Painted turtle. **FLOWER:** Apple blossom. **TREE:** White pine. **GEM:** Chlorastrolite. **STONE:** Petoskey stone. **LEGAL HOLIDAYS:** New Year's Day, 1 January; Birthday of Martin Luther King, Jr., 3d Monday in January; Lincoln's Birthday, 12 February; Washington's Birthday, 3d Monday in February; Memorial Day, last Monday in May; Independence Day, 4 July; Labor Day, 1st Monday in September; Columbus Day, 2d Monday in October; Veterans Day, 11 November; Thanksgiving Day, 4th Thursday in November; Christmas Day, 25 December. **TIME:** 7 AM EST = noon GMT; 6 AM CST = noon GMT.

¹LOCATION, SIZE, AND EXTENT

Located in the eastern north-central US, Michigan is the 3d-largest state E of the Mississippi River and ranks 23d in size among the 50 states.

The total area of Michigan (excluding Great Lakes waters) is 58,527 sq mi (151,585 sq km), of which land takes up 56,954 sq mi (147,511 sq km) and inland water 1,573 sq mi (4,074 sq km). The state consists of the upper peninsula adjoining three of the Great Lakes—Superior, Huron, and Michigan—and the lower peninsula, projecting northward between Lakes Michigan, Erie, and Huron. The upper peninsula extends 334 mi (538 km) E-W and 215 mi (346 km) N-S; the lower peninsula's maximum E-W extension is 220 mi (354 km), and its greatest N-S length is 286 mi (460 km).

Michigan's upper peninsula is bordered on the N and E by the Canadian province of Ontario (with the line passing through Lake Superior, the St. Marys River, and Lake Huron); on the S by Lake Huron, the Straits of Mackinac separating the two peninsulas, and Lake Michigan; and on the SW and W by Wisconsin (with the line passing through the Menominee, Brule, and Montreal rivers). The lower peninsula is bordered on the N by Lake Michigan, the Straits of Mackinac, and Lake Huron; on the E by Ontario (with the line passing through Lake Huron, the St. Clair River, Lake St. Clair, and the Detroit River); on the SE by Ontario and Ohio (with the line passing through Lake Erie); on the S by Ohio and Indiana; and on the W by Illinois and Wisconsin (with the line passing through Lake Michigan and Green Bay). The state's geographic center is in Wexford County, 5 mi (8 km) NNW of Cadillac.

Among the most important islands are Isle Royale in Lake Superior; Sugar, Neebish, and Drummond islands in the St. Marys River; Bois Blanc, Mackinac, and Les Cheneaux islands in Lake Huron; Beaver Island in Lake Michigan; and Belle Isle and Grosse Ile in the Detroit River.

The state's total boundary length is 1,673 mi (2,692 km). The total freshwater shoreline is 3,121 mi (5,023 km).

²TOPOGRAPHY

Michigan's two peninsulas are generally level land masses. Flat lowlands predominate in the eastern portion of both peninsulas and in scattered areas elsewhere. The state's lowest point, 572 feet (174 meters), is found in southeastern Michigan along Lake Erie. Higher land is found in the western area of the lower peninsula, where elevations rise to as much as 1,600 feet (500 meters); the hilly uplands of the upper peninsula attain elevations of 1,800 feet (550 meters). The state's highest point, at 1,979 feet (603 meters), is Mt. Arvon, in Baraga County.

Michigan's political boundaries extend into four of the five Great Lakes, giving Michigan jurisdiction over 16,231 sq mi (42,038 sq km) of Lake Superior, 13,037 sq mi (33,766 sq km) of Lake Michigan, 8,975 sq mi (23,245 sq km) of Lake Huron, and 216 sq mi (559 sq km) of Lake Erie, for a total of 38,459 sq mi (99,608 sq km). In addition, Michigan has about 35,000 inland lakes and ponds, the largest of which is Houghton Lake, on the lower peninsula, with an area of 31 sq mi (80 sq km).

The state's leading river is the Grand, about 260 mi (420 km) long, flowing through the lower peninsula into Lake Michigan. Other major rivers that flow into Lake Michigan include the St. Joseph, Kalamazoo, Muskegon, Pere Marquette, and Manistee. On the eastern side of the peninsula, the Saginaw River and its tributaries drain an area of some 6,000 sq mi (15,500 sq km), forming the state's largest watershed. Other important rivers that flow into Lake Huron include the Au Sable, Thunder Bay, and Cheboygan. In the southeast, the Huron and Raisin rivers flow into Lake Erie. Most major rivers in the upper peninsula (including the longest, the Menominee) flow southward into Lake Michigan and its various bays. Tahquamenon Falls, in the eastern part of the upper peninsula, is the largest of the state's more than 150 waterfalls.

Most of the many islands belonging to Michigan are located in northern Lake Michigan and in Lake Huron, although the largest, Isle Royale, about 44 mi (71 km) long by 8 mi (13 km) wide, is found in northern Lake Superior. In northern Lake

Michigan, Beaver Island is the largest, while Drummond Island, off the eastern tip of the upper peninsula, is the largest island in the northern Lake Huron area.

Michigan's geological development resulted from its location in what was once a basin south of the Laurentian Shield, a landmass covering most of eastern and central Canada and extending southward into the upper peninsula. Successive glaciers that swept down from the north dumped soil from the shield into the basin and eroded the basin's soft sandstone, limestone, and shale. With the retreat of the last glacier from the area about 6000 BC, the two peninsulas, the Great Lakes, and the islands in these lakes began to emerge, assuming their present shapes about 2,500 years ago.

³CLIMATE

Michigan has a temperate climate with well-defined seasons. The warmest temperatures and longest frost-free period are found most generally in the southern part of the lower peninsula; Detroit has a normal daily mean temperature of 49°F (9°C), ranging from 23°F (–5°C) in January to 72°F (22°C) in July. Colder temperatures and a shorter growing season prevail in the more northerly regions; Sault Ste. Marie has a normal daily mean of 40°F (4°C), ranging from 13°F (–11°C) in January to 64°F (18°C) in July. The coldest temperature ever recorded in the state is –51°F (–46°C), registered at Vanderbilt on 9 February 1934; the all-time high of 112°F (44°C) was recorded at Mio on 13 July 1936. Both sites are located in the interior of the lower peninsula, away from the moderating influence of the Great Lakes.

Detroit has an average annual precipitation of 31 in (79 cm); rainfall tends to decrease as one moves northward. The greatest snowfall is found in the extreme northern areas, where cloud cover created by cold air blowing over the warmer Lake Superior waters causes frequent heavy snow along the northern coast; Houghton and Calumet, on the Keweenaw Peninsula, average 183 in (465 cm) of snow a year, more than any other area in the state. Similarly, Lake Michigan's water temperatures create a snow belt along the west coast of the lower peninsula.

Cloudy days are more common in Michigan than in most states, in part because of the condensation of water vapor from the Great Lakes. Detroit has sunshine, on average, only 32% of the days in December and January, and only 54% year-round. The annual average relative humidity at Detroit is 77% at 7 AM, dropping to 58% at 1 PM; at Sault Ste. Marie, the comparable percentages are 85% and 67%, respectively. The southern half of the lower peninsula is an area of heavy thunderstorm activity. Late spring and early summer are the height of the tornado season; there were 10 tornadoes in 1995.

⁴FLORA AND FAUNA

Maple, birch, hemlock, aspen, spruce, and fir predominate in the upper peninsula; maple, birch, aspen, pine, and beech in the lower. Once common in the state, elms have largely disappeared because of the ravages of disease, while the white pine (the state tree) and red pine, which dominated northern Michigan forests and were prime objects of logging operations, have been replaced in cutover lands by aspen and birch. The area south of a line from about Muskegon to Saginaw Bay formerly held the only significant patches of open prairie land (found chiefly in southwestern Michigan) and areas of widely scattered trees, called oak openings. Intensive agricultural development, followed by urban industrial growth, leveled much of this region's forests, although significant wooded acreage remains, especially in the less populated western regions.

Strawberries, raspberries, gooseberries, blueberries, and cranberries are among the fruit-bearing plants and shrubs that grow wild in many areas of the state, as do mushrooms and wild asparagus. The state flower, the apple blossom, calls to mind the importance of fruit-bearing trees and shrubs in Michigan, but wild flowers also abound, with as many as 400 varieties found in a single county. Protected plants include all members of the orchid, trillium, and gentian families; trailing arbutus; prince's-pine; bird's-foot violet; climbing bittersweet; flowering dogwood; mountain and Michigan hollies; and American lotus.

Michigan's fauna, like its flora, has been greatly affected by settlement and, in a few cases, by intensive hunting and fishing. Moose are now confined to Isle Royale, as are nearly all the remaining wolves, which once roamed throughout the state. The caribou and passenger pigeon have been extirpated, but the elk and turkey have been successfully reintroduced in the 20th century. There is no evidence that the state's namesake, the wolverine, was ever found in Michigan, at least in historic times. Despite intensive hunting, the deer population remains high. Other game animals include the common cottontail, snowshoe hare, raccoon, and various squirrels. In addition to the raccoon, important native furbearers are the river otter and the beaver, once virtually exterminated but now making a strong comeback.

More than 300 types of birds have been observed. Aside from the robin (the state bird), the most notable bird is Kirtland's warbler, which nests only in a 60-sq-mi (155-sq-km) section of jack-pine forest in north-central Michigan. Ruffed grouse, bob-white quail, American woodcock, and various ducks and geese are hunted extensively. Populations of ring-necked pheasant, introduced in 1895, have dropped at an alarming rate in recent decades. Reptiles include the massasauga, the state's only poisonous snake.

Whitefish, perch, and lake trout (the state fish) are native to the Great Lakes, while perch, bass, and pike are indigenous to inland waters. In 1877, the carp was introduced, with such success that it has since become a nuisance. Rainbow and brown trout have also been planted, and in the late 1960s, the state enjoyed its most spectacular success with the introduction of several species of salmon.

The first Michigan list of threatened or endangered fauna in 1976 included 64 species, 15 endangered and 49 threatened. Subsequent surveys indicated that Kirtland's warbler, the bald eagle, and the osprey were holding their own, while the greater prairie chicken, barn owl, and common tern were continuing to decline. Other endangered animals include the Indiana bat, gray wolf, Kirtland's water snake, blue pike, and five species of cisco.

⁵ENVIRONMENTAL PROTECTION

The Michigan Department of Natural Resources (DNR) is the state's 4th-largest department employing approximately 3,700 persons. It is responsible for the administration of hundreds of programs affecting every aspect of the environment. These programs are based on state and federal laws calling for the protection and management of natural resources, including: air, water, fish, wildlife, recreational activities, wetlands, forests, minerals, oil, and gas. The regulatory programs operated by the DNR conserve and manage natural resources by controlling access or limiting their use and removal. Most of these programs rely on permit or license systems such as hunting or fishing licenses, forest use permits, and air/wastewater discharge permits.

Responding to citizens' concerns and new federal legislation, Michigan enacted programs to address water and air pollution as well as waste problems. At least 10 major environmental programs were established under Michigan law during the 1970sand 1980s, directing the DNR to assume new responsibilities and authorities. These included the Wetland Protection Act of 1980, Inland Lakes and Streams Act, the Resource Recovery Act, the Solid Waste Management Act, and the Hazardous Waste Management Act. In addition, changes in administrative rules and amendments to existing statutes greatly expanded the scope of some programs such as air and water pollution control (Air

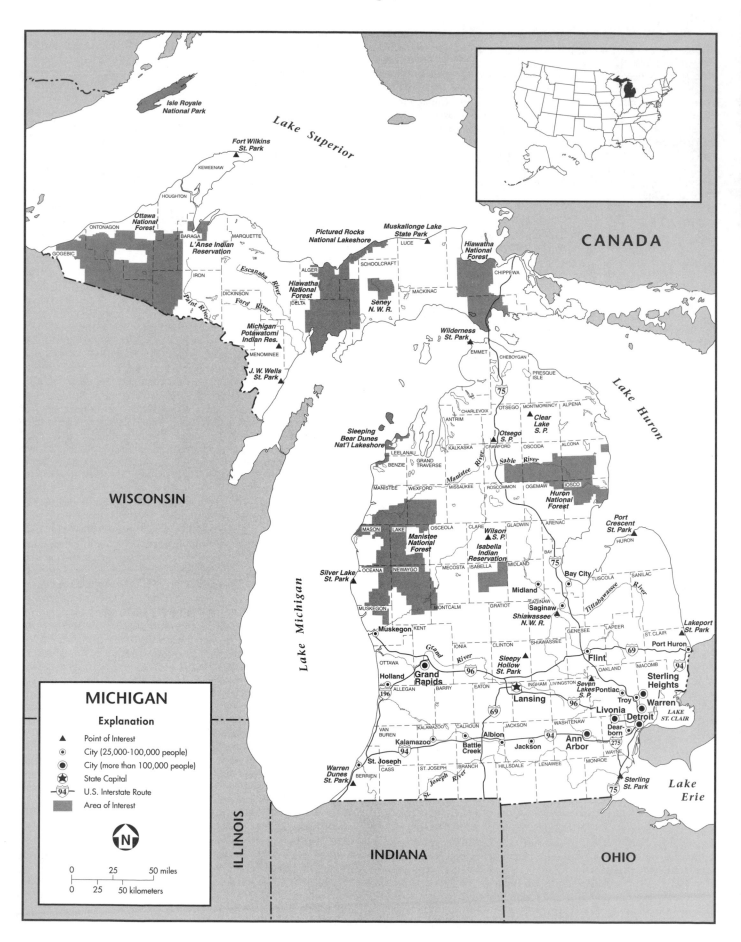

MICHIGAN

Explanation

▲ Point of Interest

⊙ City (25,000-100,000 people)

● City (more than 100,000 people)

★ State Capital

—94— U.S. Interstate Route

▨ Area of Interest

N

| 0 | 25 | 50 miles |

| 0 | 25 | 50 kilometers |

Pollution Control Act and Water Resources Commission Act). These legislated changes, coupled with reorganization measures enacted by executive order, greatly expanded the state's role in environmental protection matters and substantially increased the scope of DNR's mission.

Governor William Milliken decided Michigan would be better served if all environmental programs were under one roof. Executive Order 1973-2 transferred three programs from the Department of Public Health to the DNR, including sewage system maintenance and certification; solid waste disposal; and licensing of septic tank cleaners. Further transfers were accomplished under Executive Order 1973-2a, which changed the status of the Water Resources Commission (WRC), making it subordinate to the Natural Resources Commission (NRC). Additionally, Executive Order 1973-2a transferred the Air Pollution Control Commission to the DNR under the jurisdiction of the NRC. The Executive Order divided the DNR for the first time into two branches, the natural resources branch, and the environmental protection branch. The Executive Orders of 1973 clearly consolidated and defined the DNR's environmental protection responsibilities.

As the 1970s drew to a close, Michigan enacted two major pollution control laws: the Solid Waste Management Act and the Hazardous Waste Management Act. These acts provide the legal basis for the separate management of hazardous wastes under a detailed regulatory program. The two waste management laws substantially increased the DNR's enforcement and administrative responsibilities. In addition to these two acts, several other laws were enacted or amended by the legislature in the late 1970s and 1980s which had a major impact on the Department. For example, the Environmental Response Act provides for the identification of sites of environmental contamination throughout the state and an appropriation procedure to support the cleanup of contamination sites in the state. Other programs created by statute included the Clean Michigan Fund and the Leaking Underground Storage Tanks Act. Each of these statutes required the DNR to assume new program responsibilities and authorities in the 1980s.

As the policy body over the DNR, the Natural Resources Commission (NRC) consists of seven members appointed by the governor, with the advice of the senate. The NRC sets the overall direction of the department and hires the director to carry out its policies. The department is organized both programmatically and

Michigan Counties, County Seats, and County Areas and Populations

COUNTY	COUNTY SEAT	LAND AREA (SQ MI)	POPULATION (1996 EST)	COUNTY	COUNTY SEAT	LAND AREA (SQ MI)	POPULATION (1996 EST)
Alcona	Harrisville	679	10,799	Lapeer	Lapeer	658	85479
Alger	Munising	912	9971	Leelanau	Leland	341	18430
Allegan	Allegan	832	99019	Lenawee	Adrian	753	97133
Alpena	Alpena	568	30746	Livingston	Howell	575	137616
Antrim	Bellaire	480	20595	Luce	Newberry	905	6180
Arenac	Standish	368	16268	Mackinac	St. Ignace	1,025	11096
Baraga	L'Anse	901	8472	Macomb	Mt. Clemens	483	734625
Barry	Hastings	560	53145	Manistee	Manistee	543	22902
Bay	Bay City	447	110824	Marquette	Marquette	1,822	62017
Benzie	Beulah	322	14037	Mason	Ludington	495	27725
Berrien	St. Joseph	576	161434	Mecosta	Big Rapids	560	38460
Branch	Coldwater	508	42991	Menominee	Menominee	1,045	24551
Calhoun	Marshall	712	14112	Midland	Midland	525	80669
Cass	Cassopolis	496	50050	Missaukee	Lake City	565	13607
Charlevoix	Charlevoix	421	23503	Monroe	Monroe	557	140488
Cheboygan	Cheboygan	720	22993	Montcalm	Stanton	713	58969
Chippewa	Sault Ste. Marie	1,590	37289	Montmorency	Atlanta	550	9868
Clare	Harrison	570	28618	Muskegon	Muskegon	507	164913
Clinton	St. Johns	573	62239	Newaygo	White Cloud	847	44285
Crawford	Grayling	559	13671	Oakland	Pontiac	875	1162098
Delta	Escanaba	1,173	39047	Oceana	Hart	541	24379
Dickinson	Iron Mt.	770	27285	Ogemaw	West Branch	569	20790
Eaton	Charlotte	579	9562	Ontonagon	Ontonagon	1,311	8405
Emmet	Petoskey	468	27870	Osceola	Reed City	569	22047
Genesee	Flint	642	436128	Oscoda	Mio	568	8775
Gladwin	Gladwin	505	24615	Otsego	Gaylord	516	21343
Gogebic	Bessemer	1,105	17704	Ottawa	Grand Haven	567	215064
Grand Traverse	Traverse City	466	72072	Presque Isle	Rogers City	656	14407
Gratiot	Ithaca	570	39978	Roscommon	Roscomon	528	22847
Hillsdale	Hillsdale	603	45887	Saginaw	Saginaw	815	211808
Houghton	Houghton	1,014	36230	St. Clair	Port Huron	734	155636
Huron	Bad Axe	830	35281	St. Joseph	Centreville	503	60977
Ingham	Mason	560	285737	Sanilac	Sandusky	964	42440
Ionia	Ionia	577	60378	Schoolcraft	Manistique	1,173	8653
Iosco	Tawas City	546	24761	Shiawassee	Corunna	541	72333
Iron	Crystal Falls	1,163	13121	Tuscola	Caro	812	57837
Isabella	Mt. Pleasant	576	57118	Van Buren	Paw Paw	612	75308
Jackson	Mackson	705	154563	Washtenaw	Ann Arbor	710	295149
Kalamazoo	Kalamazoo	562	229008	Wayne	Detroit	615	2036819
Kalkaska	Kalkaska	563	15325	Wexford	Cadillac	566	28789
Kent	Grand Rapids	862	536103				
Keweenaw	Eagle River	544	20010				
Lake	Balwin	568	9874	TOTALS		56,954	9,594,350

geographically. The three program areas, each headed by a deputy director, include: resource management; environmental protection; and policy, budget, and administration. The three geographical regions split the state into the north, central, and south zones, each headed by a deputy director. The deputy directors report to the director of the DNR.

The mission of the department is to conserve and develop the state's natural resources and to protect and enhance the state's environmental quality in order to provide clean air, clean water, productive land, and healthy life. Additionally, the department seeks to provide quality recreational opportunities to the people of Michigan through the effective management of state recreational lands and parks, boating facilities, and population of fish and wildlife.

In 1995, Michigan had 78 hazardous waste sites, the 5th-highest concentration of such sites in the nation. Wetlands covered 15% of the state in 1996.

The environmental protection program area encompasses five divisions participating in the protection of the state's environmental quality. The five divisions are air quality, environmental response, surface water quality, underground storage tanks, and waste management. In many cases, the programs and statutes managed by these five divisions were transferred to the DNR in the 1970s or enacted by the legislature in the last two decades.

6POPULATION

Michigan ranked 8th among the 50 states in the 1990 census, with a population of 9,295,297. That total represented an increase of only 0.4% over the 1980 population, because from 1980 to 1985, Michigan's population declined 2.9%. The state's population increased 3.2% to an estimated 9,594,350 in 1996.

During the long prehistoric period, Michigan was inhabited by only a few thousand Indians. As late as 1810, the non-Indian population of Michigan Territory was only 4,762. The late 1820s marked the start of steady, often spectacular, growth. The population increased from 31,639 people in 1830 to 212,267 in 1840 and 397,654 in 1850. Subsequently, the state's population grew by about 400,000 each decade until 1910, when its population of 2,810,173 ranked 8th among the 46 states. Industrial development sparked a sharp rise in population to 4,842,325 by 1930, which pushed Michigan ahead of Massachusetts into 7th place.

According to the 1980 census, Michigan's population was slightly younger than the national median age and in 1989, 11.9% of residents were over 65. As of 1990, 57% of those 5 years of age or older were still living in the same house as five years before.

With 70.5% of its population classified as urban in 1990, Michigan's percentage was below the national average. Population density for the entire state in 1990 was 163.6 persons per sq mi (62.9 per sq km); half the population was concentrated in the Detroit metropolitan area.

Detroit has always been Michigan's largest city since its founding in 1701, but its growth, like the state's, was slow until well into the 19th century. The city's population grew from 21,019 in 1850 to 285,704 in 1900, when it ranked as the 13th-largest city in the country. Within the next 30 years, the booming automobile industry pushed the city up into 4th place, with a population of 1,568,662 in 1930. Since 1950, when the total reached 1,849,568, Detroit has lost population, dropping to 1,514,063 in 1970, 1,203,369 in 1980 and to 1,028,000 in 1990, when it held 7th place among US cities. The 1996 population was estimated at 992,038, putting Detroit in 10th place. As Detroit lost population, however, many of its suburban areas grew at an even greater rate, and the Detroit metropolitan area totaled an estimated 4,320,203 in 1995, up from 3,950,000 in 1960.

Other Michigan cities with estimated 1996 populations in excess of 100,000 include: Grand Rapids with a population of 190,395; Warren, 142,625; Flint, 138,164; Lansing (the capital), 119,590; Sterling Heights, 119,505; and Ann Arbor, 108,817.

7ETHNIC GROUPS

The 1990 census counted about 56,000 American Indians, more than 40% higher than in 1980. Most were scattered across the state, with a small number concentrated on the four federal reservations, comprising 16,635 acres (6,732 hectares). The Ottawa, Ojibwa, and Potawatomi were the principal groups with active tribal organizations. In 1996, the total Native American population, including Eskimos and Aleuts, was estimated at 72,000.

In 1996 the black population of Michigan totaled an estimated 1,222,000, 13% of the state's total population. In 1980, nearly two-thirds lived in Detroit, where they made up 75.7% of the population, the highest percentage in any US city of 1 million or more. Detroit, which experienced severe race riots in 1943 and 1967, has had a black mayor since 1974.

The 1990 census found that 355,393 state residents (3.8%) were foreign-born. According to estimates for 1996, this figure had risen to 491,000 (5%). There were 202,000 persons of Hispanic origin living in the state in 1990, of whom 118,424 were of Mexican descent. The state's Asian population has been increasing: as of 1990 there were 18,100 Asian Indians, 16,086 Filipinos, 17,100 Chinese, 17,738 Koreans, 13,309 Japanese, and 5,229 Vietnamese. Although state residents of first- or second-generation European descent are, almost without exception, decreasing in number and proportion, their influence remains great. Detroit continues to have numerous well-defined ethnic neighborhoods, and Hamtramck, a city surrounded by Detroit, is still dominated by its Polish population. Elsewhere in Michigan, Frankenmuth is the site of an annual German festival, and the city of Holland has an annual tulip festival that attracts about 400,000 people each spring. In the upper peninsula, the Finnish culture dominates in rural areas; in the iron and copper mining regions, descendants of immigrants from Cornwall in England, the original mining work force, and persons of Scandinavian background predominate.

8LANGUAGES

Before white settlement, Algonkian-language tribes occupied what is now Michigan, with the Menomini and Ojibwa in the upper peninsula and Ottawa on both sides of the Straits of Mackinac. Numerous place-names recall their presence: Michigan itself, Mackinaw City, Petoskey, Kalamazoo, Muskegon, Cheboygan, and Dowagiac.

Except for the huge industrial area in southeastern Michigan, English in the state is remarkably homogeneous in its retention of the major Northern dialect features of upper New York and western New England. Common are such Northern forms as *pail, wishbone, darning needle* (dragonfly), *mouth organ* (harmonica), *sick to the stomach, quarter to four* (3:45), and *dove* as past tense of *dive*. Common also are such pronunciations as the /ah/ vowel in *fog, frog,* and *on;* the /aw/ vowel in *horrid, forest,* and *orange; creek* as /krik/; *root* and *roof* with the vowel of *put;* and *greasy* with an /s/ sound. *Swale* (a marsh emptying into a stream) and *clock shelf* (mantel) are dying Northern words not carried west of Michigan. *Pank* (to pack down, as of snow) is confined to the upper peninsula, and *pasty* (meat-filled pastry) is borrowed from Cornish miners and heard in the upper peninsula and a few other areas. A minister is a *dominie* in the Dutch area around Holland and Zeeland.

Southern blacks have introduced into the southeastern automotive manufacturing areas a regional variety of English that, because it has class connotations in the North, has become a controversial educational concern. Three of its features are perhaps more widely accepted than others: the coalescence of /e/ and /i/ before a nasal consonant, so that *pen* and *pin* sound alike; the loss of /r/ after a vowel, so that *cart* and *cot* also sound alike; and the lengthening of the first part of the diphthong /ai/, so that *time* and *Tom* sound alike, as do *ride* and *rod*.

In 1990, only 6.6% of the state's population 5 years old or older spoke a language other than English at home. Other languages spoken at home, with the number of speakers, were as follows:

Spanish	137,490	Italian	38,023
Polish	64,527	Chinese	15,378
German	57,328	Indic	14,916
Arabic	40,242	Other West Germanic	13,772
French	39,794	Greek	13,431

9RELIGIONS

The Roman Catholic Church was the only organized religion in Michigan until the 19th century. Detroit's Ste. Anne's parish, established in 1701, is the second-oldest Catholic parish in the country. In 1810, a Methodist society was organized near Detroit and, after the War of 1812, as settlers poured in from the east, Presbyterian, Congregational, Baptist, Episcopal, and Quaker churches were founded. The original French Catholics, reduced to a small minority by the influx of American Protestants, were soon reinforced by the arrival of Catholic immigrants from Germany, Ireland, and, later, from eastern and southern Europe. The Lutheran religion was introduced by German and Scandinavian immigrants; Dutch settlers were affiliated with the Reformed Church in America. The first Jewish congregations were organized in Detroit by German Jews, with a much greater number of eastern European Jews arriving toward the end of the 1800s. The Orthodox Christian Church and the Islamic religion have been introduced by immigrants from the Near East during the 20th century.

Michigan had 2,338,608 Roman Catholics in 1990, and an estimated 107,116 Jews. Among Protestant denominations, a census taken in 1990 showed various Lutheran groups with a combined total of 421,029 adherents and Methodist groups with 252,129 adherents. Among other major denominations, the Presbyterian Church had 126,326 adherents; the Episcopal Church, 71,727; and the Reformed Church in America, 100,680. The Seventh Day Adventists, who had their world headquarters in Battle Creek from 1855 to 1903, numbered 37,949 in 1980; the Salvation Army, 7,896; and the Church of Jesus Christ of Latter-day Saints (Mormon), 23,475.

10TRANSPORTATION

Because of Michigan's location, its inhabitants have always depended heavily on the Great Lakes for transportation. Not until the 1820s did land transportation systems begin to be developed. Although extensive networks of railroads and highways now reach into all parts of the state, the Great Lakes remain major avenues of commerce.

The first railroad company in the Midwest was chartered in Michigan in 1830, and six years later the Erie and Kalamazoo, operating between Toledo, Ohio, and Adrian, became the first railroad in service west of the Appalachians. Between 1837 and 1845, the state government sought to build three lines across southern Michigan, before abandoning the project and selling the two lines it had partially completed to private companies. The pace of railroad construction lagged behind that in other midwestern states until after the Civil War, when the combination of federal and state aid and Michigan's booming economy led to an enormous expansion in trackage, from fewer than 800 mi (1,300 km) in 1860 to a peak of 9,021 mi (14,518 km) in 1910. With the economic decline of northern Michigan and the

resultant drop in railroad revenues, however, Class I trackage declined to 3,900 rail mi (3,218 km) by December 1995. Most railroad passenger service is provided by Amtrak, which operates five trains through the state and carried 534,668 Michigan passengers in 1995/96. Freight is carried by the state's 27 railroads. In 1995, over 88 million tons were handled, with Michigan ranking 29th in rail tonnage. The Michigan state government, through the Department of Transportation, has helped to revive the railroad system through its Rail Program.

Railroads have been used only to a limited degree in the Detroit area as commuter carriers, although efforts have been made to improve this service. In the early 1900s, more than 1,000 mi (1,600 km) of interurban rail lines provided rapid transit service in southern Michigan, but automobiles and buses drove them out of business, and the last line shut down in 1934. Street railway service began in a number of cities in the 1860s, and Detroit took over its street railways in 1922. Use of these public transportation systems declined sharply after World War II. By the 1950s, streetcars had been replaced by buses, but by 1960, many small communities had abandoned city bus service altogether. During the 1970s, with massive government aid, bus service was restored to many cities and was improved in others, and the number of riders generally increased. In fiscal year 1995/96, local public transit systems handled 82.5 million passengers, while intercity bus systems carried an estimated 350,000 passengers in 1996.

As of 1 January 1993, the state had 89,528 mi (144,140 km) of rural roads and 28,012 mi (45,099 km) of urban roads. There were 1,240 mi (1,996 km) of interstate highway open to traffic. Major expressways included I-94 (Detroit to Chicago), I-96 (Detroit to Grand Rapids), and I-75 (from the Ohio border to Sault Ste. Marie). In 1995 there were 5,314,815 registered passenger cars, 2,335,026 trucks, 22,249 buses, and 126,590 motorcycles. Licensed drivers numbered 6,658,750 during the same year.

The completion in 1957 of the Mackinac Bridge, the fourth-longest suspension span in the world, eliminated the major barrier to easy movement between the state's two peninsulas. The International Bridge at Sault Ste. Marie, the Blue-Water Bridge at Port Huron, the Ambassador Bridge at Detroit, and the Detroit-Windsor Tunnel link Michigan with Canada.

The opening of the St. Lawrence Seaway in 1959 made it possible for a large number of oceangoing vessels to dock at Michigan ports. In 1995, the port of Detroit handled 18,661,000 tons of cargo; Stoneport, 10,936,000 tons; and the limestone-shipping port of Calcite, 8,479,000.

Michigan was a pioneer in developing air transportation service. The Ford Airport at Dearborn in the 1920s had one of the first air passenger facilities and was the base for some of the first regular airmail service. In 1996, the state had 240 licensed public-use airfields, 79 heliports, and one public-use seaplane base. The major airport is Detroit Metropolitan Wayne County Airport, which in 1996 enplaned 14,524,476 passengers; handled 499,301,916 pounds of cargo, express, and package freight; and had 538,655 aircraft departures.

11HISTORY

Indian hunters and fishermen inhabited the region now known as Michigan as early as 9000 BC, these peoples were making use of copper found in the upper peninsula—the first known use of a metal by peoples anywhere in the western hemisphere. Around 1000 BC, their descendants introduced agriculture into southwestern Michigan. In the latter part of the prehistoric era, the Indians appear to have declined in population.

In the early 17th century, when European penetration began, Michigan's lower peninsula was inhabited by tribes of Native Americans who may have moved west of Lake Michigan for temporary periods during periods of war. In the upper peninsula there were small bands of Ojibwa along the St. Marys River and the Lake Michigan shore; in the west, Menomini Indians lived along the present Michigan-Wisconsin border. Both tribes were of Algonkian linguistic stock, as were most Indians who later settled in the area, except for the Winnebago of the Siouan group in the Green Bay region of Lake Michigan, and the Huron of Iroquoian stock in the Georgian Bay area of Canada. In the 1640s, the Huron were nearly wiped out by other Iroquois tribes from New York, and the survivors fled westward with their neighbors to the north, the Ottawa Indians. Eventually, both tribes settled at the Straits of Mackinac before moving to the Detroit area early in the 18th century. During the same period, the Potawatomi and Miami Indians moved from Wisconsin into southern Michigan.

For two centuries after the first Europeans came to Michigan, the Indians remained a vital force in the area's development. They were the source of the furs that the whites traded for, and they also were highly respected as potential allies when war threatened between the rival colonial powers in North America. However, after the War of 1812, when the fur trade declined and the possibility of war receded, the value of the Indians to the white settlers diminished. Between 1795 and 1842, Indian lands in Michigan were ceded to the federal government, and the Huron, Miami, and many Potawatomi were removed from the area. Some Potawatomi were allowed to remain on lands reserved for them, along with most of the Ojibwa and Ottawa Indians in the north.

The first European explorer known to have reached Michigan was a Frenchman, Etienne Brulé, who explored the Sault Ste. Marie area around 1620. Fourteen years later, Jean Nicolet explored the Straits of Mackinac and the southern shore of the upper peninsula en route to Green Bay. Missionary and fur trading posts, to which were later added military forts, were established at Sault Ste. Marie by Father Jacques Marquette in 1668, and then at St. Ignace in 1671. By the 1860s, several temporary posts had been established in the lower peninsula. In 1701, Antoine Laumet de la Mothe Cadillac founded a permanent settlement at the site of present-day Detroit.

Detroit and Michigan grew little at first, however, because the rulers of the French colony of New France were obsessed with the fur trade, which did not attract large numbers of settlers. After France's defeat in the French and Indian War, fears that the British would turn the area over to English farmers from the coastal colonies, with the consequent destruction of the Indian way of life, led the Indians at Detroit to rebel in May 1763, under the leadership of the Ottawa chief Pontiac. Other uprisings resulting from similar grievances soon spread throughout the west, but ended in failure for the Indians. Pontiac gave up his siege of Detroit after six months, and by 1764, the British were in firm control. Nevertheless, the British authorities did not attempt to settle the area. The need to protect the fur trade placed the people of Michigan solidly on the British side during the American Revolution, since a rebel triumph would likely mean the migration of American farmers into the west, converting the wilderness to cropland. The British occupied Michigan and other western areas for 13 years after the Treaty of Paris in 1783 had assigned these territories to the new United States. The US finally got possession of Michigan in the summer of 1796.

Michigan became a center of action in the War of 1812. The capture of Detroit by the British on 16 August 1812 was a crushing defeat for the Americans. Although Detroit was recaptured by the Americans in September 1813, continued British occupation of the fort on Mackinac Island, which they had captured in 1812, enabled them to control most of Michigan. The territory was finally returned to American authority under the terms of the Treaty of Ghent at the end of 1814. With the opening in 1825 of the Erie Canal, which provided a cheap, all-water link between Michigan and New York City, American pioneers turned their attention to these northern areas, and during the 1820s settlers for the first time pushed into the interior of southern Michigan.

Originally part of the Northwest Territory, Michigan had been set aside in 1805 as a separate territory, but with boundaries considerably different from those of the subsequent state. On the south, the territory's boundary was a line set due east from the southernmost point of Lake Michigan; on the north, only the eastern tip of the upper peninsula was included. In 1818 and 1834, areas as far west as Iowa and the Dakotas were added to the territory for administrative purposes. By 1833, Michigan had attained a population of 60,000, qualifying it for statehood. The territorial government's request in 1834 that Michigan be admitted to the Union was rejected by Congress, however, because of a dispute over Michigan's southern boundary. When Indiana became a state in 1816, it had been given a 10-mi (16-km) strip of land in southwestern Michigan, and Michigan now refused to accede to Ohio's claim that it should be awarded lands in southeastern Michigan, including the present site of Toledo. In 1835, Michigan militia defeated the efforts of Ohio authorities to take over the disputed area during the so-called Toledo War, in which no one was killed. Nevertheless, Ohio's superior political power in Congress ultimately forced Michigan to agree to relinquish the Toledo Strip. In return, Congress approved the state government that the people of Michigan had set up in 1835. As part of the compromise that finally brought Michigan into the Union on 26 January 1837, the new state was given land in the upper peninsula west of St. Ignace as compensation for the loss of Toledo.

Youthful Stevens T. Mason, who had led the drive for statehood, became Michigan's first elected governor, but he and the Democratic Party fell out of grace when the new state was plunged into financial difficulties during the depression of the late 1830s. The party soon returned to power and controlled the state until the mid-1850s. In Michigan, as elsewhere, it was the slavery issue that ended Democratic dominance. In July 1854, antislavery Democrats joined with members of the Whig and Free-Soil parties at a convention in Jackson to organize the Republican Party. In the elections of 1854, the Republicans swept into office in Michigan, controlling the state, with rare exceptions, until the 1930s.

Abraham Lincoln was not the first choice of Michigan Republicans for president in 1860, but when he was nominated, they gave him a solid margin of victory that fall and again in 1864. Approximately 90,000 Michigan men served in the Union army, taking part in all major actions of the Civil War. Michigan's Zachariah Chandler was one of the leaders of the Radical Republicans in the US Senate who fought for a harsh policy toward the South during Reconstruction.

Michigan grew rapidly in economic importance. Agriculture sparked the initial growth of the new state and was responsible for its rapid increase in population. By 1850, the southern half of the lower peninsula was filling up, with probably 85% of the state's population dependent in some way on agriculture for a living. Less than two decades later, exploitation of vast pine forests in northern Michigan had made the state the top lumber producer in the US. Settlers were also attracted to the same area by the discovery of rich mineral deposits, which made Michigan for a time the nation's leading source of iron ore, copper, and salt.

Toward the end of the 19th century, as timber resources were being exhausted and as farming and mining reached their peak stages of development, new opportunities in manufacturing opened up. Such well-known Michigan companies as Kellogg, Dow Chemical, and Upjohn had their origins during this period. The furniture industry in Grand Rapids, the paper industry in Kalamazoo, and numerous other industries were in themselves sufficient to ensure the state's increasing industrial importance.

But the sudden popularity of Ransom E. Olds's Oldsmobile runabout, manufactured first in Lansing, inspired a host of Michiganians to produce similar practical, relatively inexpensive automobiles. By 1904, the most successful of the new models, Detroit's Cadillac (initially a cheap car) and the first Fords, together with the Oldsmobile, had made Michigan the leading automobile producer in the country—and, later, in the world. The key developments in Michigan's auto industry were the creation of General Motors by William C. Durant in 1908; Henry Ford's development of the Model T in 1908, followed by his institution of the moving assembly line in 1913–14; and Walter P. Chrysler's formation in 1925 of the automobile corporation named after him.

Industrialization brought with it urbanization; the census of 1920 for the first time showed a majority of Michiganians living in towns and cities. Nearly all industrial development was concentrated in the southern third of the state, particularly the southeastern Detroit area. The northern two-thirds of the state, where nothing took up the slack left by the decline in lumber and mining output, steadily lost population and became increasingly troubled economically. Meanwhile, the Republican Party, under such progressive governors as Fred Warner and Chase Osborn—and, in the 1920s, under a brilliant administrator, Alexander Groesbeck—showed itself far better able than the Democratic opposition to adjust to the complexities of a booming industrial economy.

The onset of the depression of the 1930s had devastating effects in Michigan. The market for automobiles collapsed; by 1932, half of Michigan's industrial workers were unemployed. The ineffectiveness of the Republican state and federal governments during the crisis led to a landslide victory for the Democrats. In traditionally Republican areas of rural Michigan, the defection to the Democratic Party in 1932 was only temporary, but in the urban industrial areas, the faith of the factory workers in the Republican Party was, for the great majority, permanently shaken. These workers, driven by the desire for greater job security, joined the recruiting campaign launched by the new Congress of Industrial Organizations (CIO). By 1941, with the capitulation of Ford Motor, the United Automobile Workers (UAW) had organized the entire auto industry, and Michigan had been converted to a strongly pro-union state.

Eventually, the liberal leadership of the UAW and of other CIO unions in the state allied itself with the Democratic Party to provide the funds and organization the party needed to mobilize worker support. The coalition elected G. Mennen Williams governor in 1948 and reelected him for five successive two-year terms. By the mid-1950s, the Democrats controlled virtually all statewide elective offices. Because legislative apportionment still reflected an earlier distribution of population, however, the Republicans maintained their control of the legislature and frustrated the efforts of the Williams administration to institute social reforms. In the 1960s, as a result of US Supreme Court rulings, the legislature was reapportioned on a strictly equal-population basis. This shifted a majority of legislative seats into the urban areas, enabling the Democrats generally to control the legislature at that time. Since the early 1980s, the Republicans have controlled the state Senate. (In 1990 Republican John Engler narrowly won the governorship, but won a decisive victory in 1994. In that year the GOP won control of both houses of the state legislature.)

In the meantime, Republican moderates, led by George Romney, gained control of their party's organization. Romney was elected governor in 1962 and served until 1969, when he was succeeded by William G. Milliken, who held the governorship for 14 years. When Milliken chose not to run in the 1982 election, the statehouse was captured by the Democrats, ending 20 years of Republican rule. The new governor faced the immediate tasks of saving Michigan from bankruptcy and reducing the unemployment rate, which had averaged more than 15% in 1982 (60% above the US average).

The nationwide recession of the early 1980s hit Michigan harder than most other states because of its effect on the auto industry, which had already suffered heavy losses primarily as a result of its own inability to foresee the demise of the big luxury cars and because of the increasing share of the American auto market captured by foreign, mostly Japanese, manufacturers. In 1979, Chrysler had been forced to obtain $1.2 billion in federally guaranteed loans to stave off bankruptcy, and during the late 1970s and the first two years of the 1980s, US automakers were forced to lay off hundreds of thousands of workers, tens of thousands of whom left the state. Many smaller businesses, dependent on the auto industry, closed their doors, adding to the unemployment problem and to the state's fiscal problem; as the tax base shrank, state revenues plummeted, creating a budget deficit of nearly $1 billion. Two months after he took office in January 1983, Governor James J. Blanchard was forced to institute budget cuts totaling $225 million and lay off thousands of government workers; and, at his urging, the state legislature increased Michigan's income tax by 38%

As the recession eased in 1983, Michigan's economy showed some signs of improvement. The automakers became profitable, and Chrysler was even able to repay its $1.2 billion in loans seven years before it was due, rehire 100,000 workers, and make plans to build a $500-million technological center in the city of Rochester. By May 1984, Michigan's unemployment rate had begun to drop, but the state faced the difficult task of restructuring its economy to lessen its dependence on the auto industry.

By the late 1980s, there were signs that Michigan had succeeded in diversifying its economy. Fewer than one in four wage earners worked in factories in 1988, a drop from 30% in 1978. Despite continued layoffs and plant closings by auto manufacturers between 1982 and 1988, Michigan added half a million more jobs than it lost. Many of the new jobs were in small engineering and applied technology companies which found opportunities in the big manufacturers' efforts to automate. The state established a $100 million job retraining program to upgrade the skills of displaced factory workers, and contributed $5 million to a joint job training program created by General Motors and the United Automobile Workers. In the mid-1990s, the manufacture of transportation equipment was still Michigan's most important industry, with 28% of domestic automobiles produced in the state. Employment, wages, exports, and housing starts were all on the rise.

12 STATE GOVERNMENT

Michigan has had four constitutions. The first, adopted in 1835 when Michigan was applying for statehood, was followed by constitutions adopted in 1850, 1908, and 1963.

The legislature consists of a senate of 38 members, elected for terms of four years, and a house of representatives of 110 members, elected for two-year terms. The legislature meets annually for a session of indeterminate length. Special sessions may be called by the governor. Legislation may be adopted by a majority of each house, but to override a governor's veto, a two-thirds vote of the members of each house is required. A legislator must be at least 21 years of age, a US citizen, and a qualified voter of the district in which he or she resides. The legislative salary was $49,155 in 1995.

Elected executive officials include the governor and lieutenant governor (who run jointly), secretary of state, and attorney general, all serving four-year terms. Elections are held in even-numbered years between US presidential elections. The governor and lieutenant governor must be at least 30 years old. US citizens, and must have been registered voters in the state for at least four years prior to election. In 1996 the governor's salary was $121,166. The governor appoints the members of the governing boards and/or directors of 19 executive departments, with the exception of the Department of Education, whose head is appointed by the elected State Board of Education.

Legislative action is completed when a bill has been passed by both houses of the legislature and signed by the governor. A bill also becomes law if not signed by the governor after a 14-day period when the legislature is in session. The governor may stop passage of a bill by vetoing it or, if the legislature adjourns before the 14-day period expires, by refusing to sign it.

The constitution may be amended by a two-thirds vote of both houses of the legislature and a majority vote at the next general election. An amendment also may be proposed by registered voters through petition and submission to the general electorate. Every 16 years, the question of calling a convention to revise the constitution must be submitted to the voters; the question was put on the ballot in 1978 and was rejected.

To be eligible to vote in Michigan, one must be a US citizen, 18 years of age, and must have been a resident of the state and precinct for 30 days.

13POLITICAL PARTIES

From its birth in 1854 through 1932, the Republican Party dominated state politics, rarely losing statewide elections and developing strong support in all parts of the state, both rural and urban. The problems caused by the economic depression of the 1930s revitalized the Democratic Party and made Michigan a strong two-party state. Democratic strength was concentrated in metropolitan Detroit, while Republicans maintained their greatest strength in "outstate" areas, except for the mining regions of the upper peninsula, where the working class, hit hard by the depression, supported the Democrats.

Most labor organizations, led by the powerful United Automobile Workers union, have generally supported the Democratic Party since the 1930s. But in recent years, moderate Republicans have had considerable success in attracting support among previously Democratic voters.

Between 1948 and 1992, the Republican candidate for president carried Michigan in 9 out of 13 elections, but Michiganians gave Democrat Bill Clinton 44% of the vote in 1992 and 52% in 1996. In that election, Bob Dole trailed with 38% of the vote; Independent Ross Perot picked up close to 9%. In the 1994 mid-term elections, Republican governor John Engler was reelected. Three-term Democratic Senator Carl Levin was reelected in 1996. Republican Spencer Abraham was elected to the Senate in 1994, replacing retiring Democrat Donald Riegel. In 1995, the state's 16-member US House delegation consisted of 6 Democrats and 10 Republicans. There were 16 Republicans and 22 Democrats in the Michigan state senate, and 58 Democrats and 52 Republicans in the state house.

There were 333 blacks and 8 Hispanics in public office in 1994. In 1995, 35 women served in the state legislature and in elective executive office.

Among minor parties, only Theodore Roosevelt's Progressive Party, which captured the state's electoral vote in 1912, has succeeded in winning a statewide contest. George Wallace captured 10% of the total vote cast for president in 1968; Ross Perot almost doubled that showing in 1992 with 19% of the vote.

14LOCAL GOVERNMENT

In 1992 there were 2,722 separate units of local government in Michigan, including 83 counties, 534 municipal governments, 1,242 townships, 585 school districts, and 277 special districts. Each county is administered by a county board of commissioners whose members, ranging in number from 3 to 35 according to population, are elected for two-year terms. Executive authority is vested in 5 officers elected for four-year terms: the sheriff, prosecuting attorney, treasurer, clerk, and register of deeds. An increasing number of counties are placing overall administrative responsibility in the hands of a county manager or administrator.

Most cities are governed by home-rule legislation, adopted in 1909, enabling them to establish their own form of government under an adopted charter. Some charters provide for the election of a mayor, who usually functions as the chief executive officer of the city. Other cities have chosen the council-manager system. with a council appointing the manager to serve as chief executive and the office of mayor being largely ceremonial. Many villages

Michigan Presidential Vote by Political Parties, 1948–96

YEAR	ELECTORAL VOTE	MICHIGAN WINNER	DEMOCRAT	REPUBLICAN	PROGRESSIVE	SOCIALIST	PROHIBITION
1948	19	Dewey (R)	1,003,448	1,038,595	46,515	6,063	13,052
						SOC. WORKERS	
1952	20	*Eisenhower (R)	1,230,657	1,551,529	3,922	655	10,331
1956	20	*Eisenhower (R)	1,359,898	1,713,647	—	—	6,923
					SOC. LABOR		
1960	20	*Kennedy (D)	1,687,269	1,620,428	1,718	4,347	2,029
1964	21	*Johnson (D)	2,136,615	1,060,152	1,704	3,817	
							AMERICAN IND.
1968	21	Humphrey (D)	1,593,082	1,370,665	1,762	4,099	331,968
							AMERICAN
1972	21	*Nixon (R)	1,459,435	1,961,721	2,437	1,603	63,321
					PEOPLE'S		LIBERTARIAN
1976	21	Ford (R)	1,696,714	1,893,742	3,504	1,804	5,406
					CITIZENS	COMMUNIST	
1980	21	*Reagan (R)	1,661,532	1,915,225	11,930	3,262	41,597
1984	20	*Reagan (R)	1,529,638	2,251,571	1,191	—	10,055
					NEW ALLIANCE	WORKERS LEAGUE	
1988	20	*Bush (R)	1,675,783	1,965,486	2,513	1,958	18,336
					IND. (PEROT)	TISCH IND. CITIZENS	
1992	18	*Clinton (D)	1,871,182	1,554,940	824,813	8,263	10,175
1996	18	*Clinton (D)	1,989,653	1,481,212	336,670	—	27,670

*Won US presidential election

are incorporated under home-rule legislation in order to provide services such as police and fire protection.

Each county is divided into two types of townships, geographical and political. Each geographical (or congressional) township has an area of 36 sq mi (93 sq km); in sparsely populated areas, parts of two or more geographical townships may be combined into one political township. Township government, its powers strictly limited by state law, consists of a supervisor, clerk, treasurer, and up to four trustees, all elected for four-year terms and together forming the township board.

15 STATE SERVICES

Educational services are handled in part by the Department of Education, which distributes state school-aid funds, certifies teachers, and operates the School for the Deaf at Flint, the School for the Blind at Lansing, the State Technical Institute and Rehabilitation Center at Plainwell, and the state library system. The 13 state-supported colleges and universities are independent of the department's control, each being governed by an elected or appointed board. Although most of the funds administered by the Department of Transportation go for highway construction and maintenance, some allocations support improvements of railroad, bus, ferry, air, and port services.

Health and welfare services are provided by the Department of Public Health, the Department of Metal Health, the Family Independence Agency, and the Department of Civil Rights, as well as through programs administered by the Department of Labor, the Commission on Services to the Aging, the Michigan Women's Commission, the Indian Affairs Commission, the Spanish-Speaking Affairs Commission, and the Veterans Trust Fund. The state's Army and Air National Guard units are maintained by the Department of Military Affairs. Civil defense is part of the Department of State Police, and state prisons and other correctional facilities are maintained by the Department of Corrections.

Housing services are provided by the State Housing Development Authority. The Department of Labor establishes and enforces rules and standards relating to safety, wages, licenses, fees, and conditions of employment Security Commission administers unemployment benefits and assists job seekers.

16 JUDICIAL SYSTEM

Michigan's highest court is the state supreme court, consisting of 7 justices elected for eight-year terms; the chief justice is elected by the members of the court. The high court hears cases on appeal from lower state courts and also administers the state's entire court system. The 1963 constitution provided for an 18-member court of appeals to handle most of the cases that previously had clogged the high court's calendar. Unless the supreme court agrees to review a court of appeals ruling, the latter's decision is final. As of the 1990s, six appeals court justices are elected from each of four districts for six-year terms. The supreme court appoints a chief judge of the appeals court.

The major trial courts in the state as of 1997 were the 57 circuit courts, encompassing 181 judicial seats, with the judges elected for six-year terms. The circuit courts have original jurisdiction in all felony criminal cases, civil cases involving sums of more than $10,000, and divorces. Beginning in January 1998, the circuit courts will have a "family" division to better serve families and individuals. The circuit courts also hear appeals from lower courts and state administrative agencies. Probate courts have original jurisdiction in cases involving juveniles and dependents, and also handle wills and estates, adoptions, and commitments of the mentally ill. The 1963 constitution provided for the abolition of justice-of-the-peace courts and nearly all municipal courts, although the Detroit "Recorders Court" was not abolished until 1996 in a controversial move supported by the Republican

governor and legislative majority but opposed by most Democratic leaders. To replace them, 101 district courts, some consisting of two or more divisions, have been established. These courts, employing 259 judges, handle civil cases involving sums of less than $10,000, minor criminal violations, and preliminary examinations in all felony cases. Michigan had 27,600 licensed attorneys in 1996.

Prisoners in state or federal correctional facilities numbered 40,416 in 1995, or 423 per 100,000 inhabitants. Detroit received adverse publicity during the 1970s as the "murder capital of the world," with more murders and other violent crimes than any other US city. Violent crimes (murder, nonnegligent manslaughter, forcible rape, and aggravated assault) reached a peak of 2,226 offenses per 100,000 population in 1976; the city's rate subsequently declined, falling to 880.8 in 1996. Michigan had an overall 1996 crime rate of 5,182.8 per 100,000 population, including a rate of 687.8 for violent crime and 4,495 for property crime.

In 1846, Michigan became the first state to abolish capital punishment, and recent efforts to restore capital punishment have failed.

17 ARMED FORCES

In 1996, there were 1,248 active duty military personnel in Michigan. The Detroit Arsenal at Warren is the state's largest center for civilians, employing 4,144. In 1995/96 Michigan firms received over $1.2 billion in defense contracts.

As of 1 July 1996 there were an estimated 940,000 veterans of US military service living in Michigan. Of these, fewer than 500 saw service during World War I, 246,000 in World War II, 144,000 in the Korean conflict, 292,000 during the Vietnam era, and 67,000 during the Persian Gulf War. Veterans' benefits exceeded $1.06 million in 1995/96.

Approximately 39,590 personnel were allocated to Michigan's National Guard and Reserve units in 1996. In recent decades, the units have frequently been called out for riot duty and to aid in the aftermath of natural disasters such as tornadoes and heavy snowstorms. In 1993, the Michigan State Police employed 1,986 full-time sworn officers, or 2 per 10,000 residents.

18 MIGRATION

The earliest European immigrants were the French and English. The successive opening of interior lands for farming, lumbering, mining, and manufacturing proved an irresistible attraction for hundreds of thousands of immigrants after the War of 1812, principally Germans, Canadians, English, Irish, and Dutch. During the second half of the 19th century, lumbering and mining opportunities in northern Michigan attracted large numbers of Cornishmen, Norwegians, Swedes, and Finns. The growth of manufacturing in southern Michigan at the end of the century brought many Poles, Italians, Russians, Belgians, and Greeks to the state. After World War II, many more Europeans immigrated to Michigan, plus smaller groups of Mexicans, other Spanish-speaking peoples from Latin America, and large numbers of Arabic-speaking peoples, particularly in Detroit, who by the late 1970s were more numerous there than in any other US city.

The first large domestic migration into Michigan came in the early 19th century after the War of 1812. Heavy immigration took place in the 1920s and 1930s, especially from northeastern states, particularly New York and Pennsylvania, and from Ohio. Beginning in 1916, the demand for labor in Michigan's factories started the second major domestic migration to Michigan, this time by southern blacks, who settled mainly in Detroit, Flint, Pontiac, Grand Rapids, and Saginaw. During World War 11, many southern whites migrated to the same industrial areas. Between 1940 and 1970, a net total of 518,000 migrants were drawn to Michigan. The economic problems of the auto industry in the 1970s and 1980s caused a significant reversal of this trend, with the state suffering a net loss of 496,000 by out-migration in the 1970s and over 460,000 in the 1980s. Between 1990 and 1996, Michigan had a net loss of 139,169 in domestic migration and a net gain of 60,903 in international migration. In 1996, Michigan's foreign-born population totaled 491,000, or 5% of its total population. In the same year, 17,253 foreign immigrants entered the state, the 11th-highest total for any state that year.

Intrastate migration has been characterized since the late 19th century by a steady movement from rural to urban areas. Most parts of northern Michigan have suffered a loss of population since the early years of this century, although a back-to-the-land movement, together with the growth of rural Michigan as a retirement area, appeared to reverse this trend beginning in the 1970s. Since 1950, the central cities have experienced a steady loss of population to the suburbs, in part caused by the migration of whites from areas that were becoming increasingly black. As of 1990, just under three-fourths of all state residents had been born in Michigan. About 57% of the state's population age 5 and older lived in the same house in 1990 as in 1985; of those who lived in a different house in 1985, only 18% did so in another state.

19INTERGOVERNMENTAL COOPERATION

The Commission on Intergovernmental Cooperation of the Michigan legislature represents the state in dealings with the Council of State Governments and its allied organizations. Since 1935, the state has joined at least 18 interstate compacts, dealing mainly with such subjects as gas and oil problems, law enforcement, pest control, civil defense, tax reciprocity, and water resources. In 1985, Michigan, seven other Great Lakes states, and the Canadian provinces of Quebec and Ontario signed the Great Lakes Charter, designed to protect the lakes' water resources.

The International Bridge Authority, consisting of members from Michigan and Canada, operates a toll bridge connecting Sault Ste. Marie, Mich., and Sault Ste. Marie, Ontario. Federal aid to Michigan totaled over $7.1 billion in 1995/96.

20ECONOMY

On the whole, Michigan benefited from its position as the center of the auto industry during the first half of the 20th century, when Detroit and other south Michigan cities were the fastest-growing industrial areas in the US. But the state's dependence on automobile production has caused grave and persistent economic problems since the 1950s. Michigan's unemployment rates in times of recession have far exceeded the national average, since auto sales are among the hardest hit in such periods. Even in times of general prosperity, the auto industry's emphasis on labor-saving techniques and its shifting of operation from the state have reduced the number of jobs available to Michigan workers. Although the state was relatively prosperous during the record automotive production years of the 1960s and 1970s, the high cost of gasoline and the encroachment of imports on domestic car sales had disastrous effects by 1980, when it became apparent that the state's future economic health required greater diversification of industry. After manufacturing, agriculture, still dominant in the rural areas of southern Michigan, probably remains the most important element in the state's economy, although tourism, heavily promoted in recent years, now rivals agriculture as a source of income. In northern Michigan, forestry and mining continue but generally at levels far below earlier boom periods.

In the mid-1980s, Michigan's most immediate problem was the high rate of unemployment resulting from the deep decline in domestic car sales. Employment in car manufacturing dropped 16.5 percent between 1981 and 1991, and manufacturing employment as a whole dropped 6 percent in those years. Jobs in the non-manufacturing sector, on the other hand, increased 59.9

percent. Service jobs increased 5 percent and wholesale and retail trade grew 3 percent. By 1991, both the trade and service sectors employed more people than the manufacturing industry. Michigan's gross state product in 1994 was $240,390 million, to which private goods-producing industries contributed $83,310 million; private services-producing industries, $131,159; and government, $25,922.

In 1996, there were 31,799 bankruptcy filings in the state, up 29% from the previous year.

21INCOME

In 1996, Michigan had per capita personal income of $24,810, 16th among the 50 states. Total disposable personal income in 1996 was $205.1 billion, up from $197.6 billion in 1995.

In 1995, the median household income was $36,426. In 1995, about 12.2% of the population lived below the federal poverty level.

22LABOR

Michigan ranked 7th in the US in the size of its labor force in 1996, with 4,807,000 workers, of whom an average of 234,000, or 4.9%, were unemployed.

At the end of 1996, nonagricultural employment consisted of the following: mining, 7,800; construction, 169,200; manufacturing, 966,300; transportation and public utilities, 170,200; wholesale and retail trade, 1,070,000; services, 1,167,400; and government, 659,000.

The unemployment rate in Michigan exceeded the national average in the late 1970s and early 1980s. It reached a peak of 17.1% in December 1982, when the national rate was at a peak of 10.7%.

In 1995, Michigan had some 947,200 union members, or about 23.7% of the work force. Among manufacturing workers, unionization was 33.9%, the highest rate among the states. Michigan's most powerful and influential industrial union since the 1930s has been the United Automobile Workers (UAW), with nearly 751,000 members nationwide in 1995; its national headquarters is in Detroit. Under its long-time president Walter Reuther and his successors, Leonard Woodcock, Douglas Fraser, Owen Bieber, and Stephen Yokich, the union has been a dominant force in the state Democratic Party. In recent years, as government employees and teachers have been organized, unions and associations representing these groups have become increasingly influential. Under the Michigan Public Employment Relations Act of 1965, public employees have the right to organize and to engage in collective bargaining, but are prohibited from striking. However, strikes of teachers, college faculty members, and government employees have been common since the 1960s, and little or no effort was made to enforce the law. However, labor legislation passed during the Engler administration regarding public employees, especially public school teachers, has changed the way they are restricted.

Certain crafts and trades were organized in Michigan in the 19th century, with one national labor union, the Brotherhood of Locomotive Engineers, having been founded at meetings in Michigan in 1863, but efforts to organize workers in the lumber and mining industries were generally unsuccessful. Michigan acquired a reputation as an open-shop state, and factory workers showed little interest in unions at a time when wages were high. But the catastrophic impact of the depression of the 1930s completely changed these attitudes. With the support of sympathetic state and federal government officials, Michigan workers were in the forefront of the greatest labor-organizing drive in American history. The successful sit-down strike by the United Automobile Workers against General Motors in 1936–37 marked the first major victory of the new Congress of Industrial Organizations. Since then, a strong labor movement has provided manufacturing workers in Michigan with some of the most favorable working conditions in the country. As of December 1996, the average weekly earnings of production workers had reached $773.83.

23AGRICULTURE

In 1995, Michigan's agricultural income was estimated at over $3.5 billion, placing Michigan 20th among the 50 states. About 62% came from crops and the rest from livestock and livestock products; dairy products, cattle, corn, and soybeans were the principal commodities. The state in 1996 ranked 1st in output of tart cherries, 2d in prunes and plums, and 4th in apples.

The growing of corn and other crops indigenous to North America was introduced in Michigan by the Indians around 100 BC and early French settlers tried to develop European-style agriculture during the colonial era. But little progress was made until well into the 19th century, when farmers from New York and New England poured into the interior of southern Michigan. By mid-century, 34,000 farms had been established, and the number increased to a peak of about 207,000 in 1910. The major cash crop at first was wheat, until soil exhaustion, insect infestations, bad winters, and competition from huge wheat farms to the west forced a de-emphasis on wheat and a move toward agricultural diversity. Both the number of farms and the amount of farm acreage had declined by 1996 to 53,000 farms and 10,600,000 acres (4,300,000 hectares).

The southern half of the lower peninsula is the principal agricultural region, and the area along Lake Michigan is a leader in fruit growing. Potatoes are profitable in northern Michigan, while eastern Michigan (the "Thumb" area near Lake Huron) is a leading bean producer. The Saginaw Valley leads the state in sugar beets. The south-central and southeastern counties are major centers of soybean production. Leading field crops in 1996 included 216,200,000 bushels of corn for grain, valued at $518,880,000; 46,740,000 bushels of soybeans, worth $313,158,000; and 23,940,000 bushels of wheat, worth $93,366,000. Output of commercial apples totaled 725,000,000 lb (329,000,000 kg).

24ANIMAL HUSBANDRY

The same areas of southern Michigan that lead in crop production also lead in livestock and livestock products, except that the northern counties are more favorable for dairying than for crop production.

In 1997, there were an estimated 1.13 million cattle and calves, valued at $757 million. The state had an estimated 1 million hogs and pigs, valued at $95 million.

In 1995, dairy farmers had an estimated 326,000 milk cows which produced around 5.6 million lb (2.5 million kg) of milk. Poultry farmers produced nearly 1.4 billion eggs, valued at around $50 million, in 1995.

25FISHING

Commercial fishing, once an important factor in the state's economy, is relatively minor today; the commercial catch in 1995 was 14,331,000 lb (6,500,00 kg) valued at $10,143,000. Principal species landed are silver salmon and alewives.

Sport fishing continues to flourish and is one of the state's major tourist attractions. A state salmon-planting program, begun in the mid-1960s, has made salmon the most popular game fish for Great Lakes sport fishermen. The state has also sought, through breeding and stocking programs, to bring back the trout, which was devastated by an invasion of lamprey. In 1995/96, federal authorities distributed 4 million (247,737 lb or 112,374 kg) coldwater species fish and 15.9 million fish eggs within the state. In 1995/96, the state issued 1,464,027 sport fishing licenses.

A bitter dispute raged during the 1970s between state officials and Ottawa and Ojibwa commercial fishermen, who claimed that Indian treaties with the federal government exempted them from state fishing regulations. The state contended that without such regulations, Indian commercial fishing would have a devastating impact on the northern Great Lakes' fish population. A federal court in 1979 upheld the Indians' contention; but in 1985, the state secured federal court approval of a compromise settlement intended to satisfy both Indian and non-Indian groups.

26FORESTRY

In 1993, Michigan's forestland totaled 19.3 million acres (7.8 million hectares), or more than half the state's total land area. Approximately 97% of it is classified as timberland, about two-thirds of it privately owned. The major forested regions are in the northern two-thirds of the state, where great pine forests enabled Michigan to become the leading lumber-producing state in the last four decades of the 19th century. These cutover lands regenerated naturally or were reforested in the 20th century. The value of shipments by the lumber and wood products industry in 1995 exceeded $2 billion; by the paper and allied products industry, $5.4 billion.

State and national forests cover 6.3 million acres (2.5 million hectares), or more than one-sixth of the state's land area.

27MINING

Nonfuel mineral production was valued at $1.47 billion in 1995 in Michigan, virtually unchanged from 1994. The state ranked 8th nationally in value of nonfuel minerals produced during 1995, accounting for 4% of the national total. Michigan continued to lead the nation in the quantity and value of crude iron oxide pigments, magnesium chloride, and peat produced, and ranked second in the nation in the production of bromine, iron ore, and industrial sand. Michigan is second only to Minnesota in iron ore production, the most valuable commodity produced, followed by portland cement. In 1992, the production of 4.56 million metric tons of portland cement was worth $293 million. Over 53 million metric tons of construction sand and gravel were valued at $183 million. Crushed stone production, at 40.8 million metric tons, was worth $40.8 million.

In 1995, Michigan's Geological Survey Division reported that five companies drilled 46 mineral exploration and development holes. Diamond, copper, and gold exploration continue in the Upper Peninsula, and natural gas exploration in Crawford, Montmorency, Oscoda, and Otsego counties.

28ENERGY AND POWER

Michigan's energy supply is provided primarily by private utility companies. In 1994, energy consumption per capita totaled 325.1 million Btu (81.9 million kcal), which ranked Michigan 30th among the 50 states. Coal is the principal source of fuel used in generating electric power, while natural gas is the major fuel used for other energy needs.

The installed electric generating capacity of electric utilities and industrial plants at the end of 1995 was 23.8 million kW; electric energy production totaled 92.5 billion kWh. Hydroelectric plants, which had produced more than 10% of the state's electric energy in 1947, yielded less than 1% in 1995; coal-fired steam units produced 71%, nuclear-powered units 26%, and other units about 2%.

The two major electric utilities are Detroit Edison, serving the Detroit area and portions of the eastern part of the lower peninsula, and Consumers Power, serving most of the remainder of the lower peninsula. Michigan electric companies had combined retail sales in 1995 of 94.86 billion kWh. Of total sales, 30% went to residential users, 69% to commercial and industrial users, and the remainder for street and highway lighting and other public uses. Rates of the utility companies are set by the Public Service Commission.

Michigan is dependent on outside sources for most of its fuel needs. Petroleum production in 1996 totaled 10.8 million barrels, less than 1% of total US production; natural gas marketed production was 238.2 billion cu feet (6.7 billion cu m), less than one-fourth the natural gas consumed in the state. Proved petroleum reserves were 76 million barrels at the end of 1995, natural gas reserves, 1.3 trillion cu ft (36.8 billion cu m). Bituminous coal reserves (estimated at 127.7 million tons) remain in southern Michigan, but production is negligible.

[29]INDUSTRY

Manufacturing, a minor element in Michigan's economy in the mid-19th century, grew rapidly in importance until, by 1900, an estimated 25% of the state's jobholders were factory workers. The rise of the auto industry in the early 20th century completed the transformation of Michigan into one of the most important manufacturing areas in the world. In 1995, the value of shipments totaled $204 billion; new capital expenditures, $7.827 billion. The following table shows the value of shipments for major sectors in 1995:

Transportation equipment	$85,179,000,000
Fabricated metal products	18,928,600,000
Food and food products	13,251,900,000
Chemicals and chemical products	11,645,400,000
Primary metals	8,912,600,000
Rubber and plastic products	8,844,200,000
Printing and publishing	5,611,500,000
Furniture and fixtures	5,668,600,000
Paper and paper products	5,355,900,000
Electric and electronic equipment	3,807,900,000
Petroleum and coal products	1,485,600,000

Motor vehicles and equipment dominate the state's economy, with a payroll of $7.7 billion in 1991, representing more than one-fourth of the state's manufacturing payroll; the value of shipments by automotive manufacturers was $56.5 billion, or 39% of the total. Production of nonelectrical machinery, primary and fabricated metal products, and metal forgings and stampings was directly related to automobile production. From 1983 to 1991, total investment in manufacturing exceeded $5.6 billion, second only to California.

The Detroit metropolitan area is the major industrial region: this area includes not only the heavy concentration of auto-related plants in Wayne, Oakland, and Macomb counties, but also major steel, chemical, and pharmaceutical industries, among others. Flint, Grand Rapids, Saginaw, Ann Arbor, Lansing, and Kalamazoo are other major industrial centers.

Because the auto industry's "Big Three"—General Motors (GM), Ford, and Chrysler—have their headquarters in the Detroit area, Michigan has had for many years three of the nation's largest industrial corporations. In 1992, General Motors was the leader among all manufacturers in the world. The recession of 1979/80 forced Chrysler to obtain federally guaranteed loans of $1.2 billion and to borrow $150 million from the state in order to stave off bankruptcy. In 1997, Michigan hosted the headquarters of 14 Fortune 500 companies, including General Motors, Ford, and Chrysler (ranked 1st, 2d, and 9th, respectively). In 1996, there were 3,091 US patents issued to Michigan residents.

The auto industry's preponderance in Michigan manufacturing has come to be viewed in recent years as more of a liability than an asset. When times are good, as they were in the 1960s and early 1970s, automobile sales soar to record levels and Michigan's economy prospers. But when the national economy slumps, these sales plummet, pushing the state into a far deeper recession than is felt by the nation as a whole. In the 1970s, the escalating cost of gasoline and the slowness of Michigan automakers in providing small, fuel-efficient cars to meet foreign competition caused a severe decline in domestic motor vehicle sales. As of 1993, Michigan had 19 auto production facilities which accounted for about one-quarter of US car and truck production. Employment in motor vehicle manufacturing fell from 319,400 in 1981 to 266,700 in 1991.

[30]COMMERCE

In 1992, Michigan had 15,517 wholesale establishments, with sales of $125.7 billion, of which 67.3% was in durable goods. Leading categories were motor vehicles and automobile parts and supplies (accounting for nearly one-fifth of all sales by value), groceries, metals and minerals, and machinery.

In 1992, Michigan's 54,519 retail establishments had sales of $71.5 billion, 8th among the states and 3.8% of the US total. The Detroit–Ann Arbor–Flint area had retail sales of $41.6 billion in 1992, or 58% of the state's total. The importance of retail sales to the economy was greatest in northern Michigan.

With its ports open to oceangoing vessels through the St. Lawrence Seaway, Michigan is a major exporting and importing state for foreign as well as domestic markets. Exports of Michigan's manufactured goods totaled $27.6 billion in 1996, 4th in the US.

[31]CONSUMER PROTECTION

The Michigan Consumer's Council—composed of the attorney general, secretary of state, director of the Department of Commerce, and three members appointed by the governor and three by the legislature—was established in 1966 to protect consumers from harmful products, false advertising, and deceptive sales practices. The Council was dissolved in 1990 as a budget-cutting measure. Other state agencies, such as the Department of Licensing and Regulation and the Public Service Commission, also are responsible for protecting consumers.

A number of local governments have instituted consumer affairs offices, with Detroit's being especially active.

[32]BANKING

Michigan's banks in the territorial and early statehood years were generally wildcat speculative ventures. More restrained banking activities date from the 1840s, when the state's oldest bank, the Detroit Bank and Trust, was founded. A crisis that developed in the early 1930s forced Governor William Comstock to close all banks in February 1933 in order to prevent collapse of the entire banking system. Federal and state authorities supervised a reorganization and reform of the state's banks that has succeeded in preventing any major problems from arising since that time.

In 1992, insured Michigan commercial banks and savings institutions employed 52,270 persons and had total payrolls of $1.7 billion. There were 176 insured commercial banks in 1996, with assets of $112.2 billion, loans exceeding $81.7 billion, and deposits of $84.2 billion.

There were 24 federally insured savings institutions, with total assets of $25.5 billion in 1996. There were two state-chartered savings banks, with total assets of $1 billion as of 31 December 1996.

[33]INSURANCE

In 1995, 26 life insurance companies were based in Michigan. Life insurance benefit payments totaled $2.8 billion. There were 13,494,000 life insurance policies in force, valued at $361.1 billion; the average family had $100,500 worth of life insurance coverage. Property and liability companies wrote premiums of $2.2 billion in automobile physical damage coverage, and $935.5 million in homeowners' insurance.

³⁴SECURITIES

There are no securities or commodity exchanges in Michigan.

New York Stock Exchange member firms have sales offices and full-time registered representatives in the state.

³⁵PUBLIC FINANCE

The state constitution requires the governor to submit a budget proposal to the legislature each year. This executive budget, prepared by the Department of Management and Budget, is reviewed, revised, and passed by the legislature. During the fiscal year, which extends from 1 October to 30 September, if actual revenues drop below anticipated levels, the governor, in consultation with the legislative appropriations committees, must reduce expenditures to meet the constitutional requirement that the state budget be kept in balance.

In 1977, the legislature created a budget stabilization fund; a portion of tax revenues collected in good times is held in reserve to be used during periods of recession, when the funding of essential state services is threatened. In 1978, a tax limitation amendment put a lid on government spending by establishing a fixed ratio of state revenues to personal income in the state. Further efforts to limit taxes were rejected by the voters in 1980 and 1984.

The following is a summary of recommended revenues and expenditures for 1996/97 and 1997/98 (in millions of dollars):

REVENUES	1996/97	1997/98
Income tax (net)	5,926.9	6,199.0
Sales tax	5,405.0	5,660.0
Use tax	1,103.3	1,155.0
Business tax	2,288.0	2,390.0
Lottery	591.0	605.0
Federal aid	7,100.0	7,200.0
Other receipts	7,416.1	7,698.0
EXPENDITURES		
Family Independence Agency	$3,019.5	$3,102.2
School Aid Fund	8,595.5	9,136.9
Higher Education Institution	1,865.2	1,926.8
Community Health	6,866.5	7,000.2
Dept. of Corrections	1,423.1	1,463.2
Other current operations	7,644.1	7,775.0
Capital outlay	352.2	397.1
Debt service	64.2	105.6
TOTALS	$29,830.3	$30,907.0

The total state debt in 1996 was more than $3 billion, or $243.18 per capita.

³⁶TAXATION

Until the 1930s, Michigan relied mainly on the property tax for revenues to support both local and state governments. A state sales tax, first imposed in 1933, and a state income tax, first levied in 1967, are now the main sources of state revenues. Property taxes are reserved entirely to local governments.

The state income tax in 1996 was 4.4% on all income. The state sales tax was 6% on most retail purchases, except food. An inheritance tax ranging from 2% to 17% was levied on inheritances of more than $100, with the first $65,000 to the spouse and the first $10,000 to other close relatives being exempt. Other state taxes and fees are levied on corporate and financial-institution income, cigarettes, alcoholic beverages, pari-mutuel wagering, and gasoline and other fuels.

Michigan's share of the federal tax burden in 1995 was $48.3 billion; the per capita share was $5,065.

³⁷ECONOMIC POLICY

Michigan has a long tradition of promoting economic development. The Michigan Jobs Commission (MJC) is the single point of contact for all economic development and job training programs. The mission of MJC is to work with businesses, state government, and local communities to make Michigan more business-friendly.

Michigan is part of the so-called Rust Belt, the region of the country dominated by steel-based industries from the 1940s to the 1980s. To focus economic development on new industries, Michigan has taken a number of steps, including cutting taxes for individuals and businesses. In the 1990s, Michigan taxpayers, both individuals and businesses, benefited from 21 tax cuts. The result has been a robust economy with unemployment levels at an all-time low.

Michigan's Economic Development Job Training program makes nearly $40 million available to new and existing companies to train or retrain workers. Michigan's Economic Growth Authority offers generous tax breaks to firms that locate a facility in Michigan, and offers substantial employment opportunities to Michigan workers. The state's Renaissance Zone program exempts companies and individuals within designated areas throughout the state from all state and local taxes as an incentive to rebuild and revitalize specific areas.

³⁸HEALTH

Live births in 1995 totaled 134,642 for a rate of 14.1 per 1,000 people, a decrease from 17.1 per 1,000 in 1990. Infant mortality for the 12 months ending with December 1995 was 8.5 per 1,000 live births. There were 34,496 legal abortions in 1992 (down from 64,200 in 1982), or about 242 per 1,000 live births.

Major causes of death in 1995 (with their rates per 100,000 population) included heart disease, 294.8; cancer, 203.5; cerebrovascular diseases, 61.4; accidents and adverse effects, 33.2 (of which motor vehicle accidents accounted for 50%); and suicide, 4.7. The all-cause death rate of 876.1 per 100,000 population was slightly below the national rate of 880. The AIDS incidence rate for 1995 was only 11.28 per 100,000 population. The US average was 28.48 per 100,000 that same year. The HIV mortality rate of 8.4 per 100,000 was also lower than the US average.

In 1995, Michigan had 167 hospitals, not including 28 nursing homes, with 27,693 beds and a total of 1,116,516 admissions. There were 72,500 full-time, equivalent registered nurses in 1994. The average expense of hospitals for care was $929 per inpatient day and $6,169 per stay. Michigan had 18,896 nonfederal physicians at the beginning of 1994, and 5,750 licensed, active dentists in 1994. Over one-third of Michigan doctors specialized in the primary care fields in 1995.

In Michigan, 11% of residents were uninsured in 1995. There were 1.3 million Medicare and 1.2 million Medicaid recipients receiving $5.6 and $3.3 billion, respectively, in health care in 1994.

³⁹SOCIAL WELFARE

Until the 1930s, Michigan's few limited welfare programs were handled by the counties, but the relief load during the depression shifted the burden to the state and federal levels. In recent decades there have been enormous increases in social welfare programs.

In 1996, recipients of aid to families with dependent children numbered 535,700, with the average monthly payment per family being $563. In 1996, the food stamp program had an average monthly participation of 935,416 people receiving $68.89 per month. Pupils participating in the school lunch program cost the federal government $137.2 million in 1991.

With the enactment of the Personal Responsibility and Work Opportunity Reconciliation Act of 1996, the US government changed the form and regulations for many of its social welfare programs; most significantly, it replaced Aid to Families with Dependent Children (AFDC), an open-ended entitlement program, with Temporary Assistance for Needy Families (TANF), a limited system of assistance funded largely through federal block grants. The reform act also impacted the food stamp program, the Supplemental Security Income program, and the child nutrition program. The law took effect on 1 July 1997 and provided $16.38 billion in block grants for fiscal years 1997–2002. The grants are to be divided among the states based on an equation involving the numbers of former AFDC recipients in each state. Because many of the bill's provisions have yet to be implemented into state-by-state policy, it was not possible to include the details of each state's programs for this edition of this work.

In 1995, persons receiving Social Security benefits included 966,810 retired workers; the average benefit to retired workers in 1991 was $770. Under the Supplemental Security Income program, 210,265 aged, blind, and disabled persons received an average monthly allowance of $364.

40HOUSING

In 1996 there were an estimated 4,021,000 housing units in Michigan, 3,539,000 of which were occupied. Of the 1990 census, a total of 3,847,426 housing units, or 63%, were owner-occupied. During the 1980s, the housing stock increased by only 7%. As of 1990, 21% of all units had been built in 1939 or earlier. In 1996, 52,355 privately owned units, valued at $5.1 billion, were authorized for construction; of these, 43,421 were single-family. During 1995/96, Michigan received $520.4 million in aid from the US Department of Housing and Urban Development, including $149.4 million in community development block grants. A limited amount of state aid for low-income housing is available through the State Housing Development Authority.

41EDUCATION

Historically, Michigan has strongly supported public education, which helps account for the fact that the percentage of students attending public schools is one of the highest in the US. But the cost of maintaining this extensive public educational system has become a major problem in recent years because of the declining school-age population.

In 1990, 76.8% of persons 25 years and over had completed four years of high school. Of the 5,842,642 residents in this age range, 452,893 had completed eight years or less of schooling; 903,866 completed 9th to 12th grade with no diploma; 1,887,449 had graduated from high school; 1,191,518 had some college, but no degree; 392,869 received an associate's degree; 638,267 received a bachelor's degree; and 375,780 received a graduate or professional degree.

In 1993/94 there were 3,301 public schools, including 2,065 elementary schools, 1,205 secondary schools, and 31 combined elementary and secondary schools. Public school enrollment totaled l,655,825 in 1995. In 1993/94 there were 169,113 pupils in non-public schools. The largest number of these were enrolled in Catholic schools, which had 95,047 students in 1993/94. Lutherans, Seventh-Day Adventists, and Reformed and Christian Reformed churches also have maintained schools for some time; in the 1970s, a number of new Christian schools, particularly those of fundamentalist Baptist groups, were established.

In the fall of 1993, Michigan had 15 public universities and 29 community colleges; combined enrollment in 1994 was 551,307. The oldest state school is the University of Michigan, originally established in Detroit in 1817; its Ann Arbor campus was founded in 1835 and classes there began in 1841. Among the public universities, enrollment at the University of Michigan, including the Dearborn and Flint campuses, was 51,178; at Michigan State University, enrollment was 39,743; and Wayne State University's enrollment was 34,280. Michigan also has 54 independent, non-profit colleges and universities with a total enrollment of 85,412. Among the state's private colleges and universities, the University of Detroit Mercy, a Jesuit school, is one of the largest. Kalamazoo College (founded in 1833), Albion College (1835), Hope College (1866) and Alma College (1886) are some of the oldest, private liberal arts colleges in the state.

In 1994/95, per pupil expenditures for public schools amounted to $6,440, well above the US mean of $5,526. Teachers' salaries averaged $48,507 per year in 1994/95, ranking 4th in the country.

42ARTS

Michigan's major center of arts and cultural activities is the Detroit area. The city's refurbished Orchestra Hall is the home of the Detroit Symphony Orchestra as well as chamber music concerts and other musical events. The Music Hall and the Masonic Auditorium present a variety of musical productions; the Fisher Theater is the major home for Broadway productions; and the Detroit Cultural Center supports a number of cultural programs. The new Detroit Opera House is sponsored by the Michigan Opera Theatre. Nearby Meadow Brook, in Rochester, has a summer music program. At the University of Michigan, in Ann Arbor, the Power Center for the Performing Arts and Hill Auditorium host major musical, theatrical, and dance presentations.

Programs relating to the visual arts tend to be academically centered; the University of Michigan, Michigan State, Wayne State, and Eastern Michigan University have notable art schools. The Cranbrook Academy of Arts, which was created by the architect Eliel Saarinen, is a significant art center, and the Ox-bow School at Saugatuck is also outstanding. The Ann Arbor Art Fair, begun in 1959, is the largest and most prestigious summer outdoor art show in the state.

The Meadow Brook Theater at Rochester is perhaps the largest professional theater company; Detroit has a number of little theater groups. Successful summer theaters include the Cherry County Playhouse at Traverse City and the Star Theater in Flint.

The Detroit Symphony Orchestra, founded in 1914, is nationally known. Grand Rapids and Kalamazoo have regional orchestras that perform on a part-time, seasonal basis. The National Music Camp at Interlochen is a mecca for young musicians in the summer.

There are local ballet and opera groups in Detroit and in a few other communities. Michigan's best-known contribution to popular music was that of Berry Gordy, Jr., whose Motown recording company in the 1960s popularized the "Detroit sound" and featured such artists as Diana Ross and the Supremes, Smokey Robinson and the Miracles, Aretha Franklin, the Four Tops, the Temptations, and Stevie Wonder, among many others. In the 1970s however, Gordy moved his operations to California.

The state of Michigan generated federal and state funds for its arts programs in 1996. The NEA contributed $1,021,000 to the programs and $2,278,000 to the Michigan Council for the Arts and Cultural Affairs. The state provided a large share for the activities of the Council. Private sources contributed the greatest amount.

In 1991, there were 1,040 arts associations in Michigan. There were also 101 local arts associations.

In 1996, the Michigan Council for the Arts received funding from the NEA for its arts education program. Grants were received from the NEA's state and regional program, too.

43LIBRARIES AND MUSEUMS

Michigan in 1994/95 had 380 public libraries, 109 academic libraries, and numerous special libraries. In 1994/95, public libraries in the state had a total of nearly 26 million volumes and a circulation exceeding 48.5 million. The Library of Michigan in Lansing functions as the coordinator of library facilities in the state. The largest public library is the Detroit Public Library, which in 1994/95 had 2,504,416 books and print materials in its main library and 25 branches. Outstanding among its special collections are the Burton Historical Collection, a major center for genealogical research, the National Automotive History Collection, and the E. Azalia Hackley Collection, a notable source for material pertaining to African Americans in the performing arts, especially music. Grand Rapids, Kalamazoo, Lansing, Flint, and Ann Arbor are among the larger public libraries.

Among academic libraries, the University of Michigan at Ann Arbor, with 1,874,648 volumes and 69,566 periodical subscriptions in 1995/96, features the William L. Clements collection of books and manuscripts on the colonial period, the Labadie Collection relating to the history of American radicalism, and the Bentley Library's distinctive collection of books and manuscripts, particularly the one on Michigan, the largest such collection.

In 1980, the Gerald R. Ford Presidential Library was opened on U-M's Ann Arbor campus. The Michigan State University Library at East Lansing had 4,047,477 volumes and 5,101,191 microfilm units in 1995/96. At Wayne State University in Detroit, the Walter P. Reuther Library houses the largest collection of labor history records in the US, as well as primary materials relating to social, economic, and political reform and urban affairs.

The Detroit Institute of Arts is the largest art museum in the state and has an outstanding collection of African art. It is located in the Detroit Cultural Center, along with the Public Library and the Detroit Historical Museum, one of the largest local history museums in the country. The Kalamazoo Institute of Art, the Flint Institute of Art, the Grand Rapids Art Museum, and the Hackley Art Gallery in Muskegon are important art museums. The University of Michigan and the Cranbrook Academy of Arts in Bloomfield Hills also maintain important collections.

The Detroit Historical Museum heads 223 museums in the state, including the State Historical Museum in Lansing and museums in Grand Rapids, Flint, Kalamazoo, and Dearborn. In the latter city, the privately run Henry Ford Museum and Greenfield Village are leading tourist attractions. In 1996 the world's largest museum of African American history was established in Detroit. A major Holocaust Memorial Center is located in the West Bloomfield Hills area of metropolitan Detroit.

The major historical sites open to the public include the late-18th-century fort on Mackinac Island and the reconstructed early-18th-century fort at Mackinaw City. The latter site has also been the scene of an archaeological program that has accumulated one of the largest collections of 18th-century artifacts in the country. Major investigations of prehistoric Indian sites have also been conducted in recent years.

44COMMUNICATIONS

Michigan's remote position in the interior of the continent hampered the development of adequate communications services, and the first regular postal service was not instituted until the early 19th century.

Telephone service began in Detroit in 1877. By March 1993, 96.3% of the 3,557,000 occupied housing units in the state had telephones.

Michigan had 129 AM radio stations and 235 FM stations in 1996. Radio station WWJ, originally owned by the *Detroit News*, began operating in 1920 as one of the country's first commercial broadcasting stations, and the *News* also started Michigan's first television station in 1947. As of 1993 there were 40 commercial television stations and 10 educational stations in the state. There were also 28 large cable television systems serving the state in 1996.

45PRESS

The first newspaper to appear in Michigan was Father Richard's *Michigan Essay or Impartial Observer,* published in August 1917. Continuous newspaper coverage in Michigan dates from the appearance of the weekly *Detroit Gazette,* also in 1817. The state's oldest paper still being published is the *Detroit Free Press,* founded in 1831 and the state's first daily paper since 1835.

In 1997 there were 50 daily newspapers in Michigan. In addition, 23 Sunday editions were published in the state and there were also 331 weekly or other non-daily newspapers. The number of daily papers has declined in recent decades. Two of the state's largest newspapers—Knight Ridder's *Detroit Free Press* and Gannett's *Detroit News*—entered into a joint operating agreement (JOA) in 1989. The advertising, business, delivery, and production of each paper joined forces in a company called Detroit Newspapers; the editorial and news operations remain separate and report to their respective parent companies. During the struggle, the *Detroit Journal* was published weekly by locked-out newspaper workers. *The News* had the 6th-largest daily circulation of any paper in the US in 1994, and the *Free Press* ranked 7th.

The following table shows leading daily newspapers in Michigan with average daily and Sunday circulation in 1994:

AREA	NAME	DAILY	SUNDAY
Detroit	*News* and *Free Press* (m,S)	823,310	1,107,645
Flint	*Journal* (e,S)	97,007	118,968
Grand Rapids	*Press* (e,S)	139,359	191,226
Kalamazoo	*Gazette* (e,S)	61,243	78,438
Lansing	*State Journal* (e,S)	71,636	95,637
Pontiac	*Oakland Press* (e,S)	84,365	98,836
Saginaw	*News* (e,S)	54,508	64,845

46ORGANIZATIONS

The 1992 US Census of Service Industries counted 2,278 organizations in Michigan, including 406 business associations; 1,431 civic, social, and fraternal associations; and 441 other membership organizations. Few national organizations maintain their headquarters in Michigan, but the first chapters of the Kiwanis and Exchange service clubs were organized in the state.

The most important trade association headquartered in Michigan is the Motor Vehicle Manufacturers Association, with offices in Detroit. Its labor union counterpart, the United Automobile Workers, also has its international headquarters in that city.

Other organizations with headquarters in the state include the American Concrete Institute, Detroit; Society of Manufacturing Engineers, Dearborn; American Society of Agricultural Engineers, St. Joseph; and the National Association of Investment Corporations, Madison Heights.

47TOURISM, TRAVEL, AND RECREATION

Tourism has been an important source of economic activity in Michigan since the 19th century and now rivals agriculture as the second most important segment of the state's economy. In 1995, in-state visitors were estimated to have spent over $7.5 million in Michigan.

Michigan's tourist attractions are diverse and readily accessible to much of the country's population. The opportunities offered by Michigan's water resources are the number one attraction; no part of the state is more than 85 mi (137 km) from one of the Great Lakes, and most of the population lives only a few miles away from one of the thousands of inland lakes and streams. Southwestern Michigan's sandy beaches along Lake Michigan offer sunbathing and swimming. Inland lakes in southern Michigan are favored by swimmers, while the Metropolitan Beach on Lake St. Clair, northeast of Detroit, claims to be the largest artificial-lake beach in the world. Camping has enjoyed an enormous increase in popularity; in addition to the extensive public camping facilities, there are many private campgrounds.

Although the tourist and resort business has been primarily a summer activity, the rising popularity of ice fishing, skiing, and other winter sports, autumn scenic tours, hunting, and spring festivals has made tourism a year-round business in many parts of the state. Historic attractions have been heavily promoted in recent years, following the success of Dearborn's Henry Ford Museum and Greenfield Village, which attract about 1.5 million paying visitors each year. Tours of Detroit automobile factories and other industrial sites, such as Battle Creek's breakfast-food plants, are also important tourist attractions.

Camping and recreational facilities are provided by the federal government at three national forests, comprising 2.8 million acres (1.1 million hectares); three facilities operated by the National Park Service (Isle Royale National Park and the Pictured Rocks National Lakeshore and Sleeping Bear Dunes National Lakeshore); and several wildlife sanctuaries.

State-operated facilities include 64 parks and recreational areas with 172,343 acres (69,747 hectares), and state forests and wildlife areas totaling 4,250,000 acres (1,720,000 hectares). In 1996, total visitation was 24,291,957. Holland and Warren Dunes state parks, located on Lake Michigan, had the largest overall park attendances for the year; Ludington State Park, also on Lake Michigan, attracted the largest number of campers. In 1996, 2,045,767 hunting licenses and 1,740,975 fishing licenses were issued.

[48]SPORTS

Michigan has four major league professional sports teams, all of them centered in Detroit: the Tigers of Major League Baseball, the Lions of the National Football League, the Pistons of the National Basketball Association, and the Red Wings of the National Hockey League. The Tigers won the World Series in 1935, 1945, 1968, and 1984. The Pistons won the NBA Championship in 1989 and 1990. The Red Wings won the Stanley Cup in 1936, 1937, 1943, 1950, 1952, 1954, 1955, and 1997.

The state also has minor league hockey teams in Grand Rapids, Kalamazoo, and Plymouth; and baseball teams in Grand Rapids, Kalamazoo, and Lansing.

Horse racing, Michigan's oldest organized spectator sport, is controlled by the state racing commissioner, who regulates thoroughbred and harness-racing seasons at tracks in the Detroit area and at Jackson. Attendance and betting at these races is substantial, although the modest purses rarely attract the nation's leading horses. Auto racing is also popular in Michigan. The state hosts three major races: the Detroit Grand Prix, and the US 500 Indy car races, and the Michigan 500 NASCAR Winston Cup race.

Interest in college sports centers on the football and basketball teams of the University of Michigan and Michigan State University, which usually are among the top-ranked teams in the country. The University of Michigan football team won the Rose Bowl in 1948, 1951, 1965, 1981, 1989 and 1993 and was named National Champion in 1901 (with Harvard), 1902, 1904 (with Penn), 1918 (with Pittsburgh), 1923 (with Illinois), 1932, 1933, 1947, and 1948. Michigan State won the Rose Bowl in 1954, 1956, and 1988, and was named National Champion in 1952 (with Georgia Tech), 1965 (with Alabama), and 1966 (with Notre Dame). The basketball teams of Michigan and Michigan

State have each won the NCAA tournament once, in 1989 and 1979, respectively. Michigan also advanced to the championship game in 1965, 1976, 1992, and 1993.

Other colleges also have achieved national ranking in basketball, hockey, baseball, and track. Elaborate facilities have been built for these competitions; the University of Michigan's football stadium, seating 104,001, is the largest college-owned stadium in the country.

Other annual sporting events include the I-500 snowmobile race in Sault St. Marie in early February and, in July, there are yacht races from Chicago and Port Huron to Makinac Island.

[49]FAMOUS MICHIGANIANS

Only one Michiganian has held the offices of US president and vice president. Gerald R. Ford (Leslie King, Jr., b.Nebraska, 1913), the 38th US president, was elected to the US House as a Republican in 1948 and served continuously until 1973, becoming minority leader in 1965. Upon the resignation of Vice President Spiro T. Agnew in 1973, President Richard M. Nixon appointed Ford to the vice-presidency. When Nixon resigned on 9 August 1974, Ford became president, the first to hold that post without having been elected to high national office. Ford succeeded in restoring much of the public's confidence in the presidency, but his pardoning of Nixon for all crimes he may have committed as president helped cost Ford victory in the presidential election of 1976. Ford subsequently moved his legal residence to California.

Lewis Cass (b.New Hampshire, 1782–1866), who served as governor of Michigan Territory, senator from Michigan, secretary of war and secretary of state, is the only other Michigan resident nominated by a major party for president; he lost the 1848 race as the Democratic candidate. Thomas E. Dewey (1902–72), a native of Owosso, was the Republican presidential nominee in 1944 and 1948, but from his adopted state of New York.

Two Michiganians have served as associate justices of the Supreme Court: Henry B. Brown (b.Massachusetts, 1836–1913), author of the 1896 segregationist decision in *Plessy v. Ferguson*; and Frank Murphy (1890–1949), who also served as US attorney general, mayor of Detroit, governor of Michigan, and was a notable defender of minority rights during his years on the court. Another justice, Potter Stewart (1915–85), was born in Jackson but appointed to the court from Ohio.

Other Michiganians who have held high federal office include Robert McClelland (b.Pennsylvania, 1807–80), secretary of the interior; Russell A. Alger (b.Ohio, 1836–1907), secretary of war; Edwin Denby (b.Indiana, 1870–1929), secretary of the Navy, who was forced to resign because of the Teapot Dome scandal; Roy D. Chapin (1880–1936), secretary of commerce; Charles E. Wilson (b.Ohio, 1890–1961), and Robert S. McNamara (b.California, 1916), secretaries of defense; George Romney (b.Mexico, 1907–96), secretary of housing and urban development; Donald M. Dickinson (b.New York, 1846–1917) and Arthur E. Summerfield (1899–1972), postmasters general; and W. Michael Blumenthal (b.Germany, 1926), secretary of the treasury.

Zachariah Chandler (b.New Hampshire, 1813–79) served as secretary of the interior but is best remembered as a leader of the Radical Republicans in the US Senate during the Civil War era. Other prominent US senators have included James M. Couzens (b.Canada, 1872–1936), a former Ford executive who became a maverick Republican liberal during the 1920s; Arthur W. Vandenberg (1884–1951), a leading supporter of a bipartisan internationalist foreign policy after World War II; and Philip A. Hart, Jr. (b.Pennsylvania, 1912–76), one of the most influential senators of the 1960s and 1970s. Recent well-known US representatives include John Conyers, Jr. (b.1929), and Martha W. Griffiths (b.Missouri, 1912), a representative for 20 years who served as the state's lieutenant governor from 1983–91.

In addition to Murphy and Romney, important governors have included Stevens T. Mason (b.Virginia, 1811–43), who guided Michigan to statehood; Austin Blair (b.New York, 1818–94), Civil War governor; Hazen S. Pingree (b.Maine, 1840–1901) and Chase S. Osborn (b.Indiana, 1860–1949), reform-minded governors; Alexander Groesbeck (1873–1953); G. Mennen Williams (1911-88); and William G. Milliken (b.1922), governor from 1969 to January 1983. From 1974 to 1994, Detroit's first black mayor, Coleman A. Young (b.Alabama, 1918), promoted programs to revive the city's tarnished image.

The most famous figure in the early development of Michigan is Jacques Marquette (b.France, 1637–75). Other famous historical figures include Charles de Langlade (1729–1801), a leader of the Ottawa people and a French-Indian soldier in the French and Indian War and the American Revolution; the Ottawa chieftain Pontiac (1720?–69), leader of an ambitious Indian uprising; and Gabriel Richard (b.France, 1769–1832), an important pioneer in education and the first Catholic priest to serve in Congress. Laura Haviland (b.Canada, 1808–98) was a noted leader in the fight against slavery and for black rights, while Lucinda Hinsdale Stone (b.Vermont, 1814–1900) and Anna Howard Shaw (b.England, 1847–1919) were important in the women's rights movement.

Nobel laureates from Michigan include diplomat Ralph J. Bunche (1904–71), winner of the Nobel Peace Prize in 1950; Glenn T. Seaborg (b.1912), Nobel Prize winner in chemistry in 1951; and Thomas H. Weller (b.1915) and Alfred D. Hershey (b.1908), Nobel Prize winners in physiology or medicine in 1954 and 1969, respectively. Among leading educators, James B. Angell (b.Rhode Island, 1829–1916), president of the University of Michigan, led that school to the forefront among American universities while John A. Hannah (1902–91), longtime president of Michigan State University, successfully strove to expand and diversify its programs. General Motors executive Charles S. Mott (b.New Jersey, 1875–1973) contributed to the growth of continuing education programs through huge grants of money.

In the business world, William C. Durant (b.Massachusetts, 1861–1947), Henry Ford (1863–1947) and Ransom E. Olds (b.Ohio 1864–1950) are the three most important figures in making Michigan the center of the American auto industry. Ford's grandson, Henry Ford II (1917-87), was the dominant personality in the auto industry from 1945 through 1979. Two brothers, John Harvey Kellogg (1852–1943) and Will K. Kellogg (1860–1951), helped make Battle Creek the center of the breakfast-food industry. William E. Upjohn (1850–1932) and Herbert H. Dow (b.Canada, 1866–1930) founded major pharmaceutical and chemical companies that bear their names, James E. Scripps (b.England, 1835–1906), founder of the *Detroit News*, was a major innovator in the newspaper business. Pioneer aviator Charles A. Lindbergh (1902–74) was born in Detroit.

Among prominent labor leaders in Michigan were Walter Reuther (b.West Virginia, 1907–70), president of the United Automobile Workers, and his controversial contemporary, James Hoffa (b.Indiana, 1913–1975?), president of the Teamsters Union, whose disappearance and presumed murder remain a mystery.

The best-known literary figures who were either native or adopted Michiganians include Edgar Guest (b.England, 1881–1959), writer of enormously popular sentimental verses; Ring Lardner (1885–1933), master of the short story; Edna Ferber (1885–1968), best-selling novelist; Paul de Kruif (1890–1971), popular writer on scientific topics; Steward Edward White (1873–1946), writer of adventure tales; Howard Mumford Jones (1892–1980), critic and scholar; and Bruce Catton (1899–1978), Civil War historian.

Other prominent Michiganians past and present include Frederick Stuart Church (1842–1924), painter; Liberty Hyde Bailey (1858–1954), horticulturist and botanist; Albert Kahn (b.Germany, 1869–1942), noted architect and innovator in factory design; and (Gottlieb) Eliel Saarinen (b.Finland, 1873–1950), architect and creator of the Cranbrook School of Art, and his son Eero (1910–61), designer of the General Motors Technical Center in Warren and many distinctive structures throughout the US. Malcolm X (Malcolm Little, b.Nebraska, 1925–65) developed his black separatist beliefs while living in Lansing.

Popular entertainers born in Michigan include Danny Thomas (Amos Jacobs, 1914–91), David Wayne (1914-91), Betty Hutton (b.1921), Ed McMahon (b.1923), Julie Harris (b.1925), Ellen Burstyn (Edna Rae Gilhooley, b.1932), Della Reese (Dellareese Patricia Early, b.1932), William "Smokey" Robinson (b.1940), Diana Ross (b.1944), Bob Seger (b.1945), and Stevie Wonder (Stevland Morris, b.1950), along with film director Francis Ford Coppola (b.1939).

Among sports figures who had notable careers in the state were Fielding H. Yost (b.West Virginia, 1871–1946), University of Michigan football coach; Joe Louis (Joseph Louis Barrow, b.Alabama, 1914-81), heavyweight boxing champion from 1937 to 1949; "Sugar Ray" Robinson (1921-89), who held at various times the welterweight and middleweight boxing titles; and baseball Hall of Famers Al Kaline (b.Maryland, 1934) and Tyrus Raymond ("Ty") Cobb (b. Georgia, 1886–1961), who won 12 batting titles, were Detroit Tigers stars. Earvin "Magic" Johnson (b. 1959), who broke Oscar Robertson's record for most assists, was born in Lansing, Michigan.

50BIBLIOGRAPHY

Bald, F. C. *Michigan in Four Centuries*. Rev. ed. New York: Harper & Row, 1961.

Browne, William Paul. *Michigan Politics and Government: Facing Change in a Complex State*. Lincoln: University of Nebraska Press, 1995.

Catton, Bruce. *Michigan: A Bicentennial History*. New York: Norton, 1976.

Dunbar, Willis F., and George S. May. *Michigan: A History of the Wolverine State*. 3d rev. ed. Grand Rapids: Eerdmans, 1995.

Federal Writers' Project. *Michigan: A Guide to the Wolverine State*. Reprint. New York: Somerset, 1981 (orig. 1941).

Fine, Sidney. *Civil Rights and the Michigan Constitution of 1963*. Ann Arbor: Bentley Historical Library, University of Michigan, 1996.

Fuller, George N., ed. *Michigan: A Centennial History of the State*. 5 vols. Chicago: Lewis, 1939.

Hershock, Martin John. *Liberty and Power in the Old Northwest: Michigan, 1850–1867*. N.p., 1996.

The Legislative Process in Michigan: A Student's Guide. Lansing: Legislative Service Bureau, 1995.

May, George S. *Pictorial History of Michigan*. 2 vols. Grand Rapids: Eerdmans, 1967, 1969.

Michigan, State of. Department of Management and Budget. *Michigan Manual, 1983-84*. Lansing, 1984.

Michigan State University. Graduate School of Business Administration. Division of Research. *Michigan Statistical Abstract*. 18th ed. Edited by David I. Verway. East Lansing, 1984.

Moore, Elizabeth. *The State We're In: A Citizen's Guide to Michigan State Government*. Lansing: League of Women Voters of Michigan, 1995.

Rubenstein, Bruce A. *Michigan, A History of the Great Lakes State*. Wheeling, Ill.: Harlan Davidson, 1995.

Sommers, Lawrence M., ed. *Atlas of Michigan*. East Lansing: Michigan State University Press, 1977.

MINNESOTA

State of Minnesota

ORIGIN OF STATE NAME: Derived from the Sioux Indian word *minisota,* meaning "sky-tinted waters." **NICKNAME:** The North Star State. **CAPITAL:** St. Paul. **ENTERED UNION:** 11 May 1858 (32d). **SONG:** "Hail! Minnesota." **MOTTO:** *L'Etoile du Nord* (The North Star). **FLAG:** On a blue field bordered on three sides by a gold fringe, a version of the state seal is surrounded by a wreath with the statehood year (1858) the year of the establishment of Ft. Snelling (1819), and the year the flag was adopted (1893); five clusters of gold stars and the word "Minnesota" fill the outer circle. **OFFICIAL SEAL:** A farmer, with a powder horn and musket nearby, plows a field in the foreground, while in the background, before a rising sun, an Indian on horseback crosses the plains; pine trees and a waterfall represent the state's natural resources. The state motto is above, and the whole is surrounded by the words "The Great Seal of the State of Minnesota 1858." Another version of the seal in common use shows a cowboy riding across the plains. **BIRD:** Common loon. **FISH:** Walleye. **FLOWER:** Pink and white (or showy) lady slipper. **TREE:** Red (Norway) pine. **GRAIN:** Wild rice. **MUSHROOM:** Morel or sponge mushroom. **DRINK:** Milk. **GEM:** Lake Superior agate. **LEGAL HOLIDAYS:** New Year's Day, 1 January; Birthday of Martin Luther King, Jr., 3d Monday n January; Washington's and Lincoln's Birthdays, 3d Monday in February; Memorial Day, last Monday in May; Independence Day, 4 July; Labor Day, 1st Monday in September; Columbus Day, 2d Monday in October; Veterans Day, 11 November; Thanksgiving Day, 4th Thursday in November; Christmas Day, 25 December. By statute, schools hold special observances on Susan B. Anthony Day, 15 February; Arbor Day, last Friday in April; Minnesota Day, 11 May; Frances Willard Day, 28 September; Leif Erikson Day, 9 October. **TIME:** 6 AM CST = noon GMT.

¹LOCATION, SIZE, AND EXTENT

Situated in the western north-central US, Minnesota is the largest of the midwestern states and ranks 12th in size among the 50 states.

The total area of Minnesota is 84,402 sq mi (218,601 sq km), of which land accounts for 79,548 sq mi (206,029 sq km) and inland water 4,854 sq mi (12,572 sq km). Minnesota extends 406 mi (653 km) N-S; its extreme E-W extension is 358 mi (576 km).

Minnesota is bordered on the N by the Canadian provinces of Manitoba and Ontario (with the line passing through the Lake of the Woods, Rainy River, Rainy Lake, a succession of smaller lakes, the Pigeon River, and Lake Superior); on the E by Michigan and Wisconsin (with the line passing through Lake Superior and the St. Croix and Mississippi rivers); on the S by Iowa; and on the W by South Dakota and North Dakota (with the line passing through Big Stone Lake, Lake Traverse, the Bois de Sioux River, and the Red River of the North).

The length of Minnesota's boundaries totals 1,783 mi (2,870 km). The state's geographic center is in Crow Wing County, 10 mi (16 km) SW of Brainerd.

²TOPOGRAPHY

Minnesota, lying at the northern rim of the Central Plains region, consists mainly of flat prairie, nowhere flatter than in the Red River Valley of the west. There are rolling hills and deep river valleys in the southeast; the northeast, known as Arrowhead Country, is more rugged and includes the Vermilion Range and the Mesabi Range, with its rich iron deposits. Eagle Mountain, in the extreme northeast, rises to a height of 2,301 feet (701 meters), the highest point in the state; the surface of nearby Lake Superior, 602 feet (183 meters) above sea level, is the state's lowest elevation.

With more than 15,000 lakes and extensive wetlands, rivers, and streams, Minnesota has more inland water than any other state except Alaska. Some of the inland lakes are quite large: Lower and Upper Red Lake, 451 sq mi (1,168 sq km); Mille Lacs, 207 sq mi (536 sq km); and Leech Lake, 176 sq mi (456 sq km). The Lake of the Woods, 1,485 sq mi (3,846 sq km), is shared with Canada, as is Rainy Lake, 345 sq mi (894 sq km). A total of 2,212 sq mi (5,729 sq km) of Lake Superior lies within Minnesota's jurisdiction.

Lake Itasca, in the northwest, is the source of the Mississippi River, which drains about three-fifths of the state and, after meeting with the St. Croix below Minneapolis–St. Paul, forms part of the eastern boundary with Wisconsin. The Minnesota River, which flows across the southern part of the state, joins the Mississippi at the Twin Cities. The Red River of the North, which forms much of the boundary with North Dakota, is part of another large drainage system; it flows north, crosses the Canadian border above St. Vincent, and eventually empties into Lake Winnipeg in Canada.

Most of Minnesota, except for small areas in the southeast, was covered by ice during the glacial ages. When the ice melted, it left behind a body of water known as Lake Agassiz, which extended into what we now call the Dakotas and Canada and was larger than the combined Great Lakes are today; additional melting to the north caused the lake to drain away, leaving flat prairie in its wake. The glaciers also left behind large stretches of pulverized limestone, enriching Minnesota's soil, and the numerous shallow depressions that have developed into its modern-day lakes and streams.

³CLIMATE

Minnesota has a continental climate, with cold, often frigid winters and warm summers. The growing season is 160 days or more in the south-central and southeastern regions, but 100 days or less in the northern counties. Normal daily mean temperatures range from 7°F (–14°C) in January to 66°F (19°C) in July for Duluth, and from 12°F (–11°C) in January to 74°F (23°C) in July for Minneapolis–St. Paul, often called the Twin Cities. The lowest temperature recorded in Minnesota was –60°F (–51°C), at Tower on 2 February 1996; the highest, 114°F (46°C), at Moorhead on 6 July 1936.

Precipitation is heaviest in the southeast, where the mean annual precipitation is 32 in (81 cm), and lightest in the northwest, where it averages 19 in (48 cm) per year. Heavy snowfalls occur from November to April, averaging about 70 in (178 cm) annually in the northeast and 30 in (76 cm) in the southeast. Blizzards hit Minnesota twice each winter on the average. Tornadoes occur mostly in the south; on average there are 18 tornadoes in the state each year.

[4]FLORA AND FAUNA

Minnesota is divided into three main life zones: the wooded lake regions of the north and east, the prairie lands of the west and southwest, and a transition zone in between. Oak, maple, elm, birch, pine, ash, and poplar still thrive, although much of the state's woodland has been cut down since the 1850s. Common shrubs include thimbleberry, sweetfern, and several varieties of honeysuckle. Familiar among some 1,500 native flowering plants are puccoon, prairie phlox, and blazing star; the pink and white (showy) lady slipper is the state flower. White and yellow water lilies cover the pond areas, with bulrushes and cattails on the shore.

Among Minnesota's common mammals are the opossum, eastern and starnose moles, little brown bat, raccoon, mink, river otter, badger, striped and spotted skunks, red fox, bobcat, 13-lined ground squirrel (also known as the Minnesota gopher, symbol of the University of Minnesota), beaver, porcupine, eastern cottontail, moose, and white-tailed deer. The common loon (the state bird), western meadowlark, Brewer's blackbird, Carolina wren, and Louisiana water thrush are among some 240 resident bird species; introduced birds include the English sparrow and ring-necked pheasant. Teeming in Minnesota's many lakes are such game fishes as walleye, muskellunge, northern pike, and steelhead, rainbow, and brown trouts. The two poisonous snakes in the state are the timber rattler and the massasauga.

Classification of rare, threatened, and endangered species is delegated to the Minnesota Department of Natural Resources. Among rare species noted by the department are the white pelican, short-eared owl, rock vole, pine marten, American elk, woodland caribou, lake sturgeon, and paddlefish; threatened species include the bobwhite quail and piping plover. Endangered species are the gray (timber) wolf, trumpeter swan, American peregrine falcon, whooping crane, burrowing owl, and Higgins' eye pearly mussel.

[5]ENVIRONMENTAL PROTECTION

The state's northern forests have been greatly depleted by fires, lumbering, and farming, but efforts to replenish them began as early as 1876, with the formation of the state's first forestry association. In 1911, the legislature authorized a state nursery, established forest reserves and parks, and created the post of chief fire warden to oversee forestry resources and promote reforestation projects. Minnesota divides its environmental programs among three agencies: the Minnesota Pollution Control Agency, the Department of Natural Resources, and the Office of Waste Management (newly reorganized as the Office of Environmental Assistance). The Conservation Department, created in 1931, evolved into the present Department of Natural Resources, which is responsible for the management of forests, fish and game, public lands, minerals, and state parks and waters. The department's Soil and Water Conservation Board has jurisdiction over the state's 92 soil and water conservation districts. A separate Pollution Control Agency enforces air and water quality standards and oversees solid waste disposal and pollution-related land-use planning. The Environmental Quality Board coordinates conservation efforts among various state agencies.

Minnesotans dump 4,400 tons of waste a year (0.99 tons per capita) into 53 municipal landfills. In 1994, the state implemented the Minnesota Landfill Cleanup Program to ensure the proper care of 106 closed or closing municipal landfills. Beginning in 1996, the state began construction on 25 new municipal landfills and instituted a planning effort to manage all existing and closed sites. There were 37 hazardous waste sites in the state in 1995. To control the state's solid waste stream, Minnesotans have established 488 curbside recycling programs. In 1997, the state had some 9.5 million acres (3.8 million hectares) of wetlands. The Wetlands Conservation Act of 1991 set the ambitious goal of no wetland loss in the future. The Reserve Mining Co. complied with a court order in 1980 by ending the dumping of taconite wastes, a possible carcinogen, into Lake Superior. Other pollution problems came to light during the 1970s with the discovery of asbestos in drinking water from Lake Superior, of contaminants from inadequately buried toxic wastes at St. Louis Park, and of the killing by agricultural pesticides of an estimated 100,000 fish in two southeastern Minnesota brooks. During the early 1980s, the state's Pollution Control Agency approved plans by FMC, a munitions maker, to clean up a hazardous waste site at Fridley (near Minneapolis), which the Environmental Protection Agency claimed was the country's most dangerous hazardous waste area. The Minnesota Mining and Manufacturing Co. in 1983 began to remove chemical wastes from three dumps in Oakdale (a suburb of St. Paul), where the company had disposed of hazardous wastes since the late 1940s. Each cleanup project was to cost the respective companies at least $6 million.

[6]POPULATION

The 1990 census gave Minnesota a population of 4,375,099, ranking it 20th among the 50 states. The 1996 estimated population was 4,657,758, representing a population increase of 6.4% since 1990. The average population density for the state in 1990 was 55 per sq mi (21 per sq km).

Minnesota was still mostly wilderness until a land boom in 1848 attracted the first substantial wave of settlers, mainly lumbermen from New England, farmers from the Middle Atlantic states, and tradespeople from eastern cities. The 1850 census recorded a population of 6,077 in what was then Minnesota Territory. With the signing of major Indian treaties and widespread use of the steamboat, large areas were opened to settlement, and the population exceeded 150,000 by the end of 1857. Attracted by fertile farmland and enticed by ambitious recruitment programs overseas, large numbers of European immigrants came to settle in the new state from the 1860s onward. In 1880, the state population totaled 780,733; by 1920 (when overseas immigration virtually ceased), the state had 2,387,125 residents. Population growth leveled off during the 1920s and has fallen below the national average since the 1940s. As of 1980, Minnesotans were, on average, somewhat older than the nation as a whole, with a median age of 29 years. Women make up about 51% of the population.

In 1990, two out of three Minnesotans lived in metropolitan areas. The Minneapolis–St. Paul metropolitan area was the country's 16th-largest in 1990, with a population of 2,464,000, a 10.4% increase since 1980. By 1995 the population had increased another 7.3% to an estimated 2,723,137. In Minneapolis itself, the population fell by 0.7% from 1980 to 1990; in

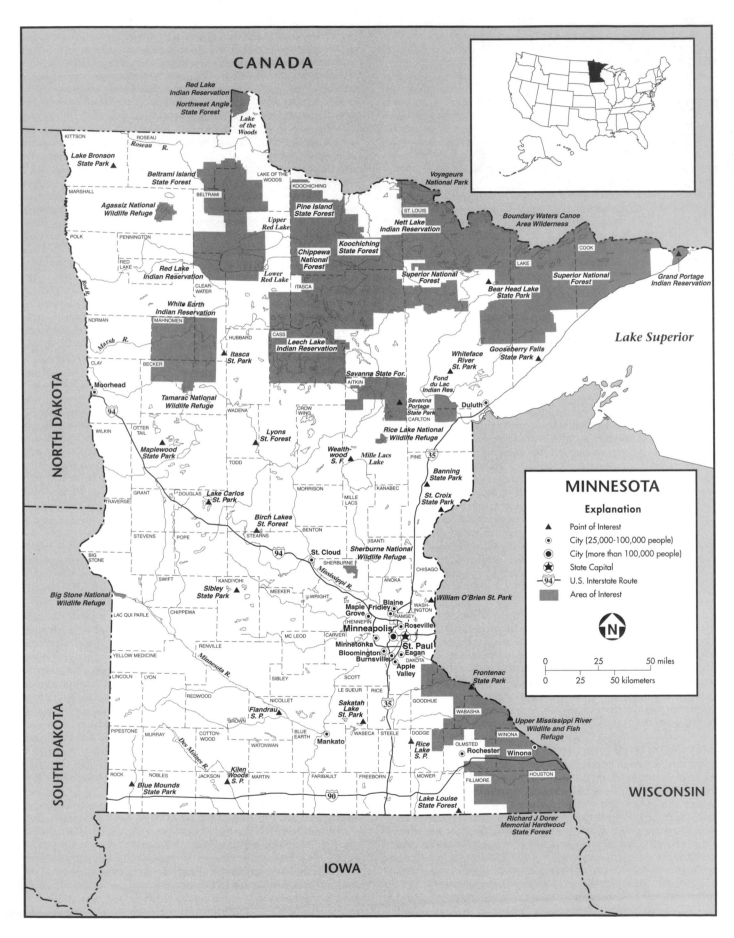

CANADA

Red Lake
Indian Reservation

Northwest Angle
State Forest

Lake
of the
Woods

KITTSON   ROSEAU   Roseau   R.

Lake Bronson
State Park ▲

MARSHALL   Beltrami Island
                  State Forest

BELTRAMI   LAKE OF THE
                  WOODS

Agassiz National
Wildlife Refuge

POLK   PENNINGTON   Upper
                                  Red Lake

RED
LAKE   Red Lake
              Indian Reservation

CLEAR-
WATER   Lower
               Red Lake

NORMAN   White Earth
                Indian Reservation   CASS

MAHNOMEN   HUBBARD

BECKER   Itasca
                St. Park ▲   ITASCA

CLAY   Tamarac National
              Wildlife Refuge

Moorhead ◉

Marsh R.

OTTER
TAIL   Maplewood
              State Park ▲

WILKIN

94

TRAVERSE   GRANT   DOUGLAS   Lake Carlos
                                                 St. Park ▲

Red R.

STEVENS   POPE   Birch Lakes
                               St. Forest

BIG
STONE

Big Stone National
Wildlife Refuge

SWIFT   KANDIYOHI   Sibley
                                  State Park ▲

LAC QUI PARLE   CHIPPEWA

YELLOW MEDICINE

Minnesota R.

LINCOLN   LYON   REDWOOD

Des Moines R.

PIPESTONE   MURRAY   COTTON-
                                   WOOD

Flandrau
S.P. ▲

WATONWAN   BLUE
                  EARTH

ROCK   NOBLES   JACKSON   Kilen
                                               Woods
                                               S. P. ▲   MARTIN

Blue Mounds
State Park ▲

90

SOUTH DAKOTA

NORTH DAKOTA

KOOCHICHING

Pine Island
State Forest

Chippewa
National
Forest

Koochiching
State Forest

Leech Lake
Indian Reservation

WADENA   CROW
                WING

Lyons
St. Forest ▲

AITKIN

MORRISON

TODD   Wealth-
              wood
              S. F. ▲   Mille Lacs
                               Lake

MILLE
LACS

BENTON

STEARNS   St. Cloud ◉

SHERBURNE

Mississippi R.

MEEKER   WRIGHT

Sherburne National
Wildlife Refuge

ANOKA

McLEOD   CARVER   HENNEPIN

Maple
Grove   Blaine
               Fridley ◉
               RAMSEY

Minneapolis ★

Minnetonka ◉   Roseville ◉
Bloomington ◉   St. Paul ★
Burnsville ◉   Eagan ◉

DAKOTA

Apple
Valley ◉

RENVILLE

SIBLEY

NICOLLET

Sakatah
Lake
St. Park ▲

LE SUEUR   RICE

Mankato ◉

BROWN   WASECA   STEELE

WASHINGTON

ISANTI

CHISAGO

PINE   35

Banning
State Park ▲

St. Croix
State Park ▲

William O'Brien St. Park ▲

KANABEC

35

GOODHUE   Frontenac
                 State Park ▲

WABASHA

DODGE   Rice
               Lake
               S. P. ▲   OLMSTED   Rochester ◉   Upper Mississippi River
                                                                      Wildlife and Fish
                                                                      Refuge

WINONA   Winona ◉

FARIBAULT   FREEBORN   MOWER   FILLMORE   HOUSTON

Lake Louise
State Forest ▲

Richard J Dorer
Memorial Hardwood
State Forest

Voyageurs
National Park

ST. LOUIS   Boundary Waters Canoe
                   Area Wilderness

Nett Lake
Indian Reservation

COOK

LAKE

Superior National
Forest

Superior National
Forest

Grand Portage
Indian Reservation ▲

Bear Head Lake
State Park ▲

Whiteface
River
St. Park ▲   Gooseberry Falls
                    State Park ▲

Lake Superior

Fond
du Lac
Indian Res.

Savanna State For.

Savanna
Portage
State Park ▲   Duluth ◉

CARLTON

Rice Lake National
Wildlife Refuge

WISCONSIN

IOWA

MINNESOTA

Explanation

▲ Point of Interest
◉ City (25,000-100,000 people)
◉ City (more than 100,000 people)
★ State Capital
─94─ U.S. Interstate Route
▨ Area of Interest

(N)

0   25   50 miles
0   25   50 kilometers

1994, the city had an estimated 354,590 residents, while St. Paul had a population of 262,071. The estimates for other leading cities were as follows: Duluth, 83,990; and Rochester, 75,769.

7ETHNIC GROUPS

Minnesota was settled during the second half of the 19th century primarily by European immigrants, chiefly Germans, Swedes, Norwegians, Danes, English, and Poles, along with the Irish and some French Canadians. The Swedish newcomers were mainly farmers; Norwegians concentrated on lumbering, while the Swiss worked for the most part in the dairy industry. In 1890, Finns and Slavs were recruited to work in the iron mines; the state's meat-packing plants brought in Balkan nationals, Mexicans, and Poles after the turn of the century. By 1930, 50% of the population was foreign-born. Among first- and second-generation Minnesotans of European origin, Germans and Scandinavians are still the largest groups. The state has more ethnic Norwegians than any other, and is 2d in number of ethnic Swedes, behind California. The other ethnic groups are concentrated in Minneapolis–St. Paul or in the iron country of the Mesabi Range, where ethnic enclaves still persist. As of 1990, the foreign born residents of Minnesota numbered 113,039, or 2.5% of the state total.

As of 1990 there were 50,000 Indians in Minnesota. Besides those living in seven small reservations and four villages, a cluster of Indian urban dwellers (chiefly Ojibwa) lived in St. Paul. The reservations with the largest 1995 estimated population were the Fond du Lac (6,676), Leech Lake (6,260), Nett Lake (2,162), and Mille Lacs (1,400) reservations. Indian lands totaled 764,000 acres (309,000 hectares) in 1982, of which 93% were tribal lands. There were only 39 black Americans in Minnesota in 1850; by 1990, blacks numbered 95,000, or 2.1% of the total population. In 1990 there were 78,000 Asian and Pacific peoples, mostly Hmong, Korean, and Vietnamese. There also were 54,000 Hispanic Americans.

8LANGUAGES

Many place-names echo the languages of the Yankton and Santee Sioux Indian tribes and of the incoming Algonkian-language Ojibwa, or Chippewa, from whom most of the Sioux fled to Dakota Territory. Such place-names as Minnesota itself, Minnetonka, and Mankato are Siouan in origin; Kabetogama and Winnibigoshish, both lakes, are Ojibwan.

English in the state is essentially Northern, with minor infiltration of Midland terms because of early movement up the Mississippi River into southern Minnesota and also up the Great Lakes into and beyond Duluth. Among older residents, traces of Scandinavian intonation persist, and on the Iron Range several pronunciation features reflect the mother tongues of mine workers from eastern Europe.

Although some minor variants now compete in frequency, on the whole Minnesota speech features such dominant Northern terms as *andirons, pail, mouth organ* (harmonica), *comforter* (tied and filled bedcover, *wishbone, clingstone peach, sweet corn, angleworm* (earthworm), *darning needle* or *mosquito hawk* (dragonfly), and *sick to the stomach.* Minnesotans call the grass strip between street and sidewalk the *boulevard* and a rubber band a *rubber binder,* and many *cook coffee* when they brew it. Three-fourths of a sample population spoke *root* with the vowel of *put;* one third, through school influence, pronounced /ah/ in *aunt* instead of the usual Northern short /a/, as in *pants.* Many younger speakers pronounce *caller* and *collar* alike.

In 1990, 3,811,700 Minnesotans 5 years old or older spoke only English at home. Other leading languages spoken at home were:

German	45,409
Spanish	42,362
Various Scandinavian	25,758
French	13,693
Vietnamese	8,314
Chinese	6,844

9RELIGIONS

Minnesota's first Christian church was organized by Presbyterians in Ft. Snelling in 1835; the first Roman Catholic church, the Chapel of St. Paul, was dedicated in 1841 at a town then called Pig's Eye but now known by the same name as the chapel. Immigrants arriving in subsequent decades brought their religions with them, with Lutherans and Catholics predominating.

As of 1990, there were 1,693,568 known Protestant adherents, including 1,069,703 Lutherans, 142,771 United Methodists, 66,715 United Presbyterians, 55,497 members of the United Church of Christ, and 31,980 Episcopalians. Roman Catholics numbered 1,110,071 in 1990, when the estimated Jewish population was 33,779. Minnesota is the headquarters for three national Lutheran religious groups: the American Lutheran Church, the Church of the Lutheran Brethren, and the Association of Free Lutheran Congregations.

10TRANSPORTATION

The development of an extensive railroad network after the Civil War was a key factor in the growth of lumbering, iron mining, wheat growing, and other industries. By the start of 1996, Minnesota had a total of 4,784 rail mi (7,697 km), of which over 70% was Class I track. In 1995, 42,748,705 tons of metallic ores originated from Minnesota, more than any other state, and accounted for 47% of the total rail tonnage originated within the state. Amtrak serves Minneapolis–St. Paul en route from Chicago to Seattle. Total Minnesota ridership in 1995/96 came to 126,967.

Planning and supervision of mass transportation in the Twin Cities metropolitan area are under the jurisdiction of the Metropolitan Transit Commission, a public corporation. The national Greyhound bus line was founded in Hibbing in 1914.

Minnesota had 130,391 mi (209,800 km) of public roads and streets in 1995 (5th-highest in US), of which 115,225 mi (185,397 km) were rural and 15,166 mi (24,402 km) municipal. Interstate highways totaled 914 mi (1,470 km); I-35 links Minneapolis–St. Paul with Duluth and I-94 connects the Twin Cities with Moorhead and Fargo, ND. In 1995 there were 2,552,004 registered automobiles, 1,314,173 trucks, and 15,562 buses; there were 2,761,121 licensed drivers in that year.

The first settlements grew up around major river arteries, especially in the southeast; early traders and settlers arrived first by canoe or keelboat, later by steamer. The port of Duluth-Superior, at the western terminus of the Great Lakes–St. Lawrence Seaway (officially opened in 1959), is the 18th-busiest US port, handling 45 million tons of domestic and international cargo in 1995, including bulk grain, coal, metallic ores, and refrigerated commodities. The ports of Minneapolis and St. Paul handle more than 6 million tons of cargo each year, with agricultural products and scrap iron moving downstream and petroleum products, chemicals, and cement moving upstream.

As of 1995, the state had 370 airports, 70 seaplane bases, 37 heliports, and 1 stolport. Minneapolis–St. Paul International Airport handled 141,060 departing flights, enplaning 10,892,061 passengers in 1994.

11HISTORY

People have lived on the land that is now Minnesota for at least 10,000 years. The earliest inhabitants—belonging to what archaeologists classify as the Paleo-Indian (or Big Game) culture—hunted large animals, primarily bison, from which they obtained food, clothing, and materials for shelter. A second identifiable cultural tradition, from around 5000 BC, was the Eastern Archaic (or Old Copper) culture. These people hunted small as well as large game animals and fashioned copper implements through a cold hammering process. The more recent Woodland Tradition (1000 BC–AD 1700) was marked by the introduction of pottery and of mound burials. From the 1870s to the early 1900s, more than 11,000 burial mounds were discovered in Minnesota—the most visible remains of prehistoric life in the area. Finally, overlapping the Woodland culture in time was the Mississippian Tradition, beginning around AD 1000, in which large villages with permanent dwellings were erected near fertile river bottoms; their residents, in addition to hunting and fishing, raising corn, beans, and squash. There are many sites from this culture throughout southern Minnesota.

At the time of European penetration in the 17th and early 18th centuries, the two principal Indian nations were the Dakota, or Minnesota Sioux, and, at least after 1700, the Ojibwa, or Chippewa, who were moving from the east into northern Minnesota and the Dakota homelands. Friendly relations between the two nations were shattered in 1736, when the Dakota slew a party of French missionaries and traders (allies of the Ojibwa) and their Cree Indian guides (distant relatives of the Ojibwa) at the Lake of the Woods, an act the Ojibwa viewed as a declaration of war. There followed more than 100 years of conflict between Dakota and Ojibwa, during which the Dakota were pressed toward the south and west, with the Ojibwa establishing themselves in the north.

Few scholars accept the authenticity of the Kensington Rune Stone, found in 1898, the basis of the claim that Minnesota was visited in 1362 by the Vikings. The first white men whose travels through the region have been documented were Pierre Esprit Radisson and his brother-in-law, Médart Chouart, Sieur de Groseilliers, who probably reached the interior of northern Minnesota in the 1650s. In 1679, Daniel Greysolon, Sieur Duluth, held council with the Dakota near Mille Lacs and formally claimed the region for King Louis XIV of France. The following year, Duluth negotiated the release of three captives of the Dakota Indians, among them a Belgian explorer and missionary, Father Louis Hennepin, who named the falls of the Mississippi (the site of present-day Minneapolis) after his patron saint, Anthony of Padua, and returned to Europe to write an exaggerated account of his travels in the region.

Duluth was in the vanguard of the French, English, and American explorers, fur traders, and missionaries who came to Minnesota during the two centuries before statehood. Among the best known was Nicolas Perrot, who built Ft. Antoine on the east side of Lake Pepin in 1686. In 1731, Pierre Gaultier de Varennes, Sieur de la Verendrye, journeyed to the Lake of the Woods, along whose shores he erected Ft. St. Charles; subsequently, he or his men ventured farther west than any other known French explorer, reaching the Dakotas and the Saskatchewan Valley. His eldest son was among those slain by Dakota Indians at the Lake of the Woods in 1736.

Competition for control of the upper Mississippi Valley ended with the British victory in the French and Indian War, which placed the portion of Minnesota east of the Mississippi under British control; the land west of the Mississippi was ceded by France to Spain in 1762. Although the Spanish paid little attention to their northern territory, the British immediately sent in fur traders and explorers. One of the best known was Jonathan Carver, who spent the winter of 1766–67 with the Dakota on the Minnesota River. His account of his travels—a mixture of personal observations and borrowings from others—quickly became a popular success.

There was little activity in the region during the Revolutionary War, and for a few decades afterward, the British continued to pursue their interests there. The North West Company built a major fur-trading post at Grand Portage, which quickly became the center of a prosperous inland trade, and other posts dotted the countryside. The company hired David Thompson away from the Hudson's Bay Company to map the area from Lake Superior west to the Red River; his detailed and accurate work, executed in the late 1790s, is still admired today. After the War of 1812, the US Congress passed an act curbing British participation in the fur trade, and the North West Company was eventually replaced by the American Fur Company, which John Jacob Astor had incorporated in 1808.

Under the Northwest Ordinance of 1787, Minnesota east of the Mississippi became part of the Northwest Territory; most of western Minnesota was acquired by the US as part of the Louisiana Purchase of 1803. The Red River Valley became a secure part of the US after an agreement with England on the northern boundary was reached in 1818.

In 1805, the US War Department sent Lieutenant Zebulon Pike and a detachment of troops to explore the Mississippi to its source. Pike failed to locate the source, but he concluded a treaty with a band of Dakota for two parcels of land along the river. Later, additional troops were sent in to establish US control, and in 1819, a military post was established in part of Pike's land, on a bluff overlooking the junction of the Mississippi and Minnesota rivers. First called Ft. St. Anthony, it was renamed in 1825 for Colonel Josiah Snelling, who supervised the construction of the permanent fort. For three decades, Ft. Snelling served as the principal center of civilization in Minnesota and the key frontier outpost in the northwest.

In 1834, Henry H. Sibley was appointed a manager of the American Fur Company on the upper Mississippi. He settled comfortably at Mendota, a trading post across the river from Ft. Snelling, and enjoyed immediate success. The company's fortunes took a downward turn in 1837, however—partly because of a financial panic but, even more important, because the first of a series of treaties with the Dakota and Ojibwa transferred large areas of Indian land to the US government and thus curtailed the profitable relationship between fur traders and Indians. The treaties opened the land for lumbering, farming, and settlement. Lumbering spawned many of the early permanent settlements, such as Marine and Stillwater, on the St. Croix River, and St. Anthony (later Minneapolis) at the falls of the Mississippi. Another important town, St. Paul (originally Pig's Eye), developed as a trading center at the head of navigation on the Mississippi.

In 1849, Minnesota Territory was established. It included all of present-day Minnesota, along with portions of North and South Dakota east of the Missouri River. Alexander Ramsey, a Pennsylvania Whig, was appointed as the first territorial governor, and in 1851, the legislature named St. Paul the capital. Stillwater was chosen for the state prison, while St. Anthony was selected as the site for the university. As of 1850, the new territory had slightly more than 6,000 inhabitants, but as lumbering grew and subsequent Indian treaties opened up more land, the population boomed, reaching a total of more than 150,000 by 1857, with the majority concentrated in the southeast corner, close to the rivers.

On 11 May 1858, Minnesota officially became the 32d state, with its western boundaries pruned from the Missouri to the Red River. Henry Sibley, a Democrat, narrowly defeated Alexander Ramsey, running as a Republican, to become the state's first governor. But under Ramsey's leadership, the fastgrowing Republican Party soon gained control of state politics and held it firmly through the early 20th century. In the first presidential election in which Minnesota participated, Abraham Lincoln, the Republican candidate, easily carried the state, and when the Civil War broke out, Minnesota was the first state to answer Lincoln's call for troops. In all, Minnesota supplied more than 20,000 men to defend the Union.

More challenging to the defense of Minnesota was the Dakota War of 1862. Grieved by the loss of their lands, dissatisfied with reservation life, and ultimately brought to a condition of near starvation, the Dakota appealed to US Indian agencies without success. The murder of five whites by four young Dakota Indians ignited a bloody uprising in which more than 300 whites and an unknown number of Indians were killed. In the aftermath, 38 Dakota captives were hanged for "voluntary participation in murders and massacres," and the Dakota remaining in Minnesota were removed to reservations in Nebraska. (Some later returned to Minnesota.) Meanwhile, the Ojibwa were relegated to reservations on remnants of their former lands.

Also during 1862, Minnesota's first railroad joined St. Anthony (Minneapolis) and St. Paul with 10 mi (16 km) of track. By 1867, the Twin Cities were connected with Chicago by rail; in the early 1870s, tracks crossed the prairie all the way to the Red River Valley. The railroads brought settlers from the eastern states (many of them Scandinavian and German in origin) to every corner of Minnesota; the settlers, in turn, grew produce for the trains to carry back to the cities of the east. The railroads soon ushered in an era of large-scale commercial farming. Wheat provided the biggest cash crop, as exports rose from 2 million bushels in 1860 to 95 million in 1890. Meanwhile, the falls of St. Anthony became the major US flour-milling center; by 1880, 27 Minneapolis mills were producing more than 2 million barrels of flour annually.

Despite these signs of prosperity, discontent grew among Minnesota farmers, who were plagued by high railroad rates, damaging droughts, and a deflationary economy. The first national farmers' movement, the National Grange of the Patrons of Husbandry, was founded in 1867 by a Minnesotan, Oliver H. Kelley, and spread more rapidly in Minnesota than in any other state. The Farmers' Alliance movement, joining forces with the Knights of Labor, exerted a major influence on state politics in the 1880s. In 1898, the Populist Party—in which a Minnesotan, Ignatius Donnelly, played a leading role nationwide—helped elect John Lind to the governorship on a fusion ticket.

Most immigrants during the 1860s and 1870s settled on the rich farmland of the north and west, but after 1880 the cities and industries grew more rapidly. When iron ore was discovered in the 1880s in the sparsely settled northeast, even that part of the state attracted settlers, many of them immigrants from eastern and southern Europe. Before the turn of the century, Duluth had become a major lake port, and by the eve of World War I, Minnesota had become a national iron-mining center.

The economic picture changed after the war. As the forests became depleted, the big lumber companies turned to the Pacific Northwest. An agricultural depression hit the region, and flour mills moved to the Kansas City area and to Buffalo, N.Y. Minnesotans adapted to the new realities in various ways. Farmers planted corn, soybeans, and sugar beets along with wheat, and new food-processing industries developed. To these were added business machines, electronics, computers, and other high-technology industries. In 1948, for the first time, the dollar value of all manufactured products exceeded total cash farm receipts. In 1950 the state's urban population exceeded its rural population for the first time. Minnesota was becoming an urban commonwealth.

In addition to heightened demand for its agricultural products, Minnesota prospered as a result of new defense-related, high-technology, and other industries that grew up following World War II. Over $1 billion was invested in plants to process low-grade iron ore, called taconite, after the state's supply of high-grade ore declined. By the 1970s, environmentalists were targeting the ore producers for polluting Lake Superior with mineral wastes, and in 1978 the Minnesota Supreme Court ordered Reserve Mining Company to comply with pollution-control standards.

A successful merger of Minnesota's Farmer-Labor and Democratic parties, engineered in 1943–44 by both local and national politicians, revived the state's progressivist tradition after World War II. Hubert Humphrey (later US vice president) and his colleagues Orville Freeman, Eugene McCarthy, and Eugenie Anderson emerged as leaders of this new coalition. Their political heir, Walter Mondale, was vice president in 1977–81 but, as the Democratic presidential candidate in 1984, lost the election in a Republican landslide, carrying only his native state and the District of Columbia.

In the 1990s, Minnesota continued its tradition of economic diversification as service industries, including finance, insurance, and real estate, became increasingly important.

In 1988, Minnesota's farmers suffered from the worst drought since the 1930s. As a result of the severe flooding of the Mississippi River in 1993, almost half of Minnesota's counties were designated as disaster areas. Again in 1997, some of the most severe flooding in the century occurred in the Red River and Minnesota River valleys.

12 STATE GOVERNMENT

The constitutional convention that assembled at St. Paul on 13 July 1857 was marked by such bitter dissension that the Democrats and Republicans had to meet in separate chambers; the final draft was written by a committee of five Democrats and five Republicans and then adopted by a majority of each party, without amendment. Since Democrats and Republicans were also unwilling to sign the same piece of paper, two separate documents were prepared, one on blue-tinted paper, the other on white. The constitution was ratified by the electorate on 13 October and approved by the US Congress on 11 May 1858. An amendment restructuring the constitution for easy reference and simplifying its language was approved in 1974; for purposes of constitutional law, however, the original document (incorporating numerous other amendments) remains authoritative.

As reapportioned by court order after the 1970 census, the Minnesota legislature consists of a 67-member senate and a 134-member house of representatives. Senators serve four years and representatives two, at annual salaries of $29,675 as of 1995. Legislators must be US citizens, must be at least 21 years of age, and must have resided in the state for one year and in the legislative district for six months preceding election.

The governor and lieutenant governor are jointly elected for four-year terms; both must be US citizens at least 25 years old, and must have been residents of Minnesota for a year before election. Other constitutional officers are the secretary of state, auditor, treasurer, and attorney general, all serving for four years. Numerous other officials are appointed by the governor, among them the commissioners of the 20 government departments and many heads and members of independent agencies.

Once a bill is passed by a majority of both houses, the governor may sign it, veto it in whole or in part, or pocket-veto it by failing to act within 14 days of adjournment. (When the legislature is in session, however, a bill becomes law if the governor fails to act on it within 3 days.) A two-thirds vote of both houses is sufficient to override a veto. Constitutional amendments require the approval of a majority of both houses of the legislature and are subject to ratification by the electorate. Those voting in state elections must be at least 18 years old and must have been US citizens for three months and residents of the district for 20 days.

[13]POLITICAL PARTIES

The two major political parties are the Democratic-Farmer-Labor Party (DFL) and the Independent-Republican Party (IR), as Minnesota's Republican Party is now officially called. The Republican Party dominated Minnesota politics from the 1860s through the 1920s, except for a period around the turn of the century. The DFL, formed in 1944 by merger between the Democratic Party and the populist Farmer-Labor Party, rose to prominence in the 1950s under US Senator Hubert Humphrey.

The DFL is the heir to a long populist tradition bred during the panic of 1857 and the early days of statehood, a tradition perpetuated by a succession of strong, though transient, third-party movements. The Grange, a farmers' movement committed to the cause of railroad regulation, took root in Minnesota in 1868; it withered in the panic of 1873, but its successors, the Anti-Monopoly Party and the Greenback Party, attracted large followings for some time afterward. They were followed by a new pro-silver group, the Farmers' Alliance, which spread to Minnesota from Nebraska in 1881 and soon became associated with the Minnesota Knights of Labor. The Populist Party also won a foothold in Minnesota, in alliance with the Democratic Party in the late 1890s.

The Farmer-Labor Party, the most successful of Minnesota's third-party movements, grew out of a socialist and isolationist movement known at first as the Non-Partisan League. Founded in North Dakota with the initial aim of gaining control of the Republican Party in that state, the league moved its headquarters to St. Paul and competed in the 1918 elections under the name Farmer-Labor Party, hastily adopted to attract what party leaders hoped would be its two main constituencies. The party scored a major success in 1922 when its candidate, Henrik Shipstead, a Glenwood dentist, defeated a nationally known incumbent, Republican Senator Frank B. Kellogg; Farmer-Labor candidate Floyd B. Olson won the governorship in 1930. The decline of the party in the late 1930s was hastened by the rise of Republican

Harold Stassen, an ardent internationalist, who won the governorship in 1938 and twice won reelection.

The first DFL candidate to become governor was Orville Freeman in 1954. The DFL held the governorship from 1963 to 1967 and from 1971 to 1978, when US Representative Al Quie (IR) defeated his DFL opponent, Rudy Perpich; however, Perpich regained the governorship for the DFL in 1982. Perpich served four terms. He lost to Independent-Republican Arne Carlson in 1990, and Carlson was re-elected in 1994.

Minnesota is famous as a breeding ground for presidential candidates. Governor Harold Stassen contended seriously for the Republican nomination in 1948 and again in 1952. Vice President Hubert Humphrey was the Democratic presidential nominee in 1968, losing by a narrow margin to Richard Nixon. During the same year, US Senator Eugene McCarthy unsuccessfully sought the Democratic presidential nomination on an antiwar platform; his surprising showings in the early primaries against the incumbent, Lyndon B. Johnson, helped persuade Johnson to withdraw his candidacy. Eight years later, McCarthy ran for the presidency as an independent, drawing 35,490 votes in Minnesota (1.8% of the total votes cast) and 756,631 votes (0.9%) nationwide. Walter Mondale, successor to Hubert Humphrey's seat when Humphrey became Johnson's vice president in 1964, was chosen in 1976 by Jimmy Carter as his vice-presidential running mate; he again ran with Carter in 1980, when the two lost their bid for reelection. In the 1984 election, Minnesota was the only state to favor the Mondale-Ferraro ticket. Minnesotans gave the Republican Party a majority in the state's house of representatives for the first time since 1970, but the Democrats retained control of the state senate. In 1994, US Senator David Durenberger retired, partly a result of having been "denounced" by the Senate in 1990, and Rod Grams, a 46-year-old Republican was elected to the seat. In 1996, Democrat Paul Wellstone successfully defended his Senate seat against a challenge by Republican Rudy Boschwitz, from whom he had won the seat in 1990. The Democrats continued to control the

Minnesota Presidential Vote by Political Parties, 1948–96

YEAR	ELECTORAL VOTE	MINNESOTA WINNER	DEMOCRAT[1]	REPUBLICAN[2]	PROGRESSIVE	SOCIALIST	SOCIALIST LABOR[3]
1948	11	*Truman (D)	692,966	483,617	27,866	4,646	2,525
1952	11	*Eisenhower (R)	608,458	763,211	2,666	—	2,383
						SOC. WORKERS	
1956	11	*Eisenhower (R)	617,525	719,302	—	1,098	2,080
1960	11	*Kennedy (D)I	779,933	757,915	—	3,077	962
1964	10	*Johnson (D)	991,117	559,624	—	1,177	2,544
							AMERICAN IND.
1968	10	Humphrey (D)	857,738	658,643	—	—	68,931
					PEOPLE'S		AMERICAN
1972	10	*Nixon (R)	802,346	898,269	2,805	4,261	31,407
					LIBERTARIAN		
1976	10	*Carter (D)	1,070,440	819,395	3,529	4,149	13,592
						CITIZENS	
1980	10	Carter (D)	954,173	873,268	31,593	8,406	6,136
1984	10	Mondale (D)	1,036,364	1,032,603	2,996	1,219	—
					MINNESOTA PROGRESSIVE		SOCIALIST WORKERS
1988	10	Dukakis (D)	1,109,471	962,337	5,109	5,403	2,155
					IND. (Perot)		CONSTITUTION
1992	10	*Clinton (D)	1,020,997	747,841	3,373	562,506	3,363
							GREEN (Nader)
1996	10	*Clinton (D)	1,120,438	766,476	8,271	257,704	24,908

*Won US presidential election.
1 Called Democratic-Farmer-Labor Party in Minnesota.
2 Since 1976, called Independent-Republican in Minnesota.
3 Appeared as Industrial Government Party on the ballot.

congressional delegation following the 1996 elections, by a margin of 6–2. In 1996, Democrat Bill Clinton won 51% of the presidential vote, Republican Bob Dole gained 35%, and Independent Ross Perot received 12%. In 1997, there were 42 Democrats serving in the Minnesota state senate, and 24 Republicans. Party representation in the state house consisted of 70 Democrats and 64 Republicans.

In 1994 there were 16 blacks and 3 Hispanics holding public office. As of 1995, there were 50 women serving in the state legislature and 3 women in elective executive office.

14LOCAL GOVERNMENT

Minnesota is divided into 87 counties and 13 regional administrations. As of 1992; the state had 1,803 townships (more than any other state), 854 municipal governments, 458 school districts, and 377 special districts.

Each of Minnesota's counties is governed by a board of commissioners, ordinarily elected for four-year terms. Other elected officials include the auditor, treasurer, recorder, sheriff, attorney, and coroner; an assessor and engineer are customarily appointed. Besides administering welfare, highway maintenance, and other state programs, the county is responsible for planning and development and, except in large cities, for property assessment. During the 1970s, counties also assumed increased responsibility for solid waste disposal and shoreline management.

Each regional development commission, or RDC, consists of local officials (selected by counties, cities, townships, and boards of education in the region) and of representatives of public interest groups (selected by the elected officials). RDCs prepare and adopt regional development plans and review applications for loans and grants.

As of 1984, 104 cities had home-rule charters; the remaining 751 were statutory cities, restricted to the systems of government prescribed by state law. In either case, the mayor-council system was the most common. Besides providing such traditional functions as street maintenance and police and fire protection, some cities operate utilities, sell liquor, or run hospitals, among other services. Each township is governed by a board of three supervisors and by other officials elected for three-year terms at the town meeting, held annually on the 2d Tuesday in March.

15STATE SERVICES

Minnesota's ombudsman for corrections investigates complaints about corrections facilities or the conduct of prison officials. A six-member Ethical Practices Board supervises the registration of some 1,300 lobbyists, monitors the financing of political campaigns, and sees that some 1,000 elected and appointed state officials observe regulations governing conflict of interest and disclosure of personal finances. Minnesota law also provides that legislative meetings of any kind must be open to the public.

The state-aided public school system is under the jurisdiction of the Department of Children, Families, and Learning, which carries out the policies of a nine-member Board of Education appointed by the governor with the advice and consent of the senate. Responsible for higher education are the University of Minnesota Board of Regents, elected by the legislature; the boards of trustees of the Minnesota State Colleges and Universities (MNSCU), appointed by the governor; and other agencies. The Department of Transportation maintains roads and bridges, enforces public transportation rates, inspects airports, and has responsibility for railroad safety.

Minnesota's Department of Health investigates health problems, disseminates health information, regulates hospitals and nursing homes, and inspects restaurants and lodgings. Health regulations affecting farm produce are administered by the Department of Agriculture. State facilities for the mentally retarded are operated by the Department of Human Services, which administers state welfare programs and provides social services to the aged, the handicapped, and others in need.

The Department of Public Safety registers motor vehicles, licenses drivers, enforces traffic laws, and regulates the sale of liquor. The Department of Military Affairs has jurisdiction over the Minnesota National Guard, and the Department of Corrections operates prisons, reformatories, and parole programs. The Housing Finance Agency aids the construction and rehabilitation of low- and middle-income housing. Laws governing occupational safety, wages and hours, and child labor are enforced by the Department of Labor and Industry, while the Department of Economic Security supervises public employment programs and administers unemployment insurance.

16JUDICIAL SYSTEM

Minnesota's highest court is the supreme court, consisting of a chief justice and eight associate justices; all are elected without party designation for six-year terms, with vacancies being filled by gubernatorial appointment. The district court, divided into 10 judicial districts, is the court of original jurisdiction. Each judicial district has at least three district judges, elected to six-year terms. The governor designates a chief judge for a three-year term.

County courts, operating in all counties of the state except two—Hennepin (Minneapolis) and Ramsey (St. Paul), which have municipal courts—assume functions formerly exercised by probate, family, and local courts. They exercise civil jurisdiction in cases where the amount in contention is $5,000 or less, and criminal jurisdiction in preliminary hearings and misdemeanors. They also hear cases involving family disputes, and have concurrent jurisdiction with the district court in divorces, adoptions, and certain other proceedings. The probate division of the county court system presides over guardianship and incompetency proceedings and all cases relating to the disposing of estates. All county judges are elected for six-year terms. Minnesota had 20,900 active attorneys in 1996.

Minnesota's 10 federal and state correctional institutions had a total population of over 4,600 in 1997, and more than 230 juvenile offenders.

Crime rates are generally below the national average. In 1996, Minnesota's total crime rate per 100,000 inhabitants was 4,497.3. There were 16,416 violent crimes (356 per 100,000 inhabitants) and 190,911 property crimes (4,141.2 per 100,000 inhabitants). Minnesota has no death penalty statute. The Crime Victims Reparations Board offers compensation to innocent victims of crime or to their dependent survivors.

17ARMED FORCES

There were 867 active duty military personnel stationed in Minnesota in 1996. Firms in the state received $960 million in defense contract awards during the same year.

As of 1 July 1996 there were 457,000 veterans living in Minnesota, including fewer than 500 who saw service in World War I, 113,000 in World War II, 75,000 during the Korean conflict, 150,000 during the Vietnam era, and 26,000 during the Persian Gulf War. Veterans in Minnesota received a total of $666 million in benefits in 1995/96.

The Minnesota National Guard and Reserve had a total authorized strength of 28,168 in 1992, of which 70% is from the Army. In 1993, the Minnesota State Patrol employed 451 full-time sworn officers, or 1 per 10,000 residents.

18MIGRATION

A succession of migratory waves began in the 17th and 18th centuries with the arrival of the Dakota and Ojibwa, among other Indian groups, followed during the 19th century by New England Yankees, Germans, Scandinavians, and finally southern and eastern Europeans. Especially since 1920, new arrivals from other states and countries have been relatively few, and the state experienced a net loss from migration of 80,000 between 1970 and 1980, but nearly halted the trend in the 1980s, when immigration nearly equaled emigration. Between 1990 and 1996, Minnesota had net gains of 66,141 in domestic migration and 34,249 in international migration. In 1996, 8,977 foreign immigrants entered the state. As of 1990, 73.6% of all Minnesota residents were native-born. About 45% of those age 5 and older lived in a different house in 1985 than in 1990, of which 18% did so in a different state.

Within the state, there has been a long-term movement to metropolitan areas and especially to the suburbs of major cities; from 1970 to 1983, the state's metropolitan population grew by nearly 1% annually. During the 1980s, the urban population increased from 66.8% to 69.9%. From 1970 to 1990, the population of the Minneapolis-St. Paul metropolitan area grew by 24%.

19INTERGOVERNMENTAL COOPERATION

Relations with the Council of State Governments are conducted through the Minnesota Commission on Interstate Cooperation. consisting of five members from each house of the state legislature and five administrative officers or other state employees; in addition, the governor, the president of the senate, and the speaker of the house are nonvoting members. Minnesota also participates in the Great Lakes Charter, which it formed with seven other states in 1985 to preserve the lakes' water supply, and in other regional compacts. In 1995/96, Minnesota received $3.5 billion in federal aid.

20ECONOMY

Furs, wheat, pine lumber, and high-grade iron ore were once the basis of Minnesota's economy. As these resources diminished, however, the state turned to wood pulp, dairy products, corn and soybeans, taconite, and manufacturing, often in such food-related industries as meat-packing, canning, and the processing of dairy products. The leading sources of income in Minnesota have shifted again in recent years. Manufacturing remains central to the state's economy, but finance, real estate, and insurance have also come to play a dominant role. The share of GSP generated by government and trade rose significantly between the late 1960s and early 1980s, while the relative contributions of manufacturing and construction declined.

Minnesota's gross state product in 1994 was $124,641 million, to which private goods-producing industries contributed $34,131 million; private services-producing industries, $76,509 million; and government, $14,001 million.

Minnesota's per capita personal income in 1995 was $23,971 which ranked 14th nationally.

In 1996, there were 18,236 filings for bankruptcy in the state, up almost 23% from the previous year.

21INCOME

In 1996, Minnesota ranked 9th among the 50 states in personal income per capita, amounting to $25,580. Total nonfarm personal income in 1992 was $89.8 billion, up by 5.9% from $84.8 billion in 1991. Total disposable personal income increased from $93.8 billion in 1995 to $100.6 billion in 1996.

Minnesota's median household income was $37,933 in 1995. Wide regional differences in personal income exist within the state; family incomes are highest in the Twin Cities area, where the state's high-income counties are clustered. On the other hand, 9.2% of all state residents lived below the poverty level in 1996, down from 12.8% in 1992.

22LABOR

In 1996, the civilian labor force totaled 2,609,000 persons, of whom an average 2,505,000 were employed and 104,000 were unemployed. The unemployment rate that year was 4.0%. As of 1995, manufacturing workers in Minnesota earned a weekly salary of $680.

Actual employment and earnings in 1995 were as follows:

	EMPLOYMENT (1,000S)	EARNINGS (MILLIONS OF DOLLARS)
Total	2,314.0	63,312.7
Agricultural services, forestry, fisheries	20.6	366.9
Mining	7.8	335.2
Construction	83.9	2,803.2
Manufacturing	426.3	15,064.1
Durable goods	243.6	8,694.0
Nondurable goods	182.7	6,370.1
Transportation, public utilities	111.0	3,746.5
Trade	580.9	11,413.0
Wholesale trade	142.1	5,313.0
Retail trade	438.8	6,100.0
Finance, insurance, real estate	138.0	5,156.3
Services	619.2	14,822.2
Government	326.3	9,605.3

The history of unionization in the state includes several long and bitter labor disputes, notably the Iron Range strike of 1916, the Teamsters' strike of 1934, and the Hormel strike of 1985–86. The earliest known unions—two printers' locals, established in the late 1850s—died out during the Civil War, and several later unions faded in the panic of 1873. The Knights of Labor were the dominant force of the 1880s; the next decade saw the rise of the Minnesota State Federation of Labor, whose increasing political influence bore fruit in the landmark Workmen's Compensation Act of 1913 and the subsequent ascension of the Farmer-Labor Party. The legislature enacted a fair employment practices law in 1955 and passed a measure in 1973 prescribing collective-bargaining procedures for public employees and granting them a limited right to strike.

As of 1995, union membership totaled 430,600, or 20.3% of all workers. Unionization among manufacturing workers was 16.8%.

23AGRICULTURE

Cash receipts from farm marketings totaled over $7.0 billion in 1995, placing Minnesota 7th among the 50 states; crops made up about 51% of the total value. For 1996, Minnesota ranked 1st in the production of sugar beets, sweet corn for processing, and green peas for processing; 2d in cultivated wild rice; 3d in flaxseed, spring wheat, and soybeans; 4th in corn, oats, barley, and sunflowers; 7th in dry edible beans, potatoes, and rye; and 8th in all hay.

The early farmers settled in the wooded hills and valleys in the southeastern quarter of the state, where they had to cut down trees and dig up stumps to make room for crops. With the coming of the railroads, farmers began planting the prairies with wheat, which by the late 1870s took up 70% of all farm acreage. In succeeding decades, wheat prices fell and railroad rates soared, fanning agrarian discontent. Farmers began to diversity, with dairy farming, oats, and corn becoming increasingly important. Improved corn yields since the 1940s have spurred the production of hogs and beef cattle and the growth of meat-packing as a major industry.

As of 1996, the state had 87,000 farms, covering 29,800,000 acres (12,065,000 hectares), or 55% of the state's total land area; the average farm had 343 acres (139 hectares). The number of people living on farms steadily declined from 624,000 in 1960 to

482,000 in 1970, and then to only 207,956, or 4.75% of the total population, by 1991. The value of farmland also dropped, from $1,197 per acre in 1982 to $954 per acre in 1996. Minnesota's farmers faced acute financial troubles during the early 1980s as a result of heavy debts, high interest rates, and generally low crop prices.

The main farming areas are in southern Minnesota, where corn, soybeans, and oats are important, and in a Red River Valley along the western border, where wheat, barley, sugar beets, and potatoes are among the chief crops. The following table shows selected major crops in 1996:

	PRODUCTION	VALUE (000)
Soybeans	124,200,000 bushels	$1,513,350
Corn for grain	868,750,000 bushels	2,085,000
Hay	5,998,000 tons	469,930
Wheat	102,382,000 bushels	439,819
Oats	15,120,000 bushels	26,460
Barley (1990)	33,280,000 bushels	79,872
Sunflowers	184,660,000 lb	22,655
Sweet corn for processing	719,400 tons	56,113
Sugar beets	7,971,000 tons	—

Agribusiness is Minnesota's largest basic industry, with about one-fourth of the state's labor force employed in agriculture or agriculture-related industries, most notably food processing.

24 ANIMAL HUSBANDRY

Excluding the northeast, livestock-raising is dispersed throughout the state, with cattle concentrated particularly in west-central Minnesota and in the extreme southeast, and hogs along the southern border.

In 1997, the state had nearly 2.75 million cattle and calves, valued at nearly $1.7 billion. The state had 4.85 million hogs and pigs, valued at nearly $475 million, (3d in the US) in 1996. Minnesota produced more turkey in 1995 than any other state except North Carolina; 854 million lb (387 million kg), worth nearly $300 million. Also during 1995, the state produced nearly 18.3 million lb (8.3 million kg) of sheep and lambs which brought in a total of nearly $15.5 million.

The state's total of 9.4 billion lb (4.3 billion kg) of milk outproduced all but four states in 1995. Production of chickens and broilers was 268 million lb (121.5 million kg), worth around $83.1 million, and the egg output was 2.8 billion in 1995.

25 FISHING

Commercial fishermen in 1995 landed 497,000 lb (225,000 kg) of fish, valued at $236,000. The catch included herring and smelts from Lake Superior, whitefish and yellow pike from large inland lakes, and carp and catfish from the Mississippi and Minnesota rivers. Sport fishing attracts some 1.5 million anglers annually to the state's 2.6. million acres (1.1 million hectares) of fishing lakes and 7,000 mi (11,000 km) of fishing streams, which are stocked with trout, bass, pike, muskellunge, and other fish by the Division of Fish and Wildlife of the Department of Natural Resources. Federal hatcheries distributed 240,243 fish (17,257 lb or 7,828 kg) and 142,411 fish eggs within the state in 1995/96.

26 FORESTRY

Forests, which originally occupied two-thirds of Minnesota's land area, have been depleted by lumbering, farming, and forest fires. As of 1992, forestland covered 18,253,000 acres (7,387,000 hectares), or 36% of the state's total land area. Most of the forestland is in the north, especially in Arrowhead Country in the northeast. Of the 14,773,000 acres (6,056,930 hectares) of commercial timberland, less than half is privately owned and more than one-third is under state, county, or municipal jurisdiction. Over half of the timber that is harvested is used in paper

products, 10% for furniture, and 30% for wood products. Mills that process raw logs account for half of all forest and forest-product employment in Minnesota. Millwork accounts for 80% of the value added in the timber industry. In 1995, respective employment figures for the lumber and paper industries were 21,700 and 16,100; the values added by manufacture were $1.5 billion and $2.1 billion; and the values of total shipments were $3.2 billion and $4.6 billion.

The state's two national forests are Superior (2,054,022 acres—831,236 hectares) and Chippewa (661,218 acres—267,586 hectares). The Department of Natural Resources, Division of Forestry, promotes effective management of the forest environment and seeks to restrict forest fire occurrence to 1,100 fires annually, burning no more than 30,000 acres (12,000 hectares) in all.

More than 3 million acres (1.2 million hectares) are planted each year with trees by the wood fiber industry, other private interests, and federal, state, and county forest services—more than enough to replace those harvested or destroyed by fire, insects, or disease.

27 MINING

The value of nonfuel mineral production in Minnesota in 1995 was estimated to be about $1.49 billion, an increase of about 4% from the $1.34 billion reported in 1994. Iron ore, Minnesota's leading mineral commodity, accounted for nearly 86% ($1.28 billion) of the state's total mineral value. Iron ore is found along a belt that runs through Itasca and St. Louis counties. The combined value of construction sand and gravel and crushed stone, the two other leading mineral commodities produced, accounted for less than 11% of Minnesota's mineral value in 1995. The estimated value of construction sand and gravel ($109 million) and crushed stone ($49.3 million) increased about 21% and 25%, respectively, over values reported in 1994. The state rose from 9th to 7th rank nationally in value of nonfuel minerals produced during the year. The changes in Minnesota's total nonfuel mineral value that occurred between 1992 and 1995 resulted mainly from the combined effects of increased iron ore shipments. Minnesota ranked 1st nationally in iron ore, 8th in construction sand and gravel, and 10th in industrial sand and gravel.

Mining employment totaled 7,600 workers in December 1996, about the same as the previous year.

28 ENERGY AND POWER

Minnesota produced 42.5 billion kWh of electricity in 1995, when installed capacity reached 9.24 million kW. Conventional thermal plants accounted for 78% of total installed capacity; most plants were coal-fired. There are three nuclear reactors, all owned by the Northern States Power Co. The retail cost of electricity increased from less than 4 cents per kWh in Minneapolis in 1979 to 7.2 cents in 1995.

Minnesota's 7 million acres (2.8 million hectares) of peat lands, the state's only known fossil fuel resource, constitute nearly half of the US total (excluding Alaska). If burned directly, the accessible fuel-quality peat deposit could substantially supplement Minnesota's energy needs.

29 INDUSTRY

Minnesota's vast wealth of natural resources, especially the state's extensive timberlands and fertile prairie, was the basis for Minnesota's early industrial development. In the late 19th century, Minneapolis was the nation's flour milling center. By the early 20th century, canning and meat packing were among the state's largest industries.

While food and food products remain an important part of the state's economy, the state's economy has diversified significantly from these early beginnings. Today, the state looks to high technology industries such as computer manufacturing, scientific instruments and medical products as well as resource-based industries such as food products and wood products.

The total value of shipments by manufacturers in 1995 exceeded $69 billion. The value of shipments by selected industry groups in 1995 was as follows:

Food and food products	14,396,800,000
Industrial machinery and equipment	10,245,700,000
Electronic and other electric equipment	5,491,800,000
Paper and allied products	4,618,700,000
Fabricated metal products	4,417,500,000
Transportation equipment	4,094,400,000
Instruments and related products	3,912,100,000

Industry is concentrated in the state's southeast region, especially in the Twin Cities area. Minnesota is the headquarters of 15 Fortune 500 companies as of 1997.

In 1995, there were 1,967 US patents issued to Minnesota residents.

30COMMERCE

Access to the Great Lakes, the St. Lawrence Seaway, and the Atlantic Ocean, as well as to the Mississippi River and the Gulf of Mexico, helps make Minnesota a major marketing and distribution center for the upper Midwest. Sales by wholesale establishments totaled $72.5 billion in 1992, of which 48.9% was in durable goods. As of 1995, the state's 14,504 wholesale trade establishments had payroll totals of $5.3 billion (13th among the 50 states). Retail sales totaled $35.6 billion (20th) in 1992. The 27,779 retail establishments in 1995 had payroll totals slightly higher than $6.1 billion (18th in the US), with eating and drinking establishments accounting for 21.2% of the total; auto dealers, 17.3%; and general merchandise stores, 15.2%. Much of this volume was concentrated in the Twin Cities metropolitan region; in 1992, Minneapolis–St. Paul had retail sales of $22.6 billion, or 63.4% of the state's total.

Manufacturing exports to foreign countries amounted to $8.9 billion in 1996 (19th among the 50 states). The manufactured exports included computers and computer software, electronic equipment, scientific instruments, and transportation equipment. Dairy products, feed grains, soybeans, and wheat were the largest agricultural commodity exports.

31CONSUMER PROTECTION

The Consumer Enforcement Division of the Minnesota Attorney General's Office enforces Minnesota's laws against false advertising, consumer fraud, and deceptive trade practices. The Consumer Services Division answers consumer questions and mediates consumer complaints, attempting to resolve the complaints through a voluntary mediation program. The Attorney General's office also produces brochures and booklets on a wide variety of consumer topics, including landlords and tenants, new-car buying, home building, credit, and debt collection.

32BANKING

As of 31 December 1995, Minnesota had 525 insured commercial banks; the total assets of the state's insured commercial banks in 1996 were $70.2 billion, including $19.0 billion in real estate loans. Deposits exceeded $48.9 billion, of which $36.9 billion were time and savings deposits.

Minnesota had 22 insured savings institutions as of 31 December 1995, with assets totaling over $5.7 billion.

33INSURANCE

Minnesotans held 3,539,000 life insurance policies valued at $254 billion as of 1995. Coverage per family averaged $137,200. Payments to beneficiaries in the same year totaled $2.8 billion, including $500 million in death payments

Property and liability insurance companies wrote premiums totaling over $4.9 billion in 1995; automotive liability insurance accounted for $1.5 billion, automobile physical damage insurance for $609 million, and homeowners' coverage for $444.1 million. No-fault automobile insurance was enacted in 1974. Minnesotans held nearly $360.1 million worth of flood insurance at the end of 1994.

34SECURITIES

The Minneapolis Grain Exchange, founded in 1881, is the state's major commodity exchange. Enforcement of statutes governing securities, franchises, and corporate takeovers (as well as charitable organizations, public cemeteries, collection agencies, and bingo) is the responsibility of the Securities Division of the Department of Commerce. New York Stock Exchange member firms have sales offices and registered representatives in Minnesota.

35PUBLIC FINANCE

Minnesota spends a relatively large amount on state government and local assistance, especially on a per capita basis. In 1992/93, Minnesota ranked 7th among the 50 states in total state and local general expenditures per capita ($4,783).

The state budget is prepared by the Department of Finance and submitted biennially by the governor to the legislature for amendment and approval. The fiscal year runs from 1 July to 30 June. The following table summarizes estimated general fund revenues and expenditures for the 1996/97 biennium (in millions of dollars):

REVENUES	
Individual income tax	$ 8,681.0
Corporate income tax	1,369.9
General sales tax	5,941.9
Motor vehicle tax	758.7
Other taxes	1,811.4
Nontax revenue	772.4
TOTAL	$19,335.3
EXPENDITURES	
Education aids	$ 6,598.5
Postsecondary education	2,146.2
Property tax aids and credits	2,411.9
Health care	2,879.6
Family support	463.2
Debt service	438.9
Other outlays	3,754.7
TOTAL	$18,693.0

As of 30 June 1993, the outstanding debt of state and local governments totaled $21 billion; the per capita debt was $4,641.

36TAXATION

In 1993, Minnesota ranked 17th among the 50 states in total receipts from state and local taxes ($12.1 billion) and 6th in state and local taxes collected per capita ($2,672). In per capita terms, Minnesota ranked 7th in individual income taxes ($734), 11th in corporate income taxes ($113), 14th in sales and excise taxes ($811), 14th in property taxes ($835), and 19th in other state and local taxes ($179).

As of 1997, corporate profits were taxed at a flat rate of 9.8%. Individual income is taxed at graduated rates that range from 6% to 8.5%. Personal exemptions and the standard deduction are the same as for federal income tax, and tax brackets are indexed for inflation. A refundable earned income credit is provided for low-income workers. The state of Minnesota also levies a 6.5% state sales tax, a gasoline tax of 20 cents per gallon, a cigarette tax of 48 cents per pack, a motor vehicle registration tax, and other selective business taxes.

Gift and inheritance taxes were repealed in 1980, and Minnesota's estate tax is offset, dollar for dollar, by a reduction in the taxpayer's federal estate tax liability.

Real property (commercial, industrial, and residential) is subject to the property tax, which accounts for 95% of total tax collections by local governing units. In Minnesota's classified property tax system, commercial, industrial, and rental properties are taxed at considerably higher rates than owned homes. Minnesota's "circuit breaker" system refunds property tax payments to homeowners and renters whose residential property taxes are high relative to their income.

According to the Tax Foundation, Minnesota residents paid $24.3 billion in federal taxes in 1995—$5,312 per capita—and received $19.0 billion in federal expenditures.

37ECONOMIC POLICY

Minnesota's Department of Trade and Economic Development offers a variety of programs to encourage expansion of existing industries and to attract new industry to the state. The Department extends loans to small businesses for capital investments which create or retain jobs. It awards grants to new or expanding companies in rural areas and provides limited guarantees to private lenders for loans given to start-up companies. A Tourism Loan Program offers low interest loans to tourism-related businesses to upgrade existing facilities or develop new ones. The Minnesota Export Finance Authority assists with the financing of small business exports. The state offers grants to depressed communities to help them retain or attract business or to rebuild their infrastructure. Minnesota's corporate income tax is structured to favor companies having relatively large payrolls and property (as opposed to sales) within the state.

38HEALTH

Shortly after the founding of Minnesota Territory, promoters attracted new settlers partly by proclaiming the tonic benefits of Minnesota's soothing landscape and cool, bracing climate; the area was trumpeted as a haven for retirees and for those afflicted with malaria or tuberculosis.

In 1995, 63,263 infants were born in Minnesota, or 13.7 per 1,000 population. below the national rate. Infant mortality was relatively low, with a rate of 6.4 per 1,000 live births in 1995. There were 15,546 legal abortions in 1992; the ratio of 237 abortions per 1,000 live births was well below the national rate. In 1995, 37,472 deaths, or 812.9 per 100,000 population (below the 879 national rate), were recorded. In 1995, 20.5% of Minnesota residents were smokers. Men smoked slightly more than women (22.5% vs. 18.6%). The projected number of deaths from smoking-related illness was 97,009 in 1995. The death rates per 100,000 population for the two leading causes, heart disease and cancer, were 225.2 and 188.6, respectively. Minnesota ranked 12th for coronary heart disease death rates in 1993; 81.4 per 100,000 population. Rates for these causes of death were below the national norms, while the death rate from cerebrovascular diseases (67.8) exceeded the national average. In 1995 there were only 204 reported AIDS cases, for a rate of 9.04 per 100,000 population. The US average was 28.48 per 100,000 in 1995.

In 1995, Minnesota had 142 hospitals, with 13,081 beds, 492,150 patient admissions. Hospital personnel included 15,485 full-time equivalent registered nurses as of 1 January 1991. The average expense to a hospital in the state for services provided in 1994 per admission was $695 per inpatient day, and the average expense per stay was $6,029. Minnesota had 12,512 federal and nonfederal physicians at the end of 1995, as well as 2,859 licensed active dentists in 1995, and 44,900 registered nurses in 1994. In fiscal 1994 there were 426,000 Medicaid recipients, who received a total of $1.98 billion in health care benefits, and 623,000 Medicare enrollees, who got $2.17 billion. Only 9.5% of Minnesota residents were uninsured in 1994, the 5th-lowest percentage in the US.

The Mayo Clinic, developed by Drs. Charles H. and William J. Mayo in the 1890s and early 1900s, was the first private clinic in the US and became a world-renowned center for surgery; today it is owned and operated by a self-perpetuating charitable foundation. The separate Mayo Foundation for Medical Education and Research, founded and endowed by the Mayo brothers in 1915, was subsequently affiliated with the University of Minnesota, which became the first US institution to offer graduate education in surgery and other branches of clinical medicine.

39SOCIAL WELFARE

The AFDC program assisted 171,900 Minnesotans in 1996, dispersing an average monthly payment of $621. That year, 294,825 Minnesotans received monthly food stamps averaging $62.18. During the same period, school children taking part in the school lunch program cost the federal government $73.1 million. In 1995, 712,570 Minnesotans received Social Security retirement benefits; the average monthly payment was $706. In 1995, 62,126 Minnesotans received Supplemental Security Income benefits averaging $324 a month. During 1995, state and federal unemployment benefits averaged $228.22 weekly.

With the enactment of the Personal Responsibility and Work Opportunity Reconciliation Act of 1996, the US government has changed the form and regulations for many of its social welfare programs; most significantly, it replaces Aid to Families with Dependent Children (AFDC), an open-ended entitlement program, with Temporary Assistance for Needy Families (TANF), a limited system of assistance funded largely through federal block grants. The reform act also impacts the food stamp program, the Supplemental Security Income program, and the child nutrition program. The law took effect on 1 July 1997 and provided $16.38 billion in block grants for fiscal years 1997–2002. The grants are to be divided among the states based on an equation involving the numbers of former AFDC recipients in each state. Because many of the bill's provisions have yet to be implemented into state-by-state policy, it was not possible to include the details of each state's programs for this edition of this work.

40HOUSING

In 1996, Minnesota had 1,956,000 year-round housing units, of which 1,732,000 were occupied. Of the 1990 census total of 1,848,445 housing units, 64% were occupied by their owners. Over 98% of the occupied housing had full plumbing. The median valuation of an owner-occupied house in 1990 was $74,000.

In 1996, 27,043 new units, valued at $2.9 billion, were authorized for construction; of these, 22,085 were owner-occupied. In 1992/93, HUD awarded Minnesota $324.7 million in grants. The median monthly cost for an owner with a mortgage was $724 in 1990, the last year for which figures are available, and $186 for an owner without a mortgage. Renters paid a median amount of $422 per month in 1990. During 1995/96, Minnesota received $318.3 million in aid from the US Department of Housing and Urban Development, including $70.3 million in community development block grants.

41EDUCATION

Minnesota's first public school system was authorized in 1849, but significant growth in enrollment did not occur until after the Civil War. Today, Minnesota has one of the best-supported systems of public education in the US. By 1990, according to state data, 334,335 Minnesotans aged 20 or older were high school graduates.

In 1995, Minnesota had an estimated 834,158 public school students, and a pupil-teacher ratio of 17.4 to 1. In 1995/96 there were 48,400 public school teachers, earning an average salary of $37,145 (22d place among the states).

Catholic parochial schools had a total enrollment of 50,769 in 1992/93; other private schools enrolled 30,862 pupils in 1992/93.

The state's public postsecondary education system is overseen by Minnesota State Colleges and Universities (MNSCU) as of 1 July 1995,and includes three areas: the state university system—with campuses at Bemidji, Mankato, Marshall, Minneapolis-St. Paul, Moorhead. St. Cloud, and Winona—which had an enrollment of 52,047 in 1992/93; the community college system, consisting of 18 two-year colleges and 3 centers, which had 35,150 students; and a statewide network of 33 area vocational-technical institutes that enrolled 35,388 students as of 1992/93. The University of Minnesota (founded as an academy in 1851), with campuses in the Twin Cities, Duluth, Morris, and Crookston, had 52,930 students in 1992/93. The state's oldest private college, Hamline University in St. Paul, was founded in 1854 and is affiliated with the United Methodist Church. In 1992/93 there were 26 private colleges, many of them with ties to Lutheran or Roman Catholic religious authorities. Carleton College, at Northfield, is a notable independent institution.

Minnesota has an extensive program of student grants, work-study arrangements, and loan programs, in addition to reciprocal tuition arrangements with Wisconsin, North Dakota, and South Dakota. In 1990/91, a total of $71 million was granted to 59,077 students to help pay their expenses at institutions of higher learning inside the state;

In 1992/93, state expenditures for education totaled $6.6 billion, with $4.7 billion for elementary and secondary education and $1.9 billion for post-secondary education. State spending on education is estimated to increase to $7.9 billion for 1994/95, with $5.8 billion of that total going towards K–12 education.

42ARTS

The new Ordway Music Theater in St. Paul, which has two concert halls, opened in January 1985. The Ordway is the home of the Minnesota Opera Company and of the St. Paul Chamber Orchestra. The privately owned, nonprofit theater was built for about $45 million and was founded by Minnesota Mining and Manufacturing Corp. and other private sources.

The Minnesota Orchestra, founded in 1903 in Minneapolis, is headed by music director Eiji Oue. Music director Hugh Wolf is in his fifth season with the St. Paul Chamber Orchestra and shares conducting duties with Christopher Hogwood and Bobbie McFerrin. The Minnesota Opera, conducted by Phillip Brunelle, and the St. Olaf College Choir, at Northfield, also have national reputations. The Tyrone Guthrie Theater, founded in Minneapolis in 1963, is one of the nation's most prestigious repertory companies and was headed by director Joe Dowling as of 1996.

The Walker Art Center in Minneapolis is an innovative museum with an outstanding contemporary collection, while the Minneapolis Institute of Arts exhibits more traditional works. The Weisman Art Museum of the University of Minnesota is in Minneapolis, and the Minnesota Museum of Art is in St. Paul.

State and regional arts groups as well as individual artists are supported by state and federal grants administered through the State Arts Board, an 11-member panel appointed by the governor.

The State of Minnesota received federal and state assistance for its arts programs in 1996. The NEA contributed $3,269,000 to the state's programs, and $1,144,000 to the Minnesota State Arts Board. The State Arts Board was also given funding from the state. Private sources amounted to $101 million. Audiences for the state's arts programs totaled 98,083,000. There were 113,000 contributing artists. The State offered arts education to 49,000 school children. Some 2,420 teachers also participated in the programs. Local art associations as well as state art associations, continue to contribute to the art education programs. Money also was generated through the NEA's state and regional programs.

43LIBRARIES AND MUSEUMS

Minnesota has 361 public libraries and library outlets, serving 97% of the state's population; about 99% of them are joined in a network of 12 regional public library systems. The total number of books and audiovisual items was 17,735,101 in 1996, when public library circulation reached 43,160,266. The largest single public library system is the Minneapolis Public Library and Information Center (founded in 1885), which had 2,083,000 volumes in 1995. The leading academic library, with 4,651,111 volumes, is that maintained by the University of Minnesota at Minneapolis. Special libraries include the James Jerome Hill Reference Library (devoted to commerce and transportation) and the library of the Minnesota Historical Society, both located in St. Paul. Nearly all public, academic, school, and special libraries participate in one of the seven library system networks that facilitate resource sharing.

There are more than 150 museums and historic sites. In addition to several noted museums of the visual arts, Minnesota is home to the Mayo Medical Museum at the Mayo Clinic in Rochester. The Minnesota Historical Society Museum offers rotating exhibits on varied aspects of the state's history. In May 1996, the Mille Lacs Indian Museum and Trading Post opened its doors. Historic sites include the Split Rock Lighthouse on the north shore of Lake Superior, Historic Fort Snelling in the Twin Cities, the boyhood home of Charles Lindbergh in Little Falls, and the Sauk Centre home of Sinclair Lewis.

44COMMUNICATIONS

As of March 1993, 97.6% of Minnesota's 1,792,000 occupied housing units had telephones. Commercial broadcasting began with the opening of the first radio station in 1922; as of 1996 there were 275 radio stations—l00 AM and 175 FM—and 29 television stations, including 7 educational stations. As of 1996, 9 major cable television systems served the state.

45PRESS

The *Minnesota Pioneer,* whose first issue was printed on a small hand press and distributed by the publisher himself on 28 April 1849 in St. Paul, vies with the *Minnesota Register* (its first issue was dated earlier but may have appeared later) for the honor of being Minnesota's first newspaper. Over the next 10 years, in any case, nearly 100 newspapers appeared at locations throughout the territory, including direct ancestors of many present-day publications. In April 1982, Minneapolis's only daily newspapers were merged into the *Minneapolis Star and Tribune.* As of 1997, the state had 13 morning dailies, 12 evening dailies, and 13 Sunday papers. The following table lists the leading dailies, with their paid circulations in 1994:

AREA	NAME	DAILY	SUNDAY
Duluth	*News–Tribune* (m,S)	52,377	80,107
Minneapolis	*Star and Tribune* (m,S)	365,847	682,318
St. Paul	*Pioneer Press* (m,S)	206,488	272,330

As of 1997, 337 weekly newspapers and 176 periodicals were being published in Minnesota. Among the most widely read magazines published in Minnesota were *Family Handyman*, appearing 10 times a year, with a paid circulation of 1,076,905; *Catholic Digest*, a religious monthly serving 575,000 readers; and *Snow Goer*, published five times a year for snowmobile enthusiasts, with a paid circulation of 75,000.

46ORGANIZATIONS

The 1992 Census of Service Industries counted 2,265 organizations in Minnesota, including 338 business associations; 1,509 civic, social, and fraternal associations; and 418 other membership organizations. The Minnesota Historical Society, founded in 1849, is the oldest educational organization in the state and the official custodian of its history. The society is partly supported by state funds, as are such other semistate organizations as the Academy of Science (which promotes interest in science among high school students), the Minnesota State Horticultural Society, and the Humane Society. The Sons of Norway and American Swedish Institute, both with headquarters in Minneapolis, seek to preserve the state's Scandinavian heritage. Among the various professional, commercial, educational, and hobbyist associations with headquarters in Minnesota are the American Collectors Association and National Scholastic Press Association, Minneapolis; American Board of Radiology, American Ophthalmological Society, and American Board of Physical Medicine and Rehabilitation, Rochester; and World Pen Pals, St. Paul.

47TOURISM, TRAVEL, AND RECREATION

With its lakes and parks, ski trails and campsites, and historical and cultural attractions, Minnesota provides ample recreational opportunities for residents and visitors alike. In-state visitors in 1993 spent nearly $4.5 million on overnight and day trips.

Besides the museums, sports stadiums, and concert halls in the big cities, Minnesota's attractions include the 220,000-acre (80,000-hectare) Voyageurs National Park, near the Canadian border; Grand Portage National Monument, in Arrowhead Country, a former fur-trading center with a restored trading post; and Pipestone National Monument, in southwestern Minnesota, containing the red pipestone quarry used by Indians to make peace pipes. Lumbertown USA, a restored 1870s lumber community, is in Brainerd, and the US Hockey Hall of Fame is in Eveleth.

The state maintains and operates 66 parks, 9240 mi (14,870 km) of trails, 10 scenic and natural areas, 5 recreation areas, and 18 canoe and boating routes. Minnesota also has 288 primary wildlife refuges. The parks had an estimated 8.0 million visitors in 1991. As of 1995 there were 1,400,326 licensed fishermen and 843,717 licensed hunters, most of whom hunted deer, muskrat, squirrel, beaver, duck, pheasant, and grouse.

An estimated 723,000 people enjoy boating each year on Minnesota's scenic waterways. Winter sports have gained in popularity, and many parks are now used heavily all year round. Snowmobiling, though it has declined somewhat since the mid-1970s, still attracts an estimated 193,000 enthusiasts annually, and cross-country skiing has rapidly accelerated in popularity.

48SPORTS

Three of the major league professional sports currently have teams in Minnesota: the Minnesota Twins of Major League Baseball, the Minnesota Vikings of the National Football League, and the Minnesota Timberwolves of the National Basketball Association. The Twins won the World Series in 1987 and 1991. The Vikings have gone to the Super Bowl four times, losing each one. The Minnesota North Stars of the National Hockey League moved to Dallas in 1993, but a new NHL team is slated to play in St. Paul for the 2000/01 season.

In collegiate sports, the University of Minnesota Golden Gophers compete in the Big Ten conference. The football team won the Rose Bowl in 1962, while the basketball team won the Big Ten title and advanced to the NCAA Final Four in 1997. The university is probably best known for its ice hockey team, which won the NCAA title three times during the 1970s and supplied the coach, Herb Brooks, and many of the players for the gold medal-winning US team in the 1980 Winter Olympics.

Other annual sporting events include the John Beargrease Sled Dog Race between Duluth and Grand Marais in January, and auto racing at the Brainerd International Raceway in July and August. Alpine and cross country skiing are popular.

49FAMOUS MINNESOTANS

No Minnesotan has been elected to the US presidency, but several have sought the office, including two who served as vice president. Hubert Horatio Humphrey (b.South Dakota, 1911–78) was vice president under Lyndon Johnson and a serious contender for the presidency in 1960, 1968, and 1972. A onetime mayor of Minneapolis, the "Happy Warrior" entered the US Senate in 1949, winning recognition as a vigorous proponent of liberal causes; after he left the vice presidency, Humphrey won reelection to the Senate in 1970. Humphrey's protégé, Walter Frederick "Fritz" Mondale (b.1928), a former state attorney general, was appointed to fill Humphrey's Senate seat in 1964, was elected to it twice, and after an unsuccessful try for the presidency, became Jimmy Carter's running mate in 1976; four years later, Mondale and Carter ran unsuccessfully for reelection, losing to Ronald Reagan and George Bush. Mondale won the Democratic presidential nomination in 1984 and chose US Representative Geraldine A. Ferraro of New York as his running mate, making her the first woman to be nominated by a major party for national office; they were overwhelmingly defeated by Reagan and Bush, winning only 41% of the popular vote and carrying only Minnesota and the District of Columbia. Warren Earl Burger (1907–95) of St. Paul was named chief justice of the US Supreme Court in 1969. Three other Minnesotans have served on the court: Pierce Butler (1866–1939), William O. Douglas (1898–1980), and Harry A. Blackmun (b.Illinois, 1908–97).

Senator Frank B. Kellogg (b.New York, 1856–1937), who as secretary of state helped to negotiate the Kellogg-Briand Pact renouncing war as an instrument of national policy (for which he won the 1929 Nobel Peace Prize), also served on the Permanent Court of International Justice. Other political leaders who won national attention include Governors John A. Johnson (1861–1909), Floyd B. Olson (1891–1936), and Harold E. Stassen (b.1907), a perennial presidential candidate since 1948 but a serious contender in his early races. Eugene J. McCarthy (b.1916), who served in the US Senate, was the central figure in a national protest movement against the Vietnam war and, in that role, unsuccessfully sought the 1968 Democratic presidential nomination won by Humphrey. McCarthy also ran for the presidency as an independent in 1976.

Several Minnesotans besides Kellogg have served in cabinet posts. Minnesota's first territorial governor, Alexander Ramsey (1815–1903), later served as a secretary of war, and Senator William Windom (1827–91) was also secretary of the treasury. Others serving in cabinet posts have included William DeWitt Mitchell (1874–1955), attorney general; Maurice H. Stans (b.1908), secretary of commerce; James D. Hodgson (b.1915), secretary of labor; and Orville Freeman (b.1918) and Bob Bergland (b.1928), both secretaries of agriculture. The first woman ambassador in US history was Eugenie M. Anderson (b.Iowa, 1909), like Humphrey an architect of the Democratic-Farmer-Labor Party.

Notable members of Congress include Knute Nelson (b.Norway, 1843–1923), who served in the Senate from 1895 to his death; Henrik Shipstead (1881–1960), who evolved into a leading Republican isolationist during 24 years in the Senate; Representative Andrew J. Volstead (1860–1947), who sponsored the 1919 prohibition act that bears his name; and Representative Walter Judd (b.1898–1994), a prominent leader of the so-called China Lobby.

The Mayo Clinic was founded in Minnesota by Dr. William W. Mayo (b.England, 1819–1911) and developed through the efforts of his sons, Drs. William H. (1861–1939) and Charles H. (1865–1939) Mayo. Oil magnate J. Paul Getty (1892–1976) was a Minnesota native, as was Richard W. Sears (1863–1914), founder of Sears, Roebuck.

Prominent literary figures, besides Sinclair Lewis, include Ignatius Donnelly (b.Pennsylvania, 1831–1901), a writer, editor, and Populist Party crusader; F. Scott Fitzgerald (1896–1940), well known for classic novels including *The Great Gatsby;* and Ole Edvart Rølvaag (b.Norway, 1876–1931), who conveyed the reality of the immigrant experience in his *Giants in the Earth*. The poet and critic Allen Tate (b.Kentucky, 1899–1979) taught for many years at the University of Minnesota.

Journalist Westbrook Pegler (1894–1969) and cartoonist Charles Schulz (b.1922) were both born in Minnesota as was radio personality and author Garrison Keillor (b.1942), who gained nationwide fame playfully satirizing his home state through the fictitious town of Lake Wobegon. Architects LeRoy S. Buffington (1847–1937) and Cass Gilbert (b.Ohio, 1859–1934) and economist Thorstein Veblen (b.Wisconsin, 1857–1929) influenced their fields well beyond the state's borders, as did Minnesota artists Wanda Gag (1893–1946) and Adolph Dehn (1895–1968).

Minnesota born entertainers include Judy Garland (Frances Gumm, 1922–69) and Bob Dylan (Robert Zimmerman, b.1941). Football star William "Pudge" Heffelfinger (1867–1954) was a Minnesota native, and Bronislaw "Bronco" Nagurski (b.Canada, 1908–1990) played for the University of Minnesota.

Daniel Greysolon, Sieur Duluth (b.France, 1636–1710), Father Louis Hennepin (b.Flanders, 1640?–1701), and Jonathan Carver (b.Massachusetts, 1710–80) were among the early explorers and chroniclers of what is now the State of Minnesota. Fur trader Henry H. Sibley (b.Michigan, 1811–91) was a key political leader in the territorial period and became the state's first governor; he also put down the Sioux uprising of 1862. Railroad magnate James J. Hill (b.Canada, 1838–1916) built one of the greatest corporate empires of his time, and Oliver H. Kelley (b.Massachusetts, 1826–1913), a Minnesota farmer, organized the first National Grange. John Ireland (b.Ireland, 1838–1918) was the first Roman Catholic archbishop of St. Paul, while Henry B. Whipple (b.New York, 1822–1901), longtime Episcopal bishop of Minnesota, achieved particular recognition for his work among Indians in the region.

The first US citizen ever to be awarded the Nobel Prize for literature was Sinclair Lewis (1885–1951), whose novel *Main Street* (1920) was modeled on life in his hometown of Sauk Centre. Philip S. Hench (b.Pennsylvania, 1896–1965) and Edward C. Kendall (b.Connecticut, 1886–1972), both of the Mayo Clinic, shared the 1950 Nobel Prize for medicine, and St. Paul native Melvin Calvin (b.1911) won the 1961 Nobel Prize for chemistry.

[50]BIBLIOGRAPHY

Blegen, Theodore C. *Minnesota: A History of the State*. Rev. ed. Minneapolis: University of Minnesota Press, 1975 (orig. 1937).

Brook, Michael. *Reference Guide to Minnesota History: A Subject Bibliography of Books, Pamphlets, and Articles in English*. St. Paul: Minnesota Historical Society, 1983.

Chrislock, Carl H. *The Progressive Era in Minnesota, 1899-1918*. St. Paul: Minnesota Historical Society, 1971.

Coen, Rena N. *Painting and Sculpture in Minnesota, 1820-1914*. A Minneapolis: University of Minnesota Press, 1976.

Federal Writers' Project. *Minnesota: A State Guide*. Reprint. New York: Somerset, n.d. (orig. 1938).

Folwell, William W. *A History of Minnesota*. 4 vols. Rev. Ed. St. Paul: Minnesota Historical Society, 1956-69 (orig. 1921-30).

Hazard, Evan B. *The Mammals of Minnesota*. Minneapolis: University of Minnesota Press, 1982.

Holmquist, June D., and Jean A. Brookins. *Minnesota's Major Historic Sites: A Guide*. 2d ed. St. Paul: Minnesota Historical Society, 1972.

Lass, William E. *Minnesota: A Bicentennial History*. New York: Norton, 1977.

Meyer, Roy. Rev. ed. *History of the Santee Sioux: United States Indian Policy on Trial*. Lincoln: University of Nebraska Press, 1993.

Mitau, G. Theodore. *Politics in Minnesota*. 2d rev. ed. Minneapolis: University of Minnesota Press, 1970.

Radicalism in Minnesota, 1900–1960: A Survey of Selected Sources. St. Paul, MN: Minnesota Historical Society Press, 1994.

Rueter, Theodore. *The Minnesota House of Representatives and the Professionalization of Politics*. Lanham, MD: University Press of America, 1994.

Schwartz, George M., and G. A. Thiel. *Minnesota's Rocks and Waters: A Geological Story*. Minneapolis: University of Minnesota Press, 1954.

Spadaccini, Victor M., ed. *Minnesota Pocket Data Book, 1985–86*. St. Paul: Blue Sky, 1983.

Stuhler, Barbara. *Gentle Warriors: Clara Ueland and the Minnesota Struggle for Woman Suffrage*. St. Paul, MN: Minnesota Historical Society Press, 1994.

Upham, Warren. *Minnesota Geographic Names: Their Origin and Historic Significance*. St. Paul: Minnesota Historical Society, 1969 (orig. 1920).

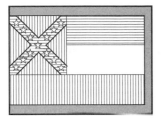

MISSISSIPPI

State of Mississippi

ORIGIN OF STATE NAME: Derived from the Ojibwa Indian words *misi sipi,* meaning great river. **NICKNAME:** The Magnolia State. **CAPITAL:** Jackson. **ENTERED UNION:** 10 December 1817 (20th). **SONG:** "Go, Mississippi." **MOTTO:** *Virtute et armis* (By valor and arms). **COAT OF ARMS:** An American eagle clutches an olive branch and a quiver of arrows in its talons. **FLAG:** Crossed blue bars, on a red field, bordered with white and emblazoned with 13 white stars—the motif of the Confederate battle flag—cover the upper left corner. The field consists of three stripes of equal width, blue, white, and red. **OFFICIAL SEAL:** The seal consists of the coat of arms surrounded by the words "The Great Seal of the State of Mississippi." **MAMMAL:** White-tailed deer. **WATER MAMMAL:** Porpoise. **BIRD:** Mockingbird. **WATERFOWL:** Wood duck. **FISH:** Largemouth or black bass. **INSECT:** Honeybee. **FLOWER:** Magnolia. **TREE:** Magnolia. **STONE:** Petrified wood. **FOSSIL:** Prehistoric whale. **BEVERAGE:** Milk. **LEGAL HOLIDAYS:** New Year's Day, 1 January; Birthdays of Robert E. Lee and Martin Luther King, Jr., 3d Monday in January; Washington's Birthday, 3d Monday in February; Confederate Memorial Day, last Monday in April; Jefferson Davis's Birthday, 1st Monday in June; Independence Day, 4 July; Labor Day, 1st Monday in September; Veterans Day, 11 November; Thanksgiving Day, 4th Thursday in November; Christmas Day, 25 December. **TIME:** 6 AM CST = noon GMT.

¹LOCATION, SIZE, AND EXTENT

Located in the eastern south-central US, Mississippi ranks 32d in size among the 50 states.

The total area of Mississippi is 47,689 sq mi (123,514 sq km), of which land takes up 47,233 sq mi (122,333 sq km) and inland water 456 sq mi (1,181 sq km). Mississippi's maximum E-W extension is 188 mi (303 km); its greatest N-S distance is 352 mi (566 km).

Mississippi is bordered on the N by Tennessee; on the E by Alabama; on the S by the Gulf of Mexico and Louisiana; and on the W by Louisiana (with the line partially formed by the Pearl and Mississippi rivers) and Arkansas (with the line formed by the Mississippi River). Several small islands lie off the coast.

The total boundary length of Mississippi is 1,015 mi (1,634 km). The state's geographic center is in Leake County, 9 mi (14 km) WNW of Carthage.

²TOPOGRAPHY

Mississippi lies entirely within two lowland plains. Extending eastward from the Mississippi River, the Mississippi Alluvial Plain, popularly known as the Delta, is very narrow south of Vicksburg but stretches as much as a third of the way across the state farther north. The Gulf Coastal Plain, covering the rest of the state, includes several subregions, of which the Red Clay Hills of north-central Mississippi and the Piney Woods of the south and southeast are the most extensive. Mississippi's generally hilly landscape ascends from sea level at the Gulf of Mexico to reach its maximum elevation, 806 feet (246 meters), at Woodall Mountain, in the extreme northeastern corner of the state.

The state's largest lakes—Grenada, Sardis, Enid, and Arkabutla—are all manmade. Numerous smaller lakes—called oxbow lakes because of their curved shape—extend along the western edge of the state; once part of the Mississippi River, they were formed when the river changed its course. Mississippi's longest inland river, the Pearl, flows about 490 mi (790 km) from the eastern center of the state to the Gulf of Mexico, its lower reaches forming part of the border with Louisiana. The Big Black River, some 330 mi (530 km) long, begins in the northeast and cuts diagonally across the state, joining the Mississippi about 20 mi (32 km) below Vicksburg. Formed by the confluence of the Tallahatchie and Yalobusha rivers at Greenwood, the Yazoo flows 189 mi (304 km) southwest to the Mississippi just above Vicksburg.

³CLIMATE

Mississippi has short winters and long, humid summers. Summer temperatures vary little from one part of the state to another. Biloxi, on the Gulf coast, averages 82°F (28°C) in July, while Oxford, in the north-central part of the state, averages 80°F (27°C). During the winter, however, because of the temperate influence of the Gulf of Mexico, the southern coast is much warmer than the north; in January, Biloxi averages 52°F (11°C) to Oxford's 41°F (5°C). The lowest temperature ever recorded in Mississippi was –19°F (–28°C) on 30 January 1966 in Corinth; the highest, 115°F (46°C), was set on 29 July 1930 at Holly Springs.

Precipitation in Mississippi increases from north to south. The north-central region averages 53 in (135 cm) of precipitation a year; the coastal region, 62 in (157 cm). Some snow falls in northern and central sections. Mississippi lies in the path of hurricanes moving northward from the Gulf of Mexico during the late summer and fall. On 17–18 August 1969, Hurricane Camille ripped into Biloxi and Gulfport and caused more than 100 deaths throughout the state. Two tornado alleys cross Mississippi from the southwest to northeast, from Vicksburg to Oxford and McComb to Tupelo. In 1995, Mississippi was hit by 45 tornadoes.

⁴FLORA AND FAUNA

Post and white oaks, hickory, maple, and magnolia grow in the forests of the uplands; various willows and gums (including the tupelo) in the Delta; and longleaf pine in the Piney Woods. Characteristic wild flowers include the green Virginia creeper, black-eyed Susan, and Cherokee rose.

Common among the state's mammals are the opossum, eastern mole, armadillo, coyote, mink, white-tailed deer, striped skunk, and diverse bats and mice. Birds include varieties of wren, thrush, warbler, vireo, and hawk, along with numerous waterfowl and seabirds, Franklin's gull, the common loon, and the wood stork among them. Black bass, perch, and mullet are common freshwater fish. Rare species in Mississippi include the hoary bat, American oystercatcher, mole salamander, pigmy killifish, Yazoo darker, and five species of crayfish. The brown or grizzly bear, cliff swallow, and eastern indigo snake are among threatened species, and the Florida panther, gray bat, red wolf, Mississippi sandhill crane, bald eagle, peregrine falcon, brown pelican, red-cockaded and ivory-billed woodpeckers, and Bayou darker are endangered.

5ENVIRONMENTAL PROTECTION

Except for the drinking water program, housed in the State Health Department, and regulation of noncommercial oil field waste disposal activities, assigned to the State Oil and Gas Board, the Mississippi Department of Environmental Quality (MDEQ) is responsible for environmental regulatory programs in the state. MDEQ regulates surface and groundwater withdrawals through its Office of Land and Water Resources and surface mining reclamation through its Office of Geology. All other environmental regulatory programs, including those federal regulatory programs delegated to Mississippi by the US Environmental Protection Agency (EPA), are administered through MDEQ's Office of Pollution Control. The state has primacy for almost all federally delegable programs; the one notable exception is the federal hazardous waste corrective action program (under the federal Hazardous and Solid Waste Amendments of 1984). MDEQ implements one of the premier Pollution Prevention programs in the nation.

In 1995, Mississippi had only 4 hazardous waste sites, ranking 45th in the nation. In 1996, wetlands accounted for 13% of the state's lands. The Natural Heritage Program identifies and inventories priority wetlands.

6POPULATION

With a 1990 census population of 2,573,216, Mississippi ranked 31st among the 50 states. After remaining virtually level for 30 years, Mississippi's population during the 1970s grew 13.7%, but increased only 2.1% from 1980 to 1990. In 1996, the population was estimated at 2,716,115, a 5.5% increase over 1990.

According to the 1990 census, 48.1% of Mississippians were male, and 51.9% female. Mississippians were less mobile than residents of most other states: 60% were living in the same house as in 1985. In 1990, the population density was 55 persons per sq mi (21 per sq km).

With a 1990 population that was 53% rural, Mississippi remains one of the most rural states in the US, although the urban population has increased fivefold since 1920, when only 13% of state residents lived in cities. Mississippi's largest city, Jackson, had an estimated 1994 population of 193,097, down 1.8% from 1990. Biloxi had an estimated population of 47,832, and Gulfport, 43,023. The Jackson metropolitan area had an estimated population of 416,297 in 1995.

7ETHNIC GROUPS

Since 1860, blacks have constituted a larger proportion of the population of Mississippi than of any other state. By the end of the 1830s, blacks outnumbered whites 52% to 48%, and from the 1860s through the early 20th century, they made up about three-fifths of the population. Because of out-migration, the proportion of black Mississippians declined to less than 36% in 1990, when the state had 1,633,000 whites, 915,000 blacks, 13,000 Asians and Pacific Islanders, and 9,000 American Indians. Of the total population, 16,000 (0.6%) were of Hispanic origin.

Until the 1940s, the Chinese, who numbered 2,532 in 1990, were an intermediate stratum between blacks and whites in the social hierarchy of the Delta Counties. There also were 3,340 Vietnamese and 2,120 Filipinos in 1990. Although the number of foreign-born almost tripled in the 1970s, Mississippi had the smallest percentage of foreign-born residents (0.8%) in 1990.

Mississippi has only a small Indian population remaining—0.3% of the state's population in 1990. Many of them live on the Choctaw reservation in the east-central region.

8LANGUAGES

English in the state is largely Southern, with some South Midland speech in northern and eastern Mississippi because of population drift from Tennessee. Typical are the absence of final /r/ and the lengthening and weakening of the diphthongs /ai/ and /oi/ as in *ride* and *oil*. South Midland terms in northern Mississippi include *tow sack* (burlap bag), *dog irons* (andirons), *plum peach* (clingstone peach), *snake doctor* (dragonfly), and *stone wall* (rock fence). In the eastern section are found *jew's harp* (harmonica) and *croker sack* (burlap bag). Southern speech in the southern half features *gallery* for porch, *mosquito hawk* for dragonfly, and *press peach* for clingstone peach. Louisiana French has contributed *armoire* (wardrobe).

In 1990, 97.2% of Mississippi residents 5 years old and older spoke only English in the home. Other languages spoken at home, and the number of people who spoke them, included Spanish, 25,061, and French, 13,215.

9RELIGIONS

Protestants have dominated Mississippi since the late 18th century. The Baptists are the leading denomination, and many adherents are fundamentalists. Partly because of the strong church influence, Mississippi was among the first states to enact prohibition and among the last to repeal it.

During 1990, membership in the two principal Protestant denominations was: Southern Baptist Convention, 869,942 known adherents, and United Methodist Church, 240,325. There were 94,948 Roman Catholics and an estimated 2,466 Jews in 1990.

10TRANSPORTATION

At the end of 1996, there were 2,841 rail mi (4,572 km) of main-line railroad track in the state, including 2,283 mi (3,674 km) operated by Class I railroads, which, in 1996, included the Burlington Northern, CSX, Illinois Amtrak, Kansas City Southern, and Norfolk Southern lines. Rail passenger service providers include the City of New Orleans, which operates over Illinois Central's rails, and serves the cities of Greenwood, Yazoo, Jackson, Hazlehurst, Brookhaven, and McComb in Mississippi on its route between Chicago and New Orleans; and the Crescent, which operates over the Norfolk Southern rail line and serves Meridian, Laurel, Hattiesburg, and Picayune in Mississippi on its route between Atlanta and New Orleans. The total Mississippi ridership was 94,930 in 1996, an increase of 10% from the previous year.

Mississippi had 73,203 mi (117,806 km) of roads—65,281 mi (105,057 km) rural and 7,922 mi (12,749 km) urban—as of 1996. In addition, there were 685 mi (1,102 km) of interstate highways. Interstate highways 55, running north–south, and 20, running east–west, intersect at Jackson. I-220 provides a loop from I-55 north of Jackson to I-20 west of Jackson. I-10 runs across the Mississippi Gulf Coast and I-110 provides a connector from I-10 to US Highway 90 in Biloxi. I-59 runs diagonally through the southeastern corner of Mississippi from Meridian to New Orleans.

As of July 1996, under all jurisdictions, there were 2,055 mi (3,307 km) of four-lane highway in the state. This figure is

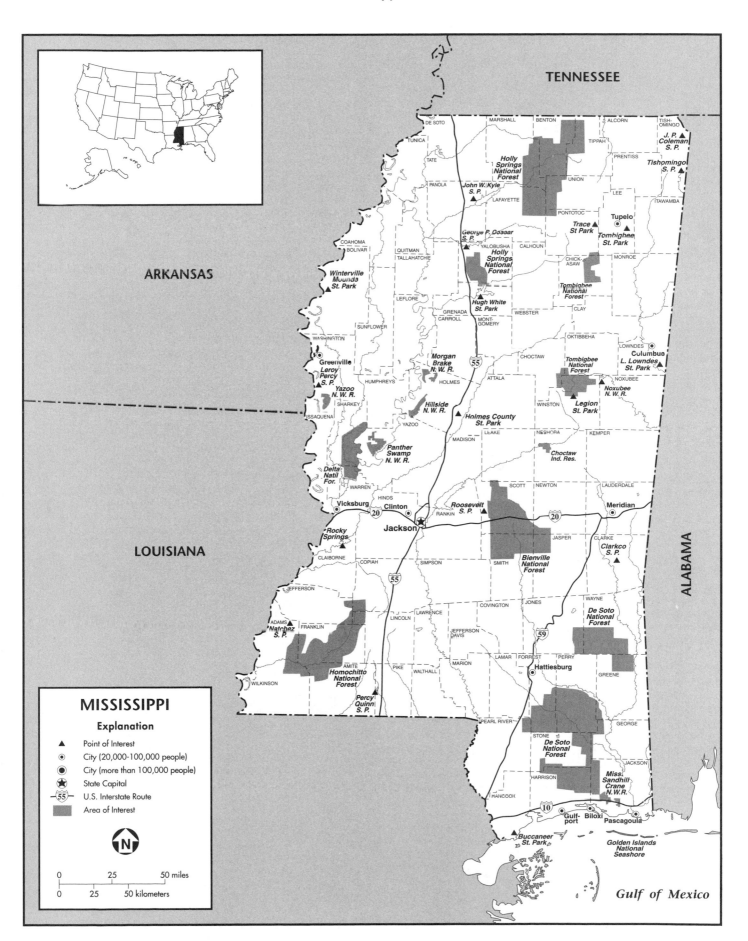

TENNESSEE

ARKANSAS

LOUISIANA

ALABAMA

MISSISSIPPI

Explanation

▲ Point of Interest

◉ City (20,000-100,000 people)

◉ City (more than 100,000 people)

★ State Capital

⌐55⌐ U.S. Interstate Route

▮ Area of Interest

Ⓝ

0   25   50 miles

0   25   50 kilometers

Gulf of Mexico

increasing daily under a "pay-as-you-go" public works program passed by the Mississippi legislature in 1987 to provide a four-lane highway within 30 minutes or 30 miles of every citizen in the state. Originally, the $1.6 billion, three-phase agenda called for the creation of four lanes for 1,077 mi (1,733 km) of highway by the year 2001. During the 1994 regular legislative session, an additional 619 miles (996 km), known as Phase IV, were added to the program at an expected cost of $1.3 billion. As of 1996, 322 mi (518 km) of new four-lane highway were in place with an additional 332 mi (534 km) under contract. In 1996, there were 1,700,132 licensed drivers in Mississippi and 2,296,975 registered motor vehicles, including 1,670,149 automobiles and 478,561 trucks.

Mississippi's ports and waterways serve a surrounding 16-state market where nearly 40% of the nation's total population is located. Mississippi has two deepwater seaports, Gulfport and Pascagoula, both located on the Gulf of Mexico. In 1996, Gulfport handled 2,104,832 tons of cargo and Pascagoula handled 28,639,978 tons. Much of Pascagoula's heavy volume consists of oil and gas imports. Other ports located on the Gulf include Port Bienville in Hancock County and Biloxi in Harrison County. Port Bienville handled 329,056.7 tons of cargo in 1996.

The Mississippi River flows along the western border of the state, linking the Gulf of Mexico to inland river states as far away as Minneapolis, Minn. The Mississippi is the largest commercial river in the country and the 3d-largest river system in the world, and it carries the majority of the nation's inland waterway tonnage (520.3 million tons in 1995). Approximately 409 mi (658 km) of the Mississippi River flow through the state, with ports in Natchez, Vicksburg, Yazoo County, Greenville, and Rosedale. In 1996, cumulative tonnage handled by the Port of Natchez was 329,407,641.5; the Port of Vicksburg handled 5,127,950 tons; the Port of Yazoo County, 443,577; the Port of Greenville, 1,873,694; and the Port of Rosedale, 538,000 tons.

To the east of Mississippi lies the Tennessee-Tombigbee (Tenn-Tom) Waterway, completed in 1984, which links the Tennessee and Ohio rivers with the Gulf of Mexico. Stretching 95 mi (153 km) through Mississippi from the northeast corner of the state down to a point just south of Columbus, the Tenn-Tom Waterway's overall length is 232 mi (373 km). Five local ports are located on the waterway: Yellow Creek, Itawamba, Amory, Aberdeen, and Columbus-Lowndes County. In 1996, cumulative tonnage handled by Yellow Creek Port was 1,265,000; Port Itawamba, 650,000; Port of Amory, 550,000; Port of Aberdeen, over 500,000; and Columbus-Lowndes County Port, 752,000. In 1996, 8.9 million tons of commodities were shipped on the Tenn-Tom Waterway, compared with 8.7 million tons in 1995 and 7.9 million tons in 1994.

In 1996, there were 76 public-use airports in Mississippi, seven with air carrier service and one designated as a reliever for the Memphis International Airport. They provide access to the nation's system of airports and are a major factor in the economic development of the state and of the communities where they are located. In addition, there are approximately 113 airports and 59 heliports in the state that are for private use.

11HISTORY

The earliest record of human habitation in the region that is now the state of Mississippi goes back perhaps 2,000 years. The names of Mississippi's pre-Columbian inhabitants are not known. Upon the appearance of the first Spanish explorers in the early 16th century, Mississippi Indians numbered some 30,000 and were divided into 15 tribes. Soon after the French settled in 1699, however, only three large tribes remained: the Choctaw, the Chickasaw, and the Natchez. The French destroyed the Natchez in 1729–30 in retaliation for the massacre of a French settlement on the Natchez bluffs.

Spanish explorers, of whom Hernando de Soto in 1540–41 was the most notable, explored the area that is now Mississippi in the first half of the 16th century. De Soto found little of the mineral wealth he was looking for, and the Spanish quickly lost interest in the region. The French explorer Robert Cavelier, Sieur de la Salle, penetrated the lower Mississippi Valley from New France (Canada) in 1682. La Salle discovered the mouth of the Mississippi and named the entire area Louisiana in honor of the French king, Louis XIV.

An expedition under French-Canadian Pierre Lemoyne, Sieur d'Iberville, established a settlement at Biloxi Bay in 1699. Soon the French opened settlements at Mobile (1702), Natchez (1716), and finally New Orleans (1718), which quickly eclipsed the others in size and importance. After losing the French and Indian War, France ceded Louisiana to its Spanish ally in 1762. The following year, Spain ceded the portion of the colony that lay east of the Mississippi to England, which governed the new lands as West Florida. During the American Revolution, the Spanish, who still held New Orleans and Louisiana, marched into Natchez, Mobile, and Pensacola (the capital) and took West Florida by conquest.

Although the US claimed the Natchez area after 1783, Spain continued to rule it. However, the Spanish were unable to change the Anglo-American character of the settlement. Spain agreed to relinquish its claim to the Natchez District by signing the Treaty of San Lorenzo on 27 October 1795, but did not evacuate its garrison there for another three years.

The US Congress organized the Mississippi Territory in 1798. Between 1798 and 1817, the territory grew enormously in population, attracting immigrants mainly from the older states of the South but also from the Middle Atlantic states and even from New England. During this period, the territory included all the land area that is today within the borders of Mississippi and Alabama. However, sectionalism and the territory's large size convinced Congress to organize the eastern half as the Alabama Territory in 1817. Congress then offered admission to the western half, which became the nation's 20th state—Mississippi—on 10 December.

Until the Civil War, Mississippi exemplified the American frontier; it was bustling, violent, and aggressive. By and large, Mississippians viewed themselves as westerners, not southerners. Nor was Mississippi, except for a few plantations around Natchez, a land of large planters. Rather, Mississippi's antebellum society and government were dominated by a coalition of prosperous farmers and small landowners. At the time of statehood, the northern two-thirds of Mississippi, though nominally under US rule since 1783, remained in the hands of the Choctaw and Chickasaw and was closed to settlement. Under intense pressure from the state government and from Andrew Jackson's presidential administration, these tribes signed three treaties between 1820 and 1832, ceding their Mississippi lands and agreeing to move to what is now Oklahoma.

The opening of fertile Indian lands for sale and settlement produced a boom of speculation and growth unparalleled in Mississippi history. Cotton agriculture and slavery—introduced by the French and carried on by the British and Spanish, but hitherto limited mostly to the Natchez area—swept over the state. As the profitability and number of slaves increased, so did attempts by white Mississippians to justify slavery morally, socially, and economically. The expansion of slavery also produced a defensive attitude which focused the minds of white Mississippians on two dangers: that the slaves outnumbered the whites and would threaten white society unless kept down by slavery; and that any attack on slavery, whether from the abolitionists or from Free-Soilers like Abraham Lincoln, was a threat to white society. The danger, they believed, was so great that no price was too high to pay to maintain slavery, even secession and civil war.

After Lincoln's election to the US presidency, Mississippi became, on 9 January 1861, the second southern state to secede. When the war began, Mississippi occupied a central place in Union strategy. The state sat squarely astride the major Confederate east-west routes of communication in the lower South, and the Mississippi River twisted along the state's western border. Control of the river was essential to Union division of the Confederacy. The military campaign fell into three phases: the fight for northeastern Mississippi in 1862, the struggle for Vicksburg in 1862–63, and the battle for east Mississippi in 1864–65. The Union advance on Corinth began with the Battle of Shiloh (Tenn.) in April 1862. The first Union objective was the railroad that ran across the northeastern corner of Mississippi from Corinth to Iuka and linked Memphis, Tenn., to Atlanta, Ga. Losses in the ensuing battle of Shiloh, which eventually led to the occupation of Corinth by Union troops, exceeded 10,000 men on each side.

The campaign that dominated the war in Mississippi—and, indeed, along with Gettysburg provided the turning point of the Civil War—was Vicksburg. Perched atop high bluffs overlooking a bend in the Mississippi and surrounded by hills on all sides, Vicksburg provided a seemingly impregnable fortress. Union forces maneuvered before Vicksburg for more than a year before Grant besieged the city and forced its surrender on 4 July 1863. Along with Vicksburg went the western half of Mississippi. The rest of the military campaign in the state was devoted to the fight for the east, which Union forces still had not secured when the conflict ended in 1865. Of the 78,000 Mississippians who fought in the Civil War, nearly 30,000 died.

Ten years of political, social, and economic turmoil followed. Reconstruction was a tumultuous period during which the Republican Party encouraged blacks to vote and hold political office, while the native white Democrats resisted full freedom for their former slaves. The resulting confrontation lasted until 1875, when, using violence and intimidation, the Democrats recaptured control of the state from the Republicans and began a return to the racial status quo antebellum. However, reconstruction left its legacy in minds of Mississippians: to the whites it seemed proof that blacks were incapable of exercising political power; to the blacks it proved that political and social rights could not long be maintained without economic rights.

The era from the end of Reconstruction to World War II was a period of economic, political, and social stagnation for Mississippi. In many respects, white Mississippians pushed blacks back into slavery in all but name. Segregation laws and customs placed strict social controls on blacks, and a new state constitution in 1890 removed the last vestiges of their political rights. Mississippi's agricultural economy, dominated by cotton and tenant farming, provided the economic equivalent of slavery for black sharecroppers. As a continuing agricultural depression ground down the small white farmers, many of them also were driven into the sharecropper ranks; in 1890, 63% of all Mississippi farmers were tenants. Whether former planter-aristocrats like John Sharp Williams or small-farmer advocates like James K. Vardaman (1908–12) and Theodore Bilbo (1916–20 and 1928–32) held office as governor, political life was dominated by the overriding desire to keep the blacks subservient. From Reconstruction to the 1960s, white political solidarity was of paramount importance. Otherwise, the whites reasoned, another Reconstruction would follow. According to the Tuskegee Institute, 538 blacks were lynched in Mississippi between 1883 and 1959, more than in any other state.

The Great Depression of the 1930s pushed Mississippians, predominantly poor and rural, to the point of desperation, and the state's agricultural economy to the brink of disaster. In 1932, cotton sank to 5 cents a pound, and one-fourth of the state's farmland was forfeited for nonpayment of taxes. World War II unleashed the forces that would later revolutionize Mississippi's economic, social, and political order, bringing the state its first prosperity in a century. By introducing outsiders to Mississippi and Mississippians to the world, the armed forces and the war began to erode the state's insularity. It also stimulated industrial growth and agricultural mechanization and encouraged an exodus of blacks to better-paying jobs in other states. By the early 1980s, according to any standard, Mississippi had become an industrial state. In the agricultural sector, cotton had been dethroned and crop diversification accomplished. Politics in Mississippi have also changed considerably since World War II. Within little more than a generation, from 1945 to 1975, legal segregation was destroyed, and black people exercised their political rights for the first time since Reconstruction. The "Mississippi Summer" civil rights campaign—and the violent response to it, including the abduction and murder of three civil rights activists in June 1964—helped persuade white Mississippians to accept racial equality. Charles Evers, the brother of slain civil rights leader Medgar Evers, was elected mayor of Fayette in 1969, becoming Mississippi's first black major since Reconstruction.

Following the 1990 redistricting that boosted the number of blacks in the Mississippi house of representatives, the Mississippi legislature was nearly 23% black in a state in which blacks constitute 33% of the population. Reformist governor Ray Mabus, elected in 1987, enacted the nation's largest teacher pay increase in 1988. Nevertheless, teacher salaries in 1992 were still, on average, the second lowest in the nation. Mississippi's economy was hard hit by the 1986 decline in oil and gas prices. Unemployment in the state rose to 13%. By 1992 it had fallen to about 8%. The 1990s saw increasing industrial diversification and rising personal incomes, although many agricultural workers in the Mississippi Delta area remained jobless due to the increasing mechanization of farm work.

12STATE GOVERNMENT

Mississippi has had four state constitutions. The first (1817) accompanied Mississippi's admission to the Union. A second constitution (1832) was superseded by that of 1868, redrafted under Republican rule to allow Mississippi's readmission to the Union after the Civil War. The state's present constitution, as amended, dates from 1890.

Mississippi's bicameral legislature includes a 52-member senate and a 122-member house of representatives. All state legislators are elected to 4-year terms. State representatives must be at least 21 years of age and senators 25. All legislators must have been Mississippi residents for four years and residents of their district for two years before election. The legislative salary was $10,000 in 1997.

The governor, lieutenant governor, secretary of state, attorney general, state treasurer, state auditor of public accounts, commissioner of insurance, and commissioner of agriculture and commerce are independently elected four-year terms. The governor (and lieutenant governor) must be at least 30 years of age, a US citizen for 20 years, and a Mississippi resident for 5 years before election. In 1996 the governor's salary was $83,160.

Constitutional amendments must first receive the approval of two-thirds of the members of each house of the legislature; a majority of voters must approve the amendment on a statewide ballot. The constitution also provides for the calling of a constitutional convention, by majority vote of each house.

Every US citizen over the age of 18 may vote in Mississippi upon producing evidence of 30 days of residence in the state. There were an estimated 1,715,913 persons registered to vote in 1996.

[13]POLITICAL PARTIES

Mississippi's major political parties are the Democratic Party and the Republican Party, each an affiliate of the national party organization, but the Republicans are weak below the national level. Mississippi Democrats have often been at odds with each other and with the national Democratic Party. In the 1830s, party affiliation in the state began to divide along regional and economic lines: woodsmen and small farmers in eastern Mississippi became staunch Jacksonian Democrats, while the conservative planters in the western river counties tended to be Whigs. An early demonstration of the power of the Democrats was the movement of the state capital from Natchez in 1821 to a new city named after Andrew Jackson. During the pre–Civil War years, the secessionists were largely Democrats; the Unionists, western Whigs.

During Reconstruction, Mississippi had its first Republican governor. After the Democrats returned to power in 1875, they systematically deprived blacks of the right to vote, specifically by inserting into the constitution of 1890 a literacy clause that could be selectively interpreted to include illiterate whites but exclude blacks. A poll tax and convoluted residency requirements also restricted the electorate. Voter registration among blacks fell from 130,607 in 1880 to 16,234 by 1896.

In 1948, Mississippi Democrats seceded from the national party over the platform, which opposed racial discrimination. That November, Mississippi voters backed the States' Rights Democratic (Dixiecrat) presidential ticket. At the national Democratic convention in 1964, the black separatist Freedom Democratic Party asked to be allotted 40% of Mississippi's seats but was turned down. A further division in the party occurred during the 1960s between the (black) Loyalist Democrats and the (white) Regular Democrats, who were finally reunited in 1976. During the 1950s and early 1960s, the segregationist White Citizens' Councils were so widespread and influential in the state as to rival the major parties in political importance.

Since the passing of the federal Voting Rights Act of 1965, black Mississippians have registered and voted in substantial numbers. According to estimates by the Voter Education Project, only 5% of voting-age blacks were registered in 1960; by 1992, 23% were registered. In 1993 there were 751 blacks holding

elected office and in 1995, 20 women served in the state legislature.

Mississippi was one of the most closely contested states in the South during the 1976 presidential election, and that again proved to be the case in 1980, when Ronald Reagan edged Jimmy Carter by a plurality of fewer than 12,000 votes. In 1984, however, Reagan won the state by a landslide, polling 62% of the vote. In the 1996 election, Republican Bob Dole won 49% of the vote; Democrat Bill Clinton received 44%; and Independent Ross Perot garnered 6%.

Elected in 1992, Mississippi's governor Kirk Fordice was the first Republican governor since Reconstruction; also Republicans were its two senators, Thad Cochran and Trent Lott. Lott became majority leader of the Senate in 1996 following the departure of Bob Dole; Cochran was reelected to a fourth term in that year's November elections. All five of its US representatives were Democrats until the 1994 mid-term elections when Republican Roger Wicker won a House seat that had been in Democratic hands since Reconstruction. Following the 1996 elections, the House delegation comprised three Republicans and two Democrats. After the 1996 elections, the state senate comprised 34 Democrats and 18 Republicans; the state house had 84 Democrats, 35 Republicans, and 3 Independents.

[14]LOCAL GOVERNMENT

Each of Mississippi's 82 counties is divided into 5 districts, each of which elects a member to the county board of supervisors. As of 1997, Mississippi had 295 municipal governments, 173 school districts, and 320 special districts. Most cities, including most of the larger ones, have a mayor and city council.

[15]STATE SERVICES

The Mississippi Ethics Commission, established by the state legislature in 1979, is composed of eight members who administer a code of ethics requiring all state officials and elected local officials to file statements of sources of income.

The Mississippi Department of Education is primarily a planning and service organization whose role is to assist local schools from kindergarten through junior college and adult education. A separate Board of Trustees of Institutions of Higher Learning administers Mississippi's public college and university

Mississippi Presidential Vote by Political Parties, 1948–96

YEAR	ELECTORAL VOTE	MISSISSIPPI WINNER	DEMOCRAT	REPUBLICAN	STATES' RIGHTS DEMOCRAT	SOCIALIST WORKERS	LIBERTARIAN
1948	9	Thurmond (SRD)	19,384	4,995	167,538	—	—
1952	8	Stevenson (D)	172,553	112,966	—	—	—
					INDEPENDENT		
1956	8	Stevenson (D)	144,453	60,683	42,961	—	—
					UNPLEDGED		
1960	8	Byrd**	108,362	73,561	116,248	—	—
1964	7	Goldwater (R)	52,616	356,512	—	—	—
					AMERICAN IND.		
1968	7	Wallace (AI)	150,644	88,516	415,349	—	—
					AMERICAN		
1972	7	*Nixon (R)	126,782	505,125	11,598	2,458	—
1976	7	*Carter (D)	381,309	366,846	6,678	2,805	2,788
					WORKERS' WORLD		
1980	7	*Reagan (R)	429,281	441,089	2,402	2,240	4,702
1984	7	*Reagan (R)	352,192	582,377	—	—	2,336
1988	7	*Bush (R)	363,921	557,890			3,329
					IND. (Perot)	NEW ALLIANCE	
1992	7	Bush (R)	400,258	487,793	85,626	2,625	2,154
1996	7	Dole (R)	394,022	439,838	52,222	—	2,809

* Won US presidential election.
** Unpledged electors won plurality of votes and cast Mississippi's electoral votes for Senator Harry F. Byrd of Virginia.

system. The Department of Health administers a statewide system of public health services, but other bodies, including the Department of Mental Health, also have important functions in this field. The Department of Public Welfare provides welfare services in the areas of assistance payments, child support, food stamp distribution, and such social services as foster home care.

Public protection is afforded by the Civil Defense Council, Military Department, Bureau of Narcotics, Department of Public Safety (including the Highway Safety Patrol), and Department of Corrections.

16JUDICIAL SYSTEM

The Mississippi supreme court consists of a chief justice, two presiding justices, and six associate justices, all elected to eight-year terms. The constitution stipulates that the supreme court must hold two sessions a year in the state capital; one session is to commence on the 2d Monday of September, the other on the 1st Monday of March. A new court of appeals was created in 1995. It consists of one chief judge, two presiding judges, and seven judges. The principal trial courts are 20 chancery courts, which try civil cases, and 22 circuit courts, which try both civil and criminal cases; their 93 judges are elected to four-year terms. Municipal court judges are appointed. Small-claims courts are presided over by justices of the peace, who need not be lawyers. Mississippi had 5,385 active attorneys.

There were 14,453 prisoners in state prisons in Mississippi as of 29 April 1997. There were 85 prisoners in the newly opened Federal Correctional Institution located in Yazoo City.

In 1995, Mississippi had a total FBI Crime Index rate of 4,514.5 per 100,000 population, including 502.8 for violent crime and 4,011.7 for property crime. The death penalty was reinstated in 1977, and since then four persons have been executed. In 1995, 49 persons were under sentence of death.

17ARMED FORCES

In 1996, there were 12,454 active duty military personnel stationed in Mississippi. There were two major US Air Force bases, Keesler (Biloxi) and Columbus. Among the four US naval installations were an oceanographic command at Bay St. Louis, an air station at Meridian, and a construction battalion center at Gulfport. In 1995/96, Mississippi received $1.9 billion in federal defense contracts.

There were 229,000 veterans of US military service living in Mississippi as of 1 July 1996. Of those who served in wartime, fewer than 500 were veterans of World War I, 65,000 of World War II, 42,000 of the Korean conflict, 69,000 of the Vietnam era, and 24,000 of the Persian Gulf War. Benefits totaling some $553 million were paid to Mississippi veterans during 1995/96.

As of 1996, the Mississippi Army National Guard and Reserve units had assigned strength of 17,757, the Air National Guard and Reserve had assigned strength of 7,737. In 1993, the Mississippi Highway State Patrol employed 469 full-time sworn officers, or two per 10,000 residents.

18MIGRATION

In the late 18th century, most Mississippians were immigrants from the South and predominantly of Scotch-Irish descent. The opening of lands ceded by the Indians beginning in the 1820s brought tens of thousands of settlers into northern and central Mississippi, and a resulting population increase between 1830 and 1840 of 175% (including an increase of 197% in the slave population).

After the Civil War, there was little migration into the state, but much out-migration, mainly of blacks. The exodus from Mississippi was especially heavy during the 1940s and 1950s, when at least 720,000 people, nearly three-quarters of them black, left the state. During the 1960s, a net total of between 267,000 and 279,000 blacks departed, while net white out-migration came to an end. Black out-migration slowed considerably during the 1970s, and more whites settled in the state than left. Also during the 1970s there was considerable intrastate migration to Hinds County (Jackson) and the Gulf Coast. Between 1980 and 1990, Mississippi had a net loss from migration of 144,128 (38% whites). Only 12 of the state's 82 counties recorded a net gain from migration during the 1980s, mostly in Rankin, DeSoto, Madison, and Hancock counties. Between 1990 and 1996, Mississippi had net gains of 31,768 in domestic migration and 4,162 in international migration. As of 1990, 77.3% of the state's residents had been born in Mississippi. About 40% of state residents age 5 and older lived in a different house in 1985 than in 1990, of which 20% did so in another state. The proportion of urban residents declined by 0.2% during the 1980s.

19INTERGOVERNMENTAL COOPERATION

The Mississippi Commission on Interstate Cooperation oversees and encourages the state's participation in interstate bodies, especially the Council of State Governments and the National Conference of State Legislatures. Mississippi also participates in the Gulf States Marine Fisheries Compact, Southern Growth Policies Compact, Southern Interstate Energy Compact, Southern Regional Education Compact, and Tennessee-Tombigbee Waterway Development Compact. Mississippi received over $2.7 billion in federal aid in 1995/96.

20ECONOMY

Between the Civil War and World War II, Mississippi's economy remained poor, stagnant, and highly dependent on the market for cotton—a bitter legacy from which the state is only now beginning to recover. As in the pre–Civil War years, Mississippi exported its raw materials and imported manufactures. In the 1930s, however, state leaders began to realize the necessity of diversifying the economy. By the mid-1960s, many more Mississippians recognized that political and economic inequality and racial conflict did not provide an environment attractive to the industries the state needed.

Once the turmoil of the 1950s and early 1960s had subsided, the impressive industrial growth of the immediate postwar years resumed. By the mid-1960s, manufacturing—attracted to the state, in part, because of low wage rates and a weak labor movement—surpassed farming as a source of jobs. During the following decade, the balance of industrial growth changed somewhat. The relatively low-paying garment, textile, and wood-products industries, based on cotton and timber, grew less rapidly in both value added and employment than a number of heavy industries, including transportation equipment and electric and electronic goods. Still, Mississippi remains a poor state. Its gross state product in 1994 was $50,587 million, consisting of private good-producing industries, $15,608 million; private services-producing industries, $27,354 million; and government, $7,625 million.

In 1995, Mississippi's per capita personal income ranked 50th in the nation with $16,683. In 1996, there were 15,743 bankruptcy filings in the state, up 33% from the previous year.

21INCOME

As it has for much of this century, Mississippi ranked last among the 50 states in per capita personal income in 1996, at $17,471. For many years Mississippi has steadily closed the gap between its low income level and the national norm. Per capita income grew from 54% of the US average in 1960 to 65% in 1970, 69% in 1975, and 73% in 1978, then leveled off at about 70% in the next several years before rising to 72% in 1995 and 1996. Measured in constant 1982 dollars, per capita income grew 25%

between 1973 and 1988, compared to 27% for the nation. Total earned income grew by 5.5% (from $30.6 in 1995 to 32.3% in 1996), compared to 5.4% for the nation. Nonfarm personal income grew at a pace slightly slower than the nation's during that period: from 1995 to 1996 it increased 4.9% compared to 5.3% for the nation. Median four-person family income in 1995 was $49,687. About 23.5% of all state residents lived below the federal poverty line in 1995, a greater reported proportion than in any other state. Per capita income growth, however, rose by 4.7% in 1995/96, the 15th fastest rate of growth in the nation. Nearly 4% (35,000) of all households in Mississippi had an income level exceeding $75,000, including 1% (9,100) whose disposable incomes were greater than $125,000 in 1990. In addition, between 1991 and 1994, the number of taxpayers reporting adjusted gross incomes of over $100,000 on their federal individual income tax returns rose from 13,512 to 20,794, an increase of 54%.

22LABOR

Data for 1996 showed a civilian labor force of approximately 1,262,000 in Mississippi, of whom 1,762,000 were employed; the unemployment rate was 5.6%.

At the end of 1996, 240,800 Mississippi residents worked in services: 239,800 in manufacturing; 230,200 in trade; 227,200 in government; 50,800 in construction; 48,700 in transportation, communication, and public utilities; 39,600 in finance, insurance, and real estate; and 4,300 in mining.

In December 1995, the average weekly earnings of Mississippi production workers in manufacturing were $435.93. Mississippi has a right-to-work law. In 1995, only about 5.2% of all workers were members of unions.

23AGRICULTURE

In 1995, Mississippi ranked 24th among the states in income from agriculture, with marketings of over $3.1 billion; crops accounted for $1.4 billion and livestock and livestock products $1.7 billion.

The history of agriculture in the state is dominated by cotton, which from the 1830s through World War II was Mississippi's principal cash crop. During the postwar period, however, as mechanized farming replaced the sharecropper system, agriculture became more diversified. In 1995 Mississippi ranked 4th in cotton and 5th in rice production, and 13th in soybeans. About 1,841,000 bales of cotton worth $652 million were harvested in 1995; the figures for 1989 were 1,556,000 bales worth $470.2 million. Soybean output in 1995 totaled 37,800,000 bushels, worth $257 million, compared to 56,425,000 bushels and $459.9 million in 1983. Rice production was 13,395,000 and 14,250,000 hundredweight in 1989 and 1990, respectively; 1990 value was $99.6 million. Mississippi led the nation in catfish production in 1995 with sales amounting to $259 million.

Federal estimates for 1995 showed some 42,000 farms with a total area of 13 million acres (5.2 million hectares). Mississippi's farm population in 1990 was approximately 56,000, down from 85,000 in 1980 and 277,000 in 1970. The richest soil is in the Delta, where most of the cotton is raised. Livestock has largely taken over the Black Belt, a fertile area in the northwest.

24ANIMAL HUSBANDRY

Cattle are raised throughout the state, though principally in the Black Belt and Delta. The main chicken-raising area is in the eastern hills.

In 1997, there were around 1.34 million cattle and calves, valued at $482 million. In 1996, there were around 4.85 million hogs and pigs, valued at $475 million. Mississippi is a leading producer of broilers, ranking 5th in 1995; nearly 3 billion lb (1.4 billion kg) of broilers, worth $1 billion, were produced in that year.

25FISHING

In 1995, Mississippi ranked 11th among the 50 states in size of commercial fish landings, 145.5 million lb (66 million kg), with a value of $41,735,000. Of this total, 128.6 million lb (58 million kg) or 88% of the catch was landed at Pascagoula-Moss Point, the nation's 7th-largest port for commercial landings in 1995. Shrimp and blue crab made up the bulk of the commercial landings. The saltwater catch also includes mullet and red snapper; the freshwater catch is dominated by buffalo fish, carp, and catfish. As of 1 January 1997, Mississippi ranked 1st among the states in catfish farming, mostly from ponds in the Yazoo River basin. There were 360 catfish farms in operation, covering about 102,000 acres (41,300 hectares) of water surface, with a combined inventory of 631.4 million fingerlings and 466.6 million stocker-sized catfish. In 1995/96, the state issued 415,858 sport fishing licenses.

26FORESTRY

Mississippi had approximately 18,595,400 acres (7,525,600 hectares) of commercial forested land in 1994, 62% of the total land area of the state. Six national forests extend over 1.1 million acres (445,000 hectares). The state's most heavily forested region is the Piney Woods in the southeast. Of the state's total commercial timberland, 90% is privately owned. Some of this land was also used for agricultural purposes (grazing). Timber production was valued at $1.1 billion in 1996.

27MINING

Mississippi's nonfuel mineral production in 1995 was valued at $125 million, a decrease of $10 million from in 1994. A $5.7 million decrease in the value of construction sand and gravel headed the decline. Construction sand and gravel was the leading nonfuel mineral in 1995, accounting for 38% of the state's total nonfuel mineral production value. Mississippi ranked 2d among the states in production of fuller's earth, 3d in bentonite, and 4th in all clay. Fuller's earth was the second most valuable nonfuel mineral commodity produced in 1995, followed by portland cement. In 1995, 1.16 million metric tons of clays were produced for a value of $41 million. Almost 10.8 million metric tons of sand and gravel produced were worth $47.5 million. A quantity of 2.2 million metric tons of crushed stone was worth $9 million. Mississippi ranked 42d nationally in mineral value.

28ENERGY AND POWER

There were 20 electric generating plants in Mississippi in 1996, with a total installed capacity of 7.28 million kw, almost all coal-fired or gas-fired. The Grand Gulf Nuclear Station boiling-water reactor, built by Mississippi Power Company in Claiborne County, continues to provide power to consumers within Mississippi.

The Tennessee Valley Authority, the nation's largest producer of electricity, has negotiated and signed a contract with CRSS, Inc., to purchase electric power from a planned lignite power plant, known as the Red Hills Power Project, to be developed in Choctaw County.

Mississippi is a major petroleum producer, ranking 13th in the US in 1995. In that year, there were 4,166 producing wells located within 45 of the state's 82 counties. Production of petroleum totaled 19,911,000 barrels, and there were proved reserves of 160 million barrels. Mississippi produced 97.3 billion cu ft of natural gas during 1995, when it ranked 18th in the nation and proved reserves were estimated at 650 billion cu ft. Most production comes from the south-central part of the state.

²⁹INDUSTRY

In 1995, the value of shipments by Mississippi manufacturers totaled $39,546.5 million.

The following table shows value of shipments in 1995 for selected major industry groups (in millions of dollars):

Food and food products	$ 4,359.0
Transportation equipment	2,963.7
Lumber and wood products	4,342.4
Electric and electronic equipment	3,032.2
Chemicals and allied products	3,375.4
Apparel and other textile products	1,544.2

The state's biggest manufacturing concern is Litton Industries' Ingalls shipyard at Pascagoula. In addition to merchant vessels, this yard builds US Navy ships, including nuclear-powered submarines.

In 1997, Mississippi was the headquarters for one Fortune 500 company, Worldcom. There were 138 US patents issued to Mississippi residents in 1995.

³⁰COMMERCE

In 1992, a federal census counted 3,868 wholesale establishments in Mississippi, with $15.8 billion in sales. Durable goods accounted for 33.9% of the sales. Retail sales totaled $14.8 billion in 1992, conducted by 15,285 establishments. Food stores accounted for 23.2% of the sales income; automotive dealers, 21%; general merchandise stores, 16.4%; eating and drinking places, 8.2%; and other establishments, 31.2%.

Exports produced in Mississippi totaled $2.6 billion in 1996, while exports shipped from the state amounted to $1.2 billion.

³¹CONSUMER PROTECTION

The Consumer Protection Division of the Office of the Attorney General, established in 1974, may investigate complaints of unfair or deceptive trade practices and, in specific cases, may issue injunctions to halt them. Under 1994 amendments, a violation of the Consumer Protection Act is now a criminal misdemeanor.

³²BANKING

Mississippi's 111 insured commercial banks had assets of $28.5 billion at the end of 1996. They held loans and leases amounting to $17.0 billion and deposits of nearly $23.4 billion, including $4.2 billion in demand deposits and $19.2 billion in time and savings deposits. At the end of 1996, Mississippi had 14 insured savings institutions with assets totaling $2.0 billion.

³³INSURANCE

At the end of 1996, 39 life insurance companies were domiciled in Mississippi. Some 3,179,000 life insurance policies were in force in 1996, worth a total of $96.1 billion. Life insurance companies paid $311.1 million to 29,000 beneficiaries in 1996. The average Mississippi family held $99,100 in life coverage, 20% below the national average and 42nd among the 50 states. In 1996, premiums written for automobile liability and physical damage insurance totaled $803.8 million.

³⁴SECURITIES

There are no securities exchanges in Mississippi. As of April 1997, there were 1,205 securities brokers and dealers registered to conduct business in Mississippi, involving 36,671 designated agents. At that time, 503 securities investment advisory firms were registered, involving 1,600 agents.

³⁵PUBLIC FINANCE

Two state budgets are prepared annually—one by the State Department of Finance and Administration, for the executive branch, and one by the Joint Legislative Budget Committee, for the legislative branch—and submitted to the legislature for reconciliation and approval. The fiscal year runs from 1 July through 30 June.

The following table shows general fund revenues and expenditures for 1994/95 (in thousands):

Revenues	
From federal government	$2,456,626
From other sources	4,020,212
Taxes	
Sales and gross receipts	2,397,900
Income	948,847
TOTAL	3,346,747
CHARGES AND MISCELLANEOUS	
Current charges	393,618
Interest earnings	79,568
Special assessments	—
Other	200,279
TOTAL	673,465
TOTAL REVENUES	$6,476,838
EXPENDITURES	
Education	$1,705,595
Health and social services	2,465,015
Financial administration	134,444
Transportation (highways)	532,763
Utilities	91,044
Public safety (police)	57,423
Natural resources	115,405
Community development	101,420
Other	559,804
TOTAL GENERAL EXPENDITURES	$6,592,804

As of 1995, the outstanding debt of state and local governments was $98 million, or $305 per capita.

³⁶TAXATION

In 1996, Mississippi collected slightly more than $3.8 billion in state taxes. As of 1996, the state income tax for both individuals and corporations ranged from 3% on the first $5,000 of net income to 5% on amounts over $10,000; the corporate income tax rate was one of the lowest in the nation. Mississippi also imposes severance taxes on oil, natural gas, and timber. A 7% retail sales tax is levied, along with taxes on inheritance, gasoline, tobacco, beer, wine, insurance premiums, and numerous other items. In 1995, Mississippians paid $6 billion in federal taxes and received nearly $14.2 billion in federal funding.

³⁷ECONOMIC POLICY

In 1936, the state began implementing a program called Balance Agriculture with Industry (BAWI), designed to attract manufacturing to Mississippi. The BAWI laws offered industry substantial tax concessions and permitted local governments to issue bonds to build plants that would be leased to companies for a 20-year period, after which the company would own them. Mississippi continues to offer low tax rates and numerous tax incentives to industry.

The Department of Economic Development is charged with encouraging economic growth in the specific fields of industrial development, marketing of state products, and development of tourism. A high-technology asset is the National Space and Technology Laboratory in Hancock County.

38HEALTH

In 1995 there were 41,344 live births in Mississippi, the birthrate was 15.3 per 1,000 population. There were 3,563 legal abortions in the state in 1995; at 86.2 per 1,000 live births, Mississippi's abortion ratio was one of the nation's lowest. In the same year, Mississippi's death rates from heart diseases (356.0 per 100,000 population), cancer (213), and cerebrovascular diseases (69.3) exceeded national rates. The state had few reported AIDS cases in 1995 (15.51 per 100,000 population). In 1993, Mississippi had the highest mortality rate related to cardiovascular disease in the nation; the coronary heart disease death rate was 108.2 per 100,000 population. Among persons ages 18–30, 20% were reported to be smokers.

Mississippi had 97 hospitals, with 11,248 beds, in 1995; the 43,879 medical personnel in 1995 included 8,523 registered nurses. The average hospital expense for services provided per stay was $4,235 in 1994, lower than any other state. In 1994 there were 3,470 active non-federal physicians. The 1994 ratio of 132 physicians per 100,000 civilian population was lower than that in every other state but Alaska. At the end of 1995, the state had 1,023 professionally active dentists. Approximately 22.4% of the state's population has no health insurance.

39SOCIAL WELFARE

Social Security, welfare, and other transfer payments were the principal source of income in 34 counties and the second most important source of income in the state. During 1996, aid to families with dependent children (AFDC) was paid to 133,000 Mississippians. Average monthly AFDC payments of $144 per family were the lowest among the 50 states. In 1996, 457,106 residents received $68.53 monthly in food stamps. In 1996, students participating in the state's school lunch program cost US taxpayers $99.7 million.

With the enactment of the Personal Responsibility and Work Opportunity Reconciliation Act of 1996, the US government changed the form and regulations for many of its social welfare programs; most significantly, it replaced Aid to Families with Dependent Children (AFDC), an open-ended entitlement program, with Temporary Assistance for Needy Families (TANF), a limited system of assistance funded largely through federal block grants. The reform act also impacted the food stamp program, the Supplemental Security Income program, and the child nutrition program. The law took effect on 1 July 1997 and provided $16.38 billion in block grants for fiscal years 1997–2002. The grants were to be divided among the states based on an equation involving the numbers of former AFDC recipients in each state. Because many of the bill's provisions have yet to be implemented into state-by-state policy, it was not possible to include the details of each state's programs for this edition of this work.

In 1995, 494,530 residents received federal Social Security benefits; their average monthly payment in that year was $634. Unemployment insurance benefits averaged $134.06 per week in 1995.

40HOUSING

The 1996, Mississippi had 1,065,000 housing units, of which 961,000 were occupied. Only 77% of the occupied units had full plumbing in 1970—the lowest rate in the US—but by 1990 the rate had increased to 97.8%. Sixty-four percent of the units were owner-occupied in 1990.

In 1996, 10,367 privately owned units, valued at $709 million, were authorized for construction; of these, 8,061 were owner-occupied.

In 1990, the last year for which figures were available, Mississippi had the lowest median home value of any state except South Dakota, at $45,600. The median monthly costs for owners (with a mortgage) and renters in 1990 were $511 and $309, respectively; both costs were lower than in any other state but West Virginia. During 1995/96, Mississippi received $227.9 million in aid from the US Department of Housing and Urban Development, including $45.1 million in community development block grants.

41EDUCATION

Only 68% of adult Mississippians 25 and older had completed high school in 1993, an improvement since 1980, when 55% of the adult population were graduates.

Mississippi's reaction to the US Supreme Court decision in 1954 mandating public school desegregation was to repeal the constitutional requirement for public schools and to foster the development of segregated private schools. In 1964, the state's schools did begin to integrate, and compulsory school attendance was restored 13 years later. In 1982, the compulsory school age was raised to 14, and as of 1997, it is now 16; also in 1982, a system of free public kindergartens was established for the first time. As of 1980, 26% of minority (nonwhite) students were in schools in which minorities represented less than 50% of the student body, and 19% were in 99–100% minority schools—a considerable degree of de facto segregation, but less so than in some northern states.

As of the fall of 1996, there were 503,602 students enrolled in public schools in Mississippi: 365,006 elementary (including kindergarten) and 138,596 secondary. At $27,689, the average salary of public classroom teachers in 1996 was 49th of all the states.

During 1996 there were 40 institutions of higher education with a total enrollment of 165,655; 8 were public universities, 15 were community colleges, and 17 (including 4 Bible colleges and theological seminaries) were private colleges. Important institutions of higher learning in Mississippi include the University of Mississippi, established in 1844, Mississippi State University, and Southern Mississippi University. Predominantly black institutions include Tougaloo College, Alcorn State University, Jackson State University, and Mississippi Valley State University.

42ARTS

Jackson has two ballet companies, a symphony orchestra, and two opera companies. Opera South, an integrated but predominantly black company, presents free operas during its summer tours and mounts two major productions yearly. The Mississippi Opera instituted a summer festival during its 1980/81 season. There are local symphony orchestras in Meridian, Starkville, Tupelo, and Greenville. The established professional theaters in the state are the Sheffield Ensemble in Biloxi and the New Stage in Jackson. The Greater Gulf Coast Arts Center has been very active in bringing arts programs into the coastal area.

A distinctive contribution to US culture is the music of black sharecroppers from the Delta, known as the blues. The Delta Blues Museum in Clarksdale has an extensive collection documenting blues history.

In 1996, the NEA contributed $532,000 to arts programs in Mississippi and $542,000 to the Mississippi Arts Commission. The commission also receives significant sums from the state. Private sources contributed $11 million between 1987 and 1991, when audiences for the state's arts programs totaled 9,795,000. There were 45,050 contributing artists. In this five-year period, the Mississippi Arts Commission contributed $4,000 to support the Delta Blues Festival and $7,000 to assist the Corinth Theatre-Arts group. In 1991, there were 18 arts associations and 30 local arts groups. In 1992, the Mississippi Arts Commission received grants from the NEA to develop its arts education programs. The commission also received grants from the NEA's State and Regional Program.

43 LIBRARIES AND MUSEUMS

There were 47 county or multicounty (regional) libraries, serving all counties in 1996/97. There were 5.3 million volumes in Mississippi libraries, and total circulation was over 8 million. The finest collection of Mississippiana is at the Mississippi State Department of Archives and History in Jackson. In the Vicksburg-Warren County Public Library are collections on the Civil War and state history and oral history collections. Tougaloo College has special collections of African materials, civil rights papers, and oral history. The Gulf Coast Research Library of Ocean Springs has a marine biology collection.

There are 61 museums, including the distinguished Mississippi State Historical Museum at Jackson. Pascagoula, Laurel, and Jackson all have notable art museums. The Mississippi Museum of Natural Science in Jackson has been designated the state's official natural science museum by the legislature. Also in Jackson is the Mississippi Agriculture and Forestry Museum. In Meridian is a museum devoted to country singer Jimmie Rodgers, and in Jackson one to pitcher Dizzy Dean.

Beauvoir, Jefferson Davis's home at Biloxi, is a state shrine and includes a museum. The Mississippi governor's mansion—completed in 1845, restored in 1975, and purportedly the 2d-oldest executive residence in the US—is a National Historical Landmark.

44 COMMUNICATIONS

In March 1993, only 86.7% of the state's 971,000 occupied housing units had telephones, the lowest rate in the US. In 1996, the state had 233 operating radio stations (98 AM, 135 FM), 21 commercial television stations, and 6 noncommercial educational stations; 4 large cable television systems also served Mississippi.

45 PRESS

In 1997, Mississippi had 23 daily newspapers: 8 morning dailies and 14 evening dailies. In addition there were 13 Sunday papers in the state. The state's leading newspaper is in Jackson, owned by the Gannett Co.: the *Clarion–Ledger,* a morning daily with a weekday circulation of 107,876 (127,393 Sunday). A monthly, *Mississippi Magazine,* is published in Edwards, and a bimonthly, *Mississippi: A View of the Magnolia State,* in Jackson.

46 ORGANIZATIONS

Among the organizations that played key roles in the civil rights struggles in Mississippi during the 1950s and 1960s were the National Association for the Advancement of Colored People (NAACP), the Congress of Racial Equality, the Southern Christian Leadership Conference, and the Student Nonviolent Coordinating Committee (SNCC, later the Student National Coordinating Committee). Of the national civil rights organizations still active in Mississippi, the NAACP is the largest, with members in every county. In contrast to the 1960s, most civil rights activities in the state are now organized around local social and economic programs, such as Head Start. The Freedom Information Service is a clearinghouse for information about civil rights activities in the state. The Citizens' Councils of America, headquartered in Jackson, is a states' rights group. The 1992 Census of Service Industries counted 598 organizations in Mississippi, including 154 business associations; 284 civic, social, and fraternal associations; and 160 other membership organizations. Among the organizations with headquarters in Mississippi are the American Association of Public Health Physicians (Greenwood); the Sons of Confederate Veterans (Hattiesburg); and the Amateur Field Trial Clubs of America (Hernando).

47 TOURISM, TRAVEL, AND RECREATION

During 1993, in-state visitors spent $2.2 million on overnight and day trips in Mississippi. Among Mississippi's major tourist attrac-

tions are its mansions and plantations, many of them in the Natchez area. McRaven, in Vicksburg, was built in 1797. The Delta and Pine Land Co. plantation near Scott is one of the largest cotton plantations in the US. At Greenwood is the Florewood River Plantation, a museum re-creating 19th-century plantation life. The Mississippi State Fair is held annually in Jackson during the second week in October.

The Natchez Trace Parkway, Gulf Islands National Seashore, and Vicksburg National Military Park—3 of the state's 5 national parks—attracted 6,493,762 visitors in 1995. There are also 6 national forests and 27 state parks. In 1995, licenses were held by 283,347 hunters and 452,986 fishermen.

48 SPORTS

There are no major league professional teams in Mississippi. Jackson has a minor league baseball team, the Generals, in the Texas League, and a minor league basketball team in the Continental Basketball Association. There is also a minor league hockey team in Biloxi. The University of Mississippi has long been prominent in college football. "Ole Miss" teams won the Sugar Bowl in 1958, 1960, 1961, 1963, and 1970, and the Cotton Bowl in 1956. The Rebels play in the southeastern conference, as do the Mississippi State Bulldogs. Southern Mississippi is a member of the Conference USA.

Other annual sporting events of interest include the Dixie National Livestock Show and Rodeo, held in Jackson in January, and the Deposit Guaranty Bank Golf Classic, held in Hattiesburg in April.

49 FAMOUS MISSISSIPPIANS

Mississippi's most famous political figure, Jefferson Davis (b.Kentucky, 1808–89), came to the state as a very young child, was educated at West Point, and served in the US Army from 1828 to 1835. He resigned a seat in Congress in 1846 to enter the Mexican War from which he returned home a hero after leading his famous regiment, the 1st Mississippi Rifles, at the Battle of Buena Vista, Mexico. From 1853 to 1857, he served as secretary of war in the cabinet of President Franklin Pierce. Davis was representing Mississippi in the US Senate in 1861 when the state withdrew from the Union. In February 1861, he was chosen president of the Confederacy, an office he held until the defeat of the South in 1865. Imprisoned for two years after the Civil War (though never tried), Davis lived the last years of his life at Beauvoir, an estate on the Mississippi Gulf Coast given to him by an admirer. There he wrote *The Rise and Fall of the Confederate Government,* completed eight years before his death in New Orleans.

Lucius Quintus Cincinnatus Lamar (b.Georgia, 1825–93) settled in Oxford in 1855 and only two years later was elected to the US House of Representatives. A supporter of secession, he served as Confederate minister to Russia in 1862. After the war, Lamar was the first Mississippi Democrat returned to the House; in 1877, he entered the US Senate. President Grover Cleveland made Lamar his secretary of the interior in 1885, later appointing him to the US Supreme Court. Lamar served as associate justice from 1888 until his death.

Some of the foremost authors of 20th-century America had their origins in Mississippi. Supreme among them is William Faulkner (1897–1962), whose literary career began in 1924 with the publication of *The Marble Faun,* a book of poems. His novels included such classics as *The Sound and the Fury* (1929), *Light in August* (1932), and *Absalom, Absalom!* (1936). Faulkner received two Pulitzer Prizes (one posthumously), and in 1949 was awarded the Nobel Prize for literature.

Richard Wright (1908–60), born near Natchez, spent his childhood years in Jackson. He moved to Memphis as a young man, and from there migrated to Chicago; he lived his last years in Paris. A powerful writer and a leading spokesman for the black Americans of his generation, Wright is best remembered for his novel *Native Son* (1940) and for *Black Boy* (1945), an autobiographical account of his Mississippi childhood.

Other native Mississippians of literary renown (and Pulitzer Prize winners) are Eudora Welty (b.1909), Tennessee Williams (Thomas Lanier Williams, 1911–83), and playwright Beth Henley (b.1952). Welty's work, like Faulkner's, is set in Mississippi; her best-known novels include *Delta Wedding* (1946), *The Ponder Heart* (1954), and *Losing Battles* (1970). Although Tennessee Williams spent most of his life outside Mississippi, some of his most famous plays are set in the state. Other Mississippi authors are Hodding Carter (b.Louisiana, 1907–72), Shelby Foote (b.1916), Walker Percy (b.Alabama, 1916–1990), and Willie Morris (b.1934).

Among the state's numerous musicians are William Grant Still (1895–1978), a composer and conductor, and Leontyne Price (Mary Leontine Price, b.1927), a distinguished opera singer. Famous blues singers are Charlie Patton (1887–1934), William Lee Conley "Big Bill" Broonzy (1898–1958), Howlin' Wolf (Chester Arthur Burnett, 1910–1976), Muddy Waters (McKinley Morganfield, 1915–83), John Lee Hooker (b.1917), and Riley "B. B." King (b.1925). Mississippi's contributions to country music include Jimmie Rodgers (1897–1933), Conway Twitty (1933–1994), and Charley Pride (b.1939). Elvis Presley (1935–77), born in Tupelo, was one of the most popular entertainers in US history.

[50]BIBLIOGRAPHY

Alampi, Gary, ed. *Gale State Rankings Reporter*. Detroit: Gale Research, Inc., 1994

Bettersworth, John K. *Your Mississippi*. Austin, Tex.: Steck-Vaughn, 1975.

Bond, Bradley G. *Political Culture in the Nineteenth-century South: Mississippi, 1830–1900*. Baton Rouge: Louisiana State University, 1995.

Brooks, Cleanth. *William Faulkner: The Yoknapatawpha Country*. New Haven: Yale University Press, 1963.

Coleman, Mary DeLorse. *Legislators, Law, and Public Policy: Political Change in Mississippi and the South*. Westport, Conn.: Greenwood Press, 1993.

Council of State Governments. *The Book of the States, 1994– 1995 Edition*. Vol. 30. Lexington, Ky.: The Council of State Governments, 1994.

Dittmer, John. *Local People: The Struggle for Civil Rights in Mississippi*. Urbana: University of Illinois Press, 1994.

FDIC, Division of Research and Statistics. *Statistics on Banking: A Statistical Profile of the United States Banking Industry*. Washington, D.C.: Federal Deposit Insurance Corporation, 1993.

Federal Writers' Project. *Mississippi: A Guide to the Magnolia State*. New York: Somerset, n.d. (orig. 1938).

Ferris, William C. *Blues from the Delta*. Garden City, N.Y.: Doubleday, 1978.

Kirwan, Albert D. *Revolt of the Rednecks: Mississippi Politics (1876-1925)*. Magnolia, Mass.: Peter Smith, 1964.

Loewen, James W., and Charles Saillis. *Mississippi: Conflict and Change*. Rev. ed. New York: Pantheon, 1982.

McLemore, Richard A., ed. *A History of Mississippi*. 2 vols. Hattiesburg: University and College Press of Mississippi, 1973.

Miles, Edwin A. *Jacksonian Democracy in Mississippi*. New York: Da Capo, 1970 (orig.1900).

Mitchell, George. *Blow My Blues Away*. Baton Rouge: Louisiana State University Press, 1971.

Schmittroth, Linda, and Mary Kay Rosteck (eds.). *Cities of the United States*. 2nd ed. Detroit: Gale Research, Inc., 1994.

Silver, James W. *Mississippi: The Closed Society*, 2d ed. New York: Harcourt, Brace, and World, 1966.

Skates, John Ray. *Mississippi: A Bicentennial History*. New York: Norton, 1979.

Sydnor, Charles S. *Slavery in Mississippi*. New York: Appleton Century, 1933.

Welty, Eudora. *One Time, One Place: Mississippi in the Depression*. New York: Random House, 1971.

Wharton, Vernon L. *The Negro in Mississippi, 1865-90*. New York: Harper and Row, 1965 (orig. 1947).

U.S. Department of Education, National Center for Education Statistics. Office of Educational Research and Improvement. *Digest of Education Statistics, 1993*. Washington, D.C.: U.S. Government Printing Office, 1993.

U.S. Department of the Interior, U.S. Fish and Wildlife Service. *Endangered and Threatened Species Recovery Program*. Washington, D.C.: U.S. Government Printing Office, 1990.

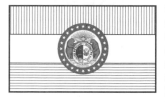

MISSOURI

State of Missouri

ORIGIN OF STATE NAME: Probably from the Iliniwek Indian word *missouri,* meaning "owners of big canoes." **NICKNAME:** The Show Me State. **CAPITAL:** Jefferson City. **ENTERED UNION:** 10 August 1821 (24th). **SONG:** "Missouri Waltz." **MOTTO:** *Salus populi suprema lex esto* (The welfare of the people shall be the supreme law). **COAT OF ARMS:** Two grizzly bears standing on a scroll inscribed with the state motto support a shield portraying an American eagle and a constellation of stars, a grizzly bear on all fours, and a crescent moon, all encircled by the words "United We Stand, Divided We Fall." Above are a six-barred helmet and 24 stars; below, the roman numeral MDCCCXX (1820), when Missouri's first constitution was adopted. **FLAG:** Three horizontal stripes of red, white, and blue, with the coat of arms, encircled by 24 white stars on a blue band, in the center. **OFFICIAL SEAL:** The coat of arms surrounded by the words "The Great Seal of the State of Missouri." **BIRD:** Bluebird. **INSECT:** Honeybee. **FLOWER:** Hawthorn blossom. **TREE:** Flowering dogwood. **ROCK:** Mozarkite (chert, or flint rock). **MINERAL:** Galena. **LEGAL HOLIDAYS:** New Year's Day, 1 January; Birthday of Martin Luther King, Jr., 3d Monday in January; Lincoln's Birthday, 12 February; Washington's Birthday, 3d Monday in February; Harry S. Truman's Birthday, 8 May; Memorial Day, last Monday in May; Independence Day, 4 July; Primary Election Day; 1st Tuesday after 1st Monday in August (every four years); Labor Day, 1st Monday in September Columbus Day, 2d Monday in October; Election Day, 1st Tuesday after 1st Monday in November (every four years); Veterans Day, 11 November; Thanksgiving Day, 4th Thursday in November; Christmas Day, 25 December. Though not a legal holiday, Missouri Day, the 3d Wednesday in October, is commemorated in schools each year. **TIME:** 6 AM CST = noon GMT.

¹LOCATION, SIZE, AND EXTENT

Located in the western north-central US, Missouri ranks 19th in size among the 50 states.

The total area of Missouri is 69,697 sq mi (180,516 sq km), of which land takes up 68,945 sq mi (178,568 sq km) and inland water 752 sq mi (1,948 sq km). Missouri extends 284 mi (457 km) E-W; its greatest N-S extension is 308 mi (496 km).

Missouri is bounded on the N by Iowa (with the line in the extreme NE defined by the Des Moines River); on the E by Illinois, Kentucky, and Tennessee (with the line passing through the Mississippi River); on the S by Arkansas (with a "boot heel" in the SE bounded by the Mississippi and St. Francis rivers); and on the W by Oklahoma, Kansas, and Nebraska (the line in the NW being formed by the Missouri River).

The total boundary length of Missouri is 1,438 mi (2,314 km). The state's geographic center is in Miller County, 20 mi (32 km) SW of Jefferson City.

²TOPOGRAPHY

Missouri is divided into four major land regions. The Dissected Till Plains, lying north of the Missouri River and forming part of the Central Plains region of the US, comprise rolling hills, open fertile flatlands, and well-watered prairie. The Osage Plains cover the western part of the state, their flat prairie monotony broken by low rounded hills. The Mississippi Alluvial Plain, in the southeastern corner, is made up of fertile black lowlands whose flood-plain belts represent both the present and former courses of the Mississippi River. The Ozark Plateau, which comprises most of southern Missouri and extends into northern Arkansas and northeastern Oklahoma, constitutes the state's largest single region. The Ozarks contain Taum Sauk Mountain, at 1,772 feet (540 meters) the highest elevation in the state. Along the St.

Francis River, near Cardwell, is the state's lowest point, 230 feet (70 meters).

Including a frontage of at least 500 mi (800 km) along the Mississippi River, Missouri has more than 1,000 mi (1,600 km) of navigable waterways. The Mississippi and Missouri rivers, the two largest in the US, respectively form the state's eastern border and part of its western border; Kansas City is located at the point where the Missouri bends eastward to cross the state, while St. Louis developed below the junction of the two great waterways. The White, Grand, Chariton, St. Francis, Current, and Osage are among the state's other major rivers. The largest lake is the artificial Lake of the Ozarks, covering a total of 93 sq mi (241 sq km).

Missouri's exceptional number of caves and caverns were formed during the last 50 million years through the erosion of limestone and dolomite by melting snows bearing vegetable acids. Coal, lead, and zinc deposits date from the Pennsylvanian era, beginning some 250 million years ago. The Mississippi Valley area is geologically active: massive earthquakes during 1811 and 1812 devastated the New Madrid area of the southeast.

³CLIMATE

Missouri has a continental climate, but with considerable local and regional variation. The average annual temperature is 50°F (10°C) in the northwest, but about 60°F (16°C) in the southeast. Kansas City has a normal daily mean temperature of 54°F (12°C), ranging from 26°F (−3°C) in January to 79°F (26°C) in July; St. Louis has an annual mean of 56°F (13°C) with 29°F (−2°C) in January and 80°F (27°C) in July.

The coldest temperature ever recorded in Missouri was −40°F (−40°C), set at Warsaw on 13 February 1905; the hottest, 118°F (48°C), at Warsaw and Union on 14 July 1954. A 1980 heat wave caused 311 heat-related deaths in Missouri, the highest toll in the country; most were elderly residents of St. Louis and Kansas City. Fifty-one more heat-related deaths occurred in St. Louis during a 1983 heat wave.

The average annual precipitation for the state is about 40 in (100 cm), with some rain or snow falling about 110 days a year. The heaviest precipitation is in the southeast, averaging 48 in (122 cm); the northwest usually receives 35 in (89 cm) yearly. Snowfall averages 20 in (51 cm) in the north, 10 in (25 cm) in the southeast. During the winter, northwest winds prevail; the air movement is largely from the south and southeast during the rest of the year. Springtime is the peak tornado season; in 1995, Missouri had 35 tornadoes.

⁴FLORA AND FAUNA

Representative trees of Missouri include the shortleaf pine, scarlet oak, smoke tree, pecan *(Carya illinoensis),* and peachleaf willow, along with species of tupelo, cottonwood, cypress, cedar, and dogwood (the state tree). American holly, which once flourished in the southeastern woodlands, is now considered rare; various types of wild grasses proliferate in the northern plains region. Missouri's state flower is the hawthorn blossom; other wild flowers include Queen Anne's lace, meadow rose, and white snakeroot. Showy and small white lady's slipper, green adder's-mouth, purslane, corn salad, dotted monardo, and prairie white-fringed orchid are rare in Missouri. Among endangered plants are the small-whorled pogonia, water sedge, Loesel's twayblade, and marsh pink; the American elm, common throughout the state, is considered endangered because of Dutch elm disease.

Indigenous mammals are the common cottontail, muskrat, white-tailed deer, and gray and red foxes. The state bird is the bluebird; other common birds are the cardinal, solitary vireo, and the prothonotary warbler. A characteristic amphibian is the plains leopard frog; native snakes include garter, ribbon, and copperhead. Bass, carp, perch, jack salmon (walleye), and crayfish abound in Missouri's waters. The chigger, a minute insect, is a notorious pest.

Listed as endangered in Missouri are the Ozark big-eared, gray, and Indiana bats, two subspecies of peregrine falcon, bald eagle, whooping crane, and eight varieties of mussel.

⁵ENVIRONMENTAL PROTECTION

Missouri's first conservation law, enacted in 1874, provided for a closed hunting season on deer and certain game birds. In 1936, the state established a Conservation Commission to protect the state's wildlife and forest resources. Today, Missouri's principal environmental protection agencies are the Department of Conservation, which manages the state forests and fish hatcheries and maintains wildlife refuges, the Department of Natural Resources, responsible for state parks, energy conservation, and environmental quality programs, including air pollution control, water purification, land reclamation, soil and water conservation, and solid and hazardous waste management. The State Environmental Improvement and Energy Resources Authority, within the Department of Natural Resources, is empowered to offer financial aid to any individual, business, institution, or governmental unit seeking to meet pollution control responsibilities.

An important environmental problem is soil erosion; the state loses 71 million tons of topsoil each year. Residents approved a 0.1% sales tax in 1984 and 1988 to create a fund to address this problem. For 1995/96, the state spent $32 million to reverse erosion. As of 1982, 42 sites in Missouri were found to have unsafe concentrations of dioxin, a highly toxic by-product of hexachlorophene, manufactured in a Verona chemical plant; in that year, an evacuation was begun (completed in 1985) of the 2,000 residents of Times Beach, a community 30 mi (48 km) west of St. Louis that was declared a federal disaster area. St. Louis ranks high among US cities for the quantities of lead and

suspended particles found in the atmosphere, but conditions improved between the mid-1970s and early 1980s.

In 1995, the state had 22 hazardous waste sites. In 1996, it had 643,000 acres (260,000 hectares) of wetlands, or about 1.4% of the state's lands.

⁶POPULATION

Missouri ranked 15th among the 50 states at the 1990 census, with a population of 5,117,073, whose density was 74.3 per sq mi (28.5 per sq km), a 4% increase over the 1980 census total of 4,917,444. The population estimate for 1996 was 5,358,692, up 4.7% from 1990; the population projection for 2000 is 5,473,000.

In 1830, the first year in which Missouri was enumerated as a state, the population was 140,455. Missouri's population just about doubled each decade until 1860, when the growth rate subsided; the population surpassed the 2 million mark at the 1880 census, 3 million in 1900 (when it ranked 5th in the US), and 4 million during the early 1950s. According to 1990 figures, the population was 51.8% female and slightly older than the national average (13.9% were 65 or older in 1989, 6th among the states). In addition, the population was slightly less mobile than the national average: almost 70% of Missourians were born in the state, and 54% of those over 5 years of age were living in the same house in 1990 as in 1985.

In 1990, 68.7% of all Missourians lived in urban areas and 31.3% in rural areas; in 1830, the population distribution had been 4% urban and 96% rural. The largest cities and their estimated 1994 populations were Kansas City, 443,878; and St. Louis, 368,215—both well below the 1980 figures. St. Louis lost 7.5% of its population since 1984, continuing the trend of the 27.2% drop during the 1970s. Kansas City lost 2.9% since 1980. The St. Louis metropolitan area, embracing parts of Missouri and Illinois, comprised an estimated 2,547,686 people in 1995, while metropolitan Kansas City, in Missouri and Kansas, had a population of 1,663,453.

⁷ETHNIC GROUPS

After the flatboat and French traders and settlers had made possible the earliest development of Missouri and its Mississippi shore, the river steamer, the Civil War, the Homestead Act (1862), and the railroad changed the character of the state ethnically as well as economically. Germans came in large numbers, developing small diversified industries, and they were followed by Czechs and Italians. The foreign-born numbered 83,633 in 1990.

Black Americans have represented a rising proportion of Missouri's population in recent decades: 9% in 1960, 10.3% in 1970, 10.5% in 1980, and 10.7% in 1990. Of 548,000 blacks in 1990, 34% lived in St. Louis (which was more than 47% black); Kansas City's black community, 128,700 in 1990, supported a flourishing jazz and urban blues culture between the two world wars, while St. Louis was the home of Scott Joplin and W. C. Handy in the early years of the century. In 1990 Missouri also had 62,000 people of Hispanic origin, including 35,860 of Mexican ancestry. The Asian community was small in 1990: 8,006 Chinese, 7,181 Filipinos, 6,452 Koreans, 6,233 Japanese, and 4,030 Asian Indians.

Only a few American Indians remained in Missouri after 1836. The 1990 census showed an Indian population of 20,000; the state has no Indian reservations.

Of those claiming descent from at least one specific ancestry group in 1990, over 1,840,000 named German, 743,232 English, and 1,037,658 Irish.

⁸LANGUAGES

White pioneers found Missouri Indians in the northern part of what is now Missouri Osage in the central portion, and Quapaw

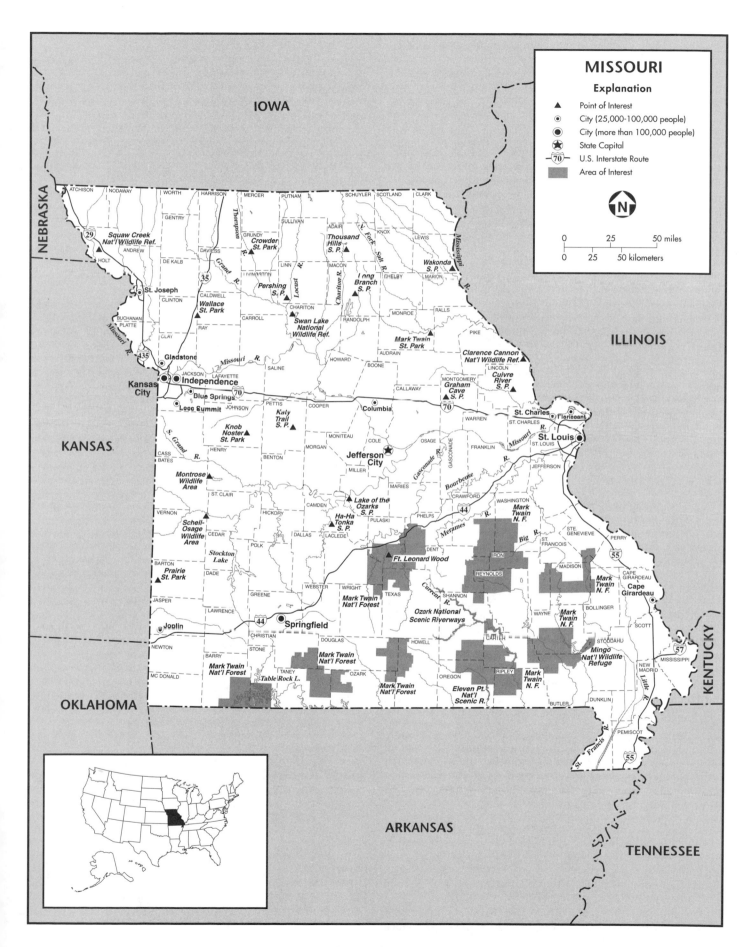

MISSOURI
Explanation
▲ Point of Interest
⊙ City (25,000-100,000 people)
◉ City (more than 100,000 people)
★ State Capital
—⟨70⟩— U.S. Interstate Route
Area of Interest

0   25   50 miles
0   25   50 kilometers

in the south. Long after these tribes' removal to Indian Territory, only a few place-names echo their heritage: Missouri itself, Kahoka, Wappapello.

Four westward-flowing language streams met and partly merged in Missouri. Northern and North Midland speakers settled north of the Missouri River and in the western border counties, bringing their Northern *pail* and *sick to the stomach* and their North Midland *fishworm* (earthworm), *gunnysack* (burlap bag), and *sick at the stomach*. But *sick in the stomach* occurs along the Missouri River from St. Louis to Kansas City and along the Mississippi south of St. Louis. South of the Missouri River, and notably in the Ozark Highlands, South Midland dominates, though with a few Southern forms, especially in the cotton-growing floodplain of the extreme southeast. *Wait on* (wait for), *light bread* (white bread), and *pullybone* (wishbone) are critical dialect markers for this area, as are *redworm* (earthworm), *towsack* (burlap bag), *snap beans* (string beans), *how* and *now* sounding like /haow/ and /naow/, and *Missouri* ending with the vowel of *me* rather than the final vowel of /uh/ heard north of the Missouri. In the extreme southeast are Southern *loaf bread, grass sack* (burlap bag), and *cold drink* as a term for a soft drink. In the eastern half of the state, a soft drink is generally *soda* or *sody*; in the western half, *pop*.

About 96% of state residents five years old or older spoke only English at home in 1990. Of those who claimed to speak another language at home, the leading languages and number of speakers were:

Spanish	59,585	Italian	9,125
German	32,286	Chinese	7,018
French	20,135	Other West Germanic	4,338

⁹RELIGIONS

Beginning in the late 17th century, French missionaries brought Roman Catholicism to what is now Missouri; the first permanent Roman Catholic church was built about 1755 at Ste. Genevieve. Immigration from Germany, Ireland, Italy, and Eastern Europe swelled the Catholic population during the 19th century, and Roman Catholicism remains the largest Christian denomination. Baptist preachers crossed the Mississippi River into Missouri in the late 1790s, and the state's first Methodist church was organized about 1806. Immigrants from Germany included not only Roman Catholics, but also many Lutherans, the most conservative of whom organized the Lutheran Church—Missouri Synod in 1847. In 1990, the Missouri Synod, with its headquarters in St. Louis, had a total US membership of 2,603,725.

In 1990, Missouri had 802,083 Roman Catholics. The principal Protestant denominations in 1990 were the Southern Baptist Convention, with 789,183 adherents; United Methodist Church, 255,111; Lutheran Church—Missouri Synod, 145,741; and the Christian Church (Disciples of Christ), 101,756. In 1990, Missouri's estimated Jewish population was 53,092.

¹⁰TRANSPORTATION

Centrally located, Missouri is the leading US transportation center. Both St. Louis and Kansas City are hubs of rail, truck, and airline transportation.

In 1836, delegates from 11 counties met in St. Louis to recommend construction of two railroad lines and to petition Congress for a grant of 800,000 acres (324,000 hectares) of public land on which to build them. More than a dozen companies were incorporated by the legislature, but they all collapsed with the financial panic of 1837. Interest in railroad construction revived during the following decade, and in 1849 a national railroad convention was held in St. Louis at which

nearly 1,000 delegates from 13 states recommended the construction of a transcontinental railroad. By 1851, three railroad lines had been chartered, and construction by the Pacific Railroad at St. Louis was under way; the Pacific line reached Kansas City in 1865, and a bridge built over the Missouri River four years later enabled Kansas City to link up with the Hannibal and St. Joseph Railroad, providing a freight route to Chicago that did not pass through St. Louis. In 1996, there were 4,500 rail mi (7,241 km) of track in the state, including 3,800 rail mi (6,114 km) of Class I track. In 1995/96, Amtrak provided eight passenger trains running directly from Chicago to St. Louis and to Kansas City, en route to San Antonio and Los Angeles, and two daily Kansas City–St. Louis round trips. Amtrak trains made eight other Missouri stops between St. Louis and Kansas City; total 1995/96 Missouri ridership was 729,192.

The first road developed in colonial Missouri was probably a trail between the lead mines and Ste. Genevieve in the early 1700s. A two-level cantilever bridge—the first in the world to have a steel superstructure—spanning the Mississippi at St. Louis was dedicated on 4 July 1874. By 1940, no place in Missouri was more than 10 miles (16 km) from a highway. As of 31 December 1995, there were 122,613 mi (197,407 km) of public roads in Missouri. The main interstate highways were I-70, linking St. Louis with Kansas City; I-44, connecting St. Louis with Springfield and Joplin; I-55, linking St. Louis with Chicago, Ill, to the north and paralleling the course of the Mississippi between St. Louis and Memphis, Tenn.; I-35, connecting Kansas City with Des Moines Iowa; and I-29, paralleling the Missouri River north of Kansas City. Motor vehicle registration for the state in 1996 was 4,761,031, including 3,394,248 passenger cars, 1,349,039 trucks, and 17,744 buses; 3,579,993 driver's licenses were in force during the same year.

The Mississippi and Missouri rivers have long been important transportation routes. Pirogues, keelboats, and flatboats plied these waterways for more than a century before the first steamboat, the *New Orleans*, traveled down the Mississippi in 1811. The Mississippi still serves considerable barge traffic, making metropolitan St. Louis an active inland port area, with 30,138,000 tons of cargo handled in 1995.

Pioneering aviators in Missouri organized the first international balloon races in 1907 and the first US-sponsored international aviation meet in 1910. Five St. Louis pilots made up the earliest US Army air corps, and a barnstorming pilot named Charles A. Lindbergh, having spent a few years in the St. Louis area, had the backing of businessmen from that city when he flew his *Spirit of St. Louis* across the Atlantic in 1927. Today, Kansas City International Airport and Lambert-St. Louis Municipal Airport are among the busiest airports in the country. These two enplaned 4,533,185 and 12,736,060 passengers, respectively, in 1995. There are 498 aviation facilities in Missouri, including airports, heliports, and seaplane bases. The state has 6,210 aircraft and 11,967 registered pilots.

¹¹HISTORY

The region we now call Missouri has been inhabited for at least 4,000 years. The prehistoric Woodland peoples left low burial mounds, rudimentary pottery, arrowheads, and grooved axes; remains of the later Mississippian Culture include more sophisticated pottery and finely chipped arrowheads. When the first Europeans arrived in the late 17th century, most of the few thousand Indians living in Missouri were relatively recent immigrants, pushed westward across the Mississippi River because of pressures from eastern tribes and European settlers along the Atlantic coast. Indians then occupying Missouri belonged to two main linguistic groups: Algonkian-speakers, mainly the Sauk, Fox, and Iliniwek (Illinois) in the northeast; and a Siouan group, including the Osage, Missouri, Iowa, Kansas, and other tribes, to the south and west. Of greatest interest to the Europeans were the Osage, among whom were warriors and runners of extraordinary ability. The flood of white settlers into Missouri after 1803 forced the Indians to move into Kansas and into what became known as Indian Territory (present-day Oklahoma). During the 1820s, the US government negotiated treaties with the Osage, Sauk, Fox, and Iowa tribes whereby they surrendered, for the most part peaceable, all their lands in Missouri. By 1836, few Indians remained.

The first white men to pass through land eventually included within Missouri's boundaries apparently were Jacques Marquette and Louis Joliet, who in 1673 passed the mouth of the Missouri River on their journey down the Mississippi; so did Robert Cavelier, Sieur de la Salle, who claimed the entire Mississippi Valley for France in 1682. Probably the first Frenchman to explore the Missouri River was Louis Armand de Lom d'Arce, Baron de Lahontan, who in 1688 claimed to have reached the junction of the Missouri and Osage rivers. The French did little to develop the Missouri region during the first half of the 18th century, although a few fur traders and priests established posts and missions among the Indians. A false report that silver had been discovered set off a brief mining boom in which no silver but some lead—available in abundance—was extracted. Missouri passed into Spanish hands with the rest of the Louisiana Territory in 1762, but development was still guided by French settlers; in 1764, the French fur trader Pierre Laclède established a trading post on the present site of St. Louis.

Although Spain fortified St. Louis and a few other outposts during the American Revolution and beat back a British-Indian attack on St. Louis in 1780, the Spanish did not attempt to settle Missouri. However, they did allow Americans to migrate freely into the territory. Spanish authorities granted free land to the new settlers, relaxed their restrictions against Protestants, and welcomed slave-holding families from southern states—especially important after 1787, when slavery was banned in the Northwest Territory. Pioneers such as Daniel Boone arrived from Kentucky, and the Chouteau fur-trading family gained a lucrative monopoly among the Osage. Spanish rule ended abruptly in 1800 when Napoleon forced Spain to return Louisiana to France. Included in the Louisiana Purchase, Missouri then became part of the US in 1803. After the Lewis and Clark expedition (1804–6) had successfully explored the Missouri River, Missouri in general—and St. Louis in particular—became the gateway to the West.

Missouri was part of the Louisiana Territory (with headquarters at St. Louis) until 1 October 1812, when the Missouri Territory (including present-day Arkansas, organized separately in 1819) was established. A flood of settlers between 1810 and 1820 more than tripled Missouri's population from 19,783 to 66,586, leading Missourians to petition the US Congress for statehood as early as 1818. But Congress, divided over the slavery issue, withheld permission for three years, finally approving statehood for Maine and Missouri under the terms of the Missouri Compromise (1820), which sanctioned slavery in the new state but banned it in the rest of the former Louisiana Territory north of Arkansas. Congress further required that Missouri make no effort to enforce a state constitutional ban on the immigration of free Negroes and mulattos; once the legislature complied, Missouri became the 24th state on 10 August 1821, Alexander McNair became the state's first governor, and Thomas Hart Benton was one of the state's first two US senators; Benton remained an important political leader for more than three decades.

Aided by the advent of steamboat travel on the Mississippi and Missouri rivers, settlers continued to arrive in the new state, whose population surpassed 1 million by 1860. The site for a new capital, Jefferson City, was selected in 1821, and five years later the legislature met there for the first time. French fur traders settled the present site of Kansas City in 1821 and established a trading post at St. Joseph in 1827. Mormons came to Independence during the early 1830s but were expelled from the state and crossed the Mississippi back into Illinois. For much of the antebellum period, the state's economy flourished, with an emphasis on cotton, cattle, minerals (especially lead and zinc), and commerce—notably the outfitting of wagon trains for the Santa Fe and Oregon trails. On the eve of the Civil War, more than half the population consisted of Missouri natives; 15% of the white population was foreign-born, chiefly German and Irish. Black slaves represented only 9% of the total population—the lowest proportion of any slave state except Delaware—while only about 25,000 Missourians were slave holders. Nevertheless, there was a great deal of proslavery sentiment in the state, and thousands of Missourians crossed into neighboring Kansas in the mid-1850s to help elect a proslavery government in that territory. State residents were also active in the guerrilla warfare between proslavery forces and Free Staters that erupted along the border with "bleeding Kansas." The slavery controversy was exacerbated by the US Supreme Court's 1857 decision in the case of Dred Scott, a slave formerly owned by a Missourian who had temporarily brought him to what is now Minnesota, where slavery was prohibited; Scott's suit to obtain his freedom was denied by the Court on the grounds that it was unconstitutional to restrict the property rights of slave holders, in a decision that voided the Missouri Compromise reached 37 years earlier.

During the Civil War, Missouri remained loyal to the Union, though not without difficulty. When the conflict began, Governor Claiborne Fox Jackson called out the state militia "to repel the invasion" of federal forces, but pro-Union leaders such as Francis P. Blair deposed Jackson on 30 July 1861. Missouri supplied some 110,000 soldiers to the Union and 40,000 to the Confederacy. As devastating as the 1,162 battles or skirmishes fought on Missouri soil—more than in any other state except Virginia and Tennessee—was the general lawlessness that prevailed throughout the state; pro-Confederate guerrilla bands led by William Quantrill and Cole Younger, as well as Unionist freebooters, murdered and looted without hindrance. In October 1864, a Confederate army under Major General Sterling Price was defeated at the Battle of Westport, on the outskirts of Kansas City, ending the main military action. Some 27,000 Missourians were killed during the war. At a constitutional convention held in January 1865, Missouri became the first slave state to free all blacks.

During Reconstruction, the Radical Republicans sought to disfranchise all citizens who failed to swear that they had never aided or sympathized with the Confederacy. But the harshness of this and other measures caused a backlash, and Liberal Republicans such as Benjamin Gratz Brown and Carl Schurz, allied with the Democrats, succeeded in ousting the Radicals by 1872. The subsequent decline of the Liberal Republicans inaugurated a period during which Democrats occupied the governorship uninterruptedly for more than three decades.

The 1870s saw a period of renewed lawlessness, typified by the exploits of Jesse and Frank James, that earned Missouri the epithet of the "robber state." Of more lasting importance were the closing of the frontier in Missouri, the decline of the fur trade and steamboat traffic, and the rise of the railroads, shifting the market economy from St. Louis to Kansas City, whose population tripled during the 1880s, while St. Louis was eclipsed by Chicago as a center of finance, commerce, transportation, and population. Missouri farmers generally supported the movement for free silver coinage, along with other Populist policies such as railroad regulation. Reform Governor Joseph W. Folk (1905–09) and his immediate successors in the statehouse, Herbert S. Hadley (1909–13) and Elliott W. Major (1913–17), introduced progressive policies to Missouri. However, the ideal of honest government was soon subverted by Kansas City's corrupt political machine, under Thomas J. Pendergast, the most powerful Democrat in the state between the two world wars. Machine politics did not prevent capable politicians from rising to prominence—among them Harry S. Truman, Missouri's first and thus far only native son to serve in the nation's highest office.

The state's economy increasingly shifted from agriculture to industry, and Missouri's rural population declined from about three-fourths of the total in 1880 to less than one-third by 1970. Although the overall importance of mining declined, Missouri remained the world's top lead producer, and the state has emerged as second only to Michigan in US automobile manufacturing. Postwar prosperity was threatened beginning in the 1960s by the deterioration of several cities, notably St. Louis, which lost 47% of its population between 1950 and 1980; both St. Louis and Kansas City subsequently undertook urban renewal programs to cope with the serious problems of air pollution, traffic congestion, crime, and substandard housing. During the early 1980s, millions of dollars in federal, state, and private funds were used to rehabilitate abandoned and dilapidated apartment buildings and houses.

Missouri was affected by the farm crisis of the 1980s, and many farms in the state failed. With the weakening of trade restrictions, the state's industries also suffered during this period. However, Missouri's economy improved in the 1990s.

Times Beach and other parts of the state were found to be contaminated by high levels of dioxin in the early 1980s. The federal government purchased the homes and businesses that had to be abandoned by residents of Times Beach and in 1991 began a cleanup program that was expected to last through 1997.

In the spring and summer of 1993, Missouri was hit by devastating floods. The Illinois, Mississippi, and Missouri rivers reached record crests, rising in some areas to twice the height considered to be flood level. Over half the state was declared a disaster area, and 19,000 people were evacuated from their homes. Damage to the state was estimated at $3 billion.

12 STATE GOVERNMENT

Missouri's first constitutional convention met in St. Louis on 12 May 1820, and on 19 July a constitution was adopted. The constitution was rewritten in 1865 and again in 1875, the latter document remaining in effect until 1945, when another new constitution was enacted and the state government reorganized.

A subsequent reorganization, effective 1 July 1974, replaced some 90 independent agencies with 13 cabinet departments and the Office of Administration.

The legislative branch, or general assembly, consists of a 34-member senate and a 163-seat house of representatives. Senators are elected to staggered four-year terms, representatives for two; the minimum age requirement for a senator is 30, for a representative 24. The legislative salary was $24,313 in 1995. The state's elected executives are the governor and lieutenant governor (who run separately), secretary of state, auditor, treasurer, and attorney general; all serve four-year terms. The governor is limited to two terms in office; he must be at least 30 years of age and must have been a US citizen for 15 years and a Missouri resident for 10 years prior to election. In 1996, the governor's salary was $98,345.

A bill becomes law when signed by the governor within 15 days of legislative passage. A two-thirds vote by both houses is required to override a gubernatorial veto. Except for appropriations or emergency measures, laws may not take effect until 90 days after the end of the legislative session at which they were enacted. Constitutional amendments require a majority vote of both houses of the legislature and ratification by the voters.

To vote in Missouri, one must be a US citizen and at least 18 years of age; there is no residency requirement.

13 POLITICAL PARTIES

The major political groups in Missouri are the Democratic Party and the Republican Party, each affiliated with the national party organization. Before 1825, the state had no organized political parties, and candidates ran as independents; however, each of Missouri's first four governors called himself a Jeffersonian Republican, allying himself with the national group from which the modern Democratic Party traces its origins. Except for the Civil War and Reconstruction periods, the Democratic Party held the governorship from the late 1820s to the early 1900s. Ten Democrats and seven Republicans served in the statehouse from 1908 through 1985. The outstanding figures of 20th century Missouri politics were both Democrats: Thomas Pendergast, the Kansas City machine boss whose commitment to construction projects bore no small relation to his involvement with a concrete manufacturing firm, and Harry S Truman, who began his political career as a Jackson County judge in the Kansas City area and in 1945 became 33d president of the US.

Missouri Presidential Vote by Political Parties, 1948–96

YEAR	ELECTORAL VOTE	MISSOURI WINNER	DEMOCRAT	REPUBLICAN	PROGRESSIVE	SOCIALIST
1948	15	*Truman (D)	917,315	655,039	3,998	2,222
1952	13	*Eisenhower (R)	929,830	959,429	—	—
1956	13	Stevenson (D)	918,273	914,289	—	—
1960	13	*Kennedy (D)	972,201	962,218	—	—
1964	12	*Johnson (D)	1,164,344	653,535	—	—
					AMERICAN IND.	
1968	12	*Nixon (R)	791,444	811,932	206,126	—
1972	12	*Nixon (R)	698,531	1,154,058	—	—
1976	12	*Carter (D)	998,387	927,443	—	—
					LIBERTARIAN	SOC. WORKERS
1980	12	*Reagan (R)	931,182	1,074,181	14,422	1,515
1984	11	*Reagan (R)	848,583	1,274,188	—	—
						NEW ALLIANCE
1988	11	*Bush (R)	1,001,619	1,084,953	434	6,656
						IND. (Perot)
1992	11	*Clinton (D)	1,053,873	811,159	7,497	518,741
1996	11	*Clinton (D)	1,025,935	890,016	10,522	217,188

*Won US presidential election.

As of 1994, Missouri had 3,067,955 registered voters; there is no party registration. After voting consistently for Republican presidential candidates in the 1980s, Missouri was carried by Democrat Bill Clinton in 1996. In 1996, Clinton won over 47% of the vote; Republican Bob Dole received 41%; and Ross Perot collected 10%. Democrat Mel Carnahan was reelected to the governorship in 1996. As of the mid-term elections in 1994, Missouri's US senators were both Republicans—Christopher Bond, re-elected in 1992, and former Governor John Ashcroft, newly elected to fill the seat formerly held by senior senator John Danforth. Following the 1996 elections, five of the US representatives were Democrats; four were Republicans. In the state senate in 1997, there were 19 Democrats and 15 Republicans; in the state house, there were 87 Democrats and 75 Republicans.

There were 185 blacks and 1 Hispanic holding elective office in Missouri in 1994. As of 1995, there were 39 women serving in the state legislature and 2 women in elective executive office. In 1994, Tim Van Zandt won 78% of the vote to become Missouri's first openly gay legislator.

14LOCAL GOVERNMENT

As of 1994, Missouri had 114 counties, 933 municipalities, 324 townships, 552 school districts, and 1,386 special districts. Elected county officials generally include a public administrator, prosecuting attorney, sheriff, collector of revenue, assessor, treasurer, and coroner. The city of St. Louis, which is administratively independent of any county, has an elected mayor, a comptroller, and a 29-member board of aldermen (including the president); the circuit attorney, city treasurer, sheriff, and collector of revenue, also elected, perform functions analogous to county officers. Most other cities are governed by an elected mayor and council.

15STATE SERVICES

Under the 1974 reorganization plan, educational services are provided through the Department of Elementary and Secondary Education and the Department of Higher Education. Within the former's jurisdiction are the state schools for the deaf, the blind, and the severely handicapped; adult education programs; teacher certification; and the general supervision of instruction in the state. The department is headed by a board of education whose eight members are appointed by the governor to eight-year terms; the board, in turn, appoints the commissioner of education, the department's chief executive officer. The Department of Higher Education—governed by a nine-member appointive board that selects the commissioner of higher education—sets financial guidelines for state colleges and universities, authorizes the establishment of new senior colleges and residency centers, and establishes academic, admissions, residency, and transfer policies. Transportation services are under the direction of the Department of Highways and Transportation, which is responsible for aviation, railroads, mass transit, water transport, and the state highway system. The Department of Revenue licenses all road vehicles and motor vehicle operators and is responsible for the administration of all state taxes and local-option sales taxes.

Health and welfare services are provided primarily through the Department of Social Services, which oversees all state programs concerning public health (including operating a chest hospital and a cancer hospital), public assistance, youth corrections, probation and parole, veterans' affairs, and the aging. The Department of Mental Health operates 5 state mental hospitals, 3 community mental health centers, and 19 other facilities throughout the state, providing care for the emotionally disturbed, the mentally retarded, alcoholics, and drug abusers. Among the many responsibilities of the Department of Consumer Affairs, Regulations, and Licensing were enforcement of antidiscrimination laws, development of low- and moderate-income

housing, and provision of financial aid to private nonprofit hospitals and higher-education facilities. In 1984, however, a constitutional amendment created a new Department of Economic Development, which inherited most of the responsibilities of the former department.

Administered within the Department of Public Safety are the Missouri State Highway Patrol, National Guard, and civil defense, veterans' affairs, highway and water safety, and alcoholic beverage control programs. The Department of Labor and Industrial Relations administers unemployment insurance benefits, workers' compensation, and other programs. The Department of Corrections and Human Resources is responsible for corrections, probation, and parole of adult offenders. The Department of Agriculture enforces state laws regarding agribusiness products. The lieutenant governor is designated as state ombudsman and volunteer coordinator.

16JUDICIAL SYSTEM

The supreme court, the state's highest court, consists of seven judges and three commissioners. Judges are selected by the governor from three nominees proposed by a nonpartisan judicial commission; after an interval of at least 12 months, the appointment must be ratified by the voters on a separate nonpartisan ballot. The justices, who serve 12-year terms, select one of their number to act as chief justice. The mandatory retirement age is 70 for all judges in state courts.

The court of appeals, consisting of 32 judges in three districts, assumed its present structure by constitutional amendment in 1970. All appellate judges are selected for 12-year terms in the same manner as the supreme court justices.

The circuit court is the only trial court and has original jurisdiction over all cases and matters, civil and municipal. Circuit court judges serve 6-year terms. Although many circuit court judges are still popularly elected, judges in St. Louis, Kansas City, and some other areas are selected on a nonpartisan basis. Many circuit courts have established municipal divisions, presided over by judges paid locally. In 1996, there were 14,755 licensed attorneys in the state, down from 16,446 in 1992.

As of 30 April 1997, the Department of Corrections had 23,140 inmates in 21 correctional and treatment centers, including inmates in the 2 mental health programs operated in cooperation with the Department of Mental Health. The total number of inmates includes those who were in work release programs at 2 community release centers located in St. Louis and Kansas City; the inmates housed in Texas jails through a cell leasing program; and those inmates who were either in the electronic monitoring program or receiving treatment at a residential treatment facility. The incarceration rate per 100,000 residents based on the number of inmates under the jurisdiction of the Department of Corrections only was 411 as of December 1996. Missouri has a death penalty and has executed 17 persons since 1977.

17ARMED FORCES

Missouri has played a key role in national defense since World War II, partly because of the influence of Missourian Stuart Symington, first as secretary of the Air Force (1947–50) and later as an influential member of the Senate Armed Services Committee. In 1996 there were 14,574 active duty military personnel stationed in the state. Installations include Ft. Leonard Wood, near Rolla, and Whiteman AFB, Knob Noster. The Defense Mapping Agency Aerospace Center is in St. Louis. Defense contract awards for 1995/96 totaled $7.1 billion. The McDonnell Douglas aerospace firm of St. Louis received $2.7 billion of that total.

There were about 579,000 veterans living in the state as of 1 July 1996. Of these fewer than 500 saw service in World War I,

158,000 in World War II, 101,000 in the Korean conflict, 183,000 during the Vietnam era, and 39,000 in the Persian Gulf War. Veterans' benefits amounted to $887 million in 1995/96.

Missouri had 21,470 Army, 13,344 Navy and Marine Corps National Guard and Reserve, and 5,063 Air National Guard and Reserve personnel in 1996. In 1993, the Missouri State Highway Patrol employed 889 full-time sworn officers, or 2 per 10,000 residents.

[18] MIGRATION

Missouri's first European immigrants, French fur traders and missionaries, began settling in the state in the early 18th century. Under Spain, Missouri received few Spanish settlers but many immigrants from the eastern US. During the 19th century, newcomers continued to arrive from the South and the East-slave-owning southerners (with their black slaves) as well as New Englanders opposed to slavery. They were joined by a wave of European immigrants, notably Germans and, later, Italians. By 1850, one out of three St. Louis residents was German-born; of all foreign-born Missourians in the late 1800s, more than half came from Germany.

More recently, the state has been losing population through migration—322,000 people were lost to net migration between 1940 and 1970, followed by a net gain of 22,000 during the 1970s and a net loss of nearly 100,000 during the 1980s. Between 1990 and 1996, Missouri had net gains of 72,301 in domestic migration and 22,419 in international migration. In 1996, 5,690 foreign immigrants arrived in the state. The dominant intrastate migration pattern has been the concentration of blacks in the major cities, especially St. Louis and Kansas City, and the exodus of whites from those cities to the suburbs and, more recently, to small towns and rural areas. As of 1990, just under 70% of all state residents had been born in Missouri. About 54% of the population age 5 and older lived in the same house in 1990 as in 1985; of those who changed residences, about 21% had lived in another state in 1985.

[19] INTERGOVERNMENTAL COOPERATION

The Commission on Interstate Cooperation, established by the state legislature in 1941, represents Missouri before the Council of State Governments and its allied organizations. Regional agreements in which the state participates include boundary compacts with Arkansas, Iowa, and Kansas and various accords governing bridges across the Mississippi and Missouri rivers. Representatives from both Missouri and Kansas take part in the Kansas City Area Transportation Authority, which operates public transportation in the metropolitan region, and the Kansas-Missouri Waterworks Compact. Missouri also belongs to the Southern Interstate Energy Compact and many other multistate bodies. Federal aid to state and local governments in 1995/96 was over $4 billion.

[20] ECONOMY

Missouri's central location and access to the Mississippi River contributed to its growth as a commercial center. By the mid–1700s, the state's first permanent settlement at Ste. Genevieve was shipping lead, furs, salt, pork, lard, bacon, bear, grease, feathers, flour and grain, and other products to distant markets. The introduction of steamboat traffic on the Mississippi, western migration along the Santa Fe and Oregon trails, and the rise of the railroads spurred the growth of commerce during the 19th century. Flour and grist mills, breweries and whiskey distilleries, and meat-packing establishments were among the state's early industrial enterprises. Lead mining has been profitable since the early 19th century. Grain growing was well established by the mid-18th century, and tobacco was a leading crop 100 years later.

Missouri's economy remains diversified, with manufacturing, farming, trade, tourism, services, government, and mining as prime sources of income. Today, automobile and aerospace manufacturing are the state's leading industries, while soybeans and meat and dairy products are the most important agricultural commodities. The state's historic past, varied topography, and modern urban attractions—notably the Gateway Arch in St. Louis—have made tourism a growth industry in recent decades. Mining, employing less than 1% of the state's nonagricultural workers, is no longer as important as it once was, although the state remains the leading US producer of lead and ranks 2d in the US in zinc production. Missouri's gross state product was $128,216 million in 1994. Private goods-producing industries contributed $35,510 million; private services-producing industries, $78,281 million; and government, $14,426 million.

The economic impact of state and local government and of defense-related federal expenditures has increased enormously since World War II.

In 1996, there were 22,103 bankruptcy filings.

[21] INCOME

With a personal income per capita of $22,864 in 1996, Missouri ranked 25th among the 50 states. Total disposable personal income for Missouri rose from $101.5 billion in 1995 to $106.7 billion in 1996. About 9.4% of state residents lived below the federal poverty level in 1995. Median household income was $34,825 in 1996.

[22] LABOR

In 1996, Missouri's civilian labor force averaged 2,898,000; 2,765,000 were employed and 132,000 (4.6%) were unemployed, below the US rate of 5.4%.

At the end of 1996, 708,600 Missourians were employed in services; 628,700 in wholesale and retail trade; 414,000 in manufacturing; 227,200 in government; 166,600 in transportation, communications, and public utilities; 151,300 in finance, insurance, and real estate; 115,400 in construction; and 5,000 in mining.

As early as the 1830s, journeyman laborers and mechanics in St. Louis, seeking higher wages and shorter hours, banded together to form trade unions and achieved some of their demands. Attempts to establish a workingman's party were unsuccessful, however, and immigration during subsequent decades ensured a plentiful supply of cheap labor. Union activity increased in the 1870s, partly because of the influence of German socialists. The Knights of Labor took a leading role in the labor movement from 1879 to 1887, the year that saw the birth of the St. Louis Trades and Labor Assembly; one year later, the American Federation of Labor came to St. Louis for its third annual convention, with Samuel Gompers presiding. The Missouri State Federation of Labor was formed in 1891, at a convention in Kansas City. By 1916, the state had 915 unions. Missouri remains a strong union state: 342,200 Missourians, representing 14.6% of the work force, belonged to labor organizations in 1995. Unionization among the manufacturing work force was 23.9%.

[23] AGRICULTURE

Missouri had 105,000 farms (2d in the US) covering 30 million acres (12.1 million hectares) in 1995. About 12,529,000 acres (5,070,000 hectares) were actually harvested in 1992. Missouri's agricultural income reached $4.4 billion in 1995, 15th among the 50 states. Of this total, about 20% came from soybeans.

In 1995, Missouri was 4th among the states in grain sorghum production and 6th in soybean and rice production. Soybean production is concentrated mainly in the northern counties and in the extreme southeast, with Mississippi County a leading producer. Stoddard County is a major source for corn and wheat production, as is New Madrid for grain sorghum.

The cash value of all crops totaled $2.4 billion in 1995, including $894 million from soybeans, $462 million from hay, $502 million from corn, $184.6 million from wheat, $110 million from grain sorghum, and $172.6 million from cotton. The value of rice production in 1995 was $50.7 million. Farmers harvested 131 million bushels of soybeans, 150 million bushels of corn, 48 million bushels of wheat, 35.8 million bushels of grain sorghum, 513,000 bales of cotton, and 6.82 million tons of hay in 1995. In 1995, 5.94 million hundredweight (269 million kg) of rice was harvested. Tobacco, oats, rye, apples, peaches, grapes, watermelons, and various seed crops are also grown in commercial quantities.

24 ANIMAL HUSBANDRY

In Missouri, hog raising is concentrated north of the Missouri River, cattle raising in the western counties, and dairy farming in the southwest.

In 1997, Missouri farms and ranches had an estimated 4.45 million cattle and calves, valued at $1.9 billion. In 1996, there were around 3.5 million hogs and pigs, valued at $294 million. During 1995, Missouri farmers produced 551 million lb (250 million kg) of turkey (ranked 4th in the nation), valued at around $231 million, and 800.5 million lb (363.1 million kg) of broilers, valued at around $280 million. Also in 1995, poultry farmers produced 1.7 million eggs, valued at $69.6 million. The state's 190,000 milk cows yielded nearly 2.7 million lb (1.2 million kg) of milk in 1995.

25 FISHING

Commercial fishing takes place mainly on the Mississippi, Missouri, and St. Francis rivers. Sport fishing is enjoyed throughout the state, but especially in the Ozarks, whose waters harbor walleye, rainbow trout, bluegill, and largemouth bass. In 1995/96, Missouri issued 1,011,279 sport fishing licenses, and the US Fish and Wildlife Service apportioned $4.8 million to the state for sport fish restoration programs. Federal hatcheries distributed over 1.8 million fish (83,904 lb or 38,058 kg) and 834,000 fish eggs within Missouri in 1995/96.

26 FORESTRY

At one time, Missouri's forests covered 30 million acres (12 million hectares), more than two-thirds of the state. As of 1992, Missouri had 14,007,000 acres (5,669,000 hectares) of forestland (31% of the land area in the state), of which more than 95% was commercial forest, 85% of it privately owned. Most of Missouri's forestland is in the southeastern third of the state. Of the commercial forests, approximately three-fourths are of the oak/hickory type; shortleaf pine and oak/pine forests comprise about 5%, while the remainder consists of cedar and bottomland hardwoods.

According to the Forestry Division of the Department of Conservation, Missouri leads the US in the production of charcoal, red cedar novelties, gunstocks, and walnut bowls and nutmeats; railroad ties, hardwood veneer and lumber, wine and bourbon casks, and other forest-related items are also produced. Timber production in 1994 totaled 133 million cubic ft (3.8 million cu m), and shipments of all lumber and wood products in 1995 were valued at $984.5 million, while shipments of paper products amounted to $3.4 billion.

More than 580,000 acres (235,000 hectares) of conservation areas, managed by the Forestry Division, are used for timber production, wildlife and watershed protection, hunting, fishing, and other recreational purposes. A state-run nursery sells seedling trees and shrubs to Missouri landowners. Missouri's one national forest, Mark Twain in the southeast, encompassed 1,481,619 acres (599,611 hectares) of National Forest System lands as of July 1994.

27 MINING

Nonfuel mineral production in Missouri was estimated at over $1,110 million in 1995, a $20 million increase over the $1,090 million reported in 1994. Estimated sales increased in 1992 for nine of the mineral commodities produced in the State. The increase in portland cement production was the most substantial, followed by construction sand and gravel, dimension stone, and crushed stone. Increases also occurred in the production of masonry cement, industrial sand and gravel, and zinc. Crushed stone, by value, has been Missouri's leading mineral commodity since 1993 when it surpassed portland cement and lead. Missouri ranked 1st of 11 states producing lead in 1995. In 1994, Missouri's lead production comprised 78% of the US market. Restrictions on the use of lead in paint and gasoline, along with prolonged labor strikes, caused lead production in Missouri to decline in the 1980s. The state also ranked 1st in fire clay production. Items of high value in 1995 included crushed stone, $337 million; lead, $267 million; portland cement, $223 million; and zinc, $49.1 million. Lead (289,000 tons), crushed stone (63 million tons), portland cement (3.98 million tons), and zinc (42,000 tons) accounted for almost 80% of the estimated total mineral value reported in 1995. Missouri ranked 10th nationally in nonfuel mineral value and continued as the nation's leading producer of lead, lime, and fire clay.

28 ENERGY AND POWER

Missouri's electric power plants had an installed generating capacity of 17,074 Mw in 1996. Electrical output totaled 67.9 billion kWh in 1996, 15% more than in 1990. Sales of electric power, both private and public, totaled 62.8 billion kWh in 1995, of which 25.6 billion kWh went to residential users, 21.8 billion kWh to commercial users, 14.6 billion kWh to industrial users, and 0.8 million kWh for other purposes. Coal-fired plants accounted for 84% of all power production, and nuclear plants for 13%, in 1996.

Fossil fuel resources are limited. Reserves of bituminous coal totaled 6 billion tons in 1995, but only a small portion (2 million tons) was considered recoverable; 699,000 tons were mined in 1996, all from 6 surface mines. Small quantities of crude petroleum are also produced commercially; in 1996, production was 115,445 barrels. The average Missouri residence paid $700 for 1,200 therms during 1996/97.

29 INDUSTRY

In 1995, the value of shipments for manufactured goods in Missouri was $82,556.6 million. The following table shows value of shipments by manufacturers for selected industries that year:

Transportation equipment	$26,137,500,000
Food and kindred products	13,536,600,000
Chemicals	8,046,900,000
Electric/electronic equipment	4,057,900,000
Fabricated metal products	4,264,300,000
Industrial machinery	4,349,000,000

St. Louis County, the city of St. Louis, and Jackson County (Kansas City) lead the state in manufacturing employment. McDonnell Douglas, with headquarters in St. Louis, was the nation's 23th-ranked industrial corporation in 1992, with sales of $17.5 billion; its aerospace products have included all the Mercury capsules and Gemini space capsules, the DC-9 and DC-10 commercial jet aircraft, and the Tomahawk cruise missile. As of 1997, the state was the headquarters for 14 Fortune 500 companies. In 1995, there were 817 US patents issued to Missouri residents.

[30]COMMERCE

Missouri has been one of the nation's leading trade centers ever since merchants in Independence (now part of the Kansas City metropolitan area) began provisioning wagon trains for the Santa Fe Trail. In 1992, Missouri had 11,236 wholesale establishments, with sales of $68.4 billion, including $33.5 billion in durable goods. Retail sales totaled $37.9 billion in 1992 from 32,185 establishments. Automotive dealers accounted for 22.2% of total retail sales; food stores, 18.2%; general merchandise stores, 15.2%; and eating and drinking places, 10.6%.

Foreign exports of Missouri products exceeded $5.4 billion in 1996.

[31]CONSUMER PROTECTION

The Missouri Department of Insurance handles consumer complaints related to insurance matters. The office has a consumer affairs division that accepts complaints regarding violations of state insurance laws and regulations, unfair claim practices, advertising, and mandated benefits, policy language, and offers. The Attorney General's office has a consumer protection provision which investigates and prosecutes allegations of fraud in connection with the sale or offer for sale (advertising) of goods and services. In addition, the Attorney General's office offers a mediation program whereby consumer complaints may be resolved informally.

[32]BANKING

The first banks in Missouri, the Bank of St. Louis (established in 1816) and the Bank of Missouri (1817), had both failed by the time Missouri became a state, and the paper notes they had distributed proved worthless. Not until 1837 did the Missouri state government again permit a bank within its borders, and then only after filling its charter with elaborate restrictions. The Bank of Missouri, chartered for 20 years, kept its reputation for sound banking by issuing notes bearing the portrait of US Senator Thomas Hart Benton, nicknamed "Old Bullion" because of his extreme fiscal conservatism. At the end of 1996, 430 commercial banks were operating in Missouri. The state's commercial banks had assets totaling $88.3 billion and deposits of nearly $75.8 billion. Assets of the state's 49 insured savings institutions at the end of 1996 totaled $15.3 billion, and mortgage loans reached $9.5 billion.

[33]INSURANCE

In 1996, 46 life insurance companies and 2 fraternal benefit societies were domiciled in Missouri. Total direct business in the state in 1996 included $1,919 million in life insurance premiums, $911 million in annuity considerations, and $2,074 million in deposit-type funds collected. About 6.8 million life insurance policies valued at $261.2 billion were in force at the end of 1996. Payouts totaled more than $3.7 billion, of which death benefit payments accounted for $781.1 million; annuity benefits, $987.8 million; and policy and contract dividends, $307.2 million.

In 1996, 57 property and casualty insurance companies were domiciled in Missouri. Direct premiums written by all property and casualty companies in Missouri totaled $5.25 billion in that year, including $1.4 billion in total (private and commercial) automotive liability insurance, $934 million in total automotive physical damage insurance, and $526.8 million in homeowners coverage. A total of $3.6 million in direct premiums were written in Missouri by property and casualty companies through the National Flood Insurance Program.

[34]SECURITIES

The Missouri Uniform Securities Act, also known as the "Blue Sky Law" and administered by the Securities Division of the Office of Secretary of State, requires the registration of stocks,

bonds, debentures, notes, investment contracts, and oil, gas, and mining interests intended for sale in the state. In cases of fraud, misrepresentation, or other failure to comply with the act, the Missouri investor has the right to sue to recover the investment, plus interest, costs, and attorney fees. Government securities, mutual funds, stocks listed on the principal national exchanges, and securities sold under specific transactional agreements are exempt from registration.

Missouri had 1,385 broker-dealers and 807 investment adviser organizations (involving 66,433 agents) in May 1997, all of whom, by law, were required to register with the state annually. Kansas City has a commodity exchange, the Board of Trade, which deals in grains, including futures and storage. The world's largest winter-wheat market is in Kansas City.

[35]PUBLIC FINANCE

The Missouri state budget is prepared by the Office of Administration's Division of Budget and Planning and submitted annually by the governor to the general assembly for amendment and approval. The fiscal year runs from 1 July to 30 June. The following table summarizes actual consolidated revenues and expenditures for 1995 (in thousands of dollars):

REVENUES	
Taxes	
Property	3,802,198
Sales and gross receipts	4,216,896
Income	2,535,063
TOTAL TAXES	10,554,157
Charges and miscellaneous	
Current charges	1,039,173
Interest earnings	922,345
Other	3,070,659
TOTAL	5,032,177
TOTAL REVENUES	$15,586,334
EXPENDITURES	
Education	$ 4,285,044
Health and social concerns	3,816,792
Financial administration	399,692
Transportation (highways)	1,159,689
Public safety (police)	391,362
Natural resources	264,780
Other (general)	2,164,687
TOTAL EXPENDITURES	$12,482,046

The debt of Missouri state government in 1995 was over $6 billion, or $1,261 per capita.

[36]TAXATION

Missouri's total state tax income revenues, traditionally low, ranked 17th in the nation in 1993. On a per capita basis, state general revenue of $968.70 ranked 26th in the US in 1993.

The Missouri personal income tax ranges from 1.5% to 6%; the corporate tax rate was 6.25% of net income. The basic state sales tax was 4.225%; cities and towns may add an additional tax (St. Louis and Kansas City added 1%). Other taxes levied by the state include charges on motor fuel, cigarettes, and alcoholic beverages along with motor vehicle and operator's license fees and taxes on credit institutions, insurance companies, and inheritances.

Property and sales taxes are the leading sources of local revenue. During 1995, Missouri contributed $30 billion in federal taxes and received $31 billion in federal funding.

37 ECONOMIC POLICY

Primary responsibility for economic development is vested in the Department of Economic Development, and especially in its Division of Community and Economic Development, which seeks outside investment in the state, promotes the national and international marketing of Missouri products, provides technical assistance to existing businesses, and maintains an office in Dusseldorf in the Federal Republic of Germany and in Tokyo, Japan. Its Enterprise Zone Program provides a variety of tax credits, exemptions, and other incentives to businesses that locate in designated areas. The division also offers grants, information, technical aid, and other public resources to foster local and regional development. Special programs are provided for the Ozarks region and to rehabilitate urban neighborhoods. Loan and bond guarantees are provided to selected businesses by the Missouri Economic Development Commission and direct loans by the Missouri Industrial Development Authority. A nonprofit Missouri Business Modernization and Technology Corporation, provides support for research and development and for the development of new technologies.

General incentives for business include the state's reputation for fiscal conservatism, wage rates no higher than the national average, and a tax structure toward which the corporate income tax contributes only about 8%.

38 HEALTH

The infant mortality rate in Missouri for the 12 months ending with December 1995 was 7.9 per 1,000 live births, just below the national norm. There were 13,390 legal abortions performed in 1992; the rate of 176 abortions per 1,000 live births was well below the US average. The birth rate was 13.7 per 1,000 population in 1995, lower than the US average.

The overall death rate of 10.4 per 1,000 population in 1996 was one of the highest in the US—a phenomenon attributable in part to the relatively high proportion of elderly Missourians in the population as a whole. Deaths from heart disease, cancer, stroke, accidents, and adverse effects (including motor vehicle accidents)—the major causes of death—were all above the national average. The age-adjusted death rate for Missouri was 1,038 per 100,000 population in 1995. The suicide rate of 13.9 per 100,000 population was also higher than the national average.

In 1995, there were 13.19 AIDS cases per 100,000 population, below the US average. Twenty-eight percent of men and 20.9% of women in Missouri were reported to be smokers.

In 1995, Missouri had 126 hospitals, with 19,337 beds; 685,415 admissions were recorded in 1995. Hospital personnel included 22,587 registered nurses. The average expense of hospitals for care in 1994 was $915 per inpatient day and $6,249 per stay, the latter above the US average. The state had 11,131 licensed physicians in 1994, and 2,866 licensed, active dentists in 1995. At least 6.7% of Missouri's population was uninsured in 1995. Twelve counties (with a combined population of 83,900) each had no physician active in patient care in 1991.

39 SOCIAL WELFARE

Some 238,000 Missourians were recipients of aid to families with dependent children in 1996; the average monthly payment of $342 per family was below the national average. In 1996, 553,930 residents received monthly food stamp allowances averaging $72.15, while the subsidy for Missouri's school lunch program amounted to $97.4 million.

With the enactment of the Personal Responsibility and Work Opportunity Reconciliation Act of 1996, the US government changed the form and regulations for many of its social welfare programs; most significantly, it replaces Aid to Families with Dependent Children (AFDC), an open-ended entitlement program, with Temporary Assistance for Needy Families (TANF), a limited system of assistance funded largely through federal block grants. The reform act also impacted the food stamp program, the Supplemental Security Income program, and the child nutrition program. The law took effect on 1 July 1997 and provided $16.38 billion in block grants for fiscal years 1997–2002. The grants were to be divided among the states based on an equation involving the numbers of former AFDC recipients in each state. Because many of the bill's provisions had yet to be implemented into state-by-state policy, it was not possible to include the details of each state's programs for this edition of this work.

Social Security recipients numbered 967,630 in 1995; retirees numbered 591,230 and received an average monthly payment of $705 in 1995. Unemployment weekly benefit checks averaged $152.46 in 1995.

40 HOUSING

In 1996, Missouri had an estimated 2,337,000 housing units, of which 2,031,000 were occupied. As of 1990, 98.8% of the year-round units had full plumbing. In 1996, 26,298 privately owned units, valued at $2.2 billion, were authorized for construction; of these, 20,107 were single-family.

The Missouri Housing Development Commission of the Department of Economic Development is empowered to make and insure loans to encourage the construction of residential housing for persons of low or moderate income; funds for mortgage financing are provided through the sale of tax-exempt notes and bonds issued by the commission. Construction of multi-unit public housing stagnated during the 1970s. In 1972, municipal authorities ordered the demolition of two apartment buildings in St. Louis's Pruitt-Igoe public housing complex, built 18 years earlier and regarded by many commentators as a classic case of the failure of such high-rise projects to offer a livable environment; the site remained vacant in the early 1980s. Only 5.5% of St. Louis's housing units in 1990 had been built during the 1980s; during the 1970s, many units were abandoned.

The median price of a single-family home in Missouri was $59,800 in 1990, the last year for which figures were available, ranking 33d among the states. The median costs for owners (including a mortgage) and renters in 1990 were $600 and $368, respectively, per month. During 1995/96, Missouri received $481.4 million in aid from the US Department of Housing and Urban Development, including $110.7 million in community development block grants.

41 EDUCATION

Although the constitution of 1820 provided for the establishment of public schools, it was not until 1839 that the state's public school system became a reality through legislation creating the office of state superintendent of common schools and establishing a permanent school fund. Missouri schools were officially segregated from 1875 to 1954, when the US Supreme Court issued its landmark ruling in Brown v. Board of Education; the state's school segregation law was not taken off the books until 1976. In that year, nearly 37% of all black students were in schools that were 99–100% black, a condition fostered by the high concentration of black Missourians in the state's two largest cities. In 1983, a desegregation plan was adopted for St. Louis-area public schools that called for 3,000 black students to be transferred from city to county schools.

In 1990, 78.7% of all Missourians 25 years of age or older were high school graduates. About 816,558 students are enrolled in Missouri's 538 public elementary and secondary school districts. Over 46,900 students graduate from high schools each year. There are 52,362 public school teachers in the state and the pupil-teacher ratio is 16:1.

Missouri had 30 public and 26 private institutions of higher education in 1991; there were 56 in all in 1991. Total full-time enrollment in the fall of 1991 was 281,914 students. The University of Missouri, established in 1839, was the first state-supported university west of the Mississippi River. It has four campuses: Columbia (site of the world's oldest and one of the best-known journalism schools), Kansas City, Rolla, and St. Louis. The Rolla campus, originally founded in 1870 as a mining and engineering school, is still one of the nation's leading universities specializing in technology. The four campuses had a combined full-time enrollment of 40,000 in 1991/92, with a majority of the students at the Columbia facility.

Lincoln University, a public university for blacks until segregation ended in 1954, is located in Jefferson City. There are five regional state universities, at Warrensburg, Maryville, Cape Girardeau, Springfield, and Kirksville, and three state colleges, at St. Louis, St. Joseph, and Joplin. Two leading independent universities, Washington and St. Louis, are located in St. Louis, as is the Concordia Seminary, an affiliate of the Lutheran Church-Missouri Synod and the center of much theological and political controversy during the 1970s. The Department of Higher Education offers grants and guaranteed loans to Missouri students.

42ARTS

Theatrical performances are offered throughout the state, mostly during the summer. In Kansas City, productions of Broadway musicals and light opera are staged at the Starlight Theater, seating 7,860 in an open-air setting. The Missouri Repertory Theater, on the University of Missouri campus in Kansas City, also has a summer season. In St. Louis, the 12,000-seat Municipal Opera puts on outdoor musicals, while the *Goldenrod,* built in 1909 and said to be the largest showboat ever constructed (seating capacity 289), is used today for vaudeville, melodrama, and ragtime shows. Other notable playhouses are the 8,000-seat Riverfront Amphitheater in Hannibal, and the 344-seat Lyceum Theater in Arrow Rock (population 89).

Leading orchestras are the St. Louis Symphony and Kansas City Symphony; Independence, Liberty, Columbia, Kirksville, St. Joseph, and Springfield also have orchestras. The Opera Theatre of St. Louis and the Lyric Opera of Kansas City are distinguished musical organizations. Springfield has a regional opera company.

Between World Wars I and II, Kansas City was the home of a thriving jazz community that included Charlie Parker and Lester Young; leading bandleaders of that time were Benny Moten, Walter Page, and, later, Count Basie. Country music predominates in rural Missouri: the Ozark Opry at Osage Beach. There are over 40 performing venues in Branson. In 1995, there were 26,385 shows (at the 38 largest venues), with combined seating capacity of 964,984. The majority of Branson theaters operate from May to October.

The state of Missouri provided $5,554,128 to support its arts programs in 1996/97. The NEA contributed $497,500 to the Missouri State Council on the Arts, and awarded $1.7 million directly to Missouri artists and arts organizations in 1995/96. Private sources accounted for $74 million. Audiences for the states' arts programs during this period totaled 40,138,000. There were 112,144 contributing artists. In 1997, there were 350 arts associations and 51 local associations in Missouri. The state provided arts education in all 550 public school districts. In 1994, the Missouri general assembly established the Missouri Cultural Trust, a state endowment for the arts, with the goal of building it into a $200 million operational endowment in 10 years. The Trust is one of only a few such trusts in the nation, and the only one that receives dedicated annual tax revenues. As of 31 December 1996, the Trust had reached $8.3 million and was earning over $25,000 in interest monthly.

43LIBRARIES AND MUSEUMS

Missouri had 38 county and 11 regional library systems in 1996/97, when the combined book stock of all public libraries in the state was 19,475,127, and their combined circulation 37,933,327. The Missouri State Library, in Jefferson City, is the center of the state's interlibrary loan network. It also serves as the only public library for the 10% of the state's population who live in areas without public libraries; it has 81,160 books. The largest public library systems, those of Kansas City and St. Louis County, had 1,887,800 and 2,013,472 volumes, respectively; the public library system of the city of St. Louis had 1,740,000. The University of Missouri-Columbia has the leading academic library, with 2,683,566 volumes in 1996/97. The State Historical Society of Missouri Library in Columbia contains 449,000 volumes. The federally-administered Harry S. Truman Library and Museum is at Independence.

Missouri has well over 150 museums and historic sites. The William Rockhill Nelson Gallery/Atkins Museum of Fine Arts in Kansas City and the St. Louis Art Museum each house distinguished general collections, while the Springfield Art Museum specializes in American sculpture, paintings, and relics of the westward movement. The Mark Twain Home and Museum in Hannibal has a collection of manuscripts and other memorabilia. Also notable are the Museum of Art and Archaeology, Columbia; the Kansas City Museum of History and Science; the Pony Express Stables Museum, St. Joseph; and the Jefferson National Expansion Memorial, Missouri Botanical Garden, St. Louis Center Museum of Science and Natural History and McDonnell Planetarium, National Museum of Transport, and a zoo, all in St. Louis. Kansas City, Springfield, and Eldon also have zoos.

44COMMUNICATIONS

In 1858, John Hockaday began weekly mail service by stagecoach between Independence and Salt Lake City, and John Butterfield, with a $600,000 annual appropriation from Congress, established semimonthly mail transportation by coach and rail from St. Louis to San Francisco. On 3 April 1860, the Pony Express was launched, picking up mail arriving by train at St. Joseph and racing it westward on horseback; the system ceased in October 1861, when the Pacific Telegraph Co. began operations. The first experiment in airmail service took place at St. Louis in 1911; Charles Lindbergh was an airmail pilot on the St. Louis-Chicago route in 1926.

As of March 1993, Missouri had approximately 1,898,000 residences with telephones. About 92.9% of all state residences had telephone service.

Radio broadcasting in Missouri dates from 1921, when a station at St. Louis University began experimental programming. On Christmas Eve 1922, the first midnight Mass ever to be put on the air was broadcast from the Old Cathedral in St. Louis. The voice of a US president was heard over the air for the first time on 21 June 1923, when Warren G. Harding gave a speech in St. Louis. FM broadcasting began in Missouri during 1948. As of 1996 there were 108 commercial AM stations and 178 FM stations in service. Missouri's first television station, KSD-TV in St. Louis, began in 1947, with WDAF-TV in Kansas City following in 1949. As of 1996, Missouri had 29 commercial and 4 noncommercial television stations; 8 commercial stations broadcast in the Kansas City area and 7 around St. Louis, with Kansas City, Joplin, St. Louis, Sedalia, and Springfield each having a noncommercial station. In 1996, the state had 9 major cable systems in service.

45PRESS

The *Missouri Gazette,* published in St. Louis in 1808 by the politically independent and controversial Joseph Charless, was the state's first newspaper; issued to 174 subscribers, the paper was partly in French. In 1815, a group of Charless's enemies raised funds to establish a rival paper, the *Western Journal*, and brought in Joshua Norvell from Nashville to edit it. By 1820 there were five newspapers in Missouri. Since that time, many Missouri newspapermen have achieved national recognition. The best known is Sam Clemens (later Mark Twain), who started out as a "printer's devil" in Hannibal at the age of 13. Hungarian-born Joseph Pulitzer began his journalistic career in 1868 as a reporter for a German-language daily in St. Louis. Pulitzer created the *St. Louis Post–Dispatch* from the merger of two defunct newspapers in 1878, endowed the Columbia University School of Journalism in New York City, and established by bequest the Pulitzer Prizes, which annually honor journalistic and artistic achievement.

As of 1997 there were 13 morning newspapers, 33 evening dailies, and 23 Sunday papers. The following table shows Missouri's leading dailies with their 1994 circulations:

AREA	NAME	DAILY	SUNDAY
Kansas City	*Star* (e,S)	285,086	425,337
St. Louis	*Post–Dispatch* (m,S)	323,374	511,991

Periodicals include the St. Louis-based *Sporting News,* the bimonthly "bible" of baseball fans; *VFW Magazine,* put out monthly in Kansas City by the Veterans of Foreign Wars; and the *Missouri Historical View,* a quarterly with offices in Columbia.

46ORGANIZATIONS

The 1992 US Census of Service Industries counted 1,464 organizations in Missouri, including 334 business associations; 805 civic, social, and fraternal associations; and 325 other membership organizations. Among the organizations with headquarters in Kansas City are the Veterans of Foreign Wars of the USA, Camp Fire Inc., People-to-People International, the American Academy of Family Physicians, the American Business Women's Association, the American Nurses Association, the Fellowship of Christian Athletes, the National Association of Intercollegiate Athletics, and Professional Secretaries International.

Headquartered in St. Louis are the American Association of Orthodontists, the American Optometric Association, the Catholic Health Association of the US, the Danforth Foundation, the International Consumer Credit Association, and the National Hairdressers and Cosmetologists Association. Other organizations are the National Council of State Garden Clubs (Clayton), the Accrediting Council on Education in Journalism and Mass Communications (Columbia), and the American Cat Fanciers Association (Branson).

47TOURISM, TRAVEL, AND RECREATION

During 1991, travelers spent more than $7.8 billion in Missouri on transportation, accommodations, meals, entertainment, recreation, and other items. About 250,000 jobs were attributable to the travel industry.

The principal attraction in St. Louis is the Gateway Arch, at 630 feet (192 meters) the tallest man-made national monument in the US. Designed by Eero Saarinen in 1948 but not constructed until 1964, three years after his death, the arch and the Museum of Westward Expansion form part of the Jefferson National Expansion Memorial on the western shore of the Mississippi River. In the Kansas City area are the modern Crown Center hotels and shopping plaza, Country Club Plaza, the Truman Sports Complex, Ft. Osage near Sibley, Jesse James's birthplace near Excelsior Springs, and Harry Truman's hometown of Independence. Memorabilia of Mark Twain are housed in and around Hannibal, in the northeast, and the birthplace and childhood home of George Washington Carver, a national monument, is in Diamond. The Lake of the Ozarks, with 1,375 mi (2,213 km) of shoreline, is one of the most popular vacation spots in mid-America. Other attractions are the Silver Dollar City handicrafts center near Branson; the Pony Express Stables and Museum at St. Joseph; Wilson's Creek National Battlefield at Republic, site of a Confederate victory in the Civil War; and the "Big Springs Country" of the Ozarks, in the southeast. The state fair is held in Sedalia each August.

As of 1996, Missouri had 27 state parks. Operated by the Department of Natural Resources, they offer camping, picnicking, swimming, boating, fishing, and hiking facilities. Lake of the Ozarks State Park is the largest, covering 16,872 acres (6,828 hectares). There were also 27 historic sites in 1994, when state parks and historic sites covered 105,000 acres (43,050 hectares); they attract nearly 15 million visitors annually. Hunting and fishing are popular recreational activities. In 1995, licenses were issued to 1,602,116 fishermen and 1,060,699 hunters.

48SPORTS

There are six major league professional sports teams in Missouri: the Kansas City Royals and St. Louis Cardinals of Major League Baseball; the Kansas City Chiefs and St. Louis Rams of the National Football League; the St. Louis Blues of the National Hockey League; and the Kansas City Wizards of Major League Soccer.

The Cardinals won the World Series in 1931, 1934, 1942, 1944, 1946, 1964, 1967 and 1982. The Royals have won the World Series once, in 1985, against their cross-state rivals, the St. Louis Cardinals. The Chiefs appeared in Super Bowl I in 1967, losing to the Green Bay Packers. They won the Super Bowl in their next appearance, in 1970. The Rams moved to St. Louis from Los Angeles after the 1994 season and now play in the 66,000-seat Trans World Dome, which opened in 1995.

Horse racing has a long history in Missouri. In 1812, St. Charles County sportsmen held two-day horse races; by the 1820s, racetracks were laid out in nearly every city and in crossroads villages. Today, thoroughbred racing can be seen during a summer and fall season at Cahokia Downs, outside St. Louis.

In collegiate sports, the University of Missouri competes in the Big 12 Conference. Other annual sporting events include the National Intercollegiate Basketball Tournament, held in Kansas City in March.

49FAMOUS MISSOURIANS

Harry S Truman (1884–1972) has been the only native-born Missourian to serve as US president or vice president. Elected US senator in 1932, Truman became Franklin D. Roosevelt's vice-presidential running mate in 1944 and succeeded to the presidency upon Roosevelt's death on 12 April 1945. The "man from Independence"—whose tenure in office spanned the end of World War II, the inauguration of the Marshall Plan to aid European economic recovery, and the beginning of the Korean conflict—was elected to the presidency in his own right in 1948, defeating Republican Thomas E. Dewey in one of the most surprising upsets in US political history. Charles Evans Whittaker (b.Kansas, 1901–73) was a federal district and appeals court judge in Missouri before his appointment as Supreme Court associate justice in 1957. Among the state's outstanding US military leaders are Generals John J. Pershing (1860–1948) and Omar Bradley (1893–1981).

Other notable federal officeholders from Missouri include Edward Bates (b.Virginia, 1793–1869), Abraham Lincoln's attorney general and the first cabinet official to be chosen from a state west of the Mississippi River; Montgomery Blair (b.Kentucky, 1813–83), postmaster general in Lincoln's cabinet; and Norman Jay Colman (b.New York, 1827–1911), the first secretary of agriculture. Missouri's best-known senator was Thomas Hart Benton (b.North Carolina, 1782–1858), who championed the interests of Missouri and the West for 30 years.

Other well-known federal legislators include Francis P. Blair, Jr. (b.Kentucky, 1821–75), antislavery congressman, pro-Union leader during the Civil War, and Democratic vice-presidential nominee in 1868; Benjamin Gratz Brown (b.Kentucky, 1826–85), senator from 1863 to 1867 and later governor of the state and Republican vice-presidential nominee (1872); Carl Schurz (b.Germany, 1829–1906), senator from 1869 to 1875 and subsequently US secretary of the interior, as well as a journalist and Union military leader; William H. Hatch (b.Kentucky, 1833–96), sponsor of much agricultural legislation as a US representative from 1879 to 1895; Richard P. Bland (b.Kentucky, 1835–99), leader of the free-silver bloc in the US House of Representatives; James Beauchamp "Champ" Clark (b.Kentucky, 1850–1921), speaker of the House from 1911 to 1919; W. Stuart Symington (b.Massachusetts, 1901–88), senator from 1953 to 1977 and earlier the nation's first secretary of the Air Force; and Thomas F. Eagleton (b.1929), senator since 1969 and, briefly, the Democratic vice-presidential nominee in 1972, until publicity about his having received electroshock treatment for depression forced him off the ticket. (Eagleton announced in 1984 that he would not seek reelection to the Senate in 1986.)

Outstanding figures in Missouri history included two pioneering fur traders: William Henry Ashley (b.Virginia, 1778–1838), who later became a US representative, and Manuel Lisa (b.Louisiana, 1772–1820), who helped establish trade relations with the Indians. Meriwether Lewis (b.Virginia, 1774–1809) and William Clark (b.Virginia, 1770–1838) explored Missouri and the West during 1804–6; Lewis later served as governor of Louisiana Territory, with headquarters at St. Louis, and Clark was governor of Missouri Territory from 1813 to 1821. Dred Scott (b.Virginia, 1795–1858), a slave owned by a Missourian, figured in a Supreme Court decision that set the stage for the Civil War. Missourians with unsavory reputations include such desperadoes as Jesse James (1847–82), his brother Frank (1843–1915), and Cole Younger (1844–1916), also a member of the James gang. Another well-known native was Kansas City's political boss, Thomas Joseph Pendergast (1872–1945), a power among Missouri Democrats until convicted of income tax evasion in 1939 and sent to Leavenworth prison.

Among notable Missouri educators were William Torrey Harris (b.Connecticut, 1835–1909), superintendent of St. Louis public schools, US commissioner of education, and an authority on Hegelian philosophy; James Milton Turney (1840–1915), who helped establish Lincoln University for blacks at Jefferson City; and Susan Elizabeth Blow (1843–1916), cofounder with Harris of the first US public kindergarten at St. Louis in 1873. Distinguished scientists include agricultural chemist George Washington Carver (1864–1943), astronomers Harlow Shapley (1885–1972) and Edwin P. Hubble (1889–1953), Nobel Prize-winning nuclear physicist Arthur Holly Compton (b.Ohio, 1892–1962), and mathematician-cyberneticist Norbert Wiener (1894–1964). Engineer and inventor James Buchanan Eads (b.Indiana, 1820–87) supervised construction during 1867–74 of the St. Louis bridge that bears his name. Charles A. Lindbergh (b.Michigan 1902–74) was a pilot and aviation instructor in the St. Louis area during the 1920s before wining worldwide acclaim for his solo New York-Paris flight.

Prominent Missouri businessmen include brewer Adolphus Busch (b.Germany, 1839–1913); William Rockhill Nelson (b.Indiana, 1847–1915), who founded the *Kansas City Star* (1880); Joseph Pulitzer (b.Hungary, 1847–1911), who merged two failed newspapers to establish the *St. Louis Post-Dispatch* (1878) and later endowed the journalism and literary prizes that bear his name; and James Cash Penney (1875–1971), founder of the J. C. Penney Co. Noteworthy journalists from Missouri include newspaper and magazine editor William M. Reedy (1862–1920), newspaper reporter Herbert Bayard Swope (1882–

1958), and television newscaster Walter Cronkite (b.1916). Other distinguished Missourians include theologian Reinhold Niebuhr (1892–1971), civil rights leader Roy Wilkins (1901–81), and medical missionary Thomas Dooley (1927–61).

Missouri's most popular author is Mark Twain (Samuel Langhorne Clemens, 1835–1910), whose *Adventures of Tom Sawyer* (1876) and *Adventures of Huckleberry Finn* (1884) evoke his boyhood in Hannibal. Novelist Harold Bell Wright (b.New York, 1872–1944) wrote about the people of the Ozarks; Robert Heinlein (1907–88) is a noted writer of science fiction, and William S. Burroughs (b.1914) an experimental novelist. Poet-critic T(homas) S(tearns) Eliot (1888–1965), awarded the Nobel Prize for literature in 1948, was born in St. Louis but became a British subject in 1927. Other Missouri-born poets include Sara Teasdale (1884–1933), Marianne Moore (1887–1972), and Langston Hughes (1902–67). Popular novelist and playwright Rupert Hughes (1872–1956) was a Missouri native, as was Zoe Akins (1886–1958), a Pulitzer Prize-winning playwright.

Distinguished painters who lived in Missouri include George Caleb Bingham (b.Virginia, 1811–79), who also served in several state offices; James Carroll Beckwith (1852–1917); and Thomas Hart Benton (1889–1975), the grandnephew and namesake of the state's famous political leader. Among the state's important musicians are ragtime pianist-composers Scott Joplin (b.Texas, 1868–1917) and John William "Blind" Boone (1864–1927); W(illiam) C(hristopher) Handy (b.Alabama, 1873–1958), composer of "St. Louis Blues," "Beale Street Blues," and other classics; composer-critic Virgil Thomson (1896–1989), known for his operatic collaborations with Gertrude Stein; jazzman Coleman Hawkins (1907–69); and popular songwriter Burt Bacharach (b.1929). Photographer Walker Evans (1903–75) was a St. Louis native.

Missouri-born entertainers include actors Wallace Beery, (1889–1949), Vincent Price (1911–93), and Edward Asner (b.1929); actresses Jean Harlow (Harlean Carpenter, 1911–37), Jane Wyman (b.1914), Betty Grable (1916–73), and Shelley Winters (b.1922); dancers Sally Rand (1904–79) and Josephine Baker (1906–75); actress-dancer Ginger Rogers (b.1911); film director John Huston (1906–84); and opera stars Helen Traubel (1903–72), Gladys Swarthout (1904–69), and Grace Bumbry (b.1937). In popular music, the state's most widely known singer-songwriter is Charles "Chuck" Berry (b.California, 1926), whose works had a powerful influence on the development of rock'n' roll.

St. Louis Cardinals stars who became Hall of Famers include Jerome Herman "Dizzy" Dean (b.Arkansas, 1911–74), Stanley Frank "Stan the Man" Musial (b.Pennsylvania, 1920), Robert "Bob" Gibson (b.Nebraska, 1935), and Louis "Lou" Brock (b.Arkansas, 1939). Among the native Missourians who achieved stardom in the sports world are baseball manager Charles Dillon "Casey" Stengel (1890–1975), catcher Lawrence Peter "Yogi" Berra (b.1925), sportscaster Joe Garagiola (b.1926), and golfer Tom Watson (b.1949).

50BIBLIOGRAPHY

Burnett, Robyn. *German Settlement in Missouri: New Land, Old Ways.* Columbia: University of Missouri Press, 1996.

Dorsett, Lyle W. *The Pendergast Machine.* New York: Oxford University Press, 1968.

Federal Writers' Project. *Missouri: A Guide to the "Show Me" State.* 1941. Rev. ed., New York: Somerset, 1981.

Foley, William E. *A History of Missouri: 1673 to 1820.* Columbia: University of Missouri Press, 1971.

Gerlach, Russel L. *Immigrants in the Ozarks.* Columbia: University of Missouri Press, 1976.

Gibson, Arrell M. *The Encyclopedia of Missouri.* New York: Somerset, 1984.

Glaab, Charles N. *Kansas City and the Railroads*. 1941. Rev. ed., New York: Somerset, 1981.

Greene, Lorenzo J., et al. *Missouri's Black Heritage*. Rev. ed. Columbia: University of Missouri Press, 1993.

Hall, Leonard. *Stars Upstream: Life Along an Ozark River*. Columbia: University of Missouri Press, 1991.

Larsen, Lawrence Harold. *Federal Justice in Western Missouri: The Judges, the Cases, the Times*. Columbia: University of Missouri Press, 1994.

March, David D. *The History of Missouri*. 4 vols. New York and West Palm Beach, Fla.: Lewis, 1967.

McCandless, Perry. *A History of Missouri: 1820 to 1860*. Columbia: University of Missouri Press, 1972.

Missouri, State of. Secretary of State. *Official Manual, 1983–84*. Jefferson City, 1983.

Nagel, Paul C. *Missouri: A Bicentennial History*. New York: Norton, 1977.

Park, Eleanore G., and Kate S. Morrow. *Women of the Mansion: Missouri, 1821-1936*. Jefferson City: Midland, 1936.

Parrish, William E. *A History of Missouri: 1860 to 1875*. Columbia: University of Missouri Press, 1973.

———, et al. *Missouri: The Heart of the Nation*. St. Louis: Forum, 1980.

Primm, James Neal. *Economic Policy in the Development of a Western State: Missouri, 1820–60*. Cambridge: Harvard University Press, 1954.

Rafferty, Milton D. *Historical Atlas of Missouri*. Norman: University of Oklahoma Press, 1982.

Sprague, Marshall. *So Vast a Land: Louisiana and the Purchase*. Boston: Little, Brown, 1974.

State Historical Society of Missouri. *Historic Missouri: A Pictorial Narrative*. Columbia, 1977.

Truman, Harry S. *Memoirs*. 2 vols. Garden City, N.Y.: Doubleday, 1955–56.

Wecter, Dixon. *Sam Clemens of Hannibal*. Boston: Houghton Mifflin, 1952.

MONTANA

State of Montana

ORIGIN OF STATE NAME: Derived from the Latin word meaning "mountainous." **NICKNAME:** The Treasure State. (ALSO: Big Sky Country.) **CAPITAL:** Helena. **ENTERED UNION:** 8 November 1889 (41st). **SONG:** "Montana." **BALLAD:** "Montana Melody." **MOTTO:** *Oro y Plata* (Gold and silver). **FLAG:** A blue field, fringed in gold on the top and bottom borders, surround the state coat of arms, with "Montana" in gold letters above the coat of arms. **OFFICIAL SEAL:** In the lower center are a plow and a miner's pick and shovel; mountains appear above them on the left, the Great Falls of the Missouri River on the right, and a state motto on a banner below. The words "The Great Seal of the State of Montana" surround the whole. **ANIMAL:** Grizzly bear. **BIRD:** Western meadowlark. **FISH:** Black-spotted (cutthroat) trout. **FLOWER:** Bitterroot. **TREE:** Ponderosa pine. **GRASS:** Bluebunch wheatgrass. **GEMS:** Yogo sapphire; Montana agate. **FOSSIL:** Duck-billed dinosaur. **LEGAL HOLIDAYS:** New Year's Day, 1 January; Birthday of Martin Luther King, Jr., 3d Monday in January; Lincoln's Birthday, 12 February; Washington's Birthday, 3d Monday in February; Memorial Day, last Monday in May; Independence Day, 4 July; Labor Day, 1st Monday in September; Columbus Day, 2d Monday in October; State Election Day, 1st Tuesday after the 1st Monday in November in even-numbered years; Veterans Day, 11 November; Thanksgiving Day, 4th Thursday in November; Christmas Day, 25 December. **TIME:** 5 AM MST = GMT.

¹LOCATION, SIZE, AND EXTENT

Located in the northwestern US, Montana is the largest of the 8 Rocky Mountain states and ranks 4th in size among the 50 states.

The total area of Montana is 147,046 sq mi (380,849 sq km), of which land takes up 145,388 sq mi (376,555 sq km) and inland water 1,658 sq mi (4,294 sq km). The state's maximum E-w extension is 570 mi (917 km); its extreme N-S distance is 315 mi (507 km).

Montana is bordered on the N by the Canadian provinces of British Columbia, Alberta, and Saskatchewan; on the E by North Dakota and South Dakota; on the S by Wyoming and Idaho; and on the w by Idaho. The total boundary length of Montana is 1,947 mi (3,133 km). The state's geographic center is in Fergus County, 12 mi (19 km) w of Lewistown. Nearly 30% of the state's land belongs to the federal government.

²TOPOGRAPHY

Montana, as mountainous in parts as its name implies, has an approximate mean elevation of 3,400 feet (1,000 meters). The Rocky Mountains cover the western two-fifths of the state, with the Bitterroot Range along the Idaho border; the high, gently rolling Great Plains occupy most of central and eastern Montana. The highest point in the state is Granite Peak, at an elevation of 12,799 feet (3,901 meters), located in south-central Montana, near the Wyoming border. The lowest point, at 1,800 feet (550 meters), is in the northwest, where the Kootenai River leaves the state at the Idaho border. The Continental Divide passes in a jagged pattern through the western part of the state, from the Lewis to the Bitterroot ranges.

Ft. Peck Reservoir is Montana's largest body of inland water, covering 375 sq mi (971 sq km); Flathead Lake is the largest natural lake. The state's most important rivers are the Missouri, rising in southwest Montana and flowing north and then east across the state, and the Yellowstone, which crosses southeastern Montana to join the Missouri in North Dakota near the Montana border. Located in Glacier National Park is the Triple Divide, from which Montana waters begin their journey to the Arctic and Pacific oceans and the Gulf of Mexico.

³CLIMATE

The Continental Divide separates the state into two distinct climatic regions: the west generally has a milder climate than the east, where winters can be especially harsh. Montana's maximum daytime temperature averages 27°F (−2°C) in January and 85°F (29°C) in July. Great Falls has a normal daily mean temperature of 45°F (7°C), ranging from 21°F (−6°C) in January to 69°F (21°C) in July. The all-time low temperature in the state, −70°F (−57°C), registered at Rogers Pass on 20 January 1954, is the lowest ever recorded in the conterminous US; the all-time high, 117°F (47°C), was set at Medicine Lake on 5 July 1937. During the winter, Chinook winds from the eastern Rocky Mountains can bring rapid temperature increases of 40–50°F within a few minutes. Great Falls receives an average annual precipitation of 15 in (38 cm), but much of north-central Montana is arid. About 57 in (145 cm) of snow descends on Great Falls each year.

⁴FLORA AND FAUNA

Montana has three major life zones: subalpine, montane, and plains. The subalpine region, in the northern Rocky Mountains, is rich in wild flowers during a short midsummer growing season. The montane flora consists largely of coniferous forests, principally alpine fir, and a variety of shrubs. The plains are characterized by an abundance of grasses, cacti, and sagebrush species.

Game animals of the state include elk, moose, white-tailed and mule deers, pronghorn antelope, bighorn sheep, and mountain goat. Notable among the amphibians is the axolotl; rattlesnakes and other reptiles occur in most of the state. Rare or threatened species include the grizzly bear, spotted bat, prairie falcon, and Arctic grayling. The black-footed ferret, Eskimo curlew, and greenback cutthroat trout are on the endangered list.

⁵ENVIRONMENTAL PROTECTION

Montana's major environmental concerns are management of mineral and water resources and reclamation of strip-mined land. The 1973 Montana Resource Indemnity Trust Act, by 1975 amendment, imposes a coal severance tax of 30% on the contract sales price, with the proceeds placed in a permanent tax trust fund. This tax, in conjunction with the Montana Environmental Policy Act (1971) and the Major Facilities Siting Act (1973) reflects the determination of Montanans to protect the beauty of the Big Sky Country while maintaining economic momentum.

In 1995, the state had 9 hazardous waste sites. Only a tiny fraction of the state's lands are wetlands. The Water Quality Bureau of the Montana Department of Health and Environmental Sciences is responsible for managing wetlands.

6POPULATION

According to the 1990 census, Montana ranked 44th among the 50 states, with a population of 799,065 and a density of only 5.5 per sq mi (2 per sq km). The 1996 estimated population was 879,372, a 10.1% increase from 1990. This trend may, in part, be exacerbated by men outnumbering women 50.1% to 49.9%, respectively. Montana's largest cities and their estimated 1994 populations are: Billings, 81,125; Great Falls, 58,202; Missoula, 45,364; Butte–Silver Bow, 34,190; Helena, 26,339; and Bozeman, 25,067

7ETHNIC GROUPS

According to the 1990 census, there were approximately 48,000 American Indians in Montana, of whom the Blackfeet and Crow are the most numerous. In 1995 there were an estimated 8,208 Blackfeet and 7,153 Crow living on or near reservations.

The foreign-born made up 1.7% of Montana's 1990 census population, a decrease of 24% since 1980. Canada, Germany, the United Kingdom, and Mexico were the leading places of origin. The black, Hispanic, and Asian populations are very small comprising 0.3%, 0.5%, and 1.5%, respectively.

8LANGUAGES

English in Montana fuses Northern and Midland features, the Northern proportion declining from east to west. Topography has given new meaning to *basin, hollow, meadow,* and *park* as kinds of clear spaces in the mountains.

In 1990, 703,198 Montanans—95% of the resident population 5 years of age or older—spoke only English at home. Other languages spoken at home included:

German	9,644	Various Native American	8,207
Spanish	8,083	French	2,572

9RELIGIONS

As of 1990, Protestant groups had 467,345 known adherents in Montana. Leading denominations included American Lutheran Church Association, 16,172; United Methodist, 19,461; and Latter-day Saints (Mormons), 28,620. Montana had 125,799 Roman Catholics in 1990 and an estimated 310 Jews in 1990.

10TRANSPORTATION

Montana's first railroad, the Utah and Northern, entered the state in 1880. Today, Montana is served by three major railroads, operating on about 3,315 rail mi (5,334 km) of track. Amtrak operated one long-distance route (Chicago–Seattle/Portland) through the state, which served 12 stations; total Montana ridership in 1996 was 97,855.

Because of its large size, small population, and difficult terrain, Montana was slow to develop a highway system. As of the beginning of 1997, the state had 69,845 mi (112,381 km) of public roads, streets, and highways. There were 1,011,423 registered motor vehicles in 1996 (up 0.8% from 1995) and 573,749 licensed drivers in 1995.

Montana had 122 public-use airports and 2,930 active aircraft in 1997. The leading airports are at Great Falls and Billings.

11HISTORY

Much of Montana's prehistory has only recently been unearthed. The abundance of fossils of large and small dinosaurs, marine reptiles, miniature horses, and giant cave bears indicates that, from 100 million to 60 million years ago, the region had a tropical climate. Beginning some 2 million years ago, however, dramatic temperature changes profoundly altered what we now call Montana. At four different times, great sheets of glacial ice moved south through Canada to cover much of the north. The last glacial retreat, about 10,000 years ago, did much to carve the state's present topographic feature. Montana's first humans probably came from across the Bering Strait; their fragmentary remains indicate a presence dating between 10,000 and 4000 BC.

The Indians encountered by Montana's first white explorers—probably French traders and trappers from Canada—arrived from the east during the 17th and 18th centuries, pushed westward into Montana by the pressure of European colonization. In January 1743, two traders, Louis-Joseph and Francois Vérendrye, crossed the Dakota plains and saw before them what they called the "shining mountains," the eastern flank of the northern Rockies. However, it was not until 1803 that the written history of Montana begins. In that year, the Louisiana Purchase gave the United States most of Montana, and the Lewis and Clark expedition, dispatched by President Thomas Jefferson in 1804 to explore the upper reaches of the Missouri River, added the rest. On 25 April 1805, accompanied by a French trapper named Toussaint Charbonneau and his Shoshoni wife, Sacagawea, Meriwether Lewis and William Clark reached the mouth of the Yellowstone River near the present-day boundary with North Dakota. Shortly thereafter, the first American trappers, traders, and settlers entered Montana.

The fur trade dominated Montana's economy until 1858, when gold was discovered near the present community of Drummond. By mid-1862, a rush of miners from the gold fields of California, Nevada, Colorado, and Idaho had descended on the state. The temporary gold boom brought not only the state's first substantial white population but also an increased demand for government. In 1863, the eastern and western sectors of Montana were joined as part of Idaho Territory, which, in turn, was divided along the Bitterroot Mountains to form the present boundary between the two states. On 26 May 1864, President Abraham Lincoln signed the Organic Act, which created Montana Territory.

The territorial period was one of rapid and profound change. By the time Montana became a state on 8 November 1889, the remnants of Montana's Indian culture had been largely confined to federal reservations. A key event in this transformation was the Battle of the Little Big Horn River on 25 June 1876, when Lieutenant Colonel George Custer and his 7th US Cavalry regiment of fewer than 700 men were overwhelmed as they attacked an encampment of 15,000 Sioux and Northern Cheyenne led by Crazy Horse and Chief Gall. The following year, after a four-month running battle that traversed most of the state of Montana, Chief Joseph of the Nez Percé tribe surrendered to federal forces, signaling the end of organized Indian resistance.

As the Indian threat subsided, stockmen wasted little time in putting the seemingly limitless open range to use. By 1866, Nelson Story had driven the first longhorns up from Texas, and by the mid-1870s, sheep had also made a significant appearance on the open range. In 1886, at the peak of the open-range boom, approximately 664,000 head of cattle and nearly a million sheep grazed Montana's rangeland. Disaster struck during the "hard winter" of 1886/87, however, when perhaps as many as 362,000 head of cattle starved trying to find the scant forage covered by snow and ice. That winter marked the end of a cattle frontier based on the "free grass" of the open range and taught the stockmen the value of a secure winter feed supply.

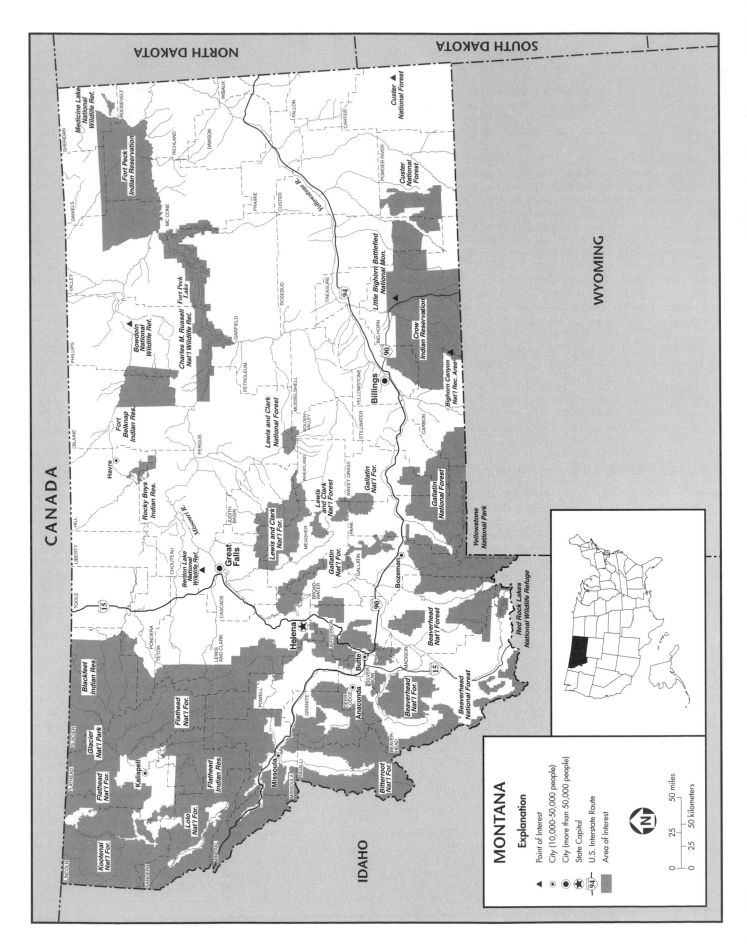

CANADA

NORTH DAKOTA

SOUTH DAKOTA

WYOMING

IDAHO

MONTANA

Explanation

◢ Point of Interest

◉ City (10,000–50,000 people)

◉ City (more than 50,000 people)

✪ State Capitol

94 U.S. Interstate Route

▨ Area of Interest

	50 miles
0 25	50 kilometers
0 25	

Medicine Lake National Wildlife Ref.

Fort Peck Indian Reservation

Fort Peck Lake

Charles M. Russell Nat'l Wildlife Ref.

Bowdoin National Wildlife Ref.

Fort Belknap Indian Res.

Rocky Boys Indian Res.

Havre

Benton Lake National Wildlife Ref.

Great Falls

Lewis and Clark Nat'l For.

Lewis and Clark National Forest

Lewis and Clark Nat'l Forest

Gallatin Nat'l For.

Gallatin Nat'l For.

Gallatin Nat'l Forest

Gallatin National Forest

Yellowstone National Park

Bozeman

Helena

Butte

Anaconda

Deer Lodge

Missoula

Kalispell

Blackfeet Indian Res.

Glacier Nat'l Park

Flathead Nat'l For.

Flathead Nat'l For.

Flathead Indian Res.

Kootenai Nat'l For.

Lolo Nat'l For.

Bitterroot Nat'l For.

Beaverhead Nat'l For.

Beaverhead National Forest

Beaverhead Nat'l Forest

Red Rock Lakes National Wildlife Refuge

Custer National Forest

Custer National Forest

Little Bighorn Battlefield National Mon.

Crow Indian Reservation

Bighorn Canyon Nat'l Rec. Area

Billings

Yellowstone R.

Missouri R.

SHERIDAN
DANIELS
ROOSEVELT
VALLEY
PHILLIPS
BLAINE
HILL
LIBERTY
TOOLE
GLACIER
FLATHEAD
LINCOLN
SANDERS
MINERAL
MISSOULA
RAVALLI
LAKE
POWELL
GRANITE
DEER LODGE
SILVER BOW
BEAVER-HEAD
MADISON
JEFFERSON
BROAD-WATER
LEWIS AND CLARK
PONDERA
TETON
CHOUTEAU
CASCADE
MEAGHER
GALLATIN
PARK
SWEET GRASS
WHEATLAND
JUDITH BASIN
FERGUS
PETROLEUM
GARFIELD
GOLDEN VALLEY
MUSSELSHELL
STILLWATER
CARBON
BIG HORN
YELLOWSTONE
TREASURE
ROSEBUD
PRAIRIE
CUSTER
DAWSON
MC CONE
RICHLAND
WIBAUX
FALLON
CARTER
POWDER RIVER
15
94
90
90
15

Construction of Montana's railroad system between 1880 and 1909 breathed new life into mining as well as the livestock industry. Moreover, the railroads created a new network of market centers at Great Falls, Billings, Bozeman, Missoula, and Havre. By 1890, the Butte copper pits were producing more than 40% of the nation's copper requirements. The struggle to gain financial control of the enormous mineral wealth of Butte Hill led to the "War of the Copper Kings," in which the Amalgamated Copper Co., in conjunction with Standard Oil gave up its copper holdings. The new company, Anaconda Copper Mining, virtually controlled the press, politics, and governmental processes of Montana until changes in the structure of the international copper market and the diversification of Montana's economy in the 1940s and 1950s reduced the company's power. Anaconda Copper was absorbed by the Atlantic Richfield Co. in 1976, and the name was changed to Anaconda Minerals in 1982.

The railroads also brought an invasion of agricultural homesteaders. Montana's population surged from 243,329 in 1900 to 548,889 by 1920, while the number of farms and ranches increased form 13,000 to 57,000. Drought and a sharp drop in wheat prices after World War I brought an end to the homestead boom. By 1926, half of Montana's commercial banks had failed. Conditions worsened with the drought and depression of the early 1930s, until the New Deal—enormously popular in Montana—helped revive farming and silver mining and financed irrigation and other public works projects.

The decades since the end of World War II have seen moderate growth in Montana's population, economy, and social services. Although manufacturing developed slowly, the state's fossil fuels industry grew rapidly during the national energy crisis of the 1970s. However, production of coal, crude oil, and natural gas leveled off after the crisis and even declined in the early 1980s.

In 1983 the Anaconda Copper Mining Company shut down its mining operations in Butte. Farm income also suffered in the 1980s as a result of falling prices, drought, and damage by insects. Growth in manufacturing and construction and recovery in the agricultural sector, have improved Montana's economy in the 1990s.

Tourism, air quality, and wildlife in parts of Montana were affected by the 1988 forest fires that burned for almost three months in Yellowstone National Park. Some Montana residents had to be evacuated from their homes.

In 1992 Montana's delegation to the US House of Representatives was reduced from two members to one, based on the results of the 1990 Census.

12STATE GOVERNMENT

Montana's original constitution, dating from 1889, was substantially revised by a 1972 constitutional convention, effective 1 July 1973. Under the present document, the state legislature consists of 50 senators, elected to staggered four-year terms, and 100 representatives, who serve for two years. In 1995 legislators received $57 per diem during regular sessions. The only elected officers of the executive branch are the governor and lieutenant governor (who run jointly), secretary of state, attorney general, superintendent of public instruction, and auditor; each serves a four-year term. In 1996 the governor's salary was $59,310.

To become law, a bill must pass both houses by a simple majority and be signed by the governor, remain unsigned for five days, or be passed over the governor's veto by a two-thirds vote of both houses. The state constitution may be amended by constitutional convention, by legislative referendum, or by voter initiative. To be adopted, each proposed amendment must be ratified at the next general election.

To vote in Montana, one must be a US citizen and at least 18 years of age; there is a county residency requirement of 30 days for registration.

13POLITICAL PARTIES

Since statehood, Democrats have generally dominated in contests for the US House and Senate, and Republicans in elections for state and local offices and in national presidential campaigns (except during the New Deal years). It is remarkable that, as of 1985, only two Montana Republicans had been elected to the US Senate. Although the erosion of Montana's rural population since the 1920s has diluted the Republicans' agrarian base, the party has gained increasing financial and organizational backing from corporate interests, particularly from the mining and energy-related industries.

The strength of the Democratic Party, on the other hand, lies in the strong union movement centered in Butte and its surrounding counties, augmented by smaller family farms throughout the state. Urbanization has also benefited the Democrats. Montanans voted overwhelmingly for Republican President Ronald Reagan in November 1984 and for Republican George Bush in 1988, but Democrat Bill Clinton carried the state in 1992. However, in 1996 Clinton lost the state to Republican Bob Dole, who won 44% of the vote to Clinton's 41%, and 14% for Independent Ross Perot.

The governor of Montana as of 1996, Marc Racicot, was a Republican. Republican Conrad Burns was elected to the Senate in 1988 and reelected in 1994, and Democrat Max Baucus won reelection in 1996. The sole US representative is a Republican. In the 1994 mid-term elections, the Republicans found themselves in control of the state senate for the first time since the presidency of Dwight Eisenhower. Following the 1996 elections, there were 34 Republicans and 16 Democrats, representing a further Democratic loss of 3 seats. The Republicans continued to control the state house with 65 seats to the Democrats' 35. In 1994, Montana had 2 Hispanic public officials. As of 1995, there were 36 women serving in the state legislature and 1 woman holding an elective executive office.

Montana Presidential Vote by Major Political Parties, 1948–96

YEAR	ELECTORAL VOTE	MONTANA WINNER	DEMOCRAT	REPUBLICAN
1948	4	*Truman (D)	119,071	96,770
1952	4	*Eisenhower (R)	106,213	157,394
1956	4	*Eisenhower (R)	116,238	154,933
1960	4	Nixon (R)	134,891	141,841
1964	4	*Johnson (D)	164,246	113,032
1968	4	*Nixon (R)	114,117	138,835
1972	4	*Nixon (R)	120,197	183,976
1976	4	Ford (R)	149,259	173,703
1980	4	*Reagan (R)	118,032	206,814
1984	4	*Reagan (R)	146,742	232,450
1988	4	*Bush (R)	168,936	190,412
1992**	3	*Clinton (D)	154,507	144,207
1996**	3	Dole (R)	167,922	179,652

*Won US presidential election.

** Independent candidate Ross Perot received 107,225 votes in 1992 and 55,229 votes in 1996.

14LOCAL GOVERNMENT

As of 1994, Montana had 54 counties, 128 municipalities, 578 special districts, and 544 school districts. Typical elected county officials are three county commissioners, attorney, sheriff, clerk and recorder, school superintendent, treasurer, public administrator assessor, and coroner. Unified city-county governments include Anaconda-Deer Lodge and Butte-Silver Bow.

[15]STATE SERVICES

The Citizens' Advocate Office, established in 1973, serves as a clearinghouse for problems, complaints, and questions concerning state government. The commissioner of higher education administers the state university system, while the superintendent of public instruction is responsible for the public schools. The Department of Highways is the main transportation agency. Health and welfare programs are the province of the Department of Public Health and Human Services.

[16]JUDICIAL SYSTEM

Montana's highest court, the supreme court, consists of a chief justice and 6 associate justices. District courts are the courts of general jurisdiction. Justice of the peace courts are essentially county courts whose jurisdiction is limited to minor civil cases, misdemeanors, and traffic violations. Montana has seven supreme court justices elected on nonpartisan ballots for eight-year terms and 37 district court judges elected for six years. There were 2,340 practicing lawyers in 1996.

Montana's crime rates in 1995 were 5,304.9 per 100,000, including 170.6 for violent crime and 5,134.4 for property crime. The state rarely enforces the death penalty; only seven convicted persons have been executed since 1930, and one since 1977. Six persons were under sentence of death in 1995.

In 1995 there were 1,683 inmates in eight state and federal correctional facilities, a rate of 193 inmates per 100,000 inhabitants. The prison population increased by over 32% between 1990 and 1995.

[17]ARMED FORCES

In 1996, there were 3,737 active duty military personnel stationed in Montana. The principal military facility in Montana is Malmstrom Air Force Base (Great Falls), a Strategic Air Command facility employing 3,676 military personnel. An estimated 94,000 veterans of US military service were living in Montana in 1996. In 1995/96, expenditures on veterans totaled $152 million.

Total defense contracts amounted to $56 million, the smallest amount of any state. There were a total of 7,743 Reserve and National Guard personnel in the state in 1996. In 1993, the Montana Highway Patrol employed 196 full-time sworn officers, or 2 per 10,000 residents.

[18]MIGRATION

Montana's first great migratory wave brought Indians from the east during the 17th and 18th centuries. The gold rush of the 1860s and a land boom between 1900 and 1920 resulted in surges of white settlement. The economically troubled 1920s and 1930s produced a severe wave of out-migration that continued through the 1960s. The trend reversed between 1970 and 1980, however, when Montana's net gain from migration was 16,000; from 1980 to 1989, the state had a net loss of 43,000 residents from migration. Between 1990 and 1996, Montana had net gains of 52,095 in domestic migration and 1,851 in international migration. In 1990, 58.9% of all Montanans had been born in the state. In 1990, about 52% of the state's resident population age 5 and older lived in the same house as in 1985. Of those who changed residences from 1985, 24% had lived in a different state.

[19]INTERGOVERNMENTAL COOPERATION

Among the interstate agreements in which Montana participates are the Interstate Oil and Gas Compact, Interstate Corrections Compact, Western Interstate Energy Compact, Western Regional Education Compact, and Yellowstone River Compact (with North Dakota and Wyoming). Federal aid to the state and local governments in 1995/96 totaled $960 million.

[20]ECONOMY

Resource industries—agriculture, mining, lumbering—dominate Montana's economy, although tourism is of increasing importance. In 1983, manufacturing contributed $4 billion to the state economy; mining, $1.6 billion; agriculture, $1.5 billion; and travel, $600 million. A pending lawsuit with the federal government over the federal lands which supplied much of the state's timber placed the timber industry's future in question, as did the selling by Champion International of its two mills and of its timber lands. While Stimson Lumber purchased the mills from Champion, it planned to rehire only two-thirds of the employers, reducing employment in the lumber and wood sector by 600 workers. The mining industry in western Montana was hurt by low international price levels. The closure of Troy Mine, which produced silver, lead and zinc, resulted in the idling of 300 workers. Residential construction rebounded in 1993 with a rise in population growth. Montana's gross state product in 1994 was $16,862 million, to which private goods-producing industries contributed $3,882 million; private services-producing industries, $10,238 million; and government, $2,742 million.

In 1996, there were 2,805 filings for bankruptcy in the state.

[21]INCOME

With a per capita personal income of $19,047 in 1996, Montana ranked 46th among the 50 states. Total disposable personal income increased to $14.6 million in 1996, up from $14.1 million in 1995. Nonfarm personal income rose from $14.7 billion in 1994 to $15.7 billion in 1995, an increase of 6.4%.

Median household income reached $27,757 in 1995. About 15.3% of the state's population lived below the federal poverty level in 1995.

Over 5.2% (17,427) of all households had a disposable income exceeding $75,000 in 1995 (including just under 1% whose disposable incomes were greater than $150,000).

[22]LABOR

Montana's labor force varies sharply with the season, swelling in the summer and shrinking in the winter. As of 1996, the civilian labor force averaged 446,577 persons, of whom 423,064 were employed and 23,511 were unemployed. The unemployment rate was 5.3% in 1996.

Montana's employment and earnings by industry, in 1995 annual averages, were:

	EARNINGS	EMPLOYMENT (JOBS)
Total	$16,052,167,000	502,590
Farm	332,107,000	27,192
Nonfarm	10,070,843,000	475,398
Private	7,980,051,000	391,788
Agricultural services, forestry, fisheries	106,544,000	7,873
Mining	279,839,000	7,118
Construction	725,962,000	29,479
Manufacturing	807,780,000	28,296
Nondurable goods	290,197,000	10,157
Durable goods	517,583,000	18,139
Transportation and public utilities	907,949,000	25,198
Wholesale trade	561,744,000	19,889
Retail trade	1,312,709,000	97,157
Finance, insurance, and real estate	514,348,000	30,863
Services	2,763,176,000	145,915
Government	2,090,792,000	83,610

In 1995, union membership was 50,800, or 15.8% of the work force. Unionization among manufacturing workers was 15.6%.

23AGRICULTURE

Montana's farms numbered 22,000 in 1996, with average acreage of 2,713 (1,098 hectares). Farm income totaled over $1.8 billion in 1995, ranking 33d in the US. In that year, Montana was the nation's 3d-leading wheat producer, with an output of 195.7 million bu, valued at $897.3 million. Other major crops were barley (2d in the US) with 62.4 million bu, valued at $193.4 million; sugar beets (6th) with 1.3 million bu, valued at $47.6 million; and hay (12th) with 5.36 million tons, valued at $350.2 million.

24ANIMAL HUSBANDRY

In 1997, Montana's farms and ranches had around 2.7 million cattle and calves, valued at $1.6 million. There were an estimated 150,000 hogs and pigs, valued at $14.4 million in 1996. During 1995, Montana farmers produced around 34.5 million lb (15.6 million kg) of sheep and lambs that grossed $25.8 million in income.

25FISHING

Montana's designated fishing streams offer some 10,000 mi (16,000 km) of good to excellent freshwater fishing. Federal hatcheries distributed about 2.2 million (67,010 lb or 30,396 kg) coldwater species (predominantly trout) fish and 10 million fish eggs within Montana in 1995/96, when the state issued 389,820 sport fishing licenses.

26FORESTRY

As of 1995, 22,419,089 acres (9,073,005 hectares) in Montana were classified as forestland. There were 10 national forests, comprising roughly 16,797,507 acres (6,797,951 hectares) in 1995. The lumbering industry produced 1.0 billion board feet that year; its product shipments were valued at $1.3 billion.

27MINING

The estimated value of nonfuel mineral production for Montana in 1995 rose to $581 million, an increase of more than 7% from that of 1994. Between 1993 and 1995, the increase in nonfuel mineral production value was a result of increases in copper, molybdenum, and portland cement. Metallic minerals—copper, gold, iron ore, lead, molybdenum, platinum group metals, silver, and zinc—accounted for 77% of the state's total nonfuel mineral production vale. Most metal mining—especially for gold, silver, and copper—occurs in the southwest region in the vicinity of Helena and Butte. In 1995, Montana ranked 22d nationally in the value of these minerals, compared with 18th in 1992.

Gold was Montana's leading mineral by value in 1995, followed by copper and portland cement. Portland cement accounted for 43% of the industrial mineral value in 1995. Montana is the only state to produce primary platinum and palladium, and is 1st in the production of talc and pyrophyllite; 2d in bentonite; 4th in copper and lead; 5th in gold, molybdenum, and zinc; and 6th in silver. Production and value in 1995 included gold, 27,100 lb or 12,300 kg ($148 million); construction sand and gravel, 8.5 million metric tons ($34.4 million); palladium, 14,100 lb or 6,400 kg ($29.2 million); platinum, 4,400 lb or 2,000 kg ($25.8 million); and zinc, 21,000 metric tons ($24.6 million).

28ENERGY AND POWER

In 1995, Montana generated 25.4 billion kWh of electricity, 42% from hydropower and 58% by coal burning; installed capacity was 5.1 million kW, excluding qualifying facilities.

In 1995, the state produced 16.5 million barrels of crude oil, leaving proved reserves of about 178 million barrels; natural gas production totaled 50.2 billion cu ft (1.4 billion cu m) with proved reserves amounting to 782 billion cu ft (22 billion cu m).

As of January 1995, coal reserves were estimated at 119.8 billion tons—1st in the US and 24% of the US total—of which bituminous coal accounted for 1.4 billion tons; subbituminous, 102.6 billion tons; and lignite, 15.8 billion tons. Production of coal in 1995 totaled 39.4 million tons.

29INDUSTRY

Montana's major manufacturing industries process raw materials from mines, forests, and farms. The total value of shipments by manufacturers in 1995 amounted to $4,898,500,000. Major sectors and their value of shipments included:

Lumber and wood products	$1,302,700,000
Food and food products	531,200,000
Printing and publishing materials	200,300,000
Stone, clay, and glass products	145,600,000
Electronic and other electric equipment	147,500,000

In 1995, there were 130 US patents issued to Montana residents.

30COMMERCE

In 1992, 1,853 wholesale establishments had sales of $5.9 billion, including $2 billion in durable goods. That year, 6,803 retail stores had sales of $6.2 billion.

In 1994, 1,901 wholesale establishments, employing 17,331 workers, had a payroll of $405.5 million, while 7,288 retailers had a payroll of $848.4 million. Montana's foreign exports in 1995 totaled $969.7 million. Wheat is the leading export item, at $626.6 million in 1995.

31CONSUMER PROTECTION

Montana's consumer protection laws are administered by the Legal and Consumer Affairs Division of the Commerce Department.

32BANKING

At the end of 1996, Montana had 100 insured commercial banks; their assets totaled $8.7 billion, and deposits were over $7.9 billion. In 1996, there were 8 insured savings and loan associations, all federally chartered, with total assets of almost $1.8 billion.

33INSURANCE

In 1996 there were 575,209 life insurance policies in force, with a total value of $31.1 billion. The average coverage per family was $94,900.

Property and liability insurers wrote premiums of $854.1 million in 1996, of which automobile physical damage accounted for $213.3 million; automotive liability insurance, $148.3 million; and homeowners coverage, $110.9 million.

34SECURITIES

There are no securities exchanges in Montana. In April 1997, 1,132 broker-dealers were registered to sell securities in the state by means of 31,428 designated agents. At that time, 287 firms were registered to market advisory services concerning investment in securities, involving 2,100 registered agents.

35PUBLIC FINANCE

The Montana state budget is prepared biennially by the Office of Budget and Program Planning and submitted by the governor to the legislature for amendment and approval. The fiscal year runs from 1 July to 30 June. The following is a summary of estimated revenues and expenditures in the general fund for 1993/94 and 1994/95 (in thousands of dollars):

REVENUES	1993/94	1994/95
Individual income taxes*	$195,896	$315,080
Corporate income taxes*	39,252	55,901
Interest income*	47,657	55,386
Mineral production taxes	23,062	23,325
Long-range bond excess	44,140	45,834
Other sources	117,264	120,523
TOTALS	$467,271	$616,049

EXPENDITURES		
University system	$103,257	$113,387
Public schools*	49,474	160,474
Social services	151,166	152,957
Corrections & human Services	76,624	78,375
Department of Revenue	20,793	19,537
Property tax reimbursements	18,336	18,336
Debt service	11,248	13,497
All other	64,692	58,768
TOTALS	$495,590	$615,331

* Effective fiscal year 1995, certain public school revenues are to be deposited in general fund, increasing general fund revenues and public school appropriations.

36 TAXATION

In 1996, Montana's personal income tax, which has been indexed to inflation since 1981, ranged from 2% to 11%. The corporate income tax was 6.75% on net income, with a minimum tax of $50; for small business corporations, $10. The state levies a property tax but no sales tax. Montana received $4.8 billion in federal funding in 1995, or $5,525 per capita. State residents paid $2 billion in federal taxes in 1995.

37 ECONOMIC POLICY

The Economic Development Division of the state's Department of Commerce offers a variety of programs aimed at improving and enhancing Montana's economic and business climate. Working closely with other state agencies and federal and private programs, the department's aim is to assist start-up and existing businesses with the technical and financial assistance necessary for their success. Relationships with local development groups, chambers of commerce, and similar organizations help Montana communities develop their full potential. Montana micro-business companies with fewer than 10 full-time equivalent employees and annual gross revenues under $500,000 can receive loans of up to $35,000. Other qualifying businesses can borrow under several other state and federal development loan programs. The Economic Development Division's trade program assists businesses in pursuing domestic and worldwide trade. The Small Business Development Center (SBDC) program and the State Data Center program both operate statewide networks of service centers.

38 HEALTH

The abortion rate was 16 per 1,000 women in 1992, and 15.7% of abortions in 1992 were obtained by out-of-state residents. The infant mortality rate per 1,000 live births was 7.4 per 1,000 population in 1995, and the death rate that year was 8.7. Major causes of death in 1995 (with their rates per 100,000 population) were heart disease, 230.2; cancer, 202.8; cerebrovascular diseases, 68; accidents and adverse effects, 43 (of which motor vehicle accidents accounted for 22.4); and suicide, 21.9. The first two rates were below national norms; the last three were above national norms. When cause-specific death rates are age-adjusted for comparison of state and national rates, Montana's cancer rates far exceeds its heart disease rate, although both remain lower than national rates of death from either of those causes.

Montana has one of the lowest AIDS rates per 100,000 population in the country. As of 1995, there had been only 178 AIDS cases reported.

There were 67 hospitals in 1997, with 2,548 beds and 93,429 admissions during the year. Hospital personnel included 2,736 registered nurses in 1991. In 1994, the average expense of a hospital providing service was $915 per inpatient day. There were 1,700 physicians in 1994, and 459 licensed, active dentists in 1995. At least 14.9% of Montana's residents were uninsured in 1995. There were 128 and 669 million Medicare and Medicaid recipients in 1994, respectively.

39 SOCIAL WELFARE

Montana played an important role in the development of social welfare. It was one of the first states to experiment with workers' compensation, enacting a compulsory compensation law in 1915; eight years later, Montana and Nevada became the first states to provide for old age pensions.

Public assistance payments to an average of 32,500 recipients with dependent children in 1996, averaged $461 per month as of 1996. In 1995, Social Security benefits went to 151,530 residents, with the average monthly payment being $698. Weekly unemployment benefit checks averaged $159.56 in 1995. In 1996, 70,754 residents received monthly food stamp allowances averaging $68.76, and the student lunch program received total federal funding of $15.5 million.

With the enactment of the Personal Responsibility and Work Opportunity Reconciliation Act of 1996, the US government changed the form and regulations for many of its social welfare programs; most significantly, it replaced Aid to Families with Dependent Children (AFDC), an open-ended entitlement program, with Temporary Assistance for Needy Families (TANF), a limited system of assistance funded largely through federal block grants. The reform act also impacted the food stamp program, the Supplemental Security Income program, and the child nutrition program. The law took effect on 1 July 1997 and provided $16.38 billion in block grants for fiscal years 1997–2002. The grants were to be divided among the states based on an equation involving the numbers of former AFDC recipients in each state. Because many of the bill's provisions had yet to be implemented into state-by-state policy, it was not possible to include the details of each state's programs for this edition of this work.

40 HOUSING

In 1996, Montana had an estimated 369,000 housing units, of which 333,000 were occupied. As of 1990, 58% of the units were owner-occupied, and 98.1% had full plumbing. In 1996, 2,678 privately owned units, valued at $209 million, were authorized for construction; of these, 1,494 were single-family. About one-third of the units were in multi-family dwellings. In 1990, the last year for which statistics are available, the median home value was $56,600; the median monthly cost for the owner (including a mortgage) was $575 that year. Renters had a median monthly cost of $311 in 1990. During 1995/96, Montana received $65.1 million in aid from the US Department of Housing and Urban Development, including $12.4 million in community development block grants.

41 EDUCATION

As of 1990, 81% of Montanans 25 years and older had completed high school, and 20% were college graduates.

Public school enrollments in fall 1996 were 114,538 for grades Pre-K–8, and 50,022 in grades 9–12. The ratio of pupils to teachers was 16:1.

As of fall 1996, 43,360 students attended institutions of higher education. Of these, the University of Montana (Missoula) enrolled 11,886+ and Montana State University (Bozeman), 11,562.

42ARTS

The C. M. Russell Museum in Great Falls honors the work of Charles Russell, whose mural *Lewis and Clark Meeting the Flathead Indians* adorns the capitol in Helena. Other fine art museums include the Museum of the Rockies in Bozeman, Yellowstone Art Center at Billings, and the Missoula Museum of the Arts.

The state of Montana generated $663,000 in financial support from federal sources from 1991 to 1996. The NEA contributed $485,000 to the state's arts programs and $610,000 to the Montana Arts Council. The Council was also given funding by the state. Private sources contributed $15 million. Audiences for Montana's arts programs totaled 11,000,000. There were 34,000 contributing artists. The Montana Arts Council received funds from the NEA for its arts education program. The state offered arts education programs to 19,000 school children. In 1996, Montana had 500 arts associations and 20 local arts groups. The Montana Arts Council assisted the Missoula Museum of the Arts and the Judith Cultural Committee. The NEA also contributed to the development of the Yellowstone Art Center and the Custer County Art and Heritage Center.

43LIBRARIES AND MUSEUMS

Montana has 82 public libraries, 28 public library branches, 6 institutional libraries, 61 special libraries, and 437 school libraries serving 56 counties. The combined book stock of all Montana public libraries is 2,607,143—3.17 volumes per capita—and their combined circulation is 4,941,329. Distinguished collections include those of the University of Montana (Missoula), with over 800,000 volumes; Montana State University (Bozeman), 569,886; and the Montana State Library and Montana Historical Society Library, both in Helena.

Among the state's 66 museums are the Montana Historical Society Museum, Helena; World Museum of Mining, Butte; Western Heritage Center, Billings; and Museum of the Plains Indian, Browning. National historic sites include Big Hole and Little Big Horn battlefields and the Grant-Kohrs Ranch at Deer Lodge, west of Helena.

44COMMUNICATIONS

In March 1993, 94.4% of the state's households had telephone service. There were 101 commercial radio stations (47 AM, 54 FM) in 1996, and 21 television stations, including 2 educational broadcasters. During the same year, Billings Tele-Communications, Inc. was the major provider of cable television service.

45PRESS

As of 1997, Montana had 6 morning dailies, 5 evening dailies, and 6 Sunday newspapers. The leading papers were the *Billings Gazette* (53,702 mornings, 59,516 Sundays) and the *Great Falls Tribune* (33,704 mornings, 40,051 Sundays).

46ORGANIZATIONS

The 1992 Census of Service Industries counted 464 organizations in Montana, including 83 business associations; 277 civic, social, and fraternal associations; and 104 other membership organizations. Among the organizations headquartered in Montana are the American Simmental Association (Bozeman) and Bikecentennial: The Bicycle Travel Association (Missoula).

47TOURISM, TRAVEL, AND RECREATION

Many tourists seek out the former gold rush camps, ghost towns, and dude ranches. Scenic wonders include all of Glacier National Park, covering 1,013,595 acres (410,202 hectares), which is the US portion of Waterton-Glacier International Peace Park; part of Yellowstone National Park, which also extends into Idaho and Wyoming; and Bighorn Canyon National Recreation Area. In 1993, in-state domestic travelers spent $6,215,000 on overnight and day trips in Montana; 588,639 anglers and 855,179 hunters were licensed in Montana in 1995.

48SPORTS

There are no major league professional sports teams in Montana, although there is minor league baseball in Billings. The University of Montana Grizzlies and Montana State University Bobcats both compete in the Big Sky Conference. Skiing is a very popular participation sport. The state has world class ski resorts in Big Sky. Other annual sporting events include the National Outdoors Speedskating Championship in Butte in January, the Governor's Cup 500 Sled Dog Race between Helena and Seely Lake in February, and the College Nationals Final Rodeo in Bozeman in June—along with several other rodeos statewide.

49FAMOUS MONTANANS

Prominent national officeholders from Montana include US Senator Thomas Walsh (b.Wisconsin, 1859–1933), who directed the investigation that uncovered the Teapot Dome scandal; Jeannette Rankin (1880–1973),the first woman member of Congress and the only US representative to vote against American participation in both world wars; Burton K. Wheeler (b.Mass., 1882–1975), US senator from 1923 to 1947 and one of the most powerful politicians in Montana history; and Michael Joseph "Mike" Mansfield (b.New York, 1903), who held the office of majority leader of the US Senate longer than anyone else.

Chief Joseph (b.Oregon, 1840?–1904), a Nez Percé Indian, repeatedly outwitted the US Army during the late 1870s; Crazy Horse (1849?–77) led a Sioux-Cheyenne army in battle at Little Big Horn. The town of Bozeman is named for explorer and prospector John M. Bozeman (b.Georgia, 1835–67).

Creative artists from Montana include Alfred Bertram Guthrie, Jr. (b.Indiana, 1901–91), author of *The Big Sky* and the Pulitzer Prize-winning *The Way West;* Dorothy Johnson (b.Iowa, 1905–84), whose stories have been made into such notable Western movies as *The Hanging Tree, The Man Who Shot Liberty Valance,* and *A Man Called Horse;* and Charles Russell (b.Missouri, 1864–1926), Montana's foremost painter and sculptor. Hollywood stars Gary Cooper (Frank James Cooper, 1901–61) and Myrna Loy (1905–93) were born in Helena. Newscaster Chet Huntley (1911–74) was born in Cardwell.

50BIBLIOGRAPHY

Farr, William, and K. Ross Toole. *Montana: Images of the Past.* Boulder, Colo.: Pruett, 1984.

Federal Writer's Project. *Montana: A State Guide Book.* Reprint. New York: Somerset, n.d. (orig. 1939).

Malone, Michael P., and Richard B. Roeder. *Montana: A History of Two Centuries.* Rev. ed. Seattle: University of Washington Press, 1991.

Small, Lawrence F., ed. *Religion in Montana: Pathways to the Present.* Billings, Mont.: Rocky Mountain College, 1992.

Spence, Clark C. *Montana: A Bicentennial History.* New York: Norton, 1978.

Toole, Kenneth R. *Montana: An Uncommon Land.* Norman: University of Oklahoma Press, 1984.

———. *Twentieth-Century Montana: A State of Extremes.* Norman: University of Oklahoma Press, 1983.

NEBRASKA

State of Nebraska

ORIGIN OF STATE NAME: From the Oto Indian word *nebrathka,* meaning "flat water" (for the Platte River). **NICKNAME:** The Cornhusker State. **CAPITAL:** Lincoln. **ENTERED UNION:** 1 March 1867 (37th). **SONG:** "Beautiful Nebraska." **MOTTO:** Equality Before the Law. **FLAG:** The great seal appears in the center in gold and silver, on a field of blue. **OFFICIAL SEAL:** Agriculture is represented by a farmer's cabin, sheaves of wheat, and growing corn, the mechanic arts by a blacksmith. Above is the state motto; in the background, a steamboat plies the Missouri River and a train heads toward the Rockies. The scene is surrounded by the words "Great Seal of the State of Nebraska, March 1st 1867." **BIRD:** Western meadowlark. **INSECT:** Honeybee. **FLOWER:** Goldenrod. **TREE:** Western cottonwood. **GRASS:** Little bluestem. **GEM:** Blue agate. **ROCK:** Prairie agate. **FOSSIL:** Mammoth. **LEGAL HOLIDAYS:** New Year's Day, 1 January; Birthday of Martin Luther King, Jr., 3d Monday in January; Presidents' Day, 3d Monday in February; Arbor Day, 22 April; Memorial Day, last Monday in May; Independence Day, 4 July; Labor Day, 1st Monday in September; Columbus Day, 2d Monday in October; Veterans Day, 11 November; Thanksgiving, 4th Thursday in November and following Friday; Christmas Day, 25 December. **TIME:** 6 AM CST = noon GMT; 5 AM MST = noon GMT.

¹LOCATION, SIZE, AND EXTENT

Located in the western north-central US, Nebraska ranks 15th in size among the 50 states. The total area of the state is 77,355 sq mi (200,349 sq km), of which land takes up 76,644 sq mi (198,508 sq km) and inland water 711 sq mi (1,841 sq km). Nebraska extends about 415 mi (668 km) E-W and 205 mi (330 km) N-S.

Nebraska is bordered on the N by South Dakota (with the line formed in part by the Missouri River); on the E by Iowa and Missouri (the line being defined by the Missouri River); on the S by Kansas and Colorado; and on the W by Colorado and Wyoming. The boundary length of Nebraska totals 1,332 mi (2,143 km). The state's geographic center is in Custer County, 10 mi (16 km) NW of Broken Bow.

²TOPOGRAPHY

Most of Nebraska is prairie; more than two-thirds of the state lies within the Great Plains proper. The elevation slopes upward gradually from east to west, from a low of 840 feet (256 meters) in the southeast to 5,426 feet (1,654 meters) in Kimball County. Rolling alluvial lowlands in the eastern portion of the state give way to the flat, treeless plain of central Nebraska, which in turn rises to a tableland in the west. The Sand Hills of the north-central plain is an unusual region of sand dunes anchored by grasses that cover about 18,000 sq mi (47,000 sq km).

The Sand Hills region is dotted with small natural lakes; in the rest of the state, the main lakes are artificial. The Missouri River—which, with its tributaries, drains the entire state—forms the eastern part of the northern boundary of Nebraska. Three rivers cross the state from west to east: the wide, shallow Platte River flows through the heart of the state for 310 mi (499 km); the Niobrara River traverses the state's northern region; and the Republican River flows through southern Nebraska.

³CLIMATE

Nebraska has a continental climate, with highly variable temperatures from season to season and year to year. The central region has an average annual normal temperature of 50°F (10°C), with a normal monthly maximum of 76°F (24°C) in July and a normal

monthly minimum of 22°F (–6°C) in January. The record low for the state is –47°F (–44°C), registered in Morrill County on 12 February 1899; the record high of 118°F (48°C) was recorded at Minden on 24 July 1936.

Normal yearly precipitation in the semiarid panhandle in the west is 17 in (43 cm); in the southeast, 30 in (76 cm). Snowfall in the state varies from about 21 in (53 cm) in the southeast to about 45 in (114 cm) in the northwest corner. Blizzards, droughts, and windstorms have plagued Nebraskans throughout their history. There were 26 tornadoes in 1995.

⁴FLORA AND FAUNA

Nebraska's deciduous forests are generally oak and hickory; conifer forests are dominated by western yellow (ponderosa) pine. The tallgrass prairie may include various slough grasses and needlegrasses, along with big bluestem, and prairie dropseed. Mixed prairie regions abound with western wheatgrass and buffalo grass. The prairie region of the Sand Hills supports a variety of bluestems, gramas, and other grasses. Common Nebraska wild flowers are wild rose, phlox, petunia, columbine, goldenrod, and sunflower. Rare species of Nebraska's flora include the Hayden penstemon, yellow ladyslipper, pawpaw, and snow trillium.

Common mammals native to the state are the pronghorn sheep, white-tailed and mule deer, badger, kit fox, coyote, striped ground squirrel, prairie vole, and several skunk species. There are more than 400 kinds of birds, the mourning dove, barn swallow, and western meadowlark (the state bird) among them. Carp, catfish, trout, and perch are fished for sport. Rare animal species include the least shrew, least weasel, and bobcat. The bald eagle, Arctic peregrine falcon, Higgins' eye pearly mussel, black-footed ferret, and northern swift fox *(Vulpes velox)* are listed as endangered species.

⁵ENVIRONMENTAL PROTECTION

The Department of Environmental Quality was established in 1971 to protect and improve the quality of the state's water, air, and land resources. The Agricultural Pollution Control Division of the Department regulates disposal of feedlot wastes and other sources of water pollution by agriculture. The Water and Waste Management Division is responsible for administering the Federal Clean Water Act, the Federal Resources Conservation and Recovery Act, portions of the Federal Safe Drinking Water Act, and the Nebraska Environmental Protection Act as it relates to water, solid waste, and hazardous materials. The state had 10 hazardous waste sites in 1996.

A program to protect groundwater from such pollutants as nitrates, synthetic organic compounds, hydrocarbons, pesticides, and other sources, was outlined in 1985. In 1996, the state spent $3.2 million on its Soil and Water Conservation Program. In 1994, the state imposed a tax on commercial fertilizers to create the Natural Resources Enhancement Fund, which distributes funds to local natural resource districts for water quality improvement programs. The Engineering Division regulates wastewater treatment standards and assists municipalities in securing federal construction grants for wastewater facilities. The Air Quality Division is responsible for monitoring and securing compliance with national ambient air quality standards.

The state has three wetlands of international importance as migrational and breeding grounds for waterfowl and nongame birds. While these areas are protected, the state has lost about 1 million acres (405,000 hectares) of wetlands since pre-European settlement times.

6POPULATION

Nebraska ranked 36th in the US in 1990 with a census population of 1,587,385, a 1.1% increase over 1980. The 1996 estimated population was 1,652,093, a 4.7% increase over 1990.

In 1990, there were 51% women and 49% men in Nebraska. Some 66% of Nebraska's population lived in urban areas in 1990, compared with 54% in 1960. The largest cities were Omaha, which ranked 48th among the nation's cities with a 1994 estimated population of 345,033; and Lincoln, with 203,076.

7ETHNIC GROUPS

Among Nebraskans reporting at least one specific ancestry in the 1990 census, 794,911 identified their ancestry as German, 208,616 as English, 272,185 as Irish, 90,043 as Czech, and 99,263 as Swedish. The 1990 population also included 57,000 black Americans (44,000 in Omaha), up from 48,389 in 1980, and 12,000 Asians and Pacific Islanders.

There were some 12,000 American Indians in Nebraska in 1990. The three Indian reservations maintained for the Omaha, Winnebago, and Santee Sioux tribes had the following estimated populations in 1995: Omaha, 5,012; Winnebago, 1,212; and Santee Sioux, 603.

8LANGUAGES

Many Plains Indians of the Macro-Siouan family once roamed widely over what is now Nebraska. Place-names derived from the Siouan language include Omaha, Ogallala, Niobrara, and Keya Paha. In 1990, about 1,300 Nebraskans claimed Indian tongues as their first languages.

Nebraska English, except for a slight South Midland influence in the southwest and some Northern influence from Wisconsin and New York settlers in the Platte River Valley, is almost pure North Midland. A few words, mostly food terms like *kolaches* (fruit-filled pastries), are derived from the language of the large Czech population. Usual pronunciation features are *on* and *hog* with the /o/ or *order, cow,* and *now* as /kaow/ and /naow/, *because* with the /ah/ vowel, *cot* and *caught* as sound-alikes, and a strong final /r/. *Fire* sounds almost like *far,* and *our* like *are; greasy* is pronounced /greezy/.

In 1990, 1,389,032 Nebraskans—95.2% of the resident population 5 years old or older—spoke only English at home.

The number of residents who spoke other languages at home included:

German	13,927	French	4,135
Spanish	24,555	Polish	2,673
Various Slavic	7,634	Various Scandinavian	1,699

9RELIGIONS

Nebraska's religious history derives from its patterns of immigration. German and Scandinavian settlers tended to be Lutheran; Irish, Polish, and Czech immigrants were mainly Roman Catholic. Methodism and other Protestant religions were spread by settlers from other midwestern states.

In 1990, the state's Catholic population numbered 335,372. Lutherans constituted the largest Protestant group with 114,944 adherents of the Missouri Synod, 128,667 of the Lutheran Church of America and 572 of the American Lutheran Churches Association. A total of 145,248 were United Methodists, and 48,591 were Presbyterians. The Jewish population was estimated at 6,732 in 1990.

10TRANSPORTATION

Nebraska's development was profoundly influenced by two major railroads, the Union Pacific and the Burlington Northern, both of which were major landowners in the state in the late 1800s. As of 1995, these lines still operated in Nebraska, together with Atchison, Topeka, and Santa Fe and six small companies. Altogether, there were nine lines with 3,578 rail mi (5,761 km) of track in the state in 1995. Amtrak had a total Nebraska ridership of 38,173 in 1995/96. Railroad freight traffic increased from 74,770,000 tons in 1970 to 168,463,000 tons in 1981, to 321,674,989 tons in 1995 (2d in the US), when the state originated 19,611,098 rail tons of farm products, more than any other state, which accounted for 53% of all rail tonnage originating within Nebraska that year.

The state's road system estimated at 92,755 mi (149,336 km) in 1995, is dominated by Interstate 80, the major east–west route and the largest public investment project in the state's history. About 93% of the driving-age population of the state—1,151,764 people—held driver's licenses in 1995. A total of 1,466,635 motor vehicles were registered in 1995, of which 848,757 were automobiles and 612,083 trucks.

There were 209 private and 93 public airports in the state in 1994. Eppley Airfield, Omaha's airport, is by far the busiest in the state, handling 21,398 aircraft departures with 1,165,479 passengers in 1994.

11HISTORY

Nebraska's first inhabitants, from about 10,000 BC, were nomadic Paleo-Indians. Successive groups were more sedentary, cultivating corn and beans. Archaeological excavations indicate that prolonged drought and dust storms before the 16th century caused these inhabitants to vacate the area. In the 16th and 17th centuries, other Indian tribes came from the East, some pushed by enemy tribes, others seeking new hunting grounds. By 1800, semisedentary Pawnee, Ponca, Omaha, and Oto, along with several nomadic groups, were in the region.

The Indians developed amiable relations with the first white explorers, French and Spanish fur trappers and traders who traveled through Nebraska in the 18th century, using the Missouri River as a route to the West. The area was claimed by both Spain and France and was French territory at the time of the Louisiana Purchase, when it came under US jurisdiction. It was explored during the first half of the 19th century by Lewis and Clark, Zebulon Pike, Stephen H. Long, and John C. Frémont.

The Indian Intercourse Act of 1834 forbade white settlement west of the Mississippi River, reserving the Great Plains as Indian

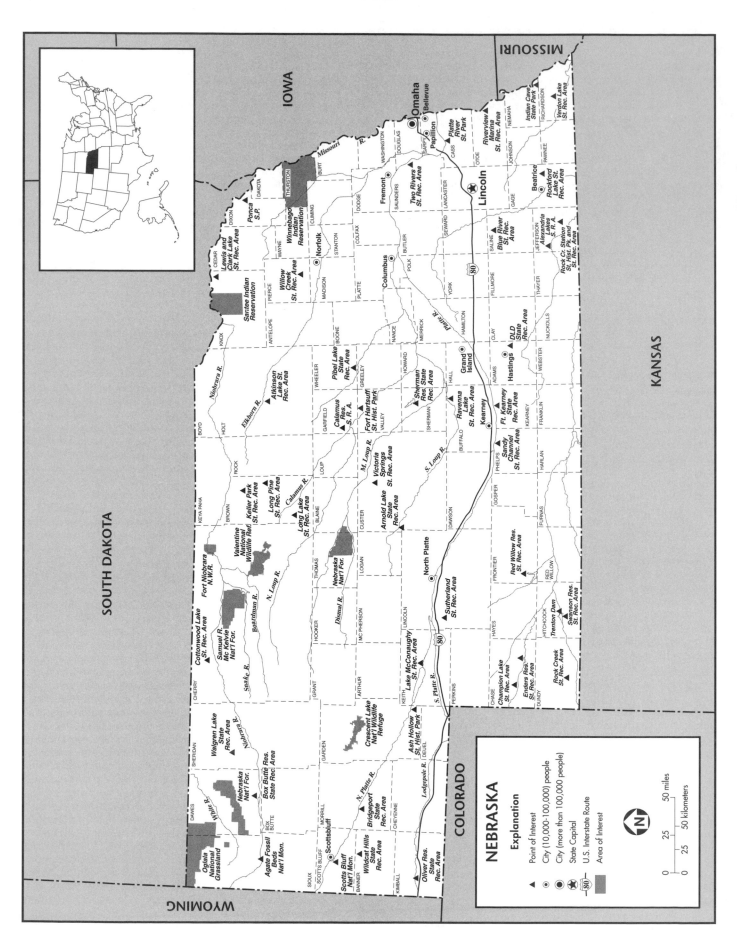

NEBRASKA

Explanation

▲ Point of Interest

◉ City (10,000-100,000) people

◉ City (more than 100,000 people)

★ State Capital

⬡ U.S. Interstate Route

▮ Area of Interest

0　25　50 miles

0　25　50 kilometers

Omaha
Bellevue
Papillion
Lincoln
Norfolk
Columbus
Fremont
Grand Island
Hastings
Kearney
North Platte
Scottsbluff
Beatrice

Lewis and Clark Lake St. Rec. Area
Ponca S.P.
Winnebago Indian Reservation
Santee Indian Reservation
Willow Creek St. Rec. Area
Two Rivers St. Rec. Area
Riverview Marina St. Rec. Area
Platte River St. Park
Indian Cave State Park
Verdon Lake St. Rec. Area
Rockford Lake St. Rec. Area
Blue River St. Rec. Area
Alexandria Lakes S.R.A.
Rock Cr. Station St. Hist. Pk. and St. Rec. Area
DLD State Rec. Area
Pibel Lake State Rec. Area
Atkinson Lake St. Rec. Area
Calamus Res. S.R.A.
Fort Hartsuff St. Hist. Park
Sherman Res. State Rec. Area
Ravenna Lake St. Rec. Area
Ft. Kearney State Rec. Area
Sandy Channel St. Rec. Area
Victoria Springs St. Rec. Area
Arnold Lake State Rec. Area
Long Pine St. Rec. Area
Keller Park St. Rec. Area
Long Lake St. Rec. Area
Valentine National Wildlife Ref.
Fort Niobrara N.W.R.
Cottonwood Lake St. Rec. Area
Samuel R. Mc Kelvie Nat'l For.
Nebraska Nat'l For.
Red Willow Res. St. Rec. Area
Sutherland St. Rec. Area
Lake McConaughy St. Rec. Area
Crescent Lake Nat'l Wildlife Refuge
Ash Hollow St. Hist. Park
Trenton Dam
Swanson Res. St. Rec. Area
Rock Creek St. Rec. Area
Enders Res. St. Rec. Area
Champion Lake St. Rec. Area
Walgren Lake State Rec. Area
Box Butte Res. State Rec. Area
Oglala National Grassland
Agate Fossil Beds Nat'l Mon.
Scotts Bluff Nat'l Mon.
Wildcat Hills State Rec. Area
Bridgeport State Rec. Area
Oliver Res. State Rec. Area

Missouri R.
Niobrara R.
Elkhorn R.
Platte R.
M. Loup R.
Loup R.
N. Loup R.
Calamus R.
Snake R.
Boardman R.
Dismal R.
S. Loup R.
N. Platte R.
S. Platte R.
Lodgepole R.
White R.

DAKOTA
THURSTON
CEDAR
DIXON
WAYNE
PIERCE
ANTELOPE
KNOX
BOYD
HOLT
ROCK
BROWN
KEYA PAHA
CHERRY
SHERIDAN
DAWES
BOX BUTTE
SIOUX
SCOTTS BLUFF
BANNER
KIMBALL
MORRILL
GARDEN
GRANT
HOOKER
THOMAS
BLAINE
LOUP
GARFIELD
WHEELER
GREELEY
BOONE
MADISON
STANTON
CUMING
BURT
WASHINGTON
DOUGLAS
SARPY
CASS
OTOE
SAUNDERS
DODGE
COLFAX
PLATTE
NANCE
MERRICK
POLK
BUTLER
SEWARD
LANCASTER
YORK
HAMILTON
HALL
HOWARD
SHERMAN
VALLEY
CUSTER
LOGAN
MC PHERSON
ARTHUR
KEITH
LINCOLN
DAWSON
BUFFALO
ADAMS
CLAY
FILLMORE
SALINE
JEFFERSON
GAGE
THAYER
NUCKOLLS
WEBSTER
FRANKLIN
KEARNEY
PHELPS
GOSPER
FRONTIER
RED WILLOW
FURNAS
HARLAN
HITCHCOCK
HAYES
PERKINS
CHASE
DUNDY
RICHARDSON
PAWNEE
JOHNSON
NEMAHA

80

Territory. Nothing prevented whites from traversing Nebraska, however, and from 1840 to 1866, some 350,000 persons crossed the area on the Oregon, California, and Mormon trails, following the Platte River Valley, a natural highway to the West. Military forts were established in the 1840s to protect travelers from Indian attack.

The Kansas-Nebraska Act of 1854 established Nebraska Territory, which stretched from Kansas to Canada and from the Missouri River to the Rockies. The territory assumed its present shape in 1861. Still sparsely populated, Nebraska escaped the violence over the slavery issue that afflicted Kansas. The creation of Nebraska Territory heightened conflict between Indians and white settlers, however, as Indians were forced to cede more and more of their land. From mid-1860 to the late 1870s, western Nebraska was a battleground for Indians and US soldiers. By 1890, the Indians were defeated and moved onto reservations in Nebraska, South Dakota, and Oklahoma.

Settlement of Nebraska Territory was rapid, accelerated by the Homestead Act of 1862, under which the US government provided 160 acres (65 hectares) to a settler for a nominal fee, and the construction of the Union Pacific, the first transcontinental railroad. The Burlington Railroad, which came to Nebraska in the late 1860s, used its vast land grants from Congress to promote immigration, selling the land to potential settlers from the East and from Europe. The end of the Civil War brought an influx of Union veterans, bolstering the Republican administration, which began pushing for statehood. On 1 March 1867, Nebraska became the 37th state to join the Union. Farming and ranching developed as the state's two main enterprises. Facing for the first time the harsh elements of the Great Plains, homesteaders in central and western Nebraska evolved what came to be known as the sod-house culture, using grassy soil to construct sturdy insulated homes. They harnessed the wind with windmills to pump water, constructed fences of barbed wire, and developed dry-land farming techniques.

Ranching existed in Nebraska as early as 1859, and by the 1870s, it was well established in the western part of the state. Some foreign investors controlled hundreds of thousands of acres of the free range. The cruel winter of 1886/87 killed thousands of cattle and bankrupted many of these large ranches.

By 1890, depressed farm prices, high railroad shipping charges, and rising interest rates were hurting the state's farmers, and a drought in the 1890s exacerbated their plight. These problems contributed to the rise of populism, a proagrian movement. Many Nebraska legislators embraced populism helping to bring about the first initiative and referendum laws in the US, providing for the regulation of stockyards and telephone and telegraph companies and instituting compulsory education.

World War I created a rift among Nebraskans as excessive patriotic zeal was directed against residents of German descent. German-language newspapers were censored, ministers were ordered to preach only in English (often to congregations that understood only German), and three university professors of German origin were fired. A Nebraska law (1919) that prohibited the teaching of any foreign language until high school was later declared unconstitutional by the US Supreme Court.

Tilling of marginal land to take advantage of farm prices that had been inflated during World War I caused economic distress during the 1920s. Nebraska's farm economy was already in peril when the dust storms of the 1930s began, and conditions worsened as drought, heat, and grasshopper invasions plagued the state. Thousands of people, particularly from the southwest counties in which dust-bowl conditions were most severe, fled Nebraska for the west coast. Some farmers joined protest movements—dumping milk, for example, rather than selling at depressed prices—while others marched on the state capital to demand a moratorium on farm debts, which they received. In the end, federal aid saved the farmers.

The onset of World War II brought prosperity to other sectors. Military airfields and war industries were placed in the state because of its safe inland location, bringing industrial growth that extended into the postwar years. Much of the new industry developed since that time is agriculture-related, including the manufacture of mechanized implements and irrigation equipment.

Farm output and income increased dramatically into the 1970s through wider use of hybrid seed, pesticides, fungicides, chemical fertilizers, close-row planting, and irrigation, but contaminated runoff adversely affected water quality and greater water use drastically lowered water-table levels. Many farmers took on large debt burdens to finance expanded output, their credit buoyed by strong farm-product prices and exports. When prices began to fall in the early 1980s, many found themselves overextended. By spring 1985, an estimated 10% of all farmers were reportedly close to bankruptcy. Since the late 1980s, farm prices have risen steadily; the average farm income in Nebraska rose more than 10% between 1989 and the mid-1990s. Increasingly, the state had fewer, larger, and more-mechanized farms. The growth of small industries and tourism also bolstered Nebraska's economy in the 1990s. Challenges facing the state included a loss of population in rural areas, urban decay, and tension among different racial and ethnic groups, including Native Americans. Water conservation to avoid depletion of the state's aquifers for irrigation purposes was also a major priority.

12STATE GOVERNMENT

The first state constitution was adopted in 1866; a second, adopted in 1875, is still in effect. A 1919–20 constitutional convention proposed—and voters passed—41 amendments; by 1982, the document had been revised an additional 138 times.

Nebraska's legislature is unique among the states; since 1934, it has been a unicameral body of 49 members elected on a nonpartisan basis. Members, who go by the title of senator, are chosen in even-numbered years for four-year terms. The legislative salary was $12,000 in 1995. Elected executives are the governor, lieutenant governor, secretary of state, auditor, treasurer, and attorney general, all of whom serve four-year terms. The governor and lieutenant governor are jointly elected; each must be a US citizen, at least 30 years old, and have been a resident of Nebraska for five years. After serving two consecutive terms, the governor is ineligible for the office for four years. In 1996 the governor's salary was $65,000.

A bill becomes law when passed by a majority of the legislature and signed by the governor. If the governor does not approve, the bill is returned with objections, and a three-fifths vote of the legislature is required to override the veto. A bill automatically becomes law if the governor does not take action within five days after receiving it.

A three-fifths majority of the legislature is required to propose an amendment to the state constitution. The people may propose an amendment by presenting a petition signed by 10% of the electorate. The amendments are then submitted for approval at the next regular election or at a special election that can be called by a four-fifths vote of the legislature.

Voters in the state must be at least 18 years of age; there is no residency requirement.

13POLITICAL PARTIES

In 1994 there were 464,955 registered Republicans, or 49% of the total number of registered voters; 389,102 registered Democrats, or 41%, and 97,897 independents, or 10%. In the 1996 elections, Republican challenger Bob Dole secured 54% of the vote; Democrat Bill Clinton, 35%; and Independent Ross

Perot, 11%. In the November 1994 elections, Democrat Bob Kerrey was re-elected to the US Senate and another Democrat, Ben Nelson, won the election for governor. In 1996, Republican Chuck Hagel won election to the Senate. Republicans won all three seats of the US House of Representatives in 1994 and 1996.

Minority elected officials as of 1994 included 6 blacks and 3 Hispanics. In 1995 there were 12 women serving in the state legislature and 1woman holding elective executive office.

Nebraska Presidential Vote by Major Political Parties, 1948–96

YEAR	ELECTORAL VOTE	NEBRASKA WINNER	DEMOCRAT	REPUBLICAN
1948	6	Dewey (R)	224,165	264,774
1952	6	*Eisenhower (R)	188,057	421,603
1956	6	*Eisenhower (R)	199,029	378,108
1960	6	Nixon (R)	232,542	380,553
1964	5	*Johnson (D)	307,307	276,847
1968	5	*Nixon (R)	170,784	321,163
1972	5	*Nixon (R)	169,991	406,298
1976	5	Ford (R)	233,692	359,705
1980	5	*Reagan (R)	166,424	419,214
1984	5	*Reagan (R)	187,866	460,054
1988	5	*Bush (R)	259,235	397,956
1992**	5	Bush (R)	217,344	344,346
1996**	5	Dole (R)	236,761	363,467

* Won US presidential election.
* * Independent candidate Ross Perot received 174,687 votes in 1992 and 71,278 votes in 1996.

14LOCAL GOVERNMENT
In 1992, Nebraska had 93 counties, 452 townships, 534 municipalities, and 797 school districts. More than 1,000 special districts covered such services as fire protection, housing, irrigation, and sewage treatment. Municipalities are governed by mayors.

15STATE SERVICES
As of 1 June 1971, the Office of Public Counsel (Ombudsman) was empowered to investigate complaints from citizens in relation to the state government. The Accountability and Disclosure Commission, established in 1977, regulates the organization and financing of political campaigns and investigates reports of conflicts of interest involving state officials.

The eight-member state Board of Education, elected on a nonpartisan basis, oversees elementary and secondary public schools and vocational education. The Board of Regents, which also consists of eight elected members, governs the University of Nebraska system. Special examining boards license architects, engineers, psychologists, and land surveyors.

The Department of Roads maintains and builds highways, and the Department of Aeronautics regulates aviation, licenses airports, and registers aviators. The Department of Motor Vehicles provides vehicle and driver services.

Public assistance, child welfare, medical care for the indigent, and a special program of services for children with disabilities are the responsibility of the Health and Human Service System, which also operates community health services, provides nutritional services, and is responsible for disease control.

The state's huge agricultural industry is aided and monitored by the Department of Agriculture, which is empowered to protect livestock, inspect food-processing areas, conduct research into crop development, and encourage product marketing.

16JUDICIAL SYSTEM
The state's highest court is the supreme court, consisting of a chief justice and 6 other justices, all of whom are initially appointed by the governor. They must be elected after serving three years, and every six years thereafter, running unopposed on their own record. Below the supreme court are the district courts; 50 judges serve 21 districts in the state. These are trial courts of general jurisdiction. County courts handle criminal misdemeanors and civil cases involving less than $5,000. In addition, there are a court of industrial relations, a worker's compensation court, two conciliation courts (family courts), two municipal courts (in Omaha and Lincoln), and juvenile courts in three counties. Nebraska's crime rate is well below the national average. In 1996, there were 4,515 practicing attorneys in the state.

In 1995, prison inmates in 9 state and federal prisons numbered 2,880, a rate of 176 inmates per 100,000 inhabitants. Six persons were executed between 1930 and 1995; 10 were under sentence of death in 1995. In 1995, Nebraska had a total crime rate of 4,544.5 per 100,000, including 382 for violent crime and 4,162.5 for property crime.

17ARMED FORCES
The US military presence in the state is concentrated near Omaha, where Offutt Air Force Base serves as the headquarters of the US Strategic Air Command. Total Air Force personnel at the base in 1995/96 was 8,704. In 1996, Nebraska firms were awarded $322 million in defense contracts. In 1996, there were 9,357 active duty military personnel stationed in Nebraska.

A total of 165,000 veterans of US military service resided in Nebraska as of 1 July 1996. Of these, fewer than 500 served in World War I; 44,000 in World War II; 31,000 in the Korean conflict; 51,000 in the Vietnam era; and 12,000 in the Persian Gulf War. In 1995/96, a total of $294 million was spent on veterans benefits.

As of 1996, Nebraska had 11,486 men and women in Reserve and National Guard Units; 7,251 Army, 2,166 Navy and Marine Corps, and 2,069 Air Force.

In 1993, the Nebraska State Patrol employed 485 full-time sworn officers, or 3 per 10,000 residents.

18MIGRATION
The pioneers who settled Nebraska in the 1860s consisted mainly of Civil War veterans from the North and foreign-born immigrants. Some of the settlers migrated from the East and easterly parts of the Midwest, but many came directly from Europe to farm the land. The Union Pacific and Burlington Northern railroads, which sold land to the settlers, actively recruited immigrants in Europe. Germans were the largest group to settle in Nebraska (in 1900, 65,506 residents were German-born), then Czechs from Bohemia, and Scandinavians from Sweden, Denmark, and Norway. The Irish came to work on the railroads in the 1860s and stayed to help build the cities. Another wave of Irish immigrants in the 1880s went to work in the packinghouses of Omaha. The city's stockyards also attracted Polish workers. The 1900 census showed that over one-half of all Nebraskans were either foreign-born or the children of foreign-born parents. For much of this century, Nebraska has been in a period of out-migration. From 1930 to 1960, the state suffered a net loss of nearly 500,000 people through migration, with more than one third of the total leaving during the dust-bowl decade, 1930– 40. This trend continues, with Nebraska experiencing a net out-migration of 27,400 for the period 1985–90. Between 1990 and 1996, the state had net gains of 7,690 in domestic migration and 9,532 in international migration. In 1996, 2,150 foreign immigrants arrived in Nebraska. About 70.2% of the state's residents were native-born Nebraskans in 1990. Some 56% of residents age 5 and older lived in the same house in 1990 as in 1985. About 23% of those who lived in a different house in 1985 did so in another state.

[19]INTERGOVERNMENTAL COOPERATION

Nebraska's Commission on Intergovernmental Cooperation represents the state in the Council of State Governments. As an oil-producing state, Nebraska is a member of the Interstate Compact to Conserve Oil and Gas. In addition, the state belongs to several regional commissions. Of particular importance are the Republican River Compact with Colorado and Kansas, the Big Blue River Compact with Kansas, the South Platte River Compact with Colorado, and the Upper Niobrara River Compact with Wyoming. The Nebraska Boundary Commission was authorized in 1982 to enter into negotiations to more precisely demarcate Nebraska's boundaries with Iowa, South Dakota, and Missouri. Nebraska is also a member of the Central Interstate Low-Level Radioactive Waste Compact, under which Nebraska, Kansas, Oklahoma, Louisiana, and Arkansas will ultimately locate a suitable disposal site that all compact members can share. In 1995/96, the state received over $1.2 billion in federal grants.

[20]ECONOMY

Agriculture is the backbone of Nebraska's economy, with cattle, corn, hogs, and soybeans leading the state's list of farm products. However, Nebraska is attempting to diversify its economy and has been successful in attracting new business, in large part because of its location near western coal and oil deposits.

Nearly one-half of the state's labor force is employed in agriculture, either directly or indirectly—as farm workers, as factory workers in the food-processing and farm-equipment industries, or as providers of related services. The service sector, which includes not only the servicing of equipment but also the high growth areas of health and business services and telemarketing, expanded at an annual rate of 4.4 percent in between 1980 and 1990. The total gross state product in 1994 was $41,357 million, to which private goods-producing industries contributed $11,311 million; private services-producing industries, $23,856 million; and government, $6,190 million. Unemployment, generally well below the national average, was only 5.7 percent in 1983 and 4.4 percent in 1984. By 1992, it had dropped to 2.9 percent. Nebraska's per capita income in 1991 was $17,780, although that figure masks as disparity between the standard of living in the metropolitan and rural areas. The average per capita income of metropolitan communities was $19,071, whereas rural counties had an average per capita income of $16,472. In 1995, Nebraska's per capita personal income was $21,477, which ranked 27th nationally. In 1996, there were 5,304 filings for bankruptcy, up 40% from the previous year.

[21]INCOME

Nebraska's per capita personal income was $23,047 in 1996, giving the state a rank of 24th in the nation. Total disposable personal income rose to $33.3 billion in 1996, from $30.9 billion in 1995.

In 1995, 9.6% of the state's population were living below the federal poverty level. Median income of all households in Nebraska in 1996 was $32,929.

[22]LABOR

Nebraska's nonfarm labor force has increased rapidly in recent decades. The labor force totaled 896,634 in 1995, of which 23,717 were unemployed. Based on the 1990 Census, 61% of all women were in the state's labor force.

In 1995, nonfarm employment and wages (in millions of dollars) for Nebraska were as follows:

	EARNINGS	EMPLOYMENT (1,000s)
Total	17,768.2	793.6
Private	14,216.4	649.8
Agricultural services, forestry, fisheries	181.6	10.6
Mining	33.3	1.3
Construction	900.7	34.6
Manufacturing	3,120.0	112.0
Transportation, public utilities	1,181.0	39.4
Wholesale trade	1,395.4	53.2
Retail trade	1,834.1	151.5
Finance, insurance, and real estate	1,468.6	50.5
Services	4,101.6	196.8
Government	3,551.7	143.8

There were approximately 40 national labor unions operating in the state in 1996; membership in unions totaled 65,400 in 1995, or 9.1% of workers. Nebraska has a right-to-work law.

[23]AGRICULTURE

With total cash receipts from farm marketings at $8.7 billion in 1995, Nebraska ranked 4th among the 50 states. That same year, it ranked 7th among the states in farm industry income ($1.6 billion). About $5.2 billion of all farm marketings came from livestock production, and $3.5 billion from cash crops.

Territorial Nebraska was settled by homesteaders. Farmers easily adapted to the land and the relatively rainy eastern region, and corn soon became their major crop. In the drier central and western prairie regions, settlers were forced to learn new farming methods to conserve moisture in the ground. Droughts in the 1890s provided impetus for water conservation. Initially, oats and spring wheat were grown along with corn, but by the end of the 19th century, winter wheat became the main wheat crop. The drought and dust storms of the 1930s, which devastated the state's agricultural economy, once again drove home the need for water and soil conservation. In 1995, a total of 8.1 million acres (3.3 million hectares) were irrigated, a 6.6% increase from 1982. In 1996, there were 56,000 farms covering 47 million acres (19 million hectares). The average farm was about 839 acres (340 hectares) in 1996.

Crop production in 1996 (in bushels) included: corn, 1.19 billion; sorghum grain, 97.8 million; wheat, 73.5 million; soybeans, 135.4 million; oats, 7.5 million; barley, 901,000; and rye, 418,000. Hay production was 7.4 million tons; and potato production, 5.9 million hundredweight, (267.6 million kg). In 1996, Nebraska ranked 3d among the states in production of corn for grain and sorghum for grain; 5th in winter wheat; and 7th in soybeans.

Farms in Nebraska are major businesses requiring large land holdings to justify investments. The value of the average farm in 1995 was $667,436, up from $590,929 in 1992, but down from $698,270 in 1982. Nebraska farms still tend to be owned by single persons or families rather than by large corporations. The strength of state support for the family farm was reflected in the passage of a 1982 constitutional amendment, initiated by petition, prohibiting the purchase of Nebraska farm and ranch lands by other than a Nebraska family farm corporation.

[24]ANIMAL HUSBANDRY

In 1991, Nebraska ranked 2d behind Texas in the US in number of cattle and calves marketed (5,508,000 head) and ranked 1st in commercial cattle slaughter (6,310,000 head). In 1991, Nebraska had a total of 6,000,000 cattle on farms, including 100,000 milk cows. Nebraska's hog-raising business is the nation's 4th largest. The state had 4.4 million hogs in 1991 and 120,000 sheep and lambs. Dairy products included 1.2 billion lb of milk in 1991.

In 1997, Nebraska ranked 2d, tied with Kansas behind Texas, in the number of cattle and calves (6.55 million head), which was valued at nearly $3.7 billion. Nebraska farmers had around 3.6 million hogs and pigs, valued at $342 million in 1996. During 1995, the state produced an estimated 11.6 million lb (5.3 million kg) of sheep and lambs, which grossed $11 million in income for Nebraska farmers. Dairy products included 1.095 billion lb (0.5 billion kg) of milk produced from around 74,000 milk cows in 1995.

25FISHING

Commercial fishing is negligible in Nebraska. The US Fish and Wildlife Service maintained 87 public fishing areas and apportioned nearly $2.5 million for sport fish restoration programs in 1995/96, when the state had 233,841 fishing-license holders. The North Platte and Valentine State Fish Hatcheries provide fish for anglers; federal hatcheries distributed over 36,100 fish and 362,750 fish eggs within the state in 1995/96.

26FORESTRY

Arbor Day, now observed throughout the US, originated in Nebraska in 1872 as a way of encouraging tree planting in the sparsely forested state. Forestland occupies 1,129,000 acres (457,000 hectares), or 2% of all Nebraska. Ash, boxelder, hackberry, cottonwood, honey locust, red and bur oaks, walnut, elm, and willow trees are common to eastern and central Nebraska, while ponderosa pine, cottonwood, eastern red cedar, and Rocky Mountain juniper prevail in the west. The state's two national forests—Nebraska and Samuel R. McKelvie—are actually primarily grassland and are managed for livestock grazing. The two national forests contain 46,000 acres (18,600 hectares) of forestland, including 16,000 acres (6,500 hectares) of planted forest.

27MINING

The value of nonfuel mineral production in Nebraska in 1995 was approximately $142 million, a decrease of about $4 million from the 1994 value of $146 million. This followed a 16% gain in value from 1993 to 1994. Nebraska accounted for about 0.5% of the national total value of nonfuel minerals produced in 1995.

All nonfuel minerals produced in Nebraska, with the exception of gemstones, were basic construction materials and production continued to reflect construction trends in the state. Most clay mining occurs in the southeast region, but sand and gravel mining takes place throughout the state. Industrial sand was used in the production of glass and had some applications outside of construction activities.

In 1995, 16 million metric tons of sand and gravel were mined, for a value of $55.2 million. That same year, 6.6 million metric tons of crushed stone and 222 metric tons of clay were mined, with values of $39.6 and $1.03 million, respectively. Nebraska ranked 41st nationally in the production of nonfuel mineral resources.

Mining employment in December 1996 was 1,200.

28ENERGY AND POWER

Total energy consumed in Nebraska in 1995 was an all-time record of 591.5 trillion Btu (149 trillion kcal). Of this amount, 222.2 trillion Btu (56 trillion kcal) were derived from petroleum, the leading fuel type; 134.1 trillion Btu (33.8 trillion kcal) came from natural gas, the chief fuel for heating homes and businesses; and 178.7 trillion Btu (45 trillion kcal) came from coal, 172 trillion Btu (43.3 trillion kcal) of it used by electric-generating units. Nuclear sources accounted for a total of 79.9 trillion Btu (20.1 trillion kcal), all of it consumed by electric utilities; and hydroelectricity, for 14.7 trillion Btu (3.7 trillion kcal). Altogether, slightly more than 43% of all energy was used to generate electricity, and 29% was used by the transportation sector. An estimated 3% of all the energy used in 1995 in Nebraska came from renewable sources, primarily hydropower and biomass in the form of ethanol.

Nebraska is the only state with an electric power system owned by the public through regional, cooperative, and municipal systems. The state's installed capacity was 5.6 million kW in 1995, when electricity generation totaled 25.3 billion kWh, a new all-time record. Electricity from coal accounted for 63.6% of the total (16.4 billion kWh). Nuclear power generation (at Brownville and Fort Calhoun) accounted for 29.6% (7.5 billion kWh), hydropower generation accounted for 5.6% (1.4 million kWh), and less than 1% of the electricity was produced from natural gas or oil units.

About 55.9% of all electricity in 1995 was sold for commercial and industrial use, 37% for residential use, and the remaining 7.1% for other uses.

Crude oil production in 1995 in Nebraska was 3.8 million barrels, a new modern-day low. Oil is produced in 17 counties, primarily in the southwest and panhandle areas of the state. Estimated consumption in 1995 totaled 41.2 million barrels. In 1995, natural-gas production in Nebraska totaled 2.2 billion cu ft (62 million cu m), less than 2% of the natural gas consumed in 1995. Nebraska, which has no commercial coal industry, used 10.4 million tons of coal in 1995, most of it for electric utilities.

29INDUSTRY

Nebraska has a small but growing industrial sector. In 1987, there were 1,876 manufacturing establishments with 90,700 employees, but only 631 employed more than 20 workers. By 1991, manufacturing employment totaled 100,500 with a payroll of $2.3 billion. The value of shipments for manufactured goods for Nebraska in 1995 was $4,898,500,000.

The following table shows value of shipments by manufacturers in selected industries in 1995:

Food and food products	$12,324,500,000
Industrial machinery and equipment	1,685,600,000
Electronic and other electric equipment	1,348,300,000
Transportation equipment	1,216,200,000
Chemicals and allied products	1,158,800,000
Instruments and related products	1,157,100,000

More than one-third (627) of all manufacturing establishments in Nebraska in 1987 were in the Omaha metropolitan area, including ConAgra, the nation's largest flour miller and a producer of broiler chickens and crop-protection chemicals. Other manufacturing centers are Lincoln (237 establishments) and the Sioux City, Iowa, metropolitan area in Nebraska (18 establishments). As of 1997, there were 6 Fortune 500 companies headquartered in Nebraska. In 1995, there were 169 US patents issued to Nebraska residents.

30COMMERCE

In 1992, Nebraska had 4,035 wholesale trade establishments, with sales of $32.5 billion. In 1994, Nebraska had 4,057 wholesale trade establishments, with annual payrolls totaling $1.3 billion.

Retail sales totaled $6.2 billion in 1992, from 6,808 establishments. Automotive dealers had retail sales of $1.4 billion that year; food stores, $1.3 billion; and general merchandise stores, $737 million. In 1994, Nebraska's 11,565 retail establishments had total annual payrolls of $1.6 billion. The automotive sector accounted for 18.4% of the total payrolls; food stores, 14.2%.

Nebraska's exports of goods produced within the state totaled $1.9 billion in 1996.

31CONSUMER PROTECTION

Nebraska has no separate state agency in charge of consumer protection. The Office of the Attorney General has a Consumers Protection Division. The Nebraska Public Service Commission regulates railroads, telephone companies, motor transport companies, and other common carriers operating in the state.

32BANKING

As of 31 December 1995 there were 336 insured commercial banks in Nebraska. That same year, state banks had assets of $26.7 billion and deposits of $22.6 billion, with $3.5 billion in demand deposits and $12.0 billion in time deposits.

There were 14 savings institutions in the state as of 31 December 1995. Total assets amounted to over $8.7 billion; $5.8 billion in mortgage loans were outstanding.

33INSURANCE

The insurance industry is important in Nebraska's economy. The major company in the state is Mutual of Omaha.

Twenty-eight life insurance companies were based in the state in 1995. In that year, 1,721,000 policies were in force, with a total value of $88.4 billion. The average amount of life insurance per family was valued at $135,200.

As of early 1995, there were 42 Nebraska-based property and liability insurance companies. The state's property and liability insurance companies earned $1.7 billion in premiums in 1995, $541 million of it from private automobile insurance. Flood insurance coverage totaled $647 million as of 1995.

34SECURITIES

The Bureau of Securities within the Department of Banking and Finance regulates the sale of securities. There are no stock exchanges in the state. Securities were sold in Nebraska by 1,037 registered broker-dealers (as of December 1996) through 34,268 listed agents; 284 investment advisory firms also were registered.

35PUBLIC FINANCE

The Nebraska state budget is prepared by the Budget Division of the Department of Administrative Services and is submitted annually by the governor to the legislature. The fiscal year runs from 1 July to 30 June. Following is a summary of annual revenues and expenditures (in thousands of dollars):

REVENUES	1991/92	1992/93	1995
Income Taxes	$ 758,032	$ 780,823	$ 864.8
Sales and Use Tax	664,202	653,455	1,187.4
Other Taxes	114,229	133,066	167.5
Charges for Services	44,440	47,965	539.9
Investment Income	36,396	24,320	419.7
Other	18,597	27,331	321.1
TOTAL REVENUES	$ 2,793,747	$ 2,866,992	$4,614.6
Other Financing Sources	44,289	38,795	
TOTAL	$ 2,838,036	$ 2,905,787	
EXPENDITURES			
Current:			
General Government	$ 69,351	$ 70,275	$119.2
Natural Resources Conservation	51,027	55,860	128.0
Culture-Recreation	13,755	14,501	19.5
Education	628,539	653,332	1,439.6
Health and Social Services	891,526	967,959	1,360.2
Public Safety	120,773	109,404	125.5
Transportation	477,160	511,154	544.5
Capital Projects	4,639	10,552	480.1
Debt Service	1,201	1,221	83.5
Other			430.7
TOTAL EXPENDITURES	$ 2,508,010	$ 2,614,905	$4,250.4

Nebraska's Constitution prohibits the state from incurring debt in excess of $100,000. However, there is a provision in the Constitution that permits the issuance of revenue bonds for highway and water conservation and management structure construction. At 30 June 1996, there was no outstanding debt for either of these purposes.

There are $10 million of bonds payable by a separate legal entity that has been blended into the financial activity of the state. These bonds do not represent a general obligation of the state and are secured by revenues from the equipment that the debt was incurred to purchase.

The Constitution also authorizes the Board of Regents of the University of Nebraska, the Board of Trustees of the Nebraska State Colleges, and the State Board of Education to issue revenue bonds to construct, purchase, or remodel educational buildings and facilities. The payment of these bonds is generally made from revenue collected from use of the buildings and facilities. At 30 June 1996, $64.9 million of bonds were outstanding.

The Legislature has authorized the creation of two financing authorities that are not subject to state Constitutional restrictions on the incurrence of debt. These financing authorities were organized to assist in providing funds for the construction of capital improvement projects at the colleges and the University. At 30 June 1996, these authorities had $48.7 million outstanding. Although the state has no legal responsibility for the debt of these financing authorities, they are considered part of the reporting entity.

36TAXATION

A constitutional amendment in 1967 prohibited the use of property tax revenues for state government. This forced the passage of both a sales and use tax and an income tax, which had long been resisted by fiscal conservatives in the state. The sales and use tax became effective in 1967, the income tax in 1968.

State income tax in 1996 was between 2.62% and 6.99%. The corporate tax was 5.58% of the first $50,000 income and 7.81% of income over $50,000, based on federal tax liability for Nebraska operations. The state sales tax was 5.0%.

Nebraska's federal income tax burden in 1996 was $7.4 billion, or $4,565 per capita, and the state's share of federal funding was $7.6 billion, or $4,698 per capita.

37ECONOMIC POLICY

The Department of Economic Development was created in 1967 to plan, promote, and develop the economy of the state. Nebraska offers loans for businesses which create or maintain employment for persons of low and moderate income. It provides tax credits to companies which increase investment and add jobs.

38HEALTH

There were 23,221 live births in the state in 1995, or 14.4 per 1,000 population. Infant mortality in 1995 was 7.4 per 1,000 live births. There were 5,214 abortions performed in the state in 1996, a ratio of 222 per 1,000 live births. The death rate in 1995 was 9.5 per 1,000 population.

A total of 168,469 discharges were documented from 101 hospitals in 1995. Hospital personnel included 7,469 registered nurses in 1995, and 2,260 licensed practical nurses in 1992. University Hospital and University of Nebraska Medical Center are in Omaha. The average expense to a hospital in the state per inpatient day was $546 in 1991. There were 3,548 physicians working in Nebraska in 1994. The personal health expenditure for Nebraska was $2,332, 12% less than the national average of 1991. At least 10% of Nebraska residents were uninsured in 1994. That year, 11 Nebraska counties were each without an active physician in patient care. In 1993, licensed, active dentists in the state numbered 1,026. The overall smoking rate in

Nebraska during 1995 was 21.1% of all adults over 18 years. An estimated 35,492 smoking-related deaths are predicted for the 110,913 persons who will become smokers (1995). Major causes of death per 100,000 residents in 1995 were heart disease (316.7), cancer (209.4), cerebrovascular diseases (72.2), pneumonia (39.3), accidents and adverse effects (35.4), and suicide (11.5). In 1995 the AIDS prevalence rate was 6.84 per 100,000, much lower than the US average.

39SOCIAL WELFARE

In 1996, 38,600 Nebraskans received an average monthly payment of $435 under the Aid to Families with Dependent Children (AFDC) program. In 1996, 101,625 persons received monthly food stamp allowances averaging $63.55, and the student lunch program received total federal funding of $30 million. A total of 281,640 residents received Social Security benefits averaging $709 a month in 1995; additionally, 21,326 Nebraskans received Supplementary Security Income assistance averaging $306 a month. Unemployment benefits had an average weekly benefit of $156.89 in 1995.

With the enactment of the Personal Responsibility and Work Opportunity Reconciliation Act of 1996, the US government has changed the form and regulations for many of its social welfare programs; most significantly, it replaces Aid to Families with Dependent Children (AFDC), an open-ended entitlement program, with Temporary Assistance for Needy Families (TANF), a limited system of assistance funded largely through federal block grants. The reform act also impacts the food stamp program, the Supplemental Security Income program, and the child nutrition program. The law took effect on 1 July 1997 and provided $16.38 billion in block grants for fiscal years 1997–2002. The grants are to be divided among the states based on an equation involving the numbers of former AFDC recipients in each state. Because many of the bill's provisions have yet to be implemented into state-by-state policy, it was not possible to include the details of each state's programs for this edition of this work.

40HOUSING

In 1996, there were some 690,000 housing units in Nebraska, 621,000 of which were occupied. In 1990, 81% of all housing units were linked to public sewers, 83% obtained water from public systems or private companies rather than wells, and 99.2% had complete plumbing facilities. In 1996, 10,091 privately owned units, valued at $681 million, were authorized for construction; of these, 5,717 were single-family. Median value for owner-occupied homes was $50,400 in 1990, when owners with a mortgage had a median monthly cost of $610. Renters had a median cost of $348 per month. During 1995/96, Nebraska received $119.4 million in aid from the US Department of Housing and Urban Development, including $31.3 million in community development block grants.

41EDUCATION

In 1997–97, there were 1,333 public schools in Nebraska: 964 were elementary schools, 349 were secondary schools, and 20 were special education schools. Public school enrollments for 1996–97 were elementary, 156,441; and secondary, 134,449; with a total public-school enrollment of 290,890 (pre-kindergarten through 12th grade).

In 1993–94, Nebraska had 261 nonpublic schools: 211 were elementary schools, 47 were secondary schools, and 3 were special education schools. Nonpublic school enrollments for 1996–97 were elementary, 26,609; and secondary, 15,185; with a total nonpublic-school enrollment of 41,794 (pre-kindergarten through 12th grade).

The University of Nebraska is the state's largest postsecondary institution, with campuses in Kearney, Lincoln, and Omaha. In 1996–97, there were also 3 state colleges, 17 independent colleges and universities, and 6 community colleges. In fall 1996, 23,887 students were enrolled at the University of Nebraska-Lincoln; 14,974 at the University of Nebraska-Omaha; 7,680 at University Omaha; 8,507 at the three state colleges; 19,651 at independent institutions of higher learning; and 41,761 at community colleges.

42ARTS

The 15-member Nebraska Arts Council, appointed by the governor, is empowered to receive federal and state funds and to plan and administer statewide and special programs in all the arts. Funds are available for arts education, organizational support, multicultural arts projects, special arts-related programs, touring, and fellowships. Affiliation with the Mid-America Arts Alliance allows the council to help sponsor national and regional events.

The Nebraska Arts Council budget from fiscal years 1992 through 1996 has remained at approximately $1.9 million annually, with one-quarter of that amount generated federally from the National Endowment for the Arts, and the remainder from state contributions and private sources. Over $1.6 million is regranted annually to arts programs and technical assistance in Nebraska.

In fiscal year 1996, the NAC administered over 540 grant applications from communities, schools, and individuals. Sixty grants supported 175 artist residencies, which utilized 150 artists and reached 198,143 students and community members, including 29,000 students of color. In addition, 60 grants for multicultural awareness arts projects impacted 103,339 persons of color; and 52 grants were awarded to rural communities for presenting 104 Nebraska performing and visual artists to audiences totaling over 40,000.

The state of Nebraska supports over 20 major art museums and art centers, 15 professional orchestras and ensembles, dance companies, opera, and theaters, and maintains over 100 local arts presenters, community theaters and volunteer exhibition spaces. Nebraska's not-for-profit arts activities is a $26-million-dollar industry annually.

43LIBRARIES AND MUSEUMS

The Nebraska Library Commission coordinates library services. In 1997, the state had 9 county libraries, and 270 public libraries. A total of 4,886,399 volumes were in the public library system in 1995; total circulation was 10,011,376.

The Joslyn Art Museum in Omaha is the state's leading museum. Other important museums include the Nebraska State Museum of History, the University of Nebraska State Museum (natural history), and the Sheldon Memorial Art Gallery, all in Lincoln; the Western Heritage Museum in Omaha; the Stuhr Museum of the Prairie Pioneer in Grand Island; and the Hastings Museum in Hastings. In all, the state had 102 museums in 1997. The Agate Fossil Beds National Monument in northwestern Nebraska features mammal fossils from the Miocene era and a library of paleontological and geologic material.

44COMMUNICATIONS

Telephone service is regulated by the Public Service Commission. About 97.4% of the state's 625,000 occupied housing units had telephones in March 1993.

In 1996, 84 FM stations and 50 AM stations were operating. There were 18 commercial TV stations, and a network of 9 PBS stations. In 1996, 3 large cable television systems operated in the state.

45PRESS

In 1997, Nebraska had 5 morning dailies, 12 evening dailies, and 7 Sunday newspapers. The leading newspaper in 1997 was the *Omaha World–Herald*, with a daily circulation of 232,336 and a Sunday circulation of 292,682. The *Lincoln Journal–Star* had a daily circulation of 78,098 and a Sunday circulation of 84,382.

46ORGANIZATIONS

The 1992 Census of Service Industries counted 787 organizations in Nebraska, including 147 business associations; 465 civic, social, and fraternal associations; and 175 other membership organizations. Among the organizations based in Nebraska are the Great Plains Council at the University of Nebraska (Lincoln), the American Shorthorn Society (Omaha), the Morse Telegraph Club (Lincoln), and the National Arbor Day Foundation (Nebraska City).

47TOURISM, TRAVEL, AND RECREATION

Expenditures by travelers in the state totaled about $1.6 billion in 1990. The 8 state parks, 9 state historical parks, 12 federal areas, and 55 recreational areas are main tourist attractions; fishing, swimming, picnicking, and sight-seeing are the principal activities. Pawnee State Recreation Area and Fremont State Recreation Area are the most popular attractions. In 1995, licenses were held by 255,133 fishers and 404,717 hunters.

48SPORTS

There are no major league professional sports teams in Nebraska. Minor league baseball's Omaha Royals play in the Triple-A American Association. The most popular spectator sport is college football. Equestrian activities, including racing and rodeos, are popular. Major annual sporting events are the NCAA College Baseball World Series and the World's Championship Rodeo, both held in Omaha. Parimutuel racing is licensed by the state.

The University of Nebraska Cornhuskers compete in the Big 12 conference. The football team often places high in national rankings and was named National Champion in 1970 (with Texas), 1971, 1994, and 1995. The Cornhuskers won the Orange Bowl in 1964, 1971, 1972, 1973, 1983, 1995, and 1997; the Cotton Bowl in 1974 (January); the Sugar Bowl in 1974 (December), 1985, and 1987; the Bluebonnet Bowl in 1976; the Liberty Bowl in 1977; the Sun Bowl in 1980; and the Fiesta Bowl in 1996.

The Nebraska basketball team won the National Invitational Tournament in 1996.

49FAMOUS NEBRASKANS

Nebraska was the birthplace of only one US president, Gerald R. Ford (Leslie King, Jr., b.1913). When Spiro Agnew resigned the vice-presidency in October 1973, President Richard M. Nixon appointed Ford, then a US representative from Michigan, to the post. Upon Nixon's resignation on 9 August 1974, Ford became the first nonelected president in US history.

Four native and adoptive Nebraskans have served in the cabinet. J. Sterling Morton (b.New York, 1832–1902), who originated Arbor Day, was secretary of agriculture under Grover Cleveland. William Jennings Bryan (b.Illinois, 1860–1925), a US representative from Nebraska, served as secretary of state and was three times the unsuccessful Democratic candidate for president. Frederick A. Seaton (b.Washington, 1909–74) was Dwight Eisenhower's secretary of the interior, and Melvin Laird (b.1922) was Richard Nixon's secretary of defense.

George W. Norris (b.Ohio, 1861–1944), the "fighting liberal," served 10 years in the US House of Representatives and 30 years in the Senate. Norris's greatest contributions were in rural electrification (his efforts led to the creation of the Tennessee Valley Authority), farm relief, and labor reform; he also promoted the unicameral form of government in Nebraska. Theodore C. Sorensen (b.1928) was an adviser to President John F. Kennedy.

Indian leaders important in Nebraska history include Oglala Sioux chiefs Red Cloud (1822–1909) and Crazy Horse (1849?–77). Moses Kinkaid (b.West Virginia, 1854–1920) served in the US House and was the author of the Kinkaid Act, which encouraged homesteading in Nebraska. Educator and legal scholar Roscoe Pound (1870–1964) was also a Nebraskan. In agricultural science, Samuel Aughey (b.Pennsylvania, 1831–1912) and Hardy W. Campbell (b.Vermont, 1850–1937) developed dry-land farming techniques. Botanist Charles E. Bessey (b.Ohio, 1845–1915) encouraged forestation. Father Edward Joseph Flanagan (b.Ireland, 1886–1948) was the founder of Boys Town, a home for underprivileged youth. Two native Nebraskans became Nobel laureates in 1980: Lawrence R. Klein (b.1920) in economics and Val L. Fitch (b.1923) in physics.

Writers associated with Nebraska include Willa Cather (b.Virginia, 1873–1947), who used the Nebraska frontier setting of her childhood in many of her writings and won a Pulitzer Prize in 1922; author and poet John G. Neihardt (b.Illinois, 1881–1973), who incorporated Indian mythology and history in his work; Mari Sandoz (1901–66), who wrote of her native Great Plains; writer-photographer Wright Morris (b.1910); and author Tillie Olsen (b.1912). Rollin Kirby (1875–1952) won three Pulitzer Prizes for political cartooning. Composer-conductor Howard Hanson (1896–1982), born in Wahoo, won a Pulitzer Prize in 1944.

Nebraskans important in entertainment include actor-dancer Fred Astaire (Fred Austerlitz, 1899–1984); actors Harold Lloyd (1894–1971), Henry Fonda (1905–82), Robert Taylor (Spangler Arlington Brugh, (1911–69), Marlon Brando (b.1924), and Sandy Dennis (1937–93); television stars Johnny Carson (b.Iowa, 1925) and Dick Cavett (b.1936); and motion-picture producer Darryl F. Zanuck (1902–79).

50BIBLIOGRAPHY

Creigh, Dorothy Weyer. *Nebraska: A Bicentennial History.* New York: Norton, 1977.

Federal Writers' Project. 1993. *Nebraska: A Guide to the Cornhusker State.* Reprint, New York: Somerset, n.d.

Hanna, Robert. *Sketches of Nebraska.* Lincoln: University of Nebraska Press, 1984.

Luebke, Frederick C. *Nebraska: An Illustrated History.* Lincoln: University of Nebraska Press, 1995.

Olson, James C., and Ronald C. Naugle. *History of Nebraska.* 3d ed. Lincoln: University of Nebraska Press, 1997.

State of Nebraska. Department of Economic Development. *Nebraska Statistical Handbook, 1993–1994.* Lincoln, 1994.

Wishart, David J. *An Unspeakable Sadness: The Dispossession of the Nebraska Indians.* Lincoln: University of Nebraska Press, 1994.

NEVADA

State of Nevada

ORIGIN OF STATE NAME: Named for the Sierra Nevada, *nevada* meaning "snow-covered" in Spanish. **NICKNAME:** The Silver State. (Also: The Sagebrush State.) **CAPITAL:** Carson City. **ENTERED UNION:** 31 October 1864 (36th). **SONG:** "Home Means Nevada." **MOTTO:** All for Our Country. **FLAG:** On a blue field, two sprays of sagebrush and a golden scroll in the upper lefthand corner frame a silver star encircled by the word "Nevada"; the scroll, reading "Battle Born," recalls that Nevada was admitted to the Union during the Civil War. **OFFICIAL SEAL:** An ore-crushing mill, ore cart, and mine tunnel symbolize Nevada's mining industry; a plow, sickle, and sheaf of wheat represent its agricultural resources. In the background are a railroad, a telegraph line, and a sun rising over the mountains. Encircling this scene are 36 stars and the state motto. The words "The Great Seal of the State of Nevada" surround the whole. **ANIMAL:** Desert bighorn sheep. **BIRD:** Mountain bluebird. **FISH:** Lahontan cutthroat trout. **FLOWER:** Sagebrush. **TREE:** Bristlecone pine and single-leaf pinon. **GRASS:** Indian ricegrass. **METAL:** Silver. **FOSSIL:** Ichthyosaur. **LEGAL HOLIDAYS:** New Year's Day, 1 January; Birthday of Martin Luther King, Jr., 3d Monday in January; Washington's Birthday, 3d Monday in February; Memorial Day, last Monday in May; Independence Day, 4 July; Labor Day, 1st Monday in September; Nevada Day, 31 October; Veterans Day, 11 November; Thanksgiving Day, 4th Thursday in November; Christmas Day, 25 December. **TIME:** 4 AM PST = GMT.

¹LOCATION, SIZE, AND EXTENT

Situated between the Rocky Mountains and the Sierra Nevada in the western US, Nevada ranks 7th in size among the 50 states.

The total area of Nevada is 110,561 sq mi (286,352 sq km), with land comprising 109,894 sq mi (284,624 sq km) and inland water covering 667 sq mi (1,728 sq km). Nevada extends 320 mi (515 km) E-W; the maximum N-S extension is 483 mi (777 km).

Nevada is bordered on the N by Oregon and Idaho; on the E by Utah and Arizona (with the line in the SE formed by the Colorado River); and on the S and W by California (with part of the line passing through Lake Tahoe). The total boundary length of Nevada is 1,480 mi (2,382 km). The state's geographic center is in Lander County, 26 mi (42 km) SE of Austin.

²TOPOGRAPHY

Almost all of Nevada belongs physiographically to the Great Basin, a plateau characterized by isolated mountain ranges separated by arid basins. These ranges generally trend north–south; most are short, up to 75 mi (121 km) long and 15 mi (24 km) wide, and rise to altitudes of 7,000–10,000 ft (2,100–3,000 m). Chief among them are the Schell Creek, Ruby, Toiyabe, and Carson (within the Sierra Nevada). Nevada's highest point is Boundary Peak, 13,143 feet (4,006 meters), in the southwest.

Nevada has a number of large lakes and several large saline marshes known as sinks. The largest lake is Pyramid, with an area of 188 sq mi (487 sq km), in the west. Nevada shares Lake Tahoe with California, and Lake Mead, created by Hoover Dam on the Colorado River, with Arizona. The streams of the Great Basin frequently disappear during dry spells; many of them flow into local lakes or sinks without reaching the sea. The state's longest river, the Humboldt, flows for 290 mi (467 km) through the northern half of the state into the Humboldt Sink. The Walker, Truckee, and Carson rivers drain the western part of Nevada. The canyon carved by the mighty Colorado, the river that forms the extreme southeastern boundary of the state, is the site of Nevada's lowest elevation, 470 feet (143 meters).

³CLIMATE

Nevada's climate is sunny and dry, with wide variation in daily temperatures. The normal daily temperature at Reno is 49°F (9°C), ranging from 32°F (0°C) in January to 69°F (21°C) in July. The all-time high, 125°F (52°C), was set at Laughlin on 29 June 1994; the record low, –50°F (–46°C), at San Jacinto on 8 January 1937.

Nevada is the driest state in the US, with overall average annual precipitation of less than 4 in (10 cm). Snowfall is abundant in the mountains, however, reaching 60 in (152 cm) a year on the highest peaks.

⁴FLORA AND FAUNA

Various species of pine—among them the single-leaf pinon, the state tree—dominate Nevada's woodlands. Creosote bush is common in southern Nevada, as are many kinds of sagebrush throughout the state. Wildflowers include shooting star and white and yellow violets.

Native mammals include the black bear, white-tailed and mule deer, pronghorn antelope, Rocky Mountain elk, cottontail rabbit, and river otter. Grouse, partridge, pheasant, and quail are the leading game birds, and a diversity of trout, char, salmon, and whitefish thrive in Nevada waters. Rare and protected reptiles are the Gila monster and desert tortoise. Listed as endangered are the Colorado squawfish, Moapa dace, Ash Meadows speckled dace, Pahrump killifish, Ash Meadows Armagosa pupfish, Devil's Hole pupfish, Warm Springs pupfish, woundfin, and bonytail chub. The Lahoutan cutthroat trout is threatened.

⁵ENVIRONMENTAL PROTECTION

Preservation of the state's clean air, scarce water resources, and no longer abundant wildlife are the major environmental challenges facing Nevada. The Department of Fish and Game sets quotas on the hunting of deer, antelope, bighorn sheep, and other game animals. The Department of Conservation and Natural Resources has broad responsibility for environmental protection, state lands, forests, and water and mineral resources. The

Division of Environmental Protection within the department has primary responsibility for the control of air pollution, water pollution, waste management, and groundwater protection. In 1995, Nevada had only one hazardous waste site, the fewest of any state in the nation. Although wetlands cover only about 1% of the mainly barren state, they are some of the most valuable lands in the state.

⁶POPULATION

Nevada ranked 39th in the US with a 1990 census population of 1,201,833, up 50.1% from 800,493 in 1980, making it the fastest-growing state in the 1980s—the third consecutive decade in which it had a population growth rate over 50%.

A population of 1,603,163 was estimated for 1996, an increase of 33.4%. Nevada had only 110,427 residents in 1940, when the current population boom began. As might be expected, Nevadans are among the most mobile Americans; as of 1990, more than 65% of the population over age 5 had lived in a different house in 1985.

With a population density of 10.9 per sq mi (4.2 per sq km) in 1990, Nevada remains one of the nation's most sparsely populated states. More than 88% of Nevada's people live in cities, the largest of which, Las Vegas, had an estimated 327,878 residents in 1994, a 27% increase in population since 1990. Reno had an estimated population of 145,029. The greater Reno metropolitan area had an estimated 290,833 residents in 1995.

⁷ETHNIC GROUPS

Some 79,000 black Americans made up about 6.5% of Nevada's population in 1990. The American Indian population was 20,000 in 1990; tribal landholdings totaled 1,138,462 acres (460,721 hectares). Major tribes are the Washo, Northern Paiute, Southern Paiute, and Shoshoni.

Some 104,828 persons, or 8.7% of all state residents, were foreign-born in 1990. About 124,000 Nevadans were of Hispanic origin, including 72,281 of Mexican ancestry.

⁸LANGUAGES

Midland and Northern English dialects are so intermixed in Nevada that no clear regional division appears; an example of this is the scattered use of both Midland *dived* (instead of *dove*) as the past tense of *dive* and the Northern /krik/ for *creek*. In 1990, 964,298, Nevadans—86.8% of the resident population 5 years old or older—spoke only English at home. Other languages spoken at home included:

Spanish*	85,474
German	8,457
Tagalog	8,007
French	5,464
Chinese	5,204
Italian	5,335
Korean	3,324
Various Native American	2,486

* Up 138% from 1980

⁹RELIGIONS

In 1990, Nevada had 156,956 Roman Catholics. Other Christian denominations in 1990 included 89,033 adherents of the Church of Jesus Christ of Latter-day Saints (Mormons); 27,889 Southern Baptists; 6,219 Lutherans of the Missouri Synod; and 8,529 Methodists. In 1990, there were an estimated 20,400 Jews living in Nevada.

¹⁰TRANSPORTATION

As of 1996, Nevada had 1,200 rail mi (1,931 km) of railroads. Amtrak provides passenger service across northern Nevada en route from Chicago to Oakland. Total Nevada ridership in 1996 was 125,000.

In 1996 there were 44,939 mi (72,323 km) of public roads and streets. As of 1 April 1997, there were 1,398,657 registered vehicles (up 52% from 1992), and 1,173,619 licensed drivers, or about 89% of the state's driving age population. The major highways, I-80 and I-15, link Salt Lake City with Reno and Las Vegas, respectively. There were about 60 public-use airfields in 1995 and 24 heliports. The leading commercial air terminals are McCarran International Airport in Las Vegas, which handled 15.2 million enplanements in 1996, and Reno-Tahoe International Airport, with 3.2 million enplanements.

¹¹HISTORY

The first inhabitants of what is now Nevada arrived about 12,000 years ago. They were fishermen, as well as hunters and food gatherers, for the glacial lakes of the ancient Great Basin were then only beginning to recede. Numerous sites of early human habitation have been found, the most famous being Pueblo Grande de Nevada (also known as Lost City). In modern times, four principal Indian groups have inhabited Nevada: Southern Paiute, Northern Paiute, Shoshoni, and Washo.

Probably the first white explorer to enter the state was the Spanish priest Francisco Garces, who apparently penetrated extreme southern Nevada in 1776. The year 1826 saw Peter Skene Ogden of the British Hudson's Bay Company enter the northeast in a prelude to his later exploration of the Humboldt River; the rival American trapper Jedediah Smith traversed the state in 1826–27. During 1843–44, John C. Frémont led the first of his several expeditions into Nevada.

Nevada's first permanent white settlement, Mormon Station (later Genoa), was founded in 1850 in what is now western Nevada, a region that became part of Utah Territory the same year. (The southeastern tip of Nevada was assigned to the Territory of New Mexico.) Soon other Mormon settlements were started there and in Las Vegas Valley. The Las Vegas mission failed, but the farming communities to the northwest succeeded, even though friction between Mormons and placer miners in that area caused political unrest. Most of the Mormons in western Nevada departed in 1857, when Salt Lake City was threatened by an invasion of federal troops.

A separate Nevada Territory was established in 1861; only three years later, on 31 October 1864, Nevada achieved statehood, although the present boundaries were not established until 18 January 1867. Two factors accelerated the creation of Nevada: the secession of the southern states, whose congressmen had been blocking the creation of new free states, and the discovery, in 1859, of the Comstock Lode, an immense concentration of silver and gold that attracted thousands of fortune seekers and established the region as a thriving mining center.

Nevada's development during the rest of the century was determined by the economic fortunes of the Comstock, whose affairs were dominated, first, by the Bank of California (in alliance with the Central Pacific Railroad) and then by the "Bonanza Firm" of John W. Mackay and his partners. The lode's rich ores were exhausted in the late 1870s, and Nevada slipped into a 20-year depression. A number of efforts were made to revive the economy, one being an attempt to encourage mining by increasing the value of silver. To this end, Nevadans wholeheartedly supported the movement for free silver coinage during the 1890s, and the Silver Party reigned supreme in state politics for most of the decade.

Nevada's economy revived following new discoveries of silver at Tonopah and gold at Goldfield early in the 20th century. A second great mining boom ensued, bolstered and extended by major copper discoveries in eastern Nevada. Progressive political ferment in this pre–World War I period added recall, referendum,

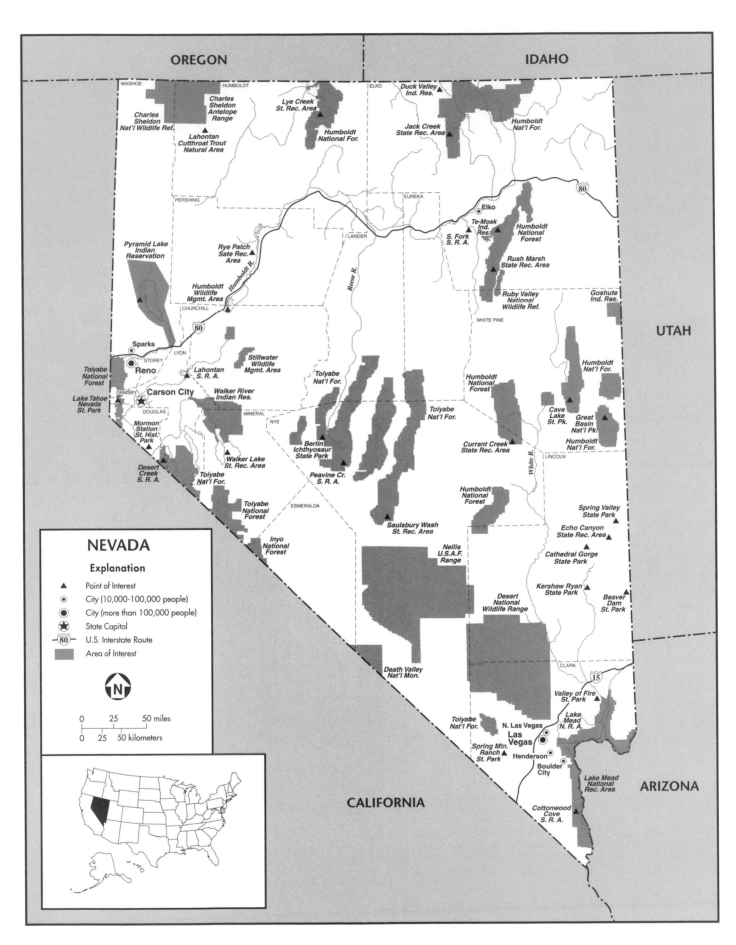

NEVADA

Explanation

▲   Point of Interest

⊙   City (10,000-100,000 people)

◉   City (more than 100,000 people)

★   State Capital

—⑧⓪—   U.S. Interstate Route

▨   Area of Interest

Ⓝ

0   25   50 miles

0   25   50 kilometers

and initiative amendments to the state constitution and brought about the adoption of women's suffrage (1914).

The 1920s was a time of subdued economic activity; mining fell off, and not even the celebrated divorce trade, centered in Reno, was able to compensate for its decline. Politically, the decade was conservative and Republican, with millionaire George Wingfield dominating state politics through a so-called bipartisan machine. Nevada went Democratic during the 1930s, when the hard times of the Depression were alleviated by federal public-works projects, most notably the construction of the Hoover (Boulder) Dam, and by state laws aiding the divorce business and legalizing gambling.

Gaming grew rapidly after World War II, becoming by the mid-1950s not only the mainstay of Nevada tourism but also the state's leading industry. Revelations during the 1950s and 1960s that organized crime had infiltrated the casino industry and that casino income was being used to finance narcotics and other rackets in major East Coast cities led to a state and federal crackdown and the imposition of new state controls.

From 1960 to 1980, Nevada was the fastest-growing of the 50 states, increasing its population by 70% in the 1960s and 64% in the 1970s. In the mid-eighties the state's population growth continued to outpace that of the nation, reaching 14% in the first half of the eighties in contrast to the national average of 4%. Much of this growth was associated with expansion of the gambling industry—centered in the casinos of Las Vegas and Reno—and of the military. In the 1980s, Nevada began to try to reduce its dependence on gambling by diversifying its economy. In an attempt to attract new businesses, particularly in the high-tech industry, the state promoted such features as its absence of state, corporate, or personal income taxes, inexpensive real estate, low wages, and its ready access by air or land to California.

In the first half of the 1990s, Nevada was once again the nation's fastest growing state, increasing its population by nearly 25%. Efforts to diversify the state's economy yielded results as its industrial base expanded. In the early 1990s, Nevada was the only state reporting an increase in manufacturing jobs. Nevadans' opposition to the Yucca Mountain nuclear waste disposal site, first proposed by Congress in 1987, continued into the 1990s. However, in 1991 the US Supreme Court ordered the state to authorize a feasibility study of the site, and preliminary preparations for excavation were begun in 1993.

12STATE GOVERNMENT

Nevada's 1864 constitution, as amended, continues to govern the state. The state legislature consists of a senate with 21 members, each elected to a four-year term, and a house of representatives with 42 members, each serving two years. The legislative salary was $130 per diem during regular sessions in 1995. Executive officials elected statewide include the governor and lieutenant governor (who run separately), secretary of state, attorney general, treasurer, and controller, all of whom serve for four years. In 1996 the governor's salary was $90,000. A two-thirds vote of the elected members of each house is required to override a gubernatorial veto.

Constitutional amendments may be submitted to the voters for ratification if they have received majority votes in each house in two successive sessions or under an initiative procedure calling for petitions signed by 10% of those who voted in the last general election. Legislative amendments need a majority vote; initiative amendments require majorities in two consecutive elections. Voters must be US citizens, be at least 18 years old, and have lived in the state for 30 days.

13POLITICAL PARTIES

Since World War II neither the Democrats nor the Republicans have dominated state politics, which are basically conservative. There are 295,111 registered Democrats, comprising 45% of the electorate, 255,897 registered Republicans, or 39%; and 98,897 independents, or 15%. In 1992, after choosing Republicans in each of the previous eight presidential elections, Nevadans elected Democrat Bill Clinton with 37% of the vote. In 1996 Clinton won 44% of the vote, while Republican Bob Dole won 43%, and Independent Ross Perot received 9%. Nevada was represented in the US Congress by two Democratic senators—Richard Bryan, reelected in 1994, and Harry Reid elected in 1992. Following the 1996 elections, both of Nevada's US Representatives are Republicans. Democrat Robert J. Miller, formerly lieutenant governor, was elected to the governorship in 1990 and reelected in 1994. In 1997 there were 12 Republicans and 9 Democrats in the state senate and 25 Democrats and 17 Republicans in the state house. Minorities in elective office in 1994 included 10 blacks and 4 Hispanics. There were 22 women serving in the state legislature in 1995 and one woman holding elective executive office.

Nevada Presidential Vote by Major Political Parties, 1948–96

YEAR	ELECTORAL VOTE	NEVADA WINNER	DEMOCRAT	REPUBLICAN
1948	3	*Truman (D)	31,290	29,357
1952	3	*Eisenhower (R)	31,688	50,502
1956	3	*Eisenhower (R)	40,640	56,049
1960	3	*Kennedy (D)	54,880	52,387
1964	3	*Johnson (D)	79,339	56,094
1968	3	*Nixon (R)	60,598	73,188
1972	3	*Nixon (R)	66,016	115,750
1976	3	Ford (R)	92,479	101,273
1980	3	*Reagan (R)	66,666	155,017
1984	4	*Reagan (R)	91,655	188,770
1988	4	*Bush (R)	132,738	206,040
1992**	4	*Clinton (D)	189,148	175,828
1996**	4	*Clinton (D)	203,974	199,244

* Won US presidential election.
** Independent candidate Ross Perot received 132,580 votes in 1992 and 43,986 votes in 1996.

14LOCAL GOVERNMENT

As of 1992, Nevada was subdivided into 16 counties, 1 independent municipality (Carson City), and 16 other municipalities constituting the 16 county seats. The state had 17 school districts and 156 special districts.

15STATE SERVICES

The Executive Ethics Commission was created in 1977 to oversee financial disclosure by state officials. The Department of Education and the University of Nevada System are the main state educational agencies. The Department of Human Resources has divisions covering public health, rehabilitation, mental hygiene and mental retardation, welfare, youth services, and programs for the elderly. Regulatory functions are exercised by the Commerce Department (insurance, banking, consumer affairs, real estate), the Public Service Commission, the Gaming Control Board, and other state agencies.

16JUDICIAL SYSTEM

Nevada's supreme court consists of a chief justice and 4 other justices. There are 38 district court judges organized into nine judicial districts. All judges are elected by nonpartisan ballot to six-year terms. In 1996 there were 3,426 practicing attorneys in the state.

Nevada's overall crime rate in 1995 was 6,579.3 per 100,000 persons, including 945.2 for violent crime and 5,634.2 for property crime. The rate for murder and nonnegligent manslaughter was 10.7 per 100,000 persons; forcible rape, 61.2; robbery, 324.6; assault, 548.7; burglary, 1,322.5; larceny-theft, 3,566.2; and motor vehicle theft, 745.4.

There were 7,289 inmates in 18 state and federal correctional facilities in 1995, a rate of 476 inmates per 100,000 inhabitants. The prison population has grown by almost 30% since 1990.

Nevada has a death penalty and has executed 34 persons since 1930, 5 since 1977. In 1995, 75 persons were under sentence of death.

17 ARMED FORCES
In 1996, there were 7,802 active duty military personnel stationed in Nevada. The largest installation is the Nellis Air Force Base near Las Vegas, with 6,538 personnel. The state has been the site of both ballistic missile and atomic weapons testing. In 1995/96, Nevada firms received $285.1 million in federal defense contracts.

As of 1 July 1996, 186,000 military veterans were living in the state, including fewer than 500 from World War I, 46,000 of World War II, 36,000 of the Korean conflict, 64,000 from the Viet Nam era, and 7,000 from the Persian Gulf War. Veterans' benefits in 1995/96 totaled $257 million.

In 1996, army reserve and national guard personnel numbered 3,551, and there were 2,058 members of the air national guard at that time. In 1993, the Nevada Highway Patrol employed 330 full-time sworn officers, or 3 per 10,000 residents.

18 MIGRATION
In 1870, about half of Nevada's population consisted of foreign immigrants, among them Chinese, Italians, Swiss, British, Irish, Germans, and French Canadians. Though their origins were diverse, their numbers were few—no more than 21,000 in all. Not until the 1940s did migrants come in large volume. Between 1940 and 1980, Nevada gained a total of 507,000 residents through migration, equal to 63% of the 1980 population; there was an additional net gain from migration of 233,000 during the 1980s, accounting for 75% of the net population increase. Between 1990 and 1996, Nevada had net gains of 293,813 in domestic migration and 28,828 in international migration.

In 1990, only about 21.8% of Nevadans had been born within the state, the lowest proportion among the states. Only 35% of Nevadans age 5 and older lived in the same house in 1990 as in 1985; for those 694,739 individuals who lived in a different house in 1985, 47% did so in another state.

19 INTERGOVERNMENTAL COOPERATION
Nevada takes part in the Colorado River Compact, the Tahoe Regional Planning Compact, and the California-Nevada Interstate Compact, under which the two states administer water rights involving Lake Tahoe and the Carson, Truckee, and Walker rivers. The state also is a signatory to the Interstate Oil and Gas Compact and the Western Interstate Energy Compact. Federal aid in 1995/96 totaled $876 million.

20 ECONOMY
Nevada is disadvantaged by aridity and a shortage of arable land but blessed with a wealth of mineral resources—gold, silver, copper, and other metals. Mining remains important, though overshadowed since World War II by tourism and gambling, which generate more than 50% of the state's income. Legalized gaming alone produces nearly half of Nevada's tax revenues. Nevada's gross state product in 1994 was $43,958 million, to which private goods-producing industries contributed $6,850 million, and private services-producing industries $4,633 million.

In 1995, Nevada's per capita income was $24,390 which ranked 10th nationally. During 1996, there were 10,531 filings for bankruptcy.

21 INCOME
Personal nonfarm income in Nevada came to $40.5 billion in 1996 (up 5.8% from 1991); per capita income averaged $25,451 (10th among the states). The median family income was $36,084 in 1995. In 1995, 11.1% of all Nevadans were below the federal poverty line.

22 LABOR
Nevada's total civilian labor force in 1996 was 844,000, of whom about 46,000 (5.4%) were unemployed.

At the end of 1996 there were 376,000 Nevadans employed in services; 180,800 in wholesale and retail trade; 107,900 in government; 76,800 in construction; 43,500 in transportation, communications, and public utilities; 39,700 in manufacturing; 39,000 in finance, insurance and real estate; and 14,500 in mining.

In 1995, 3,280 manufacturing workers belonged to unions and other employee associations, with a total of 198,830 union workers in all industries. Nevada has a right-to-work law.

23 AGRICULTURE
Agricultural income in 1996 totaled $285.6 million (47th in the US), of which $122 million was from crops and $163.6 million from livestock and animal products. Chief crops in 1996 included 1.65 million bushels of wheat, 1.5 million tons of hay, and 3.16 million hundredweight of potatoes. Nevada's barley crop in 1996 was 375,000 bushels, down from 2,700,000 in 1983. Virtually all of the state's cropland requires irrigation.

24 ANIMAL HUSBANDRY
In 1997, Nevada ranches and farms had 520,000 cattle and calves, valued at $270 million. In 1995, the state produced 4.4 million lb of sheep and lambs which brought in around $5.3 million in gross income. Also during 1995, the shorn wool production was 680,000 lb of wool. Nevada's total milk yield in 1995 was 425 million lb.

25 FISHING
There is no commercial fishing industry in Nevada. The Lahontan National Fish Hatchery distributed nearly 545,500 (90,572 lb) cutthroat trout within the state in 1995/96, when the state issued 156,131 sport fishing licenses.

26 FORESTRY
Nevada in 1992 had 8,938,000 acres (3,617,000 hectares) of forestland, of which 5,150,000 acres (2,084,000 hectares) were in the National Forest System. Less than 2.5% of all forested land in Nevada was classified as commercial timberland.

27 MINING
In 1995, the value of nonfuel mineral production in Nevada was estimated at $2.92 billion, a decrease of about 4% from that reported in 1994. A 5% drop in the estimated value of gold accounted for most of the drop. Overall, Nevada accounted for 8% of the national nonfuel mineral production value. Gold production was 210,000 kg, a 2% drop over 1994's production, but silver increased by 10 metric tons to 683 metric tons. The state's mines provided 65% and 46% of the nation's gold and silver in 1995, respectively. Nevada remained the leading state in the production of gold, silver, mercury, and barite (447,000 metric tons), and second in the production of diatomite and lithium. It was the sole producer of mined magnesite, which is used in making refractories and magnesia. Nevada also ranked

4th in perlite, 5th in gypsum, 6th in kaolin, and 8th in copper. Nevada ranked 2nd among the states in 1994 production value of nonfuel minerals.

Gold remained Nevada's most valuable mineral commodity, accounting for more than 86% of the state's total nonfuel value, about $2.52 billion. Silver and construction sand and gravel were the state's next most valuable minerals ($116 and $95 million, respectively). Mining industry employment in Nevada was 14,500 in December 1996.

28ENERGY AND POWER

Nevada had an installed electrical capacity of 5,792 Mw in 1996; 20 billion kWh of power were produced in 1995. About half the electrical energy is sold in the state; the remainder is exported, principally to California. Hoover Dam, anchored in the bedrock of Black Canyon east of Las Vegas, is the state's largest hydro-electric installation, with an installed capacity of 1,037,000 kW in 1996. The first six of the dam's eight turbines came onstream during 1936–38, while the other two were added in 1944 and 1961. In 1996, total oil production was 1,058,000 barrels.

29INDUSTRY

Industry in Nevada is limited but diversified, producing communications equipment, pet food, chemicals, and sprinkler systems, among other products. The total value of shipments by manufacturers in 1995 was $5.444 billion. Major sectors and their value of shipments in 1995 were as follows:

Printing and publishing	$ 614,400,000
Food and food products	655,100,000
Industrial machinery and equipment	415,100,000
Stone, clay, glass products	619,700,000
Fabricated metal products	300,200,000
Primary metal industries	234,400,000
Chemicals and chemical products	317,400,000

In 1995, there were 228 US patents issued to Nevada residents.

30COMMERCE

Nevada had 2,075 wholesale establishments with sales of $7.8 billion in 1992, according to the Census of Wholesale Trade. Durable goods accounted for 41.3% of wholesale sales. Retail trade amounted to $11.5 billion (35th) in 1992, conducted by 7,502 establishments. Food stores led in retail sales ($2.4 billion), followed by automotive dealers ($2.3 billion), general merchandise stores ($1.5 billion), and eating and drinking places ($1.2 billion). Foreign exports in 1996 totaled $1.3 million in goods produced within the state.

31CONSUMER PROTECTION

The Consumer Affairs Division of the Department of Commerce, with offices in Las Vegas and Carson City, protects consumers from deceptive or fraudulent sales practices and represents consumers' interests in government.

32BANKING

In 1996 there were 25 insured commercial banks in Nevada, with total assets of $32.4 billion. Outstanding loans totaled $25.3 billion (1996), deposits $9.7 billion.

33INSURANCE

Nevadans held 938,000 life insurance policies in 1995 with a total value of $55.8 billion. Life insurance per family averaged $89,900 (49th), and benefit payments totaled $450 million. Property and liability insurers wrote over $1.0 billion in premiums, of which 56% was automobile coverage.

34SECURITIES

There are no securities exchanges in Nevada. As of May 1997, 1,542 brokers and dealers were registered to perform securities transactions in Nevada, involving 53,293 registered agents. Additionally, 493 organizations were registered to vend advice regarding investment in securities, involving 4,266 agents.

35PUBLIC FINANCE

The budget is prepared biennially by the Budget Division of the Department of Administration and submitted by the governor to the legislature, which has unlimited power to change it.

REVENUES (IN THOUSANDS)	1995	1996
Gaming tax	$ 517,524	$ 566,834
Sales taxes	446,504	566,834
Federal	836,557	502,960
Other taxes	694,031	877,735
Licenses, fees, permits	175,139	729,808
Charges for sales, services	39,751	185,375
Interest income	68,387	41,458
Proceeds from debt financing	90,093	91,595
Net operating transfers	3,274	239,531
Other	43,321	4,829
TOTAL REVENUES	$ 2,914,581	$ 3,283,181
EXPENDITURES		
General government	$ 75,742	$ 75,770
Health, social service	994,633	1,061,930
Education and support	24,633	28,482
Law, justice, public safety	224,281	256,015
Regulation of business	58,925	58,819
Transportation	368,040	344,183
Recreation, resource development	77,273	80,713
Intergovernmental	482,910	608,781
Capital improvements	40,548	27,932
Debt service	107,225	138,791
Transfers to University	257,676	266,381
TOTAL EXPENDITURES	$ 2,711,886	$ 2,947,797

As of 30 June 1996, the total general obligation state debt was $1.235 billion, or $753 per capita.

36TAXATION

As of 1997, Nevada levied a 6.5% state sales and use tax (with localities levying additional amounts), along with taxes on liquor, soft drinks, cigarettes, jet fuel, and gaming. There is no personal or corporate income tax, inheritance tax, or estate tax, and real estate transfer taxes ended in 1980. Nevadans paid $1.2 billion in tax in 1996 (this figure does not include property taxes).

37ECONOMIC POLICY

Federal projects have played an especially large role in Nevada's development. During the depression of the 1930s, Hoover (Boulder) Dam was constructed to provide needed jobs, water, and hydroelectric power for the state. Other public works—Davis Dam (Lake Mohave) and the Southern Nevada Water Project—have served similar purposes. The fact that some 87% of Nevada land is owned by the US government further increases the federal impact on the economy. Gaming supplies a large proportion of state revenues.

Nevada offers a number of incentives to encourage the growth of businesses. There is no corporate or personal income tax and other state taxes are low. The Department of Commerce issues tax-exempt industrial development bonds which provide low-interest financing of new construction or improvement of manufacturing facilities and other projects. The Development Corporation, a private financial corporation certified by the US Small Business Administration, offers long-term loans for expanding or new businesses. Rural small businesses can obtain loans from the Rural Nevada Development Corporation and the Nevada Revolving Loan Fund Program.

38HEALTH

Infant mortality during the 12 months ending with December 1995 was 6.0 per l,000 live births. The overall death rate in the same year was 8.2 per 1,000 population, with heart disease, cancer, and cerebrovascular disease the leading causes of death. Deaths by accident (including motor vehicle accidents) were above the national rate. In 1995, Nevada had the highest suicide rate among the states, at 25.8 per 100,000 population. In 1993, Nevada has the 6th lowest coronary artery disease rate in the US (73.0 deaths per 100,000) yet had a cardiovascular disease mortality rate above the US average in 1995.

In 1995, Nevada had the 4th-highest smoking prevalence in the US at an overall rate of 26.3% (24.8% men and 27.8% of women). The HIV death rate was slightly lower than the national average in 1993 (11.7 per 100,000 population). The birthrate in 1995 was 16.4 per 1,000 population, slightly above the national average of 14.8. In 1992, abortions totaled 8,022, for a ratio of 357 per 1,000 live births.

In 1995, there were 20 hospitals with 3,344 beds and seven nursing homes with 256 beds. The average expense to a hospital in the state for care provided in 1994 came to $1,016 per inpatient day and $6,526 per stay. The state had 2,194 physicians in 1994, and 570 licensed active dentists in 1994.

At least 15.7% of all Nevada residents had no health insurance in 1994. Medicare and Medicaid benefits paid out in 1993/94 were $810 and $307 million, respectively.

39SOCIAL WELFARE

Aid for families with dependent children was distributed to 40,491 recipients in 1996 with average monthly payments of $408. In 1996, 96,712 residents received monthly food stamp allowances averaging $78.59. School lunch subsidies required $20.7 million in federal funds in 1996.

With the enactment of the Personal Responsibility and Work Opportunity Reconciliation Act of 1996, the US government has changed the form and regulations for many of its social welfare programs; most significantly, it replaces Aid to Families with Dependent Children (AFDC), an open-ended entitlement program, with Temporary Assistance for Needy Families (TANF), a limited system of assistance funded largely through federal block grants. The reform act also impacts the food stamp program, the Supplemental Security Income program, and the child nutrition program. The law took effect on 1 July 1997 and provided $16.38 billion in block grants for fiscal years 1997-2002. The grants are to be divided among the states based on an equation involving the numbers of former AFDC recipients in each state. Because many of the bill's provisions have yet to be implemented into state-by-state policy, it was not possible to include the details of each state's programs for this edition of this work.

During 1995, 228,810 Nevadans received Social Security benefits averaging $725 a month. Weekly unemployment benefits averaged 189.98 in 1995.

40HOUSING

In 1996, there were an estimated 646,000 housing units, of which 587,000 were occupied; more than 99.5% had full plumbing. The 1990 census counted 518,858 housing units in Nevada, up by over 52% from 1980. In 1996, 37,242 privately owned units, valued at $2.8 billion, were authorized for construction; of these, 23,810 were single-family.

From 1990 to 1993, the number of total housing units was estimated to have increased by 14.6%, more than any other state. As of 1990, over 40% of all housing units had been built in the previous decade. In 1990, the last year for which figures are available, the median cost for an owner with a mortgage was $833; renters paid a median cost of $509. The median value of a home in 1990 was $45,700. During 1995/96, Nevada received $116.9 million in aid from the US Department of Housing and Urban Development, including $15.4 million in community development block grants.

41EDUCATION

By 1990, 82.2% of Nevadans 25 years and over had completed at least high school. In 1996/97, 282,131 pupils were enrolled in Nevada's public schools: 1,790 pre-kindergarten, 22,970 kindergarten, 139,925 elementary, and 116,824 secondary. In 1994, 64,085 students were enrolled in institutions of higher learning, nearly all of them in the University of Nevada system.

42ARTS

Major exhibits are mounted by the Las Vegas Arts League and the Sierra Arts Foundation in Reno. Reno also has a symphony orchestra and an opera association.

The state of Nevada generated $634,000 in federal funds to support arts programs in 1996. The NEA contributed $431,000 to the state's programs and $694,000 to the Nevada State Council on the Arts. The state also gave substantial funding to the Arts Council.

Between 1987 and 1991, audiences for the state's arts programs totaled 7,948,000, and there were 41,326 contributing artists. During the same period, the state provided arts education programs for 12,200 school children. As of 1991, there were 200 arts associations in Nevada and 14 local arts associations. The NEA has assisted the Nevada Opera Association, the Western Folklife Center, and the Nevada State Council on the Arts through its State and Regional Program.

43LIBRARIES AND MUSEUMS

Nevada's public library system in 1996 had a combined book stock of 5,643,427 volumes and a circulation of 8,012,391. The University of Nevada had 911,567 books in its Reno campus library system and 781,734 at Las Vegas. The Nevada State Library in Carson City had 52,036.

There are some 29 museums and historic sites. Notable are the Nevada State Museum in Carson City and Las Vegas; the museum of the Nevada Historical Society and the Fleischmann Planetarium, University of Nevada, in Reno; and the Museum of Natural History, University of Nevada, at Las Vegas.

44COMMUNICATIONS

In March 1993, 94.9% of Nevada's occupied housing units had telephones. In 1996, broadcast facilities comprised 70 radio stations (26 AM, 44 FM) and 18 television stations (two were noncommercial educational). In 1996, two large cable television systems served the Las Vegas and Reno areas.

45PRESS

In 1996, the state had five morning newspapers, four evening papers, and five Sunday papers. The leading newspaper was the *Las Vegas Review–Journal,* with an all-day circulation of 148,854 and a Sunday circulation of 216,179. The *Reno Gazette–Journal,* with a daily circulation of 67,179 and Sunday circulation of 84,884, is the most influential newspaper in the northern half of the state.

46ORGANIZATIONS

The 1992 Census of Service Industries counted 299 organizations in Nevada, including 59 business associations; 175 civic, social, and fraternal organizations; and 65 other membership organizations. Notable organizations with headquarters in Nevada include the National Council of Juvenile and Family Court Judges and the Western History Association.

⁴⁷TOURISM, TRAVEL, AND RECREATION

Tourism remains Nevada's most important industry. In 1993, domestic travelers spent over $2,539,000 billion in the state. Tourists flock to "Vegas" for gambling and for the top-flight entertainers who perform there. Other Nevada attractions are Pyramid Lake, Lake Tahoe, Lake Mead, and Lehman Caves National Monument. There are 12 state parks and the Great Basin National Park, which hosted 86,635 visitors in 1995.

There are 21 state parks and recreation areas. In 1995, licenses were held by 251,122 anglers and 94,561 hunters.

⁴⁸SPORTS

There are no major league professional sports teams in Nevada. Las Vegas has a minor league baseball team, the Stars, in the Triple-A Pacific Coast League; and a minor league hockey team, the Thunder, in the International Hockey League. Las Vegas and Reno have hosted many professional boxing title bouts. Golfing and rodeo are also popular.

The basketball team at the University of Nevada-Las Vegas emerged as a national power in the late 1980s and early 1990s. The Runnin' Rebels won the National Championships in 1990. Over their 30-plus years in the NCAA, UNLV has the highest winning percentage of any team, 76.3%.

Other annual sporting events include the Bristlecone Birkebeines Cross Country Ski Race in Ely in February, the Las Vegas International Golf Tournament in October, and the Nationals Finals Rodeo staged in Las Vegas each December.

⁴⁹FAMOUS NEVADANS

Nevadans who have held important federal offices include Raymond T. Baker (1877–1935) and Eva B. Adams (b.1908), both directors of the US Mint, and Charles B. Henderson (b.California, 1873–1954), head of the Reconstruction Finance Corporation. Prominent US senators have been James W. Nye (b.New York, 1815–76), also the only governor of Nevada Territory; William M. Stewart (b.New York, 1827–1909), author of the final form of the 15th Amendment to the US Constitution, father of federal mining legislation, and a leader of the free-silver-coinage movement in the 1890s; and Francis G. Newlands (b.Mississippi, 1848–1917), author of the federal Reclamation Act of 1902.

Probably the most significant state historical figure is George Wingfield (b.Arkansas, 1876–1959), a mining millionaire who exerted great influence over Nevada's economic and political life in the early 20th century. Among the nationally recognized personalities associated with Nevada is Howard R. Hughes (b.Texas, 1905–76), an aviation entrepreneur who became a casino and hotel owner and wealthy recluse in his later years.

Leading creative and performing artists have included operatic singer Emma Nevada (Emma Wixon, 1862–1940); painter Robert Caples (1908–79); and, among writers, Dan DeQuille (William Wright, b.Ohio, 1829–98); Lucius Beebe (b.Massachusetts, 1902–66); and Walter Van Tilburg Clark (b.Maine, 1909–71).

⁵⁰BIBLIOGRAPHY

Bushnell, Eleanore, and Don W. Driggs, *The Nevada Constitution: Origin and Growth*. 5th ed. Reno: University of Nevada Press, 1980.

Driggs, Don W. *Nevada Politics and Government: Conservatism in an Open Society*. Lincoln, Neb.: University of Nebraska Press, 1996.

Hulse, James W. *The Nevada Adventure: A History*. 5th ed. Reno: University of Nevada Press, 1981.

Laxalt, Robert. *Nevada: A Bicentennial History*. New York: Norton, 1977.

Nevada, State of. Secretary of State. *Political History of Nevada*. 7th ed. Carson City, 1979.

Toll, David W. *The Complete Nevada Traveler*. Virginia City, Nev.: Gold Hill, 1981.

NEW HAMPSHIRE

State of New Hampshire

ORIGIN OF STATE NAME: Named for the English county of Hampshire. **NICKNAME:** The Granite State. **CAPITAL:** Concord. **ENTERED UNION:** 21 June 1788 (9th). **SONG:** "Old New Hampshire." **MOTTO:** Live Free or Die. **FLAG:** The state seal, surrounded by laurel leaves with nine stars interspersed, is centered on a blue field. **OFFICIAL SEAL:** In the center is a broadside view of the frigate *Raleigh;* in the left foreground is a granite boulder, in the background a rising sun. A laurel wreath and the words "Seal of the State of New Hampshire 1776" surround the whole. **STATE EMBLEM:** Within an elliptical panel appears a replica of the Old Man of the Mountains, with the state name above and motto below. **ANIMAL:** White-tailed deer. **BIRD:** Purple finch. **INSECT:** Ladybug. **FLOWER:** Purple lilac. **TREE:** White birch. **GEM:** Smoky quartz. **LEGAL HOLIDAYS:** New Year's Day, 1 January; Civil Rights Day, 3d Monday in January; Washington's Birthday, 3d Monday in February; Memorial Day, 30 May; Independence Day, 4 July; Labor Day, 1st Monday in September; Columbus Day, 2d Monday in October; Election Day, Tuesday following 1st Monday in November in even-numbered years; Veterans Day, 11 November; Thanksgiving Day, 4th Thursday in November; Christmas Day, 25 December. **TIME:** 7 AM EST = noon GMT.

[1] LOCATION, SIZE, AND EXTENT

Situated in New England in the northeastern US, New Hampshire ranks 44th in size among the 50 states. The total area of New Hampshire is 9,279 sq mi (24,033 sq km), comprising 8,993 sq mi (23,292 sq km) of land and 286 sq mi (741 sq km) of inland water. The state has a maximum extension of 93 mi (150 km) E-W and 180 mi (290 km) N-S. New Hampshire is shaped roughly like a right triangle, with the line from the far N to the extreme SW forming the hypotenuse.

New Hampshire is bordered on the N by the Canadian province of Quebec; on the E by Maine (with part of the line formed by the Piscataqua and Salmon Falls rivers) and the Atlantic Ocean; on the S by Massachusetts; and on the W by Vermont (following the west bank of the Connecticut River) and Quebec (with the line formed by Halls Stream).

The three southernmost Isles of Shoals lying in the Atlantic belong to New Hampshire. The state's total boundary line is 555 mi (893 km). Its geographic center lies in Belknap County, 3 mi (5 km) E of Ashland.

[2] TOPOGRAPHY

The major regions of New Hampshire are the coastal lowland in the southeast; the New England Uplands, covering most of the south and west; and the White Mountains (part of the Appalachian chain) in the north, including Mt. Washington, at 6,288 feet (1,917 meters) the highest peak in the northeastern US. With a mean elevation of about 1,000 feet (305 meters), New Hampshire is generally hilly, rocky, and in many areas densely wooded.

There are some 1,300 lakes and ponds, of which the largest is Lake Winnipesaukee, covering 70 sq mi (181 sq km). The principal rivers are the Connecticut (forming the border with Vermont), Merrimack, Salmon Falls, Piscataqua, Saco, and Androscoggin. Near the coast are the nine rocky Isles of Shoals, three of which belong to New Hampshire.

[3] CLIMATE

New Hampshire has a changeable climate, with wide variations in daily and seasonal temperatures. Summers are short and cool, winters long and cold. Concord has a normal daily mean temperature of 46°F (8°C), ranging from 21°F (−6°C) in January to 70°F (21°C) in July. The record low temperature, −46°F (−43°C), was set at Pittsburg on 28 January 1925; the all-time high, 106°F (41°C) at Nashua, 4 July 1911. Annual precipitation at Concord averages 36 in (91 cm); the average snowfall in Concord is 65 in (165 cm) a year, with more than 100 in (254 cm) yearly in the mountains. The strongest wind ever recorded, other than during a tornado—231 mph (372 kph)—occurred on Mt. Washington on 12 April 1934.

[4] FLORA AND FAUNA

Well forested, New Hampshire supports an abundance of elm, maple, beech, oak, pine, hemlock, and fir trees. Among wild flowers, several orchids are considered rare; three are classified as threatened. Robbins' cinquefoil was added to the federal endangered species list in 1980; and the small whorled pogonia in 1982.

Among native New Hampshire mammals are the white-tailed deer, muskrat, beaver, porcupine, and snowshoe hare. Threatened animals include the pine marten, arctic tern, purple martin, eastern bluebird, whippoorwill, and osprey. The Indiana bat, lynx, bald eagle, shortnose sturgeon, sunapee trout, and Atlantic salmon are on the state's endangered species list.

[5] ENVIRONMENTAL PROTECTION

State agencies concerned with environmental protection include the Fish and Game Department, the Department of Resources and Economic Development (DRED), and the Department of Environmental Services (DES). DRED oversees the state's forests, lands and parks and, in the late 1980s, DRED was the lead state agency in the acquisition and long-term protection of open space. DES was created in 1987, consolidating several pre-existing commissions and boards into four divisions which protect the environmental quality of air, groundwater, the state's surface waters, and solid waste. In the 1990s, DES has focused on such issues as ground-level ozone, landfill closures, groundwater remediation and protection of lakes, rivers, and other wetlands in New Hampshire.

[6]POPULATION

New Hampshire ranked 40th among the 50 states in the 1990 census, with a population of 1,109,252. The estimated 1996 population figure was 1,162,481, representing a growth since 1990 of 4.8%. Projections to 2000 foresee a population of 1,410,000, 10% more than in 1990. The population density in 1990 was 123.7 per sq mi (47.5 per sq km).

In 1990, about 49% of the population lived in rural areas and only 51% in cities and towns, well below the US average. Leading cities with their 1990 census populations are Manchester, 96,640; Nashua, 79,631; and Concord, the capital, 36,198. All three are located in the southeastern region, where more than two-thirds of all state residents live.

[7]ETHNIC GROUPS

In 1990, a total of 265,668 New Hampshirites claimed English ancestry. Those claiming French ancestry numbered 205,455, and Irish 232,409. There are also about 118,000 French Canadians. About 7,000 Black Americans, 9,000 Asians and Pacific Islanders, and 2,000 Native Americans live in New Hampshire.

[8]LANGUAGES

Some place-names, such as Ossipee, Mascoma, and Chocorua, preserve the memory of the Pennacook and Abnaki Algonkian tribes living in the area before white settlement.

New Hampshire speech is essentially Northern, with the special features marking eastern New England: loss of final /r/, *park* and *path* with a vowel between those in *cat* and *father*, and /yu/ in *tube* and *new*. *Raspberries* sounds like /rawzberries/, a wishbone is a *luckybone*, gutters are *eavespouts*, and cows are summoned by "Loo!" Canadian French is heard in the northern region.

In 1990, 91.3% of all state residents aged five and above—a total of 935,825—spoke only English at home; 51,284 residents spoke French at home.

[9]RELIGIONS

The first settlers of New Hampshire were Separatists, precursors of the modern Congregationalists (United Church of Christ) and their first church was probably built around 1633. The first Episcopal church was built in 1638, and the first Quaker meeting-house in 1701; Presbyterians, Baptists, and Methodists built churches later in the 18th century. The state remained almost entirely Protestant until the second half of the 19th century, when Roman Catholics (French Canadian, Irish, and Italian) began arriving in significant numbers, along with some Greek and Russian Orthodox Christians.

As of 1990, Protestant groups in New Hampshire had 134,632 known adherents. The leading denominations were United Church of Christ, 36,989; United Methodist, 19,328; and American Baptist, 18,663. There were 297,062 Roman Catholics and an estimated 6,680 Jews in 1990.

[10]TRANSPORTATION

New Hampshire's first railroad, between Nashua and Lowell, Massachusetts, was chartered in 1835 and opened in 1838. Two years later, Exeter and Boston were linked by rail. The state had more than 1,200 mi (1,900 km) of track in 1920, but by 1995, the total route mileage in New Hampshire was only 400 mi (640 km).

In 1995, the state had a total of 15,086 mi (24,138 km) of roads of which 12,173 mi (19,477 km) were rural and 2,913 mi (4,660 km) municipal; the main north-south highway is I-93. As of 1995, there were 731,463 automobiles, 49,445 motorcycles, 1,763 buses, and 388,802 trucks registered in the state, as well as 901,104 licensed drivers. New Hampshire had 48 airports, 41 heliports, and 5 seaplane bases. The main airport is Manchester Municipal Airport.

[11]HISTORY

The land called New Hampshire has supported a human population for at least 10,000 years. Prior to European settlement, Indian tribes of the Algonkian language group lived in the region. During the 17th century, most of New Hampshire's Indians, called Pennacook, were organized in a loose confederation centered along the Merrimack Valley.

The coast of New England was explored by Dutch, English, and French navigators throughout the 16th century. Samuel de Champlain prepared the first accurate map of the New England coast in 1604, and Captain John Smith explored the Isles of Shoals in 1614. By this time, numerous English fishermen were summering on New England's coastal banks, using the Isles of Shoals for temporary shelter and to dry their catch.

The first English settlement was established along the Piscataqua River in 1623. From 1643 to 1680, New Hampshire was a province of Massachusetts, and the boundary between them was not settled until 1740. During the 18th century, as settlers moved up the Merrimack and Connecticut river valleys, they came into conflict with the Indians. By 1760, however, the Pennacook had been expelled from the region.

Throughout the provincial period, people in New Hampshire made their living through fishing, farming, cutting and sawing timber, shipbuilding, and coastal and overseas trade. By the first quarter of the 18th century, Portsmouth, the provincial capital, had become a thriving commercial port. New Hampshire's terrain worked against Portsmouth's commercial interests, however, by dictating that roads (and later railroads) run in a north-south direction—making Boston, and not Portsmouth, New England's primary trading center. During the Revolutionary War, extensive preparations were made to protect the harbor from a British attack that never came. Although nearly 18,500 New Hampshire men enlisted in the war, no battle was fought within its boundaries. New Hampshire was the first of the original 13 colonies to establish an independent government—on 5 January 1776, six months before the Declaration of Independence.

During the 19th century, as overseas trade became less important to the New Hampshire economy, textile mills were built, principally along the Merrimack River. By midcentury, the Merrimack Valley had become the social, political, and economic center of the state. So great was the demand for workers in these mills that immigrant labor was imported during the 1850s; a decade later, French Canadian workers began pouring south from Quebec.

Although industry thrived, agriculture did not; New Hampshire hill farms could not compete against Midwestern farms. The population in farm towns dropped, leaving a maze of stone walls, cellar holes, and new forests on the hillsides. The people who remained began to cluster in small village centers.

World War I, however, marked a turning point for New Hampshire industry. As wartime demand fell off, the state's old textile mills were unable to compete with newer cotton mills in the South, and New Hampshire's mill towns became as depressed as its farm towns; only in the north, the center for logging and paper manufacturing, did state residents continue to enjoy moderate prosperity. Industrial towns in the southern counties responded to the decline in textile manufacture by making other items, particularly shoes, but the collapse of the state's railroad network spelled further trouble for the slumping economy. The growth of tourism aided the rural areas primarily, as old farms became spacious vacation homes for "summer people," who in some cases paid the bulk of local property taxes.

During the 1960s, New Hampshire's economic decline began to reverse, except in agriculture. In the 1970s and early 1980s,

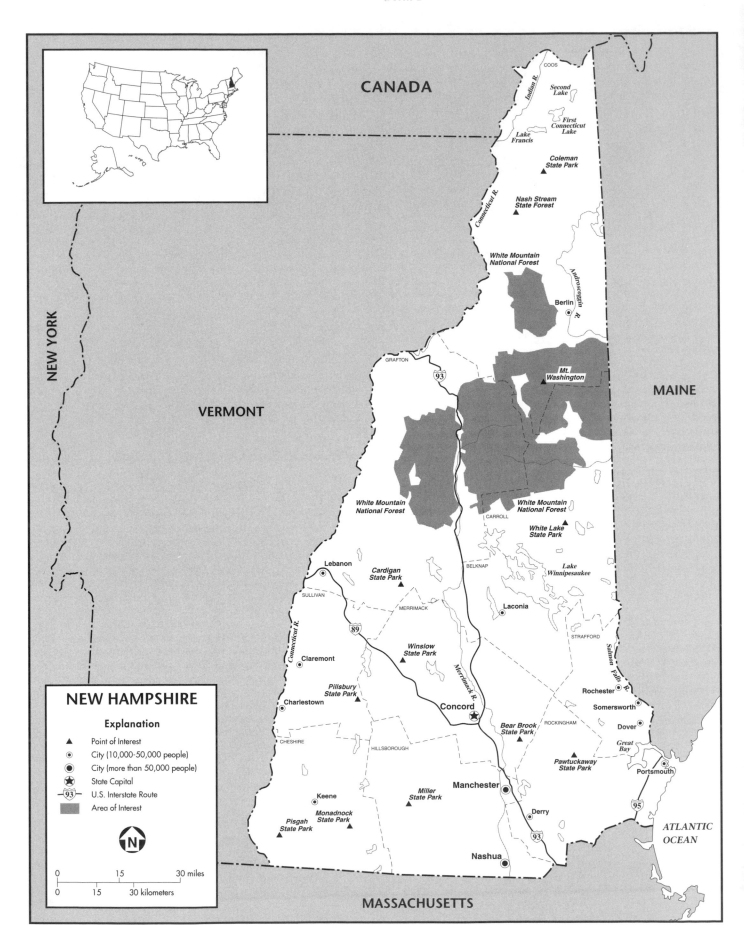

CANADA

NEW YORK

VERMONT

MAINE

MASSACHUSETTS

ATLANTIC OCEAN

COOS

Indian R.

Second Lake

First Connecticut Lake

Lake Francis

Connecticut R.

Coleman State Park ▲

Nash Stream State Forest ▲

White Mountain National Forest

Androscoggin R.

Berlin ⊙

GRAFTON

93

Mt. Washington ▲

White Mountain National Forest

White Mountain National Forest

CARROLL

White Lake State Park ▲

Lebanon ⊙

Cardigan State Park ▲

BELKNAP

Lake Winnipesaukee

Connecticut R.

SULLIVAN

MERRIMACK

Laconia ⊙

STRAFFORD

Salmon Falls R.

89

Winslow State Park ▲

Claremont ⊙

Merrimack R.

Pillsbury State Park ▲

Rochester ⊙

Somersworth ⊙

Charlestown ⊙

Concord ★

Dover ⊙

Bear Brook State Park ▲

ROCKINGHAM

Great Bay

CHESHIRE

HILLSBOROUGH

Pawtuckaway State Park ▲

Portsmouth ⊙

Keene ⊙

Miller State Park ▲

Manchester ⊙

95

Monadnock State Park ▲

Derry ⊙

Pisgah State Park ▲

93

Nashua ⊙

NEW HAMPSHIRE

Explanation

▲ Point of Interest
⊙ City (10,000-50,000 people)
⊙ City (more than 50,000 people)
★ State Capital
93 U.S. Interstate Route
▨ Area of Interest

N

0   15   30 miles
0   15   30 kilometers

growth in the state's northern counties remained modest, but the combination of Boston's urban sprawl, interstate highway construction, and low state taxes encouraged people and industry—notably high-technology businesses—to move into southern New Hampshire. The state's population doubled between 1960 and 1988, from 606,921 to 1.1 million. Most of the arrivals were younger, more affluent, and better educated than the natives. The newcomers shared the fiscally conservative views of those born in New Hampshire but tended to be more liberal on social questions such as gun control and abortion. The rise in population strained government services, prompted an increase in local taxes, and provoked concern over the state's vanishing open spaces.

Like the other New England states, New Hampshire was hard hit by the recession of the early 1990s, with the unemployment rate rising to 10% by 1992. By 1994, a recovery was underway, and about 30,000 of the more than 60,000 jobs lost during the recession had been regained. In 1990, the Seabrook nuclear plant, a focus of protest and controversy since the 1970s, began operations.

12STATE GOVERNMENT

New Hampshire's constitution, adopted in 1784 and extensively revised in 1792, is the second-oldest state-governing document still in effect. Every 10 years, the people vote on the question of calling a convention to revise it; proposed revisions must then be approved by two-thirds of the voters at a referendum. Amendments may also be placed on the ballot by a three-fifths vote of both houses of the General Court—the state legislature—which consists of a 24-member senate and a 400-seat house of representatives (larger than that of any other state). Legislators serve two-year terms, for which they are paid $200 ($100 per year).

The only executive elected statewide is the governor, who serves a two-year term and is assisted by a five-member executive council, elected for two years by district. The council must approve all administrative and judicial appointments. The secretary of state and state treasurer are elected by the legislature. The governor must be at least 30 years of age and must have been a state resident for seven years before election. In 1996, the governor's salary was $86,235.

A bill becomes law if signed by the governor, if passed by the legislature and left unsigned by the governor for five days while the legislature is in session, or if passed over a gubernatorial veto by two thirds of the legislators present in each house. US citizens at least 18 years of age who have resided in the state for 10 days are eligible to vote in New Hampshire elections.

13POLITICAL PARTIES

New Hampshire has almost always gone with the Republican presidential nominee in recent decades, but the Democratic and Republican parties have been much more evenly balanced in local and state elections. New Hampshire's quadrennial presidential preference primary, traditionally the first state primary of the campaign season, accords to New Hampshirites a degree of national political influence and a claim on media attention far out of proportion to their numbers. In the 1992 presidential election, New Hampshire voters defied their tradition and chose Democrat Bill Clinton over Republican incumbent George Bush by a scant 6,556 votes. In 1996 Clinton won 49% of the vote, Republican Bob Dole won 39%, and Independent Ross Perot received 10%. As of 1997, both of New Hampshire's senators, Judd Gregg (elected in 1992) and Robert Smith (re-elected in 1996), were Republicans. Prior to the 1994 elections, New Hampshire's delegation of US Representatives consisted of a Democrat and a Republican. However, in the 1994 congressional elections Republican's took both seats and in doing so reclaimed a seat that had been Republican since Woodrow Wilson was President.

Following the 1996 elections, both House seats remained in Republican hands. The New Hampshire state senate in 1997 contained 15 Republicans and 9 Democrats; the state house had 253 Republicans and 145 Democrats. In 1993 there were two black state representatives and in 1995, 128 women served in the state legislature.

New Hampshire Presidential Vote by Major Political Parties, 1948–96

YEAR	ELECTORAL VOTE	NEW HAMPSHIRE WINNER	DEMOCRAT	REPUBLICAN
1948	4	Dewey (R)	107,995	121,299
1952	4	*Eisenhower (R)	106,663	166,287
1956	4	*Eisenhower (R)	90,364	176,519
1960	4	Nixon (R)	137,772	157,989
1964	4	*Johnson (D)	182,065	104,029
1968	4	*Nixon (R)	130,589	154,903
1972	4	*Nixon (R)	116,435	213,724
1976	4	Ford (R)	147,635	185,935
1980	4	*Reagan (R)	108,864	221,705
1984	4	*Reagan (R)	120,347	267,050
1988	4	*Bush (R)	163,696	281,537
1992**	4	*Clinton (D)	209,040	202,484
1996**	4	*Clinton (D)	246,214	196,532

* Won US presidential election.
** Independent candidate Ross Perot received 121,337 votes in 1992, and 48,390 votes in 1996.

14LOCAL GOVERNMENT

New Hampshire has 10 counties, each governed by three commissioners. Other elected county officials include the sheriff, attorney, treasurer, registrar of deeds, and registrar of probate.

As of 1992, New Hampshire also had 13 municipalities and 221 townships, 167 school districts, and 116 special districts. Municipalities have elected mayors and councils. The basic unit of town government is the traditional town meeting, held once a year, when selectmen and other local officials are chosen.

15STATE SERVICES

The Department of Education, governed by the State Board of Education (which appoints an education commissioner), has primary responsibility for public instruction. The Department of Transportation and the Port Authority share transport responsibilities, while the Department of Health and Human Services oversees public health and mental health and welfare. There are 21 executive branch departments, not counting the governor's office, and 21 authorities, boards, and commissions, such as the Liquor Commission and the Sweepstakes Commission.

16JUDICIAL SYSTEM

All judges in New Hampshire are appointed by the governor, subject to confirmation by the executive council; appointments are to age 70, with retirement compulsory at that time. The state's highest court, the supreme court, consists of a chief justice and 4 associate justices. The main trial court is the superior court for which there were 29 judges in 1994. In 1996 an estimated 2,941 lawyers practiced in New Hampshire.

New Hampshire's total crime rate in 1995 was 2,655.4, including 114.5 for violent crime and 2,540.9 for property crime. In 1995 there were 2,200 inmates in 6 state and federal correctional facilities, a rate of 192 inmates per 100,000 inhabitants. The inmate population increased by almost 58% between 1990 and 1995.

New Hampshire imposes the death penalty but has executed only one person since 1930.

[17]ARMED FORCES

In 1996, there were 386 active duty military personnel stationed in New Hampshire. The principal military installation is the Portsmouth Naval Shipyard. Firms in the state received $567.9 million in defense contract awards in 1995/96. As of 1996, veterans living in New Hampshire numbered 134,000, of whom less than 500 were veterans of World War I, 32,000 of World War II, 22,000 of the Korean conflict, 46,000 of the Vietnam era, and 8,000 of the Persian Gulf War. Veterans benefits totaled $172 million in 1995/96.

The National Guard and Reserve had 6,661 personnel in 1996. In 1993, the New Hampshire state police employed 246 full-time sworn officers, or 2 per 10,000 residents.

[18]MIGRATION

From the time of the first European settlement until the middle of the 19th century, the population of New Hampshire was primarily of British origin. Subsequently, immigrants from Quebec and from Ireland, Italy, and other countries began arriving in significant numbers. New Hampshire's population growth since 1960 has been fueled by migrants from other states. The net gain from migration was 74,000 from 1985 to 1990. Between 1990 and 1995, New Hampshire had net gains of 5,344 in domestic migration and 4,001 in international migration. As of 1990, about 44.1% of the state's residents had been born in New Hampshire. Just under 50% of residents age five and older moved to a different house between 1985 and 1990; 39% of these moved from another state.

[19]INTERGOVERNMENTAL COOPERATION

New Hampshire participates in the American and Canadian French Cultural Exchange Commission, Atlantic States Marine Fisheries Compact, Connecticut River Valley Flood Control Compact, and various New England regional compacts. Federal grants to New Hampshire totaled $651.7 million in 1992/93.

[20]ECONOMY

New Hampshire is one of the most industrialized states in the US, ranking well above the national median in proportion of labor force employed in manufacturing and in value added by manufacture. Between 1977 and 1982, manufacturing employment rose 13%, to 107,500, as many high-technology firms moved into the southern portion of the state. Since World War II, tourism has been one of the state's fastest-growing sources of income. In 1996, there were 3,692 bankruptcy filings in the state.

The gross state product in 1994 was $29,393 million, to which private goods-producing industries contributed $7,346 million; private services-producing industries, $19,207 million; and government, $2,840 million.

[21]INCOME

In 1996, total disposable personal income amounted to $27.1 billion, up from $26 billion in 1995. New Hampshire's per capita income, which ranked 20th in the US in 1970, had slipped to 32d by 1978, largely because of rapid population growth rather than any slowdown in real economic growth. By 1996, New Hampshire ranked 8th, with a per capita personal income of $26,520. In 1995, median household income was $39,171. In 1995, 5.3% of state residents were below the federal poverty level.

[22]LABOR

New Hampshire's estimated civilian labor force totaled 624,000 in 1996. Of these, 598,000 were employed, yielding an unemployment rate of just over 4.2%. At the end of 1996, services employed 154,200 people; wholesale and retail trade,

149,000; manufacturing 101,400; government, 81,000; finance, insurance, and real estate, 29,400; transportation and public utilities, 21,000; construction, 20,500; and mining, 400.

There were 66,600 labor union members (12.6% of all workers) in 1995.

[23]AGRICULTURE

Only Rhode Island and Alaska generate less income from farming than New Hampshire. Farm income in 1996 was $152.1 million, 58% of which was in crops.

In 1996 there were about 2,400 farms occupying about 430,000 acres (174,000 hectares). Leading crops and their output in 1996 were hay, 117,000 tons, and commercial apples, 37 million lb (17 million kg).

[24]ANIMAL HUSBANDRY

Dairy and poultry products are the mainstays of New Hampshire's agriculture. In 1995, the state had 20,000 milk cows, with a total milk yield of 326 million lb (148 million kg). Poultry items included 830,000 lb (376,000 lb) of chickens, sold for $24,000; 347,000 lb (157,000 kg) of turkey, valued at $406,000, and 44 million eggs, valued at nearly $4 million.

[25]FISHING

New Hampshire's commercial catch in 1995 consisted of 12,768,000 lb (5,800,000 kg), much of it cod (2,765,000 lb or 1,254,000 kg) and lobster, worth $14,923,000. The state's 23 fish processors and wholesalers employed 429 persons in 1994. In 1995/96, the state issued 156,352 sport fishing licenses.

[26]FORESTRY

New Hampshire had 5,740,000 acres (2,323,000 hectares) of forestland in 1992, of which 4,981,000 acres (2,042,210 hectares) were considered suitable for commercial use. Of that total, 88% was privately owned. Forests cover 87% of New Hampshire, and the forest products industry employs 16,000 workers.

[27]MINING

The value of nonfuel mineral production in New Hampshire in 1995 was estimated to be $35.6 million. The total value in 1994 was $46.4 million, but the dollar values reported in 1995 were artificially low because information was withheld to protect company confidentiality.

In 1995, 5.6 million metric tons of construction sand and gravel were mined, worth $25.7 million. There were 1.98 million short tons (1.8 million metric tons) of crushed stone mined, worth $9.9 million. Dimension stone, common clay, and gem stones collected by hobbyists, accounted for the remainder of the state's mineral value. Sand and gravel are mined in every county, and dimension granite is quarried in Hillsborough, Merrimack, and Coos counties. Crude gypsum, imported into the state, was calcined at two plants to manufacture wallboard.

[28]ENERGY AND POWER

About 90% of all New Hampshire's electrical power was generated by water in the 1930s. By 1995, however, about 24% of the state's electricity came from coal-fired plants, another 7% from oil-fired plants, and 7% from hydroelectric facilities. Power production totaled 13.9 billion kWh in 1995, when installed capacity was 2.6 million kW. In 1990, the controversial nuclear power plant at Seabrook, being built by Public Service Co. of New Hampshire, began operating. Originally planned as a two-reactor, 2,300-Mw facility, Seabrook was scaled back to one, 1,150 Mw reactor whose cost was about five times the original $1 billion two-reactor estimate. Nuclear power supplied 60% of the state's electricity in 1995.

29INDUSTRY

During the provincial era, shipbuilding was New Hampshire's major industry. By 1870, cotton and woolen mills, concentrated in the southeast, employed about one-third of the labor force and accounted for roughly half the value of all manufactures. In 1992, employment in industrial and commercial machinery and computer equipment accounted for 31% of all durable goods manufacturing employment, while electronic and electrical equipment and components employment made up 20%.

The value of shipments by manufacturers in 1995 was $15.437 billion. Major sectors and their value of shipments in 1995 were as follows: industrial equipment and machinery, $3,875.9 million; electronic and other electric equipment, $2,161.8 million; instruments and related products, $1,462.5 million; rubber and plastic products, $1,065.7 million; food and food products, $1,010.2 million; and fabricated metal products, $1,000.2 million. As of 1997, there was one Fortune 500 company headquartered in New Hampshire, Tyco International. In 1995, there were 455 US patents issued to residents of New Hampshire.

30COMMERCE

New Hampshire wholesalers had $8.1 billion in sales in 1992. Retailers had sales of $11.1 billion, the leading sectors being food stores, 21.7%; automotive dealers, 18.5%; and general merchandise stores, 13.5%. Foreign exports of goods originating in New Hampshire totaled $1.5 million in 1996.

31CONSUMER PROTECTION

The Attorney General's Office is responsible for enforcing New Hampshire's consumer protection laws.

32BANKING

New Hampshire had 23 insured commercial banks in 1996. Total assets that year amounted to $10 billion, outstanding loans were $6.8 billion in 1996, and deposits were $7.6 billion in 1996. In 1996, the state's 26 insured savings institutions held total assets of $9.4 billion, including mortgage loans of $4.5 billion.

33INSURANCE

In 1995 there were 1,033,000 life insurance policies in force in New Hampshire, with a total value of $58.6 billion. The average coverage per family was $133,600, slightly below the US average.

Property and liability insurers wrote premiums amounting to $1.2 billion in 1995, of which automobile physical damage insurance accounted for $338.3 million; automotive liability insurance, $206.5 million; and homeowners' coverage, $127.2 million.

34SECURITIES

New Hampshire has no securities exchanges. There are over 1,000 broker-dealer firms registered to do business in the state, involving approximately 50,0000 agents.

35PUBLIC FINANCE

The New Hampshire state budget is drawn up biennially by the Department of Administrative Services and then submitted by the governor to the legislature for amendment and approval. The fiscal year runs from 1 July to 30 June. The following were recommended expenditures for 1994/95 (in millions of $):

Health and social services	$ 1,050.2
Transportation	344.6
Higher education	412.5
Board of Education	154.0
Other outlays	557.9

Leading sources of revenue in 1994/95, in addition to federal aid, were estimated as follows (in millions of $):

Meals and rooms tax	$ 223.0
Business profits tax	140.5
Gasoline tax	99.5
Board and care	78.2
Liquor and beer	76.0
Motor vehicle fees	56.7
Insurance tax	51.0
Cigarette tax	45.0

As of 1995, the combined debt of state and local governments was $5.7 billion, or about $5,035 per capita.

36TAXATION

New Hampshire has no general income or sales tax but does levy 7% on net corporate income. Levies on property, gasoline, alcoholic beverages, tobacco products, pari-mutuel betting, and many other items are also imposed. State tax revenues were $720.39 per capita in 1996.

During 1995, New Hampshire paid almost $4.5 billion in federal taxes and received federal benefits amounting to about $4.8 billion.

37ECONOMIC POLICY

Business incentives in New Hampshire include a generally favorable tax climate (which includes the absence of sales, personal income, and capital gains taxes), specific tax incentives and exemptions, and relatively low wage rates. The state offers loan programs aimed at encouraging economic development and job creation and at assisting small businesses. The state also participates in a joint venture with Maine and Vermont which provides loans to export companies.

38HEALTH

Infant mortality in New Hampshire for 1995 stood at just 4.8 per 1,000 live births, the lowest rate among the states. Abortions numbered 3,129 in 1992, or 196 per 1,000 live births. The death rate in 1995 was 8.0 per 1,000 population.

In 1995 there were 29 hospitals, with 3,072 beds. Hospital admissions in that year totaled 109,115. Hospital personnel in 1994 included 11,100 registered nurses. The average expense of a hospital for inpatient care in 1994 was $825 per day and $5,978 per stay, both well below the national averages. New Hampshire had 2,383 active, non-federal physicians in January 1994, and 840 active, licensed dentists in 1995.

Payments made out to Medicare and Medicaid recipients for health expenditures in 1994 were $530 million and $389 million dollars respectively.

The overall death rate in New Hampshire was 803.6 per 100,000 in 1995, lower than the national average. Although death by homicide and firearm injuries were lower than the US average, deaths by cancer, heart disease, and chronic obstructive diseases were higher.

39SOCIAL WELFARE

Like its tax revenues, New Hampshire's expenditures on welfare are low for a northeastern state. Some 24,000 New Hampshirites received an average monthly payment of $613 under the aid to families with dependent children program during 1996. That year, 52,809 residents received monthly food stamp allowances averaging $65.71, and school lunches for eligible students required a federal outlay of $12.6 million. In 1995, Social Security benefits were paid to 186,290 eligible New Hampshirites, the average monthly benefit being $724. Federal Supplemental Security Income payments averaging $323 a month were paid to 10,533 residents. Unemployment insurance benefits had an average weekly payment of $147.58 in 1995.

With the enactment of the Personal Responsibility and Work Opportunity Reconciliation Act of 1996, the US government has changed the form and regulations for many of its social welfare programs; most significantly, it replaces Aid to Families with Dependent Children (AFDC), an open-ended entitlement program, with Temporary Assistance for Needy Families (TANF), a limited system of assistance funded largely through federal block grants. The reform act also impacts the food stamp program, the Supplemental Security Income program, and the child nutrition program. The law took effect on 1 July 1997 and provided $16.38 billion in block grants for fiscal years 1997–2002. The grants are to be divided among the states based on an equation involving the numbers of former AFDC recipients in each state. Because many of the bill's provisions have yet to be implemented into state-by-state policy, it was not possible to include the details of each state's programs for this edition of this work.

40HOUSING

In 1996, there were 524,000 housing units in New Hampshire, 429,000 of which were occupied. That year, 4,926 privately owned units, valued at $516 million, were authorized for construction; of these, 4,233 were single family. Of all occupied units in 1990, 56% were owner-occupied, the remainder rented; 98.8% had full plumbing. In 1990 there were 2.62 persons per household, as opposed to 3.14 in 1970. In 1990, the last year for which figures were available, the median value of a home was $129,400, up 69.8% from 1980 after adjusting for inflation. An owner-occupied unit with a mortgage had a median monthly cost of $1,000 in 1990, when the median monthly rent was $549.

During 1995/96, New Hampshire received $122.9 million in aid from the US Department of Housing and Urban Development, including $15 million in community development block grants.

41EDUCATION

New Hampshire residents have a long-standing commitment to education. More than 82% of all adult state residents were high school graduates in 1993.

In fall 1995, enrollment in public schools and approved public academies totaled 194,171; private elementary and secondary schools had an enrollment of 18,651 in fall 1993. The number of teachers in public elementary and secondary schools in 1995/96 was 12,399, with an average salary of $39,564. The 1994/95 per pupil expenditure for elementary and secondary schools was $5,652, just above the US mean of $5,526.

The best-known institution of higher education is Dartmouth College (enrollment approximately 4,300), which originated in Connecticut in 1754 as Moor's Indian Charity School and was established at Hanover in 1769. When the state of New Hampshire attempted to amend Dartmouth's charter to make the institution public in the early 19th century, the US Supreme Court handed down a precedent-setting ruling prohibiting state violation of contract rights. The University of New Hampshire, the leading public institution, was founded at Hanover in 1866 and relocated at Durham in 1891; it has an undergraduate enrollment of just over 10,000.

42ARTS

Hopkins Center at Dartmouth College features musical events throughout the year, while the Monadnock Music Concerts are held in several towns during the summer. The New Hampshire Music Festival takes place at Meredith. Theater by the Sea at Portsmouth presents classical and modern plays, and there is a year-round student theater at Dartmouth.

Principal galleries include the Currier Gallery of Art in Manchester, the Arts and Science Center in Nashua, the University Art Galleries at the University of New Hampshire in Durham, the Dartmouth College Museum and Galleries at Hanover, and the Lamont Gallery at Phillips Exeter Academy in Exeter.

The state of New Hampshire generated $573,000 in federal funds to support its arts programs in 1996. The NEA contributed $621,000 to the state's programs, $1,206,000 to the New Hampshire State Council on the Arts, and contributed to the Monadnock Music Festival. The state and private sources also contributed substantial funding to the state's arts programs, which attracted audiences totaling around 10 million and featured well over 50,000 contributing artists. In 1996, New Hampshire had 275 arts associations and 8 local art associations. The New Hampshire State Council on the Arts contributed funds for Artist in Residence programs, visual arts exhibitions, and the development of the Hood Museum of Art at Dartmouth College.

43LIBRARIES AND MUSEUMS

New Hampshire public libraries had a total book stock of 4,593,967 volumes and a combined circulation of 8,127,467 volumes in 1995. Leading academic and historical collections include Dartmouth College's Baker Memorial Library in Hanover (2,130,672 volumes); the New Hampshire State Library (500,047) and New Hampshire Historical Society Library (60,000), both in Concord; and the University of New Hampshire's Ezekiel W. Dimond Library (1,024,911) in Durham.

Among the more than 75 museums and historic sites are the Museum of New Hampshire History in Concord and the Franklin Pierce Homestead in Hillsboro.

44COMMUNICATIONS

In March 1993, 97.2% of New Hampshire's occupied housing units—about 419,000—had telephones. In 1993, the state had 70 radio stations (23 AM, 47 FM), 4 commercial television stations, and 3 non-commercial educational stations. State residents also receive broadcasts from neighboring Massachusetts, Vermont, and Maine. A total of five major cable systems in 1996 served the state.

45PRESS

In 1997, New Hampshire had 11 daily newspapers and 4 Sunday papers. The best-known newspaper in the state is the *Manchester Union–Leader* (66,890 daily and 96,175 Sunday), published by conservative William Loeb until his death in 1981. In the capital, the Concord *Monitor* circulates 21,703 papers daily and 22,489 on Sundays.

46ORGANIZATIONS

The 1992 Census of Service Industries counted 429 organizations in New Hampshire, including 83 business associations; 275 civic, social, and fraternal associations; and 71 other membership organizations. Organizations with headquarters in New Hampshire include the Student Conservation Association (Charlestown), the American Association of Commodity Traders (Concord), the American Society of Environmental Education (Hanover), and the Natural Organic Farmers Association (Antrim).

47TOURISM, TRAVEL, AND RECREATION

Tourism ranks 2d only to manufacturing in the economy of New Hampshire. Domestic travelers spent $1.4 million on overnight stays and day trips in New Hampshire during fiscal year 1993.

Skiing, camping, hiking, and boating are the main outdoor attractions. Other attractions include Strawbery Banke, a restored village in Portsmouth; Daniel Webster's birthplace near

Franklin; the Mt. Washington Cog Railway; and the natural "Old Man of the Mountains" granite head profile in the Franconia subrange of the White Mountains, on which the state's official emblem is modeled. Hunters numbering 148,670, and fishermen numbering 156,352 received permits and licenses in 1995.

48SPORTS

There are no major league professional sports teams in New Hampshire. Major national and international skiing events are frequently held in the state, as are such other winter competitions as snowmobile races and the Annual World Championship Sled Dog Derby in Laconia. Thoroughbred, harness, and greyhound racing are the warm-weather spectator sports. The annual Whaleback Yacht Race is held in early August.

Dartmouth College competes in the Ivy League, and the University of New Hampshire belongs to the Yankee Conference, both Division I-AA conferences.

The New Hampshire International Speedway, which opened in Loudon in 1994, plays host to a NASCAR Winston Cup stock car race in July, and an Indy Racing League event in August.

49FAMOUS NEW HAMPSHIRITES

Born in Hillsboro, Franklin Pierce (1804–69), the nation's 14th president, serving from 1853 to 1857, was the only US chief executive to come from New Hampshire. Henry Wilson (Jeremiah Jones Colbath, 1812–75), US vice president from 1873 to 1875, was a native of Farmington.

US Supreme Court chief justices Salmon P. Chase (1808–73), Harlan Fiske Stone (1872–1946), and David Souter (b.1939) were New Hampshirites, and Levi Woodbury (1789–1851) was a distinguished associate justice. John Langdon (1741–1819) was the first president pro tempore of the US Senate; two other US senators from New Hampshire, George Higgins Moses (b.Maine, 1869–1944) and Henry Styles Bridges (b.Maine, 1898–1961), also held this position. US cabinet members from New Hampshire included Henry Dearborn (1751–1829), secretary of war; Daniel Webster (1782–1852), secretary of state; and William E. Chandler (1835–1917), secretary of the Navy. Other political leaders of note were Benning Wentworth (1696–1770), royal governor Meshech Weare (1713–86), the state's leader during the American Revolution; Josiah Bartlett (b.Massachusetts, 1729–95), a physician, governor, and signer of the Declaration of Independence; Isaac Hill (b.Massachusetts, 1789–1851), a publisher, governor, and US senator; and John Parker Hale (1806–73), senator, antislavery agitator, minister to Spain, and presidential candidate of the Free Soil Party. John Sununu, a former Governor of New Hampshire (b. 1939, Cuba) was chief of staff during the Bush administration.

Military leaders associated with New Hampshire during the colonial and Revolutionary periods include John Stark (1728–1822), Robert Rogers (b.Massachusetts, 1731–95), and John Sullivan (1710–95). Among other figures of note are educator Eleazar Wheelock (b.Connecticut, 1711–79), the founder of Dartmouth College; physicians Lyman Spaulding (1775–1821), Reuben D. Mussey (1780–1866), and Amos Twitchell (1781–1850), as well as Samuel Thomson (1769–1843), a leading advocate of herbal medicine; religious leaders Hosea Ballou (1771–1852), his grandnephew of the same name (1796–1861), and Mary Baker Eddy (1821–1910), founder of Christian Science; George Whipple (1878–1976), winner of the 1934 Nobel Prize for physiology or medicine; and labor organizer and US Communist Party leader Elizabeth Gurley Flynn (1890–1964).

Sarah Josepha Hale (1788–1879), Horace Greeley (1811–72), Charles Dana (1819–97), Thomas Bailey Aldrich (1836–1907), Bradford Torrey (b.Massachusetts, 1843–1912), Alice Brown (1857–1948), and J(erome) D(avid) Salinger (b.New York, 1919) are among the writers and editors who have lived in New Hampshire, along with poets Edna Dean Proctor (1829–1923), Celia Laighton Thaxter (1826–94), Edward Arlington Robinson (b.Maine, 1869–1935), and Robert Frost (b.California, 1874–1963), one of whose poetry volumes is entitled *New Hampshire* (1923). Painter Benjamin Champney (1817–1907) and sculptor Daniel Chester French (1850–1931) were born in New Hampshire, while Augustus Saint-Gaudens (b.Ireland, 1848–1907) created much of his sculpture in the state.

Vaudevillian Will Cressey (1863–1930) was a New Hampshire man. More recent celebrities include newspaper publisher William Loeb (b.New York, 1905–81) and astronaut Alan B. Shepard, Jr. (b.1923).

50BIBLIOGRAPHY

Brown, William R. *Our Forest Heritage.* Concord: New Hampshire Historical Society, 1958.

Clark, Charles E. *The Eastern Frontier: The Settlement of Northern New England, 1610–1763.* New York: Knopf, 1970.

Federal Writers' Project. *New Hampshire: A Guide to the Granite State.* Reprint. New York: Somerset, n.d. (orig. 1938).

Morison, Elizabeth Forbes, and Elting E. Morison. *New Hampshire: A Bicentennial History.* New York: Norton, 1976.

Smith, Clyde H. *New Hampshire: A Scenic Discovery.* Dublin, N.H.: Yankee Books, 1985.

Squires, J. Duane. *The Granite State of the United States: A History of New Hampshire from 1623 to the Present.* 4 vols. New York: American Historical Co., 1956.

Stacker, Ann P., and Nancy C. Hefferman. *Short History of New Hampshire.* Grantham, N.H.: Thompson and Rutter, 1985.

Taylor, William L., ed. *Readings in New Hampshire and New England History.* New York: Irvington, 1981.

NEW JERSEY

State of New Jersey

ORIGIN OF STATE NAME: Named for the British Channel Island of Jersey. **NICKNAME:** The Garden State. **CAPITAL:** Trenton. **ENTERED UNION:** 18 December 1787 (3d). **MOTTO:** Liberty and Prosperity. **COLORS:** Bluff and Jersey blue. **COAT OF ARMS:** In the center is a shield with three plows, symbolic of agriculture; a helmet above indicates sovereignty, and a horse's head atop the helmet signifies speed and prosperity. The state motto and the date "1776" are displayed on a banner below. **FLAG:** The coat of arms on a buff field. **OFFICIAL SEAL:** The coat of arms surrounded by the words "The Great Seal of the State of New Jersey." **ANIMAL:** Horse. **BIRD:** Eastern goldfinch. **INSECT:** Honeybee. **FLOWER:** Violet. **TREE:** Red oak. **MEMORIAL TREE:** Dogwood. **LEGAL HOLIDAYS:** New Year's Day, 1 January; Birthday of Martin Luther King, Jr. 3d Monday in January; Lincoln's Birthday, 12 February; Washington's Birthday, 3d Monday in February; Good Friday, March or April; Memorial Day, last Monday in May; Independence Day, 4 July; Labor Day, 1st Monday in September; Columbus Day, 2d Monday in October; Election Day, 1st Tuesday after 1st Monday in November; Veterans Day, 11 November; Thanksgiving Day, 4th Thursday in November; Christmas Day, 25 December. **TIME:** 7 AM EST = noon GMT.

¹LOCATION, SIZE, AND EXTENT

Situated in the northeastern US, New Jersey is the smallest of the Middle Atlantic states and ranks 46th among the 50 states.

The total area of New Jersey is 7,787 sq mi (20,168 sq km), of which 7,468 sq mi (19,342 sq km) constitute land and 319 sq mi (826 sq km) are inland water. New Jersey extends 166 mi (267 km) N-S; the extreme width E-W is 57 mi (92 km).

New Jersey is bordered on the N and NE by New York State (with the boundary formed partly by the Hudson River, New York Bay, and Arthur Kill, and passing through Raritan Bay); on the E by the Atlantic Ocean; on the S and SW by Delaware (with the line passing through Delaware Bay); and on the W by Pennsylvania (separated by the Delaware River). Numerous barrier islands lie off the Atlantic coast.

New Jersey's total boundary length is 480 mi (773 km), including a general coastline of 130 mi (209 km); the tidal shoreline is 1,792 mi (2,884 km). The state's geographic center is in Mercer County, near Trenton.

²TOPOGRAPHY

Although small, New Jersey has considerable topographic variety. In the extreme northwest corner of the state are the Appalachian Valley and the Kittatinny Ridge and Valley. This area contains High Point, the state's peak elevation, at 1,803 feet (550 meters) above sea level. To the east and south is the highlands region, an area of many natural lakes and steep ridges, including the Ramapo Mountains, part of the Appalachian chain. East of the highlands is a flat area broken by the high ridges of the Watchungs and Sourlands and—most spectacularly—by the Palisades, a column of traprock rising some 500 feet (150 meters) above the Hudson River. The Atlantic Coastal Plain, a flat area with swamps and sandy beaches, claims the remaining two-thirds of the state. Its most notable feature is the Pine Barrens, 760 sq mi (1,968 sq km) of pitch pines and white oaks. Sandy Hook, a peninsula more than 5 mi (8 km) long, extending northward into the Atlantic from Monmouth County, is part of the Gateway National Recreation Area.

Major rivers include the Delaware, forming the border with Pennsylvania, and the Passaic, Hackensack, and Raritan. The largest natural lake is Lake Hopatcong, about 8 mi (13 km) long.

Some 550 to 600 million years ago, New Jersey's topography was the opposite of what it is now, with mountains to the east and a shallow sea to the west. Volcanic eruptions about 225 million years ago caused these eastern mountains to sink and new peaks to rise in the northwest; the lava flow formed the Watchung Mountains and the Palisades. The shoreline settled into its present shape at least 10,000 years ago.

³CLIMATE

Bounded by the Atlantic Ocean and the Delaware River, most of New Jersey has a moderate climate with cold winters and warm, humid summers. Winter temperatures are slightly colder and summer temperatures slightly milder in the northwestern hills than in the rest of the state.

In Atlantic City, the average mean temperature is 53°F (12°C), ranging from 31°F (–1°C) in January to 75°F (24°C) in July. Precipitation is plentiful, averaging 46 in (117 cm) annually; snowfall totals about 16 in (41 cm). The annual average humidity is 81% at 7 AM, reaching a normal high of 87% in September.

Statewide, the record high temperature is 110°F (43°C), set in Runyon on 10 July 1936; the record low is –34°F (–37°C), set in River Vale on 5 January 1904. A 29.7-in. (75.4-cm) accumulation on Long Beach Island in 1947 was the greatest 24-hour snowfall in the state's recorded history. Occasional hurricanes and violent spring storms have damaged beachfront property over the years, and floods along northern New Jersey rivers especially in the Passaic River basin, are not uncommon. A serious drought occurs, on average, about once every 15 years.

⁴FLORA AND FAUNA

Although highly urbanized, New Jersey still provides a diversity of natural regions, including a shady coastal zone, the hilly and wooded Allegheny zone, and the Pine Barrens in the south. Birch, beech, hickory, and elm all grow in the state, along with black locust, red maple, and 20 varieties of oak; common shrubs include the spicebush, staggerbush, and mountain laurel. Vast stretches beneath pine trees are covered with pyxie, a small creeping evergreen shrub. Common wild flowers include meadow rue, butterflyweed, black-eyed Susan, and the ubiquitous eastern (common) dandelion. Among rare plants are Candy's lobelia, floating heart, and pennywort; the small whorled pogonia is endangered.

Among mammals indigenous to New Jersey are the white-tailed deer, black bear, gray and red foxes, raccoon, woodchuck, opossum, striped skunk, eastern gray squirrel, eastern chipmunk, and common cottontail. The herring gull, sandpiper, and little green and night herons are common shore birds, while the red-eyed vireo, hermit thrush, English sparrow, robin, cardinal, and Baltimore oriole are frequently sighted inland. Anglers prize the northern pike, chain pickerel, and various species of bass, trout, and perch. Declining or rare animals include the whippoorwill, hooded warbler, eastern hognose snake, northern red salamander, and northern kingfish. The Atlantic green turtle, barred owl, bobolink, great blue heron, pied-billed grebe, corn snake, Atlantic tomcod, Atlantic sturgeon, and native brook trout are on the state's threatened species list. Fauna on the endangered list include six types of whale, four varieties of sea turtle, the Indiana bat, bald eagle, least tern, bog turtle, timber rattlesnake, Pine Barrens treefrog, Tremblay's salamander, and shortnose sturgeon.

5ENVIRONMENTAL PROTECTION

Laws and policies regulating the management and protection of New Jersey's environment and natural resources are administered by the Department of Environmental Protection (DEP). The state devoted 1.4% of its total budget appropriations, or $225.1 million, to environmental protection in 1996/97.

The proximity of the populace to industrial plants and to the state's expansive highway system makes air pollution control a special concern in the state. New Jersey had one of the most comprehensive air pollution control programs in the US, maintaining a network of 105 air pollution monitoring stations, as well as 60 stations that monitor just for particulates and 10 that monitor for radiation.

The DEP reported that a 1984 review of water quality in the state showed that water quality degradation had been halted and that the quality of streams had been stabilized or improved. The greatest improvements had been made in certain bays and estuaries along the Atlantic coast, where the elimination of discharges from older municipal sewage treatment plants resulted in the reopening of shellfish-harvesting grounds for the first time in 20 years. However, some rivers in highly urbanized areas were still severely polluted.

Approximately 1,500 treatment facilities discharge waste water into New Jersey's surface and ground waters. Nearly 80% of these facilities comply with the requirements of federal and state clean water laws. Solid waste disposal in New Jersey became critical as major landfills reached capacity. In 1977, the state had more than 300 operating landfills; in 1991 there were about 50 landfills. The state's solid waste stream is 1,100 tons per capita. Some counties and municipalities were implementing recycling programs in 1985, and the state legislature was considering a bill to make recycling mandatory. By 1991 the state of New Jersey had 26 curbside recycling programs.

New Jersey's toxic waste cleanup program is among the most serious in the US. In 1993, 109 hazardous waste sites—more than in any other state—were listed as national priorities for cleanup with federal Superfund financing. Four New Jersey locations, including the worst site in the nation (a landfill near Pitman), were listed among the top 10 on the Superfund list. The state has received over $1 billion in Superfund money for site cleanup.

The New Jersey Spill Compensation Fund was established by the state legislature in 1977 and amended in 1980. A tax based on the transfer of hazardous substances and petroleum products is paid into the fund and used for the cleanup of spills.

New Jersey was the first state to begin a statewide search for sites contaminated by dioxin, a toxic by-product in the manufacture of herbicides.

New Jersey first acquired land for preservation purposes in 1907. Since 1961, the state has bought more than 240,000 acres (97,000 hectares) under a "Green Acres" program for conservation and recreation. In 1984, an $83-million Green Trust Fund was established to expand land acquisition. The Green Acres Program has assisted county and municipal governments in acquiring over 70,000 acres (28,000 hectares). Additionally, Green Acres is assisting nonprofit conservation groups in acquiring over 20,000 acres (8,000 hectares) in a 50% matching grant program established in 1989. The US Congress designated 1.1 million acres (445,000 hectares) in the southern part of the state as the Pinelands National Reserve in 1978. Since then, the state has purchased more than 60,000 acres (24,000 hectares in the region, bringing the state open-space holding in the Pinelands to more than 270,000 acres (109,000 hectares). As of July 1, 1993, there were approximately 790,000 acres (319,000 hectares) of preserved public open space and recreation land in New Jersey.

6POPULATION

New Jersey ranked 9th among the 50 states in the 1990 census, with a total population of 7,730,188. This yielded an average density of 1,042 per sq mi (400 per sq km), making New Jersey the most densely populated state. The 1996 population totaled an estimated 7,987,933, a 3.3% increase over 1990.

Sparsely populated at the time of the Revolutionary War, New Jersey did not pass the 1 million mark until the 1880 census. Most of the state's subsequent growth came through migration, especially from New York during the period after 1950, when the New Jersey population had stood at 4,835,329. The most significant population growth came in older cities in northern New Jersey and in commuter towns near New York and Philadelphia. The average annual population growth declined from 2.3% in the 1950s to 1.7% in the 1960s and to 0.3% in the 1970s. Total growth during the 1980s was 5%. Net migration was no longer a growth factor, as the state actually experienced a net loss from migration of 275,000 during the 1970s.

New Jersey Counties, County Seats, and County Areas and Populations

COUNTY	COUNTY SEAT	LAND AREA (SQ MI)	POPULATION (1996 EST)
Atlantic	Mays Landing	568	235,447
Bergen	Hackensack	237	846,498
Burlington	Mt. Holly	808	410,931
Camden	Camden	223	506,420
Cape May	Cape May	263	98,252
Cumberland	Bridgeton	498	135,943
Essex	Newark	127	775,089
Gloucester	Woodbury	327	244,203
Hudson	Jersey City	46	550,789
Hunterdon	Flemington	427	118,737
Mercer	Trenton	227	330,226
Middlesex	New Brunswick	316	702,458
Monmouth	Freehold	472	591,182
Morris	Morristown	470	449,218
Ocean	Toms River	641	474,102
Passaic	Paterson	187	464,833
Salem	Salem	338	67,540
Somerset	Somerset	305	269,902
Sussex	Newton	525	141,308
Union	Elizabeth	103	497,281
Warren	Belvidere	359	97,574
TOTALS		7,468	7,987,933

The state's entire population is classified as living in metropolitan areas, a distinction claimed by no other state. Ironically, most of the state's major cities have declined in population, with Newark, the state's largest city, falling from 329,248 to about

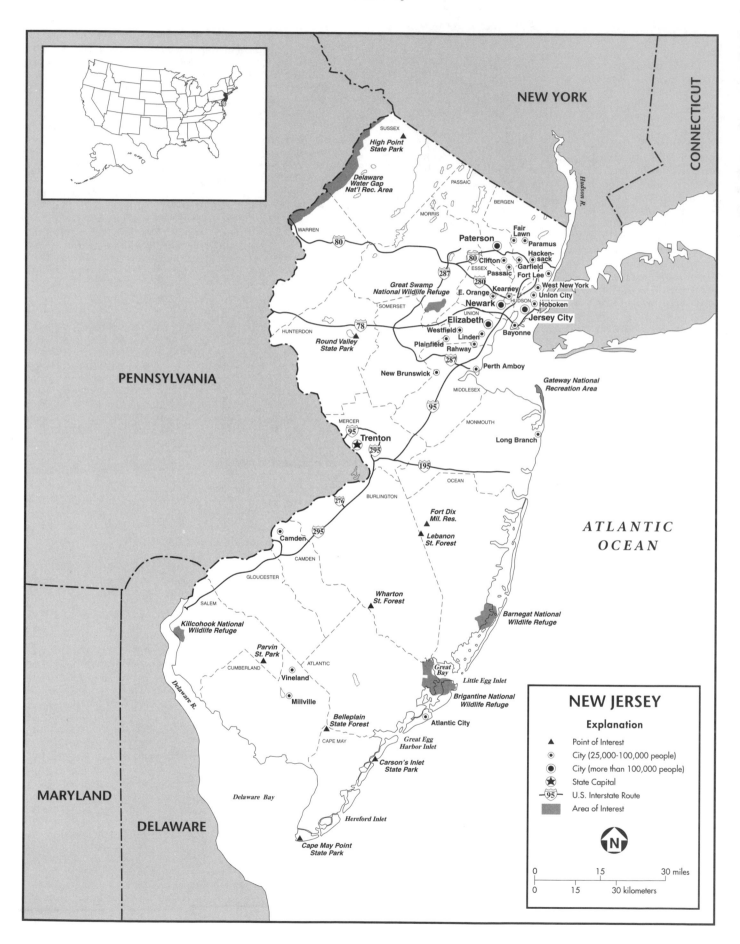

High Point
State Park

Delaware
Water Gap
Nat'l Rec. Area

SUSSEX

PASSAIC

WARREN

BERGEN

MORRIS

Paterson

Fair
Lawn

Paramus

Clifton

Hacken-
sack

Garfield

Passaic

Fort Lee

Great Swamp
National Wildlife Refuge

ESSEX

Kearney

West New York

E. Orange

Union City

Newark

HUDSON

Hoboken

SOMERSET

Elizabeth

Jersey City

Round Valley
State Park

Westfield

Linden

Bayonne

HUNTERDON

Plainfield

Rahway

Perth Amboy

New Brunswick

MIDDLESEX

Gateway National
Recreation Area

MERCER

MONMOUTH

Trenton

Long Branch

BURLINGTON

OCEAN

Fort Dix
Mil. Res.

Lebanon
St. Forest

Camden

CAMDEN

GLOUCESTER

Wharton
St. Forest

Barnegat National
Wildlife Refuge

SALEM

Killcohook National
Wildlife Refuge

Parvin
St. Park

CUMBERLAND

ATLANTIC

Vineland

Great
Bay

Little Egg Inlet

Brigantine National
Wildlife Refuge

Millville

Belleplain
State Forest

Atlantic City

CAPE MAY

Great Egg
Harbor Inlet

Carson's Inlet
State Park

Delaware Bay

Hereford Inlet

Cape May Point
State Park

PENNSYLVANIA

MARYLAND

DELAWARE

Delaware R.

NEW YORK

CONNECTICUT

Hudson R.

ATLANTIC
OCEAN

NEW JERSEY

Explanation

▲ Point of Interest

⊙ City (25,000-100,000 people)

◉ City (more than 100,000 people)

★ State Capital

95 U.S. Interstate Route

Area of Interest

0   15   30 miles

0   15   30 kilometers

275,000 between 1980 and 1990, a drop of 16.4%, and an estimated 258,751 in 1996, representing a further decline of 6%. Estimated populations of other New Jersey cities in 1994 were Jersey City, 226,022; Paterson 138,290; Elizabeth, 106,298; and Trenton, 84,441.

Parts of New Jersey are included in the New York City and Philadelphia metropolitan areas, the nation's largest and 5th largest, respectively.

7ETHNIC GROUPS

New Jersey is one of the most ethnically heterogeneous states. As of 1990, 966,610 New Jerseyites were of foreign birth. The leading countries of origin were Italy, 7.3%; Cuba, 6.5%; India, 5.4%; and Germany, 4.4%. The foreign born continue to come, including many from Colombia, Poland, the Philippines, and the Dominican Republic. Estimates for 1996 place the foreign-born population at 1,152,000 or 14.5% of the state's total population.

Blacks first came to New Jersey as slaves in the 1600s; the state abolished slavery in 1804, one of the last of the northern states to do so. Today black people constitute the state's largest (13.4%) ethnic minority, 1,037,000 as of 1990 (although 1996 estimates show a decline to 894,000). Newark, 58% black in 1990, elected its first black mayor, Kenneth Gibson, in 1970, three years after the city was torn by racial disorders that killed 26 people and injured some 1,500 others. In 1985, Gibson was in his fourth term as mayor.

There were 740,000 state residents of Hispanic origin in 1990 divided into distinct ethnic communities. The Puerto Rican population, which increased from 55,361 in 1960 to 219,942 in 1990, lived mostly in Newark, Jersey City, Elizabeth, Paterson, and Passaic. There were 72,373 Cubans in 1990, many of them in Union City and Elizabeth; their numbers were augmented by the migration of Cuban refugees in 1980. Smaller Spanish-speaking groups included Colombians and Dominicans. By 1996, the Hispanic population totaled an estimated 868,000.

The number of Asians living in New Jersey in 1990 was 273,000. The largest group of Asians is from India (54,039 in 1990). There were 51,821 Filipinos, 47,068 Chinese, 38,087 Koreans, and 19,948 Japanese. In 1996 the number of Asian/Pacific Islanders was estimated at 390,000.

American Indians numbered 15,000 in 1990; the state's total Native American population, including Eskimos and Aleuts, numbered an estimated 38,000 in 1996.Among the state's Indians is a group claiming to be descended from Dutch settlers, black slaves, British and German soldiers, and Leni-Lenape and Tuscarora Indians; incorporated as the Ramapough Mountain Indians in 1978, they live in the Ramapo hills near Ringwood and Mahwah.

8LANGUAGES

European settlers found New Jersey inhabited largely by the Leni-Lenape Indians, whose legacy can still be found in such place-names as Passaic, Totowa, Hopatcong, Kittatinny, and Piscataway.

English in New Jersey is rather evenly divided north and south between Northern and Midland dialects. Special characteristics of some New York metropolitan area speech occur in the northeast portion, such as the absence of /r/ after a vowel, a consonant like /d/ or /t/ instead of the /th/ sounds in *this* or *thin,* and pronunciations as *coop* rhyming with *stoop, food* with *good,* and *goal* and *fool; faucet* has the vowel of *father.* Dominant in the southern half are *run* (small stream), *baby coach* (baby carriage) in the Philadelphia trading area, *winnering owl* (screech owl), and *eel worm* (earthworm). Heard also are *out* as /aot/, *muskmelon* as /muskmillon/, and *keg* rhyming with *bag, scarce* with *fierce, spook* with *book,* and *haunted* with *panted.*

In 1990, 5,794,548 New Jerseyites—80.5% of the resident population 5 years old or older—spoke only English at home. Other languages spoken at home were:

Spanish	621,416	French	52,351
Italian	154,160	Chinese	47,334
Polish	69,145	Tagalog	38,107
Indic	60,248	Korean	30,712
German	56,877	Greek	28,080
Portuguese	55,285	Arabic	24,384

9RELIGIONS

With a history of religious tolerance, New Jersey has welcomed many denominations to its shores. Dutch immigrants founded a Reformed Church in 1662, the first in the state. After the English took control, Puritans came from New England and Long Island, Congregationalists from Connecticut, and Baptists from Rhode Island. Quaker settlements in Shrewsbury and western New Jersey during the early 1670s predated the better-known Quaker colony in Pennsylvania. Episcopalians, Presbyterians, German Lutherans, and Methodists arrived during the 18th century. The state's first synagogue was established in 1848, in Newark.

About the only religion not tolerated by New Jerseyites was Catholicism; the first Catholic parish was not organized until 1814, and laws excluding Catholics from holding office were on the books until 1844. The Catholics' numbers swelled as a result of Irish immigration after 1845, and even more with the arrival of Italians after 1880. Today, Roman Catholics constitute the state's single largest religious group, with a population of 3,189,315 in 1990. Passaic is the headquarters of the Byzantine-Ruthenian Rite in the Byzantine Catholic Church.

The Jewish population was estimated at 429,885 in 1990. The largest Protestant denomination in 1990 was the United Methodist, with 166,502 adherents, followed by the United Presbyterian Church, with 138,763; Episcopal, 105,607; Evangelical Lutheran Church in America, 86,825; American Baptist Convention, 82,795; and Reformed Church in America, 41,392.

10TRANSPORTATION

Ever since the first traders sought the fastest way to get from New York to Philadelphia, transportation has been of central importance to New Jersey and has greatly shaped its growth. In the mid-1820s, Hoboken engineer John Stevens built the first steam locomotive operated in the US; over the protests of the dominant stagecoach operators, his son Robert obtained a charter in 1830 for the Camden and Amboy Railroad. The line opened in 1834, and six years later it held a monopoly on the lucrative New York–Philadelphia run. Other lines—such as the Elizabeth and Somerville, the Morris and Essex, the Paterson and Hudson, and the Jersey Central—were limited to shorter runs, largely because the Camden and Amboy's influence with the legislature gave it a huge competitive advantage. Camden and Amboy stock was leased to the Pennsylvania Railroad in 1871, and the ensuing controversy over whether New Jersey transit should be entrusted to an "alien" company led to the passage of a law opening up the state to rail competition. Industry grew around the rail lines, and the railroads became a vital link in the shipment of products from New York and northern New Jersey.

As of 1995, the major freight operations were run by Conrail, representing a consolidation of several bankrupt freight carriers, including the Penn Central, Central of New Jersey, Erie-Lackawanna, Reading, Lehigh Valley, and Lehigh and Hudson River railroads. In 1995, there were 1,094 route mi (1,761 km) of track in the state; about 73% of the total was Class I track operated by Conrail. In addition, there were two regional, five local, and seven switching and terminal railroads operating in the state. About 90 daily Amtrak trains linking Newark, Trenton, and a few other New Jersey cities along the main eastern rail corridor served 1,264,308 riders in 1995/96. But the bulk of interstate passenger traffic consists of commuters to New York and Philadelphia on trains operated by the Port Authority of New York and New Jersey (PA) and the Port Authority Transit Corp. (PATCO), a subsidiary of the Delaware River Port Authority.

The New Jersey Transit Corporation, called NJ TRANSIT, is a public corporation created under the Public Transportation Act of 1979. The corporation is charged with coordinating and improving bus and rail services throughout the state. It is one of the nation's largest pubic transit agencies, providing 189 million passenger trips annually for 321,000 daily riders. It operates 591 daily trains on 12 rail lines, covering 544.9 track miles and 334 route miles, and 1,900 buses on 177 routes throughout the state. It also owns and operates the Newark City Subway, a 4.3-mile light rail system providing service through downtown Newark. NJ TRANSIT provides contracts for 61 privately-run routes and leases 224 buses to these contract carriers. In addition, approximately 800 buses are leased, at no cost, to independent private carriers.

Although associated more with the West, the first stagecoach service began in New Jersey, as part of a New York–Philadelphia trek that took some five days in 1723. For a time, colonial law required towns along the way to provide taverns for the passengers, and it was not uncommon for coach operators who were also tavern owners to find some way to prolong the journey an extra night. They traveled on roads that were barely more passable than the Leni-Lenape trails from which they originated. Improvement was slow, but by 1828, the legislature had granted 54 turnpike charters.

Road building has continued ever since. In 1995 there were 35,646 mi (57,390 km) of roads in the state, including about 381 mi (613 km) of state toll roads, and 93 mi (153 km) of interstate toll roads. Altogether, state-administered toll roads received over $545.6 million from motorists (2d only to New York), mostly from the New Jersey Turnpike and the Garden State Parkway. In 1995 there also were 3,284 mi (5,244 km) of state highways, 8,460 mi (11,485 km) of county roads, 23,862 mi (38,391 km) of municipal roads, and 40 mi (70 km) of national park and forest roads. The major highways are the New Jersey Turnpike, opened in 1952 and extending 133 mi (214 km) between Bergen and Salem counties, and the Garden State Parkway, completed in 1955 and stretching 173 mi (278 km) from the New York State line to Cape May. More than 61 billion vehicle-mi (80 billion vehicle-km) were traveled on state roads in 1995, when there were 5,403,671 licensed New Jersey drivers. New Jersey highways are congested; on average, 4,689 vehicles used each mile of the state's highways every day in 1995, compared to a US average of 1,697. Nonetheless, fatalities per 100 million miles driven in 1991 stood at 1.18, lower than the US average of 1.54.

Many bridges and tunnels link New Jersey with New York State, Pennsylvania, and Delaware. Twenty-seven bridges cross the Delaware River, connecting New Jersey with Pennsylvania and Delaware.

At the gateway to New York Harbor, ports at Elizabeth and Newark have overtaken New York City ports in cargo volume, and contribute greatly to the local economy. Operated by the Port Authority of New York and New Jersey, Port Newark has almost 4 miles of berthing space along Newark Bay, while nearby Port Elizabeth, with better than 3 miles of berths, is a major handler of containerized cargo. Private piers in Jersey City and Bayonne handle both containerized and bulk cargoes. The tonnage handled by northern New Jersey port facilities, taken as a whole, make it the largest port on the east coast, and second largest overall in the United States. The Ports of Philadelphia and Camden, Inc., headquartered in Philadelphia, operates facilities along the Delaware River including the Beckett Street and Broadway Terminals in Camden formerly operated by the South Jersey Port Corporation. The port facility at Paulsboro is the most active in the state, with 24.8 million tons of cargo (primarily petroleum) handled in 1995. The Camden ports handled some 5.9 million tons during the same period.

The state's early aviation centers were Lakehurst and Newark. Lakehurst, whose dirigible operations attracted crowds of spectators during the 1920s and 1930s, was the scene of the crash on 6 May 1937 of the *Hindenburg,* a disaster that killed 26 people and spelled the end of commercial airship flights in the US. The state's first airmail service began in 1924 from New Brunswick's Hadley Field. Newark Airport in the late 1920s billed itself as the busiest air terminal in the world. The PA took over its operation from the city of Newark in 1948. Rebuilt during the 1960s and 1970s, Newark International Airport has become the state's busiest by far; it handled 11,863,730 passengers (10th highest in the nation) and 286,675 tons of freight in 1994. Statewide in 1995 there were 114 airports, 227 heliports, and 11 seaplane bases.

[11]HISTORY

The first known inhabitants of what is now New Jersey were the Leni-Lenape (meaning "Original People"), who arrived in the land between the Hudson and Delaware rivers about 6,000 years ago. Members of the Algonkian language group, the Leni-Lenape were an agricultural people supplementing their diet with fresh-water fish and shellfish. The peace-loving Leni-Lenape believed in monogamy, educated their children in the simple skills needed for wilderness survival, and clung rigidly to a tradition that a pot of food must always be warm on the fire to welcome all strangers.

The first European explorer to reach New Jersey was Giovanni da Verrazano, who sailed into what is now Newark Bay in 1524. Henry Hudson, an English captain sailing under a Dutch flag, piloted the *Half Moon* along the New Jersey shore and into Sandy Hook Bay in the late summer of 1609, a voyage that established a Dutch claim to the New World. Hollanders came to trade in what is now Hudson County as early as 1618, and in 1660, they founded New Jersey's first town, called Bergen (now part of Jersey City). Meanwhile, across the state, Swedish settlers began moving east of the Delaware River in 1639. Their colony of New Sweden had only one brief spurt of glory, from 1643 to 1653, under Governor Johan Printz.

The Leni-Lenape lost out to the newcomers, whether Dutch, Swedish, or English, despite a series of treaties that the Europeans thought fair. State and local records describe these agreements: huge tracts of land exchanged for trinkets, guns, and alcohol. The guns and alcohol, combined with smallpox (another European import), doomed the "Original People." In 1758, when a treaty established an Indian reservation at Brotherton (now the town of Indian Mills), only a few hundred Indians remained.

England assumed control in March 1664, when King Charles II granted a region from the Connecticut River to the Delaware River to his brother James, the Duke of York. The duke, in turn, deeded the land between the Hudson and Delaware rivers, which he named New Jersey, to his court friends John Berkeley, 1st Baron Berkeley of Stratton, and Sir George Carteret, on 23 June 1664. Lord Berkeley and Sir George became proprietors, owning the land and having the right to govern its people. Subsequently, the land passed into the hands of two boards of proprietors in two provinces called East Jersey and West Jersey, with their capitals in Perth Amboy and Burlington, respectively. East Jersey was settled mainly by Puritans from Long Island and New England, West Jersey by Quakers from England. The split cost the colony dearly until 1702, when Queen Anne united East and West Jersey but placed them under New York rule. The colony did not get its own "home rule" until 1738, when Lewis Morris was named the first royal governor.

By this time, New Jersey's divided character was already established. Eastern New Jersey looked toward New York, western New Jersey toward Philadelphia. The level plain connecting those two major colonial towns made it certain that New Jersey would serve as a pathway. Along the makeshift roads that soon crossed the region—more roads than in any other colony—travelers brought conflicting news and ideas. During the American Revolution, the colony was about equally divided between Revolutionists and Loyalists. William Franklin (illegitimate son of Benjamin Franklin), royal governor from 1763 until 1776, strove valiantly to keep New Jersey sympathetic to England, but failed and was arrested. Throughout the Revolutionary period, he remained a leading Loyalist; after the war, he left for England.

Franklin's influence caused New Jersey to dally at first over independence, but in June 1776, the colony sent five new delegates to the Continental Congress—Abraham Clark, John Hart, Frances Hopkinson, Richard Stockton, and the Reverend John Witherspoon—all of whom voted for the Declaration of Independence. Two days before the Declaration was proclaimed, New Jersey adopted its first state constitution. William Livingston, a fiery anti-British propagandist, was the first elected governor of the state.

New Jersey played a pivotal role in the Revolutionary War, for the side that controlled both New York and Philadelphia would almost certainly win. George Washington and his battered troops made their winter headquarters in the state three times during the first four years of the war, twice in Morristown and once in Somerville. Five major battles were fought in New Jersey, the most important being the Battle of Trenton on 26 December 1776 and the Battle of Monmouth on 28 June 1778. At war's end, Princeton became the temporary capital of the US from 26 June 1783 to 4 November 1783.

The state languished after the Revolution, with many of its pathway towns ravaged by the passing of competing armies, its trade dependent on New York City, and its ironworks (first established in 1676) shut down because of decreased demand. The state's leaders vigorously supported a federation of the 13 states, in which all states, regardless of size, would be represented equally in one national legislative body. This so-called New Jersey Plan led to the establishment of the US Senate.

Railroads and canals brought life to the state in the 1830s and set it on a course of urbanization and industrialization. The 90-mi (145-km) Morris Canal linked northern New Jersey with the coal fields of Pennsylvania. Considered one of the engineering marvels of the 19th century, the canal rose to 914 feet (279 meters) from sea level at Newark Bay to Lake Hopatcong, then fell 760 feet (232 meters) to a point on the Delaware River opposite Easton, Pa. Old iron mines beside the canal found markets, the dyeing and weaving mills of Paterson prospered, and Newark, most affected by the emerging industries, became the state's first incorporated city in 1836. Another canal, the Delaware and Raritan, crossed the relatively flat land from Bordentown, Trenton, and New Brunswick boomed. Princeton, whose leaders fought to keep the canal away from the town, settled into a long existence as a college community built around the College of New Jersey, founded in Elizabeth in 1746 and transferred to Princeton in 1756.

The canals were doomed by railroad competition almost from the start. The Morris Canal was insolvent long before World War I, and the Delaware Canal, although operative until 1934, went into a long, slow decline after the Civil War. The first railroad, from Bordentown to South Amboy, closely paralleled the Delaware and Raritan Canal and in 1871 became an important part of the Pennsylvania Railroad. The coal brought in on railroad cars freed industry from waterpower; factories sprang up wherever the rails went. The Hudson County waterfront, eastern terminus for most of the nation's railway systems, became the most important railroad area in the US. Rail lines also carried vacationers to the Jersey shore, building an important source of income for the state.

The Civil War split New Jersey bitterly. Leaders in the Democratic Party opposed the war as a "Black Republican" affair. Prosperous industrialists in Newark and Trenton feared that their vigorous trade with the South would be impaired, Cape May hotelkeepers fretted about the loss of tourists from Virginia, and even Princeton students were divided. As late as the summer of 1863, after the Battle of Gettysburg, many state "peace Democrats" were urging the North to make peace with the Confederacy. Draft calls were vigorously opposed in 1863, yet the state sent its full quota of troops into service throughout the conflict. Most important, New Jersey factories poured forth streams of munitions and other equipment for the Union army. At war's end, political leaders stubbornly opposed the 13th, 14th, and 15th Amendments to the US Constitution, and blacks were not permitted to vote in the state until 1870.

During the last decades of the 19th century, New Jersey developed a reputation for factories capable of making the components necessary for thousands of other manufacturing enterprises. Few factories were large, although in 1873, Isaac M. Singer opened a huge sewing machine plant at Elizabeth that employed 3,000 persons. Oil refineries on the Hudson County waterfront had ever-expanding payrolls, pottery firms in Trenton thrived, and Newark gained strength from many diversified manufacturers and also saw its insurance companies become nationally powerful.

Twentieth-century wars stimulated New Jersey's industries. During World War I, giant shipyards at Newark, Kearny, and Camden made New Jersey the nation's leading shipbuilding state. The Middlesex County area refined 75% of the nation's copper, and nearly 75% of US shells were loaded in the state. World War II revived the shipbuilding and munitions industries, while chemical and pharmaceutical manufacturing, spawned by the World War I cutoff of German chemicals, showed further growth during the second world conflict. Paterson, preeminent in locomotive building during the 19th century, became the nation's foremost airplane engine manufacturing center. Training and mobilization centers at Ft. Dix and Camp Kilmer moved millions of soldiers into the front lines.

The US Census Bureau termed New Jersey officially "urban" in 1880, when the state population rose above 1 million for the first time. Urbanization intensified throughout the 20th century and especially after World War II, as people left the old cities in New Jersey and other northeastern states to buy homes in developments on former farmlands. Places like Cherry Hill, Woodbridge, Clifton, and Middletown Township have boomed since 1945, increasing their population as much as sixfold. New Jersey has also experienced many of the problems of urbanization. Its cities have declined; traffic congestion is intense in the morning, when commuters stream into urban areas to work, and again in the evening, when they return home to what once was called "the country." That country now knows the problems of urban growth: increased needs for schools, sewers, police and fire protection, and road maintenance, along with rising taxes.

The state has not surrendered to its problems, however. In 1947, voters overwhelmingly approved a new state constitution, a terse, comprehensive document that streamlined state government, reformed the state's chaotic court system, and mandated equal rights for all. Governor Alfred E. Driscoll promptly integrated the New Jersey National Guard, despite strong federal objectives; integration of all US armed forces soon followed. Voters since 1950 have passed a wide variety of multimillion-dollar bond issues to establish or rebuild state colleges. Rutgers, the state university, has been rapidly expanded. Funds have been allocated for the purchase and development of new park and forest lands. Large bond issues have financed the construction of highways, reservoirs, and rapid transit systems.

In the seventies and early eighties, New Jersey experienced a recession. The unemployment rate climbed to almost 10%. Over 270,000 people left the state. The state's cities were hit particularly hard, suffering both from the loss of manufacturing jobs and from a flight of retailing to suburban malls. The economy of New Jersey in these decades also underwent a dramatic restructuring. While the state lost over 200,000 manufacturing jobs it gained 670,000 jobs in service industries. The economy rebounded during the eighties, but began to contract again at the end of the decade, and declined further during the recession of early 1990s. In 1996 the state's unemployment rate fell below 6% for the first time in six years. Observers credited the recovery of the 1990s in part to a skilled workforce that attracted pharmaceutical, biotechnology, electronics, and other high-tech firms to the state. Tax and economic incentives have also helped bring business to the state.

Since the end of World War II, New Jersey has had no predictable political pattern. It gave huge presidential majorities to Republican Dwight D. Eisenhower and Democrat Lyndon B. Johnson, narrowly supported Democrat John F. Kennedy, favored Republican Gerald Ford over Democrat Jimmy Carter by a small margin, and gave two big majorities to Ronald Reagan. For more than 20 years, the state's two US senators, Clifford B. Case (R) and Harrison A. Williams (D), were recognized as like-minded liberals. Democrat Bill Bradley, former Princeton University and New York Knickerbockers basketball star, was elected to Case's seat in 1978.

Republican Governor Thomas Kean, who served from 1983–89, helped to improve the public image of New Jersey, long perceived as dominated by smoke-belching factories and troubled cities. Kean was succeeded by Democrat Jim Florio who sought to redistribute wealth throughout the state by doubling the income tax of those in the top bracket, raising the sales tax, lowering property taxes for middle- and low-income homeowners and renters, and shifting state aid from public schools in affluent areas to schools in poor and moderate income communities. In 1992, Florio lost his bid for reelection to Republican Christine Todd Whitman, who promised to lower income taxes by 30%. As soon as she took office, Whitman implemented a 5% cut and pushed through another 10% cut as part of her budget package in 1993.

12STATE GOVERNMENT

New Jersey's first state constitution took effect in 1776. A second constitution was written in 1844, and a third in 1947. This last document, as amended, continues to govern the state today.

The state legislature consists of a 40-member senate and an 80-member general assembly. Senators, elected to four-year terms, must be at least 30 years of age and have been New Jersey residents for four years and district residents for a year. Assembly members, elected to two-year terms, must be at least 21 years of age and have been New Jersey residents for two years and district residents for a year. Both houses of the legislature meet in unlimited annual sessions. The legislative salary was $35,000 in 1995.

New Jersey is one of only two states—the other is Maine—in which the governor is the only elective administrative official. Given broad powers by the state constitution, the governor appoints the heads, or commissioners, of the 20 major state departments with the advice and consent of the senate; not subject to senate approval are more than 500 patronage positions. The governor is also commander-in-chief of the state's armed forces, submits the budget to the legislature each January, presents an annual message on the condition of the state, and may grant pardons and, with the aid of the Parole Board, grant

executive clemency. Elected to a four-year term in the odd-numbered year following the presidential election, the governor may run for a second term but not for a third until four years have passed. A candidate for governor must be at least 30 years old and must have been a US citizen for 20 years and a New Jersey citizen for 7 years in order to qualify for the ballot. In 1996 the governor's salary was $85,000.

A bill may be introduced in either house of the legislature. Once passed, it goes to the governor, who may sign it, return it to the legislature with recommendations for change, or veto it in its entirety. A two-thirds majority in each house is needed to override a veto.

Amendments to the state constitution may originate in either house. If, after public hearings, both houses pass the proposal by a three-fifths vote, the amendment is placed on the ballot at the next general election. If approved by a majority, but by less than a three-fifths vote in both houses, the amendment is referred to the next session of the legislature, at which time, if again approved by a majority, it is placed on the ballot. The amendment goes into effect 30 days after ratification by the electorate.

To vote in New Jersey, one must be at least 18 years old, a US citizen, and a New Jersey resident for 30 days before the election.

13POLITICAL PARTIES

From the 1830s through the early 1850s, Democrats and Whigs dominated the political life of New Jersey. Exercising considerable, though subtle, influence in the decade before the Civil War was the Native American (Know-Nothing) Party, an anti-immigrant, anti-Catholic group that won several assembly and senate seats. Wary of breaking ties with the South and ambivalent about the slavery issue, New Jerseyites, especially those in Essex and Bergen counties, did not lend much support to the abolitionist cause. Early Republicans thus found it advantageous to call themselves simply "Opposition;" the state's first Opposition governor was elected in 1856. Republicans controlled the state for most of the 1860s; but with heavy support from business leaders, the Democrats regained control in 1869 and held the governorship through 1896. They were succeeded by a series of Progressive Republican governors whose efforts were largely thwarted by a conservative legislature. Sweeping reforms—including a corrupt-practices act, a primary election law, and increased support for public education—were implemented during the two years that Woodrow Wilson, a Democrat, served as governor before being elected to the presidency. Between 1913 and 1985, Democrats held the statehouse almost two-thirds of the time.

As of 1994 there were 1,175,041 registered Democrats, comprising 29% of the total number of registered voters; 817,837 Republicans, or 20%; and 2,067,459 independents, or 51%. In 1997, the state senate contained 24 Republicans and 16 Democrats, while the General Assembly consisted of 49 Republicans and 29 Democrats. In the 1996 presidential voting, Democrat Bill Clinton defeated Republican Bob Dole, picking up 54% of the vote to Dole's 36%. Independent Ross Perot garnered 9%. In 1993, New Jersey elected its first woman as governor, Republican Christine Todd Whitman. In the 1996 elections, the Republicans retained a slim 7-6 majority among New Jersey's 13 US representatives. Democratic representative Robert G. Torricelli won the Senate seat vacated by Democrat Bill Bradley. New Jersey's other senator is Frank R. Lautenberg, who was elected in 1994.

In 1994, there were 211 blacks and 37 Hispanics holding public office. In 1995, 16 women served in the state legislature.

New Jersey's unenviable reputation for corruption in government dates back at least to 1838, when ballot tampering resulted in the disputed election of five Whigs to the US House of Representatives. (After a House investigation, the Whigs were barred and their Democratic opponents given the seats.) Throughout the rest of the century, corruption was rampant in local elections: Philadelphians, for example, were regularly imported to vote in Atlantic City elections, and vote buying was a standard election-day procedure in Essex and Hudson counties. Wilson's 1911 reform bill eliminated some of these practices, but not the bossism that had come to dominate big-city politics. Frank Hague of Jersey City controlled patronage and political leaders on the local, state, and national level from 1919 to 1947; during the 1960s and 1970s, Hague's successor John V. Kenny, Jersey City mayor Thomas Whelan, and Newark mayor Hugh Addonizio, along with numerous other state and local officials, were convicted of corrupt political dealings. From 1969 to mid-1975, federal prosecutors indicted 148 public officials, securing 72 convictions. Brendan Byrne, who had never before held elective office, won the governorship in 1973, mainly on the strength of a campaign that portrayed him as the "judge who couldn't be bought." On the national level, New Jersey Representative Peter Rodino gained a reputation for honesty and fairness when he chaired the House Judiciary Committee's impeachment hearings against Richard Nixon. However, the state's image suffered a further blow in 1980, when, as a result of the FBI's "ABSCAM" investigation, charges of influence peddling were brought against several state officials, including members of the Casino Control Commission, whose function was to prevent corruption and crime in Atlantic City's gambling establishments.

Later in the year, New Jersey Democrat Harrison Williams became the nation's first US senator to be indicted, on charges of bribery and conspiracy, as a result of the ABSCAM probe. He was convicted in 1981 and sentenced to prison. As a result of the same investigation, US Representative Frank Thompson, Jr., was convicted in 1980 on bribery and conspiracy charges. A New Jerseyite, Raymond Donovan, was named secretary of labor by President Ronald Reagan in 1981, but he resigned in 1985 after being indicted late in 1984 for allegedly seeking to defraud the New York City Transit Authority while serving as vice president of the Schiavone Construction Company in Secaucus.

[14]LOCAL GOVERNMENT

As of 1992, New Jersey had 21 counties, 320 municipal governments, 247 townships, 550 school districts, and 374 special districts.

Counties are classified by population and location. First-class counties (3 in 1994) have populations exceeding 600,000; second-class counties (9), populations of 200,000–600,000; third-class counties (6), populations of 50,000–200,000 but no Atlantic shore; fourth-class counties (0), under 50,000 population, no Atlantic shore; fifth-class counties (3), population more than 100,000, Atlantic shore; and sixth-class counties (0), less than 100,000 population, Atlantic shore. These classes determine the number of members on the main county governing body, the board of freeholders, which may range from three to nine. Elected to staggered three-year terms, the freeholders administer county and state programs. Under the Optional County Charter Law of 1972, four counties have an elected county executive, and one county has an appointed county manager. Other county officers are the clerk, sheriff, surrogate, prosecutor, boards of election and taxation, county counsel, administrator, medical examiner, chief probation officer, and jury commissioner.

Cities, boroughs, and towns may employ the mayor-council system, council-manager system, commission system, or other forms of their own devising. Most townships and villages are governed by committee or by a council and a mayor with limited powers. Cities, too, are classed by population and location: first-class cities are those over 150,000 in population; second-class, 12,000–150,000; third-class, all others except ocean resorts; and fourth-class, ocean resorts.

The budgets of all local units are supervised by the New Jersey Department of Community Affairs, which also offers municipal aid programs. By state law, all local budgets must be balanced,

New Jersey Presidential Vote by Political Parties, 1948–96

YEAR	ELECTORAL VOTES	NEW JERSEY WINNER	DEMOCRAT	REPUBLICAN	PROGRESSIVE		SOCIALIST	PROHIBITION	SOCIALIST LABOR	SOCIALIST WORKERS
1948	16	Dewey (R)	895,455	981,124	42,683		10,521	10,593	3,354	5,825
1952	16	*Eisenhower (R)	1,015,902	1,373,613	5,589		8,593	—	5,815	3,850
					CONSTITUTION					
1956	16	*Eisenhower (R)	850,337	1,606,942	5,317		—	9,147	6,736	4,004
					CONSERVATIVE					
1960	16	*Kennedy (D)	1,385,415	1,363,324	8,708		—	—	4,262	11,402
1964	17	*Johnson (D)	1,867,671	963,843	—		—	—	7,075	8,181
					AMERICAN IND.	PEACE & FREEDOM				
1968	17	*Nixon (R)	1,264,206	1,325,467	262,187		8,084	—	6,784	8,667
					PEOPLE'S	AMERICAN				
1972	17	*Nixon (R)	1,102,211	1,845,502	—		5,355	34,378	4,544	2,233
					US LABOR	LIBERTARIAN				COMMUNIST
1976	17	Ford (R)	1,444,653	1,509,688	7,716		1,650	9,449	3,686	1,662
1980	17	*Reagan (R)	1,147,364	1,546,557	8,203		—	20,652	2,198	2,555
						WORKERS WORLD				
1984	16	*Reagan (R)	1,261,323	1,933,630	—		8,404	6,416	—	1,564
					NEW ALLIANCE	PEACE & FREEDOM			CONSUMER	SOCIALIST
1988	16	*Bush (R)	1,320,352	1,743,192	5,139		9,953	8,421	3,454	2,587
					IND. (PEROT)			IND. (BRADFORD)		TAXPAYERS
1992	15	*Clinton (D)	1,436,206	1,356,865	3,513		521,829	6,822	4,749	2,670
1996	15	*Clinton(D)	1,652,329	1,103,078	—		262,134	14,763	GREEN (Nader) 32,465	

* Won US presidential election.

and budgetary increases ("budget caps") are limited to 5% a year for most items.

[15]STATE SERVICES

The constitution of 1947 limited the number of state government departments to 20, and that was the total in 1985. New Jersey in 1974 became the first state to establish a Public Advocate Department, empowered to provide legal assistance for indigent criminal defendants, mental patients, and any citizen with a grievance against a government agency or regulated industry. A Code of Ethics, adopted by the legislature in 1976, seeks to prevent state employees from using their positions for personal gain. By executive order, more than 500 state executive officials must file financial disclosure statements.

The Education Department administers state and federal aid to all elementary and secondary schools, oversees pupil transportation, and has jurisdiction over the state library, museum, and historical commission. State-run colleges and universities and higher education policy are the province of the Department of Higher Education. All state-maintained highways and bus and rail transportation are the responsibility of the Department of Transportation, which also operates New Jersey Transit, whose function is to acquire and operate public transportation services.

The Human Services Department administers welfare, Medicaid, mental health, and mental retardation programs, as well as veterans' institutions and programs and other state-supported social services. Alcohol, drug abuse, and many other health-related programs are monitored by the Health Department, which also oversees hospitals and compiles statewide health statistics.

The Office of the Attorney General, officially titled the Department of Law and Public Safety, is the statewide law enforcement agency. Its functions include criminal justice, consumer affairs, civil rights, alcoholic beverage control, and gaming enforcement; also within this department are the State Police, State Racing Commission, Violent Crimes Compensation Board, and a number of regulatory boards. The Defense Department controls the Army and Air National Guard. Correctional institutions, training schools, treatment centers, and parole offices are administered by the Corrections Department.

The Department of Energy monitors the supply and use of fuel and administers the state master plan for energy use and conservation; its Board of Public Utilities has broad regulatory jurisdiction, ranging from garbage collection to public broadcasting. Other agencies are the departments of agriculture, banking, civil service, commerce and economic development, community affairs, environmental protection, insurance, labor and industry, state, and treasury.

[16]JUDICIAL SYSTEM

All judges in New Jersey, except municipal court judges, are appointed by the governor with the consent of the senate. Initial terms for supreme and superior court judges are seven years; after reappointment, judges may serve indefinitely.

The supreme court, the state's highest, consists of six associate justices and a chief justice, who is also the administrative head of the state court system. As the court of highest authority, the supreme court hears appeals on constitutional questions and on certain cases from the superior court, which comprises three divisions: chancery, law, and appellate. The chancery division has original jurisdiction over general equity cases, most probate cases, and divorce actions. All other original cases are tried within the law division. The appellate division hears appeals from the chancery and law divisions, from lower courts, and from most state administrative agencies. A state tax court, empowered to review local property tax assessments, equalization tables, and state tax determinations, has been in operation since 1979; by

statute, it may have from 6 to 12 judges. Municipal court judges, appointed by local governing bodies for three-year terms, hear minor criminal matters, motor vehicle cases, and violations of municipal ordinances. In 1996 there were 48,320 practicing attorneys in the state.

The legislature approved a sweeping reform of the state's criminal law code in 1978. Strict sentencing standards were established, and one result was an overcrowding of the state's prison system. Governor Brendan Byrne signed a law in 1981 imposing a minimum three-year sentence on anyone committing a crime with a gun. In 1982, Governor Thomas Kean signed legislation establishing a death penalty by lethal injection; New Jersey became the ninth state to use that method, although the sentence has yet to be imposed.

According to the FBI Crime Index, in 1995 New Jersey had a total crime rate of 4,703.7 per 100,000 persons, including 599.8 for violent crime and 4,103.9 for property crime. Specific rates included murder and nonnegligent homicide, 5.1; forcible rape, 24.3; robbery, 283; aggravated assault, 287.4; burglary, 875.2; larceny-theft, 2,597.1; and motor vehicle theft, 631.6. Prisoners under jurisdiction of state and federal correctional authorities in New Jersey numbered 19,387 in 1995.

[17]ARMED FORCES

In 1996, there were 6,568 active duty military personnel in New Jersey. The largest installation in the state is McGuire Air Force Base in Wrightstown, with 4,818 active duty personnel. The US Coast Guard operates a training center in Cape May. New Jersey firms received over $2.5 billion in defense contracts awards in 1996.

Of the 726,000 estimated veterans living in New Jersey on 1 July 1992, World War I veterans numbered less than 500; World War II, 229,000, Korean Conflict, 129,000; Vietnam era, 200,000; and Persian Gulf War, 34,000. Veterans' benefits in 1996 totaled $763 million.

In 1996, 17,746 persons served in the New Jersey Army Reserve and National Guard and 6,246 in the Air National Guard and Reserve.

In 1993, the New Jersey State Police employed 1,631 full-time sworn officers, or 3 per 10,000 residents.

[18]MIGRATION

New Jersey's first white settlers were intercolonial migrants: Dutch from New Amsterdam, Swedes from west of the Delaware River, and Puritans from New England and Long Island. By 1776, New Jersey's population was about 138,000, of whom perhaps 7% were black slaves.

Population growth lagged during the early 19th century, as discouraged farmers left their worn-out plots for more fertile western soil; farmers in Salem County, for example, went off to found new Salems in Ohio, Indiana, Iowa, and Oregon. Not until the rapid industrial growth of the mid-1800s did New Jersey attract great waves of immigrants. Germans and Irish were the first to arrive, the latter comprising 37% of Jersey City's population by 1870. The late 1800s and early 1900s brought newcomers from Eastern Europe, including many Jews, and a much larger number of Italians to the cities. By 1900, 43% of all Hudson County residents were foreign-born. More recently, migration from Puerto Rico and Cuba has been substantial. In 1990, 143,974 New Jersey residents age 5 and older had lived in Puerto Rico in 1985. In 1996, 1,152,000 New Jersey residents, or 14%, were foreign born. In the same year, 63,303 foreign immigrants entered the state. As of 1994, the number of undocumented immigrants was estimated at between 98 and 168, the sixth highest total of any state.

From World War I on, there has been a steady migration of blacks from southern states; Newark's black population grew by

130,000 between 1950 and 1970. Black as well as Hispanic newcomers settled in major cities just as whites were departing for the suburbs. New Jersey's suburbs were also attractive to residents of New York City, Philadelphia, and other adjacent areas, who began a massive move to the state just after World War II; nearly all of these suburbanites were white. From 1940 to 1970, New Jersey gained a net total of 1,360,000 residents. Between 1970 and 1990, however, the state lost about 250,000 residents through migration. Between 1990 and 1996, New Jersey had a net loss of 264,086 in domestic migration and a net gain of 233,584 in internation migration. While the black, Hispanic, and Asian populations were still rising, whites were departing from New Jersey in increasing numbers. As of 1990, some 54.8% of the state's residents had been born in New Jersey. About 60% of the state's residents age 5 and older lived in the same house in 1990 as in 1985; of those who had changed their residence, 21% lived in a different state in 1985.

¹⁹INTERGOVERNMENTAL COOPERATION

New Jersey participates in such regional bodies as the Interstate Sanitation Commission, Atlantic States Marine Fisheries Commission, and Mid-Atlantic Regional Fisheries Management Council. Of primary importance to the state are its relations with neighboring Pennsylvania and New York. With Pennsylvania, New Jersey takes part in the Delaware Valley Regional Planning Commission, Delaware River Joint Toll Bridge Commission, and Delaware River Port Authority; with New York, the Port Authority of New York and New Jersey, the Palisades Interstate Park Commission, and the Waterfront Commission, established to eliminate corruption and stabilize employment at the Hudson River ports. The Delaware River Basin Commission manages the water resources of the 12,750-sq mi (33,000-sq km) basin under the jurisdiction of Delaware, New Jersey, New York, and Pennsylvania. The Delaware River and Bay Authority operates a bridge and ferry between New Jersey and Delaware. In 1996, the state received over $6.5 billion in federal assistance.

²⁰ECONOMY

New Jersey was predominantly agricultural until the mid-1800s, when the rise of the railroads stimulated manufacturing in northern New Jersey and opened the Jersey shore to resort development. The steady growth of population in the 1900s fostered the growth of service-related industries, construction, and trade, for which the state's proximity to New York and Philadelphia had long been advantageous.

Manufacturing accounted for about one-fourth of nongovernment employment in 1984. Although petroleum refining, chemicals and pharmaceuticals, food processing, apparel, fabricated metals, electric and electronic equipment, and other machinery all important, the state is more noteworthy for the diversity of its manufacturers than for any dominant company or product. The service sector of the economy, led by wholesale and retail trade, continued to grow rapidly during the early 1980s. The heaviest concentrations of jobs are in and near metropolitan New York and Philadelphia, but employment opportunities in the central and north-central counties have been increasing. Fresh market vegetables are the leading source of farm income.

During the 1970s, New Jersey's economy followed national trends, except that the mid-decade recession was especially severe. Conditions in most areas improved in the latter part of the decade, particularly in Atlantic City, with the construction of gambling casinos and other entertainment facilities. Manufacturing in the central cities declined, however, as industries moved to suburban locations. The 1981/82 recession was followed by an economic boom that was especially pronounced in New Jersey. By 1984, state unemployment was below the national average, as the construction and services industry set the pace. In 1984 alone,

employment rose by 116,000, or 3.7%. New Jersey's gross state product in 1994 was $254,945 million, to which private goods-producing industries contributed $47,597 million; private services-producing industries, $179,468; government, $27,880 million. New Jersey's per capita income in 1995 was $29,848 which was 2nd in the US. In 1996, there were 34,091 filings for bankruptcy.

²¹INCOME

In 1996, total disposable personal income amounted to $212.2 billion, up from $204 billion in 1995. Per capita personal income increased 4.1% from 1995 to 1996, to $31,053. New Jersey's per capita personal income in 1996 ranked 2d among the 50 states. Median household income was $43,924 in 1995.

New Jerseyites living below the federal poverty line in 1995 were 7.8% of the population.

²²LABOR

The civilian labor force was estimated at 4,124,400 in 1996. About 3,869,000 were employed and 255,100 unemployed, for an overall unemployment rate of 6.2%.

New Jersey Department of Labor 1995 unemployment insurance covered employment wage data show the following:

	COVERED ANNUAL WAGES	EMPLOYMENT IN THOUSANDS
Total	$34,534	3,504.8
Private Sector	33,890	2,972.3
Agricultural services, forestry	20,120	27.0
Mining	43,644	2.0
Construction	37,353	122.6
Manufacturing	42,171	498.0
Nondurable goods	43,532	300.4
Durable goods	40,103	197.6
Transportation and public utilities	31,327	149.9
Wholesale trade	43,700	263.8
Retail trade	17,820	582.0
Finance, insurance, and real estate	45,469	220.6
Services	31,979	1,006.3
Government	38,122	532.7

About 70,000 persons were federal employees in 1996. Although migrant workers are still employed at south Jersey tomato farms and fruit orchards, the number of farm workers coming into the state is declining with the increased use of mechanical harvesters.

The state's first child labor law was passed in 1851, and in 1886, workers were given the right to organize. Labor's gains were slow and painful, however. In Paterson, no fewer than 137 strikes were called between 1881 and 1900, every one of them a failure. A 1913 strike of Paterson silkworkers drew nationwide headlines but, again, few results. Other notable strikes were a walkout at a Carteret fertilizer factory in 1915 during which six picketers were killed by guards, a yearlong work stoppage by Passaic textile workers in 1926, and another Paterson silkworkers' strike in 1933, this one finally leading to union recognition and significant wage increases. That year, the state enacted a law setting minimum wages and maximum hours for women. This measure was repealed in 1971, in line with the trend toward nonpreferential labor standards. As of 1994, 129,800 New Jerseyites who worked in the manufacturing industries belonged to labor unions, of which there were 14 national unions operating in the state in 1993.

²³AGRICULTURE

New Jersey is a leading producer of fresh fruits and vegetables. Its total farm income was $927 million in 1995. In 1996, according to the New Jersey Agricultural Statistics Services, New Jersey ranked 2d in the US in the production of cultivated blueberries and peaches, 3d in cranberries, 5th in lettuce, 8th in fresh market tomatoes, and 12th overall in fresh market vegetables.

Some 840,000 acres (about 340,000 hectares) were in 9,200 farms in 1996. The major farm counties are: Warren for grain and milk production, Gloucester and Cumberland for fruits and vegetables, Atlantic for blueberries, Burlington for nursery production and berries, Salem for processing vegetables, and Monmouth for nursery and equine.

In 1996, New Jersey produced 288,200 tons of fresh market vegetables worth $138 million. Leading crops (in hundredweight units) were: bell peppers, 1,100,000; cabbage, 759,000; sweet corn, 720,000; tomatoes, 697,000; and head lettuce, 364,000. New Jersey farmers also produced 80,490 tons of vegetables for processing. Fruit crops in 1996 (in pound units) included apples, 60,000,000, and peaches, 77,000,000. Blueberry production in 1996 totaled 34.0 million pounds while cranberry and strawberry production were 45.5 million and 1.6 million pounds respectively. The expansion of housing and industry has increased the value of farm acreage and buildings in New Jersey to $8,172 per acre, the highest in the nation.

24ANIMAL HUSBANDRY

In 1997, New Jersey had an estimated 68,000 cattle and calves, valued at $53.7 million. During 1996, New Jersey farmers had an estimated 21,000 hogs and pigs valued at $2.3 million. In 1995, the state produced 770,000 lb of sheep and lambs which brought in $1.1 million in gross income. In addition, poultry farmers produced 1.98 million lb of turkey, 3.5 million lb of chickens, and 444 million eggs in 1995. The state's total milk yield was 320 million lb in 1995.

25FISHING

New Jersey had a commercial fish catch of 177,177,000 lb (10th in the US) in 1995, worth $95.5 million. Cape May–Wildwood was the 18th-largest fishing port in the US by volume, bringing in 75.4 million lb of fish, worth $30.5 million. Clams, scallops, swordfish, tuna, squid, lobster, and flounder are the most valuable species. In 1995, landings of surf clams totaled 46.3 million lb; ocean quahog (a species of clam), 21.8 million lb; and Atlantic mackerel, 4.8 million lb.

The US Fish and Wildlife Service of the Department of the Interior maintains a total of 190,000 acres (76,900 hectares) on 12 different sites with boating access, and apportioned nearly $2 million for sport fish restoration programs in 1995/96.

Recreational fishermen catch finfish and shellfish along the Atlantic coast and in the rivers and lakes of northern New Jersey. In 1995/96, the state issued 241,741 sport fishing licenses.

26FORESTRY

About 42% of New Jersey's land area, or 2,007,000 acres (822,870 hectares), was forested in 1992. Of that, 93% was classified as commercial timberland, 83% of it privately owned. The forests of New Jersey are important for their function in conservation and recreation. Wood that is harvested contributes to specialty markets and quality veneer products.

As of 1992, the Bureau of Parks maintained 272,000 acres (110,000 hectares) of state land, nearly 70% of that in 11 state forests. The bureau also operates 40 state parks, 12 natural areas, and a recreation area. These account for 6% of the state's land, far above the US average of 0.4%.

27MINING

The value of nonfuel mineral production in New Jersey in 1995 was estimated to be $289 million, virtually unchanged from 1994. In 1995, 20.6 million metric tons of crushed stone were produced, for a total value of $163 million, up $154 million from the previous year. Other mineral resources mined or recovered included construction sand and gravel, (15 million metric tons, worth $93.7 million), industrial sand and gravel (1.7 million metric tons, worth $30.1 million), common and fire clays, greensand, peat, titanium, and zircon concentrates. New Jersey continued to be the only state that produced greensand, also known as the mineral glauconite, which is processed and sold mainly as a water softening filtration medium to remove soluble iron and manganese from well water. A secondary use is as an organic conditioner for soils. The state ranked 37th among the states in total nonfuel mineral production value.

The New Jersey Geological Survey reported that large-scale capital projects contributed up to 5% of the improved performance level for the construction sector in 1995. Since aggregate producers rely heavily on a healthy construction industry, the trends in that industry affect the state's mineral industry. Combined public agency and private sector construction activity in 1995 was estimated at $5.9 billion.

28ENERGY AND POWER

Although it contains some of the largest oil refineries in the US, New Jersey produces little of its own energy, importing much of its electric power and virtually all of its fossil fuels.

In 1996, there were 31 electric generating plants in New Jersey; installed capacity totaled 14.77 million kW. Power production amounted to 27 billion kWh in 1995. Per capita energy consumption in 1994 was 322.3 million Btu.

New Jersey had four nuclear reactors in operation in 1996. Two of them, at Salem, are operated by Public Service Electric and Gas (PSE&G), the state's largest utility. A smaller unit is at Toms River. Another reactor, at Hope Creek, began operation in 1986. Nuclear generating stations accounted for 62% of the electric power generated in the state in 1995, up from only 16.5% in 1983.

29INDUSTRY

New Jersey's earliest industries were glassmaking and ironworking. In 1791, Alexander Hamilton proposed the development of a planned industrial town at the Passaic Falls. The Society for Establishing Useful Manufactures, an agency charged with developing the town, tried but failed to set up a cotton mill at the site, called Paterson, in 1797. By the early 1800s, however, Paterson had become the country's largest silk manufacturing center; by 1850, it was producing locomotives as well. On the eve of the Civil War, industry already had a strong foothold in the state. Newark had breweries, hat factories, and paper plants; Trenton, iron and paper; Jersey City, steel and soap; and Middlesex, clays and ceramics. The late 1800s saw the birth of the electrical industry, the growth of oil refineries on Bayonne's shores, and emerging chemical, drug, paint, and telephone manufacturing centers. All these products retain their places among the state's diverse manufactures.

In 1995, the value of shipments for manufactured goods totaled $92,382,500,000. The following table shows value of shipments for selected industries in 1995 (in million dollars):

Chemicals	$ 24,431.5
Food	9,407.6
Printing & Publishing	7,602.0
Instruments	4,659.2
Petroleum products	6,434.9
Industrial machinery	5,370.7
Fabricated metals	4,321.4
Electronic equipment	5,019.5
Rubber & misc. plastics	4,484.0
Paper products	3,646.5
Transportation equipment	4,716.3

Nearly every major US corporation has facilities in the state. As of 1997, there were 23 Fortune 500 companies headquartered in New Jersey. Numerous corporations have moved their headquarters from New York to New Jersey since 1960. In 1995, there were 3,067 US patents issued to New Jersey residents.

30COMMERCE

With one of the nation's busiest ports and many regional distribution centers, New Jersey is an important commercial state.

In 1992, New Jersey had 18,444 wholesale establishments, with sales of $176 billion, including $86 billion in durable goods. Retail sales were conducted by 48,648 establishments and totaled $63.1 billion (9th) in 1992. The major sales categories were food stores, 20.7%; automotive dealers, 20.6%; and general merchandise stores, 10.5%. The state's wholesale trade is largely concentrated near manufacturing centers and along the New Jersey Turnpike.

Bergen, Union, and Essex counties accounted for more than one half of wholesale trade. Other large shopping centers are in Burlington, Eatontown, Lawrenceville, Livingston, Menlo Park, and Woodbridge. Three of the nation's largest supermarket chains have their headquarters in New Jersey: Great Atlantic and Pacific Tea Co. (A&P) in Montvale, Supermarkets General (Pathmark) in Woodbridge, and Grand Union in Elmwood Park. The toy store chain Toys R Us is headquartered in Rochelle Park.

Port Newark and the Elizabeth Marine Terminal, foreign-trade zones operated by the Port Authority of New York and New Jersey, have been modernized and enlarged in recent years, and together account for most of the cargo unloaded in New York Harbor. In 1996, New Jersey exported $13.1 billion of its own manufactures to foreign countries. The leading exports were chemicals, nonelectrical machinery, and electrical equipment. Exporters located in New Jersey had shipments valued at $18.5 billion (9th) in 1996.

31CONSUMER PROTECTION

Consumer fraud cases are handled by the Division of Consumer Affairs of the Department of Law and Public Safety, which maintains regional offices in Camden and Newark. The Offices of Consumer Protection and Weights and Measures, the Bureau of Securities, and 34 professional and occupational boards that license 57 occupations and professions, work together to protect New Jerseyites from fraud and deceit.

32BANKING

The colonies' first bank of issue opened in Gloucester in 1682. New Jersey's first chartered bank, the Newark Banking and Insurance Co., was the first of many banks to open in that city. By the mid-1800s, Newark was indisputably the financial center of the state. For the most part, commercial banking in New Jersey is overshadowed by the great financial centers of New York City and Philadelphia.

As of December 31, 1996, there were 68 insured commercial banks having their principal office in New Jersey. Deposits of these banks exceeded $70.4 billion. The state's 31 state chartered savings banks had assets of $20.9 billion and mortgage loans of $9.6 billion. The 61 savings and loan associations had assets of $27.7 billion and mortgage loans of $14.6 billion. In addition, New Jersey has 14 state chartered trust companies which had assets on the same date of $4.6 billion and fiduciary responsibility over $75.3 billion in assets.

Regulation of all state chartered banks, savings banks, savings and loan associations and limited purpose trust companies is the responsibility of the Department of Banking and Insurance. National banks are regulated by the Office of Comptroller of the Currency. The principal regulator of federally chartered savings and loan associations is the Office of Thrift Supervision.

33INSURANCE

For the year-end 1996, there were 70 property/casualty insurance companies headquartered in the state along with 17 life/health domestic insurers. Some 6.7 million life insurance policies, worth $525.0 billion, were in force in 1995. The average family had $178,300 in life coverage, 44% above the national average. More than 7.0 billion in benefits were paid to policy holders and their beneficiaries, including $1.4 billion in death payments.

Property and liability premiums totaling over $11.1 billion were written in 1996, including $4.0 billion in automobile liability coverage, $1.8 billion in automobile physical damage insurance, and $919.3 million in homeowners' insurance. More than $18.1 billion in flood insurance was in force in 1996.

No-fault automobile insurance has been compulsory in New Jersey since 1973. All insurance agents, brokers, and companies in the state are licensed and regulated by the Department of Banking and Insurance.

34SECURITIES

There are no stock or commodity exchanges in New Jersey. Regulation of securities trading in the state is under the control of the Bureau of Securities of the Division of Consumer Affairs, within the Department of Law and Public Safety.

As of June 1996, 2,200 broker-dealers were registered to sell securities within New Jersey, involving 105,177 agents; registered investment advisory companies numbered 1,145.

35PUBLIC FINANCE

The annual budget, prepared by the Treasury Department's Division of Budget and Accounting, is submitted by the governor to the legislature for approval. The fiscal year runs from 1 July to 30 June.

The following is a summary of recommended revenues and expenditures for all state funds in 1997/98 (in thousands):

REVENUES	
Sales tax	$ 4,557,000
Income tax	4,830,000
Corporation tax	4,134,640
Other taxes	2,149,000
Casino and lottery revenue	1,072,661
Other receipts and transfers	2,320,526
TOTAL	16,063,827
APPROPRIATIONS	
Education, of which:	$ 5,077,997
Higher education	(1,122,448)
Human services	3,965,385
Transportation	730,510
Debt service	491,210
Law and public safety	357,372
Corrections	728,537
Environmental protection	256,101
Community affairs	892,342
Other net appropriations	2,798,950
TOTAL	16,420.852

The public debt of state government as of 1996 was $3.7 billion.

36TAXATION

Revenues from state taxes in 1998 were expected to exceed $16 billion. The personal income tax is the largest single source generating $4.8 billion with a 6% retail sales tax the second largest at $4.4 billion. Taxes based on the net income of business corporations and banks generate $1.4 billion. Various excise taxes on tobacco, alcoholic beverages, motor fuels, and petroleum products generate $1 billion. Revenues from casino gambling and lottery sales account for $970 million.

The personal income tax is based on gross income which allows deductions only for extraordinary medical expenses, alimony and separate maintenance payments, and property taxes paid. The taxpayer and spouse are each allowed a $1,000 personal exemption; each dependent child is allowed $1,500. Property taxes paid or their equivalent for tenants (18% of rent) are deductible up to maximums of $2,500 in 1996, $5,625 in 1997, and $10,000 in 1998. Tax rates for joint filers are imposed at graduated rates starting with 1.4% of the first $20,000 in taxable income, 1.75% of the next $30,000; 2.45% on taxable income between $50–70,000; 3.5% between $70–80,000; 5.25% between $80–150,000, and 6.37% on income over $150,000. Rates for single filers are similar with the top rate applying to taxable income over $75,000.

The 566 New Jersey municipalities are dependent on the local property tax, state grants, and state aid for their finances. Only Atlantic City and a few shore communities have a local sales tax. Property taxes generated $12.2 billion in 1996 and have been growing at an average rate of 4.18% per year between 1992–96.

Non-senior citizens with gross incomes under $40,000 are eligible for a Homestead Rebate of 490 (homeowner) or $30 (tenant). Citizens age 65 and over with incomes under $100,000 are eligible for rebates ranging from $100–500 (homeowners) and $35–500 (tenants). Over $323 million in property tax relief is provided through this program each year. In addition, about $60 million per year is directed towards offsetting local property tax bills for senior citizens, veterans, and surviving spouses.

37ECONOMIC POLICY

New Jersey's controlled budget and relatively low business tax burden have helped encourage new businesses to enter the state. In addition, the state Department of Commerce and Economic Development administers a number of development programs designed to retain and attract business and jobs. The state's Economic Development Authority (EDA) is an independent authority established to provide financing programs, including loans, loan guarantees, and tax-free and taxable bond packages.

The Urban Enterprise Zone Program seeks to revitalize urban areas by granting tax incentives and relaxing some government regulations. The Office of Business Development identifies and assists firms that have expansion needs or are experiencing difficulties.The Economic Development Marketing Office fosters New Jersey's business-friendly environment through marketing and advertising initiatives, including targeted industry assistance programs. The Division of Development for Small Businesses, Women and Minority Businesses supports the start-up, growth and expansion of smaller firms and women and minority-owned enterprises. The Division of International Trade seeks to boost the state's exports and bring more foreign companies into the state. Other offices within the department promote tourism and motion picture production.

Each of the state's 567 municipalities is "qualified" to adopt ordinances that authorize property tax exemptions and abatements for commercial and industrial properties in areas in need of rehabilitation. The state's basic corporate tax rate is 9%. New Jersey has also phased out the net-worth portion of the corporation business tax and has repealed the retail gross receipts tax, the unincorporated business tax, and the sales tax on production machinery and equipment.

38HEALTH

During the 12 months ending with December 1995, the infant mortality rate in New Jersey was 7.3 per 1,000 live births. The birthrate in 1995 was 14.5 per 1,000 women aged 15–44 years, below the national average. There were 38,168 abortions in 1992; the abortion rate of 318 per 1,000 live births was below the national norm. Another factor contributing to the low birthrate was a marriage rate of just 7.5 per 1,000 population in 1991, compared to the national rate of 9.8. Partly because the marriage rate was so low, New Jersey's divorce rate, 3.0 per 1,000 residents, was also below the national rate of 4.7.

The leading causes of death in the state are heart disease and cancer, for both of which New Jersey ranks above the national average. Mortality rates per 100,000 residents in 1995 were as follows: diseases of the heart, 303.3; cancer, 231.9; cerebrovascular disease, 53.4; accidents and adverse effects, 29.1 (including motor vehicle accidents, 10.6); and suicide, 7.3. In 1990, New Jersey ranked higher than any other state in the proportion of breast cancer deaths per 100,000 women, at 32.9.

As of 1991, 120 hospitals of all types had 37,897 beds; 1,168,793 patients were admitted that year. Hospital personnel in 1991 included 28,595 registered nurses. Average expenses of hospital care in 1991, $680 per inpatient day and $5,136 per stay, were below the US averages. There were 20,277 active nonfederal physicians in 1991 and 6,084 licensed active dentists in 1995. The state's only medical school, the University of Medicine and Dentistry of New Jersey, is a public institution that combines three medical schools, one dental school, a school of allied professions, and a graduate school of biomedical sciences.

39SOCIAL WELFARE

Through the Department of Human Services, New Jersey administers the major federal welfare programs, as well as several programs specifically designed to meet the needs of New Jersey minority groups. Among the latter in 1991 was the Cuban-Haitian Entrant Program. Additional assistance went to refugees from such areas as Southeast Asia and Eastern Europe.

In 1996, aid to families with dependent children served 293,800 New Jerseyites with an average monthly payment of $488. In 1996, 540,626 residents received monthly food stamp allowances averaging $78.27. Under the school lunch program, $111.1 million was spent to feed eligible students.

With the enactment of the Personal Responsibility and Work Opportunity Reconciliation Act of 1996, the US government changed the form and regulations for many of its social welfare programs; most significantly, it replaced Aid to Families with Dependent Children (AFDC), an open-ended entitlement program, with Temporary Assistance for Needy Families (TANF), a limited system of assistance funded largely through federal block grants. The reform act also impacted the food stamp program, the Supplemental Security Income program, and the child nutrition program. The law took effect on 1 July 1997 and provided $16.38 billion in block grants for fiscal years 1997–2002. The grants were to be divided among the states based on an equation involving the numbers of former AFDC recipients in each state. Because many of the bill's provisions have yet to be implemented into state-by-state policy, it was not possible to include the details of each state's programs for this edition of this work.

Of the eligible Social Security beneficiaries who received more than $11.6 billion in 1996, retired workers and their spouses and children received $8.3 billion, and survivors, $2.1 billion; disabled workers and their spouses and children received $1.2 billion. In 1995, 144,004 persons received supplemental security income averaging $356 a month.

Unemployment benefits averaged $252.63 per week in 1995.

40HOUSING

Before 1967, New Jersey took a laissez-faire attitude toward housing. With each locality free to fashion its own zoning ordinances, large tracts of rural land succumbed to "suburban sprawl"—single-family housing developments spread out in two huge arcs from New York City and Philadelphia. Meanwhile, the tenement housing of New Jersey's central cities was left to deteriorate. Because poor housing was at least one of the causes of the Newark riot in 1967, the state established the Department of Community Affairs to coordinate existing housing aid programs and establish new ones. The state legislature also created the Mortgage Finance Agency and Housing Finance Agency to stimulate home buying and residential construction. In an effort to halt suburban sprawl, local and county planning boards were encouraged during the 1970s to adopt master plans for controlled growth. Court decisions in the late 1970s and early 1980s challenged the constitutionality of zoning laws that precluded the development of low-income housing in suburban areas.

In 1996, the state had an estimated 3,155,000 housing units, of which 2,861,000 were occupied. As of 1990, 59% of all housing units were owner occupied and 99.5% had full plumbing. In 1996, 24,173 privately-owned units, valued at $2.1 billion, were authorized for construction; of these, 20,853 were single family. The median monthly cost to the owner of a mortgaged home in 1990, the last year for which figures are available, was $1,105 (higher than any other state); the median cost to a renter was $592. In 1990, the median home value was $162,300, up 69.8% from 1980. During 1996, New Jersey received $770.5 million in aid from the US Department of Housing and Urban Development, including $114.6 million in community development block grants.

41EDUCATION

Public education in New Jersey dates from 1828, when the legislature first allocated funds to support education; by 1871, a public school system was established statewide. In 1990, the state was above the US norm in the proportion of persons over age 25 who were high school graduates (77%), and above the US norm in the percentage of persons with four or more years of college (census).

In 1996–97, New Jersey had 619 school districts. There were 2,310 public schools, of which 1,855 were elementary and 327 were secondary, 46 were vocational and 82 were for children with disabilities. The total public school enrollment in 1996–97, 1,218,578, represented a 3.0% increase in a single year and was the second year of enrollment increase. In 1996–97, the student body was 62.2% white, 18.4% black, and 13.7% Hispanic. There were 56,612 elementary and 26,979 secondary school teachers in 1995–96. The pupil-teacher ratio in the state in 1995-96 was 13.9, which compared favorably with the national average of 17.2. Enrollment in 1,055 private schools and academies in 1995-96 totaled about 214,872.

Total expenditures for education in 1996 were $14.2 billion. The state ranked first nationwide in expenditures per pupil ($9,075) in 1994.

Rutgers, the state university, began operations as Queen's College in 1766 and was placed under state control in 1956. Encompassing the separate colleges of Rutgers, Douglass, Livingston, and Cook, among others, the university had a total enrollment of 48,000 in 1989–90. Altogether, 223,748 students were enrolled in 1989–90 in the state's 12 public four-year colleges and 18 two-year community colleges. Enrollment at 26 private colleges totaled 43,128 in 1989–90. The major private university in the state and one of the nation's leading institutions is Princeton University, founded in 1746, with an enrollment of 4,500 undergraduate students in 1990–91. Other major private universities are Seton Hall (1856), 10,000; Stevens Institute of Technology (1870), 1,600; and Fairleigh Dickinson (1942), 20,000 on three main campuses.

The New Jersey Department of Higher Education offers tuition aid grants and scholarships to state residents who attend colleges and universities in the state. Guaranteed loans for any qualified resident are available through the New Jersey Higher Education Assistance Authority.

Total expenditures for education in 1993–94 were $5 billion. The state ranked 3d nationwide in expenditures per pupil (based on average daily attendance); per capita expenditures, $1,296.58, were the 4th highest of the 50 states.

42ARTS

During the late 1800s and early 1900s, New Jersey towns, especially Atlantic City and Newark, were tryout centers for shows bound for Broadway. The New Jersey Theater Group, a service organization for nonprofit professional theaters, was established in 1978; in 1997, 20 theaters—including the Tony Award-winning McCarter Theater at Princeton and Paper Mill Playhouse in Millburn—are members of the Theater Group.

Around the turn of the century, Ft. Lee was the motion picture capital of the world. Most of the best-known "silents"—including the first, *The Great Train Robbery*, and episodes of *The Perils of Pauline*—were shot there, and in its heyday the state film industry supported 21 companies and 7 studios. New Jersey's early preeminence in cinema, an era that ended with the rise of Hollywood, stemmed partly from the fact that the first motion picture system was developed by Thomas Edison at Menlo Park in the late 1880s. The state created the New Jersey Motion Picture and Television Commission in 1977; in the next six years, production companies spent $57 million in the state. Notable productions during this period included two Woody Allen pictures, *Broadway Danny Rose* and *The Purple Rose of Cairo*.

The state's long history of support for classical music dates at least to 1796, when William Dunlap of Perth Amboy wrote the libretto for *The Archers*, the first American opera to be commercially produced. There are currently over 60 professional and community orchestras throughout the state. The state's leading orchestra is the New Jersey Symphony, which makes its home in the new New Jersey Performing Arts Center in Newark; there are other symphony orchestras in Plainfield and Trenton. The New Jersey State Opera performs in Newark's Symphony Hall while the Opera Festival of New Jersey makes its home in Lawrenceville. Noteworthy dance companies include the American Repertory Ballet, New Jersey Ballet, and the Nai N. Chen Dance Company.

The jazz clubs of northern New Jersey and the seaside rock clubs in Asbury Park have helped launch the careers of many local performers. Famous stars perform in the casinos and hotels of Atlantic City. The state of New Jersey generated $93,491,415 in federal and state funds to support its arts programs from 1987 to 1991. The NEA contributed $6,283,450 to the state's arts programs and $3,073,965 to the New Jersey State Council on the Arts. The state also contributed $84,134,000. Private sources amounted to $247 million. Audiences for the state's arts programs totaled 73,166,000. There were 439,127 contributing artists. The state offered arts education programs to 24,300 school children.

In 1997, 123 arts organizations and 450 local arts groups received $9.3 million in support from the NJSCOA.

The NEA contributed $2,500 to the Montclair Art Museum and $32,000 to the Crossroads, Inc. In 1992, the State Council on the Arts received $187,500 from the NEA's arts education program and $516,000 from the state and regional program. The Crossroads Theatre Company received $500,000 from the NEA's Challenge grant program to initiate an Associate Artists Program. An NEA Arts Plus grant of $150,000 was given to the Festival of Music and Artsgenesis. NEA support to New Jersey reached an all-time high of $2.8 million in 1995. The agency's budget was cut in 1996 and New Jersey received $1.01 million.

[43]LIBRARIES AND MUSEUMS

Statewide, 311 public libraries in 1991 housed more than 27.5 million volumes and recorded a circulation of 39.3 million. The Newark Public Library was the largest municipal system with 1,219,951 volumes and 11 branches. Distinguished by special collections on African-American studies, art and archaeology, economics, and international affairs, among many others, Princeton University's library is the largest in the state, with 4,427,435 volumes in 1991; Rutgers University ranked 2d with 3,800,000. The New Jersey State Library in Trenton contained 428,200 volumes, mostly on the state's history and government. One of the largest business libraries, emphasizing scientific and technical data, is the AT&T Bell Laboratories' library system, based in Murray Hill.

New Jersey has more than 145 museums, historic sites, botanical gardens and arboretums. Among the most noteworthy museums are the New Jersey Historical Society in Newark and New Jersey State Museum in Trenton; the Newark Museum, containing both art and science exhibits; Princeton University's Art Museum and Museum of Natural History; and the Jersey City Museum. Also of interest are the early waterfront homes and vessels of Historic Gardner's Basin in Atlantic City, as well as Grover Cleveland's birthplace in Caldwell; the Campbell Museum in Camden (featuring the soup company's collection of bowls and utensils); Cape May County Historical Museum; Clinton Historical Museum Village; US Army Communications-Electronics Museum at Ft. Monmouth; Batsto Village, near Hammonton; Morristown National Historic Park (where George Washington headquartered during the Revolutionary War); Sandy Hook Museum; and one of the most popular attractions, the Edison National Historic Site, formerly the home and workshop of Thomas Edison, in West Orange. In 1984, the grounds at the Skylands section of Ringwood State Park were designated as the official state botanical garden.

[44]COMMUNICATIONS

Many communications breakthroughs—including Telstar, the first communications satellite—have been achieved by researchers at Bell Labs in Holmdel, Whippany, and Murray Hill. Three Bell Labs researchers shared the Nobel Prize in physics (1956) for developing the transistor, a device that has revolutionized communications and many other fields. In 1876, at Menlo Park, Thomas Edison invented the carbon telephone transmitter, a device that made the telephone commercially feasible.

The first mail carriers to come to New Jersey were, typically enough, on their way between New York and Philadelphia. Express mail between the two cities began in 1737, and by 1764, carriers could speed through the state in 24 hours. In colonial times, tavern keepers generally served as the local mailmen. The nation's largest bulk-mail facility is in Jersey City. In March 1993, 94.1% of the state's 2,879,000 occupied housing units had telephones.

Because the state lacks a major television broadcasting outlet, New Jerseyites receive more news about events in New York City and Philadelphia than in their own towns and cities. In 1993 there were 114 radio stations (36 AM, 78 FM) and 14 television stations, none of which commanded anything like the audiences and influence of the stations across the Hudson and Delaware rivers. The state government operates 5 television stations under the Public Broadcasting Authority. In 1978, in cooperation with public television's WNET (licensed in Newark but operated in New York), these stations began producing New Jersey's first nightly newscast. In 1996, cable television service was provided by 25 large systems.

[45]PRESS

If New Jersey is a state without a clear identity, the lack of a powerful press must be at least partly responsible. Queen Anne in 1702 banned printers from the colony; the state's first periodical, founded in 1758, died two years later. New Jersey's first daily paper, the *Newark Daily Advertiser,* did not arrive until 1832.

Although several present-day newspapers, most notably the Newark *Star–Ledger,* have amassed considerable circulation, none have been able to muster statewide influence or match the quality or prestige of the nearby *New York Times* or *Philadelphia Inquirer,* both of which are read widely in the state, along with other New York City and Philadelphia papers. In 1997, there were 13 morning dailies, six evening and 16 Sunday papers. The following table shows leading New Jersey dailies with their 1994 circulation:

AREA	NAME	DAILY	SUNDAY
Atlantic City	*Press* (m,S)	74,194	95,745
Hackensack	*Record* (e,S)	153,661	210,061
Newark	*Star–Ledger* (m,S)	433,317	641,393
Trenton	*Times*	85,893	95,036

Numerous scholarly and historical works have been published by the university presses of Princeton and Rutgers, Prentice-Hall's offices are in Englewood Cliffs, and those of Silver Burdett, a textbook publisher, are in Morristown. Several New York City publishing houses maintain their production and warehousing facilities in the state. Periodicals published in New Jersey include *Home, Medical Economics, New Jersey Monthly, Personal Computing,* and *Tiger Beat.*

[46]ORGANIZATIONS

The 1992 Census of Service Industries counted 1,482 organizations in New Jersey, including 295 business associations; 802 civic, social, and fraternal associations; and 385 other membership organizations.

Princeton is the headquarters of several education-related groups, including the Educational Testing Service, Graduate Record Examinations Board, Independent Educational Services, and Woodrow Wilson National Fellowship Foundation. Seeing Eye of Morristown was one of the first organizations to provide seeing-eye dogs for the blind. Other medical and health-related organizations are National Industries for the Blind (Wayne) and the American Association of Veterinary State Boards (Teaneck). Birthright USA, an anti-abortion counseling service, has its headquarters in Woodbury; the National Council on Crime and Delinquency is in Ft. Lee.

Among the many trade and professional organizations are the Hobby Industry Association of America in Elmwood Park, Science Fiction Writers of America in Wharton, and American Littoral Society in Highlands. Hobby and sports groups include the US Golf Association and World Amateur Golf Council in Far Hills, US Equestrian Team in Gladstone, and National Intercollegiate Women's Fencing Association in Upper Montclair.

[47]TOURISM, TRAVEL, AND RECREATION

Tourism is a leading industry in New Jersey, accounting for a sizeable part of the state's revenues. The Jersey shore has been a popular attraction since 1801, when Cape May began advertising itself as a summer resort.

Of all the shore resorts, the largest has long been Atlantic City, which by the 1890s was the nation's most popular resort city and by 1905 was the first major city with an economy almost totally dependent on tourism. That proved to be its downfall, as improvements in road and air transportation made more modern resorts in other states easily accessible to easterners. By the early 1970s, the city's only current claims to fame were the Miss America pageant and the game of Monopoly, whose standard version uses its street names. In an effort to restore Atlantic City to its former luster and revive its economy, New Jersey voters approved a constitutional amendment in 1976 to allow casinos in the resort. Some 33 million people visit Atlantic City annually. Casino taxes were earmarked to reduce property taxes of senior citizens.

State attractions include 10 ski areas in northwestern New Jersey (on Hamburg Mountain alone, more than 50 slopes are available), canoeing and camping at the Delaware Water Gap National Recreation Area, three national wildlife refuges, 31 public golf courses, and 30 amusement parks, including Great Adventure in central Jersey.

State parks, forests, historic sites, and other areas attracted almost 5,392,774 visitors in 1996. New Jersey's inland lakes, 14,000 mi (22,500 km) of trout streams, and 26 towns with saltwater fishing facilities attracted the state's 364,566 fishing license holders in 1995. Licenses were also held by 321,135 hunters.

[48]SPORTS

New Jersey did not have a major league professional team until 1976, when the New York Giants of the National Football League moved across the Hudson River into the newly completed Giants Stadium in the Meadowlands Sports Complex at East Rutherford. The NFL's New York Jets began playing their home games at the Meadowlands in 1984. The Brendon Byrne Arena, located at the same site, is the home of the New Jersey Nets of the National Basketball Association and the New Jersey Devils of the National Hockey League. As New York teams who no longer play in their home state, the Giants and the Jets are scorned by some New York sports purists. When the Giants won the Superbowl in 1987, New York's then mayor, Ed Koch, refused them the tickertape parade, traditionally given to local sports champions on the grounds that since they play in New Jersey they are not a New York team.

The state did celebrate a championship it could call its own, however, when the Devils won the Stanley Cup in 1995.

The Meadowlands is also the home of a dual thoroughbred-harness-racing track. Other racetracks are Garden State Park (Cherry Hill), Monmouth Park (Oceanport), and Atlantic City Race Course for Thoroughbreds, and Freehold Raceway for harness racing. Auto racing is featured at speedways in Trenton, Atlantic City, Bridgeport, Englishtown, and elsewhere. Trenton also has a minor league baseball team, the Thunder, in the Eastern League. New Jersey has several world-class golf courses, including Baltusrol, the site of the 1980 US Open. Numerous championship boxing matches have been held in Atlantic City.

New Jersey is historically significant in the births of two major national sports. Princeton and Rutgers played what is claimed to be the first intercollegiate football game on 6 November 1869 at New Brunswick. (Princeton was named national champion several times around the turn of the century, for the last time in 1911). The first game of what we know today as baseball was also played in New Jersey: at the Elysion Field in Hoboken between the Knickerbockers and the New York Nine on 19 June 1846. Several important college games are held at Giants Stadium each fall, including one post-season game, the Garden State Bowl. In college basketball Seton Hall placed high in the rankings repeatedly in the late eighties and early nineties. In 1989 they made it to the finals, losing to Michigan by one point in overtime. Rutgers had a formidable team in the seventies, making it to the final four in 1976.

Other annual sporting events include the New Jersey Offshore Grand Prix Ocean Races held at Point Pleasant Beach in July, the National Marbles Tournament in Wildwood, and the Striped Boss Derby at Long Beach Island.

[49]FAMOUS NEW JERSEYITES

While only one native New Jerseyite, (Stephen) Grover Cleveland (1837–1908), has been elected president of the US, the state can also properly claim (Thomas) Woodrow Wilson (b.Virginia, 1856–1924), who spent most of his adult life there. Cleveland left his birthplace in Caldwell as a little boy, winning his fame and two terms in the White House (1885–89, 1893–97) as a resident of New York State. After serving as president, he retired to Princeton, where he died and is buried. Wilson, a member of Princeton's class of 1879, returned to the university in 1908 as a professor and became its president in 1902. Elected governor of New Jersey in 1910, Wilson pushed through a series of sweeping reforms before entering the White House in 1913. Wilson's two presidential terms were marked by his controversial decision to declare war on Germany and his unsuccessful crusade for US membership in the League of Nations after World War I.

Two vice presidents hail from New Jersey: Aaron Burr (1756–1836) and Garret A. Hobart (1844–99). Burr, born in Newark and educated at what is now Princeton University, is best remembered for killing Alexander Hamilton in a duel at Weehawken in 1804. Hobart was born in Long Branch, graduated from Rutgers College, and served as a lawyer in Paterson until elected vice president in 1896; he died in office.

Four New Jerseyites have become associate justices of the US Supreme Court: William Paterson (b.Ireland, 1745–1806), Joseph P. Bradley (1813–92), Mahlon Pitney (1858–1924), and William J. Brennan, Jr. (1906-1997). Among the relatively few New Jerseyites to serve in the US cabinet was William E. Simon (1927), secretary of the treasury under Gerald Ford.

Few New Jerseyites won important political status in colonial years because the colony was so long under New York's political and social domination. Lewis Morris (b.New York, 1671–1746) was named the first royal governor of New Jersey when severance from New York came in 1738. Governors who made important contributions to the state included William Livingston (b.New York, 1723–90), first governor after New Jersey became a state in 1776; Marcus L. Ward (1812–84), a strong Union supporter; and Alfred E. Driscoll (1902–75), who persevered in getting New Jersey a new state constitution in 1947 despite intense opposition from the Democratic Party leadership. Other important historical figures are Molly Pitcher (Mary Ludwig Hays McCauley, 1754?–1832), a heroine of the American Revolution, and Zebulon Pike (1779–1813), the noted explorer.

Two New Jersey persons have won the Nobel Peace Prize: Woodrow Wilson in 1919, and Nicholas Murray Butler (1862–1947) in 1931. A three-man team at Bell Laboratories in Murray Hill won the 1956 physics award for their invention of the transistor: Walter Brattain (b.China, 1902–87), John Bardeen (b.Wisconsin, 1908–91), and William Shockley (b.England, 1910). Dr. Selman Waksman (b.Russia, 1888–1973), a Rutgers University professor, won the 1952 prize in medicine and physiology for the discovery of streptomycin. Dickinson Woodruff (1895–1973) won the medicine and physiology prize in 1956, and Joshua Lederberg (b.1925) was a co-winner in 1958. Theoretical physicist Albert Einstein (b.Germany, 1879–1955), winner of a Nobel Prize in 1921, spent his last decades in Princeton. One of the world's most prolific inventors, Thomas Alva Edison (b.Ohio, 1847–1931) patented over 1,000 devices from workshops at Menlo Park and West Orange. David Dinkins (b. 1927), first African-American mayor of New York was born in Trenton, New Jersey. Norman Schwarzkopf (b. 1934), commander of US forces in Desert Storm (Gulf War), was born August 22, 1934 in Trenton, New Jersey. Michael Chang (b. 1972), 1989 French Open tennis champion, was born in Hoboken.

The state's traditions in the arts began in colonial times. Patience Lovell Wright (1725–86) of Bordentown was America's first recognized sculptor. Jonathan Odell (1737–1818) was an anti-Revolutionary satirist, while Francis Hopkinson (b.Pennsylvania, 1737–91), lawyer, artist, and musician, lampooned the British. Authors of note after the Revolution included William Dunlap (1766–1839), who compiled the first history of the stage in America; James Fenimore Cooper (1789–1851), one of the nation's first novelists; Mary Mapes Dodge (b.New York, 1838–1905), noted author of children's books; Stephen Crane (1871–1900), famed for *The Red Badge of Courage* (1895); and Albert Payson Terhune (1872–1942), beloved for his collie stories.

Quite a number of prominent 20th-century writers were born in or associated with New Jersey. They include poets William Carlos Williams (1883–1963) and Allen Ginsberg (1926-1997); satirist Dorothy Parker (1893–1967); journalist-critic Alexander Woollcott (1887–1943); Edmund Wilson (1895–1972), influential critic, editor, and literary historian; Norman Cousins (1912–90); Norman Mailer (b.1923); Thomas Fleming (b.1927); John McPhee (b.1931); Philip Roth (b.1933); Imamu Amiri Baraka (LeRoi Jones, b.1934); and Peter Benchley (b.New York, 1940).

Notable 19th-century artists were Asher B. Durand (1796–1886) and George Inness (b.New York, 1825–94). The best-known 20th-century artist associated with New Jersey was Ben Shahn (1898–1969); cartoonist Charles Addams (1912–88) was born in Westfield. Noted photographers born in New Jersey include Alfred Stieglitz (1864–1946) and Dorothea Lange (1895–1965). Important New Jersey composers were Lowell Mason (b.Massachusetts, 1792–1872), called the "father of American church music," and Milton Babbitt (b.Pennsylvania, 1916), long active at Princeton. The state's many concert singers include Anna Case (1889–1984), Paul Robeson (1898–1976), and Richard Crooks (1900–72). Popular singers include Francis Albert "Frank" Sinatra (b.1915), Sarah Vaughan (1924-1990), Dionne Warwick (b.1941), Paul Simon (b.1942), and Bruce Springsteen (b.1949). Jazz musician William "Count" Basie (1904–84) was born in Red Bank.

Other celebrities native to New Jersey are actors Jack Nicholson (b.1937), Michael Douglas (b.1944), Meryl Streep (b.1948), and John Travolta (b.1954). Comedians Lou Costello (1906–59), Ernie Kovacs (1919–62), Jerry Lewis (b.1926), and Clerow "Flip" Wilson (b.1933) were also born in the state. New Jersey-born athletes include figure skater Richard "Dick" Button (b.1929), winner of two Olympic gold medals.

50BIBLIOGRAPHY

Amick, George. *The American Way of Graft*. Princeton, NJ: Center for Analysis of Public Issues, 1987.

Cohen, David. *The Folklore and Folklife of New Jersey*. New Brunswick, NJ.: Rutgers University Press, 1983.

Cunningham, John T. *This is New Jersey*. 4th ed. New Brunswick, N.J.: Rutgers University Press, 1994.

Federal Writers' Project. *New Jersey: A Guide to the Present and Past*. Reprint. New York: Somerset, n.d. (orig. 1939).

Fleming, Thomas. *The Forgotten Victory: The Battle for New Jersey*. New York: Reader's Digest, 1973.

——. *New Jersey: A Bicentennial History*. New York: Norton, 1977.

Gillette, William. *Jersey Blue: Civil War Politics in New Jersey, 1854-1865*. New Brunswick, N.J.: Rutgers University Press, 1995.

League of Women Voters of New Jersey. *New Jersey: Spotlight on New Jersey Government*.6th ed. New Brunswick, N.J.: Rutgers University Press, 1992.

Link, Arthur F. *The Road to the White House*. Princeton, N.J.: Princeton University Press, 1947.

McPhee, John. *The Pine Barrens*. New York: Farrar, Straus & Giroux, 1981.

A New Jersey Anthology. Newark: New Jersey Historical Society, 1994.

New Jersey, State of Economic Policy Council and Office of Economic Policy. *1985 Economic Outlook for New Jersey*. Trenton, 1984.

Roberts, Russell. *Discover the Hidden New Jersey*. New Brunswick, N.J.: Rutgers University Press, 1995.

Rosenthal, Alan, and John Blydenburgh (eds.). *Politics in New Jersey*. New Brunswick, N.J.: Rutgers University Press, 1975.

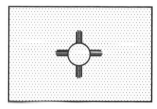

NEW MEXICO

State of New Mexico

ORIGIN OF STATE NAME: Spanish explorers in 1540 called the area "the new Mexico." **NICKNAME:** Land of Enchantment. **CAPITAL:** Santa Fe. **ENTERED UNION:** 6 January 1912 (47th). **SONGS:** "O Fair New Mexico"; "Así Es Nuevo México." **MOTTO:** *Crescit eundo* (It grows as it goes). **FLAG:** The sun symbol of the Indians of Zia Pueblo appears in red on a yellow field. **OFFICIAL SEAL:** An American bald eagle with extended wings grasps three arrows in its talons and shields a smaller eagle grasping a snake in its beak and a cactus in its talons (the emblem of Mexico; and thus symbolic of the change in sovereignty over the state). Below the scene is the state motto; the words "Great Seal of the State of New Mexico 1912" surround the whole. **ANIMAL:** Black bear. **BIRD:** Roadrunner (chaparral bird). **FISH:** Cutthroat trout. **FLOWER:** Yucca. **VEGETABLES:** Frijol; chile. **TREE:** Piñon. **FOSSIL:** *Coelophysis* dinosaur. **GEM:** Turquoise. **LEGAL HOLIDAYS:** New Year's Day, 1 January; Birthday of Martin Luther King, Jr., 3d Monday in January; Lincoln's Birthday, 12 February; Washington's Birthday, 3d Monday in February; Memorial Day, 30 May; Independence Day, 4 July; Labor Day, 1st Monday in September; Columbus Day, 2d Monday in October; Veterans Day, 11 November; Thanksgiving Day, 4th Thursday in November; Christmas Day, 25 December. **TIME:** 5 AM MST = noon GMT.

¹LOCATION, SIZE, AND EXTENT

New Mexico is located in the southwestern US. Smaller only than Montana of the eight Rocky Mountain states, it ranks 5th in size among the 50 states. The area of New Mexico is 121,593 sq mi (314,926 sq km), of which land comprises 121,335 sq mi (314,258 sq km) and inland water 258 sq mi (668 sq km). Almost square in shape except for its jagged southern border, New Mexico extends about 352 mi (566 km) E-W and 391 mi (629 km) N-S.

New Mexico is bordered on the N by Colorado; on the E by Oklahoma and Texas; on the S by Texas and the Mexican state of Chihuahua (with a small portion of the south-central border formed by the Rio Grande); and on the W by Arizona. The total boundary length of New Mexico is 1,434 mi (2,308 km).

The geographic center of the state is in Torrance County, 12 mi (19 km) SSW of Willard.

²TOPOGRAPHY

The Continental Divide extends from north to south through central New Mexico. The north–central part of the state lies within the Southern Rocky Mountains, and the northwest forms part of the Colorado Plateau. The eastern two-fifths of the state fall on the western fringes of the Great Plains.

Major mountain ranges include the Southern Rockies, the Chuska Mountains in the northwest, and the Caballo, San Andres, San Mateo, Sacramento, and Guadalupe ranges in the south and southwest. The highest point in the state is Wheeler Peak, at 13,161 feet (4,011 meters); the lowest point, 2,817 feet (859 meters), is at Red Bluff Reservoir.

The Rio Grande traverses New Mexico from north to south and forms a small part of the state's southern border with Texas. Other major rivers include the Pecos, San Juan, Canadian, and Gila. The largest bodies of inland water are the Elephant Butte Reservoir and Conchas Reservoir, both created by dams.

The Carlsbad Caverns, the largest known subterranean labyrinth in the world, penetrate the foothills of the Guadalupes in the southeast. The caverns embrace more than 37 mi (60 km) of connecting chambers and corridors and are famed for their stalactite and stalagmite formations.

³CLIMATE

New Mexico's climate ranges from arid to semiarid, with a wide range of temperatures. Average January temperatures vary from about 35°F (2°C) in the north to about 55°F (13°C) in the southern and central regions. July temperatures range from about 78°F (26°C) at high elevations to around 92°F (33°C) at lower elevations. The record high temperature for the state is 122°F (50°C), set most recently on 27 July 1994 at Lakewood; the record low, –50°F (–46°C), was set on 1 February 1951 at Gavilan.

Average annual precipitation ranges from under 10 in (25 cm) in the desert to over 20 in (50 cm) at high elevations. Nearly one-half the annual rainfall comes during July and August, and thunderstorms are common in the summer. Snow is much more frequent in the north than in the south; Albuquerque gets about 10 in (25 cm) of snow a year, and the northern mountains receive up to 100 in (254 cm).

⁴FLORA AND FAUNA

New Mexico is divided into the following six life zones: lower Sonoran, upper Sonoran, transition, Canadian, Hudsonian, and arctic-alpine.

Characteristic vegetation in each zone includes, respectively, desert shrubs and grasses; piñon/juniper woodland, sagebrush, and chaparral; ponderosa pine and oak woodlands; mixed conifer and aspen forests; spruce/fir forests and meadows; tundra wild flowers and riparian shrubs. The yucca has three varieties in New Mexico and is the state flower. Six types of aster are considered threatened; several cacti are on the endangered list.

Indigenous animals include pronghorn antelope, javelina, and black-throated sparrow in the lower Sonoran zone; mule and white-tailed deer, ringtail, and brown towhee in the upper Sonoran zone; elk and wild turkey in the transition zone; black bear and hairy woodpecker in the Canadian zone; pine marten and blue grouse in the Hudsonian zone; and bighorn sheep, pika, ermine, and white-tailed ptarmigan in the arctic-alpine zone. Among notable desert insects are the tarantula, centipede, and vinegaroon. The coatimundi, Baird's sparrow, and brook stickleback are among rare animals. Threatened species include the

Arizona shrew and Mexican tetra. The black-footed ferret, river otter, gray wolf, Gila monster, and Socorro isopod are on the endangered list.

5ENVIRONMENTAL PROTECTION

Agencies concerned with the environment include the New Mexico Environment Department (NMED), the Environmental Improvement Board, the Water Quality Control Commission, and the Energy, Minerals and Natural Resources Department. As the state's leading environmental agency, the NMED's mission is to preserve, protect, and perpetuate New Mexico's environment for present and future generations. The Department is comprised of four divisions, 14 bureaus, four districts, and 17 field offices. Each entity is responsible for different areas and functions of environmental protection (or administrative support) concerning air, water, and land resources. Under the authority of state/federal laws and regulations, the NMED fulfills its mission through the judicious application of statewide regulatory, technical assistance, planning, enforcement, educational, and related functions in the service of its citizens. As of 1996, New Mexico had 11 hazardous waste sites. In 1996, it had 482,000 acres (0.6%) of wetlands.

6POPULATION

In 1990, New Mexico had a census population of 1,515,069, 37th in the US, with a population density of 12.5 persons per sq mi (4.8 per sq km). The estimated population in 1996 was 1,713,407 (an 13% increase over 1990). About 73% of the population was urban and 27% rural in 1990. In 1995, an estimated 522,328 people, about one-third of New Mexico's population, lived in the Albuquerque metropolitan area in Bernalillo County. Albuquerque itself had 411,994 residents in 1994, and Santa Fe, the 2d-largest city and the state capital, had 62,514 inhabitants.

7ETHNIC GROUPS

New Mexico has two large minorities: Indians and Hispanics.

There were 134,000 American Indians in the state in 1990, 8.9% of the total population. Part of Arizona's great Navaho reservation extends across the border into New Mexico. There are 2 Apache reservations, 19 Pueblo villages (including one for the Zia in Sandoval County), and lands allotted to other tribes. Indian lands cover 8,152,895 acres (3,299,477 hectares), 10.5% of New Mexico's area (second only to Arizona in proportion of Indian lands). In 1995, the most populous Pueblos (with estimated populations) were Acoma (6,344), Santo Domingo (4,246), and Isleta (4,170). The Zuni Pueblo was estimated at 8,759.

The Hispanic population is an old one, descending from Spanish-speaking peoples who lived there before the territory was annexed by the US. This group, with a much smaller one of immigrants from modern Mexico, makes up 38.2% of New Mexicans.

About 14,000 Asians and Pacific Islanders and 30,000 black Americans live in the state. The people of New Mexico are proud of their ethnoracial civic harmony, though there have been local conflicts between Anglos and Hispanics.

8LANGUAGES

New Mexico has large Indian and Spanish-speaking populations. But just a few place-names, like Tucumcari and Mescalero, echo in English the presence of the Apache, Zuni, Navaho, and other tribes living there. Numerous Spanish borrowings include *vigas* (rafters) in the northern half, and *canales* (gutters) and *acequia* (irrigation ditch) in the Rio Grande Valley. New Mexico English is a mixture of dominant Midland, with some Northern features (such as *sick to the stomach)* in the northeast, and Southern and

South Midland features such as *spoonbread* and *carry* (escort) in the eastern agricultural fringe.

In 1990, 896,049 New Mexicans—64.5% of the resident population 5 years of age and older—spoke only English at home. Other languages spoken at home included the following:

Spanish	388,186
Various Native American	79,087
German	6,000
French	3,402
Italian	1,880
Chinese	1,686

9RELIGIONS

The first religions in New Mexico were practiced by Pueblo and Navaho Indians. Franciscan missionaries arrived at the time of Coronado's conquest in 1540, and the first Roman Catholic church in the state was built in 1598. Roman Catholicism has long been the dominant religion, though from the mid-1800s there has also been a steady increase in the number of Protestants. The first Baptist missionaries arrived in 1849, the Methodists in 1850, and the Mormons in 1877.

The state's Roman Catholic churches had 467,356 members in 1990. Major Protestant denominations in 1990 included 158,873 Southern Baptists and 54,664 United Methodists.

The Jewish population was estimated at 6,075 in 1990. Other faiths in the state include the Pentecostals.

10TRANSPORTATION

Important early roads included El Camino Real, extending from Mexico City, Mexico, up to Santa Fe and the Santa Fe Trail, leading westward from Independence, Missouri. By 1995, New Mexico had 61,289 mi (98,675 km) of public roads and streets, including 1,000 mi (1,610 km) of interstate highway.

In 1995, 1,483,727 road vehicles were registered in the state, of which 832,075 were automobiles, 648,217 trucks, 31,180 motorcycles, and 3,435 buses.

Rail service did not begin in New Mexico until 1879. New Mexico had 2,067 rail mi (3,328 km) of track in 1995, with Class I road making up about 92% of that total; the main rail lines serving the state are the Southern Pacific, the Atchison, Topeka & Santa Fe, and the Burlington Northern. Amtrak provided passenger service en route from Chicago to Los Angeles and from New Orleans to Los Angeles. Total New Mexico ridership was 76,001 in 1995/96.

In 1995 there were 149 airports, 21 heliports, and 1 seaplane base. Albuquerque International is the state's main airport with 41,484 aircraft departures and 2,938,786 enplaned passengers during 1994.

11HISTORY

The earliest evidence of human occupation in what is now New Mexico, dating from about 20,000 years ago, has been found in Sandia Cave near Albuquerque. This so-called Sandia man was later joined by other nomadic hunters—the Clovis and Folsom people from the northern and eastern portions of the state, and the Cochise culture, which flourished in southwestern New Mexico from about 10,000 to 500 BC. The Mogollon people tilled small farms in the southwest from 300 BC to about 100 years before Columbus came to the New World. Also among the state's early inhabitants were the Basket Makers, a seminomadic people who eventually evolved into the Anasazi, or Cliff Dwellers. The Anasazi, who made their home in the Four Corners region (where present-day New Mexico meets Colorado, Arizona, and Utah), were the predecessors of the modern Pueblo Indians.

The Pueblo people lived along the upper Rio Grande, except for a desert group east of Albuquerque, who lived in the same

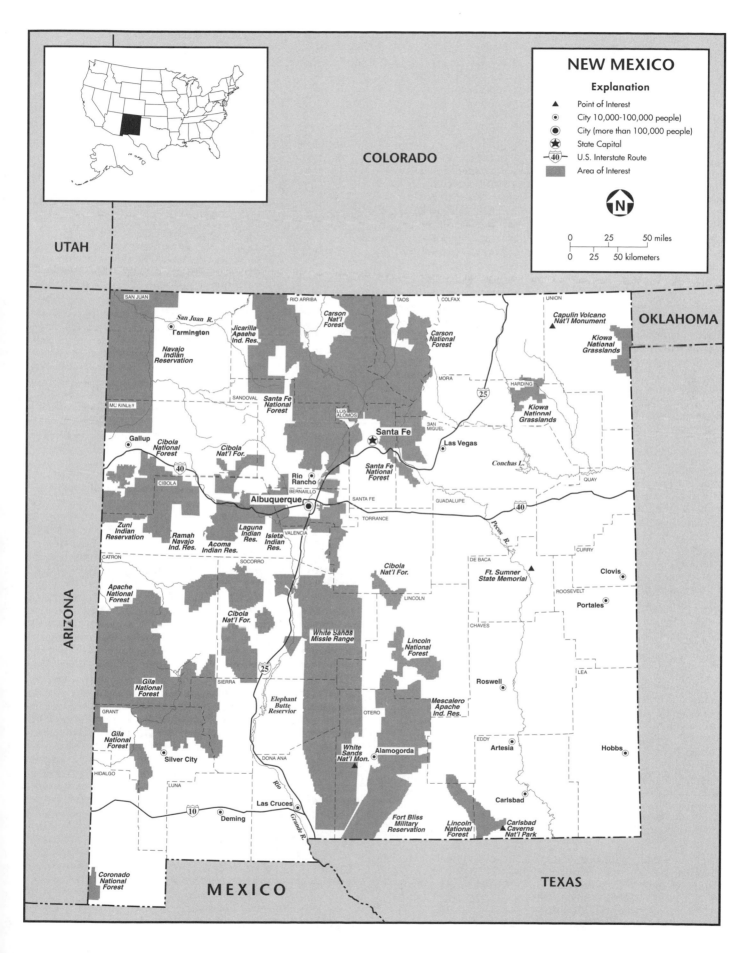

NEW MEXICO

Explanation

▲ Point of Interest
⊙ City 10,000-100,000 people)
⦿ City (more than 100,000 people)
★ State Capital
—40— U.S. Interstate Route
▨ Area of Interest

kind of apartment-like villages as the river Pueblos. During the 13th century, the Navaho settled in the Four Corners area to become farmers, sheepherders, and occasional enemies of the Pueblos. The Apache, a more nomadic and warlike group who came at about the same time, would later pose a threat to all the non-Indians who arrived in New Mexico during the Spanish, Mexican, and American periods.

Francisco Vásquez de Coronado led the earliest major expedition to New Mexico, beginning in 1540, 80 years before the Pilgrims landed at Plymouth Rock. In 1598, Don Juan de Onate led an expedition up the Rio Grande, where, one year later, he established the settlement of San Gabriel, near present-day Espanola; in 1610, the Spanish moved their center of activity to Santa Fe. For more than two centuries, the Spaniards, who concentrated their settlements, farms, and ranches in the upper Rio Grande Valley, dominated New Mexico, except for a period from 1680 to about 1693, when the Pueblo Indians temporarily regained control of the region.

In 1821, Mexico gained its independence from Spain, and New Mexico came under the Mexican flag for 25 years. The unpopularity of government officials sent from Mexico City and the inability of the new republic to control the Apache led to the revolt of 1837, which was put down by a force from Albuquerque led by General Manuel Armijo. In 1841, as governor of the Mexican territory, Armijo defeated an invading force from the Republic of Texas, but he later made a highly controversial decision not to defend Apache Pass east of Santa Fe during the Mexican-American War, instead retreating and allowing US forces under the command of General Stephen Watts Kearny to enter the capital city unopposed on 18 August 1846.

Kearny, without authorization from Congress, immediately attempted to make New Mexico a US territory. He appointed the respected Indian trader Charles Bent, a founder of Bent's Fort on the Santa Fe Trail, as civil governor, and then led his army on to California. After Kearny's departure, a Mexican and Indian revolt in Taos resulted in Bent's death; the suppression of the Taos uprising by another US Army contingent secured American control over New Mexico, although the area did not officially become a part of the US until the Treaty of Guadalupe-Hidalgo ended the Mexican-American War in 1848.

New Mexico became a US territory as part of the Compromise of 1850, which also brought California into the Union as a free state. Territorial status did not bring about rapid or dramatic changes in the lives of those who were already in New Mexico. However, an increasing number of people traveling on the Santa Fe Trail—which had been used since the early 1820s to carry goods between Independence, Mo., and Santa Fe—were Americans seeking a new home in the Southwest. One issue that divided many of these new settlers from the original Spanish-speaking inhabitants was land. Native New Mexicans resisted, sometimes violently, the efforts of new Anglo residents and outside capital to take over lands that had been allocated during the earlier Spanish and Mexican periods. Anglo lawyers such as Thomas Benton Catron acquired unprecedented amounts of land from native grantees as payment of legal fees in the prolonged litigation that often accompanied these disputes. Eventually, a court of private land claims, established by the federal government, legally processed 33 million acres (13 million hectares) of disputed land from 1891 to 1904.

Land disputes were not the only cause of violence during the territorial period. In 1862, Confederate General Henry Hopkins Sibley led an army of Texans up the Rio Grande and occupied Santa Fe; he was defeated at Glorieta Pass in northern New Mexico by a hastily assembled army that included volunteers from Colorado and New Mexico and Union regulars, in a battle that has been labeled the Gettysburg of the West. The so-called Lincoln County War of 1878–81, a range war pitting cattlemen

against merchants and involving, among other partisans, William H. Bonney (Billy the Kid), helped give the territory the image of a lawless region unfit for statehood.

Despite the tumult, New Mexico began to make substantial economic progress. In 1879, the Atchison, Topeka & Santa Fe Railroad entered the territory. General Lew Wallace, who was appointed by President Rutherford B. Hayes to settle the Lincoln County War, was the last territorial governor to enter New Mexico by stagecoach and the first to leave it by train.

By the end of the 19th century, the Indian threat that had plagued the Anglos, like the Spanish-speaking New Mexicans before them, had finally been resolved. New Mexicans won the respect of Theodore Roosevelt by enlisting in his Rough Riders during the Spanish-American War, and when he became president, he returned the favor by working for statehood. New Mexico finally became a state on 6 January 1912, under President William H. Taft.

In March 1916, irregulars of the Mexican revolutionary Pancho Villa crossed the international boundary into New Mexico, killing, robbing, and burning homes in Columbus. US troops under the command of General John J. Pershing were sent into Mexico on a long and unsuccessful expedition to capture Villa, while National Guardsmen remained on the alert in the Columbus area for almost a year.

The decade of the 1920s was characterized by the discovery and development of new resources. Potash salts were found near Carlsbad, and important petroleum reserves in the southeast and northwest were discovered and exploited. Oil development made possible another important industry, tourism, which began to flourish as gasoline became increasingly available. This period of prosperity ended, however, with the onset of the Great Depression.

World War II revived the economy, but at a price. In 1942, hundreds of New Mexicans stationed in the Philippines were among the US troops forced to make the cruel "Bataan march" to Japanese prison camps. Scientists working at Los Alamos ushered in the Atomic Age with the explosion of the first atomic bomb at White Sands Proving Ground in June 1945.

The remarkable growth that characterized the Sunbelt during the postwar era has been most noticeable in New Mexico. Newcomers from many parts of the country moved to the state, a demographic shift with profound social, cultural, and political consequences. Spanish-speaking New Mexicans, once an overwhelming majority, became a minority. As of the 1990 census, Hispanics account for 38% of the state's population. In that year, New Mexico had a higher percentage of both Hispanics and Indians than any other state.

Defense-related industries have been a mainstay of New Mexico's economy in the postwar period. Income from this sector declined in the early 1990s due to reductions in military spending following the end of the Cold War. However, this decline has been offset by New Mexico's diversification into nonmilitary production, including such high-tech projects as Intel's Rio Rancho plant, which, in the mid-1990s, was the world's largest computer-chip factory. Tourism also played a major role in New Mexico's economy in the 1990s, and the state remains a leading center of space and nuclear research.

In the 1994 midterm elections, the only three-term governor in New Mexico's history, Democrat Bruce King, was removed from office in the Republican tide that swept the nation.

[12]STATE GOVERNMENT

The constitution of New Mexico was drafted in 1910, approved by the voters in 1911, and came into effect when statehood was achieved in 1912. A new constitution drawn up by a convention of elected delegates was rejected by the voters in 1969.

The legislature consists of a 42-member senate and a 70-member house of representatives. Senators serve four-year terms, and house members serve two-year terms. The legislature meets every year, for 60 calendar days in odd-numbered years and 30 calendar days in even-numbered years.

The executive branch consists of 10 elected officials, including the governor, lieutenant governor, secretary of state, auditor, treasurer, attorney general, and commissioner of public lands. These 7 are elected for four-year terms; none may serve two successive terms. In 1996 the governor's salary was $90,000. Three elected members of the Corporation Commission, which has various regulatory and revenue-raising responsibilities, serve six-year terms.

In general, constitutional amendments must be approved by majority vote in each house and by a majority of the electorate. Amendments dealing with voting rights, school lands, and linguistic requirements for education can be proposed only by three-fourths of each house, and subsequently must be approved by three-fourths of the total electorate and two-thirds of the electorate in each county.

In order to vote in state elections, a person must be 18 years of age, a US citizen, and a state resident for at least 42 days.

13POLITICAL PARTIES

Although Democrats hold a very substantial edge in voter registration—there were 412,023 registered Democrats and only 239,736 registered Republicans in 1994—New Mexico has been a "swing state" in US presidential elections since it entered the Union. Between 1948 and 1992, New Mexicans voted for Democratic presidential candidates four times and Republican presidential candidates eight times, choosing in every election except 1976 and 1992 the candidate who was also the presidential choice of voters nationwide. In 1996, Democratic incumbent Bill Clinton captured 49% of the vote; Republican Bob Dole received 42%; and Independent Ross Perot collected 6%. New Mexico's senators in 1997 were Democrat Jeff Bingaman, elected in 1994 to his third term, and Republican Peter V. Domenici who was elected to his fifth term in 1996. New Mexico's US House delegation consists of three Republicans. As of 1997 there were 25 Democrats and 17 Republicans in the state senate and 42 Democrats and 28 Republicans in the state house. There were three black elected officials and 716 Hispanics

holding public office in 1994. As of 1995, 23 women served in the state legislature and two women held elective executive office.

14LOCAL GOVERNMENT

There are 33 counties in New Mexico. Each is governed by commissioners elected for two-year terms. Municipalities are incorporated as cities, towns, or villages. As of 1992, there were 98 municipalities, 94 school districts, and 116 special districts.

The Indian Reorganization Act of 1934 reaffirmed the right of Indians to govern themselves, adopt constitutions, and form corporations to do business under federal law. Indians also retain the right to vote in state and federal elections. Pueblo Indians elect governors from each of 19 pueblos, and they form a coalition called the All-Indian Pueblo Council. The Apache elect a tribal council headed by a president and vice-president. The Navaho—one-third of whom live in New Mexico—elect a chairman, vice-chairman, and council members from their reservation in New Mexico and Arizona.

15STATE SERVICES

Agencies supervising the state transportation system include the Department of Aviation, the Civil Air Patrol, the State Highway Commission, the Department of Motor Transportation, the Department of Motor Vehicles, and the Traffic Safety Commission.

Welfare services are provided through the Human Services Department. Related service agencies include the Office of Indian Affairs and Human Rights Commission. Health services are provided by the Department of Health and Environment. The various public protection agencies include the Office of Civil and Defense Mobilization of the Attorney General's Office, the State Human Rights Commission, the Department of Corrections, and the New Mexico State Police.

The state's natural resources are protected by the Fish and Wildlife Service, the State Forest Conservation Commission, the Environmental Improvement Division of the Department of Health and Environment, the Water Quality Control Commission, and the State Park and Recreation Commission.

16JUDICIAL SYSTEM

The judicial branch consists of a supreme court, an appeals court, district courts, probate courts, magistrate courts, and other inferior courts as created by law.

New Mexico Presidential Vote by Political Parties, 1948–96

YEAR	ELECTORAL VOTE	NEW MEXICO WINNER	DEMOCRAT	REPUBLICAN	PROGRESSIVE
1948	4	*Truman (D)	105,240	80,303	1,037
1952	4	*Eisenhower (R)	105,435	132,170	225
					CONSTITUTION
1956	4	*Eisenhower (R)	106,098	146,788	364
1960	4	*Kennedy (D)	156,027	153,733	570
1964	4	*Johnson (D)	194,015	132,838	1,217
					AMERICAN IND.
1968	4	*Nixon (R)	130,081	169,692	25,737
					AMERICAN
1972	4	*Nixon (R)	141,084	235,606	8,767
					SOC. WORKERS
1976	4	Ford (R)	201,148	211,419	2,462
					LIBERTARIAN
1980	4	*Reagan (R)	167,826	250,779	4,365
1984	4	*Reagan (R)	201,769	307,101	4,459
1988	4	*Bush (R)	244,497	270,341	3,268
1992**	5	*Clinton (D)	261,617	212,824	1,615
1996**	5	*Clinton (D)	273,495	232,751	2,996

* Won US presidential election.

** Independent candidate Ross Perot received 91,895 votes in 1992 and 32,257 votes in 1996.

The supreme court is composed of a chief justice and four associate justices; the appeals court, created to take over some of the supreme court's caseload, is composed of ten judges. All are elected for eight-year terms.

The state's 33 counties are divided into 13 judicial districts, served by 61 district judges, each elected for a six-year term. District courts have unlimited general jurisdiction and are commonly referred to as trial courts. They also serve as courts of review for decisions of lower courts and administrative agencies. Each county has a probate court, served by a probate judge who is elected from within the county for a two-year term. In 1996 there were 4,480 active attorneys in the state.

In 1995, New Mexico had a total crime rate of 6,428 per 100,000 persons, including 819.2 for violent crime and 5,608.8 for property crime. For murder and manslaughter, the rate was 8.8 for 100,000 persons; forcible rape, 56.6; robbery, 154.3; aggravated assault, 599.3; burglary, 1,487.1; larceny-theft, 3,648.5; and motor vehicle theft, 513.2.

In 1995, there were 3,991 inmates held in 8 state and federal correctional facilities, a rate of 237 inmates per 100,000 inhabitants. The inmate population increased by 28% between 1990 and 1995.

New Mexico imposes the death penalty but has not executed anyone for over 25 years.

17ARMED FORCES

In 1992, there were 14,402 active-duty military personnel stationed in New Mexico, 13,406 of whom were in the Air Force. That year, there were 11,343 Reserve and National Guard personnel in the state. The major installations are Kirtland Air Force Base in the Albuquerque area, Holloman Air Force Base at Alamogordo, and White Sands Missile Range north of Las Cruces. Defense contract awards totaled $676 million in 1995/96.

There were about 170,000 veterans living in New Mexico in 1996. Of these fewer than 500 had served in World War I, 43,000 in World War II, 29,000 in the Korean conflict, 60,000 during the Vietnam era, and 12,000 in the Persian Gulf War. In 1995/96 total federal expenditures for veterans' programs amounted to $359 million. In 1993 the New Mexico State Police employed 419 full-time sworn officers, or 3 per 10,000.

18MIGRATION

Prior to statehood, the major influx of migrants came from Texas and Mexico; many of these immigrants spoke Spanish as their primary language.

Wartime prosperity during the 1940s brought a wave of Anglos into the state. New Mexico experienced a net gain through migration of 78,000 people during 1940–60, a net loss of 130,000 during the economic slump of the 1960s, and another net gain of 154,000 between 1970 and 1983. In the 1980s, New Mexico had a net gain from migration of 63,000 residents, accounting for 28% of the state's population increase during those years. Between 1990 and 1996, the state had net gains of 67,825 in domestic migration and 6,361 in international migration. in 1996, 5,780 foreign immigrants entered New Mexico. As of 1994, the number of undocumented immigrants was estimated between 14 and 25. However, the proportion of native-born state residents only nominally fell from 51.8% in 1980 to 51.7% in 1990. About 48% of residents age 5 and older in 1990 lived in a different house than in 1985, of which 30% did so in another state.

19INTERGOVERNMENTAL COOPERATION

New Mexico participates in the Interstate Oil and Gas Compact; Interstate Mining Compact; Western Corrections Compact; Western Interstate Energy Compact; compacts governing use of the Rio Grande and the Canadian, Colorado, La Plata, and Pecos rivers; and other interstate agreements. In 1995/96, New Mexico received a total of $1.9 billion in government grants.

20ECONOMY

New Mexico was primarily an agricultural state until the 1940s, when military activities assumed major economic importance. Currently, major industries include primary metals (mining), petroleum, and food. Tourism also continues to flourish. Major employers range from Kirtland Air Force Base, to Los Alamos National Laboratory, Honeywell, Inc.

In 1994, the total gross state product for New Mexico was $37,832 million, to which private goods-producing industries contributed $10,342 million; private service-producing industries, $20,593 million; government, $6,897 million.

In 1995, New Mexico's per capita income was $18,206 which ranked 47th nationally. In 1996, there were 5,870 bankruptcy filings, up 35% from the previous year.

21INCOME

In 1996, per capita personal income in New Mexico was $18,770, 48th among the 50 states. Total disposable personal income was $28.6 billion in 1996, up from $27.3 billion in 1995. Median household income was $25,991 in 1995.

About 25.3% of the population lived below the federal poverty level in 1995. In 1995, median household income in New Mexico was $25,991.

22LABOR

In 1996, the total civilian labor force of New Mexico was estimated at 799,800. Of that total, 735,400 were employed and 64,400 (8.1%) unemployed. According to the US Bureau of Economic Analysis, the 1995 earning and employment pattern in the state of New Mexico was as follows:

	EARNINGS ($000)	EMPLOYMENT
Total	21,436,654	903,412
Farm	288,801	20,465
Nonfarm	21,147,853	882,947
Private	15,643,829	694,321
Agricultural services	148,020	12,203
Mining	755,549	21,539
Construction	1,545,357	59,763
Manufacturing	1,666,300	52,058
Nondurable goods	513,712	17,327
Durable goods	1,152,588	34,731
Transportation, communication, and Utilities	1,289,617	36.269
Wholesale trade	898,120	31,468
Retail trade	2,392,975	163,452
Finance, insurance, and real estate	977,297	53,915
Services	5,970,594	263,654
Government	5,504,024	188,626

About 6.4% of private sector employees in New Mexico were covered by unions and 24.9% of public sector workers were covered by unions in 1995.

23AGRICULTURE

The first farmers of New Mexico were the Pueblo Indians, who raised corn, beans, and squash. Wheat and barley were introduced from Europe, and indigo and chiles came from Mexico.

In 1996, New Mexico's total farm marketings were $1.4 billion (35th in the US). About 32% came from crops and 68% from livestock products. Leading crops included hay and wheat. In 1996, hay production was 1,577,000 tons, valued at $193,002,000, and wheat production was 4,070,000 bushels, valued at $21,164,000. The state also produced 14,700,000 bushels of corn for grain, and 2,560,000 hundredweight of potatoes in 1996.

24ANIMAL HUSBANDRY

Meat animals, especially cattle, represent the bulk of New Mexico's agricultural income. In 1997, there were nearly 1.5 million cattle and calves, valued at $819.5 million. In 1996, there were an estimated 5,000 hogs and pigs, valued at $500,000 on New Mexico farms. During 1995, New Mexico farms and ranches produced around 13.9 million lb of sheep and lambs which brought in a gross income of nearly $13 million. The main stock-raising regions are in the east, northeast, and northwest.

25FISHING

There is no commercial fishing in New Mexico. The native cutthroat trout is prized by sport fishermen, however, and numerous species have been introduced into state lakes and reservoirs. In 1995–96, according to the US Fish and Wildlife Service, seven national hatchery facilities distributed over one million fish and 588,000 fish eggs within the state.

26FORESTRY

Although lumbering ranks low as a source of state income, the forests of New Mexico are of crucial importance because of the role they play in water conservation and recreation.

In 1993, 20% of New Mexico's land area—15.2 million acres—was forestland. Of the state total, 8,362,000 acres (3,384,000 hectares) were federally owned or managed; 878,000 acres (355,000 hectares) were owned by the state; and 6,043,000 acres (2,446,000 hectares) were privately owned.

27MINING

In national standing, New Mexico ranked 11th in total nonfuel mineral value. In 1995, nonfuel mineral production was valued at $1,080 million, up 16% from 1994. Copper is the third most widely used metal, after iron and aluminum, and one that is employed in electrical and telecommunications products, building construction, industrial machinery, transportation, consumer products, and in strategic military applications. In 1995, New Mexico remained third, behind Arizona and Utah, of 13 copper-producing states. Copper and potash again led other mineral commodities, with respective values of $725 million and $200 million or 86% of the state's total nonfuel mineral value. Value totals of masonry cement, gold, and salt fell, while all other mineral commodity totals increased or remained about the same.

The state continued to lead the country in perlite production with the largest output of six states, and the main markets for New Mexico's perlite were its uses in building construction, as filter aids, as a filler, and in agriculture. New Mexico also ranked first in production of potash and zeolites, second in pumice and crude mica, sixth in molybdenum, and ninth in silver. According to the state, about 95% of the potash finds its way as a soil amendment in agriculture; the remaining 5% is used in industry for such things as manufacturing television tubes, chinaware, soaps, and synthetic rubber.

28ENERGY AND POWER

New Mexico is a major producer of oil and natural gas, and has significant reserves of low-sulfur bituminous coal.

In 1994, the state consumed, per capita, 344 million Btu of energy. The residential sector used 81 trillion Btu, the commercial, 96 trillion; industrial, 198 trillion; and transportation, 217 trillion. Chief sources were petroleum, 228 trillion Btu; natural gas, 221 trillion Btu; and coal, 278 trillion Btu.

Most of New Mexico's natural gas and oil fields are located in the southeastern counties of Eddy, Lea, and Chaves, and in the northwestern counties of McKinley and San Juan. In 1995, 70 million barrels of crude petroleum were produced, and there were proven reserves of 730 million barrels. Natural gas marketed production in 1995 totaled 1.5 trillion cu feet.

In 1995, 26.1 million tons of coal were mined.

29INDUSTRY

The value of shipments by manufacturers in New Mexico exceeded $12.5 billion in 1995.

The following table shows the value of shipments for selected industries in 1995:

Electronic and electric equipment	$6,644,300,000
Food and food products	775,500,000
Instruments and related products	507,900,000
Industrial machinery	132,000,000
Primary metal industries	1,119,800,000

More than 50% of the manufacturing jobs in the state are located in and around Albuquerque, in Bernalillo County. Other counties with substantial manufacturing activity include Santa Fe, San Juan, Otero, McKinley, and Dona Ana. Leading manufacturing employers include Honeywell and G.E. Aircraft (Albuquerque), Intel Corp. (Rio Rancho), Levi Strauss Co. (Roswell/Albuquerque), Transportation Manufacturing Corp. (Roswell), and Digital Equipment Corp. (Albuquerque).

Manufacturing has been largely reliant on the vagaries of federal defense expenditures, which have been falling in recent years. In 1992, however, several companies not as dependent upon defense expenditures were expanding: Intel (computer chips), Philips Semiconductors (computer chip production equipment), General Mills (cereal processing), and Transportation Manufacturing Corp. (buses).

In 1995, there were 276 US patents issued to New Mexico residents.

30COMMERCE

In 1992, New Mexico's 1,515 wholesale establishments had sales of nearly $6.3 billion. In 1995, wholesale establishments in the state registered total personal incomes of $898 million. Leading sectors of wholesale trade included petroleum and petroleum products; food and food products; machinery, equipment, and supplies; lumber and construction materials; and farm products. Retail sales totaled $11.3 billion in 1992, 37th among the states. In 1995, retail establishments had total personal incomes of $2.4 billion. Leading sectors of retail trade included food stores and eating and drinking establishments, 41.1%, and automotive dealers, 19.19%.

New Mexico's foreign exports totaled $971 million in 1996, 45th in the US.

31CONSUMER PROTECTION

Consumer protection in New Mexico is regulated by the Attorney General's Consumer Protection Division. This office may commence civil and criminal proceedings, represent the state before regulatory agencies, administer consumer protection programs, and handle consumer complaints.

32BANKING

New Mexico's first bank, the First National Bank of Santa Fe, was organized in 1870. After the turn of the century, banking establishments expanded rapidly in the state, mainly because of growth in the livestock industry.

In 1996 there were 68 insured commercial banks in New Mexico, with total assets of $15.4 billion, and total deposits of $11.9 billion. In 1996, 10 insured savings institutions had total assets of $1.4 billion.

33INSURANCE

There were two life insurance companies in 1995, and three property/casualty insurance companies in 1992.

In 1995, 1,436,000 life insurance policies were in force in the state, and their total value was $67.5 billion; $490.2 million in benefits were paid. The average family had $107,900 in life insurance.

The $1.47 billion of property and liability insurance premiums written in the state in 1995 included $740.3 million in automobile liability and damage insurance and $147.6 million in homeowners' insurance.

The insurance industry is regulated by the State Insurance Board.

34SECURITIES

There are no securities exchanges in New Mexico. In March 1994, 823 broker-dealer organizations were registered to conduct securities transactions in the state, involving 22,463 agents. There were also 221 registered securities investment advisory firms that provided services through 1,673 agents.

35PUBLIC FINANCE

The governor of New Mexico submits a budget annually to the legislature for approval. The fiscal year runs 1 July–30 June.

The following is a summary of estimated general revenues and expenditures for 1996–97 and 1997–98, in millions:

REVENUES	1996/97	1997/98
Gross receipts tax*	$ 1,282,600	$ 1,344,400
Income taxes	841,600	895,400
Mineral severance taxes	182,200	156,500
Other taxes and license fees	211,400	180,500
Other receipts	408,900	415,600
TOTALS	$2,926,700	$2,992,000
EXPENDITURES		
Public schools	$ 1,309,873	$2,862,259
Higher education	485,082	N/A
Health and human services	583,270	N/A
Public safety	180,071	N/A
Other expenses	410,167	139,183
TOTALS	$2,968,463	$3,001,442

* Includes governmental gross receipts and compensating taxes.

Outstanding debt of the state totaled $210 million as of June 30, 1993.

36TAXATION

The state of New Mexico levies a gross receipts tax on property and services, various excise taxes, personal and corporate income taxes, property taxes, and mineral severance taxes. As of 1996, personal income tax rates ranged from 1.7% on taxable income under $8,000 to 8.5% on income over $100,000.

In 1995, New Mexicans' federal income tax bill amounted to $3.9 billion.

37ECONOMIC POLICY

The Economic Development Division of the Department of Commerce and Industry promotes industrial and community development through such measures as tax-free bonds for manufacturing facilities; tax credits for investment and for job training, venture capital funds; and community development block grants. The state also seeks export markets for New Mexico's products and encourages use of the state by the film industry.

38HEALTH

In 1995 there were 26,914 live births in New Mexico, or 16 per 1,000 population. In 1995, there were 4,574 legal abortions, or 170 per 1,000 live births. In 1995 there were 12,500 deaths in the state (7.4 per 1,000 population). The infant death rate was 6.0 per 1,000 live births for the 12 months ending with December 1994. Deaths from heart disease and cancer were far below the national average.

New Mexico has the distinction of being the state with the lowest death rate from cardiovascular diseases. The rate per 100,000 population in 1993 was 149.4. For the year ending on 30 June 1995, AIDS was documented in 13.79 people per 100,000 population. The cancer mortality rate of 160 per 100,000 population was less than the US average.

There were half a million smokers in 1995. For those persons 0–17 who will become smokers, the estimated number of deaths is 33,367 (1995 estimate).

There were 36 hospitals in 1995, with 3,569 beds and 154,353 admissions; personnel included 12,400 registered nurses. The state had 4,030 active non-federal physicians in 1995, and 725 active dentists in 1995.

39SOCIAL WELFARE

In 1996, a total of 102,000 people received aid to families with dependent children. The monthly average allotment per family was $458. In 1996, 235,060 residents received monthly food stamp allowances averaging $70.59. Eligible students participating in the school lunch program cost the federal government $46.2 million. Weekly unemployment benefits averaged $153.05 in 1995.

In 1995, Social Security benefits averaging $674 a month were paid to 258,460 New Mexicans; additionally, 44,755 residents received monthly allowances averaging $323 from the federally administered Supplemental Security Income. The state maintains the Carrie Tingley Crippled Children's Hospital in Truth or Consequences, the Meadows Home for the Aged in Las Vegas, the Miners Hospital of New Mexico in Raton, and the New Mexico School for the Visually Handicapped in Alamogordo.

With the enactment of the Personal Responsibility and Work Opportunity Reconciliation Act of 1996, the US government has changed the form and regulations for many of its social welfare programs; most significantly, it replaces Aid to Families with Dependent Children (AFDC), an open-ended entitlement program, with Temporary Assistance for Needy Families (TANF), a limited system of assistance funded largely through federal block grants. The reform act also impacts the food stamp program, the Supplemental Security Income program, and the child nutrition program. The law took effect on 1 July 1997 and provided $16.38 billion in block grants for fiscal years 1997–2002. The grants are to be divided among the states based on an equation involving the numbers of former AFDC recipients in each state. Because many of the bill's provisions have yet to be implemented into state-by-state policy, it was not possible to include the details of each state's programs for this edition of this work.

40HOUSING

In 1996, New Mexico had an estimated 684,000 housing units, 602,000 of which were occupied; fewer than 4% of the units lacked full plumbing. Over 27% of all housing units in New Mexico were built in the 1980s. In 1996, 10,180 privately-owned units valued at just over $1 billion, were authorized for construction; of these, 8,842 were single family.

In 1990, the last year for which figures are available, the median monthly cost for an owner with a mortgage in New Mexico was $651, and $163 for an owner without a mortgage. The median monthly rent was $372. Median monthly costs for mortgage holders and renters in the greater Santa Fe area were $835 and $486, respectively; for the Albuquerque area the costs were $739 and $402, respectively, in 1990. During 1996, New Mexico received $121.6 million in aid from the US Department of Housing and Urban Development, including $23.5 million in community development block grants.

41EDUCATION

Of 928,000 New Mexicans 25 years old and older in 1990, 77.0% had completed high school, and 20.9% had completed college.

The public school system had 303,792 students in 1995. New Mexico's graduation rate of 71.7% ranked 32d in 1987. Direct expenditures per pupil for public elementary and secondary schools was $4,881 in the 1994–95 school year.

New Mexico had 16 institutions of higher education in 1990. The leading public institutions are the University of New Mexico, with its main campus at Albuquerque, and New Mexico State University in Las Cruces. College teachers averaged $36,398 in yearly salary in 1990/91.

42ARTS

New Mexico is a state rich in Indian, Spanish, Mexican, and contemporary art. Major exhibits can be seen at the University of New Mexico Art Museum in Albuquerque, and the Art Museum of the Harwood Foundation in Taos. Taos itself is an artists' colony of renown. The Santa Fe Opera, one of the nation's most distinguished regional opera companies, has its season during July and August.

The state of New Mexico generated $649,000 in federal funds in 1996. The National Endowment for the Arts (NEA) contributed $1,153,000 to the state's arts programs and $1,261,000 to the New Mexico Arts Division; the state and private sources also contributed funding. Private source contributed $38 million. Audiences for the state's arts programs totaled 4,334,940. There were 52,306 contributing artists. The state offered arts education programs to 26,600 school children. In 1995, New Mexico had 200 arts associations and 55 local arts groups. The New Mexico Arts Division has contributed funding to promote multicultural arts programs which reflect the Spanish and American Indian cultural influences of the area. The Arts Division also sponsors the Dance on Tour Initiative to help traveling dance companies. The New Mexico Symphony Orchestra received funding from the NEA; the NEA also contributed to the Institute of American Indian Arts. New Mexico's Arts Division received NEA funding for arts programs and grants from the NEA's state and regional program.

43LIBRARIES AND MUSEUMS

Public libraries in New Mexico had a combined total of 3,821,064 volumes and a circulation of 7,527,129 volumes in 1996-97. The largest municipal library is the Albuquerque Public Library. The largest university library is that of the University of New Mexico, with 1,647,787 volumes. There is a scientific library at Los Alamos and a law library at Santa Fe.

New Mexico has 99 museums. Especially noteworthy are the Maxwell Museum of Anthropology at Albuquerque; the Museum of New Mexico, Museum of International Folk Art, and Institute of American Indian Arts Museum, all in Santa Fe; and several art galleries and museums in Taos. Historic sites include the Palace of the Governors (1610), the oldest US capitol and probably the nation's oldest public building, in Santa Fe; Aztec Ruins National Monument, near Aztec; and Gila Cliff Dwellings National Monument, 44 mi (71 km) north of Silver City. A state natural history museum, in Albuquerque, opened in 1985.

44COMMUNICATIONS

The first regular monthly mail service between New Mexico and the other US states began in 1849. In March 1993, 89.1% of the state's 578,000 occupied housing units had telephones. In 1993 there were 61 AM radio stations and 91 FM stations. There were 178 commercial and 4 educational television stations in 1996, as well as three large cable systems.

45PRESS

The first newspaper published in New Mexico was *El Crepúsculo de la Libertad* (Dawn of Liberty), a Spanish-language paper established at Santa Fe in 1834. *The Santa Fe Republican,* established in 1847, was the first English-language newspaper.

In 1997 there were 17 daily newspapers (including 5 morning and 12 evening and 13 Sunday) in the state. The leading dailies include the *Albuquerque Journal,* with a morning circulation in 1997 of 116,134 (168,818 on Sundays); and the *Santa Fe New Mexican,* with a morning circulation of 23,979 (26,329 on Sundays).

46ORGANIZATIONS

The 1992 Census of Service Industries counted 509 organizations in New Mexico, including 106 business associations; 286 civic, social, and fraternal associations; and 117 other membership organizations. National organizations with headquarters in New Mexico include the National Association of Consumer Credit Administrators (Santa Fe); and the American Indian Law Students Association, the National Indian Youth Council, and Futures for Children, all located in Albuquerque.

47TOURISM, TRAVEL, AND RECREATION

The development of New Mexico's recreational resources has made tourism a leading economic activity. Hunting, fishing, camping, boating, and skiing are among the many outdoor attractions. In 1995 there were 348,451 hunting-license holders and 264,738 fishing-license holders.

The state has a national park—Carlsbad Caverns—and 13 national monuments: Aztec Ruins, Bandelier, Capulin Mountain, Chaco Canyon, El Morro (Inscription Rock), Fort Union, Gila Cliff Dwellings, Gran Quivira, Pecos, and White Sands. In 1984, the US House of Representatives designated 27,840 acres (11,266 hectares) of new wilderness preserves in New Mexico's San Juan basin, including a 2,720-acre (1,100-hectare) "fossil forest." Tourism is actively encouraged by the state. Outlay expenditures to attract visitors and maintain services were close to $19 million for 1995.

48SPORTS

New Mexico has no major league professional sports teams, though Albuquerque does have a minor league baseball team in the Class AAA Pacific Coast League. Thoroughbred and quarter-horse racing with pari-mutuel betting is an important spectator sport. Sunland Park, south of Las Cruces, has a winter-long schedule; from May to August there is racing and betting at Ruidoso Downs, La Mesa Park, and the Downs at Santa Fe.

The Lobos of the University of New Mexico compete in the Western Athletic Conference, while the Aggies of New Mexico State belong to the Big West Conference. New Mexico State finished third in the 1970 NCAA basketball tournament.

Other annual sporting events include the Great Overland Windsail Race in Lordsburg in June, the Rodeo de Santa Fe in July, and the International Balloon Fiesta in Albuquerque in October.

49FAMOUS NEW MEXICANS

Among the earliest Europeans to explore New Mexico were Francisco Vasquez de Coronado (b.Spain, 1510–54) and Juan de

Oñate (b.Mexico, 1549?–1624?), the founder of New Mexico. Diego de Vargas (b.Spain, 1643–1704) reconquered New Mexico for the Spanish after the Pueblo Revolt of 1680, which was led by Popé (d.1685?), a San Juan Pueblo medicine man. Later Indian leaders include Mangas Coloradas (1795?–1863) and Victorio (1809?–80), both of the Mimbreño Apache. Two prominent native New Mexicans during the brief period of Mexican rule were Manuel Armijo (1792?–1853), governor at the time of the American conquest, and the Taos priest José Antonio Martinez (1793–1867).

Army scout and trapper Christopher Houston "Kit" Carson (b.Kentucky, 1809–68) made his home in Taos, as did Charles Bent (b.Virginia, 1799–1847), one of the builders of Bent's Fort, a famous landmark on the Santa Fe Trail. A pioneer of a different kind was Jean Baptiste Lamy (b.France, 1814–88), the first Roman Catholic bishop in the Southwest; his life inspired Willa Cather's novel *Death Comes for the Archbishop*. Among the more notorious of the frontier figures in New Mexico was Billy the Kid (William H. Bonney, b.New York, 1859–81); his killer was New Mexico lawman Patrick Floyd "Pat" Garrett (b.Alabama, 1850–1908).

Notable US senators from New Mexico were Thomas Benton Catron (b.Missouri, 1840–1921), a Republican who dominated New Mexico politics during the territorial period; Albert Bacon Fall (b.Kentucky, 1861–1944), who later, as secretary of the interior, gained notoriety for his role in the Teapot Dome scandal; Dennis Chavez (1888–1962), the most prominent and influential native New Mexican to serve in Washington; Carl A. Hatch (b.Kansas, 1889–1963), best known for the Hatch Act of 1939, which limited partisan political activities by federal employees; and Clinton P. Anderson (b.South Dakota, 1895–1975) who was also secretary of agriculture.

New Mexico has attracted many artists and writers. Painters Bert G. Phillips (b.New York, 1868–1956) and Ernest Leonard Blumenschein (b.Ohio 1874–1960) started the famous Taos art colony in 1898. Mabel Dodge Luhan (b.New York, 1879–1962) did much to lure the creative community to Taos through her writings; the most famous person to take up residence there was English novelist D. H. Lawrence (1885–1930). Peter Hurd (1940–84) was a muralist, portraitist, and book illustrator. New Mexico's best-known artist is Georgia O'Keeffe (b.Wisconsin, 1887–1986). Maria Povera Martinez (1887?–1980) was known for her black-on-black pottery.

Other prominent persons who have made New Mexico their home include rocketry pioneer Robert H. Goddard (b.Massachusetts, 1882–1945), Pulitzer Prize-winning editorial cartoonist Bill Mauldin (b.1921), novelist and popular historian Paul Horgan (b.New York, 1903), novelist N. Scott Momaday (b.Oklahoma, 1934), and golfer Nancy Lopez-Melton (b.California, 1957). Al Unser Sr., four-time winner of the Indianapolis 500, was born in Albuquerque, New Mexico, 29 May 1939.

⁵⁰BIBLIOGRAPHY

Beck, W. A. *New Mexico: A History of Four Centuries*. Reprint. Norman: University of Oklahoma Press, 1979.

Enchanted Lifeways: The History, Museums, Arts & Festivals of New Mexico. Compiled by the New Mexico Office of Cultural Affairs. Santa Fe, N. Mexico.: New Mexico Magazine, 1995.

Federal Writers' Project. *New Mexico: A Guide to the Colorful State*. Reprint. New York: Hastings House, 1962.

New Mexico, University of. Bureau of Business and Economic Research. *New Mexico Statistical Abstract, 1984*. Albuquerque, 1984.

Reeve, Frank, and Alice Cleaveland. *New Mexico: Land of Many Cultures*. Rev. ed. Boulder, Colo.: Pruett, 1979.

Religion in Modern New Mexico. Edited by Richard W. Etulain and Ferenc M. Szasz. Albuquerque: University of New Mexico Press, 1997.

Samora, Julian, and Patricia Vandel Simon. *A History of the Mexican-American People*. Rev. ed. Notre Dame, Ind.: University of Notre Dame Press, 1993.

Simmons, Marc. *New Mexico: A Bicentennial History*. New York: Norton, 1977.

NEW YORK

State of New York

ORIGIN OF STATE NAME: Named for the Duke of York (later King James II) in 1664. **NICKNAME:** The Empire State. **CAPITAL:** Albany. **ENTERED UNION:** 26 July 1788 (11th). **SONG:** "I Love New York" (unofficial). **MOTTO:** *Excelsior* (Ever upward). **COAT OF ARMS:** Liberty and Justice stand on either side of a shield showing a mountain sunrise; surmounted on the shield is an eagle on a globe. In the foreground are a three-masted ship and a Hudson River sloop, both representing commerce. Liberty's left foot has kicked aside a royal crown. Beneath the shield is the state motto. **FLAG:** Dark blue with the coat of arms in the center. **OFFICIAL SEAL:** The coat of arms surrounded by the words "The Great Seal of the State of New York." **ANIMAL:** Beaver. **BIRD:** Bluebird. **FISH:** Brook or speckled trout. **FLOWER:** Rose. **TREE:** Sugar maple. **FRUIT:** Apple. **BEVERAGE:** Milk. **GEM:** Garnet. **FOSSIL:** Prehistoric crab (Eurypterus remipes). **LEGAL HOLIDAYS:** New Year's Day, 1 January; Birthday of Martin Luther King, Jr., 3d Monday in January; Lincoln's Birthday, 12 February; Washington's Birthday, 3d Monday in February; Memorial Day, last Monday in May; Flag Day, 2d Sunday in June; Independence Day, 4 July; Labor Day, 1st Monday in September; Columbus Day, 2d Monday in October; General Election Day, 1st Tuesday after the 1st Monday in November; Veterans Day, 11 November; Thanksgiving Day, 4th Thursday in November; Christmas Day, 25 December. **TIME:** 7 AM EST = noon GMT.

¹LOCATION, SIZE, AND EXTENT

Located in the northeastern US, New York State is the largest of the three Middle Atlantic states and ranks 30th in size among the 50 states.

The total area of New York is 49,108 sq mi (127,190 sq km), of which land takes up 47,377 sq mi (122,707 sq km) and the remaining 1,731 sq mi (4,483 sq km) consist of inland water. New York's width is about 320 mi (515 km) E-W, not including Long Island, which extends an additional 118 mi (190 km) SW-NE; the state's maximum N-S extension is about 310 mi (499 km). New York State is shaped roughly like a right triangle: the line from the extreme NE to the extreme SW forms the hypotenuse, with New York City as the right angle.

Mainland New York is bordered on the NW and N by the Canadian provinces of Ontario (with the boundary line passing through Lake Ontario and the St. Lawrence River) and Quebec; on the E by Vermont (with part of the line passing through Lake Champlain and the Poultney River), Massachusetts, and Connecticut; on the S by the Atlantic Ocean, New Jersey (part of the line passes through the Hudson River), and Pennsylvania (partly through the Delaware River); and on the W by Pennsylvania (with the line extending into Lake Erie) and Ontario (through Lake Erie and the Niagara River).

Two large islands lie off the state's SE corner. Long Island is bounded by Connecticut (through Long Island Sound) to the N, Rhode Island (through the Atlantic Ocean) to the NE, the Atlantic to the S, and the East River and the Narrows to the W. Staten Island (a borough of New York City) is separated from New Jersey by Newark Bay in the N, Raritan Bay in the S, and Arthur Kill channel in the W, and from Long Island by the Narrows to the E. Including these two islands, the total boundary length of New York State is 1,430 mi (2,301 km). Long Island, with an area of 1,396 sq mi (3,616 sq km), is the largest island belonging to one of the 48 coterminous states.

The state's geographic center is in Madison County, 12 mi (19 km) S of Oneida.

²TOPOGRAPHY

Two upland regions—the Adirondack Mountains and the Appalachian Highlands—dominate the topography of New York State.

The Adirondacks cover most of the northeast and occupy about one-fourth of the state's total area. The Appalachian Highlands, including the Catskill Mountains and Kittatinny Mountain Ridge (or Shawangunk Mountains), extend across the southern half of the state, from the Hudson River Valley to the basin of Lake Erie. Between these two upland regions, and also along the state's northern and eastern borders, lies a network of lowlands, including the Great Lakes Plain; the Hudson, Mohawk, Lake Champlain, and St. Lawrence valleys; and the coastal areas of New York City and Long Island.

The state's highest peaks are found in the Adirondacks: Mt. March, 5,344 feet (1,629 meters), and Algonquin Peak, 5,114 feet (1,559 meters). Nestled among the Adirondacks are many scenic lakes, including Lake Placid, Saranac Lake, and Lake George. The region is also the source of the Hudson and Ausable rivers. The Adirondack Forest Preserve covers much of this terrain, and both public and private lakes are mainly for recreational use.

The highest peak in the Catskills is Slide Mountain, at 4,204 feet (1,281 meters). Lesser upland regions of New York include the Hudson Highlands, projecting into the Hudson Valley; the Taconic Range, along the state's eastern border; and Tug Hill Plateau, set amid the lowlands just west of the Adirondacks.

Three lakes—Erie, Ontario, and Champlain—form part of the state's borders. The state has jurisdiction over 594 sq mi (1,538 sq km) of Lake Erie and 3,033 sq mi (7,855 sq km) of Lake Ontario. New York contains some 8,000 lakes; the largest lake wholly within the state is Oneida, about 22 mi (35 km) long, with a maximum width of 6 mi (10 km) and an area of 80 sq mi (207 sq km). Many smaller lakes are found in the Adirondacks and in the Finger Lakes region in west-central New York, renowned for its vineyards and great natural beauty. The 11 Finger Lakes themselves (including Owasco, Cayuga, Seneca, Keuka,

Canadaigua, and Skaneateles) are long and narrow, fanning southward from a line that runs roughly from Syracuse westward to Geneseo.

New York's longest river is the Hudson, extending from the Adirondacks to New York Bay for a distance of 306 mi (492 km). The Mohawk River flows into the Hudson north of Albany. The major rivers of central and western New York State—the Black, Genesee, and Oswego—all flow into Lake Ontario. Rivers defining the state's borders are the St. Lawrence in the north, the Poultney in the east, the Delaware in the southeast, and the Niagara in the west. Along the Niagara River, Niagara Falls forms New York's most spectacular natural feature. The falls, with an estimated mean flow rate of more than 1,585,000 gallons (60,000 hectoliters) per second, are both a leading tourist attraction and a major source of hydroelectric power.

About 2 billion years ago, New York State was entirely covered by a body of water that periodically rose and fell. The Adirondacks and Hudson River Palisades were produced by undersea volcanic action during this Grenville period. At about the same time, the schist and other crystalline rock that lie beneath Manhattan were formed. The Catskills were worn down by erosion from what was once a high, level plain. Glaciers from the last Ice Age carved out the inland lakes and valleys and determined the surface features of Staten Island and Long Island.

³CLIMATE

Although New York lies entirely within the humid continental zone, there is much variation from region to region. The three main climatic regions are the southeastern lowlands, which have the warmest temperatures and the longest season between frosts; the uplands of the Catskills and Adirondacks, where winters are cold and summer cool; and the snow belt along the Great Lakes Plain, one of the snowiest areas of the US. The growing (frost-free) season ranges from 100 to 120 days in the Adirondacks, Catskills, and higher elevations of the hills of southwestern New York to 180–200 days on Long Island.

Among the major population centers, New York City has an annual mean temperature of 55°F (13°C), with a normal maximum of 62°F (17°C) and a normal minimum of 47°F (8°C). Albany has an annual mean of 47°F (8°C), with a normal maximum of 58°F (14°C) and a normal minimum of 37°F (3°C). The mean in Buffalo is 48°F (9°C), the normal maximum 56°F (13°C), and the normal minimum 39°F (4°C). The record low temperature for the state is –52°F (–47°C), recorded at Stillwater Reservoir in the Adirondacks on 9 February 1934 and at Old Forge on 18 February 1979; the record high is 108°F (42°C), registered at Troy on 22 July 1926.

Annual precipitation ranges from over 50 in (127 cm) in the higher elevations to about 30 in (76 cm) in the areas near Lake Ontario and Lake Champlain, and in the lower half of the Genesee River Valley. New York City has an annual mean snowfall of 29 in (74 cm), while Albany gets 65 in (165 cm); in the snow belt, Buffalo receives 92 in (234 cm) of snow. Rochester 86 in (218 cm), and Syracuse 110 in (279 cm). Although New York City has fewer days of precipitation than other major populated areas (120 days annually, compared with 168 for Buffalo), more of New York City's precipitation comes in the form of rain: 41 in (104 cm), compared with 29 in (74 cm) for Albany and Buffalo. Buffalo is the windiest city in the state, with a mean hourly wind speed of about 12 mph (19 km/hr). Tornadoes are rare, but hurricanes and tropical storms sometimes cause heavy damage to Long Island.

⁴FLORA AND FAUNA

New York has some 150 species of trees. Post and willow oak, laurel magnolia, sweet gum, and hop trees dominate the Atlantic shore areas, while oak, hickory, and chestnut thrive in the Hudson and Mohawk valleys and the Great Lakes Plain. Birch, beech, basswood, white oak, and commercially valuable maple are found on the Appalachian Plateau and in the foothills of the Adirondack Mountains. The bulk of the Adirondacks and Catskills is covered with red and black spruce, balsam fir, and mountain ash, as well as white pine and maple. Spruce, balsam fir, paper birch, and mountain ash rise to the timberline, while only the hardiest plant species grow above it. Larch, mulberry, locust, and several kinds of willow are among the many varieties that have been introduced throughout the state. Apple trees and other fruit-bearing species are important in western New York and the Hudson Valley.

Common meadow flowers include several types of rose (the state flower), along with dandelion, Queen Anne's lace, goldenrod, and black-eyed Susan. Wild sarsaparilla, Solomon's seal, Indian pipe, bunchberry, and goldthread flourish amid the forests. Cattails grow in profusion along the Hudson, and rushes cover the Finger Lakes shallows. Among protected plants are all species of fern, bayberry, lotus, all native orchids, five species of rhododendron (including azalea), and trillium.

Some 600 species of mammals, birds, amphibians, and reptiles are found in New York, of which more than 450 species are common. Mammals in abundance include many mouse species, the snowshoe hare, common and New England cottontails, woodchuck, squirrel, muskrat, and raccoon. The deer population was estimated in 1983 at 500,000, making them a pest causing millions of dollars annually in crop damage. The wolverine, elk, and moose were all wiped out during the 19th century, and the otter, mink, marten, and fisher populations were drastically reduced; but the beaver, nearly eliminated by fur trappers, had come back strongly by 1940.

More than 260 bird species have been observed. The most common year-round residents are the crow, hawk, and several types of woodpecker. Summer visitors are many, and include the bluebird (the state bird). The wild turkey, which disappeared during the 19th century, was successfully reestablished in the 1970s. The house (or English) sparrow has been in New York since its introduction in the 1800s.

The common toad, newt, and several species of frog and salamander inhabit New York waters. Garter snakes, water snakes, grass snakes, and milk snakes are common; rattlesnakes formerly thrived in the Adirondacks. There are 210 known species of fish; 130 species are found in the Hudson, 120 in the Lake Ontario watershed. Freshwater fish include species of perch, bass, pike, and trout (the state fish). Oysters, clams, and several saltwater fish species are found in Long Island Sound. Of insect varieties, the praying mantis is looked upon as a friend (since it eats insects that prey on crops and trees), while the gypsy moth has been singled out as an enemy in periodic state-run pest-control programs.

In 1992, the following species were classified as endangered: the Indiana bat, gray wolf, Eskimo curlew, northern and southern bald eagles, American and Arctic peregrine falcons, and shortnose sturgeon. The northeastern beach tiger beetle is threatened.

There were nine national wildlife refuges in 1991, covering a total of 26,420 acres (10,692 hectares).

⁵ENVIRONMENTAL PROTECTION

New York was one of the first states to mount a major conservation effort. In the 1970s, well over $1 billion was spent to reclaim the state from the ravages of pollution. State conservation efforts date back at least to 1885, when a forest preserve was legally established in the Adirondacks and Catskills. Adirondack Park was created in 1892, Catskill Park in 1904. Then, as now, the issue was how much if any state forestland would be put to commercial use. Timber cutting in the forest preserve was

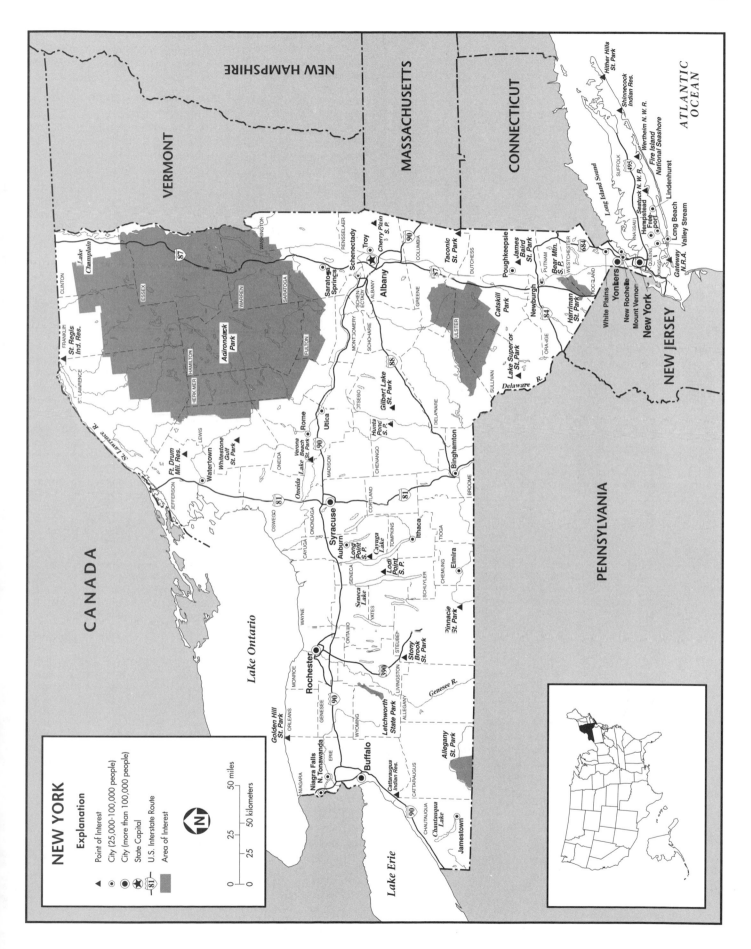

NEW YORK

Explanation

▲ Point of Interest

⊙ City (25,000-100,000 people)

◉ City (more than 100,000 people)

★ State Capital

[81] U.S. Interstate Route

▨ Area of Interest

0 25 50 miles

0 25 50 kilometers

CANADA

Lake Ontario

Lake Erie

ATLANTIC OCEAN

Long Island Sound

NEW HAMPSHIRE

VERMONT

MASSACHUSETTS

CONNECTICUT

NEW JERSEY

PENNSYLVANIA

St. Lawrence R.

Lake Champlain

Adirondack Park

Catskill Park

St. Regis Ind. Res.

Ft. Drum Mil. Res.

Cattaraugus Indian Res.

Golden Hill St. Park

Whitestone Gulf St. Park

Verona Beach St. Park

Gilbert Lake St. Park

Hunts Pond S. P.

Lake Superior St. Park

Long Point S.P.

Lodi Point S. P.

Stony Brook St. Park

Pinnacle St. Park

Letchworth State Park

Allegany St. Park

Cherry Plain St. P.

Taconic St. Park

James Baird St. Park

Bear Mtn. S. P.

Harriman St. Park

Seneca Lake

Cayuga Lake

Oneida Lake

Chautauqua Lake

Delaware R.

Genesee R.

Niagra Falls

N. Tonawanda

Buffalo

Rochester

Watertown

Syracuse

Auburn

Ithaca

Elmira

Binghamton

Rome

Utica

Saratoga Springs

Schenectady

Troy

Albany

Poughkeepsie

Newburgh

White Plains

New Rochelle

Mount Vernon

Yonkers

New York

Long Beach

Valley Stream

Gateway N.R.A.

Lindenhurst

Fire Island National Seashore

Wertheim N. W. R.

Seatuck N. W. R.

Shinnecock Indian Res.

Hither Hills St. Park

Hempstead

Freeport

Jamestown

CLINTON

FRANKLIN

ST. LAWRENCE

JEFFERSON

LEWIS

ESSEX

WARREN

HAMILTON

HERKIMER

FULTON

SARATOGA

WASHINGTON

ONEIDA

MADISON

MONTGOMERY

SCHENECTADY

SCHOHARIE

RENSSELAER

COLUMBIA

GREENE

ALBANY

DUTCHESS

ULSTER

ORANGE

SULLIVAN

PUTNAM

ROCKLAND

WESTCHESTER

DELAWARE

OTSEGO

CHENANGO

BROOME

CORTLAND

TOMPKINS

TIOGA

CHEMUNG

SCHUYLER

STEUBEN

YATES

SENECA

CAYUGA

ONONDAGA

OSWEGO

WAYNE

ONTARIO

LIVINGSTON

ALLEGANY

CATTARAUGUS

CHAUTAUQUA

ERIE

NIAGARA

ORLEANS

GENESEE

WYOMING

MONROE

WASHINGTON

SUFFOLK

NASSAU

QUEENS

[87] [90] [87] [84] [88] [81] [90] [390] [90] [684]

legalized in 1893, but the constitution of 1895 forbade the practice. By the late 1930s, the state had spent more than $16 million on land purchases and controlled 2,159,795 acres (874,041 hectares) in the Adirondacks and some 230,000 acres (more than 93,000 hectares) in the Catskills. The constitutional revision of 1894 expressly outlawed the sale, removal, or destruction of timber on forestlands. That requirement was modified by constitutional amendment in 1957 and 1973, however, and the state is now permitted to sell forest products from the preserves in limited amounts.

All state environmental programs are run by the Department of Environmental Conservation (DEC), established in 1970. The department oversees pollution control programs, monitors environmental quality, manages the forest preserves, and administers fish and wildlife laws (including the issuance of hunting and fishing licenses). The state's national parks totaled 35,914 acres (14,534 hectares). State parks and recreational areas totaled 258,000 acres (104,000 hectares). Wetlands covered 2.4 million acres of the state as of 1996. About one-half of the 160 species identified as endangered or threatened by the Department of Environmental Conservation are wetland-dependent.

Because of budget cuts by New York City, the state took over the operation of the city's air-monitoring network in 1978. The chief problem areas are Buffalo, where levels of particles (especially from the use of coke in steelmaking) are high, and New York City, where little progress has been made in cutting carbon monoxide emissions from motor vehicles.

Despite air-quality efforts, acid rain has been blamed for killing fish and trees in the Adirondacks, Catskills, and other areas. In 1984, the legislature passed the first measure in the nation designed to reduce acid rain, calling for a cut of 12% in sulfur dioxide emissions by 1988 and further reductions after that.

Before the 1960s, the condition of New York's waters was a national scandal. Raw sewage, arsenic, cyanide, and heavy metals were regularly dumped into the state's lakes and rivers, and fish were rapidly dying off. Two Pure Waters Bond Acts during the 1960s, the Environmental Quality Bond Act of 1972, and a state fishery program have helped reverse the damage. The state has also taken action against corporate polluters, including a $7-million settlement with General Electric over that company's discharge of toxic polychlorinated biphenyls (PCBs) into the Hudson. In addition, the state and federal government spent perhaps $45 million between 1978 and 1982 on the cleanup of the Love Canal area of Niagara Falls, which was contaminated by the improper disposal of toxic wastes, and on the relocation of some 400 families that had lived there. Remaining problems include continued dumping of sewage and industrial wastes into New York Bay and Long Island Sound, sewage overflows into the Lower Hudson, industrial dumping in the Hudson Valley, nuclear wastes in West Valley in Cattaraugus County, and contamination of fish in Lake Erie. Toxic pollutants, such as organic chemicals and heavy metals, appear in surface and ground water to an extent not yet fully assessed.

By 1995 the state had 80 hazardous waste sites. New York ranks 4th in the number of hazardous waste sites in the country. A 1982 law requires a deposit on beer and soft-drink containers sold in the state, to encourage return and recycling of bottles and cans.

[6]POPULATION

New York is no longer the most populous state, having lost that position to California in the 1970 census. However, New York City remains the most populous US city, as it has been at least since 1790. The 1990 census figures showed a population in New York State of 17,990,455, a rise of 2.5% since the 1980 census. The state's estimated population in 1996 was 18,184,774, up 1.1% from 1990.

In 1990, New York's population was 52.3% female and 47.7% male; 84% lived in urban areas. In 1990, 91.1% lived in metropolitan areas (7th highest in the nation). In 1990, the state's population density was 381 per sq mi (146 per sq km).

New York Counties, County Seats, and County Areas and Populations

COUNTY	COUNTY SEAT	LAND AREA (SQ MI)	POPULATION (1996 EST.)
Albany	Albany	584	296,087
Allegany	Belmont	1,032	51,282
Bronx	Bronx	42	1,193,775
Broome	Binghamton	712	201,533
Cattaraugus	Little Valley	1,306	85,680
Cayuga	Auburn	695	82,062
Chautauqua	Mayville	1,064	140,800
Chemung	Elmira	411	93,282
Chenango	Norwich	897	52,121
Clinton	Plattsburgh	1,043	80,537
Columbia	Hudson	628	63,613
Cortland	Cortland	500	48,573
Delaware	Delhi	1,440	47,287
Dutchess	Poughkeepsie	804	262,675
Erie	Buffalo	1,046	954,021
Essex	Elizabethtown	1,806	37,789
Franklin	Malone	1,648	49,335
Fulton	Johnstown	497	53,965
Genesee	Batavia	495	61,206
Greene	Catskill	648	47,291
Hamilton	Lake Pleasant	1,721	5,232
Herkimer	Herkimer	1,416	65,968
Jefferson	Watertown	1,273	113,844
Kings	Brooklyn	70	2,273,966
Lewis	Lowville	1,283	27,799
Livingston	Geneseo	633	65,898
Madison	Wampsville	656	71,508
Monroe	Rochester	663	721,996
Montgomery	Fonda	404	51,894
Nassau	Mineola	287	1,303,389
New York	New York	22	1,533,774
Niagara	Lockport	526	221,219
Oneida	Utica	1,819	236,437
Onondaga	Syracuse	785	466,675
Ontario	Canandaigua	644	99,634
Orange	Goshen	826	324,422
Orleans	Albion	391	44,979
Oswego	Oswego	954	125,446
Otsego	Cooperstown	1,004	61,470
Putnam	Carmel	231	90,983
Queens	Queens	109	1,980,643
Rensselaer	Troy	655	155,098
Richmond	Staten Island	59	398,748
Rockland	New City	175	278,136
St. Lawrence	Canton	2,728	114,759
Saratoga	Ballston Spa	810	194,837
Schenectady	Schenectady	206	147,599
Schoharie	Schoharie	624	33,012
Schuyler	Watkins Glen	329	19,108
Seneca	Waterloo	327	32,530
Steuben	Bath	1,396	99,201
Suffolk	Riverhead	911	1,356,896
Sullivan	Monticello	976	70,346
Tioga	Owego	519	52,520
Tompkins	Ithaca	477	96,152
Ulster	Kingston	1,131	167,082
Warren	Town of Queensbury*	882	61,490
Washington	Hudson Falls**	836	60,777
Wayne	Lyons	605	94,324
Westchester	White Plains	438	893,412
Wyoming	Warsaw	595	44,357
Yates	Penn Yan	339	24,300
TOTALS		47,377	18,184,774

* Mail Lake George.
** Mail Fort Edward.

First in the state as well as the nation in population was New York City, with 7,323,000 residents in 1990 and an estimated population of 7,333,253 in 1994. As of 1990, Brooklyn had a population of 2,301,000; Queens, 1,952,000; Manhattan, 1,488,000; the Bronx, 1,204,000; and Staten Island, 379,000. Other leading cities, with their estimated 1994 populations were Buffalo, 312,965; Rochester, 231,170; Yonkers, 183,490; and Syracuse, 159,895. Albany, the state capital, had a population of 104,828. All these cities have lost population since the 1970s.

With 18,087,000 people, the tri-state New York City metropolitan area remained the nation's largest in 1990; Buffalo, the 33d largest, had an estimated 1,189,000 people; Rochester, the 39th largest, had an estimated 1,002,000.

The growth of New York City has been remarkable. In 1790, when the first national census was taken, the city had 49,401 residents. By 1850, its population had boomed to 696,115; by 1900, to 3,437,202, double that of Chicago, the city's closest rival. Manhattan alone housed more people in 1900 than any city outside New York. The data for 1990 are equally impressive. If Brooklyn, Queens, Manhattan, and the Bronx had each been a separate city, they would still have ranked 3d, 4th, 6th, and 7th in the nation, respectively.

7ETHNIC GROUPS

During the 19th and 20th centuries, New York has been the principal gateway for European immigrants. In the great northern migration that began after World War I, large numbers of blacks also settled there; more recently there has been an influx of Hispanic Americans and, to a lesser extent, of Asians. Today, New York has the largest black and Puerto Rican population of all the states, and the 2d-largest Asian community and number of foreign-born.

According to the US Bureau of the Census, New York had 63,000 Indians in 1990, the 9th highest Indian population in the nation. In 1996, the total number of Native Americans, including Eskimos and Aleuts, was estimated at 73,000. In the same year, there were an estimated 16,014 Indians living on or adjacent to the reservations of the following seven tribes: the Cayuga, Oneida, Onondaga, Seneca, and Tuscarora nations, the St. Regis Mohawk Tribe, and the Tonawanda Band of Senecas.

Blacks have been in New York since 1624. All black slaves were freed by a state law in 1827. Rochester was a major center of the antislavery movement; Frederick Douglass, a former slave, settled and published his newspaper *North Star* there, while helping to run the Underground Railroad. After World War I, blacks moving into New York City displaced the Jews, Italians, Germans, and Irish then living in Harlem, which went on to become the cultural capital of black America. The black population of New York State was 2,859,000 as of 1990—15.9% of the state's population, and 1st among the states in the number of blacks. In 1996, New York's black population totaled an estimated 3,082,000 (16.8%). In 1990 almost three of every four blacks lived in New York City; with 2,101,000, New York had more black people than any other US city.

The Hispanic population as of 1990 was 2,214,000, of whom 1,786,000 (81%) were in New York City. Puerto Ricans numbered 762,429 (34% of Hispanics in the state). Cubans, Dominicans, Colombians, Central Americans, and Mexicans are also present in growing numbers, including a large but undetermined number of illegal immigrants. By 1996 the Hispanic population totaled an estimated 2,541,000.

The Asian and Pacific Islander population was 694,000 in 1990, 2d only to California. Among state residents were 236,876 Chinese, 80,430 Asian Indians, 93,145 Koreans, 64,202 Filipinos, 39,859 Japanese, and 12,116 Vietnamese. Three-quarters of all of the Asians in the state lived in New York City, which has the 2d-largest Chinatown in the US. Estimates placed the Asian/Pacific Islander population at 893,000 by 1996, a 29% increase over 1990.

In 1990 there were 2,851,861 foreign-born New Yorkers, 15.8% of the population and more than any state except California. By 1996, the estimated total was 3,232,000 (17.6%). The leading countries of birth, with both 1990 and (where available) 1996 estimated totals, were the Dominican Republic, 241,941 (337,000); Italy, 190,305; Jamaica, 146,829 (197,000); China, 128,133 (198,000); the former Soviet Union, 98,576; and Germany, 92,322. Among persons who reported at least one specific ancestry group, 2,898,888 named German; 2,837,904 Italian; 2,800,128 Irish; 1,566,019 English; 1,181,077 Polish; and 596,875 Russian. These figures do not distinguish the large numbers of European Jewish immigrants who would identify themselves as Jews rather than by their country of origin.

The ethnic diversity of the state is reflected in such Manhattan neighborhoods as Harlem, Chinatown, Little Italy, and "Spanish," or East, Harlem, with its large Puerto Rican concentration. Many of the more successful ethnics have moved to the suburbs; on the other hand, new immigrants still tend to form ethnic communities, often in the outer boroughs, such as Asians and South Americans in certain parts of Queens and Russian Jews in south Brooklyn. Outside New York City there are also important ethnic enclaves in the Buffalo metropolitan area, with its large populations of Polish and Italian origin.

8LANGUAGES

Just as New York for three centuries has channeled immigrant speakers of other languages into the English-speaking population, so it has helped to channel some of their words into English, with much more rapid dissemination because of the concentration of publishing and communications industries in New York City.

Little word-borrowing followed contacts by European settlers with the unfriendly Iroquois, who between the 14th and 17th centuries had dispersed the several Algonkian tribes of Montauk, Delaware, and Mahican Indians. In New York State, the effect on English has been almost entirely the adoption of such place-names as Manhattan, Adirondack, Chautauqua, and Skaneateles.

Although the speech of metropolitan New York has its own characteristics, in the state as a whole the Northern dialect predominates. New York State residents generally say /hahg/ and /fahg/ for *hog* and *fog*, /krik/ for *creek*, *greasy* with an /s/ sound, and *half* and *path* with the vowel of *cat*. They keep the /r/ after a vowel, as in *far* and *cord*; sharply differentiate *horse* and *hoarse* by pronouncing the former with the vowel of *haw* and the latter with the vowel of *hoe*; and call a clump of hard maples a *sugarbush*.

There are many regional variations. In the Hudson Valley, *horse* and *hoarse* tend to be pronounced alike, and a sugarbush is called a *sap bush*. In the eastern sector, New England *piazza* for porch and *buttonball* for sycamore are found, as is the Hudson Valley term *nightwalker* for a large earthworm. In the Niagara peninsula, Midland *eavespout* (gutter) and *bawl* (how a calf sounds) have successfully moved north from Pennsylvania to invade Northern speech. In the North Country, some Canadian influence survives in *stook* (shock), *boodan* (liver sausage), and *shivaree* (wedding celebration). In the New York City area, many speakers pronounce *bird* almost as if it were /boyd/, do not sound the /h/ in *whip* or the /r/ after a vowel—although the trend now is toward the /r/ pronunciation—may pronounce initial /th/ almost like /t/ or /d/, stand *on line* (instead of in a line) while waiting to buy a huge sandwich they call a *hero* and may even pronounce *Long Island* with an inserted /g/ as /long giland/. From the high proportion of New York Yiddish speakers (nearly 40% of all those in the US in 1990) have come such terms as *schlock*, *schmaltz,* and *chutzpah.*

Serious communication problems have arisen in New York City, especially in the schools, because of the major influx since World War II of Spanish speakers from the Caribbean region, speakers of so-called black English from the South, and, more recently, Asians, in addition to the ever-present large numbers of speakers of other languages. As a result, schools in some areas have emphasized teaching English as a second language.

According to the 1990 census, 76.7% of all New Yorkers 5 years of age or older spoke only English at home, well below the national average of 86.2%. The following table shows other major languages spoken at home by New York State residents:

Spanish	1,848,825	Korean	80,394
Italian	400,218	Russian	78,310
Chinese	247,334	Tagalog	46,276
French	236,099	Arabic	44,060
German	128,525	Other Slavic	34,931
Polish	120,923	Portuguese	33,089
Yiddish	117,323	South Slavic	26,377
Greek	87,608	Hungarian	23,394

[9]RELIGIONS

Before the 1800s, Protestant sects dominated the religious life of New York, although religion did not play as large a role in the public life of New Netherland as it did in New England, with its Puritan population. The first Jews were permitted by the Dutch to settle in New Amsterdam in 1654, but their numbers remained small for the next 200 years. Both the Dutch and later the English forbade the practice of Roman Catholicism. Full religious freedom was not permitted until the constitution of 1777, and there was no Roman Catholic church in upstate New York until 1797. During the early 19th century, Presbyterian, Methodist, Universalist, Baptist, and Quaker pioneers carried their faith westward across the state. Many Protestant churches took part enthusiastically in the abolitionist movement, and the blacks who fled northward out of slavery formed their own Protestant churches and church organizations.

For Roman Catholics and Jews, the history of the 19th century is the story of successive waves of immigration: Roman Catholics first from Ireland and Germany, later from Italy and Poland, Jews first from Germany, Austria, and England, later (in vast numbers) from Russia and other Eastern European nations. The Jews who settled in New York City tended to remain there, the Roman Catholic immigrants were more dispersed throughout the state, with a large German and Eastern European group settling in Buffalo. Irish Catholics were the first group to win great political influence, but since World War II, Jews and Italian Catholics have played a leading role, especially in New York City.

As of 1990 New York had 7,280,488 Roman Catholic church members. The Jewish population of New York State was estimated at 1,843,240 in 1990.

Membership of leading Protestant denominations in 1990 included United Methodist, 466,586; Episcopal, 231,690; United Presbyterian, 199,519; Evangelical Lutheran Church in America, 187,551; Lutheran Church-Missouri Synod, 90,837; Reformed Church in America, 79,865; and United Church of Christ 73,353.

Because of diversified immigration, New York City has small percentages but significant numbers of Buddhists, Muslims, Hindus, and Orthodox Christians. There is also a wide variety of religious-nationalist sects and cults, including the World Community of Islam in the West, also called the Nation of Islam (Black Muslims), the Hare Krishna group, and the Unification Church of the Reverend Sun Myung Moon.

[10]TRANSPORTATION

New York City is a major transit point for both domestic and international passenger and freight traffic. The Port of New York and New Jersey is the nation's 2d-busiest harbor; in 1994, more than 18.7 million passengers enplaned at New York City's two major airports, Kennedy International and La Guardia, both in Queens. New York City is connected with the rest of the state by an extensive network of good roads, although road and rail transport within the metropolitan region is sagging with age.

The first railroad in New York State was the Mohawk and Hudson, which made its initial trip from Albany to Schenectady on 9 August 1831. A series of short intercity rail lines, built during the 1830s and 1840s, were united into the New York Central in 1853. Cornelius Vanderbilt gained control of the New York Central in 1867, and by 1873 had connected New York with Chicago. Under Vanderbilt and his son William, rail links were also forged between New York and Boston, Buffalo, Montreal, and western Pennsylvania.

The height of the railroads' power and commercial importance came during the last decades of the 19th century. After World War I, road vehicles gradually replaced the railroads as freight carriers. In 1995, New York ranked 14th in total rail mileage, with 3,826 mi (6,160 km). In 1996, there were 6 Class I lines, 3 regional, 25 local, 4 switching and terminal railroads, and 6 tourist operations.

The decline in freight business, and the railroads' inability to make up the loss of passenger traffic, led to a series of reorganizations and failures: the best known is the merger of the New York Central with the Pennsylvania Railroad, and the subsequent bankruptcy of the Penn Central. Today, much of New York's rail network is operated by Conrail, a federally assisted private corporation that among its operations provides commuter service up the Hudson and to New Jersey and Connecticut. In 1997 CSX Transportation and Norfolk & Southern Railroad were in the process of acquiring Conrail. The National Railroad Passenger Corporation (Amtrak) owns and operates lines along the eastern corridor from Boston through New York City to Washington, D.C. In 1995/96, it regularly operated 110 daily trains through New York State, stopping at 25 stations; ridership was 7,590,708. New York City's Penn Station is the busiest station in the entire Amtrak system. The Long Island Railroad, an important commuter carrier, is run by the Metropolitan Transportation Authority (MTA), which also operates the New York City subways; ridership in 1995 was 97.7 million. Ridership on the Metro North Commuter Railroad was 62.6 million in 1995. Construction of the New York City subway system began in 1900; service started on 27 October 1904. The route network is about 230 mi (370 km) long, of which 137 mi (220 km) are underground; ridership on New York City's subways in 1995 was 1.8 billion.

The only other mass-transit rail line in the state is Buffalo's 6.4 mi (10.3 km) light rail system, of which 5.2 mi (8.4 km) is underground; total ridership in 1995 was 29 million. In 1984, regular trolley service resumed in Buffalo for the first time since 1950 on the other 1.2 mi (1.9 km) of track, running through the downtown shipping district. Among cities served by municipal, county, or metropolitan-area bus systems are Albany, Binghamton, Buffalo, Elmira, and Syracuse.

In 1996, 9,235,437 motor vehicles were registered in New York State, including 7,093,452 automobiles, 32,895 buses, and 929,164 trucks. In addition 162,933 motorcycles were registered. As of 1995, the state had 112,060 mi (180,304 km) of roads and highways, of which 14.7% were state roads, 18.2% were county roads, 50.9% were town roads, and 16.1% were city and municipal streets. Of the total mileage, 1,396 mi (2,246 km) consisted of interstate highway. Two-thirds of the mileage was rural. That same year, local, state, and federal authorities spent over $2.8 billion on highway maintenance. The major toll road, and the nation's longest toll superhighway, is the Thomas E. Dewey Thruway, operated by the New York State Thruway Authority, which extends 559 mi (900 km) from just outside New

York City to Buffalo and the Pennsylvania border in southwestern New York, and received over $316.6 million from motorists in 1995. Altogether, state-administered toll road and crossing facilities received over $865.8 million from motorists, more than any other state. Toll-free expressways include the Adirondack Northway (I-87), from Albany to the Canadian border, and the North–South Expressway (I-81), from the Canadian to the Pennsylvania border. Total expenditures on highways from state government in 1995 came to over $4.7 billion, with maintenance accounting for 17% of that amount. Although New York was third after California and Texas in the total number of traffic injuries (288,667), it ranked first in the number of nonfatal pedestrian injuries (20,680) in 1995.

A number of famous bridges and tunnels connect the five boroughs of New York City with each other and with New Jersey. The Verrazano–Narrows Bridge, opened to traffic in 1964, spans New York Harbor between Brooklyn and Staten Island. Equally famous, and especially renowned for their beauty, are the Brooklyn Bridge (1883), the city's first suspension bridge, and the George Washington Bridge (1931). The Holland (1927) and Lincoln (1937–57) tunnels under the Hudson River link Manhattan with New Jersey, and provided 57% of the state's receipts from state-administered toll road and crossing facilities in 1995. Important links among the five boroughs include the Triborough Bridge, Manhattan Bridge, Williamsburg Bridge, Queensboro Bridge, Bronx-Whitestone Bridge, Throgs Neck Bridge, Brooklyn-Battery Tunnel, and Queens-Midtown Tunnel. The Staten Island Ferry conveys passengers and autos between the borough and lower Manhattan.

Until the early 1800s, almost all the state's trade moved on the Atlantic Ocean, Hudson River, and New York Bay. This waterway transportation system was expanded starting in the 1820s. Off the Hudson, one of the country's major arteries, branched the main elements of the New York Barge Canal System: the Erie Canal, linking the Atlantic with Lake Erie, and New York City with Buffalo; the Oswego Canal, connecting the Erie Canal with Lake Ontario; the Cayuga and Seneca Canal, connecting the Erie Canal with Cayuga and Seneca lakes; and the Champlain Canal, extending the state's navigable waterways from the Hudson to Lake Champlain, and so to Vermont and Quebec Province. By 1872, New York's canal system was carrying over 6 million tons of cargo a year; but an absolute decline in freight tonnage began after 1890 (the relative decline had begun 10 years earlier, with the rise of the railroads). By the mid-1980s, the canals carried less than 10% of the tonnage for 1880.

Buffalo, on Lake Erie, is the most important inland port. In 1995, it handled 1,872,534 tons of cargo. The 53% drop in traffic from 1983 to 1991, as well as the 70% decline in freight totals from 1972 to 1982 is testimony to Buffalo's decline as an industrial center. Albany, the major port on the Hudson, handled 5,802,920 tons of cargo, and Port Jefferson, on Long Island Sound, handled 2,018,078 tons in 1995.

It would be hard to exaggerate the historic and economic importance of New York Harbor—haven for explorers, point of entry for millions of refugees and immigrants, and the nation's greatest seaport until recent years, when it was passed by Greater New Orleans and Houston in terms of cargo tonnage. Harbor facilities, including those of Bayonne, Jersey City, and Newark, N.J., add up to 755 mi (1,215 km) of frontage, with some 700 piers and wharves. The entire port is under the jurisdiction of the Port Authority of New York and New Jersey. In 1995, it handled 119,341,574 tons of cargo, valued at over $59.6 billion. The port ranked 1st nationally in the value of exports handled, at over $19.5 billion, and 3d overall in the value of imports handled, at over $40.1 billion. In 1995, the port had 3,125 ship arrivals, and

was served by 1,000 trucking companies, 80 steamship lines, and 12 intermodal rail terminals.

At the beginning of 1996, New York State had 437 airfields, including 327 airports, 91 heliports, and 19 seaplane bases. By far the busiest airports in the state are John F. Kennedy International and La Guardia, both in New York City. In 1995, Kennedy handled 15,189,894 enplaned passengers, 165,084 aircraft departures, and 814,634 tons of freight, while La Guardia handled 10,299,701 enplaned passengers, 163,756 departures, and 15,242 tons of freight. The Greater Buffalo International Airport, the largest in the state outside New York City, handled 1,470,928 passengers and 24,629 departures in 1995, and 5,938 tons of freight.

[11]HISTORY

The region now known as New York State has been inhabited for about 10,000 years. The first Indians probably came across the Bering Strait and most likely reached New York via the Niagara Peninsula. Remains have been found in southwestern New York of the Indians called Mound Builders (for their practice of burying their dead in large mounds), who cultivated food crops and tobacco. The Mound Builders were still living in the state well after AD 1000, although by that time most of New York was controlled by later migrants of the Algonkian linguistic group. These Algonkian tribes included the Mahican in the northeast, the Wappinger in the Hudson Valley and on Long Island, and the Leni-Lenape (or Delaware) of the Delaware Valley.

Indians of the Iroquoian language group invaded the state from the north and west during the early 14th century. In 1570, after European explorers had discovered New York but before the establishment of any permanent European settlements, the main Iroquois tribes—the Onondaga, Oneida, Seneca, Cayuga, and Mohawk—established the League of the Five Nations. For the next 200 years, members of the League generally kept peace among themselves but made war on other tribes, using not only traditional weapons but also the guns they were able to get from the French, Dutch, and English. In 1715, a sixth nation joined the League—the Tuscarora, who had fled the British in North Carolina. For much of the 18th century, the Iroquois played a skillful role in balancing competing French and British interests.

The first European known to have entered New York Harbor was the Florentine navigator Giovanni da Verrazano, on 17 April 1524. The Frenchman Samuel de Champlain began exploring the St. Lawrence River in 1603. While Champlain was aiding the Huron Indians in their fight against the League in 1609, the English mariner Henry Hudson, in the service of the Dutch East India Company, entered New York Bay and sailed up the river that would later bear his name, reaching about as far as Albany. To the Dutch the area did not look especially promising, and there was no permanent Dutch settlement until 1624, three years after the Dutch West India Company had been founded. The area near Albany was first to be settled. The Dutch were mainly interested in fur trading, and agriculture in the colony—named New Netherland—was slow to develop. New Amsterdam was founded in 1626, when Director-General Peter Minuit bought Manhattan (from the Indian word *manahatin*, "hill island") from the Indians for goods worth—as tradition has it—about $24.

New Amsterdam grew slowly, and by 1650 had no more than 1,000 people. When the British took over New Netherland in 1664, only 8,000 residents lived in the colony. Already, however, the population was remarkably diverse: there were the Dutch and English, of course, but also French, Germans, Finns, Swedes, and Jews, as well as black slaves from Angola. The Swedes lived in what had been New Sweden, a territory along the Delaware River ceded to the Netherlands during the administration of Peter Stuyvesant. Equally famed for his wooden leg and his hot temper, Stuyvesant had become director general of the New Netherland colony in 1647. Three years later, after skirmishes with the English settlers of New England, the colony gave up all claims to the Connecticut Valley in the Treaty of Hartford.

Though small and weak, New Netherland was an annoyance to the English. The presence of Dutch traders in New York Bay made it difficult for England to enforce its monopolies under the Navigation Acts. Moreover, the Dutch colony was a political barrier between New England and two other English colonies, Maryland and Virginia. So, in 1664, King Charles II awarded "all the land from the west side of the Connecticutte River to the East Side of De La Ware Bay" to his brother, the Duke of York and Albany, the future King James II. The British fleet arrived in New York Bay on 18 August 1664. Stuyvesant wanted to fight, but his subjects refused, and the governor had no choice but to surrender. The English agreed to preserve the Dutch rights of property and inheritance, and to guarantee complete liberty of conscience. Thus New Netherland became New York. It remained an English colony for the next 112 years, except for a period in 1673 when Dutch rule was briefly restored.

The first decades under the English were stormy. After repeated demands from the colonists, a general assembly was called in 1683. The assembly adopted a Charter of Liberties and Privileges, but the document, approved by James before his coronation, was revoked after he became king in 1685. The assembly itself was dissolved in 1686, and James II acted to place New York under the dominion of New England. The plan was aborted by the Glorious Revolution of 1688, when James was forced to abdicate. Power in New York fell to Jacob Leisler, a German merchant with local backing. Leisler ruled until 1691, when a new royal governor arrived and had Leisler hanged for treason.

The succeeding decades were marked by conflict between the English and French and by the rising power of the provincial assembly in relations with the British crown. As early as 1690, a band of 150 Frenchmen and 100 Indians attacked and burned Schenectady. New York contributed men and money to campaign against the French in Canada in 1709 and 1711 (during Queen Anne's War) and in 1746 (during King George's War). In 1756, the English determined to drive the French out of the region once and for all. After some early reverses, the English defeated the French in 1760. The Treaty of Paris (1763), ending the French and Indian War, ceded all territory east of the Mississippi to England, except for New Orleans and two islands in the mouth of the St. Lawrence River. The Iroquois, their power weakened during the course of the war, signed treaties giving large areas of their land to the New York colony.

The signing of the Treaty of Paris was followed by English attempts to tighten control over the colonies, in New York as elsewhere. New York merchants vehemently protested the Sugar Act and Stamp Act, and the radical Sons of Liberty made their first appearance in the colony in October 1765. Later, in 1774, after Paul Revere brought news of the Boston Tea Party to New York City, British tea was also dumped into that city's harbor. Nevertheless, New York hesitated before committing itself to independence. The colony's delegates to the Continental Congress in Philadelphia were not permitted by the Third Provincial Congress in New York to vote either for or against the Declaration of Independence on 4 July 1776. The Fourth Provincial Congress, meeting at White Plains, did ratify the Declaration five days later. On 6 February 1778, New York became the second state to ratify the Articles of Confederation.

Nearly one-third of all battles during the Revolutionary War took place on New York soil. The action there began when troops under Ethan Allen captured Fort Ticonderoga in May 1775, and Seth Warner and his New England forces took Crown Point. Reverses came in 1776, however, when George Washington's forces were driven from Long Island and

Manhattan by the British; New York City was to remain in British hands for the rest of the war. Troops commanded by British General John Burgoyne recaptured Ticonderoga in July 1777, but were defeated in October at Saratoga, in a battle that is often considered the turning point of the war. In 1778, General Washington made his headquarters at West Point, which General Benedict Arnold tried unsuccessfully to betray to the British in 1780. Washington moved his forces to Newburgh in 1782, and marched into New York City on 25 November 1785, the day the British evacuated their forces. On 4 December, he said farewell to his officers at Fraunces Tavern in lower Manhattan, a landmark that still stands.

Even as war raged, New York State adopted its first constitution on 20 April 1777. The constitution provided for an elected governor and house of assembly, but the franchise was limited to property holders. The first state capital was Kingston, but the capital was moved to Albany in January 1797. After much debate, in which the Federalist Alexander Hamilton played a leading role, the state ratified the US Constitution (with amendments) on 26 July 1788. New York City served as the seat of the US government from 11 January 1785 to 12 August 1790, and the first US president, George Washington, was inaugurated in the city on 30 April 1789.

George Clinton was the state's first elected governor, serving from 1777 to 1795 and again from 1801 to 1804. The achievements under his governorship were considerable. Commerce and agriculture expanded, partly because of Clinton's protectionist policies and partly because of the state's extremely favorable geographical situation.

The end of the War of 1812 signaled the opening of an era of unprecedented economic expansion for the state. By this time, the Iroquois were no longer a threat (most had sided with the British during the Revolutionary War, and many later fled to Canada). Migrants from New England were flocking to the state, which the census of 1810 showed was the most populous in the country. Small wonder that New York was the site of the early 19th century's most ambitious engineering project: construction of the Erie Canal. Ground was broken for the canal in 1817, during the first term of Governor De Witt Clinton, the nephew of George Clinton; the first vessels passed through the completed canal in 1825.

Actually, New York had emerged as the nation's leading commercial center before the canal was even started. The textile industry had established itself by the mid-1820s, and the dairy industry was thriving. The effects of the canal were felt most strongly in foreign trade—by 1831, 50% of US imports and 27% of US exports passed through the state—and in the canal towns of Utica, Syracuse, Rochester, and Buffalo, where business boomed.

Commercial progress during this period was matched by social and cultural advancement. New York City became a center of literary activity during the 1820s, and by the 1840s was already the nation's theatrical capital. A new state constitution drafted in 1821 established universal white male suffrage, but retained the property qualifications for blacks. Slavery was abolished as of 4 July 1827 (few slaves actually remained in the state by this time), and New Yorkers soon took the lead in the growing antislavery movement. The first women's rights convention in the US was held in Seneca Falls in 1848—though women would have to wait until 1917 before winning the right to vote in state elections. Also during the 1840s, the state saw the first of several great waves of European immigration. The Irish and Germans were the earliest major arrivals during the 19th century, but before World War I they would be joined—not always amicably—by Italians and European Jews.

New Yorkers voted for Abraham Lincoln in the presidential election of 1860 and were among the readiest recruits to the

Union side. Enthusiasm for the conflict diminished during the next two years, however. When the military draft reached New York City on 11 July 1863, the result was three days of rioting in which blacks were lynched and the homes of prominent abolitionists were burned. But New York was not a wartime battleground, and overall the war and Reconstruction were very good for business.

The decades after the Civil War ushered in an era of extraordinary commercial growth and political corruption. This was the Gilded Age, during which entrepreneurs became multimillionaires and New York was transformed from an agricultural state to an industrial giant. In 1860, the leading manufactures in the state were flour and meal, men's clothing, refined sugar, leather goods, liquor, and lumber; 90 years later, apparel, printing and publishing, food, machinery, chemicals, fabricated metal products, electrical machinery, textiles, instruments, and transportation equipment had become the dominant industries.

The key to this transformation was the development of the railroads. The boom period for railroad construction started in the 1850s and reached its high point after 1867, when "Commodore" Cornelius Vanderbilt, who had been a steamboat captain in 1818, took over the New York Central. During the 1860s, native New Yorkers like Jay Gould and Russell Sage made their fortunes through investment and speculation. Especially during the century's last two decades, corporate names that today are household words began to emerge: Westinghouse Electric in 1886, General Electric (as Edison Electric) in 1889, Eastman Kodak in 1892. In 1882, another native New Yorker, John D. Rockefeller, formed the Standard Oil Trust; although the trust would eventually be broken up, the Rockefeller family would help shape New York politics for many decades to come.

The period immediately following the Civil War also marked a new high in political influence for the Tammany Society (or "Tammany Hall"), founded in 1789 as an anti-Federalist organization. From 1857 until his exposure by the press in 1871, Democrat William March "Boss" Tweed ruled Tammany and effectively dominated New York City by dispersing patronage, buying votes, and bribing legislators and judges. Tammany went into temporary eclipse after the Tweed Ring was broken up, and Republicans swept the state in 1872. The first result was a series of constitutional changes, including one abolishing the requirement that blacks hold property in order to vote. A new constitution approved in 1894, and effective in 1895, remains the basic law of New York State today.

During the Union's first 100 years, New York's political life had projected into national prominence such men as Alexander Hamilton, John Jay, George and De Witt Clinton, Martin Van Buren, and Millard Fillmore. The state's vast population—New York held more electoral votes than any other state between 1812 and 1972—coupled with its growing industrial and financial power, enhanced the prestige of state leaders during the nation's second century. Grover Cleveland, though born in New Jersey, became mayor of Buffalo, then governor of New York, and finally the 22d US president in 1885. Theodore Roosevelt was governor of New York, then became vice president and finally president of the US in 1901. In 1910, Charles Evans Hughes resigned the governorship to become an associate justice of the US Supreme Court; he also served as secretary of state, and in 1930 was appointed chief justice of the US. By the 1920s, Tammany had rebounded from the Tweed Ring breakup and from another scandal during the 1890s to reach its peak of prestige: Alfred E. Smith, a longtime member of Tammany, as well as an able and popular official, was four times elected governor and in 1928 became the first Roman Catholic candidate to be nominated by a major party for the presidency of the US. That year saw the election of Franklin D. Roosevelt as governor of New York.

The 1930s, a period of depression, ushered in a new wave of progressive government. From 1933 until 1945, FDR was in the White House. Roosevelt's successor in the statehouse was Herbert H. Lehman, whose Little New Deal established the basic pattern of present state social welfare policies that had begun on a much more modest scale during Smith's administration. The Fusion mayor of New York City at this time—propelled into office by yet another wave of exposure of Tammany corruption—was the colorful and popular Fiorello H. La Guardia.

The decades since World War II have seen extraordinary expansion of New York social services, including construction of the state university system, but also an erosion of the state's industrial base. Fiscal crises are not new to the state—reformers in the 1920s railed against New York City's "spendthrift" policies—but the greatly increased scale of government in the 1970s made the fiscal crisis of 1975 unprecedented in its scope and implications. The city's short-term debt grew from virtually zero to about $6 billion between 1970 and 1975, although its government reported consistently balanced budgets. Eventually a package totaling $4.5 billion in aid was needed to avoid bankruptcy. The decreasing pace of population and industrial growth during the 1950s and 1960s, and the decline during the 1970s, also led to a dimming of New York's political fortunes. The single dominant political figure in New York since World War II, Nelson A. Rockefeller (governor, 1958–73), tried and failed three times to win the Republican presidential nomination before his appointment to the vice-presidency in 1974. Unable to overcome the hostility of his party's conservative wing, he was not renominated for the vice-presidency in 1976. In 1984, however, US Representative Geraldine Ferraro of Queens was the Democratic Party's vice-presidential standard-bearer, and Governor Mario M. Cuomo emerged as an influential Democratic spokesman. After serving for 12 years, Cuomo was replaced in 1995 by State Senator George Pataki, the first Republican to be elected governor since 1970.

From the late seventies through the late eighties, New York enjoyed an economic boom, particularly in finance, insurance, real estate and construction. The state budget increased in constant dollars by 20%. While much of that increase compensated for cuts in federal aid to states and was directed at education, municipalities, schools and prisons, some went to meet new needs such as homelessness and AIDS victims. Prosperity did not reach all sectors of the economy or the population, however. In 1984, 25% of the residents of New York City lived below the poverty line. The collapse of the stock market in October of 1987, in which the market plunged 36% in two months, not only forced a retrenchment on Wall Street but also signaled the end of the boom and the beginning of a recession that was quite severe in New York, exacerbated by the curtailment of federal funding by the Reagan and Bush administrations. Unemployment peaked in 1992, and by 1994 a recovery was under way. In that year the US Census Bureau announced that New York, which had the nation's second largest population in 1990, had dropped to third place behind California and Texas.

In 1994, Occidental Chemical Corporation agreed to pay $98 million in damages for the dumping of hazardous wastes at Love Canal in Buffalo, ending 16 years of legal battles with the largest legal settlement in New York's history. Both New York and the federal government had paid the costs of moving families from the area when it was found that their health was threatened by leaking chemical wastes in the 1970s and early 1980s.

12STATE GOVERNMENT

New York has had four constitutions, adopted in 1777, 1822, 1846, and 1895. The 1895 constitution was extensively revised in 1938, and the basic structure of state government has not changed since then, although the document had been amended

197 times by the end of 1983. In 1993 the Temporary State Commission on Constitutional Revision was created in anticipation of a referendum on a constitutional convention in 1997.

The legislature consists of a 61-member senate and 150-member assembly. Senators and assembly members serve two-year terms and are elected in even-numbered years. The legislative salary was $57,500 in 1995. Each house holds regular annual sessions; special sessions may be called by the governor or initiated by petition of two-thirds of the membership of each body.

Either senators or assembly members may introduce or amend a bill; the governor may introduce a budget bill. To pass, a bill requires a majority vote in both houses; a two-thirds majority is required to override the governor's veto. Members of both the senate and assembly must be US citizens and must have resided in the state for five years and in their district for 12 months.

The state's only elected executives are the governor, lieutenant governor, comptroller, and attorney general. Each serves a four-year term. The governor and lieutenant governor are jointly elected; there is no limit to the number of terms they may serve. The governor must be at least 30 years old, a US citizen, and a resident of the state for five years prior to the date of election. The lieutenant governor is next in line for the governorship (should the governor be unable to complete his term in office) and presides over the senate. In 1996 the governor's salary was $130,000.

The governor appoints the heads of 15 of the 20 major executive departments, 13 of them with the advice and consent of the senate. The exceptions are the comptroller and attorney general, who are elected by the voters; the commissioner of education, who is named by the Regents of the University of the State of New York; the commissioner of social services, elected by the Board of Social Services; and the chief of the Executive Department, which the governor heads ex officio.

A bill becomes law when passed by both houses of the legislature and signed by the governor. While the legislature is in session, a bill may also become law if the governor fails to act on it within 10 days of its receipt. The governor may veto a bill or, if the legislature has adjourned, may kill a bill simply by taking no action on it for 30 days.

A proposed amendment to the state constitution must receive majority votes in both houses of the legislature during two successive sessions. Amendments so approved are put on the ballot in November and adopted or rejected by majority vote. The constitution also provides that the voters must be permitted every 20 years to decide whether a convention should be called to amend the present constitution. To vote in New York State, one must be a US citizen, at least 18 years of age, and a resident of the election district for 30 days. New York State has a permanent personal registration system; a registered voter who fails to vote in any general election during a two-year period must reregister.

13POLITICAL PARTIES

In addition to the Democratic and Republican parties, the major political groups, there has always been a profusion of minor parties in New York, some of which have significantly influenced the outcomes of national and state elections.

Party politics in the state crystallized into their present form around 1855. Up to that time, a welter of parties and factions—including such short-lived groups as the Anti-Masons, Bucktails, Clintonians, Hunkers, and Barnburners (split into Hardshell and Softshell Democrats), Know-Nothings (Native American Party), Wooly Heads and Silver-Grays (factions of the Whigs), and the Liberty Party—jockeyed for power in New York State.

Roughly speaking, the Democratic Party evolved out of the Democratic Republican factions of the old Republican Party and had become a unified party by the 1850s. The Democratic power

base was—and has remained—the big cities, especially New York City. The most important big-city political machine from the 1860s through the 1950s, except for a few brief periods, was the Tammany Society ("Tammany Hall"). Tammany controlled the Democratic Party in New York City and, through that party, the city itself.

The Republican Party in New York State emerged in 1855 as the heir of the Whigs, the Liberty Party, and the Softshell Democratic faction. The Republican Party's power base includes the state's rural counties, the smaller cities and towns, and (though not so much in the 1970s and early 1980s as in earlier decades) the New York City suburbs. Although New York Republicans stand to the right of the Democrats on social issues, they have usually been well to the left of the national Republican Party. The liberal "internationalist" strain of Republicanism was personified during the 1960s by Governor Nelson Rockefeller, US Senator Jacob Javits, and New York City Mayor John V. Lindsay (who later became a Democrat).

The disaffection of more conservative Republicans and Democrats within the state led to the formation of the Conservative Party in 1963. At first intended as a device to exert pressure on the state Republican establishment, the Conservative Party soon became a power in its own right, electing a US senator, James Buckley, in 1970. Its power decreased in the late 1970s as the Republican Party embraced some of its positions. The Conservative Party has its left-wing counterpart in the Liberal Party, which was formed in 1944 by dissidents in the American Labor Party who claimed the ALP was Communist-influenced. Tied strongly to labor interests, the Liberals have normally supported the national Democratic ticket. Their power, however, has waned considerably in recent years.

Minor parties have sometimes meant the difference between victory and defeat for major party candidates in state and national elections. The Liberal Party line provided the victory margin in the state, and therefore the nation, for Democratic presidential candidate John F. Kennedy in 1960. Other significant, though not victorious, minor-party presidential candidates have included the American Labor Party with Henry Wallace in 1948 (8% of the vote), the Courage Party with George Wallace in 1968 (5%), and the Liberal Party with John Anderson in 1980 (7%). Among radical parties, the Socialists qualified for the presidential ballot continuously between 1900 and 1952, reaching a peak of 203,201 votes (7% of the total) in 1920.

In 1994, the state had 4,256,952 registered Democrats, or 47%; 2,776,954 registered Republicans, or 31%; and 1,999,188 independents, or 22%. Democrat Mario M. Cuomo was defeated in his run for a fourth term as governor in November 1994 by Republican George Pataki. In 1997 New York's US senators were Alphonse D'Amato, a Republican serving his third term, and Democrat Daniel Moynihan who was also serving his third term. After the 1996 elections, New York's US representatives included 18 Democrats and 13 Republicans. Republicans held 35 seats in the state senate while Democrats held 26. In the state assembly there were 95 Democrats and 55 Republicans. Minority representation in 1994 included 299 black elected officials and 83 Hispanics in public office. As of 1995, there were 38 women serving in the state legislature.

In the November 1980 presidential elections, Republican nominee Ronald Reagan (with Conservative Party backing) won the state's 41 electoral votes, apparently because John Anderson, running in New York State on the Liberal Party line, siphoned enough votes from the Democratic incumbent, Jimmy Carter, to give Reagan a plurality. Reagan carried the state again in 1984, despite the presence on the Democratic ticket of US Representative Geraldine Ferraro of Queens as the running mate of Walter Mondale; Ferraro was the first woman candidate for president or vice president on a major party ticket. New Yorkers chose

Democratic nominees Michael Dukakis and Bill Clinton in 1988 and 1992, respectively. Clinton captured 59% of the vote in 1996 while Republican Bob Dole won 31% of the vote and Independent Ross Perot picked up 8%.

In November 1993, New York City mayor David Dinkins, a Democrat and New York's first black mayor, who had served since 1990, was defeated by Republican Rudolph Giuliani.

[14]LOCAL GOVERNMENT

The state constitution, endorsing the principle of home rule, recognizes many different levels of local government. In 1992, New York had 57 counties, 619 municipal governments, 929 towns, and 713 school districts. In addition, there were 980 special districts, of which 900 were for fire prevention. With the exception of some counties within New York City, each county has a county attorney and a district attorney, a sheriff, a fiscal officer usually called a treasurer, a county clerk, and a commissioner of social services.

Cities are contained within counties, with one outstanding exception: New York City is made up of five counties, one for each of its five boroughs. Traditionally, counties are run by an elected board of supervisors or county legislature; however, a growing number of counties have vested increased powers in a single elected county executive.

Towns are run by a town board; the most important board member is the town supervisor, who is the board's presiding officer and acts as town treasurer. A group of people within a town or towns may also incorporate themselves into a village, with their own elected mayor and elected board of trustees. Some villages have administrators or managers. Members of the village remain members of the town, and must pay taxes to both jurisdictions. The constitution grants the state legislature the power to decide which taxes the local governments may levy and how much debt they may incur.

New York City is governed by a mayor and city council, but much practical power resides in the Board of Estimate. On this board sit the city's three top elected officials—the mayor, comptroller, and city council president. The board also includes the five borough presidents, elected officials who represent (and, to a limited extent, govern) each of the five boroughs. New York City government is further complicated by the fact that certain essential services are provided not by the city itself but by independent "authorities." The Port Authority of New York and New Jersey, for example, operates New York Harbor, sets interstate bridge and tunnel tolls, supervises the city's bus and air terminals, and operates the city's largest office complex, the World Trade Center; it is responsible not to the mayor but to the governors of New York and New Jersey. Similarly, the Metropolitan Transportation Authority, which controls the city's subways and some of its commuter rail lines, is an independent agency responsible to the state rather than the city.

[15]STATE SERVICES

Educational services are provided through the Education Department. Under this department's jurisdiction are the State Library, the State Museum, the State Archives, the New York State School for the Blind at Batavia, and the New York State School for the Deaf at Rome. The Education Department also issues licenses for 20 professions, including architecture, engineering and land surveying, massage, pharmacy, public accountancy, social work, and various medical specialties. The state university system is administered by a separate agency headed by a chancellor.

Transportation services are under the direction of the Department of Transportation, which has responsibility for

New York Presidential Vote by Political Parties, 1948–96

YEAR	ELECTORAL VOTE	NEW YORK WINNER	DEMOCRAT	LIBERAL[1]	REPUBLICAN	PROGRESSIVE[2]	SOCIALIST	SOCIALIST WORKERS	PEACE AND FREEDOM
1948	47	Dewey (R)	2,557,642	222,562	2,841,163	509,559	40,879	2,675	—
1952	45	*Eisenhower (R)	2,687,890	416,711	3,952,815	64,211	2,664	2,212	—
1956	45	*Eisenhower (R)	2,458,212	292,557	4,340,340	—	—	—	—
1960	45	*Kennedy (D)	3,423,909	406,176	3,446,419	—	—	14,319	—
1964	43	*Johnson (D)	4,570,670	342,432	2,243,559		SOC. LABOR 6,118	3,228	—
1968	43	Humphrey (D)	3,066,848	311,622	3,007,932	AMERICAN IND.[3] 358,864	8,432	11,851	24,517
1972	41	*Nixon (R)	2,767,956	183,128	3,824,642	CONSERVATIVE[4] 368,136	4,530	7,797	COMMUNIST 5,641
1976	41	*Carter (D)	3,244,165	145,393	2,825,913	2,724,878	LIBERTARIAN 12,197	6,996	10,270
1980	41	*Reagan (R)	2,728,372	467,801	2,637,700	256,131	52,648	RIGHT TO LIFE 24,159	CITIZENS 23,186
1984	36	*Reagan (R)	3,001,285	118,324	3,376,519	288,244	11,949	—	COMMUNIST 4,226
1988	36	Dukakis (D)	3,255,487	92,395	2,838,414	243,457	12,109	NEW ALLIANCE 15,845	20,497
1992[5]	22	*Clinton (D)	3,346,894	97,556	2,041,690	177,000	13,451	15,472	11,318
1996[5]	33	*Clinton (D)	3,649,630	106,547	1,738,707	183,392	12,220	FREEDOM[4] 11,393	GREEN (NADER) 75,956

* Won US presidential election.

[1] Supported Democratic candidate except in 1980, when John Anderson ran on the Liberal line.

[2] Ran in the state as the American Labor Party.

[3] Appeared on the state ballot as the Courage Party.

[4] Supported Republican candidate.

[5] Independent candidate Ross Perot received 1,090,721 votes in 1992 and 503,458 votes in 1996.

highways, aviation, mass transit, railroads, water transport, transportation safety, and intrastate rate regulation. The Department of Motor Vehicles licenses all road vehicles, motor vehicle dealers, motor vehicle operators, and driving schools.

Human services are provided through several state departments. Among the programs and facilities operated by the Department of Health are three research and treatment facilities; the New York State Veterans' Home at Oxford, Roswell Park Memorial Institute at Buffalo, and Helen Hayes Hospital at West Haverstraw. The state provides care for the mentally ill, retarded, and alcoholics and other substance-dependent persons through the Department of Mental Hygiene. In 1985, it maintained 30 psychiatric centers, and 18 developmental centers for retardation and developmental disabilities. The Department of Social Services supervises and sets standards for locally administered public and private welfare and health programs, including Medicaid and Aid to Families with Dependent Children; it has special responsibilities for the blind and visually handicapped and over Indian affairs. Other human services are provided through the Division of Veterans' Affairs, the Division of Human Rights, the Division for Youth, and the Office for the Aging, all within the Executive Department.

Public protection services include state armed forces, corrections, and consumer protection. Included within the Division of Military and Naval Affairs, in the Executive Department, are the Army National Guard, Air National Guard, Naval Militia, State Civil Defense Commission, and Disaster Preparedness Commission. The Division of State Police operates within the Executive Department, while prisons are administered by the separate Department of Correctional Services, which in 1985 operated 46 correctional facilities. The State Consumer Protection Board (Executive Department) coordinates the consumer protection activities of the various agencies and departments. The major legal role in consumer protection is played by the attorney general.

Housing services are provided through the Division of Housing and Community Renewal of the Executive Department, and through the quasi-independent New York State Housing Finance Agency, State of New York Mortgage Agency, and New York State Urban Development Corporation. The Division of Economic Opportunity (Department of State) acts as the state representative of the economically disadvantaged in dealing with local, state, and federal agencies. The Department of Commerce has an Office of Minority and Women's Business.

Natural resources protection services are centralized in the Department of Environmental Conservation. The administration of the state park and recreation system is carried out by the Office of Parks, Recreation and Historic Preservation, in the Executive Department. The Department of Agriculture and Markets serves the interests of farmers and also administers the state's Pure Food Law. Energy is the province of the Department of Public Service. The quasi-independent Power Authority of the State of New York finances, builds, and operates electricity-generating and transmission facilities.

The Department of Labor provides most labor services for the state. Its responsibilities include occupational health and safety, human resource development and allocation, administration of unemployment insurance and other benefit programs, and maintenance of labor standards, including enforcement of minimum wage and other labor laws. The Employment Relations Board tries to settle labor disputes and prevent work stoppages.

16 JUDICIAL SYSTEM

New York's highest court is the court of appeals, in Albany, with appellate jurisdiction only. The court of appeals consists of a chief judge and six associate judges, appointed by the governor and approved by the senate for 14-year terms. Below the court of appeals is the supreme court, with over 590 justices in 12 judicial districts. The supreme court of New York State does not sit as one body; instead, most supreme court justices are assigned original jurisdiction in civil and criminal matters, while 24 justices are assigned to one of the court's four appellate divisions. Supreme court justices are elected by district and serve 14-year terms.

The New York court of claims, which sits in Albany, consisted in 1992 of 18 judges appointed by the governor to nine-year terms, along with 46 judges sitting as acting Supreme Court justices in felony trials. This special trial court hears civil cases involving claims by or against the state.

Outside New York City, each county has its own county court to handle criminal cases, although some are delegated to be handled by lower courts. County court judges are elected to 10-year terms. Many counties have a surrogate's court to handle such matters as wills and estates; surrogates are elected to 10-year terms except in New York City counties, where they are elected to 14-year terms. Each county has its own family court. In New York City, judges are appointed by the mayor for 10-year terms; elsewhere they are elected for 10 years. A county's district attorney has authority in criminal matters. Most cities (including New York City) have their own court systems; in New York City, the mayor appoints judges of city criminal and family courts. Village police justices and town justices of the peace handle minor violations and other routine matters. There are 103,230 attorneys practicing in the state.

The Department of Correctional Services maintains correctional facilities throughout the state, as well as regional parole offices. In 1995, 68,471 inmates were in state and federal facilities, at a rate of 378 inmates per 100,000 inhabitants.

New York had a violent crime rate in 1996 of 841.9 per 100,000 inhabitants, down from 1,122 in 1992. About 54% of all crimes reported to the police in the state occurred in New York City, which had an FBI Crime Index total of 444,758 crimes. FBI data for the New York metropolitan area showed a violent crime rate of 1,392.8 per 100,000 population, well above the national average of 684.6. The property crime rate of 4,276.7 was somewhat below the national average of 4,593. In New York City alone there were 1,177 cases of murder or nonnegligent manslaughter, 2,374 forcible rapes, 59,280 robberies, 52,322 aggravated assaults, 73,889 cases of burglary, 183,037 cases of larceny-theft, and 72,679 motor vehicle thefts. In all areas there was a substantial decline since 1992.

New York abolished the death penalty in 1965 and reinstated it in 1995. No one has been executed under the new law and the last execution in the state occurred under the old law in 1963.

17 ARMED FORCES

In 1996, there were 20,383 active-duty military personnel stationed in New York, more than half of whom were at Fort Drum. Approximately 5,500 active duty personnel were at the US Military Academy at West Point, which was founded in 1802.

In 1995/96, New York firms received $3.5 billion in defense contracts. In 1996 there were 1,515,000 veterans of US military service in the state. Of these, 1,171,000 had seen service during wartime. Allowing for overlapping (some veterans served in more than one war), the estimates for living veterans of wartime service were as follows: World War I, 1,000; World War II, 451,000; Korea, 252,000; Vietnam era, 414,000; Persian Gulf War, 99,000. Veterans' benefits totaling $2.4 billion were paid to New Yorkers during 1995/96.

In 1996 the Army Reserve and National Guard had 40,380 personnel; the Air Force Reserve and National Guard, 9,134; and Navy and Marine Corps Reserve and National Guard, 13,851. About 10% of all US police employees work in the state. In 1993, the New York State Police employed 3,957 sworn officers, or 2 per 10,000 residents.

18MIGRATION

Since the early 1800s, New York has been the primary port of entry for Europeans coming to the US. The Statue of Liberty—dedicated in 1886 and beckoning "your tired, your poor, /Your huddled masses yearning to breathe free" to the shores of America—was often the immigrants' first glimpse of America. The first stop for some 20 million immigrants in the late 19th and early 20th centuries was Ellis Island, where they were processed, often given Americanized names, and sent onward to an uncertain future.

The first great wave of European immigrants arrived in the 1840s, impelled by the potato famine in Ireland. By 1850, New York City had 133,730 Irish-born inhabitants, and by 1890, 409,224. Although smaller in number, German immigration during this period was more widespread; during the 1850s, German-speaking people were the largest foreign-born group in Rochester and Buffalo, and by 1855 about 30,000 of Buffalo's 74,000 residents were German.

The next two great waves of European immigration—Eastern European Jews and Italians—overlapped. Vast numbers of Jews began arriving from Eastern Europe during the 1880s, by which time some 80,000 German-speaking Jews were already living in New York City. By 1910, the Jewish population of the city was about 1,250,000, growing to nearly 2,000,000 by the mid-1920s. The flood of Italians began during the 1800s, when the Italian population of New York City increased from 75,000 to more than 200,000; in 1950, nearly 500,000 Italian-born immigrants were living in the state. Migration from the 1840s onward followed a cyclical pattern: as one group dispersed from New York City throughout the state and the nation, it was replaced by a new wave of immigrants.

Yankees from New England made up the first great wave of domestic migration. Most of the migrants who came to New York between 1790 and 1840 were Yankees; it has been estimated that by 1850, 52,000 natives of Vermont (20% of that state's population) had become residents of New York. There was a slow, steady migration of African Americans from slave states to New York before the Civil War, but massive black migration to New York, and especially to New York City, began during World War I and continued well into the 1960s. The third great wave of domestic migration came after World War II, from Puerto Rico. Nearly 40,000 Puerto Ricans settled in New York City in 1946, and 58,500 in 1952/53. By 1960, the census showed well over 600,000 New Yorkers of Puerto Rican birth or parentage. As of 1990, Puerto Rican-born New Yorkers numbered 143,974. Nearly 41,800 state residents in 1990 had lived in Puerto Rico in 1985. Many other Caribbean natives—especially Dominicans, Jamaicans, and Haitians—followed. In 1996, there were a reported 3,232,000 state residents who were foreign-born (about 17% of the state's population). In the same year, 154,095 foreign immigrants entered New York, the second highest total of any state (surpassed only by California) and 17% of the total immigration for that year. As of 1994, it was estimated that between 462 and 539 undocumented immigrants were living in New York, a figure second only to that for California.

The fourth and most recent domestic migratory trend is unique in New York history—the net outward migration from New York to other states. During the 1960s, New York suffered a net loss of more than 100,000 residents through migration; between 1970 and 1980, the estimated net loss was probably in excess of 1,500,000, far greater than that in any other state: probably 80% of the migration was from New York City. From 1980 to 1990, net loss from migration exceeded 340,000. Between 1990 and 1996, New York had a net loss of 1,276,953

in domestic migration. These general estimates hide a racial movement of historic proportions: during the 1960s, while an estimated net total of 638,000 whites were moving out of the state, 396,000 blacks were moving in; during 1970–75, according to Census Bureau estimates, 701,000 whites left New York, while 60,000 blacks were arriving. According to a private study, a net total of 700,000 whites and 50,000 blacks left the state during 1975–80. It appears that many of the white emigrants went to suburban areas of New Jersey and Connecticut, but many also went to two Sunbelt states, Florida and California. Overwhelmingly, the black arrivals came from the South. During the 1980s, the black population of the New York City area increased by 16.4%.

Intrastate migration has followed the familiar pattern of rural to urban, urban to suburban. In 1790, the state was 88% rural; the rural population grew in absolute terms (though not as a percentage of the total state population) until the 1880s, when the long period of decline began. New York's farm population decreased by 21% during the 1940s, 33% during the 1950s, 38% during the 1960s, and 49% during the 1970s. By 1990, 84% of all New Yorkers lived in urban areas. Meanwhile, the suburban population has grown steadily. In 1950, 3,538,620 New Yorkers (24% of the state total) lived in suburbs; by 1980, this figure had grown to 7,461,161 (42% of all state residents). It should be remembered, of course, that this more than doubling of the suburban population reflects natural increase and direct migration from other states and regions, as well as the intrastate migratory movement from central cities to suburbs. As of 1990, 67.5% of all state residents had been born in New York. About 62% of residents age 5 and older in 1990 lived in the same house as in 1985. For those who lived in a different house in 1985, only 13% did so in another state.

19INTERGOVERNMENTAL COOPERATION

New York State is a member of the Council of State Governments and its allied organizations. The state participates in many interstate regional commissions (and in commissions with the Canadian provinces of Ontario and Quebec). Among the more active interstate commissions are the Atlantic States Marine Fisheries Commission, Delaware River Basin Commission, Great Lakes Basin Commission, Interstate Oil and Gas Compact Commission, Lake Champlain Bridge Commission, New England Interstate Water Pollution Control Commission, Northeastern Forest Fire Protection Commission, and Ohio River Valley Water Sanitation Commission. In 1985, New York joined seven other Great Lakes states and two Canadian provinces in the Great Lakes Charter, for the purpose of protecting the lakes' water reserves.

The three most important interstate bodies for the New York metropolitan area are the Palisades Interstate Park Commission, Interstate Sanitation Commission, and Port Authority of New York and New Jersey. The Palisades Interstate Park Commission was founded in 1900 (with New Jersey) in order to preserve the natural beauty of the Palisades region. The Interstate Sanitation Commission (with New Jersey and Connecticut; established in 1961) monitors and seeks to control pollution within the tri-state Interstate Sanitation District. The Port Authority of New York and New Jersey, created in 1921 and the most powerful of the three, is a public corporation with the power to issue its own bonds. Its vast holdings include 4 bridges, 2 tunnels, 6 airports and heliports, 3 motor vehicle terminals, 7 marine terminals, the trans-Hudson rapid transit system, an industrial park in the Bronx, and the 110-story twin-towered World Trade Center in lower Manhattan.

Federal aid to New York state and local governments totaled $24.6 billion in 1995/96, higher than for any other state, except California.

[20] ECONOMY

From the Civil War through the 1950s, New York State led the nation in just about every category by which an industrial economy can be measured. With the rise of California and the growth of other Sunbelt states, New York can no longer be described in such superlatives.

The state is no stranger to economic transitions. In the colonial and early national periods, New York was a leading wheat-growing state. When the wheat crop, declined dairying and lumbering became the state's mainstays. New York then emerged as the national leader in wholesaling, retailing, and manufacturing—and remained so well into the 1960s. By 1973, however, the state was running neck and neck with California by most output measures, or had already been surpassed. The total labor force, the number of workers in manufacturing, and the number of factories all declined during the 1960s and 1970s.

New York City's manufacturing base and its skilled laborers have been emigrating to the suburbs and to other states since World War II. Between 1969 and 1976, the city lost 600,000 jobs. About 1 in 8 New York City residents received some form of public assistance (including Medicaid and Supplemental Security Income benefits) in 1982. With the departure of much of the middle class has come a shrinking of the city's tax base, a factor that contributed to the fiscal crisis of 1975, when a package of short-term aid from Congress, the state government, and the labor union pension funds saved the city from default.

The early 1980s saw the state's fortunes on the rise. A shift in dependence from manufacturing to services, and particularly to finance, helped the state and New York City weather the 1981–82 recession. In 1983, the state's three largest industrial and commercial employers (excluding public utilities) were all banks based in New York City. From 1980 to 1990, the state's economy acquired approximately one million jobs, in contrast to 50,000 the previous decade. New York City gained 164,000 jobs from 1980 through 1984, 76,000 in 1984 alone. Financial services led the city's economic expansion, adding 100,000 jobs from 1980 to 1987. Long Island also experienced growth in the first half of the decade, benefiting from the defense build-up by the federal government in the early and mid-eighties. The expanding economy moved New York from 10th place in per capita income in 1980 to 5th place in 1990, when the state's per capita income reached $21,073.

New York's economy not only grew during the eighties but also underwent a restructuring. Manufacturing witnessed a decline in its share of total employment from 20% in 1980 to 14 percent in 1990, and manufacturing jobs declined 21% over the course of the decade. Apparel, industrial machinery and equipment, and primary metals accounted for 40% of the total loss of jobs. Industrial output, however, increased 10.1% between 1980 and 1987. Productivity gains produced both the rise in output and the decline in employment. Construction boomed from 1982–89, increasing its share of employment from 2.9% to 3.8%. The service sector, particularly business-related, health care, education and social services grew 52% in the decade, increasing services' share of employment from 24% in 1980 to 29% in 1990. Finance, insurance, and the real estate industry expanded 64%. The surge in financial services employment ended with the crash of the stock market in October of 1987, in which stock prices dropped 36% in two months. The crash prompted the layoff of 9,000 employees on Wall Street and a downsizing of the banking and securities industries.

In 1994, New York's gross state product was $570,994 million, to which private goods-producing industries contributed $90,055 million; private services-producing industries, $415,842 million; and government, $65,097 million.

[21] INCOME

With a per capita income of $28,782 in 1996, New York ranked 4th among the 50 states. New York's total nonfarm personal income for that year was $520.0 billion, 2d behind California, and 8.1% of the US total. From 1973 to 1983, total personal income grew by less than 6% in constant dollars, but increased by 20% from 1984 to 1988.

In 1995, 16.5% of the population of New York State had money incomes below the poverty line, compared to 13.8% nationally. The New York City area had a poverty rate of 15% in 1995. New York's reputation for "Wall Street millionaires" is not entirely deserved: in 1992, only some 3.3% of all New York households had disposable incomes exceeding $75,000, a proportion lower than four other states and the District of Columbia. As of 1990, however, New York did have 74 residents whose assets each exceeded $260 million, more than any other state. During 1996, there were 55,339 bankruptcy filings, up 21% from 1995.

[22] LABOR

The state ranks 3d to California and Texas in the size of its labor force. The civilian labor force totaled 8,639,000 in 1996, of whom 8,100,000 (93.8%) were employed and 540,000 (6.2%) were unemployed.

The labor force participation rate of women increased from 42.0% in 1974 to 52.8% in 1995. Over the same period, participation rates for men declined from 75.9% to 70.1%. Among minority groups, the unemployment rate in 1996 was 11.7% for blacks and 9.7% for Hispanics.

Estimates of nonagricultural payroll jobs for 1996 are shown below for major industry groups, along with 1995 payrolls covered by unemployment insurance:

INDUSTRY	1996 JOBS (IN 1,000S)	1995 PAYROLLS (MILLIONS)
Total nonfarm	7,917.1	$270.3
Total private sector	6,534.8	222.2
Manufacturing	921.8	37.1
Durable goods	486.3	20.1
Nondurable goods	435.5	17.1
Mining	4.6	0.2
Construction	254.1	8.9
Transportation, public utilities	402.2	15.7
Wholesale trade	425.6	18.1
Retail trade	1,195.1	19.4
Finance, insurance, real estate	721.0	47.3
Services	2,610.4	74.1
Government	1,382.3	48.1

The average weekly manufacturing wage for production workers was $521 in 1996.

At the turn of the century, working conditions in New York were among the worst in the country. The flood of immigrants into the labor market and the absence of labor laws to protect them led to the development in New York City of cramped, ill-lit, poorly ventilated, and unhealthy factories—the sweatshops for which the garment industry became notorious. Since that time working conditions in the garment factories have improved, primarily through the efforts of the International Ladies' Garment Workers Union and, later, its sister organization, the Amalgamated Clothing and Textiles Workers Union.

According to the US Department of Labor, 2,050,000 workers belonged to unions in 1994. That figure represented nearly 28.9% of the manufacturing work force. In 1993, 16 of 97 large national unions had their headquarters in New York City. Under the Taylor Law, public employees do not have the right to strike. Penalties for striking may be exacted against both the unions and their leaders.

[23]AGRICULTURE

New York ranked 27th in farm income in 1995, with cash receipts from farming at over $2.8 billion. About 66% came from livestock products, mostly dairy goods. In 1996, the state ranked 2d in the production of corn for silage, 2d in apples, 3d in tart cherries and cauliflower, 3d in snap beans, 6th in onions, 10th in oats, and 18th in hay.

Corn was the leading crop for the Indians and for the European settlers of the early colonial period. During the early 1800s, however, wheat was the major crop grown in eastern New York. With the opening of the Erie Canal, western New York (especially the Genesee Valley) became a major wheat-growing center as well. By the late 1850s, when the state's wheat crop began to decline, New York still led the nation in barley, flax, hops, and potato production and was a significant grower of corn and oats. The opening of the railroads took away the state's competitive advantage, but as grain production shifted to the Midwest, the state emerged as a leading supplier of meat and dairy products.

New York remains an important dairy state, but urbanization has reduced its overall agricultural potential. In 1992, 11.1% of the state's land area was devoted to crop growing; in 1996, there were only 36,000 farms, with 7.7 million acres (3.1 million hectares).

The west-central part of the state is the most intensively farmed. Chautauqua County, in the extreme southwest, leads the state in grape production, while Wayne County, along Lake Ontario, leads in apples and cherries. The dairy industry is concentrated in the St. Lawrence Valley; grain growing dominates the plains between Syracuse and Buffalo. Potatoes are grown mostly in Suffolk County, on eastern Long Island.

The following table shows area, production, and value of leading field crops in 1996:

CROP	AREA (ACRES)	PRODUCTION		VALUE
Hay	1,510,000	3,468,000	tons	$285,072,000
Corn, grain	630,000	67,410,000	bushels	215,712,000
Corn, silage	510,000	7,905,000	tons	203,949,000
Potatoes	29,000	7,980,000	cwt	55,062,000
Oats	90,000	4,275,000	bushels	9,405,000
Wheat	160,000	6,450,000	bushels	27,413,000

Farms in 1996 also produced 941,200 tons of vegetables. Leading vegetable crops were cabbage, onions, sweet corn, and snap beans. State vineyards produced 184,000 tons of grapes for wine and juice in 1996, while the apple crop totaled 1.05 billion lb.

[24]ANIMAL HUSBANDRY

The St. Lawrence Valley is the state's leading cattle-raising region, followed by the Mohawk Valley and Wyoming County, in western New York. The poultry industry is more widely dispersed. In 1997, an estimated 1.54 million cattle and calves were worth around $1.15 billion. There were around 70,000 hogs and pigs, worth $6.44 million in 1996. During 1995, around 21.9 million lb of chickens and broilers were produced, and nearly 13 million lb of turkey, worth $5.4 million.

New York is a leading dairy state. In 1995, New York was 3d in the US in milk production with 11.6 million lb of milk from 703,000 milk cows, and the state produced nearly 25.6 million lb of butter and 35.9 million gallons of ice cream.

Also during 1995, New York farmers produced around 4 million lb of sheep and lambs, which brought in around $3.9 million in gross income. The state produced around 1 billion eggs, valued at $55.8 million in 1995. Duck raising is an industry of local importance on Long Island.

[25]FISHING

Fishing, though an attraction for tourists and sportsmen, plays only a marginal role in the economic life of the state. In 1995, the commercial catch by New York fishers was 53,210,000 lb, less than 1% of the US total and far below the 1880 peak of 335,000,000 lb. The catch was valued at $76,501,000. Important species for commercial use are menhaden and, among shellfish, clams and oysters. Virtually all of New York's commercial fishing takes place in the Atlantic waters off Long Island. Montauk, on the eastern end of Long Island, is the state's leading fishing port.

Pollution and poor wildlife management have seriously endangered the state's commercial and sport fishing in the ocean, rivers, and lakes. Commercial fishing for striped bass in the Hudson River was banned in 1976 because of contamination by polychlorinated biphenyls (PCBs). Commercial fishing in the river for five other species—black crappie, brown bullhead, carp, goldfish, and pumpkinseed—was banned in 1985. Also banned in 1985 was commercial fishing for striped bass in New York Harbor and along both shores of western Long Island.

In recent decades, however, the Department of Environmental Conservation has taken an active role in restocking New York's inland waters. The US Fish and Wildlife Service distributes large numbers of lake trout and Atlantic salmon fingerlings and rainbow and brook trout fry throughout the state. In 1995/96, federal hatcheries distributed 751,346 fish (44,340 lb) and 535,565 fish eggs within the state. New York issued 1,082,129 sport fishing licenses in 1995/96.

[26]FORESTRY

About 60% of New York's surface area is forestland. The most densely forested counties are Hamilton, Essex, and Warren in the Adirondacks, and Delaware, Greene, and Ulster in the Catskills. The total forested area was about 18,713,000 acres (7,573,000 hectares) in 1992, of which 84% was classified as commercial forest, meaning it was available for the harvest of wood products such as sawlogs, veneer, and pulpwood or firewood. In 1996, the Division of Lands and Forests harvested timber from 15,526 acres (6,283 hectares) of state forestland, bringing in revenue of $4,075,405.

The state Department of Environmental Conservation manages about 3,000,000 acres (1,200,000 hectares) in the Catskills and Adirondacks as Forest Preserves, and an additional 800,000 acres in State Forests and Wildlife Management Areas (where timber harvesting is allowed as part of their management plans). The Saratoga Tree Nursery distributed 1,200,000 tree seedlings and 250,000 shrub seedlings in 1996.

[27]MINING

The value of nonfuel mineral production in New York in 1995 was estimated to be $820 million, a decrease of $72 million from that of 1994. In 1995, crushed stone replaced salt as New York's leading nonfuel mineral, based on value. About 90% of the total value came from industrial minerals and mineral products, primarily crushed stone, salt, construction sand and gravel, portland cement, and wollastonite. The value of crushed stone in 1995 was $219 million; salt, $190 million; construction sand and gravel, $134 million; and portland cement, $125 million.

Other commodities produced included masonry cement, clays, garnet, gypsum, peat, industrial sand, dimension stone, talc, and byproduct lead and silver. The combined value of abrasive garnet, crude gypsum, lead, industrial sand and gravel, silver, talc and pyrophyllite, wollastonite, zinc, and peat in 1995 was $122,000,000.

Nationally, the state ranked 13th overall in the value of nonfuel minerals produced. New York was the only state in the nation that produced wollastonite and one of only two states where garnet was mined. Major uses of wollastonite (a type of calcium silicate) are as a filler in ceramic tile, marine wallboard, paint, plastics, and refractory liners in steel mills.

28ENERGY AND POWER

Although New York State's fossil fuel resources are limited, the state ranked 9th in the US in electric power production in 1995. About one-fifth of the state's annual electric power output came from hydroelectric plants built and operated by the Power Authority of the State of New York. Almost 8% came from oil-fired units, 20% from coal-fired units, 23% from gas-fired units, and 23% from nuclear power plants.

Installed capacity in the state in 1996 was 32.5 million kW. Electrical output totaled nearly 101.2 billion kWh in 1995.

The largest nonfederal hydroelectric plant in the US is the Niagara Power Project, which had a capacity of 2,090,000 kW at the beginning of 1996. The New York side of the St. Lawrence River Power Project had a capacity of 912,000 kW in 1996.

Both plants were built and are operated by the Power Authority of the State of New York, which also built and operates a pumped-storage plant in Schoharie County (1,040,000 kW) and a nuclear power plant on Lake Ontario near Oswego (800,000 kW). Other nuclear plants in the state include two reactors at Indian Point (one operated by Consolidated Edison, and one by the State Power Authority), and units operated by the Niagara Mohawk Power Co. and the Rochester Gas & Electric Co.

The State Energy Research and Development Authority manages the only commercial nuclear fuel reprocessing plant in the US, at West Valley in Cattaraugus County.

Sales of public and private electric power totaled 130 billion kWh in 1995, of which 41% went to commercial users, 19% to industrial purchasers, 31% to residential users, and 9% for other purposes.

Electric bills for New York City are the highest in the nation, and customers in Buffalo and Rochester also pay above the national median. New York's per capita energy expenditure of $1,710 (47th) in 1994 was well below the national average of $1,938.

Estimated reserves of petroleum in New York State are much less than 1% of the US total. Oil output in 1996 was 309,000 barrels—again, a tiny fraction of the national total. Because New York has a large number of motor vehicles and because more than half of all occupied housing units in the state are heated by oil, the state is a very large net importer of petroleum products.

The state's estimated natural gas reserves as of December 1995 were 197 billion cu feet; marketed production in 1995 totaled 18.4 billion cu feet. Although the state's natural gas output has risen steadily since 1966, both production and reserves represent only a tiny fraction of US totals. About 33% of natural gas sold in the state in 1995 was used for residential purposes.

29INDUSTRY

Until the 1970s, New York was the nation's foremost industrial state, ranking 1st in virtually every general category. However, US Commerce Department data show that by 1975 the state had slipped in manufacturing to 2d in number of employees, payroll, and value added, 4th in value of shipments of manufactured goods, and 6th in new capital spending. By 1982, it had risen back to 3d in value of shipments and new capital spending, but manufacturing jobs declined by 2% between 1982 and 1987. Employment in manufacturing fell by 1% in 1987–89, and by another 3.5% in 1989–90. Important sectors are instruments and related products, industrial machinery and equipment, electronic and electric equipment, printing and publishing, and textiles.

The Buffalo region, with its excellent transport facilities and abundant power supply, is the main center for heavy industry in the state. Plants in the region manufacture iron and steel, aircraft,

automobile parts and accessories, and machinery, as well as flour, animal feed, and various chemicals. The Buffalo area's biggest private industrial employer, Bethlehem Steel, closed its Lackawanna plant in 1983. Republic Steel also closed its plant, and General Motors cut employment at its Tonawanda facility by two-thirds. Light industry is dispersed throughout the state. Rochester is especially well known for its photographic (Kodak) and optical equipment (Bausch & Lomb) and office machines (Xerox); the city is the world headquarters of the Eastman Kodak Co., a world leader in photography with sales of $15.968 billion in 1997. The state's leadership in electronic equipment is in large part attributable to the International Business Machines Corp. (IBM), which was founded in 1911 at Endicott, near Binghamton. In 1997, IBM ranked as the 6th-leading US industrial corporation, with sales of $75.9 billion. Its world headquarters is at Armonk, in Westchester County, and it has important facilities at Endicott, Kingston, and Poughkeepsie. The presence of two large General Electric plants has long made Schenectady a leader in the manufacture of electric machinery.

New York City excels not only in the apparel and publishing trades but also in food processing, meat packing, chemicals, leather goods, metal products, and many other manufactures. In addition, the city serves as headquarters for many large industrial corporations whose manufacturing activities often take place entirely outside New York. In all, 61 *Fortune* 500 firms had their headquarters in New York State in 1997.

In 1995, there were 5,371 US patents issued to New York residents.

30COMMERCE

New York was 2d in sales from wholesale trade in 1992; the sales from wholesale trade in the New York City metropolitan area (including portions of nearby New Jersey, Connecticut, and Pennsylvania) alone exceeded that of any state. The state ranked 3d in retail trade, behind California and Texas.

In 1992, state wholesale sales totaled $287.7 billion, or 8.9% of the US total. The most valuable categories of goods traded were petroleum and petroleum products, apparel, piece goods and notions, groceries and related products, jewelry, watches, diamonds and other precious stones, woven goods, grain, machinery, equipment and supplies, minerals and metals, and electrical goods. Except for apparel, woven goods, jewelry, and perhaps electrical goods, this list appears to reflect the importance of New York City as a port and transportation center rather than the makeup of state or city industries.

According to the Census of Retail Sales of 1992, 110,771 retail establishments in New York had sales of $118.9 billion (3d), or 6.3% of the US total. Retail sales from food stores accounted for 20.5%; automotive dealers, 16%; eating and drinking places, 10.8%; general merchandise stores, 10.2%; apparel and accessory stores, 7.9%; and others, 45.4%. Retail sales in the New York City metropolitan area totaled $140.7 billion in 1992, or 7.4% of the US total.

The state's long border with Canada, its important ports on Lakes Erie and Ontario, and its vast harbor on New York Bay ensure it a major role in US foreign trade. About 24% of US waterborne imports and exports pass through the New York Customs District (including New York City, Albany, and Newark and Perth Amboy, N.J.), which handled about $23.5 billion in merchandise exports in 1994. Exports of goods originating within New York totaled $34.2 billion in 1996, 3d among the states. Exporters located within the state shipped merchandise valued at nearly $45 billion in 1996.

31CONSUMER PROTECTION

The State Consumer Protection Board in the Executive Department was created in 1970, and is headed by an executive director appointed by the governor with the advice and consent of the senate. The board coordinates the activities of all state agencies performing consumer protection functions, represents consumer interests before federal, state, and local bodies (including the Public Service Commission), and encourages consumer education and research, but it has no enforcement powers. These are vested in the Bureau of Consumer Frauds and Protection within the Department of Law, under the direction of the attorney general. The Department of Public Service has regulatory authority over several areas of key interest to consumers, including gas, electric, and telephone rates. Especially during the 1960s and 1970s, consumer groups complained that the department was more sensitive to the interests of the utility companies than to those of consumers.

State law outlaws unfair or deceptive trade practices and provides for small-claims courts, where consumers can take action at little cost to themselves. New York licenses and regulates automobile repair services, permits advertising of prescription drug prices, and requires unit pricing. A "cooling-off" period for home purchase contracts is mandated, and standards have been established for mobile-home construction. New York has no-fault automobile insurance. In 1974, the legislature outlawed sex discrimination in banking, credit, and insurance policy transactions; the state's fair-trade law, which allowed price fixing on certain items, was repealed in 1975. The Fair Credit Reporting Act passed in 1977, allows consumers access to their credit bureau files. A 1984 "lemon law" entitles purchasers of defective new cars to repairs, a refund, or a replacement under specified circumstances. A similar law for used cars requires a written warranty for most essential mechanical components.

Extremely influential both within the state and throughout the US is the Consumers Union (CU), established as a nonprofit corporation at Mt. Vernon in 1936. CU derives its income solely from sales of its magazine, *Consumer Reports,* and other publications. The magazine embraces many consumer interests, but the bulk of each issue consists of product reports on items as varied as stereos and canned chili. Product tests are conducted by CU's own research staff. Ratings of products may not be cited in advertising or used by product manufacturers or distributors for any commercial purpose.

32BANKING

New York City is the major US banking center. Banking is one of the state's leading industries, ranking 1st in the US in assets and employing 234,582 people in 4,432 establishments as December 1992. Five of the nations's ten largest banks were located in New York in 1992: Citicorp, with assets of $213.7 billion; Chemical Banking Corp., $139.6 billion; J.P. Morgan & Co., $102.9 billion; Chase Manhattan Corp., $95.9 billion; and Bankers Trust New York Corp., $72.4 billion.

In 1996 there were 278 insured depository institutions in New York. Among these were 166 commercial banks, 28 of which were Federal Reserve members. As of 1996, New York's commercial banks held total assets of $922.8 billion; deposits totaled $547.3 billion. New York led the nation in both categories.

There were 112 insured savings banks in 1996, 57 state-chartered, and 55 federally chartered. In 1996, savings banks held assets of $129.5 billion.

33INSURANCE

Like banking, insurance is big business in New York. Three of the ten top US life insurance companies—Metropolitan Life, New York Life, and Equitable Life Assurance—had their headquarters in New York, and the industry employed 277,000 workers in the state in 1990.

Premiums written in the state at the end of 1995 totaled $28.8 billion for all types of insurance by both state and out-of-state companies. That same year, New Yorkers paid $7.8 billion for life insurance, $5.2 billion for health insurance, and $9.0 billion for automobile insurance. Automobile insurance is compulsory for all owners of motor vehicles in the state. A no-fault system is in effect.

In 1995, New Yorkers held 13.5 million life insurance policies with a value of $953.3 billion (2d in the US). The average amount of life insurance per family increased from $111,600 in 1991 to $136,100 in 1995. At the end of 1995, 86 companies were licensed to sell life insurance in the state. A total of 208 New York fire and casualty companies were licensed in the state at the end of 1994.

34SECURITIES

New York City is the capital of the US securities market. In 1994, nearly 11% of all broker-dealers in the US were registered to conduct business in the state. The New York Stock Exchange (NYSE) is by far the largest organized securities market in the nation; in 1997, over 50 million individual investors and 10,000 institutional investors bought and sold securities issued by nearly 3,000 companies. The NYSE began as an agreement among 24 brokers, known as the Buttonwood Agreement, in 1792; the exchange adopted its first constitution in 1817 and took on its present name in 1863. A clear sign of the growth of the NYSE is the development of its communications system. Stock tickers were first introduced in 1867; a faster ticker, installed in 1930, was capable of printing 500 characters a minute. By 1964, this was no longer fast enough, and a 900-character-a-minute ticker was introduced. Annual registered share volume increased from 1.8 billion in 1965 to 7.6 billion in 1978 following the introduction in 1976 of a new data line capable of handling 36,000 characters a minute. In 1997, there were 480 firms with seats on the NYSE. In June of that year, the New York Stock Exchange converted stock quotes to sixteenths of a dollar, or increments of 6.25 cents. In January 2000, it plans to switch to a decimal system. The New York Futures Exchange was incorporated in 1979 as a wholly owned subsidiary of the NYSE and began trading in 1980. It also deals in options on futures.

The American Stock Exchange (AMEX) is the 2d-leading US securities market, but the AMEX ranks far below the NYSE in both volume and value of securities. The AMEX traces its origins to the outdoor trading in unlisted securities that began on Wall and Hanover streets in the 1840s, the exchange was organized as the New York Curb Agency in 1908; the exchange moved indoors, but continued to use the hand signals developed by outdoor traders. The AMEX adopted its current name in 1953. Constitutional changes in 1976 for the first time permitted qualified issues to be traded on both the AMEX and the NYSE as well as on other exchanges. This Intermarket Trading System (ITS) began in 1978. In 1996, the hand signals used in trading on the AMEX for over 100 years were replaced by a computerized communication system.

The National Association of Securities Dealers Automated Quotations (NASDAQ), created in 1971, is a highly active exchange for over-the-counter securities. New York City is also a major center for trading in commodity futures. Leading commodity exchanges are the New York Coffee and Sugar Exchange; the New York Cocoa Exchange; the New York Cotton Exchange; the Commodity Exchange, Inc. (COMEX), specializing in gold, silver, and copper futures; and the New York Mercantile Exchange, which trades in futures for potatoes, platinum, palladium, silver coins, beef, and gold, among other items. Bonds may be issued in New York by cities, counties, towns, villages, school districts, and fire districts, as well as by quasi-independent authorities.

35 PUBLIC FINANCE

New York State and New York City have the 2d- and 3d-largest budgets (behind California), respectively, of all states or municipalities in the US. The wide range of services offered, combined with a shrinking tax base, led to serious financial trouble for both the state and the city during the mid-1970s.

The New York State budget is prepared by the Division of the Budget and submitted annually by the governor to the legislature for amendment and approval. The fiscal year runs from 1 April to 31 March.

Under the Rockefeller administration, the state budget expanded rapidly from about $1.8 billion in 1958/59 to $8.5 billion in 1973/74. This trend has continued. The following is a summary of estimated state revenues and expenditures for 1995 (in thousands), on a cash basis:

REVENUES	1989/90	1995
Taxes		
Property	$18,399,741	26,918,482
Sales and gross receipts	15,711,965	16,705,003
Income	21,429,387	17,589,489
TOTAL	$58,764,950	61,212,974
CHARGES AND MISCELLANEOUS		
Current charges	$ 9,319,800	3,649,034
Interest earnings	4,515,693	5,013,139
Special assessments	78,494	2,108,352
Other	3,104,029	19,013,611
TOTAL	17,078,016	29,784,136
TOTAL REVENUES	$90,348,861	90,997,110
EXPENDITURES		
Education	$25,411,219	17,494,460
Health and social concerns	16,002,105	31,808,624
Financial administration	1,338,885	2,798,889
Transportation (highways)	4,796,385	3,046,882
Utilities	9,669,421	4,169,888
Public safety (police)	3,391,355	2,620,442
Natural resources	395,636	322,292
Other	52,050,594	19,110,581
TOTAL GENERAL EXPENDITURES	$90,332,396	81,371,988

As of 1995, the total debt of state and local governments in New York was $68.5 billion, or $3,775 per capita.

36 TAXATION

On a per capita basis, New York's state taxes are well above the national average, but far from the highest. In fiscal year 1995, New York ranked 7th, with per capita local taxes of $1,890.96. In fiscal year 1993, combined state and local revenues ranked 2d to Alaska's. Personal income tax is the state's largest source of revenue. Personal income tax rates in 1997 ranged from 4% to 6.85%. The basic corporate tax was 9% on net income. The state imposes a 4% sales tax, but cities and towns may levy an additional tax. The estate tax ranges from 2% of the first $50,000 to a maximum of 21% on amounts over $10,100,000. Other taxes include charges on motor fuel, cigarettes, alcoholic beverages, petroleum gross receipts, and motor vehicle and highway usage, plus a bank tax, unincorporated business tax, insurance taxes, pari-mutuel taxes, and a real estate transfer tax. State tax receipts in fiscal year 1996 totaled approximately $32.2 billion.

37 ECONOMIC POLICY

New York has created a number of incentives for business to foster new jobs and encourage economic prosperity. Among these are government-owned industrial park sites, state aid in the creation of county and city master plans, state recruitment and screening of industrial employees, programs for the promotion of research and development, and state help in bidding on federal procurement contracts. Through Empire State Development, New York State provides a full range of technical assistance. Representatives of the Division of International Commerce call on firms in Canada, Asia, and Europe; the division maintains offices in London, Tokyo, Montreal, Toronto, and Frankfurt, Germany. The Strategic Business Division, through its ten regional offices, encourages the retention and expansion of existing facilities and the attraction of new job-creating investments. Other divisions aid small business and minority and women's business.

The state administers a number of financial programs to attract or retain businesses. Among these are low interest loans and grants for small businesses or for firms that create substantial numbers of jobs; grants and low cost loans for the development of industrial parks; and working capital loans to help companies at risk of downsizing. The state awards both grants and loans to manufacturing companies to encourage productivity improvements and modernization. It also seeks to encourage economic development in distressed rural communities with low interest loans for small businesses located in such areas. To promote technological innovation, the state provides debt and equity financing for technology based start-up companies.

38 HEALTH

Health presents a mixed picture in New York State. The state has some of the finest hospital and medical education facilities in the US, but it also has large numbers of the needy with serious health problems.

Infant deaths per 1,000 live births were 7.7 in 1994. The birthrate of 15.1 was equivalent to the national rate. New York State was one of the first states to liberalize its abortion laws, in 1970. A total of 149,594 legal abortions were performed in the state in 1994, of which 103,896 were in New York City. The 1994 state ratio of 536 legal abortions to 1,000 live births was higher than that of any other state, except California.

The death rate of 914 per 100,000 residents in 1994 reflected New York's older-than-average population. The state ranks above the national average in deaths due to heart disease and malignant neoplasms (cancer), but below the national average in deaths due to cerebrovascular diseases, suicide, and accidents. In 1992, New Yorkers had the highest rate of mortality from coronary heart disease in the US according to the American Heart Association. Stroke death rates were low (23.1 per 100,000) in the same year. Major causes of death in 1994 (with their rates per 100,000 population) included heart disease, 342.5; cancer, 213.0; cerebrovascular diseases, 44.4; accidents and adverse effects, 23.4; and suicide, 8.4. The AIDS rate was 45.2 per 100,000 residents in 1994.

Major public health issues in the 1990s included emerging infections such as multidrug resistant TB, chronic diseases such as those related to smoking, HIV/AIDS, violent and abusive behavior, and the care of vulnerable populations.

New York City was heavily hit by the outbreak, first recognized in 1981, of AIDS, usually fatal in time. As of 1994, nearly 84,331 of all reported AIDS cases (19.1% of the US total) had been in New York, more than in any other state.

In 1995, New York State had 286 hospitals, with 93,074 beds, more than any other state. In 1995, hospitals in New York recorded 2,506,198 admissions, performed 1,674,516 surgical operations, had an occupancy rate of 72.1% (2d highest in the nation), and employed 434,819 persons with a total payroll of $15.8 billion. Medical personnel licensed to practice in the state included 60,184 active nonfederal physicians (1996), 191,895 active registered nurses (1996), and 16,534 dentists (1996).

About 85% of all New Yorkers are covered by hospital and surgical insurance. The average daily expense per inpatient per day by hospitals in 1995 was $909; the average cost per patient stay was $8,077.

39SOCIAL WELFARE

A 1938 New York constitutional provision mandated that the care and support of the needy shall be a state concern. Social welfare is a major public enterprise in the state; the growth of poverty relief programs has been enormous. The number of persons qualifying under the Aid for Families with Dependent Children program was 1.2 million in 1996, when the average payment was $687 per person per month. In 1996, 2.1 million residents received monthly food stamp allowances averaging $81.56.

The cost to the federal government for the National School Lunch Program was $390.2 million in 1991.

With the enactment of the Personal Responsibility and Work Opportunity Reconciliation Act of 1996, the US government has changed the form and regulations for many of its social welfare programs; most significantly, it replaces Aid to Families with Dependent Children (AFDC), an open-ended entitlement program, with Temporary Assistance for Needy Families (TANF), a limited system of assistance funded largely through federal block grants. The reform act also impacts the food stamp program, the Supplemental Security Income program, and the child nutrition program. The law took effect on 1 July 1997 and provided $16.38 billion in block grants for fiscal years 1997–2002. The grants are to be divided among the states based on an equation involving the numbers of former AFDC recipients in each state. Because many of the bill's provisions have yet to be implemented into state-by-state policy, it was not possible to include the details of each state's programs for this edition of this work.

Federal Social Security benefits were paid to 2.9 million New Yorkers in 1995, averaging $768 a month; additionally, 588,538 residents received monthly payments averaging $402 from Supplementary Security Income. The average weekly unemployment benefit was $207.71 in 1995.

40HOUSING

Census data show that housing in New York State differs in many ways from the national housing pattern. In 1996, the state had an estimated 7,332,000 housing units, of which 6,672,000 were occupied. As of 1990, about 46% of New York's housing units were in New York City. The first striking feature of the state's housing stock is its age: over 35% of year-round housing units in the state (40% in the city) were in structures built in 1939 or before compared with the US average of 18.4%. In Buffalo, 68% were built in 1939 or before. Only 9.4% of New York State's dwelling units were built between 1980 and 1990; only 6.8% of New York City's and 1.8% of Buffalo's were built during those years, while the US average was 20.7%.

A second striking feature of housing in the state is the dominance of multi-unit dwellings. New York State had the lowest percentage of owner-occupied housing (47.9%) of all states in the US in 1990. From 1990 to 1992, 27,200 new housing units were completed in the New York City area, of which less than one-third were one-family houses. During the same period, however, a total of 92,400 new units were completed in the greater New York City area (including suburban New Jersey and Connecticut), of which nearly two-thirds were one-family houses. In 1990, the last year for which figures are available, the median monthly cost for an owner with a mortgage in the New York City area of New York was $1,147 and $400 for

an owner without a mortgage. The median rent was $579 per month. Housing differences in New York City offer far greater contrasts than units per structure: the posh apartment houses of Manhattan and the hovels of the South Bronx both count as multi-unit dwellings. Characteristic of housing in New York is a system of rent controls that began in 1943.

The tight housing market—which may have contributed to the exodus of New Yorkers from the state—was not helped by the slump in housing construction from the mid-1970s to the mid-1980s. In 1972, permits were issued for 111,282 units valued at $2.1 billion. By 1975, however, only 32,623 units worth $756 million were authorized; in 1982 there were only 25,280 units worth $1.1 billion, and in 1996, 34,895 units valued at $3.1 billion were authorized. In New York City, more units were demolished than built every year from 1974 to 1981. The drop in construction of multi-unit dwellings was even more noticeable: from 64,959 units in 1972 to 11,740 units in 1982. In 1993, only 7,723 multi-unit dwellings were authorized. The overall decline in construction was coupled with a drastic drop in new public housing.

Direct state aid for housing is limited. Governmental and quasiindependent agencies dealing with housing include the Division of Housing and Community Renewal of the Executive Department, which makes loans and grants to municipalities for slum clearance and construction of low-income housing, is responsible for supervising the operation of 427 housing developments (1984), and administers rent-control and rent-stabilization laws; the New York State Housing Finance Agency, empowered to issue notes and bonds for various construction projects, not limited to housing; the State of New York Mortgage Agency, which may purchase existing mortgage loans from banks in order to make funds available for the banks to make new mortgage loans, and which also offers mortgage insurance; and the New York State Urban Development Corporation (UDC), a multi-billion dollar agency designed to raise capital for all types of construction, including low-income housing. During 1995/96, New York received $2.6 billion in aid from the US Department of Housing and Urban Development, including $440 million in community development block grants.

41EDUCATION

The Board of Regents and the State Education Department govern education from prekindergarten to graduate school, and are constitutionally responsible for setting educational policy, standards, and rules—and are legally required to ensure that the entities they oversee carry them out. The board and department also oversee 38 licensed professions, provide vocational and educational services to people with disabilities, guide local government records programs, and operate the State Archives, Library, and Museum.

The percentage of high school graduates—87.5% from 1992 through 1994—among New Yorkers ages 18 through 24 was slightly above the US average. The percentage of New York college graduates—23.7%—was above the US average.

In the fall of 1995, a total of 2,77,876 students were enrolled in public elementary and secondary schools in the state; of these, nearly 7.8% were in kindergarten, 45.3% in grades 1–6, 41.5% in grades 7–12, and nearly 5.4% in ungraded classes. Public schools in the state employed 229,335 professionals in the fall of 1995, of whom 197,591 were classroom teachers. The average dropout rate for public high schools in the state was 4.1% in 1994. New York State had 2,149 nonpublic elementary and secondary schools in the fall of 1995, with enrollment of 477,889.

There were 251 institutions of higher learning in 1995/96, 76 of them public two year institutions. Enrollment in all institutions of higher learning totaled 1,016,639 in the fall of 1995. Of that total, 356,575 degree-credit students were enrolled full-time at public colleges and universities, and 301,942 at private institutions. About 21% of all full-time students were in public two-year colleges. A total of 203,000 undergraduate and graduate degrees were confirmed in 1994/95.

There are two massive public university systems: the State University of New York (SUNY) and the City University of New York (CUNY). Established in 1948, SUNY in 1995 was the largest university system in the country, with 4 university centers, 7 health sciences centers, 13 university colleges of arts and sciences, 4 specialized colleges, 6 agricultural and technical colleges, 5 statutory colleges (allied with private universities), and 30 locally sponsored community colleges. SUNY's total enrollment in the fall of 1995 was 382,859. Of the university centers, Buffalo enrolled 24,493 students; Albany, 15,996; and Binghamton, 9,281 undergraduates. The City University of New York was created in 1961, although many of its 19 component institutions were founded much earlier. CUNY's total degree-credit enrollment in the fall of 1995 was 205,835, of whom 118,901 were full-time university students. Under an open-enrollment policy adopted in 1970, every New York City resident with a high school diploma is guaranteed the chance to earn a college degree within the CUNY system (which CUNY campus the student attends is determined by grade point average).

The oldest private university in the state is Columbia University, founded in New York City as Kings College in 1754. Columbia had 19,302 students in 1995/96; another 2,218 (all women) were enrolled in Barnard College in 1995/96, and there were approximately 4,585 students (male and female) in Columbia University Teachers College in 1995/96. Other major private institutions are Cornell University in Ithaca (1865), with 20,625 students in 1995/96; Fordham University in Manhattan and the Bronx (1841), 13,909; New York University in Manhattan (1831), 35,835; Rensselaer Polytechnic Institute in Troy (1824), 6,553; St. John's University in Queens (1870), 17,393; Syracuse University (1870), 18,804; and the University of Rochester (1850), 9,457. Among the state's many smaller but highly distinguished institutions are Hamilton College, the Juilliard School, the New School for Social Research, Rockefeller University, Sarah Lawrence College, Vassar College, and Yeshiva University.

The educational work of New York State is vested in the Education Department, under the direction of the Regents of the University of the State of New York. The Board of Regents consists of 16 persons elected by the state legislature to 5-year terms. The commissioner of education, who heads the state Education Department and is appointed by the Regents, also serves as president of the University of the State of New York (which should not be confused with SUNY). Unique features of education in the state are the "Regents exams," uniform subject examinations administered to all high school students, and the Regents Scholarships Tuition Assistance Program (TAP), a higher-education aid program. Recipients of these awards must be in full-time attendance at an approved institution in New York State and must have resided in the state at least one year before enrollment. The state passed a "truth in testing" law in 1979, giving students the right to see their graded college and graduate school entrance examinations, as well as information on how the test results were validated.

During 1995, the public school system consisted of 709 districts; New York City constituted a single district. Receipts of all public school systems in the state totaled $25.9 billion in 1995, of which nearly $10.1 billion came from state sources and $1.5 billion from federal sources. Teachers' salaries averaged $48,115 in 1995/96.

42ARTS

New York City is the cultural capital of the state, and leads the nation in both the creative and the performing arts. The state's foremost arts center is Lincoln Center for the Performing Arts, in Manhattan. Facilities at Lincoln Center include Avery Fisher Hall (which opened as Philharmonic Hall in 1962), the home of the New York Philharmonic; the Metropolitan Opera House (1966), where the Metropolitan Opera Company performs; and the New York State Theater, which presents both the New York City Opera and the New York City Ballet. Also at Lincoln Center are the Juilliard School and the Library and Museum of the Performing Arts. The best-known arts center outside New York City is the Saratoga Performing Arts Center at Saratoga Springs. During the summer, the Saratoga Center presents performances by the New York City Ballet and the Philadelphia Orchestra. Artpark, a state park at Lewiston, has a 2,324-seat theater for operas and musicals, and offers art exhibits during the summer. Classical music, opera, and plays are performed at the Chautauqua Festival, which has been held every summer since 1874.

The state of New York generated $942,000 in federal funds to support arts programs in 1996. The NEA contributed $13,956,000 to the state's programs and $12,416,000 to the New York State Council on the Arts. The state gave the Council on the Arts funding and received contributions from private sources. Private sources gave $899 million. Audiences for the state's arts programs totaled 220,142,000. There were 1,503,041 contributing artists. The state offered arts education programs to about 978,000 school children. In 1996, the state of New York had 2,000 arts associations and 90 local art groups. The New York State Council on the Arts contributed to the Arts Connection of New York City and to the National Book Foundation.

In 1995/96, the NEA provided for arts education programs administered by the New York State Council on the Arts. The Council on the Arts also received monies from the NEA's state and Regional Program. Other programs receiving state and federal assistance include: the Ballet Hispanics; Chamber Music America, Inc.; Cooper Union for the Advancement of Science; Glimmerglass Opera, Inc.; House Foundation for the Arts; Joyce Foundation, Inc.; Manhattan Theatre Club; New York City Opera, Inc.; and the Paul Taylor Dance Foundation.

In addition to its many museums, New York City has more than 350 galleries devoted to the visual and plastic arts. The city's most famous artists' district is Greenwich Village, which still holds an annual outdoor art show, although after the 1950s many artists moved to SoHo (Manhattan on the West Side between Canal and Houston Streets), NoHo (immediately north of Houston Street), the East Village, and Tribeca (between Canal Street and the World Trade Center). By the early 1980s, artists seeking space at reasonable prices were moving to Long Island City in Queens, to areas of Brooklyn, or out of the city entirely, to places such as Hoboken and Paterson in New Jersey. During the late 1940s and early 1950s, abstract painters—including Jackson Pollock, Mark Rothko, and Willem de Kooning—helped make the city a center of the avant garde.

At the same time, poets such as Frank O'Hara and John Ashbery sought verbal analogues to developments in the visual arts, and an urbane, improvisatory literature was created. New York has enjoyed a vigorous poetic tradition throughout its history, most notably with the works of Walt Whitman (who served as editor of the *Brooklyn Eagle* from 1846 to 1848) and through Hart Crane's mythic vision of the city in his long poem *The Bridge*. The emergence of New York as the center of the US publishing and communications industries fostered the growth of a literary marketplace, attracting writers from across the country and the world. Early New York novelists included Washington Irving, Edgar Allan Poe, and Herman Melville; among the many who made their home in the city in the 20th century were Thomas Wolfe and Norman Mailer. The simultaneous growth of the Broadway stage made New York City a vital forum for playwriting, songwriting, and theatrical production.

There are more than 35 Broadway theaters—large theaters in midtown Manhattan presenting full-scale, sometimes lavish productions with top-rank performers. "Off Broadway" productions are often of high professional quality, though typically in smaller theaters, outside the midtown district, often with smaller casts and less costly settings. "Off-Off Broadway" productions range from small experimental theaters on the fringes of the city to performances in nightclubs and cabarets. The New York metropolitan area has hundreds of motion picture theaters—more than 65 in Manhattan alone, not counting special series at the Museum of Modern Art and other cultural institutions. In the 1970s, New York City made a determined and successful effort to attract motion picture production companies.

New York's leading symphony orchestra is the New York Philharmonic, whose history dates back to the founding of the Philharmonic Society of New York in 1842. Among the principal conductors of the orchestra have been Gustav Mahler, Josef Willem Mengelberg, Wilhelm Furtwangler, Arturo Toscanini, Leonard Bernstein, Pierre Boulez, and Zubin Mehta. Leading US and foreign orchestras and soloists appear at both Avery Fisher Hall and Carnegie Hall, built in 1892 and famed for its acoustics. Important orchestras outside New York City include the Buffalo Philharmonic, which performs at Kleinhans Music Hall, the Rochester Philharmonic, and the Eastman Philharmonia, the orchestra of the Eastman School of Music (University of Rochester).

New York City is one of the world centers of ballet. Of special renown is the New York City Ballet, whose principal choreographer until his death in 1983 was George Balanchine. Many other ballet companies, including the American Ballet Theatre and the Alvin Ailey American Dance Theatre, make regular appearances in New York. Rochester, Syracuse, Cooperstown, Chautauqua, and Binghamton have opera companies, and Lake George has an opera festival. Jazz and popular artists perform at more than 60 night spots in New York City. The Westbury Music Fair (Long Island) presents a wide-ranging annual program of musical entertainment, and many leading US performers play the Catskill resorts regularly. New York City is a major link in the US songwriting, music-publishing, and recording industries.

The New York State Council on the Arts is the nation's leading state arts funding mechanism. Its appropriation averages about 25% of the total for all state arts agencies.

43 LIBRARIES AND MUSEUMS

New York State has three of the world's largest libraries, and New York City has several of the world's most famous museums. The state had 761 public libraries, 263 academic and research libraries, and 142 state institutional libraries in 1991. The New York State Library in Albany coordinated 23 public library systems covering every county in the state, with book holdings of 63,819,417 volumes and a combined circulation of 116,716,286 volumes. The public libraries received $557,244,875 during that year, of which $3,538,476 came from the federal government, $58,971,261 from the state government, and the rest from local sources.

The leading public library systems and their operating statistics as of 1996 were the New York Public Library, 11,615,172 volumes and 11,392,565 circulation; Brooklyn Public Library, 6,395,664 volumes and 10,144,433 circulation; Queens Borough Public Library, 8,668,948 volumes and 14,829,837 circulation; Suffolk Cooperative system, 8,670,848 volumes and 1,647,401 circulation; and Buffalo and Erie County system, 3,663,678 volumes and 8,666,198 circulation.

Chartered in 1895, the New York Public Library (NYPL) is the most complete municipal library system in the world. The library's main building, at 5th Avenue and 42d St., is one of the city's best-known landmarks; 78 operating branch libraries and three bookmobiles serve the needs of Manhattan, the Bronx, and Staten Island. The NYPL is a repository for every book published in the US, with a book stock of 8 million volumes in 1991. The NYPL also operates the Library and Museum of the Performing Arts at Lincoln Center; the Schomburg Center for Research in Black Culture; and the Science, Industry, and Business Library that opened in May 1996.

Two private university libraries—at Columbia University (6,142,293 volumes in 1991) and Cornell University (5,468,870)–rank among the world's major libraries. Other major university libraries in the state, with their 1991 book holdings, are Syracuse University, 2,178,144; New York University, 2,037,636; the State University of New York at Buffalo, 2,154,507; and the University of Rochester, 2,250,337.

There are about 622 museums in New York State; about 150 are major museums, of which perhaps 80% are in New York City. In addition, some 579 sites of historic importance are maintained by local historical societies. Major art museums in New York City include the Metropolitan Museum of Art, with more than one million art objects and paintings from virtually every period and culture; the Cloisters, a branch of the Metropolitan Museum devoted entirely to medieval art and architecture; the Frick collection; the Whitney Museum of American Art; the Brooklyn Museum; and two large modern collections, the Museum of Modern Art and the Solomon R. Guggenheim Museum (the latter designed by Frank Lloyd Wright in a distinctive spiral pattern). The Jewish Museum, the Museum of the American Indian, and the museum and reference library of the Hispanic Society of America specialize in cultural history.

The sciences are represented by the American Museum of Natural History, famed for its dioramas of humans and animals in natural settings and for its massive dinosaur skeletons; the Hayden Planetarium; the New York Botanical Garden and New York Zoological Society Park (Bronx Zoo), both in the Bronx. Also of interest are the Museum of the City of New York, the Museum of the New-York Historical Society, the South Street Seaport Museum, and the New York Aquarium.

The New York State Museum in Albany contains natural history collections and historical artifacts. Buffalo has several museums of note, including the Albright-Knox Art Gallery (for contemporary art), the Buffalo Museum of Science, and the Buffalo and Erie County Historical Society museum.

Among the state's many other fine museums, the Everson Museum of Art (Syracuse), the Rochester Museum and Science Center, the National Baseball Hall of Fame and Museum (Cooperstown), and the Corning Museum of Glass deserve special mention. Buffalo, New Rochelle, Rochester, Syracuse, and Utica have zoos.

44 COMMUNICATIONS

New York City is the hub of the entire US communications network. Postal service was established in New York State in 1692; at the same time, the first General Letter Office was begun in New York City. By the mid-19th century, postal receipts in the state accounted for more than 20% of the US total. "Fast mail" service by train started in the 1870s, with the main routes leading from New York City to either Chicago or St. Louis via Indianapolis and Cincinnati. Mail was carried by air experimentally from Garden City to Mineola, Long Island, in 1911; the first regular airmail service in the US started in 1917, between New York City and Washington, D.C., via Philadelphia.

Telephone service in New York is provided primarily by the New York Telephone Co., but also by 40 smaller companies throughout the state. As of March 1993, 93.7% of New York's 6,875,000 occupied housing units had telephones.

Until 31 December 1983, New York Telephone was part of the Bell System, whose parent organization was the American Telephone and Telegraph Co. (AT&T). Effective 1 January 1984, as the result of a US Justice Department antitrust suit, AT&T divested itself of 22 Bell operating companies, which regrouped into seven independent regional telephone companies to provide local telephone service in the US. One of these companies, NYNEX, is the parent company of New York Telephone. AT&T, which continued to supply long-distance telephone services to New Yorkers (along with competitive carriers such as MCI, ITT, and GTE), is headquartered in New York City.

Domestic telegraph service is provided by the Western Union Telegraph Co., ITT World Communications, RCA Global Communications, and Western Union International. All four companies have their headquarters in New York City. New York State had 161 AM stations and 309 FM stations operating in 1996. New York City operates its own radio stations, WNYC-AM and FM, devoted largely to classical music and educational programming. There were 55 television stations (including 13 noncommercial educational) in the state in 1993; of these, 9 were operating in New York City. The city is the headquarters for most of the major US television networks, including the American Broadcasting Co. (now part of Walt Disney Corp.), Columbia Broadcasting System (owned by the Westinghouse Corp.), National Broadcasting Co. (owned by General Electric), Westinghouse Broadcasting (Group W), Metromedia, and the Public Broadcasting Service (PBS). Thirteen educational television stations serve all the state's major populated areas, and the metropolitan area's PBS affiliate, WNET (licensed in Newark, N.J.), is a leading producer of programs for the network. As of 1996, 35 large cable television systems served the state.

45PRESS

A pioneer in the establishment of freedom of the press, New York is the leader of the US newspaper, magazine, and book-publishing industries. The first major test of press freedom in the colonies came in 1734, when a German-American printer, John Peter Zenger, was arrested on charges of sedition and libel. In his newspaper, the *New-York Weekly Journal*, Zenger had published articles criticizing the colonial governor of New York. Zenger's lawyer, Andrew Hamilton, argued that because the charges in the article were true, they could not be libelous. The jury's acceptance of this argument freed Zenger and established the right of the press to criticize those in power. Two late decisions involving a New York newspaper also struck blows for press freedom. In *New York Times v. Sullivan* (1964), the US Supreme Court ruled that a public official could not win a libel suit against a newspaper unless he could show that its statements about him were not only false but also malicious or in reckless disregard of the truth. In 1971, the *New York Times* was again involved in a landmark case when the federal government tried—and failed—to prevent the newspaper from publishing the Pentagon Papers, a collection of secret documents concerning the war in Viet Nam.

All of New York City's major newspapers have claims to fame. The *Times* is the nation's "newspaper of record," excelling in the publication of speeches, press conferences, and government reports. It is widely circulated to US libraries and is often cited in research. The *New York Post,* founded in 1801, is the oldest US newspaper published continuously without change of name. The *New York Daily News* has the largest daily and Sunday circulation of all general-interest newspapers in the US. The *Wall Street Journal,* published Monday through Friday, is a truly national paper, presenting mostly business news in four regional editions. Many historic New York papers first merged and then—bearing compound names like the *Herald-Tribune, Journal-*

American, and *World-Telegram & Sun*—died in the 1950s and 1960s.

In 1997, New York had 33 morning newspapers, 32 evening papers, two all-day papers, and 38 Sunday editions. The following table shows leading papers in New York, with their average daily and Sunday circulations in 1997:

AREA	NAME	DAILY	SUNDAY
Albany	*Times–Union* (m,S)	100,831	156,644
Buffalo	*News* (all day,S)	272,995	361,344
Long Island	*Newsday*	555,203	643,421
New York City	*Daily News* (m,S)	758,509	1,010,504
	Post (all day)	418,255	—
	Times (m,S)	1,157,656	1,746,707
	Wall Street Journal	1,841,188	—
Syracuse	*Post-Standard* (m)	86,175	—
	Herald-Journal (e)	73,119	—
	Herald–Amer./Post–Stand. (S)	—	204,628

The leading newspaper chain is the Gannett group. All the major news agencies have offices in New York City, and the Associated Press has its headquarters there.

Many leading US magazines are published in New York City, including the newsmagazines *Time* and *Newsweek,* business journals like *Fortune, Forbes,* and *Business Week,* and hundreds of consumer and trade publications. *Reader's Digest* is published in Pleasantville. Two weeklies closely identified with New York are of more than local interest. While the *New Yorker* carries up-to-date listings of cultural events and exhibitions in New York City, the excellence of its journalism, criticism, fiction, and cartoons has long made it a literary standard-bearer for the entire nation. *New York* magazine influenced the writing style and graphic design of the 1960s and set the pattern for a new wave of state and local magazines that avoided boosterism in favor of independent reporting and commentary. Another weekly, the *Village Voice* (actually a tabloid newspaper), became the prototype for a host of alternative or "underground" journals during the 1960s.

New York City is also the center of the nation's book-publishing industry. New York publishers include McGraw–Hill, Macmillan, Simon & Schuster, and Random House; many book publishers are subsidiaries of other companies.

46ORGANIZATIONS

The 1992 Census of Service Industries counted 4,297 organizations in New York, including 815 business associations; 2,395 civic, social, and fraternal associations; and 1,087 other membership organizations.

The United Nations is the best-known organization to have its headquarters in New York. The UN Secretariat, completed in 1951, remains one of the most familiar landmarks of New York City. Hundreds of US nonprofit organizations also have their national headquarters in New York City. General and service organizations operating out of New York City include the American Field Service, Boys Clubs of America, Girls Clubs of America, Girl Scouts of the USA, Young Women's Christian Associations of the USA (YWCA), and Associated YM-YWHAs of Greater New York (the Jewish equivalent of the YMCA and YWCA). Among the cultural and educational groups are the American Academy of Arts and Letters, Authors League of America, Children's Book Council, Modern Language Association of America, and PEN American Center.

Among the environmental and animal welfare organizations with headquarters in the city are the American Society for the Prevention of Cruelty to Animals (ASPCA), Friends of Animals, Fund for Animals, National Audubon Society, Bide-A-Wee Home Association, Environmental Defense Fund, and American Kennel Club.

Many medical, health, and charitable organizations have their national offices in New York City, including Alcoholics Anonymous, American Foundation for the Blind, National Society to Prevent Blindness, CARE, American Cancer Society, United Cerebral Palsy Associations, Child Welfare League of America, American Diabetes Association, National Multiple Sclerosis Society, Muscular Dystrophy Association, and Planned Parenthood Federation of America.

Leading ethnic and religious organizations based in the city include the American Bible Society, National Conference of Christians and Jews, Hadassah, United Jewish Appeal, American Jewish Committee, American Jewish Congress, National Association for the Advancement of Colored People (NAACP), United Negro College Fund, Congress of Racial Equality, and National Urban League.

There are many commercial, trade, and professional organizations headquartered in New York City. Among the better known are the Actors' Equity Association, American Arbitration Association, American Booksellers Association, American Federation of Musicians, American Institute of Chemical Engineers, American Society of Civil Engineers, American Society of Composers, Authors, and Publishers (ASCAP), American Society of Journalists and Authors, American Insurance Association, Magazine Publishers Association, American Management Associations, American Society of Mechanical Engineers, and American Institute of Physics.

Sports organizations centered in New York City include the National Football League, the American and the National Leagues of Professional Baseball Clubs, National Basketball Association, and the US Tennis Association. There are also several influential political and international-affairs groups: the American Civil Liberties Union, Council on Foreign Relations, Trilateral Commission, United Nations Association of the USA, and US Committee for UNICEF.

Major organizations with their headquarters outside New York City include the Consumers Union of the United States (Mt. Vernon), US Chess Federation (New Windsor), and the Thoroughbred Racing Association (Lake Success). Virtually every other major US organization has one or more chapters within the state.

47TOURISM, TRAVEL, AND RECREATION

New York State is a popular destination for both domestic and foreign travelers. Although New York City is the primary attraction, each of the major state regions has features of interest.

Foreign visitors are not the only curiosity seekers who come to New York. Domestic travelers spent $19,950,000 on overnight and day trips within the state in 1993.

A typical visit to New York City might include a boat ride to the Statue of Liberty—a three-hour boat ride around Manhattan; visits to the World Trade Center, the Empire State Building, the UN, Rockefeller Center, and the New York Stock Exchange; walking tours of the Bronx Zoo, Chinatown, and the theater district; and a sampling of the city's many museums, restaurants, shops, and shows.

Second to New York City as a magnet for tourists comes Long Island, with its beaches, racetracks, and other recreational facilities. Attractions of the Hudson Valley include the US Military Academy (West Point), the Franklin D. Roosevelt home at Hyde Park, Bear Mountain State Park, and several wineries. North of Hudson Valley is Albany, with its massive government center, Governor Nelson A. Rockefeller Plaza, often called the Albany Mall; Saratoga Springs, home of an arts center, racetrack, and spa; and the Adirondack region, with its forest preserve, summer and winter resorts, and abundant hunting and fishing. Northwest of the Adirondacks, in the St. Lawrence River, are the Thousand Islands—actually some 1,800 small islands extending over about

50 mi (80 km), and popular among freshwater fishermen and summer vacationers.

Scenic sites in central New York include the resorts of the Catskills and the scenic marvels of the Finger Lakes region, including Taughannock Falls in Trumansburg, the highest waterfall east of the Rockies. Further west lie Buffalo and Niagara Falls. South of the Niagara Frontier is the Southwest Gateway, among whose dominant features are Chautauqua Lake and Allegany State Park, the state's largest.

The Office of Parks, Recreation and Historic Preservation operates state parks, historic sites, and boat-launching sites. In 1995, a total of 60,124,135 people visited the state parks and historic sites. In that year also, state residents held 1,441,275 hunting licenses and 1,085,119 fishing licenses. The state park system generated $36,939,909 in revenues in 1995.

48SPORTS

New York has ten major league professional sports teams: the New York Yankees and the New York Mets of major league baseball; the New York Giants, the New York Jets (although the Giants' and Jets' stadiums are located in New Jersey), and the Buffalo Bills of the National Football League; the New York Knickerbockers (usually called the Knicks) of the National Basketball Association; the New York Islanders, the New York Rangers and the Buffalo Sabres of the National Hockey League; and the New York-New Jersey Metro Stars of Major League Soccer.

The Yankees have a record of excellence spanning most of this century. They won the American League Pennant 34 times and the World Series 23 times, most recently in 1996, when they defeated the Atlanta Braves in six games. Other championship streaks include the American League Pennant in 1927 and 1928; 1936–39; 1941–43; 1949–53; 1955–58; and 1960–64. In the 28 years between 1936 and 1964, the Yankees competed in 23 World Series, winning 16. The Mets have played in three World Series, winning in 1969 and 1986. The Giants won Super Bowls in 1987 and 1991, and the Jets did so in 1969 in a memorable upset victory over the Baltimore Colts. The Buffalo Bills won the American Football Conference Championship in 1991, 1992, 1993, and 1994, losing the Super Bowl each time. The Knicks won the NBA championship in 1973, and lost in the NBA finals in 1951, 1952, 1953, 1972, and 1994. The Islanders won the Stanley Cup in 1980, 1981, 1982, and 1983. The Rangers won it in 1928, 1933, 1940, and 1994.

Three New York teams, the Nets, Giants, and Jets, moved to New Jersey during the 1970s and 1980s. The Giants and Jets remained, in name, New York teams, (unlike the Nets who are now the New Jersey Nets) although the move remains controversial. In 1986, when the Giants won the Super Bowl, then-mayor of New York Ed Koch, refused them the ticker-tape parade through the city traditionally given in honor of championship teams on the grounds that, their name not withstanding, they are a New Jersey team.

The state also has eight minor league baseball teams, four minor league hockey teams, and a minor league basketball team in Albany.

Horse racing is important to New York State, both as a sports attraction and because of the tax revenues that betting generates. The main thoroughbred race tracks are Aqueduct in Queens, Belmont in Nassau County, and the Saratoga Race Course in Saratoga Springs. Belmont is the home of the Belmont Stakes, one of the three jewels in the Triple Crown of US racing. Saratoga Springs also has a longer harness-racing season at their Saratoga Equine Sports Center facility. Thoroughbred racing is also offered at the Finger Lakes track in Canandaigua. The top tracks for harness racing are Roosevelt Raceway (Westbury, Long Island), Yonkers Raceway, and Monticello Raceway (in the Catskills).

The New York City Off-Track Betting Corporation (OTB), which began operations in April 1971, takes bets on races at the state's major tracks, as well as on some out-of-state races. Off-track betting services operate on a smaller scale on Long Island and in upstate New York.

New York City hosts several major professional tennis tournaments every year: the US Open and the WCT Invitational in Forest Hills, Queens; the Colgate Grand Prix Masters (men) and the Avon Championships (women), both at Madison Square Garden.

Among other professional sports facilities, the Watkins Glen automobile racetrack was, until recently, the site of a Grand Prix race every October. It now hosts a NASCAR Winston Cup race in August. Lake Placid, an important winter-sports region, hosted the 1932 and 1980 Winter Olympics, and continues to host amateur winter sports competitions, such as bobsled racing and ski jumping. New York City's Madison Square Garden is a leading venue for professional boxing and hosts many other sporting events.

In collegiate sports, basketball is perhaps most popular. Historically, the City College of New York produced many nationally ranked teams including the NCAA champions of 1950; that year they also won the NIT (National Invitational Basketball Tournament). St. John's and Syracuse have produced more contemporary nationally prominent teams including the 1989 St. John's team that won the NIT.

The US Military Academy at West Point (Army) won college football national championships in 1944 and 1945, and ranks 12th all time among Division I-A teams with more than 600 victories.

In 1978, New York became the first state to sponsor a statewide amateur athletic event, the Empire State Games. More than 50,000 athletes now compete for a place in the finals, held each summer; the Winter Games, held each March in Lake Placid, host more than 1,000.

The New York City marathon, which is held in October, has become one of the largest, most prestigious marathons in the world.

Other annual sporting events include the Intercollegiate Rowing Association Championship in Syracuse in June, the Adirondack Hot Air Balloon Festival in Glens Falls in September, and the Westminster Kennel Club Dog Show in New York City in February. The Baseball Hall of Fame is located in Cooperstown.

[49]FAMOUS NEW YORKERS

New York State has been the home of five US presidents, eight US vice presidents (three of whom also became president), many statesmen of national and international repute, and a large corps of writers and entertainers.

Martin Van Buren (1782–1862), the 8th US president, became governor of New York in 1828. He was elected to the vice presidency as a Democrat under Andrew Jackson in 1832, and succeeded Jackson in the election of 1836. An unpopular president, Van Buren ran for reelection in 1840 but was defeated, losing even his home state. The 13th US president, Millard Fillmore (1800–74), was elected vice president under Zachary Taylor in 1848. He became president in 1850 when Taylor died. Fillmore's party, the Whigs, did not renominate him in 1852; four years later, he unsuccessfully ran for president as the candidate of the Native American (or Know-Nothing) Party.

Chester Alan Arthur (1829–86), a transplanted New Yorker born in Vermont, became the 21st US president when James Garfield was assassinated. New York's other US presidents had more distinguished careers. Although he was born in New Jersey, Grover Cleveland (1837–1908) served as mayor of Buffalo and as governor of New York before his election to his first presidential term in 1884; he was again elected president in 1892. Theodore

Roosevelt (1858–1919), a Republican, was elected governor in 1898. He won election as vice president under William McKinley in 1900, and became the nation's 26th president after McKinley was murdered in 1901. Roosevelt pursued an aggressive foreign policy, but also won renown as a conservationist and trustbuster. Reelected in 1904, he was awarded the Nobel Peace Prize in 1906 for helping to settle a war between Russia and Japan. Roosevelt declined to run again in 1908. However, he sought the Republican nomination in 1912 and, when defeated, became the candidate of the Progressive (or Bull Moose) Party, losing the general election to Woodrow Wilson.

Franklin Delano Roosevelt (1882–1945), a fifth cousin of Theodore Roosevelt, first ran for national office in 1920, when he was the Democratic vice-presidential choice. A year after losing that election, FDR was crippled by poliomyelitis. He then made an amazing political comeback: he was elected governor of New York in 1928 and served until 1932, when US voters chose him as their 32d president. Reelected in 1936, 1940, and 1944, FDR is the only president ever to have served more than two full terms in office. Roosevelt guided the US through the Great Depression and World War II, and his New Deal programs greatly enlarged the federal role in promoting social welfare.

In addition to Van Buren, Fillmore, and Theodore Roosevelt, five US vice presidents were born in New York: George Clinton (1739–1812), who was also New York State's first elected governor; Daniel D. Tompkins (1774–1825); William A. Wheeler (1819–87); Schuyler Colfax (1823–85); and James S. Sherman 1855–1912). Two other US vice presidents, though not born in New York, were New Yorkers by the time they became vice president. The first was Aaron Burr (1756–1836), perhaps best known for killing Alexander Hamilton in a duel in 1804; Hamilton (b.Nevis, West Indies, 1757–1804) was a leading Federalist, George Washington's treasury secretary, and the only New York delegate to sign the US Constitution in 1787. The second transplanted New Yorker to become vice president was Nelson Aldrich Rockefeller (1908–79). Born in Maine, Rockefeller served as governor of New York State from 1959 to 1973, was for two decades a major force in national Republican politics, and was appointed vice president by Gerald Ford in 1974, serving in that office through January 1977. Alan Greenspan (b. 1926), a chairman of the Federal Reserve, was born in New York City.

Two native New Yorkers have become chief justices of the US: John Jay (1745–1829) and Charles Evans Hughes (1862–1948). A third chief justice, Harlan Fiske Stone (1872–1946), born in New Hampshire, spent most of his legal career in New York City and served as dean of Columbia University's School of Law. Among New Yorkers who became associate justices of the US Supreme Court, Benjamin Nathan Cardozo (1870–1938) is noteworthy. Ruth Bader Ginsberg (b. 1933) was President Bill Clinton's first appointment to the Supreme Court.

Other federal officeholders born in New York include US secretaries of state William Henry Seward (1801–72), Hamilton Fish (1808–93), Elihu Root (1845–1937), Frank B. Kellogg (1856–1937), and Henry L. Stimson (1867–1950). Prominent US senators have included Robert F. Wagner (1877–1953), who sponsored many New Deal laws; Robert F. Kennedy (1925–68), who though born in Massachusetts was elected to represent New York in 1964; Jacob K. Javits (1904–86), who served continuously in the Senate from 1957 through 1980; and Daniel Patrick Moynihan (b.1927), a scholar, author, and former federal bureaucrat who has represented New York since 1977. Colin Powell (b. 1937), first African American to lead the Armed Forces, attended the City University of New York.

The most important—and most colorful—figure in colonial New York was Peter Stuyvesant (b.Netherlands, 1592–1672); as director general of New Netherland, he won the hearty dislike of the Dutch settlers. Signers of the Declaration of Independence in 1776 from New York were Francis Lewis (1713–1803); Philip Livingston (1716–78); Lewis Morris (1726–98), the half-brother of the colonial patriot Gouverneur Morris (1752–1816); and William Floyd (1734–1821).

Other governors who made important contributions to the history of the state include DeWitt Clinton (1769–1828); Alfred E. Smith (1873–1944); Herbert H. Lehman (1878–1963); W. Averell Harriman (1891–1986), who has also held many US diplomatic posts; and Thomas E. Dewey (1902–71). Mario M. Cuomo (b.1932) served three terms as governor from 1982–94. Robert Moses (b.Connecticut, 1888–1981) led in the development of New York's parks and highway transportation system. One of the best-known and best-loved mayors in New York City history was Fiorello H. La Guardia (1882–1947), a reformer who held the office from 1934 to 1945. Edward I. Koch (b.1924) was first elected to the mayoralty in 1977.

Native New Yorkers have won Nobel prizes in every category. Winners of the Nobel Peace Prize besides Theodore Roosevelt were Elihu Root in 1912 and Frank B. Kellogg in 1929. The lone winner of the Nobel Prize for literature was Eugene O'Neill (1888–1953) in 1936. The chemistry prize was awarded to Irving Langmuir (1881–1957) in 1932, John H. Northrop (1891–1987) in 1946, and William Howard Stein (1911–80) in 1972. Winners in physics include Carl D. Anderson (b.1905-1991) in 1936, Robert Hofstadter (b.1915) in 1961, Richard Phillips Feynman (1918–88) and Julian Seymour Schwinger (1918–94) in 1965, Murray Gell-Mann (b.1929) in 1969, Leon N. Cooper (b.1930) in 1972, Burton Richter (b.1931) in 1976, and Steven Weinberg (b.1933) and Sheldon L. Glashow (b.1923) in 1979.

The following New Yorkers have been awarded the Nobel Prize for physiology or medicine: Hermann Joseph Muller (1890–1967) in 1946, Arthur Kornberg (b.1918) in 1959, George Wald (b.1906) in 1967, Marshall Warren Nirenberg (b.1927) in 1968, Julius Axelrod (b.1912) in 1970, Gerald Maurice Edelman (b.1929) in 1972, David Baltimore (b.1938) in 1975, Baruch Samuel Blumberg (b.1925) and Daniel Carlton Gajdusek (b.1923) in 1976, Rosalyn Sussman Yalow (b.1921) in 1977, and Hamilton O. Smith (b.1931) in 1978.

The Nobel Prize for economic science was won by Kenneth J. Arrow (b.1921) in 1972, Milton Friedman (b.1912) in 1976, Richard Stone (b.1928) in 1984, and Robert Fogel (b. 1926) in 1993. New York is also the birthplace of national labor leader George Meany (1894–1980) and economist Walter Heller (1915–87). Other distinguished state residents were physicist Joseph Henry (1797–1878), Mormon leader Brigham Young (b.Vermont, 1801–77), botanist Asa Gray (1810–88), inventor-businessman George Westinghouse (1846–1914), and Jonas E. Salk (b.1914), developer of a poliomyelitis vaccine. Melvin Schwartz (b. New York City, 1932) was a co-recipient of the 1988 Nobel prize in physics. Gertrude Belle Elron (b. 1918), Nobel Prize winner in medicine 1988, was born in New York City. Leon Max Laderman (b. 1922) was a co-recipient of the 1988 Nobel Prize in physics.

Writers born in New York include the storyteller and satirist Washington Irving (1783–1859); poets Walt Whitman (1819–92) and Ogden Nash (1902–71); and playwrights Eugene O'Neill (1888–1953), Arthur Miller (b.1915), Paddy Chayefsky (1923–81), and Neil Simon (b.1927). Two of America's greatest novelists were New Yorkers: Herman Melville (1819–91), who was also an important poet, and Henry James (1843–1916), whose short stories are equally well known. Other novelists include James Fenimore Cooper (b.New Jersey, 1789–1851), Henry Miller (1891–1980), James Michener (b.1907), J(erome) D(avid) Salinger (b.1919), Joseph Heller (b.1923), James Baldwin (1924–87), and Gore Vidal (b.1925). Lionel Trilling (1905–75) was a well-known literary critic; Barbara Tuchman (1912–89), a

historian, has won both scholarly praise and popular favor. New York City has produced two famous journalist-commentators, Walter Lippmann (1889–1974) and William F. Buckley, Jr. (b.1925), and a famous journalist-broadcaster Walter Winchell (1897–1972).

Broadway is the showcase of American drama and the birthplace of the American musical theater. New Yorkers linked with the growth of the musical include Jerome Kern (1885–1945), Lorenz Hart (1895–1943), Oscar Hammerstein 2d (1895–1960), Richard Rodgers (1902–79), Alan Jay Lerner (1918–86), and Stephen Sondheim (b.1930). George Gershwin (1898–1937), whose Porgy and Bess raised the musical to its highest artistic form, also composed piano and orchestral works. Other important US composers from New York include Irving Berlin (b.Russia, 1888–1989), Aaron Copland (1900–90), Elliott Carter (b.1908), and William Schuman (1910–92). New York was the adopted home of ballet director and choreographer George Balanchine (b.Russia, 1904–83); his associate Jerome Robbins (b.1918) was born in New York City, as was choreographer Agnes De Mille (b.1905). Leaders in the visual arts include Frederic Remington (1861–1909), the popular illustrator Norman Rockwell (1894–1978), Willem de Kooning (b.Netherlands, 1904), and the photographer Margaret Bourke-White (1906–71).

Many of America's best-loved entertainers come from the state. A small sampling would include comedians Groucho Marx (Julius Marx, 1890–1977), Mae West (1892–1980), Eddie Cantor (Edward Israel Iskowitz, 1892–1964), James "Jimmy" Durante (1893–1980), Bert Lahr (Irving Lahrheim, 1895–1967), George Burns (1896–1996), Milton Berle (Berlinger, b.1908), Lucille Ball (1911–1989), Danny Kaye (David Daniel Kominsky, 1913–87), and Sid Caesar (b.1922); comedian-film directors Mel Brooks (Melvin Kaminsky, b.1926) and Woody Allen (Allen Konigsberg, b.1935); stage and screen stars Humphrey Bogart (1899–1957), James Cagney (b.1904-1986), Zero Mostel (Samuel Joel Mostel, 1915–77), and Lauren Bacall (Betty Joan Perske, b.1924); pop, jazz, and folk singers Cab Calloway (1907–90), Lena Horne (b.1917), Pete Seeger (b.1919), Sammy Davis, Jr. (1925–90), Harry Belafonte (b.1927), Joan Baez (b.1941), Barbra Streisand (b.1942), Carly Simon (b.1945), Arlo Guthrie (b.1947), Billy Joel (b.1951), and Mariah Carey, Grammy Award-winning pop singer, (b.1969); and opera stars Robert Merrill (b.1919), Maria Callas (Kalogeropoulos, 1923–77), and Beverly Sills (Belle Silverman, b.1929). Also noteworthy are producers Irving Thalberg (1899–1936), David Susskind (1920–87), Joseph Papp (1921–91), and Harold Prince (b.1928) and directors George Cukor (1899–1983), Stanley Kubrick (b.1928), John Frankenheimer (b.1930), Peter Bogdanovich (b.1939), and actor Tom Cruise (b. 1962 in Syracuse, New York).

Among many prominent sports figures born in New York are first-baseman Lou Gehrig (1903–41), football coach Vince Lombardi (1913–70), pitcher Sanford "Sandy" Koufax (b.1935), and basketball stars Kareem Abdul-Jabbar (Lew Alcindor, b.1947) and Julius Erving (b.1950). Orel Leonard Hershiser IV (b. 1958), who set the record for most consecutive scoreless innings pitched, was born in Buffalo, New York.

50BIBLIOGRAPHY

Auletta, Ken. The Streets Were Paved with Gold. New York: Random House, 1980.

Barlow, Elizabeth, Frederick Law Olmsted's New York. New York: Praeger, 1972.

Bellush, Jewel, and Stephen M. David. Race and Politics in New York City. New York: Praeger, 1971.

Berle, Beatrice Bishop. 80 Puerto Rican Families in New York City. New York: Arno Press, 1975.

Berrol, Selma Cantor. The Empire City: New York and Its Peo-

ple, 1624-1996. Westport, Conn.: Praeger, 1997.

Bliven, Bruce. *New York.* New York: Norton, 1981.

Brown, Claude. *Manchild in the Promised Land.* New York: Macmillan, 1965.

Caro, Robert A. *The Power Broker: Robert Moses and the Fall of New York.* New York: Vintage, 1975.

Colby, Peter W. (ed.). *New York State Today: Politics, Government, Public Policy.* 2d ed. Albany: State University of New York Press, 1989.

Cuomo, Mario M. *Diaries of Mario M. Cuomo: The Campaign for Governor.* New York: Random House, 1984.

Edmiston, Susan, and Linda D. Cirino, *Literary New York: A History and Guide.* Boston, Houghton Mifflin, 1976.

Ellis, David M. *New York: State and City.* Ithaca: Cornell University Press, 1979.

Ellis, David M., James A. Frost, Harold C. Syrett, and Harry J. Carman. *A History of New York State.* Rev. ed. Ithaca: Cornell University Press, 1967.

Ellis, David M., James A. Frost, and William B. Fink. *New York: The Empire State.* 4th ed. Englewood Cliffs, N.J.: Prentice-Hall, 1975.

Federal Writers' Project. *New York City Guide.* New York: Somerset, n.d. (orig. 1939).

Flick, Alexander C. (ed.). *History of the State of New York.* Port Washington, N.Y.: Ira J. Friedman, 1969 (orig. 1860).

Furer, Howard B. *New York: A Chronological and Documentary History:1524-1970.* Dobbs Ferry, N.Y.: Oceana Publications, 1974.

Galie, Peter J. *The New York State Constitution: A Reference Guide.* New York, Greenwood Press, 1991.

———. *Ordered Liberty: A Constitutional History of New York.* New York: Fordham University Press, 1996.

Hacker, Andrew, *The New Yorkers: A Profile of an American People.* New York: Mason/Charter, 1975.

Heckscher, August, with Phyllis Robinson. *When La Guardia was Mayor: New York's Legendary Years.* New York: Norton, 1978.

Henderson, Mary C. *The City and the Theatre: New York Playhouses from Bowling Green to Times Square.* Clifton, N.J.: J. T. White, 1975.

Hevesi, Alan G. *Legislative Politics in New York State.* New York: Praeger, 1975.

Homberger, Eric. *The Historical Atlas of New York City: A Visual Celebration of Nearly 400 Years of New York City's History.* New York: H. Holt and Co., 1996.

Howe, Irving. *World of Our Fathers.* New York: Harcourt Brace Jovanovich, 1976.

Irving, Washington. *A History of New York.* Edited by Michael L. Black and Nancy B. Black. Boston: Twayne Publishers, 1984.

Kammen, Michael. *Colonial New York: A History.* Millwood, N.Y.: Kraud, 1975.

Kennedy, William. *O Albany!* New York: Viking, 1983.

Kenney, Alice P. *Stubborn for Liberty: The Dutch in New York.* Syracuse: Syracuse University Press, 1975.

Koch, Edward I., and William Rauch. *Mayor: An Autobiography.* New York: Simon & Schuster, 1984.

Kouwenhoven, John A. *The Columbia Historical Portrait of New York: An Essay in Graphic History.* New York: Harper & Row, 1972 (orig. 1952).

League of Women Voters of New York State. *A Guide to New York State Government.* Edited by Mary Jo Fairbanks. Croton-on-Hudson, N.Y.: Policy Studies Associates, 1995.

Lopez, Manual D. *New York: A Guide to Information and Reference Sources.* Metuchen, N.J.: Scarecrow, 1980.

Myers, Gustavus. *The History of Tammany Hall.* New York: Burt Franklin, 1967 (orig. 1901).

Nelson A. Rockefeller Institute of Government, in cooperation with the New York State Division of the Budget. *New York State Statistical Yearbook, 1984-1985.* Albany: Rockefeller Institute, 1985.

Newfield, Jack, and Paul DuBrul. *Abuse of Power: The Permanent Government and the Fall of New York.* New York: Viking, 1977.

Peirce, Neal R. *The Megastates of America: People, Politics, and Power in the Ten Great States.* New York: Norton, 1972.

Ravitch, Diane. *The Great School Wars: New York City 1805-1973.* New York: Basic Books, 1974.

Schneider, David Moses, and Albert Deutsch. *The History of Public Welfare in New York State.* Montclair, N.J.: Patterson, Smith, 1969.

Talese, Gay. *The Kingdom and the Power.* New York: World, 1969.

Torres, Andrés. *Between Melting Pot and Mosaic: African Americans and Puerto Ricans in the New York Political Economy.* Philadelphia: Temple University Press, 1995.

Zimmerman, Joseph F. *The Government and Politics of New York State.* New York: New York University Press, 1981.

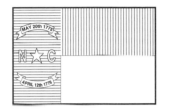

NORTH CAROLINA

State of North Carolina

ORIGIN OF STATE NAME: Named in honor of King Charles I of England. **NICKNAME:** The Tar Heel State and Old North State. **CAPITAL:** Raleigh. **ENTERED UNION:** 21 November 1789 (12th). **SONG:** "The Old North State." **MOTTO:** *Esse quam videri* (To be rather than to seem). **FLAG:** Adjacent to the fly of two equally sized bars, red above and white below, is a blue union containing a white star in the center, flanked by the letters N and C in gold. Above and below the star are two gold scrolls, the upper one reading "May 20th 1775," the lower one "April 12th 1776." **OFFICIAL SEAL:** Liberty, clasping a constitution and holding aloft on a pole a liberty cap, stands on the left, while Plenty sits beside a cornucopia on the right; behind them, mountains run to the sea, on which a three-masted ship appears. "May 20, 1775" appears above the figures; the words "The Great Seal of the State of North Carolina" and the state motto surround the whole. **MAMMAL:** Gray squirrel. **BIRD:** Cardinal. **FISH:** Channel bass. **DOG:** Plott hound. **REPTILE:** Eastern box turtle. **INSECT:** Honeybee. **FLOWER:** Dogwood. **TREE:** Pine. **VEGETABLE:** Sweet potato. **BEVERAGE:** Milk. **SHELL:** Scotch bonnet. **PRECIOUS STONE:** Emerald. **ROCK:** Granite. **LEGAL HOLIDAYS:** New Year's Day, 1 January; Birthday of Martin Luther King, Jr., 3d Monday in January; Easter Monday, March or April; Memorial Day, last Monday in May; Independence Day, 4 July; Labor Day, 1st Monday in September; Veterans Day, 11 November; Thanksgiving Day, 4th Thursday in November, and the day following; Christmas Eve, 24 December; Christmas Day, 25 December. **TIME:** 7 AM EST = noon GMT.

¹LOCATION, SIZE, AND EXTENT

Located in the southeastern US, North Carolina ranks 28th in size among the 50 states.

The total area of North Carolina is 52,669 sq mi (136,413 sq km), of which land accounts for 48,843 sq mi (126,504 sq km) and inland water 3,826 sq mi (9,909 sq km). North Carolina extends 503 mi (810 km) E–W; the state's maximum N–S extension is 187 mi (301 km).

North Carolina is bordered on the N by Virginia; on the E by the Atlantic Ocean; on the S by South Carolina and Georgia; and on the W by Tennessee. A long chain of islands or sand banks, called the Outer Banks, lies off the state's Atlantic coast. The total boundary line of North Carolina is 1,270 mi (2,044 km), including a general coastline of 301 mi (484 km); the tidal shoreline extends 3,375 mi (5,432 km). The state's geographic center is in Chatham County, 10 mi (16 km) NW of Sanford.

²TOPOGRAPHY

North Carolina's three major topographic regions belong to the Atlantic Coastal Plain, the Piedmont Plateau, and the Appalachian Mountains.

The Outer Banks, narrow islands of shifting sandbars, screen most of the coastal plain from the ocean. Treacherous navigation conditions and numerous shipwrecks have earned the name of "Graveyard of the Atlantic" for the shoal waters off Cape Hatteras, which, like Cape Lookout and Cape Fear, juts out from the banks into the Atlantic. Cape Hatteras Lighthouse is the tallest in the US, rising 208 feet (63 meters). The shallow Pamlico and Albemarle sounds and broad salt marshes lying behind the Outer Banks serve as valuable habitats for marine life but as further hindrances to water transportation.

On the mainland, the coastal plain extends westward from the sounds for 100 to 140 mi (160–225 km) and upward from sea level to nearly 500 feet (150 meters). Near the ocean, the outer coastal plain is very flat, and often swampy; this region contains all the natural lakes in North Carolina, the largest being Lake

Mattamuskeet (67 sq mi or 174 sq km), followed by lakes Phelps and Waccamaw. The inner coastal plain is more elevated and better drained. Infertile sand hills mark its southwestern section, but the rest of the region constitutes the state's principal farming country.

The Piedmont is a rolling plateau of red clay soil roughly 150 mi (240 km) wide, rising from 30 to 600 feet (90 to 180 meters) in the east to 1,500 feet (460 meters) in the west. The fall line, a sudden change in elevation, separates the piedmont from the coastal plain and produces numerous rapids in the rivers that flow between the regions.

The Blue Ridge, a steep escarpment that parallels the Tennessee border, divides the piedmont from North Carolina's westernmost region, containing the highest and most rugged portion of the Appalachian chain. The two major ranges are the Blue Ridge itself, which averages 3,000–4,000 feet high (900–1,200 meters), and the Great Smoky Mountains, which have 43 peaks higher than 6,000 feet (1,800 meters). Several smaller chains intersect these two ranges; one of them, the Black Mountains, contains Mt. Mitchell, at 6,684 feet (2,037 meters) the tallest peak east of the Mississippi River.

No single river basin dominates North Carolina. The Hiwassee, Little Tennessee, French Broad, Watauga, and New rivers flow from the mountains westward to the Mississippi River system. East of the Blue Ridge, the Chowan, Roanoke, Tar, Neuse, Cape Fear, Yadkin, and Catawba drain the piedmont and coastal plain. The largest artificial lakes are Lake Norman on the Catawba, Lake Gaston on the Roanoke, and High Rock Lake on the Yadkin.

³CLIMATE

North Carolina has a humid, subtropical climate. Winters are short and mild, while summers are usually very sultry; spring and fall are distinct and refreshing periods of transition. In most of North Carolina, temperatures rarely go above 100°F (38°C) or fall below 10°F (−12°C), but differences in altitude and proximity to the ocean create significant local variations. Average January temperatures range from 36°F (21°C) to 48°F (9°C), with an average daily maximum January temperature of 51°F (11°C) and minimum of 29°F (–2°C). Average July temperatures range from 68°F (20°C) to 80°F (27°C), with an average daily high of 87°F (31°C) and a low of 66°F (19°C). The coldest temperature ever recorded in North Carolina was –34°F (–37°C), registered on 21 January 1985 on Mt. Mitchell; the hottest, 110°F (43°C), occurred on 21 August 1983 at Fayetteville.

In the southwestern section of the Blue Ridge, moist southerly winds rising over the mountains drop more than 80 in (203 cm) of precipitation per year, making this region the wettest in the eastern states; the other side of the mountains receives less than half that amount. The piedmont gets between 44 and 48 in (112 to 122 cm) of precipitation per year, while 44 to 56 in (112 to 142 cm) annually fall on the coastal plain. Average winter snowfalls vary from 50 in (127 cm) on Mt. Mitchell to only a trace amount at Cape Hatteras. In the summer, North Carolina weather responds to the Bermuda High, a pressure system centered in the mid-Atlantic. Winds from the southwest bring masses of hot humid air over the state; anticyclones connected with this system frequently lead to upper-level thermal inversions, producing a stagnant air mass that cannot disperse pollutants until cooler, drier air from Canada moves in. During late summer and early autumn, the eastern region is vulnerable to high winds and flooding from hurricanes. Hurricane Diana struck the Carolina coast in September 1984, causing $36 million in damage. A series of tornadoes in March of that year killed 61 people, injured over 1,000, and caused damage exceeding $120 million. In 1995, 26 tornadoes were recorded in the state. Hurricanes Hugo (1989) and Fran (1996) caused major damage.

4FLORA AND FAUNA

North Carolina has approximately 300 species and subspecies of trees and almost 3,000 varieties of flowering plants. Coastal plant life begins with sea oats predominating on the dunes and saltmeadow and cordgrass in the marshes, then gives way to wax myrtle, yaupon, red cedar, and live oak further inland. Black-water swamps support dense stands of cypress and gum trees. Pond pine favors the peat soils of the Carolina bays, while longleaf pine and turkey oak cover the sand hills and other well-drained areas. Weeds take root when a field is abandoned in the piedmont, followed soon by loblolly, shortleaf, and Virginia pine; sweet gum and tulip poplars spring up beneath the pines, later giving way to an oak-hickory climax forest. Dogwood decorates the understory, but kudzu—a rank, weedy vine introduced from Japan as an antierosion measure in the 1930s—is a less attractive feature of the landscape. The profusion of plants reaches extraordinary proportions in the mountains. The deciduous forests on the lower slopes contain Carolina hemlock, silver bell, yellow buckeye, white basswood, sugar maple, yellow birch, tulip poplar, and beech, in addition to the common trees of the piedmont. Spruce and fir dominate the high mountain peaks. There is no true treeline in the North Carolina mountains, but unexplained treeless areas called "balds" appear on certain summits. The branched arrowhead is an endangered plant.

The white-tailed deer is the principal big-game animal of North Carolina, and the black bear is a tourist attraction in the Great Smoky Mountains National Park. The wild boar was introduced to the mountains during the 19th century; beavers have been reintroduced and are now the state's principal furbearers. The largest native carnivore is the bobcat.

North Carolina game birds include the bobwhite quail, mourning dove, wild turkey, and many varieties of duck and goose. Trout and smallmouth bass flourish in North Carolina's clear mountain streams, while catfish, pickerel, perch, crappie, and largemouth bass thrive in fresh water elsewhere. The sounds

and surf of the coast yield channel bass, striped bass, flounder, and bluefish to anglers. Among insect pests, the pine bark beetle is a threat to the state's forests and forest industries.

The gray wolf, elk, eastern cougar, and bison are extinct in North Carolina; the American alligator, protected by the state, has returned in large numbers to eastern swamps and lakeshores. Endangered species (all on the federal list) include the Florida manatee, Indiana and gray bats, bald eagle, American and Arctic peregrine falcons, eastern brown pelican, ivory woodpecker, and Atlantic ridley and hawksbill turtles. Threatened species include the noonday snail.

5ENVIRONMENTAL PROTECTION

State actions to safeguard the environment began in 1915 with the purchase of the summit of Mt. Mitchell as North Carolina's first state park. North Carolina's citizens and officials worked actively (along with those in Tennessee) to establish the Great Smoky Mountains National Park during the 1920s, the same decade that saw the establishment of the first state agency for wildlife conservation. In 1937, a state and local program of soil and water conservation districts began to halt erosion and waste of natural resources.

Interest in environmental protection intensified during the 1970s. In 1971, the state required its own agencies to submit environmental impact statements in connection with all major project proposals; it also empowered local governments to require such statements from major private developers. Voters approved a $150 million bond issue in 1972 to assist in the construction of wastewater treatment facilities by local governments. The Coastal Management Act of 1974 mandated comprehensive land-use planning for estuaries, wetlands, beaches, and adjacent areas of environmental concern. The most controversial environmental action occurred mid-decade, when a coalition of state officials, local residents, and national environmental groups fought the proposed construction of a dam that would have flooded the New River Valley in northwestern North Carolina. Congress quashed the project when it designated the stream as a national scenic river in 1976.

Air quality in most of North Carolina's eight air-quality-control regions is good, although the industrialized areas of the piedmont and mountains experience pollution from vehicle exhausts and coal-fired electric generating plants. Water quality ranges from extraordinary purity in numerous mountain trout streams to serious pollution in major rivers and coastal waters. Soil erosion and municipal and industrial waste discharges have drastically increased the level of dissolved solids in some piedmont streams, while runoffs from livestock pastures and nitrates leached from fertilized farmland have overstimulated the growth of algae in slow-moving eastern rivers. Pollution also has made certain areas of the coast unsafe for commercial shell-fishing. About 5.7 million acres (2.3 million hectares) of the state are wetlands. About 70% of North Carolina's rare and endangered plants and animals are considered wetland-dependent.

The Department of Environment, Health and Natural Resources, the state's main environmental agency, issues licenses to industries and municipalities and seeks to enforce clean air and water regulations. In 1995, the state had 23 hazardous waste sites.

6POPULATION

North Carolina had 6,628,367 inhabitants in 1990 (10th in the US), a 12.7% increase over 1980. The estimated population in 1996 was 7,322,870, up 10.4% over 1990. At the time of the first census in 1790, North Carolina ranked 3d among the 13 states, with a population of 393,751, but it slipped to 10th by 1850. In the decades that followed, North Carolina grew slowly by natural increase and suffered from net out-migration, while

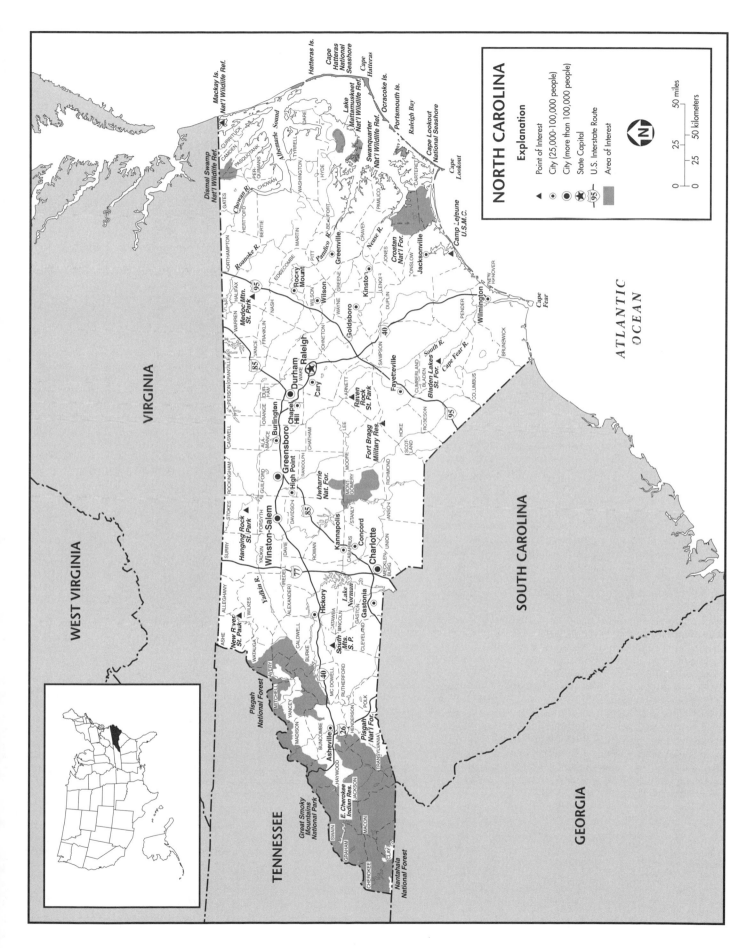

the rest of the nation expanded rapidly. Outmigration abated after 1890, however, and North Carolina's overall growth rate in the 20th century has been slightly greater than that of the nation as a whole.

As of 1990, the state's population had a median age of 33.1. North Carolina's estimated population density was 136 per sq mi (52 per sq km) in 1990. About 50.4% of North Carolinians lived in urban areas in 1990, compared with 75.2% of all Americans. Most North Carolinians live in and around a relatively large number of small and medium-sized cities and towns, many of which are concentrated in the Piedmont Crescent, between Charlotte, Greensboro, and Raleigh. Leading cities in 1994 were Charlotte, 437,797; Raleigh, 236,707; Greensboro, 196,167;

Winston-Salem, 155,128; and Durham, 143,439. The Charlotte metropolitan area had an estimated 1,289,177 people in 1995.

[7]ETHNIC GROUPS

North Carolina's white population is descended mostly from English settlers who arrived in the east in the 17th and early 18th centuries and from Scottish, Scots-Irish, and German immigrants who poured into the piedmont in the middle of the 18th century. Originally very distinct, these groups assimilated with one another in the first half of the 19th century to form a relatively homogeneous body of native-born white Protestants. By 1860, North Carolina had the lowest proportion of foreign-born whites of any state; more than a century later, in 1990, only 1.7%

North Carolina Counties, County Seats, and County Areas and Populations

COUNTY	COUNTY SEAT	LAND AREA (SQ MI)	POPULATION (1996 Est)	COUNTY	COUNTY SEAT	LAND AREA (SQ MI)	POPULATION (1996 Est)
Alamance	Graham	433	115,514	Jones	Trenton	470	9,501
Alexander	Taylorsville	259	30,192	Lee	Sanford	259	47,483
Alleghany	Sparta	234	9,849	Lenoir	Kinston	402	59,355
Anson	Wadesboro	533	24302	Lincoln	Lincolnton	298	56,235
Ashe	Jefferson	426	23,792	Macon	Franklin	517	38,057
Avery	Newland	247	15,626	Madison	Marshall	451	27,114
Beaufort	Washington	826	44,027	Martin	Williamston	461	18,242
Bertie	Windsor	701	20,722	McDowell	Marion	437	38,057
Bladen	Elizabethtown	879	30,330	Mecklenburg	Charlotte	528	597,589
Brunswick	Bolivia	861	63,225	Mitchell	Bakersville	222	14,719
Buncombe	Asheville	659	191,800	Montgomery	Troy	490	24,144
Burke	Morganton	505	80,986	Moore	Carthage	701	68,483
Cabarrus	Concord	364	113,165	Nash	Nashville	540	87,991
Caldwell	Lenoir	471	74,683	New Hanover	Wilmington	185	143,513
Camden	Camden	241	6,523	Northampton	Jackson	538	21,280
Carteret	Beaufort	525	58,773	Onslow	Jacksonville	763	144,533
Caswell	Yanceyville	427	21,585	Orange	Hillsborough	400	108,795
Catawba	Newton	396	129,104	Pamlico	Bayboro	341	12,188
Chatham	Pittsboro	708	43,870	Pasquotank	Elizabeth City	228	34,036
Cherokee	Murphy	452	21,934	Pender	Burgaw	875	36,601
Chowan	Edenton	181	14,099	Perquimans	Hertford	246	10,913
Clay	Hayesville	214	8,132	Person	Roxboro	398	32,793
Cleveland	Shelby	468	91,381	Pitt	Greenville	656	119,064
Columbus	Whiteville	939	51,975	Polk	Columbus	238	16,226
Craven	New Bern	702	86,352	Randolph	Asheboro	789	117,455
Cumberland	Fayetteville	657	284,800	Richmond	Rockingham	477	45,665
Currituck	Currituck	256	16,766	Robeson	Lumberton	949	113,169
Dare	Manteo	391	26,803	Rockingham	Wentworth	569	89,575
Davidson	Lexington	548	137,395	Rowan	Salisbury	519	121,785
DAvie	Mocksville	267	30,243	Rutherford	Rutherfordton	568	59,723
Duplin	Kenansville	819	42,802	Sampson	Clinton	947	50,675
Durham	Durham	298	197,352	Scotland	Laurinburg	319	35,404
Edgecombe	Tarboro	506	56,166	Stanly	Albemarle	396	54,850
Forsyth	Winston-Salem	412	284,207	Stokes	Danbury	452	42,062
Franklin	Louisburg	494	42,872	Surry	Dobson	539	65,848
Gaston	Gastonia	357	182,623	Swain	Bryson City	526	12,008
Gates	Gatesville	338	9,911	Transylvania	Brevard	378	27,499
Graham	Robbinsville	289	7,616	Tyrrell	Columbia	407	3,820
Granville	Oxford	534	41,622	Union	Monroe	639	102,372
Greene	Snow Hill	266	17,660	Vance	Henderson	249	41,312
Guilford	Greensboro	651	379,201	Wake	Raleigh	854	534,075
Halifax	Halifax	724	57,183	Warren	Warrenton	427	18,039
Harnett	Lillington	601	79,052	Washington	Plymouth	332	13,956
Haywood	Waynesville	555	50,387	Watauga	Boone	314	40,357
Henderson	Hendersonville	375	77,940	Wayne	Goldsboro	554	111,581
Hertford	Winton	356	22,447	Wilkes	Wilkesboro	752	61,884
Hoke	Racford	391	28,471	Wilson	Wilson	374	67,809
Hyde	Swanquarter	624	5,413	Yadkin	Yadkinville	336	34,161
Iredell	Statesville	574	106,383	Yancey	Burnsville	314	16,380
Jackson	Sylva	490	29,668				
Johnston	Smithfield	795	98,289	TOTALS		48,843	7,322,870

(115,077) of North Carolina residents were foreign-born, mostly from Germany, the United Kingdom, and Mexico.

According to the 1990 federal census there were some 80,000 Native Americans living in North Carolina, the 7th-largest number in any state, and the largest number in any state east of the Mississippi. The Lumbee of Robeson County and the surrounding area are the major Indian group. Their origins are mysterious, but they probably descend from many small tribes, decimated by war and disease, that banded together in the Lumber River swamps in the 18th century. The Lumbee have no language other than English, have no traditional tribal culture, and are not recognized by the Bureau of Indian Affairs. The Haliwa, Waccamaw Siouan, Coharie, and Person County Indians are smaller groups in eastern North Carolina who share the Lumbee's predicament. The only North Carolina Indians with a reservation, a tribal language and culture, and federal recognition are the Cherokee, whose ancestors hid in the Smokies when the majority of their tribe was removed to Indian Territory (now Oklahoma) in 1838. The North Carolina Cherokee have remained in the mountains ever since, living in a community that now centers on the Qualla Boundary Reservation near Great Smoky Mountains National Park.

The 1,456,000 blacks in North Carolina made up 22% of its total population in 1990. Black slaves came to North Carolina from the 17th century through the early 19th; like most white immigrants, they usually arrived in North Carolina after previous residence in other colonies. Although black slaves performed a wide variety of tasks and lived in every county of the state, they were most often field laborers on the large farms in the eastern region. The distribution of black population today still reflects the patterns of plantation agriculture: the coastal plain contains a much higher than average concentration of black inhabitants. The overall proportion of blacks in North Carolina rose throughout the 19th century but fell steadily in the 20th, until about 1970, as hundreds of thousands migrated to northern and western states. Some of the earliest demonstrations of the civil rights movement, most notably a 1960 lunch counter sit-in at Greensboro, took place in the state.

8LANGUAGES

Although most of the original Cherokee Indians were removed to Indian Territory around 1838, descendants of those who resisted and remained have formed a strong Indian community in the Appalachian foothills. Among Indian place-names are Pamlico, Nantahala, and Cullasaja.

Many regional language features are widespread, but others sharply distinguish two subregions: the western half, including the piedmont and the Appalachian Highlands, and the eastern coastal plain. Terms common to South Midland and Southern speech occur throughout the state: both *dog irons* and *firedogs* (andirons), *bucket* (pail), *spicket* (spigot), *seesaw, comfort* (tied and filled bedcover), *pullybone* (wishbone), *ground squirrel* (chipmunk), *branch* (small stream), *light bread* (white bread), *polecat* (skunk), and *carry* (escort). Also common are *greasy* with the /z/ sound, *new* as /nyoo/ and *due* as /dyoo/, *swallow* it as / swaller it/, *can't* rhyming with *paint*, *poor* with the vowel sound / aw/, and *horse* and *hoarse* with different vowels.

Distinct to the western region are *snake feeder* (dragonfly), *blinds* (roller shades), *poke* (paper bag), *redworm* (earthworm), *a little piece* (a short distance), *plum peach* (clingstone peach), *sick on the stomach* (also found in the Pee Dee River Valley), *boiled* as /bawrld/, *fog* as /fawg/, *Mary* sounding like *merry* and *bulge* with the vowel of *good*. Setting off eastern North Carolina are *lightwood* (kindling), *mosquito hawk* (dragonfly), *earthworm, press peach* (instead of plum peach), *you-all* as second-person plural, and *sick in the stomach*. Distinctive eastern pronunciations include the loss of /r/ after a vowel, *fog* as /fagh/, *scarce* and

Mary with the vowel of *gate, bulge* with the vowel sound /ah/. Along the coast, peanuts are *goobers* and a screech owl is a *shivering owl*.

In 1990, 5,931,435 North Carolinians—96.1% of the population 5 years of age and older—spoke only English at home. Other languages spoken at home, and the number of speakers, included the following:

Spanish	105,963	Korean	6,053
French	37,590	Japanese	4,949
German	24,689	Italian	4,801
Chinese	7,252	Arabic	4,300

9RELIGIONS

The majority of North Carolinians are Protestant. The churches of the Southern Baptist Convention reported 1,446,228 adherents in 1990; the United Methodist Church claimed 605,362; the American Zion Church had 312,693; and the Presbyterian Church USA, 205,548. In 1990, the state had 149,483 Roman Catholics and an estimated 28,870 Jews.

The Church of England was the established church of colonial North Carolina but was never a dominant force among the early immigrants. Scottish Presbyterians settled in the upper Cape Fear Valley, and Scots-Irish Presbyterians occupied the piedmont after 1757. Lutheran Evangelical Reformed Germans later moved into the Yadkin and Catawba valleys of the same region. The Moravians, a German sect, founded the town of Salem (later merging with Winston to become Winston-Salem) in 1766 as the center of their utopian community at Wachovia. Methodist circuit riders and Separate Baptists missionaries won thousands of converts among blacks and whites, strengthening their appeal in the Great Revival of 1801. In the subsequent generation, a powerful evangelical consensus dominated popular culture. After the Civil War, blacks left the white congregations to found their own churches, but the overall strength of Protestantism persisted. When many North Carolinians left their farms at the end of the 19th century, they moved to mill villages that were well supplied with churches, often at the mill owners' expense.

White church organizations have generally kept out of state politics except where matters of personal morality are concerned. In recent years, however, individual Protestant leaders have worked to reject the Equal Rights Amendment and to deny state-funded abortions to the poor. Resurgent political activism among fundamentalist Christians is a growing and prominent feature of contemporary North Carolina politics.

10TRANSPORTATION

The history of North Carolina's growth and prosperity has been inextricably linked to the history of transportation in the state, and especially the history of highway development. North Carolina has the largest state-maintained highway system in the nation. To provide and maintain this system, North Carolina relies strictly on user-related sources of funds, such as motor fuel taxes and state license and registration fees.

The early settlers widened and improved the Indian trails into bridle trails and then dirt roads. In colonial times, waterways were the avenues of commerce. Almost all products moved on rivers and streams within the state, and most manufactured goods arrived by sea. When it became necessary to transport goods farther inland, local laws were passed which directed that a road be built to the nearest landing. By this piecemeal process, the state slowly acquired a system of dirt roads.

As the population of the state grew, so did the demand for roads. From 1830 onward, a new element was introduced into the picture—railroads, representing the newest and most efficient means of travel. In the 1850s, transportation took yet another turn when the state invested in plank roads, which did not prove financially practical.

With the coming of the Civil War, transportation improvements in North Carolina ground to a halt. During the war, the existing railroads were used heavily for military purposes. Renovations and improvements were delayed during the early years of the Reconstruction period because of poor economic conditions in the state. By 1870, the state gave up on assistance to railroads and left their further development to private companies. In 1895, the Southern Railway acquired a 99-year lease on the piedmont section of the North Carolina Railroad, while eastern routes fell to the Atlantic Coast Line and the Seaboard Air Line Railway.

In the early years of the 20th century, the principal emphasis was on the further development of the investor-owned railroads. By 1911, there were railroads covering 4,608 mi (7,414 km) and by 1937, this figure had increased only slightly, to a total of 4,763 (7,663 km). Today, North Carolina has more than 3,600 route mi (5,792 km) of railroad track. Nearly 140 mi (225 km) of track are state-owned. Twenty-six private railroad companies operate in North Carolina, transporting more than 88 million tons of rail freight through the state each year. Amtrak provides passenger service to most large North Carolina cities. The *Carolinian* and *Piedmont*, both state-owned trains, provide daily, round-trip passenger-rail service between Charlotte and Raleigh. The *Carolinian* also offers continuing service to the Northeast. Each year more than 325,000 rail passengers begin or end their trips at one of North Carolina's 16 Amtrak stations.

By the second decade of the century, the building of roads received new emphasis. It was during this period that North Carolina earned the label, "the Good Roads State." In 1915, the Highway Commission was created, and in 1921 the General Assembly approved a $40 million state highway bond to construct a system of hard-surface roads connecting each of the 100 county seats with all of the others. The new hard-surface roads soon proved ideal for automobiles and trucks. More highway bonds were approved to pay for a statewide system of paved highways, giving the state more roads by the end of the decade than any other southern state except Texas. The state government took over the county roads in 1931.

To date, North Carolina has almost 78,000 mi (125,000 km) of highways: primary highways (US and interstate) 11,948 mi (19,236 km); secondary roads, 59,463 mi (95,735 km); and urban streets (state-maintained), 6,288 mi (10,124 km). Total public road length in 1995 was 96,809 mi (158,760 km). There are more than 6.3 million vehicles registered and 5.5 million licensed drivers in North Carolina. The major interstate highways are I-95, which stretches north-south across the coastal plain, and I-85, which parallels it across the piedmont. I-40 leads from the mountains to the coast at Wilmington, and I-26 and I-77 handle north-south traffic in the western section. I-73 and I-74 add 325 miles of interstate highway and will handle north-south traffic in the eastern section of the state.

In 1994, *Transportation 2001*, a plan to speed up highway construction and complete key corridors, eliminate the road maintenance backlog, and develop a master plan for public transportation, was unveiled. A $950 million highway bond was approved in 1996 by North Carolina voters, to accelerate construction of urban loops and intrastates and to pave secondary roads. *Transit 2001*, the master plan to improve public transportation was unveiled in February 1997. A major incentive will be placed on high-speed rail service from Raleigh to Charlotte, reducing travel time to two hours by 2000.

There are nine types of public transportation currently operating in North Carolina: human service transportation, rural general public transportation, urban transit, regional transit, vanpool and carpool programs, intercity busses, intercity rail passenger service, pupil transportation, and passenger ferry service. There are 17 publicly owned urban transit systems operating in North Carolina. More than 33 million passengers rode nearly 17.6 million city-bus miles (28.3 km) between July 1994 and June 1995. About three million North Carolinians have access to rural public transportation services operating in 45 counties and towns.

The Atlantic Intracoastal Waterway follows sounds, rivers, and canals down the entire length of eastern North Carolina. The North Carolina ferry system, the second largest in the nation, transports more than 23 million passengers and 820,000 vehicles each year. Twenty-four ferry vessels move passengers and vehicles between the state's coastal communities. Seventeen of the vessels feature the colors and seals of North Carolina's public and private colleges and universities to promote the ferry system.

North Carolina has 75 publicly owned and nearly 300 privately owned airports. Fifteen airports have regularly scheduled airline service; four are international. There are more than 6,000 private aircraft based in the state, flown by more than 15,000 certified pilots. More than 36 million passengers fly to and from North Carolina each year, and more than 650 million pounds of air freight originate annually in the state. There are three major airline hubs in North Carolina. More than 429,000 airlines and 472,000 general aviation flights depart each year from North Carolina's larger airports at Asheville, Charlotte, Fayetteville, Greensboro, Kinston, Raleigh/Durham, Wilmington, and Winston-Salem.

11HISTORY

Paleo-Indian peoples came to North Carolina about 10,000 years ago. These early inhabitants hunted game with spears and gathered nuts, roots, berries, and freshwater mollusks. Around 500 BC, with the invention of pottery and the development of agriculture, the Woodland Culture began to emerge. The Woodland way of life—growing corn, beans, and squash, and hunting game with bows and arrows—prevailed on the North Carolina coast until the Europeans arrived.

Living in North Carolina by this time were Indians of the Algonkian-, Siouan-, and Iroquoian-language families. The Roanoke, Chowanoc, Hatteras, Meherrin, and other Algonkian-speaking tribes of the coast had probably lived in the area the longest; some of them belonged to the Powhatan Confederacy of Virginia. The Siouan groups were related to larger tribes of the Great Plains. Of the Iroquoian-speakers, the Cherokee probably had lived in the mountains since before the beginning of the Christian era, while the Tuscarora had entered the upper coastal plain somewhat later. After their defeat by the colonists in the Tuscarora War of 1711–13, the tribe fled to what is now upper New York State to become the sixth member of the Iroquois Confederacy.

Contact with whites brought war, disease, and enslavement of the Algonkian and Siouan tribes. Banding together, the survivors probably gave rise to the present-day Lumbee and to the other Indian groups of eastern North Carolina. The Cherokee tried to avoid the fate of the coastal tribes by selectively adopting aspects of white culture. In 1838, however, the federal government responded to the demands of land-hungry whites by expelling most of the Cherokee to Indian Territory along the so-called Trail of Tears.

European penetration began when Giovanni da Verrazano, a Florentine navigator in French service, discovered the North Carolina coast in 1524. Don Lucas Vásquez de Ayllón led an unsuccessful Spanish attempt to settle near the mouth of the Cape Fear River two years later. Hernando de Soto tramped over the North Carolina mountains in 1540 in an unsuccessful search for gold, but the Spanish made no permanent contribution to the colonization of North Carolina.

Sixty years after Verrazano's voyage, North Carolina became the scene of England's first experiment in American empire. Sir

Walter Raleigh, a courtier of Queen Elizabeth I, gained the queen's permission to send out explorers to the New World. They landed on the Outer Banks in 1584 and returned with reports so enthusiastic that Raleigh decided to sponsor a colony on Roanoke Island between Albemarle and Pamlico sounds. After a second expedition returned without founding a permanent settlement, Raleigh sent out a third group in 1587 under John White as governor. The passengers included White's daughter Eleanor and her husband, Ananias Dare. Shortly after landfall, Eleanor gave birth to Virginia Dare, the first child born of English parents in the New World. Several weeks later, White returned to England for supplies, but the threat of the Spanish Armada prevented his prompt return. By the time White got back to Roanoke in 1590, he found no trace of the settlers—only the word "Croatoan" carved on a tree. The fate of this "Lost Colony" has never been satisfactorily explained.

The next English venture focused on the more accessible Jamestown colony in the Chesapeake Bay area of Virginia. England tended to ignore the southern region until 1629, when Charles I laid out the territory between 30° and 36°N, named it Carolana for himself, and granted it to his attorney general, Sir Robert Heath. Heath made no attempt to people his domain, however, and Carolana remained empty of whites until stragglers drifted in from the mid-17th century onward. Events in England transformed Virginia's outpost into a separate colony. After the execution of Charles I in 1649, England had no ruling monarch until a party of noblemen invited Charles II back to England in 1660. Charles thanked eight of his benefactors three years later by making them lord proprietors of the province, now called Carolina. The vast new region eventually stretched from northern Florida to the modern boundary between North Carolina and Virginia, and from the Atlantic to the Pacific Ocean.

The proprietors divided Carolina into three counties and appointed a governor for each one. Albemarle County embraced the existing settlements in northeastern North Carolina near the waters of Albemarle Sound; it was the only one that developed a government within the present state boundaries. From the beginning, relations between the older pioneers and their newly imposed government were stormy. The English philosopher John Locke drew up the Fundamental Constitutions of Carolina, but his political blueprints proved unworkable. The proprietors' arbitrary efforts to collect royal customs touched off factional violence, culminating in Culpepper's Rebellion of 1677, one of the first American uprisings against a corrupt regime.

For a few years afterward, local residents had a more representative government, until the proprietors attempted to strengthen the establishment of the Anglican Church in the colony. In 1711, Cary's Rebellion was touched off by laws passed against the colony's Quakers. During the confusion, Tuscarora Indians launched a war against the white intruders on their lands. The whites won the Tuscarora War in 1713 with assistance from South Carolina, but political weakness in the north persisted. Proprietary officials openly consorted with pirates—including the notorious Edward Teach, alias Blackbeard—and royal inspectors questioned the fitness of proprietary government. South Carolina officially split off in 1719 and received a royal governor in 1721. Ten years later, all but one of the proprietors relinquished their rights for £2,500 each, and North Carolina became a royal colony. The remaining proprietor, Lord Granville, gave up his governing rights but retained ownership of one-eighth of the original grant; the Granville District thus included more than half of the unsettled territory in the North Carolina colony.

In the decades that followed, thousands of new settlers poured into North Carolina; by 1775 the population had swollen to 345,000, making North Carolina the 4th most populous colony. Germans and Scots-Irish trekked down the Great Wagon Road from Pennsylvania to the piedmont. Scottish Highlanders spread over the upper Cape Fear Valley as more Englishmen filled up the coastal plain. Backcountry settlers practiced self-sufficient farming, but eastern North Carolinians used slave labor to carve out rice and tobacco plantations. The westerners were often exploited by an eastern-dominated colonial assembly that sent corrupt and overbearing officials to govern them. Organizing in 1768 and calling themselves Regulators, unhappy westerners first petitioned for redress and then took up arms. Royal Governor William Tryon used eastern militia to crush the Regulators in a two-hour pitched battle at Alamance Creek in 1771.

The eastern leaders who dominated the assembly opposed all challenges to their authority, whether from the Regulators or from the British ministry. When England tightened its colonial administration, North Carolinians joined their fellow colonists in protests against the Stamp Act and similar impositions by Parliament. Meeting at Halifax in April 1776, the North Carolina provincial congress resolved in favor of American independence, the first colonial representative body to do so. Years later, citizens of Mecklenburg County recalled a gathering in 1775 during which their region declared independence, but subsequent historians have not verified their claim. The two dates on the North Carolina state flag nevertheless commemorate the Halifax Resolves and the "Mecklenburg Declaration of Independence."

Support for Britain appeared among recent Scottish immigrants, who answered the call to aid the royal governor but were ambushed by patriot militia at Moore's Creek Bridge on 27 February 1776. The incident effectively prevented a planned British invasion of the South. There was little further military action in North Carolina until late in the War for Independence, when Gen. Charles Cornwallis invaded the state from South Carolina in the fall of 1780. Guerrilla bands harassed his troops, and North Carolina militia wiped out a Loyalist detachment at King's Mountain. Pursuing the elusive American army under Gen. Nathanael Greene, Cornwallis won a costly victory at Guilford Courthouse in March 1781 but could neither eliminate his rival nor pacify the countryside. For the rest of 1781, Cornwallis wearied his men in marches and countermarches across North Carolina and Virginia before he finally succumbed to a trap set at Yorktown, Va., by an American army and a French fleet.

Numerous problems beset the new state. The government had a dire need of money, but when the victors sought to pay debts by selling land confiscated from the Loyalists, conservative lawyers objected strenuously, and a bitter political controversy ensued. Suspicious of outside control, North Carolina leaders hesitated before joining the Union. The state waited until November 1789 to ratify the US Constitution—a delay that helped stimulate the movement for adoption of a Bill of Rights. North Carolina relinquished its lands beyond the Great Smokies in 1789 (after an unsuccessful attempt by settlers to create a new state called Franklin), and thousands of North Carolinians migrated to the new western territories. The state did not share in the general prosperity of the early federal period. Poor transportation facilities hampered all efforts to expand commercial agriculture, and illiteracy remained widespread. North Carolina society came to appear so backward that some observers nicknamed it the "Rip Van Winkle state."

In 1815, state senator Archibald D. Murphey of Orange County began to press for public schools and for improved transportation to open up the piedmont. Most eastern planters resisted Murphey's suggestions, partly because they refused to be taxed for the benefit of the westerners and partly because they feared the destabilizing social effects of reform. As long as the east controlled the general assembly, the ideas of Murphey and his sympathizers had little practical impact, but in 1835, as a result of reforms in the state constitution, the west obtained reapportionment and the political climate changed. North Carolina initiated a program of state aid to railroads and other public works, and established the first state-supported system of common schools in the South.

Like other southern whites, North Carolina's white majority feared for the security of slavery under a national Republican administration, but North Carolinians reacted to the election of Abraham Lincoln with caution. When South Carolina and six other states seceded and formed the Confederate States of America in 1861, North Carolina refused to join, instead making a futile attempt to work for a peaceful settlement of the issue. However, after the outbreak of hostilities at Ft. Sumter, S.C., and Lincoln's call for troops in April 1861, neutrality disappeared and public opinion swung to the Confederate side. North Carolina became the last state to withdraw from the Union, joining the Confederacy on 20 May 1861.

North Carolina provided more troops to the Confederacy than any other state, and its losses added up to more than one-fourth of the total for the entire South, but support for the war was mixed. State leaders resisted the centralizing tendencies of the Richmond government, and even Governor Zebulon B. Vance opposed the Confederacy's conscription policies. North Carolina became a haven for deserters from the front lines in Virginia. William W. Holden, a popular Raleigh editor, organized a peace movement when defeat appeared inevitable, and Unionist sentiment flourished in the mountain counties; nevertheless, most white North Carolinians stood by Vance and the dying Confederate cause. At the war's end, Gen. Joseph E. Johnston surrendered the last major Confederate army to Gen. William T. Sherman at Bennett House near Hillsborough on 26 April 1865.

Reconstruction was marked by a bitter political and social struggle in North Carolina. United in the Conservative Party, most of the prewar slaveholding elite fought to preserve as much as possible of the former system, but a Republican coalition of blacks and nonslaveholding white Unionists defended freedmen's rights and instituted democratic reforms for the benefit of both races. After writing a new constitution in 1868, Republicans elected Holden as governor, but native whites fought back with violence and intimidation under the robes of the Ku Klux Klan. Holden's efforts to restore order were ineffectual, and when the Conservatives recaptured the general assembly in 1870, they impeached him and removed him from office. Election of a Conservative governor in 1876 signaled the end of the Reconstruction era.

Once in power, the Conservatives—or Democrats, as they renamed themselves—slashed public services and enacted legislation to guarantee the power of landlords over tenants and sharecroppers. They cooperated with the consolidation of railroads under northern ownership, and they supported a massive drive to build cotton mills on the swiftly flowing streams of the piedmont. By 1880, industry had surpassed its prewar level. But it was not until the turn of the century that blacks and their white allies were entirely eliminated as contenders for political power.

As the Industrial Revolution gained ground in North Carolina, small farmers protested their steadily worsening condition. The Populist Party expressed their demands for reform, and for a brief period in the 1890s shared power with the Republican Party in the Fusion movement. Under the leadership of Charles Brantley Aycock, conservative Democrats fought back with virulent denunciations of "Negro rule" and a call for white supremacy. In 1900, voters elected Aycock governor and approved a constitutional amendment that barred all illiterates from voting, except for those whose ancestors had voted before 1867. This literacy test and "grandfather clause" effectively disenfranchised blacks, while providing a temporary loophole for uneducated whites. To safeguard white rights after 1908 (the constitutional limit for registration under the grandfather clause), Aycock promised substantial improvements in the school system to put an end to white illiteracy.

In the decades after Aycock's election, an alliance of business interests and moderate-to-conservative Democrats dominated North Carolina politics. The industrial triumvirate of textile, tobacco, and furniture manufacturers, joined by banks and insurance companies, controlled the state's economy. The Republican Party shrank to a small remnant among mountain whites as blacks were forced out of the electorate.

In the years since World War II, North Carolina has taken its place in the booming Sunbelt economy. The development of Research Triangle Park—equidistant from the educational facilities of Duke University, North Carolina State University, and the University of North Carolina at Chapel Hill—has provided a home for dozens of scientific laboratories for government and business. New industries, some of them financed by foreign capital, have appeared in formerly rural areas, and a prolonged population drain has been reversed.

The process of development has not been smooth or uniform, however. The late 1980s and early 1990s saw a shift in employment patterns as financial and high-technology industries boomed while jobs in the state's traditional industries, notably textiles and tobacco, declined. North Carolina possesses both the largest percentage of manufacturing jobs in the country and the lowest manufacturing wages. In 1990, 30% of all jobs paid annual wages below the poverty line for a family of four. The excellence of many of North Carolina's universities contrasts with the inferior education provided by its primary and secondary public schools. North Carolina students' SAT scores placed them last nationally in 1989.

Racial tensions have created divisions within the state, which has one of the highest levels of Ku Klux Klan activity in the country. While Charlotte integrated its schools peacefully in 1971 through court-ordered busing, the militancy of black activists in the late 1960s and early 1970s provoked a white backlash. That backlash, along with the identification of the Democratic party in the early seventies with liberal causes and with opposition to the Vietnam War, helped the conservative wing of the Republican party gain popularity in a state whose six military bases had given it a hawkish tradition. In 1972, North Carolina elected its first Republican US senator (Jesse A. Helms) and governor (James E. Holshouser, Jr.) since Fusion days, and Republican strength has continued to build. After the election of November 1994, Republicans held 8 of the state's 12 House seats. In 1990 Harvey Gantt, the liberal black mayor of Charlotte, challenged Helms, who had earned a reputation as the most conservative member of the Senate, in his bid for re-election to a fourth term. Helms won by a margin of 8% of the vote. Gantt mounted another unsuccessful challenge against Helms in 1996.

Rising crime rates were among the leading public policy issues in the 1990s. The state legislature enacted laws imposing tough penalties on adults who supply guns to minors, and mandating life imprisonment without parole for three-time violent offenders.

In 1996 hurricanes Bertha and Fran caused millions of dollars worth of damage and together killed 30 people.

12STATE GOVERNMENT

North Carolina has operated under three constitutions, adopted in 1776, 1868, and 1971, respectively. The first was drafted hurriedly under wartime pressures and contained several inconsistencies and undemocratic features. The second, a product of Reconstruction, was written by native white Republicans and a sprinkling of blacks and northern-born Republicans. When conservative whites regained power, they left the basic framework of this constitution intact, though they added the literacy test, poll tax, and grandfather clause to it.

A century after the Civil War, the document had become unwieldy and partially obsolete. A constitutional study commission submitted to the general assembly in 1969 a rewritten constitution, which the electorate ratified, as amended, in 1971. As of the end of 1983, 16 other amendments had been added, one of which permits the governor and lieutenant governor to serve two successive four-year terms.

Under the 1971 constitution, the general assembly consists of a 50-member senate and a 120-member house of representatives. Senators must be at least 25 years old, must be qualified voters of the state, and must have been residents of the state for at least two years prior to election. Representatives must be qualified voters of the state and must have lived in their district for at least a year; the constitution establishes 21 as the minimum age for elective office. All members of the general assembly serve two-year terms. The legislative salary was $13,951 in 1995.

The governor and lieutenant governor (who run separately) must be 30 years old; each must have been a US citizen for five years and a state resident for two. In 1996 the governor's salary was $98,576. North Carolina's chief executive has powers of appointment, supervision, veto, and budgetary recommendation. The voters also elect a secretary of state, treasurer, auditor, superintendent of public instruction, attorney general, and commissioners of agriculture, insurance, and labor to four-year terms. These officials preside over their respective departments and sit with the governor and lieutenant governor as the council of state. The governor appoints the heads of the 10 other executive departments.

Bills become law when they have passed three readings in each house of the general assembly, and take effect 30 days after adjournment. Constitutional amendments may be proposed by a convention called by a two-thirds vote of both houses and a majority of the voters, or may be submitted directly to the voters by a three-fifths consent of each house. In either case, the proposed amendments must be ratified by a popular majority before becoming part of the constitution.

Prospective voters in North Carolina must be US citizens who are at least 18 years old and have never been convicted of a felony (unless their rights have been restored by law). They must have lived in North Carolina for one year and in their home precinct for 30 days prior to the election.

¹³POLITICAL PARTIES

Prior to the Civil War, Whigs and Democrats were the two major political groups in North Carolina. The Republican Party emerged during Reconstruction as a coalition of newly enfranchised blacks, northern immigrants, and disaffected native whites, especially from nonslaveholding areas in the mountains. The opposing Conservative Party, representing a coalition of antebellum Democrats and former Whigs, became the Democratic Party after winning the governorship in 1876; from that time and for most of the 20th century, North Carolina was practically a one-party state.

Beginning in the 1930s, however, as blacks reentered the electorate as supporters of the New Deal and the liberal measures associated with Democratic presidents, the Republican Party attracted new white members who objected to national Democratic policies. Republican presidential candidates picked up strength in the 1950s and 1960s, and Richard Nixon carried North Carolina in 1968 and 1972, when Republicans also succeeded in electing Governor James E. Holshouser, Jr., and US Senator Jesse A. Helms. The Watergate scandal cut short this movement toward a revitalized two-party system, and in 1976, Jimmy Carter became the first Democratic presidential candidate to carry the state since 1964.

Republican presidential candidate Ronald Reagan narrowly carried North Carolina in 1980, and a second Republican senator, John P. East, was elected that year. In 1984, the Republican Party had its best election year in North Carolina. Reagan won the state by a landslide, Helms won a third term—defeating Governor James B. Hunt in the most expensive race in Senate history (more than $26 million was spent)—and Republican James G. Martin, a US representative, was elected governor, succeeding Hunt. In 1990, Helms was reelected to the Senate, defeating black mayor Harvey Gantt in a bitterly contested race. In 1996 Gantt challenged Helms again, and once again Helms was the victor. Lauch Faircloth, a Republican, captured the other Senate seat in 1992. In 1996, Republican Bob Dole won 49% of the vote in the presidential election, Democrat Bill Clinton won 44%, and Independent Ross Perot won 7%. James B. Hunt won re-election to the governorship in 1996. Following the November 1996 elections, 6 of North Carolina's 12 US Representatives were Republicans. In the state legislature, 30 of the state senators were Democrats and 20 were Republicans. There were 61 Republicans

North Carolina Presidential Vote by Political Parties, 1948–96

YEAR	ELECTORAL VOTE	NORTH CAROLINA WINNER	DEMOCRAT	REPUBLICAN	STATES' RIGHTS DEMOCRAT	PROGRESSIVE
1948	14	*Truman (D)	459,070	258,572	69,652	3,915
1952	14	Stevenson (D)	652,803	558,107	—	—
1956	14	Stevenson (D)	590,530	575,069	—	—
1960	14	*Kennedy (D)	713,136	655,420	—	—
1964	13	*Johnson (D)	800,139	624,841	—	—
						AMERICAN IND.
1968	13	*Nixon (R)	464,113	627,192	—	496,188
						American
1972	13	*Nixon (R)	438,705	1,054,889	—	25,018
					LIBERTARIAN	
1976	13	Carter (D)	927,365	741,960	2,219	5,607
1980	13	*Reagan (R)	875,635	915,018	9,677	—
1984	13	*Reagan (R)	824,287	1,346,481	3,794	—
						NEW ALLIANCE
1988	13	*Bush (R)	890,167	1,237,258	1,263	5,682
						IND. (Perot)
1992	14	Bush (R)	1,114,042	1,134,661	5,171	357,864
1996	14	Dole (R)	1,107,849	1,225,938	8,740	168,059

*Won US presidential election.

and 59 Democrats in the state assembly. In 1994, 2,313,520 voters (61%) were registered as Democrats, 1,217,114 (32%) as Republicans, and 2,86,746 as Independents.

Minor parties have had a marked influence on the state. George Wallace's American Independent Party won 496,188 votes in 1968, placing second with more than 31% of the total vote. In 1992, Independent Ross Perot captured 14% of the vote.

Minority representation in North Carolina politics has been growing. In 1993 there were 468 blacks holding public office; in 1993 Melvin Watt, an African American, was elected to the US House of Representatives. In 1995, 27 women served in the state legislature.

14LOCAL GOVERNMENT

As of 1992, North Carolina had 100 counties, 516 municipalities, and 321 special districts.

Counties have been the basis of local government in North Carolina for more than 300 years, and are still the primary governmental units for most citizens. All counties are led by boards of commissioners; commissioners serve either two- or four-year terms, and most are elected at large rather than by district. Most boards elect their own chairman from among their own members, but voters in some counties choose a chairman separately. More than half the counties employ a county manager to supervise day-to-day operations of county government. Counties are subdivided into townships, but these are for administrative convenience only; they do not exercise any independent government functions.

County and municipal governments share many functions, but the precise allocation of authority varies in each case. Although the city of Charlotte and Mecklenburg County share a common school system, most often schools, streets, sewers, garbage collection, police and fire protection, and other services are handled separately. Most cities use the council-manager form of government, with council members elected from the city at large. Proliferation of suburban governments is hampered by a 1972 constitutional amendment that forbids the incorporation of a new town or city within 1 mi (1.6 km) of a city of 5,000–9,999 people, within 3 mi (4.8 km) of a city of 10,000–24,999, within 4 mi (6.4 km) of a city of 25,000–49,999, and within 5 mi (8 km) of a city of 50,000 or more unless the general assembly acts to do so by a three-fifths vote of all members of each house.

15STATE SERVICES

The Department of Public Instruction administers state aid to local public school systems, a board of governors directs the 16 state-supported institutions of higher education, and the Department of Community Colleges administers the 58 community colleges. The Department of Cultural Resources offers a variety of educational and enrichment services to the public, maintaining historical sites, operating two major state museums, funding the North Carolina Symphony, and providing for the State Library. The Department of Transportation plans, builds, and maintains state highways; registers motor vehicles; develops airport facilities; administers public transportation activities; and operates 15 ferries.

Within the Department of Human Resources, the Division of Mental Health, Mental Retardation, and Substance Abuse Services operates 4 regional psychiatric hospitals, 5 regional mental retardation centers, and 3 alcoholic rehabilitation centers; it also coordinates 41 area mental health programs that include community mental health centers, group homes for the mentally retarded and emotionally disturbed, shelter workshops, halfway houses, a special-care facility, and 2 reeducation programs for emotionally disturbed children and adolescents. The Division of Social Services administers public assistance programs, and other

divisions license medical facilities, promote public health, administer programs for juvenile delinquents and the vocationally handicapped, and operate a school for the blind and visually impaired and three schools for the deaf.

The Department of Crime Control and Public Safety includes the Highway Patrol and the National Guard, while the Department of Correction manages the prison system. Local law enforcement agencies receive assistance from the Department of Justice's State Bureau of Investigation and the Police Information Network. The Community Assistance Division of the Department of Natural Resources and Community Development offers a variety of planning services to local government in the areas of housing, neighborhood renewal, and fiscal resources. The Department of Labor administers the state Occupational Safety and Health Act; inspects boilers, elevators, amusement rides, mines, and quarries; offers conciliation, mediation, and arbitration services to settle labor disputes; and enforces state laws governing child labor, minimum wages, maximum working hours, and uniform wage payment.

16JUDICIAL SYSTEM

North Carolina's general court of justice is a unified judicial system that includes appellate courts (supreme court and court of appeals) and trial courts (superior court and district court). District court judges are elected to four-year terms; judges above that level are elected for eight years.

The state's highest court, the supreme court, consists of a chief justice and 6 associate justices. It hears cases from the court of appeals as well as certain cases from lower courts. The court of appeals comprises 12 judges who hear cases in 3-judge panels. Superior courts, in 44 districts, have original jurisdiction in most major civil and criminal cases. There are over 80 superior court judges appointed by the governor to eight-year terms. All superior court justices rotate between the districts within their divisions. District courts try misdemeanors, civil cases involving less than $5,000, and all domestic cases. They have no juries in criminal cases, but these cases may be appealed to superior court and be given a jury trial de novo; in civil cases, jury trial is provided on demand. In 1996 North Carolina had 12,113 active attorneys.

North Carolina had 25,576 prisoners in state and federal institutions in 1995. In 1995 North Carolina's overall crime rate per 100,000 persons was 5,639.5, including 646.4 for violent crime and 4,993.1 for property crime. The 9.4 murders per 100,000 population were somewhat above the national average of 8.2 while the 32.2 forcible rapes were slightly lower than the national average of 37.1.

North Carolina punishes crime severely. From 1930 to 1992, the state ranked 5th in number of persons executed (273). The US Supreme Court invalidated North Carolina's death penalty statute in 1976, and the sentences of all inmates then on death row reverted to life imprisonment. The state passed a new capital punishment statute in 1977 that apparently met the Court's objections, and two persons were executed in 1984—the state's first executions since 1961. One of the prisoners executed that year, Velma Barfield, was the first woman executed in the US since 1962 and the first in North Carolina since 1944.

In 1995 there were 139 persons under sentence of death and 2 were executed.

17ARMED FORCES

North Carolina holds the headquarters of the 3d Army at Ft. Bragg in Fayetteville and a major training facility for the Marine Corps at Camp Lejeune in Jacksonville. The Marine Corps air stations at Cherry Point and New River and Seymour Johnson Air Force Base in Goldsboro are the state's other important military installations. North Carolina firms received $1.4 billion in defense contract awards in 1995/96.

In 1996, there were 96,250 active duty military personnel stationed in North Carolina, more than 70,000 of whom were at Ft. Bragg.

There were 703,000 veterans living in North Carolina as of 1 July 1996; fewer than 500 saw service in World War I, 178,000 in World War II, 117,000 in the Korean Conflict, 232,000 during the Viet Nam era, and 49,000 in the Persian Gulf War. Veterans' benefits totaled $1.1 billion in 1995/96.

The strength of the Reserve and National Guard was 43,186 in 1996: Army, 30,002; Navy and Marine Corps, 8,707; and Air Force, 4,477.

In 1993, the North Carolina State Highway Patrol employed 1,236 full-time sworn officers, or 2 per 10,000 residents.

[18]MIGRATION

For most of the state's history, more people have moved away every decade than have moved into the state, and population growth has come only from net natural increase. In 1850, one-third of all free, native-born North Carolinians lived outside the state, chiefly in Tennessee, Georgia, Indiana, and Alabama. The state suffered a net loss of population from migration in every decade from 1870 to 1970.

Before 1890, the emigration rate was higher among whites than among blacks; since then, the reverse has been true, but the number of whites moving into North Carolina did not exceed the number of white emigrants until the 1960s. Between 1940 and 1970, 539,000 more blacks left North Carolina than moved into the state; most of these emigrants sought homes in the North and West. After 1970, however, black out-migration abruptly slackened as economic conditions in eastern North Carolina improved. Net migration to North Carolina was estimated at 278,000 (6th among the states) from 1970 to 1980, at 83,000 (9th among the states) from 1980 to 1983; and 347,000 (5th among the states) from 1985 to 1990. Between 1990 and 1996, the state had net gains of 367,655 in domestic migration and 36,687 in international migration. In 1996, 7,011 foreign immigrants arrived in North Carolina. In 1990, 70.4% of all state residents had been born in North Carolina, down from 76.1% in 1980. About 46% of residents age 5 and older lived in a different house in 1985 than in 1990, of which 27% did so in another state.

[19]INTERGOVERNMENTAL COOPERATION

North Carolina adheres to at least 17 interstate compacts, including 4 that promote regional planning and development. The oldest of the 4, establishing the Board of Control for Southern Regional Education, pools the resources of southern states for the support of graduate and professional schools. The Southeastern Forest Fire Protection Compact promotes regional forest conservation, while the Southern Interstate Energy Compact fosters cooperation in nuclear power development. The Southern Growth Policies Board, formed in 1971 at the suggestion of former North Carolina Governor Terry Sanford, collects and publishes data for planning purposes from its headquarters in Research Triangle Park. The Tennessee Valley Authority operates three dams in western North Carolina to aid in flood control, generate hydroelectric power, and assist navigation downstream on the Tennessee River; most of the electricity generated is exported to Tennessee. Total federal aid in 1996 was nearly $5.2 billion.

[20]ECONOMY

North Carolina's economy was dominated by agriculture until the closing decades of the 19th century, with tobacco the major cash crop; today, tobacco is still the central factor in the economy of the coastal plain. In the piedmont, industrialization accelerated after 1880 when falling crop prices made farming less attractive. During the "cotton mill crusade" of the late 19th and early 20th centuries, local capitalists put spinning or weaving mills on swift streams throughout the region, until nearly every hamlet had its own factory. Under the leadership of James B. Duke, the American Tobacco Co. (now American Brands, with headquarters in New York City) expanded from its Durham headquarters during this same period to control, for a time, virtually the entire US market for smoking products. After native businessmen had established a successful textile boom, New England firms moved south in an effort to cut costs, and the piedmont became a center of southern industrial development.

As more and more Tar Heels left agriculture for the factory, their per capita income rose from 47% of the national average in 1930 to almost 83% in 1983. The biggest employers are the textile and furniture industries. Wages in these labor-intensive fields remain comparatively low in all states, but especially low in North Carolina. As of 1992, North Carolina led the nation in the proportion of manufacturing workers in its nonagricultural work force, but ranked 32d in per capita income in 1989.

Since the 1950s, state government has made a vigorous effort to recruit outside investment and to improve the state's industrial mix. Major new firms now produce electrical equipment, processed foods, technical instruments, fabricated metals, plastics, and chemicals. The greatest industrial growth, however, has come not from wholly new industries but from fields related to industries that were firmly established. Apparel manufacture spread across eastern North Carolina during the 1960s as an obvious extension of the textile industry, and other new firms produce chemicals and machinery for the textile and furniture business.

The major test for North Carolina's continued economic growth will be whether the state can break out of the low-skill, low-wage trap. Despite recent improvements, North Carolina remains well below the national average in total personal income and gross state product. In 1996 the per capita personal income was $22,101, placing North Carolina 32d in the nation. The gross state product in 1994 was $181,521 million, to which private goods–producing industries contributed $65,142 million; private services–producing industries, $92,155 million; and government, $24,224 million. During 1996, there were 22,196 filings for bankruptcy, up 39% from 1995.

[21]INCOME

In 1996 North Carolina's per capita personal income averaged $22,101, 32d among the 50 states. Measured in current dollars, per capita income increased by 63.3% between 1986 and 1995, faster than the 53.3% national increase and faster than the 59% increase as in the Southeast region as a whole. North Carolina's total nonfarm personal income of $149 billion in 1995 (up 8.0% from $138 billion in 1994) represented 2.5% of the US total.

Median household income was $31,979 in 1995, when 12.6% of North Carolina residents were below the poverty line.

[22]LABOR

North Carolina is unusual for combining a predominantly industrial and service-related work force with a dispersed pattern of rural residence. North Carolina's civilian labor force numbered 3,796,000 in 1996. The overall unemployment rate in 1996 was 4.3%, compared to 5.4% nationally.

The following employment and wages were tabulated in North Carolina during 1995:

	AVERAGE ANNUAL EMPLOYMENT (1,000S)	ANNUAL WAGES PAID ($MILLIONS)	AVERAGE WEEKLY WAGES/WORKER
Agricultural services, forestry, fisheries	42.3	693.3	$315
Mining	3.6	1,132.1	697
Construction	174.9	4,216.6	464
Manufacturing	862.3	23,928	534
Transportation, Public Utilities	162.4	5,461.3	647
Wholesale trade	181.4	5,982.6	634
Retail trade	620.2	8,637.4	268
Finance, insurance, and real estate	144.9	4,807.4	638
Services	713.4	16,132.4	435
Government	533.6	13,830.4	498

North Carolina working conditions have brought the state considerable notoriety in recent years. As of December 1996, the average North Carolina factory worker received a wage of $466.91 per week. Only 2.9% of all manufacturing workers belonged to a labor organization in 1995, and only 4.2% of all workers were union members (2d lowest among the states).

North Carolina has a right-to-work law, and public officials are legally barred from negotiating a collective bargaining agreement. The major symbol of resistance to unionization in recent decades has been J. P. Stevens & Co., a textile firm found guilty of illegal labor practices 21 times between 1966 and 1979, the highest conviction rate in US history. The Amalgamated Clothing and Textile Workers Union won the right to represent employees at seven J. P. Stevens mills in Roanoke Rapids but waged a 17-year battle to use it; not until 1980 was a contract finally approved. In the interim, Stevens was found guilty of refusing to bargain in good faith by the National Labor Relations Board and a US court of appeals, and union supporters had turned to a national boycott of Stevens products as an additional source of pressure on the company. Despite this settlement, Stevens maintained it would continue to block organizational efforts at its other plants. In 1983, a $1.2-million settlement resolved the eight remaining complaints of unfair labor practices brought against Stevens by the union.

23AGRICULTURE

Farm marketings in North Carolina totaled nearly $7 billion in 1996, 8th among the 50 states, with 46% from crop marketings. North Carolina led the nation in the production of tobacco and sweet potatoes, ranked 4th in peanuts, and was also a leading producer of corn, grapes, pecans, apples, tomatoes, and soybeans. Farm life plays an important role in the culture of the state.

The number of hired and family workers on North Carolina farms was 83,835 in 1990 (down from 590,000 in 1950). According to state government statistics, the number of farms fell from 301,000 in 1950 to 58,000 in 1996, while the number of acres in farms declined from 17,800,000 to 9,200,000 (7,203,000 to 3,723,000 hectares). At 158 acres (64 hectares), the average North Carolina farm was only one-third the size of the average US farm—a statistic that in part reflects the smaller acreage requirements of tobacco, the state's principal crop. The relatively large number of family farm owner-operators who depend on a modest tobacco allotment to make their small acreages profitable is the basis for North Carolina's opposition to the US government's antismoking campaign and its fight to preserve tobacco price supports.

Although farm employment continues to decline, a significant share of North Carolina jobs—perhaps more than one-third—are still linked to agriculture either directly or indirectly. North Carolina's most heavily agricultural counties are massed in the coastal plain, the center of tobacco, corn, and soybean production, along with a bank of northern piedmont counties on the Virginia border. Virtually all peanut production is in the eastern part of the state, while tobacco, corn, and soybean production spills over into the piedmont. Cotton is grown in scattered counties along the South Carolina border and in a band leading northward across the coastal plain. Beans, tomatoes, cucumbers, strawberries, and blueberries are commercial crops in selected mountain and coastal plain locations. Apples are important to the economy of the mountains, and the sand hills are a center of peach cultivation.

In 1996, tobacco production was 590,683,000 lb, 37.7% of US production. Production and value data for North Carolina's other principal crops were as follows: corn, 85,500,000 bushels, $290,700,000; soybeans, 34,800,000 bushels, $233,160,000; peanuts, 363,750,000 lb, $95,666,000; and sweet potatoes, 4,340,000 hundredweight, $52,514,000.

24ANIMAL HUSBANDRY

North Carolina farms and ranches had 1.19 million cattle and calves in 1997, valued at $476 million. In 1996, the state had around 9.3 million hogs and pigs, valued at $855.6 million. During 1995, North Carolina led the nation in turkey production with 1.4 billion lb of turkey, worth $582 million; the state was 4th in broiler production with 3.4 billion lb, worth $1.16 billion; the state was also 9th in egg production with 3.152 billion eggs, worth $203 million. Milk cows numbered 87,000 in 1995 and they produced 1.4 million lb of milk.

25FISHING

North Carolina's fishing industry ranks 2d only to Virginia's among the South Atlantic states, but its overall economic importance has declined. The record landing for the state was in 1981, a total of 432 million lb; the 1995 catch was only 184.7 million lb, valued at $110.9 million. North Carolina had 10,050 commercial fishing boats and vessels in 1994. Flounder, menhaden, and sea trout are the most valuable finfish; shrimp, crabs, and clams are the most sought-after shellfish. The state's 219 fish processors and wholesalers employed 1,988 persons in 1994. In 1995/96, the state issued 571,273 sport fishing licenses.

26FORESTRY

As of 1992, forests covered 19,277,549 acres (7,801,624 hectares) in North Carolina, or about 62% of the state's land area. North Carolina's forests constitute 2.8% of all US forestland, and fully 97.5% of the state's wooded areas have commercial value. The largest tracts are found along the coast and in the Western Mountains, where most counties are more than 70% tree-covered. Hardwoods make up 53% of the state's forests. Mixed stands of oak and pine account for an additional 14%. The remaining 33% is pine and other conifers. More than 90% of the acreage harvested for timber is reforested.

National forests embrace 6% of North Carolina's timberlands, and state and local governments own another 2%. The remainder is privately owned.

In the days of wooden sailing vessels, North Carolina pine trees supplied large quantities of "naval stores"—tar, pitch, and turpentine for waterproofing and other nautical purposes. Today, the state produces mainly saw logs, pulpwood, veneer logs, and Christmas trees.

North Carolina has about 2,900 forest product manufacturing plants, and leads the nation in hardwood veneer and plywood production, as well as furniture production. In 1995, the lumber, furniture, and paper industries employed 43,900, 79,300, and 23,800 persons, respectively. The value added by manufacture and the value of shipments for the lumber industry that year was $2,124.8 million and $5,458.6 million, respectively; for the furniture industry, $3,433.5 million and $5,577 million.

27MINING

The estimated 1995 value of minerals produced in North Carolina increased 5% over that of 1994, rising from $709 million to $742 million. The recovery was led by significant increases in the value of the state's leading mineral commodities, crushed stone and phosphate rock, along with smaller increases in feldspar, dimension stone, talc, gemstones, and pyrophyllite. Crushed stone, valued at $380 million (8% more than in 1994, was the state's leading mineral commodity. Production was estimated at 57.2 million metric tons and accounted for over 51% of the total value of mineral production. Phosphate rock, in Beaufort County, and lithium minerals, mined in the Kings Mountain area of Gaston and Cleveland counties, were the next most valuable mineral commodities mined. In 1995, North Carolina continued to lead the nation in the production of lithium compounds. The only other domestic lithium production was from geothermal brine deposits in Nevada. North Carolina also ranked 1st in the production of feldspar, crude mica, and olivine, 3d in phosphate, 5th in talc and pyrophyllite, and 7th in industrial sand and gravel. Clay production amounted to 2.25 million metric tons, valued at $10.1 million. Two categories of clay, common clay, and shale and kaolin, were produced, the kaolin as a byproduct of feldspar and mica operations in Avery and Cleveland counties. Production of feldspar was 483,000 metric tons (valued at $17.7 million), while mica production was 68 million metric tons (valued at $3.2 million).

28ENERGY AND POWER

Except for a modest volume of hydroelectric power, the energy consumed in North Carolina comes from outside sources. The state used 2,214.2 trillion Btu of energy in 1994, of which 36% came from petroleum, 26% from coal, 9% from natural gas, 16% from nuclear power, 4% from hydropower, and the remainder imported from other states. Residential users consumed about 23% of North Carolina's energy in that year, commercial users 17%, industrial users 34%, and transportation 26%.

Installed electrical capacity totaled 21.6 million kW in early 1996, and production reached 96.1 billion kWh in 1995. The two Brunswick stations in Southport and the Harris plant in Wake County, operated by Carolina Power & Light, and the two Duke Power McGuire stations at Cowens Ford Dam were the only nuclear power units in operation at the start of 1996.

No petroleum or natural gas has been found in North Carolina, but major companies have expressed interest in offshore drilling. There is no coal mining, and proved coal reserves are minor, at only 10.7 million tons.

29INDUSTRY

North Carolina has had a predominantly industrial economy for most of the 20th century. Today, the state remains the nation's largest manufacturer of textiles, cigarettes, and furniture. The textile industry was the largest manufacturing sector in 1991, followed by tobacco manufacturers, chemicals and allied products, industrial machinery, food products, electronics/electrical equipment, furniture and fixtures, and rubber and plastics products. The total value of shipments by manufacturers exceeded $152 billion in 1995. The following table shows value of shipments by manufacturers for selected industries in 1995:

Textile mills	$22,742,500,000
Tobacco manufacturers	14,226,900,000
Chemicals and allied products	20,345,600,000
Industrial machinery	14,648,500,000
Electronic/electrical equipment	12,505,600,000
Furniture and fixtures	6,756,500,000
Rubber and misc. plastics	6,902,700,000
Paper and paper products	5,577,000,000

The industrial regions of North Carolina spread out from the piedmont cities; roughly speaking, each movement outward represents a step down in the predominant level of skills and wages and a step closer to the primary processing of raw materials. Burlington Industries (the world's largest textile company), Blue Bell Inc., Cannon Mills, and Cone Mills are major US textile corporations based in Greensboro; Fieldcrest Mills has its headquarters in Eden. The furniture industry is centered in the High Point-Thomasville and Hickory-Statesville areas. Charlotte's factories produce electrical appliances, textiles, and chemicals and machinery for the textile industry. Broad rural areas of the piedmont also have many industrial installations: Gaston County near Charlotte contains the largest concentration of textile factories in the US.

In 1997, North Carolina was the headquarters for seven Fortune 500 companies: Nationsbank Corp., First Union Corp., Lowe's, Duke Power, Wachovia Corp., Nucor, and Carolina Power and Light.

In 1995, 1,230 US patents were issued to North Carolina residents.

30COMMERCE

North Carolina had 13,351 wholesale establishments in 1992 with sales of over $76.3 billion, including $34.4 billion in durable goods. Wholesaling is concentrated in the Piedmont Crescent. Retail sales by 44,164 establishments in 1992 totaled $49.6 billion (11th). The leading retail sales sectors in 1992 were automotive dealers, 21.5%; food stores, 19.9%; general merchandise stores, 11.9%; and eating and drinking places, 10.1%.

The state ports at Wilmington and Morehead City handle a growing volume of international trade. In 1995 $4.4 billion worth of export goods were exported from Wilmington and $7.4 billion were imported. North Carolina exported over $15.7 billion worth of its goods to foreign markets in 1996 (10th in the US).

31CONSUMER PROTECTION

The Consumer Protection Section of the Department of Justice has as its function the protection of North Carolina consumers from unfair and deceptive trade practices and dishonest and unethical business competition. Although it assists in the resolution of disputes, investigates cases of consumer fraud, and initiates action to halt proscribed trade practices, it does not represent individual consumers in court. It also represents the public before the North Carolina Utilities Commission.

32BANKING

North Carolina had 61 insured commercial banks in 1996 with assets of $180 billion and deposits of $94 billion. There were 65 FDIC-insured savings institutions in 1996, with assets of $8.9 billion and total deposits of $7.1 billion.

33INSURANCE

In 1995, 19 life insurance companies were domiciled in North Carolina. North Carolina families held, on average, $126,500 in life insurance coverage in 1995, about 1% above the US average. The 10,329,000 policies in effect that year had a combined value of $365 billion. North Carolinians paid life insurance premiums totaling $2.7 billion in 1995, and received $2.8 billion in benefits, including $908.7 million in death benefits. Also in 1995, policy holders paid property and liability companies $6.0 billion in premiums, including $2.1 billion in automobile liability coverage, $923.3 million in automobile physical damage insurance, and $642.8 million in homeowners' policies.

34SECURITIES

There are no securities exchanges in North Carolina. The Securities Division of the Office of Secretary of State is authorized to protect the public against fraudulent issues and sellers of securities.

35PUBLIC FINANCE

The North Carolina budget is prepared biennially by the governor and reviewed annually by the Office of State Budget and Management, in consultation with the Advisory Budget Commission, an independent agency composed of five gubernatorial appointees, five members from the senate, and five from the house of representatives. It is then submitted to the general assembly for amendment and approval. The fiscal year runs from 1 July to 30 June. The following is a summary of projected consolidated revenues and recommended expenditures for 1992/93, 1993/94, and 1994/95 (in millions):

	1992/93	1993/94	1994/95
REVENUES			
General fund	$ 8,209.5	$ 9,378.6	$11,425,714
Individual income tax	(3,921.4)	(4,124.4)	(4,699,115)
Corporate income tax	(643.0)	(511.6)	(906,007)
Sales and use tax	(2,391.1)	(2,455.7)	(5,571,600)
Franchise tax	(416.8)	(455.9)	(248,992)
Federal funds	3,617.6	4,516.4	2,921,279
Highway fund	1,318.4	1,363.3	5,474,293
Other receipts	1,363.2	1,456.5	2,269,417
TOTALS	$14,508.7	$16,714.8	$22,091,333
EXPENDITURES			
Education	$ 6,034.7	$ 6,472.1	$7,761,071
Human resources	4,244.2	5,283.7	5,604,217
Transportation	1,614.3	1,716.6	1,818,036
Other outlays	2,615.5	3,242.4	5,253,289
TOTALS	$14,508.7	$16,714.8	$20,436,713

North Carolina's total state indebtedness was $4.5 billion as of 1995, or $632.04 per capita.

36TAXATION

The state's total tax revenues were $11.88 billion, a per capita share of $1,622.60.

In 1996, the personal income tax ranged from 6.0% to 7.75%. Most corporate incomes faced a 7.75% levy on net income. The state sales and use tax is 4%. Prescription drugs and certain other articles are exempt from sales tax, but food is not. As of 1996, the cigarette tax was 5 cents per pack, and the gasoline tax was 21.6 cents per gallon. The state also levies inheritance, estate, gift, insurance, beverage, and franchise taxes.

North Carolina taxpayers contributed $24.1 billion to the federal treasury in 1995 and received $30.6 billion in federal funding in 1995.

37ECONOMIC POLICY

North Carolina's government has actively stimulated economic growth ever since the beginning of the 19th century. During the administration of Governor Luther H. Hodges (1954–61), the state began to recruit outside investment directly, developing such forward-looking facilities as Research Triangle Park. Since the 1970s, other policies and legislation have been aimed at the fostering of development in rural areas, where per capita income is lower and unemployment is higher than elsewhere in the state. In 1996, under the administration of Governor James B. Hunt, the General Assembly adopted the William S. Lee Quality Jobs and Business Expansion Act. The act groups North Carolina's 100 counties into Enterprise Tiers, and provides for graduated tax credit amounts, depending upon Enterprise Tier location, for specific company activities including job creation, machinery and equipment investment, worker training, and research and development.

The state also actively participates in programs involving industrial revenue bonds, state and federally assisted loan and grant programs, business energy loans, and assistance to local communities with shell buildings that can be customized to meet the needs of a company in a shorter period of time.

38HEALTH

Health conditions and health care facilities in North Carolina vary widely from region to region. In the larger cities—and especially in proximity to the excellent medical schools at Duke University and the University of North Carolina at Chapel Hill—quality health care is as readily available as anywhere in the US.

Around 16.5% of North Carolinians were uninsured in 1995. The one million Medicare and 985,000 Medicaid recipients in North Carolina received respectively $3.7 and $2.7 billion dollars in health care in 1994.

The birthrate in North Carolina dropped from 24.1 live births per 1,000 population in 1960 to 15.3 per l,000 in 1977 and to 14.3 in 1982, before rising to 14.1 in 1995, still below the national average. In the year ending with February 1995, 9.3 infants per 1,000 live births died before their first birthday. There were 35,253 legal abortions in 1992, or 339 per 1,000 live births. There were 14.36 AIDS cases per 100,000 population, lower than the 28.48 US average of 1995. The leading causes of death in North Carolina are similar to those in the rest of the US, although, as of 1991, North Carolinians died less frequently from heart disease and cancer than other Americans, and more frequently from cerebrovascular disease, accidents, and suicide. The 1996 death rate of 925.1 per 100,000 was above the national average. Many of North Carolina's residents between the ages of 18 and 30 were smokers in 1995. Projected deaths caused by smoking–related illness numbered 165,692. North Carolina had the highest percentage (30.2%) of male smokers in the United States in 1995 (21.8% for women).

A particularly serious public health problem in North Carolina is byssinosis, or brown lung disease. Caused by prolonged inhalation of cotton dust, byssinosis cripples the lungs of longtime textile workers, producing grave disability and even death. According to a study in 1980, the Brown Lung Association estimated that some 25,000 present or former North Carolina textile workers showed symptoms of byssinosis, and that between 10,000 and 15,000 North Carolinians were disabled by it; textile industry estimates ran to less than one-tenth of those figures.

The 119 hospitals in North Carolina contained 20,362 beds in 1995. Average hospital expenses were $806 per inpatient day and $5,701 per stay in 1994, both figures below the US average.

The number of physicians was 17,527 in 1995; the number of professionally active registered nurses was 55,800 in 1994. There were 3,016 active licensed dentists in 1994. One–third of all doctors in North Carolina are classified as primary care physicians in 1995. The state acted to increase the supply of doctors in eastern North Carolina in the 1970s by the establishment of a new medical school at East Carolina University in Greenville. Medical schools and superior medical research facilities are also located at Duke University Medical Center in Durham, UNC Hospitals at the University of North Carolina in Chapel Hill, and the Bowman Gray School of Medicine at Wake Forest University in Winston-Salem.

39SOCIAL WELFARE

North Carolina's social welfare programs are modest by national standards. Aid to families with dependent children (AFDC) benefited 282,000 persons in 1996; the average payment was

$297 per family per month, well below the national average. In the same year, the school lunch program cost was $149.4 million, and 631,061 residents received monthly food stamp allowances averaging $72.20.

With the enactment of the Personal Responsibility and Work Opportunity Reconciliation Act of 1996, the US government has changed the form and regulations for many of its social welfare programs; most significantly, it replaces Aid to Families with Dependent Children (AFDC), an open-ended entitlement program, with Temporary Assistance for Needy Families (TANF), a limited system of assistance funded largely through federal block grants. The reform act also impacts the food stamp program, the Supplemental Security Income program, and the child nutrition program. The law took effect on 1 July 1997 and provided $16.38 billion in block grants for fiscal years 1997–2002. The grants are to be divided among the states based on an equation involving the numbers of former AFDC recipients in each state. Because many of the bill's provisions have yet to be implemented into state-by-state policy, it was not possible to include the details of each state's programs for this edition of this work.

Social Security benefits were paid to nearly 1.2 million North Carolina residents in 1995, averaging $681 a month. The Supplemental Security Income program assisted 190,790 aged, disabled, and blind recipients that year, averaging payments of $293 a month. The average weekly unemployment insurance benefit was $189.62.

⁴⁰HOUSING

In 1996 there were an estimated 3,119,000 units of year-round housing in North Carolina, of which 2,730,000 were occupied. In 1996, 66,997 privately owned units, valued at $6 billion, were authorized for construction; of these, 51,796 were single-family. During 1996, North Carolina received $407.1 million in aid from the US Department of Housing and Urban Development, including $75.2 million in community development block grants. The proportion of houses built within the previous 10 years (28.6%) was much higher than the proportion built before 1939 (9.9%). Most housing units had the customary amenities of the average American home: 98.5% had complete plumbing facilities; 65.4% utilized water from a public system or a private company; 49.8% were connected to a public sewer.

⁴¹EDUCATION

North Carolina's commitment to education has been strengthened in recent years with legislative and financial support for improving student achievement through high standards; teacher accountability; an emphasis on teaching the basics of reading, writing and mathematics; and moving state control of schools to the local, community level.

Legislation passed in 1996 allowed for the state's first public charter schools, up to 100 of them, and the first ones approved began operating in 1997.

The state received a strong ranking, placing it in the top 12 states in the nation educationally, in the first national report card on state-by-state performance ever issued. That work was released in 1997 by *Education Week* magazine and the Pew Charitable Trusts.

School leaders received strong evidence of the public's support of public schools in 1996 when voters overwhelmingly approved $1.8 billion in a statewide bond referendum to build and renovate schools. By comparison, in 1953, the school construction needs, approved in a statewide referendum, were $50 million.

North Carolina has a rich educational history, having started the first state university in the United States, in 1795, and the first free system of common schools in the South in 1839. North Carolina led the nation in the construction of rural schools in the 1920s.

In 1957, Charlotte, Greensboro, and Winston-Salem were the first cities in the South to admit black students voluntarily to formerly all-white schools. But, as was the case throughout the South, widespread desegregation took much longer. In 1971, the US Supreme Court, in the landmark decision *Swann v. Charlotte-Mecklenburg Board of Education*, upheld the use of busing to desegregate that school system. The remainder of the state soon followed suit.

North Carolina piloted a public kindergarten program in 1969, established a statewide testing program in 1977, (requiring since 1978 that students pass a competency test before graduating), and increased high school graduation requirements in 1983, becoming the first state to require that students pass Algebra I in order to earn a diploma.

Each school district has a five-year state board – approved technology plan. From 1995 to mid-1997, $62 million had been used to buy and upgrade school technology; today, North Carolina schools have one computer per six students.

Total public school enrollment in 1996 was 1,172,894 in the state's 117 school districts. The state's school systems employed 137,247 full-time personnel. In 1996, North Carolina led the nation in the highest number of nationally certified teachers.

North Carolina has been active in providing special programs for gifted students. Governor's School, a summer residential program for the gifted, was founded in 1963. Other talented students are served by the highly regarded North Carolina School of the Arts in Winston-Salem, which began operating in 1965, and the North Carolina School of Science and Mathematics, located in Durham, which opened in 1980.

The University of North Carolina (UNC) was chartered in 1789 and opened at Chapel Hill in 1795. The UNC system now embraces 16 campuses under a common board of governors; total enrollment stood at 152,483 in 1996. The three oldest and largest campuses, all of which offer research and graduate as well as undergraduate programs, are UNC-Chapel Hill, North Carolina State University in Raleigh (the first land-grant college for the study of agriculture and engineering), and UNC-Greensboro. North Carolina's 58 community colleges and the NC Center for Applied Textile Technology in Belmont enrolled approximately 780,000 students in 1996.

Duke University in Durham is North Carolina's premier private institution and takes its place with the Chapel Hill and Raleigh public campuses as the third key facility in the Research Triangle. In addition to the public institutions and community colleges, there are also 35 private, four-year schools, of which Wake Forest University in Winston-Salem and Davidson College in Davidson are most noteworthy. Additionally, the state has two private junior colleges, plus seven theological seminaries for a total of 118 institutions of higher learning.

⁴²ARTS

North Carolina has been a pioneer in exploring new channels for state support of the arts. It was the first state to fund its own symphony, to endow its own art museum, to found a state school of the arts, to create a statewide arts council, and to establish a cabinet-level Department of Cultural Resources. Its state arts council, created in 1964, reaches the pubic through a network of over 100 community arts councils and over 600 arts organizations each year. The North Carolina Symphony, based in Raleigh, gives free concerts to more than 150,000 public school children, and performs 175 concerts annually. The North Carolina Museum of Art, which is visited by about 230,000 people each year, features one of the finest collections of early European master paintings in the country. The museum's collection spans 5,000 years and includes work by Dutch masters, Renaissance masterpieces, Egyptian artifacts, classical statues, and tribal and contemporary art.

The North Carolina Arts Council's Grassroots Arts Program established in 1977, was the nation's first per capita funding program for the local arts initiatives in which decision making remained at the local level. The program has invested over $21 million in community-based programming over the past 20 years.

For 30 years, the North Carolina Arts Council has supported artists in the schools to teach, perform, and encourage creative expression. The council was instrumental in funding two of the first arts-based curriculum experiments in the state; there are now 27 elementary schools teaching core curriculum through the arts and interdisciplinary instruction.

In 1996/97, the state of North Carolina provided $5,384,268 in state funds to support arts programs, and the National Endowment for the Arts contributed $1,224,400. In 1997 North Carolina had 2,177 arts organizations; 34,091 artists working in all disciplines; and over 18,000,000 citizens and visitors participating in the arts programs.

At least 200 arts-related festivals are held in North Carolina each year. Summer dance and music festivals, as well as professional theaters and historical outdoor dramas, galleries and museums, and the crafts community all serve as anchors for the state's $9.2 billion tourism industry. North Carolina's Pulitzer Prize–winning playwright Paul Green created the genre of historical drama with the 1937 production of *The Lost Colony*, which celebrates its 60th season in 1997. North Carolina's nine outdoor historical dramas (double the number of any other state), had more than $2 million in ticket sales in 1995.

Based for 20 years in Durham, the American Dance Festival has commissioned new dance works, preserved dance history, trained dancers, and presented the best in contemporary dance. The African American Dance Ensemble, based in North Carolina, performs for over 350,000 people across the US each year. Flat Rock Playhouse, the state theater of North Carolina, performed for over 60,000 people from 46 states in 1996, generating ticket sales of $930,000.

Folk and traditional arts thrive across North Carolina in all disciplines. The North Carolina Folk Heritage Awards are given to recognize the state's leading folk artists. Penland School of Crafts, the John C. Campbell Folk School, the Southern Highland Guild, Qualla Arts and Crafts Mutual, Inc., the Core Sound Waterfowl Museum and the North Carolina Pottery Center are but a few of the organizations in North Carolina that help to keep the craft traditions alive. A 1994 economic impact study found that $122 million was spent on crafts in a 20–county region of western North Carolina alone.

43LIBRARIES AND MUSEUMS

Public libraries, open in nearly every North Carolina community, are linked together through the State Library, ensuring that users in all parts of the state can have access to printed, filmed, and recorded materials. Total volumes in public libraries numbered 13,992,298 in 1995/96, when circulation reached 34,915,578. Major university research libraries are located at the Chapel Hill, Raleigh, and Greensboro campuses of the University of North Carolina and at Duke University in Durham. The North Carolina Collection and Southern Historical Collection at the Chapel Hill campus are especially noteworthy.

North Carolina had 174 museums and historical sites in 1996/97. Established in 1956, the North Carolina Museum of Art, in Raleigh, is one of only two state-supported art museums in the US (the other is in Virginia); the museum had an attendance of 240,718 in 1991. The North Carolina Museum of History is in Raleigh. The Department of Cultural Resources administers 20 state historical sites and Tryon Place Restoration in New Bern. The Museum of Natural History in Raleigh is maintained by the state Department of Agriculture; smaller science museums exist in Charlotte, Greensboro, and Durham.

44COMMUNICATIONS

Government postal service in North Carolina began in 1755 but did not become regular until 1771, with the establishment of a central post office for the southern colonies. Mails were slow and erratic, and many North Carolinians continued to entrust their letters to private travelers until well into the 19th century. Rural free delivery in the state began on 23 October 1896 in Rowan County.

Telephone service began in Wilmington and Raleigh in October 1879, and long distance connections between Wilmington and Petersburg, Va., began later that same year. There were 20 telephone companies in North Carolina in 1982; in March 1996, 93% of the state's 2,646,000 occupied housing units had telephones.

There were 206 AM radio stations in North Carolina in 1996, and 170 FM stations. Commercial television stations numbered 34, and there were 11 noncommercial stations. As of 1996, cable television service was provided by 20 large systems.

45PRESS

As of 1997, North Carolina had 21 morning newspapers, 29 evening dailies, and 35 Sunday papers. The following table shows the circulation of the largest dailies as of 1997:

AREA	NAME	DAILY	SUNDAY
Charlotte	*Observer* (m,S)	240,170	303,106
Greensboro	*News & Record* (m,e,S)	95,973	124,031
Raleigh	*News & Observer* (m,S)	151,159	201,357
Winston–Salem	*Journal* (m,S)	92,998	104,334

The *Charlotte Observer* won a 1981 Pulitzer Prize for its series on brown lung disease. The (Raleigh) *News & Observer* won a 1996 Pulitzer Prize for its series on the hog industry in North Carolina.

North Carolina has been the home of several nationally recognized "little reviews" of literature, poetry, and criticism, including *The Rebel, Crucible, Southern Poetry Review, The Carolina Quarterly, St. Andrews Review, The Sun, Pembroke Magazine*, and *Miscellany*. The *North Carolina Historical Review* is a quarterly scholarly publication of the Division of Archives and History.

46ORGANIZATIONS

The 1992 Census of Service Industries counted 1,608 organizations in North Carolina, including 392 business associations; 800 civic, social, and fraternal associations; and 416 other membership organizations.

The North Carolina Citizens Association serves as the voice of the state's business community. A teachers' organization, the North Carolina Association of Educators, is widely acknowledged as one of the most effective political pressure groups in the state, as is the North Carolina State Employees Association. Every major branch of industry has its own trade association, most of which are highly effective lobbying bodies. Carolina Action, the North Carolina Public Interest Research Group, the Kudzu Alliance, and the Brown Lung Association represent related consumer, environmental, antinuclear power, and public health concerns. Among the national organizations headquartered in the state are the Improved Benevolent Protective Order of Elks of the World, the Association of Professors of Medicine, Winston-Salem; the Institute for Southern Studies, Durham; the Tobacco Association of the US, Raleigh; and the US Power Squadrons, Raleigh.

47 TOURISM, TRAVEL, AND RECREATION

Travelers spent $2.2 billion in North Carolina in 1995. Tourists are attracted by North Carolina's coastal beaches, by golf and tennis opportunities in the piedmont (including the world-famous golf courses at Pinehurst), and parks and scenery in the North Carolina mountains. Sites of special interest are the Revolutionary War battlegrounds at Guilford Courthouse and Moore's Creek Bridge; Bennett Place, near Hillsborough, where the last major Confederate army surrendered; Ft. Raleigh, the site of the Lost Colony's misadventures; and the Wright Brothers National Memorial at Kitty Hawk. Cape Hatteras and Cape Lookout national seashores, which protect the beauty of the Outer Banks, together cover 58,563 acres (23,700 hectares) and received over 3 million visitors in 1996. The Blue Ridge Parkway, a scenic motor route operated by the National Park Service that winds over the crest of the Blue Ridge in Virginia, North Carolina, and Georgia, attracts millions of visitors to North Carolina yearly. Another popular attraction, Great Smoky Mountains National Park, straddling the North Carolina-Tennessee border, annually attracts about 9 million visitors to North Carolina. In 1995, North Carolina's 27 state parks received more than 11,974,118 visitors. In the same year, licenses were held by 621,802 anglers and 458,765 hunters.

48 SPORTS

There are three major league professional sports teams in North Carolina: The Charlotte Hornets of the National Basketball Association, the Carolina Panthers of the National Football League, and the Carolina Hurricanes of the National Hockey League, who relocated to Raleigh from Hartford, Conn., in 1997. Minor league baseball's Carolina League is based in North Carolina, and six minor league teams call the state home. Additionally, there is minor league hockey in Charlotte and Raleigh. Two other professional sports that figure prominently in the state are golf and stock-car racing. The Greater Greensboro Open, the Kemper Open in Charlotte, and the Hall of Fame Classic at Pinehurst are major tournaments on the Professional Golfers' Association tour. The North Carolina Motor Speedway in Rockingham hosts the Carolina 500 annually, while the Charlotte Motor Speedway is the home of the World 600, the most lucrative race after the Daytona 500 on the National Association for Stock Car Auto Racing (NASCAR) Winston Cup circuit.

College basketball is the ruling passion of amateur sports fans in North Carolina. Organized in the Atlantic Coast Conference, the University of North Carolina at Chapel Hill, North Carolina State University, Wake Forest University, and Duke University consistently field nationally ranked basketball teams. North Carolina won the NCAA Championships in 1957, 1982, and 1993, North Carolina State captured the title in 1974 and 1983, and Duke won back-to-back championships in 1991 and 1992.

Other annual sporting events include the Stoneybrook Steeplechase in Southern Pines in April. The National Hollerin' Contest in Spivey's Corner tests farmers' ability to call livestock, and the State Championship Horse Show is held in Raleigh in September.

49 FAMOUS NORTH CAROLINIANS

Three US presidents had North Carolina roots, but all three reached the White House from Tennessee. Andrew Jackson (1767–1845), the 7th president, was born in an unsurveyed border region, probably in South Carolina, but studied law and was admitted to the bar in North Carolina before moving to frontier Tennessee in 1788. James K. Polk (1795–1849), the 11th president, was born in Mecklenburg County but grew up in Tennessee. Another native North Carolinian, Andrew Johnson (1808–75), was a tailor's apprentice in Raleigh before moving to Tennessee at the age of 18. Johnson served as Abraham Lincoln's vice president for six weeks in 1865 before becoming the nation's 17th president when Lincoln was assassinated. William Rufus King (1786–1853), the other US vice president from North Carolina, also served for only six weeks, dying before he could exercise his duties.

Three native North Carolinians have served as speaker of the US House of Representatives. The first, Nathaniel Macon (1758–1837), occupied the speaker's chair from 1801 to 1807 and served as president pro tem of the US Senate in 1826–27. The other two were James K. Polk and Joseph G. "Uncle Joe" Cannon (1836–1926), who served as speaker of the House from 1903 to 1911, but as a representative from Illinois.

Sir Walter Raleigh (or Ralegh, b.England, 1552?–1618) never came to North Carolina, but his efforts to found a colony there led state lawmakers to give his name to the new state capital in 1792. Raleigh's "Lost Colony" on Roanoke Island was the home of Virginia Dare (1587–?), the first child of English parents to be born in America. More than a century later, the infamous Edward Teach (or Thatch, b.England, ?–1716) made his headquarters at Bath and terrorized coastal waters as the pirate known as Blackbeard.

Principal leaders of the early national period included Richard Caswell (b.Maryland, 1729–89), Revolutionary War governor; William Richardson Davie (b.England, 1756–1820), governor of the state and founder of the University of North Carolina; and Archibald De Bow Murphey (1777–1832), reform advocate, legislator, and judge. Prominent black Americans of the 19th century who were born or who lived in North Carolina were John Chavis (1763–1838), teacher and minister; David Walker (1785–1830), abolitionist; and Hiram Revels (1827–1901), first black member of the US Senate.

North Carolinians prominent in the era of the Civil War and Reconstruction included antislavery author Hinton Rowan Helper (1829–1909), Civil War governor Zebulon B. Vance (1830–94), Reconstruction governor William W. Holden (1818–92), and "carpetbagger" judge Albion Winegar Tourgee (b.Ohio, 1838–1905). Among major politicians of the 20th century are Furnifold McLendell Simmons (1854–1940), US senator from 1901 to 1931; Charles Brantley Aycock (1859–1912), governor from 1901 to 1905; Frank Porter Graham (1886–1972), University of North Carolina president, New Deal adviser, and US senator, 1949–50; Luther H. Hodges (b.Virginia, 1898–1974), governor from 1954 to 1960, US secretary of commerce from 1961 to 1965, and founder of Research Triangle Park; Samuel J. Ervin, Jr. (1896–1985), US senator from 1954 to 1974 and chairman of the Senate Watergate Investigation; Terry Sanford (b.1917), governor from 1961 to 1965, US presidential aspirant, and president of Duke University; and Jesse Helms (b.1921), senator since 1973. Civil rights leader Jesse Jackson (b.1941) began his career as a student activist in Greensboro. The most famous North Carolinian living today is probably evangelist Billy Graham (b.1918).

James Buchanan Duke (1856–1925) founded the American Tobacco Co. and provided the endowment that transformed Trinity College into Duke University. The most outstanding North Carolina-born inventor was Richard J. Gatling (1818–1903), creator of the "Gatling gun," the first machine gun. The Wright brothers, Wilbur (b.Indiana, 1867–1912) and Orville (b.Ohio, 1871–1948), achieved the first successful powered airplane flight at Kitty Hawk, on the Outer Banks, on 17 December 1903. Psychologist Joseph Banks Rhine (b.Pennsylvania, 1895–1980) was known for his research on extrasensory perception. Kary Mullis, 1993 winner of the Nobel Prize for chemistry, was born in Lenoir, North Carolina.

A number of North Carolinians have won fame as literary figures. They include Walter Hines Page (1855–1918), editor and diplomat; William Sydney Porter (1862–1910), a short-story writer who used the pseudonym O. Henry; playwright Paul Green (1894–1984); and novelists Thomas Wolfe (1900–38) and Reynolds Price (b.1933). Major scholars associated with the state have included sociologist Howard W. Odum (b.Georgia, 1884–1954) and historians W. J. Cash (1901–41) and John Hope Franklin (b.Oklahoma, 1915). Journalists Edward R. Murrow (1908–65), Tom Wicker (b.1926), and Charles Kuralt (1934–97) were all North Carolina natives. Harry Golden (Harry L. Goldhurst, b.New York, 1903–81), a Jewish humorist, founded the *Carolina Israelite*.

Jazz artists Thelonious Monk (1918–82), John Coltrane (1926–67), and Nina Simone (b.1933) were born in the state, as were pop singer Roberta Flack (b.1939), folksinger Arthel "Doc" Watson (b.1923), bluegrass banjo artist Earl Scruggs (b.1924), and actor Andy Griffith (b.1926). North Carolina athletes include former heavyweight champion Floyd Patterson (b.1935), NASCAR driver Richard Petty (b.1937), football quarterbacks Sonny Jurgenson (b.1934) and Roman Gabriel (b.1940), baseball pitchers Gaylord Perry (b.1938) and Jim "Catfish" Hunter (b.1946), and basketball player Meadowlark Lemon (b.1932), long a star with the Harlem Globetrotters. Michael Jordan (b. Brooklyn, N.Y., 1963) played college basketball at the University of North Carolina, and went on to fame as a National Basketball Association star.

50BIBLIOGRAPHY

Chafe, William H. *Civilities and Civil Rights: Greensboro, North Carolina and the Black Struggle for Freedom.* New York: Oxford University Press, 1980.

Clay, James W., Douglas M. Orr, Jr., and Alfred W. Stuart (eds.). *North Carolina Atlas: Portrait of a Changing Southern State.* Chapel Hill: University of North Carolina Press, 1975.

Fleer, Jack D. *North Carolina Government & Politics.* Lincoln, Nebr.: University of Nebraska, 1994.

Jones, H.G. *North Carolina History: An Annotated Bibliography.* Westport, Conn.: Greenwood Press, 1995.

Lefler, Hugh T., and Albert Ray Newsome. *North Carolina: The History of a Southern State.* 3d ed., rev. Chapel Hill: University of North Carolina Press, 1973.

Nathans, Sydney. *The Quest for Progress: The Way We Lived in North Carolina, 1870–1920.* Chapel Hill: University of North Carolina Press, 1983.

Powell, William S. *North Carolina: A Bicentennial History.* New York: Norton, 1977.

—Powell, William S. *The North Carolina Gazetteer.* Chapel Hill: University of North Carolina Press, 1968.

State of North Carolina. Office of State Budget and Management. *North Carolina State Government Statistical Abstract, 1984.* 5th ed. Raleigh, 1984.

NORTH DAKOTA

State of North Dakota

ORIGIN OF STATE NAME: The state was formerly the northern section of Dakota Territory; *dakota* is a Siouan word meaning "allies." **NICKNAME:** Peace Garden State. **CAPITAL:** Bismarck. **ENTERED UNION:** 2 November 1889 (39th). **SONG:** "North Dakota Hymn." **MARCH:** "Spirit of the Land." **MOTTO:** Liberty and Union, Now and Forever, One and Inseparable. **FLAG:** The flag consists of a blue field with yellow fringes; on each side is depicted an eagle with outstretched wings, holding in one talon a sheaf of arrows, in the other an olive branch, and in his beak a banner inscribed with the words "*E Pluribus Unum.*" Below the eagle are the words "North Dakota"; above it are 13 stars surmounted by a sunburst. **OFFICIAL SEAL:** In the center is an elm tree; beneath it are a sheaf of wheat, a plow, an anvil, and a bow and three arrows, and in the background an Indian chases a buffalo toward a setting sun. The depiction is surrounded by the state motto, and the words "Great Seal State of North Dakota October 1st 1889" encircle the whole. **BIRD:** Western meadowlark. **FISH:** Northern pike. **FLOWER:** Wild prairie rose. **TREE:** American elm. **GRASS:** Western wheatgrass. **BEVERAGE:** Milk. **STONE:** Teredo petrified wood. **LEGAL HOLIDAYS:** New Year's Day, 1 January; Birthday of Martin Luther King, Jr., 3d Monday in January; George Washington's Birthday, 3d Monday in February; Good Friday, March or April; Memorial Day, last Monday in May; Independence Day, 4 July; Labor Day, 1st Monday in September; Veterans Day, 11 November; Thanksgiving Day, 4th Thursday in November; Christmas Day, 25 December. **TIME** 6 AM CST = noon GMT; 5 AM MST = GMT.

¹LOCATION, SIZE, AND EXTENT

Located in the western north-central US, North Dakota ranks 17th in size among the 50 states.

The total area of North Dakota is 70,703 sq mi (183,121 sq km), comprising 69,300 sq mi (179,487 sq km) of land and 1,403 sq mi (3,634 sq km) of inland water. Shaped roughly like a rectangle, North Dakota has three straight sides and one irregular border on the E. Its maximum length E-W is about 360 mi (580 km), its extreme width N-S about 210 mi (340 km).

North Dakota is bordered on the N by the Canadian provinces of Saskatchewan and Manitoba; on the E by Minnesota (with the line formed by the Red River of the North); on the S by South Dakota; and on the W by Montana. The total boundary length is 1,312 mi (2,111 km). The state's geographic center is in Sheridan County, 5 mi (8 km) SW of McClusky.

²TOPOGRAPHY

North Dakota straddles two major US physiographic regions: the Central Plains in the east and the Great Plains in the west. Along the eastern border is the generally flat Red River Valley, with the state's lowest point, 750 feet (229 meters); this valley was once covered by the waters of a glacial lake. Most of the eastern half of North Dakota consists of the Drift Prairie, at 1,300–1,600 feet (400–500 meters) above sea level. The Missouri Plateau occupies the western half of the state, and has the highest point in North Dakota—White Butte, 3,506 (1,069 meters)—in the Slope Country of the southwest. Separating the Missouri Plateau from the Drift Prairie is the Missouri Escarpment, which rises 400 feet (122 meters) above the prairie and extends diagonally from northwest to southeast.

North Dakota has two major rivers: the Red River of the North, flowing northward into Canada; and the Missouri River, which enters in the northwest and then flows east and, joined by the Yellowstone River, southeast into South Dakota.

³CLIMATE

North Dakota lies in the northwestern continental interior of the US. Characteristically, summers are hot, winters very cold, and rainfall sparse to moderate, with periods of drought. The average annual temperature is 40°F (4°C), ranging from 7°F (–14°C) in January to 69°F (21°C) in July. The record low temperature, –60°F (–51°C), was set at Parshall on 15 February 1936; the record high, 121°F (49°C), at Steele on 6 July 1936.

The average yearly precipitation is about 18 in (46 cm). The total annual snowfall averages 40 in (102 cm) at Bismarck.

⁴FLORA AND FAUNA

North Dakota is predominantly a region of prairie and plains, although the American elm, green ash, box elder, and cottonwood grow there. Cranberries, juneberries, and wild grapes are also common. Indian, blue, grama, and buffalo grasses grow on the plains; the wild prairie rose is the state flower.

Once on the verge of extinction, the white-tailed and mule deers and pronghorn antelope have been restored. The elk and grizzly bear, both common until about 1880, had disappeared by 1900; bighorn sheep, reintroduced in 1956, are beginning to flourish. North Dakota claims more wild ducks than any other state except Alaska, and it has the largest sharptailed grouse population in the US. The black-footed ferret and northern swift fox are listed by federal authorities as endangered in North Dakota.

⁵ENVIRONMENTAL PROTECTION

North Dakota has little urban or industrial pollution. An environmental issue confronting the state in the mid-1980s and early 1990s was how to use its coal resources without damaging the land through strip mining or polluting the air with coal-fired industrial plants. Major environmental issues confronting the state are importation of non-hazardous and hazardous solid wastes for treatment or disposal, non-point surface water pollution from agricultural and native land, groundwater contamination by fuel storage tanks and by irrigation, and air pollution by energy conversion plants.

North Dakota has little urban air pollution with one exception: motor vehicle traffic is causing excess ambient carbon monoxide in an area within the city of Fargo. The major industrial sources of air contaminants within the state are seven coal-fired electrical generating plants, a coal gasification plant, a refinery, and agricultural commodity processing facilities. The ambient air quality has been in compliance with federal standards, although an epidemiologic study has associated certain air contaminants with a higher incidence of respiratory illness among persons living in the vicinity of coal-burning plants.

To conserve water and provide irrigation, nearly 700 dams have been built, including Garrison Dam, completed in 1960. The Garrison Diversion Project, authorized by the US Congress in 1965, was intended to draw water from Lake Sakakawea, the impoundment behind Garrison Dam.

North Dakota's municipal solid waste stream is estimated at 1,350 tons per day (4.3 lb per person). The state has 16 municipal landfills. Diversion of household waste to recycling grew to 125 million lb for 1996, or about 12.5% of the waste stream. Yard wastes, household appliances, and scrap tires are also diverted for compost, recycling, or fuel, respectively.

[6] POPULATION

North Dakota ranked 47th in the US with a 1990 census population of 638,800 representing a decrease of 2.1% since 1980. The estimated population in 1996 was 643,539. The population density in 1990 was 9.3 per sq mi (3.5 per sq km), making it the fifth most sparsely populated state. North Dakota is one of the most rural states in the US, with 62% of its population living outside metropolitan areas as of 1990. Leading cities as of 1990 were Fargo, with a population of 79,715; Bismarck, the capital, 52,592; and Grand Forks, 50,168.

[7] ETHNIC GROUPS

As of 1990, about 94.6% of the state's population was white. The American Indian population was 26,000, or about 4.1% of the total, and there were some 4,000 blacks, representing 0.6% of the population. Among Americans of European origin, the leading groups were Germans, who made up 50% of the total population, and Norwegians, who made up 29%. Only about 1.5% of the state's population was foreign-born as of 1990, predominantly from neighboring Canada.

[8] LANGUAGES

Although a few Indian words are used in the English spoken near the reservations where Ojibwa and Sioux live in North Dakota, the only general impact of Indian speech on English is in such place-names as Pembina, Mandan, Wabek, and Anamoose.

A few Norwegian food terms like *lefse* and *lutefisk* have entered the Northern dialect that is characteristic of North Dakota, and some Midland terms have intruded from the south.

In 1990, 92.1% of the population 5 years old or older spoke only English at home; German, the next most frequently used language, was spoken by 24,453 residents.

[9] RELIGIONS

As of 1990 there were an estimated 310,713 adherents of Protestant groups, representing nearly one-half of the state's total population. Leading denominations were the Evangelical Lutheran Church in America with 179,711 adherents; Lutheran Church–Missouri Synod, 25,691; United Methodist Church, 23,850; and United Presbyterian Church, 11,960. As of 1990, the state had 173,432 Roman Catholics, representing more than one-fifth of the total population, and an estimated 483 Jews.

[10] TRANSPORTATION

In 1996, there were 4,406 mi (6,511 km) of rail trackage in North Dakota. Railroad lines, the largest of which were the Burlington Northern Santa Fe (BNSF) and the CP rail system (Soo Line), transported over 44.4 million tons of freight by rail in 1995. Farm products and coal accounted for most of the tonnage originated and carried within the state. Amtrak passenger service was provided by the Chicago–Seattle/Portland route. Total North Dakota ridership on Amtrak was 61,110 in 1995.

There were 86,831 mi (140,050 km) of public roads, streets, and highways in North Dakota in 1995. There were also 677,276 registered motor vehicles and 448,781 licensed drivers in the state.

In 1996, there were 300 private airports, 93 public airports, and 51 heliports in North Dakota. There are approximately 150 scheduled aircraft arrivals and departures daily in the state. About 8,000 tons of freight are transported annually by air in North Dakota.

[11] HISTORY

Human occupation of what is now North Dakota began about 13,000 BC in the southwestern corner of the state, which at that time was covered with lush vegetation. Drought drove away the aboriginal hunter-gatherers, and it was not until about 2,000 years ago that Indians from the more humid regions to the east moved into the easternmost third of the Dakotas. About AD 1300 the Mandan Indians brought an advanced agricultural economy up the Missouri River. They were joined by the Hidatsa and Arikara about three or four centuries later. Moving from the Minnesota forests during the 17th century, the Yanktonai Sioux occupied the southeastern quarter of the state. Their cousins west of the Missouri River, the Teton Sioux, led a nomadic life as hunters and mounted warriors. The Ojibwa, who had driven the Sioux out of Minnesota, settled in the northeast.

European penetration of the Dakotas began in 1738, when Pierre Gaultier de Varennes, Sieur de la Vérendrye, of Trois Riviéres in New France, traded for furs in the Red River region. Later the fur trade spread farther into the Red and Missouri river valleys, especially around Pembina, where the North West Company and the Hudson's Bay Company had their posts. After the Lewis and Clark expedition (1804–06) explored the Missouri, the American Fur Company traded there, with buffalo hides the leading commodity.

In 1812, Scottish settlers from Canada moved up the Red River to Pembina. This first white farming settlement in North Dakota also attracted numerous métis, half-breeds of mixed Indian and European ancestry. An extensive trade in furs and buffalo hides, which were transported first by heavy carts and later by steamboats, sprang up between Pembina, Ft. Garry (Winnipeg, Canada), and St. Paul, Minn.

Army movements against the Sioux during and after the Civil War brought white men into central North Dakota, which in 1861 was organized as part of the Dakota Territory, including the present-day Dakotas, Montana, and Wyoming. The signing of treaties confining the agricultural Indians to reservations, the arrival of the Northern Pacific Railroad at Fargo in 1872, and its extension to the Missouri the following year led to the rise of homesteading on giant "bonanza farms." Settlers poured in, especially from Canada. This short-lived "Great Dakota boom" ended in the mid-1880s with drought and depressed farm prices. As many of the original American and Canadian settlers left in disgust, they were replaced by Norwegians, Germans, and other Europeans. By 1910, North Dakota, which had entered the Union in 1889, was among the leading states in percentage of foreign-born residents.

From the time of statehood onward, Republicans dominated politics in North Dakota. Their leader was Alexander McKenzie,

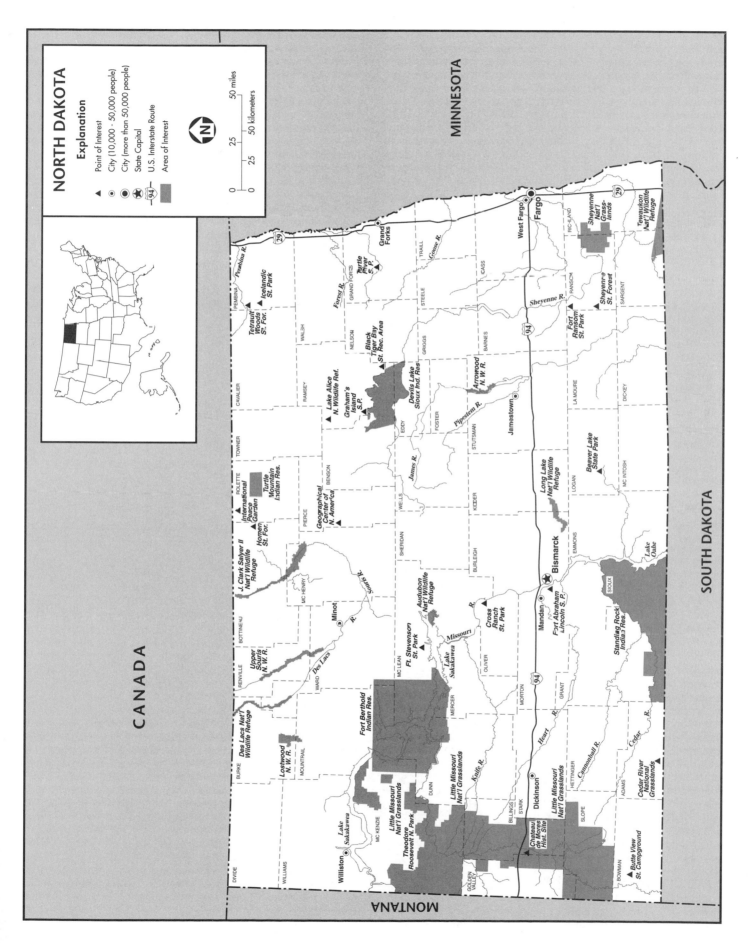

NORTH DAKOTA

Explanation

▲ Point of Interest
⊙ City (10,000 - 50,000 people)
◉ City (more than 50,000 people)
✪ State Capital
94 U.S. Interstate Route
Area of Interest

0   25   50 miles
0   25   50 kilometers

CANADA

MONTANA

SOUTH DAKOTA

MINNESOTA

DIVIDE
BURKE
RENVILLE
BOTTINEAU
ROLETTE
TOWNER
CAVALIER
PEMBINA

WILLIAMS
MOUNTRAIL
WARD
MC HENRY
PIERCE
BENSON
RAMSEY
WALSH

MC KENZIE
DUNN
MERCER
OLIVER
SHERIDAN
WELLS
EDDY
NELSON
GRAND FORKS

BILLINGS
STARK
MORTON
GRANT
BURLEIGH
KIDDER
STUTSMAN
FOSTER
GRIGGS
STEELE
TRAILL

GOLDEN VALLEY
SLOPE
HETTINGER
ADAMS
BOWMAN
SIOUX
EMMONS
LOGAN
LA MOURE
BARNES
CASS

MC INTOSH
DICKEY
SARGENT
RANSOM
RICHLAND

Williston
Minot
Dickinson
Mandan
Bismarck ✪
Jamestown
Grand Forks
West Fargo
Fargo

Des Lacs Nat'l Wildlife Refuge
Lostwood N.W.R.
Upper Souris N.W.R.
J. Clark Salyer II Nat'l Wildlife Refuge
International Peace Garden
Turtle Mountain Indian Res.
Homen St. For.
Geographical Center of N. America
Tetrault Woods St. For.
Icelandic St. Park
Pembina R.
Forest R.
Turtle River S.P.
Lake Alice N. Wildlife Ref.
Graham's Island S.P.
Black Tiger Bay St. Rec. Area
Devils Lake Sioux Ind. Res.
Arrowwood N.W.R.
Pipestem R.
Long Lake Nat'l Wildlife Refuge
Beaver Lake State Park
Sheyenne R.
Sheyenne St. Forest
Fort Ransom St. Park
Sheyenne Nat'l Grass-lands
Tewaukon Nat'l Wildlife Refuge

Fort Berthold Indian Res.
Lake Sakakawea
Ft. Stevenson St. Park
Audubon Nat'l Wildlife Refuge
Cross Ranch St. Park
Fort Abraham Lincoln S.P.
Standing Rock Indian Res.
Lake Oahe
Little Missouri Nat'l Grasslands
Theodore Roosevelt N. Park
Chateau de Mores Hist. Site
Cedar River National Grasslands
Butte View St. Campground

Missouri R.
Knife R.
Heart R.
Cannonball R.
Cedar R.
James R.
Souris R.
Goose R.
Sheyenne R.

Souris R.

a Canadian immigrant who built a reputation as an agent of the railroads, protecting them from regulation. Between 1898 and 1915, the "Second Boom" brought an upsurge in population and railroad construction. In politics, Republican Progressives enacted reforms, but left unsolved the basic problem of how North Dakota farmers could stand up to the powerful grain traders of Minneapolis–St. Paul. Agrarian revolt flared in 1915, when Arthur C. Townley organized the Farmers' Nonpartisan Political League. Operating through Republican Party machinery, Townley succeeded in having his gubernatorial candidate, Lynn J. Frazier, elected in 1916. State-owned enterprises were established, including the Bank of North Dakota, the Home Building Association, the Hail Insurance Department, and a mill and grain elevator. However, the league was hurt by charges of "socialism" and, after 1917, by allegations of pro-German sympathies in World War I, as well as of mismanagement. In 1921, Frazier and Attorney General William Lemke were removed from office in the nation's first recall election.

The 1920s, a period of bank failures, low farm prices, drought, and political disunity, saw the beginnings of an exodus from the state. Matters grew even worse during the depression of the 1930s. Elected governor by hard-pressed farmers in 1932, William Langer took spectacular steps to save farms from foreclosure and to raise grain prices, until a conflict with the Roosevelt administration led to his removal from office on charges that he had illegally solicited political contributions.

World War II brought a quiet prosperity to North Dakota that lasted into the following decades. The Republican Party generally continued to control the state legislature, although Democrats held the governorship from 1960 until 1981. The Arab oil embargo of 1973 and the rise of oil prices throughout the decade spurred drilling for oil, encouraged the mining of lignite for electrical generation, and led to the construction of the nation's first coal gasification plant, at a cost of $2 billion, in a lignite mining area near Beulah. In the 1980s, however, North Dakota's economy suffered a setback when oil prices dropped. In addition, a drought that began in 1987 damaged over 5.3 million acres of land by 1988 and persisted into the 1990s.

The state's economy was boosted by the 1991 repeal of the "blue laws" enforcing the closing of all retail businesses on Sundays. Agricultural production was strong in the late 1980s and early 1990s. However, severe storms and flooding in 1994 damaged about $600 million in crops.

12STATE GOVERNMENT

North Dakota is governed by the constitution of 1889, as amended. Statewide elected officials include governor and lieutenant governor, secretary of state, auditor, treasurer, attorney general, superintendent of public instruction, commissioners of labor, insurance, taxation, and agriculture, and three public service commissioners. In 1996 the governor's salary was $69,648. The legislature, which convenes every two years beginning on the first Tuesday in January, is bicameral, with a 49-member senate and a 98-member house of representatives. Senators are elected to staggered four-year terms, while representatives serve for two years. In 1995 legislators received a per diem salary during regular sessions of $90 per calendar day. A two-thirds vote of the elected members of each house is required to override a gubernatorial veto.

Voters in North Dakota must be US citizens, at least 18 years of age, and must have been residents of the state at least 30 days prior to the election. Advance registration is not required.

13POLITICAL PARTIES

Between 1889 and 1960, Republicans held the governorship for 58 years. North Dakota politics were not monolithic, however, for aside from the Populist and Democratic opposition, the Republican Party was itself torn by factionalism, with Progressive and Nonpartisan League challenges to the conservative, probusiness party establishment. Between 1960 and 1980, the statehouse was in Democratic hands. In the early and mid-nineties, the Republican party increased its influence at the state level, gaining dominance in both houses of the state legislature, having wrestled control of the senate away from the Democrats in the November 1994 election. Following the 1996 election, the state senate had 30 Republicans and 19 Democrats. The state house was dominated by the Republicans, who held 72 seats, while the Democrats had 26.

In November 1996, North Dakotans cast 45% of the total popular vote for Republican Bob Dole, 40% for Democrat Bill Clinton, and 12% for Independent Ross Perot. Edward Schafer, a Republican, won the governorship in 1992 and was reelected in 1996. North Dakota's senators in 1997 were Kent Conrad, a Democrat elected in 1992 to fill a seat vacated by the death of Quentin D. Burdick and reelected to a full term in 1994, and Democrat Byron Dorgan, who was also elected in 1992. North Dakota's US Representative is Democrat Earl Pomeroy who was reelected in 1996. There were 22 women serving in the state legislature and 5 women holding elective executive office in 1995.

North Dakota Presidential Vote by Major Political Parties, 1948–96

YEAR	ELECTORAL VOTE	N. DAKOTA WINNER	DEMOCRAT	REPUBLICAN
1948	4	Dewey (R)	95,812	115,139
1952	4	*Eisenhower (R)	76,694	191,712
1956	4	*Eisenhower (R)	96,742	156,766
1960	4	Nixon (R)	123,963	154,310
1964	4	*Johnson (D)	149,784	108,207
1968	4	*Nixon (R)	94,769	138,669
1972	3	*Nixon (R)	100,384	174,109
1976	3	Ford (R)	136,078	153,470
1980	3	*Reagan (R)	79,189	193,695
1984	3	*Reagan (R)	104,429	200,336
1988	3	*Bush (R)	127,739	166,559
1992**	3	Bush (R)	99,168	136,244
1996**	3	Dole (R)	106,905	125,050

*Won US presidential election.

** Independent candidate Ross Perot received 71,084 votes in 1992 and 32,515 votes in 1996.

14LOCAL GOVERNMENT

North Dakota in 1992 had 2,765 units of local government, including 53 counties, 364 municipalities designated as cities, 1,350 townships, 275 school districts, and 722 special districts. Typical elected county officials are the sheriff, court clerk, county judge, county justice, and state's attorney.

15STATE SERVICES

Educational services are under the jurisdiction of the Department of Public Instruction and the Board of Higher Education; there are state schools for the deaf, blind, handicapped, and mentally retarded. Health and welfare agencies include the State Health Department, Veterans Affairs Department, Social Service Board, and Indian Affairs Commission. Agricultural services include an extensive program of experiment and extension stations. The state bank, mill, and grain elevator established under Nonpartisan League influence remain to this day.

16JUDICIAL SYSTEM

North Dakota has a supreme court of five justices, seven district courts, and a system of local (county) courts. Supreme court justices are elected for 10-year terms, district court judges for 6-year terms. In 1996 there were 1,335 practicing attorneys in the state.

According to the FBI Crime Index, in 1995 North Dakota had a total crime rate of 2,866.3 crimes per 100,000 population (86.7 violent, 2,779.6 property). There were 677 inmates held in correctional facilities.

North Dakota does not have a death penalty.

[17]ARMED FORCES

In 1996, there were 9,503 active-duty military personnel in North Dakota, the majority of whom were stationed at the Strategic Air Command bases at Minot and Grand Forks. North Dakota firms received $106 million in defense contract awards in 1995/96. As of 1996, 58,000 veterans were living in North Dakota, including fewer than 500 from World War I, 15,000 from World War II, 10,000 from the Korean conflict, 18,000 from the Viet Nam era, and 5,000 from the Persian Gulf War. A total of $103 million was spent on major veterans' benefit programs in the state in 1995/96.

In 1996, North Dakota had 6,966 reserve and national guard personnel. In 1993, the North Dakota Highway Patrol employed 122 full-time sworn officers, or 2 per 10,000 residents.

[18]MIGRATION

During the late 19th century, North Dakota was largely settled by immigrants of German and Scandinavian stock. The state reached a peak population in 1930, but then suffered steady losses until well into the 1970s because of out-migration. This trend has shown some signs of abating, however. From 1980 to 1983, the state's population grew 4.3%, in part because of a net gain in migration of about 5,000 people. From 1985 to 1990, North Dakota had a net loss of 44,142 from migration. Between 1990 and 1996, the state had a net loss of 18,905 in domestic migration and 3,123 in international migration. As of 1990, 73.2% of state residents had been born in North Dakota.

About 57% of residents age 5 and older lived in the same house in 1990 as in 1985. Of those who lived in a different house in 1985, 23% did so in a different state. During the 1980s, the urban population grew to outnumber the rural population, rising from 48.8% to 53.3% of the total population.

[19]INTERGOVERNMENTAL COOPERATION

North Dakota participates in such interstate agreements as the Yellowstone River Compact, Western Interstate Energy Compact, and Interstate Oil and Gas Compact. A Minnesota–North Dakota Boundary Compact was ratified in 1961.

Federal assistance in 1992/93 totaled $734 million.

[20]ECONOMY

North Dakota has been and still is an important agricultural state, especially as a producer of wheat, much of which finds its way onto the world market. Many segments of the economy are affected by agriculture; for example, a substantial wholesale trade is involved in moving grain and livestock to market. Like other midwestern farmers, North Dakotans suffered from high interest rates and a federal embargo on grain shipments to the Soviet Union in the early 1980s. Farm numbers have continued to decline, posing a threat to the vitality of the state's rural lifestyle. Growth industries for the state include petroleum and the mining of coal, chiefly lignite; North Dakota has more coal resources than any other state. Manufacturing is concentrated to a great extent on farm products and machinery. North Dakota's gross state product in 1994 was $17,250 million, to which private goods–producing industries contributed $4,613 million; private services–producing industries, $10,299 million; and government, $2,337 million. North Dakota's per capita personal income was $18,625 in 1995, which ranked 43d nationally. During 1996, there were 1,688 bankruptcy filings.

[21]INCOME

In 1996, North Dakota ranked 38th among the 50 states in per capita personal income, with $20,710. Total nonfarm personal income reached $11.7 billion in 1995, an increase of 7.5% from 1994. Total disposable personal income rose from $10.6 billion in 1995 to $11.8 billion in 1996. The median household income was $29,089 in 1995. As of 1995, 12% of all North Dakotans lived below the federal poverty level.

[22]LABOR

North Dakota's labor force numbered 343,000 in 1996, of whom 11,000 (3.1%) were unemployed. At the end of 1996, North Dakota's nonfarm labor force was distributed as follows: 86,300 worked in services; 83,400 in wholesale and retail trade; 72,400 in government; 21,900 in manufacturing; 18,700 in transportation, communications, and public utilities; 14,300 in finance, insurance, and real estate; 13,700 in construction; and 4,000 in mining.

As of 1995, only 10% of all North Dakotans in the workforce belonged to labor unions. A right-to-work law is in force.

[23]AGRICULTURE

North Dakota's farm marketings totaled $3.5 billion in 1995 (22d in the US). Typically, North Dakota is the number one producer of hard spring wheat, durum wheat, sunflowers, barley, oats, flax, all dry edible beans, and pinto beans. In 1995, North Dakota led the nation in all those commodities as well as in overall wheat production. The state ranked second in navy beans and honey, third in sugarbeets, and fourth in rye.

The total number of farms has declined over the years as the average size of farming operations has increased. In 1995, the state had approximately 32,000 farms and ranches occupying 40.3 million acres (16.3 million hectares) and producing 300 million bushels of wheat, 101 million bushels of barley, 1.74 billion lb of sunflowers, 21.6 million bushels of oats, 6.1 hundredweight of dry edible beans, 54 million bushels of corn, 4.2 million tons of sugar beets, and 28.2 million hundredweight of potatoes. The average farm is 1,259 acres (510 hectares).

[24]ANIMAL HUSBANDRY

North Dakota farms and ranches had an estimated 1.9 million cattle and calves, valued at $1.14 billion in 1997. During 1996, there were around 200,000 hogs and pigs, worth $19.2 million. North Dakota farmers produced nearly 8.5 million lb of sheep and lambs, which brought in $6.7 million in gross income in 1995, and nearly 13 million lb of turkey were produced in that same year. Poultry farmers also sold 675,000 lb of chickens and produced 47 million eggs in 1995.

[25]FISHING

There is little commercial fishing in North Dakota. In 1995/96, the state issued 122,863 sport fishing licenses, and federal hatcheries distributed over 72,200 lb of fish within the state.

[26]FORESTRY

The dispersed forests on the rolling prairie are not a dominant feature of the landscape; North Dakota's climate is more favorable to grassland ecosystems. At the time of settlement, native forests covered about 700,000 acres (283,000 hectares). In 1992, there were 462,000 acres (187,000 hectares) of forestland, with an additional 504,500 acres (204,200 hectares) classified as protective shelterbelts, windbreaks, woody draws, and other woody areas. Agricultural clearing, inundation by reservoirs, and other land use changes have resulted in a 9% reduction in total forestland since 1954. Farmers are the largest group of landholders with 66% of forest acreage.

27MINING

The value of nonfuel minerals produced in North Dakota in 1995 was about $24.5 million, down from the $25.3 million reported in 1994. The state ranked 49th nationally in nonfuel mineral value, accounting for 0.01% of the nation's total. Construction sand and gravel accounted for more than 81% of the value ($20,000,000) of North Dakota's nonfuel mineral output, from a production of 7,000,000 metric tons. Recovered elemental sulfur is the second most important mineral produced in North Dakota, in terms of value. Sulfur and other byproducts such as krypton, xenon, anhydrous ammonia, and liquid nitrogen are recovered during natural gas processing at five plants in the western part of the state. Lapidary and collectible materials such as petrified wood, agates, jasper, and flint are also found in North Dakota.

28ENERGY AND POWER

Power stations in North Dakota generated 28.8 billion kWh of electricity in 1995 and had 4.6 million kW of installed electric generating capacity. Energy consumption per capita in 1991 amounted to 538.2 million Btu (5th among the states); energy expenditure per capita was $2,573 in 1994 (4th).

Recoverable coal reserves totaled 1,668 million short tons in 1995, when North Dakota produced 30,112,000 tons of coal. Proved petroleum reserves in 1995 totaled 233,000,000 barrels; production was 32,317,000 barrels in 1996. In 1995, natural gas reserves totaled 463 billion cu feet; marketed production was 49.5 billion cu feet.

29INDUSTRY

By number of employees, the leading manufacturing industries in North Dakota in 1995 were food and food products; industrial machinery and equipment; printing and publishing; electronic and other electric equipment; transportation equipment; and fabricated metal products. Value of shipments of manufactures in 1995 were estimated at over $4.38 billion. The following table shows value of shipments by selected industries in 1995:

Food and related products	$1,570,600,000
Industrial machinery	1,183,900,000
Transportation equipment	396,700,000
Printing and publishing	151,800,000

In 1995, 66 US patents were issued to North Dakota residents.

30COMMERCE

In 1992, North Dakota had 2,086 wholesale establishments, with sales of $7.6 billion. The leading wholesale lines by sales volume were farm-product raw materials, machinery, equipment, and supplies (especially farm machinery), groceries and related products, and petroleum and petroleum products. The state's 4,790 retail establishments recorded $4.7 billion (49th) in sales during 1992. Exports of North Dakota origin totaled $706.8 million in 1996.

31CONSUMER PROTECTION

Allegations of consumer fraud and other illegal business practices are handled by the Consumer Protection Division of the State Attorney General's Office.

32BANKING

As of 1996, North Dakota's 123 insured commercial banks had assets of $8.5 billion, and the state's 3 savings institutions had $5.5 billion in assets.

33INSURANCE

In 1995, North Dakota had 394,000 life insurance policies in force, worth $31.2 billion. The average life insurance per family was $124,800. The total life insurance benefits paid out were $302.8 million. Direct premiums written by property and casualty insurers in 1995 totaled $631 million.

34SECURITIES

North Dakota has no securities exchanges.

35PUBLIC FINANCE

General fund revenues and appropriated expenditures (estimated) are given below for 1995–97 and 1997–99.

	1995–97	1997–99
REVENUES		
Sales and use taxes	$ 528,098,731	$ 566,192,000
Income taxes	311,382,072	336,093,000
Insurance premium tax	35,247,560	34,000,000
Oil & gas production tax	30,648,134	36,528,000
Gaming tax	23,444,235	22,625,000
Oil extraction tax	23,237,950	24,781,648
Cigarette & tobacco tax	45,748,767	45,490,000
Coal severance tax	22,331,993	22,311,000
Coal conversion tax	24,305,245	24,713,000
Bank of North Dakota profits	50,296,005	32,000,000
State mill profits	1,000,000	2,000,000
Other revenues*	51,903,936	50,888,872
Other transfers	37,917,801	45,360,000
TOTALS	$1,373,339,740	$1,441,463,326
EXPENDITURES		
Grants & general government	99,918,490	112,061,044
Education	769,128,539	847,833,814
Health and human services	327,901,612	363,840,767
Regulatory & nat. resources	52,689,864	54,970,268
Public safety	43,207,812	57,118,726
Agriculture, economic development extension, and research	54,097,937	58,570,445
TOTALS	$1,346,944,260	$1,494,395,064

*Other revenues include business privilege tax, interest income, departmental collections, mineral leasing fees, and gas tax administration.

Total expenditures for 1995–97 (including federal and special funds) totaled approximately $3.6 billion, including $500 million for transportation, a total of $1.1 billion for health and human services, and a total of $1.3 billion for education. The recommended total appropriation for 1997–99 is $4 billion. North Dakota has the only state-owned bank and state-owned mill.

36TAXATION

As of 1994, the personal income tax ranged from 2.67% to 12.0%, or 14% of adjusted federal income tax liability on the optional short form, Form 375. The corporate tax rate ranged from 3% to 10.5%. The state also taxed oil and gas production, gasoline, insurance premiums, alcoholic beverages, tobacco products, mineral leases, and coal severance. There is a general sales and use tax of 5%.

In 1995, North Dakotans paid $1.8 million in federal income tax.

37ECONOMIC POLICY

The North Dakota Department of Economic Development and Finance seeks to attract new industry, retain and expand existing industry, promote start-up businesses, and develop markets for state products. The state uses a local approach to provide business incentives, including job-training, financing, and tax-abatement programs.

38HEALTH

The birthrate in 1995 was 13.27 per l,000 population. The mortality rate for all major causes in North Dakota for 1995 was higher than the national average. For 100,000 population, 304.3 residents died of heart disease.

As of January 1997 the state had 46 general acute hospitals, with 3,339 beds, and 4 specialty hospitals (mental health, rehabilitation) with 402 beds. The expense to a hospital for services provided per inpatient day in 1995 averaged $515 and was among the lowest in the US. Medical personnel licensed in the state included 1,300 physicians who provided direct patient care (1997); 7,789 registered nurses (1997); and 289 licensed dentists (1996). Fifteen counties in the state (with a combined population of 49,000) were without a county resident physician in patient care at the end of 1995.

The Centers for Disease Control estimate that in 1992 there were 169 abortions per 1,000 live births. Of the 1,493 abortions performed in 1992, 31.9% were obtained by out-of-state residents. Only 10 provisional cases of AIDS were reported in 1996.

39SOCIAL WELFARE

Benefits averaging $517 a month under the Aid to Families with Dependent Children program (AFDC) were paid to 13,600 recipients in 1996. In the same year, 39,825 residents received monthly food stamp allowances averaging $67.51, and the school lunch program received federal funding of $12.3 million. In 1995, Social Security benefits were paid to 115,540 North Dakotans, averaging $676 a month. The weekly unemployment insurance benefit was $166.08 in North Dakota in 1995.

With the enactment of the Personal Responsibility and Work Opportunity Reconciliation Act of 1996, the US government has changed the form and regulations for many of its social welfare programs; most significantly, it replaces Aid to Families with Dependent Children (AFDC), an open-ended entitlement program, with Temporary Assistance for Needy Families (TANF), a limited system of assistance funded largely through federal block grants. The reform act also impacts the food stamp program, the Supplemental Security Income program, and the child nutrition program. The law took effect on 1 July 1997 and provided $16.38 billion in block grants for fiscal years 1997–2002. The grants are to be divided among the states based on an equation involving the numbers of former AFDC recipients in each state. Because many of the bill's provisions have yet to be implemented into state-by-state policy, it was not possible to include the details of each state's programs for this edition of this work.

40HOUSING

In 1996, North Dakota had some 287,000 housing units, 243,000 of which were occupied. In the same year, 2,324 new units were authorized for construction at a value of $181 million; of these, 1,479 were single-family units. In 1990, the last year for which figures are available, the median home value was $50,800. That year, owners (with a mortgage) and renters had median monthly costs of $608 and $313, respectively. During 1995/96, North Dakota received $73.6 million in aid from the US Department of Housing and Urban Development, including $16.3 million in community development block grants.

41EDUCATION

As of 1990, three-quarters (76.7%) of all adults were high school graduates, and 18.1% had at least four years of college. In 1996/97, 117,816 students were enrolled in public schools, including 80,139 students in prekindergarten to grade 8 and 37,677 in grades 9–12. Average salary for public school teachers (1996/97) was $27,709.

In fall 1996, 40,078 students were enrolled in North Dakota's higher educational institutions, which number 20. The chief universities are the University of North Dakota in Grand Forks, with 11,274 students, and North Dakota State University in Fargo, with 9,598 students. North Dakota is first in the nation for the number of students per capita enrolled in college, and nearly one in three North Dakotans have a college degree. The North Dakota Student Financial Assistance Program offers scholarships for North Dakota college students, and the state Indian Scholarship Board provides aid to Native Americans attending college in the state.

42ARTS

The Council on the Arts, a branch of the North Dakota state government, provides grants to local artists and groups, encourages visits by out-of-state artists and exhibitions, and provides information and other services to the general public. Two popular musical events are the Old Time Fiddlers Contest (at Dunseith in June) and the Medora Musical (Medora, June through Labor Day); the latter features Western songs and dance. The State of North Dakota generated $484,000 in federal funds for its arts programs in 1996. The National Endowment for the Arts (NEA) contributed $429,000 to the state's arts programs and $481,000 to the North Dakota Council on the Arts. The state also provided the council with funding.

From 1987 to 1991, arts program audiences totaled 4,175,000 people, and there were 54,973 contributing artists. The state offered arts education to 13,500 school children. In 1995, North Dakota had 150 arts associations and 35 local arts groups. The North Dakota Council on the Arts provided funds to bring the state's artists into the schools. The council also sponsored the performance of a new dramatic work at the Trollwood Performing Arts School. The NEA contributed support to the Annual United Tribes Indian Art Expo and for the development of a Native American art exhibition at Mandan Depot.

The North Dakota Council on the Arts receives funding from the NEA for the development of the state's art education programs, and grants from the NEA's State & Regional Program.

43LIBRARIES AND MUSEUMS

During 1996, North Dakota public libraries had 1,946,578 volumes and a total circulation of 4,260,640. The leading academic library was that of the University of North Dakota (Grand Forks), with 1,121,953 items.

Among the most notable of the state's 47 museums are the Art Galleries and Zoology Museum of the University of North Dakota and the North Dakota Heritage Center at Bismarck, which has an outstanding collection of Indian artifacts. Theodore Roosevelt National Park contains relics from the Elkhorn ranch where Roosevelt lived in the 1880s.

44COMMUNICATIONS

In March 1993, 97.1% of North Dakota's 242,000 occupied housing units had telephones. There were 74 radio stations (34 AM, 40 FM) in 1996. As of 1993, 18 commercial television stations and 6 public television stations were in operation. There were two large cable service providers as of 1996.

45PRESS

As of 1997, there were six morning dailies, and four evening dailies. There were also six Sunday papers in the state. The leading dailies were the *Fargo Forum*, with an all-day circulation of 54,363, Sunday, 68,346; the *Grand Forks Herald*, 36,718 morning, 37,508 Sunday; the *Minot Daily News*, 25,843 evening, 27,080 Sunday; and the *Bismarck Tribune*, 30,550 evening, 32,746 Sunday. In addition, there were 67 weekly newspapers and 15 periodicals. The leading historical journal is *North Dakota Horizons,* a quarterly founded in 1971.

46ORGANIZATIONS

The 1992 Census of Service Industries counted 440 organizations in North Dakota, including 83 business associations; 257 civic, social, and fraternal associations; and 100 other membership organizations. Two of the state's largest organizations are the Friends (Service Club) and the Northwest Farm Managers Association, both headquartered in Fargo.

47TOURISM, TRAVEL, AND RECREATION

In 1993, domestic travelers spent an estimated $828 million in North Dakota. State parks and other state recreational areas received 1,420,621 visitors in 1995. In the same year, including for-profit facilities only, the state had 229 hotels, motels, and similar facilities, and 12 recreational vehicle parks and camps.

Among the leading tourist attractions is the International Peace Garden, covering 2,200 acres (890 hectares) in North Dakota and Manitoba and commemorating friendly relations between the US and Canada. Ft. Abraham Lincoln State Park, south of Mandan, has been restored to evoke the 1870s, when General Custer left the area for his "last stand" against the Sioux. The most spectacular scenery in North Dakota is found in the Theodore Roosevelt National Park. The so-called "badlands," an integral part of the park, consist of strangely colored and intricately eroded buttes and other rock formations. Hunting and fishing are major recreational activities in North Dakota. In 1995, there were 414,063 licensed hunters and 141,867 licensed fishermen in the state.

48SPORTS

There are no major professional sports teams in North Dakota. In collegiate football, the University of North Dakota Sioux and the North Dakota State University Bison compete in the North Central Conference. The University of North Dakota also competes in collegiate ice hockey, winning NCAA championships in 1959, 1963, 1980, 1982, 1987, and 1997.

Other annual sporting events include the Governor's Cup Walleye Fishing Tournament in July, and several rodeos throughout the state.

49FAMOUS NORTH DAKOTANS

Preeminent among North Dakota politicians known to the nation was Gerald P. Nye (b.Wisconsin, 1892–1971), a US senator and a leading isolationist opponent of President Franklin D. Roosevelt's foreign policy, as was Senator William Langer (1886–1959). Another prominent senator, Porter J. McCumber (1858–1933), supported President Woodrow Wilson in the League of Nations battle. US Representative William Lemke (1878–1950) sponsored farm-relief legislation and in 1936 ran for US president on the Union Party ticket. Usher L. Burdick (1879–1960), a maverick isolationist and champion of the American Indian, served 18 years in the US House of Representatives.

Vilhjalmur Stefansson (b.Canada, 1879–1962) recorded in numerous books his explorations and experiments in the high Arctic. Orin G. Libby (1864–1952) made a significant contribution to the study of American history. Other North Dakota-nurtured writers and commentators include Maxwell Anderson (b.Pennsylvania, 1888–1959), a Pulitzer Prize–winning playwright; Edward K. Thompson (b.Minnesota, 1907), editor of *Life* magazine and founder-editor of *Smithsonian;* radio and television commentator Eric Severeid (1912–1992); and novelist Larry Woiwode (b.1941).

To the entertainment world North Dakota has contributed band leaders Harold Bachman (1892–1972), Lawrence Welk (1903–92), and Tommy Tucker (Gerald Duppler, 1908–89); jazz vocalist Peggy Lee (Norma Delores Egstrom, b.1920) and country singer Lynn Anderson (b.1947); and actresses Dorothy Stickney (b.1900) and Angie Dickinson (Angeline Brown, b.1931).

Sports personalities associated with the state include outfielder Roger Maris (1934–85), who in 1961 broke Babe Ruth's record for home runs in one season.

50BIBLIOGRAPHY

Crawford, Lewis F. *History of North Dakota.* 3 vols. Chicago: American Historical Society, 1931.

Federal Writers' Project. *North Dakota: A Guide to the Northern Prairie State.* Reprint. New York: Somerset, 1980 (orig. 1938).

Goodman, L. R., and R. J. Eidem. *The Atlas of North Dakota.* Fargo: North Dakota Studies, Inc., 1976.

Hoover, Herbert T. *The Sioux and Other Native American Cultures of the Dakotas: An Annotated Bibliography.* Westport, Conn.: Greenwood Press, 1993.

North Dakota Economic Development Commission. *North Dakota Growth Indicators.* Bismarck, 1984.

Raaen, Aagot. *Grass of the Earth: Immigrant Life in Dakota Country.* St. Paul, Minn.: Minnesota Historical Society Press, 1994.

Robinson, Elwyn B. *History of North Dakota.* Lincoln: University of Nebraska Press, 1966.

Tweton, D. Jerome, and Theodore Jelliff. *North Dakota—The Heritage of a People.* Fargo: North Dakota Institute for Regional Studies, 1976.

———, and Daniel F. Rylance. *The Years of Despair: North Dakota in the Depression.* Grand Forks: Oxcart Press, 1973.

University of North Dakota. Bureau of Business and Economic Research. *Statistical Abstract of North Dakota 1983.* Grand Forks: University of North Dakota Press, 1983.

Wilkins, Robert P., and Wynona H. *North Dakota: A Bicentennial History.* New York: Norton, 1977.

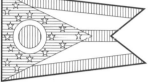

OHIO

State of Ohio

ORIGIN OF STATE NAME: From the Iroquois Indian word *oheo*, meaning "beautiful." **NICKNAME:** The Buckeye State. **CAPITAL:** Columbus. **ENTERED UNION:** 1 March 1803 (17th). **SONG:** "Beautiful Ohio." **MOTTO:** With God All Things Are Possible. **FLAG:** The flag is a burgee, with three red and two white lateral stripes; at the staff is a blue triangular field covered with 17 stars (signifying Ohio's order of entry into the Union) grouped around a red disk superimposed on a white circular O. **OFFICIAL SEAL:** In the foreground are a sheaf of wheat and a sheaf of 17 arrows; behind, a sun rises over a mountain range, indicating that Ohio is the 1st state west of the Alleghenies. Surrounding the scene are the words "The Great Seal of the State of Ohio." **ANIMAL:** White-tailed deer. **BIRD:** Cardinal. **INSECT:** Ladybug. **FLOWER:** Scarlet carnation. **TREE:** Buckeye. **BEVERAGE:** Tomato juice. **STONE:** Ohio flint. **LEGAL HOLIDAYS:** New Year's Day, 1 January; Birthday of Martin Luther King, Jr., 3d Monday in January; Presidents' Day, 3d Monday in February; Memorial Day, last Monday in May; Independence Day, 4 July; Labor Day, 1st Monday in September; Columbus Day, 2d Monday in October; Veterans Day, 11 November; Thanksgiving Day, 4th Thursday in November; Christmas Day, 25 December. **TIME:** 7 AM EST = noon GMT.

¹LOCATION, SIZE, AND EXTENT

Located in the eastern north-central US, Ohio is the 11th largest of the 12 midwestern states and ranks 35th in size among the 50 states.

The state's total area is 41,330 sq mi (107,044 sq km), of which land comprises 41,004 sq mi (106,201 sq km) and inland water 326 sq mi (823 sq km). Ohio extends about 210 mi (338 km) E-W; its maximum N-S extension is 230 mi (370 km).

Ohio is bordered on the N by Michigan and the Canadian province of Ontario (with the line passing through Lake Erie); on the E by Pennsylvania and West Virginia (with the Ohio River forming part of the boundary); on the S by West Virginia and Kentucky (with the entire line defined by the Ohio River); and on the W by Indiana.

Five important islands lie off the state's northern shore, in Lake Erie: the three Bass Islands, Kelleys Island, and Catawba Island. Ohio's total boundary length is 997 mi (1,605 km).

The state's geographic center is in Delaware County, 25 mi (40 km) NNE of Columbus.

²TOPOGRAPHY

Ohio has three distinct topographical regions: the foothills of the Allegheny Mountains in the eastern half of the state; the Erie lakeshore, extending for nearly three-fourths of the northern boundary; and the central plains in the western half of the state.

The Allegheny Plateau in eastern Ohio consists of rugged hills and steep valleys that recede gradually as the terrain sweeps westward toward the central plains. The highest point in the state is Campbell Hill (1,550 feet/470 meters), located in Logan County about 50 mi (80 km) northwest of Columbus.

The Erie lakeshore, a band of level lowland that runs across the state to the northwestern corner on the Michigan boundary, is distinguished by sandy beaches. The central plains extend to the western boundary with Indiana. In the south, undulating hills decline in altitude as they reach the serpentine Ohio River, which forms the state's southern boundary with Kentucky and West Virginia. The state's lowest point is on the banks of the Ohio River in the southwest, where the altitude drops to 433 feet (132 meters) above sea level.

Most of Ohio's 2,500 lakes are situated in the east, and nearly all are reservoirs backed up by river dams. The largest, Pymatuning Reservoir, on the Pennsylvania border, has an area of 14,650 acres (5,929 hectares). Grand Lake (St. Marys), located near the western border, covering 12,500 acres (5,059 hectares), is the largest lake wholly within Ohio.

Ohio has two drainage basins separated by a low ridge extending from the northeast corner to about the middle of the western border with Indiana. North of the ridge, more than one-third of Ohio's area is drained by the Maumee, Portage, Sandusky, Cuyahoga, and Grand rivers into Lake Erie. South of the ridge, the remaining two-thirds of the state is drained mainly by the Muskingum, Hocking, Raccoon, Scioto, Little Miami, and Miami rivers into the Ohio River, which winds for about 450 (725 km) along the eastern and southern borders.

Ohio's bedrock of sandstone, shale, and limestone was formed during the Paleozoic era some 300–600 million years ago. The oldest limestone rocks are found in the Cincinnati anticline, a ridge of sedimentary rock layers about 3,000 feet (900 meters) thick that extends from north to south in west-central Ohio. Inland seas filled and receded periodically to form salt and gypsum, also creating peat bogs that later were pressurized into the coal beds of southeastern Ohio. At the end of the Paleozoic era, the land in the eastern region uplifted to form a plateau that was later eroded by wind and water into hills and gorges.

About 2 million years ago, glaciers covering two-thirds of the state leveled the western region into plains and deposited fertile limestone topsoil. As the glaciers retreated, the melting ice formed a vast lake, which overflowed southward into the channels that became the Ohio River. Perhaps 15,000 years ago, during the last Ice Age, the glacial waters ran off and reduced Lake Erie to its present size. Limestone rocks in Glacier Grooves State Park on Kelleys Island bear the marks of the glaciers' movements.

³CLIMATE

Lying in the humid continental zone, Ohio has a generally temperate climate. Winters are cold and summers mild in the eastern highlands. The southern region has the warmest temperatures and longest growing season—198 days on the average,

473

compared with 150 to 178 days in the remainder of the state. More than half of the annual rainfall occurs during the growing season, from May to October.

Among the major cities, Columbus, in the central region, has an annual mean temperature of 51°F (11°C), with a normal maximum of 61°F (16°C) and a normal minimum of 42°F (6°C). Cleveland, in the north, has an annual mean of 50°F (10°C), with a normal maximum of 59°F (15°C) and minimum of 41°F (5°C). The mean temperature in Cincinnati, in the south, is 53°F (12°C), the normal maximum 63F (17°C), and the normal minimum 43°F (6°C). Cleveland has an average of 127 days per year in which the temperature drops to 32° (0°C) or lower, Columbus 124 days, and Cincinnati 99 days. The record low temperature for the state is –39°F (–39°C), set at Milligan on 10 February 1899. The record high is 113°F (45°C), registered near Gallipolis on 21 July 1934.

Cleveland has an average annual snowfall of 52 in (132 cm), while Columbus receives 28 in (71 cm), and Cincinnati 24 in (61 cm). Cincinnati has the most total precipitation, with 40 in (102 cm), compared with 37 in (94 cm) for Columbus and 35 in (89 cm) for Cleveland. Because of its proximity to Lake Erie, Cleveland is the windiest city, with winds that average 11 mph (18 km/hr).

[4]FLORA AND FAUNA

More than 2,500 plant species have been found in Ohio. The southeastern hill and valley region supports pitch pine, bigleaf magnolia, and sourwood, with undergrowths of sassafras, witch-hazel, pawpaw, hornbeam, and various dogwoods. At least 14 species of oak, 10 of maple, 9 of poplar, 9 of pine, 7 of ash, 7 of elm, 6 of hickory, 5 of birch, and 2 of beech grow in the state, along with butternut, eastern black walnut, wild black cherry, black locust, and sycamore. A relative of the horse chestnut (introduced to Ohio from Asia), the distinctive buckeye—first called the Ohio buckeye and now the official state tree—is characterized by its clusters of cream-colored flowers that bloom in spring and later form large, brown, thick-hulled nuts. The yellow-fringed orchid, northern wild monkshood, and wild kidney bean are threatened species, while painted trillium, white lady's-slipper, and rock elm are among more than 200 endangered plants.

The Buckeye State is rich in mammals. White-tailed deer, badger, mink, raccoon, red and gray foxes, coyote, beaver, eastern cottontail, woodchuck, least shrew, and opossum are found throughout the state's five wildlife districts; the bobcat, woodland jumping mouse, and red-backed mole are among many species with more restricted habitats. Common birds include the eastern great blue heron, green-winged teal, mourning dove, eastern belted kingfisher, eastern horned lark, blue-gray gnatcatcher, eastern cowbird, and a great variety of ducks, woodpeckers, and warblers; the cardinal is the state bird, and the ruffed grouse, mostly confined to the Allegheny Plateau, is a favorite game species. Bass, pickerel, perch, carp, pike, trout, catfish, sucker, and darter thrive in Ohio's lakes and streams. The snapping, midland painted, and spiny soft-shelled turtles, five-lined skink, northern water snake, midland brown snake, eastern hognose, and eastern milk snake appear throughout Ohio. The northern copperhead, eastern massasauga (swamp rattler), and timber rattlesnake are Ohio's only poisonous reptiles. Fowler's toad, bullfrog, green pickerel frog, and marbled and red-backed salamanders are common native amphibians.

Acting on the premise that the largest problem facing wildlife is the destruction of their habitat, the Division of Wildlife of the Department of Natural Resources has instituted an ambitious endangered species program. Among the numerous animals categorized by the state as endangered are the river otter, bobcat, Allegheny woodrat, sharp-shinned hawk, king rail, upland sandpiper, common tern, spotted turtle, five species of salamander, Ohio lamprey, shortnose gar, Great Lakes muskellunge, northern madtom, Tippecanoe darter, and Allegheny crayfish.

[5]ENVIRONMENTAL PROTECTION

Early conservation efforts in Ohio were aimed at controlling the ravages of spring floods and preventing soil erosion. After the Miami River floods of March 1913, which took 361 lives and resulted in property losses of more than $100 million in Dayton alone, the Miami Conservancy District was formed; five earth dams and 60 mi (97 km) of river levees were completed by 1922, at a cost of $40 million, to hold back cresting water. In the Muskingum Conservancy District in eastern Ohio, construction of flood-control dams has prevented spring flooding and the washing away of valuable topsoil into the Ohio River.

In recent years, the state's major environmental concerns have been to reverse the pollution of Lake Erie, control the air pollution attributable to industries and automobiles, clean up dumps for solid and hazardous wastes, improve water quality, and prevent pollution. Of recent concern is the problem with so-called "brownfields"—polluted industrial sites whose cleanup costs present barriers to development.

The state's regulatory agency for environmental matters is the Ohio Environmental Protection Agency, established in 1972. The agency has long-range programs to deal with pollution of air, water, and land resources. Ohio EPA also coordinates state, local, and federal funding of environmental programs. In 1995, Ohio EPA's budget was approximately $107 million.

Since 1972, antipollution efforts in Lake Erie have focused on reducing the discharge of phosphorus into the lake from sewage and agricultural wastes; sewage treatment facilities have been upgraded with the aid of more than $750 million in federal grants, and efforts have been made to promote reduced-tillage farming to control runoff. By the early 1980s, numerous beaches had been reopened, and sport fishing was once again on the increase. Since 1972, Ohio industries spent more than $5 billion on efforts to control air pollution. Peak ozone levels have dropped by 25% overall and by up to 50% in some urban areas. Lead levels in the outdoor air have dropped 97% since 1978 and particulate levels have dropped 80%. From 1967 to 1983, through the efforts of local health departments and with the eventual help of the EPA, over 1,300 open garbage dumps were closed down and more than 200 sanitary landfills constructed to replace them.

In 1980, Ohio passed its first legislation aimed at controlling hazardous wastes, and by early 1985, with the aid of more than $11 million in federal Superfund grants, cleanup had been completed or begun at 16 major sites. In 1994, there were 34 hazardous waste sites in Ohio.

Another agency, the Ohio Department of Natural Resources, is responsible for the development and use of the state's natural resources. The state's parks and recreational areas totaled 208,000 acres (84,000 hectares). The department also assists in soil conservation, issues permits for dams, promotes conservation of oil and gas, and allocates strip-mining licenses.

In 1994, Ohio allocated 0.77% of its budget to environmental and natural resources, and ranked 14th in the nation in total spending for environmental protection.

[6]POPULATION

Ohio ranked 7th in population among the 50 states at the 1990 census, with a population of 10,847,115. From 1980 to 1990, Ohio's population only increased 0.5%; the state fell from 6th place in 1980 and is now behind Illinois. In 1996 Ohio's population was 11,172,782, an increase of 3% over 1990.

Ohio's population grew slowly during the colonial period and totaled 45,365 persons in 1800. Once the territory became a state

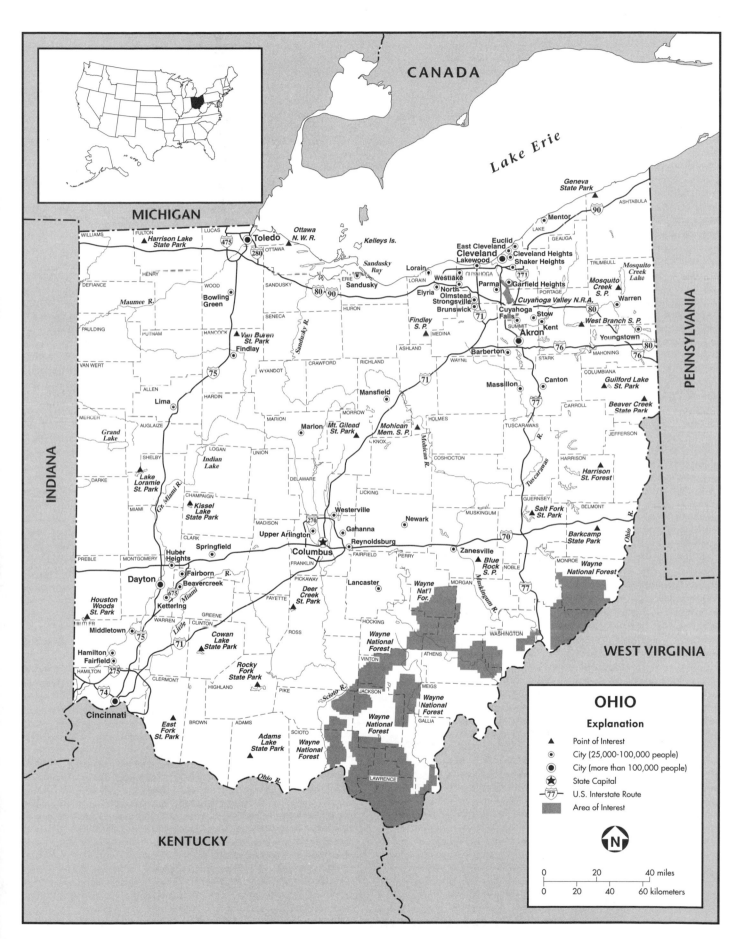

Lake Erie

MICHIGAN

PENNSYLVANIA

INDIANA

WEST VIRGINIA

KENTUCKY

WILLIAMS
FULTON
Harrison Lake State Park
LUCAS
Toledo
Ottawa N. W. R.
Kelleys Is.

Geneva State Park
Mentor
ASHTABULA

HENRY
OTTAWA
Sandusky Bay
Sandusky
ERIE
Lorain
Westlake

Cleveland
East Cleveland
Euclid
Cleveland Heights
Shaker Heights
Lakewood

LAKE
GEAUGA
TRUMBULL
Mosquito Creek Lake

DEFIANCE
WOOD
Bowling Green
SANDUSKY
HURON
Elyria
North Olmstead
Strongsville
Brunswick
Parma
Garfield Heights
CUYAHOGA
Mosquito Creek S. P.
Warren

PAULDING
PUTNAM
HANCOCK
Van Buren St. Park
SENECA
Cuyahoga Valley N.R.A.
Cuyahoga Falls
Stow
Kent
PORTAGE
West Branch S. P.
80

Maumee R.
Findlay
CRAWFORD
RICHLAND
Findley S. P.
MEDINA
WAYNE
Barberton
Akron
SUMMIT
STARK
Youngstown
MAHONING
76

VAN WERT
ALLEN
HARDIN
Mansfield
Massillon
Canton
COLUMBIANA
77

Lima
MERCER
AUGLAIZE
WYANDOT
MARION
MORROW
KNOX
HOLMES
TUSCARAWAS
CARROLL
Guilford Lake St. Park
Beaver Creek State Park
JEFFERSON

Grand Lake
SHELBY
LOGAN
UNION
Marion
Mt. Gilead St. Park
Mohican Mem. S. P.
COSHOCTON
R.
HARRISON
Harrison St. Forest

Indian Lake
Lake Loramie St. Park
CHAMPAIGN
DELAWARE
Mohican R.
MUSKINGUM
GUERNSEY
BELMONT
Salt Fork St. Park

DARKE
MIAMI
Kissel Lake State Park
MADISON
LICKING
Westerville
Newark
Barkcamp State Park

PREBLE
CLARK
Springfield
Upper Arlington
Gahanna
Reynoldsburg
Columbus
FRANKLIN
FAIRFIELD
PERRY
Zanesville
Blue Rock S.P.
NOBLE
MONROE
70
Wayne National Forest

Huber Heights
MONTGOMERY
Fairborn
Beavercreek
Lancaster
HOCKING
Wayne Nat'l For.
MORGAN
WASHINGTON

Dayton
Kettering
675
Miami
GREENE
Deer Creek St. Park
PICKAWAY
Wayne National Forest
ATHENS

Houston Woods St. Park
BUTLER
Middletown
WARREN
CLINTON
Cowan Lake State Park
FAYETTE
ROSS
VINTON
Wayne National Forest
MEIGS

Hamilton
Fairfield
HAMILTON
275
CLERMONT
Rocky Fork State Park
HIGHLAND
PIKE
Scioto R.
JACKSON
Wayne National Forest
GALLIA

Cincinnati
East Fork St. Park
BROWN
ADAMS
Adams Lake State Park
Wayne National Forest
SCIOTO
LAWRENCE

Ohio R.

75
71
74
90
80
280
475
77
71
270

Sandusky R.
Gt. Miami R.
Little Miami R.
Tuscarawas R.
Muskingum R.
Ohio R.

OHIO

Explanation

▲ Point of Interest

⊙ City (25,000-100,000 people)

◉ City (more than 100,000 people)

★ State Capital

—77— U.S. Interstate Route

▨ Area of Interest

| 0 | 20 | 40 miles |

| 0 | 20 | 40 | 60 kilometers |

in 1803, settlers flocked to Ohio and the population quintupled to 230,760 by 1810, The state's population doubled again by 1820, approached 2,000,000 in 1850, and totaled 3,198,062 by 1880. Ohio's annual rate of population increase slowed considerably after 1900, when its population was 4,157,545; nevertheless, in the period between 1900 and 1960, the total population more than doubled to 9,706,397. A slow rate of population increase during the 1970s, and a population decline during 1980–85, resulted from a net migration loss and a declining birthrate.

In 1990, Ohio's population was 51.5% female and 74.1% urban. The population density was 265 persons per sq mi (102 per sq km) in 1990.

As of the 1990 census, Columbus became Ohio's largest city, with a population of 632,910, trading 2d place with Cleveland, which had 505,616 residents. Whereas Columbus increased its population by 12% during the 1980s, Cleveland lost population by 11.9%. The 1994 estimated populations of the two cities were Columbus, 635,913, and Cleveland, 492,901. Cincinnati and other large cities also lost population during this period, largely because of the shift of the middle class from the inner cities to the suburbs or to other states. In 1994, Cincinnati's estimated population was 358,170, followed by Toledo, 322,550; Akron, 221,886; Dayton, 178,540; and Youngstown, 91,775.

Ohio's three most populous cities and their suburbs ranked among the 30 largest metropolitan areas in the US in 1990. In 1995, metropolitan Cleveland (including Akron and Lorain) had an estimated population of 2,903,808; metropolitan Cincinnati (including some portions of Kentucky and Indiana), 1,907,438; and the metropolitan area of Columbus, 1,437,512.

7ETHNIC GROUPS

Ohio was first settled by migrants from the eastern states and from the British Isles and northern Europe, especially Germany. Cincinnati had such a large German population that its public schools were bilingual until World War I. With the coming of the railroads and the development of industry, Slavic and other south Europeans were recruited in large numbers.

By 1990, however, only about 2.4% of Ohioans were foreign-born, the major places of origin being Germany, Italy, and the

Ohio Counties, County Seats, and County Areas and Populations

COUNTY	COUNTY SEAT	LAND AREA (SQ MI)	POPULATION (1996)	COUNTY	COUNTY SEAT	LAND AREA (SQ MI)	POPULATION (1996)
Adams	West Union	586	28,093	Logan	Bellefontaine	458	45,608
Allen	Lima	405	108,440	Lorain	Elyria	495	281,231
Ashland	Ashland	424	51,372	Lucas	Toledo	341	452,691
Ashtabula	Jefferson	703	102,207	Madison	London	467	41,184
Athens	Athens	508	61,162	Mahoning	Youngstown	417	260,107
Auglaize	Wapakoneta	398	47,059	Marion	Marion	403	65,323
Belmont	St. Clairsville	537	70,002	Medina	Medina	422	138,943
Brown	Georgetown	493	39,358	Meigs	Pomeroy	432	23,938
Butler	Hamilton	469	323,579	Mercer	Celina	457	40,890
Carroll	Carrollton	393	28,522	Miami	Troy	410	96,941
Champaign	Urbana	429	37,910	Monroe	Woodsfield	458	15,268
Clark	Springfield	398	147,472	Montgomery	Dayton	458	566,312
Clermont	Batavia	456	169,670	Morgan	McConnelsville	420	14,599
Clinton	Wilmington	410	38,645	Morrow	Mt. Gilead	406	30,481
Columbiana	Lisbon	534	111,406	Muskingum	Zanesville	654	84,349
Coshocton	Coshocton	566	36,131	Noble	Caldwell	399	12,134
Crawford	Bucyrus	403	47,290	Ottawa	Port Clinton	253	40,535
Cuyahoga	Cleveland	459	1,401,522	Paulding	Paulding	419	20,344
Darke	Greenville	600	54,259	Perry	New Lexington	412	33,834
Defiance	Defiance	414	40,059	Pickaway	Circleville	503	52,727
Delaware	Delaware	443	83,245	Pike	Waverly	443	27,156
Erie	Sandusky	264	78,913	Portage	Ravenna	493	149,571
Fairfield	Lancaster	506	119,182	Preble	Eaton	426	42,633
Fayette	Washington Ct. House	405	28,395	Putnam	Ottawa	484	35,199
Franklin	Columbus	542	1,013,724	Richland	Mansfield	497	128,151
Fulton	Wauseon	407	41,180	Ross	Chillicothe	692	74,407
Gallia	Gallipolis	471	32,820	Sandusky	Fremont	409	62,732
Geauga	Chardon	408	86,054	Scioto	Portsmouth	614	80,905
Greene	Xenia	415	139,936	Seneca	Tiffin	553	60,368
Guernsey	Cambridge	522	40,509	Shelby	Sidney	409	46,837
Hamilton	Cincinnati	412	857,616	Stark	Canton	574	374,406
Hancock	Findlay	532	68,562	Summit	Akron	412	530,571
Hardin	Kenton	471	31,629	Trumbull	Warren	612	227,069
Harrison	Cadiz	400	16,001	Tuscarawas	New Philadelphia	569	87,803
Henry	Napoleon	415	29,901	Union	Marysville	437	37,396
Highland	Hillsboro	553	39,388	Van Wert	Van Wert	410	30,426
Hocking	Logan	423	28,413	Vinton	McArthur	414	12,068
Holmes	Millersburg	424	36,786	Warren	Lebanon	403	134,791
Huron	Norwalk	495	59,563	Washington	Marietta	640	63,827
Jackson	Jackson	420	32,352	Wayne	Wooster	557	108,556
Jefferson	Steubenville	410	77,037	Williams	Bryan	422	37,950
Knox	Mt. Vernon	529	51,702	Wood	Bowling Green	619	117,546
Lake	Painesville	231	223,301	Wyandot	Upper Sandusky	406	22,718
Lawrence	Ironton	457	64,258				
Licking	Newark	686	137,584	TOTALS		41,004	11,172,782

United Kingdom. Ethnic clusters persist in the large cities, and some small communities retain a specific ethnic flavor, such as Fairport Harbor on Lake Erie, with its large Finnish population.

As of 1990 there were 1,155,000 blacks, representing 10.6% of the population. Most lived in the larger cities, especially Cleveland, which in 1990 was 46.6% black. Historically, Ohio was very active in the antislavery movement. Oberlin College, established in 1833 by dissident theological students, admitted blacks from its founding and maintained a "station" on the Underground Railroad. Cleveland elected its first black mayor in 1967.

Some 140,000 people in Ohio were of Hispanic origin in 1990. The largest number were of Mexican descent, but there were also many Puerto Ricans. American Indians numbered about 20,000. In 1990, 16,829 Chinese, 12,726 Filipinos, 13,999 Japanese, and 13,041 Koreans were living in Ohio.

Except for small Iroquoian groups like the Erie and Seneca, most of the Indian population before white settlement comprised four Algonkian tribes: Delaware, Miami, Wyandot, and Shawnee. Indian place-names include Ohio, Coshocton, Cuyahoga, and Wapakoneta.

8LANGUAGES

Ohio English reflects three post-Revolutionary migration paths. Into the Western Reserve south of Lake Erie came Northern speech from New York and Connecticut. Still common there are the Northern pronunciation of the *ow* diphthong, as in *cow*, with a beginning like the /ah/ vowel in *father*, and the use of that /ah/ in *fog* and *college*, *crik/* is more common than /kreek/ for *creek*. A dragonfly is a *devil's darning needle;* doughnuts may be *fried cakes;* a boy throws himself face down on a sled in a *bellyflop(per);* and a tied and filled bedcover is a *comforter.*

Most of nonurban Ohio has North Midland speech from Pennsylvania. Generally, except in the northern strip, *cot* and *caught* are sound-alikes, and *now* is /naow/, south of Columbus, because of the influence of South Midland patterns from Kentucky and extreme southern Pennsylvania, corn bread may be *corn pone,* lima beans are *butter beans,* and a tied quilt is a *comforter. Spouting,* yielding to *gutters,* barely reaches across to Indiana; and *sick at the stomach, dived,* and *wait on me* are competing with expanding Northern *to the stomach, dove,* and *wait for me.* A new Midland term, *bellybuster,* originated around Wheeling and has spread north to compete with *bellyflop.* Northern and Midland merge in the mixed dialect west of Toledo.

From Kentucky, South Midland speakers took *you-all* into Ohio River towns, and in the southwestern tip of the state can be heard their *evening* for *afternoon, terrapin* for *tortoise,* and *frogstool* for *toadstool.* Recent northward migration has introduced South Midland speech and black English, a southern dialect, into such industrial centers as Cleveland, Toledo, and Akron.

Localisms have developed. For the grass strip between sidewalk and street, Akron has *devil-strip* and Cleveland has *treelawn.* Foreign-language influence appears in such Pennsylvania Germanisms as *clook* (hatching hen), *snits* (dried apples), *smearcase* (cottage cheese), and *got awake.*

Of Ohioans aged 5 years or older 94.6% spoke only English at home in 1990. Other languages spoken at home, and the number of speakers, were as follows:

Spanish	139,194	French	46,075
German	80,975	Hungarian	18,219
Italian	41,179	Chinese	15,475
Polish	26,207	Various southern Slavic	21,948
Other Slavic	22,170		

9RELIGIONS

The first religious settlement in Ohio territory was founded among Huron Indians in 1751 by a Roman Catholic priest near what is now Sandusky. Shortly afterward, Moravian missionaries converted some Delaware Indians to Christianity; the first Protestant church was founded by Congregationalist ministers at Marietta in 1788. Dissident religious sects such as the Shakers, Amish, and Quakers moved into Ohio from the early 18th century onward, but the majority of settlers in the early 19th century were Presbyterians, Methodists, Baptists, Disciples of Christ, and Episcopalians.

The first Roman Catholic priest to be stationed permanently in Ohio was Father Edward Fenwick, who settled in Cincinnati in 1817. When the Protestant settlers there did not allow him to build a Catholic church in the town, he founded Christ Church (now St. Francis Church) just outside Cincinnati. In 1821, Father Fenwick became the first Catholic bishop in Ohio. The large influx of Irish and German immigrants after 1830 greatly increased the Catholic constituency in Cleveland, Cincinnati, Columbus, and Toledo. Among the German immigrants were many Lutherans and large number of Jews, who made Cincinnati a center of Reform Judaism. In the mid-19th century, Cincinnati had the nation's third-largest Jewish community; the Union of American Hebrew Congregations, the most important Reform body, was founded there in 1873, and Hebrew Union College, a rabbinical training school and center of Jewish learning, was founded two years later.

In 1990, Ohio had a Roman Catholic population of 2,141,777. During the same year, the state's Jewish population was estimated at 124,832. Leading Jewish communities were in Cleveland, Cincinnati, and Columbus.

Adherents of all Protestant groups totaled 3,171,021 in 1990. The largest Protestant denominations and their adherents in 1990 were United Methodist, 656,107; United Presbyterian, 205,721; United Church of Christ, 195,349; Lutheran Church, Missouri Synod, 86,336; Evangelical Lutheran Church in America 320,021; Southern Baptist Convention, 188,219; Christian Church and Churches of Christ, 135,830; American Baptist USA, 127,219; and Episcopal, 69,302.

10TRANSPORTATION

Sandwiched between two of the country's largest inland water systems, Lake Erie and the Ohio River, Ohio has long been a leader in water transport. With its numerous terminals on the Ohio River and deepwater ports on Lake Erie, Ohio ranks as one of the major US states for shipping.

The building of railroads in the mid-19th century greatly improved transportation within the state by connecting inland counties with Lake Erie and the Ohio River. The Mad River and Lake Erie Railroad, between Dayton and Sandusky, was completed in 1844, and two years later, it was joined with the Little Miami Railroad, to provide through service to Cincinnati. Also in 1846, Cleveland was connected by rail with Columbus and Pittsburgh. Railroad building in the state reached a peak in the 1850s; at the outbreak of the Civil War, Ohio had more miles of track than any other state. By 1900, railroads were by far the most important system of transport.

In 1996, Class I railroads operated 4,503 rail mi (7,250 km) of track in the state; 6,114 mi (9,844 km) of track was in service, utilized by 26 railroads, including 3 Class I railroads. In 1995, the state handled 5,184,006 rail carloads, 4th in the US. Freight service on branch lines to counties has been maintained through a state subsidy program.

Mass transit in Ohio's cities began in 1859 with horse-drawn carriages carrying paying passengers in Cleveland and Cincinnati, which added a cable car on rails about 1880. The electric trolley car, introduced to Cleveland in 1884, soon became the most popular mass transit system for the large cities. Inter-urban electric railways carried passengers to and from rural towns that had been bypassed by the railroads; there were 2,809 mi (4,521 km) of interurban track in the state by 1907. The use of electric railways declined with the development of the motor car in the 1920s, and by 1939, for example, the seven interurban lines serving Columbus had been abandoned. Today, suburbanites commute to their workplaces in Columbus and other cities by automobile and bus lines. In 1995/96, Amtrak operated four regularly scheduled trains through Ohio on 631 mi (1,016 km) of track, with a total ridership in the state of 162,392 passengers.

Rough roads were used by settlers in the early 19th century. The National Road was built from Wheeling, W.Va., to Zanesville in 1826, and was extended to Columbus by 1833. The increasing use of the automobile in the 1930s led to massive state and federal road-building programs in Ohio as elsewhere. The major interstate highways across Ohio connect Cleveland and the Toledo area in the north (I-80, I-90); link Columbus with Dayton, Zanesville, and Wheeling (I-70) and with Cincinnati and Cleveland (I-71); and extend north–south from Cleveland and Akron to Marietta in the east (I-77), and from Toledo to Dayton and Cincinnati in the west (I-75).

In 1996, Ohio had 113,542 mi (182,806 km) of roads; 79,198 mi (124,289 km) rural and 33,070 mi (53,243 km) urban, including 1,572 mi (2,531 km) of interstate highways. In 1995, 7,193,203 automobiles, 2,584,252 trucks, and 217,917 motorcycles were registered in the state, and there were 7,772,757 licensed drivers.

Inland waterways have long been important for transport and commerce in Ohio. The first settlers traveled into Ohio by flatboat down the Ohio River to establish such towns as Marietta and Cincinnati. Lake Erie schooners brought the founders of Cleveland and Sandusky. Steamboat service began on the Ohio River in 1811, and at Lake Erie ports in 1818. The public demand for water transportation in the interior of the state, where few rivers were navigable, led to construction of the Ohio and Erie Canal from Cincinnati to Dayton; both were opened to traffic in 1827 but not completed for another 14 years. The canals gave Ohio's farmers better access to eastern and southern markets. Water transportation is still a principal means of shipping Ohio's products through the St. Lawrence Seaway to foreign countries, and the method by which millions of tons of cargo, particularly coal, are moved via the Ohio River to domestic markets.

Ohio's ports rank among the busiest of the 50 states in volume. In 1995, the state's most active ports were Cleveland, with 15,393,496 tons of cargo handled; Lorain, 14,964,284 tons; and Toledo, 14,074,499 tons.

Ohioans consider Dayton to be the birthplace of aviation because it was there that Wilbur and Orville Wright built the first motor-powered airplane in 1903. In 1996 there were 568 airports in the state. The major air terminal is the Greater Cincinnati airport (actually located across the Ohio River in Kentucky), which enplaned 5,487,388 passengers on 81,728 departing flights in 1994. Hopkins International in Cleveland enplaned 4,830,570 passengers from 77,923 aircraft departures in 1994.

11 HISTORY

The first people in Ohio, some 11,000 years ago, were hunters. Their stone tools have been found with skeletal remains of long-extinct mammoths and mastodons. Centuries later, Ohio was inhabited by the Adena people, the earliest mound builders. Their descendants, the Hopewell Indians, built burial mounds, fortifications, and ceremonial earthworks, some of which are now preserved in state parks.

The first European travelers in Ohio, during the 17th century, found four Indian tribes: Wyandot and Delaware in northern Ohio, Miami and Shawnee in the south. All were hunters who followed game trails that threaded the dense Ohio forest. All together, these four tribes numbered about 15,000 people. European exploration was begun by a French nobleman, Robert Cavelier, Sieur de la Salle, who, with Indian guides and paddlers, voyaged from the St. Lawrence River to the Ohio, which he explored in 1669–70. In the early 1700s, French and English traders brought knives, hatchets, guns, blankets, tobacco, rum, and brandy to exchange for the Indians' deer and beaver skins.

Both the French and the English claimed possession of Ohio, the French claim resting on La Salle's exploration, while the British claimed all territory extending westward from their coastal colonies. To reinforce the French claim, Celeron de Bienville led an expedition from Canada to Ohio in 1749 to warn off English traders, win over the Indians, and assert French possession of the land. Traveling by canoe, with marches overland, he found the Indians better disposed at that time to the English than to the French. The following year, a company of Virginia merchants sent Christopher Gist to map Ohio trade routes and to make friendship and trade agreements with the tribes. The clash of ambitions brought on the French and Indian War—during which the Indians fought on both sides—ending in 1763 with French defeat and the ceding of the vast western territory to the British. During the Revolutionary War, the American militiaman George Rogers Clark, with a small company of woodsmen-soldiers, seized British posts and trading stations in Ohio, and, in the Battle of Piqua, defeated Indian warriors allied with the British. It was largely Clark's campaigns that won the Northwest Territory for the US.

The new nation had a huge public domain, extending from the Allegheny Mountains to the Mississippi River. To provide future government and development of the territory northwest of the Ohio River, the US Congress enacted the Land Ordinance of 1785 and the Northwest Ordinance of 1787. The Land Ordinance created a survey system of rectangular sections and townships, a system begun in Ohio and extended to all new areas in the expanding nation. The farsighted Northwest Ordinance provided a system of government under which territories could achieve statehood on a basis equal with that of the original colonies. When a specified area had a population of 60,000 free adult males, it could seek admission to the Union as a state.

The first permanent settlement in Ohio was made in 1788 by an organization of Revolutionary War veterans who had received land warrants as a reward for their military service. They trekked by ox-drawn wagons over the mountains and by flatboat down the Ohio River to the mouth of the Muskingum, where they built the historic town of Marietta. John Cleves Symes, a New Jersey official, brought pioneer settlers to his Miami Purchase in southwestern Ohio; their first settlement, in 1789, eventually became the city of Cincinnati. Access to the fertile Ohio Valley was provided by the westward-flowing Ohio River, which carried pioneer settlers and frontier commerce. Flatboats made a one-way journey, as families floated toward what they hoped would be new settlements. Keelboats traveled both downstream and upstream—an easy journey followed by a hard one. The keelboat trade, carrying military supplies and frontier produce, created an enduring river lore. Its legendary hero is burly, blustering Mike Fink, "half horse and half alligator," always ready for a fight or a frolic, for riot or rampage.

Increasing settlement of the Ohio Valley aroused Indian resistance. War parties raided outlying villages, burned houses, and drove families away. Two military expeditions against the Indians were shattered by Chief Little Turtle and his Miami warriors. Then, in 1793, Maj. Gen. "Mad Anthony" Wayne took command in the West. He built roads and forts in the Miami Valley, and trained a force of riflemen. On a summer morning in 1794, Wayne routed allied tribesmen, mostly Miami and

Shawnee, in the decisive Battle of Fallen Timbers. In the ensuing Treaty of Greenville, Indian leaders surrendered claim to the southern half of Ohio, opening that large domain to uncontested American occupation.

When, in 1800, Connecticut ceded to the US a strip of land along Lake Erie claimed by its colonial charter and called the Western Reserve, that region became a part of the Northwest Territory. Now the future seemed unclouded, and from the older colonies came a great migration to the promised land. By 1802, Ohio had enough population to seek statehood, and in November, a constitutional convention assembled at Chillicothe. In 25 days and at a total cost of $5,000, the 35 delegates framed a constitution that vested most authority in the state legislature and gave the vote to all white male taxpayers. On 1 March 1803, Ohio joined the Union as the 17th state.

Beyond Ohio's western border, Indians still roamed free. In 1811, the powerful Shawnee chief Tecumseh led a tribal resistance movement (supported by the British) seeking to halt the white man's advance into the new territory and to regain lands already lost to the Americans. Ohio militia regiments led by Gen. William Henry Harrison repulsed an Indian invasion near Toledo in the battle of Tippecanoe on 7 November 1811. Control of Lake Erie and of Great Lakes commerce was at stake when Commodore Oliver Hazard Perry won a decisive naval victory over a British fleet in western Lake Erie during the War of 1812. Tecumseh was slain in the Battle of Thames in Canada on 5 October 1813.

With peace restored in 1815, "Ohio fever" spread through New England. In a great migration, people streamed over the mountains and the lakes to a land of rich soil, mild climate, and beckoning opportunities. Across the Atlantic, especially in England, Ireland, and Germany, thousands of immigrants boarded ship for America. At newly opened land offices, public land was sold at $1.25 an acre. Forest became fields, fields became villages and towns, towns became cities. By 1850, Ohio was the 3d most populous state in the Union.

Having cleared millions of acres of forest, Ohioans turned to economic development. Producing more than its people consumed, the state needed transportation routes to eastern markets. The National Road extended across the central counties in the 1830s, carrying stagecoach passengers and wagon commerce from Pennsylvania and Maryland. The Ohio canal system, created between 1825 and 1841, linked the Ohio River and Lake Erie, providing a waterway to the Atlantic via New York's Erie Canal. In 1826, state lands were valued at $16 million; 15 years later, their value exceeded $100 million. The chief products were wheat, corn, pork, beef, salt, wool, and leather. By 1850, when farm and factory production outstripped the capacity of mule teams and canal barges, railroad building had begun. In the next decade, railroads crisscrossed the state.

In 1861, Ohio, like the rest of the nation, was divided. The northern counties, teeming with former New Englanders, were imbued with abolitionist zeal. But Ohio's southern counties had close ties with Virginia and Kentucky across the river. From southeastern Ohio came Clement L. Vallandigham, leader of the Peace Democrats—called Copperheads by their opponents—who defended states' rights, opposed all of President Lincoln's policies, and urged compromise with the Confederacy. While Ohio surpassed its quota by providing a total of 320,000 Union Army volunteers, the Copperhead movement grew strong enough to nominate Vallandigham for state governor in 1863. Responding to the news of Vallandigham's defeat by the rugged Unionist John Brough, Lincoln telegraphed: "Ohio has saved the nation." Ohio became directly involved in the war for two weeks in 1863, when Confederate Gen. John Hunt Morgan led a Kentucky cavalry force on a daring but ineffectual raid through the southern counties.

Ohio gave the Union its greatest generals—Ulysses S. Grant, William Tecumseh Sherman, and Philip H. Sheridan—each of whom won decisive victories at crucial times. Also essential to the Union cause was the service of Ohio men in Lincoln's cabinet, including Treasury Secretary Salmon P. Chase and War Secretary Edwin M. Stanton.

Mid-19th-century Ohio was primarily an agricultural state, but war demands stimulated Ohio manufacturing, and in the decade following the war, the state's industrial products surpassed the value of its rich farm production. The greatest commercial development came in northern Ohio, where heavy industry grew dramatically. To Toledo, Cleveland, and Youngstown via Lake Superior came iron ore that was converted into iron and steel with coal from the Ohio Valley. In the 1870s, John D. Rockefeller of Cleveland organized the Standard Oil Co., which soon controlled oil refining and distribution throughout the nation. At the same time, B. F. Goodrich of Akron began making fire hose, the first rubber product in an industry whose prodigious growth would make Akron the "rubber capital of the world." In the middle of the state, the capital city, Columbus, became a center of the brewing, railroad equipment, and farm implement industries. Cincinnati factories made steamboat boilers, machine tools, meat products, railroad cars, and soap. Dayton became known for its paper products, refrigerators, and cash registers. With industrial growth came political power. In the next half century, Ohio virtually took possession of the White House. Presidents Grant, Rutherford B. Hayes, James A. Garfield, Benjamin Harrison, William McKinley, William Howard Taft, and Warren G. Harding were all Ohioans.

The four great business pursuits—agriculture, commerce, mining, and manufacturing—were remarkably balanced in Ohio. Its ethnic strains were various. Following the earlier English, Irish, and German influx came Italian, Czech, Dutch, Finnish, Greek, Hungarian, Polish, Russian, Serbian, and Ukrainian immigrants, along with a growing number of blacks from the rural South. Thus Ohio provided an advantageous background for a president; to any segment of the nation, an Ohio candidate did not seem alien. In the 1920 campaign, both the Republican and Democratic nominees—Harding and James M. Cox—were Ohio men. Norman Thomas, a perennial Socialist candidate, was likewise an Ohioan.

During World War I, Ohio's heavy industry expanded and its cities grew. Progressivism developed in Toledo and Cleveland, under their respective mayors, Samuel M. "Golden Rule" Jones and Tom L. Johnson, whose reforms resulted in the city manager form of government that spread to other Ohio cities. In the postwar 1920s, Ohio's oil, rubber, and glass industries kept pace with accelerating automobile production. Yet none of these industries was immune to the prolonged depression of the 1930s. Widespread unemployment and a stagnant economy were not relieved until the outbreak of World War II. The war swept 641,000 Ohioans into military service and gave Ohio industry military contracts totaling $18 billion.

The state's economy prospered after World War II, with highway building, truck and tractor production, aircraft manufacture, and airport construction leading the field. The completion of the St. Lawrence Seaway in 1959 made active ocean ports of Toledo and Cleveland. Major problems during this period involved pollution created by the dumping of industrial wastes (especially in Lake Erie) and urban decay resulting from the departure of middle-class families to the suburbs, an exodus that left the central cities to growing numbers of the poor and underprivileged. Related to these problems were troubles in the Ohio school system. Deteriorating neighborhoods produced inadequate revenues for schools and public services, and attempts at racial integration brought controversy and disturbance. When political office went to minority leaders—in 1967, Carl Stokes of

Cleveland became the first black mayor of any major US city—friction and tension continued. A further shock to Ohioans was the shooting of 13 students, 4 of whom died, at Kent State University on 4 May 1970 by national guardsmen who had been sent to the campus to preserve order during a series of demonstrations against US involvement in Indochina.

During the early 1980s, Ohio was still beset by serious social and economic problems. The state's population was static. The unemployment rate in 1982 and 1983 reached 14%. The decline in manufacturing jobs was only partly offset by the employment brought by a growing service sector. Ohio's huge coal reserves were of limited use because of their content of sulfur, an atmospheric pollutant.

In 1983, the state established the Thomas Edison Program, which provided start-up companies with venture capital funds. It also introduced substantial conservancy programs embracing the watersheds of the Muskingum and Miami rivers which became models for such undertakings in other states, and participated in programs that, to a significant extent, reversed the pollution of Lake Erie. Ohio has strengthened its state universities and developed a system of community colleges that brought vocational training within the reach of most of its citizens.

Economic progress in the 1980s slowed toward the end of the decade, and unemployment once again rose in the recession of the early 1990s, reaching 6.9% in 1992. Within two years it had recovered to 4.9%. In March 1995, Ohio was the site of the largest work stoppage in the auto industry in a quarter century, when almost 178,000 employees were laid off in response to a 17-day strike by auto workers at two General Motors plants in Dayton. In the same year, Dayton's Wright-Patterson Air Force Base was the setting for the negotiations preceding the historic signing of the Bosnia peace agreement.

12STATE GOVERNMENT

The Ohio constitution of 1803 was replaced by a second constitution in 1851. Amendments proposed by a constitutional convention in 1912 and subsequently approved by the voters so heavily revised the 1851 constitution as to make it virtually a new document. This modified constitution, with subsequent amendments, provides for county and municipal home rule, direct primary elections, recall of elected officials, and constitutional amendments by initiative and referendum.

Ohio's general assembly consists of a 99-member house of representatives, elected for two years, and a senate of 33 members serving four-year terms (half the members are chosen every two years). Regular sessions of the legislature convene the first Monday in January of off-numbered years, and a second session is called on the same date of the following year. The legislative salary was $42,426 in 1995. Each house may introduce legislation, and both houses must approve a bill before it can be signed into law by the governor. The governor's veto of a bill can be overridden by three-fifths majority votes of both houses.

Officials elected statewide are the governor and lieutenant governor (elected jointly), secretary of state, attorney general, auditor, and treasurer, all of whom serve four-year terms. Effective in 1959, a constitutional amendment changed the governor's term from two to four years and forbade a governor from serving more than two successive terms. The governor appoints the heads of 22 executive department, as well as the adjutant general and members of most statutory boards. In 1996, the governor's salary was $115,762.

The constitution may be amended legislatively by a three-fifths vote of each house; the proposed amendment must then receive majority approval by the voters at the next general election. Amendments may also be proposed by petition of 10% of the electors who voted for governor in the last general election; a majority vote in a subsequent referendum is required for passage.

The constitution provides that every 20 years (from 1932 onward), the voters must be given the chance to choose whether a constitutional convention should be held. Voters rejected this option in 1932, 1952, 1972, and again in 1992.

To vote in Ohio, one must be a US citizen, 18 years of age or older, and have been a resident of the county and voting precinct for at least 30 days.

13POLITICAL PARTIES

Ohio has sent seven native sons and one other state resident to the White House—equaling Virginia as the "mother of presidents." The state's two major political parties, Democratic and Republican, have dominated the political scene since 1856.

Ohioans scattered their votes among various political factions until 1836, when they rallied behind state resident William Henry Harrison and the Whig Party; they again supported Harrison in 1840, helping him win his second bid for the presidency. Whigs and Democrats divided the votes in 1844, 1848, and 1852; in 1856, however, Ohio supported the newly formed Republican Party, and after the Civil War, 7 of the country's next 12 presidents were Ohio-born Republicans, beginning with Grant and ending with Harding. From 1856 to 1984, Ohioans voted for the Republican candidate in all presidential elections except those in which the following 6 Democrats were elected: Woodrow Wilson (twice), Franklin D. Roosevelt (three times), Harry S Truman, Lyndon B. Johnson, Jimmy Carter, and Bill Clinton. In 1920, when the presidential candidates of both major parties were Ohioans, the Republican, Warren G. Harding, carried Ohio as well as the nation.

Political bossism flourished in Ohio during the last quarter of the 19th century, when the state government was controlled by Republicans Mark Hanna in Cleveland and George B. Cox in Cincinnati. Hanna played an influential role in Republican national politics; in 1896, his handpicked candidate, William McKinley, was elected to the presidency. But the despotism of the bosses and the widespread corruption in city governments led to public demands for reform. In Toledo, a reform mayor, Samuel "Golden Rule" Jones, began to clean house in 1897. Four years later, another group of reformers, led by Mayor Tom L. Johnson, ousted the Hanna machine and instituted honest government in Cleveland. At the time, journalist Lincoln Steffens called Cleveland "the best-governed city in the US" and Cincinnati "the worst." The era of bossism ended for Cincinnati in 1905, when the voters overthrew the Cox machine, elected a reform mayor on a fusion ticket, and instituted reforms that in 1925 made Cincinnati the first major US city with a nonpartisan city-manager form of government.

With the decline of big-city political machines, ticket splitting has become a regular practice among Ohio voters in state and local contests. Overall, between 1946 and 1992, Republicans served seven terms as governor and Democrats served eight terms. Governor Frank J. Lausche, a Democrat, was elected to an unprecedented five two-year terms (1945–47, 1949–57), and Republican James A. Rhodes served four four-year terms (1963–71, 1975–83). In 1982, Ohioans elected a Democratic governor, Richard F. Celeste, and Democrats swept all state offices and won control of both houses of the state legislature. Two years later, Republicans lost the majority they had enjoyed in the state's congressional delegation but regained control of the state senate. Following the November 1996 elections, there were 8 Democrats and 11 Republicans serving as US Representatives. In 1992 both Ohio senators—John Glenn, elected to a fourth term in 1992, and Howard Metzenbaum, elected to a third term in 1988—were Democrats. However, in 1994 Metzenbaum retired and a Republican, Mike DeWine, took the seat. DeWine faced Metzenbaum's son-in-law, Joel Hyatt, a lawyer who had never held elected office. Republican George Voinovich won the governorship in

1990 and again in 1994. In the November 1996 elections, Republicans remained dominant in the state senate, with 21 seats as opposed to the Democrats' 12; and they retained the control they had won over the House in 1994 for the first time in 22 years, increasing their majority to 60-39, from the previous 55 seats to 43.

In general, third parties have fared poorly in Ohio since 1856. Exceptions were the 1968 presidential election, in which American Independent Party candidate George Wallace garnered nearly 12% of Ohio's popular vote, and the 1992 presidential election, when Independent Ross Perot captured 21% of the vote. A more typical voting pattern was displayed in the 1976 presidential election, when the two major parties together received 97.7% of the total votes cast, and only 2.3% of the votes were split among minor parties and independents. Of the state's 5,222,041 registered voters, nearly 80% voted, and Democrat Jimmy Carter won an extremely close election by only 11,116 votes.

The result was not nearly so close in 1980, when Ronald Reagan, the Republican presidential nominee, won 51% of the popular vote to 41% for Jimmy Carter (with 6% going to John Anderson and 2% to minor party candidates), or in 1984, when Reagan won 59% of the popular vote to defeat Walter Mondale in the state. Republican George Bush won 55% of the vote in 1988. In 1992, however, Bush lost the state to Democratic nominee Bill Clinton, who captured 40% of the vote to Bush's 38%. In 1996, Clinton won 47% of the vote, Republican Bob Dole won 41%, and Independent Ross Perot received 11%.

In 1994, there were 219 blacks and 4 Hispanics holding public office. As of 1995, there were 32 women serving in the state legislature and 2 women in elective executive office.

14LOCAL GOVERNMENT

Local government in Ohio is exercised by the 88 counties, 942 cities and villages, and more than 1,300 townships. In 1992 there were 666 school districts and 513 special districts.

Each county is administered by a board of three commissioners, elected to four-year terms, whose authority is limited by state law. The county government is run by eight officials elected to four-year terms: the auditor or financial officer, whose duties include levying taxes; the clerk of courts, who is elected as clerk of the court of common pleas and also serves as clerk of the county court of appeals; the coroner, who must be a licensed physician; an engineer; a prosecuting attorney; the recorder, who keeps records of deeds, mortgages, and other legal documents; a sheriff; and the treasurer, who collects and disburses public funds.

Within each county are incorporated areas with limited authority to govern their own affairs. Thirty voters in an area may request incorporation of the community as a village. A village reaching the population of 5,000 automatically becomes a city, which by law must establish executive and legislative bodies. There are three types of city government: the mayor-council plan, which is the form adopted by a majority of the state's approximately 200 cities; the city-manager form, under which the city council appoints a professional manager to conduct nonpartisan government operations; and the commission type, in which a board of elected commissioners administers the city government.

In practice, most large cities have adopted a home-rule charter which permits them to select the form of government best suited to their requirements.

Cleveland experimented with the city-manager form of government from 1924 to 1932, at which time public disclosures of municipal corruption led the city's voters to return to the mayor-council plan. In 1967, Cleveland became the first major US city to elect a black mayor; Carl Stokes served two two-year terms but retired from politics in 1971. Cleveland again attracted national attention in 1978 when its 31-year-old mayor, Dennis J. Kucinich, publicly disputed the city's financial policies with members of the city council, and the city defaulted on $15 million in bank loans. Mayor Kucinich narrowly survived a recall election; in 1979, he was defeated for reelection by the state's lieutenant governor, George Voinovich.

Cincinnati has retained the city-manager form of government since 1925. The mayor, elected by the city council from among its nine members, has no administrative duties. Instead, the council appoints a city manager to an indefinite term as chief executive. Columbus, the state capital since 1816, has a mayor-council form of government.

Townships are governed by three trustees and a clerk, all elected to staggered four-year terms. These elected officials oversee zoning ordinances, parks, road maintenance, fire protection, and other matters within their jurisdiction.

Ohio Presidential Vote by Political Parties, 1948–96

YEAR	ELECTORAL VOTE	OHIO WINNER	DEMOCRAT	REPUBLICAN	PROGRESSIVE	SOC. LABOR	COMMUNIST	LIBERTARIAN
1948	25	*Truman (D)	1,452,791	1,445,684	37,487	—	—	—
1952	25	*Eisenhower (R)	1,600,367	2,100,391	—	—	—	—
1956	25	*Eisenhower (R)	1,439,655	2,262,610	—	—	—	—
1960	25	Nixon (R)	1,944,248	2,217,611	—	—	—	—
1964	26f	*Johnson (D)	2,498,331	1,470,865	—	—	—	—
					AMERICAN IND.			
1968	26	*Nixon (R)	1,700,586	1,791,014	467,495	—	—	—
					AMERICAN			
1972	25	*Nixon (R)	1,558,889	2,441,827	80,067	7,107	6,437	—
						SOC. WORKERS		
1976	25	*Carter (D)	2,011,621	2,000,505	15,529	4,717	7,817	8,961
					CITIZENS			
1980	25	*Reagan (R)	1,745,103	2,203,139	8,979	4,436	5,030	49,604
1984	25	*Reagan (R)	1,825,440	2,678,560	—	—	—	5,886
						WORKER'S LEAGUE	NEW ALLIANCE	
1988	25	*Bush (R)	1,939,629	2,416,549	—	5,432	12,017	11,989
					IND. (Perot)	POPULIST/AMERICA FIRST		
1992	21	*Clinton (D)	1,984,942	1,894,310	1,036,426	4,698	6,411	7,252
1996	21	*Clinton (D)	2,148,222	1,859,883	483,207	—	—	12,851

* Won US presidential election.

[15]STATE SERVICES

The State Department of Education administers every phase of public school operations, including counseling and testing services, the federal school lunch program, and teacher education and certification. The department also oversees special schools for the blind and deaf. The department's chief administrator is the superintendent of public instruction.

Health and welfare services are provided by several departments. The Department of Health issues and enforces health and sanitary regulations. Violations of health rules are reviewed by a Public Health Council of seven members, including three physicians and a pharmacist. The Department of Mental Health administers mental health institutions; develops diagnostic, prevention, and rehabilitation programs; and trains mental health professionals. The Department of Human Services helps the poor through aid to families with dependent children, public assistance payments, food stamps, and Medicaid. The Bureau of Employment Services and the Bureau of Workers' Compensation administer labor benefit programs.

Public protection services include those of the State Highway Patrol and the Bureau of Motor Vehicles, both within the Department of Highway Safety; the Department of Rehabilitation and Correction, which operates penal institutions; the Department of Youth Services, which administers juvenile correction centers; and the Environmental Protection Agency.

[16]JUDICIAL SYSTEM

The supreme court of Ohio, the highest court in the state, reviews proceedings of the lower courts and of state agencies. The high court has a chief justice and six associate justices elected to six-year terms. Below the supreme court are 12 courts of appeals, which exercise jurisdiction over their respective judicial districts. Each court has at least three judges elected to six-year terms; the district including Cleveland has nine appeals court judges, and the Cincinnati district has six.

Trial courts include 88 courts of common pleas, one in each county; judges are elected to six-year terms. Probate courts, domestic relations courts, and juvenile courts often function as divisions of the common pleas courts. In 1957, a system of county courts was established by the legislature to replace justices of the peace and mayor's courts at the local level. Large cities have their own municipal, juvenile, and police courts. In 1996, an estimated 30,821 attorneys practiced in the state.

In 1997, state and federal prisons in Ohio had over 46,000 inmates. According to the FBI Crime Index, Ohio's crime rates rank well below the national averages. According to FBI data for 1995, the state's crime rates per 100,000 population were as follows: murder and nonnegligent manslaughter, 5.4; forcible rape, 43.4; robbery, 178.7; aggravated assault, 255.0; burglary, 838.8; larceny, 2,669.0; and motor vehicle theft, 414.9.

Ohio imposes the death penalty but has not executed anyone in recent times. In 1995, 155 persons were under sentence of death.

[17]ARMED FORCES

In 1996, there were 8,448 active duty military personnel stationed in Ohio, the vast majority of whom (7,078) were at Wright-Patterson Air Force Base near Dayton. In 1995/96, the Defense Department awarded $2.7 billion in defense contracts to Ohio companies.

In 1996, Ohio had 1,177,000 living veterans, of whom fewer than 500 had served in World War I, 327,000 in World War II, 188,000 during the Korean conflict, 355,000 during the Viet Nam era, and 84,000 during the Persian Gulf War. In 1995/96, the Veterans Administration expended $1.3 billion in pensions, medical assistance, and other major veterans' benefits.

Reservists and National Guard personnel in Ohio numbered 53,093 in 1996. In 1993, the Ohio State Highway Patrol employed 1,369 full-time sworn officers, or 1 per 10,000 residents.

[18]MIGRATION

After the Ohio country became a US territory in 1785, Virginians, Connecticut Yankees, and New Jerseyites began arriving in significant numbers; tens of thousands of settlers from New England, Pennsylvania, and some southern states thronged into Ohio in subsequent decades. The great migration from the eastern states continued throughout most of the 19th century, and was bolstered by new arrivals from Europe. The Irish came in the 1830s, and many Germans began arriving in the 1840s. Another wave of European immigration brought about 500,000 people a year to Ohio during the 1880s, many of them from southern and eastern Europe. Former slaves left the South for Ohio following the Civil War, and a larger migratory wave brought blacks to Ohio after World War II to work in the industrial cities. In the 1910s, many emigrants from Greece, Albania, and Latvia settled in Akron to work in the rubber industry.

The industrialization of Ohio in the late 19th and the 20th centuries encouraged the migration of Ohioans from the farms to the cities. The large number of Ohioans who lived in rural areas and worked on farms declined steadily after 1900, with the farm population decreasing to under 1,000,000 during World War II and then to fewer than 400,000 by 1979. A more recent development has been the exodus of urbanites from Ohio's largest cities. From 1970 to 1990, Cleveland lost 245,000 residents, Cincinnati 90,000, Dayton 61,000, Akron 52,000, and Toledo 50,000. Columbus was the only major city to gain residents—93,000—during this period. Ohio lost more than 1 million people through migration during the period 1970–83. Net migration loss for the state from 1985 to 1990 came to 72,000. Between 1990 and 1996, Ohio had a net loss of 69,296 in domestic migration and a net gain of 35,997 in international migration. In 1996, 10,237 foreign immigrants arrived in Ohio. As of 1994, the number of undocumented immigrants was estimated at between 7 and 36. As of 1990, 74.1% of state residents had been born in Ohio. About 42% of Ohioans age 5 and older lived in a different house in 1985 than in 1990, of which just 15% did so in another state. In 1990, about three-fourths of the reported instrastate residence changes from 1985 took place within the same county.

[19]INTERGOVERNMENTAL COOPERATION

The Ohio Commission on Interstate Cooperation represents the state in dealings with the Council of State Governments and its allied organizations. Ohio is a signatory to interstate compacts covering the Ohio River Valley, Pymatuning Reservoir, and the Great Lakes Basin, including the Great Lakes Charter signed in February 1985. The state also participates in the Interstate Mining Compact, the Interstate Oil and Gas Compact, and other compacts.

Federal aid to Ohio for all purposes exceeded $8.7 billion in the 1995/96 fiscal year.

[20]ECONOMY

Ohio's economy has shown remarkable balance over the years. In the mid-19th century, Ohio became a leader in agriculture, ranking 1st among the states in wheat production in 1840, and 1st in corn and wool by 1850. With industrialization, Ohio ranked 4th in value added by manufacturing in 1900.

Coal mining in the southeastern part of the state and easy access to Minnesota's iron ore via the Great Lakes contributed to the growth of the iron and steel industry in the Cleveland–Youngstown area; Ohio led the nation in the manufacture of machine tools and placed 2d among the states in steel production in the early 1900s. Automobile manufacturing and other new industries developed after World War I. Hit hard by the depression of the 1930s, the state diversified its industrial foundation and enjoyed prosperity during and after World War II, as its population increased and its income grew.

In the 1970s, however, growth began to lag. By 1980, per capita income in Ohio had fallen well behind the national average. While the gross national product in constant dollars grew 99% from 1960 to 1980, the gross state product expanded only 66%. Manufacturing, which traditionally accounts for more than one-third of the gross state product, was shrinking, as demand for durable goods declined. Manufacturing employment peaked at 1.4 million in 1969; by 1982, the total was down to 1.1 million, and it was believed that many of these jobs would be permanently lost because of a reorientation of Ohio's economy from manufacturing toward services. With unemployment reaching peak levels, the state was forced to borrow from the federal government to fund the soaring cost of unemployment benefits.

In 1982, manufacturing accounted for 27% of the state's total employment, down from 39% in 1970. Steel was produced primarily in Youngstown, automotive and aircraft parts in Cleveland, automobile tires and other rubber products in Akron, and office equipment in Dayton. Recessionary trends in 1980 led to the closing of a US Steel plant in Youngstown and of two Firestone tire and rubber factories in the Akron area, and to widespread layoffs in the auto parts industry. This bad economic news was partially offset when in 1983 the Honda Motor Co. opened Japan's first US automobile assembly plant at Marysville near Columbus, where Honda had already been manufacturing motorcycles. Honda suppliers also began establishing plants in the state.

Despite its shrinking size, manufacturing remains the dominant industry in Ohio. The industry centers on durable goods. Among manufacturers, transportation equipment and industrial machinery are the largest employers. Both durable and nondurable goods (instruments, chemicals, printing and lumber) have enjoyed the greatest gains in employment between 1987 and 1993. However, durable goods' share of the gross state product, particularly primary metals, motor vehicles, and industrial machinery, fell 4.5% between 1977 and 1990 while nondurable goods industries' share of the gross state product remained constant and services, particularly business services, increased their share by 2.5%. The close tie of the growing service industries to manufacturing suggests that manufacturing is not declining in its importance to the state economy but rather that manufacturers are increasingly contracting out for services which they formerly performed themselves.

In 1994, Ohio's gross state product was $274,844 million, to which private goods–producing services contributed $88,869 million; private services–producing industries, $156,352 million; and government, $29,623 million. Ohio's per capita personal income in 1995 was $22,514, which ranked 21st nationally. During 1996, there were 44,494 bankruptcy filings, up 29% from 1995.

21INCOME

Ohio had a personal nonfarm income in 1995 of $250.3 billion. In 1996, Ohio placed 21st in per capita personal income, with an average of $23,537. In constant dollars, per capita income increased by nearly 7% from 1973 to 1983, then rose by almost 14% from 1984 to 1988.

In 1995, Ohio had a median household income of $34,941. In the same year, 11.5% of all Ohioans lived below the national poverty line.

22LABOR

In 1996, Ohio's civilian labor force averaged 5,643,000. In that year there were an average of 5,365,000 wage and salary earners, for an unemployment rate of 4.9%.

At the beginning of 1997, nonfarm employment was estimated as follows: mining, 13,800; construction, 215,700; manufacturing, 1,084,200; transportation, communications, and public utilities, 232,800; wholesale and retail trade, 1,317,700; finance, insurance, and real estate, 279,300; services, 1,434,200; and government, 756,700.

As of the end of 1996, the Cleveland metropolitan area accounted for 19.5% of the state's labor force; Columbus, 14%; and Cincinnati, 14.3%. In December 1996, the unemployment rate in metropolitan areas ranged from 2.9% in Columbus and 4.2% in Dayton to more than 6.8% in Steubenville-Wierton.

The first workers' organization in Ohio was formed by Dayton mechanics in 1811. The Ohio Federation of Labor was founded in 1884; the American Federation of Labor (AFL) was founded in Columbus in 1886, and Ohio native William Green became president of the AFL in 1924. But it was not until the 1930s that labor unions in Ohio were formed on a large scale. In 1934, the United Rubber Workers began to organize workers in Akron; through a successful series of sit-down strikes at the city's rubber plants, the union grew to about 70,000 members by 1937. In that year, the United Steelworkers struck seven steel plants in the Youngstown area and won the right to bargain collectively for 50,000 steelworkers. The number of union members increased from about 25% of the state's nonfarm employees in 1939 to 32% in 1980, when about 1.4 million workers belonged to labor organizations (5th in the US). In 1995, 885,200 workers—18.5% of the labor force—belonged to labor unions.

Progressive labor legislation in the state began in 1852 with laws regulating working hours for women and children and limiting men to a 10-hour workday. In 1890, Ohio became the first state to establish a public employment service. Subsequent labor legislation included a workers' compensation act in 1911, and child labor and minimum wage measures in the 1930s. In 1983, a law was passed giving public employees, other than police officers and fire fighters, a limited right to strike.

23AGRICULTURE

Despite increasing urbanization and industrialization, agriculture retains its economic importance. In 1996, Ohio ranked 13th in farm value including land and buildings. Ohio ranked 15th in net farm income among the 50 states in 1995. In that year, the state's production of crops, dairy products, and livestock was valued at nearly $4.6 billion.

Mechanization of agriculture contributed to the decline of Ohio's farm population from 1,089,000 in 1940 to 225,000 by 1996, and to a decrease in the number of farms from 234,000 to 72,000 over the same period. The average size of farms increased from 94 acres (38 hectares) in 1940 to 210 acres (85 hectares) in 1996. As of 1996, Ohio had a farm population of about 114,000 farm workers.

Grain is grown and cattle and hogs are raised on large farms in the north-central and western parts of the state, while smaller farms predominate in the hilly southeastern region. Truck farming has continued to expand near the large cities.

Ohio was the 2d-leading producer of tomatoes for processing in 1996 with 307,650 tons. Field crops in 1996 (in bushels) included corn for grain, 305,250,000; soybeans, 157,150,000; wheat, 51,870,000; and oats, 5,130,000. The most valuable crops included soybeans, with sales of $956,034,000, and corn, $924,095,000. Ohio farmers also produced 3,400,000 tons of hay and 79,000 tons of sugar beets in 1996.

[24]ANIMAL HUSBANDRY

Cattle and hogs are raised in the central and western regions. In 1997, Ohio had 1.46 million cattle and calves, worth $876 million. In 1996, Ohio farmers had 1.5 million hogs and pigs, valued at $135 million. During 1995, Ohio farmers produced nearly 11.9 million lb of sheep and lambs.

Dairying is common in most regions of the state, but especially in the east and southeast. In 1995, Ohio ranked 8th among the states in the number of milk cows, which produced 4.6 billion lb of milk. The poultry industry is dispersed throughout the state. Ohio ranked 2d among the states in production of eggs with nearly 6 billion eggs in 1995. Poultry farmers in Ohio also produced 192 million lb of turkey and sold 55 million lb of chickens in 1995.

[25]FISHING

Commercial fishing, which once flourished in Lake Erie, has declined during the 20th century. Only 4,722,000 lb of fish, worth $2,639,000, were landed in 1995, up from 3,980,000 lb and $917,000 in 1984, but far from the record catch of 31,083,000 lb in 1936.

A statewide fish hatchery system annually produces and stocks up to 30 million fry and yearling size fish—mostly walleye, saugeye, trout, catfish, bass, sunfish, muskellunge, and pike. In 1995/96 the state issued 990,387 sport fishing licenses.

[26]FORESTRY

In 1992, Ohio had 7,863,000 acres (3,182,000 hectares) of forestland, representing 30% of the state's total land area, but less than 1% of all US forests. Although scattered throughout the state, hardwood forests are concentrated in the hilly region of the southeast. Commercial timberlands in 1992 totaled 7,567,400 acres (3,062,500 hectares), of which 93% was privately owned.

The state's lumber and wood products industry supplies building materials, household furniture, and paper products. In 1995, shipments of paper and allied products were valued at $6.9 billion, lumber and wood products at $2.9 billion, and furniture at $1.9 billion. In 1992 there were about 778,000 acres (315,000 hectares) of federal, state, county, and municipal timberland in Ohio.

[27]MINING

The value of nonfuel mineral production in Ohio in 1995 was $880 million, essentially the same as that of 1994. During 1995, substantially increased values of lime, construction sand and gravel, and clay minerals were offset mainly by 10% and 12% decreases, respectively, in crushed stone and portland cement values. Crushed stone and construction sand and gravel were the leading mineral commodities produced in Ohio. The combined production of these two commodities (about 108 million metric tons) accounted for 50%, or about $446 million of the state's nonfuel value. Nationally, Ohio ranked 8th in crushed stone and 4th in construction sand and gravel production. Crushed stone, the state's leading mineral commodity, showed a production total of about 58.5 million metric tons, up 3.7% from 1994. In 1995, Ohio led the nation in lime production (2,030,000 metric tons worth $121,000,000). Nationally, Ohio ranked 14th in the value of nonfuel mineral production, accounting for slightly more than 2% of the US total.

[28]ENERGY AND POWER

Ohio has abundant energy resources. The state government estimates that Ohio's coal reserves are sufficient to meet demand for 500 years and that oil and natural gas reserves are also ample.

In 1995, Ohio ranked 5th among all states in electric power production. In that year, installed electric power capacity was 29.5 million kW, and electrical output totaled 137.9 billion kWh.

With an energy consumption of 356.1 million Btu per capita, Ohio ranked 23d among the 50 states in 1994. Total energy consumption amounted to 3,954.1 trillion Btu (3d highest after Texas and California), of which industries consumed 41%, residential users 22%, commercial establishments 15%, and transportation 22%. Coal was the source of about 35% of all energy consumed, petroleum 30%, dry natural gas 22%, nuclear power 3%, and other sources about 10%.

In the 1880s, petroleum was discovered near Lima and natural gas near Toledo, both in the northwest; these fossil fuels have since been found and exploited in the central and eastern regions. In 1996, the state produced 8,306,000 barrels of crude petroleum; proved reserves were estimated at approximately 53,000,000 barrels.

About 126.3 billion cu feet of natural gas were extracted in 1995, with reserves estimated at 1,054 billion cu feet. At the end of 1995 there were 34,520 producing gas wells. In the same year, Ohio's gas utilities served 3,226,248 customers, of whom 92% were residential users.

Coalfields lie beneath southeastern Ohio, particularly in Hocking, Athens, and Perry counties. In 1992, Ohio ranked 11th in the US in coal production, with a total output of 29,889,000 tons. In 1991, 122 surface mines produced two-thirds of the state's coal; 11 underground mines supplied the remainder. A potential energy source is the rich bed of shale rock, underlying more than half of Ohio, which was estimated to contain more than 200 trillion cu feet of natural gas; but much research is needed before the gas could be extracted economically.

As of 1997, two nuclear facilities, Perry in Lake County and Davis-Besse in Ottawa County were in operation. In January 1985, three Ohio utilities halted construction of the Zimmerman nuclear power plant, after spending $1.7 billion on the project; plans were announced to convert the plant to coal use, at an estimated cost of another $1.7 billion. In June 1985, a nuclear reactor at Oak Park was closed down after an accident involving the failure of 14 pieces of equipment; no radiation release or major damage was reported.

[29]INDUSTRY

Ohio has been a leading manufacturing state since the mid-1800s, and in 1981, despite a recessionary slump, it ranked 4th among the states in value of manufacturing shipments.

During the last two decades of the 19th century, Ohio became the nation's leader in machine-tool manufacturing, the 2d-leading steel producer, and a pioneer in oil refining and in the production of automobiles and automotive parts, such as rubber tires.

In recent decades, Ohio has become important as a manufacturer of glassware, soap, matches, paint, business machines, refrigerators—and even comic books and Chinese food products. In 1995, the value of manufacturing shipments was estimated at $222.92 billion.

The following table shows the estimated value of shipments for selected industries in 1995:

Motor vehicles and equipment	$48,307,300,000
Blast furnace and steel mill products	12,560,500,000
Miscellaneous plastics products	9,610,900,000
Metal forgings and stampings	7,439,700,000
Petroleum refining	3,773,300,000
Metalworking machinery	5,448,500,000
Soap cleaners and toilet goods	5,061,400,000
General industrial machinery	4,075,100,000
Fabricated structural metal products	4,075,700,000

In 1997, Ohio was the headquarters to 29 Fortune 500 companies. In 1995, 3,041 US patents were issued to Ohio residents.

30COMMERCE

Ohio is a major commercial state. In 1992, 19,305 wholesale establishments had sales of $127.3 billion, including $68.3 billion in durable goods. The chief categories of wholesale goods traded are groceries and related products, machinery, equipment. and supplies, motor vehicles and automotive parts, metals and minerals (except petroleum), petroleum and oil products. chemicals, electrical goods, grains and other agricultural raw materials, hardware, plumbing, and heating equipment, and lumber and construction materials. Retail sales amounted to $79 billion (7th) in 1992. The principal retail store groups and their sales percentages, among establishments with payrolls, were automotive, 21%; food stores, 19%; and general merchandise, 13.6%.

In 1996, Ohio ranked 7th in the US as an exporter of goods originating within the state, with exports worth $22.7 billion, or 3.6% of the US total. Transportation equipment, nonelectric machinery, chemicals, electric and electronic equipment, primary metals, fabricated metal products, stone, clay, and glass products, and rubber and plastic products account for most of the export value.

31CONSUMER PROTECTION

Agencies involved in consumer protection include the Agriculture Department's Division of Foods, Dairies and Drugs, which operates inspection programs to protect consumers, and the Commerce Department's Division of Banking and its Division of Savings and Loans, which regulate commercial banks and savings and loan associations, respectively. The Ohio Consumers' Counsel acts to protect the interests of residential consumers of public utilities and works to educate consumers about utility issues and resolve consumer complaints. The Attorney General's Office resolves consumer complaints and enforces consumer protection laws.

32BANKING

Ohio's first banks, in Marietta and Chillicothe, were incorporated in 1808, and a state bank was authorized in 1845. There were 260 insured commercial banks in Ohio in 1996, with total assets of $157.8 billion, including $112.6 billion in outstanding loans and leases. Their deposits totaled $104.3 billion, including time and savings deposits of $84.5 billion. In 1996 there were 160 savings institutions in the state, with total assets of more than $47.4 billion. At the end of 1995, the Resolution Trust Corporation had resolved 18 institutions at a cost of $664 million.

33INSURANCE

In 1996, 52 life insurance companies had headquarters in Ohio. In 1995, Ohio and out-of-state life insurance companies received premiums totaling $10.9 billion and paid benefits of more than $4.2 billion, including $1.1 billion in death benefits; premium receipts for life insurance policies were $3.3 billion. The average Ohio family had $101,100 in life insurance in 1991. There were 17,517,000 life insurance policies in force in the state in 1991, worth $438.6 billion.

In early 1996, 177 property and casualty insurance companies were domiciled in Ohio. In 1995, Ohio and out-of-state companies wrote direct premiums of nearly $8.2 billion, which included $4.3 billion in automobile liability and physical damage insurance.

34SECURITIES

The Cincinnati Stock Exchange (CSE) was organized on 11 March 1885 by 12 stockbrokers who agreed to meet regularly to buy and sell securities. In the mid-1990s, the Cincinnati Stock Exchange moved to Chicago and ceased operations in Ohio.

The Ohio securities marketplace is overseen by the Ohio Division of Securities of the Ohio Department of Commerce. The division provides investor protection, enhances capital formation, and protects the integrity of the securities marketplace by administering and enforcing the Ohio Securities Act, which was enacted in 1913. It requires that all securities sold in Ohio be registered with the division or properly exempted from registration and requires that each person transacting business in securities in Ohio be licensed by the division. It also imposes anti-fraud standards in connection with the sale of securities.

35PUBLIC FINANCE

The state budget is prepared on a biennial basis by the Office of Budget and Management. It is submitted by the governor to the state legislature, which must act on it by the close of the current fiscal year (30 June).

The general assembly has nearly total discretion in allocating general revenues, which are used primarily to support education, welfare, mental health facilities, law enforcement, property tax relief, and government operations. The assembly also allocates money from special revenue funds by means of specific legislative acts. More than one-half of all state expenditures come from the general fund.

The general fund for the 1995 biennium was $34.9 billion, compared with the 1991–93 total of $27.7 billion. The following table summarizes state general revenues and expenditures for the fiscal year 1994/95 (in millions):

REVENUES	
Sales and use taxes	$ 8,387.3
Personal income tax	9,541.8
Corporation franchise tax	1,805.5
Public utility excise tax	1,230.8
Cigarette tax	547.6
Alcoholic beverages taxes	101.7
Miscellaneous taxes	949.8
Federal aid	7,579.1
Other income	526.4
TOTAL	$30,670.0
EXPENDITURES	
Primary and secondary education	$ 6,740.1
Human services	7,218.6
Higher education	3,757.6
Tax relief	1,567.5
Justice and corrections	2,102.3
General state government	591.8
Development, transportation, and environment	455.7
Other state expenses	279.9
Federal welfare match	7,983.0
TOTAL	$30,696.5

36TAXATION

Ohio ranked 8th among the 50 states in total state tax revenues collected during 1992/93, but was 29th in per capita state and local taxation as of 1993, with an average tax burden of $2,059.

In 1996, the state personal income tax ranged from 0.693% to 7.004%. The state sales and use tax was 5% on retail sales (excepting groceries and prescription drugs), rental of personal property, and selected services. The corporate franchise tax rate was between 5.1% and 8.9% The public utility excise tax, on intrastate business receipts of public utilities, was 4.75% for most utilities. Other taxes include those on cigarettes, alcoholic beverages, and gasoline. The state also imposes taxes on estates, banks and insurance companies, dealers in intangibles (stockbrokers), coal and other minerals, and pari-mutuels. In 1996, Ohio's state tax receipts from its own sources totaled $12.9 billion.

Ohio residents paid more than $50.8 billion in federal income tax in 1995.

37ECONOMIC POLICY

Although Ohio seeks to attract new industries, a substantial portion of the state's annual economic growth stems from the expansion of existing businesses.

Ohio offers numerous business incentives to spur industrial development. The state encourages capital investment by offering private developers property tax abatements for commercial redevelopment. A 1976 state law permits municipal corporations to exempt certain property improvements from real property taxes for periods of up to 30 years. The state's guaranteed-loan program for industrial developers provides repayment guarantees on 90% of loans up to $1 million. The state also offers revenue bonds to finance a developer's land, buildings, and equipment at interest rates below the going mortgage interest rates.

The Ohio Department of Development (ODOD) administers plans for economic growth in cooperation with city and county governments. It informs companies about opportunities and advantages in the state and promotes the sale of Ohio's exports abroad. In the 1980s, the department instituted research and development programs at state universities in such fields as biotechnology, clean coat technologies, welding and joining technologies, robotics, polymers, and artificial intelligence.

38HEALTH

Ohio's birthrate fell from 23.8 live births per 1,000 population in 1960 to 15.1 in 1977, rising to 15.3 in 1982, and standing at 13.8 in 1995. In the latter year there were 154,064 live births. The infant death rate for the 12 months ending February 1995 was 8.4 per 1,000 live births, about the same as the national rate. In 1992, 36,019 legal abortions were performed in Ohio, a rate of 222 per 1,000 live births.

Ohio ranks above the national average in deaths due to heart disease and cancer, but below the US average for deaths caused by accidents, cerebrovascular diseases, and suicide. The major causes of death in 1995 (with rates per 100,000 population) included heart disease, 317.4; malignant neoplasms, 226.1; cerebrovascular diseases, 60.0; accidents, and adverse effects, 29.1; motor vehicle accidents, 12.4; and suicide, 9.7. The HIV mortality rate was 6.3 per 100,000, less than half the national average. In 1993 Ohio had a high coronary heart disease mortality rate of 111.3 per 100,000. Death by stroke was less common at 26.5 per 100,000 population during the same year. Ohio had the 3d-highest smoking prevalence rate among persons aged 18–30 years.

Ohio had 180 hospitals with 35,325 beds in 1995, when 1,358,106 patients were admitted. At the beginning of 1994, the state had 23,509 active nonfederal physicians; in 1994 there were 5,893 licensed practicing dentists. During 1994, there were 99,800 professionally active registered nurses in the state. Medicare and Medicaid benefits paid out in fiscal 1994 were $6.5 billion and $4.9 billion, respectively. The average expense to hospitals for care per inpatient day was $1,008, and the average cost per stay was $6,103. In 1995, 13.5% of Ohio residents were uninsured.

39SOCIAL WELFARE

The growth of welfare programs in the state was remarkably rapid during the 1970s and early 1980s. From 1970 to 1978, for example, Aid to Families with Dependent Children (AFDC) nearly tripled, to $446 million; by 1996, there were 552,000 AFDC recipients; the average payment per family was $421.

With the enactment of the Personal Responsibility and Work Opportunity Reconciliation Act of 1996, the US government has changed the form and regulations for many of its social welfare programs; most significantly, it replaces Aid to Families with Dependent Children (AFDC), an open-ended entitlement program, with Temporary Assistance for Needy Families (TANF), a limited system of assistance funded largely through federal block grants. The reform act also impacts the food stamp program, the Supplemental Security Income program, and the child nutrition program. The law took effect on 1 July 1997 and provided $16.38 billion in block grants for fiscal years 1997–2002. The grants are to be divided among the states based on an equation involving the numbers of former AFDC recipients in each state. Because many of the bill's provisions have yet to be implemented into state-by-state policy, it was not possible to include the details of each state's programs for this edition of this work.

Social Security benefits were paid to 1.9 million Ohioans in 1995, averaging $736 a month. That year, Supplemental Security Income payments were made to 284,195 eligible persons, averaging $362 a month. In 1996, 1.04 million residents received monthly food stamp allowances averaging $74.19. In 1991, the school lunch program cost the federal government about $163.2 million. The average weekly unemployment insurance benefit payment was $196.78 in 1995.

40HOUSING

In 1996, Ohio had an estimated 4,545,000 housing units, 4,219,000 of which were occupied. In the same year, 49,280 privately owned units, valued at just over $15 billion, were authorized for construction; of these, 35,719 were single-family. As of 1990, about 63% of the state's housing units were occupied by their owners and 37% were rented. About 74% of the housing units were built in 1940 or later; 20% were built in the 1970s, and 12% in the 1980s. In 1990 the median monthly mortgage and selected carrying costs for owner-occupied housing units with mortgages was $625, and the median monthly rent was $379. The median home value was $63,500, down 10.9% from 1980 after adjusting for inflation. During 1995/96, Ohio received $811.4 million in aid from the US Department of Housing and Urban Development, including $190.4 million in community development block grants.

41EDUCATION

Ohio claims a number of "firsts" in US education: the first kindergarten, established by German settlers in Columbus in 1838; the first junior high school, also at Columbus, in 1909; the first municipal university, the University of Cincinnati, founded in 1870; and the first college to grant degrees to women, Oberlin, in 1837. The state's earliest school system was organized in Akron in 1847.

Of the total adult population age 25 years and over in 1990, 78.6% were high school graduates, and 18.4% had completed at least four years of postsecondary study. In 1996/97, the state's 3,674 public elementary and secondary schools enrolled an estimated 1,812,497 pupils, 93,568 of whom were in secondary job training programs; in the same year there were 120,633 public school teachers. In 1995/96, Ohio's public school teachers received an average annual salary of $38,064, 21st highest among the 50 states. Roman Catholic parochial schools had 147,065 elementary school pupils and 44,054 high school pupils in 1995/96.

In 1995/96, public schools enrolled 280,671 blacks, accounting for almost 15.5% of all public school pupils.

There are 12 state universities, including Ohio State University (Columbus), Ohio University (Athens), Miami University (Oxford), and other state universities at Akron, Bowling Green, Cincinnati, Cleveland, Dayton, Kent, Toledo, Wilberforce, and Youngstown. The largest, Ohio State, was chartered in 1870 and also has campuses at Lima, Mansfield, Marion, Newark, and

Wooster. Ohio has 45 public two-year colleges. Well-known private colleges and universities include Antioch (Yellow Springs), Case Western Reserve (Cleveland), Kenyon (Gambier), Muskingum (New Concord), Oberlin, Wittenberg (Springfield), and Wooster.

Ohio residents enrolled as full-time students at an eligible institution within the state may apply for instructional grants from the Student Assistance Office of the Ohio Board of Regents. Guaranteed loans are provided through the Ohio Student Loan Commission.

42ARTS

The earliest center of artistic activities in Ohio was Cincinnati, where a group of young painters did landscapes and portraits as early as 1840. The state's first art gallery was established there in 1854; the Cincinnati Art Academy was founded in 1869, and the Art Museum in 1886. Famous American artists who worked in Cincinnati during part of their careers include Thomas Cole, a founder of the "Hudson River School" of landscape painting, who was raised in Steubenville; Frank Duveneck, dean of the Cincinnati Academy; and Columbus-born George Bellows, whose realistic "Stag at Sharkey's" is displayed at the Cleveland Museum of Art (founded in 1913). Other notable centers for the visual arts include the Akron Art Institute, Columbus Museum of Art, Dayton Art Institute, Toledo Museum of Art, and museums or galleries in Marion, Oberlin, Springfield, Youngstown, and Zanesville.

Cincinnati also was an early center for the theater; the Eagle Theater opened there in 1839, and shortly afterward, the first showboat on the Ohio River began making regular stops at the city. The first US minstrel show appeared in Ohio in 1842; Al Field's famous minstrels, formed in Columbus in 1886, successfully toured the US for 41 years. As of 1984, Ohio had three professional theatrical companies: the Cincinnati Playhouse, the Cleveland Playhouse, and the Great Lakes Shakespeare Festival. The Ohio Community Theater Association included groups in Akron, Canton, Columbus, Mansfield, Toledo, and Youngstown.

Ohio's foremost orchestras are the Cincinnati Symphony, which was founded in 1895 and reorganized in 1909 with Leopold Stokowski as conductor, and the Cleveland Symphony, founded in 1918; especially since 1946, when George Szell began his 24-year tenure as conductor and music director, the Cleveland Orchestra has been considered one of the finest in the world. Blossom Music Center, the orchestra's summer home, between Cleveland and Akron, has been a center for both classical and popular music in northeast Ohio since its opening in 1968. The Cincinnati Pops Orchestra acquired a new summer home in 1984 at the newly opened Riverbend Music Center. The nation's first college music department was organized at Oberlin College in 1865; the Cincinnati Conservatory of Music was established in 1867, and the Cleveland Institute of Music in 1920. There are civic symphony orchestras in Columbus, Dayton, Toledo, and Youngstown. Operas are performed by resident companies in Cleveland, Columbus, Cincinnati, Toledo, and Dayton. The State of Ohio generated $1,055,000 from federal sources in support of its arts programs in 1996. The NEA contributed $2,216,000 to the state's programs and $2,532,000 to the Ohio Arts Council. The state and private sources contributed funds as well. From 1987 to 1991, audiences for the state's programs totaled 119,159,000; there were 423,623 participating artists. During the same period, the state of Ohio provided about 57,200 school children with arts education programs. In 1995, the state had 2,100 arts associations and 98 local arts groups. The Ohio Arts Council contributes funds for artists to visit the schools. In 1992, the council received monies from the NEA's arts education grant program and from the State and Regional program.

43LIBRARIES AND MUSEUMS

Ever since early settlers traded coonskins for books and established, in 1804, the Coonskin Library (now on display at the Ohio Historical Center in Columbus), Ohioans have stressed the importance of the public library system. In 1995, the state public library system had 41,012,204 volumes, and a circulation of 133,384,332.

Major public library systems include those of Cincinnati, with 4,566,725 volumes in 1996; Cleveland, 2,864,276; Dayton, 1,586,317; and Columbus, 2,310,808. Leading academic libraries include those of Ohio State University, with 7,100,284 books and bound periodicals; Case Western Reserve University, 2,181,240 books; and the University of Cincinnati, 3,655,920 books and bound periodicals. The State Library of Ohio in Columbus, founded in 1817, provides research and information services for Ohio's state government and agencies with more than two million books and periodicals.

Among the state's more than 257 museums are the Museum of Art, Natural History Museum, and Western Reserve Historical Society Museum in Cleveland; the Museum of Natural History, Art Museum, and Taft Museum in Cincinnati; the Dayton Art Institute; and the Center of Science and Industry and Ohio Historical Center in Columbus. The Zanesville Art Center has collections of ceramics and glass made in the Zanesville area. Also noteworthy are the US Air Force Museum near Dayton, the Neil Armstrong Air and Space Museum at Wapakoneta, and the Ohio River Museum in Marietta. Cincinnati has a conservatory of rare plants, while Cleveland has botanical gardens and an aquarium; both cities have zoos.

Historical sites in Ohio include the Schoenbrunn Village State Memorial, a reconstruction of the state's first settlement by Moravian missionaries, near New Philadelphia; the early-19th-century Piqua Historical Area, with exhibits of Indian culture; and the Fort Meigs reconstruction at Perrysburg. Archaeological sites include the "great circle" mounds, built by the Hopewell Indians at present-day Newark, and Inscription Rock, marked by prehistoric Indians, on Kelleys Island.

44COMMUNICATIONS

In March 1993, 95% of Ohio's 4,262,000 occupied housing units had telephones.

Many of the state's radio stations were established in the early 1920s, when the growth of radio broadcasting was fostered by the availability of low-priced sets manufactured by Crosley Radio of Cincinnati. In 1996 there were 118 AM stations, 257 FM stations, and 42 commercial and 12 noncommercial television stations. There were also 24 large cable television systems serving the state.

45PRESS

The first newspaper published in the region north and west of the Ohio River was the *Centinel of the North–Western Territory*, which was written, typeset, and printed in Cincinnati by William Maxwell in 1793. The oldest newspaper in the state still published under its original name is the *Scioto Gazette*, which appeared in 1800. The oldest extant weekly, the *Lebanon Western Star*, began publication in 1807, and the first daily, the *Cincinnati Commercial Register*, appeared in 1826. By 1840 there were 145 newspapers in Ohio.

Two of the state's most influential newspapers, the Cleveland *Plain Dealer* and the Cincinnati *Enquirer*, were founded in 1841. In 1878, Edward W. Scripps established the Cleveland *Penny Press* (later called the *Press*), the first newspaper in what would become the extensive Scripps-Howard chain; he later added to his newspaper empire the Cincinnati *Post* (1881) and the Columbus *Citizen* (1899), as well as papers in Akron, Toledo, and Youngstown.

In 1997 there were 17 morning daily newspapers, 67 daily evening papers, one all-day daily, and 36 Sunday papers. The following table lists leading Ohio newspapers with their daily circulation in 1997:

AREA	NAME	DAILY	SUNDAY
Akron	*Beacon Journal* (e,S)	152,760	218,436
Cincinnati	*Enquirer* (m,S)	205,591	352,893
	Post (e)	79,652	—
Cleveland	*Plain Dealer* (m,S)	398,398	528,818
Columbus	*Dispatch* (e,S)	268,670	401,612
Dayton	*Daily News* (e,S)	161,016	217,976
Toledo	*Blade* (e,S)	145,899	201,155
Youngstown	*Vindicator* (e,S)	83,117	124,275

46ORGANIZATIONS

The 1992 Census of Service Industries counted 3,330 organizations in Ohio, including 480 business associations; 2,152 civic, social, and fraternal associations; and 698 other membership organizations.

Service organizations with headquarters in Ohio include the Army and Navy Union, USA, at Lakemore, and the National Exchange Club, in Toledo. Among the state's cultural associations are the American Classical League, at Oxford, and the Guild of Carilloneurs in North America and the Music Teachers National Association, both in Cincinnati.

Commercial and professional organizations include the American Ceramic Society and Order of United Commercial Travelers of America, both in Columbus; American Society for Metals, in Metals Park; and Association for Systems Management and Brotherhood of Locomotive Engineers, both in Cleveland.

Sports associations operating out of Ohio are the Lighter-Than-Air Society and Professional Bowlers Association, Akron; American Motorcyclist Association, Westerville; Amateur Trapshooting Association, Vandalia; and Indoor Sports Club, Napoleon. The International Brotherhood of Magicians has its headquarters in Kenton.

47TOURISM, TRAVEL, AND RECREATION

Leading tourist attractions include Ohio's presidential memorials and homes: the William Henry Harrison Memorial at North Bend, Ulysses S. Grant's birthplace at Point Pleasant, the James A. Garfield home at Mentor, the Rutherford B. Hayes home at Fremont, the William McKinley Memorial at Canton, the Taft National Historic Site in Cincinnati, and the Warren G. Harding home in Marion. Also of interest are the Thomas A. Edison birthplace at Milan, and Malabar Farm, in Richland County, home of author and conservationist Louis Bromfield.

Beaches and parks in the Lake Erie region are especially popular with tourists during the summer. Among the many attractions in the northern region are the Crosby Gardens in Toledo, reconstructions of Auglaize Village near Defiance and of Harbour Town in Vermilion, the Marblehead Lighthouse, and the Lake Erie Nature and Science Center in Cleveland. The Portside Festival Marketplace is located in downtown Toledo, with many shops and restaurants along the banks of the Maumee River. The Cuyahoga Valley National Recreation Area is a popular attraction, linking the urban center of Cleveland and Akron.

The eastern Allegheny region has several ski resorts for winter sports enthusiasts. Popular tourist attractions include the Amish settlement around Millersburg, the National Road-Zane Grey Museum near Zanesville, and the restored Roscoe Village on the Ohio-Erie Canal. The southern region offers scenic hill country, the Paramount Kings Island entertainment complex at Kings Mills, and the showboat *Majestic,* the last of the original floating theaters, in Cincinnati.

In the western region, tourist sites include the Wright brothers' early flying machines in Dayton's Carillon Park, the Ohio Caverns at West Liberty, and the Zane Caverns near Bellefontaine. The central region is "Johnny Appleseed" country; the folk hero (a frontiersman whose real name was John Chapman) is commemorated in Mansfield by the blockhouse to which he directed settlers in order to save them from an Indian raid. At Columbus are the reconstructed Ohio Village and the Exposition Center, site of the annual Ohio State Fair, held for 13 days in mid-August.

Ohio has state parks which comprise 204,274 acres (84,000 hectares). Among the most visited state parks are Alum Creek, East Harbor and Kelleys Island (both on Lake Erie), Grand Lake, St. Marys, Hocking Hills, Hueston Woods, Mohican, Pymatuning (on the Pennsylvania border), Rocky Fork, Salt Fork, Scioto Trail, and West Branch.

The most popular sport fish are bass, catfish, bullhead, carp, perch, and rainbow trout. The deer-shooting season is held in late November; hunters are limited to one deer per season. However, because of the growing deer population in Ohio, hunters have been able to take two deer per season recently. Also the season times vary for shotgun, primitive arms, and bows. The bow season lasts several months. Licenses were held by 1,140,568 hunters and 994,019 anglers in 1995.

48SPORTS

There are five major league professional sports teams in Ohio: the Cleveland Indians and the Cincinnati Reds of Major League Baseball, and the Columbus Crew of Major League Soccer, the Cincinnati Bengals of the National Football League, and the Cleveland Cavaliers of the National Basketball Association.

The state is also home to Triple-A minor league baseball teams in Columbus and Toledo, and a Double-A team in Akron. In addition, there is minor league hockey in Cleveland, Columbus, Dayton, and Toledo.

The Cincinnati Reds (traditionally short for Redstockings) were the first professionally organized baseball team, playing their first season 1869. Their record was 64–0. The Reds won the World Series in 1919, 1940, 1975, 1976, and in 1990. The Indians won the World Series in 1920 and 1948. In 1995, the Indians won their first American League pennant since 1954, but lost to the Atlanta Braves in the World Series. The Cleveland Browns, who moved to Baltimore in 1995, won four NFL titles, football's championship prior to the Super Bowl, the last in 1964. An expansion or relocation NFL team will play as the Browns in a new stadium in Cleveland beginning in 1999. The Bengals won the American Football Conference Championship in both 1981 and 1988, but lost each year's Super Bowl.

Akron has been headquarters for the Professional Bowlers Association (PBA) since its founding in 1958. The PBA's top tournament is played there each year, and the PBA Hall of Fame is also located in Akron. The World Series of Golf is played annually in Akron, and the Memorial Golf Tournament in Columbus.

Major horse-racing tracks include Cleveland's Thistledown, Cincinnati's River Downs, Columbus's Scioto Downs, and other tracks at Toledo, Lebanon, Grove City, and Northfield. The Cleveland Gold Cup race is held annually at Thistledown, as is the Ohio Derby. The Little Brown Jug classic for three-year-old pacers takes place every year at the Delaware Fairgrounds, and the Ohio State race for two-year-old trotters is held during the state fair at Columbus.

In collegiate sports, Ohio State University has long been a football power, winning 25 Big Ten titles (through 1996). Ohio State won the Rose Bowl in 1950, 1955, 1958, 1969, 1974, and 1997. The Buckeyes were named national champions in 1942, 1954 (with UCLA), 1957 (with Auburn), and 1968. Ohio State also has won NCAA championships in baseball, basketball, fencing, golf, gymnastics, and swimming, while Cincinnati and Dayton universities have had highly successful basketball teams. The Pro Football Hall of Fame is located in Canton, where the sport was first organized professionally in 1920.

Other annual sporting events include the grand tournament of the American Trapshooting Association in Vandalia, the Grand Prix or Cleveland Indy car race, and the All-American Soap Box Derby in Akron, a nationally covered event in which 9- to 15-year-olds compete.

[49]FAMOUS OHIOANS

Ohio has been the native state of seven US presidents and the residence of another. Inventions by Ohioans include the incandescent light, the arc light, and the airplane.

William Henry Harrison (b.Virginia, 1773–1841), the 9th US president, came to Ohio as a US Army ensign in territorial times. After serving in the Indian wars under Gen. Anthony Wayne, he became secretary of the Northwest Territory. As the territorial delegate to Congress, he fostered the Harrison Land Act, which stimulated settlement of the public domain. Named territorial governor in 1800, Harrison conducted both warfare and peace negotiations with the Indians. After the defeat of British and Indian forces in 1813, he became known as the "Washington of the West." After settling at North Bend on the Ohio River, he began a political career that carried him to the White House in 1841. Harrison caught a chill from a cold March wind and died of pneumonia exactly one month after his inauguration.

From 1869 to 1881, the White House was occupied by three Ohioans. All were Republicans who had served with distinction as Union Army generals. The first, Ulysses Simpson Grant (Hiram Ulysses Grant, 1822–85), the 18th US president, was an Ohio farm boy educated at West Point. After service in the Mexican War, he left the US Army, having been charged with intemperance. He emerged from obscurity in 1861, when he was assigned to an Illinois regiment. Grant rose quickly in command; after victories at Shiloh and Vicksburg, he was commissioned major general. In 1864, he directed the Virginia campaign that ended with Confederate surrender, and this rumpled, slouching, laconic man became the nation's hero. In 1868, he was elected president, and he was reelected in 1872. His second term was rocked with financial scandals, though none were directly connected to Grant. After leaving the presidency in 1877, he went bankrupt, and to discharge his debts, he wrote his memoirs. That extraordinary book was completed four days before his death from throat cancer in 1885. Grant is buried in a monumental tomb in New York City.

Rutherford B. Hayes (1822–93), the 19th US president, was born in Delaware, Ohio, and educated at Kenyon College and Harvard Law School. Following Army service, he was elected to Congress, and in 1876 became the Republican presidential nominee. In a close and disputed election, he defeated New York's Governor Samuel J. Tilden. Hayes chose not to run for reelection, returning instead to Ohio to work on behalf of humanitarian causes. In 1893, Hayes died in Fremont, where the Hayes Memorial was created—the first presidential museum and library in the nation.

James A. Garfield (1831–81), 20th US president, was born in a log cabin in northern Ohio. Between school terms, he worked as a farmhand and a mule driver on the Ohio Canal. After holding several Civil War commands, he served in Congress for 18 years. Elected president in 1880, he held office but a few months; he was shot by a disappointed office seeker in the Washington, D.C. railroad station on 2 July and died 11 weeks later.

Benjamin Harrison (1833–1901), 23d US president and grandson of William Henry Harrison, was born in North Bend. After graduation from Miami University, he studied law and

began to practice in Indianapolis. Military command in the Civil War was followed by service in the US Senate and the Republican presidential nomination in 1888. As president, Harrison gave impetus to westward expansion, moved toward annexation of Hawaii, and enlarged the civil-service system.

US presidents in the 20th century include three more native Ohioans. William McKinley (1843–1901) was born in Niles. Elected in 1896 as the 25th president, he established the gold standard and maintained tariff protection for US manufactures. Early in his second term, while greeting a throng of people, he was shot to death by a young anarchist. William Howard Taft (1857–1930), of Cincinnati, was the 27th US president. He gained a national reputation in 1904 as President Theodore Roosevelt's secretary of war; five years later, he succeeded Roosevelt in the White House. Defeated in 1912, Taft then left Washington for a law professorship at Yale. In 1921, under President Warren G. Harding (1865–1923), he became US chief justice, serving in that office until a month before his death. Harding, the last Ohioan to win the White House, was born in Blooming Grove. He went into politics from journalism, after serving as editor of the *Marion Star*. After eight years in the US Senate, he was a dark-horse candidate for the Republican presidential nomination in 1920. He won the election from James M. Cox (1870–1957), another Ohio journalist-politician, and became the 29th US president. Harding, who died in office, was surrounded by graft and corruption in his own cabinet.

Three US vice presidents were natives of Ohio. Thomas A. Hendricks (1819–85) was elected on the Democratic ticket with Grover Cleveland in 1884. Charles W. Fairbanks (1852–1918) served from 1905 to 1909 under Theodore Roosevelt. Charles Gates Dawes (1865–1951) became vice president under Calvin Coolidge in 1925, the same year the Dawes Plan for reorganizing German finances brought him the Nobel Peace Prize; from 1929 to 1932, he served as US ambassador to Great Britain.

Three Ohioans served as chief justice on the Supreme Court: Salmon P. Chase (b.New Hampshire, 1808–73), Morrison R. Waite (b.Connecticut, 1816–88), and Taft. Most notable among nearly 40 cabinet officers from Ohio were Secretary of State Lewis Cass (b.New Hampshire, 1783–1866), Treasury Secretaries Chase and John Sherman (1823–1900), and Secretary of War Edwin M. Stanton (1814–69). William Tecumseh Sherman (1820–91) was a Union general in the Civil War whose Georgia campaign in 1864 helped effect the surrender of the Confederacy. Although disappointed in his quest for the presidency, US Senator Robert A. Taft (1889–1953) was an enduring figure, best remembered for his authorship of the Taft-Hartley Labor Management Relations Act of 1947.

Nobel Prize winners from Ohio include Dawes and physicists Arthur Compton (1892–1962) and Donald Glaser (b.1926). Notable Pulitzer Prize winners include novelist Louis Bromfield (1896–1956), dramatist Russell Crouse (1893–1966), historian Paul Herman Buck (1899–1979), and historian and biographer Arthur Schlesinger, Jr. (b.1917). Ohio writers of enduring fame are novelists William Dean Howells (1837–1920), Zane Grey (1875–1939), and Sherwood Anderson (1876–1941), whose short story collection *Winesburg, Ohio* was set in his hometown of Clyde; poets Paul Laurence Dunbar (1872–1906) and Hart Crane (1899–1932); and humorist James Thurber (1894–1961). Toni Morrison (b. 1931), winner of the 1988 Pulitzer Prize for literature and the 1993 Nobel Prize for literature, was born in Lorain, Ohio. Among Ohio's eminent journalists are Whitelaw Reid (1837–1912), satirists David R. Locke (1833–88) and Ambrose Bierce (1842–1914), columnist O. O. McIntyre (1884–1938), newsletter publisher W. M. Kiplinger (1891–1967), and James Reston (b.Scotland, 1909), an editor and columnist for the *New York Times* along with author-commentator Lowell Thomas (1892–1981). Important in the art world were painters Thomas

Cole (b.England, 1801–48), Frank Duveneck (b.Kentucky, 1848–1919), and George Bellows (1882–1925), as well as architects Cass Gilbert (1859–1934) and Philip Johnson (b.1906). Defense lawyer Clarence Darrow (1857–1938) was also an Ohioan.

Ohio educators whose books taught reading, writing, and arithmetic to the nation's schoolchildren were William Holmes McGuffey (b.Pennsylvania, 1800–73), Platt R. Spencer (1800–64), and Joseph Ray (1807–65). In higher education, Horace Mann (b.Massachusetts, 1796–1859) was the first president of innovative Antioch College, and William Rainey Harper (1856–1906) founded the University of Chicago.

Several Ohio-born inventor-scientists have furthered the nation's industrial progress. Thomas A. Edison (1847–1931) produced the incandescent lamp, the phonograph, and the movie camera. Charles Brush (1849–1929) invented the arc light. John H. Patterson (1844–1922) helped develop the cash register. The Wright brothers, Orville (1871–1948) and Wilbur (b.Indiana, 1867–1912), made the first flight in a powered aircraft. Charles F. Kettering (1876–1958) invented the automobile self-starter. Ohio's leading industrialist was John D. Rockefeller (b.New York, 1839–1937), founder of Standard Oil of Ohio. Harvey S. Firestone (1868–1938) started the tire company that bears his name. Edward "Eddie" Rickenbacker (1890–1973), an ace pilot in World War I, was president of Eastern Airlines.

The most notable Ohioans in the entertainment field are markswoman Annie Oakley (Phoebe Anne Oakley Mozee, 1860–1926); movie actors Clark Gable (1901–60) and Roy Rogers (Leonard Slye, b.1912); movie director Stephen Spielberg (b.1947); comedian Bob Hope (Leslie Townes Hope, b.England, 1903); actors Paul Newman (b.1925), Hal Holbrook (b.1925), and Joel Grey (b.1932); jazz pianist Art Tatum (1910–56); and composer Henry Mancini (1924–94).

Leading sports figures from Ohio are boxing champion Jim Jeffries (1875–1953), racing driver Barney Oldfield (1878–1946), baseball pitcher Cy Young (1867–1955), baseball executive Branch Rickey (1881–1965), baseball star Peter "Pete" Rose (b.1941) who broke Ty Cobb's record for the most hits, track star Jesse Owens (b.Alabama, 1912–80), jockey George Edward "Eddie" Arcaro (b.1916), and golfer Jack Nicklaus (b.1940).

Astronauts from Ohio include John Glenn (b.1921), the first American to orbit the earth, who was elected US senator from Ohio in 1974; and Neil Armstrong (b.1930), the first man to walk on the moon.

[50]BIBLIOGRAPHY

Bromfield, Louis. *The Farm*. New York: Harper, 1933.

Condon, George E. *Cleveland: The Best Kept Secret*. Garden City, N.Y.: Doubleday, 1967.

Curtin, Michael F. *The Ohio Politics Almanac*. Kent: Kent State University Press, 1996.

Downes, Randolph C. *Frontier Ohio: 1788-1803*. Columbus: Ohio State Archaeological and Historical Society, 1935.

Ellis, William D. *The Cuyahoga*. New York: Holt, 1966.

Feagler, Dick. *Feagler's Cleveland*. Cleveland: Gray & Co., 1996.

Federal Writers' Project. *The Ohio Guide*. Reprint. New York: Somerset, n.d. (orig. 1940).

Galbreath, Charles B. *History of Ohio*. 5 vols. Chicago and New York: American Historical Society, 1925.

A Geography of Ohio. Edited by Leonard Peacefull. Kent: Kent State University Press, 1996.

Havighurst, Walter. *Ohio: A Bicentennial History*. New York: Norton, 1976.

Hopkins, Charles E. *Ohio the Beautiful and Historic*. Boston: Page, 1931.

Howe, Henry, *Historical Collections of Ohio*. 2 vols. Columbus: Henry Howe & Son, 1889.

Howells, William Dean. *A Boy's Town*. New York: Harper, 1890.

Hulbert, Archer B. *The Ohio River: A Course of Empire*. New York and London: Putnam, 1906.

Jones, Robert L. *The History of Agriculture in Ohio to Eighteen Eighty*. Kent: Kent State University Press, 1983.

Leech, Margaret. *In the Days of McKinley*. New York: Harper & Row, 1959.

Longworth de Chambrun, Clara. *Cincinnati: The Story of the Queen City*. New York: Scribner, 1939.

McCormick, Richard P. *The Second American Party System: Party Formation in the Jacksonian Era*. Chapel Hill: University of North Carolina Press, 1966.

Morgan, H. Wayne. *From Hayes to McKinley*. Syracuse, N.Y.: Syracuse University Press, 1969.

The National Road. Edited by Karl Raitz. Baltimore, Md.: Johns Hopkins University Press, 1996.

Notestein, Lucy. *Wooster of the Middle West*. New Haven, Conn.: Yale University Press, 1937.

Ohio Politics. Edited by Alexander P. Lamis. Kent: Kent State University Press, 1994.

Ohio State. Department of State. *Constitution of the State of Ohio*. Columbus: Anderson, 1979.

Ohio State. Secretary of State. *Official Roster, 1983-1984*. Columbus, 1984.

Patterson, James T. *Mr. Republican: A Biography of Robert A. Taft*. Boston: Houghton Mifflin, 1972.

Reid, Whitelaw. *Ohio in the War: Her Statesmen, Generals, and Soldiers*. 2 vols. Cincinnati: Moore, Wilstach & Baldwin, 1868.

Roseboom, Eugene Holloway, and Francis P. Weisenburger. *A History of Ohio*. New York: Prentice-Hall, 1934.

Thurber, James. *My Life and Hard Times*. New York: Harper, 1933.

Warner, Hoyt Landon. *Progressivism in Ohio 1897–1917*. Columbus: Ohio State University Press, 1964.

Wittke, Carl, ed. *History of the State of Ohio*. 6 vols. Columbus: Ohio State Archaeological and Historical Society, 1941-44.

OKLAHOMA

State of Oklahoma

ORIGIN OF STATE NAME: Derived from the Choctaw Indian words *okla humma*, meaning "land of the red people." **NICKNAME:** The Sooner State. **CAPITAL:** Oklahoma City. **ENTERED UNION:** 16 November 1907 (46th). **SONG:** "Oklahoma!" **POEM:** "Howdy Folks." **MOTTO:** *Labor omnia vincit* (Labor conquers all things). **FLAG:** On a blue field, a peace pipe and an olive branch cross an Osage warrior's shield, which is decorated with small crosses and from which seven eagle feathers descend; the word "Oklahoma" appears below. **OFFICIAL SEAL:** Each point of a five-pointed star incorporates the emblem of an Indian nation: (clockwise from top) Chickasaw, Choctaw, Seminole, Creek, and Cherokee. In the center, a frontiersman and Indian shake hands before the goddess of justice; behind them are symbols of progress, including a farm, train, and mill. Surrounding the large star are 45 small ones and the words "Great Seal of the State of Oklahoma 1907." **ANIMAL:** American buffalo (bison). **BIRD:** Scissor-tailed flycatcher. **FISH:** White bass (sand bass). **REPTILE:** Collared lizard (mountain boomer). **FLORAL EMBLEM:** Mistletoe. **TREE:** Redbud. **GRASS:** Indian grass. **STONE:** Barite rose (rose rock). **LEGAL HOLIDAYS:** New Year's Day, 1 January; Birthday of Martin Luther King, Jr., 3d Monday in January; Washington's Birthday, 3d Monday in February; Memorial Day, last Monday in May; Independence Day, 4 July; Labor Day, 1st Monday in September; Columbus Day, 2d Monday in October; Veterans Day, 11 November; Thanksgiving Day, 4th Thursday in November; Christmas Day, 25 December. **TIME:** 6 AM CST = noon GMT.

¹LOCATION, SIZE, AND EXTENT

Situated in the western south-central US, Oklahoma ranks 18th in size among the 50 states.

The total area of Oklahoma is 69,956 sq mi (181,186 sq km), of which land takes up 68,655 sq mi (177,817 sq km) and inland water 1,301 sq mi (3,369 sq km). Oklahoma extends 464 mi (747 km) E-W including the panhandle in the NW, which is about 165 mi (266 km) long. The maximum N-S extension is 230 mi (370 km).

Oklahoma is bordered on the N by Colorado and Kansas; on the E by Missouri and Arkansas; on the s and sw by Texas (with part of the line formed by the Red River); and on the extreme w by New Mexico. The total estimated boundary length of Oklahoma is 1,581 mi (2,544 km). The state's geographic center is in Oklahoma County, 8 mi (13 km) N of Oklahoma City.

²TOPOGRAPHY

The land of Oklahoma rises gently to the west from an altitude of 287 feet (87 meters) at Little River in the southeastern corner to a height of 4,973 feet (1,516 meters) at Black Mesa, on the tip of the panhandle. Four mountain ranges cross this Great Plains state: the Boston Mountains (part of the Ozark Plateau) in the northeast, the Quachitas in the southeast, the Arbuckles in the south-central region, and the Wichitas in the southwest. Much of the northwest belongs to the High Plains, while northeastern Oklahoma is mainly a region of buttes and valleys.

Not quite two-thirds of the state is drained by the Arkansas River, and the remainder by the Red River. Within Oklahoma, the Arkansas is joined by the Verdigris, Grand (Neosho), and Illinois rivers from the north and northeast, and by the Cimarron and Canadian rivers from the northwest and west. The Red River, which marks most of the state's southern boundary, is joined by the Washita, Salt Fork, Blue, Kiamichi, and many smaller rivers. There are few natural lakes but many artificial ones, of which the largest is Lake Eufaula, covering 102,500 acres (41,500 hectares).

³CLIMATE

Oklahoma has a continental climate with cold winters and hot summers. Normal daily mean temperatures in Oklahoma City range from 37°F (3°C) in January to 82°F (28°C) in July. The record low temperature of −27°F (−33°C) was set at Watts on 18 January 1930; the record high, 120°F (49°C), occurred at Tipton on 29 June 1994.

Dry, sunny weather generally prevails throughout the state. Precipitation varies from an average of 15 in (38 cm) annually in the panhandle to over 50 in (127 cm) in the southeast. Snowfall averages 9 in (23 cm) a year in Oklahoma City, which is also one of the windiest cities in the US, with an average annual wind speed of 12.8 mph (20.6 km/hr).

Oklahoma is tornado-prone. One of the most destructive windstorms was the tornado that tore through Ellis, Woods, and Woodward countries on 9 April 1947, killing 101 people and injuring 782 others. In 1995, Oklahoma had 79 tornadoes.

⁴FLORA AND FAUNA

Grasses grow in abundance in Oklahoma. Bluestem, buffalo, sand lovegrass, and grama grasses are native, with the bluestem found mostly in the eastern and central regions, and buffalo grass most common in the western counties, known as the "short grass country." Deciduous hardwoods stand in eastern Oklahoma, and red and yellow cactus blossoms brighten the Black Mesa area in the northwest.

The white-tailed deer is found in all counties, and Rio Grande wild turkeys are hunted across much of the state. Pronghorn antelope inhabit the panhandle area, and elk survive in the Wichita Mountains Wildlife Refuge, where a few herds of American buffalo (bison) are also preserved. The bobwhite quail, ring-necked pheasant, and prairie chicken are common game birds. Native sport fish include largemouth, smallmouth, white, and spotted bass; catfish; crappie; and sunfish.

Among the state's endangered or threatened species of wildlife are the leopard darter, Ozark big-eared bat, red wolf, black-footed ferret, Indiana bat, southern bald eagle, whooping crane, ivory-billed and red-cockaded woodpeckers, Bauchman's warbler, American peregrine falcon, Eskimo curlew, and American alligator.

[5]ENVIRONMENTAL PROTECTION

The Department of Pollution Control, created in 1968, is the executive arm of the Oklahoma Pollution Control Coordinating Board. The department has overall responsibility for coordinating all pollution control activities by other state agencies and for developing a comprehensive water quality management program for Oklahoma.

The Department of Health is responsible for the monitoring of air quality standards; the enforcement of regulations covering control of industrial and solid waste; the enforcement of regulations covering radioactive materials at the Kerr-McGee processing facility at Gore and elsewhere; and the maintenance of standards at all public waterworks and sewer systems. The Water Resources Board has broad statutory authority to protect the state's waters.

Toxic industrial wastes remain an environmental concern, and old mines in the Tar Creek area of northeastern Oklahoma still exude groundwater contaminated by zinc, iron, and cadmium. Three hazardous waste sites placed on the EPA's National Priorities List for Superfund cleanup were Compass Industries, Sand Springs Petro Chemical Complex, and Criner.

Lands devastated by erosion during the droughts of the 1930s were purchased by the federal government and turned over to the Soil Conservation Service for restoration. When grasses were firmly established in the mid-1950s, the land was turned over to the US Forest Service and is now leased for grazing. In 1996, the state had 950,000 acres of wetlands—about 2% of the land. There are 11 hazardous waste sites in Oklahoma.

[6]POPULATION

Oklahoma ranked 28th among the states in the 1990 census with a total population of 3,145,585, an increase of 4% over the census total of 3,025,300 in 1980, when Oklahoma ranked 26th among the 50 states. The estimated population in 1996 was 3,300,902, a 4.9% increase over 1990. In 1990, Oklahoma had a population density of 45.8 per sq mi (17.6 per sq km).

In 1990, 67.7% of all Oklahomans lived in urban areas. The largest city is Oklahoma City, which in 1994 had an estimated 463,201 inhabitants in the inner city (up from 403,484 in 1984) and a 1995 estimated population of 1,015,174 in the metropolitan statistical area (up from 861,000 in 1980). Tulsa, the 2d-largest city, had a 1994 estimated populations of 373,851 in the inner city (up from 360,919 in 1980) and a 1995 estimated population of 746,500 in the metropolitan area (up from 657,173 in 1980). Lawton ranked 3d with a 1994 estimate of 86,078 in the city (80,054 in 1980).

[7]ETHNIC GROUPS

According to the 1990 Census, Oklahoma has more American Indians—252,420—than any other state.

Black slaves came to Oklahoma (then known as Indian Territory) with their Indian masters after Congress forced the resettlement of Indians from the southeast to lands west of the Mississippi River in 1830. By the time of the Civil War, there were 7,000 free Negroes in Oklahoma. After the depression of the 1930s, blacks left the farms and small towns and concentrated in Oklahoma City and Tulsa. More than 51% of the state's black population, 234,000 in 1990, lived in Oklahoma City and Tulsa.

Mexicans came to Oklahoma during the 19th century as laborers on railroads and ranches, and in coal mines. Later they worked in the cotton fields until the depression of the 1930s and subsequent mechanization reduced the need for seasonal labor. Today, most 1st- and 2d-generation Mexicans live in Oklahoma City, Tulsa, and Lawton. Most of the 86,000 persons classified as of Hispanic origin in the 1990 census said they were of Mexican descent.

Italians, Czechs, Germans, Poles, Britons, Irish, and others of European stock also came to Oklahoma during the 19th century. Foreign immigration has been small since that time, however, and in 1990, less than 3% of the population consisted of the foreign-born. Persons claiming at least one specific ancestry group in 1990 included English, 441,391; German, 714,184; and Irish, 641,733.

[8]LANGUAGES

Once the open hunting ground of the Osage, Commanche, and Apache Indians, what is now Oklahoma later welcomed the deported Cherokee and other transferred eastern tribes. The diversity of tribal and linguistic backgrounds is reflected in numerous place-names such as Oklahoma itself, Kiamichi, and Muskogee. Almost equally diverse is Oklahoma English, with its uneven blending of features of North Midland, South Midland, and Southern dialects.

In 1990, 2,775,957 Oklahomans—95% of the resident population 5 years or older—spoke only English at home. Other languages spoken at home, and the number of people who spoke them, included Spanish, 64,562; various Native American, 19,158; and German, 15,195.

[9]RELIGIONS

Protestant groups predominate in Oklahoma, and Protestant fundamentalists constitute a third of the population. This group was influential in keeping the state "dry"—that is, banning the sale of all alcoholic beverages—until 1959 and resisting legalization of public drinking until 29 counties voted to permit the sale of liquor by the drink in 1985.

The leading Protestant groups in 1990 included Southern Baptist, 964,615; United Methodist, 326,294; Church of Christ, 85,193; Assembly of God, 88,780; Christian Church (Disciples of Christ), 58,901; and Episcopal, 18,908. There were 143,640 Roman Catholics in 1990 and an estimated 9,980 Jews in 1990.

Oral Roberts, a popular minister, has established a college and faith-healing hospital in Tulsa, and his "Tower of Faith" broadcasts by radio and television have made him a well-known preacher throughout the US.

[10]TRANSPORTATION

In 1930, the high point for railroad transportation in Oklahoma, there were 6,678 mi (10,747 km) of railroad track in the state. As of 31 December 1995 there were 3,474 rail mi (5,593 km) of track; Burlington Northern had the most track, followed by the Atchison, Topeka & Santa Fe. Kansas City Southern, Southern Pacific, and Union Pacific were other Class I railroads operating in the state in 1995. In 1979, Amtrak terminated the state's last passenger train. Inter-urban transit needs, formerly served by streetcars (one of the most popular routes operated between Oklahoma City and Norman), are now supplied by buses.

The Department of Transportation is responsible for construction and maintenance of the state road system, which in 1995 included state roads and highways, and interstate highways. The main east-west highways are I-44, connecting Tulsa and Oklahoma City, and I-40; the major north-south route is I-35, which links Oklahoma City with Topeka, Kansas and Dallas-Ft. Worth, Texas. Overall in 1995, Oklahoma had 112,517 mi (181,152 km) of roadway. A total of 2,856,079 motor vehicles were registered in 1995, including 1,629,491 automobiles and 1,211,802 trucks. There were 2,155,558 licensed drivers.

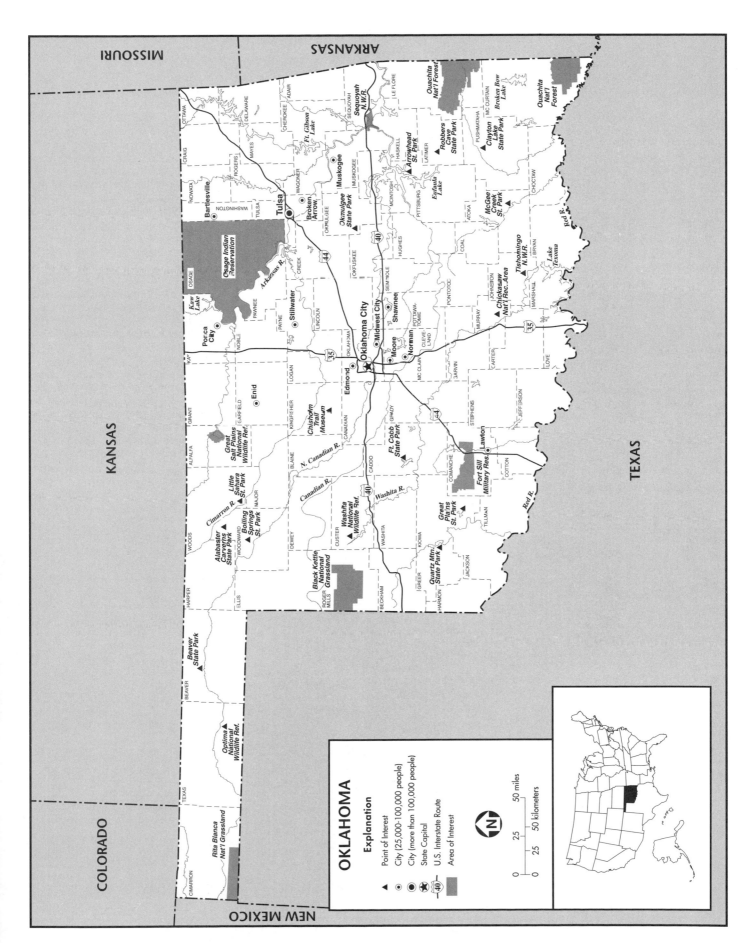

OTTAWA
CRAIG
NOWATA
WASHINGTON
OSAGE
KAY
GRANT
ALFALFA
WOODS
HARPER
BEAVER
TEXAS
CIMARRON

CHEROKEE
DELAWARE
MAYES
ROGERS
TULSA
PAWNEE
NOBLE
GARFIELD
KINGFISHER
BLAINE
DEWEY
ELLIS

ADAIR
SEQUOYAH
MUSKOGEE
WAGONER
CREEK
LINCOLN
PAYNE
LOGAN
CANADIAN
CADDO
CUSTER
WASHITA
ROGER MILLS
BECKHAM
GREER
HARMON
JACKSON
TILLMAN

HASKELL
LE FLORE
LATIMER
PITTSBURG
MCINTOSH
OKMULGEE
OKFUSKEE
SEMINOLE
OKLAHOMA
CLEVELAND
MC CLAIN
GRADY
COMANCHE
COTTON
KIOWA

PUSHMATAHA
MC CURTAIN
CHOCTAW
ATOKA
COAL
HUGHES
PONTOTOC
POTTAWATOMIE
GARVIN
MURRAY
CARTER
STEPHENS
JEFFERSON
LOVE
MARSHALL
BRYAN
JOHNSTON

Ft. Gibson Lake
Sequoyah N.W.R.
Ouachita Nat'l Forest
Clayton Lake State Park
Broken Bow Lake
Ouachita Nat'l Forest
Robbers Cave State Park
Arrowhead St. Park
Muskogee
Okmulgee State Park
Eufaula Lake
McGee Creek St. Park
Tishomingo N.W.R.
Broken Arrow
Tulsa
Bartlesville
Osage Indian Reservation
Kaw Lake
Arkansas R.
Stillwater
Ponca City
Enid
Chisholm Trail Museum
Oklahoma City
Midwest City
Shawnee
Moore
Norman
Edmond
Chickasaw Nat'l Rec. Area
Lake Texoma
Red R.
Great Salt Plains National Wildlife Ref.
Little Sahara St. Park
Cimarron R.
Alabaster Caverns State Park
Bolling Springs St. Park
N. Canadian R.
Canadian R.
Washita R.
Washita National Wildlife Ref.
Ft. Cobb State Park
Lawton
Fort Sill Military Res.
Great Plains St. Park
Quartz Mtn. State Park
Black Kettle National Grassland
Beaver State Park
Optima National Wildlife Ref.
Rita Blanca Nat'l Grassland

44
40
35

OKLAHOMA

Explanation

▲ Point of Interest
⊙ City (25,000-100,000 people)
◉ City (more than 100,000 people)
★ State Capital
40 U.S. Interstate Route
■ Area of Interest

N

0 25 50 miles
0 25 50 kilometers

The opening of the McClellan–Kerr Arkansas River Navigation System in 1971 linked Oklahoma with the Mississippi River and thus to Gulf coast ports. Catoosa (Tulsa), chief port on the system, handled 1,473,584 tons of cargo in 1995.

Oklahoma had 325 airports, 89 heliports, and 1 seaplane base in early 1995. Tulsa International Airport, which enplaned 1,529,384 passengers in 1995, and Will Rogers World Airport in Oklahoma City, which enplaned 1,656,837 passengers, are the state's largest airports.

11 HISTORY

There is evidence—chiefly from the Spiro Mound in eastern Oklahoma, excavated in 1930—that an advanced Indian civilization inhabited the region around AD 900–1100. By the time the Spanish conquistadores, led by Hernando de Soto and Francisco Vasquez de Coronado, arrived there in the 16th century, however, only a few scattered tribes remained. Two centuries later, French trappers moved up the rivers of Oklahoma.

Except for the panhandle, which remained a no-man's-land until 1890, all of present-day Oklahoma became part of US territory with the Louisiana Purchase in 1803. Under the Indian Removal Act of 1830, Indian tribes from the southeastern US were resettled in what was then known as Indian Country. Although 4,000 Indians died along the "Trail of Tears" (from Georgia to Oklahoma) between the time of removal and the Civil War, the Five Civilized Tribes—Cherokees, Chickasaw, Choctaw, Creek, and Seminole—prospered in the new land. The eastern region that they settled, comprising not quite half of modern Oklahoma and known as Indian Territory since the early 19th century (although not formally organized under that name until 1890), offered rich soil and luxurious vegetation. White settlers also came to farm the land, but their methods depleted the soil, preparing the way for the dust bowl of the 1930s. Meanwhile, the increasing movement of people and goods between Santa Fe and New Orleans spurred further growth in the region. Military posts such as Ft. Gibson, Ft. Supply, and Ft. Towson were established between 1824 and the 1880s, with settlements growing up around them.

During the early Civil War period, the Five Civilized Tribes—some of whose members were slaveholders—allied with the Confederacy. After Union troops captured Ft. Gibson in 1863, the Union Army controlled one-half of Indian Territory. From the end of the Civil War to the 1880s, the federal government removed the eastern tribes from certain lands that were especially attractive to the railroads and to interested white settlers. Skirmishes between the Indians and the federal troops occurred, culminating in a massacre of Cheyenne Indians on 27 November 1868 by Colonel George Custer and his 7th Cavalry at the Battle of the Washita.

Amid a clamor for Indian lands, Congress opened western Oklahoma—formerly reserved for the Cherokee, Cheyenne, Fox, and other tribes—to homesteaders in 1889. Present-day Oklahoma City, Norman, Guthrie, Edmond, and Stillwater represent the eastern boundary for the 1889 "run" on Oklahoma lands; eight more runs were to follow. The greatest was in 1893, when about 100,000 people stormed onto the newly opened Cherokee outlet. The drive to get a land claim was fierce, and thousands of "Sooners" staked their claims before the land was officially opened. The western region became Oklahoma Territory, governed by a territorial legislature and a federally appointed governor in 1890; Guthrie was named the capital. Most of eastern Oklahoma continued to be governed by the Five Civilized Tribes.

Although an Oklahoma statehood bill was introduced in Congress as early as 1892, the Five Civilized Tribes resisted all efforts to unite Indian Territory until their attempt to form their own state was defeated in 1905. Congress passed an enabling act

in June 1906, and Oklahoma became the 46th state on 16 November 1907 after a vote of the residents of both territories. Oklahoma City was named the state capital in 1910.

When President Theodore Roosevelt signed the statehood proclamation, Oklahoma's population was about 1,500,000—75% rural, 25% urban—most of them drawn by the state's agricultural and mineral resources. The McAlester coal mines had opened in 1871, and lead and zinc were being mined in Ottawa County. But it was oil that made the state prosperous. Prospecting began in 1882, and the first commercial well was drilled at Bartlesville in 1897. The famous Glenn Pool gusher, near Tulsa, was struck in 1905. Oil wells were producing more than 40 million barrels annually when Oklahoma entered the Union, and the state led all others in oil production until 1928.

Generally, the decade of the 1920s was a tumultuous period for Oklahoma. A race riot in Tulsa in 1921 was put down by the National Guard; the Ku Klux Klan claimed close to 100,000 Oklahomans that same year. The Klan was outlawed when Governor John C. Walton declared martial law in 1923, during a period of turmoil and violence that culminated in Walton's impeachment and conviction on charges of incompetence, corruption, and abuse of power. The 1930s brought a destructive drought, dust storms, and an exodus of "Okies," many of them to California. Colorful Governor William "Alfalfa Bill" Murray led the call for federal relief for the distressed dust bowl region—though he insisted on his right to administer the funds. When Oklahoma oil fields were glutting the market at 15 cents a barrel, Murray placed 3,106 producing wells under martial law from August 1931 to April 1933. Kansas, New Mexico, and Texas also agreed to control their oil production and under the leadership of Governor E. W. Marland, the Interstate Oil Compact was created in 1936 to conserve petroleum and stabilize prices.

Oklahoma's first native-born governor, Robert Kerr, later to be senator for 14 years, held the statehouse during World War II and brought the state national recognition by promoting Oklahoma as a site for military, industrial, and conservation projects. Under early postwar governors Roy Turner, Johnston Murray, and Raymond Gary, tax reductions attracted industry, major highways were built, a loyalty oath for state employees was declared unconstitutional, and Oklahoma's higher educational facilities were integrated. The term of Governor Howard Edmondson saw the repeal of prohibition in 1959, the establishment of merit and central purchasing systems, and the introduction of a state income tax withholding plan.

Oil and gas again brought increased wealth to the state in the 1960s, 1970s, and early 1980s, as state revenues from oil and gas increased from $72 million in 1972 to $745 million in 1982. Nearly $1 billion was spent for new highways, schools, and state offices; new police were hired; and teacher salaries were raised to nationally competitive levels. Unemployment fell to 3.6% in 1981 while an influx of job seekers from other states made Oklahoma one of the fastest growing states in the nation in the early 1980s.

In 1983, as oil prices fell in the face of a growing worldwide oil glut, the oil boom suddenly ended. Between 1982 and 1986, jobs in the extraction of oil and gas dropped by 50%. The failure of 24 banks, home mortgage foreclosures, and mounting distress among the state's farmers added to Oklahoma's financial woes. Falling state revenues and a balanced budget requirement in the state constitution compelled Governor George Nigh in 1983 to cut appropriations and to preside over a series of tax increases that lost for Oklahoma its claim to one of the lowest tax burdens in the nation.

The oil bust did not entirely devastate the Oklahoma economy. Those industries with a national rather than a regional base, such as distribution, transportation, food processing, and light manufacturing, continued to prosper, and the state's leaders made a concerted effort to diversify Oklahoma's industries even further by attracting both private enterprise and defense contracts. By the end of the decade, the economy had begun to recover, and recovery continued into the 1990s.

On 19 April 1995, the Alfred P. Murrah Federal Building in Oklahoma City was destroyed in a bomb blast that claimed 168 lives and constituted the most serious act of terrorism in the history of the United States.

12 STATE GOVERNMENT

Oklahoma's first and only constitutional convention began its deliberations in Guthrie on 20 November 1907.

The Oklahoma legislature consists of two chambers, a 48-member senate and a 101-member house of representatives. To serve in the legislature, senators must be 25 years of age, and representatives 21. Senators hold office for four years, representatives for two. The legislative salary in 1995 was $32,000. Elected executive officials include the governor, lieutenant governor, attorney general, state treasurer, superintendent of public instruction, and commissioner of insurance, all of whom serve four-year terms, and three corporation commissioners, who serve staggered six-year terms. The governor must be a US citizen at least 31 years of age, and must have been a qualified voter in Oklahoma for at least 10 years preceding election. In 1996 the governor's salary was $70,000.

Any member of either house may introduce legislation. A bill passed by the legislature becomes law if signed by the governor, if left unsigned by the governor for five days while the legislature is in session, or if passed over the governor's veto by two-thirds of the elected members of each house or three-fourths in the case of emergency bills. Constitutional amendments may be placed on the ballot by majority vote in both houses, by initiative petition of 15% of the electorate, or by constitutional convention.

To vote in Oklahoma, one must be a US citizen, at least 18 years of age, and registered. There is no minimum state residence requirement.

13 POLITICAL PARTIES

The history of the two major political groups in Oklahoma, the Democratic and Republican parties, dates back to 1890, when Indian Territory and Oklahoma Territory were separately organized. Indian Territory was dominated by Democrats, reflecting the influence of southern immigrants, while Oklahoma Territory was primarily Republican because of immigration from the northern states. When the two territories joined for admission to the Union in 1907, Democrats outnumbered Republicans, as they have ever since. Democrats have continued to dominate the lesser state offices, but the Republicans won the governorship three times between 1962 and 1990, and the Republican presidential nominee outpolled his Democratic counterpart in ten of twelve presidential elections between 1948 and 1992. The best showing by a minor party in a recent presidential race was 25% garnered by Independent Ross Perot in 1992.

As of 1994, the Democratic Party had 1,452,949 registered voters, or 63% of the total, while registered Republicans numbered 775,754, or 34% of the total; there were 73,576 registered Independents, or 3% of the total.

Oklahomans cast 48% of their popular vote for Republican Bob Dole in the 1996 presidential election, 40% for Bill Clinton, and 11% for Ross Perot. Democrat Don Nickles won election to his third term in the Senate in 1992, while Republican David Boren was reelected to a third term in 1990, but his seat came open in 1994 after Boren resigned to become president of the University of Oklahoma. His Senate seat was won by Republican James M. Inhofe, who rode the nationwide Republican surge of November 1994 to victory. In 1996 Inhofe retained the seat against a challenge by James H. Boren, a cousin of the former

senator. Following the 1996 elections, Oklahoma's entire six-member delegation of US representatives consisted of Republicans. (Republicans gained two seats in the 1994 election and an additional one in 1996.) In November 1994, the governor's office was won by Republican Frank Keating, a former official in the administration of President Ronald Reagan.

There are 33 Democrats and 15 Republicans in the state senate and 65 Democrats and 36 Republicans in the state house. In 1994, there were 123 blacks and 1 Hispanic holding public office. As of 1995, 16 women served in the state legislature, and 3 women held statewide elective executive office.

Oklahoma Presidential Vote by Political Parties, 1948–96

YEAR	ELECTORAL VOTE	OKLAHOMA WINNER	DEMOCRAT	REPUBLICAN
1948	10	*Truman (D)	452,782	2687,817
1952	8	*Eisenhower (R)	430,939	518,045
1956	8	*Eisenhower (R)	385,581	473,769
1960	8	Nixon (R)	370,111	533,039
1964	8	*Johnson (D)	519,834	412,665
1968	8	*Nixon (R)	301,658	449,697
1972	8	*Nixon (R)	247,147	759,025
1976	8	Ford (R)	532,442	545,708
1980	8	*Reagan (R(	402,026	695,570
1984	8	*Reagan (R)	385,080	861,530
1988	8	*Bush (R)	483,423	678,367
1992**	8	Bush (R)	473,066	592,929
1996**	8	Dole (R)	488,105	582,315

* Won US presidential election.

** Independent candidate Ross Perot received 319,878 votes in 1992 and 130,788 votes in 1996.

14 LOCAL GOVERNMENT

As of 1992, local governmental units in Oklahoma included 77 counties, 588 incorporated cities and towns, and several hundred unincorporated areas. There were 605 school districts and 524 special districts.

County government consists of three commissioners elected by districts, a county clerk, assessor, treasurer, sheriff, surveyor, and (in most counties) superintendent of schools. Towns of 1,000 population or more may incorporate as cities. Any city of 2,000 or more people may vote to become a home-rule city, determining its own form of government, by adopting a home-rule charter. Cities electing not to adopt a home-rule charter operate under aldermanic, mayor-council, or council-manager systems. A large majority of home-rule cities have council-manager systems.

15 STATE SERVICES

The Oklahoma Department of Education, functioning under a six-member appointed Board of Education and an elected superintendent of public instruction, has responsibility for all phases of education through the first 12 grades. Postsecondary study is under the general authority of the Oklahoma State Regents for Higher Education and 16 separate boards of regents associated with one or more institutions. Vocational and technical education, a federal-state cooperative program, is administered in Oklahoma under the Department of Vocational and Technical Education. The Department of Transportation has authority over the planning, construction, and maintenance of the state highway system. The Oklahoma Corporation Commission regulates transportation and transmission companies, public utilities, motor carriers, and the oil and gas industry, while the Oklahoma Aeronautics Commission participates in financing airports.

The Department of Health has as a major function the control and prevention of communicable diseases; it administers community health program funds and licenses most health-related facilities. The Department of Human Services oversees the care of neglected children, delinquent youths, and the mentally retarded and operates various facilities and programs for the handicapped, the elderly, and the infirm.

Protective services are supplied through the Oklahoma Military Department, which administers the Army and Air National Guard; the Department of Corrections, overseeing the state penitentiary and reformatory, nine adult correctional centers, and eight community treatment centers; and the Department of Public Safety, with general safety and law enforcement responsibilities, among which are licensing drivers and patrolling the highways. Natural resource protection services are centered principally in the Oklahoma Conservation Commission. The Department of Wildlife Conservation and the Wildlife Conservation Commission administer the game and fish laws.

16JUDICIAL SYSTEM

In 1967, following some of the worst judicial scandals in the history of the state, in which one supreme court justice was imprisoned for income tax evasion and another impeached on charges of bribery and corruption, Oklahoma approved a consti-tutional amendment to reform the state's judicial system. Under the new provisions, the supreme court, the state's highest court, consists of nine justices initially elected to six-year terms, but with additional terms pursuant to nonpartisan, noncompetitive elections; if a justice is rejected by the voters, the vacancy is filled by gubernatorial appointment, subject to confirmation by the electorate. The court's appellate jurisdiction includes all civil cases (except those which it assigns to the courts of appeals), while its original jurisdiction extends to general supervisory control over all inferior courts and agencies created by law.

The highest appellate court for criminal cases is the court of criminal appeals, a five-member body filled in the same manner as the supreme court. Courts of civil appeals, created by the legis-lature in 1968, are located in Tulsa and Oklahoma City; each has six elective judges with powers to hear civil cases assigned to them by the supreme court. When final, their decisions are not appealable to any other state court, a system unique to Oklahoma.

District courts have original jurisdiction over all justiciable matters and some review powers over administrative actions. There are 26 districts with 71 district judges, 77 associate and 76 special judges, who are elected to four-year terms. Municipal courts hear cases arising from local ordinances. A total of 13,869 attorneys lived and practiced in the state in 1996. As of 1996, over 19,500 prisoners were under the jurisdiction of state and federal authorities. Between 1990 and 1995 the inmate population increased by over 40%.

In 1995 the FBI reported a crime index total of 5,596.8 crimes per 100,000 population, including rates of 664.1 for violent crime and 4,932.7 for property crime. Oklahoma law permits capital punishment by lethal injection for several felony crimes; three persons were executed in 1995.

17ARMED FORCES

In 1996, there were 28,138 active-duty military personnel stationed in Oklahoma, the majority of whom were at Ft. Sill, near Lawton, the training facility for the Artillery Branch, with 16,010 military personnel in 1996. A total of $771 million in prime military contracts was received by local businesses in 1996.

As of 1 July 1996, about 342,000 veterans were living in Oklahoma, of whom fewer than 500 saw service in World War I, 97,000 in World War II, 63,000 in the Korean conflict, 117,000 during the Vietnam era, and 21,000 in the Persian Gulf War. Veterans' benefits for 1996 were $739 million.

The Oklahoma Reserve and National Guard had 24,739 assigned personnel as of September 1992; Army, 15,852; Air Force 5,625; and Navy and Marine Corps, 3,662. In 1993, the

Oklahoma Highway Patrol employed 800 full-time sworn officers, or 3 per 10,000 residents.

18MIGRATION

Early immigrants to what is now Oklahoma included explorers, adventurers, and traders who made the country conscious of the new territory, and Indian tribes forcibly removed from the East and Midwest. The interior plains of Oklahoma remained basically unchanged until white settlers came in the late 1880s.

Coal mining brought miners from Italy to the McAlester and Krebs area in the 1870s, and Poles migrated to Bartlesville to work in the lead and zinc smelters. British and Irish coal miners came to Indian Territory because they could earn higher wages there than in their native countries, and Czechs and Slovaks arrived from Nebraska, Kansas, Iowa, and Texas when railroad construction began. Mexicans also worked as railroad laborers, ranch hands, and coal miners before statehood. The oil boom of the early 20th century brought an influx of workers from the eastern and midwestern industrial regions. In 1907, the population of Oklahoma was 75% rural and 25% urban; by 1990, however, 67.7% of all inhabitants resided in urban areas. Oklahoma lost population during the 1930s because of dust bowl and drought conditions, and the trend toward out-migration continued after World War II; from 1940 through 1960, the net loss from migration was 653,000. Migration patterns were reversed, however, after 1960. From 1960 to 1970 nearly 21,000 more people moved into the state than out of it. In the period 1970–80, a total of 293,500 more people came than left, the migration accounting for nearly two-thirds of Oklahoma's total increase of 466,000 persons in that decade. From 1980 to 1983, Oklahoma ranked 4th among the states with a total net gain from migration of 186,000 people. From 1985 to 1990, a net migration loss of about 95,500 was reported. Between 1990 and 1996, the state had net gains of 34,037 in domestic migration and 18,622 in international migration. In 1996, 3,511 foreign immigrants arrived in Oklahoma. As of 1990, 63.5% of state residents had been born in Oklahoma. About 48% of residents age 5 and older lived in a different house in 1985 than in 1990, of which 20% did so in a different state.

19INTERGOVERNMENTAL COOPERATION

Oklahoma participates in a number of regional intergovern-mental agreements, among them the Arkansas River Compact, Arkansas River Basin Compact, Canadian River Compact, Inter-state Oil and Gas Compact, Red River Compact, South Central Interstate Forest Fire Protection Compact, Southern Growth Policies Compact, and Southern Interstate Energy Compact. Oklahoma also takes part in the Ozarks Regional Commission along with Arkansas, Kansas, Louisiana, and Missouri.

Federal grants in 1996 totaled over $2.4 billion.

20ECONOMY

Primarily an agricultural state through the first half of the 20th century, Oklahoma has assumed a broader economic structure since the 1950s. Manufacturing heads the list of growth sectors, followed by wholesale and retail trade, services, finance, insurance, and real estate. Oil and gas extraction continues to play a major role, with Oklahoma ranking 5th among the states in value of mineral fuel production in 1982. All but two of the state's 77 counties produced some oil or gas in 1981. The oil industry boomed from the mid-1970s through the mid-1980s. In 1985, however, the boom ended. Prices dropped from $27 a barrel to $13 a barrel within a month in 1985. Oklahoma's unemployment rate, which averaged about 3% in the early 1980s, jumped to 9% in 1983, and then fell to 7% in 1985, and rose again, to 8%, in 1986. Since then, the economy has undergone a slow but steady recovery. Oklahoma's gross state product has risen from $45 billion in 1982 dollars to $49 billion in 1993. Its unemployment rate dropped to just over 6% in 1993, after a brief increase during the national recession of the early 1990s to 7.5%.

In 1994, Oklahoma's gross state product was $66,189 million, to which private goods-producing industries contributed $18,312 million; private services-producing industries, $36,986 million; government, $10,891 million. Oklahoma's per capita personal income in 1995 was $18,580, which ranked 44th in the nation. During 1996, there were 18,451 bankruptcy filings.

²¹INCOME

In 1996 the average per capita personal income in Oklahoma was $19,350, 44th among the states. Total disposable personal income in 1996 was $56 billion, up from $53.7 billion in 1995; median household income increased from $30.6 billion in 1991 to $31.9 billion in 1992. As of 1995, 17.1% of all state residents were below the federal poverty line.

²²LABOR

The civilian labor force in 1996 was estimated at 1,577,000 persons, of whom 64,000, or 4.1%, were unemployed. This was an increase from the 1,548,000 persons in the labor force in 1995.

At the end of 1996, Oklahoma's nonfarm employment was distributed as follows: mining, 30,700; construction, 50,800; manufacturing, 174,000; transportation and public utilities, 77,100; wholesale and retail trade, 329,000; finance, insurance, and real estate, 67,800; services, 371,800; and government, 277,100.

There were about 116,900 labor union members in 1995. Union membership, at 9.3% of all nonagricultural workers, was well below the national average of 14.9%.

²³AGRICULTURE

Agriculture remains an important economic activity in Oklahoma, even though its relative share of personal income and employment has declined since 1950. Total farm income, estimated at $3.7 billion, ranked 19th in the US in 1996. Crop marketings contributed $1.1 billion, livestock $2.6 billion.

As of 1996, Oklahoma had 72,000 farms and ranches covering 34,000,000 acres (13,760,000 hectares). The state ranked 8th in the US for wheat production in 1996, with 93,100,000 bushels (down from 201,600,000 in 1990) worth $460.8 million (down from $518 million in 1990). Peanut production ranked 7th in 1996, with 194,400,000 lb, valued at $58,320,000. Other 1996 crop figures include hay, 4,520,000 tons, $265,600,000; sorghum for grain, 28,910,000 bushels, $78,830,000; soybeans, 7,410,000 bushels, $50,018,000; corn for grain, 24,650,000 bushels, $78,880,000; oats, 600,000 bushels, $1,920,000; and barley, 69,000 bushels, $221,000.

Virtually all of Oklahoma's wheat production is located in the western half of the state; cotton (130,000 bales in 1996) is grown in the southwest corner. Sorghum-producing regions include the panhandle, central to southwestern Oklahoma, and the northeast corner of the state.

²⁴ANIMAL HUSBANDRY

In 1997, there were 5.4 million cattle and calves (4th in the US), worth $2.376 billion. During 1996, Oklahoma farmers had 1.32 million hogs and pigs, valued at $145 million. In 1995, the state produced around 5.4 million lb of sheep and lambs which brought in nearly $5 million in gross income. Also during 1995, poultry farmers produced 876.6 million lb of broilers and chickens, and 897 million eggs valued at $64 million. Oklahoma dairy farmers had an estimated 1.3 billion lb of milk.

²⁵FISHING

Commercial fishing is of minor importance in Oklahoma. The prolific white bass (sand bass), Oklahoma's state fish, is abundant in most large reservoirs. Smallmouth and spotted bass, bluegill, and channel catfish have won favor with fishermen. Rainbow trout are stocked year round in the Illinois River, and walleye and sauger are stocked in most reservoirs. In 1995/96, the state issued 551,517 sport fishing licenses.

²⁶FORESTRY

While Oklahoma is not generally known as a forested state, a significant amount of forest is found there. Oklahoma's forests cover approximately 10 million acres (4.1 million hectares) or nearly one-fourth of the state's land area. Approximately 65% of this is commercially productive forest land. These forests are about 95% privately owned. They are intensively utilized for lumber, plywood, paper, fuelwood, and other products. They also provide high quality drinking water for the state's two largest cities, excellent wildlife habitat, substantial protection against soil erosion, and numerous recreational opportunities.

Oklahoma's forests play a vital role in the economy in the eastern half of the state, contributing more than $1 billion annually. Timber is the eighth most valuable agricultural commodity in Oklahoma. Much of the timber harvested in Oklahoma is shipped to processing plants in western Arkansas. Nearly two million acres of the loblolly-shortleaf pine and shortleaf pine-oak forests support several major wood processing plants in the southeastern corner of the state. Hardwood processing is scattered over the entire forested area in smaller sawmills. In the late 1980s and early 1990s, Oklahoma's eastern redcedar forests and woodlands supported a surge in processing plants.

As of 1993 nearly 90 million cu ft (2.5 million cu m) of roundwood was being harvested in eastern Oklahoma annually. Since that time, the Oklahoma Department of Agriculture's Forestry Division reports a dramatic increase in harvesting activity, in both pine and hardwood forest types. In 1994 more than 200 sawmills were known to be active in the state. Four major new processing facilities have been started or expanded in eastern Oklahoma and western Arkansas. These mills are active in all areas of the state except the panhandle. The value of shipments by the paper industry in Oklahoma was $2 billion in 1995, and shipments by the lumber and wood products industry had a value of $441 million.

²⁷MINING

Large deposits of limestone are found throughout northeastern Oklahoma, while gypsum is extracted in the northwest, the westcentral region, and the four southwesternmost counties. Oklahoma had been a leading producer of lead and zinc until the 1970s.

The value of nonfuel mineral production in Oklahoma in 1995 was estimated at $374 million, a $34 million increase over the $340 million reported in 1994. Increases in the production of crushed stone and iodine caused most of the rise in the mineral value in 1995. Crushed stone continued as the state's leading mineral commodity, accounting for over 39% of the total nonfuel mineral value in 1995. Oklahoma remained the only state producing crude iodine, which constituted almost 5.2% of the state's total nonfuel mineral value, or $19.6 million for the production of 1,830 metric tons. The state remained first of 20 states producing crude gypsum, with 2.75 million metric tons worth $17.5 million in 1995. Estimated production and value of portland cement was 1.7 million metric tons worth $103 million. Combined values of crushed stone, portland cement, gypsum, and construction sand and gravel accounted for almost 79% of the estimated total mineral value reported in 1995. That year,

Oklahoma ranked 34th in the US in nonfuel mineral value, a drop from its rank of 30th in 1984.

28ENERGY AND POWER

Electric power production in Oklahoma in 1995 was 47.9 billion kWh, based on an installed capacity of 13.8 million kW. That year, electric energy sales in the state totaled 41.3 billion kWhs of which 11.6 billion kWh went for industrial purposes, 11.2 billion kWh for commercial purposes, and 16.3 billion kWh for residential uses. Coal-fired steam units accounted for 29.7 billion kWh of electricity produced in 1995, natural gas-fired units 15.5 billion kWh, and hydroelectricity 2.7 billion kWh. There were no nuclear power plants as of 1 January 1996.

Oklahoma is rich in fossil fuel resources, producing oil, natural gas, and coal. Crude oil production declined from 223.6 million barrels in 1968, to 150.5 million barrels in 1978, to 85.4 million barrels in 1996. Proved reserves of crude oil were estimated at 676 million barrels at the close of 1995. In 1995, Oklahoma's natural gas output exceeded 1.8 trillion cu ft (3d in the US), leaving reserves of 13.438 trillion cu ft. Consumption of natural gas in the state in 1994 was 572 billion cu ft.

Production of bituminous coal fell from a record high of 6.1 million tons in 1978 to 1.7 million tons in 1996. Of 11 coal mines in the state, all but one were surface mines. Reserves totaling 1.5 billion tons are concentrated in eastern Oklahoma.

29INDUSTRY

Oklahoma's earliest manufactures were based on agricultural and petroleum production. As late as 1939, the food-processing and petroleum-refining industries together accounted for one-third of the total value added by manufacture. Although resource-related industries continue to predominate, manufacturing was much more diversified in 1991. The total value of shipments of manufactured goods in 1995 was more than $33 billion. The following table shows the value of shipments by manufacturers for selected industries:

Transportation equipment	$5,009,700,000
Petroleum and coal products	3,509,300,000
Food and kindred products	3,379,000,000
Electric and electronic equipment	2,998,000,000
Fabricated metal products	2,864,900,000
Rubber and miscellaneous plastics products	2,343,700,000
Chemical and allied products	1,576,700,000

In 1997, four Fortune 500 companies were headquartered in Oklahoma: Fleming, Phillips Petroleum, Williams, and Mapco. In 1995, 606 US patents were issued to Oklahoma residents.

30COMMERCE

In 1992, Oklahoma had 5,993 wholesale establishments, with sales of $26.4 billion (including $8.9 billion in durable goods.)

Wholesale establishments had personal income totaling $2.3 billion in 1995. Retail sales totaled $21.2 billion (29th) in 1992. Retail establishments had personal incomes totaling $4.2 billion in 1995, ranking 39th in the US. Automotive dealers accounted for 24.8% of the total sales in 1992, followed by food stores, 19.7%; general merchandise stores, 15.5%; and eating and drinking places, 10.2%. The value of foreign exports produced within Oklahoma in 1996 was $2.4 billion.

31CONSUMER PROTECTION

A Uniform Consumer Credit Code, passed in 1969, prohibits discrimination because of sex or marital status. It is administered by the Commission on Consumer Credit, which also maintains a program of consumer education and has the power to require lawful and businesslike procedures by lending agencies. The attorney general is responsible for enforcing the state's Consumer Protection Act.

32BANKING

In 1996, Oklahoma had 342 insured commercial banks. That same year, the state's insured commercial banks had assets totaling $34.5 billion and deposit liabilities of $28.8 billion. Thirteen insured savings institutions had combined assets of $5.8 billion as of 1996. The failure of the Penn Square Bank in 1982 led to a series of mergers between strong institutions and distressed smaller ones and a 1983 revision of the state's banking laws which allowed for the restructuring of the industry. Concurrently, Oklahoma's banks were adversely affected by proposals to ease restrictions on reciprocal interstate banking in Missouri and Texas.

The State Banking Department has the responsibility for supervising all state-chartered banks, savings and loan associations, credit unions, and trust companies.

33INSURANCE

In 1995, 43 life insurance companies were headquartered in Oklahoma. During that same year, Oklahomans purchased $10.5 million of ordinary life insurance and received benefit payments of $1.161 billion, including $347.2 million in death payments. Life insurance policies in force in 1995 numbered nearly 2.5 million, with a total value of $119.1 billion and an average value per family of $91,800 billion. Property and liability companies wrote premiums totaling $2.9 billion in 1991.

The state Insurance Commission has responsibility for supervising and licensing all domestic and foreign insurance companies doing business in Oklahoma. The commission must approve certain life, accident, and health insurance policy forms before such contracts can be offered for sale to the public.

34SECURITIES

There are no stock or commodity exchanges in Oklahoma. New York Stock Exchange member firms maintained sales offices and had full-time registered representatives to provide service to Oklahomans who are shareowners of public corporations.

35PUBLIC FINANCE

The Oklahoma budget is prepared by the director of state finance and submitted by the governor to the legislature each February. Article 10, section 23 of the Oklahoma Constitution requires a balanced budget. The constitution establishes a "Rainy Day" Fund into which general revenue fund revenues in excess of the certified estimate are deposited for emergency appropriation at a later date. All funds are "appropriated" pursuant to the constitution. In addition, state law authorizes a cash-flow reserve fund that can be up to 10% of the approved budget. The fiscal year is 1 July–30 June.

The following table summarizes consolidated state revenues and expenditures for 1995/96 (in millions):

REVENUES	
Receipts from federal government	$ 2,396.0
Income tax	
personal	1,530.9
corporate	169.8
Total income tax	1,700.7
Severance tax	319.8
Sales and use taxes	1,202.0
Motor fuels taxes	349.1
Tobacco tax	78.0
Other receipts	2,431.0
TOTAL	$ 8,476.6

EXPENDITURES	
Public education	$ 1,394.8
Human services	1,457.8
Higher education	882.2
Transportation	777.0
Other social services & health	2,760.4
Other outlays	901.5
TOTAL	$ 8,173.7

The total indebtedness of state and local governments in Oklahoma was $536.5—or $162.6 per capita—in mid-1997.

36TAXATION

As of 1994, the state income tax ranged from 0.5% to 7.0% on amounts over $10,000. The corporate tax on net income was 6.0%. The state levies a sales and use tax of 4.5%, and many municipalities levy their own sales taxes of 1–4%. Property taxes remain the principal source of revenue for local governments. The motor fuels tax was increased from 6.58 cents to 9 cents per gallon of gasoline in 1984, the first such increase in 36 years. In 1996, the gasoline tax in Oklahoma was 17 cents per gallon. The severance tax on oil and gas is 7% of gross value; on uranium, 5%; and on asphalt and minerals, up to 1%. The gas conservation excise tax is 7 cents per million cu ft.

Oklahoma's federal income tax burden in 1995 was $12.8 billion, while the state received a total of $16 billion in federal government funding.

37ECONOMIC POLICY

Pro-business measures in Oklahoma include a comparatively low property tax rates, limits on annual increases in property tax rates, and requirements that tax increases be submitted to a vote of the people or pass the legislature with a 75% vote.

Business incentives include cash rebates of up to 5% for 10 years for qualifying basic firms that add at least $2.5 million of new payroll in the state over a three-year period. This incentive, known as the Oklahoma Quality Jobs Program, was adopted in July 1993. Since that time, more than 110 firms have received in excess of $23 million in incentive payments while adding more than 18,000 jobs to the Oklahoma economy. More than 55,000 jobs were planned to be added by the year 2005.

Other incentives include a new job tax credit of $1,000 per year for 5 years for new manufacturing jobs in state enterprise zones; a 30% investment tax credit for investment in qualifying agricultural processing ventures or cooperatives; and free customized training for qualifying firms from the Oklahoma Department of Vocational and Technical Education through its Training in Industry Program (TIP).

38HEALTH

In 1995 there were 45,365 births, for a birthrate of 13.8 per 1,000. The infant mortality rate was 8.3 per 1,000 live births. The death rate for 1995 was 9.9. A total of 28,616 marriages were performed in 1995, at a rate of 8.7 per 1,000 inhabitants; 21,753 divorces were granted, for a rate of 6.6 per 1,000 residents. There were 9,881 legal abortions performed in Oklahoma in 1992, a ratio of 208 per 1,000 live births. The leading causes of death in 1992–94 in Oklahoma and their age-adjusted 3-year death rates in 1991 were heart disease, 163.3 per 100,000 population; cancer, 133.2; accidents, 36.4; and stroke and cerebrovascular disease, 28.8.

Oklahoma had 110 hospitals in 1995, providing 10,993 beds and recording 364,729 admissions. The average expense of a hospital for services provided per inpatient day was $848. Oklahoma had 4,965 licensed non-federal physicians in 1994, and 1,617 active dentists in 1995. The Health Sciences Center of the University of Oklahoma is located in Oklahoma City. At least

22.3% of Oklahoma residents were uninsured in 1995. While payments for Medicare recipients increased 14% from 1993 to 1994, Medicaid payments dropped by 6% in the same time interval.

39SOCIAL WELFARE

Benefits in aid to families with dependent children were received by 110,000 persons in 1996, averaging $380 per month. In 1996, 353,790 residents received monthly food stamp allowances averaging $72.48, and some children received school lunches, requiring a federal expenditure of $75.4 million.

With the enactment of the Personal Responsibility and Work Opportunity Reconciliation Act of 1996, the US government has changed the form and regulations for many of its social welfare programs; most significantly, it replaces Aid to Families with Dependent Children (AFDC), an open-ended entitlement program, with Temporary Assistance for Needy Families (TANF), a limited system of assistance funded largely through federal block grants. The reform act also impacts the food stamp program, the Supplemental Security Income program, and the child nutrition program. The law took effect on 1 July 1997 and provided $16.38 billion in block grants for fiscal years 1997–2002. The grants are to be divided among the states based on an equation involving the numbers of former AFDC recipients in each state. Because many of the bill's provisions have yet to be implemented into state-by-state policy, it was not possible to include the details of each state's programs for this edition of this work.

Social Security benefits were paid to 574,750 retired persons, survivors, and disabled workers in 1993; monthly payments to retired workers averaged $687. Federal Supplemental Security Income payments were made to 74,281 aged, disabled, and blind persons that year. In 1995, the average weekly unemployment insurance benefit payment was $172.52.

40HOUSING

Indian tepees and settlers' sod houses dotted the Oklahoma plains when the "eighty-niners" swarmed into the territory; old neighborhoods in cities and towns of Oklahoma still retain some of the modest frame houses they built. Oklahomans continue to prefer single-family dwellings, despite a recent trend toward condominiums. Modern underground homes and solar-heated dwellings can be seen in the university towns of Norman and Stillwater.

In 1996 there were an estimated 1,442,000 year-round housing units. That year, 10,640 privately owned units, valued at $980 million, were authorized for construction. In 1990, about 12.4% of all housing units dated from 1939 or earlier and 22% from the 1980s; only 10% were without one or more complete bathrooms. As of 1990, the last year for which figures are available, the median home value was $48,100, with a median monthly cost for an owner (including mortgage) of $573. The median monthly rent was $340 in 1990. During 1995/96, Oklahoma received $247.3 million in aid from the US Department of Housing and Urban Development, including $60.2 million in community development block grants.

41EDUCATION

Oklahoma's educational enterprise is the largest expenditure item in the state budget. Oklahoma ranks 46th among the states in terms of per-pupil expenditure. In higher education, Oklahoma ranks 45th in per pupil expenditure. The state spends $4,097 for each elementary and secondary school student.

About 76.7% of all Oklahomans 25 years of age or older were high school graduates in 1990; during the same year, 31.2% of adult state residents had at least one year of college, almost the same as the US average. In 1995, Oklahoma's public school enrollment totaled 616,500.

Public higher education institutions include 2 comprehensive institutions, 6 regional campuses, 18 senior and junior colleges, and a professional college. The comprehensive institutions, the University of Oklahoma (Norman) and Oklahoma State University (Stillwater), have more than 20,800 students each and offer major graduate-level programs. The 16 private colleges and universities in Oklahoma increased their enrollment to 19,270 in 1990. Well-known institutions include Oral Roberts University and the University of Tulsa.

[42]ARTS

Major arts centers are located in Tulsa and Oklahoma City, but there are many arts and crafts museums throughout the state. The Oklahoma Arts and Humanities Council, now known as the State Arts Council of Oklahoma, was created by the Oklahoma legislature in 1965.

Oklahoma City's leading cultural institution is the Oklahoma City Philharmonic. The Tulsa Philharmonic, Tulsa Ballet Theater, and Tulsa Opera all appear at the Tulsa Performing Arts Center, a municipally owned and operated facility; this six-level center consists of a 2,500-seat concert hall, 450-seat theater, and two multilevel experimental theaters.

There are five other ballet companies located in Oklahoma City, Bartlesville, Clinton, Lawton, and Norman. The intermingling of Native American, American West, and Euro-American art traditions infuse all aspects of Oklahoma culture. Native American contributions to the arts include achievements in art and sculpture, as well as the international acclaim accorded to ballerinas Maria and Marjorie Tallchief, Rosella Hightower, and Moscelyne Larkin.

The state of Oklahoma generated $575,000 in federal funds to support arts programs in 1996. The NEA contributed $478,000 to the programs and $917,000 to the State Arts Council of Oklahoma, and the state contributed funding to the Arts Council with grants from private sources. In 1995, the State Arts Council received monies from the NEA to develop its arts education programs, as well as assistance from the NEA's State and Regional Program. The NEA has also contributed funds to assist the Metropolitan Library Commission of Oklahoma Country, the Red Earth Native American Cultural Festival, and the Theater of North Tulsa.

From 1987 to 1991, Oklahoma's arts programs attracted a total audience of about 13,640,000 people. Contributing artists numbered 116,015. The state offered arts education programs to 63,000 school children.

By 1996, there were 400 arts associations and 70 local art groups in Oklahoma. The State Arts Council provided funds for the state's International Festival and performances by touring companies.

[43]LIBRARIES AND MUSEUMS

Six multi-county, 2 city-county, and 6 county libraries serve 42 counties, while 4 bookmobiles aid in serving counties without libraries of their own. In 1996/97 a total of 5,634,594 volumes occupied public library shelves; total circulation was 16,241,260. The Five Civilized Tribes Museum Library in Muskogee has a large collection of Indian documents and art, while the Cherokee archives are held at the Cherokee National Historical Society in Tahlequah. The Morris Swett Library at Ft. Sill has a special collection on military history, particularly field artillery. The Oklahoma Department of Libraries in Oklahoma City has holdings covering law, library science, Oklahoma history, and other fields. Large academic libraries include those of the University of Oklahoma (Norman), with 2,106,398 volumes in

1996, and Oklahoma State University Library (Stillwater), with 1,760,761.

Oklahoma has 108 museums and historic sites. The Philbrook Art Center in Tulsa houses important collections of Indian, Renaissance, and Oriental art. Also in Tulsa are the Thomas Gilcrease Institute of American History and Art. Major museums in Norman are the University of Oklahoma's Museum of Art and the Stovall Museum of Science and Industry. The Oklahoma Art Center, National Cowboy Hall of Fame and Western Heritage Center, Oklahoma Heritage Association, Oklahoma Historical Society Museum, Oklahoma Museum of Art, State Museum of Oklahoma, and the Omniplex Science Museum are major attractions in Oklahoma City. Other museums of special interest include the Museum of the Great Plains in Lawton, the Will Rogers Memorial in Claremore, Cherokee National Museum in Tahlequah, and the Woolaroc Museum in Bartlesville.

[44]COMMUNICATIONS

The Butterfield Stage and Overland Mail delivered the mail to Millerton on 18 September 1858 as part of the first US transcontinental postal route. After the Civil War, the early railroads delivered mail and parcels to the Oklahoma and Indian territories.

In March 1996, 91.9% of Oklahoma's occupied housing units had telephones. In 1993, Oklahoma had 58 AM and 118 FM radio stations, 22 commercial and 5 educational television channels, and two major cable television systems.

[45]PRESS

In 1997, Oklahoma had 17 morning dailies, 27 evening dailies, and 35 Sunday newspapers. Leading dailies and their circulation in 1997 were as follows:

AREA	NAME	DAILY	SUNDAY
Oklahoma City	*Oklahoman* (m)	219,158	312,732
	Oklahoman and Times (m)	212,671	—
Tulsa	*Tulsa World* (m,S)	162,111	227,884

As of 1997 there were 153 newspapers that appeared weekly or up to three times a week; most had circulations of less than 10,000 copies.

Tulsa and Oklahoma City each have monthly city-interest publications, and the University of Oklahoma has a highly active university press.

[46]ORGANIZATIONS

The 1992 census of service industries counted 960 organizations in Oklahoma, including 221 business associations; 485 civic, social, and fraternal associations; and 254 other membership organizations. Among the organizations headquartered in Oklahoma are the Football Writers Association of America (Edmond); the International Professional Rodeo Association (Pauls Valley); the Amateur Softball Association of America and the International Softball Federation, both in Oklahoma City; and the American Association of Petroleum Geologists, the Gas Processors Association, and the US Jaycees, all located in Tulsa.

[47]TOURISM, TRAVEL, AND RECREATION

Tourism has become a growing sector of Oklahoma's economy. Domestic travelers spent $2.7 billion on overnight and day trips in 1993. Oklahoma's 45 state parks and recreational areas draw some 16 million visitors annually. The national park service maintains one facility in Oklahoma—Chickasaw National Recreation Area, centering on artificial Lake Arbuckle.

The state also maintains and operates the American Indian Hall of Fame, in Anadarko; Black Kettle Museum, in Cheyenne; the T. B. Ferguson Home in Watonga; the Murrell Home, south of Tahlequah; the Pawnee Bill Museum, in Pawnee; the Pioneer

Woman Statue and Museum, in Ponca City; the Chisholm Trail Museum, in Kingfisher; and the Western Trails Museum, in Clinton.

Licenses were held by 295,442 hunters and 994,019 fishermen in 1995, using state resources. National wildlife refuges include Optima, Salt Plains, Sequoyah, Tishomingo, Washita, and Wichita Mountains; they have a combined area of 140,696 acres (56,938 hectares).

48SPORTS

Oklahoma has no major league professional sports teams. The class-AAA baseball 89ers play in Oklahoma City. Sports on the college level are still the primary source of pride for Oklahomans. As of 1994, the University of Oklahoma Sooners had won six national football titles. They won the Orange Bowl in 1954, 1956, 1958, 1959, 1968, 1976, 1979, 1980, 1981, 1986, and 1987. They have also produced championships in wrestling, baseball, and gymnastics. The Oklahoma State University Cowboys have captured NCAA and Big Eight titles in basketball, baseball, and golf, and are a perennial national contender in wrestling.

Oklahoma City hosts the International Finals of Rodeo every December. In golf, Tulsa has been the site of several US Open tournaments. The Softball Hall of Fame is in Oklahoma City.

Other annual sporting events include the World Championship Quarterhorse Show in Oklahoma City in November.

49FAMOUS OKLAHOMANS

Carl Albert (b.1908), a McAlester native, has held the highest public position of any Oklahoman. Elected to the US House of Representatives in 1947, he became majority leader in 1962 and served as speaker of the House from 1971 until his retirement in 1976. Patrick Jay Hurley (1883–1963), the first Oklahoman appointed to a cabinet post, was secretary of war under Herbert Hoover and later ambassador to China.

William "Alfalfa Bill" Murray (b.Texas, 1869–1956) was president of the state constitutional convention and served as governor from 1931 to 1935. Robert S. Kerr (1896–1963), founder of Kerr-McGee Oil, was the state's first native-born governor, serving from 1943 to 1947; elected to the US Senate in 1948, he became an influential Democratic leader. A(lmer) S(tillwell) Mike Monroney (1902–80) served as US representative from 1939 to 1951 and senator from 1951 to 1969.

Oklahomans have been prominent in literature and the arts. Journalist and historian Marquis James (b.Missouri, 1891–1955) won a Pulitzer Prize in 1930 for his biography of Sam Houston and another in 1938 for Andrew Jackson; John Berryman (1914–72) won the 1965 Pulitzer Prize in poetry for 77 Dream Songs, 1964; and Ralph Ellison (1914–94) won the 1953 National Book Award for his novel Invisible Man. The popular musical Oklahoma! by Richard Rodgers and Oscar Hammerstein 2d is based on Green Grow the Lilacs by Oklahoman Lynn Riggs (1899–1954). N(avarre) Scott Momaday (b.1934), born in Lawton, received a Pulitzer Prize in 1969 for House Made of Dawn. Woodrow Crumbo (b.1912) and Allen Houser (b.1914) are prominent Indian artists born in the state.

Just about the best-known Oklahoman was William Penn Adair "Will" Rogers (1879–1935), the beloved humorist and writer who spread cheer in the dreary days of the Depression. Part Cherokee, Rogers was a horse rider, trick roper, and stage and movie star until he was killed in a plane crash in Alaska. Among his gifts to the American language are the oft-quoted expressions "I never met a man I didn't like" and "All I know is what I read in the newspapers." Other prominent performing artists include singer-songwriter Woody Guthrie (1912–67), composer of "This Land Is Your Land," among other classics; ballerina Maria Tallchief (b.1925); popular singer Patti Page (b.1927); and operatic soprano Roberta Knie (b.1938). Famous Oklahoma actors include (Francis) Van Heflin (1910–71), Ben Johnson (b.1918), Jennifer Jones (b.1919), Tony Randall (b.1920), James Garner (James Baumgardner, b.1928), and Cleavon Little (b.1939). Paul Harvey (b.1918) is a widely syndicated radio commentator. James Francis "Jim" Thorpe (1888–1953) became known as the "world's greatest athlete" after his pentathlon and decathlon performances at the 1912 Olympic Games; of Indian ancestry, Thorpe also starred in baseball, football, and other sports. Bud Wilkinson (b.Minnesota, 1916) coached the University of Oklahoma football team to a record 47-game unbeaten streak in the 1950s. Baseball stars Paul Warner (1903–65) and his brother Lloyd (1906–82), Mickey Mantle (1931–95), Wilver Dornel "Willie" Stargell (b.1941), and Johnny Bench (b.1947) are native Oklahomans.

50BIBLIOGRAPHY

Bicha, Karel D. The Czechs in Oklahoma. Norman: University of Oklahoma Press, 1980.

Blessing, Patrick. The British and Irish in Oklahoma. Norman: University of Oklahoma Press, 1980.

Brown, Kenny L. Italians in Oklahoma. Norman: University of Oklahoma Press, 1978.

Fischer, John. From the High Plains. New York: Harper & Row, 1978.

Franklin, Jimmie Lewis. Blacks in Oklahoma. Norman: University of Oklahoma Press, 1980.

Gibson, Arrell M. The Oklahoma Story. Norman: University of Oklahoma Press, 1978.

Goble, Danney. Progressive Oklahoma: The Making of A New Kind of State. Norman: University of Oklahoma Press, 1980.

Morgan, Anne, H. Wayne, and Anne Hodges. Oklahoma: A Bicentennial History. New York: Norton, 1977.

Morgan, Anne and H. Wayne. Oklahoma: New Views of the Forty-sixth State. Norman: University of Oklahoma Press, 1982.

Rohrs, Richard. Germans in Oklahoma. Norman: University of Oklahoma Press, 1980.

Smith, Michael. Mexicans in Oklahoma. Norman: University of Oklahoma Press, 1980.

Stein, Howard F., and Robert F. Hill, eds. The Culture of Oklahoma. Norman: University of Oklahoma Press, 1993.

Strain, Jack M. An Outline of Oklahoma Government. Edmond, Okla.: Central State University, 1978.

Strickland, Rennard. Indians in Oklahoma. Norman: University of Oklahoma Press, 1980.

Tobias, Henry J. Jews in Oklahoma. Norman: University of Oklahoma Press, 1980.

OREGON

State of Oregon

ORIGIN OF STATE NAME: Unknown; name first applied to the river now known as the Columbia. **NICKNAME:** The Beaver State. **CAPITAL:** Salem. **ENTERED UNION:** 14 February 1859 (33d). **SONG:** "Oregon, My Oregon." **DANCE:** Square dance. **MOTTO:** The Union. **COLORS:** Navy-blue and gold. **FLAG:** The flag consists of a navy-blue field with gold lettering and illustrations. Obverse: the shield from the state seal, supported by 33 stars, with the words "State of Oregon" above and the year of admission below. Reverse: a beaver. **OFFICIAL SEAL:** A shield, supported by 33 stars and crested by an American eagle, depicts mountains and forests, an elk, a covered wagon and ox team, wheat, a plow, a pickax, and the state motto; in the background, as the sun sets over the Pacific, an American merchant ship arrives as a British man-o'-war departs. The words "State of Oregon 1859" surround the whole. **ANIMAL:** American beaver. **BIRD:** Western meadowlark. **FISH:** Chinook salmon. **INSECT:** Oregon swallowtail butterfly. **FLOWER:** Oregon grape. **TREE:** Douglas fir. **ROCK:** Thunderegg (geode). **GEM:** Sunstone. **LEGAL HOLIDAYS:** New Year's Day, 1 January; Birthday of Martin Luther King, Jr., 3d Monday in January; Lincoln's Birthday, 1st Monday in February; Washington's Birthday, 3d Monday in February; Memorial Day, last Monday in May; Independence Day, 4 July; Labor Day, 1st Monday in September; Veterans Day, 11 November; Thanksgiving Day, 4th Thursday in November; Christmas Day, 25 December. Designated as commemoration days are Oregon's Admission into the Union, 14 February, and Columbus Day, 12 October. **TIME:** 5 AM MST = noon GMT; 4 AM PST = noon GMT.

¹LOCATION, SIZE, AND EXTENT

Located on the Pacific coast of the northwestern US. Oregon ranks 10th in size among the 50 states.

The total area of Oregon is 97,073 sq mi (251,419 sq km), with land comprising 96,184 sq mi (249,117 sq km) and inland water 889 sq mi (2,302 sq km). Oregon extends 395 mi (636 km) E–W; the state's maximum N–S extension is 295 mi (475 km).

Oregon is bordered on the N by Washington (with most of the line formed by the Columbia River); on the E by Idaho (with part of the line defined by the Snake River); on the S by Nevada and California; and on the W by the Pacific Ocean. The total boundary length of Oregon is 1,444 mi (2,324 km), including a general coastline of 296 mi (476 km); the tidal shoreline extends 1,410 mi (2,269 km). The state's geographic center is in Crook County, 25 mi (40 km) SSE of Prineville.

²TOPOGRAPHY

The Cascade Range, extending north-south, divides Oregon into distinct eastern and western regions, each of which contains a great variety of landforms.

At the state's western edge, the Coast Range, a relatively low mountain system, rises from the beaches, bays, and rugged headlands of the Pacific coast. Between the Coast and Cascade ranges lie fertile valleys, the largest being the Willamette Valley, Oregon's heartland. The two-thirds of the state lying east of the Cascade Range consists generally of arid plateaus cut by river canyons, with rolling hills in the north-central portion giving way to the Blue Mountains in the northeast. The Great Basin in the southeast is characterized by fault-block ridges, weathered buttes, and remnants of large prehistoric lakes.

The Cascades, Oregon's highest mountains, contain nine snow-capped volcanic peaks more than 9,000 ft (2,700 m) high, of which the highest is Mt. Hood, at 11,235 ft (3,424 m). A dormant volcano, Mt. Hood last erupted in 1865. (Mt. St. Helens, which erupted in 1980, is only 60 mi—97 km—to the northwest, in Washington.) The Blue Mountains include several

rugged subranges interspersed with plateaus, alluvial basins, and deep river canyons. The Klamath Mountains in the southwest form a jumble of ridges where the Coast and Cascade ranges join.

Oregon is drained by many rivers, but the Columbia, demarcating most of the northern border with Washington, is by far the biggest and most important. Originating in Canada, it flows more than 1,200 mi (1,900 km) to the Pacific Ocean. With a mean flow rate of 250,134 cu ft per second, the Columbia is the 3d-largest river in the US. It drains some 58% of Oregon's surface by way of a series of northward-flowing rivers, including the Deschutes, John Day, and Umatilla. The largest of the Columbia's tributaries in Oregon, and longest river entirely within the state, is the Willamette, which drains a fertile valley more than 100 mi (160 km) long. Better than half of Oregon's eastern boundary with Idaho is formed by the Snake River, which flows through Hells Canyon, one of the deepest canyons in North America.

Oregon has 19 natural lakes with a surface area of more than 3,000 acres (1,200 hectares), and many smaller ones. The largest is Upper Klamath Lake, which covers 58,922 acres (23,845 hectares) and is quite shallow. The most famous, however, is Crater Lake, which formed in the crater created by the violent eruption of Mt. Mazama several thousand years ago and is now a national park. Its depth of 1,932 ft (589 m)—greater than any other lake in the US—and its nearly circular expanse of bright-blue water, edged by the crater's rim, make it a natural wonder.

³CLIMATE

Oregon has a generally temperate climate, but there are marked regional variations. The Cascade Range separates the state into two broad climatic zones: the western third, with relatively heavy precipitation and moderate temperatures, and the eastern two-thirds, with relatively little precipitation and more extreme temperatures. Within these general regions, climate depends largely on elevation and land configuration.

In January, normal daily mean temperatures range from more than 45°F (7°C) in the coastal sections to between 25°F (–4°C) and

28°F (–2°C) in the southeast. In July, the normal daily means range between 65°F (18°C) and 70°F (21°C) in the plateau regions and central valleys and between 70°F (21°C) and 78°F (26°C) along the eastern border. Oregon's record low temperature, –54°F (–48°C), was registered at Seneca on 10 February 1933; the all-time high, 119°F (48°C), at Pendleton on 10 August 1898.

The Cascades serve as a barrier to the warm, moist winds blowing in from the Pacific, confining most precipitation to western Oregon. The average annual rainfall varies from less than 8 in (20 cm) in the drier plateau regions to as much as 200 in (508 cm) at locations on the upper west slopes of the Coast Range. In the Blue Mountains and the Columbia River Basin, totals are about 15 in (38 cm) to 20 in (51 cm). In Portland, fog is common, and the sun shines, on average, during only 49% of the daylight hours—one of the lowest such percentages for any major US city. From 300 in (760 cm) to 550 in (1,400 cm) of snow falls each year in the highest reaches of the Cascades.

4FLORA AND FAUNA

With its variety of climatic conditions and surface features, Oregon has a diverse assortment of vegetation and wildlife, including 78 native tree species. The coastal region is covered by a rain forest of spruce, hemlock, and cedar rising above dense underbrush. A short distance inland, the stands of Douglas fir—Oregon's state tree and dominant timber resource—begin, extending across the western slopes to the summit of the Cascade Range. Where the Douglas fir has been destroyed by fire or logging, alder and various types of berries grow. In the high elevations of the Cascades, Douglas fir gives way to pines and true firs. Ponderosa pine predominates on the eastern slopes, while in areas too dry for pine the forests give way to open range, which, in its natural state, is characterized by sagebrush, occasional juniper trees, and sparse grasses. The state's many species of smaller indigenous plants include Oregon grape—the state flower—as well as salmonberry, huckleberry, blackberry, and many other berries. The Malheur wire-lettuce and MacFarlane's four-o'clock are endangered.

More than 130 species of mammal are native to Oregon, of which 28 are found throughout the state. Many species, such as the cougar and bear, are protected, either entirely or through hunting restrictions. The bighorn sheep, once extirpated—deliberately exterminated—in Oregon, has been reintroduced in limited numbers; the Columbian white-tailed deer, with an extremely limited habitat along the Columbia River, is still classified as endangered. Deer and elk are popular game mammals, with herds managed by the state: mule deer predominate in eastern Oregon, black-tailed deer in the west. Among introduced mammals, the nutria and opossum are now present in large numbers. At least 60 species of fish are found in Oregon, including five different salmon species, of which the Chinook is the largest and the coho most common. Salmon form the basis of Oregon's sport and commercial fishing, although dams and development have blocked many spawning areas, causing a decline in numbers and heavy reliance on hatcheries to continue the runs. Hundreds of species of birds inhabit Oregon, either year-round or during particular seasons. The state lies in the path of the Pacific Flyway, a major route for migratory waterfowl, and large numbers of geese and ducks may be found in western Oregon and marshy areas east of the Cascades. Extensive bird refuges have been established in various parts of the state. The bald eagle, southern sea otter, and Oregon silver-spot butterfly are considered threatened, while the brown pelican, short-tailed albatross, California condor, Aleutian Canada goose, American and Arctic peregrine falcons, and Borax Lake chub are classified as endangered.

5ENVIRONMENTAL PROTECTION

Oregon has been among the most active states in environmental protection. In 1938, the polluted condition of the Willamette River led to the enactment, by initiative, of one of the nation's first comprehensive water pollution control laws, which helped restore the river's quality for swimming and fishing. An air pollution control law was enacted in 1951, and air and water quality programs were placed under the new Department of Environmental Quality (DEQ) in 1969. This department is Oregon's major environmental protection agency, enforcing standards for air and water quality and solid and hazardous waste disposal. A vehicle inspection program has been instituted to reduce exhaust emissions in the Portland area and in Rogue Valley. The DEQ also operates an asbestos program to protect the public from asbestos in buildings that are being demolished or remodeled. The DEQ monitors 18 river basins for water quality and issues permits to businesses, industries, and government bodies that discharge waste water into public waters. As of March 1993, DEQ was aware of 1,359 groundwater contamination sites. In 1995, Oregon had 12 hazardous waste sites.

During the summer of 1995, Portland, the state's largest city, had 15 days when ozone levels were in the moderate range and none in the unhealthful range. In 1973, the legislature enacted what has become known as the Oregon Bottle Bill, the first state law prohibiting the sale of nonreturnable beer or soft-drink containers. The DEQ estimates that more than 95% of beverage containers are returned for recycling and that in 1993, 30% (974,687 tons) of the state's solid waste was recovered for recycling. In 1995, the agency estimated a 32% rate of recycling for rigid plastic containers. The success of the Bottle Bill was partly responsible for the passage, in 1983, of the Recycling Opportunity Act, which reduces the amount of solid waste generated. Furthermore, all cities with 5,000 or more residents are required to provide curbside recycling services.

6POPULATION

Oregon ranked 29th among the 50 states at the 1990 census, with a population of 2,842,321. Like other western states, Oregon experienced a more rapid population growth than that of the US as a whole in the 1970s, when population expanded 26%. The 1990 census figure represented a 7.9% increase over the 1980 census population; the 1996 population estimate, 3,203,735, represents a 12.7% increase over the 1990 population. Oregon's estimated population density in 1990 was 29.6 per sq mi (11.3 per sq km), less than half the national average.

As of 1990, about 52% of all Oregonians lived in the Portland region, while much of the remainder also lived in the Willamette Valley, particularly in and around Salem and Eugene. The city of Portland had an estimated 450,777 residents in 1994; the Portland Consolidated Metropolitan Statistical Area (which includes Vancouver, Wash.) had an estimated 1995 population of 1,710,260. The estimated population of Eugene was 118,122; Salem, 115,912.

7ETHNIC GROUPS

Oregon's Indians number some 38,000, with most of the population living in urban areas. The state's four reservations (with estimated 1995 population) are the Umatilla (2,154), Siletz (1,778), Spokane (1,416), and Kalispel (170). Important salmon fishing rights in the north are reserved under treaty. About 46,000 black Americans lived in Oregon in 1990, most of them in the Portland area. People of Hispanic descent numbered about 113,000 in the same year. In 1990 there were 14,796 Chinese, 14,142 Japanese, 9,355 Koreans, 9,114 Filipinos, 8,130 Vietnamese, 3,287 Laotians, and 2,726 Asian Indians. French Canadians have lived in Oregon since the opening of the territory, and they have continued to come in a small but steady migration.

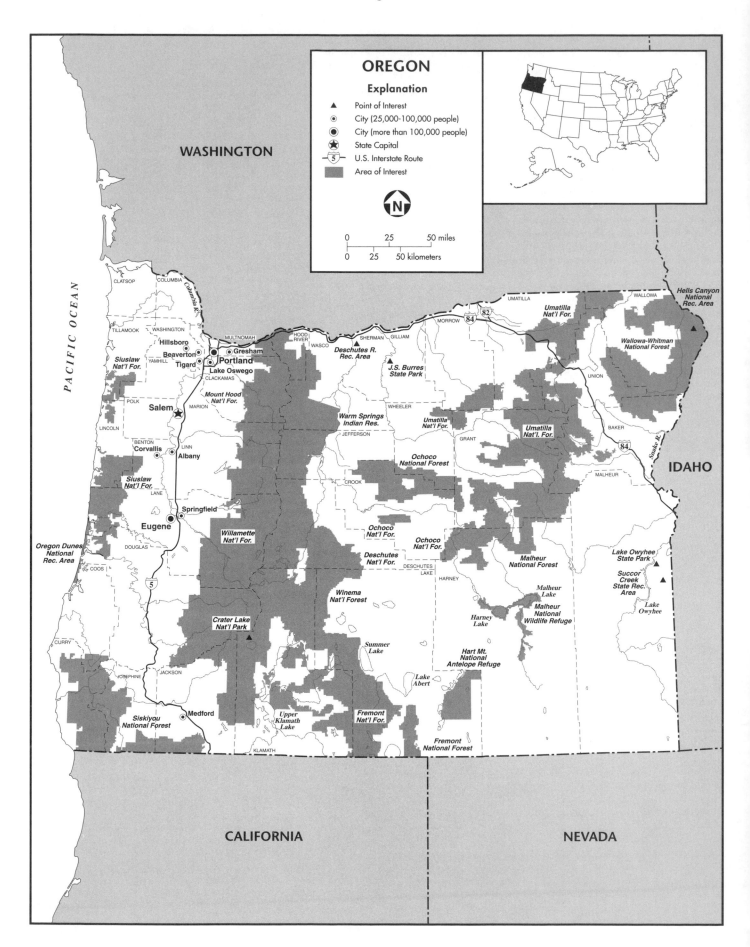

OREGON

Explanation

▲ Point of Interest
⊙ City (25,000-100,000 people)
◉ City (more than 100,000 people)
★ State Capital
⑤ U.S. Interstate Route
▨ Area of Interest

Ⓝ

0   25   50 miles
0   25   50 kilometers

WASHINGTON

PACIFIC OCEAN

CLATSOP
COLUMBIA
Columbia R.
TILLAMOOK
WASHINGTON
Hillsboro
Beaverton
Tigard
Portland
Gresham
Lake Oswego
Siuslaw Nat'l For.
YAMHILL
CLACKAMAS
MULTNOMAH
HOOD RIVER
Deschutes R. Rec. Area
WASCO
SHERMAN
GILLIAM
Umatilla Nat'l For.
UMATILLA
MORROW
84
82
WALLOWA
Hells Canyon National Rec. Area
Wallowa-Whitman National Forest
POLK
Mount Hood Nat'l For.
Salem
MARION
J.S. Burres State Park
Warm Springs Indian Res.
WHEELER
Umatilla Nat'l For.
GRANT
UNION
Umatilla Nat'l For.
BAKER
84
Snake R.
LINCOLN
BENTON
Corvallis
LINN
Albany
JEFFERSON
Ochoco National Forest
IDAHO
Siuslaw Nat'l For.
LANE
Springfield
Eugene
CROOK
Ochoco Nat'l For.
Ochoco Nat'l For.
MALHEUR
Oregon Dunes National Rec. Area
DOUGLAS
Willamette Nat'l For.
Deschutes Nat'l For.
DESCHUTES
Malheur National Forest
Lake Owyhee State Park
COOS
5
Winema Nat'l Forest
LAKE
HARNEY
Malheur Lake
Succor Creek State Rec. Area
Lake Owyhee
Crater Lake Nat'l Park
Summer Lake
Malheur National Wildlife Refuge
Harney Lake
CURRY
JOSEPHINE
JACKSON
Medford
Upper Klamath Lake
Fremont Nat'l For.
Hart Mt. National Antelope Refuge
Lake Abert
Siskiyou National Forest
KLAMATH
Fremont National Forest

CALIFORNIA   NEVADA

In all, the 1990 census counted some 139,307 Oregonians of foreign birth, accounting for 4.9% of the population.

8LANGUAGES

Place-names such as Umatilla, Coos Bay, Klamath Falls, and Tillamook reflect the variety of Indian tribes that white settlers found in Oregon territory.

The midland dialect dominates Oregon English, except for an apparent Northern dialect influence in the Willamette Valley. Throughout the state, *foreign* and *orange* have the /aw/ vowel, and *tomorrow* has the /ah/ of *father*.

In 1990, 2,448,772 Oregonians—92.7% of the population 5 years old or older—spoke only English at home. Other languages spoken at home included:

Spanish	83,087	Vietnamese	7,468
German	19,289	Japanese	6,724
French	10,854	Russian	5,325
Chinese	10,099	Korean	5,574

9RELIGION

Just over one-third of Oregon's population is affiliated with an organized religion, well below the national average. The leading Christian denominations were the Roman Catholic church, with 279,650 members in 1990, and the Church of Jesus Christ of Latter-day Saints (Mormon), with 89,601 adherents in 1994. Other major Protestant groups, with their 1990 adherents were United Methodist, 42,209; Assemblies of God, 46,902; and United Presbyterian, 38,086. Jewish Oregonians were estimated to number 10,691 in 1990.

10TRANSPORTATION

With the state's major deepwater port and international airport, Portland is the transportation hub of Oregon. The state has 2,600 rail mi (4,200 km) of track and is served by two major rail systems: Union Pacific and Burlington Northern/Santa Fe. Lumber and wood products are the major commodities originating in Oregon. Farm products and chemicals are the major commodities terminating in Oregon, primarily at the Port of Portland. Amtrak provides passenger service north-south through Portland, Salem, and Eugene. Total Amtrak ridership in 1995/96 was 483,648.

Starting with pioneer trails and toll roads, Oregon's roads and highways had become a network extending 95,275 mi (156,613 km) by 1996. The main interstate highways are I-5, running the length of the state north-south connecting the major cities, and I-84, running northwest from Ontario in eastern Oregon and then along the northern border. In 1996 there were 3.4 million registered vehicles, including 2.8 million passenger cars, registered in Oregon, with 2.5 million licensed drivers.

The Columbia River forms the major inland waterway for the Pacific Northwest, with barge navigation possible for 464 mi (747 km) upstream to Lewiston, Idaho, via the Snake River. Wheat from eastern Oregon and Washington is shipped downstream to Portland for reloading onto oceangoing vessels. The Port of Portland owns five major cargo terminals and handled more than 10.5 million tons of cargo in 1996, with imports valued at $3.6 billion and exports valued at $5.5 billion. Oregon also has several important coastal harbors, including Astoria, Newport, and Coos Bay.

In 1996, Oregon had more than 500 airfields (100 public, 400 private), of which the largest and busiest, Portland International Airport, handled 109,500 departures and enplaned 6.3 million passengers.

11HISTORY

The land now known as Oregon has been inhabited for at least 10,000 years, the age assigned to woven brush sandals found in caves along what was once the shore of a large inland lake. Later, a variety of Indian cultures evolved. Along the coast and lower Columbia River lived peoples of the Northern Coast Culture, who ate salmon and other marine life, built large dugout canoes and cedar plank houses, and possessed a complex social structure, including slavery, that emphasized status and wealth. East of the Cascade Range were hunter-gatherers who migrated from place to place as the food supply dictated.

The first European to see Oregon was probably Sir Francis Drake. In 1578, while on a raiding expedition against the Spanish, Drake reported sighting what is believed to be the Oregon coast before being forced to return southward by "vile, thicke and stinking fogges." For most of the next 200 years, European contact was limited to occasional sightings by mariners, who considered the coast too dangerous for landing. In 1778, however, British Captain James Cook, on his third voyage of discovery, visited the Northwest and named several Oregon capes. Soon afterward, American ships arrived in search of sea otter and other furs. A Yankee merchant captain, Robert Gray, discovered the Columbia River (which he named for his ship) in 1792, contributing to the US claim to the Northwest.

The first overland trek to Oregon was the Lewis and Clark Expedition, which traveled from St. Louis to the mouth of the Columbia, where it spent the winter of 1805/6. In 1811, a party of fur traders employed by New York merchant John Jacob Astor arrived by ship at the mouth of the Columbia and built a trading post named Astoria. The venture was not a success and was sold three years later to British interests, but some of the Astor party stayed, becoming Oregon's first permanent white residents. For the next 20 years, European and US interest in Oregon focused on the quest for beaver pelts. Agents of the British North West Company (which merged in 1821 with the Hudson's Bay Company) and some rival American parties explored the region, mapped trails, and established trading posts. Although Britain and the US had agreed to a treaty of joint occupation in 1818, the de facto governor from 1824 to the early 1840s was Dr. John McLoughlin, the Hudson's Bay Company chief factor at Ft. Vancouver in Washington.

Another major influence on the region was Protestant missionary activity, which began with the arrival of Jason Lee, a Methodist missionary, in 1834. Lee started his mission in the Willamette Valley, near present-day Salem. After a lecture tour of the East, he returned to Oregon in 1840 with 50 settlers and assistants. While Lee's mission was of little help to the local Indians, most of whom had been killed off by white men's diseases, it served as a base for subsequent American settlement and as a counterbalance to the Hudson's Bay Company.

The first major wagon trains arrived by way of the Oregon Trail in the early 1840s. On 2 May 1843, as a "great migration" of 875 men, women, and children was crossing the plains, about 100 settlers met at the Willamette Valley community of Champoeg and voted to form a provisional government. That government remained in power until 1849, when Oregon became a territory, three years after the Oregon Treaty between Great Britain and the US established the present US-Canadian boundary. As originally constituted, Oregon Territory included present-day Washington and much of Montana, Idaho, and Wyoming. A constitution prepared by an elected convention was approved in November 1857, and after a delay caused by North-South rivalries, on 14 February 1859, Congress voted to make Oregon, reduced to its present borders, the 33d state.

Oregon remained relatively isolated until the completion of the first transcontinental railroad link in 1883. State politics, which had followed a pattern of venality and influence buying, underwent an upheaval in the early 1900s. Reformers led by William S. U'Ren instituted what became known as the "Oregon

System" of initiative, referendum, and recall, by which voters could legislate directly and removed corrupt elected officials.

Oregon's population grew steadily in the 20th century as migration into the state continued. Improved transportation helped make the state the nation's leading lumber producer and a major exporter of agricultural products. Development was also aided by hydroelectric projects, many undertaken by the federal government. The principal economic changes since World War II have been the growth of the aluminum industry, a rapid expansion of the tourist trade, and the creation of a growing electronics industry. The dominant industries in the Oregon economy, however, remained those centered on its abundant natural resources— timber, agriculture, and coal. These industries suffered in the late 1970s and 1980s when interest rates skyrocketed, reducing demand for houses and therefore for wood. Employment in the lumber and wood industry dropped from 81,000 jobs in 1979 to 64,000 in 1985. High interest rates, by boosting the value of the dollar, also lowered foreign demand for lumber and produce.

It was hoped that the construction of high-technology plants in the mid-1980s would help immunize Oregon from the fluctuating fortunes of the extractive and agricultural industries. However, a slump in the computer industry delayed the building of planned facilities in the state. By the early 1990s, Oregon did boast a burgeoning electronics industry, although the greatest job growth had occurred in the service sector. Agricultural industries had also helped boost the state's economy. By 1994, unemployment stood at a 25-year low of 5%.

By the late 1980s and early 1990s, the struggle between environmentalists and the timber industry over logging in Oregon's remaining rainforests had become a major public policy debate. Federal legislation passed in 1993 set limits on commercial exploitation of older forests that were home to the spotted owl.

In 1990 Democrat Barbara Roberts became the first woman to be elected governor of Oregon.

12STATE GOVERNMENT

The Oregon constitution—drafted and approved in 1857, effective in 1859, and amended more than 170 times—governs the state today. The first decade of the 20th century saw the passage of numerous progressive amendments, including provisions for the direct election of senators, the rights of initiative, referendum, recall, and a direct primary system.

The constitution establishes a 60-member house of representatives, elected for 2 years, and a senate of 30 members, serving 4-year terms. Major executive officials include the governor, secretary of state, attorney general, state treasurer, superintendent of public instruction, and commissioner of labor and industries, all elected for 4 years. The governor, who may serve no more than 8 years in any 12-year period, must be a US citizen, must be at least 30 years of age, and must have been a resident of the state for 3 years before assuming office. In 1996 the governor's salary was $80,000. Much policy in Oregon is set by boards and commissions whose members are appointed by the governor, subject to confirmation by the senate.

Bills become law when approved by a majority of house and senate and either signed by the governor or left unsigned for 5 days when the legislature is in session or for 20 days after it has adjourned. Measures presented to the voters by the legislature or by petition become law when approved by a majority of the electorate. The governor may veto a legislative bill, but the legislature may override a veto by a two-thirds vote of those present in each house. Proposed constitutional amendments require voter approval to take effect, and they may be placed on the ballot either by the legislature or by initiative petition.

US citizens over age 18 are entitled to vote, subject to residency requirements of 20 days.

13POLITICAL PARTIES

Oregon has two major political parties, Democratic and Republican. Partly because of the role the direct primary system plays in choosing nominees, party organization is relatively weak. There is a strong tradition of political independence, evidenced in 1976 when Oregon gave independent presidential candidate Eugene McCarthy 3.9% of the vote—his highest percentage in any state—a total that probably cost Jimmy Carter Oregon's 6 electoral votes. Another independent, John Anderson, won 112,389 votes (9.5%) in the 1980 presidential election.

Oregon's Presidential Vote by Political Parties, 1948–96

YEAR	ELECTORAL VOTE	OREGON WINNER	DEMOCRAT	REPUBLICAN	PROGRESSIVE	SOCIALIST	LIBERTARIAN
1948	6	Dewey (R	243,147	260,904	14,978	5,051	—
1952	6	*Eisenhower (R)	270,579	420,815	3,665	—	—
1956	6	Eisenhower (R)	329,204	406,393	—	—	—
1960	6	Nixon (R	367,402	408,065	—	—	—
1964	6	*Johnson (D)	501,017	282,779	—	—	—
						AMERICAN IND.	
1968	6	*Nixon (R)	358,866	408,433	—	49,683	—
						AMERICAN	
1972	6	*Nixon (R)	392,760	486,686	—	46,211	—
1976	6	Ford (R	490,407	492,120	—	—	—
						CITIZENS	
1980	6	*Reagan (R)	456,890	571,044	—	13,642	25,838
1984	7	*Reagan (R)	536,479	685,700	—	—	—
					NEW ALLIANCE		
1988	7	Dukakis (D)	678,367	483,423	2,985	—	6,261
						IND. (PEROT)	
1992	7	*Clinton (D)	621,314	475,757	3,030	354,091	4,277
					PACIFIC (NADER)		
1996	7	*Clinton (D)	649,641	538,152	49,415	121,221	8,903

* Won US presidential election.

As of 1994 there were 792,115 registered Democrats (45% of the total number of registered voters) and 641,914 registered Republicans (36%), along with 340,420 independents and minor-party members (19%). Democrat Barbara Roberts was elected governor in 1990. She did not run for reelection in 1994, and Dr. John Kitzhaber, a Democrat who designed Oregon's health care rationing system, defeated Republican congressman Denny Smith to become governor. Oregonians elected two US senators in 1996. In a special election in January, Democrat Ron Wyden was chosen to serve the remainder of Robert Packwood's term after Packwood resigned from the Senate due to allegations of sexual misconduct. In the November election, Republican Gordon Smith won the seat vacated by five-term senator Mark Hatfield. All but one of the five US representatives are Democrats.

As of 1997, there are 20 Republicans and 10 Democrats in the state senate, and 31 Republicans and 29 Democrats in the state house. Oregon voters gave Democratic presidential incumbent Bill Clinton 47% of the popular vote in November 1996, while Republican Bob Dole received 39% and Independent Ross Perot captured 9%. In 1994, there were 10 blacks and 5 Hispanics holding public office. As of 1995, 24 women served in the state legislature and 1 woman held statewide elective executive office.

14LOCAL GOVERNMENT

As of 1992, Oregon had 36 counties, 239 municipal governments, 340 school districts, and 835 special districts. Towns and cities enjoy home rule, the right to choose their own form of government and enact legislation on matters of local concern. In 1958, home rule was extended to counties. Most of Oregon's larger cities have council-manager forms of government. Typical elected county officials are three to five commissioners, assessor, district attorney, sheriff, and treasurer.

The state constitution gives voters strong control over local government revenue by requiring voter approval of property tax levies.

15STATE SERVICES

Special offices within the governor's office include the Office of the Citizens' Representative, the state Affirmative Action Office, and the Long-Term Care Ombudsman. The Oregon Government Ethics commission is a citizens' panel, established in 1974, to investigate conflicts of interest involving public officials and to levy civil penalties for infractions. Responsibility for educational matters is divided among the Board of Education, which oversees primary and secondary schools and community colleges; the Board of Higher Education, which controls the state college and university system; and the Educational Coordinating Commission, which monitors programs and advises the governor and legislature on policy.

State highways, airfields, and public transit systems are under the jurisdiction of the Department of Transportation, which is headed by an appointed commission. The largest state agency is the Department of Human Resources; nearly one-fourth of the state's budget and work force is committed to this department's 250 programs, which include corrections, children's services, adult and family services, health, mental health, and vocational rehabilitation. State agencies involved in environmental matters include the Department of Environmental Quality, the Department of Land Conservation and Development, and the departments of Energy, Forestry, and Water Resources. State-owned lands are administered through the Land Board.

16JUDICIAL SYSTEM

Oregon's highest court is the supreme court, consisting of 7 justices who elect one of their number to serve as chief justice. It accepts cases on review from the 10-judge court of appeals, which has exclusive jurisdiction over all criminal and civil appeals from lower courts and over certain actions of state agencies. Circuit courts (with 97 circuit judges as of 1997) are the trial courts of original jurisdiction for civil and criminal matters. The 30 more-populous counties also have district courts, which hear minor civil, criminal, and traffic matters; there are 63 district court judges. In 1998, the circuit courts and district courts will be merged; the circuit courts will then be the only state-level trial courts, with 160 judges. Thirty localities retain justices of the peace, also with jurisdiction over minor cases. State judges and local justices of the peace are elected by nonpartisan ballot for six-year terms. In 1996, an estimated 9,172 attorneys practiced in the state.

Oregon's penal system is operated by the Oregon Department of Corrections. There were 7,837 inmates in state correctional facilities as of 1 May 1997, or 246 per 100,000 in population. As measured by the FBI Crime Index, Oregon's crime rate was above the national average in 1995, but violent crime was only three-quarters of the national average. Property crimes, particularly theft (4,253 per 100,000 population) were higher than the national average. Oregon imposes the death penalty, and there were 20 persons under sentence of death in 1995.

17ARMED FORCES

In 1996, there were 874 active duty military personnel stationed in Oregon. The US Coast Guard does maintain search-and-rescue facilities, and the Army Corps of Engineers operates a number of hydroelectric projects in the state. Military contract awards in 1995/96 totaled $202 million.

As of 1 July 1996, some 368,000 military veterans were living in Oregon, of whom fewer than 500 served in World War I; 101,000 in World War II; 58,000 during the Korean conflict; 124,000 during the Vietnam era; and 22,000 in the Persian Gulf War. Federal veterans' benefits totaled $603 million in 1995/96.

Reserve and national guard personnel numbered 18,570 in September 1992, with 10,414 in the army, 4,567 in the navy and marine corps, and 3,589 in the air force. In 1993, the Oregon State Police employed 785 full-time sworn officers, or 3 per 10,000 residents.

18MIGRATION

The Oregon Trail was the route along which thousands of settlers traveled to Oregon by covered wagon in the 1840s and 1850s. This early immigration was predominantly from midwestern states. After the completion of the transcontinental railroad, northeastern states supplied an increasing proportion of the newcomers.

Foreign immigration began in the 1860s with the importation of Chinese contract laborers, and reached its peak about 1900. Germans and Scandinavians (particularly after 1900) were the most numerous foreign immigrants; Japanese, who began arriving in the 1890s, met a hostile reception in some areas. Canadians have also come to Oregon in significant numbers. Nevertheless, immigration from other states has predominated. Between 1970 and 1980, the state's net gain from migration was about 341,000; from 1980 to 1983, however, the state suffered a net loss of about 37,000, and from 1985 to 1990, the net migration gain was 123,500. Between 1990 and 1996, Oregon had net gains of 221,395 in domestic migration and 42,405 in international migration. In 1996, 7,554 foreign immigrants arrived in Oregon. As of 1994, it was estimated that between 21 and 27 undocumented immigrants were living in the state. In 1990, 46.6% of state residents had been born in Oregon. About 54% of residents age 5 and older lived in a different house in 1985 than in 1990, of which 26% did so in another state.

Oregon's urban population grew from 67.9% of the total population in 1980 to 70.5% in 1990.

[19]INTERGOVERNMENTAL COOPERATION

Oregon participates in such regional accords as the Columbia River Compact, Klamath River Compact (with California), Pacific Marine Fisheries Compact, and several western groups concerned with corrections, education, and energy matters.

While Oregon receives federal assistance for a variety of programs, federal involvement is particularly heavy in the areas of energy and natural resources, through federal development, operation, and marketing of hydroelectric power and federal ownership of forest and grazing lands. Approximately 49% of Oregon's land area is owned by the federal government. Federal aid to Oregon was more than $2.7 billion in 1995/96.

[20]ECONOMY

Since early settlement, Oregon's natural resources have formed the basis of its economy. Vast forests have made lumber and wood products the leading industry in the state. Since World War II, however, the state has striven to diversify its job base. The aluminum industry has been attracted to Oregon, along with computer and electronics firms, which now constitute the fastest-growing manufacturing sector. Development, principally in the "Silicon Forest" west of Portland, was expected to bring as many as 3,000 jobs a year during the mid- and late 1980s. Meanwhile, the trend in employment has been toward white-collar and service jobs, with agriculture and manufacturing holding a declining share of the civilian labor force. Tourism and research-related businesses growing out of partnerships between government and higher education are on the rise.

Despite diversification efforts, 60% of manufacturing jobs outside the Portland area were in the lumber and wood products field in 1982. As a result, the state's economy remains dependent on the health of the US construction industry. Jobs are plentiful when US housing starts rise, but unemployment increases when nationwide construction drops off. Employment in the lumber and wood industry plummeted from 81,000 in 1979 to 56,000 in 1982 and then increased to 64,000 in 1985. The cyclical changes in demand for forest products are a chronic problem, with rural areas and small towns particularly hard hit by the periodic closing of local lumber and plywood mills.

In 1995, the per capita personal income was $21,611, 26th in the US. Oregon's gross state product in 1994 was $74,366 million, to which private goods-producing industries contributed $20,572 million; private services-producing industries, $44,283 million; and government, $9,511 million. During 1996, there were 16,709 bankruptcy filings.

[21]INCOME

Per capita personal income in Oregon in 1996 was $22,668, 27th among the 50 states. Total personal disposable income was $61.5 billion in 1996, up from $57.8 billion in 1995.

Median household income in 1995 was $36,374. About 11.2% of all Oregonians were living below the federal poverty level during that year.

[22]LABOR

Oregon's civilian labor force numbered 1,721,000 in 1996, out of which 1,619,000 were employed, giving the state an unemployment rate of 5.9%.

At the end of 1996, mining employed 1,900 persons; construction, 76,300; manufacturing, 232,100; transportation and public utilities, 74,400; wholesale and retail trade, 388,700; finance, insurance, and real estate, 92,900; services, 406,600; and government, 241,400.

In 1995, 266,800 Oregon workers—20.1% of all employees—were members of a labor union; the rate was 15.1% among manufacturing workers. Average weekly earnings of production workers were $540.29 in December 1996.

[23]AGRICULTURE

Oregon ranked 28th in the US in agricultural output in 1995, with cash receipts of $3.4 billion. Crops accounted for 80% of the total. While wheat has been Oregon's leading crop since the state was first settled, in recent years nursery and greenhouse products, valued at more than $420 million, have taken over the number-one spot. Additionally, more than 170 farm and ranch commodities are commercially produced in the state. Oregon leads the nation in the production of hazelnuts, peppermint oil, blackberries, black raspberries, boysenberries, loganberries, several grass and seed crops, and Christmas trees.

Farmland covers about 17.5 million acres (7 million hectares), or 28% of Oregon's total area. Oregon's average farm is 455 acres (184 hectares), the same size as the national average. In 1995, the state had some 38,500 farms. Quantity and value of selected crops in 1995 were as follows:

	VOLUME	VALUE (MILLIONS)
Nursery and greenhouse	36,000 acres	$420
Hay	3.3 m. tons	304
Wheat	60.4 m. bushels	287
Grass seed	553.6 m. lb	236
Potatoes	24.7 thou. cwt	166

In recent years, the growth of Oregon's wine industry has become noteworthy.

[24]ANIMAL HUSBANDRY

Most beef cattle are raised on the rangeland of eastern Oregon, while dairy operations are concentrated in the western portion of the state. Sheep and poultry are also raised largely in the west.

Cattle and calf production is Oregon's leading agricultural activity in terms of value, although income varies greatly with market conditions. Ranchers lease large tracts of federally owned grazing land under a permit system.

In 1997, Oregon ranches and farms had around 1.45 million cattle and calves, worth an estimated $754 million. During 1995, the state produced nearly 22 million lb (10 million kg) of sheep and lambs, which brought in nearly $13.5 million in gross income, and the shorn wool production was 2.4 million lb (1.1 million kg) of wool. The 1995 milk output was estimated at 1.7 billion lb (0.8 billion kg). Oregon's poultry farmers produced nearly 113 million lb (51 million kg) of chickens and broilers in 1995, and 709 million eggs.

[25]FISHING

Oregon's fish resources have long been of great importance to its inhabitants. For centuries, salmon provided much of the food for Indians, who gathered at traditional fishing grounds when the salmon were returning upstream from the ocean to spawn.

In 1995, Oregon ranked 6th among the states in the total amount of its commercial catch, at 238,764,000 lb (108,303,000 kg), valued at $77,766,000. The catch included salmon, especially chinook and silver; groundfish such as flounder, rockfish, and lingcod; shellfish such as shrimp and oysters; and albacore tuna. Salmon landings totaled 2.8 million lb (1.3 million kg), valued at $3.6 million; sablefish, 7 million lb (3 million kg), $9.3 million; dungeness crab, 11.9 million lb (5.4 million kg); and shrimp, 12.1 million lb (5.5 million kg). Newport, Astoria, and Coos Bay–Charleston were the leading commercial fishing ports in 1995, with landings of 112 million, 89 million, and 21 million lb (51 million, 40 million, and 9.5 million kg), respectively. Oregon's commercial fishing fleet consisted of 2,436 boats and vessels in 1994, and supplied the state's 87 fish processing and wholesale plants.

Sport fishing, primarily for salmon and trout, is a major recreational attraction. In 1995/96, the state issued 709,934 sport fishing licenses. An estimated 209,000 coastal residents, along with 13,000 inland Oregonians and 81,000 residents of other states, participated in 700,000 recreational marine fishing trips in 1995, catching some 1,576,000 fish (mainly rockfish).

Hatchery production of salmon and steelhead has taken on increased importance, as development has destroyed natural fishspawning areas. About 2.7 million fish and 4.8 million fish eggs were distributed by federal hatcheries in 1995/96.

26FORESTRY

Oregon's total land area is 62 million acres (25 million hectares). Almost half of this, 28.5 million acres (11.5 million hectares), is forested. Oregon's forests are divided into two major geographic regions. Douglas-fir is a primary conifer species in western Oregon, with western hemlock and sitka spruce found along the coast. In eastern Oregon, ponderosa pine is the main species. Several species of true fir, larch, and lodgepole pine also grow east of the Cascades. Noncommercial forests are found along the crest of the Cascade Range and in the high-desert country of eastern Oregon. These species include alpine fir, mountain hemlock and western juniper.

Over 60% of Oregon's forests are publicly owned. Most of these are federal lands. Federal timber harvest levels have steadily declined over the last several years as timber sales have been appealed and forest set-asides for habitat protection have increased. Reduced revenues have affected local services and infrastructure—where a percentage of harvest tax dollars are reinvested—and the overall structure and funding of federal agencies. The Oregon Department of Forestry manages about 786,000 acres (318,000 hectares) of forest land. About 654,000 acres (265,000 hectares) are managed by the department for the counties, and a further 132,000 acres (53,000 hectares) are Common School Fund forest lands, managed for the State Land Board. State forest lands are not managed with the same "multiple-use" strategy as lands managed by the US Forest Service. According to statute, state lands are managed to produce sustainable revenue for counties, schools, and local taxing districts. About 77% of the state's forest land, or 21.6 million acres (8.7 million hectares), is land capable of producing timber for commercial harvest. However, less than 60% of this commercial land is available for full-yield timber production. The remaining forest land base contains commercial forest, but at reduced levels, and provides vital environmental and recreational functions.

Forest land available for commercial timber management has decreased over the last 25 years, and this trend is expected to continue through the 1990s. Estimates show that Oregon's commercial land base has decreased by more than 24% since 1945. Private forest land has been lost due to urban expansion and other non-timber uses. Private forest lands, however, have assumed a much more important role as Oregon's timber supplier due to harvest limitations placed on federal forest land. Timber harvest levels on non-industrial forest lands—parcels typically smaller than 5,000 acres (2,000 hectares) and owned by individuals, not corporations—have more than doubled since 1981, and harvest levels on industry-owned forest lands have also increased during the same period. The relative percentage of overall harvest, however, emphasizes the importance of Oregon's private forest lands. In 1993, Oregon's total roundwood harvest of 1.9 billion cu ft (53.8 million cu m) was greater than any other state's, and contributed 8.3% to the national total. One interesting element of the private timber harvest is that nearly all of the timber harvested from private forest lands is second-growth—trees originating from 1920 to 1940. Private forest lands are being reforested and will play a major role in sustaining Oregon's long-term timber supply. Oregon law has required reforestation following timber harvesting since 1941. Oregon was the first state to pass a Forest Practices Act, in 1971. About 100 million seedlings are planted in Oregon each year.

27MINING

The estimated value of Oregon's nonfuel mineral production in 1995 was $261 million, up 8% from 1994. Industrial minerals account for nearly all of the nonfuel mineral production value, with less than 1% coming from the mining of metals. Crushed stone (by value) was Oregon's leading nonfuel mineral commodity, accounting for more than 40% of the state's total nonfuel mineral value in 1995. In 1995, Oregon produced 21.5 million metric tons of crushed stone, worth $105 million, up 16% from 1994. Construction sand and gravel production rose from 18.4 million metric tons ($86.6 million) to 17.5 million metric tons ($81.4 million) between 1994 and 1995. The state's nonfuel mineral production value ranked 38th in the nation. Oregon was the nation's sole producer of nickel. It ranked first nationally in the quantity of pumice produced, third in the quantity of diatomite, and was a significant producer of processed natural zeolites, which are processed and sold for ammonia absorbent in aquarium systems, animal feed supplement, anticaking agents, fungicide carriers, odor control, and wastewater treatment.

28ENERGY AND POWER

Oregon ranks 2d in the US in hydroelectric power development, and hydropower supplies nearly half of the state's energy needs. Multipurpose federal projects, including four dams on the Columbia River and eight in the Willamette Basin, and projects owned by private or public utilities, give Oregon a hydroelectric capacity of over 8,000,000 kW. In recent decades, low-cost power from dams has proved inadequate to meet the state's energy needs, and nuclear and coal-fired steam plants have been built to supply additional electric power. Hydropower provided 92% of electricity in 1995; coal and gas-fired thermal plants produced nearly 8%. Oregon's total electric power production in 1995 was 44 billion kWh; installed capacity was 9.8 million kW. The Bonneville Power Administration, the federal power-marketing agency, operates a power distribution grid interconnecting Oregon, Washington, and parts of Idaho and Montana.

About 15% of Oregon's total energy is provided by natural gas, the majority of which comes from Canada and the southwestern US.

Energy consumption per capita was 336.3 million Btu (84.4 million kcal) in 1994 (29th in the US), and energy expenditures per capita amounted to $1,791 (42d in the US).

29INDUSTRY

Manufacturing in Oregon is dominated by the lumber and wood products industry. In 1995, the total value of shipments of manufactured goods was $42,338,000,000. More than half of Oregon's industrial workers are employed in the Portland area. The Willamette Valley is the site of one of the nation's largest canning and freezing industries.

The following table shows value of shipments by manufacturers for selected industry groups in 1995:

Lumber and wood products	$ 10,596,500,000
Preserved fruits and vegetables	1,736,300,000
Primary metal products	2,010,300,000
Papermill products	3,537,400,000
Electronic components and accessories	4,675,200,000
Transportation equipment	3,107,100,000

In 1997, Oregon was the headquarters of 6 Fortune 500 companies: Nike, Thrifty Payless Holdings, Pacificorp, Fred Meyer, Willamette Industries, and US Bancorp. During 1995, 847 US patents were issued to Oregon residents.

30COMMERCE

Wholesalers numbered 6,455 in 1992, with sales of $42.4 billion. Retail establishments in 1992 had combined sales of $24.2 billion, of which automotive dealers accounted for 21.7%; food stores, 18%; general merchandise stores, 16.5%; and restaurants and taverns, 10.2%.

Exports moving through Oregon customs districts in Portland were valued at almost $10.2 billion in 1995, with imports valued at more than $7.9 billion. Oregon's foreign exports of its own products in 1996 were valued at $8.9 billion.

31CONSUMER PROTECTION

The Consumer Advisory Council of the Department of Justice coordinates consumer services carried on by other government agencies, conducts studies and research in consumer services, and advises executive and legislative branches in matters affecting consumer interests. Also responsible for consumer protection are the Department of Agriculture (weights and measures); the Real Estate, Corporation, and Insurance divisions of the Department of Commerce; and the public utility commissioner.

32BANKING

Consolidations and acquisitions have transformed Oregon's banking system from one characterized by a large number of local banks into one dominated by two large chains—the US National Bank of Oregon and Wells Fargo.

In all, the state had 43 insured commercial banks in 1996, with total assets of $30.4 billion and deposits of $22.9 billion. There were 10 insured savings institutions in 1996, with combined assets of nearly $10.5 billion. By 1996, the Resolution Trust Corporation had resolved three institutions at a cost of $393 million.

33INSURANCE

As of April 1997, Oregon had a total of 53 insurance companies operating in the state, consisting of the following: life and health, 6; property and casualty, 14; health maintenance organizations (HMOs), 10; health, medical, dental, or indemnity corporations (HMDIs), 12; fraternal, 1; title insurers, 3; multiple employer welfare arrangement, 1; and exempt insurers (member-based insurance), 6. Direct premiums written for all types of insurance amounted to over $6.3 billion in 1995, and losses paid at the end of 1995 totaled $1.2 million. At the end of 1995, Oregonians held 2,120,000 life insurance policies valued at $129.8 billion.

The average life insurance per family was $100,700, 19% below the national average. Flood insurance in force in 1991 totaled $1.138 billion.

34SECURITIES

There are no securities or commodities exchanges in Oregon. New York Stock Exchange member firms had sales offices and registered representatives in Oregon to provide services to Oregonians owning shares of public corporations.

35PUBLIC FINANCE

Oregon's biennial budget, covering a period from 1 July of each odd-numbered year to 30 June of the next odd-numbered year, is prepared by the Executive Department and submitted by the governor to the legislature for amendment and approval. Unlike some state budgets, Oregon's is not contained in a single omnibus appropriations bill; instead, each agency appropriation is considered as a separate measure. When the legislature is not in session, fiscal problems are considered by an emergency board of 17 legislators; this board may adjust budgets, allocate money from a special emergency fund, and establish new expenditure limitations, but it cannot enact new general fund appropriations. The Oregon constitution prohibits a state budget deficit and

requires that all general obligation bond issues be submitted to the voters.

The following table summarizes revenues and expenditures for the 1993–95 budget period and for 1995 (in millions of dollars):

	1993–95 ADOPTED	1995 ACTUAL
REVENUES—ALL FUNDS		
Individual taxes	$ 5,379.0	$ 2,797.6
Business taxes	1,983.4	312.0
Federal funds	4,669.2	—
Interest	3,496.2	3,372.1
Loan repayments	1,414.6	—
Bond sales	954.9	—
Charges for services	1,341.3	1,090.0
Liquor and other sales income	387.9	175.6
Licenses and fees	535.6	504.2
Other receipts	2,323.0	4,608.9
Tobacco taxes	220.0	—
Lottery distributions	330.3	—
Motor fuels taxes	688.3	—
TOTAL	$ 23,723.7	12,985,916

	1993–95 ADOPTED	1995 ACTUAL
EXPENDITURES—ALL FUNDS		
Education	$ 6,169.9	3,085.7
Human resources	4,347.5	2,912.7
Public safety	711.9	395.7
Natural resources	995.5	—
Transportation	1,554.1	251.3
Other		6,384.4
TOTAL		$ 11,029.9

As of 1995, the total state and local government debt was $5.5 billion. The per capita state debt was $1,745.

36TAXATION

Oregon's chief source of general revenue is the personal income tax, adopted in 1929; as of 1994, the tax ranged from 5.0% to 9.0%. A corporate income tax of 6.6% is also levied. Local governments rely on the property tax. Oregon does not have a general sales tax, although it does tax sales of gasoline and cigarettes.

The state constitution gives voters the right to vote on any substantial tax increase, either by the state or by local governments. State tax measures may be placed on the ballot by the legislature or by petition; local levies must be voted on yearly unless voter approval has been secured for a tax base that may increase by 6% a year without an additional vote.

In 1995, Oregon had a federal income tax burden of $14.2 million and a per capita burden of $4,552.

37ECONOMIC POLICY

Oregon actively seeks balanced economic growth in order to diversify its industrial base, reduce its dependence on the wood products industry, and provide jobs for a steadily growing labor force. The Economic Development Department offers a variety of financial assistance and incentives to companies which create jobs, particularly for low income residents. It extends loans and issues industrial development bonds for manufacturing, processing and tourism-related facilities in Oregon. The bonds are exempt from federal taxes. The Department enables banks to make loans to projects that carry higher than conventional risk by creating reserve accounts which function as insurance for the banks. To promote new technologies, the Oregon Resource and Technology Development Corporation invests in applied research. The state offers tax credits to encourage businesses to use pollution control facilities, to invest in energy conservation and to employ renewable energy resources.

38HEALTH

In 1995 there were 42,811 live births in Oregon, a rate of 13.6 per 1,000 population. The 1995 infant mortality rate was 4.7 infant deaths per 1,000 live births. In 1992, 12,685 legal abortions were performed in Oregon, a rate of 302 abortions per 1,000 births. The AIDS rate per 100,000 population was 16.40, 42% below the national average in 1995. Major causes of death, with rates per 100,000 population, were heart disease, 240.1; cancer, 214.7; cerebrovascular diseases, 77.7; accidents and adverse effects, 43.5 (of which motor vehicle accidents accounted for 18.9); and suicide, 15.8. The overall death rate of 898.4 per 100,000 population has recently risen to above the national average. Oregon had the 10th-lowest cardiovascular disease mortality rate (164.8 per 100,000 population) in 1992. Stroke was much more common. At least 21.8% of Oregon residents over 18 smoked in 1995.

In 1995, Oregon had 64 hospitals, with 6,402 beds. The average expense to a hospital providing services in the state in 1994 was $1,077 per inpatient day and $5,492 per stay. There were 6,434 active nonfederal physicians in 1994. In 1994, the state had 2,075 active, licensed dentists. Professionally active registered nurses totaled 24,400 during 1994, or 791 employed registered nurses per 100,000 population. Some 13.9% of Oregon residents were uninsured in 1995. The only medical and dental schools in the state are at the University of Oregon Health Sciences University in Portland.

39SOCIAL WELFARE

The Department of Human Resources was created in 1971 to coordinate social service activities. Public assistance payments consist largely of Aid to Families with Dependent Children (AFDC) and medical assistance. AFDC payments were made to 92,000 Oregonians in 1996, with an average monthly payment of $565. Social Security benefits were paid to 544,480 eligible Oregonians in 1995, averaging $732 a month. Federal Supplemental Security Income payments were made to 47,124 residents, averaging $341 a month. In 1996, 287,607 residents received monthly food stamp allowances averaging $75.15. Students enrolled in the school lunch program were subsidized by $47.3 million in federal funds. In 1995 the state's unemployment insurance program paid $183.97 per week on average to eligible recipients.

With the enactment of the Personal Responsibility and Work Opportunity Reconciliation Act of 1996, the US government has changed the form and regulations for many of its social welfare programs; most significantly, it replaces Aid to Families with Dependent Children (AFDC), an open-ended entitlement program, with Temporary Assistance for Needy Families (TANF), a limited system of assistance funded largely through federal block grants. The reform act also impacts the food stamp program, the Supplemental Security Income program, and the child nutrition program. The law took effect on 1 July 1997 and provided $16.38 billion in block grants for fiscal years 1997–2002. The grants are to be divided among the states based on an equation involving the numbers of former AFDC recipients in each state. Because many of the bill's provisions have yet to be implemented into state-by-state policy, it was not possible to include the details of each state's programs for this edition of this work.

40HOUSING

In general, owner-occupied homes predominate in Oregon, and there are few urban slums. During the 1970s and early 1980s,

however, a growing percentage of new construction went for rental units. Between 1970 and 1980, the proportion of the housing stock in single-family units fell from 77% to 68%. In 1996 there were an estimated 1,309,000 housing units in Oregon, of which 1,216,000 were occupied. That year, 27,814 privately owned units, valued at $2.7 billion, were authorized for construction. In 1990, the last year for which figures were available, the median home value was $67,100, down 25.8% from 1980. The median monthly costs for owners (with a mortgage) and renters in 1990 were $650 and $408, respectively.

During 1995/96, Oregon received $232.1 million in aid from the US Department of Housing and Urban Development, including $37.3 million in community development block grants. The Housing Division of the Department of Commerce offers housing purchase assistance (through interest rates below the prevailing market) and construction subsidies to build units for disabled and for low- and moderate-income renters.

41EDUCATION

Oregon has emerged as a leader in a growing nationwide movement to build a superior system of public education. Passed by Oregon's legislature in 1991, the Educational Act for the 21st Century set into motion an extensive restructuring of the state's kindergarten through 12th grade public school system. The Act's goals are to produce the best-educated citizens in the nation and the world. Key components of the Act include: raising academic standards for all students, increasing student skills and abilities needed in the workplace, involving parents in decision-making, assessing student performance, requiring accountability for results, emphasizing early childhood education, providing learning opportunities in partnership with communities, and giving local schools more freedom and autonomy.

In the 1995/96 school year, there were 914 public elementary schools and 232 public secondary schools, with a combined enrollment of 499,361. In school year 1995/96, there were 342 private (mainly independent, nonparochial) elementary and secondary schools and enrollment totaled 38,150 students.

Higher education in Oregon comprises 16 community colleges, 19 independent institutions, and a state higher education system of 8 institutions. The state system had a fall 1993 total enrollment of 59,545 students. University of Oregon in Eugene had the highest regular enrollment (16,593), followed by Portland State University in Portland (14,486) and Oregon State University in Corvallis (14,101).

The Oregon State Scholarship Commission administers an extensive financial aid program for state college students.

Major private higher education institutions include Willamette University, Salem; George Fox College, Newberg; Linfield College, McMinnville; and University of Portland, Reed College, Lewis & Clark College, and Oregon Graduate Institute of Science and Technology, all in Portland.

42ARTS

The Portland Art Museum, with an associated art school, is the city's center for the visual arts. The University of Oregon in Eugene has an art museum specializing in Oriental art.

The state's most noted theatrical enterprise is the annual Shakespeare Festival in Ashland, with a complex of theaters drawing actors and audiences from around the nation. The Oregon Symphony is situated in Portland, and Salem and Eugene have small symphony orchestras of their own.

The Oregon Arts Commission operates a program of direct-mail marketing of fine art prints created by artists from the Northwest. The Commission and the Department of Education jointly administer a program of Young Writers Fellowships.

The total amount of federal aid to Oregon for the support of its arts programs was $781,000 in 1996. The Oregon Arts

Commission received $922,000 from the NEA. Arts organizations in the state also received $1,483,000. The state, as well as private sources, contributed funding. Audiences for the state's programs numbered about 32,573,000 people. There were 154,137 contributing artists. The state provided art education programs for 82,000 school children. In 1995, the state had 300 arts associations and 60 local arts groups. The Oregon Arts Commission assisted the Budges Teen Theatre and the Eugene Ballet. The NEA contributed to the Oregon Shakespeare Festival and to the Oregon Symphony Association. The Oregon Arts commission receives grants to develop the state's art education programs.

The Commission also received funds from the NEA's state and regional program.

43LIBRARIES AND MUSEUMS

In 1996/97, Oregon had over 600 academic, public, and special libraries, including branches; the total book stock of all public libraries was 7,333,827, and their combined circulation was 27,835,910. Most cities and counties in Oregon have public library systems, the largest being the Multnomah County library system in Portland, with 14 branches and 1,367,010 volumes in 1996/97. The State Library in Salem, with over 1.3 million volumes in 1991/92, serves as a reference agency for state government.

Oregon has 79 museums, historic sites, botanical gardens and arboretums. Historical museums emphasizing Oregon's pioneer heritage appear throughout the state, with Ft. Clatsop National Memorial—featuring a replica of Lewis and Clark's winter headquarters—among the notable attractions. The Oregon Historical Society operates a major historical museum in Portland, publishes books of historical interest, and issues the *Oregon Historical Quarterly*. In Portland's Washington Park area are the Oregon Museum of Science and Industry, Washington Park Zoo, Western Forestry Center, and an arboretum and other gardens.

44COMMUNICATIONS

As of March 1993, 92.8% of Oregon's 1,214,000 households had telephones. Oregon had 88 AM and 114 FM commercial radio stations in 1996; 6 of the state's 23 commercial television stations were in Portland. A state-owned broadcasting system, which includes 8 television stations, provides educational radio and television programming. As of 1996, 7 large cable television systems served Oregon.

45PRESS

Oregon's first newspaper was the weekly *Oregon Spectator*, which began publication in 1846. Early newspapers engaged in what became known as the "Oregon style" of journalism, characterized by intemperate, vituperative, and fiercely partisan comments. As of 1997, 17 daily and 59 weekly newspapers were published in Oregon. The state's largest newspaper, the *Oregonian*, published in Portland, is owned by the Newhouse group. The following table lists leading Oregon newspapers with their 1997 circulations:

AREA	NAME	DAILY	SUNDAY
Eugene	*Register–Guard* (e,S)	75,881	79,428
Portland	*Oregonian* (m,S)	349,193	445,293
Salem	*Statesman–Journal* (m)	60,131	70,322

46ORGANIZATIONS

The 1992 Census of Service Industries counted 1,013 organizations in Oregon, including 256 business associations; 536 civic, social, and fraternal associations; and 221 other membership organizations. Among the many forestry-related organizations in Oregon are the International Woodworkers of America (AFL-CIO), Association of Western Pulp and Paper Workers, Pacific Lumber Exporters Association, Western Forest Industries Association, and Western Wood Products Association, all with their headquarters in Portland.

47TOURISM, TRAVEL, AND RECREATION

Oregon's abundance and variety of natural features and recreational opportunities make the state a major tourist attraction. Travel and tourism is the state's 3d-largest employer, generating thousands of jobs. Domestic travelers spent $3,795,000 on overnight and day trips in 1993. The Travel Information Council of the Department of Transportation maintains an active tourist advertising program, and Portland hotels busily seek major conventions.

Among the leading attractions are the rugged Oregon coast, with its offshore salmon fishing; Crater Lake National Park; the Rogue River, for river running and fishing; the Columbia Gorge, east of Portland; the Cascades wilderness; and Portland's annual Rose Festival. Oregon has one national park, Crater Lake, and three other areas—John Day Fossil Beds National Monument, Oregon Caves National Monument and Ft. Clatsop National Memorial—managed by the National Park Service. The US Forest Service administers the Oregon Dunes National Recreation Area, on the Oregon coast; the Lava Lands Visitor Complex near Bend; and the Hells Canyon National Recreation Area, east of Enterprise. Oregon has one of the nation's most extensive state park systems: 225 parks and recreation areas cover 90,000 acres (36,400 hectares).

48SPORTS

Oregon's lone major professional team, based in Portland, is the Trail Blazers, winners of the National Basketball Association championship in 1977. The Portland Beavers compete in baseball's class–AAA Pacific Coast League.

Horse racing takes place at Portland Meadows in Portland and, in late August and early September, at the Oregon State Fair in Salem; there is greyhound racing at the Multnomah Kennel Club near Portland. Parimutuel betting is permitted at the tracks, but off-track betting is prohibited.

The University of Oregon and Oregon State University belong to the Pacific 10 Conference. The Oregon State Ducks won the Rose Bowl in 1942 and appeared in it but lost in 1965. Oregon was a surprise winner at the PAC-10 in 1994, and made its first Rose Bowl appearance in 37 years. The Ducks lost to Penn State in the 1995 Rose Bowl.

Other annual sporting events include sled dog races in Bend and Union Creek, the All-Indian Rodeo in Tygh Valley in May (one of many rodeos), and the Cycle Oregon Bike Ride.

49FAMOUS OREGONIANS

Prominent federal officeholders from Oregon include Senator Charles McNary (1874–1944), a leading advocate of federal reclamation and development projects and the Republican vice-presidential nominee in 1940; Senator Wayne Morse (b.Wisconsin, 1900–1974), who was an early opponent of US involvement in Viet-Nam; Representative Edith Green (1910–1984), a leader in federal education assistance; and Representative Al Ullman (b.Montana, 1914–1986), chairman of the House Ways and Means Committee until his defeat in 1980. Recent cabinet members from Oregon have been Douglas McKay (1893–1959), secretary of the interior; and Neil Goldschmidt (b.1940) secretary of transportation.

A major figure in early Oregon history was sea captain Robert Gray (b.Rhode Island. 1755–1806), discoverer of the Columbia River. Although never holding a government position, fur trader Dr. John McLoughlin (b.Canada, 1784–1857) in effect ruled Oregon from 1824 to 1845; he was officially designated the "father of Oregon" by the 1957 state legislature. Also of importance in the early settlement was Methodist missionary Jason Lee (b.Canada, 1803–45). Oregon's most famous Indian was Chief Joseph (1840?–1904), leader of the Nez Percé in northeastern Oregon; when tension between the Nez Percé and white settlers erupted into open hostilities in 1877, Chief Joseph led his band of about 650 men, women, and children from the Oregon-Idaho border across the Bitterroot Range evading three army detachments before being captured in northern Montana.

Other important figures in the early days of statehood were Harvey W. Scott (b.Illinois 1838–1910), longtime editor of the Portland *Oregonian,* and his sister, Abigail Scott Duniway (b.Illinois, 1823–1915), the Northwest's foremost advocate of women's suffrage, a cause her brother strongly opposed. William Simon U'Ren (b.Wisconsin, 1859–1949) was a lawyer and reformer whose influence on Oregon politics and government endures to this day. Journalist and Communist John Reed (1887–1920), author of *Ten Days That Shook the World,* an eyewitness account of the Bolshevik Revolution, was born in Portland, and award-winning science-fiction writer Ursula K. LeGuin (b.California, 1929) is a Portland resident. Linus Pauling (1901–94), two-time winner of the Nobel Prize (for chemistry in 1954, for peace in 1962), was another Portland native. Other scientists prominent in the state's history include botanist David Douglas (b.Scotland, 1798–1834), who made two trips to Oregon and after whom the Douglas fir is named; and geologist and paleontologist Thomas Condon (b.Ireland, 1822–1907), discoverer of major fossil beds in eastern Oregon.

[50]BIBLIOGRAPHY

Blair, Karen J. *Northwest Women: An Annotated Bibliography of Sources on the History of Oregon and Washington Women, 1787–1970.* Pullman, Wash.: Washington State University Press, 1997.

Cogswell, Philip. *Capitol Names: Individuals Woven into Oregon's History.* Portland: Oregon Historical Society, 1977.

Corning, Howard. *Dictionary of Oregon History.* Portland: Binfords & Mort, 1956.

Dodds, Gordon B. *Oregon: A Bicentennial History.* New York: Norton, 1977.

Federal Writers' Project. *Oregon: End of the Trail.* 1941. Reprint, New York: Somerset, n.d.

Johansen, Dorothy, and Charles Gates. *Empire of the Columbia: A History of the Pacific Northwest.* 2d ed. New York: Harper & Row, 1967.

Loy, William. *Atlas of Oregon.* Eugene: University of Oregon Books, 1976.

Parkman, Francis, Jr. *The Oregon Trail.* New York: Penguin, 1982.

Throckmorton, Arthur L. *Oregon Argonauts: Merchant Adventurers on the Western Frontier.* Portland: Oregon Historical Society, 1961.

Vaughan, Thomas, and Terrence O'Donnell. *Portland: A Historical Sketch and Guide.* Portland: Oregon Historical Society, 1976.

PENNSYLVANIA

Commonwealth of Pennsylvania

ORIGIN OF STATE NAME: Named for Admiral William Penn, father of the founder of Pennsylvania. **NICKNAME:** The Keystone State. **CAPITAL:** Harrisburg. **ENTERED UNION:** 12 December 1787 (2d). **MOTTO:** Virtue, Liberty, and Independence. **COAT OF ARMS:** A shield supported by two horses displays a sailing ship, a plow, and three sheaves of wheat; an eagle forms the crest. Beneath the shield an olive branch and a cornstalk are crossed, and below them is the state motto. **FLAG:** The coat of arms appears in the center of a blue field. **OFFICIAL SEAL:** OBVERSE: A shield displays a sailing ship, a plow, and three sheaves of wheat, with a cornstalk to the left, an olive branch to the right, and an eagle above, surrounded by the inscription "Seal of the State of Pennsylvania." REVERSE: A woman representing Liberty holds a wand topped by a liberty cap in her left hand and a drawn sword in her right, as she tramples a lion representing Tyranny; the legend "Both Can't Survive" encircles the design. **ANIMAL:** White-tailed deer. **BIRD:** Ruffed grouse. **DOG:** Great Dane. **FISH:** Brook trout. **INSECT:** Firefly. **FLOWER:** Mountain laurel. **TREE:** Hemlock. **BEAUTIFICATION AND CONSERVATION PLANT:** Penngift crownvetch. **BEVERAGE:** Milk. **FOSSIL:** Phacops rana. **LEGAL HOLIDAYS:** New Year's Day, 1 January; Birthday of Martin Luther King, Jr., 3d Monday in January; Presidents' Day, 3d Monday in February; Memorial Day, last Monday in May; Flag Day, 14 June; Independence Day, 4 July; Labor Day, 1st Monday in September; Columbus Day, 2d Monday in October; Veterans Day, 11 November; Thanksgiving Day, 4th Thursday in November; Christmas Day, 25 December. **TIME:** 7 AM EST = noon GMT.

¹LOCATION, SIZE, AND EXTENT

Located in the northeastern US, the Commonwealth of Pennsylvania is the 2d largest of the three Middle Atlantic states and ranks 33d in size among the 50 states.

The total area of Pennsylvania is 45,308 sq mi (117,348 sq km), of which land occupies 44,888 sq mi (116,260 sq km) and inland water 420 sq mi (1,088 sq km). The state extends 307 mi (494 km) E-W and 169 mi (272 km) N-S. Pennsylvania is rectangular in shape, except for an irregular side on the E and a break in the even boundary in the NW where the line extends N-E for about 50 mi (80 km) along the shore of Lake Erie.

Pennsylvania is bordered on the N by New York; on the E by New York and New Jersey (with the Delaware River forming the entire boundary); on the SE by Delaware; on the S by Maryland and West Virginia (demarcated by the Mason-Dixon line); on the W by West Virginia and Ohio; and on the NW by Lake Erie. The total boundary length of Pennsylvania is 880 mi (1,416 km). The state's geographical center lies in Centre County, 2.5 mi (4 km) SW of Bellefonte.

²TOPOGRAPHY

Pennsylvania may be divided into more than a dozen distinct physiographic regions, most of which extend in curved bands from east to south. Beginning in the southeast, the first region (including Philadelphia) is a narrow belt of coastal plain along the lower Delaware River; this area, at sea level, is the state's lowest region. The next belt, dominating the southeastern corner, is the Piedmont Plateau, a wide area of rolling hills and lowlands. The Great Valley, approximately 10–15 mi (16–24 km) in width, runs from the middle of the state's eastern border to the middle of its southern border. The eastern, central, and western parts of the Great Valley are known as the Lehigh, Lebanon, and Cumberland valleys, respectively. West and north of the Great Valley, the Pocono Plateau rises to about 2,200 feet (700 meters). Next, in a band 50–60 mi (80–100 km) wide most of the way from the

north-central part of the eastern border to the west-central part of the southern border are the Appalachian Mountains, a distinctive region of parallel ridges and valleys.

The Allegheny High Plateau, part of the Appalachian Plateaus, makes up the western and northern parts of the state. The Allegheny Front, the escarpment along the eastern edge of the plateau, is the most striking topographical feature in Pennsylvania, dissected by many winding streams to form narrow, steep-sided valleys; the southwestern extension of the Allegheny High Plateau contains the state's highest peak, Mt. Davis, at 3,213 feet (979 meters). A narrow lowland region, the Erie Plain, borders Lake Erie in the extreme northwestern part of the state.

According to federal sources, Pennsylvania has jurisdiction over 735 sq mi (1,904 sq km) of Lake Erie; the state government gives a figure of 891 sq mi (2,308 sq km). Pennsylvania contains about 250 natural lakes larger than 20 acres (8 hectares), most of them in the glaciated regions of the northeast and northwest. The largest natural lake within the state's borders is Conneaut Lake, about 30 mi (48 km) south of the city of Erie, with an area of less than 1.5 sq mi (39 sq km); the largest manmade lake is Lake Wallenpaupack, in the Poconos, occupying about 9 sq mi (23 sq km). Pennsylvania claims more than 21 sq mi (54 sq km) of the Pymatuning Reservoir, on the Ohio border.

The Susquehanna River and its tributaries drain more than 46% of the area of Pennsylvania, much of it in the Appalachian Mountains. The Delaware River forms Pennsylvania's eastern border and, like the Susquehanna, flows southeastward to the Atlantic Ocean. Most of the western part of the state is drained by the Allegheny and Monongahela rivers, which join at Pittsburgh to form the Ohio. The Beaver, Clarion, and Youghiogheny rivers are also important parts of this system.

During early geological history, the topography of Pennsylvania had the reverse of its present configurations, with mountains in the southeast and a large inland sea covering the rest of the state. This sea, which alternately expanded and contracted, interwove layers of vegetation (which later became coal) with layers of sandstone and shale.

³CLIMATE

Although Pennsylvania lies entirely within the humid continental zone, its climate varies according to region and elevation. The regions with the warmest temperatures and the longest growing seasons are the low-lying southwest Ohio valley and the Monongahela valley in the southeast. The region bordering Lake Erie also has a long growing season, as the moderating effect of the lake prevents early spring and late autumn frosts. The first two areas have hot summers, while the Erie area is more moderate. The rest of the state, at higher elevations, has cold winters and cool summers.

Among the major population centers, Philadelphia has an annual mean temperature of 54°F (12°C), with a normal minimum of 45°F (7°C) and a normal maximum of 64°F (18°C). Pittsburgh has an annual mean of 50°F (10°C), with a minimum of 41°F (5°C) and a maximum of 60°F (16°C). In the cooler northern areas, Scranton has a normal annual mean ranging from 41°F (5°C) to 59°F (15°C); Erie, from 42°F (6°C) to 58°F (14°C). The record low temperature for the state is –42°F (–41°C), set at Smethport on 5 January 1904; the record high, 111°F (44°C), was reached at Phoenixville on 10 July 1936.

Philadelphia has about 41 in (104 cm) of precipitation annually, and Pittsburgh has 36 in (91 cm). Pittsburgh, however, has much more snow—45 in (114 cm), compared with 22 in (56 cm) for Philadelphia. The snowfall in Erie, in the snow belt, exceeds 54 in (137 cm) per year, with heavy snows sometimes experienced late in April. In Philadelphia, the sun shines an average of 57% of the time; in Pittsburgh, 49%.

The state has experienced several destructive floods. On 31 May 1889, the South Fork Dam near Johnstown broke after a heavy rainfall, and its rampaging waters killed 2,200 people and devastated the entire city in less than 10 minutes. On 19–20 July 1977, Johnstown experienced another flood, resulting in 68 deaths. Three tornadoes raked the southwestern part of the commonwealth on 23 June 1944, killing 45 persons and injuring another 362. Rains from Hurricane Agnes in June 1972 resulted in floods that caused 48 deaths and more than $1.2 billion worth of property damage in the Susquehanna Valley.

⁴FLORA AND FAUNA

Maple, walnut, poplar, oak, pine, ash, beech, and linden trees fill Pennsylvania's extensive forests, along with sassafras, sycamore, weeping willow, and balsam fir (Abies fraseri). Red pine and paper birch are found in the north, while the sweet gum is dominant in the extreme southwest. Mountain laurel (the state flower), June-berry, dotted hawthorn, New Jersey tea, and various dogwoods are among the shrubs and small trees found in most parts of the state, and dewberry, wintergreen, wild columbine, and wild ginger are also common. The wild red rose is classified as threatened, the small whorled pogonia as endangered.

Numerous mammals persist in Pennsylvania, among them the white-tailed deer (the state animal), black bear, red and gray foxes, opossum, raccoon, muskrat, mink, snowshoe hare, common cottontail, and red, gray, fox, and flying squirrels. Native amphibians include the hellbender, Fowler's toad, and the tree, cricket, and true frogs; among reptilian species are the five-lined and black skinks and five varieties of lizard. The ruffed grouse, a common game species, is the official state bird; other game birds are the wood dove, ring-necked pheasant, bobwhite quail, and mallard and black ducks. The robin, cardinal, English sparrow, red-eyed vireo, cedar waxwing, tufted titmouse, yellow-shafted flicker, barn swallow, blue jay, and killdeer are common nongame birds. More than 170 types of fish have been identified

in Pennsylvania, with brown and brook trout, grass pickerel, bigeye chub, pirate perch, and white bass among the common native varieties.

In 1978, the Pennsylvania Game Commission and the US Fish and Wildlife Service signed a cooperative agreement under which the federal government provides two dollars for each dollar spent by the state to determine the status of and improve conditions for threatened or endangered species. On the endangered list are the brown (grizzly) bear, Indiana bat, Delmarva Peninsula fox squirrel, eastern cougar, bald eagle, American and Arctic peregrine falcons, Kirkland's warbler, orange-footed pearly mussel, and pink mucket pearly mussel.

⁵ENVIRONMENTAL PROTECTION

Pennsylvania's environment was ravaged by uncontrolled timber cutting in the 19th century, and by extensive coal mining and industrial development until recent times. Pittsburgh's most famous landmarks were its smokestacks, and it was said that silverware on ships entering the port of Philadelphia would tarnish immediately from the fumes of the Delaware River. The anthracite-mining regions were filled with huge, hideous culm piles, and the bituminous and anthracite fields were torn up by strip-mining. In 1979, a different kind of threat to Pennsylvania's environment received worldwide attention when the nuclear power plant at Three Mile Island seriously malfunctioned.

In 1895, Pennsylvania appointed its first commissioner of forestry, in an attempt to repair some of the earlier damage. Gifford Pinchot, who twice served as governor of Pennsylvania, was the first professionally trained forester in the US (he studied at the École National Forestiere in Paris), developed the US Forest Service, and served as Pennsylvania forest commissioner from 1920 to 1922. In 1955, the state forests were put under scientific management.

In 1972, Pennsylvania voters ratified a state constitutional amendment adopted 18 May 1971, acknowledging the people's "right to clean air, pure water, and to the preservation of the natural, scenic, historic, and esthetic values of the environment" and naming the state as trustee of these resources. Passage of the amendment came only two years after establishment of the Pennsylvania Department of Environmental Resources, which in the 1990s was reorganized into two separate entities. The Department of Conservation and Natural Resources (DCNR) was established on 1 July 1995 to maintain and preserve the state's 116 state parks, manage the 2.1 million acres of state forest land, and provide information on the state's ecological and geologic resources. The DCNR also oversees environmental education and provides assistance and grants for preserving rivers, community trails, parks, and recreation. The Pennsylvania Department of Environmental Protection was established to protect the state's air, land, and water from pollution and to provide a cleaner environment for the health and safety of Pennsylvania's citizens.

As of the early 1990s, sewage and industrial wastes were the major pollutants in areas with high industrial and population concentrations. In western and parts of central Pennsylvania, drainage from abandoned bituminous coal mines created serious water quality problems; active mines in this region were also potentially polluting. A similar situation prevailed in the anthracite areas of northeastern Pennsylvania. Oil and gas well operations, located primarily in the northwestern portion of the commonwealth, were additional pollution sources. The state has 102 hazardous waste sites, the second-highest concentration of such sites in the nation. In 1996, there were 404,000 acres of wetlands in the state.

In March 1979, Pennsylvania suffered the worst nuclear-power accident in US history when a nuclear reactor on Three Mile Island malfunctioned and radioactive gases escaped. A

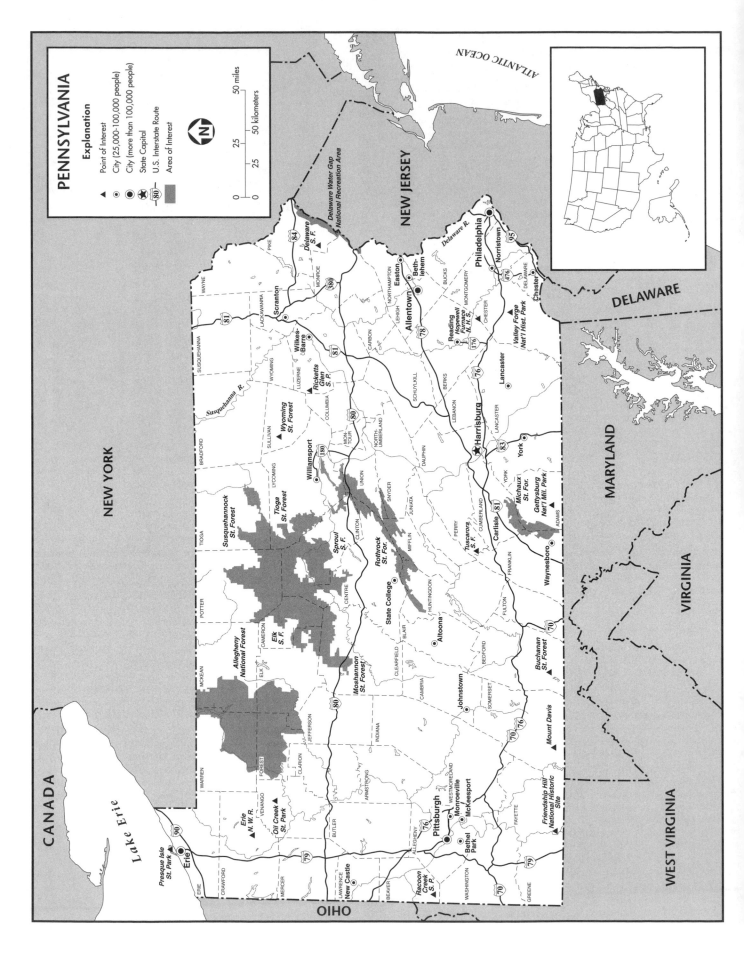

PENNSYLVANIA

Explanation

▲ Point of Interest
⊙ City (25,000-100,000 people)
◉ City (more than 100,000 people)
★ State Capital
—80— U.S. Interstate Route
▨ Area of Interest

50 miles
50 kilometers
0 25 50

CANADA

Lake Erie

NEW YORK

OIHO

Presque Isle St. Park
Erie
Erie N.W.R.
Oil Creek St. Park
New Castle
Racoon Creek S.P.

WARREN
McKEAN
POTTER
TIOGA
BRADFORD
SUSQUEHANNA
WAYNE
PIKE

Allegheny National Forest
Susquehannock St. Forest
Tioga St. Forest
Wyoming St. Forest
Elk S.F.
Sproul S.F.
Moshannon St. Forest
Rothrock St. For.
Tuscarora S.F.
Michaux St. For.
Buchanan St. Forest

ELK
CAMERON
FOREST
VENANGO
JEFFERSON
CLARION
ARMSTRONG
BUTLER
LAWRENCE
MERCER
CRAWFORD
ERIE

Delaware S.F.
MONROE
Delaware Water Gap National Recreation Area

Scranton
LACKAWANNA
WYOMING
SULLIVAN
LYCOMING
CLINTON
CENTRE
Williamsport
Ricketts Glen S.P.
Wilkes-Barre
LUZERNE
COLUMBIA
MONTOUR
NORTH-UMBERLAND
UNION
SNYDER
MIFFLIN
JUNIATA
PERRY

State College
Altoona
HUNTINGDON
BLAIR
CLEARFIELD
CAMBRIA
INDIANA
Johnstown
SOMERSET
Mount Davis
Friendship Hill National Historic Site
FAYETTE
GREENE
WASHINGTON
BEAVER

Pittsburgh
Monroeville
McKeesport
Bethel Park
WESTMORELAND
ALLEGHENY

NEW JERSEY
ATLANTIC OCEAN

Easton
Beth-lehem
NORTHAMPTON
LEHIGH
Allentown
CARBON
SCHUYLKILL
DAUPHIN
Harrisburg
York
YORK
Carlisle
CUMBERLAND
FRANKLIN
FULTON
BEDFORD
Waynesboro
Gettysburg Nat'l Mil. Park
ADAMS

Reading
Hopewell Furnace N.H.S.
BERKS
LEBANON
LANCASTER
Lancaster
CHESTER
Valley Forge Nat'l Hist. Park
MONTGOMERY
BUCKS
Norristown
Philadelphia
DELAWARE
Chester

Delaware R.
Susquehanna R.

DELAWARE
MARYLAND
VIRGINIA
WEST VIRGINIA

84
380
81
81
80
180
80
79
76
70
76
70
90
95
476
78
76
176
83
81
70
79

second reactor was shut down immediately even though it was not damaged. The cleanup of radioactive waste cost about $1 billion, and it was not until late 1985 that the undamaged unit was placed back in operation.

An oil spill at Marcus Hook, near the Delaware Border, released 435,000 gallons of crude oil into the Delaware River in September 1985; damage to birds and wetlands was more extensive in Delaware than in Pennsylvania.

⁶POPULATION

As recently as 1940, Pennsylvania was the second most populous state in the US. By the 1980 census, however, the state had slipped to 4th place, with a population of 11,863,895; it dropped to 5th place in 1990 with a population of 11,881,643. The 1996 estimate was 12,056,112, up 1.5% from 1990.

As of 1990, 48% of the population was male, 52% female; 68.9% of all Pennsylvanians lived in urban areas. The population density in 1990 was 265.1 per sq mi (102 per sq km), making Pennsylvania the 8th most densely populated state in the US. There are fewer young people and more persons aged 65 or over represented in the state's population than in the US as a whole: as of 1989, 19.7% of the state's population was under age 18, while 15.1% was over 65. Population projections by the US Census Bureau suggest that Pennsylvania will experience a 1.6% population increase between 1990 and 2000.

The largest city in the state, Philadelphia, was the 5th-largest US city as of 1990, with a population of 1,585,577; the estimated 1994 population was 1,524,249. Philadelphia's population has declined since 1970, when 1,949,996 people lived there. The population of its metropolitan area also declined during the 1970s, but then increased from 4,716,559 in 1980 to 4,922,257 in 1990 and an estimated 4,950,866 in 1995. Further, the larger Philadelphia–Wilmington, Del.–Trenton, N.J. consolidated metropolitan area increased from 5,680,509 in 1980 to an estimated 5,967,323. Pittsburgh's population declined from 616,806 in 1950 to an estimated 358,883 in 1994 in the city proper; the Pittsburgh metropolitan area population went from 2,348,000 in 1970 to 2,139,000 in 1990.

The 1994 estimated populations of Pennsylvania's other major cities were Erie, 108,398; Allentown, 105,339; Reading, 78,246; Scranton, 77,964; Bethlehem, 72,821; Lancaster, 55,551; Harrisburg, 54,238; Altoona, 52,521; and Wilkes-Barre, 45,645.

⁷ETHNIC GROUPS

During the colonial period, under the religious tolerance of a Quaker government, Pennsylvania was a haven for dissident sectarians from continental Europe and the British Isles. Some German sectarians, including the Amish, have kept up their traditions to this day. An initially friendly policy toward the Indians waned in the late 18th century under the pressures of population growth and the anxieties of the French and Indian War. The famous Carlisle Indian School (1879–1918) educated many leaders from various tribes throughout the US. In Pennsylvania itself, however, there were only 15,000 American Indians as of 1990.

Modest numbers of black slaves were utilized as domestics, field workers, and iron miners in colonial Pennsylvania.

Pennsylvania Counties, County Seats, and County Areas and Populations

COUNTY	COUNTY SEAT	LAND AREA (SQ MI)	POPULATION (1996 EST.)	COUNTY	COUNTY SEAT	LAND AREA (SQ MI)	POPULATION (1996 EST.)
Adams	Gettysburg	521	84,921	Lancaster	Lancaster	952	450,834
Allegheny	Pittsburgh	727	1,296,037	Lawrence	New Castle	363	95,780
Armstrong	Kittanning	646	73,872	Lebanon	Lebanon	363	117,179
Beaver	Beaver	436	187,009	Lehigh	Allentown	348	297,802
Bedford	Bedford	1,017	49,322	Luzerne	Wilkes-Barre	891	321,309
Berks	Reading	861	352,353	Lycoming	Williamsport	1,237	119,083
Blair	Hollidaysburg	527	131,450	McKean	Smethport	1,237	48,156
Bradford	Towanda	1,152	62,352	Mercer	Mercer	672	122,155
Bucks	Doylestown	610	578,715	Mifflin	Lewistown	413	47,006
Butler	Butler	789	167,732	Monroe	Stroudsburg	609	119,581
Cambria	Ebensburg	691	158,500	Montgomery	Norristown	486	708,782
Cameron	Emporium	398	5,745	Montour	Danville	131	18,044
Carbon	Jim Thorpe	384	58,783	Northhampton	Easton	376	257,719
Centre	Bellefonte	1,106	131,489	Northumberland	Sunbury	461	95,897
Chester	West Chester	758	410,744	Perry	New Bloomfield	557	43,727
Clarion	Clarion	607	42,205	Philadelphia	Philadelphia	136	1,478,002
Clearfield	Clearfield	1,149	79,640	Pike	Milford	550	38,139
Clinton	Lock Haven	891	37,130	Potter	Coudersport	1,081	17,103
Columbia	Bloomsburg	486	64,079	Schuylkill	Pottsville	782	153,630
Crawford	Meadville	1,011	89,175	Snyder	Middleburg	329	38,034
Cumberland	Carlisle	547	207,042	Somerset	Somerset	1,073	80,517
Dauphin	Harrisburg	528	246,807	Sullivan	Laporte	451	6,145
Delaware	Media	184	547,592	Susquehanna	Montrose	826	42,002
Elk	Ridgeway	830	35,141	Tioga	Wellsboro	1,131	41,510
Erie	Erie	804	280,570	Union	Lewisburg	317	40,826
Fayette	Uniontown	794	145,628	Venango	Franklin	679	58,820
Forest	Tionesta	428	4,942	Warren	Warren	885	44,624
Franklin	Chambersburg	774	127,035	Washington	Washington	858	206,708
Fulton	McConnellsburg	438	14,435	Wayne	Honesdale	731	44,718
Greene	Waynesburg	577	42,054	Westmoreland	Greensburg	1,033	376,297
Huntingdon	Huntingdon	877	44,977	Wyoming	Tunkhannock	399	29,362
Indiana	Indiana	829	90,073	York	York	906	368,322
Jefferson	Brookville	657	46,624				
Juniata	Mifflintown	392	21,793	TOTALS		45,150	12,056,112
Lackawanna	Scranton	461	213,323				

Antislavery sentiment was stirred in the 18th century through the efforts of a Quaker, John Woolman, and other Pennsylvanians. The Gradual Abolition of Slavery Act was passed in 1780, and the important antislavery newspaper *The Liberator* appeared in Philadelphia in 1831. Today, black Americans are concentrated in the large cities. Pennsylvania's black population in 1990 was 1,090,000, amounting to 9.2% of the state's population as a whole. Philadelphia was almost 40% black in 1990, Pittsburgh 25%. By 1996, the state's black population had risen to an estimated 1,310,000 (10.8%).

The late 19th and early 20th centuries brought waves of immigrants from Ireland, Wales, various Slavic nations, and the eastern Mediterranean and the Balkans. Many of the new immigrants settled in the east-central anthracite coal-mining region. In 1990, 3.1% of all Pennsylvania residents were foreign-born; Italy, Germany, the United Kingdom, India, the former Soviet Union, Korea, and Poland were the leading countries of origin. In the valleys surrounding Pittsburgh there are still self-contained ethnic enclaves, and there has been increased interest in preserving distinctive ethnic traditions.

Hispanic Americans in Pennsylvania numbered 232,000 in 1990 and an estimated 286,000 in 1996. Most were Puerto Ricans, with smaller numbers of Cubans and Central Americans. In 1990, the Asian population included 25,908 Chinese, 25,800 Koreans, 19,769 Asian Indians, 14,474 Filipinos, and 14,126 Vietnamese.

8LANGUAGES

Once home to several Algonkian tribes, Pennsylvania still has such Algonkian place-names as Punxsutawney, Aliquippa, Pocono, Towanda, Susquehanna, and Shamokin. An Iroquoian tribe gave its name to the Conestoga region. The word came to identify first the pioneers' covered wagons manufactured in the area and then, in shortened form, a cheap cigar called a *stogie*.

Although not quite homogeneous, Pennsylvania's North Midland dialect is significant as the source of much midwestern and western speech. The only non-Midland sector is the northern tier of counties, settled from southern New York State, where features of the northern dialect predominate.

On the whole, Pennsylvania North Midland is distinguished by the presence of *want off* a tram or bus, *snake feeder* (dragonfly), *run* (small stream), *waterspouts* and *spouts* (gutters), and *creek* as /krik/. With these features are found others that commonly occur in Southern Pennsylvania, such as *corn pone*, *roasting ears*, and *spiket* (spigot). Western Pennsylvania, however, contrasts with the eastern half by the dominance of /nawthing/ for *nothing*, /greezy/ for *greasy*, /kao/ for *cow*, *sugar tree* (sugar maple), *hap* (quilt), and *clothes press* (closet), as well as by the influential merging of the /ah/ vowel and the /aw/ vowel so that *cot* and *caught* sound alike. Southern Pennsylvania has *flannel cakes* for pancakes and *ground hackie* for chipmunk. Within this region, Philadelphia and its suburbs have distinctive *baby coach* for baby carriage, *pavement* for sidewalk, *hoagie* for a large sandwich, the vowel of *put* in *broom* and *Cooper*, and the vowel of *father* in *on* and *fog*. In the east and northeast, a doughnut is a *cruller*, one is *sick in the stomach*, and *syrup* has the vowel of *sit*.

In much of central Pennsylvania, descendants of the colonial Palatinate German population retain their speech as Deutsch, often misnamed Pennsylvania Dutch, which has influenced English in the state through such loanwords as *toot* (bag), *rainworm* (earthworm), *snits* (dried apples), and *smearcase* (cottage cheese).

In 1990, 10,278,294 Pennsylvanians—92.7% of the population 5 years old or older—spoke only English at home. Other languages spoken at home included:

Spanish	213,096	French	45,515
(up 52% from 1980)		Chinese	24,857
Italian	103,844	Greek	17,982
(down 27% from 1980)		Korean	18,116
German	78,499	Indic	17,401
Other West Germanic	56,517	Russian	13,929
Polish	55,344	Various southern Slavic	11,936
		Other Slavic	40,540

9RELIGIONS

With a long history of toleration, Pennsylvania has been a haven for numerous religious groups.

The first European settlers were Swedish Lutherans; German Lutherans began arriving 1703. William Penn brought the Quakers to Pennsylvania during the 1680s, and the climate of religious liberty soon attracted other dissident groups, including German Mennonites, Dunkars, Moravians, and Schwenkfelders; French Huguenots; Scots-Irish Presbyterians; and English Baptists. Descendants of the 16th-century Anabaptists, the Mennonites for the most part settled as farmers; they and the Quakers were the first religious groups openly to advocate abolition of slavery and to help runaway slaves to freedom via the Underground Railroad. The Amish-Mennonite followers of Jacob Amman continue to dress in black clothing, shun the use of mechanized tools, automobiles and electrical appliance, and observe Sundays by singing 16th-century hymns.

The Presbyterians, who built their first church in the state in 1704, played a major role both in the establishment of schools in the colony and in the later development of Pittsburgh and other cities in the western part of the state. Methodists held their first services in Philadelphia in 1768; for many years thereafter, Methodist circuit riders proselytized throughout the state.

Immigration during the 19th century brought a major change in patterns of worship. The Quakers gradually diminished in number and influence, while Roman Catholic and Greek Orthodox churches and Jewish synagogues opened in many of the mining and manufacturing centers. The bulk of the Jewish migration came, after 1848, from Germany and, after 1882, from East Europe and Russia. The Gilded Age saw the founding of a new group in Pittsburgh by clergyman Charles Taze Russell; first called the Russellites, members of this group are known today as Jehovah's Witnesses.

As of 1990, Roman Catholic constituted the largest religious group in the state, with a total population of 3,675,250. The largest Protestant denomination in 1990 was the United Methodists, with 722,871 adherents. Other Protestant groups were the Evangelical Lutheran Church in America, 682,111; United Presbyterians, 388,774; German Reformed (United Church of Christ), 284,275; and Episcopalians, 138,152. The historically important Mennonites had 50,009 adherents in 1990; Friends USA (Quakers), 12,081; and Moravians, 11,724. The Jewish population living in Pennsylvania as of 1990 was 329,651.

10TRANSPORTATION

Like so many of its industrial assets, Pennsylvania's well-developed road and rail networks are showing signs of old age. Nevertheless, the state remains an important center of transportation, and its ports are among the busiest in the US.

The early years of railroad building left Pennsylvania with more miles of track than any other state. The first railroad charter, issued in 1819, provided for a horse-drawn railroad from the Delaware Valley to the headwaters of the Lehigh River. The state authorized construction of a line between Columbia and Philadelphia in 1828, and partial service began four years later as part of the State Works. The roadbed was state-owned, and private rail car companies paid a toll to use the rails. During this time, Pennsylvanians John Jervis and Joseph Harrison were developing steam-powered locomotives. Taking advantage of the new technology were separate rail lines connecting Philadelphia with Germantown (1834), Trenton, N.J. (1838), and Reading (1839), with the Lehigh Valley (1846), and with New York City (1855). In December 1852, the Pennsylvania Central completed lines connecting Philadelphia and Pittsburgh. Five years later, the Pennsylvania Railroad purchased the State Works, eliminating state competition and tolls. By 1880, the company (which had added many smaller coal hauling lines to its holdings) was the world's largest corporation, with more than 30,000 employees and $400 million in capital. Although railroad revenues declined with the rise of the automobile, the Pennsylvania Railroad remained profitable until the 1960s, when the line merged with the New York Central to form the Penn Central. In 1970, the Penn Central separated its real estate holdings from its transportation operation, on which it declared bankruptcy.

As of 1995, the major (Class I) lines using the state's 5,379 rail mi (8,660 km) of track were the Consolidated Rail Corp., or Conrail (which took over much of Penn Central's business), CSX Transportation, and Norfolk Southern. In 1995, Pennsylvania had 62 railroads in operation, more than any other state. Coal accounted for most of the 174.8 million tons carried by rail that year—in both tonnage originated and terminated within the state. Amtrak operates 95 daily trains through Pennsylvania, offering passenger service to Philadelphia, Pittsburgh, and other cities along the east–west route, and from Philadelphia to New York and Washington, D.C., along the northeast corridor. Amtrak's total Pennsylvania ridership in 1995/96 was 4,295,642.

Mass transit systems exist in metropolitan Philadelphia and Pittsburgh, in Bucks, Chester, Delaware, Montgomery, and Philadelphia counties, and in Altoona, Allentown, Erie, Harrisburg, Johnstown, Lancaster, Reading, Scranton, State College, and Wilkes-Barre. The Philadelphia Rapid Transit System, the state's first subway, was established in 1902 and is operated by the Southeastern Pennsylvania Transportation Authority, (SEPTA), which also runs buses, trolleys, trackless trolleys, and commuter trains in Bucks, Chester, Delaware, Montgomery, and Philadelphia counties. In 1985, a 1.1-mile (1.8-km) subway was opened in Pittsburgh as part of a 10.5-mile (16.9-km) light-rail (trolley) transit system linking downtown Pittsburgh with the South Hills section of the city.

Throughout its history, Pennsylvania has been a pioneer in road transportation. One of the earliest roads in the colonies was a "king's highway," connecting Philadelphia to Delaware in 1677; a "queen's road" from Philadelphia to Chester opened in 1706. A flurry of road building connected Philadelphia with other eastern Pennsylvania communities between 1705 and 1735. The first interior artery, the Great Conestoga Road, was opened in 1741 and linked Philadelphia with Lancaster. Indian trails in western Pennsylvania were developed into roadways, and a thoroughfare to Pittsburgh was completed in 1758. During the mid-1700s, a Lancaster County artisan developed an improved wagon for transporting goods across the Alleghenies; called a Conestoga wagon after the region from which it came, this vehicle later became the prime means of transport for westward pioneers. Another major improvement in land transportation came with the opening in 1792 of the Philadelphia and Lancaster Turnpike, one of the first stone-surfaced roads in the US. The steel-cable suspension bridge built by John Roebling over the Monongahela River at Pittsburgh in 1846 revolutionized bridge building, leading to the construction of spans longer and wider than had previously been thought possible. During the 1920s, Pennsylvania farmers were aided by the building of inexpensive rural roads connecting them with their markets.

A major development in automotive transport, the limited-access highway came to fruition with the Pennsylvania Turnpike, which opened in 1940 and was the first high-speed, multilane

highway in the US. In 1995, this 470-mi (756-km) toll highway received $297.6 million from motorists, or 74% of the total receipts for state-administered toll road and crossing facilities in Pennsylvania. In 1995, Pennsylvania had 118,648 mi (191,023 km) of public roads, including 85,376 mi (137,455 km) of rural roads and 33,272 mi (53,568 km) of urban streets. In addition, 1,588 mi (2,557 km) of interstate highways crossed the state. In 1995, total road and highway expenditures from all units of government came to almost $4.2 billion, with 37% of that amount for maintenance. Besides the Turnpike, the major highways are I-80 (Keystone Shortway), crossing the state from East Stroudsburg to the Ohio Turnpike; I-81, from the New York to the Maryland border via Scranton, Wilkes–Barre, and Harrisburg; and I-79, from Erie to the West Virginia border via Pittsburgh. As of 1995 there were 8,480,526 motor vehicles registered, including 6,013,649 automobiles, 2,433,003 trucks, and 33,874 buses. The total of 8,154,055 licensed drivers as of 1995 was the 5th highest in the US.

Blessed with access to the Atlantic Ocean and the Great Lakes and with such navigable waterways as the Delaware, Monongahela, Allegheny, and Ohio rivers, Pennsylvania was an early leader in water transportation, and Philadelphia, Pittsburgh, and Erie all developed as major ports. The peak period of canal building came during the 1820s and 1830s, which saw the completion of the Main Line of Public Works, used to transport goods between Philadelphia and Pittsburgh from 1834 to 1854. This system used waterways and a spectacular portage railroad that climbed over and cut through, via a tunnel, the Allegheny Mountains. Monumental as it was, the undertaking was largely a failure. Built too late to challenge the Erie Canal's domination of east–west trade, the Main Line was soon made obsolete by the railroads, as was the rest of the state's 800-mi (1,300-km) canal system.

Philadelphia, Pittsburgh, and Erie are the state's major shipping ports. The Philadelphia Harbor (including ports in the Philadelphia metropolitan area) handled 40.6 million tons of cargo in 1995. Although no longer the dominant gateway to the Mississippi, Pittsburgh is still a major inland port, and handled 48.8 million tons of cargo that year. Erie is the state's port on the Great Lakes, with just over 1 million tons of cargo handled in 1995.

As of 31 December 1994, Pennsylvania had 752 airfields, including 482 airports, 290 heliports, 8 seaplane bases, and 3 stolports. The busiest air terminal in the state, Greater Pittsburgh Airport, enplaned 8,996,598 passengers in 1994; Philadelphia International Airport was next with 7,612,424 enplaned passengers.

¹¹HISTORY

Soon after the glacier receded from what is now Pennsylvania, about 20,000 years ago, nomadic hunters from the west moved up the Ohio River, penetrated the passes through the Allegheny Mountains, and moved down the Susquehanna and Delaware rivers. By about AD 500, the earliest Indians, already accustomed to fishing and gathering nuts, seeds, fruit, and roots, were beginning to cultivate the soil, make pottery, and build burial mounds. Over the next thousand years, the Indians became semisedentary, or only seasonal, nomads.

Woodland Indians living in Pennsylvania, mostly of the Algonkian language family, were less inclined toward agriculture than other Indian tribes. The first Europeans to sail up the Delaware River found the Leni-Lenape ("original people"), who, as their name signified, had long occupied that valley, and whom the English later called the Delaware. Other Algonkian tribes related to the Leni-Lenape were the Nanticoke, who ranged along the Susquehanna River, and the Shawnee, who were scattered throughout central Pennsylvania. The other major Indian language group in Pennsylvania was Iroquoian. This group included the Susquehanna (Conestoga), living east of the Susquehanna River and south to the shores of Chesapeake Bay; the Wyandot, along the Allegheny River; and the Erie, south of Lake Erie. Proving that tribes related by language could be deadly enemies, the Iroquoian Confederacy of the Five Nations, located in what is now New York, destroyed the Iroquoian-speaking Erie in the 1640s and the Susquehanna by 1680. The confederacy conquered the Leni-Lenape by 1720 but failed to destroy them.

The first European to reach Pennsylvania was probably Cornelis Jacobssen, who in 1614 entered Delaware Bay for Dutch merchants interested in the fur trade. In 1638, the Swedes began planting farms along the Delaware River; they lived in peace with the Leni-Lenape and Susquehanna, with whom they traded for furs. Under Governor Johan Printz, the Swedes expanded into present-day Pennsylvania with a post at Tinicum Island (1643) and several forts along the Schuylkill River. The Dutch conquered New Sweden in 1655, but surrendered the land in 1664 to the English, led by James, Duke of York, the brother of King Charles II and the future King James II.

The English conquest was financed partly by Admiral William Penn, whose son, also named William, subsequently joined the Society of Friends (Quakers), a radical Protestant sect persecuted for espousing equality and pacifism. Dreaming of an ideal commonwealth that would be a refuge for all persecuted peoples, Penn asked Charles II, who had not paid the debt owed to Penn's father, to grant him land west of the Delaware. The Duke of York willingly gave up his claim to that land, and Charles II granted it in 1681 as a proprietary colony to the younger Penn and named it Pennsylvania in honor of Penn's father.

As proprietor of Pennsylvania, Penn was given enormous power to make laws and wars (subject to approval by the king and the freeman of Pennsylvania), levy taxes, coin money, regulate commerce, sell land, appoint officials, administer justice, and construct a government. From the beginning, Penn virtually gave up his lawmaking power and granted suffrage to property holders of 50 acres or £50. Even before coming to Pennsylvania, he forged his first Frame of Government, a document that went into effect 25 April 1682 but lasted less than a year. Under it, a 72-member council, presided over by a governor, monopolized executive, legislative, and judicial power, although a 200-member assembly could veto or amend the council's legislation. Arriving in the colony in October 1682, Penn approved the location and layout of Philadelphia, met with the Leni-Lenape to acquire land and exchange vows of peace, called for elections to select an assembly, and proposed a Great Law that ranged from prescribing weights and measures to guaranteeing fundamental liberties.

When the First Frame proved unwieldy, Penn on 2 April 1683 approved a Second Frame, which created an 18-member council and a 36-member assembly. A conspicuous friend of the deposed James II, Penn lost control of Pennsylvania from 1692 to 1694, and it was during this period that the legislature began to assert its rights. Penn returned to the colony in 1699, and on 28 October 1701 approved yet another constitution, called the Charter of Privileges. This document lodged legislative power in an annually elected unicameral assembly, executive power in a governor and council, which he now appointed, and judicial power in appointed provincial judges and an elected county judiciary. The Charter of Privileges remained in force until 1776.

As Pennsylvania's government evolved, its population grew steadily. Most of the first immigrants were from the British Isles and Germany. From 1681 to 1710, numerous English and Welsh Quaker migrants populated a 25-mi (40-km) zone surrounding Philadelphia. By 1750, most German immigrants were settled in a semicircular zone some 25–75 mi (40–120 km) from Philadelphia. A third and outermost ring, extending roughly 75 mi

(120 km) west and north of the Germans, was populated beginning in 1717 by the Scots-Irish, who were indifferent farmers, but known as aggressive pioneers. By 1776, each of the major groups—which remained quite distinct—constituted roughly a third of the 300,000 Pennsylvanians. Minorities included about 10,000 Scots, 10,000 Irish Catholics, 8,000 French Huguenots, 8,000 black slaves (despite Quaker hostility to slavery), and 1,000 Jews.

A key issue during the pre-Revolutionary period was the size and extent of the colony. Conflicting colonial charters, reflecting vague English ideas of American geography, brought all of Pennsylvania's boundaries except the Delaware River into dispute. After a protracted struggle, Pennsylvania and Maryland agreed upon a basis for Charles Mason and Jeremiah Dixon to run the famous line (1763–67) that divided North and South. Although Virginia and Pennsylvania both claimed the area around Pittsburgh, a joint commission agreed in 1779 to extend the Mason-Dixon line west the full five degrees prescribed in Penn's original charter. Five years earlier, the Penn family had abandoned to New York land north of the 42d parallel. This was confirmed as Pennsylvania's northern border in 1782, when the US Congress rejected Connecticut's claim to the Wyoming Valley area, where skirmishes (called the Yankee-Pennamite wars) had been going on since the 1760s.

Pennsylvania moved rapidly toward independence after the British victory in the French and Indian War. The Proclamation of 1763, preventing settlement west of the Alleghenies, outraged western Pennsylvania, while the Stamp Act (1765), Townshend Acts (1767), and Tea Act (1773) incensed Philadelphians. Although the Continental Congress began meeting in Philadelphia in September 1774, Pennsylvania revolted reluctantly. In July 1776, only three Pennsylvania delegates to the Second Continental Congress voted for independence, while two were opposed and two absented themselves from the vote. Nevertheless, the Declaration of Independence was proclaimed from Independence Hall, Pennsylvania's State House, on 4 July 1776. As the headquarters of the Congress, Philadelphia was an important British target. The American defeat at the Battle of Brandywine Creek on 11 September 1777 led to the British occupation of the city. The provisional capital was moved first to Lancaster and then to York, where the Articles of Confederation were drafted. Following battles at Germantown and Whitemarsh, General George Washington set up winter headquarters at Valley Forge, remaining there from December 1777 to June 1778. Faced with the threat of French naval power intervening on behalf of the Americans, the British evacuated Philadelphia during the spring of 1778, and Congress reconvened there on 2 July. Philadelphia would serve as the US capital until 1783, and again from 1790 to 1800.

With independence, Pennsylvania adopted the state constitution of 1776, which established a powerful unicameral assembly elected annually by all freemen supporting the Revolution, a weak administrative supreme executive council (with a figurehead president), an appointed judiciary, and a council of censors meeting every seven years in order to take a census, reapportion the assembly, and review the constitutionality of state actions. In 1780, Pennsylvania passed the first state law abolishing slavery. Seven years later, Pennsylvania became the second state to ratify the US Constitution and join the Union. In 1790, Pennsylvania adopted a new constitution, modeled on the federal one, allowing all taxpaying males to vote. This document provided for a powerful governor, elected for a three-year term and eligible to succeed himself twice, a bicameral legislature (with senators elected every four years and a house elected annually), and an appointed judiciary.

Opposition to national taxes was evidenced by two disturbances in the 1790s. In 1794, western Pennsylvania settlers, opposed to a federal excise tax on distilled spirits, waged the Whiskey Rebellion. The insurrection was soon quashed by state troops under federal command. The levying of a federal property tax inspired the unsuccessful Fries Rebellion (1799) among Pennsylvania Germans.

By 1800, the first stages of industrialization were at hand. Pittsburgh's first iron furnace was built in 1792, and the increasing use of coal as fuel made its mining commercially feasible. The completion of the Main Line of Public Works, a canal and rail system connecting Philadelphia with Pittsburgh, was a major development of the early 19th century, which was otherwise a period of political turmoil and shifting party alliances.

By 1838, Pennsylvania adopted a new constitution curtailing the governor's power (he could serve only two three-year terms in a nine-year period), making many judgeships elective for specific terms, restricting the charter of banks, and disenfranchising black people. The 1840s saw not only an influx of Irish immigrants but also the rise of the Native American (Know-Nothing) Party, an anti-Catholic movement. The antislavery crusade, which gave birth to the Republican Party, influenced state politics during the following decade.

Although a Pennsylvania Democrat, James Buchanan, carried the state and won the presidency in 1856, the Republicans captured Pennsylvania for Abraham Lincoln in 1860, partly by their strong support for a protective tariff. Protectionism attracted Pennsylvania because, in addition to its enormously productive farms, it was heavily industrialized, leading the nation in the production of iron, lumber, textiles, and leather.

Pennsylvania rallied to the Union cause, supplying some 338,000 men, a figure exceeded only by New York. The state was the scene of the Battle of Gettysburg (1–3 July 1863), a turning point in the war for the Union cause. Under General George Gordon Meade, the Union troops (one-third of whom were Pennsylvanians) defeated Confederate forces under General Robert E. Lee, who was then forced to lead a retreat to Virginia.

The Civil War left the Republican Party dominant in Pennsylvania, but, in the postwar years, the Republicans were themselves dominated by industry, particularly the Pennsylvania Railroad. Between 1890 and 1900, the state was the nation's chief producer of coal, iron, and steel, and for much of that period the main source of petroleum and lumber. Farmers' sons and daughters joined immigrants from abroad in flocking to the anthracite and bituminous coal regions and to Philadelphia, Pittsburgh, and other urban centers to work in mines, mills, and factories. As the state's industrial wealth increased, education, journalism, literature, art, and architecture flourished in Philadelphia and Pittsburgh. The 1876 Centennial Exhibition at Philadelphia illustrated America's advancement in the arts and industry.

Pennsylvania adopted a reform constitution in 1873, increasing the size of the senate and house to reduce the threat of bribery, prescribing rules to prevent treachery in legislation and fraud at the polls, equalizing taxation, limiting state indebtedness, restricting the governor to one four-year term in eight years, and creating the office of lieutenant governor. None of this, however, seriously hampered the Republican political machine, led by Simon Cameron, Matthew Quay, and Boies Penrose, which dominated the state from the 1860s to the 1920s. Though Progressive reforms were enacted in subsequent years, the Penrose machine grew ever more efficient, while industrial leaders—supported both by the Pennsylvania state government and by society at large—smashed labor's efforts to unite, particularly in the great steel strike of 1919.

During the nationwide boom years of the 1920s, Pennsylvania did little more than hold its own economically, and its industrial growth rate was low. The state's share of the nation's iron and steel output no longer exceeded that of the rest of the country

combined. Coal, textiles, and agriculture—all basic to the state's economy—were depressed. When Penrose died in 1921, at least five factions sought to control the powerful Pennsylvania Republican Party. In this confusion, Gifford Pinchot, a Progressive disciple of Theodore Roosevelt, won the governorship for 1923–27 and reorganized the state's administration, but failed in his attempt to enforce prohibition and to regulate power utilities.

The disastrous depression of the 1930s brought major changes to Pennsylvania. Serving again as governor (1931–35), Pinchot fought for state and federal relief for the unemployed. The Republican organization's lack of enthusiasm for Pinchot and Progressivism helped revive the state Democratic Party long enough to secure the election in 1934—for the first time since 1890—of its gubernatorial nominee, George H. Earle. As governor, Earle successfully introduced a Little New Deal, supporting labor, regulating utilities, aiding farmers, and building public works. With government support, coal miners, steelworkers, and other organized labor groups emerged from the Depression strong enough to challenge industry. Full employment and prosperity returned to Pennsylvania with the unprecedented demands on it for steel, ships, munitions, and uniforms during World War II.

Despite their professed opposition to government control, the Republican administrations (1939–55) that succeeded the Earle regime actually espoused and even enlarged Earle's program. They regulated industry, improved education, and augmented social services, at the same time increasing state bureaucracy, budgets, and taxes. Markets, transportation, banks, factories, machinery, and skilled labor remained abundant, and two Democratic governors were able to attract new industries to the state during the 1950s and early 1960s. However, the economy was still not healthy in 1963, when Republican William W. Scranton entered the statehouse (1963–67). Scranton continued both to enlarge state responsibilities (through increased taxes) and to secure federal aid for economic and social programs. He was rewarded with four years of steady economic growth. Pennsylvania's unemployment level, 2nd highest in the nation from 1950 to 1962, had dropped below the national average by 1966. The 1873 constitution was extensively revised at a constitutional convention held in 1967–68, during the administration of Raymond P. Shafer (1967–71), Scranton's Republican successor.

Pennsylvania faced an unresolved financial crisis in 1971 when Democrat Milton J. Shapp became governor. During his first term (1971–75), Shapp weathered the storm by securing passage of a state income tax. He virtually eliminated state patronage by signing union contracts covering state employees. Not only did he continue to attract business to Pennsylvania, but he also championed the consumer with no-fault auto insurance, adopted in 1974. Shapp's second term, however, was wrecked by his pursuit of the 1976 presidential nomination and by rampant corruption among Pennsylvania Democrats. Shapp's successor, Republican Richard L. Thornburgh, had scarcely been seated in the governor's chair before the release of radioactive gases resulting from the malfunction of one of the two nuclear reactors at Three Mile Island in March 1979 confronted him—and others—with vexing questions concerning the safety and wisdom of atomic power. Nevertheless, in September 1985, during Thornburgh's second term, and following six years of cleanup of radioactive waste, the undamaged reactor at Three Mile Island was restarted.

In the mid-1980s, Pennsylvania found itself confronted with the problem of completing the transition from a manufacturing to a service economy. While some parts of the state, namely southeastern Pennsylvania and Philadelphia, had successfully negotiated the transition, the economies of Pittsburgh, Lehigh Valley, Scranton, and Wilkes-Barre, on the other hand, remained centered on the depressed steel and coal industries. Under Governor Robert Casey, who took office in 1987, Pennsylvania created an organization called the Governor's Response Team to assist ailing industries in the state. The team helped companies obtain low-interest loans and subsidized companies which sought to retrain their workers. In the first year of its existence, the team reached out to assist 214 companies, saved 10,000 existing jobs, and created 10,000 new ones.

In the mid-1990s, steel was no longer the mainstay of industry in Pennsylvania, although the state still led the nation in production of specialty steel. Important manufacturing sectors included food processing and chemicals, especially pharmaceuticals. Philadelphia had become a center for high-technology industries, while Pittsburgh was a mecca for corporate headquarters. The state remained one of the nation's most populous, ranking 5th both in the 1990 census and 1995 estimates.

12STATE GOVERNMENT

The 1873 constitution, substantially reshaped by a constitutional convention in 1967–68, is the foundation of state government in Pennsylvania.

The general assembly consists of a 50-member senate, elected to staggered four-year terms, and a 203-member house of representatives, elected every two years. Each house meets annually, and there are no limits to the length of each session. To qualify for the general assembly, a person must be a US citizen and have been a Pennsylvania resident for at least four years and a district resident for at least one; senators must be at least 25 years of age, representatives at least 21. The legislative salary was $47,000 in 1995.

As head of the executive branch and chief executive officer of the state, the governor of Pennsylvania has the power to appoint heads of administrative departments, boards, and commissions, to approve or veto legislation, to grant pardons, and to command the state's military forces. The governor, who may serve no more than two four-year terms in succession, must be a US citizen, be at least 30 years of age, and have been a Pennsylvania resident for at least seven years before election. Elected with the governor is the lieutenant governor, who serves as president of the senate and chairman of the board of pardons, and assumes the powers of the governor if the governor becomes unable to continue in that office. In 1996, the governor's salary was $105,000.

Other Pennsylvania officials also elected for four years are the auditor general, who oversees all state financial transactions; the state treasurer, who receives and keeps records of all state funds; and the attorney general, who heads the Department of Justice. All other department heads, or secretaries, are appointed by the governor and confirmed by a majority of the senate.

A bill may be introduced in either house of the general assembly. After the measure is passed by majority vote in each house, the governor has 10 days in which to sign it, refuse to sign it (in which case it becomes law), or veto it. Vetoes may be overridden by a two-thirds vote of the elected members of each house. A bill becomes effective 60 days after enactment.

A proposed constitutional amendment must be approved by a majority of both house and senate members in two successive legislatures before it can be placed on the ballot. If approved by a majority of the voters in a general election, the amendment then becomes part of the constitution.

To vote in state elections, a person must be a US citizen, be at least 18 years old, and have been a resident of Pennsylvania and of the district for at least 30 days preceding the election. Registration may take place at any time up to 30 days before an election; mail registration is allowed.

13POLITICAL PARTIES

The Republican Party totally dominated Pennsylvania politics from 1860, when the first Republican governor was elected, to the early 1930s. During this period, there were 16 Republican and only 2 Democratic administrations. Most of the Republicans were staunchly probusiness, though one Republican Progressive, Gifford Pinchot, was elected governor in 1922 and again in 1930. A Democrat, George Earle, won the governorship in 1934, in the depths of the Depression, but from 1939 through 1955, Republicans again held the office without interruption. Only since the mid-1950s has Pennsylvania emerged as a two-party state, with Democrats electing governors in 1954, 1958, 1970, 1974, 1986 and 1990, and Republicans winning the governorships in 1962, 1966, 1978, 1982, and 1994. Both US Senate seats were held by Republicans from 1968 to 1991. In November of 1991, a little-known Democrat and former college president named Harris Wofford defeated former governor Richard Thornburgh for the seat of Senator John Heinz, who died in 1991. In 1994, Republican Rick Santorum, a Congressman from the Pittsburgh area, defeated Wofford. Pennsylvania's other senator, Republican Arlen Specter, is currently serving his third term. In 1997, Pennsylvania's 21 US House seats were held by 11 Democrats and 10 Republicans. Following the 1996 elections, there were 30 Republicans and 20 Democrats in the state senate, and 104 Republicans and 99 Democrats in the state house.

As of 1994 there were 3,043,757 registered Democrats, or 51% of the total number of registered voters; 2,567,643 Republicans, or 43%; and 381,602 Independents, or 6%. Democratic voters were heavily concentrated in metropolitan Philadelphia and Pittsburgh. Pennsylvania, a pivotal state for Jimmy Carter in 1976, was swept by the Republican tide in the 1980 presidential election; Ronald Reagan, the Republican nominee, won nearly 50% of the popular vote. In 1984, President Reagan received 53% of the popular vote, while Democrat Walter Mondale received 46%. In 1988, Republican and former vice president George Bush won 51% of the popular vote. Democratic nominee Bill Clinton garnered 45% of the vote in 1992; Bush received 36%; and Independent Ross Perot collected 18%. In 1996, Clinton won 49% of the vote, Republican Bob Dole won 40%, and 10% went to Perot.

In 1994 there were 158 blacks and 8 Hispanics holding public office. As of 1995, there were 30 women serving in the state legislature and 2 women in statewide elective executive office.

14LOCAL GOVERNMENT

As of 1992, Pennsylvania had 66 counties, 1,022 municipal governments, 1,548 townships, 516 school districts, and 2,006 authorities (special districts). Under home-rule laws, municipalities may choose to draft and amend their own charter.

Pennsylvania counties are responsible for state law enforcement, judicial administration, and the conduct of state elections: counties also are involved in public health, regional planning, and solid waste disposal. Counties can also maintain hospitals, homes for the aged, community colleges, libraries, and other community facilities. The chief governing body in each county is a three-member board of commissioners, each elected to a four-year term. Other elected officials generally include the sheriff, district attorney, prothonotary (notary), clerk of courts, register of wills, recorder of deeds, two jury commissioners, three auditors or a controller, and treasurer. Among the appointed officials is a public defender. Counties are divided by law into nine classes, depending on population. The only first-class county, Philadelphia, is also the only city-county in the state; its county offices were merged with the city government in 1952, pursuant to the home-rule charter of 1951.

There are four classes of cities. The only first-class city, Philadelphia, is governed by a mayor and 17-member city council.

Other elected officials are the controller, district attorney, sheriff, register of wills, and three city commissioners. Major appointed officials include managing director, director of finance, city representative, and city solicitor. Both Pittsburgh, the only second-class city, and Scranton, the only second-class-A city, are governed under mayor-council systems that give the mayors strong discretionary powers.

Boroughs are governed under mayor-council systems giving the council strong powers. Other elected officials are the tax assessor, tax collector, and auditor or controller. The state's first-class townships, located mostly in metropolitan areas, are governed by elected commissioners who serve four-year overlapping terms. Second-class townships, most of them located in rural areas, have three supervisors who are elected at large to six-year terms. Other elected officials may include a tax assessor, tax collector. three auditors or a controller, and treasurer.

15 STATE SERVICES

Executive agencies under the governor's jurisdiction are the Pennsylvania Council on Aging, Human Relations Commission, Governor's Council on the Hispanic Community, Commission for Women, and State Ethics Commission. The Liquor Control Board operates state liquor stores and claims to be the world's largest single purchaser of liquors and wines.

The Department of Education administers the school laws of Pennsylvania, oversees community colleges, licenses and regulates private schools, and administers the state public library program. Educational policy is the province of the State Board of Education, a panel with 17 members appointed by the governor to six-year terms. Also within the department are various boards that make policies for and review developments within the state's higher educational system.

The Department of Transportation maintains state-operated highways, mass transit, rail service, and aviation facilities. The State Highway and Bridge Authority and the Pennsylvania Turnpike Commission also have transport-related responsibilities. Agencies and departments providing health and welfare services include the Department of Aging, Department of Community and Economic Development, and Department of Health. All public assistance, social service, mental health, and mental retardation programs are administered by the Department of Public Welfare.

The Office of Attorney General has divisions on criminal law, legal services, and public protection. The National Guard, Bureau for Veterans' Affairs, and state veterans' homes are under the Department of Military Affairs; the Pennsylvania State Police is a separate state agency. The Pennsylvania Commission on Crime and Delinquency, created in 1978, allocates federal funds for crime control, juvenile justice, and delinquency prevention. The Pennsylvania Emergency Management Agency (formerly the State Council of Civil Defense) provides assistance in emergency situations resulting from natural or manmade disasters.

All state park and forest preservation programs, ecological and geological resource information programs, and community conservation partnerships are under the supervision of the Department of Conservation and Natural Resources. Land and water environmental protection programs are under the supervision of the Department of Environmental Protection. The Governor's Energy Council seeks to augment the state's energy security through the planned development and conservation of energy resources. The Department of Labor and Industry administers safety, employment, and industrial standards; operates vocational rehabilitation and workers' compensation programs; and mediates labor disputes.

16 JUDICIAL SYSTEM

Since 1968, all Pennsylvania courts have been organized under the Unified Judicial System. The highest court in the state is the supreme court, which, having been established in 1722, is the oldest appellate court in the US. The supreme court consists of 7 justices, elected to 10-year terms; the justice with the longest continuous service on the court automatically becomes chief justice. In general, the supreme court hears appeals from the commonwealth court. A separate appellate court, called the superior court, hears appeals from the courts of common pleas. There are 15 superior court judges, also elected to 10-year terms,

Pennsylvania Presidential Vote by Political Parties, 1948–96

YEAR	ELECTORAL VOTE	PENNSYLVANIA WINNER	DEMOCRAT	REPUBLICAN	PROGRESSIVE	SOCIALIST	PROHIBITION	SOC. LABOR
1948	35	Dewey (R)	1,752,426	1,902,197	55,161	11,325	10,538	1,461
						SOC. WORKERS		
1952	32	*Eisenhower (R)	2,146,269	2,415,789	4,222	1,508	8,951	1,377
1956	32	*Eisenhower (R)	1,981,769	2,585,252	—	2,035	—	7,447
1960	32	*Kennedy (D)	2,556,282	2,439,956	—	2,678	—	7,158
1964	29	*Johnson (D)	3,130,954	1,673,657	—	10,456	—	5,092
					PEACE & FREEDOM		AMERICAN IND.	
1968	29	Humphrey (D)	2,259,403	2,090,017	7,821	4,862	378,582	4,977
								AMERICAN
1972	27	*Nixon (R)	1,796,951	2,714,521	—	4,639	—	70,593
					COMMUNIST			US LABOR
1976	27	*Carter (D)	2,328,677	2,205,604	1,891	3,009	25,344	2,744
						LIBERTARIAN	SOC. WORKERS	
1980	27	*Reagan (R)	1,937,540	2,261,872	5,184	33,263	20,291	—
1984	25	*Reagan (R)	2,228,131	2,584,323	21,628	6,982	—	—
					CONSUMER		NEW ALLIANCE	POPULIST
1988	25	*Bush (R)	2,194,944	2,300,087	19,158	12,051	4,379	3,444
								IND. (Perot)
1992	23	*Clinton (D)	2,239,164	1,791,164		21,477	4,661	902,667
1996	23	*Clinton (D)	2,215,819	1,801,169	—	28,000	—	430,984

*Won US presidential election.

as are the commonwealth and common pleas, which have original jurisdiction over all civil and criminal cases not otherwise specified. As of 1994 there were 366 judges in 60 courts of common pleas, one for each judicial district.

In counties other than Philadelphia, misdemeanors and other minor offenses are tried by district justices, formerly known as justices of the peace. The Philadelphia municipal court consists of 22 judges, all of whom must be lawyers; the 6 judges who constitute the Philadelphia traffic court need not be lawyers. Pittsburgh's magistrates court, appointed by the mayor, comprises 5 to 8 judges who need not be lawyers. All of Pennsylvania's judges, except traffic court judges and Pittsburgh's magistrates, are initially elected on a partisan ballot and thereafter on a nonpartisan retention ballot.

Pennsylvania's overall crime rate in 1995 was 3,364.9 per 100,000 people; the violent crime rate was 427.3, the property crime rate 2,937.6. Rates for specific crimes were as follows: murder and nonnegligent manslaughter, 6.3; forcible rape, 25.2; robbery, 189.3; aggravated assault, 206.5; burglary, 561.8; larceny-theft, 1,1,963.1; and motor vehicle theft, 412.7. All these figures were well below the national norms.

In 1995, there were 29,666 inmates held in state and federal correctional facilities, a rate of 246 inmates per 100,000 population. Between 1990 and 1995, the inmate population increased by almost 43%.

Pennsylvania imposes the death penalty and executed two persons in 1995.

[17]ARMED FORCES
In 1996, there were 3,268 active-duty military personnel stationed in Pennsylvania. The US Army War College is in Carlisle, and there are army depots in Chambersburg, Harrisburg, and Scranton. Defense contracts worth $3.6 billion were awarded to Pennsylvania firms in 1995/96.

As of 1 July 1996, there were 1,349,000 veterans living in the state, of whom fewer than 500 served in World War I, 424,000 in World War II, 225,000 in the Korean conflict, 377,000 during the Viet Nam era, and 84,000 in the Persian Gulf War. Veterans' benefits exceeded $1.7 billion in 1995/96.

In 1996, 62,967 Pennsylvanians served in the reserve and national guard; the army had 40,159 personnel, the navy and marine corps 13,970, and the air force had 8,838 members. In 1993, the Pennsylvania State Police employed 4,123 full-time sworn officers, or 3 per 10,000 residents.

[18]MIGRATION
When William Penn's followers arrived in Pennsylvania, they joined small groups of Dutch, Swedish, and Finnish immigrants who were already settled along the Delaware River. By 1685, 50% of Pennsylvania's European population was British. In 1683, the Frankfort Land Co. founded the Mennonite community of Germantown on 6,000 acres (2,400 hectares) east of the Schuylkill River. One hundred years later there were 120,000 Germans, about one-fourth of the state's census population; the Moravians, from Saxony, settled primarily in Bethlehem and Nazareth, and the Amish in Lancaster and Reading.

During the 19th century, more immigrants settled in Pennsylvania than in any other state except New York. Between 1840 and 1890, the anthracite mines in east-central Pennsylvania attracted the Irish, Welsh, and Slavs; Scots-Irish, Italian, Austrian, Hungarian, and Polish (and, after 1880, Russian) immigrants worked the western coal fields. The cities attracted Italian, French, and Slavic workers. East European and Russian Jews settled in Philadelphia and Pittsburgh between 1882 and 1900. By the turn of the century, the urban population surpassed the rural population.

During the 20th century, these patterns have been reversed. The trend among whites, particularly since World War II, has been to move out—from the cities to the suburbs, and from Pennsylvania to other states. Blacks, who began entering the state first as slaves and then as freemen, continued to migrate to the larger cities until the early 1970s, when a small out-migration began. Overall, between 1940 and 1980, Pennsylvania lost a net total of l,759,000 residents through migration; it lost an additional 98,000 residents between 1980 and 1983. From 1985 to 1990, Pennsylvania had a net migration gain of nearly 21,000. Between 1990 and 1996, the state had a net loss of 122,290 in domestic migration and 77,345 in international migration. In 1996, about 3% of Pennsylvania's population (421,000) was foreign-born. In the same year, 16,938 foreign immigrants arrived in the state. As of 1994, it was estimated that there were between 10 and 53 undocumented immigrants in Pennsylvania.

As of 1990, 80.2% of state residents were native-born, the highest proportion among the states. In 1990, about 37% of state residents age 5 or older lived in a different house than in 1985, of which only about 18% did so in another state.

[19]INTERGOVERNMENTAL COOPERATION
Pennsylvania participates in such regional bodies as the Atlantic States Marine Fisheries Commission, Susquehanna River Basin Commission, Ohio River Valley Sanitation Commission, Wheeling Creek Watershed Protection and Flood Prevention Commission, and Great Lakes Basin Commission. In 1985, Pennsylvania, seven other Great Lakes states, and the Canadian provinces of Quebec and Ontario signed the Great Lakes Compact to protect the lakes' water reserves.

Some of the most important interstate agreements concern commerce and development along the Delaware River. The Delaware River Basin Commission involves the governors of Delaware, New Jersey, New York, and Pennsylvania in the utilization and conservation of the Delaware and its surrounding areas. Through the Delaware River Port Authority, New Jersey and Pennsylvania control an interstate mass transit system. The two states also are signatories to the Delaware River Joint Toll Bridge Compact and Delaware Valley Urban Area Compact.

During 1995/96, Pennsylvania received over $101.1 billion in federal grants (4th among the 50 states).

[20]ECONOMY
Dominated by coal and steel, Pennsylvania is an important contributor to the national economy, but its role has diminished considerably in this century. The state reached the height of its economic development by 1920, when its western oil wells and coal fields made it the nation's leading energy producer. By that time, however, Pennsylvania's oil production was already on the decline, and demand for coal had slackened. No longer did the state dominate US steel production: Pennsylvania produced 60% of the US total in 1900, but only 30% in 1940 and 24% in 1960. Philadelphia, a diversified manufacturing center, began to lose many of its textile and apparel factories. The Depression hastened the decline. Industrial production in 1932 was less than half the 1929 level, and mineral production, already in a slump throughout the 1920, dropped more than 50% in value between 1929 and 1933. By 1933, 37% of the workforce was unemployed.

Massive federal aid programs and the production of munitions stimulated employment during the 1940s, but some sections of the state have never fully recovered from the damage of the Depression years. Declines in coal and steel production and the loss of other industries to the Sunbelt have not been entirely counterbalanced by gains in other sectors, despite a steady expansion of machinery production, increased tourism, and the growth of service-related industries and trade. Manufacturing, the second largest employer in Pennsylvania—providing 1 million jobs in the early nineties—lost about 350,000 jobs during the eighties. The outlook for the steel industry remained uncertain in the 1980s and 1990s, as Pennsylvania's aging factories faced severe competition from foreign producers. Services, in contrast, added about 375,000 jobs, reaching a total of 1.4 million in 1990. The fastest growing service industries were concentrated in the medical and health fields.

Pennsylvania's gross state product in 1994 was $294,431 million, to which private goods-producing industries contributed $74,479 million; private services-producing industries, $188,167 million; and government, $31,785 million. Pennsylvania's per capita personal income in 1996 was $24,668, 18th in the US. In 1996, there were $32,502 bankruptcy filings, up 33% from 1995.

21INCOME

Although Pennsylvania is one of the nation's most industrialized states, its wage earners tend to receive less than their counterparts in other states.

Per capita personal income in 1996 was $24,668—18th among the 50 states and slightly above the US average. Total personal disposable income grew from $248 billion in 1995 to $258 billion in 1996. Median household income in 1995 was $34,524.

About 12.2% of all Pennsylvanians were below the federal poverty line in 1995.

22LABOR

In 1996, Pennsylvania's civilian labor force averaged 5,903,000, of whom 5,590,000 were employed. At the end of 1996, the largest area of nonfarm employment was in the services industry, with 1,622,400, followed by wholesale and retail trade, 1,260,100; manufacturing, 926,700; government, 735,200; finance, insurance, and real estate, 310,000; transportation and public utilities, 275,100; construction, 199,800; and mining, 18,800.

A survey of employers in 1996 revealed the following nonfarm employment pattern for Pennsylvania:

Total nonagricultural wages and salaries	100%
Goods-producing	21.7
Mining	0.4
Contract construction	3.8
Manufacturing	17.5
Durable goods	10.0
Primary metal industries	1.4
Industrial machinery and equipment	2.0
Other durable goods	6.6
Nondurable goods	7.5
Apparel & other textile prods.	0.8
Food & kindred products	1.6
Other nondurable goods	5.1
Services-producing	78.3
Transportation and public utilities	5.1
Wholesale trade	4.9
Retail trade	17.8
Finance, insurance, and real estate	5.8
Services and miscellaneous	31.1
Government	13.6
Federal government	2.4
State and local government	11.2

Pennsylvania had 720,900 government workers in 1996.

The average unemployment for the state in 1996 was 5.3%. The history of unionism in Pennsylvania dates back to 1724, when Philadelphia workers organized the Carpenters' Company, the first crafts association in the colonies. Its Carpenters' Hall gained fame as the site of the First Continental Congress in 1774; the carpenters were also responsible for the first strike in the US, in 1791. The nation's first labor union was organized by Philadelphia shoemakers in 1794. By 1827, the Mechanics' Union of Trade Associations, the country's first central labor body, was striking for a 10-hour workday and was the impetus behind the formation of the Organized Workingman's Party. Nine years later there were no fewer than 58 labor organizations in Philadelphia and 13 in Pittsburgh, but the Panic of 1837 resulted in a sharp decline of union strength and membership for many years. Union ranks were further depleted by the Civil War, despite the efforts of Pennsylvania labor leader William Sylvis, who later became an important figure in the national labor reform movement. After the Civil War ended, the Noble Order of the Knights of Labor was established in Philadelphia in 1869.

The coal fields were the sites of violent organizing struggles. In 1835, low wages and long hours sparked the first general mine strikes, which, like a walkout by anthracite miners in 1849, proved unsuccessful. During the 1850s and 1870s, a secret society known as the Molly Maguires led uprisings in the anthracite fields, but its influence ended after the conviction of its leaders for terrorist activities. The demise of the Molly Maguires did not stop the violence, however. Eleven persons were killed during a mine strike at Connellsville in 1891, and a strike by Luzerne County miners in 1897 resulted in 20 deaths. Finally, a five-month walkout by anthracite miners in 1902 led to increased pay, reduced hours, and an agreement to employ arbitration to settle disputes.

Steelworkers, burdened for many years by 12-hour workdays and 7-day workweeks, called several major strikes during this period. An 1892 lockout at Andrew Carnegie's Homestead steel mill led to a clash between workers and Pinkerton guards hired by the company; after several months, the strikers went back to work, their resources exhausted. A major strike in 1919, involving half of the nation's steelworkers, shut down the industry for more than three months, but it too produced no immediate gains. The Steel Workers Organizing Committee, later the United Steelworkers, finally won a contract and improved benefits from US Steel in 1937, although other steel companies held out until the early 1940s, when the Supreme Court forced recognition of the union.

As of 1995, nearly 26.7% of Pennsylvania's manufacturing employees belonged to unions, the 6th highest such percentage in the US. The most important union in the state is the United Steelworkers of America, headquartered in Pittsburgh.

23AGRICULTURE

Pennsylvania ranked 18th among the 50 states in agricultural income in 1995, with receipts of nearly $3.7 billion.

During the colonial period, German immigrants farmed the fertile land in southeastern Pennsylvania, making the state a leader in agricultural production. Unlike farmers in other states, who worked the soil until it was depleted and then moved on, these farmers carefully cultivated the same plots year after year, using crop rotation techniques that kept the land productive. As late as 1840, the state led the nation in wheat production, thanks in part to planting techniques developed and largely confined to southeastern Pennsylvania. However, westward expansion and the subsequent fall in agricultural prices hurt farming in the state, and many left the land for industrial jobs in the cities. Today, most farms in the state produce crops and dairy items for Philadelphia and other major eastern markets.

As of 1995 there were about 50,000 farms averaging 154 acres (62 hectares) in size. The leading farm areas were all in southeastern Pennsylvania. Lancaster County is by far the most productive, followed by the counties of Chester, Berks, Franklin, Adams, and Lebanon.

The following table shows leading field crops in 1995:

	OUTPUT (BUSHELS)	VALUE
Hay (tons)	4,409,000	$415,596,000
Corn for grain	94,080,000	348,096,000
Soybeans	9,450,000	58,118,000
Wheat	10,175,000	42,226,000
Oats	9,440,000	16,048,000
Barley	5,175,000	9,056,000

In 1991, Pennsylvania was a major producer of mushrooms, and greenhouse and nursery crops. Other crops were fresh vegetables, potatoes, strawberries, apples, pears, peaches, grapes, and cherries (sweet and tart). The value of fresh market vegetables exceeded $32 million in 1995; of vegetables for processing, $8.4 million.

24ANIMAL HUSBANDRY

Most of Pennsylvania's farm income stems from livestock production, primarily in Lancaster County.

In 1997, there were an estimated 1.75 million cattle and calves, valued at nearly $1.3 billion. During 1996, there were around 950,000 hogs and pigs, worth $93 million. In 1995 the state produced 7.5 million lb of sheep and lambs, which brought in $5.24 million in gross income.

Pennsylvania is a leading producer of chickens in the US, selling 72.5 million lb in 1995. An estimated 10.6 billion lb of milk (4th among the 50 states) was produced from 642,000 milk cows in 1995.

25FISHING

Although there is little commercial fishing in Pennsylvania—the 1995 catch of 506,000 lb was worth only $496,000—the state's many lakes and streams make it a popular area for sport fishing. All recreational fishing in the state is supervised by the Fish Commission, established in 1866 and one of the oldest conservation agencies in the US. Walleye, trout, and salmon were the leading species. In 1995/96, Pennsylvania issued 1,164,989 sport fishing licenses, and the US Fish and Wildlife Service apportioned over $5.1 million to the state for sport fish restoration programs.

26FORESTRY

Pennsylvania's richly diverse forests dominate the landscape, covering 59.2% (16,992,700 acres) of the total land area. For the northeastern United States, public ownership is high at 25% (4,193,300 acres), mostly owned by the commonwealth. The 1989 Forest Inventory identified 90 different tree species; most of the 2,076 species of native vascular plants are forest related. Eagles and ospreys are making a comeback, there is a resident elk herd (the largest east of the Mississippi), coyotes have moved in, and river otters and fishers have been reintroduced. Some species of forest birds which are experiencing declines regionally have increasing populations in Pennsylvania's forests.

The forest products industry and forest-based recreation are very important to Pennsylvania's economy. Ten commercial tree species dominate the average annual net growth, producing 74% of the wood grown each year. In 1993, the total roundwood harvest was 589.2 million cu ft, or 2.6% of the US total. Pennsylvania leads the nation in the volume of export grade hardwoods produced. The value of shipments for the lumber and wood products industry totaled $3,578.5 million in 1995. The paper industry had shipments valued at $8,808.2 million that year.

Camping, fishing, hiking, and hunting are traditional Pennsylvania pastimes and the clean streams, vistas, and flora and fauna of the forest provide a focal point for these activities.

27MINING

The value of nonfuel mineral production in Pennsylvania in 1995 was about $1,050 million, up 6% from 1994. The most valuable nonfuel mineral was crushed stone, which amounted to 83.5 million short tons, worth $518 million (2d in US). Other important minerals were portland cement, 5.61 million short tons ($314 million); lime, 1.62 million short tons ($101 million); and construction sand and gravel, 15.1 million short tons ($86.8 million). Pennsylvania ranked 12th among the states in value of nonfuel minerals, accounting for 3% of the U.S. value. Although no metals were mined in Pennsylvania, it retained its position as the nation's 3d leading producer of steel, processing about 8.3 million short tons through September 1995. Mining employment, including coal mines, totaled 18,800 persons in December 1996, reflecting 200 fewer workers than in December 1995.

28ENERGY AND POWER

Installed capacity of Pennsylvania's electric power plants in 1991 was 36.9 million kw, all of it privately owned. Total energy consumption in 1994 reached 3,830.7 trillion Btu. Coal supplied 35% of the state's energy needs; petroleum, 35%; natural gas, 19%; and nuclear power, hydropower, and other sources, 11%. That year, energy consumption was 317.6 million Btu per capita. In 1994, energy expenditures per capita averaged $1,952.

Pennsylvania's nuclear power production dropped abruptly on 28 March 1979, when a malfunction at the 906,000-kw Unit 2 plant operated by Metropolitan Edison (a subsidiary of General Public Utilities) at Three Mile Island near Harrisburg caused the reactor's containment building to fill up with radioactive water. Some radioactive steam was vented into the atmosphere, and thousands of residents of nearby areas were temporarily evacuated. A 12-member panel appointed by President Jimmy Carter to investigate the accident found serious flaws in the design of the plant's safety systems and in federal regulation of the nuclear power industry. Metropolitan Edison's 819,000-kw Unit I plant was also shut down after the accident but was reopened in fall 1985. Remaining nuclear plants in Pennsylvania are the Peach Bottom Units 2 and 3 (combined capacity 2,090,000 kw), 85% of which is owned jointly by Philadelphia Electric and Public Service Electric and Gas; Beaver Valley Units 1 and 2 (combined capacity 1,640,000 kw), at Shippingport, 69% owned by Duquesne Light and Ohio Edison; Susquehanna Units 1 and 2 (2,100,000 kw), 90% owned by Pennsylvania Power & Light; and Moser 1 (1,055,000 kw), owned by Philadelphia Electric.

Electric energy sales in the state in 1995 exceeded 125.6 billion kwh, of which 38% was industrial, 34% residential, 27% commercial, and 1% for other purposes.

The nation's first oil well was struck in Titusville in 1859, and for the next five decades Pennsylvania led the nation in oil production. Reserves totaled 11 million barrels in 1995, and output dropped to 1.7 million barrels in 1996. The state's natural gas production in 1995 was 111 billion cu ft; estimated reserves as of 1995 were 1,482 billion cu ft. Virtually all the state's commercial oil and gas reserves lie beneath the Allegheny High Plateau, in western Pennsylvania.

Coal is the state's most valuable mineral commodity, accounting for more than two-thirds of all mine income; the state's output in 1995 represented 6% of US production. In 1995, Pennsylvania's mining companies produced 61,576,000 tons of coal. Pennsylvania is the only major US producer of anthracite coal, with an output of 4,682,000 tons in 1995; bituminous coal production totaled 61,576,000 tons. Bituminous coal is mined in Washington, Clearfield, Greene, Cambria, Armstrong, Somerset, Clarion, Allegheny, and 19 other counties in the western part of the state; anthracite mining is concentrated in Schuylkill, Luzerne, Lackawanna, Northumberland, Carbon, Columbia,

Sullivan, and Dauphin counties in the east. In 1995, there were 459 active coal mines, 96 underground and 363 surface. Recoverable reserves as of 1995 were almost 687 million tons of bituminous (5th in the US) and 49 million tons of anthracite, 96% of the US total.

29INDUSTRY

At different times throughout its history, Pennsylvania has been the nation's principal producer of ships, iron, chemicals, lumber, oil, textiles, glass, coal, and steel. Although it is still a major manufacturing center, Pennsylvania's industrial leadership has diminished steadily during this century.

The first major industry in colonial Pennsylvania was shipbuilding, centered in Philadelphia. Iron works, brick kilns, candle factories, and other small crafts industries also grew up around the city. By 1850, Philadelphia alone accounted for nearly half of Pennsylvania's manufacturing output, with an array of products including flour, preserved meats, sugar, textiles, shoes, furniture, iron, locomotives, pharmaceuticals, and books. The exploitation of the state's coal and oil resources and the discovery of new steel-making processes helped build Pittsburgh into a major industrial center.

From 1977 to 1991, value added by manufacture increased from $36 billion to $64.9 billion, and the value of shipments of manufactured goods grew from $79.8 billion to $134 billion. In 1995, the value of shipments for manufactured goods was $164.88 billion.

The following table shows the value of shipments for selected industries in 1995:

Basic steel and blast furnace products	$11,690,400,000
Electronic components and accessories	9,406,000,000
Drugs	8,759,800,000
Petroleum refining	7,296,900,000
Stone, clay, and glass products	5,775,500,000
Commercial printing	3,867,700,000
Preserved fruits and vegetables	2,719,800,000
Motor vehicles and equipment	2,532,100,000
Measuring and controlling devices	2,249,800,000
Textile mill products	1,861,400,000
Construction and related machinery	1,739,000,000
Railroad equipment	1,537,000,000
Ladies' outerwear	1,535,000,000
Metalworking machinery	1,481,900,000

In 1997, Pennsylvania was headquarters for 32 Fortune 500 companies. During 1995, 2,963 US patents were issued to Pennsylvania residents.

30COMMERCE

A major component in Philadelphia's early economy, trade remains important to the state.

According to federal data, sales from wholesale trade in 1992 totaled $126.4 billion, 6th highest in the US. The main items sold were groceries and related products; machinery, equipment, and supplies; motor vehicles and automotive parts and supplies; metals and minerals (excluding petroleum); electrical goods; and petroleum and petroleum products.

Pennsylvania ranked 5th in the US in sales from retail trade in 1992, with almost $87.8 billion. The top categories were automotive dealers, 20.3%; food stores, 19.9%; and general merchandise stores, 11.6%. Philadelphian John Wanamaker opened the world's first department store in 1876; by 1992, Pennsylvania had 566 department stores, about 33% of them in the Philadelphia and Pittsburgh metropolitan areas.

During the colonial era, Philadelphia was one of the busiest Atlantic ports and the leading port for the lucrative Caribbean trade. Philadelphia remains one of the country's leading foreign trade centers; the main import suppliers are the United Kingdom,

Indonesia, Saudi Arabia, Venezuela, and Algeria. During 1995, the Philadelphia Customs District—which includes ports in Delaware and New Jersey, as well as Pennsylvania—processed import cargo worth almost $18.3 billion, of which fully 85% consisted of coal, coke, and other mineral fuels. Also passing through the Philadelphia Customs District were exports worth over $6.7 billion. In 1996, total exports of Pennsylvania goods had a value of $14.4 billion (12th in the US).

31CONSUMER PROTECTION

The Bureau of Consumer Protection is part of the Public Protection Division of the Office of Attorney General. The Bureau investigates and mediates complaints. Also within the Office of Attorney General is the Office of the Consumer Advocate and the Charitable Trusts and Organizations section. Pennsylvanians are encouraged to report instances of fraud, waste, or mismanagement of state funds through a toll-free telephone service run by the Auditor General. Additionally, the Department of Insurance and the Banking Commission protect state residents against insurance fraud and banking fraud, respectively.

32BANKING

Philadelphia is the nation's oldest banking center, and Third Street between Chestnut and Walnut has been called the cradle of American finance. The first chartered commercial bank in the US was the Bank of North America, granted its charter in Philadelphia by the federal government in December 1781 and by Pennsylvania in April 1782. The First Bank of the US was headquartered in Philadelphia from its inception in 1791 to 1811, when its charter was allowed to expire. Its building was bought by Stephen Girard, a private banker whose new institution quickly became one of the nation's largest banks. Girard's bank was closed after he died in 1831, but a new Girard Bank was opened in 1832; it merged with Philadelphia National Bank in 1926.

By the early 1800s, Philadelphia had reached its zenith as the nation's financial center. It was the home of the Bank of Pennsylvania, founded in 1793; the Bank of Philadelphia (1804); the Farmers and Mechanics Bank (1809); the Philadelphia Savings Fund Society (1816), the first mutual savings bank; and, most powerful of all, the Second Bank of the US (1816). After 1823, under the directorship of Nicholas Biddle, this bank became an international leader and the only rival to New York City's growing banking industry. When President Jackson vetoed the bank's recharter in 1831, Philadelphia lost its preeminence as a banking center.

Pittsburgh also rose to prominence during the Gilded Age, in great part because of the efforts of its most successful financier, Andrew Mellon. In March 1982, the state legalized multibank holding companies; subsequently, the Mellon Bank acquired Centre County Bank of State College, Girard Bank, and Northwest Bank. Other major institutions are Pittsburgh National Bank, part of PNC Financial, and Philadelphia National Bank. First Pennsylvania, in financial difficulty for several years, was saved from possible failure early in 1980 through a loan package engineered by the Federal Deposit Insurance Corporation.

As of 31 December 1996, Pennsylvania had 216 insured commercial banks with $184.1 billion in deposits and $243.4 billion in assets. The 160 savings institutions held $45.4 billion in assets and $32.2 billion in deposits as of 31 December 1996.

33INSURANCE

In 1995, there were 14,091,000 policies in force, with a total value of $628.7 billion. The average coverage per family was

$131,900. There were 37 life insurance companies headquartered in Pennsylvania in 1995.

Property and liability insurers wrote premiums amounting to $12.5 billion in 1995, of which automobile physical damage insurance accounted for $1.863 billion; automobile liability insurance, $3.898 billion; and homeowners insurance, $1.131 billion. A total of 202 property and casualty insurance companies were headquartered in Pennsylvania in 1995.

34SECURITIES

Formally established in 1790, the Philadelphia Stock Exchange (PHLX) is the oldest stock exchange in the US. It was also the nation's most important exchange until the 1820s, when the New York Stock Exchange eclipsed it. Since World War II, the Philadelphia exchange has merged with stock exchanges in Baltimore (1949), Washington, D.C. (1953), and Pittsburgh (1969). As the primary odd-lot market for Government National Mortgage Association securities and as a leading market for odd-lot government securities and stock options, PHLX ranks after only the New York and American exchanges in trading volume. PHLX was the first exchange in the US to trade foreign currency options (1982) and the National Over-the-Counter Index (1985).

In March 1997, Pennsylvania had 2,256 brokers and dealers registered to do business in the state through 104,179 designated agents and investment advisory services were provided by 963 firms (4,252 registered agents).

Sales of securities are regulated by the Pennsylvania Securities Commission, which also licenses all securities dealers, agents, and investment advisors in the state.

35PUBLIC FINANCE

Pennsylvania's budget is prepared annually by the Office of Budget and submitted by the governor to the general assembly for amendment and approval. By law, annual operating expenditures may not exceed available revenues and surpluses from prior years. The fiscal year runs from 1 July to 30 June.

The following table shows general revenues and expenditures for the state government in 1995/96 in millions:

REVENUES	
Taxes:	
Property	9,517
Sales and gross receipts	12,055
Income	5,165
TOTAL TAXES	26,737
CHARGES AND MISCELLANEOUS:	
Current charges	1,312
Interest earnings	153
Special assessments	2,497
Other	227
TOTAL	4,189
TOTAL REVENUES	$30,926
EXPENDITURES	
Education	$ 7,418
Health and social concerns	13,651
Transportation (highways)	2,345
Public safety (police)	349
Natural resources	604
Housing and community development	2,621
Financial administration	—
Other	737
TOTAL GENERAL EXPENDITURES	$30,567

The state debt as of the end of 1995/96 exceeded $5 billion, or $418 per capita.

36TAXATION

Pennsylvania's personal income tax, adopted in 1971, is levied at a rate of 2.8%. Business taxes include a corporate net income tax of 9.99%, capital stock and franchise tax, and taxes on public utilities, insurance premiums, and financial institutions. Pennsylvania's 6% sales and use tax exempts essential items like clothing, groceries, and medicines. Programs such as the Target Jobs Tax Credit and the Employment Incentive Payment program provide tax credits for hiring welfare recipients or persons from specified groups that have special employment needs or high unemployment rates.

In 1995/96, Pennsylvanians paid $5.4 billion in state income taxes.

37ECONOMIC POLICY

The Bureau of Economic Assistance directs and controls the Commerce Department's economic assistance activities, including the administration and management of the Revenue Bond and Mortgage Program, the Pennsylvania Industrial Development Authority, the Job Training Partnership Act, and the Pennsylvania Capital Loan Fund. Among the activities of the Bureau of Domestic and International Commerce are supervising projects encouraging industrial development, attracting both domestic and foreign investment to the state, and providing export assistance to Pennsylvania companies.

The Pennsylvania Industrial Development Authority Board and the Pennsylvania Minority Business Development Authority provide loans to businesses that want to build new facilities or renovate and expand older ones. The Office of Minority Business Enterprise seeks to strengthen minority businesses by helping them obtain contracts with the state. The Small Business Action Center aids small businesses by providing a network of informational sources. The Bureau of Technological Development directs all phases of the Department of Commerce's scientific and technological activities and monitors advanced technology initiatives and growth throughout the state. Additional services are provided by the Bureau of Statistics, Research and Planning, the Bureau of Appalachian Development, the Bureau of Travel Development, the Bureau of Motion Picture and Television Development, the Bureau of Management and Administration, the Financial Analysis Office, and the Nursing Home Loan Agency.

In 1987, Governor Robert Casey created a Pennsylvania Development Partnership whose 45 members drew up a strategic investment plan to diversify Pennsylvania's economy. The plan included measures to encourage particular industries, such as hardwood and food processing, and to promote the development of new technologies. In addition to offering guidelines for the state's economic policy, the Partnership put together a Response Team which assists ailing Pennsylvania companies or firms from out of state that wish to locate in Pennsylvania.

38HEALTH

Pennsylvania's infant mortality rate in 1994 was 8.1 per 1,000 live births. There were 39,050 legal abortions performed in 1995. Death rates for the leading causes of death—heart disease, cancer, and stroke—were well above the US average. Rates in 1995 per 100,000 population were as follows: heart disease, 359.7; cancer, 250.7; cerebrovascular disease, 68.6; accidents, 35.3; and suicide, 12.1. The overall death rate in 1995 was 1,050 per 100,000 population, one of the highest among the states. A high percentage of Pennsylvania residents aged 18–30 smoke; in 1995, estimated deaths from smoking-related illnesses totaled 274,359.

Statewide in 1995 there were 225 hospitals of all types, with 44,554 beds. The average expense per stay in Pennsylvania hospitals in 1995 was $5,707, and the average expense per inpatient day was $976. In 1996, there were 28,807 physicians and 8,206 dentists in the state. In 1995/96, 1,650,359 Medicaid recipients and 2,055,000 Medicare enrollees received $6.2 billion and $10.1 billion in benefits, respectively.

The University of Pennsylvania School of Medicine, which originated as the medical school of the College of Philadelphia in 1765, is the nation's oldest medical school. One of the nation's newest is the Hershey Medical Center of Pennsylvania State University. Other medical schools in Pennsylvania are the University of Pittsburgh School of Medicine, Temple University's School of Medicine, the Medical College of Pennsylvania, and Allegheny University, the last three in Philadelphia. The state also aids colleges of osteopathic medicine, podiatric medicine, and optometry—all in Philadelphia. Among the many medical certification boards located in Philadelphia are the boards of allergy and immunology, internal medicine, ophthalmology, and surgery.

39SOCIAL WELFARE

During 1991, 553,000 Pennsylvanians received aid to families with dependent children, with an average monthly payment of $497. In 1996, 1.12 million residents received monthly food stamp allowances averaging $72.76. Some $174.4 million in federal funds were spent on subsidized school lunches.

With the enactment of the Personal Responsibility and Work Opportunity Reconciliation Act of 1996, the US government has changed the form and regulations for many of its social welfare programs; most significantly, it replaces Aid to Families with Dependent Children (AFDC), an open-ended entitlement program, with Temporary Assistance for Needy Families (TANF), a limited system of assistance funded largely through federal block grants. The reform act also impacts the food stamp program, the Supplemental Security Income program, and the child nutrition program. The law took effect on 1 July 1997 and provided $16.38 billion in block grants for fiscal years 1997–2002. The grants are to be divided among the states based on an equation involving the numbers of former AFDC recipients in each state. Because many of the bills provisions have yet to be implemented into state-by-state policy, it was not possible to include the details of each state's programs for this edition of this work.

In 1995, Social Security benefits were paid to 23 million residents, averaging $740 a month. Supplemental Security Income was paid to 264,564 Pennsylvanians in 1995, averaging $379 a month. The average weekly unemployment benefit in Pennsylvania was $219.48 in 1995.

40HOUSING

In 1996, there were 5,107,000 housing units in Pennsylvania, 4,567,000 of which were occupied. That year, 37,895 units, valued at $3.5 billion, were authorized for construction; of these, 32,439 were owner-occupied. About 27% of the state's housing units were in Philadelphia, while 15% were in Pittsburgh. The median monthly cost for an owner-occupied housing unit with a mortgage in 1990, the last year for which figures are available, was $682; for a nonmortgaged unit the cost was $226. The median monthly rent for a renter-occupied unit was $404. In 1990, the median home value was $69,700, up 12.2% from 1980. During fiscal year 1996, Pennsylvania received $1.2 billion in aid from the US Department of Housing and Urban Development, including $268.4 million in community development block grants.

Faced with a decaying housing stock, Philadelphia during the 1970s and 1980s encouraged renovation of existing units along with the construction of new ones, effectively revitalizing several neighborhoods.

41EDUCATION

Pennsylvania lagged behind many of its neighbors in establishing a free public school system. From colonial times until the 1830s, almost all instruction in reading and writing took place in private schools. Called "dame schools" in the cities and "neighborhood schools" in rural areas, they offered primary courses, usually taught by women in their own homes. In addition, the Quakers, Moravians, and Scots-Irish Presbyterians all formed their own private schools, emphasizing religious study. Many communities also set up secondary schools, called academies, on land granted by the state; by 1850, there were 524 academies, some of which later developed into colleges. A public school law passed in 1834 was not mandatory in the school districts but was still unpopular. Thaddeus Stevens, then a state legislator, is credited with saving the law from repeal in 1835. Two years later, more than 40% of the state's children were in public schools.

As of 1990, 78.6% of the population 25 years old and older had completed four years of high school, and 18.6% had finished four or more years of college. In 1996, 105,981 students graduated from public high schools.

During the 1995/96 school year, 983,602 students were enrolled in public elementary schools, and 803,931 in secondary schools. Enrollment in private elementary schools was 253,341; in private secondary schools, 81,649. In 1995/96, Pennsylvania had 727 Roman Catholic elementary and high schools, which accounted for about 67% of all nonpublic school enrollment.

Enrollment in the 14 state-owned colleges in fall 1996 totaled 93,711. Indiana University of Pennsylvania, established in 1872, accounted for about 15% of this enrollment, with 13,680 students. Four universities have nonprofit corporate charters but are classified as state-related: Pennsylvania State University, Temple University, the University of Pittsburgh, and Lincoln University. Of these, Penn State is by far the largest, with a fall 1996 enrollment of 77,318. Founded in 1855 as the Farmers' High School of Pennsylvania, Penn State now has its main campus at University Park and 23 smaller campus locations statewide. In 1997 there were 15 community colleges and one technical institute.

The eight state-aided private institutions (receiving designated grants from the legislature) had a combined enrollment of 40,702 in 1996. The largest of these schools is the University of Pennsylvania, founded in 1740 by Benjamin Franklin as the Philadelphia Academy and Charitable School; among its noteworthy professional schools is the Wharton School of Business. The state's many private colleges and universities, which may also receive state aid through a per-pupil funding formula, include Bryn Mawr College (founded in 1880), Bucknell University (1846) in Lewisburg, Carnegie-Mellon University (1900) in Pittsburgh, Dickinson College (1733) in Carlisle, Duquesne University (1878) in Pittsburgh, Haverford College (1833), Lafayette College (1826), Lehigh University (1865), Swarthmore College (1864), and Villanova University (1842). Enrollment at all private colleges and universities in the state totaled 176,669 in fall 1996. The Pennsylvania Higher Education Assistance Agency offers higher education grants, guarantees private loans, and administers work-study programs for Pennsylvania students.

During the 1994/95 school year, Pennsylvania's total public school revenue receipts exceeded $11.9 billion. That year, per-pupil expenditures were $6,916.

42ARTS

Philadelphia was the cultural capital of the colonies, and rivaled New York as a theatrical center during the 1800s. In 1984, Philadelphia had five fully developed resident theaters, ranking 3d in the nation after New York and California. A number of regional and summer-stock theaters are scattered throughout the state, the most noteworthy being in Bucks County, Lancaster, and Pittsburgh. The National Choreographic Center was established in the mid-1980s in Carlisle in conjunction with the Central Pennsylvania Youth Ballet School.

Pennsylvania's most significant contribution to the performing arts has come through music. One of America's first important songwriters, Stephen Foster, grew up in Pittsburgh. The Pittsburgh Symphony, which began performing in 1896, first achieved prominence under Victor Herbert. Temporarily disbanded in 1910, the symphony was revived under Fritz Reiner in 1927; subsequent music directors have included William Steinberg and André Previn. Even more illustrious has been the career of the Philadelphia Orchestra, founded in 1900. Among this orchestra's best-known permanent conductors have been Leopold Stokowski and Eugene Ormandy, both of whom recorded extensively. Ormandy was succeeded in 1980 by Riccardo Muti. An important dance company, the Pennsylvania Ballet, is based in Philadelphia, which also has the Curtis Institute of Music, founded in 1924. Opera companies include the Pennsylvania Opera Theater, Pittsburgh Opera, and Opera Company of Philadelphia.

Expressions '80, a minorities arts festival in Philadelphia that attracted artists from a six-state area, was the first regional festival of its kind in the Northeast. The Pennsylvania Writers Collective, an initiative program of the Pennsylvania Council on the Arts, supports the work of the state's creative writers. Contributions from the NEA to the state's arts programs totaled $2,154,000. The NEA also gave $3,070,000 to the Pennsylvania Council on the Arts. The state and various private sources also provided funding for the council's activities.

Audiences for the state's art programs totaled 126,192,000 between 1987 and 1991. In 1991, the state had 3,000 arts associations and 75 local arts groups. There were 404,112 contributing artists.

The NEA has contributed to the Carnegie Museum of Art, the Philadelphia Orchestra, and the Central Pennsylvania Friends of Jazz. In 1996, the Association of Professional Vocal Ensembles (Chorus America) received funding from the NEA as well. The Pittsburgh Cultural District promotes the expansion of the city's economy and arts programs.

43LIBRARIES AND MUSEUMS

Pennsylvania's public libraries stocked 26,219,331 volumes during 1996/97, with a total circulation of 53,985,078. The largest public library in the state, and one of the oldest in the US, is the Free Library of Philadelphia, with 6,682,777 volumes in 48 branches. The Carnegie Library in Pittsburgh has 1,987,799 volumes and 17 branches. Harrisburg offers the State Library of Pennsylvania, which had 983,949 volumes in 1996/97. The Alverthorpe Gallery Library in Jenkintown contains the Rosenwald collection of illustrated books dating from the 15th century.

Philadelphia is the site of the state's largest academic collection, the University of Pennsylvania Libraries, with 4,209,747 volumes. Other major academic libraries are at the University of Pittsburgh, 3,296,893 volumes; Penn State, 2,500,000; Temple, 2,146,396; Carnegie-Mellon, 852,241; and Swarthmore, 680,000.

Pennsylvania has 339 museums and public gardens, with many of the museums located in Philadelphia. The Franklin Institute, established in 1824 as an exhibition hall and training center for inventors and mechanics, is a leading showcase for science and technology. Other important museums are the Philadelphia Museum of Art, Academy of Natural Sciences, Pennsylvania Academy of the Fine Arts, Afro-American Historical and Cultural Museum, American Catholic Historical Society, American Swedish Historical Foundation Museum, and Museum of American Jewish History.

The Carnegie Institute in Pittsburgh is home to several major museums, including the Carnegie Museum of Natural History and the Museum of Art. Also in Pittsburgh are the Buhl Planetarium and Institute of Popular Science and the Frick Art Museum. Other institutions scattered throughout the state include the Moravian Museum, Bethlehem; US Army Military History Institute, Carlisle; Erie Art Center, Museum, and Old Custom House; Pennsylvania Lumber Museum, Galeton; Pennsylvania Historical and Museum Commission and William Penn Memorial Museum, Harrisburg; Pennsylvania Dutch Folk Culture Society, Lenhartsville; Schwenkfelder Museum, Pennsburg; and Railroad Museum of Pennsylvania, Strasburg.

Several old forts commemorate the French and Indian War, and George Washington's Revolutionary headquarters at Valley Forge is now a national historical park. Brandywine Battlefield (Chadds Ford) is another Revolutionary War site. Gettysburg National Military Park commemorates the Civil War. Other historic sites are Independence National Historical Park, Philadelphia; the Daniel Boone Homestead, Birdsboro; John Brown's House, Chambersburg; James Buchanan's home, Lancaster; and Ft. Augusta, Sunbury, a frontier outpost.

44COMMUNICATIONS

Philadelphia already had mail links to surrounding towns and to Maryland and Virginia by 1737, when Benjamin Franklin was named deputy postmaster of the city, but service was slow and not always reliable. During the remainder of the century, significant improvements in delivery were made, but some townspeople devised ingenious ways of transmitting information even faster than the mails. Philadelphia stock exchange brokers, for instance, communicated with agents in New York by flashing coded signals with mirrors and lights from a series of high points across New Jersey, thereby receiving stock prices on the same day they were transacted. By 1846, the first telegraph service in the state linked Harrisburg and Lancaster.

In 1993, 97.5% of Pennsylvania's 4,736,000 households had telephones.

Pittsburgh's KDKA became the world's first commercial radio station in 1920. By 1996, it was one of 178 AM and 272 FM radio stations. In addition, there were 46 television stations, nine of which were noncommercial, educational stations. Philadelphia alone had 12 AM, 17 FM, and 7 television stations. Pittsburgh had 8 AM, 16 FM, and 7 television stations. WQED in Pittsburgh pioneered community-sponsored educational television when it began broadcasting in 1954. In 1996 there were 46 large cable television systems in service.

45PRESS

Benjamin Franklin may have been colonial Pennsylvania's most renowned publisher, but its first was Andrew Bradford, whose *American Weekly Mercury*, established in 1719, was the third newspaper to appear in the colonies. Founded nine years later, the *Pennsylvania Gazette* was purchased by Franklin in 1730 and served as the springboard for *Poor Richard's Almanack*.

During the 1800s, newspapers sprang up in all the major cities and many small communities. By 1880, Pittsburgh had 10 daily newspapers—more than any other city its size. After a series of mergers and closings, however, it is left with only one paper today—the *Post-Gazette*. Philadelphia has two newspapers, the *Inquirer* and the *Daily News*. The *Inquirer*, founded in 1829, has won numerous awards for its investigative reporting.

In 1997, Pennsylvania had 45 morning newspapers, 46 evening newspapers, 3 all-day dailies, and 42 Sunday papers. The following table shows the circulation of some of the leading dailies in 1997:

AREA	NAME	DAILY	SUNDAY
Allentown	*Morning Call* (m)	133,735	186,557
Harrisburg	*Patriot News* (m,S)	64,283	174,106
Philadelphia	*Inquirer* (m,S)	446,842	391,740
	Daily News (e)	184,906	—
Pittsburgh	*Post-Gazette* (m)	240,043	440,504
Wilkes-Barre	*Citizens' Voice* (m)	38,122	31,001
	Times Leader (m)	48,352	71,755

Farm Journal and *Current History,* both monthlies, are published in Philadelphia, and there are monthlies named for both Philadelphia and Pittsburgh. Of more specialized interest are the gardening, nutrition, and health magazines and books from Rodale Press in Emmaus, and automotive guides from the Chilton Co. in Radnor.

46ORGANIZATIONS

The 1992 US Census of Service Industries counted 4,631 organizations in Pennsylvania, including 499 business associations; 3,325 civic, social, and fraternal associations; and 807 other membership organizations.

Philadelphia is the home for two major service organizations: Big Brothers/Big Sisters of America and the Grand United Order of Odd Fellows. Cultural and educational organizations in that city include the American Academy of Political and Social Science, American Philosophical Society, and Middle States Association of Colleges and Schools. The Association for Children with Learning Disabilities is located in Pittsburgh, the College Placement Council in Bethlehem, and the American Philatelic Society in State College. Also in State College is the Environmental Coalition on Nuclear Power. The Society for Animal Rights, a humane organization, is in Clarks Summit.

Commercial and trade groups in the state include the American Mushroom Institute, Kennett Square; Insurance Institute of America, Malvern; and Society of Automotive Engineers, Warrendale. The Gray Panthers, a senior citizens' activist group, and Women's Strike for Peace are in Philadelphia. Valley Forge is the home of the Patriotic Order of the Sons of America.

Among the many sports organizations headquartered in Pennsylvania are the US Squash Racquets Association, in Bala-Cynwyd; National Trotting and Pacing Association, Hanover; Pop Warner Football and US Rowing Association, Philadelphia; and Little League Baseball, Williamsport.

47TOURISM, TRAVEL, AND RECREATION

Domestic travelers spent more than $10,060,000 in Pennsylvania in 1993. Travel and tourism was the state's 2d-largest employer.

Philadelphia—whose Independence National Historical Park has been called the most historic square mile in America—offers the Liberty Bell, Independence Hall, Carpenter's Hall, and many other sites. North of Philadelphia, in Bucks County, is the town of New Hope, with its numerous crafts and antique shops. The Lancaster area is "Pennsylvania Dutch" country, featuring tours and exhibits of Amish farm life. Gettysburg contains not only the famous Civil War battlefield but also the home of Dwight D. Eisenhower, opened to the public in 1980. Among the most popular sites are Chocolate World and Hersheypark in the town of Hershey and Valley Forge National Historic Park. Annual parades and festivals include the Mummers Parade on 1 January in Philadelphia and the Kutztown Folk Festival, commemorating Pennsylvania Dutch life, held the first week of July.

No less an attraction are the state's outdoor recreation areas. By far the most popular for both skiing and camping are the Delaware Water Gap and the Poconos, also a favorite resort region. The state park system, includes 106 parks, 11 state forests, and 3 environmental education centers. In 1995,

2,433,557 Pennsylvania hunting licenses and 1,787,160 trout stamps were sold.

48SPORTS

Pennsylvania has seven major league professional sports teams: the Philadelphia Phillies and the Pittsburgh Pirates of major league baseball, the Philadelphia Eagles and the Pittsburgh Steelers of the National Football League, the Philadelphia 76ers of the National Basketball Association, and the Pittsburgh Penguins and Philadelphia Flyers of the National Hockey League.

The Phillies won the World Series in 1980; they won the National League Championship in 1993, but lost the World Series to the Toronto Blue Jays. The Pirates won it in 1909, 1925, 1960, 1971, and 1979. The Steelers established a legendary football dynasty in the 1970s, winning Super Bowls in 1975, 1976, 1979, and 1980. They also played in the 1996 Super Bowl, losing to the Dallas Cowboys. The Eagles won the NFL championship in 1981, but lost to Oakland in that year's Super Bowl. The 76ers won the NBA championship in 1947, 1956, 1967, and 1983, and lost the championship series in 1977, 1980, and 1982. The Flyers won the Stanley Cup in 1974 and 1975 and lost in the finals in 1976, 1980, 1985, 1987, and 1997. The Penguins won the Stanley Cup in 1991 and 1992.

There are also minor league baseball teams in Harrisburg, Scranton, Wilkes-Barre, and Erie, and minor league hockey teams in Hershey, Johnstown, and Philadelphia.

Horse racing is conducted at Keystone Race Track in Bucks County, Penn National Race Course in Dauphin County, and Commodore Downs in Erie County. Harness-racing tracks include Liberty Bell Park in northeast Philadelphia, the Meadows in Washington County, and Pocono Downs in Luzerne County. Each June, Pennsylvania hosts a major auto race, the Pocono 500. The Penn Relays, an important amateur track meet, are held in Philadelphia every April.

In collegiate sports, football is most prominent. The University of Pittsburgh Panthers were named national champions in 1918, 1937, and 1976. Penn State was named champion in 1982 and 1986 and joined the Big Ten in 1990. The Nittany Lions won the Rose Bowl in 1995, the Sugar Bowl in 1983, the Orange Bowl in 1969, and the Cotton Bowl in 1972. Villanova won the NCAA basketball championship in 1985.

Other annual sporting events include the US Pro Indoor Tennis Championship in Philadelphia in January and February. Each summer, Williamsport hosts baseball's Little League World Series.

49FAMOUS PENNSYLVANIANS

Johan Printz (b.Sweden, 1592–1663), the 400-lb, hard-drinking, hard-swearing, and hard-ruling governor of New Sweden, was Pennsylvania's first European resident of note. The founder of Pennsylvania was William Penn (b.England, 1644–1718), a Quaker of sober habits and deep religious beliefs. Most extraordinary of all Pennsylvanians, Benjamin Franklin (b.Massachusetts, 1706–90), a printer, author, inventor, scientist, legislator, diplomat, and statesman, served the Philadelphia, Pennsylvania, and US governments in a variety of posts.

Only one native Pennsylvanian, James Buchanan (1791–1868), has ever become US president. Buchanan was a state assemblyman, five-term US representative, two-term US senator, secretary of state, and minister to Russia and then to Great Britain before entering the White House as a 65-year-old bachelor in 1857. As president, he tried to maintain the Union by avoiding extremes and preaching compromise, but his toleration of slavery was abhorrent to abolitionists and his desire to preserve the Union was obnoxious to secessionists. Dwight D. Eisenhower (b.Texas, 1890–1969) retired to a farm in Gettysburg after his presidency was over. George M. Dallas (1792–1864), Pennsylvania's only US vice president, was James K. Polk's running mate.

The six Pennsylvanians who have served on the US Supreme Court have all been associate justices: James Wilson (1742–98), Henry Baldwin (1780–1844), Robert C. Grier (1794–1870), William Strong (1808–95), George Shiras, Jr. (1832–1924), and Owen J. Roberts (1875–1955). Controversial supreme court nominee Robert Heron Bock (b. Pennsylvania 1927) served as a federal judge for many years.

Many other Pennsylvanians have held prominent federal positions. Albert Gallatin (b.Switzerland, 1761–1849), brilliant secretary of the treasury under Thomas Jefferson and James Madison, later served as minister to France and then to Great Britain. Richard Rush (1780–1859) was Madison's attorney general and John Quincy Adams's secretary of the treasury. A distinguished jurist, Jeremiah Sullivan Black (1810–83) was Buchanan's attorney general and later his secretary of state. John Wanamaker (1838–1922), an innovative department store merchandiser, served as postmaster general under Benjamin Harrison. Philander C. Knox (1853–1921) was Theodore Roosevelt's attorney general and William Howard Taft's secretary of state. Financier Andrew C. Mellon (1855–1937) was secretary of the treasury under Warren G. Harding, Calvin Coolidge, and Herbert Hoover. Recent Pennsylvanians in high office include Richard Helms (b.1913), director of the US Central Intelligence Agency from 1966 to 1973, and Alexander Haig (b.1924), former commander of NATO forces in Europe, chief of staff under Richard Nixon, and Ronald Reagan's first choice for secretary of state.

Three US senators, Simon Cameron (1799–1889), Matthew Quay (1833–1904), and Boies Penrose (1860–1921), are best known as leaders of the powerful Pennsylvania Republican machine. Senator Joseph F. Guffey (1870–1959) sponsored legislation to stabilize the bituminous coal industry. After serving as reform mayor of Philadelphia, Joseph S. Clark (1901–1990) also distinguished himself in the Senate, and Hugh Scott (b.1900) was Republican minority leader from 1969 to 1977. Outstanding representatives from Pennsylvania include Thaddeus Stevens (1792–1868), leader of radical Republicans during the Civil War era; David Wilmot (1814–68), author of the proviso attempting to prohibit slavery in territory acquired from Mexico; and Samuel J. Randall (1828–90), speaker of the House of Representatives from 1876 to 1881.

Other notable historical figures were Joseph Galloway (b.Maryland, 1729?–1803), a loyalist; Robert Morris (b.England, 1734–1806), a Revolutionary financier; and Betsy Ross (Elizabeth Griscom, 1752–1836), the seamstress who allegedly stitched the first American flag. Pamphleteer Thomas Paine (b.England, 1737–1809), pioneer Daniel Boone (1734–1820), and General Anthony Wayne (1745–96) also distinguished themselves during this period. In the Civil War, General George B. McClellan (1826–85) led the Union army on the Peninsula and at the Battle of Antietam, while at the Battle of Gettysburg, Generals George Gordon Meade (b.Spain, 1815–72) and Winfield Scott Hancock (1824–86) both showed their military prowess.

Important state governors include John W. Geary (1819–73), Samuel W. Pennypacker (1843–1916), Robert E. Pattison (b.Maryland, 1850–1904), Gifford Pinchot (b.Connecticut 1865–1946), James H. Duff (1883–1969), George H. Earle (1890–1974), Milton J. Shapp (b.Ohio, 1912), William W. Scranton (b.Connecticut, 1917), George M. Leader (b.1918), and Richard L. Thornburgh (b.1932).

Pennsylvanians have won Nobel Prizes in every category except literature. General George C. Marshall (1880–1959), chief of staff of the US Army in World War II and secretary of state when the European Recovery Program (Marshall Plan) was adopted, won the 1953 Nobel Peace Prize. Simon Kuznets (b.Russia, 1901–85) received the 1971 Nobel Prize in economic

science for work on economic growth, and Herbert A. Simon (b.Wisconsin, 1916) received the 1978 award for work on decision making in economic organizations; in 1980, Lawrence R. Klein (b.Nebraska, 1920) was honored for his design and application of econometric models. In physics, Otto Stern (b.Germany, 1888–1969) won the 1943 prize for work on the magnetic momentum of protons. In chemistry, Theodore W. Richards (1868–1928) won the 1914 Nobel Prize for determining the atomic weight of many elements, and Christian Boehmer Anfinsen (b.1916) won the 1972 award for pioneering studies in enzymes. In physiology or medicine, Philip S. Hench (1896–1965) won in 1950 for his discoveries about hormones of the adrenal cortex, Haldane K. Hartline (1903–83) won in 1967 for work on the human eye, and Howard M. Temin (1934–94) was honored in 1975 for the study of tumor viruses.

Many other Pennsylvanians were distinguished scientists. Ebenezer Kinnersly (1711–78) studied electricity, and Benjamin Franklin's grandson Alexander Dallas Bache (1806–67) was an expert on magnetism. Caspar Wistar (b.Germany, 1761–1818) and Thomas Woodhouse (1770–1809) pioneered the study of chemistry, while William Maclure (b.Scotland, 1763–1840) and James Mease (1771–1846) were early geologists. David Rittenhouse (1732–96) was a distinguished astronomer. John Bartram (1699–1777) and his son William (1739–1823) won international repute as botanists. Benjamin Rush (1745–1813) was Pennsylvania's most distinguished physician. Philip Syng Physick (1768–1837) was a leading surgeon, and Nathaniel Chapman (b.Virginia, 1780–1853) was the first president of the American Medical Association. Rachel Carson (1907–64), a marine biologist and writer, became widely known for her crusade against the use of chemical pesticides. Noted inventors born in Pennsylvania include steamboat builder Robert Fulton (1765–1815) and David Thomas (1794–1882), the father of the American anthracite iron industry.

Pennsylvania played a large role in the economic development of the US. In addition to Mellon, outstanding bankers include Stephen Girard (b.France, 1750–1831), Nicholas Biddle (1786–1844), Anthony J. Drexel (1826–93), and John J. McCloy (1895–1985). Andrew Carnegie (b.Scotland, 1835–1919) and his lieutenants, including Henry Clay Frick (1849–1919) and Charles M. Schwab (1862–1939), created the most efficient steel-manufacturing company in the 19th century. Wanamaker, Frank W. Woolworth (b.New York, 1852–1919), and Sebastian S. Kresge (1867–1966) were pioneer merchandisers.

Other prominent businessmen born in Pennsylvania are automobile pioneer Clement Studebaker (1831–1901), chocolate manufacturer Milton S. Hershey (1857–1945), and retired Chrysler chairman Lee A. Iacocca (b.1924).

Pennsylvania labor leaders include Uriah S. Stephens (1821–82) and Terence V. Powderly (1849–1924), leaders of the Knights of Labor; Philip Murray (b.Scotland, 1886–1952), president of the CIO; and David J. MacDonald (1902–79), leader of the steelworkers. Among economic theorists, Henry George (1839–97) was the unorthodox advocate of the single tax. Florence Kelley (1859–1932) was an important social reformer, as is Bayard Rustin (1910–1987).

Important early religious leaders, all born in Germany, include Henry Melchior Muhlenberg (1711–87), organizer of Pennsylvania's Lutherans; Count Nikolaus Ludwig von Zinzendorf (1700–1760), a Morovian leader; and Johann Conrad Beissel (1690–1768), founder of the Ephrata Cloister. Charles Taze Russell (1852–1916), born a Congregationalist, founded the group that later became Jehovah's Witnesses. Among the state's outstanding scholars are historians Henry C. Lee (1825–1909), John Bach McMaster (1852–1932), Ellis Paxson Oberholtzer (1868–1936), and Henry Steele Commager (b.1902); anthropologist Margaret Mead (1901–78); behavioral psychologist

B(urrhus) F(rederic) Skinner (1904–1990); urbanologist Jane Jacobs (b.1916); and language theorist Noam Chomsky (b.1928). Thomas Gallaudet (b.1787–1851) was a pioneer in education of the deaf.

Pennsylvania has produced a large number of distinguished journalists and writers. In addition to Franklin, newspapermen include John Dunlap (b.Ireland, 1747–1812), Benjamin Franklin Bache (1769–98), William L. McLean (1852–1931), and Moses L. Annenberg (1878–1942). Magazine editors were Sarah Josepha Buell Hale (b.New Hampshire, 1788–1879), Cyrus H. K. Curtis (b.Maine, 1850–1933), Edward W. Bok (b.Netherlands, 1863–1930), and I(sidor) F(einstein) Stone (1907–1989). Ida M. Tarbell (1857–1944) was perhaps Pennsylvania's most famous muckraker. Among the many noteworthy Pennsylvania-born writers are Charles Brockden Brown (1771–1810), Bayard Taylor (1825–78), novelist and physician Silas Weir Mitchell (1829–1914), Charles Godfrey Leland (1824–1903), Owen Wister (1860–1938), Richard Harding Davis (1864–1916), Gertrude Stein (1874–1946), Mary Roberts Rinehart (1876–1958), Hervey Allen (1889–1949), Christopher Morley (1890–1957), Conrad Richter (1890–1968), John O'Hara (1905–70), Donald Barthelme (1931–89), and John Updike (b.1932). James Michener (b.New York, 1907) was raised in the state. Pennsylvania playwrights include James Nelson Barker (1784–1858), Maxwell Anderson (1888–1959), George S. Kaufman (1889–1961), Marc Connelly (1890–1980), Clifford Odets (1906–63), and Ed Bullins (b.1935). Among Pennsylvania poets are Francis Hopkinson (1737–91), Philip Freneau (b.New York, 1753–1832), Thomas Dunn English (1819–1902), Thomas Buchanan Read (1822–72), and Wallace Stevens (1879–1955).

Composers include Stephen Collins Foster (1826–64), Ethelbert Woodbridge Nevin (1862–1901), Charles Wakefield Cadman (1881–1946), and Samuel Barber (1910–81). Among Pennsylvania painters prominent in the history of American art are Benjamin West (1738–1820), renowned as the father of American painting; Charles Willson Peale (1741–1827), who was also a naturalist; Thomas Sully (b.England, 1783–1872); George Catlin (1796–1872); Thomas Eakins (1844–1916); Mary Cassatt (1845–1926); Man Ray (1890–1976); Andrew Wyeth (b.1917); and Andy Warhol (1927–87). Outstanding sculptors include William Rush (1756–1833), George Grey Barnard (1863–1938), and Alexander Calder (1898–1976).

Pennsylvania produced and patronized a host of actors, including Edwin Forrest (1806–72) Lionel (1878–1954), Ethel (1879–1959), and John (1882–1942) Barrymore; W. C. Fields (William Claude Dukenfield, 1880–1946); Ed Wynn (Isaiah Edwin Leopold, 1886–1966); William Powell (1892–1987); Ethel Waters (1896–1977); Janet Gaynor (1906–84); James Stewart (1908–97); Broderick Crawford (1911–1986); Gene Kelly (b.1912); Charles Bronson (Charles Buchinsky, b.1922); Mario Lanza (1925–59); Shirley Jones (b.1934); and comedian Bill Cosby (b.1937). Film directors Joseph L. Mankiewicz (1909–1993), Arthur Penn (b.1922), and Sidney Lumet (b.1924) and film producer David O. Selznick (1902–65) also came from Pennsylvania.

Pennsylvania has produced outstanding musicians. Four important Pennsylvania-born vocalists are Marian Anderson (b.1897–1993), Blanche Thebom (b.1919), Marilyn Horne (b.1934), and Anna Moffo (b.1934). Pianists include the versatile Oscar Levant (1906–72) and jazz interpreters Earl "Fatha" Hines (1905–83) and Erroll Garner (1921–77). Popular band leaders include Fred Waring (1900–84), Jimmy Dorsey (1904–57) and his brother Tommy (1905–56), and Les Brown (b.1912). Perry Como (b.1913), Daryl Hall (b.1949), and John Oates (b.New York, 1948) have achieved renown as popular singers. Dancers and choreographers from Pennsylvania include Martha Graham (1893–1991), Paul Taylor (b.1930), and Gelsey Kirkland (b.1952).

Of the many outstanding athletes associated with Pennsylvania, Jim Thorpe (b.Oklahoma, 1888–1953) was most versatile, having starred in Olympic pentathlon and decathlon events and football. Baseball Hall of Famers include Honus Wagner (1874–1955), Stan Musial (b.1920), and Roy Campanella (1921–1993). Outstanding Pennsylvania football players include Harold "Red" Grange (1903–91), George Blanda (b.1927), John Unitas (b.1933), Joe Namath (b.1943), and Tony Dorsett (b.1954). Other stars include basketball's Wilt Chamberlain (b.1936); golf's Arnold Palmer (b.1929), tennis's Bill Tilden (1893–1953); horse racing's Bill Hartack (b.1932); billiards' Willie Mosconi (b.1913); swimming's Johnny Weissmuller (1904–84); and track and field's Bill Toomey (b.1939).

Pennsylvania has also been the birthplace of a duchess—Bessie Wallis Warfield, the Duchess of Windsor (1896–1986)—and of a princess—Grace Kelly, Princess Grace of Monaco (1929–82).

[50] BIBLIOGRAPHY

Billinger, Robert D. *Pennsylvania's Coal Industry.* Gettysburg: Pennsylvania Historical Association, 1954.

Binder, Frederick Moor. *Coal Age Empire: Pennsylvania Coal and its Utilization to 1860.* Harrisburg: Pennsylvania Historical and Museum Commission. 1974

Blockson, Charles L. *African Americans in Pennsylvania: A History and Guide.* Baltimore: Black Classic, 1994.

Bremer, Francis J., and Dennis B. Downey (eds.). *A Guide to the History of Pennsylvania.* Westport, Conn.: Greenwood, 1994.

Bridenbaugh, Carl. *Cities in Revolt: Urban Life in America, 1743–76.* New York: Knopf, 1955.

Cochran, Thomas C. *Pennsylvania: A Bicentennial History.* New York: Norton, 1978.

Commonwealth of Pennsylvania. Bureau of Statistics. Research, and Planning. *1984 Pennsylvania Statistical Abstract.* 26th ed. Harrisburg, 1984.

Federal Writers' Project. *Pennsylvania: A Guide to the Keystone State.* Reprint. New York: Somerset, 1980 (orig. 1940).

Klein, Philip S., and Ari Hoogenboom. *A History of Pennsylvania.* Rev. ed. University Park: Pennsylvania State University Press, 1980.

Miller, E. Willard, ed. *A Geography of Pennsylvania.* University Park: Pennsylvania State University Press, 1995.

Murphy, Raymond E., and Marion Murphy. *Pennsylvania: A Regional Geography.* Harrisburg: Pennsylvania Book Service, 1937.

Pennsylvania, Commonwealth of. Department of General Services. *The Pennsylvania Manual, 1995.* Vol 112. Harrisburg, 1995.

Pennsylvania Chamber of Commerce. *Pennsylvania Government Today.* State College, Pa: Pennsylvania Valley Publishers, 1973.

Soderland, Jean R., and Richard S. Dunn (eds.). *William Penn and the Founding of Pennsylvania, 1680-1684: A Documentary History.* Philadelphia: University of Pennsylvania Press, 1983.

Wallace, Paul A. W. *Pennsylvania: Seed of a Nation.* New York: Harper & Row, 1962.

RHODE ISLAND

State of Rhode Island and Providence Plantations

ORIGIN OF STATE NAME: Named for Rhode Island in Narragansett Bay, which was likened to the isle of Rhodes in the Mediterranean Sea. **NICKNAME:** The Ocean State. (ALSO: Little Rhody.) **CAPITAL:** Providence. **ENTERED UNION:** 29 May 1790 (13th). **SONG:** "Rhode Island." **MOTTO:** Hope. **COAT OF ARMS:** A golden anchor on a blue field. **FLAG:** In the center of a white field is a golden anchor and, beneath it, a blue ribbon with the state motto in gold letters, all surrounded by a circle of 13 gold stars. **OFFICIAL SEAL:** The anchor of the arms is surrounded by four scrolls, the topmost bearing the state motto: the words "Seal of the State of Rhode Island and Providence Plantations 1636" encircle the whole. **ANIMAL:** Quahaug. **BIRD:** Rhode Island Red. **FLOWER:** Violet. **TREE:** Red maple. **MINERAL:** Bowenite. **ROCK:** Cumberlandite. **LEGAL HOLIDAYS:** New Year's Day, 1 January; Birthday of Martin Luther King, Jr., 3d Monday in January; Washington's Birthday, 3d Monday in February; Memorial Day, last Monday in May; Independence Day, 4 July; Victory Day, 2d Monday in August; Labor Day, 1st Monday in September; Columbus Day, 2d Monday in October; Election Day, 1st Tuesday after 1st Monday in November, in even-numbered years; Veterans Day, 11 November; Thanksgiving Day, 4th Thursday in November; Christmas Day, 25 December. **TIME:** 7 AM EST = noon GMT.

¹LOCATION, SIZE, AND EXTENT

One of the six New England states in the northeastern US, Rhode Island is the smallest of all the 50 states. Rhode Island occupies only 0.03% of the total US area, and could fit inside Alaska, the largest state, nearly 486 times.

The total area of Rhode Island is 1,212 sq mi (3,139 sq km), of which land comprises 1,055 sq mi (2,732 sq km), and inland water 157 sq mi (407 sq km). The state extends 37 mi (60 km) E-W and 48 mi (77 km) N-S.

Rhode Island is bordered on the N and E by Massachusetts; on the S by the Atlantic Ocean (enclosing the ocean inlet, Narragansett Bay); and on the W by Connecticut (with part of the line formed by the Pawcatuck River). Three large islands—Prudence, Aquidneck (officially known as Rhode Island), and Conanicut—are situated within Narragansett Bay. Block Island, with an area of about 11 sq mi (28 sq km), lies some 9 mi (14 km) SW of Pt. Judith, on the mainland. There are 38 islands in all.

The total boundary length of Rhode Island is 160 mi (257 km). The state's geographic center is in Kent County, 1 mi (1.6 km) SSW of Cranston.

²TOPOGRAPHY

Rhode Island comprises two main regions. The New England Upland Region, which is rough and hilly and marked by forests and lakes, occupies the western two-thirds of the state, while the Seaboard Lowland, with its sandy beaches and salt marshes, occupies the eastern third. The highest point in the state is Jerimoth Hill, at 812 feet (247 meters), in the northwest.

Rhode Island's principal river, the Blackstone, flows from Woonsocket past Pawtucket and thence into the Providence River, which, like the Sakonnet, is an estuary of Narragansett Bay; the Pawcatuck River flows into Block Island Sound. The state has 38 islands, the largest being Aquidneck (Rhode Island), with an area of about 45 sq mi (117 sq km).

³CLIMATE

Rhode Island has a humid climate, with cold winters and short summers. The average annual temperature is 50°F (10°C). At Providence the temperature ranges from an average of 28°F (–2°C) in January to 73°F (23°C) in July. The record high temperature, 104°F (40°C), was registered in Providence on 2 August 1975; the record low, –23°F (–31°C), at Kingston on 11 January 1942. In Providence, the average annual precipitation is 45 in (114 cm); snowfall averages 37 in (94 cm) a year. Rhode Island's weather is highly changeable, with storms and hurricanes an occasional threat. On 21 September 1938, a hurricane and tidal wave took a toll of 262 lives; Hurricane Carol, on 31 August 1954, left 19 dead, and property damage was estimated at $90 million. A blizzard on 6–7 February 1978 dropped a record 28.6 in (73 cm) of snow on the state, as measured at Warwick, and caused 21 storm-attributed deaths.

⁴FLORA AND FAUNA

Though small, Rhode Island has three distinct life zones; sand-plain lowlands, rising hills, and highlands. Common trees are the tuliptree, pin and post oaks, and red cedar. Cattails are abundant in marsh areas, and 40 types of fern and 30 species of orchid are indigenous to the state. The small whorled pogonia is endangered.

Urbanization and industrialization have taken their toll of native mammals. Swordfish, bluefish, lobsters, and clams populate coastal waters; brook trout and pickerel are among the common freshwater fish. The Indiana bat, peregrine and Arctic falcons, bald eagle, and shortnose sturgeon are on the federal endangered list.

⁵ENVIRONMENTAL PROTECTION

The Department of Environmental Management coordinates all of the state's environmental protection and management programs. The Air, Solid Waste, and Hazardous Materials Section enforces controls on solid waste disposal, hazardous waste management facilities, industrial air pollution, and site remediation; the Water Quality Management Section regulates waste-treatment facilities, the discharge of industrial and oil wastes into state waters and public sewer facilities, groundwater protection, freshwater wetlands, dam maintenance, and home sewage disposal systems; the Natural Resources Management Section oversees fish, wildlife and estuarine resources, forest management, parks and recreation, and the enforcement of conservation laws; Planning and Administrative Services assists industry in pollution prevention, administers recycling programs, administers land preservation programs, and coordinates land acquisitions. The department also oversees water supply management.

In 1995, there were 12 hazardous waste sites in the state. In 1996, 10% of the state's area was wetland.

⁶POPULATION

Rhode Island ranked 43rd in population among the 50 states with a 1990 census total of 1,003,464 (a 5.9% increase from 1980). In 1996, the population was estimated at 990,225, a 1.3% decline from 1990. Rhode Island was, at 960.3 persons per sq mi (369 per sq km), the nation's 2d most densely populated state, after New Jersey. According to the 1990 census, 86% of all Rhode Islanders lived in urban areas. Providence, the capital, is the leading city, with an estimated population in 1994 of 150,639 (compared to the 1940 peak of 253,504). Other cities include Pawtucket, 69,002; and Woonsocket, 40,752. In 1995, the Providence-Warwick-Pawtucket metropolitan area had an estimated population of 907,801, down from 917,178 in 1990.

⁷ETHNIC GROUPS

Rhode Island's black population numbered 39,000 in 1990, or less than 4% of the state total. Among other minority groups, the 1990 census counted 46,000 persons of Hispanic origin, 4,000 Native Americans, 3,417 Cambodians, 3,037 Chinese, and 2,040 Laotians. The foreign born made up 9.5% of the population in 1990.

⁸LANGUAGES

Many place-names in Rhode Island attest to the early presence of Mahican Indians: for instance, Sakonnet Point, Pawtucket, Matunuck, Narragansett.

English in Rhode Island is of the Northern dialect, with the distinctive features of eastern New England: absence of final /r/, and a vowel in *part* and *bath* intermediate between that in *father* and that in *bat*.

Rhode Island's immigrant past is reflected in the fact that in 1990, 18% of the state's residents reported speaking a language other than English in the home. The leading languages, and the number of people speaking them, were Portuguese, 39,947; Spanish, 35,492; French, 31,669; and Italian, 20,619.

⁹RELIGIONS

The first European settlement in Rhode Island was founded by an English clergyman, Roger Williams, who left Massachusetts to find freedom of worship. The Rhode Island Charter of 1663 proclaimed that a "flourishing civil state may stand and best be maintained with full liberty in religious concernments." Rhode Island has maintained this viewpoint throughout its history, and has long been a model of religious pluralism. The first Baptist congregation in the US was established in 1638 in Providence. In Newport stands the oldest synagogue (1763) and the oldest Quaker meetinghouse (1699) in the US.

Contemporary Rhode Island is the most Catholic state in the US, reflecting heavy immigration from Italy, Ireland, Portugal, and French Canada. There were 633,427 Roman Catholics and an estimated 16,101 Jews in 1990. The only large Protestant denominations were Episcopalians, 31,865, and American Baptist USA, 21,703.

¹⁰TRANSPORTATION

As of 1995, Providence & Worcester was the only freight-hauling railroad in operation, utilizing 81 rail mi (130 km) of track; in 1995 chemicals accounted for most of the 571,880 tons of freight brought into or hauled from the state. In 1996, Amtrak operated 16 daily trains through Rhode Island. Ridership, at three stops, was 423,447 in 1995/96. In 1995 there were 5,893 mi (9,488 km) of public highways and roads; 699,210 motor vehicles were registered in 1995, and 670,360 drivers' licenses were in force. The major route through New England, I-95, crosses Rhode Island. The Rhode Island Public Transit Authority provides commuter bus service connecting urbanized areas. Some of the best deepwater ocean ports on the east coast are in Narragansett Bay. The port at Providence handled over 6.9 million tons of cargo in 1995.

There were 26 airfields in early 1995. Theodore Francis Green Airport is the major air terminal, with 1,081,215 enplaned passengers in 1994.

¹¹HISTORY

Before the arrival of the first white settlers, the Narragansett Indians inhabited the area from what is now Providence south along Narragansett Bay. Their principal rivals, the Wampanoag, dominated the eastern shore region.

In 1524, Florentine navigator Giovanni da Verrazano, sailing in the employ of France, became the first European to explore Rhode Island. The earliest permanent settlement was established at Providence in 1636 by English clergyman Roger Williams and a small band of followers who left the repressive atmosphere of the Massachusetts Bay Colony to seek freedom of worship. Other nonconformists followed, settling Portsmouth (1638), Newport (1639), and Warwick (1642). In 1644, Williams journeyed to England, where he secured a parliamentary patent uniting the four original towns into a single colony, the Providence Plantations. This legislative grant remained in effect until the Stuart Restoration made it prudent to seek a royal charter. The charter, secured for Rhode Island and the Providence Plantations from Charles II in 1663, guaranteed religious liberty, permitting significant local autonomy, and strengthened the colony's territorial claims. Encroachments by white settlers on Indian lands led to the Indian uprising known as King Philip's War (1675–76), during which the Indians were soundly defeated.

The early 18th century was marked by significant growth in agriculture and commerce, including the rise of the slave trade. Having the greatest degree of self-rule, Rhode Island had the most to lose from British efforts after 1763 to increase the mother country's supervision and control over the colonies. On 4 May 1776, Rhode Island became the first colony formally to renounce all allegiance to King George III. Favoring the weak central government established by the Articles of Confederation, the state quickly ratified them in 1778, but subsequently resisted the centralizing tendencies of the federal constitution. Rhode Island withheld ratification until 29 May 1790, making it the last of the original 13 states to join the Union.

The principal trends in 19th-century Rhode Island were industrialization, immigration, and urbanization. The state's royal charter (then still in effect) contained no procedure for its amendment, gave disproportionate influence to the declining rural towns, and conferred almost unlimited power on the legislature. In addition, suffrage was restricted by the general assembly to owners of real estate and their eldest sons. Because earlier, moderate efforts at change had been virtually ignored by the assembly, political reformers decided to bypass the legislature and convene a People's Convention. Thomas Wilson Dorr, who led this movement, became the principal draftsman of a progressive "People's Constitution," ratified in a popular referendum in December 1841. A coalition of Whigs and rural

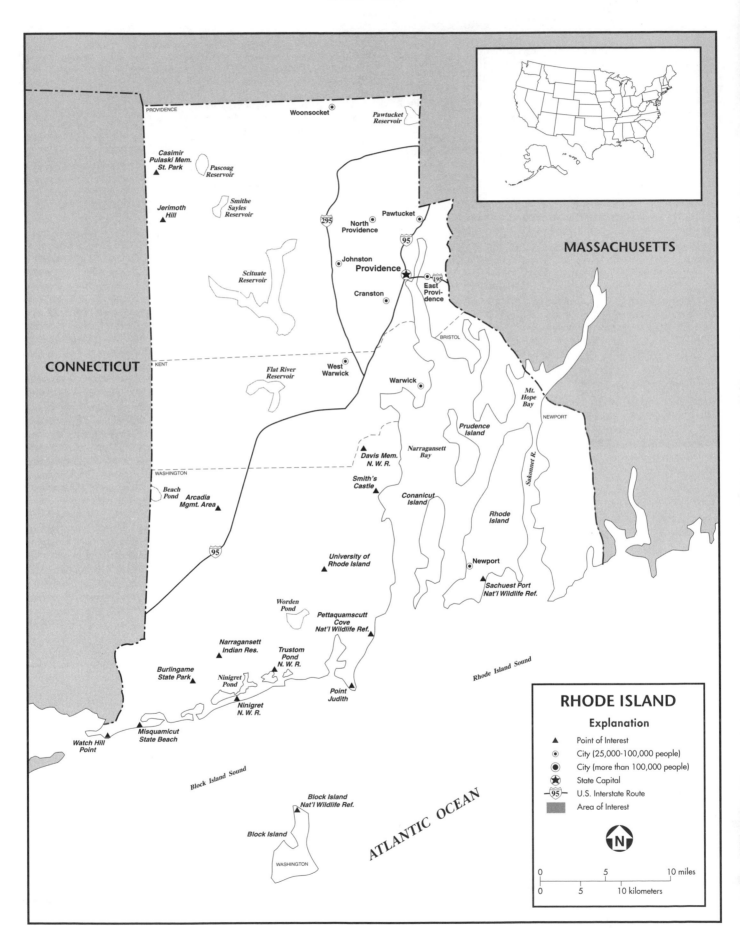

CONNECTICUT

MASSACHUSETTS

PROVIDENCE

Woonsocket

Pawtucket
Reservoir

Casimir
Pulaski Mem.
St. Park

Pascoag
Reservoir

Smithe
Sayles
Reservoir

Jerimoth
Hill

295

North
Providence

Pawtucket

95

Johnston

Providence

Scituate
Reservoir

Cranston

East
Provi-
dence

195

BRISTOL

KENT

West
Warwick

Flat River
Reservoir

Warwick

Mt.
Hope
Bay

NEWPORT

Prudence
Island

WASHINGTON

Davis Mem.
N. W. R.

Narragansett
Bay

Beach
Pond

Arcadia
Mgmt. Area

Smith's
Castle

Conanicut
Island

Rhode
Island

Sakonnet R.

95

University of
Rhode Island

Newport

Sachuest Port
Nat'l Wildlife Ref.

Worden
Pond

Pettaquamscutt
Cove
Nat'l Wildlife Ref.

Narragansett
Indian Res.

Trustom
Pond
N. W. R.

Burlingame
State Park

Ninigret
Pond

Point
Judith

Rhode Island Sound

Ninigret
N. W. R.

Misquamicut
State Beach

Watch Hill
Point

Block Island Sound

Block Island
Nat'l Wildlife Ref.

ATLANTIC OCEAN

Block Island

WASHINGTON

RHODE ISLAND

Explanation

▲ Point of Interest

⊙ City (25,000-100,000 people)

◉ City (more than 100,000 people)

★ State Capital

95 U.S. Interstate Route

Area of Interest

N

0   5   10 miles

0   5   10 kilometers

Democrats used force to suppress the movement now known as Dorr's Rebellion, but they bowed to popular pressure and made limited changes via a new constitution, effective May 1843.

The latter half of the 19th century was marked by continued industrialization and urbanization. Immigration became both more voluminous and more diverse. Politically the state was dominated by the Republican Party until the 1930s. The Democrats, having seized the opportunity during the New Deal, consolidated their power during the 1940s, and from that time onward have captured most state and congressional elections. Present-day Rhode Island, though predominantly Catholic and Democratic, retains an ethnic and cultural diversity surprising in view of its size but consistent with its pluralist traditions. Rhode Island's residents have begun to move out from the cities to the suburbs, and in 1980 the state lost its ranking as the most urban state in the country to New Jersey. In the mid-1990s Rhode Island was still the nation's second most densely populated state, with more than three-quarters of its residents living within 15 miles of the capital city of Providence.

Since the 1950s, manufacturing jobs have been held by 30% of the work force; in the 1990s, many of these were still low-paid jobs in the jewelry and textile industries. Rhode Island experienced a real estate boom in the 1980s thanks to federal savings and loan deregulation and the state's proximity to the thriving Boston metropolitan area. However, real estate values declined at the end of the decade, and Rhode Island entered the 1990s with a banking crisis that forced its government to spend taxpayer dollars propping up uninsured financial institutions. The state was also hard hit by the recession of the early 1990s. By 1994, a slow recovery was under way, with unemployment fluctuating between 6% and 8%. As of 1997, unemployment had recovered to around 5%, partly due to new opportunities in the financial and electronic industries.

In 1991 Hurricane Bob caused $125 million in property damage.

12STATE GOVERNMENT

Rhode Island is governed under the constitution of 1842. Through 1983 there had been 43 amendments to this document.

Legislative authority is vested in the general assembly, a bicameral body composed of 50 senators and 100 representatives. All legislators are elected for two-year terms from districts that are apportioned equally according to population after every federal decennial census. Legislators must be qualified voters in the state and must thus have been residents of the state and their district for 30 days prior to election. Among the more important checks enjoyed by the assembly is the power to override the governor's veto by a three-fifths vote of its members and the power to establish all courts below the supreme court.

The chief officers of the executive branch are the governor, lieutenant governor, attorney general, secretary of state, and general treasurer. All are elected for four-year terms as of 1994. The governor and lieutenant governor must be qualified voters in Rhode Island and must have been residents of the US and the state for 30 days prior to election. In 1996 the governor's salary was $69,900.

Constitutional amendments are enacted by majority vote of the whole membership of each house of the legislature, and by a simple majority at the next general election. Voters must be US citizens, 18 years old or over, and have been residents of the state at least 30 days prior to an election.

13POLITICAL PARTIES

For nearly five decades, Rhode Island has been one of the nation's most solidly Democratic states. It has voted for the Republican presidential candidate only four times since 1928, elected only one Republican (former governor John Chafee) to the US Senate

since 1934, and sent no Republicans to the US House from 1940 until 1980, when one Republican and one Democrat were elected. (They were reelected in 1982 and 1984.) Also in 1980, Rhode Island was one of only six states to favor Jimmy Carter. However, in 1984, Republican Edward DiPrete was elected governor, and Ronald Reagan narrowly carried the state in the presidential election. In the 1996 presidential election, Democratic incumbent Bill Clinton captured 60% of the popular vote; Republican Bob Dole received 27%; and Independent Ross Perot collected 11%. In 1994, Republican Lincoln C. Almond was elected governor and Republican John H. Chafee won a fourth term in the US Senate. In 1996, Democrat Jack Reed won the Senate seat vacated by Claiborne Pell after 36 years in office. Both US representatives were Democrats in 1997. Among state officeholders, there were 41 Democrats and 9 Republicans in the state senate, and 84 Democrats and 16 Republicans in the state house.

In 1994 there were 12 black elected officials and 1 Hispanic holding public office. As of 1995, 36 women served in the state legislature and 1 woman was in an elective executive position.

Rhode Island Presidential Vote by Major Political Parties, 1948–96

YEAR	ELECTORAL VOTE	RHODE ISLAND WINNER	DEMOCRAT	REPUBLICAN
1948	4	*Truman (D)	188,736	135,787
1952	4	*Eisenhower (R)	203,293	210,935
1956	4	*Eisenhower (R)	161,790	225,819
1960	4	*Kennedy (D)	258,032	147,502
1964	4	*Johnson (D)	315,463	74,615
1968	4	Humphrey (D)	246,518	122,359
1972	4	*Nixon (R)	194,645	220,383
1976	4	*Carter (D)	227,636	181,249
1980	4	Carter (D)	198,342	154,793
1984	4	*Reagan (R)	197,106	212,080
1988	4	Dukakis (D)	225,123	177,761
1992**	4	*Clinton (D)	213,299	131,601
1996**	4	*Clinton (D)	233,050	104,683

*Won US presidential election.

** Independent candidate Ross Perot received 105,045 votes in 1992 and 43,723 votes in 1996.

14LOCAL GOVERNMENT

Rhode Island is subdivided into 8 municipalities and 31 towns, the main units of local government. The state's 5 counties are merely units of judicial administration. There are three school districts and 83 special districts.

Many smaller communities retain the New England town meeting form of government, under which the town's eligible voters assemble to enact the local budget, set the tax levy, and approve other local measures. Larger cities and towns are governed by a mayor and/or city manager and a council.

15STATE SERVICES

The Board of Regents for Elementary and Secondary Education and the Board of Governors for Higher Education oversee all state educational services. Railroads, motor vehicle administration, and highway and bridge management come under the jurisdiction of the Department of Transportation. Health and welfare services are provided through the Department of Children, Youth, and Families, the Department of Elderly Affairs, the Department of Health, the Department of Mental Health, Retardation, and Hospitals, and the Department of Human Services.

[16]JUDICIAL SYSTEM

The five-member supreme court is the state's highest appellate tribunal; it may also issue, upon request, advisory opinions on the constitutionality of a questioned act to the governor or either house of the legislature. Supreme court justices are chosen by the legislature and, like other state judges, hold office for life ("during good behavior"), but in actuality they can be removed by a mere resolution of the general assembly. In 1935, all five justices were ousted in this manner when a Democratic legislature replaced a court previously appointed by Republicans. In 1994, Chief Justice Thomas Fay resigned under impeachment pressure.

The second judicial level consists of the 19-member superior court and the 11-member family court. The former, the state's trial court, hears all jury trials in criminal cases and in civil matters involving more than $5,000, but can also hear nonjury cases. The family court deals with divorce, custody, juvenile crime, adoption, and related cases. Superior, family, and district court judges are appointed by the governor with the consent of the senate.

District courts do not hold jury trials. Civil matters that involve $5,000 or less, small claims procedures, and nonjury criminal cases, including felony arraignments and misdemeanors, are handled at the district level. All cities and towns appoint judges to operate probate courts for wills and estates. Providence and a few other communities each have a municipal or police court. Practicing attorneys in Rhode Island numbered 3,420 in 1996.

According to the FBI Crime Index for 1992, the crime rate of 4,244.5 per 100,000 persons, significantly below the national average of 5,277.6. There were 3,608 prisoners in state and federal prisons in 1995, or 310 prisoners per 100,000 in population. Rhode Island does not have a death penalty.

[17]ARMED FORCES

In 1996, there were 3,047 active duty military personnel stationed in Rhode Island, 2,837of whom were at the US Naval Education and Training Center and Naval War College in Newport. Rhode Island firms received $333 million in defense contracts during 1991/92. A total of 108,000 US veterans were living in the state in 1992, of whom less than 500 saw military service during World War I, 35,000 during World War II, 19,000 in the Korean conflict, 31,000 during the Vietnam era, and 6,000 in the Persian Gulf War. Veterans' benefits totaled $180 million in 1995/96.

In 1996, the state had 7,403 reserve and national guard personnel. In 1993, the Rhode Island State Police employed 182 full-time sworn officers, or 2 per 10,000 residents.

[18]MIGRATION

During the 19th and early 20th centuries, the major immigrant groups who came to work in the state's growing industries were Irish, Italian, and French-Canadian. Significant numbers of British, Portuguese, Swedish, Polish, and German immigrants also moved to Rhode Island. Between 1940 and 1970, however, 2,000 more people left the state than moved to it, and between 1970 and 1983 there was a net loss of about 42,000. From 1985 to 1990, there was a net gain from migration of nearly 34,000. Between 1990 and 1996, Rhode Island had a net loss of 59,791 in domestic migration and a net gain of 11,088 in international migration. In 1996, 3,098 foreign immigrants arrived in the state, many of whom were from Southeast Asia and Eastern Europe. As of 1990, 63.4% of state residents had been born in Rhode Island. In 1990, 57% of Rhode Island's population age 5 and older lived in the same house as in 1985. Of those who lived in a different house in 1985, 28% did so in another state. During the 1980s, the urban proportion of the population remained virtually unchanged, dropping from 87% to 86%.

[19]INTERGOVERNMENTAL COOPERATION

Rhode Island participates in many interstate regional bodies, including the Atlantic States Marine Fisheries Commission, New England Corrections Commission, New England Interstate Water Pollution Control Commission, and Northeastern Forest Fire Protection Commission.

Federal aid to Rhode Island state and local governments exceeded $1.1 billion in 1995/96.

[20]ECONOMY

Rhode Island's economy is based overwhelmingly on industry; agriculture, mining, forestry, and fishing make only small contributions. The state's leading manufactured products are jewelry, silverware, machinery, primary metals, textiles, and rubber products. Unemployment rates in Rhode Island exceeded those of the US throughout the 1970s, and the state's economic growth lagged behind that of the nation as a whole. Unemployment fell dramatically in 1983 and 1984, rose again to 8.7% in 1992, and fell to around 5% in 1996. Rhode Island's chief economic problem, its concentration of manufacturing industries paying low wages, persists. Manufacturing employment declined 23% between 1983 and 1992, while service jobs increased 36%. Rhode Island's gross state product in 1994 was $23,867 million, to which private goods-producing industries contributed $5,187 million; private services-producing industries, $15,823 million; and government, $2,857 million. Rhode Island's per capita personal income in 1995 was $23,844, 17th in the US. In 1996, there were 4,328 bankruptcy filings in the state.

[21]INCOME

With a personal income per capita of $24,765 in 1996, Rhode Island ranked 17th among the 50 states. Total disposable personal income rose from $20.7 billion in 1995 to $21.5 billion in 1996. Median household income was $35,359 in 1995. That same year, 10.6% of the population lived below the federal poverty line.

[22]LABOR

In 1996, the civilian labor force for the state totaled 496,000. At 25,000, unemployment averaged 5.1% in 1996.

At the end of 1996, nonfarm employment was as follows: services, 151,600; wholesale and retail trade, 100,100; manufacturing, 82,500; government, 63,100; finance, insurance, and real estate, 24,800; transportation and utilities, 15,800; construction, 14,100; and mining, 100.

In 1995, some 78,100 Rhode Islanders belonged to labor unions.

[23]AGRICULTURE

The state's total receipts from farm marketings were $80 million in 1995, 49th in the US; Alaska was 50th. Rhode Island had only about 700 farms in 1996, with an average size of just 90 acres, with the smallest area devoted to crops (21,000 acres, or 8,500 hectares) of any state. Nursery and greenhouse products were the main agricultural commodity. Total crop marketings amounted to $70 million in 1995.

[24]ANIMAL HUSBANDRY

In 1997, Rhode Island had around 7,000 cattle and calves, valued at $4.83 million. During 1996, there were some 2,800 hogs and pigs, valued at $269,000. In 1995, the state produced 32.5 million lb of milk and 34 million eggs.

[25]FISHING

The commercial catch in 1995 was 121.9 million lb, valued at $68.4 million. Point Judith is the main fishing port, with landings of 89.6 million lb in 1995, ranking 14th in the US for size of catch that year. The commercial fishing fleet consisted of 3,168 boats and vessels in 1994, supplying the state's 94 processing and wholesale plants. The most valuable edible fish and shellfish caught are whiting, fluke and yellowtail flounders, cod, scup lobster, squid, and clams. Landings of Atlantic mackerel in 1995 totaled 12.2 million lb, 65% of the national total.

In 1995/96, Rhode Island issued 35,832 sport fishing licenses. Federal hatcheries distributed nearly 286,000 Atlantic salmon and 150,000 salmon eggs within the state.

26FORESTRY

In 1993, forests and woodlands covered 404,800 acres (163,800 hectares), 60% of the state's land area. Some 372,000 acres (160,000 hectares) were usable as commercial timberland.

27MINING

The value of nonfuel mineral production in Rhode Island in 1995 was estimated to be $29.5 million, a $3.2 million increase over that of 1994. Crushed stone (1.5 million metric tons, worth $11.4 million) and construction sand and gravel (2.9 million metric tons, worth $18.1 million) accounted for virtually all of the state's production. Small amounts of industrial sand and gemstones were also mined.

28ENERGY AND POWER

Rhode Island is part of the New England regional power grid and imports most of its electric power. The state's installed capacity was 512,000 kw in 1996, and power production totaled 653 million kwh in 1995; both figures were the lowest in the US. Electric utility sales in Rhode Island in 1995 were 6.5 billion kwh, of which 2.4 billion kwh went for residential users, 2.6 billion kwh for commercial purchasers, and nearly all the rest for industry. The total number of gas utility customers for 1995 was 224,778.

29INDUSTRY

The Industrial Revolution began early in Rhode Island. The first spinning jenny in the US was built at Providence in 1787; three years later, in Pawtucket, Samuel Slater opened a cotton mill, one of the first modern factories in America. By the end of the 18th century, textile, jewelry, and metal products were being manufactured in the state.

In 1992, 89,800 residents were employed in manufacturing, (down 23% from 1983); of that total, 23,193 were engaged in miscellaneous manufacturing, primarily jewelry and toys. Over 1,000 manufacturers in the state produce finished jewelry and jewelry parts. Prominent manufacturing firms in the state include AT Cross and Shaeffer (pens), Fort (novelty gift and collector items), and Swarovski (rhinestones and crystal boutique items). Hasbro, one of the world's largest toy manufacturers, is headquartered in Pawtucket.

Electronic and related products manufactured in the state include online lottery machines, circuit boards, and meteorological, navigational, and medical equipment. Chemicals and allied products made in the state include pigments and dyes, drugs and biomedical products, and liquid and aerosol consumer products.

The total value of shipments of manufactured products in 1995 was $10,073,900. The following table shows value of shipments for the state's principal industrial sectors during 1995:

Fabricated metal products	$1,084,600,000
Primary metal industries	995,400,000
Rubber and plastic products	832,600,000
Costume jewelry and notions	886,400,000
Jewelry, silverware, and plated ware	510,800,000

30COMMERCE

Wholesalers in 1992 had sales of $6.6 billion, including $3.4 billion in durable goods. In that year, retail establishments had sales of $6.7 billion (43d). Of this total, 21% came from food store sales, 15.7% from automotive dealers, 10.7% from general merchandise stores, 11.4% from eating and drinking places, and 41.2% from other establishments. Foreign exports of manufactured goods were $918.8 million in 1996.

31CONSUMER PROTECTION

The consumer unit of the public protection division of the Department of the Attorney General, the Consumer's Council, and the consumer affairs division within the Department of Business Regulation bear primary responsibility for enforcing consumer laws and regulations.

32BANKING

In 1996, Rhode Island had 8 commercial banks with combined assets of $16.9 billion; deposits totaled $9.1 billion, and outstanding loans were over $11.6 billion in 1996. In 1996 there were six savings institutions, whose combined assets reached $6.1 billion.

33INSURANCE

In mid-1991, the state had five life insurance companies; the 804,000 policies held by state residents had an aggregate value of over $62.7 billion. The average amount of life insurance per family was $142,400.

34SECURITIES

Rhode Island has no securities exchanges. As of April 1997, there were 1,351 broker-dealers, involving 45,708 designated agents, and 475 investment adviser companies with 4,315 representatives.

35PUBLIC FINANCE

The annual budget is prepared by the State Budget Office in conjunction with the governor, and submitted to the legislature for approval. The fiscal year runs from 1 July to 30 June.

The following is a summary of general revenues and expenditures in 1995 in thousands:

	1995
REVENUES	
Taxes:	
Property	1,193,087
Sales and gross receipts	768,656
Income	612,566
TOTAL	2,574,309
Charges and miscellaneous	
Current charges	277,406
Other	1,304,722
TOTAL	1,582,128
TOTAL RESOURCES	$4,156,437
EXPENDITURES	
Education	$885,077
Health	241,221
Transportation (highway)	266,080
Public Safety (police)	28,672
Natural resources	34,548
Financial administration	181,590
Utilities	39,110
Other	2,588,842
TOTAL GENERAL EXPENDITURES	$4,265,140

36TAXATION

As of 1996, Rhode Island levied a state income tax equal to 27.5% of the taxpayer's federal income tax liability. The basic corporate tax rate was 9.0%. The sales and use tax was 7.0% on most items.

37ECONOMIC POLICY

The Rhode Island Economic Development Corporation (RIEDC) exists to preserve and expand Rhode Island businesses, and to attract new businesses to the state. Some of the services available to businesses through RIEDC are: job training assistance; financial assistance; government contracting assistance; site selection; and exporting assistance.

38HEALTH

Rhode Island's birthrate of 12.9 per 1,000 persons in 1995 was lower than the national rate of 14.8. Despite the state's heavy Catholic population, the ratio of 490 abortions to 1,000 live births in 1992 was the nation's 3d highest. As of 1995, the infant mortality rate was 6.9 per 1,000 live births. Death rates from heart disease (334.1 per 100,000 population) and cancer (250.4)—the leading causes of death in 1995—were well above the national averages. The death rate of 962.5 per 100,000 ranked above the national rate of 879.

Although there were only 137 AIDS cases from January to June 1995, the overall incidence of 29.19 per 100,000 population was above the US average of 28.48 in 1995. In 1995, Rhode Island had one of the highest smoking rates in the US for persons aged 18–30. Projected deaths due to smoking-related illness numbered 23,503 for 1995.

The state had 3,302 active nonfederal and federal physicians in 1995, and 575 active dentists in 1995. There were 11 hospitals, with 2,718 beds in 1995; hospital personnel included 9,600 registered nurses in 1994.

About 15.4% of Rhode Island residents were uninsured in 1995. Nearly 30% of physicians specialized in primary care during 1995. There were 166 million Medicare and 115 million Medicaid recipients in 1994.

39SOCIAL WELFARE

Aid to families with dependent children was paid to 60,600 Rhode Islanders in 1996,with an average monthly allotment of $632. In 1991, Social Security benefits were paid to 189,930 persons, averaging $718 a month. In 1996, 90,873 residents received monthly food stamp allowances averaging $71.49, and the school lunch program received total federal funding of $115 million. State and local governments are generous providers of public welfare; the $648.73 spent per capita for this purpose in 1991 ranked the state 5th in the nation. Weekly unemployment benefits averaged $225.73 in 1995.

With the enactment of the Personal Responsibility and Work Opportunity Reconciliation Act of 1996, the US government has changed the form and regulations for many of its social welfare programs; most significantly, it replaces Aid to Families with Dependent Children (AFDC), an open-ended entitlement program, with Temporary Assistance for Needy Families (TANF), a limited system of assistance funded largely through federal block grants. The reform act also impacts the food stamp program, the Supplemental Security Income program, and the child nutrition program. The law took effect on 1 July 1997 and provided $16.38 billion in block grants for fiscal years 1997–2002. The grants are to be divided among the states based on an equation involving the numbers of former AFDC recipients in each state. Because many of the bills provisions have yet to be implemented into state-by-state policy, it was not possible to include the details of each state's programs for this edition of this work.

40HOUSING

In 1996, there were an estimated 424,000 housing units, 374,000 of which were occupied. That year, 2,462 privately owned units, valued at $219 million, were authorized for construction; of these, 2,077 were owner-occupied. As of 1990, 99.5% of year-round units had full plumbing. Much of the new residential construction has taken place in the suburbs south and west of Providence. In 1990, the last year for which figures were available, Rhode Island ranked sixth in median home value, at $133,500. Owners with a mortgage who occupied their houses had a median monthly cost of $891, while owners without a mortgage paid a median of $290 in costs per month. Median monthly rent in 1990 was $489. During 1995/96, Rhode Island received $189.9 million in aid from the US Department of Housing and Urban Development, including $18.1 million in community development block grants.

41EDUCATION

Only 73.2% of adult Rhode Islanders were high school graduates in 1990, the lowest such percentage for any northern state.

As of September 1995, 149,802 students were enrolled in public schools. Some 23,036 were in private schools in the fall of 1991, most of them Catholic schools. More than 78,273 students were enrolled in the state's 13 institutions of higher education in fall 1990. Leading institutions included Brown University (1764) in Providence, with 6,873 students in fall 1990; the University of Rhode Island (1892), in Kingston, with 11,233; and Providence College (1917), with 5,533. The Rhode Island School of Design (1877), with 1,795 students in 1990, is located in Providence.

42ARTS

Newport and Providence have notable art galleries and museums. Theatrical groups include the Trinity Repertory Company in Providence. The Rhode Island Philharmonic performs throughout the state. Newport is the site of the internationally famous Newport Jazz Festival and the Newport Music Festival.

The state of Rhode Island's arts funding from 1992 to 1997 amounted to $5,234,354. The NEA contributed $1,189,661 to the state's programs and $3,539,690 to the Rhode Island State Council on the Arts. The state gave the council $4,321,319. The New England Foundation for the Arts gave the Arts Council $16,000 in support of local arts councils in 1994/95. Audiences for arts programs totaled about 20,932,735. There were 45,877 contributing artists. The state provided arts education programming grants that reached 126,451 school children. By 1997, the state of Rhode Island had 1,000 arts associations and 6 local arts councils. The State Council on the Arts assisted the Groundwerx Dance Theatre and the Rhode Island Labor & Ethnic Heritage Festival. In 1996, the NEA gave $4,600 to the Rhode Island Philharmonic Orchestra, $40,000 to Trinity Repertory Company, and $82,000 to the Rhode Island School of Design. In 1997, the Rhode Island State Council on the Arts received a total of $77,000 for arts education programs. The NEA contributed $300,000 to the State Arts Council through its State and Regional Program. In 1996/97, the Arts Council, in partnership with the Rhode Island Foundation, received $136,640 from the NEA's Expansion Arts Program.

43LIBRARIES AND MUSEUMS

In 1996, Rhode Island had 120 public, academic, and special libraries. In 1996/97, public libraries had a book stock of 3,253,298, and a combined circulation of 5,657,359. The Providence Public Library maintains several special historical collections. The Brown University Libraries, containing more than 2.6 million books and periodicals, include the Annmary Brown Memorial Library, with its collection of rare manuscripts, and the

John Carter Brown Library, with an excellent collection of early Americana.

Among the state's more than 52 museums and historic sites are the Haffenreffer Museum of Anthropology in Bristol, the Museum of Art of the Rhode Island School of Design in Providence, the Roger Williams Park Museum, also in Providence, the Nathanael Greene Homestead in Coventry, and the Slater Mill Historic Site in Pawtucket. Providence has the Roger Williams Park Zoo.

44COMMUNICATIONS

The first automated post office in the US postal system was opened in Providence in 1960. As of March 1993, 94.7% of the state's 391,000 occupied housing units had telephones. In 1996, the state had 16 AM and 17 FM radio stations. Rhode Island had seven television stations, including one public broadcasting affiliate operated by the state's Public Telecommunications Authority. The state had three large cable television systems in 1996.

45PRESS

The *Rhode Island Gazette,* the state's first newspaper, appeared in 1732. In 1850, Paulina Wright Davis established *Una,* one of the first women's rights newspapers in the country.

In 1997, Rhode Island had six daily newspapers. The following table shows the circulation for the state's leading dailies in 1997:

AREA	NAME	DAILY	SUNDAY
Newport	*Daily News*	14,233	—
Providence	*Journal-Bulletin*	171,733	—
Providence	*Journal*	—	254,012

46ORGANIZATIONS

The 1992 US Census of Service Industries counted 351 organizations in Rhode Island, including 51 business associations; 223 civic, social, and fraternal associations; and 77 other membership organizations. Among the organizations with headquarters in Rhode Island are the US Surfing Federation (Barrington); the Rooster Class Yacht Racing Association (Wakefield); the Foundation for Gifted and Creative Children and the Foster Parents Plan USA (both in Warwick); the American Mathematical Society and the Manufacturing Jewelers and Silversmiths of America (both in Providence); and the US International Sailing Association and US Yacht Racing Union (both in Newport).

47TOURISM, TRAVEL, AND RECREATION

Travel and tourism generated $1.1 billion in revenue in the early 1990s. Historic sites—especially the mansions of Newport and Providence—and water sports (particularly the America's Cup yacht races) are the main tourist attractions. Block Island is a popular resort. During 1995, licenses were issued to 34,325 hunters and 51,709 fishermen who visited the state. Rhode Island's state parks and recreational areas total 8,063 acres (3,263 hectares).

48SPORTS

Rhode Island has no major league professional sports teams. Pawtucket has a AAA minor league baseball team and Providence has a minor league team in the American Hockey League. Providence College has competed successfully in collegiate basketball, winning National Invitational Tournament titles in 1961 and 1963, and advancing to the NCAA Final Four in 1973, 1987, and 1997.

Historically, Rhode Island has played an important part in the development of both yachting and tennis. The Newport Yacht Club hosted the America's Cup, international sailing's most prestigious event, from 1930 until 1983, when an Australian

yacht won the race. It was the first time since 1851 the cup had been won by a non-American. The cup was returned to America in 1987, but by a yacht from San Diego, where the race is now held. Lawn tennis was first played in America at the Newport Casino, which was also the site of the United States Tennis championship from 1881 until 1915. Today it is home to the International Tennis Hall of Fame. The Yachting Hall of Fame is located in Newport as well. Dog racing at Lincoln and Jai Alai at Newport are popular spectator sports with pari-mutuel betting.

Other annual sporting events include the Tennis Hall of Fame Championships in Newport in July, the Annual Tuna Tournament near Galilee and Narragansett in September, the Rhode Island Marathon in Newport in November, and summer college baseball league play on Martha's Vineyard.

49FAMOUS RHODE ISLANDERS

Important federal officeholders from Rhode Island have included US Senators Nelson W. Aldrich (1841–1915), Henry Bowen Anthony (1815–84), Theodore Francis Green (1867–1966), and John O. Pastore (b.1907), and US Representative John E. Fogarty (1913–67). J. Howard McGrath (1903–66) held the posts of US senator, solicitor general, and attorney general.

Foremost among Rhode Island's historical figures is Roger Williams (b.England, 1603?–83), apostle of religious liberty and founder of Providence. Other significant pioneers, also born in England, include Anne Hutchinson (1591–1643), religious leader and cofounder of Portsmouth, and William Coddington (1601–78), founder of Newport. Other 17th-century Rhode Islanders of note were Dr. John Clarke (b.England, 1609–76), who secured the colony's royal charter, and Indian leader King Philip, known also as Metacomet (1639?–76). Important participants in the War for Independence were Commodore Esek Hopkins (1718–1802) and General Nathanael Greene (1742–86). The 19th century brought to prominence Thomas Wilson Dorr (1805–54), courageous leader of Dorr's Rebellion; social reformer Elizabeth Buffum Chace (1806–99); and naval officers Oliver Hazard Perry (1785–1819), who secured important US victories in the War of 1812, and his brother, Matthew C. Perry (1794–1858), who led the expedition that opened Japan to foreign trade in 1854. Among the state's many prominent industrialists and inventors are Samuel Slater (b.England, 1768–1835), pioneer in textile manufacturing, and silversmith Jabez Gorham (1792–1869). Other significant public figures include Unitarian theologian William Ellery Channing (1780–1842); political boss Charles R. Brayton (1840–1910); Roman Catholic bishop and social reformer Matthew Harkins (b.Massachusetts, 1845–1921); and Dr. Charles V. Chapin (1856–1941), pioneer in public health.

Rhode Island's best-known creative writers are Gothic novelists H. P. Lovecraft (1890–1937) and Oliver La Farge (1901–63), and its most famous artist is portrait painter Gilbert Stuart (1755–1828). Popular performing artists include George M. Cohan (1878–1942), Nelson Eddy (1901–67), Bobby Hackett (1915–76), Van Johnson (b.1916), and Spalding Gray (b.1941).

Important sports personalities include Baseball Hall of Famers Hugh Duffy (1866–1954), Napoleon Lajoie (1875–1959), and Charles "Gabby" Hartnett (1900–1972).

50BIBLIOGRAPHY

Carroll, Charles. *Rhode Island: Three Centuries of Democracy.* 4 vols. New York: Lewis, 1932.

Conley, Patrick T. *Democracy in Decline: Rhode Island's Constitutional Development, 1775–1841.* Providence: Rhode Island Historical Society, 1977.

———. *Rhode Island Profile.* Providence: Rhode Island Publications Society, 1983.

Conley, Patrick T., and Matthew J. Smith. *Catholicism in Rhode Island.* Providence: Diocese of Providence, 1976.

Federal Writers' Project. *Rhode Island: A Guide to the Smallest State*. Reprint. New York: Somerset, n.d. (orig. 1937).

James, Sydney V. *Colonial Rhode Island: A History*. White Plains, N.Y.: Kraus International, 1975.

McLoughlin, William G. *Rhode Island: A Bicentennial History*. New York: Norton, 1978.

Providence Journal-Bulletin. *1985. Journal-Bulletin Rhode Island Almanac*. 99th ed. Providence, n.d.

Rhode Island, Department of Economic Development, Economic Research Division. *Rhode Island: Basic Economic Statistics 1982–1983*. Providence, 1983.

Rhode Island, Secretary of State. *Rhode Island Manual 1983–84*. Edited by Edward F. Walsh. Providence, 1983.

Steinberg, Sheila, and Cathleen McGuigan. *Rhode Island: An Historical Guide,* Providence: Rhode Island Bicentennial Commission, 1976.

SOUTH CAROLINA

State of South Carolina

ORIGIN OF STATE NAME: Named in honor of King Charles I of England. **NICKNAME:** The Palmetto State. **CAPITAL:** Columbia. **ENTERED UNION:** 23 May 1788 (8th). **SONG:** "Carolina" and "South Carolina on My Mind." **POET LAUREATE:** Helen von Kolnitz Hyer. **MOTTO:** *Animis opibusque parati* (Prepared in mind and resources); *Dum spiro spero* (While I breathe, I hope). **COAT OF ARMS:** A palmetto stands erect, with a ravaged oak (representing the British fleet) at its base; 12 spears, symbolizing the first 12 states, are bound crosswise to the palmetto's trunk by a hand bearing the inscription "Quis separabit" (Who shall separate?). Two shields bearing the inscriptions "March 26" (the date in 1776 when South Carolina established its first independent government) and "July 4," respectively, hang from the tree; under the oak are the words "Meliorem lapsa locavit" (Having fallen, it has set up a better one) and the year "1776." The words "South Carolina" and the motto *Animis opibusque parati* surround the whole. **FLAG:** Blue field with a white palmetto in the center and a white crescent at the union. **OFFICIAL SEAL:** The official seal consists of two ovals showing the original designs for the obverse and the reverse of South Carolina's great seal of 1777. LEFT (OBVERSE): same as the coat of arms. RIGHT (REVERSE): as the sun rises over the seashore, Hope, holding a laurel branch, walks over swords and daggers; the motto *Dum spiro spero* is above her, the word "Spes" (Hope) below. **ANIMAL:** White-tailed deer. **BIRD:** Carolina wren. **WILD GAME BIRD:** Wild turkey. **FISH:** Striped bass. **FLOWER:** Yellow jessamine. **TREE:** Palmetto. **GEM:** Amethyst. **STONE:** Blue granite. **LEGAL HOLIDAYS:** New Year's Day, 1 January; Birthday of Martin Luther King, Jr., 3d Monday in January; Lee's Birthday, 19 January; Washington's Birthday, 3d Monday in February; Jefferson Davis's Birthday, 3 June; Independence Day, 4 July; Labor Day, 1st Monday in September; Election Day, 1st Tuesday after 1st Monday in November (even-numbered years); Veterans Day, 11 November; Thanksgiving Day, 4th Thursday in November; Christmas Eve, 24 December, when declared by the governor; Christmas Day, 25 December; day after Christmas. **TIME:** 7 AM EST = noon GMT.

¹LOCATION, SIZE, AND EXTENT

Situated in the southeastern US, South Carolina ranks 40th in size among the 50 states.

The state's total area is 31,113 sq mi (80,583 sq km), of which land takes up 30,203 sq mi (78,226 sq km) and inland water 910 sq mi (2,357 sq km). South Carolina extends 273 mi (439 km) E-W; its maximum N-S extension is 210 mi (338 km).

South Carolina is bounded on the N and NE by North Carolina; on the SE by the Atlantic Ocean; and on the SW and W by Georgia (with the line passing through the Savannah and Chattooga rivers).

Among the 13 major Sea Islands in the Atlantic off South Carolina are Bull, Sullivans, Kiawah, Edisto, Hunting, and Hilton Head, the largest island (42 sq mi—109 sq km) on the Atlantic seaboard between New Jersey and Florida. The total boundary length of South Carolina is 824 mi (1,326 km), including a general coastline of 187 mi (301 km); the tidal shoreline extends 2,876 mi (4,628 km). The state's geographic center is located in Richland County, 13 mi (21 km) SE of Columbia.

²TOPOGRAPHY

South Carolina is divided into two major regions by the fall line that runs through the center of the state from Augusta, Ga., to Columbia and thence to Cheraw, near the North Carolina border. The area northwest of the line, known as the upcountry, lies within the Piedmont Plateau; the region to the southeast, called the low country, forms part of the Atlantic Coastal Plain. The rise of the land from ocean to the fall line is very gradual: Columbia, 120 mi (193 km) inland, is only 135 feet (41 meters) above sea level. In the extreme northwest, the Blue Ridge Mountains cover

about 500 sq mi (1,300 sq km); the highest elevation, at 3,560 feet (1,085 meters), is Sassafras Mountain.

Among the many artificial lakes, mostly associated with electric power plants, is Lake Marion, the state's largest, covering 173 sq mi (48 sq km). Three river systems—the Pee Dee, Santee, and Savannah—drain most of the state. No rivers are navigable above the fall line.

³CLIMATE

South Carolina has a humid, subtropical climate. Average temperatures range from 68°F (20°C) on the coast to 58°F (14°C) in the northwest, with colder temperatures in the mountains. Summers are hot: in the central part of the state, temperatures often exceed 90°F (32°C), with a record of 111°F (44°C) set at Camden on 28 June 1954. In the northwest, temperatures of 32°F (0°C) or less occur from 50 to 70 days a year; the record low for the state is –20°F (–29°C), set at Caesars Head Mountain on 18 January 1977. The daily mean temperature at Columbia is 44°F (7°C) in January and 81°F (27°C) in July.

Rainfall is ample throughout the state, averaging 49 in (124 cm) annually at Columbia and ranging from 38 in (97 cm) in the central region to 52 in (132 cm) in the upper piedmont. Snow and sleet (averaging 2 in—5 cm—a year at Columbia) occur about three times annually, but more frequently and heavily in the mountains. South Carolina had 54 tornadoes in 1995.

⁴FLORA AND FAUNA

Principal trees of South Carolina include palmetto (the state tree), balsam fir, beech, yellow birch, pitch pine, cypress, and several types of maple, ash, hickory, and oak; longleaf pine grows mainly south of the fall line. Rocky areas of the piedmont contain a wide mixture of moss and lichens. The coastal plain has a diversity of land formations—swamp, prairie, savannah, marsh, dunes—and, accordingly, a great number of different grasses, shrubs, and vines. Azaleas and camellias, not native to the state, have been planted profusely in private and pubic gardens. Bunched arrowhead and persistent trillium are endangered plants.

South Carolina mammals include white-tailed deer (the state animal), black bear, opossum, gray and red foxes, cottontail and marsh rabbits, mink, and woodchuck. Three varieties of raccoon are indigenous, one of them unique to Hilton Head Island. The state is also home to Bachman's shrew, originally identified in South Carolina by John Bachman, one of John J. Audubon's collaborators. Common birds include the mockingbird and Carolina wren (the state bird). among endangered animals—all of which appear on the federal list—are the brown pelican, bald eagle, Bachman's warbler, eastern cougar, Florida manatee, shortnose sturgeon, American alligator, Atlantic leatherback and ridley turtles, and several whale species.

⁵ENVIRONMENTAL PROTECTION

The Department of Health and Environmental Control, established in 1973, is South Carolina's primary environmental protection agency. The agency's responsibilities were broadened in 1993 by Government Restructuring which brought all natural resources permitting under the DHEC umbrella. The former Land Resources Commission and Water Resources Commission were dissolved by restructuring. The Department's areas of responsibility now include all programs dealing with surface and ground water protection; air quality; solid, hazardous, infectious and nuclear waste; mining; dam safety; public drinking water protection; shell fish; public swimming pool inspection; and environmental laboratory certification.

South Carolina has an aggressive environmental compliance program in all media. Recent convictions for criminal violations have moved the state to the national forefront in this area.

The state has implemented an innovative river basin planning program for the modeling, permitting and protection of its surface water resources. South Carolina's five major river basins are to be studied, modeled, and subsequent permits renewed on a five-year rotating basis. The state's goal is to use the environmental permitting process to assess and control the overall health of the basin systems.

South Carolina, as the rest of the nation, is preparing to implement an aggressive air quality permitting program. The state has in place an industrial fee system to support the air program which will include both stationary and mobile source activities.

In 1992, South Carolina passed the Solid Waste Management and Policy Act requiring county and regional solid waste planning to be in conformance with the State Solid Waste Management Plan. The state has in place innovative programs for source reduction, waste minimization, and recycling. Regulations have been approved for municipal and industrial waste land disposal systems, incineration, construction, and land clearing debris and other solid waste activities.

South Carolina is undergoing an aggressive Regulatory Reform effort. Coupled with "streamlined permitting," customer-friendly programs promote economic development without sacrificing environmental protection.

⁶POPULATION

South Carolina in 1990 ranked 25th in population among the 50 states, with 3,486,703 residents, representing a 12% increase over the 1980 census. From 1990 to 1995, the population increased by 6.1% to an estimated total of 3,698,746. The population density in 1990 was 115.8 per sq mi (44.5 per sq km). In 1990, South Carolina was 51.6% female, and 48.4% male. In

1990, the median age was 32. The number of residents between 5 and 17 years of age accounted for 19% of the population, while those aged 65 and older accounted for 11.4% of the state's population.

The urban share of the population was 54.6% in 1990. The largest cities, with 1990 populations, were Columbia, 104,101; Charleston, 76,854; Greenville, 59,808; and Spartanburg, 42,721. In 1995, the Charleston metropolitan area had an estimated 506,420 residents, and the Columbia metropolitan area had 481,718.

⁷ETHNIC GROUPS

The white population of South Carolina is mainly of Northern European stock; the great migratory wave from Southern and Eastern Europe during the late 19th century left South Carolina virtually untouched. As of 1990, only 1.4% of South Carolinians were foreign-born.

Black Americans made up about 30% of the state's population in 1990. In the coastal regions and offshore islands there still can be found some vestiges of African heritage, notably the Gullah dialect. South Carolina has always had an urban black elite, much of it of mixed racial heritage. After 1954, racial integration proceeded relatively peacefully, with careful planning by both black and white leaders.

The 1990 census counted 8,000 American Indians. In 1983, a federal appeals court upheld the Indians' claim that 144,000 acres (58,275 hectares) of disputed land still belonged to the Catawba tribe, who numbered an estimated 1,597 in 1995. There were also 8,316 Mexicans, 6,028 Filipinos, 4,282 Puerto Ricans, 3,279 Japanese, and 3,198 Koreans in South Carolina.

⁸LANGUAGES

English settlers in the 17th century encountered first the Yamasee Indians and then the Catawba, both having languages of the Hokan-Siouan family. Few Indians remain today, and a bare handful of their place-names persist: Cherokee Falls, Santee, Saluda.

South Carolina English is marked by a division between the South Midland of the upcountry and the plantation Southern of the coastal plain, where dominant Charleston speech has extensive cultural influence even in rural areas. Many upcountry speakers of Scotch-Irish background retain /r/ after a vowel, as in *hard*, a feature now gaining acceptance among younger speakers in Charleston. At the same time, a longtime distinctive Charleston feature, a centering glide after a long vowel, so that *date* and *eight* sound like /day-uht/ and /ay-uht/, is losing ground among younger speakers.

Along the coast and on the Sea Islands, some blacks still use the Gullah dialect, based on a Creole mixture of pre-Revolutionary English and African speech. The dialect is rapidly dying in South Carolina, though its influence on local pronunciations persists.

In 1990, 96.5% of all state residents 5 years of age and older reported speaking English at home. Other languages spoken at home included:

Spanish	44,427	Tagalog	2,976
French	22,339	Greek	2,940
German	14,053	Italian	2,735

⁹RELIGIONS

South Carolina is predominantly Protestant, and has been since colonial days. The Protestant denominations with more than 100,000 members in 1990 were Southern Baptist; Baptist Educational and Missionary Convention (black), 894,390; and United Methodist, 308,915. The Episcopal Church had great influence during colonial times, but in 1990 it had only 48,655 members.

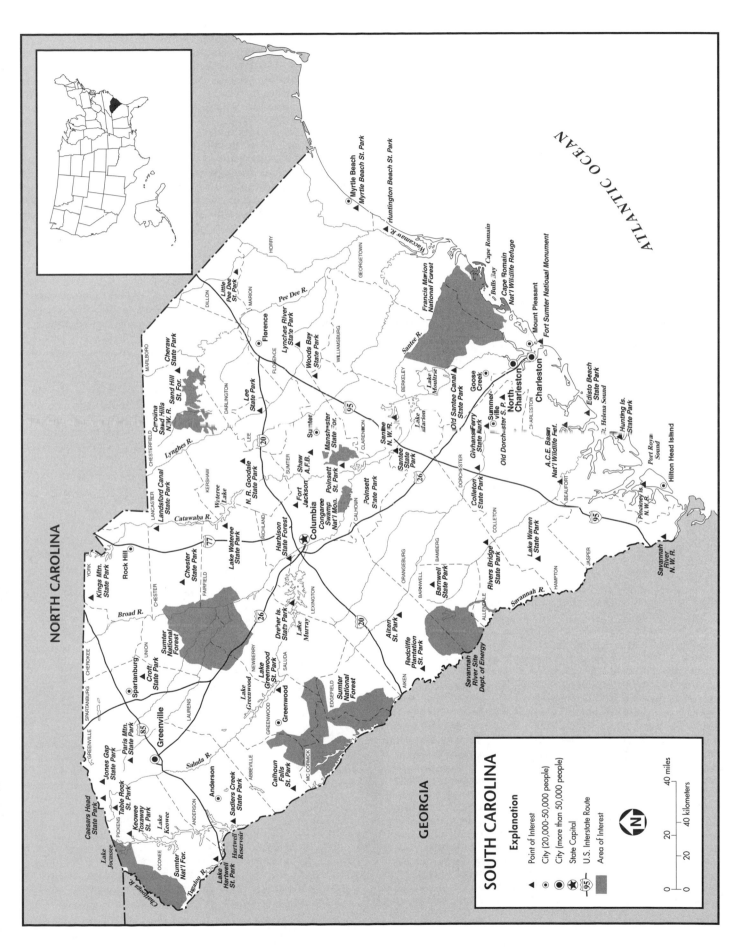

ATLANTIC OCEAN

NORTH CAROLINA

GEORGIA

SOUTH CAROLINA

Explanation

▲ Point of Interest
⊙ City (20,000–50,000 people)
◉ City (more than 50,000 people)
✪ State Capital
95 U.S. Interstate Route
▆ Area of Interest

40 miles
40 kilometers
20
20
0
0

As of 1990, the state also had 78,768 Roman Catholics and an estimated 8,558 Jews.

10TRANSPORTATION

Since the Revolutionary War, South Carolina has been concerned with expanding the transport of goods between the upcountry and the port of Charleston and the midwestern US. Several canals were constructed north of the fall line, and the 136-mi (219-km) railroad completed from Charleston to Hamburg (across the Savannah River from Augusta, Ga.) in 1833 was the longest in the world at that time. Three years earlier, the *Best Friend of Charleston* had become the first American steam locomotive built for public railway passenger service; by the time the Charleston–Hamburg railway was completed, however, the *Best Friend* had blown up, and a new engine, the *Phoenix,* had replaced it. Many other efforts were made to connect Charleston to the interior by railway, but tunnels through the mountains were never completed. Today, most freight service is furnished by Norfolk Southern and CSX Transportation. In 1995, there were 2,372 rail mi (3,818 km) of track, utilized by two Class I, nine local, and five switching and terminal railroads. About 29% (4,305,656 tons) of the rail tonnage in 1995 originating within the state was lumber and wood products, and also that year, coal represented 39% (10,876,443 tons) of the rail tonnage terminated in South Carolina. Amtrak passenger trains pass north–south through the state, providing limited service to Charleston, Columbia, and other cities. In 1995/96, South Carolina ridership amounted to 151,985.

The public road network in 1995 was made up of 53,570 mi (86,248 km) of rural roads, 10,543 mi (16,974 km) of urban roads, and 829 mi (1,335 km) of interstate highways in operation. Highway I-26, running northwest–southeast from the upcountry to the Atlantic, intersects I-85 at Spartanburg, I-20 at Columbia, and I-95 on its way toward Charleston. There were 1,865,265 passenger vehicles, 953,078 trucks, and 14,988 buses registered in 1995, when the number of licensed drivers totaled 2,542,139. City bus service carried 6,162,985 passengers in the state during 1994, 96% in the Charleston and Columbia systems.

The state has three deepwater seaports. Charleston is one of the major ports on the Atlantic, handling over 11.1 million tons of cargo in 1995, and the harbors of Georgetown and Port Royal also handle significant waterborne trade. The Atlantic Intracoastal Waterway, crossing the state slightly inward form the Atlantic Ocean, is a major thoroughfare.

South Carolina's 140 airports handled 2,294,778 passengers in 1994. Charleston, Columbia, and Greenville–Spartanburg are the major airports within the state: many travelers also enter South Carolina via the air terminals at Savannah, Augusta, and Atlanta, Ga., and at Charlotte, N.C. In 1994, the state registered 1,566 active aircraft and 6,354 pilots.

11HISTORY

Prior to European settlement, the region now called South Carolina was populated by several Indian groups. Indians of Iroquoian stock, including the Cherokee, inhabited the northwestern section, while those of the Siouan stock—of whom the Catawba were the most numerous—occupied the northern and eastern regions. Indians of Muskogean stock lived in the south.

In the early 1500s, long before the English claimed the Carolinas, Spanish sea captains explored the coast. The Spaniards made an unsuccessful attempt to establish a settlement in 1526 at Winyah Bay, near the present city of Georgetown. Thirty-six years later, a group of French Huguenots under Jean Ribault landed at a site near Parris Island, but the colony failed after Ribault returned to France. The English established the first permanent settlement in 1670 under the supervision of the eight lords proprietors who had been granted "Carolana" by King Charles II. At first the colonists settled at Albemarle Point on the Ashley River: 10 years later, they moved across the river to the present site of Charleston.

Rice cultivation began in the coastal swamps, and black slaves were imported as field hands. The colony flourished, and by the mid-1700s, new areas were developing inland. Germans, Scotch-Irish, and Welsh, who differed markedly from the original aristocratic settlers of the Charleston area, migrated to the southern part of the new province. Although the upcountry was developing and was taxed, it was not until 1770 that the settlers there were represented in the government. For the most part, the colonists had friendly relations with the Indians. In 1715, however, the Yamasee were incited by Spanish colonists at St. Augustine, Fla., to attack the South Carolina settlements. The settlers successfully resisted, with no help from the proprietors.

The original royal grant had made South Carolina a very large colony, but eventually the separate provinces of North Carolina and Georgia were established, two moves that destined South Carolina to be a small state. The colonists were successful in having the proprietors overthrown in 1719 and the government transferred to royal rule by 1721.

Skirmishes with the French, Spanish, Indians, and pirates, as well as a slave uprising in 1739, marked the pre-Revolutionary period. South Carolina opposed the Stamp Act of 1765 and took an active part in the American Revolution. The first British property seized by American Revolutionary forces was Ft. Charlotte in McCormick County in 1775. Among the many battles fought in South Carolina were major Patriot victories at Ft. Moultrie in Charleston (1776), Kings Mountain (1780), and Cowpens (1781), the last two among the war's most important engagements. Delegates from South Carolina, notably Charles Cotesworth Pinckney, were leaders at the federal constitutional convention of 1787. On 23 May 1788, South Carolina became the 8th state to ratify the Constitution.

Between the Revolutionary War and the Civil War, two issues dominated South Carolinians' political thinking: tariffs and slavery. Senator John C. Calhoun took an active part in developing the nullification theory by which a state claimed the right to abrogate unpopular federal laws. Open conflict over tariffs during the early 1830s was narrowly averted by a compromise on the rates, but in 1860, on the issue of slavery, no compromise was possible. At the time of secession, on 20 December 1860, more than half the state's population consisted of black slaves. The first battle of the Civil War took place at Ft. Sumter in Charleston Harbor on 12 April 1861. Federal forces soon captured the Sea Islands, but Charleston withstood a long siege until February 1865. In the closing months of the war, Union troops under General William Tecumseh Sherman burned Columbia and caused widespread destruction elsewhere. South Carolina contributed about 63,000 soldiers to the Confederacy out of a white population of some 291,000. Casualties were high: nearly 14,00 men were killed in battle or died after capture.

Federal troops occupied South Carolina after the war. During Reconstruction, as white South Carolinians saw it, illiterates, carpetbaggers, and scalawags raided the treasury, plunging the state into debt. The constitution was revised in 1868 by a convention in which blacks outnumbered whites by 76 to 48; given the franchise, blacks attained the offices of lieutenant governor and US representative. In 1876, bands of white militants called Red Shirts, supporting the gubernatorial candidacy of former Confederate General Wade Hampton, rode through the countryside urging whites to vote and intimidating potential black voters. Hampton, a Democrat, won the election, but was not permitted by the Republican incumbent to take office until President Rutherford B. Hayes declared an end to Reconstruction and withdrew federal troops from the state in April 1877.

For the next 100 years, South Carolina suffered through political turmoil, crop failures, and recessions. A major political change came in the 1880s with a large population increase upcountry and the migration of poor whites to cities. These trends gave farmers and industrial workers a majority of votes, and they found their leader in Benjamin Ryan "Pitchfork Ben" Tillman, a populist who stirred up class and racial hatreds by attacking the "Charleston ring." Tillman was influential in wresting control of the state Democratic Party from the coastal aristocrats; he served as governor from 1890 to 1894 and then as US senator until his death in 1918. However, his success inaugurated a period of political and racial demagoguery that saw the gradual (though not total) disfranchisement of black voters.

The main economic transformation since 1890 has been the replacement of rice and cotton growing by tobacco and soybean cultivation and truck farming, along with the movement of tenant farmers, or sharecroppers, from the land to the cities. There they found jobs in textile mills, and textiles became the state's leading industry after 1900. With the devastation of the cotton crop by the boll weevil in the 1920s, farmers were compelled to diversify their crops, and some turned to cattle raising. Labor shortages in the North during and after World War II drew many thousands of blacks to Philadelphia, Washington, D.C., New York, and other cities.

In the postwar period, industry has taken over the dominant role formerly held by agriculture in South Carolina's economy, and the focus of textile production has shifted from cotton to synthetic fabrics. In the 1990s the major industries were textiles and chemicals, and foreign investment played a major role in the state's economy. BMW, the German automobile company, developed their North American plant in Greenville.

Public school desegregation after the *Brown vs. Board of Education* ruling of 1954 proceeded peaceably, but very slowly, and blacks were gradually accepted alongside whites in the textile mills and other industries. In 1983, for the first time in 95 years, a black state senator was elected; the following year, four blacks were elected to the reapportioned senate. Despite these changes, most white South Carolinians remain staunchly conservative in political and social matters. In the postwar period, the Democrats' traditional control of the state weakened, and, beginning with Barry Goldwater, Republican presidential candidates have carried the state in every election except that of 1976, in which Southerner Jimmy Carter prevailed. Well-known conservative Republican Strom Thurmond has represented South Carolina in the US Senate since 1954.

In 1989, Hurricane Hugo, the tenth-strongest hurricane to hit the United States coast in the 20th century, struck South Carolina, bringing 135-mph (217 kph) winds. Ripping roofs off buildings and sweeping boats onto city streets, the storm killed 37 people and produced over $700 million worth of property damage. Seven South Carolina counties were declared disaster areas. In 1993, flooding, followed by a record-breaking drought, caused an estimated $226 million in crop damage.

In response to a Supreme Court ruling, The Citadel, one of only two state-supported military schools in the country, admitted its first female cadet, Shannon Faulkner, in 1995. Faulkner left the institution after only six days. In 1997 two of four women attending the institution quit, alleging hazing and sexual harassment by their male peers.

12STATE GOVERNMENT

South Carolina has had seven constitutions, dating from 1776, 1778, 1790, 1861, 1865, 1868, and 1895, respectively. Beginning in 1970, most articles of the 1895 constitution were rewritten. The present document had been amended 444 times by 1983.

The general assembly consists of a senate of 46 members, elected for four-year terms, and a house of representatives of 124 members, elected for two years. Senators must be 25 years of age, representatives 21; all legislators must be qualified voters in the districts they represent. The legislative salary was $10,400 in 1995. Officials elected statewide include the governor and lieutenant governor (who run separately), attorney general, secretary of state, comptroller general, treasurer, adjutant general, secretary of agriculture, and superintendent of education, all elected to four-year terms. Eligibility requirements for the governor include a minimum age of 30, US citizenship for at least five years, and a five-year state residency. In 1996 the governor's salary was $106,078.

Most state agencies are governed by boards of at least five members appointed by the governor, but some of the largest agency boards are elected by the general assembly. Outside of his own office, the governor appoints very few department heads. South Carolina has nearly 130 agencies, boards, and commissions.

Legislative sessions are held annually. Bills may be introduced in either house, except for revenue measures, which are reserved to the house of representatives. The governor has a regular veto and an item veto on appropriation matters, either of which may be overridden by a two-thirds vote of those present in each house of the legislature; bills automatically become law after five days if the governor takes no action. The constitution may be amended by a two-thirds vote of each house of the general assembly and by a majority of those casting their ballots at the next general election. To take effect, however, the amendment must then be ratified by a majority vote of the next general assembly.

Citizens 18 years of age and older who have been state residents for 30 days are eligible to vote.

13POLITICAL PARTIES

South Carolina's major political organizations are the Democratic and Republican parties. From the end of Reconstruction, the Democratic Party dominated state politics. Dissatisfaction with the national party's position on civil rights in 1948 led to the formation of the States' Rights Democrat faction, whose candidate, South Carolina Governor J. Strom Thurmond, carried the state in 1948. Thurmond's subsequent switch to the Republicans while in the US Senate was a big boost for the state's Republican Party, which since 1964 has captured South Carolina's eight electoral votes in seven of the eight presidential elections. In 1996, Republican Bob Dole won nearly 50% of the popular vote, to Democrat Bill Clinton's 44% and Independent Ross Perot's 6%. South Carolina's US senators are Democrat Ernest F. Hollings, whose term expires in 1999, and Republican Strom Thurmond, who was reelected in 1996 at the age of 93—the oldest senator in the country's history (Hollings is also the oldest junior senator serving). As of 1997, there were 2 Democrats and 4 Republicans serving as US representatives. The state senate had 26 Democrats and 20 Republicans; while in the state house there were 70 Republicans, 53 Democrats, and 1 independent. In 1994, there were 450 black elected officials. As of 1995, 21 women served in the state legislature, and 1 woman held an elective executive office.

Voters do not register according to political party in South Carolina. Instead, at primary elections, they simply take an oath that they have not participated in another primary. In 1994 there were 1,537,140 registered voters.

14LOCAL GOVERNMENT

As of 1992, South Carolina had 46 counties, 269 incorporated municipalities, 91 school districts, and 291 special districts of various types. Ten regional councils provide a broad range of technical and advisory services to county and municipal governments.

Under legislation enacted in 1975, all counties and municipalities have the same powers, regardless of size. Most municipalities operate under the mayor-council or city manager system; more than half the counties have a county administrator or manager. Customarily, each county has a council or commission, attorney, auditor, clerk of court, coroner, tax collector, treasurer, and sheriff. Many of these county officials are elected, but the only municipal officers elected are the mayor and the members of the council.

While the state shares revenues from many different sources with the counties and, municipalities, these local units derive virtually all their direct revenue from the property tax. In recent years, the state's school districts have rapidly increased their own property tax levies, squeezing the counties' and municipalities' revenue base.

15 STATE SERVICES

The State Ethics Commission establishes rules covering possible conflicts of interest, oversees election campaign practices, and provides for officeholders' financial disclosure.

The Department of Education administers state and federal aid to the public schools, while the State Commission on Higher Education oversees the public colleges and universities, and the State Board for Technical and Comprehensive Education is responsible for postsecondary technical training schools. The state also runs special schools for the deaf and blind. Complementing both public and higher education is a state educational television network, under the jurisdiction of the South Carolina Educational Television Commission. Transportation services are provided by the Department of Highways and Public Transportation, which maintains most major roads, issues drivers' licenses, and has jurisdiction over the Highway Patrol. The Department of Commerce Division of Aeronautics oversees airport development.

Through a variety of agencies, South Carolina offers a broad array of human services in the fields of mental health, mental retardation, vocational rehabilitation, veterans' affairs, care of the blind, and adoptions. An ombudsman for the aging handles complaints about nursing homes, which are licensed by the state. The South Carolina Law Enforcement Division provides technical aid to county sheriffs and municipal police departments. Emergency situations are handled by the Office of Disaster Assistance and the National Guard.

The State Housing Authority is authorized to subsidize interest rates on mortgages for middle- and low-income families. The Employment Security Commission oversees unemployment compensation and job placement, while the Department of Labor offers arbitration and mediation services and enforces health and safety standards. The Human Affairs Commission looks into unfair labor practices based on sex, race, or age.

16 JUDICIAL SYSTEM

South Carolina's unified judicial system is headed by the chief justice of the supreme court, who, along with four associate justices, is elected by the general assembly to a 10-year term. The supreme court is the final court of appeal. A five-member intermediate court of appeals for criminal cases was established in 1979, but legal questions (specifically, about the election of general assembly members to four of the five seats) prevented the court from convening until 1981; the court became a permanent constitutional court in 1984.

Sixteen circuit courts hear major criminal and civil cases. As of 1996 there were over 30 circuit court judges, all of them elected by the general assembly to six-year terms. The state also has a system of family courts for domestic and juvenile cases. In addition, there are magistrates' courts (justices of the peace) in all counties, municipal courts, and county probate judges. In 1996, there were 6,743 attorneys practicing in the state.

The state penal system is rapidly becoming centralized under the state Department of Corrections; there is a separate state system for juvenile offenders. In 1996 there were 18,329 inmates in state and federal correctional institutions, or 499 prisoners per 100,000 in population. South Carolina's total crime rate for 1996 of 6,063.8 crimes per 100,000 inhabitants exceeded the national average of 5,277.6. South Carolina has a death penalty statute. In May of 1997 there were 71 inmates on death row. Between 1912 and 1962 there were 241 executions, and there have been 11 since 1962.

17 ARMED FORCES

In 1996, there were 33,842 active duty military personnel. Ft. Jackson, in Columbia, is the Army's largest major training center, with 11,569 military personnel in 1996. Air Force bases at Charleston and Sumter are major installations. Parris Island has long been one of the country's chief Marine Corps training bases.

South Carolina Presidential Vote by Political Parties, 1948–96

YEAR	ELECTORAL VOTE	SOUTH CAROLINA WINNER	DEMOCRAT	REPUBLICAN	STATES' RIGHTS DEMOCRAT	LIBERTARIAN
1948	8	Thurmond (SRD)	34,423	5,386	102,607	—
1952	8	Stevenson (D)	172,957	168,043	—	—
					UNPLEDGED	—
1956	8	Stevenson (D)	136,278	75,634	88,509	—
1960	8	*Kennedy (D)	198,121	188,558	—	—
1964	8	Goldwater (R)	215,723	309,048	—	—
					AMERICAN IND.	
1968	8	*Nixon (R)	197,486	254,062	215,430	
					AMERICAN	
1972	8	*Nixon (R)	1,868,824	477,044	10,075	—
1976	8	*Carter (D)	450,807	346,149	2,996	—
						LIBERTARIAN
1980	8	*Reagan (R)	430,385	441,841	—	4,975
1984	8	*Reagan (R)	344,459	615,539	—	4,359
1988	8	*Bush (R)	370,554	606,443	—	4,935
					IND. (Perot)	
1992	8	Bush (R)	479.514	577,507	138,872	2,719
1996	8	Dole (R)	506,283	573,458	64,386	4,271

* Won US presidential election.

South Carolina firms received $1.01 billion in defense contract awards during 1995/96.

Veterans in South Carolina as of 1 July 1996 totaled 376,000, including less than 500 from World War I, 92,000 from World War II, 63,000 from the Korean conflict, 130,000 who served during the Vietnam era, and 31,000 from the Persian Gulf War. Veterans' benefits during 1995/96 amounted to $593 million.

National Guard and Reserve units had 32,124 personnel in 1996. In 1993, the South Carolina Highway Patrol employed 995 full-time sworn officers, or 3 per 10,000 residents.

[18]MIGRATION

The original European migration into South Carolina consisted mostly of German, Welsh, and Scotch-Irish settlers. During the 19th century, many of the original settlers emigrated westward to Alabama, Mississippi, and Texas. In the 20th century, many blacks left the state for cities in the North. Between 1940 and 1970, South Carolina's net loss from migration was 601,000. During 1970–80, however, the state enjoyed a net gain of 210,000; in the 1980s, the net gain from migration was nearly 200,000.

As of 1990, 68.4% of state residents had been born in South Carolina. Between 1990 and 1996, the state had net gains of 48,119 in domestic migration, and 11,264 in international migration. In 1996, 2,151 foreign immigrants arrived in South Carolina. About 55% of the residents age 5 and older lived in the same house in 1990 as in 1985. Some three-fourths of those who reported living in a different house in 1985 (from 1990) had done so elsewhere within South Carolina.

[19]INTERGOVERNMENTAL COOPERATION

The South Carolina Interstate Cooperation Commission represents the state before the Council of State Governments. South Carolina also participates in the Atlantic States Marine Fisheries Compact, Southeastern Forest Fire Protection Compact, Southern Growth Policies Compact, Southern Interstate Energy Compact, and Southern Regional Education Compact.

In 1995/96, the state received $3 billion in federal funds.

[20]ECONOMY

During its early days, South Carolina was one of the country's richest areas. Its economy depended on foreign commerce and agriculture, especially indigo, rice, and later cotton. After the Civil War, the state suffered severe economic depression. Not until the 1880s did the textile industry—today the state's major employer—begin to develop.

Textiles and farming completely dominated the economy until after World War II, when efforts toward economic diversification attracted paper, chemical, and other industries to the state. During the postwar period, the state spent sizable amounts to improve its three ports, especially the harbor facilities of Charleston.

By 1992, manufacturing had become the most important sector in the South Carolina economy. Almost 25% of the labor force worked in manufacturing, well above the national average of 17%. The top ten manufacturers in the state employed over 40,000 workers. The Westinghouse Savannah River Site military base accounts for a significant portion of the state's manufacturing base. Employment at those facilities grew significantly during the 1980s when the Reagan administration increased military expenditures. In the early 1990s, however, the federal government began cutting staff at the bases and was considering phasing them out.

Largely because of its legacy of low-wage industries and an unorganized and poorly educated work force, the state continues to fall below national norms by most economic measures. Nevertheless, during the 1970s and early 1980s, real per capita income increased faster than in the nation as a whole. Rising foreign and domestic investment, coupled with an abundance of first-class tourist facilities along the coast, contributed to the continuing growth of South Carolina's economy in the 1980s and were only temporarily hurt by the national recession of the early nineties. South Carolina's per capita personal income in 1995 was $18,998, placing it 39th in the nation.

South Carolina's gross state product in 1994 was $79,925 million, to which private goods-producing industries contributed $26,505 million; private services-producing industries, $40,738 million; and government, $12,682 million.

During 1996, there were 9,778 filings for bankruptcy, up 31% from 1995.

[21]INCOME

South Carolina ranked 41st among the 50 states in 1996 with a per capita personal income of $19,755.

Total nonfarm income rose from $65.7 billion in 1994 to $69.8 billion in 1995, an increase of 6.2%. Total disposable income increased from $61.9 billion in 1995 to $64.6 billion in 1996. Median family income averaged $34,400 in 1993. In 1995, an estimated 19.9% of all residents were living below the federal poverty level.

Counties with sizable military or other federal facilities generally ranked highest in per capita income, while counties having majority black populations ranked among the lowest.

[22]LABOR

In 1996, South Carolina had a nonagricultural civilian labor force of 1,848,000, of whom 1,737,000 were employed and 111,000 were unemployed. The unemployment rate of 6% was above the 1996 national average of 5.4%. At the end of 1996, the nonagricultural employment distribution was as follows: mining, 1,900; construction, 90,300; manufacturing, 364,400; transportation and utilities, 74,200; wholesale and retail trade, 409,200; finance, insurance, and real estate, 72,300; and government, 300,700.

South Carolina has one of the lowest work stoppage rates in the nation and only a small percentage of the total labor force is organized. Manufacturing workers' membership in labor unions was only 2.9% of the manufacturing work force in 1995, and only 3.3% of all workers were union members that year, the lowest rate of any state. Textile, clothing, and ladies' garment workers' unions make up the bulk of the membership, followed by transportation and electrical workers. Several large textile companies have made major efforts to prevent their workers from organizing unions; conflicts between management and workers have continued for years, but without serious violence. A right-to-work law was enacted in the 1950s.

[23]AGRICULTURE

Agriculture is an integral part of the state's economy. The total cash receipts for agriculture and forestry average about $2 billion per year, but that figure represents only a fraction of the impact of agriculture and agribusiness in the state. Agriculture (food and fiber) along with forestry and forestry products contribute about 25% to the gross state product (GSP). Some 18% of all jobs in South Carolina are from agriculture and agribusiness. As of 1996 there were about 21,500 farms in the state, occupying 5 million acres (2 million hectares) with an average size of 233 acres (94 hectares). Agriculture in South Carolina supplies not only food for consumption, but also cotton for clothing and soybean oil for newsprint ink.

The main farming area is a 50-mi (80-km) band across the upper coastal plain. The Pee Dee region in the east is the center for tobacco production. Cotton is grown mostly south of the fall line, and feed crops thrive in the coastal and sand hill counties.

Tobacco is the leading crop by value; in 1996, farmers in the state produced 111.8 million lb (50.7 million kg) of tobacco on 50,000 acres (20,200 hectares) with a value of $203.6 million. Soybean and cotton production in that year were 14 million bushels and 450,000 bales, respectively. There were 21,000 acres (8,500 hectares) of peach tree orchards in 1996, but severe late spring freezes all but wiped out the crop that year. Peach production in 1995 was 215 million lb (97.5 million kg). South Carolina ranked 3d in ornamental horticulture, floriculture, and turf grass sales in 1996, with $170 million in cash receipts. The horticultural industry provided over 18,000 full-time jobs and $2.5 million in wages that year.

South Carolina farmers and agribusinesses also produce apples, barley, beans, berries, canola, corn, cucumbers, hay, kiwifruit, mushrooms, oats, peanuts, pecans, popcorn, rye, sorghum, sweet potatoes, tea, turf grasses, tomatoes, ornamental trees, and wheat. As more people relocate and retire to the state, demand for agricultural products is increasing in order to supply restaurant, hotel, and landscaping businesses. The South Carolina Department of Agriculture operates three state farmers' markets in Columbia, Florence, and Greenville.

[24]ANIMAL HUSBANDRY

In 1997, there were an estimated 520,000 cattle and calves, worth $213 million. During 1996, there were around 300,000 hogs and pigs, valued at $26.7 million. Dairy farmers produced around 391 million lb (177 million kg) of milk from 27,000 milk cows in 1995. Poultry farmers produced nearly 1.3 billion eggs, worth some $70 million in 1995, and 16.5 million lb (7.5 million kg) of chicken, 680.4 million lb (308.6 million kg) of broilers, and 184.8 million lb (83.8 million kg) of turkey.

[25]FISHING

The state's oceanfront saltwater inlets and freshwater rivers and lakes provide ample fishing opportunities. Major commercial fishing is restricted to saltwater species of fish and shellfish, mainly shrimp, crabs, clams, and oysters. In 1995, the commercial catch totaled 24.2 million lb (11 million kg), valued at $25,621,000. In 1995/96, federal hatcheries distributed 47.6 million fish and 1.3 million fish eggs within the state, which had issued 500,804 sport fishing licenses at that time.

[26]FORESTRY

South Carolina had 12,645,557 acres (5,117,657 hectares) of forestland in 1993—about 66% of the state's area and 1.7% of all US forests. The state's two national forests, Francis Marion and Sumter, comprised 4% of the forested area. Nearly all of South Carolina's forests are classified as commercial timberland, 91% of it privately owned. Several varieties of pine, loblolly, longleaf and shortleaf, are the major source of timber and of pulp for the paper industry. Shipments of lumber and wood products were valued at $1.59 billion in 1994; shipments of paper and allied products, $3.74 billion. The total value of the forest products industry in 1994 was $5.9 billion (3d-largest industry in South Carolina).

[27]MINING

The estimated 1995 value of nonfuel mineral commodities produced in South Carolina decreased by 2% from $433 million in 1994 to $426 million, 30th in the nation. The modest increases in construction and industrial sand and gravel did not completely offset decreases in portland cement, kaolin clay, and gold values.

Crushed stone was the leading mineral commodity produced in South Carolina again in 1995. Some 1.4 million metric tons were produced, valued at $140 million, down in tonnage from the 20 million metric tons in 1994, but a significant rise from the value of $128 million at that time. The crushed stone consisted

primarily of granite and limestone with minor amounts of dolomite, marl, and shell. Two companies in Orangeburg County and one in Dorchester County produced cement. Its estimated value of $127 million, $16 million less than that of 1994, accounted for 29.8% of the total value of nonfuel minerals produced. Gold was produced by four companies in Chesterfield, Fairfield, McCormick, and Lancaster Counties. Construction sand and gravel was the 3d-most-valuable nonfuel mineral produced in 1995, with 9.7 million metric tons, valued at $31 million. Clay was the 4th-most-valuable mineral commodity produced, accounting for 5.4% of the total value produced in 1995. Common clay and shale, fuller's earth, and kaolin were the varieties of clay mined. South Carolina continued to be the 2d-leading state in the production of kaolin. Industrial sand and gravel production totaled 812,000 metric tons, valued at $19.6 million. South Carolina in 1995 ranked 1st of the states in vermiculite production, 3d in kaolin, fourth in crude mica, 7th in common clays, and 9th in gold.

[28]ENERGY AND POWER

Although it lacks fossil fuel resources, South Carolina produces more electricity than it consumes. Installed electric capacity totaled 18 million kW in 1995, when power production reached 78.4 billion kwh.

About 63% of electric output came from nuclear reactors, 33% from coal-fired plants, and 3% from hydropower. Sales of electric energy in 1995 amounted to 64.3 billion kWh. Major power suppliers are six private companies and the state-owned Public Service Authority, known as Santee-Cooper. Gas utilities sold 147 million cu ft (4.2 million cu m) of natural gas—all of it imported—to some 461,354 customers in 1995.

South Carolina is heavily engaged in nuclear energy. As of 1996, four nuclear plants were producing electricity. The vast Savannah River plant in Aiken County produces most of the plutonium for the nation's nuclear weapons; Chem-Nuclear Systems in Barnwell County stores about half of the country's low-level nuclear wastes; and a Westinghouse plant in Richland County makes fuel assemblies for nuclear reactors.

[29]INDUSTRY

South Carolina's principal industry beginning in the 1880s was textiles, but many textile mills were closed during the 1970s and early 1980s because of the importation of cheaper textiles from abroad. The economic slack was made up, however, by the establishment of new industries, especially paper and chemical manufactures, and by increasing foreign investment in the state. Overseas investments totaled $1,162 million in South Carolina in 1992, or more than 45% of total industrial investment in the state. Investment in metalworking and chemicals accounted for $1,091.7 million and $800 million, respectively, in 1992. Principal overseas investment came from Switzerland, Germany, the United Kingdom, and Japan. South Carolina's major manufacturing centers are concentrated north of the fall line and in the piedmont.

The total value of shipments for manufactured goods in 1995 was $66,902,500,000. The following table shows value of shipments for selected industries.

Chemical and allied products	$12,302,900,000
Textile mill products	10,724,000,000
Industrial machinery and equipment	8,051,600,000
Paper and paper products	5,140,500,000
Rubber and plastic products	4,709,000,000
Electronic and other electric equipment	4,128,400,000

In 1997, Sonoco Products was the only Fortune 500 company headquartered in South Carolina. During 1995, 497 US patents were issued to South Carolina residents.

30COMMERCE

South Carolina had 5,564 wholesale establishments in 1992, with sales of $21.3 billion. Tobacco wholesale markets and warehouses are centered in the Pee Dee region, while soybean sales and storage facilities cluster around the port of Charleston; truck crops, fruits, and melons are sold in large quantities at the state farmers' market in Columbia. Sales from 22,836 retail establishments in 1992 totaled $24.7 billion, of which food stores accounted for 20.9%, automotive dealers, 20.5%; general merchandise stores, 12.1%; eating and drinking places, 10.7%; and other outlets, 35.8%.

In 1995, foreign imports from the Charleston customs district were valued at $10.4 billion, and overseas exports at $10.1 billion. Foreign exports of South Carolina's own products were valued at $6.7 billion in 1996.

31CONSUMER PROTECTION

The Department of Consumer Affairs, established in 1974, has the authority to take, process, and investigate consumer complaints for probable basis and merit, represent the public at regulatory proceedings, and enforce consumer credit laws and consumer-related licensing laws.

32BANKING

In 1996, the state's 73 commercial banks had total assets of $32.3 billion and deposits of more than $24.7 billion; outstanding loans amounted to $15.0 billion. The largest commercial bank in 1995 was NationsBank (Columbia), with assets of $7,595,716,000. There were 30 insured savings institutions with assets totaling $7.3 billion and mortgage loans of $4.6 billion.

33INSURANCE

The South Carolina Department of Insurance licenses and supervises the insurance companies doing business in the state. Most of these represent national insurance organizations. In 1995, life insurance in force in the state totaled $174 billion, or approximately $121,200 per household (total coverage divided evenly among all households in the state); premiums paid totaled $1.3 billion; and payments to beneficiaries totaled $482 million. Property and casualty companies wrote premiums totaling $3.4 billion in 1995. A tort system of automobile insurance is in effect.

34SECURITIES

There are no securities exchanges in South Carolina, but as of May 1997 there were 1,459 broker-dealers registered there, involving some 55,043 designated agents; registered investment advisors numbered 540, with 6,227 agents. Enforcement of the state Securities Act is vested in the securities commissioner within the Office of the Attorney General.

35PUBLIC FINANCE

South Carolina's governor submits the annual budget to the General Assembly in January as the basis for enactment of an appropriation bill, effective for the fiscal year beginning July 1.

The state constitution requires that budget appropriations not exceed expected revenues. A General Reserve Fund (equaling three percent of General Fund revenues) is maintained to cover operating deficits. In addition, approximately 25% of projected revenue growth is set-aside and may be used as a surplus at the end of the fiscal year. Many tax revenues are earmarked for specific purposes and are deposited in accounts other than the General Fund: all gasoline taxes and related charges are designated for highways, and a portion of the sales tax goes directly to public education. In addition, public education accounts for more than half of all General Fund expenditures. The state shares tax collections with its subdivisions—counties and municipalities—which determine how their share of the money will be spent.

The following table summarizes General Fund revenues and expenditures for fiscal year 1995:

REVENUES	FY 1995
Retail sales tax	1,794,120
Individual income tax	1,655,954
Corporate income tax	250,214
Other receipts	8,376,628
TOTALS	$12,076,916

EXPENDITURES	
Education	3,537,053
Health	623,469
Debt service	180,061
Other outlays	7,282,520
TOTALS	$11,623,103

In 1995, South Carolina's public debt totaled $5.0 billion (including local and state governments), or $4,414.13 per capita.

36TAXATION

South Carolinians bear a tax burden that is lighter than most other states'. As of 1997, the chief levies were a personal income tax ranging from 2.5% to 7%; a corporate income tax of 5% (4.5% for banks, 6% for savings and loan associations); a broad-based 5% sales tax; and taxes on gasoline, alcoholic beverages, business licenses, insurance, and gifts and estates. In addition to the property tax, municipalities and counties may impose business license fees, plus charges for such services as garbage collection and water supply. Particularly in the tourist-attraction coastal areas, there are some local option sales and accommodations taxes.

Taxes remitted to the federal government totaled $11 billion in 1995; South Carolina received more than $17.4 billion in federal funding in 1995.

37ECONOMIC POLICY

The Department of Commerce seeks to encourage economic growth and to attract new industries; it has been successful in attracting foreign companies, especially to the Piedmont. The state's Small Business Development Center and Governor's Office of Minority Business help small companies to get started.

The state exempts all new industrial construction from local property taxes (except the school tax) for five years. Moreover, industrial properties are assessed very leniently for tax purposes. State and local governments have cooperated in building necessary roads to industrial sites, providing water and sewer services, and helping industries to meet environmental standards. Counties are authorized to issue industrial bonds at low interest rates. Generally conservative state fiscal policies, relatively low swage rates, and an anti-union climate also serve as magnets for industry.

38HEALTH

South Carolina's infant mortality rate has improved significantly in recent years but was still higher than the nation's rate in 1995: 9.0 per 1,000 live births, up slightly from the previous year. In South Carolina there were 196 abortions per 1,000 live births, and 9% of the 32,253 abortions performed in 1992 were obtained by out-of-state residents. Impeding efforts to further improve health standards are a shortage of doctors (especially in rural areas and small towns), inadequate public education, poor housing, and improper sanitation.

As of 1995, the leading causes of death were heart disease, which caused 30.4% of all deaths; cancer, 22.1%; stroke, 12.1%; and accidents and adverse effects, 4.8%. The state has mounted major programs to detect heart disease and high blood pressure, reduce infant mortality, and expand medical education. In 1995, the birthrate of 13.9 per 1,000 population was below the US average; the state's death rate of 14.8 per 1,000 in 1995 was also below the norm.

In 1995, South Carolina's health facilities included 66 general hospitals and 8 nursing homes. At least 16% of South Carolina residents were uninsured. Nonfederal medical personnel in 1995 included 7,999 active physicians, and 1,597 dentists.

In 1995 there were 27.16 AIDS cases per 100,000 population, slightly below the US average. Since the first appearance of AIDS in the US, there have been a total of 4,875 cases in South Carolina.

In the population of South Carolina residents 18–30 years of age, 22% were smokers in 1995.

39SOCIAL WELFARE

Aid to 121,700 persons with dependent children averaged $240 a month per family in 1996. In 1996, 358,341 residents received monthly food stamp allowances averaging $69.61. In that year, virtually every school in the state participated in the school lunch program, at a federal cost of $94.7 million.

With the enactment of the Personal Responsibility and Work Opportunity Reconciliation Act of 1996, the US government changed the form and regulations for many of its social welfare programs; most significantly, it replaced Aid to Families with Dependent Children (AFDC), an open-ended entitlement program, with Temporary Assistance for Needy Families (TANF), a limited system of assistance funded largely through federal block grants. The reform act also impacted the food stamp program, the Supplemental Security Income program, and the child nutrition program. The law took effect on 1 July 1997 and provided $16.38 billion in block grants for fiscal years 1997–2002. The grants were to be divided among the states based on an equation involving the numbers of former AFDC recipients in each state. Because many of the bill's provisions have yet to be implemented into state-by-state policy, it was not possible to include the details of each state's programs for this edition of this work.

In 1995, 624,920 people received Social Security benefits, averaging $682 a month; additionally, Federal Supplemental Security Income payments were made to 111,095 persons, averaging $300 a month. In 1995, unemployment insurance benefits averaged a weekly payment of $161.55.

40HOUSING

In 1996 there were an estimated 1,567,000 year-round housing units, 1,351,000 of which were occupied. That year, 29,403 privately owned units, valued at $2.4 billion, were authorized for construction; of these, 22,511 were single-family. About 98.6% of all occupied units had full plumbing. The median value of an owner-occupied house was $61,100 in 1990, the last year for which figures were available, up by 9.7% from 1980 after adjusting for inflation. During 1995/96, South Carolina received $243.4 million in aid from the US Department of Housing and Urban Development, including $40.7 million in community development block grants. In 1990, over 16.5% of the state's housing units consisted of mobile homes or trailers, a greater proportion than in any other state except Wyoming.

South Carolina has made a determined effort to upgrade housing. The State Housing Authority, created in 1971, is empowered to issue bonds to provide mortgage subsidies for low- and middle-income families.

41EDUCATION

For decades, South Carolina ranked below the national averages in most phases of education, including expenditures per pupil, median years of school completed, teachers' salaries, and literacy levels. During the 1970s, however, significant improvements were made through the adoption of five-year achievement goals, enactment of a statewide educational funding plan, provision of special programs for exceptional children and of kindergartens for all children, measurement of students' achievements at various stages, and expansion of adult education programs. As a result, South Carolina high school graduates now score only slightly lower than the national averages on standardized examinations. South Carolina's educational funding is higher in relation to per capita income than that of most other states. As of 1990, more than 68.9% of all residents 25 years or older had completed high school and 16.2% had attended college.

In 1995/96 there were 633,494 pupils enrolled in public schools. South Carolina ranked below the national average in pupil/teacher ratio in public schools with 16.2 pupils per teacher in 1996.

Higher education institutions in 1996/97 enrolled 176,957 students, of whom 84% were attending public institutions. The state has three major universities: the University of South Carolina, with 25,489 students (1996/97) at its main campus in Columbia; Clemson University (16,526 students), at Clemson; and the Medical University of South Carolina (2,296 students), in Charleston. In addition, there are 7 four-year state colleges, as well as 7 four-year and two-year branches of the University of South Carolina. The state also has 23 four-year private colleges and universities, of which only Bob Jones University in Greenville enrolled more than 3,851 students in 1996/97; most are church-affiliated. The Lutheran Theological Southern Seminary in Columbia is the only major private graduate institution. There were 4 private junior colleges, with a total enrollment of 1,314, in 1996/97. South Carolina has an extensive technical education system, supported by both state and local funds. Tuition grants are offered for needy South Carolina students enrolled in private colleges in the state.

42ARTS

South Carolina's three major centers for the visual arts are the Gibbes Art Gallery in Charleston, the Columbia Museum of Art and Science, and the Greenville County Museum of Art. Local theater groups in the larger municipalities produce five or six plays a year; Columbia's Town Theater claims to be the nation's oldest continuous community playhouse. Perhaps South Carolina's best-known musical event is the Spoleto Festival—held annually in Charleston during May and June and modeled on the Spoleto Festival in Italy—at which artists of international repute perform in original productions of operas and dramas. The South Carolina Arts Commission, created in 1967, has developed apprenticeship programs in which students learn from master artists.

The state of South Carolina generated $1,084,000 in federal funds for its arts programs in 1996. The NEA contributed $637,000 to the state's arts programs, and $893,000 to the South Carolina Arts Commission. The state also gave the Commission funding, along with private sources. The state's arts programs drew a total audience of 17,354,000 people during this period. There were 78,100 contributing artists. Arts education programs were offered to about 195,110 school children. In 1996, the state of South Carolina had 200 arts associations and 48 local arts groups. The South Carolina Arts Commission has provided funds for the Youth Art League and the Camp Baskerville art programs. The NEA contributed financial support for the Spoleto Festival in Charleston, South Carolina; The Marlboro Civic Center Foundation; and the ETV Endowment of South Carolina

($30,000). In 1996, the South Carolina Arts Commission received grants from the NEA to develop the state's art education programs. The Commission also received monies from the NEA's state and regional Program.

43LIBRARIES AND MUSEUMS

Public libraries in South Carolina had a combined book stock of 6,817,395 volumes and a total circulation of 16,122,660 in 1995/96. The State Library in Columbia works to improve library services throughout the state and also provides reference and research services for the state government. The University of South Carolina and Clemson University libraries, with more than 3,000,000 and 2,200,000 volumes, respectively, have the most outstanding academic collections. Special libraries are maintained by the South Carolina Historical Society in Charleston and the Department of Archives and History in Columbia; the South Caroliniana Society at the University of South Carolina is a friends' group devoted to the USC library.

There are 126 museums and historic sites, notably the State Museum in Columbia, with collections reflecting all areas of the state; Charleston Museum (specializing in history, natural history, and anthropology); and the University of South Carolina McKissick Museums (with silver, lapidary, and military collections) also in Columbia. Charleston is also famous for its many old homes, streets, churches, and public facilities; at the entrance to Charleston Harbor stands Ft. Sumter, where the Civil War began. Throughout the state, numerous battle sites of the American Revolution have been preserved; many antebellum plantation homes have been restored, especially in the low country. Restoration projects have proceeded in Columbia and Charleston, where the restored Exchange Building, dating to the Revolutionary War, was opened to the public in 1981.

Among the state's best-known botanical gardens are the Cypress, Magnolia, and Middleton gardens in the Charleston area. Edisto Garden in Orangeburg is renowned for its azaleas and roses, and Brookgreen Gardens near Georgetown displays a wide variety of plants, animals, and sculpture.

44COMMUNICATIONS

In March 1993, 89.1% of South Carolina's 1,300,000 occupied housing units had telephones. The state had 219 radio stations (94 AM, 125 FM) and 22 commercial television stations in 1996. South Carolina has one of the most highly regarded educational television systems in the nation, with 10 stations serving the public schools, higher education institutions, state agencies, and the general public through a multichannel closed-circuit network and seven open channels. In 1996, 7 large cable systems provided television programming.

45PRESS

Of the leading morning newspapers still published in South Carolina, the *Charleston Post and Courier* (with a paid daily circulation of 108,162 and 122,953 on Sunday in 1997) was founded in 1803, the *Spartanburg Herald-Journal* (61,166 daily, and 68,761 Sunday) in 1872, the *Greenville News* (101,635 daily, and 139,931 Sunday) in 1874, and *The* (Columbia) *State* (122,053 daily, and 160,381 Sunday) in 1891. Overall, as of 1997, South Carolina had 11 morning newspapers, 4 evening dailies, and 14 Sunday newspapers.

46ORGANIZATIONS

The 1992 US Census of Service Industries counted 804 organizations in South Carolina, including 163 business associations; 454 civic, social, and fraternal associations; and 187 other membership organizations. National organizations with headquarters in the state include the Association of Social and Behavioral Scientists, in Orangeburg, and the International Studies Association and the US Collegiate Sports Council, in Columbia.

47TOURISM, TRAVEL, AND RECREATION

Domestic travelers spent $4,831,000 in South Carolina during 1993. About 75% of out-of-state tourist revenue is spent by vacationers in Charleston and at the Myrtle Beach and Hilton Head Island resorts. The Cowpens National Battlefield and the Ft. Sumter and Kings Mountain national military sites are popular tourist attractions. State parks attracted a total of 10,564,824 visitors in 1995.

48SPORTS

There are no major league professional sports teams in South Carolina. Minor league baseball teams are located in Spartanburg, Greenville, Columbia, and Charleston. There is also minor league hockey in Florence and North Charleston. Several steeplechase horse races are held annually in Camden, and important professional golf and tennis tournaments are held at Hilton Head Island.

In collegiate football, the Clemson Tigers won the AP and UPI polls in 1981; the University of South Carolina of the Southeastern Conference and South Carolina State of the Mid-Eastern Athletic Conference also have football programs. Fishing, water-skiing, and sailing are popular participant sports. There are two major stock car races held at Darlington each year: The TranSouth 500 in April and the Southern 500 on Labor Day weekend.

Other annual sporting events include Polo Games held from February through Easter in Aiken, and the Governor's Annual Frog Jumping Contest held in Springfield on the Saturday, before Easter.

49FAMOUS SOUTH CAROLINIANS

Many distinguished South Carolinians made their reputations outside the state. Andrew Jackson (1767–1845), the 7th US president, was born in a border settlement probably inside present-day South Carolina, but studied law in North Carolina before establishing a legal practice in Tennessee. Identified more closely with South Carolina is John C. Calhoun (1782–1850), vice president from 1825 to 1832; Calhoun also served as US senator and was a leader of the South before the Civil War.

John Rutledge (1739–1800), the first governor of the state and a leader during the America Revolution, served a term as US chief justice but was never confirmed by the Senate. Another Revolutionary leader, Charles Cotesworth Pinckney (1746–1825), was also a delegate to the US constitutional convention. A strong Unionist, Joel R. Poinsett (1779–1851) served as secretary of war and as the first US ambassador to Mexico; he developed the poinsettia, named after him, from a Mexican plant. Benjamin R. Tillman (1847–1918) was governor, US senator, and leader of the populist movement in South Carolina. Bernard M. Baruch (1870–1965), an outstanding financier, statesman, and adviser to presidents, was born in South Carolina. Another presidential adviser, James F. Byrnes (1879–1972), also served as US senator, associate justice of the Supreme Court, and secretary of state. The state's best-known recent political leader is J(ames) Strom Thurmond (b.1902), who ran for the presidency as a States' Rights Democrat ("Dixiecrat") in 1948, winning 1,169,134 popular votes and 39 electoral votes, and has served in the Senate since 1955.

Famous military leaders native to the state are the Revolutionary War General Francis Marion (1732?–95), known as the Swamp Fox, and James Longstreet (1821–1904), a Confederate lieutenant general during the Civil War, Mark W. Clark (b.New York, 1896–1984), US Army general and former president of the Citadel, lived in South Carolina after 1954. General William C.

Westmoreland (b.1914) was commander of US forces in Viet-Nam.

Notable in the academic world are Francis Lieber (b.Germany, 1800–1872), a political scientist who taught at the University of South Carolina and, later, Columbia University in New York City, and wrote for the US the world's first comprehensive code of military laws and procedures; Mary McLeod Bethune (1875–1955), founder of Bethune-Cookman College in Florida and of the National Council of Negro Women; John B. Watson (1878–1958), a pioneer in behavioral psychology; and Charles H. Townes (b.1915), awarded the Nobel Prize in physics in 1964. South Carolinians prominent in business and the professions include architect Robert Mills (1781–1855), who designed the Washington Monument and many other buildings; William Gregg (b.Virginia, 1800–1867), a leader in establishing the textile industry in the South; David R. Coker (1870–1938), who developed many varieties of pedigreed seed; and industrial builder Charles E. Daniel (1895–1964), who helped bring many new industries to the state.

South Carolinians who made significant contributions to literature include William Gilmore Simms (1806–70), author of nearly 100 books; Julia Peterkin (1880–1961), who won the Pulitzer Prize for *Scarlet Sister Mary;* DuBose Heyward (1885–1940), whose novel *Porgy* was the basis of the folk opera *Porgy and Bess;* and James M. Dabbs (1896–1970), a writer who was also a leader in the racial integration movement.

Entertainers born in the state include singer Eartha Kitt (b.1928) and jazz trumpeter John Birks "Dizzy" Gillespie (1917–1993). Tennis champion Althea Gibson (b.1927) is another South Carolina native.

[50]BIBLIOGRAPHY

Alampi, Gary, ed. *Gale State Rankings Reporter.* Detroit: Gale Research, Inc., 1994.

Barry, John M. *Natural Vegetation of South Carolina.* Columbia: University of South Carolina Press, 1979.

Cauthen, Charles E. *South Carolina Goes to War, 1860–65.* Chapel Hill: University of North Carolina Press, 1950.

Council of State Governments. *The Book of the States, 1994–1995 Edition.* Vol. 30. Lexington, Kentucky: The Council of State Governments, 1994.

FDIC, Division of Research and Statistics. *Statistics on Banking: A Statistical Profile of the United States Banking Industry.* Washington, D.C.: Federal Deposit Insurance Corporation, 1993.

Graham, Cole Brease. *South Carolina Politics & Government.* Lincoln, Nebr.: University of Nebraska Press, 1994.

Jones, Lewis P. *South Carolina: A Synoptic History for Laymen.* Orangeburg, S.C.: Sandlapper Publishing, 1979.

Lander, Ernest M. *A History of South Carolina, 1856–1960.* 2d ed. Columbia: University of South Carolina Press, 1970.

McCaslin, Richard B. *Photographic History of South Carolina in the Civil War.* Fayetteville, Ark.: University of Arkansas Press, 1994.

Rogers, George C. *A South Carolina Chronology, 1497–1992.* Columbia, S.C.: University of South Carolina Press, 1994.

Schmittroth, Linda, and Mary Kay Rosteck, ed. *Cities of the United States.* 2d ed. Detroit: Gale Research, Inc., 1994.

Sirmans, M. Eugene. *Colonial South Carolina: A Political History, 1663–1763.* Chapel Hill: University of North Carolina Press, 1966.

South Carolina, State of. Division of Research and Statistical Services. *South Carolina Statistical Abstract, 1984.* Columbia, 1984.

Taylor, Rosser H. *Ante-Bellum South Carolina: A Social and Cultural History.* New York: Da Capo Press, 1970.

US Department of Education, National Center for Education Statistics. Office of Educational Research and Improvement. *Digest of Education Statistics, 1993.* Washington, D.C.: US Government Printing Office, 1993.

US Department of the Interior, US Fish and Wildlife Service. *Endangered and Threatened Species Recovery Program.* Washington, D.C.: US Government Printing Office, 1990.

Wallace, David Duncan. *History of South Carolina.* 4 vols. New York: American Historical Society, 1934.

Wood, Peter H. *Black Majority: Negroes in Colonial South Carolina from 1670 through the Stono Rebellion.* New York: Knopf, 1974.

Wright, Louis B. *South Carolina: A Bicentennial History.* New York: Norton, 1976.

Zuczek, Richard. *State of Rebellion: Reconstruction in South Carolina.* Columbia, S.C.: University of South Carolina Press, 1996.

SOUTH DAKOTA

State of South Dakota

ORIGIN OF STATE NAME: The state was formerly the southern part of Dakota Territory; *dakota* is a Sioux word meaning "friend." **NICKNAME:** Mt. Rushmore State or the Coyote State. **CAPITAL:** Pierre. **ENTERED UNION:** 2 November 1889 (40th). **SONG:** "Hail, South Dakota." **MOTTO:** Under God the People Rule. **COAT OF ARMS:** Beneath the state motto, the Missouri River winds between hills and plains; symbols representing mining (a smelting furnace and hills), commerce (a steamboat), and agriculture (a man plowing, cattle, and a field of corn) complete the scene. **FLAG:** The state seal, centered on a white or light-blue field and encircled by a serrated sun, is surrounded by the words "South Dakota" above and "The Mount Rushmore State" below. **OFFICIAL SEAL:** The words "State of South Dakota Great Seal 1889" encircle the arms. **ANIMAL:** Coyote. **BIRD:** Chinese ring-necked pheasant. **FISH:** Walleye. **INSECT:** Honeybee. **FLOWER:** Pasqueflower. **TREE:** Black Hills spruce. **GRASS:** Western wheatgrass. **GEM:** Fairburn agate. **MINERAL:** Rose quartz. **LEGAL HOLIDAYS:** New Year's Day, 1 January; Birthday of Martin Luther King, Jr., 3d Monday in January; Washington's Birthday, 3d Monday in February; Memorial Day, last Monday in May; Independence Day, 4 July; Labor Day, 1st Monday in September; Columbus Day, 2d Monday in October; Veterans Day, 11 November; Thanksgiving Day, 4th Thursday in November; Christmas Day, 25 December. **TIME** 6 AM CST = noon GM; 5 AM MST = noon GMT.

¹LOCATION, SIZE, AND EXTENT

Situated in the western north-central US, South Dakota ranks 16th in size among the 50 states.

The state has a total area of 77,121 sq mi (199,730 sq km), comprising 75,896 sq mi (196,715 sq km) of land and 1,164 sq mi (3,015 sq km) of inland water. Shaped roughly like a rectangle with irregular borders on the E and SE, South Dakota extends about 380 mi (610 km) E-W and has a maximum N-S extension of 245 mi (394 km).

South Dakota is bordered on the N by North Dakota; on the E by Minnesota and Iowa (with the line in the NE passing through the Bois de Sioux River, Lake Traverse, and Big Stone Lake, and in the SE through the Big Sioux River); on the S by Nebraska (with part of the line formed by the Missouri River and Lewis and Clark Lake); and on the W by Wyoming and Montana.

The total boundary length of South Dakota is 1,316 mi (2,118 km). The state's geographic center is in Hughes County, 8 mi (13 km) NE of Pierre. The geographic center of the US, including Alaska and Hawaii, is at 44°58′N, 103°46′W, in Butte County, 17 mi (27 km) W of Castle Rock.

²TOPOGRAPHY

The eastern two-fifths of South Dakota is prairie, belonging to the Central Lowlands. The western three-fifths falls within the Missouri Plateau, part of the Great Plains region; the High Plains extend into the southern fringes of the state. The Black Hills, an extension of the Rocky Mountains, occupy the southern half of the state's western border; the mountains, which tower about 4,000 feet (1,200 meters) over the neighboring plains, include Harney Peak, at 7,242 feet (2,207 meters) the highest point in the state. East of the southern Black Hills are the Badlands, a barren, eroded region with extensive fossil deposits. South Dakota's lowest elevation, 962 feet (293 meters), is at Big Stone Lake, in the northeastern corner. Flowing south and southeast, the Missouri River cuts a huge swath through the heart of South Dakota before forming part of the southeastern boundary. Tributaries of the Missouri include the Grand, Cheyenne, Bad, Moreau, and White rivers in the west and the James, Vermillion,

and Big Sioux in the east. The Missouri River itself is controlled by four massive dams—Gavins Point, Ft. Randall, Big Bend, and Oahe—which provide water for irrigation, flood control, and hydroelectric power. Major lakes in the state include Traverse, Big Stone, Lewis and Clark, Francis Case, and Oahe.

³CLIMATE

South Dakota has an interior continental climate, with hot summers, extremely cold winters, high winds, and periodic droughts. The normal January temperature is 12°F (–11°C); the normal July temperature, 74°F (23°C). The record low temperature is –58°F (–50°C), set at McIntosh on 17 February 1936; the record high, 120°F (49°C), at Gannvalley on 5 July 1936.

Normal annual precipitation averages 24 in (61 cm) in Sioux Falls in the southeast, decreasing to less than 13 in (33 cm) in the northwest. Sioux Falls receives an average of 39 in (99 cm) of snow per year.

⁴FLORA AND FAUNA

Oak, maple, beech, birch, hickory, and willow are all represented in South Dakota's forests, while thickets of chokecherry, wild plum, gooseberry, and currant are found in the eastern part of the state. Pasqueflower (*Anemone ludoviciana*) is the state flower; other wild flowers are beardtongue, bluebell, and monkshood.

Familiar native mammals are the coyote (the state animal), porcupine, raccoon, bobcat, buffalo, white-tailed and mule deer, white-tailed jackrabbit, and black-tailed prairie dog. Nearly 300 species of birds have been identified; the sage grouse, bobwhite quail, and ring-necked pheasant are leading game birds. Trout, catfish, pike, bass, and perch are fished for sport. South Dakota's list of threatened animals includes the river otter, mountain lion, northern swift fox, black bear, peregrine falcon, longnose sucker, brown snake, and Blandings turtle. The black-footed ferret, interior least tern, and pearl dace are endangered.

⁵ENVIRONMENTAL PROTECTION

The mission of the Department of the Environment and Natural Resources is to provide environmental services in a customer-

555

oriented manner that promotes economic development; conserves natural resources; helps municipalities, industry, and citizens comply with regulations; and protects public health and the environment.

6POPULATION

South Dakota ranked 45th in the US with a 1990 census population of 696,004; the 1996 population was estimated to be 732,405, representing a 5.2% increase over 1990. The average population density in 1990 was 9.2 per sq mi (3.5 per sq km).

About 30% of all South Dakotans lived in metropolitan areas in 1990, up from only 16% in 1983. The leading cities as of 1994 were Sioux Falls, with an estimated 109,174 residents; and Rapid City, with 57,609.

7ETHNIC GROUPS

According to the 1990 census, South Dakota's population included some 51,000 American Indians. Many lived on the 5,099,000 acres (2,063,500 hectares) of Indian lands in 1982, but Rapid City also had a large Indian population. The state's largest reservations (with estimated 1995 population) include the Pine Ridge (38,426), Rosebud (24,217), and Cheyenne River (11,813). As of 1990, the state had 3,000 black Americans and 3,000 Asian-Pacific peoples. Of the South Dakotans who reported at least one specific ancestry in the 1990 census, 355,102 listed German, 106,361 Norwegian, 87,657 Irish, 68,345 English, and 36,844 Dutch. In the same year, 7,731 South Dakotans—1.1% of the population—were foreign-born.

8LANGUAGES

Despite hints given by such place-names as Dakota, Oahe, and Akaska, English has borrowed little from the language of the Sioux still living in South Dakota. *Tepee* is such a loanword, and *tado* (jerky) is heard near Pine Ridge. South Dakota English is transitional between the Northern and Midland dialects. Diffusion throughout the state is apparent, but many terms contrast along a curving line from the southeast to the northwest corner.

In 1990, 641,226 South Dakotans—93.5% of the resident population 5 years of age or older—spoke only English at home. Other languages spoken at home included:

German	17,537
Various Native American	9,969
Spanish	5,033
Various Scandinavian	2,509
Various Slavic	1,351

9RELIGIONS

Leading Protestant denominations in 1990 were the South Dakota Evangelical Lutheran Church in America, with 114,690 adherents; and Lutheran Church—Missouri Synod, 32,968. The state had 143,776 Roman Catholics and an estimated 135 Jews in 1990.

10TRANSPORTATION

A total of 2,424 mi (3,903 km) of railroad track are operated in South Dakota by 10 railroads. The Burlington Northern/Santa Fe (BNSF) and CP Rail System were Class I railroads in operation in 1996, when over 87.9 million tons of freight were hauled in the state. The freight was primarily agricultural products (originating) and coal. Class I trackage amounted to 973 mi (1,567 km). The remaining 1,451 mi (2,336 km) of track were operated by eight other regional and shortline railroads.

Public highways, streets, and roads covered 83,375 mi (134,183 km) in 1996, when the state had 747,768 registered motor vehicles and 529,408 licensed drivers. There were a total of 73 public approved airfields, of which Joe Foss Field at Sioux Falls was the most active, with 49,974 departures in 1996.

11HISTORY

People have lived in what is now South Dakota for at least 25,000 years. The original inhabitants, who hunted in the northern Great Plains until about 5000 BC, were the first of a succession of nomadic groups, followed by a society of semisedentary mound builders. After them came the prehistoric forebears of the modern riverine groups—Mandan, Hidatsa, and Arikara—who were found gathering, hunting, farming, and fishing along the upper Missouri River by the first European immigrants. These groups faced no challenge until the Sioux, driven from the Minnesota woodlands, began to move westward during the second quarter of the 18th century, expelling all other Native American groups form South Dakota by the mid-1830s.

Significant European penetration of South Dakota followed the Lewis and Clark expedition of 1804–06. White men came to assert US sovereignty, to negotiate Indian treaties, to "save Indian souls," and to traffic in hides and furs. Among the most important early merchants were Manuel Lisa, who pressed up the Missouri from St. Louis, and Pierre Chouteau, Jr., whose offices in St. Louis dominated trade on both the upper Mississippi and upper Missouri rivers from 1825 until his death in 1865, by which time all major sources of hides and furs were exhausted, negotiations for Indian land titles were in progress, and surveyors were preparing ceded territories for non-Indian settlers.

The Dakota Territory, which included much of present-day Wyoming and Montana as well as North and south Dakota, was established in 1861, with headquarters first at Yankton (1861–83) and later at Bismarck (1883–89). The territory was reduced to just the Dakotas in 1868; six years later, a gold rush brought thousands of prospectors and settlers to the Black Hills. South Dakota emerged as a state in 1889, with the capital in Pierre. Included within the state were nine Indian reservations, established, after protracted negotiations and three wars with the Sioux, by Indian Office personnel. Five reservations were established west of the Missouri for the Teton and Yanktonai Sioux, and four reserves east of the Missouri for the Yankton and several Isanti Sioux tribes. Sovereignty was thus divided among Indian agents, state officials, and tribal leaders, a division that did not always make for efficient government. Through the late 19th and early 20th centuries, South Dakotans had limited economic opportunities, for they depended mainly on agriculture. Some 30,000 Sioux barely survived on farming and livestock production, supplemented by irregular government jobs and off-reservation employment. The 500,000 non-Indians lived mainly off cattle-feeding enterprises and small grain sales east of the Missouri, mineral production (especially gold) in the Black Hills, and various service industries at urban centers throughout South Dakota.

The period after World War I saw extensive road building, the establishment of a tourist industry, and efforts to subdue and harness the waters of the Missouri. Like other Americans, South Dakotans were helped through the drought and depression of the 1930s by federal aid. Non-Indians were assisted by food relief, various work-relief programs, and crop-marketing plans, while Indians enjoyed an array of federal programs often called the "Indian New Deal." The economic revival brought about by World War II persisted into the postwar era. Rural whites benefited from the mechanization of agriculture, dam construction along the Missouri, rural electrification, and arid-land reclamation. Federal programs were organized for reservation Indians, relocating them in urban centers where industrial jobs were available, establishing light industries in areas already

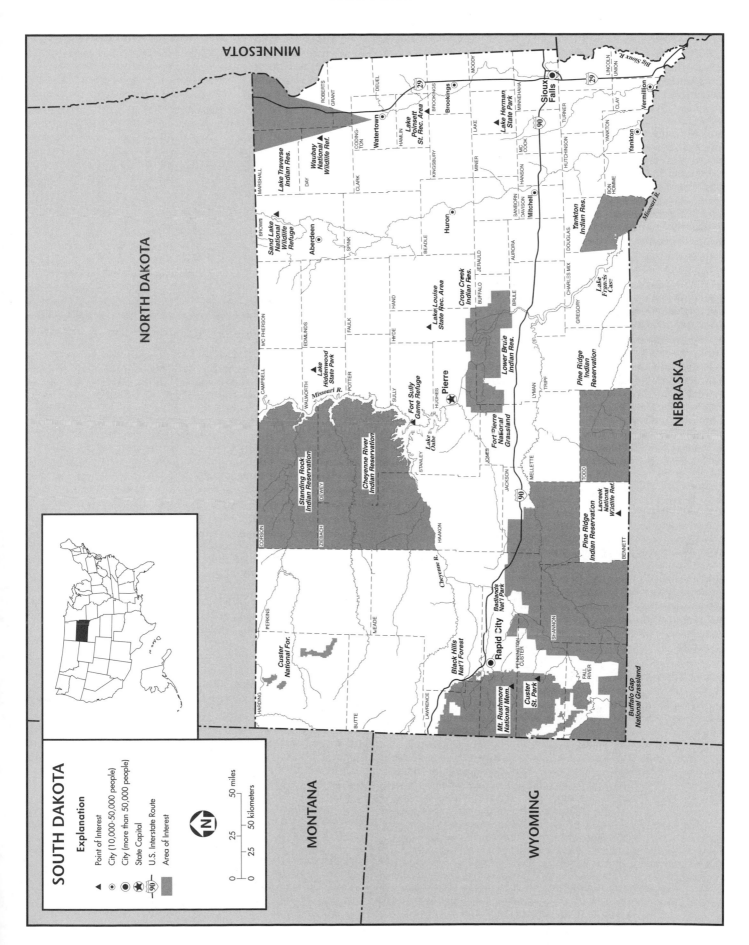

South Dakota

Explanation

▲ Point of Interest
⊙ City (10,000–50,000 people)
◉ City (more than 50,000 people)
✪ State Capital
90 U.S. Interstate Route
■ Area of Interest

0   25   50 miles
0   25   50 kilometers

heavily populated by Indians, and improving education and occupational opportunities on reservations.

Meanwhile, the Sioux continued to bring their historic grievances to public attention. For 70 days in 1973, some 200 armed Indians occupied Wounded Knee, on the Pine Ridge Reservation, where hundreds of Sioux had been killed by US cavalry 83 years earlier. In 1980, reviewing one of several land claims brought by the Sioux, the US Supreme Court upheld compensation of $105 million for land in the Black Hills taken from the Indians by the federal government in 1877. But members of the American Indian Movement (AIM) opposed this settlement and demanded the return of the Black Hills to the Sioux. The economic plight of South Dakota's Indians worsened during the 1980s after the federal government reduced job training programs, and conditions on reservations remained bad in the 1990s, with unemployment in some cases as high as 70%.

In sharp contrast, the state economy as a whole has shown strength under the direction of Republican Governor William Janklow, elected in 1978 and reelected in 1982 and, after an eight-year hiatus, in 1994. Janklow, noted for his strong opposition to Indian claims, developed the state's water resources, revived railroad transportation, and attracted new industry to South Dakota, including Citicorp, the largest bank-holding company in the US, which set up a credit-card operation in Sioux Falls and bought controlling interest in the American State Bank of Rapid City. In the 1990s, farm income has risen; record corn and soybean yields were reported in 1994, in spite of major flooding the year before that resulted in parts of the state being declared disaster areas. Manufacturing also prospered, expanding by up to 10% each year in the early 1990s. Legalized casino gambling has become an important source of government revenue since it was authorized in 1989.

12STATE GOVERNMENT

South Dakota is governed by the constitution of 1889, which had been amended 92 times as of December 1983. The legislature consists of a 35-seat senate and 70-seat house of representatives, all of whose members serve two-year terms. As of 1995 the legislative salary was $4,267 in odd-numbered years, and $3,733 in even-numbered years. Chief executive officials are the governor, lieutenant governor, secretary of state, attorney general, treasurer, auditor, and commissioner of school and public lands, all of them elected for four-year terms. Voters must be US citizens and at least 18 years of age. In 1996 the governor's salary was $82,700.

13POLITICAL PARTIES

For the most part, South Dakota has voted Republican in presidential elections, even when native-son George McGovern was the Democratic candidate in 1972. Conservatism runs strong at the local level, although between the two world wars, populist groups gained a broad agrarian following. South Dakotans chose George Bush in 1988 and again in 1992, and in 1996 they gave Republican Bob Dole 46% of the vote, while Bill Clinton collected 43% and Ross Perot captured under 10%. Thomas Daschle won a second term in the Senate in 1992. In 1996, South Dakota's US representative, Tim Johnson, a Democrat, won the US Senate seat of Larry Pressler, who was seeking a fourth term. Johnson's replacement in the House, John Thune, is a Republican. There are 22 Republicans and 13 Democrats in the state senate, and 49 Republicans and 21 Democrats in the state house.

In 1993, there were three blacks holding elective office. As of 1995, 19 women served in the state legislature and 3 women held statewide elective executive office.

South Dakota Presidential Vote by Major Political Parties, 1948–96

YEAR	ELECTORAL VOTE	SOUTH DAKOTA WINNER	DEMOCRAT	REPUBLICAN
1948	4	Dewey (R)	117,653	129,651
1952	4	*Eisenhower (R)	90,426	203,857
1956	4	*Eisenhower (R)	122,288	171,569
1960	4	Nixon (R)	128,070	178,417
1964	4	*Johnson (D)	163,010	130,108
1968	4	*Nixon (R)	118,023	149,841
1972	4	*Nixon (R)	139,945	166,476
1976	4	Ford (R)	147,068	151,505
1980	4	*Reagan (R)	103,855	198,343
1984	3	*Reagan (R)	116,113	200,267
1988	3	*Bush (R)	145,560	165,415
1992**	3	Bush (R)	124,888	136,718
1996**	3	Dole (R)	139,333	150,543

* Won US presidential election.

** Independent candidate Ross Perot received 73,295 votes in 1992 and 31,250 votes in 1996.

14LOCAL GOVERNMENT

As of 1992, South Dakota had 1,786 units of local government, including 64 counties, 310 municipalities, 969 townships, 180 school districts, and 262 special districts. Typical county officials include a treasurer, auditor, state's attorney, sheriff, register of deeds, and clerk of courts.

15STATE SERVICES

The Department of Education and Cultural Affairs oversees all elementary, secondary, higher, vocational, and cultural education programs.

The Department of Social Services administers a variety of welfare programs, the Department of Labor aids the unemployed and underemployed, and the Department of Vocational Rehabilitation serves disabled South Dakotans. Special agencies within the executive branch include the Office of Indian Affairs and Office of Energy Policy.

16JUDICIAL SYSTEM

South Dakota has a supreme court with 5 justices, and eight circuit courts with 36 judges; all are elected on a nonpartisan ballot to staggered eight-year terms. South Dakota had 1,503 attorneys practicing in the state in 1996.

In 1995, South Dakota's crime index total was 3,060.6 crimes per 100,000 inhabitants, including 207.5 for violent crimes and 2,853.1 for property crimes—well below the national averages of 684.6 for violent crime and 4,593.7 for property crime.

In 1995 there were 1,882 inmates in state and federal correctional facilities, a rate of 258 inmates per 100,000 inhabitants. South Dakota imposes the death penalty but has only executed one person since 1930.

17ARMED FORCES

In 1996 there were 3,313 active duty military personnel stationed in South Dakota, almost all of whom (3,207) were at Ellsworth Air Force Base, near Rapid City, the state's only defense installation. South Dakota firms received $109.9 million in federal defense contracts in 1995/96. As of 1 July 1996, about 73,000 veterans were living in the state, including fewer than 500 from World War I, 19,000 from World War II, 14,000 from the Korean conflict, 21,000 from the Vietnam era, and 7,000 from the Persian Gulf War. Veterans' benefits totaled $210 million during 1995/96.

South Dakota's National Guard and Reserve numbered 7,157 in 1996. In 1993, South Dakota employed 156 full-time sworn officers, or 2 per 10,000 residents.

18MIGRATION
Since the 1930s, more people have left South Dakota than have settled in the state. Between 1940 and 1990, the net loss from migration amounted to almost 340,000. Between 1990 and 1996, South Dakota had net gains of 7,224 in domestic migration and 2,729 in international migration. As of 1990, just over 70% of all South Dakotans had been born within the state. About 55% of residents age 5 and older lived in the same house in 1990 as in 1985; some 25% of those residents who reported living in a different house in 1985 did so in another state. In 1980, the urban population stood at 46.4%, but had grown to equal the rural population (at 50%) by 1990.

19INTERGOVERNMENTAL COOPERATION
South Dakota participates in the Belle Fourche River Compact (with Wyoming), the Interstate Oil and Gas Compact, and the Western Interstate Energy Compact, among other organizations; there are, in addition, boundary compacts with Minnesota and Nebraska. In 1995/96, South Dakota received $867 million in federal aid.

20ECONOMY
Agriculture dominates South Dakota's economy. Grains and livestock are the main farm products, and processed foods and farm equipment are leading manufactured items. Mining and tourism are also important. South Dakota's gross state product in 1994 was $17,250 million, to which private goods-producing industries contributed $4,613 million; private service-producing industries, $10,299 million; and government, $2,337 million. During 1996, there were 1,912 bankruptcy filings.

21INCOME
Per capita income in 1996 was $19,755, ranking South Dakota 41st among the 50 states. Total nonfarm personal income increased 8.4% to $13.8 billion in 1995, up from $12.6 billion in 1994. Total disposable personal income rose from $12.8 billion in 1995 to $14.2 billion in 1996. Median household income was $29,578 in 1995, with 14.5% of all South Dakotans below the federal poverty level (national average 13.8%).

22LABOR
The state's civilian labor force numbered 389,617 in 1996, of whom 377,100 were employed and 12,517, or 3.2%, were unemployed. Federal surveys revealed the following earnings and worker estimates in South Dakota:

	1996 EARNINGS (MILLIONS OF $)	1995 WORKERS (THOUSANDS)
Total	$11,108.6	471.9
Farm	1,166.8	38.2
Nonfarm	9,941.8	433.7
Private	8,247.0	363.2
Agricultural services, forestry, fisheries	166.0	5.4
Mining	106.8	3.1
Construction	608.5	23.1
Manufacturing	1,457.0	48.5
Nondurable goods	1,026.0	16.8
Durable goods	431.0	31.7
Transportation and public utilities	768.3	20.5
Wholesale trade	668.3	21.3
Retail trade	1,156.5	84.5
Finance, insurance, and real estate	660.8	31.6
Services	2,654.8	125.2
Government	1,694.8	70.5

In 1995, 9.1% of the South Dakota manufacturing workers belonged to labor unions. The state has a right-to-work law.

23AGRICULTURE
South Dakota ranked 21st among the 50 states in 1995 in agricultural income, with receipts of $3.6 billion. In 1996 there were an estimated 32,500 farms and ranches in the state, covering about 44.0 million acres (17.8 million hectares).

Leading crops and their values during 1996 were hay, 8.2 million tons, $538.0 million; wheat, 139.3 million bushels, $547.5 million; corn for grain, 370.0 million bushels, $814.0 million; soybeans, 90.8 million bushels, $590.1 million; oats, 21.6 million bushels, $38.9 million; and barley, 6.4 million bushels, $16.3 million.

24ANIMAL HUSBANDRY
The livestock industry is of great importance in South Dakota, particularly in the High Plains. In 1997 the state had an estimated 3.8 million cattle and calves, valued at around $2.2 billion. During 1996, there were 1.2 million hogs and pigs, valued at $120 million. In 1995 the state produced 43.2 million lb (19.6 million kg) of sheep and lambs, 87.36 million lb (39.63 million kg) of turkeys, 481 million eggs, and 4.36 million lb (1.98 million kg) of chickens. Dairy farmers produced nearly 1.6 billion lb (0.7 billion kg) of milk from around 118,000 milk cows in 1995.

25FISHING
Virtually all fishing is recreational. Sport fishing is popular; the state manages the maintenance of 5 million angler days of recreation per year. In 1995/96, South Dakota issued 206,092 sport fishing licenses. Federal hatcheries distributed nearly 6 million fish (66% walleye) within the state in 1995/96.

26FORESTRY
In terms of geography and forests, east meets west in South Dakota in a rather dramatic way. The Prairie Plains in the east gradually give way to the grasslands of the Great Plains in the west as elevation increases by some 1,500 ft (450 m) between the Minnesota border and Rapid City.

The forests in the Plains regions are primarily associated with water-reservoirs, lakes, and the dominating Missouri River and its major tributaries such as the Cheyenne, Big White, Moreau, Grand, and Bad rivers. Collectively these forests make up only 10% of the total forest land in the state and consist primarily of tree species associated with the eastern hardwood forests—elm, ash, basswood, and so forth. In the far western portion of the state and spilling over into northeastern Wyoming are the Black Hills. The forests in the Black Hills and at higher elevations west of the 103d meridian to the southeast and north of the "Hills" are typically "western," consisting principally of ponderosa pine. About 90% of the forest land in South Dakota occurs west of the 103d meridian, and most of it is in the Black Hills. Three counties, Pennington, Lawrence, and Custer, account for most of the State's forest area, which totals roughly 1.7 million acres (0.6 million hectares).

The public sector owns 64% of South Dakota's forest land. The Black Hills and Custer National Forests administer about 90% of the public forest land. The rest is under the jurisdiction of the State and the US Department of the Interior, Bureau of Land Management (BLM). Most of the state-owned land is in the Custer State Park. East of Rapid City the 226,300 acres (91,500 hectares) of forest land is primarily privately owned.

Nonreserved timberland is the primary component of the state's forestland and occupies 1,670,000 acres (676,000 hectares). Woodland covers an additional 17,400 acres (7,000 hectares). Of the forest land, 1% contained primarily in national parks is reserved from harvesting wood products. Ponderosa pine is the state's predominant species, occupying 1.4 million acres (0.6 million hectares) or 82% of the total forestland. The second-most-predominant species group occurs in the bottomland hardwood group, elm/ash, and makes up only 6% or 95,700 acres (38,700 hectares).

Sawtimber stands occupy 964,700 acres (390,400 hectares), which is more than half the total forested area; 675,000 acres (273,000 hectares) of this area is found in national forests. Poletimber stands account for a fifth of the timberland base, and sapling and seedling stands account for an additional 118,700 acres (48,000 hectares) of timberland. Nonstocked areas total 65,500 acres (26,500 hectares), which is 3% of the total timberland. The majority of these nonstocked lands are privately owned.

South Dakota's timberland is not very productive when compared to other western states. Of timberland, 73% or 1.2 million (486,000 hectares) acres falls in the 20 to 49 cu ft (0.6 to 1.4 cu m) per acre per year productivity class. Just 16% of the state's timberland has the potential to produce greater than 50 cu ft (1.42 cu m) per acre per year. However, this is not to say that the state's timberland and in particular the Black Hills area has not been a good timber-producer. The Black Hills has, for nearly a century, been successfully producing and supplying sawlogs, fuelwood, pulpwood, posts, and poles.

27 MINING
The estimated value of nonfuel mineral production for South Dakota in 1995 was $317 million, a decrease of over $6 million from the $323 million reported in 1994, and down $20 million from the record $337 million of 1993. In terms of value, gold remained the leading commodity followed by portland cement, construction sand and gravel, and dimension stone. South Dakota ranked in the top six nationally in the production of gem stones, gold, mica, and dimension stone. In 1993 the major gold mining operations processed 677,376 oz or 19,200 kg (worth $223,000,000) of gold. In 1995, 4 metric tons (worth $707,000) of silver were recovered. All the major gold operations were within a 7-mi (11.3-km) radius of Lead, in Lawrence County.

In 1995, South Dakota quarries produced 6,500,000 metric tons of construction sand and gravel, and 5,400,000 metric tons of crushed stone, with respective values of $21,100,000 and $24,300,000. South Dakota ranked 4th of 14 gold-producing states, 5th in iron ore and crude mica, 7th in feldspar, and 8th in dimension stone. Milbank Granite, a dark to medium red granite found in the northeastern part of the state, has been quarried continuously since 1907 and is the major source of dimension stone in the state. The state ranked 36th in the country in terms of the value of nonfuel mineral production, accounting for slightly less than 1% of the national total.

28 ENERGY AND POWER
In 1995, South Dakota had an installed electrical capacity of 2.97 million kW and produced 8.8 billion kWh of electricity, more than half of it sold to customers in other states. Over 68% of the power output came from hydroelectric sources and almost all the remainder from coal-fired plants. Utilities in South Dakota sold 1,252 million cu ft (35 million cu m) of natural gas to 140,833 customers during 1995.

South Dakota has very modest fossil-fuel resources. Lignite reserves were 366,100,000 tons; production of lignite and petroleum was negligible in 1995, however.

29 INDUSTRY
The total value of shipments of manufactured goods in 1995 was $9,212,500,000. The following table shows value of shipments by selected industries in 1995:

Food products	$1,972,900,000
Electronics	511,400,000
Printing	225,100,000
Industrial machinery and equipment	4,258,100,000
Instruments and related products	501,500,000

In 1997, South Dakota was headquarters to one Fortune 500 company, Gateway 2000. During 1995, there were 40 US patents issued to South Dakota residents.

30 COMMERCE
Wholesalers in South Dakota numbered 1,809 in 1992 and had sales totaling $6.5 billion (including $1.8 billion in durable goods). Of the state's $5.1 billion in sales from retail trade that year, automotive dealers contributed 23.2%; food stores, 17.7%; general merchandise stores, 13.4%; eating and drinking places, 9.6%; and other establishments, 36.1%. The state's exports were valued at $443.3 million in 1996.

31 CONSUMER PROTECTION
The Division of Consumer Protection of the Office of the Attorney General enforces South Dakota's Deceptive Trade Practices Act, prosecutes cases of fraud and other illegal activities, and registers Charitable Solicitation organizations and Buying Clubs. Disputes are mediated between consumers and businesses.

32 BANKING
South Dakota in 1996 had 116 insured commercial banks with total assets of $28.6 billion and total deposits of $11.8 billion. In 1996 there were 6 savings institutions with total assets of $924 million, mortgage loans of $476 million, and savings deposits of $668 million.

33 INSURANCE
During 1995, 626 life insurance companies were licensed to do business in South Dakota. The 601,000 policies in force had a combined value of $30.3 billion. Benefit payments totaled $265.6 million in 1995. Automobile insurance accounted for 38.5% of the $762.7 million in premiums written by property and casualty insurance companies in 1995.

34 SECURITIES
As of April 1997, there were 314 investment advisory firms registered in the state, and 2,706 agents. At the end of 1996, over 22,809 agents were registered to sell securities.

35 PUBLIC FINANCE
The governor must submit the annual budget to the state legislature by 1 December; the fiscal year begins the following 1 July. The legislature may amend the budget at will, but the governor has an item veto. For 1996, general revenues were $624,416,792 (est.) and expenditures totaled $624,146,738 (est.).

36 TAXATION
South Dakota has no personal or corporate income tax, with the exception of a 6% tax levied on financial institutions. Personal property taxes have been reduced since 1978. A state sales and use tax of 4% supplies more than two-thirds of South Dakota's general-fund receipts. Taxes are also levied on gasoline sales, alcoholic beverages, tobacco products, mineral severance, inheritances, insurance premiums, and other items.

Federal income taxes in South Dakota totaled $2 billion in 1995.

37ECONOMIC POLICY

Efforts to attract industry to South Dakota and to broaden the state's economic base are under the jurisdiction of the Governor's Office of Economic Development. Among the advantages noted by the agency are the absence of corporate or personal income taxes, the low level of property taxes, the availability of community development corporations to finance construction of new facilities, various property tax relief measures, inventory tax exemptions, personal property tax exemptions, and a favorable labor climate in which work stoppages are few and union activity is limited by a right-to-work law. South Dakota is one of the few states to have enacted a statute of limitations on product liability—in this case, six years—a measure cited as further proof of the state's attempt to create an atmosphere conducive to manufacturing.

38HEALTH

The birthrate in 1995 stood at 15.0 per 1,000 population (above the national rate of 14.8), while the death rate was 9.9 per 1,000 population (above the US rate of 8.8). Infant mortality in 1995 was 9.5 per 1,000 live births. In 1992 only 1,038 licensed abortions were performed, for a rate of 7 per 1,000 women, the lowest in the US. In 1995, 22% of persons 18–30 years of age were smokers. The estimated number of deaths from smoking-related diseases are 14,626 as of 1995. Death caused by coronary heart disease was 99.4 per 100,000 population. Stroke-related deaths ranked 15th-lowest in the country.

In 1996, the state had 58 hospitals, with 3,442 beds. South Dakota had 1,182 active physicians (active nonfederal physicians, 1,138), of which 1,099 were licensed in the state. The state also had 414 active dentists. That year, 17 counties were without a full-time physician in patient care. The average expense for patients in a community hospital in 1994 was $470 per day and $4,979 per stay, both lower than the national average. Benefits paid out to Medicare and Medicaid recipients were $357 million and $284 million, respectively, in 1994 for health services.

39SOCIAL WELFARE

Payments in aid for dependent children went to 16,800 South Dakotans in 1991, averaging $478 a month. In 1995, 135,580 residents received Social Security benefits averaging $664 a month. Federally administered Supplemental Security Income aided 13,631 South Dakotans, averaging $295 a month. In 1996, 48,843 residents received monthly food stamp allowances averaging $69.53, and the school lunch program received total federal funding of $17.1 million. The average weekly unemployment insurance benefit was $144.92 in 1995.

With the enactment of the Personal Responsibility and Work Opportunity Reconciliation Act of 1996, the US government has changed the form and regulations for many of its social welfare programs; most significantly, it replaces Aid to Families with Dependent Children (AFDC), an open-ended entitlement program, with Temporary Assistance for Needy Families (TANF), a limited system of assistance funded largely through federal block grants. The reform act also impacts the food stamp program, the Supplemental Security Income program, and the child nutrition program. The law took effect on 1 July 1997 and provided $16.38 billion in block grants for fiscal years 1997–2002. The grants are to be divided among the states based on an equation involving the numbers of former AFDC recipients in each state. Because many of the bill's provisions have yet to be implemented into state-by-state policy, it was not possible to include the details of each state's programs for this edition of this work.

40HOUSING

In 1996, there were an estimated 311,000 housing units, of which 269,000 were occupied. As of 1990, 98% of the occupied units had full plumbing. In 1996, 3,648 privately owned units, valued at $278 million, were authorized for construction; of these, 2,418 were single-family. In 1990, the last year for which figures are available, the median value of a home in South Dakota was $5,200, lowest among the states. The median monthly costs for owners (with a mortgage) and renters were $569 and $306, respectively, in 1990. During 1995/96, South Dakota received $77.9 million in aid from the US Department of Housing and Urban Development, including $11.5 million in community development block grants.

41EDUCATION

As of 1990 77.1% of South Dakotans 25 years of age or older were high school graduates and 17.2% had four or more years of college.

Fall 1996 enrollment in public schools totaled 133,725: 92,281 in grades K–8; and 41,644 in grades 9–12. Private-school enrollment included 11,640 students in grades K–8 and 5,853 in grades 9–12. There are 8 state-supported colleges and universities, of which the largest was the University of South Dakota; and South Dakota State University. In addition, the state had 12 private institutions of higher education.

42ARTS

The South Dakota Arts Council, located at Pierre, and the South Dakota Humanities Council, at Brookings, aid and coordinate arts and humanities activities throughout the state. Artworks and handicrafts are displayed at the Dacotah Prairie Museum (Aberdeen), South Dakota Art Center (Brookings), Sioux Indian Museum and Crafts Center (Rapid City), Civic Fine Arts Association (Sioux Falls), Cultural Heritage Center (Pierre), and W. H. Over Museum (Vermillion). Symphony orchestras include the South Dakota Symphony in Sioux Falls and the Rapid City Symphony Orchestra.

The state of South Dakota generated considerable funding for its arts programs from a variety of sources. The NEA gave $392,000 to the programs and $893,000 to the South Dakota Arts Council. The state also gave the Council $1,707,722.

The state's arts programs drew audiences totaling about 8,529,000 people. Contributing artists numbered 65,339. South Dakota provided about 50,000 of its school children with arts education programs. In 1996, the state had 350 arts associations and 40 local arts groups. The South Dakota Arts Council also sponsors the "Dakota Visions '91" art exhibition and a folk arts program by the Freeman Academy Heritage Archives Museum. The NEA contributed to the American Indian Services, to the State Historical Preservation Center in Pierre, to the South Dakota Symphony Orchestra for 1996, and to artists' residencies through the Arts Corps organization.

In 1996, the South Dakota Arts Council received $285,000 to support the state's art education programs from the NEA's state and regional program.

43LIBRARIES AND MUSEUMS

In 1994, South Dakota had 118 public libraries with a combined total of 2,278,053 volumes and 5,042,183 circulation. Leading collections, each with more than 100,000 volumes, were those of South Dakota State University (Brookings), Northern State College and Alexander Mitchell Library (Aberdeen), Augustana College (Sioux Falls), the University of South Dakota (Vermillion), the South Dakota State Library (Pierre), and the Sioux Falls and Rapid City public libraries.

South Dakota has 81 museums and historic sites, including the Cultural Heritage Museum (Pierre), Siouxland Heritage

Museums and Delbridge Museum of Natural History (Sioux Falls), and the Shrine to Music Museum (Vermillion). Badlands National Park and Wind Cave National Park also display interesting exhibits.

44COMMUNICATIONS

In March 1993, 93.5% of South Dakota's 271,000 occupied housing units had telephones. Commercial broadcasters included 75 of 93 radio stations (35 AM, 58 FM) and 28 television stations, 9 of which were noncommercial educational stations. Cable television service was mainly provided by Midcontinent Cable Company in the Sioux Falls area.

45PRESS

In 1997, South Dakota had 4 morning newspapers, 7 evening papers, and 4 Sunday papers. Leading newspapers included the *Rapid City Journal,* evenings 33,157, Sundays 35,462; and the Sioux Falls *Argus Leader,* mornings 49,847, Sundays 73,167.

46ORGANIZATIONS

The 1992 Census of Service Industries counted 395 organizations in South Dakota, including 79 business associations; 235 civic, social, and fraternal associations, and 81 other membership organizations. Among the organizations headquartered in South Dakota are the National Buffalo Association (Custer) and the National Trail Council (Brookings).

47TOURISM, TRAVEL, AND RECREATION

Domestic travelers spent an estimated $834 million in South Dakota in 1993. Most of the state's tourist attractions lie west of the Missouri River, especially in the Black Hills region. Mt. Rushmore National Memorial consists of the heads of four US presidents-George Washington, Thomas Jefferson, Abraham Lincoln, and Theodore Roosevelt—carved in granite in the mountainside. Wind Cave National Park and Jewel Cave National Monument are also in the Black Hills region. Just to the east is Badlands National Monument, consisting of fossil beds and eroded cliffs almost bare of vegetation. In 1995, South Dakota had 534,232 licensed hunters and 300,628 licensed fishers.

48SPORTS

There are no major league professional sports teams in South Dakota. The University of South Dakota Coyotes and the Jackrabbits of South Dakota State both compete in the North Central Intercollegiate Athletic Conference. Skiing and hiking are popular in the Black Hills. Other annual sporting events include the Black Hills Motorcycle Classic in Sturgis, and many rodeos, including the Days of '76 in Deadwood.

49FAMOUS SOUTH DAKOTANS

The only South Dakotan to win high elective office was Hubert H. Humphrey (1911–78), a native of Wallace who, after rising to power in Minnesota Democratic politics, served as US senator for 16 years before becoming vice president under Lyndon Johnson (1965–69).

Other outstanding federal officeholders from South Dakota were Newton Edmunds (1819–1908), second governor of the

Dakota Territory; Charles Henry Burke (b.New York, 1861–1944), who as commissioner of Indian affairs improved education and health care for Native Americans; and Vermillion-born Peter Norbeck (1870–1936), a Progressive Republican leader, first while governor (1917–21) and then as US senator until his death. The son of a German-American father and a Brulé Indian mother, Benjamin Reifel (1906-1990) was the first American Indian elected to Congress from South Dakota; he later served as the last US commissioner of Indian affairs. George McGovern (b.1922) served in the US Senate from 1963 through 1980; an early opponent of the war in Viet Nam, he ran unsuccessfully as the Democratic presidential nominee in 1972.

Associated with South Dakota are several distinguished Indian leaders. Among them were Red Cloud (b.Nebraska 1822–1909), an Oglala warrior; Spotted Tail (b.Wyoming, 1833?–1881), the Brulé chief who was a commanding figure on the Rosebud Reservation; Sitting Bull (1834–90), a Hunkpapa Sioux most famous as the main leader of the Indian army that crushed George Custer's Seventh US Cavalry at the Battle of the Little Big Horn (1876) in Montana; and Crazy Horse (1849?–1877), an Oglala chief who also fought at Little Big Horn.

Ernest Orlando Lawrence (1901–58), the state's only Nobel Prize winner, received the physics award in 1939 for the invention of the cyclotron. The business leader with the greatest personal influence on South Dakota's history was Pierre Chouteau, Jr. (b.Missouri, 1789–1865), a fur trader after whom the state capital is named.

South Dakota artists include George Catlin (b.Pennsylvania, 1796–1872), Karl Bodmer (1809–93), Harvey Dunn (1884–1952), and Oscar Howe (1915–83). Gutzon Borglum (b.Idaho, 1871–1941) carved the faces on Mt. Rushmore. The state's two leading writers are Ole Edvart Rölvaag (b.Norway, 1876–1931), author of *Giants in the Earth* and other novels, and Frederick Manfred (b.Iowa, 1912–94), a Minnesota resident who served as writer-in-residence at the University of South Dakota and has used the state as a setting for many of his novels.

50BIBLIOGRAPHY

Amerson, Robert. *From the Hidewood: Memories of a Dakota Neighborhood.* St. Paul: Minnesota Historical Society Press, 1996.

Federal Writers' Project. *South Dakota: A Guide to the State.* 1938. Reprint, New York: Somerset, 1952.

Kingsbury, George W. *History of Dakota Territory.* 2 vols. Chicago: Clarke, 1915.

Milton, John R., ed. *The Literature of South Dakota.* Vermillion: Dakota Press, 1976

———. *South Dakota: A Bicentennial History.* New York: Norton, 1977.

Nelson, Paula. *The Prairie Winnows Out Its Own: The West River Country of South Dakota in the Years of Depression and Dust.* Iowa City: University of Iowa Press, 1996.

Parker, Watson. *Gold in the Black Hills.* Norman: University of Oklahoma Press, 1966.

Schell, Herbert. *History of South Dakota.* 3d ed. Lincoln: University of Nebraska Press, 1975.

Shaff, Howard and Audrey. *Six Wars at a Time.* Sioux Falls, S.D.: Center for Western Studies at Augustana College, 1985.

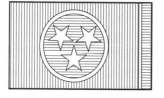

TENNESSEE

State of Tennessee

ORIGIN OF STATE NAME: Probably from Indian name *Tenase,* which was the principal village of the Cherokee. **NICKNAME:** The Volunteer State. **CAPITAL:** Nashville. **ENTERED UNION:** 1 June 1796 (16th). **SONGS:** "When It's Iris Time in Tennessee"; "The Tennessee Waltz"; "My Homeland, Tennessee"; "Rocky Top." **PUBLIC SCHOOL SONG:** "My Tennessee." **POET LAUREATE:** Richard M. "Pek" Gunn. **POEM:** "Oh Tennessee, My Tennessee." **FOLK DANCE:** Square dance. **MOTTO:** Agriculture and Commerce. **SLOGAN:** Tennessee—America at Its Best. **FLAG:** On a crimson field separated by a white border from a blue bar at the fly, three white stars on a blue circle edged in white represent the state's three main general divisions—East, Middle, and West Tennessee. **OFFICIAL SEAL:** The upper half consists of the word "Agriculture," a plow, a sheaf of wheat, a cotton plant, and the roman numeral XVI, signifying the order of entry into the Union; the lower half comprises the word "Commerce" and a boat. The words "The Great Seal of the State of Tennessee 1796" surround the whole. The date commemorates the passage of the state constitution. **WILD ANIMAL:** Raccoon. **BIRD:** Mockingbird. **INSECTS:** Ladybug, firefly. **CULTIVATED FLOWER:** Iris. **WILD FLOWER:** Passion flower. **TREE:** Tulip poplar. **GEM:** Freshwater pearl. **ROCKS:** Limestone, agate. **LEGAL HOLIDAYS:** New Year's Day, 1 January; Birthday of Martin Luther King, Jr., 3d Monday in January; Washington's Birthday, 3d Monday in February; Good Friday, March or April; Decoration Day, last Monday in May; Independence Day, 4 July; primary and county elections, 1st Thursday in August in even-numbered years; Labor Day, 1st Monday in September; Columbus Day, 2d Monday in October; General Election Day, 1st Tuesday after 1st Monday in November in even-numbered years; Veterans Day, 11 November; Thanksgiving Day, 4th Thursday in November; Christmas Day, 25 December. **TIME:** 7 AM EST = noon GMT; 6 AM CST = noon GMT.

¹LOCATION, SIZE, AND EXTENT

Situated in the eastern south-central US, Tennessee ranks 34th in size among the 50 states.

The total area of the state is 42,144 sq mi (109,152 sq km), of which land occupies 41,155 sq mi (106,591 sq km) and inland water 989 sq mi (2,561 sq km). Tennessee extends about 430 mi (690 km) E-W and 110 mi (180 km) N-S.

Tennessee is bordered on the N by Kentucky and Virginia; on the E by North Carolina; on the S by Georgia, Alabama, and Mississippi; and on the W by Arkansas and Missouri (with the line formed by the Mississippi River). The boundary length of Tennessee totals 1,306 mi (2,102 km). The state's geographic center lies in Rutherford County, 5 mi (8 km) NE of Murfreesboro.

²TOPOGRAPHY

Long, narrow, and rhomboidal, Tennessee is divided topographically into six major physical regions: the Unaka Mountains, the Great Valley of East Tennessee, the Cumberland Plateau, the Highland Rim, the Central Basin, and the Gulf Coastal Plain. In addition, there are two minor physical regions: the Western Valley of the Tennessee River and the Mississippi Flood Plains.

The easternmost region is the Unaka Mountains, part of the Appalachian chain. The Unakas actually include several ranges, the most notable of which is the Great Smoky Mountains. The region constitutes the highest and most rugged surface in the state and covers an area of about 2,600 sq mi (6,700 sq km). Several peaks reach a height of 6,000 feet (1,800 meters) or more: the tallest is Clingmans Dome in the Great Smokies, which rises to 6,643 feet (2,025 meters) and is the highest point in the state.

Lying due west of the Unakas is the Great Valley of East Tennessee. Extending from southwestern Virginia into northern Georgia, the Great Valley is a segment of the Ridge and Valley province of the Appalachian Highlands, which reach from New York into Alabama. This region, consisting of long, narrow ridges with broad valleys between them, covers more than 9,000 sq mi (23,000 sq km) of Tennessee. Since the coming of the Tennessee Valley Authority (TVA) in 1933, the area has been dotted with artificial lakes and dams, which supply electric power and aid in flood control.

The Cumberland Plateau, which extends in its entirety from southern Kentucky into central Alabama, has an area of about 5,400 sq mi (14,000 sq km) in Middle Tennessee. The plateau is a region of contrasts, including both the Cumberland Mountains, which rise to a height of 3,500 feet (1,100 meters), and the Sequatchie Valley, the floor of which lies about 1,000 feet (300 meters) below the surface of the adjoining plateau.

The Highland Rim, also in Middle Tennessee, is the state's largest natural region, consisting of more than 12,500 sq mi (32,400 sq km) and encircling the Central Basin. The eastern section is a gently rolling plain some 1,000 feet (300 meters) lower than the Cumberland Plateau. The western part has an even lower elevation and sinks gently toward the Tennessee River.

The Central Basin, an oval depression with a gently rolling surface, has been compared to the bottom of an oval dish, of which the Highland Rim forms the broad, flat brim. With its rich soil, the region has attracted people from the earliest days of European settlement and is more densely populated than any other area in the state.

The westernmost of the major regions is the Gulf Coastal Plain. It embraces practically all of West Tennessee and covers an area of 9,000 sq mi (23,000 sq km). It is a broad plain, sloping gradually westward until it ends abruptly at the bluffs overlooking the Mississippi Flood Plains. In the northwest corner is Reelfoot Lake, the only natural lake of significance in the state, formed by a series of earthquakes in 1811 and 1812. The state's lowest point, 182 feet (55 meters) above sea level, is on the banks of the Mississippi in the southwest.

Most of the state is drained by the Mississippi River system. Waters from the two longest rivers—the Tennessee, with a total length of 652 mi (1,049 km), and the Cumberland, which is 687 mi (1,106 km) long—flow into the Ohio River in Kentucky and join the Mississippi at Cairo, Ill. Formed a few miles north of Knoxville by the confluence of the Holston and French Broad rivers, the Tennessee flows southwestward through the Great Valley into northern Alabama, then curves back into the state and flows northward into Kentucky. Other tributaries of the Tennessee are the Clinch, Duck, Elk, Hiwassee, and Sequatchie rivers. The Cumberland River rises in southeastern Kentucky, flows across central Tennessee, and then turns northward back into Kentucky; its principal tributaries are the Harpeth, Red, Obey, Caney Fork, and Stones rivers and Yellow Creek. In the western part of the state, the Forked Deer and Wolf rivers are among those flowing into the Mississippi, which forms the western border with Missouri and Arkansas.

[3]CLIMATE

Generally, Tennessee has a temperate climate, with warm summers and mild winters. However, the state's varied topography leads to a wide range of climatic conditions.

The warmest parts of the state, with the longest growing season, are the Gulf Coastal Plain, the Central Basin, and the Sequatchie Valley. In the Memphis area in the southwest, the average date of the last killing frost is 20 March, and the growing season is about 235 days. Memphis has an annual mean temperature of 62°F (17°C), 40°F (4°C) in January, and 83°F (28°C) in July. In the Nashville area, the growing season lasts about 225 days. Nashville has an annual mean of 59°F (15°C), ranging from 36°F (2°C) in January to 79°F (26°C) in July. The Knoxville area has a growing season of 220 days. The city's annual mean temperature is 60°F (16°C), with averages of 41°F (5°C) in January and 78°F (26°C) in July. In some parts of the mountainous east, where the temperatures are considerably lower, the growing season is as short as 130 days. The record high temperature for the state is 113°F (45°C), set at Perryville on 9 August 1930; the record low, –32°F (–36°C), was registered at Mountain City on 30 December 1917.

Severe storms occur infrequently. The greatest rainfall occurs in the winter and early spring, especially March; the early fall months, particularly September and October, are the driest. Average annual precipitation is 49 in (124 cm) in Memphis and 46 in (117 cm) in Nashville. Snowfall varies and is more prevalent in East Tennessee than in the western section; Nashville gets about 11 in (28 cm) a year, Memphis only 6 in (15 cm). Tennessee had 39 tornadoes in 1995.

[4]FLORA AND FAUNA

With its varied terrain and soils, Tennessee has an abundance of flora, including at least 150 kinds of native trees. Tulip poplar (the state tree), shortleaf pine, and chestnut, black, and red oaks are commonly found in the eastern part of the state, while the Highland Rim abounds in several varieties of oak, hickory, ash, and pine. Gum maple, black walnut, sycamore, and cottonwood grow in the west, and cypress is plentiful in the Reelfoot Lake area. In East Tennessee, rhododendron, mountain laurel, and wild azalea blossoms create a blaze of color in the mountains. More than 300 native Tennessee plants, including digitalis and ginseng have been utilized for medicinal purposes. Glade cress, Duck River bladderpod, and American yellowwood are listed as threatened plants; Cumberland rosemary is classified as endangered.

Tennessee mammals, of which there were 81 species in 1984, include the raccoon (the state animal), white-tailed deer, black bear bobcat, muskrat, woodchuck, opossum, and red and gray foxes; the European wild boar was introduced by sportsmen in 1912. As of 1984, 259 bird species resided in Tennessee. Bobwhite quail, ruffed grouse, mourning dove, and mallard duck are the most common game birds. The state's 56 amphibian species include numerous frogs, salamanders, newts, and lizards; 58 reptile species include three types of rattlesnake. Of the 186 fish species in Tennessee's lakes and streams, catfish, bream, bass, crappie, pike, and trout are the leading game fish.

Tennessee's Wildlife Resources Agency conducts an endangered and threatened species protection program. Among threatened species are the river otter, Cooper's hawk, Bewick's wren, northern pike snake, Tennessee cave salamander, blue sucker, amber darter, and silverjaw minnow. The snail darter, cited by opponents of the Tellico Dam, is probably Tennessee's most famous threatened species. The eastern cougar, gray and Indiana bats, Bachman's sparrow, Mississippi kite, lake sturgeon, Ohio River muskellunge, and Cumberland minkey face and Appalachian monkey face pearly mussels are on the endangered list.

[5]ENVIRONMENTAL PROTECTION

Tennessee is historically an agricultural state but is geologically varied with mountains in the east, rolling hills in the central part of the state, and the wide floodplain of the Mississippi in the west.

The Great Smoky Mountains in east Tennessee are sensitive to changes in air quality. In 1997 the state forged an agreement with the US National Park Service and the US Forest Service to ensure that the process for issuing permits for new industries in the area take into account both business and environmental concerns.

The first conservationists were agricultural reformers who, even before the Civil War, recommended terracing to conserve the soil and curtail erosion. Such conservation techniques as crop rotation and contour plowing were discussed at county fairs and other places where farmers gathered. In 1854, the legislature established the State Agricultural Bureau, which sought primarily to protect farmlands from floods. The streams of west Tennessee were extensively channeled for flood control beginning in the late 1800s, with a negative impact on both habitat and cropland. As of the late 1990s, the state is working with local citizens and the US Army Corps of Engineers to reverse this process by restoring the natural meandering flow to the tributaries of the Mississippi.

The Department of Environment and Conservation is responsible for air, land, and water protection in Tennessee. The department also manages the state park system and state natural areas. In 1996, Tennessee had approximately one million acres of wetlands. The Tennessee Wetland Act of 1986 authorized the acquisition of wetlands through the use of real estate taxes. In 1997, the state created four new natural areas.

When many of the first environmental laws were written in the 1970s, pollution of the air and water was widespread and severe. The early laws focused on tough enforcement tools and strict compliance measures to address this problem. In 1993, the Division of Pollution Prevention Assistance was established to provide information and support to industries attempting to reduce their pollution and waste. In 1995, there were 18 hazardous waste sites in Tennessee.

[6]POPULATION

Tennessee, with a population of 4,877,185, ranked 17th among the 50 states at the 1990 census, with a density of 118.3 persons per sq mi (45 per sq km). Estimates for 1996 show Tennessee with a population of 5,319,654, a 9.1% increase over 1990, and projections to 2000 foresee a population of 5,424,000.

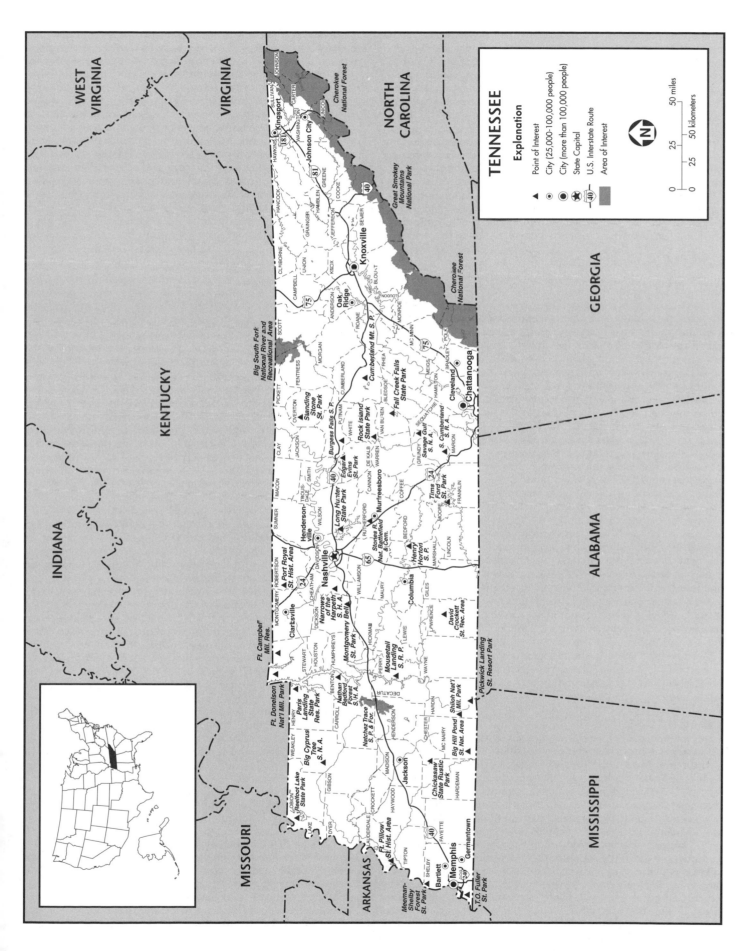

The first permanent white settlements in the state were made in the 1760s, when people from North Carolina and Virginia crossed the Unaka Mountains and settled in the fertile valleys. Between 1790 and 1800, the population increased threefold, from 35,690 to 105,600, and it doubled during each of the next two decades. After the Civil War, the population continued to increase, though at a slower rate, tripling between 1870 and 1970.

A pronounced urban trend became apparent after World War II. In 1960, for the first time in the state's history, census figures showed slightly more people living in urban than in rural areas. By 1990, 67.7% of all Tennesseans lived in metropolitan areas. Memphis is the state's largest city; in 1994, it had an estimated population of 614,289. Nashville (Davidson County) had 504,505; followed by Knoxville, 169,311; and Chattanooga, 152,259. The Memphis metropolitan area, including parts of Arkansas and Mississippi, had an estimated 1,068,891 residents in 1995, while metropolitan Nashville had 1,093,836.

7ETHNIC GROUPS

For nearly a century after the earliest white settlements, Tennessee was inhabited by three ethnoracial populations: whites of English and Scotch-Irish descent, Cherokee Indians, and black Americans. Settlers crossing the Appalachians met Indian resistance as early as the late 1700s. Eventually, however, nearly all the Cherokee were forced to leave; in 1990 there were only about 10,000 Indians in the state.

Blacks, originally brought into the state as slaves to work in the cotton fields of West Tennessee, made up about 10% of the population in 1790. White Tennesseans were divided on the issue of slavery. The small farmers of the eastern region were against it, and in the late 1820s and 1830s there were more antislavery societies in Tennessee than in any other southern state except North Carolina. The planters and merchants of southwest Tennessee, however, linked their sentiments and interests with those of the proslavery planters of the Mississippi Valley. The introduction of the cotton gin gave impetus to the acquisition of more slaves; by 1840, blacks accounted for 26% of the population, and Memphis had become a major market for the shipment of black slaves to large plantations farther south.

Immediately after the Civil War, many blacks, now free, migrated from Virginia and North Carolina to East Tennessee to become farmers, artisans, and owners of small businesses. After 1880, however, the black proportion of the population declined steadily. In 1990 there were about 778,000 blacks in Tennessee, 16% of the total.

Descendants of European immigrants make up about half the population of Tennessee, the largest groups being of English and German descent. In 1990, only 59,114 residents—1.2% of the population—were foreign-born.

8LANGUAGES

White settlers found Tennessee inhabited by Cherokee Indians in the eastern mountains, Shawnee in most of the eastern and central region, and Chickasaw in the west—all of them speakers of Hokan-Siouan languages. Subsequently removed to Indian Territory, they left behind such place-names as Chickamauga, Chattanooga, and Chilhowee, as well as Tennessee itself.

Tennessee English represents a mixture of North Midland and South Midland features brought into the northeastern and north-central areas, of South Midland and Southern features introduced by settlers from Virginia and the Carolinas, and of a few additional Southern terms in the extreme western fringe, to which they were carried from Mississippi and Louisiana. Certain pronunciations exhibit a declining frequency from the Appalachians to the Mississippi River, such as /r/ after a vowel in the same syllable, as in *form* and *short,* and a rounded /aw/ before /r/

in *arm* and *barbed.* Others occur statewide, such as the /ah/ vowel in *forest* and *foreign, coop* and *Cooper* with the vowel of *book,* and simplification of the long /i/ vowel, so that *lice* sounds like *lass.* Common are such non-Northern terms as *wait on* (wait for), *pullybone* (along with Northern *wishbone),* *nicker* (neigh), *light bread* (white bread), and *snake feeder* (dragonfly), as well as *Jew's harp, juice harp,* and *French harp* (all for harmonica). In eastern Tennessee are found *goobers* (peanuts), *tote* (carry), *plum peach* (clingstone peach), *ash cake* (a kind of cornbread), *fireboard* (mantel), *redworm* (earthworm), *branch* (stream), and *peckerwood* (woodpecker). Appearing in western Tennessee are *loaf bread, cold drink* (soft drink), and *burlap bag.* In Memphis, a large, long sandwich is a *poorboy.*

In 1990, 4,413,193 Tennesseans 5 years old and over—97% of the population in that age group—spoke only English at home. Speakers of other languages were as follows:

Spanish	49,661	Chinese	5,024
German	17,716	Arabic	2,800
French	20,444	Korean	3,775

9RELIGIONS

Baptist and Presbyterian churches were organized on the frontier soon after permanent settlements were made. Many divisions have occurred in both groups. The Cumberland Presbyterian Church, which spread into other states, was organized near Nashville in 1810 because of differences within the parent church. Both the Baptists and the Presbyterians divided over slavery. Methodist circuit riders arrived with the early settlers, and they quickly succeeded in attracting many followers. Controversies over slavery and other sectional issues also developed within the Methodist Church and, as with the Baptists and Presbyterians, divisions emerged during the 1840s. The Methodists, however, were able to resolve their differences and regroup. The United Presbyterian Church and the Presbyterian Church in the US finally ended their 122-year separation in 1983, reuniting to form the Presbyterian Church (USA).

Two other Protestant groups with large followings in the state had their origin on the Tennessee frontier in the first half of the 19th century: the Disciples of Christ and the Church of Christ. Both groups began with the followers of Thomas and Alexander Campbell and Barton W. Stone, among others, who deplored formal creeds and denominations and sought to return to the purity of early Christianity. As their numbers grew, these followers divided into Progressives, who supported missionary societies and instrumental music in church, and Conservatives, who did not. In 1906, a federal census of religions listed the Conservatives for the first time as the Church of Christ and the Progressives as the Disciples of Christ. The latter, now the Christian Church (Disciples of Christ) had 20,986 known adherents in 1990.

Protestant groups had a total of 2,830,239 known adherents in 1990. By far the largest group was the Southern Baptist Church. The United Methodists were second, followed by the Churches of Christ, and the Presbyterian Church in the US. In 1990, there were 137,203 Roman Catholics and an estimated 17,474 Jews in the state.

Tennessee has long been considered part of the Bible Belt because of the influence of fundamentalist Protestant groups that believe in the literal accuracy of the Bible.

10TRANSPORTATION

Memphis, Nashville, Knoxville, and Chattanooga are the focal points for rail, highway, water, and air transportation. All are located on important rivers and interstate highways, and all have airports served by the major airlines.

Railroad building began in Tennessee as early as the 1820s. During the 1850s, the basis for 20th-century rail transportation was laid: the Louisville and Nashville Railroad linked Tennessee to the northern states, and the Memphis and Charleston line established ties with the East Coast. In 1995, Tennessee had 2,634 rail mi (4,217 km) of track, of which about 83% was Class I track; railroad employees numbered 4,931 in 1995. No east-west passenger trains operate in the state today (Amtrak serves Memphis on the Chicago–New Orleans route), but considerable freight is hauled. In 1995/96, total Tennessee ridership on Amtrak passenger trains came to 37,401.

The first roads—such as the Natchez Trace, which connected Nashville with the southwestern part of the state—often followed Indian trails. Many roads in the early 1800s were constructed by private individuals or chartered turnpike companies. The introduction of the automobile shortly after the beginning of the 20th century brought the development of modern roads and highways. After 1916, the federal government began to share the high cost of highway construction, and the 1920s were a decade of extensive road building.

In 1995, Tennessee had 68,403 mi (110,129 km) of rural roads and 14,801 mi (23,830 km) of urban roads. The major interstate highway is I-40, crossing east-west from Knoxville to Nashville and Memphis. In 1997, 5,793,717 motor vehicles were registered in the state, and 3,826,470 Tennesseans held drivers' licenses.

The principal means of transportation during Tennessee's early history was water, and all the early settlements were built on or near streams. The introduction of steamboats on the Cumberland River in the early 19th century helped make Nashville the state's largest city and its foremost trading center. By mid-century, however, Memphis, on the Mississippi River, had surpassed Nashville in population and trade, largely because of cotton. Tennessee has about 1,000 mi (1,600 km) of navigable waterways. The completion in 1985 of the 234-mi (377-km) Tennessee-Tombigbee Waterway gave Tennessee shippers a direct north-south route for all vessels between the Tennessee River and the Gulf of Mexico via the Black Warrior River in Alabama. Although none of the waterway runs through Tennessee, the northern terminus is on the Tennessee River near the common borders of Tennessee, Alabama, and Mississippi. In 1995, the ports of Memphis and Nashville handled 15,949,945 and 3,748,978 tons of freight, respectively.

In December 1996 there were 155 public and private airports, 105 heliports, 9 stolports, and 2 seaplane bases in the state. Memphis International Airport is the world's busiest cargo-handling facility, moving 1,712,066 metric tons of goods in 1995. It was also the state's major air terminal in terms of enplanement, with 3,762,863 passengers in 1995, while Nashville International retains the lead in terms of aircraft operations, with 287,858 departures in 1996.

11HISTORY

The lower Tennessee Valley was heavily populated with hunter-gatherers some 10,000 years ago. Their descendants, called Paleo-Indians, were succeeded by other native cultures, including the Archaic Indians, Woodland Indians, and Early Mississippians. When the first Spanish arrived in the early 16th century, Creek Indians were living in what is now East Tennessee, along with the Yuchi. About 200 years later, the powerful Cherokee—the largest single tribe south of the Ohio River, occupying parts of North Carolina, South Carolina, Georgia, and East Tennessee—drove the Creek and Yuchi out of the area and established themselves as the dominant tribe. Their settlements, varying in size from a dozen families to more than 200, were known as the Upper or Overhill Towns. The Cherokee retained their tribal dominance until they were forced out by the federal government in the 1830s. In West Tennessee, the Chickasaw were the major group. They lived principally in northern Mississippi but used Tennessee

lands as a hunting ground. Shawnee occupied the Cumberland Valley in Middle Tennessee until driven north of the Ohio River by the Cherokee and Chickasaw.

Explorers and traders from continental Europe and the British Isles were in Tennessee for well over 200 years before permanent settlements were established in the 1760s. Hernando de Soto, a Spaniard, came from Florida to explore the area as early as 1540. He was followed during the 17th century by the French explorers Jacques Marquette, Louis Jolliet, and Robert Cavelier, Sieur de la Salle. Englishmen were not far behind: by the mid-1700s, hundreds—perhaps thousands—had crossed the Appalachian barrier and explored the transmontane country beyond, which was claimed first by the colony of Virginia and later assigned to North Carolina. They came in search of pelts, furs, and whatever else of value they might find. A fiercely independent breed, they were accustomed to hardship and unwilling to settle in a civilized community. Perhaps the best known was Daniel Boone, who by 1760 had found his way into present-day Washington County.

With the conclusion of the French and Indian War in 1763, many people from North Carolina and Virginia began to cross the Alleghenies. Elisha Walden was among those who first led groups of "long hunters" into the wilderness. By 1770, small pockets of white settlement were developing in the valley between the Unaka and Cumberland mountains. In the two decades that followed, more than 35,000 people settled on soil soon to become the State of Tennessee.

Two major areas of settlement developed. The larger one—in the northeast along the Holston, Nolichucky, and Watauga rivers—was organized as the Watauga Association in 1791. The second major area was in the Cumberland Basin, where James Robertson, under the sponsorship of the Transylvania Company (formed by eastern land speculators), established a settlement he called Nashborough (now Nashville) in 1779. There more than 250 adult males signed the Cumberland Compact, which established a government. They pledged to abide by the will of the majority and expressed their allegiance to North Carolina.

The Revolutionary War did not reach as far west as Tennessee, but many of the frontiersmen fought in the Carolinas and Virginia. The most famous battle involving these early Tennesseans was that of Kings Mountain, in South Carolina, where Colonel John Sevier and others defeated a superior force of British soldiers and captured more than 1,000 prisoners. Hardly was the Revolution over when Tennesseans began to think about statehood for themselves. As early as 1784, leaders in three mountain counties—Greene, Sullivan, and Washington—established the Free State of Franklin. John Sevier was chosen as governor, and an assembly was formed. Only after border warfare developed and factionalism weakened their cause did Franklin's leaders abandon their plans and return their allegiance to North Carolina. But the spirit of independence—indeed, defiance—persisted.

In 1790, less than two years after Franklin collapsed, North Carolina ceded its western lands to the US. Tennessee became known as the Southwest Territory, with William Blount, a prominent North Carolina speculator and politician, as its governor. During his six-year tenure, a government was organized and a capital established at Knoxville. The population doubled to more than 70,000 in 1795, and steps were taken to convert the territory into a state. When the territorial legislature presented Congress with a petition for statehood, a lively debate ensued in the US Senate between Jeffersonian Democratic-Republicans, who urged immediate admission, and Federalists, who opposed it. The Jeffersonians triumphed, and on 1 June 1796, President George Washington signed a bill admitting Tennessee as the 16th state. Sevier became governor of the new state, Blount was elected to the US Senate, and Andrew Jackson became the state's first US representative.

Sevier dominated state politics for the first two decades of statehood, and he had little difficulty in thwarting the ambitions of Andrew Jackson and others who sought to challenge his leadership. Tennessee's population, about 85,000 when Sevier became governor, was more than 250,000 when he left the statehouse in 1809. Under Sevier's governorship, Nashville, Knoxville, and other early settlements became thriving frontier towns. Churches and schools were established, industry and agriculture developed, and Tennessee became a leading iron producer.

Andrew Jackson's rise to prominence came as a result of the Battle of New Orleans, fought at the conclusion of the War of 1812. Jackson, who had little difficulty raising troops in a state where volunteers for military service have always been abundant, lost only about a half dozen of his men, while British casualties exceeded 2,000. He returned to Nashville a hero, built a fine house that he named The Hermitage, received thousands of congratulatory messages, and conferred with friends about his political and military future. In 1823, Jackson was elected to the US Senate. Defeated the following year in a four-man race for the presidency, he ran again, this time successfully, in 1828, serving in that office for eight years.

Jackson alienated himself from many people in the state after 1835, when he announced his support of Martin Van Buren for president instead of Knoxvillian Hugh Lawson White, an avowed candidate. A majority of Tennesseans joined the new Whig Party, which arose in opposition to Jackson's Democratic Party, and voted in the 1836 presidential election for White instead of for Van Buren. The Whigs won every presidential election in Tennessee from 1836 to 1852, including the election of 1844, which sent Tennessean James Knox Polk, a Democrat, to the White House. Polk's term (1845–49) brought another war, this one with Mexico. Although Tennessee's quota was only 2,800, more than 25,000 men volunteered for service. Among the heroes of that war were William Trousdale and William B. Campbell, both of whom later were elected governor.

Social reform and cultural growth characterized the first half of the 19th century. A penitentiary was built, and the penal code made somewhat more humane. Temperance newspapers were published, temperance societies formed, and laws passed to curtail the consumption of alcoholic beverages. In 1834, a few women, embracing the feminist cause, were influential in giving the courts, rather than the legislature, the right to grant divorces. Many important schools were established, including the Nashville Female Academy, the University of Nashville, and more than two dozen colleges.

More than most other southern states, antebellum Tennessee was divided over the issue of slavery. Slaves had accompanied their owners into Tennessee in the 18th century, and by 1850, they constituted about one-fourth of the state's population. Although slaveholders lived in all sections of the state, they predominated in the west, where cotton was grown profitably, as well as in Middle Tennessee. In East Tennessee, where blacks made up less than 10% of the population, antislavery sentiment thrived. Most of those who supported emancipation urged that it be accomplished peacefully, gradually, and with compensation to the slave owners. Frances Wright, the Scottish reformer, founded the colony of Nashoba near Memphis in the 1820s as a place where freed blacks could learn self-reliance. After a few years the colony failed, however, and Wright took her colonists to Haiti. At the constitutional convention of 1834, hundreds of petitions were presented asking that the legislature be empowered to free the slaves. But while the convention endorsed several measures to democratize the constitution of 1796—abolishing property qualifications as a condition for holding office, for example—it decided against emancipation.

Considerable economic growth took place during this period. West Tennessee became a major cotton-growing area immediately after it was purchased form the Chickasaw in 1818, and Memphis, established in 1821, became the principal cotton-marketing center. The Volunteer State's annual cotton crop grew from less than 3,000 bales in 1810 to nearly 200,000 bales by midcentury. The counties of the Highland Rim produced tobacco in such abundance that, by 1840, Tennessee ranked just behind Kentucky and Virginia in total production. East Tennessee farmers practiced greater crop diversification, growing a variety of fruits and vegetables for market. Silk cultivation flourished briefly in the 1830s and 1840s.

Tennessee became a major battleground during the Civil War, as armies from both North and South crossed the state several times. Most Tennesseans favored secession. But the eastern counties remained staunchly Unionist, and many East Tennesseans crossed over into Kentucky to enlist in the Union Army. General Albert Sidney Johnston, the Confederate commander of the western theater, set up lines of defense across the northern border of the state and built forts on both the Cumberland and Tennessee rivers. In February 1862, Ft. Donelson and Ft. Henry were taken by General Ulysses S. Grant and naval Captain Andrew H. Foote, thereby opening the state to Union armies. Within two weeks Nashville was in the hands of the enemy. Northern troops pushed farther south and west, taking key positions on the Mississippi River. Less than two months later, on 6 April, Union forces near the Mississippi state line engaged Johnston's army in the Battle of Shiloh. Both sides suffered tremendous losses, including Johnston himself, who bled to death after sustaining a thigh wound. In the meantime President Abraham Lincoln had established a military government for the conquered state and appointed Andrew Johnson to head it. Johnson, who had served two terms as governor a decade earlier, had been elected to the US Senate in 1858; he remained there in 1861, the only southern senator to do so, refusing to follow his state into the Confederacy. In 1864, he was elected vice president under Lincoln.

Johnson's governorship did not mean the end of Confederate activities in Tennessee. Late in December 1862, Confederate forces made the first of two vigorous attempts to rid the state of the invader. General Braxton Bragg, who replaced Johnston as Confederate commander, established himself at Murfreesboro, 30 mi (48 km) southwest of Nashville, and threatened to retake the capital city. But at the Battle of Stones River, Union troops under General William S. Rosecrans forced Bragg to retreat to the southeast. Fighting did not resume until 19–20 September 1863, when the Confederates drove Union troops back to Chattanooga in the Battle of Chickamauga, one of the bloodiest engagements of the war. The second major Confederate drive occurred in November and December 1864, when General John B. Hood, commanding the Confederate Army of Tennessee, came out of Georgia and attacked the Union forces at Franklin and Nashville. Hood's army was destroyed, and these battles were the last major engagements in the state.

Returning to the Union in 1866, Tennessee was the only former Confederate state not to have a military government during Reconstruction. Economic readjustment was not as difficult as elsewhere in the South, and within a few years agricultural production exceeded antebellum levels. Extensive coal and iron deposits in East Tennessee attracted northern capital, and by the early 1880s, flour, woolen, and paper mills were established in all the urban areas. By the late 1890s, Memphis was a leading cotton market and the nation's foremost producer of cottonseed oil. Politically, the Democratic Party became firmly entrenched, and would remain so until the 1950s.

As the 20th century dawned, the major issue in Tennessee was the crusade against alcohol, a movement with deep roots in the 19th century. Though the major cities still were "wet," earlier legislation had dried up the rural areas and small towns, and the

Tennessee Anti-Saloon League and Women's Christian Temperance Union (WCTU) kept the matter in the public eye. In 1908, with "wet" forces controlling the state government, Edward Ward Carmack—a rabid prohibitionist, powerful politician, newspaper editor, and former US senator—was shot and killed in the street of Nashville. His assailants were convicted but pardoned immediately by the governor. In the following year, with Carmack as a martyr to their cause, "dry" forces enacted legislation that, in effect, imposed prohibition on the entire state. The dominant Democratic Party was divided and demoralized to such an extent that a Republican governor was elected—only the second since Reconstruction. The prohibition movement helped promote the cause of women's suffrage. A proposed state constitutional amendment giving women the right to vote failed in 1915, but in 1919, they were granted the franchise in municipal elections. One year later, Tennessee became the 36th state to ratify the 19th Amendment to the US Constitution, thereby granting women the right to vote nationwide.

The 1920s brought a resurgence of religious fundamentalism. When, in 1925, the legislature enacted a measure that prohibited the teaching of the theory of evolution in the public schools, a high school teacher named John T. Scopes decided to challenge the law. Three-time presidential candidate and fundamentalist spokesman William Jennings Bryan arrived in the tiny town of Dayton to aid in Scopes's prosecution, while the great civil liberties lawyer Clarence Darrow came from Chicago to lead the defense. The Scopes trial gave the Volunteer State unwanted notoriety throughout the civilized world. Scopes was convicted, and it was not until 1967 that the law was repealed.

The 1930s brought depression, but they also brought the Tennessee Valley Authority. Before TVA, residents of the Tennessee River Valley could boast of the beauty of the landscape, but of little else. The soil was so thin that little other than subsistence agriculture was possible, and many people lived on cash incomes of less than $100 a year. There were some senators, such as George Norris of Nebraska and Tennessee's own Kenneth D. McKellar, who saw great possibilities in valley development. Harnessing the Tennessee River with dams could not only generate electricity inexpensively but also greatly improve navigation; aid flood control, soil conservation, and reforestation; and produce nitrate fertilizer. Efforts to establish such a program failed, however, until Franklin D. Roosevelt included it in his New Deal. The law establishing the TVA was passed a few weeks after Roosevelt's inauguration in 1933, and dam construction began almost immediately. Before TVA, people in the valley consumed only 1.5 billion kWh of electricity annually; but consumption increased to 11.5 billion kWh by 1945 and to 57.5 billion kWh by 1960. Fewer than 2% of rural families in Tennessee had electricity in 1933; but by the late 1930s, power lines were being strung into remote areas, bringing to practically everyone the advantages that hitherto only urban residents had enjoyed. Inexpensive power became a magnet for industry, and industrial employment in the region nearly doubled in two decades. The building of a plant for the production of atomic weapons at Oak Ridge in 1942 was due in large measure to the availability of TVA power.

The TVA notwithstanding, the depression caused many manufacturers to close or curtail operations, and farm prices declined drastically. Cotton, which had earlier brought farmers more than 30 cents a pound, declined to 5.7 cents, and the prices of corn, tobacco, and other crops fell proportionately. The state still was in the grip of financial depression when World War II began. Thousands of men volunteered for service before conscription was introduced; when the US entered the war in 1941, several training posts were established in Tennessee. Tennessee firms manufacturing war materiel received contracts amounting to $1.25 billion and employed more than 200,000

people during the war. Industrial growth continued during the postwar period, while agriculture recovered and diversified. The chemical industry, spurred by high demand during and after World War II, became a leading sector, along with textiles, apparel, and food processing. Cotton and tobacco continued to be major crops, but by the early 1970s, soybeans had taken the lead, accounting for 22% of estimated farm income in 1980. Beef and dairy production also flourished.

Democratic boss Edward H. Crump, who ran an efficient political machine in Memphis, dominated state politics for most of the period between 1910 and the early 1950s, an era that saw the elevation of many Tennessee Democrats to national prominence. Considerable progress was made toward ending racial discrimination during the postwar years, although the desegregation of public schools was accomplished only after outbursts of violence at Clinton, Nashville, and Memphis. The killing of civil rights leader Martin Luther King, Jr., in Memphis in 1968 resulted in rioting by blacks in that city. The most notable political development during the 1970s was the resurgence of the Republican Party, making Tennessee one of the few true two-party states in the South.

The early 1980s saw the exposure of corruption in high places: former governor Ray Blanton and several aides were convicted for conspiracy to sell liquor licenses, and banker and former gubernatorial candidate Jacob F. "Jake" Butcher was convicted for fraud in the aftermath of the collapse of his banking empire. On the brighter side, there was a successful World's Fair in 1982, the Knoxville International Energy Exposition, and a fairly resilient state economy, bolstered by the much-heralded openings of the Nissan truck-assembly plant in Smyrna in 1983 and the General Motors Saturn plant in Spring Hill in 1990.

Manufacturing in Tennessee continued to grow throughout the 1980s, aided by the completion of the Tennessee–Tombigbee Waterway in 1985. The state gained nearly 45,000 manufacturing jobs between 1982 and 1992, many of them in the automotive and other transport-related industries. Tennessee's unemployment rate fell to a 16-year low of 4.7% in 1994.

The state legislature passed school reform laws in 1992 and, in 1993, a health-care package mandating the creation of TennCare, an insurance program designed to replace Medicaid coverage for 1.5 million uninsured residents of the state.

12 STATE GOVERNMENT

Tennessee's first constitution was adopted in 1796, just before the state was admitted to the Union. It vested executive authority in a governor, elected for two years, who had to be at least 25 years of age and own at least 500 acres (202 hectares) of land. The governor could approve or veto bills adopted by the legislature, as commander-in-chief of the militia, and could grant pardons and reprieves, among other powers. Legislative power was placed in a general assembly, consisting of a house and senate, whose members served terms of two years. Candidates for the legislature were required to fulfill residence and age requirements and to own at least 200 acres (81 hectares). Property qualifications were not required for voting, and all freemen—including free blacks—could vote.

The basic governmental structure established in 1796 remains the fundamental law today. The constitution has been revised several times, however. The spirit of Jacksonian democracy prompted delegates at the constitutional convention of 1834 to remove property qualifications as a requirement for public office, reapportion representation, transfer the right to select county officials from justices of the peace to the voters, and reorganize the court system. At the same time, though, free blacks were disfranchised. In 1870, another constitutional convention confirmed the abolition of slavery and the enfranchisement of black men but imposed a poll tax as a requirement for voting.

Membership of the house was fixed at 99, and of the senate at 33—numbers retained today. The legislative salary in 1995 was $16,500.

Yet another constitutional convention was held in 1953. Delegates increased the gubernatorial term from two to four years, gave the governor the power of item veto, eliminated the poll tax, authorized home rule for cities, and provided for the consolidation of county and city functions. Later conventions extended the term of state senators from two to four years, sought to improve and streamline county government, and placed a constitutional limit on state spending. A limited convention in 1965 required the apportionment of the legislature according to population. This change greatly increased the weight of urban, and particularly black, votes.

The governor appoints a cabinet of 21 members. The speaker of the state senate automatically becomes lieutenant governor; the secretary of state, treasurer, and comptroller of the treasury are chosen by the legislature. In 1996 the governor's salary was $85,000.

Legislation is enacted after bills are read and approved three times in each house and signed by the governor. If the governor vetoes a measure, the legislature may override the veto by majority vote of both houses. Not more often than once every six years the legislature may submit to the voters the question of calling a convention to amend the constitution. If the vote is favorable, delegates are chosen. Changes proposed by the convention must be approved by a majority vote in a subsequent election. Individual amendments also may be considered by the legislature from time to time, but the process is cumbersome.

People may vote in state and national elections if they are US citizens, are at least 18 years of age, and have registered at least 30 days before the election.

[13]POLITICAL PARTIES

The major political groups are the Democratic and Republican parties. Minor parties have seldom affected the outcome of an election in Tennessee.

When Tennessee entered the Union in 1796, it was strongly loyal to the Democratic-Republican Party. The Jacksonian era brought a change in political affiliations, and for more than 20 years, Tennessee had a vibrant two-party system. Jackson's followers formed the Democratic Party, which prevailed for a decade over the National Republican Party led by John Quincy Adams and Henry Clay. But by 1835, Tennesseans had become disillusioned with Jackson, and they joined the new Whig Party in large numbers. A Whig governor was elected in that year, and Whig presidential nominees consistently garnered Tennessee's electoral votes until the party foundered over the slavery issue in the 1850s.

After the Civil War and Reconstruction, Tennessee was part of the solid Democratic South for nearly a century. Only three Republican governors were elected during that period, and only then because bitter factionalism had divided the dominant party. East Tennessee remained a Republican stronghold. However, the 2d Congressional district, which includes Knoxville, was the only district in the country to elect a Republican continuously from 1860 on. Republicans Warren G. Harding and Herbert Hoover carried the state in the presidential elections of 1920 and 1928. But whereas the 1920s saw a tendency away from one-party domination, Franklin D. Roosevelt and the New Deal brought the Volunteer State decisively back into the Democratic fold. Tennesseans voted overwhelmingly Democratic in the four elections that Roosevelt won (1932–44).

After World War II, the one-party system in Tennessee was shaken anew. Dwight D. Eisenhower narrowly won the state in 1952 and 1956, although Tennessee Senator Estes Kefauver was the Democratic vice-presidential nominee in the latter year. Tennesseans chose Richard Nixon all three times he ran for president. In fact, between 1948 and 1976, the only Democratic nominees to carry the state came from the South (Lyndon Johnson and Jimmy Carter) or from a border state (Harry Truman).

In state elections, the Republicans made deep inroads into Democratic power during the 1960s and 1970s. In 1966, Howard Baker became the first popularly elected Republican US senator in the state history. In 1970, voters elected Winfield Dunn as the first Republican governor in more than 50 years, and in the same year, they sent Republican Bill Brock to join Baker in the

Tennessee Presidential Vote by Political Parties, 1948–96

YEAR	ELECTORAL VOTE	TENNESSEE WINNER	DEMOCRAT	REPUBLICAN	STATES' RIGHTS DEMOCRAT	SOCIALIST	PROGRESSIVE	PROHIBITION
1948	11	*Truman (D)	270,402	202,914	73,815	1,288	1,864	—
					CONSTITUTION	—		
1952	11	*Eisenhower (R)	443,710	446,147	379	—	887	1,432
1956	11	*Eisenhower (R)	456,507	462,288	19,820	—	—	789
					NATL. STATES' RIGHTS			
1960	11	Nixon (R)	481,453	556,577	11,298	—	—	2,450
1964	11	*Johnson (D)	635,047	508,965	—	—	—	—
					AMERICAN IND.			
1968	11	*Nixon (R)	351,233	472,592	424,792	—	—	—
							AMERICAN	
1972	10	*Nixon (R)	357,293	813,147	—	—	30,373	—
								LIBERTARIAN
1976	10	*Carter (D)	825,897	633,969	2,303	—	5,769	1,375
					NATL. STATESMAN		CITIZENS	
1980	10	*Reagan (R)	783,051	787,761	5,0211	—	1,112	7,116
1984	11	*Reagan (R)	711,714	990,212	—	—	978	3,072
1988	11	*Bush (R)	679,794	947,233	—	—	1,334	2,041
					IND. (Perot)			
1992	11	*Clinton (D)	933,521	841,300	199,968	1,356	727	1,847
1996	11	*Clinton (D)	909,146	863,530	105,918	—	—	5,020

*Won US presidential election.

Senate. The Democrats regained the governorship in 1974 and Brock's seat in 1976, but Republicans again won the governorship in 1978 when Lamar Alexander defeated Jacob F. "Jake" Butcher. In 1982, Alexander became the first Tennessee governor to be elected to two successive four-year terms. Ned McWherter, a Democrat, was elected governor in 1990. Republican Don Sundquist became governor in 1994. In 1994, Dr. Bill Frist, a heart surgeon, was elected to the US Senate on the Republican ticket, defeating Democrat James Sasser. Democrat Harlan Matthews was appointed to fill the seat vacated by Albert Gore in 1992 when Gore became vice president. In 1994, Republican Fred Thompson defeated Jim Cooper for the remaining two years of Gore's term. US representatives included five Republicans and four Democrats after the November 1996 elections. There are 18 Democrats and 15 Republicans in the state senate and 61 Democrats and 38 Republicans in the state house. Tennessee voters, who gave Republican George Bush 57.4% of the vote in 1988, chose Bill Clinton in 1992. In 1996, Clinton received 48% of the vote to Republican Bob Dole's 46%; Independent Ross Perot collected under 6%.

In 1993, there were 168 blacks in public office. As of 1995, 18 women served in the state legislature.

14LOCAL GOVERNMENT

Local government in Tennessee is exercised by 93 counties and more than 300 municipalities. The county, a direct descendant of the Anglo-Saxon shire, has remained remarkably unaltered in Tennessee since it was brought from Virginia and North Carolina in frontier days. The constitution specifies that county officials must include at least a register, trustee (the custodian of county funds), sheriff, and county clerk, all of whom hold office for four years and may succeed themselves. Other officials have been added by legislative enactment: county executives (known for many years as county judges or county chairmen), tax assessors, county court clerks, and superintendents of public schools.

City government is of more recent origin than county government and is, in fact, a creature of the state. There are three forms of municipal government: mayor-council (or mayor-alderman), council-manager, and commission. The mayor-council system is the oldest and by far the most widely employed. There were 339 municipalities in 1992, as well as 14 school districts and 477 special districts.

15STATE SERVICES

The commissioner of education oversees the public schools as well as special, higher, and vocational-technical education. Highways, aeronautics, mass transit, and waterways are the responsibility of the Department of Transportation. The Department of Safety, including the State Highway Patrol, is charged with enforcing the safety laws on all state roads and interstate highways. Railroad regulation and the setting of railroad rates are the duties of the Public Service Commission. Public protection services are provided by the Military Department, which includes the Army and Air National Guard. The Department of Correction maintains prisons for adult offenders, a work-release program, and correctional and rehabilitation centers for juveniles.

The Department of Health and Environment licenses medical facilities, provides medical care for the indigent, operates tuberculosis treatment centers, and administers pollution control programs. The Department of Mental Health and Mental Retardation supervises mental hospitals, mental health clinics, and homes for retarded children. The Department of Human Services administers aid to the blind, aged, disabled, and families with dependent children, and determines eligibility for families receiving food stamps. The Department of Employment Security administers unemployment insurance and provides job training and placement services. State laws governing workers' compensation, occupational and mine safety, child labor, and wage standards are enforced by the Department of Labor.

16JUDICIAL SYSTEM

The supreme court is the highest court in the state. It consists of five justices, not more than two of whom may reside in any one grand division of the state—East, Middle, or West Tennessee. The justices are elected by popular vote for terms of 8 years and must be at least 35 years of age. The court has appellate jurisdiction only, holding sessions in Nashville, Knoxville, and Jackson. The position of chief justice rotates every 19 months.

Immediately below the supreme court are two appellate courts (each sitting in three divisions), established by the legislature to relieve the crowded high court docket. The court of appeals has appellate jurisdiction in most civil cases. The court of criminal appeals hears cases from the lower courts involving criminal matters. Judges on both appellate courts are elected for eight-year terms.

Circuit courts have original jurisdiction in both civil and criminal cases. Tennessee still has chancery courts, vestiges of the English courts designed to hear cases where there was no adequate remedy at law. They administer cases involving receiverships of corporations, settle disputes regarding property ownership, hear divorce cases, and adjudicate on a variety of other matters. In some districts, judges of the circuit and chancery courts, all of whom are elected for eight-year terms, have concurrent jurisdiction.

At the bottom of the judicial structure are general sessions courts. A comprehensive juvenile court system was set up in 1911. Other courts created for specific services include domestic relations courts and probate courts. There were 13,247 attorneys practicing in Tennessee in 1996.

As of 1995, federal and state prisons in Tennessee had 11,280 inmates, or 248 per 100,000. Tennessee's inmate population rose by over 56% between 1990 and 1995, one of the largest increases in the nation.

According to the FBI Crime Index, Tennessee's crime rates ranked above the national averages for a number of crimes. For murder, its rate was 10.6; the national rate was 9.1. Its rate of forcible rape crimes was 47.1; the national rate was 38.9. Tennessee's rate of aggravated assault was 490.5, in contrast to the national rate of 458.7. Burglary occurred at a rate of 1,143.2, whereas the national rate was 1,048.2.

17ARMED FORCES

In 1996, there were 5,824 active duty military personnel stationed in Tennessee, most of whom (4,763) were at Millington Naval Air Station near Memphis.

Tennessee supplied so many soldiers for the War of 1812 and the Mexican War that it became known as the Volunteer State. During the Civil War, more than 100,000 Tennesseans fought for the Confederacy and about half that number for the Union. In World War I, some 91,000 men served in the armed forces, and in World War II, 316,000 Tennesseans saw active duty. As of 1 July 1996, 512,000 veterans were living in Tennessee, of whom less than 500 served in World War I, 131,000 in World War II, 85,000 in the Korean conflict, 171,000 during the Viet Nam era, and 38,000 during the Persian Gulf War. Veterans' benefits totaled $1.03 billion in fiscal year 1996.

The reserve and national guard had 35,507 personnel in 1996—two-thirds of whom were in the army—organized into more than 135 units with activities in 88 cities and towns. Tennessee's Air Force Reserve and National Guard had more than 4,825 members in the same year, while navy and marine corps personnel numbered 6,907. In 1993, the Tennessee Department of Safety employed 745 full-time sworn officers, or 2 per 10,000 residents.

18MIGRATION

The first white settlers in Tennessee, who came across the mountains from North Carolina and Virginia, were almost entirely of English extraction. They were followed by an influx of Scotch-Irish, mainly from Pennsylvania. About 3,800 German and Irish migrants arrived during the 1830s and 1840s. In the next century, Tennessee's population remained relatively stable, except for an influx of blacks immediately following the Civil War. There was a steady out-migration of blacks to industrial centers in the North during the 20th century. The state suffered a net loss through migration of 462,000 between 1940 and 1970, but gained over 465,000 between 1970 and 1990. Between 1990 and 1996, Tennessee had net gains of 271,078 in domestic migration and 17,713 in international migration. In 1996, 4,343 foreign immigrants arrived in Tennessee.

The major in-state migration has been away from rural areas and into towns and cities. Blacks, especially, have tended to cluster in large urban centers. The population of Memphis, for example, is more than 54% black. In 1990, some 69.2% of state residents had been born within Tennessee, and about 54% of residents age 5 and older lived in the same house as in 1985. Of those who reported living in a different house in 1985, 24% did so in a different state.

19INTERGOVERNMENTAL COOPERATION

Tennessee participates in such interstate agreements as the Interstate Mining Compact, Southeastern Forest Fire Protection Compact, Southern Growth Policies Compact, and Southern Interstate Energy Compact. There are boundary accords with Arkansas, Kentucky, and Virginia, and an agreement with Alabama, Florida, Kentucky, and Mississippi governing development of the Tennessee-Tombigbee waterway.

Federal aid to Tennessee was about $45 billion in 1995/96.

20ECONOMY

Tennessee's economy is based primarily on industry. Since the 1930s, the number of people employed in industry has grown at a rapid rate, while the number of farmers has declined proportionately. Wage rates and average weekly earnings are well below the national average. The principal manufacturing areas are Memphis, Nashville, Chattanooga, Knoxville, and Kingsport-Bristol. With the construction in the 1980s of a Nissan automobile and truck plant and a General Motors automobile facility, both in the area southeast of Nashville, Tennessee is becoming an important producer of transportation equipment. The new GM plant employs 6,000 persons.

Income from agricultural products now comes more from dairy and beef cattle and soybeans than from tobacco, cotton, and corn, which were the leading money crops for many years. Tourism is the third major contributor to the state's economy. Tennessee's gross state product in 1994 was $126,539 million, to which private goods-producing industries contributed $37,353 million; private services-producing industries, $73,638 million; and government, $15,547 million. Tennessee's per capita personal income in 1995 was $21,038, 32nd in the US. In 1996, there were 48,748 bankruptcy filings.

21INCOME

With a per capita income of $21,038 in 1995, Tennessee ranked 32d in the US. In 1995, nonfarm personal income amounted to $110.3 billion, up from $102.8 billion in 1994. Total personal income rose from $103.4 billion in 1994 to $110.6 billion in 1995, an increase of 7%. From 1980 to 1995, total personal income grew by over 58% in constant (1992) dollars, while real per capita income increased by over 38% during that period.

In 1995, median family income was $44,312. In that year, about 15.5% of all Tennesseans were below the federal poverty line.

22LABOR

In 1996, Tennessee had an average civilian labor force of 2,751,000. The overall unemployment rate for that year was 5.2%. The Nashville and Memphis metropolitan areas accounted for 22.7% and 19.4% of the labor force, respectively.

In 1995, 9.5% of the state's workers were union members. Tennessee has a right-to-work law. Average weekly earnings of production workers were $477.76 in December 1996.

23 AGRICULTURE

Tennessee ranked 31st among the 50 states in 1995 with farm receipts of over $2.1 billion. There were 80,000 farms in 1996.

From the antebellum period to the 1950s, cotton was the leading crop, followed by corn and tobacco. But during the early 1960s, soybeans surpassed cotton as the principal source of income. In 1996, 40.25 million bushels of soybeans, valued at $281.75 million, were harvested. Tobacco production in 1996 was 114 million lb. The main types of tobacco are burley, a fine leaf used primarily for cigarettes, and eastern and western dark-fired, which are used primarily for cigars, pipe tobacco, and snuff. The corn harvest in 1996 was about 78.9 million bushels, valued at $240.6 million. In 1996, cotton production was 674,000 bales, valued at $229 million.

24ANIMAL HUSBANDRY

Cattle are raised throughout the state, but principally in middle and east Tennessee. In 1930, fewer than a million cattle and calves were raised on Tennessee farms; by early 1992, however, there were 2.2 million head of beef cattle.

In 1997, there were an estimated 2.4 million cattle and calves, valued at nearly $900 million. During 1996, hogs and pigs numbered around 400,000 and were valued at $34.4 million. In 1995, Tennessee farmers produced 654,000 lb of sheep and lambs, valued at $418,000, and poultry farmers produced 572 million lb of broilers, worth nearly $186 million, and 254 million eggs, valued at $16.7 million. Tennessee dairy farmers produced 1.745 billion lb of milk from some 126,000 milk cows.

25FISHING

Fishing is a major attraction for sport but plays a relatively small role in the economic life of Tennessee. There are 17 TVA lakes and 7 other lakes, all maintained by the Army Corps of Engineers; 10 of these lakes span an area of 10,000 acres (4,000 hectares) or more, and there are thousands of miles of creeks and mountain streams, all of which attract anglers. Tennessee has no closed season, except on trout.

In the 1970s, pollution from industrial waste dumping killed millions of fish and seriously endangered sport fishing. By the 1980s, however, industrial establishments in the state were complying more fully with the 1974 Water Pollution Act. Federal hatcheries distributed 1,150,459 fish (312,877 lb) and 6,390,842 fish eggs within Tennessee in 1995/96, when the state issued 954,148 sport fishing licenses.

26FORESTRY

Forests covered 13,612,000 acres (5,509,000 hectares) in 1992, or about 52% of the state's total land area. Commercial timberlands in 1992 totaled 13,275,000 acres (5,372,000 hectares). In 1992, 86% of the forested area was privately owned, 10% federally owned, 3% state-owned, and 1% municipally owned. The counties of the Cumberland Plateau and Highland Rim are the major sources of timber products, and in Lewis, Perry, Polk, Scott, Sequatchie, Unicoi, and Wayne counties, more than 75% of the total area is commercial forest.

About 89% of Tennessee's timber is in hardwoods, and nearly one-half of that is in white and red oak. Of the softwoods, pine—shortleaf, loblolly, Virginia, pitch, and white—accounts for 80%. Red cedar accounts for about 5% of the softwood supply.

Tennessee produces about $4.8 billion worth of wood products each year. Wood products manufacturing is the state's 4th largest basic industry. Approximately 60,000 Tennesseans are employed in the wood products industry, which has an annual payroll of $880 million and accounts for 1 of every 11 dollars paid to factory workers and managers in Tennessee. The wood products industry in Tennessee falls into three main categories: paper and similar products, employing 36% of the workers and producing 46% of the dollars; lumber and similar products, employing 34% of the workers and producing 30% of the dollars; and furniture, employing 30% of the workers and producing 24% of the dollars. Tennessee leads the nation in the production of hardwood flooring, log homes, and pencils, and is among the top three hardwood-lumber-producing states. Manufacturing uses only about a third of the wood grown by forests in Tennessee each year. The remaining two-thirds continues to accumulate on aging trees or is lost through decomposition of diseased and dead trees. The most common method of cutting timber in Tennessee has long been "high-grading," that is, cutting only the most valuable trees and leaving those of inferior quality and value. Clearcutting, patch cutting, and group selection are silviculturally preferable, but, with the exception of clearcutting on industry lands, are rarely practiced.

27MINING

The 1995 value of nonfuel mineral production in Tennessee increased by over $57 million from that of 1994, to $659 million. The 18% increase followed a previous 18% increase between 1993 and 1994. However, Tennessee's mineral value was still below the record high of $664.6 million established in 1990. Crushed stone and zinc, by value the leading commodities, provided most of the increased nonfuel mineral value in both 1994 and 1995. Nationally, Tennessee continued to rank 18th in the total value of nonfuel minerals produced in 1995. In 1991, Tennessee led the nation in the value of natural gemstones produced, which increased from $23.1 million in 1994 to $35.4 million in 1995. Gemstone production consisted almost entirely of cultured freshwater pearls and mother-of-pearl derived from freshwater mussel shells. Crushed stone has been the leading nonfuel mineral commodity produced in Tennessee since 1981. In 1995, production was 52.2 million metric tons, 6% more than the 49.2 million metric tons produced in 1994. The value of crushed stone produced represented 43.6% ($287,000,000) of the total value of nonfuel minerals produced. Major rock types quarried to produce crushed stone were limestone, dolomite, and sandstone. Zinc, the state's leading nonfuel mineral commodity until 1981, remained the second leading mineral produced. Zinc was mined in Knox and Jefferson counties. Estimated clay production (excluding common, fuller's earth, and kaolin) decreased by almost 12,000 metric tons to 653,000 metric tons. Despite the decrease in production, the estimated value of clay produced climbed from $28.6 million to $29.3 million. The production of construction sand and gravel decreased from 8.7 million metric tons valued at $38 million in 1994 to 7.6 million metric tons valued at $33.4 million in 1995. The quantity of industrial sand and gravel produced increased from 660,000 metric tons to 768,000 metric tons between 1994 and 1995, with respective values of $11.6 and $13.2 million.

28ENERGY AND POWER

The Tennessee Valley Authority (TVA) is the principal supplier of power in the state, providing electricity to more than 100 cities and 50 rural cooperatives. In 1995, Tennessee's installed electrical generating capacity was 18 million kW, virtually all of it publicly owned; electrical output totaled 82.3 billion kWh (99% public). Since electric energy sales amounted to 85.3 billion kWh that year, Tennessee imported about 3.5% of its electricity from neighboring states. There was one nuclear power facility in operation as of December 1996.

Between 1978 and 1995, declining demand for coal, conservationist opposition to surface mining, and other factors led to a drop in coal production from 10 million tons to 3.2 million tons. Reserves in 1995 totaled 68 million tons of recoverable coal. Surface mining, which had marred thousands of acres of land and which accounted for 59% of coal production in 1978, accounted for only 39% by 1995. Surface mine operators are now required to reclaim mined land. Most of the coal mined in the state is used for producing electricity, although some is used for home heating.

Tennessee produced 381,000 barrels of crude oil in 1996; natural gas reserves were negligible. In 1995, Tennessee's gas utilities served 908,678 customers, of whom 89% were residential users. Energy consumption per capita for 1994 was 377.3 million Btu; energy expenditures per capita were $1,971.

29INDUSTRY

On the eve of the Civil War, only 1% of Tennessee's population was employed in manufacturing, mostly in the iron, cotton, lumber, and flour-milling industries. Rapid industrial growth took place during the 20th century, however, and by 1981, Tennessee ranked 3d among the southeastern states and 15th in the US in value of shipments, with $41.3 billion. In 1982, Tennessee's four major metropolitan areas, Memphis, Nashville, Knoxville, and Chattanooga, employed 49% of all the state's industrial workers.

From 1987 to 1992, 54 industrial and commercial machinery manufacturers announced new plant locations in Tennessee while 366 existing companies in the industry expanded plant facilities. The state ranks 4th nationally in auto production. Automotive jobs went from 3,000 in the early 1980s to more than 22,000 jobs in 1996. The state is the leading noncoastal state for foreign investment. Of the total value of shipments for manufactured goods, $96.208 billion in 1995, transportation equipment accounted for $17.718 billion; food and food products, $11.731 billion; chemicals and allied products, $9.038 billion; industrial machinery and equipment, $8.582 billion; electronic and other electric equipment, $6.106 billion; and rubber and plastic products, $5.745 billion.

In 1997, Tennessee was headquarters to four Fortune 500 companies: Columbia/HCA Healthcare, Federal Express, Eastman chemical, and Service Merchandise. During 1995, there were 722 patents issued to Tennessee residents.

30COMMERCE

Tennessee has been an important inland commercial center for some 60 years. In 1992, the state's sales from wholesale trade amounted to $59.7 billion. In 1992, Tennessee's retail sales totaled $37.5 billion (19 in the US). The principal retail groups and their sales percentages were: automotive dealers, 23.6%; food stores, 18.7%; general merchandise stores, 13.9%; and eating and drinking places, 10%. Tennessee's foreign exports of goods originating in the state totaled nearly $8 billion in 1996.

31CONSUMER PROTECTION

The Tennessee Division of Consumer Affairs is a division of the State Department of Commerce and Insurance. Its mission is to serve and protect consumers from deceptive business practices.

The division's activities include consumer complaint mediation, litigation for violations of the Tennessee Consumer Protection Act, consumer education, investigation, registration of health clubs, and influence on legislation.

32BANKING
The first bank in Tennessee was the Bank of Nashville, chartered in 1807. Four years later, the Bank of the State of Tennessee was chartered at Knoxville; branches were established at Nashville, Jonesboro, Clarksville, and Columbia. In 1817, nearly a dozen more banks were chartered in various frontier towns. The Civil War curtailed banking operations, but the industry began again immediately after cessation of hostilities.

In 1996, Tennessee had 240 FDIC-insured commercial banks with total assets of $66.6 billion. The state also had 25 savings institutions with total assets of $6.8 billion, mortgage loans of $3.9 billion, and total deposits of $4.7 billion.

33INSURANCE
In 1995, 35 property/casualty and 31 life insurance companies had home offices in Tennessee. Some 6,786,000 life insurance policies worth $237.8 billion were in force in 1995, when the average Tennessee family held $115,400 in coverage. Some $1,856 million in benefits was paid to Tennesseans during the same year, including $698.3 million in death payments. Property and liability insurers wrote premiums totaling nearly $4.7 billion, of which $1,206.6 million was automobile liability insurance, $844.3 million was automobile physical damage insurance, and $465.8 million was homeowners' coverage.

34SECURITIES
There are no securities exchanges in Tennessee. As of 30 April 1997, 1,435 broker-dealers, 50,159 securites agents, and 435 investment advisers were registered with the Tennessee Department of Commerce.

35PUBLIC FINANCE
The state budget is prepared annually by the Budget Division of the Tennessee Department of Finance and Administration and submitted by the governor to the legislature every January. The fiscal year lasts from 1 July to 30 June.

The following table summarizes estimated general fund revenues and proposed state-funded appropriations for 1995 (in thousands):

REVENUES
Sales and use tax	$3,360,568
Income tax	594,583
Other taxes	2,547,153
Other receipts	6,397,608
TOTAL	$12,899,912

APPROPRIATIONS
Primary and secondary education	$4,302,667
Health and environment	560,550
Corrections	424,429
Other outlays	8,144,728
TOTAL	$13,432,374

36TAXATION
The Tennessee state government ranked 22nd in the US in general revenues in 1995 with $11.5 billion. It was 48th in per capita state and local taxation, however, with an average tax burden in 1995 of $1,123.98.

The major source of general state revenue is a sales and use tax, first levied in 1947; in 1995, the maximum rate was 8.75%, of which the state collected 6% and municipalities up to 2.75%.

Other taxes include a 6% levy on dividend and interest income, a 6% corporate income tax, and levies on inheritances, alcoholic beverages, tobacco, gross receipts, motor vehicle registration, and other items. Tennessee is one of a few states that do not impose a tax on salaries and wages. Counties and municipalities depend on real property taxes as their major source of income.

In 1995, Tennesseans paid approximately $9.5 billion in federal personal income taxes.

37ECONOMIC POLICY
Since World War II, Tennessee has aggressively sought new business and industry. The Department of Economic and Community Development helps prospective firms locate industrial sites in communities throughout the state, and its representatives work with firms in Canada, Europe, and the Far East, as well as with domestic businesses. The department also administers special Appalachian regional programs in 50 counties and directs the state Office of Minority Business Enterprise.

Tennessee's right-to-work law and relatively weak labor movement constitute important industrial incentives. The counties and municipalities, moreover, offer tax exemptions on land, capital improvements, equipment, and machinery. In the early 1980s, two automobile manufacturers were among the Japanese and US firms that established production in Tennessee: Nissan opened a 2,600-employee plant in Smyrna, and General Motors built a plant in Spring Hill, south of Nashville, to produce the Saturn automobile.

38HEALTH
Tennessee's birthrate fell from 23 live births per 1,000 population in 1960 to 13.9 in 1995, when there were 73,173 live births. Between 1982 and 1992, the ratio of legal abortions to live births fell from 372 to 245 for every 1,000 births; about 18,029 legal abortions were performed in 1992. The infant mortality rate in 1995 was 9.6 per 1,000 live births. The HIV/AIDS mortality rate of 9.7 per 100,000 was lower than the US average of 16.4 in 1995. In the same year, the rate of infection was 13.68 per 100,000.

The major causes of death in Tennessee in 1995 (with rates per 100,000 population) were heart disease, 308.2; cancer, 220.9; cerebrovascular diseases, 79.8; accidents, 47.3; and suicide, 13.0. The age-adjusted death rate overall in 1996, 576.3 per 100,000 population, was slightly above the US average. Tennessee was ranked 42nd in cardiovascular disease mortality rate in 1993. Only one other state had a higher cerebrovascular mortality rate than Tennessee in 1995. Of all Tennessee residents aged 18 or older, 27.9% of men and 25.2% of women were regular smokers, for an overall smoking rate of 26.5% in 1995.

There were 126 hospitals, with 19,159 beds, in 1995, and 732,615 patients were admitted. The average expense of hospitals for care per admission in 1994 was $870 per inpatient day and $5,621 per stay, both below the national average. Around 16.6% of Tennessee residents went uninsured in 1995. The nearly 753,000 Medicare and 939,000 Medicaid recipients had $3.7 and $1.9 billion, respectively, paid out for health services in 1994.

Tennessee has four medical schools: two in Nashville (Vanderbilt University and Meharry Medical School), one at Johnson City (East Tennessee State University), and one at Memphis (University of Tennessee). In 1995, the state had 13,301 federal and nonfederal physicians and 2,663 licensed, active dentists.

39SOCIAL WELFARE
Aid to families with dependent children (AFDC) averaged $226 a month per family in 1996, when there were 265,300 eligible residents. In 1996, 637,773 residents received average monthly

food stamp allowances of $70.76; the school lunch program cost the federal government $108.9 million.

With the enactment of the Personal Responsibility and Work Opportunity Reconciliation Act of 1996, the US government has changed the form and regulations for many of its social welfare programs; most significantly, it replaces Aid to Families with Dependent Children (AFDC), an open-ended entitlement program, with Temporary Assistance for Needy Families (TANF), a limited system of assistance funded largely through federal block grants. The reform act also impacts the food stamp program, the Supplemental Security Income program, and the child nutrition program. The law took effect on 1 July 1997 and provided $16.38 billion in block grants for fiscal years 1997–2002. The grants are to be divided among the states based on an equation involving the numbers of former AFDC recipients in each state. Because many of the bill's provisions have yet to be implemented into state-by-state policy, it was not possible to include the details of each state's programs for this edition of this work.

In 1995, Social Security benefits averaging $680 per month were paid to 926,110 Tennesseans. Supplemental Security Income payments were made to 179,676 eligible state residents, averaging $316 per month. Unemployment benefits in Tennessee averaged $150.11 a week in 1995.

40HOUSING

In 1996, there were an estimated 2,184,000 occupied housing units in the state, 2,003,000 of which were owner-occupied. That year, 40,522 privately owned units, valued at $3.3 billion, were authorized for construction in the state; of these, 28,217 were single-family. The median monthly cost for owners with a mortgage payment in 1990 (the last year for which figures are available) was $594; the median value of a home in 1990 was $58,400, up 3.4% from 1980. The median monthly apartment rent in 1990 was $357. During 1995/96, Tennessee received $367.6 million in aid from the US Department of Housing and Urban Development, including $51.8 million in community development block grants.

41EDUCATION

The state assumed responsibility for education in 1873, when the legislature established a permanent school fund and made schools free to all persons between the ages of 6 and 21. In 1917, an eight year elementary and four-year secondary school system was set up. Thirty years later, enactment of the state sales and use tax enabled state authorities to increase teachers' salaries by about 100% and to provide capital funds for a variety of expanded educational programs. In the early 1980s, Tennessee further improved its educational system by offering incentive pay to its teachers. Today, 54% of the consolidated state budget is spent on education.

The 21st Century Schools Program adopted by the Tennessee General Assembly in 1992 has provided K-12 public schools with nearly $1 billion in new state dollars—an increase of 90%. The program repeals 3,700 state rules and regulations, gives communities wide discretion over education decision-making, makes local school systems more accountable for results, and has funded 5,450 high-tech classrooms in Tennessee's public schools. Local school systems are using the new state funds to decrease class size, buy new textbooks for students, furnish supplies for teachers, and provide state-of-the-art technology. In 1996/97, Tennessee pioneered a statewide network connecting every public school to museums, libraries, and databases available on the World Wide Web. The state's high school curriculum prepares every student for college, a technical career, or both. Tennessee's Literacy 2000 initiative (begun in 1987) improved the adult literacy rate by 24% in its first four years. More than two of three

adult Tennesseans hold a high school diploma. Public school expenditures per pupil were $4,713 in 1995/96.

The Department of Education administers 1,562 public schools for grades K-12 and a variety of public educational services. In 1996 there were 875,670 students enrolled in the public elementary schools.

The University of Tennessee system, with principal campuses at Knoxville, Memphis, Martin, and Chattanooga, enrolled some 32,400 students in 1992/93. Components of the State University and Community College System of Tennessee included Memphis State University (the largest, with 20,449 students in 1991/92), Tennessee Technological University at Cookeville, East Tennessee State University at Johnson City, Austin Peay State University at Clarksville, Tennessee State University at Nashville, and Middle Tennessee State University at Murfreesboro, along with 14 two-year community colleges enrolling 73,652 students on campuses throughout the state. Well-known private colleges are Vanderbilt University at Nashville (with 5,547 students in 1992/93), the University of the South at Sewanee (1,142), and Rhodes College at Memphis (1,414). Vanderbilt has schools of medicine, law, divinity, nursing, business, and education, as well as an undergraduate program. Loan and grant programs are administered by the Tennessee Student Assistance Corporation.

42ARTS

Each of Tennessee's major cities has a symphony orchestra. The best known are the Memphis Symphony and the Nashville Symphony, the latter of which makes its home in the Tennessee Performing Arts Center. Included in this complex are three performing arts theaters and the State Museum. The major operatic troupes are Opera Memphis, Nashville Opera, and Knoxville Opera. Nashville is known as "Music City, USA"; the Grand Ole Opry, Country Music Hall of Fame, Ryman Auditorium, and numerous recording studios are located there. Among the leading art galleries are the Dixon Gallery and the Brooks Museum of Art in Memphis, the Cheekwood Museum of Art in Nashville, the Knoxville Museum of Art, and the Hunter Museum of Art in Chattanooga. Professional dance and theater groups are located in both urban and rural areas.

Arts program funds for the state of Tennessee totaled more than $25 million for 1987–1996, with federal, state, and private-sector funds. The state's arts programs attract a total audience of more than 5 million each year. The Tennessee Arts Commission, in partnership with the Tennessee Department of Education and the Tennessee Performing Arts Center, offers arts education programs to one-third of the state's 900,000 public school students. In 1996, Tennessee had more than 300 arts groups. The Tennessee Arts Commission provided support for such groups as the Tennessee Repertory Theatre, the Fort Sanders Education Development Center of Knoxville, and the West Tennessee Regional Art Center. The NEA has also recently provided funding recently for the Jellico Children's Theatre ($5,000) and the Jubilee Community Arts ($25,000). The Memphis Arts Council is active in promoting the cultural and economic growth of the city. Members help to encourage new businesses to relocate in Memphis based on the city's cultural advantages. Similar groups work in Tennessee's other urban centers, as well as dozens of suburban and rural areas. In 1997, the Tennessee Arts Commission received $53,500 from the NEA to support the state's arts education programs. The commission also received $354,000 from the NEA.

43LIBRARIES AND MUSEUMS

Libraries and library associations were formed soon after Tennessee became a state. The Dickson Library at Charlotte was founded in 1811, and the Nashville Library Company in 1813. Not until 1854, however, was the first state-maintained library established. Andrew Johnson, the governor, requested a library appropriation of $5,000, telling legislators that he wanted other Tennesseans to have the opportunities that had been denied him. Today, the institution he founded, the State Library at Nashville, with more than 540,741 volumes, has a renowned collection of state materials and is the repository for state records. In all, there are more than 190 public libraries and nearly 82 academic libraries in Tennessee. Their combined book stock exceeds 7.6 million, and their total circulation is over 18.1 million volumes. The largest libraries are the Vanderbilt University Library at Nashville (2,026,237 volumes), Memphis-Shelby County Library (1,676,931), Memphis State University Libraries (975,071), University of Tennessee at Knoxville Library (925,180), Knoxville-Knox County Library (560,159), Chattanooga-Hamilton County Library (381,928), and East Tennessee State University Library at Johnson City (536,403).

Tennessee has more than 109 museums and historic sites. The Tennessee State Museum in Nashville displays exhibits on pioneer life, military traditions, evangelical religion, and presidential lore. The Museum of Appalachia, near Norris, attempts an authentic replica of early Appalachian life, with more than 20,000 pioneer relics on display in several log cabins. Displays of solar, nuclear, and other energy technologies are featured at the American Museum of Science and Energy, at Oak Ridge. There are floral collections at the Goldsmith Civic Garden Center in Memphis and the Tennessee Botanical Gardens and Fine Arts Center in Nashville.

44COMMUNICATIONS

The first postal service across the state, by stagecoach, began operations in the early 1790s.

As of March 1993, 92.8% of Tennessee's 2,006,000 occupied housing units had telephones.

Tennessee had 172 AM stations and 178 FM stations in 1996. There were 35 television stations in operation in 1993, including 7 noncommercial educational stations. In 1996, 12 large cable systems served the state.

45PRESS

In 1997, there were 12 morning newspapers, 15 evening dailies, and 13 Sunday papers. The following table lists leading Tennessee newspapers with their daily circulation in 1994:

AREA	NAME	DAILY	SUNDAY
Chattanooga	*News-Free Press* (e,S)	41,696	115,549
Knoxville	*News-Sentinel* (e,S)	119,529	174,375
Memphis	*Commercial Appeal* (m,S)	178,181	267,935
Nashville	*Banner* (e)	49,478	—
	Tennessean (m,S)	149,292	284,571

Several dozen trade publications, such as *Southern Lumberman*, appear in Nashville, the state's major publishing center, where there is also a thriving religious publishing industry.

46ORGANIZATIONS

The 1992 US Census of Service Industries counted 1,258 organizations in Tennessee, including 252 business associations; 678 civic, social, and fraternal associations; and 328 other membership organizations.

Nashville is a center for Tennessee cultural and educational organizations. Among them are the American Association for State and Local History, Country Music Association, and Gospel Music Association.

Several national and regional trade associations are based in Tennessee, including the Walking Horse Breeders' and Exhibitors' Association (Lewisburg) and the Walking Horse Trainers' Association (Shelbyville). Knoxville is the headquarters of the Burley (Tobacco) Stabilization Corporation, and Springfield is the home of the Eastern Dark-Fired Tobacco Growers Association. The offices of the Southern Cotton Association, National Cotton Council of America, and Southern Hardwood Lumber Manufacturing Association are in Memphis, as is the headquarters of the American Contract Bridge League.

47TOURISM, TRAVEL, AND RECREATION

The natural beauty of Tennessee, combined with the activity of the Department of Tourist Development, has made tourism a major industry in the state. Tennessee was the first state to create a government department devoted solely to the promotion of tourism. In 1991/92, the state spent $7.7 million to attract tourists. In 1993, domestic visitors spent $6,779,000 on day trips and overnight stays in the state.

Leading tourist attractions include Fort Loudoun, built by the British in 1757; the American Museum of Science and Energy at Oak Ridge; the William Blount Mansion at Knoxville; the Beale Street Historic District in Memphis, home of W. C. Handy, the "father of the blues"; Graceland, the Memphis estate of Elvis Presley; and Opryland USA and the Grand Ole Opry at Nashville. There are three presidential homes—Andrew Johnson's at Greeneville, Andrew Jackson's Hermitage near Nashville, and James K. Polk's at Columbia. Pinson Mounds, near Jackson, offers outstanding archaeological treasures and the remains of an Indian city. Reservoirs and lakes attract thousands of anglers and water sports enthusiasts.

There are 33 state parks, almost all of which have camping facilities. Altogether, they cover 88,160 acres (35,678 hectares). Among the most visited state parks are the Meeman-Shelby Forest in Shelby County, Montgomery Bell in Dickson County, Cedars of Lebanon in Wilson County, and Natchez Trace in Henderson and Carroll counties. Extending from North Carolina, the Great Smoky Mountains National Park covers 241,207 acres (97,613 hectares) in Tennessee and drew nearly 5 million visitors in 1995.

Licenses were held by 928,058 hunters and 1,170,503 fishermen in 1995.

48SPORTS

Tennessee has one major league professional sports team, the National Football League's Oilers, who relocated to Nashville from Houston before the 1997 season. Nashville has also been awarded a National Hockey League expansion franchise, which will begin play in the city's new arena in 1999. Minor league baseball teams that compete in the Class-AAA Southern League are the Knoxville Vols, Chattanooga Lookouts, and Memphis Chicks.

Tennessee's colleges and universities provide the major fall and winter sports. The University of Tennessee Volunteers and Vanderbilt University Commodores, in the Southeastern Conference, compete in football, basketball, and baseball. Austin Peay and Tennessee Technological universities belong to the Ohio Valley Conference. The University of Tennessee won the Sugar Bowl in 1943, 1971, 1986, and 1991. The Volunteers were named national champions in 1951. The University of Tennessee's women's basketball team, the Lady Vols, won NCAA titles in 1987, 1989, 1991, 1996, and 1997. Other annual sporting events include the Iroquois steeplechase in Nashville in May.

49FAMOUS TENNESSEANS

Andrew Jackson (b.South Carolina, 1767–1845), the 7th president, moved to Tennessee as a young man. He won renown in the War of 1812 and became the first Democratic president in 1828. Jackson's close friend and associate, James Knox Polk (b.North Carolina, 1795–1849), came to Tennessee at the age of 10. He was elected the nation's 11th president in 1844 and served one term. Andrew Johnson (b.North Carolina, 1808–75) also a Democrat, remained loyal to the Union during the Civil War and was elected vice president with Abraham Lincoln in 1864. He became president upon Lincoln's assassination in 1865 and served out his predecessor's second term. Impeached because of a dispute over Reconstruction policies and presidential power, Johnson escaped conviction by one vote in 1868. Albert Gore, Jr. (b.Washington, D.C., 1948), was elected vice president in 1992 and 1996 on the Democratic ticket with Bill Clinton; Gore, whose father was a prominent US senator from Tennessee, had previously served in the Senate as well.

Supreme Court justices from Tennessee include John Catron (b.Pennsylvania, 1786–1865), Howell Jackson (1832–95), James C. McReynolds (b.Kentucky, 1862–1946), and Edward T. Sanford (1865–1930). Tennesseans who became cabinet officials include Secretary of State Cordell Hull (1871–1955), secretaries of war John Eaton (1790–1856) and John Bell (1797–1869), Secretary of the Treasury George Campbell (b.Scotland, 1769–1848), and attorneys general Felix Grundy (b.Virginia, 1777–1840) and James C. McReynolds.

Other nationally prominent political figures from Tennessee are Cary Estes Kefauver (1903–63), two-term US senator who ran unsuccessfully for vice president in 1956 on the Democratic ticket; Albert Gore (b.1907), three-term member of the US Senate; and Howard Baker (b.1925), who in 1966 became the first popularly elected Republican senator in Tennessee history. Three Tennesseans have been speaker of the US House of Representatives: James K. Polk, John Bell, and Joseph W. Byrns (1869–1936). Nancy Ward (1738–1822) was an outstanding Cherokee leader, and Sue Shelton White (1887–1943) played a major role in the campaign for women's suffrage.

Tennessee history features several military leaders and combat heroes. John Sevier (b.Virginia, 1745–1815), the first governor of the state, defeated British troops at Kings Mountain in the Revolution. David "Davy" Crockett (1786–1836) was a frontiersman who fought the British with Jackson in the War of 1812. Sam Houston (b.Virginia, 1793–1863) also fought in the War of 1812 and was governor of Tennessee before migrating to Texas. Nathan Bedford Forrest (1821–77) and Sam Davis (1842–63) were heroes of the Civil War. Sergeant Alvin C. York (1887–1964) won the Medal of Honor for his bravery in World War I.

Cordell Hull was awarded the Nobel Peace Prize in 1945 for his work on behalf of the United Nations. In 1971, Earl W. Sutherland, Jr. (b.Kansas 1915–75), a biomedical scientist at Vanderbilt University, won a Nobel Prize for his discoveries concerning the mechanisms of hormones. Outstanding educators include Philip Lindsey (1786–1855), a Presbyterian minister and first president of the University of Nashville, and Alexander Heard (b.Georgia, 1917), nationally known political scientist and chancellor of Vanderbilt University.

Famous Tennessee writers are Mary Noailles Murfree (1850–1922), who used the pseudonym Charles Egbert Craddock; influential poet and critic John Crowe Ransom (1888–1974); author and critic James Agee (1909–55), posthumously awarded a Pulitzer Prize for his novel *A Death in the Family;* poet Randall Jarrell (1914–65), winner of two National Book Awards; and Wilma Dykeman (b.1920), novelist and historian. Peter Taylor

(Trenton, Tenn., 1917–94) won a Pulitzer in 1987 for *A Summons to Memphis.* Sportswriter Grantland Rice (1880–1954) was born in Murfreesboro.

Tennessee has long been a center of popular music. Musician and songwriter William C. Handy (1873–1958) wrote "St Louis Blues" and "Memphis Blues," among other classics. Bessie Smith (1898?–1937) was a leading blues singer. Elvis Presley (b.Mississippi, 1935–77) fused rhythm-and-blues with country-and-western styles to become one of the most popular entertainers in US history. Other Tennessee-born singers are Dinah Shore (1917–1994), Aretha Franklin (b.1942), and Dolly Parton (b.1946). Morgan Freeman, star of movies including *Driving Miss Daisy,* was born in Memphis in 1937.

50BIBLIOGRAPHY

Abernethy, Thomas P. *From Frontier to Plantation in Tennessee.* Reprint. Westport, CT: Greenwood Press, 1979 (orig. 1932).

Atkins, Jonathan M. *Parties, Politics, and the Sectional Conflict in Tennessee, 1832–1861.* Knoxville: University of Tennessee Press, 1997.

Connelly, T. L. *Civil War Tennessee: Battles and Leaders.* Knoxville: University of Tennessee Press, 1979.

Corlew, Robert E. *Statehood for Tennessee.* Nashville: Tennessee Bicentennial Commission, 1976.

———. *Tennessee: A Short History.* 2d ed. Knoxville: University of Tennessee Press, 1981.

Dykeman, Wilma. *Tennessee: A Bicentennial History.* New York: Norton, 1975.

Federal Writers' Project: *Tennessee: A Guide to the State.* New York: Somerset, n.d. (orig. 1939).

Folmsbee, Stanley J., Robert E. Crolew, and Enoch Mitchell. *History of Tennessee.* 4 vols. New York: Lewis, 1960.

Goehring, Eleanor E. *Tennessee Folk Culture: An Annotated Bibliography.* Knoxville: University of Tennessee Press, 1982.

Greene, Lee S., et al. *Government in Tennessee.* 4th ed. Knoxville: University of Tennessee Press, 1982.

Hsiung, David C. *Two Worlds in the Tennessee Mountains: Exploring the Origins of Appalachian Stereotypes.* Lexington: University Press of Kentucky, 1997

Hubbard, Preston. *Origins of the TVA.* New York: Norton, 1968.

Lewis, Thomas M. N., and Madeline Kneberg. *Tribes That Slumber: Indians of the Tennessee Region.* Knoxville: University of Tennessee Press, 1958.

Mooney, Chase. *Slavery in Tennessee.* Bloomington: Indiana University Press, 1957.

Patterson, Christine P. *Haunting Memories: Echoes and Images of Tennessee's Past.* Knoxville: University of Tennessee Press, 1996.

Smith, Samuel B., ed. *Tennessee History: A Bibliography.* Knoxville: University of Tennessee Press, 1974.

Tennessee, State of. Secretary of State. *Tennessee Blue Book 1983/84.* Nashville, 1983.

Tennessee, University of. College of Business Administration. Center for Business and Economic Research. *Tennessee Statistical Abstract 1984/85.* Knoxville, 1984.

TEXAS

State of Texas

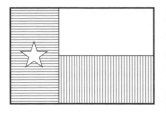

ORIGIN OF STATE NAME: Derived from the Caddo word *tavshas,* meaning "allies" or "friends." **NICKNAME:** The Lone Star State. **CAPITAL:** Austin. **ENTERED UNION:** 29 December 1845 (28th). **SONG:** "Texas, Our Texas." **ALSO:** "The Eyes of Texas." **MOTTO:** Friendship. **FLAG:** At the hoist is a vertical bar of blue with a single white five-pointed star; two horizontal bars of white and red cover the remainder of the flag. **OFFICIAL SEAL:** A five-pointed star encircled by olive and live oak branches, with the words "The State of Texas" surrounding. **BIRD:** Mockingbird. **FISH:** Guadalupe bass. **FLOWER:** Bluebonnet. **TREE:** Pecan. **GRASS:** Sideoats grama. **DISH:** Chili. **GEM:** Topaz. **STONE:** Petrified palmwood. **SEASHELL:** Lightning whelk. **LEGAL HOLIDAYS:** New Year's Day, 1 January; Confederate Heroes Day, 19 January; Birthday of Martin Luther King, Jr., 3d Monday in January; Washington's Birthday, 3d Monday in February; Texas Independence Day, 2 March: San Jacinto Day, 21 April; Memorial Day, last Monday in May; Emancipation Day, 19 June; Independence Day, 4 July; Lyndon B. Johnson's Birthday, 27 August; Labor Day, 1st Monday in September; Columbus Day, 2d Monday in October; General Election Day, 1st Tuesday after 1st Monday in November; Veterans Day, 11 November; Thanksgiving Day, 4th Thursday in November; Christmas Day, 25 December. **TIME:** 6 AM CST = noon GMT.

¹LOCATION, SIZE, AND EXTENT

Located in the west south-central US, Texas is the largest of the 48 conterminous states. Texas's US rank slipped to 2d when Alaska entered the Union in 1959.

The total area of Texas is 266,807 sq mi (691,030 sq km), of which land comprises 262,017 sq mi (678,624 sq km) and inland water 4,790 sq mi (12,406 sq km). The state's land area represents 8.8% of the US mainland and 7.4% of the nation as a whole. The state's maximum E-W extension is 801 mi (1,289 km); its extreme N-S distance is 773 mi (1,244 km).

Texas is bordered on the N by Oklahoma and Arkansas (with part of the line formed by the Red River); on the E by Arkansas and Louisiana (with part of the Louisiana line defined by the Sabine River); on the SE by the Gulf of Mexico; on the SW by the Mexican states of Tamaulipas, Nuevo León, Coahuila, and Chihuahua (with the line formed by the Rio Grande); and on the W by New Mexico. The state's geographic center is in McCulloch County, 15 mi (24 km) NE of Brady.

Large islands in the Gulf of Mexico belonging to Texas are Galveston, Matagorda, and Padre. The boundary length of the state totals 3,029 mi (4,875 km), including a general Gulf of Mexico coastline of 367 mi (591 km); the tidal shoreline is 3,359 mi (5,406 km).

²TOPOGRAPHY

Texas's major physiographic divisions are the Gulf Coastal Plain in the east and southeast; the North Central Plains, covering most of central Texas; the Great Plains, extending from west-central Texas up into the panhandle; and the mountainous trans-Pecos area in the extreme west.

Within the Gulf Coastal Plain are the Piney Woods, an extension of western Louisiana that introduces into East Texas for about 125 mi (200 km), and the Post Oak Belt, a flat region of mixed soil that gives way to the rolling prairie of the Blackland Belt, the state's most densely populated region. The Balcones Escarpment (so-called by the Spanish because its sharp profile suggests a balcony), a geological fault line running from the Rio Grande near Del Rio across central Texas, separates the Gulf Coastal Plain and Rio Grande Plain from the North Central

Plains and south-central Hill Country, and in so doing, divides East Texas from West Texas, watered Texas from dry Texas, and (culturally speaking) the Old South from the burgeoning West.

The North Central Plains extend from the Blackland Belt to the Cap Rock Escarpment, a natural boundary carved by erosion to heights of nearly 1,000 feet (300 meters) in some places. Much of this plains region is rolling prairie, but the dude ranches of the Hill Country and the mineral-rich Burnet-Llano Basin are also found here. West of the Cap Rock Escarpment are the Great Plains, stretching north–south from the Panhandle Plains to the Edwards Plateau, just north of the Balcones Escarpment. Along the western edge of the panhandle and extending into New Mexico is the Llano Estacado (Staked Plains), an extension of the High Plains lying east of the base of the Rocky Mountains.

The trans-Pecos region, between the Pecos River and the Rio Grande, contains the highest point in the state: Guadalupe Peak, with an altitude of 8,751 feet (2,667 meters), part of the Guadalupe Range extending southward from New Mexico into western Texas for about 20 mi (32 km). Also in the trans-Pecos region is the Diablo Plateau, which has no runoff to the sea and holds its scant water in lakes that often evaporate entirely. Farther south are the Davis Mountains, with a number of peaks rising above 7,000 feet (2,100 meters), and Big Bend country (surrounded on three sides by the Rio Grande), whose canyons sometimes reach depths of nearly 2,000 feet (600 meters). The Chisos Mountains, also exceeding 7,000 feet (2,100 meters) at some points stand just north and west of the Rio Grande.

For its vast expanse, Texas boasts few natural lakes. Caddo Lake, which lies in Texas and Louisiana, is the state's largest natural lake, though its present length of 20 mi (32 km) includes waters added by dam construction in Louisiana. Two artificial reservoirs—Amistad (shared with Mexico), near Del Rio, and Toledo Bend (shared with Louisiana) on the Sabine River—have respective storage capacities exceeding 3 million and 4 million acre-feet, and the Sam Rayburn Reservoir (covering 179 sq mi/ 464 sq km) has a capacity of 2.9 million acre-feet. All together, the state contains close to 200 major reservoirs, eight of which can store more than 1 million acre-feet of water. From the air,

Texas looks as well-watered as Minnesota, but the lakes are artificial and much of the soil is dry.

One reason Texas has so many reservoirs is that it is blessed with a number of major river systems, although none is navigable for more than 50 mi (80 km) inland. Starting from the west, the Rio Grande, a majestic stream in some places but a trickling trough in others, imparts life to the Texas desert and serves as the international boundary with Mexico. Its total length of 1,896 mi (3,051 km), including segments in Colorado and New Mexico, makes the Rio Grande the nation's 2d-longest river, exceeded only by the Missouri-Mississippi river system. The Colorado River is the longest river wholly within the state, extending about 600 mi (970 km) on its journey across central and southeastern Texas to the Gulf of Mexico. Other important rivers include the Nueces, in whose brushy valley the range cattle industry began; the San Antonio, which stems from springs within the present city limits and flows, like most Texas rivers, to the Gulf of Mexico; the Brazos, which rises in New Mexico and stretches diagonally for about 840 mi (1,350 km) across Texas; the Trinity, which serves Ft. Worth and Dallas; the San Jacinto, a short river but one of the most heavily trafficked in North America, overlapping the Houston Ship Channel, which connects the Port of Houston with the Gulf; the Neches, which makes an ocean port out of Beaumont; the Sabine, which has the largest water discharge (6,800,000 acre-feet) at its mouth of any Texas river; the Red, forming part of the northern boundary; and the Canadian, which crosses the Texas panhandle from New Mexico to Oklahoma, bringing moisture to the cattle raisers and wheat growers of that region. In all, Texas has about 3,700 identifiable streams, many of which dry up in the summer and flood during periods of rainfall.

Because of its extensive outcroppings of limestone, extending westward from the Balcones Escarpment, Texas contains a maze of caverns. Among the better-known caves are Longhorn Cavern in Burnet County; Wonder Cave, near San Marcos; the Caverns of Sonora, at Sonora; and Jack Pit Cave, in Menard County, which, with 19,000 feet (5,800 meters) of passages, is the most extensive cave yet mapped in the state.

About 1 billion years ago, shallow seas covered much of Texas. After the seas receded, the land dropped gradually over millions of years, leaving a thick sediment that was then compressed into a long mountain range called the Ouachita Fold Belt. The sea was eventually restricted to a zone in West Texas called the Permian Basin, a giant evaporation pan holding gypsum and salt deposits hundreds of feet deep. As the mountain chain across central Texas eroded and the land continued to subside, the Rocky Mountains were uplifted, leaving deep cuts in Big Bend country and creating the Llano Estacado. The Gulf of Mexico subsided rapidly, depositing sediment accumulations several thousand feet deep, while salt domes formed over vast petroleum and sulfur deposits. All this geologic activity also deposited quicksilver in the Terlingua section of the Big Bend, built up the Horseshoe Atoll (a buried reef in west-central Texas that is the largest limestone reservoir in the nation), created uranium deposits in southern Texas, and preserved the oil-bearing Jurassic rocks of the northeast.

³CLIMATE

Texas's great size and topographic variety make climatic description difficult. Brownsville, at the mouth of the Rio Grande, has had no measurable snowfall during all the years that records have been kept, but Vega, in the panhandle, averages 23 in (58 cm) of snowfall a year. Near the Louisiana border, rainfall exceeds 56 in (142 cm) annually, while in parts of extreme West Texas, rainfall averages less than 8 in (20 cm).

Generally, a maritime climate prevails along the Gulf coast, with continental conditions inland; the Balcones Escarpment is the main dividing line between the two zones, but they are not completely isolated from each other's influence. Texas has two basic seasons—a hot summer that may last from April through October, and a winter that starts in November and usually lasts until March. When summer ends, the state is too dry for autumn foliage, except in East Texas. Temperatures in El Paso, in the southwest, range from a mean January minimum of 29°F (−2°C) to a mean July maximum of 96°F (36°C); at Amarillo, in the panhandle, from 23°F (−5°C) in January to 91°F (33°C) in July; and at Galveston, on the Gulf, from 48°F (9°C) in January to 88°F (31°C) in August. Perhaps the most startling contrast is in relative humidity, averaging 34% at noon in El Paso, 44% in Amarillo, and 72% in Galveston. In the Texas panhandle, the average date of the first freeze is 1 November; in the lower Rio Grande Valley, 16 December. The last freeze arrives in the panhandle on 15 April, and in the lower Rio Grande Valley on 30 January. The valley thus falls only six weeks short of having a 12-month growing season, while the panhandle approximates the growing season of the upper Midwest.

Record temperatures range from −23°F (−31°C) at Seminole, on 8 February 1933, to 120°F (49°C) at Seymour in north-central Texas on 12 August 1936. The greatest annual rainfall was 109 in (277 cm), measured in 1873 at Clarksville, just below the Red River in northeast Texas; the least annual rainfall, 1.786 in (4.47 cm), was recorded at Wink, near the New Mexico line, in 1956. Thrall, in central Texas, received 38.2 in (97 cm) of rain in 24 hours on 9–10 September 1921. Alvin, in Brazoria County on the Gulf Coast, had 43 in (109 cm) of rain on 25–26 July 1979, a national record for the most rainfall during a 24-hour period. Romero, on the New Mexico border, received a record 65 in (165 cm) of snow in the winter of 1923/24, and Hale Center, near Lubbock, measured 33 in (84 cm) during one storm in February 1956. The highest sustained wind velocity in Texas history, 145 mph (233 km/hr), occurred when Hurricane Carla hit Matagorda and Port Lavaca along the Gulf coast on 11 September 1961.

Hurricanes strike the Gulf coast about once every decade, usually in September or October. A hurricane on 19–20 August 1886 leveled the port of Indianola; the town (near present-day Port Lavaca) was never rebuilt. Galveston was the site of the most destructive storm in US history: on 8–9 September 1900, a hurricane blew across the island of 38,000 residents, leaving at least 6,000 dead (the exact total has never been ascertained) and leveling most of the city. A storm of equal intensity hit Galveston in mid-August 1915, but this time, the city was prepared; its new seawall held the toll to 275 deaths and $50 million worth of property damage. Because of well-planned damage-prevention and evacuation procedures, Hurricane Carla—at least as powerful as any previous hurricane—claimed no more than 34 lives. More recent hurricanes have frequently passed over the coastal area with no loss of life at all. Texas also lies in the path of "Tornado Alley," stretching across the Great Plains to Canada. The worst tornado in recent decades struck downtown Waco on 11 May 1953, killing 114 persons, injuring another 597, and destroying or damaging some 1,050 homes and 685 buildings. At least 115 tornadoes—the greatest concentration on record—occurred with Hurricane Beulah during 19–23 September 1967; the 67 tornadoes on 20 September set a record for the largest number of tornadoes on one day in the state. Texas had a total of 232 tornadoes during 1995.

Floods and droughts have also taken their toll in Texas. The worst flood occurred on 26–28 June 1954, when Hurricane Alice moved inland up the Rio Grande for several hundred miles, dropping 27 in (69 cm) of rain on Pandale above Del Rio. The Rio Grande rose 50 to 60 feet (15–18 meters) within 48 hours, as a wall of water 86 feet (26 meters) high in the Pecos River canyon fed it from the north. A Pecos River bridge built with a 50-foot (15-meter) clearance was washed out, as was the international

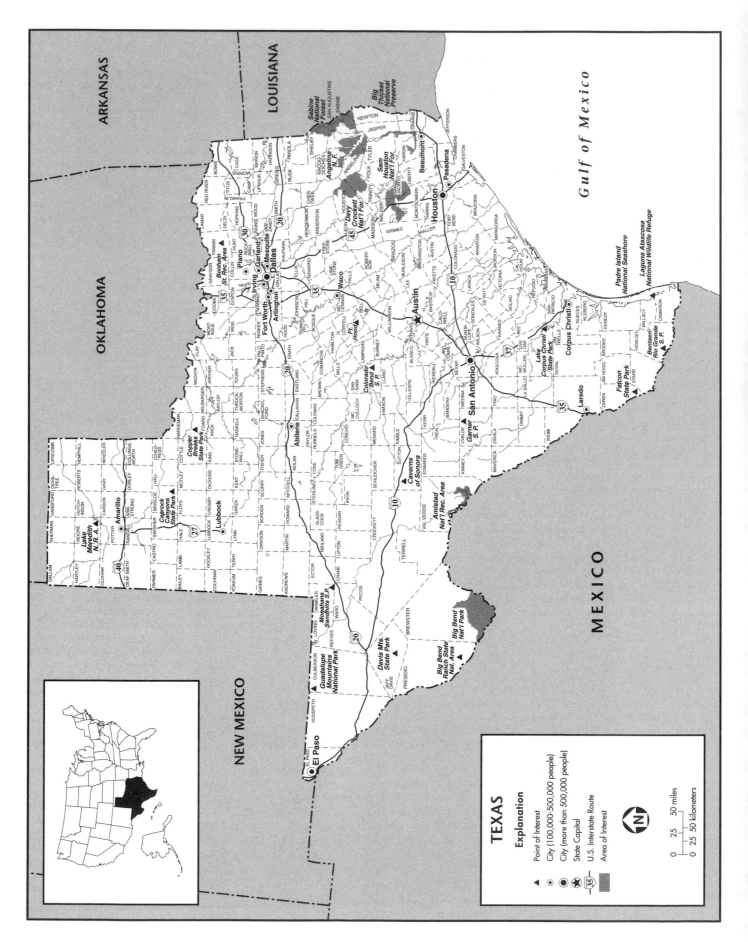

ARKANSAS

LOUISIANA

Gulf of Mexico

OKLAHOMA

MEXICO

NEW MEXICO

TEXAS

Explanation

▲ Point of Interest

⊙ City (100,000-500,000 people)

◉ City (more than 500,000 people)

★ State Capital

U.S. Interstate Route

Area of Interest

0   25   50 miles
0   25   50 kilometers

N

bridge linking Laredo with Mexico. Periodic droughts afflicted Texas in the 1930s and 1950s.

4FLORA AND FAUNA

More than 500 species of grasses covered Texas when the Spanish and Anglo-Americans arrived. Although plowing and lack of soil conservation destroyed a considerable portion of this rich heritage, grassy pastureland still covers about two-thirds of the state. Bermuda grass is a favorite ground cover, especially an improved type called Coastal Bermuda, introduced after World War II. The prickly pear cactus is a mixed blessing: like the cedar and mesquite, it saps moisture and inhibits grass growth, but it does retain moisture in periods of drought and will survive the worst dry spells, so that (with the spines burned off) it can be of great value to ranchers as cattle feed in difficult times. The bean of the mesquite also provides food for horses and cattle when they have little else to eat, and its wood is a favorite in barbecues and fireplaces.

Texas has more than 20 native trees, of which the catclaw, flowering mimosa, huisache, black persimmon, huajillo, and weeping juniper (unique to the Big Bend) are common only in Texas. Cottonwood grows along streams in almost every part of the state, while cypress inhabits the swamps. The flowering dogwood in East Texas draws tourists to that region every spring, and the largest bois d'arc trees in the US are grown in the Red River Valley. Probably the most popular shade tree is the American (white) elm, which, like the gum tree, has considerable commercial importance. The magnolia is treasured for its grace and beauty; no home of substance in southeastern Texas would have a lawn without one. Of the principal hardwoods, the white oak is the most commercially valuable, the post oak the most common, and the live oak the most desirable for shade; the pecan is the state tree. Pines grow in two areas about 600 mi (970 km) apart—deep East Texas and the trans-Pecos region. In southeast Texas stands the Big Thicket, a unique area originally covering more than 3 million acres (1.2 million hectares) but now reduced to about one-tenth that by lumbering. Gonzales County, in south-central Texas, is the home of palmettos, orchids, and other semitropical plants not found anywhere else in the state. Texas wild rice and several cactus species are classified as endangered throughout the state.

Possibly the rarest mammal in Texas is the red wolf, which inhabits the marshland between Houston and Beaumont, one of the most thickly settled areas of the state; owing to human encroachment and possible hybridization with coyotes, the red wolf is steadily disappearing despite efforts by naturalists throughout the US to save it. On the other hand, Texans claim to have the largest number of white-tailed deer of any state in the Union, an estimated 3 million. Although the Hill Country is the white-tailed deer's natural habitat, the species has been transplanted successfully throughout the state.

Perhaps the most unusual mammal in Texas is the nine-banded armadillo. Originally confined to the Rio Grande border, the armadillo has gradually spread northward and eastward, crossing the Red River into Oklahoma and the Mississippi River into the Deep South. It accomplished these feats of transport by sucking in air until it becomes buoyant and then swimming across the water. The armadillo is likewise notable for always having its young in litters of identical quadruplets. The chief mammalian predators are the coyote, bobcat, and mountain lion.

Texas attracts more than 825 different kinds of birds, with bird life most abundant in the lower Rio Grande Valley and coastal plains. Argument continues as to whether Texas is the last home of the ivory-billed woodpecker, which lives in inaccessible swamps, preferably in cutover timber. Somewhat less rare is the pileated woodpecker, which also inhabits the forested lowlands. Other characteristic birds include the yellow-trimmed hooded warbler, which frequents the canebrakes and produces one of the most melodious songs of any Texas bird; the scissor-tailed flycatcher, known popularly as the scissor-tail; Attwater's greater prairie chicken, now declining because of inadequate protection from hunters and urbanization; the mockingbird, the state bird; and the roadrunner, also known as paisano and chaparral. Rare birds include the Mexican jacana, with a flesh comb and bright yellow-green wings; the white-throated swift, one of the world's fastest flyers; the Texas canyon wren, with a musical range of more than an octave; and the Colima warbler, which breeds only in the Chisos Mountains. In the Aransas National Wildlife Refuge, along the central Gulf coast, lives the whooping crane, which has long been on the endangered list. Controversy surrounds the golden eagle, protected by federal law but despised by ranchers for allegedly preying on lambs and other young livestock.

Texas has its fair share of reptiles, including more than 100 species of snake, 16 of them poisonous, notably the deadly Texas coral snake. There are 10 kinds of rattlesnake, and some parts of West Texas hold annual rattlesnake roundups. Disappearing with the onset of urbanization are the horned toad, a small iguana-like lizard; the vinegarroon, a stinging scorpion; and the tarantula, a large, black, hairy spider that is scary to behold but basically harmless.

In addition to providing protection for the animals on federal lists of threatened and endangered species, the state has its own wildlife protection programs. Among the animals classified as non-game (not hunted) and therefore given special consideration are the lesser yellow bat, spotted dolphin, reddish egret, white-tailed hawk, wood stork, Big Bend gecko, rock rattlesnake, Louisiana pine snake, white-lipped frog, giant toad, toothless blindcat, and blue sucker. Along with the red wolf, Attwater's greater prairie chicken, and ivory-billed woodpecker, endangered species include the American alligator, jaguar, ocelot, Eskimo curlew, Houston toad, Big Bend gambusia, Comanche Springs pupfish, and fountain darter.

Texas has 15 National Wildlife Refuges, with a total of 302,731 acres (122,511 hectares). The Texas Parks and Wildlife Department administers an additional 19 wildlife management areas.

5ENVIRONMENTAL PROTECTION

Conservation in Texas officially began with the creation of a State Department of Forestry in 1915; 11 years later, this body was reorganized as the Texas Forest Service, the name it retains today. The state's Soil Conservation Service was created in 1935.

The scarcity of water is the one environmental crisis every Texan must live with. Much of the state has absorbent soils, a high evaporation rate, vast areas without trees to hold moisture, and a rolling terrain susceptible to rapid runoff. The Texas Water Commission and Water Development Board direct the state's water supply and conservation programs. Various county and regional water authorities have been constituted, as have several water commissions for river systems. Probably the most complete system is that of the three Colorado River authorities—lower, central, and upper. The oldest of these is the Lower Colorado River Authority, created in 1934 by the Texas legislature to "control, store, preserve, and distribute" the waters of the Colorado River and its feeder streams. The authority exercises control over a 10-county area stretching from above Austin to the Gulf coast, overseeing flood control, municipal and industrial water supplies, irrigation, hydroelectric power generation, soil conservation, and recreation.

The most powerful conservation agency in Texas is the Railroad Commission. Originally established to regulate railroads, the commission extended its power to regulate oil and natural gas by virtue of its jurisdiction over the transportation of those products by rail and pipeline. In 1917, the state legislature empowered the commission to prevent the waste of oil and gas. The key step in conservation arrived with the discovery of oil in East Texas in 1930. With a national depression in full swing and the price of oil dropping to $1 a barrel, the commission agreed to halt ruinous overproduction, issuing the first proration order in April 1931. In a field composed of hundreds of small ownerships, however, control was difficult to establish; oil was bootlegged, the commission's authority broke down, Governor Ross S. Sterling declared martial law, and the state's conservation edicts were not heeded until the federal government stepped in to enforce them. Today, the Railroad Commission acts to eliminate wasteful drilling procedures and decides which equipment and techniques are permissible. In addition, the commission requires careful accounting of all production and sales.

As in other states, hazardous wastes have become an environmental concern in Texas. In 1984, for example, a suit was brought against eight oil and chemical companies, including both Exxon and Shell Oil, alleging that they had dumped hazardous wastes at four sites in Harris County. The agency that oversees compliance with hazardous-waste statutes is the Hazardous and Solid Waste Division of the Texas Water Commission. In 1995, Texas had 27 hazardous waste sites. The state has lost about one-half of its original wetlands, which now cover about 7.6 million acres (3.1 million hectares), or 4.4% of the land.

⁶POPULATION

According to 1990 census figures, Texas ranked 3d behind California and New York, with a population of 16,986,510, with a density of just 64.9 persons per sq mi (24.9 per sq km). The state had placed 4th at the 1970 census, with a population of 11,196,730, but had surpassed Pennsylvania in 1974. The estimated population in 1996 was 19,128,261, a 12.6% increase over 1990.

At the first decennial census of 1850, less than five years after Texas had become a state, the population totaled 212,592. It reached 1,600,000 by the early 1880s (when the state ranked 11th), passed 4,000,000 during World War I, and jumped to 7,700,000 in 1950. The slowest period of growth occurred during the Depression decade (1930–40) when the population rose only 10%, and the state was surpassed by California. The growth rate ranged between 17% and 27% for each decade from the 1940s through the 1970s, and was 19.4% between 1980 and 1990.

The ratio between the sexes has changed during the 20th century. In 1920, the state had 155,000 more men than women; 40 years later, women outnumbered men by 90,000; and in 1990, the female lead was 223,000. At the same time, the Texas population has grown steadily older, a phenomenon linked to declining birthrates and increased life expectancies. In 1870, only one out of 68 Texans was 65 years of age or older; by 1990, the proportion was one out of 10. Surprisingly for a state whose population has grown so fast, about 65% of all state residents were born in Texas.

In 1990, about 82% of all Texans lived in metropolitan areas. The largest, Dallas-Ft. Worth (which traded places with Houston-Galveston-Brazoria in the national rank of the most populated metropolitan areas from 1980 to 1990), had an estimated 4,449,875 people in 1995. Close behind was the Houston-Galveston-Brazoria area, with 4,164,393 residents. San Antonio had an estimated 1,460,809. Houston, the largest city in Texas and 4th largest in the US, had an estimated 1994 population of 1,702,086. Next was Dallas, with 1,022,830; followed by San Antonio, 998,905; El Paso, 579,307; Ft. Worth, 451,814; Austin, 514,013; and Corpus Christi, 275,419. With the exception of El Paso, in the far western corner of the trans-Peco region, most of the larger cities are situated along the Gulf coast or on or near an axis that extends north-south from Wichita Falls to Corpus Christi, in the heart of the Blackland Belt.

⁷ETHNIC GROUPS

Hispanic Americans constitute the largest ethnic minority in Texas, about 25.5% of the population in 1990. Black Americans accounted for 11.9%, and most of the rest were "Anglos"—a term denoting all whites except Spanish-surnamed or Spanish-speaking individuals. Although many Indian groups have lived in Texas, few Indians remain.

As white settlers pushed toward Texas during the 19th century, many Indian groups moved west and south into the region. The most notable tribes were the Comanche, Wichita, Kiowa, Apache, Choctaw, and Cherokee. Also entering in significant numbers were the Kickapoo and Potawatomi from Illinois, the Delaware and Shawnee from Missouri, the Quapaw from Arkansas, and the Creek from Alabama and Georgia. One of the few Texas tribes that has survived to the present time as an identifiable group is the Alabama-Coushatta, who inhabit a 4,351-acre (1,761-hectare) reservation in Polk County, 90 mi (145 km) northeast of Houston. The Tigua, living in Texas since the 1680s, were recognized by a federal law in 1968 that transferred all responsibility for them to the state of Texas. The two Indian reservations number about 500 persons each. Overall, at the 1990 census, there were 66,000 American Indians, including 339 Eskimos and 89 Aleuts living in Texas; however, over 815,000 residents claimed American Indian ancestry. In 1996, estimates placed the total number of Native Americans, including Eskimos and Aleuts, at 166,000.

Blacks have been integral to the history of Texas ever since a black Moor named Estevanico was shipwrecked near present-day Galveston in 1528. By 1860, Texas had 182,921 blacks, or 30% of the total population, of whom only 355 were free. Once emancipated, blacks made effective use of the franchise, electing two of their number to the state senate and nine to the house in 1868. After the return of the Democratic Party to political dominance, however, the power of blacks steadily diminished. Since then, their numbers have grown, but their proportion of the total population has dwindled, although Houston and Dallas were, respectively, about 28% and 29% black at the 1990 census. In 1990, 2,022,000 blacks lived in the state, which ranked 3d behind New York and California.

Hispanic Americans, the largest minority in Texas, numbered 4,340,000 in 1990 (2d only to California), and an estimated 5,959,000 in 1996. Mostly of Mexican ancestry, they are nevertheless a heterogeneous group, divided by history, geography, and economic circumstances. Hispanics have been elected to the state legislature and to the US Congress. In 1980, the Houston independent school district, the state's largest, reported more Hispanic students than Anglos for the first time in its history.

Altogether, Texas has nearly 30 identifiable ethnic groups. Certain areas of central Texas are heavily Germanic and Czech. The first permanent Polish colony in the US was established at Panna Maria, near San Antonio, in 1854. Texas has one of the largest colonies of Wends in the world, principally at Serbin in central Texas. Significant numbers of Danes, Swedes, and Norwegians have also settled in Texas. As of 1990, foreign-born Texans numbered 1,524,436, with Mexico, Vietnam, El Salvador, and Germany the leading countries of origin. The same census counted 55,023 Chinese, 40,053 Filipinos, 40,506 Asian Indians, 35,281 Koreans, and 23,729 Japanese. Of the 60,649 Vietnamese, many were refugees who resettled in Texas beginning in 1975. In 1996 foreign-born Texans numbered an estimated 2,081,000.

Texas Counties, County Seats, and County Areas and Populations

COUNTY	COUNTY SEAT	LAND AREA (SQ MI)	POPULATION (1996 EST.)	COUNTY	COUNTY SEAT	LAND AREA (SQ MI)	POPULATION (1996 EST.)
Anderson	Palestine	1,077	52,174	Duval	San Diego	1,795	13,383
Andrews	Andrews	1,501	14,338	Eastland	Eastland	924	18,064
Angelina	Lufkin	807	76,069	Ector	Odessa	903	123,398
Aransas	Rockport	280	21,803	Edwards	Rocksprings	2,120	3,374
Archer	Archer City	907	8,247	Ellis	Waxahachie	939	97,054
Armstrong	Claude	910	2,162	El Paso	El Paso	1,014	684,446
Atascosa	Jourdanton	1,218	35,044	Erath	Stephenville	1,080	30,815
Austin	Bellville	656	22,768	Falls	Marlin	770	17,727
Bailey	Muleshoe	827	6,789	Fannin	Bonham	895	27,614
Bandera	Bandera	793	14,287	Fayette	La Grange	950	21,185
Bastrop	Bastrop	895	46,819	Fisher	Roby	897	4,449
Baylor	Seymour	862	4,153	Floyd	Floydada	992	8,334
Bee	Beeville	880	27,833	Foard	Crowell	703	1,719
Bell	Belton	1,055	222,450	Ft. Bend	Richmond	876	306,832
Bexar	San Antonio	1,248	1,318,322	Franklin	Mt. Vernon	294	9,320
Blanco	Johnson City	714	7,774	Freestone	Fairfield	888	17,476
Borden	Gail	900	807	Frio	Pearsall	1,133	15,824
Bosque	Meridian	989	16,756	Gaines	Seminole	1,504	14,719
Bowie	Boston	891	84,969	Galveston	Galveston	399	240,653
Brazoria	Angleton	1,407	220,854	Garza	Post	895	4,729
Brazos	Bryan	588	131,904	Gillespie	Fredericksburg	1,061	19,635
Brewster	Alpine	6,169	9,221	Glasscock	Garden City	900	1,407
Briscoe	Silverton	887	1,917	Goliad	Goliad	859	6,586
Brooks	Falfurrias	942	8,493	Gonzales	Gonzales	1,068	17,608
Brown	Brownwood	936	36,746	Gray	Pampa	921	23,335
Burleson	Caldwell	668	15,288	Grayson	Sherman	934	100,589
Burnet	Burnet	994	29,753	Gregg	Longview	273	112,138
Caldwell	Lockhart	546	30,514	Grimes	Anderson	799	22,192
Calhoun	Port Lavaca	540	20,711	Guadalupe	Seguin	713	73,253
Callahan	Baird	899	12,580	Hale	Plainview	1,005	36,548
Cameron	Brownsville	905	315,015	Hall	Memphis	876	3,750
Camp	Pittsburg	203	10,913	Hamilton	Hamilton	836	7,570
Carson	Panhandle	924	6,714	Hansford	Spearman	921	5,372
Cass	Linden	937	30,621	Hardeman	Quanah	688	4,808
Castro	Dimmitt	899	8,535	Hardin	Kountze	898	47,574
Chambers	Anahuac	616	22,789	Harris	Houston	1,734	3,126,966
Cherokee	Rusk	1,052	42,484	Harrison	Marshall	908	59,685
Childress	Childress	707	7,580	Hartley	Channing	1,462	5,210
Clay	Henrietta	1,085	10,450	Haskell	Haskell	901	6,247
Cochran	Morton	775	4,083	Hays	San Marcos	678	81,744
Coke	Robert Lee	908	3,437	Hemphill	Canadian	903	3,648
Coleman	Coleman	1,277	9,700	Henderson	Athens	888	65,664
Collin	McKenney	851	372,445	Hidalgo	Edinburg	1,569	495,594
Collingsworth	Wellington	909	3,269	Hill	Hillsboro	968	29,968
Colorado	Columbus	964	18,757	Hockley	Levelland	908	23,931
Comal	New Braunfels	555	67,687	Hood	Granbury	425	34,976
Comanche	Comanche	930	13,465	Hopkins	Sulphur Springs	789	30,455
Concho	Paint Rock	992	3,186	Houston	Crockett	1,234	21,962
Cooke	Gainesville	893	32,254	Howard	Big Spring	901	32,836
Coryell	Gatesville	1,057	74,446	Hudspeth	Sierra Blanca	4,566	3,265
Cottle	Paducah	895	1,975	Hunt	Greenville	840	67,906
Crane	Crane	782	4,514	Hutchinson	Stinnett	871	24,425
Crockett	Ozona	2,806	4,372	Irion	Mertzon	1,052	1,718
Crosby	Crosbyton	898	7,349	Jack	Jacksboro	920	7,285
Culberson	Van Horn	3,815	3,210	Jackson	Edna	844	13,687
Dallam	Dalhart	1,505	6,269	Jasper	Jasper	921	32,954
Dallas	Dallas	880	2,000,192	Jeff Davis	Ft. Davis	2,258	2,155
Dawson	Lamesa	903	15,172	Jefferson	Beaumont	937	243,733
Deaf Smith	Hereford	1,497	19,519	Jim Hogg	Hebbronville	1,136	5,036
Delta	Cooper	278	4,293	Jim Wells	Alice	867	39,725
Denton	Denton	911	348,453	Johnson	Cleburne	731	110,344
DeWitt	Cuero	910	19,657	Jones	Anson	931	18,692
Dickens	Dickens	907	2,317	Karnes	Karnes City	753	12,567
Dimmet	Carrizo Springs	1,307	10,475	Kaufman	Kaufman	788	62,116
Donley	Clarendon	929	3,863	Kendall	Boerne	663	19,639

Texas Counties, County Seats, and County Areas and Populations

COUNTY	COUNTY SEAT	LAND AREA (SQ MI)	POPULATION (1996 EST.)	COUNTY	COUNTY SEAT	LAND AREA (SQ MI)	POPULATION (1996 EST.)
Kenedy	Sarita	1,389	438	Refugio	Refugio	771	7,903
Kent	Jayton	878	864	Roberts	Miami	915	988
Kerr	Kerrville	1,107	41,406	Robertson	Franklin	864	15,522
Kimble	Junction	1,250	4,215	Rockwall	Rockwall	128	34,153
King	Guthrie	914	336	Runnels	Ballinger	1,056	11,410
Kinney	Brackettville	1,359	3,402	Rusk	Henderson	932	45,596
Kleberg	Kingsville	853	30,325	Sabine	Hemphill	486	10,443
Knox	Benjamin	845	4,425	San Augustine	San Augustine	524	8,051
Lamar	Paris	919	45,255	San Jacinto	Coldspring	572	19,957
Lamb	Littlefield	1,013	14,989	San Patricio	Sinton	693	68,334
Lampasas	Lampasas	714	17,163	San Saba	San Saba	1,136	6,024
La Salle	Cotulla	1,517	6,063	Schleicher	Eldorado	1,309	3,088
Lavaca	Hallettsville	971	18,872	Scurry	Snyder	900	18,248
Lee	Giddings	631	14,442	Shackelford	Albany	915	3,296
Leon	Centerville	1,078	14,190	Shelby	Center	791	22,677
Liberty	Liberty	1,174	63,294	Sherman	Stratford	923	2,818
Limestone	Groesbeck	931	20,829	Smith	Tyler	932	165,002
Lipscomb	Lipscomb	933	3,081	Somervell	Glen Rose	188	5,986
Live Oak	George West	1,057	10,195	Starr	Rio Grande City	1,226	53,974
Llano	Llano	939	12,861	Stephens	Breckenridge	894	9,798
Loving	Mentone	671	141	Sterling	Sterling City	923	1,411
Lubbock	Lubbock	900	232,035	Stonewall	Aspermont	925	1,813
Lynn	Tahoka	888	6,588	Sutton	Sonora	1,455	4,449
McCulloch	Brady	1,071	8,694	Swisher	Tulia	902	8,495
McLennan	Waco	1,031	201,775	Tarrant	Ft. Worth	868	1,305,185
McMullen	Tilden	1,163	799	Taylor	Abilene	917	122,130
Madison	Madisonville	473	11,984	Terrell	Sanderson	2,357	1,237
Marion	Jefferson	385	10,430	Terry	Brownfield	886	13,093
Martin	Stanton	914	4,957	Throckmorton	Throckmorton	912	1,797
Mason	Mason	934	3,598	Titus	Mt. Pleasant	412	24,909
Matagorda	Bay City	1,127	38,192	Tom Green	San Angelo	1,515	102,580
Maverick	Eagle Pass	1,287	46,563	Travis	Austin	989	683,967
Medina	Hondo	1,331	35,363	Trinity	Groveton	692	12,454
Menard	Menard	902	2,361	Tyler	Woodville	922	20,283
Midland	Midland	902	116,016	Upshur	Gilmer	587	34,909
Milam	Cameron	1,019	23,972	Upton	Rankin	1,243	3,816
Mills	Goldthwaite	748	4,767	Uvalde	Uvalde	1,564	25,343
Mitchell	ColoradoCity	912	9,002	Val Verde	Del Rio	3,150	43,131
Montague	Montague	928	18,030	Van Zandt	Canton	855	42,579
Montgomery	Conroe	1,047	245,845	Victoria	Victoria	887	81,541
Moore	Dumas	905	19,427	Walker	Huntsville	786	54,417
Morris	Daingerfield	256	13,262	Waller	Hempstead	514	26,195
Motley	Matador	959	1,330	Ward	Monahans	836	11,994
Nacogdoches	Nacogdoches	939	56,533	Washington	Brenham	610	28,610
Navarro	Corsicana	1,068	41,290	Webb	Laredo	3,363	176,792
Newton	Newton	935	14,259	Wharton	Wharton	1,086	40,224
Nolan	Sweetwater	915	16,370	Wheeler	Wheeler	905	5,344
Nueces	Corpus Christi	847	315,722	Wichita	Wichita Falls	606	128,064
Ochiltree	Perryton	919	8,791	Wilbarger	Vernon	947	14,308
Oldham	Vega	1,485	2,270	Willacy	Raymondville	589	19,419
Orange	Orange	362	84,488	Williamson	Georgetown	1,137	198,286
Palo Pinto	Palo Pinto	949	25,463	Wilson	Floresville	807	28,867
Panola	Carthage	812	22,899	Winkler	Kermit	840	8,043
Parker	Weatherford	902	76,073	Wise	Decatur	902	40,451
Parmer	Farwell	885	10,403	Wood	Quitman	689	33,321
Pecos	Ft. Stockton	4,776	16,349	Yoakum	Plains	800	8,325
Polk	Livingston	1,061	44,906	Young	Graham	919	17,528
Potter	Amarillo	902	108,636	Zapata	Zapata	999	11,100
Presidio	Marfa	3,857	7,966	Zavala	Crystal City	1,298	12,322
Rains	Emory	243	7,869				
Randall	Canyon	917	97,379	TOTALS		262,017	19,128,261
Reagan	Big Lake	1,173	4,254				
Real	Leakey	697	2,724				
Red River	Clarksville	1,054	13,959				
Reeves	Pecos	2,626	14,993				

⁸LANGUAGES

The Indians of Texas are mostly descendants of the Alabama-Coushatta who came to Texas in the 19th century. The few Indian place-names include Texas itself, Pecos, Waco, and Toyah.

Most of the regional features in Texas English derive from the influx of South Midland and Southern speakers, with a noticeable Spanish flavor from older as well as more recent loans. Settlers from the Gulf Coast states brought such terms as *snap beans* (green beans), the widespread *pail* (here probably of Southern rather the Northern origin), and *carry* (escort), with a 47% frequency in north Texas and 22% in the south. Louisiana *praline* (pecan patty) is now widespread, but *banquette* (sidewalk) appears only in the extreme southeast corner.

Southern and South Midland terms were largely introduced by settlers from Arkansas, Missouri, and Tennessee; their use ranges from northeast to west, but with declining frequency in the trans-Pecos area. Examples are *clabber cheese* (cottage cheese), *mosquito hawk* (dragonfly), *croker sack* (burlap bag), *mouth harp* (harmonica), *branch* (stream), and *dog irons* (andirons). A dialect survey showed *pallet* (bed on the floor) with a 90% overall frequency; *light bread* (white bread) and *pullybone* (wishbone), each 78%; and *you-all*, more than 80%. General Midland terms also widespread in the state are *sook!* (call to calves), *blinds* (roller shades), *piece* (a certain distance), and *quarter till five* (4:45).

Some terms exhibit uneven distribution. Examples include *mott* (clump of trees) in the south and southwest, *sugan* (a wool-filled comforter for a cowboy's bedroll) in the west, Midland *draw* (dry streambed) in the west and southwest, South Midland *peckerwood* (woodpecker) in most of the state except west of the Pecos, *poke* (paper bag) in the central and northern areas, and *surly* (euphemism for bull) in the west. A curious result of dialect mixture is the appearance of a number of hybrids combining two different dialects, such as *freeseed* peach from *freestone* and *clearseed*, *fire mantel* and *mantel board* from *fireboard* and *mantel*, *flapcakes* from *flapjacks* and *pancakes*, and *horse doctor* from *horsefly* and *snake doctor*. The large sandwich is known as a *torpedo* in San Antonio and a *poorboy* in Houston.

Texas pronunciation is largely South Midland, with such characteristic forms as /caow/, and /naow/ for *cow* and *now* and /dyoo/ for *due*, although /doo/ is now more common in urban areas. In the German settlement around New Braunfels are heard a few loanwords such as *smearcase* (cottage cheese), *krebbel* (doughnut), *clook* (setting hen), and *oma* and *opa* for grandmother and grandfather.

Spanish has been the major foreign-language influence. In areas like Laredo and Brownsville, along the Rio Grande, as many as 90% of the people may be bilingual; in northeast Texas, however, Spanish is as foreign as French. In the days of the early Spanish ranchers, standard English adopted *hacienda, ranch, burro, canyon,* and *lariat;* in the southwestern cattle country are heard *la reata* (lasso), *remuda* (group of horses), and *resaca* (pond), along with the *acequia* (irrigation ditch), *pilon* (something extra, as a trip), and *olla* (water jar). The presence of the large Spanish-speaking population was a major factor in the passage of the state's bilingual education law, as a result of which numerous school programs in both English and Spanish are now offered; in a ruling issued in January 1981, US District Judge William Wayne Justice ruled that by 1987, the state must expand such programs to cover all Spanish-speaking students. About one-sixth of all Texas counties—and a great many cities—are named for Mexicans or Spaniards or after place-names in Spain or Mexico.

In 1990, 11,635,518 Texans—74.6% of the population 5 years old or older—spoke only English at home. Other languages most commonly spoken at home included:

Spanish	3,443,106	Chinese	52,220
German	90,659	Indic	37,065
French	64,585	Korean	26,228
Vietnamese	57,736	Tagalog	22,256

⁹RELIGIONS

Because of its Spanish heritage, Texas originally was entirely Roman Catholic except for unconverted Indians. Consequently, the early history of Texas is almost identical with that of the Roman Catholic Church in the area. Under the Mexican Republic, the Catholic Church continued as the sole recognized religious body. In order to receive the generous land grants given by the Mexicans, Anglo-American immigrants had to sign a paper saying that they followed the Catholic religion. With an average grant of 4,605 acres (1,864 hectares) as bait, many early Protestants and atheists must have felt little hesitancy about becoming instant Catholics.

The Mexican government was careless about enforcing adherence to the Catholic faith in Texas, however, and many Baptists, Methodists, and Presbyterians drifted in from the east. The Methodist practice of having itinerant ministers range over frontier areas was particularly well suited to the Texas scene and, in 1837, the church hierarchy sent three preachers to the new republic. The first presbytery had been formed by that date, and Baptists had organized in Houston by 1840. Swedish and German immigrants brought their Lutheranism with them; the first German Lutheran synod was organized in Houston in 1851.

Geographically, Texas tends to be heavily Protestant in the north and east and Catholic in the south and southwest. Leading Protestant denominations and their known adherents in 1990 were Southern Baptist Convention, 3,259,395; United Methodist Church, 1,004,318; Churches of Christ, 380,948; Episcopal Church, 169,112; Assembly of God, 162,232; Presbyterian Church in the US, 200,969; Christian Church (Disciples of Christ), 105,495; Baptists Missionary Association of America, 125,323; Lutheran Church-Missouri Synod, 134,280; and Evangelical Lutheran Church in America, 155,276. Roman Catholics numbered 3,574,728 in 1990 and there were an estimated 107,980 Jews.

¹⁰TRANSPORTATION

Texas ranks 1st among the 50 states in total railroad mileage, highway mileage, and number of airports, and 2d only to California in motor vehicle registrations and in number of general aviation aircraft.

Transportation has been a severe problem for Texas because of the state's extraordinary size and sometimes difficult terrain; one of the more unusual experiments in US transport history was the use of camels in southwestern Texas during the mid-1800s. The Republic of Texas authorized railroad construction as early as 1836, but the financial panic of 1837 helped kill that attempt. Not until 1853 did the state's first railroad—from Harrisburg (now incorporated into Houston) to Stafford's Point, 20 mi (32 km) to the west—come into service. At the outbreak of the Civil War, 10 railroads were operating, all but 2 connected with seaports. Texas lacked sufficient capital to satisfy its railroad-building needs until the war was over, although the state legislature in 1852 had offered railroad companies eight sections (5,120 acres/2,072 hectares) of land per mile of road construction and doubled that offer two years later; the state generally held to the 10,240-acre (4,144-hectare) figure until all grants ceased in 1882. In all, Texas granted more than 50,000 sq mi (130,000 sq km) to railroad companies.

In 1870, Texas had fewer than 600 mi (970 km) of track; 10 years later, it had 3,026 mi (4,870 km); in 1890, 6,045 mi (9,729 km); and by 1920, 16,049 mi (25,828 km). A peak was reached in 1932, when there were 17,078 mi (27,484 km) of track; by the end of 1995, trackage had dwindled to 10,758 rail mi (17,320 km), with 84% of the total being Class I railroad. Total rail mileage in Texas still ranks higher than any other state, and 46% more than 2d-ranked Illinois. Five carriers—Atchison, Topeka & Santa Fe, Burlington Northern, Kansas City Southern, Southern Pacific, and Union Pacific—control about 85% of the mileage. The only rail passenger service in Texas is provided by Amtrak, which runs two routes—the Sunset Limited (New Orleans–Los Angeles) from Beaumont through Houston and San Antonio to El Paso, and the Texas Eagle (Chicago–San Antonio). In 1995/96, Amtrak carried 147,944 passengers within Texas.

In mid-1983, Dallas area voters approved the creation of the Dallas Area Rapid Transit system (DART), to serve the city and 13 suburbs; 160 mi (257 km) of surface rail routes were to be constructed and bus service doubled at an expense of some $8.9 billion over a 26-year period. Ft. Worth has the state's only true subway—a 1-mi (1.6-km) line from a parking lot to a downtown shipping and office center—although Dallas-Ft. Worth Regional Airport has its own rail shuttle system.

In 1995, Texas had 296,186 mi (476,859 km) of public roadway, 72% of it rural. Texas has by far the most mileage of any state, and has almost 74% more public road mileage than California which ranked 2d in 1996. In 1995, expenditures on roads and highways by federal, state, and local governments came to over $6.2 billion, 2d only to California. The leading interstate highways are I-10 and I-20, respectively linking Houston and the Dallas–Ft.Worth Areas with El Paso in the west, and I-35 and I-45, connecting Dallas–Ft. Worth with, respectively, San Antonio (via Austin) and Galveston (via Houston). There were 13,035,449 licensed drivers in 1997 (2d highest). Registered motor vehicles in 1995 included 8,604,958 automobiles, 130,117 motorcycles, 5,005,001 trucks, and 71,776 buses.

River transport did not become commercially successful until the end of the 19th century, when the Houston Ship Channel was dredged along the San Jacinto River and Buffalo Bayou for more than 50 mi (80 km), and another channel was dredged down the Neches River to make a seaport out of Beaumont. With 13 major seaports and many shallow-water ports, Texas has been a major factor in waterborne commerce since the early 1950s. The Port of Houston is the nation's second most active harbor, with over 135.2 million tons of cargo handled in 1995. The Gulf Intracoastal Waterway begins in Brownsville, at the mouth of the Rio Grande, and extends across Texas for 423 mi (681 km) on its way to Florida and its connections with a similar waterway on the Atlantic. In 1995, the waterway transported 78.3 million short tons of cargo.

After American entry into World War I, Texas began to build airfields for training grounds; when the war ended, many US fliers returned to Texas and became civilian commercial pilots, carrying air mail (from 1926), dusting crops, and mapping potential oil fields. In 1997, the state had over 1,600 landing facilities. There were 1,271 airports and 392 heliports in 1994. The Dallas–Ft. Worth Regional Airport, the nation's largest air terminal and its 2d busiest in 1994, serviced nearly half of the aircraft departures in Texas, with another sixth handled by Houston Intercontinental Airport.

11HISTORY

Although a site near Lewisville, in Denton County, contains artifacts that might be more than 37,000 years old, the generally accepted date for the earliest human presence in the region now known as Texas is the Llano civilization, dating from 12,000 years ago. Prehistoric Indians in Texas failed to develop as complex technologies as their neighbors to the west and east. When the first Europeans arrived in the 16th century, the Indians had developed little in the way of pottery or basketry, and had shown little interest in agriculture except in the extreme east and northeast, and possibly west of the Pecos. They were still largely hunter-gatherers on whom the more technologically complex cultures of Mexico and the southeastern US had little effect.

Along the Gulf coast and overlapping into northeastern Mexico were the Coahuiltecan and Karankawa peoples. They lived in a hostile environment, consuming berries in season, animal dung, spiders, and an occasional deer, bison, or jabalina. In central Texas lived the Tonkawa, who hunted buffalo, slept in tepees, used dogs for hauling, and had a communal structure akin to that of the Plains Indians. Unlike the Karankawa, who were tall, the Tonkawa were of average height, tattooed, and dressed in breech-clouts—long for men, short for women. They proved extremely susceptible to European diseases and evidently died out, whereas the Karankawa migrated to northern Mexico.

About two dozen tribes of Caddo in eastern and northeastern Texas were at the time of European penetration the most technologically complex Indians living within the state's present borders. Having developed agriculture, the Caddo were relatively sedentary and village oriented. Those belonging to the Hasinai Confederation called each other *tayshas,* a term that translates as "allies" or "friends." When the Hasinai told Spanish explorers that they were *tayshas,* the Spaniards wrote the word as *Tejas,* which in time became *Texas.* The Caddo lived in the gentle portion of Texas, where woods, wild fruits, and berries abound, and where game was plentiful until the advent of European civilization. Life was so good, in fact, that several members of an expedition under Robert Cavelier, Sieur de la Salle, reaching Matagorda Bay on 15 February 1685, chose to desert to the Caddo rather than remain with their fellow Frenchmen. Henri de Tonti, who entered the region somewhat later, reported that one Caddo tribe had a woman as chief. The Caddo were also unusual in their belief that three women had created the world.

In trans-Pecos Texas, to the west, lived a fourth Indian group, the Jumano, probably descendants of the Pueblo cultures. Some of the Jumano were nomadic hunters in the Davis and Chisos mountains. Others became farmers along the Rio Grande and the lower Rio Conchos, making and using some pottery and raising good crops of corn, beans, squash, and possibly cotton. Probably the successive droughts so common to the region began to thin out their ranks, and the coming of the Spanish removed them from the historical picture altogether.

The first European to enter Texas was Spanish explorer Alonso Alvarez de Pineda, who sailed into the mouth of the Rio Grande in 1519. Basically, the Spanish left the Texas Indians alone for more than 150 years. Sometimes an accident placed Spaniards in Texas, or sometimes they entered by design, but generally, the Spanish looked on Texas as too remote from Florida and the Mexico highlands—where most of their colonizing occurred—for successful settlement. A remarkable episode of this period involves the survivors of the Pánfilo de Narváez expedition, which had been commissioned to occupy the Gulf of Mexico coast from Mexico to Florida. Four shipwrecked men, led by Álvar Nunez Cabeza de Vaca, were washed ashore on a Texas sandbar on 6 November 1528: three were Spaniards, and one was the Moor Estevanico. For eight years, they wandered virtually naked among the Texas Indians, sometimes as slaves and sometimes as free men, alternately blistered by the summer sun and freezing under winter ice storms. Using a deer bone as a needle, Cabeza removed an arrowhead from deep in an Indian's chest—a bit of surgical magic that earned him treatment as a demigod, for a time. Finally, the four Europeans reached the west coast of Mexico, from where Cabeza de Vaca returned home a hero. The other two Spaniards remained in Mexico, but Estevanico joined the Fray Marcos de Niza expedition as a guide, dying at the hands of Pueblo Indians in New Mexico in 1539. The trail he helped blaze through the High Plains of West Texas served as the route for the expedition a year later by Francisco Vásquez de Coronado. The first Texas towns and missions were begun by Spaniards in West Texas, outside present-day El Paso. Ysleta del Sur was founded in 1682, almost a decade before the earliest East Texas missions. But Ysleta was 500 mi (800 km) from anything else resembling a settlement in Texas, and the Spanish considered it a part of New Mexico.

What changed the Spaniards' attitude toward the colonization of Texas was the establishment of Ft. St. Louis by La Salle on the Gulf coast in 1685. Four years later, Capt. Alonso de León, governor of Coahuila, sent out an expedition to expel the French. Father Damien Massanet, a Coahuilan priest, accompanied the León expedition and was charged with establishing a mission near wherever the captain built a fort. During the next several decades these two men and their successors established a string of mission-forts across Texas. After fear of the French presence eased, Spain tended to neglect these establishments. But when the French entered Louisiana in force during the early 18th century, Spanish fears of French expansion were re-ignited. In 1718, the Spanish began to build a mission, San Antonio de Valero, and a fort, San Antonio de Bexar, at the site of the present city of San Antonio. As a halfway post between Mexico and the Louisiana border, San Antonio grew to be Texas's most important city during the Spanish period.

Until the 19th century, the US showed little interest in Texas. But the purchase of Louisiana Territory from the French by the US government in 1803 made Texas a next-door neighbor, and "filibusters" (military adventurers) began to filter across the border into Spanish territory. The best known is Philip Nolan, an Irish-born intriguer who started spending time in Texas as early as 1790. Ostensibly, he was trading horses with the Indians, but the Spanish associated him with Aaron Burr's schemes to excise the Spanish southwest from its owners. In the summer of 1800, the Spanish governor of Texas, Juan Bautista Elguezábal, ordered that Nolan should be arrested if he returned. In December of that year, Nolan returned with a small force of 20 men and built a fort near Nacogdoches; he was killed fighting the Spanish on 4 March 1801. Nolan is remembered for having drafted the first Anglo-American map of Texas.

In 1810–11, the Mexicans launched their revolution against Spain, and though only an outpost, Texas as a Spanish-Mexican colony was naturally involved. In 1813, Texas formally declared its independence of Spain and its intention of becoming a Mexican state, with its capital at San Antonio. Various Anglo-Americans entered the new state to serve on behalf of Mexico. Pirates also aided the Mexican cause: on Galveston Island, Luis Aury preyed on Spanish shipping, and after 1816, his place was taken by Jean Laffite, who privateered against both Spanish and US shipping until the US Navy drove him out.

The Spanish finally gave up on Mexico in 1821, leaving Texas as a Mexican province with a non-Indian population of about 7,000. The only towns of significant size were Goliad, San Antonio (commonly called Bexar), and Nacogdoches. A year earlier, Moses Austin of Missouri had received permission from Spanish authorities to introduce Anglo-American colonists into Texas, presumably as a barrier against aggression by the US. When Spanish rule ended, his son, Stephen F. Austin, succeeded his late father as head of the colonization movement, securing permission from the new Mexican government to settle 300 families in the area between the lower Colorado and Brazos rivers. After Austin had settled his "Old Three Hundred" in 1821, he received permission to settle more, and within a decade, his colonists numbered more than 5,000. The Mexicans invested Austin with the responsibilities and privileges of an *empresario*: authority to run commerce, maintain militia, administer justice, and hand out land titles. Other *empresarios* made similar arrangements. Green DeWitt, also of Missouri, settled several hundred families farther west and founded the town of Gonzales in 1825. Hayden Edwards received a grant to settle 800 families near Nacogdoches. Mexicans were also permitted to organize colonies. Texas thus began a pattern of growth from the outside that has continued to the present day.

Between 1821 and 1835, the population of non-Indian Texas expanded to between 35,000 and 50,000. Most new settlers were Anglo-Americans who often brought their prejudices against Mexico with them, whether they were from the North or the South. They disliked Mexican culture, Mexican folkways, Mexican justice—and the Protestants among them resented the omnipresence of the Roman Catholic Church. All of these Anglo-American settlers had ties to the US, and many undoubtedly longed for the time when they would live under the American flag again. The ineptitude of the Mexican government made the situation even worse. In 1826, Hayden Edwards organized the Republic of Fredonia and tried to drive the Mexicans from East Texas, but in the end, he had to flee the province himself. Troubled by the rising spirit of rebellion, the Mexican Congress enacted the Law of 1830, which forbade most immigration and imposed duties on all imports. Anglo-Americans in Texas responded with the same anger that New Englanders had once shown when Britain imposed tax restrictions on the original American colonies.

At first, the Anglo-Texans insisted they were opposing Mexican political excesses, not the Mexican nation. Their hope lay with Gen. Antonio López de Santa Anna, who was leading a liberal revolution against President Anastasio Bustamante. Skirmishes between the Anglo-Texans and Mexican officials remained sporadic and localized until 1833 when Santa Anna became president of Mexico and almost immediately dropped his liberal stance. Texans sent Austin to Mexico City to petition Santa Anna to rescind the Law of 1830, to allow the use of English in public business, and to make Texas (then an appendage of Coahuila) a separate state. After several months in Mexico City, Austin was arrested on his way back to Texas and was imprisoned for a year. When Santa Anna tried to enforce customs collections, colonists at Anahuac, led by William Barret Travis, drove the Mexican officials out of town. Santa Anna's answer was to place Texas under military jurisdiction. When the Mexican military commander, Col. Domingo de Ugartechea, sent his soldiers to Gonzales to take a cannon there from the colonists, the Anglo-Texan civilians drove them off on 2 October 1835, in a battle that is generally considered to mark the start of the Texas Revolution.

On 3 November, a provisional government was formed. It called not for independence but for a return to the liberal Mexican constitution of 1824. Three commissioners, one of them Austin, were sent to Washington, D.C., to request aid from the US. Sam Houston, who only six years earlier had resigned the governorship of Tennessee (when his wife left him) and had come to Texas after stays in Oklahoma and Arkansas, was named commander in chief of the upstart Texas army. Hostilities remained at a standstill until February 1836, when Santa Anna led an army across the Rio Grande. The Mexicans concentrated outside San Antonio at a mission-fort called the Alamo, where 187 or so Texans, commanded by Col. William Barret Travis, had holed up in defense. The Mexicans besieged the Alamo until 6 March, when Santa Anna's forces, now numbering more than 4,000, stormed the fortress. When the battle ended, all the Alamo's defenders, including several native Mexicans, were dead. Among those killed were Travis and two Americans who became legends—James Bowie and Davy Crockett.

Four days before the battle of the Alamo, other Texans gathered at Washington-on-the-Brazos and issued a declaration of independence. As so often happens, a fight that had started on principle—in this case, a constitutional issue—grew into a fight for independence. The men who died at the Alamo believed they were fighting for restoration of the constitution of 1824. But three weeks after the Alamo fell, on 27 March 1836, the Mexicans killed 342 Texans who had surrendered at Goliad, thinking they would be treated as prisoners of war. Coming on the heels of the Alamo tragedy, the "Goliad massacre" persuaded Texans that only total victory or total defeat would solve their problems with Santa Anna. The Texas army under Sam Houston retreated before Santa Anna's oncoming forces, which held a numerical advantage over Houston's of about 1,600 to 800. On 21 April 1836, however, the Texans surprised the Mexicans during their siesta period at San Jacinto (east of present-day Houston). Mexican losses were 630 killed, 280 wounded, and 730 taken prisoner, while the Texans had only 9 killed and 30 wounded. This decisive battle—fought to the cry of "Remember the Alamo, remember Goliad!"—freed Texas from Mexico once and for all.

For 10 years, Texas existed as an independent republic, recognized by the US, Belgium, France, the United Kingdom, the Netherlands, and several German states. Sam Houston, the victorious commander at San Jacinto, became the republic's first nationally elected president. Although Texans are proud of their once-independent status, the fact is that the republic limped along like any new nation, strife-torn and short of cash. It was unable to reach agreement with Mexico on a treaty to clarify the border. Moreover, its original $1-million public debt increased eightfold in a decade, and its paper money depreciated alarmingly. Consequently, when Texas joined the Union on 29 December 1845, the date of the US congressional resolution recognizing the new state (the Lone Star flag, the republic's official banner, was not actually lowered and a governor inaugurated until 19 February 1846), its citizens looked on the action as a rescue. The annexation in great measure provoked the Mexican War, which in turn led to the conclusion of the Treaty of Guadalupe Hidalgo on 2 February 1848. Under the treaty, Mexico dropped its claim to the territory between the Rio Grande and the Nueces River. Later, in accordance with the Compromise of 1850, Texas relinquished, for $10 million, its claim on lands stretching into New Mexico, Colorado, Wyoming, Oklahoma, and Kansas.

With the coming of the Civil War, Texas followed its proslavery southern neighbors out of the Union into the Confederacy; Governor Houston, who opposed secession, was ousted from office. The state saw little fighting, and Texas thus suffered from the war far less than most of the South. The last battle of the war was fought on Texas soil at Palmito Ranch, near Brownsville, on 13 May 1865—more than a month after Gen. Robert E. Lee's surrender at Appomattox Court House in Virginia.

During Reconstruction, Texas was governed briefly by a military occupation force and then by a Republican regime; the so-called carpetbag constitution of 1869, passed during this period, gave the franchise to blacks, a right that the Ku Klux Klan actively sought to deny them. Texas was allowed to rejoin the Union on 30 March 1870. Three years later, Republican Governor Edmund J. Davis was defeated at the polls by Richard Coke, and a Democratic legislature wrote a new constitution, which was approved by the voters in 1876.

While most southern states were economically prostrate, the Texas economy flourished because of the rapid development of the cattle industry. Millions of Texas cattle walked the trails to northern markets, where they were sold for hard cash, providing a bonanza for the state. The widespread use of barbed wire to fence cattle ranches in the 1880s ended the open range and encouraged scientific cattle breeding. By 1900, Texas began to transform its predominantly agricultural economy into an industrial one. This process was accelerated by the discovery of the Spindletop oil field—the state's first gusher—near Beaumont in 1901, and by the subsequent development of the petroleum and petrochemical industries. World War I saw the emergence of Texas as a military training center. The rapid growth of the

aircraft industry and other high-technology fields contributed to the continuing industrialization of Texas during and after World War II.

Texas politics remained solidly Democratic during most of the modern era, and the significant political conflict in the state was between the liberal and conservative wings of the Democratic Party. Populist-style reforms were enacted slowly during the governorships of James E. Ferguson—impeached and removed from office during his second term in 1917—and of his wife, Miriam A. "Ma" Ferguson (1925–27, 1933–35), and more rapidly during the two administrations of James V. Allred (1935–39). During the 1960s and 1970s, the Republican Party gathered strength in the state, electing John G. Tower as US senator in 1961 and William P. Clements, Jr., as governor in 1978—the first Republicans to hold those offices since Reconstruction. In general, the state's recent political leaders, Democrats was well as Republicans, have represented property interests and taken a conservative line.

On the national level, Texans have been influential since the 1930s, notably through such congressional leaders as US House Speaker Sam Rayburn and Senate Majority Leader Lyndon B. Johnson. Johnson, elected vice president under John F. Kennedy, was riding in the motorcade with the president when Kennedy was assassinated in Dallas on 22 November 1963. The city attained further national notoriety when Kennedy's alleged killer, Lee Harvey Oswald, was shot to death by Jack Ruby, a Dallas nightclub operator, two days later. Johnson served out the remainder of Kennedy's term, was elected to the presidency by a landslide in 1964, and presided over one of the stormiest periods in US history before retiring to his LBJ ranch in 1969. Memorials to him include the Lyndon B. Johnson Library at Austin and the renamed Lyndon B. Johnson Space Center, headquarters for the US manned spaceflight program, near Houston.

The most prominent Texan on the national scene since Johnson has been Republican George Bush, who, in 1980, after failing in his bid for the Republican presidential nomination, became Ronald Reagan's running mate; Reagan and Bush won in 1980 and were reelected in 1984. Bush ran for and won the presidency in 1988, but was defeated in his 1992 bid for re-election by Bill Clinton. Bush's son, George W. Bush, was elected governor of Texas in 1994, succeeding Democrat Ann Richards, the second woman governor in Texas history.

Texas benefited from a booming oil industry in the seventies. The economy grew at an average of 6% a year, more than twice the national average. The boom collapsed in the early eighties as overproduction caused world oil prices to plummet. The state's annual rate of population growth, 60% of which came from migration, dropped from 4% in 1982 to 1.3% in 1985. By 1986, the state had become a net exporter of population. Scrambling to make up the $100 million in revenues that the government estimated it lost for every $1 dollar decline in the price of a barrel of oil, the government in 1985 imposed or raised fees on everything from vanity license plates to day-care centers. The state also took steps to encourage economic diversification by wooing service, electronics, and high-technology companies to Texas. In 1985, the government and the University of Texas at Austin persuaded Microchips and Computer Corporation, which translates basic scientific research into computer innovations, to settle in Austin. In the late eighties, a number of Texas's financial institutions collapsed, brought down by the slump in the oil industry and by unsound real estate loans.

Since 1986, oil prices have increased and stabilized, and the state has reaped the benefits of diversification efforts spurred by the oil price collapse earlier in the decade. Although the petroleum industry was still the state's leading economic sector in the mid-1990s, high-technology and service sector jobs had played a major role in rebuilding the Texas economy and reversing the population decline of the previous decade. High-tech companies were concentrated in the "Silicon Hills" area surrounding Austin.

In the mid-1990s, Texas had the 2d-largest population of any state. The high rate of migration into Texas which accompanied the oil boom had a profound effect on the state's population distribution and political profile. Newcomers to the state have tended to share the fiscally conservative values of native Texans but take more liberal positions on issues such as abortion, civil rights, and homosexuality.

On 19 April 1993, the 51-day confrontation between the FBI and the Branch Davidian cult near Waco ended tragically when the group's compound burned to the ground, killing at least 72 persons.

12STATE GOVERNMENT

Texas has been governed directly under eight constitutions: the Mexican national constitution of 1824, the Coahuila-Texas state constitution of 1827, the independent Republic of Texas constitution of 1836, and the five US state constitutions of 1845, 1861, 1866, 1869, and 1876. This last document, with more than 250 amendments, is the foundation of the state government today. An attempt to replace it with eight propositions that in effect would have given Texas a new constitution was defeated at the polls in November 1975.

The state legislature consists of a senate of 31 members elected to four-year terms, and a house of representatives of 150 members elected to two-year terms. The legislature meets on the 2d Tuesday in January of odd-numbered years for sessions of as many as 140 calendar days; the governor may also call special sessions, each limited to 30 calendar days. Senators and representatives receive the same pay, pursuant to a constitutional amendment of 1975: $7,200 per year and $95 per diem living expenses while the legislature is in session. The constitution requires that senators be 26 years of age and residents of the state for five years prior to election; for representatives, the requirements are 21 years of age and two years of residency.

The state's chief executives are the governor and lieutenant governor, separately elected to four-year terms. Other elected executives, also serving for four years, are the attorney general, comptroller, treasurer, commissioner of agriculture, and commissioner of the general land office. The remaining cabinet members are appointed by the governor, who also appoints members of the many executive boards and commissions. The governor, whose salary was $99,122 as of 1996, must be a US citizen, at least 30 years of age, and must have resided in the state for at least five years prior to election. A uniquely important executive agency is the Texas Railroad Commission, established in 1891 and consisting of three members, elected for six-year terms, who regulate the state's oil and gas production, coal and uranium mining, and trucking industry, in addition to the railroads. The commission thus wields extraordinary economic power, and the alleged influence by the regulated industries over the commission has been a major source of political controversy.

To become law, a bill must be approved by a majority of members present and voting in each house, with a quorum of two-thirds of the membership present, and either signed by the governor or left unsigned for 10 days while the legislature is in session or 20 days after it has adjourned. A gubernatorial veto may be overridden by a two-thirds vote of members present in the house of origin, followed by either a vote of two-thirds of members present in the lower house or two-thirds of the entire membership of the senate (the difference is the result of differing interpretations of an ambiguity in the state constitution). Overrides are rare: the vote in April 1979 by state legislators to override the new Republican governor's veto of a minor wildlife regulation measure affecting only one county was the first

successful attempt in 38 years—and the last one as of July 1985. A constitutional amendment requires a two-thirds vote of the membership of each house and ratification by the voters at the next election.

In order to vote in Texas, one must be a US citizen and 18 years of age or over; there is a 30-day residency requirement.

13POLITICAL PARTIES

The Democratic Party has dominated politics in Texas. William P. Clements, Jr., elected governor in 1978, was the first Republican since Reconstruction to hold that office. No Republican carried Texas in a presidential election until 1928, when Herbert Hoover defeated Democrat Al Smith, a Roman Catholic at a severe disadvantage in a Protestant fundamentalist state. Another Roman Catholic, Democratic presidential candidate John Kennedy, carried the state in 1960 largely because he had a Texan, Lyndon Johnson, on his ticket.

Prior to the Civil War, many candidates for statewide office ran as independents. After a period of Republican rule during Reconstruction, Democrats won control of the statehouse and state legislature in 1873. The major challenge to Democratic rule during the late 19th century came not from Republicans but from the People's Party, whose candidates placed second in the gubernatorial races of 1894, 1896, and 1898, aided by the collapse of the cotton market; imposition of a poll tax in 1902 helped disfranchise the poor white farmers and laborers who were the base of Populist support. The Populists and the Farmers' Alliance probably exercised their greatest influence through a Democratic reformer, Governor James S. Hogg (1891–95), who fought the railroad magnates, secured lower freight rates for farmers and shippers, and curbed the power of large landholding companies. Another Democratic governor, James E. "Farmer Jim" Ferguson, was elected on an agrarian reform platform in 1914 and reelected in 1916, but was impeached and convicted the following year for irregular financial dealings. Barred from holding state office, he promoted the candidacy of his wife, Miriam "Ma" Ferguson, whose first term as governor (1925–27) marked her as a formidable opponent of the Ku Klux Klan. During her second term (1933–35), the state's first New Deal reforms were enacted, and prohibition was repealed. The Fergusons came to represent the more liberal wing of the Democratic Party in a state where liberals have long been in the minority. After the progressive administration of Governor James V. Allred, during which the state's first old-age assistance program was enacted, conservative Democrats, sometimes called "Texas Tories," controlled the state until the late 1970s.

There is no voter registration by party in Texas; as of November 1993, the state had 8,439,874 registered voters. Republican and native son George Bush captured 56% of the vote in the 1988 presidential election and 41% in the 1992 election. In 1996, Republican Bob Dole won 49% of the presidential vote, Democrat Bill Clinton gained 44%, and 7% went to Independent Ross Perot. In the November 1994 elections, the former president's son, George W. Bush, Jr., upset Ann Richards to become governor. Republican Kay Bailey Hutchison was elected in 1993 to fill the seat vacated by Democratic Senator Lloyd Bentsen, who resigned to become secretary of the treasury in the Clinton administration. In 1994, Hutchinson won re-election to a full term. Republican Phil Gramm was re-elected to the Senate in 1996. Going into 1997, Democrats held 17 seats in the US House of Representatives and the Republicans 13. The Democrats continued to control the state house after the November 1996 elections, by a margin of 82 to 68, but the Republicans won a slim majority of 16–14 in the state senate.

Aside from the Populists, third parties have played a minor role in Texas politics. The Native American (Know-Nothing) Party helped elect Sam Houston governor in 1859. In 1968,

George Wallace of the American Independent Party won 19% of the Texas popular vote and in 1992 native son Ross Perot picked up 22% of the vote.

Following passage of the federal Voting Rights Act of 1965, registration of black voters increased to about 11.5% of the total population of voters. Between 1895 and 1967, no black person served as a state legislator. In 1993, however, there were 472 blacks holding elective office. Hispanic elected officials in 1994 numbered 2,215. Democrat Henry Cisneros, former mayor of San Antonio, served as Secretary of Housing and Urban Development in the Clinton Administration. As of 1995, 33 women served in the state legislature and 2 women held elective executive office.

14 LOCAL GOVERNMENT

The Texas constitution grants considerable autonomy to local governments. As of 1992, Texas had 254 counties, a number that has remained constant since 1931. In 1983 there were 1,171 municipal governments, about 1,100 school districts (down from 8,600 in 1910), and at least 2,266 special districts.

Each county is governed by a commissioners' court of five members, consisting of four commissioners elected by precinct and a county judge or administrator elected at large. Other elected officials generally include a county clerk. attorney, treasurer, assessor-collector, and sheriff.

15 STATE SERVICES

For a state of its size and population, Texas provides rather limited statewide services to its citizens. It has no ombudsman, ethics commission, consumer protection division, department of housing, or unified environmental protection agency.

Educational services in the public schools are administered by the Texas Education Agency, which is run by a commissioner of education appointed by an elected State Board of Education; the State Textbook Committee, appointed by the board, oversees textbook purchases statewide. The Coordinating Board for the State College and University System, consisting of appointed members, oversees public higher education. Transportation facilities are regulated by the State Highway and Public Transportation Commission, the Texas Railroad Commission, and the Texas Aeronautics Commission.

Health and welfare services are offered by the Department of Health and the Department of Human Resources, while public protection is the responsibility of the National Guard, Texas Department of Corrections, and Texas Youth Council, which maintains institutions for juvenile offenders. Labor services are provided by the Texas Employment Commission and the Department of Labor and Standards.

16 JUDICIAL SYSTEM

The Texas judiciary comprises the supreme court, the state court of criminal appeals, 14 courts of appeals, and more than 380 district courts.

The highest court is the supreme court, consisting of a chief justice and eight justices, who are popularly elected to staggered six-year terms. As of September 1996, each justice received a salary of $94,686 annually, and the chief justice earned an additional $2,784. The court of criminal appeals, which has final jurisdiction in most criminal cases, consists of a presiding judge and eight judges, also elected to staggered six-year terms.

Justices of the courts of appeals are elected to six-year terms and sit in 14 judicial districts; each court has a chief justice and at least two associate justices. Chief justices receive annual salaries from the state ($98,482 in 1996). There were 386 district court judges in 1996, each elected to a four-year term, and receiving state salaries of $85,217 each, plus supplemental payments by local subdivisions. County, justice of the peace, and municipal courts handle local matters.

On 31 December 1995, there were 129,457 offenders incarcerated within the Texas Department of Criminal Justice facilities, or 691 per 100,000. Texas has a much lower crime rate than the national average, according to the 1995 US Department of Justice Uniform Crime Report and the 1995 Texas Department of Public Safety's (DPS) Texas Crime Report. Overall, according to the Texas DPI Crime Index, Texas had a 1995 crime rate of 5,684.5 per 100,000 population, 663.7 for violent crimes and 5,020.8 for property crimes. Rates for specific crimes were murder, 9.0; forcible rape, 45.5; robbery, 179.8; aggravated assault, 429.3; burglary, 1,082.2; larceny-theft, 3,378.1; and motor vehicle theft, 560.5. Texas criminal law provides for capital punishment by lethal intravenous injection for certain violent crimes. Between 7 December 1982 and 6 May 1997, 116

Texas Presidential Vote by Political Parties, 1948–96

YEAR	ELECTORAL VOTE	TEXAS WINNER	DEMOCRAT	REPUBLICAN	STATES' RIGHTS DEMOCRAT	PROGRESSIVE	PROHIBITION
1948	23	*Truman (D)	750,700	282,240	106,909	3,764	2,758
					CONSTITUTION		
1952	24	*Eisenhower (R)	969,227	1,102,818	1,563	—	1,983
1956	24	*Eisenhower (R)	859,958	1,080,619	14,591	—	—
1960	24	*Kennedy (D)	1,167,935	1,121,693	18,170	—	3,868
1964	25	*Johnson (D)	1,663,185	958,566	5,060	—	—
					AMERICAN IND.		
1968	25	Humphrey (D)	1,266,804	1,227,844	584,269	—	—
					AMERICAN	SOC. WORKERS	
1972	26	*Nixon (R)	1,154,289	2,298,896	6,039	8,664	—
1976	26	*Carter (D)	2,082,319	1,953,300	11,442	1,723	—
					LIBERTARIAN		
1980	26	*Reagan (R)	1,881,147	2,510,705	37,643	—	—
1984	29	*Reagan (R)	1,949,276	3,433,428	—	—	—
						NEW ALLIANCE	
1988	29	*Bush (R)	2,352,748	3,036,829	30,355	7,208	—
					POPULIST/AMERICA FIRST		IND. (Perot)
1992	32	Bush (R)	2,281,815	2,496,071	19,699	505	1,354,781
1996	32	Dole (R)	2,549,683	2,736,167	20,256	—	378,537

* Won US presidential election.

persons were executed in Texas, by far the highest number in the nation. There were over 62,000 attorneys practicing in Texas in 1997.

17ARMED FORCES

In few states do US military forces and defense-related industries play such a large role as in Texas, which as of 30 September 1992 had 115,246 military personnel and 51,712 civilians employed at major US military bases. In 1995/96 Texas received prime defense contract awards worth more than $8.8 billion.

Ft. Sam Houston, at San Antonio, is headquarters of the US 5th Army, while Ft. Bliss, at El Paso, is the home of the US Army Air Defense Center. Ft. Hood, near Killeen, is headquarters of the 3d Army Corps and other military units, with 43,328 military personnel in 1996. It is the state's single largest defense installation. Ft. Sam Houston is also the headquarters of the US Army Health Services Command and the site of the Academy of Health Sciences, the largest US military medical school, enrolling more than 25,000 officers and enlisted personnel and providing correspondence courses for another 30,000 students. Brooke Army Medical Center, the 2d-largest US Army hospital, is located at the same installation. William Beaumont Army Medical Center, at El Paso, is one of the nation's largest US Army hospitals and one of its most modern medical treatment centers.

Four principal Air Force bases are located near San Antonio: Brooks, Kelly, Lackland, and Randolph. Other major air bases are Dyess (Abilene); Ellington (southwest of Houston); Goodfellow (San Angelo); Laughlin (Del Rio); Reese (Lubbock); and Sheppard (Wichita Falls). All US-manned spaceflights are controlled from the Lyndon B. Johnson Space Center, operated by the National Aeronautics and Space Administration. Naval air training stations are located at Corpus Christi, Beeville, Dallas, and Kingsville. The Inactive Ships Maintenance Facility, at Orange, is home port for some of the US Navy's "mothball fleet."

Texas was a major military training center during World War II, when about one out of every 10 soldiers was trained there. Some 750,000 Texans served in the US armed forces during that war; the state's war dead numbered 23,022. Military veterans living in the state as of 1 July 1996 totaled 1,617,000, including fewer than 500 who served in World War I, 404,000 in World War II, 271,000 during the Korean conflict, 579,000 during the Viet Nam era, and 110,000 in the Persian Gulf War. Expenditures on Texas veterans exceeded $2.9 billion in 1995/96.

The Texas Army National Guard has dual status as a federal and state military force; its assigned strength plus Army Reserve personnel was 58,271 as of 1996. The Air Force National Guard and Reserve had 16,537 personnel. The Texas State Guard—an all-volunteer force available either to back up National Guard units or to respond to local emergencies—had some 2,500 members.

The famous Texas Rangers, a state police force first employed in 1823 (though not formally organized until 1835) to protect the early settlers, served as scouts for the US Army during the Mexican War. Many individual rangers fought with the Confederacy in the Civil War; during Reconstruction, however, the rangers were used to enforce unpopular carpetbagger laws. Later, the rangers put down banditry on the Rio Grande. The force was reorganized in 1935 as a unit of the Department of Public Safety and is now called on in major criminal cases, helps control mob violence in emergencies, and sometimes assists local police officers. The Texas Rangers have been romanticized in fiction and films, but one of their less glamorous tasks has been to intervene in labor disputes on the side of management. In 1993 the Texas Department of Public Safety employed 2,700 full-time sworn officers, or 2 per 10,000 residents.

18MIGRATION

Estimates of the number of Indians living in Texas when the first Europeans arrived range from 30,000 to 130,000. Eventually, they all were killed, fled southward or westward, or were removed to reservations. The first great wave of white settlers, beginning in 1821, came from nearby southern states, particularly Tennessee, Alabama, Arkansas, and Mississippi; some of these newcomers brought their black slaves to work in the cotton fields. During the 1840s, a second wave of immigrants arrived directly from Germany, France, and eastern Europe.

Interstate migration during the second half of the 19th century was accelerated by the Homestead Act of 1862 and the westward march of the railroads. Particularly notable since 1900 has been the intrastate movement from rural areas to the cities; this trend was especially pronounced from the end of World War II, when about half the state's population was rural, to the late 1970s, when nearly four out of every five Texans made their homes in metropolitan areas.

Texas's net gain from migration between 1940 and 1980 was 1,821,000, 81% of that during the 1970-80 period. A significant proportion of postwar immigrants were seasonal laborers from Mexico, remaining in the US either legally or illegally. By 1990, Texas had a foreign-born population of 1,524,436, representing 9% of the total. During 1980-83, Texas had the highest net migration gain—922,000—in the nation. From 1985 to 1990, the net gain from migration was 36,700. Between 1990 and 1996, the state had net gains of 428,300 in domestic migration and 491,931 in international migration. In 1996, 83,385 foreign immigrants arrived in Texas. In the same year, the state's foreign-born population was 2,081,000, or 11% of the total population. As of 1994, the number of undocumented immigrants was estimated at between 300,000 and 427,000, the third-highest total in the nation. As of 1990, 64.7% of all Texans were native born. Only 49% of residents age 5 and older in 1990 were living in the same house as in 1985. Of those who were living in a different house in 1985, about 85% did so within Texas.

19INTERGOVERNMENTAL COOPERATION

The Texas Advisory Commission on Intergovernmental Relations—including three state senators, three representatives, and (ex officio) the lieutenant governor and the speaker of the state house of representatives—works to improve coordination between state, local, and federal governments. The Texas Commission on Interstate Cooperation, similarly constituted but with greater legislative participation, represents Texas before the Council of State Governments. Texas is a member of the Interstate Mining Compact and Interstate Oil and Gas Compact. The state is also a signatory to the Gulf States Marine Fisheries Compact, Southern Interstate Energy Compact, and Southern Regional Education Compact, and to accords apportioning the waters of the Canadian, Peeks, and Saline rivers and the Rio Grande.

During 1995/96, Texas received just over $13 billion in federal aid.

20ECONOMY

Traditionally, the Texas economy has been dependent on the production of cotton, cattle, timber, and petroleum. In recent years, cotton has declined in importance, cattle ranchers have suffered financial difficulties because of increased production costs, and lumber production has remained relatively stable. But in the 1970s, as a result of rising world petroleum prices, oil and natural gas emerged as by far the state's most important resource. The decades since World War II have also witnessed a boom in the electronics, computer, transport equipment, aerospace, and communications industries, which has placed Texas 2d only to

California in manufacturing among all the states of the Sunbelt region.

The Lone Star State's robust economy in the early 1980s was due chiefly to a plentiful labor market, high worker productivity, diversification of new industries, and less restrictive regulation of business activities than in most other states. The result was a steady increase in industrial production, construction values, retail sales, and personal income, coupled with a relatively low rate of unemployment. Between 1972 and 1982, the Texas economy grew 6 percent a year, twice the national average. Texas was also helped by a booming oil industry. In 1982, however, Texas began to be affected by worldwide recession. In addition, lower energy demand, worldwide overproduction of oil, and the resulting fall in prices, caused a steep decline in the state's petroleum industry. Unemployment in Texas increased from 6.9% in 1982 to 8% in 1983, a period during which the national rate fell 0.1%. Much of this unemployment was among persons who came to Texas seeking jobs, particularly from northern industrial states. The rise and fall in the oil industry's fortunes affected other industries as well. Thousands of banks had speculated in real estate in the early eighties. By the late eighties, many of their investments had become worthless, and numerous banks were declared insolvent.

In the wake of the oil-centered recession, Texas began attempts to diversify. The state government has successfully wooed high-tech industries to locate in Texas. The percentage of economic activity contributed by the energy industry dropped from 20% to 10% between 1980 and 1990. Electronics, telecommunications, food processing, services and retail trade, on the other hand, saw substantial growth in the late 1980s and helped Texas through the national recession of 1990. Texas's gross state product in 1994 was $479.774 billion, to which private goods-producing industries contributed $135,902 million; private services-producing industries, $285,163 million; and government, $58,709 million. Texas's per capita personal income was $21,206 in 1995, placing it 30th in the nation. During 1996, there were 61,515 bankruptcy filings, up 27% from the previous year.

21INCOME

In 1994, personal nonfarm income in Texas amounted to $358.8 billion, or more than 6.4% of the US total; per capita personal income during the same year reached $19,716, 32d among the states. The state's personal income enjoyed a real growth of 24% from 1981 to 1990, compared with a national growth average of 32%. From 1991 to 1996, however, real total personal income grew by 20.2%, whereas the nation's growth was just over 15% during those years.

Major sources of earnings in 1994 are represented in the following table (in millions):

Total, of which:	$275,630.3
Farm	3,586.4
Agricultural services, forestry, fisheries, and other	1,768.1
Mining	11,302.9
Construction	15,354.5
Manufacturing	41,955.3
Transportation and public utilities	23,787.4
Wholesale and retail trade	45,591.6
Finance, insurance, and real estate	16,705.7
Services	72,153.7
Government	43,224.7

The median household income in Texas was $32,039 in 1995. In the same year, 17.4% of all Texans were living below the federal poverty line. Famed for its cattle barons and oil millionaires, Texas was the home of an estimated 150,000 of the nation's wealthiest households (about 2.4% of the state's total).

Among metropolitan areas in 1994, per capita personal income for Dallas was $24,480; Houston, $23,046; Ft. Worth-Arlington, $21,412; Galveston-Texas City, $20,107; Tyler, $19,994; and Austin, $20,611.

22LABOR

With a civilian labor force of 9,748,000 in 1996, Texas ranked 2nd among the 50 states; of that total, 9,200,000 were employed, with an unemployment rate of 5.6%. In February 1997, the metropolitan areas with the lowest unemployment rates were Bryan-College Station (2.5%), Austin-San Marcos (3.4%), and San Angelo (3.6%). Areas with the highest unemployment rates included El Paso (11.8%), Laredo (12.3%), Brownsville-Harlingen-San Benito (12.9%), and McAllen-Edinburg-Mission (21.7%). The largest number of unemployed persons lived in south Texas and the Rio Grande Valley; many of the unemployed and under-employed workers were Mexican aliens, some of them legal residents of the US, others not.

At the end of 1996, the greatest nonagricultural employment was in services (2,251,300), followed by wholesale and retail trade (2,069,100); government (1,509,500); manufacturing (1,050,300); transportation and public utilities (500,700); finance, insurance, and real estate (447,500); construction (438,600); and mining (153,800).

Organized labor has never been able to establish a strong base in Texas, and a state right-to-work law continues to make unionization difficult. The earliest national union, the Knights of Labor, declined in Texas after failing to win a strike against the railroads in 1886, when the Texas Rangers served as strike breakers. That same year, the American Federation of Labor (AFL) began to organize workers along craft lines. One of the more protracted and violent disputes in Texas labor history occurred in 1935, when longshoremen struck Gulf coast ports for 62 days. The Congress of Industrial Organizations (CIO) succeeded in organizing oil-field and maritime workers during the 1930s. As of 1995, labor union membership in manufacturing industries in the state represented 8.9% of the manufacturing workforce. Unionization for all employment sectors was 6.5%.

Manufacturing workers earned an average weekly wage of $531.47 in December 1996.

23AGRICULTURE

Texas ranked 2nd among the 50 states in agricultural production in 1995, with farm marketings totaling over $13 billion; crops accounted for 36% of the total. Texas leads the nation in output of cotton, grain sorghum, watermelons, cabbages, and spinach.

Since 1880, Texas has been the leading producer of cotton (producing both Upland and American-Pima), which accounted for 24% of total US production and 12% of the state's farm marketings in 1995. After 1900, Texas farmers developed bumper crops of wheat, corn, and other grains by irrigating dry land and transformed the "great Sahara" of West Texas into one of the nation's foremost grain-growing regions. Texans also grow practically every vegetable suited to a temperate or semitropical climate. Since World War II, farms have become fewer and larger, more specialized in raising certain crops and meat animals, more expensive to operate, and far more productive.

About 130 million acres (52.6 million hectares) are devoted to farms and ranches, representing more than three-fourths of the state's total area. The number of farms declined from 420,000 in 1940 to fewer than 185,000 in 1978, but rose to 205,000 in 1996. The average farm was valued at $550 per acre in 1995. During the 1940–70 period, the farm population decreased from 2,160,000 persons to 471,000; as of 1990, there were over 192,000 people (1.1% of the state's population) living on Texas farms and ranches.

Productive farmland is located throughout the state. Grains are grown mainly in the temperate north and west, and vegetables and citrus fruits in the subtropical south. Cotton has been grown in all sections, but in recent years, it has been extensively cultivated in the High Plains of the west and the upper Rio Grande Valley. Grain sorghum, wheat, corn, hay, and other forage crops are raised in the north-central and western plains regions. Rice is cultivated along the Gulf coast, and soybeans are raised mainly in the High Plains and Red River Valley.

Major crops in 1996 are shown in the following table:

	HARVESTED ACRES (000)	PRODUCTION (000)	VALUE (000 DOLLARS)
Upland cotton	4,000	4,350 bales	$1,394,784
Wheat	2,900	75,400 bushels	380,770
Hay	4,350	7,815 tons	707,865
Sorghum, grain	3,800	102,144 bushels	601,920
Corn	1,800	201,600 bushels	655,200
Rice	298	18,465 cwt	192,036
Vegetables, fresh	111.7	24,162 tons	257,884
Soybeans	270	7,020 bushels	47,736

The major vegetables and fruits, in terms of value, are onions, cabbages, watermelons, carrots, potatoes, cantaloupes, green peppers, honeydew melons, spinach, cucumbers, and lettuce. Cottonseed, barley, oats, peanuts, pecans, sugar beets, sugarcane, and sunflowers are also produced in commercial quantities.

The total value of farmland and buildings alone was estimated at $71 billion in 1995, higher than any other state.

Irrigated farmland in 1992 totaled 4.9 million acres (2 million hectares), of which about 65% was in the High Plains; other areas dependent on irrigation included the lower Rio Grande Valley and the trans-Pecos region. Approximately 80% of the irrigated land is supplied with water pumped from wells. Because more than half of the state's irrigation pumps are fueled by natural gas, the cost of irrigation increased significantly as gas prices rose during the 1970s. Texas's water use for irrigation was 5th among the states in 1990, at nearly 8.5 billion gallons.

24ANIMAL HUSBANDRY

About 60% of cattle fattened for market are kept in feedlots located in the Texas panhandle and northwestern plains. In 1997, Texas ranked 1st in number of cattle and calves with around 14.1 million, valued at $6.2 billion. During 1996, Texas farms had around 500,000 hogs and pigs, valued at $43 million. In 1995, Texas ranked 1st in the production of sheep and lambs with 83.47 million lb, valued at $64.3 million; Texas also ranked 1st in shorn wool production with nearly 13.5 million lb of wool.

About 90% of the dairy industry is located in eastern Texas. In 1995, milk production was around 6 billion lb from 401,000 milk cows. Poultry production included 1.7 billion lb of broilers, valued at around $646 million (ranked 6th among the states), and 3.95 billion eggs were produced, valued at $218 million.

Breeding of Palominos, Arabians, Appaloosas, Thoroughbreds, and quarter horses is a major industry in Texas. The animals are most abundant in the most heavily populated areas, and it is not unusual for residential subdivisions of metropolitan areas to include facilities for keeping and riding horses.

25FISHING

Texas in 1995 recorded a commercial catch of 94,674,000 lb, valued at $198,876,000 (5th). The leading commercial fishing ports are Brownsville-Port Isabel, Aransas Pass-Rockport, and Freeport.

Shrimp accounted for about 81% of the total volume of the catch in 1995; other commercial shellfish include blue crabs and oysters. Species of saltwater fish with the greatest commercial value are yellowfin tuna, red snapper, swordfish, and flounder.

Texas had 4,578 commercial fishing vessels and boats in 1994, and 147 fish processing and wholesale plants employing 1,919 persons. Early in 1980, the US government banned shrimp fishing for 45 days, effective in the summer of 1981, in order to conserve shrimp supplies. Texas has since continued to close the Gulf to shrimping from about 1 June to 15 July.

The state manages fish stocks and habitats to maintain 40.4 million freshwater and 14.5 million marine angler days per year. In 1995/96, Texas issued over 1,755,976 sport fishing licenses. Among the most sought-after native freshwater fish are largemouth and white bass, crappie, sunfish, and catfish.

26FORESTRY

Texas forestland in 1994 covered 23,000,000 acres (9,308,100 hectares), representing more than 3% of the US total and about 14% of the state's land area. Commercial timberland comprised 11,773,800 acres (4,764,857 hectares), of which 94% was privately owned. Included in this total are 3,767,400 acres (1,524,667 hectares) of timberland owned by the forest products industry and 7,223,000 acres (2,923,148 hectares) owned by non-industrial private individuals, farmers, and corporations. Timberlands managed by the federal government covered 668,500 acres (46,500 hectares). Timberland increased by some 208,500 acres (84,400 hectares) between 1986 and 1992. Most forested land, including practically all commercial timberland, is located in the Piney Woods region of east Texas.

In 1994, Texas timberlands yielded a harvest of 660.1 million cu ft of pine (up 12% from 1993) and 207.4 million cu ft of hardwoods (an increase of 11% over 1993). In 1994, 17% more pine was harvested than was grown. Meanwhile, hardwood harvests represented 96% of growth. In 1994, trees were planted on 92,208 acres (37,317 hectares) to help sustain the forest resource of the state.

Primary forest products manufactured in 1994 included 1.54 billion bd ft of lumber (87% softwood), 2.6 billion sq ft of plywood and waferboard, and 5.5 million cords of pulpwood (64% softwood). Texas wood-treating plants processed 24.5 million cu ft of timber products in 1994. Major treated products included 233,512 utility poles, 2.0 million crossties, 144.7 million bd ft of lumber, and 241,216 fence posts.

The estimated value of the industrial timber harvested in 1994 was $682,975,000, but that represents only a small fraction of the economic impact of the state's wood-based industry. In 1995, the value of shipments from the forest products industry totaled $14.1 billion, including $5.2 billion in lumber and wood products, $6.9 in paper and allied products, and $2 billion in furniture and fixtures. In 1995, lumber and paper manufacturing together employed 66,600 workers and paid over $1.6 billion in wages and salaries.

The Texas Forest Service, a member of the Texas A&M University System, provides direct, professional forestry assistance to private landowners, manages several state and federal reforestation and forest stewardship incentives programs, coordinates pest control activities, and assists in protecting against wildfires statewide. In addition, the state agency has an urban and community forestry program, forest products laboratory, two tree nurseries, and a genetics laboratory.

As of 1994 there were four national forests in Texas—Angelina, Davy Crockett, Sabine, and Sam Houston—with a total area of 637,134 acres (257,848 hectares). Texas also has five state forests: the E. O. Siecke, W. Goodrich Jones, I. D. Fairchild, John Henry Kirby, and Paul N. Masterson Memorial State Forests.

27MINING

According to estimates, 1995 nonfuel mineral production in Texas was valued at $1,660 million, $12 million higher than the

1994 total. Declines in value occurred only for sales of crude helium, Grade-A helium, and Frasch sulfur; all other nonfuel mineral commodities posted gains or held steady. Texas continued to rank 6th in overall mineral value. In 1995, Texas ranked 1st in crushed stone, 7th in dimension stone, 8th in kaolin, and 9th in fuller's earth. About 88% of Texas's common clay was used to make brick, portland cement, and structural concrete, and for highway surfacing. Output rose from the 1994 total of 2.19 million metric tons to 2.41 million metric tons. About 85% of the state's nonfuel mineral production value came from industrial minerals, especially portland cement, crushed stone, construction sand and gravel, salt, and lime. In 1995, Texas ranked 1st in crushed stone and magnesium metal; 2nd in portland cement, sodium sulfate, construction sand and gravel, salt, Frasch sulfur, zeolites, talc, pyrophyllite, crude helium, and ball clays; 3d in grade-A helium and crude gypsum; and 6th in industrial sand and gravel.

The following table details some of the mineral production and value in 1995:

	QUANTITY	UNIT	VALUE ($1000s)
Portland cement	8,990,000	metric tons	$475,000
Clays	2,410,000	metric tons	17,700
Crude gypsum	1,890,000	metric tons	9,360
Lime	1,360,000	metric tons	87,200
Salt	11,800,000	metric tons	99,700
Construction sand and gravel	55,600,000	metric tons	245,000
Industrial sand and gravel	1,540,000	metric tons	37,400
Crushed stone	83,600,000	short tons	343,000

28ENERGY AND POWER

Texas is an energy-rich state. Its vast deposits of petroleum and natural gas liquids account for nearly 30% of US proved liquid hydrocarbon reserves. Texas is also the largest producer and exporter of oil and natural gas to other states, and it leads the US in electric power production.

As of 31 December 1995, Texas power plants had a combined installed capacity of 68 million kW; their power output was 261.7 billion kWh, 8.7% of the US total. Gas-fired steam plants accounted for 39% of the production; coal, slightly less than 47%; oil less than 1%, and others 13%. In 1995, domestic sales of electricity totaled 262.3 million kWh, of which industrial plants used 34%, homes 35%, businesses 26%, and other consumers 5%. Major suppliers of electricity were Central Power & Light, Community Public Service, Dallas Power & Light, El Paso Electric, Gulf States Utilities, Houston Lighting & Power, Southwestern Electric Power, Southwestern Electric Service, Southwestern Public Service, Texas Electric Service, Texas Power & Light, Texas-New Mexico Power, and West Texas Utilities.

The state's first oil well was drilled in 1866 at Melrose in East Texas, and the first major oil discovery was made in 1894 at Corsicana, northwest of Melrose, in Navarro County. The famous Spindletop gusher, near Beaumont, was tapped on 10 January 1901. Another great oil deposit was discovered in the panhandle in 1921, and the largest of all, the East Texas field, in Rusk County, was opened in 1930. Subsequent major oil discoveries were made in West Texas, starting in Scurry County in 1948. Thirty years later, the state's crude-oil production exceeded 1 billion barrels. In 1983, production was 908.2 million barrels, averaging 2.5 million barrels per day. Production in 1996 was 543.3 million barrels (including over 1 million barrels from offshore wells), averaging 1.49 million barrels per day. Proved petroleum reserves at the end of 1995 were estimated at more than 5.7 billion barrels, representing almost 26% of total US reserves.

In 1995, Texas produced more than 6.3 trillion cu ft of natural gas, representing 32% of total US production. As of 31 December 1995, proved natural gas reserves were estimated at 36.5 trillion cu ft, 22% of the US total.

Coal production totaled 52.7 million tons in 1995, all from 14 surface mines. Almost 99% of the coal was lignite, nearly all of it used as fuel for electric generating plants close to the mines. Recoverable coal reserves were estimated at 940 million tons in 1995. As of 1996, four nuclear reactors—South Texas Project 1 and 2, in Matagorda County, and Comanche Peak 1 and 2, in Somervell County—were in operation. In 1994, energy consumption per capita in Texas was 564.1 million Btu, 3d highest in the nation. Energy expenditures per capita—$2,566—were 5th highest in 1994.

29INDUSTRY

Before 1900, Texas had an agricultural economy based, in the common phrase, on "cotton, cows, and corn." When the first US Census of Manufactures was taken in Texas in 1849, there were only 309 industrial establishments, with 1,066 wage earners; payrolls totaled $322,368, and the value added by manufacture was a mere $773,896. The number of establishments increased tenfold by 1899, when the state had 38,604 wage earners and a total value added of $38,506,130. During World War II, the value added passed the $1-billion mark, and by 1982, the total was $53.4 billion.

In 1995, the value of all shipments by manufacturers was $265 billion. The following table shows value of shipments for the state's principal industrial sectors during 1995:

Petroleum and coal products	$39,899,100,000
Chemicals and allied products	59,984,800,000
Food and food products	28,709,000,000
Electric and electronic equipment	24,912,000,000
Transportation equipment	14,317,100,000
Fabricated metal products	11,930,400,000
Primary metals	9,396,800,000
Instruments and related products	7,004,700,000
Printing and publishing	7,508,900,000
Rubber and plastics products	7,722,200,000
Paper and allied products	6,901,000,000
Apparel and other textile products	4,890,600,000
Stone, clay, and glass products	5,264,200,000
Lumber and wood products	5,180,000,000

Three of the state's leading industrial products—refined petroleum, industrial organic chemicals, and oil-field machinery—all stem directly from the petrochemical sector. Major oil refineries are located at Houston and other Gulf ports. Aircraft plants include those of North American Aviation and Chance-Vought at Grand Prairie, General Dynamics near Ft. Worth, and Bell Aircraft's helicopter division at Hurst. In 1997, Texas was the headquarters to 36 Fortune 500 companies, including Exxon, which ranked as the third-largest industrial corporation. During 1995, there were 4,335 US patents issued to Texas residents.

30COMMERCE

Texas ranked 3d among the 50 states in wholesale trade, with total sales of $281.3 billion in 1992. Sales of durable goods accounted for 40% of wholesale trade. Trade from wholesaling is an important source of personal income. The leading wholesaling centers are the Houston, Dallas-Ft. Worth, San Antonio, El Paso, Lubbock, Midland, Amarillo, Austin, and Corpus Christi metropolitan areas.

Texas ranked 2d behind California in retail sales, which amounted to $130.7 billion in 1992. Of the retail sales total, automotive dealers accounted for 22.9%; food stores, 20.2%;

general merchandise stores, 14.5%; restaurants and taverns, 10.3%; gasoline service stations, 6.9%; furniture and home furnishing stores, 4.7%; and others, 20.5%.

An amendment to the state constitution permits counties to vote on whether to allow sales of liquor by the drink. As of 31 August 1982, distilled spirits were legal in all or part of 167 counties; 2 counties permitted beverages with an alcohol content of 14% or less; 11 counties permitted only 4% beer; and 74 counties were wholly dry.

Foreign exports through the five customs districts in Texas during 1995 totaled $65.3 billion, imports $74.6 billion. The leading items shipped through Texas ports to foreign countries were grains, chemicals, fertilizers, and petroleum refinery products; principal imports included crude petroleum, minerals and metals (especially aluminum ores), liquefied gases, motor vehicles, bananas, sugar, and molasses. Exports of the state's own products were valued at $66.9 billion in 1996. Texas ranked 2d among the 50 states in 1996 as a producer of goods for export.

31CONSUMER PROTECTION

The attorney general's Consumer Protection Division protects consumers and the legitimate business community by filing civil lawsuits under the Deceptive Trade Practices Act (DTPA) and other related statutes. The division is best known for its work in traditional areas of consumer protection litigation: false and deceptive advertising, defective merchandise, and home or appliance repair scams, for example. In addition, four specialized sections within the division protect Texas citizens in ways that go beyond the usual consumer issues. These are the Antitrust, Charitable Trusts, Insurance Practices, and Public Agency Representation sections.

The attorney general's litigation activities are supplemented by a highly effective mediation program that is available to Texas consumers who have complaints amenable to informal resolution. The Consumer Protection Division also disseminates a wide range of public information materials to educate consumers about their rights, alert them to trends in deceptive or unfair business practices, and prevent losses due to fraud before they occur. Over the years, the division has succeeded in winning funds for consumer education as part of the settlement of consumer protection litigation.

32BANKING

Texas has more banks than any other state and ranked 5th among the 50 states in commercial bank assets in 1996.

Banking was illegal in the Texas Republic and under the first state constitution, reflecting the widespread fear of financial speculation like that which had caused the panic of 1837. Because both the independent republic and the new state government found it difficult to raise funds or obtain credit without a banking system, they were forced to borrow money from merchants, thus permitting banking functions and privileges despite the constitutional ban. A formal banking system was legalized during the latter part of the 19th century.

At the end of 1996, Texas had 877 insured commercial banks; commercial bank assets totaled $205.2 billion, with 17 banks having assets of $1 billion or more. As of 31 December 1996, there were 445 state banks and 432 national banks for a total of 468 Federal Reserve members. In 1996, bank loans and leases outstanding by insured commercial banks amounted to $106.5 billion, of which commercial and industrial loans accounted for $36.8 billion and real estate loans $39.6 billion.

At the end of 1996, Texas had 52 insured savings institutions with combined assets of $62.3 billion; these associations held $33.7 billion in outstanding loans and $33.4 billion in capital deposits. Between 1986 and 1989, the number of bank closings in

Texas rose from 26 per year to 134, or 64.7% of all US bank closings. By 1993, the number of failed banks fell to 10. In 1994 and 1995, no banks failed, but in 1996, there were 2 banks closed. Today, 98% of the 445 banks in the state banking system are in good condition. The statistics for the national banks in Texas parallel state banking system numbers.

33INSURANCE

As of May 1997, Texas had 519 domestic life/health, property/casualty and title insurance companies and 67 domestic health maintenance organizations.

The industry's most recent state-by-state comparison showed Texas ranked 2d (behind Arizona) in number of domestic life companies in 1995 with 236, and 2d (behind Vermont) in the number of domestic property/casualty companies with 255.

In 1995, Texas life insurance in force with both domestic and foreign (out-of-state) companies totaled $741.2 billion. The number of life insurance policies and certificates in force as of 31 December 1995 was 15,293,368.

Property and casualty premiums written in 1995 totaled $17.9 billion, including $7.5 billion for private passenger auto and $2.3 billion for homeowners coverage.

The insurance industry is regulated by the Texas Department of Insurance. TDI is headed by the commissioner of insurance, who is appointed by the governor and confirmed by the state senate for two-year terms beginning 1 February of odd-numbered years. Governor George W. Bush appointed Elton Bomer as commissioner in 1995 and reappointed him in 1997.

34SECURITIES

Although there are no securities exchanges in Texas, several thousand broker-dealers are registered to conduct securities transactions, with the number of designated agents approaching 100,000. Securities investment advice is professionally marketed by registered firms. The State Securities Board, established in 1957, oversees the issuance and sale of stocks and bonds in Texas.

35PUBLIC FINANCE

The Texas budget operates on a "pay as you go" basis in that expenditures cannot exceed revenue during the budget cycle. The state's budget period runs on a biennial basis from September 1 of each odd-numbered year to August 31 of the following odd-numbered year.

The state legislature meets from approximately January to May every odd-numbered year and writes a budget for the next two years. The appropriations committee in the house, and the finance committee in the senate are responsible for budget development. The primary legislative entity responsible for oversight of the budget when the legislature is not in session is the 10-member legislative budget board. Chaired by the lieutenant governor, the board prepares the initial budget which will be considered by the legislature.

The governor's office of budget and planning also prepares a budget for the Legislature's consideration. The governor has line-item veto authority over the budget and must sign the appropriations bill before it becomes law. The comptroller of public accounts must also sign the bill certifying that sufficient revenue will be available to fund the budget.

After running large budget surpluses in the early 1980s, the state experienced several years of budget shortfalls in the wake of falling oil prices. As the state's economy has diversified, the budget has shown greater ability to withstand minor economic fluctuations. Revenue and expenditure for 1996/97 are presented below:

REVENUES	FY 1996/97 (IN MILLIONS)
Major Taxes	
Sales tax	$6,380.6
Oil production and regulation taxes	267.9
Natural gas production tax	415.5
Motor fuels taxes	1,344.7
Motor vehicle sales and rental taxes	1,115.1
Corporation franchise tax	152.6
Cigarette and tobacco taxes	341.9
Alcoholic beverage tax	246.0
Insurance company taxes	490.5
Utility taxes	132.9
Inheritance tax	100.5
Hotel and motel tax	98.1
Other taxes	290.3
TOTAL TAXES	11,376.7
Other Major Revenue Sources	
Federal Funds	6,983.2
Interest income	5,339.9
Licenses and fees	2,276.5
Contributions to employee benefits	104.4
Sales of goods and services	127.6
Land income	
Rent, royalties, and sales	155.1
Other revenue sources	880.1
Net lottery proceeds	1,077.0
TOTAL NET REVENUE	$28,320.3
EXPENDITURES	
Salaries and wages	$3,846.0
Employee benefits	
Employee benefit payments	1,507.1
Supplies and materials	307.4
Other expenditures	860.9
Public assistance payments	8,385.4
Intergovernmental payments	
Foundation school program grants	5,468.5
Other public education grants	1,211.3
Grants to higher education	386.9
Other grants	620.3
Travel	61.4
Professional services and fees	490.8
Payment of interest— debt service	280.1
Highway construction	1,711.1
Capital outlay	346.6
Repairs and maintenance	101.5
Communication and utilities	225.9
Rentals and leases	125.9
Claims and judgments	26.9
Costs of goods sold	93.5
Printing and reproduction	28.1
TOTAL NET EXPENDITURES	$25,545.4

36TAXATION

Texas's total tax collections amounted to almost $37.9 billion in 1996. The principal source of state tax revenue is the 6.25% sales and use tax. Other major sources of revenue are oil and natural-gas production taxes, motor fuel taxes, motor vehicle sales and rental tax, and cigarette and tobacco taxes. Other state levies include the corporation franchise tax, alcoholic beverage tax, public utility taxes, inheritance tax, and a tax on telephones.

Local property tax rates per $100 of assessed valuation varied widely throughout the state. The city sales tax is a major source of revenue for the municipalities. Although the state and local tax burden is well below the US average, tax collections per capita nearly tripled between 1972 and 1982. In 1978, Texans approved a constitutional amendment limiting further tax increases. The legislature responded the following year by passing a tax-cut package totaling about $400 million, including a comprehensive property tax reform bill and a public education bill to provide greater equity between rich and poor school districts. In 1984, the legislature significantly increased taxes for the first time in 13 years. Taxes on cigarettes and alcoholic beverages were increased, and various exemptions to the sales tax, including those on amusement admissions, cable television, and laundry and dry cleaning, were eliminated. Federal income collections in Texas during 1996 exceeded $92 billion.

37ECONOMIC POLICY

Texas state government has historically been pro business: regulation is less restrictive than in many states, and there is no corporate income tax. The state government actively encourages outside capital investment in Texas industries, and the state's industrial productivity has produced a generally high return on investment.

The Texas Economic Development Commission (formerly the Texas Industrial Commission) helps businesses locate or expand their operations in the state. A private organization, the Texas Industrial Development Council, in Bryan, also assists new and developing industries.

38HEALTH

Medical care ranges from adequate to excellent in the state's largest cities, but many small communities are without doctors and hospitals. Texas suffers from a general shortage of health care personnel: although the number of students enrolled in medical education programs more than doubled during the 1970s, many hospitals were functioning without adequate numbers of registered nurses, laboratory technicians, and therapists in the 1980s.

The infant mortality rate as of 1995 was 6.5 per 1,000 live births. In 1994, there were 83,419 legal abortions—19 per 1,000 women of childbearing age and 293 for each 1,000 live births. Rates for live births (17.2 per 1,000 population), marriages (9.5), and divorces (5.2) all exceeded the national norms in 1990.

The overall death rate in 1995 was 7.5 per 1,000 population. Texas ranked below the national average in deaths due to heart disease, cancer, and cerebrovascular diseases, but above average in deaths from accidents and suicide. The leading causes of death in 1995, with their rates per 100,000 population, were heart disease, 223.5; cancer, 169.5; cerebrovascular disease, 52.5; accidents, 34.4.

There were 5,859 new cases of AIDS in Texas in 1994. The overall AIDS rate is near the US national average. According to the CDC, nearly 5.4 million Texans 18–30 years of age smoke; this translates to 21.5% of the population 18–30 in 1995.

In 1994, Texas's 526 hospitals, with a total of 74,900 beds, admitted 2,048,600 patients and had 22,142,800 outpatient visits. In 1995, hospital personnel numbered 320,500, including 64,500 registered nurses and 2,900 medical and health care trainees. The average expense to a hospital for care provided per inpatient day was $1,950 in 1995, when the average hospital stay in Texas was 6.2 days and the expenses per stay totaled $12,050. Texas had 26,037 active, nonfederal licensed physicians in 1995. Twenty-three Texan counties (with a combined population of 59,943) each were without an active physician in patient care at the end of 1995. In 1995, Texas had 7,452 active, licensed dentists.

There are 8 medical schools, 2 dental colleges, and 64 schools of nursing in the state. The University of Texas has medical colleges at Dallas, Houston, Galveston, San Antonio, and Tyler. The University of Texas Cancer Center at Houston is one of the nation's major facilities for cancer research. Houston is also noted as a center for cardiovascular surgery. On 3 May 1968, Houston surgeon Denton Cooley performed the first human heart transplant in the US.

39SOCIAL WELFARE

In 1996, payments to families with dependent children were made to 714,500 Texans; the monthly payment per family averaged $226. In 1996, 2.37 million residents received monthly food stamp allowances averaging $75.18. Eligible schoolchildren enjoyed school-provided lunches, at a federal cost of $514.2 million.

With the enactment of the Personal Responsibility and Work Opportunity Reconciliation Act of 1996, the US government has changed the form and regulations for many of its social welfare programs; most significantly, it replaces Aid to Families with Dependent Children (AFDC), an open-ended entitlement program, with Temporary Assistance for Needy Families (TANF), a limited system of assistance funded largely through federal block grants. The reform act also impacts the food stamp program, the Supplemental Security Income program, and the child nutrition program. The law took effect on 1 July 1997 and provided $16.38 billion in block grants for fiscal years 1997–2002. The grants are to be divided among the states based on an equation involving the numbers of former AFDC recipients in each state. Because many of the bill's provisions have yet to be implemented into state-by-state policy, it was not possible to include the details of each state's programs for this edition of this work.

Social Security benefits were paid to 2.5 million Texans in 1995, averaging $698 a month. Federally administered Supplemental Security Income payments were made to 404,097 Texans, averaging $296 a month. Unemployment benefits in Texas averaged $186.97 a week in 1995.

40HOUSING

The variety of Texas architectural styles reflects the diversity of the state's topography and climate. In the early settlement period, Spanish-style adobe houses were built in southern Texas. During the 1840s, Anglo-American settlers in the east erected primitive log cabins. These were later replaced by "dog-run" houses, consisting of two rooms linked by an open passageway covered by a gabled roof, so-called because pet dogs slept in the open, roofed shelter, as did occasional overnight guests. During the late 19th century, southern-style mansions were built in East Texas, and the familiar ranch house, constructed of stone and usually stuccoed or whitewashed, with a shingle roof and a long porch, proliferated throughout the state; the modern ranch house in southwestern Texas shows a distinct Mexican-Spanish influence. Climate affects such modern amenities as air conditioning: a new house in the humid eastern region is likely to have a refrigeration-style cooler, while in the dry west and south, an evaporating "swamp cooler" is the more common means of making hot weather bearable.

In 1996, Texas had an estimated 7,348,000 year-round housing units, of which 6,677,000 were occupied. That year, 118,823 privately owned units, valued at nearly $10 billion, were authorized for construction; of these, 83,103 were single-family units. In 1990, the last year for which figures are available, the median home value was $59,600, down 4% from 1980 (in terms of 1990 dollars). The median monthly costs for owners (with a mortgage) and renters in 1990 were $712 and $395, respectively. From 1990 to 1992, the Dallas-Ft. Worth area had 55,900 new housing unit completions, while the Houston-Galveston-Brazoria area had 41,700 completions.

During 1995/96, Texas received $1.1 billion in aid from the US Department of Housing and Urban Development, including $278.8 million in community development block grants.

41EDUCATION

In 1995/96 Texas had 6,643 public school campuses with an enrollment of 3,740,260.

Although public instruction began in Texas as early as 1746, education was slow to develop during the period of Spanish and Mexican rule. The legislative foundation for a public school system was laid by the government of the Republic of Texas during the late 1830s, but funding was slow to develop. After annexation, in 1846, Galveston began to support free public schools, and San Antonio had at least four free schools by the time a statewide system of public education was established in 1854. Free segregated schooling was provided for black children beginning in the 1870s; their schools were ill-maintained and underfinanced. School desegregation was accomplished during the 1960s, nonviolently for the most part.

In 1990, more than 62% of the population 25 years old and over had completed at least four years of high school, and nearly 16.9% had four or more years of college. More than 20% had fewer than eight years of school, however, and the state's median of 12.4 school years lagged behind the US average. Enrollment in Texas's 6,643 public schools in 1995/96 was 2,750,204 in grades K–8 and 990,056 in grades 9–12. Teachers numbered 240,371 in 1995/96, and the average salary was $32,001. Institutions of higher education in 1994 included 35 public senior colleges and universities, 50 public community college campuses, and more than 38 private institutions with a combined enrollment of 923,197. Fall 1994 enrollment in Texas's community colleges was 400,323 students. The leading public universities are Texas A&M (College Station), which opened in 1876 and enrolled 43,256 students in the fall of 1994, and the University of Texas (Austin), founded in 1883, with 47,957 students enrolled in the same year; each institution is now the center of its own university system, including campuses in several other cities. Oil was discovered on lands owned by the University of Texas in 1923, and beginning in 1924, the university and Texas A&M shared more than $1 billion in oil-related rentals and royalties. Another state-supported institution, the University of Houston, enrolled 31,298 on its main campus in 1994, and Texas Tech University (Lubbock) enrolled 24,083.

The first private college in Texas was Rutersville, established by a Methodist minister in Fayette County in 1840. The oldest private institution still active in the state is Baylor University (1845), at Waco, with a 1994 enrollment of 12,240. Other major private universities include Hardin-Simmons (Abilene), Rice (Houston), Southern Methodist or SMU (Dallas), and Texas Christian, or TCU (Ft. Worth). Well-known black-oriented institutions of higher learning include Texas Southern University in Houston, and Prairie View A&M University.

Tuition charges to Texas colleges are among the lowest in the nation. The Texas Student Assistance Corp. administers a guaranteed-loan program and tuition equalization grants for needy students.

42ARTS

Although Texas has never been regarded as a leading cultural center, the arts have a long history in the state. The cities of Houston and Matagorda each had a theater before they had a church, and the state's first theater was active in Houston as early as 1838. Stark Young founded the Curtain Club acting group at the University of Texas in Austin in 1909, and the little-theater movement began in that city in 1921. The performing arts now flourish at Houston's Theater Center, Jones Hall of Performing Arts, and Alley Theater, as well as at Dallas's Theater Center, National Children's Theater, and Theater Three. The Margo Jones repertory company in Dallas has a national reputation, and there are major repertory groups in Houston and San Antonio. During the late 1970s, Texas also emerged as a center for motion picture production.

Texas has 5 major symphony orchestras—the Dallas Symphony (with Eduardo Mata as music director), Houston

Symphony, San Antonio Symphony, Austin Symphony, and Ft. Worth Symphony—and 25 orchestras in other cities. The Houston Grand Opera performs at Jones Hall; other opera companies perform regularly in Beaumont, Dallas, El Paso, Ft. Worth, and San Antonio. All these cities also have resident dance companies, as do Abilene, Amarillo, Austin, Corpus Christi, Denton, Galveston, Garland, Longview, Lubbock, Midland-Odessa, and Pampa.

Popular music in Texas stems from early Spanish and Mexican folk songs, Negro spirituals, cowboy ballads, and German-language songfests. Texans pioneered a kind of country and western music that is more outspoken and direct than Nashville's commercial product, and a colony of country-rock songwriters and musicians were active in the Austin area during the 1970s. Texans of Mexican ancestry have also fashioned a Latin-flavored music that is as distinctly "Tex-Mex" as the state's famous chili.

Arts program funds for the state of Texas amounted to $1,084,000 in the period from 1991 to 1996. The NEA contributed $3,340,000 to the programs and $3,316,000 to the Texas Commission on the Arts. The state also provided the Commission with funding.

Between 1987 and 1991, the state's arts programs attracted a total audience of about 22,539,000 and had 134,054 contributing artists. In the same period, the state provided about 50,000 of its school children with art education programs. In 1996, the state of Texas had 2,093 arts associations and 140 local arts groups. The Texas Commission on the Arts received grants from the NEA's state and regional program.

43LIBRARIES AND MUSEUMS

In 1995, the latest year for which data has been received, Texas public libraries served 246 counties and 16,313,265 people, and answered 16,368,226 reference questions, both in person and on the phone. During the same reporting period, there was a total collection of library materials of 51,502,286 and 73,012 subscriptions. Library materials include 36,619,252 print items, 14,847,068 items in microform, audio-visual, and film format, and 35,969 items in machine readable format. The total number of books and other materials checked out of Texas public libraries was 70,161,608, and this number does not include information printed or downloaded by patrons from electronic sources in the libraries.

Funding for public libraries in Texas comes from local cities, counties, school districts, and state and federal sources, with additional funding from donations, gifts, and corporate and foundation grants. The largest municipal libraries in Texas include the Houston Public Library with 7,317,762 items, and the Dallas Public Library with 7,235,235 items. The University of Texas at Austin, noted for outstanding collections in the humanities and in Latin American studies, had 7,176,889 volumes in 1995. The Lyndon B. Johnson Presidential Library is also located in Austin, as is the Lorenzo de Zavala State Archives and Library Building. Other notable academic libraries include those of Texas A&M University, with over 2,000,000 volumes, and the University of Houston, Rice University, Southern Methodist University, and Texas Tech University, all with collections of over 1,000,000 volumes.

Among the state's 367 museums are Austin's Texas Memorial Museum; the Dallas Museum of Fine Arts and the Dallas Museum of Art; and the Amon Carter Museum of Western Art, the Ft. Worth Art Museums, and Kimbell Art Museum, all in Ft. Worth. Houston has the Museum of Fine Arts, Contemporary Arts Museum, and at least 30 galleries. Both Dallas-Ft. Worth and Houston have become major centers of art sales.

National historic sites in Texas are Ft. Davis (Jeff Davis County), President Johnson's boyhood home and Texas White House (Blanco and Gillespie counties), and the San Jose Mission

(San Antonio). Other historic places include the Alamo, Dwight D. Eisenhower's birthplace at Denison, the Sam Rayburn home in Bonham, and the John F. Kennedy memorials in Dallas. A noteworthy prehistoric Indian site is the Alibates Flint Quarries National Monument, located in Potter County and accessible by guided tour.

44COMMUNICATIONS

The US Postal Service had about 42,000 employees and 1,495 post offices in Texas in March 1985. In March 1993, 92% of the 6,480,000 occupied housing units in Texas had telephones. Dallas was one of Western Union's first US communications satellite stations, and it leads the state as a center for data communications.

The state has not always been in the communications vanguard, however. Texas passed up a chance to make a handsome profit from the invention of the telegraph when, in 1838, inventor Samuel F. B. Morse offered his newfangled device to the republic as a gift. When the Texas government neglected to respond, Morse withdrew the offer.

Texas had 735 radio stations (281 AM, 454 FM) in 1996 and 106 commercial and 20 educational television stations in 1996. Twelve Texan television stations broadcast in Spanish. The state's first radio station, WRR, was established by the city of Dallas in 1920. The first television station, WBAP, began broadcasting in Ft. Worth in 1948. Cable television service was provided in 1996 by 31 large systems.

45PRESS

The first newspaper in Texas was a revolutionary Spanish-language sheet published in May 1813 at Nacagdoches. Six years later, the *Texas Republican* was published by Dr. James Long in the same city. In 1835, the *Telegraph and Texas Register* became the official newspaper of the Texas Republic, and it continued to publish until 1877. The first modern newspaper was the *Galveston News* (1842), a forerunner of the *Dallas Morning News* (1885). Other pioneering papers still in continuous publication include the *San Antonio Express* and the *Houston Post*.

By 1997, Texas had 90 morning, evening, and all-day dailies and 72 Sunday papers. The newspapers with the largest daily circulations were as follows:

AREA	NAME	DAILY	SUNDAY
Austin	*American-Statesman* (all day,S)	182,925	242,236
Dallas	*Morning News* (m,S)	494,266	803,610
Houston	*Chronicle* (all day,S)	551,553	764,443
San Antonio	*Express News*(all day,S)	222,413	387,506

In 1997, there were 437 weekly newspapers. The *Texas Almanac,* a comprehensive guide to the state, has been issued at regular intervals since 1857 by the A. H. Belo Corp., publishers of the *Dallas Morning News.* Leading magazines include the *Texas Monthly* and *Texas Observer,* both published in Austin.

46ORGANIZATIONS

The 1992 Census of Service Industries counted 4,458 organizations in Texas, including 969 business associations; 2,576 civic, social, and fraternal associations; and 913 other membership organizations.

Irving is the home of one of the nation's largest organizations, the Boy Scouts of America. Important medical groups are the American Heart Association, in Dallas, and the National Association for Retarded Citizens, Arlington. Professional societies include the American Association of Petroleum Landmen, Ft. Worth. The Noncommissioned Officers Association has its home office in San Antonio; the Airline Passengers Association is in Dallas. Among the many organizations devoted to horse breeding are the American Quarter Horse Association, Amarillo; Palomino

Horse Breeders of America, Mineral Wells; and the National Cutting Horse Association and American Paint Association, both in Ft. Worth. Ft. Worth is also the home of the Texas Longhorn Breeders Association of America.

47TOURISM, TRAVEL, AND RECREATION

Recent tourism statistics indicate that of the tourists that visited Texas in the 1990s, millions were foreigners, including nearly 200,000 Canadians and over 2 million Mexicans.

Each of the state's seven major tourist regions offers outstanding attractions. East Texas has one of the state's oldest cities, Nacogdoches, with the nation's oldest public thoroughfare and a reconstruction of the Old Stone Fort, a Spanish trading post dating from 1779. Jefferson, an important 19th-century inland port, has many old homes, including Excelsior House. Tyler, which bills itself as the "rose capital of the world," features a 28-acre (11-hectare) municipal rose garden and puts on a Rose Festival each October. The Gulf Coast region of southeastern Texas offers the Lyndon B. Johnson Space Center, the Astrodome sports stadium and adjacent Astroworld amusement park, and a profusion of museums, galleries, and shops, all in metropolitan Houston; Spindletop Park, in Beaumont, commemorating the state's first great oil gusher; Galveston's sandy beaches, deep-sea fishing, and Sea-Arama Marineworld; and the Padre Island National Seashore.

To the north, the Dallas-Ft. Worth metropolitan area (including Arlington) has numerous cultural and entertainment attractions, including the Six Flags Over Texas amusement park and the state fair held in Dallas each October. Old Abilene Town amusement park, with its strong western flavor, is also popular with visitors. The Hill Country of south-central Texas encompasses many tourist sites, including the state capitol in Austin, Waco's Texas Ranger Museum (Ft. Fisher), the Lyndon B. Johnson National Historic Site, and frontier relics in Bastrop and Bandera.

South Texas has the state's most famous historic site—the Alamo, in San Antonio, which also contains HemisFair Plaza and Brackenridge Park. The Rio Grande Valley Museum, at Harlingen, is popular with visitors, as is the King Ranch headquarters in Kleberg County. The Great Plains region of the Texas panhandle offers Palo Duro Canyon—Texas's largest state park, covering 16,402 acres (6,638 hectares) in Armstrong and Randall counties—the Prairie Dog Town at Lubbock, Old West exhibits at Matador, and the cultural and entertainment resources of Amarillo. In the extreme northwestern corner of the panhandle is the XIT Museum, recalling the famous XIT Ranch, at one time the world's largest fenced ranch, which formerly covered more than 3 million acres (1.2 million hectares). Outstanding tourist sites in the far west are the Big Bend and Guadalupe Mountains national parks, the Jersey Lilly Saloon and Judge Roy Bean visitor center in Langtry, and metropolitan El Paso.

Texas's growing park system attracted 24,248,552 visitors in 1994/95. In addition to Palo Duro Canyon, notable state parks include Big Creek (Ft. Bend County), Brazos Island (Cameron County), Caddo Lake (Harrison County), Dinosaur Valley (Somervell County), Eisenhower (Grayson County), Galveston Island, and Longhorn Cavern (Burnet County). State historical parks include San Jacinto Battleground (east Harris County), Texas State Railroad (Anderson and Cherokee counties), and Washington-on-the-Brazos (Washington County).

Hunting and fishing are extremely popular in Texas. White-tailed deer are hunted as a way of cutting the wildlife population; thousands of jabalina and wild turkeys are shot. During 1995, licenses were issued to 1,526,602 hunters and 2,454,864 anglers.

48SPORTS

Texas has eight major league professional sports teams: the Texas Rangers and Houston Astros of Major League Baseball; the Dallas Cowboys of the National Football League; the Dallas Stars of the National Hockey League; the Houston Rockets, San Antonio Spurs, and Dallas Mavericks of the National Basketball Association; and the Dallas Burn of Major League Soccer. The Cowboys are, by far, the most consistently successful of Texas's teams. They have won the Super Bowl five times—in 1972, 1978, 1993, 1994, and 1996. They have appeared in it and lost an additional three times. The Houston Rockets won consecutive NBA Championships in 1994 and 1995. Houston lost the Oilers of the NFL, who moved to Tennessee after the 1996 season.

Pari-mutuel betting on horse races was legalized in Texas in the early 1990s, and Thoroughbred tracks are open near Houston and Dallas. Quarter horse racing is also popular and rodeo is a leading spectator sport. Participant sports popular with Texans include hunting, fishing, horseback riding, boating, swimming, tennis, and golf. State professional and amateur golf tournaments are held annually, as are numerous rodeos. The Texas Sports Hall of Fame was organized in 1951; new members are selected each year by a special committee of the Texas Sports Writers Association.

49FAMOUS TEXANS

Two native sons of Texas have served as president of the US. Dwight D. Eisenhower (1890–1969), the 34th president, was born in Denison, but his family moved to Kansas when he was two years old. Lyndon Baines Johnson (1908–73), the 36th president, was the only lifelong resident of the state to serve in that office. Born near Stonewall, he occupied center stage in state and national politics for a third of a century as US representative, Democratic majority leader of the US Senate, and vice president under John F. Kennedy, before succeeding to the presidency after Kennedy's assassination. Reelected by a landslide, Johnson accomplished much of his Great Society program of social reform but saw his power and popularity wane because of the war in Viet Nam. His wife, Claudia Alta Taylor "Lady Bird" Johnson (b.1912), was influential in environmental causes as First Lady.

Texas's other native vice president was John Nance Garner (1868–1967), former speaker of the US House of Representatives. George Bush (b.Massachusetts, 1924), who founded his own oil development company and has served in numerous federal posts, was elected vice president in 1980 on the Republican ticket and reelected in 1984, then elected to the presidency in 1988. Tom C. Clark (1899–1977) served as an associate justice on the US Supreme Court from 1949 to 1967; he stepped down when his son Ramsey (b.1927) was appointed US attorney general, a post the elder Clark had also held.

Another prominent federal officeholder from Texas was Jesse H. Jones (1874–1956), who served as chairman of the Reconstruction Finance Corporation and secretary of commerce under Franklin D. Roosevelt. Oveta Culp Hobby (b.1905), publisher of the *Houston Post,* became the first director of the Women's Army Corps (WAC) during World War II and the first secretary of the Department of Health, Education, and Welfare under President Eisenhower. John Connally (1917–1993), a protégé of Lyndon Johnson's, served as secretary of the US Navy under Kennedy and, as governor of Texas, was wounded in the same attack that killed the president; subsequently, he switched political allegiance, was secretary of the treasury under Richard Nixon, and had been active in Republican Party politics. Other federal officials from Texas include "Colonel" Edward M. House (1858–1938), principal advisor to President Wilson, and Leon Jaworski (1905–82), the Watergate special prosecutor whose investigations led to President Nixon's resignation. Lloyd Bentsen, a senator and a secretary of the treasury, was born 11 February 1921 in Mission, Texas.

The state's most famous legislative leader was Sam Rayburn (1882–1961), who served the longest tenure in the nation's history as speaker of the US House of Representatives—17 years in three periods between 1940 and 1961. James Wright (b.1922) was Democratic majority leader of the House in the 1970s and early 1980s, and Barbara C. Jordan (1936–96) won national attention as a forceful member of the House Judiciary Committee during its impeachment deliberations in 1974.

Famous figures in early Texas history include Moses Austin (b.Connecticut, 1761–1821) and his son, Stephen F. Austin (b.Virginia, 1793–1836), often called the "father of Texas." Samuel "Sam" Houston (b.Virginia, 1793–1863), adopted as a youth by the Cherokee, won enduring fame as commander in chief of the Texas revolutionary army, as president of the Texas Republic, and as the new state's first US senator; earlier in his career, he had been governor of Tennessee. Mirabeau Bonaparte Lamar (b.Georgia, 1798–1859), the second president of the republic, founded the present state capital (now called Austin) in 1839. Anson Jones (b.Massachusetts, 1798–1858) was the last president of the republic.

Noteworthy state leaders include John H. Reagan (b.Tennessee, 1818–1905), postmaster general for the Confederacy; he dominated Texas politics from the Civil War to the 1890s, helping to write the state constitutions of 1866 and 1875, and eventually becoming chairman of the newly created Texas Railroad Commission. The most able Texas governor was probably James Stephen Hogg (1851–1906), the first native-born Texan to hold that office. Another administration with a progressive record was that of Governor James V. Allred (1899–1959), who served during the 1930s. In 1924 Miriam A. "Ma" Ferguson (1875–1961) became the first woman to be elected governor of a state, and she was elected again in 1932. With her husband, Governor James E. Ferguson (1871–1944), she was active in Texas politics for nearly 30 years. Texas military heroes include Audie Murphy (1924–71), the most decorated soldier of World War II (and later a film actor), and Admiral of the Fleet Chester W. Nimitz (1885–1966).

Figures of history and legend include James Bowie (b.Kentucky, 1796?–1836), who had a reputation as a brawling fighter and wheeler-dealer until he died at the Alamo: he is popularly credited with the invention of the bowie knife. David "Davy" Crockett (b.Tennessee, 1786–1836) served three terms as a US representative from Tennessee before departing for Texas; he, too, lost his life at the Alamo. Among the more notorious Texans was Roy Bean (b.Kentucky, 1825–1903), a judge who proclaimed himself "the law west of the Pecos." Gambler, gunman, and desperado John Wesley Hardin (1853–95) boasted that he "never killed a man who didn't deserve it." Bonnie Parker (1910–34) and Clyde Barrow (1909–34), second-rate bank robbers and murderers who were shot to death by Texas lawmen, achieved posthumous notoriety through the movie *Bonnie and Clyde* (1967).

Many Texas businessmen have profoundly influenced the state's politics and lifestyle. Clint Murchison (1895–1969) and Sid Richardson (1891–1959) made great fortunes as independent oil operators and spread their wealth into other enterprises: Murchison became owner-operator of the successful Dallas Cowboys professional football franchise, and Richardson, through the Sid Richardson Foundation, aided educational institutions throughout the Southwest. Oilman H(aroldson) L(afayette) Hunt (b.Illinois, 1889–1974), reputedly the wealthiest man in the US, was an avid supporter of right-wing causes. Howard Hughes (1905–79), an industrialist, aviation pioneer, film producer, and casino owner, became a fabulously wealthy eccentric recluse in his later years. Stanley Marcus (b.1905), head

of the famous specialty store Neiman-Marcus, became an arbiter of taste for the world's wealthy and fashionable men and women. Rancher Richard King (b.New York, 1825–85) put together the famed King Ranch, the largest in the US at his death. Charles Goodnight (b.Illinois, 1836–1929) was an outstanding cattleman. H. Ross Perot, billionaire computer software developer and independent presidential candidate in 1992 and 1996, was born 27 June 1930 in Dallas.

Influential Texas historians include folklorist John A. Lomax (b.Mississippi, 1867–1948); Walter Prescott Webb (1888–1963), whose books *The Great Plains* and *The Great Frontier* helped shape American thought; and J. Frank Dobie (1888–1964), well-known University of Texas educator and compiler of Texas folklore. Dan Rather (b.1931) has earned a nationwide reputation as a television reporter and anchorman. Frank Buck (1884–1950), a successful film producer, narrated and appeared in documentaries showing his exploits among animals.

William Sydney Porter (b.North Carolina, 1862–1910) apparently embezzled funds from an Austin bank, escaped to Honduras, but returned to serve a three-year jail term—during which time he began writing short stories, later published under the pen name O. Henry. Katherine Anne Porter (1890–1980) also won fame as a short-story writer. Fred Gipson (b.1908) wrote *Hound Dog Man* and *Old Yeller*, praised by critics as a remarkable evocation of a frontier boy's viewpoint. Two novels by Larry McMurtry (b.1936), *Horsemen, Pass By* (film title, *Hud*) and *The Last Picture Show*, became significant motion pictures. Robert Rauschenberg (b.1925) is a leading contemporary painter. Elisabet Ney (b.Germany, 1833–1907), a sculptor, came to Texas with a European reputation and became the state's first determined feminist; she wore pants in public, and seldom passed up an opportunity to transgress Texans' Victorian mores. E. Donnall Thomas, 1990 co-recipient of the Nobel Prize in medicine, was born 15 March 1920 in Mart, Texas.

Prominent Texans in the entertainment field include Mary Martin (1913–1990), who reigned over the New York musical comedy world for two decades; her son, Larry Hagman (b.1931), star of the *Dallas* television series; actress Debbie Reynolds (b.1931); movie director King Vidor (1894–1982); and Joshua Logan (1903–1988), director of Broadway plays and Hollywood movies. Texans who achieved national reputations with local repertory companies were Margo Jones (1912–55) and Nina Vance (1914–80), who founded and directed theater groups in Dallas and Houston, respectively; and Preston Jones (1936–79), author of *A Texas Trilogy* and other plays.

Among Texas-born musicians, Tina Turner (b.1941) is a leading rock singer, as was Janis Joplin (1943–70). Willie Nelson (b.1933) wedded progressive rock with country music to start a new school of progressive "outlaw" music. Bob Wills (b.Oklahoma, 1905–75) was the acknowledged king of western swing. Musicians Trini Lopez (b.1937), Freddy Fender (Baldemar Huerta, b.1937), and Johnny Rodriguez (b.1951) have earned popular followings based on their Mexican-American music. Charlie Pride (b.Mississippi, 1938) became the first black country-western star. Other country-western stars born in Texas are Waylon Jennings (b.1937) and Kenny Rogers (b.1938). In the jazz field, pianist Teddy Wilson (1912–86) was a member of the famed Benny Goodman trio in the 1930s. Trombonist Jack Teagarden (1905–64) and trumpeter Harry James (1916–83) have also been influential.

The imposing list of Texas athletes is headed by Mildred "Babe" Didrikson Zaharias (1913–56), who gained fame as an All-American basketball player in 1930, won two gold medals in track and field in the 1932 Olympics, and was the leading woman golfer during the 1940s and early 1950s. Another Texan, John Arthur "Jack" Johnson (1878–1946), was boxing's first black heavyweight champion. Texans who won fame in football include quarterbacks Sammy Baugh (b.1914), Don Meredith (b.1938), and Roger Staubach (b.Ohio, 1942); running back Earl Campbell (b.1955); and coaches Dana X. Bible (1892–1980). Darrell Royal (b.Oklahoma, 1924), and Thomas Wade "Tom" Landry (b. 1924). Tim Brown (b. Dallas, Texas 1966), a wide receiver in the NFL, won the Heisman Trophy in 1987 as a member of the Fighting Irish of Notre Dame. Among other Texas sports greats are baseball Hall of Famers Tris Speaker (1888–1958) and Rogers Hornsby (1896–1963); golfers Ben Hogan (1912–97), Byron Nelson (b.1912), and Lee Trevino (b.1939); auto racing driver A(nthony) J(oseph) Foyt (b.1935); and jockey William Lee "Willie" Shoemaker (b.1931). Nolan Ryan, pitching giant, was born 31 January 31 1947 in Refugio, Texas.

⁵⁰BIBLIOGRAPHY

Arbingast, Stanley A., et al. *Atlas of Texas.* Austin: University of Texas Press, 1979.

Bainbridge, John. *The Super-Americans.* New York: Doubleday. 1961.

Binkley, William C. *The Texas Revolution.* Austin: Texas State Historical Association, 1979.

Buenger, Walter L. (ed.) *Texas History.* Boston: American Press, 1983.

Caro, Robert A. *The Years of Lyndon Johnson: The Path to Power.* New York: Knopf, 1982.

Chipman, Donald E. *Spanish Texas, 1519-1821.* Austin: University of Texas Press, 1992.

Conaway, James. *The Texans.* New York: Knopf, 1976.

Connor, Seymour V. (ed.). *The Saga of Texas.* 6 vols. Austin: Steck-Vaughn, 1965.

Dobie, J. Frank. *Coronado's Children.* New York: Grosset & Dunlap, 1963.

——. *The Longhorns.* Boston: Little, Brown, 1941.

Duke, Cordia Sloan, and Joe B. Frantz. *6000 Miles of Fence: Life on the XIT Ranch of Texas.* Austin: University of Texas Press, 1981.

Federal Writers' Project. *Texas: A Guide to the Lone Star State.* Reprint. New York: Somerset, n.d. (orig. 1940).

Fehrenbach, T. R. *Lone Star: A History of Texas and the Texans.* New York: Crown, 1983.

Frantz, Joe B. *Texas: A Bicentennial History.* New York: Norton, 1976.

Frantz, Joe B., and Julian E. Choate, Jr. *The American Cowboy.* Norman: University of Oklahoma Press, 1955.

Friend, Llerena. *Sam Houston: The Great Designer.* Austin: University of Texas Press, 1954.

Gambrell, Herbert. *Anson Jones: The Last President of Texas.* Austin: University of Texas Press, 1964.

Handbook of Texas. 3 vols. Edited by Walter Prescott Webb and H. Bailey Carroll, with supplement edited by Eldon Stephen Brandon. Austin: Texas State Historical Association. 1952–76.

Horgan, Paul. *Great River: The Rio Grande in North American History.* New York: Holt, Rinehart & Winston, 1954.

Jordan, Terry G. *Immigration to Texas.* Boston: American Press, 1981.

Lack, Paul D. *The Texas Revolutionary Experience: A Political and Social History, 1835-1836.* College Station: Texas A&M University Press, 1992.

Newcomb, W. W., Jr. *The Indians of Texas: From Prehistoric to Modern Times.* Austin: University of Texas Press, 1969.

Nunn, W. C. *Texas under the Carpetbaggers.* Austin: University of Texas Press, 1962.

Richardson, Rupert N., et al. *Texas: The Lone Star State.* 4th ed. Englewood Cliffs, N.J.: Prentice-Hall, 1981.

Sibley, Marilyn McAdams. *The Port of Houston: A History.* Austin: University of Texas Press, 1968.

Spratt, John S. *The Road to Spindletop: Economic Change in Texas, 1875–1901.* Austin: University of Texas Press, 1983.

Texas Almanac and State Industrial Guide, 1984–85. 50th ed. Dallas: A. H. Belo Corp., 1983.

Texas Fact Book, 1984. Edited by Joseph E. Pluta. Rita J. Wright and Midred C. Anderson. Austin: University of Texas, 1983.

Texas Government Today. Pacific Grove, Calif.: Brooks/Cole Pub. Co., 1992.

Tinkle, Lon. *Thirteen Days to Glory.* New York: McGraw-Hill, 1958.

Webb, Walter Prescott. *The Texas Rangers: A Century of Frontier Defense.* Austin: University of Texas Press, 1965.

Wright, Rita J. *Texas Sources: A Bibliography.* Austin: University of Texas, 1976.

UTAH

State of Utah

ORIGIN OF STATE NAME: Named for the Ute Indians. **NICKNAME:** The Beehive State. **CAPITAL:** Salt Lake City. **ENTERED UNION:** 4 January 1896 (45th). **SONG:** "Utah. We Love Thee." **MOTTO:** Industry. **COAT OF ARMS:** In the center, a shield, flanked by American flags, shows a beehive with the state motto and six arrows above, sego lilies on either side, and the numerals "1847" (the year the Mormons settled in Utah) below. Perched atop the shield is an American eagle. **FLAG:** Inside a thin gold circle, the coat of arms and the year of statehood are centered on a blue field, fringed with gold. **STATE SEAL:** The coat of arms with the words "The Great Seal of the State of Utah 1896" surrounding. **ANIMAL:** Rocky Mountain elk. **BIRD:** Sea gull. **FISH:** Rainbow trout. **INSECT:** Honeybee. **FLOWER:** Sego lily. **TREE:** Blue spruce. **GEM:** Topaz. **EMBLEM:** Beehive. **LEGAL HOLIDAYS:** New Year's Day, 1 January; Birthday of Martin Luther King, Jr., 3d Monday in January; Lincoln's Birthday, 12 February; Washington's Birthday, 3d Monday in February; Memorial Day, last Monday in May; Independence Day, 4 July; Pioneer Day, 24 July; Labor Day, 1st Monday in September; Columbus Day, 2d Monday in October; Veterans Day, 11 November; Thanksgiving Day, 4th Thursday in November; Christmas Day, 25 December. **TIME:** 5 AM MST = noon GMT.

¹LOCATION, SIZE, AND EXTENT

Located in the Rocky Mountain region of the western US, Utah ranks 11th in size among the 50 states.

The area of Utah totals 84,899 sq mi (219,899 sq km), of which land comprises 82,073 sq mi (212,569 sq km) and inland water 2,826 sq mi (7,320 sq km). Utah extends 275 mi (443 km) E-W and 345 mi (555 km) N-S.

Utah is bordered on the N by Idaho; on the NE by Wyoming; on the E by Colorado; and on the S by Arizona (with the two borders joined at Four Corners); and on the W by Nevada. The total boundary length of Utah is 1,226 mi (1,973 km). The state's geographic center is in Sanpete County, 3 mi (5 km) N of Manti.

²TOPOGRAPHY

The eastern and southern two-thirds of Utah belong to the Colorado Plateau, a region characterized by deep river canyons; erosion has carved much of the plateau into buttes and mesas. The Rocky Mountains are represented by the Bear River, Wasatch, and Uinta ranges in the north and northeast. These ranges, rising well above 10,000 feet (3,000 meters), hold the highest point in Utah—Kings Peak in the Uintas—at an altitude of 13,528 feet (4,123 meters).

The arid, sparsely populated Great Basin dominates the western third of the state. Drainage in this region does not reach the sea, and streams often disappear in the dry season. To the north are the Great Salt Lake, a body of hypersaline water, and the Great Salt Lake Desert (containing the Bonneville Salt Flats), both remnants of a vast prehistoric lake that covered the region during the last Ice Age. The lowest point in Utah—2,000 feet (610 meters) above sea level—occurs at Beaverdam Creek in Washington County, in the southwest corner of the state.

The western edge of the Wasatch Range, or Wasatch Front, holds most of Utah's major cities. It also attracts the greatest rainfall and snowfall, particularly in the north. Two regions rich in fossil fuels are the Kaiparowits Plateau, in southern Utah, and the Overthrust Belt, a geologic structural zone underlying the north-central part of the state.

The largest lake is the Great Salt Lake, which at the end of 1984 covered 2,250 sq mi (5,827 sq km) and was 34% larger than in 1976. In 1984, as a result of increased precipitation, the lake rose to 4,209.25 feet (1.283 meters) above sea level, its highest level since 1877; the lake has been rising steadily since 1963, causing severe flooding, and its waters, diluted by runoff, have lost some salinity. Other major bodies of water are Utah Lake, Bear Lake (shared with Idaho), and Lake Powell, formed by the Glen Canyon Dam on the Colorado River. Other important rivers include the Green, flowing into the Colorado; the Sevier, which drains central and southern Utah; and the Bear, which flows into the Great Salt Lake.

³CLIMATE

The climate of Utah is generally semiarid to arid. Temperatures are favorable along the Wasatch Front, where there are relatively mild winters. At Salt Lake City, the normal daily mean temperature is 52°F (11°C), ranging from 28°F (–2°C) in January to 78°F (26°C) in July. The record high temperature, 117°F (47°C), was set at St. George on 5 July 1985; the record low temperature, –69°F (–56°C), in Peter's Sink, on 1 February 1985. The average precipitation varies from less than 5 in (12.7 cm) in the west to over 40 in (102 cm) in the mountains, with Salt Lake City receiving 15 in (38 cm) per year. The annual snowfall is about 59 in (150 cm) and remains on the higher mountains until late summer.

⁴FLORA AND FAUNA

Botanists have recognized more than 4,000 floral species in Utah's six major life zones. Common trees and shrubs include four species of pine and three of juniper; aspen, cottonwood, maple, hawthorn, and chokecherry also flourish, along with the Utah oak, Joshua tree, and blue spruce (the state tree). Among Utah's wildflowers are sweet William and Indian paintbrush; the sego lily is the state flower. Endangered plants include four varieties of cactus (purple-spined hedgehog, spineless hedgehog, Siler pincushion, and Wright fishhook), Rydberg milk-vetch, clay phacelia, and the dwarf bear-poppy.

Mule deer are the most common of Utah's large mammals; other mammals include pronghorn antelope, Rocky Mountain bighorn sheep, lynx, grizzly and black bears, and white- and black-tailed jackrabbits. Among native bird species are the great horned owl, plain titmouse, and water ouzel; the golden eagle and great white pelican are rare species; and the sea gull (the state bird) is a spring and summer visitor from the California coast. The pygmy rattler is found in southwest Utah, and the Mormon cricket is unique to the state.

Among Utah's endangered fauna (as listed by the US government) are the grizzly bear, bald eagle, Utah prairie dog, bonytail and humpback chubs, Colorado River squawfish, and woundfin. Many birds and fish have been killed or imperiled by the inundation of freshwater marshes with salt water from the flooding Great Salt Lake.

[5] ENVIRONMENTAL PROTECTION

Divisions of the Department of Natural Resources oversee water and mineral resources, parks and recreation, state lands and forests, and wildlife. The Department of Agriculture is concerned with soil conservation and pesticide control. The Department of Environmental Quality has separate divisions dealing with air quality, drinking water systems, water quality, and regulation of water pollution, radioactive, hazardous, and solid wastes.

Air pollution is a serious problem along the Wasatch Front where 70% of the state's population reside. Automobiles are a major contributor to the high levels of ozone and carbon monoxide impacting the communities in the Salt Lake, Weber, and Utah counties. Also of considerable concern is the quality of drinking water.

As of 1995, the Division of Environmental Health has identified 16 sites in Utah where uncontrolled dumping and abandoned materials pose a potential threat. Other environmental issues of concern in the state are transportation safety of hazardous materials, chemical warfare agent storage and disposal, a proposed nuclear fuel storage site in the western part of the state, and interstate transportation of hazardous waste for disposal. Another environmental problem is the pollution of Great Salt Lake by industrial waste. In 1996, the lake and its surrounding wetlands were designated a Hemispheric Reserve in the Western Hemisphere Shorebird Reserve Network. The move was taken in recognition of the area's importance to migratory waterfowl and shorebirds.

[6] POPULATION

At the 1990 census, Utah had a population of 1,722,850, 35th in the US. The estimated 1996 population was 2,000,494, representing a growth of 16.1% since 1990. Utah's estimated population density was 21 per sq mi (8 per sq km) in 1990. Because of the consistently high birthrate, Utahns tend to be much younger than the US population as a whole: more than 9% of state residents were under 5 years of age in 1990, and 36% were younger than 18 years of age.

About 87% of all Utahns live in cities and towns, mostly along the Wasatch Front. Salt Lake City is Utah's most populous urban center, with an estimated 1994 population of 171,849 in the city proper and a 1995 estimate of 1,199,323 —over 60% of state residents—in its metropolitan region. Other major cities included Provo, 88,519; Ogden, 67,763; and Orem, 74,402.

[7] ETHNIC GROUPS

Hispanic Americans constitute the largest ethnic minority in Utah, with a 1990 population at 85,000.

American Indians are the 3d-largest minority group in Utah, numbering 24,000 in 1990. Indian lands covered 2,331,000 acres (943,000 hectares) in 1982, all but 35 acres (14 hectares) of which were tribal landholdings. The Uintah and Ouray Indian reservation, in the northeast (estimated 1995 population 3,205), and the Navaho Indian reservation, in the southeast, are the largest. Far smaller are the Skull Valley and Goshute reservations, in the west.

About 33,000 Asians and Pacific Islanders lived in Utah in 1990, the largest group (8,455) being Japanese-Americans. There were 5,487 Chinese and 2,450 Vietnamese. Utah also had 12,000 black Americans in 1990. Until 1978, blacks were denied full church membership as Mormons.

Utah had 58,600 residents who were foreign-born in 1990. Among persons reporting at least one specific ancestry in 1990, 749,665 persons claimed English descent, 299,414 German, 163,048 Danish, 136,645 Irish, and 103,715 Swedish.

[8] LANGUAGES

Forebears of the Ute, Goshute, and Paiute contributed to English only a few place-names, such as Utah itself, Uinata (and Uintah), Wasatch, and Tavaputs.

Utah English is primarily that merger of Northern and Midland carried west by the Mormons, whose original New York dialect later incorporated features from southern Ohio and central Illinois. Conspicuous in Mormon speech in the central valley, although less frequent now in Salt Lake City, is a reversal of vowels, so that *farm* and *barn* sound like *form* and *born* and, conversely, *form* and *born* sound like *farm* and *barn*.

In 1990, 92.2% of all state residents 5 years of age or older spoke only English at home. Other languages spoken at home, and the number of people who spoke them, included Spanish, 51,945, and German, 11,233.

[9] RELIGIONS

The dominant religious group in Utah is the Church of Jesus Christ of Latter-day Saints, popularly known as the Mormons. The church was founded by Joseph Smith, Jr., in 1830, the same year he published the *Book of Mormon*, the group's sacred text. The Mormons' arrival in Utah climaxed a long pilgrimage that began in New York State and led westward to Missouri, then back to Illinois (where Smith was lynched), and finally across Iowa, Nebraska, and Wyoming to Salt Lake City in 1847. The Latter-day Saints had 1,236,242 members in Utah in 1990. The Mormon Church and its leadership continue to play a central role in the state's political, economic, and cultural institutions. Among other assets in the state, the church owns Zion Cooperative Mercantile Institute (the largest department store in Salt Lake City), one of the leading newspapers, one television station, and holdings in banks, insurance companies, and real estate.

Other leading Christian denominations and their 1990 memberships include various Baptist groups, Presbyterians (6,658), and Episcopal (5,436). In 1990 there were 66,316 Roman Catholics and an estimated 2,950 Jews.

[10] TRANSPORTATION

Utah, where the golden spike was driven in 1869 to mark the completion of the first transcontinental railroad, had 1,420 rail mi (2,286 km) of track in 1995. Major railroads are the Union Pacific and Southern Pacific. Amtrak provides passenger service to Salt Lake City, Ogden, Milford, Provo, Helper, and Thompson and carried 44,976 riders in 1995/96.

The Utah Transit Authority, created in 1970, provides bus service for Salt Lake City, Provo, and Ogden. Utah in 1995 had 41,044 mi (66,081 km) of public roads and streets; there were 1,446,886 registered motor vehicles and 1,255,460 licensed drivers. The state has 940 mi (1,513 km) of interstate highways. The main east–west and north–south routes—I-80 and I-15, respectively—intersect at Salt Lake City. Utah had 88 airports in early 1995. By far the busiest was Salt Lake City International Airport, handling 90,510 departures in 1994 and enplaning 7,828,969 passengers.

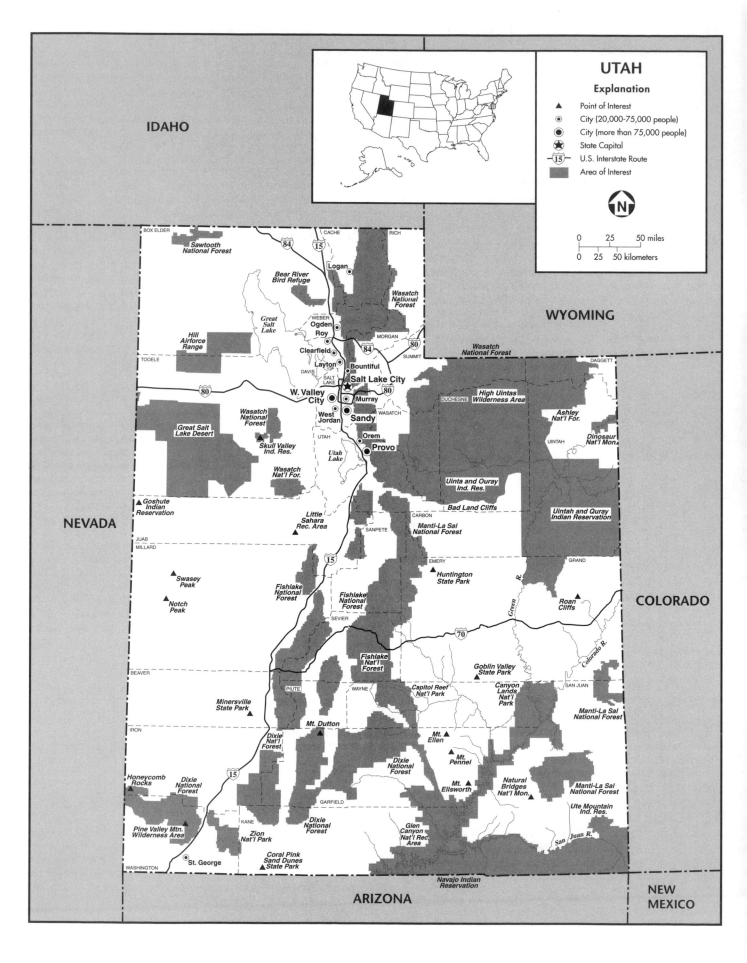

¹¹HISTORY

Utah's historic Indian groups are primarily Shoshonean: the Ute in the eastern two-thirds of the state, the Goshute of the western desert, and the Southern Paiute of southwestern Utah. The Athapaskan-speaking Navaho of southeastern Utah migrated from western Canada, arriving not long before the Spaniards. The differing lifestyles of each group remained essentially unchanged until the introduction of the horse by the Spanish sometime after 1600. White settlement from 1847 led to two wars between whites and Indians—the Walker War of 1853–54 and the even more costly Black Hawk War of 1865–68—resulting finally in the removal of many Indians to reservations.

Mexicans and Spaniards are the first non-Indians known to have entered Utah, with Juan María Antonio Rivera reportedly arriving near present-day Moab as early as 1765. In July 1776, a party led by two Franciscan priests, Francisco Atanasio Domínguez and Silvestre Vélez de Escalanta, entered Utah from the east, traversed the Uinta basin, crossed the Wasatch Mountains, and visited the Ute encampment at Utah Lake. Trade between Santa Fe, the capital of the Spanish province of New Mexico, and the Indians of Utah was fairly well established by the early 1800s.

Until 1848, the 1,200-mi (1,900-km) Spanish Trail, the longest segment of which lies in Utah, was the main route through the Southwest. Following this trail, mountain men competing for fur explored vast areas of the American West, including most of Utah's rivers and valleys. In the 1840s, Utah was traversed by California-bound settlers and explorers, the most notable being John C. Frémont.

When Joseph Smith, Jr., founder of the Church of Jesus Christ of Latter-day Saints (Mormons), was lynched at Carthage, Ill., in June 1844, Brigham Young and other Mormon leaders decided to move west. By April 1847, the pioneer company of Mormons, including three blacks, was on its way to Utah, the reports of Frémont having influenced their choice of the Great Basin as a refuge. Advance scouts entered the Salt Lake Valley on 22 July, and the rest of the company two days later. Planting and irrigation were begun immediately. Natural resources were regarded as community property, and the church organization served as the first government.

After the Treaty of Guadalupe-Hidalgo (1848) gave the US title to much of the Southwest, the Mormons established the provisional state of Deseret. Congress refused to admit Deseret to the Union, choosing instead to create Utah Territory "with or without slavery." The territory encompassed, in addition to present-day Utah, most of Nevada and parts of Wyoming and Colorado; land cessions during the 1860s left Utah with its present boundaries.

The territorial period lasted for 46 years, marked by immigration, growth, and conflict. Reports that Utahns were in rebellion against federal authority led President James Buchanan to send an expeditionary force under Albert Sidney Johnston to Utah in 1857. On 11 September, Mormon militiamen and their Indian allies, caught up in an atmosphere of war hysteria, massacred some 120 California-bound migrants at Mountain Meadows—the darkest event in Utah history and the only major disaster of the so-called Utah War. Peace was attained in June 1858, and Alfred Cumming assumed civil authority, replacing Brigham Young as territorial governor. Cumming's appointment signaled the beginning of prolonged hostility between Mormon leaders and federal authorities.

Almost 98% of Utah's total population was Mormon until after 1870, and the Mormon way of life dominated politics, economics, and social and cultural activities. As church president, Brigham Young remained the principal figure in the territory until his death in 1877. He contracted in 1868 with the Union Pacific to lay part of the track for the transcontinental railroad in Utah, and on 10 May 1869, the Central (now Southern) Pacific and Union Pacific were joined at Promontory. During the 1870s, new rail lines connected many settlements with the capital, Salt Lake City, spurring commerce and mining. Young had discouraged mining until agriculture and manufacturing were firmly established. Not until 1863, with the rediscovery of silver-bearing ore in Bingham Canyon, did the boom in precious metals begin. Those connected with mining, mostly non-Mormons, began to exert influence in the territory's business, politics, and social life.

Several factors made the non-Mormon minority fearful of Mormon domination: communitarian economic practices, lack of free public schools, encouragement of immigration of Mormon converts, church authoritarianism, and the mingling of church and state. But the most sensational reason was the Mormon practice of polygamy. Congress passed the Anti-Bigamy Act in 1862, but it was generally not enforced. After the Edmunds Act of 1882 was upheld by the US Supreme Court, arrests for polygamy greatly increased. Finally, in 1887, the Edmunds-Tucker Act dissolved the Mormon Church as a corporate entity, thereby threatening the survival of all Mormon institutions.

In fall 1890, Mormon president Wilford Woodruff issued a manifesto renouncing the practice of polygamy. The following year, the Republican and Democratic parties were organized in Utah, effectively ending political division along religious lines. A constitutional convention was held in 1895, and statehood became a reality on 4 January 1896. The new state constitution provided for an elected governor and a bicameral legislature, and restored the franchise to women, a privilege they had enjoyed from 1870 until 1887, when the Edmunds-Tucker Act had disfranchised Utah women and polygamous men.

The early 20th century saw further growth of the mineral industry. Many of those who came to mine copper and coal were foreign immigrants. Militant union activity had begun slowly during the 1890s, until an explosion that killed 200 miners at Scofield on 1 May 1900 dramatized the plight of the miners and galvanized radical organizers in the state. It was in Utah in 1915 that a Swedish miner and songwriter named Joe Hill, associated with the Industrial Workers of the World ("Wobblies"), was executed for the murder of a Salt Lake City grocer and his son, a case that continues to generate controversy because of the circumstantial quality of the evidence against him.

Gradually, modern cities emerged, along with power plants, interurban railroads, and highways. By 1920, nearly half the population lived along the Wasatch Front. The influx of various ethnic groups diversified the state's social and cultural life, and the proportion of Mormons in the total population declined to about 68% in 1920.

Utah businesses enjoyed the postwar prosperity of the 1920s. On the other hand, mining and agriculture were depressed throughout the 1920s and 1930s, decades marked by increased union activity, particularly in the coal and copper industries. The depression of the 1930s hit Utah especially hard. Severe droughts hurt farmers in 1931 and 1934, and high freight rates limited the expansion of manufacturing. With the coming of World War II, increased demand for food revived Utah's agriculture, and important military installations and war-related industries brought new jobs to the state.

In the years since World War II, the state's population has more than doubled, while per capita income has declined relative to the national average—both trends indicative of a very high birthrate. Politics generally reflect prevailing Mormon attitudes and tend to be conservative. The state successfully opposed plans for storing nerve gas bombs in Utah and for the location in the western desert of an MX missile racetrack system. In 1967 work began on the Central Utah Project, a dam and irrigation program still under way in the 1990s and intended to assure an adequate water supply for the state through the year 2020.

Utah had one of the nation's fastest growing economies in the 1990s and one of its lowest rates of unemployment. The state's leading industry was the manufacture of transport equipment, including aircraft parts and parts for missiles and rockets. In 1994, Utah had a budget surplus. At the close of the 20th century, Utahns were divided over the issue of protecting the state's natural areas from residential and commercial development.

12STATE GOVERNMENT

The state legislature, as established in the constitution of 1896, consists of a 29-member senate and a 75-seat house of representatives; senators serve for four years, representatives for two. In 1995 the legislators received a per diem salary of $85 during regular sessions.

The chief executive officers, all elected for four-year terms, include the governor, lieutenant governor (who also serves as secretary of state), attorney general, treasurer, and auditor. The governor must be at least 30 years of age and must have been a US citizen and state resident for at least five years. In 1996 the governor's salary was $82,000. Gubernatorial vetoes may be overridden by two-thirds of the elected members of each house of the legislature.

Amending the constitution requires a two-thirds vote of the legislature and ratification by majority vote at the next general election. Voters must be US citizens, at least 18 years of age, and have been residents of the state 30 days prior to voting day. The Utah Constitutional Revision Commission has been a permanent commission since 1977, recommending and drafting proposed constitutional changes. In 1994 Utah's voters approved constitutional amendment dealings with the rights of crime victims.

13POLITICAL PARTIES

The Republican and Democratic parties, each affiliated with the national party organization, are the state's leading political groups. In November 1996, Utahns cast 54% of their presidential votes for Republican Bob Dole; 33% for Democrat Bill Clinton; and just under 10% for Independent Ross Perot. There were 965,211 registered voters in 1994. In the midterm elections of 1994, Orrin Hatch was reelected to a fourth term in the US Senate. Utah's other US senator is Republican Robert F. Bennett, last elected in 1992. As of that election, Utah's US House delegation consisted of three Republicans. Following the 1996 elections, the state house had 55 Republicans and 20 Democrats, while the state senate had 20 Republicans and 9 Democrats.

Minorities hold few elected positions. In 1994, one Hispanic held elected office. As of 1995, 15 women served in the state legislature and 2 women held elective executive office.

Utah Presidential Vote by Major Political Parties, 1948–96

YEAR	ELECTORAL VOTE	UTAH WINNER	DEMOCRAT	REPUBLICAN
1948	4	*Truman (D)	149,151	124,402
1952	4	*Eisenhower (R)	135,364	194,190
1956	4	*Eisenhower (R)	118,364	215,631
1960	4	Nixon (R)	169,248	205,361
1964	4	*Johnson (D)	219,628	181,785
1968	4	*Nixon (R)	156,665	238,728
1972	4	*Nixon (R)	126,284	323,643
1976	4	Ford (R)	182,110	337,908
1980	4	*Reagan (R)	124,266	439,687
1984	5	*Reagan (R)	155,369	469,105
1988	5	*Bush (R)	207,343	428,442
1992**	5	Bush (R)	183,429	322,632
1996**	5	Dole (R)	221,633	361,911

* Won US presidential election.

** Independent candidate Ross Perot received 203,400 votes in 1992 and 66,461 votes in 1996.

14LOCAL GOVERNMENT

Utah has 29 counties, governed by elected commissioners. Other elected county officials include clerk-auditor, sheriff, assessor, recorder, treasurer, county attorney, and surveyor. There were 228 municipal governments in 1992, as well as 40 school districts and 329 special districts.

15STATE SERVICES

The Department of Public Education is responsible for public instruction, and the Utah State Board of Regents oversees the state college and university system. Highways and airports are the responsibility of the Department of Transportation.

The Department of Community and Economic Development supports economic and technological development programs in the state. Agencies dealing with the elderly, disabled, family services, mental health, assistance payments, and youth corrections are under the Department of Social Services. The Department of Health oversees public health and health care for the indigent. Other state departments deal with natural resources, business, labor, agriculture, corrections, and public safety.

16JUDICIAL SYSTEM

Utah's highest court is the supreme court, consisting of a chief justice and 4 other justices, each serving a 10-year term. As of 1994 there were 35 district court judges, each one serving a 6-year term. Supreme court justices and district court judges are appointed by the governor with the consent of the state senate. Appointments must be ratified by the voters at the next general election. In 1984, to ease the supreme court's caseload, Utahns approved a constitutional amendment allowing the legislature to create an intermediate court. An estimated 4,393 attorneys practiced in the state in 1996.

In 1995, the FBI reported a crime-index total of 6,090.8 crimes per 100,000 inhabitants, above average for the states. This included rates of 5,762 per 100,000 inhabitants for property crimes and a relatively low 328.8 per 100,000 for violent crimes, about one-half the national average. Utah has a death penalty statute providing for execution by lethal injection or firing squad. In 1977 it executed (by firing squad) a prisoner, Gary Gilmore, thus becoming the first state in a decade to carry out a sentence of capital punishment. Prisoners under jurisdiction of state and federal correctional facilities numbered 3,643 in 1996, or 182 per 100,000.

17ARMED FORCES

In 1996, there were 5,022 active duty military personnel stationed in Utah, the majority of whom (4,334) were at Hill Air Force Base near Ogden and, in the Great Salt Lake Desert, Tooele Army Depot. Dugway Proving Ground—where nerve gas tests have been conducted—and the USAF Utah Test and Training Range are near the Nevada line. State firms were awarded $394.7 million in federal contracts during the same year.

As of 1 July 1996, 136,000 veterans were living in Utah, of whom fewer than 500 were veterans of World War I, 39,000 of World War II, 24,000 of the Korean Conflict, 44,000 of the Viet Nam era, and 9,000 of the Persian Gulf War. Veterans' benefits in 1996 totaled $258 million.

Utah's reserve and national guard had 15,641 personnel in 1996: 62% Army, 9,678; Air Force, 3,966; and Navy and Marine Corps, 997.

In 1993, the Utah Highway Patrol employed 341 full-time sworn officers, or 2 per 10,000 residents.

18MIGRATION

After the initial exodus of Latter-day Saints from the eastern US to Utah, Mormon missionaries attracted other immigrants to the state, and some 90,000 foreign converts arrived between 1850 and 1905. Many non-Mormons were recruited from overseas to work in the mines, especially during the early 20th century. Utah had a net gain from migration of 176,000 between 1940 and 1985. From 1985 to 1990, there was a net loss from migration of 10,500. Between 1990 and 1996, the state had net gains of 80,935 in domestic migration and 17,278 in international migration. In 1996, 4,250 foreign immigrants arrived in Utah. As of 1990, 67.2% of Utahns were native-born, and 53% (age 5 and older) were living in the same house as in 1985. About 75% of those who lived in a different house in 1985 had resided elsewhere in Utah.

19INTERGOVERNMENTAL COOPERATION

Utah participates in several regional agreements, including the Bear River Compact (with Idaho and Wyoming), Colorado River Compact, and the Upper Colorado River Basin Compact. The state is also a signatory to the Interstate Oil and Gas Compact, Western Corrections Compact, and Western Interstate Energy Compact. Federal aid in 1996 amounted to over $1.4 billion.

20ECONOMY

Trade replaced government as the leading employer in Utah in 1980, employing 143,693 workers in September 1984 when 129,772 were employed by government. Nearly 14% of personal income in the state was derived from government sources in 1995. With more than 70% of Utah lands under US control and some 37,750 civilian workers on federal payrolls—and others employed by defense industries or the military—the federal presence in Utah is both a major economic force and a controversial political issue. On the one hand, elected officials have sought federal funds for mammoth reclamation and power projects. On the other hand, they resent many federal programs concerned with social welfare, land use, or environmental protection. Utah suffered disproportionately from cuts in the federal military budget in the late eighties and early nineties. Between 1993 and 1994, federal defense jobs declined 17%.

Since 1965, employment has shifted away from agriculture, transportation, and communications toward government, trade, and service occupations, and to a lesser extent, manufacturing. Mining employment, a source of high wages for semi-skilled labor has also declined. The percentage of Utah's workforce employed in mining dropped from 7% in 1957 to under 2% in 1985.

In 1994, the gross state product was $41,657 million, to which private goods-producing industries contributed $10,067 million; private service-producing industries, $24,932 million; and government, $6,659 million. Utah's per capita personal income in 1995 was $18,232, 46th nationally.

During 1996, there were 9,299 filings for bankruptcy.

21INCOME

In 1996, Utahns' total disposable personal income reached $32.8 billion, up from $30.6 billion in 1995. Total earned income rose from $23.4 billion in 1993 to $25.4 billion in 1994, an increase of 8.5%. Personal per capita income in 1996 averaged $19,156 (45th among the 50 states). Median household income was $32,039 in 1995, when 8.4% of all Utahns were below the federal poverty line.

22LABOR

In 1996, Utah's civilian labor force averaged 998,000, of whom 964,000 were employed and 35,000 unemployed, with a resulting unemployment rate of 3.5%.

The Utah Department of Employment Security in 1995 revealed the following nonagricultural earnings and employment patterns for Utah:

	WAGES IN (MILLIONS OF 1995 DOLLARS)	EMPLOYMENT (THOUSANDS OF JOBS)
Nonfarm total	21,096.1	907.9
Private sector	17,062.7	744.2
Mining	339.2	8.1
Construction	1,342.6	57.8
Manufacturing	3,543.7	123.9
Nondurable goods	1,023.9	41.7
Durable goods	2,519.8	82.2
Transportation and public utilities	1,670.2	51.5
Wholesale trade	1,368.4	45.8
Retail trade	2,365	174.3
Finance, insurance, and real estate	1,317.3	47.7
Services	5,116.3	238.3
Government	4,033.4	163.7

Utah's union movement weakened in the 1980s as mining and heavy manufacturing industries mechanized, which resulted in the elimination of thousands of jobs. In 1995, 72,700, or 9%, of Utah's workers belonged to labor unions. Utah has a right to-work law, enacted in 1955.

23AGRICULTURE

Despite a dry climate and unpromising terrain, Utah ranked 36th in the US in value of farm marketings in 1996, with $838 million. Crops accounted for $225 million; livestock and livestock products for $613 million. The first pioneers in Utah settled in fertile valleys near streams, which were diverted for irrigation. Today, Utah farmers and ranchers practice comprehensive soil and water conservation projects to help maximize crop yields and protect the natural resources. A farmland preservation movement is under way to protect valuable food-producing land from urban sprawl. In 1995 there were some 13,200 farms and ranches, covering 11,100,000 acres (4,500,000 hectares). The chief crops in 1995 were hay, 2.6 million tons; wheat, 8.9 million bushels; tart cherries, 22 million lb.

24ANIMAL HUSBANDRY

Livestock and livestock products account for over three-fourths of Utah's agricultural income. In 1997, there were an estimated 930,000 cattle and calves, valued at nearly $493 million on Utah farms and ranches. During 1996, hogs and pigs numbered 163,000 and were valued at around $16 million. In 1995, Utah farms produced nearly 28 million lb of sheep and lambs and 3.5 million lb of shorn wool. Dairy farms had around 88,000 milk cows, which produced 1.47 billion lb of milk.

25FISHING

Fishing in Utah is for recreation only. The state maintains egg-taking facilities at Bear Lake, Swan Creek, St. Charles, and Big Spring Creek to support 5.2 million angler days annually. Federal hatcheries distributed 1,463,134 fish (87,927 lb) and 859,667 fish eggs within Utah in 1995/96. In the same period, Utah issued 514,976 sport fishing licenses.

26FORESTRY

In 1992, Utah had 16,234,000 acres (6,655,940 hectares) of forestland. Of that, 7,989,733 acres (3,233,341 hectares) were in the state's nine national forests—Ashley, Cache, Caribou, Dixie, Fishlake, Manti-La Sal, Sawtooth, Uinta, and Wasatch. Only 3,078,000 acres (1,245,666 hectares) were classed as commercial timberland.

27MINING

The total value of nonfuel mineral production in Utah was approximately $1.84 billion in 1995, an increase of about 21% from the previous year. The state maintained its 4th-place ranking nationally, however, in the output of nonfuel minerals. Approximately 80% of the value of production in the state was attributed to the metals sector that included copper, gold, iron, magnesium, molybdenum, and silver. In addition, Utah mines produced significant quantities of beryllium, cement, magnesium compounds, sand and gravel, and salt. In 1995, Utah was 2d in the nation in the output of copper, 3d in gold, and was the only US source of mined beryllium during the year. The largest operating beryllium mine in the world is in Juab County, located at Spor Mountain. The state ranked 4th domestically in the production of iron ore.

[28]ENERGY AND POWER

During 1995, electric utilities in the state had an installed capacity of 5.1 million kw and produced 32.1 billion kwh of power. A total of 30.9 billion kwh was derived from fossil-fueled steam units, and 1.2 billion kwh from hydroelectric and other units.

Proved oil reserves totaled 216 million barrels in 1995, and production was 19.4 million barrels in 1996. Reserves of natural gas in 1995 amounted to 1,580 billion cu ft, marketed production, 241.3 billion cu ft. Early in 1980 there were large new natural gas finds in northeastern Utah. The state's recoverable reserves of bituminous coal were estimated at nearly 375 million tons in 1995, production reached 25.2 million tons. Utah is the only coal producing state whose entire production comes from underground mines.

[29]INDUSTRY

Utah's diversified manufacturing is concentrated geographically in Salt Lake City, Weber, Utah, and Cache counties. In 1995, the leading sectors for manufacturing employment were transportation equipment, food and food products, instruments and related products, and printing and publishing. Utah has one truck-assembly plant, in Ogden.

The total value of shipments by manufacturers in 1995 was 420 billion. The following table shows value of shipments for selected industries in 1995:

Motor vehicles and equipment	$1,642,6000,000
Medical instruments and supplies	906,900,000
Fabricated structural metal products	773,600,000
Printing and publishing	1,120,200,000
Food and food products	3,131,200,000

In 1997, Utah was the headquarters for two Fortune 500 companies, American Stores and Smith's Food & Drug Centers. During 1995, there were 539 US patents issued to Utah residents.

[30]COMMERCE

In 1992, Utah had 3,231 wholesale establishments, with sales of $15.3 billion. Utah's wholesale business had personal income exceeding $1.4 billion in 1995, when income from retail sales surpassed $2.5 billion. Retail sales in 1992 totaled $12.4 billion, 34th among the states. Retail and wholesale trading establishments are heavily concentrated in the Salt Lake City-Ogden metropolitan area. The leading wholesale trade categories were machinery, electrical goods, hardware, professional equipment, and construction materials. Foreign exports of Utah's manufactured goods totaled $2.3 billion in 1996. Exports of all goods originating in Utah were $3.3 billion.

[31]CONSUMER PROTECTION

The Division of Consumer Protection in the Department of Commerce is charged with protecting Utah's consumers. The Division investigates and mediates complaints and allegations of unfair, deceptive, or fraudulent business practices. The Division conducts ongoing consumer education programs to teach consumers how to recognize consumer fraud and how to avoid becoming a victim.

[32]BANKING

Utah in 1996 had 35 insured commercial banks with total assets of $22.5 billion, outstanding loans and leases of $14.2 billion, and deposits of $11.0 billion. Utah also had 15 insured industrial loan corporations with total assets of $13.5 billion, outstanding loans and leases of $12.9 billion, and deposits of $3.9 billion. There were 4 insured savings and loan associations in 1996, with total assets of $7.4 billion.

[33]INSURANCE

Utahns held some 1,270,000 life insurance policies in 1995; their total value was $76.5 billion, and the average coverage per family was $121,000. Total benefit payments of $839.8 million included $192.1 million in death payments, $92.8 million in dividends, and $209.6 million in annuities.

[34]SECURITIES

Utah had 1,332 brokerage firms licensed to do business in the state as of 30 June 1996 via 48,501 broker-dealers' agents. Securities investment advisory services are provided by 475 firms through 4,482 representatives.

[35]PUBLIC FINANCE

The annual budget is prepared by the State Budget Office and submitted by the governor to the legislature for amendment and approval. The fiscal year runs from 1 July through 30 June.

The following table summarizes state revenues and expenditures for 1995 and 1996 (in thousands):

REVENUES	1995	1996
General sales tax	$1,061,870	$1,170,120
Individual income tax	1,026,803	1,139,080
Motor fuel tax	196,422	206,904
Corporate income tax	157,901	176,781
Other taxes	327,090	329,502
Federal aid	1,193,140	1,266,632
Other receipts	100,435	107,438
Departmental Collections	158,454	149,868
TOTALS	$ 4,222,115	$ 4,546,325

EXPENDITURES BY FUNCTION	1995	1996
Education:		
Public education	$ 1,301,530	$ 1,479,309
Higher education	409,083	432,816
Human services, corrections, health, and environmental quality	1,296,189	1,394,764
Transportation and public safety	502,937	548,900
General government	252,313	247,819
Debt service	86,572	94,426
Capital projects	177,937	207,418
Natural resources	78,440	86,899
Community and economic development	71,883	82,585
Business, labor, and agriculture	34,550	36,307
TOTAL EXPENDITURES[a]	$ 4,211,434	$ 4,611,243

[a]Note: This does not include transfers made to other funds, except general fund appropriations transferred to the colleges and universities, which are included as higher education expenditures.

[36]TAXATION

The main source of state revenue is a 5% general sales and gross receipts tax. As of 1994, personal income tax rates ranged from 2.55% to 7.2%; the corporate income tax rate was 5%. Taxes are also levied on motor fuels, alcoholic beverages, tobacco products, and other items. Property taxes are the main source of local revenue.

Utah's total federal income tax burden was $6.9 million in 1990, while federal funding in the state totaled $8.5 million in 1995.

37ECONOMIC POLICY

The economic development of Utah has been dominated by two major forces: the relatively closed system of the original Mormon settlers and the more wide-open, speculative ventures of the state's later immigrants. The Mormons developed agriculture, industry, and a cooperative exchange system that excluded non-Mormons. The church actively opposed mining, and it was mostly with non-Mormon capital, by non-Mormon foreign immigrants, that the state's mineral industry was developed.

In the 1980s and 1990s, these conflicts were supplanted by a widespread fiscal conservatism that supports business activities and opposes expansion of government social programs at all levels. One Utah politician, J. Bracken Lee, who served as governor from 1949 to 1957, and as mayor of Salt Lake City from 1960 to 72, became nationally famous for his call to repeal the federal income tax.

The Department of Community and Economic Development is the state agency responsible for the expansion of tourism and industry. The department's economic development programs include the Technology Finance Corporation, which uses private venture capital to provide loans for new technological investments.

38HEALTH

Health conditions in Utah are exceptionally good. In 1995 death rates per 100,000 population for heart disease (145.1), cancer (108.6), cerebrovascular disease (39.8), and accidents (29.0) were lower than US rates, while the suicide rate (14.4) was above the national norm. The infant mortality rate—5.2 per 1,000 live births in 1993/94—is among the lowest in the US, and the overall death rate (5.5 per 1,000 persons in 1991) is well below the national average of 8.5. In 1990, Utah had the lowest proportion of smoking-attributable mortalities of any state, at 13.4% of all deaths. The birthrate—20.2 per 1,000 persons —was 2d only to Alaska among the 50 states. A total of 4,786 legal abortions were performed in 1995, when the abortion rate was 85.9 per 1,000 live births.

In 1995 there were 42 hospitals in the state, with 3,876 beds and admissions totaling 167,312. The average expense to a hospital in Utah for services provided per inpatient day was $1,115 in 1994. Hospital personnel in 1995 included 31,300 nurses, for a rate of 594 per 100,000 civilian population. In the same year, there were 3,525 active nonfederal licensed physicians and 1,184 active licensed dentists.

39SOCIAL WELFARE

With the enactment of the Personal Responsibility and Work Opportunity Reconciliation Act of 1996, the US government has changed the form and regulations for many of its social welfare programs; most significantly, it replaces Aid to Families with Dependent Children (AFDC), and open-ended entitlement program, with Temporary Assistance for Needy Families (TANF), a limited system of assistance funded largely through federal block grants. The reform act also impacts the food stamp program, the Supplemental Security Income program, benefits for legal immigrants, the Child Support Enforcement program, and the child nutrition program. The law took effect on 1 July 1997 and provided $16.38 billion in block grants for fiscal years 1997-2002. The grants are to be divided among the states based on an equation involving the numbers of former AFDC recipients in each state. Because many of the bill's provisions have yet to be implemented into state-by-state policy, it was not possible to include the details of each state's programs for this edition of this

work. In 1996, 110,011 residents received monthly food stamp allowances averaging $65.85. Some 41,000 residents received AFDC payments averaging $498 a month per family. The national school lunch program cost the federal government $39.1 million in 1996.

In 1995, 224,370 Utahns received a total of $1.3 billion in Social Security benefits averaging $726 a month. That year, federal Supplemental Security Income payments were made to 20,462 residents, averaging $339 a month. In 1995, weekly unemployment benefits in Utah were $191.74 per week.

40HOUSING

In 1996, there were an estimated 658,000 housing units in Utah, of which 617,000 were occupied. That year, 23,481 privately owned units, valued at $2.1 billion, were authorized for construction; of these, 16,663 were single family. As of 1990, 61% of all housing units were owner-occupied. As of 1993, Utah had an estimated 3.15 persons per household, more than any other state. The median monthly costs for owners (with a mortgage) and renters in 1990, the last year for which figures are available, were $667 and $369, respectively. In 1990, the median home value was $68,900, down 24.3% from 1980 (in terms of 1990 dollars). During 1995/96, Utah received $104.1 million in aid from the US Department of Housing and Urban Development, including $23.6 million in community development block grants.

41EDUCATION

Utahns are among the nation's leaders in educational attainments. In 1990, Utah had the 2d-highest proportion of adult high school graduates, 87.5% (Alaska was 1st); nearly 22.4% had four years or more of college, and fewer than 1% had four years or less of grade school.

In fall 1995, Utah public schools had an enrollment of 473,666. There were 19,864 teachers in 1995/96, when per pupil expenditures reached $3,470.

Enrollment at Utah's higher educational institutions totaled 121,303 in 1990/91. Major public institutions include the University of Utah, with 24,770 students in 1990/91; Utah State University, 12,087; and Weber State College, 11,117. Brigham Young University (Provo), founded in 1875 and affiliated with the Latter-day Saints, is the main private institution, with 26,894 students.

42ARTS

Music has a central role in Utah's cultural life. Under the baton of former director Maurice Abravanel and current director Joseph Silverstein, the Utah Symphony (Salt Lake City) has become one of the nation's leading orchestras. The Mormon Tabernacle Choir has won world renown, and Ballet West is ranked among the nation's leading dance companies. Opera buffs enjoy the Utah Opera Company, founded in 1976.

The Utah Arts Council sponsors exhibitions, artists in the schools, rural arts and folk arts programs, and statewide arts competitions in cooperation with arts organizations throughout the state. In addition, the partially state-funded Utah Arts Festival is held each year in Salt Lake City. In 1985, Utah had 24 art museums and galleries, including Utah State University's Nora Eccles Harrison Museum in Logan and the LDS Church Museum of Art and History in Salt Lake City. Other major facilities are the Brigham Young University Art Museum Collection, Provo; Museum of Fine Arts of the University of Utah, Salt Lake City; and the Springville Art Museum.

In 1996, the NEA contributed $668,000 to the state's programs, $744,000 to the Utah Arts Council, and funding to Salt Lake City's Ballet West. In addition, the state and private sources gave substantial contributions to the Arts Council. The

NEA has also provided funds to the Sundance Institute for Film and Television, the Utah Arts Council for art education programs, and the Utah Opera Company (through the challenge grant program).

Between 1987 and 1991, Utah's arts programs attracted a total audience of about 18,685,540; contributing artists numbered 171,722. During the same period, Utah provided arts education programs to 137,000 school children. As of 1996, Utah had 450 arts associations and 60 local arts groups. In 1992, the Utah Arts Council provided funding for the Utah Shakespearean Festival and for the New Hope Multi-Cultural Center of Salt Lake City.

43LIBRARIES AND MUSEUMS

In 1996, Utah had 69 public libraries with a circulation of 17,710,711 items. The combined book stock of public libraries was 5,497,495. The Salt Lake County library system had 1,565,648 volumes (not including Salt Lake City, whose system has 655,000 volumes); the Weber County system (including Ogden) has 355,000. The leading academic libraries are the University of Utah (Salt Lake City), 3,250,000; and Brigham Young University (Provo), 2,371,000. Other collections are the Latter-day Saints' Library-Archives and the Utah State Historical Society Library, both in Salt Lake City. During 1994, Utah had at least 58 museums, notably the Utah Museum of Natural History and Utah Museum of Fine Arts, Salt Lake City; Hill Aerospace Museum near Ogden; College of Eastern Utah Prehistoric Museum, Price; and Museum of Peoples and Cultures, Provo. Some are maintained as museums, including Beehive House and Wheeler Historic Farm, Salt Lake City, and Brigham Young's Winter Home, St. George.

44COMMUNICATIONS

In March 1993, 95.8% of Utah's 544,000 occupied houses had telephones.

A total of 93 radio stations broadcast in Utah in 1996; 40 were AM stations, 53 FM (145 of them noncommercial). There were 12 television stations in 1996, including 3 public stations. Cable television service was provided by four large systems in 1996.

45PRESS

Utah in 1997 had six daily newspapers and six Sunday papers. The following table shows leading daily newspapers in 1997:

AREA	NAME	DAILY	SUNDAY
Ogden	*Standard-Examiner* (e,S)	62,186	65,627
Provo	*Daily Herald* (e,S)	32,699	33,779
Salt Lake City	*Deseret News* (e,S)	63,108	67,065
	Tribune (m,S)	127,805	161,802

46ORGANIZATIONS

The 1992 Census of Service Industries counted 355 organizations in Utah, including 80 business associations; 194 civic, social, and fraternal associations; and 81 other membership organizations, including research associations. Salt Lake City is the world headquarters of the Church of Jesus Christ of Latter-day Saints (Mormon). The city is also home to the Mental Retardation Association of America and to Executive Women International.

47TOURISM, TRAVEL, AND RECREATION

Temple Square, Pioneer Trail State Park, and Hogle Zoological Gardens are leading attractions of Salt Lake City, about 11mi (18 km) east of the Great Salt Lake. At the Bonneville Salt Flats, experimental automobiles have set world land-speed records.

Under federal jurisdiction are 13 national parks—the Arches, Bryce Canyon, Canyonlands, Capitol Reef, and Zion—Glen Canyon National Recreation Area, 7 national monuments—including the controversial new Grand Staircase-Escalante National Monument—and 1 national historical site, Golden Spike. Under state control are 6 state parks, 7 state natural areas, 13 state recreation areas, 8 state historic areas, and 8 water-use areas. Mountain and rock climbing, skiing, fishing, and hunting are major forms of recreation. Licenses were held by 414,127 hunters and 544,210 anglers in 1995.

48SPORTS

Utah has one major league professional sports team, the Utah Jazz of the National Basketball Association, which moved from New Orleans at the close of the 1979 season. The Jazz advanced to the NBA Finals for the first time in 1997, but lost to the Chicago Bulls. Basketball is also popular at the college level. The University of Utah's Running Utes won the NCAA championship in 1944 and the National Invitation Tournament in 1947, while the Cougars of Brigham Young won NIT titles in 1951 and 1966, and were named college football's national champions in 1984.

Salt Lake City is also home to minor league baseball and hockey teams, and the Utah Starzz of the new Women's National Basketball Association.

Other annual sporting events include the Easter Jeep Sandhill Climb in Moab, the Ute Stampede (a rodeo) in Nephi in July, and various skiing events at Utah's world class resort in Park City. Salt Lake city will host the Winter Olympics in 2002.

49FAMOUS UTAHNS

George Sutherland (b.England, 1862–1942) capped a long career in Utah Republican politics by serving as an associate justice of the US Supreme Court (1922–38). Other important federal office-holders from Utah include George Dern (b.Nebraska, 1872–1936), President Franklin D. Roosevelt's secretary of war from 1933 to 1936; Ezra Taft Benson (b.Idaho, 1899), a high official of the Mormon Church and President Dwight Eisenhower's secretary of agriculture; and Ivy Baker Priest (1905–75), US treasurer during 1953–61. Prominent in the US Senate for 30 years was Republican tariff expert Reed Smoot (1862–1941), also a Mormon Church official. The most colorful politician in state history. J(oseph) Bracken Lee (b.1899), was mayor of Price for 12 years before serving as governor during 1949–57 and mayor of Salt Lake City during 1960–72. Jacob "Jake" Garn (b.1932), first elected to the US Senate in 1974, was launched into space aboard the space shuttle in 1985.

The dominant figure in Utah history is undoubtedly Brigham Young (b.Vermont, 1801–77), the great western colonizer. As leader of the Mormons for more than 30 years, he initiated white settlement of Utah in 1847 and, until his death, exerted almost complete control over life in the territory. Other major historical figures include Eliza R. Snow (b.Massachusetts, 1804–87), Mormon women's leader; Wakara, anglicized Walker (c.1808–55), the foremost Ute leader of the early settlement period; Colonel Patrick Edward Conner (b.Ireland, 1820–91), founder of Camp Douglas and father of Utah mining; George Q. Cannon (b.England, 1827–1901), editor, businessman, political leader, and a power in the Mormon Church for more than 40 years; and Lawrence Scanlan (b.Ireland, 1843–1915), first Roman Catholic bishop of Salt Lake City, founder of schools and a hospital.

Utah's most important scientist is John A. Widtsoe (b.Norway, 1872–1952), whose pioneering research in dryland farming revolutionized agricultural practices. Noted inventors are gunsmith John M. Browning (1855–1926) and television innovator Philo T. Farnsworth (1906–71). Of note in business are mining entrepreneurs David Keith (b.Canada, 1847–1918), Samuel Newhouse (b.New York, 1853–1930), Susanna Emery-Holmes (b.Missouri, 1859–1942), Thomas Kearns (b.Canada, 1862–1918), and Daniel C. Jackling (b.Missouri, 1869–1956). Labor leaders include William Dudley "Big Bill" Haywood

(1869–1928), radical Industrial Workers of the World organizer, and Frank Bonacci (b.Italy, 1884–1954), United Mine Workers of America organizer.

Utah's artists and writers include sculptors Cyrus E. Dallin (1861–1944) and Mahonri M. Young (1877–1957), painter Henry L. A. Culmer (b.England, 1854–1914), author-critic Bernard A. DeVoto (1897–1955), poet-critic Brewster Ghiselin (b.Missouri, 1903), folklorist Austin E. Fife (b.Idaho, 1909), and novelists Maurine Whipple (b.1904), Virginia Sorensen (b.1912), and Edward Abbey (b.1927–1989).

Actors from Utah are Maude Adams (1872–1953), Robert Walker (1918–1951, Loretta Young (b.1913), Laraine Day (b.1920). Donald "Donny" Osmond (b.1957) and his sister Marie (b.1959) are Utah's best-known popular singers. Emma Lucy Gates Bowen (1880–1951), an opera singer, founded her own traveling opera company, and William F. Christensen (b.1902) founded Ballet West. Maurice Abravanel (b.Greece, 1903–1993) conducted the Utah Symphony for many years. Other musicians of note include jazz trumpeter Ernest Loring "Red" Nichols (1905–1965).

Sports figures include former world middleweight boxing champion Gene Fullmer (b.1931), former Los Angeles Rams tackle Merlin Olsen (b.1940), and NFL quarterback Steve Young (b.1961) of the San Francisco 49ers.

50 BIBLIOGRAPHY

Alexander, Thomas. *Mormons and Gentiles: A History of Salt Lake City.* Boulder, Colo.: Pruett Publishing, 1984.

Alter, J. Cecil. *Utah, the Storied Domain: A Documentary History.* 3 vols. Chicago: American Historical Society, 1932.

Arrington, Leonard J., and Davis Bitton. *The Mormon Experience: A History of the Latter-day Saints.* 2d ed. Urbana: University of Illinois Press, 1992.

Ellsworth, Samuel G. *Utah's Heritage.* Salt Lake City: Peregrine Smith, 1984.

Papanikolas, Helen Z., ed. *The Peoples of Utah.* Salt Lake City: Utah State Historical Society, 1981 (orig. 1976).

Peterson, Charles S. *Utah: A Bicentennial History.* New York: Norton, 1977.

Poll, Richard D., et al. *Utah's History.* Provo, Utah: Brigham Young University Press, 1978.

Utah History Encyclopedia. Salt Lake City: University of Utah Press, 1994.

Verdoia, Ken. *Utah: The Struggle for Statehood.* Salt Lake City: University of Utah Press, 1996.

VERMONT

State of Vermont

ORIGIN OF STATE NAME: Derived from the French words *vert* (green) and *mont* (mountain). **NICKNAME:** The Green Mountain State. **CAPITAL:** Montpelier. **ENTERED UNION:** 4 March 1791 (14th). **SONG:** "Hail, Vermont!" **MOTTO:** Freedom and Unity. **COAT OF ARMS:** Rural Vermont is represented by a pine tree in the center, three sheaves of grain on the left, and a cow on the right, with a background of fields and mountains; a deer crests the shield. Below are crossed pine branches and the state name and motto. **FLAG:** The coat of arms on a field of dark blue. **OFFICIAL SEAL:** Bisecting Vermont's golden seal is a row of wooded hills above the state name; the upper half has a spearhead, pine tree, cow, and two sheaves of wheat, while two more sheaves and the state motto fill the lower half. **ANIMAL:** Morgan horse. **BIRD:** Hermit thrush. **FISH:** Brook trout (cold water); walleye pike (warm water). **INSECT:** Honeybee. **FLOWER:** Red clover. **TREE:** Sugar maple. **BEVERAGE:** Milk. **POET LAUREATE:** Louise Gluck. **LEGAL HOLIDAYS:** New Year's Day, 1 January; Birthday of Martin Luther King, Jr., 3d Monday in January; Lincoln's Birthday, 12 February; Washington's Birthday, 3d Monday in February; Town Meeting Day, 1st Tuesday in March; Memorial Day, 30 May; Independence Day, 4 July; Bennington Battle Day, 16 August; Labor Day, 1st Monday in September; Columbus Day, 2d Monday in October; Veterans Day, 11 November; Thanksgiving Day, 4th Thursday in November; Christmas Day, 25 December. **TIME:** 7 AM EST = noon GMT.

¹LOCATION, SIZE, AND EXTENT

Situated in the northeastern US, Vermont is the 2d largest of the 6 New England states, and ranks 43d in size among the 50 states.

Vermont's total area of 9,614 sq mi (24,900 sq km) consists of 9,249 sq mi (23,955 sq km) of land and 365 sq mi (945 sq km) of inland water. Vermont's maximum E–W extension is 90 mi (145 km); its maximum N–S extension is 158 mi (254 km). The state resembles a wedge, wide and flat at the top and narrower at the bottom.

Vermont is bordered on the N by the Canadian province of Quebec; on the E by New Hampshire (separated by the Connecticut River); on the S by Massachusetts; and on the W by New York (with part of the line passing through Lake Champlain and the Poultney River).

The state's territory includes several islands and the lower part of a peninsula jutting south into Lake Champlain from the Canadian border, collectively called Grand Isle County. Vermont's total boundary length is 561 mi (903 km). Its geographic center is in Washington County, 3 mi (5 km) E of Roxbury.

²TOPOGRAPHY

The Green Mountains are the most prominent topographic region in Vermont. Extending north–south from the Canadian border to the Massachusetts state line, the Green Mountains contain the state's highest peaks, including Mansfield, 4,393 feet (1,339 meters), the highest point in Vermont; Killington, 4,235 feet (1,293 meters); and Elbow Mountain (Warren), 4,135 feet (1,260 meters). A much lower range, the Taconic Mountains, straddles the New York–Vermont border for about 80 mi (129 km). To their north is the narrow Valley of Vermont; farther north is the Champlain Valley, a lowland about 20 mi (32 km) wide between Lake Champlain—site of the state's lowest point, 95 feet (29 meters) above sea level—and the Green Mountains. The Vermont piedmont is a narrow corridor of hills and valleys stretching about 100 mi (161 km) to the east of the Green

Mountains. The Northeast Highlands consist of an isolated series of peaks near the New Hampshire border.

Vermont's major inland rivers are the Missisquoi, Lamoille, and Winooski. The state includes about 66% of Lake Champlain on its western border and about 25% of Lake Memphremagog on the northern border.

³CLIMATE

Burlington's normal daily mean temperature is 45°F (7°C), ranging from 16°F (–9°C) in January to 71°F (22°C) in July. Winters are generally colder and summer nights cooler in the higher elevations of the Green Mountains. The record high temperature for the state is 105°F (41°C), registered at Vernon on 4 July 1911; the record low, –50°F (–46°C), at Bloomfield, 30 December 1933. Burlington's average annual precipitation of 33 in (84 cm) is less than the statewide average of 40 in (102 cm). Annual snowfall ranges from 55 to 65 in (140–165 cm) in the lower regions, and from 100 to 125 in (254–318 cm) in the mountain areas.

⁴FLORA AND FAUNA

Common trees of Vermont are the commercially important sugar maple (the state tree), the butternut, white pine, and yellow birch. Other recognized flora include 15 types of conifer, 130 grasses, and 192 sedges. Among endangered plants in Vermont are the alpine woodsia, white adder's-mouth, and small whorled pogonia.

Native mammalian species include white-tailed deer, coyote, red fox, and snowshoe hare. Several species of trout are prolific. Characteristic birds include the raven *(Corvus corax)*, gray or Canada jay, and saw-whet owl. Among endangered animals in Vermont are the Canada lynx, pine marten, and lake sturgeon.

⁵ENVIRONMENTAL PROTECTION

All natural resource regulation, planning, and operation are coordinated by the Agency of Environmental Conservation. The state is divided into 14 soil and water conservation districts operated by local landowners with the assistance of the state Natural Resources Conservation Council. Several dams on the Winooski and Connecticut rivers' drainage basins help control flooding. Legislation enacted in 1972 bans the use of throwaway beverage containers in Vermont, in an effort to reduce roadside litter. Billboards were banned in 1968. In the 1980s and early 1990s, the effects of acid rain became a source of concern in Vermont, as in the rest of the Northeast. In 1995, the state had 8 hazardous waste sites. By some estimates, as much as 35%, in some estimates, of Vermont's wetlands have been lost since colonization. Currently, about 5% of the state is wetlands, and the government has established the Vermont Wetlands Conservation Strategy.

⁶POPULATION

Vermont ranked 49th among the 50 states in population in 1993, and had a 1990 census total of 562,758. Population estimates for 1996 put the total at 588,654, an increase of 4.6%.

In 1990, Vermont's population was 68% rural, the highest percentage of all states; the rural population increased 12% between 1970 and 1980, and the urban population increased 21%. The population density was 60.8 per sq mi (23.3 per sq km) in 1990.

According to 1994 estimates, Burlington had 39,435 residents; Rutland, 17,921; and Montpelier, 8,254.

⁷ETHNIC GROUPS

There were slightly over 33,000 residents reporting French Canadian ancestry in 1990. These Vermonters are congregated chiefly in the northern counties and in such urban centers as Burlington, St. Albans, and Montpelier. Italians make up a little over 5% of the population reporting at least one specific ancestry group. The foreign-born numbered 17,544—3.1% of the population—in 1990.

The 1990 census counted few non-Caucasians. There were 3,000 Asians and Pacific Islanders, and about 2,000 each of blacks and American Indians.

⁸LANGUAGES

A few place-names and very few Indian-language speakers remain as evidence of the early Vermont presence of the Algonkian Mohawk tribe and of some Iroquois in the north. Vermont English, although typical of the Northern dialect, differs from that of New Hampshire in several respects, including retention of the final /r/ and use of *eavestrough* in place of eavespout.

In 1990, 491,112 Vermonters—94.2% of the population aged 5 and over—spoke only English at home. Other languages spoken at home included:

French	17,171	Spanish	3,196
German	2,716	Italian	1,289

⁹RELIGIONS

From the early days of settlement to the present, Congregationalists (whose church is now called the United Church of Christ) have played a dominant role in the state. They are the second leading Protestant denomination in the state, with 24,461 known adherents in 1990. Other major Protestant groups include the United Methodists, 9,628; American Baptists, 8,286; and Episcopalians, 9,628. The largest single religious organization in Vermont is the Roman Catholic Church, with 143,938 members in 1990. There is a small Jewish population (estimated at 4,400 in 1990) most of which lives in Burlington.

Vermont was the birthplace of both Joseph Smith and Brigham Young, founders of the Church of Jesus Christ of Latter-day Saints. The state had 2,855 Mormons in 1990.

¹⁰TRANSPORTATION

Vermont's first railroad, completed in 1849, served more as a link to Boston than as an intrastate line; it soon went into receivership, as did many other early state lines. From a high of nearly 1,100 mi (1,770 km) of track in 1910, trackage shrank to 497 rail mi (800 km) in 1995, none of it Class I line. Ten railroads together transported 8.7 million tons of freight within the state in 1995. Glass and stone made up 76% of the rail tonnage originating within the state, and petroleum accounted for 24% of the rail tonnage terminated within Vermont that year. In 1995/96, Amtrak provided passenger service to eight stations, with a total Vermont ridership of 72,841.

Of the 13,944 mi (22,440 km) of streets, roads, and highways in 1995, counties and towns had jurisdiction over 11,266 mi (18,138 km), the state over 2,838 mi (4,569 km), and the federal government over 80 mi (129 km). A total of 615,237 motor vehicles were registered in 1995, when there were 493,952 licensed drivers.

In early 1995, Vermont had 17 public use airports. Burlington International Airport, the state's major air terminal, had 3,876 air carrier and 22,120 commuter aircraft departures in that year.

¹¹HISTORY

Vermont has been inhabited continuously since about 10,000 BC. Archaeological finds suggest the presence of a pre-Algonkian group along the Otter River. Algonkian-speaking Abnaki settled along Lake Champlain and in the Connecticut Valley, and Mahican settled in the southern counties between AD 1200 and 1790. In 1609, Samuel de Champlain crossed the lake that now bears his name, becoming the first European explorer of Vermont. From the 1650s to the 1760s, French, Iroquois Indians from New York, Dutch, and English passed through the state over trails connecting Montreal with Massachusetts and New York. However, few settled there. In 1666 the French built and briefly occupied Ft. Ste. Anne on Isle La Motte, and in 1690 there was a short-lived settlement at Chimney Point. Ft. Dummer, built in 1724 near present-day Brattleboro, was the first permanent settlement.

Governor Benning Wentworth of New Hampshire, claiming that his colony extended as far west as did Massachusetts and Connecticut, had granted 131 town charters in the territory by 1764. In that year, the crown declared that New York's northeastern boundary was the Connecticut River. Owners of New Hampshire titles, fearful of losing their land, prevented New York from enforcing its jurisdiction. The Green Mountain Boys, organized by Ethan Allen in 1770–71, scared off the defenseless settlers under New York title and flouted New York courts.

Shortly after the outbreak of the Revolutionary War, Ethan Allen's men helped capture Ft. Ticonderoga, and for two years frontiersmen fought in the northern theater. On 16 August 1777, after a skirmish at Hubbardton, a Vermont contingent routed German detachments sent by British General Burgoyne toward Bennington—a battle that contributed to the general's surrender at Saratoga, N.Y. There were several British raids on Vermont towns during the war.

Vermont declared itself an independent republic with the name "New Connecticut" in 1777, promulgated a constitution abolishing slavery and providing universal manhood suffrage, adopted the laws of Connecticut, and confiscated Tory lands. Most Vermonters preferred to join the US, but the dominant Allen faction, with large holdings in the northwest, needed free trade with Canada, even at the price of returning to the British Empire. Political defeat of the Allen faction in 1789 led to negotiations that settled New York's claims and secured Vermont's admission to the Union on 4 March 1791.

With 30,000 people in 1781 and nearly 220,000 in 1810, Vermont was a state of newcomers spread evenly over the hills in

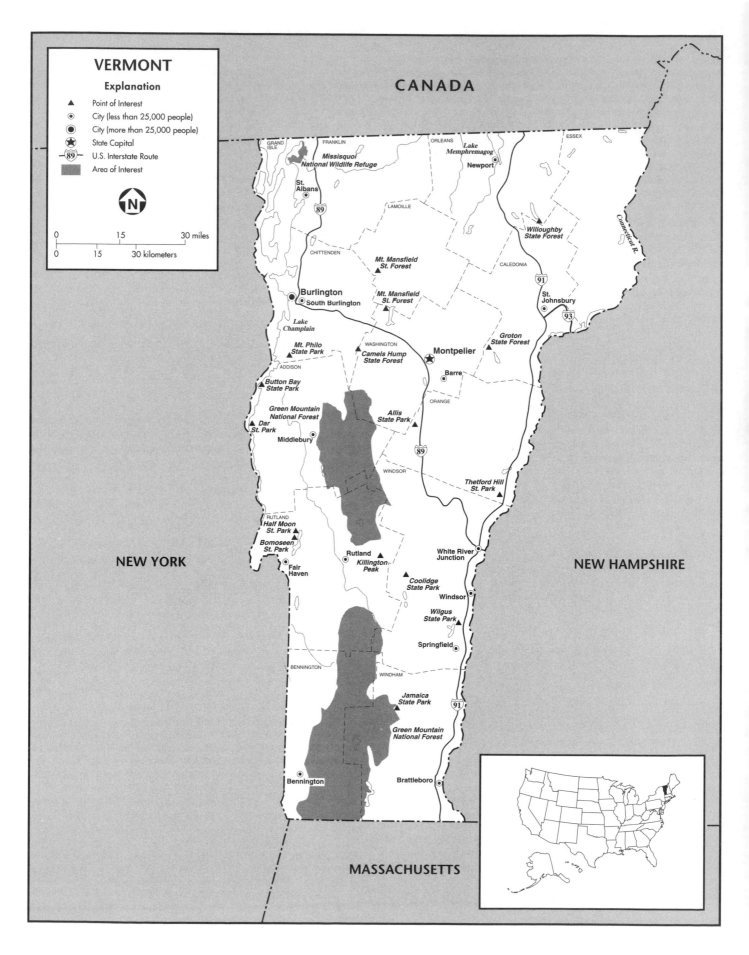

VERMONT

Explanation

▲ Point of Interest
⊙ City (less than 25,000 people)
◉ City (more than 25,000 people)
★ State Capital
—89— U.S. Interstate Route
▨ Area of Interest

N

0   15   30 miles
0   15   30 kilometers

CANADA

GRAND ISLE
FRANKLIN
ORLEANS
ESSEX

Missisquoi National Wildlife Refuge

Lake Memphremagog
Newport

St. Albans

LAMOILLE

Willoughby State Forest

CHITTENDEN

Mt. Mansfield St. Forest

CALEDONIA

Burlington
South Burlington

Mt. Mansfield St. Forest

Lake Champlain

St. Johnsbury

WASHINGTON

Mt. Philo State Park

Camels Hump State Forest

Groton State Forest

ADDISON

Montpelier

Barre

Button Bay State Park

Green Mountain National Forest

ORANGE

Allis State Park

Dar St. Park

Middlebury

Thetford Hill St. Park

WINDSOR

RUTLAND

Half Moon St. Park

White River Junction

Bomoseen St. Park

Rutland
Killington Peak

NEW YORK

Fair Haven

Coolidge State Park

NEW HAMPSHIRE

Windsor

Wilgus State Park

Springfield

BENNINGTON

WINDHAM

Jamaica State Park

Green Mountain National Forest

Bennington

Brattleboro

Connecticut R.

MASSACHUSETTS

self-sufficient homesteads. Second-generation Vermonters developed towns and villages with water-powered mills, charcoal-fired furnaces, general stores, newspapers, craft shops, churches, and schools. Those who ran these local institutions tended to be Congregationalist in religion and successively Federalist, Whig, and Republican in party politics. Dissidents in the early 1800s included minority Protestants suffering legal and social discrimination, hardscrabble farmers, and Jacksonian Democrats.

Northwestern Vermonters smuggled to avoid the US foreign trade embargo of 1808, and widespread trade continued with Canada during the War of 1812. In September 1814, however, Vermont soldiers fought in the Battle of Plattsburgh, N.Y., won by Thomas Macdonough's fleet built at Vergennes the previous winter. The Mexican War (1846–48) was unpopular in the state, but Vermont, which had strongly opposed slavery, was an enthusiastic supporter of the Union during the Civil War.

The opening of the Champlain-Hudson Canal in 1823, and the building of the early railroad lines in 1846–53, made Vermont more vulnerable to western competition, caused the demise of many small farms and businesses, and stimulated emigration. The remaining farmers' purchasing power steadily increased, as they held temporary advantages in wool, then in butter and cheese-making, and finally in milk production. The immigration of the Irish and French Canadians stabilized the population, and the expansion of light industry bolstered the economy.

During the 20th century, and especially after World War II, autos, buses, trucks, and planes took over most passengers and much freight from the railroads. Manufacturing, especially light industry, prospered in valley villages. Vermont's picturesque landscape began to attract city buyers of second homes. Still rural in population distribution, Vermont became increasingly suburban in outlook, as new highways made the cities and hills mutually accessible, and the state absorbed an influx of young professionals from New York and Massachusetts. Tourism thrived, especially in the Green Mountains and other ski resort areas. Longtime Vermonters, accustomed to their state's pristine beauty, were confronted in the 1980s with the question of how much development was necessary for the state's economic health. The newcomers changed the political landscape as well. Whereas Vermont had long been dominated by the Republican Party, by the mid-eighties fully a third of the electorate voted Democratic. In 1990, Vermont elected as its sole congressional representative a democratic socialist, Bernie Sanders, who called for reduced limits on campaign spending, a sharply progressive income tax, national health care, and 50% cuts in military spending over five years. Sanders's victory reflected, in part, voters' frustration with a downturn in the New England economy in the late eighties. He was reelected in 1996.

In the early 1990s Vermont had the nation's highest percentage of women in its state legislature. With two-thirds of its population living in towns of 2,500 or fewer, it was the nation's most rural state. In 1993 Vermont passed legislation barring smoking in all public buildings, including most restaurants and hotels.

12STATE GOVERNMENT

A constitution establishing Vermont as an independent republic was adopted in 1777. This document, as revised and amended, still governs the state.

The general assembly consists of a 150-member house of representatives and a 30-member senate. All legislators are elected to two-year terms. State elective officials include the governor, lieutenant governor (elected separately), treasurer, secretary of state, auditor of accounts, and attorney general, all of whom serve two-year terms. In 1996 the governor's salary was $80,724.

The legislature meets in odd-numbered years for two-year sessions. All bills require a majority vote in each house for passage. Bills can be vetoed by the governor, and vetoes can be overridden by a two-thirds vote of each legislative house. A constitutional amendment must first be passed by a two-thirds vote in the senate, followed by a majority in the house during the same legislative session. It must then receive majority votes in both houses before it can be submitted to the voters for approval.

Voters must be US citizens and 18 years of age; there is no minimum residency requirement.

13POLITICAL PARTIES

The Republican Party, which originally drew strength from powerful abolitionist sentiment, gained control of Vermont state offices in 1856 and for more than 100 years dominated state politics. No Democrat was elected governor from 1853 until 1962.

In 1994 there were 373,442 registered voters. In 1984, Democrat Madeleine M. Kunin was elected as Vermont's first woman governor and only the third Democratic governor in the state's history. Kunin served as governor for three terms, followed in 1990 by Republican Richard Snelling and in 1992 by Democrat Howard Dean. Vermont's delegation to the House of Representatives consists of one Independent. In 1997, Democrats controlled the state senate, with 17 seats out of 30. In the state house of representatives, the Democrats held 88 seats; the Republicans had 58; Independents had 1; and Progressive Coalition members held 3. In 1997 Vermont had one Republican US senator, James Jeffords, elected in 1988 and reelected in 1994, and one Democratic US senator, Patrick Leahy, who was elected to his fourth term in 1992.

Vermont has often shown its independence in national political elections. In 1832, it was the only state to cast a plurality vote for the Anti-Masonic presidential candidate, William Wirt; in 1912, the only state besides Utah to vote for William Howard Taft; and in 1936, the only state besides Maine to prefer Alf Landon to Franklin D. Roosevelt. In 1996, Vermonters gave 53% of their presidential vote to Democratic incumbent Bill Clinton; 31% to Republican Bob Dole; and 12% to Independent Ross Perot.

Minority representation in public office in 1996 consisted of one black serving in the state legislature, in which women held 45 seats.

Vermont Presidential Vote by Major Political Parties, 1948–96

YEAR	ELECTORAL VOTE	VERMONT WINNER	DEMOCRAT	REPUBLICAN
1948	3	Dewey (R)	45,557	75,926
1952	3	*Eisenhower (R)	43,355	109,717
1956	3	*Eisenhower (R)	42,549	110,390
1960	3	Nixon (R)	69,186	98,131
1964	3	*Johnson (D)	108,127	54,942
1968	3	*Nixon (R)	70,255	85,142
1972	3	*Nixon (R)	68,174	117,149
1976	3	Ford (R)	77,798	100,387
1980	3	*Reagan (R)	81,891	94,598
1984	3	*Reagan (R)	95,730	135,865
1988	3	*Bush (R)	115,775	124,331
1992**	3	*Clinton (D)	133,592	88,122
1996**	3	*Clinton(D)	137,894	80,352

* Won US presidential election.
** Independent candidate Ross Perot received 65,991 votes in 1992 and 31,024 votes in 1996.

14LOCAL GOVERNMENT

As of 1992, there were 14 counties, 50 municipal governments, and 237 townships in Vermont, as well as 276 school districts and 104 special districts. County officers, operating out of shire towns (county seats), include the probate courts judge, assistant judges of the county court, county clerk, state's attorney, high bailiff, treasurer, and sheriff. All cities have mayor-council systems. Towns are governed by three selectmen, who serve staggered three-year terms; one is elected at each annual town meeting, held on the 1st Tuesday in March. Larger towns also have town managers.

[15]STATE SERVICES

Vermont's Department of Education oversees public elementary, secondary, higher education, and adult education programs. The Agency of Transportation includes the Department of Motor Vehicles, Transportation Board, and Hazardous Materials Committee. The Agency of Human Services coordinates programs for nursing homes, veterans' affairs, social welfare, employment and training, health, corrections, and parole. The Agency of Development and Community Affairs administers federal housing programs and offers aid to localities.

[16]JUDICIAL SYSTEM

Vermont's highest court is the supreme court, which consists of a chief justice and 4 associate justices. Other courts include the superior, district, family, and environmental courts, with 30 judges. All judges are appointed by the governor to six-year terms, subject to senate confirmation, from a list of qualified candidates prepared by the Judicial Nominating Board, which includes representatives of the governor, the legislature, and the Vermont bar. There are also 28 assistant judges and 19 probate court judges, all of them elected to four-year terms. There were 2,730 practicing attorneys in August 1997.

In 1996 there were 1,095 inmates in stage and federal correctional facilities, a rate of 143 inmates per 100,000 inhabitants.

There is no death penalty.

[17]ARMED FORCES

In 1996, there were 127 active duty military personnel stationed in Vermont. In 1995/96, the government awarded $225 million in defense contracts to Vermont firms, principally Lockheed Martin ($208 million). Of the estimated 62,000 veterans living in Vermont in 1996, 138 served in World War I, 17,000 in World War II, 10,000 in the Korean conflict, 20,000 during the Viet Nam era, and 4,000 in the Persian Gulf War. Veterans' benefits in 1996 totaled $113 million. There were 5,789 reserve and national guard members in 1992. In 1993, the Vermont Department of Public Safety employed 289 full-time sworn officers, or 5 per 10,000 residents—the second-highest ratio in the country.

[18]MIGRATION

The earliest Vermont settlers were farmers from southern New England and New York; most were of English descent, although some Dutch settlers moved to Vermont from New York. French Canadians came beginning in the 1830s; by 1850, several thousand had moved into Vermont. As milling, quarrying, and mining grew during the 19th century, other Europeans arrived—small groups of Italians and Scots in Barre, and Poles, Swedes, Czechs, Russians, and Austrians in the Rutland quarry areas. Irish immigrants built the railroads in the mid-19th century. Steady out-migrations during the 19th and early 20th centuries kept population increases down, and in the decades 1910–1920 and 1930–1940, the population dropped. During the 1960s, the population of blacks more than doubled, though they still accounted for only 0.34% of the population in 1990. Between 1970 and 1983, 45,000 migrants settled in Vermont. From 1985 to 1990, Vermont had a net gain from migration of nearly 21,400. Between 1990 and 1996, the state had net gains of 6,025

in domestic migration and 2,724 in international migration. As of 1990, 57.2% of state residents had been born within Vermont, and 52% of those age 5 and older were living in the same house as in 1985. Nearly 70% of those who lived in a different house in 1985 did so elsewhere within Vermont. At 32.2%, Vermont's urban population in 1990 was the lowest among the states and had fallen from 33.8% in 1980.

[19]INTERGOVERNMENTAL COOPERATION

Vermont participates in New England compacts on corrections, higher education, water pollution control, police, and radiological health protection. The state also takes part in the Connecticut River Valley Flood Control Compact, Lake Champlain Bridge Compact, and Interstate Pest Control Compact.

Federal aid to Vermont totaled $641 million in 1996.

[20]ECONOMY

During its early years of statehood, Vermont was overwhelmingly agricultural, with beef cattle, sheep, and dairying contributing greatly to the state's income. After World War II, agriculture was replaced by manufacturing and tourism as the backbone of the economy. Durable goods manufacturing (primarily electronics and machine parts), construction, wholesale and retail trade, and other service industries have shown the largest growth in employment during the 1980s. Vermont's gross state product in 1994 was $13,282 million, to which private goods-producing industries contributed $3,217 million; private services-producing industries, $8,428 million; and government, $1,637 million. Vermont's per capita personal income was $22,124, 30th in the US. During 1995, there were 1,368 bankruptcy filings.

[21]INCOME

Vermont ranked 30th in per capita personal income with $22,124 in 1996. Total personal disposable income that year was $11.4 billion (up from $10.9 billion in 1995.) Total earned income grew by 3.7% to $8.5 billion in 1995, up from $8.2 billion in 1994. About 7.6% of all Vermonters were below the federal poverty line in 1995. Median household income that same year was $35,802.

[22]LABOR

According to the US Department of Labor, 324,000 Vermonters were in the labor force on average during 1996, of whom 310,000 were employed. The unemployment rate that year was 4.6%. About 30% of the labor force lived in the Burlington area, which had an unemployment rate of 3.8% at the beginning of 1997.

At the beginning of 1997, nonagricultural employment was as follows: mining, 700; construction, 13,000; manufacturing, 46,300; transportation and public utilities, 12,000; wholesale and retail trade, 65,000; finance, insurance and real estate, 12,500; services, 81,200; and government, 45,700.

There were 23,900 manufacturing workers who were members of labor unions in Vermont in 1995.

[23]AGRICULTURE

Although Vermont is one of the nation's most rural states, its agricultural income was only $472.3 million in 1995, 44th among the 50 states. More than 80% of that came from livestock and livestock products, especially dairy products. The leading crops in 1996 were corn for silage, 1,254,000 tons; hay, 507,000 tons; and apples, 37.5 million lb.

[24]ANIMAL HUSBANDRY

The merino sheep and the Morgan horse (a breed developed in Vermont) were common sights on pastures more than a century ago, but today they have been for the most part replaced by dairy cattle. In 1995, Vermont dairy farms had around 157,000 milk cows that produced 2.538 billion lb of milk. In 1997, the state had 300,000 cattle and calves, valued at $237 million.

25FISHING

Sport fishermen can find ample species of trout, perch, walleye pike, bass, and pickerel in Vermont's waters, many of which are stocked by the Department of Fish and Game. Maintenance stocking by the US Fish and Wildlife Service amounted to 3,025,520 fish (9,608 lb) and 2,639,430 fish eggs in 1995/96, when the state issued 100,397 sport fishing licenses. There is little commercial fishing.

26FORESTRY

The Green Mountain State is covered by 4,538,000 acres (1,837,000 hectares) of forestland—77% of the state's total land area—much of it owned or leased by lumber companies. More than 25% of all manufacturing establishments in the state depend on the lumber industry. Shipments of forest products in 1995 included paper and paper products, $468 million, and lumber and wood products, $403.2 million. Vermont is the nation's leading producer of maple syrup; the 1993 output was 550,000 gallons.

The largest forest reserve in Vermont is the Green Mountain National Forest, with over 340,000 acres (136,000 hectares) managed by the US Forest Service.

27MINING

The value of nonfuel mineral production in Vermont in 1995 was estimated to be $67.7 million, a $4.4 million increase over that of 1994. Leading mineral commodities, in terms of value, were dimension stone ($28,900,000 for 102,000 metric tons), crushed stone ($27,800,000 for 4,900,000 metric tons), and construction sand and gravel ($11,000,000 for 2,900,000 metric tons). Nationally, the state ranked 3d in talc and pyrophyllite, and 4th in dimension stone. Dimension stone, the state's leading mineral commodity produced, accounted for more than 42% of the state's mineral production value. Granite is quarried near Barre, and slate is found in the southwest. The West Rutland-Proctor area has the world's largest marble reserve, the Danby quarry.

28ENERGY AND POWER

Because of the state's lack of fossil fuel resources, utility bills are higher in Vermont than in most states. During 1995, 64 plants with a capacity of 1,135,000 kw generated 4.8 billion kwh of power, more than 79% of which was produced by the state's lone nuclear plant at Vernon, operated by Vermont Yankee Nuclear Power Corp.

29INDUSTRY

The estimated value of shipments of manufactured goods was $8.9 billion in 1995.

Scales, machine tools, and electronic components are important manufactured items. The following table shows estimated value of shipments of manufacturers for selected industries in 1995:

Electronic and other electric equipment	$3,904,700,000
Food and food products	1,021,900,000
Printing and publishing	548,900,000
Paper and paper products	468,000,000
Fabricated metal products	411,100,000
Industrial machinery and equipment	410,900,000

During 1995, there were 173 US patents issued to Vermont residents.

30COMMERCE

Wholesale trade in 1992 was nearly $4.5 billion. Retail trade totaled $4.6 billion (48th), of which the leading sectors were food stores, 23.6%; automotive dealers, 18.7%; and eating and drinking places, 9.3%. Foreign exports of Vermont manufacturers were estimated at $3.3 billion for 1996.

31CONSUMER PROTECTION

The Consumer Protection Division of the Attorney General's Office handles most consumer complaints. The Vermont Public Service Department's Consumer Affairs Division monitors utility rates, and the Agency of Human Services' Office on Aging protects the rights of the state's senior citizens.

32BANKING

In 1996, there were 13 state-chartered commercial banks. As of 31 December 1996, Vermont's state-chartered commercial banks had assets of $4.9 billion and deposits exceeding 46.3 billion. There were four savings institutions at the end of 1996.

33INSURANCE

Three life insurance and 370 property/casualty insurance companies have their home offices in Vermont. As of 1995, life insurance premiums worth nearly $185 million were paid by Vermonters. Automobile insurance premiums written in the state in 1995 totaled $243.2 million; homeowners insurance premiums, $72.4 million.

34SECURITIES

There are no stock or commodity exchanges in Vermont. Securities were sold by 1,090 brokers and dealers (39,820 agents) registered to do business in Vermont as of May 1997.

35PUBLIC FINANCE

The budgets for two fiscal years are submitted by the governor to the general assembly for approval during its biennial session. The fiscal year runs from 1 July to 30 June.

The following table shows estimated general revenues and expenditures for the year 1995 (in thousands):

REVENUES	
From own sources	2,073,665
Taxes	
Property	633,266
Sales and gross receipts	502,839
Income	298,557
SUBTOTAL	$ 1,434,662
CHARGES AND MISCELLANEOUS	
Current charges	$ 242,504
Interest earnings	176,297
Special assessments	27,953
Other	192,269
SUBTOTAL	$ 639,023
TOTAL	$ 2,073,685
EXPENDITURES	
Education	$ 610,672
Transportation (highways)	157,005
Public safety (police)	68,237
Natural resources	54,308
Utilities	1,162
Financial administration	111,600
Health and social concerns	568,304
Other	442,277
TOTAL	$ 2,013,565

The total outstanding debt of state and local governments in Vermont was $1.7 billion, or $2,850 per capita, as of 1995.

36 TAXATION

Vermont ranked 47th in the US in state tax receipts in 1991, with $685 million; the tax burden was $1,207.30 per capita. The state imposes personal and corporate income taxes, sales and use taxes, a bank franchise tax, and an estate tax. Taxes are also levied on beverages, certain electrical energy, generators, insurance, meals and rooms, real estate transfers, and tobacco products, among other items.

In 1995, Vermonters paid $1.7 million in federal income taxes.

37 ECONOMIC POLICY

Incentives for industrial expansion include state and municipally financed industrial sites, state employment development and training funds, revenue bond financing, tax credits for investment in research and development and in capital equipment; loans and loan guarantees for construction and equipment, and financial incentives for locating plants in areas of high unemployment. There are also exemptions from inventory taxes and sales tax on new equipment and raw materials.

38 HEALTH

In 1995 there were 6,448 live births (11.6 per 1,000 resident population) in Vermont. In 1995, the infant mortality rate was 6 per 1,000 live births, one of the nation's lowest. There were 2,170 legal abortions in 1995.

Heart disease was the leading cause of death in 1995, though the rate of 278.4 per 100,000 population was below the US average. In 1995, there were 94 motor vehicle traffic fatalities in the state. Vermont's suicide rate of 12.8 per 100,000 population exceeded the national rate of 1995 and was the 4th highest among the New England states in 1994. In 1993, Vermont ranked 25th for coronary heart disease death rate. The state's AIDS rate of 4.6 per 100,000 population in 1995 was one of the lowest in the country.

Vermont had 14 hospitals operating in 1995. In 1994, average hospital expenses per inpatient stay ($5,400) and per day ($651) were below the US average. The state had 1,204 active, nonfederal licensed physicians in 1994 and 325 professionally active dentists in 1996.

Most Vermont residents had health insurance. In 1994, 8.6% had no form of insurance. Both Medicare and Medicaid reimbursements increased from 1993 to 1994.

39 SOCIAL WELFARE

In 1996, aid to families with dependent children (AFDC) paid an average monthly allotment of $738 to 25,800 residents. In 1996, 56,459 residents received monthly food stamps averaging $64.65; the school lunch program received total funding of $8.2 million. Weekly unemployment benefits averaged $165.82 in 1995.

In 1995, Social Security benefits averaging $562 a month were paid to approximately 90,000 Vermonters; additionally, Supplemental Security Income payments averaging $332 were paid to 13,015 residents.

With the enactment of the Personal Responsibility and Work Opportunity Reconciliation Act of 1996, the US government has changed the form and regulations for many of its social welfare programs; most significantly, it replaces Aid to Families with Dependent Children (AFDC), an open-ended entitlement program, with Temporary Assistance for Needy Families (TANF), a limited system of assistance funded largely through federal block grants. The reform act also impacts the food stamp program, the Supplemental Security Income program, and the child nutrition program. The law took effect on 1 July 1997 and provided $16.38 billion in block grants for fiscal years 1997–

2002. The grants are to be divided among the states based on an equation involving the numbers of former AFDC recipients in each state. Because many of the bills provisions have yet to be implemented into state-by-state policy, it was not possible to include the details of each state's programs for this edition of this work.

40 HOUSING

As rustic farmhouses gradually disappear, modern units (many of them vacation homes for Vermonters and out-of-staters) are being built to replace them. In 1996, there were an estimated 289,000 housing units in Vermont, 223,000 of which were occupied. That year, 2,308 privately owned units, valued at $201 million, were authorized for construction; of these, 1,872 were single family. About 36.5% of the housing stock dates before 1940; 97.7% of all housing units have complete plumbing facilities. The median monthly cost for an owner with a mortgage in 1990, the last year for which figures are available, was $718; renters had a median monthly cost of $446. Vermont's median housing costs are the second-lowest in New England, after Maine. During 1995/96, Vermont received $64.1 million in aid from the US Department of Housing and Urban Development, including $7 million in community development block grants.

41 EDUCATION

As of 1997, some 82.1% of Vermonters above the age of 25 were high school graduates, and 26.4% had completed at least four years of postsecondary study.

During the 1996/97 school year, 106,341 students were enrolled in Vermont's public schools. The total 1990/91 enrollment in the state's 22 two- and four-year colleges was 36,398. The state college system includes colleges at Castleton, Johnson, and Lyndonville, a technical college at Randolph Center, and the Community College of Vermont system with 12 branch campuses. The University of Vermont (Burlington) is a state-supported institution combining features of both a private and a state facility. Founded in 1791, it is the oldest higher educational institution in the state.

Notable private institutions include Bennington College, Champlain College (Burlington), Landmark College (Putney) serving students with ADHD and learning disabilities, Marlboro College (Marlboro), and Norwich University (Northfield), the oldest private military college in the US. The School for International Training (Brattleboro) is the academic branch of the Experiment in International Living, a student exchange program. Other notable institutions include St. Michael's College (Winooski) and Trinity College (Burlington).

The Vermont Student Assistance Corp. offers scholarships, incentive grants, and guaranteed loans for eligible Vermont students.

42 ARTS

The Vermont State Crafts Centers at Frog Hollow (Middlebury) and Windsor display the works of Vermont artisans. The Vermont Symphony Orchestra, in Burlington, makes extensive statewide tours. Marlboro College is the home of the summer Marlboro Music Festival, directed by pianist Rudolf Serkin. Among the summer theaters in the state are those at Dorset and Weston, and the University of Vermont Shakespeare Festival. The Middlebury College Bread Loaf Writers' Conference, founded in 1926, meets each August in Ripton.

In 1996, the NEA contributed $595,000 to arts programs in Vermont and $611,000 to the Vermont Council on the Arts. Between 1987 and 1991, the state's arts programs attracted a total audience of 4,172,000 and had 41,279 contributing artists. During the same period, Vermont provided 18,600 school children with arts education programs. In 1996, the state had 100 arts associations and 5 local arts groups. The Council on the Arts has received grants through the NEA's State and Regional Program.

43 LIBRARIES AND MUSEUMS

During 1995/96, the state's public libraries held 2,435,183 volumes and had a combined circulation of 3,479,152. The largest academic library was at the University of Vermont, with a book stock of 1,031,962.

Vermont has 87 museums and more than 65 historic sites. Among them are the Bennington Museum, with its collection of Early American glass, pottery, furniture, and Grandma Moses paintings, and the Art Gallery–St. Johnsbury Athenaeum, featuring 19th-century American artists. The Shelburne Museum, housed in restored Early American buildings, contains collections of American primitives and Indian artifacts. The Vermont Museum, in Montpelier, features historical exhibits concerning Indians, the Revolutionary War, rural life, and railroads and industry. Old Constitution House in Windsor offers exhibits on Vermont history.

44 COMMUNICATIONS

In March 1993, about 223,000 homes (93.5%) had telephones. There were 16 AM and 42 FM radio stations and 7 television stations (including 4 public stations) in operation in 1996. In the same year, Adelphia Cable was the state's major cable provider.

45 PRESS

In 1997 there were 99 daily papers, and 3 Sunday papers. The leading daily in 1991 was the *Burlington Free Press* (53,433 mornings, 66,537 Sundays). *Vermont Life* magazine is published quarterly under the aegis of the Agency of Development and Community Affairs.

46 ORGANIZATIONS

The 1992 Census of Service Industries counted 325 "selected membership" organizations in Vermont, including 60 business associations, 194 civic, social, and fraternal associations, and 71 other membership organizations. Associations headquartered in Vermont largely reflect the state's agricultural interests. Among these are Gardens for All (the National Association for Gardening) in Burlington, the Ayrshire Breeders' Association of America (Brattleboro), and the International Maple Syrup Institute (Fairfax).

47 TOURISM, TRAVEL, AND RECREATION

With the building of the first ski slopes in the 1930s (Woodstock claims the first ski area in the US) and the development of modern highways, tourism became a major industry in Vermont. Domestic travelers spent $1,030,000 in Vermont in 1993. In the winter, the state's ski areas offer some of the finest skiing in the East. In 1995 state residents held 163,547 hunting and 135,360 fishing licenses.

48 SPORTS

Vermont has no major league professional sports teams. Skiing is, perhaps, the most popular participation sport and Vermont ski areas have hosted national and international ski competitions in both Alpine and Nordic events. World Cup races have been run at Stratton Mountain, and the national cross-country championships have been held near Putney.

49 FAMOUS VERMONTERS

Two US presidents, both of whom assumed office upon the death of their predecessors, were born in Vermont. Chester Alan Arthur (1829–86) became the 21st president after James A. Garfield's assassination in 1881 and finished his term. A machine politician, Arthur became a civil-service reformer in the White House. Calvin Coolidge (1872–1933), 28th president, was born in Plymouth Notch but pursued a political career in Massachusetts. Elected vice president in 1920, he became president on the death of Warren G. Harding in 1923 and was elected to a full term in 1924.

Other federal officeholders have included Matthew Lyon (1750–1822), a US representative imprisoned under the Sedition Act and reelected from a Vergennes jail; Jacob Collamer (1791–1865), who, after serving three terms in the US House, was US postmaster general and then a US senator; Justin Smith Morrill (1810–98), US representative and senator who sponsored the Morrill tariff in 1861 and the Land Grant College Act in 1862; Levi Parsons Morton (1824–1920), Benjamin Harrison's vice president from 1889 to 1893; George Franklin Edmunds (1828–1919), a US senator who helped draft the Sherman Antitrust Act; Redfield Proctor (1831–1908), secretary of war, US senator, state governor, and the founder of a marble company; John Garibaldi Sargent (1860–1939), Coolidge's attorney general; Warren Robinson Austin (1877–1963), US senator and head of the US delegation to the UN; and George David Aiken (1892–1984), US senator from 1941 to 1977.

Important state leaders were Thomas Chittenden (1730–97), leader of the Vermont republic and the state's first governor; Ethan Allen (1738–89), a frontier folk hero, leader of the Green Mountain Boys, and presenter of Vermont's claim to independence to the US Congress in 1778; Ira Allen (1751–1814), the brother of Ethan, who led the fight for statehood; Cornelius Peter Van Ness (b.New York, 1782–1852), who served first as Vermont chief justice and then as governor; and Erastus Fairbanks (1792–1864), a governor and railroad promoter.

Vermont's many businessmen and inventors include Thaddeus Fairbanks (1796–1886), inventor of the platform scale; Thomas Davenport (1802–51), inventor of the electric motor; plow and tractor manufacturer John Deere (1804–86); Elisha G. Otis (1811–61), inventor of a steam elevator and elevator safety devices; and Horace Wells (1815–48), inventor of laughing gas. Educator John Dewey (1859–1952) was born in Burlington. Donald James Cram (b. 1919), a professor of chemistry at the University of California at Los Angeles, was awarded a Nobel Prize in chemistry in 1987.

Robert Frost (b.California, 1874–1963) maintained a summer home near Ripton, where he helped found Middlebury College's Bread Loaf Writers' Conference. He was named poet laureate of Vermont in 1961. In 1992, Louise Gluck became the first Vermont woman to win a Pulitzer Prize for poetry. A famous Vermont performer is crooner and orchestra leader Rudy Vallee (Hubert Prior Rudy Vallee, 1901–1986).

50 BIBLIOGRAPHY

Bassett, T. D. S. *Vermont.* Hanover, N.H.: University Press of New England, 1983.

Bearse, Ray, ed. *Vermont: A Guide to the Green Mountain State.* Boston: Houghton Mifflin, 1968.

Crockett, Walter H. *History of Vermont.* 5 vols. New York: Century, 1921.

Hill, Ralph Nading. *Vermont: A Special World.* Montpelier: Vermont Life, 1969.

Morrissey, Charles T. *Vermont: A Bicentennial History.* New York: Norton, 1981.

Sherman, Micheal, and Jennie Versteeg (eds.). *We Vermonters: Perspectives on the Past.* Montpelier: Vermont Historical Society, 1992.

VIRGINIA

ORIGIN OF STATE NAME: Named for Queen Elizabeth I of England, the "Virgin Queen." **NICKNAME:** The Old Dominion. **CAPITAL:** Richmond. **ENTERED UNION:** 25 June 1788 (10th). **SONG EMERITUS:** "Carry Me Back to Old Virginia" was formally retired from use in 1997 but has not yet been replaced. **MOTTO:** *Sic semper tyrannis* (Thus ever to tyrants). **FLAG:** On a blue field with a white border at the fly, the state seal is centered on a white circle. **OFFICIAL SEAL:** OBVERSE: the Roman goddess Virtus, dressed as an Amazon and holding a sheathed sword in one hand and a spear in the other, stands over the body of Tyranny, who is pictured with a broken chain in his hand and a fallen crown nearby. The state motto appears below, the word "Virginia" above, and a border of Virginia creeper encircles the whole. REVERSE: the Roman goddesses of Liberty, Eternity, and Fruitfulness, with the word "Perseverando" (By persevering) above. **ANIMAL:** Foxhound. **BIRD:** Cardinal. **FLOWER:** Dogwood. **TREE:** Dogwood. **SHELL:** Oyster. **LEGAL HOLIDAYS:** New Year's Day, 1 January; Lee-Jackson Day and Birthday of Martin Luther King, Jr., 3d Monday in January; Washington's Birthday, 3d Monday in February; Memorial Day, last Monday in May; Independence Day, 4 July; Labor Day, 1st Monday in September; Columbus Day and Yorktown Victory Day, 2d Monday in October; Election Day, 1st Tuesday after 1st Monday in November; Veterans Day, 11 November; Thanksgiving Day, 4th Thursday in November; Christmas Day, 25 December. **TIME:** 7 AM EST = noon GMT.

¹LOCATION, SIZE, AND EXTENT

Situated on the eastern seaboard of the US, Virginia is the 4th largest of the South Atlantic states and ranks 36th in size among the 50 states.

The total area of Virginia is 40,767 sq mi (105,586 sq km), of which land occupies 39,704 sq mi (102,833 sq km) and inland water 1,063 sq mi (2,753 sq km). Virginia extends approximately 440 mi (710 km) E-W, but the maximum point-to-point distance from the state's noncontiguous Eastern Shore to the western extremity is 470 mi (756 km). The maximum N-S extension is about 200 mi (320 km).

Virginia is bordered on the NW by West Virginia; on the NE by Maryland and the District of Columbia (with the line passing through the Potomac River and Chesapeake Bay); on the E by the Atlantic Ocean; on the S by North Carolina and Tennessee; and on the W by Kentucky. The state's geographic center is in Buckingham County, 5 mi (8 km) SW of the town of Buckingham.

Virginia's offshore islands in the Atlantic include Chincoteague, Wallops, Cedar, Parramore, Hog, Cobb, and Smith. The boundaries of Virginia, including the Eastern Shore at the tip of the Delmarva Peninsula, total 1,356 mi (2,182 km), of which 112 mi (180 km) is general coastline; the tidal shoreline extends 3,315 mi (5,335 km).

²TOPOGRAPHY

Virginia consists of three principal physiographic areas: the Atlantic Coastal Plain, or Tidewater; the Piedmont Plateau, in the central section; and the Blue Ridge and Allegheny Mountains of the Appalachian chain, in the west and northwest.

The long, narrow Blue Ridge rises sharply from the piedmont, reaching a maximum elevation of 5 ͅ 9 feet (1,746 meters) at Mt. Rogers, the state's highest poir ͅ ͅ ween the Blue Ridge and the Allegheny Mountains of t. ͅ lachian chain in the northwest lies the Valley of Virgi. ͅ sisting of transverse

ridges and six separate valleys. The floors of these valleys ascend in altitude from about 300 feet (90 meters) in the northern Shenandoah Valley to 2,400 feet (730 meters) in the Powell Valley. The Alleghenies average 3,000 feet (900 meters) in height.

The Piedmont, shaped roughly like a triangle, varies in width from 40 mi (64 km) in the far north to 180 mi (290 km) in the extreme south. Altitudes in this region range from about 300 feet (90 meters) at the fall line in the east to a maximum of about 1,000 feet (300 meters) at the base of the Blue Ridge in the southwest. The Tidewater, which declines gently from the fall line to sea level, is divided by four long peninsulas cut by the state's four principal rivers—the Potomac, Rappahannock, York, and James—and the Chesapeake Bay. On the opposite side of the bay is Virginia's low-lying Eastern Shore, the southern tip of the Delmarva Peninsula. The Tidewater has many excellent harbors, notably the deep Hampton Roads estuary. Also in the southeast lies the Dismal Swamp, a drainage basin that includes Lake Drummond, about 7 mi (11 km) long and 5 mi (8 km) wide near the North Carolina border. Other major lakes in Virginia are Smith Mountain—at 31 sq mi (80 sq km) the largest lake wholly within the state—Claytor, and South Holston. The John H. Kerr Reservoir, covering 76 sq mi (197 sq km), straddles the Virginia–North Carolina line.

³CLIMATE

A mild, humid coastal climate is characteristic of Virginia. Temperatures, most equable in the Tidewater, become increasingly cooler with the rising altitudes as one moves westward. The normal daily mean temperature at Richmond is about 58°F (14°C), ranging from 36°F (2°C) in January to 78°F (26°C) in July. The record high, 110°F (43°C), was registered at Balcony Falls (near Glasgow) on 15 July 1954; the record low, –30°F (–34°C), was set at Mountain Lake on 22 January 1985. The frost-free growing season ranges from about 140 days in the mountains of the extreme west to over 250 in the Norfolk area.

Precipitation at Richmond averages 44 in (112 cm) a year; the average snowfall amounts to nearly 15 in (38 cm) at Richmond but only 8 in (20 cm) at Norfolk.

4FLORA AND FAUNA

Native to Virginia are 12 varieties of oak, 5 of pine, and 2 each of walnut, locust, gum, and popular. Pines predominate in the coastal areas, with numerous hardwoods on slopes and ridges inland; isolated stands of persimmon, ash, cedar, and basswood can also be found. Characteristic wild flowers include trailing arbutus, mountain laurel, and diverse azaleas and rhododendrons. The Virginia round-leaf birch and small whorled pogonia are endangered.

Among indigenous mammalian species are white-tailed (Virginia) deer, elk, black bear, bobcat, woodchuck, raccoon, opossum, nutria, red and gray foxes, and spotted and striped skunks, along with several species each of moles, shrews, bats, squirrels, deermice, rats, and rabbits; the beaver, mink, and river otter, once thought to be endangered, have returned in recent decades. Principal game birds include the ruffed grouse (commonly called pheasant in Virginia), wild turkey, bobwhite quail, mourning dove, woodcock, and Wilson's snipe. Tidal waters abound with croaker, hogfish, gray and spotted trout, and flounder; bass, bream, bluegill, sunfish, perch, carp, catfish, and crappie live in freshwater ponds and streams. Native reptiles include such poisonous snakes as the northern copperhead, eastern cottonmouth, and timber rattler.

Endangered species in Virginia include the eastern cougar; Delmarva fox squirrel; Indiana, gray, and Virginia big-eared bats; southern bald eagle; red-cockaded and ivory-billed woodpeckers; Bachman's warbler; shortnose sturgeon; Virginia fringed mountain snail; Madison cave isopod; five species of pearly mussels; three species of pigtoe; and the tan riffle shell. Threatened species are the slender and spotfin chubs and yellowfin madtom. Of more than 60 rare or endangered species in the state, at last one-fourth are found in the Dismal Swamp.

5ENVIRONMENTAL PROTECTION

The Virginia Department of Environmental Quality (DEQ), established in 1993, is under the jurisdiction of the Secretary of Natural Resources. The mission of the DEQ is to protect the environment of Virginia in order to promote the health and well-being of the citizens of the Commonwealth. The DEQ administers state and federal environmental programs; issues environmental permits and ensures compliance with regulations; and coordinates planning among Virginia's environmental programs. The DEQ provides staff support to assist the State Water Control Board in administering the federal Clean Water Act and enforcing state laws to improve the quality of surface water and groundwater for aquatic life and human health; the State Air Pollution Control Board in administering the federal Clean Air Act and enforcing state laws and regulations to improve air quality; and the Waste Management Board in administering waste management programs created by legislation such as the Resource Conservation and Recovery Act and the Virginia Waste Management Act. The Commission of Game and Inland Fisheries manages land wildlife and freshwater fish resources, while the Marine Resources Commission manages the wetlands, commercial fishery resources, and the use of the marine environment in the Tidewater area. Virginia has implemented programs to improve air quality in the Northern Virginia, Richmond, and Hampton Roads regions; to enhance water quality monitoring for streams and lakes statewide; to continue restoration efforts for the Chesapeake Bay; and to promote voluntary cleanups of contaminated industrial sites. In 1995, the state had 24 hazardous waste sites. About 1 million acres of the state is wetlands. These areas are regulated by the Virginia Water Protection Permit.

6POPULATION

Virginia ranked 12th among the 50 states at the 1990 census with a population of 6,187,358, a 15% increase over 1980. By 1996, the population was estimated at 6,675,451, a 7.9% increase over 1990. The population density in 1990 was 156.3 per sq mi (60 per sq km).

From the outset, Virginia was the most populous of the English colonies, with a population that doubled every 25 years and totaled more than 100,000 by 1727. By 1790, the time of the first US census, Virginia's population of 821,287 was about 21% of the US total and almost twice that of 2d-ranked Pennsylvania. Although surpassed by New York State at the 1820 census, Virginia continued to enjoy slow but steady growth until the Civil War, when the loss of its western counties (which became the new state of West Virginia) and the wartime devastation caused a decline of 23% for the decade of the 1860s. The population passed the 2-million mark in 1910, and the number of Virginians doubled between 1920 and 1970. The population growth rates for the five decades since 1940 were 23.9%, 19.5%, 17.2%, 15%, and 15.7%, in each case above the US average.

In 1990, 72.5% of all Virginians lived in metropolitan areas, the largest of which in 1995 was the Norfolk–Virginia Beach–Newport News area, with an estimated 1,540,446 people; the Richmond-Petersburg metropolitan area had 927,435 people. Virginia's most populous cities with their estimated 1994 populations were that year were Virginia Beach, 430,295; Norfolk, 241,426; Richmond, 201,108; Arlington, 174,603; Newport News, 179,127; Chesapeake, 180,577; Hampton, 139,628; Portsmouth, 103,464; and Roanoke, 96,643.

7ETHNIC GROUPS

When the first federal census was taken in 1790, more than 306,000 blacks—of whom only 12,000 were free—made up more than one-third of Virginia's total population. After emancipation, blacks continued to be heavily represented, accounting in 1870 for 512,841 (42%) of the 1,225,163 Virginians. Blacks numbered 1,163,000 in 1990—but their proportion of the total estimated population was less than 19%. Virginia's estimated black population in 1996 was 1,392,000. Richmond was 55% black in 1990, and Norfolk and Newport News had black populations of 39% and 33%, respectively.

In 1990, Virginia had 160,000 Hispanic residents, chiefly Mexicans and Salvadorans. (The estimated 1996 total was 168,000.) The 1990 census counted some 159,000 Asians and Pacific Islanders, including 35,605 Filipinos, 32,362 Koreans, 20,857 Chinese, 20,271 Vietnamese, 14,937 Asian Indians, and 12,385 Japanese. An estimated 372,000 Virginians—6% of all state residents—were of foreign birth in 1996, compared with 177,000 in 1980. The Native American population, including Eskimos and Aleuts, was 14,000 during the same year.

8LANGUAGES

English settlers encountered members of the Powhatan Indian confederacy, speakers of an Algonkian language, whose legacy includes such place-names as Roanoke and Rappahannock.

Although the expanding suburban area south of the District of Columbia has become dialectically heterogeneous, the rest of the state has retained its essentially Southern speech features. Many dialect markers occur statewide, but subregional contrasts distinguish the South Midland of the Appalachians from the Southern of the piedmont and Tidewater. General are *batter bread* (a soft corn cake), *batter cake* (pancake), *comfort* (tied and filled bedcover), and *polecat* (skunk). Widespread pronunciation

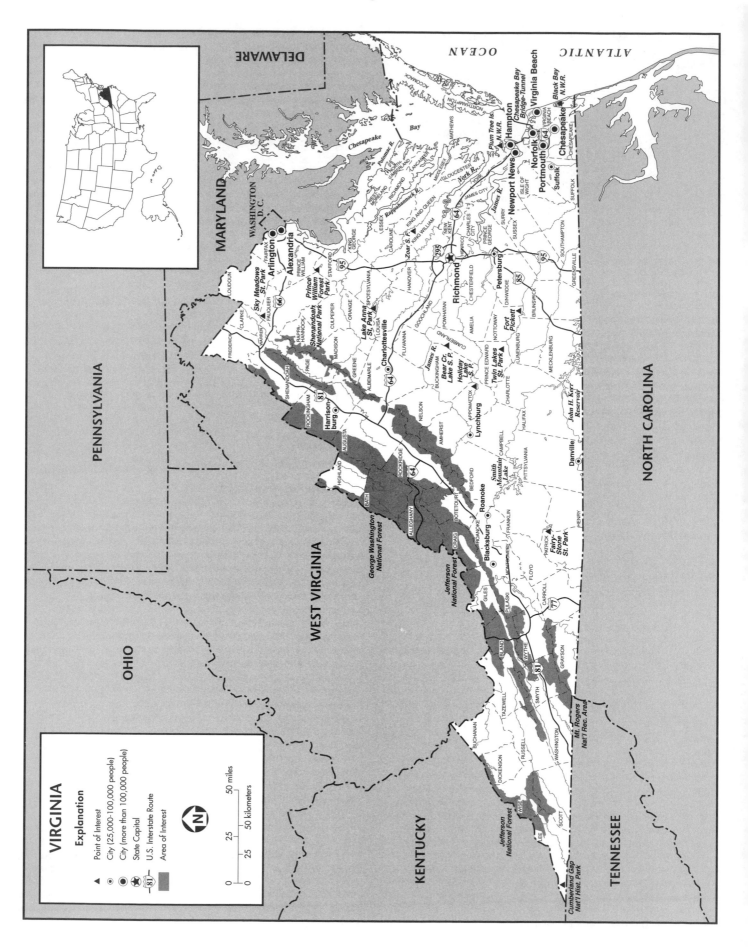

features include *greasy* with a /z/ sound; *yeast* and *east* as sound-alikes, *creek* rhyming with *peek*, and *can't* with *paint; coop* and *bulge* with the vowel of *book;* and *forest* with an /ah/ sound.

The Tidewater is set off by *creek* meaning a saltwater inlet, *fishing worm* for earthworm, and *fog* as /fahg/. Appalachian South Midland has *redworm* for earthworm, *fog* as /fawg/, *wash* as /wawsh/, *Mary* and *merry* as sound-alikes, and *poor* with the vowel of *book.* The Richmond area is noted also for having two variants of the long /i/ and /ow/ diphthongs as they occur before voiceless and voiced consonants, so that the vowel in the noun *house* is quite different from the vowel in the verb *house,* and the vowel in *advice* differs from that in *advise.* The Tidewater exhibits similar features.

In 1990, Virginia residents five years of age and over who spoke only English at home numbered 5,327,898, or 92.7% of the total. Other languages spoken at home, and the number of people who spoke them, included:

Spanish	152,663	Tagalog	21,018
French	40,353	Vietnamese	19,025
German	32,069	Chinese	18,037
Korean	25,736		

⁹RELIGIONS

The Anglican Church (later the Episcopal Church), whose members founded and populated Virginia Colony in the early days, was the established church during the colonial period. The first dissenters to arrive were Scotch-Irish Presbyterians in the late 17th century; they were followed by large numbers of German Lutherans, Welsh Baptists, and English Quakers, who settled in the Valley of Virginia in the early 18th century. The general

Virginia Counties, County Seats, and County Areas and Populations

COUNTY	COUNTY SEAT	LAND AREA (SQ MI)	POPULATION (1996 EST)	COUNTY	COUNTY SEAT	LAND AREA (SQ MI)	POPULATION (1996 EST)
Accomack	Accomac	476	32,065	King William	King William	278	12,333
Albemarle	Charlottesville	725	74,189	Lancaster	Lancaster	133	11,418
Allegheny	Covington	446	12,586	Lee	Jonesville	437	24,257
Amelia	Amelia	357	9,912	Loudoun	Leesburg	521	123,333
Amherst	Amherst	478	30,065	Louisa	Louisa	497	23,321
Appomattox	Appomattox	336	12,879	Lunenburg	Lunenburg	432	11,104
Arlington	Arlington	26	175,334	Madison	Madison	322	12,405
Augusta	Staunton	989	59,515	Mathews	Mathews	87	8,967
Bath	Warm Springs	537	4,959	Mecklenburg	Boydton	616	30,946
Bedford	Bedford	747	52,768	Middlesex	Saluda	134	9,396
Bland	Bland	359	6,934	Montgomery	Christiansburg	390	75,443
Botetourt	Fincastle	545	27,813	Nelson	Lovingston	475	13,529
Brunswick	Lawrenceville	563	16,458	New Kent	New Kent	213	12,047
Buchanan	Grundy	504	30,033	Northampton	Eastville	226	12,098
Buckingham	Buckingham	583	14,388	Northumberland	Heathsville	185	11,226
Campbell	Rustburg	505	48,946	Nottoway	Nottoway	317	15,230
Caroline	Bowling Green	536	21,319	Orange	Orange	342	24,512
Carroll	Hillsville	478	27,703	Page	Luray	313	22,891
Charles City	Charles City	181	6,887	Patrick	Stuart	481	18,075
Charlotte	Charlotte	476	12,218	Pittsylvania	Chatham	995	55,774
Chesterfield	Chesterfield	434	242,686	Powhatan	Powhatan	261	19,794
Clarke	Berryville	178	12,543	Prince Edward	Farmville	354	18,751
Craig	New Castle	330	4,839	Prince George	Prince George	266	28,401
Culpeper	Culpeper	382	31,981	Prince William	Manassas	3392	249,278
Cumberland	Cumberland	300	7,845	Pulaski	Pulaski	318	34,290
Dickenson	Clintwood	331	17,381	Rappahannock	Washington	267	7,206
Dinwiddie	Dinwiddie	507	22,961	Richmond	Warsaw	193	8,496
Essex	Tappahannock	263	9,373	Roanoke	Salem	251	81,585
Fairfax	Fairfax	393	902,492	Rockbridge	Lexington	603	19,006
Fauquier	Warrenton	651	51,765	Rockingham	Harrisonburg	865	62,432
Floyd	Floyd	381	12,832	Russell	Lebanon	479	29,134
Fluvanna	Palmyra	290	16,887	Scott	Gate City	536	22,949
Franklin	Rock Mount	683	43,574	Shenandoah	Woodstock	512	33,612
Frederick	Winchester	415	52,459	Smyth	Marion	452	33,076
Giles	Pearisburg	362	16,349	Southampton	Courtland	603	17,682
Gloucester	Gloucester	225	33,659	Spotsylvania	Spotsylvania	404	74,106
Goochland	Goochland	281	16,586	Stafford	Stafford	271	82,488
Grayson	Independence	446	16,420	Surry	Surry	281	6,406
Greene	Standardsville	157	12,972	Sussex	Sussex	496	10,088
Greensville	Emporia	300	10,954	Tazewell	Tazewell	522	47,070
Halifax	Halifax	816	37,581	Warren	Front Royal	219	29,879
Hanover	Hanover	468	76,781	Washington	Abingdon	578	48,498
Henrico	Richmond	238	232,810	Westmoreland	Montross	250	16,549
Henry	Martinsville	283	56,326	Wise	Wise	405	39,494
Highland	Monterey	416	2,543	Wythe	Wytheville	460	26,357
Isle of Wight	Isle of Wight	319	28,391	York	Yorktown	122	55,010
James City	Williamsburg	153	41,340	Independent Cities		1,605	2,332,619
King and Queen	King and Queen	317	6,390				
King George	King George	180	16,379	TOTALS		39,704	6,675,451

assembly's adoption in 1785 of the Virginia Statute for Religious Freedom, drafted by Thomas Jefferson, disestablished the Episcopal Church and made religious toleration the norm in Virginia. Although the Episcopal and Presbyterian churches retained the allegiance of the landed gentry during the 19th century, the Methodists and Baptists became the largest church groups in the state.

Protestant denominations combined had the greatest number of known adherents in 1990, when the leading groups were the Southern Baptist Convention, with 742,860 adherents; United Methodist Church, 490,789; Episcopal Church, 129,070; and Presbyterian Church in the US, 138,554. As of 1990, there were 384,285 Roman Catholics in Virginia, and the Jewish population was estimated at 66,564.

10 TRANSPORTATION

Virginia has one of the nation's most extensive highway systems, one of the leading ports—Hampton Roads—and two of the nation's busiest air terminals.

Virginia was a leader in early railroad development. Rail lines were completed between Richmond and Fredericksburg in 1836, from Portsmouth to Roanoke in 1837, and from Richmond to Washington, D.C., in 1872. Virginia's 1,290 mi (2,076 km) of track formed a strategic supply link for both the Confederate and Union armies during the Civil War. Railroads remained the primary system of transportation until the rise of the automobile in the 1920s. As of 1997, there were 13 rail companies operating in the state, three of them Class I railways with combined trackage of 3,188 rail mi (5,133 km). Principal (Class I) railroads are Conrail, CSX, and Norfolk Southern. These three, combined with nine local and one switching and terminal railroad carried over 170 million tons of freight by rail. In 1996, more rail-tons of coal terminated in Virginia than in any other state. Amtrak passenger trains served 21 communities, with total Virginia ridership of 897,225 in 1994/95, up 2.5% from 875,713 in 1993/94.

Virginia's road network, at first built mainly for hauling tobacco to market, had expanded across the Blue Ridge by 1782, to the Cumberland Gap by 1795, and into the Shenandoah Valley by means of the Valley Turnpike in 1840. As of 1995, Virginia had 69,142 mi (111,319 km) of public roads, 5,613.133 registered vehicles, and 4,628,886 licensed drivers. Major interstate highways are I-95 extending north–south from Washington, D.C., via Richmond to the North Carolina border (and, eventually, to Florida); I-81, connecting northern Virginia with the southwest; and I-64, linking the Hampton Roads area with West Virginia via Clifton Forge and Covington in the west. The 18-mi (29-km) Chesapeake Bay Bridge–Tunnel, completed in 1964, connects the Eastern Shore with the southeastern mainland. Popular scenic highways include the Blue Ridge Parkway, Colonial National Historical Parkway, and George Washington Memorial Parkway.

Virginia's District of Columbia suburbs are linked to the nation's capital by the Washington Metropolitan Area Transit Authority's bus and rail systems. Norfolk, Newport News–Hampton, and Richmond have extensive bus systems.

Virginia's Hampton Roads has one of the largest and strongest commercial port complexes in the world. Three state-owned general cargo marine terminals—Newport News Marine Terminal, Norfolk International Terminals, and Portsmouth Marine Terminal— share the harbor with more than 20 privately owned bulk terminals. The Hampton Roads harbor has the greatest volume of total tonnage on the US east coast and leads the world in coal exports, handling an average of 65– 70 million tons each year. Located on a naturally deep, ice-free harbor, 18 miles from the open sea, Virginia's ports have the largest land-side intermodal facilities on the US east coast. Each general cargo terminal in the port has on-site rail connections that offer single and double-stack train service from the docks. Virginia's mid-Atlantic location and transportation infrastructure offer users of the port access to two-thirds of the US population within 24 hours. In addition to the marine terminals, the Virginia Inland Port (VIP) terminal, just west of Washington, D.C., in Front Royal, Virginia, offers daily rail service to the marine terminals in Hampton Roads and allows direct access to the international trade routes of the 75 international shipping lines calling at the Ports. In addition to the movement of international export and import cargo, the VIP is a full-service domestic rail ramp for Norfolk Southern's domestic service.

Virginia's 405 aircraft facilities included 69 licensed public-use airports, 239 private airports, 96 heliports, and 1 public-use seaplane base. Each year, some 6 million passengers enplane at Dulles International Airport; over 7 million enplane at Washington National Airport, at Arlington, a major center for domestic flights.

11 HISTORY

Distinctively fluted stone points found at Flint Run in Front Royal and at the Williamson Site in Dinwiddie County testify to the presence in what is now the Commonwealth of Virginia of nomadic Paleo-Indians after 8000 BC. Climatic changes and the arrival of other Indian groups about 3500 BC produced the Archaic Culture, which lasted until about AD 500. These Indians apparently were great eaters of oysters, and shell accumulations along riverbanks mark their settlement sites. The Woodland Period (AD 500–1600) marked the Indians' development of the bow and arrow and sophisticated pottery. At the time of English contact, early in the 17th century, Tidewater Virginia was occupied principally by Algonkian-speakers, planters as well as hunters and fishers, who lived in pole-framed dwellings forming small, palisaded towns. The piedmont area was the home of the Manahoac, Monacan, and Tutelo, all of Siouan stock. Cherokee lived in Virginia's far southwestern triangle.

The first permanent English settlement in America was established at Jamestown on 13 May 1607 in the new land named Virginia in honor of Elizabeth I, the "Virgin Queen." The successful settlement was sponsored by the London Company (also known as the Virginia Company), a joint-stock venture chartered by King James I in 1606. The charter defined Virginia as all of the North American coast between 30° and 45°N and extending inland for 50 mi (80 km). A new royal charter in 1609 placed Virginia's northern and southern boundaries at points 200 mi (320 km) north and south of Point Comfort, at the mouth of the James River, and extended its territory westward to the Pacific; a third charter issued in 1612 pushed Virginia eastward to embrace the Bermuda Islands. Thus, Virginia at one time stretched from southern Maine to California and encompassed all or part of 42 of the present 50 states, as well as Bermuda and part of the Canadian province of Ontario.

Upon landing at Jamestown, the 100 or more male colonists elected from among 12 royally approved councillors a governor and captain general, Edward Maria Wingfield. Much internal strife, conflict with the Indians, and a "starving time" that reduced the settlers to eating their horses caused them to vote to leave the colony in 1610, but just as they were leaving, three supply ships arrived; with them came Thomas West, Baron De La Warr (Lord Delaware), who stayed to govern the Virginia Colony until 1611. Finally, however, it was the energy, resourcefulness, and military skill of Captain John Smith that saved the colony from both starvation and destruction by the Indians. He also charted the coast and wrote the first American book, *A True Relation,* which effectively publicized English colonization of the New World.

Smith's chief Algonkian adversary was Powhatan, emperor of a confederacy in eastern Virginia that bore his name. Although Smith was taken prisoner by Powhatan, he was able to work out a tenuous peace later cemented by the marriage in 1614 of the emperor's favorite daughter, Pocahontas, to John Rolfe, a Jamestown settler who founded the colonial tobacco industry.

Three events marked 1619 as a red-letter year in Virginia history. First, women were sent to the colony in large numbers. Any man marrying one of a shipment of 90 "young maids" had to pay 120 lb of tobacco for the cost of her transportation. The women were carefully screened for respectability, and none had to marry if she did not find a man to her liking. The second key event was the arrival in Jamestown of the first blacks, probably as indentured servants, a condition from which slavery in the colony evolved (the first legally recognized slaveholder, in the 1630s, was Anthony Johnson, himself black). The third and most celebrated event of 1619 was the convening in Jamestown of the first representative assembly in the New World, consisting of a council chosen by the London Company and a house of burgesses elected by the colonists. Thus, self-government through locally elected representatives became a reality in America and an important precedent for the English colonies.

King James I, for whom the colonial capital was named, was at first content with colonization under the London Company's direction. But in 1624, he charged the company with mismanagement and revoked its charter. Virginia remained a royal colony until 1776, although royal governors such as Sir Francis Wyatt and Sir George Yeardley continued to convoke the general assembly without the Crown's assent. A serious challenge to self-government came in 1629–35 with Governor John Harvey's "executive offenses"—including the knocking out of a councillor's teeth and the detaining of a petition of protest to the king—which sparked a rebellion led by Dr. John Pott. Harvey was bloodlessly deposed by the council—which, significantly, turned to the house of burgesses for confirmation of the action the council had taken.

Despite serious setbacks because of Indian massacres in 1622 and 1644, the colony's population expanded rapidly along the James, York, Rappahannock, and Potomac rivers, and along the Eastern Shore. In 1653, the general assembly attempted to collect taxes from the Eastern Shore, although that area had no legislative representation. At a mass meeting, Colonel Thomas Johnson urged resistance to taxation without representation. The resulting Northampton Declaration embodied this principle, which would provide the rallying cry for the American Revolution; the immediate result was the granting of representation to the Eastern Shore.

Virginia earned the designation Old Dominion through its loyalty to the Stuarts during England's Civil War, but the superior military and naval forces of Oliver Cromwell compelled submission to parliamentary commissioners in 1652. In the eight years that followed, the house of burgesses played an increasingly prominent role. Colonial governors, while at least nominally Puritan, usually conducted affairs with an easy tolerance that did not mar Virginia's general hospitality to refugee Cavaliers from the mother country.

With the restoration of the royal family in 1660, Sir William Berkeley, an ardent royalist who had served as governor before the colony's surrender to the Commonwealth, was returned to that office. In his first administration, his benign policies and appealing personality had earned him great popularity, but during his second term, his dictatorial and vindictive support of royal prerogatives made him the most hated man in the colony. When he seemed unable to defend the people against Indian incursions in 1676, they sought a general of their own. They found him in young Nathaniel Bacon, a charismatic planter of great daring and eloquence, whose leadership attracted many

small planters impatient by this time with the privileged oligarchy directing the colony. Bacon's war against the Indians became a populist-style revolt against the governor, who fled to the Eastern Shore, and reform legislation was pushed by the burgesses. Berkeley regained control of the capital briefly, only to be defeated by Bacon's forces; but Jamestown was burned by the retreating Bacon, who died of fever shortly afterward. Berkeley's subsequent return to power was marked by so many hangings of offenders that the governor was summoned to the court of Charles II to answer for his actions. Bacon's Rebellion was cited as a precedent when the colonies waged war against George III a century later.

The 17th century closed on a note of material and cultural progress with the gubernatorial administration of Francis Nicholson. The College of William and Mary, the second institution of higher learning in America, was chartered in 1693, and Middle Plantation (renamed Williamsburg in 1722), the site of the college, became the seat of government when the capital was moved from Jamestown in 1699. The new capital remained small, although it was crowded when the legislature was in session. A new era of cultural and economic progress dawned with the administration of Alexander Spotswood (1710–22), sometimes considered the greatest of Virginia's colonial governors. He discouraged the colony's excessively heavy dependence on a single crop, tobacco; promoted industry, especially ironwork; took a humane interest in blacks and Indians' strengthened fortification; ended the depredations of the notorious pirate Edward Teach, better known as Blackbeard; and, by leading his "Knights of the Golden Horseshoe" across the Blue Ridge, dramatized the opening of the transmontane region.

In the decades that followed, eastern Virginians moving into the Valley of Virginia were joined by Scotch-Irish and Germans moving southward from Maryland and Pennsylvania. Virginians caught up in western settlement lost much of their awe of the mother country during the French and Indian War (1756–63). A young Virginia militiaman, Colonel George Washington, gave wise but unheeded advice to Britain's Major General Edward Braddock before the Battle of Monongahela, and afterward emerged as the hero of that action.

Virginia, acting independently and with other colonies, repeatedly challenged agents of the Crown. In 1765, the House of Burgesses, swept by the eloquence of Patrick Henry, adopted five resolutions opposing the Stamp Act, through which the English Parliament had sought to tax the colonists for their own defense. In 1768, Virginia joined Massachusetts in issuing an appeal to all the colonies for concerted action. The following year, Virginia initiated a boycott of British goods in answer to the taxation provisions of the hated Townshend Acts. In 1773, the Old Dominion became the first colony to establish an intercolonial Committee of Correspondence. And it joined the other colonies at the First Continental Congress, which met in Philadelphia in 1774 and elected Virginia's Peyton Randolph president.

Virginia was the first colony to instruct its delegates to move for independence at the Continental Congress of 1776. The congressional resolution was introduced by one native son, Richard Henry Lee, and the Declaration of Independence was written by another, Thomas Jefferson. In the same year, Virginians proclaimed their government a commonwealth and adopted a constitution and declaration of rights, prepared by George Mason. The declaration became the basis for the Bill of Rights in the US Constitution. Virginians were equally active in the Revolutionary War. George Washington was commander in chief of the Continental Army, and other outstanding Virginia officers were George Rogers Clark, Hugh Mercer, Henry "Light Horse Harry" Lee, William Campbell, Isaac Shelby, and an adopted son, Daniel Morgan. In addition, the greatest American naval hero was a Scottish-born Virginian, John Paul Jones.

Virginia itself was a major battlefield, and it was on Virginia soil, at Yorktown on 19 October 1781, that British General Charles Cornwallis surrendered to Washington, effectively ending the war.

During the early federal period, Virginia's leadership was as notable as it had been during the American Revolution. James Madison is honored as the "father of the Constitution," and Washington, who was president of the constitutional convention, became the first US president in 1789. Indeed, Virginians occupied the presidency for all but 4 of the nation's first 28 years. Far more influential than most presidents was another Virginian, John Marshall, who served as US chief justice for 34 years, beginning in 1801.

During the first half of the 19th century, Virginians became increasingly concerned with the problem of slavery. From the early 1700s, the general assembly had repeatedly prohibited the importation of slaves, only to be overruled by the Crown, protecting the interests of British slave traders. In 1778, no longer subject to royal veto, the legislature provided that any slave brought into the state would automatically be freed upon arrival. (There was no immediate legal termination of the bondage of those already enslaved, or of their offspring.) The number of free blacks grew tenfold by 1810, and though some became self-supporting farmers and artisans, many could find no employment. Fearing that unhappy free blacks might incite those who were still slaves to rebellion, the general assembly in 1806 decreed that each slave emancipated in due course must then leave Virginia within a year or after reaching the age of 21. Nat Turner's slave revolt—which took the lives of at least 55 white men, women, and children in Southampton County in 1831—increased white fears of black emancipation. Nevertheless, legislation to end slavery in Virginia failed adoption by only seven votes the following year.

The slavery controversy did not consume all Virginians' energies in the first half of the 19th century, an era that saw the state become a leading center of scientific, artistic, and educational advancement. But this era ended with the coming of the Civil War, a conflict about which many Virginians had grave misgivings. Governor John Letcher was a Union man, and most of the state's top political leaders hoped to retain the federal tie. Even after the formation at Montgomery, Alabama, of the Confederate States of America, Virginia initiated a national peace convention in Washington, D.C., headed by a native son and former US president, John Tyler. A statewide convention, assembled in Richmond in April 1861, adopted an ordinance of secession only after President Abraham Lincoln sought to send troops across Virginia to punish the states that had already seceded and called upon the commonwealth to furnish soldiers for that task. Virginia adopted secession with some regret and apprehension but with no agonizing over constitutional principles, for in ratifying the Constitution the state had reserved the right to secede. Shortly afterward, Richmond, the capital of Virginia since 1780, became the capital of the Confederacy. It was also the home of the Tredegar Ironworks, the South's most important manufacturer of heavy weaponry.

Robert E. Lee, offered field command of the Union armies, instead resigned his US commission in order to serve his native state as commander of the Army of Northern Virginia and eventually as chief of the Confederate armies. Other outstanding Virginian generals included Thomas Jonathan "Stonewall" Jackson, J. E. B. "Jeb" Stuart, Joseph E. Johnston, and A. P. Hill. Besides furnishing a greater number of outstanding Confederate generals than any other state, the Old Dominion supplied some of the Union's military leaders, George H. Thomas, the "Rock of Chickamauga," among them. More than 30 Virginians held the rank of brigadier general or major general in the federal forces.

Virginia became the principal battlefield of the Civil War, the scene of brilliant victories won by General Lee's army at Bull Run (about 30 mi—48 km—southwest of Washington, D.C.), Fredericksburg, and Chancellorsville (Spotsylvania County). But the overwhelming numbers and industrial and naval might of the Union compelled Lee's surrender at Appomattox on 9 April 1865. Virginia waters were the scene of one of the most celebrated naval engagements in world history, the first battle of the ironclads, when the USS *Monitor* and CSS *Virginia (Merrimac),* rebuilt in the Portsmouth Shipyard, met at Hampton Roads. The war cost Virginia one-third of its territory when West Virginia was admitted to the Union as a separate state on 20 June 1863. Richmond was left in ruins, and agriculture and industry throughout the commonwealth were destroyed. Union General Philip H. Sheridan's systematic campaign of demolition in the Shenandoah Valley almost made good his boast that a crow flying over the valley would have to carry its own rations.

In 1867, Virginia was placed under US military rule. A constitutional convention held in Richmond under the leadership of carpetbaggers and scalawags drafted a constitution that disqualified the overwhelming majority of white Virginians from holding office and deprived about 95% of them of the right to vote. In this crisis, a compromise was negotiated under which white Virginians would accept Negro suffrage if they themselves were permitted to vote and hold office. The amended constitution, providing for universal manhood suffrage, was adopted in 1869, and Virginia was readmitted to the Union on 26 January 1870.

Although the bankrupt state was saddled with a debt of more than $45 million, the Conservative Democrats undertook repayment of the entire debt, including approximately one-third estimated to be West Virginia's share. Other Democrats, who came to be known as Readjusters, argued that the commonwealth could not provide education and other essential services to its citizens unless it disclaimed one-third of the debt and reached a compromise with creditors concerning the remainder. William Mahone, a railroad president and former Confederate major general, engineered victory for the Readjusters in 1880 with the aid of the Republicans. His election to the US Senate that year represented another success for the Readjuster-Republican coalition, which was attentive to the needs of both blacks and underprivileged whites.

Throughout the 1880s and 1890s, life in public places in Virginia continued in an unsegregated fashion that sometimes amazed visitors from northern cities. As the 19th century neared an end, however, Virginia moved toward legal separation of the races. In 1900, the general assembly by a one-vote majority enacted segregation on railroad cars. The rule became applicable the following year to streetcars and steamboats. In 1902, the Virginia constitutional convention enacted a literacy test and poll tax that effectively reduced the black vote to negligible size.

Two decades later, just when the Old Dominion seemed permanently set in the grooves of conservatism, two liberals, each with impeccable old-line backgrounds, found themselves battling for the governorship in a Democratic primary campaign that changed the course of Virginia's political history. Harry F. Byrd defeated G. Walter Mapp in the election of 1925 and immediately after taking office launched the state on an era of reform. In a whirlwind 60 days, the general assembly revised the tax system, revised balloting procedures, and adopted measures to lure industry to Virginia. The Anti-Lynch Act of 1927 made anyone present at the scene of a lynching who did not intervene guilty of murder; there has not been a lynching in Virginia since its passage. Byrd also reorganized the state government, consolidating nearly 100 agencies into 14 departments. Later, as US senator, Byrd became so renowned as a conservative that many people forgot his earlier career as a fighting liberal.

Following the depression of the 1930s, Virginia became one of the most prosperous states of the Southeast. It profited partly from national defense contracts and military and naval expansion, but also from increased manufacturing and from what became one of the nation's leading tourist industries. Few states made so great a contribution as Virginia to the US effort in World War II. More than 300,000 Virginians served in the armed forces; 9,000 lost their lives, and 10 were awarded the Medal of Honor. Virginians were proud of the fact that General George C. Marshall was a Virginia resident and a graduate of Virginia Military Institute, and even delighted in the knowledge that both General Dwight D. Eisenhower, commander in the European theater, and General Douglas MacArthur, commander in the Pacific, were sons of Virginia mothers.

The postwar period brought many changes in the commonwealth's public life. During the first administration of Governor Mills E. Godwin, Jr. (1966–70), the state abandoned its strict pay-as-you-go fiscal policy, secured an $81-million bond issue, and enacted a sales tax. Much of the increased revenue benefited the public school system; funding for the four-year colleges was greatly expanded, and a system of low-tuition community colleges was instituted.

In 1970, A. Linwood Holton, Jr., became the first Republican governor of Virginia since 1874. Pledging to "make today's Virginia a model in race relations," Holton increased black representation on state boards and in the higher echelons of government. He reversed the policies of his immediate predecessors, who had generally met the US Supreme Court's desegregation ruling in 1954 with a program of massive resistance, eschewing violence but adopting every legal expedient to frustrate integration. By the mid-1970s, public school integration in Virginia had been achieved to a degree not yet accomplished in many northern states.

The northeast and Virginia Beach/Norfolk area of Virginia boomed in the early 1980s, spurred by an expansion of federal jobs and a national military build-up. The population in Virginia Beach grew by 50% between 1980 and 1990, and the population % in that decade. Non-agricultural employment rose by 29 %between 1980 and 1988. The economies of rural parts of the state to the west and south, however, remained stagnant.

In the late1980s, Virginia was hit by a recession. Douglas Wilder, the nation's first black governor and a moderate Democrat, responded to a significant shortfall in state revenues by refusing to raise taxes and by insisting on maintaining a $200 million reserve fund. Instead, Wilder reduced the budgets and staff of state services and of the state's college and university system. Wilder's cuts created particular hardship for the less affluent counties that relied heavily on state aid for their funding of schools, libraries, and road maintenance. Wilder, limited by law to one term in office, was succeeded in 1993 by conservative Republican Richard Allen. In 1994, nationwide attention was focused on the US Senate race in which the Democratic incumbent, Charles S. Robb defeated Republican challenger Oliver North, known for his role in the Iran-contra affair of the 1980s.

In the mid-1990s Virginia's economy was strong, thanks to its diversified base of agriculture, manufacturing, and service industries (the latter dominated by federal government employment). Pollution from industry and agricultural chemicals remained a significant concern, and the state was investing in cleanup efforts in the Chesapeake Bay.

In 1994, the Walt Disney Company abandoned its much-publicized plan to build a history theme park, "Disney's America," in Virginia, following strong opposition from residents, environmentalists, and historians.

Heavy flooding caused millions of dollars in property damage in 1995.

[12]STATE GOVERNMENT

Since 1776, Virginia has had six constitutions, all of which have expanded the power of the executive branch. The last constitution, framed in 1970 and effective 1 July 1971, governs the state today. As of the end of 1993, this document had been amended 23 times.

The general assembly consists of a 40-member senate, elected to four-year terms, and a 100-member house of delegates, serving for two years. Senators and delegates must be at least 21 years of age and residents of their district. The assembly convenes annually on the 2d Wednesday in January for 60-day sessions in even-numbered years and 30-day sessions in odd-numbered years, with an option to extend the annual session for a maximum of 30 days or declare a special session by two-thirds vote of both houses. In 1995, legislative salaries were $18,000 for state senators and $17,640 for delegates.

The governor, lieutenant governor, and attorney general, all serving four-year terms, are the only officials elected statewide; the governor, who must be at least 30 years of age and a state resident for five years, may not serve two successive terms. In 1996, the governor's salary was $80,724. Most state officials—including the secretaries of administration and finance, commerce and resources, education, human resources, public safety, and transportation—are appointed by the governor but must be confirmed by both houses of the legislature. Bills become law when signed by the governor or left unsigned for 7 days while the legislature is in session; a bill dies if left unsigned for 30 days after the legislature has adjourned. A two-thirds majority in each house is needed to override a gubernatorial veto. The constitution may be amended by constitutional convention or by a two thirds vote of two successive sessions of the general assembly; ratification by the electorate is required.

A qualified voter must be a US citizen, be at least 18 years old, and have registered in the precinct of residence at least 31 days before the election. Elections for state offices are held in odd-numbered years.

[13]POLITICAL PARTIES

Virginia has exercised a unique role in US politics as the birthplace not only of representative government but also of one of America's two major parties. The modern Democratic Party traces its origins to the original Republican Party (usually referred to as the Democratic-Republican Party, or the Jeffersonian Democrats), led by two native sons of Virginia, Thomas Jefferson and James Madison. Virginians have also been remarkably influential in the political life of other states: a survey published in 1949 showed that 319 Virginia natives had represented 31 other states in the US Senate and House of Representatives.

From the end of Reconstruction through the 1960s, conservative Democrats dominated state politics, with few exceptions. Harry F. Byrd was the state's Democratic political leader for 40 years, first as a reform governor (1926–30) and then as a conservative senator (1933–95). During the 1970s, Virginians, still staunchly conservative, turned increasingly to the Republican Party, whose presidential nominees carried the state in every election from 1952 through 1984 except for 1964. Linwood Holton, the first Republican governor since Reconstruction, was elected in 1969. His Republican successor, Mills E. Godwin, Jr., the first governor since the Civil War to serve more than one term, had earlier won election as a Democrat. The election in 1977 of another Republican, John N. Dalton, finally proved that Virginia had become a two-party state. In 1981, however, the governorship was won by Democrat Charles S. Robb, who appointed a record number of blacks and women to state offices. Robb, prohibited by law from seeking a consecutive second term, was succeeded by Democrat Gerald L. Baliles in 1985, when Virginians also elected L. Douglas Wilder as lieutenant governor and Mary Sue Terry as attorney general; Wilder became the highest-ranking black state official in the US, and Terry was the first woman to win a statewide office in Virginia. Wilder was elected governor in 1989, followed by Republican George Allen in 1993. Robb subsequently won election to the US Senate in 1988 and re-election in 1994, and John Warner, a Republican, was elected to a fourth term in the Senate in 1996. In the November 1994 elections, Robb's Republican opponent was Oliver North, a former Marine and Reagan White House aide who gained famed for his role in the Iran-contra affair. In 1996, Bob Dole won 47% of the presidential vote, Bill Clinton received 45%, and Ross Perot gained 7%. After the 1996 elections, Virginia's delegation to the US House of Representatives consisted of six Democrats and five Republicans. Control of the state senate was split between the two major parties, each of whom contributed half of the body's 40 members. Democrats controlled the state house, 52–46. As of 1993, there were 155 blacks holding public office. In 1995, 16 women served in the state legislature and one woman held an elective executive office.

14LOCAL GOVERNMENT

As of 1992, Virginia had 95 counties and 230 municipal governments. In all, there were 455 local government units, as well as 129 special districts.

During the colonial period, most Virginians lived on plantations and were reluctant to form towns. In 1705, the general assembly approved the formation of 16 "free boroughs." Although only Jamestown, Williamsburg, and Norfolk chose at that time to avail themselves of the option and become independent municipalities, their decision laid the foundation for the independence of Virginia's present-day cities from county government. In 1842, Richmond became the commonwealth's first charter city. Today, 41 cities elect their own officials, levy their own taxes, and arc unencumbered by any county obligations. The 189 incorporated towns remain part of the counties.

In general, counties are governed by elected boards of supervisors, with a county administrator or executive handling day-to-day affairs; other typical county officials are the clerk of the circuit court (chief administrator of the court), county treasurer,

commissioner of the revenue, commonwealth's attorney, and sheriff. Incorporated towns have elected mayors and councils.

15STATE SERVICES

Under the jurisdiction of the secretary of education are the Department of Education, which administers the public school system, and the State Council of Higher Education, which coordinates the programs of the state-controlled colleges and universities. The secretary of transportation oversees the Department of Highways and Transportation, Department of Transportation Safety, Department of Aviation, Virginia Port Authority, Department of Military Affairs (National Guard), Division of Motor Vehicles, and State Office of Emergency Services.

Within the purview of the secretary of human resources are the Department of Health, Department of Mental Health and Mental Retardation, Department of Health Regulatory Boards, Department of Social Services, and Department of Rehabilitative Services, as well as special offices dealing with problems that affect women, children, the elderly, and the disabled. The departments of State Police, Corrections, Criminal Justice Services, Fire Programs, and Alcoholic Beverage Control are under the aegis of the secretary of public safety.

The secretary of commerce and resources oversees the departments of Housing and Community Development, Labor and Industry, Commerce, Agriculture and Consumer Services, and Conservation and Economic Development, as well as a profusion of boards, councils, offices, divisions, and commissions. The secretary of administration and finance exercises jurisdiction over budgeting, telecommunications, accounting, computer services, taxation, the state treasury, records, and personnel, as well as over the State Board of Elections. Regulatory functions are concentrated in the quasi-independent State Corporation Commission, consisting of three commissioners elected by the legislature to staggered six-year terms. The commission regulates all public utilities; licenses banks, savings and loan associations, credit unions, and small loan companies; enforces motor carrier and certain aviation laws and sets railroad rates; supervises the activities of insurance companies; and enforces laws governing securities and retail franchising.

Virginia Presidential Vote by Political Parties, 1948–96

YEAR	ELECTORAL VOTE	VIRGINIA WINNER	DEMOCRAT	REPUBLICAN	STATES' RIGHTS DEMOCRAT	PROGRESSIVE	SOCIALIST	SOCIALIST LABOR
1948	11	*Truman (D)	200,786	172,070	43,393	2,047	726	234
1952	12	*Eisenhower (R)	268,677	349,037	—	—	504	1,160
					CONSTITUTION			
1956	12	*Eisenhower (R)	267,760	386,459	42,964	—	444	351
					VA. CONSERVATIVE			
1960	12	Nixon (R)	362,327	404,521	4,204	—	—	397
1964	12	*Johnson (D)	558,038	481,334`	—	—	—	2,895
					AMERICAN IND.		PEACE & FREEDOM	
1968	12	*Nixon (R)	442,387	590,319	320,272	—	1,680	4,671
					AMERICAN			
1972	12	*Nixon (R)	438,887	988,493	19,721	—	—	9,918
						LIBERTARIAN	US LABOR	SOC. WORKERS
1976	12	Ford (R)	813,896	836,554	16,686	4,648	7,508	17,802
							Citizens	
1980	12	*Reagan (R)	752,174	989,609	—	12,821	**14,024	1,9861
1984	12	*Reagan (R)	796,250	1,337,078	—	—	—	—
					NEW ALLIANCE			
1988	12	*Bush (R)	859,799	1,309,162	14,312	8,336	—	—
							IND. (PEROT)	IND. (LAROUCHE)
1992	13	Bush (R)	1,038,650	1,150,517	3,192	5,730	348,639	11,937
1996	13	Dole (R)	1,091,060	1,138,350	—	9,174	159,861	—

* Won US presidential election.
**Candidates of the nationwide Citizens and Socialist Workers parties were listed as independents on the Virginia ballot; another independent, John Anderson, won 95,418 votes.

[16]JUDICIAL SYSTEM

The highest judicial body in the commonwealth is the supreme court, consisting of a chief justice and six other justices elected to 12-year terms by the General Assembly. The court of appeals has ten judges serving 8-year terms. The state is divided into 31 judicial circuits/districts. Each city and county has a circuit court, a general district court, and a juvenile and domestic relations district court. Circuit court judges are elected by the legislature for eight-year terms. General district courts hear all misdemeanors, including civil cases involving $1,000 or less, and have concurrent jurisdiction with the circuit courts in claims involving $1,000 to $15,000. General district courts also hold preliminary hearings concerning felony cases. Each of the 31 judicial districts has a juvenile and a domestic relations court, with judges elected by the general assembly to six-year terms. Each city or county has at least one local magistrate. In 1996, an estimated 16,350 attorneys practiced in the state.

Virginia's state and federal prisons had 28,827 inmates in 1996, or 421 per 100,000 in population. Between 1990 and 1995, the inmate population rose by almost 55%. According to the FBI Crime Index, the state's crime rates per 100,000 population, below the national average in every category, were as follows in 1995: murder and nonnegligent manslaughter, 7.6; forcible rape, 27.2; robbery, 131.7; aggravated assault, 194.9; burglary, 595.2; larceny-theft, 2,740; and motor vehicle theft, 292.6. A capital punishment statute providing for death by electrocution or lethal injection is in effect; two prisoners were executed in the early 1980s, the first executions since 1962. During 1996, Virginia executed 5 prisoners using lethal injection. The last execution by electrocution was in 1994.

[17]ARMED FORCES

In 1996, there were 89,010 active duty military personnel stationed in Virginia. The Hampton Roads area, one of the nation's major concentrations of military facilities, includes Langley Air Force Base in Hampton, the Norfolk naval air station and shipyard, the naval air station at Virginia Beach, the Marine Corps air facility and command and staff college at Quantico, and Forts Eustis, Belvoir, and Lee. Norfolk is the home base of the Atlantic Fleet, and several major army and air commands are in Virginia. Virginia's major defense establishments also include an army base at Arlington. In 1996, Virginia ranked 2d among the 50 states in value of federal defense contracts, receiving awards worth $9.6 billion.

As of 1 July 1996, 698,000 veterans of US military service lived in Virginia. Of these, fewer than 500 saw service during World War I, 159,000 in World War II, 119,00 during the Korean conflict, 259,000 during the Vietnam era, and 45,000 in the Persian Gulf War. Veterans' benefits allocated to Virginia totaled $11 billion in 1996.

Reserve and National Guard units comprised some 46,760 personnel in 1996: 27,411 in the Army, 15,259 in the Navy and Marine Corps, and 4,090 in the Air Force. In 1993, the Virginia State Police employed 1,647 full-time sworn officers, or 3 per 10,000 residents.

[18]MIGRATION

Virginia's earliest European immigrants were English—only a few hundred at first, but 4,000 between 1619 and 1624, of whom fewer than 1,200 survived epidemics and Indian attacks. Despite such setbacks, Virginia's population increased, mostly by means of immigration, from about 5,000 in 1634 to more than 15,000 in 1642, including 300 blacks. Within 30 years, the population had risen to more than 40,000, including 2,000 blacks. In the late 17th and early 18th centuries, immigrants came not only from England but also from Scotland, Wales, Ireland, Germany, France, the Netherlands, and Poland. In 1701, about 500 French Huguenots fled Catholic France to settle near the present site of Richmond, and beginning in 1714, many Germans and Scotch-Irish moved from Pennsylvania into the Valley of Virginia.

By the early 19th century, Virginians were moving westward into Kentucky, Ohio, and other states; the 1850 census showed that 388,000 former Virginians (not including the many thousands of slaves sold to other states) were living elsewhere. Some of those who left—Henry Clay, Sam Houston, Stephen Austin—were among the most able men of their time. The Civil War era saw the movement of thousands of blacks to northern states, a trend that accelerated after Reconstruction and again after World War I. Since 1900, the dominant migratory trend has been intra-state, from farm to city. Urbanization has been most noticeable since World War II in the Richmond and Hampton Roads areas. At the same time, the movement of middle-income Virginians to the suburbs and increasing concentrations of blacks in the central cities have been evident in Virginia as in other states. During the 1980s, the urban population grew from 66% to 69.4% of the total population.

Between 1940 and 1970, Virginia enjoyed a net gain from migration of 325,000. In the 1970s, the net gain was 239,000, and during 1985–90, 377,000 (4th highest among the states for that period). Between 1990 and 1996, Virginia had net gains of 61,397 in domestic migration and 93,847 in international migration. In 1996, 372,000, or about 6%, of the state's population was foreign-born. In the same year, 21,375 foreign immigrants arrived in Virginia, the 8th highest total of any state. As of 1994, the number of undocumented immigrants was estimated at between 37 and 63. In 1990, 54.2% of state residents had been born in Virginia, down from 59.9% in 1980. Just under one-half of Virginians age five and older in 1990 lived in the same house as in 1985. Some 31% of residents who lived in a different house in 1985 did so in another state (mostly Maryland, New York, or Pennsylvania).

[19]INTERGOVERNMENTAL COOPERATION

Regional bodies in which Virginia participates include the Atlantic States Marine Fisheries Commission, Ohio River Valley Water Sanitation Commission, Southern Growth Policies Board, Southern Interstate Energy Board, and Washington Metropolitan Area Transit Authority. In 1996, Virginia received federal aid exceeding $3.4 billion.

[20]ECONOMY

Early settlements in Virginia depended on subsistence farming of native crops such as corn and potatoes. Tobacco, the leading export crop during the colonial era, was joined by cotton during the early statehood period. Although cotton was never "king" in Virginia, as it was in many other southern states, the sale of slaves to Deep South plantations was an important source of income for Virginians, especially during the 1830s, when some 118,000 slaves were exported for profit. Eventually, a diversified agriculture developed in the piedmont and the Shenandoah Valley. Manufacturing became significant during the 19th century, with a proliferation of cotton mills, tobacco-processing plants, ironworks, paper mills, and shipyards.

Services and trade and government are important economic sectors today. Because of Virginia's extensive military installations and the large number of Virginia residents working for the federal government in the Washington, D.C., metropolitan area, the federal government plays a larger role in the Virginia economy than in any other state except Hawaii. In 1992, federal civilian employment reached 178,000, and military personnel stationed in Virginia totaled 170,000. The industries that experienced the most growth in the 1980s and early 1990s were printing, transportation equipment, and electronic and other electrical equipment. Virginia has a high concentration of high-technology industry, with 158,000 people employed in 3,600 companies. The two largest high-tech fields are computer and data processing services and electronic equipment. Virginia's per capita personal income in 1996 was $24,925, 14th in the US. During 1996, there were 35,955 bankruptcy filings, up 27% from 1995.

²¹INCOME

Virginia's per capita personal income in 1996 averaged $24,925, 14th among the 50 states and highest in the Southeast region. Total personal disposable income grew to $143.1 billion in 1996, up from $137 billion in 1995.

Median household income was $36,222 in 1995. In 1995, 10.2% of all state residents were below the federal poverty level.

²²LABOR

In 1996, Virginia's civilian labor force averaged 3,389,000 persons. At the end of 1996, nonagricultural employment distribution in Virginia was as follows: mining, 10,100; construction, 173,900; manufacturing, 396,500; transportation and utilities, 164,900; wholesale and retail trade, 746,600; finance, insurance, and real estate, 162,900; services, 918,900; and government, 605,700. In 1992, Virginia's civilian labor force averaged 3,363,000 persons, of whom 51.4% were male and 48.6% female.

Virginia had an unemployment rate of 4.5% in February 1997, below the national average of 5.9%. A right-to-work law is in effect. Although the state has no equal-employment statute, an equal-pay law does prohibit employers from wage discrimination on the basis of sex, and the Virginia Employment Contracting Act established as state policy the elimination of racial, religious, ethnic, and sexual bias in the employment practices of government agencies and contractors. The labor movement has grown slowly, partly because of past practices of racial segregation that prevented workers from acting in concert. Union membership among workers totaled 201,000 in 1996, or only 6.8% of all employment. In December 1996, weekly earnings of production workers on manufacturing payrolls averaged $538.59.

²³AGRICULTURE

Virginia ranked 30th among the 50 states in 1991 with farm marketings of more than $2.2 billion. The commonwealth is an important producer of tobacco, soybeans, peanuts, cotton, tomatoes, potatoes, and peaches. There were an estimated 47,000 farms in 1995.

The Tidewater is an important farming region, as it has been since the early 17th century. Crops grown include corn, wheat, tobacco, cotton, peanuts and truck crops. Truck crops and soybeans are cultivated on the Eastern Shore. The piedmont is known for its apples and other fruits, while the Shenandoah Valley is one of the nation's main apple growing regions. In 1995, Virginia ranked 5th among states in peanuts, 6th in tobacco, and 6th in apples. The following table shows data for leading crops in 1995:

	ACRES(1,000s)	PRODUCTION	VALUE
Tobacco	44,170	81,269,000 lb	$ 147,051,000
Hay	1,1250,000	2,571,000,000 tons	221,388,000
Soybeans	490,000	11,280,000 bushels	75,576,000
Corn for grain	430,000	30,525,000 bushels	96,154,000
Peanuts	90,000	206,925,000 lb	62,078,000
Wheat	300,000	17,600,000 bushels	64,240,000
Apples	*22,842	400,000,000 lb	38,752,000
Tomatoes	3,800	1,406,000 hundredweight	43,586,000
Barley	100,000	6,720,000 bushels	11,424,000
Potatoes (1990)	9,000	2,040,000 hundredweight	22,032,000
Peaches (1992)	2,344	26,000,000 lb	5,570,000
Sweet potatoes	500	85,000 hundredweight	901,000
Cotton	107,000	137,000(480lb bales)	51,905,000

²⁴ANIMAL HUSBANDRY

In 1997, Virginia farms and ranches had 1.83 million cattle and calves, valued at $805.2 million. During 1996, the state had around 390,000 hogs and pigs, valued at nearly $37 million. The state produced 6.4 million lb of sheep and lambs in 1995, and 358,000 lb of shorn wool.

Dairy farmers produced 1.95 billion lb of milk from 129,000 milk cows in 1995. That same year, poultry farmers produced 916 million eggs, worth around $68.3 million; 441.8 million lb of turkey, worth almost $199 million; nearly 1.2 billion lb of broilers, valued at $401 million; and 18.4 million lb of chicken sold for nearly $1.9 million in 1995.

²⁵FISHING

The relative importance of Chesapeake Bay and Atlantic fisheries to Virginia's economy has lessened considerably in recent decades, although the state continues to place high in national rankings. In 1995, Virginia's commercial fish landings totaled 777.6 million lb (3d in the US), worth $113.7 million (9th). Landings at the Hampton Roads port in 1995 totaled 12.6 million lb, valued at $26.6 million. The bulk of the catch consists of shellfish such as crabs, scallops, and clams, and finfish such as flounder and menhaden. The blue crab catch exceeded 3 million tons in 1995, or 15% of the US total. Both saltwater and freshwater fish are avidly sought by sport fishermen. A threat to Virginia fisheries has been the chemical and oil pollution of the Chesapeake Bay and its tributaries. In 1996, the state issued 634,115 fishing licenses.

²⁶FORESTRY

As of 1992, Virginia had 15,858,000 acres (6,418,000 hectares) of forestland, representing more than 62% of the state's land area and 2.1% of all US forests. Virtually every county has some commercial forestland and supports a wood products industry.

In 1993, 774.2 million cu ft of lumber were produced. Shipments of lumber and wood products were valued at $2.9 billion in 1995.

Pine volume increased 6% during 1985–91. Reforestation programs initiated by the Division of Forestry in 1971 have paid landowners to plant pine seedlings, and state-funded tree nurseries produce 60–70 million seedlings annually. In 1993, the Division of Forestry was responsible for the reforesting of 87,000 acres (35,200 hectares). The division's tree seed orchards have developed improved strains of loblolly, shortleaf, white, and Virginia pine for planting in cutover timberland.

For recreational purposes, there were over 2 million acres (800,000 hectares) of forested public lands in 1992, including Shenandoah National Park, Washington and Jefferson National Forests, 24 state parks, and 8 state forests.

²⁷MINING

Virginia is one of the nation's most diverse producers of industrial minerals. In 1995, the state ranked 24th nationally in total nonfuel mineral production value. The value of nonfuel mineral production in Virginia in 1995 was about $517 million, a rise from $465 million in 1993 and $502 million in 1994. In 1995, the combined output of crushed stone, portland cement, and lime accounted for 84% of the total value. Crushed stone was the leading mineral commodity produced in Virginia, accounting for about 66% of the state's value of nonfuel mineral production. Virginia ranked 2d in the nation in production of crude vermiculite and was also second in feldspar, 4th in iron oxide pigments, 7th in talc, 8th in fuller's earth, and 9th in lime.

²⁸ENERGY AND POWER

Virginia's installed electric utility net generating capacity was approximately 17,600 kW in 1996. Production of electricity totaled 56.6 billion kWh, almost all of it provided by private utilities. Electric power is supplied to the eastern, northeastern, and central parts of the state chiefly by Virginia Power; to the central and southwestern regions by American Electric Power; to the far southwest by Old Dominion Power; to the northwest by Potomac Edison; and to the Eastern Shore by Delmarva Power and Light. Sales of electric power in 1996 amounted to 87.5 billion kWh: 40% residential, 21% industrial, 28% commercial, and 11% other.

Virginia has one major oil refinery at Yorktown that uses imported petroleum. The state is supplied with natural gas by three major interstate pipeline companies. Liquefied natural gas plants operate in Chesapeake, Roanoke, and Lynchburg, and a synthetic gas plant is in service at Chesapeake. There is one underground natural gas storage facility in Scott and Washington Counties, and a second was under development during 1997 in Saltville.

Coal-fired steam units accounted for 49% of electric power production in 1996. Oil-fired plants produced 1%, nuclear 47%, and gas 2%. Hydroelectric power gave the state a net power gain in 1996 of 556 million kWh (1%). The state has two nuclear power reactors, both owned by Virginia Power.

Virginia's 328 coal mines (246 underground), all in the Appalachian Mountains area, produced 36.8 million tons in 1996, 43.6% of the US total. All the coal was bituminous.

Virginia's 1,821 gas wells produced 54.3 billion cu ft of natural gas (63% from coal-bed methane) in 1996. The state's 39 oil wells produced 13,363 barrels of oil in 1996.

29 INDUSTRY

Beginning with the establishment of a glass factory at Jamestown in 1608, manufacturing grew slowly during the colonial era to include flour mills and, by 1715, an iron foundry. During the 19th century, the shipbuilding industry flourished, and many cotton mills, tanneries, and ironworks were built; light industries producing a wide variety of consumer goods developed later.

In general, manufacturing has shown more consistent growth in Virginia than at the national level. The strength of the Commonwealth's diversified manufacturing sector is shown in its 10.2% employment increase between 1970 and 1993. During this time period, national manufacturing employment declined by 8.3%. The following table shows value of shipments by leading industry groups in 1995:

Food and food products	$ 9,933,500,000
Tobacco products	9,155,100,000
Chemical and allied products	8,021,700,000
Electronic and other electric equipment	4,528,000,000
Transportation equipment	7,446,300,000
Textile mill products	3,466,700,000
Paper and allied products	4,604,700,000
Fabricated metal products	2,854,500,000
Printing and publishing	4,310,100,000
Industrial machinery	4,488,300,000
Rubber and miscellaneous plastic products	4,161,400,000
Lumber and wood products	2,918,200,000
Apparel and other textile products	1,960,700,000
Furniture and fixtures	1,649,600,000

Richmond is a principal industrial area for tobacco processing, paper and printing, clothing, and food products; nearby Hopewell is a locus of the chemical industry. Newport News, Hampton, and Norfolk are centers for shipbuilding and the manufacture of other transportation equipment. In the western part of the state, Lynchburg is a center for electrical machinery, metals, clothing, and printing, and Roanoke for food, clothing, and textiles. In the south, Martinsville has a concentration of furniture and textile-manufacturing plants, and textiles are also dominant in Danville.

In 1997, Virginia was the headquarters for 16 Fortune 500 companies. During 1995, there were 947 US patents issued to Virginia residents.

30 COMMERCE

Virginia's wholesale trade in 1992 totaled $51,453 million, conducted by 9,290 establishments. Retail sales in 1992 amounted to $48 billion (12th). The leading retail sales categories among establishments with payroll were food stores, 26.5%; automotive dealers 26%; merchandise stores, 15.4%; and eating and drinking places, 12.6%.

Virginia, a major container shipping center, handled import and export cargo worth nearly $23 billion combined in 1995, almost all through the Hampton Roads estuary. Coal is the leading exported commodity and residual fuel oil the principal import. Exports of goods originating within Virginia totaled $12.2 billion in 1996.

31 CONSUMER PROTECTION

The Department of Agriculture and Consumer Services, Division of Consumer Protection, regulates food processors and handlers, product labeling, the use of pesticides, and product safety, and is also responsible for enforcement of consumer protection laws. The Office of the Attorney General is responsible for representing citizens in a variety of consumer protection issues.

32 BANKING

In 1996, Virginia's 157 commercial banks reported combined assets of $77.8 billion and total deposits of $56.3 billion. Insured commercial banks had outstanding loans amounting to $48 billion, of which 20% went for commercial and industrial purposes and 50% for real estate. There were 32 savings institutions in 1996. As of the end of 1995, the Resolution Trust Corporation had resolved 18 institutions with combined assets of $11.5 billion at a resolution cost of $2.3 billion.

33 INSURANCE

Virginians held 7,111,681 life insurance policies worth $438.8 billion in 1996; the average coverage per family was $116,500, 13% above the national norm. Benefit payments totaled over $3.1 billion, of which death payments accounted for $983.9 million, annuities $733 million, policy and contract dividends $347.6 million, and other disbursements $1.1 billion.

In 1996, property and casualty companies wrote premiums of $5.6 billion, including $1.9 billion in automotive liability insurance, $970.4 million in automobile physical damage insurance, and $497.2 million in homeowners' coverage.

34 SECURITIES

There are no securities exchanges in Virginia. As of March 1997, 1,792 broker-dealers were registered to conduct securities transactions in the Commonwealth through 87,103 registered agents. Investment advice on securities was provided by 1,522 registered advisors.

35 PUBLIC FINANCE

Consolidated revenues and expenditures budgeted for the 1994–96 biennium were as follows (in $100,000s):

REVENUES	
General fund:	
Carry forwards	$ 254.2
Personal income tax	8,432.9
Corporate income tax	641.2
Sales and use tax	4,080.8
Other revenues	944.2
Transfers	748.5
TOTAL GENERAL FUND	$ 15,101.8

Nongeneral fund:

Balance forward	$ 165.1
Grants and donations	6,494.0
Institutional revenue	4,846.7
Taxes	3,244.2
Sales of property and commodities	513.3
Rights and privileges	1,001.5
Bond proceeds	128.5
Other receipts	1,082.1
TOTAL NONGENERAL FUND	$ 17,475.4
TOTAL REVENUES	$ 32,577.2

EXPENDITURES

Education	$ 13,200.7
Transportation	4,172.1
Public safety	2,221.3
Human resources	8,441.4
Natural resources	321.0
Commerce and trade	1,151.0
Administration	774.0
Finance	591.1
Capital outlays	457.3
Other outlays	1,037.4
TOTAL EXPENDITURES	$ 32,267.3

As of 30 June 1995, debts incurred by state and local governments totaled $8.72 billion.

36TAXATION

Virginia collected $7.6 billion in state taxes, or $1,165.51 per capita, which was 40th among the 50 states. Total state and local tax collections were $13.4 billion, or $2,068.30 per capita, which was 29th among the f50 states.

As of 1997, state income tax rates ranged from 2% to 5.75% on amounts over $17,000. The basic corporate income tax rate is 6%, and the state sales and use tax rate is 3.5%, with a local 1% option added by counties and independent cities. The gasoline tax is 17.5 cents per gallon, and the cigarette tax is 2.5 cents per pack statewide, with varying local-option rates. Virginians remitted $25 billion in income taxes to the federal government for taxable year 1995.

37ECONOMIC POLICY

The state government actively promotes a pro-business climate. Conservative traditions, low tax rates, low wage rates, a weak labor movement, and excellent access to eastern and overseas markets are the general incentives for companies to relocate into Virginia. Five duty-free foreign trade zones have been established in Virginia.

The Virginia Economic Development Corp. (VEDCORP), a privately financed and privately capitalized lending facility operating under special charter from the general assembly, extends low-interest loans to creditworthy companies to purchase land, buildings, and machinery if conventional financing is not available. The state also issues revenue bonds to finance industrial projects—a popular method of financing because the return to investors is tax-free. The bonds are issued for small as well as large companies and may be used to finance the installation of pollution control equipment. Localities allow total or partial tax exemptions for such equipment and for certified solar energy devices. The Virginia Small Business Financing Authority's loan guarantee program helps small companies obtain working capital by guaranteeing up to $150,000 of a bank loan.

Counties, cities, and incorporated towns may form local industrial development authorities to finance industrial projects and various other facilities, and may issue their own revenue bonds to cover the cost of land, buildings, machinery, and equipment. The authority's lease of the property normally includes an option to buy at a nominal price on the expiration of the lease. In addition, some 110 local development corporations have been organized. The Virginia Department of Housing and Community Development offers grants for projects which will generate employment in economically depressed areas, and the Virginia Coalfield Economic Development Authority extends loans to new or growing companies in southwestern Virginia. For minority-owned entrepreneurships, Virginia maintains the Office of Minority Business Enterprises to give advice on special problems.

38HEALTH

Virginia's live-birth rate was 114.0 per 1,000 population in 1995, below the national rate of 14.8. The infant mortality rate in 1995 was 7.7 deaths per 1,000 live births. A total of 25,548 legal abortions were performed in 1995. Virginia's death rate of 8 per 1,000 population was below the US average of 8.8 during 1995. Virginia's death rates in 1991 for the leading causes of death—heart disease, cancer, and stroke—were likewise below the national norms. In 1995, 26.3% of persons aged 18–30 were smokers.

During 1994, 1,156 new cases of AIDS were reported. The prevalence of AIDS, 17.55 cases per 100,000, was lower than the national average in 1995. Virginia's age-adjusted death rates for the leading causes of death were: diseases of the heart, 137.2 per 100,000 population; cancer, 132.7; and stroke, 29.4.

In 1994, Virginia's 102 general hospitals had 21,763 beds and recorded 694,166 admissions, with 5,645,594 outpatient visits. The average expense of hospitals for care in 1994 amounted to $5,518 per admission; Virginia had 15,075 active physicians at the end of 1996; and 59,383 licensed registered nurses in 1997. There were 3,654 active dentists in 1995.

39SOCIAL WELFARE

Payments averaging $347 a month per family were given to 166,000 residents. In 1996, 537,531 residents received monthly food stamp allowances averaging $69.69. During the same fiscal year, the school lunch program involved a federal outlay of $104.5 million.

In 1995, Social Security benefits were paid to 949,290 residents, averaging $689 a month. Federal Supplemental Security Income payments were made to 130,310 aged, blind, or disabled persons that year, averaging $314 a month. The average weekly unemployment benefit check in Virginia was $169.63 a week in 1995.

With the enactment of the Personal Responsibility and Work Opportunity Reconciliation Act of 1996, the US government has changed the form and regulations for many of its social welfare programs; most significantly, it replaces Aid to Families with Dependent Children (AFDC), an open-ended entitlement program, with Temporary Assistance for Needy Families (TANF), a limited system of assistance funded largely through federal block grants. The reform act also impacts the food stamp program, the Supplemental Security Income program, and the child nutrition program. The law took effect on 1 July 1997 and provided $16.38 billion in block grants for fiscal years 1997–2002. The grants are to be divided among the states based on an equation involving the numbers of former AFDC recipients in each state. Because many of the bills provisions have yet to be implemented into state-by-state policy, it was not possible to include the details of each state's programs for this edition of this work.

40HOUSING

In 1996, Virginia had an estimated 2,705,000 housing units, 2,476,000 of them occupied. According to the 1990 census, 61%

of all housing units were owner-occupied. In 1996, 45,919 privately owned units, valued at $3.9 billion, were authorized for construction; of these, 35,163 were single family. In 1990, the last year for which figures are available, the median monthly cost for owners with a mortgage throughout Virginia was $831; renters had a median cost of $495. The median monthly costs for owners (including mortgage) and renters for some of Virginia's more populous areas were: Roanoke, $602 and $364; Richmond, $746 and $459; Norfolk, $822 and $481; and Arlington, $1,240 and $703. During 1996, Virginia received $400.1 million in aid from the US Department of Housing and Urban Development, including $78.2 million in community development block grants.

41EDUCATION

Although Virginia was the first English colony to found a free school (1634), the state's public school system developed very slowly. Thomas Jefferson proposed a system of free public schools as early as 1779, but it was not until 1851 that such a system was established—for whites only. Free schools for blacks were founded after the Civil War, but they were poorly funded until recent years. Opposition by white Virginians to the US Supreme Court's desegregation order in 1954 was marked in certain communities by public school closings and the establishment of all-white private schools. In Prince Edward County, the most extreme case, the school board abandoned public education and left black children without schools from 1959 to 1963. By the 1970s, however, school integration was an accomplished fact throughout the commonwealth.

About 75.9% of all state residents 25 years of age or older were high school graduates in 1990, and more than 25% had at least 4 years of college. Under a Literacy Passport program adopted in 1990, students must pass writing tests in reading, writing, and math in order to enter high school. In 1993/94 school year, Virginia had 1,796 public schools, with 1,045,471 pupils; there were 293 private schools in 1993/94, with an estimated 64,710 pupils.

Virginia has had a distinguished record in higher education since the College of William and Mary was founded at Williamsburg (then called Middle Plantation) in 1693, especially after Thomas Jefferson established the University of Virginia at Charlottesville in 1819. In 1993/94, 74 colleges and universities in the state enrolled more than 351,600 students, almost three-fifths of them full-time; 23 community colleges on 36 campuses had 212,018 students in the fall of 1993. In addition to the University of Virginia and the College of William and Mary—with enrollments of 21,394 and 7,586, respectively, in 1993/94—public state-supported institutions include Virginia Polytechnic Institute and State University, Blacksburg; Virginia Commonwealth University, Richmond; Virginia Military Institute, Lexington; Old Dominion University, Norfolk; and George Mason University, Fairfax. Well-known private institutions include the Hampton Institute, Hampton; Randolph-Macon College, Ashland; University of Richmond; Sweet Briar College, Sweet Briar; and Washington and Lee University, Lexington. Tuition assistance grants and scholarships are provided through the State Council of Higher Education, while the Virginia Student Assistance Authority provides guaranteed student loans.

42ARTS

Richmond, Norfolk, and the northern Virginia metropolitan area are the principal centers for the creative and the performing arts in Virginia, although the arts flourish throughout the state. Richmond's Landmark Theatre (formerly known as The Mosque) has been the scene of concerts by internationally famous orchestras and soloists for generations. Theatre Virginia, located at the Virginia Museum of Fine Arts, presents new plays and classics with professional casts. The Barksdale Theatre and its repertory company present serious plays and occasionally give first performances of new works. In Norfolk, the performing arts are strikingly housed in Scope, a large auditorium designed by Pier Luigi Nervi; Chrysler Hall, an elegant structure with gleaming crystal; and the Wells Theatre, an ornate building where John Philip Sousa, Will Rogers, and Fred Astaire once performed. The internationally recognized Virginia Opera Association is housed in the recently constructed Harrison Opera House.

Wolf Trap Foundation for the Performing Arts, in northern Virginia, provides theatrical, operatic, and musical performances featuring internationally celebrated performers. The John F. Kennedy Center for the Performing Arts in nearby Washington, DC is heavily patronized by Virginians. The College of William and Mary's Phi Beta Kappa Hall in Williamsburg is the site of the Virginia Shakespeare Festival, an annual summer event inaugurated in 1979. Abingdon is the home of the Barter Theatre, the first state-supported theatre in the United States, whose alumni include Ernest Borgnine and Gregory Peck. This repertory company has performed widely in the US and at selected sites abroad.

Virginia's arts programs were supported by federal and state funds amounting to $8,025,23 from 1994 to 1996. The state's arts programs attracted audiences totaling 12,469,657 people from 1994–1996. There were 119,462 contributing artists. Arts education programs were offered to 132,870 of the state's school children. By 1997, Virginia had 544 arts organizations. The Virginia Commission for the Arts supported the Virginia Center for the Creative Arts and programs for the schools involving all artistic disciplines. The NEA gave $13,500 to the Carter Family Memorial Music Center and $50,000 to the Signature Theatre in 1997. In 1997, the Virginia Commission for the Arts received $57,000 from the NEA to develop the state's arts education programs. The Commission also received $351,922 from the Endowment for its other grant programs.

43LIBRARIES AND MUSEUMS

A total of 92 county, city, town, and regional library systems served 98% of the population in 1996–97; their combined book stock reached 20,086,440 volumes, and their combined circulation was 44,505,441. The Virginia State Library in Richmond and the libraries of the University of Virginia (Charlottesville) and the College of William and Mary (Williamsburg) have the personal papers of such notables as Washington, Jefferson, Madison, Robert E. Lee, William H. McGuffey, and William Faulkner. The University of Virginia also has an impressive collection of medieval illuminated manuscripts, and the library of colonial Williamsburg has extensive microfilms of British records.

There were 260 museums in 1996/97. In Richmond, the Virginia Museum of Fine Arts, the first state museum of art in the US, has a collection that ranges from ancient Egyptian artifacts to mobile jewelry by Salvador Dali. The Science Museum of Virginia has a 280-seat planetarium that features a simulated excursion to outer space. Other museums in Richmond are Wilton, the Randolphs' handsome 18th-century mansion, and the Maymont and Wickham-Valentine houses, elaborate 19th-century residences; Agecroft Hall and Virginia House, Tudor manor houses that were moved from England, are also open to the public. Norfolk has the Chrysler Museum, with its famous glassware collection; Myers House, an early Federal period home with handsome art and furnishings; and the Hermitage Foundation Museum, noted for its Oriental art. The Mariners Museum in Newport News has a superb maritime collection, and the much smaller but quite select exhibits of the Portsmouth Naval Shipyard Museum are also notable. Perhaps the most extensive "museum" in the US is Williamsburg's mile-long Duke of Gloucester Street, with such remarkable restorations as the Christopher Wren Building of the College of William and Mary,

Bruton Parish Church, the Governor's Palace, and the colonial capital.

More historic sites are maintained as museums in Virginia than in any other state. These include Washington's home at Mt. Vernon (Fairfax County), Jefferson's residence at Monticello (Charlottesville), and James River plantation houses such as Berkeley, Shirley, Westover, Sherwood Forest, and Carter's Grove. The National Park Service operates a visitors' center at Jamestown.

44COMMUNICATIONS

The state's communications network has expanded steadily since the first postal routes were established in 1738. Airmail service from Richmond to New York and Atlanta began in 1928.

According to the FCC, in March 1993, 93.8% of Virginia's 2,287,000 occupied housing units had telephones. In 1993, broadcasters operated 138 AM radio stations and 163 FM stations. In the same year, Virginia had 25 commercial and 11 educational television stations, and 17 large cable television systems.

45PRESS

Although the Crown forbade the establishment of a printing press in Virginia Colony, William Parks was publishing the *Virginia Gazette* at Williamsburg in 1736. Three newspapers were published regularly during the Revolutionary period, and in 1780 the general assembly declared that the press was "indispensable for the right information of the people and for the public service." The oldest continuously published Virginia daily, tracing its origins to 1784, is the *Alexandria Gazette*. The first Negro newspaper, *The True Southerner*, was started by a white man in 1865; several weeklies published and edited by blacks began soon after. By 1900 there were 180 newspapers in the state, but the number has declined drastically since then because of fierce competition, mergers, and rising costs.

In 1997, Virginia had 15 morning dailies, 12 evening, and 12 Sunday papers.

AREA	NAME	DAILY	SUNDAY
Norfolk	*Virginian-Pilot* (e,S)	188,678	239,274
Richmond	*Times–Dispatch* (m,S)*	211,992	249,902
Newport News	*Daily Press* (m,e,S)	102,037	124,903
Fairfax	*Journal*	54,636	----------

*Absorbed Richmond's News Leader in 1992.

46ORGANIZATIONS

The 1992 US Census of Service Industries counted 1,940 organizations in Virginia, including 541 business associations; 852 civic, social, and fraternal associations; and 547 other membership organizations. Service and educational groups headquartered in the state include the United Way of America, American Astronautical Society, American Society for Horticultural Science, American Geological Institute, and American Physical Therapy Association, all located in Alexandria; and the National Honor Society, Music Educators National Conference, and National Art Education Association, located in Reston.

Veterans' organizations include the Veterans of World War I of the USA and the Retired Officers Association, Alexandria; and the Military Order of the Purple Heart, Springfield. The United Daughters of the Confederacy has national offices in Richmond. Among the business and professional groups based in Virginia are the American Gas Association, Arlington; and the National Automobile Dealers Association, McLean.

Sports societies headquartered in the state include the American Canoe Association, Lorton; Boat Owners Association of the US, Alexandria; and National Rowing Foundation and the Walking Association, both lin Arlington.

Other groups operating out of Virginia include the Future Farmers of America and the National Sojourners, Alexandria; American Automobile Association, Falls Church; Federation of Homemakers and National Alliance of Senior Citizens, Arlington; Association of Former Intelligence Officers, McLean; and the Moral Majority, Lynchburg.

47TOURISM, TRAVEL, AND RECREATION

In 1993, domestic travelers spent $9.0 billion in Virginia on daytrips and overnight stays. Attractions in the coastal region alone include the Jamestown and Yorktown historic sites, the Williamsburg restoration, and the homes of George Washington and Robert E. Lee. Also featured are the National Aeronautics and Space Administration's Langley Research Center, Assateague Island National Seashore, and the resort pleasures of Virginia Beach.

The interior offers numerous Civil War Sites, including Appomattox; Thomas Jefferson's Monticello; Booker T. Washington's birthplace near Smith Mountain Lake; and the historic cities of Richmond, Petersburg, and Fredericksburg. In the west, the Blue Ridge Parkway and Shenandoah National Park, traversed by the breathtaking Skyline Drive, are favorite tourist destinations, as are Cumberland Gap and, in the Lexington area, the Natural Bridge, the home of Confederate General Thomas "Stonewall" Jackson, the George C. Marshall Library and Museum, and the Virginia Military Institute. A number of historic sites in Arlington and Alexandria attract many visitors to the Washington, D.C., area.

The state's many recreation areas include state parks, national forests, a major national park, scenic parkways, and thousands of miles of hiking trails and shoreline. State parks attracted 4,572,548 visitors in 1995. Some of the most-visited sites are Mt. Rogers National Recreational Area, Prince William Forest Park, Chincoteague National Wildlife Refuge, and the Kerr Reservoir. Part of the famous Appalachian Trail winds through Virginia's Blue Ridge and Appalachian mountains. The commonwealth has more than 1,500 mi (2,400 km) of well-stocked trout streams. Virginians held 853,833 hunting and 914,756 fishing licenses in 1995.

48SPORTS

Although Virginia has no major-league professional sports team, it does support two class AAA baseball teams: the Richmond Braves and Norfolk Tides. There is also minor league hockey in Richmond, Roanoke, and Norfolk.

In collegiate sports, the University of Virginia belongs to the Atlantic Coast Conference, and Virginia Military Institute competes in the Southern Conference. Virginia won college basketball's NIT Tournament in 1980 and 1992; Virginia Tech won the NIT in 1973.

Stock car racing is also popular in the state. The Richmond International Raceway and Martinsville Speedway host four NASCAR Winston Cup races each year.

Participant sports popular with Virginians include tennis, golf, swimming, skiing, boating, and water skiing. The state has at least 180 public and private golf courses.

49FAMOUS VIRGINIANS

Virginia is the birthplace of eight US presidents and many famous statesmen, noted scientists, influential educators, distinguished writers, and popular entertainers.

The first president of the US, George Washington (1732–99), also led his country's armies in the Revolutionary War and presided over the convention that framed its Constitution. Washington—who was unanimously elected president in 1789 and served two four-year terms, declining a third—was not, as has sometimes been assumed, a newcomer to politics: his political career began at the age of 27 with his election to the house of burgesses.

Thomas Jefferson (1743–1826), the nation's 3d president, offered this as his epitaph: "author of the Declaration of Independence and the Virginia Statute for Religious Freedom, and father of the University of Virginia." After serving as secretary of state under Washington and vice president under John Adams, he was elected president of the US in 1800 and reelected in 1804. Honored now as a statesman and political thinker, Jefferson was also a musician and one of the foremost architects of his time, and he has been called the first American archaeologist.

Jefferson's successor, James Madison (1751–1836), actually made his most important contributions before becoming chief executive. As a skillful and persistent negotiator throughout the Constitutional Convention of 1787, he earned the designation "father of the Constitution"; then, as coauthor of the Federalist papers, he helped produce a classic of American political philosophy. He was more responsible than any other statesman for Virginia's crucial ratification vote. Secretary of State during Jefferson's two terms, Madison occupied the presidency from 1809 to 1817.

Madison was succeeded as president in 1817 by James Monroe (1758–1831), who was reelected to a second term starting in 1821. Monroe—who had served as governor, US senator, minister to France, and secretary of state—is best known for the Monroe Doctrine, which has been US policy since his administration. William Henry Harrison (1773–1841) became the 9th president in 1841 but died of pneumonia one month after his inauguration; he had been a governor of Indiana Territory, a major general in the War of 1812, and a US representative and senator from Indiana. Harrison was succeeded by Vice President John Tyler (1790–1862), a native and resident of Virginia, who established the precedent that, upon the death of the president, the vice president inherits the title as well as the duties of the office.

Another native of Virginia, Zachary Taylor (1784–1850), renowned chiefly as a military leader, became the 12th US president in 1849 but died midway through his term. The eighth Virginia-born president, (Thomas) Woodrow Wilson (1856–1924), became the 28th president of the US in 1913 after serving as governor of New Jersey.

John Marshall (1755–1835) was the third confirmed chief justice of the US and is generally regarded by historians as the first great American jurist, partly because of his establishment of the principle of judicial review. Five other Virginians—John Blair (1732–1800), Bushrod Washington (1762–1829), Philip P. Barbour (1783–1841), Peter V. Daniel (1784–1860), and Lewis F. Powell, Jr. (b.1907)—have served as associate justices.

George Washington's cabinet included two Virginians, Secretary of State Jefferson and Attorney General Edmund Randolph (1753–1813), who, as governor of Virginia, had introduced the Virginia Plan—drafted by Madison and calling for a House of Representatives elected by the people and a Senate elected by the House—at the Constitutional Convention of 1787. Among other distinguished Virginians who have served in the cabinet are James Barbour (1775–1842), secretary of war; John Y. Mason (1799–1859), secretary of the Navy and attorney general; Carter Glass (1858–1946), secretary of the treasury, author of the Federal Reserve System, and US senator for 26 years; and Claude Augustus Swanson (1862–1939), secretary of the Navy and earlier, state governor and US senator.

Other prominent US senators from Virginia include Richard Henry Lee (1732–94), former president of the Continental Congress; James M. Mason (b.District of Columbia, 1798–1871), who later was commissioner of the Confederacy to the United Kingdom and France; John W. Daniel (1842–1910), a legal scholar and powerful Democratic Party leader; Thomas S. Martin (1847–1919), US Senate majority leader; Harry F. Byrd (1887–1966), governor of Virginia from 1926 to 1930 and US senator from 1933 to 1965; and Harry F. Byrd, Jr. (b.1914), senator from 1965 to 1982. In 1985, Virginia was represented in the senate by Republican John W. Warner (b.District of Columbia, 1927), former secretary of the Navy, and Republican Paul S. Trible, Jr. (b.Maryland, 1946), a US representative from 1976 to 1982.

Some native-born Virginians have become famous as leaders in other nations. Joseph Jenkins Roberts (1809–76) was the first president of the Republic of Liberia, and Nancy Langhorne Astor (1879–1964) was the first woman to serve in the British House of Commons.

Virginia's important colonial governors included Captain John Smith (b.England, 1580?–1631), Sir George Yeardley (b.England, 1587?–1627), Sir William Berkeley (b.England, 1606–77), Alexander Spotswood (b.Tangier, 1676–1740), Sir William Gooch (b.England, 1681–1751), and Robert Dinwiddie (b.Scotland, 1693–1770).

Virginia signers of the Declaration of Independence, besides Jefferson and Richard Henry Lee, were Carter Braxton (1736–97); Benjamin Harrison (1726?–1791), father of President William Henry Harrison; Francis Lightfoot Lee (1734–97); Thomas Nelson, Jr. (1738–89); and George Wythe (1726–1806). Wythe is also famous as the first US law professor and the teacher, in their student days, of Presidents Jefferson, Monroe, and Tyler, and Chief Justice Marshall. Virginia furnished both the first president of the Continental Congress, Peyton Randolph (1721–75), and the last, Cyrus Griffin (1748–1810).

Other notable Virginia governors include Patrick Henry (1736–99), the first governor of the commonwealth, though best remembered as a Revolutionary orator; Westmoreland Davis (1859–1942); Andrew Jackson Montague (1862–1937); and Mills E. Goodwin, Jr. (b.1914). A major historical figure who defies classification is Robert "King" Carter (1663–1732), greatest of the Virginia land barons, who also served as acting governor of Virginia and rector of the College of William and Mary.

Chief among Virginia's great military and naval leaders besides Washington and Taylor are John Paul Jones (b.Scotland, 1747–92); George Rogers Clark (1752–1818); Winfield Scott (1786–1866); Robert E. Lee (1807–70), the Confederate commander who earlier served in the Mexican War and as superintendent of West Point; Joseph E. Johnston (1807–91); George H. Thomas (1816–70); Thomas Jonathan "Stonewall" Jackson (1824–63); James Ewell Brown "Jeb" Stuart (1833–64); and George C. Marshall (b.Pennsylvania, 1880–1959). Virginians' names are also written high in the history of exploration. Daniel Boone (b.Pennsylvania, 1734–1820), who pioneered in Kentucky and Missouri, was once a member of the Virginia general assembly. Meriwether Lewis (1774–1809) and William Clark (1770–1838), both native Virginians, led the most famous expedition in US history, from St. Louis to the Pacific coast (1804–6). Richard E. Byrd (1888–1957) was both an explorer of Antarctica and a pioneer aviator.

Woodrow Wilson and George C. Marshall both received the Nobel Peace Prize, in 1919 and 1953, respectively. Distinguished Virginia-born scientists and inventors include Matthew Fontaine Maury (1806–73), founder of the science of oceanography; Cyrus H. McCormick (1809–84), who perfected the mechanical reaper; and Dr. Walter Reed (1851–1902) who proved that yellow fever was transmitted by a mosquito. Among educators associated with the state are William H. McGuffey (b.Pennsylvania, 1800–1873), a University of Virginia professor who designed and edited the most famous series of school readers in American history; and Booker T. Washington (1856–1915), the nation's foremost black educator.

William Byrd II (1674–1744) is widely acknowledged to have been the most graceful writer in English America in his day, and Jefferson was a leading prose stylist of the Revolutionary period. Edgar Allen Poe (b.Massachusetts, 1809–49), who was taken to Richmond at the age of three and later educated at the University of Virginia, was the father of the detective story and one of America's great poets and short-story writers. Virginia is the setting of historical romances by three natives: John Esten Cooke (1830–86), Thomas Nelson Page (1853–1922), and Mary Johnston (1870–1936). Notable 20th-century novelists born in Virginia include Willa Cather (1873–1947), Ellen Glasgow (1874–1945), and James Branch Cabell (1879–1958). Willard Huntington Wright (1888–1939), better known as S. S. Van Dine, wrote many detective thrillers. Twice winner of the Pulitzer Prize for biography and often regarded as the greatest American master of that genre was Douglas Southall Freeman (1886–1953). Other important historians were Lyon Gardiner Tyler (1853–1935), son of President Tyler and also an eminent educator; Philip A. Bruce (1856–1933); William Cabell Bruce (1860–1946); Virginius Dabney (b.1901); and Alf J. Map, Jr. (b.1925). Some contemporary Virginia authors are poet Guy Carlton Drewry (b.1901); television writer-producer Earl Hamner (b.1923); novelist William Styron (b.1925); and journalists Virginia Moore (1903–1993) and Tom Wolfe (Thomas Kennerly Wolfe, Jr., b. 1931).

Celebrated Virginia artists include sculptors Edward V. Valentine (1838–1930) and Moses Ezekiel (1844–1917), and painters George Caleb Bingham (1811–79) and Jerome Myers (1867–1940). A protégé of Jefferson's, Robert Mills (b.South Carolina, 1781–1855), designed the Washington Monument.

The roster of Virginians prominent in the entertainment world includes Bill "Bojangles" Robinson (1878–1949), Francis X. Bushman (1883–1966), Freeman Gosden (1899–1982), Randolph Scott (1903–1987), Joseph Cotten (b.1905), Margaret Sullavan (1911–60), John Payne (1912–1989), George C. Scott (b.1927), Shirley MacLaine (b.1934), and Warren Beatty (b.1938).

Outstanding musical performers include John Powell (1882–1963), whose fame as a pianist once equaled his prominence as a composer. Virginia's most eminent contemporary composer is Thea Musgrave (b.Scotland, 1928). Popular musical stars include Kathryn Elizabeth "Kate" Smith (1907–1986), Pearl Bailey (1918–1990), Ella Fitzgerald (b.1918–1996), June Carter (b.1929), Roy Clark (b.1933), and Wayne Newton (b.1942).

The Old Dominion's sports champions include golfers Bobby Cruickshank (b.1896), Sam Snead (b.1912), and Chandler Harper (b.1914); tennis star Arthur Ashe (1943–1993); football players Clarence "Ace" Parker (b.1912), Bill Dudley (b.1921), and Francis "Fran" Tarkenton (b.1940); and baseball pitcher Eppa Rixey (1891–1963). At age 15, Olympic swimming champion Melissa Belote (b.1957) won three gold medals. Helen Chenery "Penny" Tweedy (b.1922) is a famous breeder and racer of horses from whose stables have come Secretariat and other champions. Equestrienne Jean McLean Davis (b.1929) won 65 world championships.

50BIBLIOGRAPHY

Ashe, Dora J. (comp.). *Four Hundred Years of Virginia, 1584–1984: An Anthology.* Lanham, Md.: University Press of America, 1985.

Bruce, Philip Alexander. *Economic History of Virginia in the Seventeenth Century.* 2 vols. New York: Johnson Reprints. n.d. (orig. 1896).

Bruce, Philip Alexander. *Social Life of Virginia in the Seventeenth Century.* Lynchburg, Va.: J. P. Bell, 1927.

Buni, Andrew. *The Negro in Virginia Politics, 1902–65.* Charlottesville: University Press of Virginia. 1967.

Dabney, Virginius. *Richmond: The Story of a City.* Rev. and enl. Charlottesville: University Press of Virginia, 1990.

Dabney, Virginius. *Virginia: The New Dominion.* Charlottesville: University Press of Virginia, 1983 (orig. 1971).

Davis, Richard Beale. *Intellectual Life in Jefferson's Virginia, 1790–1830.* Knoxville: University of Tennessee Press, 1972.

Diversity and Accommodation: Essays on the Cultural Composition of the Virginia Frontier. Knoxville: University of Tennessee Press, 1997.(orig. 1964).

Federal Writers' Project. *Virginia: A Guide to the Old Dominion.* New York: Somerset, 1980 (orig. 1940).

Freeman, Douglas Southall. *George Washington.* 7 vols. New York: Scribner, 1948–57.

Friddell, Guy. *What Is It About Virginia?* Richmond: Dietz, 1983 (orig. 1966).

Gottmann, Jean. *Virginia in Our Century.* Charlottesville: University Press of Virginia, 1969.

Malone, Dumas. *Jefferson and His Time.* Vols. 1 and 2. Boston: Little, Brown, 1948, 1951.

Mapp, Alf J., Jr. *Frock Coats and Epaulets: The Men Who Led the Confederacy.* Lanham, Md.: Madison Books, 1996.

———. *The Virginia Experiment: The Old Dominion's Role in the Making of America, 1607–1781.* 3d ed. Lanham, Md.: Hamilton Press, 1987.

Moger, Allen W. *Virginia: Bourbonism to Byrd, 1870–1925.* Charlottesville: University Press of Virginia, 1968.

Morgan, Edmund S. *American Slavery, American Freedom: The Ordeal of Colonial Virginia.* New York: Norton, 1975.

Morton, Richard L. *Colonial Virginia.* 2 vols. Chapel Hill: University of North Carolina Press, 1960.

Pratt, Robert A. *The Color of their Skin: Education and Race in Richmond, Virginia, 1954-89.* Charlottesville: University Press of Virginia, 1992.

Ragsdale, Bruce A. *A Planters' Republic: The Search for Economic Independence in Revolutionary Virginia.* Madison, Wis.: Madison House, 1996.

Rubin, Louis D., Jr. *Virginia: A Bicentennial History.* New York: Norton, 1977.

Shade, William G. *Democratizing the Old Dominion: Virginia and the Second Party System, 1824-1861.* Charlottesville: University Press.

Stanard, Mary Newton. *The Story of Virginia's First Century.* Philadelphia: Lippincott, 1938.

Virginia, Commonwealth of. Division of Industrial Development. *Virginia Facts and Figures 1984.* Richmond, 1984.

Wertenbaker, Thomas J. *Norfolk, Historic Southern Port.* 2d ed. Durham, N.C.: Duke University Press, 1962.

Wertenbaker, Thomas J. *Torchbearer of the Revolution.* Princeton, N.J.: Princeton University Press, 1940.

Wright, Louis B. *The First Gentlemen of Virginia.* Charlottesville: University Press of Virginia, 1940.

WASHINGTON

State of Washington

ORIGIN OF STATE NAME: Named for George Washington. **NICKNAME:** The Evergreen State. **CAPITAL:** Olympia. **ENTERED UNION:** 11 November 1889 (42d). **SONG:** "Washington, My Home." **DANCE:** Square dance. **MOTTO:** Alki (Chinook for *By and by*). **FLAG:** The state seal centered on a dark green field. **OFFICIAL SEAL:** Portrait of George Washington surrounded by the words "The Seal of the State of Washington 1889." **BIRD:** Willow goldfinch. **FISH:** Steelhead trout. **FLOWER:** Western rhododendron. **TREE:** Western hemlock. **GEM:** Petrified wood. **LEGAL HOLIDAYS:** New Year's Day, 1 January; Birthday of Martin Luther King, Jr., 3d Monday in January; Presidents' Day, 2d Monday in February; Memorial Day, last Monday in May; Independence Day, 4 July; Labor Day, 1st Monday in September; Veterans Day and State Admission Day, 11 November; Thanksgiving Day, 4th Thursday in November; Christmas Day, 25 December. **TIME:** 4 AM PST = noon GMT.

¹LOCATION, SIZE, AND EXTENT

Located on the Pacific coast of the northwestern US, Washington ranks 20th in size among the 50 states.

The total area of Washington is 66,582 sq mi (176,477 sq km), of which land takes up 66,511 sq mi (172,263 sq km) and inland water 1,627 sq mi (4,214 sq km). The state extends about 360 mi (580 km) E-W and 240 mi (390 km) N-S.

Washington is bounded on the N by the Canadian province of British Columbia (with the northwestern line passing through the Juan de Fuca Strait and the Haro and Georgia straits); on the E by Idaho (with the line in the southwest passing through the Snake River); on the S by Oregon (with most of the line defined by the Columbia River); and on the W by the Pacific Ocean.

Islands of the San Juan group, lying between the Haro and Rosario straits, include Orcas, San Juan, and Lopez; Whidbey is a large island in the upper Puget Sound. The state's boundary length totals 1,099 mi (1,769 km), including 157 mi (253 km) of general coastline; the tidal shoreline extends 3,026 mi (4,870 km). Washington's geographic center is in Chelan County, 10 mi (16 km) WSW of Wenatchee.

²TOPOGRAPHY

Much of Washington is mountainous. Along the Pacific coast are the Coast Ranges extending northward from Oregon and California. This chain forms two groups: the Olympic Mountains in the northwest, mainly on the Olympic Peninsula between the Pacific Ocean and Puget Sound, and the Willapa Hills in the southwest. The highest of the Olympic group is Mt. Olympus, at 7,965 feet (2,428 meters). About 100 mi (160 km) inward from the Pacific coast is the Cascade Range, extending northward from the Sierra Nevada in California. This chain, 50–100 mi (80–100 km) wide, has peaks generally ranging up to 10,000 feet (3,000 meters), except for such volcanic cones as Mt. Adams, Mt. Baker, Glacier Peak, Mt. St. Helens, and Mt. Rainier, which at 14,410 feet (4,392 meters) is the highest peak in the state.

Between the Coast and Cascade ranges lies a long, troughlike depression—the Western Corridor—where most of Washington's major cities are concentrated. The northern section of this lowland is carved by Puget Sound, a complex, narrow arm of the Pacific wending southward for about 80 mi (130 km) and covering an area of 561 sq mi (1,453 sq km). Of all the state's

other major regions, only south-central Washington, forming part of the Columbia Plateau, is generally flat.

The Cascade volcanoes were dormant, for the most part, during the second half of the 19th century and most of the 20th. Early in 1980, however, Mt. St. Helens began to show ominous signs of activity. On 18 May, the volcano exploded, blasting more than 1,300 feet (400 meters) off a mountain crest that had been 9,677 feet (2,950 meters) high. Tremendous plumes of steam and ash were thrust into the stratosphere, where prevailing winds carried volcanic dust thousands of miles eastward. The areas immediately surrounding Mt. St. Helens were deluged with ash and mudflows, choking local streams and lakes, particularly Spirit Lake. About 150 sq mi (388 sq km) of trees and brush were destroyed; the ash fall also damaged crops in neighboring agricultural areas and made highway travel extremely hazardous. The eruption left 57 people dead or missing. Eruptions of lesser severity followed the main outburst; the mountain continued to pose a serious danger to life in the area as the estimated cost of the damage to property, crops, and livestock approached $3 billion. Another minor eruption, on 14 May 1984, shot ash 4 miles (6 km) high and caused a small mudflow down the mountain's flanks, but no injuries or other damage occurred. East of the Cascade Range, much of Washington is a plateau underlain by ancient basalt lava flows. In the northeast are the Okanogan Highlands; in the southeast, the Blue Mountains and the Palouse Hills. All these uplands form extensions of the Rocky Mountain system.

Among Washington's numerous rivers, the longest and most powerful is the Columbia, entering Washington from Canada in the northeast corner and flowing for more than 1,200 mi (1,900 km) across the heart of the state and then along the Oregon border to the Pacific. In average discharge, the Columbia ranks 2d only to the Mississippi, with 262,000 cu feet (7,400 cu meters) per second. Washington's other major river, the Snake, enters the state from Idaho in the southeast and flows generally westward, meeting the Columbia River near Pasco.

Washington has numerous lakes, of which the largest is the artificial Franklin D. Roosevelt Lake, covering 123 sq mi (319 sq km). Washington has some 90 dams, providing water storage, flood control, and hydroelectric power. One of the largest and most famous dams in the US is Grand Coulee on the upper Columbia River, measuring 550 feet (168 meters) high and 4,173 feet (1,272 meters) long, with a storage capacity of more than 9.7 million acre-feet (11,960 cu m).

³CLIMATE

The Cascade Mountains divide Washington not only topographically but also climatically. Despite its northerly location, western Washington is as mild as the middle and southeastern Atlantic coast; it is also one of the rainiest regions in the world. Eastern Washington, on the other hand, has a much more continental climate, characterized by cold winters, hot summers, and sparse rainfall. Since the prevailing winds are from the west, the windward (western) slopes of the state's major mountains intercept most of the atmospheric moisture and precipitate it as rain or snow. Certain coastal areas, receiving more than 200 in (500 cm) of rain a year, support dense stands of timber in a temperate rain forest. But in the dry southeastern quadrant, there are sagebrush deserts.

Average January temperatures in western Washington range from a minimum of 20°F (–7°C) on the western slope of the Cascades to a maximum of 48°F (9°C) along the Pacific coast; July temperatures range from a minimum of 44°F (7°C) on the western slope of the Cascades to a maximum of 80°F (27°C) in the foothills. In the east the temperature ranges are much more extreme: in January, from 8°F (–13°C) in the northeastern Cascades to 40°F (4°C) on the southeastern plateau; in July, from 48°F (9°C) on the eastern slope of the Cascades to 92°F (33°C)in the south-central portion of the state. The normal daily mean temperature in Seattle is 52°F (11°C), ranging from 40°F (4°C) in January to 65°F (18°C) in July; Spokane averages 47°F (8°C), ranging from 27°F (–3°C) in January to 69°F (21°C) in July. The lowest temperature ever recorded in the state is –48°F (–44°C), set at Mazama and Winthrop on 30 December 1968; the highest, at Ice Harbor Dam on 5 August 1961, was 118°F (48°C).

The average annual precipitation in Seattle is 43 in (109 cm), falling most heavily from October through March; Spokane receives only 17 in (43 cm), more than half of that from November through February. Snowfall in Seattle averages 13 in (33 cm) annually; in Spokane, 51 in (130 cm). Paradise Ranger Station holds the North American record for the most snowfall in one season, when 1,122 in (2,850 cm) of snow fell during the winter of 1971–72. High mountain peaks, such as Mt. Adams, Mt. Baker, and Mt. Rainier, have permanent snowcaps or snowfields of up to 100 feet (30 meters) deep.

⁴FLORA AND FAUNA

More than 1,300 plant species have been identified in Washington. Sand strawberries and beach peas are found among the dunes, while fennel and spurry grow in salt marshes; greasewood and sagebrush predominate in the desert regions of the Columbia Plateau. Conifers include Sitka spruce, Douglas fir, western hemlock, and Alaska cedar; big-leaf maple, red alder, black cottonwood, and western yew are among the characteristic deciduous trees. Wild flowers include the deerhead orchid and wake-robin; the western rhododendron is the state flower.

Forest and mountain regions support Columbia black-tailed and mule deer, elk, and black bear; the Roosevelt elk, named after President Theodore Roosevelt, is indigenous to the Olympic Mountains. Other native mammals are the Canadian lynx, red fox, and red western bobcat. Smaller native mammals—western fisher, raccoon, muskrat, porcupine, marten, and mink—are plentiful. The whistler (hoary) marmot is the largest rodent. Game birds include the ruffed grouse, bobwhite quail, and ring-necked pheasant. Sixteen varieties of owl have been identified; other birds of prey include the prairie falcon, sparrow hawk, and golden eagle. The bald eagle is more numerous in Washington than in any other state except Alaska. Washington is also a haven for marsh, shore, and water birds. Various salmon species thrive in coastal waters and along the Columbia River, and the octopus, hair seal, and sea lion inhabit Puget Sound.

Animals driven away from the slopes of Mt. St. Helens by the volcanic eruption in 1980 have largely returned, and as of July 1984, 26 species of mammals and 101 species of birds were observed inhabiting the mountain again. The number of elk and deer in the vicinity was roughly the same as prior to the eruption, although the mountain goat population reportedly had been killed off. Earlier, on 17 August 1982, the Mt. St. Helens National Volcanic Monument was created by an act of Congress; it includes about 110,000 acres (44,500 hectares) of the area that had been devastated by the original eruption.

Endangered wildlife in the state includes the northern Rocky Mountain wolf, Columbian white-tailed deer, woodland caribou, southern sea otter, American peregrine falcon, Aleutian Canada goose, and short-tailed albatross.

⁵ENVIRONMENTAL PROTECTION

The mission of the Department of Ecology (established in 1970) is to protect, preserve, and enhance Washington's environment and promote the wise management of our air, land, and water for the benefit of current and future generations. To fulfill this mission, the Department of Ecology: administers permit and authorization programs which ensure that pollutant discharges, waste management and clean-up, and resource uses are properly controlled; provides technical assistance on pollution control or resource development issues; and provides financial assistance through grant and loan programs to local governments for waste water and solid waste facilities. The Department of Ecology also reviews federal and state actions and plans for consistency with state laws and regulations for natural resource protection, maintains an ongoing program to monitor the quality of air and water resources, hazardous waste management, and toxic and nuclear clean-up actions; and reviews local government-permitting actions relating to the state's shorelands and to solid waste facilities. Furthermore, the Department of Ecology directly administers an automobile inspection program for the Seattle, Vancouver (Washington), and Spokane areas, an Estuarine Sanctuary program at Padilla Bay, the Conservation Corps employment program, and the Youth Corps litter control program.

Among other state agencies with environmental responsibilities are the State Conservation Commission, Environmental Hearings Office, State Parks and Recreation Commission, Department of Health, Department of Fish and Wildlife, and Department of Natural Resources.

Principal air pollutants in the state are particulate emissions, carbon monoxide, hydrocarbons, lead, and dioxides of nitrogen. Fuel combustion and industrial processes are responsible for most of the first two pollutants, transportation (especially the automobile) for most of the last four. Significant progress has been made since 1988 in reducing the amount of criteria air pollutants released to the air. In 1988, the total number of days air quality did not meet health standards was 25. In 1994, the total number of days was 15.

More than 6,500 sites in Washington are suspected or confirmed to be contaminated with toxic chemicals. At the Hanford Nuclear Site alone, contamination includes 1,500 places where radioactive and chemical wastes were disposed to the soil. Clean-up is well underway or completed at a majority of the-high priority sites.

Washington state has the highest overall recycling rate of any state in the United States. More than 39% of the state's total solid waste was recycled in 1995, compared to 23% in 1987. In the mid-1980s, Bellingham began the state's first curbside recycling collection program. Seattle soon started its own program after being forced to close a municipal landfill and facing fierce

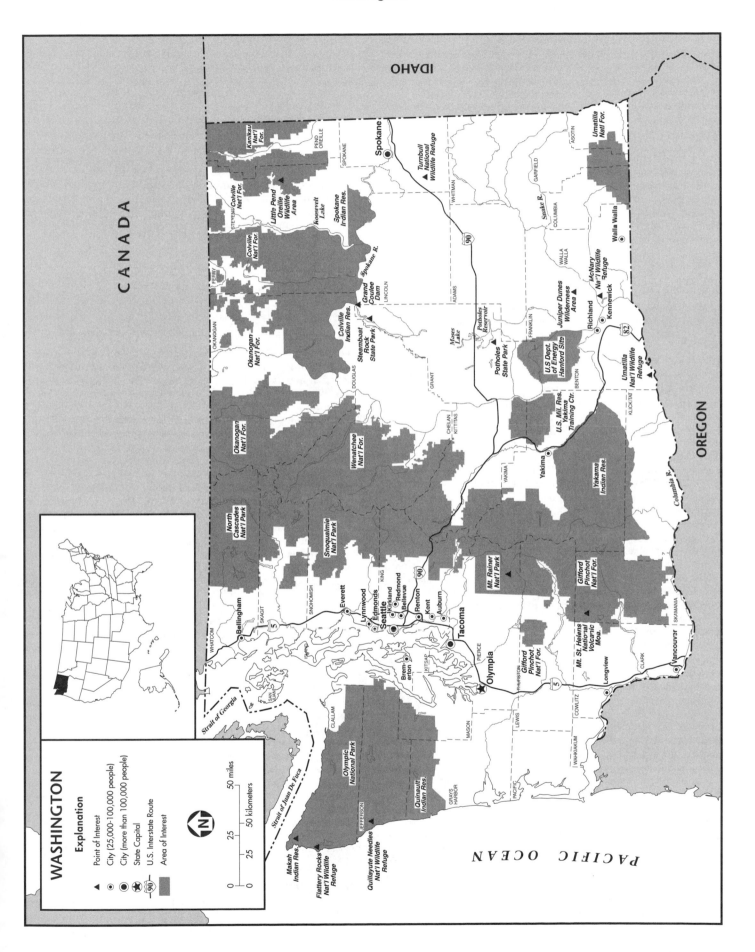

opposition to construction of a garbage incinerator. In 1989, the state legislature passed the Waste-Not Washington Act which defined a clear solid-waste management strategy.

6POPULATION

Washington was the nation's 18th-most-populous state at the 1990 census, with 4,866,692 residents. The estimated population in 1996 was 5,516,800, an increase over 1990 that follows the 21% increase from 1970–80, and the 17.8% rise from 1980–90. Washington's estimated population density in 1990 was 73.1 per sq mi (28 per sq km). From 1940 to 1980 alone, the state's population more than doubled. About 76% of Washington's population was urban at the 1990 census and 24% rural.

Most Washingtonians live in the Western Corridor, a broad strip in western Washington running north-south between the Coast and Cascade ranges. The leading city in the Western Corridor is Seattle, with an estimated 1996 population of 534,700. Other leading cities with their 1996 population estimates are Spokane, 187,700; Tacoma, 185,000; Bellevue, 84,239; Everett, 76,685; Yakima, 61,976; Bellingham, 57,119; and Vancouver, 51,847. Olympia, the state capital, had 37,960 residents in 1996. The Seattle-Tacoma-Bremerton metropolitan area had an estimated 1995 population of 3,056,800.

7ETHNIC GROUPS

Washington is ethnically and racially heterogeneous. As of 1990, foreign-born Washingtonians made up only 6.6% of the state's population, with Mexico, Canada, the Philippines, Korea, and Germany being the leading countries of origin. The largest minority group consists of Hispanic Americans, numbering 215,000 according to the 1990, census and 211,000 according to 1996 estimates. Most of the state's Spanish-speaking residents have come since World War II. Black Americans numbered 150,000 in 1990 and an estimated 174,000 in 1996. Black immigration dates largely from World War II and postwar recruitment for defense-related industries.

Japanese-Americans have been farmers and small merchants in Washington throughout the 20th century. During World War II, the Nisei of Washington were interned. Chinese-Americans, imported as laborers in the mid-1800s, endured a wave of mob violence during the 1880s. According to the 1990 census, there were 49,222 Filipinos, 43,378 Japanese, 33,954 Chinese, 32,918 Koreans, and 17,004 Vietnamese in Washington. Immigration from Southeast Asia was an important factor during the late 1970s and early 1980s. In 1996 there were an estimated 281,000 Asian/Pacific Islanders in Washington.

There were 81,000 American Indians, Eskimos, and Aleuts living in Washington in 1990, 6th-highest in the nation. This figure increased to an estimated 103,000 in 1996. The most-populous reservation is the Puyallup Reservation (estimated 1995 population 14,282). Indian lands in the state cover some 2.5 million acres (1 million hectares). A dispute developed in the 1970s over Indian fishing rights in the Puget Sound area; a decision in 1974 by US District Judge George Boldt that two 120-year-old treaties guaranteed the Indians 50% of the salmon catch in certain rivers was essentially upheld by the US Supreme Court in 1979.

8LANGUAGES

Early settlers took from Chinook jargon some words like *potlatch* (gift-dispensing feast), *skookum* (strong), and *tillicum* (friend). Other language influences came from the many Indian tribes inhabiting Washington, especially such place-names as Chehalis, Walla Walla, Puyallup, Humptulips, and Spokane. Northern and Midland dialects dominate, with Midland strongest in eastern Washington and the Bellingham area, Northern elsewhere. In the urban areas, minor eastern variants have been lost; in rural

sections, however, older people have preserved such terms as *johnnycake* (corn bread) and *mouth organ* (harmonica). One survey showed Northern *quarter to* dominant in the state with 81%, with Midland *quarter till* having only a 5% response; Northern *angleworm* (earthworm) had 63%, but Midland *fishworm* and *fishing worm* only 17%. The north coast of the Olympic Peninsula, settled by New Englanders who sailed around Cape Horn, retains New England /ah/ in *glass* and *aunt*. In Seattle, *fog* and *frog* are Midland /fawg/ and /frawg/, but *on* is Northern /ahn/; *cot* and *caught* sound alike, as in Midland; but the final /y/, as in *city* and *pretty*, has the Northern /ee/ sound rather than the Midland short /i/ as in *pit*.

In 1990, English was the language spoken at home by 91% of Washington residents 5 years old and older. Other languages spoken at home and the number of people 5 years old and older speaking them were:

Spanish	143,647	Korean	23,190
German	39,011	Japanese	17,626
French	19,883	Vietnamese	15,488
Chinese	26,378	Various Scandinavian	13,626
Tagalog	24,574		

9RELIGIONS

First settled by Protestant missionaries, Washington remains a predominantly Protestant state. As of 1990, there were 1,052,281 known adherents of Protestant groups. The leading denominations were the Church of Jesus Christ of Latter-day Saints (Mormon), 150,634; United Methodist, 89,499; Evangelical Lutheran Church in America, 132,528; and United Presbyterian, 72,273. In 1990, there were 526,546 Roman Catholics and an estimated 33,689 Jews.

10TRANSPORTATION

As of 1997, Washington had 3,114 rail mi (5,014 km) of railroad lines. In 1995, the state ranked 1st in rail tonnage of farm products terminated, at 26,676,524 tons. Amtrak provides service from Seattle down the coast to Los Angeles, and eastward via Spokane to St. Paul, Minn., and Chicago. There were 663,717 Amtrak passengers in 1995/96; more than 59% of them boarded trains in Seattle.

Washington had 79,712 mi (128,257 km) of public highways, roads, and streets in 1997, of which 764 mi (1,229 km) formed part of the interstate highway system. Principal interstate highways include I-90, connecting Spokane and Seattle, and I-5, proceeding north-south from Vancouver in British Columbia through Seattle and Tacoma to Vancouver, Wash., and Portland, Ore. In 1996, the state had 3,765,378 licensed drivers and 4,595,834 registered motor vehicles, including 3,179,663 automobiles.

Washington's principal ports include Seattle, Tacoma, and Anacortes, all part of the Puget Sound area and belonging to the Seattle Customs District; and Longview, Kalama, and Vancouver, along the Columbia River and considered part of the Portland (Ore.) Customs District. In 1995, Seattle and Tacoma ranked 4th ($34.3 billion) and 8th ($20.5 billion), respectively, in total value of cargo handled. State-operated ferry systems transported 13.6 million passengers and 10.6 million vehicles across Puget Sound in 1995.

In 1995, Washington had 310 airports and 100 heliports. Seattle-Tacoma (SEATAC) International Airport, by far the busiest, handled 22.8 million arriving and departing passengers in 1995.

11HISTORY

The region now known as the State of Washington has been inhabited for at least 9,000 years, the first Americans having crossed the Bering Strait from Asia and entered North America via the Pacific Northwest. Their earliest known remains in Washington—some burned bison bones and a human skeleton—date from approximately 7000 BC. Clovis points, a type of arrowhead, have been unearthed and determined to be approximately 30,000 years old.

The Cascades impeded communications between coastal Indians and those of the eastern plateau, and their material cultures evolved somewhat differently. Coastal Indians—belonging mainly to the Nootkin and Salishan language families—lived in a land of plenty, with ample fish, shellfish, roots, and berries. Timber was abundant for the construction of dugout canoes, villages with wooden dwellings, and some stationary wooden furniture. Warfare between villages was fairly common, with the acquisition of slaves the primary objective. The coastal Indians also emphasized rank based on wealth, through such institutions as the potlatch, a gigantic feast with extravagant exchanges of gifts. The plateau (or "horse") Indians, on the other hand, paid little attention to class distinctions. Social organization was simpler and intertribal warfare less frequent here than on the coast. After the horse reached Washington around 1730, the plateau tribes (mainly of the Shahaptian language group) became largely nomadic, traveling long distances in search of food. Housing was portable, often taking the form of skin or mat teepees. In winter, circular pit houses were dug for protection from the wind and snow.

The first Europeans known to have sailed along the Washington coast were 18th-century Spaniards; stories of earlier voyages to the area by Sir Francis Drake in 1579 and Juan de Fuca in 1592 are largely undocumented. In 1774, Juan Pérez explored the northwestern coastline to the southern tip of Alaska; an expedition led by Bruno Heceta and his assistant, Juan Francisco de la Bodega y Quadra, arrived a year later. Men from this expedition made the first known landing on Washington soil, at the mouth of the Hoh River, but the venture ended in tragedy when the Indians seized the landing boat and killed the Spaniards.

English captain James Cook, on his third voyage of exploration, arrived in the Pacific Northwest in 1778 while searching for a northwest passage across America. He was the first of numerous British explorers and traders to be attracted by the luxuriant fur of the sea otter. Cook was followed in 1792 by another Englishman George Vancouver, who mapped the Pacific coast and the Puget Sound area. In the same year, an American fur trader and explorer, Captain Robert Gray, discovered the mouth of the Columbia River. As the maritime fur trade began to prosper, overland traders moved toward the Northwest, the most active organizations being the British Hudson's Bay Company and the Canadian North West Company.

American interest in the area also increased. Several US maritime explorers had already visited the Northwest when President Thomas Jefferson commissioned an overland expedition to inspect the territory acquired from France through the Louisiana Purchase (1803). That expedition, led by Meriwether Lewis and William Clark, first sighted the Pacific Ocean in early November 1805 from the north bank of the Columbia River in what is now Pacific County. In time, as reports of the trip became known, a host of British and American fur traders followed portions of their route to the Pacific coast, and the interest of missionaries was excited. In 1831, a delegation visited Clark in St. Louis, Mo., where he was then superintendent of Indian affairs, to persuade him to send teachers who could instruct the Indians in the Christian religion. When news of the visit became known, there was an immediate response from the churches.

The first missionaries to settle in Washington were Marcus and Narcissa Whitman, representing the Protestant American Board of Missions; their settlement, at Waiilatpu in southeastern Washington (near present-day Walla Walla), was established in 1836. Although the early Protestant missions had scant success in converting the Indians, the publicity surrounding their activities encouraged other Americans to journey to the Pacific Northwest, and the first immigrant wagons arrived at Waiilatpu in 1840. The Indian population became increasingly hostile to the missionaries, however, and on 29 November 1847, Marcus and Narcissa Whitman and 12 other Americans were massacred.

As early as 1843, an American provisional government had been established, embracing the entire Oregon country and extending far into the area that is now British Columbia, Canada. Three years later, after considerable military and diplomatic maneuvering, a US-Canada boundary along the 49th parallel was established by agreement with the British. Oregon Territory, including the present state of Washington, was organized in 1848. In the early 1850s, residents north of the Columbia River petitioned Congress to create a separate "Columbia Territory." The new territorial status was granted in 1853, but at the last minute the name of the territory (which embraced part of present-day Idaho) was changed to Washington.

President Franklin Pierce appointed Isaac I. Stevens as the first territorial governor. Stevens, who served at the same time as a US superintendent of Indian affairs, negotiated a series of treaties with the Northwest Indian tribes, establishing a system of reservations. Although the Indian situation had long been tense, it worsened after the treaties were concluded, and bloody uprisings by the Yakima, Nisqualli, and Cayuse were not suppressed until the late 1850s. Court battles over fishing rights spelled out in those treaties were not substantially resolved until 1980.

On the economic front, discoveries of gold in the Walla Walla area, in British Columbia, and in Idaho brought prosperity to the entire region. The completion in 1883 of the Northern Pacific Railroad line from the eastern US to Puget Sound encouraged immigration, and Washington's population, only 23,955 in 1870, swelled to 357,232 by 1890. In the political sphere, Washington was an early champion of women's suffrage. The territorial legislature granted women the vote in 1883; however, the suffrage acts were pronounced unconstitutional in 1887.

Cattle and sheep raising, farming, and lumbering were all established by the time Washington became the 42d state in 1889. The Populist movement of the 1890s found fertile soil in Washington, and the financial panic of 1893 further stimulated radical labor and Granger activity. In 1896, the Fusionists—a coalition of Populists, Democrats, and Silver Republicans—swept the state. The discovery of gold in the Klondike, for which Seattle was the primary departure point, helped dim the Fusionists' prospects, and for the next three decades the Republican Party dominated state politics.

In 1909 Seattle staged the Alaska-Yukon-Pacific Exposition, celebrating the Alaska gold rush and Seattle's new position as a major seaport. World War I brought the state several major new military installations, and the Puget Sound area thrived as a shipbuilding center. The war years also saw the emergence of radical labor activities, especially in the shipbuilding and logging industries. Seattle was the national headquarters of the Industrial Workers of the World (IWW) and became, in 1919, the scene of the first general strike in the US, involving about 60,000 workers. The towns of Centralia and Everett were the sites of violent conflict between the IWW and conservative groups.

Washington's economy was in dire straits during the depression of the 1930s, when the market for forest products and field crops tumbled. The New Deal era brought numerous federally funded public works projects, notably the Bonneville and Grand Coulee dams on the Columbia River, providing hydroelectric power for industry and water for the irrigation of desert lands. Eventually, more than 1 million acres (400,000 hectares) were reclaimed for agricultural production. During World War II,

Boeing led the way in establishing the aerospace industry as Washington's primary employer. Also during the war, the federal government built the Hanford Reservation nuclear research center; the Hanford plant was one of the major contractors in the construction of the first atomic bomb and later became a pioneer producer of atomic-powered electricity.

In 1962, "Century 21," the Seattle World's Fair, again promoted the area, as the Alaska-Yukon-Pacific Exposition had a half-century earlier. The exhibition left Seattle a number of buildings—including the Space Needle and Coliseum—that have since been converted into a civic and performing arts center. The 1960s and 1970s, a period of rapid population growth (with Seattle and the Puget Sound area leading the way), also witnessed an effort by government and industry to reconcile the needs of an expanding economy with an increasing public concern for protection of the state's unique natural heritage. An unforeseen environmental hazard emerged in May 1980 with the eruption of Mt. St. Helens and the resultant widespread destruction.

Washington experienced a deep recession in 1979. The industries of logging and lumber, which lost market share to mills in the Southeast and in Canada, were particularly hard hit. Employment in wood products dropped 30% between 1978 and 1982. Nuclear waste also became an issue with the publication of a study in 1985 claiming that plutonium produced at the Hanford bomb fuel facility had leaked into the nearby Columbia River. This claim was confirmed in 1990 by the federal government, which, together with the state, started a clean-up program expected to continue past the year 2000. The state's economy, strengthened by the expansion of Microsoft Corporation, Boeing, and Weyerhauser Paper in the 1980s, was still hampered by falling agricultural prices and weakness in the timber industry.

Speaker of the House Tom Foley, a Democrat and 30-year congressional veteran, lost his House seat in the 1994 mid-term elections in which Republicans prevailed in seven of the state's nine congressional districts.

12 STATE GOVERNMENT

Washington's constitution of 1889, as amended, continues to govern the state today. The legislative branch consists of a senate of 49 members elected to four-year terms, and a house of representatives with 98 members serving for two years. The legislative salary in 1995 was $25,900. Executives elected statewide include the governor and lieutenant governor (who run separately), secretary of state, treasurer, attorney general, auditor, and officers for education, insurance, and land. The governor and lieutenant governor, who serve four-year terms, must be qualified voters in the state. In 1996 the governor's salary was $121,000.

A bill becomes law if passed by a majority of the elected members of each house and then signed by the governor or left unsigned for 5 days while the legislature is in session or 20 days after it has adjourned; a two-thirds vote of members present in each house is sufficient to override a gubernatorial veto. Constitutional amendments require a two-thirds vote of the legislature and ratification by the voters at the next general election.

Voters in Washington must be US citizens, at least 18 years of age; the residency requirement is 30 days.

13 POLITICAL PARTIES

Washington never went for a full-fledged Democrat in a presidential election until 1932, when Franklin D. Roosevelt won the first of four successive victories in the state. Until then, Washington had generally voted Republican, the lone exceptions being 1896, when the state's Populist voters carried Washington for William Jennings Bryan, and 1912, when a plurality of the voters chose Theodore Roosevelt on the Progressive ticket.

In recent decades, the state has tended to favor Republicans in presidential elections, but Democrats have more than held their own in other contests. Washingtonians elected a Democratic governor, Dixy Lee Ray, in 1976, but in 1980 they chose a Republican, John Spellman; in 1984, they returned to the Democratic column, electing Booth Gardner. Mike Lowry, also a Democrat, was elected governor in 1992. In November 1994, Slade Gorton, a Republican, was reelected to a third term in the senate. Washington's other senator, Democrat Patty Murray, was

Washington Presidential Vote by Political Parties, 1948–96

YEAR	ELECTORAL VOTE	WASHINGTON WINNER	DEMOCRAT	REPUBLICAN	PROGRESSIVE	SOCIALIST	PROHIBITION	SOCIALIST LABOR	CONSTITUTION
1948	8	*Truman (D)	476,165	386,315	31,692	3,534	6,117	1,113	—
1952	9	*Eisenhower (R)	492,845	599,107	2,460	—	—	633	7,290
1956	9	*Eisenhower (R)	523,002	620,430	—	—	—	7,457	
1960	9	Nixon (R)	599,298	629,273	—	—	—	10,895	1,401
1964	9	*Johnson (D)	779,699	470,366	—	—	—	7,772	—
					PEACE & FREEDOM		AMERICAN IND.		
1968	9	Humphrey (D)	616,037	588,510	1,669	—	96,900	491	—
					PEOPLE'S	LIBERTARIAN			AMERICAN
1972	9	*Nixon (R)	568,334	837,135	2,644	1,537	–	1,102	58,906
1976	9	Ford (R)	717,323	777,732	1,124	5,042	8,585	—	5,046
					CITIZENS			SOC. WORKERS	
1980	9	*Reagan (R)	650,193	865,244	9,403	29,213	—	1,137	—
1984	9	*Reagan (R)	807,352	1,051,670	1,891	8,844	—	—	
					NEW ALLIANCE		WORKER'S WORLD		
1988	9	Dukakis (D)	933,516	903,835	3,520	17,240	1,440	1,290	—
					IND. (PEROT)		TAXPAYERS	NATURAL LAW	POPULIST
1992	11	*Clinton (D)	993,037	731,234	541,780	7,533	2,354	2,456	4,854
					IND. (NADER)				
1996	11	*Clinton (D)	1,123,323	840,712	201,003	12,522	60,322	—	

* Won US presidential election.

elected in 1992. Following the 1996 elections, four of Washington's nine US Representatives were Democrats. A stunning Republican victory in the 1994 mid-term elections saw, for the first time since 1860, a sitting Speaker of the US House of Representatives, Thomas S. Foley, lose his seat in the House. The winner was a little-known Republican, George Nethercutt, who called for change and received support from conservative national talk show hosts and former Presidential candidate Ross Perot. There were 26 Republicans and 20 Democrats serving in the state senate, and 56 Republicans and 42 Democrats in the state house. The rise of the Democratic Party after World War II was linked to the careers of two US senators—Henry Jackson, who held his seat from 1953 until his death in 1983, and Warren Magnuson, defeated in 1980 after serving since 1945. Democratic incumbent Bill Clinton won 50% of the vote in the 1996 presidential election; Republican Bob Dole received 37%, and Independent Ross Perot received 9%.

In 1994, there were 19 blacks and 14 Hispanics holding public office. As of 1997, 56 women served in the state legislature, the most women legislators in any state; in 1995, 4 women held elective executive office in Washington.

14LOCAL GOVERNMENT

As of 1992, Washington had 39 counties, 268 municipal governments, 296 school districts, and 1,157 special districts, including public utility, library, port, water, hospital, cemetery, and sewer districts.

Counties may establish their own institutions of government by charter; otherwise, the chief governing body is an elected board of three commissioners. Other elected officials generally include the sheriff, prosecuting attorney, coroner, auditor, treasurer, and clerk. Cities and towns are governed under the mayor-council or council-manager systems. Larger cities, Seattle among them, generally have their own charters and elected mayors.

15STATE SERVICES

The Public Disclosure Commission, consisting of five members appointed by the governor and confirmed by the senate, provides disclosure of financial data in connection with political campaigns, lobbyists' activities, and the holdings of elected officials and candidates for public office. Each house of the legislature has its own board of ethics.

Public education in Washington is governed by a Board of Education and superintendent of public instruction; the Council for Postsecondary Education coordinates the state's higher educational institutions. The Department of Transportation oversees the construction and maintenance of highways, bridges, and ferries and assists locally owned airports.

The Department of Social and Health Services, the main human resources agency, oversees programs for adult corrections, juvenile rehabilitation, public and mental health, Medicaid, nursing homes, income maintenance, and vocational rehabilitation. Also involved in human resources activities are the Human Rights Commission, Department of Labor and Industries, Employment Security Department, Department of Veterans Affairs, and Council on Child Abuse and Neglect. Public protection services are provided by the Washington State Patrol, the Department of Emergency Services (civil defense), and the Military Department (Army and Air National Guard).

16JUDICIAL SYSTEM

The state's highest court, the supreme court, consists of 9 justices serving six-year terms; 3 justices are elected by nonpartisan ballot in each even-numbered year. The chief justice is elected to a four-year term by members of the court. The courts' senior judge holds the title of associate chief justice. Appeals of superior court decisions are usually heard in the court of appeals, whose 20 judges are elected to staggered six-year terms. The superior courts, consisting in 1997 of 163 judges elected to four-year terms in 30 judicial districts, are the state's felony trial courts. There are 213 judges in the 176 district and municipal courts; they hear traffic and misdemeanor matters. An estimated 19,472 attorneys practiced in the state in 1996.

Prisoners in state or federal correctional facilities numbered 11,751 in 1996. In 1995, Washington's crime index total was 6,269.8 per 100,000 inhabitants, including a rate of 484.3 for violent crime, and 5,785.5 for property crime. Washington imposes the death penalty and as of 1995 had 9 persons under sentence of death.

17ARMED FORCES

In 1996, there were 36,429 active duty military personnel stationed in Washington, nearly half of whom were at Fort Lewis near Tacoma. Other chief facilities in Washington include a Trident nuclear submarine base at Bangor, Whidbey Island Naval Air Station, McChord Air Force Base (Tacoma), and Fairchild Air Force Base (Airway Heights). In 1995/96, federal defense contract awards exceeded $2.3 billion, less than half the amount received during 1983/84. Veterans living in Washington as of 1 July 1996 numbered 625,000, of whom fewer than 500 saw service during World War I, 147,000 during World War II, 103,000 in the Korean conflict, 232,000 during the Vietnam era, and 37,000 in the Persian Gulf War. During 1995/96, veterans' benefits totaled $907 million. In 1996, Reserve and National Guard units had 36,532 personnel. In 1993, the Washington State Patrol employed 995 full-time sworn officers, or 2 per 10,000 residents.

18MIGRATION

The first overseas immigrants to reach Washington were Chinese laborers, imported during the 1860s; Chinese continued to arrive into the 1880s, when mob attacks on Chinese homes forced the territorial government to put Seattle under martial law and call in federal troops to restore order. The 1870s and 1880s brought an influx of immigrants from western Europe—especially Germany, Scandinavia, and the Netherlands—and from Russia and Japan.

In recent decades, Washington has benefited from a second migratory wave even more massive than the first. From 1970 to 1980, the state ranked 7th among the states in net migration with a gain of 719,000. From 1985 to 1990, the net migration gain was 317,832 (6th among the states). Many of those new residents were drawn from other states by Washington's defense- and trade-related industries. In addition, many immigrants from Southeast Asia arrived during the late 1970s. Between 1990 and 1996, Washington had net gains of 316,218 in domestic migration and 87,040 in international migration. In 1996, the foreign-born population totaled 386,000, or 7% of the state's total population. In the same year, 18,833 immigrants from foreign countries entered Washington, the 10th-highest total of any state for that year. As of 1994, the number of undocumented immigrants was estimated at 45. As of 1990, 48.2% of state residents had been born in Washington, and 46% of all residents age 5 and older lived in the same house as in 1985. Of those who lived in a different house in 1985 (from 1990), 27% did so in another state. Urban residents amounted to 76.4% of the population in 1990, up from 73.6% in 1980.

19INTERGOVERNMENTAL COOPERATION

Washington participates in the Columbia River Compact (with Oregon), Pacific Marine Fisheries Compact, Western Corrections Compact, Western Interstate Energy Compact, Western Regional Education Compact, Interstate Compact for the Supervision of Parolees and Probationers, Agreement on Qualification of Educational Personnel, Interstate Compact on Placement of Children, Multistate Tax Compact, and Driver License Compact, among other interstate bodies.

Federal aid in 1995/96 totaled over $4.2 billion.

20ECONOMY

The mainstays of Washington's economy are wholesale and retail trade, manufacturing (especially aerospace equipment, shipbuilding, food processing, and wood products), agriculture, lumbering, and tourism. Between 1971 and 1984, employment increased in such sectors as lumber and wood products, metals and machinery, food processing, trade, services, and government, while decreasing in aerospace—which remains, nevertheless, the state's single leading industry. Foreign trade, especially with Canada and Japan, was an important growth sector during the 1970s and early 1980s. The eruption of Mt. St. Helens in 1980 had an immediate negative impact on the forestry industry—already clouded by a slowdown in housing construction—crop growing, and the tourist trade. Washington's unemployment rate hovered around 6.2% in the late 1980s and early 1990s, with a brief improvement in 1990, when it dropped to 4.9%.

In 1994, the gross state product was $143.9 billion; private goods-producing industries contributed $31.7 billion; private services-producing industries, $90.5 billion; and government, $21.7 billion. During 1996, there were 28,630 bankruptcy filings, up 35% from 1995.

Leading manufacturers are the Boeing Aerospace Co. and Microsoft, Inc.

21INCOME

With a personal income per capita of $25,838 in 1996, Washington ranked 15th among the 50 states. Total personal disposable income was $120.3 billion in 1996, up from $113.6 billion in 1995. Median household income in 1995 was $35,568.

During 1995, 12.5% of all state residents were listed below the federal poverty level.

22LABOR

In 1996, Washington's civilian labor force averaged 2,887,000, of whom 2,699,000 were employed and 188,000 unemployed, yielding an overall unemployment rate of 6.5%. Of those actually employed in 1995, 55% were males and 45% were females. The Department of Labor and Industries administers laws pertaining to conditions of work; its concerns include industrial safety, health, and insurance, as well as employment standards.

Total nonfarm employment averaged 2,411,900 for 1996. Of that total, mining accounted for 3,400; construction, 127,200; manufacturing, 344,100 (durable goods employment alone averaged 234,700); transportation and public utilities, 122,900; wholesale trade, 145,100; retail trade, 445,800; finance, insurance, and real estate, 123,800; services, 649,200; and government, 450,400.

Although state and federal authorities suppressed radical labor activities in the mines around the turn of the century, in the logging camps during World War I, and in Seattle in 1919, the impulse to unionize remained strong in Washington. The state's labor force is still one of the most organized in the US, although (in line with national trends) the unions' share of the nonfarm work force declined from 45% in 1970 to 34% in 1980. In 1995, 477,100 workers belonged in a union, or 21% of the workforce (4th in the US). Unionization among manufacturing workers was 29.3% (3d). In December 1996, Washington workers in the manufacturing sector earned an average of $608.53 weekly.

23AGRICULTURE

Orchard and field crops dominate Washington's agricultural economy, which yielded $5.8 billion in farm marketings in 1995,

12th among the 50 states. Fruits and vegetables are raised in the humid and in the irrigated areas of the state, while wheat and other grains grow in the drier central and eastern regions.

Washington is the nation's leading producer of apples. The estimated 1995 crop, representing 47% of the US total, totaled 2.5 million tons. Among leading varieties, delicious apples ranked 1st, followed by golden delicious and winesap. The state also ranked 1st in production of hops, red raspberries, pears, and cherries; and 2d in grapes and apricots. Other preliminary crop figures for 1995 included wheat, 153.7 million bushels, valued at $733 million; potatoes, 80.8 million hundredweight (3,665 million kg), $553.8 million; barley, 20.8 million bushels, $59.5 million; and corn for grain, 19.3 million bushels, $64.9 million. Sugar beets, peaches, and various seed crops are also grown in Washington.

24ANIMAL HUSBANDRY

In 1997, Washington's farms and ranches had 1.2 million cattle and calves, valued at $756 million. During 1996, the state had approximately 35,000 hogs and pigs, valued at $3.85 million. The state produced 4.9 million lb (2.2 million kg) of sheep and lambs, which brought in $2.93 million in gross income in 1995.

Washington dairy farmers had 266,000 milk cows that produced 5.3 billion lb (2.4 billion kg) of milk in 1995. Poultry farmers sold 18.4 million lb (8.3 million kg) of chicken for nearly $1.9 million, and produced 197.5 million lb (89.5 million kg) of broilers, valued at $68 million in 1995; that same year, 1.455 billion eggs were produced, valued at $93 million.

25FISHING

In 1995, Washington's production of food fish reached 343 million lb (156 million kg), valued at $115.4 million. The record catch was 527.8 million lb (239.4 million kg) in 1994. Oyster landings in 1995 amounted to over 4.9 million lb (2.2 million kg), 76% of the Pacific region's total. The shellfish catch in 1995 also included 21.3 million lb (9.7 million kg) of crab and 8.6 million lb (3.9 million kg) of shrimp. Most production of farm-raised oysters occurs in Washington, although there are some smaller operations in the other Pacific coastal states. Salmon landing were 24.4 million lb (11.1 million kg), valued at $9.5 million, of which pink salmon accounted for 42%; chum, 28%; silver, 12%; sockeye, 9%; and chinook, 9%. Washington had 4,055 commercial fishing vessels in 1994. The leading fishing ports, by value of landings in 1995, were Westport, $25 million; Bellingham, $15 million; Anacortes-LaConner, $11 million; and Seattle, $10 million. In 1994, on average, over 4,000 workers were employed in the state's 115 fish processing plants, and 473 were engaged in 122 wholesale plants.

In 1995/96, federal hatcheries distributed over 37.1 million fish in Washington's streams and lakes. Planted species included mainly salmon and trout. In 19995/96, Washington issued 820,940 fishing licenses and received over $4.1 million in federal funds for sport-fish restoration programs.

26FORESTRY

Washington's forests, covering 20,483,000 acres (8,289,000 hectares), are an important commercial and recreational resource. Some 16,238,000 acres (6,572,000 hectares) are classified as commercial forestland. The largest federal forests are Wenatchee, Mt. Baker–Snoqualmie, and Okanogan.

Forest production is Washington's second-largest manufacturing industry. In 1995, the industry employed more than 56,400 people, generated $12.7 billion in revenue, and paid $57 million in state taxes. Lumber and wood products continue to be the larger of the two forest products sectors, employing 35,400 people, creating $8.7 billion in revenue, and paying $39 million in state taxes. The value of shipments for the lumber and wood products industry in 1995 was nearly $7.4 billion, and the paper industry's shipments were valued at almost $6.1 billion. Together, these two industries contributed 19.5% to the state's total value of manufactured shipments in 1995.

Restrictions on federal timberlands to protect the Northern spotted owl, which became effective in late 1990, reflect diverse public demands on forest values. The regulations impact Washington's forest industry and forest-based employment due to the sharp decline of federal timber supply. However, this scarcity of timber created by forest preservation practices will enhance the value of the state's timber resource. This will spur the trend toward more efficient wood use and higher value-added products.

Public ownership accounts for about 60% of Washington's forest, with the remaining 40% owned by the forest industry and other private owners. Lumber and plywood, logs for export, various chip products, pulp logs, and shakes and shingles are leading forest commodities. The largest forest industry company is Weyerhauser, with headquarters in Tacoma.

Federal, state, and private nurseries in Washington planted more than 148,000 acres (59,892 hectares) in fiscal year 1996. Since 1975, more acres have been planted or seeded than have been cut down. Washington's forest-fire control program covers some 12.5 million acres (5.1 million hectares). In 1995 there were 886 fires that burned 4,035 acres (1,633 hectares). Leading causes of forest fires in lands under the jurisdiction of the Department of Natural Resources are (in order of frequency) burning debris, lightning, recreation, children, smokers, incendiary logging, and railroad operations.

27MINING

The estimated value of nonfuel mineral production for Washington in 1995 was $613 million, a 7% increase from that of 1994. Increases in the production values of magnesium metal (25%) and crushed stone (35%) more than offset the drop estimated for portland cement, gold, and construction sand and gravel. Washington ranked 20th nationally in nonfuel mineral production value in 1995, unchanged since 1992. In 1995, crushed stone production was 20.6 million metric tons, valued at $118 million. That same year, construction sand and gravel quarried amounted to 38 million metric tons, valued at $162 million, and 242,000 metric tons of clays were worth $1.07 million. Industrial minerals accounted for 60% of the state's total nonfuel mineral production value. Washington ranked 2d in magnesium metal in 1995, 5th in construction sand and gravel, 6th in gold, and 10th in silver. In 1995, the state's seven aluminum smelters produced a total of 986,000 metric tons of aluminum ingot, from imported ores, 30% of the national total.

28ENERGY AND POWER

End-use energy consumption in the state totaled 1,289 trillion Btu (325 trillion kcal) in 1994, of which 14.4% went to residential customers, 10.2% to commercial users, 28.6% to industrial users, and 46.8% for transportation. Transportation's share of the energy consumed has increased steadily, owing to large increases in the number of people, cars, and miles driven per vehicle; declines in the real cost of fuel; and major increases in airplane travel. Transportation consumption is derived almost exclusively from petroleum, which is the major energy source in the state.

Washington has no indigenous sources of petroleum or natural gas, but it does have the largest hydroelectric generation base of any state in the nation, with a net generation capability of 24.26 million kW in 1995. Electric plants in Washington generated 95,671 million kWh in 1995, 85.7% of that from hydroelectric facilities, which are largely publicly owned and operated. Almost all of the 4,868 short tons (4,416 metric tons) of coal mined in

the state in 1995 were burned to generate electricity. Washington's petroleum refinery capacity is the 5th-largest in the nation. The state has also been a pioneer in pursuing efficiency as a source of new energy. Significant savings have been captured since 1983.

Washington is one of the beneficiaries of the hydropower system owned by various federal entities and marketed by Bonneville Power Administration. While this results in both low power costs and the lowest power-related air emissions per capita of any state, there are associated responsibilities to ensure protection and preservation of fish.

29INDUSTRY

The 1980s were Washington's busiest years in terms of technology company start-ups. The build-up began in the 1970s and peaked in the middle of the following decade. Software and computer-related businesses accounted for most of the activity but more traditional manufacturing companies were also emerging. Even today, computers, software, and related activities make up the largest single portion in Washington technology companies. Manufacturing of all types is another strong element.

Washington technology companies cross borders and many are world leaders. Boeing's airplane sales make that company one of the nation's leading exporters. Microsoft has offices around the world and its products are in use on every continent. However, even small firms benefit from foreign trade and over half of Washington's technology companies are in overseas markets. Less than 12% deal only within the state, and more are reporting foreign sales each year.

Aerospace/transportation equipment is the largest industry in Washington state, employing more than 80,000 people.

Boeing's long-range commercial outlook remains optimistic despite a $4.1 billion net loss by the world's airline industry in 1993. The aerospace giant predicts demand for new passenger jets will grow by 5.2% over the next two decades. A total of more than 14,000 new jets worth $980 billion is envisioned requiring output of 700 planes per year.

Some 70% of the state's biotech firms have been founded since 1980, mostly still in the research and development stage. More than two-thirds are developing products for human health care. Most of the firms not focused on medical treatment are developing products and processes for the state's natural resource sectors: agriculture, food processing, forestry, veterinary medicine, marine industries, and environmental waste clean-up and management.

Washington state is one of the top 15 film-production states in the US. Film and video have grown to represent at least a $100-million-a-year industry. Washington state has approximately 1,500 film and video businesses which provide jobs for about 5,000 state residents. From 1983–93, at least $219 million was spent in Washington to make feature films, television movies, TV series or episodes, TV commercials, documentaries, industrial films and music videos. In 1993, out-of-state producers shot 145 film and video projects in Washington, contributing more than $40 million to the state's economy. In addition, $45 million is generated by in-state film and video companies for an estimated $80–100 million annual industry.

The total value of shipments for manufactured goods in 1995 was $69 billion. The value of shipments for selected industries that year was: transportation equipment, $21,156.7 million; food and food products, $8,827.1 million; lumber and wood products, $7,366.8 million; paper and paper products, $6,098.6 million; petroleum and coal products, $4,307.1 million; primary metal industries, $3,355.1 million; and industrial machinery and equipment, $3,052.9 million.

In 1997, Washington was the headquarters for eight Fortune 500 companies: Boeing, Costco, Weyerhauser, Microsoft, Paccar, Nordstrom, Safeco, and Washington Mutual.

During 1995, 1,231 US patents were issued to Washington residents.

30COMMERCE

Wholesalers in 1992 had sales of $62.5 billion, including $31.3 billion in durable goods. Total retail sales in 1992 reached $40.9 billion (15th among all the states), of which food stores accounted for 20%; automotive dealers, 19.8%; and general merchandise stores, 13.3%. The Seattle-Tacoma-Bremerton area had retail sales of $26.4 billion in 1992, or 64.5% of the state's total.

In 1996, exports of goods originating from the state had a value of $26.5 billion, 5th in the US. Exporters in the state shipped goods valued at $25.5 billion in 1996. The Seattle-Bellevue-Everett metropolitan area handled exports valued at $21.7 billion in 1994. The leading exports were aircraft and aircraft parts (accounting for more than one-half of the total), machinery, lumber and logs, fish and fish products, grains, motor vehicles and parts, fruits and vegetables, wood pulp, and paper products. Principal imports included crude petroleum, lumber, natural gas, passenger cars, truck chassis and bodies, newsprint, aluminum oxide, motorcycles, radios, and television sets.

31CONSUMER PROTECTION

The Office of the Attorney General, which enforces the state's 1961 Consumer Protection Act, investigates consumer complaints and, when necessary, seeks court action in connection with retail sales abuses, unfair automobile sales techniques, false advertising, and other fraudulent or deceptive practices. In 1996, the consumer protection division handled 272,944 telephone inquiries and 21,757 written complaints, and recovered close to $5.5 million for consumers.

Responsibilities of the Department of Agriculture include food inspection and labeling, sanitary food handling and storage, and accurate weights and measures.

32BANKING

As of 31 December 1996, Washington had 61 insured state-chartered commercial banks. In 1996, there were 14 state-chartered savings institutions. Washington also had 5 state-chartered foreign banking offices and 8 trust companies. Total assets under regulation for state-chartered institutions aggregated $47.8 billion.

33INSURANCE

Washingtonians held 3.4 million life insurance policies with a total face value of $213.6 billion in 1995, when the average life insurance coverage per family was $100,100. Benefits paid by life insurance companies in 1995 totaled $3,527 million, including $500.2 million in death payments, $1,179 million in annuities, and $273.7 million in policy dividends. During the same year, property and liability companies wrote premiums totaling more than $4.7 billion, of which $777.9 million was automobile physical damage insurance, $1.7 billion was automotive passenger liability insurance, and $511.4 million was homeowners coverage. Flood insurance valued at $1,516 million was in force in 1995.

The Office of the Insurance Commissioner and State Fire Marshal regulates insurance company operations, reviews insurance policies and rates, and examines and licenses agents and brokers. It also conducts fire safety inspections in hospitals, nursing homes, and other facilities, investigates fires of suspicious origin, and regulates the manufacture, sale, and public display of fireworks.

34SECURITIES

The Spokane Stock Exchange (founded 1897), specializing in mining stocks, is no longer operating. As of December 1996, 1,686 broker-dealers and 64,472 agents were registered to conduct business in the state. Professional securities investment advice was available from 941 registered firms and 8,142 representatives in 1996.

35PUBLIC FINANCE

Washington's biennial budget is prepared by the Office of Financial Management and submitted by the governor to the legislature for amendment and approval. The fiscal year runs from 1 July through 30 June.

The following table shows estimated revenues and expenditures for 1995/96 (in thousands):

REVENUES	
Retail sales and use taxes	$ 4,471,074
Business and occupation taxes	1,654,502
Property taxes	1,107,303
Excise taxes	836,448
Motor vehicle and fuel taxes	676,717
Other taxes	1,077,665
Licenses, permits, and fees	477,637
Timber sales	169,961
Other contracts and grants	438,088
Federal grants-in-aid	4,566,501
Charges for services	654,637
Unemployment compensation contributions	602,631
Interest income	286,655
Miscellaneous revenue	417,981
TOTAL REVENUES	$ 17,437,800

EXPENDITURES	
Current:	
General government	$ 1,025,772
Human services	7,093,752
Natural resources and recreation	498,159
Transportation	861,378
Education	6,921,873
Capital outlays	975,260
Debt service:	
Principal	306,912
Interest	299,866
TOTAL EXPENDITURES	$ 17,982,972

State government units in Washington had a public debt (general long-term obligations) in 1996 of $6.8 billion; the per capita debt was $1,234.

36TAXATION

Taxes, licenses, permits, and fees account for about three-quarters of Washington state government revenues. In 1992, the state tax burden per capita was $2,326, 12th among the 50 states.

Washington has no individual or corporate income tax. As of 1 July 1996, the state levied a general sales tax of 6.5%; a gasoline tax of 23 cents per gallon; a cigarette tax of 82.5 cents a pack; a liquor excise tax of 13.1% on sales to restaurants and 19.7% on sales to individuals; an estate and transfer tax in the amount of credit allowed under federal estate tax; an insurance premium tax of 0.95% for ocean marine/trade insurers and 2% for all other insurers; a business and occupation tax on gross receipts with the most common rates being 0.4%, 0.506%, 1.829% and 2.0%; a motor vehicle excise tax of 2.2%; a 6.0% excise tax on the value of the timber harvest from private land and 5.0% on timber harvested from public lands; and taxes on public utilities and parimutuel income. The state property tax is dedicated to the public schools.

In 1995, Washington remitted more than $23 billion in income to the federal government, and received nearly $28.8 billion in federal funding.

37ECONOMIC POLICY

The Department of Trade and Economic Development seeks to promote a healthy state economy and to expand markets for Washington's products. The state has no corporate or personal income tax and no tax on interest, dividends or capital gains. The department offers a tax credit program for companies which expand or locate in high unemployment areas and issues industrial development bonds with federal tax-exempt status for new capital construction. It extends loans to projects in distressed and timber-dependent areas and offers low interest loans to small and medium-sized Washington State forest products companies. The state helps communities finance infrastructure improvements to retain existing businesses or to attract new companies and provides special services for small and minority-owned enterprises. In an effort to encourage international trade, Washington created nine foreign trade zones.

38HEALTH

The birthrate in 1995 was 14.2 per 1,000 population, slightly below the US average; the infant mortality rate in 1995 was 4.7 per 1,000 live births, substantially below the national norm. There were 27,573 abortions performed in 1992, or 347 for every 1,000 live births. The death rate, 760.8 per 100,000 population, was below the national average in 1996, and the rates for heart disease and cancer were lower than average. The AIDS rate per 100,000 was 41%; below the national average; only 93 cases were reported in 1994.

Leading causes of death in 1995 were heart disease (208.6 deaths per 100,000), cancer (183 deaths per 100,000 population), accidents and adverse effects (34.9 deaths per 100,000), and suicide (14.4 deaths per 100,000).

As of 1995 there were 88 general hospitals, with 10,399 beds. The average cost per day in community hospitals during 1994 was $1,206, with average hospital expenses of $5,909 per stay. In fiscal 1994, 668,000 Medicaid recipients and 671,000 Medicare enrollees accepted $1.6 billion and $2.3 billion in benefits, respectively. The per capita personal health expenditure was slightly lower than the US average of $2,648 (1991). At least 12.7% of Washington residents were uninsured in 1994.

Licensed health professionals as of 1995 included 44,300 registered nurses. In 1995 there were 14,609 active, nonfederal physicians; in 1995, there were 3,279 active, licensed dentists.

39SOCIAL WELFARE

Most of the state and federal funds for income maintenance go to Aid to Families with Dependent Children (AFDC) and Supplemental Security Income (SSI) programs. In 1996, 276,000 persons received AFDC payments, averaging $642 a month per family. Social Security benefits in 1995 were paid to 793,150 residents, averaging $748 a month. Additionally, Supplemental Security Income payments averaging $372 were made to 91,654 residents. In 1996, 476,391 residents received monthly food stamp allowances averaging $74.50. The school lunch program received total funding of $85.3 million. The average weekly unemployment benefit payment was $204.53 per week in 1995.

With the enactment of the Personal Responsibility and Work Opportunity Reconciliation Act of 1996, the US government has changed the form and regulations for many of its social welfare programs; most significantly, it replaces Aid to Families with Dependent Children (AFDC), an open-ended entitlement program, with Temporary Assistance for Needy Families (TANF), a limited system of assistance funded largely through federal block grants. The reform act also impacts the food stamp program, the Supplemental Security Income program, and the child nutrition program. The law took effect on 1 July 1997 and provided $16.38 billion in block grants for fiscal years 1997–2002. The grants are to be divided among the states based on an equation involving the numbers of former AFDC recipients in each state. Because many of the bill's provisions have yet to be implemented into state-by-state policy, it was not possible to include the details of each state's programs for this edition of this work.

40HOUSING

In 1996, there were an estimated 2,250,000 housing units in Washington, 2,084,000 of which were occupied. That year 39,597 privately owned units, valued at $3.8 billion, were authorized for construction; of these, 27,015 were single-family. In 1990, 58% of the units were owner-occupied, and more than 99% had full plumbing. About 23% of all housing units in Washington were built in the 1980s. In 1990, the last year for which figures are available, the median monthly cost for an owner-occupied housing unit was $738; median rent was $445. According to the 1990 census, Seattle had 249,032 units, of which 11.9% were built since 1980. From 1990 to 1992, the Seattle-Tacoma area saw 68,300 new housing unit completions, of which 54% were single-family houses. The median value of a one-family house in the state was $93,400, down 1.8% from 1980 (in terms of 1990 dollars). During 1995/96, Washington received $315.5 million in aid from the US Department of Housing and Urban Development, including $54.2 million in community development block grants.

41EDUCATION

Washingtonians rank exceptionally high by most educational standards. As of 1990, more than 87% of all Washingtonians 25 years of age or older were high school graduates, and 24% had four or more years of college. Washington ranked 3rd among the 50 states in state aid for education with an average expenditure of $1,313 per capita in 1993–94. It placed 4th among the states in the number of public school pupils (20.5) per teacher as of the fall 1995 enrollment. The state was 19th in average yearly salaries for public school teachers in 1994–95. Current expenditures for public schools in 1995–96 were $5,708 per pupil (21st).

As of 1995–96, there were an estimated 951,696 pupils enrolled in public kindergartens, elementary schools, and high schools. Enrollment in private schools was 70,205 in 1993–94.

As of 1995–96, Washington had 32 colleges and universities (8 public, 24 private) and 32 community colleges. The largest institutions are the University of Washington (Seattle), founded in 1861 and enrolling 33,719 students in 1994, and Washington State University (Pullman) with 19,314 students. Other public institutions, and their 1993 enrollments, include the following: Eastern Washington University (Cheney), 8,431; Central Washington University (Ellensburg), 8,423; Western Washington University (Bellingham), 10,302; and Evergreen State College (Olympia), 3,433. Private institutions include Gonzaga University (Spokane), with 4,642 students in 1992; Pacific Lutheran University (Tacoma), 3,451 students; Seattle University, 4,844; Seattle Pacific College, 3,351; University of Puget Sound (Tacoma), 4,048; Walla Walla College, 1,734; and Whitworth College (Spokane), 1,735. Community colleges enrolled 159,249 students in 1994–95. Total enrollment in public and private institutions of higher education in 1994–95 was 244,722 and 60,984, respectively.

42ARTS

The focus of professional performance activities in Washington is Seattle Center, home of the Seattle Symphony, Pacific Northwest Ballet Company, and Seattle Repertory Theater. The Seattle

Opera Association (founded 1964), which also performs there throughout the year, is one of the nation's leading opera companies, offering five operas each season and presenting Richard Wagner's "Ring" cycle at the Pacific Northwest Festival in July. Tacoma and Spokane have notable local orchestras.

Among Washington's many museums, universities, and other organizations exhibiting works of art on a permanent or periodic basis are the Seattle Art Museum, with its Modern Art Pavilion, and the Henry Art Gallery of the University of Washington at Seattle. Others include the Washington State University Museum of Art at Pullman; the Whatcom Museum of History and Art (Bellingham); the Tacoma Art Museum; the State Capitol Museum (Olympia); and the Cheney Cowles Memorial Museum of the Eastern Washington State Historical Society (Spokane). The State Arts Commission, established in 1961, supports nonprofit arts groups as well as professional arts organizations and an artists-in-schools program.

The state of Washington received for its arts programs federal funds totaling $812,000 in 1996. The NEA also gave $1,972,000 to the state's arts programs, and $2,360,000 to the Washington State Arts Commission. Contributions to the arts also came from state and private sources. The state's arts programs attracted audiences totaling 34,407,210 people. There were 63,602 contributing artists. The state provided arts education programs for 2,158,840 school children. In 1996, the state of Washington had 230 arts associations and 74 local arts groups. The Washington State Arts Commission contributed funds to support the Latin American Folk Art Exhibit and the Seattle Repertory Company. The NEA has contributed to the Otherworld Media radio organization and to the Tears of Joy Theatre, which sponsors the International Children's Festival. In 1992, the Washington State Arts Commission received funding from the NEA to support the state's arts education programs. The NEA also gave the Arts Commission grants from the state and regional programs.

43LIBRARIES AND MUSEUMS

In 1995, Washington's system of public libraries held more than 17,313,390 volumes and had a combined circulation of nearly 52.2 million. Of Washington's 39 counties, 29 were served by the state's 19 county and multicounty libraries. Total library income in 1995 came to $161,417,045, most of that total derived from public funds.

The leading public library system is the Seattle Public Library, with 22 branches and 2,007,421 volumes in 1995. The principal academic libraries are at the University of Washington (Seattle) and Washington State University (Pullman), with 8,547,391 and 3,250,286 volumes, respectively. Olympia is the home of the Washington State Library, with a collection of 758,088 books and more than 1 million documents.

Washington has 153 museums and historic sites. The Washington State Historical Society Museum (Tacoma) features Native American and other pioneer artifacts; the State Capitol Museum (Olympia) and Cheney Cowles Memorial Museum (Spokane) also have important historical exhibits, as do the Thomas Burke Memorial Washington State Museum (Seattle) and the Pacific Northwest Indian Center (Spokane). Mt. Rainier National Park displays zoological, botanical, geological, and historical collections. The Pacific Science Center (Seattle) concentrates on aerospace technology; the Seattle Aquarium is a leading attraction of Waterfront Park. Also in Seattle is Woodland Park Zoological Gardens, while Tacoma has the Point Defiance Zoo and Aquarium.

44COMMUNICATIONS

As of March 1993, 97.3% of Washington's 2,060,000 households had telephones. During 1996, Washington had 227 radio stations (186 commercial)—98 AM, 129 FM—and 27 commercial and 6 educational television stations (including 7 commercial stations and 1 public station located in Seattle), while 13 large cable systems served the state.

45PRESS

In 1997, Washington had 11 morning newspapers (including all-day papers), 12 evening dailies, and 16 Sunday papers. The following table shows the leading newspapers with their 1997 circulations:

AREA	NAME	DAILY	SUNDAY
Seattle	*Post-Intelligencer* (m,S)	202,156	506,216*
	Times (e,S)	235,963	506,216*
Spokane	*Spokesman–Review* (m,S)	118,770	147,328
Tacoma	*News Tribune Ledger* (e,S)	129,382	148,396

*Sunday edition is a combination of *Post-Intelligencer* and *Times*.

46ORGANIZATIONS

The 1992 Census of Service Industries counted 1,727 organizations in Washington, including 326 business associations; 1,068 civic, social, and fraternal associations; and 333 other membership organizations.

Among the associations with headquarters in Washington are the American Plywood Association and the American Academy on Mental Retardation (Tacoma); the Center for the Defense of Free Enterprise and the Citizens Committee for the Right to Keep and Bear Arms (Bellevue); the Pacific International Trapshooting Association (Puyallup); the Northwest Mining Association (Spokane); and the Northwest Fisheries Association, the International Association for the Study of Pain, the International Conference of Symphony and Opera Musicians, and the Mountaineers, all located in Seattle.

47TOURISM, TRAVEL, AND RECREATION

Seattle Center—featuring the 605-foot (184-meter) Space Needle tower, Opera House, and Pacific Science Center—helps make Washington's largest city one of the most exciting on the West Coast. Nevertheless, scenic beauty and opportunities for outdoor recreation are Washington's principal attractions for tourists from out of the state.

Mt. Rainier National Park, covering 235,404 acres (95,265 hectares), encompasses not only the state's highest peak but also the most extensive glacial system in the conterminous US. Glaciers, lakes, and mountain peaks are also featured at North Cascades National Park (504,780 acres—204,278 hectares), while Olympic National Park (908,720 acres—367,747 hectares) is famous as the site of Mt. Olympus and for its dense rain forest and rare elk herds. Washington also offers two national historic parks (San Juan Island and part of Klondike Gold Rush), two national historic sites (Fort Vancouver and the Whitman Mission), and three national recreation areas (Coulee Dam, Lake Chelan, and Ross Lake). State parks, including the popular Deception Pass, received 47,186,082 visitors in 1995.

Hunting is a highly popular pastime. Licenses were held by 777,807 hunters and 1,008,889 fishers in 1995.

Tourism is the 4th largest industry in Washington state, after aerospace/transportation equipment, agriculture, and timber. Domestic travelers spent $5.3 million in 1993 on overnight and day trips in Washington. Washington has been consistently ranked among the nation's top 10 tourist destination states.

Part of the state's strategy currently under development focuses on regional appeal and off-season activities. Areas such as the Yakima Valley, the Columbia River Gorge, the Olympic Peninsula and the Methow Valley were rural, undervisited tourist markets that have been able to draw travelers by promoting the region as opposed to a city within the region. High seasonality was one of the biggest problems facing Washington State. Spring, fall, and winter traditionally have not drawn as many tourists as the summer.

48SPORTS

Washington is home to three major league professional sports teams, all of which play in Seattle. The Mariners, of major league baseball; the Seahawks, of the National Football League; and the Supersonics, of the National Basketball Association. The Supersonics won the NBA Championship in 1979. The Mariners reached the American League Championship Series in 1995. In collegiate sports, the Huskies of the University of Washington won the Rose Bowl in 1960, 1961, 1978, 1982, and 1992. Skiing, boating, and hiking are popular participant sports.

Other annual sporting events include outboard hydroplane races in Electric City in June, and the Ellensburg Rodeo in September.

49FAMOUS WASHINGTONIANS

Washington's most distinguished public figure was US Supreme Court Justice William O. Douglas (b.Minnesota, 1898–1980), who grew up in Yakima and attended Whitman College in Walla Walla. In addition to his 37-year tenure on the Court, an all-time high, Douglas was the author of numerous legal casebooks as well as 27 other volumes on various subjects. Other federal officeholders from Washington include Lewis B. Schwellenbach (b.Wisconsin, 1894–1948), secretary of labor under Harry Truman, and Brockman Adams (b.Georgia, 1927), secretary of transportation under Jimmy Carter. Serving in the US Senate from 1945 to 1981, Warren G. Magnuson (b.Minnesota, 1905) held the chairmanship of the powerful Appropriations Committee. A fellow Democrat, Henry M. "Scoop" Jackson (1912–83) was first elected to the House in 1940 and to the Senate in 1952. Influential on the Armed Services Committee, Jackson ran unsuccessfully for his party's presidential nomination in 1976. William E. Boeing (b.Michigan, 1881–1956) pioneered Washington's largest single industry, aerospace technology.

Notable governors include Isaac I. Stevens (b.Massachusetts, 1818–62), Washington's first territorial governor; after serving as Washington's territorial representative to Congress, he died in the Civil War. Elisha P. Ferry (b.Michigan, 1825–95), territorial governor from 1872 to 1880, was elected as Washington's first state governor in 1889. John R. Rogers (b.Maine, 1838–1901), Washington's only Populist governor, was also the first to be elected for a second term. Clarence D. Martin (1886–1955) was governor during the critical New Deal period. Daniel J. Evans (b.1925) is the youngest man ever elected governor of Washington and also is the only one to have served three consecutive terms (1965–77).

Dixy Lee Ray (1914–93), governor from 1977 to 1981 and the only woman governor in the state's history, was a former head of the federal Atomic Energy Commission and a staunch advocate of nuclear power. Other notable women were Emma Smith DeVoe (b.New Jersey, 1848–1927), a leading proponent of equal suffrage, and Bertha Knight Landes (b.Massachusetts, 1868–1943), elected mayor of Seattle in 1926; Landes, the first woman to be elected mayor of a large US city, was also an outspoken advocate of moral reform in municipal government.

Thomas Stephen Foley, former Speaker of the House, was born on 6 March 1929 in Spokane.

Several Washington Indians attained national prominence. Seattle (1786–1866) was the first signer of the Treaty of Point Elliott, which established two Indian reservations; the city of Seattle is named for him. Kamiakin (b.Idaho, c.1800–80) was the leader of the Yakima tribe during the Indian Wars of 1855, and Leschi (d.1858) was chief of the Nisqualli Indians and commanded the forces west of the Cascades during the 1855 uprising; Leschi was executed by the territorial government after the uprising was suppressed.

Washington authors have made substantial contributions to American literature. Mary McCarthy (1912-1989) was born in Seattle, and one of her books, *Memories of a Catholic Girlhood* (1957), describes her early life there. University of Washington professor Vernon Louis Parrington (b.Illinois, 1871-1929) was the first Washingtonian to win a Pulitzer Prize (1928), for his monumental *Main Currents in American Thought*. Another University of Washington faculty member, Theodore Roethke (b.Michigan, 1908–63), won the Pulitzer Prize for poetry in 1953. Seattle-born Audrey May Wurdemann (1911–60) was awarded a Pulitzer Prize for poetry in 1934 for *Bright Ambush*. Max Brand (Frederick Schiller Faust, 1892–1944) wrote hundreds of Western novels. Norman Ramsey (b. Washington, 1915) 1989 Nobel Prize recipient for physics. Hans Georg Dehmelt (b. Germany, 1922) was a recipient of the 1989 Nobel Prize for physics as a member at the University of Washington. George Herbert Hitchings, Nobel Prize winner in medicine 1988, was born April 18, 1905 in Hoquiam, Washington.

Singer-actor Harry Lillis "Bing" Crosby (1904–77), born in Tacoma, remained a loyal alumnus of Spokane's Gonzaga University. Modern dance choreographers Merce Cunningham (b.1919) and Robert Joffrey (1930–88) are both Washington natives. Photographer Edward S. Curtis (b.Wisconsin, 1868–1952) did most of the work on the North American Indian series while residing in Seattle. Modern artists Mark Tobey (b.Wisconsin, 1890–1976) spent much of his productive life in Seattle, and Robert Motherwell (1915–91) was born in Aberdeen. Washington's major contribution to popular music is rock guitarist Jimi Hendrix (1943–70).

50BIBLIOGRAPHY

Bancroft, H. H. *History of Washington, Idaho, and Montana*. San Francisco: History Co., 1890.

Blair, Karen J. *Northwest Women: An Annotated Bibliography of Sources on the History of Oregon and Washington Women, 1787–1970*. Pullman, Wash.: Washington State University Press, 1997.

Clark, Norman H. *Washington: A Bicentennial History*. New York: Norton, 1976.

Douglas, William O. *Of Men and Mountains*. New York: Harper & Row, 1950.

Drury, Clifford M. *Marcus and Narcissa Whitman and the Opening of Old Oregon*. 2 vols. Glendale, Calif.: Clark, 1973.

Ficken, Robert E. *Lumber and Politics: The Career of Mark E. Reed*. Seattle: University of Washington Press, 1980.

Johansen, Dorothy O., and Charles M. Gates. *Empire of the Columbia: A History of the Pacific Northwest*. 2d ed. New York: Harper & Row, 1967.

Kirk, Ruth. *Washington State: National Parks, Historic Sites, Recreation Areas, and Natural Landmarks*. Seattle: University of Washington Press, 1974.

Lee, W. Storrs, ed. *Washington State: A Literary Chronicle*. New York: Funk & Wagnalls, 1969.

Meany, Edmond S. *History of the State of Washington*. New York: Macmillan, 1909.

Meinig, D. W. *The Great Columbia Plain: A Historical Geography, 1805–1910*. Seattle: University of Washington Press, 1968.

Seeberger, Edward D. *Sine Die: A Guide to the Washington State Legislative Process*. Seattle, Wash.: Washington State University Press, 1997.

Snowden, Clinton A. *History of Washington*. 6 vols. New York: Century History, 1911.

Stewart, Edgar I. *Washington, Northwest Frontier*. 4 vols. New York: Lewis, 1957.

WEST VIRGINIA

State of West Virginia

ORIGIN OF STATE NAME: The state was originally the western part of Virginia. **NICKNAME:** The Mountain State. **CAPITAL:** Charleston. **ENTERED UNION:** 20 June 1863 (35th). **SONGS:** "The West Virginia Hills"; "West Virginia, My Home Sweet Home"; "This Is My West Virginia." **MOTTO:** *Montani semper liberi* (Mountaineers are always free). **COAT OF ARMS:** A farmer stands to the right and a miner to the left of a large ivy-draped rock bearing the date of the state's admission to the Union. In front of the rock are two hunters' rifles upon which rests a Cap of Liberty. The state motto is beneath and the words "State of West Virginia" above. **FLAG:** The flag has a white field bordered by a strip of blue, with the coat of arms in the center, wreathed by rhododendron leaves; across the top of the coat of arms are the words "State of West Virginia." **OFFICIAL SEAL:** The obverse is the same as the coat of arms; the reverse is no longer in common use. **ANIMAL:** Black bear. **BIRD:** Cardinal. **FISH:** Brook trout. **FLOWER:** *Rhododendron maximum* ("big laurel"). **TREE:** Sugar maple. **FRUIT:** Apple. **COLORS:** Old gold and blue. **LEGAL HOLIDAYS:** New Year's Day, 1 January; Birthday of Martin Luther King, Jr., 3d Monday in January; Lincoln's Birthday, 12 February; Washington's Birthday, 3d Monday in February; Memorial Day, last Monday in May; West Virginia Day, 20 June; Independence Day, 4 July; Labor Day, 1st Monday in September; Columbus Day, 2d Monday in October; Veterans Day, 11 November; Thanksgiving Day, 4th Thursday in November; Christmas Day, 25 December. **TIME:** 7 AM EST = noon GMT.

¹LOCATION, SIZE, AND EXTENT

Located in the eastern US, in the South Atlantic region, West Virginia ranks 41st in size among the 50 states.

The area of West Virginia totals 24,231 sq mi (62,758 sq km), including 24,119 sq mi (62,468 sq km) of land and 112 sq mi (290 sq km) of inland water. The state extends 265 mi (426 km) E-W; its maximum N-S extension is 237 mi (381 km). West Virginia is one of the most irregularly shaped states in the US, with two panhandles of land—the northern, narrower one separating parts of Ohio and Pennsylvania, and the eastern panhandle separating parts of Maryland and Virginia.

West Virginia is bordered on the N by Ohio (with the line formed by the Ohio River), Pennsylvania, and Maryland (with most of the line defined by the Potomac River); on the E and S by Virginia; and on the W by Kentucky and Ohio (with the line following the Ohio, Big Sandy, and Tug Fork rivers).

The total boundary length of West Virginia is 1,180 mi (1,899 km). The geographical center of the state is in the Elk River Public Hunting Area in Braxton County, 4 mi (6 km) E of Sutton.

²TOPOGRAPHY

West Virginia lies within two divisions of the Appalachian Highlands. Most of the eastern panhandle, which is crossed by the Allegheny Mountains, is in the Ridge and Valley region. The remainder, or more than two-thirds of the state, is part of the Allegheny Plateau, to the west of a bold escarpment known as the Allegheny Front, and tilts toward the Ohio River.

The mean elevation of West Virginia is 1,500 feet (457 meters), higher than any other state east of the Mississippi River. Its highest point, Spruce Knob, towers 4,863 feet (1,482 meters) above sea level. Major lowlands lie along the rivers, especially the Potomac, Ohio, and Kanawha. A point on the Potomac River near Harpers Ferry has the lowest elevation, only 240 feet (73 meters) above sea level. West Virginia has no natural lakes.

Most of the eastern panhandle drains into the Potomac River. The Ohio and its tributaries—the Monongahela, Little Kanawha, Kanawha, Guyandotte, and Big Sandy—drain most of the Allegheny Plateau section. Subterranean streams have carved out numerous caverns—including Seneca Caverns, Smoke Hole Caverns, and Organ Cave—from limestone beds.

During the Paleozoic era, when West Virginia was under water, a 30,000-foot (9,000-meter) layer of rock streaked with rich coal deposits was laid down over much of the state. Alternately worn down and uplifted during succeeding eras, most of West Virginia is thus a plateau where rivers have carved deep valleys and gorges and given the land a rugged character.

³CLIMATE

West Virginia has a humid continental climate, with hot summers and cool to cold winters. The climate of the eastern panhandle is influenced by its proximity to the Atlantic slope and is similar to that of nearby coastal areas. Mean annual temperatures vary from 56°F (13°C) in the southwest to 48°F (9°C) at higher elevations. The yearly average is 53°F (12°C). The highest recorded temperature, 112°F (44°C), was at Martinsburg on 10 July 1936; the lowest, –37°F (–38°C), at Lewisburg on 30 December 1917.

Prevailing winds are from the south and west, and seldom reach hurricane or tornado force. Precipitation averages 45 in (114 cm) annually and is slightly heavier on the western slopes of the Alleghenies. Accumulations of snow may vary from about 20 in (51cm) in the western sections to more than 50 in (127 cm) in the higher mountains.

⁴FLORA AND FAUNA

With its varied topography and climate, West Virginia provides a natural habitat for more than 3,200 species of plants in three life zones: Canadian, Alleghenian, and Carolinian. Oak, maple, poplar, walnut, hickory, birch, and such softwoods as hemlock, pine, and spruce are the common forest trees. Rhododendron, laurel, dogwood, redbud, and pussy willow are among the more than 200 flowering trees and shrubs. Rare plant species include the box huckleberry, Guyandotte beauty, and Kate's mountain clover. The Cranberry Glades, an ancient lake bed similar to a glacial bog, contains the bog rosemary and other plant species common in more northern climates.

West Virginia fauna includes at least 56 species and subspecies of mammals and more than 300 types of birds. The gray wolf, puma, elk, and bison of early times have disappeared. The white-tailed (Virginia) deer and the black bear (both protected by the state) as well as the wildcat are still found in the deep timber of the Allegheny ridges; raccoons, skunks, woodchucks, opossums, gray and red foxes, squirrels, and cottontail rabbits remain numerous. Common birds include the cardinal, tufted titmouse, brown thrasher, scarlet tanager, catbird, and a diversity of sparrows, woodpeckers, swallows, and warblers. Major game birds are the wild turkey, bobwhite quail, and ruffed grouse; hawks and owls are the most common birds of prey. Notable among more than 100 species of fish are smallmouth bass, rainbow trout, and brook trout (the state fish). The copperhead and rattlesnake are both numerous and poisonous. The southern bald eagle, American and Arctic peregrine falcons, Indiana and Virginia big-eared bats, flat-spired three-toothed snail, and tuberculed-blossom and pink mucket pearly mussels are on the endangered list.

⁵ENVIRONMENTAL PROTECTION

Major responsibility for environmental protection in West Virginia rests with the Division of Environmental Protection (DEP). The DEP was established in October 1991 and became West Virginia's leading environmental agency in July 1992, with the consolidation of the state's major environmental regulatory programs. Today, the DEP is responsible for the oversight of the state's Abandoned Mine Lands, Air Quality, Mining and Reclamation, Oil and Gas, Waste Management, and Water Resources programs.

A new DEP program is the Office of Environmental Advocate. The office was created to improve public access and input into DEP functioning.

Environmental issues confronting the state of West Virginia include the restoration of about 2,000 miles of streams that are being impacted by acid mine damage. To combat the problem, the state has created a Stream Restoration program, which is using a variety of treatment methods, including limestone drum technology, to improve water quality. The first treatment station is under construction in the Blackwater River watershed, with plans to construct a second station in the Middlefork River watershed. The state is in the midst of an initiative that focuses on better planning and management of West Virginia's five major watersheds. In 1996, less than one percent of West Virginia's land was designated wetlands.

West Virginia is embarking on a new air permitting program to comply with Title V of the federal Clean Air Act. An estimated 800 West Virginia businesses and industries will be required to obtain permits under this new program. The state is seeking US Environmental Protection Agency approval to redesignate five counties as being in compliance with Clean Air Act requirements for ozone.

The proper disposal of solid waste is being addressed through requirements for landfills to meet environmental safety standards by the end of 1994, or face closure. West Virginia also mandates that cities with populations of 10,000 or more develop recycling programs. In 1997, the state had seven hazardous waste sites.

⁶POPULATION

With a 1990 census total of 1,793,477, West Virginia ranked 34th among the 50 states in population. In 1996, the population was estimated at 1,825,754, a 1.8% increase over 1990. The density in 1990 was 74.5 persons per sq mi (28.6 per sq km).

The state's population grew rapidly in the 1880s and 1890s, as coal mining, lumbering, and railroads expanded to meet the needs of nearby industrial centers, but the pace of expansion slowed in the early 20th century. The population peaked at 2,005,552 in 1950; then mass unemployment, particularly in the coal industry, caused thousands of families to migrate to midwestern cities. An upswing began in the 1970s.

In 1990, when nearly 75% of the US population lived in urban areas, only 36.1% of West Virginia's population was urban—a smaller proportion than any other state but Vermont. In 1994, Charleston, the largest city, had an estimated 56,553 residents; Huntington, 53,789; Wheeling, 33,969; and Parkersburg, 33,102. The Huntington–Ashland metropolitan region, which includes parts of eastern Kentucky and southern Ohio, had an estimated population of 317,489 in 1995; the Charleston region had 255,139.

⁷ETHNIC GROUPS

Nearly all Indian inhabitants had left the state before the arrival of European settlers. In the 1990 census, about 2,000 Indians were counted.

The 56,000 blacks in the state in 1990 constituted about 3.1% of the population. The majority lived in industrial centers and coal-mining areas. Only 15,712 West Virginians, or 0.9% of the population, were foreign-born in 1990. Most of these residents came from Italy, the UK, Germany, and India. There were 8,000 Hispanic Americans and 7,000 persons of Asian and Pacific origin. Persons reporting at least one specific ancestry group in 1990 included 269,798 English, 468,927 Germans, 348,448 Irish, and 74,877 Dutch.

⁸LANGUAGES

With little foreign immigration and with no effect from the original Iroquois and Cherokee Indians, West Virginia maintains Midland speech. There is a secondary contrast between the northern half and the southern half, with the former influenced by Pennsylvania and the latter by western Virginia.

The basic Midland speech sounds the /r/ after a vowel as in *far* and *short*, and has /kag/ for *keg*, /greezy/ for *greasy*, *sofy* instead of sofa, and *nicker* in place of neigh. The northern part has /yelk/ for *yolk*, /loom/ for *loam*, an /ai/ diphthong so stretched that *sat* and *sight* sound very much alike, *run* for creek, and *teeter (totter)* for seesaw. The southern half pronounces *here* and *hear* as /hyeer/, *aunt* and *can't* as /aint/ and /kaint/, and uses *branch* for creek, and *tinter* for teeter.

In 1990, 1,642,729 West Virginians—97.4% of the population 5 years of age or over—spoke only English at home. Other languages spoken at home included Spanish, 13,337; Italian, 4,691; French, 7,695; and German, 5,280.

⁹RELIGIONS

Throughout its history, West Virginia has been overwhelmingly Protestant. Most settlers before the American Revolution were Anglicans, Presbyterians, Quakers, or members of German sects, such as Lutherans, German Reformed, Dunkers, and Mennonites. The Great Awakening had a profound effect on these settlers, and they avidly embraced its evangelism, emotionalism, and emphasis on personal religious experience. Catholics were mostly immigrants from Ireland and southern and eastern Europe.

In 1990, the major Protestant denominations and the number of their adherents were United Methodist, 182,731; American Baptist USA, 132,325; and Presbyterian Church US, 37,586. The Catholic population was 108,529 in 1990; the Jewish population was estimated at 2,181. Leading fundamentalist denominations in 1990 were the Church of God, 19,814, and the Church of the Nazarene, 25,811.

¹⁰TRANSPORTATION

West Virginia has long been plagued by inadequate transportation. The first major pre–Civil War railroad line was the

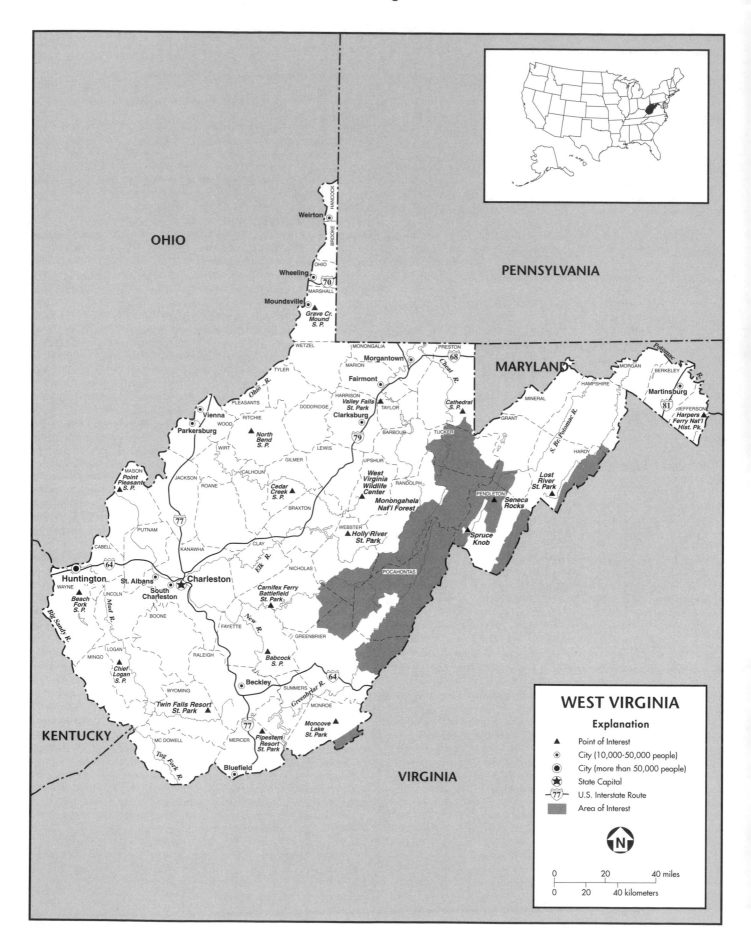

OHIO

PENNSYLVANIA

MARYLAND

KENTUCKY

VIRGINIA

Weirton
HANCOCK
BROOKE
OHIO
Wheeling
70
MARSHALL
Moundsville
Grave Cr.
Mound
S. P.

WETZEL
MONONGALIA
PRESTON
TYLER
Morgantown
MARION
Fairmont
68
Cheat R.
Cathedral
S. P.
MORGAN
BERKELEY
Martinsburg
81
HAMPSHIRE
MINERAL
Potomac
HARRISON
TAYLOR
Valley Falls
St. Park
Clarksburg
PLEASANTS
Vienna
RITCHIE
DODDRIDGE
Parkersburg
WOOD
North
Bend
S. P.
WIRT
GILMER
LEWIS
79
BARBOUR
TUCKER
GRANT
Harpers
Ferry Nat'l
Hist. Pk.
JEFFERSON
S. Br. Potomac R.
HARDY
MASON
Point
Pleasant
S. P.
JACKSON
ROANE
CALHOUN
UPSHUR
West
Virginia
Wildlife
Center
RANDOLPH
Lost
River
St. Park
Cedar
Creek
S. P.
BRAXTON
Monongahela
Nat'l Forest
Seneca
Rocks
PENDLETON
PUTNAM
77
WEBSTER
Holly River
St. Park
Spruce
Knob
CABELL
KANAWHA
Elk R.
CLAY
NICHOLAS
Huntington
64
St. Albans
Charleston
South
Charleston
POCAHONTAS
WAYNE
LINCOLN
Beach
Fork
S. P.
Mud R.
BOONE
Carnifex Ferry
Battlefield
St. Park
New R.
FAYETTE
GREENBRIER
Big Sandy R.
LOGAN
MINGO
Chief
Logan
S. P.
RALEIGH
Babcock
S. P.
WYOMING
Beckley
SUMMERS
Greenbrier R.
64
Twin Falls Resort
St. Park
MONROE
77
Moncove
Lake
St. Park
McDOWELL
MERCER
Pipestem
Resort
St. Park
Tug Fork R.
Bluefield

WEST VIRGINIA

Explanation

▲ Point of Interest
◉ City (10,000-50,000 people)
● City (more than 50,000 people)
★ State Capital
77 U.S. Interstate Route
Area of Interest

N

0   20   40 miles
0   20   40 kilometers

Baltimore and Ohio (B&O), completed to Wheeling in 1852. Later railroads, mostly built between 1880 and 1917 to tap rich coal and timber resources, also helped open up interior regions to settlement. Today, the railroads still play an important part in coal transportation. In 1995, Conrail, CSX, and Norfolk Southern were the state's Class I operators; total rail mileage in 1995 was 2,589 mi (4,168 km). West Virginia had the 2d highest (after Wyoming) amount of originated rail-tons of coal in 1995, at 104.5 million tons, which accounted for 95% of all rail tonnage originating within the state that year. Amtrak provides passenger service for parts of the state; in 1995/96, it had a total West Virginian ridership of 51,523.

At the end of 1992 there were 31,678 mi (50,970 km) of public roads under the state system, 650 mi (1,046 km) under federal control, and 2,411 mi (3,879 km) of other municipal and rural roads. The West Virginia Turnpike was completed from Charleston to Princeton in 1955. In 1995, the state had 552 mi (889 km) of interstate highways, not including the Appalachian Corridor highway system. There were 1,425,209 registered motor vehicles in the state in 1995, and 1,304,539 licensed drivers. Greyhound buses had a ridership of 179,000 in 1994, when the state's 17 public transit systems had an estimated daily ridership of 17,956.

Major navigable inland rivers are the Ohio, Kanawha, and Monongahela; each has locks and dams. In 1994, West Virginia had 67 airports, 29 heliports, and 10 seaplane bases. Yeager Airport in Charleston is the state's main air terminal.

11 HISTORY

Paleo-Indian cultures in what is now West Virginia existed some 15,000 years ago, when hunters pursued buffalo and other large game. About 7000 BC, they were supplanted by Archaic cultures, marked by pursuit of smaller game. Woodland (Adena) cultures, characterized by mound-building and agriculture, prevailed after about 1000 BC.

By the 1640s, the principal Indian claimants, the Iroquois and Cherokee, had driven out older inhabitants and made the region a vast buffer land. When European settlers arrived only a few Shawnee, Tuscarora, and Delaware Indian villages remained, but the area was still actively used as hunting and warring grounds, and European possession was hotly contested.

The fur trade stimulated early exploration. In 1671, Thomas Batts and Robert Fallam explored New River and gave England a claim to the Ohio Valley, to which most of West Virginia belongs. France also claimed the Ohio Valley by virtue of an alleged visit by Robert Cavelier, Sieur de la Salle, in 1669. England eventually prevailed as a result of the French and Indian War.

Unsubstantiated tradition credits Morgan Morgan, who moved to Bunker Hill in 1731, with the first settlement in the state. By 1750, several thousand settlers were living in the eastern panhandle. In 1769, following treaties with the Iroquois and Cherokee, settlers began to occupy the Greenbrier, Monongahela, and upper Ohio valleys, and movement into other interior sections continued into the Revolutionary War, although wars with Indians occurred sporadically until the 1790s. The area that is now West Virginia was part of Virginia at the time of that state's entry into the Union, 25 June 1788.

Serious differences between eastern and western Virginia developed after the War of 1812. Eastern Virginia was dominated by a slaveholding aristocracy, while small diversified farms and infant industries predominated in western Virginia. Westerners bristled under property qualifications for voting, inadequate representation in the Virginia legislature, and undemocratic county governments, as well as poor transportation, inadequate schools, inequitable taxes, and economic retardation. A constitutional convention in 1829–30 failed to effect changes, leaving the

westerners embittered. Another convention in 1850–51 met the west's political demands but exacerbated economic differences.

When Virginia seceded from the Union in 1861, western counties remaining loyal to the Union set up the Reorganized Government and consented to the separation of present-day West Virginia from Virginia. After approval by Congress and President Lincoln, West Virginia entered the Union on 20 June 1863 as the 35th state. West Virginia won control over Jefferson and Berkeley counties in the eastern panhandle in 1871, giving it a greater share of the Baltimore and Ohio Railroad lines in the state.

Both Bourbon Democratic and Republican governors after the Civil War sought to improve transportation, foster immigration, and provide tax structures attractive to business. Industrialists such as Democrats Henry Gassaway Davis and Johnson N. Camden, who amassed fortunes in coal, oil, railroads, and timber, sat in the US Senate and dominated party affairs in West Virginia. Similarly, industrialists Nathan Goff, Jr., and Stephen B. Elkins—Davis's son-in-law—wielded preponderant influence in the Republican Party from the 1870s until 1911. Native industrialists often collaborated with eastern interests to give the state a colonial economy dominated by absentee owners. Although Republican governors of the early 20th century were dominated by Elkins, they were attuned to Progressive ideas and were instrumental in the adoption of the direct primary, safety legislation for the coal mines, revision of corporate tax laws, and improvements in highways and education.

The Great Depression of the 1930s, from which West Virginia suffered acutely, ushered in a Democratic era. West Virginians embraced the New Deal and Fair Deal philosophies of presidents Franklin D. Roosevelt and Harry S Truman.

World Wars I and II produced significant changes in West Virginia, particularly through stimulation of chemical, steel, and textile industries in the Kanawha and Ohio valleys and the eastern panhandle. These industries lessened the state's dependence on extractive industries, historically the backbone of its economy, and gave cities and towns a more cosmopolitan character.

Overshadowing the economic diversification was the plight of the coal-mining areas, where, after World War II, mechanization and strip-mining displaced thousands of miners and resulted in a large exodus to other states. By 1960, West Virginia was considered one of the most economically depressed areas of the country, primarily because of conditions in the mining regions. The antipoverty programs of the Kennedy and Johnson administrations provided some relief, but much of it was temporary, as was a brief upsurge in coal mining during the late 1970s.

Over the last several decades, West Virginia's manufacturing and mining sectors have shrunk dramatically. Automation, foreign competition, and the recession of the early 1980s caused employment in steel, glass, and chemical manufacturing and in coal mining to drop by a third between 1979 and 1985, when the state had the highest rate of unemployment in the nation.

West Virginia's economy has improved in the 1990s. Coal and timber production have expanded, and trade and tourism have been boosted by the completion of Interstate Highway 64 in 1988. The state has won a number of federal projects (including the FBI's new fingerprint identification division), aided by the tenure of Robert C. Byrd as chairman of the US Senate Appropriations Committee from 1988 to 1995.

12 STATE GOVERNMENT

Since becoming a state, West Virginia has had two constitutions. The first, adopted in 1863, served until 1872, when the present constitution was adopted. As of the end of 1994, 64 amendments to this constitution had become law.

The legislature consists of a senate with 34 members and a house of delegates with 100 members. Senators and delegates must be at least 25 and 18 years old, respectively. Both must have been residents of the state and of their districts for at least one year before taking their seats. Senators are elected to staggered four-year terms, and delegates serve for two years. The legislature meets annually in 60-day sessions. The legislative salary in 1995 was $15,000.

Elected officials of the executive branch of government are the governor, secretary of state, auditor, attorney general, commissioner of agriculture, and treasurer, all elected for four-year terms. The governor, who may serve no more than two terms in succession, must be at least 30 years old and have been a resident of the state for at least five years. In 1996, the governor's salary was $72,000.

Bills passed by the legislature become law when signed by the governor. Those he vetoes may become law if repassed by majorities of both house memberships—except for revenue and appropriations bills, which require a two-thirds majority of both houses. Either house may propose an amendment to the state constitution. If both houses approve it by a two-thirds majority, it is submitted to the voters at the next regular election or at a special election for adoption by majority vote.

The right to vote in an election is extended to all citizens over 18 years old who have registered and who have resided in their respective counties for 30 days.

13POLITICAL PARTIES

The Republican Party presided over the birth of West Virginia, but the Democrats have generally been in power for the past five decades. In 1940, a strong New Deal faction, headed by Matthew M. Neely and supported by organized labor, formed the "statehouse machine," which became a dominant factor in state politics. Only two Republicans, Cecil H. Underwood (1957–61) and Arch Moore, Jr. (1969–77, 1985–89), have been governor since 1933.

West Virginia Presidential Vote by Major Political Parties, 1948–96

YEAR	ELECTORAL VOTE	WEST VIRGINIA WINNER	DEMOCRAT	REPUBLICAN
1948	8	*Truman (D)	429,188	316,251
1952	8	Stevenson (D)	453,578	419,970
1956	8	*Eisenhower (R)	381,534	449,297
1960	8	*Kennedy (D)	441,786	395,995
1964	7	*Johnson (D)	538,087	253,953
1968	7	Humphrey (D)	374,091	307,555
1972	6	*Nixon (R)	277,435	484,964
1976	6	*Carter (D)	435,914	314,760
1980	6	Carter (D)	367,462	334,206
1984	6	*Reagan (R)	328,125`	405,483
1988	6	Dukakis (D)	341,016	310,065
1992**	5	*Clinton (D)	331,001	241,974
1996**	5	*Clinton (D)	327,812	233,946

* Won US presidential election.

** Independent candidate Ross Perot received 108,829 votes in 1992, and 71,639 in 1996.

In 1984, West Virginia had 996,689 registered voters, of whom 675,106 were Democrats, 300,147 were Republicans, and 21,436 belonged to minor parties or were unaffiliated. Since the New Deal, Republican presidential candidates have carried West Virginia only in 1956, 1972, and 1984. In 1996 Democrat Bill Clinton won 51.5% of the vote, Republican Bob Dole received close to 37%, and Independent Ross Perot garnered 11%. West Virginia is even more firmly Democratic in elections for other offices. Both Robert C. Byrd, who has served in the Senate since 1959 and was majority leader from 1977 to 1980, and John D.

Rockefeller IV, who won a third term as Senator in 1996, are Democrats. West Virginia's three US Representatives are Democrats. In addition, both the state senate and state house are dominated by Democrats. Following the 1996 elections, there were 25 Democrats and 9 Republicans in the state senate, and 74 Democrats and 26 Republicans in the state house. In 1993 there were 21 blacks in public office, including one in the state legislature. As of 1995, 20 women served in the state legislature.

14LOCAL GOVERNMENT

West Virginia has 55 counties. The chief county officials are the three commissioners, elected for six-year terms, who serve on the county court; the sheriff, assessor, county clerk, and prosecuting attorney, elected for four-year terms; and the five-member board of education, elected for six-year terms. The sheriff is the principal peace officer but also collects taxes and disburses funds of the county court and board of education.

The 231 cities, towns, and villages, as of 1992, were divided into classes according to population. The minimum requirement for incorporation was a population of 100; the minimum for incorporation as a city was 2,000. There were 55 school districts and 350 special districts.

15STATE SERVICES

The Board of Education determines policy for public elementary and secondary schools, and the Board of Regents governs the state's colleges and universities. The Department of Highways is responsible for construction and operation of state roads. Services of the Department of Health center around treatment of alcoholism and drug abuse, mental health, environmental health services, maternal and child care, family planning, and control of communicable diseases. The Department of Human Services administers a variety of economic, medical, and social services.

In the area of public protection, the Department of Public Safety enforces criminal and traffic laws, the Office of Emergency Services oversees civil defense and other emergency activities, and the Department of Corrections oversees prisons and other such facilities. The Public Service Commission regulates utilities. The Housing Development Fund concentrates on housing for low- and middle-income families and the elderly. The Department of Natural Resources has the major responsibility for protection of forests, wildlife, water, and other resources, for reclamation projects, and for operation of state parks and recreational facilities.

Responsibility in labor matters is shared by the Department of Labor, Department of Employment Security, Department of Mines, Workers' Compensation Fund, and Labor-Management Relations Board.

16JUDICIAL SYSTEM

The highest court in West Virginia, the supreme court of appeals, has five justices, including the chief justice, elected for 12-year terms. The court has broad discretionary appellate jurisdiction in both civil and criminal cases, and original jurisdiction in certain other cases.

As of 1996, West Virginia was divided into 31 judicial circuits, each with from 1 to 7 judges, for a total of 62, elected for eight-year terms. Each circuit served from one to four counties and had jurisdiction over civil cases in amounts that exceeded $300 and criminal cases. Circuit courts also had jurisdiction over juveniles, domestic relations, and certain administrative appeals. Family law specialists conduct most domestic relations hearings.

Local courts include the county magistrate and municipal courts. Magistrate courts have original jurisdiction in criminal matters but may not convict or sentence in felony cases. All judges down to the magistrate level are popularly elected by partisan ballot. Municipal, police, or mayor's courts have authority to enforce municipal ordinances; unlike other courts, these are not part of the unified court system. Appeals from municipal and magistrate courts are to circuit courts, and from circuit courts are to the supreme court.

As of 1997, there were 1,549 prisoners in state or federal correctional facilities, or 120 per 100,000.

In total crimes per 100,000 population in 1995, West Virginia's total crime rate was 2,458 per 100,000 persons, in contrast to the national average of 5,277. West Virginia's violent crime rate of 210.2 was about one-third the US average of 684.6. The state abolished the death penalty in 1965. In 1996, there were 3,700 attorneys practicing in the state.

17ARMED FORCES

In 1996, there were 518 active duty military personnel stationed in West Virginia. The state has no military bases, academies, or training facilities. The Naval Telecommunications Station (Sugar Grove) is the main receiving facility for the Navy's global high-frequency radio communications and for point-to-point circuits destined for Washington, D.C. In 1995/96, defense contracts awarded West Virginia totaled $199.3 million.

In 1996, West Virginia had about 197,000 veterans, of whom fewer than 500 served in World War I, 60,000 in World War II, 35,000 in the Korean conflict, 59,000 in the Vietnam era, and 15,000 in the Persian Gulf War. In 1995/96, veterans received $463 million in benefits. There were 13,432 reserve and national guard personnel in 1996. In 1993, the West Virginia State Police employed 492 full-time sworn officers, or 3 per 10,000 residents.

18MIGRATION

West Virginia has considerable national and ethnic diversity. Settlers before the Civil War consisted principally of English, German, Scotch-Irish, and Welsh immigrants, many of whom came by way of Pennsylvania. A second wave of immigration from the 1880s to the 1920s brought thousands of Italians, Poles, Austrians, and Hungarians to the coal mines and industrial towns, which also attracted many blacks from the South. In 1980, 79% of the residents of the state were born in West Virginia (4th highest among states).

Between 1950 and 1970, West Virginia suffered a 13% loss in population, chiefly from the coal-mining areas; but between 1970 and 1980, population rose by almost 12%. According to federal estimates, the state had a net migration gain of 71,000 in the 1970s and a net migration loss of about 81,000 in the 1980s. Between 1990 and 1996, West Virginia had net gains of 18,451 in domestic migration and 2,786 in international migration. As of 1990, 77.3% of state residents had been born in West Virginia, and 64% (age 5 or older) were living in the same house as in 1985. About 80% of those who reported living in a different house in 1985 did so within West Virginia.

19INTERGOVERNMENTAL COOPERATION

The West Virginia Commission on Interstate Cooperation participates in the Council of State Governments. West Virginia is a member of 23 regional compacts, including the Ohio River Valley Water Sanitation and Potomac River Basin compacts, Southern Regional Education Board, Southern States Energy Board, and Southern States Governors' Association. In 1995/96, federal grants to West Virginia totaled over $2 billion.

20ECONOMY

Agriculture was the backbone of West Virginia's economy until the 1890s, when extractive industries (including coal, oil, natural gas, and timber) began to play a major role. World War I stimulated important secondary industries, such as chemicals, steel, glass, and textiles. The beauty of West Virginia's mountains and forests attracted an increasing number of tourists in the 1980s, but the state's rugged topography and relative isolation from major markets continued to hamper its economic development. In 1994, West Virginia's gross state product totaled $34,654 million, to which private goods-producing industries contributed $11,210 million; private services-producing industries, $18,776 million; and government, $4,668 million. West Virginia's per capita personal income in 1996 was $18,444, 49th in the nation.

During 1996 there were 6,013 filings for bankruptcy, up 43% from 1995.

21INCOME

West Virginia's total disposable personal income was $30.1 billion in 1996, up from $29 billion in 1995. The state's per capita personal income of $18,444 ranked 49th in the US, down from 43d in 1980. In 1995, about 16.7% of all West Virginians lived below the federal poverty line. That same year, median household income was $24,880.

22LABOR

West Virginia's labor force averaged 808,000 in 1996. Unemployment averaged 7.5% in 1996; the number of unemployed persons in 1996 averaged 61,000. At the end of 1996, nonagricultural employment was as follows: mining, 24,500; construction, 35,100; manufacturing, 80,600; transportation and public utilities, 39,200; wholesale and retail trade, 165,700; services, 191,100; and government, 140,800.

Important milestones in the growth of unionism were the organization of the state as District 17 of the United Mine Workers of America (UMWA) in 1890 and the formation of the State Federation of Labor in 1903. The coal miners fought to gain union recognition by coal companies, and instances of violence were not uncommon in the early 1900s. Wages, working conditions, and benefits for miners improved rapidly after World War II. Membership in unions in 1980 was 222,000, or 34% of the work force, compared to 47% in 1970, an indication of the UMWA's waning strength. In 1995, 104,500 workers belonged to labor unions, 16.3% of the workforce.

23AGRICULTURE

With estimated farm marketings of $386.3 million ($312.1 million from livestock and poultry), West Virginia ranked 46th among the 50 states in 1995. Poultry, meat animals, and dairy dominate the farm economy in the Mountain State.

Until about 1890 small, diversified farms were dominant, but, as in other states, farms have grown larger and the farm population has dropped, from 533,000 in 1940 to 78,000 in 1970, to 23,700 in 1990. In 1996, the state had 3,700,000 acres (1,498,000 hectares), or 24% of its land, devoted to farming. Its 20,000 farms averaged 185 acres (75 hectares) in size. Major farm sections are the eastern panhandle, a tier of counties along the Virginia border, the upper Monongahela Valley, and the Ohio Valley. Leading crops produced in 1996 were hay, 1,066,000 tons; corn for grain, 4,200,000 bushels; corn for silage, 320,000 tons; commercial apples, 115,000,000 lb; and tobacco, 2,500,000 lb.

24ANIMAL HUSBANDRY

In 1997, there were an estimated 450,000 cattle and calves, valued at $184.5 million. During 1996, the state had 19,000 hogs and pigs, valued at around $1.8 million. During 1995, poultry farmers produced 391.2 million lb of broilers valued at $131 million, and 90 million lb of turkey, valued at $40.6 million. The dairy industry yielded 266 million lb of milk and 239 million eggs.

[25]FISHING

West Virginia fishing has little commercial importance. In 1995/96, federal hatcheries distributed nearly 352,500 coldwater and warmwater species of fish within the state. Fishing licenses issues in that year numbered 310,968.

[26]FORESTRY

In 1994, West Virginia had four-fifths, or 12.1 million acres (4.9 million hectares), of its land area in forestland and, of this, 11.9 million acres (4.8 million hectares) are classified as timberland, making West Virginia the third most forested state in the nation.

In 1997, West Virginia's timber resource was the largest and of the highest quality of any time in the past 75 or more years, with 64% of its timberland being sawtimber size. Sawtimber volumes average 6,500 board feet per acre. About 92% of West Virginia forest species are hardwoods, with approximately 77% of the timberland being of the oak-hickory forest type. In all, West Virginia's forests contain more than 100 species of trees.

During the early 1900s, West Virginia became a lumbering giant. From 1908 to 1911, some 1,500 mills produced up to 1.5 billion bd ft of lumber annually to feed the nation's needs. By 1920, the state was first in the production of cherry and chestnut lumber and 13th in total production. After the extensive logging and resulting debris came forest fires which devastated the remaining forest resource and caused extensive soil erosion. In the early 1930s, a cooperative fire prevention program was initiated in the state and later in the early 1950s, an educational and forestry technical assistance program was created to help forest landowners manage and protect their forests. The maturing forests of West Virginia languished in their contribution to the state's economy until the 1980s when annual production, which had averaged around 350 to 450 million bd ft per year, began to increase significantly.

Production increased to 600 million bd ft in 1988, 680 million bd ft in 1989, and 1 billion bd ft by 1997. The forest industry's impact on the state's economy was $2.1 billion in 1992 and $3 billion by 1997. Employment in the forest industry is second only to the chemical and primary metal manufacturing industries. In 1995, approximately 1 billion bd ft of timber was harvested. However, it was estimated that growth still exceeded removals by a ratio of 1.34 to 1. Even more important, the sawtimber inventory increased from 18 to 76 billion bd ft between 1949 and 1996.

The state is encouraging the professional management of its forests so they will continue to produce a sustained array of benefits, such as wood products, jobs, clean water, oxygen, scenery, and diverse recreational opportunities like hunting, hiking, and tourism.

[27]MINING

The value of nonfuel mineral production in West Virginia in 1995 was about $194 million (40th). Increased production was reported for portland cement and crushed stone. Other commodities with increased values that year were salt, lime, and common clays. In 1995, crushed stone accounted for about 55% ($107,000,000 for 13,100,000 metric tons) of the state's total value of nonfuel minerals. In 1995, construction sand and gravel production was 1.3 million short tons, worth $5.7 million.

[28]ENERGY AND POWER

West Virginia has long been an important supplier of energy in the form of electric power and fossil fuels. In 1995, installed capacity was 14.4 million kw. Net generation of electric energy was 77.3 billion kwh, of which 99% was produced by coal-fired steam units. Out of 25.9 billion kwh of electricity sold in the state in 1995, 35% went to residential customers, 23% to commercial, and 42% to industrial consumers. The state's power facilities are all privately owned. The John Amos Plant, on the Kanawha River, is one of the world's largest investor-owned generating plants.

Major coal-mining regions lie within a north-south belt some 60 mi (97 km) wide through the central part of the state and include the Fairmount, New River-Kanawha, Pocahontas, and Logan-Mingo fields. In 1995, West Virginia was 2d to Wyoming in coal production, with 843 mines producing 167.1 million tons (16% of the national total), all of it bituminous and 68% of it mined underground. Demonstrated reserves came to 37 billion tons. In 1995, West Virginia produced 2 million barrels of oil and 166 billion cu ft of natural gas. Proved petroleum reserves in 1995 totaled 25 million barrels; natural gas, 2.5 trillion cu ft.

[29]INDUSTRY

Known for its rich natural resources and strong industrial presence, West Virginia enjoyed an 11.2% increase in value added by manufacturing between 1987 and 1991 with a 3.5% reduction in manufacturing employment. The value of shipments by manufacturers in 1995 was $17,764.5 million. The values of shipments by selected industry in 1995 were as follows: chemicals and allied products, $7,367.9 million; primary metals, $3,623.3 million; fabricated metal products, $1,360.0 million; lumber and wood products, $880.7 million; and food and food products, $746.6 million.

Major industrial areas are the Kanawha, Ohio, and Monongahela valleys and the eastern panhandle. The largest industrial corporations with headquarters in West Virginia are Weirton Steel and Wheeling-Pittsburgh. Other major industrial companies with operations in West Virginia include E. I. du Pont de Nemours, Union Carbide, Ravenswood Aluminum, and Rhone Poulenc. During 1995, there were 161 US patents issued to West Virginia residents.

[30]COMMERCE

In 1992, West Virginia's 2,427 wholesale trade establishments had sales of $7.8 billion. Retail sales of $11.2 billion in 1993 placed the state 39th among the 50 states. Sales in food stores made up 22.7% of the total; automotive dealers, 21%; general merchandise group stores, 14.5%; eating and drinking places, 8.5%; and other retailers, 33.3%.

In 1996, West Virginia exported $2.2 billion worth of products originating in the state.

[31]CONSUMER PROTECTION

The state attorney general's office, Division of Consumer Protection and Antitrust, is empowered to investigate, arbitrate, and litigate complaints by consumers alleging unfair and deceptive trade practices, and violations of the West Virginia Consumer Credit and Protection Act, the West Virginia Antitrust Act, and the Pre-need Funeral Contracts Act. There are 6 lawyers and 22 support staff.

The Public Service Commission, consisting of three members, regulates rates, charges, and services of utilities and common carriers. Since 1977, it has included one member who is supposed to represent the "average" wage earner.

[32]BANKING

West Virginia had 113 commercial banks at the end of 1996, with assets worth $22.2 billion. Nine savings institutions had assets of $1.1 billion in 1996.

[33]INSURANCE

In 1991, one life insurance company, 3 property and casualty insurance companies, and 11 farmers mutual fire insurance companies were domiciled in West Virginia. Life insurance in force in 1996 had a total value of $59.7 billion. In the same year, life insurance companies collected life insurance premiums of $529.6 million and annuity considerations of $223.2 million, and paid direct benefits of $763.7 million.

Property and casualty firms collected $1.5 billion in premiums in 1996, and paid direct losses of $955.7 million. The insurance commissioner of West Virginia has responsibility for regulating the insurance industry.

34SECURITIES
There are no securities exchanges in West Virginia. As of April 1997, West Virginia had 1,145 broker-dealers registered to do business in the state, with 33,692 agents. There were 352 investment advisor firms registered in West Virginia, with approximately 2,552 registered representatives.

35PUBLIC FINANCE
The state constitution requires the governor to submit to the legislature within 10 days after the opening of a regular legislative session a budget for the ensuing fiscal year (1 July–30 June). The budget for fiscal year 1995 was as follows (in millions):

REVENUES
General revenue fund	$ 5,628.0
Federal funds	1,000.9
TOTAL	$ 6,628.9

EXPENDITURES
Education	$ 1,993.6
Health and welfare	1,784.9
Transportation	662.6
Other governmental costs	1,814.4
Capital outlay	519.4
Debt service	147.1
TOTAL	$ 6,922.0

Total public debts of the state and local governments in 1996 were nearly $2.5 billion. Per capita debt in 1996 was $1,414.

36TAXATION
West Virginia's diversified tax base yielded receipts of more than $2.6 billion in 1994/95. Personal income taxes, ranging from 3.0% to 6.5%, accounted for $718 million; the corporate income tax of 9% yielded $145.4 million; and consumer sales taxes of 6% on goods and services including food raised $793.5 million. West Virginia has a business and occupations tax on gross income; the West Virginia Business and Occupation Tax is imposed on public utilities and generators of electric power. Counties and localities mainly tax real and personal property. The federal income tax burden per capita in 1996 was $3,413.

37ECONOMIC POLICY
The West Virginia Development Office supports business and industry in the state and assists new companies with site location and employee training programs as well as with the construction of plants and access roads and the provision of essential services. The West Virginia Economic Development Authority may make loans of up to 50% of the costs of land, buildings, and equipment at low interest rates for a normal term of 15 years. Tax incentives include a credit of 10% on industrial expansion and revitalization, applicable to the business and occupations tax over a 10-year period.

The Development Office helps small business by investing in venture capital companies and by offering loans for venture capital purposes.

38HEALTH
West Virginia's birthrate was 11.6 per 1,000 in 1995. That year, 2,606 abortions were performed. The death rate in West Virginia, 11 per 1,000 population in 1995, was exceeded by only two other states, Florida and Pennsylvania. AIDS was rarely reported in West Virginia, which has the 8th lowest rate of the disease per 100,000 in the country.

In 1995, West Virginia had one of the highest death rates from cardiovascular disease of any state, at 376.3 per 100,000. Other leading causes of death were cancer, stroke, accidents, chronic obstructive pulmonary diseases, pneumonia and flu, and diabetes. Pneumoconiosis (black lung) is an occupational hazard among coal miners.

In 1996, the state's 66 hospitals—including 3 state-run facilities—had 7,269 beds and 265,243 admissions. There were 3,149 active, nonfederal physicians and nearly 14,000 registered nurses in 1996, and 830 active, licensed dentists.

Medical education is provided by medical schools at West Virginia University and Marshall University and at the West Virginia School of Osteopathic Medicine.

An estimated 16.2% of West Virginia residents had no health insurance in 1994.

39SOCIAL WELFARE
Although rich in resources, West Virginia is generally poor. In 1996, 98,400 persons received an average monthly payment of Aid to Families with Dependent Children (AFDC) totaling $312. Residents receiving food stamp allowances numbered 299,719. The school lunch program had a federal cost of $37.8 million.

With the enactment of the Personal Responsibility and Work Opportunity Reconciliation Act of 1996, the US government has changed the form and regulations for many of its social welfare programs; most significantly, it replaces AFDC, an open-ended entitlement program, with Temporary Assistance for Needy Families (TANF), a limited system of assistance funded largely through federal block grants. The reform act also impacts the food stamp program, the Supplemental Security Income program, and the child nutrition program. The law took effect on 1 July 1997 and provided $16.38 billion in block grants for fiscal years 1997–2002. The grants are to be divided among the states based on an equation involving the numbers of former AFDC recipients in each state. Because many of the bills provisions have yet to be implemented into state-by-state policy, it was not possible to include the details of each state's programs for this edition of this work.

Social Security benefits in 1995 were paid to 382,340 persons, averaging $690 a month. Federal Supplemental Security Income payments to 64,365 aged, blind, and disabled persons that year averaged $344 a month. Unemployment benefits in West Virginia averaged $172.07 per week.

40HOUSING
In 1996, West Virginia had an estimated 791,000 housing units, 712,000 of which were occupied. Of these units, 96.8% had full plumbing. In 1996, 3,616 privately owned units, valued at $276 million, were authorized for construction; of these 2,908 were single-family dwellings. In 1990, West Virginia had the lowest median monthly costs of any state for both owners (with a mortgage) and renters, at $498 and $303, respectively. The median home value in 1990 was $47,900, down by 21.6% from 1980 after adjusting for inflation. During 1995/96, West Virginia received $171 million in aid from the US Department of Housing and Urban Development, including $27.7 million in community development block grants.

41EDUCATION

West Virginia has generally ranked below national standards in education. In 1990, 68.4% of adult West Virginians were high school graduates, a criterion by which the state outranked only three other states.

In 1995, the state's public schools enrolled 306,451 students. In the 1995/96 school year, there were 20,915 teachers in public elementary and secondary schools with an average salary of $32,155. Expenditure per pupil in elementary and secondary public schools was $6,048 in the 1994/95 school year.

The state supports West Virginia University, Marshall University, and the West Virginia College of Graduate Studies (all offering graduate work), as well as 3 medical schools, 8 four-year colleges, and 4 two-year institutions. Public higher educational institutions enrolled 53,610 students in the fall of 1990. There were 10 private colleges with 10,304 students.

42ARTS

West Virginia is known for the quilts, pottery, and woodwork of its mountain artisans. Huntington Galleries, the Sunrise Foundation at Charleston, and Oglebay Park, Wheeling, are major art centers. The Science and Culture Center at Charleston features West Virginia and Appalachian artists at work. The Mountain State Art and Craft Fair is held each summer at Ripley. Musical attractions include the Charleston Symphony Orchestra, the Wheeling Symphony, and a country music program at Wheeling.

West Virginia supported its arts programs with federal funds amounting to $547,000 in 1996. The NEA gave $490,000 to the state's arts programs and $446,000 to the West Virginia Department of Education's Division of Culture and History.

Between 1987 and 1991, the state's arts programs attracted a total audience of 12,268,000 people. There were 39,339 contributing artists. During the same period, West Virginia provided arts education for about 24,600 of its school-aged children aided by the Department of Education's Arts and Humanities Section. By 1996, the state had 150 arts associations and 30 local arts groups. The NEA has given grants to the Ecotheater, the Friends of West Virginia Public Radio, and the state's Division of Culture and History.

43LIBRARIES AND MUSEUMS

In 1996/97, West Virginia's public libraries had 4,780,182 volumes and a circulation of 16,966,006. The largest was the Kanawha County Public Library system at Charleston, with 608,617 volumes. Of college and university libraries, the largest collection was West Virginia University's 1,705,623 volumes.

There were 48 museums in 1996, including the State Museum and the Sunrise Museum in Charleston, and Oglebay Institute-Mansion Museum in Wheeling. Point Pleasant marks the site of a battle between colonists and Indians, and Harpers Ferry is the site of John Brown's raid. Wheeling is the location of the Oglebay's Good Children's Zoo.

44COMMUNICATIONS

Of the 715,000 households in the state in March 1993, only 89.4% had telephones. In 1996, broadcasting facilities included 67 AM and 99 FM radio stations, 15 commercial television stations, and 3 public television stations; 7 large cable television systems also operated.

45PRESS

In 1997, West Virginia had 21 daily newspapers and 13 Sunday newspapers. The following table shows leading West Virginia newspapers with their 1997 circulations:

AREA	NAME	DAILY	SUNDAY
Charleston	Gazette (m,S)	53,346	—
	Daily Mail (e,S)	43,898	104,647*
Huntington	Herald–Dispatch (m,S)	39,282	45,245
Wheeling	News Register (d,S)	20,730	52,056

*The Sunday Gazette Daily Mail is a combination of the two dailies.

46ORGANIZATIONS

The 1992 US Census of Service Industries counted 601 organizations in West Virginia, including 83 business associations; 427 civic, social, and fraternal associations; and 91 other membership organizations. The Black Lung Association, based in Beckley, promotes safe working conditions in coal mines and benefits for disabled miners. The headquarters of the Appalachian Trail Conference is in Harpers Ferry, and the American Association of Zoological Parks and Aquariums is in Oglebay.

47TOURISM, TRAVEL, AND RECREATION

In 1995, 1.9 million tourists visited West Virginia's national parks. Nine million visitors sought out the 26 state parks and recreation areas. Major attractions are Harpers Ferry National Historical Park, New River Gorge National River, the Naval Telecommunications Station at Sugar Grove, and White Sulphur Springs, a popular mountain resort. Among state parks and state forests are Cass Scenic Railroad, which includes a restoration of an old logging line, and Prickett's Fort, with re-creations of pioneer life. State parks drew 9,081,870 visitors in 1995. That year, licenses were held by 782,634 hunters and 708,354 anglers.

48SPORTS

No major league professional teams are based in West Virginia, but there is one minor league baseball team in Charleston and minor league hockey in Wheeling and Huntington. West Virginia University's basketball team won a National Invitation Tournament championship in 1942 and was NCAA Division 1 runner-up in 1959. In football, West Virginia produced a string of national contenders in the late 1980s and early 1990s. They went to the Gator Bowl in 1982 and 1989, and the Sugar Bowl in 1994, losing all three games. West Virginia won the Peach Bowl in 1981.

Horseracing tracks operate in Chester and Charles Town. Greyhound races are run in Wheeling and Charleston. Other popular sports are skiing and white-water rafting.

49FAMOUS WEST VIRGINIANS

Among West Virginians who have served in presidential cabinets are Nathan Goff, Jr. (1843–1920), navy secretary; William L. Wilson (1843–1900), postmaster general; John Barton Payne (1855–1935), interior secretary; and Newton D. Baker (1871–1937), secretary of war during World War I. Lewis L. Strauss (1896–1974) was commerce secretary and chairman of the Atomic Energy Commission, and Cyrus R. Vance (b.1917) served as secretary of state. John W. Davis (1873–1955), an ambassador to Great Britain, ran as the Democratic presidential nominee in 1924. Prominent members of the US Senate have included Matthew M. Neely (1874–1958), who was also governor, Harley M. Kilgore (1893–1956), and Robert C. Byrd (b.1917).

Thomas J. "Stonewall" Jackson (1824–63) was a leading Confederate general during the Civil War. Brigadier General Charles E. "Chuck" Yeager (b.1923), a World War II ace, became the first person to fly faster than the speed of sound.

Major state political leaders, all governors (though some have held federal offices), have been E. Willis Wilson (1844–1905), Henry D. Hatfield (1875–1962), Arch A. Moore, Jr. (b.1923), and John D. "Jay" Rockefeller IV (b.New York, 1937).

The state's only Nobel Prize winner has been Pearl S. Buck (Pearl Sydenstricker, 1893–1973), who won the Nobel Prize for literature for her novels concerning China. Alexander Campbell (b.Ireland, 1788–1866), with his father, founded the Disciples of Christ Church and was president of Bethany College in West Virginia. Major labor leaders have included Walter Reuther (1907–70), president of the United Automobile Workers, and Arnold Miller (b.1923), president of the United Mine Workers.

Musicians include George Crumb (b.1929), a Pulitzer Prize-winning composer, and opera singers Eleanor Steber (1916–1990) and Phyllis Curtin (b.1922). Melville Davisson Post (1871–1930) was a leading writer of mystery stories. Important writers of the modern period include Mary Lee Settle (b.1918) and John Knowles (b.1926). Jerry West (b.1938) was a collegiate and professional basketball star, and a pro coach after his playing days ended; Rod Hundley (b.1934) and Hal Greer (b.1936) also starred in the National Basketball Association. Mary Lou Retton (b.1968) won a gold medal in gymnastics at the 1984 Olympics. Another West Virginian of note is Anna Jarvis (1864–1948), founder of Mother's Day.

50BIBLIOGRAPHY

Conley, Phil, and William Thomas Doherty. *West Virginia History.* Charleston: Education Foundation, 1974.

Federal Writers' Project. *West Virginia: A Guide to the Mountain State.* Reprint. New York: Somerset, 1980 (orig. 1941).

Forbes, Harold M. *West Virginia History: Bibliography and Guide to Studies.* Morgantown: West Virginia University Press, 1981.

Rice, Otis K. *West Virginia: The State and Its People.* Parsons, W. Va.: McClain, 1972.

———. *West Virginia: A History.* 2d ed. Lexington, Ky.: University of Kentucky Press, 1993.

West Virginia Politics and Government. Edited by Richard A. Brisbin, Jr., et al. Lincoln, Nebr.: University of Nebraska Press, 1996.

West Virginia Research League, Inc. *1984 Statistical Handbook.* Charleston, 1984.

Williams, John Alexander. *West Virginia: A Bicentennial History.* New York: Norton, 1976.

Willis, Todd C. (ed.). *West Virginia Blue Book, 1984.* Charleston: Jarrett, 1984.

WISCONSIN

State of Wisconsin

ORIGIN OF STATE NAME: Probably from the Ojibwa word *wishkonsing,* meaning "place of the beaver." **NICKNAME:** The Badger State (unofficial). **CAPITAL:** Madison. **ENTERED UNION:** 29 May 1848 (30th). **SONG:** "On, Wisconsin!" **MOTTO:** Forward. **COAT OF ARMS:** Surrounding the US shield is the shield of Wisconsin, which is divided into four parts symbolizing agriculture, mining, navigation, and manufacturing. Flanking the shield are a sailor, representing labor on water; and a yeoman or miner, labor on land. Above is a badger and the state motto; below, a horn of plenty and a pyramid of pig lead. **FLAG:** A dark-blue field, fringed in yellow on three sides, surrounds the state coat of arms on each side, with "Wisconsin" in white letters above the coat of arms and "1848" below. **OFFICIAL SEAL:** Arms surrounded by the words "Great Seal of the State of Wisconsin" and 13 stars below. **ANIMAL:** Badger. **WILDLIFE ANIMAL:** White-tailed deer. **DOMESTIC ANIMAL:** Dairy cow. **BIRD:** Robin. **SYMBOL OF PEACE:** Mourning dove. **FISH:** Muskellunge. **INSECT:** Honeybee. **FLOWER:** Wood violet. **TREE:** Sugar maple. **ROCK:** Red granite. **MINERAL:** Galena. **SOIL:** Antigo silt loam. **LEGAL HOLIDAYS:** New Year's Day, 1 January; Birthday of Martin Luther King, Jr., 3d Monday in January; Lincoln and Washington Day, 3d Monday in February; Good Friday, March or April; Memorial Day, last Monday in May; Independence Day, 4 July; Labor Day, 1st Monday in September; Primary Day, 2d Tuesday in September in even-numbered years; Columbus Day, 2d Monday in October; Election Day, 1st Tuesday after 1st Monday in November in even-numbered years; Veterans Day, 11 November; Thanksgiving Day, 4th Thursday in November; Christmas Day, 25 December. **TIME:** 6 AM CST = noon GMT.

¹LOCATION, SIZE, AND EXTENT

Located in the eastern north-central US, Wisconsin ranks 26th in size among the 50 states.

The total area of Wisconsin is 56,153 sq mi (145,436 sq km), of which 54,426 sq mi (140,963 sq km) is land and 1,727 sq mi is (4,473 sq km) inland water. The state extends 295 mi (475 km) E-w and 320 mi (515 km) N-s.

Wisconsin is bordered on the N by Lake Superior and the state of Michigan (with the northeastern boundary formed by the Menominee River); on the E by Lake Michigan; on the s by Illinois; and on the w by Iowa and Minnesota (with the line defined mainly by the Mississippi and St. Croix rivers).

Important islands belonging to Wisconsin are the Apostle Islands in Lake Superior, and Washington Island in Lake Michigan. The state's boundaries have a total length of 1,379 mi (2,219 km). Wisconsin's geographic center is in Wood County, 9 mi (14 km) SE of Marshfield.

²TOPOGRAPHY

Wisconsin can be divided into four main geographical regions, each covering roughly one-quarter of the state's land area. The most highly elevated of these is the Superior Upland, below Lake Superior and the border with Michigan. It has heavily forested rolling hills but no high mountains. Elevations range from about 700 feet (200 meters) to slightly under 2,000 feet (600 meters). A second upland region, called the Driftless Area, has a more rugged terrain, having been largely untouched by the glacial drifts that smoothed out topographical features in other parts of the state. Elevations here reach more than 1,200 feet (400 meters). The third region is a large, crescent-shaped plain in central Wisconsin; its unglaciated portion is a sandstone plain, broken by rock formations that from a distance appear similar to the buttes and mesas of Colorado. Finally, in the east and southeast along Lake Michigan lies a large, glaciated lowland plain, fairly smooth

in the Green Bay–Winnebago area but more irregular on the Door Peninsula and in the south.

Wisconsin's mean altitude is 1,050 feet (320 meters), with elevations generally higher in the north. The Gogebic Range, extending westward from Michigan's Upper Peninsula into northern Wisconsin, was an important center of iron mining in the early days of statehood. Timms Hill, in north-central Wisconsin, is the state's highest point, at 1,952 feet (595 meters). The lowest elevation is 581 feet (177 meters), along the Lake Michigan shoreline.

There are well over 8,000 lakes in Wisconsin. Lakes Michigan and Superior form part of the northern and eastern borders; the Wisconsin mainland has at least 575 mi (925 km) of lakeshore and holds jurisdiction over 10,062 sq mi (26,061 sq km) of lake waters. By far, the largest inland lake is Lake Winnebago, in eastern Wisconsin, covering an area of 215 sq mi (557 sq km).

The Mississippi River, which forms part of the border with Minnesota and the entire border with Iowa, is the main navigable river. The major river flowing through the state is the Wisconsin, which follows a south-southwest course for 430 mi (692 km) before meeting the Mississippi at the Iowa border. Other tributaries of the Mississippi are the St. Croix River, also part of the Minnesota border, and the Chippewa and Black rivers. Located on the Black River are Big Manitou Falls, at 165 feet (50 meters) the highest of the state's many waterfalls. Waters from the Fox River and its major tributary, the Wolf, flow into Green Bay and then into Lake Michigan, as does the Menominee, which is part of the Michigan state line.

Except in the Driftless Area, glaciation smoothed out many surface features, gouged out new ones, and left deposits of rock and soil creating distinctively shaped hills and ridges. Oval mounds, called drumlins, are still scattered over the southeast; and moraines, formed by deposits left at the edges of glaciers, are a prominent feature of eastern, central, and northwestern Wisconsin. In one section, called the Dells, the Wisconsin River has cut a gorge through 8 mi (13 km) of sandstone, creating caves and interesting rock formations.

³CLIMATE

Wisconsin has a continental climate. Summers are warm and winters very cold, especially in the upper northeast and north-central lowlands, where the freeze-free (growing) season is around 80 days. The average annual temperature ranges from 39°F (4°C) in the north to about 50°F (10)°C) in the south. At Danbury, in the northwest, the average January daily temperature over a 34-year period was 8°F (–13°C), and the average July daily temperature 68°F (20°C); at Racine, in the southeast, these figures were 21°F (–6°C) and 72°F (22°C), respectively. Over a 30-year period ending in 1990, Milwaukee had average daily temperatures ranging from 12°F (–11°C) to 26°F (–3°C) in January and from 62°F (17°C) to 80°F (27°C) in July. Among major US metropolitan areas, only Minneapolis–St. Paul is colder than Milwaukee. The lowest temperature ever recorded in Wisconsin was –54°F (–48°C), at Danbury on 24 January, 1922; the highest, 114°F (46°C), at Wisconsin Dells on 13 July 1936.

Annual precipitation in the state ranges from about 34 in (86 cm) for parts of the northwest to about 28 in (71 cm) in the south-central region and the areas bordering Lake Superior and Lake Michigan. Normal annual precipitation in Milwaukee is 31 in (79 cm); April, June, and July are the rainiest months in Milwaukee. Milwaukee's annual snowfall averages 47 in (119 cm); the average wind speed is 12 mph (19 km/hr).

⁴FLORA AND FAUNA

Common trees of Wisconsin include four oaks—bur, black, white, and red—along with black cherry and hickory. Jack, red, and white pine, yellow birch, eastern hemlock, mountain maple, moosewood, and leatherwood grow in the north, with black spruce, black ash, balsam fir, and tamarack concentrated in the northern lowlands. Characteristic of southern Wisconsin's climax forests are sugar maple (the state tree), white elm, basswood, and ironwood, with silver maple, black willow, silver birch, and cottonwood on low, moist land. Prairies are thick with grasses; bogs and marshes are home to white and jack pines and jack oak. Forty-five varieties of orchid have been identified, as well as 20 types of violet, including the wood violet (the state flower). Threatened plants include lenticular sedge, ram's-head lady's-slipper, blue ash, prairie white-fringed orchid, prairie bush-clover, and snow trillium. Lake cress, harbinger-of-spring, pink milkwort, wild petunia, Lake Huron tansy, mountain cranberry, northern wild monkshood, and dwarf bilberry are listed as endangered.

White-tailed deer, black bear, woodchuck, snowshoe hare, chipmunk, and porcupine are mammals typical of forestlands. The striped skunk, red and gray foxes, and various mice are characteristic of upland fields, while wetlands harbor such mammals as the muskrat, mink, river otter, and water shrew. The badger, dwelling in grasslands and semi-open areas, is rarely seen today. Game birds include the ring-necked pheasant, bobwhite quail, Hungarian partridge, and ruffed grouse; among 336 bird species native to Wisconsin are 42 kinds of waterfowl and 6 types of shorebird that are also hunted. Reptiles include 23 varieties of snake, 13 types of turtle, and 4 kinds of lizard. Muskellunge (the state fish), northern pike, walleye, and brook trout are native to Wisconsin waterways.

Among threatened animals are the red-shouldered hawk, greater prairie chicken, glass lizard, Blanding's turtle, pickerel frog, and longear sunfish. The pine marten, Canada lynx, timber wolf, bald eagle, barn owl, osprey, queen snake, massasauga, slender madtom, and Higgins' eye pearly mussel are on the endangered list. The Bureau of Endangered Resources in the Department of Natural Resources develops programs designed to aid the recovery of threatened or endangered flora and fauna.

⁵ENVIRONMENTAL PROTECTION

Conservation has been a concern in Wisconsin for more than a century. In 1867, a legislative commission reported that depletion of the northern forests by wasteful timber industry practices and frequent forest fires had become an urgent problem, partly because it increased the hazards of flooding. In 1897, a forestry warden was appointed and a system of fire detection and control was set up. A reforestation program was instituted in 1911; at about the same time, the state university began planting rows of trees in plains areas to protect soil from wind erosion, a method that was widely copied in other states. Fish and game wardens were appointed in the 1880s. In 1927, the state began a program to clean its waters of industrial wastes, caused especially by pulp and paper mills and canneries. The legislature enacted a comprehensive antipollution program in 1966.

The present Department of Natural Resources (DNR), organized in 1967, brings together conservation and environmental protection responsibilities. The department supervises air, water, and solid-waste pollution control programs and deals with the protection of forest, fish, and wildlife resources.

Southeastern Wisconsin has experienced serious air quality problems since the 1970s. Reductions in industrial emissions have been offset by increases in emissions from transportation sources and consumer products. Six counties in the area must reduce ozone enough to meet health standards early in the next century.

Since water pollution became a serious problem in the 1920s, pulp and paper mills, cheese factories, and canneries have taken major steps to control and prevent harmful water pollution. Communities built new or upgraded existing sewage treatment plants to reduce the flow of sewage into rivers and streams. Pulp and paper mills spent millions of dollars to reduce suspended solids and other pollutants in their industrial effluent. Water quality and fisheries visibly improved, but problems caused by persistent toxic chemicals, such as PCBs (polychlorinated biphenyls) and mercury, arose that had to be addressed next. In the 1980s, the state identified five Areas of Concern on Lakes Michigan and Superior where toxic pollutants harmed fish or wildlife or impaired human use of the waterways. Efforts are underway to identify sources of contamination and clean-up options at these sites and inland areas suffering similar problems. Regulations controlling the discharge of toxic substances from both water and air were passed in the late 1980s.

Contaminated stormwater and run-off from agriculture, development, and other sources remain the most serious threats to Wisconsin's lakes, rivers, and streams. The state currently is adopting rules to limit stormwater contamination in large municipalities, construction sites over five acres, and 10,000 industrial facilities. The DNR also formed a citizen advisory committee in 1994 to overhaul the state's animal waste regulations. Wetland protection regulations were upgraded in the late 1980s, and in 1991 the state became the first in the nation to legislate wetlands protection. In 1996, 15% of Wisconsin was wetlands.

Wisconsin passed a comprehensive groundwater protection law in 1984 to safeguard underground water supplies that serve two-thirds of the state's 5.2 million people. The law requires identification and clean-up of groundwater-damaging contamination sources, such as abandoned, leaking landfills; underground gasoline storage tanks; and illegal, hazardous waste dumps. The law also requires the state to establish groundwater protection and enforcement standards for various substances. Wisconsin has identified over 16,000 contamination sites that must be cleaned up to prevent environmental contamination and safety hazards. Over one-third of these sites have been cleaned up

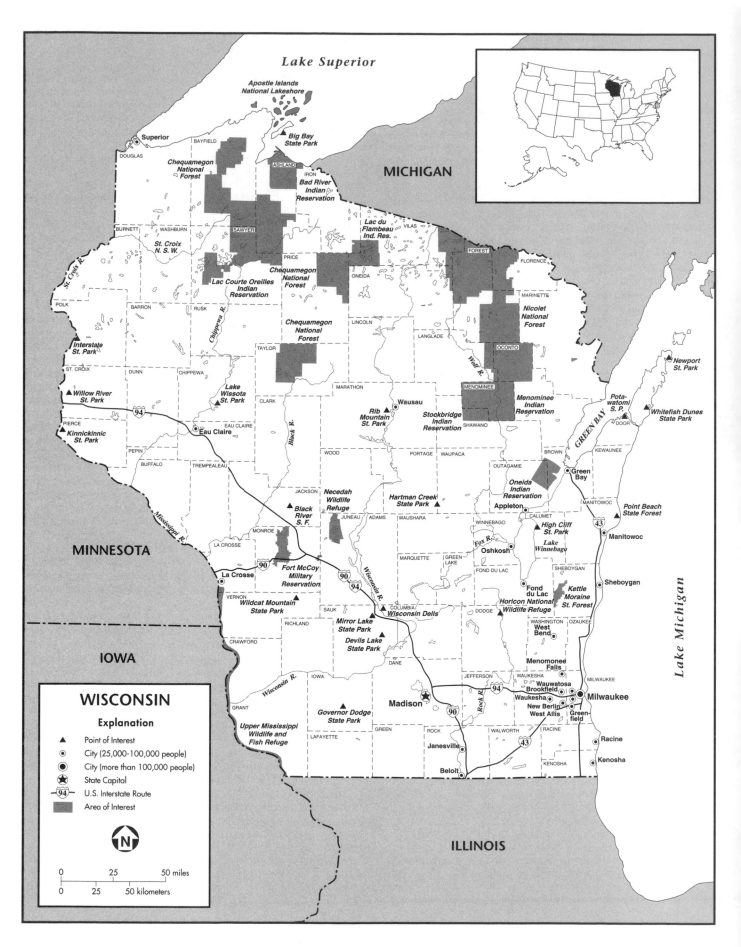

and no further action is deemed necessary. The state is developing a comprehensive rule package designed to guide the investigation and clean-up of these sites.

In 1996, Wisconsin began administering a new program whereby owners of contaminated property could petition the state for clean-up waivers if they were able to demonstrate that contamination was being cleaned up by natural processes. Property owners would then be able to redevelop within strict guidelines and monitoring. By mid-1997, 51 properties had applied for such liability releases, 30 of which were approved.

During the 1980s, groundwater monitoring programs found pesticide and nitrate problems in many private wells. Best-management practices, citing considerations and limits on the application of various agricultural pesticides, are being used to prevent this problem from worsening.

Bacterial contamination of Wisconsin drinking water supplies did not pose much of a problem in the state until 1993, when 400,000 Milwaukee residents became ill from inadequately treated water drawn from Lake Michigan. The water was found to contain the protozoan Cryptosporidium. Water treatment procedures were changed immediately at 21 community drinking water treatment plants that drew water from the Great Lakes. The state also began a two-year Cryptosporidium monitoring effort to determine the presence and distribution of this protozoan in state waterways.

In the 1980s, more than 800 landfills in the state closed because they could not meet new federal environmental protection requirements. To ease the burden on the state's remaining landfills, Wisconsin passed a comprehensive waste reduction and recycling law, 1989 Wisconsin Act 335. The law required local units of government to set up effective programs to recycle more than 11 different items by 1995. State grants collected from a tax on businesses were awarded to local governments to aid in setting up local recycling programs, with a total of nearly $30 million in grants awarded in 1994. The legislature is expected to decide a permanent funding mechanism in a future legislative session.

⁶POPULATION

Wisconsin ranked 16th in population among the 50 states in 1990, with a census population of 4,891,769. The population was estimated at 5,159,795 for 1996, a 5.5% increase over the 1990 census.

During the 18th and early 19th centuries, the area that is now Wisconsin was very sparsely settled by perhaps 20,000 Indians and a few hundred white settlers, most of them engaged in the fur trade. With the development of lead mining, the population began to expand, reaching a total of 30,945 (excluding Indians) by 1840. During the next two decades, the population increased rapidly to 775,881, as large numbers of settlers from the East and German, British, and Scandinavian immigrants arrived. Subsequent growth has been steady, if slower. In the late 19th century, industry expanded and, by 1930, the population became predominantly urban.

The 1990 census showed a population increase of 4.0% since 1980, below the national average. Average population density in 1990 was 90.1 per sq mi (34.6 per sq km). Of the 1990 population, about 50.9% were females and 49.1% males. About 13.4% of the population was 65 years of age or older in 1990, somewhat above the US average.

Almost two-thirds (65.7%) of all Wisconsinites lived in urban areas in 1990, most of them in the heavily urbanized southeastern region. Milwaukee, the largest city in Wisconsin and, as of 1990, the 17th-largest in the US, had a population of 628,088 in 1990 and an estimated population of 617,044 in 1994. Other large cities, with their 1994 population estimates, were Madison, 194,586; Green Bay, 102,708; Racine, 86,014; and Kenosha,

85,122. The state's largest metropolitan area, Milwaukee-Racine, had an estimated 1,640,831 residents as of 1995.

⁷ETHNIC GROUPS

As early as 1839, Wisconsin attracted immigrants from Norway, Sweden, Denmark, and Finland, soon to be followed by large numbers of Germans and Irish. In 1850, the greatest number of foreign-born persons were English-speaking, but within a decade, the Germans had eclipsed them. Industrial development brought Belgians, Greeks, Hungarians, Lithuanians, Italians, and especially Poles, who continued to come steadily until the restriction of immigration in the early 1920s; in the 1930 census, Poles were the largest foreign-born group. In 1990, foreign-born residents numbered 121,547 (2.5% of the total).

Black Americans were in the region as early as 1822. Before World War I, however, there were no more than 3,000 blacks. Migration during and after that war brought the number to 10,739 by 1930; by 1990, blacks were the largest racial minority in the state, numbering 245,000 (5% of Wisconsin's population). Most black Wisconsinites live in Milwaukee, which was 30% black in 1990.

Asians are few in number: in 1990 there were 15,942 Hmong, 7,147 Chinese, 6,499 Koreans, 5,297 Laotians, and 4,942 Filipinos. As of 1990 there were 93,000 state residents of Hispanic origin, of whom 51,339 were of Mexican ancestry and 15,493 of Puerto Rican descent.

Wisconsin had 39,000 American Indians in 1990. The principal tribes are Oneida, Menominee, Ojibwa (Chippewa), and Winnebago. There were 11 reservations, the largest being that of the Menominee, which comprised Menominee County (345 sq mi 896 sq km) and had an estimated population of 4,452 in 1995. Indian reservations covered 634 sq mi (1,642 sq km).

⁸LANGUAGES

Early French and English fur traders found in what is now Wisconsin several Indian tribes of the Algonkian family: Ojibwa along Lake Superior, Sauk in the northeast, Winnebago and Fox south of them, and Kickapoo in the southwest. Numerous Indian place-names include Antigo, Kaukauna, Kewaunee, Menomonie, Oshkosh, Wausau, and Winnebago.

Wisconsin English is almost entirely Northern, like that of the areas that provided Wisconsin's first settlers—Michigan, northern Ohio, New York State, and western New England. Common are the Northern *pail, comforter* (tied and filled bedcover), *sick to the stomach, angleworm* (earthworm), *skip school* (play truant), and *dove* as the past of *dive*. Pronunciation features are *fog, frog,* and *on* with the vowel sound /ah/; and *orange, forest,* and *foreign* with the /aw/ vowel sound. Northern *fried cakes* is now yielding to *doughnuts,* and *johnnycake* is giving way to *corn bread.* Milwaukee has *sick in the stomach* and is known for the localism *bubbler* (drinking fountain). A small exception to Northern homogeneity is the cluster of South Midland terms brought by Kentucky miners to the southwestern lead-mining district, such as *dressing* (sweet sauce for a pudding), *eaves spout* as a blend of *eavestrough* and Midland *spouting, branch* for stream, and *fishworm* for earthworm.

In 1990, 94.2% of the state population 5 years old and older spoke only English in the home. Other languages spoken at home and the number of speakers included:

Spanish	75,931	French	14,242
German	61,929	Various Scandinavian	10,386
Polish	20,143	Italian	8,661

⁹RELIGIONS

The largest religious groups in Wisconsin are Roman Catholics and Lutherans.

The first Catholics to arrive were Jesuit missionaries seeking to convert the Huron Indians in the 17th century. Protestant settlers and missionaries of different sects, including large numbers of German Lutherans, came during the 19th century, along with Protestants from the east. Jews settled primarily in the cities.

These groups often had conflicting aims. Evangelical sects favored strict blue laws and temperance legislation, which was enacted in many communities. The use of Protestant prayers and the King James Bible in public schools was another source of public discord until these practices were declared unconstitutional by the state supreme court in 1890. A constitutional amendment allowing parochial school students to ride in public school buses was defeated in 1946, amid great controversy; 19 years later, however, it was enacted with little opposition. By that time, religious conflicts appeared to be on the decline.

As of the end of 1990, there were 1,554,278 Roman Catholics (one-half of the population) in Wisconsin. Of Protestant denominations in 1990, the Evangelical Lutheran Church in American had the most members, 460,168; followed by the Lutheran Church-Missouri Synod, 248,876; and the United Methodists, 152,426. There were an estimated 34,605 Jews in 1990, 76% of them in Milwaukee.

10TRANSPORTATION

Wisconsin's first rail line was built across the state, from Milwaukee to Prairie du Chien, in the 1850s. Communities soon began vying with one another to be included on proposed railroad routes. Several thousand farmers mortgaged property to buy railroad stock; the state had to rescue them from ruin when companies went bankrupt. By the late 1860s, two railroads—the Chicago and North Western, and the Chicago, Milwaukee, and St. Paul—had become dominant in the state. However, Chicago emerged as the major rail center of the Midwest because of its proximity to eastern markets. In 1920, there were 35 railroads operating on 11,615 mi (18,700 km) of track; by 1996 there were just 10 railroads operating on 4,170 rail mi (6,714 km) of track, with only 40% for Class I lines. The state was 3d-highest in the amount of terminated rail-tons of metallic ores in 1995, at 15.3 million tons. That same year, 7 shortlines hauled 124,648,000 tons of freight. Amtrak provides passenger rail service to Milwaukee, Tomah, and several other cities throughout Wisconsin. Under a three-year contract signed in May 1997, the Hiawatha service between Chicago and Milwaukee provided 4 round trips daily. The Hiawatha had 328,755 passengers in 1996.

As of 1 January 1995, Wisconsin had 111,500 mi (178,400 km) of roadway; about 55% of this mileage consisted of town roads, 28% state or county highways, 11% city streets, 4% village streets, and 1% park and forest roads. The private passenger vehicle continues to be the dominant mode of travel. In 1997, Wisconsin had 3,601,619 licensed drivers and 3,845,415 registered vehicles (2,386,133 automobiles and 1,459,282 trucks).

Public transit includes large bus systems in Milwaukee and Madison. In 1996, Milwaukee County Transit System gave 60,029,178 people rides, and Madison Metro gave rides to 9,971,456 people.

The opening of the St. Lawrence Seaway in 1959 allowed oceangoing vessels access to Wisconsin via the Great Lakes but failed to stimulate traffic to the extent anticipated. Overall, the state has 15 cargo-handling ports. The port of Superior (shared with Duluth, Minn.) on Lake Superior is the busiest of all US Great Lakes ports. Its chief commodities are iron ore and coal; in 1996, it handled 37,182,106 tons of cargo. Other important Wisconsin ports, all on Lake Michigan, were Milwaukee, Green Bay, Port Washington, Oak Creek, Manitowoc, and Sturgeon Bay; coal was the chief commodity. On the Mississippi River, Prairie du Chien and La Crosse are the main ports. Ferry service across Lake Michigan is offered from Manitowoc to Ludington, Michigan.

As of 1 January 1997, Wisconsin had 691 airports. In 1996, 4,114,213 passengers enplaned at Wisconsin airports, with 2,729,311 being at Milwaukee's General Mitchell International Airport. In 1995, 33,964 tons of cargo and freight were enplaned at Wisconsin airports.

11HISTORY

The region that is now Wisconsin has probably been inhabited since the end of the glacial period, 10,000 years ago. Some of the earliest inhabitants were ancestors of the Menominee; these early immigrants from the north built burial mounds, conical ones at first, then large effigy mounds shaped like different animals. Other peoples arrived from the south and east, including ancestors of the Winnebago Indians (about AD 1400) and a tribe that built flat-top earthen pyramids. During the 17th century, the Ojibwa, Sauk, Fox, Potawatomi, Kickapoo, and other tribes came to Wisconsin. These tribes engaged in agriculture, hunting, and fishing, but with the arrival of Europeans, they became increasingly dependent on the fur trade—a dependence that had serious economic consequences when the fur trade declined in the early 19th century.

The first European believed to have reached Wisconsin was Jean Nicolet, who in 1634 landed on the shores of Green Bay while in the service of Samuel de Champlain. Two decades later, Médard Chouart des Groseilliers and Pierre Esprit Radisson, both fur traders, explored northern Wisconsin; in 1673, the Jesuit priest Jacques Marquette and the explorer Louis Jolliet crossed the whole area that is now Wisconsin, via the Fox and Wisconsin rivers, on their way to the Mississippi. Other Jesuits established missions, and French fur traders opened up posts. The French were succeeded by the British after the French and Indian War (the British ruled Wisconsin as part of Quebec Province from 1774 to 1783). Although ceded to the US in 1783, it remained British in all but name until 1816, when the US built forts at Prairie du Chien and Green Bay.

Under the Ordinance of 1787, Wisconsin became part of the Northwest Territory; it was subsequently included in the Indiana Territory, the Territory of Illinois, and then the Michigan Territory. In the early 1820s, lead mining brought an influx of white settlers called "Badgers." Indian resistance to white expansion collapsed after the 1832 Black Hawk War, in which Sauk and Fox Indians fleeing from Illinois were defeated and massacred by white militia near the site of present-day La Crosse, at the Battle of Bad Axe. Subsequently, the Winnebago and other tribes were removed to reservations outside the state, while the Ojibwa, Menominee, and some eastern tribes were among those resettled in reservations inside Wisconsin.

The Wisconsin Territory was formed in 1836. Initially it included all of Iowa and Minnesota, along with a portion of the Dakotas, but in 1838, these areas became part of a newly organized Iowa Territory. The 1830s also saw the beginning of a land boom, fueled by migration of Yankees from New England and southerners who moved to the lead-mining region of southwestern Wisconsin. The population and economy began to expand rapidly. Wisconsin voters endorsed statehood in 1846, and Congress passed enabling legislation that year. After a first constitution was rejected by the voters, a revised document was adopted on 13 March 1848, and on 29 May, President James K. Polk signed the bill that made Wisconsin the 30th state.

Transportation and industry did not develop as rapidly as proponents of statehood had expected. A canal was opened at the portage between the Fox and Wisconsin rivers in 1851, but the waterway was not heavily used. Railroads encountered difficulties in gaining financing, then suffered setbacks in the panic of 1857.

Wisconsinites took a generally abolitionist stand, and it was in Wisconsin—at Ripon, on 28 February 1854—that the Republican Party was formally established in the state. The new party developed an efficient political machine and later used much of its influence to benefit the railroads and lumber industry, both of which grew in importance in the decade following the Civil War. In that war, 96,000 Wisconsin men fought on the Union side, and 12,216 died. During the late 19th century, Wisconsin was generally prosperous; dairying, food processing, and lumbering emerged as major industries, and Milwaukee grew into an important industrial center.

Wisconsin took a new political turn in the early 20th century with the inauguration of Republican Robert "Fighting Bob" La Follette as governor and the dawning of the Progressive Era. An ardent reformer, La Follette fought against conservatives within his own party. In 1903, the legislature, under his prodding, passed a law providing for the nation's first direct statewide primary; other measures that he championed during his tenure as governor (1901–06) provided for increased taxation of railroads, regulation of lobbyists, creation of a civil service, and establishment of a railroad commission to regulate intrastate rates.

La Follette was also a conspicuous exponent of what came to be called the "Wisconsin idea": governmental reform guided by academic experts and supported by an enlightened electorate. Around the time he was governor, the philosophy of reform was energetically promoted at the University of Wisconsin (which had opened at Madison, the state capital, in 1849), and many professors were drafted to serve on government commissions and boards. In 1901, Wisconsin became the first state to establish a legislative reference bureau, intended to help lawmakers shape effective, forward-looking measures.

After La Follette left the governor's office to become a US senator, his progressivism was carried on by Republican governors James O. Davidson (1906–11) and especially by Francis E. McGovern (1911–15). During one session in 1911, legislators enacted the first state income tax in the US and one of the first workers' compensation programs. Other legislation passed during the same year sought to regulate the insurance business and the use of water power, create forest reserves, encourage farmer cooperatives, limit and require disclosure of political campaign expenditures, and establish a board of public affairs to recommend efficiency measures for state and local governments. This outburst of activity attracted national attention, and many states followed in Wisconsin's footsteps.

While serving as US senator (1906–25), La Follette opposed involvement in World War I and was one of only six senators to vote against US entry into the war; as a result, he was censured by the state legislature and the faculty of the University of Wisconsin, and there was a move to expel him from the Senate. His renomination and reelection in 1922 served to vindicate him, however, and he carried Wisconsin when he ran in 1924 for president on the national League for Progressive Political Action ticket.

After his death in 1925, the reform tradition continued in Wisconsin. A pioneering old-age pension act was passed in 1925; seven years later, Wisconsin enacted the nation's first unemployment compensation act, with the encouragement of La Follette's son Philip, then serving his first term as governor. When Wisconsin went Democratic in November 1932, turning Philip out of office, he and his brother, Robert, Jr., a US senator, temporarily left the state Republican organization and in 1934 formed a separate Progressive Party; that party, with the support of President Franklin Roosevelt and the Socialists, swept the 1934 elections and returned both brothers to office. During his second and third terms as governor, Philip La Follette successfully pressed for the creation of state agencies to develop electric power, arbitrate labor disputes, and set rules for fair business competition; his so-called Little New Deal corresponded to the New Deal policies of the Roosevelt administration.

After World War II, the state continued a trend toward increased urbanization, and its industries prospered. The major figure on the national scene in the postwar era was Senator Joseph R. McCarthy, who served 10 years in the Senate, launching unsubstantiated attacks in the early 1950s on alleged communists and other subversives in the federal government. After McCarthy's censure by the US Senate in 1954 and death in 1957, the Progressive tradition began to recover strength, and the liberal Democratic Party grew increasingly influential in state politics. There was student unrest at the University of Wisconsin during the 1960s and early 1970s, and growing discontent among Milwaukee's black population. A major controversy in the 1970s concerned a court-ordered busing plan, implemented in 1979, aimed at decreasing racial imbalances in Milwaukee's public schools. In 1984, the Milwaukee school board filed suit in federal court, charging that the policies of the state and suburban schools had resulted in an unconstitutionally segregated school system that restricted blacks to city schools. Two years later, the city school board and 9 suburban districts agreed on a plan by which minority students from the city would transfer voluntarily to the 9 suburbs, and suburban students would attend Milwaukee schools.

Wisconsin's economy, with its strong manufacturing and agricultural sectors, remained sound throughout the 1980s and into the 1990s. The dairy industry, traditionally a mainstay of the economy, was linked to two different environmental issues. The first was the 1993 contamination of Milwaukee's drinking water with harmful bacteria that made thousands of people sick and killed some of them. Some claimed that the organisms had come from agricultural runoff containing animal wastes. The second issue was the use of bovine growth hormone to bolster milk production.

Flooding of the Mississippi River in 1993 cause massive damage in Wisconsin. Forty-seven counties were declared federal disaster areas, four people were killed, and financial losses totaled $900 million.

12 STATE GOVERNMENT

Wisconsin's first constitutional convention, meeting in Madison in October 1846, was marked by controversy between conservative Whigs and allied Democrats on the one hand, and progressive Democrats with a constituency made up of miners, farmers, and immigrants on the other. The latter, who favored the popular election of judges and exemption of homesteads from seizure for debt, among other provisions, carried the day, but this version of the constitution failed to win ratification. A second constitutional convention, convened in December 1847, agreed on a new draft which made few major changes. This document, ratified by the electorate in 1848 and amended 127 times as of the end of 1993, remains in effect today.

The Wisconsin legislature consists of a senate with 33 members elected for four-year terms, and an assembly of 99 representatives elected for two-year terms. Legislators must be state residents for one year prior to election, and residents of their districts at least 10 days before the election. Voters elect an assembly and half the senate membership in even-numbered years. Regular legislative sessions begin in January. Each house elects its own presiding officer and other officers from among its members. The legislative salary in 1995 was $38,056.

There are six elected state officers: governor and lieutenant governor (elected jointly), secretary of state, state treasurer, attorney general, and superintendent of public instruction. Since 1970, all have been elected for four-year terms. The governor and lieutenant governor must be US citizens and qualified voters; there are no additional age or residency requirements. In 1996 the governor's salary was $101,861. As the chief executive officer, the governor exercises authority by the power of appointment, by presenting a budget bill and major addresses to the legislature, and by the power to veto bills and call special legislative sessions. Of 15 administrative departments in the executive branch, two—the Department of Justice, and the Department of Public Instruction—are headed by the attorney general and the superintendent of public instruction, respectively. Eight departments are headed by secretaries appointed by the governor with the advice and consent of the senate, while the Department of Military Affairs is headed by the adjutant general, who is appointed by the governor alone; part-time boards appoint the heads of the four remaining departments. There were also 18 independent agencies in 1983, of which 5 were headed by individual commissioners and 13 by commissions or boards.

A bill may be introduced in either house of the legislature, but must be passed by both houses to become law. The governor has six days (Sundays excluded) to sign or veto a measure. If the governor fails to act and the legislature is still in session, the bill automatically becomes law. Vetoes can be overridden by a two-thirds majority of both houses. Constitutional amendments may be introduced in either house. They must be approved by a simple majority of both houses in two successive legislatures and then ratified by a majority of the electorate at a subsequent election.

Voters must be US citizens 18 years of age or older and must have resided in the state for at least 10 days before the election. The residency requirement is waived in voting for US president and vice-president. Wisconsin has a statewide primary open to all without respect to party affiliation, a procedure that was challenged by the national Democratic Party. As a result, in 1984, for the first time, the Democratic party presidential primary results were not used to select delegates to the national convention.

13POLITICAL PARTIES

The Democratic Party dominated politics until the late 1850s; then the newly founded Republican Party held sway for almost 100 years. More recently, the Democrats have held a substantial edge at the state level.

Jacksonian democracy was strong in Wisconsin in the early days, and until 1856 all territorial and state governors were Democrats, except for one Whig. In 1854, however, a coalition of Whigs, antislavery Democrats, and Free Soilers formed a Republican Party in the state—a key event in the establishment of the national Republican Party. Republicans quickly gained control of most elective offices; from 1856 to 1959 there were only three Democratic governors. The Republican Party was dominated in the late 19th century by conservatives, who were sympathetic to the railroads and the lumbering industry but whose stands on pensions and jobs for Union veterans and ability to win federal funds for the state attracted support from farmers and small business. Then, in the 1890s, Progressives within the party, led by Robert La Follette, began a successful battle for control that culminated in La Follette's election as governor in 1900.

The La Follette brand of progressivism remained strong in the state, although not always under the umbrella of Republicanism. In 1924, La Follette ran for president on the Progressive ticket; 10 years later, his sons, Robert and Philip, also broke away from the GOP, to head a Progressive Party slate. However, their newly organized national third party faded and folded when Philip La Follette failed to be reelected governor, and World War II made isolationism unpopular. The Progressives rejoined the GOP in 1946.

Socialist parties have won some success in Wisconsin's political history. Socialists worked with progressive Republicans at the state level to pass important legislation in the early 20th century. In 1910, the Socialists scored two major political victories in Wisconsin: Emil Seidel was elected mayor of Milwaukee, becoming the first Socialist mayor of a major US city, and Victor Berger became the first Socialist ever elected to Congress.

There is no statewide system of registration by parties; registered voters numbered 3,602,787 in 1994.

Democratic incumbent Bill Clinton won 49% of the vote in the 1996 presidential election; Republican Bob Dole received 38%, and Independent Ross Perot collected 10%. Wisconsin's senators, both Democrats, are Russell Feingold, elected in 1992, and Herbert Kohl, reelected in 1994. Wisconsin's US House

Wisconsin Presidential Vote by Political Party, 1948–96

YEAR	ELEC. VOTE	WISCONSIN WINNER	DEMOCRAT	REPUBLICAN	PROGRESSIVE	SOCIALIST	SOC. WORKERS	SOCIALIST LABOR
1948	12	*Truman (D)	647,310	590,959	25,282	12,547	—	399
1952	12	*Eisenhower (R)	622,175	979,744	2,174	1,157	1,350	770
					CONSTITUTION			
1956	12	*Eisenhower (R)	586,768	954,844	6,918	754	564	710
1960	12	Nixon (R)	830,805	895,175	—	—	1,792	1,310
1964	12	*Johnson (D)	1,050,424	638,495	—	—	1,692	1,204
1968	12	*Nixon (R)	748,804	809,997	—	—	1,222	1,338
					AMERICAN IND.	AMERICAN		
1972	11	*Nixon (R)	810,174	989,430	127,835	47,525	—	998
						SOCIALIST		LIBERTARIAN
1976	11	*Carter (D)	1,040,232	1,004,967	8,552	4,298	1,691	3,814
							Citizens	
1980	11	*Reagan (R)	981,584	1,088,845	**1,519	—	7,767	29,135
1984	11	*Reagan (R)	995,740	1,198,584	—	—	—	4,883
					POPULIST	SOC. WORKERS	NEW ALLIANCE	
1988	11	Dukakis (D)	1,126,794	1,047,499	3,056	2,574	1,953	5,157
						IND. (Perot)	TAXPAYERS	
1992	11	*Clinton (D)	1,041,066	930,855	2,311	544,479	1,772	2,877
							IND. (Nader)	
1996	11	*Clinton (D)	1,071,971	845,029	—	227,339	28,723	7,929

*Won US presidential election.
**Listed as Constitution Party on Wisconsin ballot.

delegation consists of 4 Republicans and 5 Democrats. After the November 1996 elections, there were 17 Democrats and 16 Republicans in the state senate, and 47 Democrats and 52 Republicans in the state assembly. Wisconsin's governor, Tommy Thompson, who was reelected to an unprecedented third four-year term in 1994, is a Republican.

In 1994 there were 30 blacks and 2 Hispanics holding public office. As of 1995, 32 women served in the state legislature.

¹⁴LOCAL GOVERNMENT

Wisconsin has 72 counties, 583 municipal governments, 1,266 townships, and 440 school districts. There were also 377 special districts, each providing a certain local service, such as sewerage or fire fighting, usually across municipal lines.

Each county is governed by a board of supervisors (which in the most populous counties has more than 40 members), elected for two years, except in Milwaukee County where the term is four years. Eight counties, including Milwaukee County, have elected county executives, serving four-year terms; 10 had an appointed administrator or similar official. Other county officials include district attorneys, sheriffs, clerks, treasurers, coroners, registers of deeds, and surveyors.

Towns are civil subdivisions of counties equivalent to townships in other states. Each town is a unit of 6 sq mi (16 sq km) marked off for governmental purposes. Cities and villages have home-rule powers limited by legislative review. Each incorporated village must have at least 150 residents; each incorporated city, 1,000.

Most cities are governed by a mayor-council system; about 6% of all cities have a council-manager system, which was first authorized in Wisconsin in 1923. Executive power in a village is vested in an elected president who presides over an elected board but has no veto power.

Wisconsin towns are generally small units with populations under 2,500. Each town is governed by a board of supervisors elected every two years; a town supervisor carries out policies set at an annual April town meeting.

¹⁵STATE SERVICES

A six-member Ethics Board, appointed by the governor, administers an ethics code for public officials and employees and investigates complaints against them. The board may refer cases for criminal prosecution.

The Department of Public Instruction administers public elementary and secondary education in the state, and the Board of Regents of the University of Wisconsin System has jurisdiction over all public higher education. A Board of Vocational, Technical, and Adult Education supervises programs in these areas.

The Transportation Department plans, constructs, and maintains highways and licenses motor vehicles and drivers. Physical and mental health, corrections, public and medical assistance, service to the aged, children's services, and vocational rehabilitation fall within the purview of the Department of Health and Social Services. The Department of Industry, Labor, and Human Relations enforces antidiscrimination laws in employment as well as minimum standards for wages and working conditions, provides training for the unemployed and disadvantaged, and sets safety standards for buildings.

Public protection in general is provided by the Department of Justice, which is responsible for investigating crimes of statewide magnitude and offering technical assistance to local law enforcement agencies. Regulations to protect consumers are administered and enforced by the Trade and Consumer Protection Division of the Department of Agriculture, Trade, and Consumer Protection, in cooperation with the Justice Department. The Army and Air National Guard are under the Department of Military Affairs.

The Department of Development has responsibilities in the areas of community, economic, and housing development, promotion of trade and tourism, and small and minority business assistance.

¹⁶JUDICIAL SYSTEM

The judicial branch is headed by a supreme court, consisting of seven justices, elected statewide on a nonpartisan basis for terms of 10 years. Vacancies are filled by gubernatorial appointment until an open election day becomes available. The justice with the greatest seniority serves as chief justice. The supreme court, which is the final authority on state constitutional questions, hears appeals at its own discretion and has original jurisdiction in limited areas.

The state's next-highest court is the court of appeals, established by constitutional amendment in 1977. Its 13 judges are elected by district on a nonpartisan basis and serve staggered six-year terms. Vacancies are filled by the governor until a successor is elected. Judges sit in panels of 3 for most cases, although some cases can be heard by a single judge. Decisions by the court of appeals may be reviewed by the supreme court.

The circuit court, the trial court of general jurisdiction, also hears appeals from municipal courts. Circuit court boundaries coincide with county boundaries, except that 3 judicial circuits comprise 2 counties each; thus, there are 69 judicial circuits. Trial judges are elected by district on a nonpartisan basis for six-year terms. All justices at the circuit court level or higher must have at least five years' experience as practicing attorneys and be less than 70 years old in order to qualify for office. Vacancies are filled by the governor until a successor is elected.

Wisconsin's 200 municipal courts have jurisdiction over local matters. Municipal judges are elected for terms of two or four years, generally serve on a part-time basis, and need not be attorneys. In 1996 there were 12,292 practicing attorneys in the state.

Wisconsin's crime rate in 1995 was 3,886 per 100,000 population, well below the national average of 5,277.6. The violent crime rate was 281.1 per 100,000 population in the state; during the same period, the national average was 684.6.

Inmates in federal and state prisons totaled 10,632 in 1996, or 209 per 100,000. Wisconsin's prison population increased by almost 55% between 1990 and 1995, one of the highest rates in the nation. Wisconsin does not have a death penalty.

¹⁷ARMED FORCES

In 1996, there were 376 active duty military personnel in Wisconsin. Prime military contracts amounted to $551 million in the same fiscal year.

A total of 3,932 Wisconsinites were killed in World War I, 7,980 in World War II, 800 in Korea, and 1,142 in Vietnam. An estimated 502,000 veterans were living in Wisconsin as of 1 July 1996. Of these fewer than 500 saw service in World War I; 134,000 in World War II; 81,000 in the Korean conflict; 152,000 in the Viet Nam era; and 34,000 in the Persian Gulf War. Wisconsin veterans received benefits exceeding $700 million in 1995/96.

Wisconsin's Reserve and National Guard units had 29,274 officers and enlisted members in 1996: 19,815 in the Army; 5,076 in the Navy and Marine Corps; and 4,383 in the Air Force. In 1993 the Wisconsin State Patrol employed 482 full-time sworn officers, or 1 per 10,000 residents.

¹⁸MIGRATION

Until the early 19th century, Wisconsin was inhabited mainly by Indians; the French and British brought few permanent settlers. In the 1820s, southerners began to arrive from the lower Mississippi, and in the 1830s easterners poured in from New York, Ohio, Pennsylvania, and New England.

Foreign immigrants began arriving in the 1820s, either directly from Europe or after temporary settlement in eastern states. Most of the early immigrants were from Ireland and England. Germans also came in large numbers, especially after the Revolution of 1848, and by 1860 they were predominant in the immigrant population, which was proportionately larger than in any other state except California. The state soon became a patchwork of ethnic communities—Germans in the counties near Lake Michigan, Norwegians in southern and western Wisconsin, Dutch in the lower Fox Valley and near Sheboygan, and other groups in other regions.

After the Civil War, and especially in the 1880s, immigration reached new heights, with Wisconsin receiving a large share of Germans and Scandinavians; the proportion of Germans declined, however, as new immigrants arrived from Finland and Russia and from southern and eastern Europe, especially Poland, before World War I. Despite this overseas immigration, Wisconsin suffered a net population loss from migration beginning in 1900, as Wisconsinites moved to other states. Between 1970 and 1983 alone, this loss totaled 154,000. From 1985 to 1990, the net loss from migration amounted to 3,150. Between 1990 and 1996, Wisconsin had net gains of 88,942 in domestic migration and 18,308 in international migration. In 1996, 3,607 foreign immigrants arrived in Wisconsin. As of 1990, 76.4% of state residents had been born in Wisconsin; only six other states had a higher percentage.

A significant trend since 1970 has been the decline in population in Milwaukee and other large cities; at the same time, suburbs have continued to grow, as have many other areas, especially in parts of northern Wisconsin. From 1985 to 1990, the net loss from migration amounted to 3,150. About 57% of residents age 5 and older in 1990 were living in the same house as in 1985. Of those who lived in a different house in 1985, 70% did so elsewhere within Wisconsin, predominately within the same county.

19INTERGOVERNMENTAL COOPERATION

The Commission on Interstate Cooperation represents the state in its dealings with the Council of State Governments. Wisconsin also participates in the Education Commission of the States, Great Lakes Basin Commission, Minnesota-Wisconsin Boundary Area Commission, and Mississippi River Parkway Commission. In 1985, Wisconsin, seven other Great Lakes states, and the Canadian provinces of Quebec and Ontario signed the Great Lakes Compact to protect the lakes' water reserves.

In 1995/96, Wisconsin received nearly $3.7 billion in federal aid.

20ECONOMY

With the coming of the first Europeans, fur trading became a major economic activity; as more settlers arrived, agriculture prospered. Although farming—preeminently dairying—remains important, manufacturing is the mainstay of today's economy. Wisconsin's industries are diversified, with nonelectrical machinery and food products the leading items. Other important industries are paper and pulp products, transportation equipment, electrical and electronic equipment, and fabricated metals. Economic growth has been concentrated in the southeast. There, soils and climate are favorable for agriculture; a skilled labor force is available to industry; and capital, transportation, and markets are most readily accessible.

As happened to the country at large, Wisconsin in 1981–82 experienced the worst economic slump since the Great Depression, with the unemployment rate rising to 11.7% in late

1982. Manufacturing was hard hit, and the loss of jobs in this sector was considered permanent. In 1994, Wisconsin's gross state product was $125,321 million, to which private goods-producing services contributed $43,566 million; private service-producing industries, $67,765 million; and government, $13,990 million. Wisconsin's per capita personal income in 1995 was $22,261, 22d in the nation. During 1996, there were 16,137 bankruptcy filings, up 27% from 1995.

21INCOME

In 1996, Wisconsin ranked 23d among the 50 states in per capita personal income, which was $23,269. Personal disposable income rose from $97.7 billion in 1995 to $102.5 billion in 1996. Median household income in 1996 was $40,955.

An estimated 8.5% of the population lived below the federal poverty level in 1995, down from 10.8% in 1992.

22LABOR

As of 1996, the civilian labor force (annual average) numbered 2,918,000 persons, of whom 2,815,000 (96.5%) were employed, and 103,000 (3.5%) were unemployed, slightly above the national rate. Of all nonfarm workers, 601,200 were employed in manufacturing as of 1996, primarily in the Milwaukee area.

Income and employment for Wisconsin during 1995 were as follows:

	EARNINGS (MILLIONS OF DOLLARS)	EMPLOYMENT (THOUSANDS OF JOBS)
Total	$80,827.0	2,677.4
Farm	297.5	27.6
Nonfarm	80,529.5	2,649.8
Private	69,443.9	2,262.9
Agricultural services, forestry, fisheries	495.8	17.9
Mining	118.4	2.5
Construction	4,889.3	104.8
Manufacturing	23,366.7	604.7
Nondurable goods	8,787.6	239.1
Durable goods	14,579.1	365.6
Transportation and public utilities	4,928.0	121.3
Wholesale trade	4,865.2	128.9
Retail trade	7,398.7	475.7
Finance, insurance, and real estate	5,154.9	140.4
Services	18,226.9	666.7
Government	11,085.6	386.9

Labor began to organize in the state after the Civil War. The Knights of St. Crispin, a shoemakers' union, grew into what was at that time the nation's largest union, before it collapsed during the Panic of 1873. In 1887, unions of printers, cigarmakers, and iron molders organized the Milwaukee Federated Trades Council, and in 1893 the Wisconsin State Federation of Labor was formed. A statewide union for public employees was established in 1932. In 1977, the state's legislature granted public employees (except public safety personnel) the right to strike, subject to certain limitations. As of 1995, labor union membership was approximately 429,000, or 17.7% of all nonfarm employment.

23AGRICULTURE

Farm marketings in 1995 amounted to $5.6 billion, 10th among the 50 states; over $3.9 billion in farm marketings came from dairy products and livestock. Wisconsin led the US in 1996 in the production of snap beans for processing, cranberries, processing beets, corn for silage, and cabbage for kraut. It also ranked 2d in sweet corn and peas, 3d in oats and carrots, 5th in fall potatoes, 6th in tart cherries, 7th in hay, and 9th in corn for grain.

In the early years, Wisconsin developed an agricultural economy based on wheat, some of which was exported to eastern states and overseas via the port of Milwaukee. Farmers also grew barley and hops, finding a market for these products among early

Milwaukee brewers. After the Civil War, soil exhaustion and the depredations of the chinch bug forced farmers to turn to other crops, including corn, oats, and hay, which could be used to feed hogs, sheep, cows, and other livestock.

Although agricultural income has continued to rise in recent years and the average size of farms has increased, farm acreage and the number of farms have declined. In 1996 there were 16.8 million acres (6.8 million hectares) of land in farms, nearly 50% of the total land area, distributed among 79,000 farms, a decline of 3,000 from 1986. Farmland is concentrated in the southern two-thirds of the state, especially in the southeast. Potatoes are grown mainly in central Wisconsin, cranberries in the Wisconsin River Valley, and cherries in the Door Peninsula.

Leading field crops (in bushels) in 1996 were corn for grain, 333,000,000; oats 17,400,000; soybeans, 32,190,000; wheat, 5,725,000; and barley, 3,975,000. About 6,050,000 tons of dry hay and 11,245,000 tons of corn for silage were harvested in 1995. Potato production was 31,590,000 hundredweight (14,329,224,000 kg). In 1996, Wisconsin farmers produced for processing 701,200 tons of sweet corn, 231,760 tons of snap beans, 88,070 tons of green peas, 1,860,000 barrels of cranberries, and 6,100,000 lb (2,767,000 kg) of tart cherries, along with 49,000,000 lb (22,000,000 kg) of commercial apples, and 413,000 lb (187,000 kg) of mint for oil. Some 24,100 tons of cucumber pickles were produced in 1996; 51,480 tons of beets for canning and 63,000 tons of cabbage for kraut were also grown.

24ANIMAL HUSBANDRY

Aided by the skills of immigrant cheesemakers and by the encouragement of dairy farmers who emigrated from New York—especially by the promotional effort of the agriculturist and publisher William D. Hoard—Wisconsin turned to dairying in the late 19th century. In 1995, Wisconsin ranked first in the number of milk cows with 1.49 million milk cows which produced nearly 23 billion lb (10.4 kg) of milk, and the state produced almost one third of the nation's cheese. Dairy farms are prominent in nearly all regions, but especially in the Central Plains and Western Uplands. Wisconsin ranchers also raise livestock for meat production.

In 1997, the state had 3.7 million cattle and calves, valued at $2.627 billion. During 1996, Wisconsin farms had about 800,000 hogs and pigs, valued at $76 million. Poultry farmers sold 7 million lb (3 million kg) of chicken in 1995. Also during 1995, there were 849 million eggs produced, valued at $30.6 million.

25FISHING

In 1995, Wisconsin ranked 25th among the 50 states in the value of its commercial fishing; 8,034,000 lb (3,644,000 kg) of fish were landed (not including Mississippi River landings), at a total value of $5,139,000. In 1995/96, federal hatcheries distributed over 7.8 million fish and 6.2 million fish eggs into Wisconsin's waters. The muskellunge is the premier game fish of Wisconsin's inland waters; Coho and chinook salmon, introduced to Lake Michigan, now thrive there. The largest concentration of lake sturgeon in the US is in Lake Winnebago. In 1995/96, the state issued 1,357,428 fishing licenses.

26FORESTRY

Wisconsin was once about 85% forested. Although much of the forest was depleted by forest fires and wasteful lumber industry practices, vast areas reseeded themselves naturally, and more than 820,000 acres (332,000 hectares) have been replanted. In 1992, Wisconsin had 15,513,000 acres (6,278,000 hectares) of forest, covering 45% of the state's land area; 70% of all forestlands are privately owned. Hardwoods make up about two-thirds of the

sawtimber. The most heavily forested region is in the north. The timber industry reached its peak in the late 19th century. In 1995, the lumber and paper industries employed 31,600 and 46,500 persons, respectively, with manufactured shipments valued at $3.8 billion and $14.5 billion.

Wisconsin's woods have recreational as well as commercial value. Two national forests—Chequamegon and Nicolet, both located in northern Wisconsin—cover 1,504,202 acres (608,731 hectares). The 10 state forests cover 471,329 acres (190,741 hectares).

Forest management and fire control programs are directed by the Department of Natural Resources. The US Forest Service operates a Forest Products Laboratory at Madison, in cooperation with the University of Wisconsin.

27MINING

The estimated value of nonfuel mineral commodities produced in Wisconsin rose 8% from $409 million in 1994 to $441 million in 1995. In 1995, nearly 33% of the nonfuel mineral value was attributed to metal production; higher metal values were the main cause for Wisconsin's increased mineral value. Wisconsin ranked 29th nationally in nonfuel mineral production value in 1995, compared with 30th in 1994. Crushed stone continued to be the leading mineral commodity produced in Wisconsin (28.2 million metric tons), followed by construction sand and gravel (31 million short tons), and lime (543,000 metric tons). These three accounted for an estimated 56% of the state's total mineral value. Crushed stone alone accounted for over 25% of Wisconsin mineral sales in 1995, while construction sand and gravel was worth $101,000,000, and lime had a value of $32,800,000.

28ENERGY AND POWER

The state's first hydroelectric plant was built at Appleton in 1882; many others were built later, especially along the Wisconsin River. Because Wisconsin itself has no coal, oil, or natural gas resources, the state has been active in developing alternative energy resources to increase its energy independence. Biomass energy is being developed for the production of ethanol; and waste wood is being used for utility generation and as fuel in industrial processes. Hydropower is a significant source of electricity generation in the paper industry and for electric utility generation.

In 1996, utility electric generation totaled 51.6 billion kwh, and total utility installed generating capacity was 11,800 million kW. As of 1 January 1996, there were 20 steam-generating plants, accounting for 62% of the state's total utility generating capacity, and 45 turbine or internal combustion generating plants, accounting for 21% of the utility generating capacity. The 75 hydroelectric plants accounted for about 4% of the installed capacity. The remaining 13% of generation capacity is nuclear power in three installations: Point Beach Units 1 and 2, operated by Wisconsin Electric Power Company; and the Kewaunee plant, operated by the Wisconsin Public Service Co.

29INDUSTRY

Industrial activity is concentrated in the southeast, especially the Milwaukee metropolitan area. Milwaukee has lost some of its luster as a brewery center; Miller and Pabst still have breweries there, but Schlitz beer is no longer made in Wisconsin, and Blatz and Old Style are brewed by G. Heileman in La Crosse.

Of the state's three biggest paper and lumber products firms, Consolidated Paper is located in Wisconsin Rapids, and Fort Howard Paper in Green Bay. Johnson & Son (wax products) and J. I. Case (agricultural equipment), the latter a subsidiary of Tenneco, are in Racine. Oscar Mayer (meat-packing and food products), located in Madison, is now a subsidiary of General Foods. Parker Pen Co. is in Janesville.

In 1995, the total value of shipments for manufactured goods in Wisconsin was $109,593,100,000. The value of shipments for selected industries were as follows:

INDUSTRY	1995 SHIPMENTS ($ MILLIONS)
Food and food products	$19,573
Industrial machinery and equipment	16,793
Paper and allied products	14,487
Transportation equipment	10,762
Electronic and other electric equipment	8,254
Fabricated metal products	7,346

As of 1997, Wisconsin was headquarters for eight Fortune 500 companies: Northwestern Mutual Life, Johnson Controls, Manpower, Case, American Family Insurance Group, Aid Association for Lutherans, Harnischfeger Industrial, and Roundy's. During 1995, there were 1,409 US patents issued to Wisconsin residents.

30 COMMERCE

Wholesale trade in 1992 totaled $47.6 billion. Retail sales for 1992 amounted to $38.4 billion, ranking 16th in the nation. Statewide, automotive dealers accounted for 21.6% of retail sales; food stores, 17.9%; general merchandise stores, 12.9%; eating and drinking places, 9.6%; and other establishments, 38.1%.

The state engages in foreign as well as domestic trade through the Great Lakes ports of Superior-Duluth, Milwaukee, Green Bay, and Kenosha. Iron ore and grain are shipped primarily from Superior-Duluth, while Milwaukee handles the heaviest volume of general merchandise. Wisconsin exported about $10.6 billion in goods (14th in the US) in 1996. Greater Milwaukee is a foreign-trade zone, where goods can enter duty-free under certain conditions.

31 CONSUMER PROTECTION

The Department of Agriculture, Trade, and Consumer Protection monitors food production, inspects meat, and administers grading programs; its Trade and Consumer Protection Division administers laws governing product safety and trade practices, in cooperation with the state Department of Justice. The Office of the Commissioner of Banking administers laws governing consumer credit, and the Department of Transportation's Motor Vehicles Division investigates complaints from buyers of new and used automobiles. The Department of Justice's Office of Consumer Protection Division provides protection against deceptive and fraudulent business practices through its consumer protection unit.

32 BANKING

As of 1996 there were 387 insured commercial banks in the state. Employment in banking was about 25,017 as of 1996. Commercial banks had assets totaling $61.4 billion and deposits exceeding $47.7 billion. There were 52 savings institutions with assets of over $23.4 billion. The Office of the Commissioner of Banking licenses and charters banks, loan and collection companies, and currency exchanges. The Office of the Commissioner of Savings and Loan supervises state-chartered savings and loan associations. The Office of the Commissioner of Credit Unions enforces laws relating to credit unions.

33 INSURANCE

There were 4,428,000 life insurance policies worth $224.3 billion in force in 1995; benefits paid totaled over $2.5 billion. The average family had $114,100 in life insurance. In 1995, automobile insurance premiums written in Wisconsin totaled $2.0 billion; homeowner premiums that year reached $354.4 million.

The Office of the Commissioner of Insurance licenses insurance agents, enforces state and federal regulations, responds to consumer complaints, and develops consumer education programs and literature. The office also operates the State Life Insurance Fund, which sells basic life insurance (maximum $10,000) to state residents; and the Local Government Property Insurance Fund, which insures properties of local government units on an optional basis.

34 SECURITIES

Wisconsin has no securities exchanges. As of May 1997, 1,527 brokers and dealers were registered to conduct business in the state by means of 60,603 designated representatives. Professional securities investment advice was available through 801 firms (3,115 registered agents) in May 1997. The sale of securities is regulated by the Department of Financial Institutions, Division of Securities.

35 PUBLIC FINANCE

Budget estimates are prepared by departments and sent to the governor or governor-elect in the fall of each even-numbered year; the following January, the governor presents a biennial budget to the legislature, which passes a budget bill, often after many amendments. Most appropriations are made separately for each year of the biennium. The fiscal year begins 1 July. Revenues and expenditures for 1996 were as follows (in thousands of dollars):

	1996
REVENUES	
Taxes	
Property	3,894,791
Sales and gross	2,949,576
Receipts	
Income	4,793,454
TOTAL	11,637,821
Charges and miscellaneous	
Current charges	2,109,590
Interest earnings	5,446,036
Special assessments	667,382
Other	3,982,531
TOTAL REVENUES	$23,843,360
EXPENDITURES	
Education	$ 5,978,715
Health and social concerns	5,623,499
Transportation (highway)	2,146,487
Public safety (police)	82,503
Natural resources	2,057,321
Housing and community development	575,240
Financial administration	50,048
Other	2,191,850
TOTAL GENERAL EXPENDITURES	$18,705,663

Expenditures by state and local governments alike have risen dramatically since 1960. At one time, the state was constitutionally prohibited from borrowing money; this provision was at first circumvented by the use of private corporations and then, in 1969, eliminated by constitutional amendment. As of 1995, state indebtedness exceeded $8.2 billion.

36 TAXATION

In 1995, state taxes amounted to $1,762.5 per capita. The largest single source of state revenue is the income tax on individuals.

Most local tax revenue comes from property taxes, and most of that goes for education.

In 1996, personal income tax rates on net taxable income ranged from 4.9% to 6.93%. The corporate tax rate was 7.9% of net income. The general sales tax in 1996 was 5%. Other state taxes are those on gasoline, cigarettes, liquor, wine, beer, motor vehicles, insurance companies, estates (limited to the amount of credit allowed under the federal estate tax), real estate transfers, and public utilities.

In 1996, total federal income receipts from Wisconsin were nearly $11.6 billion, or $2,046 per capita.

37ECONOMIC POLICY

The state seeks to promote the relocation of new industries to Wisconsin, as well as the expansion of existing ones, by providing advice and assistance through the Department of Development and some 280 local development corporations. It supports businesses that promise to substantially improve the economy of a community or the state; extends loans to small businesses; helps with the training or retraining of employees; and offers financial assistance for applied research that results in a new product or production process. To revitalize economically depressed areas, the state provides tax benefits to businesses locating or expanding operations in such areas and helps finance local economic development projects. Communities are authorized to issue tax-exempt bonds to enable industries to finance new equipment. In addition, all machinery and equipment used in goods production is tax-exempt under state law. Taxes on raw materials, work in progress, waste-treatment equipment, and finished goods inventories were eliminated entirely as of 1981.

38HEALTH

There were 13.2 live births per 1,000 population in 1995, a rate well below the national average. The infant mortality rate was 7.4 per 1,000 live births.

There were 15,549 legal abortions performed in Wisconsin during 1992, a ratio of 220 abortions for every 1,000 live births. State law prohibits the use of public funds for abortions, except in cases of incest or rape or for grave health reasons. The state does provide funds for family-planning counseling.

The death rate in 1996 was 880.8 per 100,000 population. As of 1991, Wisconsin ranked above the nation as a whole in death rates for heart disease, cerebrovascular disease and cancer, but below the national averages for accidents and suicide. Leading causes of death in 1995 were heart disease (281.4 deaths per 100,000 population), cancer (206.3), and cerebrovascular disease (69.8). Wisconsin ranked 31st out of 52 for coronary heart disease mortality rate in 1993. The overall smoking rate was 21.8% (24.5% of men and 19.3% of women) in 1995.

As of 1995, Wisconsin had 127 hospitals, with 14,553 beds. Hospital personnel included 45,100 nonfederal registered nurses in 1994. The average expense of hospitals for care in 1994 came to $5,536 per stay and $802 per inpatient day.

At the end of 1994 there were 10,349 active, nonfederal physicians. In 1994, the state had 2,977 active, licensed dentists. Medical degrees are granted by the University of Wisconsin at Madison and by the Medical College of Wisconsin (formerly part of Marquette University).

The Division of Health, a branch of the State Department of Health and Social Services, has responsibility for planning and supervising health services and facilities, enforcing state and federal regulations, administering medical assistance programs, and providing information to the public. State laws provide for generic drug substitution and require continuing physician education.

39SOCIAL WELFARE

Recipients of aid to families with dependent children totaled 184,200 in 1996, when monthly payments per family average $466.

In 1996, 283,255 residents received monthly food stamp allowances averaging $58.16. Also in 1996, participation in the national school lunch program had a federal cost of $76.9 million. Social Security benefits were paid to 883,500 persons, averagin $737 a month. In addition, Supplemental Security Income funds averaging $371 a month were disbursed to 111,585 aged, disabled, and blind persons that year. The average weekly unemployment benefit in Wisconsin was $198.84 in 1995.

With the enactment of the Personal Responsibility and Work Opportunity Reconciliation Act of 1996, the US government has changed the form and regulations for many of its social welfare programs; most significantly, it replaces Aid to Families with Dependent Children (AFDC), an open-ended entitlement program, with Temporary Assistance for Needy Families (TANF), a limited system of assistance funded largely through federal block grants. The reform act also impacts the food stamp program, the Supplemental Security Income program, and the child nutrition program. The law took effect on 1 July 1997 and provided $16.38 billion in block grants for fiscal years 1997–2002. The grants are to be divided among the states based on an equation involving the numbers of former AFDC recipients in each state. Because many of the bill's provisions have yet to be implemented into state-by-state policy, it was not possible to include the details of each state's programs for this edition of this work.

40HOUSING

In 1996, there were an estimated 2,188,000 housing units, 1,910,000 of which were occupied. That year, 33,296 privately owned units, valued at $3 billion, were authorized for construction; of these, 21,811 were single-family. Rural areas had a higher proportion of deficient housing than urban areas, and substandard conditions were three times as common in units built before 1940.

As of 1990, the last year for which figures are available, the median home value was $62,500, down by 19% from 1980, after adjusting for inflation. Median monthly costs for owners (with a mortgage) and renters in 1990 were $678 and $399, respectively, throughout the state. During 1995/96, Wisconsin received $332.8 million in aid from the US Department of Housing and Urban Development, including $83.5 million in community development block grants.

The Department of Veterans Affairs makes home loans to veterans. The Housing Finance Authority, created by the legislature in 1971, raises money through the sale of tax-exempt bonds and makes loans directly or indirectly to low- and moderate-income home buyers. Wisconsin's state building code, developed in 1913 to cover construction of all dwellings with three or more units, was revised in the late 1970s to cover new one- and two-family dwellings. Local housing codes prescribing standards for structural upkeep and maintenance in existing buildings are in force in all large cities and in many smaller cities and villages.

41EDUCATION

Wisconsin has a tradition of leadership in education. The state's constitution, adopted in 1848, provided for free public education; however, there was no state tax for schools until 1885. A compulsory education law was passed in 1879 and strengthened in 1903 and 1907. The first kindergarten in the United States was established in Watertown, Wisconsin, in 1856.

General public elementary and secondary education is administered by 426 local school districts, under the overall supervision of the Department of Public Instruction, which is headed by a state superintendent elected on a nonpartisan basis. As of 1990, 78.6% of all Wisconsinites 25 years or older had completed high school, well above the US average. In 1996–97, Wisconsin's elementary and secondary schools had a total enrollment of 1,024,399 students, of whom 879,259 (or 86%) attended the state's 2,063 public schools. There were 54,713 classroom teachers in the public school system, a pupil/teacher ratio of 16.1.

The University of Wisconsin (UW) system is comprised of 13 degree-granting campuses, 13 two-year centers, and the University of Wisconsin-Extension, which has outreach and continuing education activities on all 26 UW campuses and in all 72 Wisconsin counties. During the 1996–97 academic year, 149,142 students were enrolled for courses system-wide. All 13 universities award bachelors' and masters' degrees. University of Wisconsin-Madison and University of Wisconsin-Milwaukee also confer doctoral degrees.

UW-Madison, one of the world's largest and most respected institutions of higher learning, was chartered by the state's first legislature in 1848. During the 1996–97 academic year, UW-Madison enrolled 39,306 students, of whom 28,392 (or 72%) were undergraduates. UW-Milwaukee, the system's second-largest campus, enrolled 21,877 undergraduates and 3,942 graduate students during the year. The 11 other universities, which grant bachelors' and masters' degrees, are Eau Claire, Green Bay, La Crosse, Oshkosh, Parkside (at Kenosha-Racine), Platteville, River Falls, Stevens Point, Stout (at Menomonie), Superior, and Whitewater. Also part of the University of Wisconsin system are 13 two-year centers with total enrollment of 17,325 during 1996–97.

Wisconsin's private institutions of higher education encompass a broad range of schools. There are 21 colleges and universities, including leading institutions such as Marquette University, Lawrence University, Ripon College, and Beloit College. In addition, there are 4 technical and professional schools, and 5 theological seminaries. The enrollments of the private institutions reached 50,011 in 1996–97. Wisconsin also has a system of technical colleges, the Wisconsin Technical College System, with an enrollment of 431,405 in 1995–96. In 1911, the legislature enacted the first system of state support for vocational, technical, and adult education in the nation. One in eight Wisconsin citizens attends a technical college. The system included 16 technical colleges, each governed by a local board. At the same time, each college is part of a statewide system governed by an independent board.

42ARTS

Wisconsin offers numerous facilities for drama, music, and other performing arts, including a four-theater Performing Arts Center in Milwaukee, and the Dane County Exposition Center in Madison. Milwaukee has a repertory theater, and there are many other theater groups around the state. Summer plays are performed at an unusual garden theater at Fish Creek in the Door Peninsula; there is also an annual music festival at that site. The Pro Arte String Quartet in Madison and the Fine Arts Quartet in Milwaukee have been sponsored by the University of Wisconsin, which has also supported many other musical activities. Milwaukee is the home of the Florentine Opera Company, the Milwaukee Ballet Company, and the Milwaukee Symphony.

The Wisconsin Arts Board, consisting of 15 members appointed by the governor for three-year terms, aids artists and performing groups and assists communities in developing arts programs. Wisconsin supported its arts programs with federal funding amounting to $543,000 in 1996. The NEA gave the state's arts programs $768,000. It also contributed $1,595,000 to the Wisconsin Arts Board. State and private sources contributed funding to supplement federal assistance. Wisconsin also

provided arts education for children. In 1996, the state had 1,154 arts associations and 193 local groups. The Wisconsin Arts Board sponsored the "Rise to the Sky" project for local schools and the development of arts education programs at the Wisconsin Folk Museum. The NEA has contributed to the Oneida Tribe and the Madison Civic Center. The Wisconsin Arts Board received funding from the NEA to support the state's arts education programs. The Arts Board also received grants through the NEA's state and regional program. Wisconsin's Chippewa Valley Museum, Inc. has received funds to expand its activities concerning American Indian art.

43LIBRARIES AND MUSEUMS

In 1996, the state had about 379 public libraries, with a total of 16.5 million volumes and circulation of 44 million. The Milwaukee Public Library, founded in 1878, maintained 12 branches and had 2,121,280 bound volumes as of 1983; the Madison Public Library had 7 branches and over 600,000 volumes. The largest academic library is that of the University of Wisconsin at Madison, with 4.5 million bound volumes and 3 million microfiche units. The best-known special library is that of the State Historical Society of Wisconsin at Madison, with 3.5 million books and 60,000 cu feet (1,700 cu m) of government publications and documents.

Wisconsin had 197 museums and historical sites in 1996. The State Historical Society maintains a historical museum in Madison and other historical sites and museums around the state. The Milwaukee Public Museum contains collections on history, natural history, and art. The Milwaukee Art Center, founded in 1888, a major museum of the visual arts, emphasizes European works of the 17th to 19th centuries. The Madison Art Center, founded in 1901, has European, Japanese, Mexican, and American paintings and sculpture, as well as 17th-century Flemish tapestries. The Charles Allis Art Library in Milwaukee, founded in 1947, houses collections of Chinese porcelains, French antiques, and 19th-century American landscape paintings. Other leading art museums include the Elvehjem Museum of Art in Madison and the Theodore Lyman Wright Art Center at Beloit College.

The Circus World Museum at Baraboo occupies the site of the original Ringling Brothers Circus. Other museums of special interest include the Dard Hunter Paper Museum (Appleton), the National Railroad Museum (Green Bay), and the Green Bay Packer Hall of Fame. More than 500 species of animals are on exhibit at the Milwaukee County Zoological Park; Madison and Racine also have zoos. Historical sites in Wisconsin include Villa Louis, a fur trader's mansion at Prairie du Chien; the Old Wade House in Greenbush; Old World Wisconsin, an outdoor ethnic museum near Eagle; Pendarvis, focusing on lead mining at Mineral Point; and the Taliesin estate of architect Frank Lloyd Wright, in Spring Green.

44COMMUNICATIONS

About 97.4% of the state's 1,898,000 households had telephones in March 1993. In 1996 there were 104 AM and 172 FM radio stations. The state also had 32 commercial television stations and 8 noncommercial stations. In 1996, 11 large cable television systems served the state.

45PRESS

The state's first newspaper was the *Green Bay Intelligencer,* founded in 1833. Some early papers were put out by rival land speculators, who used them to promote their interests; among these was the *Milwaukee Sentinel,* launched in 1837 and a major daily newspaper today. As immigrants poured in from Europe in succeeding decades, German, Norwegian, Polish, Yiddish, and Finnish papers sprang up. Wisconsin journalism has a tradition of political involvement. The *Milwaukee Leader,* founded as a Socialist daily by Victor Berger in 1911, was denied the use of the US mails because it printed antiwar articles; the *Madison Capital Times,* still important today, also started as an antiwar paper. Founded in 1882 by Lucius Nieman, the *Milwaukee Journal* won a Pulitzer Prize in 1919 for distinguished public service and remains the state's largest-selling and most influential newspaper.

In 1997, Wisconsin had 11 morning papers, 23 evening papers, and 20 Sunday papers. The following table shows leading dailies with their 1997 circulations:

AREA	NAME	DAILY	SUNDAY
Green Bay	*Press–Gazette* (e,S)	57,126	66,864
Madison	*Wisconsin State Journal* (m,S)	86,289	96,686
Milwaukee	*Journal Sentinel* (m)	286,741	462,168

As of 1997 there were also 27 semiweekly newspapers and weeklies, as well as 318 periodicals directed to a wide variety of special interests. Among the largest are *Hoard's Dairyman,* founded by William D. Hoard in 1885, with a paid semimonthly circulation of 139,600; *Model Railroader,* monthly 224,732; *Bowling Magazine,* monthly 150,000; *Coin Prices,* bimonthly 83,011; *Coin,* monthly 15,044; and *Old Cars Weekly,* 85,000. Other notable periodicals are the *Wisconsin Magazine of History,* published quarterly in Madison by the state historical society; and *Wisconsin Trails,* another quarterly, also published in Madison.

46ORGANIZATIONS

The 1992 Census of Service Industries counted 1,407 organizations in Wisconsin, including 351 business associations; 755 civic, social, and fraternal associations; and 301 other membership organizations. The State Historical Society of Wisconsin, founded in 1846, is one of the largest organizations of its kind; it has a museum, a library, and research collections in Madison and is a prominent publisher of historical articles and books. The Forest Products Research Society, in Madison, has an international membership of about 5,000.

Other national organizations based in Wisconsin include the American Bowling Congress, American Society of Agronomy, Conservation Education Association, Crop Science Society of America, Experimental Aircraft Association, Master Brewers Association of the Americas, Model Railroad Industry Association, National Funeral Directors Association, Wilderness Watch, and World Council of Credit Unions.

47TOURISM, TRAVEL, AND RECREATION

The state has ample scenic attractions and outdoor recreational opportunities. In addition to the famous Wisconsin Dells gorge, visitors are attracted to the Cave of the Mounds at Blue Mounds, the sandstone cliffs along the Mississippi River, the rocky Lake Michigan shoreline of the Door Peninsula, the lakes and forests of the Rhinelander and Minocqua areas in the north, and Lake Geneva, a resort, in the south. Several areas in southern and northwestern Wisconsin, preserved by the state as the Ice Age National Scientific Reserve, still exhibit drumlins, moraines, and unusual geological formations.

There are three national parks in Wisconsin: Apostle Islands National Lakeshore, on Lake Superior, and the St. Croix and Lower St. Croix scenic riverways; visits totaled 379,941 in 1995. In 1995, there were 48 state parks, covering 65,483 acres (26,193 hectares); and 4,208 campsites. Some 12,252,000 people visited state parks and recreational areas in 1991. In 1995, 1,420,500 fishing licenses and 1,814,096 hunting licenses were issued.

48SPORTS

Wisconsin has three major league teams: the Milwaukee Brewers of Major League Baseball, the Green Bay Packers of the National Football League, and the Milwaukee Bucks of the National Basketball Association. The Brewers won the American League Pennant in 1982, but lost the World Series to St. Louis. The Packers won five league championships prior to the establishment of the Super Bowl, and then won Superbowls I, II, and XXXI in 1967, 1968, and 1997, respectively. The Bucks won the NBA Championship in 1971. Milwaukee is the site of the annual Miller High Life Open in professional bowling, and of the Greater Milwaukee Open in professional golf. There are also numerous minor league baseball, basketball, and hockey teams in the state.

The University of Wisconsin Badgers compete in the Big Ten Conference. Badger ice hockey teams won the NCAA championship in 1973, 1977, 1981, 1983, and 1990. In football, they won the Rose Bowl in 1994 after losing their three previous appearances, in 1953, 1960, and 1963. Basketball teams from Marquette University in Milwaukee won the NCAA Division I title in 1977 and the National Invitation Tournament championship in 1970.

Other annual sporting events include ski jumping tournaments in Iola, Middleton, and Wetsby; the World Championship Snowmobile Derby in Eagle River in January; American Birkebeiner Cross-Country Race at Cable and Hayward in February; and the Great Wisconsin Dells Balloon Race in the Dells.

49FAMOUS WISCONSINITES

Wisconsinites who have won prominence as federal judicial or executive officers include Jeremiah Rusk (b.Ohio, 1830–93), a Wisconsin governor selected as the first head of the Agriculture Department in 1889; William F. Vilas (b.Vermont, 1840–1908), who served as postmaster general under Grover Cleveland; Melvin Laird (b.Nebraska, 1922–1992), a congressman who served as secretary of defense from 1969–73; and William Rehnquist (b.1924), named to the Supreme Court in 1971.

The state's best-known political figures achieved nationwide reputations as members of the US Senate. John C. Spooner (b.Indiana, 1843–1919) won distinction as one of the inner circle of Senate conservatives before he retired in 1907 amid an upsurge of Progressivism within his party. Robert La Follette (1855–1925) embodied the new wave of Republican Progressivism—and, later, isolationism—as governor and in the Senate. His sons, Robert, Jr. (1895–1953), and Philip (1897–1965), carried on the Progressive tradition as US senator and governor, respectively. Joseph R. McCarthy (1908–57) won attention in the Senate and throughout the nation for his anti-communist crusade. William Proxmire (b.Illinois, 1915), a Democrat, succeeded McCarthy in the Senate and eventually became chairman of the powerful Senate Banking Committee. Representative Henry S. Reuss (b.1912), also a Democrat, served in the House for 28 years and was chairman of the Banking Committee. Democrat Clement Zablocki (1912–83), elected to the House in 1948, was chairman of the Foreign Affairs Committee. Victor L. Berger (b.Transylvania, 1860–1929), a founder of the Social-Democratic Party, was first elected to the House in 1910; during World War I, he was denied his seat and prosecuted because of his antiwar views.

Besides the La Follettes, other governors who made notable contributions to the state include James D. Doty (b.New York, 1799–1865), who fought to make Wisconsin a separate territory and became the territory's second governor; William D. Hoard (b.New York, 1836–1918), a tireless promoter of dairy farming, as both private citizen and chief executive; James O. Davidson (b.Norway, 1854–1922), who attempted to improve relations between conservatives and progressives; Francis E. McGovern (1866–1946), who pushed through the legislature significant social and economic reform legislation; and Walter J. Kohler (1875–1940), an industrialist who, as governor, greatly expanded the power of the office.

Prominent figures in the state's early history include the Jesuit Jacques Marquette (b.France, 1637–75) and the explorer Louis Jolliet (b.Canada, 1645–1700); and the Sauk Indian leader Black Hawk (b.Illinois, 1767–1838), who was defeated in the Battle of Bad Axe. John Bascom (b.New York, 1827–1911) was an early president of the University of Wisconsin. Charles Van Hise (1857–1918), a later president, promoted the use of academic experts as government advisers; John R. Commons (b.Ohio, 1862–1945), an economist at the university, drafted major state legislation. Philetus Sawyer (b.Vermont, 1816–1900), a prosperous lumberman and US senator, led the state Republican Party for 15 years, before Progressives won control. Carl Schurz (b.Germany, 1829–1906) was a prominent Republican Party figure in the years immediately before the Civil War. Lucius W. Nieman (1857–1935) founded the *Milwaukee Journal,* and Edward P. Allis (b.New York, 1824–89) was an important iron industrialist.

Wisconsin was the birthplace of several Nobel Prize winners, including Herbert S. Gasser (1888–1963), who shared a 1944 Nobel Prize for research into nerve impulses; William P. Murphy (1892–1987), who shared a 1934 prize for research relating to anemia; John Bardeen (1908–91), who shared the physics award in 1956 for his contribution to the development of the transistor; and Herbert A. Simon (b.1916), who won the 1978 prize in economics. Stephen Babcock (b.New York, 1843–1931) was an agricultural chemist who did research important to the dairy industry. In addition, Wisconsin was the birthplace of the child psychologist Arnold Gesell (1880–1961), and of naturalist and explorer Chapman Andrews (1884–1960). John Muir (b.Scotland, 1838–1914), another noted naturalist and explorer, lived in Wisconsin in his youth. Conservationist Aldo Leopold (1887–1948) taught at the University of Wisconsin and wrote *A Sand County Almanac.*

Frederick Jackson Turner (1861–1932), historian of the American frontier, was born in Wisconsin, as were the economist and social theorist Thorstein Veblen (1857–1929) and the diplomat and historian George F. Kennan (b.1904). Famous journalists include news commentator H. V. Kaltenborn (1878–1965), award-winning sports columnist Red Smith (Walter Wellesley Smith, 1905–82), and television newsman Tom Snyder (b.1936).

Thornton Wilder (1897–1975), a novelist and playwright best known for *The Bridge of San Luis Rey* (1927), *Our Town* (1938), and *The Skin of Our Teeth* (1942), each of which won a Pulitzer Prize, heads the list of literary figures born in the state. Hamlin Garland (1860–1940), a novelist and essayist, was also a native, as were the poet Ella Wheeler Wilcox (1850–1919) and the novelist and playwright Zona Gale (1874–1938). The novelist Edna Ferber (b.Michigan, 1887–1968) spent her early life in the state.

Wisconsin is the birthplace of architect Frank Lloyd Wright (1869–1959) and the site of his famous Taliesin estate (Spring Green), Johnson Wax Co. headquarters (Racine), and first Unitarian Church (Madison). The artist Georgia O'Keefe (1887–1986) was born in Sun Prairie. Wisconsin natives who have distinguished themselves in the performing arts include Alfred Lunt (1893–1977), Frederic March (Frederick Bickel, 1897–1975), Spencer Tracy (1900–1967), Agnes Moorehead (1906–74), and Orson Welles (1915–85). Magician and escape artist Harry Houdini (Ehrich Weiss, b.Hungary, 1874–1926) was raised in the state, and piano stylist Liberace (Wlad Ziu Valentino Liberace, 1919–1987) was born there. Speed skater Eric Heiden (b.1958), a five-time Olympic gold medalist in 1980, is another Wisconsin native.

50BIBLIOGRAPHY

Abrams, Lawrence and Kathleen. *Exploring Wisconsin.* Skokie, Ill.: Rand McNally, 1983.

Current, Richard N. *The History of Wisconsin.* Vol. 2: *The Civil War Era, 1848–73.* Madison: State Historical Society of Wisconsin, 1976.

Current, Richard N. *Wisconsin: A Bicentennial History.* New York: Norton, 1977.

Dictionary of Wisconsin Biography. Madison: State Historical Society of Wisconsin, 1960.

Epstein, Leon D. *Politics in Wisconsin.* Madison: University of Wisconsin Press, 1958.

Federal Writers' Project. *Wisconsin: A Guide to the Badger State.* Reprint, New York: Somerset, n.d.

Gara, Larry. *A Short History of Wisconsin.* Madison: State Historical Society of Wisconsin, 1962.

Klement, Frank L. *Wisconsin in the Civil War: The Home Front and the Battle Front, 1861–1865.* Madison: State Historical Society of Wisconsin, 1997.

Nesbit, Robert C. *Wisconsin: A History.* Madison: University of Wisconsin Press, 1973.

Pederson, Jane Marie. *Between Memory and Reality: Family and Community in Rural Wisconsin, 1870–1970.* Madison: University of Wisconsin Press, 1992.

Risjord, Norman K. *Wisconsin: The Story of the Badger State.* Madison: Wisconsin Trails, 1995.

Ritzenthaler, Robert E. *Prehistoric Indians of Wisconsin.* Milwaukee: Milwaukee Public Museum, 1953.

Smith, Alice E. *The History of Wisconsin.* Vol. 1,: *From Exploration to Statehood.* Madison: State Historical Society of Wisconsin, 1973.

State of Wisconsin, Legislative Reference Bureau. *Blue Book.* Madison, n.d.

Still, Bayrd. *Milwaukee: The History of a City.* Madison: State Historical Society of Wisconsin, 1948.

Thelen, David P. *Robert M. La Follette and the Insurgent Spirit.* Boston: Little, Brown, 1976.

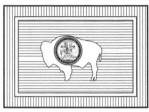

WYOMING

State of Wyoming

ORIGIN OF STATE NAME: Derived from the Delaware Indian words *maugh-wau-wa-ma,* meaning "large plains." **NICKNAME:** The Equality State, and The Cowboy State. **CAPITAL:** Cheyenne. **ENTERED UNION:** 10 July 1890 (44th). **SONG:** "Wyoming." **MOTTO:** Equal Rights. **FLAG:** A blue field with a white inner border and a red outer border (symbolizing, respectively, the sky, purity, and the Indians) surrounds a bison with the state seal branded on its side. **OFFICIAL SEAL:** A female figure holding the banner "Equal Rights" stands on a pedestal between pillars topped by lamps symbolizing the light of knowledge; two male figures flank the pillars, on which are draped banners that proclaim "Livestock," "Grain," "Mines," and "Oil." At the bottom is a shield with an eagle, star, and Roman numerals XLIV, flanked by the dates 1869 and 1890. The whole is surrounded by the words "Great Seal of the State of Wyoming." **ANIMAL:** Bison. **BIRD:** Meadowlark. **FLOWER:** Indian paintbrush. **TREE:** Cottonwood. **GEM:** Jade. **LEGAL HOLIDAYS:** New Year's Day, 1 January; Birthday of Martin Luther King, Jr., 3d Monday in January; Presidents' Day, 3d Monday in February; Memorial Day, last Monday in May; Independence Day, 4 July; Labor Day, 1st Monday in September; Columbus Day, 2d Monday in October; Election Day, 1st Tuesday after 1st Monday in November in even-numbered years; Veterans Day, 11 November; Thanksgiving Day, 4th Thursday in November; Christmas Day, 25 December. **TIME:** 5 AM MST = noon GMT.

¹LOCATION, SIZE, AND EXTENT

Located in the Rocky Mountain region of the northwestern US, Wyoming ranks 9th in size among the 50 states.

The total area of Wyoming is 97,809 sq mi (253,325 sq km), of which land comprises 96,989 sq mi (251,201 sq km) and inland water 820 sq mi (2,124 sq km). Shaped like a rectangle, Wyoming has a maximum E-W extension of 365 mi (587 km); its extreme distance N-S is 265 mi (426 km).

Wyoming is bordered on the N by Montana; on the E by South Dakota and Nebraska; on the S by Colorado and Utah; and on the W by Utah, Idaho, and Montana. The boundary length of Wyoming totals 1,269 mi (2,042 km). The state's geographic center lies in Fremont County, 58 mi (93 km) ENE of Lander.

²TOPOGRAPHY

The eastern third of Wyoming forms part of the Great Plains; the remainder belongs to the Rocky Mountains. Much of western Wyoming constitutes a special geomorphic province known as the Wyoming Basin. It represents a westward extension of the Great Plains into the Rocky Mountains, separating the Middle and Southern Rockies. Extending diagonally across the state from northwest to south is the Continental Divide, which separates the generally eastward-flowing drainage system of North America from the westward-flowing drainage of the Pacific states.

Wyoming's mean elevation is 6,700 feet (2,042 meters), 2d only to Colorado's among the 50 states. Gannett Peak, in western Wyoming, at 13,804 feet (4,207 meters), is the highest point in the state. With the notable exception of the Black Hills in the northeast, the eastern portion of Wyoming is generally much lower. The lowest point in the state—3,100 feet (945 meters)— occurs in the northeast, on the Belle Fourche River.

Wyoming's largest lake—Yellowstone—lies in the heart of Yellowstone National Park. In Grand Teton National Park to the south are two smaller lakes, Jackson and Jenny. All but one of Wyoming's major rivers originate within its boundaries and flow into neighboring states. The Green River flows into Utah; the Yellowstone, Big Horn, and Powder rivers flow into Montana;

the Snake River, into Idaho; the Belle Fourche and Cheyenne rivers, into South Dakota; and the Niobrara and Bear rivers, into Nebraska. The lone exception, the North Platte River, enters Wyoming from Colorado and eventually exits into Nebraska.

³CLIMATE

Wyoming is generally semiarid, with local desert conditions. Normal daily temperatures in Cheyenne range from 15°F (–9°C) to 38°F (3°C) in January, and 55°F (13°C) to 82°F (28°C) in July. The record low temperature, –66°F (–54°C), was set 9 February 1933 at Riverside; the record high, 114°F (46°C), 12 July 1900 at Basin. Normal precipitation in Cheyenne is 13 in (33 cm) a year, most of that falling between March and September; the snowfall in Cheyenne averages 52 in (132 cm) annually. In 1991 there were 23 tornadoes.

⁴FLORA AND FAUNA

Wyoming has more than 2,000 species of ferns, conifers, and flowering plants. Prairie grasses dominate the eastern third of the state; desert shrubs, primarily sagebrush, cover the Great Basin in the west. Rocky Mountain forests consist largely of pine, spruce, and fir.

The mule deer is the most abundant game mammal; others include the white-tailed deer, pronghorn antelope, elk, and moose. The jackrabbit, antelope, and raccoon are plentiful. Wild turkey, bobwhite quail, and several grouse species are leading game birds; more than 50 species of nongame birds also inhabit Wyoming all year long. There are 78 species of fish, of which rainbow trout is the favorite game fish. Endangered mammals include the black-footed ferret and the otter. The grizzly bear population in Yellowstone National Park was on the decline in the mid-1980s.

⁵ENVIRONMENTAL PROTECTION

The state's principal environmental concerns are conservation of scarce water resources and preservation of air quality. The

Environmental Quality Council, a 7-member board appointed by the governor, hears and decides all cases arising under the regulations of the Department of Environmental Quality. The department enforces measures to prevent pollution of Wyoming's surface water and groundwater, and it administers 21 air-monitoring sites to maintain air quality. Wyoming typically spends the most money per capita on the environment and natural resources relative to all the states in the union. Programs to dispose of hazardous waste and assure safe drinking water are administered by the federal Environmental Protection Agency. In 1995, the state had 3 hazardous waste sites. Wetlands cover about 1.25 million acres of Wyoming and are administered and protected by the Wyoming Wetlands Act.

6POPULATION

Wyoming ranks 50th in the US in population and 49th in population density; only Alaska is more sparsely populated. However, during the 1970s Wyoming was the third-fastest-growing state; its population grew by 41%, from 332,416 at the 1970 census to 469,557 according to the 1980 census, largely from migration. The growth rate reversed during the 1980s, shrinking the population to 453,588 in 1990 (–3.4%). In 1996 Wyoming had an estimated population of 481,400, a 6.1% increase over 1990. The population density in 1990 was 4.7 per sq mi (1.8 per sq km). Leading cities with their 1994 estimated populations were Cheyenne, 53,559; Casper, 49,192; and Laramie, 27,223.

7ETHNIC GROUPS

There were some 9,000 Indians in Wyoming at the 1990 census. The largest tribe is the Arapaho. Wind River (1995 estimated population 9,177) is the state's only reservation; tribal lands covered 1,793,000 acres (726,000 hectares) in 1982.

There were 4,000 black Americans living in Wyoming in 1990, and 3,000 of Asian-Pacific Island descent, about half of whom were of Japanese or Chinese descent. In 1990, 94.2% of the population was white and mostly of European descent, the largest groups being German, English, and Irish.

8LANGUAGES

Some place-names—Oshoto, Shoshoni, Cheyenne, Uinta—reflect early contacts with regional Indians.

Some terms common in Wyoming, like *comforter* (tied quilt) and *angleworm* (earthworm), evidence the Northern dialect of early settlers from New York State and New England, but generally Wyoming English is North Midland with some South Midland mixture, especially along the Nebraska border. Geography has changed the meaning of *hole, basin, meadow,* and *park* to signify mountain openings.

In 1990, 394,904 Wyomingites—94.3% of the residents 5 years old or older—spoke only English at home. The number of residents who spoke other languages at home included:

Spanish	13,790	Various Native American	1,654
German	2,688	French	1,558

9RELIGIONS

Wyoming's churchgoing population is preponderantly Protestant. There were 156,480 known adherents of Christian denominations other than Roman Catholic in 1990. The largest denominations were Catholic, with 59,565 members; Mormon, 45,793; United Methodist, 13,099; Episcopal, 9,894; Southern Baptist Convention, 18,674; Evangelical Lutheran Church in America, 9,088; and United Presbyterian, 8,749. Wyoming also had an estimated 330 Jews in 1990.

10TRANSPORTATION

Wyoming is served chiefly by the Burlington Northern–Santa Fe, the Chicago and Northwestern, and Union Pacific railroads. The total trackage of these three Class I railroads in 1996 was 1,856 rail mi (2,987 km), an increase of 241 miles (387 km) since 1992. This is due to double- and triple-tracking primarily to haul coal from the Powder River Basin. Double- and triple-tracking is expected to continue through at least the year 2000. In 1995, coal was the top commodity in both rail tonnage originated (230.3 million tons, or 93%) and terminated (8.8 million tons, or 89%) within the state. Amtrak passenger rail service in and through the state was discontinued on 10 May 1997. Public highways and rural and urban roads, totaling 34,128 miles (54,912 km) cross the state. As of October 1996, there were 601,336 registered motor vehicles and 360,921 licensed drivers.

As of June 1996, Wyoming had 698 active aircraft, 1,923 active licensed pilots, and 96 airports and heliports.

11HISTORY

The first human inhabitants of what is now Wyoming probably arrived about 11,500 BC. The forebears of these early Americans had most likely come by way of the Bering Strait and then worked their way south. Sites of mammoth kills south of Rawlins and near Powell suggest that the area was well populated. Artifacts from the period beginning in 500 BC include, high in the Big Horn Mountains of northern Wyoming, the Medicine Wheel monument, a circle of stones some 75 ft (23 m) in diameter with 28 "spokes" that were apparently used to mark the seasons.

The first Europeans to visit Wyoming were French Canadian traders. The Vérendrye brothers, Francois and Louis-Joseph, probably reached the Big Horn Mountains in 1743; nothing came of their travels, however. The first effective discovery of Wyoming was made by an American fur trader, John Colter, earlier a member of the Lewis and Clark expedition. In 1806–7, Colter traversed much of the northwestern part of the state, probably crossing what is now Yellowstone Park, and came back to report on the natural wonders of the area. After Colter, trappers and fur traders crisscrossed Wyoming. By 1840, the major rivers and mountains were named, and the general topography of the region was well documented.

Between 1840 and 1867, thousands of Americans crossed Wyoming on the Oregon Trail, bound for Oregon or California. Migration began as a trickle, but with the discovery of gold in California in 1848, the trickle became a flood. In 1849 alone it is estimated that more than 22,000 "forty-niners" passed through the state via the Oregon Trail. Fort Laramie in the east and Fort Bridger in the west were the best-known supply points; between the two forts, immigrants encountered Independence Rock, Devil's Gate, Split Rock, and South Pass, all landmarks on the Oregon Trail. Although thousands of Americans crossed Wyoming during this period, very few stayed in this harsh region.

The event that brought population as well as territorial status to Wyoming was the coming of the Union Pacific Railroad. Railroad towns such as Cheyenne, Laramie, Rawlins, Rock Springs, and Evanston sprang up as the transcontinental railroad leapfrogged across the region in 1867 and 1868; in the latter year, Wyoming was organized as a territory. The first territorial legislature distinguished itself in 1869 by passing a women's suffrage act, the first state or territory to do so. Wyoming quickly acquired the nickname the Equality State.

After hostile Indians had been subdued by the late 1870s, Wyoming became a center for cattlemen and foreign investors who hoped to make a fortune from free grass and the high price of cattle. Thousands of Texas longhorn cattle were driven to the southeastern quarter of the territory. In time, blooded cattle, particularly Hereford, were introduced. As cattle "barons" dominated both the rangeland and state politics, the small

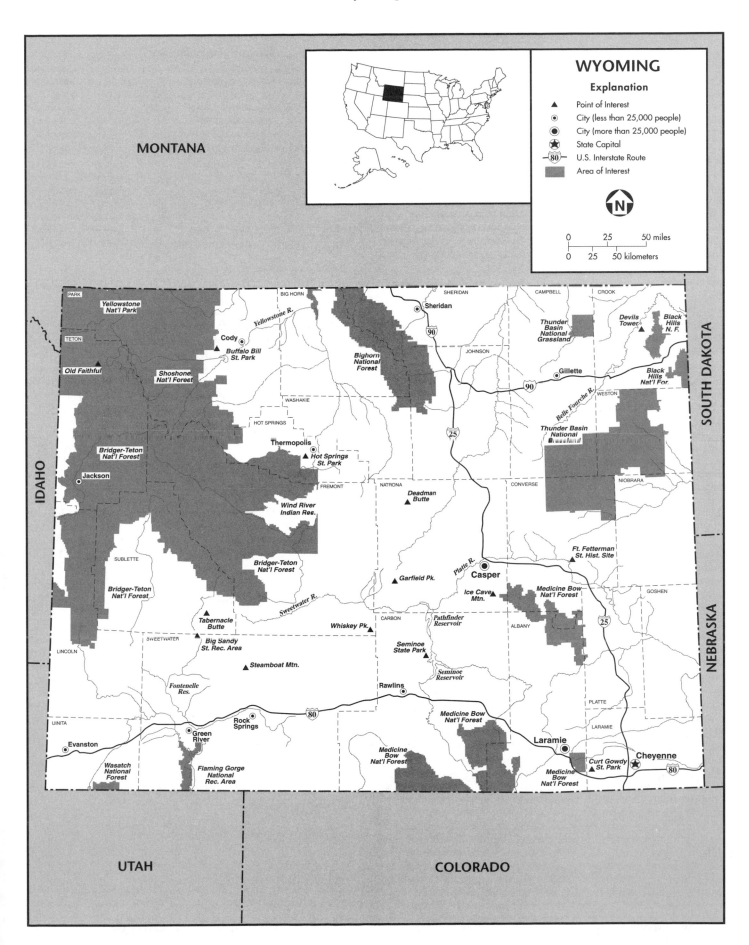

WYOMING

Explanation

▲ Point of Interest

⊙ City (less than 25,000 people)

◉ City (more than 25,000 people)

★ State Capital

—⑧⓪— U.S. Interstate Route

▨ Area of Interest

Ⓝ

| 0 | 25 | 50 miles |
| 0 | 25 | 50 kilometers |

MONTANA

IDAHO

SOUTH DAKOTA

NEBRASKA

UTAH

COLORADO

PARK

Yellowstone Nat'l Park

TETON

Old Faithful ▲

BIG HORN

Yellowstone R.

Cody ⊙

Buffalo Bill ▲ St. Park

Shoshone Nat'l Forest

WASHAKIE

HOT SPRINGS

Thermopolis ⊙

Hot Springs ▲ St. Park

Bridger-Teton Nat'l Forest

Jackson ⊙

FREMONT

Wind River Indian Res.

Bridger-Teton Nat'l Forest

Bridger-Teton Nat'l Forest

SUBLETTE

Tabernacle ▲ Butte

LINCOLN

SWEETWATER

Big Sandy ▲ St. Rec. Area

Steamboat Mtn. ▲

Sweetwater R.

Whiskey Pk. ▲

Fontenelle Res.

UINTA

Evanston ⊙

Green River ⊙

Rock Springs ⊙

Wasatch National Forest

Flaming Gorge National Rec. Area

SHERIDAN

Sheridan ⊙

⑨⓪

CAMPBELL

CROOK

Thunder Basin National Grassland

Devils Tower ▲

Black Hills N. F.

JOHNSON

Bighorn National Forest

⑨⓪

Gillette ⊙

Black Hills Nat'l For.

Belle Fourche R.

WESTON

Thunder Basin National Grassland

NIOBRARA

②⑤

NATRONA

Deadman ▲ Butte

CONVERSE

Garfield Pk. ▲

Ft. Fetterman ▲ St. Hist. Site

Platte R.

Casper ◉

Ice Cave ▲ Mtn.

Medicine Bow Nat'l Forest

GOSHEN

CARBON

Pathfinder Reservoir

ALBANY

②⑤

Seminoe State Park ▲

Seminoe Reservoir

Rawlins ⊙

⑧⓪

Medicine Bow Nat'l Forest

PLATTE

LARAMIE

Laramie ◉

Curt Gowdy ▲ St. Park

Cheyenne ★

⑧⓪

Medicine Bow Nat'l Forest

Medicine Bow Nat'l Forest

rancher and cowboy found it difficult to go into the ranching business. However, overgrazing, low cattle prices, and the dry summer of 1886 and harsh winter of 1886/87 all proved disastrous to the speculators. The struggle between the large landowners and small ranchers culminated in the so-called Johnson County War of 1891–92, in which the large landowners were arrested by federal troops after attempting to take the law into their own hands.

Wyoming became a state in 1890, but growth remained slow. Attempts at farming proved unsuccessful in this high, arid region, and Wyoming to this day remains a sparsely settled ranching state. What growth has occurred has been primarily through the minerals industry, especially the development of coal, oil, and natural gas resources during the 1970s because of the national energy crisis. However, the world's oil glut in the early 1980s slowed the growth of the state's energy industries; in 1984, the growth of the state's nonfuel mineral industry slowed as well.

Wyoming's population, which had risen 41% during the minerals boom of the 1970s, declined, leaving the state ranking 50th in population in the 1990 census, having ceded 49th place to Alaska in the decade since 1980. In the 1990s, Wyoming's economy has been spurred by a rise in oil prices and expanding coal production, as well as increased tourism.

In the summer of 1988, wild fires raged through Yellowstone National Park, damaging nearly one-third of the park's total area.

¹²STATE GOVERNMENT

Wyoming's state constitution was approved by the voters in November 1889 and accepted by Congress in 1890.

The legislature consists of a 30-member senate and a 60-member house of representatives. Senators are elected to staggered four-year terms. The entire house of representatives is elected every two years for a two-year term. In 1995 the legislative salary was $125 per diem during regular sessions.

Heading the executive branch are five elected officials: the governor, secretary of state, auditor, treasurer, and superintendent of public instruction. Each serves a four-year term and, under Wyoming's cabinet form of government, each is also a member of seven state boards and commissions. In 1996 the governor's salary was $95,000.

Voters must be US citizens, at least 18 years of age, bona fide residents of Wyoming, not convicted of a felony, and not mentally incompetent.

¹³POLITICAL PARTIES

The Republicans currently dominate Wyoming politics at the federal level, with Democrats more likely to be elected for state office, where federal land management issues are less prominent. There are 125,336 registered Republicans, or 54%; 83,091 registered Democrats, or 36%; and 25,806 independents, or 11%. The governor, Jim Geringer, who was elected in 1994, is a Republican. Both of Wyoming's senators, Craig Thomas and Mike Enzi (elected in 1996 to succeed Alan Simpson), are Republicans, as is Wyoming's US Representative, Barbara Cubin.

In the state senate, there are 21 Republicans and 9 Democrats; in the state house, there are 43 Republicans and 17 Democrats. Republican Bob Dole received just under 50% of the vote in the 1996 presidential election, while Democratic incumbent Bill Clinton won nearly 37%, and Independent Ross Perot garnered 12%.

In 1993 there was one black holding elective office. As of 1995, 19 women served in the state legislature and 2 women were in elective executive positions.

Wyoming Presidential Vote by Major Political Parties 1948–96

YEAR	ELECTORAL VOTE	WYOMING WINNER	DEMOCRAT	REPUBLICAN
1948	3	*Truman (D)	52,354	47,947
1952	3	*Eisenhower (R)	47,934	81,049
1956	3	*Eisenhower (R)	49,554	74,573
1960	3	Nixon (R)	63,331	77,451
1964	3	*Johnson (D)	80,718	61,998
1968	3	*Nixon (R)	45,173	70,927
1972	3	*Nixon (R)	44,358	100,464
1976	3	Ford (R)	62,239	92,717
1980	3	*Reagan (R)	49,427	110,700
1984	3	*Reagan (R)	53,370	133,241
1988	3	*Bush (R)	67,113	106,867
1992**	3	Bush (R)	68,160	79,347
1996**	3	Dole (R)	77,934	105,388

* Won US presidential election.
** Independent candidate Ross Perot received 51,263 votes in 1992 and 25,928 votes in 1996.

¹⁴LOCAL GOVERNMENT

In 1992 Wyoming was subdivided into 23 counties, 97 municipalities, 56 school districts, and 373 special districts and authorities.

Each county has a clerk, treasurer, assessor, sheriff, attorney, coroner, a district court clerk, three commissioners, and from one to five county judges or justices of the peace.

¹⁵STATE SERVICES

The Board of Education has primary responsibility for educational services in Wyoming. Transportation services are provided by the Wyoming Department of Transportation; health and welfare matters fall under the jurisdiction of the Departments of Health and Family Services. Among the many state agencies concerned with natural resources are the Department of Environmental Quality, Board of Land Commissioners, Oil and Gas Conservation Commission, and Water Development Commission. The Department of Employment is responsible for labor services.

¹⁶JUDICIAL SYSTEM

Wyoming's judicial branch consists of a supreme court with a chief justice and 4 other justices, 9 district courts with 17 judges, and county judges and justices of the peace. Supreme court justices are appointed by the governor but must stand for retention at the next general election; once elected, they serve eight-year terms. There were 1,203 attorneys practicing in Wyoming in 1996.

Wyoming's prison population totalled 1,458 in 1996, or 301 per 100,000 in population. Wyoming's total crime rate in 1995 was 4,320.2 per 100,000 persons, including 254.2 for violent crime and 4,066 for property crime. Wyoming has a death penalty, but as of 1995 there were no persons under sentence of death.

¹⁷ARMED FORCES

In 1996, there were 3,592 active duty military personnel stationed in Wyoming, nearly all of whom (3,505) were at Wyoming's only US military installation—the Francis E. Warren Air Force Base at Cheyenne. Total defense contracts awarded that year totaled $91.5 million.

There were about 46,000 military veterans living in Wyoming in 1996. Of these, fewer than 500 were veterans of World War I, 12,000 of World War II, 8,000 of the Korean conflict, 17,000 of the Vietnam era, and 3,000 of the Persian Gulf War. Veterans' benefits totaled $102 million in 1995/96. In 1996, 4,152 persons were members of the National Guard.

In 1993, the Wyoming Highway Patrol employed 142 full-time sworn officers, or 3 per 10,000 residents.

[18]MIGRATION

Many people have passed through Wyoming, but relatively few have come to stay. Not until the 1970s, a time of rapid economic development, did the picture change. Between 1970 and 1983, Wyoming gained a net total of 45,500 residents through migration. In the 1980s, the state's total population grew only by 1.1%, primarily offset by the net loss from migration of 52,000 persons. Between 1990 and 1996, Wyoming had net gains of 5,420 in domestic migration and 1,438 in international migration.

As of 1990, 42.6% of the state's residents were born in Wyoming, up from 38.7% in 1980. About half of all residents age 5 and older in 1990 were living in the same house as in 1985. Of those who reported living in a different house in 1985, 30% did so in another state. The urban population increased from 62.8% of the state's total in 1980 to 65% in 1990.

[19]INTERGOVERNMENTAL COOPERATION

Emblematic of Wyoming's concern for water resources is the fact that it belongs to seven compacts with neighboring states concerning the Bear, Belle Fourche, Colorado, Snake, Upper Niobrara, and Yellowstone rivers.

Wyoming has also joined the Interstate Oil and Gas Compact, the Western Interstate Energy Compact, and numerous other multistate bodies, including the Council of State Governments. Federal aid in 1995/96 totaled $708 million.

[20]ECONOMY

The economic life of Wyoming is largely sustained by agriculture—chiefly feed grains and livestock—and mining, including petroleum and gas production. Mining and petroleum production mushroomed during the 1970s, leading to a powerful upsurge in population. In the early 1980s, unemployment remained low, per capita income was high, and the inflation rate declined.

The absence of personal and corporate income taxes has helped foster a favorable business climate. In 1994, Wyoming had a gross state product of $15,660 million, to which private goods-producing services contributed $6,304 million; private services-producing industries, $7,318 million; and government, $2,038 million.

During 1996, there were 1,738 bankruptcy filings, up 44% from 1995.

[21]INCOME

In personal income per capita, Wyoming ranked 7th among the 50 states in 1980, but fell to 35th place by 1996 with personal income per capita of $21,245. In 1994, Teton County had a personal per capita income level of $37,427, 70% higher than the US average. In 1995, 12.2% of the state's residents lived below the federal poverty level. That same year, median household income was $31,529.

[22]LABOR

In 1996, Wyoming's civilian labor force averaged 257,617. Of the 1996 total, about 241,691 were employed and 12,926 were unemployed; the unemployment rate was 5%.

Employment and wages in 1995 were officially reported as follows:

	ANNUAL AVERAGE EMPLOYMENT	TOTAL PAYROLL ($MILLIONS)	AVERAGE WEEKLY WAGE PER WORKER
Total	212,217	$4,743.2	$430
Private	159,235	3,455.3	417
Agriculture	2,946	45.4	296
Mining	16,947	740.1	840
Construction	14,195	337.8	458
Manufacturing	9,720	258.2	511
Transportation, communications, public utilities	11,231	355.0	608
Wholesale trade	7,447	199.4	515
Retail trade	44,231	531.1	231
Finance, insurance, and real estate	7,855	199.6	489
Services	44,662	788.7	340
Government	59,982	1,287.9	467

In 1995, 22,200 employees belonged to labor unions, representing 11.2% of the work force in that year.

[23]AGRICULTURE

Agriculture—especially livestock and grain—is one of Wyoming's most important industries. In 1996, Wyoming had about 9,100 farms and ranches covering almost 34.6 million acres (14 million hectares). The state's average of 3,802 acres (1,539 hectares) per farm ranked 2d in the US after Arizona. The value of the lands and buildings of Wyoming's farms and ranches in 1996 was over $7.1 billion. Total farm marketings in 1995 amounted to $726 million (39th in the US). Of this, livestock and animal products accounted for $544 million; crops, $182 million.

Field crops in 1996 included barley, 10,320,000 bu; wheat, 7,110,000 bu; oats, 1,696,000 bu; potatoes, 224,000 cwt; sugar beets, 994,000 tons; dry beans, 765,000 cwt; and hay, ,208,000 tons.

[24]ANIMAL HUSBANDRY

For most of Wyoming's territorial and state history, cattle ranchers have dominated the economy, even though the livestock industry is not large by national standards. In 1997, Wyoming had 1.49 million cattle and calves, valued at $894 million. During 1996, there were 82,000 hogs and pigs, valued at $9 million. Wyoming farms and ranches produced 40.4 million lb (18.3 million kg) of sheep and lambs, and 6.4 million lb (2.9 million kg) of shorn wool in 1995. In 1995, Wyoming farmers sold 32,000 lb (14,500 kg) of chicken and produced 84.6 million lb (38.4 million kg) of milk.

[25]FISHING

There is no important commercial fishing in Wyoming. Fishing is largely recreational, and fish hatcheries and fish-planting programs keep the streams well stocked. Wyoming's streams anually provide 1.3 million angler days and 3.4 million fish; lakes generate 1.6 million angler days and a harvest of 4.1 million fish. In 1995/96, the state issued 276,989 fishing licenses. That year, federal hatcheries distributed over 859,000 fish and 937,000 fish eggs within the state.

[26]FORESTRY

Wyoming has 9,847,600 acres (3,985,300 hectares) of forested land, equal to 15.9% of the state's land area. Of this, 3,912,500 acres (1,583,400 hectares) are usable as commercial timberland. The state's 10 national forests, of which Shoshone, Bridger, and Teton were the largest, covered 9,258,719 acres (3,748,469 hectares) in 1993. Shipments by the lumber industry were valued at $82 million in 1995, with nearly 40% marketed to midwestern states. In 1996, 63.7% of the timber for sawmills came from national forests, 31.1% from state and private forests, and 5.2% from other public forests. Ponderosa pine accounted for 49.5% of the 1995 cut; lodgepole pine, 40.6%; Douglas fir and larch, 3.3%; Engelmann spruce, 3.3%; and other species, 3.3%.

27MINING

The estimated value of nonfuel mineral production for Wyoming in 1995 was nearly $976 million, an increase of about $96 million over the $880 million reported in 1994. Gains in the production value of clays and crushed stone more than offset declines in the value of portland cement and gemstones. In 1995, Wyoming produced 2,590,000 metric tons of clays, worth $152,000,000, as well as 5,300,000 metric tons of crushed stone, valued at $31,500,000. No metal production has been reported since 1984. Wyoming ranked 13th nationally in the value of nonfuel mineral production. Wyoming continued to rank first in the nation in bentonite production. In 1995, major uses of Wyoming bentonite were as pet waste absorbent, drilling mud, pelletizing iron ore, in foundry sand, and as a waterproof sealant. Wyoming continued to lead the nation in soda ash production from the world's largest known resource of trona, a natural sodium carbonate-bicarbonate. Trona mined in Wyoming was used to produce soda ash, caustic soda, sodium sulfite, sodium bicarbonate, sodium cyanide, and calcined trona. Grade A helium production increased slightly; of the four states that produced grade-A helium, Wyoming ranked second. Three commodities—clays, grade-A helium, and soda ash—accounted for over 90% of the state's nonfuel mineral production.

28ENERGY AND POWER

Wyoming is comparatively energy-rich, ranking 1st among the states in coal production and 7th in output of both crude oil and natural gas. The state's production of petroleum declined in the early 1990s as the result of declining reserves. Wyoming's 1995 oil output of 73.6 million barrels was 55% below that of the peak year 1970.

The state's proved reserves of petroleum were estimated at 3.69 billion barrels in 1995. In that year, reserves of natural gas were estimated at 12.17 trillion cu ft (0.34 trillion cu m), and natural gas production totaled 899.1 billion cu ft (25.5 billion cu m).

Wyoming has the three largest producing coal mines in the US and total recoverable coal reserves estimated at 6,724 million tons. In 1970, Wyoming's coal production accounted for only 1% of the US total. By 1994 the state's production had risen to 23.7% of national production, and to 25.6% by 1995. The Black Thunder mine in the Powder River Basin is the largest coal producer in the nation, with an output of 36.1 million tons in 1995. In 1995, the state's 29 active mines produced 263.8 million tons of coal.

Electric power production in 1995 totaled 39.7 billion kWh; installed capacity was 6.3 million kW. In 1994, consumption of electricity totaled 8.7 billion kWh; although total energy consumption was only 410.3 trillion Btu (42d), per capita consumption was 861.9 million Btu, third nationally behind Alaska and Louisiana. However, exported energy is counted as intrastate consumption, thus inflating per capita energy usage.

29INDUSTRY

Although manufacturing increased markedly in Wyoming from 1977 to 1991—value of shipments by manufacturers more than doubled from $1,287 million to $2,733 million—it remains insignificant by national standards. Total value added by manufacture

in 1995 was $2.7 billion. The following table shows value of shipments for major sectors in 1995:

Lumber and wood products	$165,700,000
Industrial machinery and equipment	116,900,000
Printing and publishing	82,500,000
Chemicals and allied products	730,500,000
Food and food products	296,500,000

During 1995, 74 US patents were issued to Wyoming residents.

30COMMERCE

In 1992, sales from wholesale trade were about $2.5 billion, and retailers had sales of $3.6 billion. Of the 1992 total, automotive dealers accounted for 20.7%; food stores, 19%; gasoline service stations, 13.9%; general merchandise stores, 13%; and other retailers, 33.4%. Wyoming's exports of products to other countries were valued at $480.5 million in 1996.

31CONSUMER PROTECTION

The Office of Consumer Affairs serves as a business regulation office, and works in conjunction with federal consumer protection agencies and other attorney general offices.

32BANKING

In 1996, Wyoming had 53 insured commercial banks with total assets of $8.3 billion, including $5.6 billion in time and savings deposits and $5.5 billion in outstanding loans. There were also 4 insured savings institutions with assets of $303 million.

33INSURANCE

In 1995, there were 398,000 policies in force in Wyoming with a total value of $19.8 billion. The average coverage per family was $103,500 in 1995.

Property and liability insurers wrote premiums amounting to $407.7 million in 1995, of which automobile liability insurance accounted for $106.1 million; automobile physical damage, $92.7 million; and homeowner's insurance, $48.9 million.

34SECURITIES

Securities transactions are conducted by nearly 1,000 firms and their thousands of agents registered to do business in Wyoming.

35PUBLIC FINANCE

Wyoming's biennial budget is prepared by the governor and submitted to the legislature at the beginning of each even-numbered calendar year. The fiscal year is 1 July–30 June.

The following is an estimate of general fund revenues and expenditures for 1997/98 biennium:

GENERAL FUND REVENUES

Taxes	
Sales and use	$ 438,700,000
Mineral severance	121,900,000
Other taxes	38,800,000
Licenses and permits	3,608,000
Fines and forfeitures	9,700,000
Use of property	5,200,000
Interest	56,300,000
Charges for sales and services	52,539,416
Revenues from others	317,211,744
Federal	570,642,651
TOTAL REVENUES	$ 1,614,601,811

EXPENDITURES

Current

General government	$ 103,261,329
Regulations	6,721,438
Education	597,605,208
Health services	568,818,467
Law, justice, and safety	122,628,185
Employment	56,142,217
Regulation of business and professionals	85,114,013
Social services	169,789,125
TOTAL EXPENDITURES	$1,710,079,982

36 TAXATION

In 1996, the Wyoming Department of Revenue collected a total of $591.6 million in tax revenue. Sales and gross receipts tax revenues accounted for $320 million; use taxes, $48.6 million; cigarette taxes, $5.9 million; estate taxes, $4.6 million; lodging taxes, $2.6 million; severance taxes, $206 million; railroad car tax, $1.0 million; and public utility assessments, $2.0 million. Wyoming has no personal or corporate income tax.

Ad valorem taxes (taxes on real, personal, and minerals, collected by the county treasurers) totaled $450 million. The state retail sales tax is 4%.

37 ECONOMIC POLICY

State policy in Wyoming has traditionally favored fiscal, social, and political conservatism. A pro-business and pro-family climate has generally prevailed. For example, Wyoming does not have a state personal income tax, a state business income tax, nor a business inventory tax. Not until 1969 was the minerals industry compelled to pay a severance tax on the wealth it was extracting from Wyoming soils. The state's leading industry is tourism, (the federal government owns over 50% of Wyoming's land), and Wyoming is first among US states in coal and trona production. The Wyoming Department of Commerce, Division of Economic and Community Development encourages entrepreneurship, emphasizes community development, and supports retention and expansion of existing Wyoming businesses. Grant and loan programs also assist Wyoming communities and businesses.

38 HEALTH

Wyoming's birthrate—13.2 per 1,000 population in 1995—was less than the national rate of 14.8 in 1995 and substantially less than the state's 1985 birthrate of 18.5. In 1995, the state's death rate—7.8 per 1,000 population—was well below the national average. The death rates for heart disease, cancer, and cerebrovascular diseases were well below the national norm, but accidental deaths were above it. More than half of the unintentional injury deaths in 1993 were related to motor vehicles. Wyoming has the lowest number, ratio, and rate of abortions of all the states—296 in 1992, or 44 for every 1,000 live births, which was equivalent to 3 abortions per 1,000 women of childbearing years.

In 1995, Wyoming's 29 hospitals, with 2,776 beds, admitted 47,989 patients and had 831,723 outpatient visits. Hospital personnel included 1,995 registered nurses in 1995. In 1995, the state had 757 licensed physicians. Active licensed dentists in the state amounted to 232 in 1996. At least 17.7% of Wyoming residents were uninsured in 1995.

Among residents aged 18–30, 23.2% are reported to be smokers. The projected number of deaths due to smoking-related illness was 10,134 in 1995. The AIDS prevalence in Wyoming is one of the lowest in the nation (2.73 per 100,000 population). The total number of AIDS cases since before 1985 is 121.

39 SOCIAL WELFARE

In 1996, 13,500 Wyoming residents received aid to families with dependent children, with an average monthly payment of $390 per family. Federal Supplementary Security Income payments were made to 5,512 persons, averaging $304 per month in 1995; additionally, 69,610 Social Security recipients were paid an average monthly allotment of $698. In 1996, 33,013 residents received monthly food stamp allowances averaging $71.07; the school lunch program received total funding of $8.8 million.

With the enactment of the Personal Responsibility and Work Opportunity Reconciliation Act of 1996, the US government has changed the form and regulations for many of its social welfare programs; most significantly, it replaces Aid to Families with Dependent Children (AFDC), an open-ended entitlement program, with Temporary Assistance for Needy Families (TANF), a limited system of assistance funded largely through federal block grants. The reform act also impacts the food stamp program, the Supplemental Security Income program, and the child nutrition program. The law took effect on 1 July 1997 and provided $16.38 billion in block grants for fiscal years 1997–2002. The grants are to be divided among the states based on an equation involving the numbers of former AFDC recipients in each state. Because many of the bill's provisions have yet to be implemented into state-by-state policy, it was not possible to include the details of each state's programs for this edition of this work.

Unemployment benefits averaged $179.63 per week in Wyoming in 1995.

40 HOUSING

In 1996 there were an estimated 207,000 housing units in Wyoming, of which 181,000 were occupied. That year, 2,192 privately owned units, valued at $200 million, were authorized for construction; of these, 1,649 were single-family.

During the 1980s, the median home value fell by 35.2%, from $95,000 in 1980 to $61,600 in 1990 (in terms of 1990 dollars). The median monthly cost for an owner-occupied home with a mortgage was $612 in 1990, the last year for which figues were available; renters had a median monthly cost of $333.

In 1995/96, Wyoming received $47.4 million in aid from the US Department of Housing and Urban Development, including $6.2 million in community development block grants.

41 EDUCATION

Nearly 86.4% of all adults in the state were high school graduates according to the 1990 census; and more than 22.3% were college graduates.

In 1994/95, student enrollment was 100,314. There were 6,746 public-school teachers in 1994/95. In 1993/94, Wyoming ranked 2d among the states in school expenditures per capita—$1,375.00. Public-school teachers' salaries averaged $32,181 in 1994/95.

In the fall of 1994, 17,993 full- and part-time students were enrolled in Wyoming's seven community colleges. The state controls and funds the University of Wyoming in Laramie (9,111 enrolled students in 1994) and the seven community colleges. There are no private colleges or universities, although the National Outdoor Leadership School, based in Lander, offers courses in mountaineering and ecology.

42 ARTS

The Wyoming Council on the Arts, consisting of 10 members appointed by the governor to three-year terms, funds local activities and organizations in the visual and performing arts, including painting, music, theater, and dance. Wyoming supported its arts programs with federal funds amounting to $676,000 in 1996. The NEA contributed $397,000 to the programs and $583,000 to the Wyoming Arts Council. The state and private sources also contributed to the Arts Council. The state of Wyoming offered arts education programs to 33,100 school children. By 1996, the state had 60 arts associations and 100 local arts groups. The Wyoming Arts Council sponsored arts programs at the Desert School of Wamsutter and the Crest Hill School Writing Center in Casper, Wyoming. The NEA has contributed to the Grand Teton Music Festival and the Buffalo Bill Historical Center in Cody, Wyoming. In 1996, the Wyoming Arts Council received funding from the NEA for the state's arts education programs. The Arts Council also received grants through the NEA's state and regional program.

[43]LIBRARIES AND MUSEUMS

Wyoming was served by 23 county public library systems, with over 2 million volumes, in 1996. Public library circulation exceeded 3 million during the same period. The University of Wyoming, in Laramie, had 1,157,531 volumes in 1996.

There are at least 47 museums and historic sites, including the Wyoming State Museum in Cheyenne; the Buffalo Bill Historical Center (Cody), which exhibits paintings by Frederic Remington; and the anthropological, geological, and art museums of the University of Wyoming at Laramie.

[44]COMMUNICATIONS

In March 1995, 180,561 Wyoming households—94.3% of the total—had telephones.

In 1997, Wyoming had 67 radio stations, 31 AM and 36 FM, plus 13 commercial television stations. Two large cable television systems serve the Casper and Cheyenne communities.

[45]PRESS

There were 9 daily newspapers and 4 Sunday newspapers in Wyoming in 1997. The major daily and its 1997 circulation was the *Casper Star-Tribune*, 31,570 (35,089 on Sunday).

[46]ORGANIZATIONS

The 1992 Census of Service Industries counted 291 organizations in Wyoming, including 66 business associations; 178 civic, social, and fraternal associations; and 47 other membership organizations. The National Association for Outlaw and Lawman History, headquartered in Laramie, is one of the few national organizations with headquarters in the state.

[47]TOURISM, TRAVEL, AND RECREATION

There are 2 national parks in Wyoming—Yellowstone and Grand Teton—and 11 state parks. Devils Tower and Fossil Butte are national monuments, and Fort Laramie is a national historic site. The national parks drew 6,332,524 visitors in 1995.

Yellowstone National Park, covering 2,219,791 acres (898,349 hectares), mostly in the northwestern corner of the state, is the oldest (1872) and largest national park in the US. The park features some 3,000 geysers and hot springs, including the celebrated Old Faithful. Just to the south of Yellowstone is Grand Teton National Park, 309,993 acres (125,454 hectares).

Adjacent to Grand Teton is the National Elk Refuge, the feeding range of the continent's largest known herd of elk. Devils Tower, a rock formation in the northeast, looming 5,117 feet (1,560 meters) high, is the country's oldest national monument (1906). Hunting and fishing are important recreational industries in Wyoming. In 1995, licenses were sold to 241,486 hunters and 336,402 fishers.

[48]SPORTS

There are no major league professional sports teams in Wyoming. Participation sports in Wyoming are typically Western. Skills developed by ranch hands in herding cattle are featured at rodeos held throughout the state. Cheyenne Frontier Days is the largest of these rodeos. Skiing is also a major sport, with Jackson Hole being the largest, best-known resort.

In collegiate sports, the University of Wyoming competes in the Western Athletic Conference. They won the Sun Bowl in 1956 and 1958; and they appeared in, but lost, the Holiday Bowl in 1987 and 1988.

[49]FAMOUS WYOMINGITES

The most important federal officeholder from Wyoming was Willis Van Devanter (b.Indiana, 1859–1941), who served on the US Supreme Court from 1910 to 1937. Many of Wyoming's better-known individuals are associated with the frontier: John Colter (b.Virginia, 1775?–1813), a fur trader, was the first white man to explore northwestern Wyoming; and Jim Bridger (b.Virginia, 1804–81), perhaps the most famous fur trapper in the West, centered his activities in Wyoming. Late in life, William F. "Buffalo Bill" Cody (b.Iowa, 1846–1917) settled in the Big Horn Basin and established the town of Cody. A number of outlaws made their headquarters in Wyoming. The most famous were "Butch Cassidy" (George Leroy Parker, b.Utah, 1866–1908) and the "Sundance Kid" (Harry Longabaugh, birthplace in dispute, 1863?–1908), who, as members of the Wild Bunch, could often be found there.

Two Wyoming women, Esther Morris (b.New York, 1814–1902) and Nellie Taylor Ross (b.Missouri, 1880–1979), are recognized as the first woman judge and the first woman governor, respectively, in the US; Ross also was the first woman to serve as director of the US Mint. Few Wyoming politicians have received national recognition, but Francis E. Warren (b.Massachusetts, 1844–1929), the state's first governor, served 37 years in the US Senate and came to wield considerable influence and power.

Without question, Wyoming's most famous businessman was James Cash Penney (b. Missouri, 1875–1971). Penney established his first "Golden Rule" store in Kemmerer and eventually built a chain of department stores nationwide. The water-reclamation accomplishments of Elwood Mead (b.Indiana, 1858–1936) and the botanical work in the Rocky Mountains of Aven Nelson (b.Iowa, 1859–1952) were highly significant. Jackson Pollock (1912–56), born in Cody, was a leading painter in the abstract expressionist movement.

[50]BIBLIOGRAPHY

Athearn, Robert G. *Union Pacific Country*. New York: Rand McNally, 1971.

Gressley, Gene M. *Bankers and Cattlemen*. New York: Knopf, 1966.

Larson, T. A. *History of Wyoming*. 2d ed., rev. Lincoln: University of Nebraska Press, 1978.

———. *Wyoming: A History*. New York: Norton, 1984.

Lavender, David. *Westward Vision: The Story of the Oregon Trail*. New York: McGraw-Hill, 1963.

Mead, Jean. *Wyoming in Profile*. Boulder, Colo.: Pruett, 1982.

Woods, L. Milton. *The Wyoming Country Before Statehood*. Worland, Wyo.: Worland Press, 1971.

Wyoming, Department of Administration and Fiscal Control, Division of Research and Statistics. *Wyoming Data Handbook 1983*. 6th ed. Cheyenne, 1983.

DISTRICT OF COLUMBIA

District of Columbia

ORIGIN OF NAME: From "Columbia," a name commonly applied to the US in the late 18th century, ultimately deriving from Christopher Columbus. **BECAME US CAPITAL:** 1 December 1800. **MOTTO:** *Justitia omnibus* (Justice for all). **FLAG:** The flag, based on George Washington's coat of arms, consists of three red stars above two horizontal red stripes on a white field. **OFFICIAL SEAL:** In the background, the Potomac River separates the District of Columbia from the Virginia shore, over which the sun is rising. In the foreground, Justice, holding a wreath and a tablet with the word "Constitution," stands beside a statue of George Washington. To her left is the Capitol; to her right, an eagle and various agricultural products. Below is the District motto and the date 1871; above are the words "District of Columbia." **BIRD:** Wood thrush. **FLOWER:** American beauty rose. **TREE:** Scarlet oak. **LEGAL HOLIDAYS:** New Year's Day, 1 January; Birthday of Martin Luther King, Jr., 3d Monday in January; Washington's Birthday, 3d Monday in February; Memorial Day, last Monday in May; Independence Day, 4 July; Labor Day, 1st Monday in September; Columbus Day, 2d Monday in October; Veterans Day, 11 November; Thanksgiving Day, 4th Thursday in November; Christmas Day, 25 December. **TIME:** 7 AM EST = noon GMT.

¹LOCATION, SIZE, AND EXTENT

Located in the South Atlantic region of the US, the District of Columbia has a total area of 69 sq mi (179 sq km), of which land takes up 63 sq mi (163 sq km) and inland water 6 sq mi (16 sq km). The District is bounded on the N, E, and S by Maryland, and on the W by the Virginia shore of the Potomac River. The total boundary length is 37 mi (60 km).

For statistical purposes, the District of Columbia (coextensive since 1890 with the city of Washington, D.C.) is considered part of the Washington, D.C., metropolitan area, which since 1985 has embraced Calvert, Charles, Frederick, Montgomery, and Prince George's counties in Maryland, and Arlington, Fairfax, Loudoun, Prince William, and Stafford counties in Virginia, along with a number of other Virginia jurisdictions, most notably the city of Alexandria.

²TOPOGRAPHY

The District of Columbia, an enclave of western Maryland, lies wholly within the Atlantic Coastal Plain. The major topographical features are the Potomac River and its adjacent marshlands; the Anacostia River, edged by reclaimed flatlands to the south and east; Rock Creek, wending its way from the northwestern plateau to the Potomac; and the gentle hills of the north. The District's average elevation is about 150 feet (46 meters). The highest point—410 feet (125 meters)—is in the northwest, at Tenleytown; the low point is the Potomac, only 1 foot (30 cm) above sea level.

³CLIMATE

The climate of the nation's capital is characterized by chilly, damp winters and hot, humid summers. The normal daily mean temperature is 58°F (14°C), ranging from 35°F (2°C) in January to 80°F (27°C) in July. The record low, –15°F (–26°C), was set on 11 February 1899; the all-time high, 106°F (41°C), on 20 July 1930. Precipitation averages 39 in (99 cm) yearly; snowfall, 17 in (43 cm). The average annual relative humidity is 73% at 7 AM and 52% at 1 PM.

⁴FLORA AND FAUNA

Although most of its original flora has been obliterated by urbanization, the District has long been known for its beautiful parks, where about 1,800 varieties of flowering plants and 250 shrubs grow. Boulevards are shaded by stately sycamores, pin and red oaks, American lindens, and black walnut trees. Famous among the introduced species are the Japanese cherry trees around the Tidal Basin. Magnolia, dogwood, and gingko are also characteristic. The District's fauna is less exotic, with squirrels, cottontails, English sparrows, and starlings predominating.

⁵ENVIRONMENTAL PROTECTION

The Environmental Regulation Administration (ERA) administers district and federal laws, regulations and mayoral initiatives governing the environment and natural resources of the District of Columbia and the surrounding metropolitan area. The main duty is the protection of human health and the environment as they relate to pesticides, hazardous waste, underground storage tanks, water, air, soils, and fisheries programs. The ERA is responsible for administrating over 30 statutes and regulations. In 1996, the District had about 250 acres of wetlands, all palustrine (marsh) or riverine.

⁶POPULATION

The District of Columbia outranked three states in population in 1990, with a census total of 606,900, a decline of almost 5% from 1980. The population density was 9,882 per sq mi (3,815 per sq km). Considered as a city, the District ranked 19th in the US in 1990. Its 1996 population was estimated at 543,213, a 10.5% decline from 1990. Even as the capital's population has declined, the number of Washington, D.C., metropolitan area residents has been increasing, from 3,040,000 in 1970 to 3,251,000 in 1980 and to 3,924,000 in 1990 (8th in US). The District's population is 100% urban and extremely mobile; only 39.3% of all residents were born in the District.

⁷ETHNIC GROUPS

Black Americans have long been the largest ethnic group in the District of Columbia, accounting for 65.8% of the population in 1990, the 4th highest percentage of any major US city after Gary,

Indiana; Detroit, Michigan; and Atlanta, Georgia. Blacks accounted for about 26.6% of the metropolitan area population in 1990, a proportion that has been relatively constant for more than 200 years. District ethnic minorities in 1990 included 33,000 Hispanics, 12,353 Russians, 8,547 Salvadorans, 3,184 Jamaicans, and 2,574 Chinese. There also were about 1,000 American Indians living in the District. Only 9.7% of the population was foreign-born in 1990, but contributing to Washington's ethnic diversity are the many foreign-born residents attached to foreign embassies and missions.

Between 1970 and 1980, the population of groups other than white and black almost quadrupled within the Washington metropolitan area, reaching 134,209 in 1980. Southeast Asians made up a significant proportion of the immigrants, as did Mexicans and Central and South Americans. By 1990 this group numbered 303,707, due mainly to an increase in the number of Asian immigrants.

8LANGUAGES

Dialectically, the Washington, D.C., area is extremely heterogeneous. In 1990, 87% of all District of Columbia residents 5 years of age or older spoke only English at home. Other languages spoken at home included Spanish, Chinese, French, Italian, German, and Greek.

9RELIGIONS

As of 1990, Washington D.C. had 77,532 Roman Catholics. The leading Protestant denominations in 1990 were Episcopal, 16,273; American Baptist Convention, 33,744; United Methodist, 18,321; and Southern Baptist Convention, 17,597. Data on some predominantly black Protestant groups were unavailable. The Jewish population in 1990 was estimated at 25,400 in the District. Washington's resident foreign population includes followers of numerous other religions.

10TRANSPORTATION

Union Station, located north of the Capitol, is the District's one rail terminal, from which Amtrak provides passenger service to the northeast corridor and southern points. In 1995/96, Amtrak operated about 75 trains per day into Union Station, with a total ridership of 3,140,399. In all, four railroads operate 26 rail mi (42 km) of track. The Washington Metropolitan Area Transit Authority, or Metro, operates bus and subway transportation within the city and its Maryland and Virginia suburbs. About 40% of working District residents commute by public transportation. In 1994/95, the federal Transit Authority awarded grants of $199 million for the Metro.

Within the District as of 1995 were 1,421 mi (2,288 km) of public streets and roads; 242,695 motor vehicles were registered, and 338,549 driver's licenses were in force. The District had a higher rate of nonfatal traffic injuries to both motorists and pedestrians than any state in 1995—299.5 and 37.1 people per 100 million vehicle miles, respectively. Three major airports handle the District's commercial air traffic: Washington National Airport, just south of the city in Virginia; Dulles International Airport in Virginia; and Baltimore–Washington International Airport in Maryland. Of these, Washington National was the busiest airfield in 1994, handling 6,982,998 enplaned passengers; Baltimore–Washington enplaned 5,524,703, and Dulles International 4,230,348.

11HISTORY

Algonkian-speakers were living in what is now the District of Columbia when Englishmen founded the Jamestown, Va., settlement in 1607. The first white person known to have set foot in the Washington area was the English fur trader Henry Fleete, who in 1622 was captured by the Indians and held there for

several years. Originally part of Maryland Colony, the region had been carved up into plantations by the latter half of the 17th century.

After the US Constitution (1787) provided that a tract of land be reserved for the seat of the federal government, both Maryland and Virginia offered parcels for that purpose; on 16 July 1790, Congress authorized George Washington to choose a site not more than 10 mi (16 km) square along the Potomac River. President Washington made his selection in January 1791 and then appointed Andrew Ellicott to survey the area and employed Pierre Charles L'Enfant, a French military engineer who had served in the Continental Army, to draw up plans for the federal city. L'Enfant's masterful design called for a wide roadway (now called Pennsylvania Avenue) to connect the Capitol with the President's House (Executive Mansion, now commonly called the White House) a mile away, and for other widely separated public buildings with spacious vistas. However, L'Enfant was late in completing the engraved plan of his design, and he also had difficulty in working with the three commissioners who had been appointed to direct a territorial survey; for these and other reasons, L'Enfant was dismissed and Ellicott carried out the plans. Construction was delayed by lack of adequate financing. Only one wing of the Capitol was completed, and the President's House was still under construction when President John Adams and some 125 government officials moved into the District in 1800. Congress met there for the first time on 17 November, and the District officially became the nation's capital on 1 December. On 3 May 1802, the city of Washington was incorporated (the District also included other local entities), with an elected council and a mayor appointed by the president.

Construction proceeded slowly, while the city's population grew to about 24,000 by 1810. In August 1814, during the War of 1812, British forces invaded and burned the Capitol, the President's House, and other public buildings. These were rebuilt within five years, but for a long time, Washington remained a rude, rough city. In 1842, English author Charles Dickens described it as a "monument raised to a deceased project," consisting of "spacious avenues that begin in nothing and lead nowhere." At the request of its residents, the Virginia portion was retroceded in 1846, thus confining the federal district to the eastern shore of the Potomac. The Civil War brought a large influx of Union soldiers, workers, and escaped slaves, and the District's population rose sharply from 75,080 in 1860 to 131,700 by the end of the decade, spurring the development of modern Washington.

In 1871, Congress created a territorial form of government; this territorial government was abolished three years later because of alleged local extravagances, and in 1878, a new form of government was established, headed by three commissioners appointed by the president. During the same decade, Congress barred District residents from voting in national elections or even for their own local officials. In the 1890s, Rock Creek Park and Potomac Park were established, and during the early 1900s, city planners began to rebuild the monumental core of Washington in harmony with L'Enfant's original design. The New Deal period brought a rise in public employment, substantial growth of federal facilities, and the beginnings of large-scale public housing construction and slum clearance. After World War II, redevelopment efforts concentrated on demolishing slums in the city's southwest section. The White House was completely renovated in the late 1940s, and a huge building program coincided with the expansion of the federal bureaucracy during the 1960s.

Because it is the residence of the president, Washington, D.C., has always been noted for its public events, in particular the Presidential Inauguration and Inaugural Ball. The District has also been the site of many historic demonstrations: the appearance in 1894 of Coxey's Army—some 300 unemployed

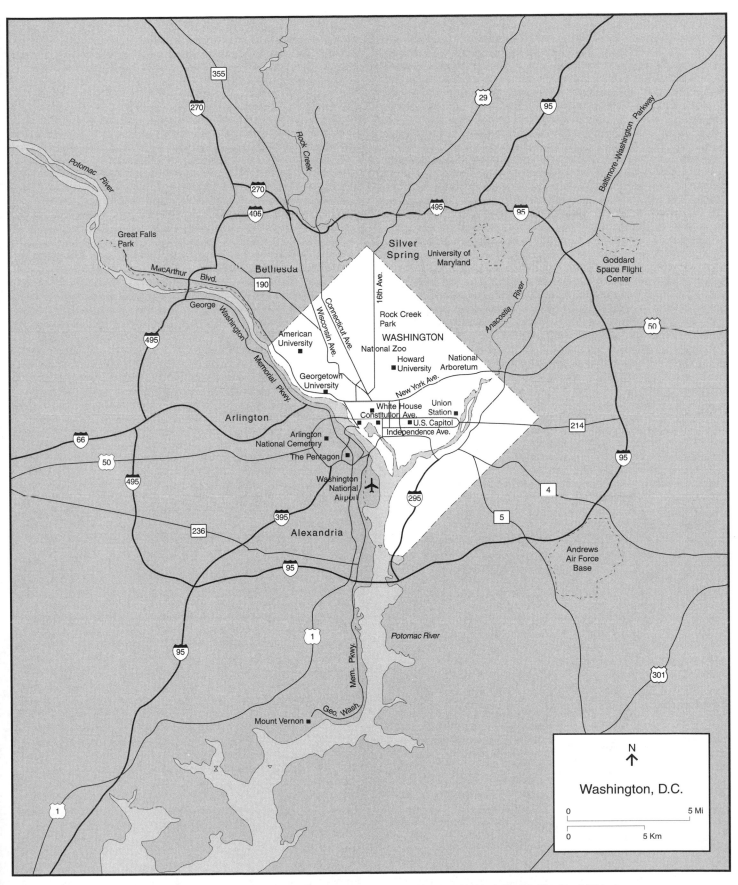

LOCATION: 38° 47' to 39°N; 76° 55' to 77° 07'W. **BOUNDARIES:** Maryland line, 25 mi (40 km); Virginia line, 12 mi (19 km).

workers; the demonstrations in 1932 of the Bonus Marchers—17,000 Army veterans demanding that the government cash their bonus certificates; the massive March on Washington by civil rights demonstrators in 1963; the march on the Pentagon in 1967 by antiwar activists and later Vietnam-era protests; and, in 1995, the Million Man March organized by the controversial Nation of Islam leader Louis Farrakhan.

In recent years, the District's form of government has undergone significant changes. The 23d Amendment to the US Constitution, ratified on 3 April 1961, permits residents to vote in presidential elections, and beginning in 1971, the District was allowed to send a nonvoting delegate to the US House of Representatives. Local self-rule began in 1975, when an elected mayor and council took office. The District has both prospered and suffered in the last two decades. In spite of an expanding economy, the city has been wracked by poverty, drug-bred crime, and even gang warfare. In 1989, the federal government mandated $80 million for a program to combat drug abuse in the nation's capital. Crime in Washington has included corruption in high places. In the mid-1980s, the federal government launched an investigation into allegations of bribery, fraud, and racketeering in the award of millions of dollars in municipal and federal contracts. The investigation produced the conviction of 11 city officials. In 1990, the District's mayor of twelve years, Marion Barry, was videotaped smoking crack and was convicted of possessing cocaine. Barry was succeeded that year by Sharon Pratt Dixon, a black lawyer and former power company executive, but re-elected in 1994.

Since the 1970s, many of Washington's residents have supported statehood for the District of Columbia. A proposal for statehood won the majority of votes in a 1980 election, and the name "New Columbia" was approved by voters two years later. In 1992, the US House of Representatives passed a measure approving statehood for the capital, but the Senate refused to consider it.

12STATE GOVERNMENT

The District of Columbia is the seat of the federal government and houses the principal organs of the legislative, executive, and judicial branches. The District of Columbia committees of the US Senate and House of Representatives oversee affairs within Washington, D.C. The District elects a delegate to the US House who participates in discussions and votes on bills within the District of Columbia Committee but may not vote on measures on the floor of the House. In 1978, Congress approved a constitutional amendment granting the District two US senators and at least one representative; however, the amendment failed to become law because it was not ratified by the necessary 38 state legislatures by August 1985.

Elected delegates drafted a constitution for the proposed State of New Columbia in 1982. It was approved by voters within the District, and a petition for statehood has been pending in Congress since 1983.

13POLITICAL PARTIES

Washington, D.C., is the headquarters of the Democratic and Republican parties, the nation's major political organizations. The District itself is overwhelmingly Democratic: in 1994, out of 340,953 registered voters, 263,574 were Democrats (77%); 28,544 were Republicans (8%); and 48,835 (14%) were independents or members of other groups. The District has a 30-day residency requirement for voters. Residents of the District, permitted to vote for president since 1964, have unfailingly cast their ballots for the Democratic nominee, as they did in 1996, giving Bill Clinton 85% of the vote, Republican Bob Dole 9%, and Independent candidates Ralph Nader and Ross Perot 3% and 2% respectively.

The first mayor, Walter Washington, was defeated for reelection in 1978 by Marion S. Barry, Jr., who was reelected in 1982 and again in 1986. Sharon Pratt Dixon was elected mayor in 1990. In 1994, Marion S. Barry Jr., returning to political life after serving a six-month jail term for a 1990 drug conviction, defeated Republican Carol Schwartz in the mayoral contest. Schwartz previously lost to Barry in the mayoral election of 1986.

Eleanor Holmes Norton serves as the District's delegate to the House of Representatives.

D.C. Presidential Vote by Major Parties, 1964–96

YEAR	ELECTORAL VOTE	D.C. WINNER	DEMOCRAT	REPUBLICAN
1964	3	*Johnson (D)	169,796	28,801
1968	3	Humphrey (D)	139,566	31,012
1972	3	McGovern (D)	127,627	35,226
1976	3	*Carter (D)	137,818	27,873
1980	3	Carter (D)	124,376	21,765
1984	3	Mondale (D)	180,408	29,009
1988	3	Dukakis (D)	159,407	27,590
1992	3	*Clinton (D)	192,619	20,698
1996	3	*Clinton (D)	158,220	17,339

* Won US presidential election.

Blacks have played a dominant role in District politics. As of 1993 the mayor, the delegate to the House of Representatives, both statehood senators, and the statehood representative were black. In the same year, the District of Columbia had a total of 198 African-American elected officials.

14LOCAL GOVERNMENT

Local government in the District of Columbia operates under authority delegated by Congress. In 1973, for the first time in more than a century, Congress provided the District with a home-rule charter, allowing Washington, D.C., residents to elect their own mayor and a city council of 13 members, all serving four-year terms. Residents of the District approved the charter on 7 May 1974, and a new elected government took office on 1 January 1975.

The mayor has traditionally been the District's chief executive, and the council is the legislative branch; however, under constitutional authority, Congress can enact laws on any subject affecting the District, and all legislation enacted by the District is subject to congressional veto. In response to both a managerial and budgetary crisis, Congress passed the District of Columbia Financial Responsibility and Management Assistance Act of 1995. This law established a Control Board that has broad powers to review all actions of the D.C. government and must approve the financial plans and budget for the city before submission to Congress. Home rule was further eroded when in 1997 Congress took responsibility for most major agencies away from the mayor and gave them to the Control Board.

The council consists of 13 members: the council chairman, 4 members elected at large, and 8 elected by wards. The 12-member Board of Education consists of 8 officials elected by ward and 4 elected at-large, including 1 at-large member elected by students. They serve for four years. The charter also provides for 36 neighborhood advisory commissions, whose seats (321 in all) are filled through nonpartisan elections.

15STATE SERVICES

Public education in the District is the responsibility of a chief executive officer and board of trustees appointed by the Control Board and the University of the District of Columbia Board of Trustees. The elected Board of Education is left with very little authority. Transportation services are provided through the Department of Transportation and the Washington Metropolitan Area Transit Authority, while health and welfare services fall within the jurisdiction of the Department of Human Resources. The Office of Consumer and Regulatory Affairs, Department of Corrections, District of Columbia National Guard, and Metropolitan Police Department provide public protection services, and the Department of Housing and Community Development is the main housing agency. Employment and job training programs are offered through the Department of Employment Services.

[16]JUDICIAL SYSTEM

All judges in Washington, D.C., are nominated by the president of the US from a list of persons recommended by the District of Columbia Nomination Commission, and appointed upon the advice and consent of the Senate. The US Court of Appeals for the District of Columbia functions in a manner similar to that of a state supreme court; it also has original jurisdiction over federal crimes. The court consists of a chief judge and 8 associate judges, all serving 15-year terms. The Superior Court of the District of Columbia, the trial court, consisted in late 1994 of five divisions and 59 judges, also serving for 15 years. Washington, D.C., is the site of the US Supreme Court and the US Department of Justice. The District of Columbia is the only US jurisdiction where the US Attorney's Office, an arm of the Justice Department, and not the local government, prosecutes criminal offenders for nonfederal crimes. An estimated 31,097 attorneys practiced in the District in 1996.

According to the FBI Crime Index, the violent crime rate in the District of Columbia was 2,661.4.8 per 100,000 population in 1995, several times greater than the national average of 684.6. The total crime rate was 12,173 per 100,000 population, more than double the national rate of 5,277.6. Crimes in the District during 1996 included 360 cases of murder and nonnegligent manslaughter, 292 forcible rapes, 6,864 robberies, and 7,228 aggravated assaults. In all, there were 67,441 crimes reported.

D.C. prisoners in state and federal institutions numbered 9,763 in 1996, or 1,444 per 100,000.

[17]ARMED FORCES

In 1996, there were 14,519 active-duty military personnel stationed in the District of Columbia, the vast majority of whom (12,157) were at the Pentagon, the headquarters of the US Department of Defense, which covers 34 acres (14 hectares) of Arlington, Virginia, across the Potomac. An Air Force installation (Bolling AFB), the Army's Fort McNair, and Walter Reed Medical Center were also within the District. Firms in the District received $1.4 billion in federal defense contract awards over $25,000 in 1995/96.

As of 1 July 1996, about 49,000 veterans of US military service were living in the District, of whom fewer than 500 served in World War I, 15,000 in World War II, 10,000 during the Korean conflict, 14,000 during the Viet Nam era, and 4,000 in the Persian Gulf War. Veterans' benefits totaled $1.07 billion during 1995/96.

Because Washington is often the scene of political demonstrations and because high federal officials and the District's foreign embassy personnel pose special police-protection problems, the ratio of police personnel to residents is higher than in any state; in 1993, its 4,271 police employees represented a rate of 7.0 per 10,000 population. There were 4,277 Army National Guard and Reserve personnel in 1996, as well as 5,987 Navy and Marine Corps and 250 Air Force Reserve and National Guard personnel.

[18]MIGRATION

The principal migratory movements have been an influx of southern blacks after the Civil War and, more recently, the rapid growth of the Washington, D.C., metropolitan area, coupled with a shrinkage in the population of the District itself. Between 1950 and 1970, the District suffered a net loss from migration of as much as 260,000, much of it to Maryland and Virginia; there was, however, an estimated net inflow of 87,000 blacks in this period. Net emigration totaled between 150,000 and 190,000 during the 1970s, and roughly 23,000 more during 1981–83.

From 1985 to 1990, the District had a net loss from migration of over 30,000. Between 1990 and 1996, there was a net loss of 109,142 in domestic migration and a net gain of 1,897 in international migration. In 1996, 3,784 foreign immigrants arrived in Washington, D.C. In 1990, only 39.3% of the District's residents were native-born. About 46% of residents age 5 and older in 1990 lived in a different house in 1985, of which 45% did so outside the District.

[19]INTERGOVERNMENTAL COOPERATION

The District of Columbia, a member of the Council of State Governments and its allied organizations, also participates in such interstate regional bodies as the Commission on Mental Health, Interstate Commission on Juveniles, Vehicle Equipment Safety Commission, Washington Metropolitan Area Transit Authority Commission, and Potomac Valley Commission. Counties and incorporated cities in the Washington area are represented on the Metropolitan Washington Council of Governments, established in 1957.

The District relies heavily on federal assistance, which came to over $2.5 billion in 1995/96.

[20]ECONOMY

Between 1980 and 1990, the number of jobs in the service sector grew 43.5%. Other sectors, however, suffered in that decade. Employment in transportation, communications, and utilities declined 6.6%; jobs in the federal government declined 3.6%; wholesale and retail trade employment decreased 2.8%; and jobs in finance, insurance and real estate declined 2%. Nevertheless, the city enjoyed an economic boom in the 1980s which increased its office space from 52,000 sq ft in 1985 to 69,000 sq ft in 1990.

The District's total gross product in 1994 was $48,028 million in 1989, to which private goods-producing industries contributed $1,716 million; private services-producing industries, $27,064 million; and government, $19,248 million. During 1996, there were 1,950 bankruptcy filings.

[21]INCOME

With a per capita personal income of $34,932 in 1996, the District of Columbia outranked every state except Connecticut and New Jersey. The proportion of District of Columbia residents below the federal poverty line increased from 17% to 18.6% between 1969 and 1979, and to 22.2% by 1995.

[22]LABOR

In 1995, the civilian labor force in the District of Columbia averaged 285,500, of whom 260,100 were employed and 25,400 were unemployed. The same year, the District's unemployment rate was 8.9%. There were 146,300 women in the District's labor force in 1995, representing 51% of the total, and the teenage unemployment rate was 35.2% in 1995.

In 1995, nonfarm payroll employment by industry in the District of Columbia totaled 642,600—387,700 jobs were in the private sector and 254,900 in the public sector. The service sector was the largest, with 263,900 job; services accounted for 41% of the overall total and 68% of the private sector total. Following services were trade; finance, insurance and real estate; transportation, communications, and public utilities; manufacturing; construction; and mining. The District of Columbia serves as the headquarters of many labor organizations. The following summarizes employment for major industry groups in the District of Columbia:

	EMPLOYMENT
Total nonfarm industry employment	642,600
Private sector	387,700
Services	263,900
Trade	52,200
Finance, insurance and real estate	29,900
Transportation, communications, and public utilities	19,900
Manufacturing	13,000
Construction	8,700
Mining	100
Public sector	254,900
Federal	206,700
State	44,000
Local	4,200

23AGRICULTURE

There is no commercial farming in the District of Columbia.

24ANIMAL HUSBANDRY

The District of Columbia has no livestock industry.

25FISHING

There is no commercial fishing in the District of Columbia. Recreational fishing is accessible via a boat-launching facility on the Anacostia River. The Mammoth Spring National Fish Hatchery in Arkansas distributed 1,200 channel catfish within the district in 1995/96.

26FORESTRY

There is no forestland or forest products industry in the District of Columbia.

27MINING

There is no mining in the District of Columbia, although a few mining firms have offices there.

28ENERGY AND POWER

The District of Columbia had an installed electric-energy capacity of 868,000 kW in 1995 from four oil-fired plants, all privately owned. Electrical output during the same year totaled 189 million kWh.

29INDUSTRY

Value of shipments by manufacturers in 1995 reached $2,051.3 million. Within the District is the Government Printing Office (established by Congress in 1860), which operates one of the largest printing plants in the US. Also in the District is the Washington Post Co., publisher of the newspaper of that name and of *Newsweek* magazine; the company also owns television stations.

During 1995, there were 66 US patents issued to residents of the District of Columbia.

30COMMERCE

Sales from wholesaling totaled $3.3 billion in 1992. Retail sales totaled $3.6 billion that same year. Among retail establishments with payrolls, eating and drinking establishments accounted for 28.5% of sales; food stores, 17.8%; apparel and accessory stores, 10%; gasoline service stations, 5.8%; and general merchandise stores, 5.7%.

Alexandria, Virginia, which lies within the Washington, D.C. Customs District, imported goods worth $1.2 billion in 1995, and exported $2.3 billion in merchandise.

31CONSUMER PROTECTION

The Department of Consumer and Regulatory Affairs has primary responsibility for consumer protection in the District.

The Department regulates businesses; land and building use; occupational and professional standards; rental housing and condominiums; health and social service care facilities; and the natural environment.

32BANKING

Banking in the District of Columbia began with the chartering of the Bank of Alexandria in 1792 and the Bank of Columbia in 1793; both banks terminated in the early 19th century. The oldest surviving bank in the District is the National Bank of Washington, founded as the Bank of Washington in 1809.

Overall, there were 13 insured commercial banks in 1996, with assets totaling $9.8 billion, and outstanding loans of $3.9 billion. The same year, one insured savings institution had assets of $265 million, and outstanding mortgage loans of $101 million.

33INSURANCE

In 1991, District of Columbia policyholders held life insurance policies worth $67.9 billion. The average coverage per family was $271,700, far higher than in any state. Benefits totaled $870 million, of which death payments made up $220.5 million. Property and casualty insurers wrote premiums worth $826 million in the District in 1995, of which $116.3 million was automotive liability insurance, $77 million was automobile physical damage insurance, and $56.8 million was homeowners' coverage.

34SECURITIES

There are no securities exchanges in the District of Columbia.

35PUBLIC FINANCE

The budget for the District of Columbia is prepared by the mayor's office and reviewed by the city council, but is subject to review and approval by Congress. The fiscal year runs from 1 October through 30 September.

The local tax base is limited by a shortage of taxable real estate, much of the District being occupied by government buildings and federal reservations. Moreover, Congress has not allowed the District to tax the incomes of people who work in Washington but live in the suburbs, an objective the District government has urgently sought.

36TAXATION

In 1996, the District of Columbia's personal income tax ranged from 6% to 9.5%. The basic corporate tax was 9.5%, plus a 5% surtax. The District levies a 5.75% general sales and use tax, plus real and personal property taxes, an inheritance tax, and various excise taxes.

37ECONOMIC POLICY

The District's Office of Business and Economic Development (OBED) administers a revolving loan fund that helps small businesses in need of investment capital. The Local Development Corporation administers the federal Small Business Administration's loan guarantee program for plant and equipment. OBED also assists business in applying for federal urban development action grant funds. Federal community development block grant funds are available as well. By District law, 35% of all construction and procurement contracts by District government agencies must go to minority-owned business enterprises.

The $98.7-million Washington Convention Center opened in December 1982.

38HEALTH

Health conditions in the nation's capital are no source of national pride. The infant mortality rate of 20.1 per 1,000 live births exceeded that of every state in 1994. Legal abortions outnumber live births in the District, a distinction that no states and few cities share; 17,698 abortions and 9,014 births occurred within the District in 1995. That same year, 53.2% of abortions were obtained by out-of-state residents. The District also had an overall death rate of 1,209.2 per 100,000 population, higher than any state. In addition, the death rate from cardiovascular diseases ranked 3d highest in the nation, at 226.6 per 100,000 in 1993. The death rates for cerebrovascular diseases, accidents and adverse effects, motor vehicle accidents, and suicide, however, were below the US rate. Firearm-related deaths in the District, 48.5 per 100,000, far exceeded the national rate of 13.7 in 1995. The homicide rate of 56.8 per 100,000 also remains the highest in the country.

In 1995 there were 12 hospitals with 3,725 beds. The average expense of hospitals for care in that year was $1,304 per inpatient day (second only to Alaska) and $9,021 per stay—the highest in the US. Medical personnel licensed to practice in the District in 1995 included 4,296 federal and nonfederal physicians and 8,000 registered nurses. At the beginning of 1994, there were 641 nonfederal physicians per 100,000 civilians in the District—a ratio much higher than in any of the states. In 1994, the District had 1,428 employed nurses per 100,000 population, more than in any of the states. Almost 20% of the population of the District of Columbia had no health insurance in 1995. The 127,000 Medicaid recipients in 1994 had $550 million paid for health services.

³⁹SOCIAL WELFARE

In 1996, aid to families with dependent children was received by 70,000 residents, with the average monthly payment per family being $513, and 92,751 District residents received monthly food stamp allowances averaging $85.31. In the same year, the school lunch program received total funding of $15.5 million. Medicaid recipients in 1990 totaled 113,192, and the 1990 cost of the program was $405 million, of which an estimated 48.5% was paid by federal funds.

With the enactment of the Personal Responsibility and Work Opportunity Reconciliation Act of 1996, the US government has changed the form and regulations for many of its social welfare programs; most significantly, it replaces Aid to Families with Dependent Children (AFDC), an open-ended entitlement program, with Temporary Assistance for Needy Families (TANF), a limited system of assistance funded largely through federal block grants. The reform act also impacts the food stamp program, the Supplemental Security Income program, and the child nutrition program. The law took effect on 1 July 1997 and provided $16.38 billion in block grants for fiscal years 1997–2002. The grants are to be divided among the states based on an equation involving the numbers of former AFDC recipients in each state. Because many of the bill's provisions have yet to be implemented into state-by-state policy, it was not possible to include the details of each state's programs for this edition of this work.

In 1996, Social Security totaling $537 million was paid to eligible residents, and Supplemental Security Income expenditures, totaled $80.8 million. Unemployment insurance totaled $112 million in 1990. Weekly unemployment benefits averaged $231.75 in 1995.

⁴⁰HOUSING

The District of Columbia in 1996 had an estimated 271,000 housing units, of which 232,000 were occupied. Some 38% of the units dated from 1939 or earlier. Over 99% of all occupied units had full plumbing. At 10.3%, the District of Columbia had the third-largest ratio of condominiums (after Hawaii and Florida) in 1990, when they numbered 28,628. In 1993, 305 new units, valued at $20.5 million, were authorized. Housing prices

were high; the median monthly cost for an owner (including mortgage) in 1990, the last year or which figures were available, was $950; renters had a median monthly cost of $479. The median home value was $123,900 in 1990, higher than in all but eight of the states. During 1995/96, the District of Columbia received $286.7 million in aid from the US Department of Housing and Urban Development, including $25.7 million in community development block grants.

⁴¹EDUCATION

The District of Columbia's first public schools were opened in 1805. In the fall of 1995, there were 176 public schools with a total enrollment of 79,802 students—88.52% black, 6.12% Hispanic, 4.02% white, 1.32% Asian or Pacific Islander, and 0.02% American Indian or Alaskan native. Of this number, 49,563 were in elementary schools, 13,839 in junior high schools, 15,484 in senior high schools, and 828 in special classes. Per-pupil expenditure was $7,085 in 1994/95.

Until 1954, public schools for whites and blacks were operated separately. The school system remains virtually segregated; in 1980, only 700 minority-group students were attending schools with less than 50% minority enrollment, while 95% attended schools of 90% to 100% minority-group enrollment. Most white and many black students attend private schools. Attendance in 1990/91 was 10,067, including 4,846 in Catholic schools, and 53% of nonpublic students were black. In 1990 over 70.9% of all residents 25 years of age or older were high school graduates, and 31.1% were college graduates.

The District had 18 institutions of higher education in 1991/92, 17 private and 1 public. Some of the best-known private universities, with 1991/92 enrollment, are American, 11,007; Georgetown, 11,861; George Washington, 19,210; and Howard, 10,724. The University of the District of Columbia, created in 1976 from the merger of 3 institutions, has an open admissions policy for District freshman undergraduate students. Its 5 academic colleges had 10,691 undergraduate and 731 graduate students in the fall of 1991; 66% were attending part-time. The US Department of Agriculture Graduate School also operates within the District.

⁴²ARTS

The John F. Kennedy Center for the Performing Arts, officially opened on 8 September 1971, is the District's principal performing arts center. Its five main halls—the Opera House, Concert Hall, Eisenhower Theater, Terrace Theatre, and American Film Institute Theater—display gifts from at least 30 foreign governments, ranging from stage curtains and tapestries to sculptures and crystal chandeliers. Major theatrical productions are also presented at the Arena Stage-Kreeger Theater, National Theatre, Folger Theatre, and Ford's Theatre. Rep, Inc. is one of the few professional black theatres in the US; the New Playwrights' Theatre of Washington is a nonprofit group presenting new plays by American dramatists.

The District's leading symphony is the National Symphony Orchestra, which performs from October through April at the Concert Hall of the Kennedy Center. On a smaller scale, the Phillips Collection, National Gallery of Art, and Library of Congress offer concerts and recitals. The Washington Opera performs at the Kennedy Center's Opera House.

During the summer months, the Carter Barron Amphitheater presents popular music and jazz. Concerts featuring the US Army, US Navy, and US Marine Corps bands and the Air Force Symphony Orchestra are held throughout the District.

The District of Columbia supported its arts programs in 1996 with federal funds amounting to $564,000. The NEA gave $1,690,000 to the District's arts programs and $4,271,000 to the District of Columbia Commission on the Arts and Humanities.

The NEA also supports the District of Columbia Commission on the Arts and Humanities through the State and Regional Program.

43LIBRARIES AND MUSEUMS

Washington, D.C., is the site of the world's largest library, the Library of Congress, with a 1996/97 collection of more than 80 million items, including 26 million books and pamphlets. The Library, which is also the cataloging and bibliographic center for libraries throughout the US, has on permanent display a 1455 Gutenberg Bible, Thomas Jefferson's first draft of the Declaration of Independence, and Abraham Lincoln's first two drafts of the Gettysburg Address. Also in its permanent collection are the oldest known existing film (Thomas Edison's *The Sneeze,* lasting all of three seconds), maps believed to date from the Lewis and Clark expedition, original musical scores by Charles Ives, and huge libraries of Russian and Chinese texts. The Folger Shakespeare Library contains not only rare Renaissance manuscripts but also a fullsize re-creation of an Elizabethan theater. The District's own public library system has a main library and 27 branches—including the Martin Luther King Memorial Library—with 2,195,676 volumes in 1996/97.

The Smithsonian Institution—endowed in 1826 by an Englishman, James Smithson, who had never visited the US—operates a vast museum and research complex that includes the National Air and Space Museum, National Museum of Natural History, National Museum of History and Technology, many of the District's art museums, and the National Zoological Park. Among the art museums operated by the Smithsonian are the National Gallery of Art, housing one of the world's outstanding collections of Western art from the 13th century to the present; the Freer Gallery of Art, housing a renowned collection of Near and Far Eastern treasures, along with one of the largest collections of the works of James McNeill Whistler, whose Peacock Room is one of the museum's highlights; the National Collection of Fine Arts; the National Portrait Gallery; and the Hirshhorn Museum and Sculpture Garden. Among the capital's other distinguished art collections are the Phillips Collection, the oldest museum of modern art in the US; the Museum of African Art, located in the Frederick Douglass Memorial Home; and the Corcoran Gallery of Art, devoted primarily to American paintings, sculpture, and drawings of the last 300 years. Washington is also the site of such historic house-museums as Octagon House, Decatur House, Dumbarton Oaks, and the Woodrow Wilson House. Many national associations maintain exhibitions relevant to their areas of interest. The US National Arboretum, US Botanic Garden, and National Aquarium are in the city.

44COMMUNICATIONS

Washington, D.C., is the headquarters of the US Postal Service. As of March 1993, about 87.2% of the 235,000 households had telephones. In 1996, the District had 6 AM and 12 FM radio stations and 6 commercial and 2 public television stations. District Cablevision also provided service in 1996.

45PRESS

Because the District of Columbia is the center of US government activity, hundreds of US and foreign newspapers maintain permanent news bureaus there. The District has one major newspaper, the *Washington Post.* In 1994, the *Post,* a morning paper, had an average daily circulation of 834,641 and a Sunday circulation of 1,140,564. The *Washington Times,* also published on weekday mornings, had a circulation of 100,932 (72,663 on Sunday). Press clubs active within the District include the National Press Club, Gridiron Club, American Newspaper Women's Club, Washington Press Club, and White House Correspondents Association.

There are more than 30 major Washington-based periodicals. Among the best known are the *National Geographic, U.S. News & World Report, Smithsonian,* and *New Republic.* Important periodicals covering the workings of the federal government are the *Congressional Quarterly* and its companion, *CQ Weekly Report.*

46ORGANIZATIONS

The 1992 US Census of Service Industries counted 1,126 organizations in the District of Columbia, including 493 business associations; 231 civic, social, and fraternal associations; and 402 other membership organizations. Service and patriotic organizations with headquarters in the District include the Air Force Association, Daughters of the American Revolution, and the 4-H Program. Among the cultural, scientific, and educational groups are the American Film Institute, American Theatre Association, Federation of American Scientists, American Association for the Advancement of Science, National Academy of Sciences, National Geographic Society, Association of American Colleges, American Council on Education, National Education Association, American Association of University Professors, American Association of University Women, and US Student Association.

Among the environmental and animal protection organizations in the District are the Animal Welfare Institute, Humane Society of the US, and National Wildlife Federation. Medical, health, and charitable organizations include the American Red Cross. Groups dealing with the elderly include the National Association of Retired Federal Employees and the American Association of Retired Persons. Among ethnic and religious bodies with headquarters in the District are the National Association of Arab Americans, B'nai B'rith International, and the US Catholic Conference.

Trade, professional, and commercial organizations include the American Advertising Federation, American Federation of Police, American Youth Hostels, National Aeronautic Association, Air Line Pilots Association, American Bankers Association, National Cable Television Association, Chamber of Commerce of the US, American Chemical Society, International Association of Firefighters, Health Insurance Association of America, American Council of Life Insurance, National Association of Manufacturers, American Petroleum Institute, and National Press Club.

Virtually every major public interest group maintains an office in Washington, D.C. Notable examples are the Consumer Federation of America, National Consumers League, National Abortion Rights Action League, National League of Cities, Common Cause, US Conference of Mayors, National Organization for Women, and National Rifle Association of America.

Among the important world organizations with headquarters in the District are the Organization of American States, International Monetary Fund, and International Bank for Reconstruction and Development.

47TOURISM, TRAVEL, AND RECREATION

The District of Columbia is one of the world's leading tourist centers, with nearly 16 million visitors in 1995. Domestic travelers spend about $3.169 million in the District each year, supporting thousands of jobs. The Washington Monument, Lincoln Memorial, Jefferson Memorial, Vietnam Veterans Memorial, White House, Capitol, US Supreme Court Building, Smithsonian Institution, Library of Congress, Ford's Theater, National Archives, National Gallery of Art, and Kennedy Center for the Performing Arts are only a few of the capital's extraordinary attractions. The most popular site is the Smithsonian's Air and Space Museum, followed by its Museum of Natural History and Museum of American History. National Park Service sites had 15,827,775 visitors in 1995. Across the Potomac, in Virginia, are Arlington National Cemetery, site of the Tomb of the Unknown Soldier and the grave of John F. Kennedy, and George Washington's home at Mt. Vernon.

48SPORTS

There are four major league professional sports teams in Washington D.C., the Redskins of the National Football League, the Wizards (formerly the Bullets), of the National Basketball Association (NBA), and the Capitals of the National Hockey League, and DC United of Major League Soccer. Hockey and basketball will be played in downtown Washington at the MCI Arena, which was scheduled to open for the 1997–98 season. The Redskins began the 1997 season in the new Jack Kent Cooke Stadium in Landover, Maryland. The Redskins have reached football's Super Bowl five times, winning in 1983, 1988, and 1992. The Bullets won the NBA championship in 1978.

In collegiate sports the Georgetown Hoyas were a dominant force in basketball during the 1980s, reaching the NCAA championship game in 1982, 1984, and 1985, and winning the title in 1984.

49FAMOUS WASHINGTONIANS

Although no US president has been born in the District of Columbia, all but George Washington (b. Virginia, 1732–99) lived there while serving as chief executive. Seven presidents died in Washington, D.C., including three during their term of office: William Henry Harrison (b. Virginia, 1773–1841), Zachary Taylor (b. Virginia, 1784–1850), and Abraham Lincoln (b. Kentucky, 1809–65). In addition, John Quincy Adams (b. Massachusetts, 1767–1848), who served as a congressman for 17 years after he left the White House, died at his desk in the House of Representatives; and William Howard Taft (b. Ohio, 1857–1930) passed away while serving as US chief justice. Retired presidents Woodrow Wilson (b. Virginia, 1856–1924) and Dwight D. Eisenhower (b. Texas, 1890–1969) also died in the capital. Federal officials born in Washington, D.C., include John Foster Dulles (1888–1959), secretary of state; J(ohn) Edgar Hoover (1895–1972), director of the FBI; and Robert C. Weaver (b.1907), who as secretary of housing and urban development during the administration of President Lyndon B. Johnson was the first black American to hold cabinet rank. Walter E. Fauntroy (b.1933) was the District's first delegate to Congress in the 20th century, appointed when that office was reestablished in 1971.

Among the outstanding scientists and other professionals associated with the District were Cleveland Abbe (b. New York, 1838–1916), a meteorologist who helped develop the US Weather Service; inventor Alexander Graham Bell (b. Scotland, 1842–1922), president of the National Geographic Society (NGS) in his later years; Henry Gannett (b. Maryland, 1846–1914), chief geographer with the US Geological Survey, president of the NGS and a pioneer in American cartography; Charles D. Walcott (b. New York, 1850–1927), director of the Geological Survey and secretary of the Smithsonian Institution; Emile Berliner (b. Germany, 1851–1929), a pioneer in the development of the phonograph; Gilbert H. Grosvenor (b. Turkey, 1875–1966), editor in chief of *National Geographic* magazine; and Charles R. Drew (1904–50), developer of the blood bank concept. Leading business executives who have lived or worked in the District include William W. Corcoran (1798–1888), banker and philanthropist, and Katharine Graham (b. New York, 1917), publisher of the *Washington Post* and chairman of its parent company; the two *Post* reporters who received much of the credit for uncovering the Watergate scandal are Carl Bernstein (b.1944), a native Washingtonian, and Robert "Bob" Woodward (b. Illinois, 1943). Mary Elizabeth "Tipper" Gore (b. 1948), wife of Vice President Al Gore, was born in Washington, D.C. Washingtonians who achieved military fame include Benjamin O. Davis (1877–1970), the first black to become an Army general, and his son, Benjamin O. Davis, Jr. (b.1912), who was the first black to become a general in the Air Force. John Shalikashvili (b. Poland, 1936) was the first foreign born commander in chief of the joint chiefs of staff.

The designer of the nation's capital was Pierre Charles L'Enfant (b. France, 1754–1825), whose grave is in Arlington National Cemetery; also involved in laying out the capital were surveyor Andrew Ellicott (b. Pennsylvania, 1754–1820) and mathematician-astronomer Benjamin Banneker (b. Maryland, 1731–1806), a black who was an early champion of equal rights. Among Washingtonians to achieve distinction in the creative arts were John Philip Sousa (1854–1932), bandmaster and composer; Herblock (Herbert L. Block, b. Illinois, 1909), political cartoonist; and playwright Edward Albee (b.1928), winner of the Pulitzer Prize for drama in 1967 and 1975. Famous performers born in the District of Columbia include composer-pianist-bandleader Edward Kennedy "Duke" Ellington (1899–1974) and actress Helen Hayes (Helen Hayes Brown, 1900–92). Alice Roosevelt Longworth (b. New York, 1884–1980) dominated the Washington social scene for much of this century.

50BIBLIOGRAPHY

Cary, Francine Curro, ed. *Urban Odyssey: A Multicultural History of Washington, D.C.* Washington, D.C.: Smithsonian Institution, 1996.

Federal Writer's Project. *Washington, D.C.: A City and Capital.* Reprint. New York: Somerset, n.d. (orig. 1942).

Greene, Constance M. *Washington: A History of the Capital.* Princeton, N.J.: Princeton University Press, 1976.

Gurney, Gene, and Harold Wise. *The Official Washington, D.C., Directory.* New York: Crown, 1977.

Gutheim, Frederick. *Worthy of the Nation: The Planning and Development of the National Capital City.* Washington, D.C.: Smithsonian, 1977.

Lewis, David L. *District of Columbia: A Bicentennial History.* New York: Norton, 1976.

Moore, John L. *Speaking of Washington: Facts, Firsts, and Folklore.* Washington, D.C.: Congressional Quarterly, 1993.

Shidler, Atlee E. *Trends and Issues in the Greater Washington Region: A Preliminary Report.* Washington, D.C.: Center for Municipal and Metropolitan Research, 1979.

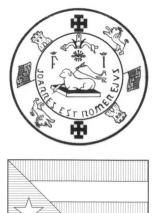

PUERTO RICO

Commonwealth of Puerto Rico
Estado Libre Asociado de Puerto Rico

ORIGIN OF NAME: Spanish for "rich port." **NICKNAME:** Island of Enchantment. **CAPITAL:** San Juan. **BECAME A COMMONWEALTH:** 25 July 1952. **SONG:** *La Borinquena.* **MOTTO:** *Joannes est nomen ejus.* (John is his name.) **FLAG:** From the hoist extends a blue triangle, with one white star; five horizontal stripes—three red, two white—make up the balance. **OFFICIAL SEAL:** In the center of a green circular shield, a lamb holding a white banner reclines on the book of the Apocalypse. Above are a yoke, a cluster of arrows, and the letters "F" and "I," signifying King Ferdinand and Queen Isabella, rulers of Spain at the time of discovery; below is the commonwealth motto. Surrounding the shield, on a white border, are the towers of Castile and lions symbolizing Spain, crosses representing the conquest of Jerusalem, and Spanish banners. **ANIMAL:** Coqui. **BIRD:** Reinita. **FLOWER:** Maga. **TREE:** Ceiba. **LEGAL HOLIDAYS:** New Year's Day, 1 January; Three Kings Day (Epiphany), 6 January; Birthday of Eugenio Maria de Hostos, 11 January; Birthday of Martin Luther King, Jr., 3d Monday in January; Washington's Birthday, 3d Monday in February; Abolition Day, 22 March; Good Friday, March or April; Birthday of José de Diego, 16 April; Memorial Day, last Monday in May; Independence Day, 4 July; Birthday of Luis Muñoz Rivera, 17 July; Constitution Day, 25 July; Birthday of José Celso Barbosa, 27 July; Labor Day, 1st Monday in September; Anniversary of the "Grito de Lares," 23 September; Discovery of America, 12 October; Veterans Day, 11 November; Discovery of Puerto Rico Day, 19 November; Thanksgiving Day, 4th Thursday in November, Christmas Day, 25 December. **TIME:** 8 AM Atlantic Standard Time = noon GMT.

¹LOCATION, SIZE, AND EXTENT

Situated on the NE periphery of the Caribbean Sea, about 1,000 mi (1,600 km) SE of Miami, Puerto Rico is the easternmost and smallest island of the Greater Antilles group. Its total area is 3,515 sq mi (9,104 sq km), including 3,459 sq mi (8,959 sq km) of land and 56 sq mi (145 sq km) of inland water.

Shaped roughly like a rectangle, the main island measures 111 mi (179 km) E-W and 36 (58 km) N-S. Offshore and to the E are two major islands, Vieques and Culebra.

Puerto Rico is bounded by the Atlantic Ocean to the N, the Virgin Passage and Vieques Sound to the E, the Caribbean Sea to the S, and the Mona Passage to the W. Puerto Rico's total boundary length is 378 mi (608 km).

²TOPOGRAPHY

About 75% of Puerto Rico's land area consists of hills or mountains too steep for intensive commercial cultivation. The Cordillera Central range, separating the northern coast from the semiarid south, has the island's highest peak, Cerro de Punta (4,389 feet–1,338 meters). Puerto Rico's best-known peak, El Yunque (3,496 feet–1,066 meters), stands to the east, in the Luquillo Mountains (Sierra de Luquillo). The north coast consists of a level strip about 100 mi (160 km) long and 5 mi (8 km) wide. Principal valleys are located along the east coast, from Fajardo to Cape Mala Pascua, and around Caguas, in the east-central region. Off the eastern shore are two small islands: Vieques, with an area of 51 sq mi (132 sq km), and Culebra, covering 24 sq mi (62 sq km). Uninhabited Mona Island (19 sq mi–49 sq km), off the southwest coast, is a breeding ground for wildlife.

Puerto Rico has 50 waterways large enough to be classified as rivers, but none is navigable by large vessels. The longest river is the Rio de la Plata, extending 46 mi (74 km) from Cayey to Dorado, where it empties into the Atlantic. There are few natural lakes but numerous artificial ones, of which Dos Bocas, south of Arecibo, is one of the most beautiful. Phosphorescent Bay, whose luminescent organisms glow in the night, is a tourist attraction on the south coast.

Like many other Caribbean islands, Puerto Rico is the crest of an extinct submarine volcano. About 45 mi (72 km) north of the island lies the Puerto Rico Trench, at over 28,000 feet (8,500 meters) one of the world's deepest chasms.

³CLIMATE

Tradewinds from the northeast keep Puerto Rico's climate equable, although tropical. San Juan has a normal daily mean temperature of 80°F (27°C), ranging from 77°F (25°C) in January to 82°F (28°C) in July; the normal daily minimum is 73°F (23°C), the maximum 86°F (30°C). The lowest temperature ever recorded on the island is 39°F (4°C), at Aibonito, the highest 103°F (39°C), at San Lorenzo. The recorded temperature in San Juan has never been lower than 60°F (16°C) or higher than 98°F (37°C).

Rainfall varies by region. Ponce, on the south coast, averages only 32 in (81 cm) a year, while the highlands average 108 in (274 cm); the rain forest on El Yunque receives an annual average of 183 in (465 cm). San Juan's average annual rainfall is 54 in (137 cm), the rainiest months being May through November.

The word "hurricane" derives from *hurakán,* a term the Spanish learned from Puerto Rico's Taino Indians. Nine hurricanes have struck Puerto Rico in this century, the most recent in 1989. On 7 October 1985, torrential rains created a mud slide that devastated the hillside barrio of Mameyes, killing hundreds of people; not only was this Puerto Rico's worst disaster of the century, but it was the single most destructive landslide in US history.

⁴FLORA AND FAUNA

During the 19th century, forests covered about three-fourths of Puerto Rico. Today, however, only one-fourth of the island is forested. Flowering trees still abound, and the butterfly tree, African tulip, and flamboyán (royal poinciana) add bright reds and pinks to Puerto Rico's lush green landscape. Among hardwoods, now rare, are nutmeg, satinwood, Spanish elm, and Spanish cedar. Pre-Columbian peoples cultivated yucca, yams, peanuts, hot peppers, tobacco, and cotton. Pineapple guava, tamarind, and cashews are indigenous, and such fruits as mamey, jobo guanábana, and quenepa are new to most visitors. Coconuts, coffee, sugarcane, plantains, mangoes, and most citrus fruits were introduced by the Spanish.

The only mammal found on the island by the conquistadores was a kind of barkless dog, now extinct. Virtually all present-day mammals have been introduced, including horses, cattle, cats, and dogs. The only troublesome mammal is the mongoose, brought in from India to control reptiles in the cane fields and now wild in remote rural areas. Mosquitoes and sand flies are common pests, but the only dangerous insect is the giant centipede, whose sting is painful but rarely fatal. Perhaps the island's best-known inhabitant is the golden coquí, a tiny tree frog whose call of "ko-kee, ko-kee" is heard all through the night; it is a threatened species. Marine life is extraordinarily abundant, including many tropical fish, crabs, and corals. Puerto Rico has some 200 bird species, many of which live in the rain forest. Thrushes, orioles, grosbeaks, and hummingbirds are common, and the reinita and pitirre are distinctive to the island. Several parrot species are rare, and the Puerto Rican parrot is endangered. Also on the endangered list are the yellow-shouldered blackbird and the Puerto Rican plain pigeon, Puerto Rican whippoorwill, Culebra giant anole, Puerto Rican boa, and Monita gecko. The Mona boa and Mona ground iguana are threatened. There were three national wildlife refuges, covering a total of 2,425 acres (981 hectares), in the early 1980s.

⁵ENVIRONMENTAL PROTECTION

US environmental laws and regulations are applicable in Puerto Rico. Land-use planning, overseen by the Puerto Rico Planning Board, is an especially difficult problem, since residential, industrial, and recreational developers are all competing for about 30% of the total land area on an island that is already more densely populated than any state of the US except New Jersey. Pollution from highland latrines and septic systems and from agricultural and industrial wastes is a potential hazard; the rum industry, for example, has traditionally dumped its wastes into the ocean. Moreover, the US requirement that sewage receive secondary treatment before being discharged into deep seas may be unrealistic in view of the commonwealth government's claim, in the late 1970s, that it could not afford to build secondary sewage treatment facilities when 45% of its population lacks primary sewage treatment systems. As of 1997, sewage discharges into the ocean remained a problem.

About 300,000 tons of hazardous waste are generated annually, and 16,000 tons of chemical substances are released into the air, water, and soil each year. As of 1996, the island had nine hazardous waste sites. Wetlands on the island have been devastated by development, but in recent years, efforts have been mounted to save and expand these resources.

⁶POPULATION

Puerto Rico's population was estimated at 3,782,862 in 1996, up 7.4% from 3,528,000 in 1990. With a population density of 1,025 per sq mi (465 per sq km), Puerto Rico is one of the most densely populated areas of the world.

In 1990, Puerto Rico's population was 48.4% male and 51.6% female. Over 27% of the population was under 15 years of age. The birthrate declined steadily from 38.9 live births per 10,000 population in 1950 to 18.2 in 1991. The death rate, on the other hand, was 7.4 per 1,000 population in both 1990 and 1991.

According to the 1990 census, the population was 71% urban and 29% rural. San Juan is Puerto Rico's capital and largest city,

with an estimated 1996 population of 433,705, followed by Bayamon, 231,845; Ponce, 189,988; Carolina, 188,427; and Mayagüez, 100,937.

⁷ETHNIC GROUPS

Three main ethnic strands reflect the heritage of Puerto Rico: the Taino Indians, most of whom fled or perished after the Spanish conquest; black Africans, imported as slaves under Spanish rule; and the Spanish themselves. With an admixture of Dutch, English, Corsicans, and other Europeans, Puerto Ricans today enjoy a distinct Hispanic-Afro-Antillean heritage.

Less than two-thirds of all ethnic Puerto Ricans live on the island. Virtually all the remainder reside on the US mainland; in 1990 there were 1,955,323 people who identified themselves as Puerto Rican in the 50 states, where they made up less than 17% of the US Hispanic population. The state of New York had almost half the US ethnic Puerto Rican population (762,429).

⁸LANGUAGES

Spanish is the official language of Puerto Rico; English is required in schools as a second language. From 1898 through the 1920s, US authorities unsuccessfully sought to make English the island's primary language.

Taino Indian terms that survive in Puerto Rican Spanish include such place-names as Arecibo, Guayama, and Mayagüez, as well as *hamaca* (hammock) and *canoa* (canoe). Among many African borrowings are food terms like *quimbombó* (okra), *guince* (banana), and *mondongo* (a spicy stew).

⁹RELIGIONS

During the first three centuries of Spanish rule, Roman Catholicism was the only religion permitted in Puerto Rico. More than 80% of the population was still Roman Catholic at the end of 1992, and the Church maintains numerous hospitals and schools on the island. Most of the remaining Puerto Ricans belong to other Christian denominations, which have been allowed on the island since the 1850s. By 2010, Protestants may outnumber Roman Catholics in Puerto Rico, according to some projections. Pentecostal churches have attracted a significant following, particularly among the urban poor of the barrios.

¹⁰TRANSPORTATION

Puerto Rico's inland transportation network consists primarily of roads and motor vehicles. A system of public buses operated by the Metropolitan Bus Authority (MBA) provides intercity passenger transport in the capital of San Juan and nearby cities. The *públicos,* a privately owned jitney service of small buses and cars, offers transportation between fixed destinations in cities and towns.

In December 1995, Puerto Rico had 14,515 mi (23,359 km) of state highways and municipal roads. In 1996, the territory had 1.5 million registered motor vehicles and 1.6 million licensed drivers.

The Puerto Rico Highway and Transportation Authority (PRHTA) is developing a rail transit system, known as the *Tren Urbano,* at an estimated cost of $1.142 billion. *Tren Urbano* is expected to serve about 115,000 passengers per day along a 105-mi (17-km), 30-minute route, passing through service and business centers.

In 1996/97, the PRHTA invested nearly $750 million to complete the strategic highway network system around the island, as well as other roads that connect small towns with the nearby cities. The PR-10 Expressway crosses from the north to the central moutainous region. The PR-53 toll road, scheduled for completion during 1997, will provide a new route for the towns of the northeast. The Baldorioty de Castro Expressway allows rapid travel between the main airport and the capital.

San Juan, the island's principal port and a leading containerized cargo-handling facility, handled 15,480 million tons of cargo in 1996. Crude oil and gasoline were the leading items. Ponce handled 1,140 million tons, and Mayagüez, 407,000 tons. Ferries link the main island with the islands of Vieques and Culebra.

Puerto Rico receives flights from 38 US mainland cities, and from the Virgin Islands, the British West Indies, Jamaica, the Dominican Republic, Great Britain, France, Spain, and the Netherlands. Luis Muñoz Marin International Airport in San Juan enplaned 4,699,220 passengers and 145,607 tons of freight in 1996. There are also 425 active aircraft and 1,690 active pilots in the territory. Other leading air terminals are located at Ponce, Mayagüez, and Aguadilla. There were 11 airports in Puerto Rico at the end of 1996.

11HISTORY

Archaeological finds indicate that at least three Indian cultures flourished on the island now known as Puerto Rico long before its discovery by Christopher Columbus on 19 November 1493. The first group, belonging to the Archaic Culture, is believed to have come from Florida. Having no knowledge of agriculture or pottery, it relied on the products of the sea; the remains of its members have been found mostly in caves. The second group, the Igneri, came from northern South America. Descended from Arawak stock, the Igneri brought agriculture and pottery to the island; their remains are found mostly in the coastal areas. The third culture, the Taino, also of Arawak origin, combined fishing with agriculture. A peaceful, sedentary tribe, the Taino were adept at stonework and lived in many parts of the island; Taino relics have been discovered not only along the coastal perimeter but also high in the mountains, where the Taino performed ritual games in ball parks that have been restored in recent times. To the Indians, the island was known as Boriquén.

Columbus, accompanied by a young nobleman named Juan Ponce de León, landed at the western end of the island—which he called San Juan Bautista (St. John the Baptist)—and claimed it for Spain. Not until colonization was well under way would the island acquire the name Puerto Rico (literally, "rich port"), with the name San Juan Bautista applied to the capital city. The first settlers arrived on 12 August 1508, under the able leadership of Ponce de León, who sought to transplant and adapt Spanish civilization to Puerto Rico's tropical habitat. The small contingent of Spaniards compelled the Taino, numbering perhaps 30,000, to mine for gold; the rigors of forced labor and the losses from rebellion reduced the Taino population to about 4,000 by 1514, by which time the mines were nearly depleted. With the introduction of slaves from Africa, sugarcane growing became the leading economic activity. Since neither mining nor sugarcane was able to provide sufficient revenue to support the struggling colony, the treasury of New Spain began a subsidy, known as the *situado,* which until the early 19th century defrayed the cost of the island's government and defense.

From the early 16th century onward, an intense power struggle for control of the Caribbean marked Puerto Rico as a strategic base of the first magnitude. After a French attack in 1528, construction of La Fortaleza (still in use today as the governor's palace) was begun in 1533, and work on El Morro fortress in San Juan commenced six years later. The new fortifications helped repel a British attack led by Sir Francis Drake in 1595; a second force, arriving in 1598 under George Clifford, Earl of Cumberland, succeeded in capturing San Juan, but the British were forced to withdraw by tropical heat and disease. In 1625, a Dutch attack under the command of Boudewijn Hendrikszoon was repulsed, although much of San Juan was sacked and burned by the attackers. By the 18th century, Puerto Rico had become a haven for pirates, and smuggling was the major

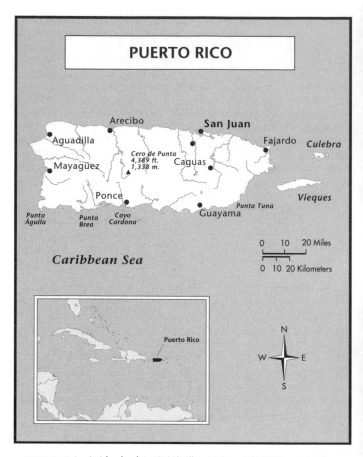

LOCATION: (main island only): 18°04'15" to 18°31'N; 65°35'30" to 67°15'9'W.
BOUNDARIES: Total coastline, 378 mi (608 km).

economic activity. A Spanish envoy who came to the island in 1765 was appalled, and his report to the crown inaugurated a period of economic, administrative, and military reform. The creation of a native militia helped Puerto Rico withstand a fierce British assault on San Juan in 1797, by which time the island had more than 100,000 inhabitants.

Long after most of the Spanish colonies in the New World had obtained independence, Puerto Rico and Cuba remained under Spanish tutelage. Despite several insurrection attempts, most of them inspired by the liberator, Simón Bolivar, Spain's military might concentrated on these islands precluded any revolution.

Puerto Rico became a shelter for refugees from Santo Domingo, Haiti, and Venezuela who were faithful to Spain, fearful of disturbances in their own countries, or both. As in Cuba, the sugar industry developed in Puerto Rico during this period under policies that favored foreign settlers. As a result, a new landowner class emerged—the *hacendados*—who were instrumental in strengthening the institution of slavery on the island. By 1830, the population was 300,000. Sugar, tobacco, and coffee were the leading export crops, although subsistence farming still covered much of the interior. Sugar found a ready market in the US, and trade steadily developed, particularly with the northeast.

The 19th century also gave birth, however, to a new Puerto Rican civil and political consciousness. Puerto Rican participation in the short-lived constitutional experiments in Spain (1812–14 and 1820–23) fostered the rise of a spirit of liberalism, expressed most notably by Ramón Power y Giralt, at one time vice president of the Spanish Cortes (parliament). During these early decades, Spain's hold on the island was never seriously threatened. Although the Spanish constitution of 1812 declared that the people of Puerto Rico were no longer colonial subjects but were full-fledged citizens of Spain, the crown maintained an alert, centralized, absolutist government with all basic powers concentrated in the captain general.

Toward the middle of the 19th century, a *criollo* generation with strong liberal roots began a new era in Puerto Rican history. This group, which called for the abolition of slavery and the introduction of far-reaching economic and political reforms, at the same time developed and strengthened Puerto Rican literary tradition. The more radical reformers espoused the cause of separation from Spain and joined in a propaganda campaign in New York on behalf of Cuban independence. An aborted revolution, beginning in the town of Lares in September 1868 (and coinciding with an insurrection in Spain that deposed Queen Isabella II), though soon quelled, awakened among Puerto Ricans a dormant sense of national identity. "El Grito de Lares" (the Cry of Lares) helped inspire a strong anti-Spanish separatist current that was unable to challenge Spanish power effectively but produced such influential leaders as Ramón Emeterio Betances and Eugenio Maria de Hostos.

The major reform efforts after 1868 revolved around abolitionism and *autonomia,* or self-government. Slavery was abolished in 1873 by the First Spanish Republic, which also granted new political rights to the islanders. The restoration of the Spanish monarchy two years later, however, was a check to Puerto Rican aspirations. During the last quarter of the century, leaders such as Luis Muñoz Rivera sought unsuccessfully to secure vast new powers of self-government. By this time, Puerto Rico was an island with a distinct Antillean profile, strong Hispanic roots, and a mixed population that, borrowing from its Indian-Spanish-African background and an influx of Dutch, English, Corsicans, and other Europeans, had developed its own folkways and mores.

The imminence of war with the US over Cuba, coupled with autonomist agitation within Puerto Rico, led Spain in November 1897 to grant to the island a charter with broad powers of self-rule. Led by Luis Muñoz Rivera, Puerto Ricans began to establish new organs of self-government; but no sooner had an elected government begun to function in July 1898 than US forces, overcoming Spanish resistance, took over the island. A cease-fire was proclaimed on 13 August, and sovereignty was formally transferred to the US with the signing in December of the Treaty of Paris, ending the Spanish-American War. The US government swept aside the self-governing charter granted by Spain and established military rule from 1898 to 1900. Civilian government was restored in 1900 under a colonial law, the Foraker Act, that gave the federal government full control of the executive and legislative branches, leaving some local representation in the lower chamber, or house of delegates. Under the Jones Act, signed into law by President Woodrow Wilson on 2 March 1917, Congress extended US citizenship to the islanders and granted them an elective senate, but still reserved vast powers over Puerto Rico to the federal bureaucracy.

The early period of US rule saw an effort to Americanize all insular institutions, even to the point of superseding the Spanish language as the vernacular. In the meantime, American corporate capital took over the sugar industry, developing a plantation economy so pervasive that, by 1920, 75% of the population relied on the cane crop for its livelihood. Glaring irregularities of wealth resulted, sharpening social and political divisions. This period also saw the development of three main trends in Puerto Rican political thinking. One group favored the incorporation of Puerto Rico into the US as a state; a second group, fearful of cultural assimilation, favored self-government; while a third group spoke for independence.

The Depression hit Puerto Rico especially hard. With a population approaching 2 million by the late 1930s and with few occupational opportunities outside the sugar industry, the island's economy deteriorated, and mass unemployment and near-starvation were the results. Controlling the Puerto Rican legislature from 1932 to 1940 was a coalition of the Socialist Party, led by Santiago Iglesias, a Spanish labor leader who became a protégé of the American Federation of Labor, and the Republican Party, which had traditionally espoused statehood and had been founded in Puerto Rico by José Celso Barbosa, a black physician who had studied in the US. The coalition was unable to produce any significant improvement, although under the New Deal a US government effort was made to supply emergency relief for the "stricken island."

Agitation for full political and economic reform or independence gained ground during this period. A violent challenge to US authority in Puerto Rico was posed by the small Nationalist Party, led by Harvard-educated Pedro Albizu Campos. A broader attack on the island's political and economic ills was led by Luis Muñoz Marin and the Popular Democratic Party (PDP), founded in 1938; within two years, the PDP won control of the senate. Under Muñoz Marin, a new era began in Puerto Rico. Great pressure was put on Washington for a change in the island's political status, while social and economic reform was carried to the fullest extent possible within the limitations of the Jones Act. Intensive efforts were made to centralize economic planning, attract new industries through local tax exemptions (Puerto Rico was already exempt from federal taxation), reduce inequality of income, and improve housing, schools, and health conditions. Meanwhile, a land distribution program helped the destitute peasants who were the backbone of the new party. All these measures—widely publicized as Operation Bootstrap—coupled with the general US economic expansion after World War II, so transformed Puerto Rico's economy that income from manufacturing surpassed that from agriculture by 1955 and was five times as great by 1970. Annual income per capita rose steadily from $296 in 1950 to $1,384 in 1970.

The PDP, the dominant force in Puerto Rican politics from 1940 to 1968, favored a new self-governing relationship with the US, distinct from statehood or independence. The party succeeded not only in bringing about significant social and economic change but also in obtaining from Congress in 1950 a law allowing Puerto Ricans to draft their own constitution with full local self-government. This new constitution, approved in a general referendum on 3 March 1952, led to the establishment on 25 July of the Commonwealth of Puerto Rico (Estado Libre Asociado de Puerto Rico), which, according to a resolution approved in 1953 by the United Nations Committee on Information from Non-Self-Governing Territories, was constituted as an autonomous political entity in voluntary association with the United States.

An island-wide plebiscite in 1967 showed that 60% of those voting favored continuation and improvement of the commonwealth relationship, 39% preferred statehood, and less than 1% supported independence; the turnout among eligible voters was 65%. The result of the plebiscite, held to support a movement for additional home-rule powers, met with indifference from the US executive branch and outright opposition from the pro-statehood minority in Puerto Rico. Consequently, efforts to obtain passage by Congress of a "Compact of Permanent Union between Puerto Rico and the United States," although approved at the subcommittee level by the House of Representatives, failed to produce any change in the commonwealth arrangement.

The result was renewed agitation for either statehood or independence, with growing internal political polarization. The island's Republican Party rearranged itself after the plebiscite as the New Progressive Party (NPP), and came to power in 1968 as a result of a split in PDP ranks that led to the creation of the splinter People's Party. The two major blocs have been evenly balanced since that time, with the PDP returning to power in 1972 but losing to the NPP in 1976 and again, by a very narrow margin, in 1980, before regaining the governorship in 1984. The independence movement, in turn, divided into two wings: the moderates favored social democracy, while the radicals pursued close ties with the Fidel Castro regime in Cuba. Capitalizing on the increased power of Third World countries in the United Nations, and with Soviet support, the radicals challenged US policies and demanded a full transfer of sovereign rights to the people of Puerto Rico. Their position won the support of the UN Special Committee on the Situation with Regard to the Implementation of the Declaration on the Granting of Independence to Colonial Countries and Peoples (more generally known as the Committee of 24), which on 15 August 1979 reaffirmed "the inalienable right of the people of Puerto Rico to self-determination and independence...." The US government replied that the people of Puerto Rico had already exercised their right of self-determination in the 1967 plebiscite, and noted that Congress in 1979 had restated its "commitment to respect and support the right of the people of Puerto Rico to determine their own political future through peaceful, open and democratic processes."

More advanced than most Caribbean countries in education, health, and social development, Puerto Rico suffered from growing political tensions in the early 1980s, with occasional terrorist attacks on US military installations and personnel. These tensions may have been exacerbated by the national recession of 1980–81, which had a particularly severe impact on Puerto Rico. The commonwealth's gross national product declined by 6% in 1982 and 1983, and federal budget cuts ended a jobs program and reduced access to food stamps. At the same time, the island's economy experienced a structural shift. Whereas 50% of jobs in Puerto Rico had been in agriculture in 1940, by 1989 that figure had dropped to 20%. Manufacturing jobs, in contrast, rose from 5 to 15% of total employment between 1940 and 1989. Although Puerto Rico's economy began to expand in the mid-1980s, growing at an annual rate of 3.6%, the island continued to depend heavily on the federal government, which in 1989 employed 25% of Puerto Rican workers.

Puerto Rico's political status remains a source of controversy. Statehood would give Puerto Rico representation in the US Congress and would make the island eligible for billions of dollars more a year in food stamps, medical insurance, and income support payments, which are currently set at levels far below those of states. However, statehood would also incur the loss of tax benefits. Under current federal tax law for the commonwealth, individuals pay no federal income tax. More importantly, corporations pay no federal tax on profits, which has persuaded many companies, particularly manufacturers of pharmaceuticals, chemicals, and electronics, to build plants in Puerto Rico. In a 1993 plebiscite, a slight majority of Puerto Rican voters chose to maintain the island's status as an American commonwealth rather than opt for statehood or independence.

In 1989, Hurricane Hugo caused 12 deaths and $1 billion in damage in Puerto Rico. In 1994, the island suffered its worst drought in almost 30 years, and narrowly avoided serious damage to its beaches and wildlife when over half a million gallons (2.3 million liters) of heavy oil were spilled by a barge that ran aground on a coral reef.

Pedro Rosselló was reelected governor in 1994.

12 STATE GOVERNMENT

Since 1952, Puerto Rico has been a commonwealth of the US, governed under the Puerto Rican Federal Relations Act and under a constitution based on the US model. The Puerto Rican constitution specifically prohibits discrimination "on account of race, color, sex, birth, social origin or condition, or political ideas." The constitution had been amended six times as of the end of 1983.

The commonwealth legislature comprises a senate (Senado) of 29 members, 2 from each of 8 senatorial districts and 11 elected at large, and a house of representatives (Cámara de Representantes) of 52 members, 1 from each of 40 districts and 11 at large. Each senate district consists of five house districts. If a single party wins two-thirds or more of the seats in either house, the number of seats can be expanded (up to a limit of 9 in the senate and 17 in the house) to assure representation for minority parties. Senators must be at least 30 years of age, representatives 25. Legislators must have been commonwealth residents for two years and district or municipal residents for one year. All legislators serve four-year terms.

The governor, who may serve an unlimited number of four-year terms, is the only elected executive. Candidates for the governorship must be US citizens for at least five years, must be at least 35 years of age, and must have resided in Puerto Rico for at least five years.

A bill becomes law if approved by both houses and either signed by the governor or left unsigned for 10 days while the legislature is in session. A two-thirds vote of the elected members of each house is sufficient to override a gubernatorial veto. The governor can employ the item veto or reduce amounts in appropriations bills. The governor also has the power to declare martial law in cases of rebellion, invasion, or immediate danger of rebellion or invasion. The constitution may be amended by a two-thirds vote of the legislature and ratification by popular majority vote.

Residents of Puerto Rico may not vote in US presidential elections. A Puerto Rican who settles in one of the 50 states automatically becomes eligible to vote for president; conversely, a state resident who migrates to Puerto Rico forfeits such eligibility. Puerto Rico has no vote in the US Senate or House of Representatives, but a nonvoting resident delegate, elected every four years, may speak on the floor of the House, introduce legislation, and vote in House committees.

Qualified voters must be US citizens, be at least 18 years of age, and have registered 50 days before a general election; absentee registration is not allowed.

13 POLITICAL PARTIES

Taking part in Puerto Rican elections during the mid-1980s were two major and three smaller political parties. The Popular Democratic (PDP), founded in 1938, favors the strengthening and development of commonwealth status. The New Progressive Party (NPP), created in 1968 as the successor to the Puerto Rican Republican Party, is pro-statehood. Two smaller parties, each favoring independence for the island, are the Puerto Rican Independence Party, founded in the mid-1940s and committed to democratic socialism, and the more radical Puerto Rican Socialist Party, which has close ties with Cuba. A breakaway group, the Renewal Party, led by the mayor of San Juan, Hernán Padilla, left the NPP and took part in the 1984 elections.

In 1980, Governor Carlos Romero Barceló of the NPP, who had pledged to actively seek Puerto Rico's admission to the Union if elected by a large margin, retained the governorship by a plurality of fewer than 3,500 votes, in the closest election in the island's history, while the PDP won control of the legislature and 52 out of 78 mayoralty contests. Former governor Rafael Hernández Colón defeated Romero Barceló's bid for reelection in 1984 by more than 54,000 votes. Colón was reelected in 1988 and was succeeded in 1992 by Pedro Rosselló, a New Progressive and a supporter of statehood, who was reelected in 1996.

The question of Puerto Rico's status remains controversial. Governor Rosselló called a plebiscite in November of 1993 to enable voters to choose between independence, commonwealth or statehood. A narrow majority of Puerto Rican voters decided to maintain the island's status as an American commonwealth. However, they conditioned their vote on a demand that the terms of the island's commonwealth status be modified. Such modifications would include eliminating the federal limits on food stamps and expanding Supplemental Security Income to encompass elderly and handicapped Puerto Ricans. Puerto Rican voters also requested that recent changes in Federal Tax Law 936, which had lowered by 60% the exemptions corporations could claim from taxes on profits, be removed and that the law be restored to its original form. Although Puerto Ricans have no vote in US presidential elections, the island does send voting delegates to the national conventions of the Democratic and Republican parties. In 1980, for the first time, those delegates were chosen by presidential preference primary.

Puerto Rico's political parties have generally committed themselves to peaceful change through democratic methods. One exception was the pro-independence Nationalist Party, whose followers were involved in an attempt to assassinate US President Harry S Truman in 1950 and in an outbreak of shooting in the House of Representatives that wounded five congressman in 1954. A US-based terrorist group, the Armed Forces of Puerto Rican National Liberation (FALN), claimed credit during the late 1970s for bombings in New York and other major cities. FALN members briefly took over the Statue of Liberty in New York Harbor on 25 October 1977. Another group, the Macheteros, apparently based on the island, claimed responsibility for an attack on a US Navy bus in 1980 and for blowing up eight US Air Force planes at a Puerto Rico Air National Guard installation early in 1981.

14 LOCAL GOVERNMENT

The Commonweath of Puerto Rico had 78 municipalities in 1992, each governed by a mayor and municipal assembly elected every four years. In fact, these governments resemble US county governments in that they perform services for both urban and rural areas. Many of the functions normally performed by municipal governments in the US—for instance, fire protection, education, water supply, and law enforcement—are performed by the commonwealth government directly.

15 STATE SERVICES

The executive branch of Puerto Rico's highly centralized government is organized into departments, agencies, and public corporations. The departments are as follows: addiction services, agriculture, commerce, consumer affairs, finance, health, housing, justice, labor and human resources, natural resources, public instruction, recreation and sports, social services, state, and transportation and public works. Lodged within the Office of the Governor are the Bureau of Budget and Management, Planning Board, Commission to Combat Crime, Commission on Women's Affairs, and Environmental Quality Board, as well as offices of economic opportunity, energy, youth affairs, cultural affairs, labor affairs, child development, and development of the disabled, and commissions for the protection and strengthening of the family and of agricultural planning and action.

Puerto Rico is more heavily socialized than any US state. Almost one-fourth of all those employed work for the commonwealth government, which operates hotels, marine transports, the telephone company, and all sugar mills, among other enterprises.

16 JUDICIAL SYSTEM

Puerto Rico's highest court, the Supreme Court, consists of a chief justice and six associate justices, appointed, like all other judges, by the governor with the consent of the senate and serving until compulsory retirement at age 70. The court may sit in separate panels for some purposes, but not in cases dealing with the constitutionality of commonwealth law, for which the entire body convenes. Decisions of the Supreme Court of Puerto Rico regarding US constitutional questions may be appealed to the US Supreme Court.

The nine superior courts are the main trial courts; superior court judges are appointed to 12-year terms. In 1994 there were 111 superior court justices in 12 districts. Superior courts heard appeals from the 38 district courts, which had 111 judges. These courts have original jurisdiction in civil cases not exceeding $10,000 and in minor criminal cases. District courts also hear preliminary motions in more serious criminal cases. Municipal judges, serving for five years, and justices of the peace, in rural areas, decide cases involving local ordinances.

San Juan is the seat of the US District Court for Puerto Rico, which has the same jurisdiction as federal district courts on the US mainland.

Puerto Rico Gubernatorial Vote by Political Parties, 1948–1996

YEAR	WINNER	POPULAR DEMOCRAT (PDP)	NEW PROGRESSIVE (NPP)	REPUBLICAN	PUERTO RICAN INDEPENDENCE	SOCIALIST	LIBERAL REFORMIST
1948	Luis Muñoz Marín (PDP)	392,033	—	88,819	66,141	64,121	28,203
1952	Luis Muñoz Marín (PDP)	429,064	—	85,172	125,734	21,655	—
1956	Luis Muñoz Marín (PDP)	433,010	—	172,838	86,386	—	—
1960	Luis Muñoz Marín (PDP)	457,880	—	252,364	24,103		
						CHRISTIAN ACTION	
1964	Roberto Sanchez Vitella (PDP)	487,280	—	284,627	22,201	26,867	—
						PEOPLE'S	
1968	Luis A Ferré (NPP)	367,903	390,623	4,057	24,713	87,844	
							PR UNION
1972	Rafael Hernández Colón (PDP)	609,670	524,039	—	52,070	2,910	1,608
1976	Carlos Romero Barceló (NPP)	634,941	682,607	—	58,556	9,761	—
1980	Carlos Romero Barceló (NPP)	756,434	759,868	—	87,275	5,225	—
							RENEWAL
1984	Rafael Hernández Colón (PDP)	822,040	767,710	—	61,101	—	68,536
1988	Rafael Hernández Colón (PDP)	865,309	813,448	—	96,230	—	—
1992	Pedro Rosselló (NPP)	845,372	919,029	—	76,357	—	—
1996	Pedro Rosselló (NPP)	1,006,331	875,852	—	75,304	—	—

* Residents of Puerto Rico are barred from voting in US presidential elections.

Crimes totaled 106,088 in 1995, including 22,450 violent crimes and 83,638 property crimes. The death penalty is constitutionally forbidden. In 1996 there were an estimated 8,338 active attorneys.

[17]ARMED FORCES

In 1996, there were 2,420 active-duty military personnel stationed in Puerto Rico. Principal of the four US military installations in Puerto Rico are the Roosevelt Roads Naval Reservation, near Ceiba, and the Naval Security Station at Sabana Seca. Ft. Buchanan, an army base, is near San Juan. Use of Vieques for training maneuvers, including shelling and bombing, forced many of that island's residents to move; aerial and naval target practice on Culebra by the US Navy was halted by protests and legal action. Defense contracts totaled $274 million in 1995/96.

As of 1996, 129,000 veterans of US military service were living on the island. Puerto Ricans suffered 731 combat deaths in Korea and 270 in Viet Nam.

Reserve and national guard personnel in Puerto Rico totaled 18,123 in 1996, with the army accounting for the vast majority (16,306).

[18]MIGRATION

Although migration from Puerto Rico to the US mainland is not an entirely new phenomenon—several Puerto Rican merchants were living in New York City as early as 1830—there were no more than 70,000 islanders in the US in 1940. Mass migration, spurred by the booming postwar job market in the US, began in 1947. The out-migration was particularly large from 1951 through 1959, when the net outflow of migrants from the island averaged more than 47,000 a year. According to the 1990 census, 1,955,323 ethnic Puerto Ricans were living in the 50 states, including 1,190,533 native-born Puerto Ricans; at least 32 cities had Puerto Rican communities of 5,000 or more. Puerto Ricans are found in significant numbers not only in New York State but also in New Jersey, Illinois, Pennsylvania, California, Florida. Connecticut, and Massachusetts.

During the 1970s, in part because of the economic decline of many US urban centers, the migration trend slowed; official estimates show that the net flow of migrants from the island totaled only 65,900. But with the Puerto Rican economy worsening in the early 1980s, the net migration from early 1980 to mid-1983 was about 90,000. From 1990 to 1992, there was a net loss from migration of about 40,000.

One striking aspect of the US-Puerto Rico migration pattern is its fluidity. As US citizens, Puerto Ricans can move freely between the island and the mainland. Even in 1953, when the heaviest net outflow was recorded—74,603—fully 230,307 persons emigrated from the US mainland to Puerto Rico, as 304,910 Puerto Ricans were migrating the other way. In 1990, 213,886 people living on the US mainland said that they had lived in Puerto Rico in 1985, while 128,558 people living in the commonwealth in 1990 said that they had lived on the mainland in 1985 (about 45% in New York). This extreme mobility, though sensitive to the job market, would not be possible were it not for the increased income available to Puerto Ricans on both the island and the US mainland, and the fact that Puerto Ricans who come to the continental US generally preserve their ties of family and friendship with those in the commonwealth, thus finding it easy to return, whether for a short stay at Christmastime or for a new job on the island. In 1996, Puerto Rico admitted 8,560 immigrants from countries other than the US.

[19]INTERGOVERNMENTAL COOPERATION

A member of the US Council of State Governments, Puerto Rico subscribes to the Compact for Education, the Interstate Compact for the Supervision of Parolees and Probationers, the Southern Interstate Energy Compact, and the Southern Growth Policies Compact. In its relations with the US government, the commonwealth is in most respects like a state, except in the key areas of taxation and representation. US laws are in effect, federal agencies regulate aviation and broadcasting, and Puerto Ricans participate in such federally funded programs as Social Security and food stamps. US aid to Puerto Rico totaled $3.3 billion in 1995/96.

[20]ECONOMY

In 1940, annual income per capita was $118, and agricultural workers made as little as 6 cents an hour. By 1978, income per capita was $2,600, and the average hourly farm wage at least $1.65—in each case, far below the US average, but also in each case a vast improvement over former times.

At the end of 1996, Puetro Rico's employment distribution was as follows: 313,300 in government; 196,400 in wholesale and retail trade; 176,800 in services; 152,100 in manufacturing; 51,800 in construction; 42,700 in finance, insurance, and real estate; 22,100 in transportation and public utilities; 900 in mining.

The island's most important industrial products are apparel, textiles, pharmaceuticals, petroleum products, rum, refined sugar, computers, instruments, and office machines. Tourism is the backbone of a large service industry, and the government sector has also grown. Tourist revenues and remittances from workers on the US mainland largely counterbalance Puerto Rico's chronic trade deficit. Federal funds to the government and directly to the people have been important to the Puerto Rican economy but fell from over 30% to nearly 20% of GNP during the 1980s (an upturn to about 23% in 1990 was due to hurricane relief).

Puerto Rico's major problem is lack of jobs for an expanding population, a problem exacerbated when rising unemployment in the US persuades Puerto Ricans to return to the island. From its former dependence on subsistence agriculture, Puerto Rico became a center for low-wage textile manufacturing, then a home for refining cheap crude oil from abroad—mainly Venezuela. The sharp rise of overseas oil prices that began in 1973 devastated this economic sector. Since then, high-technology industries have become a major presence on the island.

During 1996, there were 10,808 bankruptcy filings, up almost 36% from 1995.

[21]INCOME

Per capita personal income in Puerto Rico was $7,882 in 1996, far lower than in any of the 50 states during that year, but far exceeding that of its Caribbean neighbors. Total net income increased from $1.3 billion in 1960 to $5 billion in 1972, $9 billion in 1980, and $24.5 billion in 1996. Average family income on the island in 1996 was $27,587.

[22]LABOR

Puerto Rico's civilian labor force in March 1997 numbered 1,297,000, of whom 1,129,000 were employed, yielding an unemployment rate of 12.9%.

In March 1997, agriculture, forestry, and fishing accounted for about 3.1% of employment; mining, 0.1%; construction, 5.5%; manufacturing, 15.3%; wholesale and retail trade, 19.5%; finance, insurance, and real estate, 3.0%; transportation, communication, and public utilities, 5.5%; services, 25.5%; and government, 22.5%.

Approximately 7% of the labor force belonged to trade unions in 1997. Wages tend to adhere closely to the US statutory minimum, which applies to Puerto Rico. In December 1996, the average weekly earnings of production workers was $321.12.

23AGRICULTURE

Total farm income in 1996 was $663 million. In 1940, agriculture employed 43% of the work force; by 1996, about 3.5% of the Puerto Rican labor force had agricultural jobs. Nowhere is this decline more evident than in the sugar industry. Production peaked at 1,300,000 tons in 1952, when 150,000 cane cutters were employed; by 1978, however, production was 300,000 tons, fewer than 20,000 cutters were in the fields, and the industry was heavily subsidized. In 1996, production fell below 40,000 tons. The hilly terrain makes mechanization difficult, and manual cutting contributes to production costs that are much higher than those of Hawaii and Louisiana. Despite incentives and subsidies, tobacco is no longer profitable, and coffee production—well adapted to the highlands—falls far short of domestic consumption, although about 10% of the best quality crops are exported to Asia, Europe, and the US. In 1995/96, some 26.5 million lb (12 million kg) of coffee were produced by Puerto Rican farmers, with a value of $56 million. Plantains are an important crop, with an average annual farm value of $35 million. Ornamental plants, exotic fruits, mangoes, vegetables, and bananas are also grown on plots and on former sugar cane fields.

24ANIMAL HUSBANDRY

By the close of 1995 there were 429,000 cattle and 196,000 hogs and pigs on Puerto Rico farms and ranches. Production of meat animals in 1995 included 39.69 million lb (18,000 metric tons) of beef, and 33.075 million lb (15,000 metric tons) of pork. Sales of cattle and calves amounted to $51.6 million in 1992; hogs and pigs, $11.6 million.

Leading dairy and poultry products in 1995 were 822.465 million lb (373,000 metric tons) of milk, 39,690 lb (18 metric tons) of eggs, and 136.71 million lb (62,000 metric tons) of broilers. In 1995 there were about 14 million chickens on Puerto Rican poultry farms. Dairy and poultry sales in 1992 totaled $197.7 million and $98.9 million, respectively.

25FISHING

Although sport fishing, especially for blue marlin, is an important tourist attraction, the waters surrounding Puerto Rico are too deep to lend themselves to commercial fishery. Tuna brought in from African and South American waters and processed on the western shore provides much of the canned tuna sold in eastern US markets. Landings in 1995 amounted to 3,892,000 lb, valued at $7.05 million. Leading species by quantity (and value) included: snappers, 1,119,000 lb ($2.3 million); tuna, 135,100 lb ($179,300); dolphinfish (or mahi-mahi), 223,600 lb ($325,600); spiny lobster, 288,600 lb ($1.22 million); mackerel, 204,000 lb ($337,700); and conch (snail) meats, 221,900 lb ($499,800). In 1994, 86% of the total catch came from marine fishing.

Five aquacultural projects covering some 550 acres (220 hectares) were operating in 1992, including the largest freshwater prawn farm in the Americas. Other species produced by Puerto Rican aquaculture include saltwater shrimp, red tilapia fish, and ornamental species.

26FORESTRY

Puerto Rico lost its self-sufficiency in timber production by the mid-19th century, as population expansion, increasing demand for food, and extraction of native and endemic woods for export led to massive deforestation. Today, Puerto Rico must import nearly all of its wood and paper products. The public forest system covers 86,095 acres (34,842 hectares), of which 58,249 acres (23,573 hectares) are part of the Puerto Rico State Forest system and 27,846 acres (11,269 hectares) are part of the Caribbean National Forest.

27MINING

The estimated value of nonfuel mineral commodities produced in Puerto Rico was $84.8 million in 1995, excluding the value of crushed stone, which accounts for approximately 30% of the commonwealth's mineral value and is the island's second leading mineral commodity. In 1995, 10.9 million metric tons of crushed stone were produced, for a value of $80.8 million. Even with crushed stone being excluded, Puerto Rico's mineral value was greater than that of seven mainland states. Cement is the most valuable mineral commodity produced. Lime ($3,650,000) and clay ($370,000) production in 1995 posted changes of 23% and 9.4%, respectively, from the values reported in 1994.

A multiyear study of the island's known and undiscovered mineral resources indicated that at least 11 different types of metallic mineral deposits, including copper, iron, gold, manganese, silver, molybdenum, zinc, lead, and other minerals, occur on the island in additon to the industrial minerals (cement, stone, clay, and sand and gravel) currently being produced.

28ENERGY AND POWER

Puerto Rico is almost totally dependent on imported crude oil for its energy needs. The island has not yet developed any fossil fuel resources of its own, and its one experimental nuclear reactor, built on the south coast at Rincon in 1964, was shut down after a few years. Solar-powered hot-water heaters have been installed in a few private homes and at La Fortaleza. Inefficiency in the public transport system has encouraged commonwealth residents to rely on private vehicles, thereby increasing the demands for imported petroleum. Of Puerto Rico's total energy requirement, about 90% was supplied by liquid fuels. In 1996, Puerto Rico imported 5,290,000 barrels of refined petroleum products.

29INDUSTRY

Value added by manufacture surpassed $8.6 billion in 1982, more than double the total for 1977. In 1949, about 55,200 Puerto Rican workers were employed in industrial jobs, 26% of them in sugar refining. By 1992, despite the loss of many jobs in the sugar industry, the number was 158,181 with a total payroll of $2.7 billion. The leading employment categories in 1992 were apparel and textiles, 30,700; chemicals and allied products, 25,400; food and kindred products, 21,000; electric and electronic equipment, 18,400; and instruments, 15,900. The growth areas were electric and electronic equipment, up 47% from 1977, and instruments and related products, up 60%.

According to the 1992 Census of Manufactures, the value of shipments amounted to $31 million, of which chemicals and allied products accounted for $13.3 billion; food and kindred products, $5.2 billion; and electronic and electric equipment, $2.8 billion.

As of 1992, there were more than 90 pharmaceutical plants representing 20 of the world's leading drug and health companies. The largest included Johnson & Johnson (Rio Piedras), Abbott Chemicals (Barceloneta), Bristol-Myers Squibb (Humacao), Warner-Lambert (Vega Baja), and Schering-Plough (Manati). In 1991, Baxter International (medical devices) was one of the commonwealth's largest non–locally based manufacturers, with 10 plants; Westinghouse Electric (electric components) had 15; Sara Lee (men's underwear), 6; and Motorola (radio equipment), 4. The Coca-Cola Company operates the world's largest soft drink concentrate and base manufacturing facility in Puerto Rico.

Puerto Rico has two foreign free-trade zones, in Mayagüez and San Juan. In January 1987, the Puerto Rico Industrial Incentives Act was passed to make more manufacturing and export service industries eligible for tax exemptions.

During 1995, 22 US patents were issued to Puerto Rico residents.

30COMMERCE

Wholesale trade in Puerto Rico in 1992 involved 2,651 establishments and major distributors, with sales of $10,187.7 million. Merchant wholesalers accounted for 90.8% of establishments and 83.4% of wholesale trade. Durable goods accounted for only 34.1% of sales.

Retail trade during the same year involved 13,534 establishments, the major sectors being food and apparel stores. Total retail sales in 1992 amounted to $11,707 million. Two large shopping centers, Plaza las Americas and Plaza Carolina, are in the San Juan area. The San Juan area alone had retail sales of nearly $3.3 billion in 1992, or over 28.1% of the total.

Foreign trade is a significant factor in Puerto Rico's economy. Trade between the US and Puerto Rico is unrestricted. In 1994, the island's imports were $17.2 billion and exports $22.7 billion. During 1994, the US received 88.5% of Puerto Rico's exports and supplied about 66.8% of its import. The principal reason for the relative decline in imports from the continental US has been the heavy volume and cost of oil imports, especially from Venezuela, auto imports and other goods from Japan, and, in general, the stimulus to foreign imports created by a strong US dollar.

31CONSUMER PROTECTION

Consumer protection is the responsibility of Puerto Rico's cabinet-level Department of Consumer Affairs.

32BANKING

Puerto Rico's first bank began operations in 1850. As of 31 December 1996, there were 20 commercial banks in Puerto Rico (1 national, 4 foreign, and 15 domestic) and 2 major government banks. Most of the savings banks have converted to a commercial charter; thus, there are only 2 savings banks still in operation on the island, with total combined assets of approximately $300 million. Banco Popular de Puerto Rico continues to be the largest domestic bank (with assets of nearly $8 billion in mid-1991) followed by Banco Santander Puerto Rico (assets of $3.1 billion in mid-1991). Both are subsidiaries of bank holding companies, the former incorporated in Puerto Rico, the latter in Spain.

Since 1992, a new type of institution has flourished in Puerto Rico, promoted by the government: the international banking entity. As of 31 December 1996, there were 19 international banking entities in Puerto Rico with total combined assets of $22 billion.

The credit union industry is also thriving in Puerto Rico. Although total combined assets for credit unions were only about $3.5 million as of 31 December 1996, there were 187 credit unions throughout the island.

US corporations no longer operate tax-free in Puerto Rico. Amendments made to the US Internal Revenue Code tax laws require the payment of federal taxes on a portion of their income.

In addition to the Government Development Bank, founded in 1948, the Economic Development Bank for Puerto Rico, created in 1985, fosters the development of local businesses engaged in agriculture, manufacturing, commerce, and other services, thus decreasing the need to import goods and services.

33INSURANCE

More than 200 Puerto Rican insurance companies collected revenues of $82.4 million (life insurance companies, $18.1 million; property and casualty, $64.3 million) in 1990/91, enforcing policies exceeding $1.5 billion. Due to Hurricane Hugo, the insurance industry suffered underwriting losses of $19.5 million in 1989. The largest life insurance company in 1990 was Seguro de Service de Salud de Puerto Rico, Inc., with written premiums exceeding $275 million.

34SECURITIES

There are no securities exchanges in Puerto Rico. Bonds issued by the Government Development Bank, exempt from federal income taxes and from the income taxes of all US states and cities, are offered for sale on the world securities market. There are several hundred broker-dealer firms registered to do business in Puerto Rico. Approximately 100 organizations providing security investment advice are registered in Puerto Rico.

35PUBLIC FINANCE

Puerto Rico's annual budget is prepared by the Bureau of Budget and Management and submitted by the governor to the legislature, which has unlimited power to amend it. The fiscal year extends from 1 July to 30 June.

The following table shows Puerto Rico's revenues and expenditures for 1995/96 (in millions of US$):

REVENUES	1995/96
Income taxes	$ 3,370
Excise taxes	1,304
Other taxes	574
Transfers, reimbursement, and sales of fixed assets	138
Capital investment fund	505
Intergovernmental transfers	2,861
Special state fund	304
Balance	473
TOTAL	$ 9,529

EXPENDITURES	1989/90
General government	$ 654
Public safety	959
Health	1,236
Public housing and welfare	2,402
Education and culture	2,332
Economic development	300
Aid to municipalities	343
Special pension contributions	23
Transportation and communications	157
Debt service	413
Other debt	357
TOTAL	$ 9,176

Of expenditures, 3.3% were assigned to economic development and 26.2% to public housing and welfare; education accounted for 25.4% of the central government's expenditures.

In 1959/60, transfers from the US government amounted to $44 million, or less than 13% of all revenues. By 1972/73, receipts from the US government represented 23% of all revenues; by 1977/78, more than 29%. In 1995/96 intergovernmental transfers from the US government amounted to $2.9 billion, or 30.0% of the commonwealth government's receipts.

36TAXATION

The Puerto Rican Federal Relations Act stipulates that the commonwealth is exempt from US internal revenue laws. The federal income tax is not levied on permanent residents of Puerto Rico, but federal Social Security and unemployment taxes are deducted from payrolls, and the commonwealth government collects an income tax. Corporations in Puerto Rico are also taxed, though some companies fall under Section 936 financing.

Section 936 of the Internal Revenue Code exempts certain corporations from paying taxes for periods ranging from 10 to 25 years, allowing subsidiaries of US corporations virtual exemption from US corporate income taxes. The exemption was passed in 1976 to encourage economic development on the island. At the time of repatriation of profits to the US stockholder, the Puerto Rican government imposes a "tollgate" of 5–10%. As of 1991, deposits of Section 936 funds in local commercial, investment, and savings banks amounted to $9 billion.

Property, excise, and franchise taxes are also levied by the government. Excise taxes on new and used cars are an important source of revenue for the government.

[37]ECONOMIC POLICY

Inaugurated during the 1940s, Operation Bootstrap had succeeded by 1982 in attracting investments from more than 500 US corporations. The principal Puerto Rican agencies responsible for this transformation are the Administración de Fomento Económico, known as Fomento (Development), and its subsidiary, the Puerto Rico Industrial Development Co., which help select plant sites, build factories, hire and train workers, and arrange financing. Fomento reorganized certain industries, taking a direct role, for example, in promoting export sales of Puerto Rican rum. At first, Fomento brought in apparel and textile manufacturers, who needed relatively unskilled workers. More recently, with the improvement in Puerto Rico's educational system, Fomento has emphasized such technologically advanced industries as pharmaceuticals and electronics. Industrialization has also required heavy investment in roads, power, water facilities, and communications systems.

The primary incentives to investment in Puerto Rico have been lower wage scales than in the continental US and the exemption of up to 90% of corporate profits from island corporate and property taxes for five years, with a descending rate of exemption that can last as long as 235 years in some regions. The commonwealth government created a 218-acre (88-hectare) free-trade zone in the San Juan area that allows companies to assemble imports duty free in government-built warehouses for export from the island. Under the US Tax Reform Act of 1976, US companies may repatriate earnings from their Puerto Rican subsidiaries free of federal taxation.

[38]HEALTH

Health conditions in Puerto Rico have improved remarkably since 1940, when the average life expectancy was only 46 years. A resident of Puerto Rico born in the period from 1990 to 1995 could expect to live 75.3 years. Infant mortality declined from 113 per 1,000 live births in 1940 to 10.8 in 1990–95. The leading causes of death in 1940 were diseases brought on by malnutrition or infection: diarrhea, enteritis, tuberculosis, and pneumonia. There were 30,032 deaths in Puerto Rico in 1995. The most common causes of death that year were heart disease (23%); cancer (15%); and diabetes mellitus (7.5%). Puerto Rico had the 9th-lowest mortality rate from cardiovascular diseases in 1991, with 8,646 deaths in 1992. Stroke was far more common, with a death rate of 31.1 per 100,000.

In 1991, Puerto Rico had 56 hospitals, with 9,688 beds; average daily occupancy was 6,792. Outpatient visits came to 3,294,721. Medical personnel included 7,095 active nonfederal physicians in 1991. In 1992, the commonwealth had 202 nonfederal physicians per 100,000 population, a higher ratio than in 15 states. In 1993, there were 797 licensed active dentists. Some 885,405 Medicaid recipients and 446,172 Medicare enrollees collected $158 million and $555 million in benefits, respectively, in 1991/92.

[39]SOCIAL WELFARE

Since the mid-1960s, residents of Puerto Rico have been eligible for most of the programs that apply throughout the 50 states. About one-fourth of the commonwealth's budget is appropriated for public housing and welfare. Federal grants, transfers, and expenditures in Puerto Rico amounted to nearly one-quarter of the GNP in 1990. The school lunch program received $117.7 million in 1996.

With the enactment of the Personal Responsibility and Work Opportunity Reconciliation Act of 1996, the US government has changed the form and regulations for many of its social welfare programs; most significantly, it replaces Aid to Families with Dependent Children (AFDC), an open-ended entitlement program, with Temporary Assistance for Needy Families (TANF), a limited system of assistance funded largely through federal block grants. The reform act also impacts the food stamp program, the Supplemental Security Income program, and the child nutrition program. The law took effect on 1 July 1997 and provided $16.38 billion in block grants for fiscal years 1997–2002. The grants are to be divided among the states based on an equation involving the numbers of former AFDC recipients in each state. Because many of the bill's provisions have yet to be implemented into state-by-state policy, it was not possible to include the details of each state's programs for this edition of this work.

Because unemployment is high and wages are low, Social Security benefits are below the US average. In 1995, benefits averaging $465 per month were paid to 613,390 residents. Island residents are not eligible for Supplemental Security Income. Weekly unemployment benefits averaged $91.85 in 1995. In 1996, 149,944 residents received $97 million in Aid to Families with Dependent Children.

[40]HOUSING

In 1990, there were a total of 1,184,382 housing units with 2.97 persons per unit, up from 867,697 units in 1980, when there were 3.66 persons per occupied unit. The total value of housing construction in 1992 was an estimated $632 million, down from $754 million in 1991. In 1993, 9,785 new units valued at $381.7 million were authorized. During 1995/96, Puerto Rico received $386.7 million in aid from the US Department of Housing and Urban Development, including $132.3 million in community development block grants.

[41]EDUCATION

Puerto Rico has made enormous strides in public education. In 1900, only 14% of the island's school-age children were actually in school; the proportion had increased to 50% by 1940 and 85% by the late 1970s. The government encouraged school attendance among the poor in the 1940s and 1950s by providing inexpensive shoes, free lunches, school uniforms, and small scholarships. Today, education is compulsory for children between 6 and 16 years of age, and nearly two out of ten commonwealth budget dollars goes to education.

In the 1995/96 academic year there were 621,370 students attending public school. Instruction is carried out in Spanish, but English is taught at all levels. In 1994/95, there were 1,584 public schools, of which 994 were elementary schools, 341 were secondary schools, 196 were combined elementary/secondary schools, and 53 were other types.

Puerto Rico had 14 public institutions of higher education in 1995/96, including 10 four-year institutons. The main state-supported institution of higher learning is the University of Puerto Rico, with its main campus at Rico Piedras. The system also included doctorate-level campuses at Mayagüez and San Juan (for medical sciences); four year colleges at Auredibo, Cayey, Humacao, and Ponce; and two-year colleges at Aguadilla and Carolina. The 40 private institutions in 1995/96 included Inter-American University, with campuses at Hato Rey, San German, and other locations, and the Catholic University of Puerto Rico, at Ponce. In 1994/95, 156,439 students were enrolled at higher education institutions in Puerto Rico, of whom 113,285 were full-time students.

42ARTS

The Tapia Theater in Old San Juan is the island's major showcase for local and visiting performers, including the Taller de Histriones group and *zarzuela* (comic opera) troupes from Spain. The Institute of Puerto Rican Culture produces an annual theatncal festival. The Fine Arts Center features entertainment ranging from ballet, opera, and symphonies to drama, jazz, and popular music.

Puerto Rico has its own symphony orchestra and conservatory of music. Both were formerly directed by Pablo Casals, and the annual Music Festival Casals, which he founded, still attracts world-renowned musicians to the island each May. The Opera de Camara tours several houses. Puerto Rico supports both a classical ballet company (the Ballets de San Juan), and the Areyto Folkloric Group, which performs traditional folk dances. Salsa, a popular style pioneered by Puerto Rican musicians like Tito Puente, influenced the development of pop music on the US mainland during the 1970s. Puerto Rico generated $805,000 in federal funds to support its arts programs in 1996. The NEA contributed $461,000 to its programs and $696,000 to the Institute of Puerto Rican Culture. The NEA has also contributed to the arts education programs developed by the Institute of Puerto Rican Culture, and supported the Opera de Camara in Old San Juan and the Ballet Concierto de Puerto Rico. The Puerto Rican Community Foundation, Inc., has received funding through the NEA's challenge grant program.

43LIBRARIES AND MUSEUMS

In 1996/97, Puerto Rico's public libraries contained about 609,391 volumes and had a combined circulation of 479,133. The University of Puerto Rico Library at Rio Piedras held 587,270 books; the library of the Puerto Rico Conservatory of Music, in San Juan, has a collection of music written by Puerto Rican and Latin American composers. La Casa del Libro, also in San Juan, is a library-museum of typographic and graphic arts. Among the 21 museums in 1996/97, the Museo de Arte de Ponce (Luis A. Ferre Foundation) has paintings, sculptures, and archaeological artifacts, as well as a library. The Marine Station Museum in Mayagüez exhibits Caribbean marine specimens and sponsors research and field trips.

44COMMUNICATIONS

The Puerto Rico Telephone Co. was founded in 1914 by two German sugar brokers, Sosthenes and Hernand Behn, best known today as the creators of International Telephone and Telegraph (ITT). In 1974 the Puerto Rican government bought the phone company from ITT. In 1997, there were an estimated 1.296 million telephone lines on the island. Two companies provide cellular service to an estimated 33,000 subscribers. As of 1997, the Puerto Rican government was negotiating the sale of the Puerto Rico Telephone Co. to private entities.

On 12 September 1996, Law 213 (known as Puerto Rico's Telecommunications Act of 1996) was enacted. The Act created the Puerto Rico Telecommunications Regulatory Board with jurisdiction over all telecommunications companies providing services on the island.

WKAQ, the island's first radio station, came on the air in 1923, and the first television station, WKAQ-TV, began broadcasting in 1954. As of 1991 there were 65 AM and 41 FM radio stations and 33 television stations. As of 1997, there were six cable television service companies.

45PRESS

Puerto Rico has three major Spanish-language dailies: 1997 circulation for *El Nuevo Dia* was 223,112 mornings, 239,999 Sundays; and for *El Vocero,* 198,897 mornings. The English-language *San Juan Star,* with a circulation of 33,429 mornings and 35,003 Sundays, won a Pulitzer Prize in 1961. *El Reportero* is an evening Spanish-language newspaper.

46ORGANIZATIONS

Important organizations on the island include the Puerto Rico Medical Association, Puerto Rico Manufacturers' Association, and Puerto Rico Bar Association. Also maintaining headquarters in Puerto Rico are the Association of Island Marine Laboratories of the Caribbean, Puerto Rico Rum Producers Association, Caribbean Hotel Association, and Caribbean Studies Association.

US-based agencies such as the National Puerto Rican Forum and the Puerto Rican Community Development Project assist Puerto Ricans living on the mainland. "Hometown clubs" consisting of "absent sons" *(hilos ausentes)* of various Puerto Rican towns are a typical feature of the barrios in New York and other cities in the continental US.

47TOURISM, TRAVEL, AND RECREATION

Only government and manufacturing exceed tourism in importance to the Puerto Rican economy. The industry has grown rapidly, from 65,000 tourists in 1950 to 1,088,000 in 1970, to 3,700,000 in 1992 with an average of $547 spent per visit. Tourism decreased slightly in the mid-1990s. The beautiful reefs and waters still draw tourists from all over the world. In 1992 the tourism industry employed thousands of people. Tourism accounts for about 5% of the island's gross national product.

Many hotels are located in San Juan, though the eastern part of the island also features hotels and resorts. Most tourists come for sunning, swimming, deep-sea fishing, and the fashionable shops, night clubs, and casinos of San Juan's Condado Strip. Attractions of old San Juan include two fortresses, El Morro and San Cristobal, San Jose Church (one of the oldest in the New World), and La Fortaleza, the governor's palace. The government has been encouraging tourists to journey outside of San Juan to such destinations such as the Arecibo Observatory (with its radio telescope use for research astronomy, ionospheric studies, and radar mapping), the rain forest of El Yunque, Phosphorescent Bay, colonial-style San German, and the bird sanctuary and mangrove forest on the shores of Torrecilla Lagoon. The 53-acre (21-hectare) San Juan harbor fortifications are a national historic site.

48SPORTS

Baseball is very popular in Puerto Rico. There is a 15-team professional winter league, in which many ball players from American and National league teams participate. Horse racing, cockfighting, boxing, and basketball are also popular. Puerto Rico, which has its own Olympic Committee, sent a delegation to the 1980 Olympics in Moscow despite the US boycott. Other annual sporting events include the Copa Velasco Regatta, the first leg of the Caribbean Ocean Racing Triangle, and the International Billfish Tournament in San Juan.

49FAMOUS PUERTO RICANS

Elected to represent Puerto Rico before the Spanish Cortes in 1812, Ramón Power y Giralt (1775–1813), a liberal reformer, was the leading Puerto Rican political figure of the early 19th century. Power, appointed vice president of the Cortes, participated in the drafting of the new Spanish constitution of 1812. Ramón Emeterio Betances (1827–98) became well known not only for his efforts to alleviate a cholera epidemic in 1855 but also for his crusade to abolish slavery in Puerto Rico and as a leader of a separatist movement that culminated in 1868 in the "Grito de Lares." Eugenio Maria de Hostos (1839–1903), a writer, abolitionist, and educator, spent much of his adult life in Latin America, seeking to establish a free federation of the West Indies to replace colonial rule in the Caribbean. Luis Muñoz

Rivera (1859–1916), a liberal journalist, led the movement that obtained for Puerto Rico the Autonomic Charter of 1897, and he headed the cabinet that took office in 1898. With the island under US rule, Muñoz Rivera served between 1911 and 1916 as Puerto Rico's resident commissioner to the US Congress. Other important Puerto Rican historical figures include Juan Alejo Arizmendi (1760?–1814), the first Puerto Rican–born bishop, appointed to the See of San Juan; José de Diego (1866–1918), a noted poet and gifted orator who, under the Foraker Act, became the first speaker of the island house of delegates and was a champion of independence for Puerto Rico.

The dominant political figure in 20th-century Puerto Rico was Luis Muñoz Marin (1898–1980), founder of the Popular Democratic Party in 1938 and president of the Puerto Rico senate from 1940 to 1948. Muñoz, the first native-born elected governor of the island (1948–64), devised the commonwealth relationship that has governed the island since 1952. Another prominent 20th-century figure, Antonio R. Barceló (1869–1939), led the Unionista Party after Muñoz Rivera's death, was the first president of the senate under the Jones Act, and was later the leader of the Liberal Party. In 1946, Jesús T. Pinero (1897–1952) became the first Puerto Rican appointed governor of the island by a US president; he had been elected as resident commissioner of Puerto Rico to the US Congress two years before. Pedro Albizu Campos (1891–1965), a Harvard Law School graduate, presided over the militant Nationalist Party and was until his death the leader of forces that advocated independence for Puerto Rico by revolution. In 1945, Gilberto Concepción de Gracia (1909–68), also a lawyer, helped found the more moderate Puerto Rican Independence Party. Herman Badillo (b.1929) was the first person of Puerto Rican birth to be a voting member of the US House of Representatives, as congressman from New York, and Maurice Ferré (b.1935), elected mayor of Miami in 1973, was the first native-born Puerto Rican to run a large US mainland city. Hernán Padilla (b.1938), mayor of San Juan, became the first Hispanic American elected to head the US Conference of Mayors (1984).

Women have participated actively in Puerto Rican politics. Ana Roqué de Duprey (1853–1933) led the Asociación Puertorriquena de Mujeres Sufragistas, organized in late 1926, while Milagros Benet de Mewton (1868–1945) presided over the Liga Social Sufragista, founded in 1917. Both groups actively lobbied for the extension of the right to vote to Puerto Rican women, not only in Puerto Rico but in the US and other countries as well. Felisa Rincón de Gautier (b.1897), mayor of San Juan from 1946 to 1968, was named Woman of the Americas in 1954, the year she presided over the Inter-American Organization for Municipalities. Carmen Delgado Votaw (b.1935) was the first person of Puerto Rican birth to be elected president of the Inter-American Commission of Women, the oldest international organization in the field of women's rights.

Manuel A. Alonso (1822–89) blazed the trail for a distinctly Puerto Rican literature with the publication, in 1849, of *El Gibaro*, the first major effort to depict the traditions and mores of the island's rural society. Following him in the development of a rich Puerto Rican literary tradition were, among many others, that most prolific of 19th-century Puerto Rican writers, Alejandro Tapia y Rivera (1826–82), adept in history, drama, poetry, and other forms of literary expression; essayist and critic Manuel Elzaburu (1852–92); novelist Manuel Zeno Gandia (1855–1930); and poets Lola Rodriguez de Tió (1843–1924) and

José Gautier Benitez (1848–80). The former's patriotic lyrics, popularly acclaimed, were adapted to become Puerto Rico's national anthem. Among 20th-century Puerto Rican literary figures are poets Luis Lloréns Torres (1878–1944), Luis Palés Matos (1898–1959), and Julia de Burgos (1916–1953) and essayists and critics Antonio S. Pedreira (1898–1939), Tomás Blanco (b.1900), José A. Balseiro (b.1900), Margot Arce (b.1904), Concha Meléndez (b.1904), Nilita Vientós Gastón (b.1908), and Maria T. Babin (b.1910–1989). In the field of fiction, René Marqués (1919–79), Abelardo Diaz Alfaro (b.1919), José Luis González (b.1926), and Pedro Juan Soto (b.1928) are among the best known outside Puerto Rico.

In the world of entertainment, Academy Award winners José Ferrer (b.1912–1992) and Rita Moreno (b.1931) are among the most famous. Notable in classical music are cellist-conductor Pablo Casals (b.Spain, 1876–1973), a longtime resident of Puerto Rico; pianist Jesús Maria Sanromá (1902–84); and opera star Justino Diaz (b.1940). Well-known popular musicians include Tito Puente (b.New York, 1923) and José Feliciano (b.1945).

Roberto Clemente (1934–72), one of baseball's most admired performers and a member of the Hall of Fame, played on 12 National League All-Star teams and was named Most Valuable Player in 1966.

[50]BIBLIOGRAPHY

Babin, Maria Teresa. *The Puerto Ricans' Spirit: Their History, Life and Culture.* New York: Collier, 1971.

Carr, Raymond. *Puerto Rico: A Colonial Experiment.* New York: Vintage, 1984.

Colonial Dilemma: Critical Perspectives on Contemporary Puerto Rico. Boston: South End Press, 1993.

Fernandez, Ronald. *The Disenchanted Island: Puerto Rico and the United States in the Twentieth Century.* Westport, Conn.: Praeger, 1996.

Hostos, Adolfo de. *Diccionario Historico Bibliografico Comentado de Puerto Rico.* San Juan: Academia Puertorriquena de la Historia, 1976.

Morales Carrion, Arturo. *Puerto Rico and the Non-Hispanic Caribbean.* Rio Piedras: University of Puerto Rico, 1971.

———. *Puerto Rico: A Political and Cultural History.* New York: Norton, 1984.

Morris, Nancy. *Puerto Rico: Culture, Politics, and Identity.* Westport, Conn.: Praeger, 1995.

Puerto Rico Federal Affairs Administration. *Puerto Rico, U.S.A.* Washington, DC., 1979.

US Commission on Civil Rights. *Puerto Ricans in the Continental United States: An Uncertain Future.* Washington, D.C., 1976.

US Department of Commerce. *Economic Study of Puerto Rico.* 2 vols. Washingtion, D.C., 1979.

Vivo, Paquita. *The Puerto Ricans: An Annotated Bibliography.* New York: Bowker, 1973.

Votaw, Carmen Delgado. *Puerto Rican Women: Some Biographical Profiles.* Washington, D.C.: National Conference of Puerto Rican Woman, 1978.

Wagenheim, Kal. *Puerto Rico: A Profile.* 2d ed. New York: Praeger, 1975.

———, and Olga Jimenez de Wagenheim (eds.). *The Puerto Ricans: A Documentary History.* Maplewood, N.J.: Waterfrom Press, 1988.

Wells, Henry. *The Modernization of Puerto Rico.* Cambridge, Mass.: Harvard University Press, 1969.

UNITED STATES
CARIBBEAN DEPENDENCIES

NAVASSA

Navassa, a 5-sq-km (2-sq-mi) island between Jamaica and Haiti, was claimed by the US under the Guano Act of 1856. The island, located at 18°24′N and 75°1′W, is uninhabited except for a lighthouse station under the administration of the coast guard.

VIRGIN ISLANDS OF THE UNITED STATES

The Virgin Islands of the United States lie about 64 km (40 mi) N of Puerto Rico and 1,600 km (1,000 mi) SSE of Miami, between 17°40′ and 18°25′N and 64°34′ and 65°3′N. The island group extends 82 km (51 mi) N–S and 80 km (50 mi) E–W with a total area of at least 353 sq km (136 sq mi). Only 3 of the more than 50 islands and cays are of significant size: St. Croix, 218 sq km (84 sq mi) in area; St. Thomas, 83 sq km (32 sq mi); and St. John, 52 sq km (20 sq mi). The territorial capital, Charlotte Amalie, on St. Thomas, has one of the finest harbors in the Caribbean.

St. Croix is relatively flat, with a terrain suitable for sugarcane cultivation. St. Thomas is mountainous and little cultivated, but it has many snug harbors. St. John, also mountainous, has fine beaches and lush vegetation; about two-thirds of St. John's area has been declared a national park. The subtropical climate, with temperatures ranging from 21° to 32°C (70–90°F) and an average temperature of 25°C (77°F), is moderated by northeast trade winds. Rainfall, the main source of fresh water, varies widely, and severe droughts are frequent. The average yearly rainfall is 114 cm (45 in), mostly during the summer months.

The population of the US Virgin Islands was 96,569 at the time of the 1980 census, about triple the 1960 census total of 32,099, and was estimated at 98,942 in 1992. St. Croix has two principal towns: Christiansted and Frederiksted. Economic development has brought an influx of new residents, mainly from Puerto Rico, other Caribbean islands, and the US mainland. Most of the permanent inhabitants are descendants of slaves who were brought from Africa in the early days of Danish rule, and about 80% of the population is black. English is the official and most widely spoken language.

Some of the oldest religious congregations in the Western Hemisphere are located in the Virgin Islands. A Jewish synagogue there is the second oldest in the New World, and the Lutheran Congregation of St. Thomas, founded in 1666, is one of the three oldest congregations in the US. As of 1993, Baptists made up an estimated 42% of the population, Roman Catholics 34%, and Episcopalians 17%.

There are nearly 900 km (550 mi) of roads in the US Virgin Islands. Cargo-shipping services operate from Baltimore, Jacksonville, and Miami via Puerto Rico. In addition, weekly shipping service is available from Miami. Both St. Croix and St. Thomas have airports, with St. Croix's facility handling the larger number of jet flights from the continental US and Europe.

Excavations at St. Croix in the 1970s uncovered evidence of a civilization perhaps as ancient as AD 100. Christopher Columbus, who reached the islands in 1493, named them for the martyred virgin St. Ursula. At this time, St. Croix was inhabited by Carib Indians, who were eventually driven from the island by Spanish soldiers in 1555. During the 17th century, the archipelago was divided into two territorial units, one controlled by the British, the other (now the US Virgin Islands) controlled by Denmark.

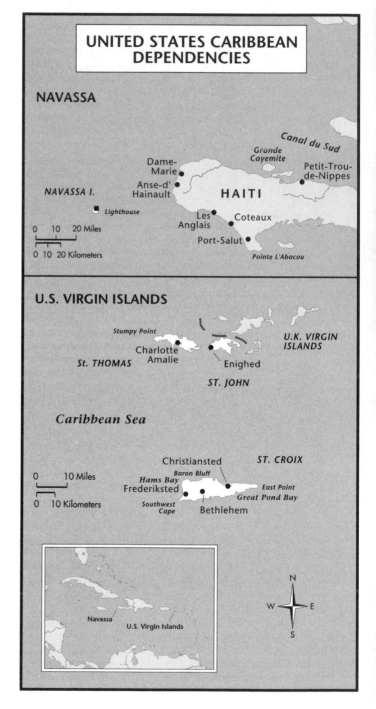

The separate history of the latter unit began with the settlement of St. Thomas by the Danish West India Company in 1672. St. John was claimed by the company in 1683, and St. Croix was purchased from France in 1733. The holdings of the company were taken over as a Danish crown colony in 1754. Sugarcane, cultivated by slave labor, was the backbone of the islands' prosperity in the 18th and early 19th centuries. After brutally suppressing several slave revolts, Denmark abolished slavery in the colony in 1848. A long period of economic decline followed, until Denmark sold the islands to the US in 1917 for $25 million. Congress granted US citizenship to the Virgin Islanders in 1927. In 1931, administration of the islands was transferred from the Department of the Navy to the Department of the Interior, and the first civilian governor was appointed. In the late 1970s, the Virgin Islands government began to consider ways to expand self-rule. A UN delegation in 1977 found little interest in independence, however, and a locally drafted constitution was voted down by the electorate in 1979.

The chief executive of the Virgin Islands is the territorial governor, elected by direct popular vote (prior to 1970, territorial governors were appointed by the US president). Constitutionally, the US Congress has plenary authority to legislate for the territory. Enactment of the Revised Organic Act of the Virgin Islands on 22 July 1954 vested local legislative power—subject to veto by the governor—in a unicameral legislature. Since 1972, the islands have sent one nonvoting representative to the US House of Representatives. Courts are under the US federal judiciary; the two federal district court judges are appointed by the US president. Territorial court judges, who preside over misdemeanor and traffic cases, are appointed by the governor and confirmed by the legislature. The district court has appellate jurisdiction over the territorial court.

Tourism has supplanted agriculture as the islands' principal economic activity. The number of tourists rose dramatically throughout the late 1960s and early 1970s, from 448,165 in 1964 to 1,116,127 in 1972/73, but has stagnated since that time. Today, tourism accounts for more than 70% of GDP and 70% of the employment. Rum remains an important manufacture, with petroleum refining (on St. Croix) a major addition in the late 1960s. Economic development is promoted by the US-government-owned Virgin Islands Corp. The island's primary export is refined petroleum products. Raw crude oil constitutes the Virgin's Island's most expensive import.

The territorial Department of Health provides hospital and medical services, public health services, and veterinary medicine. Education is compulsory. The College of the Virgin Islands is the territory's first institution of higher learning. There are 58,931 telephones and 98,000 radios in use on the islands. In 1988 the Virgin Islands had 12 radio stations (4 AM, 8 FM) and 4 television stations.

UNITED STATES
PACIFIC DEPENDENCIES

AMERICAN SAMOA

American Samoa, an unincorporated and unorganized insular US territory in the South Pacific Ocean, comprises that portion of the Samoan archipelago lying E of longitude 171°w. (The rest of the Samoan islands comprise the independent state of Western Samoa.) While the Samoan group as a whole has an area of 3,121 sq km (1,205 sq mi), American Samoa consists of only seven small islands (between 14° and 15°s and 168° and 171°w) with a total area (land and water) of 197 sq km (76 sq mi). Five of the islands are volcanic, with rugged peaks rising sharply, and two are coral atolls.

The climate is hot and rainy; normal temperatures range from 24°c (75°F) in August to 32°c (90°F) during December–February; mean annual rainfall is 330 cm (130 in), the rainy season lasting from December through March. Hurricanes are common. The native flora includes flourishing tree ferns, coconut, hardwoods, and rubber trees. There are few wild animals.

As of 1992, the estimated population was 51,115, an increase of 37% over the 1986 population estimate of 37,500. However, the total population has remained relatively constant for many years because of the substantial number of Samoans who migrate to the United States. The inhabitants, who are concentrated on the island of Tutuila, are almost pure Polynesian. English is the official language, but Samoan is also widely spoken. Most Samoans are Christians.

The capital of the territory, Pago Pago, on Tutuila, has one of the finest natural harbors in the South Pacific and is a duty-free port. Passenger liners call there on South Pacific tours, and passenger and cargo ships arrive regularly from Japan, New Zealand, Australia, and the US west coast. There are regular air and sea services between American Samoa and Western Samoa, and scheduled flights between Pago Pago and Honolulu.

American Samoa was settled by Melanesian migrants in the 1st millennium BC. The Samoan islands were visited in 1768 by the French explorer Louis-Antoine de Bougainville, who named them the Îles des Navigateurs as a tribute to the skill of their native boatmen. In 1889, the US, the UK, and Germany agreed to share control of the islands. The UK later withdrew its claim, and under the 1899 Treaty of Berlin, the US was internationally acknowledged to have rights extending over all the islands of the Samoan group lying east of 171°w, while Germany was acknowledged to have similar rights to the islands west of that meridian. The islands of American Samoa were officially ceded to the US by the various ruling chiefs in 1900 and 1904, and on 20 February 1929 the US Congress formally accepted sovereignty over the entire group. From 1900 to 1951, the territory was administered by the US Department of the Navy, and thereafter by the Department of the Interior. The basic law is the Constitution of 1966.

The executive branch of the government is headed by a governor who, along with the lieutenant governor, is elected by popular vote; before 1977, the two posts were appointed by the US government. Village, county, and district councils have full authority to regulate local affairs.

The legislature (Fono) is composed of the House of Representatives and the Senate. The 15 counties elect 18 matais (chiefs) to four-year terms in the senate, while the 20 house members are elected for two-year terms by popular vote within the counties. The secretary for Samoan affairs, who heads the Department of Local Government, is appointed by the governor. Under his administration are three district governors, the county chiefs, village mayors, and police officials. The judiciary, an independent branch of the government, functions through the high court and five district courts. Samoans living in the islands as of 17 April 1900 or born there since that date are nationals of the US.

The economy is primarily agricultural. Small plantations occupy about one-third of the land area; 70% of the land is communally owned. The principal crops are bananas, breadfruit, taro, papayas, pineapples, sweet potatoes, tapioca, coffee, cocoa, and yams. Hogs and poultry are the principal livestock raised; dairy cattle are few. The principal cash crop is copra. More than half of the total labor force is employed by the federal and territorial government. The largest employers in the private sector, with more than 15% of the labor force, are two modern tuna canneries supplied with fish caught by Japanese, US, and Taiwanese fishing fleets.

Samoans are entitled to free medical treatment, including hospital care. Besides district dispensaries, the government maintains a central hospital, a tuberculosis unit, and a leprosarium. US-trained staff physicians work with Samoan medical practitioners and nurses. The LBJ Tropical Medical Center opened in 1986.

Education is a joint undertaking between the territorial government and the villages. School attendance is compulsory for all children from 6 through 18, and about 99% of the population 10 years of age and over is literate. The villages furnish the elementary-school buildings and living quarters for the teachers; the territorial government pays teachers' salaries and provides buildings and supplies for all but primary schools. Since 1964, educational television has served as the basic teaching tool in the school system. In the early 1990s total enrollment in elementary and secondary schools was 12,258. American Samoa Community College enrolled 582 in the early 1990s.

Radiotelegraph circuits connect the territory with Hawaii, Fiji, and Western Samoa. Every village in American Samoa has telephone service.

GUAM

The largest and most populous of the Mariana Islands in the Western Pacific, Guam (13°28'N and 144°44'E) has an area, including land and water, of 540 sq km (208 sq mi) and is about 48 km (30 mi) long and from 6 to 12 km (4–7 mi) wide. The island is of volcanic origin; in the south, the terrain is mountainous, while the northern part is a plateau with shallow fertile soil. The central part of the island (where the capital, Agana, is located) is undulating country.

Guam lies in the typhoon belt of the Western Pacific and is occasionally subject to widespread storm damage. In May 1976, a typhoon with winds of 306 km/hr (190 mph) struck Guam, causing an estimated $300 million in damage and leaving 80% of the island's buildings in ruins. Guam has a tropical climate with little seasonal variation. Average temperature is 26°c (79°F); rainfall is substantial, reaching an annual average of more than

200 cm (80 in). Endangered species in 1987 included the giant Micronesian kingfisher and Marianas crow.

The 1992 population, excluding transient US military and civilian personnel and their families, was estimated at 142,271, a growth of 21% over the 1986 estimate of 117,500. The increase was attributed largely to the higher birthrate and low mortality rate. The present-day Chamorro, who comprise about 47% of the permanent resident population, descend from the intermingling of the few surviving original Chamorro with the Spanish, Filipino, and Mexican settlers, plus later arrivals from the US, UK, Korea, China, and Japan. Filipinos (25%) are the largest ethnic minority. English is the official language, although Chamorro is taught in the primary schools. The predominant religion is Roman Catholicism.

The earliest known settlers on Guam were the original Chamorro, who migrated from the Malay Peninsula to the Pacific around 1500 BC. When Ferdinand Magellan landed on Guam in 1521, it is believed that as many as 100,000 Chamorro lived on the island; by 1741, their numbers had been reduced to 5,000—most of the population either had fled the island or been killed through disease or war with the Spanish. A Spanish fort was established in 1565, and from 1696 until 1898, Guam was under Spanish rule.

Under the Treaty of Paris that ended the Spanish-American War in 1898, the island was ceded to the US and placed under the jurisdiction of the Department of the Navy. During World War II, Guam was occupied by Japanese forces; the US recaptured the island in 1944 after 54 days of fighting. In 1950, the island's administration was transferred from the Navy to the US Department of the Interior. Under the 1950 Organic Act of Guam, passed by the US Congress, the island was established as an unincorporated territory of the US; Guamanians were granted US citizenship, and internal self-government was introduced.

The governor and lieutenant governor have been elected directly since 1970. A 21-member unicameral legislature elected for two years by adult suffrage is empowered to legislate on all local matters, including taxation and appropriations. The US Congress reserves the right to annul any law passed by the Guam legislature, but must do so within a year of the date it receives the text of any such law.

Judicial authority is vested in the district court of Guam, and appeals may be taken to the regular US courts of appeal and ultimately to the US Supreme Court. An island superior court and other specialized courts have jurisdiction over certain cases arising under the laws of Guam. The judge of the district court is appointed by the US president; the judges of the other courts are appointed by the governor. Guam's laws were codified in 1953.

Guam is one of the most important US military bases in the Pacific, and the island's economy has been profoundly affected by the large sums of money spent by the US defense establishment. During the late 1960s and early 1970s, when the US took the role of a major combatant in the Viet-Nam conflict, Guam served as a base for long-range US bombers on sorties over Indochina.

Prior to World War II, agriculture and animal husbandry were the primary activities. By 1947, most adults were wage earners employed by the US armed forces, although many continued to cultivate small plots to supplement their earnings. Since World War II, agriculture has generally contributed less than 1% of the GNP, partly because a considerable amount of arable land is taken up by military installations. Fruits and vegetables are grown and pigs and poultry are raised for local consumption, but most food is imported. Current fish catches are insufficient to meet local demand.

Tourism has become a major industry and sparked a boom in the construction industry in the mid-1980s. The number of visitors grew rapidly from 6,600 in 1967 to over 900,000 per year by the 1990s.

The Guam Rehabilitation Act of 1963 has funded the territory's capital improvement program. Further allocations in 1969 and 1977 provided over $120 million for additional capital improvements and development of the island's power installations. More than $200 million of federal funds were authorized for typhoon relief in 1977/78.

Guam's trade usually shows large deficits. The bulk of Guam's trade is with the US, Micronesia, and Japan.

US income tax laws are applicable in Guam; all internal revenue taxes derived by the US from Guam are paid into the territory's treasury. US customs duties, however, are not levied. Guam is a duty-free port. In its trade with the US mainland, Guam is required to use US shipping.

Typical tropical diseases are practically unknown today in Guam. Tuberculosis, long the principal killer, was brought under control by the mid-1950s. The Guam Memorial Hospital has a capacity of 147 beds. Village dispensaries serve both as public health units and first-aid stations. In addition, there are a number of physicians in private practice. Specialists from the US Naval Hospital in Guam, assisting on a part-time basis, have made possible a complete program of curative medicine.

School attendance is compulsory from the age of 6 through 16. The yearly graduates from the islands' schools number over 1,000. The University of Guam and Guam Community College offer higher education courses of study.

HOWLAND, BAKER, AND JARVIS ISLANDS

Howland Island (0°48′N and 176°38′W), Baker Island (0°14′N and 176°28′W), and Jarvis Island (0°23′S and 160°1′W) are three small coral islands, each about 2.6 sq km (1 sq mi) in area, belonging to the Line Islands group of the Central Pacific Ocean. All are administered directly from Washington as US unincorporated territories. Howland was discovered in 1842 by US sailors, claimed by the US in 1857, and formally proclaimed a US territory in 1935–36. It was worked for guano by US and British companies until about 1890.

Baker, 64 km (40 mi) S of Howland, and Jarvis, 1,770 km (1,100 mi) E of Howland, also were claimed by the US in 1857, and their guano deposits were similarly worked by US and British enterprises. The UK annexed Jarvis in 1889. In 1935, the US sent colonists from Hawaii to all three islands, which were placed under the US Department of the Interior in 1936 and are administered as part of the National Wildlife Refuge system. Baker was captured by the Japanese in 1942 and recaptured by the US in 1944. The three islands lack fresh water and have no permanent inhabitants. They are visited annually by the US Coast Guard. A lighthouse on Howland Island is named in honor of the US aviatrix Amelia Earhart, who vanished en route to the island on a round-the-world flight in 1937.

JOHNSTON ATOLL

Johnston Atoll, located in the North Pacific 1,151 km (715 mi) SW of Honolulu, consists of two islands, Johnston (16°44′N and 169°31′W) and Sand (16°45′N and 169°30′W), with a total land and water area of about 2.6 sq km (1 sq mi). The islands are enclosed by a semicircular reef. It was discovered by English sailors in 1807 and claimed by the US in 1858. For many years, it was worked for guano and was a bird reservation. Commissioned as a naval station in 1941, it remains an unincorporated US territory under the control of the US Department of the Air Force. In recent years, it has been used primarily for the testing of nuclear weapons.

There are approximately 1,500 people living on the atoll. The atoll's population was composed entirely of government personnel and contractors.

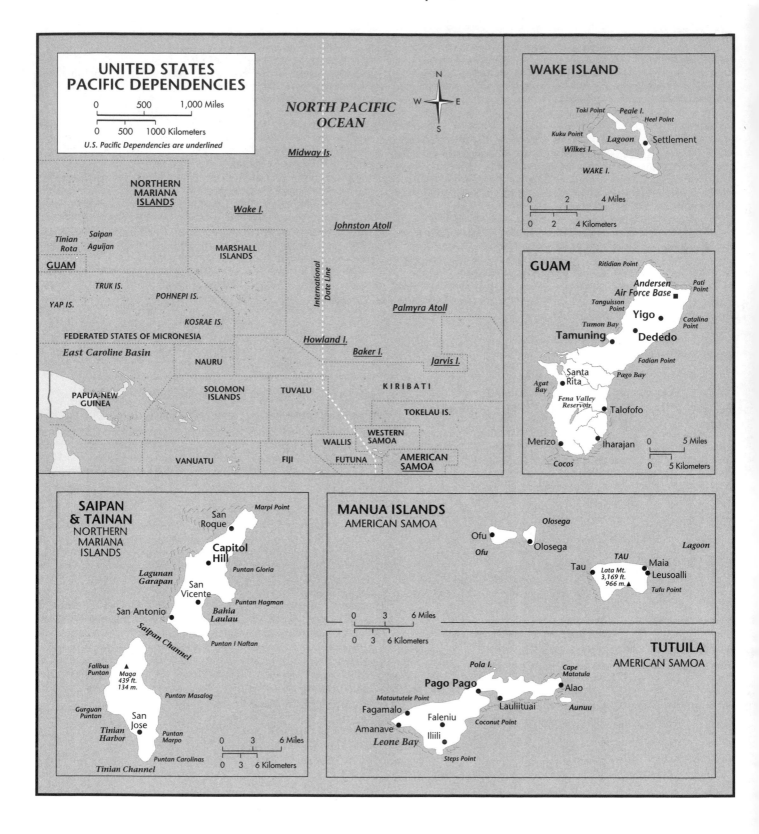

MIDWAY

The Midway Islands (28°12'–17'N and 177°19'–26'W) consist of an atoll and two small islets, Eastern Island (177°20'W) and Sand Island (177°22'–24'W), 2,100 km (1,300 mi) WNW of Honolulu. Total land and water area is 5 sq km (2 sq mi). Their population was 468 at the 1980 census, a decline from 2,220 in 1970 because of the cessation of US military involvement in Indochina. Fewer than 500 military personnel live on the base.

Discovered and claimed by the US in 1859 and formally annexed in 1867, Midway became a submarine cable station early in the 20th century and an airlines station in 1935. Made a US naval base in 1941, Midway was attacked by the Japanese in

December 1941 and January 1942. In one of the great battles of World War II, a Japanese naval attack on 3–6 June 1942 was repelled by US warplanes. There is a naval station at Midway, and the islands are important nesting places for seabirds. Midway is a US unincorporated territory under the administrative control of the US Department of the Navy.

NORTHERN MARIANAS

The Northern Marianas, a US commonwealth in the Western Pacific Ocean, is comprised of the Mariana Islands excluding Guam (a separate political entity). Located between 12° and 21°N and 144° and 146°E, it consists of 16 volcanic islands with a total land area of about 475 sq km (183.5 sq mi). Only six of the islands are inhabited, and most of the people live on the three largest islands—Rota, 85 sq km (33 sq mi); Saipan, 122 sq km (47 sq mi); and Tinian, 101 sq km (39 sq mi).

The climate is tropical, with relatively little seasonal change; temperatures average 21–29°C (70–85°F), and relative humidity is generally high. Rainfall averages 216 cm (85 in) per year. The southern islands, which include Rota, Saipan, and Tinian, are generally lower and covered with moderately heavy tropical vegetation. The northern islands are more rugged, reaching a high point of 959 m (3,146 ft) on Agrihan, and are generally barren due to erosion and insufficient rainfall. Insects are numerous and ocean birds and fauna are abundant.

The Northern Marianas had an estimated population of 47,168 in 1992. Three-fourths of the population is descended from the original Micronesian inhabitants, known as Chamorros. There are also many descendants of migrants from the Caroline Islands and smaller numbers of Filipino and Korean laborers and settlers from the US mainland. English is the official language and Chamorro and Carolinian are taught in school. About 90% of the people are Roman Catholic.

It is believed that the Marianas were settled by migrants from the Philippines and Indonesia. Excavations on Saipan have yielded evidence of settlement around 1500 BC. The first European to reach the Marianas, in 1521, was Ferdinand Magellan. The islands were ruled by Spain until the Spanish defeat by the US in the Spanish-American War (1898). Guam was then ceded to the US and the rest of the Marianas were sold to Germany. When World War I broke out, Japan took over the Northern Marianas and other German-held islands in the Western Pacific. These islands (the Northern Marianas, Carolines, and Marshalls) were placed under Japanese administration as a League of Nations mandate on 17 December 1920. Upon its withdrawal from the League in 1935, Japan began to fortify the islands, and in World War II they served as important military bases. Several of the islands were the scene of heavy fighting during the war. In the battle for control of Saipan in June 1944, some 23,000 Japanese and 3,500 US troops lost their lives in one day's fighting. As each island was occupied by US troops, it became subject to US authority in accordance with the international law of belligerent occupation. The US planes that dropped atomic bombs on Hiroshima and Nagasaki, bringing an end to the war, took off from Tinian.

On 18 July 1947, the Northern Mariana, Caroline, and Marshall islands formally became a UN trust territory under US administration. This Trust Territory of the Pacific Islands was administered by the US Department of the Navy until 1 July 1951, when administration was transferred to the Department of the Interior. From 1953 to 1962, the Northern Marianas, with the exception of Rota, were administered by the Department of the Navy.

The people of the Northern Marianas voted to become a US commonwealth by a majority of 78.8% in a plebescite held on 17 June 1975. A covenant approved by the US Congress in March 1976 provided for the separation of the Northern Marianas from the Caroline and Marshall island groups, and for the Marianas' transition to a commonwealth status similar to that of Puerto Rico. The islands became internally self-governing in January 1978. On 3 November 1986, US President Ronald Reagan proclaimed the Northern Marianas a self-governing commonwealth; its people became US citizens. The termination of the trusteeship had been approved by the UN Trusteeship Council in May 1986 but technically required approval from the UN Security Council. Approval from the council was latter obtained.

A governor and a lieutenant governor are popularly elected for four-year terms. The legislature consists of 9 senators elected for four-year terms and 14 representatives elected for two-year terms. A district court handles matters involving federal law and a commonwealth court has jurisdiction over local matters.

The traditional economic activities were subsistence agriculture, livestock raising, and fishing, but much agricultural land was destroyed or damaged during World War II and agriculture has never resumed its prewar importance. Today, government employment and tourism are the mainstays of the economy. Tourism has increased 7.5% over the last decade. The construction industry is also expanding, and there is some small-scale industry, chiefly handicrafts and food processing.

The Northern Marianas is heavily dependent on federal funds; the US government provided $228 million for capital developments, government operations, and special programs between 1986 and 1992. The US also pays to lease property on Saipan, Tinian, and Farallon de Medinilla islands for defense purposes. The principal exports are milk and meat; imports include foods, petroleum, construction materials, and vehicles. US currency is the official medium of exchange.

Health care is primarily the responsibility of the commonwealth government and has improved substantially since 1978. Tuberculosis, once the major health problem, has been controlled. There is a hospital on Saipan and health centers on Tinian and Rota. The largest hospital in the commonwealth is a 74 bed, 110,000 square foot facility.

Education is free and compulsory for children between the ages of 8 and 14, and literacy is high.

PALMYRA ATOLL

Palmyra, an atoll in the Central Pacific Ocean, containing some 50 islets with a total area of some 10 sq km (4 sq mi), is situated about 1,600 km (1,000 mi) ssw of Honolulu at 5°52′N and 162°5′w. It was discovered in 1802 by the USS *Palmyra* and formally annexed by the US in 1912, and was under the jurisdiction of the city of Honolulu until 1959, when Hawaii became the 50th state of the US. It is now the responsibility of the US Department of the Interior. The atoll is privately owned by the Fullard-Leo family of Hawaii.

Kingman Reef, NW of Palmyra Atoll at 6°25′N and 162°23′N, was discovered by the US in 1874, annexed by the US in 1922, and became a naval reservation in 1934. Now abandoned, it is under the control of the US Department of the Navy.

WAKE ISLAND

Wake Island, actually a coral atoll and three islets (Wake, Peale, and Wilkes) about 8 km (5 mi) long by 3.6 km (2.25 mi) wide, lies in the North Pacific 3,380 km (2,100 mi) w of Honolulu at 19°17′N and 166°35′E. The total land and water area is about 8 sq km (3 sq mi). Discovered by the British in 1796, Wake was long uninhabited.

In 1898, a US expeditionary force en route to Manila landed on the island. The US formally claimed Wake in 1899. It was made a US naval reservation in 1934 and became a civil aviation station in 1935. Captured by the Japanese on 23 December 1941, Wake was subsequently the target of several

US air raids. It was surrendered by the Japanese in September 1945 and has thereafter remained a US unincorporated territory under the jurisdiction, since 1972, of the Department of the Air Force.

Less than 200 US Air Force personnel and approximately 250 Thai contractors inhabit Wake Island. It is a stopover and fueling station for civilian and military aircraft flying between Honolulu, Guam, and Japan.

UNITED STATES OF AMERICA

CAPITAL: Washington, D.C. (District of Columbia). **FLAG:** The flag consists of 13 alternate stripes, 7 red and 6 white; these represent the 13 original colonies. Fifty 5-pointed white stars, representing the present number of states in the Union, are placed in 9 horizontal rows alternately of 6 and 5 against a blue field in the upper left corner of the flag. **OFFICIAL SEAL:** OBVERSE: An American eagle with outstretched wings bears a shield consisting of 13 alternating white and red stripes with a broad blue band across the top. The right talon clutches an olive branch, representing peace; in the left are 13 arrows, symbolizing military strength. The eagle's beak holds a banner with the motto *"E pluribus unum"* (From many, one); overhead is a constellation of 13 five-pointed stars in a glory. REVERSE: Above a truncated pyramid is an all-seeing eye within a triangle; at the bottom of this triangle appear the roman numerals MDCCLXXVI (1776). The pyramid stands on a grassy ground, against a backdrop of mountains. The words *"Annuit Coeptis"* (He has favored our undertakings) and, on a banner, *"Novus Ordo Seclorum"* (A new order of the ages) surround the whole. **ANTHEM:** *The Star-Spangled Banner.* **MOTTO:** In God We Trust. **MONETARY UNIT:** The dollar ($) of 100 cents is a paper currency with a floating rate. There are coins of 1, 5, 10, 25, and 50 cents and 1 dollar, and notes of 1, 2, 5, 10, 20, 50, and 100 dollars. Although issuance of higher notes ceased in 1969, a limited number of notes of 500, 1,000, 5,000, and 10,000 dollars remain in circulation. **WEIGHTS AND MEASURES:** The imperial system is in common use; however, the use of metrics in industry is increasing, and the metric system is taught in public schools throughout the US. Common avoirdupois units in use are the avoirdupois pound of 16 oz or 453.5924277 gm; the long ton of 2,240 lb or 35,840 oz; and the short ton, more commonly used, of 2,000 lb or 32,000 oz. (Unless otherwise indicated, all measures given in tons are in short tons.) Liquid measures: 1 gallon = 231 cu in = 4 quarts = 8 pints. Dry measures: 1 bushel = 4 pecks = 32 dry quarts = 64 dry pints. Linear measures: 1 ft = 12 in; 1 statute mi = 1,760 yd = 5,280 ft. Metric equivalent: 1 m = 39.37 in. **FEDERAL HOLIDAYS:** New Year's Day, 1 January; Birthday of Martin Luther King, Jr., 3d Monday in January; Lincoln's Birthday, 12 February (only in the northern and western states); Washington's Birthday, 3d Monday in February; Memorial or Decoration Day, last Monday in May; Independence Day, 4 July; Labor Day, 1st Monday in September; Columbus Day, 2d Monday in October; Election Day, 1st Tuesday after the 1st Monday in November; Veterans or Armistice Day, 11 November; Thanksgiving Day, 4th Thursday in November; Christmas, 25 December. **TIME:** Eastern, 7 AM = noon GMT; Central, 6 AM = noon GMT; Mountain, 5 AM = noon GMT; Pacific (includes the Alaska panhandle), 4 AM = noon GMT; Yukon, 3 AM = noon GMT; Alaska and Hawaii, 2 AM = noon GMT; western Alaska, 1 AM = noon GMT.

¹LOCATION, SIZE, AND EXTENT

Located in the Western Hemisphere on the continent of North America, the US is the fourth-largest country in the world. Its total area, including Alaska and Hawaii, is 9,372,607 sq km (3,618,773 sq mi). The conterminous US extends 4,662 km (2,897 mi) ENE–WSW and 4,583 km (2,848 mi) SSE–NNW. It is bordered on the N by Canada, on the E by the Atlantic Ocean, on the S by the Gulf of Mexico and Mexico, and on the W by the Pacific Ocean, with a total boundary length of 17,563 km (10,913 mi). Alaska, the 49th state, extends 3,639 km (2,261 mi) E–W and 2,185 km (1,358 mi) N–S. It is bounded on the N by the Arctic Ocean and Beaufort Sea, on the E by Canada, on the S by the Gulf of Alaska, Pacific Ocean and Bering Sea, and on the W by the Bering Sea, Bering Strait, Chukchi Sea, and Arctic Ocean, with a total boundary length of 13,161 km (8,178 mi). The 50th state, Hawaii, consists of islands in the Pacific Ocean extending 2,536 km (1,576 mi) N–S and 2,293 km (1,425 mi) E–W, with a general coastline of 1,207 km (750 mi).

²TOPOGRAPHY

Although the northern New England coast is rocky, along the rest of the eastern seaboard the Atlantic Coastal Plain rises gradually from the shoreline. Narrow in the north, the plain widens to about 320 km (200 mi) in the south and in Georgia merges with the Gulf Coastal Plain that borders the Gulf of Mexico and extends through Mexico as far as the Yucatán. West of the Atlantic Coastal Plain is the Piedmont Plateau, bounded by the Appalachian Mountains. The Appalachians, which extend from southwest Maine into central Alabama—with special names in some areas—are old mountains, largely eroded away, with rounded contours and forested, as a rule, to the top. Few of their summits rise much above 1,100 m (3,500 ft), although the highest, Mt. Mitchell in North Carolina, reaches 2,037 m (6,684 ft).

Between the Appalachians and the Rocky Mountains, more than 1,600 km (1,000 mi) to the west, lies the vast interior plain of the US. Running south through the center of this plain and draining almost two-thirds of the area of the continental US is the Mississippi River. Waters starting from the source of the Missouri, the longest of its tributaries, travel almost 6,450 km (4,000 mi) to the Gulf of Mexico. The eastern reaches of the great interior plain are bounded on the north by the Great Lakes, which are thought to contain about half the world's total supply of fresh water. Under US jurisdiction are 57,441 sq km (22,178 sq mi) of Lake Michigan, 54,696 sq km (21,118 sq mi) of Lake Superior, 23,245 sq km (8,975 sq mi) of Lake Huron, 12,955 sq km (5,002 sq mi) of Lake Erie, and 7,855 sq km (3,033 sq mi) of Lake Ontario. The five lakes are now accessible to oceangoing vessels from the Atlantic via the St. Lawrence Seaway. The basins of the Great Lakes were formed by the glacial ice cap that moved down over large parts of North America some 25,000 years ago. The glaciers also determined the direction of flow of the Missouri River and, it is believed, were responsible for carrying soil from what is now Canada down into the central agricultural basin of the US. The great interior plain consists of two major subregions: the fertile Central Plains, extending from the Appalachian highlands to a line drawn approximately 480 km (300 mi) west of the Mississippi, broken by the Ozark Plateau; and the more arid Great Plains, extending from that line to the foothills of the Rocky Mountains. Although they appear flat, the Great Plains rise gradually from about 460 m (1,500 ft) to more than 1,500 m (5,000 ft) at their western extremity.

The Continental Divide, the Atlantic-Pacific watershed, runs along the crest of the Rocky Mountains. The Rockies and the ranges to the west are parts of the great system of young, rugged mountains, shaped like a gigantic spinal column, that runs along western North, Central, and South America from Alaska to Tierra del Fuego, Chile. In the continental US, the series of western ranges, most of them paralleling the Pacific coast, are the Sierra Nevada, the Coast Ranges, the Cascade Range, and the Tehachapi and San Bernardino mountains. Between the Rockies and the Sierra Nevada–Cascade mountain barrier to the west lies the Great Basin, a group of vast arid plateaus containing most of the desert areas of the US, in the south eroded by deep canyons. The coastal plains along the Pacific are narrow, and in many places the mountains plunge directly into the sea. The most extensive lowland near the west coast is the Great Valley of California, lying between the Sierra Nevada and the Coast Ranges. There are 71 peaks in these western ranges of the continental US that rise to an altitude of 4,267 m (14,000 ft) or more, Mt. Whitney in California at 4,418 m (14,494 ft) being the highest. The greatest rivers of the Far West are the Colorado in the south, flowing into the Gulf of California, and the Columbia in the northwest, flowing to the Pacific. Each is more than 1,900 km (1,200 mi) long; both have been intensively developed to generate electric power, and both are important sources of irrigation.

Separated from the continental US by Canadian territory, the state of Alaska occupies the extreme northwest portion of the North American continent. A series of precipitous mountain ranges separates the heavily indented Pacific coast on the south from Alaska's broad central basin, through which the Yukon River flows from Canada in the east to the Bering Sea in the west. The central basin is bounded on the north by the Brooks Range, which slopes down gradually to the Arctic Ocean. The Alaskan Peninsula and the Aleutian Islands, sweeping west far out to sea, consist of a chain of volcanoes, many still active. The state of Hawaii consists of a group of Pacific islands formed by volcanoes rising sharply from the ocean floor. The highest of these volcanoes, Mauna Loa, at 4,168 m (13,675 ft), is located on the largest of the islands, Hawaii, and is still active.

The lowest point in the US is Death Valley in California, 86 m (282 ft) below sea level. At 6,194 m (20,320 ft), Mt. McKinley in Alaska is the highest peak in North America. These topographic extremes suggest the geological instability of the Pacific Coast region. Major earthquakes destroyed San Francisco in 1906 and Anchorage, Alaska, in 1964, and the San Andreas Fault in California still causes frequent earth tremors. Washington State's Mt. St. Helens erupted in 1980, spewing volcanic ash over much of the Northwest.

[3]CLIMATE

The eastern continental region is well watered, with annual rainfall generally in excess of 100 cm (40 in). It includes all of the Atlantic seaboard and southeastern states and extends west to cover Indiana, southern Illinois, most of Missouri, Arkansas, Louisiana, and easternmost Texas. The eastern seaboard is affected primarily by the masses of air moving from west to east across the continent rather than by air moving in from the Atlantic. Hence its climate is basically continental rather than maritime. The midwestern and Atlantic seaboard states experience hot summers and cold winters; spring and autumn are clearly defined periods of climatic transition. Only Florida, with the Gulf of Mexico lying to its west, experiences moderate differences between summer and winter temperatures. Mean annual temperatures vary considerably between north and south: Boston, 11°C (51°F); New York City, 13°C (55°F); Charlotte, N.C., 16°C (61°F); Miami, Fla., 24°C (76°F). The Gulf and South Atlantic states are often hit by severe tropical storms originating in the Caribbean in late summer and early autumn.

The prairie lands lying to the west constitute a subhumid region. Precipitation usually exceeds evaporation by only a small amount; hence the region experiences drought more often than excessive rainfall. Dryness generally increases from east to west. The average midwinter temperature in the extreme north—Minnesota and North Dakota—is about –13°C (9°F) or less,

Outlying Areas of the US[1]

NAME	AREA SQ MI	SQ KM	CAPITAL	YEAR OF ACQUISITION	POPULATION 1980	POPULATION 1992
Puerto Rico	3,515	9,104	San Juan	1898	3,196,520	3,797,082
Virgin Islands of the US	136	352	Charlotte Amalie	1917	96,569	101,809
Trust Territory of the Pacific Islands, of which:	713	1,847	Saipan	1947	132,929	62,943
Northern Marianas[2]	182	471	Saipan[3]	–	16,780	47,168
Republic of Palau[2]	191	495	Koror[3]	–	12,116	15,775
Other Pacific territories:						
American Samoa	77	199	Pago Pago	1899	32,297	51,115
Guam	209	541	Agaña	1898	105,979	142,271
Midway Islands	2	5	–	1867	468	453
Wake Island	3	8	–	1899	302	381

[1]Excludes minor and uninhabited islands.

[2]Although governed under separate constitutional arrangements by the mid–1980s, these territories formally remained part of the Trust Territory of the Pacific Islands pending action by the US Congress, the US president, and the UN Security Council.

[3]Centers of constitutional government. The entire Trust Territory of the Pacific Islands is administered from Saipan.

UNITED STATES

0   200   400 Miles

0   200   400 Kilometers

ALASKA

0   250   500 Miles

0   250   500 Kilometers

HAWAII

0   75   150 Miles

0   75   150 Kilometers

LOCATION: Conterminous US: 66°57′ to 124°44′w; 24°33′ to 49°23′n. Alaska: 130°w to 172°28′e; 51° to 71°23′n. Hawaii: 154°48′ to 178°22′w 18°55′ to 28°25′n.
BOUNDARY LENGTHS: Conterminous US: Canada, 6,416 km (3,987 mi); Atlantic Ocean, 3,330 km (2,069 mi); Gulf of Mexico coastline, 2,625 km (1,631 mi); Mexico, 3,111 km (1,933 mi); Pacific coastline, 2,081 km (1,293 mi). Alaska: Arctic Ocean coastline, 1,706 km (1,060 mi); Canada, 2,475 km (1,538 mi); Pacific coastline, including the Bering Sea and Strait and Chukchi coastlines, 8,980 km (5,580 mi). Hawaii: coastline, 1,207 km (750 mi).

while the average July temperature is 18°C (65°F). In the Texas prairie region to the south, January temperatures average 10–13°C (50–55°F) and July temperatures 27–29°C (80–85°F). Rainfall along the western border of the prairie region is as low as 46 cm (18 in) per year in the north and 64 cm (25 in) in the south. Precipitation is greatest in the early summer—a matter of great importance to agriculture, particularly in the growing of grain crops. In dry years, the prevailing winds may carry the topsoil eastward (particularly from the southern region) for hundreds of miles in clouds that obscure the sun.

The Great Plains constitute a semiarid climatic region. Rainfall in the southern plains averages about 50 cm (20 in) per year and in the northern plains about 25 cm (10 in), but extreme year-to-year variations are common. The tropical air masses that move northward across the plains originate on the fairly high plateaus of Mexico and contain little water vapor. Periods as long as 120 days without rain have been experienced in this region. The rains that do occur are often violent, and a third of the total annual rainfall may be recorded in a single day at certain weather stations. The contrast between summer and winter temperatures is extreme throughout the Great Plains. Maximum summer temperatures of over 43°C (110°F) have been recorded in the northern as well as in the southern plains. From the Texas panhandle north, blizzards are common in the winter, and tornadoes at other seasons. The average minimum temperature for January in Duluth, Minn., is –19°C (–3°F).

The higher reaches of the Rockies and the mountains paralleling the Pacific coast to the west are characterized by a typical alpine climate. Precipitation as a rule is heavier on the western slopes of the ranges. The great intermontane arid region of the West shows considerable climatic variation between its northern and southern portions. In New Mexico, Arizona, and southeastern California, the greatest precipitation occurs in July, August, and September, mean annual rainfall ranging from 8 cm (3 in) in Yuma, Ariz., to 76 cm (30 in) in the mountains of northern Arizona and New Mexico. Phoenix has a mean annual temperature of 22°C (71°F), rising to 33°C (92°F) in July and falling to 11°C (52°F) in January. North of the Utah-Arizona line, the summer months usually are very dry; maximum precipitation occurs in the winter and early spring. In the desert valleys west of Great Salt Lake, mean annual precipitation adds up to only 10 cm (4 in). Although the northern plateaus are generally arid, some of the mountainous areas of central Washington and Idaho receive at least 152 cm (60 in) of rain per year. Throughout the intermontane region, the uneven availability of water is the principal factor shaping the habitat.

The Pacific coast, separated by tall mountain barriers from the severe continental climate to the east, is a region of mild winters and moderately warm, dry summers. Its climate is basically maritime, the westerly winds from the Pacific Ocean moderating the extremes of both winter and summer temperatures. Los Angeles in the south has an average temperature of 13°C (56°F) in January and 21°C (69°F) in July; Seattle in the north has an average temperature of 4°C (39°F) in January and 18°C (65°F) in July. Precipitation in general increases along the coast from south to north, extremes ranging from an annual average of 4.52 cm (1.78 in) at Death Valley in California (the lowest in the US) to more than 356 cm (140 in) in Washington's Olympic Mountains.

Climatic conditions vary considerably in the vastness of Alaska. In the fogbound Aleutians and in the coastal panhandle strip that extends southeastward along the Gulf of Alaska and includes the capital, Juneau, a relatively moderate maritime climate prevails. The interior is characterized by short, hot summers and long, bitterly cold winters, and in the region bordering the Arctic Ocean a polar climate prevails, the soil hundreds of feet below the surface remaining frozen the year round. Although snowy in winter, continental Alaska is relatively dry.

Hawaii has a remarkably mild and stable climate with only slight seasonal variations in temperature, as a result of northeast ocean winds. The mean January temperature in Honolulu is 23°C (73°F); the mean July temperature 27°C (80°F). Rainfall is moderate—about 71 cm (28 in) per year—but much greater in the mountains; Mt. Waialeale on Kauai has a mean annual rainfall of 1,168 cm (460 in), highest in the world.

The lowest temperature recorded in the US was –62°C (–79.8°F) at Prospect Creek Camp, Alaska, on 23 January 1971; the highest, 57°C (134°F) at Greenland Ranch, in Death Valley,

Calif., on 10 July 1913. The record annual rainfall is 1,878 cm (739 in) recorded at Kukui, Maui in 1982; the previous record for a one-year period was 1,468 cm (578 in) recorded at Fuu Kukui, Maui, in 1950; for a 24-hour period, 98.3 cm (38.7 in) at Yankeetown, Fla., on 5–6 September 1950; in 1 hour, 30 cm (12 in), at Holt, Mo., on 22 June 1947, and on Kauai, Hawaii, on 24–25 January 1956.

[4]FLORA AND FAUNA

About 29% of the US (including Alaska and Hawaii) was forestland, 26% was grassland pasture, 20% was arable cropland, 2% was irrigated land, and the remaining 25% encompassed military, urban, and designated recreational and wilderness areas, among other lands.

At least 7,000 species and subspecies of indigenous US flora have been categorized. The eastern forests contain a mixture of softwoods and hardwoods that includes pine, oak, maple, spruce, beech, birch, hemlock, walnut, gum, and hickory. The central hardwood forest, which originally stretched unbroken from Cape Cod to Texas and northwest to Minnesota—still an important timber source—supports oak, hickory, ash, maple, and walnut. Pine, hickory, tupelo, pecan, gum, birch, and sycamore are found in the southern forest that stretches along the Gulf coast into the eastern half of Texas. The Pacific forest is the most spectacular of all because of its enormous redwoods and Douglas firs. In the southwest are saguaro (giant cactus), yucca, candlewood, and the Joshua tree.

The central grasslands lie in the interior of the continent, where the moisture is not sufficient to support the growth of large forests. The tall grassland or prairie (now almost entirely under cultivation) lies to the east of the 100th meridian. To the west of this line, where rainfall is frequently less than 50 cm (20 in) per year, is the short grassland. Mesquite grass covers parts of west Texas, southern New Mexico, and Arizona. Short grass may be found in the highlands of the latter two states, while tall grass covers large portions of the coastal regions of Texas and Louisiana and occurs in some parts of Mississippi, Alabama, and Florida. The Pacific grassland includes northern Idaho, the higher plateaus of eastern Washington and Oregon, and the mountain valleys of California.

The intermontane region of the Western Cordillera is for the most part covered with desert shrubs. Sagebrush predominates in the northern part of this area, creosote in the southern, and saltbrush near the Great Salt Lake and in Death Valley.

The lower slopes of the mountains running up to the coastline of Alaska are covered with coniferous forests as far north as the Seward Peninsula. The central part of the Yukon Basin is also a region of softwood forests. The rest of Alaska is heath or tundra. Hawaii has extensive forests of bamboo and ferns. Sugarcane and pineapple, although not native to the islands, now cover a large portion of the cultivated land.

Small trees and shrubs common to most of the US include hackberry, hawthorn, serviceberry, blackberry, wild cherry, dogwood, and snowberry. Wildflowers bloom in all areas, from the seldom-seen blossoms of rare desert cacti to the hardiest alpine species. Wildflowers include forget-me-not, fringed and closed gentians, jack-in-the-pulpit, black-eyed Susan, columbine, and common dandelion, along with numerous varieties of aster, orchid, lady's slipper, and wild rose.

An estimated 1,500 species and subspecies of mammals characterize the animal life of the continental US. Among the larger game animals are the white-tailed deer, moose, pronghorn antelope, bighorn sheep, mountain goat, black bear, and grizzly bear. The Alaskan brown bear often reaches a weight of 540–630 kg (1,200–1,400 lbs). Some 25 important furbearers are common, including the muskrat, red and gray foxes, mink, raccoon, beaver, opossum, striped skunk, woodchuck, common cottontail, snowshoe hare, and various squirrels. Human encroachment has transformed the mammalian habitat over the last two centuries. The American buffalo (bison), millions of which once roamed the plains, is now found only on select reserves. Other mammals, such as the elk and gray wolf, have been restricted to much smaller ranges.

Year-round and migratory birds abound. Loons, wild ducks, and wild geese are found in lake country; terns, gulls, sandpipers, herons, and other seabirds live along the coasts. Wrens, thrushes, owls, hummingbirds, sparrows, woodpeckers, swallows, chickadees, vireos, warblers, and finches appear in profusion, along with the robin, common crow, cardinal, Baltimore oriole, eastern

State Areas, Entry Dates, and Populations

| | TOTAL AREA | | | | ORDER OF | | | POPULATION | |
	SQ MI	SQ KM	RANK	CAPITAL	ENTRY	DATE OF ENTRY	AT ENTRY†	CENSUS 1980	CENSUS 1990
Alabama	51,705	133,916	19	Montgomery	22	14 December 1819	127,901	3,894,025	4,040,587
Alaska	591,004	1,530,699	1	Juneau	49	3 January 1959	226,167	401,851	550,043
Arizona	114,000	295,260	6	Phoenix	48	14 February 1912	204,354	2,716,598	3,665,228
Arkansas	53,187	137,754	27	Little Rock	25	15 June 1836	57,574	2,286,357	2,350,725
California	158,706	411,048	3	Sacramento	31	9 September 1850	92,597	23,667,764	29,760,021
Colorado	104,091	269,595	8	Denver	38	1 August 1876	39,864	2,889,735	3,294,394
Connecticut*	5,018	12,997	48	Hartford	5	9 January 1788	237,946	3,107,564	3,287,116
Delaware*	2,044	5,294	49	Dover	1	7 December 1787	59,096	594,338	666,168
Florida	58,664	151,940	22	Tallahassee	27	3 March 1845	87,445	9,746,961	12,937,926
Georgia*	58,910	152,577	21	Atlanta	4	2 January 1788	82,548	5,462,982	6,478,316
Hawaii	6,471	16,760	47	Honolulu	50	21 August 1959	632,772	964,691	1,108,229
Idaho	83,564	216,431	13	Boise	43	3 July 1890	88,548	944,127	1,006,749
Illinois	56,345	145,933	24	Springfield	21	3 December 1818	55,211	11,427,409	11,430,602
Indiana	36,185	93,719	38	Indianapolis	19	11 December 1816	147,178	5,490,212	5,544,159
Iowa	56,275	145,752	25	Des Moines	29	28 December 1846	192,214	2,913,808	2,776,755
Kansas	82,277	213,097	14	Topeka	34	29 January 1861	107,206	2,364,236	2,477,574
Kentucky	40,409	104,659	37	Frankfort	15	1 June 1792	73,677	3,660,324	3,685,296
Louisiana	47,752	123,678	31	Baton Rouge	18	30 April 1812	76,556	4,206,116	4,219,973
Maine	33,265	86,156	39	Augusta	23	15 March 1820	298,335	1,125,043	1,227,928
Maryland*	10,460	27,091	42	Annapolis	7	28 April 1788	319,728	4,216,933	4,781,468
Massachusetts*	8,284	21,456	45	Boston	6	6 February 1788	378,787	5,737,093	6,016,425
Michigan	58,527	151,585	23	Lansing	26	26 January 1837	212,267	9,262,044	9,295,297
Minnesota	84,402	218,601	12	St. Paul	32	11 May 1858	172,023	4,075,970	4,375,099
Mississippi	47,689	123,514	32	Jackson	20	10 December 1817	75,448	2,520,770	2,573,216
Missouri	69,697	180,515	19	Jefferson City	24	10 August 1821	66,586	4,916,762	5,117,073
Montana	147,046	380,849	4	Helena	41	8 November 1889	142,924	786,690	799,065
Nebraska	77,355	200,349	15	Lincoln	37	1 March 1867	122,993	1,569,825	1,578,385
Nevada	110,561	286,353	7	Carson City	36	31 October 1864	42,491	800,508	1,201,833
New Hampshire*	9,279	24,033	44	Concord	9	21 June 1788	141,885	920,610	1,109,252
New Jersey*	7,787	20,168	46	Trenton	3	18 December 1787	184,139	7,365,011	7,730,188
New Mexico	121,593	314,926	5	Santa Fe	47	6 January 1912	327,301	1,303,302	1,515,069
New York*	49,108	127,190	30	Albany	11	26 July 1788	340,120	17,558,165	17,990,455
North Carolina*	52,669	136,413	28	Raleigh	12	21 November 1789	393,751	5,880,415	6,628,637
North Dakota	70,702	183,118	17	Bismarck	39	2 November 1889	190,983	652,717	638,800
Ohio	41,330	107,045	35	Columbus	17	1 March 1803††	43,365	10,797,603	10,847,115
Oklahoma	69,956	181,186	18	Oklahoma City	46	16 November 1907	657,155	3,025,487	3,145,585
Oregon	97,073	251,419	10	Salem	33	14 February 1859	52,465	2,633,156	2,842,321
Pennsylvania*	45,308	117,348	33	Harrisburg	2	12 December 1787	434,373	11,864,720	11,003,464
Rhode Island*	1,212	3,139	50	Providence	13	29 May 1790	68,825	947,154	1,003,464
South Carolina*	31,113	80,583	40	Columbia	8	23 May 1788	393,751	3,120,730	3,486,703
South Dakota	77,116	199,730	16	Pierre	40	2 November 1889	348,600	690,768	696,004
Tennessee	42,144	109,153	34	Nashville	16	1 June 1796	35,691	4,591,023	4,877,185
Texas	266,807	691,030	2	Austin	28	29 December 1845	212,592	14,225,513	16,986,510
Utah	84,899	219,888	11	Salt Lake City	45	4 January 1896	276,749	1,461,037	1,722,850
Vermont	9,614	24,900	43	Montpelier	14	4 March 1791	85,425	511,456	562,758
Virginia*	40,767	105,586	36	Richmond	10	25 June 1788	747,610	5,346,797	6,187,358
Washington	68,139	176,480	20	Olympia	42	11 November 1889	357,232	4,132,353	4,866,692
West Virginia	24,231	62,758	41	Charleston	35	20 June 1863	442,014	1,950,186	1,793,477
Wisconsin	56,153	145,436	26	Madison	30	29 May 1848	305,391	4,705,642	4,891,769
Wyoming	97,809	253,325	9	Cheyenne	44	10 July 1890	62,555	469,557	453,588

†Census closest to entry date.
††Date fixed in 1953 by congressional resolution.
*One of original 13 colonies.

and western meadowlarks, and various blackbirds. Wild turkey, ruffed grouse, and ring-necked pheasant (introduced from Europe) are popular game birds.

Lakes, rivers, and streams teem with trout, bass, perch, muskellunge, carp, catfish, and pike; sea bass, cod, snapper, and flounder are abundant along the coasts, along with such shellfish as lobster, shrimp, clams, oysters, and mussels. Garter, pine, and milk snakes are found in most regions. Four poisonous snakes survive, of which the rattlesnake is the most common. Alligators appear in southern waterways, and the Gila monster makes its home in the Southwest.

Numerous laws and lists designed to protect threatened and endangered flora and fauna are in force in the US. Generally, each species listed as protected by the federal government is also protected by the states, but some states may list species not included on federal lists or on the lists of neighboring states. (Conversely, a species threatened throughout most of the US may be abundant in one or two states.) As of June 1996, the US Fish and Wildlife Service listed 751 endangered US species, including 64 mammals, 90 birds, 105 fish, and 432 plants; and 209 threatened species, including 94 plants. The agency listed another 522 endangered and 43 threatened foreign species by international agreement.

Endangered plants (and number of species) included: aster, 32; cactus, 19; pea, 18; mustard, 14; mint, 12; mallow, 11; bellflower and pink family, 9 each; snapdragon, 8; and buckwheat, 6. Threatened species, likely to become endangered if recent trends continue, include such plants as Rydberg milk-vetch, northern wild monkshood, Lee pincushion cactus, and Lloyd's Mariposa cactus. Among the endangered floral species (in imminent danger of extinction in the wild) are the Virginia round-leaf birch, San Clemente Island broom, Texas wild-rice, Furbish lousewort, Truckee barberry, Sneed pincushion cactus, spineless hedgehog cactus, Knowlton cactus, persistent trillium, dwarf bear-poppy, and small whorled pogonia.

Threatened fauna include the grizzly bear, southern sea otter, Newell's shearwater, American alligator, eastern indigo snake, bayou darter, several southwestern trout species, and Bahama and Schaus swallowtail butterflies. Among endangered fauna are the Indiana bat, key deer, black-footed ferret, northern swift fox, San Joaquin kit fox, jaguar, jaguarundi, Florida manatee, ocelot, Florida panther, Utah prairie dog, Sonoran pronghorn, Delmarva Peninsula fox squirrel, gray wolf (except in Minnesota, where it is threatened), red wolf, numerous whale species, bald eagle (endangered in most states, but only threatened in the Northwest and the Great Lakes region), Hawaii creeper, Everglade kite, brown pelican, California clapper rail, red-cockaded woodpecker, blunt-nosed leopard lizard, American crocodile, desert slender salamander, Houston toad, humpback chub, several species of pupfish, 17 US species of pearly mussel, Socorro isopod, Kentucky cave shrimp, and mission blue butterfly. Several species on the federal list of endangered and threatened wildlife and plants are found only in Hawaii.

5ENVIRONMENTAL PROTECTION

During the 1960s and 1970s, numerous laws and lists designed to protect the environment and to preserve endangered flora and fauna were adopted throughout the US. The Environmental Protection Agency (EPA), created in 1970, is an independent body with primary regulatory responsibility in the fields of air and noise pollution, water and waste management, and control of toxic substances. Other federal agencies with environmental responsibilities are the Forest Service and Soil Conservation Service within the Department of Agriculture, the Fish and Wildlife Service and the National Park Service within the Department of the Interior, the Department of Energy, and the Nuclear Regulatory Commission. In addition to the 1969 legislation, landmark

federal laws protecting the environment include the Clean Air Act Amendments of 1970 and 1990, controlling automobile and electric utility emissions; the Water Pollution Act of 1972, setting clean-water criteria for fishing and swimming; and the Endangered Species Act of 1973, protecting wildlife near extinction. A measure enacted in December 1980 established a $1.6-billion "Superfund," financed largely by excise taxes on chemical companies, to clean up toxic waste dumps such as the one in the Love Canal district of Niagara Falls, N.Y. In 1995, there were 1,270 hazardous waste sites on the Superfund's national priority list.

In 1997, the expenditure estimate for the Environmental Protection Agency was $6.5 billion. In 1995, the EPA employed 17,500 workers. The environmental industry in the US employed 1.3 million workers and generated $180 billion in revenues in 1995.

The most influential environmental lobbies include the Sierra Club (founded in 1892; 550,000 members in 1995) and its legal arm, the Sierra Club Legal Defense Fund. Large conservation groups include the National Wildlife Federation (1936; 4,400,000), the National Audubon Society (1905; 600,000), and the Nature Conservancy (1917; 705,000). Greenpeace USA (founded in 1979) has gained international attention by seeking to disrupt hunts for whales and seals.

Among the environmental movement's most notable successes have been the inauguration (and mandating in some states) of recycling programs; the banning in the US of the insecticide dichlorodiphenyltrichloroethane (DDT); the successful fight against construction of a supersonic transport (SST); and the protection of more than 40 million hectares (100 million acres) of Alaska lands (after a fruitless fight to halt construction of the trans-Alaska pipeline); and the gradual elimination of chlorofluorocarbon (CFC) production by 2000.

Outstanding problems include acid rain (precipitation contaminated by fossil fuel wastes); inadequate facilities for solid waste disposal; air pollution from industrial emissions (the US leads the world in carbon dioxide emissions from the burning of fossil fuels); the contamination of homes by radon, a radioactive gas that is produced by the decay of underground deposits of radium and can cause cancer; runoffs of agricultural pesticides, pollutants deadly to fishing streams and very difficult to regulate; continued dumping of raw or partially treated sewage from major cities into US waterways; falling water tables in many western states; the decrease in arable land because of depletion, erosion, and urbanization; the need for reclamation of strip-mined lands and for regulation of present and future strip mining; and the expansion of the US nuclear industry in the absence of a fully satisfactory technique for the handling and permanent disposal of radioactive wastes.

6POPULATION

According to census figures for 1990, the population of the US (including the 50 states and Washington, D.C.) was 248,718,301 (up from 226,542,199 in 1980), of whom 51.3% were female and 48.7% male. At the time of the first federal census, in 1790, the population of the country was 3,929,214. Between 1800 and 1850, the population almost quadrupled; between 1850 and 1900, it tripled; and between 1900 and 1950, it almost doubled. During the 1960s and 1970s, however, the growth rate slowed steadily, declining from 2.9% annually in 1960 to 2% in 1969 and to less than 1% in the 1980s. The population was estimated at 263,064,000 in mid-1995. In 1995, 7.5% of the population were under 5 years of age; 18.7% were 5 to 17; 61% were 18 to 64; and 12.7% were 65 or older. The median age of the population increased from 16.7 years in 1820 to 22.9 years in 1900 and to 34.3 years in 1995. The US Bureau of the Census projected a population of 274,634,000 for the year 2000.

By 1994, metropolitan areas had a total population of 207.6

million, representing a 4.9% increase over 1990. Suburbs have absorbed most of the shift in population distribution since 1950. In 1994 there were 8 cities with more than 1 million population: New York, 7,333,000; Los Angeles, 3,449,000; Chicago, 2,732,000; Houston, 1,702,000; Philadelphia, 1,524,000; San Diego, 1,152,000; Phoenix, 1,049,000; and Dallas, 1,023,000.

7ETHNIC GROUPS

The majority of the population of the US is of European origin, with the largest groups having primary ancestry traceable in 1990 to the UK (31,391,758), Germany (45,583,922), and Ireland (22,721,252); many Americans reported multiple ancestries. Major racial and national minority groups include blacks (either of US or Caribbean parentage), Chinese, Filipinos, Japanese, Mexicans, and other Spanish-speaking peoples of the Americas. Whites comprised 83.9% of the US population in 1990; blacks, 12.3%; Asians and Pacific Islanders, 3%; Native Americans (Amerindians—more commonly known as Indians, Eskimos, and Aleuts), 0.8%. Responding to a census question that cut across racial lines, 9% of Americans in 1990 described themselves as of Hispanic origin. Inequality in social and economic opportunities for ethnic minorities became a key public issue in the post–World War II period.

Some Indian societies survived warfare with land-hungry white settlers and retained their tribal cultures. Their survival, however, has been on the fringes of North American society, especially as a result of the implementation of a national policy of resettling Indian tribes on reservations. In 1890, according to the official census count, there were 248,253 Indians; in 1940, 333,909; and in 1990, 1,959,234 (including also Eskimos and Aleuts). Groups of Indians are found most numerously in the southwestern states of Oklahoma, Arizona, New Mexico, and California. The 1960s and 1970s saw successful court fights by Indians in Alaska, Maine, South Dakota, and other states to regain tribal lands or to receive cash settlements for lands taken from them in violation of treaties during the 1800s.

The black population in 1992 was estimated at 31,439,000. Some 53% of blacks still resided in the South in 1990, the region that absorbed most of the slaves brought from Africa in the 18th and 19th centuries. Two important regional migrations of blacks have taken place: (1) a "Great Migration" to the North, commencing in 1915, and (2) a small but then unprecedented westward movement beginning about 1940. Both migrations were fostered by wartime demands for labor and by postwar job opportunities in northern and western urban centers. More than three out of four black Americans live in metropolitan areas, constituting, as of 1990, 81% of the population of Gary, Ind., 66% of Washington, D.C., 67% of Atlanta, 76% of Detroit, 62% of New Orleans, 59% of Newark, N.J., and 59% of Baltimore; in New York City, which had the largest number of black residents (2,102,512), 28.7% of the population was black. Large-scale federal programs to ensure equality for blacks in voting rights, public education, employment, and housing were initiated after the historic 1954 Supreme Court ruling that barred racial segregation in public schools. By 1966, however, in the midst of growing and increasingly violent expressions of dissatisfaction by black residents of northern cities and southern rural areas, the federal Civil Rights Commission reported that integration programs were lagging. Throughout the 1960s, 1970s, and 1980s, the unemployment rate among nonwhites in the US was at least double that for whites, and school integration proceeded slowly, especially outside the South.

Included in the population of the US in 1992 were 8,364,000 persons whose lineage can be traced to Asian and Pacific nationalities, chiefly Chinese, Filipino, Japanese, Indian, Korean, and Vietnamese. The Chinese population is highly urbanized and concentrated particularly in cities of over 100,000 population,

mostly on the West Coast and in New York City. The Japanese population has risen steadily from a level of 72,157 in 1910. Hawaii has been the most popular magnet of Japanese emigration; the Japanese population of Hawaii accounted in 1990 for 23.6% of the state's residents and 31% of the nation's total number of Japanese. Most Japanese in California were farmers until the outbreak of World War II, when they were interned and deprived of their landholdings; after the war, most entered the professions and other urban occupations.

Mexican settlement is largely in the Southwest. Spanish-speaking Puerto Ricans, who often represent an amalgam of racial strains, have largely settled in the New York metropolitan area, where they partake in considerable measure of the hardships and problems experienced by other immigrant groups in the process of settling in the US. Since 1959, many Cubans have settled in Florida and other eastern states. As of 1992 there were 24,268,000 Hispanic Americans, of whom 60% were of Mexican ancestry, 12% Puerto Rican, and 5% Cuban.

8LANGUAGES

The primary language of the US is English, enriched by words borrowed from the languages of Indians and immigrants, predominantly European.

When European settlement began, Indians living north of Mexico spoke about 300 different languages now held to belong to 58 different language families. Only 2 such families have contributed noticeably to the American vocabulary: Algonkian in the Northeast and Aztec-Tanoan in the Southwest. From Algonkian languages, directly or sometimes through Canadian French, English has taken such words as *moose, skunk, caribou, opossum, woodchuck,* and *raccoon* for New World animals; *hickory, squash,* and *tamarack* for New World flora; and *succotash, hominy, mackinaw, moccasin, tomahawk, toboggan,* and *totem* for various cultural items. From Nahuatl, the language of the Aztecs, terms such as *tomato, mesquite, coyote, chili, tamale, chocolate,* and *ocelot* have entered English, largely by way of Spanish. A bare handful of words come from other Indian language groups, such as *tepee* from Dakota Siouan, *catalpa* from Creek, *sequoia* from Cherokee, *hogan* from Navaho, and *sockeye* from Salish, as well as *cayuse* from Chinook.

Professional dialect research, initiated in Germany in 1878 and in France in 1902, did not begin in the US until 1931, in connection with the *Linguistic Atlas of New England* (1939–43). This kind of research, requiring trained field-workers to interview representative informants in their homes, subsequently was extended to the entire Atlantic Coast, the north-central states, the upper Midwest, the Pacific Coast, the Gulf states, and Oklahoma. As of 1985, only the New England atlas, the *Linguistic Atlas of the Upper Midwest* (1973–76), and the first two fascicles of the *Linguistic Atlas of the Middle and South Atlantic States* (1980) had been published, along with three volumes based on Atlantic Coast field materials; nearing publication were atlases of the north-central states, the Gulf states, and Oklahoma. In other areas, individual dialect researchers have produced more specialized studies. The definitive work on dialect speech, the American Dialect Society's monumental *Dictionary of American Regional English,* began publication in 1985.

Dialect studies confirm that standard English is not uniform throughout the country. Major regional variations reflect patterns of colonial settlement, dialect features from England having dominated particular areas along the Atlantic Coast and then spread westward along the three main migration routes through the Appalachian system. Dialectologists recognize three main dialects—Northern, Midland, and Southern—each with subdivisions related to the effect of mountain ranges and rivers and railroads on population movement.

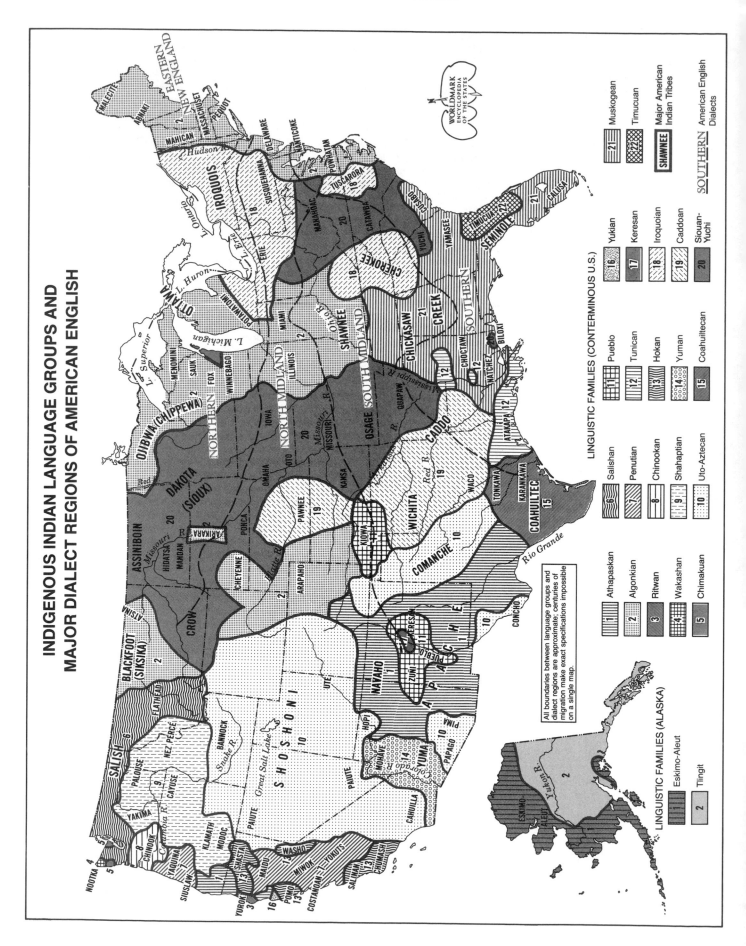

INDIGENOUS INDIAN LANGUAGE GROUPS AND
MAJOR DIALECT REGIONS OF AMERICAN ENGLISH

The Northern dialect is that of New England and its derivative settlements in New York; the northern parts of Ohio, Indiana, Illinois, and Iowa; and Michigan, Wisconsin, northeastern South Dakota, and North Dakota. A major subdivision is that of New England east of the Connecticut River, an area noted typically by the loss of /r/ after a vowel, and by the pronunciation of *can't, dance, half,* and *bath* with a vowel more like that in *father* than that in *fat.* Generally, however, Northern speech has a strong /r/ after a vowel, the same vowel in *can't* and *cat,* a conspicuous contrast between *cot* and *caught,* the /s/ sound in *greasy, creek* rhyming with *pick,* and *with* ending with the same consonant sound as at the end of *breath.*

Midland speech extends in a wide band across the US: there are two main subdivisions, North Midland and South Midland. North Midland speech extends westward from New Jersey, Delaware, and Pennsylvania into Ohio, Illinois, southern Iowa, and northern Missouri. Its speakers generally end *with* the consonant sound that begins the word *thin,* pronounce *cot* and *caught* alike, and say *cow* and *down* as /caow/ and daown/. South Midland speech was carried by the Scotch–Irish from Pennsylvania down the Shenandoah Valley into the southern Appalachians, where it acquired many Southern speech features before it spread westward into Kentucky, Tennessee, southern Missouri, Arkansas, and northeast Texas. Its speakers are likely to say *plum peach* rather than *clingstone peach* and *snake doctor* rather than *dragonfly.*

Southern speech typically, though not always, lacks the consonant /r/ after a vowel, lengthens the first part of the diphthong in *write* so that to Northern ears it sounds almost like *rat,* and diphthongizes the vowels in *bed* and *hit* so that they sound like /beuhd/ and /hiuht/. *Horse* and *hoarse* do not sound alike, and *creek* rhymes with *meek. Corn bread* is *corn pone,* and *you-all* is standard for the plural.

In the western part of the US, migration routes so crossed and intermingled that no neat dialect boundaries can be drawn, although there are a few rather clear population pockets.

The 1990 census recorded that of 229,875,493 Americans 5 years of age or over, 198,101,862 spoke only English at home; the remaining 31,773,631 spoke a language other than English. The principal foreign languages and their speakers were as follows:

Spanish	17,310,043	Greek	387,359
French	1,920,621	Arabic	353,203
German	1,544,793	Various Native North American	331,634
Chinese	1,316,956	Russian	241,092
Italian	1,307,068	Yiddish	212,951
Tagalog	841,827	Various Scandinavian	198,261
Polish	723,161	Various Southern Slavic	170,301
Korean	625,814	Hungarian	147,621
Indic	553,882	Other Indo–European	576,196
Vietnamese	506,500	Other Slavic	270,609
Portuguese	429,440	Other West Germanic	232,075
Japanese	426,876		

The majority of Spanish speakers live in the Southwest, Florida, and eastern urban centers. Refugee immigration since the 1950s has greatly increased the number of foreign-language speakers from Latin America and Asia.

Very early English borrowed from neighboring French speakers such words as *shivaree, butte, levee,* and *prairie;* from German, *sauerkraut, smearcase,* and *cranberry;* from Dutch, *stoop, spook,* and *cookie;* and from Spanish, *tornado, corral, ranch,* and *canyon.* From various West African languages, blacks have given English *jazz, voodoo,* and *okra.*

Educational problems raised by the presence of large blocs of non-English speakers led to the passage in 1976 of the Bilingual Educational Act, enabling children to study basic courses in their first language while they learn English. A related school problem is that of black English, a Southern dialect variant that is the vernacular of many black students now in the north and elsewhere.

9 RELIGIONS

US religious traditions are predominantly Judeo-Christian, and most Americans identify themselves as Protestants (of various denominations), Roman Catholics, or Jews. As of 1995, 163 million Americans, about 63% of the total population, reported affiliation with a religious group. The largest Christian denomination is the Roman Catholic Church, with 1995 membership estimated at 59.9 million in 19,787 local congregations with some 50,000 clergy. Immigration from Ireland, Italy, Eastern Europe, French Canada, and the Caribbean accounts for the predominance of Roman Catholicism in the Northeast, Northwest, and some parts of the Great Lakes region, while Hispanic traditions and more recent immigration from Mexico and other Latin American countries account for the historical importance of Roman Catholicism in California and throughout most of the sunbelt. More than any other US religious body, the Roman Catholic Church maintains an extensive network of parochial schools.

Jewish immigrants settled first in the Northeast, where the largest Jewish population remain; in 1992, nearly 6 million Jews (or 3.7% of those reporting religious affiliation in the US) were affiliated with over 3,400 local congregation served by 6,500 clergy.

As of 1992, 94,612,579 persons in the US reported affiliation with a Protestant denomination. Baptists predominate below the Mason-Dixon line and west to Texas. By far the nation's largest Protestant group, the Southern Baptist Convention had 15,398,642 adherents in 1992; the American Baptist Churches in the USA claimed some 1,516,503 adherents. A concentration of Methodist groups extends westward in a band from Delaware to eastern Colorado; the largest of these groups, the United Methodist Church, had 8,646,595 adherents in 1992. Lutheran denominations, reflecting in part the patterns of German and Scandinavian settlement, are most highly concentrated in the north-central states, especially Minnesota and the Dakotas. Two Lutheran synods, the Lutheran Church in America and the American Lutheran Church, merged in 1987 to form the Evangelical Lutheran Church in America, with 5,212,785 adherents in 1992. In June 1983, the two major Presbyterian churches, the northern-based United Presbyterian Church in the USA and the southern-based Presbyterian Church in the US, formally merged as the Presbyterian Church (USA), ending a division that began with the Civil War. In 1992, this group reported 3,796,766 adherents. Other Protestant denominations and their estimated adherents in 1992 were the Episcopal Church 2,504,683; Churches of Christ 1,651,103; and the United Church of Christ, 1,530,178. One Christian group, the Church of Latter-day Saints (Mormon), which claimed 4,672,850 members in 1992, was organized in New York in 1830 and, since migrating westward has played a leading role in Utah's political, economic, and religious life. Notable during the 1970s and early 1980s was a rise in the fundamentalist, evangelical, and Pentecostal movements. In 1992, Pentecostal churches reported 10,281,559 adherents, representing over 6% of the population reporting religious affiliation.

Several million Muslims followers of various Asian religious, a multiplicity of small Protestant groups, and a sizable number of cults also participate in US religious life.

10 TRANSPORTATION

Railroads have lost not only the largest share of intercity freight traffic, their chief source of revenue, but passenger traffic as well. Despite an attempt to revive passenger transport through the development of a national network (Amtrak) in the 1970s, the rail sector has continued to experience heavy losses and declining revenues. In 1994 there were 13 Class I rail companies in the US, with a total of 190,000 employees and operating revenues of $30.8 billion. In 1993, Amtrak carried 21.8 million passengers.

The most conspicuous form of transportation is the automobile, and the extent and quality of the US road-transport system are without parallel in the world. Over 200 million vehicles—a record number—were registered in 1995, including more than 134.9 million passenger cars and some 65.4 million commercial vehicles. In 1992, there were some 4.4 million motorcycles registered as well. In 1995, auto manufacturers in the US produced 6.3 million passenger cars and 5.6 million trucks and buses. Motor vehicle imports and exports in 1995 amounted to 4.7 million and 1.2 million, respectively. Canada accounted for 44% of the imports and 54% of the exports in 1995. In 1995, 31% of the world's motor vehicles were registered in the US, down from 36% in 1985.

The US has a vast network of public roads, whose total length as of 1993 was 6,284,488 km (3,904,992 mi). Of that total, 80% was rural. About 83% was paved, including 85,267 km (52,982 mi) of expressways. During the 1970s, about $10 billion was spent annually on highway construction. By the late 1970s, new highway construction had slowed, and an increasing share of highway funds was allocated to the improvement of existing roads.

Major ocean ports or port areas are New York, the Delaware River areas (Philadelphia), the Chesapeake Bay area (Baltimore, Norfolk, Newport News), New Orleans, Houston, and the San Francisco Bay area. The inland port of Duluth on Lake Superior handles more freight than all but the top-ranking ocean ports. The importance of this port, along with those of Chicago and Detroit, was enhanced with the opening in 1959 of the St. Lawrence Seaway. Waterborne freight consists primarily of bulk commodities such as petroleum and its products, coal and coke, iron ore and steel, sand, gravel and stone, grains, and lumber. The US merchant marine industry has been decreasing gradually since the 1950s. In 1996, the US had the 11th-largest registered merchant shipping fleet in the world (by GRT), with 309 privately-owned vessels of more than 1,000 gross registered tons with a combined GRT of 10,376. The total US merchant fleet, including government-owned vessels, was 502 ships (with a total of 13,118,000 GRT).

In 1995, the US had 26 international scheduled airlines. Revenue passengers carried by the airlines in 1940 totaled 2.7 million; by 1995, the figure was 527 million. The US in 1992 had 17,846 airports, of which 5,545 were public. US domestic and international carriers performed some 853,389 million passenger-km (530,270 million passenger-mi) of service in 1995, along with 19,615 million freight ton-km (12,188 million freight ton-mi). At the end of1994, the US had 630,188 active pilots with private licenses and 417,016 with commercial licenses, including 117,434 licensed for airline transport. An estimated 170,600 general aviation aircraft flew a total of 22,300,000 hours in 1994.

11HISTORY

The first Americans—distant ancestors of the American Indians—probably crossed the Bering Strait from Asia at least 12,000 years ago. By the time Christopher Columbus came to the New World in 1492 there were probably no more than 2 million Native Americans living in the land that was to become the US.

Following exploration of the American coasts by English, Portuguese, Spanish, Dutch, and French sea captains from the late 15th century onward, European settlements sprang up in the latter part of the 16th century. The Spanish established the first permanent settlement at St. Augustine in the future state of Florida in 1565, and another in New Mexico in 1599. During the early 17th century, the English founded Jamestown in Virginia Colony (1607) and Plymouth Colony in present-day Massachusetts (1620). The Dutch established settlements at Ft. Orange (now Albany, N.Y.) in 1624, New Amsterdam (now New York City) in 1626, and at Bergen (now part of Jersey City, N.J.) in 1660; they conquered New Sweden—the Swedish colony in Delaware and New Jersey—in 1655. Nine years later, however, the English seized this New Netherland Colony and subsequently monopolized settlement of the East Coast except for Florida, where Spanish rule prevailed until 1821. In the Southwest, California, Arizona, New Mexico, and Texas also were part of the Spanish empire until the 19th century. Meanwhile, in the Great Lakes area south of present-day Canada, France set up a few trading posts and settlements but never established effective control; New Orleans was one of the few areas of the US where France pursued an active colonial policy.

From the founding of Jamestown to the outbreak of the American Revolution more than 150 years later, the British government administered its American colonies within the context of mercantilism: the colonies existed primarily for the economic benefit of the empire. Great Britain valued its American colonies especially for their tobacco, lumber, indigo, rice, furs, fish, grain, and naval stores, relying particularly in the southern colonies on black slave labor.

The colonies enjoyed a large measure of internal self-government until the end of the French and Indian War (1745–63), which resulted in the loss of French Canada to the British. To prevent further troubles with the Indians, the British government in 1763 prohibited the American colonists from settling beyond the Appalachian Mountains. Heavy debts forced London to decree that the colonists should assume the costs of their own defense, and the British government enacted a series of revenue measures to provide funds for that purpose. But soon, the colonists began to insist that they could be taxed "only with their consent," and the struggle grew to become one of local versus imperial authority.

Widening cultural and intellectual differences also served to divide the colonies and the mother country. Life on the edge of the civilized world had brought about changes in the colonists' attitudes and outlook, emphasizing their remoteness from English life. In view of the long tradition of virtual self-government in the colonies, strict enforcement of imperial regulations and British efforts to curtail the power of colonial legislatures presaged inevitable conflict between the colonies and the mother country. When citizens of Massachusetts, protesting the tax on tea, dumped a shipload of tea belonging to the East India Company into Boston harbor in 1773, the British felt compelled to act in defense of their authority as well as in defense of private property. Punitive measures—referred to as the Intolerable Acts by the colonists—struck at the foundations of self-government.

In response, the First Continental Congress, composed of delegates from 12 of the 13 colonies—Georgia was not represented—met in Philadelphia in September 1774, and proposed a general boycott of English goods, together with the organizing of a militia. British troops marched to Concord, Mass., on 19 April 1775 and destroyed the supplies that the colonists had assembled there. American "minutemen" assembled on the nearby Lexington green and fired "the shot heard round the world," although no one knows who actually fired the first shot that morning. The British soldiers withdrew and fought their way back to Boston.

Voices in favor of conciliation were raised in the Second Continental Congress that assembled in Philadelphia on 10 May 1775, this time including Georgia; but with news of the Restraining Act (30 March 1775), which denied the colonies the right to trade with countries outside the British Empire, all hopes for peace vanished. George Washington was appointed commander in chief

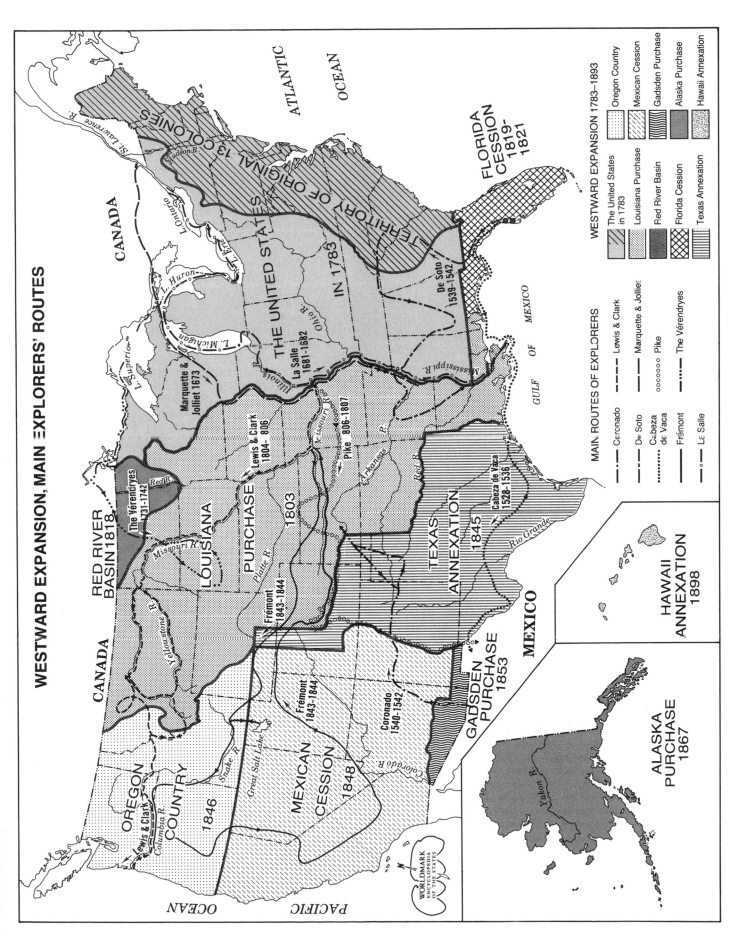

WESTWARD EXPANSION, MAIN EXPLORERS' ROUTES

WESTWARD EXPANSION 1783–1893

- The United States in 1783
- Oregon Country
- Louisiana Purchase
- Mexican Cession
- Red River Basin
- Gadsden Purchase
- Florida Cession
- Alaska Purchase
- Texas Annexation
- Hawaii Annexation

MAIN ROUTES OF EXPLORERS

- Coronado
- Lewis & Clark
- De Soto
- Marquette & Jolliet
- Cabeza de Vaca
- Pike
- Frémont
- The Vérendryes
- La Salle

CANADA

ATLANTIC OCEAN

TERRITORY OF ORIGINAL 13 COLONIES

FLORIDA CESSION 1819–1821

THE UNITED STATES IN 1783

De Soto 1539–1542

La Salle 1681–1682

Marquette & Jolliet 1673

L. Superior
L. Michigan
L. Huron
L. Ontario
L. Erie
Hudson R.
St. Lawrence R.
Ohio R.
Illinois R.

GULF OF MEXICO

Mississippi R.

Lewis & Clark 1804–1806

Pike 1806–1807

LOUISIANA PURCHASE 1803

RED RIVER BASIN 1818

The Vérendryes 1731–1742

Red R.

Missouri R.
Yellowstone R.
Platte R.

Frémont 1843–1844

Cabeza de Vaca 1528–1536

TEXAS ANNEXATION 1845

Arkansas R.
Red R.

Rio Grande

MEXICO

GADSDEN PURCHASE 1853

OREGON COUNTRY 1846

Lewis & Clark
Columbia R.
Snake R.
Great Salt Lake

MEXICAN CESSION 1848

Frémont 1843–1844

Coronado 1540–1542

Colorado R.

PACIFIC OCEAN

WORLDMARK ENCYCLOPEDIA OF THE STATES

HAWAII ANNEXATION 1898

ALASKA PURCHASE 1867

Yukon R.

of the new American army, and on 4 July 1776, the 13 American colonies adopted the Declaration of Independence, justifying the right of revolution by the theory of natural rights.

British and American forces met in their first organized encounter near Boston on 17 June 1775. Numerous battles up and down the coast followed. The British seized and held the principal cities but were unable to inflict a decisive defeat on Washington's troops. The entry of France into the war on the American side eventually tipped the balance. On 19 October 1781, the British commander, Cornwallis, cut off from reinforcements by the French fleet on one side and besieged by French and American forces on the other, surrendered his army at Yorktown, Va. American independence was acknowledged by the British in a treaty of peace signed in Paris on 3 September 1783.

The first constitution uniting the 13 original states—the Articles of Confederation—reflected all the suspicions that Americans entertained about a strong central government. Congress was denied power to raise taxes or regulate commerce, and many of the powers it was authorized to exercise required the approval of a minimum of nine states. Dissatisfaction with the Articles of Confederation was aggravated by the hardships of a postwar depression, and in 1787—the same year that Congress passed the Northwest Ordinance, providing for the organization of new territories and states on the frontier—a convention assembled in Philadelphia to revise the articles. The convention adopted an altogether new constitution, the present Constitution of the United States, which greatly increased the powers of the central government at the expense of the states. This document was ratified by the states with the understanding that it would be amended to include a bill of rights guaranteeing certain fundamental freedoms. These freedoms—including the rights of free speech, press, and assembly, freedom from unreasonable search and seizure, and the right to a speedy and public trial by an impartial jury—are assured by the first 10 amendments to the constitution, adopted on 5 December 1791; the constitution did however recognize slavery, and did not provide for universal suffrage. On 30 April 1789 George Washington was inaugurated as the first president of the US.

During Washington's administration, the credit of the new nation was bolstered by acts providing for a revenue tariff and an excise tax; opposition to the excise on whiskey sparked the Whiskey Rebellion, suppressed on Washington's orders in 1794. Alexander Hamilton's proposals for funding the domestic and foreign debt and permitting the national government to assume the debts of the states were also implemented. Hamilton, the secretary of the treasury, also created the first national bank, and was the founder of the Federalist Party. Opposition to the bank as well as to the rest of the Hamiltonian program, which tended to favor northeastern commercial and business interests, led to the formation of an anti-Federalist party, the Democratic-Republicans, led by Thomas Jefferson.

The Federalist Party, to which Washington belonged, regarded the French Revolution as a threat to security and property; the Democratic-Republicans, while condemning the violence of the revolutionists, hailed the overthrow of the French monarchy as a blow to tyranny. The split of the nation's leadership into rival camps was the first manifestation of the two-party system, which has since been the dominant characteristic of the US political scene. (Jefferson's party should not be confused with the modern Republican Party, formed in 1854.)

The 1800 election brought the defeat of Federalist President John Adams, Washington's successor, by Jefferson; a key factor in Adam's loss was the unpopularity of the Alien and Sedition Acts (1798), Federalist-sponsored measures that had abridged certain freedoms guaranteed in the Bill of Rights. In 1803, Jefferson achieved the purchase from France of the Louisiana Territory, including all the present territory of the US west of the Missis-

sippi drained by that river and its tributaries; exploration and mapping of the new territory, notably through the expeditions of Meriwether Lewis and William Clark, began almost immediately. Under Chief Justice John Marshall, the US Supreme Court, in the landmark case of *Marbury v. Madison,* established the principle of federal supremacy in conflicts with the states and enunciated the doctrine of judicial review.

During Jefferson's second term in office, the US became involved in a protracted struggle between Britain and Napoleonic France. Seizures of US ships and the impressment of US seamen by the British navy led the administration to pass the Embargo Act of 1807, under which no US ships were to put out to sea. After the act was repealed in 1809, ship seizures and impressment of seamen by the British continued, and were the ostensible reasons for the declaration of war on Britain in 1812 during the administration of James Madison. An underlying cause of the War of 1812, however, was land-hungry westerners' coveting of southern Canada as potential US territory.

The war was largely a standoff. A few surprising US naval victories countered British successes on land. The Treaty of Ghent (24 December 1814), which ended the war, made no mention of impressment and provided for no territorial changes. The occasion for further maritime conflict with Britain, however, disappeared with the defeat of Napoleon in 1815.

Now the nation became occupied primarily with domestic problems and westward expansion. Because the US had been cut off from its normal sources of manufactured goods in Great Britain during the war, textiles and other industries developed and prospered in New England. To protect these infant industries, Congress adopted a high-tariff policy in 1816.

Three events of the late 1810s and the 1820s were of considerable importance for the future of the country. The federal government in 1817 began a policy of forcibly resettling the Indians, already decimated by war and disease, in what later became known as Indian Territory (now Oklahoma); those Indians not forced to move were restricted to reservations. The Missouri Compromise (1820) was an attempt to find a nationally acceptable solution to the volatile dispute over the extension of black slavery to new territories. It provided for admission of Missouri into the Union as a slave state but banned slavery in territories to the west that lay north of 36°30′. As a result of the establishment of independent Latin American republics and threats by France and Spain to reestablish colonial rule, President James Monroe in 1923 asserted that the Western Hemisphere was closed to further colonization by European powers. The Monroe Doctrine declared that any effort by such powers to recover territories whose independence the US had recognized would be regarded as an unfriendly act.

From the 1820s to the outbreak of the Civil War, the growth of manufacturing continued, mainly in the North, and was accelerated by inventions and technological advances. Farming expanded with westward migration. The South discovered that its future lay in the cultivation of cotton. The cotton gin, invented by Eli Whitney in 1793, greatly simplified the problems of production; the growth of the textile industry in New England and Great Britain assured a firm market for cotton. Hence, during the first half of the 19th century, the South remained a fundamentally agrarian society based increasingly on a one-crop economy. Large numbers of field hands were required for cotton cultivation, and black slavery became solidly entrenched in the southern economy.

The construction of roads and canals paralleled the country's growth and economic expansion. The successful completion of the Erie Canal (1825), linking the Great Lakes with the Atlantic, ushered in a canal-building boom. Railroad building began in earnest in the 1830s, and by 1840, about 3,300 mi (5,300 km) of track had been laid. The development of the telegraph a few years later gave the nation the beginnings of a modern telecommunications network. As a result of the establishment of the factory system, a laboring class appeared in the North by the 1830s, bringing with it the earliest unionization efforts.

Western states admitted into the Union following the War of 1812 provided for free white male suffrage without property qualifications and helped spark a democratic revolution. As eastern states began to broaden the franchise, mass appeal became an important requisite for political candidates. The election to the presidency in 1928 of Andrew Jackson, a military hero and Indian fighter from Tennessee, was no doubt a result of this widening of the democratic process. By this time, the US consisted of 24 states and had a population of nearly 13 million.

The relentless westward thrust of the US population ultimately involved the US in foreign conflict. In 1836, US settlers in Texas revolted against Mexican rule and established an independent republic. Texas was admitted to the Union as a state in 1845, and relations between Mexico and the US steadily worsened. A dispute arose over the southern boundary of Texas, and a Mexican attack on a US patrol in May 1846 gave President James K. Polk a pretext to declare war. After a rapid advance, US forces captured Mexico City, and on 2 February 1848, Mexico formally gave up the unequal fight by signing the Treaty of Guadalupe Hidalgo, providing for the cession of California and the territory of New Mexico to the US. With the Gadsden Purchase of 1853, the US acquired from Mexico for $10 million large strips of land forming the balance of southern Arizona and New Mexico. A dispute with Britain over the Oregon Territory was settled in 1846 by a treaty that established the 49th parallel as the boundary with Canada. Thenceforth the US was to be a Pacific as well as an Atlantic power.

Westward expansion exacerbated the issue of slavery in the territories. By 1840, abolition of slavery constituted a fundamental aspect of a movement for moral reform, which also encompassed woman's rights, universal education, alleviation of working class hardships, and temperance. In 1849, a year after the discovery of gold had precipitated a rush of new settlers to California, that territory (whose constitution prohibited slavery) demanded admission to the Union. A compromise engineered in Congress by Senator Henry Clay in 1850 provided for California's admission as a free state in return for various concessions to the South. But enmities dividing North and South could not be silenced. The issue of slavery in the territories came to a head with the Kansas-Nebraska Act of 1854, which repealed the Missouri Compromise and left the question of slavery in those territories to be decided by the settlers themselves. The ensuing conflicts in Kansas between northern and southern settlers earned the territory the name "bleeding Kansas." in 1860, the Democratic Party, split along northern and southern lines, offered two presidential candidates. The new Republican Party, organized in 1854 and opposed to the expansion of slavery, nominated Abraham Lincoln. Owing to the defection in Democratic ranks, Lincoln was able to carry the election in the electoral college, although he did not obtain a majority of the popular vote. To ardent supporters of slavery, Lincoln's election provided a reason for immediate secession. Between December 1860 and February 1861, the seven states of the Deep South— South Carolina, Mississippi, Florida, Alabama, Georgia, Louisiana, and Texas—withdrew from the Union and formed a separate government, known as the Confederate States of America, under the presidency of Jefferson Davis. The secessionists soon began to confiscate federal property in the South. On 12 April 1861, the Confederates opened fire on Ft. Sumter in the harbor of Charleston, S.C., and thus precipitated the US Civil War. Following the outbreak of hostilities, Arkansas, North Carolina, Virginia, and Tennessee joined the Confederacy.

For the next four years, war raged between the Confederate and Union forces, largely in southern territories. An estimated 360,000 men in the Union forces died of various causes, including 110,000 killed in battle. Confederate dead were estimated at 250,000, including 94,000 killed in battle. The North, with great superiority in manpower and resources, finally prevailed. A Confederate invasion of the North was repulsed at the battle of Gettysburg, Pa. in July 1863; a Union army took Atlanta in September 1864; and Confederate forces evacuated Richmond, the Confederate capital, in early April 1865. With much of the South in Union hands, Confederate Gen. Robert E. Lee surrendered to Gen. Ulysses S. Grant at Appomattox Courthouse in Virginia on 9 April.

The outcome of the war brought great changes in US life. Lincoln's Emancipation Proclamation of 1863 was the initial step in freeing some 4 million black slaves; their liberation was completed soon after the war's end by amendments to the Constitution. Lincoln's plan for the reconstruction of the rebellious states was compassionate, but only five days after Lee's surrender, Lincoln was assassinated by John Wilkes Booth as part of a conspiracy in which US Secretary of State William H. Seward was seriously wounded.

During the Reconstruction era (1865–77), the defeated South was governed by Union Army commanders, and the resultant bitterness of southerners toward northern Republican rule, which enfranchised blacks, persisted for years afterward. Vice President Andrew Johnson, who succeeded Lincoln as president, tried to carry out Lincoln's conciliatory policies but was opposed by radical Republican leaders in Congress, who demanded harsher treatment of the South. On the pretext that he had failed to carry out an act of Congress, the House of Representatives voted to impeach Johnson in 1868, but the Senate failed by one vote to convict him and remove him from office. It was during Johnson's presidency that Secretary of State Seward negotiated the purchase of Alaska (which attained statehood in 1959) from Russia for $7.2 million.

The efforts of southern whites to regain political control of their states led to the formation of terrorist organizations like the Ku Klux Klan, which employed violence to prevent blacks from voting. By the end of the Reconstruction era, whites had reestablished their political domination over blacks in the southern states and had begun to enforce patterns of segregation in education and social organization that were to last for nearly a century.

In many southern states, the decades following the Civil War were ones of economic devastation, in which rural whites as well as blacks were reduced to sharecropper status. Outside the South, however, a great period of economic expansion began. Transcontinental railroads were constructed, corporate enterprise spurted ahead, and the remaining western frontier lands were rapidly occupied and settled. The age of big business tycoons dawned. As heavy manufacturing developed, Pittsburgh, Chicago, and New York emerged as the nation's great industrial centers. The Knights of Labor, founded in 1869, engaged in numerous strikes, and violent conflicts between strikers and strikebreakers were common. The American Federation of Labor, founded in 1886, established a nationwide system of craft unionism that remained dominant for many decades. During this period, too, the woman's rights movement organized actively to secure the vote (although woman's suffrage was not enacted nationally until 1920), and groups outraged by the depletion of forests and wildlife in the West pressed for the conservation of natural resources.

During the latter half of the 19th century, the acceleration of westward expansion made room for millions of immigrants from Europe. The country's population grew to more than 76 million by 1900. As homesteaders, prospectors, and other settlers tamed the frontier, the federal government forced Indians west of the

Mississippi to cede vast tracts of land to the whites, precipitating a series of wars with various tribes. By 1890, only 250,000 Indians remained in the US, virtually all of them residing on reservations.

The 1890s marked the closing of the US frontier for settlement and the beginning of US overseas expansion. By 1892, Hawaiian sugar planters of US origin had become strong enough to bring about the downfall of the native queen and to establish a republic, which in 1898, at its own request, was annexed as a territory by the US. The sympathies of the US with the Cuban nationalists who were battling for independence from Spain were aroused by a lurid press and by expansionist elements. A series of events climaxed by the sinking of the USS *Maine* in Havana harbor finally forced a reluctant President William McKinley to declare war on Spain on 25 April 1898. US forces overwhelmed those of Spain in Cuba, and as a result of the Spanish-American War, the US added to its territories the Philippines, Guam, and Puerto Rico. A newly independent Cuba was drawn into the US orbit as a virtual protectorate through the 1950s. Many eminent citizens saw these new departures into imperialism as a betrayal of the time-honored US doctrine of government by the consent of the governed.

With the marked expansion of big business came increasing protests against the oppressive policies of large corporations and their dominant role in the public life of the nation. A demand emerged for strict control of monopolistic business practice through the enforcement of antitrust laws. Two US presidents, Theodore Roosevelt (1901–9), a Republican and Woodrow Wilson (1913–21), a Democrat, approved of the general movement for reform, which came to be called progressivism. Roosevelt developed a considerable reputation as a trustbuster, while Wilson's program, known as the New Freedom, called for reform of tariffs, business procedures, and banking. During Roosevelt's first term, the US leased the Panama Canal Zone and started construction of a 42-mi (68-km) canal, completed in 1914.

US involvement in World War I marked the country's active emergence as one of the great powers of the world. When war broke out in 1914 between Germany, Austria-Hungary, and Turkey on one side and Britain, France, and Russia on the other, sentiment in the US was strongly opposed to participation in the conflict, although a large segment of the American people sympathized with the British and the French. While both sides violated US maritime rights on the high seas, the Germans, enmeshed in a British blockade, resorted to unrestricted submarine warfare. On 6 April 1917, congress declared war on Germany. Through a national draft of all able-bodied men between the ages of 18 and 45, some 4 million US soldiers were trained, of whom more than 2 million were sent overseas to France. By late 1917, when US troops began to take part in the fighting on the western front, the European armies were approaching exhaustion, and US intervention may well have been decisive in ensuring the eventual victory of the Allies. In a series of great battles in which US soldiers took an increasingly major part, the German forces were rolled back in the west, and in the autumn of 1918 were compelled to sue for peace. Fighting ended with the armistice of 11 November 1918. President Wilson played an active role in drawing up the 1919 Versailles peace treaty, which embodied his dream of establishing a League of Nations to preserve the peace, but the isolationist bloc in the Senate was able to prevent US ratification of the treaty.

In the 1920s, the US had little enthusiasm left for crusades, either for democracy abroad or for reform at home; a rare instance of idealism in action was the Kellogg-Briand Pact (1928), an antiwar accord negotiated on behalf of the US by Secretary of State Frank B. Kellogg. In general, however, the philosophy of the Republican administrations from 1921 to 1933 was expressed in the aphorism "The business of America is business," and the 1920s saw a great business boom. The years 1923–24 also witnessed the unraveling of the Teapot Dome scandal: the revelation that President Warren G. Harding's secretary of the interior, Albert B. Fall, had secretly leased federal oil reserves in California and Wyoming to private oil companies in return for gifts and loans.

The great stock market crash of October 1929 ushered in the most serious and most prolonged economic depression the country had ever known. By 1933, an estimated 12 million men and women were out of work; personal savings were wiped out on a vast scale through a disastrous series of corporate bankruptcies and bank failures. Relief for the unemployed was left to private charities and local governments, which were incapable of handling the enormous task.

The inauguration of the successful Democratic presidential candidate, Franklin D. Roosevelt, in March 1933 ushered in a new era of US history, in which the federal government was to assume a much more prominent role in the nation's economic affairs. Proposing to give the country a "New Deal," Roosevelt accepted national responsibility for alleviating the hardships of unemployment; relief measures were instituted, work projects were established, the deficit spending was accepted in preference to ignoring public distress. The federal Social Security program was inaugurated, as were various measures designed to stimulate and develop the economy through federal intervention. Unions were strengthened through the National Labor Relations Act, which established the right of employees' organizations to bargain collectively with employers. Union membership increased rapidly, and the dominance of the American Federation of Labor was challenged by the newly formed Congress of Industrial Organizations, which organized workers along industrial lines.

The depression of the 1930s was worldwide, and certain nations attempted to counter economic stagnation by building large military establishments and embarking on foreign adventures. Following German, Italian, and Japanese aggression, World War II broke out in Europe during September 1939. In 1940, Roosevelt, disregarding a tradition dating back to Washington that no president should serve more than two terms, ran again for reelection. He easily defeated his Republican opponent, Wendell Willkie, who, along with Roosevelt, advocated increased rearmament and all possible aid to victims of aggression. The US was brought actively into the war by the Japanese attack on the Pearl Harbor naval base in Hawaii on 7 December 1941. The forces of Germany, Italy, and Japan were now arrayed over a vast theater of war against those of the US and the British Commonwealth; in Europe, Germany was locked in a bloody struggle with the Soviet Union. US forces waged war across the vast expanses of the Pacific, in Africa, in Asia, and in Europe. Italy surrendered in 1943; Germany was successfully invaded in 1944 and conquered in May 1945; and after the US dropped the world's first atomic bombs on Hiroshima and Nagasaki, the Japanese capitulated in August. The Philippines became an independent republic soon after the war, but the US retained most of its other Pacific possessions, with Hawaii becoming the 50th state in 1959.

Roosevelt, who had been elected to a fourth term in 1944, died in April 1945 and was succeeded by Harry S Truman, his vice president. Under the Truman administration, the US became an active member of the new world organization, the United Nations. The Truman administration embarked on large-scale programs of military aid and economic support to check the expansion of communism. Aid to Greece and Turkey in 1948 and the Marshall Plan, a program designed to accelerate the economic recovery of Western Europe, were outstanding features of US postwar foreign policy. The North Atlantic Treaty (1949) established a defensive alliance among a number of West European nations and the US. Truman's Point Four program gave technical and scientific aid to developing nations. When, following the North Korean attack on South Korea on 25 June 1950, the UN Security Council resolved that members of the UN should proceed to the aid of South Korea. US naval, air, and ground forces were immediately dispatched by President Truman. An undeclared war ensued, which eventually was brought to a halt by an armistice signed on 27 June 1953.

In 1952, Dwight D. Eisenhower, supreme commander of Allied forces in Europe during World War II, was elected president on the Republican ticket, thereby bringing to an end 20 years of Democratic presidential leadership. In foreign affairs, the Eisenhower administration continued the Truman policy of containing the USSR and threatened "massive retaliation" in the event of Soviet aggression, thus heightening the Cold War between the world's two great nuclear powers. Although Republican domestic policies were more conservative than those of the Democrats, the Eisenhower administration extended certain major social and economic programs of the Roosevelt and Truman administrations, notably Social Security and public housing. The early years of the Eisenhower administration were marked by agitation (arising in 1950) over charges of Communist and other allegedly subversive activities in the US—a phenomenon known as McCarthyism, after Republican Senator Joseph R. McCarthy of Wisconsin, who aroused much controversy with unsubstantiated allegations that Communists had penetrated the US government, especially the Army and the Department of State. Even those who personally opposed McCarthy lent their support to the imposition of loyalty oaths and the blacklisting of persons with left-wing backgrounds.

A major event of the Eisenhower years was the US Supreme Court's decision in *Brown v. Board of Education of Topeka* (1954) outlawing segregation of whites and blacks in public schools. In the aftermath of this ruling, desegregation proceeded slowly and painfully. In the early 1960s, sit-ins, "freedom rides," and similar expressions of nonviolent resistance by blacks and their sympathizers led to a lessening of segregation practices in public facilities. Under Chief Justice Earl Warren, the high court in 1962 mandated the reapportionment of state and federal legislative districts according to a "one person, one vote" formula. It also broadly extended the rights of defendants in criminal trials to include the provision of a defense lawyer at public expense for an accused person unable to afford one, and established the duty of police to advise an accused person of his or her legal rights immediately upon arrest.

In the early 1960s, during the administration of Eisenhower's Democratic successor, John F. Kennedy, the Cold War heated up as Cuba, under the regime of Fidel Castro, aligned itself with the Soviet Union. Attempts by anti-Communist Cuban exiles to invade their homeland in the spring of 1961 failed despite US aid. In October 1962, President Kennedy successfully forced a showdown with the Soviet Union over Cuba in demanding the withdrawal of Soviet-supplied "offensive weapons"—missiles—from the nearby island. On 22 November 1963, President Kennedy was assassinated while riding in a motorcade through Dallas, Texas; hours later, Vice President Lyndon B. Johnson was inaugurated president. In the November 1964 elections, Johnson overwhelmingly defeated his Republican opponent, Barry M. Goldwater, and embarked on a vigorous program of social legislation unprecedented since Roosevelt's New Deal. His "Great Society" program sought to ensure black Americans' rights in voting and public housing, to give the underprivileged job training, and to provide persons 65 and over with hospitalization and other medical benefits (Medicare). Measures ensuring equal opportunity for minority groups may have contributed to the growth of the woman's rights movement in the late 1960s. This same period also saw the growth of a powerful environmental protection movement.

US military and economic aid to anti-Communist forces in Viet-Nam, which had its beginnings during the Truman administration (while Viet-Nam was still part of French Indochina) and was increased gradually by presidents Eisenhower and Kennedy, escalated in 1965. In that year, President Johnson sent US combat troops to South Viet-Nam and ordered US bombing raids on North Viet-Nam, after Congress (in the Gulf of Tonkin Resolution of 1964) had given him practically carte blanche authority to wage war in that region. By the end of 1968, American forces in Viet-Nam numbered 536,100 men, but US military might was unable to defeat the Vietnamese guerrillas, and the American people were badly split over continuing the undeclared (and, some thought, ill-advised or even immoral) war, with its high price in casualties and materiel. Reacting to widespread dissatisfaction with his Viet-Nam policies, Johnson withdrew in March 1968 from the upcoming presidential race, and in November, Republican Richard M. Nixon, who had been the vice president under Eisenhower, was elected president. Thus, the Johnson years—which had begun with the new hopes of a Great Society but had soured with a rising tide of racial violence in US cities and the assassinations of civil rights leader Martin Luther King, Jr., and US Senator Robert F. Kennedy, among others—drew to a close.

President Nixon gradually withdrew US ground troops from Viet-Nam but expanded aerial bombardment throughout Indochina, and the increasingly unpopular and costly war continued for four more years before a cease-fire—negotiated by Nixon's national security adviser, Henry Kissinger—was finally signed on 27 January 1973 and the last US soldiers were withdrawn. The most protracted conflict in American history had resulted in 46,163 US combat deaths and 303,654 wounded soldiers, and had cost the US government $112 billion in military allocations. Two years later, the South Vietnamese army collapsed, and the North Vietnamese Communist regime united the country.

In 1972, during the last year of his first administration, Nixon initiated the normalization of relations—ruptured in 1949—with the People's Republic of China and signed a strategic arms limitation agreement with the Soviet Union as part of a Nixon-Kissinger policy of pursuing détente with both major Communist powers. (Earlier, in July 1969, American technology had achieved a national triumph by landing the first astronaut on the moon.) The Nixon administration sought to muster a "silent majority" in support of its Indochina policies and its conservative social outlook in domestic affairs. The most momentous domestic development, however, was the Watergate scandal, which began on 17 June 1972 with the arrest of five men associated with Nixon's reelection campaign, during a break-in at Democratic Party headquarters in the Watergate office building in Washington, D.C. Although Nixon was reelected in 1972, subsequent disclosures by the press and by a Senate investigating committee revealed a complex pattern of political "dirty tricks" and illegal domestic surveillance throughout his first term. The president's apparent attempts to obstruct justice by helping his aides cover up the scandal were confirmed by tape recordings (made by Nixon himself) of his private conversations, which the Supreme Court ordered him to release for use as evidence in criminal proceedings. The House voted to begin impeachment proceedings, and in late July 1974, its Judiciary Committee approved three articles of impeachment. On 9 August, Nixon became the first president to resign the office. The following year, Nixon's top aides and former attorney general, John N. Mitchell, were convicted of obstruction and were subsequently sentenced to prison.

Nixon's successor was Gerald R. Ford, who in October 1973 had been appointed to succeed Vice President Spiro T. Agnew when Agnew resigned following his plea of *nolo contendere* to charges that he had evaded paying income tax on moneys he had received from contractors while governor of Maryland. Less than a month after taking office, President Ford granted a full pardon to Nixon for any crimes he may have committed as president. In August 1974, Ford nominated Nelson A. Rockefeller as vice president (he was not confirmed until December), thus giving the country the first instance of a nonelected president and an appointed vice president serving simultaneously. Ford's pardon of Nixon, as well as continued inflation and unemployment, probably contributed to his narrow defeat by a Georgia Democrat, Jimmy Carter, in 1976.

President Carter's forthright championing of human rights—though consistent with the Helsinki accords, the "final act" of the Conference on Security and Cooperation in Europe, signed by the US and 34 other nations in July 1974—contributed to strained relations with the USSR and with some US allies. During 1978–79, the president concluded and secured Senate passage of treaties ending US sovereignty over the Panama Canal Zone. His major accomplishment in foreign affairs, however, was his role in mediating a peace agreement between Israel and Egypt, signed at the Camp David, Md., retreat in September 1978. Domestically, the Carter administration initiated a national energy program to reduce US dependence on foreign oil by cutting gasoline and oil consumption and by encouraging the development of alternative energy resources. But the continuing decline of the economy because of double-digit inflation and high unemployment caused his popularity to wane, and confusing shifts in economic policy (coupled with a lack of clear goals in foreign affairs) characterized his administration during 1979 and 1980; a prolonged quarrel with Iran over more than 50 US hostages seized in Tehran on 4 November 1979 contributed to public doubts about his presidency. Exactly a year after the hostages were taken, former California Governor Ronald Reagan defeated Carter in an election that saw the Republican Party score major gains throughout the US. The hostages were released on 20 January 1981, the day of Reagan's inauguration.

Reagan, who survived a chest wound from an assassination attempt in Washington, D.C. in 1981, used his popularity to push through significant policy changes. He succeeded in enacting income tax cuts of 25 percent, reducing the maximum tax rate on unearned income from 70 percent to 50 percent, and accelerating depreciation allowances for businesses. At the same time, he more than doubled the military budget, in constant 1985 dollars, between 1980 and 1989. Vowing to reduce domestic spending, Reagan cut benefits for the working poor, reduced allocations for food stamps and Aid to Families With Dependent Children by 13 percent, and decreased grants for the education of disadvantaged children. He slashed the budget of the Environmental Protection Agency and instituted a flat rate reimbursement system for the treatment of Medicare patients with particular illnesses, replacing a more flexible arrangement in which hospitals had been reimbursed for "reasonable charges."

Reagan's appointment of Sandra Day O'Connor as the first woman justice of the Supreme Court was widely praised and won unanimous confirmation from the Senate. However, some of his other high-level choices were extremely controversial—none more so than that of his secretary of the interior, James G. Watt, who finally resigned on October 1983. In framing his foreign and defense policy, Reagan insisted on a military buildup as a precondition for arms-control talks with the USSR. His administration sent money and advisers to help the government of El Salvador in its war against leftist rebels, and US advisers were also sent to Honduras, reportedly to aid groups of Nicaraguans trying to overthrow the Sandinista government in their country. Troops were also dispatched to Lebanon in September 1982, as part of a multinational peacekeeping force in Beirut, and to Grenada in October 1983 to oust a leftist government there.

Reelected in 1984, President Reagan embarked on his second term with a legislative agenda that included reduction of federal budget deficits (which had mounted rapidly during his first term in office), further cuts in domestic spending, and reform of the federal tax code. In military affairs, Reagan persuaded Congress to fund on a modest scale his Strategic Defense Initiative, commonly known as Star Wars, a highly complex and extremely costly space-based antimissile system. In 1987, the downing of an aircraft carrying arms to Nicaragua led to the disclosure that a group of National Security Council members had secretly diverted $48 million that the federal government had received in payment from Iran for American arms to rebel forces in Nicaragua. The disclosure prompted the resignation of two of the leaders of the group, Vice Admiral John Poindexter and Lieutenant Colonel Oliver North, as well as investigations by House and Senate committees and a special prosecutor, Lawrence Walsh. The congressional investigations found no conclusive evidence that Reagan had authorized or known of the diversion. Yet they noted that because Reagan had approved of the sale of arms to Iran and had encouraged his staff to assist Nicaraguan rebels despite the prohibition of such assistance by Congress, "the President created or at least tolerated an environment where those who did know of the diversion believed with certainty that they were carrying out the President's policies."

Reagan was succeeded in 1988 by his vice president, George Bush. Benefiting from a prolonged economic expansion, Bush handily defeated Michael Dukakis, governor of Massachusetts and a liberal Democrat. On domestic issues, Bush sought to maintain policies introduced by the Reagan administration. His few legislative initiatives included the passage of legislation establishing strict regulations of air pollution, providing subsidies for child care, and protecting the rights of the disabled. Abroad, Bush showed more confidence and energy. While he responded cautiously to revolutions in Eastern Europe and the Soviet Union, he used his personal relationships with foreign leaders to bring about comprehensive peace talks between Israel and its Arab neighbors, to encourage a peaceful unification of Germany, and to negotiate broad and substantial arms cuts with the Russians. Bush reacted to Iraq's invasion of Kuwait in 1990 by sending 400,000 soldiers to form the basis of a multinational coalition which he assembled and which destroyed Iraq's main force within seven months.

One of the biggest crises that the Bush administration encountered was the collapse of the savings and loan industry in the late eighties. Thrift institutions were required by law to pay low interest rates for deposits and long-term loans. The creation of money market funds for the small investor in the eighties which paid higher rates of return than savings accounts prompted depositors to withdraw their money from banks and invest it in the higher-yielding mutual funds. To finance the withdrawals, banks began selling assets at a loss. The deregulation of the savings and loan industry, combined with the increase in federal deposit insurance from $40,000 to $100,000 per account, encouraged many desperate savings institutions to invest in high-risk real-estate ventures, for which no state supervision or regulation existed. When the majority of such ventures predictably failed, the federal government found itself compelled by law to rescue the thrifts at a cost to taxpayers of over $100 billion.

In his bid for reelection in 1992, Bush faced not only Democratic nominee Bill Clinton, Governor of Arkansas, but also third-party candidate Ross Perot, a Dallas billionaire who had made his fortune in the computer industry. In contrast to Bush's first run for the presidency, when the nation had enjoyed an unusually long period of economic expansion, the economy in 1992 was just beginning to recover from a recession. Although data released the following year indicated that a healthy rebound had already begun in 1992, the public perceived the economy during election year as weak. Clinton took advantage of this perception in his campaign, focusing on the financial concerns of what he called "the forgotten middle class." He also took a more centrist position on many issues than more traditional Democrats, promising fiscal responsibility and economic growth. Clinton defeated Bush, winning 43 percent of the vote to Bush's 38 percent. Perot garnered 18 percent of the vote.

At its outset, Clinton's presidency was plagued by numerous setbacks, most notably the failure of his controversial healthcare reform plan, drawn up under the leadership of first lady Hillary Rodham Clinton. Major accomplishments included the passage, by a narrow margin, of a deficit-reduction bill calling for tax increases and spending cuts and Congressional approval of the North American Free Trade Agreement, which removed or reduced tariffs on most goods moving across the borders of the United States, Canada, and Mexico. Although supporters and critics agreed that the treaty would create or eliminate relatively few jobs—two hundred thousand—the accord prompted heated debate. Labor strenuously opposed the agreement, seeing it as accelerating the flight of factory jobs to countries with low labor costs such as Mexico, the third largest trading partner of the US. Business, on the other hand, lobbied heavily for the treaty, arguing that it would create new markets for American goods and insisting that competition from Mexico would benefit the American economy.

By the fall of 1994, many American workers, still confronting stagnating wages, benefits, and living standards, had yet to feel the effects of the nation's recovery from the recession of 1990/91. The resulting disillusionment with the actions of the Clinton administration and the Democrat-controlled Congress, combined with the widespread climate of social conservatism resulting from a perceived erosion of traditional moral values led to an overwhelming upset by the Republican party in the 1994 midterm elections. The GOP gained control of both houses of Congress for the first time in over 40 years, also winning 11 gubernatorial races, for control of a total of 30 governorships nationwide. The Republican agenda—increased defense spending and cuts in taxes, social programs, and farm subsidies—had been popularized under the label "Contract with America," the title of a manifesto circulated during the campaign.

The ensuing confrontation between the nation's Democratic president and Republican-controlled Congress came to a head at the end of 1995, when Congress responded to presidential vetoes of appropriations and budget bills by refusing to pass stopgap spending measures, resulting in major shutdowns of the federal government in November and December. The following summer, however, the president and Congress joined forces to reform the welfare system through a bill replacing Aid to Families with Dependent Children with block grants through which welfare funding would largely become the province of the states.

The nation's economic recovery gained strength as the decade advanced, with healthy growth, falling unemployment, and moderate interest and inflation levels. Public confidence in the economy was reflected in a bull market on the stock exchange, which gained 60% between 1995 and 1997. Bolstered by a favorable economy at home and peace abroad, Clinton's faltering popularity rebounded and in 1996 he became the first Democratic president elected to a second term since Franklin D. Roosevelt in 1936, defeating the Republican candidate, former Senate majority leader Robert Dole, and Independent Ross Perot, whose electoral support was greatly reduced from its 1992 level. The Republicans retained control of both houses of Congress. In 1997, President Clinton signed into law a bipartisan budget plan designed to balance the federal budget by 2002, for the first time since 1969, through a combination of tax and spending cuts.

12FEDERAL GOVERNMENT

The Constitution of the United States, signed in 1787, is the nation's governing document. In the first 10 amendments to the Constitution, ratified in 1791 and known as the Bill of Rights, the federal government is denied the power to infringe on rights generally regarded as fundamental to the civil liberties of the people. These amendments prohibit the establishment of a state religion and the abridgment of freedom of speech, press, and the right to assemble. They protect all persons against unreasonable searches and seizures, guarantee trial by jury, and prohibit excessive bail and cruel and unusual punishments. No person may be required to testify against himself, nor may he be deprived of life, liberty, or property without due process of law. The 13th Amendment (1865) banned slavery; the 15th (1870) protected the freed slaves' right to vote; and the 19th (1920) guaranteed the franchise to women. In all, there have been 26 amendments, the last of which, in 1971, reduced the voting age to 18. The Equal Rights Amendment (ERA), approved by Congress in 1972, would have mandated equality between the sexes; only 35 of the required 38 states had ratified the ERA by the time the ratification deadline expired on 30 June 1982.

The US has a federal form of government, with the distribution of powers between the federal government and the states constitutionally defined. The legislative powers of the federal government are vested in Congress, which consists of the House of Representatives and the Senate. There are 435 members of the House of Representatives. Each state is allotted a number of representatives in proportion to its population as determined by the decennial census. Representatives are elected for two-year terms in every even-numbered year. A representative must be at least 25 years old, must be a resident of the state represented, and must have been a citizen of the US for at least seven years. The Senate consists of two senators from each state, elected for six-year terms. Senators must be at least 30 years old, must be residents of the states from which they are elected, and must have been citizens of the US for at least nine years. One-third of the Senate is elected in every even-numbered year.

Congress legislates on matters of taxation, borrowing, regulation of international and interstate commerce, formulation of rules of naturalization, bankruptcy, coinage, weights and measures, post offices and post roads, courts inferior to the Supreme Court, provision for the armed forces, among many other matters. A broad interpretation of the "necessary and proper" clause of the Constitution has widened considerably the scope of congressional legislation based on the enumerated powers.

A bill that is passed by both houses of Congress in the same form is submitted to the president, who may sign it or veto it. If the president chooses to veto the bill, it is returned to the house in which it originated with the reasons for the veto. The bill may become law despite the president's veto if it is passed again by a two-thirds vote in both houses. A bill becomes law without the president's signature if retained for 10 days while Congress is in session. After Congress adjourns, if the president does not sign a bill within 10 days, an automatic veto ensues.

The president must be "a natural born citizen" at least 35 years old, and must have been a resident of the US for 14 years. Under the 22nd Amendment to the Constitution, adopted in 1951, a president may not be elected more than twice. Each state is allotted a number of electors based on its combined total of US senators and representatives, and, technically, it is these electors who, constituted as the electoral college, cast their vote for president, with all of the state's electoral votes customarily going to the candidate who won the largest share of the popular vote of the state (the District of Columbia also has three electors, making a total of 538 votes). Thus, the candidate who wins the greatest share of the popular vote throughout the US may, in rare cases, fail to win a majority of the electoral vote. If no candidate gains a majority in the electoral college, the choice passes to the House of Representatives.

The vice president, elected at the same time and on the same ballot as the president, serves as ex officio president of the Senate. The vice president assumes the power and duties of the presidency on the president's removal from office or as a result of the president's death, resignation, or inability to perform his duties. In the case of a vacancy in the vice-presidency, the president nominates a successor, who must be approved by a majority in both houses of Congress. The Congress has the power to determine the line of presidential succession in case of the death or disability of both the president and vice president.

Under the Constitution, the president is enjoined to "take care that the laws be faithfully executed." In reality, the president has a considerable amount of leeway in determining to what extent a law is or is not enforced. Congress's only recourse is impeachment, to which it has resorted only twice, in proceedings against presidents Andrew Johnson and Richard Nixon. Both the president and the vice president are removable from office after impeachment by the House and conviction at a Senate trial for "treason, bribery, or other high crimes and misdemeanors." The president has the power to grant reprieves and pardons for offenses against the US except in cases of impeachment.

The President nominates and "by and with the advice and consent of the Senate" appoints ambassadors, public ministers, consuls, and all federal judges, including the justices of the Supreme Court. As commander in chief, the president is ultimately responsible for the disposition of the land, naval, and air forces, but the power to declare war belongs to Congress. The president conducts foreign relations and makes treaties with the advice and consent of the Senate. No treaty is binding unless it wins the approval of two-thirds of the Senate. The president's independence is also limited by the House of Representatives, where all money bills originate.

The president also appoints as his cabinet, subject to Senate confirmation, the secretaries who head the departments of the executive branch. As of 1997, the executive branch included the following cabinet departments: Agriculture (created in 1862), Commerce (1913), Defense (1947), Education (1980), Energy (1977), Health and Human Services (1980), Housing and Urban Development (1965), Interior (1849), Justice (1870), Labor (1913), State (1789), Transportation (1966), and Treasury (1789), and Veterans' Affairs (1989). The Department of Defense—headquartered in the Pentagon, the world's largest office building—also administers the various branches of the military: Air Force, Army, Navy, defense agencies, and joint-service schools. The Department of Justice administers the Federal Bureau of Investigation, which originated in 1908; the Central Intelligence Agency (1947) is under the aegis of the Executive office. Among the several hundred quasi-independent agencies are the Federal Reserve System (1913), serving as the nation's central bank, and the major regulatory bodies, notably the Environmental Protection Agency (1970), Federal Communications Commission (1934), Federal Power Commission (1920), Federal Trade Commission (1914), and Interstate Commerce Commission (1887).

Regulations for voting are determined by the individual states for federal as well as for local offices, and requirements vary from state to state. In the past, various southern states used literacy tests, poll taxes, "grandfather" clauses, and other methods to disfranchise black voters, but Supreme Court decisions and congressional measures, including the Voting Rights Act of 1965, more than doubled the number of black registrants in Deep South states between 1964 and 1992. In 1960, only 29.1% of the black voting-age population was registered to vote; by 1994, that percentage had risen to 64%.

13 POLITICAL PARTIES

Two major parties, Democratic and Republican, have dominated national, state, and local politics since 1860. These parties are made up of clusters of small autonomous local groups primarily concerned with local politics and the election of local candidates to office. Within each party, such groups frequently differ drastically in policies and beliefs on many issues, but once every four years, they successfully bury their differences and rally around a candidate for the presidency. Minority parties have been formed at various periods in US political history, but most have generally allied with one of the two major parties, and none has achieved sustained national prominence. The most successful minority party in recent decades—that of Texas billionaire Ross Perot in 1992—was little more than a protest vote. Various extreme groups on the right and left, including a small US Communist Party, have had little political significance on a national scale; in 1980, the Libertarian Party became the first minor party since 1916 to appear on the ballot in all 50 states. Independent candidates have won state and local office, but no candidate has won the presidency without major party backing.

Traditionally, the Republican Party is more solicitous of business interests and gets greater support from business than does the Democratic Party. A majority of blue-collar workers, by contrast, have generally supported the Democratic Party, which favors more lenient labor laws, particularly as they affect labor unions; the Republican Party often (though not always) supports legislation that restricts the power of labor unions. Republicans favor the enhancement of the private sector of the economy, while Democrats generally urge the cause of greater government participation and regulatory authority, especially at the federal level.

Within both parties there are sharp differences on a great many issues; for example, northeastern Democrats in the past almost uniformly favored strong federal civil rights legislation, which was anathema to the Deep South; eastern Republicans in foreign policy are internationalist-minded, while midwesterners of the same party constituted from 1910 through 1940 the hard core of isolationist sentiment in the country. More recently, "conservative" headings have been adopted by members of both parties who emphasize decentralized government power, strengthened private enterprise, and a strong US military posture overseas, while the designation "liberal" has been applied to those favoring an increased federal government role in economic and social affairs, disengagement from foreign military commitments, and the intensive pursuit of nuclear-arms reduction.

President Nixon's resignation and the accompanying scandal surrounding the Republican Party hierarchy had a telling, if predictable, effect on party morale, as indicated by Republican losses in the 1974 and 1976 elections. The latent consequences of the Viet-Nam and Watergate years appeared to take their toll on both parties, however, in growing apathy toward politics and mistrust of politicians among the electorate. As of 1992, Democrats enjoyed a large advantage over Republicans in voter registration, held both houses of congress, had a majority of state governorships, and controlled most state legislative bodies. The centers of Democratic strength were the South and the major cities; most of the solidly Republican states were west of the Mississippi. Ronald Reagan's successful 1980 presidential bid cut into traditional Democratic strongholds throughout the US, as Republicans won control of the US Senate and eroded state and local Democratic majorities.

The 1984 election marked a turning point for women in national politics. Geraldine A. Ferraro, a Democrat, became the first female vice-presidential nominee of a major US political party; no woman has ever captured a major-party presidential nomination. Also in the 1984 presidential election, the candidacy of Jesse L. Jackson, the first black ever to win a plurality in a statewide presidential preference primary, marked the emergence of black Americans as a political force, especially within the Democratic Party.

On the strength of an economic recovery, President Reagan won reelection in November 1984, carrying 49 of 50 states (with a combined total of 525 electoral votes) and 58.8% of the popular vote; the Republicans retained control of the Senate, but the Democrats held on to the House. Benefiting from a six-year expansion of the economy, Republican George Bush won 54% of the vote in 1988. As Reagan had, Bush successfully penetrated traditionally Democratic regions. He carried every state in the South as well as the industrial states of the north.

Bush's approval rating reached a high of 91% in March of 1991 in the wake of the Persian Gulf War. By July of 1992, however, that rating had plummeted to 25%, in part because Bush appeared to be disengaged from domestic issues, particularly the 1991 recession. Bill Clinton, governor of Arkansas and twenty years younger than Bush, presented himself to the electorate as a "New Democrat." He took more moderate positions than traditional New Deal Democrats, including calling for a middle-class tax cut, welfare reform, national service, and such traditionally Republican goals as getting tough on crime. The presidential race took on an unpredictable

dimension with the entrance of Independent Ross Perot, a Texas billionaire. Perot, who attacked the budget deficit and called for shared sacrifice, withdrew from the race in July and then re-entered it in October. Clinton won the election with 43% of the vote, Bush received 38%, and Perot captured 18%, more than any third-party presidential candidate since Theodore Roosevelt in 1912. The Republicans gained nine seats in the House of Representatives while the Democrats picked up one seat in the Senate.

Aided by a growing climate of conservatism on moral issues and popular discontent with the pace of economic recovery from the recent recession, the Republicans accomplished an historic upset in the 1994 midterm elections, gaining control of both houses of Congress for the first time since 1952. They gained 52 seats in the House, for a majority of 230–204, and 8 seats in the Senate, for a majority that came to 53–47 once Democrat Richard Shelby of Alabama changed parties shortly after the election. The Republicans also increased their power at the state level, winning 11 governorships, for a national total of 30. The number of state legislatures under Republican control increased from 8 to 19, with 18 controlled by the Democrats and 12 under split control.

US Popular Vote for President by National Political Parties, 1948–1996

YEAR	WINNER	TOTAL VOTES CAST	% OF ELIGIBLE VOTERS	DEMOCRAT	REPUBLICAN	PROHI-BITION	SOC. LABOR	SOC. WORKERS	SOCIALIST	PROGRES-SIVE	STATES' RIGHTS DEMOCRAT	CONSTI-TUTION	OTHER[1]
1948	Truman (D)	48,692,442	51	24,105,587	21,970,017	103,489	29,038	13,614	138,973	1,157,057	1,169,134		5,533
1952	Eisenhower (R)	61,551,118	62	27,314,649	33,936,137	73,413	30,250	10,312	20,065	140,416	—	17,200	8,676
1956	Eisenhower (R)	62,025,372	59	26,030,172	35,585,245	41,937	44,300	7,797	2,044	—	2,657	108,055	203,165
											NATL. STATES' RIGHTS		
1960	Kennedy (D)	68,828,960	63	34,221,344	34,106,761	44,087	47,522	40,166	—	—	209,314	—	159,856
												UNPLEDGED DEM.	
1964	Johnson (D)	70,641,104	62	43,126,584	27,177,838	23,266	45,187	32,701	—	—	6,953	210,732	17,843
									COMMUNIST	PEACE & FREEDOM	AMERICAN IND.		
1968	Nixon (R)	73,203,370	61	31,274,503	31,785,148	14,915	52,591	41,390	1,076	83,720[2]	9,901,151	—	48,876
										LIBERTARIAN		AMERICAN	
1972	Nixon (R)	77,727,590	55	29,171,791	47,170,179	12,818	53,811	94,415[2]	25,343	3,671	—	1,090,673	104,889
							US LABOR						
1976	Carter (D)	81,552,331	54	40,829,046	39,146,006	15,958	40,041	91,310	58,992	173,019	170,531	160,773	866,655[3]
						CITIZENS	RESPECT FOR LIFE						
1980	Reagan (R)	86,495,678	54	35,481,435	43,899,248	230,377	32,319	40,105	43,871	920,859	41,172	6,539	5,799,753[4]
							POPULIST			IND. ALLIANCE			
1984	Reagan (R)	92,652,793	53	37,577,137	54,455,074	72,200	66,336	24,706	36,386	228,314	46,852	13,161	132,627[5]
1988	Bush(R)	91,594,809	50	41,809,074	48,886,097	30,905	47,047	15,604	—	432,179	217,219	3,475	153,209
						US TAX-PAYER							
1992	Clinton(D)	104,426,659	55	44,909,889	39,104,545	43,398	107,002	23,091	39,163	291,628	73,708	3,875	19,830,360[6]
						US TAX-PAYER	GREEN			LIBERTARIAN	NATURAL LAW	AMERICAN	
1996	Clinton (D)	96,277,223	49	47,402,357	39,198,755	184,658	684,902	8,476	4,765	485,798	113,668	1,847	8,196,762[7]

[1]Includes votes for state parties, independent candidates and unpledged electors.
[2]Total includes votes for several candidates in different states under the same party label.
[3]Includes 756,631 votes for Eugene McCarthy, an independent.
[4]Includes 5,719,437 votes for John Anderson, an independent.
[5]Includes 78,807 votes for Lyndon H. LaRouche, an independent.
[6]Includes 19,742,267 votes for Ross Perot, an independent.

As of 1995, 8 women served in the US Senate, and 47 women held seats in the US House of Representatives. As of 1994, the US had 8,015 black elected officials, including the mayors of some of the nation's largest cities. In 1992 a black woman, Democrat Carol Moseley Braun of Illinois, won election to the Senate, becoming the first black senator. There were 40 blacks and 17 Hispanics in the House as of 1995.

In 1996 Bill Clinton became the first Democratic president since Franklin Roosevelt to be elected to a second term, with 49% of the popular vote to 41% for Republican Bob Dole, and 8% for Ross Perot, who once again ran as an Independent. Republicans retained control of the House and Senate.

14 LOCAL GOVERNMENT

Governmental units within each state comprise counties, municipalities, and such special districts as those for water, sanitation, highways, parks. and recreation. There are more than 3,000 counties in the US; more than 19,000 municipalities, including cities, villages, towns, and boroughs; nearly 15,000 school districts; and at least 31,000 special districts. Additional townships, authorities, commissions, and boards make up the rest of the nearly 85,000 local governmental units.

The states are autonomous within their own spheres of government, and their autonomy is defined in broad terms by the 10th Amendment to the US Constitution, which reserves to the states such powers as are not granted to the federal government and not denied to the states. The states may not, among other restrictions, issue paper money, conduct foreign relations, impair the obligations of contracts, or establish a government that is not republican in form. Subsequent amendments to the Constitution and many Supreme Court decisions added to the restrictions placed on the states. The 13th Amendment prohibited the states from legalizing the ownership of one person by another (slavery); the 14th Amendment deprived the states of their power to determine qualifications for citizenship; the 15th Amendment prohibited the states from denying the right to vote because of race, color, or previous condition of servitude; and the 19th, from denying the vote to women.

Since the Civil War, the functions of the state have expanded. Local business—that is, business not involved in foreign or interstate commerce—is regulated by the state. The states create subordinate governmental bodies such as counties, cities, towns, villages, and boroughs, whose charters they either issue or, where home rule is permitted, approve. States regulate employment of children and women in industry, and enact safety laws to prevent industrial accidents. Unemployment insurance is a state function, as are education, public health, highway construction and safety, operation of a state highway patrol, and various kinds of personal relief. The state and local governments still are primarily responsible for providing public assistance, despite the large part the federal government plays in financing welfare.

Each state is headed by an elected governor. State legislatures are bicameral except Nebraska's, which has been unicameral since 1934. Generally, the upper house is called the senate, and the lower house the house of representatives or the assembly. Bills must be passed by both houses, and the governor has a suspensive veto, which usually may be overridden by a two-thirds vote.

The number, population, and geographic extent of the more than 3,000 counties in the US—including the analogous units called boroughs in Alaska and parishes in Louisiana—show no uniformity from state to state. The county is the most conspicuous unit of rural local government and has a variety of powers, including location and repair of highways, county poor relief, determination of voting precincts and of polling places, and organization of school and road districts. City governments, usually headed by a mayor or city manager, have the power to levy taxes; to borrow; to pass, amend, and repeal local ordinances; and to grant franchises for public service corporations. Township government through an annual town meeting is an important New England tradition.

During the late 1960s and 1970s and again in the late 1980s and early 1990s, a number of large cities began to suffer severe fiscal crises brought on by a combination of factors. Loss of tax revenues stemmed from the migration of middle-class residents to the suburbs and the flight of many small and large firms seeking to avoid the usually higher costs of doing business in urban areas. Low-income groups, many of them unskilled blacks and hispanic migrants, came to constitute large segments of city populations, placing added burdens on locally funded welfare, medical, housing, and other services without providing the commensurate tax base for additional revenues.

15 STATE SERVICES

All state governments provide services in the fields of education, transportation, health and social welfare, public protection (including state police and prison personnel), housing, and labor. The 1970s saw an expansion of state services in four key areas: energy, environment, consumer protection, and governmental ethics. Each state provides some form of consumer advocacy, either through a separate department or agency or through the office of the attorney general. State government in the 1970s and early 1980s also showed the effects of the so-called post-Watergate morality. Laws mandating financial disclosure by public officials, once rare, had become common by 1983. Also notable were "sunshine laws," opening legislative committee meetings and administrative hearings to the public, and the use of an ombudsman either with general jurisdiction or with special powers relating, for example, to the problems of businesses, prisoners, the elderly, or racial minorities. Other trends in state administration, reflected on the federal level, include the separation of education from other services and the consolidation of social welfare programs in departments of human resources.

Federal aid to state, local, and territorial governments was estimated at more than $178 billion in 1991/92. The largest outlays were for Medicaid, $67.8 billion; aid to families with dependent children, $15.5 billion; highways, $14.9 billion; housing assistance payments, $8.0 billion; compensatory education for the disadvantaged, $6.1 billion; urban mass transit, $3.5 billion; unemployment insurance, $3.2 billion; community development block grants, $3.1 billion; and public housing assistance, $3.0 billion.

California received more aid than any other state, $19.7 billion, followed by New York state, $19.3 billion. Texas, Pennsylvania, Ohio, Illinois, Florida, and Michigan each received over $6 billion in federal grants.

16 JUDICIAL SYSTEM

The Supreme Court, established by the US Constitution, is the nation's highest judicial body, consisting of the chief justice of the US and eight associate justices. All justices are appointed by the president with the advice and consent of the Senate. Appointments are for life "during good behavior," otherwise terminating only by resignation or impeachment and conviction.

The original jurisdiction of the Supreme Court is relatively narrow; as an appellate court, it is open to appeal from decisions of federal district courts, circuit courts of appeals, and the highest courts in the states, although it may dismiss an appeal if it sees fit to do so. The Supreme Court, by means of a writ of certiorari, may call up a case from a district court for review. Regardless of how cases reach it, the Court enforces a kind of unity on the decisions of the lower courts. It also exercises the power of judicial review, determining the constitutionality of state laws, state constitutions, congressional statutes, and federal regulations, but only when these are specifically challenged.

The Constitution empowers Congress to establish all federal courts inferior to the Supreme Court. On the lowest level and handling the greatest proportion of federal cases are the district courts—, including one each in Puerto Rico, Guam, the Virgin Islands, the Northern Mariana Islands, and the District of Columbia—where all offenses against the laws of the US are tried. Civil actions that involve cases arising under treaties and laws of the US and under the Constitution, where the amount in dispute is greater than $5,000, also fall within the jurisdiction of the district courts. District courts have no appellate jurisdiction; their decisions may be carried to the courts of appeals, organized into 13 circuits. These courts also hear appeals from decisions made by administrative commissions. For most cases, this is usually the last stage of appeal, except where the court rules that a statute of a state conflicts with the Constitution of the US, with federal law, or with a treaty. Special federal courts include the Court of Claims, Court of Customs and Patent Appeals, and Tax Court.

State courts operate independently of the federal judiciary. Most states adhere to a court system that begins on the lowest level with a justice of the peace and includes courts of general trial jurisdiction, appellate courts, and, at the apex of the system, a state supreme court. The court of trial jurisdiction, sometimes called the county or superior court, has both original and appellate jurisdiction; all criminal cases (except those of a petty kind) and some civil cases are tried in this court. The state's highest court, like the Supreme Court of the US, interprets the constitution and the laws of the state.

The grand jury is a body of from 13 to 24 persons that brings indictments against individuals suspected of having violated the law. Initially, evidence is presented to it by either a justice of the peace or a prosecuting county or district attorney. The trial or petit jury of 12 persons is used in trials of common law, both criminal and civil, except where the right to a jury trial is waived by consent of all parties at law. It judges the facts of the case, while the court is concerned exclusively with questions of law. The United States accepts the compulsory jurisdiction of the International Court of Justice with reservations.

17 ARMED FORCES

The armed forces of the United States of America in 1996 numbered 1.5 million on active duty and 1.7 million in the Ready Reserve, a category of participation that allows regular training with pay and extended active duty periods for training. The Standby and Retired Reserve includes about 278,000 experienced officers and NCOs who can be recalled in a national emergency. Membership in all of these forces is voluntary and has been since 1973 when conscription expired in the death throes of the Viet Nam war. The active duty force includes 192,200 women who serve in all grades and all occupational specialties except direct ground combat units and some aviation billets.

From plans drawn in 1989–90 the armed forces are reducing their personnel numbers and force structure by about one-third because of the diminished threat of a nuclear war with the former Soviet Union or a major conflict in central Europe. Despite the interlude of the Gulf War, 1990–91, the force reductions will continue in the 1990s, which in turn will force some restructuring of the active duty forces. Their emphasis will be on rapid deployment to deter or fight major regional conflicts much like the Gulf War, in Korea, elsewhere in the Middle East, or Latin America (e.g. Cuba). The essence of the conventional force debate is whether the US can or should maintain forces to fight two regional conflicts simultaneously.

For the purposes of administration, personnel management, logistics, and training, the traditional four military services in the Department of Defense remain central to strategic planning. The US Army numbers 495,000 (67,100 women) soldiers on active duty, divided roughly between 7 heavy (armored or mechanized) divisions, six light (infantry airborne, airmobile) divisions, and five independent brigades as well as two armored cavalry regiments, 7 aviation brigades, and 17 air defense battalions. Army special operations missions go to 5 Special Forces groups, an airborne ranger regiment, an aviation group, and a psychological warfare group with civil affairs and communications support units. The Army has 10,497 main battle tanks, 5,371 infantry fighting vehicles, almost 20,000 other tracked vehicles, almost 6,000 towed or self-propelled artillery, 300 aircraft, and 5,331 armed and transport helicopters. Also in the process of reorganization, the Army National Guard (387,100; 30,500 women) will emphasize the preparation of combat units up to division size for major regional conflicts while the Army Reserve (596,700; 114,100 women) will prepare individuals to fill active units or provide combat support or service support/technical/medical units upon mobilization. In addition, the National Guard retains a residual state role in suppressing civil disturbances and providing disaster relief.

The US Navy (426,700; 55,400 women) has shifted from its role in nuclear strategic deterrence and control of sea routes to Europe and Asia to the projection of naval power from the sea. Naval task forces normally combine three combat elements: air, surface, and subsurface. The Navy mans 95 nuclear-powered attack submarines with one configured for special operations; most of these boats can launch cruise missiles at land targets.

Naval aviation is centered on 12 carriers (6 nuclear-powered) and 13 carrier aircraft wings. Including its armed ASW helicopters and armed long-range ASW patrol aircraft—as well as a large fleet of communications and support aircraft—the Navy controls 1,735 aircraft and 421 armed helicopters. Naval aviation reserves provide 5 more wings for carrier deployment. The surface force includes 31 cruisers (21 with advanced anti-air suites), 52 destroyers, 49 frigates, 41 amphibious ships, 21 mine warfare ships, and 25 patrol and coastal combatants. More ships are kept in ready reserve or are manned by surface line reserve units. The fleet support force numbers 102 specialized ships for global logistics that are not base-dependent.

The Marine Corps, a separate naval service, is organized into three active divisions and three aircraft wings of the Fleet Marine Force, which also include 3 Force Service Support groups. The Marine Corps (173,900; 7,600 women) emphasizes amphibious landings, but trains for a wide-range of contingency employments. It can draw upon some 43,000 reserve Marines in a fourth division and aircraft wing as well as individual ready reservists. The Marine Corps has 403 main battle tanks, 1,500 other mobile warfare tracked and wheeled combat vehicles, and about 1,000 artillery pieces, which makes it more formidable than most armies. It flies 280 aircraft and 493 helicopters as well.

The US Air Force (388,200; 62,100 women) provides 3,500 aircraft, all but about 300 now dedicated to non-strategic roles in support of forward deployed ground and naval forces. The Air Force stresses the missions of air superiority and interdiction with complementary operations in electronic warfare and reconnaissance, but it also mans a transport fleet of around 1,200 aircraft. Air Force personnel manage the US radar and satellite early-warning and intelligence effort. The Air Force Reserve and Air National Guard (roughly 186,000 active reserves) provide a wide range of flying and support units, and their flying squadrons have demonstrated exceptional readiness and combat skills on contingency missions. Air Force reserves, for example, provide the backbone of the air refueling and transport fleets.

The armed forces are deployed in functional unified or specified commands for actual missions. The Strategic Command controls the strategic nuclear deterrence forces: 1000 ICMBs (2,450 warheads), 25 Navy fleet ballistic missile submarines with 504 missiles (6,000 warheads) and 270 operational long-range bombers (2,400 missiles and bombs). These forces are undergoing reduction to conform with the START arms limitation treaty of 1991, as amended in 1992, so that by the year 2003 the US will have only 500 ICMBs, 1,728 SLBMs, and 95 nuclear-armed bombers. Strategic Command is complemented by Space Command/North American Air Defense Command. The conventional forces are assigned to a mix of geographic and functional commands: Atlantic Command, European Command, Central Command, Southern Command and Pacific Command as well as Transportation Command and Special Operations Command. The Army also maintains a Forces Command for ground forces in strategic reserve in the US. Major operational units are deployed to Germany, Korea, and Japan as part of collective security alliances. About one-third of active duty personnel are assigned to overseas billets (1–3 years) or serve in air, naval, and ground units that serve short tours on a rotational basis. The US has one battalion in Egypt and observes with four other peacekeeping missions.

Patterns of defense spending reflect the movement away from Cold War assumptions and confrontation with the former Soviet Union and the People's Republic of China. During the 1980s when defense spending hovered around $300 billion a year and increased roughly 30 percent over the decade, defense spending absorbed roughly 6 percent of the gross domestic spending, 25 percent of federal spending, and 16 percent of net public spending. In the early 1990s when the defense budget slipped back to the $250–$260 billion level, the respective percentages were 4.5, 18, and 11, the lowest levels of support for defense since the Korean War (1950). US military assistance abroad shows similar trends. From 1981 to 1991 the US sold $118 billion in arms abroad and provided some outright grants, military training, and other support services, most in dollar value to its NATOs allies, Sau'di Arabia, Israel, South Korea, and Japan. This spending is also declining. However, should the Czech Republic, Hungary, and Poland become full members of NATO, the US defense costs are expected to rise in order to support these countries' efforts to meet NATO military standards.

[18]MIGRATION

Between 1840 and 1930, some 37 million immigrants, the overwhelming majority of them Europeans, arrived in the US. Immigration reached its peak in the first decade of the 20th century, when nearly 9 million came. Following the end of World War I, the tradition of almost unlimited immigration was abandoned, and through the National Origins Act of 1924, a quota system was established as the basis of a carefully restricted policy of immigration. Under the McCarran Act of 1952, one-sixth of 1% of the number of inhabitants from each European nation residing in the continental US as of 1920 could be admitted annually. In practice, this system favored nations of northern and western Europe, with the UK, Germany, and Ireland being the chief beneficiaries. The quota system was radically reformed in 1965, under a new law that established an annual ceiling of 170,000 for Eastern Hemisphere immigrants and 120,000 for entrants from the Western Hemisphere; in October 1978, these limits were replaced by a worldwide limit of 290,000, which was lowered to 270,000 by 1981. A major 1990 overhaul set a total annual ceiling of 700,000 (675,000 beginning in fiscal 1995), of which 480,000 would be family sponsored and 140,000 employment based.

A direct result of the immigration law revisions has been a sharp rise in the influx of Asians (primarily Chinese, Filipinos, Indians, Japanese, and Koreans), of whom 2,738,157 entered the country during 1981–90, as compared with 153,249 during the entire decade of the 1950s.

Since 1961, the federal government has supported and financed the Cuban Refugee Program. More than 500,000 Cubans were living in southern Florida by 1980, when another 125,000 Cuban refugees arrived. Between 1975 and 1978, following the defeat of the US-backed Saigon government, several hundred thousand Vietnamese refugees came to the US. Under the Refugee Act of 1980, a ceiling for the number of admissible refugees is set annually. In 1995, there were 99,490 refugees that were resettled in the US. The ceiling for refugees in 1996 was 90,000. The net immigration rate in 1996 was 3.1 migrants per 1,000 population.

Large numbers of aliens—mainly from Latin America, especially Mexico—have illegally established residence in the US after entering the country as tourists, students, or temporary visitors engaged in work or business. In November 1986, Congress passed a bill allowing illegal aliens who had lived and worked in the US since 1982 the opportunity to become permanent residents. By the end of fiscal year 1992, 2,650,000 of a potential 2,760,000 eligible for permanent residence under this bill had attained that status. In 1994 the number of illegal alien residents was estimated at 3,850,000, of which 1,600,000 were believed to be in California.

The major migratory trends within the US have been a general westward movement during the 19th century; a long-term movement from farms and other rural settlements to metropolitan areas, which showed signs of reversing in some states during the 1970s; an exodus of southern blacks to the cities of the North and Midwest, especially after World War I; a shift of whites from central cities to surrounding suburbs since World War II; and, also during the post–World War II period, a massive shift from the North and East to the Sunbelt region of the South and Southwest.

[19]INTERNATIONAL COOPERATION

The US, whose failure to join the League of Nations was a major cause of the failure of that body, is a charter member of the UN, having joined on 24 October 1945. The US participates in ECE, ECLAC, ESCAP, and all the nonregional specialized agencies except UNESCO, from which it withdrew at the end of 1984, charging the agency with mismanagement and with bias against Western nations; there are also policy differences between the US and several other UN agencies. The US contributes about 25% of the total funds required for the upkeep of the UN, far more than does any other nation. In the mid-1980s, the US participated in more than 70 intergovernmental organizations, including the Asian Development Bank, OECD, the IMF and IBRD (World Bank), and international councils and commissions on various industries. The US also participates actively in the Permanent Court of Arbitration. Hemispheric agencies include the Inter-American Committee on the Alliance for Progress, IDB, OAS, IADB, and PAHO.

NATO is the principal military alliance to which the US belongs. The ANZUS alliance is a mutual defense pact between Australia, New Zealand, and the US; in 1986, following New Zealand's decision to ban US nuclear-armed or nuclear-powered ships from its ports, the US renounced its ANZUS treaty security commitments to New Zealand. The nation is a signatory of GATT but refused to sign the Law of the Sea because of unwillingness to relinquish rights over seabed mining; in keeping with international practice, however, the US does maintain a 200-mi coastal economic zone. In 1986, the US approved the 1948 UN convention against genocide.

[20]ECONOMY

In variety and quantity, the natural resources of the US probably exceed those of any other nation, with the possible exception of the former Soviet Union. The US is among the world's leading exporters of coal, wheat, corn, and soybeans. However, because of its vast economic growth, the US depends increasingly on foreign sources for a long list of raw materials. The extent of US dependence on oil imports was dramatically demonstrated during the 1973 Arab oil embargo, when serious fuel shortages developed in many sections of the country.

By the middle of the 20th century, the US was a leading consumer of nearly every important industrial raw material. The industry of the US produced about 40% of the world's total output of goods, despite the fact that the country's population comprised about 6% of the world total and its land area about 7% of the earth's surface. In recent decades, US production has continued to expand, though at a slower rate than that of most other industrialized nations. The value of US exports of manufactured goods increased from $12.7 billion to $154.2 billion between 1960 and 1995.

In absolute terms the US far exceeds every other nation in the size of its gross national product (GNP), which more than tripled between 1970 and 1983 to $3.3 trillion. In 1996 per capita GNP was estimated at $25,989 (in 1992 dollars). In 1995 the nation's gross domestic product (GDP)—the total output of goods and services produced by labor and property in the US—reached a record $7.2 trillion in current dollars. The following table shows major components of the GDP for 1970, 1980, and 1993 (in billions of dollars):

	1970	1980	1993
Agriculture, forestry, fisheries	29.8	66.7	107.3
Mining	18.7	112.6	89.4
Construction	51.1	128.7	234.2
Manufacturing	253.1	588.3	1,118.3
Transportation and public utilities	88.0	242.2	559.3
Wholesale and retail trade	168.8	436.6	1,005.5
Finance, insurance, real estate	146.3	418.4	1,180.6
Services	120.5	377.0	1,264.8
Government and government enterprises	134.2	324.2	781.6
TOTALS	1,010.7	2,708.0	6,341.0

Inflation is has not been as significant factor in the US economy in the 1990s as it was in the 1970s and 1980s. The US inflation rate tends to be lower than that of the majority of industrialized nations. For the period 1970–78, for example, consumer prices increased by an annual average of 6.7%, less than in every other Western country except Austria, Luxembourg, Switzerland, and West Germany, and well below the price increase in Japan. The double-digit inflation of 1979–81 came as a rude shock to most Americans, with economists and politicians variously blaming international oil price rises, federal monetary policies, and US government spending.

The following table shows the erosion of the purchasing power of the dollar between 1950 and 1995:

	PRODUCER PRICES (1982=$1.00)	CONSUMER PRICES (1982–84=$1.00)
1950	3.546	4.151
1955	3.279	3.732
1960	2.994	3.373
1965	2.933	3.166
1970	2.545	2.574
1975	1.718	1.859
1980	1.136	1.215
1985	0.955	0.928
1990	0.839	0.766
1992	0.812	0.713
1995	0.760	0.656

The US entered the post–World War II era with the world's largest, and strongest, economy. Public confidence in both business and government was strong, the nation enjoyed the largest peacetime trade surplus in its history, and the gross national product grew to a record $482.7 billion by the end of the 1950s.

In the sixties the country enjoyed the most sustained period of economic expansion it had known, accompanied by rising productivity and low unemployment. Real income rose 50% during the decade, and US investment in foreign countries reached $49 billion in 1965, up from $11.8 billion in 1950. Big business and big government were both powerful forces in the economy during this period, when large industrial corporations accounted for vast portions of the national income, and the federal government expanded its role in such areas as social welfare, scientific research, space technology, and development of the nation's highway system.

After two decades of prosperity, Americans experienced an economic downturn in the 1970s, a period known for the unprecedented combination of lagging economic growth and inflation that gave birth to the term *stagflation*. Foreign competitors in Japan and Europe challenged the global dominance of American manufacturers, and oil crises in 1973–74 and 1979 shook public confidence in the institutions of both government and business. The forced bail-outs of Chrysler and Lockheed were symbolic of the difficult transition to a new economic era, marked by the growing importance of the service sector and the ascendancy of small businesses.

During Ronald Reagan's first presidential term, from 1980 to 1984, the nation endured two years of severe recession followed by two years of robust recovery. The inflation rate was brought down, and millions of new jobs were created. The economic boom of the early and mid-eighties, however, coincided with a number of alarming developments. Federal budget deficits, caused by dramatic increases in the military budget and by rising costs of entitlement programs such as Medicaid and Medicare, averaged more than $150 billion annually. By 1992, the total deficit reached $290 billion, or $1,150 for every American. In addition, corporate debt rose dramatically, and household borrowing grew twice as fast as personal income. The eighties also witnessed a crisis in the banking industry, caused by a combination of factors, including high inflation and interest rates, problem loans to developing countries, and speculative real-estate ventures that caused thousands of banks to fail when the real-estate boom of the early eighties collapsed.

The disparity between the affluent and the poor widened in the course of the decade. The share of the nation's income received by the richest 5% of American families rose from 18.6% in 1977 to 24.5% in 1990, while the share of the poorest 20% fell from 5.7% to 4.3%. Externally, the nation's trade position deteriorated, as a high level of foreign investment combined with an uncompetitive US dollar to create a ballooning trade deficit. In 1990, the American economy plunged into a recession. Factors contributing to the slump included rising oil prices following Iraq's invasion of Kuwait, a sharp increase in interest rates, and declining availability of credit. Output fell 1.6% and 1.7 million jobs were cut. Unemployment rose from 5.2% in 1989 to 7.5% in 1991.

The recovery that began in March 1991 inaugurated a sustained period of expansion that, as of mid-1997, was the third longest since World War II, characterized by moderation in the key areas of growth, inflation, unemployment, and interest rates. Real GDP growth, which fluctuated between 2% and 3.5% throughout the period, was 2.4% for 1996. After peaking at 7.5%, unemployment declined steadily throughout the early and mid-1990s, falling to 5.6% in 1995, 5.3% at the end of 1996, and, as of May 1997, reaching a 24-year low of 4.8%. After 1993/94, inflation mostly remained under 3%. One exception to the generally moderate character of the economy was the stock market, which rose 60% between 1995 and 1997, buoyed by the combination of low unemployment and low inflation, as well as strong corporate earnings. Further cause for optimism was the bipartisan balanced-budget legislation enacted and signed into law in 1997. The plan, combining tax and spending cuts over a five-year period, was aimed at balancing the federal budget by 2002 for the first time since 1969.

As the 21st century neared, significant economic concerns—aside from the inevitable worry over how long the boom could last without an eventual downturn—included the nation's sizable trade deficit, the increasing medical costs of an aging population, and the failure of the strong economy to improve conditions for the poor, whose real income had fallen 16% between 1973 and 1993.

21INCOME

Total earned income was $3.42 trillion in 1995. The GDP amounted to $7.25 trillion in 1995, or $26,980 per capita. Per capita income in 1996 was $24,231, up from $23,196 in 1995, a 4.5% increase. The price index for personal consumption expenditures increased by 2.2% for the same period; the US Central Intelligence Agency estimates that the average annual inflation rate from 1985–95 was 3.2%.

The median household disposable income in 1995 was $34,076; New Jersey, Alaska, Hawaii, and New Hampshire had the highest median household disposable incomes (above $42,000). That year, among the lowest (under $26,000) were Alabama, Arkansas, New Mexico, and West Virginia. In 1995, 9% of the nation's families lived below the federal poverty line (down from 14.5% in 1992), while 10.8% had incomes of $100,000 or more. Pockets of concentrated unemployment in the central cities, especially among young blacks and Hispanics, constituted one of the nation's most serious social and economic problems. In 1994, by race, 9.5 million blacks, or 28% of all blacks in the US were considered by the federal government as impoverished, comprising 28% of the total. Nearly 22.7 million whites, or 10.5% of the white population, lived in poverty, but made up 66% of all US residents living in poverty. Among persons of Hispanic origin (who may be of any race), 7.9 million or 28% lived in poverty, representing 23% of the nation's total impoverished population.

The World Bank estimates that the wealthiest 10% of the population is responsible for 20% of consumption. Private consumption per capita in 1993 was estimated at $18,507; approximately 8.4% was spent on food; 6.5% on clothing; 13.6% on rent; 3.0% on fuel and power; 12.0% on health care; 7.0% on education; 14.3% on transportation and communication; 8.7% on consumer durables; and 26.5% on other consumption.

22LABOR

About 117,600,000 persons constituted the country's civilian and military labor force in 1992. During 1992, a recession year, the unemployment rate reached 7.4%. A federal survey in January 1997 revealed the following nonfarm employment patterns:

	EMPLOYEES	AVE. HOURLY EARNINGS (EST.)
Agricultural services	3,036,000	n/a
Mining	553,000	$16.18
Construction	7,792,000	$15.69
Manufacturing	20,591,000	$13.07
Durable goods	12,467,000	n/a
Nondurable goods	8,124,000	n/a
Transportation and public utilities	8,724,000	$14.76
Wholesale and retail trade	25,892,000	
Wholesale trade	4,824,000	$13.15
Retail trade	21,068,000	$8.22
Finance, insurance, and real estate	8,007,000	$13.04
Services	46,073,000	$12.21
Private households	946,000	n/a
Other service industries	45,127,000	n/a
Professional services	30,923,000	n/a
Public administration	5,715,000	n/a

As of 1991, federal, state, and local governments employed 18,554,000 persons. Agriculture engaged 3,115,372 Americans during 1992.

Earnings of workers vary considerably with type of work and section of country. The national average wage was $12.37 per hour for industrial workers in 1995. The average workweek for nonfarm employees in 1995 was 34.5 hours, with workers in manufacturing averaging the longest workweek with an average of 44.7.

There were 39 national labor unions with over 100,000, the largest being the National Educational Association with 2,000,000 members. In 1990, 16.1% of the nonagricultural work force belonged to labor unions, down from 18.8% in 1984. The most important federation of organized workers in the US is the American Federation of Labor–Congress of Industrial Organizations (AFL–CIO), whose affiliated unions had 14,100,000 members in 1992. The major independent industrial and labor unions and their estimated 1993 memberships are the International Brotherhood of Teamsters, 1,700,000, and the United Automobile Workers, 1,197,000. Most of the other unaffiliated unions are confined to a single establishment or locality. US labor unions exercise economic and political influence not only through the power of strikes and slowdowns but also through the human and financial resources they allocate to political campaigns (usually on behalf of Democratic candidates) and through the selective investment of multibillion-dollar pension funds.

The National Labor Relations Act of 1935 (The Wagner Act), the basic labor law of the US, was considerably modified by the Labor-Management Relations Act of 1947 (the Taft-Hartley Act) and the Labor-Management Reporting and Disclosure Act of 1959 (the Landrum-Griffin Act). Closed-shop agreements, which require employers to hire only union members, are banned. The union shop agreement, however, is permitted; it allows the hiring of nonunion members on the condition that they join the union within a given period of time.

In the mid-1990s, 19 states had right-to-work laws, forbidding the imposition of union membership as a condition of employment. Under the Taft-Hartley Act, the president of the US may postpone a strike for 90 days in the national interest. The act of 1959 requires all labor organizations to file constitutions, bylaws, and detailed financial reports with the secretary of labor, and stipulates methods of union elections. The National Labor Relations Board seeks to remedy or prevent unfair labor practices and supervises union elections, while the Equal Employment Opportunity Commission seeks to prevent discrimination in hiring, firing, and apprenticeship programs.

The number of work stoppages and of workers involved reached a peak in the late 1960s and early 1970s, declining steadily thereafter. In 1995 there were 31 major stoppages involving 191,500 workers, the lowest number at least since World War II; a major stoppage was defined as one involving 1,000 workers or more for a minimum of one day or shift.

23AGRICULTURE

In 1995, the US produced a substantial share of the world's agricultural commodities, including soybeans, 48%; corn for grain (maize), 38%; cotton, 23%; wheat, 11%; and tobacco, 8%. Much US farm produce is exported. Agricultural exports reached $45.7 billion in 1996.

The gross farm income of $210.4 billion in 1995 included $185.75 billion in farm marketings; $7.2 billion in government payments; $0.5 billion in the value of products consumed on the farm; and $9.4 billion in the rental value of dwellings. Average net farm income was $34.8 billion.

Between 1930 and 1992, the number of farms in the US declined from 6,546,000 to an estimated 1,925,000. The total amount of farmland increased from 399 million hectares (986 million acres) in 1930 to 479 million hectares (1.18 billion acres) in 1959 but declined to 378 million hectares (945.5 million acres) in 1992. From 1930 to 1992, the size of the average farm tripled from 61 to 196 hectares (from 151 to 491 acres), a result of the consolidation effected by large-scale mechanized production. The farm population, which comprised 35% of the total US population in 1910, declined to 25% during the Great Depression of the 1930s and dwindled to 1.8% by 1991.

A remarkable increase in the application of machinery to farms took place during and after World War II. Tractors, trucks, milking machines, grain combines, corn pickers, and pickup bailers became virtual necessities in farming. In 1920 there was less than one tractor in use for every 400 hectares (1,000 acres) of cropland harvested; by 1991 there were 15. Two other elements essential to US farm productivity are chemical fertilizers and irrigation. The percentage of farm acreage under irrigation increased from 4.8% in 1987 to 5.3% in 1992.

Substantial quantities of corn, the most valuable crop produced in the US, are grown in almost every state; its yield and price are important factors in the economies of the regions where it is grown. The following table reports figures for production of selected US crops in 1995, and their percent of world production:

	PRODUCTION (1,000 METRIC TONS)	AS % OF WORLD PRODUCTION
Wheat	530,000	11.2
Corn for grain	506,000	37.8
Rice, milled	351,000	1.7
Soybeans	125,000	47.6
Cotton	85,600	23.0

In 1994, the total farm cash receipts (in millions) of $179,669 million were made up of corn, $15,031, soybeans, $13,404; wheat, $7,794; cotton (lint and seed), $5,730; hay, $3,579; tobacco, $2,646; sorghum, $1,654; rice, $1,231; vegetables, $13,033; fruits and tree nuts, $10,146; and livestock, $88,107.

24ANIMAL HUSBANDRY

The livestock population in 1995 included an estimated 103.3 million head of cattle (approximately 9% of which were milk cows), 59.6 million hogs, and 8.9 million sheep and lambs. In 1994, US farms produced 7,018 million broilers (chickens), and 289 million turkeys, and 73.9 billion eggs. Beef production in 1994 amounted to 19.4 billion kg (42.7 billion lb); pork, 11.1 billion kg (24.5 billion lb); and mutton and lamb, 284 million kg (626 million lb). Milk production totaled 70.64 billion kg (155.6 billion lb) in 1995, with California, Iowa, Minnesota, New York, Texas, and Wisconsin together accounting for much of the total. Wisconsin, Minnesota, and California account for much of US butter production, which totaled 600 million kg (1,296 million lb) in 1994; in that year, the US produced 3.06 billion kg (6.73 billion lb).

25FISHING

The 1995 commercial catch was 4.5 billion kg (9.9 billion lb), excluding the weight of mollusk shells. Food fish make up 78% of the catch, and nonfood fish, processed for fertilizer and oil, 22%. Commercial landings by US fishermen valued at $3.77 billion in 1995. The commercial fishing fleet comprised some 78,000 vessels and boats in 1992. Domestic aquaculture yielded 58.3 million trout, weighing a total of 23.7 million kg (52.1 million lb), and valued at $52.7 million; and 295. 1 million catfish with a total value of $225.5 million.

Alaska pollock, with landings of 1.5 billion kg (3.26 billion lb), was the most important species in quantity and 2d in value for 1993 among the commercial fishery landings in the US. Other species' rankings for quantity (and value) in 1993 included: salmon, 3d (2d); crab, 4th (1st); flounder, 5th (8th); cod (Atlantic and Pacific), 6th (5th); shrimp, 7th (3rd); and lobsters (American), 11th (6th). Menhaden was the second most important species in quantity, but was low in value.

Pollution is a problem of increasing concern to the US fishing industry; dumping of raw sewage, industrial wastes, spillage from oil tankers, and blowouts of offshore wells are the main threats to the fishing grounds. Overfishing is also a threat to the viability of the industry in some areas, especially Alaska.

26FORESTRY

US forest and woodlands covered about 301 million hectares (754 million acres) in 1992. Major forest regions include the eastern, central hardwood, southern, Rocky Mountain, and Pacific coast areas. The National Forest System accounts for approximately 27% of the nation's forestland. Large private lumber companies control extensive tracts of land in Maine, Oregon, and several other states.

Domestic production of roundwood during 1991 amounted to 495.8 million cu m (17,507 million cu ft), of which softwoods accounted for roughly 80%. The US, the world's 2d-leading producer of newsprint, attained an output of 6.2 million metric tons in 1991. To satisfy its needs, the US imported 6.8 million metric tons of newsprint in 1991, primarily from Canada, the major world producer. Other forest products in 1991 included 58.9 million metric tons of wood pulp, 72.7 million metric tons of paper and paperboard (excluding newsprint), 30.4 million cu m (1,073 million cu ft) of wood-based panels, 6.8 million cu m (240 million cu ft) of particleboard, and 17.3 million cu m (611 million cu ft) of plywood. Rising petroleum prices in the late 1970s sparked a revival in the use of wood as home heating fuel, especially in the Northeast. Fuelwood and charcoal production amounted to 85.9 million cu m in 1991.

Throughout the 19th century, the federal government distributed forestlands lavishly as a means of subsidizing railroads and education. By the turn of the century, the realization that the forests were not inexhaustible led to the growth of a vigorous conservation movement, which was given increased impetus during the 1930s and again in the late 1960s. Federal timberlands are no longer open for private acquisition, although the lands can be leased for timber cutting and for grazing. In recent decades, the states also have moved in the direction of retaining forestlands and adding to their holdings when possible. As of 30 September 1992, the US Forest Service managed 77.2 million hectares (191 million acres) of forest, including 13.8 million hectares (34 million acres) of designated wilderness.

27MINING

Rich in a variety of mineral resources, the US is a world leader in the production of many important mineral commodities, such as aluminum, cement, copper, pig iron, lead, molybdenum, phosphates, potash, salt, sulfur, uranium, and zinc. In 1992, mining in the US employed some 637,000 persons at 30,828 establishments. The total US nonfuel mineral production value in 1992 was $31,174 million. The leading mineral-producing states are Texas, Louisiana, Oklahoma, and New Mexico, which are important for petroleum and natural gas, and Kentucky, West Virginia, and Pennsylvania, important for coal. Iron ore supports the nation's most basic nonagricultural industry, iron and steel manufacture. Domestic demand for iron ore is satisfied by imports from Canada and Venezuela. The major domestic sources are in the Lake Superior area: Minnesota and Michigan lead all other states in iron ore yields. In 1991, the US ranked 1st in the mining of salt, phosphate, and elemental sulfur; 2d in lead, gold, and silver; 3d in uranium and nitrogen in ammonia; 4th in potash and cement; and 6th in iron ore.

MAJOR LAND-USE REGIONS AND MINERAL RESOURCES

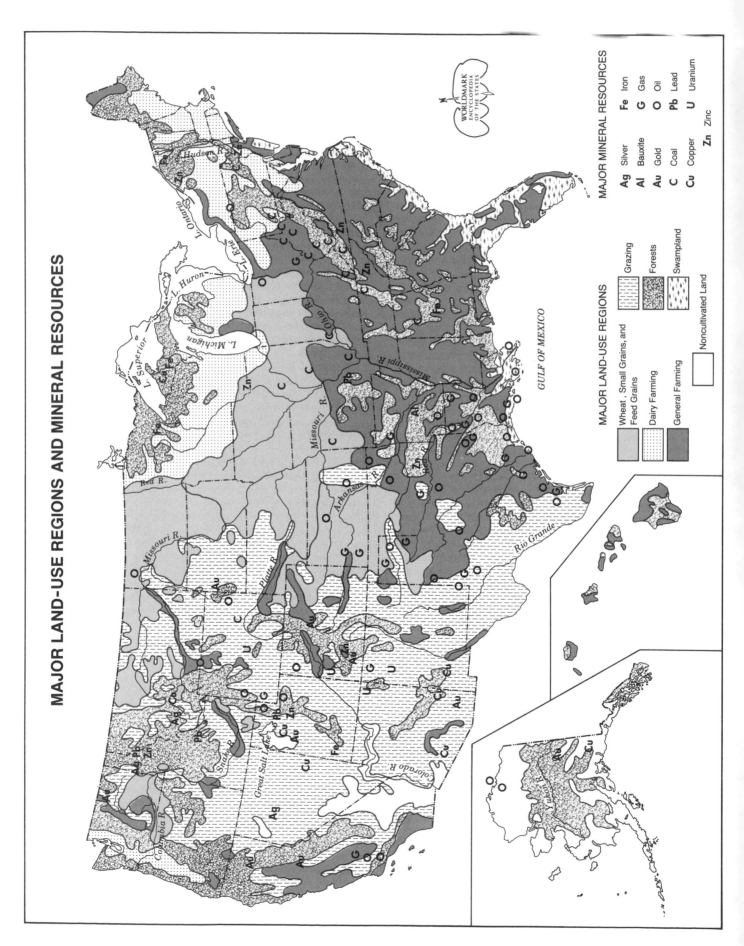

MAJOR LAND-USE REGIONS

Wheat, Small Grains, and Feed Grains

Dairy Farming

General Farming

Grazing

Forests

Swampland

Noncultivated Land

MAJOR MINERAL RESOURCES

Ag	Silver	**Fe**	Iron
Al	Bauxite	**G**	Gas
Au	Gold	**O**	Oil
C	Coal	**Pb**	Lead
Cu	Copper	**U**	Uranium
		Zn	Zinc

WORLDMARK ENCYCLOPEDIA OF THE STATES

GULF OF MEXICO

Hudson R.
L. Ontario
L. Erie
L. Huron
L. Michigan
L. Superior
Red R.
Missouri R.
Ohio R.
Mississippi R.
Arkansas R.
Rio Grande
Platte R.
Snake R.
Great Salt Lake
Columbia R.
Colorado R.
Yukon R.

The following table shows volume (in metric tons, except cement) for selected mineral production in 1995 (excluding fossil fuels):

	VOLUME
Cement*	76,100,000 short tons
Iron ore	62,000,000 tons
Phosphate	46,000,000 tons
Salt*	39,200,000 tons
Sulfur, elemental	3,010,000 tons
Potash	1,470,000 tons
Copper	1,890,000 tons
Zinc	600,000 tons
Lead	374,000 tons

*Includes Puerto Rico

28ENERGY AND POWER

The US, with about 4.6% of the world's population, consumed 24.3% of the world's energy in 1995. The US is also the world's leading energy producer, accounting for about 19.1% of the world's primary energy production in 1995. In 1995, the US produced 24% of the world's coal, 25% of its natural gas, but only 10.4% of its crude oil. Coal supplied about 23.9% of primary energy in 1995; nuclear sources, 8.8%; natural gas, 27%; waterpower, 1.2%; petroleum, 39%; and geothermal, wind, photovoltaic, and solar energy, 0.1%. Increased use of natural gas was the most spectacular development in the commercial marketing of fuel after World War II; between 1950 and 1971, its share of total US energy production doubled from 20% to 40%, although by 1995 the proportion had declined to 28%. Coal accounted for 31.8% of US energy production (Btu basis) that year; crude oil, 20.1%; liquefied natural gas, 3.5%; nuclear electric power, 10.4%; hydroelectricity, 4.8%; geothermal, wind, solar, and other energy, 1.4%.

Mineral fuel production in the US dates to the early 1800s; by 1810–19 US coal production was about 230,000 tons, and fuelwood production equivalent to 26 million tons of coal. In 1854, a refinery opened in Brooklyn, New York, to process shale and coal to kerosene. In 1859, the US recorded its first oil production, and in 1870, John D. Rockefeller established the Standard Oil Company in Cleveland, Ohio, which controlled 90% of the Western oil market from 1880 to 1910, and was split into 33 independent companies in 1911 under the Sherman Antitrust Act. In 1957, the nuclear portion of domestic electricity generation accounted for less than 0.05% of the nation's total; by 1992 it accounted for 22.1%.

Proved reserves of crude oil totaled an estimated 29.6 billion barrels at the start of 1996 (2.9% of the world's total). Reserves of natural gas were about 163.8 trillion cu ft (4.6 trillion cu m) in 1996, equivalent to about 3.3% of the world's proved reserves. Recoverable coal reserves amounted to 265,167 million tons at the start of 1996 (44% anthracite and bituminous), equivalent to 23.3% of the world's total. Mineral fuel production in 1995 included an estimated 636.1 million tons of hard coal (2d after China) and 393.5 million tons of lignite (1st); 538.5 billion cu m (18.9 trillion cu ft) of natural gas (2d after Russia), and 382.5 million tons of crude oil (2d after Saudi Arabia). The 1973 Arab oil embargo and subsequent fuel shortages prompted a host of governmental measures aimed at increasing development of oil and gas resources, including an easing of restrictions on oil drilling on the continental shelf.

In 1995, public utilities and private industrial plants generated 3,367 billion kWh of electricity. Conventional steam and internal combustion plants produced most of the electricity. Coal-fired generation accounted for 50.9%; natural gas, 14.8%; and oil, 2.3%. Nuclear power and hydroelectricity contributed 20% and 9.1%, respectively. Other sources of electricity generation in 1995 included wood/waste, 1.9%; geothermal, 0.5%; other gaseous fuels, 0.4%; and wind/solar power, 0.1%. Installed generating capacity at electric utilities totaled 733.1 million kW in 1994. In 1995, nuclear-powered generators in operation had an estimated total capability of 1,165 million kW and generated 673.4 billion kWh of electricity (up from 51.8 million kW and 251.1 billion kWh in 1980). Because of cost and safety problems, the future of the nuclear power industry in the US was in doubt in the late 1980s. The number of operable nuclear power units totaled 109 in 1995, an increase of only nine units since 1986.

During the 1980s, some attention was focused on the development of solar power, synthetic fuels, geothermal resources, and other energy technologies. Such energy conservation measures as mandatory automobile fuel-efficiency standards and tax incentives for home insulation were promoted by the federal government, which also decontrolled oil and gas prices in the expectation that a rise in domestic costs to world-market levels would provide a powerful economic incentive for consumers to conserve fuel. Since the mid-1980s, net petroleum imports have risen from 4.29 million barrels per day in 1985 to 7.06 million barrels daily in 1994, which is still below the record level of 8.56 million barrels per day set in 1977.

29INDUSTRY

Although the US remains one of the world's preeminent industrial powers, manufacturing no longer plays as dominant a role in the economy as it once did.

Between 1979 and 1991, manufacturing employment fell from 20.9 million to 18.4 million, or from 21.8% to 16.2% of national employment. In 1988, manufacturing's gross product amounted to nearly $949 billion. Throughout the 1960s, manufacturing accounted for about 29% of total national income; by 1987, the proportion was down to about 19%. In 1989, manufacturing accounted for about 22.7% of GDP.

Leading industrial centers are the metropolitan areas of Chicago, Los Angeles, New York, Detroit, and Philadelphia. The Midwest leads all other regions by virtue of its huge concentration of heavy industry, including the manufacturing of automobiles, trucks, and other vehicles.

In 1991, personal income derived from manufacturing earnings in durable goods amounted to nearly $399.3 billion; for nondurable goods, $657 billion. Leading manufacturing industries of durable goods in 1989 (as a percentage of all manufacturing) included: non-electrical machinery (18.9%), electric and electronic equipment (9.8%), motor vehicles and equipment (5%), and other transportation equipment (6.9%). The principal manufacturing industries of nondurable goods in 1989 and their contribution to the output of the manufacturing sector were: chemicals and allied products (8.1%), food and kindred products (7.6%), printing and publishing (4.9%), and petroleum and coal products (4.8%).

Large corporations are dominant especially in sectors such as steel, automobiles, pharmaceuticals, aircraft, petroleum refining, computers, soaps and detergents, tires, and communications equipment. The 500 largest firms, as ranked by *Fortune* magazine in 1993, had over $2.4 trillion in sales and assets of over $2.7 trillion, and registered just $62.6 billion in profits. Fourteen companies had profits exceeding $1 billion in 1992, led by Philip Morris ($4.94 billion), Exxon ($4.77 billion), and General Electric ($4.73 billion). Companies with the largest amount of sales in 1992 were General Motors, $132.8 billion; Exxon, $103.5 billion; Ford, $100.8 billion; International Business Machines (IBM), $64.1 billion; General Electric, $62.2 billion; Mobil, $57.4 billion; Philip Morris, $50.2 billion; DuPont, $37.6 billion; and Chevron, $37.5 billion. Although General Motors led in sales, it also led in losses, at nearly $23.5 billion. Ford and IBM reported losses of $7.3 and $4.9 billion, respectively, in 1992. The growth of multinational activities of US corporations has been rapid in recent decades, with capital expenditures by US-owned foreign affiliates peaking at $42.4 billion in 1980 before declining to $37.7 billion in 1983.

The history of US industry has been marked by the introduction of increasingly sophisticated technology in the manufacturing process. Advances in chemistry and electronics have revolutionized many industries through new products and methods: examples include the impact of plastics on petrochemicals, the use of lasers and electronic sensors as measuring and controlling devices, and the application of microprocessors to computing machines, home entertainment products, and a variety of other industries. Science has vastly expanded the number of metals available for industrial purposes, notably such light metals as aluminum, magnesium, and titanium. Integrated machines now perform a complex number of successive operations that formerly were done on the assembly line at separate stations. Those industries have prospered that have been best able to make use of the new technology, and the economies of some states—in particular California and Massachusetts—are largely based on it. On the other hand, certain industries—especially clothing and steelmaking—have suffered from outmoded facilities that (coupled with high US labor costs) force the price of their products above the world market level. In 1991, the US was the world's 2d-leading steel producer (after Japan) at 79.7 million metric tons, but also the world's 2d-largest steel importer (after Germany) at 14.3 million metric tons. Employment in the steel industry has fallen from 521,000 in 1974 to 190,000 in 1992. Automobile manufacturing was another ailing industry in the 1980s: passenger car production fell from 7,098,910 in 1987 to 5,438,579 in 1991, while commercial vehicle production declined from 3,825,776 in 1987 to 3,371,942 in 1991. Moreover, included among the cars assembled domestically were an increasing number of vehicles produced by US subsidiaries of foreign firms and containing a substantial proportion of foreign-made parts.

30COMMERCE

Retail sales in the US exceeded $1,949 billion ($7,643 per capita) in 1992, with California, Florida, New York, and Texas leading in volume. The growth of great chains of retail stores, particularly in the form of the supermarket, was one of the most conspicuous developments in retail trade following the end of World War II. Nearly 100,000 single-unit grocery stores went out of business between 1948 and 1958; the independent grocer's share of the food market dropped from 50% to 30% of the total in the same period. In 1987, there were just 137,584 grocery retailers in the US.

Multiunit chain stores account for over one-third of the total retail trade, but in certain kinds of retail business (variety and department store trade) the chain is the dominant mode of business organization. With the great suburban expansion of the 1960s emerged the planned shopping center, usually designed by a single development organization and intended to provide different kinds of stores in order to meet all the shopping needs of the particular area. Franchised businesses now account for about 40% of all retail sales in the US, and are projected to exceed 50% of retail sales by 2000.

Installment credit is a major support for consumer purchases in the US. Most US families own and use credit cards. Credit cards accounted for 35% of the $385 billion in consumer loans made to individuals by insured commercial banks in 1992.

The US advertising industry is the world's most highly developed. Particularly with the expansion of television audiences, spending for advertising has increased almost annually to successive record levels. Advertising expenditures in 1992 nearly reached an estimated $131.74 billion, up from $66.58 billion in 1982 and $11.96 billion in 1960. From 1990 to 1991, advertising expenditures decreased by $2.24 billion, due to recession. Of the 1992 total, about 58% was spent in national media and 42% in local media. Newspaper advertising accounted for 23.4%, television advertising 58%, and radio advertising 6.6%. Direct mail advertising (chiefly letters, booklets, catalogs, and handbills) accounted for 19.3%, magazines 5.3%, and other media 23%.

Exports of domestic merchandise, raw materials, agricultural and industrial products, and military goods amounted in 1995 to nearly $787 billion, up from $394 billion in 1990. Total imports for 1995 were valued at $891.6 billion, a record high, leaving a deficit of more than $105 billion; in 1987, the net merchandise trade deficit reached $159.6 billion. One import category that proliferated between the late 1970s and the mid-1990s was telecommunications apparatus—mainly television sets and video cassette recorders from Japan—which increased some ninefold between 1975 and 1985. Road vehicles accounted for nearly 14% of imports in 1992. One rapidly growing export category was computers, which rose from $1.2 billion in 1970 to $30.9 billion in 1992; grain exports rose from $2.6 billion to a peak of $19.5 billion in 1981, but declined to $11.47 billion in 1992.

Leading merchandise export by value in 1995 (in billions) included: transportation equipment, $27.7; machinery, $182.7; and agricultural products, $54.9.

Leading merchandise imports by value in 1995 (in billions) included: transportation equipment, $75.1; machinery, $241.7; and petroleum products, $52.8.

Principal trading partners in 1992 (and the respective US merchandise exports and imports in millions of dollars) were:

	EXPORTS	IMPORTS
Canada	90,423	100,724
Japan	46,856	96,858
Mexico	40,469	35,588
UK	22,410	22,000
Germany	20,348	28,750
France	14,579	14,658
Taiwan	14,470	24,599
South Korea	13,859	16,657
Netherlands	13,427	5,729
Belgium–Luxembourg	9,964	4,697
Singapore	9,526	11,316
Hong Kong	9,027	9,800
Australia	8,731	3,666
Italy	8,573	12,205
China	7,453	25,702
Brazil	5,741	7,615
Venezuela	5,316	8,180

31CONSUMER PROTECTION

Consumer protection has become a major government enterprise during the 20th century. The Federal Trade commission (FTC), established in 1914, administers laws governing the granting and use of credit and the activities of credit bureaus; it also investigates unfair or deceptive trade practices, including price fixing and false advertising. The Securities and Exchange Commission, created in 1934, seeks to protect investors, while the Consumer Product Safety Commission, created in 1972, has the authority to establish product safety standards and to ban hazardous products. Overseeing the safety of air and highway transport is the National Transportation Safety Board, established in 1975. The Consumer Information Center Program of the General Services Administration (Pueblo, Colo.) and the Food Safety and Inspection Service and Food and Nutrition Service of the Department of Agriculture also serve consumer interests. Legislation that would have established a Department of Consumer Affairs failed to win congressional approval several times during the 1970s, however.

Public interest groups have been exceptionally effective in promoting consumer issues. The Consumer Federation of

America (CFA; founded in 1967), with 220 member organizations, is the largest US consumer advocacy body; its concerns include product pricing, credit, and the cost and quality of health care, education, and housing. The CFA also serves as a clearinghouse for consumer information. Consumers Union of the US, founded in 1936, publishes the widely read monthly Consumer Reports, which tests, grades, and comments on a variety of retail products. The National Consumers League, founded in 1899, was a pioneer in the consumer movement, focusing especially on labor laws and working conditions. Much of the growth of consumerism in the 1970s resulted from the public relations efforts of one man—Ralph Nader. Already a well-known consumer advocate concerned particularly with automobile safety, Nader founded Public Citizen in 1971 and an affiliated litigation group the following year. As of 1994, Public Citizen claimed 100,000 supporters; its activities include research committees on tax reform, health care, work safety, and energy.

Other avenues open to consumers in most states include small claims courts, generally open to claims between $100 and $1,500 at modest legal cost. Complaints involving professional malpractice may be brought to state licensing or regulatory boards. Supported by the business community, the US Better Business Bureau provides general consumer information and arbitrate some customer-company disputes.

The US government publishes two helpful consumer guides. A listing of the publications is available from the government called, the "Consumer Information Catalog." This catalog is a free listing of about 200 of the best federal consumer publications. The federal publications range from planning a diet to financial planning. The publication, published quarterly by the Consumer Information Center of the US General Services Administration is available in most public libraries.

32BANKING

The Federal Reserve Act of 1913 provided the US with a central banking system. The Federal Reserve System dominates US banking, is a strong influence in the affairs of commercial banks, and exercises virtually unlimited control over the money supply.

Each of the 12 federal reserve districts contains a federal reserve bank. A board of nine directors presides over each reserve bank. Six are elected by the member banks in the district: of this group, three may be bankers; the other three represent business, industry, or agriculture. The Board of Governors of the Federal Reserve System (usually known as the Federal Reserve Board) appoints the remaining three, who may not be officers, directors, stockholders, or employees of any bank and who are presumed therefore to represent the public.

The Federal Reserve Board regulates the money supply and the amount of credit available to the public by asserting its power to alter the rediscount rate, by buying and selling securities in the open market, by setting margin requirements for securities purchases by altering reserve requirements of member banks in the system, and by resorting to a specific number of selective controls at its disposal. The Federal Reserve Board's role in regulating the money supply is held by economists of the monetarist school to be the single most important factor in determining the nation's inflation rate.

Member banks increase their reserves or cash holdings by rediscounting commercial notes at the federal reserve bank at a rate of interest ultimately determined by the Board of Governors. A change in the rediscount rate, therefore, directly affects the capacity of the member banks to accommodate their customers with loans. Similarly, the purchase or sale of securities in the open market, as determined by the Federal Open Market Committee, is another device whereby the amount of credit available to the public is expanded or contracted. The same effect is achieved in some measure by the power of the Board of Governors to raise or lower the reserves that member banks must keep against demand deposits. Credit tightening by federal authorities in early 1980 pushed the prime rate—the rate that commercial banks charge their most creditworthy customers—above 20% for the first time since the financial panics of 1837 and 1839, when rates reached 36%. As federal monetary policies eased, the prime rate dropped below 12% in late 1984 and has remained low.

Combined assets of all commercial banks as of 31 December 1992 exceeded $5.5 trillion. Net loans and leases amounted to nearly $2 trillion; aggregate domestic deposits were $2,698,954 million dollars; deposits with banks in foreign countries, foreign governments, and official institutions were $101,170 million.

The nation's leading commercial bank-holding companies on the basis of total assets as of 1990 were Citicorp—the largest commercial bank in the US, with (in thousands) $112,586,000 in deposits, followed by Bank America, $77,027,000 in deposits.

Under the provisions of the Banking Act of 1935, all members of the Federal Reserve System (and other banks that wish to do so) participate in a plan of deposit insurance (up to $100,000 for each individual account as of 1994) administered by the Federal Deposit Insurance Corporation (FDIC). As of 1992, the deposits of 14,146 commercial banks were insured by the FDIC. All national banks, of which there were 4,013 in 1990, are regulated members of the Federal Reserve System; most of the 361 mutual savings banks are registered by the FDIC. State banks, of which there were 1,021 in 1990, are also regulated by the FDIC.

Savings and loan associations are insured by the Federal Savings and Loan Insurance Corporation (FSLIC). Individual accounts were insured up to a limit of $100,000. Savings and loans failed at an alarming rate in the 1980s. In 1989 the government signed legislation that created the Resolution Trust Corporation. The RTC's job is to handle the savings and loans bailout, expected to cost taxpayers $345 billion through 2029.

33INSURANCE

At the end of 1991, 2,105 companies were dispensing ordinary life, group, industrial, and other kinds of life insurance policies. The overwhelming majority of US families have some life insurance with a legal reserve company, the Veterans Administration, or fraternal, assessment, burial, or savings bank organizations. As of 31 December 1992, life insurance policies in force totaled $10.4 trillion. Payments to policyholders totaled $218.6 billion.

Hundreds of varieties of insurance may be purchased. Besides life, the more important include accident, fire, hospital and medical expense, group accident and health, automobile liability, automobile damage, workers' compensation, ocean marine, and inland marine. Americans buy more life and health insurance than any other group except Canadians and Japanese. Of the world's ten largest insurers in 1991, three—Prudential Insurance, Metropolitan Life, and Aetna Life and Casualty—were American. During the 1970s, many states enacted a "no fault" form of automobile insurance, under which damages may be awarded automatically, without recourse to a lawsuit.

Life insurance company assets totaled $1,551 billion on 31 December 1991. The property and liability insurance industry had about $601.4 billion in assets in 1991. Premiums written totaled $223 billion, including private automotive coverage, $82.8 billion; accident and health coverage, $5.1 billion; workers' compensation coverage, $31.3 billion; homeowners' insurance, $19.3 billion; commercial multiperil policies, $17 billion; and fire insurance, $7.2 billion.

34SECURITIES

When the New York Stock Exchange opened in 1817 its trading volume was 100 shares a day. In 1992, 51.4 billion shares with a value of $1.7 trillion were traded on the NYSE. The two other major stock markets in the US are AMEX and NASDAQ. The total shares traded on these markets were 103.4 billion in 1992. The 51.4 billion shares traded on the NYSE represented 49.7% of the total shares traded. AMEX's 3.6 billion shares represented 3.5%; NASDAQ's 48.4 billion shares represented 46.8% of the total.

As of 1990 51 million people, 21.1% of the population, owned stock or mutual funds; up from 13.5% in 1980. Nearly 30 million people owned stocks listed on the NYSE and 26 million owned mutual funds, up 130% since 1985.

35 PUBLIC FINANCE

Under the Budget and Accounting Act of 1921, the president is responsible for preparing the federal government budget. In fact, the budget is prepared by the Office of Management and Budget (established in 1970), based on requests from the heads of all federal departments and agencies and advice from the Board of Governors of the Federal Reserve System, the Council of Economic Advisers, and the Treasury Department. The president submits a budget message to Congress in January. Under the Congressional Budget Act of 1974, the Congress establishes, by concurrent resolution, targets for overall expenditures and broad functional categories, as well as targets for revenues, the budget deficit, and the public debt. The Congressional Budget Office monitors the actions of Congress on individual appropriations bills with reference to those targets. The president exercises fiscal control over executive agencies, which issue periodic reports subject to presidential perusal. Congress exercises control through the comptroller general, head of the General Accounting Office, who sees to it that all funds have been spent and accounted for according to legislative intent. The fiscal year runs from 1 October to 30 September.

The public debt, subject to a statutory debt limit, rose from $43 billion in 1939/40 to more than $3.3 trillion in 1993. In fiscal year 1991/92, the federal deficit reached $290 million, a record high. President Clinton introduced a taxing and spending plan to reduce the rate of growth of the federal deficit when he began his term in 1993. The Clinton Administration calculated the package of tax increases and spending would cut the deficit by $500 billion over a four year period. The following table shows actual revenues and expenditures of the federal government for fiscal years 1991 and 1992 in billions of dollars.

	1991	1992
REVENUE AND GRANTS		
Tax revenue	1,027.00	1,052.92
Non-tax revenue	89.55	91.73
Capital revenues	0.22	0.15
Grants	43.15	11.91
TOTALS	1,159.92	1,156.71
EXPENDITURES AND LENDING MINUS REPAYMENTS	1991	1992
General public services	105.46	115.23
Defense	308.86	297.37
Public order and safety	13.82	16.11
Education	24.72	25.33
Health	196.54	231.11
Social security	373.49	411.32
Housing and community	36.55	38.40
Recreations, cultural and religious affairs	3.72	3.08
Economic affairs and services	144.07	87.93
Other expenditures	220.40	217.83
Adjustments	1.42	1.43
Lending minus repayments	3.38	0.82
TOTALS	1,433.43	1,445.96
Deficit/Surplus	−272.51	−289.25

36 TAXATION

Measured as a proportion of the GDP, the total US tax burden is less than that in most industrialized countries. Federal, state, and local taxes are levied in a variety of forms. The greatest source of revenue for the federal government is the personal income tax, which is paid by citizens and resident aliens on their worldwide income.

The Tax Reform Act of 1986, which took full effect in 1988, reduced 14 graduated tax brackets, ranging from 11% to 50%, to two brackets, 15% and 28%, in taxing individual income. In 1993, the 15% rate applied to the first $22,100 in taxable income of a single person, $18,450 of a married person filing separately, $36,900 of a married couple filing jointly, and $29,600 of a head of household. There was also a maximum rate of 31% for income over a certain amount, ranging from $44,575 for married taxpayers filing separately to $88,150 for joint returns. The 1986 law also eliminated the capital gains exclusion, reduced other deductions, and curtailed the number of value of tax shelters. The top corporate tax rate was reduced from 46% to 34%, and the investment tax credit was eliminated. Excise taxes are levied on certain motor vehicles, personal air transportation, some motor fuels (excluding gasohol), alcoholic beverages, tobacco products, tires and tubes, telephone charges, and gifts and estates.

37 ECONOMIC POLICY

By the end of the 19th century, regulation rather than subsidy had become the characteristic form of government intervention in US economic life. The abuses of the railroads with respect to rates and services gave rise to the Interstate Commerce Commission in 1887, which was subsequently strengthened by numerous acts that now stringently regulate all aspects of US railroad operations.

The growth of large-scale corporate enterprises, capable of exercising monopolistic or near-monopolistic control of given segments of the economy, resulted in federal legislation designed to control trusts. The Sherman Antitrust Act of 1890, reinforced by the Clayton Act of 1914 and subsequent acts, established the federal government as regulator of large-scale business. This tradition of government intervention in the economy was reinforced during the Great Depression of the 1930s, when the Securities and Exchange Commission and the National Labor Relations Board were established. The expansion of regulatory programs accelerated during the 1960s and early 1970s with the creation of the federal Environmental Protection Agency, Equal Employment Opportunity Commission, Occupational Safety and Health Administration, and Consumer Product Safety Commission, among other bodies. Subsidy programs were not entirely abandoned, however. Federal price supports and production subsidies have made the government a major force in stabilizing US agriculture. Moreover, the federal government has stepped in to arrange for guaranteed loans for two large private firms—Lockheed in 1971 and Chrysler in 1980—where thousands of jobs would have been lost in the event of bankruptcy.

As the 1980s began, there was a general consensus that, at least in some areas, government regulation was contributing to inefficiency and higher prices. Thus, the Carter administration moved to deregulate the airline, trucking, and communications industries; subsequently, the Reagan administration relaxed government regulation of bank savings accounts and automobile manufacture as it decontrolled oil and gas prices. The Reagan administration also sought to slow the growth of social-welfare spending and attempted, with only partial success, to transfer control over certain federal social programs to the states and to reduce or eliminate some programs entirely.

Some areas of federal involvement, however, seem safely entrenched. Old age and survivors' insurance, unemployment insurance, and other aspects of the Social Security program have been accepted areas of governmental responsibility since the 1930s. Federal responsibility has also been extended to insurance of bank deposits, to mortgage insurance, and to regulation of stock transactions. The government fulfills a supervisory and regulatory role in labor-management relations. Labor and management customarily disagree on what the role should be, but neither side advocates total removal of government from this field.

From the end of World War II until the end of 1952, US government transfers of capital abroad represented an annual average of about $5,470 million, or 88.3% of the overall national average, while private investments averaged roughly $730 million a year, or about 11.7%. Portfolio investment represented less than $150 million a year, or only 2.5% of the annual aggregate.

After 1952, however, direct private investment began to increase, and portfolio investment rose markedly. In the late 1950s, new private direct investment was increasing yearly by $2 billion or more, while private portfolio investment and official US government loans were climbing by a minimum annual amount of $1 billion each. During the 1960–73 period, the value of US-held assets abroad increased by nearly 12% annually; from the mid-1970s, they rose most years by at least 15%, reaching $887.4 billion in 1983. Through 1980, direct private investments abroad represented the largest share of US overseas assets; since 1981, however, foreign lending by US banks has come to dominate US investment holdings. The rapid rise of US bank lending abroad gave the US a vital economic as well as political stake in the financial stability of developing nations, especially in Latin America, since a serious default by a principal debtor nation would threaten all creditor institutions.

The US share of global wealth creation fell from over 40 percent in 1970 to slightly more than a third in the early nineties. This shift indicated not that the competitiveness of US industries had declined but rather that faster technological, transport and information transfer had enabled other countries to catch up, thus limiting US economy's global market share. In 1994, US productivity and costs were comparable to those of its major competitors in both manufacturing and services industries.

During the 1980s, the Reagan and Bush administrations sought to implement a variety of "supply side" reforms—to limit government intrusion in markets by reducing taxation and regulation. These measures were intended to promote saving and investment and thus raise productivity and long term growth. Contrary to the government's projections, however, the personal savings ratio continued to fall, from 7.9 percent in 1980 to 4 percent in 1989 and 1993. Gross private investment's share of US GDP declined from 17.3 percent in 1980 to 12.9 percent in 1992. The decline in savings relative to investment created a market receptive to foreign savings which transformed the US from a large creditor to a large debtor and increased its vulnerability to economic fluctuations in other countries. Whereas the US had a current account credit of 14.5 percent of GDP in 1980, in the early nineties it had a current account deficit of 2 percent of GDP. The trade deficit in 1992 was largely in goods and investment. In 1992, the US traded goods deficit consisted of a $49 billion deficit with Asia excluding Japan, $50 billion with Japan itself, and $10 billion with Canada. The US had a surplus of $7 billion with eastern and western Europe and a $6 billion surplus with Latin America.

In 1993, Congress approved the North American Free Trade Agreement, which extended the Free Trade Agreement between Canada and the United States to include Mexico. NAFTA, by eliminating tariffs and other trade barriers, created a free trade zone with a combined market size of $6.5 trillion and 370 million consumers. The effect on employment was uncertain—estimates varied from a loss of 150,000 jobs over the next ten years to a net gain of 200,000. Labor intensive goods-producing industries, such as apparel and textiles, were expected to suffer, while it was predicted that capital goods industries would benefit. It was anticipated that US automakers would benefit in the short run by taking advantage of the low wages in Mexico and that US grain farmers and the US banking, financial, and telecommunications sectors would gain enormous new markets.

38HEALTH

The US health care system is among the most advanced in the world. In 1993, health expenditures were to have reached a projected $903.3 billion, equivalent to 14.4% of GDP. Escalating health care costs resulted in several proposals for a national health care program in the 1970s, early 1980s, and early 1990s. During 1991, the US Census Bureau estimated that 35.4 million US residents (14% of the population) were without any form of health insurance. At the end of 1991, over 40 such proposals had been aired by politicians, medical and business groups, labor unions, and academicians. Most reform measures rely either on market-oriented approaches designed to widen insurance coverage through tax subsidies, on a federally controlled single-payer plan, or on mandatory employer payments for insurance coverage.

Life expectancy for someone born in 1992 was a US record high 75.7 years. Males could expect to live 72.3 years, females 79.0 years. By race and gender, white females had the highest US average expected lifespan, with 79.7 years; next came black females, 73.9; white males, 73.2; and black males, 65.5. The female and male life expectancies for all other races in 1992 were 75.6 and 67.8 years, respectively. Infant mortality has fallen from 3,830 per 100,000 live births in 1945 to 848.7 in 1992. In 1990, 1,429,577 legal abortions were obtained in the US, for a rate of 24 per 1,000 women ages 15–44 and a ratio of 345 per 1,000 live births.

The overall death rate is comparable to that of most nations—8.5 per 1,000 population in 1992. Leading causes of death (number, rate per 100,000 population, and percent of total deaths) in 1992 were: heart disease, 720,480, 282.5 (33.1%); cancer, 521,090, 204.3 (23.9%); cerebrovascular diseases, 143,640, 56.3 (6.6%); chronic obstructive pulmonary diseases, 91,440, 35.8 (4.2%); accidents and adverse effects, 86,310, 33.8 (4.0%); pneumonia and influenza, 76,120, 29.8 (3.5%); diabetes mellitus, 50,180, 19.7 (2.3%); human immunodeficiency virus (HIV) infection, 33,590, 13.2 (1.5%); suicide, 29,760, 11.7 (1.4%); and homicide and legal intervention, 26,570, 10.4 (1.2%). Other leading causes of death in 1992 included chronic liver disease and cirrhosis, nephritis, septicemia, arteriosclerosis, and from certain conditions originating in the perinatal period. Cigarette smoking has been linked to heart and lung disease; about 20% of all deaths in the US were attributed to cigarette smoking in 1990. First identified in 1981, HIV infection (resulting in acquired immune deficiency syndrome—AIDS) has risen; by 1992, there were just under 250,000 AIDS cases reported in the US.

Medical facilities in the US included 6,634 hospitals in 1991 (down 4.3% from 1981), with 1,202,000 beds (down 11.8%). There were 653,062 physicians as of 1 January 1992, for a ratio of 255 per 100,000 population (or 209 active physicians in patient care per 100,000 population). Of the total number of active classified physicians, the largest areas of activity were internal medicine, 14.9%; family practice, 8.8%; pediatrics, 6.9%; and psychiatry, 6.1%. As of March 1992, there were 2,239,816 registered nurses (82.7% employed in nursing), for a ratio of 726 employed nurses per 100,000 population. Dentists numbered 156,738 in 1993.

Per capita health care expenditures have risen from $247 in 1967 to about $3,380 in 1993. National health care spending is projected to rise to $1.6 trillion by 2000 ($5,712 per capita) comprising over 16% of GDP. Hospital care represented 38% of national health care spending in 1991, even though hospitals' proportion of total health care expenditures has fallen slightly since 1980. Hospital costs amounted to over $225 billion in 1991, equivalent to about $5,360 per admission or $752.10 per inpatient day. In fiscal 1992, services provided for 30.9 million Medicaid recipients required $90.8 billion in federal expenditures, while 35.6 million Medicare enrollees received benefit payments of $129.1 billion. Medicare payments have lagged behind escalating hospital costs; in 1991, over 60% of hospitals lost money on Medicare patients. In addition, the Federal Hospital Insurance Trust Fund, which pays for Medicare's hospital expenditures, is projected to be exhausted by 2002. Meanwhile, the elderly population in the US is projected to increase to 13% of the total population by 2000, and to 18% by 2020, thus exacerbating the conundrum of health care finance.

[39] SOCIAL WELFARE

Social welfare programs in the US depend on both the federal government and the state governments for resources and administration. Old age, survivors', disability, and the Medicare (health) programs are administered by the federal government; unemployment insurance, dependent child care, and a variety of other public assistance programs are state administered, although the federal government contributes to all of them through grants to the states. State public expenditures for all social welfare programs—including income maintenance, health, education, and welfare services—reached $156.3 billion in 1992, representing 21.2% of all state outlays. Federal expenditures on social welfare rose during the first four years of the Reagan presidency, but his administration did succeed in slowing the growth rate from 15% in 1980 to 13.7% in 1981 and 6.3% in 1982. Eligibility requirements for many social programs were tightened, operating budgets were slashed, and some programs—notably public-sector employment under the Comprehensive Employment and Training Act (CETA)—were eliminated entirely.

In 1990, 13,285,000 Americans received $18.5 billion under the aid to families with dependent children (AFDC) program. Attempts to get clients "off the welfare rolls and onto the payrolls" have foundered on the reality that many of them are not easily employable, especially in a tight job market. Moreover, the job training and day care facilities necessary to allow some poor people to find and hold jobs are often no less expensive than direct public assistance.

With the enactment of the Personal Responsibility and Work Opportunity Reconciliation Act of 1996, the US government changed the form and regulations for many of its social welfare programs; most significantly, it replaced Aid to Families with Dependent Children (AFDC), an open-ended entitlement program, with Temporary Assistance for Needy Families (TANF), a limited system of assistance funded largely through federal block grants. The reform act also impacted the food stamp program, the Supplemental Security Income program, and the child nutrition program. The law took effect on 1 July 1997 and provided $16.38 billion in block grants for fiscal years 1997–2002. The grants were to be divided among the states based on an equation involving the numbers of former AFDC recipients in each state. Because many of the bill's provisions had not been implemented into policy by the state-by-state , it was not possible to include the details of each state's programs for this edition of this work.

The Food and Nutrition Service of the US Department of Agriculture oversees several food assistance programs. In 1991, eligible Americans took part in the food stamp program, at a cost to the federal government of $17,388,720. Eligible pupils participated in the school lunch program, at a federal cost of $3.3 billion. During the same year, the federal government also expended money for school breakfasts, on nutrition programs for the elderly, and in commodity aid for the needy. The present Social Security program differs greatly from that created by the Social Security Act of 1935, which provided that retirement benefits be paid to retired workers aged 65 or older. Since 1939, Congress has attached a series of amendments to the program, including provisions for workers who retire at age 62, for widows, for dependent children under 18 years of age, and for children who are disabled prior to age 18. Disabled workers between 50 and 65 years of age are also entitled to monthly benefits. Other measures increased the number of years a person may work; among these reforms was a 1977 law banning mandatory retirement in private industry before age 70. The actuarial basis for the Social Security system has also changed. In 1935 there were about nine US wage earners for each American aged 65 or more; by the mid–1990s, however, the ratio was closer to three to one.

In 1940, the first year benefits were payable, $35 million was paid out. By 1983, Social Security benefits totaled $268.1 billion, paid to more than 40.6 million beneficiaries. The average monthly benefit for a retired worker with no dependents in 1960 was $74; in 1983, the average benefit was $629.30. Under legislation enacted in the early 1970s, increases in monthly benefits are pegged to the inflation rate, as expressed through the Consumer Price Index. Employers, employees, and the self-employed are legally required to make contributions to the Social Security fund. Wage and salary earners pay Social Security taxes under the Federal Insurance Contributions Act (FICA). As the amount of benefits and the number of beneficiaries have increased, so has the maximum FICA payment, which for 1984 was $2,533, based on a rate of 6.7% on earnings up to $37,800, plus another 0.3% supplied from general revenues; the 1960 maximum was $144. In 1990, Social Security Taxes leveled off at 7.65% on earnings up to $51,300. Among workers with many dependents, the Social Security tax deduction can now exceed the federal income tax deduction.

In January 1974, the Social Security Administration assumed responsibility for assisting the aged, blind, and disabled under the Supplemental Security Income program. In 1991, some 5,118,470 disabled Americans—1,464,684 aged, 3,569,237 disabled, and 84,549 blind—received over $18 billion. Medicare, another program administered under the Social Security Act, provides hospital insurance and voluntary medical insurance for persons 65 and over, with reduced benefits available at age 62. Medicare hospital insurance covered some 29,866,000 Americans in 1990. Medicaid is a program that helps the needy meet the costs of medical, hospital, and nursing-home care.

The laws governing unemployment compensation originate in the states. Therefore, the benefits provided vary from state to state in duration (generally from 26 to 39 weeks) and amount (ranging from $111 to $222 weekly in 1991); the national average was about $170 per week. Workers' Compensation payments in 1992 amounted to $34 billion; federal and state outlays for vocational rehabilitation exceeded $1.2 billion in 1983.

Private philanthropy plays a major role in the support of relief and health services. The private sector plays an especially important role in pension management.

The federal agency ACTION, established in 1971, coordinates several US social service agencies. Chief among these is Volunteers in Service to America—VISTA—which was created in 1964 to marshal human resources against economic and environmental problems. ACTION also administers activities for the young and the aged, including the Retired Senior Volunteer Program and the Foster Grandparent Program, enlisting elderly persons to work with children who have special physical, mental, or emotional needs.

40 HOUSING

The housing resources of the US far exceed those of any other country, with 102,264,000 housing units as of April 1990, 91,946,000 of which were occupied. In 1991, 57.2% of all US homes were occupied by their owners, 31.9% were rented, 8.3% were vacant, and 2.6% were occupied seasonally. The majority of rental tenants are found in the large metropolitan areas. As of 1990, an estimated 94 million year-round households possessed and used electrical appliances. Of these, 90.3% had color television sets; 71.7% had washing machines; 64.7% had clothes dryers; 42.7% had electric dishwashers; 29.1% had room air conditioners; and 36.6% had central air conditioning. As of 1980, about 22% of all housing units in the US had been built before 1940; 8% during 1940–49; 13% during 1950–59; 15% from 1960 to 1969; 23% during 1970–79; and 19% since 1980. The median construction year was 1964.

Construction of housing following World War II set a record-breaking pace; 1986 was the 38th successive year during which construction of more than one million housing units was begun. In that year, 1,810,000 new units were started, the highest number in eight years. After 1986, however, housing starts dropped for five years in succession, hitting 1,014,000 in 1991 and then climbing to 1,200,000 in 1992. The great bulk of the housing stock, as well as of homes produced, consists of one-family houses. Perhaps the most significant change in the housing scene has been the shift to the suburbs made possible by the widespread ownership of automobiles.

41 EDUCATION

Education is compulsory in all states and a responsibility of each state and the local government. However, federal funds are available to help meet special needs at primary, secondary, or higher levels. Generally, formal schooling begins at the age of six and continues up to age 17. But, each state specifies the age and circumstances for compulsory attendance.

"Regular" schools which educate a person towards a diploma or degree include both public and private schools. Public schools are controlled and supported by the local authorities as well as state or federal governmental agencies. Private schools are controlled and supported by religious or private organizations. Elementary schooling is from grade 1 to grade 8. High schools cover grades 9 through 12. Colleges include junior or community colleges, offering two-year associate degrees; regular four-year colleges and universities; and graduate or professional schools. The school year begins in September and ends in June.

The enrollment rate of three- to five-year olds in preprimary schools was 37% in 1970. It went up to 56% in 1991. Persons 25 years old and over completing college education was 11% in 1970 and 21% in 1992.

The total number of children enrolled in public and private elementary and secondary schools in 1996 was 51.7 million; that year, public schools had 45.8 million, and private schools, 8.9 million. It was projected that by the year 2000, public schools would have 47.7 million students and private schools 6 million students. Students in grades 9–12 numbered 14.4 million in 1996, with 13 million in public and 1.3 million in private schools. Colleges had 14.4 million students enrolled, 11.3 in public and 3.1 million in private colleges. In 1994/95, there were 3,688 higher education institutions, 1,473 of which were two-year and 2,215 were four-year colleges and universities. The literacy rate is estimated to be 98% (males 97% and females 98%).

42 ARTS

The nation's arts centers are emblems of the importance of the performing arts in US life. New York City's Lincoln Center for the Performing Arts, whose first concert hall opened in 1962, is now the site of the Metropolitan Opera House, three halls for concerts and other musical performances, two theaters, the New York Public Library's Library and Museum of the Performing Arts, and The Juilliard School. The John E Kennedy Center for the Performing Arts in Washington, D.C., opened in 1971; it comprises two main theaters, two smaller theaters, an opera house and a concert hall.

The New York Philharmonic, founded in 1842, and conducted by Zubin Mehta in 1994, is the nation's oldest professional musical ensemble. Other leading orchestras include those of Boston (conducted by Seiji Ozawa), Chicago, Cleveland (Christoph von Dohnanyi), Los Angeles (Carlo Maria Giulini), Philadelphia (Ricardo Muti), Pittsburgh (Andre Previn), St. Louis (Leonard Slatkin), and Washington, D.C. (the National Symphony, led by Mstislav Rostropovich). Particularly renowned for artistic excellence are the Lyric Opera of Chicago, San Francisco Opera, Opera Company of Boston, Santa Fe Opera, New York City Opera, and Metropolitan Opera.

The recording industry is an integral part of the music world. In 1992, 407 million US-made CD's (singles and albums) and 366 million prerecorded cartridges were sold. Popular music (mostly rock), performed in halls and arenas in every major city and on college campuses throughout the US, dominates record sales.

Though still financially insecure, dance is winning an increasingly wide following. The American Ballet Theater, founded in 1940, is the nation's oldest dance company still active today; the New York City Ballet is equally acclaimed. Other important companies include those of Martha Graham, Merce Cunningham, Alvin Ailey, Paul Taylor, and Twyla Tharp, as well as the Feld Ballet, Joffrey Ballet, and Pilobolus.

Drama remains a principal performing art, not only in New York City's renowned theater district but also in regional, university, summer, and dinner theaters throughout the US. Television and the motion picture industry have made film the dominant modern medium. The US has about 6,777 motion picture theater establishments and 999 drive-in motion picture establishments according to the 1987 economic censuses. The censuses only surveyed tax paying establishments. In 1992 films registered boxoffice receipts of $4 billion, based on a paying audience of 964 million.

In 1992, the NEA generated a total budget of $162,990,861. Of the total $8,194,011 were obligated for dance programs, $3,549,235 for design arts, $16,052,300 for expansion arts, $3,181,000 for folk arts, $4,600,766 for literature, $11,079,583 for museums, $14,901,80 for music, $5,680,786 for opera-musical theater, $4,084,975 for presenting and commissioning, $9,374,900 for theater, $5,583,625 for visual arts, $8,285,530 for arts in education, $2,419,946 for local art agencies, $30,840,085 for state and regional programs, $6,156,300 for under-served communities, $3,786,296 for advancement, $269,964 for challenge and $1,023,879 for policy, planning, research and budget activities.

In addition, 1993 total funds amounted to $174,459,382. Program funds totaled $119,984,248. Treasury funds amounted to $16,954,650. Challenge grants totaled $13,186,980. Administrative funds were $24,333,534.

Twenty percent of the arts programs sponsored by the NEA affected the nation as a whole. The NEA contributed $1.5 million to WNET/Channel 13 in New York for the "Behind the Scenes" television program in 1992. The NEA also contributed $100,000 to the Dance Theatre Workshop National Performance Network, $160,000 to the "Meet the Composer" program, $150,000 to the University of Virginia at Charlottesville for the Mayor's Institute on City Design, and the establishment of 8Y media arts centers across the nation.

In the area of film, the NEA gave $150,000 to Vanguard Film to make nationally distributed films on the history of the blues. The NEA gave $110,000 to the Mexican Museum of San Francisco to begin a national tour of Mexican art.

In 1991 the NEA provided $75,000 for the development of PEN syndicated fiction which exposes fiction writing to national audiences through newspapers and radio presentations.

The NEA's regional programs to promote the arts include $25,000 given to the Southern Arts Federation, Inc. of Atlanta, Georgia, $20,000 to the Walker Arts Center, Inc. of Minneapolis, Minnesota, $610,000 in awards to visual arts in 6 regions of the United States and of manual support for the Western States Arts Federation Books Awards. Thirty percent of the NEA's funds are used to promote arts programs on the regional and national level.

43 LIBRARIES AND MUSEUMS

Of the 32,414 libraries in the US in 1993, 9,050 were public, with 6,215 branches; 4,619 were academic; 1,871 were government; 1,925 were medical; and a number were religious, military, legal, and specialized independent collections.

The country's vast public library system is administered by municipality. The largest of these are the New York Public Library (11.5 million), the Queens Borough Public library (15 million), the Miami-Dade Public Library System (10 million), the Brooklyn Public Library (9.8 million), the Los Angeles Public Library (8 million), and the Chicago Public Library (7.5 million).

The foremost library in the country is the Library of Congress, with holdings of more than 80 million items (including more than 29 million books and pamphlets) in the mid–1990s. Other great libraries are the public libraries in New York, Philadelphia, Boston, Cleveland, and Baltimore, and the John Crerar and Newberry libraries in Chicago. Noted special collections are those of the Pierpont Morgan Library in New York; the Huntington Library in San Marino, Calif.; the Folger Shakespeare Library in Washington, D.C.; the Hoover Library at Stanford University; and the rare book divisions of Harvard, Yale, Indiana, Texas, and Virginia universities. Among the leading university libraries, as judged by the extent of their holdings in 1993, are those of Harvard, Yale, Illinois (Urbana-Champaign), Michigan (Ann Arbor), California (Berkeley), Columbia, Stanford, Cornell, California (Los Angeles), Chicago, Wisconsin (Madison), and Washington (Seattle)—each having more than 4 million bound volumes. In 1997, Cleveland, Chicago, and San Francisco all opened new, multimillion dollar libraries.

There are about 5,000 nonprofit museums in the US. The most numerous type is the historic building, followed in descending order by college and university museums, museums of science, public museums of history, and public museums of art. Eminent US museums include the American Museum of Natural History, the Metropolitan Museum of Art, and the Museum of Modern Art, all in New York City; the National Gallery of Art and the Smithsonian Institution in Washington, D.C.; the Boston Museum of Fine Arts; the Art Institute of Chicago and the Chicago Museum of Natural History; the Franklin Institute and Philadelphia Museum of Art, both in Philadelphia; and the M. H. de Young Memorial Museum in San Francisco. Also of prominence are the Cleveland Museum of Art, the St. Louis Museum of Art, and the Baltimore Museum of Art.

44 COMMUNICATIONS

All major electric communications systems are privately owned but regulated by the Federal Communications Commission. The US uses wire and radio services for communications more extensively than any other country in the world. In 1995 over 98% of all US households had telephones, utilizing some 148 million main telephone lines.

Radio serves a variety of purposes other than broadcasting. It is widely used by ships and aircraft for safety; it has become an important tool in the movement of buses, trucks, and taxicabs. Forest conservators, fire departments, and the police operate with radio as a necessary aid; it is used in logging operations, surveying, construction work, and dispatching of repair crews. In 1995, broadcasting stations on the air comprised over 10,000 radio stations (both AM and FM) and, as of 1 May 1993 1,541 television stations. In 1995 over 98% of all US households owned at least one TV set. As of 1995, there were an estimated 540 million radios and 208 million television sets in use.

The Post Office Department of the US was replaced on 1 July 1971 by the US Postal Service, a financially autonomous federal agency. In 1992 160 billion pieces of mail passed through 39,613 post offices, branches and substations with about 711,369 employees. In addition to mail delivery, the Postal Service provides registered, certified, insured, express and COD mail service, issues money orders, and operates a postal savings system. Since the 1970s, numerous privately owned overnight mail and package delivery services have been established.

45 PRESS

In 1995 there were 1,586 daily newspapers in the US, with a combined circulation of over 60 million. Circulation has hovered around the 60 million mark since the early 1980s. Twenty large newspaper chains account for almost 60% of the total daily circulation. The following newspapers, all in the English language, reported average daily circulation of approximately 500,000 or more in 1995:

USA Today	2,000,000
Wall Street Journal	1,823,200
Chicago Tribune	1,297,220
New York Times	1,170,860
Los Angeles Times	1,104,650
Detroit Free Press	900,000
Washington Post	852,260
New York Daily News	734,277
Arizona Republic	587,910
Houston Chronicle	570,000
Long Island/New York Newsday	564,754
Cleveland Plain Dealer	550,000
Dallas Morning News	536,150
Miami Herald	518,030
San Francisco Chronicle	509,540
Boston Globe	500,000
Chicago Sun-Times	496,030
Baltimore Sun	494,500
Philadelphia Inquirer	486,300

Modern Maturity, published bi-monthly by AARP, had a circulation 22 million in 1995. The two general circulation magazines that appealed to the largest audiences were Reader's Digest (about 17 million), and TV Guide (about 15 million). Time and Newsweek were the leading news magazines, with a weekly circulation of 4,630,140 and 3,100,000 respectively.

The US book-publishing industry consists of the major book companies (mainly in the New York metro area), nonprofit university presses distributed throughout the US, and numerous small publishing firms. In 1994, 51,863 book titles were published in the US.

The US Constitution provides for freedom of speech and of the press in its Bill of Rights, and the government supports these rights. Citizens enjoy a wide range of opinions in all media, where debate, editorial opinion, and government opposition viewpoints are represented in some form or another. Nearly all media are privately owned.

As of 1996, there were some 85 million personal computers and over 8 million Internet hosts.

46 ORGANIZATIONS

The 1992 Census of Service Industries counted 72,386 membership organizations, embracing 41,789 civic, social, and fraternal associations, 14,337 business associations, 5,864 professional associations, and 10,596 other bodies.

A number of industrial and commercial organizations exercise considerable influence on economic policy. The National Association of Manufacturers and the US Chamber of Commerce, with numerous local branches, are the two central bodies of business and commerce. Various industries have their own associations, concerned with cooperative research and questions of policy alike.

Practically every profession in the US is represented by one or more professional organizations. Among the most powerful of these are the American Medical Association, comprising regional, state, and local medical societies; the American Bar Association, also comprising state and local associations; the American Hospital Association; and the National Education Association.

Many private organizations are dedicated to programs of political and social action. Prominent in this realm are the National Association for the Advancement of Colored People (NAACP), the Urban League, the American Civil Liberties Union (ACLU), Common Cause, and the Anti-Defamation League. The League of Women Voters, which provides the public with nonpartisan information about candidates and election issues, sponsored televised debates between the major presidential candidates in 1976, 1980, 1984, 1988, and 1992. The National Organization for Women, and the National Rifle Association have each mounted nationwide lobbying campaigns on issues affecting their members. During 1981–82, political action committees (PACs), affiliated with corporations, labor unions, and other groups, gave $83 million to candidates for the House and Senate—an increase of 50% over 1979/80. Probably the best-financed and most influential PAC by the mid–1980s was the National Conservative Political Action Committee (NCPAC), which provided $9.8 million to President Reagan's reelection campaign in 1984. In 1988 there were 4,268 PAC's that disbursed $364.2 million to candidates for the House and Senate and other elected offices.

The great privately endowed philanthropic foundations and trusts play an important part in encouraging the development of education, art, science, and social progress in the US. In the early 1980s there were nearly 32,401 foundations, with combined assets exceeding $142 billion. Foundations, donations, and charitable bequests in 1983 provided a total of $81 billion in grants. Prominent foundations include the Carnegie Corporation and the Carnegie Endowment for International Peace, the Ford Foundation, the Guggenheim Foundation, the Mayo Association for the Advancement of Medical Research and Education, and the Rockefeller Foundation. Private philanthropy was responsible for the establishment of many of the nation's most eminent libraries, concert halls, museums, and university and medical facilities; private bequests were also responsible for the establishment of the Pulitzer Prizes. Merit awards offered by industry and professional groups include the "Oscars" of the Academy of Motion Picture Arts and Sciences, the "Emmys" of the National Academy of Television Arts and Sciences, and the "Grammys" of the National Academy of Recording Arts and Sciences.

Funds for a variety of community health and welfare services are funneled through United Way campaigns, which raises annually $2 billion. The American Red Cross has over 3,000 chapters, which paid for services and activities ranging from disaster relief to blood donor programs. Private organizations supported by contributions from the general public lead the fight against specific diseases.

The Boy Scouts of America, the Girl Scouts of the USA, rural 4–H Clubs, and the Young Men's and the Young Women's Christian Associations are among the organizations devoted to recreation, sports, camping, and education.

The largest religious organization in the US is the National Council of the Churches of Christ in the USA, which embraces 32 Protestant and Orthodox denominations, whose adherents total more than 42 million. Many organizations, such as the American Philosophical Society, the American Association for the Advancement of Science, and the National Geographic Society, are dedicated to the enlargement of various branches of human knowledge. National, state, and local historical societies abound, and there are numerous educational, sports, and hobbyist groups.

The larger veterans' organizations are the American Legion, the Veterans of Foreign Wars of the US, the Catholic War Veterans, and the Jewish War Veterans. Fraternal organizations, in addition to such international organizations as the Masons, include indigenous groups such as the Benevolent and Protective Order of Elks, the Loyal Order of Moose, and the Woodmen of the World. Many, such as the Ancient Order of Hibernians in America, commemorate the national origin of their members. One of the largest fraternal organizations is the Roman Catholic Knights of Columbus.

47 TOURISM, TRAVEL, AND RECREATION

Foreign visitors to the US numbered approximately 42,723,000 in 1991. Of these visitors, 44% came from Canada, 18% from Mexico, 18% from Europe, and 12% from Eastern Asia and the Pacific. In 1991, travelers to the US from all foreign countries spent $45.5 billion, and another $18.8 billion for fares on US carriers to and from their home countries. There were 3,080,000 hotel rooms with 5,544,000 beds. With a few exceptions, such as Canadians entering from the Western Hemisphere, all visitors to the US are required to have passports and visas.

A total of $39.4 billion was spent by US tourists abroad on 41,835,000 trips.

With the advent of a new, more environmentally conscious political administration in 1992, ecotourism is expected to grow. Among the most striking scenic attractions in the US are the Grand Canyon in Arizona; Carlsbad Caverns in New Mexico; Yosemite National Park in California; Yellowstone National Park in Idaho, Montana, and Wyoming; Niagara Falls, partly in New York; and the Everglades in Florida. The US had a total of 49 national parks as of August 1987. Popular coastal resorts include those of Florida, California, and Cape Code in Massachusetts. Historical attractions include the Liberty Bell and Constitution Hall in Philadelphia; the Statue of Liberty in New York City; the White House, the Capitol, and the monuments to Washington, Jefferson, and Lincoln in the District of Columbia; the Williamsburg historical restoration in Virginia; various Revolutionary and Civil War battlefields and monuments in the East and South; the Alamo in San Antonio; and Mt. Rushmore in South Dakota. Among many other popular tourist attractions are the movie and television studios in Los Angeles; the cable cars in San Francisco; casino gambling in Las Vegas and in Atlantic City, N.J.; thoroughbred horse racing in Kentucky; the Grand Ole Opry in Nashville, Tenn.; the many jazz clubs of New Orleans; and such amusement parks as Disneyland (Anaheim, Calif.) and Walt Disney World (near Orlando, Fla.). For abundance and diversity of entertainment—theater, movies, music, dance, and sports—New York City has few rivals. In April, 1993, Amtrak began the country's first regularly scheduled transcontinental passenger service, from Los Angeles to Miami.

Americans' recreational activities range from the major spectator sports—professional baseball, football, basketball, ice hockey, and soccer, horse racing, and collegiate football and basketball—to home gardening. Participant sports are a favorite form of recreation, including jogging, aerobics, tennis, and golf. Skiing is a popular recreation in New England and the western mountain ranges, while sailing, power boating, rafting, and canoeing are popular water sports. In 1994, the United States hosted the World Cup Soccer Championship.

48 SPORTS

Baseball, long honored as the national pastime, is the nation's leading professional team sport, with two major leagues having 28 teams (2 in Canada). In 1992, the Toronto Blue Jays became the first non-US team to win the World Series. In addition, there is an extensive network of minor league baseball teams, each of them related to a major league franchise. The National Basketball Association, created in 1946, included 27 teams, which drew nearly 18 million fans during the 1993/94 season. In 1993,14 million Americans attended regular season games of the National football League's 28 teams. Attendance at National Hockey League (NHL) games exceeded 17.5 million in 1993/94; of 26 NHL teams, 8 were Canadian, as were most of the players. The North American Soccer League (NASL), which appeared to be growing popular in the late 1970s, discontinued outdoor play in 1985. Indoor soccer continued however with the Major Indoor Soccer League but their operations ceased after the 1992 season. In 1994, however, soccer's World Cup games were played in nine US cities, with the final match held in Los Angeles. Radio and television contracts are integral to the popular and financial success of all professional team sports. In 1994, a strike by baseball players caused the World Series to be canceled for the first time since 1904; hockey players also held strikes in 1992 and 1994.

Several other professional sports are popular nationwide. Thoroughbred racing, which lured some 45 million Americans to the track in 1993, is among the nation's most popular spectator sports. Annual highlights of thoroughbred racing are the three jewels of the Triple Crown—Kentucky Derby, Preakness, and Belmont Stakes—most recently won by Seattle Slew in 1977 and by Affirmed in 1978. In 1993, nearly $9.4 billion was legally wagered on thoroughbred horse racing. Harness racing is also popular; in 1993, attendance was over 11.7 million and involved over $1.4 billion in wagering. Attendance at greyhound racetracks exceeded 26 million in 1993. The prize money that Henry Ford won on a 1901 auto race helped him start his now-famous car company two years later; since then, automobile manufacturers have backed sports car, stock car, and motorcycle racing at tracks throughout the US. From John L. Sullivan to Muhammad Ali, the personality and power of the great boxing champions have drawn millions of spectators to ringside. Glamour and top prizes also draw national followings for tennis and golf, two professional sports in which women are nationally prominent. Other professional sports include bowling and rodeo.

Football has been part of US college life since the game was born on 6 November 1869 with a New Jersey match between Rutgers and Princeton. The National Collegiate Athletic Association (NCAA) and National Association of Intercollegiate Athletics (NAIA) coordinate collegiate football and basketball. Colleges recruit top athletes with sports scholarships in order to win media attention, and to keep the loyalty of the alumni, thereby boosting fund-raising. Baseball, hockey, swimming, gymnastics, crew, lacrosse, track and field, and a variety of other sports also fill the intercollegiate competitive program

The Amateur Athletic Union (AAU), a national nonprofit organization founded in 1888, conducts the AAU/USA Junior Olympics, offering competition in 22 sports in order to help identify candidates for international Olympic competition. St. Louis hosted the 1904 summer Olympics; Los Angeles was home to the games in 1932 and 1984. The winter Olympic games were held in Squaw Valley, Calif., in 1960, and at Lake Placid, N.Y., in 1932 and 1980. Atlanta hosted the summer Olympic games in 1996.

49 FAMOUS AMERICANS

Printer, publisher, inventor, scientist, statesman, and diplomat, Benjamin Franklin (1706–90) was America's outstanding figure of the colonial period. George Washington (1732–99), leader of the colonial army in the American Revolution, became first president of the US and is known as the "father of his country." Chief author of the Declaration of Independence, founder of the US political party system, and third president was Thomas Jefferson (1743–1826). His leading political opponents were John Adams (1735–1826), second president, and Alexander Hamilton (b.West Indies, 1755–1804), first secretary of the treasury, who secured the new nation's credit. James Madison (1751–1836), a leading figure in drawing up the US Constitution, served as fourth president. John Quincy Adams (1767–1848), sixth president, was an outstanding diplomat and secretary of state.

Andrew Jackson (1767–1845), seventh president, was an ardent champion of the common people and opponent of vested interests. Outstanding senators during the Jackson era were John Caldwell Calhoun (1782–1850), spokesman of the southern planter aristocracy and leading exponent of the supremacy of states' rights over federal powers; Henry Clay (1777–1852), the great compromiser, who sought to reconcile the conflicting views of the North and the South; and Daniel Webster (1782–1852), statesman and orator, who championed the preservation of the Union against sectional interests and division. Abraham Lincoln (1809–65) led the US through its most difficult period, the Civil War, in the course of which he issued the Emancipation Proclamation. Jefferson Davis (1808–89) served as the only president of the short-lived Confederacy. Stephen Grover Cleveland (1837–1908), a conservative reformer, was the strongest president in the latter part of the 19th century. Among the foremost presidents of the 20th century have been Nobel Peace Prize winner Theodore Roosevelt (1858–1919); Woodrow Wilson (1856–1924), who led the nation during World War I and helped establish the League of Nations; and Franklin Delano Roosevelt (1882–1945), elected to four terms spanning the Great Depression and World War II. The presidents during the 1961–88 period have been John Fitzgerald Kennedy (1917–63), Lyndon Baines Johnson (1908–73), Richard Milhous Nixon (1913–94), Gerald Rudolph Ford (Leslie Lynch King, Jr., b.1913), Jimmy Carter (James Earl Carter, Jr., b.1924), and Ronald Wilson Reagan (b.1911), George Herbert Walker Bush (b. 1924), and William Jefferson Clinton (b. 1946).

Of the outstanding US military leaders, four were produced by the Civil War: Union generals Ulysses Simpson Grant (1822–85), who later served as the eighteenth president, and William Tecumseh Sherman (1820–91); and Confederate generals Robert Edward Lee (1807–70) and Thomas Jonathan "Stonewall" Jackson (1824–63). George Catlett Marshall (1880–1959), army chief of staff during World War II, in his later capacity as secretary of state under President Harry S Truman (1884–1972), formulated the Marshall Plan, which did much to revitalize Western Europe. Douglas MacArthur (1880–1964) commanded the US forces in Asia during World War II, oversaw the postwar occupation and reorganization of Japan, and directed UN forces in the first year of the Korean conflict. Dwight D. Eisenhower (1890–1969) served as supreme Allied commander during World War II, later becoming the thirty-fourth president.

John Marshall (1755–1835), chief justice of the US from 1801 to 1835, established the power of the Supreme Court through the principle of judicial review. Other important chief justices were Edward Douglass White (1845–1921), former president William Howard Taft (1857–1930), and Earl Warren (1891–1974), whose tenure as chief justice from 1953 to 1969 saw important decisions on desegregation, reapportionment, and civil liberties.

The justice who enjoyed the longest tenure on the court was William O. Douglas (1898–1980), who served from 1939 to 1975; other prominent associate justices were Oliver Wendell Holmes (1841–1935), Louis Dembitz Brandeis (1856–1941), and Hugo Lafayette Black (1886–1971).

Indian chiefs renowned for their resistance to white encroachment were Pontiac (1729?–69), Black Hawk (1767–1838), Tecumseh (1768–1813), Osceola (1804?–38), Cochise (1812?–74), Geronimo (1829?–1909), Sitting Bull (1831?–90), Chief Joseph (1840?–1904), and Crazy Horse (1849?–77). Other significant Indian chiefs were Hiawatha (fl. 1500), Squanto (d.1622), and Sequoya (1770?–1843). Historical figures who have become part of American folklore include pioneer Daniel Boone (1734–1820); silversmith, engraver, and patriot Paul Revere (1735–1818); frontiersman David "Davy" Crockett (1786–1836); scout and Indian agent Christopher "Kit" Carson (1809–68); James Butler "Wild Bill" Hickok (1837–76); William Frederick "Buffalo Bill" Cody (1846–1917); and the outlaws Jesse Woodson James (1847–82) and Billy the Kid (William H. Bonney, 1859–81).

Inventors and Scientists

Outstanding inventors were Robert Fulton (1765–1815), who developed the steamboat; Eli Whitney (1765–1825), inventor of the cotton gin and mass production techniques; Samuel Finley Breese Morse (1791–1872), who invented the telegraph; and Elias Howe (1819–67), who invented the sewing machine. Alexander Graham Bell (b.Scotland, 1847–1922) gave the world the telephone. Thomas Alva Edison (1847–1931) was responsible for hundreds of inventions, among them the long-burning incandescent electric lamp, the phonograph, automatic telegraph devices, a motion picture camera and projector, the microphone, and the mimeograph. Lee De Forest (1873–1961), the "father of the radio," developed the vacuum tube and many other inventions. Vladimir Kosma Zworykin (b.Russia, 1889–1982) was principally responsible for the invention of television. Two brothers, Wilbur Wright (1867–1912) and Orville Wright (1871–1948), designed, built, and flew the first successful motor-powered airplane. Amelia Earhart (1898–1937) and Charles Lindbergh (1902–74) were aviation pioneers. Pioneers in the space program include John Glenn (b.1921), the first US astronaut to orbit the earth, and Neil Armstrong (b.1930), the first man to set foot on the moon.

Benjamin Thompson, Count Rumford (1753–1814), developed devices for measuring light and heat, and the physicist Joseph Henry (1797–1878) did important work in magnetism and electricity. Outstanding botanists and naturalists were John Bartram (1699–1777); his son William Bartram (1739–1823); Louis Agassiz (b.Switzerland, 1807–73); Asa Gray (1810–88); Luther Burbank (1849–1926), developer of a vast number of new and improved varieties of fruits, vegetables, and flowers; and George Washington Carver (1864–1943), known especially for his work on industrial applications for peanuts. John James Audubon (1785–1851) won fame as an ornithologist and artist.

Distinguished physical scientists include Samuel Pierpont Langley (1834–1906), astronomer and aviation pioneer; Josiah Willard Gibbs (1839–1903), mathematical physicist, whose work laid the basis for physical chemistry; Henry Augustus Rowland (1848–1901), who did important research in magnetism and optics; and Albert Abraham Michelson (b.Germany, 1852–1931), who measured the speed of light and became the first of a long line of US Nobel Prize winners. The chemists Gilbert Newton Lewis (1875–1946) and Irving Langmuir (1881–1957) developed a theory of atomic structure.

The theory of relativity was conceived by Albert Einstein (b.Germany, 1879–1955), generally considered the greatest mind in the physical sciences since Newton. Percy Williams Bridgman (1882–1961) was the father of operationalism and studied the effect of high pressures on materials. Arthur Holly Compton (1892–1962) made discoveries in the field of X rays and cosmic rays. The physical chemist Harold Clayton Urey (1893–1981) discovered heavy hydrogen. Isidor Isaac Rabi (b.Austria, 1898–1988), nuclear physicist, did important work in magnetism, quantum mechanics, and radiation. Enrico Fermi (b.Italy, 1901–54) created the first nuclear chain reaction, in Chicago in 1942, and contributed to the development of the atomic and hydrogen bombs. Also prominent in the splitting of the atom were Leo Szilard (b.Hungary, 1898–1964), J. Robert Oppenheimer (1904–67), and Edward Teller (b.Hungary, 1908). Ernest Orlando Lawrence (1901–58) developed the cyclotron. Carl David Anderson (1905–91) discovered the positron. Mathematician Norbert Wiener (1894–1964) developed the science of cybernetics.

Outstanding figures in the biological sciences include Theobald Smith (1859–1934), who developed immunization theory and practical immunization techniques for animals; the geneticist Thomas Hunt Morgan (1866–1945), who discovered the heredity functions of chromosomes; and neurosurgeon Harvey William Cushing (1869–1939). Selman Abraham Waksman (b.Russia, 1888–1973), a microbiologist specializing in antibiotics, was co-discoverer of streptomycin. Edwin Joseph Cohn (1892–1953) is noted for his work in the protein fractionalization of blood, particularly the isolation of serum albumin. Philip Showalter Hench (1896–1965) isolated and synthesized cortisone. Wendell Meredith Stanley (1904–71) was the first to isolate and crystallize a virus. Jonas Edward Salk (1914–95) developed an effective killed-virus poliomyelitis vaccine, and Albert Bruce Sabin (1906–93) contributed oral, attenuated live-virus polio vaccines.

Adolf Meyer (b.Switzerland, 1866–1950) developed the concepts of mental hygiene and dementia praecox and the theory of psychobiology; Harry Stack Sullivan (1892–1949) created the interpersonal theory of psychiatry. Social psychologist George Herbert Mead (1863–1931) and behaviorist Burrhus Frederic Skinner (1904–90) have been influential in the 20th century.

A pioneer in psychology who was also an influential philosopher was William James (1842–1910). Other leading US philosophers are Charles Sanders Peirce (1839–1914); Josiah Royce (1855–1916); John Dewey (1859–1952), also famous for his theories of education; George Santayana (b.Spain, 1863–1952); Rudolf Carnap (b.Germany, 1891–1970); and Willard Van Orman Quine (b.1908). Educators of note include Horace Mann (1796–1859), Henry Barnard (1811–1900), and Charles William Eliot (1834–1926). Noah Webster (1758–1843) was the outstanding US lexicographer, and Melvil Dewey (1851–1931) was a leader in the development of library science. Thorstein Bunde Veblen (1857–1929) wrote books that have strongly influenced economic and social thinking. Also important in the social sciences have been sociologists Talcott Parsons (1902–79) and William Graham Sumner (1840–1910) and anthropologist Margaret Mead (1901–78).

Social Reformers

Social reformers of note include Dorothea Lynde Dix (1802–87), who led movements for the reform of prisons and insane asylums; William Lloyd Garrison (1805–79) and Frederick Douglass (Frederick Augustus Washington Bailey, 1817–95), prominent abolitionists; Elizabeth Cady Stanton (1815–1902) and Susan Brownell Anthony (1820–1906), leaders in the women's suffrage movement; Clara Barton (1821–1912), founder of the American Red Cross; economist Henry George (1839–97), advocate of the single-tax theory; Eugene Victor Debs (1855–1926), labor leader and an outstanding organizer of the Socialist movement in the US; Jane Addams (1860–1935), who pioneered in settlement

Presidents of the US

	NAME	BORN	DIED	OTHER MAJOR OFFICES HELD	RESIDENCE AT ELECTION
1	George Washington	Westmoreland County, Va., 22 February 1732	Mt. Vernon, Va., 14 December 1799	Commander in Chief, Continental Army (1775–83)	Mt. Vernon, Va.
2	John Adams	Braintree (later Quincy), Mass., 30 October 1735	Quincy, Mass., 4 July 1826	Representative, Continental Congress (1774–77); US vice president (1797–97)	Quincy, Mass.
3	Thomas Jefferson	Goochland (now Albemarle) County, Va., 13 April 1743	Monticello, Va., 4 July 1826	Representative, Continental Congress (1775–76); governor of Virginia (1779–81); secretary of state (1790–93); US vice president (1797–1801)	Monticello, Va.
4	James Madison	Port Conway, Va., 16 March 1751	Montpelier, Va., 28 June 1836	Representative, Continental Congress (1780–83; 1786–88); US representative (1789–97); secretary of state (1801–9)	Montpelier, Va.
5	James Monroe	Westmoreland County, Va. 28 April 1758	New York, N.Y., 4 July 1831	US senator (1790–94); governor of Virginia (1799–1802); secretary of state (1811–17); secretary of war (1814–15)	Leesburg, Va.
6	John Quincy Adams	Braintree (later Quincy), Mass., 11 July 1767	Washington, D.C., 23 February 1848	US senator (1803–8); secretary of state (1817–25); US representative (1831–48)	Quincy, Mass.
7	Andrew Jackson	Waxhaw, Carolina frontier, 15 March 1767	The Hermitage, Tenn., 8 June 1845	US representative (1796–97); US senator (1797–98)	The Hermitage, Tenn.
8	Martin Van Buren	Kinderhook, N.Y., 5 December 1782	Kinderhook, N.Y., 24 July 1862	US senator (1821–28); governor of New York (1829); secretary of state (1829–31); US vice president (1833–37)	New York
9	William Henry Harrison	Charles City County, Va., 9 February 1773	Washington, D.C., 4 April 1841	Governor of Indiana Territory (1801–13); US representative (1816–19); US senator (1825–28)	North Bend, Ohio
10	John Tyler	Charles City County, Va., 29 March 1790	Richmond, Va., 18 January 1862	US representative (1816–21); governor of Virginia (1825–27); US senator (1827–36); US vice president (1841)	Richmond, Va.
11	James K. Polk	Mecklenburg County, N.C., 2 November 1795	Nashville, Tenn., 15 June 1849	US representative (1825–39); governor of Tennessee (1839–41)	Nashville, Tenn.
12	Zachary Taylor	Orange County, Va., 24 November 1784	Washington, D.C., 9 July 1850	—	Louisiana
13	Millard Fillmore	Cayuga County, N.Y., 7 January 1800	Buffalo, N.Y., 8 March 1874	US representative (1833–35; 1837–43); US vice president (1849–50)	Buffalo, N.Y.
14	Franklin Pierce	Hillsboro, N.H., 23 November 1804	Concord, N.H., 8 October 1869	US representative, (1833–37); US senator (1837–43)	Concord, N.H.
15	James Buchanan	Mercersburg, Pa., 23 April 1791	Lancaster, Pa., 1 June 1868	US representative (1821–31); US senator (1834–45); secretary of state (1845–49)	Lancaster, Pa.
16	Abraham Lincoln	Hodgenville, Ky., 12 February 1809	Washington, D.C., 15 April 1865	US representative (1847–49)	Springfield, Ill.
17	Andrew Johnson	Raleigh, N.C., 29 December 1808	Carter Station, Tenn., 31 July 1875	US representative (1843–53); governor of Tennessee (1853–57; 1862–65); US senator (1857–62); US vice president (1865)	Greeneville, Tenn.
18	Ulysses S. Grant	Point Pleasant, Ohio, 27 April 1822	Mount McGregor, N.Y., 23 July 1885	Commander, Union Army (1864–65); secretary of war (1867–68)	Galena, Ill.
19	Rutherford B. Hayes	Delaware, Ohio, 4 October 1822	Fremont, Ohio, 17 January 1893	US representative (1865–67); governor of Ohio (1868–72; 1876–77)	Fremont, Ohio
20	James A. Garfield	Orange, Ohio, 19 November 1831	Elberon, N.J., 19 September 1881	US representative (1863–80)	Mentor, Ohio
21	Chester A. Arthur	Fairfield, Vt., 5 October 1829	New York, N.Y., 18 November 1886	US vice president (1881)	New York, N.Y.
22	Grover Cleveland	Caldwell, N.J., 18 March 1837	Princeton, N.J., 24 June 1908	Governor of New York (1882–84)	Albany, N.Y.
23	Benjamin Harrison	North Bend, Ohio 20 August 1833	Indianapolis, Ind., 13 March 1901	US senator (1881–87)	Indianapolis, Ind.

PARTY	% OF POPULAR VOTE	% OF ELECTORAL VOTE[1,2]	TERMS IN OFFICE[5]	VICE PRESIDENTS	NOTABLE EVENTS	
Federalist	—	50.0	30 April 1789–4 March 1793	John Adams	Federal government organized; Bill of Rights enacted (1791); Whiskey Rebellion suppressed (1794); North Carolina, Rhode Island, Vermont, Kentucky, Tennessee enter Union.	1
Federalist	—	25.7	4 March 1797–4 March 1801	Thomas Jefferson	Alien and Sedition Acts passed (1798); Washington, D.C., becomes US capital (1800)	2
Dem.–Rep.	—	26.4[3] 92.0	4 March 1801–4 March 1805	Aaron Burr George Clinton	Louisiana Purchase (1803); Lewis and Clark Expedition (1803–6); Ohio enters Union.	3
Dem.–Rep.	—	69.7 58.9	4 March 1809–4 March 1818 4 March 1813–4 March 1817	George Clinton Elbridge Gerry	War of 1812 (1812–14); protective tariffs passed (1816); Louisiana, Indiana enter Union.	4
Dem.–Rep.	—	84.3	4 March 1817–4 March 1821 4 March 1821–4 March 1825	Daniel D. Tompkins Daniel D. Tompkins	Florida purchased from Spain (1819–21); Missouri Compromise (1820); Monroe Doctrine (1823); Mississippi, Illinois, Alabama, Maine, Missouri enter Union.	5
National Republican	30.9	38.0[4]	4 March 1825–4 March 1829	John C. Calhoun	Period of political antagonisms, producing little legislation; road and canal construction supported; Erie Canal opens (1825).	6
Democrat	56.0 54.2	68.2 76.6	4 March 1829–4 March 1833	John C. Calhoun Martin Van Buren	Introduction of spoils system; Texas Republic established (1836); Arkansas, Michigan enter Union.	7
Democrat	50.8	57.8	4 March 1837–4 March 1841	Richard M. Johnson	Financial panic (1837) and subsequent depression.	8
Whig	52.9	79.6	4 March 1841–4 April 1841	John Tyler	Died of pneumonia one month after taking office.	9
Whig	—	—	4 April 1841–4 March 1845	—	Monroe Doctrine extended to Hawaiian Islands (1842); Second Seminole War in Florida ends (1842).	10
Democrat	49.5	61.8	4 March 1845–4 March 1849	George M. Dallas	Boundary between US and Canada set at 49th parallel (1846); Mexican War (1846–48), ending with Treaty of Guadalupe Hidalgo (1848); California gold rush begins (1848); Florida, Texas, Iowa, Wisconsin enter Union.	11
Whig	47.3	56.2	4 March 1849–9 July 1850	Millard Fillmore	Died after 16 months in office.	12
Whig	—	—	9 July 1850–4 March 1853	—	Fugitive Slave Law (1850); California enters Union.	13
Democrat	50.8	85.8	4 March 1853–4 March 1857	William R. King	Gadsden Purchase (1853); Kansas–Nebraska Act (1854); trade opened with Japan (1854).	14
Democrat	45.3	58.8	4 March 1857–4 March 1861	John C. Breckinridge	John Brown's raid at Harpers Ferry, Va. (now W. Va.; 1859); South Carolina secedes (1860); Minnesota, Oregon, Kansas enter Union.	15
Republican	39.8 55.0	59.4 91.0	4 March 1861–4 March 1865 4 March 1865–15 April 1865	Hannibal Hamlin Andrew Johnson	Confederacy established, Civil War begins (1851); Emancipation Proclamation (1863); Confederacy defeated (1865); Lincoln assassinated (1865); West Virginia, Nevada attain statehood.	16
Republican	—	—	15 April 1865–4 March 1869	—	Reconstruction Acts (1867); Alaska purchased from Russia (1867); Johnson impeached but acquitted (1868); Nebraska enters Union.	17
Republican	52.7 55.6	72.8 78.1	4 March 1869–4 March 1873 4 March 1873–4 March 1877	Schuyler Colfax Henry Wilson	Numerous government scandals; financial panic (1873); Colorado enters Union.	18
Republican	48.0	50.1	4 March 1877–4 March 1881	William A. Wheeler	Federal troops withdrawn from South (1877); civil service reform begun.	19
Republican	48.3	58.0	4 March 1881–19 Sept. 1881	Chester A. Arthur	Shot after 4 months in office, dead 2½ months later.	20
Republican	—	—	19 Sept. 1881–4 March 1885	—	Chinese immigration banned despite presidential veto (1882); Civil Service Commission established by Pendleton Act (1883).	21
Democrat	48.5	54.6	4 March 1885–4 March 1889	Thomas A. Hendricks	Interstate Commerce Act (1887)	22
Republican	47.8	58.1	4 March 1889–4 March 1893	Levi P. Morton	Sherman Silver Purchase Act (1890); North Dakota, South Dakota, Montana, Washington, Idaho, Wyoming enter Union.	23

Presidents of the US

	NAME	BORN	DIED	OTHER MAJOR OFFICES HELD	RESIDENCE AT ELECTION
24	Grover Cleveland	Caldwell, N.J., 18 March 1837	Princeton, N.J., 24 June 1908	Governor of New York (1882–84)	New York, N.Y.
25	William McKinley	Niles, Ohio, 29 January 1843	Buffalo, N.Y., 14 September 1901	US representative (1877–83; 1885–91); governor of Ohio (1892–96)	Canton, Ohio
26	Theodore Roosevelt	New York, N.Y., 27 October 1858	Oyster Bay, N.Y., 6 January 1919	Governor of New York (1899–1900); US vice president (1901)	Oyster Bay, N.Y.
27	William H. Taft	Cincinnati, Ohio, 15 September 1857	Washington, D.C., 8 March 1930	Governor of Philippines (1901–4); secretary of war (1904–8); chief justice of the US (1921–30)	Washington, D.C.
28	Woodrow Wilson	Staunton, Va., 28 December 1856	Washington, D.C., 3 February 1924	Governor of New Jersey (1911–13)	Trenton, N.J.
29	Warren G. Harding	Blooming Grove, Ohio, 2 November 1865	San Francisco, Calif., 2 August 1923	US senator (1915–21)	Marion, Ohio
30	Calvin Coolidge	Plymouth Notch, Vt., 4 July 1872	Northampton, Mass., 5 January 1933	Governor of Massachusetts (1919–20); US vice president (1921–23)	Boston, Mass.
31	Herbert Hoover	West Branch, Iowa, 10 August 1874	New York, N.Y., 20 October 1964	Secretary of commerce (1921–29)	Stanford, Calif.
32	Franklin D. Roosevelt	Hyde Park, N.Y., 30 January 1882	Warm Springs, Ga., 12 April 1945	Governor of New York (1929–1933)	Hyde Park, N.Y.
33	Harry S Truman	Lamar, Mo., 8 May 1884	Kansas City, Mo., 26 December 1972	US senator (1935–45); US vice president (1945)	Independence, Mo.
34	Dwight D. Eisenhower	Denison, Tex., 14 October 1890	Washington, D.C., 28 March 1969	Supreme allied commander in Europe (1943–44); Army chief of staff (1945–48)	New York
35	John F. Kennedy	Brookline, Mass., 29 May 1917	Dallas, Tex., 22 November 1963	US representative (1947–52); US senator (1953–60)	Massachusetts
36	Lyndon B. Johnson	Stonewall, Tex., 27 August 1908	Johnson City, Tex., 22 January 1973	US representative (1937–48); US senator (1949–60); US vice president (1961–63)	Johnson City, Tex.
37	Richard M. Nixon	Yorba Linda, Calif., 9 January 1913	New York, N.Y., 22 April 1994	US representative (1947–51); US senator (1951–53); US vice president (1953–61)	New York, N.Y.
38	Gerald R. Ford	Omaha, Neb., 14 July 1913	—	US representative (1949–73); US vice president (1973–74)	Grand Rapids, Mich.
39	Jimmy Carter	Plains, Ga., 1 October 1924	—	Governor of Georgia (1951–75)	Plains, Ga.
40	Ronald Reagan	Tampico, Ill., 6 February 1911	—	Governor of California (1967–76)	Los Angeles, Calif.
41	George Bush	Milton, Mass., 12 June 1924		US representative (1967–71) Vice president (1980–88)	Houston, Texas
42	Bill Clinton	Hope, Arkansas, 19 August 1946		Attorney general of Arkansas (1977–79) Governor of Arkansas (1979–81; 1983–92)	Little Rock, Arkansas

[1]Percentage of electors actually voting.

[2]In the elections of 1789, 1792, 1796, and 1800, each elector voted for two candidates for president. The candidate receiving the highest number of votes was elected president; the next highest, vice president. Percentages in table are of total vote cast. From 1804 onward, electors were required to designate which vote was for president and which for vice president, and an electoral majority was required.

PARTY	% OF POPULAR VOTE	% OF ELECTORAL VOTE[1,2]	TERMS IN OFFICE[5]	VICE PRESIDENTS	NOTABLE EVENTS	
Democrat	46.1	62.4	4 March 1893–4 March 1897	Adlai E. Stevenson	Financial panic (1893); Sherman Silver Purchase Act repealed (1893); Utah enters Union.	24
Republican	51.0	60.6	4 March 1897–4 March 1901	Garret A. Hobart Theodore Roosevelt	Spanish–American War (1898); Puerto Rico, Guam, Philippines ceded by Spain; independent Republic of Hawaii annexed; US troops sent to China to suppress Boxer Rebellion (1900); McKinley assassinated.	25
Republican	56.4	70.6	14 Sept. 1901–4 March 1905 4 March 1905–4 March 1909	Charles W. Fairbanks	Antitrust and conservation policies emphasized; Roosevelt awarded Nobel Peace Prize (1906) for mediating settlement of Russo–Japanese War; Panama Canal construction begun (1907); Oklahoma enters Union.	26
Republican	51.6	66.5	4 March 1909–4 March 1913	James S. Sherman	Federal income tax ratified (1913); New Mexico, Arizona enter Union.	27
Democrat	41.8 49.2	81.9 52.2	4 March 1913–4 March 1917 4 March 1917–4 March 1921	Thomas R. Marshall Thomas R. Marshall	Clayton Antitrust Act (1914); US Virgin Islands purchased from Denmark (1917); US enters World War I (1917); Treaty of Versailles signed (1919) but not ratified by US; constitutional amendments enforce prohibition (1919), enfranchise women (1920).	28
Republican	60.3	76.1	4 March 1921–2 Aug. 1923	Calvin Coolidge	Teapot Dome scandal (1923–24).	29
Republican	54.1	71.9	3 Aug. 1923–4 March 1925 4 March 1925–4 March 1929	Charles G. Dawes	Kellogg–Briand Pact (1928).	30
Republican	58.2	83.6	4 March 1929–4 March 1933	Charles Curtis	Stock market crash (1929) inaugurates Great Depression.	31
Democrat	57.4 60.8 54.7 53.4	88.9 98.5 84.6 81.4	4 March 1933–20 Jan. 1937 20 Jan. 1937–20 Jan. 1941 20 Jan. 1941–20 Jan. 1945 20 Jan. 1945–12 April 1945	John N. Garner John N. Garner Henry A. Wallace Harry S Truman	New Deal social reforms; prohibition repealed (1933); US enters World War II (1941)	32
Democrat	—	—	12 April 1945–20 Jan. 1949 20 Jan. 1949–20 Jan. 1953	Alben W. Barkley	United Nations founded (1945); US nuclear bombs dropped on Japan (1945); World War II ends (1945); Philippines granted independence (1946); Marshall Plan (1945); Korean conflict begins (1950); era of McCarthyism.	33
Republican	55.1 57.4	83.2 86.1	20 Jan. 1953–20 Jan. 1957 20 Jan. 1957–20 Jan. 1961	Richard M. Nixon Richard M. Nixon	Korean conflict ended (1953); Supreme Court orders school desegregation (1954); Alaska, Hawaii enter Union.	34
Democrat	49.7	56.4	20 Jan. 1961–22 Nov. 1963	Lyndon B. Johnson	Conflicts with Cuba (1961–62); aboveground nuclear test ban treaty (1963); Kennedy assassinated.	35
Democrat	61.1	90.3	22 Nov. 1963–20 Jan. 1965 20 Jan. 1965–20 Jan. 1969	Hubert H. Humphrey	Great Society programs; Voting Rights Act (1965); escalation of US military role in Indochina; race riots, political assassinations.	36
Republican	43.4 60.7	55.9 96.7	20 Jan. 1969–20 Jan. 1973	Spiro T. Agnew Spiro T. Agnew Gerald R. Ford	First lunar landing (1969); arms limitation treaty with Soviet Union (1972); US withdraws from Viet–Nam (1973); Agnew resigns in tax scandal (1973); Nixon resigns at height of Watergate scandal (1974).	37
Republican	—	—	9 Aug. 1974–20 Jan. 1977	Nelson A. Rockefeller	First combination of unelected president and vice president; Nixon pardoned (1974).	38
Democrat	50.1	55.2	20 Jan. 1977–20 Jan. 1981	Walter F. Mondale	Carter mediates Israel-Egypt peace accord (1978); Panama Canal treaties ratified (1979); tensions with Iran (1979–81).	39
Republican	50.8 58.8	90.9 97.6	20 Jan. 1981–20 Jan. 1985 20 Jan. 1985–20 Jan. 1989	George H. Bush George H. Bush	Defense buildup; social spending cuts; rising trade and budget deficits; tensions with Nicaragua.	40
Republican	54.0	79.2	20 Jan. 1989–20 Jan. 1993	J. Danforth Quayle	Multi-national force repelled Iraqi invaders from Kuwait; savings and loan crisis; 1991 recession.	41
Democrat	43.0 49.2	69.7 70.4	20 Jan. 1993–20 Jan. 1997 20 Jan. 1997–	Albert Gore, Jr.	Passed North American Free Trade Agreement; enacted crime bill banning assault weapons; sent troops to Haiti to restore first democratically elected Haitian president to power after military coup.	42

[3]Electoral vote tied between Jefferson and Aaron Burr; elections decided in House of Representatives.

[4]No candidate received a majority; election decided in House.

[5]In the event of a president's death or removal from office, his duties are assumed to devolve immediately upon his successor, even if he does not immediately take the oath of office.

Chief Justices of the US, 1789–1996

	NAME	BORN	DIED	APPOINTED	SUPREME COURT TERM	MAJOR COURT DEVELOPMENTS
1	John Jay	New York City 12 December 1745	Bedford, N.Y., 17 May 1829	Washington	October 1789 June 1795	Organized court, established procedures.
2	John Rutledge	September 1739	Charleston, S.C., 18 July 1800	Washington		Presided for one term in 1795, but Senate refused to confirm his appointment.
3	Oliver Ellsworth	Windsor, Conn., 29 April 1745	Windsor, Conn. 26 Nov. 1807	Washington	March 1796 December 1800	
4	John Marshall	Fauquier County, Va., 24 September 1755	Philadelphia, Pa. 6 July 1835	Adams	February 1801 July 1835	Established principle of judicial review (*Marbury v. Madison*, 1803); formulated concept of implied powers (*McCulloch v. Maryland*, 1819).
5	Roger Brooke Taney	Calvert County, Md., 17 March 1777	Washington, D.C., 12 October 1864	Jackson	March 1836 October 1864	Held that slaves could not become citizens, ruled Missouri Compromise illegal (*Dred Scott v. Sanford*, 1857).
6	Salmon Portland Chase	Cornish, N.H., 13 January 1808	New York, N.Y. 7 May 1873	Lincoln	December 1864 May 1873	Ruled military trials of civilians illegal (*Ex parte Milligan*, 1866); Chase presided at A. Johnson's impeachment trial.
7	Morrison Remick Waite	Old Lynne, Conn., 29 November 1816	Washington, D.C., 23 March 1888	Grant	March 1874 March 1888	Held that businesses affecting the "public interest" are subject to state regulation (*Munn v. Illinois*, 1877).
8	Melville Weston Fuller	Augusta, Me., 11 February 1833	Sorvento, Me., 4 July 1910	Cleveland	October 1888 July 1910	Issued first opinions on cases under the Sherman Antitrust Act. (*US v. E.C. Knight Co.*, 1895; *Northern Securities Co. v. US*, 1904); held the income tax unconstitutional (*Pollock v. Farmers' Loan*, 1895).
9	Edward Douglass White	Lafourche Parish, La., 3 November 1845	Washington, D.C., 19 May 1921	Taft	December 1910 May 1921	Further qualified the Sherman Antitrust Act (*Standard Oil Co. v. US*, 1911) by applying the "rule of reason."
10	William Howard Taft	Cincinnati, Ohio 15 September 1857	Washington, D.C., 8 March 1930	Harding	July 1921 February 1930	Held against congressional use of taxes for social reform (*Bailey v. Drexel Furniture*, 1922).
11	Charles Evans Hughes	Glens Falls, N.Y., 11 April 1862	Osterville, Mass., 27 August 1948	Hoover	February 1930 June 1941	Upheld constitutionality of National Labor Relations Act, Social Security Act, invalidated National Industrial Recovery Act (*Schechter v. US*, 1935); F Roosevelt's attempt to pack Court opposed.
12	Harlan Fiske Stone	Chesterfield, N.H., 11 October 1872	Washington, D.C., 22 April 1946	F Roosevelt	July 1941 April 1946	Upheld Court's power to invalidate state laws (*Southern Pacific Co. v. Arizona*, 1945).
13	Frederick Moore Vinson	Louisa, Ky., 22 January 1890	Washington, D.C., 8 September 1953	Truman	June 1946 September 1953	Overturned federal seizure of steel mills (*Youngstown Sheet and Tube Co. v. Sawyer*, 1952), Vinson dissenting.
14	Earl Warren	Los Angeles, Calif., 19 March 1891	Washington, D.C., 9 July 1974	Eisenhower	October 1953 June 1969	Mandated public school desegregation (*Brown v. Topeka, Kans., Board of Education*, 1954) and reapportionment of state legislatures (*Baker v. Carr*, 1962); upheld rights of suspects in police custody (*Miranda v. Arizona*, 1966).
15	Warren Earl Burger	St. Paul, Minn., 17 September 1907		Nixon	June 1969 August 1986	Legalized abortion (*Roe v. Wade*, 1973); rejected claim of executive privilege in a criminal case (*US v. Nixon*, 1974); first female justice (1981).
16	William Hubbs Rehnquist	Shorewood Village, Wis., 1 October 1924		Nixon	September 1986	Applied constitutional prohibition against taking of property without compensation to invalidate government regulation of property. (*Nollan v. California Coastal Commission*, 1987).

house work; Robert Marion La Follette (1855–1925), a leader for progressive political reform in Wisconsin and in the US Senate; Margaret Higgins Sanger (1883–1966), pioneer in birth control; Norman Thomas (1884–1968), Socialist Party leader;and Martin Luther King, Jr. (1929–68), a central figure in the black civil rights movement and winner of the Nobel Peace Prize in 1964.

Religious leaders include Roger Williams (1603–83), an early advocate of religious tolerance in the US; Jonathan Edwards (1703–58), New England preacher and theologian; Elizabeth Ann Seton (1774–1821), the first American canonized in the Roman Catholic Church; William Ellery Channing (1780–1842), a founder of American Unitarianism; Joseph Smith (1805–44), founder of the Church of Jesus Christ of Latter-day Saints (Mormon) and his chief associate, Brigham Young (1801–77); and Mary Baker Eddy (1821–1910), founder of the Christian Science Church. Paul Tillich (b.Germany, 1886–1965) and Reinhold Niebuhr (1892–1971) were outstanding Protestant theologians of international influence.

Famous US businessmen include Éleuthère Irénée du Pont de Nemours (b.France, 1771–1834), John Jacob Astor (Johann Jakob Ashdour, b.Germany, 1763–1848), Cornelius Vanderbilt (1794–1877), Andrew Carnegie (b.Scotland, 1835–1919), John Pierpont Morgan (1837–1913), John Davison Rockefeller (1839–1937), Andrew William Mellon (1855–1937), Henry Ford (1863–1947), and Thomas John Watson (1874–1956).

Literary Figures

The first US author to be widely read outside the US was Washington Irving (1783–1859). James Fenimore Cooper (1789–1851) was the first popular US novelist. Three noted historians were William Hickling Prescott (1796–1859), John Lothrop Motley (1814–77), and Francis Parkman (1823–93). The writings of two men of Concord, Mass.—Ralph Waldo Emerson (1803–82) and Henry David Thoreau (1817–62)—influenced philosophers, political leaders, and ordinary men and women in many parts of the world. The novels and short stories of Nathaniel Hawthorne (1804–64) explore New England's Puritan heritage. Herman Melville (1819–91) wrote the powerful novel *Moby-Dick*, a symbolic work about a whale hunt that has become an American classic. Mark Twain (Samuel Langhorne Clemens, 1835–1910) is the best-known US humorist. Other leading novelists of the later 19th and early 20th centuries were William Dean Howells (1837–1920), Henry James (1843–1916), Edith Wharton (1862–1937), Stephen Crane (1871–1900), Theodore Dreiser (1871–1945), Willa Cather (1873–1947), and Sinclair Lewis (1885–1951), first US winner of the Nobel Prize for literature (1930). Later Nobel Prize–winning US novelists include Pearl Sydenstricker Buck (1892–1973), in 1938; William Faulkner (1897–1962), in 1949; Ernest Hemingway (1899–1961), in 1954; John Steinbeck (1902–68), in 1962; Saul Bellow (b.Canada, 1915), in 1976; and Isaac Bashevis Singer (b.Poland, 1904–91), in 1978. Among other noteworthy writers are James Thurber (1894–1961), F(rancis) Scott (Key) Fitzgerald (1896–1940), Thomas Wolfe (1900–1938), Richard Wright (1908–60), Eudora Welty (b.1909), John Cheever (1912–82), Norman Mailer (b.1923), James Baldwin (1924–87), John Updike (b.1932), and Philip Roth (b.1933).

Noted US poets include Henry Wadsworth Longfellow (1807–82), Edgar Allan Poe (1809–49), Walt Whitman (1819–92), Emily Dickinson (1830–86), Edwin Arlington Robinson (1869–1935), Robert Frost (1874–1963), Wallace Stevens (1879–1955), William Carlos Williams (1883–1963), Marianne Moore (1887–1972), Edward Estlin Cummings (1894–1962), Hart Crane (1899–1932), and Langston Hughes (1902–67). Ezra Pound (1885–1972) and Nobel laureate Thomas Stearns Eliot (1888–1965) lived and worked abroad for most of their careers. Wystan Hugh Auden (b.England, 1907–73), who became an American citizen in 1946, published poetry and criticism. Elizabeth Bishop (1911–79), Robert Lowell (1917–77), Allen Ginsberg (1926–97), and Sylvia Plath (1932–63) are among the best-known poets since World War II. Robert Penn Warren (1905–89) won the Pulitzer Prize for both fiction and poetry and became the first US poet laureate. Carl Sandburg (1878–1967) was a noted poet, historian, novelist, and folklorist. The foremost US dramatists are Eugene (Gladstone) O'Neill (1888–1953), who won the Nobel Prize for literature in 1936; Tennessee Williams (Thomas Lanier Williams, 1911–83); Arthur Miller (b.1915); and Edward Albee (b.1928). Neil Simon (b.1927) is among the nation's most popular playwrights and screenwriters.

Artists

Two renowned painters of the early period were John Singleton Copley (1738–1815) and Gilbert Stuart (1755–1828). Outstanding 19th-century painters were James Abbott McNeill Whistler (1834–1903), Winslow Homer (1836–1910), Thomas Eakins (1844–1916), Mary Cassatt (1845–1926), Albert Pinkham Ryder (1847–1917), John Singer Sargent (b.Italy, 1856–1925), and Frederic Remington (1861–1909). More recently, Edward Hopper (1882–1967), Georgia O'Keeffe (1887–1986), Thomas Hart Benton (1889–1975), Charles Burchfield (1893–1967), Norman Rockwell (1894–1978), Ben Shahn (1898–1969), Mark Rothko (b.Russia, 1903–70), Jackson Pollock (1912–56), Andrew Wyeth (b.1917), Robert Rauschenberg (b.1925), and Jasper Johns (b.1930) have achieved international recognition.

Sculptors of note include Augustus Saint-Gaudens (1848–1907), Gaston Lachaise (1882–1935), Jo Davidson (1883–1952), Daniel Chester French (1850–1931), Alexander Calder (1898–1976), Louise Nevelson (b.Russia, 1899–1988), and Isamu Noguchi (1904–88). Henry Hobson Richardson (1838–86), Louis Henry Sullivan (1856–1924), Frank Lloyd Wright (1869–1959), Louis I. Kahn (b.Estonia, 1901–74), and Eero Saarinen (1910–61) were outstanding architects. Contemporary architects of note include Richard Buckminster Fuller (1895–1983), Edward Durrell Stone (1902–78), Philip Cortelyou Johnson (b.1906), and Ieoh Ming Pei (b.China, 1917). The US has produced many fine photographers, notably Mathew B. Brady (1823?–96), Alfred Stieglitz (1864–1946), Edward Steichen (1879–1973), Edward Weston (1886–1958), Ansel Adams (1902–84), and Margaret Bourke-White (1904–71).

Entertainment Figures

Outstanding figures in the motion picture industry are D. W. (David Lewelyn Wark) Griffith (1875–1948), Sir Charles Spencer "Charlie" Chaplin (b.England, 1889–1978), Walter Elias "Walt" Disney (1906–66), and George Orson Welles (1915–85). John Ford (1895–1973), Howard Winchester Hawks (1896–1977), Frank Capra (b.Italy, 1897), Sir Alfred Hitchcock (b.England, 1899–1980), and John Huston (1906–87) were influential motion picture directors; Mel Brooks (Kaminsky, b.1926), George Lucas (b.1944), and Steven Spielberg (b.1947) have achieved remarkable popular success. Woody Allen (Allen Konigsberg, b.1935) has written, directed, and starred in comedies on stage and screen. World-famous American actors and actresses include the Barrymores, Ethel (1879–1959) and her brothers Lionel (1878–1954) and John (1882–1942); Humphrey Bogart (1899–1957); James Cagney (1899–1986); Spencer Tracy (1900–1967); Helen Hayes Brown (b.1900); Clark Gable (1901–60); Joan Crawford (Lucille Fay LeSueur, 1904–77); Cary Grant (Alexander Archibald Leach, b.England, 1904–86); Greta Garbo (Greta Louisa Gustafsson, b.Sweden, 1905–90); Henry Fonda (1905–82) and his daughter, Jane (b.1937); John Wayne (Marion Michael Morrison, 1907–79); Bette (Ruth Elizabeth) Davis (1908–89); Katharine Hepburn (b.1909); Judy Garland (Frances Gumm, 1922–69); Marlon Brando (b.1924); Marilyn Monroe

(Norma Jean Mortenson, 1926–62); and Dustin Hoffman (b.1937). Among other great entertainers are W. C. Fields (William Claude Dukenfield, 1880–1946), Al Jolson (Asa Yoelson, b.Russia, 1886–1950), Jack Benny (Benjamin Kubelsky, 1894–1974), Fred Astaire (Fred Austerlitz, 1899–1987), Bob (Leslie Townes) Hope (b.England, 1903), Bing (Harry Lillis) Crosby (1904–78), Frank (Francis Albert) Sinatra (b.1915), Elvis Aaron Presley (1935–77), and Barbra (Barbara Joan) Streisand (b.1942). The first great US "showman" was Phineas Taylor Barnum (1810–91).

Composers and Musicians

The foremost composers are Edward MacDowell (1861–1908), Charles Ives (1874–1954), Ernest Bloch (b.Switzerland, 1880–1959), Virgil Thomson (1896–1989), Roger Sessions (1896–1985), Roy Harris (1898–1979), Aaron Copland (1900–90), Elliott Carter (b.1908), Samuel Barber (1910–81), John Cage (1912–92), and Leonard Bernstein (1918–90). George Rochberg (b.1918), George Crumb (b.1929), Steve Reich (b.1936), and Philip Glass (b.1937) have won more recent followings. The songs of Stephen Collins Foster (1826–64) have achieved folk-song status. Leading composers of popular music are John Philip Sousa (1854–1932), George Michael Cohan (1878–1942), Jerome Kern (1885–1945), Irving Berlin (Israel Baline, b.Russia, 1888–1989), Cole Porter (1893–1964), George Gershwin (1898–1937), Richard Rodgers (1902–79), Woody Guthrie (1912–67), Stephen Joshua Sondheim (b.1930), Paul Simon (b.1941), and Bob Dylan (Robert Zimmerman, b.1941). Preeminent in the blues traditions are Leadbelly (Huddie Ledbetter, 1888–1949), Bessie Smith (1898?–1937), and Muddy Waters (McKinley Morganfield, 1915–83). Leading jazz figures include the composers Scott Joplin (1868–1917), James Hubert "Eubie" Blake (1883–1983), Edward Kennedy "Duke" Ellington (1899–1974), and William "Count" Basie (1904–84), and performers Louis Armstrong (1900–1971), Billie Holiday (Eleanora Fagan, 1915–59), John Birks "Dizzy" Gillespie (1917–93), Charlie "Bird" Parker (1920–55), John Coltrane (1926–67), and Miles Davis (1926–91).

Many foreign-born musicians have enjoyed personal and professional freedom in the US; principal among them were pianists Artur Schnabel (b.Austria, 1882–1951), Arthur Rubinstein (b.Poland, 1887–1982), Rudolf Serkin (b.Bohemia, 1903–91), Vladimir Horowitz (b.Russia, 1904–89), and violinists Jascha Heifetz (b.Russia, 1901–87) and Isaac Stern (b.USSR, 1920). Among distinguished instrumentalists born in the US are Benny Goodman (1909–86), a classical as well as jazz clarinetist, and concert pianist Van Cliburn (Harvey Lavan, Jr., b.1934). Singers Paul Robeson (1898–1976), Marian Anderson (1897–1993), Maria Callas (Maria Kalogeropoulos, 1923–77), Leontyne Price (b.1927), and Beverly Sills (Belle Silverman, b.1929) have achieved international acclaim. Isadora Duncan (1878–1927) was one of the first US dancers to win fame abroad. George Balanchine (b.Russia, 1904–83), Agnes De Mille (1905–93), Jerome Robbins (b.1918), Paul Taylor (b.1930), and Twyla Tharp (b.1941) are leading choreographers; Martha Graham (1893–1991) pioneered in modern dance.

Sports Figures

Among the many noteworthy sports stars are baseball's Tyrus Raymond "Ty" Cobb (1886–1961) and George Herman "Babe" Ruth (1895–1948); football's Samuel Adrian "Sammy" Baugh (b.1914), Jim Brown (b.1936), Francis A. "Fran" Tarkenton (b.1940), and Orenthal James Simpson (b.1947); and golf's

Robert Tyre "Bobby" Jones (1902–71) and Mildred "Babe" Didrikson Zaharias (1914–56). William Tatum "Bill" Tilden (1893–1953) and Billie Jean (Moffitt) King (b.1943) have starred in tennis; Joe Louis (Joseph Louis Barrow, 1914–81) and Muhammad Ali (Cassius Marcellus Clay, b.1942) in boxing; William Felton "Bill" Russell (b.1934) and Wilton Norman "Wilt" Chamberlain (b.1936) in basketball; Mark Spitz (b.1950) in swimming; Eric Heiden (b.1958) in speed skating; and Jesse Owens (1913–80) in track and field.

50 BIBLIOGRAPHY

Ahlstrom, Sydney E. *A Religious History of the American People.* New Haven: Yale University Press, 1972.

Barone, Michael. *The Almanac of American Politics.* Washington, D.C.: National Journal, 1992.

Becker, Carl Lotus. *The Declaration of Independence: A Study in the History of Political Ideas.* New York: Knopf, 1960.

Bennett, Lerone. *Before the Mayflower: A History of Black America.* 6th ed. New York: Penguin, 1993.

Brown, Richard Maxwell. *No Duty to Retreat: Violence and Values in American History and Society.* New York: Oxford University Press, 1991.

Commager, Henry Steele (ed.). *Documents of American History.* Englewood Cliffs, N.J.: Prentice-Hall, 1988.

Glassborow, Jilly, Gillian Freeman (eds.). *Atlas of the United States.* New York: Macmillan, 1986.

Hart, James David (ed.). *Oxford Companion to American Literature.* New York: Oxford University Press, 1983.

Harvard Encyclopedia of American Ethnic Groups. Cambridge: Harvard University Press, 1980.

Josephy, Alvin M., Jr. *Now That the Buffalo's Gone: A Study of Todya's American Indians.* Norman, Okla.: Univ. of Oklahoma Press, 1984.

Kammen, Michael (ed.). *The Origins of the American Constitution: A Documentary History.* New York: Penguin, 1986.

———. *People of Paradox: An Inquiry Concerning the Origins of American Civilization.* New York: Oxford University Press, 1980.

Martis, Kenneth C. *The Historical Atlas of Political Parties in the United States Congress 1789–1989.* New York: Macmillan, 1989.

McNickle, D'Arcy. *Native American Tribalism: Indian Survivals and Renewals.* New York: Oxford University Press, 1993.

Mencken, Henry Louis. *The American Language.* New York: Knopf, 1963.

Morison, Samuel Eliot. *The Oxford History of the American People.* New York: New American Library, 1972.

Nevins, Allan. *Ordeal of the Union.* New York: Collier Books, 1992.

Reed, Carroll E. *Dialects of American English.* Amherst: University of Massachusetts Press, 1977.

Robinson, Cedric J. *Black Movements in America.* New York: Routledge, 1997.

Tocqueville, Alexis de. *Democracy in America.* New York: Knopf, 1994.

United States Government Manual. Washington, D.C.: US Government Printing Office, 1935-date.

US Bureau of the Census. *Historical Statistics of the United States, Colonial Times to 1970.* Washington, D.C.: US Government Printing Office, 1879-date.

Who's Who in America: A Biographical Dictionary of Notable Living Men and Women. Chicago: Marquis, 1899—.

GLOSSARY

ANTEBELLUM: before the US Civil War.

BLUE LAWS: laws forbidding certain practices (e.g., conducting business, gaming, drinking liquor), especially on Sundays.

CAPITAL BUDGET: a financial plan for acquiring and improving buildings or land, paid for by the sale of bonds.

CAPITAL PUNISHMENT: punishment by death.

CIVILIAN LABOR FORCE: all persons 16 years of age or older who are not in the armed forces and who are now holding a job, have been temporarily laid off, are waiting to be reassigned to a new position, or are unemployed but actively looking for work.

CLASS I RAILROAD: a railroad having gross annual revenues of $83.5 million or more in 1983.

COMMERCIAL BANK: a bank that offers to businesses and individuals a variety of banking services, including the right of withdrawal by check.

COMPACT: a formal agreement, covenant, or understanding between two or more parties.

CONSOLIDATED BUDGET: a financial plan that includes the general budget, federal funds, and all special funds.

CONSTANT DOLLARS: money values calculated so as to eliminate the effect of inflation on prices and income.

CONTINENTAL CLIMATE: the climate typical of the US interior, having distinct seasons, a wide range of daily and annual temperatures, and dry, sunny summers.

COUNCIL-MANAGER SYSTEM: a system of local government under which a professional administrator is hired by an elected council to carry out its laws and policies.

CREDIT UNION: a cooperative body that raises funds from its members by the sale of shares and makes loans to its members at relatively low interest rates.

CURRENT DOLLARS: money values that reflect prevailing prices, without excluding the effects of inflation.

DEMAND DEPOSIT: a bank deposit that can be withdrawn by the depositor with no advance notice to the bank.

ELECTORAL VOTES: the votes that a state may cast for president, equal to the combined total of its US senators and representatives and nearly always cast entirely on behalf of the candidate who won the most votes in that state on Election Day.

ENDANGERED SPECIES: a type of plant or animal threatened with extinction in all or part of its natural range.

FEDERAL POVERTY LEVEL: a level of money income below which a person or family qualifies for US government aid.

FISCAL YEAR: a 12-month period for accounting purposes.

FOOD STAMPS: coupons issued by the government to low-income persons for food purchases at local stores.

GENERAL BUDGET: a financial plan based on a government's normal revenues and operating expenses, excluding special funds.

GENERAL COASTLINE: a measurement of the general outline of the US seacoast. See also TIDAL SHORELINE.

GREAT AWAKENING: during the mid–18th century, a Protestant religious revival in North America, especially New England.

GROSS STATE PRODUCT: the total value of goods and services produced in the state.

GROWING SEASON: the period between the last 32°F (0°C) temperature in spring and the first 32°F (0°C) temperature in autumn.

HOME-RULE CHARTER: a document stating how and in what respects a city, town, or county may govern itself.

INSTALLED CAPACITY: the maximum possible output of electric power at any given time.

MAYOR-COUNCIL SYSTEM: a system of local government under which an elected council serves as a legislature and an elected mayor is the chief administrator.

MEDICAID: a federal-state program that helps defray the hospital and medical costs of needy persons.

MEDICARE: a program of hospital and medical insurance for the elderly, administered by the federal government.

METROPOLITAN AREA: in most cases, a city and its surrounding suburbs.

NO-FAULT INSURANCE: an automobile insurance plan that allows an accident victim to receive payment from an insurance company without having to prove who was responsible for the accident.

NORTHERN, NORTH MIDLAND: major US dialect regions.

OMBUDSMAN: a public official empowered to hear and investigate complaints by private citizens about government agencies.

PER CAPITA: per person.

POCKET VETO: a method by which a state governor (or the US president) may kill a bill by taking no action on it before the legislature adjourns.

PROVED RESERVES: the quantity of a recoverable mineral resource (such as oil or natural gas) that is still in the ground.

PUBLIC DEBT: the amount owed by a government.

RELIGIOUS ADHERENTS: the followers of a religious group, including (but not confined to) the full, confirmed, or communicant members of that group.

RETAIL TRADE: the sale of goods directly to the consumer.

REVENUE SHARING: the distribution of federal tax receipts to state and local governments.

RIGHT-TO-WORK LAW: a measure outlawing any attempt to require union membership as a condition of employment.

SAVINGS AND LOAN ASSOCIATION: a bank that invests the savings of depositors primarily in home mortgage loans.

SERVICE INDUSTRIES: industries that provide services (e.g., health, legal, automotive repair) for individuals, businesses, and others.

SOCIAL SECURITY: as commonly understood, the federal system of old age, survivors, and disability insurance.

SOUTHERN, SOUTH MIDLAND: major US dialect regions.

STOLPORT: an airfield for short-takeoff-and-landing (STOL) aircraft, which require runways shorter than those used by conventional aircraft.

SUNBELT: the southernmost states of the US, extending from Florida to California.

SUPPLEMENTAL SECURITY INCOME: a federally administered program of aid to the aged, blind, and disabled.

TIDAL SHORELINE: a detailed measurement of the US seacoast that includes sounds, bays, other outlets, and offshore islands.

TIME DEPOSIT: a bank deposit that may be withdrawn only at the end of a specified time period or upon advance notice to the bank.

VALUE ADDED BY MANUFACTURE: the difference, measured in dollars, between the value of finished goods and the cost of the materials needed to produce them.

WHOLESALE TRADE: the sale of goods, usually in large quantities, for ultimate resale to consumers.

ABBREVIATIONS AND ACRONYMS

AD—Anno Domini
AFDC—aid to families with dependent children
AFL–CIO—American Federation of Labor–Congress of Industrial Organizations
AM—before noon
AM—amplitude modulation
American Ind.—American Independent Party
Amtrak—National Railroad Passenger Corp.
b.—born
BC—Before Christ
Btu—British thermal unit(s)
bu—bushel(s)
c.—circa (about)
C—Celsius (Centigrade)
CIA—Central Intelligence Agency
cm—centimeter(s)
Co.—company
comp.—compiler
Conrail—Consolidated Rail Corp.
Corp.—corporation
CST—Central Standard Time
cu—cubic
cwt—hundredweight(s)
d.—died
D—Democrat
e—evening
E—east
ed.—edition, editor
e.g.—exempli gratia (for example)
EPA—Environmental Protection Agency
est.—estimated
EST—Eastern Standard Time
et al.—et alii (and others)
etc.—et cetera (and so on)
F—Fahrenheit
FBI—Federal Bureau of Investigation
FCC—Federal Communications Commission
FM—frequency modulation
Ft.—fort
ft—foot, feet
GDP—gross domestic products
gm—gram
GMT—Greenwich Mean Time
GNP—gross national product
GRT—gross registered tons
Hist.—Historic

I—interstate (highway)
i.e.—id est (that is)
in—inch(es)
Inc.—incorporated
Jct.—junction
K—kindergarten
kg—kilogram(s)
km—kilometer(s)
km/hr—kilometers per hour
kw—kilowatt(s)
kwh—kilowatt-hour(s)
lb—pound(s)
m—meter(s); morning
m^3—cubic meter(s)
mi—mile(s)
Mon.—monument
mph—miles per hour
MST—Mountain Standard Time
Mt.—mount
Mtn.—mountain
mw—megawatt(s)
N—north
NA—not available
Natl.—National
NATO—North Atlantic Treaty Organization
NCAA—National Collegiate Athletic Association
n.d.—no date
N.F.—National Forest
N.W.R.—National Wildlife Refuge
oz—ounce(s)
PM—after noon
PST—Pacific Standard Time
r.—reigned
R—Republican
Ra.—range
Res.—reservoir, reservation
rev. ed.—revised edition
s—south
S—Sunday
Soc.—Socialist
sq—square
St.—saint
UN—United Nations
US—United States
USIA—United States Information Agency
w—west

NAMES OF STATES AND OTHER SELECTED AREAS

	Standard Abbreviation(s)	Postal Abbreviation		Standard Abbreviation(s)	Postal Abbreviation
Alabama	Ala.	AL	Nebraska	Nebr. (Neb.)	NE
Alaska	*	AK	Nevada	Nev.	NV
Arizona	Ariz.	AZ	New Hampshire	N.H.	NH
Arkansas	Ark.	AR	New Jersey	N.J.	NJ
California	Calif.	CA	New Mexico	N.Mex. (N.M.)	NM
Colorado	Colo.	CO	New York	N.Y.	NY
Connecticut	Conn.	CN	North Carolina	N.C.	NC
Delaware	Del.	DE	North Dakota	N.Dak. (N.D.)	ND
District of Columbia	D.C.	DC	Ohio	*	OH
Florida	Fla.	FL	Oklahoma	Okla.	OK
Georgia	Ga.	GA	Oregon	Oreg. (Ore.)	OR
Hawaii	*	HI	Pennsylvania	Pa.	PA
Idaho	*	ID	Puerto Rico	P.R.	PR
Illinois	Ill.	IL	Rhode Island	R.I.	RI
Indiana	Ind.	IN	South Carolina	S.C.	SC
Iowa	*	IA	South Dakota	S.Dak. (S.D.)	SD
Kansas	Kans. (Kan.)	KS	Tennessee	Tenn.	TN
Kentucky	Ky.	KY	Texas	Tex.	TX
Louisiana	La.	LA	Utah	*	UT
Maine	Me.	ME	Vermont	Vt.	VT
Maryland	Md.	MD	Virginia	Va.	VA
Massachusetts	Mass.	MA	Virgin Islands	V.I.	VI
Michigan	Mich.	MI	Washington	Wash.	WA
Minnesota	Minn.	MN	West Virginia	W.Va.	WV
Mississippi	Miss.	MS	Wisconsin	Wis.	WI
Missouri	Mo.	MO	Wyoming	Wyo.	WI
Montana	Mont.	MT			

*No standard abbreviation

ISBN 0-7876-0080-6

90000

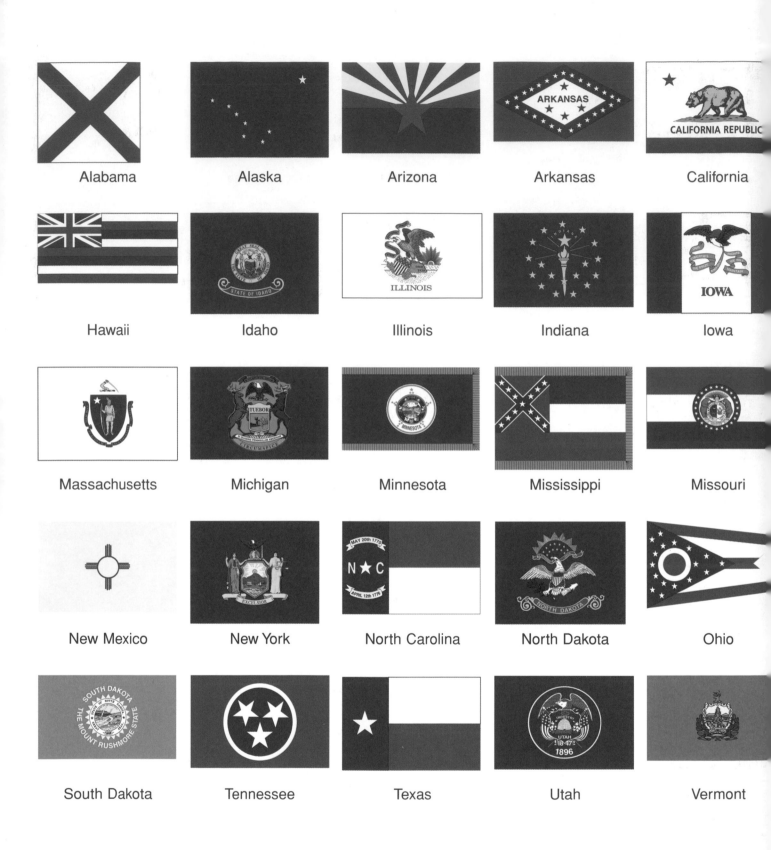

Alabama

Alaska

Arizona

Arkansas

California

Hawaii

Idaho

Illinois

Indiana

Iowa

Massachusetts

Michigan

Minnesota

Mississippi

Missouri

New Mexico

New York

North Carolina

North Dakota

Ohio

South Dakota

Tennessee

Texas

Utah

Vermont